THE BLACKWELL ENCYCLOPEDIA OF
Industrial Archaeology

𝔹

THE BLACKWELL ENCYCLOPEDIA OF
Industrial Archaeology

Edited by
Barrie Trinder

Editorial Board

Axel Föhl
David H. Shayt
Stuart Smith
Michael Stratton
Robert Vogel

BLACKWELL
Reference

First published 1992

Blackwell Publishers
108 Cowley Road, Oxford OX4 1JF, UK

238 Main Street, Suite 501
Cambridge, Massachusetts 02142, USA

British Library Cataloguing in Publication Data
The Blackwell encyclopedia of industrial archaeology.
   I. Trinder, Barrie, 1939–
   609.41
   ISBN 0-631-14216-9

Library of Congress Cataloging-in-Publication Data
The Blackwell encyclopedia of industrial archaeology/edited by Barrie Trinder
   editorial board. Axel Föhl . . . [et al.].
   1000 p. 246 cm.
   Includes bibliographical references and index.
   ISBN 0-631-14216-9
   1. Industrial archaeology—Encyclopedias.   I. Trinder. Barrie Stuart.
   T37.E53   1992
   609--dc20
                           91–41700
                              CIP

Typeset and printed at The Alden Press, Oxford

Contents

Contributors, consultants
and translators

Contributors

Institutions shown in italic indicate current (1992) affiliations. Institutions shown in square brackets are those to which contributors were affiliated when their entries were written.

Judith Alfrey
Ironbridge Institute

Christopher Andrae
Historica Research Ltd., London, Ontario

Rafael Aracil
Department of Economic History, University of Barcelona

Maria José Baragaño
Associacion Española del Patrimonio Industriala, Austurias

Hans-Peter Bärtschi,
ARIAS, Winterthur

Jean-François Belhoste
Cellule du Patrimoine Industriel, Inventaire général des monuments et des richesses artistiques de la France, Paris

Sarah Bendall
Emmanuel College, Cambridge

Ivor J. Brown,
Wakefield, West Yorkshire

Carlos Caicoya
Associacion Española del Patrimonio Industriala, Austurias

Eusebi Casanelles
Museu de la Ciencia i de la Tecnica de Catalunya, Barcelona

Kate Clark
Ironbridge Gorge Museum

Paul Collins
Ironbridge Institute

José M. Lopes Cordeiro
Unidade de Arqueologia, Universidade do Minho, Braga

Neil Cossons
The Science Museum, London

Jeff Cox
School of Applied Science, University of Wolverhampton

Nancy Cox
School of Humanities and Social Science, University of Wolverhampton

David Crossley
Division of Continuing Education, University of Sheffield

Simon Derry
British Broadcasting Corporation

Maria Fine
Athens

Axel Föhl
Rheinisches Amt für Denkmalpflege, Landschaftsverband Rheinland, Bonn

Robert Forsythe
Irvine, Strathclyde

Andres Garcia
Associacion Española del Patrimonio Industriala, Austurias

Piotr Gerber
Institute of Architectural Studies, Technical University of Wrocław

Horia Giurgiuman
Hermann Pfauter GmbH & Co., Ludwigsburg
[Polytechnic of Cluj-Napoca]

Christopher Green
Berwick-upon-Tweed Borough Museum and Art Gallery
[Ironbridge Institute]

Sarah Hill
Waterstones Ltd., Shrewsbury
[Ironbridge Institute]

Rolf Höhmann
Technische Hochschule, Darmstadt

Deryck Holdsworth
Department of Geography, Pennsylvania State University

John R. Hume
Historic Scotland, Edinburgh

Jane Hutchins
Museum of Fine Arts, Boston, Massachusetts

Ole Hyldtoft
Institute of Economic History, University of Copenhagen

Maite Ibañez
Instituto para la Promocion de la Investigacion, Universidade de Deusto, Bilbao

Jan Kesik
History Department, Wrocław University

Mihály Kubinsky
Department of Architecture, University of Sopron

vi

Mercedes Lopez
Escuela de Ingenieros de Caminos, Madrid

Michael Mende
Hochschule für Bildende Künst, Braunschweig

Norbert Mendgen
Staatliches Konservatoramt Saarland, Saarbrücken

Marie Nisser
University of Uppsala

Trefor M. Owen
Bangor, Gwynedd
[Welsh Folk Museum, St Fagans]

John Powell
Ironbridge Gorge Museum

Tim Putnam
Design History Department, Middlesex University

Larissa Rimell
Matlock, Derbyshire
[Thwaite Mills, Leeds]

Jerzy Rozpedowski
Department of Archaeology, Technical University of Wrocław

Alberto Santaña
Universidade de Deusto, Bilbao

David H. Shayt
National Museum of American History, Smithsonian Institution, Washington DC

Paul Smith
Cellule du Patrimoine Industriel, Inventaire général des monuments et des richesses artistiques de la France, Paris

Stuart B. Smith
[Ironbridge Gorge Museum]

Michael Stratton
Ironbridge Institute

Julian Temple
Brooklands Museum

Robert Thorne
Alan Baxter Associates, London
[English Heritage, London Division]

Louise Trottier
National Museum of Science and Technology, Ottawa

Barrie Trinder
Ironbridge Institute

Jurrie Van Dalen
Boom Pers, Meppel

Robert M. Vogel
Gothic Engineering and Machine Works, Washington DC
[National Museum of American History, Smithsonian Institution, Washington DC]

Peter Wakelin
Cadw, Cardiff
[School of Humanities and Social Science, University of Wolverhampton]

Mark Watson
Historic Scotland, Edinburgh

J. N. Westwood
Centre for Russian and East European Studies, University of Birmingham

Helena E. Wright
National Museum of American History, Smithsonian Institution, Washington DC

Marta Zabala
Instituto para la Promocion de la Investigacion, Universidade de Deusto, Bilbao

Consultants

The editors acknowledge with gratitude the contributions of the following people who have provided advice and comments on the topics indicated in brackets.

Astrid Baldinger, *Industriearchäologie, Brugg (Switzerland)*; Francizka Bollerey, *Department of the History of Architecture and Town Planning, University of Delft (Germany, industrial communities)*; Louis Cullen, *Department of Economic History, Trinity College, Dublin (Ireland)*; John Dunstan, *Centre for Russian and East European Studies, University of Birmingham (Eastern Europe)*; Keith Falconer, *Royal Commission on the Historical Monuments of England (recording)*; Geir Helgen, *Fylkeskonservatoren i Buskurud, Drammen (Norway)*; Nanna Hermansson, *Södermanlands Museum, Nyköping, Sweden (Iceland)*; David Higgins, *University of Liverpool (ceramics)*; Kari Hoël, *University of Trømso (Norway)*; Stephen Hughes, *Royal Commission on the Historical Monuments of Wales (recording)*; Pepa Zalewa Kileva, *Eter, Gabrovo (Bulgaria)*; Roberta Morelli, *Rome (Italy)*; Massimo Negri, *Milan (Italy)*; Ole Øverås, *Riksantikvaren, Oslo (Norway)*; Cassie Palamar, *Alberta Culture and Multi-Culturalism, Edmonton (Alberta)*; Danielle Pesce, *Rome (Italy)*; Carlo Poni, *Department of Economic Science, Universita Degli Studi di Bologna (Italy)*; Ornella Selvafolta, *Faculty of Architecture, Politecnico di Milano (Italy)*; Martin Smith, *Department of Classics, University College of North Wales, Bangor (Albania)*; J. D. Storer, *Telford, Shropshire (air transport, transport museums)*; Peter Swittaleck, *Federal Office for the Protection of Monuments, Vienna (Austria)*; Torill Thømt, *Hallingdal Folkemuseum, Nesbyen (Norway)*; Ragnheiour Thorarinsdottir, *Arbaejarsafn Reykajavik Museum (Iceland)*

Translators

The following have been responsible for translations into English.

Anthea Bell: Germany, Hungary (articles by Mihály Kubinsky), Switzerland; Hildi Hawkins: Finland; Paul Smith: France (articles by Jean-François Belhoste); Barrie Trinder: Canada (articles by Louise Trottier), Romania; Stephen Ulph: Spain.

Preface

The compilation of this encyclopedia has taken nearly eight years, and my first acknowledgement must be to my family who have patiently endured my preoccupation with the project during that period.

It has been a pleasure to work with the staff of Blackwell Publishers, particularly with Janet Godden, who first suggested the project, Alyn Shipton who has encouraged it since he joined the company, and Caroline Bundy who has overseen its transformation from an unwieldy pile of typescripts into a book.

The encyclopedia has been compiled at the Ironbridge Institute and I am grateful to the Ironbridge Gorge Museum Trust who have encouraged the project from the time it was first suggested. Particular thanks are due to the Museum's Librarian, John Powell, and to the Institute's secretarial staff, Janet Markland and Carol Sampson, without whose cheerful assistance the book would never have materialized. Some acknowledgement is also appropriate to the designers and manufacturers of the IBM XT 286 computer on which the text has been edited.

It is a matter of some satisfaction that twelve of the contributors to the encyclopedia are graduates of the Ironbridge Institute, and that two-thirds of those who have written articles for it have been at the Institute – as staff, students, conference delegates, guest lecturers or visitors – during the past eight years.

I acknowledge with gratitude the enthusiastic support of my fellow editors. It has been helpful to be able to call at any time on the expertise of my colleague, Michael Stratton, and Stuart Smith has made many wise suggestions relating to the history of technology while bearing the burdens of the day-to-day management of a large industrial museum. Axel Föhl has given the encyclopedia a wider European perspective. Robert M. Vogel and David H. Shayt, in addition to providing the articles on the United States, have helped to make the technological articles comprehensible in the light of North American experience.

I am grateful to all who have allowed me the use of their photographs and drawings, and particularly to Manfred Hamm for the view of Völklingen on the front cover. I have been fortunate to work with an able team of contributors, largely through contacts made at the meetings of the International Committee for the Conservation of the Industrial Heritage (TICCIH). My thanks are due to all of them, but I wish to record my gratitude to three in particular, Neil Cossons, Louise Trottier and Peter Wakelin, for their patience in discussing the principles on which the encyclopedia is based, and for their confidence that this was a worthwhile venture.

Barrie Trinder
September 1992

Illustration acknowledgements

The editors and publishers gratefully acknowledge the following for supplying illustrations and granting permission for their use. The illustrations are listed according to the relevant entry.

Every effort has been made to trace all copyright holders of the illustrations that appear in this book. However, if copyright has been infringed, we shall be pleased, on being satisfied as to the owner's title, to make proper acknowledgement in future editions.

Aerofilms Ltd: *Snowdonia, Wales*; Alberta Culture and Multi-Culturalism: *Alberta*; Architekturno-Etnograficzeskij Kompleks 'Eter': *Eta*; Collection of Dr Mark Baldwin: *floating mill*; Ballarat Historical Park Association: *Sovereign Hill*; Beaton Institute, Steel Project: *Cape Breton Island*; Bodleian Library, Oxford: *Randle Holme*; Public Archives, Canada: *Montreal*; Carlsberg Foundation: *Copenhagen*; Catalyst, The Museum of the Chemical Industry: *Halton*; Citroën: *motorcar factory*; CDEM: *Marseilles*; John Clark: *rivet, Sydney*; Kate Clark: *New South Wales*; P. Corbierre, Inventaire général: *helve hammer*; José M. Lopes Cordiero: *crane*; CPRE Collection, Institute of Agricultural History and Museum of English Rural Life, University of Reading: *Düsseldorf, photography*; Collection of Dr Jeff Cox: *gasworks, rolling mill, steel*; David Crossley: *excavation*; C. Decamps, Inventaire général: *public utility*; Simon Derry: *Banska Stiavnica, Príbram, Renaissance, Rožňava*; Deutsches Museum, Munich: *electric power, museum, steam locomotive*; Elton Collection, Ironbridge Gorge Museum: *iconography, international and national exhibitions, jigging, Menai Bridges, north-lit shed*; La Fonderie, Brussels: *Brussels*; P. Fortin, Inventaire général: *water power*; Piotr Gerber: *Maurzyce, Pelješac, Sielpia Wielka, Tarnowskie Gory*; Hagley Museum and Library, Pictorial Collections: *nylon*; Derek R. Hall: *Berat*; Historic American Engineering Record, National Park Service: *blast furnace, lighthouse, oil tanker, Pennsylvania, recording*; Hydro-Quebec: *Shawinigan*; Illustrated London News: *London*; Collection of l'Inventaire général, Paris: *Nantes*; Irish Distillers Ltd: *Midleton*; Ironbridge Gorge Museum Trust: *embankment, transfer of technology, water frame*; S. Januszewski: *Wieliczka*; Albert Kahn Associates: *motorcar factory*; Mihály Kubinsky: *Budapest*; Jet Lowe, HAER: *California, New York, Sault Ste Marie, Utah, viaduct*; M. Maumont, Inventaire général: *chocolate*; Craig Meredith: *Rio Tinto*; Ministère des Affaires Culturelles due Québec: *Bourlamaque*; National Board of Antiquities, Finland: *Kotka*; National Buildings Record, Royal Commission on the Historical Monuments of England: *Black Country*; National Monuments Record, Royal Commission on the Historical Monuments of England (Crown Copyright): *textile mill*; New Zealand Historic Places Trust: *time-ball station*; Novosti: *Moscow, Union of Soviet Socialist Republics*; Siem Pama: *garden city, Rotterdam*; J. M. Perin, Inventaire général: *Cevennes*; John Powell: *Ironbridge*; Private collection (Paris): *Paris*; Lauri Putkonen: *Pietarsaari*; Renault: *Paris*; E. Revault, CNMHS: *tobacco*; Royal Commission on Ancient and Historical Monuments in Wales: *aqueduct, hybrid railway, plateway*; Royal Commission on the Historical Monuments of England: *landscape, shoddy, textile mill*; Royal Commission on the Historical Monuments of England, Watkins Collection: *George Middleton Watkins*; Saarstahl GMBH: *Völklingen*; Science Museum, London: *lathe, museum*; Jørgen Sestoft: *Horsens, Mølleåen, Nivå*; Smithsonian Institution: *condensed milk, steam hammer*; Smithsonian Institution, Engineering Archives: *United States of America*; J. C. Stamm, Inventaire général: *Sedan*; Douglas Stoddart: *Oporto*; Michael Stratton: *Athens, ceramics, Colorado, Lávrion, Laxey, Rome, skyscraper, Trieste, Turin, Venice*; Sulzer Brothers Ltd, Winterthur: *diesel locomotive, rack railway*; Geoffrey Thornton, New Zealand Historic Places Trust: *Oturehua*; Hugh Torrens: *Leningrad*; Barrie Trinder: *adaptive reuse, airship, arcade, Basque country, Bilbao, boat lift, Boom, bridge, Chiemsee, Dannemora, Dublin, flourmill, forge, Forges du St Maurice, France, gasholder, Grand Canal, iron bridge, Klevfos, lime kiln, La Louvière, Lucerne, Luxembourg, Malakoff tower, Oslo, Parys Mountain, Pennines, Perthshire, phosphorus, port, power station, Quebec City, railway freight depot, Røros, Ruhrgebiet, Saint-Louis-Arzviller, Sentinel, Stoke-on-Trent, Sweden, Vienna, windmill, Wuppertal*; Ville de Chicoutimi, Caroline Bergeron: *Chicoutimi*; Robert M. Vogel, Smithsonian Institution: *Alabama, Ohio*; Mark Watson: *coal mining, Edinburgh, Glasgow, Istanbul*; E. G. Webb: *Western Australia*; Lyn Willies: *pyrites*; Michael Worthington: *Portugal*.

Abbreviations

Units

ac.	acre
amp	ampere
cm	centimetre
cu. ft.	cubic foot
cwt.	hundredweight
ft.	foot
ft.lb.	foot-pound
gall.	gallon
ha	hectare
hl	hectolitre
hp	horse power
in.	inch
km	kilometre
km/h	kilometre per hour
kW	kilowatt
l	litre
lb.	pound
lbf.	pound force
m	metre
m/s	metres per second
MW	megawatt
mi.	miles
m.p.h.	miles per hour
oz.	ounce
p.s.i.	pounds per square inch
rev./min.	revolutions per minute
s	second
sq. mi.	square mile
t	tonne
t.	ton
V	volt
yd.	yard

General

a.c.	alternating current
AEG	Allgemeine Elektricitäts-Gesellschaft
AIA	Association for Industrial Archaeology (Great Britain)
B & O	Baltimore & Ohio
BLS	Bern-Lötschberg-Simplon-Bahn
BPP	*British Parliamentary Papers*
C & O	Chesapeake and Ohio
CILAC	Comité d'information et de liaison pour l'Archéologie, l'étude et la mise en valeur du patrimoine industriel (Committee for information and liaison concerning the archaeology, study and value of the industrial heritage)
DB	Deutsche Bundesbahn
d.c.	direct current
DCL	Distillers Company Ltd.
DDR	Deutsches Demokratische Republik (German Democratic Republic)
DIEN	Dutch Industrial Heritage Documentation Centre
EcHR	*Economic History Review*
EEC	European Economic Community
EFTA	European Free Trade Association
ESPI	Education Service of the Plastics Industry (UK)
FS	Ferrovie dello Stato (Italian State Railways)
GCR	Great Central Railway
GER	Great Eastern Railway
GJR	Grand Junction Railway
GLIAS	Greater London Industrial Archaeology Society
GM	General Motors (United States of America)
GWR	Great Western Railway
HABS	Historic American Buildings Survey
HAER	Historic American Engineering Record
HB&M	Historic Buildings and Monuments (Scotland)
HMSO	Her Majesty's Stationery Office (United Kingdom)
IA	*Industrial Archeology* (journal of SIA)
IAR	*Industrial Archaeology Review*
ICCROM	International Centre for the Study of the Preservation and the Restoration of Cultural Property
ICOM	International Council of Museums
ICOMOS	International Council on Monuments and Sites
ICI	Imperial Chemical Industries (Great Britain)
ILN	*Illustrated London News*
IUPAC	International Union of Pure and Applied Chemistry
JRCHS	*Journal of the Railway and Canal Historical Society*
L&MR	Liverpool & Manchester Railway
LBSCR	London, Brighton & South Coast Railway
LMSR	London, Midland & Scottish Railway
LNER	London & North Eastern Railway
LNWR	London & North Western Railway
LYR	Lancashire & Yorkshire Railway
MV	motor vessel
nd	no date
NER	North Eastern Railway
NIRM	National Record of Industrial Monuments
NMAH	National Museum of American History

r	reigned
RCHME	Royal Commission on the Historical Monuments of England
RIBA	Royal Institute of British Architects
RN	Royal Navy
ROM	Royal Ontario Museum
RR	railroad
RRS	Royal Research Ship
S&DR	Stockton and Darlington Railway
SBB	Schweizerische Bundesbahn (Swiss Federal Railways)
SCB	Schweizerische Centralbahn (Swiss Central Railway)
SIA	Society for Industrial Archaeology (North America)
SIAI	Societa Italiana per l'Archaeologia Industriale (Italian Society for Industrial Archaeology)

SMC	Scottish Museums Council
SNCV	Société National de Chemins de Fer Vicinaux (Belgium)
TH	*Textile History*
T&C	*Technology and Culture*
TICCIH	The International Committee for the Conservation of the Industrial Heritage
TNS	*Transactions of the Newcomen Society*
UNESCO	United Nations Educational, Scientific and Cultural Organization
VVIA	Vlaamse Vereniging voor Industriële Archeologie (Flemish Association for Industrial Archaeology)
WIH	*World Industrial History*
WMS	*West Midland Studies*

Symbols used on Maps

Bold type indicates an article entry.

Flensburg town

Bremen large town

━ ▪ ━ ▪ national boundary

▪ ━ ▪ ▪ regional boundary

━┼━┼━ principal railway

━⊥⊥⊥⊥⊥ principal canal

)(passes

Introduction

Articles on places

This encyclopedia provides a guide to the monuments, settlements, landscapes and museums holding artefacts of the industrial societies which evolved in the West from the mid-eighteenth century. This material has been organized through the compilation of lists of headword subjects, chiefly regions, towns or sites, for each of the following countries:

Albania
Australia
Austria
Belgium
Bulgaria
Canada
Czechoslovakia
Denmark
England
Finland
Germany
Greece
Hungary
Iceland
Ireland
Italy
Netherlands
New Zealand
Norway
Poland
Portugal
Romania
Scotland
Spain
Sweden
Switzerland
Turkey
Union of Soviet Socialist Republics
United States of America
Wales
Yugoslavia

Most of the national sections have been compiled by or with the guidance of scholars from the countries concerned, and deal with sites within the political boundaries that existed until 1991. Contributors have enjoyed a degree of latitude in the way in which material is organized, whether in the form of relatively lengthy articles on provinces or geographical regions, as with the United States, or large numbers of short articles, as in Portugal, or combinations of the two approaches, as in Canada, England and Germany.

A list of headwords relating to each country appears after the appropriate national article. The maps which appear with the national articles provide in graphic form guides to the information on the countries concerned. They give locations for all the regions, cities, sites, physical features and transport systems which comprise separate entries, and they also indicate other important places and features mentioned in articles.

A national article identifies the country concerned in terms of its location and its history, specifying any significant changes in frontiers that have occurred since the mid-seventeenth century. It considers the country's manufacturing inheritance from the pre-industrial period, and defines significant periods of industrialization, drawing attention to the most characteristic features of the industrial archaeology of the country concerned, and to those aspects of it which are of international significance. The article also provides a review of conservation legislation, of museums, of official and voluntary bodies concerned with the conservation of the industrial heritage, and of maps and other sources of value in the investigation of industrial history.

National contributions reflect varying approaches to the discipline in different countries, and in particular the extent to which the subject of Industrial Archaeology has been moulded by its relationship with other fields of study. The influence of the history of technology is perhaps particularly evident in the United States entries, that of the history of architecture in those for Finland, that of social and economic history in the English section. Other differences can be observed between those countries where conservation of the remains of industrial enterprises is conceived primarily in terms of sites, or of finding new uses for redundant buildings, and those where it is seen as a study of landscapes or regions.

National sections inevitably reflect the state of industrial archaeological scholarship in the countries concerned, and the extent to which it has been possible to gain information about such scholarship at an academic institution in the English Midlands. Most of the world's industrial regions have not been surveyed with the thoroughness reflected in the inventories compiled by HAER in some parts of the United States, nor with the attention to detail shown in articles like those on Glasgow or Rotterdam. An element of preferential weighting has been given to areas on which the current literature in English is sparse at the expense of some which are already well-documented. An attempt has been made to provide some information on the industrial heritage in those countries, like the former Yugoslavia, where industrial archaeology is scarcely recognized. It was particularly difficult during the period when the encyclopedia was being compiled to gain information about current scholarship in the then USSR and in Albania.

In addition to the articles organized on a national basis there are single articles on the following small countries and dependent territories:

Channel Islands   Isle of Man
Cyprus   Luxembourg
Gibraltar   Malta

Articles relating to sites begin with references to the country concerned, and usually to the county, department, region, province or state in which the site is located. Some articles on border towns like Rheinfelden or Sault Ste Marie make reference to features in more than one country, as do articles on rivers such as the Rhine and the Moselle.

Articles on technology

As a secondary element, the encyclopedia provides definitions for the terms used in entries relating to countries, regions, towns or sites. These entries have been conceived in eighteen subject groups, relating principally to various branches of industrial technology and to aspects of industrial archaeology. As far as possible technical terms relating to processes have been standardized. The contents of the eighteen groups are detailed in the appendix. The main areas are as follows:

1. Transport
2. Civil Engineering
3. Mechanical Engineering
4. Extractive Industries
5. Coal
6. Iron and Steel
7. Manufacturing Industries
8. Textiles
9. Energy and Power
10. Communications
11. Service Industries
12. Industrial Communities
13. Chemicals
14. Public Utilities
15. Architecture
16. Sources
17. Interpretation
18. Theory

Biographical articles

To provide a framework of reference for the remainder of the encyclopedia there are a number of biographical entries which identify those people who are mentioned frequently in the various articles. No attempt has been made to give comprehensive coverage of every individual of comparable importance in the history of industry or technology. The biographies cover only those aspects of the lives of the individuals concerned which are relevant to this encyclopedia. Factors which have determined the selection of biographical entries include the widespread use of the name of an individual to refer to a process or

product, as with William Brunton or Leo Hendrik Baekeland; the involvement of an individual with many industries, as with Bryan Donkin, Sir William Siemens or Frederick Winslow Taylor; or where there are possibilities of confusion of individuals with kinsmen, as with Sir John Rennie; or with persons with similar names, as with Robert Stephenson and Robert Stevenson.

Some biographical entries refer to individuals who have made significant contributions to the development of the discipline of Industrial Archaeology. Some living persons are included, but as a matter of policy there are no entries within this field for editors or contributors.

CONTEXTS

The scope of the encyclopedia

The scope of industrial archaeology has been debated at length. The stance of the editors, detailed in the entry on industrial archaeology, is that the core of the discipline is the study of the physical remains of the large-scale mining, manufacturing and service enterprises that had their origins in the British Industrial Revolution of the eighteenth century, but that industrial archaeological studies extend further in time, in geographical coverage and in the extent of their overlap with other disciplines. The encyclopedia deals principally with what can be seen – standing buildings, landscapes and artefacts – and with what can be learned about the industrial past from studying them. The decisions on the scope of the encyclopedia have been pragmatic rather than philosophical judgements, determined by an evaluation of what has been editorially practical in the late 1980s and early 1990s.

Limits in time

The technological and historical coverage of the encyclopedia concentrates on the period from 1650 to 1950, which makes it possible to give adequate coverage to those pre-industrial manufactures which provide a context for the Industrial Revolution. The mid-seventeenth century is also a logical starting date from the viewpoint of the political historian, being the time of the political and financial revolutions in England, and of the conclusion of the Thirty Years War in continental Europe. The time span of the encyclopedia ends in 1950 when much of the economic structure created during the classic period of industrialization in Europe and North America was still in place, when most steel was made by processes which originated in the late nineteenth century, most railways were worked by steam power, intercontinental travel was largely by steamship, and textile manufactures still flourished in areas like Lancashire, New England, the Zürcher Oberland and Flanders. The jet engine had yet to be applied to commercial air transport; the computer was in its early infancy. Even in the most developed countries there still were communities which awaited electrification. Authorities responsible for the conservation and recording of historic monuments recognize the significance of this date. In France the national survey of the industrial heritage has a cut-off date of 1950, while in Britain the structures of the 1950s are beginning to be accorded recognition through listing. The time span 1650–1950 is not applied inflexibly, so that, for example, the medieval or earlier origins of Europe's principal non-ferrous mining regions are appropriately recognized.

Geographical limits

The encyclopedia is concerned with Europe, Canada, the United States and Australasia. There have been as yet no convincing attempts to align the approach of the western industrial archaeologist with studies of the development of manufacturing technologies in Asia, pre-colonial Australasia, Africa or Latin America. It would be valuable to be able to study the characteristic industrial structures of colonial regimes, mining settlements in Africa or railway termini in India, but there is, as yet, an inadequate foundation of secondary studies to make this possible. Nevertheless reference is made where appropriate to sites beyond the encyclopedia's geographical limits, for example, to some locations of historic ships, and to some museums holding historic aircraft.

Subject limits

It can be argued that industrial archaeology is the study of the physical remains of *all* aspects of the history of the industrial societies of recent centuries, and this view would be upheld by many of the contributors to this work. Nevertheless in practice there are certain areas of study which, following established practice, are left to other specialists, and not discussed in detail in this encyclopedia. Three are of particular concern.

The study of *polite architecture* – the design of public buildings, places of worship and large private dwellings – is by convention the province of the architectural historian. No attempt has been made in this volume to give comprehensive coverage to these aspects of architectural history. Industrial architecture is given specific consideration, architectural terms used in the encyclopedia are defined, and due attention is given to industrialized constructional techniques and to some dwellings built by entrepreneurs, like the Villa Hugel or Cragside. The significance of some classes of public buildings is considered in service industries (see section 11 in the appendix).

Installations and equipment relating to *armed forces* – the province of the military historian – are not described in detail, although it is impossible to consider the development of ships or aircraft without reference to examples built for wartime use, and the best monuments of shipbuilding throughout the world are in naval establishments. Military artefacts are regarded primarily as products of a branch of mechanical engineering (see armaments). No attempt has been made to cover fortifications or related structures, except in relation to air transport, where civil airports and military air bases have common components.

Nor does the encyclopedia discuss in detail the development of *agriculture*, although attention is drawn to some collections of agricultural machinery, regarded here primarily as products of a branch of mechanical engineering; to the production of fertilizers – part of the chemical industry; and to the processing of various foodstuffs, which is regarded as a branch of manufacturing industry.

Museums

The limits of industrial archaeology are particularly significant in considering museums. One objective of the encyclopedia is to draw attention to museums which have collections of importance in the study of industrial archaeology. Such museums range from large, often national institutions, of which some may not be primarily industrial museums, to small museums dealing with such specialized subjects as brushes, dredging or matches. Not every museum of social or local history is included, although some of no particular note are mentioned to provide points of reference in communities in which there are features of interest to industrial archaeologists. Military and agricultural museums, for reasons explained above, are mentioned only if there are specific reasons why industrial archaeologists should be interested in their collections. There are many museums of motor cars. Only the most significant have been mentioned, and no attempt has been made to include the many museums of firefighting equipment and postage stamps. Some museums whose collections have no relation to industrial archaeology are mentioned because they are located in adapted industrial buildings.

Chronological context

Industrial Archaeology is a relatively young discipline. The impetus for international co-operation within the discipline which has made possible this encyclopedia has derived from the series of conferences which began at Ironbridge in 1973, from which the TICCIH organization subsequently evolved. The generation chiefly represented at the conference, most of whom grew up during World War II or were products of the post-war baby boom, has been responsible for the majority of the articles. Most have experience, if only as childhood memories, of the technological processes with which this book is concerned, and have seen them transformed into subjects for museums. Most have become industrial archaeologists by chance, having academic qualifications in other subjects and practising the discipline within curatorial or teaching posts. Some contributors are drawn from the first generation of professional industrial archaeologists, now mostly entering their thirties, some of whom have specific qualifications in industrial archaeology. The contributors are from varied professions: museum curators, conservation architects, heritage consultants, university and polytechnic lecturers, those involved in the recording of industrial monuments, those concerned with securing legislative protection for the industrial heritage, and people working in such industries as mining, mechanical engineering and printing. Academic backgrounds are equally varied. Contributors include people holding degrees in Archaeology, Architecture, Chemistry, Engineering, Ethnography, Geography and History.

The encyclopedia is, like any reference work, a child of its time. Consideration of the project began during the summer of 1984. The first articles were written in 1986, the majority in 1988 and 1989, the last in 1990. Since it was planned, attitudes to the long term significance of industrialization within world history have changed. It is more difficult now than it was in 1984 to see the growth of mining and manufacturing since the eighteenth century as wholly beneficial developments. Ambitious schemes, like the James Bay project of Hydro Québec, now tend to be discussed as much in terms of the environmental harm which they may cause as in terms of their potential economic and social benefits. The national frameworks within which the articles on places in Eastern Europe were planned have changed since 1989. Germany has been unified, but the legacies of the two former regimes are still significant when considering the industrial heritage, and some outdated references, for example, to West Berlin, have been retained for the sake of clarity. The Union of Soviet Socialist Republics has ceased to exist while the encyclopedia has been in the final stages of production. The articles have been left unaltered, since it is unlikely that there will be substantial changes at the sites discussed in the immediate future. Other East European articles have been updated as much as possible.

Elsewhere it has been difficult to keep up to date with the pace of economic change. The earlier articles have been updated where possible, but the industrial landscape is constantly changing. The editors of this volume are not endowed with prophetic gifts, and, regrettably, it is certain that by the time this work comes into use, some significant structures mentioned here will have been demolished, some sites described may by now have been conserved, others will have been destroyed, while some, not mentioned here, may have been newly recognized as significant.

CONVENTIONS

Usages

Usages in *The Times Atlas of the World* (London, 7th edn, 1985, rev. 1988) have been followed for the spellings of place names except where there are universally accepted English names which differ from those used locally (e.g. Munich, Prague). Cross references are provided to the current name or names used in the countries concerned, and to any other forms (e.g. Aix-la-Chapelle, Breslau, Danzig, Karl Marxstadt) which may be current in historical literature. Place names are not anglicized when they occur in the titles of books or organizations, e.g. *Københavns møller* or *La Société du Port de Montréal*.

Various standard terms have been applied to physical features mentioned in the text, including fjord and lake. These terms are always used, except in the quotation of such proper names as Lough Neagh.

The word 'wagon' is used to indicate railway vehicles. Four-wheeled, animal-drawn, freight-carrying vehicles using roads are referred to as 'waggons'.

The terms 'World War I' and 'World War II' are used in a conventional West European sense to refer to the conflicts which took place from 1914–18 and from 1939–45, although it is acknowledged that for the United States, the USSR and some other countries these conflicts had different limits.

Chemical symbols and formulae are quoted where there are possibilities of ambiguity in the identification of elements or compounds, and the conventional Latin names are provided for the less common species of animals and plants.

References to individuals of significance in industrial history or industrial archaeology usually include their dates, although it has not been possible to identify in this way every architect mentioned, nor, indeed, some relatively obscure inventors. Titled persons are identified as far as possible in terms which are unambiguous. For the sake of brevity some individuals may be described by their titles even if the reference is to a period before the title was bestowed or inherited.

Attribution of articles

The signatures of authors who have co-ordinated the entries on particular countries appear below the appropriate national articles, and similarly for those responsible for the eighteen areas relating to technology and industrial archaeology with the principal articles of the sections concerned. Authors' names are given for most articles in excess of 150 words. Shorter articles will usually have been written by the co-ordinating author for the country or section concerned, or by the general editor.

When an article is followed by more than one signature, two or three individuals have made significant, but not necessarily equal, contributions to it. There are two major articles where the division of labour requires further explanation. The article on France was written by Jean-François Belhoste, except for the short sections on the tobacco and match industries which were written by Paul Smith. The article on Paris was written by Paul Smith, but the section on the city's museums is the work of Jean-François Belhoste.

Alphabetization systems

The Times Atlas of the World has been followed in the transliteration of place names in Albanian, Bulgarian, Greek, Russian, Serbo-Croat and Turkish.

French, Belgian, Québecois and Swiss place names beginning with 'Saint' or 'Sainte' are alphabetized as such. Spanish, Portuguese and Italian place names beginning with the abbreviation 'S' are treated for purposes of alphabetization as the English word 'saint'.

The definite article in place names in English (The Hague, The Lake District) is ignored for purposes of alphabetization.

German and Dutch names beginning with 'von' or 'van' are alphabetized under the word which follows, unless established usage dictates otherwise.

The Scots or Irish prefixes 'Mac', 'Mc' and 'M' are treated for purposes of alphabetization as if they were spelt out 'Mac'.

For purposes of alphabetization all accented letters are

treated as English unaccented letters. The Scandinavian letters æ, Ý and å are treated as the English ae, o and a. The Polish ę, ł and ǫ are treated as the English e, l and o.

Anglo-American vocabulary

In as far as this encyclopedia is a dictionary, it is an English dictionary, and subtleties of meaning applied to such terms as 'warehouse' and 'gallery' apply principally to English usage. Notable differences of English and American usage, as with 'car', 'railroad' or 'truck', are explained under the appropriate headwords, and explanations are provided for some terms like 'hydraulic' and 'sluice' which give rise to particular problems in translations from continental European languages into English.

Reference to 'state' support of a venture will normally mean support by the government of one of the 50 states which form the United States of America, or to one of the states of Australia or of other countries with similar systems of government. Financial support from public authorities as distinct from private organizations will be described as 'government' support if a distinction between national, regional or local government is immaterial, or as 'national government support' when referring to most countries, or 'federal' support if referring to the United States or Australia.

Translations

Titles of books and the names of museums are usually given in the original languages, in a romanized form if the original language is cyrillic, but an English translation usually appears in parentheses. In a few cases where the meaning is obvious the translation may be omitted.

Cross references

The cross-referencing system is easily followed. Cross-references are indicated by the use of small capitals, with a large capital for the initial letter of the entry referred to, for example: GEORGE WESTINGHOUSE. Most cross-references give the title of the article referred to in the wording in which it appears in bold type (excluding such parenthesized matter as dates, titles or countries) at the head of the entry, although in some cases the word may be in a slightly different form (e.g. in the plural) where this is grammatically necessary. The terms see or See also also cross refer to other entries in the encyclopedia.

An article about a place where there are remains of a relatively rare technology, a Catalan forge, for example, will cross refer to CATALAN FORGE, but many references to relatively common industrial archaeological features, railway stations, blast furnaces or textile mills, do not merit cross referencing.

Dates and measurements

All dates quoted are in New Style following the Gregorian calendar as adopted in Great Britain from 1752, and in other countries at different dates, as late as 1917 in Russia. Absolute consistency cannot be guaranteed for seventeenth and eighteenth century dates in some coun-tries, but since dates are usually quoted only to the nearest year this is unlikely to lead to significant errors.

Metric measurements are usually quoted, with the imperial equivalent in brackets. In a few cases where the imperial measurement concerned is widely known and quoted, as with some railway gauges, the order may be reversed, and occasionally where an imprecise measurement is quoted the equivalent may be omitted.

When measurements are quoted in metric tonnes or imperial tons equivalents are not normally given, since the variation is slight. Precise historical figures are quoted in imperial if an original measurement would have been in imperial, as in the displacement of a ship, the output of a furnace or the capacity of a vehicle. Estimates by historians of output in the past are usually quoted in metric.

The following equivalents have been used:

1 inch	2.54 centimetres
1 foot	30.8 centimetres
1 yard	0.9144 metres
1 mile	1.609 kilometres
1 acre	0.4047 hectares
1 square mile	259.0 hectares
1 cubic foot	0.0283 cubic metres
1 cubic yard	0.7646 cubic metres
1 gallon	4.4546 litres
1 ounce	28.35 grammes
1 pound	0.4536 kilogrammes
1 hundredweight	50.802 kilogrammes
1 ton	1.016 tonnes
1 millimetre	0.0394 inches
1 centimetre	0.3937 inches
1 metre	1.0936 yards
1 kilometre	0.6214 miles
1 hectare	2.4748 acres
1 square kilometre	0.3861 square miles
1 cubic metre	1.3080 cubic yards
1 litre	0.2200 gallons
1 gramme	0.0353 ounces
1 kilogramme	2.2046 pounds
1 tonne	0.9842 tons

Locomotive wheel arrangements are described according to British and American conventions rather than those used in continental Europe. For details see electric locomotive, steam locomotive. Conventions relating to ships' tonnages are described under sea transport.

Superlatives

An indication in the text that a structure or machine is the first or largest of its kind indicates that it is so to the best of the editors' knowledge. A claim which is historic but demonstrably wrong, for example, the first iron bridge, will normally be qualified within the text. Some superlatives (e.g. the first mousetrap factory to be adapted as apartments) are not capable of verification, and may be quoted simply because they give a valid impression of a particular site.

Architectural vocabulary

Architectural terms employed in the encyclopedia are defined in short articles listed in section 15 of the appendix. As far as possible the use of such terms is standardized within the text.

Bibliography

The bibliography comprises a single alphabetical list of all works referred to in the text which are of significance in the study of industrial archaeology, and which have been used in the compilation of this encyclopedia. Many are primarily concerned with disciplines other than industrial archaeology, but provide significant information on the subjects concerned. The bibliography is not intended to be comprehensive, particularly with respect to countries where the industrial archaeological literature is already extensive. No attempt has been made, for example, to list all the general or regional surveys of industrial archaeological sites in Britain; reference is made only to those which have been utilized in preparing the encyclopedia, and those which are of particular significance in the development of the discipline.

Books in the bibliography which relate to a particular article are listed in abbreviated form under the heading *Bibliography: General* after the article concerned. Pamphlets, articles, trail guides and similar publications which relate to a particular article are listed under the heading *Bibliography: Specific* following the article concerned, and are not included in the bibliography.

The bibliography has been updated to include some publications which have appeared in the first half of 1991. The inclusion of a recent publication in the list of books relating to an article does not necessarily mean that the article takes account of its conclusions.

Locations

Locations of places mentioned in site articles, normally distances from the place which is the subject of the headword, are usually quoted. The reference is to the approximate distance from the headword place unless otherwise indicated. If no distance is quoted, it may be assumed that the place mentioned is an integral part of the town or area being described, and that the provision of precise distances is impracticable – as in Ironbridge.

As far as possible addresses are listed for all sites [S], museums [M] and sources of information [I] mentioned in articles. The addresses quoted are for correspondence, and in a few cases are at different locations from the sites for which the institutions concerned may be responsible.

The opening hours of museums and conserved sites may be seasonal, and some may be accessible only by appointment. Even great national museums may be closed on certain days of the week. Since this is an encyclopedic dictionary and not a directory or gazetteer no attempt has been made to provide consistent information about opening hours, and readers intending to visit sites should obtain up-to-date information from the addresses provided.

Where operating industrial premises are mentioned the text will normally make it clear whether there are facilities for the public, although there may well be significant structures which can be seen without gaining access. In areas like Stoke-on-Trent many factories are open to the public but arrangements change frequently, and up-to-date information should be obtained from tourist offices or similar sources.

A

Aachen (Aix-la-Chapelle), North Rhine-Westphalia, Germany   Even before Roman times, the hot saline springs of Aachen were in use, and they remain important features today. There are over sixty springs, and with a temperature of 70°C they are among the hottest in Europe. The neo-Classical Elisenbrunnen building is the centre of the city's spa facilities.

Since the Middle Ages Aachen has had a large woollen manufacturing industry, stimulated by local sheep-rearing and plentiful water supplies. The manufacture of brass, deriving from the presence of zinc in the vicinity (see below), led to needle manufacturing, which declined after the expulsion of Protestant manufacturers in the seventeenth century. In the nineteenth century industry was stimulated by coal mining and by the building of the railway from Cologne to Aachen in 1841. Many nineteenth-century textile factories in the city have been preserved, including those of Marx & Auerbach, of 1861, and Kelleter, of 1810. In 1817 there were forty textile factories and eleven making needles and cards.

The centre of coal mining in the nineteenth century lay 20 km (12 mi.) to the north in the Würm area around the towns of Wurselen, Herzogenrath and Alsdorf. Coal was also mined in the Inde area around Eschweiler, 14 km (9 mi.) E. Pithead buildings of c.1820 remain in Kohlscheid and Herzogenrath; as well as a twin headstock at the Anna pit, Alsdorf, 14 km (9 mi.) N. of Aachen, which has steam winding engines and an electrically-operated hoist of 1907, with a museum. The engine house for a Newcomen pumping engine of 1793 remains at Eschweiler.

Stolberg, 10 km (6 mi.) E., has been a centre of brass manufacturing since the seventeenth century. In 1648 almost 20000 'zentner' (approximately 1000 tonnes) per annum was being made in sixty-five furnaces, using copper from Scandinavia and eastern Germany, and the local zinc ore. Many 'copper yards' (Kupferhöfe) remain: they are castle-like complexes with dwellings, furnaces and buildings used for manufacturing, laid out around central courtyards. Some furnaces are preserved in Stolberg-Atsch (*see* VIEILLE MONTAGNE).

In the rural area south of Aachen, in Aachen-Hahn, Aachen-Schmidt and Kornelimünster, many rubble masonry kilns bear witness to the former importance of lime-burning.

Industrial art is featured in the Burg Frankenberg Museum in Aachen, and there is an important museum of newspapers in the city.

BIBLIOGRAPHY
General
Dahmen, 1930; Fehl *et al.*, 1991; Fischer, 1949; Hansmann and Zahn, 1971; Petri, 1979; Salber, 1987; Schunder, 1968; Voppel, 1965.
Specific
Schumacher, M. Zweckbau und Industrieschloss. Fabrikbauten der Rheinisch-Westfälischen Textilindustrie vor der Gründungzeit (Functional buildings and industrial castles: factory buildings of pre-industrial textile manufactures in the Rhineland and Westphalia). In *Tradition: Zeitschrift für Firmengeschichte und Unternehmerbiographie* (Tradition: papers in business history and biography). xv. Stuttgart, 1970.

LOCATIONS
[M] Burg Frankenberg Museum, Bismarckstrasse 68, 5100 Aachen.
[M] Internationales Zeitungsmuseum der Stadt Aachen (International Museum of Newspapers of the City of Aachen), Pontstrasse 13, 5100 Aachen.

AXEL FÖHL

Aalst (Alost), Oost Vlaanderen, Belgium   A market town on the River Dender, 31 km (19 mi.) NW of Brussels, celebrated for its hop market, its maltings and its breweries; and for its railway station by P. J. Cluysenaer, built in 1851–6, in brick with a crenellated four-storey tower, arcaded front with segmental brick arches springing from stone columns, and decorative medallions above the capitals. One of the last passementerie workshops in Flanders is on J. Ringoirkaai. A locomotive preservation society, whose collection includes Belgian tramway locomotives and a Prussian P8 4–6–0, is based in Aalst; and the Reisclub Étappe operates trips in two traditional barges.

BIBLIOGRAPHY
General
Linters, 1985, 1986a, 1986b; Viaene, 1986.

LOCATIONS
[I] Belgische Vrienden van de Stoomlokomotief (Belgian Friends of Steam Locomotives), Ten Berg 101, 9300 Aalst.
[M] Museum Oud Hospitaal, Sint-Martensplein, 9300 Aalst.
[I] Reisclub Étappe, H. Hartlaan 30, 9300 Aalst.

abattoir   A slaughterhouse for cattle, to which anyone can take beasts to be killed, whether or not it is publicly owned. In England the Public Health Amendment Act 1890 obliged local authorities to inspect slaughterhouses and encouraged them to set up municipal abattoirs. Such establishments were set up in many European cities in the nineteenth century, but changes in health legislation have rendered them obsolete, and some have been adapted to new uses as exhibition halls and offices (*see* GENEVA; GRAZ; LYONS).

BIBLIOGRAPHY
General
Winstanley, 1983.

Abbaretz, Loire-Atlantique, France   The blast furnace at La Jahotière ironworks, 30 km (18 mi.) NE of Nantes, was built in 1827 by Achille de Jouffroy d'Abbans, son of one of the inventors of steam navigation. It was one of the first blast furnaces in France in which coke was used, its promoter having visited England and brought back skilled workers from Staffordshire. The complex was intended to incorporate an English-type forge, but only the blast furnace was actually built. It remained in operation, not without difficulty, until 1850.

The furnace stack still stands some 14 m (46 ft.) high, with remnants of its gas-recovery system, and its blowing engine house with its chimney stack. The former coke stores have been adapted as workers' housing. The architectural style of the surrounding storehouses and agricultural buildings is notable for its polychrome decoration.

This modern ironworks was heir to a Breton ironmaking tradition, which was particularly prosperous in the seventeenth and eighteenth centuries. From 1620 about fifteen ironworks, mostly located on large seigneurial estates, were built in the region, usually incorporating a blast furnace, a finery-and-chafery forge and a slitting mill. Many remnants of these works survive, some with nineteenth-century additions. At Paimpont are two blast furnaces with a slitting mill building and the ruins of an English-type forge set up in the 1820s. At Salles-de-Rohan, Perret, are a blast furnace and a forge building with its finery chimney. There are blast furnaces at La Nouée and La Poitevinière, and a finery forge chimney at La Hunaudière, Sion. At Moisdon-la-Rivière the charcoal store houses a permanent exhibition on these ironworks of the Châteaubriant region. Most retain the former ironmasters' mansions and workers' housing, and several, including La Jahotière, are now protected historic monuments.

BIBLIOGRAPHY
General
Andrieux, 1987; Belhoste *et al.* 1984.

JEAN-FRANÇOIS BELHOSTE

Abbeville, Somme, France   Josse Van Robais, a cloth manufacturer from Middelburg in the Netherlands, came to France to begin making cloth at Abbeville in 1686 when the exclusive privileges hitherto held by the Dijonval manufactory at SEDAN came to an end. The choice of Abbeville was probably related to its location near the mouth of the Somme, where it was easily accessible for the merino wools imported from Spain that were essential for the production of high-quality broadcloth.

Manufacturing activity was at first scattered throughout the town. A site some way out of Abbeville was also used, a Dutch-type wind-powered fulling mill being installed. Subsequently the manufacturing processes were concentrated in a single factory on the banks of the Somme, erected between 1710 and 1712 by Josse Van Robais II, son of the founder. The building was designed to house all the essential stages in the production of fine broadcloth, from the washing and dyeing of the wools to the finishing operations of napping and shearing. Only spinning continued to be done outside the new buildings in several houses in the town, whilst cloth was fulled at a water-powered mill at Ansennes on the River Bresle, 25 km (15 mi.) S. of Abbeville, which had replaced the old windmill towards the end of the seventeenth century.

Behind the main building of the manufactory a field about 100 m (110 yd.) long ran down to the Somme. Here there were six lines of TENTER FRAMES (*rames*) on which the cloth was left to dry. It was from this spectacular sight that the concern gained its name, the 'Rames Manufacture'.

The Van Robais continued the manufacture until 1810 when it was bought by the Grandins from Elbeuf. In 1855 it was purchased by J. Vayson who restored the building and installed power looms for carpet-weaving. During the twentieth century the building has been used mainly for storage. It now belongs to the town and is a protected monument.

The factory, which was erected around 1710, was probably much modified *c.*1740. There are four main buildings, a large central block with two long side wings, 70 m and 84 m (230 ft. and 275 ft.) long, forming a courtyard which is closed off from the Chaussée d'Hocquet by a monumental porch. Most of the weaving and finishing operations were concentrated in these buildings. On either side of them were two other groups of buildings: stables, storehouses, a repair workshop and a pigeon tower on one side, and dwellings and shops for drying the warp on the other. A steam engine was installed there during the nineteenth century. The fourth main building, on the river bank, housed the shops for scouring and dyeing the wool.

Today the buildings around the courtyard are more or less intact: the stone entrance with its two little shelters for the gatekeepers; the central building of three storeys with a clerestory, in brick, with a projecting part in stone; the two long, brick workshop buildings, their timber frames still in place, their roofs slightly modified to accommodate another floor. At the centre of the complex to the west some outbuildings have been demolished, but the old pigeon tower has been restored.

BIBLIOGRAPHY
General
Courtecuisse, 1920.
Specific
Belhoste, J.-F. Les Manufactures de drap fin en France au XVIIᵉ et XVIIIᵉ siècles (Broadcloth manufactures in France during the seventeenth and eighteenth centuries). In *Revue de l'Art*, LXV, 1984.

Chaplain, J.-M. Avoir ce qui manque aux autres; la manufacture de draps fins Van Robais d'Abbeville au XVIIIè siècle face au milieu local (To have what others lack; the Van Robais broadcloth manufacture at Abbeville during the eighteenth century and the local environment). In *Mouvement Social*, cxxv, 1983.

JEAN-FRANÇOIS BELHOSTE

Aberdeen, Grampian, Scotland   The 'Granite City' owes its crisp appearance to the quarries in and around the city and to building regulations that required almost every building, including Art Deco cinemas, to be granite-clad. Berryden Woollen Mills, now a business centre, has both nineteenth-century weaving sheds and a reinforced-concrete range of 1950 clad in granite. Three granite quarries remain open.

Aberdeen harbour, formed by the diversion of the River Dee, was developed by JOHN SMEATON and THOMAS TELFORD. Victoria Wet Dock dates from 1840–8, and Albert Basin, otherwise the Fish Dock, from 1870. Girdleness Lighthouse, by ROBERT STEVENSON, of 1833, has lanterns at two stages. The Dee is spanned by the Wellington flat-link chain suspension bridge of 1829–31 by Sir Samuel Brown (1776–1852). Several warehouses and fish-curing houses remain. Aberdeen shipbuilders built fast barques, schooners and tea clippers. The Hall Russell company was formed in 1868 by the amalgamation of two existing firms; the yard now makes oil-support and fishery-protection vessels. The engine works has a steel frame slotted into older granite walls, and contains some line shafting and hand-operated jib cranes, together with a three-storey smithy with corner chimney, and a later boiler shop with thermal window, similarly steel-framed. Aberdeen Maritime Museum covers shipbuilding, fishing and the oil industry.

William McKinnon and Co.'s Spring Garden Iron Works, founded in 1789, still functions as a foundry and little-altered engineering complex. Products include granite-polishing machinery and sugar- and bone-crushing machinery. Parts are of considerable antiquity, altered in the mid-nineteenth century to receive cast-iron stanchions, travelling cranes and timber roofs.

In the early nineteenth century Aberdeen had flax mills of a scale unparalleled outside Leeds. The principal survivor is Broadford Works, now spinning acrylic yarns. It was founded in 1808 by Scott Brown and Co., and sold in 1811 to Maberly and Co., now Richards plc. Gas lighting was installed in 1815 and power looms in 1824, making it the first long-lived linen power loom factory. The complex includes Scotland's oldest iron-framed building, a four-storey mill, with cruciform columns built in 1808, extended with cylindrical columns c.1820–30, and again c.1864. Single brick-arched construction persisted until 1913–14 in the new spinning mill, a brick-clad building, rare for Aberdeen. At the same time reinforced concrete was used to frame two other brick-clad buildings, the weaving mill and the crenellated flax store of 1911–12.

Grandholm works is a water-powered flax-spinning mill built in 1793–4, with cast-iron columns, beams and joists, carrying flagstone floors, possibly inserted c.1812. It was converted to woollen spinning by J. & J. Crombie and is now the biggest integrated woollen mill in Scotland, with weaving sheds of 1877–1931, and spinning sheds built in 1900 and 1919. Mules and non-continuous cards are still used, and there is a water turbine of 1938. There is a small works museum.

The woollen mill at Garlogie, 16 km (10 mi.) W., was demolished in 1934, but its single-cylinder beam engine of the 1830s has miraculously survived, together with a Francis turbine.

At Inverurie, 24 km (15 mi.) NW, the papermill founded in the 1850s is dominated by a square 29 m (92 ft.) tower producing acid for boiling wood chips, erected c.1890 when pulp was beginning to displace rags in paper-making. The buildings of the Great North of Scotland Railway's locomotive and carriage works of c.1900 are now in multiple use.

Peterhead, 45 km (28 mi.) NE of Aberdeen, and Fraserburgh, 60 km (39 mi.) N. of Aberdeen, have been major fishing ports since the herring steam-trawler boom of the 1880s.

Cruden Bay brick and tile works of 1902, 11 km (7 mi.) S. of Peterhead, the most northerly in Britain, remains in use. The Oatmeal Mill at Sandhaven, 3 km (2 mi.) W. of Fraserburgh, is being restored to work by water power. At Cults, 6 km (4 mi.) SW of Aberdeen, the St Devenick footbridge, now disused, is a suspension bridge of 1837 with single chains and Doric cast-iron pylons. At Methlick, 32 km (24 mi.) NW of Aberdeen, are an arched iron bridge of 1844 and a cast-iron girder bridge of 1864.

BIBLIOGRAPHY
General
Hay and Stell, 1986; Hume, 1977.

LOCATION
[M] Aberdeen Maritime Museum, c/o Aberdeen Art Gallery, Schoolhill, Aberdeen AB9 1FQ.

MARK WATSON

Aberystwyth, Dyfed, Wales   The chief distribution centre from the sixteenth to the nineteenth centuries for the Mid Wales lead field, one of the most productive in Britain. Hundreds of mines worked in Aberystwyth's hinterland, and many, such as Frongoch, Bryndyfi and Cwmystwyth, have left adits and shafts, hushing dams, leats and reservoirs, processing plant and spoil heaps. One mine, Bryntail, 36 km (23 mi.) E., is preserved by the state; another, Llywernog, 19 km (12 mi.) E., as a museum. Most ore was carried by road to Aberystwyth and shipped to coalfields. Local foundries supplied equipment to the mines. Aberystwyth was a resort from the late eighteenth century, but expanded after the arrival of the Cambrian Railway in 1864, with hotels, a pier, a cliff railway, and the Vale of Rheidol railway with its 59.7 cm (1 ft. $11\frac{1}{2}$ in.) gauge, built in 1902 for both mineral and tourist traffic.

BIBLIOGRAPHY
General
Lewis, 1967; Rees, 1975.

Specific
Lewis, W. J. *Born on a Perilous Rock: Aberystwyth past and present.* Aberystwyth: Cambrian News, 1980.

LOCATION
[M, S] Llywernog Silver-Lead Mine, Ponterwyd, Aberystwyth, Dyfed SY23 3AB.

accommodation bridge A bridge, not intended for public use, that meets the needs of occupiers of land on either side of a canal, railway or other means of transport. Accommodation bridges often reflect the house styles of the companies that built them.

accounts Accounts are one of the principal forms of BUSINESS RECORDS used by industrial archaeologists. The development of new means of accounting was one of the chief features of the revolution in management of manufacturing concerns which began in eighteenth-century England. Accounting literature before the nineteenth century was concerned with the systems of 'master and steward' accounting which had evolved on landed estates, mercantile systems used chiefly in export trading, and systems developed by clothiers and other entrepreneurs concerned with domestic industry. None related closely to the needs of manufacturers and there gradually developed systems where there were regular, comparable periodic returns, means of detecting error or fraud, distinctions between capital and revenue expenditure and between interest on investment and profits, and means of costing which could form the basis of management decisions. Nineteenth-century handbooks on accounting and business practice, with such titles as *The Young Merchant's Guide*, are often helpful to historians working on business records.

Accounts surviving from nineteenth-century or earlier undertakings are likely to include some in which transactions are entered in the order in which they occur, often with sales and purchases recorded separately; these are called journals, day books, waste books or cash books. A ledger, essentially a book that remains in the same place, is the principal account book in which all creditor and debtor accounts are set down.

BIBLIOGRAPHY
General
Larson, 1948; Pollard, 1965.

BARRIE TRINDER

accumulator A word with two meanings in industrial archaeology:

1. A means of providing constant pressure in a hydraulic power system and of storing the energy of the system. It was developed by WILLIAM ARMSTRONG in 1851, and superseded the gravity hydraulic power reservoir. A ram or piston in a cylinder compresses the fluid in the hydraulic system. On top of the ram a yoke carries ballasted bins to create an artificial head of water. Control chains on the bins actuate pumps to maintain the head. Accumulator houses, often crenellated, survive in many ports.
2. A type of electric battery.

BIBLIOGRAPHY
General
McNeil, 1968, 1972.

acetylene *See* ETHYNE.

acids *See* HYDROCHLORIC ACID; NITRIC ACID; PHENOL; SULPHURIC ACID.

Adamov, Central Moravia, Czechoslovakia The ironworks at Adamov probably began operation in the late sixteenth century, and by the mid-seventeenth century its foundry was producing cannon and castings for water systems. The surviving blast furnace dates from 1752 but was altered in the 1840s. The 'Kamenak' or pattern shop has been restored and converted into a museum of the iron industry. The wealth of documentary and map evidence makes proposals to convert the whole site into an open-air museum a possibility.

BIBLIOGRAPHY
Specific
Kreps, M. and Merta, J. *Stará Hut, Adamova* (The old furnace, Adamova). Brno: State Technical Museum, 1973.

adaptive reuse The adaptation of disused industrial buildings to fulfil new functions has become common since the 1960s. This process, which in the USA and more recently in Europe is now widespread, is often seen as the only means by which an otherwise redundant building can be retained. Adaptive reuse should not be confused with preservation for archaeological or historical reasons, although it is sometimes possible to retain a significant part of the original fabric as part of the new conversion. If the historic structure is incapable of renovation, because of inadequate floor load or headroom, or because of fire regulations, only the façade of the building may be retained. Such 'façadism' is now widespread. Adaptive reuse has developed its own architectural sub-style, leading to the construction of new buildings designed to look like converted mills or warehouses.

The archetypal reuse project was the conversion in the early 1960s of the Ghiradelli chocolate factory in San Francisco (*see* CALIFORNIA) into a complex of shops, restaurants, galleries, cinemas and offices. Waterfront warehouses, textile mills and railway stations have been widely converted to new uses. In the textile town of Lowell, which in the 1850s was the second city in MASSACHUSETTS, the industrial heart is now a National Historic Park, with mills used for new manufacturing purposes, chiefly electronics, and for offices, shops and recreational facilities. In Britain, the conversion of Bush's tea bond, a warehouse in Bristol where only the outer façade was retained, into offices and galleries, was an early example of waterfront rehabilitation. The Albert Dock, LIVERPOOL, and riverside warehouses in London's

Figure 1 The concrete grain silos of the Quaker Oats Co. at Akron, Ohio, abandoned in 1970 and adapted as a hotel ten years later, after windows had been created by one of the largest concrete sawing jobs ever performed on a commercial building. The silos formed part of a milling complex originally established in 1856 by Ferdinand Schumacher (1822–1908), pioneer of breakfast cereals.
Barrie Trinder

Docklands have been reused with the encouragement of specially constituted urban development corporations. The Central Station, MANCHESTER, is now an exhibition centre; the Gare d'Orsai in Paris, a museum; while Mount Royal Station, Baltimore, houses a lecture hall, a library, artists' studios, and the gallery of the Maryland Institute College of Art.

For examples of the adaptive reuse of industrial structures see figures 1, 32, 39, 53, 54, 66, 87, 170.

BIBLIOGRAPHY
General
Finegold, 1978; Kidney, 1976.

NEIL COSSONS

Adelaide, South Australia, Australia   The capital of the state, Adelaide was first permanently settled in 1836 by the South Australian Land Company as a MODEL COMMUNITY, without convicts. Laid out by Lt. Col. William Light (1784–1838) on the St Vincent Gulf, 12 km (8 mi.) from the wharves at Port Adelaide, elements of his plan remain in the fine parkland and squares of the modern city. The town was principally a port for agricultural produce, until its main period of growth, stimulated by copper mining, in the third quarter of the nineteenth century. The earliest tramways in Australia were built in Adelaide in the 1870s, and electrified from 1906. The suburban railway network was begun in 1865, and the rail link to Melbourne established in 1883. Munitions factories built during World War II became the basis for the growth of electronics manufactures. The cast-iron Albert Bridge of 1878–9 was designed by J. H. Granger and H. E. Worsley. The Palm House in the botanical gardens was prefabricated by Hoefer of Bremen and erected in 1876. The South Australian Maritime Museum, spread over seven sites through the port, includes a lighthouse of 1869, a sailmaker's and ship chandler's premises of 1884, and a bonded warehouse of 1854, as well as the steam tug *Yelta* of 1949. Other historic vessels at Port Adelaide include the *Falie*, a 215-tonne Dutch-built ketch of 1919; the 168-tonne iron schooner *Nelcebee* of 1883, which was prefabri-

5

cated at Rutherglen, Scotland, and assembled in Australia; and the *Santiago*, a 484-tonne iron barque built in Scotland in 1856.

BIBLIOGRAPHY
General
Brouwer, 1985; Donovan and Kirkman, 1986; Hammerton, 1986; Heritage of Australia, 1981; McCarty and Schedvin, 1978; Williams, 1974.

LOCATIONS
[M] Migration and Settlement Museum, 82 Kintore Avenue, Adelaide, SA 5000.
[M] Railway Museum, Railway Terrace, Mile End South, Adelaide.
[M] South Australian Maritime Museum, 117 Lipson Street, Port Adelaide SA 5015.
[M] The South Australian Museum, North Terrace, Adelaide, SA 5006.

KATE CLARK

adit A type of mine in which a horizontal or nearly horizontal tunnel is driven to gain access to minerals, whether bedded or stoped. An adit often slopes upwards at a gradient of about 1:250 to meet a mineral vein, the tunnel permitting both drainage and the easy removal of waste material and minerals. Though a SOUGH might be referred to as an adit, an adit does not necessarily have the drainage functions implied by the term sough. Adits are also referred to as 'drift mines', and known by many dialect words.

aerial ropeway A means of transporting goods across such obstacles as rivers or hilly ground, and up and down steep slopes, with less capital outlay than with a railway or road. Aerial ropeways have been widely used from the late nineteenth century to transport the produce of mines and quarries, to carry concrete and remove spoil on construction sites, and on a smaller scale in textile printing works, dye works, refrigerated warehouses and chemical plants.

The simplest type, invented by C. Hodgson in England about 1868, comprises an endless rope which both supports and moves the carriages: it is carried on pulleys mounted on pylons. It was used where not more than 50 tonnes an hour were to be moved, with individual loads not exceeding 300 kg (6 cwt.). The maximum gradient was 1 in 3, and the maximum length of span 200 m (600 ft.). The Gourjon system much used in France was a variation on this principle.

Hodgson also devised the fixed carrying-rope system which comprises one or two fixed ropes on which run carrier boxes with steel-grooved wheels, from which the carriages are suspended. The drive is provided by a haulage rope, attached to winding drums at the termini. The principle of operating aerial ropeways automatically by electric power, or 'téléphérage', was devised by H. C. Fleming Jenkin (1833–85) in 1882 and demonstrated at Glynde, Sussex, England, in 1885. For economy of operation, particularly for passenger traffic, pairs of carriages could be balanced (*see* CABLE CAR). Special forms

of carrier were devised for sacks, casks, timber, textile goods and sugar cane, and for tipping minerals.

For aerial ropeways for passengers, *see* CABLE CAR.

BIBLIOGRAPHY
General
Hipkins, 1896; Wallis-Tayler, 1898.
Specific
Annales des Ponts et Chaussées, XIV, 1887.

BARRIE TRINDER

aeroplane A heavier-than-air craft, deriving from the first successful powered flight by Orville and Wilbur Wright (1871–1948; 1867–1912) in the USA in 1903. The normal term in the USA is 'airplane'.

For the first three decades of aviation history wood was the principal structural material employed in aeroplanes. The wood was initially bamboo, but later spruce, which combined a reasonable degree of strength with straight graining. Early aircraft designs were essentially 'box' structures, incorporating wooden rectangular frames braced with steel wires both internally and externally to provide extra strength. The airframe was covered with fabric made airtight and taut by treatment with 'dope' to create the surfaces upon which lift could be generated. Biplane rather than monoplane structures dominated aircraft design until the mid-1930s, since these offered the strongest form of construction with the materials then available.

'Stressed skin' manufacturing techniques, also known as 'semi-monocoque', came to be widely used in the 1930s, deriving from established boat-building methods already employed in the manufacture of FLYING BOATS. This significant advance gave the advantage of a more spacious fuselage, relatively free from internal bracing wires, and the aircraft skin now became an integral structural part of the aircraft. This new method of design was accompanied by the change from wooden to metal construction. Although few obvious changes were immediately apparent, since biplanes were still being built and structures remained wire-braced for some time, by the late 1930s the transfer to metal was almost complete. New monoplanes like the British Vickers Supermarine Spitfire fighter and the American Douglas DC2 airliner appeared with metal-alloy fuselage frames and wing spars, and fully stressed skin fuselages and wings. The late 1930s also saw great improvements in aircraft performance as designers were stimulated by the pressures of military expansion.

Despite the technical advances made in aircraft engineering during World War II, and the advent of jet and turbo-prop engines, the basic form of aircraft structures has remained unaltered since the 1930s. Improvements have been made to stressed-skin techniques – for example the introduction of 'sandwich' structures and composite materials from the early 1940s – but generally established pre-war convention has prevailed, and aluminium alloy has remained the principal material used by aircraft manufacturers.

Preserved aircraft (other than AIRLINERS) of particular significance in the history of aircraft construction are:

- Wright Flyer, 1903: NASM, Washington DC.
- Blériot XI, 1909: Musée de l'Air, Paris.
- Vickers Vimy, 1919: Science Museum, London.
- De Havilland DH 60 Moth, 1925: Shuttleworth Collection, Old Warden.
- Junkers F13, 1928: Deutsches Museum, Munich.
- Douglas DC2, 1933: Swiss Transport Museum, Lucerne.
- Supermarine Spitfire 1, 1940: RAF Museum, Hendon, London.
- De Havilland DH 98 Mosquito, 1940: Mosquito Museum, London Colney, Hertfordshire.
- Caproni-Campini CC.1, 1940: Museum of the History of Italian Military Aviation, Vigna di Valle. (This was the second jet aircraft to fly.)
- De Havilland DH 104 Dove, 1946: Mosquito Aircraft Museum, London Colney, Hertfordshire. (The first successful application of metal-to-metal bonding in aircraft construction, the Redux process.)
- Bell X-1, 1947: NASM, Washington DC.

Aircraft have been of great importance in developing areas of sparse population and difficult terrain. The best collection of craft used for this purpose is probably that in the National Aviation Museum, OTTAWA.

Piston engines used in aeroplanes have been either air-cooled or liquid-cooled, the latter tending to be most often used in military aircraft. Civil types were more often powered by air-cooled rotary, radial and in-line engines. The evolution of the piston engine began with such types as the 25 hp three-cylinder 'Anzani', used by Louis Blériot (1872–1936) in 1909, and ended with the huge 2300 hp fourteen-cylinder Bristol 'Hercules' sleeve valve radial of World War II. Jet engines were introduced during World War II and by the late 1950s had come to dominate commercial flying. They give far greater power than any piston engine, and have been developed as turbo-props and as centrifugal, axial-flow or fan engines. The most important collections of aircraft engines are held at Bristol; Cosford; the Science Museum, London; Krakow; Prague; the Royal Museum of Scotland; and the National Air and Space Museum, Washington (*see* AIRCRAFT MUSEUMS).

See also AIRLINER; ELEVATOR; FLYING BOAT.

BIBLIOGRAPHY
General
Brent, 1933; Dornier, 1983; Gunston, 1989a, 1989b; Howard, 1988; Jackson, 1987; Mikerry, 1979; Nemecek, 1986; Pearcy, 1988; Postma, 1979; Pratt & Whitney Aircraft, 1952; Rolls Royce Ltd, 1969; Wragg, 1973.

JULIAN TEMPLE

Agricola, Georgius (Bauer, Georg; 1494–1555) A physician and student of mining and geology in Saxony, whose *De Re Metallica*, published posthumously in 1556, provides the first descriptions of numerous mining and metal-smelting technologies, many of which remained in use long after his death. His works are illustrated with numerous woodcuts.

See also figure 65.

BIBLIOGRAPHY
General
Agricola, 1556.

Aigle, Vaud, Switzerland   A town 12 km ($7\frac{1}{2}$ mi.) S. of Montreux, with two industrial museums, one concerned with clockmaking (particularly enamelling techniques), and one with winemaking.

BIBLIOGRAPHY
General
Keller, 1979.
LOCATIONS
[M] Museum of Clockmaking and Enamels, Route de Malagnon 15, 6982 Aigle.
[M] Wine Museum, Château d'Aigle, 6982 Aigle.

air brake   GEORGE WESTINGHOUSE's design for a compressed-air brake for locomotives was used on the Pennsylvania RR, USA, in 1869, and in 1872 a 'plain automatic brake' which was fail-safe on carriages was introduced. The locomotive has an air pump and air reservoirs, from which pressured air passes to cylinders on the vehicles in the train through triple valves. When the brake control is applied, air is admitted to the brake cylinders, thereby applying the brakes. The system was used in North America, most of continental Europe, and on the GER and LBSCR in Britain, on most electrified railways, and is now almost universal.

aircraft beacon   Flares and lamps illuminated runways in the early days of flying. Once out of sight of the airfields, aircraft first followed railway lines for route guidance until fifteen NEON beacons flashing MORSE were established in England and France in 1920. Croydon airport (*see* LONDON) was equipped with neon beacons and runway lights in 1928.

aircraft factory   A group of buildings used for the construction of aeroplanes, ideally in series production. Early aircraft were generally assembled in buildings built for other purposes: adapted factories, garages, stables and railway viaduct arches (*see* LONDON). Short Brothers Ltd in Britain appears to have been the first company to have built a series of aeroplanes. Their initial premises were railway viaduct arches in Battersea, London. In 1909 the company established what was claimed to be the world's first aircraft factory at Leysdown in the Isle of Sheppey, Kent. Handley Page Ltd, established in June of the same year, the first limited-liability company set up exclusively to design and manufacture aeroplanes, claimed that its factory at Barking, Essex, opened later the same year, was Britain's first purpose-built aircraft factory.

Massive increases in aircraft production during World War I led to the construction of many large, purpose-built factories, usually located near major population centres.

Towards the end of the war the British government was responsible for a series of short-lived 'National Aircraft Factories'.

The inter-war period saw a trend towards relocation on new rural or suburban sites so that all the main functions, including final assembly and flight testing, could be combined at one location. The rapid military expansion of the late 1930s ensured that many original sites were retained, but also led to the construction of 'shadow factories' (see COVENTRY) designed to accommodate increased production in wartime and intended to be run by major aircraft or motor manufacturers.

Mass production dominated both world wars. The ultimate example was the factory built by the Ford Motor Co. at Willow Run, west of Detroit, Michigan, which featured a double production line, capable of manufacturing 6800 B-24 bombers in 1941 alone. At its peak the factory completed a new B-24 every hour. Although aircraft manufacture does not readily lend itself to moving ASSEMBLY LINE methods, an exception was the track for building training aircraft employed by Miles Aircraft Ltd at Woodley, Berkshire, England, in 1940–3.

Post-war rationalization of the industry and recent moves towards international collaboration in an increasingly expensive business have resulted in many factory closures, although significant numbers of former aircraft factory buildings have survived after adaptation to new uses.

Significant surviving British aircraft factories include these:

Brooklands, Weybridge, Surrey The Vickers Aviation Ltd head office of the 1920s, now disused, formerly part of a factory which operated from 1915 until 1988.

Filton, Bristol An assembly hall designed by Eric Ross for construction of the Brabazon airliner. Filton is still in use, by British Aerospace.

Hendon, London The hangar and office of the Grahame-White Co. are the oldest listed aircraft factory structures in Britain.

Kingston upon Thames, Surrey The former Sopwith Aviation Co. and Hawker Aircraft Ltd factory and offices of the 1920s survive in Canbury Park Road: they are now used by Kingston Polytechnic.

Woodley, Berkshire The home of the former head office, of 1938, of Phillips & Powis Aircraft and Miles Aircraft, and of the former production hangar of c.1935 which from 1940 housed the world's first moving assembly line for aircraft manufacture.

BIBLIOGRAPHY
General
Ashmead, 1956; Hayward, 1989; Temple, 1987.

JULIAN TEMPLE

aircraft museum There are more than seven hundred aircraft museums and collections of aircraft on public display throughout the world, excluding many private collections. Aircraft, particularly commercial airliners, are difficult to display in museums as they take up a great deal of space and are generally too fragile for the public to be allowed unsupervised access. The question of whether aircraft preserved in museums should continue to be flown is much debated in some museums, particularly those in the private sector. The three principal aviation museums are generally recognized to be the French Air and Space Museum at Le Bourget, Paris; the National Air and Space Museum of the Smithsonian Institution, Washington DC; and the United States Air Force Museum, Wright Patterson AFB, Dayton, Ohio. The museums listed below all include exhibits of particular significance either to the history of aircraft construction (see AEROPLANE), or to that of commercial aviation (see AIRLINER). Collections consisting principally of military aircraft are otherwise excluded.

Argentina
Transport Museum, Lujan, Buenos Aires.

Canada
National Aviation Museum, PO Box 9724, Ottawa Terminal, Ottawa, Ontario K1G 5A3.
Western Canada Aviation Museum, Hangar T-2, 958 Ferry Road, Winnipeg, Manitoba, RH3 OY8.

Czechoslovakia
Military Museum, Air and Space Section, Kbely, Prague 9, 19706.
National Technical Museum, Kostelni 42, 170 00 Prague 7.

England
Aerospace Museum, Cosford, Shifnal, Shropshire WV7 3EX.
Bristol Industrial Museum, Prince's Wharf, Prince Street, Bristol BS1 4RN.
Brooklands Museum, The Clubhouse, Brooklands Road, Weybridge, Surrey KT13 0QN.
Imperial War Museum, Duxford Airfield, Cambridge CB2 4QR.
Mosquito Aircraft Museum, Box 107, Salisbury Hall, London Colney, St Albans AL2 1BU.
Royal Air Force Museum, Hendon, London NW9 5LL.
Science Museum, Exhibition Road, South Kensington, London SW7 2DD; and Wroughton Airfield, Wroughton, Swindon, Wiltshire.
Shuttleworth Collection, Old Warden Aerodrome, Biggleswade, Bedfordshire SG18 9ER.
Southampton Hall of Aviation, Albert Road South, Southampton, Hampshire.

Finland
Suomen Ilmailumseo (National Aviation Museum), PL 42, 01531 Helsinki-Vantqaa-Lento.

France
Air and Space Museum, Aéroport du Bourget 93, Paris.

Germany
Deutsches Museum, Museumsinsel 1, 8000 Munich 22.
Dornier Museum, Munich.

Italy

Museum of the History of Italian Military Aviation, Erroport di Vigna di Valle, Vigna di Valle 00062.

New Zealand

Museum of Transport and Technology, Great North Road, Western Springs, Auckland 21.

Poland

Museum of Aviation and Space, 30-969 Krakow 28.

Portugal

Air Museum, Alverca do Ribatejo, 2615.

Scotland

Royal Museum of Scotland, East Fortune Airfield, Edinburgh, East Lothian EH39 5LF.

Sweden

Tekniska Museet, Museivägen 7, N. Djurgården, Stockholm.

Switzerland

Swiss Transport Museum, Lidostrasse 5, Lucerne CH-6006.

United States of America

Cradle of Aviation Museum, Mitchel Field, Garden City, New York 11530.

Douglas Historical Foundation, California.

Henry Ford Museum and Greenfield Village, The Edison Institute, 20900 Oakwood Boulevard, Dearborn, Michigan 48121.

Museum of Flight, 9404 East Marginal Way South, Seattle, Washington 98108.

National Air and Space Museum, Smithsonian Institution, Washington DC 20560.

New England Air Museum, Bradley International Airport, Windsor Locks, Connecticut 06096.

Pima Air Museum, 6400 South Wilmot Road, Tucson, Arizona 85706.

United States Air Force Museum, Wright Patterson Air Force Base, Dayton, Ohio 45433.

BIBLIOGRAPHY
General
Ogden, 1978, 1983, 1988; Riley, 1985.

JULIAN TEMPLE

Aire-sur-la-Lys, Pas-de-Calais, France The Nord-Pas-de-Calais region, made up of parts of the former provinces of Flanders and Artois, shares with Belgium a long brewing tradition. In 1875 there were some 1900 breweries, most of them small-scale with local markets, in the department of Nord. The progressive adoption of low-temperature fermentation, a faster form of fermentation but one requiring more capital investment, led to concentration in the industry towards the end of the nineteenth century. Maltings tended to become independent establishments.

The Lys brewery at Aire-sur-Lys, 50 km (30 mi.) W. of Lille, was built in 1900. Today it is used only as a depot for bottled drinks, but with the exception of the boiler chimney, most of its buildings remain intact. The old stables, essential features of breweries of the time when beer had to be delivered fresh, are probably older, dating from c.1880. The architecture of the whole is remarkable: the façades are decorated with a combination of stone and brick with Flemish-style gables.

Several other brewing and malting buildings survive at Aire-sur-la-Lys, notably those of the Verhille-Bataille brewery, which closed in 1958. One of its buildings, erected in 1839, is decorated with a sundial adorned with the brewer's emblems. The Cossort maltings was transformed into a corn mill before 1934, but retains elements of its old malt kilns. Throughout the Lille region are many such old brewery buildings, often architecturally attractive, readily reused for storage purposes. A beer museum has recently been opened at Armentières, 20 km (12 mi.) W. of Lille, in the old maltings and brewery of Motte-Cordonnier, which was subsequently taken over by Sébastien Artois.

BIBLIOGRAPHY
General
Boissé *et al.*, 1990; Grenier and Weiser-Benedetti, 1979.

JEAN-FRANÇOIS BELHOSTE

air furnace A reverberatory furnace used for melting pig iron or cast-iron scrap before casting it into moulds (*see* FOUNDRY). The air furnace was known in England by 1718 when one was in use at Coalbrookdale, but it was largely superseded by the CUPOLA within the next hundred years. Air furnaces have remained in use for melting exceptionally large pieces of iron, and for making large castings.

BIBLIOGRAPHY
General
Gale, 1971.

BARRIE TRINDER

airliner An aeroplane designed for the carriage of passengers and mail. The first commercial air services immediately after World War I were operated with military aircraft, but purpose-built civilian transport planes were developed in many countries during the 1920s, although to many it seemed that the future of commercial flying might lie with the AIRSHIP or the FLYING BOAT. High standards of luxury were set in aircraft like the German Junkers G-31, sometimes called the 'flying dining car', and the British HP-42, a four-engined biplane introduced in 1931 for both European and Empire routes. The first air stewardesses were employed by Boeing Air Transport, later United Air Lines, in the USA in 1930. By the early 1930s low-wing, all-metal monoplanes were being developed; examples include the Junkers Ju52 of 1933, the Lockheed Electra of 1933–4, the Boeing 247 of 1934, and the Douglas DC2 and DC3, also of 1934 and carrying about twenty passengers. By 1939 four-engine, all-metal monoplanes like the Armstrong Whitworth Ensign and the Fokker-Wulf Fw200 Kondor were coming into service, offering the prospect of carrying up to forty passengers across the North Atlantic, or between Europe and Australia. Transcontinental flying vastly expanded during World War II, principally with four-engined bombers like the Avro Lancaster and Consolidated Liberator; and the first generation of post-war airliners, like the Boeing 377 Stratocruiser of 1949–50 (which could carry up to eighty passengers) and the Douglas DC-4 Skymaster, were based on bombers and military transports. The first turbo-prop (see AEROPLANE) airliner, the Vickers Viscount, flew in 1948, and the first pure jetliner, the De Havilland Comet, in the same year; but it was the Boeing 707 jetliner, which had a capacity of up to 180 passengers and first flew in 1954, that was to revolutionize transcontinental travel after its first commercial crossing of the Atlantic in 1958.

Some significant aircraft types whose design pre-dates World War II are still flying. Douglas DC3s are listed by Pearcy (1988), and Junkers Ju52 still fly from ZURICH. The most significant preserved commercial airliners from the period before 1960 are as follows:

- Aero A10, 1922: Czech Military Museum, Prague, Czechoslovakia.
- Avro 504K, 1918: Shuttleworth Collection, Bedford, England.
- Avro Lancaster I, 1942: RAF Museum, London, England; National Aviation Museum, Ottawa, Canada.
- Avro York C.1, 1944: Imperial War Museum, Duxford, England; Cosford Aerospace Museum, England.
- Boeing 40B-4, 1927: Henry Ford Museum, Dearborn, Michigan, USA.
- Boeing 80A, 1928: Museum of Flight, Seattle, Wash., USA.
- Boeing 247D, 1933: NASM, Washington DC; 1934: National Aviation Museum, Ottawa, Canada.
- Boeing 307 Stratoliner, 1939: Pima Air Museum, Tucson, Ariz., USA.
- Bristol Britannia 312, 1957: Cosford Aerospace Museum, England.
- Convair 240, 1948: NASM, Washington DC, USA.
- Curtiss JN-4 Jenny, 1918: Cradle of Aviation Museum, New York City, USA.
- De Havilland DH60X Moth, 1925: Shuttleworth Collection, Bedford, England.
- De Havilland DH104 Dove, 1949: Mosquito Museum, London Colney, England.
- De Havilland DH106 Comet IV, 1958: Science Museum, Wroughton, Swindon, England.
- Dornier Wal, 1922: Transport Museum, Lujan, Buenos Aires, Argentina.
- Dornier Do 24T.3, 1937: Dornier Museum, Munich, Germany.
- Douglas DC2, 1934: Douglas Historical Foundation, Calif., USA.
- Douglas DC3 Dakota, 1939: Henry Ford Museum, Dearborn, Michigan, USA; 1942: National Aviation Museum, Ottawa, Canada.
- Douglas DC4 Skymaster, 1941: Air Museum, Alverca, Lisbon, Portugal.
- Farman F.60 Goliath, 1919: Le Bourget, Paris, France.
- Fokker F.VIIB, 1925: Kingsford Smith Memorial, Australia.
- Fokker F.XIA, 1930: Western Canada Aviation Museum, Manitoba, Canada.
- Fokker Universal, 1928: New England Air Museum, Conn., USA.
- Ford 4-AT Trimotor, 1928: Henry Ford Museum, Dearborn, Michigan, USA.
- Junkers F.13, 1924: Technical Museum, Stockholm, Sweden.
- Junkers Ju52/3M, 1930: Deutsches Museum, Munich, Germany.
- Junkers W 34, 1932: National Aviation Museum, Ottawa, Canada.
- Lockheed 5B Vega, 1929: Henry Ford Museum, Dearborn, Michigan, USA.
- Lockheed 10A Electra, 1935: Nevada Air Museum, Nevada, USA; 1937: National Aviation Museum, Ottawa, Canada.
- Lockheed 12A, 1937: National Aviation Museum, Ottawa, Canada.
- Lockheed Constellation, 1947: Science Museum, Wroughton, Swindon, England.
- Short Sandringham IV, 1946: Southampton Hall of Aviation, England.
- Short S.45 Solent 4, 1949: Museum of Transport, Auckland, New Zealand.
- Sikorsky VS-44A, 1942: New England Air Museum, Conn., USA.
- Vickers 657 Viking 1, 1946: Aerospace Museum, Cosford, England.
- Vickers 701 Viscount, 1952: Imperial War Museum, Duxford, England.

See also AIRCRAFT MUSEUMS.

BIBLIOGRAPHY

General
Cluett *et al.*, 1980; Davies, 1972; Dornier, 1983; Dyos and Aldcroft, 1969; Hudson, 1972; Jackson, A. J., 1987; Jackson, G., 1983; Nemecek, 1986; Pearcy, 1988; Postma, 1979; Turner, 1968; Veale, 1945.

Specific
Smith, R. K. The intercontinental airliner and the essence of airplane performance. In *T & C*, XXIV, 1983.

JULIAN TEMPLE

airplane *See* AEROPLANE.

airport An area of land (or in the case of FLYING BOATS, water) where passenger and freight transport planes can land and take off; the aviation equivalent of a seaport. An airport is equipped with facilities for controlling and maintaining aircraft and handling fare-paying passengers and freight, and, if it is concerned with international traffic, with premises for customs and immigration purposes. An 'aerodrome' is likely to lack scheduled passenger services, while the terms 'airfield' and 'airbase' apply primarily to military installations.

From the primitive landing grounds used by aviation pioneers before 1914, aerodromes like Brooklands, Surrey, and Hendon, near London, developed into large military bases in World War I. After 1918 some military bases were converted into civilian airports, often adapting existing buildings. This pattern was repeated in Britain after World War II, as military sites like Bournemouth and East Midlands became available for civilian use.

The first regular international air passenger service began with flights to Paris from Hounslow Heath, London, in August 1919. The service was transferred in 1920 to Croydon Airport, which was largely rebuilt in 1928 as the principal airport for London, with one of the first combined passenger-terminal and control-tower buildings. One of the few purpose-built city-centre air terminals was built at Victoria, LONDON, in 1939, but has since been adapted to new uses.

Newark Airport, N.J., opened in 1928, was one of the first municipal airports in the USA, had the first hard-surfaced airport runway in the USA, and was the world's busiest airport by 1930. Britain's first municipal airport opened at Wythenshawe, Manchester, in May 1929, and most major cities in Europe and North America had their own airports by 1939. There has been a tendency to concentrate investment, and most large modern airports are products of continuous rebuilding and expansion on sites originally developed more than fifty years ago; some contain buildings of the inter-war period that have been little altered, and more original buildings remain at smaller airports.

An airport consists of runways (which may be grass, tarmac or concrete), passenger and freight terminal buildings, a CONTROL TOWER, and HANGARS. Examples of the last two components are listed under the headwords concerned. Other outstanding airport buildings are the former 'Flight Ticket Office' of 1911 at Brooklands, Surrey, and the 'Beehive' terminal at Gatwick of 1936. At Glendale, Calif., the pre-World War II Grand Central Air Terminal remains intact, although it ceased operation in 1959; and the pre-war terminal at Le Bourget, Paris, is now a museum, as is the 1930s terminal on Treasure Island in San Francisco Bay, Calif.

Airports, like railway stations, stimulated hotel building, and good examples of the inter-war period survive at Croydon, London, and Jersey, CHANNEL ISLANDS. Aero clubhouses of distinction remain at Brooklands, Surrey, and Woodley, Berkshire.

See also AIRCRAFT BEACON; AIR-TRAFFIC CONTROL; RADAR.

BIBLIOGRAPHY
General
Bayer-Desimond, 1931; Butler, 1985; Cluett *et al.*, 1980; Davies, 1972; Hubbard, 1930; Stroud, 1980; Wood, 1940.
Specific
Dawbarn, G. The main principles of planning civil aerodromes. In Hening, R. and Chitty, A. M. Notes on the planning of an airport. In *Architectural Record of Design & Construction*, VII, 1937.
Guillerme, A. International airports. In *A Future for our Past*, XXVIII, Strasbourg: Council of Europe, 1986.

JULIAN TEMPLE

airship A powered, lighter-than-air craft, which, unlike a BALLOON, can be steered or directed, which is why it is often called a 'dirigible'. A 'rigid' airship has gas-filled cells mounted within a lightweight metal frame; a 'blimp' is a powered non-rigid or unframed dirigible. The French General Meusnier designed an airship in 1784. Henri Giffard in 1852 built a steam-powered craft and Charles Renard and A. C. Krebs demonstrated *La France* on flights as long as 8 km (5 mi.) in 1884. Practical airships only appeared at the beginning of the twentieth century, in France, Britain, and especially Germany, where Count Ferdinand von Zeppelin established a factory on Lake Constance in 1898 from which the first rigid Zeppelin flew in 1900. In 1910–14 five Zeppelins operated a circular service from FRIEDRICHSHAFEN through Baden-Baden, Frankfurt am Main, Düsseldorf, Hamburg, Potsdam, Leipzig and Gotha. World War I demonstrated the potential of airships for carrying passengers and freight over long distances. For a time in the 1920s the regular transoceanic services provided by Zeppelins, with high standards of food, comfort and internal design, seemed to provide a pattern for future international travel, but the crash of the experimental British R101 in 1930 and the spectacular destruction by fire of the Zeppelin *Hindenburg* at Lakehurst, N.J., in 1937 effectively marked the end of the commercial hydrogen-filled craft. At that time HELIUM, which is non-inflammable, was not available in sufficient quantities.

The Zeppelin Museum, Friedrichshaven, contains many airship parts and shows superb archive film of voyages of the 1920s and 30s. A Zeppelin gondola remains in the Autotron Theme Park, Rosmalen, The Netherlands; and a propeller from the *Graf Zeppelin* in the Aerospace Museum, Rio de Janeiro. Other Zeppelin parts, models and archives are in the Deutsches Museum, Munich. Parts of British airships survive in the Science Museum, the RAF Museum, and Brooklands Museum (*see* AIRCRAFT MUSEUM).

Airships were used by Roald Amundsen (1872–1928) and Umberto Nobile (1885–1978) in exploration of Arctic regions in the 1920s, and a mooring mast survives at VÅDSO.

Airships operated from more than eighty principal locations. The outstanding remains are the 358 m (1175 ft.) Goodyear Airship Dock of 1929 at Akron, OHIO (figure 2), and the two airship hangars at Cardington (*see* BEDFORD). A concrete airship shed of 1917 survives at Augusta, Sicily; and a shed at Recife, Brazil, built for German airships in 1935, remains in good condition. Other sheds survive at Moffatt Field, Calif., at DARMSTADT and at Cherbourg. In Paris an airship hangar at Chalais Meudon, converted from a building used in the Paris Exhibition of 1878, is now a museum store. A German Zeppelin shed shipped to Japan in 1921 remains at Kasumiga-ura.

BIBLIOGRAPHY
General
Collier, 1974; Countryman, 1982; Deighton, 1978; Hildebrandt, 1908; Horton, 1973; Hudson, 1972; Mikerry, 1979.

JULIAN TEMPLE

Figure 2   The Goodyear airship dock at Akron, Ohio, built in 1929
Barrie Trinder

air-traffic control   The means by which aircraft traffic flow is regulated within internationally accepted air corridors, control zones and control areas. Radio communication with aircraft only became common in the mid-1940s, and today's air-traffic control systems derive from a Conference on International Civil Aviation of 1944, which committed every major country to provide an air-traffic control service.

See also AIRCRAFT BEACON; CONTROL TOWER.

air transport   *See* AEROPLANE; AIRCRAFT MUSEUM; AIRLINER; AIRPORT; AIRSHIP; BALLOON; FLYING BOAT.

Ajka, Veszprém, Hungary   A town in a district with many aluminium mines and smelters, 27 km (17 mi.) SW of Veszprém. There is a mining museum in the engine house of the coal mine, 128 m (420 ft.) deep, which operated during 1904–59. The steel headstock of 1912 remains, with the Schlick steam engine of 1903, as well as a smaller engine of 1904 which operated an aerial ropeway.

BIBLIOGRAPHY
General
Kiss *et al.*, 1981.

LOCATION
[M] Mining Museum, Csingervolgy, H-8403 Ajka.

akvavit   A Danish term used elsewhere ('aquavit' in Norwegian and Swedish), referring to a spirit made from grain alcohol, distilled like gin, and given a slight flavour with caraway, which is often called 'Snaps' in Denmark. In Germany this drink is called Kornbranntwein. All Danish akvavit is made in ÅLBORG.

Alabama, United States of America   Dubbed the 'Cotton State' in tribute to its chief agricultural product, Alabama has in fact compiled the most illustrious record of heavy industry in the American South. An impressive roster of industrial heritage sites testifies to the vigour with which the state has made use of its human and natural resource endowments.

By the third decade of the nineteenth century the bituminous coal seams that underlaid some 20 per cent of the state were being exploited for export, and soon thereafter for charging the first of many blast furnaces throughout the state. Almost equally as abundant as coal in north-central Alabama are limestone and red haematite iron ore, of which there are rich veins, heavy with silica, making a pig iron well-suited for foundry purposes. After the Civil War, Alabama rose from the ashes to become a major international producer of cast-iron water pipes, stoves and, later, steel products.

As with its British namesake, Birmingham in Alabama stood at the heart of the region's heavy industry, especially in iron and steel. Another name that acknowledges its roots is Bessemer, a Birmingham suburb, more recently known for its production of dynamite. Together with iron

Figure 3 One of the blast furnaces which forms part of the Sloss Furnaces National Historic Landmark, Birmingham, Alabama
Robert M. Vogel, Smithsonian Institution

and steel in raw and finished forms, cement, tin, graphite, bauxite and precious metals issued from many works in and around the 'Pittsburgh of the South' into the twentieth century, much of it moving by rail to Mobile, Alabama's only seaport.

The state capital, Montgomery, served as the chief agricultural processing hub, its rail lines crowned by the Romanesque Union Station, with its great wide-spanned train shed, an excellent late-nineteenth-century study in iron-truss bridgework applied to commercial architecture.

Alabama's early experience with smelting iron with charcoal is celebrated at Tannehill Furnace, Birmingham.

Active from 1830, Tannehill's slave-served furnace provided iron for Confederate forces in the Civil War. An attempt was made in 1976 to make iron in one of Tannehill's three stone furnaces, but with only semi-molten success.

In Birmingham proper is the world's first preservation project for a major twentieth-century urban ironworks, Sloss Furnaces, built in 1927–9. On its closure in 1970 the Sloss plant passed into enlightened civic hands: resources were found to save for the public the LANDMARK furnace stacks and all the auxiliary equipment, including blowing engines, forge shops, slag heaps, charging ramps,

13

company offices, crew quarters and maintenance facilities. The whole site was opened to the public in 1983 as an interpretation park.

High atop Red Mountain, an 18.3 m (60 ft.) cast-iron statue of Vulcan overlooks the city. Cast for the Louisiana Purchase Exposition of 1904 in St Louis, and owned today by the city government, Vulcan is the largest and therefore probably the heaviest cast-iron statue in the world. The enormous anvil at his side probably enjoys the same status among world anvils.

In north Alabama a pair of 3.2 km (2 mi.) wide, straight-crested concrete dams service power plants on the Tennessee River, both monuments to the federal assistance given to states in the 1920s in flood control and the generation of electric power. Both the Wheeler and the Wilson dams remain vital to their original missions.

BIBLIOGRAPHY
General
Jackson, 1988.
Specific
White, M. L. *The Birmingham District: an industrial history and guide.* Birmingham, Ala.: Birmingham Historical Society, 1981.

LOCATIONS
[M] Alabama Mining Museum, Allbritton Avenue, Dora, AL 35062.
[M] Iron and Steel Museum of Alabama, Tannehill, Route 1 Box 124, McCalla, AL 35111.
[S] Montgomery Union Station and Train Shed, Water & Lee Streets, Montgomery, AL.
[S] Sloss Furnaces National Historic Landmark, 1st Avenue at 32nd Street, Birmingham, AL 35222.
[S] Vulcan Park, 400 Graymont Avenue West, Birmingham, AL 35204.

DAVID H. SHAYT

Åland Islands, Ahvenanmaa, Finland The Åland Islands lie at the southern end of the Gulf of Bothnia, the capital, Mariehamn (Maarianhamina) being located 135 km (84 mi.) W. of Turku, and the same distance NE of Stockholm. The islands form a province of Finland but the language is Swedish. Mariehamn was the base of the fleet of ocean-going sailing ships owned by Gustaf Erikson which remained in commercial operation for some years after 1945, the last of its kind in the world. In 1939 Erikson was working eleven steel and thirty-seven wooden sailing vessels. The maritime museum at Mariehamn includes the *Pommern*, a 4050-tonne, steel, four-masted barque, built at Glasgow in 1903. Jan Karlsgården, an open-air museum at Sund, includes a windmill, sawmill and fulling mill.

BIBLIOGRAPHY
General
Brouwer, 1985; Mead and Jaatinen, 1975.

LOCATIONS
[M] Åland Sjöfartsmuseum (Maritime Museum), Mariehamn, Åland Islands.
[M] Jan Karlsgården, Katelholm, 22530 Sund, Åland Islands.

BARRIE TRINDER

Alaska, United States of America As the largest state of the Union – one-fifth the size of all the others combined: 1 478 458 km² (570 833 sq. mi.) – and its second most recent (1959), Alaska remains one of the great frontier lands of the continent. Its industry has been dominated by the extraction of vast mineral and animal resources, shipped south for commercial processing. Fishing, whaling, sealing, gold mining, oil extraction and copper mining have prospered in place of secondary manufacturing activities.

Alaska had been a commercial outpost of tsarist Russia since the 1740s. Its purchase by the USA in 1867 for $7 200 000 was widely viewed as folly – a distant icy land populated by unusual peoples – until gold was discovered three decades later. The Klondike gold rush of the late 1890s brought Alaska to the attention of the world, especially the footloose with the means to reach the goldfields in the Alaska panhandle. Today the remains of the fevered quest may be seen strewn along the beaches and rusting in the woods above Juneau, the state capital. Steam mine hoists and impulse turbine wheels sit on their original moorings, abandoned industrial track runs for miles through the wilderness, and ore cars and the ruins of stamp mills poke through the trees. The state's remoteness from the rest of the country has blessed such remains with protective isolation, but confounded plans to preserve and interpret them. Critical aspects are under Park Service care, through their regional centre and museum in Skagway. Near Fox a gold dredge of 1928 sits beached and preserved, accorded LANDMARK status in 1986 by the American Society of Mechanical Engineers.

The abandoned Kennecott copper mine in central

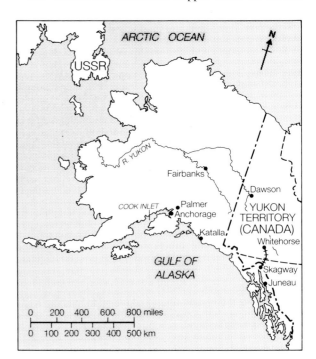

Alaska

Alaska drives home the bittersweet nature of site preservation in such a lost world. Spilling down a mountainside, the ore-dressing structures, dating from the early twentieth century, contain many of their original machines, and stand as important examples of isolated industry, serving workers' needs with shops and housing, and with skip cars and cableways still in place to transport the ore. The National Park Service wrestles with the mammoth logistical and conservation problems the site presents. How much of a site is worth preserving if no one visits it?

The completion in 1977 of the above-ground trans-Alaska oil pipeline, crossing 1300 km (800 mi.) of mountainous terrain, was the climax of eighty years of oil and gas exploration and recovery in Alaska. The first wells were drilled in 1898 at Cook Inlet, and seven years later commercial oil production began at Katalla.

The 177 km (110 mi.) White Pass and Yukon narrow-gauge railway opened in 1900 as an avenue to the wealth of the region's interior, stretching from Skagway to Whitehorse in the Yukon territory. The line shut down in 1982, bereft of freight and passenger traffic, but reopened in 1988 as a seasonal excursion line, offering one of the most majestic train rides on the continent.

LOCATIONS
[S] Klondike Gold Rush National Historical Park, PO Box 517, Skagway, AK 99840.
[M] Museum of Alaska Transportation and Industry, Mile 40.2, Glenn Highway, Palmer, AK 99645.

DAVID H. SHAYT

Albania Between 1506 and 1912 Albania was a province of the Ottoman Empire. Independence was gained in 1912, but between then and 1944 there were successive occupations by Greece, Montenegro (*see* YUGOSLAVIA), Italy and Germany. The autumn of 1944 marked the liberation of Albania under the leadership of the Albanian Communist Party, and in particular of Enver Hoxha, its First Secretary, who ruled until his death in 1984. With a population of only one million, Albania entered a 45-year stage of history as a socialist state. Hoxha aimed to transform the backward and feudal economy into an advanced industrial-agrarian society.

Albania is a small country covering only 2 875 000 ha (11 100 sq. mi.). Over three-quarters of the land is mountainous, making communications difficult. Forests cover about 40 per cent of the country. The extensive swamps that existed before World War II have been drained to provide fertile agricultural land. Albania is one of the few oil-producing countries in Europe, and has important deposits of coal, chromium, copper, and iron ore. There are also vast water-power resources, notably the Enver Hoxha hydro-electric power station at Koman on the Drin River.

Albania differs from much of Europe in that it is still undergoing its first industrial revolution. While much of Western Europe was building textile mills and mining deeper for coal, Albania was struggling for its independence against the Ottoman Empire. Throughout the eighteenth and nineteenth centuries the country was

Albania

ruled by feudal-military despots, and had a socio-economic system that hindered economic development through corruption, religious conflicts, class struggles and blood feuds, the last still accounting in the early twentieth century for about a quarter of all deaths. In the north the heads of the clans controlled all property and held despotic powers. In the south 95 per cent of the population were peasants, 4 per cent were petty tradesmen and priests, and the remaining 1 per cent held official civil and military posts and owned all the good land. Trade was still mostly by barter, and coins were rarely used.

Discussion of traditional pre-industrial manufactures in Albania is limited by the paucity of sources, and also by the way in which Albanian politicians have manipulated the image of the country. Albania puts history into its own interpreted political context, giving great emphasis to recent centuries as a period of struggle for national independence. Industrial archaeology is not recognized as a topic for study.

In the late eighteenth century about half the gross national product was consumed in taxes, but in certain towns craftsmen and merchants did prosper. Albanian business houses had offices in Venice and Trieste, and traded with Italy and Austria. They specialized particularly in ornaments, weapons and folk crafts. Shkodër, Prizen and Gjakova were famous for filigree work in non-ferrous metals. Elbasan and Tiranë were known for the casting of non-ferrous metals. Rugs and carpets were made in Luma and Has, and Gjirokastra, Dibra and Berat were noted for stone carving. Heavy industry scarcely existed.

Between the two world wars Albania was the poorest country in Europe. It was virtually an Italian colony. There were no more than thirty qualified technicians in the whole country and only six doctors. The average life expectancy was about thirty-eight years, and the people lived in utter poverty. This is the picture that emerges from current Albanian history books, which emphasize the contrast between Albania under foreign control and Albania under the leadership of the Albanian Communist Party. It is difficult to find accounts of successful economic activity before World War II. Certainly the People's Socialist Republic of Albania has been responsible for astonishing achievements since 1944, but this does not mean that there was no industrial activity at all before that date. It is claimed that industry in 1938 accounted for only 4 per cent of gross national product, and that the total annual volume of industrial production of that time is now turned out in two days. Government figures are readily available to illustrate the rapid acceleration of industrial achievement under the Communist regime.

Myrdal and Kessle (1978) sum up the situation: 'The Albania which used to be a god-forgotten country that couldn't even support its own population, a country that exported oranges and imported marmalade, whose oil wells were owned by foreigners and whose school system, too, was controlled by foreigners, is today self-supporting in foodstuffs and exports industrial products. Instead of increasing its tobacco plantations, selling tobacco and importing grain to sow, investment in tobacco is being reduced, the cultivation of cereals raised, and copper wire exported.'

By 1990 Albania supplied its own oil, fuel and electric power. It is a major exporter of chromium ore. It meets almost 90 per cent of its needs for consumer goods and spare parts. The oil refineries, steel works, hydro-electric power stations, chemical fertilizer factories, textile mills, and plants making building materials, knitwear, food-stuffs, plastics, rubber, ceramics, glassware and pharmaceutical products are all projects that were set up during the years of socialist administration.

Albania has not achieved industrialization alone. Financial and technical help from other Communist countries has been of major importance. The influence of the USSR was paramount between 1948 and 1961, and that of China between 1961 and 1978. Throughout the period of industrialization Albania has become increasingly self-reliant. When the Soviet Union withdrew its engineers in 1961, together with drawings, maps and the results of geological surveys, Albania learned not to rely on foreign experts.

Transport in the modern sense has no lengthy history in Albania. The national railway network was established only in 1947. Foreigners are not allowed to travel on public transport, but diesel trains can be seen from the road, and steam locomotives may be heard shunting at Durrës. The private car is banned, so that apart from industrial, commercial and military vehicles, and cars used by government officials, the roads are traffic-free.

The importance of museums and the study of 'the national characteristics in the various aspects of our culture and arts' and their relevance to present-day 'cultural-artistic work with the masses' are acknowledged by a quotation from Enver Hoxha in the introduction to the guidebook to Albania's only museum. A few museums did exist in Albania before 1944, and several archaeological sites were excavated, mainly during the period of Italian occupation, when Roman artefacts and sites were used in an effort to convince the Albanians of their strong historic links with Italy. A coherent conservation policy was not introduced until after the liberation, in 1944. In 1948 the first archaeological-ethnographic museum was established, and in 1976 the Centre for Archaeological Research was set up in Tiranë. Divided into three sections, prehistory, Illyrian antiquity and medieval history, it became responsible for archaeological research and museums throughout the country. *Iliria* is the main organ of Albanian archaeology; and *Monumentet*, published by the Ministry of Education and Culture, contains reports on the restoration of buildings.

Museums in Albania are now organized at three levels – national, district and local – with strong links between them. The national museums are based in Tiranë. Each of the country's twenty-six districts runs an ethnographical museum, and hundreds of small local museums are still springing up. The curator in a particular town is responsible not only for the museum, but also for historic buildings and conservation areas. Albania has achieved a remarkable success in setting up so comprehensive a service in so short a space of time. There is no formal training for curators, but they are each expected to have a degree in archaeology, history or some other relevant subject. Experts from abroad are frequently consulted as Albania is still developing its own expertise. Museums in Albania are highly political, displaying quotations from Enver Hoxha and Karl Marx, but the Atheist Museum at Shkodër, which ridiculed religion, was closed in the late 1980s because it was felt to be 'no longer appropriate'.

The most dynamic aspect of Albanian conservation policy is the concept of the 'museum city', dating from 1961, which has been applied at Berat, Krujë and Gjirokastra. These cities are each divided into three zones. In the central zone buildings must be preserved and not altered in any way, although where buildings had been demolished before designation, it is not the policy to reconstruct. In the second zone external appearances must be preserved, but interiors may be altered. Beyond these inner zones new buildings may be constructed but they must harmonize with the rest of the town. Most houses in the museum cities are privately owned, but their owners receive substantial government funding for the preservation of the buildings. The policy, administered by the Institute of Monuments of Culture, established for the purpose in 1965, is highly effective and has achieved remarkable results.

The classical and medieval contributions to Albania's historic landscape better lend themselves to tourist

Figure 4 The Mohawk tipple, part of the surface installations of a colliery in the Crowsnest Pass, Alberta
Alberta Culture and Multi-Culturalism

development than do the relics of early industry. The Albturist itineraries include visits to selected factories, and their coaches pass through industrial areas.

See also BERAT; DURRËS; ELBASAN; FIER; FIERZE; GJIRO-KASTRA; KORCË; KRUJË; MALIQ; SARANDË; TIRANË.

BIBLIOGRAPHY
General
8 Nentori, 1980, 1982, 1984; Myrdal and Kessle, 1978; Ward, 1983.
Specific
Farnell, G. and Scarce, J. Museums in Albania. *Museums Journal*, 83, 1983.
Hall, D. Foreign tourism under socialism – the Albanian 'Stalinist' model. *Annals of Tourism Research*, 11, 1984.
Smith, M. F. ed. Archaeology in Albania, 1973–83. *Archaeological Reports*, 30, 1983–4.

LOCATIONS
[I] *Monumentet*, Rruga Alqui Kondi 7, Tiranë.
[I] Qendra e Kerkimeve Arkeologjike (Centre for Archaeological Research), Tiranë.

LARISSA RIMELL

Alberta, Canada   The most westerly of Canada's prairie provinces, Alberta was settled by Europeans from the early twentieth century, and became a province within the Canadian federation in 1905. It owes much of its wealth to its wheat-producing prairies, grain elevators being a characteristic feature of the Albertan landscape, and to its oil and gas deposits. Refineries in Edmonton produce more than half of Canada's petroleum products. The Athabasca and Slave Rivers are still used in carrying freight to the Arctic regions.

The Provincial Museum has extensive displays illustrating the natural resources of Alberta and the material culture of the various groups who have settled there, including a notable harness shop of the early colonial period.

Fort George, established by fur traders of the North-West Company on the Saskatchewan River in 1792, and used for processing meat into pemmican until c.1800, was excavated from 1965 and has provided evidence of the fur trade and the material culture of the pioneering period. A different pioneering period is illustrated at the Ukrainian Cultural Heritage Village, 50 km (30 mi.) E. of Edmonton.

Medicine Hat has vast reserves of natural gas, and some original wells survive. Gas was used to heat glasshouses, of which some extensive examples remain. Since c.1885 Medicine Hat has been the prime source of ceramic products in western Canada, with beehive-shaped kilns surviving on several sites. The surviving Medalta complex includes four downdraught kilns. Much early working-class housing surrounds a town centre with many commercial buildings of c.1895–1910.

The 3.2 km (2 mi.) Brooks Aqueduct, 3 km (2 mi.) SE of Brooks, now a National Historic Site, was built in 1915 by the Canadian Pacific Railway to convey irrigation water, and was then the longest concrete structure of its kind.

The Crowsnest Pass in south-west Alberta was an important coal-mining region, from 1898 when it was reached by a line of the Canadian Pacific Railway, until 1983 when the last mine closed. The 18 km (11 mi.) length of the pass between Coleman and Lundbreck is rich in company towns, halls built by various ethnic communities, the remains of surface installations, and the ruins of the International Coal & Coke Company site where there were once 216 coke ovens. The Frank Slide Interpretive Centre commemorates the destruction of the coal-mining town of Frank by a slide of rock from Turtle Mountain, with the loss of about seventy lives on 29 April 1903. A pair of large limekilns, preserved at Hillcrest, was built to use rock loosened by the slide. At the Leitch Collieries

Provincial Historic Site are the conserved remains of the surface buildings of a mine forced out of business in 1915. It is proposed to develop Greenhill Mine, which operated from 1913 until 1957, as the centre of an écomusée for the Pass.

At Drumheller, 105 km (65 mi.) NE of Calgary, the screen system at the Atlas coal mine is the only example preserved in Canada.

The Oil Sands Interpretive Centre at Fort McMurray, 380 km (240 mi.) NE of Edmonton, illustrates the history of the extraction of bitumen from the Athabasca Oil Sands, identified in the 1870s but not exploited commercially until hot-water separation techniques were developed by Dr Karl Clark in the 1920s. Displays show how bitumen is refined to form synthetic crude oil, how the community of Fort McMurray has developed, and how similar deposits are exploited elsewhere in the world. From a special viewpoint visitors can watch mining in progress. Bitumount, an oil extraction plant on the east bank of the Athabasca River, 125 km (77 mi.) N. of Fort McMurray, was designated a Provincial Historic Resource in 1974.

Two important transport displays opening in 1992 are a collection of horse-drawn carriages at Cardston, and a large collection of cars, bicycles, motorcycles, agricultural machinery and steam engines at Wetaskiwin.

BIBLIOGRAPHY
General
Kroetsch, 1969.
Specific
Alberta Culture. *Crowsnest Pass: historical resources development proposal*. Edmonton: Alberta Culture, 1980.
Alberta Culture. *Medicine Hat Natural Gas Interpretive Centre: feasibility study*. Edmonton: Alberta Culture, 1986.
Alberta Culture. *Brooks Aqueduct: development concept and facility development programme*. Edmonton: Alberta Culture, 1987.
Babaian, S. *The Coal Mining Industry in the Crow's Nest Pass*. Edmonton: Alberta Culture, 1985.
Earthscape Consultants. *Bitumount: historic resource development proposal*. Edmonton, 1984.

LOCATIONS
[I] Alberta Culture and Multiculturalism, 8820-112 Street, Edmonton, Alberta, T6G 2P8.
[S] Fort George and Buckingham House, 51 Street and 50 Avenue, Elk Point, Alberta.
[M,S] Fort McMurray Oil Sands Interpretive Centre, 515 MacKenzie Boulevard, Fort McMurray, Alberta T9H 4X3.
[M] Foster Wheels, Reynolds-Alberta Museum, 4705-50th Avenue, Wetaskiwin, Alberta T2G 0k6.
[M] Provincial Museum of Alberta, 12845-102 Avenue, Edmonton, Alberta.
[M] Remington-Alberta Carriage Centre, 339 Main Street, Cardston, Alberta.

DERYCK HOLDSWORTH and BARRIE TRINDER

Ålborg, Jutland, Denmark   The city of Ålborg, sited at an important crossing point of the Limfjorden, is the regional centre for North Jutland. It is one of the oldest Danish towns, and the pre-industrial history of the city is illustrated by fine houses built for merchants and craftsmen, like No. 9 Østerå, dating from 1624, and the brewhouse of 1791 at 8 Østergade in Nørre Sundby, the twin city north of the Limfjorden. In the course of industrialization Ålborg gained a varied economic structure, and as early as the 1850s two of the city's firms took leading innovative roles in the tobacco and distilling industries. Today the name of Ålborg is still connected with the famous Danish drink aquavit.

During the Second Industrial Revolution (*see* DENMARK) Ålborg–Nørre Sundby gained several large industrial plants, among them two bacon factories, a steel shipyard, and factories producing sulphuric acid and fertilizers. The most important new industry was the manufacture of PORTLAND CEMENT. Five large works were founded around 1900, exploiting rich deposits of limestone near to the surface, and taking advantage of easy sea transport. The first, Rørdal, was built by the engineering firm of F. L. Smidth & Co., who developed there a continuous shaft kiln, the Ålborg kiln; introduced M. Davidson's TUBE MILL; and, in 1899, installed the first rotary kiln in Europe.

Today Rørdal is the only cement works in operation. Among other industrial buildings are the production plant of Danish Distilleries (De Danske Spritfabrikker), built at the harbour in a neo-Classical style in 1929–31, and the tobacco factory of C. W. Obel built at the harbour in 1938, in the International Modern style. A more developed form of this style is the motor works of Carl Christensen of 1957 at Riihimäkivej, designed by Arne Jacobsen (1902–71). The Danish Technical Museum has recently established a branch in the same street with communications as its main theme, incorporating collections of telegraphs, telephones, radios, television equipment and computers.

At Hobro, 46 km (30 mi.) S., is the Bie brewery of 1851, a good example of the minor provincial breweries that once flourished in almost every Danish town, which is now under legal protection.

BIBLIOGRAPHY
General
Johansen, 1987; Sestoft, 1979.
Specific
Bender, H. *Ålborgs industrielle udvikling 1735–1940* (The industrial development of Ålborg 1735–1940). Ålborg, 1987.
Bertelsen, O. *Geologi i Ålborgområdet* (Geology in the Ålborg region). Copenhagen, 1987.
Gormsen, G. H. I. Bies Bryggeri i Hobro (The brewery of H. I. Bie in Hobro). In *Fabrik og Bolig*, I, 1983.
Witt, T. Ålborg og fabrikkerne i 1890'erne (Ålborg and the factories of the 1890s). In *Ålborgbogen*, 1979–80.

LOCATION
[M] Ålborgs Historiske Museum (Historical Museum), Algade 48, 9100 Ålborg.

OLE HYLDTOFT

Albstadt, Baden-Württemberg, Germany   The Swabian Jura was long regarded as a district from which people tended to emigrate, agriculture being unprofitable because of the karst rocks and the lack of water. After the Franco-Prussian War of 1870–1 jobs were created in Albstadt, 64 km (40 mi.) S. of Stuttgart, in the manufacture of military uniforms and knitwear. There are many textile factories in the area, which extended 8 km (5 mi.) from north to south between Onstmettingen and Ebingen, as well as small mechanical engineering works connected with them. Ebingen has some well-preserved examples of industrial architecture, in styles ranging from the Romanticism of the 1870s to the International Modernism of the 1920s.

LOCATION
[M] Town Museum and Art Gallery, Kirchengraben 11, 7470 Albstadt.

Alcanena, Ribatejo, Portugal   The village that has been the centre of the Portuguese leather industry since the eighteenth century, 90 km (55 mi.) NE of Lisbon. There is a factory with a ducal crest dating from 1792. There were once over eighty leather works in Alcanena and neighbouring Moreira. Minde, 8 km (5 mi.) N., was a centre for woollen manufactures before the Methuen Treaty of 1703 (*see* PORTUGAL).

Alcobaça, Estremadura, Portugal   A town at the confluence of the Rivers Alcoa and Baça, 95 km (60 mi.) N. of Lisbon, well known for its Cistercian monastery, the huge kitchen of which has a pyramid-shaped chimney set on eight cast-iron columns dating from *c*.1750, one of the first structural uses of cast iron in Europe. A cotton factory, where the first spinning jennies used in Portugal were installed in 1789, was destroyed by the Napoleonic armies during the Peninsular Wars (1808–14).

BIBLIOGRAPHY
Specific
Lenços & Colchas de Chita de Alcobaça (Printed bedspreads and handkerchiefs of Alcobaça). Lisbon: IPPC.

alcohol   *See* AKVAVIT; BEER; BRANDY; BREWERY; CIDER; DISTILLING; ETHANOL; GIN; METHANOL; PORT WINE; RUM; SCHNAPPS; SPIRITS; VODKA; WHISKY; WINE.

ale   A term which, used loosely, is synonymous with beer. Ale may be distinguished from beer by having greater strength and by containing hops. Standard containers held less ale than beer: before 1688 a barrel held 32 gallons of ale but 36 gallons of beer. The word was also applied to a celebration or festival.

BIBLIOGRAPHY
General
Connor, 1987.

Alenquer, Estremadura, Portugal   An important nineteenth-century industrial centre, 40 km (25 mi.) N. of Lisbon, near the river of the same name. A papermill and woollen cloth factories can be seen as the former buildings of Romeira mill (1870) and the Chemina mill (1899). Local history is illustrated in the Hipólito Cabaço Museum.

LOCATION
[M] Hipólito Cabaço Museum, Rua Milne Carmo, Alenquer.

Alès, Gard, France   The coal and metalliferous mining region between Alès, 60 km (37 mi.) NW of Avignon and La Grand'Combe, 15 km (9 mi.) N., developed from the late eighteenth century and was for long the only significant centre of heavy industry in southern France. Silver and lead were mined from Roman times, but coal extraction from deep mines only began in earnest from 1774 when mining rights were granted to Baron Tubeuf. A glassworks at Rochebelle opened, using locally mined coal. The industrial take-off of the area came after the creation in 1829 of the Société des Fonderies et Forges d'Alès. Coal mining developed on a larger scale at La Grand'Combe, necessitating the construction from 1840 of one of France's earliest railways which ran to Beaucaire, on the Rhône, 67 m (41 mi.) SE. A whole new town grew up at La Grand'Combe, based on the collieries, and an associated glassworks and zinc factory.

At Salindres, 10 km (6 mi.) NE of Alès, Henry Merle opened a soda plant using local pyrites in 1855. From 1860 this plant refined aluminium by the chemical process, pioneering this technology in France.

Today industry in Alès is in crisis after the closure of the deep mines. The interpretation of the region's industrial past centres round the former 'teaching mine', opened in 1945 for training apprentices. It has 600 m (2000 ft.) of demonstration galleries showing the history of coal extraction from the nineteenth century to the present day. Several headstocks remain, a latticework construction of 1929 at the Fontanes pit, a concrete headstock of 1948 at the Destival pit, a masonry structure of *c*.1848 at the La Trouche mine, and a steel headstock of 1936 subsequently reinforced with concrete at the Ricard pit. Other industrial sites at Alès include the early-nineteenth-century furnace hall of the Rochebelle glassworks, which has recently been restored, and some vestiges of the ironworks, including the foundations of the blast furnaces. At La Grand'Combe one of the zinc works buildings of *c*.1830 survives, while the coal-fired power station of 1910 had notable architectural qualities but was demolished in 1990. There are limekilns and a kiln for calcining pyrites at Saint-Martin-de-Valgalgues. The former abbey of fonts at Saint-Julien-les-Rosiers was used in the eighteenth century for the production of 'green vitriol', ferrous sulphate used for dyeing. Many traces remain of the railways linking the mines with the factory sites, in particular a two-tiered viaduct of *c*.1850 forming an incline between the small hamlet of Champclauson and the centre of La Grand' Combe.

The region's housing is naturally linked closely to its industrial origins, with succeeding generations of barrack-type buildings, then planned estates erected by the Société des Mines de la Grand'Combe et des chemins de fer du Gard. Tenement blocks at Champclauson built between 1842 and 1848 remain in occupation.

The Béssèges coal mines, 20 km (12 mi.) N. of Alès, also retain traces of past activities, notably at Gagnières, where there are early-twentieth-century masonry headstocks.

BIBLIOGRAPHY
General
Daumas, 1980; Guiollard, 1983; Locke, 1978.
Specific
Wienin, M. Unpublished study for l'Inventaire Général.

LOCATION
[M] Musée d'Alès (Alès Museum), Château du Colombier, 30100 Alès.

JEAN-FRANÇOIS BELHOSTE

Alfeld, Lower Saxony, Germany   A town on the River Leine, 60 km (40 mi.) S. of Hanover, with what must be the most celebrated industrial building in north-west Germany, the Fagus works of Carl Benscheidt, a factory making shoemakers' lasts and leather punches, built between 1911 and 1924 to plans by Walter Gropius (*see* BAUHAUS), in collaboration with Adolf Meyer. A pioneering work of industrial architecture, it makes a striking contrast with the adjacent last and punch factory of C. Behrens, built only fifteen years earlier. The Behrens factory is of red brick, in a conservative style, but no attempt whatsoever was made to copy historical examples in the Fagus complex. The main building in particular, with its drying chambers, production plant, offices, dispatch department and staircase, is cited in most accounts of modern architecture. Pillars of pale yellow brick alternate with curtain walls which extend from near the ground to the roof. The warehouse and boilerhouse are more reminiscent of the style of PETER BEHRENS. Adjacent to the Fagus complex stands the former Kappe agricultural machinery works, designed by Gropius in 1924–5. It is now used as a warehouse but the exterior is unaltered.

In 1853 the Südbahn (southern railway) from Hanover to Kassel reached Alfeld. The station in Alfeld itself was replaced in the 1970s, but those built in the 1850s at Elze, 16 km (10 mi.) N., and Nord-stemmen, 22 km (14 mi.) N., down the Leine valley, remain, the former with tracks running between the platforms, the latter with all the buildings on an 'island' platform. The station buildings at Elze have elements of Moorish ornamentation. A small watertower stands beside the station, with a spherical tank of riveted sheet iron on a brick base.

BIBLIOGRAPHY
General
Pevsner, 1976; Wilhelm, 1983.

MICHAEL MENDE

Aljustrel, Baixo Alentejo, Portugal   A mining centre 130 km (80 mi.) SE of Lisbon, worked by the Phoenicians and the Romans, with the largest deposits of copper ore and copper and iron PYRITES in Portugal, totalling some 200 million tonnes. Between 1867 and 1881 ore was carried from the mines of São João do Deserto at Algares to the iron plant at Pedras Brancas along a narrow-gauge railway. In 1876 a bronze slab inscribed with judicial codes of the first century AD was found at the Algares mine.

alkali   A material that gives an alkaline reaction; one that is capable of neutralizing an acid. In an industrial sense it has commonly been used to mean one specific alkali, sodium carbonate or soda ash (Na_2CO_3), which is extensively used in the manufacture of glass and soap, in metal-processing, papermaking and the production of textiles. (It has also been used for potassium carbonate (K_2CO_3), which can be substituted for sodium carbonate.)

In the seventeenth and eighteenth centuries alkali was obtained from BARILLA and KELP. Many scientists experimented in the late eighteenth century with other means of producing alkali, among them Lord Dundonald (1749–1831), James Keir (1735–1820) and CARL SCHEELE. The process developed by Nicholas Leblanc (1742–1806) came to be widely adopted and was the foundation of the prosperity of the nineteenth-century British alkali industry (*see* LEBLANC PROCESS). It was superseded by the ammonia-soda process in the late nineteenth century (*see* SOLVAY, ERNEST) and from the 1890s by ELECTROLYSIS.

The pollution caused by the manufacture of sodium carbonate in Britain led to the Alkali Act of 1863, through which other processes were eventually subjected to control and inspection.

See also AMMONIA; SODA.

BIBLIOGRAPHY
General
Allen, 1906; ICI, 1950; Morgan and Pratt, 1938; Partington, 1950; Reader, 1970; Smith, 1872; Warren, 1980.

BARRIE TRINDER

Allevard, Isère, France   The iron industry of the Allevard region, in the alpine valley of the River Bréda, 30 km (19 mi.) NE of Grenoble, was already well known in the Middle Ages, thanks largely to the presence of particularly rich and abundant carbonate spathic ores ($FeCO_3$). After a period of decline in the fifteenth and sixteenth centuries, production began to rise early in the seventeenth century, largely as a result of the arrival of Italian ironworkers from the Bergamo region. About ten BERGAMASQUE FURNACES were erected, with characteristic removable front walls, at the feet of which apertures for tapping molten iron and for introducing the air blast were located one above the other. At an early date these furnaces also had TROMPES to provide the blast, an installation of this kind being mentioned in 1645.

During the eighteenth century pig iron produced from Allevard ores was used by about thirty small steelworks, located along the Fure and Morge rivers, near the towns of Rives and Voiron, 25 km (16 mi.) NW of Grenoble. It was probably the manganese content of the Allevard pig irons that made them suitable for steel production, since they were only partially decarbonized at the FINERY-AND-CHAFERY FORGES. This small region in the Dauphiné consequently remained France's leading producer of steel until the 1820s.

Most of the blast furnaces built near Allevard at the beginning of the seventeenth century disappeared before 1800 due to lack of wood. Only the furnaces located at the Gorge d'Allevard and at the Saint Hugon Carthusian monastery survived. But the Allevard ores were transported to supply furnaces further afield, for example to those of the Saint Vincent-de-Mercuze works on the opposite side of the River Isère, of the Sonnant works near Uriage, 10 km (6 mi.) SE of Grenoble, and of the Saint Gervais cannon foundry, 20 km (12 mi.) W. of Grenoble. This foundry dated from 1670, and included two Walloon-type furnaces joined together. The Grande Chartreuse monastery also owned blast furnaces at Fourvoirie and at Saint Pierre-d'Entrement, 30 km (19 mi.) N. of Grenoble.

The Allevard works was the only one in the region to survive into the nineteenth century. In 1859 it began to produce puddled steel, and in 1869 to use the Siemens-Martin OPEN-HEARTH process for steel production. The prosperity of the enterprise during the nineteenth century was based largely on its specialization in certain types of products: tyres for the wheels of railway rolling stock, springs for carriages, and armour plating for warships. At the beginning of the twentieth century the works was equipped with six new Chaplet electric furnaces, making use of the region's plentiful supplies of cheap electricity from two specially-built hydro-electric power stations opened in 1908 and 1910. The Allevard factory no longer exists, production having been transferred to the Le Cheylas works, 8 km (5 mi.) SW of Allevard on the banks of the Isère.

Elsewhere there are many remains of the iron and steel industry of the Dauphiné. At the Pelouse works at Pinsot, 3 km (2 mi.) SE of Allevard, is the masonry stack of a seventeenth-century Bergamasque furnace. An archaeological excavation of the site took place in 1988. The furnace, of sandstone, has a U-shaped plan, and is 4.3 m (14 ft.) high, with an outer shell between 1.3 and 2.2 m (4 ft. and 7 ft.) thick. Inside the structure are remains of the lining and of the boshes. The charging opening of the furnace is 1.6 m (5 ft.) square. The front wall has disappeared, but there are still remains of a small casting area in front of the furnace, measuring about 4 m² (43 sq. ft.).

Remnants of another blast furnace are to be seen at Saint Pierre-d'Entremont in the Grande Chartreuse. It is larger than the Pelouse furnace, and probably dates from c.1700. Its outer shell still has the characteristic U-shaped form. The blast furnace which still stands at Saint Vincent-de-Mercuze is a typical nineteenth-century masonry structure. It was probably built in 1845, although the site had been used for ironmaking in the eighteenth century. It is 10 m (33 ft.) high, and although it had a cylinder-type blast machine, there are still vestiges of an earlier water-supply system for TROMPES. Next to it are remains of an early-nineteenth-century ore-calcining kiln, subsequently converted into a limekiln. A larger calcining kiln may be seen at Saint Pierre d'Allevard, 13

km (8 mi.) SW of Allevard. This kiln was built c.1876 alongside the iron-ore mines exploited until 1889 by the Schneider company for its works at LE CREUSOT.

There are also notable remains at the Saint Gervais cannon foundry which remained active until 1865. There are four buildings arranged around a rectangular courtyard, the main building housing a boring shop and four reverberatory furnaces. Remains of these furnaces, with their chimney stacks, are still to be seen, as is the foundry's main reservoir. Finally there are vestiges of the old parts of the Bonpertuis steelworks, 5 km (3 mi.) N. of Rives, which is the only plant in the region still active, most of the others having disappeared in the mid-nineteenth century with the growth of steel production at SAINT-ÉTIENNE. The Bonpertuis plant still has the conical structure of a mid-nineteenth-century CEMENTATION FURNACE, a rare surviving example of this type of furnace.

BIBLIOGRAPHY
General
Belhoste, 1982, 1991; Daumas, 1980; Sütterlin, 1981.
Specific
Belhoste, J.-F. L'implantation d'une sidérurgie bergamasque en Dauphiné au début du XVIIᵉ siècle (The implanting of Bergamasque iron production in the Dauphiné in the early seventeenth century). In *Actes du colloque La siderurgia nell'antichità, Valle Camonica*, October 1988. Brescia, 1991.
Decker, M. La Fonderie de Saint-Gervais (The Saint-Gervais foundry). *Cahiers du Vieux Conflans*, CLVII, Albertville, 1983.

JEAN-FRANÇOIS BELHOSTE

Allihies (Na hAilichi), County Cork, Ireland   Centre of the copper mining region on the western extremity of Bearra Peninsula, 112 km (70 mi.) W. of Cork, which reached the peak of its prosperity in 1812–42. There are several pumphouses, one of them at great height on the side of a mountain, and a ruined Protestant chapel built by Cornish miners. The beach and many of the lanes are surfaced with washings from the dressing plant.

Alloa, Central, Scotland   *See* CLACKMANNANSHIRE.

alloy steel   *See* STEEL.

alluvial mining   Alluvial or placer mining is used for heavy minerals in secondary deposits, such as gold and tin in river terraces or rarer metals in beach sands. The techniques include sluicing, often with a high-pressure water monitor, and dredging.

alpaca   Alpaca is wool from the alpaca (*Lama pacos*) and related species of llama (*Auchenia lama*). It became an important staple in the textile industry after Sir Titus Salt (*see* BRADFORD) began to experiment with it in 1836, producing lustrous and fine fabrics, in some of which alpaca wool was mixed with cotton. Alpaca fabrics were widely used for seat coverings in RAILWAY CARRIAGES.

BIBLIOGRAPHY
General
James, 1857.

Alsemberg, Brabant, Belgium The Winderickx cardboard factory at Alsemberg in the Molenbeek valley, 12 km (8 mi.) S. of Brussels, is an iron-framed building with a Bollinckx single-cylinder horizontal steam engine, and much equipment. It originated as a papermill in 1763. The King Baudouin Foundation has supported its conversion to a museum of cardboard, paper and graphics.

BIBLIOGRAPHY
General
Linters, 1986a, 1986b; Viaene, 1986.

LOCATION
[M] Papier en Kartonfabriek Winderickx, Fabriekstraat 20, Beersel, Alsemberg.

alternator A machine for generating electric power in the form of alternating current, rather than the direct current produced by a DYNAMO. One of the first a.c. systems in Britain was installed in Paddington Station (*see* LONDON) in 1886 and employed 45-ton alternators, with 2.94 m (9 ft. 8 in.) rotating discs. The Deptford power station in London, built by Sebastian de Ferranti (1864–1930) in 1889, was one of the first to produce alternating current on a large scale. In the USA especially, fierce rivalry developed between power-supply companies using alternating current and those using direct current.

BIBLIOGRAPHY
General
Dunsheath, 1962; James, 1916.

alum Hydrated sodium (or potassium, or ammonium) aluminium sulphate ($Al_{12}(SO_4)_3$ Na_2 $SO_4.24H_2O$; $Al_{12}(SO_4)_3(NH_4)2SO_4.24H_2O$; $Al_{12}(SO_4)_3K_2SO_4.24H_2O$), obtained from aluminous shales. Roasted and lixiviated to yield aluminium sulphate, when ammonium potassium sulphate is added, alum crystallizes out. Alum is widely used as a mordant in dyeing, in making leather more supple, and in sizing paper. The principal European source from the fifteenth century was Tolfa, north of Rome, Italy, where a reddish alum was produced. Much of Europe came to rely on sources controlled by the Papacy and exported from Rome or Civitavecchia. In England in the seventeenth century alum manufacture was a royal monopoly. On the YORKSHIRE MOORS, where production began *c.*1600 and continued until *c.*1850, a blue lias shale containing both aluminium oxide and pyrites was calcined, in open heaps fired with coal, wood and furze; the iron sulphide in the pyrites oxidized to form sulphuric acid, which with the aluminium oxide formed aluminium sulphate. The calcined material was placed in pits of water to dissolve out the aluminium sulphate. The liquor was then subjected to a complex process of evaporation in which KELP and urine were added to crystallize the alum, free of unwanted iron compounds. Peter Spence in the mid-1840s perfected a means of producing alum by treating clays with sulphuric acid, and came to enjoy a near monopoly of its manufacture in Britain.

BIBLIOGRAPHY
General
Hardie and Pratt, 1966.
Specific
Morrison, A. *Alum: North-East Yorkshire's fascinating story of the first chemical industry.* Solihull: A. Morrison, 1981.

BARRIE TRINDER

aluminium (Al) An elemental metal, with a density one-third that of iron, resistance to corrosion, and high conductivity of electricity and heat. Aluminium can be rolled, cast, spun, extruded, used as paste for paint, and extruded from pellets to form tubes for toothpaste and the like. The metal was regarded as a curiosity until the late nineteenth century when it was employed for domestic utensils. Alloys of aluminium have great strength. Aluminium alloys have been particularly important in aircraft manufacture.

The chief source is BAUXITE, which is rich in aluminium oxide (usually called alumina). This is dissolved in heated caustic soda to form sodium aluminate, leaving behind iron and other impurities which do not dissolve. The addition of carbon dioxide yields aluminium hydroxide, which is heated to drive off the water, and aluminium is then isolated by ELECTROLYSIS. The process is difficult since alumina melts only at 2000 °C. In about 1886 Charles Hall (1863–1914) in the USA and Paul Héroult (1863–1914) in France discovered that a mixture of CRYOLITE and alumina would melt at just over 1000 °C, and that the metal could be isolated by electrolysis. A modern aluminium smelter consists of banks of small 'cells' for this purpose. The alumina is constantly replenished as the metal is tapped, but the cryolite remains virtually unaltered. Smelters have always been sited near large hydro-electric power stations.

BIBLIOGRAPHY
General
Alexander and Street, 1949; Jones, 1950.

BARRIE TRINDER

Älvkarleby, Uppsala, Sweden The main road north from Stockholm along the coast to Gälve crosses the River Dalälven at Älvkarleby, on a two-span arched wooden bridge near a 16 m (50 ft.) waterfall. The bridge, named after King Charles III and designed by Olof Forsgren, was completed in 1816. A hydro-electric power station designed by Erik Josephson, originally with five turbines, was built nearby by Vattenfall, the Swedish State Power Board, in 1911–15, and is open to visitors during the tourist season. The old buildings were conserved during a programme of modernization carried out at the power station from 1985.

Alvøens, Hordaland, Norway A village 12 km ($7\frac{1}{2}$ mi.) SW of Bergen. The Alvøens papermill, which worked during 1779–1981, was owned by the Fasmer family, who established a museum in an adjacent mansion. The mill made high-quality paper for banknotes and love letters. Machinery for 10 kr. notes and love letters has since been removed to the Norsk Teknisk Museum (*see* OSLO); other banknote machinery remains in the museum in the mansion. The buildings of the original papermill have now been adapted to new uses.

Amalfi, Campania, Italy   A picturesque coastal town set amidst the limestone crags of the Lattari mountains, the main street leading into the 'Valle dei Mulini' (valley of mills). There is a small working papermill in Via Genova, and a ceramic works of steel and concrete. Near the head of the valley is a pair of large mills, which are derelict. The lower has four storeys with irregular fenestration, the upper a wide central arch over a stream. Nearby is a five-storey block, designed in the form of an urban palace, with balconies and a painted representation of pilasters. A tributary stream is flanked by several smaller paperworks, the mill at Frassito incorporating a house, a series of small iron water wheels, and a spaghetti-like maze of water channels.

Amberley, West Sussex, England   Home of the Chalk Pits Museum, which features industries of southern England, in a 12 ha (30 ac.) quarry. The quarry was working before 1840, and closed in the 1960s. Surviving features include eighteen-chamber de Wit kilns of 1904. It is adjacent to Amberley railway station, and a wharf and canalized section of the River Arun. Collections include domestic radios, narrow-gauge industrial railway equipment, and twentieth-century road transport.

LOCATION
[M] Chalk Pits Museum, Houghton Bridge, Amberley, Arundel, West Sussex BN18 9LT.

American system of manufacture   American small arms assembled from INTERCHANGEABLE PARTS produced by sets of special-purpose machine tools were shown at the Great Exhibition of 1851 and led to a parliamentary investigation of the broader development of labour-saving machinery in the USA. This in turn led to the adoption of American equipment and manufacturing practice in British arsenals. Later generations of American mechanical engineers considered that it was ELI WHITNEY who, in meeting his contracts after 1802 to produce army muskets with interchangeable parts, was the originator of a distinctively American system of manufacture which had diffused from the armouries. A greater reliance on process mechanization in the USA than in the UK during the nineteenth century has been accepted by economic historians who, following Habbakuk (1962), have sought an explanation in relative factor costs.

Recent scholarship has heavily qualified this notion of an American system. The ideal of interchangeable manufacture interested a number of governments and engineers around 1800 and, among Americans, Whitney was less important than Simeon North (1765–1852) in devising machinery to approach this goal. Mechanized interchangeable manufacture in US armouries before the Civil War was pursued as a strategic objective for forty years before it became economic in terms of American factor costs, and began to diffuse into the commercial production of guns and closely related goods like sewing machines. Following Battison (1976), artefact-based research has qualified our understanding of the extent of interchangeability that was being sought, and has pushed back the date at which this interchangeability was achieved, in case after case.

Greater attention has been paid to differences than to continuities in machine-tool design and shop practice, and a detailed comparative study, as conducted by Jeremy (1981) for the textile industry, would now be likely to conclude that international differences of manufacturing practice in the nineteenth century are better understood as questions of emphasis than of fundamental principle. If anything, differences were probably greater after the turn of the century when corporate organizations seeking to exploit large markets invested in MASS PRODUCTION technology.

BIBLIOGRAPHY
General
Battison, 1976; Habbakuk, 1967; Hounshell, 1984; Jeremy, 1981; Mayr and Post, 1982; Rolt, 1986; Rosenberg, 1959; Saul, 1970; Smith, 1977; Wagoner, 1968.
Specific
Fries, R. British response to the American system. In *Technology and Culture*, XVI, 1960.
Gordon, R. Material evidence of manufacturing methods used in 'Armory Practice'. In *IA*, XIV, 1988.
Leland, O. *Master of Precision: Henry M. Leland*. Detroit, 1966.
Rosenberg, N. ed. *The American System of Manufactures*. Edinburgh: Edinburgh University Press, 1969.
Uselding, P. and Root, E. K. Forging, and the American system. In *Technology and Culture*, XV, 1974.
Woodbury, R. S. The legend of Eli Whitney and interchangeable parts. In *Technology and Culture*, I, 1960.

TIM PUTNAM

Amfissa, Stereá Ellás, Greece   Facing the Gulf of Corinth, 189 km (118 mi.) W. of Athens, Amfissa developed as a centre for leather working, particularly for the treatment of goatskins. Ten water-powered factories were established by 1914. Narrow streets are lined with open-arcaded, single-storey structures. A modest museum with machinery is being developed, and a study of the surviving workshops is in progress.

ammonia (NH_3)   A colourless gas, discovered by Joseph Priestley (1733–1804), with a range of important compounds. It was obtained in the nineteenth century in stills, from ammoniacal liquor, a by-product of the manufacture of coke and gas from coal, and usually converted immediately to ammonium sulphate ((NH_4)$_2$$SO_4$) by being bubbled into sulphuric acid. Production of 'artificial ammonia' by the Haber-Bosch process, a method published by Fritz Haber (1868–1934) and Carl Bosch (1874–1940) in 1905, was pioneered by Badische Anilin und Soda Fabrik, which began commercial production in 1913. WATER GAS is blended with PRODUCER GAS and steam under pressure, in a chromium steel vessel and in the presence of a catalyst, either iron oxide or platinum. It is essential that the gases should be purified to avoid poisoning of the catalyst. (Hydrogen can be obtained from the electrolysis of water instead of from water gas.) The perfection of the process, with the need to maintain constant temperatures and pressures, was one of the principal feats of chemical engineering of the early twentieth century.

Ammonia is the source of sodium nitrite ($NaNO_2$), used in the manufacture of many synthetic dyestuffs, of hydrogen and of nitric acid. It can be neutralized with nitric acid to form ammonium nitrate (NH_4NO_3), used as a fertilizer or explosive, and is also a source of the fertilizers calcium nitrate ($Ca(NO_3)_2$); ammonium phosphate ($(NH_4)_2HPO_4$); and ammonium sulphate ($(NH_4)_2SO_4$), which is mixed with calcium carbonate ($CaCO_3$), also formed in the process, to make 'nitro-chalk'. Ammonia was used in early commercial refrigeration systems, but has been replaced by chlorofluorocarbons, which are themselves being phased out.

BIBLIOGRAPHY
General
Morgan and Pratt, 1938; Partington, 1950; Reader, 1970.
Specific
Haber, L. F. Fritz Haber and the nitrogen problem. In *Endeavour*, 1968.

BARRIE TRINDER

ammonia-soda process *See* SOLVAY, ERNEST.

Amsterdam, Noord Holland, The Netherlands Amsterdam has always been a commercial rather than a manufacturing town. After the formation of the Zuiderzee in the thirteenth century, Amsterdam developed as a port for the newly reclaimed peat marshes at the mouth of the Amstel river, the Y. In the fifteenth century the city broke away from domination by the Hanseatic League, as shipbuilding, soapmaking and textile manufacture developed to the east. The development of European trade and the fall of Antwerp during the wars with Spain in the sixteenth century stimulated growth. Companies for trading with the East and West Indies were formed in the early sixteenth century, leading to the construction of further shipyards and warehouses. The port fell into decay as a result of English competition in the eighteenth century, and the East and West Indies companies were liquidated in the 1790s. The trade of Amsterdam collapsed completely during the French occupation. It was well into the nineteenth century before Amsterdam regained its former position as a financial and commercial centre. Until late in the century the city could only extend along the banks of the Y because of the Great North Holland Canal (*see* NOORD HOLLAND), made in 1818–23 to shorten the route to the North Sea from 150 km to 80 km (91 mi. to 49 mi.) to overcome the silting-up of the Y on the Zuiderzee side. The eastern and western docks (Oosterdok and Westerdok) were constructed in 1832–4 to prevent further silting, the first major development in the harbour since the seventeenth century.

Soon the Great North Holland Canal was too small. In 1876 the North Sea Canal linked Amsterdam to YMUIDEN, but the harbour lacked the capacity to deal with the ships coming along the new waterway. New docks and quays were built between 1879 and 1940, together with specialist facilities for bulk cargoes at Handelskade, where 2 km (1 mi.) of quays were built in 1879–83, for timber at Houthaven and for oil at Petroleumhaven, constructed in 1885–8. A new bonded warehouse, the Nieuwe Entrepôt, was built on Cruquiusweg in 1895, replacing the Entrepôt bonded warehouse complex of 1710–1840, which was converted into apartments in the 1980s. The imposing Nieuwe Amstel bascule bridge was completed in 1902. Many shipping lines established offices in the city. The nineteenth-century harbour buildings are now being redeveloped, and there are plans to build exclusive apartments where warehouses cannot be re-adapted. The Oranjesluices of 1872–95 and the adjacent pumping station are threatened by redevelopment.

Inadequate connections with the hinterland were a constraint on the development of Amsterdam as a trans-shipment port. The Merwede Canal of 1892 was not a success, and it was only the Amsterdam–Rhine Canal of 1953 that achieved a satisfactory connection. Amsterdam was a port profiting chiefly from cargoes of high value but relatively low volume, especially those from the colonies. It had an important role as a STAPLE for tea, coffee, cocoa and sugar, and was the chief tobacco market in Europe in the 1920s. Large twentieth-century ships were able to reach the port only after the sea locks at Ymuiden were enlarged in the 1930s. After World War II port activities developed to the west of the city along the North Sea Canal. The Ydoorn lighthouse east of the city dates from 1893.

Dutch maritime history is portrayed in the Maritime Museum in the Zeemagazijn of 1656, which includes a small dock containing a lugger from Vlaardingen and a steamboat of 1900. Nearby is the Kromhout shipyard, established in the 1750s, where there are slipways and buildings with cast-iron roofs. Marine engines were built in the yard until 1911 after which it concentrated on vessels for inland navigation until its closure in 1967. In the same vicinity at Oostenburg, on the premises of the East India Company, Vlissingen en Van Heel started a shipyard in 1827, building steam engines and other machinery. It was taken over by Werkspoor in 1891, which used it for manufacturing railway equipment, and made many extensions and alterations. A company museum includes models and paintings. In the 1970s economic pressures brought about the closure of the shipyards of the early twentieth century on the north bank of the Y.

The first Dutch railway between Amsterdam and Haarlem was opened in 1839 and was linked with the line to Utrecht by the Central Station of 1881–9, which has a single-span cast-iron train shed, behind a façade in the Italian Palazzo style. A 6 km (4 mi.) electric tramway terminated at the Haarlemmermeerstation of 1915, where there is a museum with a collection of eighty tramcars.

Gasworks in Amsterdam have been adapted to a variety of new uses. At the Oostergasfabriek of 1884–5, the retort house is now a creamery, one gasholder a sports hall, the pit of another a swimming pool, and the purification house, a bus garage. The purification house and offices at the Westergasfabriek of 1883–5 are protected. The water-tower of 1910 remains at the Zuidergasfabriek.

Amsterdam has long been famous for its diamond industry, many polishing works having been operated by the city's Jewish community. The industry was greatly stimulated by the discovery of diamonds in South Africa in the late nineteenth century, but from the 1920s its development was restricted by Belgian competition. The Boas works on Nieuwe Uilenburgerstraat, a former diamond-polishing factory, dating from 1876–8, is one of the most impressive industrial buildings in the city. Another late-nineteenth-century diamond factory on Anjelier straat is now an interactive science centre. The diamond workers' office of 1899 on Polaklaan is now the headquarters of the largest Dutch trade union.

The remains of the last of Amsterdam's sugar refineries, parts of which dated from the eighteenth century, were demolished in 1989. The Heineken brewery of 1868 ceased production in 1989 because of the limited possibilities for expansion. Parts are being transformed into a visitor centre explaining the technology of brewing.

Amsterdam has two remarkable cinemas, the Tuschinski of 1921 and the Cineac of 1934. Other outstanding buildings relating to the service industries are the Stock Exchange and the Bijenkorf store of 1911–13, the Hajenus Rokin cigar shop of 1914, and one of the city's first office blocks, the New York Insurance Office of 1891 on Keizersgracht, now an exclusive store. The central post office of 1899 is being transformed into luxury shops, while the reinforced concrete Olympic Stadium of 1928 remains in use.

The population of Amsterdam doubled between 1860 and 1900, when it reached 516000, and many houses built by speculators and by the public authorities remain, notably examples of 1856 at Houtmanstraat, of 1869 at Anjelierstraat, of 1915–20 at Zaanstraat, and of 1919–20 at Schwartzeplein, Takstraat. There are back-to-back houses of 1896 on Lindengracht, and the Betondorp (concrete village) of 1926–8 has been restored.

BIBLIOGRAPHY
General
Balk, 1985; Brugmans, 1973; De Jonge, 1976; DIEN database; Schade, 1980; Spangenberg and Saal, 1983.

LOCATIONS
[M] Heineken Brewery Visitor Centre, Stadhouderskade, Amsterdam.
[S] Kromhout Shipyard, Hoogte Kadijk 147, Amsterdam.
[M] Nederlands Filmmuseum, Vondelpark 3, Amsterdam.
[M] Nederlands Scheepvaart Museum (Maritime Museum), Kattenburgerplein 1, Amsterdam.
[M] Rijdend Electrisch Tram Museum (Electric Tramway Museum), Haarlemmermeerstation, Amstelveenseweg 264, Amsterdam.

[M] Technisch Museum het NINT (Technology Museum), Tolstraat 129, Amsterdam.
[M] Werkspoormuseum (Railway Museum), Oostenburgergracht 77, Amsterdam.

JURRIE VAN DALEN

Añana, Álava, Basque Country, Spain   Near to the planned medieval town of Añana, 48 km (25 mi.) S. of Bilbao, stands the saltworks known as 'La Salina', for which there is documentary evidence from the tenth century. Brine is evaporated in a series of about five thousand pans ('eras') on platforms cut from the hillsides.

Angliers, Quebec, Canada   The 100-ton log tug *T. E. Draper* is moored on the Quinze river at Angliers, 800 km (500 mi.) NE of Montreal. It worked between 1929 and 1950, in connection with the timber-floating operations of the papermaking companies Riordon Pulp & Paper and Canadian International Paper, across a network of lakes linking the Témiscamingue and Upper Outaouais regions. The *T. E. Draper* has a draught of 2.7 m (8.86 ft.) and a steel hull 18.3 m (60 ft.) long. Powered by a 240 hp Fairbank engine, and worked by a crew of seven, it could tow RAFTS containing 50000 logs. The vessel was recognized in 1979 by the Quebec government as a historic structure and is now the property of the Angliers municipality, which is responsible, together with a local society, for its interpretation.

BIBLIOGRAPHY
Specific
Beaudry-Gourd, B. *Angliers et le remorqueur 'T. E. Draper'* (Angliers and the tug 'T. E. Draper'). Collège de l'Abitibi-Témiscamingue, 1983.

Angoulême, Charente, France   The Saint-Cybard paper factory on the outskirts of Angoulême dates back to an earlier papermill, founded in 1791 on the site of the old corn mill of the abbey of Saint-Cybard. The department of Charente already ranked third in France for paper production, and in 1812 had some twenty-seven mills, which specialized in high-quality cream-laid papers for export, or for the Parisian book trade.

The Saint-Cybard papermill was purchased in 1819 by Antoine Lacroix (1774–1841). Together with his son Jean, who owned an adjacent mill, he built a completely new factory c.1835 on a branch of the River Charente, with a specially-adapted water-power system. The factory was to house the second papermaking machine in Charente; by 1844 this was the best-equipped department in France in this respect. The subsequent prosperity of the Lacroix factory was based primarily on the production of glossy paper. In 1919 it was taken over by the 'Joseph-Bardou Le Nil' company, and subsequently specialized in producing cigarette paper.

The factory closed in 1970 and was bought in 1979 by the town of Angoulême. The buildings have been reused as a regional art school, and as a paper workshop-cum-museum, which not only illustrates the history of the paper industry, but also exhibits contemporary paper creations. The buildings occupied, astride the Charente, are those of the original Lacroix factory, their façades retained and restored. The chimney stack and a water wheel are also preserved.

BIBLIOGRAPHY
Specific
André L. La Papeterie charentaise au XIXe siècle (Papermaking in Charente in the nineteenth century). *Fumée du Nil*, I. Angoulême: Atelier-Musée du Papier, 1989.
Peaucelle, D. Si Saint Cybard savait ça! (If Saint Cybard knew that!). Angoulême: *Fumée du Nil*, 0 Atelier-Musée du Papier, 1989.

LOCATION
[M] Musée Municipal (Municipal Museum), 1 rue de Friedland, 16000 Angoulême.

JEAN-FRANÇOIS BELHOSTE

Angus, Tayside, Scotland   A county to the north of the River Tay, the world leader in coarse linen manufacture in the early nineteenth century, and later in the jute industry. The Angus Folk Museum occupies weavers' cottages in Glamis, 16 km (10 mi.) N. of Dundee. The earliest water-powered spinning mills, on the Dighty, Brothock and Lunan Waters and the River Esk, were very small. Many of the sites and some buildings can be recognized. Craigo Mill, a combined bleachfield and spinning works, rebuilt in 1909 as a single-storey jute spinning mill, was the last to close, in 1988.

Montrose's first steam-powered mill started in 1805. The principal survivor, Chapel Works, built by J. & G. Paton in 1828–46, is the biggest in the county outside Dundee: now a BOND, it comprises two-, three- and four-storey mills, some fireproof, with Gothic and Romanesque detailing, and a later ropewalk.

Arbroath's first mill, Brothock Mill of 1806, became the printing works of the *Arbroath Herald* in 1936 and still stands, a narrow timber-floored building, with a late nineteenth-century extension which has a system of double brick arches. The boom occurred in the early 1820s and fireproof buildings, like Green's Mill of 1837, came in the 1830s. Sailcloth power looms were employed from 1847. Chalmers Street and St Rollox Works are weaving sheds of the 1850s and 60s. Baltic Works of 1854 is a well laid-out weaving shed with a four-storey pedimented front, now a bond. In Alma Works, of 1856, now the only linen-weaving factory in Angus, sailcloth and canvas are made by Francis Webster & Co. on British Northrop looms. Douglas Fraser & Co. diversified from sailcloth to alpargatas (jute shoes, popular in Latin America), building factories in Buenos Aires c.1890; and then to textile machinery and machine tools in the Westburn and Wellgate foundries, where there are three-storey galleried machine shops which incorporate earlier textile mills.

At Brechin, East Mill, opened in 1808, had a three-storey fireproof extension added in 1837. J. & J. Smart of Valley Works introduced power looms in the 1850s and extended their works in 1864 and 1902. D. & R. Duke's Denburn Works, designed by the Dundee engineers Robertson & Orchar, was founded in 1864, and has a four-storey Italianate campanile-towered front of 1874, now to be converted to housing.

Panmure Works, Carnoustie, which has a fine sculptured pediment to its two-storey front, was regarded as a model power-loom works from its foundation in 1857. Housing and an Italianate-towered Institute of 1863 were provided for the workpeople.

Forfar was a linen-weaving town where large power-loom factories were built in the 1860s. Three are still operated by the polypropylene company Don & Low: Strang Street Works, with a campanile tower; Canmore Works, of 1867; and St James Works. The three-storey front of Craik's Manor Works has been converted to housing.

Power looms were introduced at Kirriemuir at Marywell Brae Works in 1867, and at Garie Works in 1869. Both are weaving sheds with deep basements (used by the textile firm J. & D. Wilkie) and contain nineteenth-century calenders and press packers.

Lochside Distillery, Montrose, was founded as a brewery in the late eighteenth century. A French Gothic brewing tower was added in 1889, and the complex became a grain and malt distillery in 1957. Hillside distillery is more conventional, with stalk and double pagoda. Both it and Brechin's North Port Distillery of 1820 have closed, but Glencadam Distillery at Brechin, of 1825, still functions.

Upper Mill, Barry, 10 km (7 mi.) E. of Dundee, retains nineteenth-century water-powered plant for grinding oatmeal, and was acquired by the National Trust for Scotland in 1988. Millden's Meal Mill, Aberlemno, 8 km (5 mi.) SW of Brechin, has two pairs of stones and a restored low-breast wheel. At Angus Mill, Kirriemuir, the oatmeal stones are driven by electric power.

At Usan, 3 km (2 mi.) S. of Montrose, a conduit and a saltpan house converted to an icehouse are amongst the most substantial remains of a Scottish saltworks. A fine group of limekilns stands on an eroded promontory at Boddin.

The outstanding Bell Rock Lighthouse of 1807–12 by JOHN RENNIE and ROBERT STEVENSON is paired with a crenellated signal tower of 1813 in Arbroath, now the local museum.

The twin-basin harbour at Arbroath supports a thriving 'Smokie' industry, the haddock being smoked in tiny smokehouses. The trade migrated from Auchmithie, 5 km (3 mi.) NE. High-technology wooden fishing boats are made at two yards in Arbroath. One employs a patent slip which is crossed by an iron bascule bridge. Montrose has a small harbour and a reinforced-concrete cantilever bridge of 1928–30 by Sir E. Owen Williams (1890–1969). A wrought-iron suspension bridge of 1834 stands at Kirkton of Glenisla, 16 km (10 mi.) N. of Blairgowrie.

Montrose airfield, established by the Royal Flying Corps in 1913, retains 'Major Burke's sheds': three side-door, timber-framed hangars of Indian Army design, the oldest surviving accommodation for military aircraft in Britain. Two end-door hangars of 1917 have been moved to Bo'NESS.

The Caledonian Railway (Brechin) operates industrial

steam and diesel locomotives from Brechin station, an Italianate terminus of 1847–8 with an iron porte-cochère and a goods shed. Kerr's Miniature Railway at Arbroath, founded in 1935, has petrol and steam locomotives older than many preserved main-line locomotives. The crenellated viaduct of 1840 at Friockheim, 10 km (6 mi.) NW of Arbroath, has long lain disused.

See also DUNDEE.

BIBLIOGRAPHY
General
Hay and Stell, 1986; Hume, 1977; Whatley, 1984.
Specific
Turner, W. H. K. *The Textile Industry of Arbroath since the Early 18th Century.* Dundee: Abertay Historical Society, 1954.

LOCATIONS
[M] Angus Folk Museum, Kirkwynd Cottages, Glamis, Angus.
[S] Caledonian Railway, Brechin Station, 2 Park Road, Brechin, Angus DD9 7AF.
[S] Kerr's Miniature Railway, West Links Park, Arbroath, Angus.
[I] Montrose Aerodrome Society, c/o Ian McIntosh, 23 Glenesk Avenue, Montrose, Angus DD10 9AQ.
[I, M] Montrose Museum and Art Gallery, Panmure Place, Montrose, Angus DD10 8HE. (For Arbroath Museum, and all other Angus District Council museums.)

MARK WATSON

Anhalt/Saxony, Germany   After Saxony ceased to be a province in 1952, this territory comprised the former DDR regions of Dresden, Gera, Halle, Karl-Marx-Stadt (which in 1990 reverted to its old name of Chemnitz) and Leipzig. Its principal cities are DRESDEN, with 500 000 inhabitants; LEIPZIG, with 570 000; CHEMNITZ, with 300 000; Halle, with 250 000; and Zwickau, with 120 000.

Saxony was the most industrially diversified area of the DDR. The major industries range from textiles to the mining of bituminous coal and LIGNITE, iron ore and other minerals; there is also the chemical industry. Saxony was also an important agricultural region, the nineteenth-century centre of sugar-beet growing and the centre of the German sugar trade.

The lignite mining districts of the Magdeburg and Bitterfeld region now supply most of the former DDR's energy requirements. From 1890 an extensive chemical industry developed on the basis of this brown coal, and on the mining of bituminous coal and POTASH. Iron-smelting at Eisleben, Riesa and Gröditz, and mechanical engineering in Leipzig, Dresden and Chemnitz, are also important industries. Much archaeological evidence has been preserved of mechanized textile production dating back to the early nineteenth century in Plauen, Greiz and Zwickau, and in the west and south of Chemnitz.

BIBLIOGRAPHY
General
Berger, 1980; Föhl and Hamm, 1988; Forberger, 1982; Schmidt and Theile, 1989; Wagenbreth and Wächtler, 1983.

AXEL FÖHL

anhydrite   An important raw material in the chemical industry: rhombic calcium sulphate ($CaSO_4$). It is used in the manufacture of ammonium sulphate from AMMONIA, and is a source of sulphur dioxide for the production of sulphur and SULPHURIC ACID. It is mined under a chemical plant at Billingham (*see* TEESSIDE).

See also GYPSUM.

BIBLIOGRAPHY
General
Morgan and Pratt, 1938; Partington, 1950.

aniline   *See* PHENYLAMINE.

animal products   *See* BEES; BONE MILL; BUTCHER; DAIRY; FEATHERS; FUR; HAIR; HORN; LEATHER; TALLOW.

Anjou, Maine-et-Loire, France   Slate quarrying in the Anjou basin probably dates from the fifteenth century, when the quarries were already deep; horse gins are known to have been used for pumping. The main underground workings only began in the 1840s when steam engines could be used to overcome drainage problems.

Slate was extracted from large underground chambers dug from veins between 20 m and 200 m (65 ft. and 650 ft.) thick. The roofs of these chambers frequently collapsed, and from the end of the nineteenth century a different extraction technique was employed, from below upwards: the slate was taken from the roof and debris fell harmlessly below. Security was further improved by systematic bolt reinforcements in the walls.

Founded in 1916 at the instigation of the Bougère bank at Angers, the Saint Blaise mine at Noyant-la-Gravoyère, 40 km (25 mi.) NW of Angers, was but one of many short-lived endeavours which developed independently of the two main companies working in the basin, the Commission des Ardoisières d'Angers and the Société Ardoisière d'Anjou. The Saint-Blaise company ceased operation in 1936, prior to which it exploited twenty-two chambers, which were reached by two inclined planes going 120 m (400 ft.) deep. This particular firm sold most of its slate on the English market.

The Saint-Blaise site is now open to the public. Access is via one of the two inclined planes, passing beneath a monumental pediment. The different galleries and chambers, some of them more than 10 m (30 ft.) high and 60 m (200 ft.) long, give a good idea of the extraction techniques in use during the first half of the twentieth century. In the former boiler house, near the entrance, there is now a collection of slate-related artefacts and images. On the former 'botte' used by the slate slitters working with their mallets and chisels, a row of shelters has been rebuilt from remnants found on the site.

At Trélazé, 10 km (6 mi.) S. of Angers, another slate museum holds a collection of slitting machines and a scale model of *c*.1905 of one of the chambers, illustrating the mounting extraction process, and showing how a suspension bridge was used for boring into the vault. At Renazé (Mayenne), 90 m (66 mi.) NW of Angers, another museum has a remarkable collection of tools and vehicles. A latticework headstock has been restored at the neighbouring Longchamps slate mines, together with a brick- and metal-framed engine house and the adjacent reservoirs for compressed air, which are reused late-nineteenth century steam boilers.

In decline since the 1970s, the Anjou slate industry has left many traces in the landscape, in particular metal headstocks, the earliest dating from 1909, and even a wooden example, at La Pouèze, 19 km (12 mi.) NW of Angers, which is now a protected monument. Associated with the slate workings are several estates of workers' housing, amongst which the mid-nineteenth-century estate at Javron and the GARDEN CITY style development of 'La Promenade' at Noyant-la-Gravoyère, sixty-four houses built in 1920–4, are particularly remarkable.

Anjou is also notable for its lime industry. The presence of both limestone and coal gave birth to a lime-burning industry at Montjean-sur-Loire, 25 km (15 mi.) W. of Angers, as early as the fifteenth century, although its main period of prosperity was in the eighteenth and nineteenth centuries. Six kilns were already in existence in 1788. Two more were built between 1789 and 1830, and fifteen more between 1830 and 1882. This development was due largely to the increasing use of lime for soil improvement, a use which accounted for two-thirds of local production up to about 1914, when chemical fertilizers gradually caused the abandonment of these limeworking sites.

From the eighteenth century the Montjean kilns were permanent structures in continuous use for six or seven months of the year between April and September. Between 7 m and 14 m (23 ft. and 46 ft.) high, they were filled with alternating layers of limestone and fuel. The lime produced was removed through three openings at the base of the kiln. The kilns themselves were built of sandstone, lined with calcareous tufa, firebrick, granulate from Vendée, or other refractories.

There are remains of most of the twenty-three limekilns known to have existed since the eighteenth century. The Rivage limeworks, for example, date from 1772, and after mid-nineteenth-century modernization, remained in use until 1892. On the site of La Tranchée, on the banks of the Loire, is a battery of seven kilns set in a solid masonry structure some 28 m (92 ft.) long and 20 m (66 ft.) deep, built up against the cliff face. The battery was built in 1875 by Edmond Heusschen, a Belgian industrialist who in 1854 had founded the Mine and Limekiln Company of the Lower Loire, for the simultaneous exploitation of coal and lime at Montjean. The limestone was brought to the kilns from the Pincourt quarry by a railway installed by Heusschen, which passed through a 600 m (1970 ft.) tunnel which was a former adit. The last limekilns in the region, at Châteaupanne, closed down only in 1962. From 1911 an aerial ropeway linked these kilns to the Loire. These works, another site at Pincourt, the masonry headstocks of the La Tranchée mine (built by Heusschen in 1875), and a battery of three nineteenth-century kilns at La Veurière, Angrie, 25 km (15 mi.) NW of Angers, are now protected monuments.

BIBLIOGRAPHY
General
Kérouanton, 1988.
Specific
Cayla, P. *Mines et charbonnages de la Basse-Loire en Anjou* (Mines of the lower Loire in Anjou). Association de préfiguration pour un Écomusée d'Anjou, n.d.

LOCATION
[M] Ecomusée de Montjean-sur-Loire, 'La Forge', Place de Vallon, 49570 Montjean-sur-Loire.
[M] Saint-Jean Museum of Archaeology, Hôpital Saint-Jean, 4 boulevard Arago, 49000 Angers.

JEAN-FRANÇOIS BELHOSTE

Ankara (Angora), Turkey   A small, relatively insignificant town until 1923 when it became the Turkish capital and the symbol of Ataturk's reforms (*see* TURKEY). It has grown rapidly and in the 1980s had a population of 3.5 million. The Ethnographical Museum has collections of traditional manufactures, while the Archaeological Museum is located in a fifteenth-century bazaar. Some 12 km ($7\frac{1}{2}$ mi.) N. is the Çubuk dam and hydro-electric power station.

LOCATIONS
[M] Ethnographical Museum, Talat Pasa Boulevard, Ankara.
[M] Museum of Anatolian Civilizations, Outer Rampart of Citadel, Ankara.

annealing furnace   A furnace used to heat metal at a particular stage in its working, to hold it at a given temperature, and then to cool it at an appropriate rate in order to remove stresses set up by previous working, and to render it suitable for subsequent processes. Annealing is used particularly in such operations as cold rolling, toolmaking and cold drawing (*see* WIRE MILL), where metals can rapidly lose ductility. The form and size of furnaces vary widely. Similar processes are used in GLASS manufacture.

BIBLIOGRAPHY
General
Gale, 1971.

anthracite   A non-bituminous, clean-burning coal, often difficult to kindle, but of high calorific value, burning with little smoke. The principal deposits are in Wales and the USA, and anthracite was used as a fuel in BLAST FURNACES in both of these countries. It has also been used in malting since the seventeenth century. In the USA anthracite was widely used as domestic fuel until the 1950s, and as locomotive fuel on some railways, including the Delaware, Lackananna & Western Railroad, the route of Phoebe Snow, whose 'gown stayed white from morn to night, upon the road of anthracite'.

antimony (Sb)   An elemental metal, similar in appearance to zinc, but brittle: it can be powdered with a hammer. Antimony is used to give hardness to lead in

TYPE, batteries, bearings and cable sheathing. The chief source is stibnite (antimony sulphide, Sb_2S_3), which is found principally in China, and South and Central America, but it is also mined in Yugoslavia, Czechoslovakia and the USA.

BIBLIOGRAPHY
General
Jones, 1950; Street and Alexander, 1949.

Antwerp (Antwerpen, Anvers), Antwerp, Belgium One of the great ports of Europe, a city at the mouth of the Scheldt (Schelde), as notable for its industrial monuments as for the richness of its cultural history. Antwerp enjoyed a period of great power and influence in the sixteenth and seventeenth centuries but suffered relative decline in the eighteenth century. After the establishment of rail links with Germany, the city grew rapidly between 1880 and 1914, not just as a port, but as a centre for new, technologically-based manufactures.

Antwerp's most venerable industrial monument is the workshop of Christopher Plantin (?1520–89), who moved to the city in 1549 from Tourcoing in France and became one of the foremost printers of Renaissance Europe. His descendants, the Moretus family, continued the business until 1876, and the Plantin-Moretus Museum, established in 1877, displays the company's equipment, business records and products from the sixteenth century to the nineteenth, including a proof-reading office, a type foundry, and sixteenth- and seventeenth-century presses. Visitors are able to print one of Plantin's sonnets on a replica of a sixteenth-century press, one of the most perfect of museum souvenirs.

Antwerp's development into a modern port began with the construction of the Bonapartdok in 1811 and the Willemdok in 1812, but the main period of dock and warehouse construction came after the middle of the nineteenth century. The principal concentration of warehouses is on Godefriduskai, most of them dating from the 1860s, although many have been rebuilt after fires. The most imposing is the Entrepôt Felix, a seven-storey galleried structure of 1863, with brick-vaulted undercrofts; it had its own hydraulic power system, installed in 1885. The ornately decorated, single-storey iron transit sheds along the quays on the north bank of the Schelde, built in 1882–90 to designs by E. van Dijckkai, characteristic of ports designed to accommodate railways, are the best preserved of their kind. The ART NOUVEAU styled Magazijnen van de Zuid-natie (Warehouse of the Southern Nation), on Oude Leeuwenrui, has a concrete frame filled with brick panels. An electric windlass remains *in situ* in the garret. The Magazijn de Klok in Hessenplein is a five-storey concrete structure, with brick façades, four corner towers, and a Baroque main entrance in natural stone. The Magazijn L. Van Parijs in Zeevaartstraat, of 1934, is an extraordinary banana warehouse in the ART DECO style. Two of Antwerp's museums are located in dock buildings: the Museum of Modern Art in 'La Nationale' warehouse, a mass concrete structure of 1922, and the Photographic Museum in the 'Vlaanderen' warehouse of 1911 on Waalse Kaai, the first warehouse in the city to be constructed with a concrete frame infilled with brick panels. The history of the port is illustrated in the Maritime Museum, housed in a medieval prison tower overlooking the Schelde, restored in the nineteenth century.

The technical services depot of the port on the Noordkaai is a high, seven-bay building in brick, lit from the sides and at each end with colossal windows with semicircular headed arches. The pumping station for the Kattenkijkdok on Westkaai, of 1895, is an early steel-framed building, with polychrome-brick infill. The Nassau bridge between the Bonaparte and Willem docks is operated by the hydraulic power system installed in the port in 1878. Power for the cranes in the southern part of the docks was provided from 1882 by one of Europe's more surprising hydraulic power stations, an eccentric Baroque structure, profoundly rusticated, with twin towers housing two accumulators; it is now the base for a theatrical company. The subsequent stage in providing power in ports is represented on the Scheldekaai by an electric crane of 1907 by Demag of Duisburg. The most impressive concentration of dockside buildings associated with manufacturing is around the Binnenhaven at Merksem, north of the city, where a range of vast structures near the mouth of the Albert Canal includes the Dandelooy maltings, the Union Margarinière margarine plant, and the RIZA rice mills.

Antwerp Central Station is one of the most breathtaking railway termini in Europe. The city's first railway station was built outside the fortifications at Borgerhoutse Pont, but in 1886 it was decided to build a new line to a terminus in the city centre. The construction of the train shed for the new Central Station began in 1895, and the station buildings were constructed in 1900–5 to designs by Louis Delacenserie. The five-bay entrance to the station is flanked by two towers, and a huge lantern dome lights the area at the end of the platforms. The application of Baroque detailing hides the extensive use of steel and concrete in the station buildings. The train shed is a single vault, 185 m (607 ft.) long, 64 m (210 ft.) wide and 44 m (144 ft.) high, formed by steel ribs, infilled with glass panels, with a magnificent steel and glass screen at the outer end; it accommodates ten platforms. The impressive side elevations show how the platforms are raised high above the level of the surrounding streets. The station was extensively restored in 1975–6. The railways around the city are adorned with several water towers in vivid polychrome-brick topped by steel-plate tanks. Antwerp retains an extensive tramway system.

Two industries symbolized Antwerp's economic vitality in the decades before World War I. In 1882 a concern called NV Bell Telephone Manufacturing Company was formed in the city to produce telecommunications equipment under licence. The following year premises were opened in Boudewijnsstraat, with thirty-five workers: these have since grown into a vast manufacturing complex, the original building having been demolished to make way for a car park. In 1889 the pioneer of photography, Lievnus Gevaert (1868–1935), who was born in the city, set up a company to manufacture photographic papers, which by 1897 was exporting all over Europe. In 1904 he established a factory in Septe-straat, Mortsel, south of the centre, which by 1910 was employing over seven hundred people in an extensive range of buildings.

Antwerp's prosperity in the late nineteenth century is illustrated in its shops, notably in the Baroque store complex of 1898 at the intersection of Leysstraat and Kipdorfvest, which was extended along both streets in 1901 and 1903, and in the Grand-Bazar department store of 1885 in Groenplats. The Exchange (Handelbeurs) in Twaalfmaandenstraat has an iron and glass roof of 1858 by a Parisian company. The 'Boerentoren' in Eiermarkt, built in 1929–32 to the design of J. Van Hoenacker, is an 87 m (285 ft.) high office block, one of the first skyscrapers in Europe.

Antwerp has long been notable for its trade in diamonds, centred on the Beurs voor Diamanthandel in Pelikaanstraat, a late-nineteenth-century building in a Baroque style, with giant pilasters. The Diamond Museum explains the mining, cutting and industrial uses of precious stones.

The Brouwershuis (Brewers' house) was built in 1553 by Gilbert van Schoonbeke (1519–56) as a horse-powered pumping station supplying water to breweries. It has a magnificent council chamber, together with displays explaining the workings of the supply system.

BIBLIOGRAPHY
General
Bautens, 1984; Linters, 1986a, 1986b; Viaene, 1986.
Specific
Verhaegen, D. La Gare d'Anvers Central: un siècle d'évolution urbanistique. In *Ons Industriel Erfgoed*, I, 1982.

LOCATIONS
[M] Archief en Museum van het Vlaams Cultuurleven, Minder-broedersstraat 22, 2000 Antwerp.
[M] Museum Brouwershuis (Brewery Museum), Brouwerstraat 20, 2000 Antwerp.
[M] Museum 'Het Wiel' (The Wheel), Hopland 15–23, 2000 Antwerp.
[M] Museum Vleeshuis (Historical Museum), Vleesbouwerstraat 38–40, 2000 Antwerp.
[M] Museum voor Hedendaagse Kunst (Museum of Modern Art), Leuvenstraat 20–4, 2000 Antwerp.
[M] National Scheepvaartmuseum (Maritime Museum), Steen-plein 1, 2000 Antwerp.
[M] Plantin-Moretus Museum, Vrijdagmarkt 22, 2000 Antwerp.
[M] Poldermuseum Lillo (Lillo Polder Museum), Georges Eek-houdlaan 10, 2050 Antwerp.
[M] Provinciaal Diamant Museum (Provincial Diamond Museum), 28–30 Jezusstraat, 2000 Antwerp.
[M] Provinciaal Museum voor Fotografie (Provincial Photo-graphic Museum), Waalse Kaai 47, 2000 Antwerp.
[M] Provinciaal Museum voor Kunstambachten Sterckshof (Handicraft Museum), Hooftvunderlei 160, 1100 Deurne.
[M] Volksmuseum Deuren (Museum of Labour History), Koraal-plats 2, 2100 Deurne.

BARRIE TRINDER

apartment A set of rooms forming a dwelling, usually within a building divided into a number of such units. The term is used particularly in North America, the word FLAT being more commonly employed in England. An apartment house or building is one made up of such dwellings: particularly, in the USA, one conforming to minimum standards of sanitation. Apartments are the most common form of inner-city dwelling in most countries in continental Europe and the USA, but not in England.

apothecary The term 'apothecary' was used until *c*.1800 to describe a trader, controlled by statute or by a chartered company, who prepared and sold medicinal compounds, who would now be called a CHEMIST, pharmacist or druggist. In earlier centuries the term described someone who sold non-perishable foodstuffs, like COFFEE and COCOA. Apothecaries by tradition practised DISTIL-LING. Traditional shops, with central benches for preparing drugs, labelled cupboards topped with glass and ceramic containers, and counters keeping back customers, are preserved in many museums.

See also CHEMIST; DISPENSARY; DRUGGIST; DRUG STORE; PHARMACY.

BIBLIOGRAPHY
General
Book of Trades, 1839; Matthews, 1982, 1983a, 1983b, 1985.

applejack *See* CIDER.

apprentice house Although an apprentice is normally someone learning a craft, who is bound to his employer by an agreement covering a set period, the term 'apprentice house' usually relates to accommodation provided at English textile mills for 'parish apprentices', pauper children, often recruited from parish authorities in distant parts of the country, who were set to work in the mills but not taught particular skills. The practice had begun by the mid-1780s, but had declined by 1820. Apprentices often lived in overcrowded conditions, and surviving apprentice houses like those at Ditherington Flax Mill, SHREWSBURY, and at STYAL probably reflect the best practice.

BIBLIOGRAPHY
General
Brown, 1832; Chapman, 1967; Farey, 1811–17; Macleod *et al.*, 1988; Ure, 1835.

aquavit Norwegian and Swedish term for AKVAVIT.

aqueduct A channel for conveying water. The term can refer to a ditch conveying drinking water (*see also* LEAT) a pipe taking water to a water wheel, a viaduct carrying a WATER SUPPLY to a city, a long-distance pipeline like that from the Elan Valley in Wales to Birmingham, or, most commonly, to a bridge carrying a navigable canal.

Early masonry aqueducts were massive in appearance since they were usually sealed with about 1.3 m (4 ft.) of puddled clay, but there are examples in Britain of great elegance like those by John Rennie at Dundas (*see* BATH) and Lancaster. Iron trough aqueducts were completed at Derby and Longdon (*see* SHREWSBURY) in 1795–6, origi-

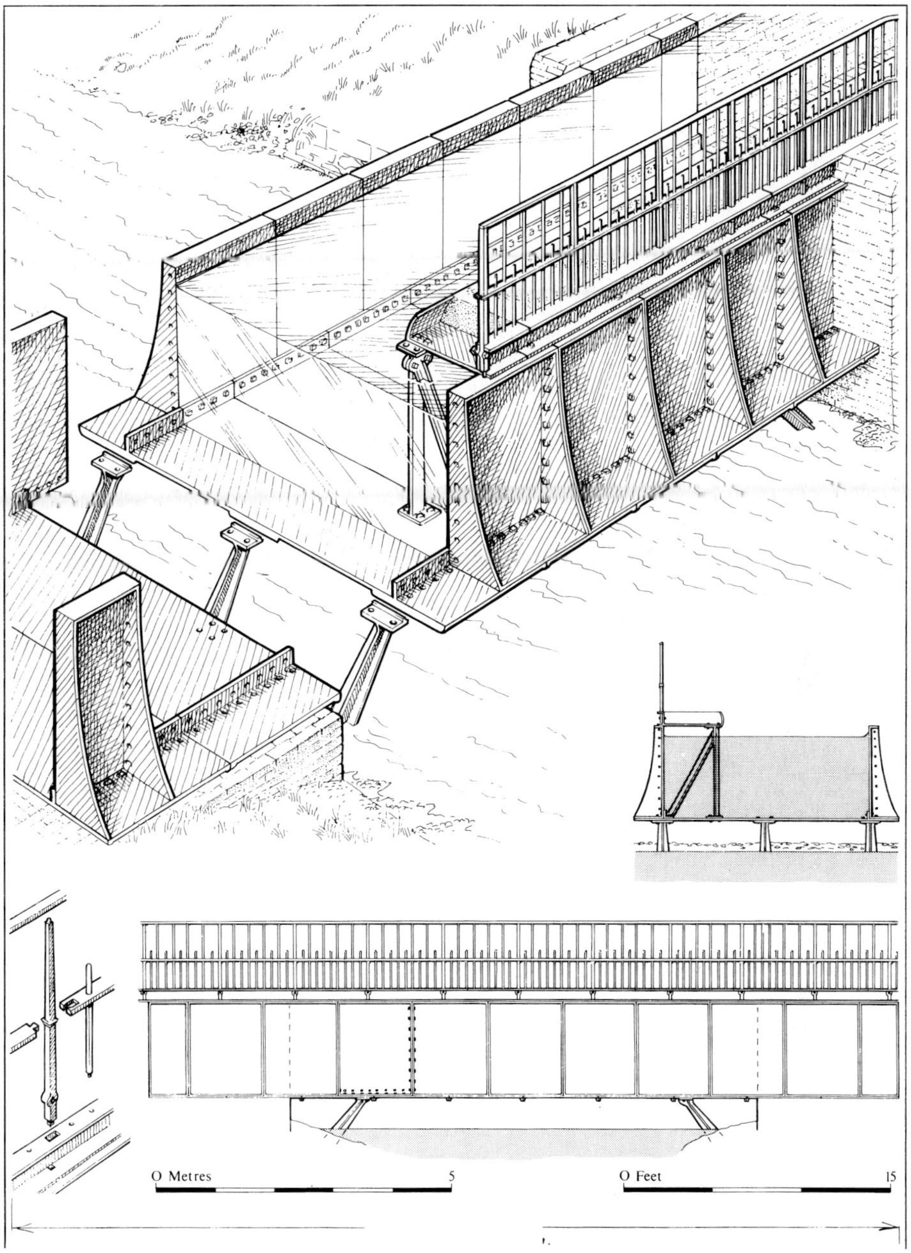

Figure 5 The Luggy Brook Aqueduct, Brithdir, on the Montgomeryshire Canal, rebuilt in this form by G. W. Buck in 1819; the side plates of the cast iron trough gradually slumped under the weight of the water, and the span was reduced with additional masonry abutments, *c*.1890. (From Stephen Hughes, *The Archaeology of the Montgomeryshire Canal*, Aberystwyth, Royal Commission on Ancient and Historical Monuments in Wales, 1988.)
Royal Commission on Ancient and Historical Monuments in Wales

nating a technique perfected in the PONTCYSYLLTE AQUE-DUCT a decade later. The Chirk Aqueduct in Wales of 1800–1 was lined with cast-iron plates, while those on the Dortmund–Ems Canal in Germany, authorized in 1886, had channels lined with sheet lead. Outstanding French examples include the 593 m (1129 yd.) Agen Aqueduct on the Canal latéral à la Garonne, authorized in 1838; and EIFFEL's Briare Aqueduct of 1896 over the Loire, 662 m (2172 ft.) long, an iron trough carried on fifteen granite piers.

Wooden aqueducts, timber troughs on masonry pillars, were relatively common in North America, on the Middlesex Canal in Massachusetts, built from 1795, and on the original line of the Welland for example. JOHN ROEBLING built a wire suspension aqueduct at Pittsburgh, USA, in 1845, and four more on the Delaware & Hudson Canal from 1847. The Barton Aqueduct built over the Manchester Ship Canal, England, in 1893, which was worked by hydraulic power, is a unique example of a swinging aqueduct.

BIBLIOGRAPHY
General
Hadfield, 1986; Vogel, 1971.

BARRIE TRINDER

31

Figure 6   The Arcade of 1890 which links Euclid Avenue and Superior Avenue, Cleveland, Ohio
Barrie Trinder

arcade   The word 'arcade' is used in industrial archaeology with at least three meanings:

1. An architectural term for a range of arches springing from upright columns. When free-standing this is sometimes called a colonnade; when attached to a wall it is properly called a blind arcade.

2. A passageway lined with shops, from which vehicles are excluded, a concept developed in Paris by 1779 and in London by 1815–19, when the Burlington Arcade was constructed to the design of Samuel Ware (1781–1860), and repeated, often with architectural distinction, in many European and American cities in the nineteenth century. One of the earliest arcades in Paris is the Passage du Grand Cerf at 145 rue St-Denis, of 1824–6. The Galérie St Hubert in Brussels, designed by J. P. Cluysenaar and built in 1846–7 in the Classical style with a magnificent cast-iron and glass roof, is one of the most distinguished in Europe. There were eight arcades in Leeds, England, by 1900, the most flamboyant of them designed by Frank Matcham. Arcades were also built in many North American cities, outstanding examples being the luxuriantly ornamented Cleveland Arcade in Cleveland, Ohio, of 1888–90 by John Eisenmann and H. G. Smith. Some of the most spectacular arcades are the Italian 'galleria' (*see* GENOA; MILAN; NAPLES). Examples in Moscow include the Upper Shopping Galleria built in 1889–93 by A. N. Pomerantsev, with over a thousand shops and a roof on Shukhov principles (*see* SHUKHOV, VLADIMIR), and the Middle Shopping Galleria by R. I. Klein, between Red Square and Khrustalny Alley, in a Russian historicist style with strong Moorish elements.

3. A place of amusement, where members of the public are able to play mechanical or electric slot machines providing peep shows, tests of skill or forecasts of the future. Amusement arcades began in the 1880s, and were a feature of seaside entertainment. The Barron company of Great Yarmouth established one of the first in England and became one of the principal manufacturers of machines. German companies produced one of the most popular machines, the Clucking Hen, while the Mills Novelty Co. of Chicago manufactured the Elk, the first fruit slot machine, *c*.1904. Since the 1920s companies in NEVADA have led the world in such machines.

BIBLIOGRAPHY
General
Kirichenko, 1977; Lindley, 1973; Marrey and Chemetov, 1976; Pevsner, 1976.

BARRIE TRINDER

Arc-et-Senans, Jura, France *See* SALINS-LES-BAINS.

arch A curved structure, which may be semicircular, elliptical or pointed, typically supporting a vertical load, as in a bridge, or an ARCADE supporting the upper storey of a building.

The masonry arch bridge has its origins in classical antiquity, and was practised with skill in medieval Europe and in the Ottoman Empire (*see* MOSTAR). The Pont Royal, Paris, of 1685, and the Loire bridge at Blois of 1724, which was designed by Jacques Jules Gabriel (1698–1782), represent the best practice of early modern Europe. Westminster Bridge, designed by Charles Labelye (1705–1781) and completed in 1750, is acknowledged to have been the first in England in which scientific theory derived from such writers as Antonio Palladio (1508–90) and Hubert Gautier (1660–1737) was applied to the principles of construction, as well as being a project that established new practices for building bridge piers in deep water. William Edwards at PONTYPRIDD in 1755 established the principle that the load on an arch could be lightened by the perforation of the SPANDRELS. The masonry arch bridge probably reached its zenith in the early nineteenth century, and some remarkable arches were constructed on main-line railways of the first generation, but gradually the high cost of the skilled labour, the need for rapid construction, and the limitations of the length of span that could be achieved led to the adoption of other forms. The Grosvenor Bridge, Chester, designed by Thomas Harrison (1744–1829) and completed in 1834 with a span of 61 m (200 ft.), was the widest stone arch until the completion of the 66 m (220 ft.) Cabin John Bridge near Washington DC in 1864. Most of the notable bridges of Australia and North America are of other types.

A masonry arch is constructed of VOUSSOIRS between two piers around centering, a wooden scaffold whose curved upper surface follows the intended shape of the arch. The centering is removed after the insertion of the keystone.

Arches can also be employed in CONCRETE BRIDGES, IRON BRIDGES, STEEL BRIDGES and WOODEN BRIDGES.

BIBLIOGRAPHY
General
Gautier, 1714, 1717; Labelye, 1739, 1751; Palladio, 1570; Prade, 1990; Ruddock, 1979.

BARRIE TRINDER

archaeometallurgy The scientific analysis, usually laboratory-based, of metal artefacts and metallic residues, like SLAGS, SLIMES, ashes and crucible fragments, which provide evidence of how metals were smelted, refined and fabricated. Studies of great virtuosity utilizing sophisticated analytical techniques have been undertaken since the 1960s, but most have been concerned with prehistoric, Roman and medieval specimens. Some individual analyses have shown the potential for such techniques in the study of the metals industries in the industrial period, but the range of data is as yet limited, and the problems of sampling and stratification on large complex sites are formidable. The Institute for Archaeo-Metallurgical Studies is part of the Institute of Archaeology in the University of London, and has published the bulletin *IAMS* since 1980. The principal learned society in the field is the Historical Metallurgy Society, which was formed as the Historical Metallurgy Group in 1963 and changed its name in 1974. Although a British organization, it has an international membership. It is affiliated to the Institute of Metals.

BIBLIOGRAPHY
General
Brothwell and Higgs, 1969; Maddin, 1988; Smith, 1988; Tylecote, 1986.
Specific
Historical Metallurgy, 1963–. IAMS, 1980–.

LOCATIONS
[I] Historical Metallurgy Society, c/o The Institute of Metals, 1 Carlton House Terrace, London SW1Y 5DB.
[I] Institute for Archaeo-Metallurgical Studies, Institute of Archaeology, University College London, 31–4 Gordon Square, London WC1H 0PY.

BARRIE TRINDER

architecture For discussion of the specific architectural characteristics of industrial buildings, *see* INDUSTRIAL ARCHITECTURE.

As far as possible architectural terms have been standardized in this encyclopedia.

For features of buildings, *see* ARCADE; ASHLAR; CAMPANILE; CLERESTORY; CRENELLATION; CUPOLA; FRETWORK; MANSARD ROOF; PEDIMENT; PILASTER; POLYCHROME; PORTE-COCHÈRE; PORTICO; PREFABRICATED HOUSE; VENETIAN WINDOW.

For architectural styles, *see* ART DECO; ART NOUVEAU; BARONIAL; BAROQUE; BEAUX-ARTS; CITY BEAUTIFUL; CLASSICAL; DORIC; EGYPTIAN; EMPIRE; FUNCTIONALIST; GARDEN CITY; GOTHIC; GREEK REVIVAL; HISTORICIST; INTERNATIONAL MODERN; IONIC; ITALIANATE; JACOBEAN; JUGENDSTIL; PALLADIAN; QUEEN ANNE; RENAISSANCE; ROMANESQUE; ROMANTIC NATIONALIST; RUNDBOGENSTIL; SECESSIONIST; TUDOR; VENETIAN GOTHIC.

For individual architects, builders and architectural critics, *see* BEHRENS, P.; BRUNEL, I. K.; EIFFEL, G.; GAUDÍ, A.; HANSOM, J. A.; HARDWICK, P.; HENNEBIQUE, F.; KAHN, A.; LATROBE, B. H.; MIES VAN DER ROHE, L.; MORRIS, W.; PAXTON, J.; SCHINKEL, K. F.; SCOTT, G. G.; SHCHUSEV, A. V.; SHUKHOV, V. G. S.; STRUTT, W.; TELFORD, T.; UNWIN, R.; WYATT, M. D.

For building materials, *see* BRICKS; COADE STONE; FAIENCE; FIREPROOF; GLASS; PREFABRICATED HOUSE; STONE; TERRACOTTA; TILES; WOOD.

Århus, Jutland, Denmark   Århus, on the east coast of Jutland, is the second largest city in Denmark, with origins in the Viking age. Its principal time of expansion was in the 1860s and 70s, when, with its well-sheltered harbour, it became the main railway centre in Jutland. Trade has always been the chief occupation of Århus, and several old merchant houses and warehouses have survived, among them the houses of Hans Broge and of Mønsted at 4 and 8 Mindegade. Like other regional centres Århus acquired a varied industrial structure, with engineering, food and textiles as the dominant sectors. Among other important factories is a large oil mill, Århus Oliefabrik, established in 1871, which has extensive premises near the railway station and at the harbour.

Of special interest is the open-air museum, Den gamle By (The Old Town), which through a great number of re-erected buildings gives an impression of an old Danish market town. Some buildings, the wool spinning mill, the steam weaving mill, the brewery, the distillery, the tobacco factory, the tannery, the printer's shop and the rope walk, illustrate early industrial activities. The old urban crafts are well represented with the workshops of a glover, a hatter, a sailmaker, a saddler, a clockmaker and a candlemaker. The museum has large collections of textiles, stoves, clocks and bicycles.

The buildings at 29 Vestergade, now under protection, for a long time housed the important tobacco factory of J. E. Schmalfeld. A current project seeks to establish a museum in the closed gasworks at Brabrand, founded in 1912.

The Danish Agricultural Museum at the estate of Gl. Estrup near Auning, 35 km (22 mi.) N., has one of the most comprehensive collections in the world of agricultural tools and equipment.

BIBLIOGRAPHY
Specific
Årbog for købstadsmuseet 'Den gamle By' (Yearbook of the Old Town), 1927ff.
Bramsen, B. *The History of the Old Town Museum in Århus.* Århus Oliefabrik A/S, 1971.
Dybdahl, V. ed. *Hus og hjem i Århus 1890–1940* (Houses and homes in Århus 1890–1940). Århus, 1977.

LOCATION
[S] Den gamle By (The Old Town), Vesterbrogade 38, 8000 Århus C.

OLE HYLDTOFT

Arizona, United States of America   In this south-western state of dramatic natural contrasts, 'tufa' appears as one of man's more unusual natural building materials: a dense volcanic stone, with roofing qualities seen most prominently in the dome of the state capitol at Phoenix.

Copper mining remains Arizona's most prominent extractive industry, the state contributing on average a half of the nation's needs. After almost a century of continuous extraction, the open-pit mines around Bisbee are some of the widest and deepest in the world. Bisbee's

cupric history and that of the great Copper Queen mine nearby are well handled at the town's historical museum. Elsewhere in the state, onyx and marble are quarried and gold and silver mined in some equally venerable settings.

In the new resort town of Lake Havasu City, an unlikely structure crosses the town's artificial waterway, a bridge covered with the stone cladding from JOHN RENNIE's London Bridge of 1831. Purchased in 1968 by an American oil company, the sheathing is secured to a look-alike reinforced concrete five-arch span. A more indigenous monument to bridge-building carries interstate auto traffic across the Grand Canyon's Colorado River in Arizona's far north-west. Navajo Arch Bridge is a high-level steel-truss arch of 1929 with a clear span of 188 m (616 ft.), passing 142 m (467 ft.) above the river. Also recommended for bridge spotters is the spidery Kaibab Trail Suspension Bridge over the Grand Canyon.

The impounding of water for irrigation, flood control and power generation has produced some of Arizona's most impressive engineering sites. Two multiple-arch dams, Bartlett of 1923 and Cave Creek of 1939, are classic examples of this novel concrete type. Roosevelt Dam of 1911 serves Phoenix's power and flood-control needs. It is considered the last major all-stone dam in the USA, but its stepped Romanesque arch, rising 85.3 m (280 ft.), has recently been threatened with encasement in concrete to increase its height and the impoundment capacity of the lake.

In 1973 the New Cornelia Tailings Dam, declared 'the world's largest dam', was completed near Ajo.

With Arizona's predominant involvement in mining and water supply, one of the more dramatic museum surprises lies in downtown Phoenix: the Hall of Flame is a national firefighting museum, containing over 130 pieces of restored firefighting equipment dating from 1725 to 1950.

BIBLIOGRAPHY
General
Jackson, 1988.

LOCATIONS
[M] Arizona Mineral Museum, Mineral Building, State Fairgrounds, Phoenix, AZ 85007.
[M] Bisbee Mining and Historical Museum, 5 Copper Queen Plaza, Bisbee, AZ 85603.
[I,S] Grand Canyon National Park, PO Box 129, Grand Canyon, AZ 86023.
[M] Hall of Flame, 6101 East Van Buren, Phoenix, AZ 85008.

DAVID H. SHAYT

Arkansas, United States of America   Arkansas's river system, some 4900 km (3000 mi.) of it navigable, is unequalled in the USA. The state borders the Mississippi River at some of its widest points, and the surrounding lands contain extensive reserves of coal, oil, bauxite, natural gas, granite and marble. Outside Murfreesboro lies the only known diamond field in North America, celebrated in a town museum.

The state name has been widely associated with a

rather modest industrial product, Arkansas stone, the hone or whetstone of choice for knife-owners and cutlers worldwide.

Since 1921 oil has been the state's chief extractive product, with the fourth largest reserves in the nation. The industry is featured at the Oil and Brine Museum at Smackover, in the heart of the oilfields.

North-western Arkansas, traditionally referred to as The Ozarks in recognition of the distinctive subculture of its hill people, contains one of the more stupendous examples of concrete bridge construction of the 1930s, the Cotter Bridge, a six-span series of rainbow arches crossing the White River. Further south the Winkley Bridge of 1912 is a fine example of a low-cost timber-decked suspension bridge, with single wire-rope cables, unwrapped. The Winkley spans 168 m (550 ft.) of the Red River, and is restricted to pedestrian traffic.

The network of railways that crisscross Arkansas intersect at Little Rock in the state's geographic centre. The magnitude of freight and passenger traffic concentrated here has yielded an array of nineteenth-century and early twentieth-century supporting works: steel-truss bridges, car shops, turntables, roundhouses and locomotive depots, all celebrated at two regional railway museums.

BIBLIOGRAPHY
General
Franks and Lambert, 1982; Jackson, 1988.

LOCATIONS
[M] Arkansas Oil and Brine Museum, Highway 7, Smackover, AR 71762.
[M] Crater of Diamonds State Park Museum, Route 1, Box 364, Murfreesboro, AR 71958.
[M] Frisco Depot Railroad Museum, Van Buren, AR 72956.
[M] Hoo-Hoo International Forestry Museum, 207 Main Street, Gurdon, AR 71743.
[M] Missouri & Arkansas Railroad Museum, 1 Railroad Avenue, Beaver, AR 72613.
[M] Patent Model Museum, 400 N. 8th Street, Fort Smith, AR 72901.

DAVID H. SHAYT

Arkwright, Richard (1732–92) The founder of the factory-based cotton textile industry was born at Preston, England, where his birthplace, Arkwright House, is preserved. He worked as a barber and wig maker, and became concerned with textile machines. By 1769 he had developed a spinning frame which he applied in a horse-powered factory at NOTTINGHAM, and from 1771 in the first water-powered cotton factory at CROMFORD, after which it was called the WATER FRAME. The frame, together with Arkwright's carding machine, was patented in 1775, although the patents were revoked ten years later. In that decade Arkwright and his partners established mills at Bakewell and Wirksworth (*see* CROMFORD), MANCHESTER, NEW LANARK and elsewhere. Controversy continues concerning his precise contribution to particular innovatory machines, but that he was primarily responsible for the radical reorganization of textile manufactures is beyond question.

BIBLIOGRAPHY
General
Fitton, 1989; Fitton and Wadsworth, 1958; Hills, 1973.
Specific
Charlton, C., Hool, D. and Strange, P. *Arkwright and the Mills at Cromford*. Cromford: Arkwright Society, 1971.
Tann, J. Richard Arkwright and technology. In *History*, LVIII, 1973.

BARRIE TRINDER

Arlberg, Vorarlberg and Tyrol, Austria A pass crossing the watershed between the Rhine and the Danube, linking Klostertal in Vorarlberg with Stanzertal in Tyrol. The road across the pass was opened to wheeled traffic in 1825; and the railway tunnel, 10.25 km (6 mi. 633 yd.) long, was constructed in 1880–3 under the direction of Julius Lott (1836–83), who is commemorated by an obelisk at the eastern end. In the main street of St Anton am Arlberg on the eastern side of the pass is an early wooden customs warehouse where dues were collected from salt carriers. The town museum contains displays relating to the construction of the tunnel.

BIBLIOGRAPHY
General
Schneider, 1963.

LOCATION
[M] The Town Museum, A-6580 St Anton am Arlberg.

Arles, Bouches-du-Rhône, France The Trinquetaille Glassworks at Arles was a bottle manufactory, opened in 1782 by a company which included Jacques Grigniard de la Haye, a member of a glassmaking dynasty from Eu, Normandy. It was built on the banks of the Rhône, along which coal was delivered from the Rive-de-Gier coalfield. The works had closed by 1809. Alongside the offices and workers' dwellings, the main glassmaking hall survives, a square building, 20 m × 20 m (66 ft. × 66 ft.), divided into three parts by internal walls, with semicircular arches. Two vaulted underground corridors intersect at the point where the furnaces were located, although all the furnaces have disappeared. The site is a protected historical monument.

BIBLIOGRAPHY
Specific
Amouric, H. and Foy, D. La Verrerie en noir de Trinquetaille à la fin du XVIIIᵉ siècle (The Trinquetaille bottle glass works at the end of the eighteenth century). In *Archéologie du Midi médiéval*, II, 1984.

LOCATION
[M] Arles Museum, 42 rue de la République, 13200 Arles.

armaments In an industrial sense the word 'armaments' means equipment, of whatever kind, for fighting forces, although originally an armament was a naval or military unit. The manufacture of armaments has profoundly influenced the mechanical engineering industry, both qualitatively, in creating demands for increased precision (as in the employment of INTERCHANGEABLE

PARTS), and, in wartime, quantitively, by stimulating the adoption of mass-production techniques, in the nineteenth century for hand guns, and in the twentieth century for aircraft and motor vehicles.

The word 'munitions' is sometimes used to mean armaments in a general sense, but it originally meant ammunition charged to GUNS. Similarly the word 'ordnance' means military supplies of all kinds, although it originally referred to CANNON and earlier machines for propelling missiles. The Board of Ordnance in England was responsible for securing supplies of all kinds for the army, while one of its sections, the Ordnance Survey, has been the principal publisher of MAPS in Britain since the early nineteenth century.

See also ARSENAL; MUSKET; PISTOL; PROOF HOUSE; RIFLE.

BARRIE TRINDER

Armstrong, Sir William George (1810–1900) The principal innovator in the use of HYDRAULIC POWER, and a leading entrepreneur in armaments manufacture and shipbuilding. Born in NEWCASTLE-UPON-TYNE and a lawyer by training, Armstrong became involved in hydraulic engineering in the 1830s, patented the HYDRAULIC CRANE in 1846, and in 1847 was appointed manager of an engineering works at Elswick-on-Tyne, 2 km (1 mi.) W. of Newcastle, which he developed as an armaments manufactory, in due course adding a yard for building warships. In 1897 he combined his armaments business with that of Sir Joseph Whitworth (1803–87). His mansion at Cragside, 42 km (26 mi.) NW of Newcastle, designed by Richard Norman Shaw (1831–1912), was lit by electricity from 1878.

BIBLIOGRAPHY
General
Saint, 1976.
Specific
Irlam, G. A. Electricity supply at Cragside. In *IAR*, XI, 1989.

Arnhem, Gelderland, The Netherlands The capital of Gelderland at a crossing point of the Rijn, and on the edge of the Hoge Veluwe heathlands, Arnhem was severely damaged in World War II. The White Mill, a water mill in Sonsbeek Park near the city centre, is preserved by the city. It has a wheel 2.5 m (8 ft.) in diameter and 1.5 m (5 ft.) wide. The Elektrum Museum illustrates the history of the generation and distribution of electricity. The first rayon factory in the Netherlands, dating from 1913, stands in Velperweg, now the headquarters of the AKZO company. Arnhem is the only Dutch town with a trolleybus system.

The Netherlands Open-Air Museum on the northern edge of the city, established in 1912 and opened in 1914, was a private institution until 1941 when it was taken over by the state, only to be privatized in the late 1980s. It occupies a 30 ha (80 ac.) site. Its original aims were related to the preservation of folk culture, but it is now regarded as the national museum in the fields of industrial, technological and social history. Many of its buildings are farmhouses in which are displayed typical Dutch household utensils: stoves, many of them tiled; pottery; coopery; pewter; and fine ironware. There are windmills for draining polders, sawing timber and grinding grain, a horse-driven oil mill of c.1830, and a papermill from the Veluwe. Workers' accommodation includes textile workers' cottages from TILBURG and a rural turf cabin. There is a traditional boatyard from Marken, a village brewery from Noord Brabant, and a clogmaker's workshop. The museum has a particularly good collection of ephemeral types of urban building, an eelmonger's hut from Amsterdam, a stall where poffertjes (waffles) were made and eaten, and a mobile cinema where electric current was provided by a traction engine. In recent years there has been a conscious attempt to portray twentieth-century Dutch life. A large farmhouse from Groningen province has been restored to its condition of the 1930s. An agricultural machinery depot from Goes has been erected, together with parts of the creamery Freia from Veenwouden in Friesland, which dates from 1897. The museum has extensive reserve collections of artefacts, and its buildings are meticulously documented. The landscape of sandy hills is not an ideal setting for buildings from polders and heathlands, but the museum communicates a vivid sense of the Dutch past.

At Otterlo, 16 km (10 mi.) NW, is a museum established by the architect G. Feenstra, where seven thousand tiles are displayed. There is a museum of constructional machinery at Ede, 22 km (14 mi.) W., and a monumental artificial silk factory of 1919 still operates near the railway station.

Heveadorp, 6 km (4 mi.) W., is a former rubber-manufacturing village, founded in 1916 by an entrepreneur from Groningen; parts of it have been restored.

Between Arnhem, Nijmegen, 15 km (9 mi.) S., Zevenaar, 10 km (6 mi.) SE, and the German border is a landscape of brickmaking, which includes the kilns, and workers' dwellings, of numerous works, most of which were founded or modernized in the 1920s, and closed in the 1960s and 70s.

BIBLIOGRAPHY
Specific
Bos J. M. *et al. Nederlands Openluchtmuseum: Guide* (Netherlands open-air museum). Arnhem, 1982.
Puijenbroek, F. van *et al. Het Nederlands Openluchtmuseum – 75 jaar.* Staatsuitgeverij 's-Gravenhage, 1987.

LOCATIONS
[M] Elektrum Museum (Electrical Museum), Kingelbeekseweg 45, Arnhem.
[M] Museum Wegenbouwmachines (Museum of Construction Machinery), Verlengde Maanderweg 129, Ede.
[M] Nederlands Openluchtmuseum (Netherlands Open-Air Museum), Hoeferlaan, Arnhem.
[M] Tegelmuseum (Tile Museum), It Noflik Ste, Eikenzoom 12, Otterlo.

JURRIE VAN DALEN and BARRIE TRINDER

arsenal A word used from the early sixteenth century to mean a naval base where ships could be repaired, and from which they could draw supplies; in Mediterranean ports like VENICE it refers to historic SHIPYARDS.

From the late sixteenth century the word was applied to a place where ARMAMENTS of any sort were stored, and where they might also be manufactured. The term implied a large establishment like the Watervliet Arsenal in the USA (*see* NEW YORK) or the Woolwich Arsenal, London, reckoned in 1876 to be the only military depot in Britain large enough to be termed an arsenal.

See also figure 160.

arsenic (As)   An element whose compounds are used as pesticides and weedkillers, and in dyeing and the manufacture of lead shot. Arsenic is found in association with copper and other ores, often in the form of arsenical iron pyrites (FeAsS). Its extraction is by crushing and calcining; the volatilized fumes are condensed in baffle chambers. The condensate is revolatilized into further baffles to produce arsenious oxide (As_2O_3). In the late nineteenth century most arsenic was produced from flue dust accumulated during the smelting of other metals. Large quantities now stored in sealed silos of mines at Boliden in northern Sweden will continue to meet current world demands.

See also MORWELLHAM; NORRLAND.

BIBLIOGRAPHY
General
Jones, 1950; Richardson, 1974.

art   For the relationship between art and industry, *see* ICONOGRAPHY.

Arta, Epirus, Greece   One of the chief towns of the region of Epirus on the river Arachthos. The river is crossed here by one of the most notable bridges in Greece: it consists of four main arches, of semicircular, almost elliptical form, with heavily constructed abutments whose weight is reduced by subsidiary arches. It has a total length of 142 m (466 ft.), and took its present form in 1606.

BIBLIOGRAPHY
Specific
Tourism in Greece: Greek popular architecture, Athens, 1974.

MARIA FINE

art castings   A term commonly applied to busts, statues, bas-reliefs and the like cast in iron, or sometimes in other metals. Such castings were made in many European foundries in the second half of the nineteenth century, probably originating from the Eisengiesserei outside the Oranienburg gate of Berlin, celebrated for its black cast-iron ornaments, varnished with a mixture of amber, linseed oil and lamp black. The Berlin foundry had produced iron replicas of gold items which contributed to the Prussian war effort in the first decade of the nineteenth century. There are collections of art castings at IRON-BRIDGE, Finspång (*see* NORRKÖPING), and ST HUBERT.

BIBLIOGRAPHY
General
Murray, 1865.

Art Deco   An architectural style stimulated by the Exposition International des Arts Décoratifs et Industriels Modernes in Paris in 1925, characterized by sharp, angular zigzag ornamentation. It was widely used in fashionable buildings of the 1920s and early 1930s, including several New York SKYSCRAPERS and British CINEMAS. It was a highly eclectic style, drawing upon such exotic sources as Mayan art, and was often executed in such manufactured materials as FAIENCE and chromium-plated steel.

BIBLIOGRAPHY
General
Whiffen and Breeze, 1984.

artificial fertilizers   A name given to various forms of fertilizer, developed after publication in 1840 of the treatise on plant physiology by Justus Liebig (1803–73). The term includes ammonium sulphate (*see* AMMONIA), basic slag (*see* BESSEMER, SIR HENRY) and sodium nitrate (*see* SALTPETRE), but chiefly refers to superphosphate, calcium dihydrogen phosphate ($Ca(H_2PO_4)_2$), manufacture of which was patented by Sir John Lawes (1814–1900) in 1842. Bones, coprolites, and from 1857 apatite (*see* PHOSPHORUS), were ground and mixed with sulphuric acid, originally on a brick floor or in a brick-lined pit. About eighty small works operated in Britain *c.*1870, but the process was mechanized from the early twentieth century, particularly through the use of the Oberphos autoclave, a double-cone, lead-lined digester developed in Baltimore, USA, which produces uniform granules of fertilizer.

BIBLIOGRAPHY
General
ICI, 1950; Morgan and Pratt, 1938.

artificial silk   The first fabric called artificial silk was made from a fibre produced in France from 1884 by extruding collodion, a form of nitro-cotton with a nitrogen content of less than 12.3 per cent, which was used in the preparation of lacquers and artificial leathers, but in the twentieth century the term has become almost synonymous with RAYON.

BIBLIOGRAPHY
General
Morgan and Pratt, 1938.

Art Nouveau   A decorative style, influential in ceramic, glass, textile, and furniture design as well as architecture, popular from the late 1880s until shortly before World War I. It was characterized by undulating forms, whiplash curves, waves and flowers, and derived some of its stylistic inspiration from the work of WILLIAM MORRIS. The name derives from a shop in Paris opened in 1895 to sell wares that were not in imitative historicist styles. Art Nouveau was influential in Belgium from 1892 through the work of Henri van de Velde (1863–1951: *see* BAUHAUS) and Baron Victor Horta (1861–1947). Louis C. Tiffany (1848–1933) was the chief exponent in the USA. In Germany, where the style was called JUGENDSTIL, the work of Hermann Obrist (1863–1927) and August Endell (1871–1925) was of particular importance. In France Art Nouveau was called 'style Guimard' after Hector Guimard (1867–1942), designer of florid ornamental arches at the entrance to many Metro stations. A Viennese variation was 'Sezessionstil' (*see* SECESSIONIST). In Italy it was called 'le stile Liberty' after the LONDON department store. In Spain, where the outstanding exponent was the architect ANTONI GAUDÍ, it was called 'Modernismo'.

BIBLIOGRAPHY
General
Haslam, 1989; Russell, 1979; Schmutzler, 1962.

BARRIE TRINDER

asbestos A mineral occurring in various forms, the commonest of them being chrysotile asbestos, a hydrated magnesium silicate $(Mg_3Si_2O_5(OH)_4)$. Known since ancient times as a curiosity, asbestos is characterized by fine, crystalline fibres with a silky lustre. A British company working in the Aosta Valley, Italy, began the commercial exploitation of the mineral in 1865, but it did not come into widespread use until the twentieth century. Recognition of the health hazards arising from its processing and use have restricted its production in recent decades. It has been mined chiefly in Canada (*see* THETFORD) and the USSR. It can be woven, and was incorporated into fireproof fabrics from the 1870s. From 1900 the short fibres, previously discarded, were used in the manufacture of asbestos cement sheeting, roofing tiles and pipes. Other uses include brake-linings and clutch facings for motor vehicles, and electrical and thermal insulation.

BIBLIOGRAPHY
General
Hudson, 1978; Jones, 1950.

Ashford, Kent, England   A market town at a crossing of the River Stour, where the South-Eastern Railway established an engineering works in 1845–7. It includes a company village, initially of seventy-two dwellings, two-storey flats of the NEWCASTLE pattern, but with the doors to the ground floors and to the first floors on opposite sides of the terraces. The works itself is now derelict. Most terraces survive, with a bath house, shops and a pub.

BIBLIOGRAPHY
Specific
Turton, B. J. The railway towns of Southern England. In *Transport History*, II, 1969.

ashlar   Squared building stone, cut in blocks with even faces, as opposed to rubble stone, which is used in buildings in unhewn form. It is also known as DIMENSION STONE.

asphalt   A solid form of BITUMEN, also called mineral pitch. Deposits in Trinidad, Neuchâtel in Switzerland, Seyssel (Ain) in France, and Limmer in North Germany are particularly important. From the mid-nineteenth century the word was used to refer to pavement or road surfaces made by mixing bitumen or pitch with sand; this material was used to surface the rue Bergère, Paris, in 1854, and Threadneedle Street, London, in 1869. Portable plants for laying hot asphalt were developed in the USA in the early twentieth century and were employed in Europe from 1919.

BIBLIOGRAPHY
General
Whitehead, 1975.

assay   A process to determine the quality or purity of metals, particularly precious metals. The right to assay was often bestowed by governments upon officers in particular towns, and access to such an office was important for jewellers and others using precious metals. In England there were offices in London, Birmingham and elsewhere. The first assay office in the USA was established in 1814, and a typical US assay office of 1871 is preserved at Boise, Idaho.
See also HALLMARK.

assembly line   The sequential arrangement of assembly processes along a moving track or line, in accordance with the flow principle previously employed in grain milling, steel rolling, meat packing, and subsequently the continuous casting of steel. Experiments with flow principles in magneto assembly at HENRY FORD's Highland Park plant in Michigan in 1913 produced dramatic increases in output and were quickly extended to integrate production throughout the plant to serve a powered final assembly line. The effectiveness of the assembly line in the MASS PRODUCTION of mechanisms depended on the utilization of INTERCHANGEABLE PARTS that could be quickly assembled, on careful production planning, and on the management of a new division of labour dominated by the pace of the line.

BIBLIOGRAPHY
General
Hounshell, 1984.
Specific
Meyer, S. *The Five Dollar Day*. Albany, NY, 1981.

Asturias, Spain   The region of Asturias in north-west Spain comprises the single province of Oviedo. It is bounded to the north by the Bay of Biscay and to the south by Castile. Its population, spread over a rugged terrain, consists largely of peasant farmers, with a concentration in its central regions of urban and industrial settlements. Asturias is one of the few regions in Spain with a continuous industrial tradition since the eighteenth century. The main fields of industrial activity have been coal mining, ironmaking, fishing and sea-borne trade. The area has suffered a gradual decline and increasing attention is being given to the monuments of past industrial activity.

The terrain in Asturias favoured the use of water power, which was employed chiefly in ironmaking. An eighteenth-century Asturian intellectual saw the iron industry as a conglomeration of artisan manufactures, sustained by water power, and capable of manufacturing keys, hoops and a whole range of other goods which could be produced by casting and forging iron.

Many of these plants have managed to survive up to the present day. Scattered over the western region of Asturias, in the urban districts of Taramundi, Oscos and Vegadeo, were many ironworks which used rich iron-ore deposits and the local coal deposits. Only foundations of the installations at La Alvariza in Belmonte, Meredo in Vegadeo and Besullo in Cangas de Narcea remain. Since 1986 the regional government has been putting into practice through the Consejería de Cultura a plan for the conservation of early ironworks at Aguillón, Mazonovo, Vega, Peizais and Teixoes, where there are more substantial remains.

See also BUSTIELLO; FELGUERA, LA; GIJÓN; PRAVIA; TRUBIA.

BIBLIOGRAPHY
General
Generalitat de Catalunya, 1988.

LOCATION
[M] Provincial Museum, Calle San Vicente 3, Oviedo.

CARLOS CAICOYA, ANDRES GARCIA and
MARIA JOSÉ BARAGAÑO

Athens (Athinai), Attikí, Greece The capital of the kingdom of Greece from 1834 was essentially a new city laid out to plans drawn up in 1832–3 by the Prussian Schaubert and the Greek Kleanthes. Athens was a small city in the early nineteenth century, with a population of only 8000 in 1823, but it grew rapidly in the second half of the century, its population reaching 42 000 in 1860, 105 000 in 1889, and, following the enforced migration of Greeks from Asia Minor in the early 1920s, 600 000 in 1928. Its present population is over 3.5 million. The port of Piraeus, 10 km (6 mi.) W., followed a similar pattern of growth in the nineteenth century, and is essentially part of the Athens conurbation.

Despite having suffered extensive redevelopment Athens preserves, both in its street plan and its buildings, evidence of different approaches to urban development. In the nineteenth century there was an attempt to create a more formal layout; the grandiose plans were only realized around Sintagma Square and Omonia Square, where there are ranges of magnificent, mostly neo-Classical buildings designed by Bavarian and Danish architects. Many buildings are decorated with small terracotta details, and balconies and canopies of cast or wrought iron abound. Trolley buses run through many of the main streets, the tram network having been removed in the 1960s.

The Stathmos Peloponnisou is the station for the metre-gauge system linking Athens with the PELOPONNESE, while the Stathmos Larissis is the station for the standard-gauge line to the north. Peloponnisou is a French Renaissance gem, with mansard roofs, tiled floors, canopies with cast-iron columns and a booking hall in virtually original condition. The subway, from Piraeus north through the centre of Athens to Kifisiá, is a development of a line of 1869 which was electrified in 1902–4. It runs along the 'Middle Wall', one of three protective works built by Themistokles in the fifth century BC. It now operates on a third rail system, with modern rolling stock, and runs underground across the city centre. Omonia Station has bright orange tiling decorating the platforms. Cast-iron columns support the canopies at Monastiraki and Kalithea stations.

A large central market, situated at the junction of Athinas and Armodiou Streets, has an iron truss roof, supported on arcaded walls, having been modelled on a Bavarian railway station.

Industry is concentrated in two belts, north and south of the city centre. In the suburb of Nea Ionia, immigrants from Asia Minor set up a rug industry in the 1920s. Ceramic manufacture was concentrated at Maroussi where sculpture, architectural detailing, and large pots are still made.

The industrial belt to the south runs along the Piraeus Road. The most important complex is the gasworks established in 1862 at the junction of Piraeus Road, Persefonis and Voutadon Streets. Much evidence remains of the processes used and the various structures display considerable architectural dignity. At the southern end of the site are two RETORT houses at right angles to each other, one surviving complete with a mechanical stoking crane. Above the retorts are tanks for the distillation of coal-tar products. Adjoining is a small steam-engine house with two horizontal engines, made in Belgium, which drove gas pumps, made in Berlin. To the northwest of this engine house are pipes for cooling gas, and the pressure house. The northernmost gasholder has ornamental iron-work finials. Adjacent to the northern group of gasholders is a long range accommodating soil filters, iron tanks filled with earth which absorbed ammonia from the gas. The south-west corner of the plant accommodates a water-gas plant made in Glasgow in 1870.

The Keramikos Factory, also on the Piraeus Road, is one of the major producers of architectural and other ceramics in the Athens region.

Hungry industrial archaeologists will appreciate the Station Restaurant, Vouliagmenis Avenue, Glyfada, close to the airport south-east of the city centre: this is housed in three railway freight wagons, built in Vienna in 1922, Cologne in 1902 and Nesseldorf in 1918. Alternatively meals may be taken in a mock railway station.

At Keratsini, south-west of the city, stands the power station established by the British; until recently this provided Athens with most of its electricity. The first power station in the city opened in 1896 at Neo Phaliron,

Figure 7 Retorts at the redundant gasworks on Piraeus Road, Athens
Michael Stratton

was later used as a substation, and is now proposed as the site of an art centre.

Piraeus focuses on a dramatic harbour congested with passenger and cargo ships and surrounded by an intriguing clutter of shipping offices, warehouses, cranes and railway stations. The largest area of warehousing is on the north-west side of the Grand Harbour and appears to have been developed in the 1920s and 30s. Concrete-framed warehouses with brick panels front the water, with grain silos behind. The outer harbour was formed by the construction of two breakwaters in 1902 and comprises naval stores, coal wharfs and a dry dock. Three railway stations contribute to the bustle of the port. The largest is the terminus of the Subway from Athens. A steel-truss overall roof is fronted by a grandiose block. Immediately to the north is the post-1945 terminus of the

40

Peloponnese Railway. West of the inner harbour is the terminus of the Northern Greek Railway, with a two-storey pavilion building and a cast-iron canopy.

Museums in Athens are concerned above all with the artefacts of classical antiquity, but the Benaki Museum has collections of such traditional manufactures as wood carvings, and the history of the last two centuries is shown in the National Historical Museum.

LOCATIONS
[M] Benaki Museum, 1 Koumbari Street, Athens.
[M] Maritime Museum of Greece, Freatis, Akti Themistocleous, Piraeus.
[M] National Historical Museum, Stadiou Street, Athens.

MARIA FINE and MICHAEL STRATTON

Atlantic cable The successful English Channel telegraph of 1850–1 inspired the laying of the first transatlantic cable in 1858. It never worked properly, and a British inquiry criticized insufficient cable trials. ISAMBARD KINGDOM BRUNEL's *Great Eastern*, in its first useful role, subsequently laid a viable cable in 1866.

BIBLIOGRAPHY
General
Kieve, 1973; Rolt, 1957.

atmospheric railway A railway provided with a cast-iron tube laid between the rails, along the top of which was a slit sealed with a leather flap; the vehicles had pistons suspended into the tube. After air had been exhausted from the tube by pumps, the vehicles were propelled along the railway by atmospheric pressure. The principle was applied on a 3 km ($1\frac{3}{4}$ mi.) section of the Dublin & Kingstown Railway, Ireland, in 1844–56; on an 8 km (5 mi.) section of the London & Croydon Railway in 1846–7; on a 24 km (15 mi.) section – later extended to a 32 km (20 mi.) section – of the South Devon Railway in 1847–8; and on a 2 km ($1\frac{1}{4}$ mi.) section of the Paris–St Germain line in 1847–60. Though the system worked in principle, the application was impractical. Starcross Pumping Station, 8 km (5 mi.) SW of Exeter, is preserved, and there are tubes from the London & Croydon line in the National Railway Museum, YORK.

BIBLIOGRAPHY
General
Hadfield, 1967.

Aube, Orne, France The Aube forge, 7 km (4 mi.) E. of l'Aigle, is one of the most interesting monuments in France of the WALLOON FORGE process, the most frequently used method of making wrought iron in France until the early years of the nineteenth century. Until the mid-seventeenth century at least, Normandy was one of the country's leading ironmaking regions. The blast furnace appeared there towards the end of the fifteenth century, first of all in the Perche and the Bray, and then, progressively, in the Ouche and the Bocage, and even as far west as the Cotentin peninsula. At the beginning of the sixteenth century many ironworkers from the Bray

emigrated to England to work in the Walloon forges then developing in the Weald. In Normandy some eighty sites have been identified as having been active at some period between 1480 and 1800. They are spread out along a more or less continuous belt of forest.

The Aube forge was active from the first half of the sixteenth century, the earliest archival mention being in 1548. During the sixteenth century a blast furnace existed on the site, and a slitting mill was installed in the vicinity before 1635. By the early eighteenth century the blast furnace had disappeared, and the works, depicted in a plan of 1731, consisted only of a finery forge. During the nineteenth century the site was acquired by the owners of a nearby wire-drawing mill at Boisthorel, who gradually adapted it for working copper as part of a brassmaking concern. A foundry was built up against the old forge building, and crushing machines and furnaces were installed for preparing and desulphurizing copper ores. This brassworks ceased operation in 1944.

The interest of the site resides in the fact that the nineteenth-century modifications had little effect on the interior layout of the old finery forge. The copper furnaces, for example, were built beneath the hoods of the old finery-and-chafery hearths. The forge hammer also survives. The forge building, as it stands today, is of timber and brick construction, measuring about 20×10 m (66 ft. $\times$ 33 ft.). Some of the timber framing is probably original. The three square chimneys, tapering towards the top, are also of brick. At the bases of these chimneys are numerous vestiges of the finery hearths, in particular the masonry foundations of the air-blast system, and the cast-iron plates of the crucibles. The base of the chafery hearth has been more drastically altered, but overall the forms and dimensions are remarkably close to those illustrated by DIDEROT. The hammer, with its wooden support structure, is also very close to these drawings. This structure, or 'harness' as it is known, is independent of the framework of the rest of the building. One of its two vertical pillars is 8 m (26 ft.) high and projects above the roof. The horizontal beam of this harness is 13 m (43 ft.) long.

Since 1983 an archaeological excavation inside the building has unearthed the bases of the finery hearths and has allowed the foundations of the hammer to be studied, in particular the system used to maintain the pile beneath the anvil. The site also retains the old copper foundry building, with its square brick chimney for the desulphurizing furnace.

Apart from the forge at Aube, many other traces of ironmaking remain in Normandy. The Varenne forge at Champsecret, 7 km (4 mi.) NE of Domfront, has three chimneys for the finery and chafery hearths, built of stone, and probably dating from the seventeenth century. The tower of the blast furnace of 1767 also survives, along with the ruins of a slitting mill, which includes a second chafery furnace. At Champ-de-la-Pierre, 30 km (19 mi.) NW of Alençon, in a place known as 'La Grande Forge', the granite stack of a nineteenth-century furnace is still to be seen. Excavation in the finery forge on this site uncovered the foundations of the hammer. Today all these sites, Aube, Varenne and Champ-de-la-Pierre, are protected monuments.

BIBLIOGRAPHY
Specific
Arnoux, M., Belhoste, J.-F., and le Cherbonnier, Y. *et al.* *Cartographie de la sidérurgie Normande* (The cartography of ironmaking in Normandy), 1990.
——— L'Homme et l'industrie en Normandie (Man and industry in Normandy). *Bulletin spécial de la Société historique et archéologique de l'Orne.* Alençon, 1990.
Gautier-Desvaux, E. La forge d'Aube, Orne: du dossier historique aux fouilles archéologiques (The Aube forge: from the historic file to the excavation). In *Actes du 5e colloque national sur le patrimoine industriel* (Transactions of the fifth national conference on the industrial heritage), *Alès, 1983. L'Archéologie industrielle en France*, 1984.

JEAN-FRANÇOIS BELHOSTE

Auckland, Central Auckland, New Zealand The main industrial centre of twentieth-century New Zealand, responsible for a third of the country's industrial production. Factories set up to produce consumer goods in the late nineteenth century include the Trenwith Brothers' footwear factory of 1870, the wooden Kapai boot factory of 1885 in Exmouth Street, and Jeffries' boot and shoe works in Airedale Street. The Chelsea Sugar Refinery, opened in 1883, is still in use. Railway workshops in Newmarket, built in 1884, are now used as store.

The Museum of Transport and Technology (MOTAT) holds New Zealand's principal industrial collections. Its trams include a horse tram built in the USA in 1883, a Baldwin steam tram locomotive, and an Auckland tramcar of 1902 built by the Brush Co. in England, as well as trolley buses of the late 1930s and late 1940s. Aircraft include an Avro Lancaster, and Short Solent and Sunderland flying boats. The engineering collection is based on Auckland's original Waterworks Pumphouses. The railway section centres round a station complex of 1920 based on the Waitakere suburban station and a short section is operational. A Ja class 4–8–2 locomotive built in DUNEDIN in 1956 is preserved. There are collections concerned with telecommunications, motorcars and electric power. A Pioneer Village contains re-erected buildings and replicas based on nineteenth-century plans, and features furniture and clothing manufacture. The Western Springs pumphouse of 1877, with a beam engine by John Key of Kirkcaldy, Scotland, forms part of the site.

LOCATION
[M] Museum of Transport and Technology of New Zealand (Inc.), PO Box 44-114, Great North Road, Western Springs, Auckland 2.

BARRIE TRINDER

Auge, Calvados, France *See* PAYS D'AUGE.

Augsburg, Bavaria, Germany Apart from monuments of its celebrated textile industry, the most interesting features of the industrial archaeology of Augsburg are connected with the city's water supplies. From 1416 artesian wells were sunk at the Rotes Tor (red gate) in Augsburg, as they were in Leipzig and Lüneburg, with wooden towers to maintain pressure in the water mains. In 1463 a wooden tower built by Hans Felber was replaced by a stone one, the height of which was increased in 1669. This tower, which has been well restored, assumed its present form in 1746, when a parapet was added at the top. A smaller tower has stood beside it since 1470, its present appearance being the result of alterations in 1556 and 1672. In 1599 two storeys to supply water were added to a nearby tower which had formerly been part of the fortifications, and a parapet was added in 1703. This splendid Baroque complex, which has been preserved complete, was complemented in the eighteenth century by the addition of nine more watertowers and nineteen pumping plants. The well-preserved complex is particularly important because of the place of these functional buildings in the development of architecture in the city as a whole.

Augsburg was an Imperial Free City until 1806, enjoying imperial privileges of which entrepreneurs took advantage to establish an extensive textile industry. Since the Middle Ages the city had been a centre of foreign trade, lying as it does at the point of intersection of the routes between Northern Europe and Italy and between Eastern and Western Europe. The great commercial firms, the Fuggers and the Welsers, made Augsburg a financial centre of the foremost importance in the sixteenth century, trading beyond as well as within Europe. Buildings like the 'Fuggerei' foundation, with its fifty-two houses, which put into practice the principle of publicly-assisted house building as early as 1523, or Elias Holl's Rathaus (town hall) in the Renaissance style, completed in 1615, survive as evidence of the importance of Augsburg at this time.

To a great extent the prosperity of the eighteenth-century textile industry in Augsburg was due to the merchant and textile printer Johann Heinrich von Schüle (b.1720). He began trading in cotton goods in 1745 and opened his own textile printing works in 1759. About 1770 about three thousand people were working for him under a putting-out system. In 1770–2 the architect Leonhard Mayr built Schüle a palatial cotton manufactory with lateral wings over 100 m (330 ft.) long. This building still stands and is one of the finest examples in Europe of such pre-industrial architecture.

Other large buildings in Augsburg provide information about the development of the local textile industry in the nineteenth century and the early twentieth century. The oldest factory of this period, the Mechanische Baumwollspinnerei und Weberei Augsburg (Augsburg Mechanical Cotton Spinning and Weaving Mill) or SWA, was built in 1840. Its hydro-electric power plant still stands by the Proviantbach. The spinning and weaving mill, Plant III, built in 1877–83 and 1895–8, has also been preserved and stands next to it. It is a good example of the type of factory modelled on a castle popular in Germany in the 1870s. The Aumühle, Plant IV of the SWA, was built in 1909–10, and is an example of the modernist style of architecture, with a reinforced concrete frame structure and large windows. As well as workers' dwellings in the Bleichstrasse – where the dramatist Bertold Brecht (1898–1956) once lived – and the Proviantbachstrasse, built in 1880 and 1900 respectively, several other buildings ranging in date between 1770 and 1910 emphasize the significance of textiles in this industrial city.

Mechanical engineering is also represented. The Augsburg plant of the Maschinenfabrik Augsburg-Nürnberg AG (Augsburg and Nuremburg Engineering Works Ltd), or M.A.N., has a works museum, illustrating its history since it was founded in 1844 as the C. Reichenbachsche Maschinenfabrik, and showing its particular importance in the construction of the DIESEL engine, developed here in 1893–7 by Rudolf Diesel (1853–1913), who had grown up in Augsburg. The firm was notable for its production of steam engines, turbines and gearboxes between 1840 and 1860, and from 1873 it also manufactured refrigeration plant and rotary printing presses.

BIBLIOGRAPHY
General
Bott, 1985; Grimm, 1985.
Specific
Ruckdeschel, W. and Klaus, L. *Technische Denkmale in Augsburg. Eine Führung durch die Stadt* (Technical monuments in Augsburg – a guide through the city). Augsburg, 1984.
Schremmer, E. The textile industry in Southern Germany, 1750–1850: some causes for the technological backwardness during the Industrial Revolution – investment approach and structure approach. In *TH*, VII, 1976.

LOCATION
[M] M.A.N. Museum, Stadtbachstrasse 1, 8900 Augsburg.

AXEL FÖHL

Augustowski Canal, Augustów, Suwałki, Poland   The Augustowski Canal is the outstanding Polish engineering achievement of the first half of the nineteenth century. It links the Niemen and Biebrza rivers through the Augustowska Forest in north-eastern Poland, some 90 km (56 mi.) N. of Białystok. The tariff war launched by Prussia in 1822 had hindered the export of Polish agricultural products from the Congress Kingdom of Poland. At the initiative of Ksawery Drucki-Lubecki a waterway to the Baltic was planned, avoiding Prussian territory. The canal was constructed between 1824 and 1829, being designed and built by the military engineers of the Congress Kingdom. Until the mid-nineteenth century the main trade on the canal was salt bound for Lithuania, but the canal has since been only of local importance as a means of transporting timber. The canal and the strip of land alongside it were put under legal protection as a site of historic importance in 1968.

The Augustowski Canal extends for some 100 km (62 mi.), of which 40 km (25 mi.) consists of man-made cuts, 26 km (16 mi.) of lakes, and 34 km (21 mi.) of stretches of the Czarna Hańcza and Netta rivers which have been canalized. There are eighteen locks. Since 1945 about 19 km (12 mi.) of the canal, including three locks, have been incorporated into the Soviet Union. The locks are 43 m (118 ft.) long, and can accommodate vessels 6 m (20 ft.) in beam. Twelve locks have brick floors, the remainder wooden floors. The lock gates are made of wood and are fitted with vertical paddles, lifted by manually operated screw devices. All the locks are provided with mooring posts, and most have plates with the name of the builder and the date of construction. Many original buildings have been preserved around the locks. Various innovative techniques were used in the construction of the canal, including the use of HYDRAULIC CEMENT. At the lock at Kużyniec the concrete base of a drawbridge, one of the first prefabricated structures in Europe, has been preserved. The section of the canal from Augustów to the Russian border is maintained in its original condition. It passes through forests and other picturesque landscapes which make it a great tourist attraction. Since the canal was not an economic success no substantial reconstruction has ever been undertaken, and it is of great historical value as an almost unaltered waterway of the early nineteenth century.

BIBLIOGRAPHY
General
Górewicz, 1971, 1974.

JAN KĘSIK

Australia   Australia had been occupied for at least 40 000 years before the arrival of colonists from Western Europe. The first permanent settlement was established by Arthur Phillip (1738–1814) at Sydney Cove in 1788, initially as a British penal colony. Further settlements were established at Port Phillip, later Melbourne, in 1803; Van Dieman's Land, later Tasmania, in 1804; Swan River in 1829; and Moreton Bay, later Brisbane, and South Australia in 1836. Reforms in 1823 meant that New South Wales came to be treated as a colony rather than a prison. In 1901 the country was united as a federation of six states and two territories, with a national parliament in the new city of CANBERRA.

Australia principally comprises the islands of the mainland and Tasmania. Much of the interior is desert, with tropical rainforest on the northern margins and more temperate grasslands on the south and east coasts.

The general theme of industrialization in Australia is one of increasing independence from Britain. The export of wool and the products of sealing and whaling dominated the early colonies. Mining developed from the 1840s, and with the processing of agricultural products was the main industry until World War I.

Some of the earliest industrial enterprises in Australia may have been the processing of foodstuffs for export by Aboriginals on the north coast. The journey to Britain took many months in a sailing ship, and so the colonies were obliged to become self-sufficient in food, and in such basic necessities as cloth, soap, leather goods and tallow. Buildings in Sydney by 1823 included a windmill and a SHOT TOWER. Woollen cloth was made at Parramatta, 32 km (20 mi.) W., in a factory established in 1815. The white colonization of the Australian interior was highly dependent upon the application of nineteenth-century

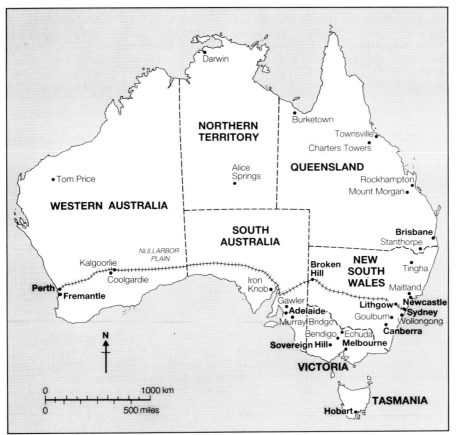

Australia

farming technology. There were many new developments in ploughs and other implements as vast tracts of land were cleared from forest. Wool, salt pork, whale oil and sealskins were processed for export to Britain, the USA, and British colonies, but there was little manufacturing for export.

The distance between Australia and other colonies such as South Africa was a limitation on the range of products that could be exported, and it was only with developments in REFRIGERATION and CANNING that a wide range of Australian products could reach overseas markets. The first meat-canning factory was built in 1847 and Australian tinned meat appeared in the Great Exhibition in London in 1851. By 1869 Britain was importing a thousand tonnes of boiled mutton, corned beef and meat extract per year. The first ice factory was set up at Rocky Point, Victoria, in 1850, and ice was being made on a large-scale commercial basis by the 1860s. Thomas Mort set up a freezing plant at Darling Harbour, Sydney, in 1878, and in 1880 the SS *Strathleven* became the first ship to carry frozen meat from Australia to Britain. Refrigeration and rail transport meant that it was possible to set up abattoirs and chilling plants in country areas and to move meat by rail to the cities and coast, rather than walking stock overland. Winemaking was another early industry, established initially by German immigrants in the Barossa

Valley, South Australia, and also in New South Wales and Victoria in the 1840s and 50s.

Coal was found at Coal River, NEWCASTLE, in 1795, and mined on a small scale until the opening of the main coalfields in eastern Australia in the 1850s. Large-scale mining expanded in LITHGOW and elsewhere with the development of the railway network. Copper was found at Burra, South Australia, in 1843, and in the mid-nineteenth century the state was the third largest producer of copper in the world. The search for gold, following its discovery in Victoria in the 1850s, had a great impact on the country as a whole. New areas were opened up for settlement, and the population grew as new colonists came in search of instant prosperity. Goldfields were also opened in New South Wales in the 1850s, in Queensland in the 1860s, and in Western Australia in the 1890s. Mining technology was very basic – alluvial deposits were washed in primitive sluices, and reefs were mined by hand or with the use of EXPLOSIVES. In the 1890s the use of CYANIDE replaced earlier processes for refining gold. Large-scale dredging for gold began in 1899.

Gold prospecting was indirectly responsible for the opening up of other geological reserves. Tin, copper and iron were found in northern Tasmania, and by the mid-1870s Australia was the world's largest tin producer with an output of up to 13 000 tonnes per annum. Miners from

CORNWALL were responsible for the development of many workings. Silver was found at Glen Osmond, SA, in 1841, and at BROKEN HILL, NSW, in 1883. Oil shale was processed in NEW SOUTH WALES from the 1860s.

Despite rich mineral resources, it proved difficult to establish viable smelting concerns in Australia. Mines were remote and overland transport expensive. It was cheaper to import pig iron as ballast than to set up blast furnaces and carry their produce overland. Iron was first smelted in Australia at the New Sheffield (later Fitzroy) works near Mittagong, NSW, in 1848, but the operation ceased in 1878. Elsewhere smelting expanded in the 1870s. An ironworks was built in northern Tasmania; the Hindmarsh Tiers furnaces were constructed in South Australia in 1873, and at LITHGOW Rutherfords leased land for a blast furnace in 1876. Remains of nineteenth-century blast furnaces survive at Lal Lal, VICTORIA, and near Launceston, TASMANIA. At Lithgow a furnace base and engine house of 1906 remain, but smelting was moved in 1926 to the steelworks at Port Kembla, the first steelworks in the southern hemisphere. At NEWCASTLE some parts remain of another major steelworks constructed in 1915.

Until the abolition in 1840 of the transportation of convicts, bridges, roads, military installations and prisons were all built by convicts, and this ready availability of cheap labour was partly responsible for the slow adoption of steam power.

Land was abundant in Australia in the early nineteenth century and the archaeology of settlement is particularly rich. Evidence survives for squatting, for penal colonies, and for settlements planned by religious groups or mining, fruit or land companies. With the exception of Sydney, most Australian cities are products of the boom in the late nineteenth century that followed the gold rushes. Several of the main coastal cities were laid out to rules promulgated by Governor Ralph Darling (1775–1858) who was in office between 1825 and 1831. The hinterland grew later and, like manufacturing, tended to accompany rather than lead the growth of these cities. In the 1880s and 90s tramways and suburban railways developed. These in turn encouraged the growth of characteristically spacious suburbs, made up of detached family houses, often BUNGALOWS, a term first used in Australia in 1876. The form of the Australian bungalow was derived from Californian models, and was broad-fronted rather than long and narrow. Already by 1911 more than half of Australian householders were owner-occupiers. By the 1960s 74 per cent of Australians lived in their own homes, the second highest proportion in the world, after Iceland.

Transport and communication form another major theme of industrial development. Exploration of the interior continued throughout the nineteenth century. The first TURNPIKE road, the Great North Road to Wiseman's Ferry and Mount Manning, was cut out of the bush north of Sydney by convicts. Overland transport was always difficult, the first towns being centred on their harbours. The railway network was built up on a state-by-state basis, as a result of which gauges were not

standardized. Under the influence of the Irish engineer F. W. Shields it had been intended to use the 5ft. 3 in. (1.6 m) gauge in New South Wales, Victoria and South Australia, but after his resignation the 4 ft. $8\frac{1}{2}$ in. (1.425 m) gauge was used in New South Wales. Subsequently the narrow 3 ft. 6 in. (1.07 m) was adopted in Queensland. The first railway in Australia, apart from some colliery installations, was that from Melbourne to Sandridge, opened in 1855. The first in New South Wales also opened in the same year, the first in South Australia in 1856, and the first in Queensland in 1863. The state systems were in due course linked up, although in most cases there were breaks of gauge at the frontiers. Victoria was linked with New South Wales in 1883, and with South Australia in 1887. The New South Wales and Queensland systems came together in 1888. During the twentieth century standard-gauge links have been completed between the major cities, a process that began with the line connecting Port Augusta, SA, with Kalgoorlie, WA, across the Nullarbor Plain, completed in 1917. A standard-gauge route from Sydney to Brisbane opened in 1930, and from Sydney to Melbourne in 1962. By 1970 the whole of the transcontinental route from Sydney to Perth was of standard gauge. Suburban railways have been important in Australia's large and dispersed cities. Electrification of the Melbourne system began in 1919, and of that in Sydney in 1926. Australia pioneered long-distance internal air transport, which has always been kept distinct from international services. Air traffic boomed in the late 1940s as large numbers of war-surplus Douglas DC3s (see AIRLINER), ideal for Australian conditions, became available. The Overland Telegraph, completed between Sydney, Melbourne and Adelaide in 1858, and the railway both crossed the centre of the continent and were seen as major achievements, both being government initiatives, a strong tradition in the early development of Australia. There are railway museums at ADELAIDE, BRISBANE, MELBOURNE and SYDNEY, and tramcar collections at Bylands, Victoria, Parramatta, NSW, and Loftus, NSW.

During World War I Australia was cut off from Britain, and was consequently obliged to manufacture many consumer goods. Multinational corporations like Ford and General Motors became established in Australia. World War II encouraged a further boost in the manufacture of consumer durables.

Industrial archaeology is seen as integral with historical archaeology, conservation priorities for which were set out in the Burra Charter, adopted in 1979 by Australia ICOMOS. The Federal Government holds a Register of the National Estate, through the Australian Heritage Commission; it is responsible for protecting Federal-owned buildings, and for sites in the Australian Capital Territory (see CANBERRA) and the Northern Territory, but otherwise the onus lies with the states. Each state has a Heritage Commission or equivalent, and its own legislation, but contributes towards the national inventory. Conservation and development control are imposed at local government level. In several states the non-governmental National Trust has produced Industrial Sites Registers, and like the National Parks Services is active in the preservation of industrial remains. The Institute of Engineers is concerned with the protection of the engineering heritage. Museums and universities undertake recording and excavation, although most professional work is done on a contract basis. Such work is published individually, or in the journal of the Australian Society for Historical Archaeology. The Historic Shipwrecks Act 1976 protects important wrecks.

Major industrial museums include the Powerhouse in SYDNEY, the Science Museum of VICTORIA and the Museum of Technology and Applied Science at Birdwood, SA. The Western Australia Maritime Museum is in Fremantle (see PERTH AND FREMANTLE), a national Maritime Museum has been opened in SYDNEY, and Queensland Museum is involved in the study of wrecks. The Queen Victoria Museum in Launceston, Tasmania, and the South Australian Museum in Adelaide cover industrial sites through guides and displays. Open-air museums that preserve industrial remains include those at Echuca, NSW, and Beechworth, Steiglitz and SOVEREIGN HILL, Victoria. Other open-air museums largely contain replicas of early colonial buildings.

Because of the size of Australia, many sites in remote areas were simply abandoned and never reoccupied. Many early settlement sites are thus well preserved, but there is a real threat to mining sites from the renewed exploitation of old workings. The pace of development in towns has caused the loss of many important industrial sites, since the recognition of the historical importance to Australia of the achievements of the nineteenth century is a very recent development.

See also ADELAIDE; BRISBANE; CANBERRA; HOBART; LITHGOW; MELBOURNE; NEWCASTLE; NEW SOUTH WALES; NORTHERN TERRITORY; PERTH AND FREMANTLE; QUEENSLAND; SOUTH AUSTRALIA; SOVEREIGN HILL; SYDNEY; TASMANIA; VICTORIA; WESTERN AUSTRALIA.

BIBLIOGRAPHY

General

Birmingham *et al.*, 1979, 1983; Brassil, 1980; Brogden, 1968; Brooke, 1984; Butlin, 1964; Carne, 1908; Cole, 1926; Connah, 1988; D'Alpuget, 1987; Freeland, 1968; Freeman *et al.*, 1985; Gillen, 1989; Glynn, 1975; Heritage of Australia, 1981; Irving, 1985; Johnson, 1980; Kerr, G. J., 1974; Kerr, J. S., 1985; Kilmartin and Thorns, 1978; King, 1984; Linge, 1979; McCarty and Schedvin, 1978; Nadel, 1957; Neutze, 1977; O'Connor, 1985; Pearson and Temple, 1983; Power, 1912; Sandercock, 1975; Schedvin and McCarty, 1976; Serle, 1972; Shann, 1930.

Specific

Allen, J. The archaeology of nineteenth-century British imperialism: an Australian case study. In *World Archaeology*, VII, 1976.
Birmingham, J. The archaeological contribution of nineteenth-century history: some Australian case studies. In *World Archaeology*, VII, 1976.
Donnachie, I. Industrial archaeology in Australia. In *IAR*, V, 1981.
Murray, T. and Allen, J. Theory and development of historical archaeology in Australia. In *Archaeology in Oceania*, XXI, 1986.
National Trust of Australia (NSW). *Industrial and Historical Archaeology*. Sydney: National Trust of Australia (NSW), 1981.

LOCATIONS
[I] Australian Society for Historical Archaeology, Box 220, Holme Building, University of Sydney, NSW 2006.

KATE CLARK

Austria The present state of Austria is bordered by Germany, Czechoslovakia, Hungary, Yugoslavia, Italy and Switzerland, and extends over some 83 850 km² (32 376 sq. mi.). It consists of nine Bundesländer, the ancient provinces of Vorarlberg, Tyrol (Tirol), Salzburg, Carinthia (Kärnten), Styria (Steiermark), Upper Austria (Oberösterreich), and Lower Austria (Neiderösterreich), together with two created in 1921, Burgenland, formerly part of Hungary, and the city of Vienna (Wien). The population totals some 7.5 million, over 99 per cent of whom speak German. About 20 per cent of the population live in VIENNA.

Until the end of World War I the provinces that now comprise the state of Austria were part of the empire of the Habsburgs which extended far into eastern Europe. In the nineteenth century it was possible to see the future for the Austrian provinces either in terms of a continuing multinational empire, or as part of a greater Germany, which would embrace all the German-speaking peoples.

In the mid-seventeenth century the Habsburgs had secured the future for absolutist government aided by the power of the Roman Catholic Church in their German-speaking provinces. Between 1648 and 1718 their empire more than doubled in extent, as the Turks were expelled from Hungary, and provinces in the Netherlands and Italy were gained by inheritance following the Treaty of Utrecht which ended the War of the Spanish Succession in 1713. The empire was saved from partition through the efforts of the Empress Maria Theresa (1717–80) in the War of the Austrian Succession between 1740 and 1748. The Habsburgs took a leading part in opposing the ambitions of revolutionary France, but much of their territory was invaded by Napoleon, who occupied Vienna in 1809. Following the Congress of Vienna in 1815 the Habsburgs gained full control of the former archiepiscopal state of SALZBURG, as well as the presidency of the confederation of German states. The authority of the empire was shaken during the revolutions of 1848, and seriously weakened by subsequent military defeats, in Italy in 1859, and in the war with Prussia in 1866. In the following year the Ausgleich (compromise) was reached, whereby Hungary became for many purposes a separate state, although still under the authority of the emperor. The provinces of Bosnia and Herzegovina were occupied in 1878, which increased the empire's involvement in the South Slav problem, which was to prove the immediate *casus belli* of World War I in 1914.

The death in 1916 of the Emperor Franz Josef (1830–1916) who had reigned since 1848, and the surrenders of Czech and Ruthenian troops on the Russian front, portended the collapse of imperial authority. As the defeat of the German army on the Western Front seemed imminent, civil unrest grew in Vienna, and in October 1918 the German-speaking members of the imperial

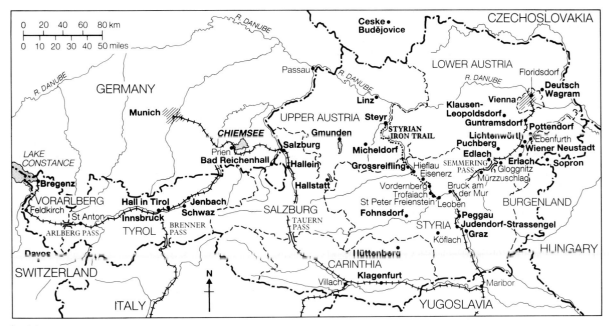

Austria

parliament proclaimed the provincial national assembly of the independent German-Austrian state. The Emperor Carl (1887–1922) abdicated on 11 November 1918 and the following day a republic was proclaimed. The new state had a weak identity. Any form of unity with the republic that had succeeded the German empire was prohibited by the Treaty of St Germain of 1919, and two other German-speaking provinces of the Habsburg Empire, Bohemia and Moravia, were incorporated within Czechoslovakia. There was a possibility for a time that Vorarlberg, the most westerly of the provinces, might become a canton of Switzerland. The Austrian republic endured an uneasy existence, facing formidable problems of economic adjustment after the demise of an empire that had shaped trading patterns in eastern Europe for many centuries. There were continual strains between the Social Democrats, who had long traditions in Vienna, and right-wing elements exemplified by the chancellor Engelbert Dollfus (1882–1934), who attempted to enforce deflation following the collapse of the Credit-Anstalt bank in 1931, and who was assassinated in July 1934.

Austria was incorporated within the German Third Reich following the Anschluss (union) of 12 March 1938, and made significant economic contributions to the German war effort. Resistance to the Nazi regime was to prove the foundation of modern Austrian national identity, and the Moscow declaration of the Allied Powers of 1943 affirmed that after the war there should be an independent Austrian state. There was heavy fighting in the eastern part of the country during the closing stages of the war, and Vienna fell to the Red Army on 13 April 1945. Austria was occupied by the victorious powers, and suffered from vast influxes of refugees, as well as from tensions that developed between the Western powers and

the Russians at the onset of the Cold War. Rebuilding was undertaken quickly, and by the Staatsvertrag (state treaty) of 1955 the occupying armies withdrew in return for a guarantee of Austria's future neutrality.

Until 1918 the Austrian provinces formed part of the economy of a multinational empire that extended over much of Europe, including territories now belonging to Italy, Czechoslovakia, Hungary, Poland, Romania, the Soviet Union and Yugoslavia. It is, as Milward and Saul (1977) have suggested, a dubious exercise to attempt to consider the economic history of any one part of the Habsburg empire separately from the rest.

Modern industrial practices were introduced to the empire relatively early, with the construction of textile mills on the British model in Bohemia and Lower Austria in the early nineteenth century, but economic growth up to World War I remained sluggish. In 1914 only 6 per cent of Europe's industrial output came from the empire, and the per capita income was only three-quarters of that in the Zollverein (see GERMANY). Less than a quarter of the empire's labour force was engaged in manufacturing industry in 1910. The empire included some 12.5 per cent of Europe's population in 1914, with eleven major language groups. The main link between the provinces was the River Danube, although at either end the connections with Germany and with the Black Sea were difficult. Serfdom continued in some form in every province of the empire except Vorarlberg and the Tyrol until the revolutions of 1848, and the low productivity of the agricultural sector is widely regarded as having been the principal reason for the sluggish economic growth of the empire. There were vast disparities of wealth between the various provinces, and after the Ausgleich (compromise) of 1867 such developments as the construction of new railways were frustrated by rivalry between Austrians and Hungarians.

Some 60 per cent of modern Austria is Alpine in character, but the country possesses one of Europe's principal sources of iron ore (see STYRIAN IRON ROAD), as well as mines of copper, lead, silver and gold, and deposits of salt. The coalfield around Köflach (see GRAZ) has long been an important source of lignite, and there are oilfields between Matzen and Gänserndorf, north of Vienna. The first oil refinery in the empire was established in Vienna as early as 1862, principally to process oil from Galicia, then a province of the empire but now the south-eastern part of POLAND.

Styria was the principal source of iron within the Habsburg Empire, producing 60 per cent of the empire's total output as late as 1880. Traditionally much of the region's iron was exported in the form of scythes, sickles and bar iron, which followed traditional routes from furnaces and forges around the Iron Mountain to the commercial centre of the trade at STEYR. Charcoal was used to fuel most furnaces until the 1870s when the Styrian firms were reorganized as the Österreichisch-Alpinen-Montangesellschaft and began to adopt coke smelting, using coal mined in Silesia to make steel by the GILCHRIST THOMAS process. There were also charcoal-fired blast furnaces in Carinthia, Salzburg and Lower Austria.

The principal concentration of mines for non-ferrous metals was along the valley of the River Inn between Kufstein and INNSBRUCK, and particularly between Brixlegg and SCHWAZ, where there were workings in the nineteenth century for copper, lead and silver, as well as some iron-ore mines. Copper was also worked on the slopes of the Jochberg and in the Ahrnthal. There were gold mines in the Hüttenwinkel-Thal and in the Gastein valley (see TAUERN), which was also a source of SERPENTINE.

The border area between Salzburg and Upper Austria was one of the empire's chief sources of salt. The Emperor Maximilian I (1493–1519) established the Salzkammergut (salt-chamber estate) by buying out private owners of saltmines, and until the end of the eighteenth century there was competition between the royal mines and those of the Archbishop of Salzburg. The area of the Salzkammergut was ill-defined, but was usually understood to be the territory within a 50 km (30 mi.) radius of Bad Ischl. The principal historic sources of salt were at HALLEIN, HALL IN TIROL, and HALLSTATT.

The cotton textile industry was established in Austria by the erection of a mill at POTTENDORF by the Englishman John Thornton of Manchester in 1801. Other mills were built in Lower Austria, while as a result of contemporary developments in Switzerland, several textile factories were constructed at Feldkirch and Thüringen in Vorarlberg. By 1843 there were 387 500 cotton spindles in Lower Austria and 141 000 in Vorarlberg, at which time textiles comprised about 40 per cent of the industrial output of the empire.

Textile manufacture stimulated the growth of engineering in the empire. Several British machine-builders were active in Austria in the early nineteenth century and in 1833 M. Fletcher and J. Punshon established a factory for building steam engines in Vienna, which was later leased to W. Norris of Philadelphia who used it for assembling locomotives.

In the early twentieth century the Austrian engineering industry was showing considerable enterprise. VIENNA and STEYR were important centres of motorcar manufacture, bicycles were amongst the products of GRAZ, and Austrian companies were celebrated for their SEWING MACHINES.

The advent of electric power had less impact on manufacturing industry in Austria than in the French Alps or Norway, but an important aluminium factory was established in the late nineteenth century at Lend-Gastein (Salzburg).

Since World War II Austria has achieved notable successes in steelmaking. The Linz-Donawitz process, in which pig-iron is decarburized by the use of an oxygen lance, was first successfully used on an experimental basis at LINZ in 1949, and has since been adopted in most steelmaking countries.

Steamship services on the DANUBE between Passau in Bavaria and the border of the Ottoman Empire at Orşova were inaugurated in 1829 when two Englishmen, John Andrews and Joseph Pritchard, were given a fifteen-year exclusive right to operate services on the river. Subsequently they formed the Donau Dampfschiffart Gesellschaft (DDSG; Danube Steamship Co.) and began time-tabled services downstream from Linz in 1837. By 1857 there were 101 steamers and 359 tugs at work on the Danube within the empire, and the river remained an important economic link until 1918. Austria was the third and last of the states bordering Lake Constance to establish a steamer service, vessels owned by the railway authorities commencing voyages from BREGENZ in 1884.

The first railway in Austria was the 53 km (33 mi.) line from Linz to České Budějovice (now in Czechoslovakia): opened in 1832, and using horse traction, it persisted until 1854. The first locomotive-worked line was the first section of the Kaiser Ferdinand's Nordbahn between Floridsdorf and DEUTSCH-WAGRAM, opened on 13 November 1837 and extended across the Danube from Floridsdorf into Vienna on 6 January 1838. Most of the early main lines were constructed under state patronage. The Kaiserin Elisabeth Bahn extended 300 km (200 mi.) from Vienna West through Linz to Salzburg. The line from Vienna to Gloggnitz, opened in 1841, became the Southern State Railway (Südbahn) in 1853, and was completed through Graz and Laibach (Ljubljana) to Trieste in 1857. By the early 1870s most of the principal towns of the empire were connected by rail. Railways were gradually built across the principal mountain passes, the SEMMERING in 1854, the BRENNER in 1867, the ARLBERG in 1883, and the TAUERN in 1909. Most of the state railways were amalgamated in 1884 to form the Kaiserlichkönigliche Österreichische Staatsbahnen (kkStB). The state lines were amalgamated with various smaller companies in 1923 to form Österreichischen Bundesbahnen (ÖBB), the Südbahn being incorporated the following year. There were numerous narrow-gauge lines giving access to remote mountain settlements, the majority of them to 760 mm (2 ft. 6 in.) gauge. Main-line electrification began in 1912 in Austria, and was completed in the post-war period. After the Anschluss the Austrian railways were absorbed in the system of the Third Reich.

The first centre of locomotive building in Austria was established in VIENNA in 1839 when the Englishman John Haswell opened a works near the south station. Locomotives were also built by private companies in Wien-Floridsdorf, WIENER NEUSTADT and LINZ.

The imperial authorities continued to construct new roads in the Austrian provinces throughout the nineteenth century. The route between Taxenbach and Rauris, and those up the Oetzthal and Passeier-Thal, were notable examples of new construction of the 1890s.

The preservation and conservation of historic buildings in Austria is the responsibility of conservators employed in each of the provinces. The terms of reference of the legislation passed in 1923 precluded its application to industrial monuments, but by 1970 some 220 had been accorded protection. A department for industrial monuments was established within the Federal Office of Historical Monuments in 1976. The Technical University of VIENNA has also been responsible for compiling lists of industrial monuments, and by 1984 some 2000 had been accorded legislative protection.

The principal collection of technological and industrial artefacts in Austria is the Technical Museum in VIENNA. Elsewhere there is a variety of museums run by local authorities, industrial companies and private bodies.

The Austrian railway authorities own some 14 600 buildings constructed between 1838 and 1914, many of which have been accorded legislative protection. There is no single national railway museum, although the Technical Museum in Vienna houses most of the country's oldest locomotives. Over 120 steam locomotives are preserved in Austria, and several of Austrian origin remain in neighbouring countries. More than twenty electric locomotives, one dating from 1912, and a handful of diesels are also preserved. Some steam locomotives have been 'plinthed' and stand in public places. The largest collection of working locomotives is at Strasshof near Vienna, while several are maintained in working order by the state railways, by the Graz Köflacher Bahn and by the Györ Sopron Ebenfurti Fsut at Pölten.

Wooden covered bridges are a characteristic feature of the Alpine landscape of the Austrian provinces. An example which crosses the River Schwechat at Alland was built in 1887 and roofed in 1898; it is 27.5 m (90 ft.) in span. It is the only remaining example in Lower Austria.

Many farms in the Alpine regions had their own water mills, and a typical example has been preserved at Elsenau in Salzburg.

As in other mountainous regions forestry has been of great importance in the Austrian provinces, and several notable monuments associated with the transport of logs have been preserved. There is a timber slide of 1784–5 at Payerbach in Lower Austria; while the Schwarzenberg Channel along the border between Austria and Czechoslo-

vakia, near St Oswald in Upper Austria, which dates from the late eighteenth century, includes a 459 m (1506 ft.) tunnel. A stone weir for pounding water for log floating at Weichselboden in Styria of 1840–6 was used until 1966 and restored in 1975, and there is a similar weir of 1756 at KLAUSEN-LEOPOLDSDORF in Lower Austria.

There is no national organization directly concerned with industrial archaeology, but the Montanhistorische Verein für Österreich (Association for the History of Mining in Austria) has been actively involved in publication and preservation.

The Bundesamt für Eich- und Vermessungswesen (Measuring and Surveying Organization) publishes maps at scales of 1:200 000, 1:100 000, 1:50 000 and 1:25 000 which cover the whole country, as well as a range of aerial photographs. More detailed maps of mountain regions at 1:25 000 are published by the Österreichischer Alpenverein (Austrian Alpine Association).

Austrian architects have been concerned to find new uses for redundant industrial buildings, and schemes to adapt locomotive roundhouses, gasholders and slaughterhouses have been amongst the most imaginative in Europe.

See also ARLBERG; BREGENZ; BRENNER; DANUBE; DEUTSCHWAGRAM; EDLACH AN DER RAX; ERLACH AN DER PITTEN; FOHNSDORF; GMUNDEN; GÖLSDORF, KARL; GRAZ; GROSSREIFLING; GUNTRAMSDORF; HALLEIN; HALL IN TIROL; HALLSTATT; HÜTTENBERG; INNSBRUCK; JENBACH; JUDENDORF-STRASSENGEL; KLAGENFURT; KLAUSEN-LEOPOLDSDORF; LICHTENWÖRTH; LINZ; MICHELDORF; PEGGAU; POTTENDORF; PUCHBERG; SALZBURG; SCHÖNERER, MATTHIAS; SCHWAZ; SEMMERING; STEYR; STYRIAN IRON ROAD; TAUERN; VIENNA; WIENER NEUSTADT.

BIBLIOGRAPHY
General
Milward and Saul, 1977; Schefold, 1986; Stadler, 1971; Wehdorn and Georgeacopol-Winischhofer, 1990; Wiskemann, 1966.

Specific
Das Bild der Industrie in Österreich (Views of industry in Austria), Innsbruck: Institut für Kunstgeschichte der Universität Innsbruck, 1988.

LOCATIONS
[I] Bundesdenkmalamt, Abteilung für technische, wirtschafts- und sozialgeschichtliche Denkmale (Monuments authority, Department for Technical, Economic and Social History), 1010-Wien, Hofburg, Schweizerhof.
[I] Montanhistorische Verein für Österreich (Association for the History of Mining in Austria), Straussgasse 1, 8700 Leoben.
[I] Österreichischer Alpenverein, 15 Wilhel-Greil-Strasse, A6010 Innsbruck.

BARRIE TRINDER

automatic loom The automatic or Draper loom resupplied its own weft pirns or bobbins, refilling its own shuttles from a cylindrical battery mounted on the frame. Developed in the USA from c. 1890 by James Northrup and built by the Draper Corporation of MASSACHUSETTS from 1894, the automatic loom greatly increased the number of looms that could be attended by each weaver. There are examples in most museums of industrial textiles.

automobile The usual formal term for 'motorcar' in North America. The word 'car' is more usual in common speech in both England and America.

Auvet, Haute-Saône, France On either side of the River Saône, between the ports of Gray and Port-sur-Saône, 50 km (30 mi.) NE of Dijon, a significant iron industry developed as early as the fifteenth century, using ores which produced iron of high quality. More than forty ironworking sites have been located in the region; most were still active in the nineteenth century. Production was interrupted by the Thirty Years War between 1618 and 1648, many furnaces being destroyed, but growth soon resumed, particularly after 1678 when Franche Comté became part of France. Much of the iron produced was sent to Lyons along the Saône, to be used by the SAINT-ÉTIENNE armaments industry. Pig iron also went north towards the metalworking establishments of the Vosges, in particular the tinplate mills of BAINS-LES-BAINS.

The Bley ironworks at Auvet, 10 km (6 mi.) NW of Gray, incorporates a blast furnace and a FINERY-AND-CHAFERY FORGE. It originally belonged to the Cisterian Abbey of Theuley, and during the sixteenth century was run by entrepreneurs from Gray. It was destroyed *c.*1640, but the blast furnace was rebuilt in 1655, the pig iron being refined at the neighbouring ironworks of Achey. At the end of the eighteenth century, during the Revolution, the blast furnace was confiscated, becoming once again the property of merchants from Gray. Between 1839 and 1841 one of them had the works completely rebuilt. The new blast furnace was still fired by charcoal, but blast was provided by a piston-type blowing engine, driven by a breast-shot water wheel. This wheel was replaced in 1856 by a steam engine, which was installed on top of the furnace, and utilized recovered heat from its throat. This innovation, the Thomas and Laurens system, was first introduced to France in 1835 at the Echalonge blast furnace, 10 km (6 mi.) SE of Auvet. The Bley furnace ceased production in 1865, and the site was then, until 1930, used as a foundry. The blast furnace stack still stands along with the casting hall, the ramp leading up to the throat of the furnace, the blowing engine house and the ironmaster's house of the 1840s.

Four other massive blast furnaces still stand in the region, at Montureux, Beaujeu, Saint Loup and Valay, while there are significant vestiges at a dozen or so other ironworking sites.

BIBLIOGRAPHY
General
Claer and Philippe, 1991.

JEAN-FRANÇOIS BELHOSTE

Avanos, Nevşehir, Turkey A town on the Red (Clay) River in the centre of Anatolia. It is an important centre of pottery manufacture; the potteries are open to the public for demonstrations of equipment and skills. There are scores of small kilns.

Aveiro, Beira Litoral, Portugal A port always regarded as the Portuguese Venice, 60 km (37 mi.) S. of Oporto, where a natural harbour and the estuary of the River Vouga provide economical and convenient means of communication. On the Vouga railway which terminates in the city there is a remarkable iron bridge between Eixo and Eiró, 8 km (5 mi.) E. Since the late nineteenth century there have been several tileworks in and around the city, celebrated for their tiled panels. The Campos ceramic plant established in 1896 will be a museum and an educational centre. There are mines nearby at Braçal, Malhada and Corõo da Mó, worked for lead and pyrites in the eighteenth century. The Aveiro lighthouse, built on a concrete plinth, dates from 1893 and is partially faced with local red sandstone.

BIBLIOGRAPHY
Specific
Neves, A. Fábrica Campos: um 'notável' exemplar de arqui-tectura industrial (The Campos factory: a fine example of industrial architecture). In *Mundo da Arte,* XIV, 1983, Coimbra.

Avesta, Kopparberg, Sweden The preserved ironworks at Avesta, on the River Dalälven, includes some of the most important surviving late-nineteenth-century plant in Europe. A copper-smelting works which had used ore from FALUN, established in 1638, was closed in 1872. Subsequently a new ironworks was built on the site by the firm known from 1883 as Avesta Jernverks AB. It had three blast furnaces, a forge for making wrought iron, BESSEMER and OPEN-HEARTH steelmaking plants, and a rolling mill. The three 16.8 m (55ft.) high charcoal-fuelled blast furnaces are preserved in the condition in which they were rebuilt between 1910 and 1916, together with the ropeway system which lifted their raw materials, and two large calcining kilns. The maximum output of the furnaces was 25.5 tonnes of iron per day, or 9010 tonnes per year. Two were last used in 1920. The third was operated for a short time in 1937–8. Many of the wooden houses of the associated settlement are still occupied, the majority of them dating from the first part of the nineteenth century (following a fire of 1803), although some are older.

The mining company Norbergand Kärrgruvan built a hydro-electric power station on the smaller of the two falls on the Dalälven in 1900; it retains its original machinery, including eight turbines. A power station was built on the larger falls in 1929–31.

BIBLIOGRAPHY
General
Nisser, 1979.
Specific
Hermelin, B. *A Few Facts on Avesta's Blast Furnace Plant.* Avesta, 1975.
Hermelin, B. *Avesta's Old Town.* Avesta, 1975.

BARRIE TRINDER

Ayrshire, Strathclyde, Scotland A coal-mining county in south-west Scotland. In the eighteenth century coal was worked in conjunction with coastal saltworks. A ruined beam-engine house on Saltcoats golf course, 9 km (6 mi.) NW of Irvine, is thought to have been built for the second Newcomen engine in Scotland in 1719. A store at St Nicholas golf course, Prestwick, was a panhouse of the 1760s, in which the salters lived above the pans. Inland Ayrshire is littered with remains of later coal mines. Barony Mine, the oldest in Scotland at the time of its closure in 1989, still has a Germanic-looking A-frame headstock.

The remains of a blast furnace of *c.*1796 are visible at Glenbuck. Most of Muirkirk Ironworks has been levelled, leaving the French Gothic-towered Ironworkers' Institute of 1885, now an outdoor centre, and traces of tramways and water-power systems. At Lugar, birthplace of WIL-LIAM MURDOCK, an institute of 1892, a baths building and terraced housing built by the Eglinton Iron Co. in the 1920s remain. Colville's Glengarnock Steelworks is now Lochshore Industrial Estate. A power house of 1908 is among the surviving structures. Famous for its industrial tank locomotives, Andrew Barclay's Caledonia Works, Kilmarnock, still functions: the first iron-framed erecting shop of *c.*1860 has cast-iron crane rails and stanchions under timber queen posts. Three shops followed, framed in a combination of cast iron and steel.

Louvred but unloved, a large tannery and shoe factory in Ayr, founded in 1793, retains courtyard pits and some plant. Part of the polychrome St Cuthbert's Boot and Shoe Factory survives to represent the defunct 'Tacketty' (hobnail boot) industry of Maybole. The 'Saxone' company began as a partnership of two Kilmarnock shoemakers in 1908.

The cotton mills at Catrine, 20 km (12 mi.) E. of Ayr, founded in 1787, closed in 1968, the great Venetian-windowed Twist Mill having been demolished in 1963. Housing and water-power installations remain. Stoneyholm Mill, Kilbirnie, 16 km (10 mi.) N. of Irvine, which is fireproof, started as a cotton mill in 1831, and since 1864 has been Knox's net and twine factory. It now uses synthetic fibres.

The lace and madras industries were concentrated at Newmilns, 11 km (7 mi.) W. of Kilmarnock and Darvel. Factories are typically small, north-lit sheds with two-storey fronts, rather than the big tenement factories of the NOTTINGHAM type. Glenbrig Mill, Irvinebank Power Loom Factory, the Louden Valley Manufacturing Co. and Hood Morton's mills, with their tiled fasciae, are typical. The Stoneygate Road Mills of Morton, Young & Borland now comprise the only madras factory in the world, having Anderston Jacquard looms driven by line shafting, and Nottingham lace looms – one, at 480 in. (12.19 m), thought to be the world's longest.

The Tam o'Shanter and Water of Ayr Hone Works still exports worldwide. The hones came first from a river bed, then a quarry, then a mine, where a winding drum of *c.*1870 remains. Heron's Mill, of 1821, cuts blocks which are faced, turned and polished in Milton Mill. The two are connected by a wire rope suspension footbridge.

Dalgarven Mill at Kilwinning, 24 km (15 mi.) N. of Ayr, is a working water-powered flour mill, now a museum. The disused Dunure Mill of *c.*1814 has Gothic details to complement the nearby Culzean Castle, by Robert Adam (1728–92). Victoria Flour Mills, Ayr, are polychrome brick roller mills of 1878.

Horse-drawn plateways, whose route may still be traced in Ayr harbour, carried coal to the coast. The four-span Laigh Milton Mill Viaduct, Gatehead, 3 km (2 mi.) W. of Kilmarnock, dating from 1812, is considered the world's oldest railway viaduct. The central 55.2 m (181 ft.) span of Ballochmyle Viaduct, 14 km (9 mi.) SE of Kilmarnock, of 1846–8, is claimed to be the world's largest masonry arch. The Kilmarnock viaduct, with twenty-three arches, is on the same line. Kilmarnock's original station of 1843 survives, having been enlarged in 1878 with a cast-iron ridge-and-furrow roof. Girvan Station has Art Deco styling of the 1930s.

Ardrossan harbour and town were laid out from 1806 by the Earls of Eglinton. A hydraulic power station with an Italianate accumulator tower operated dock cranes and a two-leaf, wrought-iron swing bridge. Troon harbour, formed from 1808 by WILLIAM JESSOPS's 210 m (230 yd.) North-East Pier, now serves a marina and the Ailsa Shipbuilding Co., which uses fabricating shops of *c.*1900 and two old dry docks, one hydraulically operated. Ayr possesses river quays, a coal basin of the 1870s, and a leading light of 1840 which is still used. Dunure is a sleepy fishing harbour, with a stone light tower. The wooden boat-building concern, Alexander Noble, operates at Girvan.

See also DALMELLINGTON; IRVINE.

BIBLIOGRAPHY
General
Hume, 1976; Tucker, 1983.

ROBERT FORSYTHE and MARK WATSON

Azores, Portugal *See* LAJES DO PICO; PONTA DELGADA.

B

Babbitt metal A specialized anti-friction metal of 80–85 per cent tin, 2–7 per cent copper and 8–9 per cent antimony or lead, used commonly in engine shaft bearings before the introduction of ball and roller bearings. It was developed by Isaac Babbitt (1799–1862) in Boston, Mass., USA.

back-to-back house A terrace consisting of a double row of houses sharing a common back wall, characteristic of industrial cities of Northern England and the Midlands from the late eighteenth century. In LEEDS, where the type was built in considerable numbers into the twentieth century, its use may have been determined by patterns of building developed on BURGAGE PLOTS and on long narrow fields which were being developed from the 1780s. A block at Newdale, Shropshire (*see* IRONBRIDGE), of *c.*1760 was built in open country with no such restraints. Legislation of 1858 and local by-laws brought an end to the construction of back-to-back houses in most cities by 1900, and only in Leeds, Bradford and surrounding areas do they survive in significant numbers.

The term is sometimes wrongly applied to TUNNEL-BACK HOUSES or nineteenth-century terraced housing in general.

BIBLIOGRAPHY
General
Beresford, 1988; Daunton, 1983; Gauldie, 1974; Horton, 1990; Muthesius, 1982; Trinder, 1982a.

Bad Ems, Rhineland-Palatinate, Germany Now best known as a spa, Bad Ems, 16 km (10 mi.) SE of Koblenz, had a tradition of lead, zinc and silver mining for over eight hundred years. The first records of mining activity are from the twelfth century. Mining licences were issued in 1743, and the first agreements with the Remy family were concluded in 1766. Mining reached its peak in the 1870s. The installation known as the Mercury pit, flooded in 1945, was never reopened, although the processing plant remained in use. It was situated on the island of Silberau, created in 1859 by the canalization of the River Lahn, and the plant closed exactly a century later. All that remains of this once extensive complex is the power station of 1903, preserved as a technological monument. Its generating hall is to be used as a public meeting place. The portal at the entrance to the municipal adit, opened in 1869, is preserved in the garden of a house. The Neuhoffnung adit, opened in 1869, lies on the road to Arzbach. Its portal dates from 1917, and other pithead buildings remain on the opposite side of the road. Several workers' settlements are further evidence of mining activities.

Bad Ems railway station, built in 1863, has a train shed of later date with double tracks, unique amongst railway stations of this size in Germany, something which can be explained only by the town's former importance as a spa, popular in the nineteenth century with Germany royalty.

The funicular railway to Malberg, built in 1886 by Maschinen-fabrik Esslingen, was the oldest and steepest railway of its kind in the Federal Republic, with a gradient of up to 54 per cent over 520 m (570 yd.) of track. It was operated by a water ballast system, but has been closed for some time.

BIBLIOGRAPHY
General
Custodis, 1990.

LOCATION
[M] Heimatsmuseum (Local History Museum), Rathaus, 5427 Bad Ems.

ROLF HÖHMANN

Baden, Aargau, Switzerland A city in north-east Switzerland notable for its engineering works. An early hydro-electric power station on the River Limmat, at Kappeler-hof, Baden, opened in 1892, is now a museum, with turbine chambers, generators and other items illustrating the early history of electric power.

At Windisch, 7 km (4 mi.) W., is a spinning plant, begun in 1828 by Heinrich Kunz, the great spinning master of the Zürich Oberland, together with its associated water-power installations.

A Sulzer tandem compound steam engine of 1904, used for generating electric power, is preserved at the Wisa Gloria factory at Lenzburg, 15 km (9 mi.) SW; and the railway station at Dietikon, 12 km ($7\frac{1}{2}$ mi.) SE, of 1846–7, has been restored to its original condition.

BIBLIOGRAPHY
General
Baldinger, 1987; INSA, 1982–91.

LOCATION
[S] Kappelerhof Power Station, 5401 Baden.

Baden-Württemberg, Germany The Federal State created in 1953 from the former states of Baden, Württemberg and Hohenzollern is now one of the most industrially flourishing areas of West Germany. Since the region was poorly situated for transport facilities, except for the Upper Rhine, and since it had negligible raw materials, industrialization could proceed only from artisan crafts, and from the plentiful supply of labour that arose from the breaking up of the agricultural estates. The result was a middle-class industrial structure which remains characteristic of the region. The textile industry was the first to develop, due to the initiatives of individual inventors and entrepreneurs. By 1900 mechanical engineering and metalworking were developing, to be followed by the now-dominant motor-manufacturing and electrical industries. While the textile industry was spread more or less evenly over the whole area, other activities were more concentrated. The central Neckar valley around the state capital of STUTTGART is the most important centre of motor manufacture, and of mechanical and electrical engineering – industries which are also of importance in MANNHEIM and Karlsruhe in the Upper Rhine plain. The Upper Rhine on the Swiss border (see BASEL) has become a centre of the chemical industry. The Black Forest (Schwarzwald) is famous for its watchmaking. There was iron-smelting at an early date in the Brenz valley in eastern Württemberg, where specialized metalworking continues.

See also ALBSTADT; FORBACH AN DER MURG; FRIEDRICHSHAFEN; GIENGEN AN DER BRENZ; GUTACH IM SCHWARZWALD; HAIGERLOCH-STETTEN; KUCHEN; LAUCHERTHAL; MANNHEIM; NECKAR; OCHSENHAUSEN; REUTLINGEN; RHEINFELDEN; RHINE; SCHRAMBERG; SCHWÄBISCH GMÜND; STUTTGART; UNTERREGENBACH; WASSERALFINGEN.

LOCATION
[I] Landesamt für Denkmalpflege Baden-Württemberg, Mörikestrasse 12, 7000 Stuttgart 1.

ROLF HÖHMANN

Bad Reichenhall, Bavaria, Germany   The installations of the largest German saltworks at Bad Reichenhall, on the Austrian border, 16 km (10 mi.) SW of SALZBURG, are both technical and architectural monuments. The old saltworks were destroyed in a fire in 1834, and rebuilt in their present form in 1844–51. Brine has been procured and processed here for some 1300 years, since Duke Theodor II of Bavaria gave to Rupertus, Bishop of Salzburg, twenty furnaces and boilers in AD 682. As early as 1440 a water-powered bucket elevator was bringing up brine from the main well shaft. Subsidiary saltworks were opened in Traunstein, 24 km (15 mi.) NW of Bad Reichenhall, in 1619, and in Rosenheim, 56 km (35 mi.) W., in 1799, and brine pipelines amounting to over 80 km (50 mi.) in length were laid. At the Karl-Theodor spring in Bad Reichenhall the techniques used to bring up brine are characteristic of engineering in the middle of the nineteenth century: two overshot water wheels, each 13 m (42 ft.) in diameter, set on marble bases, have been in uninterrupted operation since 1850, providing the drive for the pumping plant in the well shaft built by Carl Reichenbach. Some 15 m (50 ft.) lower down an undershot water wheel, working a 103 m (340 ft.) long rod with five gears on twelve bearings, brings up brine from the

Karl-Theodor spring, 40 m (130 ft.) below. It still produces 50 000 l (11 000 gall.) of brine a day.

Brine from the Berchtesgaden rock-salt mine is also processed in Bad Reichenhall. It is conveyed along an 18 km (11 mi.) pipeline. Records of the predecessors of this pipeline date from 1816.

BIBLIOGRAPHY
General
Bott, 1985; Grimm, 1985; Lossen, 1968.

LOCATION
[M] Municipal Museum, Getreidegasse 4, 8230 Bad Reichenhall.

AXEL FÖHL

Baekeland, Leo Hendrik (1863–1944)   The inventor of 'Bakelite', one of the most important PLASTICS of the early twentieth century. Baekeland's principal talent was an ability to adapt existing ideas into commercial forms. In the USA he did this with 'Velox' photographic paper, which could be developed in artificial light. In Germany from 1900 he examined the reactions of PHENOL and METHANAL, using AMMONIA and high pressure to create a mouldable, thermosetting resin. He took out his first patent for the production of plastics from this source in 1907, and set up Bakelite Gesellschaft near Berlin in 1909. Bakelite came to be widely used in electrical insulation, particularly in ignition and lighting systems for motorcars.

BIBLIOGRAPHY
General
ICI, 1962.

Bærum, Akershus, Norway   A town 12 km ($7\frac{1}{2}$ mi.) W. of Oslo. The first blast furnace in Norway was built at the Bærums verk in 1622; of this, only the lower stack remains. Ore was drawn from mines at Tanumasen in the seventeenth century, and at Sognsvannet from 1797: traces of both mines remain. An iron bridge of 1829, with diminishing circles in spandrels, removed 50 m (55 yd.) from its original site, now stands in parkland. There are more than fifty limekilns in the area, several of them preserved.

Baie Ste Clair, Ile d'Anticosti, Quebec, Canada   Baie Ste Clair, on the island of Anticosti near the north shore of the Gulf of St Lawrence, is notable for a limekiln which operated between 1897 and about 1940. It is a monument to the enterprises of the French chocolate manufacturer Henri Menier (see NOISIEL) who purchased the island in 1895 with the intention of establishing his own game and fishing reserve.

Menier followed contemporary fashions in urban planning in laying out the village, as is reflected in the location of the industrial complexes, comprising sawmills and a tinsmithing shop, as well as the dwellings and the farm buildings, which include stables, cowsheds and piggeries.

The limekiln is situated about 8 m (15 ft.) above sea level in rocky terrain running down to the shore. The kiln is 9 m (30 ft.) long, 5 m (16 ft.) from front to back and 3.5 m (11 ft.) high. The cylindrical masonry shaft, of which the bottom and exterior are in limestone bonded by mortar, incorporates an opening below a lintel with apertures for charging wood fuel, a gate and a drain; there are also stone buttresses and retaining walls protecting the hearth and keeping in the heat. The kiln was constructed by the Quebec City stone masonry contractors, the Peters company, who showed the inhabitants of the island how to make lime and mortar. These materials were still used about 1940 in the construction of the chimneys in the houses of the neighbouring village of Port Menier.

The historic importance of the Baie Ste Clair limekiln was recognized by the Quebec government in 1976, two years after the government had acquired the island of Anticosti. Since 1983 a co-ordinated programme between various provincial organizations and the municipality of the island has been directed towards archaeological research and the restoration of the kiln.

BIBLIOGRAPHY
General
Salaun, 1985.

LOUISE TROTTIER

Bailey bridge   *See* FLOATING BRIDGE.

Bains-les-Bains, Vosges, France   The wooded region to the south of the Vosges had no iron ores, but the nearby blast furnaces in the north of Franche-Comté encouraged the development of ironmaking from the sixteenth century. After an interruption during the Thirty Years' War, ironmaking, particularly the production of wire, steel and tinplate, was built up again *c.*1700, centred on the valleys of the Ourche, the Coney and the Semouse.

This was the context for the creation of the Bains-les-Bains tinplate manufacture, launched in 1733 by a group of investors from Nancy; then taken over in 1777, when Lorraine became French, by Claude Thomas Falatieu, a merchant from Lyons. During the eighteenth century it was the leading tinplate producer in France. Tinplate production ceased about 1850, and the factory was partially re-converted to nail manufacture. It finally closed down in 1951. This persistence of small-scale metal production helped to safeguard not only a large proportion of the original buildings but also the site itself within a well-preserved landscape. Apart from the water-power installations, a charcoal barn of 1779 survives, along with a tinning plant of 1836 where iron plates were scaled and dipped into basins of tin. An older building, the original tinning plant, dating from before 1737 and subsequently used for workers' housing, also survives. The master's residence and a chapel nearby also date from the establishment of the manufacture. The whole site is now a protected historical monument.

The region still conserves many other traces of its old iron and steel industries, in particular the La Hutte steelworks at Hennezel, and the nearby edge-tool works at Droiteval. Other sites, including Moulins-au-Bois, Grurupt and La Pipée, were associated with the Bains-les-Bains works, refining the wrought iron, or hammering it into sheets ready for tinplating.

BIBLIOGRAPHY
General
Malinverno *et al.,* 1989.

JEAN-FRANÇOIS BELHOSTE

bakery   Bread is baked principally from wheat and rye, but also from barley, oats, buckwheat or millet. White bread, made with flour from which most of the bran had been removed, was popularized by Napoleon's armies and baked widely in Europe by 1850. Bakers often enjoyed local monopolies for baking bread for sale. Most baking was done in the traditional BREAD OVEN.

The development of industrial-scale bakeries began in Liverpool in 1849–50 but spread slowly. The International Exhibition of Flour Mill Machinery in London in 1881 marked the beginning of mechanical baking in England, and was followed, particularly between 1890 and 1910, by a flood of innovations: flour hoists, mechanical flour sifters, mechanical mixers and dough kneaders, and steam-pipe ovens. Mechanical wrapping was introduced in the 1920s, and mechanical slicing and wrapping machines in the 1930s. Many baking firms were linked with chains of cafés. The Aerated Bread Co. in London had over a hundred branches by 1900. J. Lyons & Co., established in 1894, opened forty branches within six years. Several large commercial bakeries were established in Berlin in the early twentieth century, including Schlüterbrot-Bärenbrot on Eresburgstrasse, which dates from 1913, but has an extension in modernist style by Bruno Buch of 1927–8; and Heinrich Wittler's pumpernickel and black bread factory on Maxstrasse, the earliest part of which was designed by L. A. Ehricht in 1908.

BIBLIOGRAPHY
General
Braudel, 1981; Giedion, 1948; Hildebrandt *et al.,* 1988; Jeffreys, 1954; Kent-Jones and Mitchell, 1962; Panshar and Slater, 1956.

BARRIE TRINDER

Balaton, Hungary   The largest lake in central Europe, 90 km (55 mi.) SW of Budapest, and 75 km (47 mi.) long, for centuries important for freshwater fishing and reed cutting, and for the lavender that is processed in the Tihany peninsula on the northern shore. There are many vineyards on volcanic soils on the northern shore, where several traditional wine-producing farmsteads are protected monuments. The lake is crossed by ferry from Tihany to Szántód. The first passenger steamer on the lake, the *Helka* of 1892, is preserved as a restaurant at Balatonfüred on the northern shore. A museum portraying the history of the lake, at Siófok, 115 km (70 mi.) SW of Budapest, is named after J. Beszédes (1787–1852), a celebrated civil engineer.

At Balatonszemes, 130 km (80 mi.) SW of Budapest, the

postal museum 'From the Diligence to the Railway Post' occupies the stables of a posting station of which the inn is now a private dwelling. The 23.7 m (78 ft.) footbridge of 1931 at the railway station was the first welded-steel bridge in Hungary and the fourth in Europe.

See also SIÓ CANAL.

BIBLIOGRAPHY
General
Kiss *et al.*, 1981.

LOCATIONS
[M] Museum Beszédes József, Sió u. 2, H-8600 Siófok.
[M] Postal Museum, Bajcsy Zs. u. 46, Balatonszemes H-8636.

MIHÁLY KUBINSZKY and BARRIE TRINDER

Balearic Islands, Spain   The Balearic Islands – Majorca (Mallorca), Minorca (Menorca), Ibiza (Iviza) and Formentera – lie in the Mediterranean, the capital, Palma, being some 250 km (155 mi.) E. of VALENCIA. In the 1960s the jet airliner made the islands into a holiday resort for northern Europeans. The islands are part of Spain, but there have been traditional commercial ties with Italy, and Minorca was held by Britain in 1708–56, 1763–82, and 1798–1802. Lead, iron ore, cinnabar, marble and

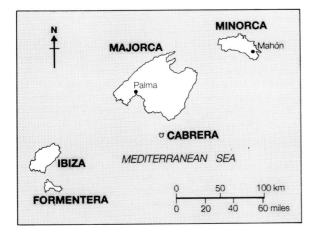

Balearic Islands

cannel coal have been worked on Majorca. The British Royal Navy established an important base at Mahón on Minorca in the eighteenth century. Surviving buildings include storehouses of 1774 and the Royal Navy's first purpose-built hospital, begun in 1712, on islands in the harbour. Minorcan distilleries still produce gin to eighteenth-century Royal Navy specifications.

BIBLIOGRAPHY
General
Baldinger, 1988; Coad, 1983, 1989.

LOCATION
[M] Maritime Museum of the Balearic Islands, Consulado de Mar, Paseo Sagrera, Palma de Mallorca.

Ball, Edmund Bruce (1903–85)   The founder-chairman of the Ironbridge Gorge Museum Trust (*see* IRONBRIDGE) in 1967–78. His charm and qualities of leadership did much to establish the museum. He read engineering at Cambridge, and worked for Glenfield & Kennedy of Kilmarnock, 'hydraulic engineers to the Empire'. He became managing director of the Lilleshall Company in Shropshire in 1959; it was this that led to his involvement with Ironbridge.

BIBLIOGRAPHY
Specific
Ironbridge Quarterly, 3, 1985.

ballast   A word with two meanings in industrial archaeology:

1. Heavy material placed in the hold of a ship that is otherwise empty or lightly loaded, in order to increase the vessel's stability. The ballast used is often gravel or other material of low value.
2. Gravel, broken stone or slag on which the tracks of a railway are laid, or the underlay of a CONCRETE or TARMACADAM road. The ballast provides a solid bed, and by its porosity prevents the accumulation of water.

ball bearing   *See* BEARING.

ball clay   A clay of high plasticity and firmness which is one of the raw materials of PORCELAINS. Ball clays result from the decomposition of GRANITE that has been washed from its point of origin and redeposited in beds of clay: the clay was originally dug out in balls. The deposits in the west of England have been worked on a large scale since the eighteenth century.

BIBLIOGRAPHY
General
Hamer, 1986; Rolt, 1974.

balloon   A gas-tight envelope, usually of a textile fabric filled with a light gas, that will rise into the air; it is usually capable of carrying a load in the form of passengers. The hot-air balloon was developed by the Montgolfier brothers, who made the first successful manned flight on 21 November 1783 in Paris. Shortly afterwards a rival Parisian pioneer, Professor J. A. C. Charles, designed a man-carrying hydrogen balloon, first flown on 1 December 1783. Both types were used for observation in nineteenth-century wars. Balloon ascents were popular means of celebrating public events in the nineteenth century, particularly the inaugurations of GASWORKS. In the twentieth century the use of balloons has been eclipsed by airships and subsequently by fixed-wing aircraft, but observation and 'barrage' balloons, whose cables acted as a deterrent against hostile aircraft, were used in World War II, and hot-air ballooning has recently been revived as an international sport.

At Farnborough, Hampshire, the Royal Aerospace Establishment Museum has ballooning archives, and a balloon basket. The Science Museum, LONDON, has the basket of a Short Brothers balloon of 1900, and a pressurized gondola from A. Piccard's balloon of 1932. There is a specialist balloon museum at Newbury, 45 km (28 mi.) S. of Oxford. The Praha Zenith Balloon of 1904 is in the National Technical Museum, PRAGUE; and several pioneering balloon artefacts are in the National Air and Space Museum, WASHINGTON DC.

BIBLIOGRAPHY
General
Hildebrandt, 1908.

LOCATION
[I,M] British Balloon Museum and Library, c/o Newbury District Museum, The Wharf, Newbury RG14 5AS.

JULIAN TEMPLE

Ballydehob (Beal an da Chab, Swantonstown), County Cork, Ireland   Centre of a copper and barytes mining region extending from Skibbereen, 14 km (8$\frac{1}{2}$ mi.) to the east, to Mount Gabriel, Schull, 8 km (5 mi.) to the west. On the road to Foilnamack, 3 km (2 mi.) S., are the remains of a substantial mine, with a capped shaft, the remnants of dressing floors, a circular chimney and the ruins of miners' cottages. The harbour is crossed by the twelve-arch Roaringwater Viaduct of the 3 ft. (0.91 m) gauge Schull & Skibbereen Light Tramway, opened in 1886 and closed in 1947.

BIBLIOGRAPHY
Specific
Newham, A. T. *The Schull and Skibbereen Tramway*. Lingfield: Oakwood Press, 1964

banana   The banana, *Musa sapientum*, was eaten in classical antiquity but became a major item of trade when cargoes were shipped from Central America to the USA in the late 1860s. The first consignment from Jamaica reached Boston, Mass., in 1872, and a company was established in the city in 1885 which came to control the banana trade between the Caribbean and the USA. Bananas were first shipped by Fyffe, Hudson & Co. from Las Palmas to London in 1878; and the first refrigerated import reached Bristol from the West Indies in 1902. Most bananas were imported to Germany through HAMBURG. The banana trade needs a complex infrastructure, with special handling facilities at ports and ripening ware-houses near to wholesale markets. Until the 1960s specially-built heated and insulated railway wagons were used to convey unripened bananas.

BIBLIOGRAPHY
General
Hudson, 1978; Prescott and Proctor, 1937.

Banbury, Oxfordshire, England   An archetypal English market town, on the Oxford Canal which opened in 1772. Banbury was a plush-weaving centre till the late nine-teenth century, and Bernhard Samuelson's foundry was one of the first manufacturers of the McCormick reaper in the 1850s. Banbury was an important railway junction during 1900–67; the marshalling yard of 1931 is now derelict. There are extensive remains of ironstone quarry-ing in the district.

At Hook Norton, 12 km (7$\frac{1}{2}$ mi.) W., a small country brewery is still working.

BIBLIOGRAPHY
General
Rolt, 1944, 1977; Trinder, 1982a.

LOCATION
[M] Banbury Museum, Horsefair, Banbury.

Banská Bystrica (Neusohl), Central Slovakia, Czechoslo-vakia   An important centre for copper and iron-ore mining and industry. A large concern was established in the 1490s using Fugger capital (*see* CZECHOSLOVAKIA) which brought about reorganization of mining concerns, creating large unified complexes. Involvement by the Fuggers ceased in 1545, but production did not decline until the seventeenth century. Several buildings asso-ciated with this mining history survive in the town centre, but there are no preserved industrial monuments nor any other signs of mining activity.

At Špania Dolina, 10 km (6 mi.) N., is a mine that may be medieval; it has extant eighteenth- and nineteenth-century buildings. Large waste heaps remain, but much of the area is covered by opencast mining.

Staré Hory, 15 km (9 mi.) N. of Banská Bystrica, was an important copper-mining centre which was developed using Fugger capital in the fifteenth century.

At Lubietová, 15 km (9 mi.) NE of Banská Bystrica, the blast furnace, one of the first in Slovakia (established *c.*1720), was supplied by the ore mines at Banská Bystrica and BANSKÁ ŠTIAVNICA.

BIBLIOGRAPHY
Specific
Vozár, J. English mechanic Isaac Potter, constructor of the first fire-engine in Slovakia. In *Studia Historica Slovaca*, VII, 1977.
Zebrak, P. Vysledy Dosavadniho Vyzkumu Pravekeho Hornictvi na Uzemi Slovenska (The results of research so far on primeval mining on Slovak territory). In *Vlastivedny Sbornik Podbrdska*, 1987.

LOCATION
[M] Museum of the History of Slovakia, Namesti Slovensko Narodneho Postvania, Banská Bystrica.

JUDITH ALFREY, TIM PUTNAM and SIMON DERRY

Banská Štiavnica (Schemnitz), Central Slovakia, Cze-choslovakia   A town that was already important as a centre for precious-metal mining in the thirteenth cen-tury, and that by the eighteenth century was a noted centre for the mining of silver, lead and iron ore. Today its significance can be seen in those buildings that have been preserved. The town centre, based on the Holy Trinity Square with its high Baroque votive monument, is surrounded by sixteenth-century houses. The town is dominated by two castles, Staré Hrad and Novy Hrad, and

Figure 8 The mining landscape in Banská Štiavnica, Slovakia
Simon Derry

several fine churches. The headstock of the Josef mine survives in the lower quarter but it is due for demolition. The town is undergoing total reconstruction which will continue well into the next century.

The museum in Banská Štiavnica has several sites. The Kammerhof, a building for testing and assaying ore, will house an exhibition of mining and the museum offices. A sixteenth-century merchant's house in the square houses the Slovakian geological and mineralogical collections. The old castle (Staré Hrad) contains paintings and sculptures relating to the town and mining and an exhibition on the history of metallurgy.

On the road to Štiavnicke Bané is the open-air museum of mining, set up between 1964 and 1973. On the surface are various buildings associated with mining: several headstocks, an administration building, a compressed-air plant, and a shed housing battery-powered locomotives for use in the mine. The main exhibit is a show mine, created using old workings where possible and new galleries where they were needed for modern standards of safety and visitor access. There are guided tours of the mine, and an exhibition which covers the history of mining from the late medieval period to the present day. The open-air museum also includes a reconstructed miner's cottage. Further development of the museum will provide holiday chalets for ex-miners and new exhibits will include a horse gin.

In Štiavnicke Bané itself there are three important buildings for the development of mining in the area, the eighteenth-century mining academy, the workshop where Newcomen engines were produced and repaired, and an early eighteenth-century powder tower. It is claimed that the workshop was one of the first outside Britain to produce a Newcomen engine, under the guidance of Isaac Potter in 1722.

Surviving remains of the water-power system include a series of reservoirs constructed between the seventeenth century and the mid-nineteenth century to provide water for powering machinery and for domestic use. The entire relict landscape surrounding the town has been designated a National Monument, and a series of educational trails have been set up, including the reservoirs and features like the Theresa mine, which has hand-mined opencast workings from the surface to a depth of 40–50 m (44–55 yd.). A 17 km (11 mi.) section of the narrow-gauge railway that brought timber to the mines at the end of the nineteenth century has been reconstructed.

BIBLIOGRAPHY
Specific
Laduba, J. Stredove Architektury na Starom Meste v Banskei Stiavnici, ich Konzevacia a Vijuzitie (Medieval architecture of the Old Town at Banská Štiavnica). In *Archaeologia Historia*, XI, 1986.
Novak, J. *Slovenske Banske Muzeum* (The Slovak Mining Museum). Banská Štiavnica: Banská Štiavnica Museum, 1976.
Vozár, J. English mechanic Isaac Potter, constructor of the first fire-engine in Slovakia. In *Studia Historica Slovaka*, VII, 1977.

LOCATION
[M] Mining Museum, Trojice Namesti and Stary Zamek, Banská Štiavnica.

SIMON DERRY

57

Barcelona, Barcelona, Catalonia, Spain   The capital of Catalonia and one of Europe's most vibrant industrial cities, with a population of 3.5 million, and a long tradition of working-class consciousness. It remains a fishing port. Its architecture is dominated by the works of ANTONI GAUDÍ and other ART NOUVEAU architects. The three chimneys of the FECSA Pobla Nou power station, the rest of which has been demolished, form one of the symbols of the city. Barcelona's primary development as an industrial city was based on textiles and engineering, but from the late nineteenth century there was the substantial growth of food-processing and consumer goods industries characteristic of great ports.

The Vapor Vell, a steam-operated textile factory of 1840, was the first large-scale industrial enterprise to be located outside the old city walls. In 1985 it became the first industrial building in Spain to be declared a national monument.

The Born covered market, a cast-iron structure of the 1880s designed by Josep Fontseré, now serves as a covered public arena for civic events.

During the first three decades of the twentieth century the growth of the wine trade led to the construction of many warehouses, known as 'cellers' or cellars. Three notable examples are the Cavas Codorniu at Sant Sadurní d'Anoia, 32 km (20 mi.) W. of Barcelona, where the main building was designed by Domenec & Muntaner, and where the printing press room is now a museum; the Celler de Pinell de Brai, the most successful of the works of Cesar Martinell, an architect who specialized in this type of building, who also designed the 'cellers' of Falset, Rocafort, Gandesa and Cervera; and the Celler de Garraf, designed by Antoni Gaudí. There is an important wine museum at Villafranca del Penedès, 40 km (25 mi.) W. of Barcelona.

Barcelona is notable for its 'harineras', vertical flour silos with elaborate external decorations. The most important are the Cervera, Vich and Manresa establishments, the last of which has become the headquarters of the Civic Guard.

Many more of Barcelona's principal industrial buildings have been adapted to new uses. The Fábrica Casaramona, one of the finest textile factories in Catalonia, is now a police station. La Sedeta, an old silk factory, is now used as a civic centre and an institute for graduate studies. A hydro-electric power station owned by Hidroeléctrica de Catalunya has been converted into the company's offices. The Cocheras de Sants, the city's former tram depot, has been converted into a civic centre. The Citadel Waterworks, a brick structure erected for the international exhibition of 1888, has been converted into an exhibition centre.

Industrial buildings of outstanding interest in the suburbs of Barcelona include the Fábrica Tecla Sala in l'Hospitalet del Llobregat, to the south, a twentieth-century factory which has been converted into a cultural centre and La Farga, an ironworks in l'Hospitalet which is now a location for fairs. The Central de Bombeo de Cornellá is a steam-powered pumping station of 1903.

Barcelona's main railway terminus, the Estaçion de Francia, completed just after World War I, has a two-bay curving train shed of steel arches, while the Estaçion del Norte retains its original ticket counter, a remarkable blend of neo-Baroque and Art Nouveau.

The Maritime Museum in the one-time royal shipyards (Reales Atarazanas) in Barcelona is located in an arsenal building which dates from the thirteenth century. It was used as a barracks from the eighteenth century, and was continually threatened with demolition from 1876 until the 1930s. The museum's exhibits include several full-size reconstructed vessels, the most important of which from an industrial archaeological viewpoint are the fishing boats from the Catalan coast. There is a rich collection of ship models, chiefly from the nineteenth century, some of which are bone and ivory models made by sailors and prisoners. Other exhibits include navigational instruments, documents and pictures, and superb eighteenth-century tiled panels depicting sailing ships.

BIBLIOGRAPHY
General
Corredor and Montaner, 1984; Generalitat de Catalunya, 1988; Marti *et al.*, 1982; Sanz and Giner, 1984.

LOCATIONS
[M] Maritime Museum, Puerta de la Paz 1, Barcelona.
[M] Museum of Ceramics, Palacio Nacional, Parc de Montjuic, Barcelona.
[M] Museum of Decorative Arts, Palacio de la Virreina, Ramla de las Flores 99, Barcelona.
[M] Museum of the History of the City of Barcelona, Plaza del Rey, Barcelona.
[M] Textile Museum, Calle Hospital 56, Barcelona.

EUSEBI CASANELLES

barge   A term loosely applied to many vessels employed in inland navigation and coastal trades, in England referring particularly to broad vessels working on rivers and unable to navigate most canals (*see* NARROW BOAT). The word also applies to some sailing vessels in the coastal trade, particularly those working in and around the Thames Estuary, England, of which *Cambria* of 1906 among others is preserved.

River barges traditionally used the current to go downstream, and employed sails where possible when proceding upstream, together with haulage by horses where towpaths were available, or gangs of men where they were not. Horse haulage was usual on early canals. Towing by steam TUGS became commonplace on the larger rivers in the nineteenth century. Steam-powered barges were built in most countries, but it was the DIESEL ENGINE that made the powered barge the norm rather than the exception. In France 1 m (39.3 in.) gauge railway tracks were installed on most canal towpaths between 1904 and 1926, from which barges were hauled by small electric locomotives. The system was abandoned in the 1960s and 70s.

In continental Europe standard sizes for barges were established in 1953, on a scale ranging from 0 (vessels under 300 tonnes) to VII (seagoing vessels), of which the most important are the Péniche (class I) and the Europa barge (class IV), of 1350 tonnes, measuring 80 m × 9.5 m × 2.5 m (262 ft. × 31 ft. × 8 ft.).

In the USA the word can mean a double-decked vessel for passengers and freight, without sails, which is towed or pushed by a steam boat.

BIBLIOGRAPHY
General
Brouwer, 1985; Ellis, 1982; Hadfield, 1986.

BARRIE TRINDER

Barger-Compascuum, Drenthe, The Netherlands Within the 180 ha (73 ac.) Nationaal Veenpark (National Peat Park), is an open-air museum of the peat-digging region, 10 km (6 mi.) SE of Emmen, near the German frontier, developed from 1966 in a village created by poor Catholic farmers from Hanover who founded a 'buckwheat colony' there in the nineteenth-century and made habitable a region of impassable bogs. Exhibits include peat-cutting tools, steam-powered cutting machines, and peat presses. A barge, and a 700 mm (2 ft. 3½ in.) gauge railway built to carry peat, now transport visitors. The village retains its original plan, with two parallel canals, and includes reconstructions of turf cottages built by the first settlers, together with brick houses of the 1930s, a bakery which uses peat as its fuel, and a windmill. Peat is still cut in the vicinity; peat litter, 'black peat' and briquettes are produced. A unique peat-processing plant remains at Klazienaveen, 8 km (5 mi.) SW; and a 900 mm (3 ft.) gauge railway operates at Erica, 10 km (6 mi.) SW. Of the once extensive peat moors of Drenthe province little remains. Only a few canals remain of more than 2000 km (1250 mi.) of waterway developed between 1850 and 1920 to serve the 'peat colonies'. Reconstructed turf huts are displayed at Schoonoord, 11 km (7 mi.) NW of Emmen.

Many oil wells have been sunk since 1943 at Schoonebeek, 16 km (10 mi.) SW of Emmen. Traditional wells remain alongside those using modern steam-injection techniques.

LOCATIONS
[M] De Zeven Marken (The Seven Marks Open-Air Museum), Tramstraat 73, Schoonoord.
[M] Nationaal Veenpark, Postweg, Barger-Compascuum.
[M] Noord Nederlandse Museum Spoorbaan (North Netherlands Railway Museum), Griendtsveen, Erica.

JURRIE VAN DALEN

barilla A source of Alkali. Ashes containing 16–24 per cent sodium carbonate were obtained by burning coastal grasses from Alicante, Málaga and Tenerife in Spain, and Aigues-Mortes in France. The grasses were gathered in September and dried in the sun before being burned in hemispherical kilns. The alkali was used in making Soap until the mid-nineteenth century.

BIBLIOGRAPHY
General
Warren, 1980.

bar iron An iron or steel bar is a rolled length of circular cross-section, between 1.6 cm ($\frac{5}{8}$ in.) and 10 cm (4 in.) in diameter: smaller sections are called rods, and larger ones rounds. The term 'bar iron' is sometimes employed loosely in historical writing as a synonym for Wrought iron.

BIBLIOGRAPHY
General
Gale, 1971.

Baronial An architectural term applied to buildings, chiefly of the mid- and late nineteenth century, and mainly in Scotland, which were Crenellated and adorned with turrets, in the style of Scottish medieval castles. The style was applied to many commercial buildings, and to some textile mills and railway stations.

Baroque A term whose original meaning was 'irregular', which is applied to the style of architecture, popular in Europe from the late seventeenth century until the revival of Classicism in the late eighteenth century, that is characterized by curvaceous forms, spatially complex compositions, a regard for individual buildings as parts of greater ensembles, and, in southern Europe, by lavish ornamentation. Baroque features were widely revived in the second half of the nineteenth century (*see* Beaux-arts).

BIBLIOGRAPHY
General
Norberg-Schulz, 1972.

barrack house A term with various meanings in industrial archaeology.

1. In the Shropshire coalfield, England, a type of single-storey house, often built in long terraces (*see* Ironbridge).
2. In northern England and Wales, a lodging shop at an isolated mine, where men slept and ate during the week but from which they returned home at weekends. An example near Stanhope, County Durham in 1842 measured 18 × 15 ft. (6 × 5 m), and accommodated forty-eight miners each of whom had a locker and a bed.
3. In Nottingham, a type of tenement block with a common open staircase.
4. Locomotive crews in England lodged overnight in enginemen's barracks.
5. In the Ruhrgebiet, the term Kasernensystem (barrack system) was applied to a dour style of working-class dwelling of the mid-nineteenth century.

BIBLIOGRAPHY
General
Chapman, 1971; Gunter, J., 1980; Gunter, R., 1973; Lewis and Denton, 1974; Trinder, 1981, 1982a.

barrage *See* Dam.

Barreiro, Estremadura, Portugal   An industrial town on the left bank of the River Tagus (Tejo) facing Lisbon, whose development started in 1861 when it became the terminus of the South & South-East Railway. The original Barreiro station on this line, a handsome, single-storey, nineteen-bay building, with a pediment, was built by P. & W. MacLellan of the Clutha Ironworks, Glasgow, in 1859. There are many important industrial plants in Barreiro, among them the Quimigal chemical works, formerly Companhia União Fabril.

At Coina, 9 km (6 mi.) S., is the site where the glass factory, the Real Fábrica de Vidros, was located between 1719 and 1747, before its transfer to MARINHA GRANDE in 1751. The site was dug in 1984–6, one of the first industrial archaeological excavations in Portugal.

barrel   A container used for wet and dry products, cylindrical in shape, wider at the middle than at the ends, and usually made by a COOPER from curved staves, bound by hoops of wood, wrought iron or steel. The word can be used synonymously with 'cask' as a general term for any container of this shape, but in England it also applies to containers of specific capacities, which vary according to commodity and date.

The standard barrel of ale contains 32 gall. (1.46 hl), and the standard barrel of beer 36 gall. (1.64 hl). In 1688 the standard for both was 34 gall. (1.55 hl). The standard for butter or soap was 32 gall. (1.46 hl), but the weights were generally reckoned to be of more importance, a barrel of butter containing 230 lb. (104 kg), and of soap 248 lb. (112 kg). The capacity of a barrel for herring or eels was 30 gall. (1.37 hl) when fully packed; for salmon 42 gall. (1.91 hl); for pilchards or mackerel, 50 gall. (1.89 hl); and for most other fish, 32 gall. (1.46 hl). A barrel of gunpowder held 1 cwt. (100 lb.; 45.4 kg); of apples, 3 bushels (1.06 hl); of BARILLA or POTASH, 2 cwt. (224 lb.; 101.6 kg); of candles, 120 lb. (54.4 kg); of raisins 1 cwt. (50.8 kg). The standard barrel of wine contained 31.5 gall. (1.19 hl), or one-eighth of a wine tun of 252 gall. (11.46 hl); and the same measure was used for honey and tar. A vinegar barrel held 34 gall. (1.29 hl).

Smaller containers were the kilderkin, with a capacity of half a barrel of 16 gall. (73 l), and the firkin, which held a quarter of a barrel or 8 gall. (36 l).

In Ireland the barrel was a measure for grain, holding 4 bushels (10 gall.) of wheat (1.8 hl); and in Wales, the Isle of Man and the Channel Islands it was a measure for lime, the capacity varying from 1.14 hl in Wales to 2.27 hl in the Channel Islands.

The unit of measurement in the oil industry is the US barrel of 1.59 hl (35 English gall., 42 US gall.).

See also HOGSHEAD; PIPE; TUN.

BIBLIOGRAPHY
General
Zupko, 1968.

BARRIE TRINDER

Barrow-in-Furness, Cumbria, England   A town which originated in the 1840s as a port for the despatch of Furness iron ore. It developed as an ironmaking, then as a shipbuilding centre, the population growing from *c.*600 in 1851 to nearly 50 000 in 1881. A planned town, the creation of Furness Railways and its manager, James Ramsden, Furness is notable for its wide streets. Many nineteenth-century terraces survive. There are late nineteenth- and early twentieth-century shipyard buildings on Barrow Island, adjacent to tenement blocks modelled on those in Dundee and Glasgow. The Vickers Co. bought the shipyard in 1899, and from 1904 built a garden suburb, Vickerstown, on Walney Island.

BIBLIOGRAPHY
General
Marshall, 1958.

Barry, South Glamorgan, Wales   A docks town, 12 km (7 mi.) SW of Cardiff, created in 1889 by DAVID DAVIES as the terminus of a railway from the RHONDDA VALLEYS: it was built to break the coal-shipping monopoly of CARDIFF. A second dock was added in 1898. In 1913 Barry set an unbroken world record for coal shipped. A scrapyard for British Rail steam locomotives from the 1950s, it has since supplied about two hundred engines to railway preservation societies and museums.

BIBLIOGRAPHY
General
Morgan, 1981; Warren, 1988.

barytes   Barium sulphate ($BaSO_4$). It is common in lead and zinc mines. Commercially important from the second half of the nineteenth century as a filler in linoleum, rubber and paper, in oil drilling, and for the manufacture of barium compounds. Barytes is commonly worked from the waste tips of lead mines.

BIBLIOGRAPHY
General
Jones, 1950; Morgan and Pratt, 1938.

basalt   A hard, fine-grained, igneous rock, which may be greenish- or brownish-black, and may contain crystals of magnetic iron or feldspar. It sometimes occurs in columnar form, as in the Giant's Causeway (*see* PORTRUSH). Some forms are used for road metals, particularly as SETTS.

BIBLIOGRAPHY
General
Challinor, 1986.

bascule bridge   A drawbridge over a waterway; essentially one that is counterbalanced, permitting it to be tilted at the abutments to allow the passage of vessels. A single-leaf bridge tilts on one side only; a double-leaf bridge is split in the centre, both sides tilting. A bridge with a hinge mechanism is called a 'heel and trunnion' design. One where the structure is rolled along its support is known as a 'rolling lift' bridge. Some bascule bridges, such as those in cities like Chicago or Cleveland, USA, are large structures that allow traffic to cross navigable waterways on the level. Tower Bridge, LONDON, a double-leaf structure of 1894, is the most ornate bascule bridge. Dutch waterways are crossed by numerous bascule bridges, and some canal companies elsewhere, including the Oxford in England and the Canal du Centre in Burgundy, have used simple forms of bascule as ACCOMMODATION BRIDGES.

See also figure 139.

BIBLIOGRAPHY
General
Jackson, 1988; Welch, 1894.

basket Baskets and hampers were extensively used in the eighteenth and nineteenth centuries as containers for manufactured goods, particularly pottery and bottles. Basketwork was also employed for the bodies of small carriages and mail carts. Baskets can be made from rushes, split wood or willow, either osier, *Salix viminalis* or sallow, *Salix cinerea* or *Salix caprea*. Willow beds on marshy land were divided into strips 2–3 m (6–10 ft.) broad. Shoots were cut after three to four years' growth, and stripped of bark by being drawn over a sharp instrument on a block. They were soaked before being woven into shape.

BIBLIOGRAPHY
General
Book of Trades, 1839.

Basle (Basel, Bâle), Basel, Switzerland   One of the most important cities of the Renaissance, and also of industrial Europe: the continent's principal railway junction, a major river port, and a leading centre for pharmaceuticals.

The Centralbahnhof, built by the Schweizerische Centralbahn, is the principal entry to Switzerland for trains from France and Germany, the latter also using the Gare Badoise, built by Karl Moser in 1913.

Basle stands at the head of navigation on the Rhine, and is the most important entrepôt for freight in Switzerland. The first steamship arrived in the city in 1832, but the growth of large-scale navigation only began in 1904 when the first barges from the Lower Rhine moored in the city. The Rhine Navigation Exhibition is concerned with the history of the waterway and its harbours.

From the 1890s Basle became the centre of the Swiss chemical industry. CIBA, the Gesellschaft für Chemische Industrie in Basel (the Basle Chemistry Industry Company), which developed from an earlier firm, began manufacturing pharmaceuticals in 1889. Five years later Hofmann-La Roche began to develop a second great chemicals empire. The Geigy company developed from a druggist's business, and later went into partnership with CIBA. The firm of Sandoz dates from 1886. In the twentieth century the chemical industry has dominated the Basel region, with its works between the French border and the Schweizerhalle. CIBA-Geigy has conserved its oldest installation, its methyl and ethylbromide plant of 1892–9, in front of its Biology Building in the Klübeckstrasse. The equipment, which is accommodated in an open-plan building, includes lead-lined iron containers and wooden distilling vessels with belt-driven agitators.

An eighteenth-century papermill in the St Albantal, which ceased production in 1955, was converted to a museum in the 1970s, and displays reconstructions of papermaking machinery from other countries together with a large collection of samples of handmade paper.

Sissach, 18 km (11 mi.) SE, and Reigoldswil, 16 km (10 mi.) S., both have museums illustrating ribbon-weaving, once the principal occupation of domestic workers in the region.

BIBLIOGRAPHY
General
Baldinger, 1987; CIBA, 1959.

LOCATIONS
[S] CIBA-Geigy, Klübeckstrasse 141, Basle.
[M] Heimatmuseum (Local History Museum), Zunzgerstrasse, 4450 Sissach, Basel-Land.
[M] Historische Sammlung (Historical Collection), Realschule, Reigoldswil, Basel-Land.
[M] Museum of the History of Pharmacy, Totengasslein 3, 4051 Basle.
[M, S] Paper Museum, Galliciani Mühle, St Albantal 35, 4051 Basle.
[M] Rhine Navigation Museum 'Our Way to the Sea', Rheinhafen Basel-Kleinhuningen, 4057 Basle.

HANS-PETER BÄRTSCHI

Basque country (Euskadi, País Vasco, Pays Basque), France and Spain   The Basque people, whose territory stretches along the shores of the Bay of Biscay in northern Spain and south-western France, have their own distinct culture and language. In Spain, four of the historic regions of the Basque country, the Euskadi, Alava, Guipúzcoa and Vizcaya, are administered by a common Basque government. Basque culture, including pre-industrial manufactures, is displayed in museums at Bayonne and Lourdes in France, and at Bermeo, BILBAO, SAN SEBASTIÁN and Vitoria in Spain. (*See* figure 9.)

LOCATIONS
[M] Archaeological Museum, Correria 116, Vitoria, Spain.
[M] Musée Basque, 1 rue Marengo, 64100 Bayonne, Pyrénées-Atlantiques, France.
[M] Musée des Pyrénées (Museum of the Pyrenees), Châteaufort, 65100 Lourdes, Hautes-Pyrénées.

Bath, Avon, England   Natural hot springs attracted the Romans to this spot, where they built the celebrated Baths and extracted lead and other minerals from the nearby Mendip Hills. In the eighteenth century Bath became a fashionable resort for the rich and famous. Demand for building materials encouraged the growth of the stone industry, and in 1731 Ralph Allen (1694–1764) built a wooden railway from the Combe Down stone quarries to the River Avon. Further expansion of stone quarrying was stimulated by the construction of the KENNET & AVON CANAL and the Great Western Railway, the building of the latter revealing huge deposits during the building of Box

Figure 9   The transporter bridge at Portugalete near Bilbao, in the Basque country, designed by the Vizcayan engineer Alberto Palacio Elisagüe and completed in 1893
Barrie Trinder

Tunnel. Most nineteenth- and twentieth-century industry is concentrated along the Lower Bristol Road. The Camden Works Museum includes large collections of engineering and foundry tools.

BIBLIOGRAPHY
General
Buchanan and Buchanan, 1980.

LOCATIONS
[M] Bath Industrial Heritage Centre, Camden Works Museum, Julian Road, Bath BA1 2RH.
[M] Bath Stone Quarry Museum, Pickwick Quarry, Corsham, Wiltshire SN13 0QR.

JOHN POWELL

bathhouse   A bathhouse may be part of a SPA where visitors drink or bathe in the waters. The name is also applied to buildings constructed in working-class areas of large cities in the second half of the nineteenth century where the public could take baths, like the 'steamies' of GLASGOW.
See also PITHEAD BATHS.

battery   The use of water-powered hammers to form sheets of metal, particularly brass and copper, for use in wire-making. The technique was developed in fifteenth-century Germany and the Low Countries, and was introduced into Britain *c*.1570 by the Society of Mineral and Battery Works with German experts. Battery is also used to fabricate hollow ware, particularly brass kettles and frying pans. A working example can be seen at HAGEN.
See also BRASS; FELTMAKING.

BIBLIOGRAPHY
General
Day, 1973; Hamilton, 1967; Plot, 1686.

Bauhaus   An academic institution which has profoundly influenced twentieth-century architecture and design. On the recommendation of Henri van de Velde (1863–1957), an exponent of ART NOUVEAU and head of the School of Arts and Crafts at Weimar, Germany, Walter Gropius (1883–1969) was appointed to head a new institute called the Bauhaus (House of Building), which opened in 1919, bringing together architects, artists and designers. In 1926 the Bauhaus moved to new premises designed by Gropius in Dessau, and became increasingly concerned with industrial design. Gropius left in 1928, and the institute was directed in 1930–3 by LUDWIG MIES VAN DER ROHE, moving to Berlin before the Third Reich brought about its end.

bauxite ($Al_2O_3 . 2H_2O$)   A hydrated oxide of aluminium, and the chief source of aluminium. Bauxite takes its name from Les Baux, near Arles, France, but there are deposits also in the USA, Canada, New Caledonia, Guyana, Hungary, and Yugoslavia.

Bavaria (Bayern), Germany   The largest state within the Federal Republic of Germany extends over 70000 km^2 (27000 sq. mi.) and in 1969 had 10.5 million inhabitants. The present federal state, the only one in the republic to describe itself as a 'free state', thus has the second largest population after North Rhine-Westphalia with its 17 million inhabitants. Historically, the old Electorate of Bavaria (the former duchy became an electorate in 1623), comprising Upper and Lower Bavaria and the Upper Palatinate, should be distinguished from the later Kingdom of Bavaria, created in 1806, which absorbed Franconia and the Palatinate on the left bank of the Rhine, so that its population increased from 1 million in 1802 to 3.5 million in 1819. At the same time it changed from being a purely Roman Catholic state to one in which a quarter of the population was Protestant. The kingdom acquired a constitution relatively early in 1818.

Bavaria and Württemberg formed a customs union in 1828, five years before the general Deutscher Zollverein (German customs union) of 1833–4. King Ludwig I (r.1825–48), whose early tendencies were liberal, played an important part in encouraging the arts and sciences. His successor Maximilian II (r.1848–64) combined reactionary power politics with internal reforms. Transport facilities developed early: the first German railway began running between Nuremberg and Fürth on 7 December 1835. Even more important was the line from Augsburg to Munich which opened in 1840. It represented one of the first stages of a German railway network. The iron and steel industry, a major one in the Upper Palatinate throughout the Middle Ages and the early modern period, reached a peak of prosperity at the beginning of the seventeenth century, particularly in the region around Amberg and Sulzbach, with an annual output of almost 300 000 tonnes of ore; but it declined almost to the point of extinction in the early nineteenth century. New technology did not reach Bavaria until around 1850: the Maxhütte ironworks was established at Burglengenfeld in 1851. The blast furnace plant at Rosenberg was brought into service in 1864 and became central to the operation of the Maxhütte works, which is still in existence in Sulzbach-Rosenberg. The importance of Augsburg as a textile centre goes back to the eighteenth century. The principal industrial towns of Bavaria are the state capital, MUNICH, which had 1.3 million inhabitants in 1969; AUGSBURG, with a population of 200 000; NUREMBERG, with 477 000; and Regensburg, with 128 000 inhabitants.

Geographically the area south of the DANUBE, which runs through Bavaria from east to west, is distinct from the area north of the river. The foothills of the Alps, and a small part of the Alpine range itself, determine the character of southern Bavaria. The Bohemian massif has moulded the north-east. Mottled sandstone, shell limestone, keuper marls and sandstones, and white Jura limestone are found in the north-west. Lower Franconia is mostly good agricultural land; sandy loam predominates in the south. The land of the Franconian hills and eastern Bavaria is not very productive. Of the minerals found in Bavaria, the iron ore near Sulzbach-Rosenberg (see THEUERN) and the rock salt of Berchtesgaden (see BAD REICHENHALL) deserve mention. The latter provides some 3 per cent of West Germany's salt requirements.

There are five oil refineries around Ingolstadt, at the end of pipelines from Marseilles, Genoa and Trieste. Ingolstadt is also a centre of motorcar manufacture. There is another oil refinery at Burghausen. Ninety per cent of Bavaria's electricity is generated in the state itself. A large propor-tion is generated at hydro-electric power stations – 1700 MW, compared with 2300 MW from thermal power plants.

Manufacturing industry is concentrated in the conurbations of Munich, Nuremberg with Fürth and Erlangen, Augsburg, Ingolstadt, Regensburg and Schweinfurt. Industry in Upper Franconia is based on smaller towns like Coburg, Hof and Selb. The main branches of industry are food manufacturing and electrical and mechanical engineering, each with some 11–13 per cent of the state's total industrial production. Regensburg and Würzburg have sizeable river harbours; the historic project of a canal link between the Rivers Main and Danube has been revived in the twentieth century. The principal airport is Munich. Nuremberg is Bavaria's second commercial airport.

See also BAD REICHENHALL; CHIEMSEE; KOCHELSEE AND WALCHENSEE; THEUERN.

BIBLIOGRAPHY
General
Bott, 1985; Grimm, 1985.

LOCATION
[I] Bayerisches Landesamt für Denkmalpflege (Bavarian authority for the protection of monuments), Pfisterstrasse 1, 8000 Munich 2.

AXEL FÖHL

bazaar The traditional place for retailing in the cities of the Ottoman Empire, where the term meant a range of premises occupied by craftsmen and stallholders. By the end of the nineteenth century it was applied in Britain and the USA to retail establishments in markets or conventional shops, which offered varied goods at low prices.

In 1891 Michael Marks (1859–1907), a Russian Jewish immigrant, opened his first 'Original Penny Bazaar' in the market at Wigan, England. He subsequently established others, entrancing places where customers could select goods from open trays, knowing that no item would cost more than a penny. Customers had to be dissuaded from thinking them places of entertainment by the sign 'Free Admission' at the doors. With his partner Thomas Spencer he subsequently established the most celebrated English CHAIN STORE company, which maintains a traditional bazaar-type stall at NEWCASTLE-UPON-TYNE.

BIBLIOGRAPHY
General
Rees, 1969.

BARRIE TRINDER

beacon Fire-baskets were used both for signalling and navigation (and were used as late as 1904 in Denmark), either on a 'swape' (a long pole supported on a fulcrum) or fore-lever, or on a LIGHTHOUSE.

beam engine The earliest and longest-surviving form of steam engine, in which the piston supplied the motion through a horizontal beam of, usually, flattened elliptical section, the beam being balanced on a wall, column or A-frame. For much of the eighteenth century beams were of wood, the elliptical cast-iron beam being devised by John Banks (?1740–1805) soon after 1795. The last beam engine was built in 1919. Considerable numbers, particularly of those used for pumping water or sewage, are preserved.

BIBLIOGRAPHY
General
Crowley, 1982.

Beamish, County Durham, England   The North of England Open-Air Museum, 14 km (8½ mi.) NW of Durham, established in the 1960s through the personal commitment of its founder-director, Frank Atkinson, and administered by a consortium of local authorities. It is concerned with the social and economic history, both urban and rural, of north-east England. It occupies an 80 ha (200 ac.) park, in which a drift mine is preserved *in situ*. A railway complex, including a passenger station, a signal box, a goods shed, coal and lime 'cells', and a 'C' class (LNER J21) 0-6-0 locomotive of 1889, exemplifies the practice of the North-Eastern Railway. Tramcars originally used in Gateshead and Sheffield convey visitors across the park. A terrace of miners' cottages, a Co-operative store of *c.*1920, and a Crowther vertical winding engine of 1855 have been re-erected. The Hetton Colliery locomotive and a model of *Locomotion No. 1* are displayed. Exhibits awaiting re-erection include the Warden Law winding-engine house and a coal drop from Seaham Harbour.

BIBLIOGRAPHY
Specific
Allen, R. E. *Beamish: the great northern experience.* Beamish: North of England Open-Air Museum.

LOCATION
[M] North of England Open-Air Museum, Beamish Hall, Stanley, County Durham.

BARRIE TRINDER

bearing   A part of a machine that bears friction, like the axlebox of a vehicle, the fulcrum of a beam engine or a support for a section of line shafting. Linings of 'plain' bearings are usually of BRASS or BABBIT METAL, and until the late eighteenth century bearings were commonly called 'brasses' or 'bushes'. Ball-bearings developed symbiotically with bicycles, and were the first 'anti-friction' as opposed to 'plain' or 'journal' bearings. The roller bearing, in which rollers on the moving 'journal' move along smooth 'races' or paths machined on the stationary part, was developed in the USA in the early twentieth century, initially for use on steam locomotives.

Bear Island (Bjørnøya), Svalbard, Norway   An island extending over some 180 km² (70 sq. mi.), and lying in the Barents Sea 800 km (500 mi.) N. of NARVIK. Mist covers the island almost permanently. The fishing har-

bour of Sørhamn is free of ice only in summer. Coal mines on the island closed in 1925, and some mining equipment remains rusting on the coast. The oldest house in the Svalbard region, dating from 1823, is a protected monument.

Beaucourt, Belfort Territory and Doubs, France   The Pays de Montbéliard, a principality incorporated into France in 1801 and today divided between the department of Doubs and the Belfort territory, is one of France's most densely industrialized regions. Its industrial vocation dates from the eighteenth century, and is intimately associated with the fortunes of a dynasty of Protestant entrepreneurs and capitalists, the Japy family, and with watch-and clockmaking. This activity developed as a cottage industry in the early years of the eighteenth century, the harsh winter months being employed in isolated settlements for the home production of 'ébauches', rough watch movements, generally finished and sold in Switzerland.

In 1776 Frédéric Japy (1749–1812), son of a successful blacksmith of the village of Beaucourt, 22 km (14 mi.) SE of Belfort, acquired and then perfected an assortment of machines which he installed in a new building on a hill above his home town. This 'fabrique' soon employed some fifty apprentices, living, eating, working and praying together. Rapidly enlarged – and apparently equipped with a horse gin, since, surprisingly, this first factory was not located on a watercourse – the enterprise produced more or less identical rough movements, which the division of labour and the use of specialized MACHINE TOOLS rendered particularly competitive. These facets of the take-off of the Japy enterprise are reminiscent of Lewis Mumford's identification of the CLOCK rather than the STEAM ENGINE as the key machine of the modern industrial age.

By 1815, the Beaucourt manufacture, now in the carefully-groomed second-generation hands of the three 'Japy Frères', directly employed more than five hundred workers, most of them unskilled. Freddy Japy, as he signed himself, writes of cripples, old men and children. It was turning out more than 150 000 movements a year, each costing the rough equivalent of a day's unskilled labour. On 1 July 1815, a fortnight after the Battle of Waterloo, the whole manufacture, now comprising six workshop buildings, sixty-three dwellings, six stables and a greenhouse full of rare and exotic plants, was burned down, not by local Luddites but by passing Prussian troops, a measure of reprisal for the sympathies of the Japys for the vanquished Napoleon.

The establishment was rebuilt within a year and a half, and by 1837 the Japy brothers owned eight different factories, along with a sales depot at Paris. The new factories, developed around mills originally purchased during the Revolution as 'national' (i.e. émigré) properties, were located in nearby villages on water-powered sites, although the supplementary power of steam engines was deemed necessary as early as 1829. Prompted by the uncertainties of the timepiece market, now witnessing lively competition from NEUCHÂTEL over the Swiss border, the Japy brothers had branched out into a widening variety of small-scale metal products made with machine tools: wood screws, steel files, locks, padlocks, hinges and other articles of household ironmongery. Taken together these sectors were soon more important than the clock and watch production from which at least two of them, screws and enamelled products, were directly derived. By 1837 the Japy factories employed over three thousand workers. Clock and watch production still relied heavily on traditional forms of domestic outwork which did not die out until the early twentieth century.

The Second Empire, of which the Japys were keen supporters, was a period of sustained growth which placed the company amongst France's three leading industrial concerns. Now a limited private partnership with twenty-six shareholders (in 1862), and run by a collegiate management including members of the third generation of Japys and prudently co-opted in laws and cousins the enterprise's dynamic, Paris-based, commercial policies were accompanied by an industrial strategy of factory enlargement and increasingly steam-powered mechanization. A new installation at l'Isle-sur-le-Doubs was developed from 1849 as a screw, nut and bolt works. Industrial development, facilitated by a much lobbied-for branch railway which reached Beaucourt in 1868, was accompanied by an extension of the Japys' paternalistic social initiatives: insurance and retirement schemes, medical services, subsidized churches, brass brands, schools and libraries, company bakeries and shops, and housing. The first 'cité ouvrière', an estate of single-family dwellings, each with its own garden and small integrated workshop, was inspired in part by developments at MULHOUSE. Built in 1864 it received special mention at the Paris Exhibition of 1867, but the experience of the practical and moral advantages of a well-housed and consequently stable workforce dated back to the firm's Lutheran-tinged origins.

The first signs of decline in the Japy 'archipelago' – the name applied to the seven industrial units scattered along the valleys of the Doubs, the Gland and the Feschotte, employing over five thousand workers living in a social environment created by the Japys – have been detected in the 1870s, when new industrial powers, the USA and later Switzerland and Germany, began to apply greater mechanization, more easily INTERCHANGEABLE PARTS and better MASS PRODUCTION techniques to clock and watch production, and subsequently to other 'democratic' items, similar to those in the voluminous Japy catalogues. Problems of inheritance and of management in an ever-burgeoning Japy clan, and the difficulties created by traditional self-financing investment habits, absorbed much energy, even if the two decades at the turn of the century were marked by frantic diversification into complementary and often innovatory sectors: agricultural machinery, gas and petrol engines, electric motors and dynamos, electric lighting equipment, cameras, gramophones, cash registers, typewriters and bicycle parts.

After a moment's hesitation in 1895, the Japy company declined to enter into the automobile adventure. A year later Armand Peugeot's Société Anonyme des Automobiles et Cycles Peugeot at Beaulieu, a suburb to the south of Montbéliard, was already producing ninety-two motorcars a year; by 1913, Peugeot was the second motorcar manufacturer in France, after Renault. The Peugeot manufacturing dynasty, already well established in the Pays de Montbéliard, its industrial origins in textiles rather than clocks, and associated with the Japys by several decades of matrimonial ties, shared religious backgrounds and common business interests, would henceforth play the roles of industrial pioneers in the region, putting a new series of Montbéliard placenames on the map: Beaulieu, producing bicycles from 1885 and motorcars from 1891; Audincourt, site of one of the first purpose-built motorcar factories in Europe, dating from 1897; and Sochaux, the Peugeot car plant opened in 1912 close to the Dijon–Mulhouse railway and the Rhône–Rhine Canal, and today one of the largest factory complexes in France.

If World War I and its defence orders gave a boost to the Peugeot factories – Sochaux quadrupled in size between 1914 and 1918 – it hastened the decline of the traditional Japy sectors and of clock and watch production in particular. The schools, the churches, the housing, including nine Japy family residences and Japy workers' housing of all descriptions, all survive, along with a rich fund of company-cum-family archives, and, of course, recycled local traditions of precision engineering and precision measuring devices. There are few vestiges, however, of the Japy factories. The Badevel works, dating from the first quarter of the nineteenth century, was demolished in 1979. The last buildings of the Berne factories at Seloncourt, of the same period, were taken down in 1982. Some of the workshop buildings of the screw, nut and bolt works at l'Isle-sur-le-Doubs, rebuilt in 1857 and notable for a precocious French use of north-lit roofs, are to be reused; while at Beaucourt, cradle of the company's history, a three-storey extension in brick and stone, added in 1893 to the buildings first put up after the fire of 1815, has recently been transformed – what fitter fate? – into 'HLM', low-cost social housing. Beneath the restored clock tower, the basement houses the Frédéric Japy museum.

BIBLIOGRAPHY
General
Lamard, 1988; Landes, 1983; Lardière, 1991.
Specific
Cohen, Y. Peugeot dans le Doubs. In *L'Usine et la ville, 1836–1936: 150 ans d'urbanisme* (The factory and the city, 1836–1986: 150 years of town and country planning). Paris: Culture technique/IFA, 1986.
Turgan, E. Etablissements Japy à Beaucourt. In *Les grandes usines, études industrielles en France et à l'étranger* (Large factories, industrial studies in France and abroad), vol. VII, Paris: Michel Lévy. 1867.

LOCATION
[M] Musée Frédéric Japy, 16 rue Frédéric Japy, 90500 Beaucourt.

PAUL SMITH

Beaulieu, Hampshire, England   Lord Montagu of Beaulieu founded the Montagu Motor Museum in the grounds of his family home in 1952. The collection grew to over a hundred vehicles in ten years, and was renamed the National Motor Museum in 1970. An innovative 'Wheels' exhibition, transporting visitors through the displays, was opened in 1985.

On the Beaulieu River, 3 km (2 mi.) SE, is the shipbuilding community of Buckler's Hard, which includes a small maritime museum.

LOCATION
[M] National Motor Museum, John Montagu Building, Beaulieu, Brockenhurst, Hampshire, SO42 7ZN.

Beaux-Arts   An architectural style, originating in the teachings of the École des Beaux Arts, Paris, and dominant internationally in the design of large commercial and public buildings in such cities as BERLIN, LONDON, VIENNA and WASHINGTON for much of the second half of the nineteenth century. RENAISSANCE and BAROQUE motifs were employed, usually in large buildings of regular plan. It is also called 'Second Empire style', and in PARIS the term 'Napoleon III style' is applied to the high buildings with MANSARD ROOFS built during Haussmann's reordering of the city.

Bedford, Bedfordshire, England   A county town, on the River Ouse. In and around it are many sites of interest to industrial archaeologists. The Britannia Ironworks of John Howard was an archetypal Victorian market-town foundry making farm machinery. Bedford was a centre of lacemaking in the nineteenth century, and there is an important Thomas Lester collection in the Cecil Higgins Gallery. A brickmaking area to the south-west grew in the nineteenth century to supply London. Fletton parish gives its name to one of the commonest English brick types. Stewartby, 7 km (4 mi.) SW, is a model village begun in 1927 by the London Brick Company and named after its chairman, P. Malcolm Stewart, who was responsible for smallholder settlements at Potton, 19 km (12 mi.) E., and Wyboston, 14 km (9 mi.) NE, both built to relieve unemployment. Most British airships were built at Cardington, 5 km (3 mi.) SE. Two airship hangars survive, together with a garden village, Shortstown, built by the manufacturers. There is a collection of historic aircraft and road vehicles at Old Warden, 12 km (7 mi.) SE.

BIBLIOGRAPHY
General
Bigmore, 1979.
Specific
Buck, A. *Thomas Lester: his lace and the East Midlands industry, 1820–1905.* Bedford: Ruth Bean, 1981.

LOCATIONS
[M] Cecil Higgins Art Gallery and Museum, Castle Close, Bedford MK40 3NY.
[M] Shuttleworth Collection, Old Warden Aerodrome, Biggleswade, Bedfordshire SG18 9ER.

BARRIE TRINDER

beer   The traditional drink of northern Europe, an effervescent beverage made by alcoholic fermentation of a solution in potable water of the extractive substance, principally of barley malt. Hops, *Humulus lupulus*, are commonly added for flavouring. Rice, wheat, oats and millet are also used in brewing. Sugar or honey may be used for sweetening.

On an industrial scale, beer is manufactured in a brewery, where MALT is first crushed in mills to form 'grist', which is mixed with hot water in a mash tun, converting the starch to malt sugars. The liquid, or 'wort', is then drained from the grist in a lauter tun, before being boiled with hops in the copper. It is then cooled to a suitable temperature for the addition of yeast, and run into vessels where the process of fermentation can take place. It is later bottled or run into BARRELS.

Beer was an important item of trade by the late seventeenth century when beer from north Germany was being taken to the East Indies, and beer made in London to France. PORT BOOKS show an extensive trade in beer in barrel and bottle along the River Severn in the 1690s. Brewing was one of the first manufactures to be organized in large units in early eighteenth-century London, and the breweries at BURTON ON TRENT, COPENHAGEN, and DUBLIN were pioneers in establishing national markets for their products.

BIBLIOGRAPHY
General
Barnard, 1889; Black, 1849; Colyer, 1880; Findlay, 1971; Fischer *et al.*, 1985; Glamann, 1962; Hinde, 1938; Mathias, 1959; Monckton, 1966; Richmond and Turton, 1989; Southby, 1885; Sykes, 1897; Thomson, 1849; Tizard, 1857; Wahl and Henius, 1908.
Specific
Mathias, P. Agriculture and the brewing and distilling industries in the eighteenth century. In *EcHR*, V, 1952–3.

BARRIE TRINDER

bees   The keeping of bees, *Apis mellifera* and *Apis dorsata*, was an important economic activity in Europe in the eighteenth and nineteenth centuries. Hives, which took many forms, were often taken to sites near to sources of nectar and placed on 'stalls', rather like market stalls. Bees might be kept primarily for HONEY or WAX. The best collection of hives and associated equipment is at the OPEN-AIR MUSEUM at Radom, Poland.

beet sugar refinery   The Prussian chemist Andreas Markgraff demonstrated in 1747 that sugar could be extracted from beet, and in 1797 his pupil Franz Achard erected a factory in Silesia. The process was developed commercially in France during the Napoleonic period, and subsequently developed with government support in Prussia, Russia, the Habsburg Empire and Belgium by 1850; and in the second half of the nineteenth century in the Netherlands, Denmark, Italy, Sweden and the USA. By 1900 about 40 per cent of the world's sugar supply came from beet. Commercial production of beet sugar in the USA began in 1879, and has subsequently become a major industry. Development on a commercial scale in Britain was delayed until the 1920s, when the proportion of British sugar made from beet increased from 0.5 per cent to nearly 20 per cent. The first British factory was built at Cantley, 18 km (11 mi.) E. of Norwich, in 1912, and nine were constructed between 1921 and 1926.

A sugar beet factory requires an extensive flat site and a water supply of up to 13.5 million l (3 million gall.) a day. There are usually single-storey buildings in which beet is washed and sliced, and large concrete silos for storing beet. The main machinery hall, usually of steel or concrete construction with large windows, houses diffusion equipment in which the beet is treated with hot water, which releases the sugar; plant for purifying the liquor with limewater and carbon dioxide; and evaporating equipment. Continuous diffusion processes have been used since the 1930s, although previously batch systems were employed. Crystals are obtained by evaporation, as in a cane sugar refinery. Hot water is produced in a large boiler plant, usually with a high chimney; and since the work is largely seasonal BARRACK HOUSE accommodation is often provided for temporary workers.

BIBLIOGRAPHY
General
Deer, 1950; Dowling, 1926; Prescott and Proctor, 1937.
Specific
Williams, H. Beet sugar factories. In *Journal of the Royal Society of Arts*, LIX, 1910.

BARRIE TRINDER

Behrens, Peter (1868–1940) A painter and designer who was influenced by WILLIAM MORRIS: he worked for a time in the ART NOUVEAU style, and became one of the principal exponents of INTERNATIONAL MODERNISM. His first industrial buildings were for AEG (*see* BERLIN; INDUSTRIAL ARCHITECTURE). His later buildings included the Mannesmann company headquarters at Düsseldorf in 1911–12; a notable range for the Höchst company at Frankfurt in 1920–4; an office block in Oberhausen for the Gutte Hoffnunghütte ironworking company; and a tobacco warehouse at LINZ in 1930. Walter Gropius (1883–1969), LUDWIG MIES VAN DER ROHE (1886–1969) and Le Corbusier (Charles-Edouard Jeanneret b.1887) were among his pupils.

BIBLIOGRAPHY
General
Buddensieg and Henning, 1978; Buderath, 1990; Pevsner, 1976.

Belfast, County Antrim, Northern Ireland Belfast was founded at the mouth of the River Lagan in the early seventeenth century and by 1750 was no more than a modest market town. Cotton mills were established in 1778 and in the course of the nineteenth century linen manufacture and engineering made Belfast one of the great industrial cities of Europe, the population rising from 53 000 in 1831 to 208 000 in 1881.

The flax industry of north-eastern Ireland grew dramatically between 1830 and 1865 with the construction of large steam-powered spinning mills. The industry was concentrated in Belfast where by 1852 there were six companies making spinning machinery. Power-loom weaving of linen began on a large scale in the early 1860s. Bleaching and finishing were similarly organized in large units. By 1900 such processes were often carried out in buildings with 'Belfast roofs', in which tarred felting was stretched over curved boards, supported by uprights set on horizontal transom beams.

There were many large spinning mills in Belfast, particularly in the Crumlin Road and Sandy Row, as well as numerous linen warehouses, some in highly individualist styles derived from the Italianate. Many have been demolished but two in Donegall Square North are listed.

Engineering, which originally grew to meet the demands of linen manufacturers for machines, extended into shipbuilding. The shipyard on Queen's Island was established in 1851, and in the years before World War I was responsible for such Atlantic liners as the *Olympic*, the *Britannic* and the *Titanic*, for the fitting out of which vast lattice girder gantries and a 150 ton floating crane were built. Most of the traditional land-based cranes were removed when new travelling cranes were installed from 1970. Working conditions were notoriously bad, seventeen lives having been lost on the *Titanic* before she left the Lagan.

The Belfast Ropework Co., established in 1876, occupied the largest ropemaking premises in the world with six rope walks each of 146 fathoms (876 ft.; 267 m), with Belfast roofs. The premises are now tenemented. Another important survival is the Clarendon No. 1 graving dock alongside Harbour Office, built in 1796–1800. The eight-storey Pacific flour mills of 1933 dominate the area around Pollock Dock.

Queen's Bridge of 1840–3, designed by Thomas Jackson Woodhouse and John Frazer, is of finely worked ashlar. It was widened in 1885, when ornamental cast-iron lampposts from the Sun Foundry, Glasgow, were added.

Belfast's imposing railway termini at Queen's Quay, Great Victoria Street and York Road have been demolished. At Greenisland, 12 km ($7\frac{1}{2}$ mi.) to the north, are some of the most important concrete structures of the inter-war period in the British Isles: two viaducts, designed by W. K. Wallace, over Valentine's Glen, built in 1931–4 to form a burrowing junction between the lines to Larne and Ballymena. The larger viaduct has three central arches each of 27 m (89 ft.) span, with a total length of 192 m (630 ft.).

Belfast's water supply is drawn largely from the Silent Valley reservoir in the Mourne Mountains, which was constructed in 1923–33, with a pedimented overflow outlet, and an octagonal valve tower in local granite. A new reservoir was created behind the Ben Crom dam in 1953–7.

The Crown Liquor Saloon in Great Victoria Street is a public house of *c.*1895, with magnificent multicoloured decorative tiles by Craven Dunnill (*see* IRONBRIDGE): it has been restored by the National Trust.

The Ulster Museum at Stranamillis opened an Engineering Hall in 1972. Large steam engines, chiefly from textile mills, are turned by electric motors. The textile gallery portrays the full sequence of linen manufacture.

The Ulster Folk Museum at Cultra, 8 km (5 mi.) NE of Belfast, is an open-air museum which includes six re-erected houses from a terrace in Rowland Street, Sandy Row, Belfast, built in 1825–30; a water-driven spade mill of c.1840 from Coalisland, County Tyrone; a water-powered scutching mill from Gorticashel Upper near Gortin, County Tyrone; and a cottage from Ballydugan, County Down, at the side of a bleach green, in the centre of which is a circular stone hut with spy-holes for the custodian.

BIBLIOGRAPHY
General
Bardon, 1982; Beckett *et al.*, 1983; Beckett and Glasscock, 1967; Blair, 1981; Brett, 1967; Dixon, 1975; Kennedy and Ollerenshaw, 1983; McCutcheon, 1980; Thompson, 1952.
Specific
Nock, O. S. The NCC section of the LMSR. In *Railway Magazine*, 467, May 1936.

LOCATIONS
[M] Ulster Folk and Transport Museum, Cultra Manor, Holywood, County Down BT18 0EU.
[M] Ulster Museum, Botanic Gardens, Stranamillis, Belfast BT9 5AB.

BARRIE TRINDER

Belgium   Belgium was one of the first countries to adopt the methods of manufacture pioneered in Britain in the eighteenth century, and by 1900 was one of the most heavily industrialized countries in the world, particularly important for coal, steel, flax, glass and zinc.

In 1650 the territory that comprises modern Belgium consisted of those provinces of the Netherlands that had remained under Spanish rule after the United Provinces gained their independence in 1581, and the principality of Liège. In 1713 Spanish rule gave way to that of the Austrian Habsburgs. Occupation by Revolutionary France in 1794 brought an end to the institutions of the *ancien régime*, which stimulated economic growth. In 1815 the former Austrian provinces and the principality of Liège were joined with the remainder of the Netherlands under the rule of King William I. The union ended in 1830 when Belgium was established as a parliamentary monarchy. Most of the country fell under German occupation in World War I, after which Belgium acquired the border territory of Eupen and Malmédy.

From its 65 km (40 mi.) North Sea coastline Belgium extends nearly 320 km (200 mi.) in a south-easterly direction into the Ardennes, and is not more than 240 km (150 mi.) wide at any point. Its population is nearly ten million, and the northern part is one of the most densely populated areas in Europe. Belgium is an association of two language groups, the Flemish-speaking Flemings in the provinces of East and West Flanders, Antwerp, Brabant and Limburg, and the French-speaking Walloons in Hainaut, Liège, Namur and Luxembourg. Brussels is

bilingual, with separate ministries for education, culture and the care of historic monuments.

By 1650 Flanders had lost the vitality that had made it one of the principal trading regions of medieval Europe, and that had produced such monuments as the thirteenth-century cloth hall at Ypres (Ieper). This decline was due largely to the closure of the River Scheldt by the Treaty of Westphalia (Munster) in 1648, which drew trade away from Antwerp.

Four coal basins were being exploited in Belgium in 1650, those around Liège, Mons (the Borinage), La Louvière (the Centre) and Charleroi. The first steam pumping engine came into use as early as 1723, but only in the Mons area did engines become common before 1800. The coal industry grew under French rule, and its growth, aided by the industrialization of Northern France and the Rhineland, continued after 1815. By 1846 the Borinage was producing 2000000 tonnes a year; the Centre, 600000 tonnes; Charleroi, 1200000 tonnes; and Liège, 1300000 tonnes. In 1900 national output reached 23000000 tonnes. Belgian coal was difficult to coke, and from 1890 such companies as Coppee and Selmet-Solvay developed ovens for making coke and recovering by-products, leading the world in this technology.

Iron ore was found in all the Belgian coal basins, but until coal could be utilized in its smelting most pig iron came from charcoal-fuelled furnaces in the Ardennes. There were concentrations of forges, rolling mills and nail manufactories in the valleys of the Sambre and the Meuse. The use of coke for smelting iron ore was introduced by the Englishmen John and James Cockerill in 1823, at the Seraing ironworks, established from 1814 in the archbishop's palace west of Liège. Puddling furnaces, hot blast, steam-driven rolling mills and other English innovations were also introduced. The Belgian iron industry was typically organized in large units like the Société Anonyme Hauts Fourneaux et Charbonnage de Marcinelle et Couillet (Marcinelle and Couillet Blast Furnace and Coal Co.) at Charleroi, and the Cockerills' concern at Seraing. Iron production grew steadily in the 1830s and 40s, and rapidly in the 50s and 60s, reaching 1000000 tonnes per annum by 1900. Cockerills built the first Bessemer steel plant on the continent in 1863. Growth in steelmaking was relatively slow until after 1892, but by 1914 Belgium was one of the world's principal producers of steel with fifteen integrated plants making 2300000 tonnes per annum.

The Belgian engineering industry in the nineteenth century produced textile machinery for the VERVIERS woollen industry, winding engines for Walloon coal mines, and railway equipment for world markets. Armaments were an important specialism. Cockerills began to roll armour plate in 1848, and small-arms manufacturing was revolutionized by the establishment of the Fabrique Nationale d'Armes de Guerre de Herstal (Herstal National Armaments Works) near Liège in 1889. The Melotte company was producing about a dozen cream separators a year in 1890, but by 1910 was employing 450 people to make 25500 a year. In the early twentieth century

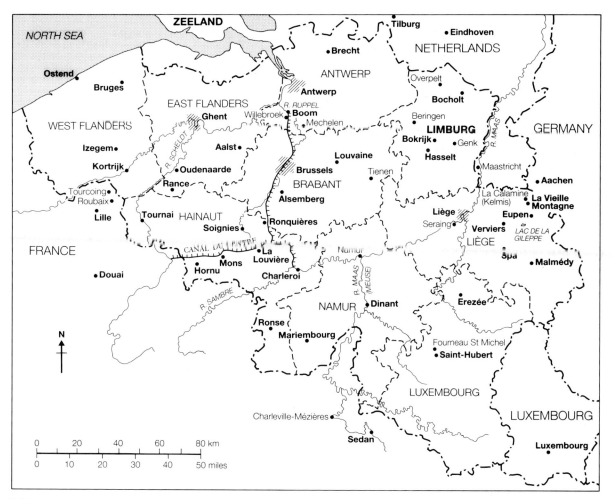

Belgium

Belgian car manufacturers like Minerva, Imperia and Excelsior led Europe both in quality and scale of production, but were overwhelmed by American-owned plants in the 1920s.

Belgium was well supplied with materials for glass-making, with sand, cheap coal, and, after the perfection of the SOLVAY process in the 1860s, soda ash. The glass industry in Hainaut and Namur was the leading international supplier of window glass by the 1850s, and the industry remained important in the twentieth century.

In the early eighteenth century linen was made in the Flanders countryside and sold in GHENT. From about 1780 specialist cotton manufacturers, supplying the same merchants, became established in the city. In 1801 Lievin Bauwens (1769–1822) introduced the first English-style mill in Ghent, and stimulated the building of many more steam-powered factories. The VERVIERS area was the first in continental Europe where the woollen industry underwent significant mechanization as the result of the import of English technology. Two huge flax mills with English machinery were built in Ghent in 1838, but faced fierce competition from domestic linen workers around KORTRIJK and OUDENAARDE, where landholdings were so small that peasant families could only survive through the by-employments associated with making linen. The flax industry remained important around Kortrijk until the 1960s. The traditional manufacture of lace in BRUSSELS and BRUGES was based on high-quality Flemish flax, particularly that from around Braine-le-Comte.

The manufacture of beaten brassware was a specialism of the DINANT region from the Middle Ages. By 1648 the principal European centre of brass production was Stolberg (see AACHEN), which drew its supplies from LA VIEILLE MONTAGNE adjacent to Kelmis. In 1806 Napoleon gave a concession for the mine to Jean-Jacques Dony who had developed a continuously-heated furnace for producing zinc. In 1816 La Vieille Montagne was declared neutral territory and did not become part of Belgium until 1919. Dony's company, La Société de la Vieille Montagne, established furnaces near Liège, and Belgium became one of the world's principal suppliers of zinc, producing 48 857 tonnes in 1860. From the 1880s new works using foreign ores were established in the north of the Campine. The last thermal zinc furnace had ceased operation by 1980. Belgium also became a leading producer of sulphuric acid, a by-product of zinc manufacture.

In 1863 ERNEST SOLVAY perfected a process for the manufacture of alkali and developed a European network of plants, but development in Belgium was restricted by the lack of raw materials.

Industrial development in Belgium owed much to canals. Brussels was linked with the sea through Willebroek from the sixteenth century, but it was not until 1827–32 that the canal was extended to CHARLEROI. By 1830 there were 1600 km (1000 mi.) of navigable waterway in the country, of which 480 km (300 mi.) were canals. In 1856 the Campine Canal was opened: it linked the River Meuse at Liège with Antwerp without entering the Netherlands. It was improved and renamed the Albert Canal in the twentieth century. The Canal du Centre near LA LOUVIÈRE was begun in the 1880s but not completed until 1917.

Roads were developed energetically in the early nineteenth century. A turnpike system existed under Austrian rule: it was abolished by the French but restored in 1814, after which it grew by 25 per cent by 1830, and doubled between 1830 and 1850. Most Belgian roads were paved.

The Belgian railway system was developed with the aim of giving manufacturers access to international markets, and originally consisted of government-financed east–west and north–south routes crossing at Mechelen. It opened in 1835. By 1880 Belgium had the densest railway system in the world. In 1885 the Société Nationale des Chemins de Fer Vicinaux (National Company of Local Railways) was established to build local lines; by 1914 it had constructed over 4000 km (2500 mi.) of routes. Belgium supplied railway equipment to many other countries, and the engineers Alfred Belpaire (1820–93) and Egide Walschaert (1820–1901) influenced locomotive practice throughout the world.

Belgium led the world in the application of concrete in civil engineering, due to the work of FRANÇOIS HENNEBIQUE and Gustav Magnel (1889–1955).

In the 1890s and 1900s Brussels, Ghent and Antwerp grew rapidly, developing new consumer goods manufactures. Wallonia was one of the world's principal heavy industrial areas, but much of Flanders was comparatively poor. In 1901 coal reserves were discovered beneath the sandy heaths of LIMBURG. Extraction did not begin until 1917, but by 1930 the new pits were producing over 7 million tonnes a year. Since 1945 heavy industry in Wallonia has declined; but Flanders, benefiting from its proximity to the coast and the prosperity of West Germany, has been relatively prosperous although the Limburg coal mines have closed.

Brewing has always been an important industry in Belgium. There were over three thousand breweries throughout the country in 1900. The traditional distilling of gin declined as a result of excise pressures from the mid-nineteenth century, but several distilleries remain.

Belgium has a long association with industrial conservation. The Museum voor Kunst en Volksvlyt (Art and Folk Life Museum) was established in Brussels in 1826 and became the Musée de l'Industrie (Museum of Industry) in 1830, but the institution no longer exists and its collections are lost. One of the first to be interested in industrial buildings was René Évrard (1907–63), founder of the Museum of Iron and Coal at Liège, who used the term 'industrial archaeology' as early as 1950. Jan Dhondt (1915–72) of the department of contemporary history at the University of Ghent fostered the growth of a concern for industrial monuments in Flanders. The protection of buildings of historic, artistic or scientific value in Belgium is based on legislation of 1931, but few industrial buildings were scheduled before 1975, when responsibility was divided between the Flemish and Walloon authorities. The regional law in Flanders of 1976 specifically mentioned industrial archaeology, and set up an office for the industrial heritage within the Department of Historic Monuments and Landscapes. Voluntary bodies concerned with conservation also follow the linguistic divide. The Vlaamse Vereniging voor Industriele Archaeologie, Vlaanderen-Brussell (VVIA: Flemish Association for Industrial Archaeology, for Flanders and Brussels) was founded in 1978, and has established an Industrial Heritage Tourist Board in Flanders. Its Walloon equivalent, the Patrimoine Industriele Wallonie-Bruxelles (Industrial Heritage in Wallonia and Brussels) was established in 1984.

Windmills and water mills in Flanders have been studied in some detail, a survey in 1978–9 revealing the survival of 300 water mills and 165 windmills. Many are listed, and some have been restored. There are several preserved railways. The railway museum at Brussels North station is small but the SNCB has preserved some steam locomotives of great significance in the history of engineering. Tramway systems still serve Brussels, Ghent and Antwerp, as well as the coastal resorts. Many conservation schemes have been proposed in recent years, ranging from the preservation of individual steam engines to écomusées like that in the Ruppel valley. Viaene's book (1986), with its accompanying maps, provides one of the most thorough national surveys of industrial monuments.

See also AALST; ALSEMBERG; ANTWERP; BOCHOLT; BOOM; BRECHT; BRUGES; BRUSSELS; CHARLEROI; DINANT; EREZÉE; EUPEN; GHENT; HASSELT; HENNEBIQUE, FRANÇOIS; HORNU; IZEGEM; KORTRIJK; LIÈGE; LIMBURG; LOUVAIN; LOUVIÈRE, LA; MALMÉDY; MARIEMBOURG; MONS; OSTEND; OUDENAARDE; RANCE; RONQUIÈRES; RONSE; ST HUBERT; SOIGNIES; SPA; TOURNAI; VERVIERS; VIEILLE MONTAGNE, LA.

BIBLIOGRAPHY
General
Bauters, 1979; Bruwier and Duvosquel, 1975; Coutant, 1986; De industrie in Belgie, 1981; Kossmann, 1978; Lebrun, 1979; Linters, 1979, 1985, 1986a, 1986b; Milward and Saul, 1973, 1977; van den Abeelen, 1973; van den Branden, 1975; Viaene, 1986.

LOCATIONS
[I] Patrimoine Industriel Wallonie-Bruxelles, quai de Maastricht 8, 4000 Liège.
[I] Vlaamse Vereniging voor Industriele Archaeologie (VVIA)

(Flemish Association for Industrial Archaeology), Postbus 30, Maria Hendrikaplein, B-9000 Ghent.

[I] VVV Industriele Erfgoed (Industrial Heritage Tourist Board), Postbus 30, Maria Hendrikaplein, B-9000 Ghent.

BARRIE TRINDER

Belgrade (Beograd), Serbia, Yugoslavia   The capital of Yugoslavia, a city with 1.2 million inhabitants at the confluence of the Rivers Sava and Danube, and an important centre for manufacturing and communications. It was ruled by the Turks during 1521–1688, 1690–1717, 1739–1806 and 1813–67. There are many important museums. The railway museum has a branch at Belgrade-Lozionica in which locomotives and rolling stock are displayed in depot buildings.

LOCATIONS
[M] Ethnographical Museum, Studentski trg 13, 11000-Belgrade.
[M] Inland Navigation Museum, ul. Kneza Miloša 82, 11000-Belgrade.
[M] Museum of Applied Arts, Vuka Karadžíca 18, 11000-Belgrade.
[M] Museum of Posts and Telecommunications, Majke Jevrosime 13, 11000-Belgrade.
[M] National Museum, ul. Vasina 1, 11000-Belgrade.
[M] Railway Museum, Nemanjina ulica 6, 11000-Belgrade.

JERZY ROZPĘDOWSKI

Bell, Alexander Graham (1847–1922)   A Scot who emigrated to Quebec in 1870 and then to the USA, the inventor of the telephone, primarily as a result of his attempts to help the deaf. He began experiments in telegraphy in Elgin in 1865, took out his first patents in 1875 and chanced on how to transmit speech in 1876. His invention was patented and demonstrated at the Philadelphia Centennial Exposition in the same year. Conversations between Boston and New York were possible by 1877. The Bell Telephone Company, formed in 1877, became the largest corporation in the USA by 1900. Late in life Bell turned to eugenics and aviation.

BIBLIOGRAPHY
General
Bruce, 1973.

Belleek, County Fermanagh, Northern Ireland   A village on the border of County Donegal, celebrated for its lustre-finish Parian porcelain, originally made with clay from Castle Caldwell, 9.5 km (6 mi.) to the NE. The pottery, an elegant three-storey, thirteen-bay building of 1857, is open to the public. Waterfalls on the River Erne were harnessed to a hydro-electric power scheme constructed as a joint venture by the two Irish governments during 1946–55.

BIBLIOGRAPHY
General
McCutcheon, 1980.

Bellis & Morcom   An engineering company from BIRM-INGHAM, England, whose chief draughtsman, Albert Charles Paine, patented in 1890 and 1892 a double-acting, triple-expansion steam engine whose main innovation was a self-lubricating system. With increased efficiency and economy, it was a serious rival to the WILLANS engine until both were superseded by the steam turbine.

BIBLIOGRAPHY
General
Law, 1965.

bell metal   An alloy of copper and tin containing 20 per cent more tin than BRONZE, and, for bells, traces of silver and antimony. A hard, casting alloy of good colour and sonority. It is used for bells and was used formerly for guns and hollow ware. Probate inventories show that cooking vessels of bell metal became popular in England from c 1690 in some areas replacing those of brass. Bell metal was also used for apothecaries' mortars.

For bell manufacture the metal was melted in a reverberatory furnace before being poured into a mould made from a mixture of red sand with a high clay content, black sand from previous castings, and horse manure, the mixture being built up over a brick and coke infilling, and the surface sealed with graphite and whitener. The mould was set in a pit. The bell was then tuned, vertical lathes being used from the mid-nineteenth century. A special 'chipping' hammer was also employed. Cast-iron and steel bells have been manufactured from the mid-nineteenth century.

BIBLIOGRAPHY
General
Elphick, 1988; Jennings, 1988; Moore, 1976.

bell pit   A type of shaft mine used until the nineteenth century, usually for coal or iron ore, and up to 10 m (30 ft.) deep. A shallow shaft was sunk and the mineral worked out, usually in a circular fashion to form a shape like a bell. The technique was employed only where seams were thick enough to justify it. Bell pits were often abandoned as the roof started to fall; a new shaft would then be sunk nearby. Former bell pits now appear in the modern landscape as saucer-shaped depressions. There are many survivals in Britain, such as those at Bentley Grange, Yorkshire, and in Shropshire (*see* CLEE HILLS); and examples are often exposed in opencast workings.

BIBLIOGRAPHY
Specific
Griffin, A. R. Bell-Pits and soughs: some East Midlands examples. In *Industrial Archaeology*, VI(4) 1969.

Belomorsk, Karelo-Finland, USSR   A town which developed rapidly after the construction of the Baltic–White Sea Canal. The inhabitants have always been regarded as one of the USSR's few sources of born seamen. The archaeological interest resides in the circumstance that, being built on islands, the town has about twenty bridges. Increasing numbers are of concrete but some timber structures

71

remain. These are of varying age, the practice having been to replace rotting bridges with structures of identical design.

BIBLIOGRAPHY
Specific
Bolshaya sovietskaya entsiklopediya (Great Soviet Encyclopaedia), vol. 4, Moscow, 1950.

Bendorf, Rhineland-Palatinate, Germany The Sayn ironworks at Bendorf, 10 km (6 mi.) N. of Koblenz, is among the major monuments of the German iron and steel industry. It was founded in 1769 by Clemens Wenzeslaus, Elector of Trier, and when Prussia absorbed the state of Nassau the plant was extended by the Royal Prussian Metallurgical Office, under the direction of Karl Ludwig Althans (1788–1864), senior inspector in charge of the Prussian mining and metalworking industries on the right bank of the Rhine. In his capacity as official buildings supervisor, Althans also had a hand in the extension of the fortress of Ehrenbreitstein and in the controlled explosions designed to deepen the River Rhine at St Goar and Bingen in 1827.

At his headquarters at Sayn, he was responsible for the building of a new BLAST FURNACE, completed in 1821, and its foundry hall, the building of which began in 1828. The blast furnace, situated on a slope, could easily be charged from above. In front of it Althans designed a foundry hall in the shape of a triple-naved basilica, originally 24 m (79 ft.) long and 29 m (95 ft.) wide, with six bays, extended by four more bays in 1844. The hall is built with cast iron made on the spot. The construction consists of hollow pillars, 6.5 m (21 ft.) high, with Doric capitals, on which are laid arched, light lattice girders. The middle nave is roofed with Gothic arches and glazed on one side to admit light from above. The front of the hall is also glazed, with cast-iron ribs arranged in a series of pointed arches. Only the side walls are of traditional masonry, with round-arched windows. Several bracket JIB CRANES are preserved inside the hall – Althans invented their ball-bearing mechanism. The remarkable architecture of this hall, built of iron and glass in the Gothic style, probably derives from the Berlin buildings committee, which had to approve all designs for state buildings. Its chairman, KARL FRIEDRICH SCHINKEL, seems to have influenced the design of this foundry hall, as the design by Althans developed from an original proposal in a heavy Greek style to the filigree-like Gothic structure in iron. The result was a building whose form and organization derived from ecclesiastical architecture, with the hearth of the blast furnace occupying, so to speak, the place of the altar.

The Sayn ironworks began by making iron pipes and cannon for the nearby fortresses of Koblenz and Ehrenbreitstein, and then made ornamental castings for fencing, handrails and staircases. In 1866, when it was the third largest ironworks in Prussia, it passed into the possession of the firm of Krupp, which blew out the blast furnace in 1878, and in 1926 gave up the business and sold it to the town of Bendorf. The buildings fell into disrepair, and parts of the blast furnace were demolished in 1958. In 1973 permission was actually given to demolish the hall, although it was already regarded as being of unusual architectural interest. A private firm acquired the site in 1976, and since then, with great commitment, has renovated the historic buildings with advice and financial grants from the appropriate government authority. Work on the reconstruction of the glazed west front of the foundry hall was completed in 1979, and the blast furnace itself and its side wings have also been restored.

BIBLIOGRAPHY
General
Custodis, 1990.
Specific
Custodis, P.-G. Zur Baugeschichte der Sayner Hütte und ihre Restaurierung (The history of the buildings of the Sayn ironworks and their restoration). In *Denkmalpflege in Rheinland-Pfalz, Jahresberichte 1976–8.* (Monuments preservation in Rhineland-Palatinate: review of the years 1976–8). Mainz, 1979.
Custodis, P.-G. *Die Sayner Hütte in Bendorf* (The Sayn ironworks at Bendorf). Cologne: Rheinische Kunstätten, 1986.
ROLF HÖHMANN

Benz, Karl Friedrich (1844–1929) Benz designed and built the first practical motorcar to be powered by an internal combustion engine. Born and educated in Karlsruhe, Benz experimented with two-stroke engines through the 1870s and in 1879 completed his first practical engine, on which he took out patents. In 1883 he established Benz & Cie, Rheinische Gasmotrenfabrik (Rhineland Gas Engine Works) in Mannheim, and patented his first motorcar, a three-wheeler (now preserved in MUNICH), in 1886. He built his first four-wheel car in 1893. He retired from active participation in his company in 1903. He remained a board member of Benz & Cie until the merger with Daimler-Motoren Gesellschaft in 1926, and of that company until his death. His house in Ladenburg, 10 km (6 mi.) E. of Mannheim, is open to the public.

benzene (C_6H_6) An aromatic hydrocarbon, obtained during the distillation of coal tar; the benzene-containing fraction is benzole. It can also be extracted from the light gas oil fraction resulting from the CRACKING of petroleum. Benzene is a source of ANILINE, PLASTICS, NYLON, weedkillers and resins.

BIBLIOGRAPHY
General
BP, 1958; Hardie and Pratt, 1966; Norman and Waddington, 1977.

Berat, Albania A 'museum city' (*see* ALBANIA) on the River Osum, with a Muslim sector on the left bank and a Christian sector on the right. Houses are built up in banks against the sides of the mountains, with all windows overlooking the river. The landscape between Berat and FIER is littered with small oil derricks. A textile mill built in 1966 with Chinese help employs 7500. Exhibits dealing

Figure 10 The 'museum city' of Berat on the River Osum in Albania
Derek R. Hall

with local history and archaeology are to be found in the museum.

BIBLIOGRAPHY
General
Ward, 1983.

LOCATION
[M] Berat Museum, Berat.

Bergamasque furnace   A type of BLAST FURNACE set between two towers, with a flat front held by wrought-iron straps. It is usually blown by a TROMPE. The form originated in the Bergamo district north-east of Milan, Italy. Bergamesque furnaces were widely used in the Mediterranean region in the seventeenth and eighteenth centuries. A modified example survives at CAPALBIO.

BIBLIOGRAPHY
General
Belhoste *et al.*, 1984; Crossley and Trinder, 1983.

Bergen, Hordaland, Norway   The principal port of western Norway, and for centuries the country's largest city and chief link with the outside world, Bergen lies on a hilly peninsula and isthmus bounded by water on every side except the north-east. Its prosperity was due to the HANSEATIC LEAGUE, which established a trading post there in the mid-fifteenth century: this came to acquire monopolistic privileges over much of the trade of northern and western Norway. The power of the League declined from 1559, but the office in Bergen functioned until 1763, and trade continued to follow the patterns that had been established until the twentieth century. Smoked and dried fish, cod-liver oil (rebarrelled in Bergen to remove sea water) and roe were taken to Bergen in the summer months, and stored in warehouses before being distributed to the more southerly parts of Europe. Steamship services to Oslo began in 1827, and from 1872 there were regular sailings to north Norway. Bergen was a prosperous city in the nineteenth century, although overtaken in population by Oslo. It remains a busy port. Fish and furs are sold on the quay, there is a constant coming and going of ferries, and a three-masted barque, the *Statsraad Lehmkuhl* of 1914, sails regularly from the harbour.

The Tysksebryggen (the German Quay), a range of painted wooden warehouses which took their present form after a fire of 1702, is perhaps the best-known group of buildings in Norway, and has been designated a World Heritage Site. The parts fronting the quay itself are used as shops, behind which stretch ranges of buildings with galleries and external staircases, extending along narrow rectangular plots.

The Hanseatisk Museum on the quay displays many items used in the traditional Bergen trades, including screw presses for filling barrels with fish, and a variety of scales and balances. Other museums include the Fiskeri-museet, for fisheries; Bergens Sjofartsmuseum, for shipping; the Teleteknisk Museum, for telecommunications, which includes generators and switchboards used in the city between 1937 and 1965; and Gamle Bergen, an open-air folk museum.

See also figure 117.

BIBLIOGRAPHY
General
Keilhau, 1951.

BARRIE TRINDER

Bergensbanen, Norway One of the world's most remarkable feats of railway building, linking Oslo with Bergen. The 470 km (290 mi.) line was completed in 1909, its summit at Taugevatn being 1301 m (4268 ft.) above sea level. There are 178 tunnels. The line was electrified in 1964. Some steam locomotives that worked it are preserved at HAMAR.

BIBLIOGRAPHY
General
Schneider, 1963.

Bergisches Land, North Rhine-Westphalia, Germany The highly-industrialized Bergisches Land lies east of the Rhine, with the River Ruhr to the north and the Sieg to the south, in the hilly country of the Rheinisches Schiefergebirge, which rises to the east. Close to the transport axis of the Rhine and to the cities of DÜSSELDORF, WUPPERTAL and COLOGNE, the textile and iron-working industries, which depended on water power, were of great importance even before the nineteenth century. There are many hammer forges around the towns of Solingen and Remscheid; some are still in use, others, like the Steffenshammer works at Remscheid and the Balkhauser Kotten works at Solingen, are preserved as museums.

In the nineteenth century Solingen's weapons and cutlery manufactures, which had flourished since medieval times, entered the factory age. Firms of international standing, such as those of J. A. Henckel and Friedrich Herder, dominate the industrial landscape with their impressive factory buildings, but smaller enterprises are still more typical of the area. Twenty-five per cent of them still make cutlery. Since c.1930 the drop forges which supplied the grinding shops have also been making motorcar parts, an industry now of great importance in Solingen. A museum displays the long development of cutlery in Solingen.

Remscheid, linked since 1897 to Solingen by the oldest steel bridge in Germany, of 107 m (351 ft.) span, also depends on the manufacture of small iron wares for its international trade. Tools, including pliers, hammers, saws and files, were manufactured by hundreds of small firms. In 1885 the Mannesmann brothers developed the process for manufacturing seamless steel tubes (*see* TUBE MILL) in the buildings of their father's file factory at Remscheid-Bliedinghausen. Wilhelm C. Röntgen, the discoverer in 1895 of X-rays, was born in Remscheid in 1845 and is commemorated in the Röntgen Museum.

The Wendenerhütte, an ironworks dating from 1728 at Wenden, 60 km (40 mi.) E. of Cologne, includes one of the best-preserved charcoal-fired blast furnaces in Europe. The FINERY AND CHAFERY forge has been restored with new water wheels and hammers.

The Upper Bergisches Land, lying further south between Cologne and Siegen, has also been a flourishing trading and industrial area since the eighteenth century. Its industries include iron-ore mining, ironworking, and textiles manufactures, which also occur further north on the Rivers Agger, Volme and Kerspe. There are still many factories of historical interest standing along the Agger. Since 1987 a branch of the Rhenish Museum of Industry, portraying the industrial development of this part of North Rhine-Westphalia, has been housed in the cotton-spinning mill at Engelskirchen, founded in 1837 by the Anglo-German firm of Ermen & Engels. Papermaking, leatherworking and mining are illustrated in the Bensberg Museum at Bergisch Gladbach.

Another branch of the Rhenish Museum of Industry (which has eight in all) houses exhibits relating to the important paper industry of the town of Bergisch Gladbach, 12 km (8 mi.) E. of Cologne, in the early-eighteenth-century Alte Dombach papermill. This mill was formerly owned by the Zanders company, which still uses some nineteenth-century buildings and some early-twentieth-century papermaking machinery.

High rainfall and the demand for drinking water from the growing industrial towns led to a DAM-building boom between 1890 and 1910 even greater than that in the EIFEL. The first West German drinking-water reservoir in the valley of the Eschbach provided Remscheid with its water from 1891. The Ronsdorf and Herbringhaus dams were built to serve Wuppertal, and a water pipeline was built to the Rhine at Benrath. Many others followed, most of them designed by Otto Intze (1843–1904), professor of hydraulic engineering at Aachen. By the time of his death he had built or designed forty-seven dams, all of them arched dams of rubble masonry, and had acquired the title of 'the father of German dam-building'.

BIBLIOGRAPHY
General
Banfield, 1846; Günter, 1970; Lunkenheimer, 1990; Schmitz, 1921; Stursberg, 1964; Werner, 1975.
Specific
Hatzfeld, L. Der Anfang der deutschen Röhrenindustrie (The beginning of the German pipe industry). In *Tradition. Zeitschrift für Firmengeschichte und Unternehmerbiographie* (Papers on business history and biography), v. Stuttgart, 1960.
Kaufmann, K. H. *Chronik der Wendener Hütte* (Chronicle of the ironworks at Wenden), 2nd edn. Wenden: Wendener Hütte EV, 1983.
Rouvé, G. Die Geschichte der Talsperren in Mitteleuropa (The history of dams in Central Europe). In Garbrecht, 1987.

[M] Röntgen Museum, Schwelmer Strasse, 5630 Remscheide-Lennep.

AXEL FÖHL

Bergslagen, Gävleborg, Kopparberg, Örebro, Uppsala and Västmanland, Sweden   A substantial although imprecisely defined region of central Sweden, bounded approximately by the cities of Gävle, Falun, Hagfors, Karlstad, Örebro and Västarås, which since prehistoric times has been concerned with the smelting and working of metals, particularly iron, silver and copper. The ironworking BRUKS in the region were the principal foundation of the Swedish economy in the eighteenth century, and many were successfully adapted to use the LANCASHIRE FORGE process from the 1830s. Some went on to produce steel in the late nineteenth century. Some of the first industrial conservation schemes in Sweden were undertaken in Bergslagen (see FALUN; LUDVIKA) but in the mid-1980s an ambitious proposal was announced for an écomusée comprising the whole region, but centring on some fifty sites, some of which had long been open to the public, in seven communities in the north-western parts of the region. The project began to operate in 1986 and the museum was formally constituted in 1988. The project incorporates the museum at LUDVIKA, the ironworks at ENGELSBERG, the STRÖMSHOLMS CANAL, Lancashire forges at Karmansbo and Ramnäs, a museum of steam locomotives in a preserved locomotive depot at GRÄNGESBERG, a water wheel built by CHRISTOPHER POLHEM at Norberg, and numerous mining and ironworking sites. The region has an unequalled wealth of industrial monuments and landscapes, with features from many centuries.

BIBLIOGRAPHY
General
Sörenson *et al.*, 1987.
Specific
Morger, K. Bergslagen. In *Teknik & Kultur*, II, 1990.
Nisser, M. Bergslagen: the conservation of Sweden's metal-working area. In S. Cantacuzino, *Architectural Conservation in Europe*. London: Architectural Press, 1975.
Sörenson, U. *The Swedish Ecomuseum: the art of engineering a landscape*. Stockholm: Swedish Institute, 1987.

LOCATION
[M] Ekomuseum Bergslagen, Box 22, S-791 21 Falun.

BARRIE TRINDER

Berlin, Germany   It has been said of Berlin as a location for industry that its only resource was and is its ability to attract people, train them, and keep them in the city. As Berlin is still the largest area of industrial concentration in Germany, it has obviously set about this task with great skill. One probable reason is that it has always been able to adapt production to the best-developed technology of any given period. First, however, the city, which became a metropolis quite late by the standards of the rest of Europe, had to be formed from the two trading centres of Cölln and Berlin, first mentioned in documents in 1237 and 1244 respectively, and develop into the capital of the German

Reich of 1871, and then into the 'Greater Berlin' of 1920. Greater Berlin was created on 27 April 1920, amalgamating eight towns, fifty-nine rural communities and twenty-seven administrative estate districts (those large estates that had not previously been included in parishes). It had a population of 3.85 million in its twenty new urban districts. The population had risen to over 4 million by 1925. By the time Nazi rule in Germany ended in 1945, Berlin could be described as 'the largest single ruinous area of Germany', and, indeed, of Europe.

Berlin's commercial and industrial history begins early, and should be seen against the background of the poverty of the natural resources of the territory of Brandenburg, later part of Prussia. As early as the eighteenth century a deliberately tolerant attitude was adopted towards minorities expelled from other countries for all kinds of reasons – generally religious – to allow them to settle in Berlin. These minorities included, for instance, Huguenots driven from France in 1685 by the Revocation of the Edict of Nantes. Specialists from the Netherlands had already been brought in to assist with the development of horticulture and canal-building in 1648, after the area had been devastated during the Thirty Years War of 1618–48. Prosperous Jewish families, particularly Jews expelled from Vienna, moved to Berlin from 1671 onwards. In 1732 King Friedrich Wilhelm I (1688–1740) of Prussia invited Protestants expelled from Salzburg into the country. Some 20000 of them, roughly the same as the number of Huguenot immigrants in the seventeenth century, took up his offer and settled in the Brandenburg area of Prussia. The textile industry in particular profited from the simultaneous arrival of Protestants from Bohemia. They settled in areas later to be included in Greater Berlin, among them Rixdorf, Nowawes and Schöneberg, forming colonies of weavers.

The improvement of transport facilities in and around Berlin began with the opening of the Spree–Oder Canal in 1699, as part of a waterways system connecting the North Sea and the Baltic. That improvement laid important foundations for the industrial development of the later imperial capital. Berlin was a city of industrial workers by 1800, when over 25000 of its 172000 inhabitants were employed in manufacturing textiles and clothing. Friedrich III of Brandenburg, who became King Friedrich I of Prussia in 1700, followed the example of Paris and London in establishing the Akademie der Künste und mechanischen Wissenschaften (Academy of Arts and Mechanical Sciences) in 1696, and the Societät der Wissenschaften (Association of Sciences) in 1700. By 1750 Berlin was a prominent seat of the German Enlightenment; such thinkers as Gotthold Lessing (1729–81), Moses Mendelssohn (1729–86) and Christoph Friedrich Nicolai (1733–1811) lived there. The university, opened in 1810, was influenced by the ideas of Karl Wilhelm von Humboldt (1767–1835) on educational reform, combining research with teaching. His brother, Friedrich Heinrich Alexander von Humboldt (1769–1859), introduced the study of natural sciences into the curriculum in 1827.

State encouragement of industry, with the aim of

creating links with the technologically more advanced economies of England and France, led to the development in the late 1830s of an independent class of industrial entrepreneurs who were to make Berlin the leading industrial city of Europe, and the largest in Germany, with the aid of capital (some from the western German states) and the further development of the waterways and railway networks. The ventures of Freund, the Cockerills, Egells and Borsig created local ironmaking and metal-working industries, which stood side by side with textile firms like that of Sieburg, while Wöhlert, Pflug and Schwartzkopff made Berlin a centre for mechanical engineering. In 1856 the locomotive manufacturer Borsig for the first time exported some of his products to Great Britain.

In 1871 two-thirds of wage-earners in Berlin were employed in trade and industry, although there were as yet few large businesses. The firms of Siemens & Halske, founded in 1847, and Allgemeine Elektricitäts-Gesellschaft (AEG: originally DEG), founded by Emil Rathenau in 1883, helped Berlin to become a leading international centre of the electrical industry. When the city's population reached a million in 1877, the chemical industry too was on its way towards a second industrial revolution, with the establishment of the firms of Schering, in 1851, and Agfa, in 1873.

By 1905 Berlin had a population of two million. The necessary steps to create an infrastructure for a population of such size had not been taken until between 1873 and 1886, when a centralized sewage-disposal system was built. In 1871-7 a ring railway was built, linking the city's main railway termini. The first municipal railway was built in 1882, and the first underground railway in 1902. In 1881 the firm of Siemens gave Berlin the first electric tramway system in the world. These various transport systems were combined into a unified network in 1896-1902. The Hobrecht Plan, drawn up in 1862, created the broad streets and imposing squares which still catch the eye today, but it did not really determine the use to be made of the various building sites, thus leaving their development to speculative builders and market forces. This led to the erection of the blocks of apartments buildings typical of Berlin, five-storey tenements extending back around several small inner courtyards. They left the city with more high-rise tenement housing than any other in the world, with the ever-recurring problems of ventilation and overcrowding: so rapid was the growth of the city that in 1918 almost 40 per cent of these apartments consisted of one room only.

No consistent efforts were made to combat these social problems until the Weimar Republic period after World War I. But in 1920 the land occupied by such large industrial firms as Siemens and Borsig, some of which had moved away from the centre more than once, was re-integrated with the city, and after 1926 there was much building activity, partly financed by the proceeds of a house-rent tax, under the city architect, Martin Wagner. Large housing estates were built in an attempt to counter the problem of poor accommodation, among them the Hufeisensiedlung in Britz by Bruno Taut, the Weisse Stadt

built in Reinickendorf by Otto Salvisberg and others, and the Siemensstadt estate. Many schools, public buildings and industrial buildings were constructed in the expressionist and modernist styles by such architects as Max Taut (1884–1967) and Bruno Taut (1880–1938), Erich Mendelsohn (1887–1933), Hans Scharoun (1893–1972) and Walter Gropius (1883–1969), and their influence on the architecture of the modern city extended beyond Berlin itself.

In 1933, with the coming of Nazi rule, internal and external decline abruptly set in. The Jewish population, which had been of particular importance in many economic and intellectual fields, was expelled or annihilated. Then came the destruction of the city by air raids, beginning in August 1940. By 1945 evacuation and casualties had lowered the population of Berlin to 2.3 million, compared with 4.3 million in 1939, and more than half the buildings had been destroyed or damaged. The city had 80 million m³ (94 million cu. yd.) of rubble, creating new hills up to 120 m (400 ft.) high in the flat Brandenburg countryside. Bertold Brecht (1898–1956) described it as 'Berlin, the rubbish dump at Potsdam'.

The period after 1945 was marked by two developments that could hardly have been envisaged: one was the rebirth of this badly damaged and devastated city; the other its division, bringing it into the areas of influence of two political systems, which reached a crisis in 1961 with the drastic measure of the construction of the Berlin Wall, 165 km (100 mi.) long, 46 km (28 mi.) of it running right through the inner-city area.

A third event that was equally hard to predict was the demolition of the Wall from November 1989; a development with repercussions on the political, industrial and social life of the 751-year-old city that cannot yet be evaluated. The period between 1949 and 1989 saw the separate development of such features of the city's infrastructure as the underground and municipal railway networks, air traffic and electricity supply, and as manufacturing centres the two halves of Berlin developed very differently with respect to innovation and modernization.

Infrastructure

The public utilities of Berlin developed gradually, initially through private enterprise, and rather later than those of such capitals as London and Paris. However, Berlin was able to learn from the mistakes of such cities. In 1825 the 'Imperial Continental Gas Association' built the first gasworks. Berlin's most magnificent thoroughfare, the Unter den Linden, was lit by gas for the first time in 1826. The first waterworks was built near the Stralauer Tor in 1856. The pressure balance tower of 1856 still stands on an eminence in the Knaackstrasse in East Berlin. Originally it had an open reservoir alongside it, and nearby stands a watertower of 1877, supported by six storeys of housing. It was extended in 1907.

Many other buildings in the city illustrate the development of water-supply and sewage-disposal systems. Particularly impressive is the largest waterworks in Berlin, which is also the oldest still operating, built alongside the Müggelsee in the south-east of the city in 1893. It has three bucket-pump engine rooms parallel to the lake shore, each containing three steam-driven pumps, passing water from the lake through sand filters. North of the Müggelsee dam stand the conveyor machine rooms A and B, with two covered pure-water containers, and twenty-two slow filters between them. The architect Richard Schultze chose the traditional Gothic style of the locality for these buildings, with pitched roofs covered with red Dutch pantiles, so that they would merge harmoniously with the forested landscape of the Mark of Brandenburg. Bucket-pump engine room B housed the Technical Water Supply and Distribution Museum of the DDR from 1987, and has a preserved, electrically-driven compound steam engine.

The sewage-disposal system also has buildings in both parts of the city, some of which are protected by conservation orders. The plan for the city's drainage drawn up in 1873 by James Hobrecht was a twelve-part radial system, including Pumping Plant III in Schönebergerstrasse, near the Landwehr Canal. It was the first plant to be built, in 1873–6, and was only taken out of operation in 1972. A steam engine with a pump has been preserved. The building, with its handsome Lombard Gothic-style chimney, now houses the collection of stone monuments of the West Berlin Monuments Preservation Authority. It has a counterpart in eastern Berlin, Pumping Plant XII in Rudolfstrasse, completed in 1893 as part of the same radial system. Prominently situated on the Hohenzollerndamm, the Wilmersdorf pumping plant built in 1903–6 is part of another system which served several western districts of the city.

There are fewer historic buildings connected with Berlin's gas supply. Two masonry gasholders in Prenzlauer Berg were demolished in 1984, but the Grossgaswerk von Berlin (Great Berlin Gasworks) still stands in Greifswalder Strasse.

The Klingenberg pulverized-coal thermal power station on the Spree in Berlin-Lichtenberg was built in 1925–6, and bears the name of the famous power station engineer Georg Klingenberg. His brother Walter Klingenberg and Werner Issels designed it. The 30 kV distribution building of the 170 MW plant, with eight towers in front of its façade, stands opposite the eleven-storey expressionist tower building, which contains an overhead water tank with a capacity of 200 m³ (7000 cu. ft.).

There are also buildings connected with electricity supply in the western part of the city, most of them expressionist transformer stations. One modernist example stands in the Hermannstrasse in Neukölln.

After 1948 West Berlin supplied all its own energy. Building of the 440 MW Ernst Reuter power station in Spandau began during the Berlin blockade, which lasted from June 1948 to May 1949, and parts for boilers and machinery weighing up to 1500 tonnes were flown in during the Berlin Airlift.

Transport

Little remains of the once numerous railway termini in Berlin. Anything left standing after World War II was demolished during the years of Germany's post-war Wirtschaftswunderjahre ('economic miracle'). A tiny part of the entrance to the 'concourse building' of the Anhalt Station, built in 1872–80, is a memento of the seven main railway stations that were in existence as early as 1867. The Hamburg Station, built in 1846, owes its survival to the fact that it had already been converted for use as a transport museum in 1906, but was given a new train shed at the time. Until 1984 it was frozen, so to speak, in the possession of the DDR state railway system, but within the territory of West Berlin. Its valuable collections illustrating the history of transport were then divided between the West Berlin Museum of Transport and Technology and the Dresden Museum of Transport. The Berlin museum includes a working replica built in 1923–4 of Die Pfalz (the Palatinate), a Crampton-type 4–2–0 of 1853, constructed by the Maffei company in Munich.

The Prussian government began building the precursor of a ring railway for freight transport in 1851. It connected the Stettin Station with the Hamburg, Potsdam, Anhalt and Frankfurt stations.

After 1867 a ring railway outside the self-contained built-up area of the city was planned, to link all eight main lines, and to provide sidings for the use of industries which had been forced out of the city centre. Passenger transport was not envisaged, but that facility was requested by the city council in 1871, when the ring railway linked the districts of Moabit, Gesundbrunnen, Friedrichsberg, Stralau, Rixdorf, Tempelhof, Schöneberg, Wedding and Treptow. The north-west stretch of the ring railway, bringing in Charlottenburg and Grunewald, was completed in 1877. By 1879 another three radial main lines had been added to the existing eight. The Civic Railway Society (Stadteisenbahngesellschaft) was founded in 1874 with the object of building independent municipal lines. It passed into the possession of the Prussian state in 1878, and by 1882 had built a four-track municipal line, 12 km (7 mi.) long, running from east to west across the city on a viaduct of 757 masonry arches.

Many station buildings of this and later lines survive. They were well renovated after 1984 when the Federal Republic bought the municipal railway system of Berlin. Stations like Nikolassee, Lichterfelde and Lehrter are preserved as monuments to the painstaking architecture practised by the well-known architects who worked on the urban railways. Until the political changes of 1989–90, Friedrichstrasse Station was a peculiarity of the system; at one and the same time it was a main-line station, a municipal railway station and an underground station, besides being a border-crossing checkpoint on the frontier between East and West Germany – a complex and fateful place.

Water transport was of great importance in the development of Berlin. The Westhafen on the Westhafen- und Hohenzollern-Kanal in the north of the city, the construction of which began in 1914, is a self-contained architectural complex. Since 1852, Berlin, with no fewer than thirteen harbours, had owned the third largest inland waterways system in Germany. The Westhafen, near Lehrter railway freight depot, was planned as the fourteenth harbour by Friedrich Krause, who succeeded

James Hobrecht as the chief of the city's civil engineering department. The buildings were designed by Wolfenstein & Lorenz. The dominant feature of the façade of the central basin, one of three, is the harbour office block: it resembles a civic hall, and has a tower on top. The first phase of the complex was finished in 1923 and the second in 1927. Some of the warehouses in Tempelhof harbour, laid out in 1901–6, also have interesting architectural features.

Berlin still has some historic monuments connected with transport before the introduction of steam, electricity and the internal combustion engine. They include the horse omnibus yard in Schwedenstrasse in Wedding, where vehicles were accommodated on the ground floor and horses on the first floor until 1928. A similar yard is situated in Monumentenstrasse in Schöneberg.

The 'Automobil-Verkehrs- und Uebungstrasse' (Automobile Traffic and Practice Road), AVUS for short, was begun in 1913 and completed in 1921: it reflects the early impact of the motorcar on city traffic and anticipated the later concept of an autobahn. It runs 10 km (6 mi.) through the Grunewald district, and was the first type of road to be devoted exclusively to motorcars.

Industrial architecture

Berlin has such a wealth of industrial buildings that only those linked with outstanding architects will be mentioned here.

One such architect was PETER BEHRENS. In Berlin he worked in association with the engineer Karl Bernhard. From 1907 to 1914 Behrens was artistic adviser to the Allgemeine-Electricitäts-Gesellschaft (AEG: the General Electricity Company), which had been established by Emil and Walther Rathenau. He was to develop what at a later date would have been called the corporate image of the firm, from the graphic design of its printed matter to the design of the products themselves, and the architectural plans for new buildings.

As well as many items – including clocks, ventilators and electric kettles – which became famous, Behrens was particularly successful with what is probably the best-known industrial building in Berlin, which is now protected by a conservation order: AEG's 'Turbinenfabrik' (turbine factory) in the Huttenstrasse in Berlin-Tiergarten. It was planned by Behrens, with Bernhard as designing engineer. The triple-jointed lattice-girder building is particularly impressive because of the inward-inclined glazed areas between the steel girders along its length, and the design of the façade – not for reasons of structural necessity – with horizontally-jointed, conically-tapering concrete structures, the roof line broken in five places and bearing the firm's trademark and the inscription 'Turbinenfabrik'. The structure, originally 123 m (400 ft.) long, and 25 m (82 ft.) wide and high, was extended another 84 m (275 ft.) in 1939.

Leaving aside the controversy as to whether, as regards the opinion of critics or the architect's own intentions, this building is to be classified as functional or monumental, the turbine factory, which is still operating after eighty years, became an early-twentieth-century symbol of modern industrial architecture in Germany. Undisputed

achievements in this field are Behrens' buildings in Wedding for the high-voltage factory in Hussitenstrasse, of 1910, and AEG's small engines factory in Voltastrasse, of 1910–13. The latter is a brick building of conventional construction, with rolled-steel columns, but the arrangement of the four groups of seven round pillars along the 195 m (640 ft.) façade is very effective. Even before its association with Behrens in 1907, AEG had employed leading architects. Founded in 1883 as DEG (Deutsche-Edison-Gesellschaft: German Edison Company), together with the firm of Siemens, it changed its name to AEG in 1887, and employed Franz Schwechten, the architect of the Anhalt Station, to build its factory in the Ackerstrasse in Wedding in 1888–9. He also designed the recently-renovated neo-Gothic gateway to the works, built in 1896 and situated in the Brunnenstrasse. This gateway, known as the management entrance, which workers were forbidden to use, has a triangular gable between compact towers. The AEG logo is set in the triangular area in a mosaic of light bulbs and porcelain insulators. Schwechten, whose work was popular with the Imperial family, had just finished building the neo-Romanesque Kaiser Wilhelm Memorial church at this time.

The designer of the innovatory Wertheim department store constructed in Leipziger Strasse in 1896–1904, Alfred Messel, also built AEG's office building on the Friedrich-Karl-Ufer. A firm operating in the ultra-modern field of the electrical industry had thus turned to the foremost artists of the day to design its buildings and present its image to the public from the time it was founded – a remarkably early example of such a procedure, and in the light of late-twentieth-century concern with corporate image a very logical one, but on a large scale the phenomenon was confined to the AEG and its guiding spirits, Emil and Walther Rathenau.

Another example of twentieth-century industrial architecture, connected with Berlin's other major electrical firm, Siemens, should be mentioned for the sake of its size. This firm, founded in 1847 as Siemens & Halske, moved to the outskirts of the city for the second time in 1898, to a site on the River Spree between Charlottenburg and Spandau. After 1914, this area was officially known as Siemensstadt (Siemens town). A large number of buildings for both manufacturing and administration had been constructed there by 1939, under the architects Janisch (d.1915) and Hans Hertlein (1881–1963). Among them was the ten-storey switch-gear building of 1926–8, which is 175 m (575 ft.) long and 45 m (150 ft.) high. Each storey of this 58-bay, steel-framed structure, is undivided internally, and could be fitted out as required. Two staircase towers in front of each of the long sides provided vertical access. Directly to the east of this building is the office block which Janisch began designing in 1912. Hertlein was in charge of the closing phase of the work. It has eight inner courtyards and was built to accommodate the firm's central administrative staff, the directors and management, which even in 1913 totalled three thousand people.

There were over six thousand staff working on the site during World War II. Today the head offices have been moved to Munich where there is a staff of only 650. Even the first phase of building, dating from 1913, contained offices for up to a hundred employees. Ribbe and Schäche (1985) provide a comprehensive account of the history and architecture of the entire Siemensstadt complex.

Two interesting examples of engineering construction in Berlin date from the post-war period. In 1975–6 the architect Ludwig Leo built an orbital canal for the Institute of Hydraulic Engineering and Shipbuilding of the Technical University, above the historic Landwehr Canal in Charlottenburg. The technical constraints influencing its design are immediately apparent. To save space, the orbital ring, which would usually be horizontal, is angled towards the vertical. In 1969–71 the same architect designed a triangular boathouse, 30 m (100 ft.) high, for the German Lifesaving Society. It accommodates eighty boats and has workshops and a life-saving station; an inclined hoist for boats is conspicuous on the bank on the Pichelsee Lake.

Industrial yards and typical factories

Typical of the commercial and industrial life of Berlin in the late nineteenth century and early twentieth century are the 'Gewerbehöfe' (industrial yards), particularly in the Kreuzberg district of the city. Proximity to the workers' dwellings, the cheap building land available behind intensively exploited sites, and, to a lesser extent, the advantage of having transport facilities available, brought all kinds of industrial firms to the Kreuzberg industrial yards. Textile and garment-making companies and the printing and metalworking industries formed notable concentrations. An example of what is called the 'Kreuzberg mixture', a typical combination of industrial building and housing, is the Urbanhof (urban yard) between Urbanstrasse and Dieffenbachstrasse in Kreuzberg, built in 1895. In all it contains three apartment blocks and two factory buildings, each five storeys high, on a site about 45 m (150 ft.) wide by 150 m (500 ft.) deep. The Erdmannshof (Erdmann yard) in Kreuzberg was designed by Karl Bernhard, engineer of the AEG turbine factory. The inner walls of its courtyards are faced, characteristically, with white-glazed tiles to lighten the interiors.

Two six-storey factories in the style of castles were built in 1882 and 1884 on sites in Köpenickerstrasse. These are just two examples of a pattern repeated over and over again in Berlin's industrial regions.

Manufactories of staple and luxury foodstuffs were plentiful in Berlin. The most striking buildings are the big breweries of this beer-drinking capital. The brewhouse and main building of what was later the Schultheiss brewery were built in 1872–96 in Stromstrasse in the Moabit area. It continued in operation until 1980. Also very striking, with their characteristic vapour outlet pipes, are the buildings of the Schloss brewery and malthouse in Tempelhof, dating from 1989, and the Schultheiss malthouse on Bessemerstrasse in Schöneberg, built in 1914, with its huge rotating ventilators. The industrial architect Bruno Buch (1883–1938) built the Groterjahn brewery in Wedding in the functionalist style in 1928–9. Despite its late date, it originally had stables for horses on its upper

storeys, reflecting the lack of space arising from the high price of building land, and at the same time being perhaps a symbol of the industrial development of Berlin, where a late start was never an obstacle to the adoption of modern technologies enabling the city to compete in international markets.

BIBLIOGRAPHY
General
Architektenverein zu Berlin *et al*, 1896; Berger, 1980; Buddensieg and Henning, 1978; Buddensieg *et al.*, 1987; Geist and Kürvers, 1980; Gut, 1984; Hildebrandt *et al.*, 1988; Huse, 1989; Korff and Rürup, 1987; Krings, 1985; Martin, 1989; Masur, 1971; Posener, 1979; Ribbe and Schäche, 1985; Schmidt and Eilhardt, 1984; Schmidt and Theile, 1989; Schneider *et al.*, 1980; Schwarz, 1981; Trost, 1987; Wagenbreth and Wächtler, 1983; Weiher, 1987; Wilhelmi *et al.*, 1987.
Specific
Die Reise nach Berlin (Journeys to Berlin), Berliner Festspiel GmbH, 1987.
Gottwald, A. and Steinle, H. *Verkehrs- und Baumuseum Berlin. Der 'Hamburger Bahnhof'* (The building and transport museum of Berlin at the Hamburg station). Berlin: Museum für Verkehr und Technik, 1984.

LOCATIONS
[M] Bauhaus-Archiv (Bauhaus Archives), Klingelhöferstrasse 14, 1000 Berlin 30.
[M] Kunstgewerbemuseum (Museum of Applied Art), Schloss Köpenick, 1170 Berlin.
[M] Märkisches Museum (Museum of Cultural History in Berlin), Am Köllnischen Park 5, 1020 Berlin.
[M] Museum für Verkehr und Technik (Transport and Technology Museum), Trebbinerstrasse 9, 1000 Berlin 61.
[M] Postmuseum der DDR, Leipziger Strasse/Mauerstrasse, 1066 Berlin.
[M] Post und Fernmeldemuseum (Post and Communications Museum), An der Urania 15, 1000 Berlin 30.
[I] Senator für Bau- und Wohnungswesen-Landeskonservator (Office for the Conservation of Buildings and Dwellings for West Berlin), Lindenstrasse 20–5, 1000 Berlin 61.

AXEL FÖHL

Berne (Bern), Bern, Switzerland   The capital of the Swiss confederacy since 1848, Bern has never been an important industrial city, although it had a small industrial museum before 1900, and some of its modern museums deal with industry. It has many arcaded shops and numerous fountains. Several spectacular bridges cross the River Aare, among them the Kornhaus Brücke of 1895–8, a 122 m (400 ft.) steel arch designed by A. and H. von Bonstetten, and the Lorraine Bridge, a single concrete arch spanning 151 m (495 ft.) and carrying four railway tracks.

LOCATIONS
[M] Bern Historical Museum, Helvetiaplatz 5, 3055 Bern.
[M] Swiss Postal, Telephone and Telegraph Museum, Helvetiaplatz 4, 3055 Bern.

Bessbrook, County Antrim, Northern Ireland   The outstanding planned industrial settlement associated with the Irish linen industry, built by John Grubb Richardson, a

Quaker, in 1846, when he was constructing a spinning mill. It is on the River Camlough 5 km (3 mi.) NW of Newry with which it was linked in 1885–1948 by an electric tramway, a tramcar from which is preserved in BELFAST at the Ulster Folk and Transport Museum. There are two squares of houses, each originally of three, four or five rooms, in blue granite, with allotments, playing fields, places of worship, schools, a dispensary, co-operative shops, and a savings bank, but no public houses or pawnshops. The Dublin–Belfast railway crosses the road to Newry 2 km (1 mi.) to the SE on a spectacular Egyptian arch of 1851 designed by Sir John Macneill (?1793–1880).

BIBLIOGRAPHY
General
Burke, 1971; Meakin, 1905; McCutcheon, 1980.

Bessemer, Sir Henry (1812–98)   An inventor, best known for his discovery of MILD STEEL although he made notable inventions in other industries. In 1856, in attempting to make WROUGHT IRON and carbon steel, Bessemer developed a new material that combined many of the qualities of cast iron and wrought iron, and that, unlike the latter, could be manufactured in large quantities. After cast iron had been melted and poured into a crucible, generally called a converter, air was blown through, creating, initially, a violent exothermic reaction as the carbon, silicon and other elements in the iron were oxidized. Bessemer patented his process, but it was unsuccessful when applied elsewhere with phosphoric irons and acidic siliceous refractories. A Swede, G. F. Goransson, was the first to make a commercial success of the Bessemer process. The acid Bessemer process was exceptionally well adapted to Swedish conditions, where non-phosphoric pig iron was easily obtained, and it was used to produce special steels in Sweden until the 1940s. The acid Bessemer process was effective with haematite irons which were non-phosphoric, and Bessemer established his own steelworks in SHEFFIELD in 1858. From the 1880s the work of SIDNEY GILCHRIST THOMAS, who demonstrated that the use of a basic lining of dolomite in a converter would remove phosphorus from the iron, enabled phosphoric irons to be used in steelmaking. Acid and basic Bessemer steelworks remained in use in many countries until the 1970s, but the process has been generally superseded.

A Bessemer converter is a pear-shaped crucible mounted on trunnions, which can be tilted for the charging of molten metal, and for the tapping of steel into ingot moulds at the end of the process. A Bessemer plant is preserved at Hagfors in Sweden and many converters have been installed in museums or retained as open-air sculptures.

BIBLIOGRAPHY
General
Bessemer, 1905; Gale, 1971; Schuhmann, 1984.
Specific
Carlberg, P. Bessemermetodens genombrott vid Edsken och

Hogbo (The Bessemer process at Edsken and Hogbo). In *Med hammare och fackla* (With hammer and tongs), XXII, 1962.

MARIE NISSER and BARRIE TRINDER

Bewdley, Worcestershire, England   A port on the River Severn, on the edge of Wyre Forest, Bewdley lost much of its trade following the growth of STOURPORT from 1772. Of interest is a stone bridge of 1798, by THOMAS TELFORD. A museum, in a former butchers' shambles, includes a working brass foundry, pewterer's and glass-blower's workshops, and displays on rope-making, basket manufacture and charcoal burning. Bewdley station is the headquarters of the Severn Valley Railway operating from Kidderminster to Bridgnorth, 25 km (16 mi.) N, with a large collection of mostly GWR and LMSR rolling stock.

BIBLIOGRAPHY
Specific
Snell, L. S. ed. *Essays towards a History of Bewdley.* Bewdley: privately published, 1973.

LOCATION
[M] Bewdley Museum, Load Street, Bewdley, Worcestershire, DY12 1BG.

Bex, Vaud, Switzerland   A resort 22 km (14 mi.) S. of Montreux. The saltmine of Le Bouillet and Le Bévieux, the last of five state mines in the Chablais region, is still in working order, and was operated by the canton of Bern from 1554. Over 50 km (30 mi.) of galleries and many underground brine reservoirs were excavated. The mine was modernized by Albrecht von Haller, who was in charge of mines in 1758–64. Mining artefacts are now displayed in the galleries, and the Salinegesellschaft (Saline Society) runs guided tours along the mine railway.

BIBLIOGRAPHY
General
Keller, 1979.

LOCATION
[M] Musée du Sel, Bex/Le Bouillet.

Beyer Garrett   A type of articulated locomotive patented in 1907 by Herbert William Garrett (1864–1913), developed and principally built by Beyer Peacock of MANCHESTER: it had two pivoting sets of frames, cylinders and driving wheels, with a boiler between them and a water tank in front, thus distributing the weight over a long wheelbase. The type was used in Africa, India and South America, with thirty-three built for the LMSR and one for the LNER in England. The largest steam locomotive built in Europe was a 4–8–2+2–8–4 of 1932 for the USSR, which weighed 262.5 tons. A Spanish 4–6–2+2–6–4 built in 1930–1 for high-speed running is preserved. The first Beyer Garrett, a Tasmanian Railways 2 ft. (0.61 m) gauge 0–4–0+0–4–0 of 1910, is preserved at YORK.

BIBLIOGRAPHY
General
Ahrons, 1927; Durrant, 1979; Ransome-Wallis, 1971; Westwood, 1983.

Specific
Hills, R. L. *Beyer Peacock*. Manchester: North-Western Museum of Science and Industry, n.d.

BARRIE TRINDER

Bezancourt, Seine-Maritime, France   It was during the fifteenth century that production techniques for flat 'crown' GLASS were developed in Upper Normandy. The blowers spun the molten glass rapidly at the ends of their irons, using centrifugal force to form the glass into a flat disc. The resulting discs, which at the end of the seventeenth century, were between 1.1 m and 1.2 m (3 ft. 7 in, and 3 ft. 11 in.) in diameter, were sold primarily for windows in Paris. In 1500 there were already ten glassworks in Normandy. By *c.*1700 there were fifteen, and by that time the large, six-crucible furnace illustrated in the article on window glass in DIDEROT's *Encyclopédie* were probably already in use. Most of these works were located in or near the forests of the earldom of Eu in northern Normandy, or near the royal beech woods around Lyons-la-Forêt.

The Landel glassworks at Bezancourt, 40 km (25 mi.) W. of Rouen, was one of four exploiting the Lyons forest in the seventeenth and eighteenth centuries. It was built between 1616 and 1631 in a square clearing at the edge of the forest, and run, in succession, by members of the Bongars, Le Vaillant and Caqueray families, Norman glassmaking dynasties which handed the privilege for making crown glass from one generation to the next. All these forest works disappeared towards the end of the eighteenth century, with the exception of the Landel factory, which continued to produce bottles and hollow glassware up to the end of the nineteenth century.

At the site remains a fine glassmaker's residence built in the mid-eighteenth century, with a detached pigeon house nearby. Several other agricultural outbuildings also survive, along with the main glassmaking hall, probably dating from the seventeenth century but much modified during the nineteenth century, when it was shortened and its timber-framed walls were replaced with brick walls. Inside, the partition separating the furnace from the area for the preparation and storage of raw material is still visible. There are also traces of a small furnace for hollow ware used in the nineteenth century and recognizable from a drawing of 1920.

BIBLIOGRAPHY
General
Levaillant de la Fieffe, 1873.
Specific
Lagabrielle, S. La Verrerie, une industrie haute-normande et son architecture (Glassmaking, an industry of Upper Normandy, and its architecture). In *L'Homme et l'Industrie en Normandie, Bulletin spécial de la Société Historique et Archéologique de l'Orne*. Alençon, 1990.

JEAN-FRANÇOIS BELHOSTE

Białogon, Kielce, Poland   The village of Białogon, now within the southern outskirts of Kielce, in the STAROPOLSKI INDUSTRIAL REGION, contains copper and engineering plants. Copper and lead have been worked there from the seventeenth century. The present plant was built *c.*1820 at the suggestion of STANISŁAW STASZIC on an old site. In 1838 twenty-seven houses for workers were completed. In 1827, with supplies of copper ore running short, the plant was turned to engineering, and a rolling mill and foundry were installed in 1831. Under the control of the Polish Bank, the plant specialized in the production of agricultural machines and industrial plant, and became the largest manufacturing complex within the Congress Kingdom of Poland. It had machine tools by Fox of Derby, now displayed at SIELPIA WIELKA. The plant was further modernized during 1836–8 and began to build steam engines. A school and twenty-two further workers' houses were added to the complex. By 1844 water and steam power at Białogon generated 175 hp, the largest power output of any plant in the Staropolski Industrial Region. The works still operates as Kielecka Fabryka Pomp 'Białogon' (the Kielce Pump Works 'Białogon'), and there is a museum within the plant. The classical planning of the complex can still readily be appreciated, as the industrial buildings are arranged in a square from which radiate five streets.

BIBLIOGRAPHY
General
Krygier, 1958; Pazdur, 1957.

LOCATION
[S] Kielecka Fabryka Pomp 'Białogon' (Kielce Pump Works 'Białogon'), Kielce-Białogon, ul. F. K. Druckiego-Lubeckiego 1.

PIOTR GERBER

bicycle   A two-wheeled vehicle, propelled by foot power applied by means of a crank, and steered by levers pivoting the front wheel. A bicycle with direct drive to a high front wheel became a successful consumer product in England in the 1870s, but was soon eclipsed by the 'safety bicycle', whose chain drive to the rear of two equal wheels permitted more efficient brakes and a saddle height closer to the ground. This bicycle became the subject of an international consumer craze in the 1880s and 90s and encouraged investment in sets of state-of-the-art machine tools for quantity production, stimulating the development of ball bearings and pneumatic tyres, and forming an important link between the tooling developed for the sewing machine and that required for the automobile.

BIBLIOGRAPHY
General
Alderson, 1972; Caunter, 1955; Hounshell, 1984; Whitt and Wilson, 1982; Woodforde, 1970.

LOCATION
[M] The National Cycle Museum, Brayford Wharf North, Lincoln LN1 1YW, England.

TIM PUTNAM

Bielsko-Biała, Katowice, Poland   An industrial town, 60 km (37 mi.) S. of Katowice, centre of the textile region,

81

Figure 11   An industrial landscape on the river at Bilbao; tugs await business in front of the Biscay blast furnaces.
Barrie Trinder

where the clothmakers' guild was established in the seventeenth century. The first power looms in Poland were installed at the Jankowski plant in 1820. The Museum of the Textile Industry is a branch of the regional museum, located in a former woollen mill of the early twentieth century. Exhibits include carding machines, self-acting mules of the late nineteenth century, winding machines and weft-winders. All the machines can still be operated.

LOCATION
[M] Muzeum Włókiennictwa (Museum of the Textile Industry), 43–300 Bielsko-Biała.

Biggar, Strathclyde, Scotland   A small town 40 km (25 mi.) SW of Edinburgh, rich in museums. Biggar Gasworks Museum is a guardianship monument (*see* SCOTLAND), outstation of National Museums of Scotland. The gasworks opened in 1839. The gasholders date from 1858 and 1879, but were subsequently altered. The horizontal retort house dates from 1914. All the plant is preserved *in situ*, with a small collection from other works.

Biggar Museum Trust has re-created at Gladstone Court Museum a series of shops of *c*.1900; and at Greenhill Covenanters' House, representations of seventeenth-century life.

LOCATIONS
[M] Biggar Gasworks Museum, c/o Department of Science, Technology and Working Life, Royal Museum of Scotland, Chambers Street, Edinburgh EH1 1JF.
[M] Gladstone Court Museum, Biggar, Strathclyde ML12 6DT.

[M] Greenhill, Moat Park, Biggar, Strathclyde ML12 6DT.

Bilbao (Bilbo), Vizcaya, Basque Country, Spain   A city nestling in the valley of the River Nervión, the lower section of which, from the city centre to the sea, some 15 km (9 mi.) downstream, is known as the Ría de Bilbao. It is situated amid impressive industrial landscapes.

Bilbao is an ancient fishing and commercial port. Its industrial development began in the 1870s with the extraction of iron ore. At first the ore was shipped to Britain, but blast furnaces, steelworks and shipyards were established in Bilbao itself, which by 1900 was the principal steelmaking and engineering centre in Spain. The river, partially canalized, is lined with bonded warehouses, sail and rope works, nitrate plants, flourmills with concrete grain silos, and, most notably, the Altos Hornos de Vizcaya (the Biscayan blast furnaces), 8 km (5 mi.) downstream from the centre, which remain a major steelmaking complex, the two current blast furnaces dating from the 1940s. The great Euskalduna shipyards are inactive, although they are still lined with cranes. Some tippler towers remain on wharves where iron ore brought by industrial railways to the riverside was transferred into the holds of ships.

The Ria de Bilbao is crossed by a variety of bridges, notable amongst them the Puente de Deusto of 1936, a double-leaf bascule bridge modelled on a Chicago proto-type, and the first of all TRANSPORTER BRIDGES, linking Getxo and Portugalete, constructed in 1890–3 by the Vizcayan engineer Alberto Palacio Elisagüe (1856–1931).

Bilbao has two contrasting railway stations. The Norte station is a six-platform terminus for broad-gauge trains, its train shed a lightweight steel structure with glass walls, a structure of great purity, with a stained-glass mural at one end; a 4–4–0T steam locomotive, *Izarra*, built in 1863 by Beyer Peacock of Manchester, is displayed in a siding in the station throat. Concordia station, the terminus of the metre-gauge line to Santander, is situated on a viaduct with a ticket hall below, in which fourteen square columns, each composed of four cruciform-section cast-iron uprights, support the platforms above. The exterior is a seven-bay glazed arcade between Baroque-style stone pavilions, the central bay of the arcade being surmounted with a wide semicircular arch, and the whole decorated with tiles and ornamental ironwork in vivid greens and yellows. It was completed in 1910 to the design of Severino Achucarro. Two metre-gauge suburban passenger lines operate on the north bank of the river, supplemented by the Funicular de Artxander.

The Elorrieta pumping station at Deusto-Bilbao dates from 1898, and was used to pump waste water from the city to the open sea. The steam engine and pumps, which remain *in situ*, were supplied by English firms, under the direction of the London engineers James Simpson & Co. To the south of the pumping station are long ranges of six-storey apartment blocks with overhanging eaves, built in the early period of the Franco dictatorship, and laid out on a monotonous grid plan.

The best-preserved monument of pre-industrial iron manufactures in Vizcaya is the forge at Pobal, 16 km (10 mi.) NW of Bilbao. There were once some 150 such works in the province, each traditionally grouped with a corn mill, a bridge, a church and a castle. Agricultural tools were forged at Pobal well into the twentieth century. The water wheel, the forge hammer and the weir, leats and reservoir tanks of the water-power system remain. Near the forge is the ancestral home of the La Guadra family, proprietors of the ironworks, and an eighteenth-century bridge which gave access to small-scale iron-ore mines.

At Balmaseda, 24 km (15 mi.) SW of Bilbao, 'boinas', the traditional berets worn by Basque men, are still manufactured in the industrial colony of La Encartada. The machines in the main fifteen-bay, three-storey building of 1892 are powered through line shafting, by Voith water turbines of 1910. Machinery supplied by Platt Brothers of Oldham, England, in 1892 remains in use, and teasles are still used in finishing processes, although seven Jacquard looms no longer operate.

At Bermeo, a fishing port 24 km (15 mi.) NE of Bilbao, townspeople are responsible for a notable museum portraying the history of the fishing industry.

La Arboleda, a late-nineteenth-century iron-ore mining village 12 km ($7\frac{1}{2}$ mi.) W. of Bilbao, stands at the centre of one of the most evocative industrial landscapes in Europe. The settlement is approached from the banks of the Rio Bilbao either by a sinuous mountain road which passes the water-filled remnant of a huge opencast working, or by a 3 km (2 mi.) funicular dating from 1921. The main part of the village consists of parallel ranks of alternating two- and three-storey houses, stretching up the hillside

from the square which contains the church of 1889, the Casa del Pueblo (People's House) and the Cooperativa Obrera (Co-operative Society). On the fringe of the settlement is a hospital, now closed, and an untidy skirt of rough, squatter-like huts. The landscape all around has been contorted by iron-ore workings. La Arboleda was the birthplace of the Spanish Communist Party, and the bar where La Passionara (Dolores Ibarruri, 1895–1988) discussed Marxism with miners still serves peppery sausages and dispenses soup from brown enamelled pots on a tiled range. Iron-ore mining has ceased, and the area has been declared a conservation area. Calcining kilns for iron ore, of several types, survive in the surrounding mining areas.

See also figure 9.

BIBLIOGRAPHY
General
Basas, 1967, 1978; Bilbao, 1984; Fullaondo, 1969, 1971; Gómez *et al.*, 1980, Gonzalez Portilla, 1981 1985, Guiard, 1917; Marti *et al.*, 1982; Silvan, 1982.

LOCATIONS
[M] Fishermen's Museum, Torrontero Emparantza, Bermeo.
[M] Vizcaya Historical Museum, Call Cruz 4, Bilbao.

MAITE IBAÑEZ, ALBERTO SANTANA and MARTA ZABALA

Billnäs, Uudenmaan lääni, Finland   In 1641 Carl Billsten founded an ironworks at Billnäs, 72 km (45 mi.) W. of Helsinki in the municipality of Pohja, and built a blast furnace and two bar-iron forges there. The works was extensively rebuilt in the late eighteenth century and became a limited company in 1898. In addition to its iron, Billnäs has also become well known for its wood products, manufacture of which started in the late nineteenth century.

The ironworks buildings on the banks of the Mustiojoki river range in date from the eighteenth century to the twentieth century, and representative workers' dwellings survive from throughout that period. A high proportion of the buildings postdate a fire of 1775. On the site of the former ironworks mansion is the château-style Villa Billnäs of 1919, designed by Lars Sonck.

Of the production buildings on the river bank, a stone-built mill of 1770 and a stone bar-iron warehouse of 1778 have survived. The power station and dam date from the 1920s. The newest production buildings are on the south bank of the river. The oldest part of the brickworks dates from the eighteenth century, although it has been enlarged many times. The carpenters' workshop dates from 1896; the so-called Ylä-Nikkari, or upper joiners' workshop, from 1918; and the brick kiln from 1901. The reinforced concrete repair shop was built in 1915–16. As at FISKARS, 8 km (5 mi.) NW, restoration with government funding has progressed since a decision was taken in 1984 to preserve the site.

BIBLIOGRAPHY
General
Ryser and Rautsi, 1986.

LAURI PUTKONEN

Billund, Jutland, Denmark A small town in Jutland, 52 km (32 mi.) NE of Esbjerg, almost entirely dependent on the Lego plastic toy factory founded in 1937 by O. Kirk Christiansen. Not surprisingly a museum of toys forms part of the company's Legoland park. Near Billund airport an ambitious museum project includes the national museum of aviation and a motorcar museum.

LOCATION
[S] Legoland, Billund.

Birkeland and Eyde process A process for the synthesis of nitric acid (HNO_3) which requires large quantities of electricity. Demonstrated in the 1890s, it was used in Norway from 1902 (*see* RJUKAN) but has since been superseded. Air was drawn through a flat circular furnace in which an electric arc raised the temperature to 3000 °C, at which some nitrogen (N) combined with oxygen (O_2) to form nitric oxide (NO). The gas was rapidly cooled and treated with steam, the formation of nitrogen dioxide (NO_2) beginning as the mixture reached 600 °C, and then passed through oxidizing and sorption towers in which nitric acid was formed, together with nitrous acid (HNO_2):

$$2NO_2 + H_2O \rightarrow HNO_2 + HNO_3$$

The acid was usually neutralized with limestone to form calcium nitrate ($Ca(NO_3)_2$), the fertilizer Norge Saltpetre; with some sodium nitrite ($NaNO_2$), used in the manufacture of synthetic dyestuffs, being produced from the most dilute gases.

BIBLIOGRAPHY
General
Morgan and Pratt, 1938; Partington, 1950.

Birmingham, West Midlands, England Birmingham, traditionally England's 'second city', has for two hundred years been the principal market centre of the English Midlands, the nodal point of the region's communications, and, as a result of its proximity to the BLACK COUNTRY, a major metalworking and engineering centre.

Water power was abundant in the Birmingham region, and in the eighteenth century there were more than fifty mills in the present area of the city. The Lloyd family, founders of Lloyds Bank, operated the Town Mill as a slitting mill in the early eighteenth century. Sarehole Mill, a corn mill of the 1760s and once used by Matthew Boulton for metal-grinding, is preserved by the museums service. Birmingham grew to prominence in the late eighteenth century when Matthew Boulton, JAMES WATT, JOHN ROEBUCK and Samuel Galton were all working there, and when the Lunar Society formed an intellectual focus for manufacturers and scientists. Boulton's twenty-one-bay Soho Manufactory of 1762, where six hundred were employed making metal 'toys', was demolished in 1862–3, but the Soho Foundry, opened by BOULTON & WATT for the manufacture of steam engines in 1796, remains in industrial use. There are memorials to Boulton, by John Flaxman (1755–1826), and to Watt and WILLIAM MURDOCK, by Sir Francis Chantrey (1781–1841), in St Mary's Church, Handsworth. Birmingham grew rapidly in the

nineteenth century, although its industries were organized on a workshop rather than a factory basis. It incorporated Handsworth, Aston and other parishes from neighbouring counties. The city was rebuilt on a vast scale after 1945, with ring roads and tower blocks.

The best evocation of Birmingham's traditional industries is in the Jewellery Quarter around St Paul's Church, north-west of the centre, where sensitive conservation policies have preserved much of the atmosphere of this region of workshops. The nearby Great Hampton Street Works, of three storeys with eight bays in the Gothic style, typifies the larger-scale factories of the nineteenth century.

The Birmingham Canal, which linked the city with the coalfield to the North-West, opened in 1768 and by 1790 Birmingham was at the crossroads of the English narrow-canal system. An extensive network survives, much of it hidden from view in the heart of the city. A walkway past Farmer's Bridge locks was opened in 1969. Birmingham remains the centre of British Rail's Inner-City passenger network, but the present New Street station dates from the 1960s. PHILIP HARDWICK's Curzon Street station of 1838, the terminus of the London & Birmingham Railway, has been adapted to office use; it stands in an area rich in railway history, where the most impressive monument is the Duddeston Viaduct, built in the 1840s to link two lines approaching the city, but never actually used. The Birmingham Railway Museum at Tyseley is a base for the restoration of steam locomotives.

Birmingham's civic identity was expressed in a series of ambitious projects in the nineteenth century. The Corinthian Town Hall of 1834 is by JOSEPH HANSOM; the spectacular Law Courts of 1887–91, with a fiery red-brick exterior and a sumptuous maze of sandy terracotta within, are by Sir Aston Webb (1849–1930) and Ingress Bell. Corporation Street was driven through a slum area at the instigation of Joseph Chamberlain (1836–1907) from 1878. The Birmingham Proof House for testing gun barrels is a Classical building of 1813 by John Horton. In the early twentieth-century Birmingham was notable for the architectural style of its public houses. The Barton Arms at 152 High Street, of 1899–1901, and the Black Horse in Bristol Road South, of 1929, are outstanding examples.

Birmingham's most significant suburb is Bournville, 6 km (4 mi.) south-west of the centre, where in 1879 the Quakers Richard and George Cadbury (1839–1922) relocated their city-centre cocoa factory in a totally rural setting. In 1894 George Cadbury acquired 120 acres for the development of a new suburb, not exclusively for his own workpeople, and the following year engaged W. Alexander Harvey as architect. Bournville is notable for its low-density housing, the sinuous curves of its roads, and its communal buildings, including two medieval timber-framed buildings moved from elsewhere. In 1900 the Bournville Village Trust was established, and has exercised a powerful influence over suburban development in the south-west quarter of the city.

Birmingham's characteristic working-class houses before the 1870s were back-to-backs, lining court developments, hidden behind long terraces fronting the main streets of areas like Duddeston and Nechells. All houses of this type have been demolished. From the 1850s FREEHOLD LAND SOCIETIES, which originated in Birmingham under the influence of James Taylor, brought more varied suburban landscapes. In the 1920s and 30s more than 100 000 houses were built in the city, slightly less than half of them by the city council. Kingstanding, 8 km (5 mi.) NW of the centre, gained a population of 30 000 by 1930, and its Odeon cinema of 1935 by Harry Weedon remains its spectacular centrepiece.

Important twentieth-century industrial plants include the IMI Kynoch explosives works at Witton, dating from the 1860s but with a fine office block of 1904; the GEC 100 ha (240 ac.) site at Witton, with an administrative block of 1922 by Wallis, Gilbert and Partners; Fort Dunlop at Erdington; and the Austin motor works at Longbridge, established in 1905 in an old printing works.

Birmingham Airport at Elmdon, 10 km (6 mi.) E., includes a 'streamlined' passenger terminal of 1939, now superseded.

The Birmingham Museum of Science and Industry, established in 1950 in an ex-electroplating factory above the Birmingham & Fazeley Canal, illustrates most aspects of the city's industries. Exhibits include the Boulton & Watt Smethwick engine of 1779, the Stanier 4–6–2 locomotive *City of Birmingham*, large collections of bicycles and motorcars, Watt copiers, and an Owens automatic bottle-making machine of c.1928.

BIBLIOGRAPHY
General
Allen, 1919; Briggs, 1963; Briggs and Gill, 1952; British Association, 1950; Broadbridge, 1974; Brook, 1977; Court, 1938; Gale, 1952; Lloyd, 1975; Pevsner and Wedgewood, 1966; Sutcliffe and Smith, 1974; Timmins, 1866; Victoria History, 1964.

Specific
Chapman, S. D. and Bartlett, J. N. The contribution of building clubs and freehold land societies to working-class housing in Birmingham. In Chapman, 1971.
Crawford, A., Dunn, M. and Thorne, R. *Birmingham Pubs, 1880–1939*. Alan Sutton, 1986.
Sutcliffe, A. The 'Midland Metropolis': Birmingham 1890–1980. In Gordon, 1986.

LOCATIONS
[M] Birmingham Museum and Art Gallery, Chamberlain Square, Birmingham B3 3DH.
[M] Birmingham Museum of Science and Industry, Newhall Street, Birmingham B3 1RZ.
[M] Birmingham Railway Museum, Warwick Road, Tyseley, Birmingham B11 2HL.
[S] Sarehole Mill, Cole Bank Road, Moseley, Birmingham B13 0BD.

BARRIE TRINDER and MICHAEL STRATTON

biscuit A hard-baked crisp dry bread, whose basic materials are flour, water or milk, and often sugar, usually baked into thin, flat cakes, and cut into rectangles or circles. Biscuits were traditionally an item of naval diet and as such were one of the first foods to be produced on an industrial scale. Biscuit mixtures were being prepared by mixing machines and baked on conveyor belts at the Victualling Yard, Deptford, London, by the 1830s.

The development of factory production of biscuits for civilian use began in the second quarter of the nineteenth century, with the rise of companies like Carrs of Carlisle, who produced light-textured biscuits using a patent aerating machine, and that of Joseph Huntley (?1806–95) and George Palmer (1818–97) who established a factory at Reading in 1841, and were the largest manufacturers of biscuits in Britain by 1860, due to astute marketing, the distribution of free samples to first-class rail travellers, and the ingenious use of decorated tins (*see* CANNING). By 1900 more than 360 types were being marketed nationally in Britain, and there was a strong Christmas trade in decorated tins. Comprehensive collections of biscuit tins are held in museums at Gloucester and Reading.

Airtight packets, with distinctive brand names, were introduced in the USA from 1899, the first brand to be so promoted being Uneeda biscuits, which remain in production.

See also figure 94.

BIBLIOGRAPHY
General
Book of Trades, 1839; Giedion, 1948; Hudson, 1980; Winstanley, 1983.

LOCATIONS
[M] Reading Museum and Art Gallery, Blagrave Street, Reading, Berkshire, England.
[M] The Robert Opie Collection, Museum of Advertising and Packaging, Albert Warehouse, Gloucester Docks, Gloucester, England.

BARRIE TRINDER

bismuth (Bi) An elemental metal with a low melting point, used to make alloys for use as fusible plugs in sprinkler systems and boilers, or as solders. Compounds of bismuth are employed in medicinal preparations. Bismuth is often a by-product of copper and lead smelting; its chief sources are South and Central America, Canada and Yugoslavia.

BIBLIOGRAPHY
General
Jones, 1950

Bitola (Monastir), Macedonia, Yugoslavia The second city of Macedonia, on the edge of the Pelagonian plain, was ruled by the Turks during 1382–1912. The old town has largely been destroyed.

Many pre-industrial technologies can be observed in the vicinity. At Wirowo (Vivrov), 25 km (15 mi.) NW, the clear, soft water of the Topolka stream is ideal for felting the woollen carpets woven in the village, and about a hundred 'wir' (swirls) survive there. In a swirl water falls from a considerable height onto the carpet for between eight and ten hours, causing certain threads to swell, giving the due fluffiness and density to the cloth. The appliance consists of a wooden runner, or 'buka', made from a halved trunk of pine or spruce, and a funnel-shaped container or 'wir', made of oak staves with gaps in between. The water passes along a slanting runner, 6–8 m (18–24 ft.) long, into the 'wir', making the carpet rotate. The water then flows between the staves into the stream running beneath. A worker standing on a wooden

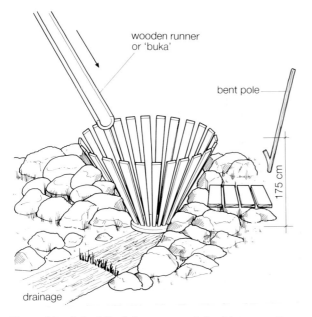

Figure 12 A 'swirl' of the type used for felting woollen carpets at Wirowo, near Bitola (from a sketch by Piotr Gerber)

platform supplies or removes carpets to be processed by means of a bent pole or 'kukaczka'. The device can be stopped by a wooden peg fixed into the runner. The process still flourishes since export demand for carpets has grown. The spinning and weaving processes were mechanized long ago, but the method of felting has remained traditional. Other features of Wirowo include a corn mill driven by a horizontal water wheel, a distillery, dyeing vats, a water-powered sawmill adapted from a corn mill, and a fulling mill driven by a vertical water wheel, with beater bars descending onto a willow trunk on which the cloth is supported on oak or beech planks.

At Bukow (Bukovo), 5 km (3 mi.) S., is a corn mill with two sets of stones, driven by horizontal paddle wheels. The original wooden runners have been replaced by halved oil drums, and the stones rotate at 125 rev./min. The mill is used to grind barley for pig fodder and to powder dried paprika.

LOCATION
[M] Municipal Museum, Trg Mali Ploštad, 97000-Bitola.

PIOTR GERBER

bitumen   A black or dark brown, solid or semi-solid

organic material, a mixture of hydrocarbons, which gradually liquefies when heated. Bitumen sometimes occurs naturally (*see* IRONBRIDGE), but is more commonly obtained as a residue during the distillation of petroleum (*see* OIL REFINERY). Uses include the insulation of cables, road surfaces, and roofing.

See also ASPHALT; TAR.

BIBLIOGRAPHY
General
BP, 1958; van der Have and Verver, 1957.

Black Country, West Midlands, England   The name given to the coalfield of South Staffordshire and North Worcestershire, between Birmingham and Wolverhampton, notable for its 10 yd. (9 m) deep seam of coal. By 1700 many smiths making locks, chains, nails and so on had settled on open heathlands and were using iron imported through BEWDLEY and local coal. Mushroom Green, Brierley Hill, is a conservation area where a chain shop, squatter cottages, and other features of the Black Country landscape are preserved.

From the late eighteenth century many blast furnaces were constructed, and in the nineteenth century the Black Country was a leading iron-producing region. No significant remains of blast furnaces survive.

From the opening of the Birmingham Canal in 1768 a dense network of canals developed, which was extended even after the opening of the railways. Much of it remains open to pleasure traffic. The principal monuments are the flight of eight locks linking the Dudley and Stourbridge Canals at Delph; the 2768 m (3027 yd.) Netherton Tunnel of 1858; and Telford's Smethwick Cutting of the 1820s, crossed by his 48 m (150 ft.) cast-iron Galton Bridge. The Smethwick pumping engine, supplied by BOULTON & WATT in 1779, is preserved in BIRMINGHAM. Its site has been excavated and forms part of a heritage trail in the Galton Valley. Numerous iron bridges, many by the Horseley ironworks of Tipton, carry towpaths across junctions.

The glass industry, established around Stourbridge in the seventeenth century, still flourishes. Several works are open to the public and products are displayed in various museums. A 26.5 m (87 ft.) high English glass cone of the late eighteenth century is preserved at the Red House works, Wordsley. The Stourbridge foundry building where the locomotives *Stourbridge Lion* (*see* WASHINGTON) and *Agenoria* (*see* YORK) were built remains in use.

The ornate office block of the Bean car factory (1919–29) survives in Hall Street, Dudley. Early motor works in Wolverhampton include those of Clyno at Pelham Street (1910–26) and Showell Road (1927–9), and of Sunbeam in Upper Villiers Street (1908–25).

The open-air collection of the Black Country Museum includes a Methodist chapel, a rolling mill, and a replica of the first Newcomen engine of 1712. The museum, established in 1966, is supported by local authorities. It is the starting point of boat trips through the 2900 m (3171 yd.) Dudley Tunnel and associated limestone caverns. Local specialisms are illustrated in the Willenhall Lock

Figure 13   The Russell Hall blast furnaces near Dudley in the heart of the Black Country, photographed in 1859; this very early photograph of an industrial subject is one of a collection taken by a Mr Mills and now in the custody of the National Buildings Record
National Buildings Record: Royal Commission on the Historical Monuments of England

Museum, the Bilston Museum, which has enamelled items made in the town from the mid-eighteenth century, and the Walsall Museum, which has collections relating to the leather industry.

BIBLIOGRAPHY
General
Allen, 1919; British Association, 1950; Broadbridge, 1974; Brook, 1977; Collins and Stratton, 1986; Court, 1938; Gale, 1979; Griffiths, 1872; Milward and Robinson, 1971; Raybould, 1973; Rowlands, 1975.
Specific
Andrew, J. H. The Smethwick engine. In *IAR*, VIII, 1985.
Benson, J. and Neville, R. G. A bibliography of the West Midlands coal industry. In *West Midlands Studies*, x, Wolverhampton: Wolverhampton Polytechnic, 1977.
Raybould, T. J. and Smith, W. A. A bibliography of the South Staffordshire iron industry. In *WMS*, XII, 1979.
Traves, R. A museum for the Black Country. In *WMS*, v, 1972.

LOCATIONS
[M] Bilston Museum and Art Gallery, Mount Pleasant, Bilston, Wolverhampton WV14 7LU.
[M] The Black Country Museum, Tipton Road, Dudley, West Midlands DY1 4SQ.
[M] Broadfield House Glass Museum, Compton Drive, Kingswinford, Brierley Hill, West Midlands DY6 9NS.
[M] The Lock Museum, Willenhall Library, Walsall Street, Willenhall, West Midlands.
[S] Stuart Crystal, Red House Glassworks, Wordsley, Stourbridge, West Midlands DY8 4AA.
[M] Walsall Museum and Art Gallery, Lichfield Street, Walsall WS1 1TR.

BARRIE TRINDER

black powder   *See* GUNPOWDER.

blacksmith   A smith who forges useful or decorative articles from WROUGHT IRON or mild STEEL. Blacksmiths have been employed to produce small forgings or to make or maintain tools in engineering works, mines and other industrial concerns, but the term is most commonly applied to an independent tradesman, of a type found in almost every community in Europe by the mid-seventeenth century, making and repairing farm tools, and shoeing horses. The trade of an independent blacksmith might overlap or develop into that of a more specialized craftsman like a nailer or chainmaker. A blacksmith specializing in shoeing horses was called a farrier. The characteristic equipment of a blacksmith consisted of a HEARTH, an anvil and block, a vice, hammers, tongs, files, punches and pincers.

See also WHITESMITH.

BIBLIOGRAPHY
General
Tunis, 1965; Webber, 1971.

Blaenau Ffestiniog, Gwynedd, Wales   An important centre in North Wales of slate production, 32 km (20 mi.) SW of Bangor. Unlike DINORWIC and other parts of SNOWDONIA, where veins followed the mountainous terrain, slate here passed under the mountainsides, and was therefore extracted through mines (called 'quarries' locally) from the 1840s. The products were exported on the FESTINIOG RAILWAY. A settlement grew up nearby from the early nineteenth century: the houses, chapels, pavements and fences are all of slate. Waste-heaps on hillsides were interspersed with workshops, tramroad inclines and aerial ropeways. Lewis and Denton (1974) made an outstanding study of the remains at the Rhosydd 'quarry'. The mines are accessible at Gloddfa Ganol and Llechwedd. Llechwedd has several large caverns, one 62 m (200 ft.) high, and an inclined railway to the deep levels. Both mines demonstrate the splitting of slates from blocks.

BIBLIOGRAPHY
General
Lindsay, 1974.
Specific
Lewis, M. J. T. and Denton, J. H. *Rhosydd Slate Quarry.* Shrewsbury: The Cottage Press, 1974.

LOCATIONS
[M,S] Llechwedd Slate Caverns, Blaenau Ffestiniog, Gwynedd LL41 3NB.
[M,S] Gloddfa Ganol Mountain Centre, Blaenau Ffestiniog, Gwynedd.

Blaenavon (Blaenafon), Gwent, Wales   A town in the South Wales coalfield, 33 km (21 mi.) NW of Cardiff, with an ironworks conserved by the state, and a coal mine conserved by a charitable trust. The ironworks was established by English ironmasters in 1788; by 1815 it had become the largest in Wales outside Merthyr Tydfil. There was little redevelopment after the associated Forgeside iron and steel works was established in the 1840s, and there are substantial remains, of five furnaces, casting houses, a water-balance lift to the furnace-bank, and tramroads to canals, mines, quarries, and a forge. There is some company housing. Scars remain on hillsides from the process of scouring for ironstone. At Big Pit visitors can see underground stables and workshops, coal-cutting and haulage machinery, and workings from the 1840s for ironstone and coal. The pithead is much as it was when production ended in 1980, with the winder, lamp room, pithead baths, smithies, railway sidings and fan house all intact.

BIBLIOGRAPHY
General
Lowe, 1977; Rees, 1969.
Specific
Atkinson, M. *Blaenafon Ironworks: a guide to its history and technology.* Torfaen, Gwent: Torfaen Museum Trust, 1983.
Rattenbury, G. *Tramroads of the Brecknock & Abergavenny Canal.* Oakham: Railway and Canal Historical Society, 1980.

LOCATIONS
[M, S] Big Pit Mining Museum, Blaenafon, Gwent NP4 9XP.
[M, S] Blaenafon Ironworks Museum, Blaenafon, Gwent.

blanket   A length of soft, woollen cloth, loosely woven to retain heat, used as a bed covering. The word has been used since the fourteenth century, the verb deriving from the noun. The traditional centre of production in England by 1700 was Witney, 18 km (12 mi.) NW of Oxford, where power-loom weaving began in the 1860s; but an increasing proportion of the growing national output in the nineteenth century came from the West Riding of Yorkshire. The main centre in the USA is Elkin, N.C., where blanket manufacture was revolutionized in the 1950s by the fibre-weaving process that dispenses with spinning. Elsewhere in the USA production of traditional woven woollen, cotton and synthetic fibre blankets continues.

BIBLIOGRAPHY
General
Plummer and Early, 1969.

Blansko, Central Moravia, Czechoslovakia   The centre of a large ironworking region. The local ironworks were taken over in 1811 by Count Hugo Francis Salm, who built a plant for making charcoal and recovering by-products from the wood, and installed a CUPOLA, although it was initially unsuccessful. The colonnade at MARIÁNSKÉ LÁZNĚ was cast here in 1889. The regional museum has displays on the early history of metallurgy.

BIBLIOGRAPHY
General
Jeníček, 1963.

LOCATION
[M] Regional Museum, Zamek, Blansko.

blast furnace   A shaft furnace, mechanically blown with one or more TUYÈRES, in which iron ore is smelted with a fuel and usually with a flux in a semi-continuous process to produce CAST IRON, usually referred to at this stage as PIG IRON. In some countries the oldest blast furnaces were built of stone and clay and were timber-clad. Later they were built entirely of stone or bricks, and from the mid-nineteenth century they could be constructed of wrought iron or steel plates, lined with REFRACTORIES and mechanically blown.

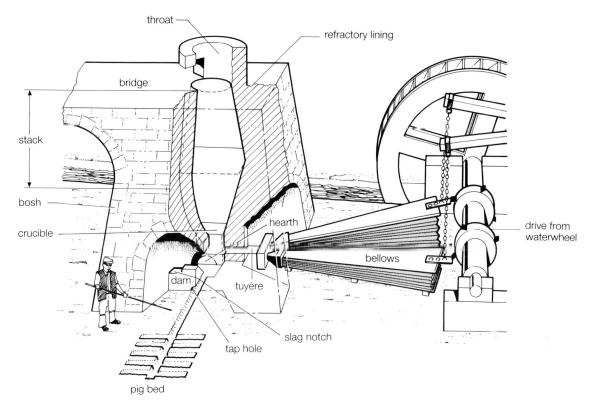

Figure 14 The parts of a characteristic British masonry stack blast furnace of the eighteenth century

Excavations in Sweden and Germany have suggested that the blast furnace was in use in some parts of Europe as early as the thirteenth century. There were blast furnaces in Italy in the fifteenth century, and from there the process spread to Carinthia. It passed from the Liège region through northern France to southern England in the late fifteenth century.

Many early blast furnaces were built into banks to obviate the need for raising materials, but since the nineteenth century, as the size of furnaces has increased, hoists and lifts have been constructed. Iron ore was often calcined (*see* CALCINING KILN) within a furnace complex, and when dependence on water power made operation seasonal, ore and charcoal (*see* CHARCOAL BARN) were often stored on the site.

Charcoal was the universal fuel of early blast furnaces, but from the early seventeenth century proposals were made for the use of coal, although none was successful until Abraham Darby I (1678–1717) (*see* IRONBRIDGE) smelted iron with coke at Coalbrookdale, England, in 1709. It was not until the 1750s that the use of coke in blast furnaces became common in Britain, but thereafter the practice quickly spread to other countries. The use of charcoal continued through the nineteenth century in Sweden, Russia and the USA, and the last Swedish charcoal-using furnace was only blown out in the 1960s. Even in coal-rich Britain the furnace at Backbarrow (*see*

LAKE DISTRICT) used charcoal until the 1920s. So much coke came to be used at blast furnaces that by the late nineteenth century it was commonplace for COKE OVENS to form parts of furnace complexes. In some regions, like North Staffordshire, England, it became common practice to use raw coal, particularly ANTHRACITE, instead of coke.

In the early eighteenth century a blast furnace might produce twenty tonnes of iron a week, but in many regions uncertain water supplies restricted operations to six or nine months of each year, sometimes even less. From the 1740s (*see* IRONBRIDGE) the period of operation was lengthened by using steam engines to recirculate the water powering the water wheels operating the bellows, and from the 1770s (*see* WILKINSON, JOHN) blowing machines were worked by steam engines, enabling continuous operation. Beam engines were used to blow furnaces until the mid-nineteenth century when engines with horizontal and vertical configurations were employed. Air was provided from conventional wooden and leather bellows until *c.*1760 when blowing machines with iron cylinders were introduced in England. From the late nineteenth century turbo-blowers were used. Air was conveyed into the furnace through tuyères. J. B. Neilson (1792–1865) patented proposals in 1828 for HOT BLAST which greatly increased the efficiency of furnaces, and by the third quarter of the nineteenth century most furnaces were closed in at the top, whether they employed hot blast

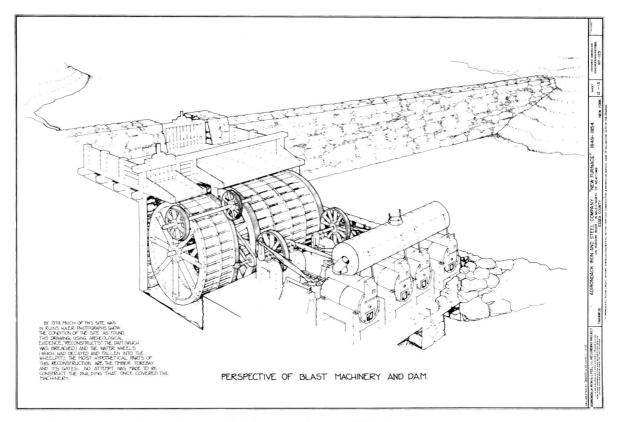

Within the drawing:

BY 1978, MUCH OF THIS SITE WAS
IN RUINS. H.A.E.R. PHOTOGRAPHS SHOW
THE CONDITION OF THE SITE AS FOUND.
THIS DRAWING, USING ARCHEOLOGICAL
EVIDENCE, "RECONSTRUCTS" THE DAM (WHICH
WAS BREACHED) AND THE WATER WHEELS
(WHICH HAD DECAYED AND FALLEN INTO THE
WHEELPIT). THE MOST HYPOTHETICAL PARTS OF
THIS RECONSTRUCTION ARE THE TIMBER FOREBAY
AND ITS GATES. NO ATTEMPT WAS MADE TO RE-
CONSTRUCT THE BUILDING THAT ONCE COVERED THE
MACHINERY.

PERSPECTIVE OF BLAST MACHINERY AND DAM

ADIRONDACK IRON AND STEEL COMPANY, "NEW FURNACE" ON HUDSON RIVER, 14 MILES NORTH OF NEWCOMB, ESSEX COUNTY   1849-1854

Figure 15   A perspective drawing by HAER of the blowing machinery and blast furnace of 1855 and the dam at the Adirondack Iron & Steel Co.'s plant near Blue Mountain Lake, New York

Historic American Engineering Record, National Park Service, Barry A. Richards, 1978

or not, thus enabling the recovery of furnace gases. In the eighteenth century furnaces were built with both square and circular plans, but from the mid-nineteenth century the latter became universal. New furnaces were built of wrought iron or steel plates lined with refractories. Furnace installations became highly complex concerns, often integrated with FORGES and steelworks (*see* STEEL), and with many facilities for utilizing by-products. From the early twentieth century ore was prepared by SINTER-ING. By the 1860s a blast furnace might produce up to 150 tonnes of iron a week. During the twentieth century output has increased dramatically, and a furnace like that at Redcar, England, is capable of an output of 10 000 tonnes a day. Scrap is now an important constituent of the charge of many furnaces.

The survival rate of blast furnaces is uneven. There are few upstanding remains of furnaces dating from before 1650, although some have been excavated (*see* WEALD). Relatively large numbers of furnaces dating from between 1650 and 1850 survive in Austria, Britain, France, Italy, Germany, Sweden and the USA, and have been listed by Crossley (1980, 1984); the remains usually include stacks and water-power systems, and sometimes charcoal barns. There remain some early twentieth-century charcoal

blast furnaces in Sweden, at AVESTA, Iggesund, Moviken and elsewhere, but survivals of large, coke-using furnaces are rare. Most working furnaces have been built since the 1950s and the majority of earlier installations have been destroyed. The Sloss Furnaces (*see* ALABAMA) and those at VÖLKLINGEN and in the RUHRGEBIET will probably be the only blast furnaces of the first half of the twentieth century to be preserved.

Blast furnaces have also been used for the smelting of non-ferrous metals but have never been the sole means of smelting the metals concerned (*see* COPPER; LEAD; ZINC).

See also BERGAMASQUE FURNACE and figures 3, 13, 23, 44, 48, 118, 136, 137, 170.

BIBLIOGRAPHY
General
Beck, 1891, 1893–5; Belhoste *et al.*, 1984; Bohm, 1972; Cleere and Crossley, 1985; Crossley, 1980, 1984; Daumas, 1962–8; Gale, 1967, 1969; Hyde, 1977; Lewis, 1976; Odelstierna, 1913; Percy, 1864; Riden, 1978, 1987; Schubert, 1957; Slotta, 1975; Sperl, 1985; Trinder, 1981; Woronoff, 1984.
Specific
Magnusson, G. The medieval blast furnace at Lapphyttan. In *ICCROM*, 1985.

MARIE NISSER and BARRIE TRINDER

bleaching The whitening of cotton and linen yarn and cloth (*see* TEXTILES) by the action of sunlight and air, usually by laying out materials on frames in an open space called a bleaching green, or by the use of chemicals, particularly chemicals like BLEACHING POWDER which contain CHLORINE. A bleach works might be a component of an integrated textile complex or a separate plant, which was usually concerned with more processes than simply bleaching. Cloths would be marked with the names of manufacturers; pieces would then be joined to go through machines, they would be cleared of odd ends of fibres by passing them over hot plates or jets of gas, and after the actual bleaching process would be mangled, dried and CALENDERED. A typical bleach works, located on a valley floor as it consumed large quantities of water, consisted of a mass of small structures around more substantial buildings where the main processes were concentrated. A steam engine might be employed to drive calenders and mangles.

bleaching powder An easily transportable substance containing available chlorine, used in bleaching. It was patented in 1800 by Charles Tennant (1768–1838) who established St Rollox Works, Glasgow. Bleaching powder was produced by the action of chlorine on hydrated lime, and was originally regarded as 'hypochlorite of lime' $(Ca(OCl)_2)$ although research now suggests a more complex formula. It was first manufactured by spreading slaked lime on the floors of large lead chambers, to which chlorine gas was admitted from above. Shovelling the powder into barrels was one of the least healthy industrial occupations. A mechanical means of manufacture – a concrete tower in which lime moves down through compartments swept by horizontal rotating rakes, as streams of chlorine gas flow upwards – was perfected in Switzerland during World War I.

BIBLIOGRAPHY
General
Morgan and Pratt, 1938; Partington, 1950.

blind-back house A house or TERRACE with windows and doors on one side only, often built facing inwards onto a BURGAGE PLOT, or sometimes on a steep slope, with no apertures on the uphill side.
See also BACK-TO-BACK HOUSE.

BIBLIOGRAPHY
General
Beresford, 1988; Lowe, 1977.

blister steel A form of CARBON STEEL made in a CEMENTATION FURNACE.

bloater A smoked herring, the term being used from the early seventeenth century. Bloaters are salted for up to 18 hours, and smoked for about 24 hours. Kippers – a term first applied to smoked salmon and not generally used for smoked herring until the late nineteenth century – are

usually treated for rather longer. Different woods, principally oak and ash, are used to provide distinctive flavours.

block A wooden pulley used in the rigging of sailing ships. Blocks were required in increasing numbers as the size of ships increased in the eighteenth century, and from the 1750s the Taylor family at Southampton, England, were using machines in their manufacture. In 1802–6 Sir Marc Brunel (1769–1849) installed forty-five machines built by HENRY MAUDSLAY at Portsmouth Dockyard; by 1808 these were making 130 000 blocks per annum, being operated by 10 machinists who had replaced 110 skilled blockmakers, a development regarded as one of the first applications of mechanized MASS PRODUCTION techniques. Examples of Maudslay's machines are preserved in the Science Museum, LONDON, and at PORTSMOUTH.

BIBLIOGRAPHY
General
Gilbert, 1965; Hudson, 1965.

bloomery A charcoal-fired furnace used for the direct reduction of iron ore to produce wrought iron or steel. The English language does not distinguish between the tiny furnaces used in prehistoric times and more recently in the Third World, and the substantial, water-powered furnaces (*see* STÜCKOFEN). The last bloomery in Britain probably ceased operation in 1720, but the process continued in AUSTRIA until late in the eighteenth century, and in the Pyrenees until the nineteenth; it was employed in North America in the early colonial period, and could still be observed in India in the 1960s. A bloom of iron produced in a water-powered bloomery could weigh as much as 150 kg (330 lb.). The bloomery process as used in the seventeenth century has been replicated at Williamsburg (*see* VIRGINIA) and was recorded in a film, *The Bloomery*, in 1985.

BIBLIOGRAPHY
General
Cleere and Crossley, 1985; Percy, 1864; Sperl, 1985; Tylecote, 1986.
Specific
Harvey, D. A progress report on the reconstruction of the American bloomery process. In Ironbridge Institute, 1986.

BARRIE TRINDER

blowing house A thatched, stone building, containing a small, stone cylindrical furnace, blown by water power, used for smelting tin ore in Cornwall. Tin concentrate and charcoal were put into the furnace in layers, and more was added as the metal melted. Metal collected in a stone trough, from which it was ladled into an iron pot with a fire beneath; damp charcoal was then thrown in, causing slag to rise to the surface where it could be skimmed off. The metal was then ladled into moulds. Later the tin was remelted and ladled into pots in which green apple wood was inserted: this caused turbulence and so separated the slag. The thatch of the blowing house was periodically burned to recover the tin in it. Blowing houses were

Figure 16 The boat lift of 1899 at Henrichenburg in the Ruhrgebiet where the Dortmund branch canal joins the Rhine–Herne Canal; it has a vertical rise of 14 m (46 ft.). The photograph was taken during restoration in 1984.
Barrie Trinder

displaced by reverberatory furnaces from the late seventeenth century, but some remained in use, particularly for streamed tin, until the mid-nineteenth century.

BIBLIOGRAPHY
General
Barton, 1968, 1971; Richardson, 1974; Stratton and Trinder, 1989.

Bluebell Railway, West Sussex, England   One of Britain's first privately-preserved standard-gauge railways. Operation of the 8 km (5 mi.) line between Horsted Keynes and Sheffield Park, formerly an LBSCR branch, began in 1960. Locomotives and rolling stock are predominantly from the Southern Railway and its constituent companies. An extension north to East Grinstead is proposed.

blueprint   *See* COPIER.

boarding house   'Board' in this sense refers to a table, and a boarding house was essentially one where food was provided for inmates, in contrast to a LODGING HOUSE where it was not. 'Boarding house' in industrial archaeology has two distinct meanings:

1. The tall narrow terraced houses built in many British seaside resorts for the accommodation of working-class and lower-middle-class visitors, traditionally managed by landladies as family businesses. The best-preserved examples tend to be in small resorts like Borth, 8 km (5 mi.) N. of ABERYSTWYTH, and Penmaenmawr, 12 km ($7\frac{1}{2}$ mi.) E. of Menai, Wales.
2. The houses in which girls from farming districts employed in New England textile mills were accommodated in cities like Lowell (*see* MASSACHUSETTS).

BIBLIOGRAPHY
General
Eno, 1976; Walton, 1978, 1983.

boat lift   A means of conveying a boat vertically between two levels of a navigable waterway. There were experiments with lifts in Britain in the 1790s and early 1800s but none was successful in the long term due to deficiencies in materials and in the understanding of them. A lift built in 1798 at Rothenfurt near FREIBERG worked until 1868 and its remains are preserved. The first boat lift of the modern era, with two counterbalanced CAISSONS, was at Anderton (see NORTHWICH), England; suggested by Sir Edward Leader Williams (1828–1910), it was designed by Edwin Clark (1814–94) and completed in 1875. It was originally worked by hydraulic power but was electrified in 1903. Clark, with his brother Latimer Clark (1822–98) and John Standfield, set up an engineering partnership responsible for other lifts including that at FONTINETTES on the Neuffosse Canal, which worked from 1888 until 1967, and the four on the Canal du Centre in Belgium (see LA LOUVIÈRE). The other outstanding lifts built before 1914 were at Henrichenburg (see RUHRGEBIET) in Germany, where the lift on the float principle with a single caisson worked from 1899 until 1962 (see figure 16); and two in Canada, one on the Severn–Trent Waterway, the other on the Peterborough Canal. Two lifts of outstanding importance were built in Germany in the inter-war period, at Niederfinow, on the Oder–Havel Canal, where a modified version of the electrified Anderton with one caisson was built in 1934 capable of raising a 1000-ton vessel 36 m (118 ft.); and at Rothensee near Magdeburg, where a lift on the float principle was completed in 1939. Major lifts built in Germany since 1950 include a new lift at Henrichenburg, which is now itself being supplemented by a lock, and a spectacular structure at Scharnebeck on the Elbe Lateral Canal, built between 1969 and 1976.

See also INCLINED PLANE and figure 78.

BIBLIOGRAPHY
General
Hadfield, 1986; Tew, 1984.
Specific
Ascenseur hydraulique des Fontinettes. In *Le Génie Civil*, VI, 1988.
Das Schiffshebewerk Niederfinow (The Niederfinow boat lift). Eberswalde, 1934.
Duer, S. The hydraulic lift at Anderton. In *Proceedings of the Institute of Civil Engineers*, XLV, 1875–6.
Reinhardt, W. The Rothensee boat elevator. In *Engineering Progress*, XV, 1934.
Wagenbreth, O. *Das älteste Schiffshebewerk* (The oldest boat lift). Eberswalde-Finow: Kulturinformationen, 1976.

BARRIE TRINDER

bobbin mill   A mill in which powered saws, lathes and machines for boring were employed to make wooden bobbins and reels for use in textile manufacture. Some mills also produced toggles for duffel coats, wooden washers, and shovel handles. Swills – hampers woven from wood stripped from the coppice poles – were used to transport bobbins, and also sold as a by-product. There were some seventy such mills in the English LAKE DISTRICT in the nineteenth century, providing for the textile manufacturers of Lancashire and Yorkshire. That at Stott Park has been preserved.

BIBLIOGRAPHY
Specific
White, P. R. Stott Park Bobbin Mill: a case study in oral history. In CILAC, 1985.

Bóbrka, Krosno, Poland   A village at the foot of the Carpathian Mountains, 170 km (106 mi.) E. of Kraków. The Ignacy Łukasiewicz Open-Air Museum of the Oil Industry was set up in 1961 at the initiative of the Association of Oil Industry Engineers and Technicians on an old oil-pumping site, built in 1854 and still in use. Over fifty exhibits illustrate the history of prospecting and oil extraction. The museum has many devices used in the industry that are unique survivals. An obelisk stands on the site with the inscription 'To commemorate the establishment of the rock-oil mine in Bóbrka, 1854 – Łukasiewicz 4 November 1879'. Many old features of the site survive, including the 'Franek' shaft, a hand-dug well of 1860, a forge of 1854 complete with its original equipment, a boiler house of 1867, an office building, and the house where IGNACY ŁUKASIEWICZ lived when he was director of the concern. There are various types of boring rigs, a manual rig of 1862, a Canadian rig of 1865 driven by a steam engine, a 'Bitkow' rig of 1922, and others. The museum has horse gins for pumping oil wells, pumping jacks, and wooden and steel lifting gear.

The museum is a branch of the regional museum in Krosno which also has collections relating to the oil industry, including scale models of shafts and refineries, boring rigs, oil and kerosene lamps, and gas lamps.

BIBLIOGRAPHY
General
Czajkowski, 1981.
Specific
Muzeum-skansen Przemysłu Naftowego im Ignacego Łukasiewicza w Bóbrce (The Ignacy Lukasiewicz Open-Air Museum of the Oil Industry in Bóbrka). In *Kwartalnik Historii Kultury Materialnej* (Quarterly Journal of the History of Material Culture), 2, 1981.

LOCATIONS
[M] Muzeum Okręgowe (Regional Museum), Krosno.
[M] Muzeum Przemysłu Naftowego im Ignacego Łukasiewicza (The Ignacy Łukasiewicz Museum of the Oil Industry, Chorkówka.

JAN KĘSIK

Bobrza, Kielce, Poland   The site of the remains of a blast furnace, on the Bobrza river, near the Kielce–Końskie road, within the STAROPOLSKI INDUSTRIAL REGION. There was an ironworks on the site in the sixteenth and seventeenth centuries of which only traces of leats and some slag remain. Construction of the plant started in 1824 on the instruction of Ksawery Drucki-Lubecki, finance minister of the Congress Kingdom. The original scheme was to build five blast furnaces in line along a slope, with six industrial buildings at the top of the slope which was to be reinforced with a strong retaining wall. A stone dam was to pound up water which would be fed through channels in the retaining wall to powerful undershot water wheels. Construction was delayed by the November Uprising of 1830 and never resumed; at the suggestion of the Polish Bank nailing machines were later installed in existing buildings. Parts of the water system survive, with ruins of the fuel store, the retaining wall (500 m (457 yd.) long and 15 m (41 ft.) high), the nail-making shop and workers' housing.

BIBLIOGRAPHY
General
Krygier, 1958.

Bocholt, Limburg, Belgium   A small town 38 km (24 mi.) NE of Hasselt on the canal from Maastricht to 's Hertogenbosch, where a brewery, whose buildings date from 1758, together with all its equipment, has been preserved as a museum. Other industrial buildings in the town include the former Reppelfabriek arsenic plant.

BIBLIOGRAPHY
General
Viaene, 1986.

LOCATION
[M] Bocholter Brouwerijmuseum, Dorpsstraat 53, 3598 Bocholt.

Bochum, North-Rhine Westphalia, Germany   *See* RUHR-GEBIET.

bog iron   Iron ore formed by bacterial action where iron-bearing surface waters meet organic materials. It is found below the turf on some moorlands, where it can accumulate at a rate of 5–10 cm every thirty years, and on lake bottoms – hence its alternative name, lake iron. Lake ores are often so fine as to need no mechanical preparation, and were often smelted in blast furnaces without a flux. Bog iron was extensively used in the Middle Ages, and was smelted on a considerable scale in Russia and Finland in the eighteenth century.

BIBLIOGRAPHY
General
Percy, 1864; Tylecote, 1986.
Specific
Braid, D. The strategic and economic importance of marsh and lake ores in the 17th and 18th centuries. In Ironbridge Institute, 1986.

boiler   A means of converting water to steam using heat. The term is most commonly applied to the source of the steam supply for a STEAM ENGINE, STEAM LOCOMOTIVE, or STEAMSHIP, in each of which heat is converted into potential energy. Early steam engine boilers of the 'haystack' type were based on brewers' coppers. Improvements, once ironworking technology made them practicable, came in the circulation of heat, 'Cornish', 'Lancashire' and 'Locomotive' boilers having increasing numbers of firetubes passing through the water. The Babcock & Willcox water-tube boiler of 1867 reversed this process by leading tubes containing water through the heat.

BIBLIOGRAPHY
General
Law, 1965.
Specific
Watkins, G. Steam power: an illustrated guide. In *IA*, IV, 1970.

boilermaker   In addition to its literal meaning, the word 'boilermaker' was applied from the early nineteenth century by builders of wooden ships, initially as a term of abuse, to skilled men employed in the construction of iron – and later of steel – ships. The English trade union, the United Society of Boilermakers, formed in 1834, came to include platers, riveters, angle-iron smiths, caulkers and holders-up amongst its members by the 1890s.

BIBLIOGRAPHY
General
Clegg *et al.*, 1964; Marsh and Ryan, 1980, 1984, 1987; Mayhew, 1849–50.
Specific
Cummings. D. C. *A Historical Survey of the Boilermakers' and Iron and Steel Ship Builders' Society from August 1834 to August 1903.* Newcastle upon Tyne: R. Robinson, 1904.
Mortimer, J. E. *A History of the Boilermakers' Society – Volume I: 1834–1906.* London: Allen & Unwin, 1973.

Bokrijk, Limburg, Belgium   Bokrijk, 7 km (4 mi.) NE of Hasselt, is an open-air museum of the Flemish provinces of Belgium, largely inspired by its first director Dr J. Weyns (1913–74). It is part of the Domein Bokrijk, a 540 ha (1334 ac.) estate, which was acquired by the Province of Limburg in 1938, and is now a centre for recreation, of which the museum forms one element. Construction began in 1953 and the public were admitted in 1958. Over a hundred buildings are now grouped to form hamlets typifying particular parts of Flanders, including some from the city of Antwerp. The museum holds extensive documentary records relating to material culture in Flanders.

Many of the buildings are farmhouses in which are displayed the typical products of Flanders: cast-iron stoves, pewter, copperware, and cranes for suspending cooking pots over fires. There is a reproduction of a cave hut from the sandy heathlands of Koersel, based on a drawing of 1918; and a house from Eksel, once occupied by Teutens, migrant workers who from bases in Limburg spent their summers working in North Germany and Denmark.

There are two horse mills from West Flanders, a tower mill from Limburg, and two post mills. A water mill from Lummen-Rekhoven, Limburg, with an undershot wheel, includes a particularly fine box housing the miller's tools. An oil mill with a horizontal crushing wheel of 1702 made oil from rape seed and linseed. The museum includes several bakehouses, and a hop oven or oasthouse from West Flanders, rectangular in plan, with walls of vertically plaited laths. A ropemaker's shop has hackles for preparing thread as well as spinning and braiding equipment. In the Kilbers farmhouse are brakes, scutchers and hackles for processing flax. In a house from Heist-op-den-Berg are some notable honey presses. Other exhibits include a tollhouse of 1725 from Gelinden on the road from Liège to St Truiden; a seventeenth-century communal brewery of typical Maasland brick construction; and a peat house from Kalmhout, Antwerp, an area once internationally known for its peat exports.

BIBLIOGRAPHY
Specific
Buys, A, *Dr Jozef Weyns: de man die Bokrijk bouwde* (Dr Jozef Weyns: the man who built Bokrijk). In *Ons Volk* (Our Folk), LVI, 1973.
25 Jaar Bokrijk (25 years of Bokrijk). In *Volkskunde* (Folk Art), LXXIX (2/3) 1978.
Weyns, J. *Bokrijk, zin en zijn* (Bokrijk: vision and reality), 1970.

LOCATION
[M] Openluchtmuseum, Provinciedomein Bokrijk, B-3600 Genk.

BARRIE TRINDER

Bologna, Emilia, Italy   Bologna's manufactures are largely dependent on agriculture, but the city has become a major centre for the study of industrial archaeology. The Communist city council has funded the restoration of large-scale models of historic machinery. The Aldini-Valeriani Museum and the University of Bologna have collaborated to create a remarkable series of working models, of which the most impressive is a half-size silk-throwing mill. Such multi-storey factories were erected in the city from the sixteenth century, and by 1700 there were about four hundred water wheels powering silk mills and other installations. The extent and achievements of such early industrialization are the subjects of a museum being developed in the redundant Gallotti brickyard alongside a canal on the edge of the city.

The old meat market north of the centre occupies a large rectangular block, with the main entrance, a formal gateway flanked by two Italianate villas, facing Via Lodovico Berti. Stalls converted into apartments line the two long sides of the market. The central area has two free-standing sheds of *c.*1900 with cast-iron columns supporting an arched brace roof.

BIBLIOGRAPHY
General
Selvafolta *et al.,* 1983.
Specific
Comune di Bologna, *Machine, scuole industria* (Mills, the origin of industry). Bologna, 1980.
Comune di Bologna, *Problemi d'acque in Bologna nell'età moderna* (Problems of water supply in Bologna in the modern era). Bologna: Instituto per la storia di Bologna (Institute for the history of Bologna), 1983.

MICHAEL STRATTON

Bolton, Greater Manchester, England   One of the principal Lancashire cotton towns, 16 km (10 mi.) NW of Manchester, situated at the confluence of streams which provided power and water for spinning and bleaching. Samuel Crompton (1753–1827), inventor of the spinning mule, was born at Firwood Fold. There are many mills of the mid-nineteenth century and later. Textile machinery

in the Tonge Moor Museum includes a carding engine from CROMFORD and a twelve-spindle hand mule. Egerton and Bank Top, textile communities built by the Ashworth family, were celebrated in the 1840s for high standards. Horwich, 9 km ($5\frac{1}{2}$ mi.) NW, is a community built around the LYR engineering works of the 1880s.

BIBLIOGRAPHY
General
Ashmore, 1969, 1982; Boyson, 1970.
Specific
Turton, B. J. Horwich: the historical geography of a Lancashire industrial town. In *Transactions of the Lancashire & Cheshire Antiquarian Society,* LXXII, 1962.

LOCATION
[M] Tonge Moor Museum, Tonge Moor Road, Bolton BL1 1SA.

Bombardier, J. Armand (1904–67)   A Québecois engineer and inventor, born in Valcourt. Bombardier was associated from 1930 with the development of vehicles that revolutionized winter transport in Canada. 'Snowmobiles', built in large numbers until about 1950, were cars adapted to be driven on snow, fitted with caterpillar tracks instead of wheels. They allowed passengers, freight and mail to be transported to all parts of Quebec throughout the province's long winters, and were of particular importance in providing medical services for isolated areas.

These vehicles were replaced by the 'Ski-doo' which has been on the market since 1959. Originally intended for recreational purposes, it now has many commercial functions, notably among the Inuit population of Canada. The Ski-doo has to a large extent been responsible for the financial success of the Bombardier company, and for its international reputation in the public transport industry, as in METRO technology.

The Musée Bombardier at Valcourt, 90 km (56 mi.) SE of Montreal, has a collection of vehicles designed by Bombardier, who by the time of his death had forty patents to his credit.

BIBLIOGRAPHY
General
Lacasse, 1988.

LOCATION
[M] Musée J. A. Bombardier, 1000 rue J. A. Bombardier, Valcourt, Quebec J0E 2L0.

LOUISE TROTTIER

Bonawe, Strathclyde, Scotland   Bonawe Ironworks, Taynuilt, 16 km (10 mi.) W. of Oban, has from 1973 been a guardianship monument (*see* SCOTLAND). It is the most complete charcoal-fuelled blast furnace in Britain. It was established in 1753 to smelt ores from the English Lake District, and ceased operation in 1873. Workers' and the manager's houses may be seen, as may charcoal and iron-ore stores and a near-intact furnace.

Craleckan furnace at Furnace on Loch Fyne, 33 km (20 mi.) W. of Oban, was founded in 1755 and closed in 1813.

95

A charcoal shed, the furnace and the blowing house beneath the charging platform all survive. An ironworks at Glen Kinglass, 23 km (15 mi.) W. of Oban, founded in 1722 and closed in 1738, is in ruins.

BIBLIOGRAPHY
General
Hay and Stell, 1986; Hume, 1977.
Specific
Lewis, J. The charcoal-fired blast furnaces of Scotland. In *Proceedings of the Society of Antiquaries of Scotland*, CXIV, 1984.

bond or **bonded warehouse**   A warehouse where goods liable to customs or excise duty are stored until it is convenient for the importer or manufacturer, who has deposited a bond with the customs authorities, to pay duty and take possession of them. Bonded warehouses are of particular importance in ports, where goods for re-export may be landed, stored and re-dispatched without paying duty; and in DISTILLING (*see also* SCOTCH WHISKY), where products may be matured in storage before the payment of duty. In England, bonding in most ports was made possible by the Warehousing Act 1803.

See also figure 39.

bone mill   Bone was an essential element in fine china (*see* PORCELAIN) and was often prepared by calcining and grinding in conjunction with flint, for example, at the Etruscan Bone and Flint Mill of 1857 at STOKE-ON-TRENT.

BIBLIOGRAPHY
General
Hamer, 1986.

Bo'ness, Central, Scotland   The Scottish Railway Preservation Society, founded in 1961, has built up a collection of locomotives and rolling stock, including a 'Scandinavian Vintage Train' from Norway. The Society moved to reclaimed land at Bo'ness in 1979, and its lines will link various proposed museum sites. Its station is the oldest train shed left in Scotland, the 1841 wrought-iron trusses and cast-iron supports having been removed from Haymarket station, Edinburgh. There is a station from Wormit, Fife, and it is planned to re-erect the cast-iron framework of the Caledonian Ironworks, once the 1888 Glasgow International Exhibition Engineering Hall (*see* GLASGOW).

The Bo'ness Heritage Area comprises several sites linked by the railway. On the foreshore by the station a Scottish township is to be erected using buildings moved from elsewhere. The most spectacular acquisitions are two aircraft hangars of 1918 from Montrose, Angus. The display will also include houses, high-street shops, and telephone boxes, products of Falkirk.

Kinneil Colliery of the 1950s is now closed and largely demolished, but the winding gear and fan house have been retained alongside a bird sanctuary. Birkhill Clay Mine, closed in 1981, will be the only preserved clay mine in Scotland. The Scottish fireclay industry formerly exported high-quality refractory bricks for blast furnaces, gasworks, glassworks, power stations and chimney linings. The mine was founded in 1913 by Mark Hurll, and No. 3 mine of 1932 is open to visitors. It has six miles of underground stoop and room workings, for the most part flooded, but part is naturally drained because it is above the water table. It is linked by a 200 m (220 yd.) incline with the rambling brick-built surface buildings, which house two pan mills and a smithy.

The New Grange Foundry of A. Ballantine & Sons in Main Street was established in 1856 and is still functioning, specializing in ornamental cast-iron work, stills, vats and oil-refining equipment. The two-storey office block and pattern shop date from the nineteenth century.

In the eighteenth century Bo'ness was Scotland's third port, but the later tidal harbour and wet dock are now disused. The Tobacco Warehouse of 1772 in Scotland's Close was later a granary and bakehouse and has been imaginatively converted to a library. The five-storey granary in North Street has been converted to flats. There is a large stone-built whisky BOND of the late nineteenth century.

Kinneil House, 2.5 km (1½ mi.) SW, was the home of the eighteenth-century entrepreneur Dr John Roebuck (1718–94), of the Prestonpans Vitriol Co. and the Carron Co. In a ruined and still overgrown cottage nearby JAMES WATT made improvements to a mine-pumping engine in 1765. It was this engine that he took to Birmingham in 1774 at the commencement of the BOULTON & WATT partnership.

LOCATIONS
[I] Bo'ness Heritage Trust, Bo'ness Station, Bo'ness, West Lothian EH51 0AD.
[S] Scottish Railway Preservation Society, Bo'ness Station, Bo'ness, West Lothian EH51 0AD.

MARK WATSON

Boom, Antwerp, Belgium   The Rupel valley between Boom, 15 km (9 mi.) S. of Antwerp, and its confluence with the River Scheldt opposite Rupelmonde, 12 km (8 mi.) SW of Antwerp, was the principal brickmaking area of Belgium, producing 1 000 000 000 bricks a year by 1900. Coal from the Charleroi collieries was delivered by canal. A steel-lattice bascule bridge stands near the lock at the confluence of the River Rupel and the old Brussels–Willebroek canal at Klein-Willebroek. The valley is filled with the remains of Hoffman kilns, which replaced various forms of intermittent kilns from the 1870s; and with pantile-roofed, rail-served drying sheds. The Frateur works at Boom-Noeveren is the headquarters of an écomusée which aims to interpret the entire brickmaking region.

BIBLIOGRAPHY
Specific
VVV, *Industriele Archeologie langs Schelde en Rupel* (Industrial archaeology along the Scheldt and the Rupel). Ghent, 1987.

LOCATION
[M] Het Ecomuseum en archief van de Boomse Baksteen

Figure 17 A late nineteenth-century kiln which forms part of the conserved Frateur brickworks, Boom, Belgium
Barrie Trinder

(Écomusée and archives of the Boom brickmaking region), Noeveren 196, 2650 Boom.

BARRIE TRINDER

boots *See* SHOES.

BOP Basic Oxygen Process, an American term for the LD PROCESS.

Bor, Serbia, Yugoslavia A mining town at the foot of the Veliki Crs mountain, 160 km (100 mi.) SE of Belgrade: the site of the largest copper mines in Europe, mostly strip mines, and the principal source of gold in Yugoslavia.

LOCATIONS
[M] Mining Museum, 12210-Bor.
[M] National Museum, 12210-Bor.

Borås, Älvsborg, Sweden An important textile centre since the sixteenth century, which by the nineteenth century specialized in the production of cotton. The technical museum is concerned chiefly with the textile industry, particularly the manufacture of ready-made clothing, while the town museum is notable for its photographic collections.

LOCATIONS
[M] Borås Museum, Ramnaparken, 502 65 Borås.

[M] Tekomuseum (Technical Museum), Skaraborgsvägen 7, 502 34 Borås.

Borders, Scotland The counties of Roxburghshire, Selkirkshire, Peeblesshire and Berwickshire in the south of Scotland are primarily rural, but their woollen industry is renowned.

One of the first jenny spinning mills in Scotland is Caerlee Mill in Innerleithen, of *c*.1790: it has four storeys and ten bays and retains an 1860s turbine.

Galashiels became the major spinning town with the conversion in 1791–1805 of five waulk (fulling) mills to carding and finishing mills. The three-storey Nether Mill of 1805 still stands, part turned into a museum by tartan weavers Peter Anderson Ltd. There is a restored Leffel water turbine, and factory tours visit the weaving shed which has some old finishing machinery. A three-storey mill of 1866 and an engine house of 1887 complete the complex. Factory tours are also given at North Wheatlands and Comelybank Mills. Mules are still used in Bristol Mill. High Tweed Mill, a three-storey, thirty-two-bay mill of 1852, which is still in the woollen industry, was the first solely steam-powered mill in Galashiels. Others followed: Mid Mill and Netherdale Mill survive, the former now a supermarket, the latter an industrial estate. Each has four storeys and nineteen bays, a central stair tower, wooden floors and an M-roof – the optimum layout for a mule mill.

Mills came to Selkirk, 8 km (5 mi.) S., in 1835–8, once water-powered sites were fully occupied in Galashiels. Ettrick Mill, founded in 1835 and doubled in size by 1850,

97

is the finest in the Borders: four-storeyed with a double attic, a Venetian-windowed pediment, and a fireproof wing, the only brick-arched mill known in the Borders. Mule spinning stopped in 1988. A large wheelhouse, a chimney and one- and two-storey weaving sheds survive. Dunsdale Mill nearby includes the original mill of 1838 and a block of 1865 with a central stair tower. Forest Mill is a short four-storey and double-attic five-bay mill with a bellcote and *in situ* shafting that may soon house a small textile museum. The three-storey hand-loom shed (in which Cheviot cloth was first woven) and the single-storey scouring and weaving sheds are bigger than the spinning mill. The four-storey Yarrow Mill of 1866, doubled in size in 1872, is of the same type as Dunsdale Mill and Netherdale Mill, and has a Scottish Baronial single-storey front of 1892. Bridgehaugh Mill of 1865 is now a fellmonger's. At Tweed Mills tweed is still woven in weaving sheds of the 1880s. St Mary's Mill, a weaving shed of 1894, is now divided for small businesses. Heather Mill, of the 1870s, still employs mules. (Some of Selkirk's single-storey mills were built for spinning rather than weaving.) Mules, some of the nineteenth century, are still needed for particular counts of yarn and for cashmere, despite high labour costs.

The Scottish Museum of Woollen Textiles in Walkerburn, 14 km (9 mi.) NW of Selkirk, was originally associated with Tweedvale Mills, a concern which in 1988 was reduced to a mill shop. Exhibits include an eighteenth-century hand-powered mule and a drop-box Jacquard loom. Terraces of workers' housing and a mill-owner's Gothic house are associated with the mill.

Hawick, 14 km (9 mi.) S., led Scotland's hosiery industry after the introduction of stocking frames in 1771. Early stocking shops have been identified behind 21 High Street, Hawick; and in Denholm, 8 km (5 mi.) NE. Wilton Mills were founded in 1811 and integrated spinning and weaving. Two of its mills survive with clock and stair towers over a system of lades. Weensland Mills are early and later nineteenth-century four-storey blocks which still house mules. Cotton's power frames were not well established in hosiery shops until the 1880s and 90s. Eastfield Mills of 1882 are single-storey with a French front. Woollen underwear, and now knitwear, have ensured continued prosperity and with it modernization of several mills. Hawick Museum has late eighteenth-century stocking and broad frames as well as more modern machinery.

Kelso Mills at Kelso comprise a large group of late eighteenth- and nineteenth-century grain mills with hoists and louvres. They now grind animal feed. Edrington Castle Mill of 1789 at Mordington, Berwickshire, is out of use but intact, with wheels. Lindean Mill, 2 km (1 mi.) N. of Selkirk, has been converted to offices and workshops which have displaced the machinery.

A Museum of Ornamental Plasterwork was opened in Peebles in 1985 by L. Grandison & Son, Scotland's foremost decorative plasterers. It offers 'hands on' experience, a recreated casting workshop of *c.*1900, and occasional casting. Scottish plaster was worked *in situ* to a greater extent than in England.

The printing works of Robert Smail & Sons in Innerleithen, 8 km (5 mi.) W. of Peebles, was founded in 1848 and was acquired by the National Trust for Scotland in 1987 as an intact example of a small town printing works where type was composed by hand and the four presses were driven by line shafting. Traquair House, Innerleithen, has its own private laird's brewhouse, with a copper installed in 1739 and restarted in 1962; it is open to the public.

The first of JOHN SMEATON's major bridges was that of five masonry arches at Coldstream of 1763–7. JOHN RENNIE built Kelso Bridge in 1800–3: it has five level spans with Doric details. Sir Samuel Brown (1776–1852) built the first large wrought-iron suspension bridge in the United Kingdom, the Union Bridge linking England and Scotland, at Hutton in 1820. This bridge and suspension bridges at Kalemouth near Jedburgh and at Melrose (1826) have stone pylons, wrought-iron link chains, and rod suspenders.

Melrose station, of 1849, was adapted in 1986 to house craft workshops and a display of railwayana. Leaderfoot Viaduct, 4 km (2½ mi.) SW, of 1865, with nineteen tall stone arched spans, is among the most dramatic in Scotland. Dunglass Viaduct, Cockburnspath, of 1846, with a 41 m (135 ft.) central span, remains in use.

BIBLIOGRAPHY
General
Biddle and Nock, 1983; Hume, 1976.

LOCATIONS
[M] Galashiels Museum, Peter Anderson Ltd, Nether Mill, Huddersfield Street, Galashiels TD1 3BA.
[M] Hawick Museum, Wilton Lodge Park, Hawick, Roxburghshire TD9 7JL.
[M,S] Robert Smail's Printing Works, High Street, Innerleithen.
[M] Scottish Museum of Woollen Textiles, Tweedvale Mills, Walkerburn, Peeblesshire EH43 6AH.
[M] The Cornice, Museum of Ornamental Plasterwork, 31 High Street, Peebles.
[M,S] Traquair House, Innerleithen, Peeblesshire EH44 6PW.

MARK WATSON

boring machine A boring machine or boring mill is a machine tool devised to cut cylindrical internal or external surfaces larger and more uniform than could be drilled or turned. Before the mid-eighteenth century cannon cast hollow were fed against a rotating cutting bar mounted at the end of a long shaft. This technique provided only mediocre support for the boring head, however, when applied to large-diameter Newcomen engine cylinders at Coalbrookdale, England, and elsewhere. Jan Verbruggen developed a means of boring solid cannon in the 1750s by feeding a rigid boring bar and cutter horizontally against the solid cannon casting while it was rotating. JOHN WILKINSON, following this practice, produced a cylinder machined accurately enough to enable JAMES WATT's engine to work, but he recognized that a boring bar supported at both ends would be more suitable for this work.

While Wilkinson's cutter was driven through a slot by a

rack running inside a hollow boring bar, the cutter could also be driven by an internal or external screw, or a longer bar fed through hollow centres. From the early nineteenth century boring bars were fitted to engine lathes, although both vertical and horizontal boring machines continued to be made for heavy work or where boring between centres was not appropriate. Eventually boring machines were built predominantly along vertical axes, the cutting tools locked in rigid crossbars above the work. Such machines are known also as vertical lathes.

BIBLIOGRAPHY
General
Rolt, 1986; Steeds, 1969.

TIM PUTNAM

Bornholm, Denmark An island in the Baltic 160 km (100 mi.) SE of Copenhagen. Its geology differs strongly from the rest of Denmark, with many Precambrian formations, overlain in the south by later sediments. The quarrying of sandstone and granite have been important for centuries. The rocks are still extracted at several places, and at Moseløkken near Sandvig in the north of the island a museum illustrating the history of Bornholm's stone industry has been established in a working quarry. Several closed quarries, with deep, calm pools of water, like Opal-søen near Sandvig and the coal mine at Rubin-søen near Hasle, have become tourist attractions.

In the transition zone between the granite and the sedimentary rocks are valuable deposits of clays, including china clay, which is exploited at Rabækkeværket, and local clays are used by Hasle Klinker- & Chamottestens-fabrik, both located near Rønne, the main city of the island. The excellent clays also stimulated the establishment of dozens of faience and terracotta factories in Rønne from 1840 onwards. The prominent firms of M. Andersen, L. Hjorth and Søholm can be visited; and recently the factory of L. Hjorth, dating from 1861, with wood-fired kilns and other early equipment, has been restored and given legal protection.

In Denmark the word Bornholm is synonymous with two other activities of the islanders. One is the making of grandfather clocks, a principal trade in Rønne from *c*.1750 until *c*.1870. The other is the production of smoked kippers, from the island's important fishing fleet. The characteristic profiles of smokehouses can be seen all over Bornholm.

On the railway line from Gudhjem to Almindingen, now closed, are four splendid and recently protected stations, built in 1915–16 to the designs of the Danish architects K. Fisker and Åge Rafn.

BIBLIOGRAPHY
Specific
Hansen, M. ed. *Geologi paa Bornholm* (Geology of Bornholm). Copenhagen, 1969.
Tornehave, B. De Bornholmske Fajance-og Terrakottafabrikker (The faience and terracotta factories of Bornholm). In *Bornholmske Samlinger*, 1980.
Tornehave, B. *Bornholmske urmagere* (Watchmakers of Bornholm). Copenhagen, 1983.

LOCATION
[M] Bornholms Museum (Historical Museum), Sct Mortensgade 29, 3700 Rønne.

OLE HYLDTOFT

bottle Although bottles have been made of leather, and some glass ones were used in antiquity, the bottle can be seen as a symbol of industrialization: a container of modest cost which enabled the widespread distribution of a variety of products. The growing trade in alcoholic beverages of the late seventeenth century was made possible by increased manufactures of bottles and corks, and by recycling. In England, bottles made in Bristol were carried up the River Severn to the cider-producing areas of Worcestershire. One vessel in 1705 conveyed upstream consignments of up to 2000 dozen (24000) bottles.

The machine that made possible the mass production of bottles was patented in 1895 by Michael Joseph Owens (1859–1923), who worked for a glassmaker, Edward Drummond Libbey (1854–1925) in Toledo, Ohio. A pump sucked a lump of heated glass from a tank into a mould, then its action was reversed to blow the glass into the shape of a bottle. A succession of pumps was arranged on a large rotary machine. By 1905 the operation was completely automatic, and a machine operated by two men could produce 25000 bottles an hour. Libbey and Owens established the Owens Bottle Machine Co. in 1903, opening a European subsidiary two years later, and marketed machines throughout the world, like that of 1928 displayed at BIRMINGHAM. Machines on the same principle were used for the mass production of drinking glasses and electric light bulbs.

BIBLIOGRAPHY
General
Boorstin, 1973.

BARRIE TRINDER

bottle oven A conical structure in brick, providing draught for KILNS used for firing or enamelling ceramics. Bottle kilns are a feature of the landscape of STOKE-ON-TRENT, where about forty remain of many hundreds that were still in use in 1945. Bottle ovens could be updraught, downdraught or muffle in form. They used large quantities of coal, causing severe atmospheric pollution, and their use is now illegal in Britain. Some kilns for calcining bone and flint (*see* BONE MILL; FLINT MILL) in Stoke-on-Trent were of similar form and remain in use.

Bouch, Sir Thomas (1822–80) A civil engineer, who was employed on the Edinburgh & Northern Railway from 1849, and devised the company's train FERRIES over the Forth and Tay estuaries. He built the elegant Hownes Gill viaduct (*see* DURHAM) in firebrick in 1856–8. He is best known in a tragic context as the designer of the first Tay

Figure 18 The gold rush boom town of Bourlamaque, Quebec, with the gold mine in the background, 1935
Ministre des Affaires Culturelles du Québec

Bridge (*see* DUNDEE), the collapse of which in 1879 led to his death from shock.

BIBLIOGRAPHY
General
Walters, 1966.

Boulton & Watt The partnership formed by JAMES WATT and Matthew Boulton (1728–1809) in 1774, with the object of developing Watt's improvements to the steam engine. Boulton was a leading TOY manufacturer in BIRMINGHAM, who in 1769 had built the Soho Manufactory, a three-storey, nineteen-bay building to the north of the city, for the manufacture of small metal products. The partners successfully developed the Watt engine and continued with general manufactures, producing Sheffield plate, coinage and, from 1805, plant for making COAL GAS. For twenty years the partners supplied only drawings and valves to customers buying engines, but in 1796 they built the Soho Foundry in Smethwick to manufacture engine parts themselves. The two sons of the founders were admitted to the partnership in 1794, and James Watt senior retired in 1800. After the death in 1848 of James Watt junior the firm was known as James Watt & Co. until the Soho Foundry was sold to another Birmingham company in 1895. The Soho Manufactory was closed in 1848 and demolished in 1863.

The records of the partnership, held in Birmingham Public Library, including drawings for most engines, and complete files of inward and outward correspondence, form one of the prime sources for the study of the Industrial Revolution of the eighteenth century.

BIBLIOGRAPHY
General
Dickinson and Jenkins, 1927; Farey, 1827; Lord, 1923; Muirhead, 1854; Roll, 1930; Tann, 1970, 1981.

Specific
Gale, W. K. V. *Boulton, Watt and the Soho Undertakings.* Birmingham: City of Birmingham Museum, 1952.
Tann, J. Boulton & Watt's organization of steam-engine production before the opening of the Soho Foundry. In *TNS*, XLIX, 1977–8.
Tann, J. Marketing methods in the international steam-engine market: the case of Boulton and Watt. In *Journal of Economic History*, XXXVIII, 1978.

LOCATION
[M] Archives Department, Birmingham Public Libraries, Central Library, Chamberlain Square, Birmingham B3 3HQ.

CHRISTOPHER GREEN

Bourlamaque, Quebec, Canada A characteristic gold-rush boom town in the Abitibi region, 530 km (330 mi.) NW of Montreal. In Quebec gold prospecting was stimulated by the completion of the transcontinental railway. Thus between 1912 and 1920 many prospectors from Ontario were drawn to the Abitibi region where they discovered gold-bearing strata along the Cadillac geological fault.

They were followed by mining companies from the USA, notably Lamaque Gold Mines, which in 1934 set up the town of Bourlamaque together with the industrial plant for exploiting and processing the ores. The company built and maintained for its employees nearly seventy log cabins, as well as community buildings, a bank, a post office, a leisure centre, a dispensary, a school and a general store.

In recent decades several developments in the locality and within the founding company have led to the merging of Bourlamaque with the neighbouring township of Val d'Or, and to the sale of the houses. This led the government of Quebec to take measures in 1979 for the protection of this historic area in collaboration with the municipal authorities, the Chamber of Commerce, the Historical Society and the residents' association.

BIBLIOGRAPHY
General
Beaudry-Gourd, 1983.

LOUISE TROTTIER

Bourne, John Cooke (1814–96) An English artist whose published works magnificently conveyed the self-assurance of the early railway age. His first volume provides the best representation of the construction of a railway before the introduction of mechanical excavation techniques. His second depicts the first stages of main-line railway operation, including freight depots, locomotive depots and signals, as well as ISAMBARD KINGDOM BRUNEL's bridges and the locomotives of Sir Daniel Gooch (1816–89). His original wash drawings are in the National Railway Museum, YORK, and at IRONBRIDGE. From the late 1840s he prepared drawings from designs by Charles Vignoles (1793–1875) for bridges in Russia.

See also figure 41.

BIBLIOGRAPHY
General
Bourne, 1839, 1846; Vignobles, 1898.
Specific
Elton, A. The Piranesi of the Age of Steam. In *Country Life Album*. London, 1965.

box girder   *See* GIRDER BRIDGE.

Brad, Hunedoara, Romania   An ancient gold-working area, 50 km (30 mi.) N. of Hunedoara, where exploitation dates back to Dacian times. The Romans appointed a 'subprocurator aurariarum' to supervise the mines. The earliest known railway vehicle, a wagon for carrying ore in the underground workings, was found in a mine at Brad. Constructed entirely of wood, and with a gauge of 48 cm (19 in.), it was constructed in the fourteenth or fifteenth century, and certainly pre-dates those from the Harz Mountains and the Nuremberg (Nürnberg) region, or any railway vehicle from England. Some wooden rails and points were found with the wagon. A full-scale model of the wagon has been exhibited since 1930 in the Transport Museum (Verkehrsmuseum) in Berlin, and there are scale models in the Technical Museum and the Railway Museum in BUCHAREST.

BIBLIOGRAPHY
General
Bălan and Mihăilescu, 1985; Schumacher, 1912.

LOCATION
[M] Museul Aurului (Gold Museum), str. Moţilor, Brad.

HORIA GIURGIUMAN

Bradford, West Yorkshire, England   An archetypal boom town of the Industrial Revolution, Bradford's population grew from 13 000 in 1801, to 104 000 in 1851, to 280 000 in 1901. The Venetian Gothic Wool Exchange by Lockwood & Mawson, completed in 1867, and the substantial warehouses of the third quarter of the nineteenth century in 'Little Germany', east of the centre, are evidence of Bradford's role as commercial capital of the worsted trade. The centre is ringed by mills, the most impressive of them being the six-storey Manningham Mill built by Listers in 1873. Bradford Industrial Museum, housed in Moorside Mills, a typical worsted spinning complex of 1875, has textile collections and exhibits relating to motorcar manufacture, important in the city until the 1950s. The Colour Museum has the best British collection of dyestuffs. Stone back-to-back terraces typified working-class housing in Bradford until the late nineteenth century.

Saltaire, 6 km (4 mi.) N., built by Sir Titus Salt (1803–76) from 1851 to designs by Lockwood & Mawson, is one of the most impressive model industrial settlements. The mill is 170 m (557 ft) long, six storeys high, and of fireproof construction. Over eight hundred spacious houses were built by 1872 in carefully planned streets, together with an institute, a school, a church and a hospital.

The National Museum of Photography, Film and Television, a branch of the Science Museum, has comprehensive collections illustrating the development of the three media as industries and of their products.

Bradford has pioneered the promotion of industrial archaeology as a means of attracting tourists.

BIBLIOGRAPHY
Specific
White, D. *et al. Titus of Salts*. Bradford: Watmough, 1976.

LOCATIONS
[M] Bradford Industrial Museum, Moorside Road, Eccleshill, Bradford BD2 3HP.
[M] Colour Museum (Society of Dyers & Colourists), 82 Grattan Road, Bradford BD1 2JB.
[M] National Museum of Photography, Film and Television, Princes View, Bradford.

BARRIE TRINDER

Braga, Minho, Portugal   A town 50 km (30 mi.) NE of Oporto, the Bracara Augusta of the Romans and later a religious centre, now the capital of an important industrial region, with a soap factory of 1894 and a bell foundry. It was once a hat-making centre. The Bom Jesus rack railway is the oldest in the Iberian Peninsula, having been built in 1884 on the Riggenbach principle (*see* RACK RAILWAY) by the Portuguese engineer Raoul Mesnier du Ponsard. A railway museum at the station includes a Beyer Peacock 2–4–0 locomotive of 1875.

At Ruães, 10 km (6 mi.) S., are the ruins of a former papermill and the buildings of a large cotton mill, now disused, where there is a steam engine. What are probably the last Jacquard looms working in Portugal are employed to weave silk cloth in a workshop in the city centre.

BIBLIOGRAPHY
General
Vilaça, 1980.

LOCATION
[M] Railway Museum, Braga.

Brăila, Brăila, Romania   The district capital and a port on the River Danube, notable for the grain silos built by Anghel Saligny (1854–1925) in 1888–9: the silos have precast concrete panels, one of the earliest uses of this technique.

BIBLIOGRAPHY
General
Hudson, 1971.

braking   A pounding operation designed to break the retted stalk of the FLAX plant from the usable fibre. The pre-industrial flax brake is a wooden bench with a hinged wooden arm brought down on bunches of retted flax. Braking machinery accomplished the same purpose by passing the stalks through rollers that crush the woody stalk covering the inner fibre.

Bramah, Joseph (1748–1814)   The pioneer of HYDRAULIC POWER, responsible for many innovations and improvements to the innovations of others. Bramah was born near Sheffield, England, and apprenticed to a carpenter in London. In 1778 he patented improvements to the water closet, which became the basis for its commercial production. His hydraulic press was patented in 1795; and his beer engine, which raised beer from cellars to bars, in 1797. He also developed security locks, planing machines, and machines for numbering banknotes.

BIBLIOGRAPHY
General
McNeill, 1968, 1972; Smiles, 1863.

Brandenburg, Germany   This province, covering the areas of the present regions of Potsdam, Frankfurt, Cottbus and Neubrandenburg, was dominated economically by the presence in its centre of Berlin. Formerly the mark of Brandenburg, it became a Prussian province in 1816, and was the original home of the Prussian monarchy. Its only industry at that time, apart from those of Berlin, was wool-spinning and cloth manufacture in the Niederlausitz area, which was absorbed by Saxony in 1816. The transport and trade of Brandenburg profited by the railway and canal network running into BERLIN.

BIBLIOGRAPHY
General
Schmidt and Theile, 1989.
Specific
Liefert, W. Zur Entwicklung des Werks- und Industriebaus in Berlin und der Mark Brandenburg (The development of works and industrial buildings in Berlin and the mark of Brandenburg). In *Jahrbuch für Brandenburgische Landesgeschichte* (Yearbook of history in the province of Brandenburg), xxx. Berlin, 1979.
Lindner, W. Technische Kulturdenkmale in der Mark Brandenburg, Teil 1 und Teil 2 (Technical monuments in the mark of Brandenburg, part 1 and part 2). In *Brandenburgische Jahrbücher* (Brandenburg yearbooks), v, vi. Berlin, 1937.

brandy   A spirit distilled from wine made from grapes, although the term is also applied to Kirsch, made from cherries in Alsace and the Black Forest, and to plum-based spirits made in Eastern Europe. Cognac, the highest-quality brandy, is, strictly speaking, the product of the French departments of Charente and Charente Maritime, and Armagnac is from the department of Gers, both being made in traditional pot stills (*see* SPIRITS). Brandy is made in most wine-producing regions from the 'marc', the remains of the grapes when the wine has been pressed from them.
See also WINE.

BIBLIOGRAPHY
General
Delamain, 1936; Ray, 1973.

brass   An important range of alloys of COPPER and ZINC with other metals. Copper lends toughness; zinc hardness and a lower melting point. Early brasses (up to 35 per cent zinc) could be cast or worked cold, but needed annealing (*see* ANNEALING FURNACE).

In the seventeenth century brass was made in pots in closed furnaces without chimneys by cementation – that is, calamine (zinc carbonate) was oxidized to form zinc oxide, which was then heated in crucibles in reducing conditions with copper and charcoal. The resulting brass was cast into plates, $1.37 \text{ m} \times 0.11 \text{ m} \times 0.06 \text{ m}$ (4 ft. 6 in. $\times 4\frac{1}{2}$ in. $\times \frac{1}{4}$ in.), in granite moulds and beaten into hollow ware or into sheets for making wire. It was also cast in iron moulds into ingots for reworking.

In England in the 1550s the Society of Mineral and Battery Works was granted a monopoly in all production concerning brass. Members introduced brassmaking and battery, but failed to make good brass. The Mines Royal Act 1689 broke the monopoly and works were established at Esher, Redbrook and BRISTOL, where Abraham Darby I introduced skilled foreigners and, probably, the use of coke. His brother-in-law introduced rollers for brass (as opposed to copper) at Tern, Shropshire, about 1712.

Both the manufacture and the use of brass changed during the eighteenth century. From 1781 brass was made in Bristol by alloying zinc and copper metals in crucibles or reverberatory furnaces, and after the development by Dony of new processes for making metallic zinc (*see* VIEILLE MONTAGNE, LA) the process using calamine declined and by 1850 was little used. Much brass was now cast, but from 1769 items like saucepans and buttons were stamped from rolled sheet. Fancy articles were cleaned in nitric acid, then painted or lacquered.

In the nineteenth century new brasses were developed with zinc contents of 38–40 per cent: these rolled easily but had to be worked hot. Muntz metal (1832) replaced copper for sheathing wooden hulls. Delta metal (about 1883), which included 4 per cent iron, was used for bearings and ships' propellers. By 1860 'leaded' brasses were found to machine better. BATTERY became periph-eral, ceasing entirely in 1927.

See also MASLIN; WHITE METAL.

BIBLIOGRAPHY
General
Day, 1973; Hamilton, 1967; Morton, 1983.

NANCY COX

Bratislava (Pozsony, Pressburg), Southern Moravia, Czechoslovakia The capital of Slovakia, which owes much of its early importance to its strategic location at a crossing of the River Danube, which stimulated commer-cial development. The town was already an important trading centre by the thirteenth century. It was also the centre of a textile-producing region, and following the introduction of mechanical spinning at the end of the eighteenth century, industry developed in the town, which expanded rapidly. The surrounding region has long been a vine-growing area, and wine production is fea-tured in a local museum.

BIBLIOGRAPHY
Specific
Kalesny, F. *The Museum of Viticulture in Bratislava*. Bratislava: Museum of Viticulture, 1977.

LOCATIONS
[M] Museum of Viticulture, 1, Radnicna, Bratislava.
[M] Slovakian National Museum, Hrad, Bratislava.

Braunschweig, Germany *See* BRUNSWICK.

Brdy Uplands, South-West Bohemia, Czechoslovakia An ironworking area from the late Middle Ages with many important industrial monuments.

Dubnik, 20 km (12 mi.) E. of Plzeň, is an early charcoal ironworking site where blast furnaces dating from 1650 worked until 1850, but have since been destroyed. There was an earlier bloomery on the site. A mill race and a pond, a rolling mill, administration offices and a hammer mill remain. The mill race dates from the sixteenth century. The hammer mill is preserved as it was recon-structed in 1800. It has three different sizes of HELVE HAMMER of the tail helve and belly helve types, driven by shafting from water wheels. It worked until after World War II, and became one of the first industrial monuments to be preserved under the monuments protection pro-gramme.

Hořovice is an old centre of the charcoal iron industry, 50 km (30 mi.) SW of Prague. The regional museum interprets the history of the local iron industry.

Jince is an ironworking settlement, 10 km (6 mi.) SE of Hořovice. The ironworks was founded in 1810 by Count Rudolf Wrbna. The blast furnace and foundry remained in use until 1874 when the ironworks was converted to a water- and steam-powered sawmill, which closed in 1951. The blast furnace was powered by two water wheels. It is now a technical monument which may be developed as a museum.

Kladno is an iron-producing centre, 20 km (12 mi.) NW of Prague, where large-scale charcoal iron manufacture was supplemented by the introduction of coke blast furnaces in 1855. Steelmaking dominated the town after 1879. A museum of mining and metallurgy opened in 1970, and there are several trails through the industrial landscape.

Komárov is an ironworking site where activity goes back for some five hundred years. It was owned by Count Wrbna, who commissioned an Englishman, Winwood, to build two reverberatory furnaces there in 1793. Unsuc-cessful, they were demolished. Wrbna introduced English piston-blowing engines, but these too were unsuccessful. Gerstner designed a wooden blower for the furnaces. In 1819 two new cupolas were installed, and two new crucible furnaces in 1824. In the 1880s bracelets and necklaces were being made at Komárov, along with busts and decorative castings such as lampposts and bridges. The works was enlarged throughout the nineteenth century but could not compete with coke-fired plants. The last charcoal blast furnace closed in the 1920s, and the foundry in the 1930s. The site was converted for the manufacture of bombs and piston rings in 1952, then turned to rubber fabrics. The foundries were recon-structed in 1963 for the five hundredth anniversary of the works, but no important buildings survive.

A sixteenth-century blast furnace on the Rezna river at Železná Ruda, 100 km (60 mi.) S. of Plzeň, has been preserved as a historical monument.

BIBLIOGRAPHY
General
Jeníček, 1963.

LOCATIONS
[M] Forge Museum, Dubnik.
[M] Museum of Iron, Budova Byv. Zamku, Dnes Posty, Komárov.
[M] Railway Museum, Jince.
[M] Sumava Museum, Železná Ruda.

JUDITH ALFREY, SIMON DERRY and TIM PUTNAM

bread oven Traditionally, a chamber of brick or refrac-tory stone, heated with faggots of brushwood, with the entrance open to let out the smoke. The ashes were raked out when the bricks were hot, and risen dough was pushed inside with a long wooden paddle called a peel. The entrance was stopped up, and the bread was baked by the residual heat from the bricks. Several are preserved in museums. Today specialist industrial-scale ovens for baking bread may be fuelled by gas, coal or electricity. Some operate continuously with the bread being taken through on conveyors.

breakfast cereals A phrase that applies to a range of products developed in the USA in the late nineteenth century, Shredded Wheat being launched in 1893, and Puffed Wheat in 1902. W. K. Kellogg (1860–1951), of the Western Health Reform Institute, Battle Creek, Michigan, devised ways of rolling grain, particularly maize, cooking it in thin crisp flakes, and presenting it as a breakfast food.

Kellogg set up a factory in 1906 to make cornflakes. It suffered fires in 1908 and 1924, but surviving buildings have been surveyed by HAER (*see* UNITED STATES OF AMERICA). Kelloggs began selling in Britain, from Canada, in 1924, and built a factory at Trafford Park (*see* MANCHESTER) in 1938. The most notable breakfast cereal factory in Britain is the Shredded Wheat works of 1926 at Welwyn (*see* GARDEN CITY).

BIBLIOGRAPHY
General
Abbott, 1976; Hudson, 1978.

breakwater A term used since the eighteenth century to describe a solid barrier, made up of timber, rubble, coursed masonry, the hulks of ships, or 'dolosse' (interlocked forty-ton concrete blocks). The breakwater is designed to protect a harbour from the force of the waves, or a beach against the erosion of sand or shingle by the tide, in which case it may be called a groyne.

Brecht, Antwerp, Belgium A brickmaking town on the Dessel–Tournhout–Schoten Canal, 22 km (14 mi.) NE of Antwerp, where twenty-one Hoffman kilns were built between 1870 and 1928. The sole remaining kiln is the focus of a 'clay diggers' trail' through a landscape of pits and other relics of brickmaking. A tower windmill, 'Bounke-Bounke', was restored in the 1970s, and a former tramway station, an eccentric building of *c.*1910, is now a restaurant.

BIBLIOGRAPHY
General
Viaene, 1986.

LOCATION
[M] Kempisch Museum, Mudaeusstraat 2, 2160 Brecht.

Bregenz, Vorarlberg, Austria The capital of Vorarlberg, and a packet station at the eastern end of Lake Constance, close to the borders of Germany and Switzerland. The Rhine enters the lake through a delta 19 km (12 mi.) to the south-west. The Vorarlberger Landesmuseum displays glass, ceramics, and blue-and-white tiled stoves characteristic of the region. The Pfänderbahn cable car provides views westward over the lake. A semi-ROUND-HOUSE locomotive shed of 1890 has been adapted as a community centre. The Verein Bregenzer Waldbahn is a PRESERVED RAILWAY with its headquarters in the village of Bezau.

LOCATIONS
[S] Verein Bregenzer Waldbahn (Bregenz Forest Railway Association), 6870 Bezau.
[M] Vorarlberger Landesmuseum (Vorarlberg Museum), Kornmarkt 1, 6900 Bregenz.

Bremen, Bremen, Germany One of the principal north German ports, Bremen was linked to Hanover by rail in 1847; as in Hanover the original station was replaced in the 1880s by a new building designed by Hubert Stier, who was also responsible for the stations in Uelzen and Kreiensen in the Northeim district, 24 km (15 mi.) N. of Göttingen. All four stations follow the Renaissance style. The buildings in Bremen and Hanover are of approximately the same size, one reason for the form they take being the necessity of laying tracks above the level of the surrounding streets: however, the four stations differ considerably in their general appearance. While Hanover central station lost its train shed in World War II, the original arched train shed still covers most of the platform at Bremen. The main station building, which forms a right angle with it, also has a round vaulted roof. The end adjoining the street has a powerful, broad gable end, which is slightly curved. The monumental effect, dynamic by comparison with the station in Hanover, is heightened by large round-arched windows, and by monumental reliefs showing images of shipping and railways in the spandrels, and by seated, colossal allegorical figures on the corner pylons. To the right and left arcading links the main buildings with pavilions. The tall and almost unbroken mass of the train shed rises behind the complex, with slender columns at either end. In Kreiensen, 16 km (10 mi.) N. of Northeim, where the station buildings stand on an island platform, the monumental effect is achieved by a passage from the Hanover platform to the Brunswick platform built in the shape of a triumphal arch.

Bremen is traditionally the main port for the importation of wool and cotton. In 1930, only shortly before its sensational failure, Norddeutsche Wollkämmerei und Kammgarnspinnerei (the North German Wool Combing and Worsted Spinning Mill) erected a large office block to plans drawn up by the Gildemeister brothers. It was called the Haus des Reiches and is now used by the revenue authorities. It is a huge cube with a sandstone façade, a clock tower on one side, and sparse but grandiose expressionist ornamentation.

The first, most important, and for long after its construction in 1884 the largest plant of what later became the woollen firm of Lahusen was in Delmenhorst, 16 km (10 mi.) W. of Bremen, which at the time belonged to Oldenburg. Production in this 24 ha (59 ac.) complex ceased in 1981, but most of the buildings remain. There were two main phases of building: in the 1880s, to plans by Wilhelm Weye in the Hanoverian RUNDBOGENSTIL; and from 1897 to 1914, to plans by Henrich Deetjen, partly, as in the New Engine House, in the Romanesque style, and partly in brick in the neo-Classical style, much favoured for factory building at that time. The new engine house, with its machinery, has been restored and is now an industrial museum.

Civil engineering works carried out on the River Weser between 1883 and 1895, supervised by Ludwig Franzius, made it navigable by ships with draughts of up to 5 m (16 ft. 5 in.). Subsequently two custom-free ports were constructed: the Freihafen I (Europe) in 1885–6, and the Freihafen II (overseas) in 1901–6. No processing of imported goods was allowed in these areas, and consequently several companies opened premises around the timber and factory harbour (Holz- und Fabrikenhafen). Several of these buildings are preserved in their original form, at least from the exterior. They include the former Bremen-Besigheim oil works (now Meistermann works) of 1904, with a brick façade broken by pilaster strips, oculi and a shallow projecting arch; the HAG coffee-roasting plant, built to designs by Hugo Wagner in 1907, an early reinforced-concrete skeleton construction, with transom-windows, and a hipped roof to soften the general impression of modernity; and finally the monumental tower of the Roland Mill, built in 1925 to designs by Carl Heinrich Behrens-Nicolai. The entrance to the dock basins has been dominated since 1914 (with a second phase of building in 1926–9), by the great granary with its almost unbroken surfaces of brickwork.

Local history is illustrated in two museums in the city.

BIBLIOGRAPHY
General
Mende and Hamm, 1990; Slotta, 1975–85.

LOCATIONS
[M] Focke Museum, Schwachhauser Heerstrasse 240, 2800 Bremen.
[M] Schloss Schönebeck Museum, Im Dorfe 3–5, 2820 Bremen.
[I] Landesamt für Denkmalpflege Bremen (Bremen Monuments Protection Department), Sandstrasse 3, 2800 Bremen.

MICHAEL MENDE

Bremerhaven, Bremen, Germany   In 1827 a treaty with Hanover, then still under the British Crown, provided for a 25 ha (60 ac.) site downriver from Bremen to be developed as a port for transatlantic shipping. The Alte Hafen (old harbour) was built by 1830, the Neue Hafen (new harbour) in 1847–51, and finally the Kaiserhäfen (imperial harbours) were laid out between 1872 and 1909. In 1931 the great Norschleuse (north sluice) came into operation, joining the Kaiserschleuse (imperial sluice) which had been completed in 1897. In their day these were two of the largest sea locks in the world, and they keep the harbours independent of the tidal flow.

There are several lighthouses in Bremerhaven, including the 'Oberfeuer', built in the Gothic style in 1853–5 to a design by Simon Loschen, and the 'Unterfeuer Bremerhaven' in the Neue Hafen, a red-and-white striped steel tower tapering at the top, with a circular superstructure, which was built in 1893. The most celebrated lighthouse in Germany, the Roter Sand, has marked the entrance to the outer Weser in the German Bight since 1885.

Bremerhaven has a series of fine industrial buildings of the inter-war period, partly in the expressionist and partly in the INTERNATIONAL MODERN style. They include the buildings of the North Sluice and the adjoining swing bridge; the engine rooms of the bascule bridges in Keilstrasse and H. H. Meier Strasse; and the unusual watertower including living accommodation at Wulsdorf, dating from 1926–7. Above a six-storey dwelling house are two reservoirs, each holding 750 m³ (981 cu. yd.), set behind a brick wall almost blank in its appearance, and twice as high as the house beneath.

The German Maritime Museum and Museum Harbour on the Alte Hafen was established in 1972–5. Another, smaller maritime museum is in Brake, 30 km (19 mi.) upstream on the west bank of the Weser. The latter is housed in a telegraph station, part of the semaphore system established in 1846 for communications between Bremen and Bremerhaven. A water-level indicator of 1903, working on the SEMAPHORE principle, remains in use in the Alte Hafen at Bremerhaven. It has a counterpart in the semaphore wind-strength indicator of 1884, next to the lighthouse of 1803 at Cuxhaven, 24 km (15 mi.) N. (*see* HAMBURG). Bremerhaven is the principal German fishing PORT, evidenced by numerous warehouses erected between 1906 and 1982.

BIBLIOGRAPHY
General
Mende and Hamm, 1990; Slotta, 1975–85.

LOCATION
[M] Deutsches Schiffahrtsmuseum (German Museum of Shipping), Van-Ronzelen-Strasse, 2850 Bremerhaven.

MICHAEL MENDE

Brenner, Tyrol, Austria   The lowest pass over the main chain of the Alps, with a summit of 1369 m (4490 ft.); it is also the boundary between North and South Tyrol, the latter now in Italy although containing many German-speakers. The carriage road (Kaiserstrasse) south from Innsbruck through Matrei, Steinach and Gries across the pass into Val d'Isarco (Eisack tal) was completed in 1772. A railway was built in 1863–7 by Karl von Etzel (1812–65), whose memorial stands on Brenner station.

BIBLIOGRAPHY
General
Schneider, 1963.

Brescia, Lombardy, Italy   A centre for armaments manufacture since the Middle Ages. The growth of Brescia's metal trades in the eighteenth and nineteenth centuries was stimulated by mining and ironmaking in the Val Camonica, 40 km (25 mi.) NW, a valley now dominated by hydro-electric power stations.

The Toscolano Valley, west of Lake Garda, 38 km (24 mi.) NE of Brescia, became a papermaking centre in the fourteenth century, utilizing the abundant water power. Only the boundary walls remain of the largest works at Maina Superiore, and there are other ruins at Canete Vage and Maina Inferiore. The most impressive surviving plant was built by the lake at Toscolano in 1905.

BIBLIOGRAPHY
Specific
Piardi, F. La valle del Toscolano (The Toscolano valley). In *Archeologia Industriale*, I, 1984.

brewery   A manufactory for BEER and allied beverages.

bricks   Small prismatic blocks used for constructional purposes, most commonly coloured red or buff, and sometimes glazed on one or more sides to give a decorative effect and render the bricks impervious to moisture. Refractory bricks are used for structures that must be resistant to heat, or to corrosion by fluxes and flue gases. They are made of different materials, most typically fireclays.

The use of brick varies from country to country. In Britain bricks were widely used for prestigious buildings from the sixteenth century, but almost universal use for housing came only in the nineteenth century. There were important traditions of brickmaking in northern Germany, the Netherlands, Belgium and northern Italy. In the nineteenth century there was a strong revival of interest in the structural possibilities of brickwork, and the decorative effects that could be achieved with it. Bricks are used much less than formerly in much of Europe, but remain highly popular in Britain.

Brickmaking remained widely dispersed with strongly regional patterns into the twentieth century. Most bricks were still hand-moulded c.1900, and fired in clamps or simple updraught kilns. The scale of brickworks supplying London – first from the MEDWAY Valley, then from Bedfordshire – increased dramatically in the nineteenth century. The largest brickworks in Britain is at the company town of Stewartby, near BEDFORD.

In early wire-cutting machines for brickmaking, clay was extruded by plungers. The process was demonstrated in England by William Irving in 1841 but the first fully operational wire-cutting machine was designed by Richard Bennett in 1879; it was soon to be supplanted by the use of screw augers. Machines for re-pressing, to produce smooth facing bricks, date from the 1870s.

Hollow extruded bricks came to be used for the floors, ceilings and partition walls of factories and tall buildings to achieve fireproof but lightweight construction. Pots had been used for fireproof construction in late-eighteenth-century Britain and France, but the principle was applied on a large scale in the late-nineteenth-century skyscrapers built in the aftermath of the Chicago Fire of 1871.

See also figures 17, 97.

BIBLIOGRAPHY
General
Dobson, 1893; Dobson and Hammond, 1903; Hamilton, 1978; Lefêvre, 1900; Lloyd, 1925; Searle, 1915, 1920, 1929, 1929–30; Woodford, 1976.
Specific
Hammond, M. D. P. Brick kilns: an illustrated survey. In *IAR*, I, 1977.

MICHAEL STRATTON

bridge Bridges, more than any other product of industry, exemplify the technological potential, the powers of imagination, and the aesthetic taste of a generation. 'Bridges define our landscape', wrote the contemporary American historian, David McCullough. The poet Robert Southey (1774–1843) considered that, 'Of all the works of man, there is not any one which unites so well with natural scenery, and so heightens its beauty, as a bridge, if any taste, or rather if no bad taste, be displayed in its structure. This is exemplified in the rude as well as in the magnificent: by the stepping stones or crossing plank of a village brook, as well as by the immortal works of Trajan'. (*See* figure 19.)

The most memorable bridges are those that achieve what previous generations could not achieve – spanning the Menai in 1826, the East River between New York and Brooklyn in 1883, or the Bosporus in the 1980s – but the beginnings in the eighteenth century of large-scale transport projects, such as canals, turnpike roads and subsequently railways, led to a need for the construction of standardized but less spectacular structures, which was equally challenging.

Types of bridge are discussed under the following headwords: ACCOMMODATION BRIDGE; AQUEDUCT; ARCH; BASCULE BRIDGE; CANTILEVER BRIDGE; CONCRETE BRIDGE; FLOATING BRIDGE; GIRDER BRIDGE; IRON BRIDGE; LIFTING BRIDGE; RAILWAY BRIDGE; SKEW BRIDGE; STEEL BRIDGE; SUSPENSION BRIDGE; TRANSPORTER BRIDGE; TRUSS BRIDGE; TUBULAR BRIDGE; VIADUCT; WOODEN BRIDGE.

BIBLIOGRAPHY
General
De Jong, 1983; De Maré, 1950; Hopkins, 1970; Mock, 1949; Plowden, 1974; Prade, 1990.

BARRIE TRINDER

Bridgewater Canal, Greater Manchester, England A canal from Worsley to MANCHESTER, 8 km (5 mi.) long, built in 1759–61 by JAMES BRINDLEY (1716–72) for Francis Egerton, 3rd Duke of Bridgewater (1736–1803). It is often, misleadingly, described as the first in Britain. It was extended to the Mersey at Runcorn in 1772, becoming a source of great wealth and a powerful influence on the transport politics of the North-West. At Worsley Delph are the twin entrances to the 73 km (36 mi.) underground canal system, which included an inclined plane of 1795–6, together with the Packet House, the starting point of the canal's celebrated passenger services, two eighteenth-century dry docks, and the Duke's memorial. Brindley's Barton Aqueduct, 4 km ($2\frac{1}{2}$ mi.) SE, was replaced in 1893 by a 180 m (600 ft.) swing aqueduct over the Manchester Ship Canal. Most of the canal is still open. Monks Hall Museum has a steam hammer made by James Nasmyth (1808–90) at the Bridgewater Foundry (which was established in 1836), together with slotting and shaping machines made during 1851–6 for the colliery workshops at Elsecar (*see* SHEFFIELD).

BIBLIOGRAPHY
General
Cantrell, 1984; Malet, 1990; Richards, 1973.
Specific
Mullineux, F. The Duke of Bridgewater's underground canals at Worsley. In *Transactions of the Lancashire & Cheshire Antiquarian Society*, LXXI, 1961.

LOCATION
[M] Monks Hall Museum, 42 Wellington Road, Eccles M30 0NP.

BARRIE TRINDER

Figure 19 The wrought-iron Parker truss bridge which carries Elm Street across the Ottaquechee River in Woodstock, Vermont: built in 1869–70 by the National Bridge & Iron Co. of Boston, Massachusetts, it became a *cause célèbre* in the late 1970s, when it was widened and strengthened rather than being demolished.
Barrie Trinder

Brienz, Bern, Switzerland   A town celebrated for wood-carving. It is on the north shore of Lake Brienz, and on Brünig railway from Interlaken to Lucerne. The 7.5 km (5 mi.) Brienzer Rothornbahn, opened in 1894, is the only wholly steam-operated rack railway in Switzerland. Seven locomotives climb to the 2350 m (7710 ft.) summit.

At Ballenberg, 6 km (4 mi.) E., the 50 ha (124 ac.) Swiss open-air museum, opened in 1978, is designed to display re-erected buildings, chiefly farmhouses from all regions of the country, although the emphasis is on the canton of Bern. Domestic industries like linen-weaving and basket-making are well illustrated.

BIBLIOGRAPHY
General
Allen, 1965.
Specific
Gschwend, M. *Ballenberg: Schweizerisches Freilichtmuseum für landliche Bau- und Wohnkultur* (Ballenberg: the Swiss open-air museum for the study of rural buildings and society). Ballenberg, 1978.

LOCATIONS
[M] Museum of the School of Woodcarving, 3855 Brienz.

[M] Schweizerisches Freilichtmuseum für landliche Bau- und Wohnkultur, Ballenberg ob Brienz.

Brighton, East Sussex, England   A fishing village that became a fashionable resort in the early nineteenth century when it was popularized by the Prince Regent (later King George IV). Brighton Pavilion, the royal residence, has an early example of the architectural use of cast iron, used here to support onion-shaped domes. There is a splendid railway station of 1841 by David Mocatta (1806–82) with a later overall roof. The railway works established by the LBSCR was closed in the 1950s and has now been demolished. There are two Victorian piers: Palace Pier and West Pier, the latter being Britain's only Grade I listed pier. In 1883 Brighton-born Magnus Volk (1851–1937) opened the first electric railway in Britain along the sea front; it survives in a slightly modified form. Restored waterworks beam engines form the main exhibit at the British Engineerium in nearby Hove.

BIBLIOGRAPHY
General
Haselfoot, 1978.

LOCATION
[M] British Engineerium, off Nevill Road, Hove, East Sussex BN3 7QA.

Brindley, James (1716–71) The outstanding engineer of the first era of canal construction in England, Brindley was responsible for the BRIDGEWATER CANAL, the Trent & Mersey, the BIRMINGHAM and the OXFORD canals. By trade a millwright, he came to build canals through involvement with the Bridgewater estate. A mill that he designed is preserved at Leek, Staffordshire. He was also a mining engineer, whose work at Wet Earth Colliery near Manchester has been investigated in detail.

BIBLIOGRAPHY
General
Banks and Schofield, 1968; Boucher, 1968; Malet, 1977.

LOCATION
[S] Brindley Mill, Mill Street, Leek, Staffordshire.

brine A solution of SALT (sodium chloride, NaCl) in water.

Brisbane, Queensland, Australia The state capital evolved from a penal colony of 1824 which closed in 1839 and was reopened for free settlement in 1842. Two buildings remain from the convict period: a windmill of 1828, subsequently converted to a treadmill, and the Commissariat stores of 1829. The polychrome-brick Exhibition Building of 1891 is now a museum. Along the Brisbane River is a range of fine warehouses and a dry dock of 1878–81 by W. D. Nisbett, in stone, with the original iron caisson, the boilers and the boilermakers' workshop surviving.

BIBLIOGRAPHY
General
Heritage of Australia, 1981; McCarty and Schedvin, 1978.

LOCATIONS
[M] Royal Historical Society of Queensland Museum, Newstead House, Newstead Park, Brisbane 4000.
[M] Steam Locomotive Museum, Redbank, Brisbane 4000.

Bristol, Avon, England Established during the Dark Ages around the bridge that was the lowest crossing point on the River Avon, Bristol had already developed into a port of some importance by 1239–47 when the River Frome was diverted to provide improved quays, one of the principal engineering projects of medieval England. A royal charter of 1373 granted county status to the city, which it retained until 1974 when it became part of Avon. Traffic handled included most vessels to or from the River Severn, plus coastal traffic and trade with Ireland and many European countries. Bristol developed strong trading links with the New World which brought it great wealth and prosperity. By 1700 it was second in size and importance only to London, but the great tidal range of the Avon and its tortuous route from the Severn made navigation difficult for ships of increasing size.

Further improvements to the harbour were discussed but it was not until 1804–9 that a scheme was implemented, to the designs of William Jessop (1745–1814): this enabled vessels to remain afloat between tides instead of settling on the mud as previously. The modified port was thus known as the 'Floating Harbour', a name which it retains. It was created by damming the River Avon close to the southern end of the Avon Gorge, and diverting river water by means of a New Cut excavated south of the main channel. Some further alterations were carried out in the 1840s and 1870s, but the Floating Harbour remains much as it was when completed in 1809. New docks were constructed downstream from Bristol at Avonmouth in 1877 and at Portishead in 1879, but too late to prevent Bristol's supremacy being ceded to Liverpool, Glasgow and Southampton.

The Floating Harbour has seen little commercial use since the 1970s, but has progressively been adapted for leisure and other uses. Many dockside features survive. The more impressive buildings include the Welsh Back granary, Bush House, alongside St Augustine's Reach, and the three red-brick bonded warehouses at Cumberland Basin. Nineteenth-century Port Authority workshops and working hydraulic plant survive (although not publicly accessible) at Underfall Yard at the western end of the complex.

Three other important survivals in Bristol are all the work of ISAMBARD KINGDOM BRUNEL. At Temple Meads stands the terminus of the broad-gauge Great Western Railway, with a crenellated frontage in medieval style and an overall roof to the train shed of mock hammerbeam construction. In Great Western Dock the SS *Great Britain*, the world's first iron-hulled, screw-driven vessel, is undergoing restoration where she was launched on 19 July 1843, following her rescue from the Falkland Islands as a hulk in 1970. Clifton Suspension Bridge was designed by Brunel, but remained unfinished when he died in 1859, and was completed as his memorial by the Institution of Civil Engineers in 1864.

BIBLIOGRAPHY
General
Buchanan and Buchanan, 1980; Buchanan and Cossons, 1969.

LOCATIONS
[M] Bristol Industrial Museum, Prince's Wharf, Prince Street, Bristol BS1 4RN.
[M] City of Bristol Museum and Art Gallery, Queens Road, Bristol BS8 1RL.
[S] SS *Great Britain*, Great Western Dock, Gas Ferry Road, Bristol BS1 6TY.

JOHN POWELL

Britannia metal An alloy of tin, antimony and copper, invented by James Vickers. It is tougher than pewter and can be polished.

British Columbia, Canada The Canadian mainland west of the Rockies, which was united with the colony on Vancouver Island in 1866, and became a province in the

Canadian federation in 1871. It was linked with the rest of Canada by the Canadian Pacific Railway, completed in 1885.

Vancouver developed as a sawmilling centre, near the mouth of the Fraser River, to which the coastal forest cut was brought by floating and later by barge to more than a dozen large mills, which dispatched by train planks, boards, building lumber, shakes, shingles, sashes, doors and prefabricated houses to the lumber-scarce prairie provinces. Almost all the mills have gone, removed in the face of urban renewal or by the relocation of forest industries on sites closer to the cut, either on VANCOUVER ISLAND or in the interior. Some prefabricated houses built by the British Columbia Mills, Timber & Trading Co. survive, together with a store from Hastings Mill, the first of the Vancouver mills.

Gold rushes on the Fraser and Cariboo Rivers in the 1850s and 60s have left many traces, particularly abandoned settlements like those at Barkerville in the Cariboo, as well as remnants of early waggon roads carved along the Fraser Canyon by the Royal Engineers of the British army.

In the Kootenay mountains in the south-east of the province, great mining discoveries were made in the 1890s around what is now the city of Trail. There are extensive remains of the communities which exploited the copper, silver, lead and zinc ores. Ghost towns like Sandon near New Denver have been largely washed away in floods, but at 1800 m (6000 ft.) above sea level in the ridges above the town mine shafts, slag heaps and expensive machines stamped with the name 'Chicago Boiler and Flume Company' are testimony to once active mines and smelters. The War Eagle Mine at Rossland displays the same phenomena, while at Greenwood there is a slag heap and a brick smoke stack, and an ore dump remains from the Granby smelter at Grand Forks. Many other sites hint at the past prosperity of the Boundary Country copper mines. The province's Museum of Mining, north of Vancouver, incorporates the Britannia Copper Mine, which operated from c.1900 until 1974, in which visitors can tour underground workings by train.

Salmon canning was the quintessential food-processing industry of the province. Salmon could only be caught at certain periods and until the technological capacity was developed to transform the fish into marketable products, fishing was of little economic importance. With the establishment of salmon-canning plants, the first of them financed by English capital based in San Francisco, it became possible to reach European markets. Steveston on the Fraser River, 8 km (5 mi.) S. of Vancouver, which had more than a dozen canneries in the late nineteenth century, became the main centre; but canneries were also built on the estuaries of such other salmon rivers as the Nass and the Skeena. Such canneries used native Indian, Chinese and Japanese labour, and built distinctive bunkhouse complexes. The canning industry is illustrated in the provincial museum at Victoria (see VANCOUVER ISLAND), but the principal interpretation site has been designated as the Gulf of Georgia Cannery at Steveston, owned by the Canadian Parks Service since 1984.

BIBLIOGRAPHY
General
Haig-Brown, 1961; Newell, 1986b, 1989; Newell and Hovis, 1985; Newell *et al.*, 1986; Ormsby, 1971; Rich, 1967; Stacey, 1982.
Specific
Holdsworth, D. W. Houses and homes in Vancouver: images of West Coast urbanism. In Stelter and Artibise, 1977.
Mills, E. G. and Holdsworth, D. W. The emergence of ready-made housing in Western Canada. In *Natural Historic Sites: Occasional Papers in History & Archeology*, 14, 68–121, 1974.
Newell, D. Survey of historic industrial tidewater sites: the case of the British Columbia salmon-canning industry. In *IA*, XIII, 1987.

LOCATIONS
[M,S] British Columbia Museum of Mining, 1255 Welch Street, North Vancouver, BC.
[M] British Columbia Provincial Museum, 601 Belleville Street, Victoria, BC, V8V 1X4.

DERYCK HOLDSWORTH

Brno (Brunn), Moravia, Czechoslovakia A medieval town on the Vienna–Wrocław highway, which became an important centre for textiles and engineering. Although an impressive variety of trades flourished in Brno in the early modern period, its modern industrial history began with the introduction of fine-woollen manufacture in 1764 by the state-sponsored Brno Fine Cloth factory, followed by the German entrepreneur Wilhelm Mundy in 1774, and the Offermann-Thomann company who attempted to introduce mechanized spinning and carding in the early 1790s (although it has also been claimed that a spinning machine was first smuggled into Brno from England in 1802). In 1816 Offermann-Thomann introduced a 12 hp steam engine from London, and by 1834 they had added a locally constructed one of 25 hp, and had eighty spinning machines. The mill employed 2000 people in 1840.

The development of the textile industry stimulated machine-building from as early as 1802. Although Brno had to compete for skilled workers with both Prague and Vienna it developed as an important engineering centre, producing such heavy items as armaments and boilers. Brno's industrial and urban growth has continued into the twentieth century and left a legacy of significant modernist architecture, including a cinema by Joseph Kranz of 1927–9; the Hotel Avion, Vesna School and Student Hostel, all by Bohuslav Fuchs; and Rozenhal's Children's Hospital, with its functionally separated pavilions.

Today several textile factories have been adapted to new uses, and there is a project to preserve a textile mill as a museum and to display a collection of textile machinery. The Technical Museum houses an interactive display of water power showing the principles of the Kaplan turbine. There is a separate engine house with reciprocal compound engine and a Parsons turbine made under licence. The museum hopes to show the work of the Zibrock Company, now one of the largest Brno employers, producing everything from automobiles to telexes and

109

Bren guns. It has many trolley buses and trams in store. The Museum manages Stará Hut foundry at ADAMOV and a Renaissance corn mill at SLOUP (*see* figure 124); and it operates a blacksmith's smithy at Tesany, and at Kuzelov a working Dutch-type windmill constructed in 1842. Some buildings connected with wine manufacture are conserved at nearby Petrov.

BIBLIOGRAPHY
General
Komlos, 1983.
Specific
Freudenberger, H. *The Industrialisation of a Central European City*. Edington, Wiltshire: Pasold Research Fund Ltd, 1977.

LOCATIONS
[M] Museum of the City of Brno, Hrad 1, Brno.
[M] Technical Museum, Orti Ulice, c.20 and Josefka Ulice, c.1.

TIM PUTNAM and SIMON DERRY

broad-gauge railway A railway of wider gauge than the standard in the country concerned or than the standard of 1.435 m (4 ft. $8\frac{1}{2}$ in.). Some systems adopted slightly wider gauges before there was an accepted standard; examples include the 5 ft. 3 in. (1.6 m) used in Ireland and South Australia, and the 5 ft. 6 in. (1.68 m) employed in India and Spain. Russia adopted 5 ft. (1.52 m) on the advice of an engineer from the USA where that gauge was used on most lines in the South before the Civil War. Several early lines in the USA were built to a 6 ft. (1.829 m) gauge and converted in the 1870s. One of the few engineers deliberately to use a significantly wider gauge was ISAMBARD KINGDOM BRUNEL, who built the GREAT WESTERN RAILWAY and its subsidiaries to a gauge of 7 ft. $0\frac{1}{4}$ in. (2.14 m), giving advantages in speed and in the capacity and comfort of vehicles. Extension of the Broad Gauge was restricted by legislation, and it was gradually given up by the GWR, the last sections being converted on 20–2 May 1892.

BIBLIOGRAPHY
General
Westwood, 1983.
Specific
Clinker, C. R. *New Light on the Gauge Conversion*. Avon Anglia, 1978.

BARRIE TRINDER

Broken Hill, New South Wales, Australia Broken Hill, 450 km (280 mi.) NE of Adelaide and 950 km (600 mi.) W. of Sydney, is one of Australia's prime sources of zinc, lead and silver. Thirteen headstocks still stand within the city boundaries. Broken Hill is linked by rail to both the east coast and the south coast. Three underground mines still operate, and public tours of surface installations are offered at the North Broken Hill Mine. There are two mining museums. In the Delprats Mine visitors can descend a 120 m (400 ft.) deep shaft to view the stopes and workings. The Gladstone Mining Museum offers a simulated mining experience within a hotel building of 1887. Silverton, 16 km (10 mi.) NW, is a classic mining ghost town, where a local history museum is based in the former gaol. The Daydream Mine, about halfway along the road from Broken Hill to Silverton, is a preserved ADIT mine where visitors can travel along 400 m (1300 ft.) of tunnels amidst old workings.

BIBLIOGRAPHY
Specific
Brown, I. J. Mining and tourism in Southern Australia. In *IAR*, XII, 1989.

LOCATIONS
[S] Daydream Mine, Broken Hill, NSW 2880.
[M,S] Delprats Mine, Broken Hill, NSW 2880.
[M] Gladstone Mining Museum, Broken Hill, NSW 2880.
[S] North Broken Hill Mine, Broken Hill, NSW 2880.
[M] Silverton Gaol and Historical Museum, Silverton, Broken Hill, NSW 2880.

KATE CLARK

Bromsgrove, Worcestershire, England A nailmaking town at the foot of the 3 km (2 mi.) 1-in-37 Lickey Incline on the Birmingham & Gloucester Railway, opened in 1840–1. In the churchyard are the graves of two enginemen killed when a locomotive exploded on 10 November 1840. A Norris of Philadelphia 4–2–0 is depicted on the headstones, although the locomotive involved was not of this type. Avoncroft, a 4 ha (10 ac.) open-air museum opened in 1967, aims to rescue buildings from destruction. It includes a nail shop, a chain shop with working OLIVER hammers, a post mill of *c*.1800, and a prefabricated house of the late 1940s.

BIBLIOGRAPHY
General
Brook, 1977; Christiansen, 1973; Long, 1987.

LOCATION
[M] Avoncroft Museum of Buildings, Stoke Heath, Bromsgrove B60 4JR.

bronze An alloy of copper and tin. It is easily melted in small coke-fired furnaces, in amounts up to 45 kg (100 lb.), or in reverberatory furnaces. Bronze is hard, easily cast and resistant to corrosion. It is widely used for guns, statuary, and domestic hollow ware. Bronze coinage was introduced in France in the 1790s, and in 1860 in Britain. Specialist bronzes were developed during the nineteenth century, for example phosphorbronze (1856).
See also BELL METAL; GUN METAL.

BIBLIOGRAPHY
General
Alexander and Street, 1949; Partington, 1950.

Brown, Joseph Rogers (1810–76) One of the most innovative of machine-tool makers, Brown was born in RHODE ISLAND, the son of a watchmaker. From 1827 he learned the trade of a textile machinist, after two years turning to the manufacture of turret (or tower) clocks. His first major innovation was the linear dividing engine, perfected in 1850; this was followed by the Vernier calliper, capable of measuring in thousandths of an inch, in 1851, and by the micrometer calliper in 1867. He employed fourteen people in 1853 when Lucien Sharpe became his partner in the firm of J. R. Brown & Sharpe. In 1855 he devised a precision gear-cutter for clock gears, and on gaining a contract to make Wilcox & Gibb sewing machines in 1861, gave up clockmaking to concentrate on machine tools. In 1861 he produced his turret screw machine, and in 1861–2 his universal MILLING MACHINE, which was patented in 1865. Perhaps his greatest achievement was the universal GRINDING MACHINE which was granted a patent in 1877, soon after his death.

BIBLIOGRAPHY
General
Roe, 1916.

brown coal *See* LIGNITE.

Bruges (Brugge), West Vlaanderen, Belgium   One of the principal cities of Europe in the late Middle Ages and Renaissance, Bruges declined in the eighteenth century, and was notable in the mid-nineteenth century for its exceptionally high incidence of pauperism. The growth of tourism in the second half of the century followed the establishment of the Ostend–Dover packet in 1846. Bruges has few industrial buildings, a yeast factory in Wulpenstraat of 1924–6 being one of the few of note, but is ringed by canals ranging in date from the Middle Ages to the twentieth century.

Bruges was one of the first European cities to make extensive use of brick, a notable early use being the Palace of the Lords of Gruuthuse, now the Gruuthusemuseum, which dates from the fifteenth century.

The original railway station was removed to RONSE. The present station is a concrete and brick structure of 1939, with symmetrical nine-bay wings on each flank of the central booking hall, whose interior is decorated with murals by R. De Pauw.

Three windmills stand along the rampart to the east of the city, St Janshuismolen: a large post mill of 1770, Bonne Chierre of 1844, and De Nieuwe Papegaai of 1709.

A section on the city's history in the Historical Museum includes reconstructions of old kitchens, and a grocer's and confectioner's of 1937, together with displays of lighting apparatus.

Zeebrugge, 12 km ($7\frac{1}{2}$ mi.) N., established in 1907, is the only deep-water port in Belgium. It is linked to Bruges by the Baudouin Canal.

LOCATIONS
[M] Gruuthusemuseum, Dijver 17, 8000 Bruges.
[M] Museum voor Geschiedenis (Historical Museum), Kruispoort ter Langestraat 191, 8000 Bruges.
[M] Stadelijk Museum voor Volkskunde (City Folk Art Museum), Balstraat 27, 8000 Bruges.

BARRIE TRINDER

bruk   A Swedish term which does not readily translate into English. A 'bruk' implies a community whose main activity was industrial, typically the making of iron, but which was also responsible for the provision of food, fuel, transport and health care for its members. Some bruks were patriarchal, under the influence of landowners; others were essentially peasant co-operatives. Bruks were characteristic of the Swedish ironworking regions of the seventeenth and eighteenth centuries, and some were laid out on regular plans based on Classical precedents. Most ceased to function when the iron industry was reorganized in the late nineteenth century, but some have retained the suffix 'bruk' in their names while turning to such new industries as the production of wood pulp.

BIBLIOGRAPHY
General
Andersson, 1978.

Brunel, Isambard Kingdom (1806–59)   The most original of the engineers of the British Industrial Revolution, Brunel was resident engineer of the first Thames Tunnel, opened in 1826, which was designed by his father Sir Marc Brunel (1769–1849), and engineer of the BROAD-GAUGE GREAT WESTERN RAILWAY and its principal subsidiaries, including the South Devon Railway which was designed on the ATMOSPHERIC RAILWAY principle. His railways incorporated ARCH bridges of great originality. He was responsible for the STEAMSHIPS *Great Western*, *Great Britain* and *Great Eastern*; for substantial improvements to BRISTOL docks, and for building the Royal Albert Bridge, Saltash (*see* PLYMOUTH). The Clifton Suspension Bridge, BRISTOL, was built, after his death, to his design. He was the greatest British exponent of timber engineering, but none of his trestle viaducts in Devon and Cornwall remains.

BIBLIOGRAPHY
General
Brunel, 1870; Pugsley, 1976; Rolt, 1957.

Brunswick (Braunschweig), Lower Saxony, Germany   The city of Brunswick was formerly the capital of the duchy of the same name. It remains one of the principal cities of North Germany. The railway between Brunswick and Wolfenbüttel was opened in 1838. The original wooden station, in the Gothic revival style, was replaced in 1843–4 by a neo-Classical building designed by Karl Theodor Ottmer. In 1960 this terminus was closed, and the buildings along the train shed, which itself was destroyed in World War II, were themselves demolished. The imposing building at the head of the platforms now serves as the entrance to a bank. The main portal is in the shape of a triumphal arch, with goddesses of victory depicted in relief hovering above the side portals with wreaths of laurel. Colossal fluted pilasters with palmette bands and other decorative features add to the palatial effect. In 1841 the railway was extended to Harzburg. The Vienenburg station has been preserved and is one of the oldest remaining in Germany, much of it dating from 1840. In the course of extensive restoration in 1985, the original wooden facing with its late neo-Classical detailing and colouring was restored, and the building known as the Kaisersaal (Emperor's Hall), constructed in 1888, was also renovated.

The yellow-brick buildings of the sugar factory of the 1860s remain on Federal Highway 1 in the suburb of Rautheim. The factory closed in 1942, but the virtually unchanged exterior is typical of that of many rural sugar factories opened between 1840 and 1880, before the introduction of the diffusion process, and then, from about 1950, of extraction towers, for removing the juice from sliced beet.

The former Ducal Brewery of the Carl Wolters company, dating from 1884, stands on the main road to Wolfenbüttel. The complex is grouped around a courtyard, shielded from the road by a high ornamental fence, and consists of a brewhouse, a warehouse, a dispatch building and some living accommodation. Like the tall detached chimney, the buildings are constructed in a traditional style of pale yellow brick. The three-dimensional effect of the brickwork, with bands of bright-red brick running through it, emphasizes the ambitious nature of the design, which is further enhanced in the brewhouse by three large round-arched windows, and a central projecting section of the façade with a shallow-pitched triangular gable.

BIBLIOGRAPHY
General
Mende and Hamm, 1990; Slotta, 1975–85.

LOCATIONS
[M] Braunschweigisches Landesmuseum (Brunswick Provincial Museum), Burgplatz 1, 3300 Brunswick.
[M] Municipal Museum, Am Löwenwall, 3300 Brunswick.

MICHAEL MENDE

Brunton, William (1771–1851) The English engineer responsible for important developments in ore-dressing, including the Brunton calciner of 1828 for extracting arsenic from tin ores, and the Brunton BUDDLE of 1841. The son of a clockmaker, he worked at NEW LANARK and for BOULTON & WATT before becoming a partner in a Birmingham foundry, and from 1825 a consulting engineer in London.

Brussels (Brussel, Bruxelles), Brussels, Belgium The Belgian capital is the hub of the national economy, comprising only 0.5 per cent of the land area of Belgium, but accommodating 10 per cent of the population. It is not only the focus of Belgian service industries, but a major centre of manufacturing. Most of the city's imposing boulevards were laid out between 1867 and 1871, following the removal of fortifications. The city retains several notable monuments of its international exhibitions, including the display halls, statues and park where the Cinquantenaire took place in 1880, marking the jubilee of the Belgian nation, and the Atomium commemorating the exhibition of 1958. The AAM (Archives d'Architecture Moderne) has been responsible for an eighteen-volume survey of the industrial archaeology of Brussels.

La Grande Place (Grote Markt) is one of the most magnificent of market places, and the surrounding streets retain shop buildings of great interest, including traditional confectioners' premises, and a shop with a cast-iron façade in the rue Marché aux Herbes, with five plate-glass windows at first-floor level. The Galéries St Hubert (St Hubertusgalerijen), running from the rue Marché aux Herbes, was designed in 1846 by J. P. Cluysenaar, and with its neo-Classical detailing, and its barrel-vaulted cast-iron and glass roof, forms one of Europe's most civilized shopping arcades. A later mark of architectural distinction is the Marché Ste Marie, in Koninklijkestraat, Schaerbeek, now a cultural centre, which has a magnificent iron and glass roof.

The industrial economy of Brussels was largely shaped by the city's canals. That from Willebroek and the sea was opened in the sixteenth century, extended through the city to Charleroi in 1827–32, and widened in the early twentieth century. By 1910 most heavy industrial plants were ranged along an axis from north-east to south-west along the canals, through the suburbs of Schaerbeek, Koekelberg, Cureghem, St-Jans-Molenbeek and Anderlecht, and included two oil refineries, the Vivinus motorcar factory and the Lever Brothers (*see* PORT SUNLIGHT) soap works. At Nederoyer-Heembeek to the north of the city the canal is spanned by the Buda lifting bridge of 1955, adjacent to the Marly Coke Ovens.

The most spectacular industrial monument in Brussels is the complex bounded by the Avenue du Port and the rue Picard, now a railway freight depot, constructed as the Gare Maritime between 1902 and 1910 by the architects C. Bosmans & H. Vand de Veld, and the public warehouse of the Tours et Taxis freight company built between 1904 and 1907 by E. Van Humbeek. The latter includes three huge freight-handling sheds with cast-iron roofs. The reconstruction of the railway system with the completion of the link between Nord and Midi stations after World War II means that there are few features of historical interest in the main railway termini in Brussels, but there are several notable suburban stations, including Schaerbeek, adjacent to the main railway depots, with an imposing clock tower of 1887 and a booking hall of 1913. The tracks adjacent to the station are spanned by a long bridge of concrete trusses of 1935. Laken station, in the royal park, north of the city, is a neo-Classical building of 1875–7, with a nearby overbridge in an ornate style, flanked by obelisks.

Brussels retains an extensive tramway system now integrated with the city's Metro, many routes now passing beneath the city centre in tunnels. A monumental building in Fernand Demetskaai, Anderlecht, constructed as a warehouse c.1880, was subsequently adapted as the power station for the tramways. A tram stop with an iron roof remains in Hippodroomlaan, Elsene, and a brick tramway depot of 1900 in Fonsynylaan, St Gillis. The history of the system is commemorated in the City Transport Museum. Situated in a typical country tram depot of 1888 is the Vicinal Museum at Schepdaal, which has a collection of over fifty vehicles, including four steam tramway locomotives, one built at Grand HORNU.

Figure 20   The canal basins in Brussels in the late 1890s, before the commencement of a programme of modernization which made the port accessible to ships of up to 4500 tons: the photograph provides evidence of the barges used on Belgian canals in the nineteenth century, and of the variety of road waggons which distributed cargoes brought to the city by water.
La Fonderie, Brussels

The history of motor transport is illustrated by the first Renault motorcar showroom in Brussels, a RUNDBOGEN-STIL building of 1912 in Bataviersstraat, Elsene, and by the Autoworld Motor Museum, one of the largest in Europe, now housed in one of the Cinquantenaire exhibition halls of 1880. It is the collection of Ghislain Mahy (b. 1907), a motor trader from Ghent, and includes vehicles from most car-producing countries, with Belgian examples from Fondu (1906–12), Germain (1897–1914), Imperia (1905–48), Minerva (1899–1958) and Nagant (1900–28).

The textile industry in Brussels, particularly lacemaking, is illustrated in the Museum of Costume and Lace. Early nineteenth-century workshops remain in Roodklooster-Abdij, Oudergem, and there is a passementerie workshop in Kapucijnenstraat. The 'Filatures d'Aoust' spinning factory of *c.*1890 remains in Bollinckxstraat, Anderlecht, and there is an elegant 1921 lingerie factory in concrete in Huart-Hamoirlaan, Schaerbeek.

Brussels is also celebrated for its role in the manufacture of food and drink. More than twenty brewery complexes have been identified in the city. Outstanding among them is the former Vandengeuvel brewery in Ninoofsesteen-weg, St-Jans-Molenbeek, the earliest parts of which date from 1850, with additions of 1929 in the ART DECO style. The history of brewing is portrayed in a museum in the Brewers' House in La Grande Place (Grote Markt). Other buildings connected with the food industry include the Victoria chocolate factory of 1896 in Deneckstraat, Koekelberg, now tenemented; the Boulangerie de l'Union Économique in T. Vincottestraat, an industrial bakery of 1908; the former sugar refinery of Charles Gräffe in Manchesterstraat, St-Jans-Molenbeek, now an arts centre; an ice factory of 1874 in IJskelderstraat, St Gillis; and an Art Deco banana warehouse of 1928 built for the fruit merchant G. Koninckx in A. Dansaertstraat. The Meuneries Bruxelloises, a grain silo of 1907 in Groendreef, was adapted as sixteen apartments as early as 1935.

Brussels is rich in monuments of manufacturing industry. A shot tower in Fabriekstraat was in use until 1940. The monumental Desmet piano factory in Waterloose Steenweg, Elsene, dates from *c.*1870, with additions of 1905. The Danckaert factory, which made woodworking machinery, in Barastraat, Anderlecht, is a reinforced concrete building with Art Deco ornamentation. In Dobbelenbergstraat stand the De Keyn paint and varnish factory, of 1850, and the Usines Peters-Lacroix, which made wallpaper. A shoe factory in Van Volxemlaan dates from 1871, but is dominated by a huge concrete warehouse built for the Bata company in 1940. The extensive Ajja tobacco factory in Vandermaelenstraat, St-Jans-Molenbeek, consists of five ranges, three of 1873 and two identical buildings of 1910.

Outstanding among buildings associated with the city's public utilities is the abattoir in Anderlecht, with an iron market hall, 100 m (330 ft.) long, 100 m (330 ft.) wide, and 20 m (66 ft.) high, and a figure of a bull at the entrance, designed by Émile Tirou and built in 1890. Another former slaughterhouse, dating from 1850, has accommodated the Gemeentelijk Museum van Elsene since 1892. Several early power-station buildings survive, including examples of 1895 in Vinkenlaan, Watermaal-Bosvoorde, of 1906 in Vilvoordelaan, Schaerbeek, and of 1911 in Voltastraat.

Brussels is closely associated with the development of the ART NOUVEAU style, which can be experienced most vividly in the museum in the home of Victor Horta (1861–1947): it can also be seen in a variety of industrial buildings, among them the 'Palais de Vin' wine depot in Huidevettersstraat of 1909, by Fernand Symons; the 'Old England' warehouse of 1899 in Hofberg, by Paul Saintenoy; the coachworks of Smutsel Frères in Pagestraat, of 1906; and in two buildings by Horta, the shop of 1909 of Wolfers, jewellers, in Arenbergerstraat (the original fittings of which are in the Royal Museum of Art and History), and the Waucquez warehouse of 1903–6 in Zandstraat, notable for its delicate wrought-iron work.

Housing of historical interest in Brussels includes Gothic apartments in O-L-V van Vaakstraat and Kruitmolendstraat, Art Nouveau examples of 1912 by Émile Hellemans in Marollenwijk, and Art Deco flats of 1925 in J. Schildknechtstraat, Laken. An apartment block of 1904 in J.-F. Navezstraat, Schaerbeek, has a mosaic portraying 'Cleanliness and Health'. The Cité Moderne, around Samenwerkersplein in St Agatha-Berchem, dates from 1922–5, and is a combination of GARDEN CITY and INTERNATIONAL MODERN styles.

La Fonderie ASBL (Foundry Association) is a voluntary body formed in 1983 to promote the establishment of a museum illustrating the social and industrial history of the Brussels region in the great hall of La Compagnie des Bronzes, where high-quality metalwork, including much of the sculpture to be seen in the city, was made. A museum has been established in the 'Cheval Noir' warehouse formerly used for the storage of beer and pig iron.

At Vilvoorde, 12 km ($7\frac{1}{2}$ mi.) N., are the five-storey former lace factory of J. Legrand, a neo-Classical market hall of 1903 and a railway museum, as well as steelworks and coke ovens. The Lammens papermill at Zaventem, 15 km (9 mi.) NE, consists of substantial brick buildings on a site where paper was first made at a converted cornmill in 1610. The mills specialized in paper for offices in Brussels. The buildings of the former leather works, 'Tanneries et Maroquineries Belges', remain alongside the railway from Brussels to Louvain. At Ruisbroek, 6 km (4 mi.) SW of Brussels on the Canal de Bruxelles à Charleroi is a range of late-nineteenth-century flourmills, with a seven-storey, twenty-bay brick main block. A bakery museum at Groot Bijgaarden, 6 km (4 mi.) W., demonstrates the manufacture of bread and pastry on an industrial scale.

See also figure 126.

BIBLIOGRAPHY
General
Culot, 1980; Viaene, 1986; Vire, 1970.

LOCATIONS
[M] Bakkerijmuseum Puratos (Puratos Bakery Museum), Industrialaan 25, 1720 Groot Bijgaarden.
[M] Biermuseum (Brewing Museum), Grote Markt 10, 1000 Brussels.
[I] Centre d'Animation et de Recherche en Histoire Ouvrière et Populaire (Centre for interpreting and researching working-class and people's history), Paleizenstraat 90, 1030 Brussels.
[I] Centrum voor Hedendaagse Sociale Geschiedenis (Centre for Modern Social History), Vrije Universiteit Brussel, Pleinlaan 1, 1050 Brussels.
[M] Filmmuseum (Film Museum), Paleis voor Schone Kunsten, Baron Hortastraat 9, 1000 Brussels.
[M] Gemeentelijk Museum van Elsene (Local History Museum of Elsene), J. Van Volsemstraat 71, 1050 Brussels.
[M] Horta Museum, Amerikastraat 15, 1050 Brussels.
[M] Koninklijke Museum voor Kunst en Geschiedenis (Royal Museum of Art and History), Jubelpark 10, 1040 Brussels.
[I] La Fonderie ASBL, rue Ransfort 27, 1080 Brussels.
[M] Museum en Archief voor Moderne Architectuur (AAM; Museum and Archives of Modern Architecture), Kluisstraat 86, 1050 Brussels.
[M] Museumstoomtrein der Twee Bruggen (Steam Train Museum of the Two Bridges), Harensesteenweg 494, 1800 Vilvoorde.
[M] Museum van de Belgische Radio en Televisie Omroep (Museum of Belgian Radio and Television), Omroep-Centrum (Broadcasting Centre), A. Reyerslaan 52, 1040 Brussels.
[M] Museum van de Belgische Spoorwegen (Musée des Chemins de Fer), Leuvenseweg 21, 1000 Brussels.
[M] Museum van de Buurtspoorwegen (Tramway Museum), Ninoofsesteenweg 184, 1750 Schepdaal.
[M] Museum van Posterijen en Telecommunicaties, Grote Zavel 40, 1000 Brussels.
[M] Museum voor Geld en Geschiedenis van de Nationale Bank van België (Museum of Money and of the History of the Belgian National Bank), Wildewoudstraat 9, 1000 Brussels.
[M] Museum voor het Kostuum en de Kant (Museum of Costume and Lace), Violetstraat 6, 1000 Brussels.
[M] Museum voor het Stedelijk Vervoert Brussel (Museum of City Transport in Brussels), Tervurenlaan 364 bis, 1140 Brussels.
[M] Museum voor Kermisorgels (Museum of Fairground Organs), Waelhemstraat 104, 1030 Brussels.
[M] Slotenmuseum (Museum of Locks), Beenhouwersstraat 70, 1000 Brussels.
[M] Spoorwegmuseum (Railway Museum), Vooruitgangstraat 86, 1000 Brussels.
[M] Stadsmuseum van Brussel (City Museum of Brussels), Peperstraat 1, 1000 Brussels.
[M] Wereldautomobielcentrum en Museum Autoworld (World Motorcar Centre and Museum), Woluwelaan 46-13 bis, 1200 Brussels.

BARRIE TRINDER

Bucharest (Bucureşti), Ilfov, Romania   The capital of Romania: a city with few outstanding industrial monuments, but the museums have important collections. The Technical Museum, founded in 1928 by the engineer DIMITRIE LEONIDA (1883–1965), has exhibits from all over Romania, including steam engines from metalliferous and salt mines, early electric motors, and an eighteenth-century chain pump or 'pater noster' from Borzas (Maramureş). The collection of the Railway Museum consists chiefly of models but includes the locomotive *43 Calugareni* which was built for the opening of the railway between Bucharest and Giurgiu (*see* ROMANIA).

The Village Museum in Bucharest is situated on an 8 ha (20 ac.) site in Herastrau Park. The concept of an open-air ethnographic museum in Romania originated with the archaeologist Alexandru Odobescu who arranged a display of peasant houses at the Paris exhibition of 1867. A series of exhibitions on this theme was arranged during the first half of the twentieth century, and the present museum was established in 1948. It now comprises over three hundred structures grouped in sixty-four units. Exhibits include an oil press of 1794, ovens for smoking fruit, a nineteenth-century cask-maker's workshop, fishing equipment in great variety, fulling mills, gold-ore crushing mills and washing plants from the Carpathians, and a pottery from Olari Horezu, notable in the early twentieth century for its high-quality wares.

BIBLIOGRAPHY

Specific

Focsa, G. *The Village Museum in Bucharest*, 3rd edn. Bucharest: Meridiane Publishing House, 1970.

Wollmann, V. Romania. In Georgeacopol-Winischhofer *et al.*, 1987.

LOCATIONS

[M] Museul Cailor Ferate (Railway Museum), Calea Griviţa 193B, Bucharest.

[M] Technical Museum 'Ing D. Leonida', Str. C. Popescu 2 – Parcul Libertătii 5, Bucharest.

[M] Village Museum, Şoseaua Kiseleff 20, Bucharest.

HORIA GIURGIUMAN

Budapest, Hungary Budapest is a settlement formed by three towns, Buda (on the right bank of the Danube), Old Buda (north of Buda) and Pest (on the left bank). Its history can be traced from pre-Roman times. Under the Emperor Hadrian Old Buda became a 'municipium', and the Romans built a pontoon bridge over the Danube to link it with Contra-Aquincum, which was to become Pest. Beyond lay the barbaric lands of the East. After the occupation of the region by the Magyars in 895, Pest became a centre of trade, particularly with the Bulgarians, and Buda the royal residence. Under King Mattias in the late fifteenth century both towns flourished, but after his death decline set in, to be followed by Turkish rule between 1541 and 1686.

After the liberation by the armies of the Habsburg Emperor Leopold I, it was more than a hundred years before the two towns recovered from the devastation. The Empress Maria Theresa, who reigned between 1740 and 1780, had a royal palace built in Buda, and a permanent pontoon bridge built over the Danube. Her son Joseph II moved the university to Pest from Tyrnau. The vigorous

urban building programme that commenced then has continued ever since. In the first half of the nineteenth century buildings for such institutions as the National Museum, the Academy of Sciences and the National Theatre were constructed, as well as the Chain Bridge in 1849, and the first railways, to Vác in 1846 and to Szolnok in 1847. The parliament still met at Pozsony (now BRATISLAVA), but in 1848 Pest became the centre of the youth movement which was engineering a national rising. This rising led to the War of Independence, involving the whole Hungarian nation, the war being suppressed in 1849 by the Austrian army, with the aid of the Tsar of Russia. In 1867 the House of Habsburg and the Hungarian nation came to the 'Compromise', the Habsburg Empire becoming the Austro-Hungarian monarchy which lasted until 1918.

That half-century brought Hungary a degree of economic prosperity which placed it among the leading nations of Europe and of the world. In 1873 the three towns of Old Buda, Buda and Pest were united and became the capital city of the kingdom of Hungary. The city became the centre of Hungarian industry, and many industrial structures, halls, stations, bridges, and buildings such as those on the banks of the Danube date from this period. After defeat in World War I, the monarchy was dissolved and Hungary became independent, the country being ruled by a regent from 1920 to 1944. Development could now keep pace with Western Europe only in certain branches of industry – locomotive construction, for example – while in others, such as its previous flourishing automobile industry, Hungary fell behind. In World War II Budapest suffered severely from two months of siege by the Red Army, and from American bombing raids. The retreating Germans destroyed the Danube bridges. Some of the scars of the war can still be seen, although intensive reconstruction has restored the city's unique beauty.

Budapest has some two million inhabitants. Pest, situated on the edge of the Hungarian plain, is connected to Buda, on the hills on the right bank of the river, by six road and two railway bridges. Budapest's first horse tramway opened in 1866. Its Ujpest terminus, a three-storey building of 1867 designed by Janos Wagner, is a preserved monument. The network was converted from horse to electric operation as early as 1887. The romantically-styled Zugliget station dating from *c*.1900 is now used as a dwelling house. Budapest had the first underground electric railway in continental Europe: a 3.7 km ($2\frac{1}{2}$ mi.) line opened in 1896 during the festivities celebrating the thousandth anniversary of the Magyar conquest. In recent decades it has been extended into a large network. A rack railway, a 2.8 km ($1\frac{1}{2}$ mi.) line up the Szabadság hill, was built in 1874, extended in 1899 and electrified in 1930.

Technological innovations of such worldwide significance as the transformer, the carburettor and the telephone exchange were made in Budapest. Even the electric motor, the invention of Ányos Jedlik, was introduced there earlier than the Siemens motor in Berlin. It was in Budapest that the Swiss Abraham Ganz opened a foundry in 1845. In 1847 he began casting railway wheels and his

Figure 21 A reinforced concrete bus depot in Budapest, a pioneering work by the engineer I. Manyhárt
Mihály Kubinszky

foundry of 1858, which was built for that purpose and operated until 1964, is now a museum where several cupolas, many cranes and other foundry equipment are displayed. He expanded into electrical engineering from 1878, producing sixty turbines a year and employing over 6000 men by 1895. An innovative reinforced-concrete assembly shop designed by Szilárd Zielinski, 17.4 m × 80 m (53 ft. × 244 ft.) and 23.27 m (71 ft.) high, remains at Kőbányai út 31. Factories for producing heavy goods vehicles were opened and textile and engineering industries followed. There had long been brickworks and breweries in the city. The nucleus of Hungarian heavy industry developed on Csepel Island in the Danube, not far from the capital.

Budapest is still the centre of Hungarian cultural life, with several universities, polytechnics, and technical colleges, as well as numerous theatres. From the beginning of the nineteenth century a neo-Classical architectural style was developed, symbolic of its cultural independence, and after the Compromise of 1867, Hungarian architecture adopted a historicist style of a kind familiar throughout Europe. At the end of the nineteenth century, when fresh efforts were being made to free the countries from the dual monarchy, it was in the applied arts, with JUGENDSTIL architecture in the lead, that Hungarian independence was emphasized. Many fine works in that style can still be seen in the city. Finnish and Scottish architects influenced this kind of building with its nationalist overtones. After a transitional period of a new kind of HISTORICISM, modern architecture began to develop in Hungary from 1930, during those years when other European countries, for political reasons, were distancing themselves from modern architectural ideas. Consequently there are some fine works by famous avant-garde architects in the capital. The most attractive architectural feature of all, however, is the view of the city from the Fishermen's Bastion, or Gellért Hill, equally appealing by day or in the evening light. From these vantage points the whole fabric of the city can be seen unfolding, with its artistic monuments, its residential areas and the industrial zones visible in the distance – and, most striking of all, the Danube bridges. Their principal features, going from north to south, are as follows.

The North Railway Bridge
A bridge carrying a single-track line once owned by an Italian company, and built by the Societa Nazionale delle Ufficine di Savigliane in 1894–6. Its steel girders were manufactured by the engineering works of Hungarian Railways. It was reinforced several times, destroyed by air raids in 1944, and rebuilt by 1955.

The Árpád Bridge
A bridge between Old Buda and northern Pest, touching the northern tip of Margaret Island, designed by Károly Széchy. Construction began in 1939, was halted in 1943 on account of the war, was resumed in 1948, and completed in 1950.

The Margaret Bridge
A bridge between Buda and Pest, touching the southern tip of Margaret Island. The neo-Baroque design, chosen by competition in 1872, was by the French engineer Ernest Gouin. The carvings on the piers are by the Parisian Thabard. The bridge was opened in 1876. Horse trams began using the bridge in 1879, and in 1900 the wing linking it to Margaret Island was completed. This part of the bridge was reinforced in 1935. On 4 November 1944, before fighting had reached the capital itself, the Pest side of the bridge was blown up without any warning while crowded with traffic. After the war it was rebuilt, reinforced and modernized, but the spirit and form of the old bridge were retained. It reopened in 1948.

The Chain Bridge

The pride of the capital and the country, this bridge was built in 1842–9 on the initiative of the great political reformer Count Stephan Széchenyi, to plans by the British engineer William Tierney Clark, the work actually being carried out by Adam Clark (no relation), and the materials being imported from England and supplied by the firms of Humber & English, Howard & Ravenhill, and Harvey. The span is 197.6 m (648 ft.). Adam Clark also constructed a 350 m (383 yd.) tunnel under Castle Hill, opened in 1856, which continues the line of the bridge. After destruction in 1945 the bridge was rebuilt in time for the centenary of its original opening. Only minor modernization (widening of the openings in the piers) was necessary, and the bridge retains its old form.

The Elizabeth Bridge

This bridge links the inner city of Pest and Gellért Hill. It is the most elegant of the Budapest bridges: a single-span suspension bridge, with a span of 298 m (946 ft.), built in 1897–1903 to plans by a team of whom the engineer Istvan Gallik was the moving spirit. It was blown up in 1945 and completion of its rebuilding was delayed until 1964 because of technical difficulties. The finished work, to designs by the engineer Pál Sávoly, gave the city another suspension bridge as fine as the Chain Bridge itself.

The Franz Joseph Bridge

The decision to build this bridge, known since 1945 as the Liberty Bridge, was taken at the same time as that to construct the Elizabeth Bridge. The work was carried out in 1894–6 to designs by the Hungarian engineer János Feketeházy, submitted in competitive tender. It is a console bridge, built of steel. It was blown up in 1945, but was the first of the Budapest bridges to be rebuilt, the work being completed in 1946.

The most southerly road bridge

This bridge was built in 1933–7 to designs by the engineer Pál Álgyay-Hubert, submitted in competitive tender. It was blown up in 1945, but rebuilt, wider than before, by 1952.

The Southern Railway Bridge

A double-track bridge built in 1872–7, a four-span steel structure, the first link between the sections of the Hungarian rail network on the right and left banks of the Danube. Frequently reinforced, it was swiftly if temporarily reconstructed after it was blown up in 1944. One track was reopened in 1948, and the second restored in 1953.

The two principal Budapest railway stations are particularly noteworthy. A station erected in 1846, which stood in the way of city development plans, was demolished. On the site grew Budapest West (Nyugati Pályaudvar), originally the terminus of the State Railway Company, which was run by the Austrians with French financial backing. The new station was constructed in 1874–7 in accordance with the new plans. The concourse is the work of Gustave Eiffel, but its architectural features are attributed to the railway's Director of Building, W. A. de Serres. The steel-roofed train shed, 146 m × 42 m (445 ft. × 128 ft.) and 24.81 m (76 ft.) high, is flanked on either side by four-storey buildings. The station was restored in 1977–88, with great respect for its historical value. The East Station (Keleti Pályaudvar), originally the Central Station of MÁV (Hungarian State Railways), has an elliptical iron and glass roof and was built by the architect Gyula Rochlitz and the engineer János Feketeházy in 1881–4: apart from minor alterations it remains in its original condition. The state railways locomotive assembly shop of 1873, a vast building with cast-iron columns and a complex roof of cast-iron latticework, remains in use at Kőbanyai út 30.

The Tiger Inn, at Nádor utca 5, was the departure point for mail coaches to Vienna and was once the residence of Louis Kossuth.

There are several market-hall buildings of note in Budapest, including those in Klauzál and Hunyadi Squares, and the Central Market Hall in Dimitrov Square. The city slaughterhouse at Soroksári út 58, designed by the Prussian architect Gyula Hennicke, is notable for its huge water tower and for statues of animals and slaughtermen on the entrance piers.

Many inner-city residential buildings in Budapest have cast-iron gallery structures in their inner courtyards, dating from their original construction.

Among the famous buildings of the Jugendstil period are the works of the architect Ödön Lechner (1845–1914): his Post Office Savings Bank, the Museum of Applied Art (Üllői út), and the Geological Institute (Népstadion út). The Zoo buildings are the works of the architects Károly Kós (1883–1977) and Dezső Zrumeczky (1884–1917). Outstanding concrete structures include the Firearms and Gas Appliances factory at Soroksári út 158, a five-storey reinforced-concrete structure of 1913–15 by Árpád Gut and Jenő Gergely; and the 24 m (73 ft.) water tank of 1911 on Margaret Island, designed by Szilárd Zielinski.

Budapest's industrial history is comprehensively illustrated in the city's museums. The Drainage Exhibition portrays the history of sewers. There is a large transport museum, and transport history is also illustrated in an exhibition devoted to the Metro, and on the museum paddle steamer Kossuth of 1913, which has displays on Danube shipping. Heavy engineering is covered in the Ganz, Lang and Csepel museums. Other museums are concerned with electrical engineering, the construction of elevators or lifts, milling, and meat preparation.

BIBLIOGRAPHY
General
Kiss *et al.*, 1981.

LOCATIONS
[M] Drainage Exhibition, 1023 Budapest Zsigmond tér. 2–4.
[M] Ganz Foundry Museum, 1027 Budapest Bem u. 20.
[M] Hungarian Museum of Electrical Technology, 1075 Budapest Kazinczy u. 21.
[M] Hungarian Trade, Restaurant and Tourism Museum, 1014 Budapest Fortuna u. 4.
[M] Industrial Milling Museum, 1095 Budapest Soroksári u. 24.
[M] *Kossuth* Museum Ship, 1051 Budapest.

[M] Lang Engineering Works Collection, 1139 Budapest Rozs-nyay u. 3.
[M] Museum of the Meat Products Industry, 1097 Budapest Gubacsi út 6/b.
[M] Postal Museum, 1061 Budapest Andrássy u. 3.
[M] Specialist Elevator Collection, 1135 Budapest Mohács u. 16/c.
[M] Technical Museum, 1117 Budapest Kaposvári u. 13.
[M] Textiles Museum, 1133 Budapest Gogol u. 9–11.
[M] Transport Museum, 1146 Budapest Városligeti körút 11.
[M] Underground Railway Exhibition, 1052 Budapest Deák tér., Underpass.
[M] Works Museum of the Csepel Ironworks, 1211 Budapest Gyepsor u. 1.

MIHÁLY KUBINSZKY

buddle   A means of separating metallic ores from waste, usually after crushing, comprising a series of containers through which water flowed, carrying away the lighter waste and leaving the ore, which could then be shovelled out. In its simplest form, a buddle was a plank of wood damming a stream. The trunk buddle, in use in England by 1800, consisted of three interconnected boxes through which water flowed. Circular buddles, either convex or concave, were used in northern England from the 1820s. Mineral-bearing material in the form of SLIME was fed onto the middle of a circular sloping platform, a rotating arm spreading material around the platform and depositing the washed slimes in a circular trough around the platform, the heaviest on the inside. The Brunton buddle, introduced in 1847, consisted of a continuous inclined canvas belt revolving round rollers. Mineral-bearing slimes fed onto the top were sprayed with water which washed away the waste. Examples at Killhope (*see* DURHAM) were driven by a water wheel. Many buddles remain in Cornwall, the most notable being those at the Basset Mines, Camborne.

BIBLIOGRAPHY
General
Palmer and Neaverson, 1987; Stratton and Trinder, 1988.

Buffon, Côte-d'Or, France   The important Buffon iron-works on the River Armançon near Montbard in northern Burgundy is in the south-western part of the Châtillon ironmaking region where there were fourteen blast furnaces in 1780. The works was established in 1768–72 by the naturalist Georges-Louis Leclerc de Buffon (1707–88), and was among the best-conceived integrated works of the time, incorporating a blast furnace, a forge and a slitting mill on the same site. The works produced iron until 1866, after which a cement firm occupied the buildings until the 1920s.

The site was restored and opened to visitors from 1979, excavations being carried out on the ore-preparation area, the blast furnace and the forge. The archaeological evidence has provided a better understanding of the evolution of building techniques and of the general organization of the works. A full-size replica of the blast-furnace bellows, along with the water wheel that powered

them, has been installed on the site, as has a scale model of the slitting mill.

The Buffon ironworks is the point of departure for a tourist circuit around northern Burgundy which illustrates different phases in the region's rich ironmaking history. East of Montbard at the Cistercian abbey of Fontenay, which dates from the late twelfth century, a building known as 'The Forge' retains a remarkably complex water-power system. It was much altered during the nineteenth century when it was used as a papermill. At Marcenay, 10 km (6 mi.) W. of Châtillon-sur-Seine, there is a blast furnace with its charcoal barn, both dating from 1742. South of Châtillon at Ampilly-le-Sec is another blast furnace in the form in which it was rebuilt in 1829, which worked until 1861. Its masonry stack and casting hall were restored in 1985. Finally, at Sainte-Colombe-sur-Seine, to the west of Châtillon, are some remains, including a dam on the Seine and workers' housing, of an important English-style FORGE, with PUDDLING FURNACES and a ROLLING MILL. It was one of the first to be built on the continent, and began work in 1822.

BIBLIOGRAPHY
General
Benoit, 1990.
Specific
Association Régionale pour la Promotion de l'Action Culturelle, Scientifique et Technique. *Route of the Forges and Mines in Burgundy*. Beaune: Office de la Culture, 1988.
Benoit, S. and Peyre, P. L'Apport de la fouille archéologique à la connaissance d'un site industriel: l'exemple des forges de Buffon (Côte-d'Or) (The contribution of archaeological evidence to the understanding of an industrial site: the Buffon ironworks). In *L'Archéologie Industrielle en France*, IX, 1984.
Benoit, S. and Rignault, B. Le Patrimoine sidérurgique du Châtillonnais (The Châtillon iron heritage). In *Mémoires de la Commission des Antiquités du Département de la Côte-d'Or*, XXXIV, 1984–6.

LOCATION
[S] Forges de Buffon, 21500 Montbard.

JEAN-FRANÇOIS BELHOSTE

building society   An organization designed to provide money for the construction of dwellings for those who do not have immediate recourse to the necessary capital. Organizations with similar aims, but whose methods vary with different legal systems, exist in most developed countries. Building clubs, by which tradesmen co-operated to build groups of houses for themselves, were operating in Leeds and other English cities by the 1780s. Early societies were 'terminating' – they had no permanent existence – and were often actuarially insecure. In 1836 the Benefit Building Societies Act extended the provisions of Friendly Society legislation to such bodies, which were subjected to further legislative control under the Building Societies Acts 1874 and 1894. Arthur Scratchley (1821–97) originated the permanent building society, which took in money from savers and provided this to borrowers. As loans were repaid, money was re-circulated to further borrowers. By the late nineteenth century there were more than two thousand such

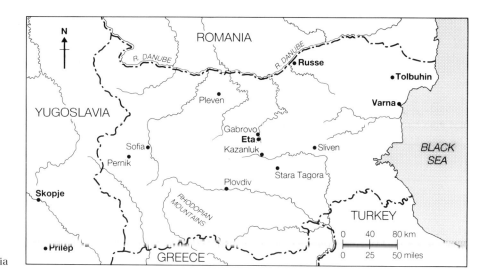

Bulgaria

societies, most of them more middle-class in their nature than the earlier terminating societies, and serving largely as savings banks. Thomas Bowkett and R. B. Starr set up more than a thousand societies designed to ease working-class access to funds for housing from the 1850s. While houses built by terminating societies are easily identified, commonly by such names as 'Union Street' or 'Club Row', permanent societies were rarely identified with particular groups of dwellings.

BIBLIOGRAPHY
General
Beresford, 1988; Cleary, 1965; Gosden, 1973; Hudson, 1953; Price, 1958; Scratchley, 1849.

BARRIE TRINDER

Bükk, Borsod-Abaúj-Zemplén and Heves, Hungary   A mountainous region NE of Eger, 60 km (40 mi.) east–west and 48 km (30 mi.) north–south, with limestone and lignite deposits supplying many cement works.

There are many ironworks in the region. At Ózd, 215 km (137 mi.) NE of Budapest, a works was established by Marton Sturmann in 1720. More furnaces were built in the nineteenth century and there is now a museum showing the history of the works, with a substantial open-air section, including a lathe of 1860, a slotting machine of 1892, and a stand from a rolling mill of 1914.

At Diósgyőr, a suburb of Miskolc, 185 km (115 mi.) NE of Budapest, are the Lenin Metallurgical Works, a large modern plant; the Dimávag engineering works; and the Central Metallurgical Museum, housed in a Baroque office and warehouse building of 1778–9. A branch of the museum at Ujmassa incorporates a preserved blast furnace of 1813–14, with a complete stone stack, approximately 10 m (33 ft.) high, which has been conserved since 1951, the first industrial monument to be accorded protection in Hungary. The 2320 m (2537 yd.) Granzenstein railway tunnel of 1869 was constructed to enable first horse-drawn, then steam trains to reach the newly-built Diósgyőr Ironworks. There is also a preserved papermill in Diósgyőr.

Eger is the centre of production of Bull's Blood, the celebrated Hungarian red wine.

BIBLIOGRAPHY
General
Kiss *et al.*, 1981.

LOCATIONS
[M] Central Metallurgical Museum, H-3517 Miskolc, Felsőhámor, Palota, u. 22.
[M] Massa-Museum, H-3517 Miskolc-Ujmassa.
[M] Museum of Metallurgy, Gyár u. 10, H-3600 Ózd.
[M] Papermill Museum, Hegyalja u. 203/1, H-3535 Miskolc-Diósgyőr.

MIHÁLY KUBINSZKY and BARRIE TRINDER

Bulgaria   The Bulgarian nation emerged in the eighth century AD in the area south of the Danube and the Maritsa valley which opens eastwards to the Black Sea. The intervening Balkan Mountains are dissected by deep valleys which provide crucial links with the north of the country. To the south the Rodopian range, running from west to east, forms the country's southern boundary. Historically the landscape was heavily forested and it is estimated that woodlands still cover about one-third of the land surface, giving Bulgaria rich timber resources.

Like the rest of the Balkan peoples the Bulgarians came under Turkish rule from the mid-fourteenth century; subsequently, though, Bulgaria remained under closer control than did the other Balkan territories of the Ottoman Empire. A cultural revival in the late eighteenth and early nineteenth centuries, the National Revival, led to a measure of political autonomy. The end of the Ottoman yoke came in 1878, when Sofia replaced Veliko Tŭrnovo as capital. Bulgaria became an independent kingdom in 1908, and a socialist republic in 1946. The grain-exporting region of South Dobrudja was ceded to Romania after World War I but was returned in 1940.

Bulgaria under Turkish rule had a predominantly agricultural economy which expanded during the favourable internal economic conditions of the nineteenth century, resulting in increased domestic and foreign trade. A mainly artisan manufacturing industry flourished in such centres as Gabrovo and Karlovo, producing a variety of goods including woollen cloth and braid, together with ironmongery and shoes destined for the Ottoman market, and especially for the Sultan's standing army which was established in 1826. Many of the historic houses open to the public in such places as Veliko Tŭrnovo, Plovdiv, Tolbuhin and Pleven were built by merchants with the profits of this lucrative trade.

Mechanized factories for the most part came only after 1900 and then only on a small scale. Some earlier attempts had been made to establish manufacturing industries, the first factory in Bulgaria having been built in Sliven in 1834. Other early factories were opened in the Plovdiv district in 1847, Stara Zagora in 1855, Karlovo in 1873, and Gabrovo in 1882. During the American Civil War a cotton mill was opened in Varna under British auspices to compensate for cotton supplies being disrupted by the hostilities.

Brown coal deposits in the Pernik area were worked from 1876, the industry being commemorated in a museum of mining in Pernik. The nineteenth century saw the emergence of a tobacco industry, tobacco cultivation having been introduced in 1880. The first factory, in Shoumen, was burned down, and its replacement is now used in part as a museum of the tobacco industry.

A distinctive Bulgarian industry centred in the 'Valley of Roses' near Kazanlŭk is the production of attar from the 'alba' and 'damascara' varieties of roses which are rich in oil. The industry is reputed to have been introduced to Bulgaria by an eighteenth-century Turkish traveller. The rose petals are gathered in May at dawn with the dew still on them. They are then baled and steam is passed through them to produce yellowish-green drops of oil which are drained off. Terrace irrigation raised production to about 1300 kg (3000 lb.) of blossom per acre, but as much as 110 kg (250 lb.) is required to produce 28.35 g (1 oz.) of oil. Production reached a peak in 1900 when exports totalled 5350 kg (105 cwt.). The Ethnology Museum in Plovdiv includes a still that was used in the production of attar.

The Danube, the only significant navigable river, provided a major line of communication in the north of the country. Bulgaria was one of the first countries to use oil engines to power ships, the first vessel so propelled having been introduced on the Danube in 1858. The construction of the first single-track railway from Russe to Varna in 1866 shortened the journey to the Black Sea and linked Bulgaria's two most important ports. The line was built by an engineer called Barclay, employed by the English firm of Gladstone. A further line was built in 1873 from Sarambey to Plovdiv and the Turkish frontier. Only in 1888, when it became part of the through route from Vienna to Istanbul, was Sofia, the new capital, linked with the railway system. A railway constructed in 1899 linked the capital with the port of Varna.

Local museums in most of the principal Bulgarian towns are concerned to a considerable extent with the country's history since 1945, and often portray relatively recent industrial developments. The National Polytechnic Museum in Sofia is the chief museum of technology.

See also ETA; RUSSE; TOLBUHIN; VARNA.

BIBLIOGRAPHY
General
Crompton, 1972; Evans, 1960; Jelavich, 1983; Milward and Saul, 1977; Roussinov, 1965.

LOCATIONS
[M] National Polytechnic Museum, 108 rue Rakovski, 1000 Sofia.
[M] Regional Museum of Ethnology, Dr Çomakov 2, Plovdiv.

TREFOR M. OWEN

bungalow A word now used in most European languages, 'bungalow' was originally applied to the peasant hut of rural Bengal (literally, 'of Bengal'), and came to mean a house for Europeans in India. In the eighteenth century there was often the connotation that it provided overnight accommodation, for a peripatetic administrator or for a stay in the hills during the hot season. By the early twentieth century it came to mean almost any house occupied by Europeans in India, whether of one or two storeys.

The first single-storey dwellings in Britain to be called bungalows were built at Birchington, 32 km (20 mi.) E. of Faversham, in 1869; these were followed by others on adjacent plots, one of which survives. In 1877 the first prefabricated timber bungalow was built nearby, and was occupied by the artist Dante Gabriel Rossetti (it was demolished in 1952); in 1878 a prefabricated, single-storey 'Bungalow Hotel' was constructed. The term came to mean a speculatively-built holiday home. From the 1890s bungalows were built at many British seaside resorts, often prefabricated buildings of CORRUGATED IRON. Some bungalows were houses of considerable scale and style, built in the countryside. In the 1920s and 30s bungalows were built in large numbers as year-round dwellings, and became symbols of what refined opinion most disliked in suburban growth, the pejorative term 'bungaloid' being employed from 1907 to refer to unplanned growth.

The bungalow became the typical suburban dwelling for millions of Americans in the first quarter of the twentieth century, the characteristic 'Californian bungalow', dating from c.1904–5, being built in great numbers from 1906. Los Angeles provides the archetypal example of the move to the single-family home in contrast to the traditional working-class apartments of eastern seaboard cities. Bungalows reached a peak of popularity around 1930, but the pace of building slackened in the Depression, and other styles became popular in the post-war period. Bungalows were fashionable in Canada, particularly in British Columbia; and became a major feature of the suburbs of Australian cities in the early twentieth century: the word 'bungalow' features in many Australian place names. Bungalows are closely associated with colonial regimes in Africa and the Caribbean. In many countries the word is now associated with second homes.

King's study (1984) is outstanding for the way in which archaeological evidence is related to social, cultural and economic change.

BIBLIOGRAPHY
General
King, 1984.

BARRIE TRINDER

bung mill A specialist concern in Canada and the USA in the nineteenth century, which employed water power to make bungs for barrels from pine, oak, maple or birch. The diameter of a standard bung is 0.32 cm ($\frac{1}{8}$ in.) smaller at the shorter end than at the larger end. Such mills also made spiles (or spigots), small plugs of red pine for stopping the vents of casks, and plugs of spruce or pine for vats.

buoy Floating moorings or wreck markers, and from the nineteenth century channel markers, sometimes equipped with bells, horns or other audible signals. There were sixteen standard types in Britain by 1939. The first light buoy, powered by acetylene (*see* ETHYNE), appeared in Scotland in 1880.

burgage plot Burgage was a particular type of tenure by which property in a town was held from a landlord for an annual rent. Burgage plots were the long, narrow building plots characteristic of planned towns of the Middle Ages throughout Europe. Frequently lines of workshops or dwellings, often BLIND-BACK HOUSES, were built along such plots, which in many towns profoundly influenced the development of the industrial landscape.

BIBLIOGRAPHY
General
Beresford, 1961.

Burton on Trent, Staffordshire, England A town famous for beer by 1600, and in the nineteenth century the principal brewing town in England, its population rising, because of the brewing, from 6000 in 1801 to 50 000 in 1901. It is near the head of navigation on the Trent, and is on the Trent & Mersey Canal. Most nineteenth-century breweries and maltings have since been demolished: the outstanding survivor is Marstons' Albion brewery of 1875 (originally Mann, Crossman and Paulin). The Bass Museum of brewing, in a joinery shop of 1866, includes a Robey steam engine of 1905. There are two cotton mills built by Sir Robert Peel (1750–1830): one, of 1787, is now part of Burton flour mills; the other is a cold store.

BIBLIOGRAPHY
General
Owen, 1978; Stuart, 1975.
Specific
The Arkwright Society, Burton on Trent, 1978.

LOCATION
[M] The Bass Museum, Horninglow Street, Burton on Trent.

bus *See* OMNIBUS.

bus depot A building, with adjacent open areas, in which motor OMNIBUSES are maintained, usually having an extensive area free from upright columns or stanchions to permit overnight storage, repair bays with inspection pits, stores for mechanical parts and tyres, and offices for handling cash collected in fares. The depot at Stockwell, LONDON, is an outstanding example.

See also figure 21.

business machines *See* CASH REGISTER; COMPUTER; COPIER; TYPEWRITER.

business records Industrial archaeological research demands, where possible, the establishment of a dialogue between archaeological evidence and that found in the records of companies, which may be classified as follows:

(a) legal records, relating to partnerships, and to property transactions;
(b) financial records, principally ACCOUNTS;
(c) administrative records, minutes, reports, and records of personnel;
(d) technical records, reports concerning the operation of plant, plans by architects and engineers, and drawings and specifications for products;
(e) correspondence with sales staff, customers and suppliers.

Material relating to more recent periods may be more voluminous than that surviving from eighteenth-century enterprises. It will not necessarily be related more easily to archaeological evidence.

The Society of American Archivists provides guidance on major firms like Firestone, the Ford Motor Co. and IBM, which maintain their own archives; while Lovett and Bishop (1978) and Rigg (1970) list collections containing substantial archives of manufacturing concerns.

BIBLIOGRAPHY
General
Larson, 1948; Lovett and Bishop, 1978; Richmond and Stockford, 1986; Rigg, 1970; Society of American Archivists, 1969.
Specific
Barker, T. C., Campbell, R. H. and Mathias, P. *Business History*. London: Historical Association, 1971.
Management and Control of Business Records. London: Business Archives Council, 1966.

BARRIE TRINDER

bus station A bus station is a building, or open area, from which motor OMNIBUSES, usually those working local or regional services, begin their journeys. In the 1920s stations were often established by the construction of ranges of bus stops across marketplaces, with offices in adjacent buildings. Some purpose-built stations were

121

constructed, like the cast-iron and glass shelter erected at Durham, England, in 1927, which is now at BEAMISH. Some bus stations are of notable architectural quality, including that alongside the George Washington Bridge, New York, erected by Pier Luigi Nervi (1891–1979) in 1960–3.

See also COACH STATION.

Bustiello, Oviedo, Asturias, Spain   Bustiello is a MODEL COMMUNITY for coal miners, in the Meires district, 14 km (9 mi.) S. of Oviedo. It is a planned town, with a uniform pattern of settlement, quite distinct from that of neighbouring mining communities where the layout was shaped by the features of the terrain. Bustiello was built in the late nineteenth century according to plans formulated by the Sociedad Hullera Española (Spanish Coalmining Company).

Bustiello is spread over three levels: the river-bank level, where most of the houses are grouped; an intermediate level, where there is just one terrace of four houses; and the upper-area level with the highway, which is almost wholly devoted to communal buildings, a school, an administrative building, a church, a store, a dispensary and the former workers' club, which since the Civil War has been the Civil Guard headquarters, with houses for the doctor, nurse and priest.

Bustiello was constructed in several phases. The first saw the completion of two rows of houses at the river-bank level. The school and the administrative building also date from an early period. Later came the construction of the intermediate level, followed by a third row of houses on the river bank. The earliest houses were of stone, later examples being of brick. Each house is a unit comprising two dwellings with ground floor, upper floor and attic. Around the side and rear of the house is a stretch of garden, a little over 200 m^2 (2100 sq. ft.) in size. The ground floor included the kitchen, a dining room and a utility room. An inside staircase led to the upper storey, where there were two rooms separated by a passage, from the far end of which a narrow stepladder gave access to the attic. Similar dwellings were built in the Cité Ouvrière at MULHOUSE, which was publicized at the Paris exhibition of 1867; they were favoured by paternalist employers because they avoided the evils of tenement blocks.

CARLOS CAICOYA

butane (C_4H_{10})   A flammable gas, the by-product of the hydrogenation of coal; also obtained from natural gas and the CRACKING of petroleum. It is used as LPG, and is a source of compounds used in making synthetic rubber, chewing gum and greaseproof paper.

BIBLIOGRAPHY
General
BP, 1958; Morgan and Pratt, 1938.

butcher   In about 1850 most butchers in England still slaughtered beasts and sold the meat from them, many keeping beasts on grazing land, but in many European countries killing of beasts by individual traders was discouraged on health grounds, and the killing was concentrated in ABATTOIRS. The trade in England was transformed by the import of chilled meat from the 1870s and of frozen meat from the 1880s. Traditional butchers sold the former, but the latter was largely handled by new chains of shops. The first of them, John Bell & Son of Glasgow, Scotland, who began to expand in the early 1880s, had over a hundred shops by 1885, and in 1889 amalgamated with T. C. & J. Eastman of New York. Six British firms each had more than a hundred stores by 1914. In 1940 A&P (*see* CHAIN STORE) in the USA introduced CELLOPHANE-wrapped meat in their stores, which began a switch in trade from traditional butchers to all-purpose foodstores.

See also PET FOOD; SAUSAGE; SLAUGHTERHOUSE.

BIBLIOGRAPHY
General
Braudel, 1981; Critchell and Raymond, 1912; Dunning, 1985; Perren, 1978; Short, 1928; Swift, 1927; Winstanley, 1983.

Bute, John 2nd Marquis of (1793–1848)   A landowner with monopolistic control over the industrialization of eastern South Wales. Unlike European aristocrats, British lords owned the minerals under their estates and commons. Bute controlled CARDIFF and the eastern third of the South Wales coalfield. He foresaw the value of the RHONDDA VALLEYS in the 1820s, and consolidated his holdings to lease mining rights in the coal boom. He built private docks and forced lessees to ship their coal there.

BIBLIOGRAPHY
General
Davies, 1981.

butter   Butter is made by sieving milk and allowing it to settle; then skimming off the cream (from the late nineteenth century removing it by a mechanical separator) and churning it, in a wooden barrel with a plunger or in a rotating barrel churn. If for immediate sale butter may be moulded with decorative sycamore stamps.

Butter is used particularly in northern Europe. It was a significant item of long-distance trade in England by 1700, conveyed in the barrel, containing 224 lb. (102 kg), or the pot, containing 20 lb. (9 kg). Much salt was used in preparing butter destined for transport.

BIBLIOGRAPHY
General
Braudel, 1981; Brears and Harrison, 1979; Connor, 1987.

Bystrzyca Kłodzka (Habelschwerdt), Wrocław, Poland   A town in Lower Silesia, 100 km (62 mi.) S. of Wrocław. A Museum of the Matchmaking Industry was established here in 1964, in a former Protestant church of the early nineteenth century. Large collections of matches, matchboxes, mechanical lighters and matchmaking equipment are on show. Displays show methods of kindling fire from the sixteenth to the nineteenth century.

BIBLIOGRAPHY
General
Kietowicz, 1968.

Specific
Muzeum Filumenistyczne w Bystrzycy Kłodzkiej, Informator (Museum of the Matchmaking Industry in Bystrzyca Kłodzka, Guide Book), 1974.

LOCATION
[M] Muzeum Filumenistyczne w Bystrzycy Kłodzkiej (Museum of the Matchmaking Industry), Bystrzyca Kłodzka, Mały Rynek 4.

C

cable Originally a ship's rope, the term now applies chiefly to electric cables. A cable consists of a multiplicity of wires, usually copper, stranded together in a bundle, and insulated. Early submarine cables usually consisted of single conductors, interwoven with insulating materials. Wires both for telegraphs and power supply were at first insulated only at support points. Early continuous insulators were glass, gummed silk and lead, but GUTTA-PERCHA became common after 1843, especially in submarine cables. Latterly rubber (from 1859), bitumen (from 1881) and jute (from 1887) were extensively used, before impregnated paper, first used in 1886, with various outer sheaths, became universal. Failures at high voltages were prevented by Luigi Emanueli's oil-filled cable of 1920.

Surviving cable-laying ships include *Thalis O. Milissios* of 1909 at Piraeus (*see* ATHENS) and *John W. Mackay* of 1922 in LONDON.

BIBLIOGRAPHY
General
Bradfield and John, 1928; Bright, 1898; Brouwer, 1985; Marland, 1964.

CHRISTOPHER GREEN

cable car A term with two meanings in industrial archaeology:

1. A form of rope haulage little used in Britain, for which reason English lacks a range of words that provide clear distinctions among types. The most significant for public transport is the 'luftseilbahn' or 'téléphérique', on which pairs of cars, balanced like those on a FUNICULAR, are attached to wheeled carriages running along a steel cable suspended between pylons, and are drawn along by a continuous haulage rope, electrically worked from the termini. The first was built at Grindelwald, Switzerland, in 1908, but operated only until 1914. The next began work at Engelberg, Switzerland, in 1927, and many have been built since, some with small cars serving villages in isolated positions, others with spans of up to 1800 m (6000 ft.) and cars carrying up to a hundred people, taking tourists to such Alpine summits as Titlis, Switzerland. The simplest form of passenger carriage by ropeway is the chair lift, 'sesselbahn' or 'télésiège', used chiefly for carrying skiers up mountain slopes on seats attached to continuously moving cables. A 'gondelbahn' works on the same principle but has enclosed cabins.

2. An American term for CABLE TRAM.

BIBLIOGRAPHY
General
Allen, 1965.

BARRIE TRINDER

cable tram The principle of the cable tram was derived from the rope haulage employed on INCLINED PLANES on RAILWAYS. A shaft on the tram's underframe passed down through a slot between the rails to the level of a moving, endless wire cable carried beneath on pulleys within a conduit. The shaft carried a mechanism that could grip the cable, allowing the tram to be hauled along at a speed determined by a steam engine in a remote winding house. Cable trams either carried their own grip mechanism, or were trailers hauled by a small four-wheeled gripper car called a 'dummy'. They were particularly suited to hilly cities; San Francisco, Edinburgh and Melbourne all had extensive systems at some time. Cable trams were liable to breakdowns through jammed slots, broken or frayed cables and winding-engine failures. Driving required considerable skill as the trams had to 'ungrip' and use momentum to negotiate curves and junctions, other traffic often causing them to stall. Most systems were converted to electric traction, although several of the San Francisco lines survive as highly functional icons.

BIBLIOGRAPHY
General
Klapper, 1961.

PAUL COLLINS

Cabo Mondego, Figueira da Foz, Beira Litoral, Portugal An important industrial plant in the Boa Viagem mountains, facing the sea and 6 km (4 mi.) E. of Figueira da Foz. The exploitation of coal began under the direction of the Marquis of POMBAL (1699–1789) in 1773 and continued until 1967. A glassworks of 1869 operated until the end of the nineteenth century and was the first in Portugal to produce green bottles on an industrial scale. The same concern possessed a ceramic works near Buarcos, 3 km (2 mi.) N. of Figueira da Foz, and a cement and lime plant which once had a remarkable set of vertical furnaces. Quarries supplied the works with limestone by railway. Now only the cement and lime plant, which includes a power station, and the workers' dwellings remain. Nearby are the ruins of the Cabo Mondego lighthouse, abandoned in 1923.

BIBLIOGRAPHY
General
Santos, 1982.

124

caboose A North American term for vehicles coupled at the ends of freight trains to carry conductors and rear-end brakemen, who can watch for hot boxes, loose loads and other problems. The word derives from a word meaning ship's galley.

caisson A word with at least two meanings in industrial archaeology:

1. A watertight enclosure built to enable the construction of the foundations of a bridge.

2. A tank containing water in which a vessel can float while being lifted up an INCLINED PLANE or in a BOAT LIFT.

Calábria, Italy The province forming the toe of Italy has relatively little industry. Water-powered corn mills were widespread, and thirteen have been recorded in detail, some of them still being in operation. Many have wheels mounted horizontally on vertical axles, fed by long stone leats running along the edges of hillsides. The greatest concentration is around Cosenza. Two of these horizontally mounted wheels can be seen in use grinding grain in San Marco Argentano, 30 km (19 mi.) N. of Cosenza, at Via Julia 37. Other examples have been studied at Vibo Valentia further south. Tropea, 70 km (45 mi.) N. of Reggio di Cannitello, was an important silk centre, using both pre-industrial and steam-powered technology. Three throwing works built during the 1880s with foreign capital survive in a derelict condition, one retaining its steam engine.

The liquorice industry had several centres in Calábria. At San Lorenzo del Vallo, 30 km (19 mi.) N. of Cosenza, water wheels that powered the grinding of roots still remain: while at Rende, 8 km (5 mi.) W. of Cosenza, is the Febbrica Zagarese, a steam-powered liquorice works dating from the late nineteenth century which closed in the 1960s.

There have been ironworks on a modest scale in Calábria since the sixteenth century, the documentation of the site at Stilo, 150 km (90 mi.) NE of Reggio di Calábria, dating from 1523. The Bourbons established works in the late eighteenth century inland from the Ionian Sea between Stilo and Catanzaro. At Mongiana in 1770 the Neapolitan architect Mario Cioffredo built a large complex with two blast furnaces. Some ruins remain, set into the hillside beside the River Alara. Extensions were undertaken in the early nineteenth century and a new armaments factory was built on the southern edge of Mongiana in the 1850s. Forges and grindstones were powered by water wheels. The entrance to the arms factory has a shallow arch supported by cast-iron Doric columns.

The Ferdinandea armaments works which commenced operation in 1798 was located in Stilo, and laid out by Teodoro Paoletti. By the 1840s four ranges of buildings surrounded the blast furnace, but after unification most of the plant was converted into a country residence. The most dramatic remaining structure is a long, barn-like range, in which ore and coal were stored on the upper floor, workmen being accommodated below.

BIBLIOGRAPHY
General
Negri *et al.*, 1983.
Specific
Matacena, G. Architettura del lavoro in Calábria Tra i secolo XV e XIX (The architecture of work in Calábria from the fifteenth century to the nineteenth), In *Edizioni Scientifische Italiane* (Italian Scientific Papers). Naples, 1983.
Morelli, R. Mulino ad acqua in Calábria (Water mills in Calábria). In *Archeologia Industriale*, II, 1984.

MICHAEL STRATTON

calamine Zinc carbonate ($ZnCO_3$), or Smithsonite, named after its discoverer, James Smithson. It is usually found in association with lead ores. It was used in the production of BRASS, for which smelting into metallic zinc was unnecessary.

calcining kiln A kiln in which metallic ores were heated before smelting, in order to drive off moisture, sulphur and carbon dioxide, separate some solid waste materials, and sometimes partially to oxidize the ore. Sometimes calcining took place at the mine (*see* YORKSHIRE MOORS) but normally it was done at the smelting works (*see* CAPALBIO). Flints, bones and other materials used in ceramic manufactures were also calcined before grinding.

Caldas da Rainha, Estremadura, Portugal A traditional ceramics centre, 75 km (47 mi.) NE of Lisbon. The Fábrica de Faianças Rafael Bordalo Pinheiro (faience factory) has been operating since the late nineteenth century. Bordalo Pinheiro's works have brought about great changes in Portuguese ceramics and he is regarded as the country's greatest sculptor working in ceramics. His clay caricatures, such as Zé Povinho (corresponding to the English John Bull) are particularly famous. Examples of his work can be seen in the Museu José Malhoa.

LOCATION
[M] Museu José Malhoa, Parque D. Carlos I, Caldas da Rainha.

calender A machine that provides the final pressed finish for TEXTILES or paper, or the person who operates the machine. The cloth or paper travels through the steel rolls of the calender: the rolls may be either hot or cold.

calico printing Calico is printed cotton cloth; the name derives from Calcutta, as India is thought to be the home of cotton printing, although South American and Egyptian examples survive from antiquity. The earliest hand methods, in use until the nineteenth century, involved cutting the pattern into wooden blocks to be impressed upon the cloth, either by hand or set in a frame and printed by machine. Copper plates and cylinders were also engraved for printing cloth. The cylinder machine was developed in Britain in the 1780s and reached America about 1810. The cloth was fed through an elaborate system of pattern, inking and drying rollers, some printing several successive colours for complicated patterns. A typical works consisted of numbers of relatively small buildings clustered around the larger structures accommodating the printing machines. There were about 170 works in England and Scotland in the 1860s. The largest each employed more than a thousand people, and most more than a hundred.

BIBLIOGRAPHY
General
BPP, 1868–9; Chapman and Chassagne, 1981; Montgomery, 1970.
Specific
Chapman, S. D. David Evans and Co.: the last of the old London textile printers. In *TH*, XIV, 1983.
Clark, H. The design and designing of Lancashire printed calicoes during the first half of the nineteenth century. In *TH*, XV, 1984.

HELENA WRIGHT

California, United States of America   In this massive state bordering the Pacific Ocean for over 1600 km (1000 mi.), the breadth of industrial archaeological topical fields is addressed in standing sites and structures, some of world-class calibre. The Far West's abundant natural endowments – temperate climate, deep-water ports, arable land, watersheds, mineral and timber resources – attracted labour and capital to California early in the nation's history.

Spanish and Mexican development of California remained agricultural and missionary from 1769 until the territory was seized from Mexico by the USA in 1846, a by-product of hostilities then under way in the South-West. Two years later north-central California exploded with eastern immigration and small-scale commercial development, when gold flakes were discovered in a creek bed. Feverish pan, hydraulic and hard-rock mining of the state's gold continued through the 1870s, establishing industrial- and materials-transport networks that enabled northern California to diversify from its gold and agricultural bases into general manufacturing, construction, and the large-scale processing of the state's other resources. The genesis years of the Rush are commemorated at the Marshall Gold Discovery site in Coloma. In the surrounding hills mining camps in various stages of abandonment and regeneration as resort towns evoke the gold frenzy that once gripped the area.

Quite as fundamental to both gold mining and the development of the state's general manufacturing was a heavy metalworking industry. Although the required pig and wrought iron came from out-of-state, foundries sprang up around the port of San Francisco to cast parts for mine cars, pumps, steam engines, boilers and all classes of light hardware. The field is represented today by the heavy metals industries south of San Francisco, and in sculpture by an imposing outdoor bronze in the city centre, a great lever-operated sheet-metal punch, worked by a gang of stout pressmen, a tribute to Peter Donohue, long-time proprietor of a major local ironworks.

The logging of western softwoods, chiefly redwood, cedar and fir, has long been a major Californian enterprise. Along the north coast, redwood harvest was widespread until steps were taken early in this century to restrict clear-cutting to specific areas, saving the tallest and lushest groves of coastal redwood in state and national parks. Today the redwood mill town of Scotia remains a unique example of the American 'company town', its life linked to the fortunes and activities of one paternal mill.

The fruits and vegetables grown in the fertile San Joaquin Valley, together with the fisheries scattered along the Pacific coast, have been served by several generations of canneries that render the goods suitable for cross-country transport, among other support activities. Converted canneries have been one of California's special contributions to the field of adaptive reuse. Museums, shopping centres and office facilities now occupy canneries in Marysville, along the waterfront in San Francisco, and in Pacific Grove, the setting for *Cannery Row*, the novel by John Steinbeck (1902–68).

California is especially well endowed with railway museums, as it has been with railways since the first transcontinental reached the state in 1869. The expansive station and train-shed architecture of the East and Midwest did not spread to the Far West, but San Francisco's LANDMARK Ferry Building of 1903 has a similar gateway presence. Once a hub of streetcar and steam ferryboat traffic, the Beaux Arts tower and terminal building now anchor San Francisco's main downtown boulevard, Market Street.

The Californian railway known most widely runs along barely 16 km (10 mi.) of track up and down the hills of San Francisco, a shade of its original 274 km (170 mi.) extent. The city's cable-car system, established in 1873, remains the nation's and the world's only in-use survival of this once popular buried-cable form of urban transit. The Carle Car Barn in the downtown serves as the source of power for the wire-rope cable, maintenance shop and cable-car museum. It overlooks the exposed cable-winding gear, now electrically powered but originally worked by steam.

The art of lighthouse engineering is well preserved in several precariously placed lights around San Francisco Bay and up the north coast. While all are now unmanned, and their Fresnel lenses mostly replaced with high-intensity lights, their distinctive architecture remains a treasured aspect of the state's built heritage. The headquarters of the non-profit United States Lighthouse Society is in San Francisco.

Heavy snowfalls in the state's higher regions combine with consistent levels of coastal rainfall to explain some of the nation's more unusual and historic examples of dam-building, for both water supply and hydro-electric power. The Hume Lake Dam of 1909, the Mulholland Dam of 1940, the Hetch Hetchy Dam of 1930, the Sweetwater Dam of 1888, the Crystal Springs Dam of 1890 and the Shasta Dam of 1945 are concrete behemoths of varying styles: they are well worth visits by water-impoundment enthusiasts, despite their remote locations.

The historic bridges of California are a remarkable mix

Figure 22   An early hydro-electric power station at Battle Creek, California
Jet Lowe, HAER

of size, type and materials. In San Francisco's Golden Gate Park the modest Alvord Lake Bridge of 1889 stands as the earliest reinforced concrete bridge in the USA, built by the concrete pioneer Ernest Ransome. Majestic examples of the open-spandrel concrete deck-arch appear along Coastal Route 1 (Bixby Creek Bridge of 1932), and in Pasadena (Colorado Street Bridge of 1913). The Oakland–San Francisco Bay Bridge of 1936 is a rare union of suspension and trussed cantilever, joining at Yerba Buena Island in the middle of the Bay. The twin spans of the Carquinez Strait Bridges of 1927–8 are a matched pair of steel cantilevers. At the Bay's entrance, the Golden Gate Bridge of 1937 offers one of the more arresting examples of engineering as fine art and as a conqueror of nature at its most treacherous. On its completion the Golden Gate Bridge held the world records for main cable diameter, at 0.9232 m ($36\frac{3}{8}$ in.), and suspended span between towers, at 1280 m (4200 ft.).

Elsewhere in California the Moffett Field Dirigible Hangar at Sunnyvale remains a gigantic monument to the nation's brief involvement with airships between 1929 and the 1940s. The 345 m (1133 ft.) steel-trussed structure was built in 1933 to house the US Navy's dirigibles, and today serves as an aircraft maintenance facility.

Two outstanding transport artefacts preserved at Long Beach are the Cunard LINER *Queen Mary*, and the colossal flying boat *Spruce Goose*, built for the eccentric millionaire Howard Hughes (1905–76). The Maritime Museum in San Francisco probably holds the best collection of historic seagoing ships in the world.

The conservatory of flowers in San Francisco's Golden Gate Park is among the nation's largest glass conservatories. The wood and glass structure, modelled in 1879 after the Crystal Palace, remains a focal point of horticultural activity. Of related interest are two Dutch windmills at the park's west end, erected in 1907 to harness the Pacific Ocean winds in powering pumps to irrigate flowerbeds and grass throughout the park.

The Hollywood area of Los Angeles is the historic centre of the world's cinema industry, although most of the active film-production facilities are now elsewhere in the

127

city, many of them open to visitors. In Hollywood itself, Mann's (Grauman's) Chinese Theater has one of the world's most exotic façades, and one of the lushest cinema interiors. It is just one of a cluster of spectacular cinemas on Hollywood Boulevard. The Paramount and other once-famous studios are now mostly used for other purposes. The golden age of film-making is portrayed in the Hollywood Wax Museum.

In Newhall stands one of the world's few preserved oil refineries. Oil production in the state began in 1873 at Lyons but shifted to Newhall in 1876, drawing from wells in nearby Pico Canyon to create fuel oil in a series of steam-injected stills to reduce the oil to burnable quality. The two surviving stills were declared National Mechanical Engineering Landmarks in 1975, and are open to the public.

The Rancho La Brea Tar Pits in the 1389 ha (3433 ac.) Black Diamond Mines Regional Park near Los Angeles resulted from the exploitation in the late nineteenth century of seepages of natural bitumen, first noted in 1769. The pit yielded bitumen for paving streets and caulking ships, as well as bones from numerous prehistoric animals. The original working, the 'great tar lake', is conserved, together with later workings in some of which methane still bubbles to the surface.

BIBLIOGRAPHY
General
Jackson, 1988; Rosten, 1945.

LOCATIONS
[M] Antique Gas and Steam Engine Museum, 2040 N. Santa Fe Avenue, Vista, CA 92083.
[S] Bodie Ghost Mining Town, Bodie, CA.
[M] California Museum of Science and Industry, 700 State Drive, Los Angeles, CA 90037.
[M] California Oil Museum, 1003 Main Street, Santa Paula, CA 93060.
[M] California State Railroad Museum, 111 I Street, Sacramento, CA 95814.
[S] Conservatory of Flowers, 9th Avenue & Lincoln Way, San Francisco, CA 94122.
[M] The Exploratorium, 3601 Lyon Street, San Francisco, CA 94123.
[M] Hollywood Wax Museum, 6767 Hollywood Boulevard, Los Angeles.
[M] Laws Railroad Museum, Silver Canyon Road, Bishop, CA 93514.
[S] Mann's Chinese Theater, 6925 Hollywood Boulevard, Los Angeles.
[M] National Maritime Museum, Hyde Street Pier, San Francisco, CA 94109.
[M] Orange Empire Railway Museum, 2201 South A Street, Perris, CA 92370.
[M] Pacific Lumber Company Museum, US Highway 101, Box 37, Scotia, CA 95565.
[M] *Queen Mary* Maritime Museum (and ship), Pier 'J', Long Beach, CA 90801.
[M] San Diego Maritime Museum, 1306 North Harbor Drive, San Diego, CA 92101.
[S] *Spruce Goose*, Howard Hughes's Flying Boat, 1126 Queens Way, Long Beach, CA 90801.
[I] United States Lighthouse Society, 244 Kearney Street, San Francisco, CA 94108.

[M] Western Railway Museum, 5848 State Highway 12, Suisun City, CA 94585.

DAVID H. SHAYT

Calvados *See* CIDER.

camera A box in which light passes through a small hole or lens to meet a larger screen or plate, either directly opposite or (by reflection) above. The image on the screen can be recorded manually by drawing, or fixed by chemicals. The earliest chemical cameras, dating from the 1830s, have a lens to focus the image onto the sensitized material within, which was exposed by hand. Refinements throughout the nineteenth century concentrated on increasing the precision of focusing and exposure. These included bellows and a focusing track in the 1850s, and hand-held, multiple-shot cameras with shutter-setting and release mechanisms by the 1880s. The size of cameras was reduced, and roll-film after 1884 (*see* PHOTOGRAPHY) made the whole process far easier. A separate family of reflex cameras, with folding internal mirrors, also developed from the 1880s, with one or two lenses. Improvements in optical glass for lenses were mainly made in Germany in the 1890s, with f-number rating internationally agreed in 1900. The first exposure meters and moving-picture cameras appeared at roughly the same time. Flash bulbs were invented in 1929.

CHRISTOPHER GREEN

campanile The Italian term for a bell tower: it was often detached from the building of which it was part. Many factory CHIMNEYS and the celebrated hydraulic tower at Grimsby (*see* LINCOLNSHIRE) were designed as campanili, sometimes closely imitating Italian originals.

Canada The present nation-state of Canada dates only from 1867, when the Confederation of four former British colonies, the present Ontario, Quebec, New Brunswick and Nova Scotia, created the nucleus for a country that now stretches from the Atlantic to the Pacific, and that occupies almost all the landmass north of the US border to the Arctic Ocean. Significant phases of this expansion included the entry of British Columbia in 1871 and of Prince Edward Island in 1873; the transformation of the former Hudson's Bay Company territory (Rupert's Land) into three prairie provinces of Alberta, Manitoba and Saskatchewan, and two territories, the Northwest Territories and the Yukon; and, in 1949, the inclusion of the former British colony of Newfoundland and Labrador.

Within a vast land, much of it barren, inhospitable and relatively inaccessible, settlement and industrial development have proceeded principally on the southern edge along the border with the USA. Only a fraction of the land is suitable for agriculture – a mere 4 per cent in British Columbia – and at almost every stage the Canadian economic reality has to cope with the prosperity and opportunity to the south and the wilderness to the north. Indeed, the Canadian state is overwhelmingly an attempt

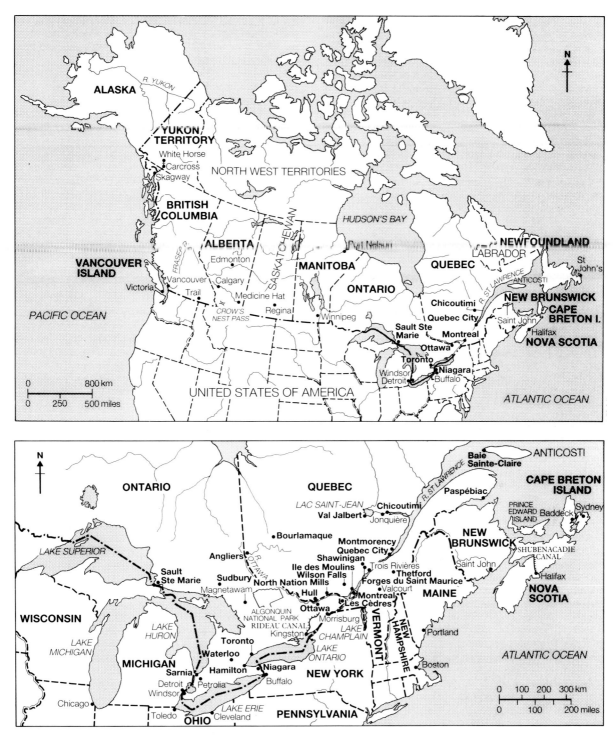

Canada (above); and (below) Quebec, Ontario and the Great Lakes

to create, bind and maintain a distinctive state in the face of vast distances, difficult terrain and marginal climate. That it has been able to do so is a reflection in large part of Canada's ability to yield a wide array of raw materials that have been in demand from the rest of the industrialized world.

129

An inventory of the industrial archaeological landmarks in Canada mirrors a history of resource exploitation and transportation. Considerable private and public investment went into developing secure routes for the harvesting, processing and export of materials. A network of rivers and lakes meant that from the beginning of European contact, the Atlantic fringe, the St Lawrence River system and the Great Lakes basin made the heart of the northern landmass accessible by water, and facilitated early penetration of resource industries; the engineering capacity to develop railways and then roads across the Appalachian lowlands, the Laurentian Shield, the Prairies and the Rockies brought access to more territories and different resources.

Much of the non-metropolitan settlement system is focused on resource development, and the dearth of major manufacturing sites is a consequence of Canada's colonial and neo-colonial status, in which materials have been moved to other places for end-processing. Many mines and mills had a half-life of a decade, others several decades: only occasionally has there been continuous resource extraction for over a century. The boom-and-bust nature of so much of the Canadian economy, dependent on demand and prices in a world market, has meant that many of Canada's production sites were destined to become industrial archaeology sooner or later. Most were abandoned, and covered by the wilderness. Rarely would a community adjust to a different economic mix, and the artefacts or site in question remain as relic features in an evolving landscape. A present- and future-orientated outlook on life and landscape has meant that until very recently most sites and artefacts did not benefit from the heritage consciousness that distinguishes the European experience.

The pre-industrial phase in Canadian history is difficult to define. A staples economy has persisted over several centuries. There is good evidence of sites of Basque whaling stations from the 1550s along the shores of the Gulf of St Lawrence, where whale oil was extracted to be barrelled for the journey to Europe; and there are long-occupied sites where cod from the Grand Banks off Newfoundland were cleaned, salted and sun-dried to be transported in schooners to Europe. Four centuries later inland sites in the same region yielded iron ore to be shipped – equally semi-processed, to concentrate its bulk – to American or European steelworks. In both periods, capital and control were external, labour was imported from outside, and the sites were destined to be abandoned once prices dropped or demand subsided. In the former, fishing outports were built in vernacular styles, modified from Irish or West Country English prototypes, the principal technological constraint being the size of the ships that could transport the product to European markets. In the latter period, prefabricated CARAVANS or 'mobile homes', and standardized bunkhouses for miners are rarely regarded as vernacular though in many ways they qualify as such, and the dominant technological contexts are the hydro-electric power systems, which enable the mines and concentrators to work, and the railways that transport the ore to

the boats. Yet is the latter type of site more industrial than the former? Rather, both could be seen as evidence of the shift from mercantile capitalism to industrial and then corporate capitalism.

Associated with the phase of mercantile capitalism was a colonial form of government that in most cases deliberately prohibited manufacturing on Canadian soil. Thus the beaver and other skins of the French and English fur-trade era went back to Paris or London for processing into hats and clothing; only the trading posts of the fur trade stand as evidence of this era, together with the canoe making, coopering and blacksmith's work regarded as the 'industrial' activities of the fort sites. Most of the forts and trading posts lasted for only a decade or so. The majority fell into ruin and only a handful remain, often as reconstructions by the Parks Service. An exception to this trend during the fur-trading period was the ironworks, LES FORGES DU ST MAURICE.

In similar fashion, most of the timbers harvested from the forests in New Brunswick, Quebec and Ontario in the nineteenth century went as squares and deals, to be cut into other forms in Britain. The logging frontier moved annually as winter crews abandoned their seasonal shanties and drove the logs down rivers and streams in spring to the great booming grounds at Quebec City, and at the mouths of the Miramichi and St John rivers in New Brunswick. Timber slides around rapids or falls would be marvels in their time, but of ephemeral value, and left to decay and disappear. The only semblance of Canadian manufacture connected with the square timber trade was the making of sailing vessels to transport wood to British markets and to participate in the coastal trade to New England and the Caribbean. Schooners were built on beaches with seasonal labour at many places in the maritime provinces. Finishing work, the addition of sails, rigging and anchors, would be done chiefly at Saint John (see NEW BRUNSWICK). Yet as British ports like Glasgow and Newcastle emerged as the major shipbuilding centres of the steam era, Saint John declined, as did Quebec City, once its connection with the timber-loading period ended. Neither place has much in the way of industrial monuments from that era, and in the myriad communities that built schooners on their beaches, there are no docks, cranes or workshops – only an occasional house that served as a seasonal bunkhouse hints at a world of work that has passed.

In the case of the east coast fisheries, early plantations established in the early eighteenth century by the French and English in Newfoundland and Quebec had developed by 1800 into a distinctive array of small 'outports' all along the shores of Atlantic Canada. The technology was simple – the drying of cod was done chiefly in the sun on raised platforms called 'flakes'. Boatbuilding developed – dories for the inshore fishery, and schooners for the Banks (see CAPE BRETON ISLAND; NEWFOUNDLAND; NOVA SCOTIA). Only since 1945 have many of the outports succumbed to new systems of production, dominated by offshore factory ships, or new freezer plants centred in a smaller number of communities.

For staple products like furs, timber and fish, there were

few production sites of considerable scale or with sophisticated technology, especially when the colonial context diminished the opportunity for the development of significant forward and backward linkages. In the case of wheat, another export staple for Ontario by the second half of the nineteenth century, a similar truncated system is evidenced – some milling for local needs, but largely the provision of transport and storage facilities. A similar pattern developed across the prairies in the early twentieth century. The small, often wooden grain elevator or SILO became a typical feature of parts of the prairies, and by 1929 there were over five thousand elevators in western Canada.

Mining, by contrast, needed significant inputs of capital and machinery in order to extract the resource, and its monuments, unlike those of fishermen or wheat farmers, are often more than the mere survival of housing.

In ONTARIO and QUEBEC, where a reasonably prosperous agrarian hinterland created a significant domestic market, a wide range of consumer industries developed, including mills and factories for the production of paper, beer, spirits, textiles, clothing, footwear, furniture, flour and agricultural implements. There are significant remains of textile communities at Marysville in NEW BRUNSWICK, MONTMORENCY and Trois Rivières in Quebec, and Cornwall and Arnprior in Ontario. Hydro-electric power became a vital factor in Canadian manufacturing in the early twentieth century, but electrical engineering was dominated by such concerns as General Electric and Westinghouse, based in the USA, just as motorcar production in Windsor (see ONTARIO) was controlled by companies from Detroit. The manufacture of consumer goods in Quebec was largely concentrated in MONTREAL, which by 1903 had the benefit of hydro-electric power from power stations on the St Maurice River. Hydro-electric power stations at SHAWINIGAN, Buckingham and elsewhere in Quebec led to the growth of chemical and pulp plants, and subsequently of aluminium smelters, like the Arvida plant of Alcan. Hydro-electric power, and often water piped from the power-station reservoirs, became staple exports from the 1940s.

Beyond the central Canadian manufacturing belt, the twentieth-century story is more of the same in terms of resource exploitation, except that development became more capital-intensive, and was tied into a railway system. In BRITISH COLUMBIA the importation of Shay engines from Michigan, of steam donkeys, which were winding frames for hauling massive trees, and of power saws and mechanical timber tugs, brought a growth in the scale of the attack on the forest. A tariff on paper imposed in 1913 led to the establishment of major American-owned newsprint mills in Canada, and most of the major newspapers in the USA came to get their paper from specific Canadian mills. Salmon canning in British Columbia brought industrial production to a number of isolated coastal sites, but these plants were seasonally operated, relying on seasonal labour accommodated in bunkhouses, of which few remain, even in relic form.

Coal mining on a large scale developed in Nova Scotia in the 1820s and in British Columbia in 1840. In both regions there were extensive company settlements by the 1870s. Successive gold rushes on the Fraser River and the Cariboo in the 1850s and 60s, and then the Dawson rush in the YUKON TERRITORY at the end of the century, did much to stimulate exploration, but quickly progressed from individual to corporate enterprises. There are extensive remains of non-ferrous mining in the south-east of BRITISH COLUMBIA and north of Vancouver, and in the company towns of MANITOBA, and Saskatchewan north of the prairie wheat belt. The mining towns of the nickel belt around SUDBURY, Ontario, persist, but little evidence remains of the silver boom town of Cobalt. Similarly in the Northwest Territories, place names like Tungsten, Copper Mine and Port Radium are evidence of past mining activity, but most of the lead and zinc ores currently produced in the Territories are obtained from a single mine at Pine Point, near the south shore of the Great Slave Lake. Of note in the Ontario segment of the Laurentian Shield are several planned company towns associated with pulpmills which show the influence of the English GARDEN CITY movement as well as that of the proponents of the CITY BEAUTIFUL in the USA. Indeed the Canadian company towns are a landscape testimony to the historical development of the resource frontier, shifting from chaotic and overly individualistic boom towns to heavily segregated company towns, and again to more planned communities where conscious separation of production site, residential and community facilities has developed. This latter model is typified by the pulp town of Corner Brook, Newfoundland, the uranium mining town of Elliot Lake, Ontario, the aluminium smelting town of Kitimat, British Columbia, and the iron-ore town of Schefferville on the Quebec/Labrador border.

In almost every province metropolitan museums carry some interpretative material and artefacts from the pre-industrial and proto-industrial phases of Canadian history, and provincial initiatives have begun towards the conservation of numerous sites that were of regional if not national significance. At the national level the Canadian Parks Service has been the leader in designating sites, but has typically been concerned with the fur trade, military history and the homes of important politicians. The Heritage Canada Foundation is a non-profit organization acting at a national level, and is moving to more sociohistorical foci, away from a concentration on grand architectural statements.

Important innovations and achievements in the fields of transport and communications have received the attention they deserve in a country whose people are so thinly spread over such vast distances. A museum on CAPE BRETON ISLAND commemorates A. G. BELL, and many preserved early railway locomotives mark important phases in the linking of towns and regions. Ironically, to celebrate the centenary of the first train to arrive in Vancouver, the Expo86 site eradicated the Canadian Pacific Railway roundhouse and other rail yards to develop the fair. Similarly in Toronto, the rail yards that served the city's industrial and warehouse district have succumbed to the Canadian National Tower for telecommunications, and to a domed football and baseball

131

stadium, symptomatic of the replacement of the railway by televised sport as the linking agent between people and places.

The national museums of Canada are in OTTAWA. The first national park, Banff in Alberta, was designated in 1887, and the Canadian Parks Service now administers over thirty national parks, as well as numerous historic parks and sites and several heritage canals.

TICCIH Canada, linked to ICOMOS, provides a national focus for industrial archaeology, publishing the journal *Machines*. The interests of the Society for Industrial Archeology cover Canada as well as the UNITED STATES OF AMERICA. The Association québécoise pour le patrimoine industriel (Aqpi) and the Ontario Society for Industrial Archaeology act as watchdogs and ginger groups in their particular provinces. The Nova Scotia Museums produce a trades and technologies newsletter called *Links*. There is a national organization for the study of canals. In Alberta, British Columbia, Nova Scotia, QUEBEC and Ontario, provincial government departments have done much to broaden the horizon of what is considered heritage, and have developed important insights on early technology and on hydro-electric power.

See also ALBERTA; ANGLIERS; BAIE STE CLAIR; BOMBARDIER, J.A.; BOURLAMAQUE; BRITISH COLUMBIA; CAPE BRETON ISLAND; CÈDRES, LES; CHICOUTIMI; FORGES DU ST MAURICE, LES; HAMILTON; HULL LANDING; ÎLE DES MOULINS; MANITOBA; MONTMORENCY; MONTREAL; NEW BRUNSWICK; NEWFOUNDLAND; NIAGARA; NORTH NATION MILLS; NOVA SCOTIA; ONTARIO; OTTAWA; PASPÉBIAC; QUEBEC; QUEBEC CITY; RIDEAU CANAL; SARNIA; SAULT STE MARIE; SHAWINIGAN; SUDBURY; THETFORD; TORONTO; VAL JALBERT; VANCOUVER ISLAND; WATERLOO; WILSON FALLS.

BIBLIOGRAPHY
General
Ball, 1987, 1988; Brown and Cook, 1974; Burnham and Burnham, 1972; Glazebrook, 1964; Harris and Matthews, 1987; Harris and Warkentin, 1974; Holdsworth, 1985; Innis, 1930, 1940; Kerr and Holdsworth, 1990; Leggatt, 1987; Sametz, 1964; Sebert, 1981; Stelter and Artibise, 1990; Stevens, 1962; Wayman, 1990.

Specific
Holdsworth, D. Dependence, diversity and the Canadian identity. In *Journal of Geography* (Western Illinois University), LXXXIII, 1986.

LOCATIONS
[I] Association québécoise pour le patrimoine industriel, CP 5225, Scc 'C', Montreal (Quebec) H2X 3N2.
[I] Canadian Canal Society, PO Box 1652, St Catharines, Ontario L2R 7K1.
[I] Heritage Canada, 306 Metcalfe Street, Ottawa, Ontario K2P 1S2.
[I] ICOMOS Canada (TICCIH), PO Box 737, Station B, Ottawa, Ontario K1P 5R4.
[I] *Links*, Nova Scotia Museums, Halifax, Nova Scotia.
[I] Ontario Society for Industrial Archaeology, c/o 88 Upper Canada Drive, North York, Ontario M2P 1S4.
[I] Parks Canada, Research Division, 1600 Liverpool Court, Ottawa, Ontario K1A 1G2.

[I] Society for Industrial Archeology, Room 5020, National Museum of American History, Smithsonian Institution, Washington DC 20560.

DERYCK HOLDSWORTH

canal An artificial channel dug to convey water for irrigation, drainage, navigation, power supply or ornamental purposes. Since the eighteenth century, in England but not in North America, the term has tended to mean an artificial navigation. Inland canals are inseparable from rivers, and are best understood as alternative courses into which river water is diverted as it runs down valleys. Where a canal crosses a watershed, water has to be obtained from streams flowing from higher altitudes than its course, either directly or through a reservoir, or by pumping water from lower levels.

Navigational canals were constructed in ancient China, the first contour canal being completed in 219 BC. The GRAND CANAL was the first canal to cross a summit. POUND LOCKS were employed in China by the eleventh century AD, and in Italy by the fifteenth century. In Europe canals were first widely used in the NETHERLANDS, where many artificial waterways served both for navigation and drainage. The first summit-level canal in Europe was the Briare Canal in France, completed in 1642, which was followed by the Canal du Midi, linking the Atlantic and the Mediterranean in 1681. There were ambitious canal projects in the seventeenth century in Prussia (*see* BERLIN) and Sweden, in Russia (*see* USSR) during the rule of Tsar Peter the Great (1672–1725), and in IRELAND in the 1730s. The building of the BRIDGEWATER CANAL in the 1760s inspired nine decades of canal building in Britain – where 6500 km (4000 mi.) of canals had been built in England and Wales by 1850 – and the construction of many canals in continental Europe and North America.

The canals of the pre-railway age were mostly built to gauges narrower than those of river barges (*see* NARROW BOAT) or TUB BOATS. They included many AQUEDUCTS, some of which were of iron, as well as INCLINED PLANES, BOAT LIFTS, and tunnels (*see* CANAL TUNNEL). In the latter part of the nineteenth century inland navigation, particularly in North America and some parts of continental Europe, received a new stimulus as rivers were improved, and their canal connections built or enlarged to take full-size river barges, which were often towed by steamboats or worked by CHAIN HAULAGE systems. Some important SHIP CANALS were built in the same period, giving ocean-going vessels access to river ports. In the twentieth century waterways have been further enlarged, so that the standard barge on the canals and rivers of Western Europe is now of 1350 tonnes, and notable new inclined planes and boat lifts have been constructed since World War II. Older canals that have not been enlarged are no longer viable for commercial traffic but many have been retained for pleasure cruising (*see* AUGUSTOWSKI CANAL; ENGLAND; THE NETHERLANDS; NEW YORK).

See also POWER CANAL; SHIP CANAL.

BIBLIOGRAPHY
General
Bentley, 1779; Bergasse, 1983; de Salis, 1904; de Vaillac, 1979; Hadfield, 1986; Priestley, 1831; Rolt, 1950; Squires, 1983.

BARRIE TRINDER

canal tunnel Drainage levels in mines were used for navigation (*see* MINING: TARNOWSKIE GÓRY) from early times, but the ability to tunnel through watersheds was something that distinguished the canal builders of the Industrial Revolution. There were 58 km (36 mi.) of canal tunnel in Great Britain by 1860, the first of which was at Preston Brook near Runcorn, opened in 1775 and 1133 m (1239 yd.) long. Standedge (*see* HUDDERSFIELD) was the longest in Britain, at 4951 m (5415 yd.). An outstanding example in France was the 2300 m (2103 yd.) Mont de Billy tunnel on the Canal de l'Aisne à la Marne, begun in 1846. The Schiffstunnel in WEILBURG is a unique river tunnel. No canal tunnel in North America exceeded a mile in length, one of the longest being the 950 m (1039 yd.) Paw Paw tunnel on the Chesapeake & Ohio Canal.

Most canal tunnels lacked towpaths. Before powered vessels became common, vessels were propelled through by 'legging': boards were placed across the hold and crew members would lie on them working the boat by 'walking' their feet along the tunnel walls. In the second half of the nineteenth century boats were hauled through the longer tunnels on busy routes by steam or electric TUGS, or by CHAIN HAULAGE.

BIBLIOGRAPHY
General
Hadfield, 1986.

BARRIE TRINDER

Canavese, Piedmont, Italy A sub-Alpine area centring on Ivrea, 50 km (30 mi.) N. of Turin, which has long been involved in ironmaking. Eight blast furnaces were active in 1750, supplying the demands of Turin, but most were closed in the nineteenth century. At Meugliano near Valchiusella a large warehouse encloses the remains of a blast furnace, and there is an arched incline to the charging area.

BIBLIOGRAPHY
Specific
Cima, C. and Pasinato, D. Altoforni Canavesani tra sette e ottocento (Blast furnaces in the Canavese region in the eighteenth century). In *Archeologia Industriale*, II, 1984.

Canberra, Australian Capital Territory, Australia The site of the Australian capital and its 2400 km² (910 sq. mi.) hinterland were designated in 1911, but it was not until 1927 that the Australian parliament began to meet there. Like most new capital cities Canberra is not primarily an industrial settlement, its main interest to industrial archaeologists arising from its GARDEN CITY plan, designed by Walter B. Griffin (1876–1937), and from the National Library.

BIBLIOGRAPHY
General
Heritage of Australia, 1981.

LOCATIONS
[I] National Library of Australia, King Edward Terrace, Canberra City, ACT 2601.
[M] Royal Australian Mint Museum, Kent and Denison Streets, Canberra, ACT 2600.

candle A rod of solid fat with a strand of twisted fibres, the wick, running through the centre. Candles were the principal means of domestic and industrial lighting before the nineteenth century. Candles were traditionally made from WAX or TALLOW, wicks being made from Turkish cotton. Wax candles were moulded by hand: they were expensive and were used chiefly in churches or by the rich. Tallow candles were made in pewter moulds or by repeated dipping in molten tallow until the desired weight for a batch was achieved. A counterbalanced device for achieving a desired batch weight was supposedly invented by HENRY MAUDSLAY.

From the early nineteenth century the manufacture of candles on an industrial scale from palm oil (*Elaeis guineensis*) was commenced by such companies as Price of London (*see* PORT SUNLIGHT). The fat was treated with lime, which separated the glycerine from the fatty acids, sulphuric acid being employed to separate the latter from the lime; it was subsequently bleached and subjected to hydraulic pressing. Candles were produced in mechanized moulding frames.

BIBLIOGRAPHY
General
Dodd, 1843; Tomlinson, 1852–4; Tunis, 1965.

cannel coal A bituminous coal which burns readily with a bright flame, its name probably being a corruption of 'candle', first applied in south Lancashire, England, where there are large deposits. Cannel coal is of particular industrial value in the production of coal gas and other derivatives; it can also be cut and polished to make ornaments.

canning Nicolas Appert (1752–1841) won a prize from Napoleon in 1809 for a new means of supplying fresh provisions to the French navy, a sequence of cooking and sealing operations which comprised the essentials of the modern canning process, although at first it was applied to glass jars. The use of tinplate for canning was patented by Peter Durand in 1810 and applied by BRYAN DONKIN, who set up a cannery at Bermondsey, London, in 1812 where cans were sealed with solder. Canned meat was being imported to England from Australia, South America and the Ottoman Empire as early as the 1840s. The canning industry in the USA developed at Baltimore, where tomatoes, peas and fish were preserved for westbound migrants. In 1861 the Baltimore canner Isaac Solomon applied Sir HUMPHRY DAVY's discovery that calcium chloride increases the temperature of boiling water to

118 °C (240 °F), and reduced the process time from 6 hours to 30 minutes. Canned food became familiar in the USA during the Civil War. The annual output of cans rose from 5 million to 30 million during the 1860s. By 1880 machines could produce 1500 cans a day.

In the early 1870s the Chicagoan J. A. Wilson devised a truncated pyramid can for corned beef, a name previously applied to slightly salted meat for short-term keeping which now came to mean 'meat compressed in cans clear of all bone and gristle'.

By 1912 canned food available in England included soups, asparagus, peas, salmon, lobsters, oysters, sardines and whole birds, and a writer commented on 'the tinned and bottled fruits now so common, though only introduced of recent years' (Beeton, 1912). By the 1920s canned food was so familiar a part of the American diet that one writer was able to proclaim, 'Canning gives the American family, especially in cities and factory towns, a kitchen garden where all good things grow, and where it is always harvest time.'

The pioneers of mass production of cans in Britain were the makers of tin boxes for the storage of biscuits, tobacco and cocoa. The tin box makers merged in 1922 when threatened with the introduction of automatic canning machinery from the USA, together forming Metal Box Ltd: this firm built a new factory at Worcester to make open-top cans ready for filling and sealing at canneries, which came into operation in 1930.

BIBLIOGRAPHY
General
Beeton, 1912; Collins, 1924; Cordeiro, 1989; Stacey, 1982; Winstanley, 1983; Woodcock, 1938.

BARRIE TRINDER

cannon A large GUN mounted on a fixed or movable carriage. Simple siege cannon, firing solid metal balls of several kilograms in weight, effectively pierced most medieval fortifications. In the more open warfare that followed, cannon were chiefly deployed firing small shot against concentrations of troops. Mobility and rate of fire became crucial although, especially at sea, accuracy at range against opposing gun positions and destructive impact were also important. While the effectiveness of cannon in battle depended greatly on drill and the calculation of position and aim, the casting and boring even of simple smooth-bore, muzzle-loaded cannon was a challenging task: the long barrels necessary to achieve a high muzzle velocity had to be straight and regular, and no heavier than necessary to contain reliably a high-explosive charge.

The manufacture of cannon (and their short-barrelled, high-trajectory variants, howitzers and mortars) stimulated the early iron industry and provided the major impetus to the development of a BORING MACHINE. From the middle of the nineteenth century sets of MACHINE TOOLS and alloy steels were exploited to produce successive generations of mobile, rifled, breech-loaded cannon firing explosive, armour-piercing shells rapidly and accurately at increasing ranges. Supplanted in anti-personnel tactics by the machine gun, such artillery became the key strategic weapon until the advent of aerial bombardment.

BIBLIOGRAPHY
General
Hughes, 1974; McNeill, 1982.

TIM PUTNAM

cantilever bridge A TRUSS BRIDGE in which one truss extends outwards from a pier, or a succession of trusses do likewise. Modern cantilever bridges originate from the 130 m (425 ft.) structure constructed over the River Main at Hassfurt between Schweinfurt and Bamberg, Germany, by Heinrich Gerber (1832–1912) in 1867, which combined an arch and a suspended span. The principle was copied in the USA. The most celebrated cantilever bridge is the FORTH BRIDGE, completed in 1890, but most large cantilever bridges are twentieth-century and in the USA.

See also figure 124.

BIBLIOGRAPHY
General
Jackson, 1988; Pottgiesser, 1985; Straub, 1949.

canvas A term applied to several types of coarse, unbleached cloth. In Britain canvas was woven from hemp or flax, made in various grades and used principally for sails, tents, bags and coverings, and as the base for TAPESTRY work and oil paintings. In the USA canvas used for sails and tents was made from cotton. Some eighteenth-century and earlier bed linen was described as canvas.

BIBLIOGRAPHY
General
Montgomery, 1984.

Capalbio, Tuscany, Italy   A small but spectacular hill-top town, 5 km (3 mi.) from the west coast, 130 km (80 mi.) NW of Rome, and 60 km (40 mi.) S. of Siena. At Pescia Fiorentina, 4 km (2½ mi.) SW, all the buildings survive of an integrated ironworks of the late eighteenth or early nineteenth century, including a blast furnace of BERGAMASQUE FURNACE layout. The works was powered by the Chiarone river, which forms the border between Tuscany and Latio. The earliest documentary evidence of the works dates from the fifteenth century. There was a blast furnace in the seventeenth century, but it was probably not used between 1649 and 1776 when the Magona, the state ironworking monopoly, leased the works and operated only the forge. Subsequently it passed to the Vivarelli Colonna family, who probably rebuilt it in its present form. In the 1840s the forge was removed elsewhere, and the furnace ceased working some time after 1864. The buildings were subsequently used for other purposes.

All the ironmaking processes were carried out in a single range of buildings about 80 m (260 ft.) long, with an aqueduct along the south-east side. The blast furnace follows conventional lines, but has been fitted into a Bergamasque layout. It has a flat front, bound with

Figure 23 The slag pit at the north end of No. 3 blast furnace at the Sydney Ironworks, Cape Breton Island; in the background is the stock yard. The blast furnace was decommissioned in June 1989.
Steel Project, Beaton Institute

wrought-iron rods, and stands between two pyramid-topped Bergamasque towers. There are substantial remains of the water TROMPES which provided blast for the furnace, and around the spectacular vaulted casting hall are wrought-iron galleries. Some traces survive of a nineteenth-century HOT BLAST system. In 1843 the forge was displaced by the insertion of a Swiss-built, water-powered blowing engine for the furnace, removed from an ironworks at Garrano. Many traces of it remain. At the south end of the range is a building, once part of the forge, in which is an olive mill, with the horizontal water wheel that drove it in a subterranean chamber below. The buildings retain many traces of the ironworking process, including blocks of iron ore, slag and conglomerate limestone, and pieces of micaceous stone from Pietrosanta which were used to line the furnace. A trust was formed in 1983 by the owner, the community of Capalbio and ICCROM to secure the conservation of the works.

Pescia Fiorentina is the best-preserved furnace of Bergamasque layout in Italy and the remains of the water trompes are probably more substantial than at any other major ironworking site. It illustrates magnificently aspects of the history of technology which cannot be observed elsewhere. It is also part of one of the most beautiful landscapes in Europe, an intrusion, by now a venerable and well-mannered one, amongst orange, fig and pine trees, richly coloured wayside flowers, and luxuriant crops of grain, olives and grapes.

BIBLIOGRAPHY
General
Breschi *et al.*, 1982; Ferragni *et al.*, 1982; Percy, 1870.

Specific
Casini, I. *Il complesso siderurgico della Pescia Fiorentina* (The ironworking complex at Pescia Fiorentina). Capalbio, 1982.

BARRIE TRINDER

Cape Breton Island, Nova Scotia, Canada   A series of connected peninsulas that form the northern part of the province of NOVA SCOTIA.

The Canadian Parks Service was responsible for the reconstruction of the fortress of Louisbourg, which portrays the military and commercial French community that oversaw all the French outport fisheries (*see* CANADA) until the French were defeated by the English at the Battle of QUEBEC. The restored site includes stores, houses, a lime kiln, a bakery, an icehouse and the governor's palace.

Coal was mined on the island from the 1720s. Mining history is commemorated in the Glace Bay Miners' Museum, 20 km (12 mi.) NE of Sydney, opened in 1967. Visitors can see underground workings, and three typical miners' dwellings illustrate living conditions in the late nineteenth century.

The 194 ha (480 ac.) steel plant at Sydney was one of three established in Canada in the early twentieth century, the others being at HAMILTON and SAULT STE MARIE in Ontario. It was built by Henry Melville Whitney, a Boston businessman, and began production in 1902. The Sydney plant was extensively modernized in the late 1980s; its blast furnace and open-hearth plant were used for the last time in 1989. Its operations have been recorded through the collection of documents, and by photography, video and oral history, by the Steel Project at the University College of Cape Breton.

The Sydney & Louisbourg Railway Museum occupies an original station building of 1895. The line worked until 1968, carrying principally fish and iron ore.

The ALEXANDER GRAHAM BELL Museum is at Baddeck, 40 km (25 mi.) W. of Sydney, where the inventor of the TELEPHONE spent his summers. The museum also houses the first hydrofoil. Bell was concerned with the first air flight in the British Empire, which took place at Baddeck in 1909.

BIBLIOGRAPHY
Specific
Fortress of Louisbourg: a Guide. Sydney, Nova Scotia: College of Cape Breton Press, 1981.

LOCATIONS
[M] Alexander Graham Bell Historic Park, Route 205, Chebucto Street, Baddeck, Nova Scotia, B0E 1B0.
[M,S] Fortress of Louisbourg National Historic Park, Louisbourg, Nova Scotia B0A 1M0.
[M,S] Glace Bay Miners' Museum, Glace Bay, Nova Scotia B1A 5T8.
[I] The Steel Project, Beaton Institute, University College of Cape Breton, PO Box 5300, Sydney, Nova Scotia B1P 6L2.

DERYCK HOLDSWORTH and MICHAEL STRATTON

Capellades, Barcelona, Catalonia, Spain The region around Capellades, 43 km (28 mi.) NW of Barcelona, was the most important papermaking area in Catalonia. The Molí de la Vila, a four-storey, eighteen-bay building of 1754, rebuilt in 1867, has been turned into a working museum demonstrating the manufacture of handmade paper. Two other private papermills in the area retain their period interiors.

BIBLIOGRAPHY
Specific
El Museo-Molino Papelero: guía par vistarlo (The papermill museum: guide for visitors). Capellades: Derección del Museo Capellades, 1983.

LOCATION
[M] Museu-Molí Paperer de Cappelades (Capellades Paper Mill Museum).

capstan A means of moving railway wagons without a locomotive. It comprises a vertically mounted cylinder in a fixed position, round which ropes or cables can be looped in order to winch wagons in and out of position in restricted spaces such as docks or warehouses. It may be operated manually or by steam or HYDRAULIC POWER.

car Originally, any kind of wheeled vehicle. In both Britain and America, the word now normally refers to a MOTORCAR. In America it also means a railway vehicle, usually qualified, as in 'Pullman car' or 'refrigerator car'.

caravan Originally a covered wagon used for the transport of goods, animals and people, and from the 1860s developed by gypsies as a mobile home. Recreational caravanning became fashionable amongst the English gentry in the 1880s and 90s, but the caravan has become increasingly important as a mobile home in the twentieth century, particularly since World War II. It developed in two directions: as recreational accommodation, and as more permanent prefabricated accommodation. In both cases mobility was a prerequisite, although in practice many large caravans have been designed to be static. The design, construction and fitment of caravans continue to reflect these sometimes conflicting requirements. Caravans were originally horse-drawn: motor caravans were introduced in c.1902, and trailer caravans in c.1912.

BIBLIOGRAPHY
General
Shercliff, 1987; Whiteman, 1973.

JUDITH ALFREY

caravanserai A place of overnight accommodation for traders in the Ottoman Empire, built at any time between the thirteenth century and the nineteenth century, which often developed into a trading centre. Originally the term meant a fortified caravan station, providing replenishment and safe lodging for traders, usually with a central courtyard surrounded by vaulted passages, storerooms, shops and sleeping quarters, all within massive masonry walls. In Arabic the buildings are called khan or hans; the usual Turkish term is kervanseray, and the Persian, caravanserai. In Turkey the development of covered markets was closely linked to caravanserai, and one of the last to be built, the Vakif Hani in ISTANBUL of 1918, was intended solely for commercial purposes. Several survive in Eastern European countries once ruled by the Turks, and some, like that at Kuşadası near Ephesus, have been turned into luxury hotels.

BIBLIOGRAPHY
General
Goknil, 1966; Hoag, 1963; Jairazbhoy, 1971; Unsal, 1973.

SIMON DERRY

car barn The North American term for TRAM DEPOT.

carbolic acid See PHENOL.

carbon dioxide (CO_2) A gas, heavier than air and colourless, with many industrial uses, being particularly important in refrigeration. It is supplied as 'dry ice', the solid form, which is made from gas collected from fermenting molasses, or as a by-product of the Haber-Bosch process (see AMMONIA), which is purified, compressed and liquefied in towers. Carbon dioxide is also used in the manufacture of aerated drinks. A heavy gas, which does not support life and is a 'waste product' of respiration, it is a hazard in mines where it accumulates in dips, and is known as 'black damp' or choke damp'.

BIBLIOGRAPHY
General
Morgan and Pratt, 1938; Partington, 1950.

carbon steel   *See* STEEL.

cardboard   A term that originally meant a grade of pasteboard, a material obtained by pasting together three or more sheets of PAPER, from which cards could be cut. By the mid-nineteenth century cardboard was used for making boxes, and the term came to be applied to materials made for this purpose, produced in increasing quantities as papermakers began to use PULP.

The pioneer of the cardboard carton was Robert Gair, owner of a paper bag factory in New York City, who from 1879 devised a press with a multiple die to cut cardboard: it had a sharp metal rule set high to cut the cardboard, and blunt rules set lower to crease it. The press could cut and crease 750 sheets an hour, each sheet producing ten carton blanks. American machinery provided the foundation for carton manufacture throughout the world.

BIBLIOGRAPHY
General
Boorstin, 1973.

Cardiff (Caerdydd), South Glamorgan, Wales   A town that was transformed during the nineteenth century from an insignificant town of under two thousand people into the largest town in Wales, commonly called the 'coal metropolis of the world'. Growth began with the connection of the MERTHYR TYDFIL iron industry to the sea at Cardiff by the Glamorganshire Canal in 1794. Development accelerated with coal exports from the 1820s as mines opened in the Taff, Aberdare and RHONDDA VALLEYS, a dock was built by the MARQUIS OF BUTE in 1839, and the Taff Vale Railway opened in 1841. By 1851 Cardiff was the largest port in Wales. During the next three decades the boom continued, especially for steam coal, aided by railway building, new docks at Cardiff and Penarth, and a Coal Exchange in 1886 which dealt in coal from South Wales and elsewhere. Congestion during the 1880s and discontent with the Butes' docks encouraged construction of new docks and rail links to other ports, including DAVID DAVIES's scheme at BARRY. In 1890 Cardiff exported as much by weight as London or Liverpool and dominated coal-dealing worldwide.

Coal exports fell quickly after 1914, and the narrow base of their trade meant that the docks gradually closed. The Pierhead Building, several substantial shipping offices and the Coal Exchange are intact in the Butetown district, alongside the Welsh Industrial and Maritime Museum. Also in Butetown are several dry docks for Cardiff's massive ship repairing trade. Spectacular Bute family residences survive at Cardiff Castle and Castell Coch. Other industries developed in Cardiff while it grew as a port, including baking and brewing, chainmaking and railwagon building. Steelmaking with imported ores began in 1891 at the New Dowlais (later East Moors) Works, the site of which is now cleared. In the twentieth century the city has become the commercial and administrative capital of Wales with an extensive civic and national centre in Cathays Park.

BIBLIOGRAPHY
General
Davies, 1981; Rees, 1975.
Specific
Daunton, M. J. *Coal Metropolis: Cardiff 1870–1914*. Leicester: Leicester University Press, 1977.
LOCATION
[M] Welsh Industrial and Maritime Museum, Bute Street, Cardiff.

PETER WAKELIN

carding machine   The tedious process of carding, often performed before industrialization by children with hand cards, was first mechanized for the cotton sector in 1738 by Lewis Paul (d.1759) in England. Revolving cylinders covered with card clothing – wire teeth set in leather – separate and straighten the fibre, producing a fine web called roving (*see* TEXTILES) or sliver. In cotton manufacture this roving moves next to the drawing process, while in wool manufacture an intermediate stage provided by the SLUBBING BILLY or later the CONDENSER must join the roving to make it strong enough to begin the spinning process. Important preserved examples for cotton are at HELMSHORE and NMAH (*see* WASHINGTON), and for wool at MAINE State Museum and the Museum of American Textile History (*see* MASSACHUSETTS).

carding mill   With the introduction of the wool carding machine in the USA and Canada, water-powered carding mills were established to card farmers' wool and provide roving (*see* TEXTILES) suitable for home spinning, greatly easing the domestic manufacture of woollens in the first four decades of the nineteenth century. There are examples at Sturbridge (*see* MASSACHUSETTS), Greenfield Village (*see* MICHIGAN) and Upper Canada Village (*see* ONTARIO).

carpenter   A worker in wood, who uses SAWS, chisels, planes, hammers and drills. In a precise sense the word normally applies to a craftsman responsible for building houses, or the roofs of houses. A joiner was strictly a finisher of a house, installing floors, skirtings and so on. A maker of FURNITURE is properly called a cabinet-maker.

BIBLIOGRAPHY
General
Book of Trades, 1839; Mayhew, 1850; Tredgold, 1895.

carpet   A woven or felted fabric, usually patterned, and before the availability of SYNTHETIC FIBRES usually of wool; it is often backed with jute or a coarse linen fabric. Carpets originated in the East, where they were used for covering floors on which people sat, or for kneeling on while praying, and were imported to Europe by the Venetians. Carpet manufacture was established in France by the mid-seventeenth century, and French migrants after 1685 were the first to practise it with success in England.

Manufacture of luxury carpets became established in TOURNAI and other cities. Most of the carpets listed in probate records in early-eighteenth-century England covered tables or cupboards, but the word later came to be applied almost exclusively to floor coverings.

Many carpets from Turkey, Iran and India were imported to Europe in the nineteenth century and subsequently. Manufacture of the traditional Brussels carpet, with an interwoven pattern of coloured WORSTED loop threads, was introduced into England at Wilton in 1749–50. From c.1735 the production of carpets on a large scale began in Kidderminster, a town which had previously specialized in woollen fabrics. The Kidderminster or Scotch carpet, known in North America as the Ingrain carpet, had a worsted warp and woollen weft, and consisted of two distinct webs, interlaced at one operation. Manufacture was gradually mechanized between 1840 and 1914, output in Britain trebling between 1850 and 1890, Glasgow and Halifax developing as major centres of production. The tapestry carpet was a pile carpet which imitated the traditional Brussels carpet: its manufacture was patented by Richard Whytock of Edinburgh in 1832. It was produced on a large scale. Axminster carpets, with tufted or velvet pile, were also made in large quantities after the development of the Axminster loom in the USA. Some oriental carpets were felted rather than woven, a practice copied in Europe, in DUNDEE, and elsewhere.

See also CARPET LOOM; RUG.

BIBLIOGRAPHY
General
Bartlett, 1969; Bradbury, 1902; James, 1857.
Specific
Smith, L. D. Industrial organization in the Kidderminster carpet trade, 1780–1860. In *TH*, xv, 1984.

BARRIE TRINDER

carpet loom Carpet weaving is the most complex form of weaving. To obtain the complicated patterns, colours and texture, from both cut and looped pile (styles known as Axminster, Brussels, Wilton, and so forth), required multiple sets of warp and weft yarns, manipulated by complicated harness motions such as dobby and JACQUARD.

Carrara, Tuscany, Italy A town 60 km (40 mi.) NW of Pisa and the centre of the finest marble outcrop in Italy, which reaches a depth of over 1000 m (3300 ft.). Quarries appear from the coast as a glistening white range of peaks. Stone has been worked from Roman times, and over three hundred quarries remain in operation, the greatest concentration being at Colonnata. Marble is now extracted from open workings by blasting and sawing and transported to the coast by a steeply graded private railway which runs 21 km (13 mi.) to the port of Marina di Carrara. From here to Forte dei Marmi cutting works extend beside the main Genoa–Pisa railway, with long sheds and overhead crane gantries.

At Pietrasanta, 18 km (11 mi.) SE of Carrara, refractory stone has been worked for lining blast furnaces (*see* CAPALBIO).

BIBLIOGRAPHY
General
Naval Intelligence Division, 1944–5.

LOCATION
[M] Exhibition of Marble Quarrying, Viale XX Settembre, Carrara.

MICHAEL STRATTON

carriage A word with at least three uses:

1. A horse-drawn road vehicle for conveying passengers, the word often being used for a vehicle with four wheels, in contrast with a trap which had two. Unqualified, the word often implies a vehicle for private use, whereas a coach was more commonly for the accommodation of the public; but in Britain a hackney carriage was one that plied for public hire, and the term is now applied to motor vehicles engaged in the same trade. The quality of carriages greatly improved in the early nineteenth century, before the coming of main-line railways.
2. Among other abstract senses, the value of transporting an object or person, for which a charge can be made.
3. A movable part of machine tools, particularly LATHES, which carries some load.

See also COACHMAKING; HANSOM, JOSEPH; RAILWAY CARRIAGE; STEAM CARRIAGE.

BIBLIOGRAPHY
General
Adams, 1837.
Specific
Cantle, G. S. The steel spring suspensions of horse-drawn carriages. In *TNS*, L, 1978–9.

cart A two-wheeled, horse-drawn open vehicle for road or farm use. Carts used on farms or by armies were also called tumbrels. Cart bodies were usually made separately from the frames.

cartridges A French patent for making a cartridge by packing shot into a paper-covered wire cage was purchased by William and Charles Eley of London in 1828. William Eley invented the waterproof percussion cap in 1837. Manufacture developed during the nineteenth century, particularly with the adoption from the 1880s of smokeless powders (*see* EXPLOSIVES).

BIBLIOGRAPHY
Specific
Thomas, D. *The Eley Story*. Birmingham: Eley, 1978.

cashmere A fabric made of hair from the Kashmir or Tibetan goat, in imitation of the tapestry Indian shawls fashionable in the late eighteenth century. Later cashmeres often had cotton, wool or silk warps with wefts of fine wool, not necessarily from goats.

BIBLIOGRAPHY
General
Montgomery, 1984.

cash register A device that records retail transactions. Its development transformed RETAILING, by providing reliable business statistics. The term was first used in the USA, *c.*1879. The cash register displaying to the customer the amount due, and later recording the transaction on a roll of paper, was the invention of James Ritty, a saloon owner of Dayton, Ohio. He sold his business in 1884 to John Henry Patterson (1844–1922) who added a cash drawer, a bell and a means of printing a receipt for customers, and developed the concern as the National Cash Register Co.

BIBLIOGRAPHY
General
Doorsin, 1973; Johnson and Lynch, 1932; Marcosson, 1945.

Castanheira de Pêra, Beira Litoral, Portugal A traditional centre of the woollen industry, 180 km (110 mi.) NE of Lisbon, with an industrial landscape along the River Pera, whose waters feed the turbines of the woollen factories, the oldest of which dates from 1860. A nearby Sarnada is the only factory making the traditional woollen cloth caps or 'barretes' worn by Portuguese fishermen.

cast iron Iron with a carbon content between 1.8 and 4.5 per cent, with various trace elements. It is used in a FOUNDRY to make castings, in which form it is strong in compression, and capable of being made into intricate shapes, but weak in tension. In the form of PIG IRON it is the product of the blast furnace. Cast iron was used in medieval China. In the West structural applications date from the eighteenth century (*see* IRON BRIDGES).

BIBLIOGRAPHY
General
Gale, 1969, 1971; Gloag and Bridgewater, 1948

Castner-Kellner cell Equipment for ELECTROLYSIS devised independently by Hamilton Y. Castner (1859–99), an American working in England, and by Austrian Carl Kellner (1850–1905). It is particularly important for the production of caustic soda from brine. A cell consists of a three-compartment slate tank, the floor being covered with MERCURY which acts as the cathode. Chlorine gas is drawn off through ceramic pipes, while the sodium dissolves in the mercury, and the mixture is drawn away to be treated with water, which reacts with the sodium to give caustic soda (NaOH) and hydrogen (H_2). Both men took out patents in 1893–5. Their ideas were brought together and applied by the Castner-Kellner Alkali Co. of Runcorn, England, in 1895.

BIBLIOGRAPHY
General
Castner-Kellner, 1945; Morgan and Pratt, 1938; Partington, 1950; Reader, 1970.

Catalan forge An efficient form of BLOOMERY used until the nineteenth century in the Basque provinces and in the French department of Ariège. In spite of the name, the use of this kind of forge was unknown in Catalonia. The Catalan forge could reduce up to 72 per cent of the iron in a sample of ore. It consisted of a furnace, a blowing machine (often a TROMPE), and a heavy hammer. Typical dimensions of a furnace were 1.04 m (41 in.) high, and 1 m (39 in.) wide at the top tapering to 0.6 m (23 in.) at the bottom. Three sides were normally of iron and the other of stone. The bottom was of refractory stone, and there was a single TUYÈRE. The first ore to be charged was reduced to powder under the hammer, and fed from one side of the furnace onto a bed of incandescent charcoal charged from the opposite side. The process was controlled by throwing on water. The lump of iron was lifted out over the side, shingled under the hammer, and heated again in the furnace prior to further hammering. A heat lasted 6–7 hours and could produce 150 kg (330 lb.) of iron.

BIBLIOGRAPHY
General
Percy, 1864; Richard, 1838; Swedish Ironmasters' Association, 1982; Tylecote, 1986.

MARIE NISSER

Catalonia (Cataluña), Spain Catalonia comprises the provinces of Barcelona, Gerona, Lérida and Tarragona in north-east Spain. Catalan culture is distinct from that of Spain and the Catalan language remains in daily use.

Catalonia developed an important manufacturing capacity during the eighteenth century, based on printed textiles, paper, the production of wrought iron, and alcoholic drinks. It was able to export these products in large quantities to Spain's American colonies after Seville lost its monopoly of such trade. The first steam engine was installed in 1804, but textile manufactures, the foundation of Catalan industrial growth in the nineteenth century, depended on water power, the lack of coal forcing entrepreneurs to locate their factories alongside rivers, and to establish industrial colonies for their workers. The industrial colonies extend through the Llobregat valley, the valley of its tributary, the Cardener, and the Ter valley in the province of Gerona. The centre of the Llobregat-Cardener industrial region is Ciudad de Manresa, 47 km (29 mi.) NW of Barcelona, where the Fábrica de Can Miranda, a water-powered factory of 1820, the oldest in Catalonia, can be visited. The Colonia de l'Ametella de la Merola still operates as a textile concern and visitors are welcomed by the management. The colony retains all its characteristic features. There are several other colonies of interest in the surrounding district. The factory at the Colonia Sedó at Esparraguera, 29 km (18 mi.) NW of Barcelona, was closed in the late 1970s and has been converted to other industrial uses, but a museum of the colony is to be established in the preserved turbine room. The factory's corkscrew-shaped chimney is of particular note. At the Colonia Guell at Sta Coloma de Cervelló, 10 km (6 mi.) N. of Barcelona, the steam-powered factory has buildings of distinguished architectural quality, while the colony's church was designed by ANTONI GAUDÍ.

The Clot del Moro Cement Works at La Pobla de Lillet, 95 km (60 mi.) N. of Barcelona, was the first in Catalonia to produce PORTLAND CEMENT. Much of it is now a range of ruins of whimsical appearance, but the engineers' house has been converted to holiday accommodation. There are plans to establish a museum for the cement industry on the site, and to reopen the line linking it with La Pobla as a museum railway.

The railway workshops at Vilanova i La Geltrú, 45 km (28 mi.) SW of Barcelona, which belong to the state's railway company, are being restored as a museum to house a large collection of railway rolling stock.

The only iron forge in Catalonia to have survived is at Ripoll, 80 km (50 mi.) N. of Barcelona, which is conserved. A forge at Bañolas, 16 km (10 mi.) N. of Gerona, which dates from the end of the seventeenth century and produced objects in copper, is also public property.

The Tobacco Factory in Tarragona is one of Catalonia's most imposing industrial buildings, having the appearance of a palace rather than a place of work. Tarragona is also notable for its 'cellars' or wine warehouses.

The Catalan museum of science and industry is at TERRASSA.

See also BARCELONA; CAPELLADES; IGUALADA.

BIBLIOGRAPHY
General
Corredor and Montaner, 1984; Generalitat de Catalunya, 1988; Marti *et al.*, 1982; Sanz and Giner, 1984.

LOCATIONS
[I] Associacio del Museu de la Ciencia i de la Técnica i d'Arqueologia Industrial de Catalunya (Association of Museums of Science, Technology and Industrial Archaeology in Catalonia), Via Laietana 39, Barcelona 08003.
[M] Provincial Archaeological Museum, Plaza del Rey 1, Tarragona.
[M] Provincial Archaeological Museum, San Pedro de Galligans, Subida Santa Lucia, Gerona.

EUSEBI CASANELLES

catalyst A substance that changes the rate of a chemical reaction without itself undergoing any permanent chemical change. The principle was discovered in 1820, and named by the Swede, Jons Jakob Berzelius (1779–1848) in 1835. Almost all major chemical processes of the last hundred years employ catalysts.

BIBLIOGRAPHY
General
Partington, 1950

catslide A house with its roof built with the rearward slope over an outshot, forming a single structural plane from ridge to eaves. The term was applied to 'salt-box' houses in New England, which had two storeys in front and one behind; and to a type of house built in the MERTHYR TYDFIL district of South Wales in association with the ironworks of Richard Crawshay (1739–1810)

from *c.*1794, which may have been based on Yorkshire precedents.

BIBLIOGRAPHY
Specific
Lowe, J. B. and Anderson, D. N. *Catslide Roofed Outshot Houses in Merthyr Tydfil and Related Areas.* Cardiff: University of Wales Institute of Science and Technology, 1973.

causey A pathway paved with flagstones for the use of PACKHORSES, particularly such a pathway crossing soft-surfaced moorlands in the PENNINES. An Act of 1691 defined the width of a causey as 3 ft. (0.91 m), but archaeological evidence shows that many were narrower. There is much documentary evidence concerning the construction of new causeys in the seventeenth and eighteenth centuries, some for specific industrial sites like lead smelters.

BIBLIOGRAPHY
General
Hey, 1980; Marshall, 1808.

caustic soda Sodium hydroxide (NaOH), a chemical of major importance in many industries, particularly in soap manufacture. It is manufactured from sodium carbonate (Na_2CO_3; *see* ALKALI) or by ELECTROLYSIS of salt.
See also SODA.

BIBLIOGRAPHY
General
Partington, 1950

Cèdres, Les, Quebec, Canada The Soulanges Canal hydro-electric power station erected in 1899 in the town of Les Cèdres, about 40 km (25 mi.) SE of Montreal, provided power for the Soulanges Canal until 1959. The canal was built in 1891 along the north shore of the St Lawrence River to provide easier navigation around the falls which separate Lake St Louis from Lake St Francis.

The power station building has been owned by the Quebec government since 1965 and is classed as a historic monument. Constructed by the Canadian General Electric Company to the design of the engineer Thomas Munro, the building is 37 m (122 ft.) long, 25 m (84 ft.) wide and 14 m (45 ft.) high, and is distinguished by its symmetrical appearance. It is constructed of red brick with ashlar dressings, resting on a plinth of limestone and covered with a black slate roof. Six tail races as well as a dike surround the central building, which is approached across a footbridge. These materials, in addition to the buttresses, the cornices, the crenellation, the turrets, the arched fanlights and the vaulting overhanging the central entrance, give to the complex a medieval atmosphere. It belongs to the 'château' tradition of architecture, popular in Canada between 1875 and 1930, which is also illustrated in some of the great hotels built by the Canadian Pacific Company in Quebec City, Ottawa, Jasper and Victoria.

The power station on the Soulanges Canal comprises two three-phase generators powered by eight turbines, as

ment: from the Hispano-Moresque pottery of fifteenth-century Spain, through the tin-glazed MAJOLICA of Italy (1475–1530) and Rhenish stoneware of Germany in the sixteenth century, to the domination of DELFTWARE made in Holland during the seventeenth century. In the eighteenth century pre-eminence passed to Meissen and Sèvres, with the mass production of utilitarian wares centring on Staffordshire in England.

By the late eighteenth century there were three basic techniques of manufacture: throwing clay on a wheel, pressing it into a previously prepared mould, and casting it in the form of a liquid slip into a plaster mould. Decoration could be applied by hand painting, dipping, or by the application of transfer prints. Transfer printing was taken up as a means of mass-produced decoration by the 1750s: a pattern was engraved on a metal plate which was inked so that the image could be transferred to paper and thence to the article itself. The technique became closely associated with wares made by Sadler & Green of Liverpool.

The major factors in promoting the establishment of large-scale ceramic works in Britain were the transporting of raw materials and products by canal and railway, the application of steam power to clay preparation, and an explosion in demand not just for tableware but for the BRICKS, pipes, and floor, roof and wall TILES needed to build the Victorian city. Brick and pipe works were widely distributed, some of the largest being established once coal-mining activity had demonstrated the presence of clay beds.

Power was widely adopted in ceramic works from the middle of the nineteenth century, several new types of machine, including presses for making stoneware pipes, being displayed at the Great Exhibition of 1851. Hydraulic tile presses were demonstrated in Germany during 1852. During the second half of the century new inventions revolutionized the techniques and scale of ceramic production, and brought massive economies in the use of labour and of fuel for kilns and driers.

Germany, Italy, Spain and France became renowned for their ceramic industries, though only in northern Italy and Germany was the use of red brick and TERRACOTTA in architecture revived on a scale comparable with Britain. The American industry was initially dependent on European skilled labour and technology; a crescendo of interest in ceramics was reached at the Centennial Exhibition held at Philadelphia in 1876. It prompted the establishment of numerous works in the eastern states, particularly New Jersey and Pennsylvania, and in the Midwest. Major brick, pipe and terracotta works were operating on the Pacific coast by the end of the century. The American ceramic industry was marked by its willingness to reinvest in new plant and to support technical training, like that provided by the University of Ohio and by Alfred University in New York state.

Ceramic products are vital in many other industries. In the 1850s bell-shaped porcelain insulators were adopted for telegraph lines. With rising demand for electrical insulators came the need for mass production and great accuracy, and techniques of moulding by hydraulic pressure were adopted. Many chemical processes, particu-larly the production of acids, can only be carried out in ceramic containers, stoneware being used for many chemical installations. Porcelain filters for drinking water were patented by Nadoud de Buffon in France in 1861.

For the technology of the ceramics industry, *see* BONE MILL; CLAY; CLAY PREPARATION MACHINES; FLINT MILL; GILDING; GLAZING; KILN; LATHE; MOULDS; POTTER'S WHEEL.

For ceramic wares, *see* BRICKS; COADE STONE; DELFTWARE; DRAINAGE PIPE; EARTHENWARE; FAIENCE; MAJOLICA; MOSAIC; PORCELAIN; POTTERY; REFRACTORIES; SALT GLAZE; SANITARY WARE; SLIPWARE; TERRACOTTA; TILES; TOBACCO PIPE.

BIBLIOGRAPHY
General
Boger, 1971; Brongniart, 1844; Chandler, 1967; Hamer, 1986; Jewitt, 1878; Searle, 1929–30.

MICHAEL STRATTON

Cernavodă, Constanţa, Romania   The site of a concrete bridge over the River Danube, for many years the longest in Europe, built in 1890–5 to designs by Anghel Saligny (1854–1925), who developed the ideas of his fellow Romanian engineer, Elie Radu (1853–1931).

BIBLIOGRAPHY
General
Bălan and Mihăilescu, 1985.

Červená Nad Vlatavou, South Bohemia, Czechoslovakia   A wrought-iron truss bridge of 1886–9, 250 m (900 ft.) long: it carries the Písek–Tábor railway across the Vltava.

BIBLIOGRAPHY
General
Dusan, 1984.

České Budějovice (Budweis), Southern Bohemia, Czechoslovakia   A thirteenth-century town on the River Vltava, prominent during the Hussite revolt and subsequently known for its wood and food products, and above all, for beer from the Budvar Brewery. České Budějovice was an important entrepôt, where traffic between Austria and Prague joined the Vltava, and it is still possible to see the tall gabled building used to store salt bound for Prague from the south. A horse-drawn railway to Linz, Austria, was built in 1822–7 and operated between 1831 and 1870. Nineteen stations have been preserved and it is possible to see how they were divided into waiting rooms, workmen's quarters, workshops and offices with separate stable blocks. Many of the 202 bridges along the meandering line survive, and one bridge near the road to Linz has been restored and laid with a 10 m (30 ft.) stretch of track. The passenger and goods terminals at České Budějovice are preserved. The Koh I Noor pencil factory has a small museum.

BIBLIOGRAPHY
General
Lewis, 1970.

Figure 25 The 'Maison rouge' silk mill at Saint-Jean-du-Gard (Gard), dating from 1838; this was the last Cevennes silk mill to remain in operation, closing down in 1964.

J. M. Perin, Inventaire général

Český Krumlov, Southern Bohemia, Czechoslovakia A historic town reservation on the River Vltava, where a spectacular five-level bridge of 1765 connects Emperor Rudolf II's castle and a monastery. Several water-powered corn mills and sawmills survive, some of which are working.

BIBLIOGRAPHY
General
Dusan, 1984.

LOCATION
[M] Regional Museum, Horni Ulice c.152, Český Krumlov.

Cevennes, Ardèche, Gard and Hérault, France The mountainous region north of Montpellier and west of ALÈS, which witnessed an economic boom in the nineteenth century based on the production of raw silk. The earliest mention of silkworm 'education' in the region, at Anduze, in Gard, dates from the thirteenth century, but the transition from a family-based seasonal activity to industrial production in purpose-built silk-reeling mills was an early-nineteenth-century development stimulated by the 'Gensoul' process, introduced c.1810. This utilized a central battery of metallic or earthenware pans, the water in them being heated by a steam boiler, isolated from the workshop. From the 1840s steam was also used for engines to turn the reels lining the workshop walls, behind the women workers busy at their pans. These workshops generally had large, arcade-like windows, good lighting being essential for the delicate manipulation of the single silk filaments unravelled from the cocoons floating in the hot water.

The raw silk was used in hosiery production, which was already a prosperous parallel industry at Ganges, in Hérault, and Le Vigan, in Gard, during the eighteenth century. Otherwise the bales of raw silk produced in these rural mills left the Cevennes for subsequent processing, going to throwing mills, many of them located in the valleys of the Ardèche, and the weavers' shops of Saint-Étienne, Troyes, Nimes and, above all, Lyons.

During the latter half of the nineteenth century some of the Cevennes mills went over to the production of cheaper floss silk, but the twentieth century was a period of long drawn-out decline, silk production ceasing entirely by the 1960s. As many as 150 mill buildings survive, however, a few still used for textile production with synthetic fibres, and many others transformed into schools, churches, cultural centres, housing, restaurants and garages well before anything was written about ADAPTIVE REUSE. Two large mills, one at Laroque, in Hérault, the other at Saint Jean-du-Gard, in Gard, are now protected monuments; whilst another, at Lasalle, in Gard, is the centre for the recently-created Cevennes 'silk trail', an interpretive cultural itinerary.

BIBLIOGRAPHY
General
Daumas, 1980; Duprat *et al.*, 1985; Durand *et al.*, 1991.
Specific
Mérian, G. and Doulcier, E. Un pré-inventaire des filatures de soie en Cevennes méridionales (A location survey of silk mills in the southern Cevennes). In *Actes du Vè colloque sur le patrimoine industriel, Alès, 1983.* Paris: CILAC, 1984.
Travier, D. La Soie dans la vie traditionnelle de la Cevenne (Silk in Cevennes traditional life). In *Actes du Vè colloque sur le patrimoine industriel, Alès, 1983.* Paris: CILAC, 1984.

PAUL SMITH

Chacim, Trás-os-Montes, Portugal   A town 225 km (140 mi.) E. of Oporto, with the remains of an important silk-throwing mill of 1778 which used a process imported from Piedmont, ITALY.

chain haulage   A means of hauling vessels along a canal, particularly through tunnels, or upstream on a river. It was used in the late nineteenth century on rivers without locks, like the Rhine, Danube, Main, Oder, Volga and Elbe. On the last, chains extended continuously for 758 km (471 mi.). A steam tug hauled itself along chains laid on the bed of a waterway, taking in the chain over rollers in its stem, passing it over hauling drums, and discarding it at the stern.

Chain haulage was abandoned from *c*.1900 as more locks were built and as self-propelled boats proliferated, but was used on the Main till the 1920s, and is still employed near St Quentin in northern France. The process is illustrated in the BERLIN Museum of Transport.

BIBLIOGRAPHY
General
Farson, 1926; Hadfield, 1986.

chains   Chains have ancient origins and many uses. For some light-duty purposes links were closed by some form of soldering, but until the advent of oxyacetylene welding in the twentieth century the traditional method of making wrought iron or steel chains was to shape the links, and then to shut them by hammer welding. A traditional chain shop, of which examples survive in the BLACK COUNTRY, has several hearths along one side, and pulleys through which completed links of a chain could be put while further links were added within the shop. From *c*.1800 wrought-iron chains displaced hemp ropes for such purposes as winding at mines and cables for ships, and factories were built to make the larger chains. Working conditions were notoriously dangerous. Precision chains for power transmission in production engineering and in BICYCLES and MOTORCYCLES, like the bush roller chain patented by Hans Renold in 1880, came into increasing use in the last quarter of the nineteenth century.

See also BROMSGROVE.

BIBLIOGRAPHY
General
Fogg, 1981; Tripp, 1956.
Specific
Gale, W. K. V. Hand-wrought chains. In *TNS*, XXIX, 1955.

BARRIE TRINDER

chain store   One of a group of similar stores under common ownership, offering similar ranges of products. Most chains depended upon aggressive advertising, and grew by taking over similar firms. The fascias and interiors of most chain stores follow company house styles. Pioneering stores often employed TILES for this purpose. Chain stores began in the food trade, with companies like the Great Atlantic & Pacific Tea Co. (A. & P.) founded in 1859 in New York by George F. Gilman (d.1901) and George H. Hartford (1833–1917), and J. J. Sainsbury, who opened his first shop in London in 1869. Most broke away from tradition by offering 'cash and carry' terms, refusing credit and not offering delivery services, in return for lower prices. Such companies grew rapidly: A. & P. had nearly 500 stores by 1912 and 15 709 by 1929; Maypole, in Britain, expanded from 185 in 1898 to 958 in 1915. Most stores concentrated on limited ranges of products reflecting changes in the food industry, among them packeted tea, butter, bacon, margarine, condensed milk and canned meat. From *c*.1950 the numbers of such shops declined with the rise of the SUPERMARKET.

Similar developments occurred before 1914 in the clothing trade, in dispensing chemists, and in the 1920s in the sale of electrical appliances. F. W. Woolworth (1852–1919) established in 1879 a company which in the US and Britain came to epitomize the chain store in the 1920s and 30s. His shops were originally five- and ten-cent stores, with inviting window displays and goods arranged on open trays, tended by low-paid sales girls.

BIBLIOGRAPHY
General
Boorstin, 1973; Boswell, 1966; Briggs, 1984; Chapman, 1974; Jeffreys, 1954; Lebhar, 1963; Mathias, 1967; Rees, 1969; Winkler, 1940.

BARRIE TRINDER

chair   The manufacture of chairs by turners working parts on LATHES was a traditional forest industry. In the CHILTERN HILLS parts were made by 'bodgers' working in the woodlands, and sent to factories to be assembled.

The making of upholstered chairs was a city trade. In London in the mid-nineteenth century chairmakers, regarded as inferior cabinet-makers, made frames for the larger types of chair, which were passed to upholsterers to be completed.

In the twentieth century mass-produced chairs have become symbols of high quality design, those works of Le Corbusier (1887–1966), Marcel Breuer (1902–81), MIES VAN DER ROHE and Michael Thonet, inventor of the bentwood chair, being regarded with particular esteem.

BIBLIOGRAPHY
General
Braudel, 1981; Mayhew, 1850.
Specific
Banham, R. Chairs as art. In Barker, 1977.

chaldron   A measure used in the shipping of coal, particularly from north-east England. From 1686 a Newcastle chaldron approximated to 53 cwt. (2700 kg) while a London chaldron was approximately 25.5 cwt. (1300 kg). From *c*.1750 the term 'chaldron wagon' was used to describe the high-sided, bottom-discharging wagon of the railways of north-east England.

BIBLIOGRAPHY
General
Lewis, 1970; Nef, 1932.

Châlette-sur-Loing, Loiret, France   The Langlée paper-mill at Châlette-sur-Loing, 5 km (3 mi.) N. of Montargis, was built between 1738 and 1740 at the instigation of a powerful group of financiers. The Duc d'Orléans, one of them, purchased the land and had the water-supply network constructed, the site being located near the junction of the Loing and Orléans canals, over both of which he had toll rights. This location had easy access to both the Seine and Loire basins, and put the new factory in an advantageous situation for supplying the Parisian printing trade.

The mill was one of the first in France to use HOLLANDERS instead of wooden mallets for reducing rags to pulp. As early as 1736 the enterprise was granted royal protection. The factory was a large-scale undertaking from the outset, with a capacity five times higher than that of any other papermill of the time. After some teething troubles it became well known, and was cited as an example by the authors of *L'Art de la Papeterie* (The art of papermaking), published by the Academy of Science in 1761, and inspiring the article on paper production in DIDEROT's *Encyclopédie* in 1765, both of which include illustrations of processes at Langlée (*see* figure 35).

In 1788, at the instigation of a new director, Léorier de Lisle, a new papermill was built nearby at Buges, the two sites being responsible for the production of many assignats of the revolutionary period. From 1798 the enterprise was in difficulty, and in 1808 Léorier sold the Langlée plant, which was used between 1816 and 1845 as a cotton-spinning mill. The site remained an attractive one to entrepreneurs, and in 1853 the factory was bought by Hiram Hutchinson, one of the American promoters of the rubber industry, who was already owner of vast rubber forests in Guyana and Bolivia. Hutchinson went into association with Charles Goodyear (1800–60), acquiring the French rights to his patent for vulcanizing RUBBER, and for manufacturing waterproof boots and shoes. Hutchinson retired in 1898 but his company continued to prosper, enlarging its range of products to include rubber tubing, driving belts, bicycle and motorcar tyres, and later concertina vestibules for railway carriages.

The Langlée factory is still in production, and despite serious fire damage in 1869, many old buildings survive. The original papermill had a large, two-storey central building, more than 130 m × 15 m (420 ft. × 50 ft.), with two single-storey side wings, 50 m × 15 m (160 ft. × 50 ft.). Papermaking was carried out primarily in the central building, in the middle of which the Hollanders were driven by water wheels, 6 m (6 ft. 6 in.) in diameter, located on a leat fed from the Loing canal. Drying lofts occupied all the upper floor. The outer shell of the ground floor of this large building survives, together with one of the two wings, notable for its original timber framework. The period of rubber manufacture has left a reinforced-concrete boiler house of 1924 and some architecturally-interesting workers' dwellings of 1925.

BIBLIOGRAPHY
General
Warschnitter, 1980.
Specific
André, L. La Papeterie de Langlée – Grande entreprise et innovation technique en France au XVIIIᵉ siècle (The Langlée paper factory: large-scale enterprise and technical innovation in eighteenth-century France). Unpublished paper.
Vincent, S. *Dossier on Langlée factory for the Inventaire Général.* Orléans.

JEAN-FRANÇOIS BELHOSTE

chalk   An opaque, soft, earthy form of LIMESTONE, occurring in south-east England, northern France and elsewhere. It can be calcined like limestone to make lime (CaO).

'Chalk' for writing on a slate or board, as in a school, is a preparation from GYPSUM.

chandler   Originally a candlestick, then an official responsible for supplying candles to a royal household, and by 1600 a retailer of groceries. Subsequently the word was used as a contraction of 'tallow chandler' (see TALLOW) to mean a maker of candles; and, in the USA, of soap and candles. Ships' chandlers deal in all kinds of supplies for ships at sea and often occupy distinctive premises in PORTS.

BIBLIOGRAPHY
General
Tunis, 1965.

Channel Islands (Les Îles Anglo-Normandes, Les Îles de la Manche)   The only portion of the Duchy of Normandy

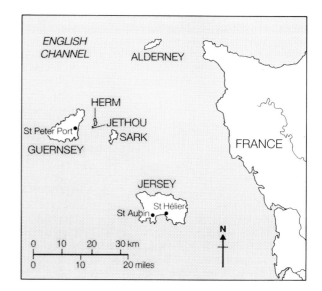

Channel Islands

still belonging to the English Crown, which has held them, except during the German occupation of 1940–5, since 1066. Jersey lies 170 km (100 mi.) from the English port of Weymouth, and 30 km (20 mi.) from the French coast. The islands of Jersey, Guernsey, Alderney, Sark, Herm and Jethou extend over some 19 000 ha (48 000 ac.) and have a total population in excess of 100 000. Most of the population live on Jersey and Guernsey, the two largest islands, whose chief sources of livelihood are tourism and finance. The islands are included among British Ordnance Survey maps.

Jersey was a source of granite in the nineteenth century, supplying stone for the construction of the Thames Embankment in London. The island has a long maritime tradition, with which was associated the manufacture of knitted garments ('jerseys') and hosiery. For much of the nineteenth century fishermen from Jersey maintained settlements at the mouth of the St Lawrence (see PASPEBIAC). Many of the island's roads were built by the British army during the Napoleonic Wars. The Jersey Railway, from the capital, St Hélier, to Corbière, opened in 1887 and closed in 1936. Its terminus in St Hélier is now the town's tourist office, and the section from St Aubin to Corbière has been adapted as a footpath. Jersey airport terminal dates from 1937, and was designed by Graham Dawbarn in steel and concrete, with a plan representing the wings of a swallow in flight. The central market in St Hélier is a cast-iron structure of 1881–2, with a central fountain. The island museum includes a twelve-person TREADMILL of 1836 from Newgate Prison, London.

The harbour at St Peter Port, Guernsey, was constructed in 1833. The town has several notable market buildings. Guernsey's seafaring history is commemorated in its Maritime Museum, and there is a telephone museum in a former manual exchange at Castel.

On Sark, shafts and waste tips remain of copper and silver mines which worked with no great success between 1834 and 1852.

BIBLIOGRAPHY
General
Lake, 1987.

LOCATIONS
[M] Guernsey Maritime Museum, Rocquaine Bay, St Peter's, Guernsey.
[M] Jersey Museum, 9 Pier Road, St Hélier, Jersey.
[M] Telephone Museum, 'Hermes', La Planque, Cobo Road, Castel, Guernsey.

BARRIE TRINDER

charcoal A form of carbon prepared by the slow combustion of wood with air excluded. It was used extensively as a fuel in industrial processes, until displaced by coal, a development that occurred in MALTING, GLASS manufacture, and the smelting of non-ferrous metals (*see* COPPER; LEAD; TIN) in England in the seventeenth century, and in ironmaking (*see* BLAST FURNACE) from 1709. Charcoal is also used in industrial processes as a filter.

Charcoal is made in a kiln, usually a temporary construction, with a central brick chimney and a covering of thatch and clay. Wood is typically cut into lengths of about 1.3 m (4 ft.), known as cords, and burned for two to three days. It is still manufactured in Portugal in horizontal clamps about 10 m (30 ft.) long. Charcoal manufacture is one of the most important forest industries, and continues in many areas. The process is replicated in some open-air museums, including the WEALD AND DOWNLAND MUSEUM. From the late eighteenth century charcoal was produced in Britain in sealed retorts, to ensure a consistent quality for gunpowder manufacture.

'Animal charcoal' is calcined bone, which, like wood charcoal, has a long history of use in filtration.

BIBLIOGRAPHY
General
Kelley, 1986.

BARRIE TRINDER

charcoal barn Part of a BLAST FURNACE complex. Extensive storage was necessary because charcoal needed protection from the elements and was usually transported in the summer when travelling conditions were best, for furnace campaign during the winter. Well-preserved examples may be seen at Duddon (*see* LAKE DISTRICT); DYFI FURNACE; CAPALBIO; Fourneau St Michel (*see* ST HUBERT); Cornwall, Pa., USA; and Högfors, Österby and Stromsberg, all in Sweden.

Charleroi, Hainaut, Belgium A city established on the River Sambre in 1666 by King Charles II of Spain, which became one of the most important centres of coal, iron, chemical and glass production in Europe in the nineteenth century. The city is bisected by the canal from Brussels, opened in 1832. The canal banks were lined with steelworks, but most of the sites are being adapted to new uses. The Solvay chemical plant, established in 1865, lies 3 km (2 mi.) SE of the centre, by Couillet-Montignies station.

Several structures recall the past importance of coal mining. The steel lattice headstock of Pit No. 25 remains on the rue de Couillet, south of Charleroi Sud station. At Marcinelle, 2 km (1 mi.) S., the twin steel headstocks of the Charbonnage de Bois-de-Gazier colliery commemorate the last great mining disaster in Belgium, in 1956, in which 261 miners died.

At Marchienne-au-Pont, 4 km ($2\frac{1}{2}$ mi.) W., remain the headstocks of pit No. 18; and the nineteenth forge, 'La Providence', a brick building containing hearths, cranes and several steam hammers, is preserved by Archéologie Industrielle de la Sambre. Typical nineteenth-century working-class dwellings are conserved in rue Joseph Wauters and chaussée de Bruxelles north of the centre, and in the Quartier de la Docherie to the north-west. The Verlipack glassworks in Jumet, 4 km ($2\frac{1}{2}$ mi.) N. of the centre, is a large modern complex specializing in bottle production: it has developed from an old plant. The glass museum is concerned with manufacturing methods and wares of all periods.

BIBLIOGRAPHY
General
Viaene, 1986.

LOCATIONS
[I] Archéologie Industrielle de la Sambre (AIS), rue Ferrer 7, 6000 Charleroi.
[M] Musée Communal des Beaux-Arts (City Museum of Fine Arts), Place Charles II, 6000 Charleroi.
[M] Musée de la Photographie (Photographic Museum), rue Huart-Chapel 19, 6000 Charleroi.
[M] Musée du Verre (Glass Museum), Boulevard Defontaine 10, 6000 Charleroi.

BARRIE TRINDER

Chartist community   The Chartist movement, which in the late 1830s and early 40s, demanded the reform of the British electoral system, is acknowledged as the first political movement of the working class. After the failure of its petitions to Parliament in 1839 and 1842, Feargus O'Connor (1794–1855) launched the Chartist Land Company, with the object of settling industrial workers on smallholdings. The appeal of the land for the working class was shown by the support generated by the Company, which had six hundred branches in 1847. Five estates, each with two- and three-acre (0.8–1.2 ha) plots, and three-room bungalow dwellings designed by O'Connor, incorporating wash houses, dairies, fuel stores and pig sties, were purchased and laid out in 1847–9. More than 250 settlers took up residence but the financial foundation of the Company was insecure and it was wound up in 1850. Most of the plots continued to be worked as smallholdings, but their distinctive school buildings ceased to be used for educational purposes. Most of the cottages remain at Heronsgate (or O'Connorville), 24 km (15 mi.) NW of London; Lowbands, 14 km (9 mi.) NW of Gloucester; Snigs End, which adjoins Lowbands; Charterville, 21 km (13 mi.) W. of Oxford; and Dodford, 3 km (2 mi.) NW of Bromsgrove.

BIBLIOGRAPHY
General
Hadfield, 1970.
Specific
MacAskill, J. The Chartist land plan. In Briggs, 1959.
Searby, P. Great Dodford and the later history of the Chartist land scheme. In *Agricultural History Review*, I, 1968.

BARRIE TRINDER

cheese   The dried curds of milk, the most easily transported source of cheap protein. Cheese was known in classical antiquity and was extensively traded in Europe by the seventeenth century. Early in the eighteenth century consignments of as much as 5 tons of cheese were being carried down the River Severn, in England.

Cheese is most commonly made from cows', goats' or sheep's milk, which is separated into its solids (curds) and a thin cloudy liquid (whey) by the addition of rennet, an extract from a calf's stomach, or of a bacterial culture. The curds are cut – manually, in a farmhouse; in a factory by a 'cheese harp' rotating in a vat – and are often subjected to pressure in a mould, traditionally a staved vessel made by a cooper, but in a factory usually of stainless steel. Cheeses are then drained and often salted before being stored until they reach maturity. Cheeses and the details of manufacturing processes vary widely.

Most cheese was made on farms until the second half of the nineteenth century when CREAMERY production began, in the Netherlands, Denmark and Canada among other countries, usually for international markets.

Processed cheese consists of one or more cheeses ground fine and mixed with an emulsifying agent.

Typical small cheesemaking plants open to the public are the Schaukäserei at Stein, Appenzell, 10 km (6 mi.) S. of ST GALLEN, and the Fromagerie Perron at St Prime de Robertval, 70 km (45 mi.) W. of CHICOUTIMI.

BIBLIOGRAPHY
General
Braudel, 1981; Brears and Harrison, 1979; Davis, 1965–75.

BARRIE TRINDER

Chełmsko Śląskie (Schomberg), Jelenia Góra, Poland   A village in the Sudeten Mountains, 110 km (68 mi.) SW of Wrocław, the centre of the Lower Silesian textile industry in the eighteenth century. In 1707 Dominik Geyer, abbot of the nearby monastery at Krzeszów, constructed a terrace of twelve weavers' houses of outstanding quality, known as the 'twelve apostles'. Eleven houses remain. Another terrace of seven houses, called the 'seven brothers', was built in the same year, but only one of these remains.

BIBLIOGRAPHY
Specific
Czerner, O. Drewniane domy podcieniowe '12 Apostołow' w Chełmsku Śląskim (The 12 Apostles wooden arcaded houses in Chełmsko Śląskie). In *Zeszyty Naukowe Politechniki Wrocławskiej* (Scientific Papers of Wrocław Technical University), 20, 1957.

chemical industry   The word 'chemistry' in its modern sense, the study of the elements of which matter is composed, and of the ways in which compounds among them are formed, was first used in the mid-seventeenth century. Many modern industrial activities depend on chemical reactions. Various manufactures are regarded as parts of 'the chemical industry': the production of substances through the destructive distillation of coal; the manufacture of drugs, fertilizers, plastics and dyestuffs; the later stages of oil refining. Some of these activities have long histories, but until the mid-nineteenth century the chemical industry essentially meant the manufacture of ALKALI. From the late nineteenth century continuous processes were developed, including those based on ELECTROLYSIS, and constant monitoring of temperatures and pressures became essential. Chemical plants became larger and more thoroughly integrated. At the same time research was showing the close links between hitherto separate manufactures, like explosives and dyestuffs. The industry grew rapidly during World War I, when demand for explosives and chlorine was particularly strong, and the production of toluene (*see* TNT) fostered links between chemical manufacturers and oil refiners.

Chemical processes have always been interdependent – the waste products of one manufacturer or of one generation have become sources of profit for others. The greater scientific awareness of the twentieth century has made it possible to see the broader implications of processes, to review sources of raw materials, to be aware of the potential uses of by-products and of their implications for the profitability of particular operations, and to shape long-term policy by research. There has consequently been a tendency towards concentration. Large multipurpose companies have grown up and huge integrated plants like those at Ludwigshafen and Leverkusen in Germany, Syracuse (N.Y.) and Billingham (*see* TEESSIDE) have been established. Since World War II the chemical industry has been increasingly concerned with petrochemicals. In 1920 less than 100 tonnes per annum of chemicals in Britain were derived from petroleum, a total which increased to 5 000 000 tonnes by 1950, and rose to 30 000 000 tonnes in the succeeding twenty years. Complex organic compounds used as dyestuffs, explosives, fuels, solvents, insecticides, detergents and plastics, as well as such basic chemicals as hydrogen and sulphur, are produced from petroleum. Most large chemical plants are now on coastal sites, such as Immingham, Fawley and Grangemouth in Britain, and Europoort (*see* ROTTERDAM) in the Netherlands, but some have developed around SALT centres like NORTHWICH, Tavaux in France and Syracuse (N.Y.).

There are few monuments of the earlier generations of the chemical industry. Most nineteenth-century plants were relatively crude, architecturally undistinguished and, by the time of their abandonment, heavily polluted. Few survive to be studied. The nature of modern processes – forests of towers and columns, and intricate networks of pipes – makes conservation difficult.

Modern chemical nomenclature was adopted at the time of the French Revolution. The conventional naming of organic compounds was changed in the 1970s. In this book, the modern IUPAC (International Union of Pure and Applied Chemistry) nomenclature has been used with cross-references to the old names.

For the main technologies used in the chemical industry, *see* ELECTROLYSIS; CASTNER-KELLNER CELL; CATALYST.

For the main branches of chemical manufacture, *see* ALKALI; AMMONIA; CELLULOSE; COAL GAS; DRUGS; EXPLOSIVES; GAS; LIMESTONE; OIL INDUSTRY; ORGANIC COMPOUNDS; PAINT; PHOSPHORUS; PLASTICS; SALT; SULPHURIC ACID; SYNTHETIC FIBRES; TEXTILES (for dyeing, bleaching).

BIBLIOGRAPHY
General
Gardner, 1978; Morgan and Pratt, 1938; Morris and Russell, 1988; Reader, 1970; Rogers, 1915; Warren, 1980.

BARRIE TRINDER

chemist A term with two meanings in industrial archaeology:

1. A later name for an APOTHECARY, a trader dispensing medicines, originally applied in England to one practising without examination by the Apothecaries' Company, but in general use since *c.*1800, and regulated by statute since 1852. The word also applied in the early nineteenth century to a trader preparing compounds for use in explosives, paints and so on. In the USA and Scotland the term DRUGGIST is used.
2. A scientist carrying out research on the CHEMICAL INDUSTRY.

See also APOTHECARY; DISPENSARY; DRUG STORE; PHARMACY.

BIBLIOGRAPHY
General
Book of Trades, 1839; Eklund, 1975; MacEwan, 1915; Matthews, 1982, 1983a, 1983b, 1985.

Chemnitz (Karl-Marx-Stadt), Saxony, Germany The Saxon industrial town of Chemnitz was renamed Karl-Marx-Stadt in 1953, but reverted to its original name in 1990. It lies some 50 km (30 mi.) W. of the Saxon ore-mining area around FREIBERG. With its 300 000 inhabitants, it is the capital of the region of the same name, which has a population of two million. The bituminous coal mines in the towns of Zwickau/Lugau and Oelsnitz were the most important in the DDR. The mining museum of the Karl Liebknecht Pit, with its headstock of 1923, was opened in 1986, and contains, among other things, two steam winding engines.

There are early relics of the Saxon textile industry in and around the city of Chemnitz. The Weissenbach calico printing works was built in 1776–8 at Plauen in the Vogtland, and was influenced by the contemporary fashion for crenellation. The Albrecht toolworks in Zeitz was built in 1782–3; the feudal magnificence of its richly-ornamented main section is combined with a plain and functional half-timbered lateral wing. These buildings of the period of manufactures were followed at the beginning of the nineteenth century by the first mechanized factories, like the cotton-spinning mill built by the Bernhard brothers in Harthau, now a part of the city of Chemnitz. As with the case of Brügelmann in Cromford (*see* DÜSSELDORF) the requisite technology was brought to the continent by a British technician. Evan Evans, who had been born in Wales and worked in Manchester, was at first employed by the Bernhard brothers in Harthau, succeeding an Englishman called Watson in 1801, but from 1806–7 he ran an engineering workshop of his own, making textile machinery. The Bernhards' mill is remarkable for the huge pilasters rising three storeys high, and bearing an architrave with a frieze above it. Many cotton mills of the 1830s have been preserved around Chemnitz, among them the seven-storey building of the Hösler factory in Altenhain, built in 1836. These mills characteristically have tall mansard roofs covering at least two production storeys, and as they generally stand in isolation in the landscape, this device makes them appear lower than they really are. It also occurs in the construction of the Meinert spinning mill of 1812 in Lugau, 16 km (10 mi.) SW, where the four Classical corner pilasters follow the same form as in the Einsiedel spinning mill. Similar plants are Greding of 1830, in Hennersdorf, and Himmelmühle of 1834, at Annaberg. In Flöha, 10 km (6 mi.) NE, the Plaue cotton spinning mill has buildings of 1800, 1850 and 1900. The spinning mill of C. F. Schmelzer in Werdau has a steam engine of 1899 from the Zwickau engineering works: since 1974, while remaining on its original site, it has belonged to the district museum of Werdau. Industrial history is among the subjects illustrated in the Schlossberg Museum.

BIBLIOGRAPHY
General
Berger, 1980; Schmidt and Theile, 1989; Wagenbreth and Wächtler, 1983.
Specific
Hentschel, W. Aus den Anfängen des Fabrikbaus in Sachsen (Factory buildings in Saxony from the beginnings). In *Wissenschaftliche Zeitschrift der Technischen Hochschule Dresden* (Scientific papers of Dresden Polytechnic), III. Dresden, 1953–4.

LOCATION
[M] Schlossberg Museum, Schlossberg 12, 9000 Chemnitz.

AXEL FÖHL

Cherepanov, Efim Alexeevich (1774–1842) and **Miron Efimovich** (1803–49) Serfs employed as mechanics in the Demidov metallurgical enterprises in the Urals, Efim Alexeevich (the father) being chief mechanic at the Nizhnii Tagil works from 1822. Together they built steam engines, including Russia's first steam locomotives. For services rendered they were granted their freedom in 1833–6.

Their first locomotive was built in 1833–4 after Miron Efimovich (the son) had been sent to look at the Liverpool & Manchester Railway. It is said that, being unskilled in the use of a pen, he memorized the details of the STEPHENSON locomotives he saw there. Other accounts say that his curiosity was frustrated by the English, who refused to show him drawings, and that in particular the circumstance that the locomotives had inside valve gear prevented him seeing how the reversing mechanism worked. It took father and son a long time to devise a method of reversing their locomotive. It had a boiler of 0.9 m (3 ft.) diameter, which refused to raise steam until the Cherepanovs installed firetubes. It then blew up, but was restored to service. Details were for a long time very meagre. It was known that it had two cylinders 0.23 m × 0.17 m (9 in. × 7 in.) and a gauge of 1.65 m (5 ft. 5 in.). A model made for a St. Petersburg exhibition in 1835 has found its way into the LENINGRAD Railway Museum. Original drawings found in the Sverdlovsk State Archive in the 1980s show that the model is inaccurate. The drawing shows that the Cherepanovs included a *Rocket*-style crenellated chimney-top, and driving wheels larger than the carrying wheels. In 1835 they built a more powerful version that could haul a 16-ton load at 16 km/h (10 m.p.h.). These locomotives in the faraway Urals aroused no interest in the capital, and foreign-built locomotives were used for the first Russian common-carrier railways.

BIBLIOGRAPHY
Specific
Virginskii, V. C. *Zhizn i deyatel'nost' russkikh bmekhanikov Cherepanovykh*. Moscow, 1956.

JOHN WESTWOOD

chewing gum A confection: a flavoured mixture of chicle, a gum extracted chiefly from the sapodilla tree, *Archas zapota*, blended by grinding and then by melting with pressurized steam, purified by centrifuge machines and fine-mesh screens, mixed with flavourings, rolled into long continuous ribbons, sometimes coated with sugar, and then packeted. Chewing-gum manufacture on an industrial scale developed in the USA in the late nineteenth century, the chief pioneer being William Wrigley (1861–1932), who set up a soap business in Chicago in 1891, diversified into baking powder and then into gum making, and introduced spearmint-flavoured gum in 1899. By 1907 Wrigley was the world's principal gum manufacturer and by 1932 he had factories in England, Canada, Australia and Germany as well as in the USA.

Chicoutimi, Quebec, Canada The Vieille Pulperie (Old Pulpmill) in the town of Chicoutimi, 211 km (131 mi.) NE of Quebec City, was one of the chief papermills which developed in Quebec between 1897 and 1943. The companies mostly concerned with the site were La Compagnie de Pulpe de Chicoutimi and the Quebec Pulp and Paper Mills Co.

The complex, designed by the architect René P. Le May, consisted of five main buildings constructed between 1897 and 1923 in which were concentrated the operations concerned with the processing of raw materials: cutting wood, stripping bark, grinding the wood, and making the pulp by mechanical means. The complex was completed by an engineering maintenance workshop which also served as a warehouse, and a transformer station.

The buildings had steel frames with ashlar walls, the windows being in a Romanesque style. Only one building, constructed in 1912, had concrete foundations. In addition to the transport infrastructure, railways and connecting roads, there were dams, sluices and penstocks which were fed by the falls on the Chicoutimi river. The Pont-Armaud power station, now administered by Hydro Québec, 5 km (3 mi.) downstream on the same river, supplied power to one of the mills.

After 1943, when the plant was sold to a papermaking multinational, the Vieille Pulperie was progressively abandoned and some buildings were demolished. Conservation and development projects, supported by the federal and provincial governments, the municipal authorities and a local voluntary group, began in 1979 with historical and archaeological research programmes as well as schemes to use buildings for interpretative and recreational purposes. An interpretation centre now occupies an engineering workshop of 1921, a theatre is

Figure 26 The pulp mill at Chicoutimi, the St Joseph Mill, constructed in 1898; note the stone facing of the mill building and the remains of the penstocks in the foreground.
Ville de Chicoutimi.
Photo: Caroline Bergeron

located in a mill of 1912, and there is a display area in the foundry.

The Saguenay–Lac St-Jean region is one of the world's largest producers of aluminium. The Aluminium Company of North America (Alcoa, which became Alcan), 14 km (9 mi.) W. of Chicoutimi, was begun in 1925 and was responsible for the creation of the city of Jonquière in 1926. Taking advantage of the water power provided by the Saguenay river, the company established a number of hydro-electric power stations, among them Shipshaw, an elegant concrete building of 1941–3, adjacent to which is the 150 m (490 ft.) Arvida Bridge, completed in 1950, the world's first aluminium bridge.

BIBLIOGRAPHY
General
Gagnon, 1984.
Specific
Gagnon, G. *La Vieille Pulperie de Chicoutimi* (The old pulpmill at Chichoutimi). Saguenayensia, 1980.

LOCATION
[M,S] La Vieille Pulperie de Chicoutimi, 300 rue Dubuc, Chicoutimi, Quebec G7H 5B8.

LOUISE TROTTIER

Chiemsee, Bavaria, Germany The largest of the Bavarian lakes. The settlements on its shores and islands are served by ships sailing from the pier at Stock, which adjoins the town of Prien, 64 km (40 mi.) SE of Munich. Stock is linked with the railway station at Prien, a distance of about 2 km (1 mi.), by the Chiemseebahn, the only steam tramway in Europe still operated with its original equipment (*see* figure 27). Most trains are worked by a tram locomotive built in 1887 by Krauss of Munich. The line is owned by the shipping company.

LOCATIONS
[I] Cheimsee-Schiffahrt Ludwig Fessler (Ludwig Fessler Chiemsee Shipping Company), Postfach 1162, 8210 Prien.
[M] Regional Museum, Friedhofweg 1, 8210 Prien.

Chiltern Hills, Bedfordshire, Buckinghamshire and Oxfordshire, England A line of chalk hills north-west of London. Chairmaking has been important in the beechwoods since the eighteenth century, and is depicted in the Wycombe Chair Museum. A rural open-air museum at Chalfont St Giles has a crenellated tollhouse of 1724. A tower mill of the 1830s and a railway centre can be seen at Quainton, 10 km (6 mi.) NW of Aylesbury; and the A423 from Bix to Henley is an outstanding example of 1930s road design.

LOCATIONS
[M] Chiltern Open-Air Museum, Newland Park, Gorelands Lane, Chalfont St Giles, Buckinghamshire HP8 4AD.
[M] Quainton Road Steam Centre, Aylesbury, Buckinghamshire.
[M] Wycombe Chair Museum, Castle Hill House, Priory Avenue, High Wycombe, Buckinghamshire.

chimney The concomitant of steam power, and the most evocative symbol of the Industrial Revolution. The purposes of an industrial chimney were to improve the combustion in the furnace (which might be the firegrate of a BOILER or a metalworking furnace) to which it was connected, by creating a natural draught; and to carry away noxious combustion gases into the high atmosphere. The principles were first formulated in Germany in the mid-seventeenth century, and first applied in Britain in the construction of FLUES at lead smelters in the 1690s. Chimneys multiplied with the steam engine. Until the early nineteenth century square sections, where smooth brickwork facilitated draughting, were favoured; but as

Figure 27 The tram locomotive of the Chiemseebahn in Bavaria, built by Krauss of Munich in 1887, crosses a public road as it leaves the station of Stock for Prien, 11 September 1990.
Barrie Trinder

heights increased, the need for round or octagonal sections, more resistant to wind pressure, was realized. Chimneys came to have a strong emotional appeal, evidenced by the queues that formed to climb the 139 m (436 ft.) stack at the St Rollox Chemical Works, Glasgow, on its completion in 1857, and by the architectural ornamentation employed, particularly the use of the CAMPANILE form, first adopted by I. K. BRUNEL on the South Devon Railway (*see* ATMOSPHERIC RAILWAY; EXETER). Chimneys have been fabricated from wrought iron and from steel, and in Spain there is a tradition of using spiral brickwork. Concrete was the characteristic material for tall chimneys by 1900. The first concrete chimney in Britain was built at Sunderland in 1875, and the Weber Co. in the USA built a thousand between 1903 and 1910. In Scotland, chimneys are known as 'stalks'.

BIBLIOGRAPHY
General
Armstrong, 1885; Bancroft, 1885; Braet, 1883; Douet, 1988; Pickles, 1971; Rawlinson, 1859.

BARRIE TRINDER

China clay A highly refractory clay, also called kaolin:

an essential raw material in the manufacture of PORCE-LAIN, which was first worked in China. Deposits in Europe, the most important of them being in CORNWALL, were not worked until the eighteenth century. China clay is now used extensively in papermaking.

BIBLIOGRAPHY
General
Rhodes, 1969.

Chippis, Valais, Switzerland The Chippis aluminium works was completed in 1908, replacing that established at SCHAFFHAUSEN in 1887. The hydro-electric plant has a capacity of 36 000 hp, and the complex remains one of the most important electro-metallurgical works in Switzerland.

BIBLIOGRAPHY
General
Barblan, 1985

Chlewiska, Radom, Poland An ironworks on the road from Szydłów to Opoczno, 40 km (25 mi.) SW of Radom, within the STAROPOLSKI INDUSTRIAL REGION. A charcoal-fired blast furnace on a private estate, built in the 1890s, it made 2600 tonnes of pig iron per annum in the early years. By 1915 it employed 195 workers; it produced castings, and puddled wrought iron as well as pig iron. It remained in use until 1941, the last charcoal-fired blast furnace in Poland, and is now administered by the Museum of Technology. All the buildings are preserved, complete with their machinery. The complex includes the blast furnace, a hoist with a Parry-type charging apparatus, a charge preparation house, a blowing house, leather and wooden bellows, steam-blowing machines, and hot-blast stoves. The works transport was by narow-gauge railway. The plant is currently under restoration and is being adapted to serve as a museum of metallurgy.

BIBLIOGRAPHY
General
Krygier, 1958.

chlorine (Cl)   An elemental gas, whose compounds have a vast range of industrial applications. In the early nineteenth century it was usually made by mixing common salt, sulphuric acid and manganese dioxide (MnO_2) in spherical lead vessels. When hydrochloric acid from the LEBLANC PROCESS became available from the late eighteenth century, this was oxidized by the use of manganese dioxide in 'chlorine stills' made of stoneware or acid-resistant stone. In a process introduced in 1866 by Walter Weldon (1832–85), the liquor from stills, previously going to waste, was treated with air, chalk and limestone, thereby recovering the manganese: this became the standard method of the late nineteenth century and early twentieth. In 1868 the Lancashire alkali maker Henry Deacon (1822–76) produced chlorine gas and water by passing hydrochloric acid gas and air over hot brickwork impregnated with a catalyst, copper chloride ($CuCl_2$). In the twentieth century chlorine has been manufactured by the electrolysis of brine. Chlorinated hydrocarbons used for insecticides and plastics are of major importance in the modern chemical industry.

See also BLEACHING POWDER.

BIBLIOGRAPHY
General
ICI, 1950; Morgan and Pratt, 1938; Partington, 1950.
Specific
Mond, L. The history of the manufacture of chlorine. In *Engineering*, 6 November 1896.

BARRIE TRINDER

chocolate   The solid product of the COCOA bean, imported to Spain from Mexico *c*.1520, and spreading to England and France in the mid-seventeenth century, where it was employed to make drinks, known as 'chocolate' until the late eighteenth century and thereafter as cocoa. Chocolate for eating was first made by apothecaries *c*.1700, and became popular during the nineteenth century. It is made by cleaning beans which are then roasted, crushed, winnowed, and pressed into a butter, which is refined and flavoured. The increase in the scale of the industry in the late nineteenth century is illustrated by the firm of J. H. Fry of BRISTOL, which employed 350 in 1866, 1000 in 1880, and 4500 in 1908.

Several chocolate factories are of considerable architectural distinction, notably the iron-framed Menier works at NOISIEL-SUR-MARNE, designed by Jules Saulnier in 1871–2 (*see* figure 28). In England the works at Bournville (*see* BIRMINGHAM), New Earswick (*see* YORK), and Somerdale, 8 km (5 mi.) SE of Bristol, are notable for GARDEN CITY style workers' housing.

Christchurch, Canterbury, New Zealand   The principal port for wool exports and the centre for manufacture of agricultural machinery. The first foundry in the province, established by John Anderson in 1857, was subsequently responsible for the construction of truss bridges for railways. The elegant foundry buildings of P. & D. Duncan and the City Foundry of Robert Buchanan both date from the early years of the twentieth century.

chromium (Cr)   An elemental metal, familiar as the shiny plating on motorcars but more important in the production of alloy STEELS, to which it adds hardness, and in refractory bricks and cements. Compounds of chromium are employed in photography, dyeing and tanning. Used in the form of ferro-chrome, it is prepared by reducing the ore, chromite ($FeO.Cr_2O_3$), in an electric furnace in the presence of carbon. The chief sources are the USSR, Turkey, Greece, and Yugoslavia.

BIBLIOGRAPHY
General
Alexander and Street, 1949; Jones, 1950.

chronometer   A precision balance-wheel mechanical CLOCK, typically accurate to a second a day. Accurate clocks were especially important in calculating longitude for maritime navigation. High precision without a pendulum depended on the maximal separation of the impulse-transmitting gear train from the regulating balance; in mid-eighteenth-century France this was achieved by a detent, or trigger, on the balance arbor, which could release a spring-locked escape wheel.

BIBLIOGRAPHY
General
Crom, 1980; Jacquet and Japis, 1970; Landes, 1983.

cider   A drink made by fermenting apple juice. It originated in northern Spain, where it is still popular in the province of Vizcaya, and spread to Normandy and subsequently to England, particularly to the counties of Somerset and HEREFORD, and in Germany to the area around Frankfurt am Main. Calvados is the spirit distilled from cider in the French department of that name, made in the same way as the American applejack.

BIBLIOGRAPHY
Specific
Quinion, M. B. *A Drink for its Time: farm cider making in the western counties.* Hereford: Museum of Cider, 1978.

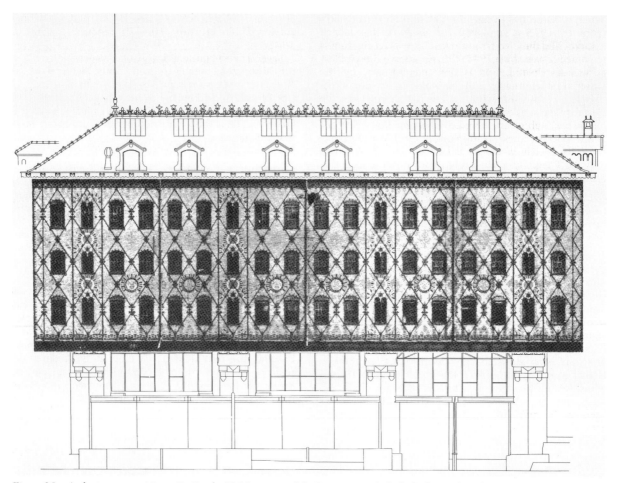

Figure 28   A photogrammetric restitution by M. Maumont of the Inventaire général of Jules Saulnier's iron-framed mill building for the Menier chocolate factory, built astride a branch of the River Marne at Noisiel in 1872
M. Maumont, Inventaire général

Ciechanowiec, Łomża, Poland   A small town in eastern Poland, 140 km (87 mi.) NE of Warsaw. In it is the Krzysztof Kluk Museum of Farming, named after the well-known eighteenth-century Polish naturalist and established in 1968. The museum is housed in an eighteenth-century palace, and exhibits include displays related to rural crafts and folk culture, with a notable section on rural weaving. The open-air part of the museum comprises buildings from the Mazowsze and Podlasie regions, including a water mill preserved *in situ*, a smithy with equipment of 1880, an early twentieth-century windmill, and horse gins of both wooden and iron construction. Displays dealing with the beginnings of agricultural engineering include a steam traction engine, a late nineteenth-century 'Perkun' internal combustion engine, and a horse-powered grain separator. Most of the machines were produced at local plants.

BIBLIOGRAPHY
General
Lorentz, 1973.

Specific
Muzeum Rolnictwa im Krzysztofa Kluka w Ciechanowcu (The Krzysztof Kluk Museum of Farming in Ciechanowiec), Warsaw, 1979.

LOCATION
[M] Muzeum Rolnictwa im Krzysztofa Kluk (The Krzysztof Kluka Museum of Farming), ul. Pałacowa 5, Ciechanowiec.

Ciechocinek, Toruń, Poland   A health resort in central Poland, 30 km (19 mi.) S. of Toruń. After the partition of Poland and the loss of the saltmines in Wieliczka and Bochnia, a new saltworks was established to make use of newly discovered sources of brine at Ciechocinek. Three salt-graduation towers designed by the mining engineer Jakub Graff have survived. The first, dating from 1827–8, is 648 m (1778 ft.) long; the second, of 1833, is 719 m (1972 ft.) long; and the third, of 1859, is 333 m (913 ft.) long. The towers are of wooden construction, made of oak baulks which rest on foundations of crushed stone. The structures are filled with faggots, and are over 15 m (41 ft.) high. Some 19 000 m³ (24 900 cu. yd.) of wood plus 50 000 m³ (65 500 cu. yd.) of faggots were used in constructing the towers. Two windmills stand on the first tower, and were formerly used for pumping brine. The technology is very simple: brine is pumped to the top of the tower, from where it runs in shallow wooden trays along the whole length of the tower. It then percolates down through the faggots filling the structure. Water evaporates and a highly concentrated brine accumulates at the bottom of the tower, ready to be fed to the saltworks. From the mid-nineteenth century the iodine-blue brine was used for medicinal purposes. Today the salt-graduation towers are used as a means of creating an iodine-rich atmosphere, as well as for graduating salt. Ciechocinek is one of the principal health resorts in Poland.

BIBLIOGRAPHY
Specific
Raczyński, M. *Materiały do historii Ciechocinka* (Materials for the history of Ciechocinek). Warsaw, 1935.
Tłoczek, J. Tężnie Ciechocińskie (The Ciechocińskie Salt Graduation Towers). In *Ochrona Zabytków* (Conservation of Historical Monuments), XI, 1958.

JAN KĘSIK

Cierny Balog, Central Slovakia, Czechoslovakia   A small traditional rural settlement, which was once a centre for forestry. There is a preserved narrow-gauge railway which was used in the transport of timber, with a wooden railway station, timber-loading sidings and locomotive depots. The timber trains, which are still functioning, can be seen working on the line that runs along the valley floor.

cigar   Tobacco leaves, from which the stalks have been removed, rolled into a cylinder. They were introduced to Europe from Cuba in the seventeenth century, and became popular in England as a result of the Peninsular War. AMSTERDAM and later EINDHOVEN became specialist centres of production.

BIBLIOGRAPHY
General
Braudel, 1981.

cigarette   Rolling tobacco in paper began in America early in the eighteenth century, spreading to Spain, and during the Peninsular War to much of Western Europe, but not on a large scale to England until the Crimean War. The first cigarette factory in England was set up in Walworth, London, in 1856. Cigarette manufacture and packaging were, more than most forms of tobacco processing, capable of mechanization, which was pioneered in the USA, and by the late nineteenth century the industry was almost entirely factory-based.

BIBLIOGRAPHY
General
Boorstin, 1973.

Cîmpia Turzii, Cluj, Romania   A town which possesses a

museum within a wire factory. The museum includes early twentieth-century wire tack machines by Malemdie & Co. of Düsseldorf, and a variety of wire-drawing equipment and lathes of American types.

BIBLIOGRAPHY
General
Wollmann, V. Romania. In Georgeacopol-Winischhofer *et al.*, 1987.

LOCATION
[M] Wire Aggregate Works, str. Laminoarelor 145, Cîmpia Turzii.

cinema   A building for the public display of cine films (US: movie film), production of which began in the 1890s.

Early cinemas were mostly conversions of other buildings, often previously connected with entertainment, like the Cirque d'Hiver in Paris (*see* CIRCUS), where films were shown from 1907, or the Lyric, Birmingham, England, a former church; but some were ornate purpose-built structures, like the Electric Palace of 1911 at HARWICH. There were 25 000 cinemas in the USA by 1916. In Britain the Cinematograph Act 1909, which required that the projections box in a cinema should be separate from the auditorium, owing to the dangers of fire caused by nitrate film, was the main stimulus to the construction of purpose-built cinemas.

When films were silent, interiors were designed to create atmospheres conducive to enjoyment of dramas in exotic settings, with organs which rose from pits in front of screens, ceilings resembling the night sky, and the walls painted and decked with sculpture. Outstanding examples in the USA from the late 1920s, all designed by John Eberson, are the Riviera, Omaha, the Avalon, Chicago, Loew's, Louisville, and the Civic, Akron, Ohio. The best in England include George Coles's Chinese-inspired Palace of 1929 at Southall, and the Granadas at Tooting and Woolwich by the Russian, Theodore Komisarjevsky (*see* LONDON).

With the coming of the 'talkies' new cinemas were often built with spectacular ceramic façades, in versions of the INTERNATIONAL MODERN style, behind which were cheaply and rapidly constructed auditoria. The Odeons, which composed the largest chain in Britain, were developed by Oscar Deutsch, an entrepreneur from Birmingham, where his first cinema, of 1930, remains at Perry Barr.

With the decline in attendances since the 1950s many cinemas have been demolished or converted to new uses, and most of those remaining in use have been reconstructed.

BIBLIOGRAPHY
General
Atwell, 1980; Ceram, 1965; Pildas, 1980; Ramsaye, 1926.
Specific
Coles, G. Modern cinemas. In *The Builder*, May 1931.

BARRIE TRINDER

circus   A traditional public show, in which the display of exotic animals was combined with feats of agility and older forms of comedy to make one of the characteristic forms of entertainment of the industrial age.

Circuses were traditionally peripatetic, often crossing national boundaries, but in the nineteenth century some established permanent quarters in cities, often in buildings converted from other uses, like Astley's Amphitheatre in Westminster Bridge Road, London, used by 'Lord' George Sanger (1827–1911) until 1893. Some premises were purpose-built. Outstanding examples are the Cirque d'Hiver, designed by Jacob Hittorf and opened in 1852 in the Place Pasdeloup, Paris, which was a polygonal building in the Classical style, with an iron roof structure; and the circus in the base of the Tower at Blackpool (*see* FYLDE). The Hippodrome, Brighton, used for many years as an indoor circus, became a music hall in 1890.

BIBLIOGRAPHY
General
Marrey and Chemetov, 1976; Sanger, 1926.
Specific
Deming, M. Der Cirque d'Hiver oder Cirque Napoleon (The Cirque d'Hiver or Napoleon Circus. In *Jacob Ignacz Hittorf: Ein Architekt aus Köln im Paris des 19 Jahrhunderts* (Jacob Ignacz Hittorf: an architect from Cologne in Paris in the nineteenth century). Cologne: Wallraf-Richartz-Museum, 1987.

BARRIE TRINDER

cistern   A tank for the storage of water. The term is most commonly applied to a tank that provides pressure for the pipe system within a house, but is also applied to large tanks for public supply (*see* ISTANBUL), to condensers in steam engines, to tanks used for soaking malt, and to tanks holding water at intermediate stages of mine-pumping operations.

City Beautiful   A movement that fostered an approach to town planning in the USA that would provide for American cities the wide boulevards and other impressive settings for public buildings characteristic of some historic European cities. The movement began with the World's Columbian Exposition in Chicago in 1893, its chief exponent being the consultant architect for the Exposition, Daniel Hudson Burnham (1846–1912).

civil engineering   Until the eighteenth century the term 'engineer' was usually applied in a military context, to mean one who devised means of taking besieged cities, or erected temporary bridges in advance of marching armies. The term 'civil engineer', meaning a professional person responsible for bridges, waterways, roads and so forth, was first adopted by JOHN SMEATON, who founded a social club, the Society of Civil Engineers, in London in 1771. The professional body in Britain, the Institution of Civil Engineers, was founded in 1818 by Henry Palmer (1795–1844), assistant to THOMAS TELFORD; Telford became the first President in 1820. The profession emerged from military origins both in France, where the Corps des Ponts et Chaussées was established in 1716, and in the USA, where the Army Corps of Engineers dates its origins from 1776. The Corps came to play a prominent part in the building of canals, ports and railways. The professional body, the American Society of Civil Engineers, was established in 1852. The parallel organization in Canada, the Canadian Society of Civil Engineers, was founded in 1887. The Verein Deutscher Ingenieure (German Society of Engineers) was established in 1856, following the organization of the medical and other professions on a national basis, to further the exchange of scientific knowledge and to enhance the professional status of engineers. The expansion of the profession has led to the formation of many specialist bodies concerned with particular aspects of civil engineering.

The principal branches of civil engineering are considered under the following headwords: AERIAL ROPEWAY; AIRPORT; BRIDGE; CRANE; DAM; ELEVATOR; HYDRAULIC POWER; INLAND NAVIGATION; LAND DRAINAGE; PORT; RAILWAY; ROAD; SEWAGE DISPOSAL; TUNNEL; WATER SUPPLY. The following terms relate to civil engineering in general: BALLAST; CUTTING; EMBANKMENT.

BIBLIOGRAPHY
General
American Society of Civil Engineers, 1970; Ball, 1987; Buchanan, 1989; Calhoun, 1960; Ludwig, 1981; Merrill, 1969; Straub, 1949.
Specific
Buchanan, R. A. The lives of the engineers. In *IAR*, XI(l) 1988.

BARRIE TRINDER

Clackmannanshire, Central, Scotland   A tiny county where in 1850 more than a third of Scotland's wool was spun, mostly to be woven into tartan. Before 1860 most mills were three-storey stone buildings of modest size. Thereafter new mills, primarily for weaving, were one- and two-storey brick structures. None is fireproof. Strude Mill, Alva, 4 km ($2\frac{1}{2}$ mi.) N. of Alloa, is an exceptional six-storey pedimented block of 1827, apparently for hand looms; it is situated between a hilly backdrop and a bungalowed foreground, and has now been converted to flats. A smaller hand-loom factory in Brook Street, Alva, is now a youth club. Four later power-loom factories are of one and two storeys, in red and white brick. The mills at Tillicoultry, 5 km (3 mi.) NE of Alloa, had a common water system of 1824, and a wooden dam rebuilt in 1857. A museum is being developed in Clock Mill, a three-storey building of 1824 with a wheel pit. In Alloa, J. & D. Paton's mills of 1825, rebuilt in 1836, which once employed a thousand people, have been converted to small business units; but Middleton Mills of 1836 and later, the first in the area to adopt self-acting mules, still function. The weaving sheds and a three-storey block of 1872 at Devonvale Mill now house 'The Big One', Britain's largest furniture centre. In Alloa, Kilncraigs Mills, the biggest woollen mill and one of the few worsted spinning mills in Scotland, now with a large trade in knitting yarns, was founded on a small scale in 1814. Expansion after 1860 has left several five-storey mills, a tall brick water tower, a sumptuous Baroque office and a six-storey block of 1934 in refined taste.

The tannery of John Tullis & Son at Tullibody, 2 km (1 mi.) NW of Alloa, is from c.1880; it is brick, with two fully louvred floors and a water tower. Once amongst the largest tanneries in Britain, it now produces plastic.

Alloa is a town of exceptional industrial archaeological interest, crisscrossed with footpaths, once wagonways which carried coal to the harbour. The wagonways were begun in 1766–8, extended in the early nineteenth century and were used until the 1930s. The Devon Colliery engine house retains the beam, entablature and pump rod of a Cornish pumping engine of 1865 by Neilson & Co. of Glasgow. Within the extensive works of United Glass Containers Ltd., founded c.1750, is one of Britain's four complete ENGLISH GLASS CONES, dating from c.1825, a 24 m (79 ft.) high structure on an octagonal arcaded stone base. The Thistle Brewery, one of Scotland's three small independent breweries, was built in 1869 by James MacLay. A four-storey, towered brick brewhouse and other louvred buildings are fronted by an eccentric office of 1896 with portholes.

BIBLIOGRAPHY
General
Hume, 1976.
Specific
McMaster, C. *Alloa Ale*, 1985.
Park, B. A. *The Woollen Mill Buildings in the Hillfoot Area*, 1984.
Swan, A. *Clackmannan and the Ochils: an illustrated architectural guide*. Edinburgh: Scottish Academic Press, 1987.

MARK WATSON

clamp   *See* KILN.

Classical   A style in architecture that derives from the buildings of ancient Greece and Rome, and is characterized by the precise use of the CORINTHIAN, DORIC and IONIC orders in columns, by entablatures (comprising architraves, friezes and cornices), by pediments, by symmetry, and by restraint in ornamentation. Classicism was revived in most European countries and in America from the late eighteenth century, and the style was applied to many industrial buildings.

See also PEDIMENT; PILASTER; PORTICO.

clay   Aluminium silicates, represented by the formula $Al_2O_3 . SiO_2 . 2H_2O$, formed by the decomposition of felspathic rock. Primary clays are located on the original site of decomposition; they are pure, they are relatively refractory, and they generally lack plasticity. Secondary clays have been deposited on different sites, and are more plastic, although containing impurities. Clays are the raw materials of the CERAMICS industry.

See also BALL CLAY; CHINA CLAY; CLAY PREPARATION MACHINES; REFRACTORIES.

BIBLIOGRAPHY
General
Rhodes, 1969; Searle, 1929.

clay preparation machines   The first use of machines in CERAMIC works was for clay preparation. The scale of production of bricks, tiles and pottery, and the need for precise standards with porcelain and insulators, encouraged the use of machines to achieve clay bodies of a consistent quality without having to wait for clays to weather over one or more winters.

The earliest machine was the pug mill, introduced in the late seventeenth century. A set of mixing blades were rotated within a cylinder, initially by horse power. After 1850 pug mills were ubiquitous in all but the most primitive of yards. Hard clays such as shales and Cornish stone could be broken down in grinding pans which might be operated wet or dry.

To create a slip for casting, clays would be mixed with water in a blunger. Filter presses were developed to separate liquid from solid matter, to remove excess water from a fluid slip or to convert a slip into a paste. They consist of a frame in which is suspended a series of bags made of cloth. Water or other liquid escapes through the pores of the bag whilst the solid or semi-solid matter is retained. To achieve a plastic clay of particularly fine and even texture, a liquid slip can be heated in a slip-pan in the form of a tank or vessel, moisture being driven off to create a paste.

The Germans initiated some key advances in clay mixing, Schlickeysen of Berlin developing an auger machine for plastic bodies in 1856. In the same year the first jaw crusher for ceramic materials was introduced in the USA.

BIBLIOGRAPHY
General
Chandler, 1967; Searle, 1925.

MICHAEL STRATTON

Clee Hills, Shropshire, England   A range of hills, rising to c.550 m (1800 ft.), between Ludlow and Bridgnorth. There are extensive remains of seventeenth- and eighteenth-century coal and iron-ore mining, with bell pits and associated squatter settlements. Also visible are the remains of three nineteenth-century railway inclines built to serve basalt quarries on the summits. The best preserved of the charcoal blast furnaces, built to use Clee Hill ores, is at Charlcott, 10 km (6 mi.) SW of Bridgnorth. This furnace, of sandstone construction, was built c.1712, and worked till the late eighteenth century. Its water supply was shared with a papermill whose remains have been incorporated into the adjacent Cinderhill Farm.

BIBLIOGRAPHY
Specific
Mutton, N. Charlcott Furnace. In *Transactions of the Shropshire Archaeological Society*, LVIII, 1967.

clerestory   A raised central section of a building, pierced with windows. The term is most commonly applied to the uppermost parts of the walls of naves in churches. It is also applied to raised sections of textile mill roofs, which provide light for attics. The first of this type appears to have been the second mill at CROMFORD, built by RICHARD

ARKWRIGHT in 1776–7, and widely copied in New England, although the type was little used in Britain. Clerestory roofs were features of many railway carriages between the mid-nineteenth and the mid-twentieth centuries, particularly those used for special purposes, like SLEEPING CARS, RESTAURANT CARS or TRAVELLING POST OFFICES.

cliff railway   A FUNICULAR, usually at a seaside resort, linking the promenade or beach with a built-up area on the cliff top. Many were built in Britain in the late nineteenth century and are still in use. Examples can be seen at Lynmouth, Saltburn, and Bridgnorth.

BIBLIOGRAPHY
General
Body and Eastleigh, 1964.

clipper   A term first used to describe US coastal vessels which ran British blockades in the War of 1812, later employed to denote a fast sailing ship, in particular one with a sharply raked stem, masts raking aft and an inclined overhanging stern. By repute the *Rainbow*, built in 1843–5 in New York for trade with China, was the first true clipper. The North American gold rushes and the opening of British ports to foreign vessels carrying China tea stimulated the building of clippers in the 1850s and 60s, the most famous of them being the *Cutty Sark* (*see* DUNBARTONSHIRE; LONDON) of 1868; but the opening of the Suez Canal (*see* SHIP CANALS) in 1869 made such vessels redundant in the tea trade, and they came to be employed in the carriage to Europe of wool from Australia, grain from San Francisco, jute from Calcutta, and nitrates from South America. Many clippers constructed in the 1870s were of iron. Apart from the *Cutty Sark*, survivors include the hulk of the *Ambassador*, an iron and wood tea clipper of 714 tons gross, built at Rotherhithe, London, in 1869, now at Estancia San Gregorio, Chile; and the *Garrick*, also of composite construction and built at Dumbarton in 1869, now an officers' club in Glasgow.

BIBLIOGRAPHY
General
Brouwer, 1985; Howe and Matthews, 1986; Knight, 1973; Lubbock, 1927, 1932, 1946; Underhill, 1938, 1958.
Specific
Carr, F. G. G. The *Cutty Sark* and the restoration of the *Cutty Sark*. In *Royal Institute of Naval Architects, Quarterly Transactions*, 1966.

BARRIE TRINDER

clock   Any of a number of devices for marking the passage of time. Sundials were widely used by the Romans and elaborate water clocks constructed for Chinese emperors around AD 1000. Mechanical clocks, which controlled an escape of force by a regulated pair of pivoted teeth alternately checking and releasing toothed wheels, were found in European bell towers from the late thirteenth century. Reliability and accuracy in a mechanical clock depended above all on allowing the oscillating regulator to control the escapement without being disturbed by impetus fed back from it; this could be achieved by increasing the mass of the regulating balance wheel or pendulum relative to the forces transmitted by the gear train, or by reducing the contact between them. By the end of the seventeenth century, movement of the pivoted escapement had been so reduced that, regulated by a pendulum, it could provide accuracy to within a second a day; this solution, however, was not appropriate for personal WATCHES or in navigation (*see* CHRONOMETER). Gravity-fed weights predominated as a power source to drive clocks prior to electrification. With the development of spring steels, smaller spring-wound movements were applied to clocks that required less force for their operation.

Clockmaking was one of the first branches of medieval metalsmithing to become recognized as a distinct trade. The use of both monumental and portable clocks increased dramatically with the growth of commerce, transport, and waged employment; clocks were found in the homes of British industrial artisans from the mid-eighteenth century. Efforts to cheapen their manufacture encouraged a division of labour and experiments with sets of MACHINE TOOLS for the making of INTERCHANGEABLE PARTS in several countries; CHRISTOPHE POLHEM's tools in Sweden date from the early eighteenth century, and factory-system production using standard parts in both wood and brass was established in Connecticut a hundred years later. Mechanical clocks, WATCHES and CHRONOMETERS, ubiquitous at the beginning of the twentieth century, have since been almost entirely superseded by synchronous a.c. electromechanical displays and digital electronic timing devices.

Clocks and watches are widely collected: collections of clock and watchmaking tools can be found at the Science Museum, London and the National Watch Museum, Prescot, in England; at the Musée International d'Horlogerie, La Chaux de Fonds, and the Musée d'Horlogerie, Le Locle, in Switzerland; and at the Smithsonian Institution, Washington, the American Clock Museum and Watch Museum, Bristol, Conn., and the Time Museum, Rockford, Ill. in the USA. Polhem's devices are in the care of the National Technical Museum, Stockholm. Names on clocks are often of their assemblers or retailers, not of those who manufactured the mechanisms.

BIBLIOGRAPHY
General
Baillie, 1951; Cipolla, 1967; Crom, 1980; Landes, 1983; Lindgren and Sorbom, 1985.
Specific
Thompson, E. P. Time, work-discipline and industrial capitalism. In *Past & Present*, XXXVIII, 1967.

TIM PUTNAM

clogs   Shoes with thick wooden soles, whose uppers might be hollowed from the same block of wood or made of leather. Clogs were characteristic of certain English industrial regions, like the textile districts of LANCASHIRE, and of the Netherlands, where mass production for sale in cities developed in some rural regions in the nineteenth century (*see* EINDHOVEN). Clogs were usually made from poplar or willow, sawn into logs, split into billets, shaped to rough size by axe and adze, then clamped to a bench and hollowed out with gouges and knives. In England clogs were often regarded as an indication of working-class status, while in continental Europe they symbolized the peasantry. Specialized forms were used as protective footware by, for example, workers in brick kilns.

Clogmakers often made pattens, which were overshoes with wooden soles beneath which were sections of wrought iron, worn to lift the wearer's shoes out of mud and dirt.

Clonakilty (Cloich na Coillte), County Cork, Ireland   A town near the south coast which had a substantial wool trade until the mid-eighteenth century, and then became the centre of linen manufacture, with four hundred looms in 1839. There are many stone warehouses around the harbour and on the banks of the river, one of which has been adapted as a public library. Shannonvale, 3 km (2 mi.) N., is a village built around the flour mill of 1788 on the Arigadeen River; for a time this was used for textiles. A large concrete silo dominates the valley. A terrace of weavers' cottages survives on the hill above the bridge.

Cloppenburg, Lower Saxony, Germany   A market town 38 km (27 mi.) SW of Bremen. It boasts one of the oldest open-air museums in Germany, founded in 1934, although most of its buildings were not added until after 1945. Besides various farmsteads from western Lower Saxony, there are several buildings illustrating rural crafts, including a blue-dye works, a smithy, a pottery and a turner's workshop, as well as a POST MILL, a Dutch windmill with a gallery, and a mill worked by a HORSE GIN. For some years the museum has concentrated on agricultural technology between 1920 and 1960, exhibiting tractors, threshing machines, reapers and binders, and on the cultivation of the marshlands, for which it has a steam-driven cable plough of 1929.

BIBLIOGRAPHY
General
Zippelius, 1974.
Specific
Kaiser, H. and Ottenjann, H. *Museumsdorf Cloppenburg: Niedersächsisches Freilichtmuseum* (The museum village at Cloppenburg: the open-air museum of Lower Saxony). Cloppenburg: Museumdorf Cloppenburg, 1978.

LOCATION
[M] Museumsdorf Cloppenburg, 4590 Cloppenburg.

cloth stove   A building in which woollen cloth is dried after fulling or bleached by heating in the presence of sulphur. It works on the same principle as a WOOLSTOVE.

clothing factory   A traditional trade in ready-made clothing was established in many European countries by the early nineteenth century, but the garments were normally secondhand items previously worn by the wealthy. There were already national markets for hosiery and felt hats in the eighteenth century, and many dressmakers' and tailors' establishments in the early nineteenth century might have fifty or more employees working by hand on ordered garments. Precedents for the mass production of garments were set by the supply of military uniforms, particularly during the American Civil War, during which developed the science of anthropometry, codified in 1880 by Daniel E. Ryan. Such research enabled manufacturers in the great American cities to produce clothing in standard sizes which fitted the wearers, in anticipation of sales rather than to order. By 1900 ready-made clothing was worn by the great majority of Americans.

The industry similarly grew rapidly in Europe in the late nineteenth century, mass production often commencing in 'sweat shops', adaptations of existing urban buildings in which low-paid, often immigrant, workers operated on piecework systems. Factory production depended on technological developments, notably the SEWING MACHINE, electric knives for cutting cloth introduced in the 1880s, and the buttonholing machine patented in 1881. Corset factories, like that which houses the museum at Market Harborough, 28 km (17 mi.) SE of LEICESTER, were some of the first purpose-built clothing factories. By the early twentieth century several very large factories had been established in LEEDS, the centre of the British clothing trade. Notable among them was that of Burton, which employed 10000 people in the 1930s. Clothing factories have been established in almost every town of consequence in the twentieth century, the majority being of modest size, and many in buildings adapted from other uses. Purpose-built factories constructed before 1950 tend to have formal brick fronts behind which are steel-framed NORTH-LIT SHEDS.

See also HATMAKING; HOSIERY; MILITARY UNIFORMS; SHAWL MANUFACTURE; SHIRT MANUFACTURE; TAILOR.

BIBLIOGRAPHY
General
Boorstin, 1973; Kidwell and Christman, 1974; Pasold, 1977.
Specific
Busfield, D. Tailoring the millions: the women workers of the Leeds clothing industry, 1880–1914. In *TH*, XVI, 1985.
Lemire, B. Developing consumerism and the ready-made clothing trade in Britain, 1750–1800. In *TH*, XV, 1984.
Thomas, J. The history of the Leeds clothing industry. In *Yorkshire Bulletin of Economic and Social Research, Occasional Paper No. 1.* Leeds, 1954.

LOCATION
[M] Harborough Museum, Adam and Eve Street, Market Harborough, Leicestershire.

BARRIE TRINDER

Cluj-Napoca, Cluj, Romania   The most important town in Transylvania, documented from as early as the 1270s. An old centre of artisan manufactures, where the number of guilds increased from eleven to thirty between 1400 and 1600. The town possesses many works of architectural importance, including the church of St Michael (built in 1349–1450), and the Banffy palace which was completed in 1785 and has housed the art museum since 1859. There is also a historical museum, and an ethnographic museum which includes an open-air section in the Hoia forest, with many exhibits illustrating the use of wood in Romanian material culture, churches, houses, peasant household utensils, mills, saws, fulling mills, oil and raisin presses, and machines for crushing mineral ores.

BIBLIOGRAPHY
General
Giurescu, 1973, 1975.

LOCATIONS
[M] Cluj Museum, 21 Str. 30 Decembrie, Cluj-Napoca.
[M] Museul de Etnografie al Transilvaniei (Ethnographical Museum of Transylvania), 21 Str. 30 Decembrie, Cluj-Napoca.
[M] Museul de Istorie al Transilvaniei (History Museum of Transylvania), St Emil Isac Nr 2, Cluj-Napoca.

HORIA GIURGIUMAN

cluster house A group of four houses in quadruplex form within a single block, of approximately square plan and set in a spacious garden. Such houses were usually provided for supervisory or skilled workers within a textile factory. The style originated in England in the 1790s, with surviving examples at Belper (*see* CROMFORD) and Darley Abbey (*see* DERBY). It was used in Cité Ouvrière at MULHOUSE in the 1850s, from where it spread to the Ruhrgebiet.

BIBLIOGRAPHY
General
Blumenfeld, 1971; Trinder, 1982a.
Specific
Arkwright Society. *Local history trail 12: Cromford.* Belper: Arkwright Society, n.d.
Peters, D. *Darley Abbey from monastery to industrial community.* Ashbourne: Moorland, 1974.

coachmaking A coach was originally a large, enclosed, four-wheeled, passenger-carrying vehicle, said to have originated in Hungary in the fifteenth century, the word deriving from the Hungarian. At first the word referred to a vehicle for royalty or eminent people but in the seventeenth century it came to imply a public conveyance.

Coachmaking was a significant industry in the most developed European countries and in the USA by the early nineteenth century. Coaches made in London were exported on a considerable scale to continental Europe, America and the Far East by *c.*1830. Firms manufacturing horse-drawn road vehicles continued to grow until *c.*1900, although with the growth of railways their products were increasingly intended for urban rather than long-distance use (*see* HORSE). The practices of coach body makers were adapted from the 1830s to the production of RAILWAY CARRIAGES, and from the 1890s to the manufacture of MOTORCARS, OMNIBUSES and other powered road vehicles. Traditional methods of coach-

building persisted in motorcar factories until displaced by the use of steel pressings in the 1920s; they are still employed by some specialist manufacturers. Railway carriages in Europe continued to have traditional coachwork until after World War II. While technology has changed, some of the terms of the trade remain in use in MOTORCAR FACTORIES.

Coachmakers were divided between those who made 'carriages' and the makers of bodies. A 'carriage', in this sense, consisted of two pairs of wheels with their axletrees, the 'perch', which connected them, and the shafts. Bodies were made from ash frames with mahogany panels, with the upper portions of highly varnished leather, and a lining of woollen cloth, silk or velvet, stuffed with horsehair. In large works there were firm demarcations between carriage makers, body makers, trimmers, painters and smiths.

See also MAIL COACH; MOTORCOACH; POST COACH; STAGE-COACH; WHEELWRIGHT.

BIBLIOGRAPHY
General
Oliver, 1981; Rolt, 1950.

BARRIE TRINDER

coach station A terminus or calling point for long-distance MOTORCOACHES, usually in a large city. Coaches would use BUS STATIONS or roadside halts in smaller towns. In most such stations coaches drive into bays, separated from waiting areas by screen-walling. Victoria Coach Station, LONDON, is an outstanding example.

Coade stone A high-quality TERRACOTTA used for reliefs, statues, garden ornaments and architectural detailing, made in Lambeth, London, from 1769 by Eleanor Coade (1733–1821). The material, which closely imitated stone in its colour and texture, received widespread fame due to Coade's employment of such major sculptors as John Bacon (1740–99). The company went out of business in the 1830s; the purchase of some of the models and moulds by John Blashfield (d. 1882) and Henry Blanchard formed the basis of the terracotta revival of the 1850s.

BIBLIOGRAPHY
General
Kelly, 1990.
Specific
Hamilton, S. B. Coade stone. In *Architectural Review*, cxvi, 1954.
Ruch, J. E. Regency Coade: a study of the Coade record books, 1813–21. In *Architectural History*, xi, 1968.

coal The principal source of energy of the first Industrial Revolution and the foundation of the economic prosperity of Britain, Western Europe and the USA in the first half of the twentieth century. Coal is carbonized vegetable matter from earlier periods of the earth's history. Coal from different sources varies substantially in its flammability, its bitumen content and its ability to be coked (*see* ANTHRACITE; CANNEL COAL; COKE; LIGNITE). The word 'coal' was often employed in seventeenth- and eighteenth-century England to refer to CHARCOAL.

Charcoal and wood fuels were used in most industrial processes until the seventeenth century, when coal came to be employed in Britain in malting, in glass manufacture, and in the smelting of tin, copper and lead, the smelting processes depending on the use of REVERBERATORY FURNACES which separated the fuel from the metal being treated. Malting, and subsequently the smelting of iron (see BLAST FURNACE), depended upon the conversion of coal to COKE. Coal-using technologies, such as reverberatory furnaces and crucibles, were developed by the craftsmen who operated them rather than by scientists, and there is little technical literature to explain some of the most critical changes of the Industrial Revolution. Great difficulties were experienced in the TRANSFER OF TECHNOLOGY to other countries.

From the mid-eighteenth century it was realized that coke and other valuable products could be obtained by the destructive distillation of coal (see COKE). The development of COAL GAS manufacture provided TAR and ammoniacal liquors (see AMMONIA) which were employed in industrial processes. The range of coal-based products increased in the early twentieth century. In the 1930s SMOKELESS FUEL and motor spirit (see PETROL) were made from coal, together with other products many of which are now obtained from petroleum sources.

BIBLIOGRAPHY
General
Ashton and Sykes, 1929; Ciekot, 1985; Curr, 1797; Flinn, 1984; Harris, 1972; JC, 1708; Morgan and Pratt, 1938; Nef, 1932; Taylor, 1848.
Specific
Harris, J. R. Skills, coal and British industry in the eighteenth century. In *History*, LXI, 1976.

BARRIE TRINDER

coal drop A development of the STAITHE, on which a coal wagon was lowered by a counterbalanced platform to the ship, where the coal was discharged, thereby avoiding breakage of the coal. It was invented by William Chapman in 1800, and first applied by Benjamin Thompson, at Bewick Main, Wallsend, England, in 1812. The drop from Seaham, County Durham, which was demolished in 1966, is stored at BEAMISH.

BIBLIOGRAPHY
General
Dunn, 1848; Lewis, 1970.
Specific
Atkinson, F. The preservation of Seaham Harbour coal drop and the history of coal transport in the North-East. In Cossons, 1975.

coal gas A term most commonly applied to the gases that are produced by the destructive distillation of coal and that are distributed for domestic and industrial use (see TOWN GAS). The calorific and illuminating qualities of coal gas were known in the late seventeenth century but WILLIAM MURDOCK, who demonstrated coal gas at Red-

ruth, England, in 1792 and lit the BOULTON & WATT works in Birmingham with it in 1802, was the first to put it to practical use. From 1805 Boulton & Watt manufactured gas-lighting plant, which was installed in many cotton factories, the drawings for such installations being an important source for the history of the textile mill. Most towns in Britain had works supplying coal gas for domestic and street lighting by 1850, as did those in other Western European countries and in the USA where coal supplies were abundant.

Coalisland, County Tyrone, Northern Ireland The centre of the east Tyrone coalfield, with many clay pits and remnants of brickworks. Also to be seen are the remains of Ducart's extension of the Coalisland Canal, a fine ashlar aqueduct of three elliptical arches over the River Torrent near Newmills, 4 km ($2\frac{1}{2}$ mi.) NW; and the remains of INCLINED PLANES at Drumreagh Eira, 2 km (1 mi.) NW, and near Farlough Lake, 3.5 km (2 mi.) W. The canal basin has been filled in but some warehouses remain. A spade mill from Coalisland can be seen in the Ulster Folk Museum (see BELFAST).

BIBLIOGRAPHY
General
McCutcheon, 1980; Rees, 1802–20.

coal mining Many aspects of the technology of coal mining are common to MINING technology generally, particularly those relating to means of access, underground haulage, hoisting, drainage, rock breaking and tunnelling. Other aspects, such as the support of excavations, ventilation and illumination, although relevant to other types of mining, have been associated particularly with coal mining, and are considered here.

Coal has been worked since Roman times, but until 1700 workings were on a small scale. Records of coal mining exist in most major coalfields from the thirteenth and fourteenth centuries, but even in Britain no more than 200 000 tonnes were being produced annually up to the mid-sixteenth century, when most manufacturing processes still used CHARCOAL. By 1700 Britain was producing about 3 million tonnes a year, and the industry grew rapidly in the eighteenth century as coal came to be used in ironmaking and other processes. The great expansion of mining in the coalfields of SAINT-ÉTIENNE, Silesia, BELGIUM, the SAARLAND and the RUHRGEBIET began between 1785 and 1850 as the use of coke in ironmaking spread to continental Europe. By 1850 Britain was producing over 50 million tonnes annually, France 5 million, Germany 6 million, and the USA 8 million. After 1900 output in Britain was surpassed by that in the USA, and later by that of Germany and Russia.

Before the seventeenth century coal workings were mainly near to the outcrops of seams. Coal was also being produced from small open pits, from adits and from shafts, many of them BELL PITS. Many shallow coal-bearing areas have been worked and reworked several times using similar methods, and dating is impossible. Modern opencast coal mining in Britain frequently exposes examples of

Figure 29 The tub circuit which receives coal raised up the shaft at the Lady Victoria Colliery, Newtongrange, which forms part of the Scottish Mining Museum
Mark Watson

early workings, but few have been subject to detailed archaeological examination. Finds of tools or other identifiable artefacts are rare. Old and shallow workings often appear as wide headings, each separated from the next by narrow ribs of solid coal. These could represent a stage in the development of coal mining that followed on from the use of bell pits and involved the use of pit props. It was certainly a less wasteful method of mining, giving a higher percentage of extraction than circular workings. Methods of mining are so dependent on local conditions of roof stability, thickness of coal, and quality and depth of the

seam that it is impossible to be specific about the chronology of development. PILLAR-AND-STALL methods were used in shallower, less gassy seams, but also in some deep and gassy mines in north-east England and Scotland. The LONGWALL method developed in Shropshire, England, during the seventeenth century. A variation was SHORT-WALL or single-entry working. Where seams are very thick – up to 10 m (30 ft.) – some, such as those in the Black Country, have been worked by a single face or lift with massive pit props made up of blocks of wood or stone. In others, a series of two or three lifts, known as the

Warwickshire system, have been used, longwall faces following each other, taking the lowermost first.

Roof support has always been important in 'soft' rock mining for coal, clay and shales. In early times waste rock was built into 'packs', and timber blocks and props were also used. From the early twentieth century effective systems of roof support were developed, with wooden props and bars, and occasionally steel supports, being used at regular intervals along faces. Behind the coalface in the areas from which coal had been extracted (the goaf), packs of stones were built in strips. Despite this there was always some convergence, and subsidence effects became apparent at the surface. In continental Europe friction-controlled steel supports came to replace wooden props, and from the 1950s hydraulic props were introduced in Britain. Hydraulic supports gave greater flexibility in mechanized mining, and allowed the cantilevering of roof beams to give a prop-free front, enabling machines to ride on heavy conveyors and load coal as well as cut it. More recently the stone packs have been replaced by hydraulic chocks which can be withdrawn and moved forwards as faces advance. In roadway supports, stone walls, brick walls, and timber props and bars backed with boards, have largely been replaced by steel arches and galvanized sheet or mesh. In shaft-sinking the timber, stone and brick linings of earlier centuries have been replaced by iron, later steel, tubing, and more recently by reinforced concrete.

Adequate ventilation is essential in all mines but particularly in coal and oil shale workings where such inflammable gases as methane are often present. Heavy carbon dioxide gas occurs naturally in shallow mines, bringing dangers of oxygen deficiency. By the seventeenth century effective systems of air circuiting were being developed in British coal mines. Two paths are always necessary, one for air to enter and one for it to leave each working place. In mines with adits for drainage and high levels or shafts for access, a natural air circuit can be formed, and its direction will often vary with the season, the warmest air, in the mine or outside it, tending to rise. This could work even in single-entry mines where a false floor was often constructed in the tunnel so that water could flow underneath. The cold water would encourage an inward flow of cool air, with the warm working area above the floor providing the outward or 'outbye' airflow. Two shafts of unequal depth connecting with the same working could have the same effect, cool air falling in one shaft and rising in the other. To aid this process buckets containing fires were often suspended in one of the shafts to induce a current of air. In the nineteenth century fire buckets were often replaced by permanent furnaces, either on the surface or in an underground return airway. These could be highly dangerous if inflammable gases were present, although various methods were developed to ensure that furnaces received only fresh air. Ventilation furnaces had ceased to be used in Britain by 1950. Alternative means of raising the temperature of air in a shaft to induce movement included the discharging of steam jets. From the early nineteenth century mechanical wind pumps were developed by such engineers as John

Buddle (1773–1843). From the 1830s ventilators or fans, mainly powered by steam, were adopted in the larger mines, notable among them the WADDLE FAN. Since 1900 large electrically driven centrifugal and axial-flow fans have gradually replaced earlier types. For small mines and remote workings in larger mines small mechanical fans called 'blow georges', working on the same principle as the corn-winnowing machine, have been employed well into the present century.

In the seventeenth century the only effective means of lighting a working place in a mine was the naked flame, and many wick types of oil lamp were employed, together with 'pine chips', tallow burners, and later candles. All these methods were dangerous if explosive gases were present. One not especially successful alternative was the phosphorescent glow from putrescent fish skins. Spedding's flint mill of 1760 produced showers of sparks, and could cause ignition. The horrifying mine explosions of the late eighteenth and early nineteenth centuries stimulated attempts to develop a safety lamp that would not ignite gas. That designed by Baron Humboldt (1769–1859) would not burn steadily, while that made by W. R. Clanny (1776–1850) needed a supply of air from a bellows. Sir HUMPHRY DAVY (1778–1829) produced the first practical design, perfected in 1815, but even this lamp gave little light and was not foolproof. A similar lamp was developed at the same time by GEORGE STEPHENSON. Davy's lamp depended mainly on the use of a fine gauze through which air but not flame would pass, and on the use of an oil lamp rather than a candle. Many improvements have been made, but what is essentially the Davy lamp is still in common use in coal mines, although now only as a means of detecting gas or in determining the presence or absence of oxygen. From the 1920s electric hand and cap lamps were introduced, and many of the problems of working in potentially explosive or gassy mines were overcome. In shallow, non-gassy workings, and in metal mines, carbide lamps were introduced before 1900. A carbide lamp has a lower chamber containing calcium carbide and an upper chamber containing water: the water drips through an adjustable needle valve onto the carbide, generating acetylene gas which passes through a tube to a burner, behind which is a reflector. Such lamps give a useful amount of illumination, and many are still in use.

Until after 1850 surface treatment of coal was rarely necessary as quality was maintained by selective working by hand underground. Until the advent of mechanized mining little more than simple screening and hand-picking was normally necessary. Mechanical jigging screens and picking belts were introduced in the 1880s, and at this time also coal washers were constructed to clean coal. Screens and washing facilities were usually built on stilts so that rail or road vehicles could be loaded beneath. Waste tips tended to be small until the development of more complicated coal preparation plants after World War II created a need for large tips, and for slurry ponds for the clarification of waste water from flotation plants.

See also figures 4, 60, 81, 92, 119, 120, 171.

BIBLIOGRAPHY
General
Griffin, 1971, 1977; Huske, 1987.

IVOR J. BROWN

cobalt (Co) An elemental metal, now used principally in special STEELS, particularly when resistance to high temperatures is required. Compounds of cobalt were formerly used as pigments to give colouring, particularly deep blue shades, to pottery, glass and enamels. Cobalt has been mined as a distinct mineral in Norway (*see* MODUM), and from silver workings at Cobalt, Ontario; but most now comes from copper deposits in central Africa.

BIBLIOGRAPHY
General
Jones, 1950.

cobbler *See* SHOES.

cobbles Small, rounded stones, or pebbles, used for surfacing a road or footpath, and usually bonded to provide a firm surface.

cocoa A drink prepared from the seed of the tropical American tree *Theobroma cacao*. The drink was called CHOCOLATE in the seventeenth century, but was known as cocoa by 1800. In the nineteenth century cocoa was much improved by the development of processes for removing the fat and was manufactured on an industrial scale.

BIBLIOGRAPHY
General
Prescott and Proctor, 1937.

coffee Coffee drinking had spread through the Turkish Empire by 1600, and was introduced in Venice *c*.1615, in Paris in the 1640s, and in London by the 1650s. Coffee was commonly drunk in bourgeois households in France and Britain by the 1780s. Supplies originally came from Mocha, Arabia, but production began in the West Indies in the eighteenth century and spread to Brazil, India and elsewhere. Coffee 'beans' are prepared for export on the plantations on which they are grown. Roasting, blending and grinding were undertaken by shopkeepers or in the home until the late nineteenth century when large-scale commercial processing companies were established, chiefly in ports like BREMEN, HAMBURG and ROTTERDAM (*see also* FRIESLAND), from the 1880s.

BIBLIOGRAPHY
General
Braudel, 1981; Franklin, 1893; Prescott and Proctor, 1937; Ukers, 1935.

Coimbra, Beira Litoral, Portugal The capital of the central area, Coimbra stands on the banks of the Mondego river: it is famous for its university, one of the oldest in Europe, whose physics laboratory, founded in 1772 during the education reforms carried out by the Marquis of POMBAL (1699–1789), possesses a remarkable collection of scientific instruments. The National Museum of Science and Technology has displays relating to industry in Portugal, as well as scientific collections. It extends through five buildings: four in the city, with the fifth, a former POSTING STATION, at Carquejo. The traditional manufactures of Coimbra are woollens, cotton, wrought iron and ceramics, but only the last remains in operation. The Museum of Transport includes a display of the city's trams.

BIBLIOGRAPHY
General
Mendes, 1984; Porto, 1982.
Specific
Mendes, J. M. A. Subsídios para a arqueologia industrial de Coimbra (A guide to the industrial archaeology of Coimbra). Coimbra: Museu Nacional Machado de Castro, 1983.

LOCATIONS
[M] Museum of the Physics Laboratory, Faculdade de Ciêcias, Coimbra.
[M] Museum of Transport, Coimbra.
[M] Museu Nacional da Ciência e da Técnica (National Museum of Science and Technology), R. dos Coutinhos 23, Coimbra.

JOSÉ M. LOPES CORDEIRO

coke The hard substance, largely carbon, that remains after the volatile substances have been removed from COAL: it burns almost without smoke, and came into use in seventeenth-century England. The first recorded use of the word is in 1669, when reference was made to 'pit coal . . . converted to the nature of charcoal'. Plot wrote in 1685 that 'the coal . . . prepared by charring, they call coaks'. Derbyshire maltsters were said by Houghton to have replaced straw with coke as their fuel *c*.1650. By 1700 coke was used, sometimes mixed with coal, in the smelting of copper, lead and tin, and by Abraham Darby of Coalbrookdale (*see* IRONBRIDGE) for the smelting of iron ore from 1709. Coke was sufficiently commonly traded in England in the 1690s for a duty to be put on 'all cynders made of Pit-coal . . . shipped or water born'.

COKE OVENS were built in England in the eighteenth century, but the establishment of GASWORKS made coke supplies abundant. In the early nineteenth century, it was the fuel of STEAM CARRIAGES and of the first generation of STEAM LOCOMOTIVES, and it was used in chemical manufacturing, in the GAY-LUSSAC TOWER and similar processes.

The 'coke push' remains one of the most dramatic events in industrial archaeology, the great orange-hot walls of lava-like coke being mechanically pushed out of the oven into gondola railcars in a cascade of fire and smoke.

BIBLIOGRAPHY
General
Houghton, 1692–1703; Mott, 1936; Mott and Wheeler, 1939; Nicol, 1923; Plot, 1685; Taylor, 1939.

DAVID H. SHAYT and BARRIE TRINDER

coke oven   An enclosed oven in which coal is converted to coke and tar, and in which other by-products are sometimes retrieved. It is particularly associated with BLAST FURNACES. Beehive ovens were patented for the production of coal tar in the seventeenth century. Tar ovens were in use in Shropshire (*see* IRONBRIDGE) by the 1740s; and from the 1780s ovens devised by Lord Dundonald were used to make coke and to extract by-products at ironworks. They were not wholly successful, and some British ironworks continued to make coke in open heaps until the early twentieth century. By the mid-nineteenth century beehive coke ovens were in increasing use, and as blast furnaces grew in size and complexity coke ovens became a normal part of the furnace installation, and systems of mechanized charging and coke removal were devised. In 1905 there were 14 259 beehive ovens in County Durham, the principal coking-coal area in England. The French and Belgians experimented with elliptical ovens in the mid-nineteenth century, and a vertically flued oven devised by E. Coppée in 1861 was widely used. Ovens from which by-products could be recovered developed in the second half of the nineteenth century. The Carve recovery oven, used by the Terrenoire Co., near Saint-Étienne, in 1866, was improved by Henry Simon in England and twenty-five Simon-Carve ovens at Crook, County Durham, which began work in 1882, were the first recovery ovens in Britain. The first in Germany were built by Albert Hussener at Gelsenkirchen in 1883, but the Otto-Hoffman kiln became the type most widely used. Recovery ovens designed by Heinrich Koppers produced TOWN GAS for distribution to communities near ironworks in Germany. The first by-product recovery ovens in the USA were built in 1893. There are remains of beehive ovens in County DURHAM and New Zealand (*see* GREYMOUTH), and a complete plant of 1898 at VÖLK-LINGEN.

BIBLIOGRAPHY
General
Mott, 1936; Trinder, 1981.

Specific
McCall, B. Beehive coke ovens at Whitfield, County Durham. In *IA*, I, 1971.

BARRIE TRINDER

Cologne (Köln), North Rhine-Westphalia, Germany Formerly a Hanseatic and Free Imperial city, and founded by the Romans, Cologne has almost a million inhabitants, and is the largest city in North Rhine-Westphalia. The economic importance of the city is connected with its situation on the Rhine, which emerges from the low mountain range 25 km (15 mi.) to the south, and flows unobstructed from that point to the North Sea, so that it has become an important transport artery. Sugar beet has been grown in the fertile farmland to the west and north-west of Cologne since 1851, and several sugar factories have sprung up. Since *c.*1890 the grain brought down the Rhine has been processed in large mills in the river ports of

Cologne, Neuss, Düsseldorf and Krefeld. To the west and north-west of Cologne, the soil bears a harvest of a different nature: the lignite-mining which has its administrative headquarters in Cologne was the progenitor of a massive concentration of electric-power generation, which made the Rhenish-Westphalian electric-power concern, based in Essen, the biggest supplier of electricity in Germany.

The mining of lignite from deep opencast pits has radically changed the entire landscape north-west of Cologne. Road and railway routes, housing, land reclamation, and in particular the drainage of the opencast mines (which are up to 500 m (1640 ft.) deep) have been seriously affected by the needs of the electricity industry. Huge brown-coal power stations, built since *c.*1910, dominate the landscape with clouds of vapour rising from their cooling towers. The phenomenon began when AEG (*see* BERLIN) built the Fortuna I power station for supplying electricity to Cologne. It was demolished in 1989. A network of large power stations on or near the lignite mines then developed. The largest is Frimmersdorf, 28 km (17 mi.) NW; with a capacity of 2600 MW it is the biggest power plant in the world. Frimmersdorf, with its Frimmersdorf West and Frimmersdorf South pits, is linked by its own industrial railway to the Niederaussem opencast mine and power station (the Fortuna-Garsdorf pit) and with Hürth-Knapsack (the Frechen mine, Hürth and Vereinigte Ville). The Rhenish-Westphalian section of Rheinbraun has an information centre at Paffendorf Castle, north-west of Bergheim, which lies 22 km (14 mi.) W. of Cologne; there are viewing points from which one can see down into the deep opencast mines and watch the huge rotary bucket excavators at work, such as that on the Aldenhoven–Düren road, 40 km (25 mi.) SW of Cologne, a point with a view of the Inden opencast mine belonging to the Weisweiler power station.

Cologne has an interesting port, with a hydraulic swing bridge of 1896 which remains in use. The large reinforced-concrete warehouse of 1909 imitates the medieval architecture of the Baltic seaports.

In 1894 Cologne's central station had the second largest platform complex in Germany, after that at FRANKFURT. It was renovated in 1986–8. The station concourse building, with a superb view of Cologne cathedral, dates from 1957.

Another communications structure of interest, one of the sixty-one stations of the Berlin–Koblenz semaphore telegraph line used by the Kingdom of Prussia from 1833 to keep its western provinces under control, has been preserved at Cologne-Flittard as a branch of the City Museum. It was replaced in 1849 by an electromagnetic line. The next station to Flittard (No. 50) along the line was on the tower of St Panteleon's Church, Cologne.

Cologne is of interest in the history of technology for its links with the OIL ENGINE and PETROL ENGINE. The works museum of the present firm of Klöckner-Humboldt-Deutz charts the course of the development on the site of the Otto four-stroke engine from 1864 through the collaboration of Eugen Langen (*see* WUPPERTAL) and Nikolaus Otto (1832–91).

BIBLIOGRAPHY
General
Günter, 1970; Herbarth, 1978; Krings, 1977; Schreiber, 1925; Stübben, 1898.

LOCATIONS
[M] Agfa Foto-Historama (Agfa-Gevaert display on the history of photography), An der Rechtsschule, 5000 Cologne.
[M] Customs Department Museum, Neuköllner Strasse 1, 5000 Cologne.
[M] Cutlery Museum, 1 Burgmauer 68, 5000 Cologne.
[M] Motorenmuseum der Klöckner-Humboldt-Deutz AG (Klöckner-Humboldt-Deutz Motorcar Museum), Deutz-Mülheimer Strasse 111, 5000 Cologne 80 (Deutz).
[M] Museum of Arts and Crafts, Overstolzenhaus, Rheingasse 8-12, 5000 Cologne.
[M] Museum of the City of Cologne, Zeughausstrasse 1-3, 5000 Cologne.

AXEL FÖHL

colonial archaeology A branch of archaeology concerned with settlements established by dominant economic and military powers in the territories of other peoples. Archaeological evidence may show the extent to which the incoming power came to dominate material culture, or the success of resistance by the host community. As a concept, colonial archaeology is not confined to European overseas settlements. Colonial archaeology is concerned with sites established in culturally alien environments, including fortresses, fur-trading posts, whaling ports, or FACTORIES opened by European trading companies in Asia. European colonies that were short-lived and unsuccessful, like some of the early eighteenth-century settlements of the Scottish Darien Company in Central America, or the seventeenth-century ironmaking settlement at Falling Creek, Va., can provide precisely dated artefacts valuable to industrial archaeologists concerned with the sites where they were produced, as can finds obtained from shipwrecks (*see* NAUTICAL ARCHAEOLOGY). Enlightening interactions between colonial archaeology and industrial archaeology in later periods are also possible. Dockyards in overseas naval bases (*see* BALEARIC ISLANDS; GIBRALTAR; MALTA) provide evidence of shipbuilding techniques of the eighteenth and nineteenth centuries which may be lacking in the home country. Studies in colonial territories may provide evidence of manufactures which have left few traces in the home countries, like the prefabricated buildings, first of timber then of cast or corrugated iron, which were produced in large numbers in nineteenth-century Britain for export to Australia and the West Indies. A further, perhaps the most important, point of contact between the two disciplines comes through the study of major industrial sites in colonial territories, like the great railway termini in India, the jute mills of the Ganges valley or the meat-processing plants of Uruguay and Argentina, which in their way were as alien to the territories in which they were built as the fur-trading posts and similar establishments of earlier centuries.

BIBLIOGRAPHY
General
Hume, 1970; Miller *et al.*, 1989; Phillipson, 1985.
Specific
Birmingham, J. M. and Jeans, D. N. The Swiss Family Robinson and the archaeology of colonialization. In *Australian Journal of Historical Archaeology*, I, 1983.

BARRIE TRINDER

colony In its industrial archaeological sense, a community whose members work at a particular mining or manufacturing establishment, in most cases a planned and relatively isolated community. The settlements associated with early cotton mills in England, described by Gaskell as 'little colonies formed under the absolute government of the employer', are typical. The term can also apply to SQUATTER SETTLEMENTS, to UTOPIAN COMMUNITIES, to concentrations of such craftsmen as hand-loom weavers, and to the communities owing allegiance to particular employers identified in Lancashire by Marshall (1968) and Joyce (1975, 1980). 'Colony' is also used to translate Werkssiedlungen, the settlements in the RUHRGEBIET constructed by employers seeking compliant and disciplined workers.

See also PAUPER COLONY; PENAL COLONY.

BIBLIOGRAPHY
General
Gaskell, 1835; Joyce, 1980; Meakin, 1905.
Specific
Ashworth, W. British industrial villages in the 19th century. In *EcHR*, 2nd series, III, 1951.
Bollerey, F. and Hartmann, K. Working class housing in the Ruhr district. In Nisser, 1981.
Chapman, S. D. Workers' housing in the cotton factory colonies. In *TH*, VII, 1976.
Gunter, R. Krupp und Essen (Krupp and Essen). In Warnke, 1970.
Joyce, P. The factory politics of Lancashire in the later nineteenth century. In *Historical Journal*, XVIII, 1975.
Marshall, J. D. Colonisation as a factor in the planting of towns in north-west England. In Dyos, 1968.
Pollard, S. The factory village in the Industrial Revolution. In *English Historical Review*, LXXIX, 1964.

BARRIE TRINDER

Colorado, United States of America As with the early industrial histories of California, Nevada and Montana, the state of Colorado owes its initial development to the discovery of metals: gold in 1858 and silver in 1875, followed by lead, tin and zinc in subsequent years. Such hill towns as Cripple Creek, Gold Hill, Telluride, Silverton, Empire, Leadville, Mill City and Breckenridge stand today as witnesses to the eastern immigrants, especially the Cornish, who swept into the region, with several individual claims quickly maturing into productions of industrial scope. Many of the old mining towns have museums commemorating their founding, with re-created frontier districts geared to mine the tourist dollar.

Two major museums embrace the broad sweep of Colorado's heritage of extractive industries: the Western

Figure 30 The Insurance Exchange Building erected by the Denver Gas & Electric Light Co., Champa Street, Denver, Colorado, in 1909–10: the faience façade is set with electric light bulbs.
Michael Stratton

Museum of Mining and Industry and the Colorado School of Mines Geology Museum. Considerable mining activity continues in the state, especially the mining of uranium, vanadium, coal and molybdenum, as well as the metals that inaugurated the state's prosperity.

Amid the grandeur of Colorado's mountains stands one of the USA's more novel suspension bridges. The Royal Gorge Bridge crosses the Arkansas River at a height of 320 m (1050 ft.), a rare example of a major bridge built intentionally as a scenic attraction. The structure, which dates from 1929, has a 372 m (1220 ft.) long roadway beneath its steel-truss towers. The span may be reached from the gorge floor by a spectacular inclined railway.

In the state capital, Denver, the High Victorian Tivoli Brewery is a robust example of its type, complete with all its internal fittings. As with other urban breweries past their prime, the fate of the Tivoli has become uncertain in recent times.

For its water supply, Denver has been serviced since 1904 by the Cheesman Dam, a curved gravity structure of granite blocks quarried on the site. Cheesman's 70 m (232 ft.) high bulk is wedged into a gap between rocky crags, backing up the South Platte River.

The Gunnison Tunnel in Montrose, with a length of 9321 m (30 582 ft.), was the longest irrigation tunnel in the USA when completed in 1909. The Moffat Tunnel of 1928 in the mountains above Denver was the western hemisphere's longest railway tunnel, passing through 9.97 km (6 mi. 350 yd.) of the Rocky Mountains. Its adjacent pilot bore became a permanent water-supply aqueduct.

BIBLIOGRAPHY
General
Jackson, 1988.

LOCATIONS
[M] Breckenridge Mining Camp Museum, 115 N., Main Street, Breckenridge, CO 80424.
[M] Clear Creek Historic Mining and Milling Museum, 23rd Avenue & Riverside Drive, Idaho Springs, CO 80452.
[M] Colorado Railroad Museum, 17155 W. 44th Street, Golden, CO 80402.
[M] Colorado School of Mines Geology Museum, 16th & Maple, Golden, CO 80401.
[M] Forney Transportation Museum, 1416 Platte Street, Denver, CO 80202.
[M] Leadville Heritage Museum, 102 E. 9th Street, Leadville, CO 80461.
[M] Manitou & Pike's Peak Cog Railway, Manitou, CO.
[M] Western Museum of Mining and Industry, 1025 Northgate Road, Colorado Springs, CO 80908.

DAVID H. SHAYT

Columbia press A hand printing press, substituting levers for the platen-screw, and using a casting of the American eagle as a counterweight. It was invented by George Clymer of Philadelphia in 1817. Many examples are preserved.

comb Combs, whether for TEXTILE manufacture or personal use were made from HORN, tortoiseshell, ivory, or from such woods as box or holly, by hand-sawing with a double saw called a stadda. In 1796 the first comb-cutting machine was made by William Bundy of London. In the twentieth century plastics have superseded other materials for comb-making.

BIBLIOGRAPHY
General
Mayhew, 1850.

combing machine   The hand wool comb consists of iron teeth, 20–25 cm (8–10 in.) long, set in a wooden or metal handle. It was heated in a small stove to ease its passage through the long, delicate wool fibres. The process was mechanized in the nineteenth century, with specific requirements resulting in several different combs. The Noble (circular motion) and Lister combs were those most prevalent in WORSTED manufacture. Samuel Lister (1815–1906), a mill-owner from BRADFORD, developed his comb for the alpaca and mohair fibres used in the plush fabrics made in the city. The French or Heilmann comb of 1845 was used for cotton and short-fibred wool, especially in continental Europe, and also proved adaptable for flax. The Nasmith comb of 1901 was perfected for combing cotton to be used for fine cotton yarns and fabrics.

BIBLIOGRAPHY
General
Burnley, 1889.

communications   The forms of communications comprehended within industrial archaeology include TRANSPORT; PRINTING; BEACON; various specialist transport applications (*see* AIRCRAFT BEACON; ROAD TRAFFIC SIGNAL; PNEUMATIC DISPATCH; RAILWAY SIGNAL), SEMAPHORE; TELECOMMUNICATIONS; TELEPHONE; TYPEWRITER; RADIO; POSTAL SERVICES; PHOTOGRAPHY; COMPUTER.

Como, Lombardy, Italy   A city 40 km (25 mi.) N. of Milan, renowned for its silk industry which was established by 1510. The region is the main Italian centre for silk throwing and weaving, and many sites relating to the industry are located around or near the shores of Lake Como. There is a silk museum at Garlate, near Lecco, 28 km (17 mi.) E. of Como. The most dramatic exhibit is the silk-throwing mill. A walk up from the lakeside in Lecco illustrates the development of factories which used water from the Torrente Gerenzone for power. Via Bovara 39 is a five-storey factory built before 1765, rebuilt in 1818–20, and now converted into apartments. It illustrates how the silk industry created the first formal factories in Italy, broadly paralleling if not preceding the Industrial Revolution in Britain. Just above, at Via Col di Lana 5, is the spinning mill Dell'Oro, established *c.*1854 but rebuilt after a fire in 1861, with further reconstruction *c.*1880 and *c.*1912. A further climb leads to Il Seminario silk mill where the courtyard of a Benedictine monastery of 1530 was converted into a silk works in 1839, and is now adapted as apartments. At Ballano, 26 km (16 mi.) N. along the shore of the lake, is the massive Cantni cotton mill built in stone in 1898–1908 in a manner akin to the woollen mills of West Yorkshire, England.

The Lecco–Colico railway has two standard types of railway station, dating from 1892, with round-arched windows and string courses in richly moulded red terracotta.

BIBLIOGRAPHY
General
Mioni *et al.*, 1981–3.
LOCATION
[M] Silk Museum, Scuola di Setificio, Como.

MICHAEL STRATTON

company mill   A term used chiefly in Yorkshire, England, in the mid-nineteenth century to describe relatively small factories operated by partnerships of independent clothiers, in which wool was prepared and finished, spinning and weaving being organized by the clothiers on other premises. Each partner would pay for work at regular prices, and take a share in the profits of the mill at the end of each year.

BIBLIOGRAPHY
General
BPP, 1840.
Specific
Goodchild, J. The Ossett Mill Company. In *TH*, I, 1968.

company store   A retail shop owned by a mining or manufacturing company, which supplies food and other necessities to workers in an industrial settlement. There often being no alternative source of supplies, high prices charged at such shops can be used as a means of reducing the level of real wages. In isolated settlements like RØROS, in Norway, such stores continued in use until the late nineteenth century. An example from the Industrial Revolution period is preserved at STYAL.

See also TRUCK SHOP.

company town   A town where the sole or principal source of manufacturing or mining employment is a single company, which may have been responsible for the provision of housing and communal amenities. In remote regions such settlements have little purpose if the initial source of employment ceases, and they tend to become ruins or museums; but elsewhere, as in the English RAILWAY TOWNS, the decline of the original economic function is matched by the growth of others. Pullman (*see* ILLINOIS) is an outstanding American example, and former coal-mining company towns are scattered throughout south-western PENNSYLVANIA.

BIBLIOGRAPHY
General
Buder, 1967.

compound engine   A steam engine that uses the same steam successively to drive pistons in high-pressure and low-pressure cylinders. The principle was first put forward by JONATHAN HORNBLOWER in 1781; it was developed in

Britain by Arthur Woolf (1776–1837) in 1804, and applied with success by William McNaught (1813–81) in 1845 who put the cylinders on either side of the beam support, thereby balancing the stresses. Many simple engines were 'McNaughted' by adding extra high-pressure cylinders. Later the compound principle was applied to horizontal engines, and with higher pressures, three-cylinder 'triple expansion' engines were developed, for industrial and marine use. Compounding was applied to some STEAM LOCOMOTIVES.

BIBLIOGRAPHY
General
Frankel, 1977; Watkins, 1968.

compressed air Compressed air has many uses in mining and civil engineering. It was first used in the caissons for the foundations of bridges in the construction of BRUNEL'S Maidenhead Bridge in the 1830s, and is used in the Greathead shield for tunnelling (*see* GREATHEAD, JAMES HENRY). It was first used in 1866 to power drills in the construction of the Hoosac Tunnel, Massachusetts, completed in 1876, and thereafter on a large scale in mining.

computer An integral part of the organization of production in most late twentieth-century industries, and a valuable aid to historical and archaeological research. It scarcely affected manufacturing before 1950, but has many antecedents. Gottfried Leibnitz (1646–1715) in 1685 devised a machine intended to be capable of 'reasoning', which is now preserved in Hanover, Germany, and there were many other seventeenth-century mechanical calculators based on gear wheels. Charles Babbage (1791–1871), taking some ideas from the JACQUARD LOOM, devised calculating machines with a form of sequence control, now in the Science Museum, LONDON. Thomas of Colmar in 1820 produced a commercial calculator based on a stepped cylinder device, which remained in production in various forms into the twentieth century. By the 1930s electromechanical calculators were being devised in Berlin, New York and Harvard; but development was accelerated by research during World War II, at Bletchley Park, England, on deciphering codes, and at the Moore School of Engineering, Pennsylvania, on artillery ballistics. At the latter, ENIAC, an 18 000-valve calculator, was completed in 1945. John von Neumann (1903–57) suggested that programmes might be stored internally, but this was first achieved by M. H. A. Newman's team, which completed MADM (Manchester Automatic Digital Machine), a 'test bed' for the principle, at the University of Manchester in 1948. The first practical computer with a stored programme was EDSAC, constructed by a team led by Maurice Wilkes (1913–) at Cambridge in 1949. The following year the British mathematician Alan Turing (1912–54) showed that a digital computing machine on the von Neumann pattern could do anything in logic that any other machine could do. The commercial potential of the computer became evident when IBM, a company whose fortunes were based

partly on the punched-card systems devised by Herman Hollerith (1860–1929) for the USA CENSUS of 1890, began to produce its IBM 701 machine in 1952, completing the first in March 1953.

See also figure 121.

BIBLIOGRAPHY
General
Feigenbaum and Feldman, 1963; Hyman, 1982; Metropolis *et al.*, 1980; Morrison, 1961; Pratt, 1987; Randall, 1975.

BARRIE TRINDER

concrete A combination of aggregate, of which sand is always a part, together with gravel, stone chippings, or crushed slag, and lime or cement to bind the aggregate. Concrete is the characteristic constructional and architectural material of the twentieth century. It was used in classical antiquity, and in the foundations of such structures as JOHN SMEATON'S Eddystone Lighthouse, off PLYMOUTH, England, but modern applications date from the mid-nineteenth century when, after the development of PORTLAND CEMENT in England, it was pioneered in France. Concrete is widely used in BRIDGES, DAMS, SEWERS, and breakwaters; in building construction, in the form of columns, beams and slabs; and even in shipbuilding.

Concrete that is simply cast in an arch is known as mass concrete: it is strong in compression but comparatively weak in tension. A concrete beam compresses on the top side while the bottom portion stretches. Reinforcing with steel overcomes this weakness since the load is transferred from the concrete to the steel rods or cables; ends of steel rods transfer the load from the reinforcement to the concrete. Joseph Monier (1823–1906) in France took out a patent in 1867 for concrete reinforced with wire netting. François Hennebique (1843–1921) was the other great European pioneer of reinforced concrete or ferroconcrete, in which the mechanical and physical properties of the two materials are used to best advantage: thin bars and strips of steel are placed so as to strengthen those parts of structures where analysis shows that the resistance of the concrete needs to be supplemented. From 1892 he developed the use of the T-section slab beam. Some six hundred structures, including water tanks, granaries, locomotive depots, theatres, office blocks, bridges, grain silos and quays were built on the Hennebique principle in Britain in the decade after its introduction in 1898. The first multi-storey reinforced concrete building in Britain, a warehouse at Swansea built in 1897–8, has been demolished. Robert Maillart (1872–1940) pioneered in Switzerland the use of columns with mushroom-shaped capitals, capable of carrying heavily loaded floors.

Pioneers in the USA included Thadden Hyatt (1816–1901), J. W. TAYLOR and ALBERT KAHN: Kahn designed the first reinforced concrete factory in America, Packard No. 10 at Detroit, in 1905. P. H. Jackson, working in California in the 1880s, developed the principle of prestressing concrete by casting it on wires that had been stretched tight: this was developed with success in France from the 1930s by Eugène Freyssinet (1879–1962).

Concrete is widely used in roadmaking. The first mass

concrete road in Britain was Blackwood Crescent, Edinburgh, laid in 1873. Reinforced concrete was used at Brooklands racing circuit in Surrey in 1907, and the first public road in reinforced concrete was completed in Chester in 1913.

See also figures 21, 91, 165, 167.

BIBLIOGRAPHY
General
Brouwer, 1983; Haegermann, 1964; Mouchel *et al.*, 1909; Stanley, 1979; Straub, 1949.
Specific
Cusack, P. François Hennebique: the specialist organisation and the success of ferro-concrete. In *TNS*, LVI, 1984.

BARRIE TRINDER

concrete bridge CONCRETE came into use for bridge construction in the late nineteenth century, and has been employed in many of the most ambitious bridges of the twentieth century.

The earliest surviving mass concrete bridge in Britain crosses the River Axe at Seaton, Devon, and dates from 1877. Glenfinnan viaduct, in Scotland, which has twenty-one arches and is 380 m (1248 ft.) long, was the largest of several mass concrete structures on the Mallaig–Fort William railway constructed in 1898. The first British reinforced concrete bridge was built in the New Forest in 1901 but has not survived.

The first major reinforced concrete bridge in the USA was the Melan Arch Bridge, Topeka, Kansas, designed by Edwin Thacher (1840–1920) and completed in 1897. Daniel Luten established several companies which constructed numerous open-spandrel deck-arch bridges, while James Marsh (1856–1936) popularized the rainbow arch design, with the arch extended above the roadway like a bowstring TRUSS BRIDGE. HENNEBIQUE'S Risorgimento Bridge, a 100 m (330 ft.) span arch of 1910–11 across the Tiber in ROME, and the Langwies viaduct on the Chur–Arosa railway in Switzerland of 1912–13, are important examples of early reinforced concrete bridges. Robert Maillart (1872–1940) was responsible for many of the outstanding twentieth-century pre-stressed bridges in Switzerland.

BIBLIOGRAPHY
General
Jackson, 1988; Prade, 1990; Straub, 1949.

BARRIE TRINDER

condensed milk The principle of condensing milk using vacuum pans was devised in the USA by Gail Borden (1809–74) who was granted a patent in 1856. Borden condensed milk by evaporating it in a vacuum pan and adding sugar. He prevented it from sticking to the pan by greasing the sides. He built a large plant at Litchfield, Conn., 60 km (100 mi.) NE of New York in 1858, and prospered from scandals concerning cow houses (*see* DAIRY) in the city, and from demand during the American Civil War. One of the key machines in the development of condensed-milk production was the Dickerson Automatic

Figure 31 The original vacuum pan for condensing milk, used in 1853 by Gail Borden and patented in 1856: it is now in the collection of the National Museum of American History in the Smithsonian Institution, Washington DC.
Smithsonian Institution

Vent Hole Filler and Sealer introduced in 1911. An example installed in a factory at Alymer, Ontario, in 1915, has been preserved in the National Museum of Science and Technology, OTTAWA, since it ceased work in 1987. Canned condensed milk was being sold in large quantities in England by the early twentieth century.

BIBLIOGRAPHY
General
Beeton, 1912; Frantz, 1951.
Specific
A Dickerson can filler retired. In *Ontario Society for Industrial Archaeology Bulletin*, VI, 1988.

condenser A word with two distinct meanings in industrial archaeology:

1. The part of a steam engine in which steam exhausted from the cylinder was converted back to water by being cooled. In a NEWCOMEN engine condensation took place within the cylinder. One of the principal innovations introduced by JAMES WATT was the separate condenser, usually situated at a lower level than the cylinder, which greatly increased the thermal efficiency of the engine.
2. A device employed from the mid-nineteenth century to extract metal from the smoke from lead smelters, avoiding the expense of long FLUES. In 1843 Joseph

Stagg used a condenser at Nenthead, County Durham, England, drawing smoke through water contained within interconnecting compartments set in a rectangular chamber. The Stokoe condenser drew smoke through a series of columns down which water fell, condensing the fumes. Kelds Head Mill, Wensleydale, England, is a well-preserved example.

BIBLIOGRAPHY
General
Stratton and Trinder, 1988.

condenser carding machine A machine used in the preparation of Wool. John Goulding's condenser, patented in 1826, revolutionized wool carding and eliminated the use of the Slubbing billy. Used at the end of the finisher carding machine, it produced roving (*see* Textiles) suitable for spinning and twisting into a continuous sliver (*see* Carding machine). Goulding, an American, protected his device with a British patent six months before he patented it at home. It was widely adopted, and in 1845 a directory of American woollen mills identified factories by the type of cloth produced and how many sets of condenser carding machines they had.

condenser cotton The Carding machine and other phases in cotton preparation produce waste, about a third of which can, after further cleaning, be spun into yarn suitable for cheaper forms of bed linen, towelling and similar purposes. In Britain a mill processing such materials, like that preserved at Helmshore, is called a condenser cotton mill.

BIBLIOGRAPHY
General
Robson, 1957.

condensing locomotive A locomotive in which exhaust steam was condensed, either to reduce smoke emission in tunnels, or to conserve water in areas of shortage. On locomotives used in Britain for urban underground lines, steam was piped into the water tank. The system developed by the Henschel company of Kassel, Germany, and employed in South Africa, Argentina and the USSR, used exhaust steam to drive turbo fans to provide draught in place of conventional blast, before piping the steam to the tender.

BIBLIOGRAPHY
General
Ahrons, 1927; Westwood, 1983.

confectionery Preparations containing sugar or honey; principally cakes, gingerbreads, sweets, candies, crystallized fruits or Jam, which are produced at an establishment called a confectionary. The trade of confectioner was commonly combined with that of baker.

The most commonly traded form of confectionery in the early industrial period was gingerbread. Numerous European towns, among them Aachen, Ashbourne and Deventer, have traditional gingerbread specialities, and

consignments of as much as 4 tons were being conveyed down the River Severn in England in 1705.

Sweets ('candies', in the USA) were being manufactured on a modest industrial scale in the nineteenth century, but were usually sold from boxes or jars. From the 1920s the market vastly increased as small, well-designed packages came to be displayed in Drug stores, at newsstands and near the checkouts of Supermarkets.

See also Chocolate.

BIBLIOGRAPHY
General
Book of Trades, 1839; Boorstin, 1973; Connor, 1987.

Connecticut, United States of America The wide geographic spread of the western states, with their borders following lines of latitude and meridians of longitude, and concentrations of urban life and industry lying between great expanses of arid terrain, contrasts with the close-ordered intensity of development in the diminutive states of the far north-east. Connecticut is one of the region's most extreme industrial examples, while being the nation's third smallest state, with an area of only 13 000 km² (5000 sq. mi.).

Connecticut has been a seedbed of industry for several centuries. An abundance of mountainous creeks furnished falling water for mills in the processing of agricultural goods and the working of timber and metals. The state's premier industry has been and remains precision manufacturing, from the smallest brass clock gears and sub-miniature ball bearings to some of the USA's most sophisticated heavy machinery.

Eighteenth-century exploitation of Connecticut's limited supplies of mineral ore is revealed at Old Newgate Copper Mine, a site mined by the British from 1707 to 1745. It was put to punitive use from 1775 to 1827, when the shaft served as a prison for the colony and later state of Connecticut. A museum at the site records the mine's infamous history amid the remains of workshops where prisoners were employed.

The manufacture both of clocks and firearms in Connecticut dates from the nation's founding, enterprises commemorated today in standing structures along the heavily industrialized seaboard. The Eli Whitney Armory site in Hamden uses the scant archaeological remains of this early supplier of rifles and pistols to the federal government to enhance Whitney's reputation as a pioneering manufacturer of interchangeable precision components. In Hartford, the state capital, the complex of structures at Colt Industries surrounds the remains of another key weapons-production site: the Samuel Colt Armory of the 1850s, source of the legendary Colt revolver that 'won the West'. Munitions are further noted as Landmarks at Remington-Union Metallic Cartridge Company in Bridgeport, its ten-storey Shot tower of 1909 being one of the few left in the country. It is still in active use dropping lead.

The towns of Winsted, Thomaston, New Haven and Waterbury contain factory structures in which many of the nation's clock movements were produced, first in wood and iron, later in brass and steel. The presence of copper ore in the state, and more critically the waves of skilled immigrants and the nearness of the New York market, propelled the production of clocks and armaments, piano keys and padlocks, brass buttons, weather vanes, cutlery and jingle bells.

Adaptive reuses of the factories that generated such output are occurring across the state. In Lakeville, the Holley Pocket Cutlery Factory of 1866 has become a swank eating establishment. The Pratt-Read Co. factory in Deep River, active since 1798 in producing goods from elephant ivory, especially piano keys, has been refitted as the Piano Works, an exclusive complex of condominium apartments. In textiles, similar structural survivals and occasional industrial revivals have occurred in the silk, twine, thread, cotton and woollen mills of Connecticut.

The USA's principal ivory-working centre flourished along the banks of the Connecticut River near Essex. Several structures remain, including an ivory piano-key bleaching shed in Deep River, and several factory sites in nearby Ivoryton.

One of the more successful state bridge preservation campaigns has saved many of Connecticut's historic spans, including the USA's largest concentration of 'water-melon seed' bridges, the lenticular truss bridges in Stamford, Collinsville, New Milford, Romford, Sharon, Meriden, Ashland, Almyville and Plainfield. Like the lenticulars, the ornate Riverside Avenue Bridge of 1871 in Greenwich, a Pratt truss of cast and wrought iron, remains in very active use.

Waterbury's Union Station of 1909 captures the pride and boosterism that once drove this metropolis, which was for long termed the 'brass city'. Surrounded by former or active brassworks, the station's monumental brick waiting room, trimmed in marble and terracotta, is surmounted by a 75 m (245 ft.) clock tower of Florentine inspiration.

The National Helicopter Museum in Bridgeport, not coincidentally, is near the works of the Sikorsky Helicopter Company, originator of many whirlybird innovations.

The country's foremost working maritime heritage site, Mystic Seaport, in Mystic, combines an active programme in historical boatbuilding with a village of associated craft revivals, and a collection of vintage sailing craft, including the *Charles W. Morgan* of 1841, the last of the nation's wooden whaling vessels. Near Burlington, the Nepaug Dam of 1914 backs up the Farmington River as a water supply for Hartford. A concrete gravity-arch dam, 34.4 m (113 ft.) in height, the Nepaug was designed specifically to provide overflow waters to the many small-scale mills lying downstream.

BIBLIOGRAPHY
General
Comp, 1974; Hall and Cooper, 1984; Jackson, 1988; Kulik *et al.*, 1982; Pool, 1982; Roth, 1981; Sande, 1971.
Specific
Cooper, C. C., Gordon, R. B. and Merrick, H. V. Archeological evidence of metallurgical innovation at the Eli Whitney Armory. In *IA*, VIII, 1982.

Starbuck, D. R. Archeological research at the Eli Whitney factory site. In *Journal of the New Haven Colony Historical Society*, XXV, 1977.
Starbuck, D. R. Industrial archeology and the Eli Whitney controversy. In *Journal of the New Haven Colony Historical Society*, XXVIII, 1981.

LOCATIONS
[M] American Clock and Watch Museum, 100 Maple Street, Bristol, CT 06010.
[M] American Silver Museum, 39 W. Main Street, Meriden, CT 06450.
[M] Connecticut Electric Railway and Trolley Museum, 58 North Road, East Windsor, CT 06088.
[M] Connecticut River Foundation at Steamboat Dock, Main Street, Essex, CT 06426.
[M] Eli Whitney Museum, 915 Whitney Avenue, Hamden, CT 06517.
[S] Kent Iron Furnace, Route 7, Kent, CT 06757.
[M] Lock Museum of America, 130 Main Street, Terryville, CT 06786.
[M] Mattatuck Museum, 144 W. Main Street, Waterbury, CT 06702.
[M,S] Mystic Seaport, Greenmanville Avenue, Mystic, CT 06355.
[M] New England Air Museum, Bradley International Airport, Windsor Locks, CT 06096.
[M,S] Old Newgate Prison and Copper Mine, Newgate Road, East Granby, CT 06026.
[M] Shore Line Trolley Museum, 17 River Street, East Haven, CT 06512.

DAVID H. SHAYT

conservation A word used in several different senses in industrial archaeology, quite apart from specialized, qualified usages, as in the conservation of heat or energy.

In a narrow, technical sense in museums, conservation refers to the specialized techniques developed for ensuring that decay is arrested, or at least slowed, in particular classes of artefacts, textiles, metal and wooden objects, and the like. In industrial museums, as in other types of museum, complex ethical issues can arise over the methods employed, over authenticity, particularly of machines in which many parts may have been replaced, and over the operation of irreplaceable machines like rare aircraft.

Conservation has been used in a broader sense since the 1960s. The concerns of the First International Congress on the Conservation of Industrial Monuments (*see* TICCIH) in 1973, were not purely with the technical problems of conserving machines, nor just with means of preserving historic industrial buildings, but with developing an appreciation of the cultural and historic value of the industrial past. Since the early 1970s industrial archaeology has been seen as one aspect of a broader programme of conservation, concerned with restoring vitality to inner-city and other economically deprived areas. Just as ecologists working for the conservation of the natural environment are now concerned not just with the survival of endangered species and particular habitats but with the positive management of habitats of all kinds, so to conserve the industrial heritage has come to mean to appreciate the historical significance and future potential of sites and landscapes, and to work to prevent their wanton destruction.

BIBLIOGRAPHY
General
Council of Europe, 1987; Feilden, 1982; ICCROM, 1974; Lambrick, 1985; Plenderleith and Werner, 1970; Thompson, 1983.

BARRIE TRINDER

continuous-chamber kiln A KILN for firing ceramics, so named because it can be kept continuously at work rather than cooled down and heated up in a wasteful cycle. Ware that had just been fired was used as a regenerator, air drawn past it being used to provide a high temperature in the burning zone; the heat from exhaust gases was used to build up the temperature of newly set bricks or other ceramics. The continuous-chamber kiln differed from a HOFFMAN KILN in that the chambers were separated by permanent partitions. The hot gases passed from one chamber to another and once cool were directed to the main exhaust flue. Many different types of flue design were patented in the late nineteenth century.

BIBLIOGRAPHY
General
Rhodes, 1968; Searle, 1929.

control tower A building from which operations at an AIRPORT or other flying field are observed, monitored and directed, incorporating radio aerials and receivers, and, since World War II, RADAR devices. The term is of American origin and has been in general use since *c.*1944. In the 1920s and 30s control towers were often incorporated within passenger terminal buildings; this is still true at some smaller airports.

A control tower of the 1930s survives at Barton, Manchester, England; and combined control towers and terminals at Croydon, London, of 1928; at Jersey, CHANNEL ISLANDS, of 1937; at Shoreham, Sussex, of 1935; and at Elmdon, Birmingham, of 1939. Early civilian examples remain within the Cuatro Vientos military base near Madrid, and at the main public airports near Washington DC and Los Angeles, Calif.

Cookstown, County Tyrone, Northern Ireland A market town, laid out along the 2 km (1¼ mi.) High Street in 1609, by the founding planter, Alan Cooke. It has been a linen manufacturing centre in the nineteenth and twentieth centuries.

There are two outstanding railway stations, both listed. The terminus of the Belfast & Ballymena Railway of 1856 is in a restrained Italianate design by Charles Lanyon, with a train shed with hipped roofs at either end, and a stone arcade on the side away from the platform. The station closed in 1959. The adjoining Great Northern station in Molesworth Street dates from 1878–9, and is of polychrome brick, with a wooden canopy carried on cast-iron brackets, and an iron archway forming the entrance to the goods yard.

Wellbrook, a beetling mill on the Ballinderry river, 5 km (3 mi.) W., was built in the 1760s and ceased commercial operation in 1961. It is a two-storey building of seven bays, of rubble construction, with a 4.8 m (16 ft.) external water wheel driving two of the seven beetling engines that remain. It has been restored by the National Trust.

BIBLIOGRAPHY
General
Gallagher and Rogers, 1986; McCutcheon, 1980; Morton, 1962.

cooper A maker of BARRELS. There were coopers in most towns in the eighteenth and nineteenth centuries, with concentrations in ports, and many were employed by large concerns manufacturing goods conveyed in barrels. The wet, butt or tight cooper made vessels for liquids; the dry cooper made casks for such commodities as sugar, tobacco and cement; and the white cooper made pails and churns, as well as cheese moulds, and sycamore shovels and spoons for dairy use. A dock cooper repaired full casks at a port, a task which usually meant fitting new hoops. A travelling cooper repaired washing and brewing utensils. Oak staves, which were an item of transatlantic trade by the early eighteenth century, were normally acquired in a cut state (*see* SAWMILL). Hoops were made of hazel, ash or wrought iron. Staves were fixed to the head hoop, and then warmed with a small portable stove before being bent and secured by the remaining hoops. A large cooperage was typically a series of lofty brick sheds with open frontages. For most purposes coopers' products were later replaced by steel, aluminium or plastic casks.

Coopers work at several open-air museums, including Colonial Williamsburg (*see* VIRGINIA) and ST FAGANS.

See also BUNG MILL; HOGSHEAD; PIPE; TUN.

BIBLIOGRAPHY
General
Book of Trades, 1839; Mayhew, 1850; Tunis, 1965.
Specific
Grant, A. The cooper in Liverpool. In *IAR*, I, 1976.

BARRIE TRINDER

co-operative movement The principal exponents of the ideals of co-operation were ROBERT OWEN and CHARLES FOURIER. UTOPIAN COMMUNITIES based on the ideas of each were established in Europe and America, but the chief influence of co-operation has been on retailing and on the marketing of farm produce.

The British co-operative movement traces its origins from the Rochdale Pioneers, themselves Owenites, who established a shop in 1844. There were 500 000 members of co-operative retail societies in Britain by 1881, and three million by 1914. Large organizations like the Royal Arsenal Society in London constructed architecturally distinguished department stores, and in the 1920s and 30s many societies developed distinctive house styles for their suburban shops. Many retail societies built housing estates. The Co-operative Wholesale Society, established in 1863 with its headquarters in Manchester, set up factories to supply retail societies, the chief concentration of these being at Pelaw, 10 km (6 mi.) N. of DURHAM. Similar co-operative retailing and wholesaling societies were set up in Germany, Sweden, Denmark and other European countries.

Co-operatives established by farmers for the production and marketing of dairy products and bacon in the late nineteenth century in such countries as Denmark, Ireland, the Netherlands and New Zealand have greatly influenced the development of the food industry. The first co-operative slaughterhouse for pigs in Denmark, set up by Peter Bojsen in 1887, is conserved at HORSENS.

BIBLIOGRAPHY
General
Cassau, 1915; Fay, 1920; Holyoake, 1870; Jeffreys, 1954; Redfern, 1913.

BARRIE TRINDER

Copenhagen (København), Denmark Copenhagen is and always has been by far the most important industrial centre in Denmark. Very appropriately, the city's name means 'the merchants' harbour'. It grew up in the early Middle Ages around a well-protected natural harbour on the Sound, at the entrance to the Baltic Sea, and at the main crossing point between Zealand and the old Danish province of Scania. In the fifteenth century the king made the city the capital, the location of the royal palace, the central administration and the royal navy. The military needs of the Crown gave rise to the earliest industrial enterprises in the form of the naval dockyards which were built up from c.1550 at Bremerholm-Gammelholm, with anchor forges, gunmaking workshops and ropeworks. The imposing gable end of the anchor forge has survived as part of the choir of Holmen's church.

In the reign of King Christian IV in the early seventeenth century the city flourished and was greatly enlarged, with new quarters to the north (New Copenhagen) and to the east on the island of Christianshavn. New harbour facilities were built, together with an arsenal, now the Museum of Arms and Uniforms. In New Copenhagen a whole new quarter (Nyboder) was laid out to accommodate the permanent personnel of the naval dockyards. Several of the colony's characteristic simple, yellow terraces are preserved, together with some later extensions. As a means of promoting trade the king also erected the Exchange, which remains one of the capital's major sights; he also set up silk and woollen cloth manufactories.

The so-called golden age of commerce of the late eighteenth century brought new prosperity to Copenhagen, as it became the centre of a booming export trade which took advantage of Denmark's neutrality in the many wars up to 1807. Several of the city's trading companies established their own shipyards, and nearly all of them built large warehouses along the waterfront. Several have been preserved, and they still dominate much of the inner harbour, although they are now converted into hotels, dwellings and conference and exhibition centres.

During the same period the naval dockyards on Holmen were greatly enlarged. Several structures remain from the mid-eighteenth century, including the entrance building and the sheer-legs used for rigging. The first Danish steam engine was installed in the anchor forge at Gammelholm in 1790.

In 1760 the state built the Royal Wool Manufactory and in 1779 founded the Royal Danish Porcelain Factory. Strong mercantilist policies also encouraged private industry, and a large textile industry became securely established in this period. Among the few surviving buildings from this time are the Royal Wool Manufactory at 7–9 Rigensgade, the silk factory at 34–6 Bredgade, and the remains of brick, lime and faience works at Kastrup on the island of Amager, east of the city.

In spite of these developments Copenhagen's economy in 1800 was essentially pre-industrial. First and foremost the city was a garrison and a centre for government and commerce. For the visitor the most prominent sign of industry was probably provided by the many windmills on the city walls and along the approach roads to the city, of which only that at Kastellet has survived. The capital suffered severely from the Danish entry into the Napoleonic Wars on the side of France, which resulted in the bombardment of the city by the English navy in 1807, the surrender of the fleet, and, in 1814, the loss of Norway. Consequently the population of Copenhagen in the following decades grew less rapidly than that of the countryside and the provincial cities of Denmark.

From about 1840 the population of the city began to grow rapidly, and trebled from 130000 to 390000 within the next fifty years. The major factor behind this growth was rapid industrial development. Most of the new industrial buildings were in a plain style with little ornamentation. The more expressive examples up to 1860 usually showed the influence of the Greek Revival, and subsequently RUNDBOGENSTIL became the dominant influence, often expressed in red bricks. Many companies and buildings from that time have survived.

Symptomatic of the new times, iron foundries and engineering works came to be of great importance. By 1850 steam engines were supplied by a dozen of the city's firms. Prominent amongst them was the company that later became Burmeister & Wain, who specialized in supplying machinery and steam engines to the city's many new factories, and later built iron steam ships. Burmeister & Wain gained its international reputation from the turn of the century, beginning the manufacture of stationary diesel engines in 1904, and in 1912 launching the first ocean-going MOTOR VESSEL. The history of Burmeister & Wain is displayed in the company's museum at Christianshavn.

Brewing, in capital-intensive, steam-powered plants, was another important industry of the period. Several breweries of the 1850s and 60s have survived, although adapted to new uses. The most successful of the new breweries was Carlsberg, founded outside the city at Valby in 1847. Through successive enlargements in the following decades, Carlsberg became one of the capital's largest industrial complexes. The company's preserved buildings, many in eccentric styles, constitute an El Dorado for both

Figure 32 Gamle
Carlsberg, a nineteenth-
century brewery within the
Carlsberg complex in
Copenhagen which has
been restored as a museum
Carlsberg Foundation

the art historian and the industrial archaeologist. Old
Carlsberg (Gamle Carlsberg), re-erected after a fire in
1867, has been restored as an important industrial
museum, and furnished with nineteenth-century equipment. The other well-known Copenhagen brewery,
Tuborg, was founded in 1873, around its own harbour
north of the city.

Until the twentieth century it was widely believed that
Denmark's industrial future lay in the development of the
applied arts, and especially with Copenhagen's two large
porcelain factories, the Royal Danish and Bing &
Grøndahl. Bing & Grøndahl was founded in 1853 at the
end of Vesterbrogade on the outskirts of the city. The
Royal Danish factory was privatized in 1883, whereupon
the new owner moved production to his faience factory at
Frederiksberg. Both porcelain factories are still in operation, and both at Vesterbrogade and Frederiksberg
several old kilns and production buildings have survived.
Bing & Grøndahl have established a museum showing
examples of the firm's products.

Other notable nineteenth-century factories include
Hirschsprung's tobacco works of 1866 at 7–9 Tordensk-
joldsgade, now part of the Royal Academy of Fine Arts,
and Holger Petersen's steam-powered weaving factory of
the 1880s in Nannagade, with its characteristic north-lit
sheds.

The rapid growth of the city demanded improvements
in public services. The earliest water-pumping station, of
1857–9, remains at Studiestræde. At the same time a

municipal gas supply became available from Vestre
Gasværk. The monumental brick gasholder of the second
gasworks, the Østre Gasværk of *c.*1880, is now used as a
theatre. The first municipal electricity plant, Gothersgades
Elværk, began operation in 1892, followed by the Vestre
Elværk in 1898 and the Østre Elværk in 1902. All three
remain although they have been much altered.

Transport facilities were of vital importance to the
capital in the period of industrialization. Copenhagen
became the starting point of the first Danish steamship
service in 1819, and the first Danish railway opened to
ROSKILDE in 1847. The present Central Railway Station is
the third on the site and dates from 1911. The only
surburban railway terminus in Copenhagen is Nørrebro
station, on the line to the north-west. It is now closed, but
the preserved station building, together with the station at
Østerbro, furnish good examples of the 'Viking', or
National Romantic, style of the early twentieth century.

Copenhagen's first horse trams began to operate in
1863, and the tramways were electrified by a municipal
undertaking at the turn of the century. The tram services
were closed down and replaced by motor buses in 1972.
At Nørrebro a tram depot has been adapted as a sports
centre, and old tramcars and buses are displayed in the
municipal transport museum at 119 Islevdalvej in
Rødovre. The main Danish tram museum, which also
covers the tramways of Århus and Odense, has been
established at Skjoldenæsholm, 20 km (12 mi.) SW of
Roskilde.

The port of Copenhagen expanded to the north in 1892–4 with the construction of the free harbour, in which reinforced concrete was extensively used. Alongside the docks ranges of large warehouses were built in the contemporary historicist style, but with modern handling equipment. Two have recently been demolished and the remainder are threatened. After 1900 the harbour was further extended to the south to serve industrial purposes.

The old city walls were pulled down in the 1850s, but in spite of this, of the rapidly growing population and its changing composition, and of the growth of manufactures, the capital retained many of its pre-industrial characteristics until c.1890. The highest density of dwellings and industrial premises remained in the city centre, and from this hub density declined at a fairly even rate as one moved further out. From the 1890s this structure disintegrated, and Copenhagen developed as a modern industrial city, with a service-dominated central business district, and several manufacturing areas, with socially-segregated residential districts. The new structure was stimulated by the larger, more extensive complexes established by new industries, by better transport facilities, new standards for dwellings, the beginnings of municipal planning, and by the continuing growth of population, which in 1950 reached 1.2 million.

The four main industrial areas became: (a) the southern part of Copenhagen harbour; (b) outer Nørrebro, near Nørrebro railway station, to the north-west; (c) an area near Frederiksberg railway station to the west; (d) the Valby area. The new building materials, reinforced concrete and steel, were extensively used in industrial complexes, and as a result industrial buildings often played pioneering roles both in technology and in architectural style in the following decades. Some points can be made by examples from the harbour area.

At Christianshavn the Danish Sugar Works (DDS) built a large new refinery in 1913. The pillars and floors of the factory were of reinforced concrete, whereas the exterior was faced with traditional red bricks, in the neo-Baroque style fashionable in the early twentieth century. North of the refinery stood the Burmeister & Wain erecting shop for diesel engines of 1923–4, a pure composition in reinforced concrete, steel and glass, which, from its rather rigid neo-Classical style, has been called the Danish counterpart to PETER BEHRENS's famous buildings in Berlin. It has now been demolished. On the Zealand side is the H. C. Ørsted municipal power station, begun in 1916, which houses the largest stationary diesel engine ever built, a 22 500 hp eight-cylinder engine, manufactured by Burmeister & Wain in 1932. To the south is a steel shipyard of 1919, Burmeister & Wain's circular iron foundry of 1920–1, and the Ford Motor Company's assembly plant of 1923–4, the last two in reinforced concrete and steel. The foreign-looking assembly plant was built to designs by ALBERT KAHN, and was the first factory in Denmark and one of the few before 1939 where the ideas of F. W. TAYLOR were put into practice.

The new municipal slaughterhouse at Halmtorvet, known as the 'White Meat City', was built in the 1930s in the functional style. Other examples of the International Modern style, in its light, Nordic form, are Copenhagen airport at Kastrup, built in 1937–9 to the designs of Wilhelm Lauritzen, and the service station by Arne Jacobsen (1902–71) of 1939 at 24 Kystvejen, Klampenborg. Such examples of the new style should not obscure the fact that most Danish industrial buildings, or at least their external elevations, were of traditional brick construction.

The rapid growth of population after 1840 created an unprecedented demand for housing, met at first by increasing the density of building in the centre. The consequent social problems stimulated several philanthropic projects. The Medical Association Dwellings (Lægeforeningens Boliger) at Østerbro, built between 1854 and 1872, provide a well-preserved example of early philanthropic housing provision. The largest colony of the co-operative, Arbejdernes Byggeforening, comprises the so-called 'potato rows' at Øster Farimagsgade. Yet the majority of workers had no option but to turn to the 'free' market in privately-owned housing. Consequently in the 1870s and 80s the inner parts of Nørrebro, Østerbro and Vesterbro developed into classic working-class districts, with high densities of population. Characteristic working-class dwellings of the late nineteenth century took the form of five- or sometimes six-storey apartment blocks along street frontages, with ranges of the same height, extending to the backs of the plots. A typical apartment consisted of two rooms and a kitchen. The best preserved area of such housing is at Vesterbro, but most of the rear wings have been demolished.

The living conditions of industrial workers form the main concern of the new Workers' Museum, which covers working life, and the culture and history of the labour movement. It is appropriately sited in the first assembly house of the trade unions, built in 1878–9, which was for decades the headquarters of Copenhagen's strong labour movement. In addition a worker's flat and a bourgeois apartment are displayed in the National Museum. A centre for the study of industrial archaeology and history through films has been established in the Institute of History and Social Science at Danmarks Lærerhøjskole.

See also MØLLEÅEN.

BIBLIOGRAPHY
General
Bech *et al.*, 1980–3; Hyldtoft, 1984; Knudsen, 1988; Nielsen, 1943–4; Sestoft, 1979; Willerslev, 1988.
Specific
Årbog for Arbejdermuseet (The Workers' Museum yearbooks). Copenhagen, 1982–4.
Ejlersen, T. *Københavns møller* (The mills of Copenhagen). In *Historiske Meddelelser om København*, 1990.
Hyldtoft, O. From fortified town to modern metropolis: Copenhagen 1840–1914. In Hammerstrom and Hall, 1979.
Hyldtoft, O. 'Arbeiterwohnungen in Kopenhagen 1840–1914' (Working-class dwellings in Copenhagen 1840–1914). In Teuteberg, 1985.
Rasmussen, S. E. *København*. Copenhagen, 1969.
Trap, J. P. *Danmark*, II–IV. Copenhagen, 1959–60.

LOCATIONS

[M] Arbejdermuseet (Worker's Museum), Römersgade 22, 1362 Copenhagen K.

[I] Institute of Economic History, Njalsgade 104, 2300 Copenhagen S.

[I] Institute of History and Social Science, Emdrupvej 101, 2400 Copenhagen NV.

[M] Københavns Bymuseum (City Museum) Vesterbrogade 59, 1620 Copenhagen V.

[M] Nationalmuseet (National Museum), Frederiksholms Kanal 12–18, 1220 Copenhagen K.

OLE HYLDTOFT

copier A means of reproducing documents quickly, without recourse to printing or conventional photographic techniques. JAMES WATT patented in 1780 a system for copying letters by pressing moist tissue paper on an original, written in special ink. The system was quite widely adopted and was used in France and the USA for commercial correspondence until the introduction of carbon paper. Sir John Herschel (1792–1871) announced the blueprinting process, whereby drawings could be copied photographically onto paper treated with ferrocyanide of potassium and iron peroxide in 1842. It became the standard means of copying engineering drawings until superseded by the Viazo process in the twentieth century. The word 'blueprint' came to be widely used, referring in a loose sense to almost any kind of plan. David Gestetner in 1885 patented in the USA a stencil system for copying typescript or manuscript. The following year David Klaber patented a flat-bed apparatus which could work with Gestetner stencils, and 'duplicators' combining these elements came onto the market in the 1890s. Chester Carlson in the USA demonstrated in 1937–8 that electricity instead of light could be used to make images, and the Haloid Co. of Rochester, N.Y., began commercial development of his theory from 1946, using the trade name 'Xerox'.

BIBLIOGRAPHY
General
Dessauer, 1971; Dessauer and Clarke, 1965; Dorlay, 1978.
Specific
Andrew, J. H. The copying of engineering drawings and documents. In *TNS*, LIII, 1981–2.

BARRIE TRINDER

copper (Cu) A metallic element, the eighth most abundant metal in the earth's crust and a constituent of over 160 minerals. It was probably worked as early as 5000 BC, but the range of copper-bearing minerals being worked has changed. As the easily worked supplies have been exhausted, ores with lower percentages of metal have been worked. All the major deposits in Europe were known and being worked by the end of the eighteenth century, including those in Britain (*see* CORNWALL; PARYS MOUNTAIN), Sweden (*see* FALUN), Norway (*see* RØROS), Germany, Greece and Spain. Isolated copper deposits in the eastern USA were worked from the mid-eighteenth century (*see* CONNECTICUT) and in the nineteenth century there were major new developments in the West and Midwest (see ARIZONA; MICHIGAN; MONTANA), and in South Australia.

Copper ores have generally been worked by STOPING, but in the twentieth century lower-grade porphyry deposits have been worked in open pits, a method employed on Parys Mountain from the mid-eighteenth century. The ore body was followed downwards leaving near-vertical sides, from which platforms were balanced, each carrying a winch mechanism. More recent open pits have been formed by following the ore body, and shelving or cutting back the surrounding strata. The waste has been moved by animals or railways, and more recently by dump trucks. Copper has also been extracted by PRECIPITATION. Some copper ores, particularly in Africa, are found as sedimentary deposits and worked like bedded minerals.

Copper ores were formerly separated from waste at the surface by hand picking, but from the nineteenth century elaborate dressing techniques were devised, involving crushing, JIGGING, and separating the ore from other minerals on shaking tables and revolving frames before it was sent to the smelter.

Techniques for smelting copper remained fundamentally unaltered for three centuries. Successive calcinings and smeltings removed arsenic and some sulphur, then repeated smelting removed iron and the remaining sulphur. Finally repeated refining produced copper that was at least 99 per cent pure. In Britain reverberatory furnaces were almost universally used, but on the continent small blast furnaces were common. Important improvements allowed the recovery of sulphur and silver from 1728 and of arsenic from 1767. The process of granulation (running molten copper into water), which was used from 1723, made subsequent smelting more efficient.

In 1850 a quarter of the world's copper production was being smelted at SWANSEA. By 1870, both the organization and the process had altered. Smelting and refining tended to migrate to the mines so that techniques could be adjusted to suit specific ores. The multi-hearth roasting furnace introduced in 1850, and the vertical Gerstenhofer kiln first used in 1865, calcined more efficiently. About 1880 the BESSEMER converter was modified for copper smelting, but REVERBERATORY FURNACES were used well into the twentieth century to produce 'fire-refined' copper. From 1865 electrolytic refining provided high-purity copper for the electrical industry. Most copper ore is now smelted near the mine into blister copper, which is exported to the using country, refined in an open-hearth furnace and then cast into sheets which are used as cathodes in an electrolytic process. The sludge deposited during electrolysis is often a source of precious metals.

In the mid-seventeenth century most copper produced in Europe was used in BRASS manufacture, wire-making and coinage. From the late eighteenth century copper sheeting was used as cladding on ships (*see* THOMAS WILLIAMS), the cladding being affixed by copper bolts manufactured by a specially developed process. Copper has also been used for cutlery, jewellery and for finework where soldering is necessary. In the form of boiler plates and tubes, copper was an important component of steam locomotives, while copper plates and rollers were used in printing both fabrics and paper. From the 1860s demand was transformed by the growth of telecommunications and later of the electricity supply industry. Electrolytic refining produced a metal with a copper content of over 99 per cent and correspondingly high conductivity. Mills were developed to draw continuous wire, producing telegraph wires, tramway wires and subsequently cables, while commutator bars and forgings were manufactured for electrical equipment.

BIBLIOGRAPHY
General
Barton, 1968, 1971; Dunell, 1925; Morton, 1983; Peters, 1907.

IVOR J. BROWN and NANCY COX

Corbeil, Essonne, France   Corn has been ground at Corbeil, 30 km (19 mi.) S. of Paris, for centuries, and there is still an important flourmill there. At the confluence of the Seine and the River Essonne, the site is particularly well placed to receive grain from the farms of the Brie and the Beauce, and then to send the flour on to Paris. A large-scale mill with twelve pairs of grinding stones was built in 1775; its granary building, known as the 'Magasin de Réserve', could store vast quantities of corn for the needs of the population of Paris. The 'American-style' grinding system, invented by Oliver Evans (1755–1819), was introduced there in 1817.

From 1830 the mill was run by the brothers Darblay, their company acquiring it in 1863. The mill soon underwent considerable modernization. Around 1880 a new metal-framed building was put up under the direction of J. Denfer, a teacher at the École Centrale des Arts et Manufactures. Between 1882 and 1886 this same engineer built a storehouse for flour, and in 1892 his former associate, the architect P. E. Friesé (1851–1917), built new flour silos to replace some old ones destroyed by fire. This building programme, creating a storage capacity of 100 000 quintals, was necessitated by the adoption, in 1886, of a new grinding system using large cylindrical rollers. In 1895 the mill could process 3200 quintals of grain per hour, one of the largest capacities in Europe. It was already electrified at this relatively early date, a 50 hp motor being employed to drive some of the cleaning apparatus. Electric lighting was used in the storehouse.

Milling today is done in a building erected in 1905, but the flour storehouses of 1882 and the silos of 1892 still stand. The first is in local gritstone, measuring 80 m × 18 m (262 ft. × 60 ft.) with eight storeys. The façade has a succession of projecting elements, each topped by a triangular pediment, with a central bull's-eye window. The building has an iron frame, with cast-iron columns topped by double brackets. This iron structure was used by Denfer to illustrate his lessons at the École Centrale and in his book of 1894 on the use of metals in architecture.

The vertical silo building, one of the first of its kind in France, was built by Friesé after study trips to CARDIFF and LIVERPOOL and to Braïla and Galatz in Romania, and after careful examination of American grain silos and elevators. It is also a gritstone structure, measuring 80 m × 16

m (260 ft × 50 ft.). It has a total of forty silos in two lines. The framework of the structure is of cast-iron columns and beams. The base of each silo slopes inwards to form a loading funnel, one of the constructional difficulties that had to be overcome. A monumental eight-storey elevator tower, more than 50 m (165 ft.) high, stands next to the silo building, linked to it by a covered passageway. The architecture of this tower is remarkable: on each elevation there are triple semicircular windows, separated by brick pilasters. The top of the tower incorporates a 600 m³ (210 000 cu. ft.) water tank, built in iron latticework and cement, according to the Monnier system which had previously been used in Liverpool and in Romania. With its decorative corbelling, the slight overhang of this top storey gives the elevator tower a belfry-like appearance. The whole site is now a protected monument.

BIBLIOGRAPHY
General
Arpin, 1948; Daumas, 1980; Denfer, 1984.
Specific
Foris, G. Les Grands Moulins de Corbeil (The great mills of Corbeil). In *La Meunerie française* (Milling in France), 1895.
Unpublished dossier for Historical Monuments.

JEAN-FRANÇOIS BELHOSTE

cordage   A collective term for strings, twines, cords, ROPES, and CABLES, particularly those used in ships (the last three terms being in ascending order of size). NETS for nautical purposes are made from cords.

BIBLIOGRAPHY
General
Lawrie, 1948.

cordite   A military propellant, manufactured at Waltham Abbey, England, from 1891. Cordite – 65 per cent nitrocotton, 30 per cent nitroglycerine and 5 per cent mineral jelly – was patented in 1889 by Sir Frederick Abel (1827–1902) and Sir James Dewar (1842–1923), and was the subject of litigation for infringement of NOBEL's Ballistite patent.

BIBLIOGRAPHY
General
Morgan and Pratt, 1938; Reader, 1970.

cordwainer   *See* SHOES.

Corinth (Kórinthos), Peloponnese, Greece   A city dating from classical times on the 6 km (3.5 mi.) wide isthmus that links the Peloponnese with the remainder of the Greek mainland. The modern city was built 7 km (4 mi.) N. of the ancient city site following an earthquake in 1858. A 'diolkos' or ship-railway was constructed across the isthmus by Periander *c.*600 BC, and may have remained in use until the ninth century AD. A canal was begun by the Emperor Nero. Construction of the present Corinth Canal was commenced by a French company in 1882, and completed by a Greek concern in 1893. Its 58 m (189 ft.) rock walls make it the most spectacular of all canals. One bridge carries both the road and the railway over the canal. Construction of the canal obliterated the remains of Nero's excavations, but part of the diolkos was excavated in 1956 and is displayed.

BIBLIOGRAPHY
General
Hadfield, 1986.

Corinthian   The lightest and most ornate of the orders of CLASSICAL architecture, in which capitals are bell-shaped and ornamented with acanthus leaves.

cork   Bark from the cork oak tree, *Quercus suber*. It is harvested in Mediterranean countries, burned to remove the outer portion, then cut into shape with very sharp knives, for use as stoppers for bottles and the like, sold wholesale by the gross. There were cork cutters in most English towns in the early nineteenth century. Cork is also used in making SHOES; in LINOLEUM; for buoyancy devices; and, until the mid-twentieth century, for thermal insulation in refrigerated warehouses.

Cork (Corgaigh), County Cork, Ireland   In the eighteenth century Cork was one of the principal ports of the Atlantic Ocean, reputed to have the world's largest market for butter, with thriving trades in grain, beef and hides, and providing Ireland's chief links with continental Europe. Its population had risen to 70 000 by the late eighteenth century. In the early nineteenth century it was a major leather-processing centre, with forty tanneries. Engineering grew rapidly. The first Irish paddle steamer was built in Cork in 1812, and there were four builders of steam engines in the city by the 1830s. Clothing manufacture prospered in the 1850s when the firm of Arnotts employed a thousand people making shirts and silk ties. In the twentieth century Cork has been the Irish base for such international concerns as the Ford Motor Co.

In 1920 the centre was burned by British irregular forces, but many buildings of industrial archaeological interest remain. The two channels of the River Lee, together with the Glasheen and Curragheen rivers which join it on the southern side, and the River Bride which flows in from the north, provided power for numerous mills. Many stone warehouses remain along the quays and on the 'island' between the two streams of the Lee. In Parnell Place stand two five-storey buildings, one of five bays and one of three, with elegant four-storey eighteenth-century houses adjoining. A large complex of mill buildings, now used for other purposes, stands on the south bank of the south channel near Wandesford Quay. On Anderson's Quay are the substantial four-storey concrete premises of J. W. Green, corn merchants, which remain in use. At the confluence of the two channels of the Lee is the elegant Custom House of 1814–18, designed by William Hargrave, adjacent to which is a range of stone, low-ceilinged bonded warehouses. Downstream from the confluence, on Victoria Quay, stand the tall concrete grain silos of R. & H. Hall.

St Patrick's Bridge, a stone structure of three elliptical arches with mouldings on the undersides, designed by Sir John Benson (1812–74) in 1859–61, is the most distinguished of the city's bridges.

Cork's once complex railway system is now greatly simplified, but the climb through the tunnel out of Kent Station (formerly Glanmire Road Station) remains one of the most memorable experiences on Irish railways. The 2–2–2 locomotive No. 36, built in 1848 for the Great Southern & Western Railway by Bury, Curtis & Kennedy of Liverpool, is displayed at the station. The Cork, Bandon & South Coast Railway linked the city with the west of County Cork between 1851 and 1961. Its outstanding remains are the two-storey, five-bay terminus building on Albert Quay, and the Chetwynd Viaduct of 1851 across the Glasheen River, 6 km (4 mi.) SW, a series of four 33 m (110 ft.) cast- and wrought-iron arches by Fox, Henderson & Co.

As in DUBLIN the construction of single-storey dwellings in Cork persisted until the late nineteenth century. A square of such cottages stands on the North Mall alongside the Lee. Maddens Buildings in Watercourse Road consist of seventy-six one-storey cottages in four parallel rows, constructed in 1886.

Collections of Cork silverware, glass, lace and crochetwork, all of high repute in the eighteenth and nineteenth centuries, are displayed in the city museum.

At Ballincollig, 8 km (5 mi.) W., are the remains of a substantial gunpowder works established in 1804, which are conserved in the Ballincollig Regional Park. The foundations of twelve pairs of mills, each with a central water-wheel pit, line the banks of the River Lee.

At Blarney, 8 km (5 mi.) NW, near the castle where the Blarney Stone reputedly gives Irishmen their eloquence, the large-scale manufacture of textiles began with the erection of a five-storey cotton spinning mill in the 1780s. By 1890 the integrated woollen concern of Martin Mahony was employing 750 workers. Many of the nineteenth-century mill buildings have been adapted as a gift-shop complex, forming as powerful an attraction to tourists as the castle. In the ground-floor restaurant cast-iron columns with lugs for power transmission systems support wooden crossbeams. Production continues in modern single-storey sheds.

At Monard, 6 km (4 mi.) N., leats, pools and a few buildings remain of a substantial water-powered spade mill established in 1790 in a deep ravine, the ravine now being crossed by a railway viaduct of 1877.

BIBLIOGRAPHY
General
Crocker, 1986; Cullen, 1987; McCutcheon, 1969, 1970, 1977.
Specific
Creedon, C. *Cork City Railway Stations, 1849–1985*, 1985.

LOCATION
[M] Cork Public Museum, Fitzgerald Park, Mardyke, Cork.

BARRIE TRINDER

Corliss, George Henry (1817–88)   An American engineer who invented in 1849 a four-valve arrangement for steam-engine cylinders. One pair at the top partially rotated to admit steam, another pair at the bottom exhausted it, thereby separating hot and cold flows, and increasing thermal efficiency. Corliss valves were used from the 1860s, especially in mill engines. Corliss engines were regarded as the best in the world, were energetically marketed from their designer's works at Providence, R. I., and were imitated by other builders on both sides of the Atlantic.

See also figure 93.

BIBLIOGRAPHY
General
Frankel, 1977.

Cornish engine RICHARD TREVITHICK's final development of the condensing single-cylinder steam engine, the first of which was installed at Wheal Prosper, Cornwall, England, in 1811–12. High-pressure steam from a cylindrical boiler, with an innovatory internal furnace flue, was admitted above the piston while exhaust steam from the previous stroke was condensed below. After Trevithick's departure to South America in 1816 the Cornish engine was developed by others. Its very high efficiency justified its high original cost, and it was widely used for pumping from mines and in waterworks well into the twentieth century. Cornish engine houses are a feature of the landscape of south-west England (*see* CORNWALL).

BIBLIOGRAPHY
General
Dickinson and Titley, 1934; Law, 1965; Ordish, 1967; Pole, 1844; Trevithick, 1872.

corn mill A building in which grain is ground, traditionally a WINDMILL or WATER MILL but occasionally operated by HORSE GINS. From the late eighteenth century steam engines were used to power corn mills, and electric power was applied from the late nineteenth century. Grain and flour were handled in sacks until suction systems were introduced in the late nineteenth century, bringing substantial changes in the layouts of mills. Grain was ground with stones until the introduction of roller milling from the 1830s. The pattern for the construction of very large mills was set in the USA by John Sargent Pillsbury (1818–1901) and Charles Alfred Pillsbury (1842–1899), whose 'A' mill of 1883 at St Anthony Falls, Minneapolis, was reckoned the largest in the world at that time. The Pillsburys also pioneered the 'purifier' (making possible the manufacture of bread flour from prairie wheat) ROLLER MILLING, and testing and control systems.

A traditional corn mill could be adapted to grind flour or to produce hulled grains for animal feedstuffs, groats or oatmeal without substantial changes in its basic operation.

See also FLOURMILL; GRAIN SILO; GRANARY; GRISTMILL; MILLSTONE.

BIBLIOGRAPHY
General
Wailes, 1967.

BARRIE TRINDER

Cornwall, England Cornwall forms the extremity of the south-west peninsula of Britain, and has been a source of minerals since prehistoric times.

The traditional centre of the tin and copper mining area around Redruth and Camborne is the de Dunstanville Monument of 1836 on Carn Brea. The landscape around is rich in engine houses, railway embankments and other relics of mining. The typical Cornish engine house is rectangular in plan, with a chimney in one corner and a massive bob wall at the other end, following the design first used by RICHARD TREVITHICK at the Wheal Prosper mine in 1811. Some three hundred such engine houses survive in the south-west peninsula. Two engines are preserved at East Pool, 3 km (2 mi.) W. of Redruth, and another at the adjacent Taylor's Shaft. There are also engines at Levant, 4 km ($2\frac{1}{2}$ mi.) N. of St Just, and Crofty Pool, 4 km ($2\frac{1}{2}$ mi.) W. of Redruth. Engine houses open to the public are at Wheal Coates, 8 km (5 mi.) N. of Redruth and Wheal Prosper, 7 km (4 mi.) W. of Helston. The most spectacular of the engine houses are those by the cliff edge at Botalleck, 3 km ($1\frac{1}{2}$ mi.) N. of St Just.

Copper ore was exported to South Wales from Hayle, where smelters were fuelled by coal brought as return freight. The harbour wall is made of copper slag. Harvey's foundry at Hayle exported engines to all parts of the world. The historic collection from Holmans, also engineers of Hayle, is displayed at the National Trust property at Poldark, 12 km (7 mi.) S. of Redruth. Ore was also exported from the spectacular harbours at Portreath, 5 km (3 mi.) NW of Redruth, and Trevaunance, 10 km (6 mi.) NE of Redruth, on the north coast. Tolgus Tin, 2 km ($1\frac{1}{2}$ mi.) NW of Redruth, is a tin-streaming plant, with a water-powered twelve-headed set of stamps, in use till 1968.

China clay has been quarried in Cornwall since its discovery by William Cookworthy (1705–80) in 1746. The views west from the B3300 Bugle–St Austell road reveal one of the most remarkable industrial landscapes in Britain. The museum at Wheal Martyn, 4 km ($2\frac{1}{2}$ mi.) N. of St Austell, located in two old clay works, gives comprehensive coverage of the industry's history. Charlestown, 3 km (2 mi.) SE of St Austell, and Pentewan, 6 km (4 mi.) S., are harbours historically associated with china clay exports.

Delabole quarry, 4 km ($2\frac{1}{2}$ mi.) W. of Camelford, a source of slate for four centuries and 150 m (500 ft.) deep, admits visitors. The Lizard peninsula is Britain's chief source of soapstone or SERPENTINE, carvings of which are still made.

The main line of the Cornwall Railway was distinguished by I. K. BRUNEL's timber-trestle viaducts. All have been replaced, but fragments of piers survive at Devoran, 8 km (5 mi.) SW of Truro, and elsewhere. A turnpike trust 'take off' stone, indicating the limits within which extra horses could be used on a vehicle, survives 3 km (2 mi.) SW of Callington on the Liskeard Road.

BIBLIOGRAPHY
General
Barton, 1961, 1967.
Specific
Booth, L. G. Timber works. In Pugsley, 1976.

LOCATIONS
[M] Royal Institution of Cornwall, County Museum, River Street, Truro TR1 2SJ.
[M] Tolgus Tin (Cornwall) Ltd, New Portreath Road, Redruth TR16 4HN.

BARRIE TRINDER

corrugated iron Wrought iron, and subsequently steel sheets, formed by machinery into uniform ridges, and coated with zinc. Corrugation provides a greater stiffness than metal of the same thickness would have in flat form. The process was first used in the 1820s and from the 1830s it was used for PREFABRICATED buildings exported from Britain, and later from other European countries.

BIBLIOGRAPHY
General
Davies, 1899.

Corsica (Corse), France The Mediterranean island of Corsica, 240 km (150 mi.) SE of Toulon, has been a French possession since 1768, prior to which it had belonged to GENOA. Its chief industrial archaeological interest lies in its ironworks.

The Querciolo forge at Vescovato in the department of Haute Corse, 30 km (18 mi.) S. of Bastia, is one of sixteen identified in the island, dating from the sixteenth to the nineteenth centuries. It employed a direct process for making iron, similar in principle to the CATALAN FORGE but differing in several important respects. The process emerged in Corsica *c.*1625, characterized by a specific mode of production and a particular organizational layout within the complexes. The process continued to be used until *c.*1840 when it died out. It was imported from the Ligurian territories which, like Corsica, belonged to Genoa.

As in the Catalan forges, blast was provided by a TROMPE, a wooden blast funnel, some 6–8 m (19–26 ft.) high, generally made from pine or chestnut. Unlike the forges in the PYRENEES these Corsican trompes had only one funnel. They seem to have appeared during the 1620s, some sixty or seventy years before the appearance of a similar system in the Ariège region. The form of the furnace and the way it was run also differed from the Catalan system. There was no permanent furnace: iron ore and charcoal were piled up in a shallow pit dug out in the furnace area. Before ore was reduced it was calcined for three hours. Because of the relatively primitive hammers, weighing only 100–150 kg (220–330 lb.), daily production was about 150–200 kg (330–440 lb.), a quarter the output of a Catalan forge.

The Querciolo forge, situated on the River Orsaticcia,

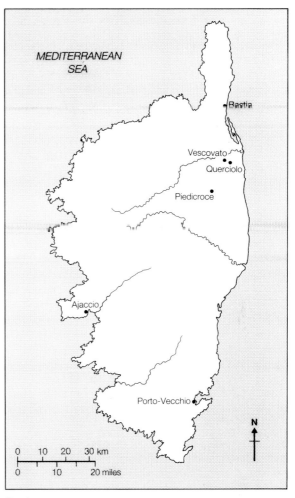

Corsica

dates from the early eighteenth century. Like most Corsican forges, it was located in the Castagniccia region, south of Bastia, on account of the abundant supplies of chestnut trees used for charcoal, and the availability of water power. The rich ores were imported from the island of Elba. The remains of the forge enable us to understand its organization. The furnace area and the hammer were located together in a workshop with rough shale walls, 11 m × 9 m (36 ft. × 29 ft.). A charcoal store and three small rooms were built up against the main workshop, one of them used as a store for finished iron bars. On the upper floor there were rooms where the forgemen could sleep. Along with the remnants of the furnace area, this site also has its trompe, exceptionally a masonry rather than a wooden structure. At the bottom of the funnel remains the 'wind chamber', a vaulted circular construction, about 2 m (6 ft. 6 in.) in diameter. Above the forge, cut out of the hillside, is the reservoir.

The form of organization of the Querciolo forge is confirmed by other, similar sites on the island. Orezza at

Piedicroce on the Fium'Alto, some 20 km (12 mi.) S. of Querciolo, is one of the best preserved, retaining its anvil and the remains of an overhead wooden aqueduct which fed the hammer wheel.

After 1840 a few blast furnaces were built in Corsica, still using the rich ores mined in Elba. The Solenzara furnaces, 30 km (18 mi.) N. of Porto-Vecchio, did not operate for long; but the important Toga works, built in the outskirts of Bastia from 1842, ended up with four blast furnaces and eight fineries. In 1851 the works was bought by the Jackson company, ironmakers from Assailly near SAINT-ÉTIENNE. The works used charcoal from Corsica and Sardinia, and ores from Elba, and sent its pig iron to Assailly. This works ceased operation in 1880, after which the buildings were taken over by L. N. Mattei, producers of tonic wine. They were almost completely demolished in 1989.

BIBLIOGRAPHY
Specific
Mattioli, M. Métallurgie proto-industrielle du fer en Corse du XVIᵉ siècle au premier tiers XIXᵉ siècle (Proto-industrial ironmaking in Corsica from the sixteenth century to the first third of the nineteenth century). In *Bulletin des Sciences Historiques et Naturelles de Corse*, special number, 1990.

JEAN-FRANÇOIS BELHOSTE

Corvol-l'Orgueilleux, Nièvre, France   The Villette paper factory at Corvol-l'Orgueilleux, 10 km (6 mi.) W. of Clamecy, was founded by the entrepreneur and banker, Etienne François Thomas-Varennes, son of a wood merchant of Clamecy. Although he lived in Paris from 1800, Thomas-Varennes still owned 1250 ha (500 ac.) of wooded estates at Villette and Sozay. In 1825, as part of his efforts to raise profits from these properties, he established a blast furnace. The construction of the paper factory dated back to 1818. It was established in a region with no earlier papermaking traditions. It consequently made use of the latest methods available – in particular, after 1822, the English papermaking machine, for which Léger Didot held the import licence in France. This machine, originally conceived by Louis Nicolas Robert, foreman of a papermill at Essonnes (Seine-et-Oise), produced paper in a continuous roll. Thomas-Varennes imported one such machine, then had two copies built, making the Corvol works the most highly mechanized in France in the 1820s. A steam-driven paper-drying machine was introduced in 1825.

In 1833 the mill went bankrupt, a consequence of a long crisis in the Parisian publishing industry. This marked the end of a period of dynamic growth, although the works continued to operate, specializing in high-quality papers, until 1971. The relative stagnation of the latter half of the nineteenth century allowed the works to evolve with little destruction. The buildings are spread out along a tributary of the River Sauzay. Only the buildings on the right bank were destroyed to make way for modern plant in the twentieth century, otherwise the site is remarkable for its architecture. Three identical two-storey buildings dominate the whole, the other buildings being single-storey. On the left bank of the river, the old offices and warehouses are arranged in a semicircle around a courtyard with an ornamental pond. The entrance is topped by a pediment and bell cupola. All the single-storey buildings have timber roofs of the 'Philibert Delorme' type, using small pieces of timber to give maximum clearance.

BIBLIOGRAPHY
Specific
Unpublished study by Monuments Historiques, Ministère de la Culture, Paris.

JEAN-FRANÇOIS BELHOSTE

Cotentin, Manche, France   The Cotentin peninsula is notable for its lime industry, which has recently been the subject of study and protective measures. Twelve sites have been protected in the department of Manche. A remarkably-preserved group of little-used nineteenth-century kilns at Regneville-sur-Mer, near Coutances, now has a small museum devoted to the local lime-burning industry and to other economic activities in this coastal region. It is also the seat of a recently-formed national association for the study of the heritage of the lime and cement industries.

See also SAINT-GOBAIN.

BIBLIOGRAPHY
Specific
Levivier, J. Les fours à chaux de Sud-Coutençais, contribution à un inventaire d'archéologie industrielle (The lime kilns of the southern Cotentin: a contribution to an industrial archaeological inventory). *Comptes rendus du 105è Congrès national des Sociétés Savantes, Caen, 1980*. Paris: Bibliothèque Nationale, 1981.

LOCATION
[I] Association Française pour l'Étude et la Protection du Patrimoine des Industries de la Chaux et du Ciment (French association for the study and protection of the heritage of the lime and cement industries), Musée du Rey, 50590 Regneville-sur-Mer.

cottage   A small rural dwelling, particularly that of a farm labourer. The word carries overtones of Arcadian peace and came to be applied to suburban residences, which might otherwise have been called VILLAS, from the eighteenth century. Cottage estates built in the late nineteenth and early twentieth centuries were substantial developments of small houses on the edges of cities, like that built by the Peabody Trust in north LONDON.

BIBLIOGRAPHY
General
Darley, 1975.
Specific
Cooper, N. The myth of cottage life. In *Country Life*, 1967.

cottage orné   An architectural term used to describe houses whose design was based on fantasized impressions of traditional cottages. Such cottages were a characteristic of the picturesque fashion of the late eighteenth century and early nineteenth century in England, the outstanding examples being those designed by John Nash (1752–1835) at Blaise Castle, 6 km (4 mi.) NW of Bristol. Other examples were built in various INDUSTRIAL COMMUNITIES.

cotton   The soft, white ball of cellulose fibre produced by the cotton plant (*Gossypium*) is processed primarily into cotton thread and yarn. Grown in warm climates, the major types of cotton are named after the regions where they are produced: Egyptian, Sea Island (with long fibres, termed long-staple), Upland, Asiatic, Peruvian. As a seed-hair fibre, cotton surrounds its seed and the fibre must be separated before it can be worked. Traditionally this operation was performed by hand until the invention of the COTTON GIN by ELI WHITNEY in the USA in 1793. The crucial role of cotton manufacture in the process of industrialization, first in Britain and then in Belgium, Switzerland, Germany, the USA and elsewhere, has long been acknowledged.

See also COTTON PRESS; DELINTING MACHINE.

BIBLIOGRAPHY
General
Baines, 1835; Copeland, 1912; Edwards, 1967; Ellison, 1968; Leigh, 1873; Mitchell, 1921.

cotton gin   A machine used to separate the cotton fibre or lint from its seeds. The traditional roller gin drew cotton fibre between two closely-spaced wooden rolls, leaving the seed behind, but sometimes crushing it and leaving particles in the cotton. ELI WHITNEY's invention of 1793 added rotating saw teeth that more effectively separated the seed. For long-staple (long-fibred) cotton the roller style was also mechanized, with the addition of a knife blade set parallel to the roller to cut out the seed.

The term 'gin' (*see* HORSE GIN) denotes both the machine and the building in which it is housed. Depending on the scale of the operation, the latter may be a small wooden shed or a large modern facility, including drying and baling equipment.

cotton press   After its seeds have been removed, cotton lint is conveyed by compressed air or brushes in continuous sequence to the press which compresses the cotton in layers to form bales. A bale is a block of compressed cotton weighing about 500 lb. (225 kg), covered with coarsely woven jute bagging and banded for shipment. The processing of cotton, including ginning (*see* COTTON GIN), pressing and baling, usually occurs on or near the plantation where it is grown.

council house   A term applied in Britain to a dwelling owned and usually erected by a local authority. From the 1890s legislation permitted borough councils in London to build 'lodging houses', a term so defined as to include separate COTTAGES and APARTMENTS for families. These powers were extended throughout the country by the Housing of the Working Classes Act 1900. The Housing and Town Planning Act 1909 accepted the principle that councils could own and administer housing, but it was not until after World War I that a succession of Acts stimulated the construction of large numbers of council houses.

BIBLIOGRAPHY
General
Daunton, 1984, 1987; Gauldie, 1974; Mowat, 1955.

counting house   The room or building, often of distinctive architectural quality, within a mine complex, ironworks, textile mill or similar concern, in which accounts were kept. The term was originally applied to the equivalent part of a royal or noble household. It also applies to booths for handling cash at markets, like the octagonal brick building of 1853 preserved at Avoncroft (*see* BROMSGROVE).

Coventry, England   A traditional textile town in the eighteenth century, specializing in ribbon and watch manufacture. The ribbon trade was organized on a factory basis from 1840. The J. & J. Cash works, a terrace of forty three-storey, half-timbered dwellings in Cash's Lane, are the outstanding survivor of several 'cottage factories'. Some watchmaking shops of the 1870s remain in Chapelfields. Bicycle manufacture was introduced in the 1870s, and car-making in the 1890s. The Singer works, Canterbury Street, built *c.*1880 for the manufacture of sewing machines, was used for car manufacture from *c.*1900 till 1936; the Swift of Coventry works, on Parkside and Mile Lane, began as a cycle factory but cars were made there *c.*1900–36; and the Standard factory, Canley Road, dates from 1910. The Massey-Ferguson plant, Banner Lane, was one of many 'shadow' factories built in anticipation of the need to increase armaments production on the eve of World War II. The Herbert Museum has collections of sewing machines, cycles, motor cycles, cars, and a textile section including Jacquard looms.

BIBLIOGRAPHY
General
Brook, 1977; Chancellor, 1969; Collins and Stratton, 1986; Lancaster and Mason, 1986; Prest, 1960.
Specific
Chaplin, R. Discovering lost new towns in the 19th century. In *Local Historian*, x, 1972.
Coventry Produces. Coventry Chamber of Commerce, 1951.

LOCATIONS
[M] Herbert Art Gallery and Museum, Jordan Well, Coventry.
[M] Museum of British Road Transport, St Agnes' Lane, Hales Street, Coventry CV1 1PN.

BARRIE TRINDER

Covilhã, Beira Baixa, Portugal   A woollen manufacturing centre, 225 km (148 mi.) NE of Lisbon, which developed around the fast-flowing streams of the area. In 1667 a factory was set up under the guidance of English experts to produce fine cloth. After the Methuen Treaty of 1703 (*see* PORTUGAL) allowed the importation of English cloth the local industry entered a crisis which lasted until the middle of the century. Under the Marquis of POMBAL

(1699–1789) a model factory was set up to provide professional training. There was an improvement in the quality of the cloth produced, and the industrial development of the town resumed, only to be interrupted by the Napoleonic invasions after 1808. Around seven thousand workers were employed in the factories in 1863. Because so much water power was available and coal was expensive there was only one steam-powered factory at that date. Many remarkable industrial buildings survive, among them the former royal cloth factory in which is located the Museum of the Woollen Industry. There are further woollen mills in the neighbouring villages of Tortozendo, 5 km (3 mi.) S., and Unhais da Serra, 10 km (6 mi.) W.; and at Paúl, 16 km (10 mi.) SW, water-powered olive presses remain in operation.

LOCATION
[M] Museum of the Woollen Industry, Covilhã.

JOSÉ M. LOPES CORDEIRO

Cowper stove A regenerative stove for heating air *en route* from the blowing engine to the blast furnace (*see* HOT BLAST). The stove had an iron shell, lined with firebricks in a honeycomb configuration: waste gases from the furnace burnt inside it, then the supply was cut off and blast air was sent through. Each furnace would require two or three stoves so that one could be used while others were being heated. The stove was invented by E. A. Cowper in 1857. Stoves at modern furnaces follow the same principle. Eighteen remain at VÖLKLINGEN.

BIBLIOGRAPHY
General
Gale, 1967, 1971; Percy, 1864.

cracking A process in an OIL REFINERY in which hydrocarbons are heated for a limited period to increase the yield of light products at the expense of the heavy. Developed by William Burton of the Standard Oil Co. (Indiana), it was first used in 1913. Continuous thermal cracking processes were developed in the next two decades, and in 1936 the first commercial process using a CATALYST was introduced by Eugene Houdry. The manufacture of PROPYLENE by thermal cracking by the Standard Oil Co. (New Jersey) in 1918 marked the beginning of the petrochemical industry. Cracking is now used in all oil refineries.

BIBLIOGRAPHY
General
BP, 1958; Harvard, 1960; Rogers, 1915.

Cracow, Poland *See* KRAKÓW.

crane A machine for raising, moving and lowering heavy objects, which may be operated by hand, by a TREADMILL, or by steam power, Hydraulic power or ELECTRIC POWER. Until the late eighteenth century cranes were principally used for lifting in QUARRIES and on quaysides (as were those that survive at Andernach, Trier

and Würzburg, Germany) and for raising the MASTS of ships, but they became essential equipment in DOCKS, where JIB CRANES were principally used, and in FOUNDRIES and steel works, in locomotive works and similar engineering plants, and in pumping stations and power stations, where beam cranes were usually employed. In 1839 James Taylor of Birkenhead, England, constructed a steam crane for use in a quarry, and subsequently built the first travelling steam crane to the design of W. W. Hulse (1821–97). HYDRAULIC CRANES were introduced in the 1840s. By the 1860s several companies specialized in crane manufacture, notably, in England, Cowans Sheldon of Carlisle, Stothert & Pitt of Bath; and Morgan Engineering of Alliance, Ohio. Electric power was first applied to cranes in 1891 in Hamburg and Manchester, and the first electric dockside cranes in England were installed at Southampton in 1893. Twenty-two had been installed in Hamburg by 1897. Purpose-built cranes were and are supplied for large-scale construction projects.

A water crane is an overhanging iron pipe or leather tube for supplying water to a steam railway locomotive or road vehicle.

See also EXCAVATOR; HYDRAULIC CRANE; JIB CRANE.

BIBLIOGRAPHY
General
Hill, 1911; Marks, 1904; Torrens, 1978.
Specific
Forbes Taylor, F. R. The winch from well-head to Goliath crane. In *Chartered Mechanical Engineer*, 1962.
Haspel, J. Der Hamburger Kaikran als Hafendenkmal (The quayside cranes in Hamburg as port monuments). In *Förderverein*, 1986.

BARRIE TRINDER

Crawshay, Richard (1739–1810) A leading Merthyr Tydfil ironmaster and founder of the Crawshay iron dynasty. Born in Yorkshire, England, he was proprietor of the Cyfarthfa Ironworks from *c.*1786. He led the adoption of Cort's puddling process, increasing his weekly bar output from 10 to 200 tons. In 1788 he installed the first Watt engine for rolling. By 1803 Cyfarthfa was among the largest ironworks in the world, with two thousand workers.

BIBLIOGRAPHY
General
Davies, 1933.

creamery A factory where milk from farms is collected. Some may be dispatched for sale as liquid milk or cream; some will be made into BUTTER, CHEESE, CONDENSED MILK or milk powder. The term, first used in the USA in the 1870s, is synonymous with one meaning of 'dairy', but may imply that a particular establishment is worked on co-operative principles (*see* CO-OPERATIVE MOVEMENT).

BIBLIOGRAPHY
General
Fay, 1920.

Figure 33 One of the two 365-ton cranes at the Leixoes harbour, Matosinhos, near Oporto, built by the French company Fives-Lille in 1888; it was originally used in the construction of the harbour and later in the handling of cargoes.
José M. Lopes Cordiero

cream separator The centrifugal cream separator consists of a bowl rotating rapidly on its own axis, in which the lighter butterfat constituents of milk are concentrated in the middle, whence they are forced out through different tubes from those further from the centre, which take the heavier liquid parts. It was the key machine in the revolution in the dairy industry of the late nineteenth century. It was developed by a Swede, Carl G. P. de Laval (1845–1913), and a Dane, L. C. Nielson, and patented in 1878.

Cregneach, Isle of Man   The first open-air museum in Britain, opened by Manx Museum and National Trust in 1938, 2 km (1½ mi.) S. of Port Erin. It is centred on a former community of crofters who lived in thatched cottages, some of whom found employment in nearby lead mines and flagstone quarries. The centrepiece is the cottage, dating from *c.*1820, of Harry Kelly, crofter and Manx Gaelic speaker, who died in 1934. Its contents include a spinning wheel and bedclothes of Manx home-spun linen and woollen cloth. The last hand loom in the parish is preserved in a loomshed attached to a weaver's cottage, and a turner's treadle lathe is preserved in another shed.

BIBLIOGRAPHY
Specific
A Guide to the Manx Open-Air Folk Museum, Cregneach, 4th edn. Douglas: Manx Museum and National Trust, 1977.

Cremona, Lombardy, Italy   An agricultural centre, famed for the manufacture of stringed instruments, above all for the productions of Stradivarius Cremonensis (1644–1737). From 1883 an extensive network of canals was built by the Consozzio Irrigazion Cremonesi to irrigate the plane of the River Po. A series of bridges was erected to improve communications between Cremona and Piacenza, 27 km (17 mi.) W. The Po bridge at Cremona of 1892 has an iron lattice structure, carrying rail traffic above a road and, originally, a tramway.

BIBLIOGRAPHY
General
Mioni *et al.,* 1981–3.

crenellation   The indentation of a parapet as in a

battlemented castle, the raised portions being called merlons. It is a feature of many kinds of INDUSTRIAL ARCHITECTURE.

creosote   An oily liquid, consisting largely of PHENOL, originally obtained from wood tar by Karl von Reichenbach (1788–1869) in 1832, and subsequently from the distillation of coal tar. It is used as an antiseptic; as a preservative for timber, particularly railway sleepers and poles for carrying cables; and as a source of phenol.

BIBLIOGRAPHY
General
Hardie and Pratt, 1966.

Crespi d'Adda, Lombardy, Italy   The grandest MODEL COMMUNITY in Italy is located 30 km (19 mi.) NE of Milan. Silvio Benigno Crespi drew upon the example of the model village created by Alessandro Rossi at Schio, providing the same range of facilities but adopting a more formal layout and lavish architectural expression. The cotton mill was built from 1878 beside a canal adjacent to the River Adda. Weaving sheds have traceried decoration in terracotta. The formal entrance passes between office blocks and faces a clock tower and one of two tall chimneys. Hydro-electric plant was installed in 1909.

The earliest apartment blocks are those in Via Mazzina, with a workers' hotel behind, four-storey, virtually four-square, and built in 1878–80. Smaller semi-detached houses for two or four families were built from 1881. The castle was built for Crespi in 1894–7 to designs by Ernesto Pirovano. An octagonal tower rises above crenellation and gargoyles, providing a look-out over the works, and, alongside the domed church, giving an inescapable paternalistic and moral directive to the workforce. Detached houses for managers were built in 1919–27, half castle, half chalet in style, also designed by Pirovano. At the end of the settlement the cemetery is dominated by the Crespi Mausoleum of 1907 by Gaetano Moretti, a massive ziggurat form executed in stone and concrete. Small standardized tombstones commemorate the workers.

This section of the River Adda, notable for the iron bridge at Paderno which dates from 1889, also has some of the most important early hydro-electric plants in Italy, which were grouped on the edge of the plain of Lombardy rather than in the Alps, to be near to Milan and other industrial centres. The stations were developed by large combines, the most important in the north being the Società Edison. Rivalry between the companies is reflected in bold engineering and highly decorative frontages. The most dramatic example is the Taccani power station at Trezzo d'Adda, 3 km (2 mi.) N. of Crespi d'Adda. It is fed directly by the river, a head being built up behind a dam with an outlet running under the peninsula formed by a loop. A short navigation canal bypasses the dam. Gaetano Moretti produced the design in 1906, to blend in with a ruined castle sited above. The three blocks for housing turbines, the control centre and transformers were faced in coarsely pitted stone, and motifs currently fashionable in Milan were used to achieve an effect of lavish monumentality. The key parts of the interior are faced with marble, with stairways lined by intricate wrought-iron work. The stencil-decorated turbine hall is hung with curtains.

Esterle, 10 km (6 mi.) NW of Trezzo, on the Adda, is a power station completed in 1914 for which Adolfo Covi was engineer. It has the appearance of an over-scaled Renaissance palace, with fresco decoration and moulded brickwork.

BIBLIOGRAPHY
General
Föhl and Hamm, 1988; Negri *et al.*, 1983.
Specific
Selvafolta, O. L'immagine del paesaggio technologica nella Lombardia del primo Novo cento (The imagery of technology in Lombardy in the first years of the century). In *Lombardia, il territorio, l'ambiete, il paesaggio* (Lombardy: land, environment, landscape). Milan: Electra, v, 1984.

MICHAEL STRATTON

Crete (Kryti), Greece   The largest of the Greek islands, with an area of more than 8259 km^2 (3189 sq. mi.), extending 260 km (162 mi.) from west to east and up to 60 km (37 mi.) from north to south, with a population just under half a million. A Byzantine possession, it was occupied in 824 by Arabs, who founded the port of Rabd-el-Kanak, which was named Candia by the Venetians, and is now the capital, Iráklion. The island reverted to Byzantine control in 861, and was held by Venice from 1204 until 1669 when it fell to the Turks. It gained autonomy in 1898 and became part of Greece in 1913. The winged lion of St Mark carved into the fortress at Iráklion is evidence of the city's Venetian past, as are the barrel-vaulted roofs of the arsenal. There is a concentration of irrigation windmills on the plateau of Lasíthi, 75 km (46 mi.) E. of Iráklion.

LOCATION
[M] Historical Museum of Crete, Mansion of A. & M. Kalokerinos, Lyssimachou Kalokerinou Street, Iráklion, Crete.

Crewe, Cheshire, England   A classic railway town, built by GJR (later LNWR) around the locomotive works. Over seven hundred houses were constructed in 1843–58, of which three short streets and some isolated examples remain. Later housing was built speculatively; some surviving examples have spectacular tiled porches. The original locomotive works has been demolished, but an enginemen's barracks, some clothing factories, and some complex multi-level track layouts at the station survive.

BIBLIOGRAPHY
General
Ashmore, 1982; Chaloner, 1950.
Specific
Chambers Edinburgh Journal, VIII, 1850.

Illustrated London News, 23 December 1843.

Cromarty, Ross and Cromarty, Scotland *See* HIGH-LANDS.

Cromford, Derbyshire, England RICHARD ARKWRIGHT built the first water-powered cotton mill at Cromford in 1771. By 1790 it formed part of a range of multi-storey spinning mills and warehouses. It was reduced from five to three storeys by a fire in the nineteenth century. The complex is being restored by the Arkwright Society. Masson Mill, on a different site, was built by Arkwright in 1784–5 and remains in production. Its elegant brick façade contrasts with the austere stone construction of the mills of the 1770s.

The village created by Arkwright – houses, a market place, an inn, a corn mill, a church and a school – remains essentially intact, and forms one of the most evocative monuments of the Industrial Revolution in Britain. The 23 km (14 mi.) Cromford Canal, now isolated from the national system, is used for boat trips. A Graham & Co. pumping engine of 1849 is preserved 3 km (2 mi.) S. of Cromford.

The Cromford & High Peak Railway, linking the canal with the Peak Forest Canal, was a typical HYBRID RAILWAY, with eight inclined planes, and was opened in 1831. After closure in 1967 it was converted to a country TRAIL, extending 45 km (28 mi.) from High Peak Junction, 3 km (2 mi.) S., to Buxton. A Butterley Co. winding engine of 1829 is preserved at Middleton Top inclined plane.

At Belper, 10 km (6 mi.) SE, the Strutt family built textile mills from 1773. The iron-framed North Mill of 1804 stands alongside the East Mill, a steel-framed, red-brick building of 1912, with terraces, CLUSTER HOUSES, nailers' shops and a Unitarian chapel built by the Strutts. The Strutts' mills at Milford, 14 km (9 mi.) SE, are demolished, but late eighteenth-century terraces still stand. Other important textile mills are in Lumsdale, 4 km (2½ mi.) NE; Lea, 3 km (2 mi.) E.; Cressbrook, 21 km (13 mi.) NW; and Calver, 18 km (11 mi.) N.

The National Tramway Museum, in a former quarry at Crich, 6 km (4 mi.) E., has a collection of tramcars from a variety of British cities and some from overseas.

Wirksworth, 4 km (2½ mi.) S., has long associations with limestone quarrying, lead mining and tape weaving. Haarlem Mill, built by Arkwright in 1777–80, was perhaps the first cotton mill in which a steam engine was employed. Conservation programmes at Wirksworth, sponsored by the Civic Trust and involving the use of REVOLVING FUNDS, have attracted international attention.

There are many remains of lead mining in the hills west of Cromford, the most notable being at Magpie Mine, and traces of smelters in Lumsdale and at Lea. The Peak District Mining Museum at Matlock Bath, 1 km (½ mi.) N., includes a Coalbrookdale Co. water engine.

Caudwell's flour mill at Rowsley, 10 km (6 mi.) NW, dates in its present form from 1874, and contains roller-milling equipment of 1885, preserved in working order, with contemporary turbines.

BIBLIOGRAPHY
General
Chapman, 1967; Charlton, Hool and Strange, 1971; Fitton and Wadsworth, 1958; Tann, 1970.
Specific
Arkwright Society Trails: *No. 1: Cromford Canal & High Peak Railway; No. 3: Leadmining; No. 8: Cromford Village; No. 10: Dethick, Lea and Holloway; No. 11: Wirksworth; No. 12: Belper; No. 16: Caudwell's Mill.* Cromford: Arkwright Society.
Rhodes, J. *Derbyshire Leadmining in the 18th century.* Sheffield: University of Sheffield, 1973.
Rimmer, A. *The Cromford & High Peak Railway.* London: Oakwood, 1985.

LOCATIONS
[I] Arkwright Society, Cromford Mills, Cromford, Matlock, Derbyshire DE4 3RQ.
[M] National Tramway Museum, Crich, Matlock, Derbyshire DE4 5DP.
[M] Peak District Mining Museum, The Pavilion, Matlock Bath, Derbyshire.

BARRIE TRINDER

cross-tie A North American term for SLEEPER.

crucible A highly REFRACTORY open-mouthed vessel, used for heating materials in various industrial processes but particularly in the manufacture of GLASS and STEEL, and in the refining of precious metals. The effectiveness of crucibles for many purposes is improved by the addition of GRAPHITE to the clay used in their manufacture.

BIBLIOGRAPHY
General
Searle, 1924.

crucible process A means of making carbon steel, perfected at Sheffield, England, in 1740 by Benjamin Huntsman (1704–76). Blister steel made in a CEMENTATION FURNACE was broken into small pieces and melted in a REFRACTORY clay crucible in a coke-fired furnace, enabling slag within the metal to be skimmed off, and allowing carbon to diffuse throughout the metal. Once the process was complete, steel in the crucible was poured into a small ingot mould. A complete plant, with a range of holes in which crucibles were placed within the furnace, can still be seen at Abbeydale, SHEFFIELD. The manufacture of crucible steel has ceased since World War II.

BIBLIOGRAPHY
General
Barraclough, 1981–4.
Specific
Barraclough, K. C. *Information Leaflet No. 8: Crucible Steel Manufacture.* Sheffield: Sheffield Museums, n.d.

crude oil PETROLEUM in the form in which it is extracted from the ground, after the removal of water or natural gas which may be physically mixed with it. Essentially crude oil comprises a long series of hydrocarbons ranging from low to high boiling points and molecular weights. Crude oils of different origins vary in their characteristics; few can be used as fuel before refining.

BIBLIOGRAPHY
General
BP, 1958.

Cruquius, Noord Holland, The Netherlands   The Cruquius pumping station, 5 km (3 mi.) S. of Haarlem, is the most celebrated in the Netherlands, one of three built in the late 1840s to drain the Haarlemmermeer, all named after great drainage engineers, the others being Van Lynden and Leeghwater. The Haarlemmermeer resulted from the flowing together of four smaller lakes in the sixteenth century. It posed a dangerous threat to the cities of Haarlem and Amsterdam in the event of storms. A commission to drain the lake was appointed in 1840, and subsequently a canal 60 km (37 mi.) long was dug around the perimeter. The first of the engines, designed by Joseph Gibbs and Arthur Dean of London, was completed in 1845. The 350 hp Cruquius engine was built in 1848–9 by Harveys of Hayle, Cornwall. It has a 3.66 m (144 in.) cylinder with an annular piston, within which is fitted a 2.13 m (84 in.) cylinder with an orthodox piston. The engine operated eleven cast-iron beams, balanced on the walls of the circular crenellated tower that houses the installation, which are connected to pumps 1.6 m (63 in.) in diameter. The three Haarlemmermeer engines became redundant in 1933. Some parts remain of the other two. The Cruquius pumping station was taken over by a foundation, as a result of an initiative by the Dutch professional engineering institution, and opened as a museum in 1934. The boilers have been removed and the boiler room houses displays relating to the struggle of the Dutch against the sea. Exhibits include a beam pumping engine of 1826 by Cockerill of Seraing.

LOCATION
[M] Museum De Cruquius (Cruquius Museum), Cruquiusdijk 27/32, Haarlemmermeer.

BARRIE TRINDER

crushing circle   A device for dressing metallic ores, comprising a circle surfaced with stone or iron over which a large wheel rolled, crushing ore-bearing materials. The wheel was stone, a truncated cone mounted on a wooden axle, with one end anchored to a buried post in the centre of the circle, the other attached to the harness of a horse which was walked round the outside of the circle. Good examples can be seen at Eldon Hill and Odin Mine, Derbyshire, England.

See also HORSE GIN.

cryolite   Sodium aluminium fluoride (Na_3AlF_6), used as a flux in smelting aluminium, and on a small scale in enamelling and as a source for fluorine. The most important deposits are at Ivittuut, GREENLAND.

cupellation   A process for recovering gold and silver from the ores of lead or other base metals. Lead was heated, in a shallow hearth fired with charcoal or wood, to 1000–1100 °C. The lead was oxidized to litharge (lead oxide, PbO) in which any other base metals present were absorbed. The litharge was in turn absorbed in a bone-ash hearth, being skimmed off or escaping as fumes, leaving the silver or gold unaltered. Cupellation was known in Roman times and was widely used until the nineteenth century.

BIBLIOGRAPHY
General
Tylecote, 1986; Percy, 1880.

cupola   A term with at least three meanings in industrial archaeology:

1. A shaft furnace, fired with coke, and blown by three or four TUYÈRES, which is used for remelting pig iron or scrap in a FOUNDRY. It operates intermittently. Though patented by JOHN WILKINSON in 1794, the design is generally attributed to his brother William (?1744–1808). Early cupolas, of which an example is displayed at IRONBRIDGE, were constructed of wrought-iron staves. Cupolas are now made from sheet steel lined with REFRACTORIES.
2. A REVERBERATORY FURNACE for smelting LEAD, normally coal-fired in Britain but wood-fired in France and Austria. The characteristic means of lead-smelting used during the Industrial Revolution, it was introduced in Britain in the seventeenth century. A typical British example of *c*.1830 had a grate measuring 1.27 m × 0.6 m (4 ft. 2 in. × 2 ft.), with a 'sole' or melting chamber, roughly octagonal in plan and measuring about 3.3 m (11 ft.) in each direction, with a curving roof. It was lined with slag, which was partially melted on the refractory brick floor and shaped as required. The furnace was charged with 16 cwt. (812 kg) of galena, which was calcined (*see* CALCINING KILN) for two hours, after which the furnace was cooled and the ore turned over. During the next heat fluorspar or lime would be added: the ore then melted quickly, the slag and ore being run off. The rich slag that remained after the ore had been removed was worked in a slag hearth. The process could be completed in six hours, but with some ores a 24-hour heat was necessary. Sometimes calcining took place in a separate furnace. Often several cupolas had flues leading into a single chimney.
3. An architectural term for a dome-shaped structure mounted on columns, often protecting a bell, frequently found on factories of the Industrial Revolution period.

BIBLIOGRAPHY
General
Gale, 1969, 1971; Percy, 1870; Tylecote, 1986.

BARRIE TRINDER

currying   The process by which leather produced by TANNING is made supple and suitable for use by shoemakers or saddlers: it entails soaking, scraping, and treatment with TALLOW or TRAIN OIL. Until the early nineteenth century in England tanners were not allowed to carry on the currying process, but most mid- and late-nineteenth-century tanneries included curriers' shops. A large urban currier's concern in the mid-nineteenth century consisted of tall louvred buildings like those used for TANNING, but there were no adjacent pits.

A currier in England might also make GLOVES, or act as a wholesaler of leather to shoemakers, and the term was sometimes applied to a leather dresser practising TAWING.

BIBLIOGRAPHY
General
Book of Trades, 1839; Mayhew, 1850.
Specific
Jenkins, J. G. *The Rhaeadr Tanner*. Cardiff: National Museum of Wales, 1973.
Thomas, S., Clarkson, L. A. and Thompson, R. *Leather Manufacture through the Ages*. Northampton: East Midlands Industrial Archaeological Conference, 1983.

customs house   A term used from the sixteenth century to describe a building in a port or at a frontier crossing point at which import and export duties are levied. Many customs houses are of considerable architectural merit: *see* DUBLIN; EXETER; LIMERICK.

cutlery   A cutler makes knives – and from the sixteenth century forks – for the table, as well as working knives, razors, swords and bayonets. Traditionally knives were made of wrought iron edged with steel. The cutting edge was normally hammered first from a steel rod, then raised to welding heat, hammered alongside a piece of iron, and shaped in a die to form the 'tang', the part around which the handle was formed. It was then hardened by being plunged into water, and tempered by re-heating until it acquired the colour appropriate to its function, ranging from light straw, indicating a temperature of 430–450 °C, to black which indicated about 600 °C. A knife would then be ground on a gritstone wheel, to remove any roughness, and 'buffed' or polished on a wheel covered in soft leather and dressed with fine sand, emery or iron oxide – a process that gave rise to 'grinder's asthma', the characteristic occupational disease of the trade. Specialist cutlers, like swordmakers and makers of fine tableware, worked in horn, fishskins and so on to produce decorative hilts and handles. Most cutlery has been produced in specialist regions like those around SHEFFIELD and SOLINGEN.

BIBLIOGRAPHY
General
Barraclough, 1976; *Book of English Trades*, 1839; Treatise, n.d.; Tunis, 1965.

BARRIE TRINDER

cutting   A lineal excavation through high ground allowing a road, railway or canal to pass through it on the level or at a reduced gradient. Except in flat terrain cuttings were essential parts of every main-line railway, being

excavated, before the development of steam-powered equipment, by the barrow-runs illustrated by J. C. BOURNE. The depth of a cutting may be exaggerated by depositing the spoil along its rims.

BIBLIOGRAPHY
General
Green and Morgan, 1924.

cyanide   A salt of hydrocyanic acid (HCN), which was isolated by J. L. Gay-Lussac (1778–1850) in 1815. All cyanides are poisonous. Potassium cyanide (KCN) and sodium cyanide (NaCN) are used in refining GOLD. Until the 1960s the industrial process used for making sodium cyanide depended on the reaction of metallic sodium with carbon and nitrogen or ammonia at $c.650$ °C:

$$2Na + 2C + 2NH_3 \rightarrow 2NaCN + 3H_2$$

The process was developed by Hamilton Y. Castner (1859–99) but not adopted until after his death.

BIBLIOGRAPHY
General
Hardie and Pratt, 1966.

Cyprus   The island of Cyprus extends 225 km (140 mi.) from east to west, and 100 km (60 mi.) from north to south at its widest point. Since the Turkish invasion of 1974 it has been divided *de facto* into Greek and Turkish sections. The island became part of the Ottoman Empire in 1571 when Nicosia, the capital, was captured from the Venetians. It was ruled by Britain from 1878 until independence was achieved in 1960.

From prehistoric times Cyprus has been an important source of copper, sulphur and pyrites. The principal workings in recent centuries have been at Troulli, 18 km (11 mi.) N. of Larnaca, at Polistis Khrysokhou and Limni. Xeros was for long the principal port for shipping ores. A salt lake, 5 km (3 mi.) SW of Larnaca, has traditionally been a government monopoly.

Manufactures in Cyprus mirror those of GREECE and

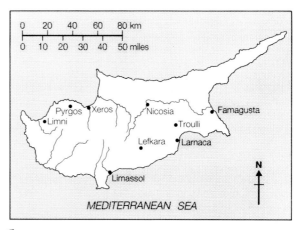

Cyprus

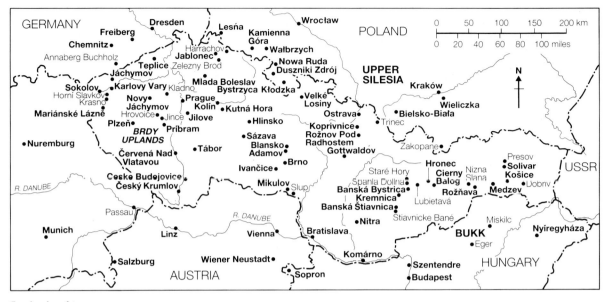

Czechoslovakia

TURKEY. Lace has traditionally been made at Lefkara, south of Nicosia, while both communities make distinctive wooden chests. Olives, citrus fruits and tobacco are grown and processed; wine has become a significant export; and Pyrgos is famous for its dried figs. In Nicosia there are several Büyükkhan, or traditional Turkish inns, while the Bedestan is a medieval Gothic church, adapted by the Turks as a covered market.

BARRIE TRINDER

Czechoslovakia   Present-day Czechoslovakia comprises three elements that were originally independent: Bohemia, Moravia and Slovakia. Bohemia and Slovakia were both part of the Great Moravian Empire in the ninth century. When this Empire broke up in the tenth century, Slovakia became part of Hungary, and Bohemia an independent kingdom which later included Moravia, and which had Prague as its capital. Bohemia became part of the Holy Roman Empire with the election of Charles IV to the imperial throne, and Prague then became the seat of an imperial court. After 1490, the Hungarian and Czech kingdoms were linked and both became part of the Habsburg Empire in 1526. The Czech and Slovak lands remained attached to opposite poles of the Empire (*see* AUSTRIA) until its dissolution in 1918, when the republic of Czechoslovakia was created. German-speaking peoples have played an important part in Czech political and economic history. Substantial parts of Bohemia were temporarily annexed by the Third Reich, and large-scale expatriation of Germans followed Hitler's defeat in 1945. From 1949 to 1991 Czechoslovakia was affiliated to the Warsaw Pact military and economic bloc as the Czechoslovak Soviet Socialist Republic, in which 'Czech' denotes

Bohemia and Moravia and 'Slovak' the autonomous region of Slovakia.

A mixed topography of upland forest and good agricultural land, generous endowments of minerals and fossil fuels, and important river connections to north-western and south-eastern Europe led to early and broad-based economic development in the Czech lands. Bohemia developed a vigorous economy in the medieval period: handicrafts, mining and metalworking contributed to the expansion of trade and the growth of both royal and estate towns, with craftsmen, miners and merchants immigrating from the German states. The Bohemian and Moravian highlands became a focus of mining for precious metals as well as lime burning, glass and ceramic manufacture, ironmaking and textiles.

Although war and the repression of movements for social and religious reform in the sixteenth and seventeenth centuries placed heavy penalties on the royal towns, rural proto-industry continued to grow throughout the upland regions, which came to be more densely settled than the agricultural lowlands. Aristocratic enterprise, Habsburg mercantilism and foreign investment combined in the eighteenth century to establish manufactories and semi-mechanized workshops which underwent intensive technical development in the early nineteenth century, giving rise to indigenous machine building and the mechanization of several branches of industry and agriculture. The emancipation of the peasantry following the revolt of 1848–9 contributed to the growth of towns, the extension of factory production and specialization in agriculture, with a concentration of investment and a dramatic expansion of output in sugar, brewing and flour milling.

The development of a state-sponsored railway network and the access to overseas markets and supplies given by the River Elbe navigation accentuated the importance of Bohemian industry in the Habsburg Empire and attracted additional foreign investment. While the textile industries of South Bohemia profited from better access to American cotton, Bohemian coal and coke supplanted Austrian charcoal in iron and steelmaking. In the 1860s textile and engineering factories began to supply less industrially developed parts of the Empire.

Towards the end of the nineteenth century, textiles gave way in importance to the production of food and heavy engineering. By 1900, Bohemia and Moravia accounted for 75 per cent of the industrial output of the Habsburg Empire, with important complexes for metallurgy (see OSTRAVA) and engineering (see BRNO; PLZEŇ; PRAGUE), glass (see JABLONEC; TEPLICE), ceramics (see KARLOVY VARY), and chemicals (along the Elbe). The population of the Czech lands increased from 7.7 million in 1870 to 10.3 million in 1913, largely in such industrial towns as Kladno, Plzeň and Ostrava, while agrarian districts suffered outmigration. Major engineering centres such as Prague and Plzeň attracted skilled workers from throughout the Czech lands and exchanged specialists on an international basis.

The predominantly mountainous character of Slovakia and its political subordination to Hungary separated and limited the impulses towards industrialization. Slovak industrialization was hindered by outside competition, and by the lack of purchasing power and capital accumulation in the home market. Although Slovakia contains important sites of mineral extraction and extensive forests, both of which have long been exploited, early industrial development had an enclave character, with weak linkages between sectors. State assistance and foreign capital were invested in a range of industries related to the land: mining, flourmills, sugar refineries, sawmills and distilleries, as well as transport. Impressive technical innovations in primary industries and the establishment of model factories in the eighteenth and nineteenth centuries, like those at Saltsin and Holič, had a relatively limited impact.

During the 1850s and 1860s, the development of railways encouraged growth in the production of iron and building materials, and also opened up markets, especially in the Ostrava region, for Slovakian ore. There was a gradual introduction of steam power in flour and sugar milling, in sawmills and in charcoal ironworks in the second half of the nineteenth century. At the end of the nineteenth century, glassworks, papermills, and new iron, steel and cement works, together with flour milling, sugar refining and distilling, dominated Slovak industry, and these were joined by textiles, furniture, chocolate and consumer goods industries chiefly serving a Hungarian market.

Post-war depression, exacerbated by a reduced home market, represented a major problem for the newly formed Czechoslovak state: industrial output in 1918 was at half its pre-war level. There were difficulties in attaining a national economic system, and recession occurred in Slovakia until new investment in food, timber, cement and paper production, in metals and in the power

industry, stimulated renewed growth in the 1920s. National identity found important expression in modernist architecture, examples of which can be seen in BRNO, PRAGUE, and Bat'a's garden city, Zlin (later GOTTWALDOV). Modern mass-production techniques were first introduced by Bat'a in 1927. State economic planning after World War II continued to provide for the rapid growth of heavy industry, accompanied by a new urbanization which has been most noticeable in Slovakia.

Mining was the original focus of Czech and Slovak industry. In Slovakia, copper was mined during the prehistoric period at Spania Dolina and BANSKÁ BYSTRICA; tin at Krupka. From the late Middle Ages, gold was mined at Celina, Sušice, JILOVE and KREMNICA, and silver at BANSKÁ ŠTIAVNICA. There were other metallurgy sites at Kysucke, Nové Město, Gemersky Sad, and Dolný Bolikov. The Fuggers, bankers of Augsburg, Germany, created large unified copper mining and smelting operations in the Banská Bystrica region. Fugger involvement finished in 1545 but production increased until the early seventeenth century when political disturbances brought about some destruction. The mining towns of Banská Štiavnica and Kremnica contain important preserved mining structures, but there are no significant remains of ore processing.

The Czech lands also have a long history of mining for tin and silver. The mines and mints at KUTNÁ HORA and PRÍBRAM were among the most important in Europe during the fourteenth century. Precious metal mines were also worked at JÁCHYMOV and Horní Blatná (see JÁCHYMOV) from the early sixteenth century. This period was one of relative stability and prosperity, and there was considerable technical progress in mining, smelting and casting. AGRICOLA worked at Jáchymov for several years and the discussion of water-powered shaft hoists and pumps in his *De Re Metallica* of 1556 was based on his experience there. His techniques of research and collection were emulated by Johann Mathesius.

Products from foundries were especially noted in an ecclesiastical context and the Slovak town of Spišské Nová Ves became an important centre of foundrymen and goldsmiths. MEDZEV, ROŽŇAVA, Nizna Slana and Vlachov were important early Slovak metalworking centres. Mining made demands on the iron industry: equipment for the mines at Banská Štiavnica and Banská Bystrica was made at Lubietova; and the first Newcomen engine outside England was introduced at Nová Baňa in 1722–4, where it was made by an Englishman, Isaac Potter, who was brought to Slovakia by the Imperial court.

Bohemian iron production had already achieved high concentrations in the eighth century where for example at Zelechovice there were twenty-four bloomeries. After the tenth century production was decentralized for a time, before a new concentration occurred in the high wooded areas by the sixteenth century. In the sixteenth century blast furnaces based on a Saxon model were introduced in the BRDY UPLANDS. These wooded mountain regions had good supplies of ore, fuel and water, and the charcoal iron industry was largely concentrated at Králův Dvůr and Karlova Hut.

191

Technical developments were furthered by the aristocracy in Bohemia and Moravia, and by the state administration in Slovakia. At Karlova Hut, Caspar Henry de Sart was casting cannon balls for the Imperial court from 1596. He moved to Strašice in 1599 and operated a water-powered forge with two hearths, also building two blast furnaces. New blast furnaces made heavy demands on the financial reserves of their owners, and it was only the feudal landholders who could make the necessary investment. Nevertheless, charcoal blast furnaces spread rapidly; by 1700 there were seventy-seven producing 7700 tonnes of pig iron per annum in Bohemia and Moravia, and they were beginning to be introduced into Slovakia. Most of the product was refined into wrought iron, although the use of cast iron grew in importance through the eighteenth century.

While the exploitation of forest products for export became progressively more important in the Slovak economy during the early modern period, spinning and weaving became the chief means of livelihood in the Czech upland districts. High-quality linen from the northern districts of Bohemia was supplied to markets in southern, western and south-western Europe, while Liberec and Jihlava became the most important of thirty centres of woollen manufacture in the Habsburg Empire in the eighteenth century. While the division between rural spinning and urban weaving, finishing and marketing was well established, the weakening of guilds and municipalities following the Thirty Years War of 1618–48 saw feudal estate holders and German merchants, and later English and Dutch merchants, transform or bypass the urban craft guilds, establishing putting-out networks throughout the countryside. By the late eighteenth century several of these networks together drew on more than a thousand domestic spinners. Centres of yarn collection, export and distribution to local weavers included Vrchlabi, Budisin, Chřibska, Friedlant, Grabstein, Jihlava, Jiřetín, Liberec, Litomyšl, Osechna, Rumburk, Sluknov, Stráž pod Raskem, and Zittau. Today, the only surviving monuments to this widespread industry are those town centres that have not been transformed by subsequent development.

In the early eighteenth century, foreign merchants began to form companies to integrate textile production on manorial estates. The alchemist Johann Becher had already set up a silk mill on a manorial estate in the 1660s, and merchants from LINZ had been involved in an estate woollen mill shortly afterwards. Count Kaunitz's installation of Swiss wool stockingers at Slavkov (Austerlitz) in 1701 lasted only twelve years, but the strategy of Englishman Robert Allason – who employed all the weavers in the town of Rumburk in 1713 to produce finished linen cloth for export to the East and West Indies – was more successful. Making substantial loans to the town's overlords, to be repaid from manorial dues of which the textile company soon supplied the lion's share, Allason increased the number of looms from 30 to 580 in eleven years, and established two bleacheries, a dye house and a finishing shop which processed the output of the whole area.

Allason's enterprise was imitated at Chřibska and Jirkov, and on the estates of Sluknov, Česká Kamenice, and Hanspach. In the development of major wool manufactories at Bela pod Bezdezem, Josefodol, Kladruby, Klášterec, Kosmonosy, Kralův Mestei, Krasna Lipa, Kuři, and Sloup, aristocratic entrepreneurs played a pre-eminent part. There were large-scale wool-finishing enterprises at Potštejn, Trutnov, and Horní Litvinov, where the Walstein works was established in 1715. By the 1770s this enterprise employed over four hundred people in various stages of yarn and cloth manufacture, supported by larger numbers of outworkers. Several of the processes were mechanized in the 1820s.

The Imperial estates fostered the development of textile industries in Slovakia, establishing a successful cotton manufactory at Sastin in 1736, which was sold to a private investor in 1754 and mechanized between 1792 and 1825. Emperor Franz Stepan established an earthenware manufactory at Holič, and Rudolf II had previously become involved in the saltworks at SOLIVAR. By the mid-eighteenth century, aristocratic enterprise was well established in mining and the iron industry and was later extended to sugar, machinery, porcelain, coal, steel and the railways. The Imperial economic commissioner Count Kinsky went so far as to break up his estates at Sloup and employ his subjects in manufactories and domestic work in glass and textiles.

These developments took place alongside the emergence of an Imperial industrial policy. While the Oriental Company of 1667–83 and the Development and Banking Commissions of the early eighteenth century bore little fruit in the context of recurrent military and fiscal crises, a programme of road and navigation improvements was instituted in the 1720s, including the Trieste–Breslau (Wrocław) highway, of which the Vienna–Brno section was completed by 1740.

The results of state-sponsored ventures in the eighteenth century were rather mixed. An attempt in 1749 to produce substitutes for imported fine woollens by transplanting Belgian weavers to the Moravian centre of the coarse woollen trade at Jihlava first fell foul of guild opposition and was subsequently plagued by unforeseen deficiencies in the quality of water, raw materials and labour when the project was resited in the remote Kladruby Castle on the Pardubice estate. Deep-seated problems of marketing and organization were never fully resolved, even after the factory's second move, in 1764, to Brno, and it closed in the 1790s, having exhausted its claims to subsidy. Nevertheless, the company's offshoots grew to make BRNO the major centre of the Empire's woollen industry in the nineteenth century.

The eighteenth century saw the re-emergence of scientific and technical education, promoted by the Jesuits at St Clement's College of Prague University in 1722, and at the Engineering School, founded in 1711, which also offered classes for craftsmen. A Slovak Mining Academy was established at Banská Štiavnica in 1735, and mining was also studied at Príbram and in Prague. The Bohemian Trade Exhibition, organized at Veltrusy Castle in 1754, was the first of a series of economic exhibitions, although

BIBLIOGRAPHY
Specific
Smith, D. L. *The Dalmellington Iron Company.* Newton Abbot:
David & Charles, 1967.

LOCATIONS
[I] Dalmellington and District Conservation Trust, Cathcartson
Interpretation Centre, Dalmellington, Strathclyde.
[I] Scottish Industrial Railway Centre, Minnivey Colliery, Burnton, Dalmellington, Strathclyde.

MARK WATSON

dam A means of diverting the flow of a natural waterway into an artificial channel, or of impounding it to control the outflow, for water-supply, irrigation, navigation or the generation of power. 'Gravity' dams impound water by their mass, the weight of earth, masonry or concrete being such that it withstands the pressure of the water behind it. Such dams have wide bases. The theoretical basis for building them was developed by M. de Sazilly in France in the 1850s. 'Arch' or 'buttress' dams depend on their shape to transmit the pressure of water to bedrocks capable of sustaining the load. An arch dam, which can only be built in a valley with solid natural walls, has a curving upstream face and transfers the pressure of the water to the sides of the valley. A buttress dam has buttresses on the downstream side to convey the pressure of the water to the foundations, and is sometimes called a 'hollow dam' from the appearance given by the buttresses. Arch dams were known in the Ancient World, and developed in Spain in the eighteenth century. The theory behind their construction was propounded by Émile Zola in France in the mid-nineteenth century. CONCRETE has been used for many of the largest twentieth-century dams.

A large dam built to increase the depth and to control the flow of a river may be termed a 'barrage'.

See also figure 165.

BIBLIOGRAPHY
General
Binnie, 1987; Burton and Dumbleton, 1928; Jackson, 1988; Smith, 1971.

BARRIE TRINDER

damask A reversible patterned fabric, usually plain-coloured, made from a variety of fibres although principally from linen, and used for bedclothes, clothing and furnishings. It was made on a draw loom, not the pedal loom employed for most other figured stuffs. The term originally applied to silk fabrics from Damascus, Syria, and is also applied to swords from Damascus combining steel and wrought iron.

BIBLIOGRAPHY
General
Kerridge, 1985; Montgomery, 1984.

dandy cart A four-wheeled railway wagon conveying a horse or horses. The cart is usually attached to the rear of a loaded downhill train on a GRAVITY RAILWAY, enabling the horse to be used to haul the empty train uphill to its starting point. Examples are preserved at YORK and at Portmadoc on the FESTINIOG RAILWAY.

Dannemora, Uppsala, Sweden The Dannemora mines lie in the northern part of the province of Uppland, 50 km (30 mi.) N. of Uppsala. Deposits of silver ore were discovered, probably in the second half of the fifteenth century. The earliest document relating to the mine, signed in 1481, granted the Archbishop of Sweden the right to a quarter of the silver mined at Dannemora. It was not, however, the silver, but the high quality of the iron ore that brought fame to the Dannemora mine. The iron ore is a magnetite containing between 30 and 50 per cent iron, encrusted in limestone. It also contains between 0.4 and 4.0 per cent manganese, and has low contents of sulphur and phosphorus. Dannemora came to be of great importance in the seventeenth century with the migration to Sweden of Walloon (*see* BELGIUM) ironworkers. The quality of the iron ore, combined with the methods used for smelting it into pig iron and for forging wrought iron from the pig iron, produced an iron of high quality, especially well suited for steelmaking.

The Dannemora mines belonged to the Crown but were acquired early in the eighteenth century by Walloon ironmasters, who used the ore almost exclusively at their own works. Until the mid-nineteenth century the export of iron ore was prohibited in Sweden. When this situation changed Dannemora ore was exported on a considerable scale, but recently the situation has again changed: Swedish ore is no longer competitive on world markets, and the closure of the Dannemora mine has been scheduled for 1992.

The iron-ore deposits are concentrated in an area over 3 km (2 mi.) long and 700 m (2300 ft.) wide, divided into three main fields. In total around eighty opencast mines have been in operation there. The largest opencast mine is Storrymningen, which is around 200 m (650 ft.) long. The known ore deposits are calculated to total some 300 million tonnes.

The mining landscape around Dannemora has been continuously transformed during five centuries, and its history is illustrated by various buildings and installations, and by the opencast pits. Of special interest is the steam engine house built by Mårten Triewald in the 1720s, which once held the first Newcomen engine in Sweden (*see* figure 34). The Dannemora steam engine was inaugurated in 1728 but was never a success. For a few years attempts were made to keep it working, but in 1736 the headstocks were dismantled and the Dannemora mines returned to traditional sources of power. Only one of the older wooden hoisting towers is preserved. The tall modern tower dates from the 1950s. Miners' dwellings from various periods can be seen in the vicinity of the mine. Some areas are no longer accessible because of the risks of subsidence.

At Österby bruk, 4 km (3 mi.) E. of Dannemora, is a WALLOON FORGE, the only one of its kind to be preserved in Sweden. It was rebuilt at the end of the eighteenth century and is equipped with two hearths and two water-driven

Figure 34 The engine house built to accommodate the Newcomen engine constructed by Mårten Triewald at Dannemora in 1728
Barrie Trinder

hammers. It ceased operation in 1906. Also preserved is a three-cylinder blowing engine of a type used at many Swedish ironworks in the nineteenth century. The bruk was established in the sixteenth century, and from 1633 was held by the de Geer family for more than a century. The manor house was built in the 1730s. Workers' houses, idyllically placed along the dam, date from the eighteenth century but have been enlarged.

See also figure 47.

BIBLIOGRAPHY
General
Nisser, 1979; Rydberg, 1981; Wahlund, 1879.

Specific
Lindqvist, S. *Technology on Trial: the introduction of power technology in Sweden, 1715–36.* Doctoral thesis, University of Uppsala, 1984.
Nisser, M. Forsmark-ett av vallonbruken kring Dannemora gruvor (Forsmark – a Walloon bruk dependent on the Dannemora mine). In *Forsmark och vallonjärnet*, Stockholm, 1987.

MARIE NISSER

Danube, River (Donau, Duna, Dunaj, Dunarea, Dunau, Dunav) Germany, Austria, Hungary, Yugoslavia, Romania, Bulgaria, Czechoslovakia   The Danube has been for centuries the commercial lifeline of Eastern Europe. It carries heavy sediments, is prone to flooding along many stretches, and was celebrated for its FLOATING MILLS. The construction of towing paths through the Carpathian Gorges (see IRON GATES) shows its importance in Roman times. Steam-boat services from Passau in Bavaria to the boundary of the Ottoman Empire at Orŝova were begun in the late 1820s by the Donau Dampfschiffahrt Gesellschaft (DDSG: see AUSTRIA). The Danube was linked with the Main and the Rhine by the King Ludwig I Canal from Bamberg to Kelheim, opened in 1845. The last tolls were abolished by the Treaty of Paris in 1856, which established a commission for the river. The International Danube Commission, set up by the Treaty of London in 1883, had greater powers and carried out programmes of dredging and other improvements (see IRON GATES). The international status of the river was confirmed by the Treaty of Versailles in 1919 and by the Statute of the Danube of 1922, but the river ceased to be open to the ships of all nations in the 1930s under the German Third Reich, and since 1948 only riparian states have been represented on the International Danube Commission. Locks have been enlarged since World War II; a new link to the Black Sea in Romania was opened in 1984; and a broad canal to the Rhine is under construction. A passenger service operates from Passau to Constanta.

See also AUSTRIA; BULGARIA; CZECHOSLOVAKIA; GERMANY; HUNGARY; ROMANIA; YUGOSLAVIA.

BIBLIOGRAPHY
General
Hadfield, 1986.

BARRIE TRINDER

Darby, Abraham (1678–1717) Abraham Darby, usually known as Abraham Darby I, was the founder of the 'dynasty of ironfounders' (Raistrick, 1953) which controlled the ironworks at Coalbrookdale (see IRONBRIDGE), Shropshire, for nearly two centuries. The son of a locksmith from the BLACK COUNTRY, he was apprenticed to a maker of malt mills in BIRMINGHAM, before moving in 1699 to BRISTOL, where he became a leading entrepreneur in the BRASS industry and began to operate an iron FOUNDRY. During the first decade of the eighteenth century he established brass and copper works at Coalbrookdale, in 1708 leasing a derelict blast furnace in which in 1709 he succeeded for the first time in smelting iron ore with coke rather than charcoal. He and his partners appear to have planned an integrated metalworking operation, smelting iron and copper and making brass at Coalbrookdale, while using water power at Tern, 8 km (5 mi.) E. of Shrewsbury, for ROLLING MILLS and BATTERY work. Their grand design was not realized but Darby established a flourishing iron foundry.

His son, Abraham Darby II (1711–63), was chiefly responsible for the great expansion in ironmaking which began in Shropshire in the 1750s and subsequently spread to other parts of Britain. His grandson, Abraham Darby III (1750–89), was chiefly responsible for building the Iron Bridge (see IRONBRIDGE). His great-grandson,

Abraham Darby IV (1805–78), was a major figure in the nineteenth-century British iron industry, having substantial interests in ironworks in South Wales, and introducing the manufacture of ART CASTINGS to the family's Coalbrookdale works.

BIBLIOGRAPHY
General
Raistrick, 1953; Trinder, 1981, 1991.
Specific
Cox, N. C. New Light on Abraham Darby I. In *IAR*, XII, 1990.

BARRIE TRINDER

Darmstadt, Hesse, Germany   The capital of southern Hesse was a centre for JUGENDSTIL architecture, examples of which are preserved in two industrial buildings: the Alter Jugendstil furniture factory, built by the architect Karl Klee in 1905, with concrete and iron construction behind a modernist façade; and the main railway station, designed by Friedrich Putzer and completed in 1912. The furniture factory is no longer used.

LOCATIONS
[M] Darmstadt Museum, Grosse Bachstrasse 2, 6100 Darmstadt.
[M] Eisenbahnmuseum (Railway Museum), Steinstrasse 7, 6100 Darmstadt.
[M] Porcelain Collection of the Grand Dukes, Prinz Georgs Palais, Schlossgarten, 6100 Darmstadt.

Dauphiné, France   Traditionally, the installation in 1869 of a 200 m (660 ft.) PENSTOCK at Lancey, 10 km (6 mi.) NE of Grenoble, by Aristide Bergès (1833–1904), is taken as marking the beginnings of the large-scale use of the hydro-electric potential of the mountain torrents of the French Alps, often known as 'white coal' (houille blanche). Bergès' penstock was destined to supply the turbine of the pulpmill of his paper factory. In fact the production of hydro-electric power became feasible only after Zénobe-Théophile Gramme (1826–1901) had perfected his dynamo, towards 1869, and after the means of transmitting high-voltage continuous current had been realized by Marcel Desprez: a 10 km (6 mi.) power line between Vizille and Grenoble, installed in 1883.

Between 1885 and 1898 sixteen waterfalls in the Dauphiné region were adapted for electricity production, representing an installed capacity of 5000 kW. One of the earliest plants was at Béconne, La-Roche-Saint-Secret, in the Drôme, 100 km (60 mi.) SW of Grenoble, an 80 kW station built in 1888 to provide power for lighting the nearby town of Dieulefit. The Cernon plant, near Chapareillan, 15 km (9 mi.) SE of Chambery, built in 1895 at the foot of a 625 m (2050 ft.) fall, and equipped with two Girard turbines, was already ten times as powerful, at 800 kW. In 1915 part of the first penstock of this plant, made of riveted plates, was replaced by a welded penstock, built by the Grenoble firm of Bouchayer and Viallet, pioneers of this technique.

The Engins power station, 5 km (3 mi.) W. of Grenoble, was the first to produce three-phase alternating current. This opened a new period in the development of hydroelectricity; between 1898 and 1930 some fifty-seven power stations were opened, with an installed capacity of 400 000 kW. From 1905 the raising of the voltage of the power-transmission lines enabled these to be extended, and grid networks to be opened, joining up local lines, and installing 60 000 V lines between regions, from 1910. Rapid growth was encouraged not only by the demand for lighting from towns but also by new electrochemical and electro-metallurgical industries, using low-voltage continuous current, close to the generating sites.

It was from 1888 at Froges, 20 km (12 mi.) NE of Grenoble, that Paul Héroult (1863–1914) was able to produce ALUMINIUM by decomposing alumina in an electric furnace. He went on to establish a works at La Praz, on the River Arc in Savoy, 20 km (12 mi.) E. of Saint-Jean-de-Maurienne. It was here that steel was obtained for the first time in an electric furnace. The process was soon taken up by the old-established steelworks at ALLEVARD, where the engineer Ernest Chaplet (1835–1909), recruited in 1904, had already designed an electric furnace for the production of steel alloys. Between 1905 and 1910 a whole new steel-production plant was opened, along with installations for producing alloys, equipped with fourteen furnaces working on the Chaplet system. Not far away, at Livet on the River Romanche, 40 km (25 mi.) SE of Grenoble, Charles Albert Keller, with some help from the Unieux ironworks at SAINT-ETIENNE, built a new steelworks with another electric furnace of his own design, in 1902–5.

Amongst the hydro-electric power stations of this period, several deserve special mention. The plant opened by Aristide's son, Maurice Bergès, at Verney, Allemont, on the Eau d'Olle, 50 km (30 mi.) E. of Grenoble, was built in 1910 to provide the town with electricity. Another station, built at La Ferrière on the Bréda, 10 km (6 mi.) S. of Allevard, was designed to provide power for the Lancey papermills. The Vernes plant of 1918 on the Romanche at Livet was built by C. A. Keller for his steelworks. Finally, the Saint-Guillerme power station, at Avris, on the Romanche, 60 km (37 mi.) SE of Grenoble, was built in 1929, and extended in 1935 when the Chambon dam was built.

The construction of this and other large dams, accompanied by the development of 150 000 volt transmission grids, led to the doubling of the region's installed capacity between 1930 and 1960. A new generation of reinforced-concrete power stations was built: among them the Sautet station of 1935 on the River Drac, 50 km (30 mi.) S. of Grenoble, and the Fond-de-France station of 1942 on the Bréda, 15 km (9 mi.) S. of Allevard.

There are significant remains on most of these sites. The pioneering power stations, such as the Béconne plant, were simple, rectangular buildings of traditional masonry construction, often with accommodation on the upper floors. At Cernon, a later and larger power station, the main building is one of the earliest to be equipped with an overhead travelling crane. The architecture of the power stations of the next period is more original. The generators, ranged in lines, imposed a pattern of long, narrow buildings, now always including an overhead crane. The window apertures are generally tall, with semicircular

arches. The development of high-voltage power lines led to the addition of distinct buildings housing the necessary transformers, often taking the shapes of towers, built up against the main generating halls. The Verney plant of 1910 is of this type, although the transformers are housed in a separate wing next to the generating hall. This power station was modernized in 1957, and although it retains many original elements, the La Ferrière power station of 1914 is far better preserved. Carefully constructed using local stone, with moulded concrete for the architraves, the framework of the roof is in wood. The transformer building is a tower, built up against the generator hall to form a symmetrical composition, with the chalet-style engineer's house on the opposite side, with its own vegetable garden. The generating hall is particularly well preserved, with brown and white floor tiling.

C. A. Keller's Vernes power station has a more monumental appearance. It is a three-storey structure, practically in the form of a cube, the transformer tower projecting very slightly from the front of the building. The result is a fortress-like façade, built in masonry, with details in moulded concrete. This was one of the first power stations to have a flat-metal-framed roof. The turbine chamber above the power station has a slight overhang, incorporating a decorative fountain, which is surrounded by a garden in the French style, with access by a double staircase.

The Saint-Guillerme plant of 1928–9 was the first Dauphiné power station in reinforced concrete. It was built by the Parisian firm, Campenon-Bernard. The building has a T-plan, its tall windows beneath a terrace roof giving it a certain elegance. It ceased to operate in 1983, but retains its four turbine-alternator sets, and all its internal transformer installations, located in the base of the T. Such installations are now rare, particularly since the development of large outdoor transformer installations in the 1930s.

At the historic site of Lancey, a 'white coal' museum was opened as early as 1925. It still has several turbines dating from the time of Aristide Bergès, and the penstocks are still in place. The museum, located in Bergès' former house, also holds some of the company's papermaking equipment, a pulp grinder, and an early-twentieth-century papermaking machine. The Bergès archives are also preserved.

The French national electricity company (Electricité de France) has recently opened another museum in the region, a collection of hydro-electric equipment, located near its new plant of Grand'Maison, and opened in 1985. Early twentieth-century turbines include examples by LESTER ALLEN PELTON, Francis and Neyret-Brenier, and there are also Gramme-type dynamos, automatic voltage regulators, switchboards and meters.

The neighbouring province of Savoy (Savoie) also makes extensive use of hydro-electric power. In particular it was the region where electrochemical and electro-metallurgical processes were pioneered, as at Praz (see above). In 1896 H. Gall built the Notre-Dame-de-Briançon works on the Isère, 20 km (12 mi.) S. of Albertville, for the production of calcium carbide, the same industrialist

200

having previously, in 1893, opened the works at Prémont, 15 km (9 mi.) E. of Saint-Jean-de-Maurienne, producing sodium and potassium chlorates. Finally, in 1909, Paul Girod opened the Ugine steelworks, 30 km (19 mi.) E. of Annecy. Following the Venthon steel alloy plant of 1900, this site utilized a new type of electric furnace. Many of the original elements of the Ugine site are still standing: the entrance pavilion, the office block, and a building known as the 'phalanstère', containing workers' accommodation and a dining hall. This works stimulated the development of one of the largest hydro-electric complexes in the French Alps: between 1904 and 1912 no fewer than seven power stations were built, three on the River Bonnant and four on the Arly. A huge artificial reservoir, 80 m (260 ft.) deep, the Girotte lake, was added in 1924, with a pumping station linked to the new Belleville power station, from which water is pumped back into the reservoir using electricity generated during off-peak periods.

See also ALLEVARD.

BIBLIOGRAPHY
General
Lyon-Caen and Ménégoz, 1989; Morsel, 1981; Veyret-Verner, 1948.
Specific
Benoît, S. De l'hydro-mécanique à l'hydro-électrique (From hydraulic power to hydro-electricity). In *La France des Electriciens 1880–1980* (The electricians' France, 1880–1980): proceedings of the second national colloquium of the Association for the History of Electricity in France. Paris: PUF 1986.
Le site de Lancey (The Lancey site). In *Actes du Ve colloque sur le patrimoine industriel, Alès, 1983*. Paris: CILAC, 1984.
Ménégoz, J. C. Quelques usines hydro-électriques anciennes des environs de Grenoble (Some old hydro-electric plants in the Grenoble region). In *Actes du Ve Colloque sur le patrimoine industriel, Alès, 1983*. Paris: CILAC, 1984.
Morsel, H. Les industries électrotechniques dans les alpes françaises du nord de 1869 à 1921 (The electro-technical industries in the northern French Alps, 1869–1921). In *Colloque, L'Industrialisation en Europe au XIXe siècle, Lyon, 1970*, Paris: CRNS, 1972.

LOCATIONS
[I] Hydrelec', Grand'Maison, BP 38114 Allemond.
[M] Musée de la Houille Blanche et de ses Industries (Museum of white coal and its industries), Lancey, 38190 Brignoud.

JEAN-FRANÇOIS BELHOSTE

Davies, David (1818–90) A Welsh industrialist from a humble background. He began as a sawyer in Llandinam, Powys; he was a railway contractor in mid-Wales in the 1850s; and he opened mines in the RHONDDA VALLEYS from 1864, establishing the first highly capitalized coal combine, Ocean Coal, in 1887. He promoted the BARRY Docks and Railway, completed in 1889, to break the Bute monopoly (*see* BUTE, JOHN). Davies became a millionaire and a Member of Parliament.

BIBLIOGRAPHY
General
Morgan, 1981.
Specific
Joby, R. S. *The Railway Builders: lives and works of the Victorian railway contractors*. Newton Abbot: David & Charles, 1983.
Thomas, I. *Top Sawyer: A biography of David Davies of Llandinam*. London, 1938.

Davos, Graubünden, Switzerland A resort on the River Landwasser which was canalized for the hydro-electric power station at Glaris, 9 km (6 mi.) SW, in the late 1890s. It is served by the metre-gauge Rhaetian Railway, whose lines include the 17 km (10 mi.) route from Klosters opened in 1890, of which 2.28 km (3.7 mi.) are in tunnels, including a series of spirals; and the 19 km (12 mi.) route from Filisur, of which 4.2 km are in a tunnel, and which includes the 210 m (690 ft.) concrete viaduct at Wiesen, 13 km (8 mi.) SW.

There is a mining museum in a former lead and zinc mine administration building at Schmelzboden, 4 km ($2\frac{1}{2}$ mi.) SW.

At Stein, 18 km (11 mi.) SW, near the road of 1696 that ascends to the Albula Pass, the remains of a blast furnace and its neighbouring forge were conserved in the 1970s.

BIBLIOGRAPHY
General
Allen, 1965; Baldinger, 1987

LOCATION
[M] Bergbaumuseum Graubünden, Schmelzboden, Davos.

Davy, Sir Humphry (1778–1829) One of the most distinguished of English scientists, Davy had a profound influence on industry. Born in CORNWALL, where he came to know the families of JOSIAH WEDGWOOD and JAMES WATT, he moved to London in 1801 to lecture on chemistry at the Royal Institution. At the same time as GEORGE STEPHENSON he developed a SAFETY LAMP for mines, announcing his discovery in 1815. He became President of the Royal Society in 1820, and encouraged the talents of Michael Faraday (1791–1867), the pioneer of electricity.

BIBLIOGRAPHY
General
Hartley, 1966.

Decazeville, Aveyron, France In 1826, at the instigation of the Duc Decazes, one of Louis XVIII's ministers, the Société des Houillères et Fonderies de l'Aveyron was founded to develop an ironworking complex, with blast furnaces, puddling furnaces and rolling mills, on the old Aubin coalfield. The town that grew up around the complex adopted its promoter's name in 1834. The site was completely modernized between 1895 and 1910 with the addition of steelmaking plant. It witnessed considerable prosperity during the 1950s but closed in 1977.

The site retains a large building housing two 250 hp Corliss-type blowing engines of 1901, built at LE CREUSOT. The shaft of a blast furnace, originally constructed at Le Creusot in 1929 and moved to Decazeville in 1959, was almost certainly the last surviving early-twentieth-century blast furnace in France. Coal mining at Decazeville ceased in 1966, but some of the surface installations remain. The blowing engines of 1901 have been afforded legal protection but a campaign to save the blast furnace proved unsuccessful.

BIBLIOGRAPHY
General
Guiollard, 1989; Reid, 1985.

Delaware, United States of America   Unlike most states, a single industrial species marks the place of Delaware in the annals of American technological enterprise. While known for its production of heavy machinery and chickens, Delaware's fame is tied chiefly to the manufacture of synthetic materials, originally explosives.

The refining and mixing of sulphur, saltpetre and charcoal into black powder is today enshrined at Elutherian Mills, a bucolic setting of gardens and mill buildings along the Brandywine River north of Wilmington, the principal city. From 1802 black powder mills under the ownership of the duPont family have operated along the Brandywine, serving the needs of the world's military and the construction industry. The du Pont company played a key role in the development of NYLON in the 1930s and 40s. The company remains one of the area's chief employers, and a giant in the chemicals industry. The Elutherian site and the adjacent Hagley Museum embrace a collection of thick-walled mill structures, water-power systems, and a re-created machine shop of the 1870s. Adjoining the Hagley Museum is one of the nation's premier library-archives in industrial history.

Bisecting Delaware and connecting Chesapeake Bay with the estuary of the Delaware River is the Chesapeake & Delaware ship canal of 1829. The completion of the Erie Canal a few years earlier had threatened to make New York the centre of trade with the West, but with the completion of the C&D Canal, new access to Philadelphia markets and manufacturers became available to Maryland and Virginia. The canal remains an active waterway, owned by the federal government and maintained by the Army Corps of Engineers.

Of some three dozen covered bridges that once stood in Delaware, two remain, the largest the 22 m (72 ft.) lattice-truss bridge of 1860 over Red Clay Creek at Wooddale.

See also figures 99, 100.

BIBLIOGRAPHY
General
Thomas, 1975.

LOCATION
[M,S] Hagley Museum and Library, PO Box 3630, Wilmington, DE 19807.

DAVID H. SHAYT

Delft, Zuid Holland, The Netherlands   One of the most beautiful towns in Europe, a classic example of a Grachtenstad, a town built around canals on reclaimed land, with a vast marketplace. The Oude Delft canal is spanned by a small iron bridge. The town centre is bounded on three sides by the provincial canal from Rotterdam to The Hague ('s-Gravenhage), opened in 1893. To the north of the centre on the line of the old fortifications is the tall 'De Roos' windmill. Delft is linked with The Hague by tramway as well as by trains from the onion-domed station.

The Delft potteries gained great repute in the seventeenth and eighteenth centuries, and the term 'Delftware' was applied to certain types of fine earthenware wherever they were made. The industry declined in the nineteenth century, but was subsequently revived, and three potteries are now operating, all open to the public. Delft pottery is displayed in the Van Meerten museum. The development of electricity and telecommunications is portrayed at a study centre at the Technical University. The Technical Exhibition Centre has a valuable collection of internal combustion engines.

The vast and largely complete yeast and spirits factory developed from 1870 dominates the area north of the centre. There is an impressive entrance hall in the main office building. Its owner, J. C. van Marken (1845–1906), formed a BUILDING SOCIETY in 1883 to develop the GARDEN SUBURB of Agneta Park, west of the railway and north of the station, the principal GARDEN CITY style development in the Netherlands. The first phase, built before 1905, consists of eighty brick cottages with steeply pitched roofs, built along a circular drive. A second stage of 1926 consists of terraces with banded windows set in sloping tiled roofs, grouped around a tree-lined lake, with communal buildings in the same style.

BIBLIOGRAPHY
General
Meakin, 1905; Ottevanger *et al.*, 1985.

LOCATIONS
[M] Electro-Technology Study Centre, Mekelweg 4, Delft.
[M] Museum Huis Lambert van Meerten, Oude Delft 199, Delft.
[M] Technisch Tentoonstelling Centrum (Technical Exhibition Centre), Rotterdamseweg 139a, Delft.

BARRIE TRINDER and JURRIE VAN DALEN

Delftware   A type of fine earthenware, named after the Dutch town of Delft and characterized by a fine blue glaze on a bluish-white ground. It is likely that it developed in the late fifteenth century as the Dutch sought to imitate Chinese and Japanese porcelain; the industry took off on a large scale about 1650. Delftware was made in England from the early seventeenth century, the chief centres of production being Lambeth, Bristol, Liverpool, Brislington and Wincanton.

BIBLIOGRAPHY
General
Garner and Archer, 1948; Searle, 1929, 1929–30.

delinting machine   The COTTON GIN cuts the longest fibre (called lint) away from the seed. This cotton is then pressed, baled and used for textile production. Some cotton seed retains a short, thick undergrowth that can be removed and utilized. These fibres are shorn by a linter or delinting machine which works like a cotton gin. These short fibres (also called linters) are used for making paper and surgical supplies, and, more importantly, as the basis of chemical cotton, the primary ingredient in the production of cellulose derivatives used in explosives, plastics, photographic film, paints, lacquers, synthetic fibres and fabric finishes. As with flax, the cotton seed is crushed to make oil, and the seed hull is pressed into cake for livestock feed. Cottonseed oil and cotton linters are often produced in the same plants.

Denmark   'You mastered England once and overran it, ruled all the North – but now men say you wane', wrote Hans Christian Andersen (1805–75) in 1850. The political history of Denmark in modern times is one of diminution. In 1658 the provinces east of the Sound were ceded to Sweden. After the Treaty of Vienna of 1814 1s Denmark's union with Norway was broken. In 1864 the Duchies of Schleswig and Holstein were annexed by Prussia, although a plebiscite in 1920 returned the northern part of Schleswig to Denmark. Iceland gained its independence from Denmark in 1943.

Denmark forms a land bridge between the Scandinavian peninsula and Central Europe, with the Baltic to the east and the North Sea to the west. The country has the distinctive character of an archipelago. The topography has largely been shaped by glacial action: a hilly landscape created by glacial moraines in the east, and a flat lowland consisting of glacial outwash plains in the west. Accordingly clay, sand, peat and in some places easily accessible chalk constitute the main mineral resources. The only exceptions from this generalization are the islands, Bornholm in the Baltic, and the Faeroe islands and Greenland in the North Atlantic.

The population of Denmark proper is 5.1 million, within an area of about 43 000 km² (16 600 sq. mi.). A bold estimate places the population in 1650 at about half a million. The official census of 1801 showed a population of 900 000; that of 1840, 1.3 million; that of 1901, 2.4 million. Most people regard Denmark as a predominantly agricultural country, and this was certainly so for a long period. Nevertheless industry has old roots. As early as 1800 more than 10 000 were engaged in manufactures. In 1840 industry and crafts accounted for 17 per cent of the gross national product, and about 1930 this sector took the lead from agriculture. Today the agricultural sector is reduced to about 5 per cent of gross national product, whereas industry accounts for about 20 per cent, after reaching a maximum of 30 per cent in 1962.

The earliest Danish industry was flint mining, and several mines of the Neolithic period have been excavated in North Jutland. The Iron Age gave birth to a new industry, the smelting of iron from bog ores, mainly in the western part of Jutland. Since Denmark was an archipelago shipping formed a central part of the lives of its people

Denmark

from earliest times. Remains of boats of the Mesolithic period have been discovered. A remarkable group of five Viking ships has been recovered near ROSKILDE and recently remains of a shipyard of the Viking age have been excavated on Falster island.

Wind- and water-power were widely used from the Middle Ages, chiefly for grinding grain. From the sixteenth century growing numbers of water mills were converted and used in the manufacture of textiles, iron and paper. The importance of wind- and water-power was increased by innovations in the late eighteenth century, particularly by the introduction of an extra gear in water mills, and by the building of new and more effective Dutch-style windmills. Further improvements, including the substitution of iron for wooden gearing, and the use of water turbines and self-regulating devices, were introduced from the mid-nineteenth century. Peak numbers of 2700 windmills and 900 water mills were recorded *c*.1900. At the same time Danish milling technology reached its zenith, with several pioneering aerodynamic studies by Poul la Cour, amongst others. Nevertheless in subsequent decades mills lost ground, chiefly to electric power. The energy crisis of the 1970s revived interest in wind power, and building upon the traditions of the early years of the century, Danish manufacturers gained a substantial share of the world market for windmills.

The first large manufacturing complexes were designed to meet the military needs of the state. In the years after 1550 the naval dockyards were established in COPENHAGEN, and north of the capital, at Ørholm, the king ordered the construction of a GUNPOWDER mill. Mercantilist policies were initiated in the seventeenth century in the reign of King Christian IV (1596–1648). Among the king's projects, many of them Dutch-inspired, were the construction of the Exchange and the establishment of woollen cloth and silk manufactories in Copenhagen. At Hellebæk near HELSINGØR a factory for small arms was established, and at MØLLEÅEN, north of Copenhagen, several old corn mills were converted to make gunpowder, copper wares, guns and paper.

A new wave of mercantilist policies swept the country from the mid-eighteenth century. Through gifts, loans, grants of monopolies and high import duties the state sought to promote native industry by encouraging the immigration of foreign entrepreneurs and skilled workers. In spite of disappointments the policy also brought many successful results. It was assisted by contemporary reforms in Danish agriculture, and by the booming overseas trade of the Copenhagen merchant houses. Among the larger new concerns was the iron, non-ferrous metals and gunpowder works at FREDERIKSVÆRK on Zealand (Sjælland). The most important growth sector was the textile industry. Woollen cloth, silk and cotton factories mushroomed, especially in Copenhagen. There were also notable developments in papermaking, sugar refining, the tobacco industry, glove making and ship-building. The first Danish steam engine was built and installed by an immigrant Scotsman in 1790 in the naval dockyard.

Nevertheless, in 1807, the year in which Denmark became involved on the French side in the Napoleonic Wars, Danish manufactures were still of an essentially pre-industrial character. During the war the English captured the Danish fleet, and in 1814 the Norwegian market was lost to Danish exporters. Among the few bright spots in the following decades was the Education Act of 1814 which introduced compulsory primary education between the ages of seven and thirteen. At a different level, the Technical University of Denmark was established in 1829, its first director being H. C. Ørsted, who in 1820 had discovered the strange power of electromagnetism.

From about 1840 the hard times yielded to a new wave of prosperity, due largely to growing exports of grain to Western Europe in a period of steadily rising prices. Progress in agriculture stimulated urban trades and industrial development. From that time Danish industry grew steadily, its progress only interrupted by short, temporary setbacks. The period up to the mid-1860s was marked by development in depth of new industries using new methods of production, mostly English-inspired. The dominance of textiles gave way to a more diversified industrial structure, with the establishment of FOUNDRIES and engineering works in nearly every Danish town, and the expansion of brickmaking, clothing manufacture and printing.

The new industries were linked closely to the diffusion of steam power which had been installed in distilleries, sawmills, foundries and engineering works by 1850, and in the 1850s spread to corn mills, weaving mills, printing works, breweries and the larger shipyards. The adoption of steam power went together with the introduction of new machinery: standard machine tools in engineering works, power looms, and cylinder presses in printing works.

The steady growth of Danish industry continued, even during the agricultural crises of the 1880s. The range of industries was widened with the growth of a modern hosiery industry and the establishment of sugar mills in the 1870s, but the most important development of this period was the founding of a strong trade union movement, which gained a firm foothold from the 1880s.

From the mid-1890s several radical innovations marked the start of a new upswing, often called the Second Industrial Revolution. Again industrial development was characterized by new production methods, new materials and new products. Most of the innovation now came from the USA and Germany. A variety of new power sources gradually replaced the old stationary steam engines. Most important were the electric motor, and petrol and diesel engines. Larger factories installed their own electricity plants, while smaller concerns took the new energy from public power stations whose networks of lines covered the country by 1914. Partly as a result of these changes new production methods were adopted with astonishing speed: milling machines and automatic lathes in engineering works, automatic looms in textile factories, typesetting in the printing trades, and refrigeration in food and drink manufacture.

Among the new industries dairies and bacon factories

grew rapidly in the late 1880s and early 1890s, due partly to the dramatic fall in grain prices in the 1880s caused by overseas competition, and partly to the invention of the continuous cream separator in 1878 by the Danish engineer L. C. Nielsen. Farmers reacted to the crisis by specializing in the production of butter and bacon, mostly for the British market. As a result by 1890 Denmark had a network of about 1200 dairies. The rapid expansion of bacon factories came a little later, but in 1900 there were about fifty in operation throughout the country.

The most characteristic new trades were the electric and electronic industries. Besides hundreds of power stations, many new and old factories began to make electric equipment, cables, electric motors, generators, dry cells, vacuum cleaners and the like. In the electronics sector the manufacture of telephone instruments and exchange equipment boomed, and in the 1920s factories producing radios were established.

The most important new constructional materials were steel and PORTLAND CEMENT, often brought together in the form of reinforced concrete. Most of the steel was imported, although Burmeister & Wain established the first Danish steelworks in 1906 with a small OPEN-HEARTH FURNACE. Production of Portland cement began in 1860, but the breakthrough came in the 1890s with the building of several large cement plants near Mariager and ÅLBORG in North Jutland. The firm of F. L. Smidth & Co. specialized in the building of cement plants in Denmark and abroad, and from 1898 had their own engineering works in Copenhagen. Several Danish contracting and engineering concerns specialized in reinforced concrete and in the following decades built many bridges, docks and piers in all parts of the world.

Developments in transport also gave birth to new products and industries. By 1900 several mechanical workshops were exporting petrol engines for fishing boats and small cargo ships. In 1912 Burmeister & Wain launched the first oceangoing motor vessel, the *Selandia*. The first Danish motorcars were built in the late 1880s, but in the 1920s several foreign firms such as Ford and General Motors established assembly line factories in Copenhagen to supply the Nordic and Baltic Markets.

Shipping continued to be important in the period of industrialization. Most Danish cities are ports, and improved harbour facilities were crucial for their growth. In 1868 the export harbour at ESBJERG was founded to stimulate direct trade with Britain. Another big step was taken in the 1890s with the building of a free harbour in Copenhagen to strengthen the capital's position as the main entrepôt for the Baltic. The first STEAMSHIP, the British-built *Caledonia*, began to trade between Copenhagen and KIEL in 1819. From 1912 the number of MOTOR VESSELS using the port grew rapidly, and in 1937 the tonnage of the motor fleet exceeded that of the steam fleet.

Denmark's first railway from Copenhagen to Roskilde was opened in 1847. The country's first iron bridge, Frederiksbroen in ODENSE, was built in 1844 to serve road traffic. In the following decades railway construction gave rise to the building of many notable bridges. Among the most significant were six reinforced concrete bridges crossing the line from Copenhagen to Helsingør, built in the 1890s, an early steel bridge of 1894 at Langelinje in Copenhagen, and two large steel bridges of the 1930s, the Little Belt Bridge (Lillebæltsbroen) between Funen and Jutland (Jylland), and the 3.2 km (2 mi.) Storestrømsbroen, connecting Zealand and Falster, the longest in Europe at the time.

Protection of selected secular buildings by the state began in 1918. The possibility of protecting the country's industrial heritage was strengthened by the Preservation of Buildings Act 1979, whose purpose is to protect the country's older buildings of architectural, historical and environmental value. The Act explicitly includes buildings that shed light on housing and working conditions and on the means of production. The administration of the law is the responsibility of the National Agency for Physical Planning (Planstyrelsen), in collaboration with owners, local authorities and country museums. The new possibilities have been exploited only to a limited extent: only about 10 per cent of the 3600 listed buildings relate to the industrial heritage, the majority of them water mills, windmills and warehouses.

In addition to these efforts, several provincial cities since 1960 have prepared local registration and conservation plans in co-operation with the National Museum and the National Agency for Physical Planning. A nationwide register of Danish factories was implemented in the 1970s and early 80s, with the support of the Research Council for the Humanities. The records are kept by the National Museum. The National Archives of Trade and Economy in ÅRHUS has rich collections of documents from various business concerns. In addition, several national and local bodies support the preservation of the industrial heritage. To some extent the different initiatives are co-ordinated by the Danish Association for the Study and Preservation of the Industrial Heritage, founded in 1979. Since 1970 there has been a growing interest in this field, with the founding of many new museums and the preservation of numbers of monuments. Museums of national status include the National Museum at Brede, north of Copenhagen (*see* MØLLEÅEN); THE TECHNICAL MUSEUM IN HELSINGØR; the Museum of Workers, Craftsmen and Industry in HORSENS, established in 1977; and the Workers' Museum in Copenhagen, opened in 1983. Recently many local history museums have shown some awareness of the industrial heritage.

A respectable number of mills has survived, due in large measure to the enthusiastic work of Anders Jespersen, an internationally recognized Danish expert on mills. Today fifty-eight windmills and forty water mills are protected by law, and six water mills and seven windmills remain in open-air museums. Many old warehouses are preserved, both in Copenhagen and in the provincial cities, where most of them were used for storing grain. Brewing in the industrial age is portrayed in the Carlsberg Museum in Copenhagen, and in Hobro and Fjerritslev in Jutland. Old dairies are preserved at Hjedding and Hjerl Hede in Jutland. The open-air museum in Århus houses an old tobacco factory and a steam-powered textile mill. Other main centres for textiles are the National Museum and the hosiery museum at Herning, Jutland. The numerous printing works are dealt with at the Graphic Museum in ODENSE, which also covers aspects of the paper industry. Old paperboard mills are preserved at Klostermølle near SILKEBORG, and at Brunnshåb near VIBORG.

Industries based on minerals or quarried materials became increasingly important during the industrial period. One of the few remaining brickworks with an open one-chamber kiln has been moved to the open-air museum at ODENSE. An early HOFFMAN KILN is preserved at NIVÅ, north of Copenhagen, and a further brick and tileworks conservation project has taken place in the Egernsund area of South Jutland. A glass museum has been established at the HOLMEGÅRD works on Zealand. Old limestone mines have been preserved at Mønsted and Daugbjerg in Jutland, and on Zealand limestone quarries can be visited at Stevns and Faxe. There are several quarries exploiting the hard rocks of Bornholm, in one of which is a museum illustrating their history. In the North Atlantic there are some remains of the coal mines once worked on the Faeroe Islands, while CRYOLITE and zinc ores have been worked on Greenland.

Several conservation projects are concerned with metals and engineering, industries that are extensively featured in the museums at Helsingør and Horsens. At Hellebæk near HELSINGØR is a well-preserved small-arms factory colony of the eighteenth century. The history of the foundry trade is treated in a company museum at Nykøbing Mors, Jutland, and an ongoing project aims to preserve the eighteenth-century foundry at FREDER-IKSVÆRK. The Burmeister & Wain company has its own museum illustrating the development of diesel engines. Several other petrol and diesel engines are displayed in the fishing and shipping museums in Esbjerg, Hirtshals and Grenå, all in Jutland. Electricity has its own museum in the hydro-electric power station at Tange, Jutland, which still operates; while the main theme of the Technical Museum in Ålborg is telecommunications.

As in most countries the transport revolution has received much attention, the principal transport museums being the Technical Museum and the Danish Maritime Museum, both in Helsingør. Viking ships are displayed in ROSKILDE. Naval history is recorded in museums at Valdemar Slot, to the south of Funen (Fünen, Fyn), and in Copenhagen. Coastal shipping is the main theme of the museum in Marstal to the south of Funen, and of those at Esbjerg, Hirtshals and Grenå. The 3046-tonne motor ferry *Zealand* (formerly *Queen Ingrid*) of 1951 is preserved in the port of Copenhagen. The central railway museum has been established by the Danish State Railways (DSB) at Odense and several local voluntary bodies operate lines at Helsingør, Bandholm on Lolland, and Bryrup in Jutland. Privately-owned museums of motorcars have been established at Nærum near Copenhagen, Ålholm on Lolland, Egeskov on Funen, and Gjern in Jutland. A current project is intended to establish a national museum of aviation at BILLUND.

Danish industrial development took place over a wide front, without dominating leading sectors. This pattern was shaped by the country's special position with regard to markets and raw materials. Until the 1950s Danish manufacturers worked principally for the home market, using imported raw materials. These features have also been the main factors dictating the location of industry. The majority of factories are in the old cities, which were centrally located in the transport network and offered concentrations of markets, workforce and capital. By far the most important industrial region is Copenhagen, where about half of Danish industry has been located. Next come the large provincial cities of Odense, Århus and Ålborg.

Some deviations from this general pattern should be noted. Most of the old water-powered mills are in rural locations, and most of the older dairies and bacon factories were built near their suppliers, typically one or two dairies to each parish, and a bacon factory to each county. The textile area around Herning in Jutland is also exceptional, since the many hosiery factories developed from a flourishing domestic manufacture, based on local supplies of wool. Extractive industries based on local resources – the Portland cement works in North Jutland, the concentrations of brickworks north of Copenhagen and around Steenstrup in the south of Funen, and Egernsund in South Jutland – represent further exceptions, as do the mines and quarries of Bornholm, the Faeroes and Greenland.

See also ÅLBORG; ÅRHUS; BILLUND; BORNHOLM; COPENHAGEN; ESBJERG; FAEROE ISLANDS; FREDERIKSVÆRK; GREENLAND; HELSINGØR; HERNING; HJEDDING; HOLMEGÅRD; HORSENS; LILLEBÆLTSBROEN; LOLLAND-FALSTER; MØLLEÅEN; NIVÅ; ODENSE; ROSKILDE; SILKEBORG; SONDERBORG; VIBORG.

BIBLIOGRAPHY
General
Boje, 1979; Cipolla, 1970; Fabrik og Bolig, 1979–; Hansen, 1970, 1972–74; Hyldtoft et al., 1981; Hyldtoft, 1984; Johansen, 1987, 1988; Milward and Saul, 1973; Nielsen, 1943–4; Sestoft, 1979.

Specific
Christensen, J. *Rural Denmark 1750–1980*. Odense.
Ejlersen, T. Møller og møllebevaring (Mills and the protection of mills). In *Nationalmuseets Arbejdsmark*, 1984.
Frednings-styrelsen. Fredede bygninger 1983 (Protected buildings, 1983). Copenhagen, 1983.
Erhvervshistorisk Årbog (Yearbook of Business History), 1949–.
Hyldtoft, O. Medvandkraft, dampmaskine og gasmotor (Power engines in Danish industry 1840–1897). In *Erhvervshistorisk Årbog*, 1987.
Såby, L. *A Guide to the Preservation of Buildings in Denmark*. Copenhagen, 1984.
Strømstad, P. ed. *Mennesket og maskinen* (Man and machine). Copenhagen, 1980.
Willersley, R. *Studier i dansk industrihistorie 1850–1880* (Studies in Danish industrial history 1850–1880). Copenhagen, 1980.

LOCATIONS
[I] Erhvervsarkivet (Business Archives), Vester Alle 12, 8000 Århus C.
[I] National Agency for Physical Planning (Planstyrelsen), Haraldsgade 53, 2100 Copenhagen Ø.
[M] National Museum, Third Department, Brede, 2800 Lyngby.

OLE HYLDTOFT

Denniston, Nelson, New Zealand A coalfield, on a

plateau 20 km ($12\frac{1}{2}$ mi.) W. of Westport. Denniston Incline, designed by Henry and Robert Young, is a self-acting railway incline almost 2 km ($1\frac{1}{2}$ mi.) long, with a gradient at its steepest of 1 in 3.4. The incline descends 550 m (1800 ft.), with twenty-six changes in grade. It was built in 1878–80 and closed in 1967. The brake drum and wagon from the incline are now at Coaltown (*see* WESTPORT).

BIBLIOGRAPHY
General
Thornton, 1982.

LOCATION
[M] Coaltown Mining Museum, Queen Street South, PO Box 216, Westport.

department store A large shop, whose nature is difficult to define. The various departments are always strongly identified. Stores are usually located in multi-storey buildings, and most are the creations of individualist entrepreneurs. The first, in the mid-nineteenth century, emphasized cheapness; subsequent examples became synonymous with luxury. Some evolved from drapery stores, one of the archetypes being Bon Marché, Paris, developed by Aristide Boucicaut from 1852, and copied in Brixton, London, in 1877, its name later being used for shops of all kinds throughout Britain. In London, Harrods developed from a Brompton grocer's shop, and the Army & Navy Stores from a military wine co-operative. The GUM store in Moscow was constructed in 1888–93 on a site previously covered by shacks and stalls.

Stock is departmentalized, but the general management system is centralized, with many common services. Department stores made expensive goods accessible, as they had not been in earlier retailing systems. Some rivalled the best museums in their attention to detailed presentation, Wanamaker's New York store of 1907 having a Louis XIV room for gowns, an oak room for antiques, and a French room for lingerie.

The chief period of growth was between 1890 and 1914. The first ELEVATOR in a department store was installed in the E. V. Haughwout store on Broadway, New York, in 1857, and by 1900 almost every department store had them. Plate-glass windows became universal, and interiors owed much to contemporary exhibition design. Many stores, like Galeries Lafayette in Paris and Liberty in LONDON, had light wells lit by domes and surrounded by galleries. The New York stores, Macy's and Wanamaker's, and Marshall Field of Chicago, were influential in both Europe and North America. The store of 1901–4 by Louis Sullivan (1856–1924) for Carson Pirie Scott & Co. in Chicago is architecturally one of the most distinguished department stores. Outstanding examples in Germany and Russia are Tietz (now Kaufhof), Düsseldorf, of 1907, by Joseph Olbricht (1867–1908); and the Muir & Merrilies store of 1908–10 on Petrovka Street, Moscow, by R. I. Klein, in which huge areas of plate glass are incorporated into a traditional Russian Gothic design.

The goods sold in department stores are well illustrated in reprinted catalogues.

See also figure 89.

BIBLIOGRAPHY
General
Adburgham, 1969, 1972, 1974, 1975; Ferry, 1960; Gibbons, 1926; Harrods, 1949; Hower, 1943; Jeffreys, 1954; Kirichenko, 1977; Lambert, 1938; Marrey, 1979; Pasdermadjam, 1954; Pevsner, 1976; Pound, 1960; Strohmeyer, 1980; Wendt and Cogan, 1952; Wiene, 1912.
Specific
Harris, N. Museums, merchandising and popular taste: the struggle for influence. In Quimby, 1978.
Porter, J. H. The development of the provincial department store 1870–1939. In *Business History*, XII, 1971.
Ullrich, R. M. Les Grands Magasins: Pariser Ingenieurarchitektur der zweiter Halfte des 19 Jahrhunderts (Les Grands Magasins: Parisian civil engineering architecture in the second half of the nineteenth century). ICOMOS, 1982.

BARRIE TRINDER

Derby, Derbyshire, England A county town, on the River Derwent, the hub of the Midland Railway system. The silk mill of Thomas Lombe (1685–1739), *c*.1717, was the first textile factory in Britain. Destroyed by fire in 1910, it was rebuilt to similar dimensions with three instead of five storeys. It is now a museum, with important sections on framework knitting, Rolls-Royce aero engines and the Midland Railway. Workers' houses of the 1840s built by Midland Railway near the station have been restored. At Darley Abbey, 3 km (2 mi.) N., there are cotton mills built by Thomas Evans from 1783, with terraces, CLUSTER HOUSES and a school of 1826, of unusual elegance.

BIBLIOGRAPHY
Specific
Peters, D. *Darley Abbey*. Hartington: Moorland, 1974.

LOCATION
[M] Derby Industrial Museum, The Silk Mill, Full Street, Derby DE1 3AR.

Derry, Northern Ireland *See* LONDONDERRY.

design registration The process of registering a design is distinct from, but closely connected with, the granting of a PATENT. Design registration usually grants to a manufacturer protection against copying for a limited period, and an identification mark will normally appear on the product itself.

In Britain legislation of 1787, 1794 and 1839 was concerned chiefly with designs for textiles, but the Copyright of Design Act 1842 provided for the registration of metal, wooden, earthenware and paper goods as well as textiles, and initiated the use of a diamond mark, indicating the date of registration. Legislation was consolidated in 1949. Records before 1910 are kept at the Public Record Office, and later examples in the Patent Offices in London and Salford.

BIBLIOGRAPHY
General
Boehm, 1967; Davenport, 1979; Myrant, 1977.
Specific
Jones, I. *Design Registration Marks*. Telford: Ironbridge Gorge
Museum Trust, 1981.

LOCATIONS
[I] Patents Office, Baskerville House, Browncross Street, New
Bailey Street, Salford M3 55U.
[I] Patents Office Library, 25 Southampton Buildings, London
WC2A 1AY.
[I] Public Record Office, Ruskin Avenue, Kew, Richmond, Surrey
TW9 4DU.

BARRIE TRINDER

detergents   Complex organic chemicals, such as alkyl-
benzenesulphonates or ethyoxylates, that can be used
instead of soap without forming a sticky and clinging
'scum'. Detergents are usually mixed with sodium sulphate and inorganic phosphates. The principle was
known in the nineteenth century, and sodium dodecylsul-
phate was used in the 1930s, but the vast increase in
production came only after 1950.

BIBLIOGRAPHY
General
Norman and Waddington, 1977.

Detmold, North Rhine-Westphalia, Germany   A small
town, once the capital of a principality, 26 km (16 mi.) SE
of Bielefeld. Detmold is the location of one of Germany's
most ambitious open-air museums, opened on an 80 ha
(200 ac.) site in 1971. The museum is dominated by vast
and magnificent Westphalian farmhouses, but also
includes woodworking workshops and a pottery, as well
as windmills and water mills, mileposts, and evidence
within the farmhouses of domestic textile manufactures.

BIBLIOGRAPHY
General
Baumeier, 1983; Zippelius, 1974.

LOCATION
[M] Westfälisches Freilichtmuseum bäuerlicher Kulturdenkmale
(Westphalian Open-Air Museum of Rural Culture and Monu-
ments), Krummes Hause, 493 Detmold.

Deutschfeistritz, Styria, Austria   *See* PEGGAU.

Deutsch-Wagram, Lower Austria, Austria   A town 16
km (10 mi.) NE of Vienna, the site of a battle in 1809 and
the terminus of the first section of the Nordbahn, opened
in 1837. There is a museum of railway relics at the
station; a pumping house of 1846 supplied water for
locomotives. A large collection of locomotives is preserved
at Strasshof, 8 km (5 mi.) NE.

LOCATIONS
[I] 'l.Osek', Heizhaus, Strasshof.
[M] Regional Museum, Gemeindeamt, Bahnhofstrass, 2232
Deutsch-Wagram, Bezirk Ganserndorf.

devil   A machine with sharp teeth, particularly one with
toothed cylinders, used for separating and cleaning fibres
in the first stages of processing wool, flax, hemp and
cotton (*see* TEXTILES), or for tearing up cloth to reduce it to
SHODDY. Also called a willower or willy, and, in the USA, a
picker.

diamond   A form of carbon, found as stones. It is likely
that these were formed in or forced into 'pipes': deep,
vertical, rock-filled holes, 200–600 m (650–1950 ft.)
across, which pierce the surrounding rocks. The pipe fill is
called 'blue ground'; this alters at the surface to a yellow
friable earth. Diamonds are mined directly from pipes and
also from alluvial deposits, the source of which must have
been pipes either eroded or yet to be discovered.

Diamonds were first brought to Europe from India, then
from Brazil after 1725, and from Australia in the
nineteenth century. The most productive localities are
now in southern Africa and the USSR. Pipes are worked to
as great a depth as possible by open pits, before underground techniques, chambering and, later, caving
methods are employed.

In ALLUVIAL MINING material is excavated, washed, and
sieved before stones are picked from the concentrate,
sometimes by hand and sometimes by a process that
exploits the fact that diamond, unlike most minerals, has a
greater affinity for grease than for water. X-ray beams,
which cause diamonds to fluoresce with a characteristic
blue light, are also used.

Apart from their popular use in jewellery and ornaments, diamonds are widely used in industry for cutting
and grinding. The chief cities in which they have been cut
are Amsterdam, London, Antwerp and New York.

An early diamond-mining centre is preserved in Pike's
County, Arkansas, the only diamond field in the USA.

BIBLIOGRAPHY
General
McLintock, 1983; Webster, 1983.

IVOR J. BROWN

Diderot, Denis (1713–84)   A polymath of the Enlightenment, whose encyclopedia magnificently portrays
French manufactures on the eve of the Industrial Revolution. In a climate of censorship, Diderot conveyed ideas of
progress and liberalism through his accounts of technology as a series of rational processes. His plates, which
have been widely reproduced, are of uneven quality; the
best, like those depicting glass manufacture and iron
smelting, are of outstanding value, although they show
French practice of the mid-eighteenth century, not technologies that were universal before the Industrial Revolu-

Figure 35 One of the illustrations of papermaking from a volume of Denis Diderot's *Encyclopédie*, published in 1765: the picture shows a shop in which ragpickers sorted materials from the pile of waste marked D into grades in the bins marked A, B and C. Diderot's illustrations were based on practices at CHÂLETTE-SUR-LOING.

tion. Many of the most important technical plates were borrowed, in slightly redrawn forms, from a similar undertaking begun by the French Académie des Sciences much earlier in the century. Most of the Academy's work was published between 1761 and 1788 under the title *Descriptions des Arts et Métiers*, by various authors.

BIBLIOGRAPHY
General
Bibliothèque Nationale, 1951; Cole and Watts, 1952; Diderot, 1751–77, 1959; Lough, 1954; Moreau, 1990; Wilson, 1957.

BARRIE TRINDER and HELENA WRIGHT

diesel engine A version of the OIL ENGINE, developed in 1892 by Rudolph Diesel (1858–1913) after a close study of thermodynamic principles. Its main feature is the smooth, spontaneous ignition of the fuel, resulting from the very high pressures (up to 1000 p.s.i.) in the cylinder. The crudest oils could be used, which made it popular, but the necessarily robust design meant that initially it could not be fitted into vehicles. At first the Diesel engine was intended for and used in stationary applications. It was applied in ocean-going MOTOR VESSELS from 1911, and to locomotives and road vehicles.

See also BARGE; DIESEL LOCOMOTIVE.

BIBLIOGRAPHY
General
Grosser, 1980; Strandh, 1979.

diesel fuel A general term for fuels produced by the oil industry for compression ignition engines (*see* DIESEL ENGINE), but it applies particularly to fuel for low- and medium-speed marine and industrial engines. In Britain, fuel suitable for high-speed engines used in road transport is called DERV (Diesel-Engine Road Vehicle).

BIBLIOGRAPHY
General
BP, 1958.

diesel locomotive The DIESEL ENGINE was first applied to railway traction in 1912 when a locomotive with a Sulzer 100 hp, four-cylinder engine, with mechanical drive to the wheels through rods, was tried in Berlin. Five diesel railcars were built in Germany before 1914.

The first diesel in revenue service was a 75 hp diesel-electric railcar which worked on the Mellersta & Sodermanlands Railway in Sweden between 1913 and 1939. The first diesel-electric SWITCHERS in the USA were built by the General Electric Co. in 1918. The first commercially successful diesel-electric in the USA was a 300 hp machine supplied by ALCO in 1923, now in the Baltimore & Ohio Transportation Museum (*see* MARYLAND). The first main-line use of diesel traction was in railcars used on the Canadian National Railway in 1925; while the first main-line diesel-electric locomotives, designed by the Russian George V. Lomonosoff (1876–1952), were set to work in

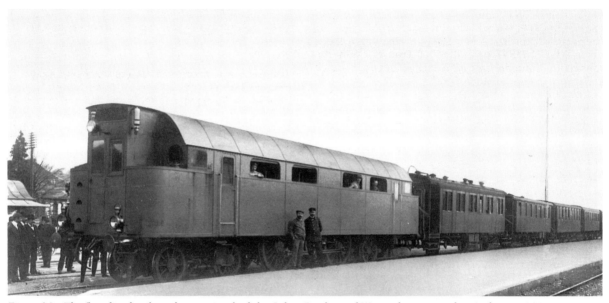

Figure 36   The first diesel railway locomotive, built by Sulzer Brothers of Winterthur, on trial in Berlin in 1912
Sulzer Brothers Ltd, Winterthur

Germany later the same year. In 1926 the first diesel-electric locomotive to enter main-line service in the USA began work on the Long Island RR. In Britain the LMSR introduced a four-car diesel MULTIPLE UNIT in 1932 and in 1933 the GWR built the first of thirty-eight successful railcars.

The most significant development in diesel traction was the introduction in the USA in 1939 of General Motors No. 103, a four-unit freight locomotive rated at 5400 hp which conclusively demonstrated the utility of diesel traction. The first diesel locomotive in regular long-distance freight haulage began work on the Santa Fe RR in 1941. In the USA in 1945 there were 38 853 steam locomotives, 842 electrics and 835 of other kinds, including diesels. By 1952 the number of steam locomotives had been reduced to 18 489, while there were 19 082 diesels. In 1961 there were 28 150 diesels, all with electric transmission, and 110 steam locomotives. Diesel traction spread rapidly in Europe in the 1950s. Some countries, including Belgium, Ireland and Denmark, imported American technology. Others, like West Germany, where hydraulic transmission was generally adopted, pursued an independent course. In countries where cheap electricity is available, like Norway, Sweden, Switzerland, and, to a large extent, France and Germany, diesel traction is used only where traffic levels are too low to justify electrification.

Wheel arrangements of diesel locomotives are classified according to the system used for ELECTRIC LOCOMOTIVES.

See also figure 80.

BIBLIOGRAPHY
General
Aston, 1957; Hinde, 1948.

BARRIE TRINDER

diligence   A carriage operating regular services for the public, with booked seats, at set fares. It was generally smaller than a STAGE COACH. After the coming of railways, the term was applied to a coach working over relatively short distances connecting with trains. The term was first used in English in the 1740s, referring to coaches linking principal cities in France. By the nineteenth century there were similar systems in most European countries ('Eilwagen' in most German states). In the Netherlands the company of Van Gend & Loos had a monopoly from 1865. In most German states diligences belonged to the government. In the Habsburg Empire a diligence normally carried two inside passengers and one in the coupé outside; in France it was usual to have six inside and three in the coupé.

See also INN; MAIL COACH; POST COACH; STAGE COACH.

BIBLIOGRAPHY
General
Murray, 1865.

dimension stone   A stone cut to specific dimensions or sizes, in contrast to rubble stone, which is used for construction in whatever shape it happens to take, or aggregate, which is crushed or used in ways in which it will be crushed in use. Dimension work or ASHLAR is masonry that employs dimension stones.

Dinant, Namur, Belgium   A town of 10 000 inhabitants which stands on the east bank of the River Meuse, 28 km (17 mi.) upstream from Namur, in a gorge created by dramatic limestone cliffs. The river is navigable up to and beyond the French frontier at Givet, 22 km (14 mi.) upstream. The Rock of Bayard, a pinnacle on the east bank about 2 km ($1\frac{1}{2}$ mi.) upstream, was separated from the adjacent cliff by a road cut through in 1698 to enable the passage of the loot-laden baggage train of the army of Louis XIV (1638–1715), King of France. From the fourteenth century *objets d'art* in copper and brass, called Dinanderie, were manufactured, and one workshop remains on the route de Givet. Bouvignes, 3 km (2 mi.) downstream, produced plainer household wares, and still makes tourist souvenirs. At Bouvignes was the nineteenth-century copper and brass mill of Warnant-Anhée, which manufactured boiler parts as well as Dinanderie. Its steam engines and other equipment are in museums in CHARLEROI and LIÈGE.

BIBLIOGRAPHY
Specific
Day, J. The continental origins of Bristol brass. In *IAR*, VII, 1984.
Willem, M, Les Laminoirs à Cuivre de Moulins Anhée: sauvetage d'un complex industriel (The copper rolling mills at Moulins-Anhée: the rescue of an industrial complex). Charleroi: Méaprint, 1989.

LOCATION
[S] Ateliers Biettlot frères, route de Givet, Dinant.

BARRIE TRINDER

Dinorwic, Llanberis, Gwynedd, Wales   The site of one of the largest slate quarries in SNOWDONIA, 12 km (7 mi.) S. of Bangor. It was begun before the 1780s, but expanded with a road to the improved harbour at Port Dinorwic in 1788. The road was replaced by a tramway in 1825, and by Padarn Railway in 1842. Unlike the area around BLAENAU FFESTINIOG, veins here are parallel with the hillsides: extraction was therefore by quarrying in terraces about 10 m (30 ft.) across, rising 600 m (2000 ft.) up the mountain. Railways were built along each level to the sawmills, workshops and spoil heaps. Up to 30 tons of waste was produced per ton of finished slates. Inclines and ropeways carried the slate down. The quarries are accessible from a museum in the water-powered workshops complex: a quadrangle containing a foundry, smithies, carpentry workshops, locomotive sheds and slate-cutting shops. Nearby, Hunslet narrow-gauge locomotives may be seen on the Llanberis Lake Railway and at Penrhyn Castle. At Llanberis is the lower terminus of the RACK RAILWAY which ascends Snowdon.

BIBLIOGRAPHY
General
Dodd, 1971; Lindsay, 1974.

LOCATIONS
[M] Penrhyn Castle Industrial Railway Museum, Bangor, Gwynedd LL57 4HN.
[M] The Welsh Slate Museum, Gilfach Ddu, Llanberis, Gwynedd LL55 4TY.
[S] Snowdon Mountain Railway, Llanberis, Gwynedd LL55 4TY.
PETER WAKELIN

dispensary   An establishment for the dispensing of medicines, essentially that of an APOTHECARY, but the word usually implies that the medicines are being provided, either as an act of individual philanthropy or by public subscription, for those unable to afford commercial prices. There were dispensaries in many COLONIES established by industrialists.

distilling   An APOTHECARY'S and later an industrial process by which a solid or liquid is converted into vapour by means of heat and then condensed into liquid form by cooling, thereby removing water and achieving a greater concentration. The term is applied to many manufacturing processes, including the destructive distillation of COAL. The most common use applies to the concentration of alcohol by distilling to make SPIRITS.

Djerdap, Serbia, Yugoslavia   *See* IRON GATES.

dobby   *See* HARNESS MOTIONS.

dock   Originally the depression made in the silt of a harbour when a ship lay dry at low tide. It came to mean an artificial basin in which a ship might be built or repaired, which formed part of a 'dockyard', and subsequently a larger basin in which ships could float at all states of the tide while being loaded and unloaded, in this case often being called a 'wet dock'. The first docks in Britain, at Rotherhithe and Blackwall in London, were constructed in the late seventeenth century but were used only for laying-by and repairing ships. Commercial docks were built by Thomas Steer in Liverpool in 1715, and by Henry Berry in Hull in 1778–9. John Rennie in the 1790s devised the essential principles of subsequent dock construction, including the use of HYDRAULIC CEMENT. His dock at Grimsby (*see* LINCOLNSHIRE), completed in 1796, was built on a timber raft and anchored with sheet piles at each end. Its floor was an inverted brick arch, resisting the upthrust of the mud beneath. These principles were utilized in LONDON in 1800–1 and elsewhere. 'Finger piers', built within docks to increase their handling capacity, were particularly popular in North America.
See also DRY DOCK.

BIBLIOGRAPHY
General
Greeves, 1980; Hunter, 1921; Jackson, 1983; Pudney, 1975.

BARRIE TRINDER

Dolaucothi, Pumsaint, Dyfed, Wales   Some of the most informative remains of gold mining in Wales, preserved by the National Trust, 50 km (30 mi.) N. of Swansea. Romans mined the site by means of opencasts, adits and caverns; these were heavily reworked until the 1930s. Many adits can be explored, and there is surface evidence of opencasting and of water control for hushing and sorting.

BIBLIOGRAPHY
Specific
Annels, A. E. and Burnham, B. C. eds *The Dolaucothi Gold Mines.* Lampeter: The National Trust for Wales, 1982.

LOCATION
[S] Dolaucothi Gold Mines, Dolaucothi, Pumsaint, Dyfed.

dolomite   A mineral ($CaMg(CO_3)_2$) commonly found in magnesian limestone regions including the Dolomite Alps in Austria and the PENNINES in England. Dolomite is used in REFRACTORIES for insulation, and as a flux in metal-working.

BIBLIOGRAPHY
General
Jones, 1950.

Dolovi-Dobrovol'skii,   Mikhail   Osipovich   (1862–1919)   An inventive electrical engineer who did much to make possible the long-distance transmission of electric power and the asynchronous electric motor. Born and educated in Russia, Dolovi-Dobrovol'skii spent much of his working life in Germany and Switzerland. What he named his 'tension distributor', developed in the 1880s, enabled d.c. electricity to be transmitted at double the tension required by the consumer. In 1888 he built a 3 hp generator using an a.c. three-phase current. A transformer and an asynchronous motor on the same principle soon followed. The motor is now displayed in the Polytechnical Museum in Moscow.

BIBLIOGRAPHY
Specific
Bol'shaya sovietskaya entsiklopediya (Great Soviet Encyclopaedia), vol. 15, Moscow, 1952.

Doły Biskupie, Kielce, Poland   The site of a paperboard plant, 'Witulin', between Starachowice and Ostrowiec Świętokrzyski, in the STAROPOLSKI INDUSTRIAL REGION. In 1885, I. Kolkowski established a masonry shop and mill on the site; in 1911 M. and J. Gombrowicz set up the paper-board plant, naming it after their son, Witold Gombrowicz, an outstanding Polish writer. Some of the buildings of 1885 survive, including a forge shop with a smith's hearth and some workers' housing. The plant still produces paper-board, using the techniques of the early twentieth century. There are manually operated board machines, crushing mills, hollanders and presses. Many machines are belt-driven, from the original water-power system of 1912. The whole plant is under legislative protection, including all surviving buildings, the water-power system, the workings of an old sandstone mine, greens for drying paper, and the communications system. It is planned to include the plant in the industrial écomusée being established in the Staropolski Industrial Region.

BIBLIOGRAPHY
Specific
Adamczyk, J. L. *Fabryka Tektury w Dołach Biskupich, dawniej 'Witulin'* (Paperboard plant in Doły Biskupie, formerly 'Witulin'). Kielce, 1982.

JAN KĘSIK

Donawitz, Styria, Austria   *See* STYRIAN IRON TRAIL.

Donetsk (Stalino, Yuzovka), Ukraine, USSR   A city now at the centre of the Donets Basin in the Ukraine, originating at the site of an ironworks established by a Welshman, John Hughes, in 1870. Although the Martins process (*see* OPEN-HEARTH FURNACE) was retained long after it had become obsolete, the works proved successful and led to the development of modern metallurgy in the Russian Empire. It is believed that many relics of late-nineteenth-century technology remain at the site, but no systematic survey appears to have been attempted, probably because many are still in use.

BIBLIOGRAPHY
Specific
Westwood, J. N. John Hughes and Russian metallurgy. In *Economic History Review*, 2nd ser., XVII(3), 1965.

LOCATION
[M] Regional Museum, Donetsk.

donkey gin   A smaller version of the HORSE GIN. Donkeys were also used extensively in TREADMILLS, to raise water.

BIBLIOGRAPHY
General
Major, 1978.

Donkin, Bryan (1768–1855)   One of the most important engineers of the Industrial Revolution, Donkin was born in Northumberland, England, but spent most of his working life in the London area after his apprenticeship to a papermaker at Dartford, Kent. In 1804 he installed the first FOURDRINIER papermaking machines to work effectively, at Frogmore, Hertfordshire, and between 1801 and 1851 he installed 191 machines in papermills, transforming the British industry. He invented the composition printing roller, and a dividing and screw-cutting machine which was of prime importance. In 1812 he devised a method of preserving meat and vegetables in airtight containers, and established a works for this purpose in Bermondsey, London – in effect, the first CANNING factory. He practised in London as a civil engineer from 1815, and was a founder member of the Institution of Civil Engineers.

Dordrecht, Zuid Holland, The Netherlands   At the confluence of the Oude Maas and the Beneden Merwede, Dordrecht is one of the busiest cities in the world for water traffic, with an average of twenty-two vessels per hour passing throughout the year. The harbour area contains many superb waterside buildings, like the six-storey, six-bay Stockholm Warehouse of 1730 in Kuipershaven. The Lange Yzeren Brug in the harbour is an elegant three-span iron bridge cast at The Hague ('s-Gravenhage) in 1856, while Scheffersplein is a square built over a canal on iron arches of 1864. The Kalkhaven is lined by several small ship-repairing yards and an iron swing bridge of 1859 spans its entrance. The Lips Museum displays the products of a lock-making company.

Across the Oude Maas in Zwijndrecht several rice mills built between 1910 and 1940 remain in use.

BIBLIOGRAPHY
General
Hadfield, 1986.

LOCATIONS
[M] Lips Museum of Locks, Merwedestraat 48, Dordrecht.
[M] Simon van Gijn Museum, 20 Nieuwe Haven, Dordrecht.

Doric The oldest and most austere of the orders of CLASSICAL architecture, widely employed in INDUSTRIAL ARCHITECTURE. The differences between Greek, Roman and Tuscan Doric are complex.

Dortmund, North-Rhine Westphalia, Germany *See* RUHRGEBIET.

Douai, Nord, France From the mid-nineteenth century the Douai region was the principal coal-producing area in France and many coal-mining sites survive. In 1988 some forty-two headstocks were extant, twenty-nine of them with winding engines in place. Perhaps ten of these structures will be preserved, among them the early-nineteenth-century masonry installation of the Sarteau colliery, Fresnes-sur-Escaut, and the engine house and lattice steel headstocks at No. 4 pit at Lens, 20 km (12 mi.) NW of Douai, which is characteristic of the headstocks constructed after World War I.

The Lewarde Historic Mining Centre at Guesnain, 8 km (5 mi.) SE of Douai, is located in the surface buildings of the Delloye colliery, which was sunk in the 1920s. First and foremost it is an open-air museum, boasting two headstocks with winding engines, a screening plant and other pithead buildings. Visitors can see the changing rooms ('la salle des pendus'), the lamp-room, coal-handling installations and the colliery offices. The history of coal-mining technology is illustrated in 450 m (1500 ft.) of exhibition gallery. The museum also deals with the history of coal as a source of energy, and has a collection of mining machinery and equipment on permanent display. The Centre is responsible for the sorting and safekeeping of the historic archives of the colliery companies of the Nord Pas-de-Calais region.

Alongside this production-based heritage, the region is rich in successive forms of workers' housing built by the coal companies: terraced cottages ('corons') of 1825–70; planned estates of 1870–1905, and GARDEN CITY style developments of 1905–39. In 1986 the land-holding company of the Nord Pas-de-Calais collieries still owned nearly 100 000 houses, most in the department of the Pas-de-Calais, and more than half of them built between 1918 and 1939. Several estates have been renovated: the Villars 'coron' at Denain, Nord, 22 km (14 mi.) E. of Douai, built *c.*1825; the Cité Foch at Hénin-Liétard, Pas-de-Calais, 12 km (7$\frac{1}{2}$ mi.) NW of Douai, of *c.*1920; and the Cité des Aviateurs at Bruay, Pas-de-Calais, 40 km (25 mi.) NW of Douai, of 1925.

BIBLIOGRAPHY
General
Daumas, 1980; Guiollard, 1989.

Specific
Kuhnmunch, A. Les archives du Centre Historique Minier. Constitution des fonds et exploitation (The archives of the Lewarde Centre. Creation and exploitation of the documents). *Actes du VIIIᵉ colloque national sur le patrimoine industriel, Lille, 7–9 mai, 1987. L'Archéologie Industrielle en France*, XVII, 1989.
LeManer, Y. Le logement ouvrier dans le bassin minier du Nord Pas-de-Calais (Workers' housing in the Nord Pas-de-Calais coalfield. *Actes du VIIIᵉ colloque national sur le patrimoine industriel, Lille, 7–9 mai, 1987. L'Archéologie Industrielle en France*, XVIII, 1989.

LOCATION
[M,S] Historic Mining Centre, Rue d'Erchin, Lewarde, 59287 Guesnain.

JEAN FRANÇOIS BELHOSTE

double way A railway track consisting of two levels of wooden rail, the topmost pinned to the lower; it was intended for flanged wheels. The first known use was in north-east England by 1760; it was also used at Coalbrookdale (*see* IRONBRIDGE) by 1767, iron rails being substituted as the top sections.

BIBLIOGRAPHY
General
Lewis, 1970; Trinder, 1981; Wood, 1825.
Specific
Broadbridge, S. R. Joseph Banks and West Midlands industry, 1767. In *Staffordshire Industrial Archaeology Society Journal*, II, 1971.

down Fine, soft FEATHERS – the first feathering of young birds, and the soft under-feathers of the breast – used for stuffing bedding. The term applies particularly to feathers of the eider duck, collected in northern NORWAY.

drainage pipe Ceramic drainage pipes are of major importance in LAND DRAINAGE and SEWAGE DISPOSAL. Porous, unglazed pipes used for land drainage, normally without sockets, are usually made from common brick clay, by extrusion. Pipes for sewage disposal are usually glazed, and have tight joints. In the USA pipes of up to 1.06 m (42 in.) can be extruded. Drainage pipes are typically fired in downdraught kilns.

BIBLIOGRAPHY
General
Lefêvre, 1900.

Drammen, Buskerud, Norway A port, 40 km (25 mi.) W. of Oslo, on either side of the River Drammens-elva, one of Norway's principal timber-floating waterways. Drammen suffered severely from fires in the nineteenth century but warehouses with adjacent seventeenth- and eighteenth-century courtyard houses on the west side of the river survived. Listed industrial buildings include a brickworks, a distillery, a glassworks and a tannery. A museum established in 1908 represents the whole county.

LOCATION
[M] Drammens Museum, Konnerudgatan 7, 3000 Drammen.

Draper loom   *See* AUTOMATIC LOOM.

dredge   *See* EXCAVATOR.

dredger   A vessel designed to remove silt from the bed of a harbour or river, and to dump it in or pump it to a place where it will not impede navigation. JOHN RENNIE designed a 29-bucket steam dredger to clear the Humber Dock in Hull, England, in the 1780s. It could handle 60 tons of silt an hour. In the nineteenth century the improvement of dredging techniques using steam shovels and grabs, and from c.1880 suction methods, made it possible for ocean-going ships to reach such ports as Glasgow, Newcastle-upon-Tyne, Amsterdam and Rotterdam. A notable preserved example is the chain dredger now at EXETER, designed in 1844 by I. K. BRUNEL for Bridgwater harbour.

BIBLIOGRAPHY
General
Brouwer, 1985; Hadfield, 1986; Jackson, 1983.

Dre-fach Felindre, Dyfed, Wales   A straggling village in west Wales, 20 km (13 mi.) N. of Carmarthen, with a rich heritage left by the woollen industry. Welsh domestic cloth manufacture was transformed into factory industry from the 1820s. Dre-fach was one of the largest centres in c.1870–1930, with forty-five weaving mills c.1900. There has been rapid decline since the 1920s but a few mills survive. There are remains of several water-powered factories, small workshops and weavers' cottages. A museum of the woollen industry is housed in the Cambrian Mills.

BIBLIOGRAPHY
General
Jenkins, 1969.

LOCATION
[M] Museum of the Woollen Industry, Cambrian Mills, Dre-fach, Llandysul, Dyfed.

Dresden, Saxony, Germany   The ancient capital of Saxony, Dresden was almost entirely destroyed by air raids in February 1945. The city was an important transport junction in the nineteenth century. The first long-distance railway in Germany, between Leipzig and Dresden, opened in 1839, and there were steamships on the Elbe from 1837. It was the centre of an area of rapid and varied industrial growth. Dresden has two important museums relating to industry, the Transport Museum of 1952, and the German Museum of Hygiene, accommodated in a building designed by the architect Wilhelm Kreis, and dating from 1928–30. Historic buildings connected with transport include the station buildings of the Leipzig–Dresden line, built in 1847 and 1862 and still standing, although not in their original form. Dresden's main station of 1892–8 is also preserved in a rather simplified form. It was built by the architects Giese & Weidner, and stands on the outskirts of the Old Town. Six lines come into the station at ground level; another six, in two groups of three, terminate at first-floor level. A triple vaulted roof covers the entire layout. A concourse building, situated away from the train shed and between the higher tracks, is reached by underpasses.

Another important building in the history of transport is the Loschwitz Bridge, which crosses the Elbe in the east of the city. Built in 1891–3 as a steel-lattice and continuous-beam structure in the form of a suspension bridge, it was called the 'Blaues Wunder' (blue wonder) because of the colour of its paint.

The passenger paddle steamer *Diesbar*, built in 1883–4, is a monument to the shipping trade on the Elbe, a service which began running from Dresden in 1837. The vessel has a two-cylinder steam engine, made by John Penn of Greenwich, London, in 1856–7, with oscillating cylinders, for which Friedrich Krupp of Essen provided the crankshaft in 1853. In 1896–7 the passenger steamer *Habsburg* (renamed *Riesa* in 1919) was launched at Dresden-Blasewitz. It was magnificently fitted out in 1910 on the occasion of a journey with Emperor Franz Joseph of Austria. It was sunk at the end of World War II, raised to the surface in 1946–7, and restored and displayed at Oderberg after 1979.

The encased gasholder in the Rieck quarter of the city, built in 1907–8 by the architect Hans Jacob Erlenwein for the gasworks which had begun operating in 1881, is an important feature of the technical infrastructure of Dresden. The round concrete structure, 75 m (250 ft.) high, has five square stairway towers, with eight floors, slightly tapering, and a dome with a lantern superstructure of steel construction, 65 m (210 ft.) in diameter. Its capacity of 110 000 m³ (3.9 million cu. ft.) illustrates the growth of the gas-supply industry in big cities in the early twentieth century, particularly when compared to the two gasholders standing beside it – two-storey structures built of brick in 1878, and only 25 m (80 ft.) high. In this connection it is remarkable that Rudolf Siegismund Blochmann constructed the first gasworks to be built in Germany without any foreign assistance in Dresden in 1828. It was only the third gasworks in Germany, and the equipment was provided by the Lauchhammer ironworks north of Dresden.

One building of particular architectural originality symbolizes the consumer-goods manufactories which were established in and around Dresden in the early twentieth century. In 1909 the architect Martin Hammitzsch built a reinforced-concrete frame structure for the Yenidze cigarette factory in the shape of a mosque 60 m (200 ft.) high. A completely glazed steel-framed dome rises above a seven-storey building on a square ground plan, and is flanked by four (originally six) pointed turrets. The chimney beside it, in red and bright yellow faience, is shaped like a minaret. Like Templeton's carpet factory in GLASGOW, the style of the building reflects the geographical origins of the raw materials (oriental tobacco in the case of this Dresden factory), and employs the shape of the building as an advertisement.

Mechanical and electrical engineering are of considerable importance in the industrial history of Dresden. In

1836 Andreas Schubert founded a mechanical engineering institute at Ubigau near Dresden; its main building still stands. Among the items designed by Schubert were the Göltzschtal viaduct (*see* GERMAN DEMOCRATIC REPUBLIC) and the first German steam railway locomotive, as well as the first passenger steamship to ply on the Elbe. The optical industry is represented by the 'tower house' built for the firm of Ernemann AG by the architects Högg and Müller between 1915 and 1923, an impressive, all-reinforced-concrete complex with a 48 m (160 ft) oval tower.

All that remains in Dresden as a record of the invention by Johann Friedrich Böttger of European hard-fired PORCELAIN is the monument commemorating the inventor, erected in 1982 at the site of his invention, the Brühl terraces. After 1710 the porcelain was made in a works in the Albrechtsburg, the residence of the Electors of Saxony, in Meissen, 24 km (15 mi.) NW of Dresden, and since that time it has been known as Meissen porcelain. The history of the industry is displayed in the residence and in the factory.

Dresden's museums illustrate many aspects of industrial history.

BIBLIOGRAPHY
General
Berger, 1980; Erler and Schmeidel, 1988; Forberger, 1982; Schmidt and Theile, 1989, 1991; Wagenbreth and Wächtler, 1983.
Specific
Erlwein, H. Der neue Gasbehälter Dresdens (The new gasholder at Dresden). In *Der Industriebau, Heft* 6 (Industrial building yearbook), 1910.
Hentschel, W. Aus den Anfängen des Fabrikbaus in Sachsen (Factory buildings in Saxony from the beginnings). In *Wissenschaftliche Zeitschrift der Technischen Hochschule Dresden* (Scientific papers of Dresden Polytechnic), III. Dresden, 1953–4.

LOCATIONS
[M,S] Albrechtsburg, Domplatz 1, 8250 Meissen.
[M] Collection of Historic Electrical Machines, Sektion Elektrotechnik der TU Dresden (Electrical Engineering Department of the Technical University of Dresden), Helmholzstrasse 9, 8027 Dresden.
[M] German Museum of Hygiene, Lingner Platz 1, 8010 Dresden.
[M] Institute and Museum for the History of the City of Dresden, Ernst Thälmann Strasse 2, 8010 Dresden.
[I] Institute of Precision Instrument-Making of the Technical University of Dresden, Barkhausen Bau, Helmholzstrasse 18, 8000 Dresden.
[I] Institut für Denkmalpflege (Institute for Monuments Protection), Augustusstrasse, Postfach 1-66, 8010 Dresden.
[M,S] Meissen State Porcelain Factory, Leninstrasse 9, 8150 Meissen.
[M] Museum of Photography, Käthe Killwitz Ufer 76, 8010 Dresden.
[M] State Art Collection: Museum of Arts and Crafts, Wasserpalais, Schloss Pillnitz, 8057 Dresden.
[M] State Art Collection: Pewter Collection, Zwinger, Sophienstrasse, 8010 Dresden.
[M] State Art Collection: Porcelain Collection, Zwinger, Sophienstrasse, 8010 Dresden.
[M] Technical Museum, Friedrich Engels Strasse 15, 8060 Dresden.

[M] Transport Museum, Johanneum, Augustusstrasse 1, 8010 Dresden.

AXEL FÖHL

dressing floor The place where metallic ores were crushed and washed to remove waste, forming a concentrate which could be used in a smelter. The dressing floor might be part of the surface installations of an individual mine, or a separate establishment taking in ores from several mines. The operation was increasingly mechanized from the mid-nineteenth century.

See also BUDDLE; CRUSHING CIRCLE; JIG; SHAKING TABLE.

dressmaker *See* TAILOR.

dried fruit Dried fruits – as terms like 'Malaga raisins' and 'currants', named after CORINTH, indicate – are traditional Mediterranean products. Most are made from the grape, *Vitis vinefera*; but apricots, peaches and plums are treated by similar methods, the last to make prunes. In the nineteenth century Greek currants and raisins were exported in sacks to England where grocers would clean them in machines, like those by Caleb Duckworth of Colne, preserved at WIGAN Pier. In the second half of the nineteenth century large-scale dried-fruit manufactures developed in CALIFORNIA around Fresno, and in Australia. Drying is traditionally by the action of the sun, but tunnel dehydrators have increasingly been used in the present century.

BIBLIOGRAPHY
General
Prescott and Proctor, 1937; Winstanley, 1983.

drift mine *See* ADIT.

drilling machine or **drill press** A machine tool designed to cut holes by feeding a rotating cutting tool against and into the supported work. Drilling is probably the earliest and most widely practised mechanical technique, and the drilling of work could be accomplished by a self-feeding bit turned by hand while braced against the body. The drilling of holes in metal requires the rotation of a hardened chisel point against the work under pressure and with considerable power and speed. Delicate watchmaking work could be controlled and powered accurately by hand; heavier industrial drilling machines had a rigid structure and brought power by belting, worm and wheel or bevel gear to a driving shaft that held a sliding spindle which could be brought to the work by winch and pulley, lever, screw or rack. Important improvements included variable-speed cone pulleys, laterally and vertically adjustable tables, and power feed. Drill presses were in all early machine shops and by 1850 were offered for sale in various sizes and incorporating special features such as radial arms and multiple spindles. The precision and efficiency of drilling in metal were greatly increased by the development of the twist drill, aided by the appearance of a universal MILLING MACHINE and subsequent improvements in tool steels.

BIBLIOGRAPHY
General
Rolt, 1986; Steeds, 1969.

TIM PUTNAM

drink   *See* AKVAVIT; BEER; BRANDY; CIDER; COCOA; COFFEE; DAIRY; GIN; PORT WINE; RUM; SCHNAPPS; SOFT DRINKS; SPIRITS; TEA; VODKA; WHISKY; WINE.

drop hammer   A hammer for shaping metal by repeated blows with dies, lifted by power and falling by gravity. When the form and section of the metal are changed the process is called drop forging. If only the form alters, the correct term is drop stamping.

BIBLIOGRAPHY
General
Gale, 1971.

druggist   One who prepares medicinal drugs.
    See also APOTHECARY; CHEMIST; DISPENSARY; DRUG STORE; PHARMACY.

drugs   *See* APOTHECARY; CHEMIST; PHARMACEUTICALS; TOBACCO.

drug store   A pharmacy, often dealing mainly with non-pharmaceutical goods, which became one of the characteristic North American institutions of the twentieth century, the modern version of the village general store. The concept was developed by Charles R. Walgreen (1875–1939), who at Tampa, Fla., in 1934, put merchandise on open display and attracted customers by lunch counters and icecream stalls. Walgreen had 493 stores by 1939.

BIBLIOGRAPHY
General
Boorstin, 1973.

Drumnaconagher, County Down, Northern Ireland Silcock's Mills, 8 km (5 mi.) W. of Ballynahinch, comprise a flax-scutching mill and a corn mill, both restored to working order by the Department of the Environment (NI). The scutch mill has a wooden, low breast-shot wheel, of 4.4 m (14 ft. 6 in.) diameter, driving a flax breaker on the ground floor, and flax-scutching and flaxseed-crushing machines at first-floor level. The corn mill has a 22 m (72 ft.) wooden breast wheel.

BIBLIOGRAPHY
General
Green, 1963; McCutcheon, 1980.

dry cleaning   The use of SOLVENTS to remove greasy stains from fabrics, understood in principle by 1800 when TURPENTINE was used, amongst other substances. The first commercial dry-cleaning plant was established in Paris in 1845, and the process spread through Europe, most English concerns coming to be known as 'clothes cleaners'. Chains of collecting agencies sending items by rail to central dry-cleaning factories were established, by W. Spindler in Berlin and J. Pullar in Perth; Pullar also operated a dyeing concern. Dry cleaning was widespread in the USA by 1910, and by the 1930s was increasingly carried out in local shops rather than centralized factories. The standard non-flammable solvent, Stoddard Solution, was developed in the 1920s. Subsequently synthetic solvents like perchlorethylene (C_2Cl_4) have been used.

dry dock   A DOCK used for repairing and sometimes for building ships, which can be emptied of water and refilled as required. Dry docks were in use by the late Middle Ages, but were much improved *c.*1800, when gates were 'mitred' or angled outwards to resist the pressure of water; floors came to be inverse masonry arches, resistant to pressures from below; and steam engines were employed for pumping.

BIBLIOGRAPHY
General
Coad, 1983, 1989; Walton, 1902.

Dublin (Baile Atha Cliath), Dublin, Ireland   Dublin flourished in the eighteenth century as a colonial capital, the leisure city for a *rentier* class. The elegance of its central area was due largely to the Commissioners for the Making of Wide and Convenient Streets, who between 1757 and 1840 laid out new thoroughfares and set standards for developers. The outstanding architect of this period was James Gandon (1743–1823). Dublin's population increased from about 9000 in 1660 to 200 000 in 1800. The city bears many marks of its former colonial status, from huge barracks to post-boxes bearing the initials of Queen Victoria, cast by firms like Andrew Handyside of Derby.
    Dublin stands at the mouth of the River Liffey, which over the centuries has been confined within retaining walls and lined by quays. Silting was reduced by the construction, following the plans of William Bligh (1754–1817), of the South Wall, completed to the Poolbeg lighthouse of 1762 in 1790, and the North Wall, built in 1820–5. The most stately of all customs houses was designed by James Gandon as part of a comprehensive development of new port facilities in 1781–91. It was burned in 1921 and later rebuilt to a different internal plan. Dublin's first docks were constructed in 1792–6 under the direction of WILLIAM JESSOP at Ringsend, at the confluence of the GRAND CANAL and the Liffey. The 10 ha (25 ac.) wet dock was the largest constructed at that date. The docks on the north bank are similarly clustered around the confluence of the Royal Canal and the Liffey. The Circular Line of the Grand Canal to the south of the city from Griffith Bridge to Ringsend is used by pleasure craft, but the former main line to the Grand Canal Harbour near the Guinness Brewery has been filled in. The

Figure 37 Single-storey and two-storey terraced housing of the first half of the nineteenth century on the banks of the Grand Canal near Portobello, Dublin; large numbers of single-storey dwellings of this sort remain in use in the city.
Barrie Trinder

Royal Canal to the north of the city is no longer navigable, but some restoration work has been done west of Drumcondra Road. Its branch from Mountjoy to Broadstone has been converted to gardens, but its City Basin remains in water.

Manufacturing has never had a dominant role in Dublin's economy but Bolands' flour mills at Ringsend represent an industry that has always been important. Distilling, which once employed some notable steam engines, has now ceased in Dublin. Some textile concerns flourished in the nineteenth century, an example of which was the Greenmount Spinning Manufactory, of which the four-storey, red and yellow brick mill together with a range of top-lit sheds have been adapted to new uses. More recent factories include the John Player tobacco works in the South Circular Road, a three-storey brick and concrete structure of nine wide bays in a debased Classical style.

For more than two centuries the Guinness Brewery has been the most important manufacturing concern in Dublin. In 1759 Arthur Guinness (1725–1803) leased a small brewery at St James's Gate, on the west wall of the city, occupying a site of 1.6 ha (4 ac.), and from 1799 he concentrated on brewing stout. By that time stout was being exported to England, where by the 1830s it could be bought in almost every town. It was obtainable worldwide by 1900. By the 1860s the brewery had become the largest in the world and by the 1960s it extended over 24 ha (59 ac.). It stretches from the banks of the Liffey, across James Street to the former site of the Grand Canal harbour. While the processes are ultra-modern, the towering four- and five-storey buildings of the late nineteenth and early twentieth centuries, of grey brick once cream-coloured, dominate thoroughfares like Rainsford Street, which are surfaced with setts whose joints are filled with barley husks. The brewery has a visitor centre located in a hopstore of 1876–82, built with local bricks and limestone, with a steel frame supplied by Ross & Walpole. Exhibits include a kieve used between 1878 and 1979, a copper of 1836, and various wooden vats. There is an extensive display relating to coopering, and detailed explanations of how malt has been brought to the brewery and stout dispatched to customers; these include videos incorporating film of boats on the Grand Canal. The tower of a nine-storey early eighteenth-century windmill is preserved within the brewery.

Of the bridges over the Liffey the oldest and most elegant is Mellows (formerly Queen's) Bridge of 1764–8, consisting of three stone arches and designed by Charles Vallancy (1721–1812). James Gandon's O'Connell (formerly Carlisle) Bridge of 1791 was completely rebuilt in the 1880s. There are three notable iron bridges. The Wellington or Halfpenny footbridge is a 43 m (140 ft.) cast-iron arch, designed by John Windsor and cast by the Coalbrookdale Co. (see IRONBRIDGE) in 1816. The Sean Heuston Bridge is an iron arch of 1821 with relief crowns cast in the spandrels; while the Rory O'More Bridge, also a single arch, with Romanesque detailing in the spandrels, was cast in 1858 by Robert Daglish of St Helens, Lancashire.

Heuston (Kingsbridge) Station, terminus of the railway to Cork, is a Renaissance palazzo designed by Sancton Woods in 1845. Connolly (Amiens) Street, the station for Belfast, in a more restrained Italianate style, was designed by W. D. Butler and completed in 1844. Broadstone Station, terminus of the Midland Great Western Railway, completed in 1850 to the design of J. S. Mulvany, is an elegant five-bay, two-storey building, with Egyptian detailing. It was closed in 1936 and the train shed is now a bus garage.

Dublin's working class was the worst-housed in the British Isles in the nineteenth century. The death rate in 1911 at 27.6 per thousand was the highest for any city in Europe, and slightly above that of cholera-stricken Calcutta. In the nineteenth century the poor lived chiefly in tenements, many of them substantial houses abandoned by the wealthy. Most housing of this kind has been replaced by blocks of flats, like those constructed by the Guinness family in the vicinity of St Patrick's Cathedral, or by municipal housing estates, the first of which was built at Inchicore in 1926. Many English-style TUNNEL-BACK HOUSES were built in Dublin, as well as large numbers of single-storey houses, which appear to derive from Irish traditions. Some are of tandem construction, like those near the Parnell Bridge on the Grand Canal, or in Geraldine Street near the City Basin of the Royal Canal; but some, like No. 9 Innisfallen Parade where Sean O'Casey (1880–1964) lived in the 1880s, appear to have been essentially one-room dwellings. Examples with barrel-vault roofs remain near the Greenmount spinning mill. Several charitable trusts provided working-class housing in Dublin, including the Artizan Dwelling Co. which constructed a grid of two-storey red-brick terraces on the site of the City Basin of the Grand Canal in 1883.

See also figures 46, 62.

BIBLIOGRAPHY
General
Cullen, 1987; Delany, 1973, 1986; Killanin and Duignan, 1967; Lynch and Vaizey, 1960; McCutcheon, 1969, 1970; Peaty, 1985.
Specific
Bowie, G. The millhouse engine in Jameson's Distillery, Bow Street, Dublin. In *IA*, ix(3) 1972.
Bowie, G. Two stationary steam engines in Power's Distillery, John's Lane, Dublin. In *IA*, xi(3) 1974.
Corran, H. S. The Guinness Museum. In *IA*, v(3) 1968.
Historic Dublin Maps. National Library of Ireland, n.d.

LOCATIONS
[M] Guinness Museum, Arthur Guinness, Son & Co. (Dublin) Ltd, The Old Hop Store, Rainsford Street, Dublin 8.
[M] National Museum of Ireland, Kildare Street, Dublin 2.

BARRIE TRINDER

Dubnik, Eastern Slovakia, Czechoslovakia   A town 20 km (12 mi.) E. of Košice, on the site of eighteenth- and nineteenth-century opal extraction. An open-air museum is proposed.

Dubrovnik (Ragusa), Croatia, Yugoslavia   One of the historic trading ports of the Adriatic, Ragusa was effectively a self-governing city state from 1526. Independence was lost with the French invasion of 1806–8, and from 1815 Ragusa was a part of the Habsburg Empire but was renamed when it became part of YUGOSLAVIA after World War I. The Maritime Museum was established in 1872 in the castle. An art museum is housed in Rupe Granary, which has sixteenth-century grain silos that are 8 m (26 ft.) deep.

BIBLIOGRAPHY
General
Carter, 1972.

LOCATIONS
[M] Maritime Museum, St John's Fortress, 50000-Dubrovnik.
[M] Municipal Museum, Knežew dvor, Prid Dvorom, 50000-Dubrovnik.
[S] Rupe Granary, Rupa, ul. od Rupa, 50000-Dubrovnik.
[M] State Archives Museum, Sponza Palace, 50000-Dubrovnik.

Duisburg, North-Rhine Westphalia, Germany   *See* RUHRGEBIET.

Dumfries and Galloway, Scotland   A primarily rural region of South-West Scotland, which nevertheless contains some industrial monuments of note.

At Gatehouse of Fleet four cotton mills – two for twisting, two for mule-spinning – were built in 1785–90. One, later a bobbin mill, is now a heritage centre. Another became a sawmill and is now a dwelling. There are rows of two-storey workers' housing.

Small water-powered woollen mills can be seen: Cumloden Waulk Mill, near Newton Stewart, now a dwelling; Kirkowan Waulk Mill of 1821, which has a shed of the 1880s that retains disused line shafting; and Barbugh Mill, originally for lint, later for blankets. Larger tweed and hosiery mills remain at Dumfries. Nithsdale Mill of 1857 has a big, polychrome mule mill of 1864, Mancunian in appearance, and an octagonal chimney stalk. Troqueer Mills of 1866 and Rosefield Mills of 1886–9 retain tweed-weaving sheds, those of the latter being in the Venetian style.

New Abbey Corn Mill, or Monksmill, dates from the late eighteenth century and has a kiln and three pairs of stones. It was restored in the 1970s and is now a guardianship monument (see SCOTLAND). The Dumfries town mills, now without their machinery, house the Robert Burns Centre. Bladnoch Distillery near Wigtown was founded in 1817 and rebuilt in 1878 with a pagoda kiln and stalk.

The first steam-powered boat, designed by William Symington (1763–1831), sailed on Dalswinton Loch in 1788. A replica has been constructed by Dumfries and Galloway College of Technology.

The large limeburning complex at Closeburn, with its

associated water system, has been excavated. Red sandstone from Dumfriesshire and granite from Kirkcudbrightshire were important exports. Dalbeattie granite was used at LIVERPOOL docks and elsewhere.

The Arrol-Johnston Motor Co. moved from Paisley to Dumfries in 1912–13, building there Scotland's largest automobile plant, on Detroit lines (see MICHIGAN), and utilizing ALBERT KAHN's system of reinforced-concrete construction. It is a three-storey, E-shaped complex, with two wings added c.1920. Production ceased in 1929 and since 1946 the complex has been occupied by a rubber company. A vast munitions factory established at Gretna in 1915 required the construction of a GARDEN CITY, accommodating 24 000 people, which was designed by RAYMOND UNWIN (1863–1940).

The New Galloway and Glenlee hydro-electric scheme of 1933–4 was then the largest in the United Kingdom, having English Electric turbines with umbrella ALTERNATORS, and the highest fish ladders in Britain. The plant was contained within striking cubist blocks designed by Sir Alexander Gibb (1872–1958). Tongland power station is open to the public.

THOMAS TELFORD built Tongland Bridge, Kirkcudbright, with its 34 m (112 ft.) span in 1804–8, and JOHN RENNIE the Bridge of Ken, New Galloway, in 1821. The Duchess Bridge at Langholm was built in 1813 and is Scotland's oldest iron bridge. Southerness Lighthouse, built in 1749 and rebuilt in the 1840s, and the Port Logan light tower of 1818–20 are no longer used.

See also WANLOCKHEAD AND LEADHILLS.

BIBLIOGRAPHY
General
Donnachie, 1971; Hume, 1976.
Specific
Blomfield, G. T. New integrated motor works in Scotland, 1889–1914. In *IAR*, v, 1981.
Butt, J. The industrial archaeology of Gatehouse of Fleet. In *IA*, III, 1966.

MARK WATSON

Dunaújváros (Sztálinváros), Fejér, Hungary   A former fishing village on the Danube, where a huge steel plant was established from 1950. The population is now 50 000. The plant is supplied with coking coal from Komlo (see PÉCS).

Dunbartonshire, Strathclyde, Scotland   A county on the northern bank of the River Clyde, north-west of Glasgow. William Denny established the Leven Shipyard, Dumbarton, in 1857, and later built the *Cutty Sark*. The shipyard closed in 1962. The Denny Ship Model Experiment Tank, the oldest private tank in the world, constructed in 1883–94, is now in the care of the Scottish Maritime Museum (see IRVINE). A narrow-gauge railway carries wax ship models along a 100 m (90 yd.) waterway. In the museum there is an original shaping machine; and the side-lever engine of the paddle steamer *Leven* is preserved.

The Forth & Clyde Canal terminated at two sea locks at Bowling, 4 km (2½ mi.) SE of Dumbarton, begun in 1768 by JOHN SMEATON, completed by Robert Whitworth in 1790 and closed in 1963. A project began in 1988 to reopen a 19 km (12 mi.) section from Glasgow to Kirkintilloch.

The Leven Valley was noted for its bleach and printfields (see CALICO PRINTING), and Kirkintilloch for the Lion and other foundries.

The Singer Kilbowie Works, Clydebank, 10 km (7 mi.) NW of Glasgow, was the largest sewing-machine factory in the world. It was opened in 1884, having been moved there by its American parent company from Glasgow. Clydebank Museum has 488 items from the Singer company's collection of industrial and domestic sewing machines. The museum also holds tools from Clydebank Shipyard, which was opened by J. & G. Thomson in 1870, and taken over by John Brown, a Sheffield armour-plater, in 1899. The yard built warships and Atlantic liners, including HMS *Hood*, SS *Aquitania*, SS *Queen Mary*, and SS *Queen Elizabeth*. The yard retains a titan cantilever crane of 1907 by Sir William Arrol & Co. and Stothert & Pitt, the oldest of the type in Scotland.

The Argyll Motor Co. in Alexandria, 14 km (8½ mi.) N. of Dumbarton, with its long Baroque office and recreation block with domed clock tower, was claimed to be the largest motorcar works in Europe, but it was never fully utilized, and closed in 1914 to become a torpedo factory.

LOCATION
[M] Clydebank District Museum, Old Town Hall, Dumbarton, Clydebank G81 1XQ.

MARK WATSON

Dundee, Tayside, Scotland   Dundee, on the north bank of the Tay estuary, is – after Glasgow – Scotland's second industrial city.

The Dighty Water and its tributaries powered Dundee's main industrial sites until the early nineteenth century; Craig, Balmuir, Benvie and Kirkton Mills, for flour, and Pitkerro Mill (now a house), for grain, survive. Milton flax mill, established in Monifieth in 1787, was internally rebuilt in 1872. Of the several bleachfields, Claverhouse is the best-preserved, having late eighteenth- and early nineteenth-century ranges, and single-storey workers' terraces at Trottick Mains.

Dundee led the world's coarse-linen industry, and then its jute industry. Some eighty mills and factories still stand. The first steam-powered mills were built in 1793. East Mill, a tannery converted in 1799 to flax-spinning, still stands and retains elements of its BOULTON & WATT engine. Dundee District Museum has in store a sun-and-planet Boulton & Watt engine of 1799 from the Douglas Bleachfield.

The boom of 1828–36 has left fourteen surviving mills, nine of them fireproof. The oldest is also the biggest: Logie Works in Brook Street. It is called the Coffin Mill. Another, Wallace Craigie Works, is still used by the family firm of the founder, William Halley, for weaving polypropylene and furnishing fabric. Verdant Works of 1833 has a timber floor and a cast-iron roof; it is remarkably little altered, and is to be a textile museum in the heart of Blackness, Dundee's earliest and best-preserved industrial area.

In Dens Works, Princes Street, Baxter Brothers had the biggest linen works in the world, founded in 1822. There four thousand people once worked in the four surviving spinning mills of 1850–66, all Venetian-towered and with Gothic cast-iron roofs. One, Upper Dens Mill, has been converted to seventy-two flats. Dundee's flax and jute mills are generally of between three and six storeys, and iron-framed to a nave-and-aisles layout, which prompted the use of Gothic cast-iron roofs in thirteen of the extant mills.

Jute, first spun mechanically in 1832, was widely adopted in the slump of the late 1830s. The first big purpose-built jute mill was Tay Works, Lochee Road, the 200 m (650 ft.) pedimented frontage of which was built in 1851–65. The mill has been converted to student accommodation. The Camperdown Works, Lochee, of the Cox Brothers, founded in 1850, is the biggest jute complex in Britain, once employing five thousand hands in the pedimented and towered High Mill of 1857–68, and in extensive carding, weaving, dyeing and calendering sheds; Cox's Stack, the works' 86 m (282 ft.) high polychrome brick campanile chimney, dominates Dundee. Camperdown Works is being converted to residential use, as are the Italianate High Mill of 1861 at Seafield Works, the French Gothic-towered Lindsay Street Mill of 1874, Blakey's Hillbank Mill of 1834, and Forebank Dyeworks of 1874.

The single-storey jute-spinning mill evolved in the 1860s and 70s to maximize efficiency. Ten still exist, of which Caldrum Works of 1872–90 is the largest, and is now used for polypropylene extrusion. Jute is still spun in the primarily single-storey Manhattan Works of 1874, Dundee Linen Works of 1874, Queen Victoria Works of 1828 and 1887, and Taybank Works of 1947; and is calendered and finished in Taybank Works of 1919, where the plant is little changed from that date, East Port Works of 1913, Riverside Works of 1905 and Camperdown Works, which has a nineteenth-century calendering machine.

Weaving was performed on the ground floors of cottages or large hand-loom factories, examples of which exist on Dons Road (later a confectionery works), and Constable and Albert Streets. Power looms were used from 1836, the oldest extant weaving sheds of 1837 being at Dudhope Works, the next being Edward Street Mill of 1851, with a four-storey fireproof front. Weaving sheds typically have roof spans of 9 m (30 ft.), three times that in typical cotton or woollen mills because here line shafting was in tunnels below the floor.

J. & C. Carmichael's Ward Foundry, established in Brown Street in 1810, made steam engines, and pioneered fan blast and reversing gears for paddlesteamers. Blackness Foundry, established in 1867 and rebuilt with steel-framed shops in 1907–14, exported textile machinery, as did the Wallace Foundry, part of which, built in 1837 for the assembling of locomotives, still survives.

Dundee Foundry in Dock Street, established in 1791, came under the ownership of Gourlay Brothers from the mid-nineteenth century, and concentrated on marine engineering. The galleried cast-iron-framed engine shop of 1870 in which the engines of RRS *Discovery* were made belongs to the Clyde tradition.

RRS *Discovery*, the timber, steam-assisted barque of Antarctic fame, returned from London to Dundee in 1986. Owned by the Maritime Trust, it is the focus of a redevelopment of the esplanade. Dundee Industrial Heritage will interpret Scott's story in a centre built on top of THOMAS TELFORD's Craig Ferry Pier. Dundee District Museums have in the McManus Galleries an industrial display relating to shipbuilding, textiles, confectionery and journalism.

Dundee's early docks by JOHN SMEATON and Telford have been infilled to carry the Tay Road Bridge. The rest are still used. Victoria Docks, started in 1833 and completed in 1869–75, is lined by transit sheds and a five-storey fireproof clocktower warehouse. Camperdown Dock dates from 1857–65, Fish Dock from 1900, and there is a 150 m (500 ft.) graving dock of the 1870s. Eastern Wharf, of 1890, was reconstructed in 1903–9 as the first reinforced-concrete wharf in Scotland, but a concrete railway bridge of 1903 on Western Wharf was the first HENNEBIQUE structure in Scotland. King George V Wharf of 1911–27 is similarly constructed.

The big Ionic Customs House and Harbour Chambers of 1842–3 stand on Dock Street. Between Marine Parade and Victoria Dock is the Panmure Yard where *Discovery* was built. It is now W. R. Stewart's hackleworks, making pinned card staves for the textile and tobacco industries. The company has a collection of early hackle-making machines and is closely involved in the restoration of HMS *Unicorn*, a 5th-rate frigate of 1824, which has iron raking struts and a wooden roof. The Harbour Workshops of 1837, used by Alex Stephen & Sons, had a steam-hauled patent slip. Forges, steam hammers and chain-testing equipment are still used there. To the east are large timber-framed, Belfast-roofed timber yards. A dockland industrial estate houses Lindsay & Low confectionery factories, Briggs's oil and asphalt refinery, both of c.1900, the steel-framed Caledon boiler shop of 1908, and the Caledon shipyard of 1917.

Morton's Bond on Exchange Street, built between 1820 and 1834, has fireproof bonded lower floors and timber upper floors for grain storage. Further bonded warehouses on Seagate include Stewarts, a neo-Classical building of 1868 converted to flats, Robertson's of 1897, now the Printmaker's Workshop, and Watson's, a reinforced-concrete BOND of 1907, the last to close, in 1987. A hydraulic lift of the 1860s still operates in an iron warehouse at 7 Commercial Street.

Keiller's, marmalade and confectionery makers, and Valentines, pioneers of the postcard, have moved from Victorian factories to the Kingsway, an outer ring road of the 1920s, but publishers D. C. Thomson occupy Renaissance offices of the 1860s and 1870s in Bank Street, and the robust Baroque Courier Building, Meadowside, of 1902. Some printing is done in the weaving shed of West

Ward Works of *c.*1860, and paper is stored in other nineteenth-century warehouses and engineering works.

Furniture factories illustrate the early adaptation of textile mills to other industries. East Brothers' Lochee Cabinet Works is a refronting of 1911 of the Balgay Linen Works of the 1860s. Justice's Ward Cabinet Works of 1911 is of four storeys and 76 m (250 ft.) long, again built in front of a jute mill of 1871. The firm now occupies the former Balgray Carpet Works of *c.*1880. Scott Street Works of 1873 produced jute cloth, hose pipes, aerated water and now, as Lord Roberts's workshop, furniture.

After World War II Dunsinane Industrial Estate was created to foster industries other than jute. Many of the factories have gone through more than one use. Prime sites went to two American corporations, NCR and Timex, whose factories of 1946 by Bennett, Beard & Williams are long, low and stylish.

Water supply was for long difficult in Dundee, but was much improved by James Leslie's Lintrathen Water scheme of 1872, with sluice chambers and water towers disguised as crenellated turrets and dovecotes.

Working-class tenement housing was of between two and five storeys, and characterized by 'platties', deck access from free-standing semi-cylindrical stair towers. Development was mostly speculative and scattered. On Court Street is a mass concrete range of 1874.

The Dundee & Newtyle Railway, opened in 1831, was a HYBRID RAILWAY line with three INCLINED PLANES, whose routes can still be seen, employing first horses and from 1833 locomotives on the level sections. Early stations survive as a barn at Newtyle, 14 km (9 mi.) NW of Dundee, and as a cottage in the grounds of King's Cross Hospital. Broughty Ferry railway station of 1849, with timber awnings and timber-sided footbridge and signal box, may be turned into a museum. Balmossie Viaduct, of 1870, has seven arches and will form part of a public walkway.

The Tay Rail Bridge is at 3264 m (10 711 ft.) the longest railway viaduct in Europe. Sir Thomas Bouch (1822–80) supervised inadequately the construction of the original bridge in 1871–8; it collapsed in 1879. The replacement, designed by William Barlow and built by William Arrol & Co. in 1882–7, utilized Bouch's wrought-iron lattice girders on wider arched plate-iron piers.

BIBLIOGRAPHY
General
Hume, 1977; Shipway, 1987; Watson, 1989.
Specific
Watson, M. Jute manufacturing: a study of Camperdown Works. In *IAR*, x, 1988.

LOCATIONS
[I] Dundee Industrial Heritage, 26 East Dock Street, Dundee.
[M] Dundee Museums and Art Galleries, Albert Square, Dundee.

MARK WATSON

Dunedin, Otago, New Zealand   A port on the east coast, the chief centre of Scottish settlement in New Zealand. It contains many buildings connected with New Zealand's basic industries. Crown Roller Mills, a seven-bay, four-storey building, dates from 1867 but was rebuilt in its present form and converted to steel roller operation in 1890. Willowbank Brewery, dating from 1862, is now New Zealand's only whisky distillery. The substantial stone malthouse of the Union Brewery has been incorporated into a motel. Donaghy's Rope and Twine Co., established in 1876, still operates its original ropewalk. Dunedin's gas-supply company of 1863 was the first in New Zealand; a monumental retort house of 1907 survives in a much altered condition, and a balance house of the 1890s remains in use.

Dunedin has an outstanding railway station of 1907 by G. A. Troup, who created polychrome effects by using dark basalt with pale cream limestone dressings. Still in use, it is now part of a precinct that includes law courts and a police station. The colonnaded street elevation has a *porte-cochère*; Doulton faience decorates the walls of the booking hall, which has a pavement with mosaics depicting locomotives.

Mosgiel, 12 km (7$\frac{1}{2}$ mi.) to the south, has a woollen mill in the Classical style by H. F. Hardy, the first in Otago, erected in Arthur J. Burns in 1871–3 and enlarged in the 1880s. A former flourmill on the site has been converted to a dyehouse, which was the first factory in New Zealand to be lit by electricity, in 1885.

BIBLIOGRAPHY
General
Thornton, 1982.

BARRIE TRINDER

Dunfermline, Fife, Scotland   A town with a reputation for its linen damask tablecloths, acquired early in the eighteenth century; major expansion came with the introduction of Jacquard looms in 1824. The Andrew Carnegie (1835–1919) Birthplace Museum, named after the Dunfermline-born philanthropist who made his fortune in the PENNSYLVANIA steel industry, is in a weaver's cottage containing a Jacquard loom. Two further hand looms, a dobby and a Jacquard, are in Dunfermline District Museum. Power looms, introduced in 1849, have not been preserved.

The town had ten linen works, characteristically north-lit weaving sheds, with handsome neo-Classical offices. Two have three-storey warehouses, with rooms for showing and designing, for making pattern cards, and for embroidery. That at St Leonard's Works, the biggest damask works in Europe, founded in 1851, was converted to flats in 1984. Some sheds still produce table linen with Northrop looms. The warehouse at Pilmuir Works, founded in 1849, was added in 1893, and is now used by Dunlop, linked to the Baroque St Margaret's Works built in the 1870s and enlarged in 1893 by a 'bridge of sighs'. Canmore of 1867 (later used for silk-weaving), Castleblair of 1868 and Victoria Works of 1876 are more typical single-storey factories.

LOCATIONS
[M] Andrew Carnegie Birthplace Museum, Moodie Street, Dunfermline, Fife KY12 7PL.

[M] Dunfermline District Museum, Viewfield Terrace, Dunfermline, Fife KY12 7HY.

MARK WATSON

duplex A system of telegraphic working dating from c.1870, used on busy lines to send messages in both directions simultaneously over the same wire. Two duplex circuits make a quadruplex.

BIBLIOGRAPHY
General
Herbert, 1916.

Durham, County, England A county between the River Tees and the River Tyne, which formed part of Britain's most productive coalfield. Mining is now concentrated on the coast, but there are many former pit villages. Engine houses are preserved at Gateshead Fell and Haswell, 10 km (6 mi.) E. of Durham City; a vertical reciprocal winding engine of 1825 at Elemore, 9 km (5 mi.) E. of Durham; and a horizontal engine of 1888 at Washington. Ironmaking was important in west County Durham in the nineteenth century. Consett is a classic steelmaking town which has since lost its industry. Whinfield coke ovens are preserved at Rowlands Gill, 7 km (4 mi.) SW of Gateshead, and traces of ovens at East Hedleyhope, 5 km (3 mi.) E. of Tow Law. Derwentcote cementation furnace, 7 km (4 mi.) NE of Consett, is a unique survival from the eighteenth century. There are impressive ranges of nineteenth-century lime kilns on the coast at Marsden.

Durham coalfield is one of the birthplaces of the English railway. Causey Arch, 14 km (9 mi.) NW of Durham, which is 32 m (100 ft.) in span, was designed by Ralph Wood in 1727 to carry the Tanfield Wagonway. The bridge has been preserved, with a replica of an eighteenth-century wagon on one end. There are many HYBRID RAILWAYS. Parts of the Stanhope & Tyne Railway, authorized in 1831, are preserved as a footpath, which includes the deep rock cuttings of the Weatherill and Crawley inclines north of Stanhope, and passes workers' cottages at the isolated settlement of Waskerley. From 1858 the line crossed Hownes Gill, 1 km ($\frac{1}{2}$ mi.) N. of Consett, on an elegant firebrick viaduct by Thomas Bouch (1822–80). Bowes Railway ran across the Team Valley to Jarrow; built by GEORGE STEPHENSON in 1836, it was closed in 1974, but a 2 km (1 mi.) section near Springwell, 17 km (10 mi.) N. of Durham, has been preserved by Tyne & Wear Industrial Monuments Trust, and displays the working of inclines. The Victoria Viaduct, Penshaw, 12 km (8 mi.) NE of Durham City, built in 1838, a five-span structure by T. E. Harrison (1808–88), was modelled on Trajan's TOLEDO bridge. A notable viaduct of 1855 carries the main line through Durham City.

There are many remains of lead mines and smelters in the west of the county, particularly in Weardale, including well-preserved flues at Castleside, 3 km (2 mi.) SW of Consett. The outstanding monument in the region, the crushing plant at Killhope, 19 km (12 mi.) W. of Stanhope, with a 10.3 m (38 ft.) diameter water wheel, has been restored. A nineteenth-century lead-working site can be seen at Allenheads, with remains of the kilns and dressing floors.

Pelaw, 10 km (6 mi.) N. of Durham, contains early twentieth-century factories by the Co-operative Wholesale Society. Team Valley Trading Estate, Birtley, was a pioneering attempt at job creation in the mid-1930s.

See also BEAMISH; SUNDERLAND.

BIBLIOGRAPHY
General
Atkinson, 1974.
Specific
Rounthwaite, T. C. *The Railways of Weardale*. London: Railway Corresponding & Travel Society, 1965.

LOCATION
[M] Tyne & Wear Industrial Monuments Trust, Sandyford House, Archbold Terrace, Newcastle-upon-Tyne NE2 1ED.

BARRIE TRINDER

Durrës (Durazzo), Albania A port and the centre of the Albanian railway network. The railway station, however, is out of bounds to foreign visitors. Steam locomotives were still working there in 1986. The local history is illustrated in the museum.

LOCATION
[M] Durrës Museum, Durrës.

Düsseldorf, North Rhine-Westphalia, Germany The impressive office blocks of industrial firms, associations and banks, which have dominated the federal state capital Düsseldorf since c.1900, bear witness to the industrial development of the nearby RUHRGEBIET. Notable architects have worked here. PETER BEHRENS, chief designer for AEG of BERLIN, built the administrative headquarters of the Mannesmann coal and steel company in 1911–12. It is an office block of five storeys on a plinth, reminiscent of the palaces of Florence, and from the first was designed to be flexible in its interior planning.

The steel framework of the 'Dreischeibenhaus', an eleven-storey tower block designed by Hentrich & Petschnigg as offices for Phönix-Rheinrohr, later Thyssen AG, was built in 1957–60. In terms of period, the Stumm building, constructed by Paul Bonatz (1877–1956) in the expressionist style in 1922–5, lies between these two buildings – as does the Wilhelm Marx building, designed by Wilhelm Kreis (1873–1955) in 1922–4, one of the first tower blocks in Germany. At the beginning of the twentieth century, the main branches of the big banks, the Deutsche Bank, the Dresdener Bank and the Commerzbank, were built in the area between Königsalle and Breite Strasse. Nearby is the 'Stahlhof' of 1908, the former headquarters of the German steelworking association.

The three bridges over the Rhine at Düsseldorf are major works of civil engineering, conceived as a family, and built in 1956–7, 1966–9 and 1971–6. The last, linking the areas of the city on the right and left banks of the Rhine, was pushed into its final position by a launchway in 1976. The first electric-powered light railway in Europe on which ran express trains was built in

479. Litter bin, advertising column & tramway stopping post, Düsseldorf. (Neg. F. Pick).

Figure 38 A tram stop in Düsseldorf photographed by Frank Pick in 1930, the year of the International Hygiene Exhibition in Dresden advertised on the posters; Pick exercised a powerful influence on the design of transport facilities in London.
CPRE Collection, Institute of Agricultural History and Museum of English Rural Life, University of Reading

1898 over the predecessor of this bridge, as part of the city tramway network which was fully electrified from 1900. Another pioneer building of European significance is the multi-storey car park of 1949–50, glazed all round, and designed by Paul Schneider-Esleben.

At Ratingen, 10 km (6 mi.) NE of Düsseldorf, is the industrial community of Cromford, established in 1784 by Johann Brügelmann around the cotton spinning mill designed for him by Rutger Flügel, and modelled on the mills built by Richard Arkwright at CROMFORD, Derbyshire. The mill has remained substantially intact during a long working life and subsequent adaptation as workers' apartments. Most of the original roof structure is intact,

there are substantial remains of heating and power-transmission systems, and excavations have revealed important evidence of the water-power system. The mansion house and workers' dwellings of the mill survive, although later extensions to the factory and the gardens worked by the inhabitants have been obliterated by modern housing developments.

BIBLIOGRAPHY
Specific
Charlton, C. The Brügelmann Mill, Cromford, Ratingen. In *World Industrial History*, IV, 1987.
Schürmann, S. Öffentliche Bauten, Geschäfts- und Verwaltungs-bauten der ersten drei Jahrzehnte des 20 Jahrhunderts in

223

Düsseldorf (Public, commercial and administrative buildings of the first three decades of the twentieth century in Düsseldorf). In *Jahrbuch der Rheinischen Denkmalpflege* (Yearbook of the Rhineland Monuments Protection Service), XXXIII. Cologne, 1989.

Die Macht der Maschine 200 Jahre Cromford-Ratingen (The power of machines: 200 years of Cromford-Ratingen). Exh. cat. Stadtmuseum Ratingen, 1984.

LOCATIONS

[M] Land Museum of the People and the Economy, Ehrenhof 1, 4000 Düsseldorf.

[M] Museum of the History of Düsseldorf, Bäckerstrasse 7–9, 4000 Düsseldorf.

[M] Rheinisches Industriemuseum, Aussenstelle Ratingen, Cromforder Allee 24, 4030 Ratingen.

AXEL FÖHL

Duszniki Zdrój (Bad Reinerz), Wrocław, Poland   A town 120 km (75 mi.) SW of Wrocław. Original buildings of a sixteenth-century water-powered papermill are preserved, and handmade paper is produced in small quantities using traditional techniques. The mill was enlarged in the seventeenth century and gained prosperity in the eighteenth when it was granted exclusive rights to supply offices in Wrocław. Paper was made from linen rags, and finished with size made from animal bones and hides. It was decided in the 1920s to convert the mill into a regional museum of papermaking, but adaptation was stopped by World War II. The scheme was revived and the museum opened in 1968. The ground floor is of brick, with the upper storeys in wood, in a Baroque style characteristic of the region. Inside the mill are displays illustrating the history of papermaking both at Duszniki and generally, and the products of the modern paper industry. There is an outstanding collection of paper moulds with watermarks.

BIBLIOGRAPHY
General
Hössle, 1935.
Specific
Tomaszewski, W. Historia zabytkowej papierni w Dusznikach (The history of the old papermill in Duszniki). In *Przegląd Papierniczy* (Papermaking Review), 1959.

LOCATION
[M] Muzeum Papiernictwa (The museum of papermaking), Duszniki Zdrój, ul.Kłodzka 42.

PIOTR GERBER

dyehouse   A building where TEXTILES are dyed, either a component of an integrated TEXTILE MILL or a specialist establishment treating fibres, yarn, thread or fabrics from other manufacturing plants. Dyehouses are usually distinguishable externally by the long ventilators in their roofs, and archaeologically by the remains of complex networks of underground pipes. Traditional dyehouses using WOAD or INDIGO were equipped with large wooden vats.

BIBLIOGRAPHY
General
Partridge, 1823; Stratton and Trinder, 1989.

dyeing   The process of impregnating materials with colours. It is employed in various manufactures, but particularly in TEXTILES where it takes place in distinctive DYEHOUSES. A range of natural dyestuffs, some of which required MORDANTS to fix colours, was employed until 1856, when Sir William Perkin (1838–1907) demonstrated mauveine. This was the first of the ANILINE dyes (*see* PHENYLAMINE), most of which were subsequently developed in Germany.

See also INDIGO; LOGWOOD; MADDER; WOAD.

BIBLIOGRAPHY
General
Beer, 1949; Berthollet, 1791; Brunello, 1973; Hummel, 1888; Hurry, 1930; Lauterbach, 1905; Martin, 1918; Partridge, 1823; Pellew, 1913; Perkins and Everest, 1918.

Dyfi Furnace, Eglwysfach, Dyfed, Wales   At Furnace, 11 km (7 mi.) SW of Machynlleth, lie the imposing remains of the structure that gave the village its name: a charcoal iron furnace which smelted Cumbrian ore for local consumption between 1755 and *c*.1800. Reused subsequently, it has been excavated and partially restored, and appears substantially as when drawn by Philip James de Loutherbourg (1740–1812) in 1804.

BIBLIOGRAPHY
General
Rees, 1975.

LOCATION
[M] Dyfi Furnace Museum, Eglwysfach, Dyfed.

dynamite   The first practical high explosive, developed by ALFRED NOBEL: a combination of nitroglycerine and kieselguhr, a diatomaceous earth. Explosive could be extruded in sticks, which were more stable than liquid nitroglycerine. The term came to be applied to the whole series of explosives based on nitroglycerine that were developed from the 1860s.

BIBLIOGRAPHY
General
Morgan and Pratt, 1938; Reader, 1970.

dynamo   A device for generating electric power, producing direct current. In 1831 Michael Faraday (1791–1867) rotated a conductor in a magnetic field, obtaining a fairly dependable current for the first time. All subsequent dynamos rely upon this principle. Faraday's conductor was a copper disc, but in 1832 Pixii replaced this with coils of wire, the armature. In most designs the armature revolved; in others, it was the magnets that turned. In the Wilde and Siemens versions electromagnets were used for the first time. Antonio Pacinotti in 1860 devised an armature with coils of wire around a ring, but this was ignored until re-invented by Z. T. Gramme in 1870, after which the design became popular until Hefner Alteneck in 1873 wound the wire over a drum. A slight modification of this system is still used in modern dynamos.

BIBLIOGRAPHY
General
Case, 1921; Dunsheath, 1962.

E

earthenware A term applied to wares having porous bodies which may or may not be covered by a glaze. The earliest earthenware was coarse in texture and baked in the sun. The development of fine earthenwares centred on Britain and the works of John Dwight (d. 1698), JOSIAH WEDGWOOD, and Josiah Spode (1754–1827) amongst others.

See also DELFTWARE; FAIENCE; MAJOLICA; SALT GLAZE; SLIPWARE, STONEWARE.

BIBLIOGRAPHY
General
Boger, 1971; Brears, 1971; Brongniart, 1844; Chaffers, 1965; Jewitt, 1878; Towner, 1957.

East Anglia, England The name usually applied to the counties of Essex, Cambridgeshire, Norfolk and Suffolk, a region superficially agricultural but with a distinctive industrial history. Many aspects of its history are illustrated in open-air museums at Stowmarket and Gressenhall. There are outstanding windmills at Drinkstone, Suffolk – a post mill of 1689 with an adjacent smock mill tower; at Tiptree, Essex, a late eighteenth-century five-storey tower; and Great Chishill, Cambridgeshire, a post mill of 1819. Water mills at Baylham, Suffolk, and at Colne Wakes, Essex, are of particular interest. Flatford Mill, Suffolk, made famous by the paintings of John Constable (1776–1837), is preserved but lacks machinery. There are many maltings in the region: a fifty-bay late nineteenth-century range may be seen at Beccles, and there are other good examples at East Dereham and Manningtree. Snape Maltings, now a concert hall, is an outstanding example of adaptive reuse. The woollen industry was important until the eighteenth century. Silk mills survive at Coggeshall (1820), Braintree (1818) and Haverhill (1828); and there is a rare survival of an 81 m × 15 m (266 ft. × 49 ft.) flax-retting pit at Hampnall, Norfolk. There are well-preserved tannery buildings at Reepham, Norfolk, and Combs, Suffolk. Many nineteenth-century market town foundries can be seen; Thomas Smithdale's works of 1869, at Panxworth, 12 km (8 mi.) NE of Norwich, and Burrells' St Nicholas Ironworks, Thetford, are good examples. The spectacular Long Shop or 'Cathedral' of 1853 at Leiston, in which Messrs Garrett erected steam engines, is now a museum. Other sites include nineteenth-century horsehair manufactories at Lavenham and Long Melford; a razor-blade factory of 1925–52 at South Creake, Norfolk; and Messrs Hobbies' fretwork factory at East Dereham. The xylonite works at Cattawade, Suffolk, dating from 1887, includes a power station with three Metro-Vickers turbines and a Bellis & Morcom steam engine. A furniture repository at Chelmsford was used from 1899 by the Wireless Telegraph & Signals Co. (later Marconi Wireless Telegraph Co. Ltd) but this building was superseded by the Marconi works of 1912 in New Street. Most British sugar beet factories are in East Anglia; Queen Adelaide works, Ely, dating from 1920, is an early example. The Hippodrome, St Peter's Road, Great Yarmouth, was purpose built for the circus in 1903.

BIBLIOGRAPHY
General
Alderton and Booker, 1980; Booker, 1974; Wailes, 1967.

LOCATIONS
[M] Museum of East Anglian Life, Stowmarket, Suffolk IP14 1DL.
[M] Norfolk Rural Life Museum, Beech House, Gressenhall, Dereham, Norfolk NR20 4DR.

BARRIE TRINDER

écomusée A French concept for which use of the French term is preferable, although the Anglicized 'ecomuseum' has some currency. An écomusée is a project that permits the population of an area to discern its own identity, through its built environment, its ecology and its geology as well as its documentary and oral history, and to make study of such topics a communal activity, not something restricted to qualified 'experts'. Political activism is seen as a likely concomitant of such activities. The idea was propounded in 1967 by the ethnologist Georges Henri Rivière (1897–1985), who defined an écomusée as 'a mirror in which the population looks to know itself better and understand the problems of its own future'. The concept was most energetically put into practice at LE CREUSOT, and since 1970 the term has been used in Belgium, Italy, Quebec, Sweden and Switzerland for innovative projects, usually directed towards the conservation and interpretation of landscapes, and involving a degree of community participation, but otherwise not necessarily conforming to Rivière's ideals.

BIBLIOGRAPHY
General
Rivière, 1989.
Specific
Écomusées Information, La Communauté Creusot-Montceau les Mines, 1983.
Hudson, K. A living museum. In *New Society*. London, 17 February 1975.
Watson, M. Écomusées. In *World Industrial History* (Ironbridge Gorge Museum Trust), I, 1984.

MARK WATSON

Edessa (Edhessa), Macedonia, Greece Water-powered cotton and woollen factories were established in Edessa, 75 km (45 mi.) W. of Thessaloníki, as in other Macedonian towns, during 1874–1912. They were located close to a dramatic 24 m (79 ft.) waterfall. Most were fitted with English machinery. The main plants are a yarn factory of 1895, a spinning mill of 1907, and a spinning and weaving mill of 1906. Several silk factories also survive. One of the main modern industries is carpet manufacture, established by refugees from Turkey after the 1920s.

BIBLIOGRAPHY
Specific
Zarkada, C. Textile factories in Edessa. In *Archaeology*, XVIII, 1986.

edge runner A type of mill in which a large wheel, often a cylindrical stone, is propelled around a trough-shaped circular track, in which may be placed solid materials to be ground, or fruits or seeds from which liquids are extracted. Such mills may be powered by animals following circular paths concentric with the tracks in which the materials to be milled are placed, as in the traditional CIDER mill. Alternatively they may be powered through shafting by water wheels, steam engines or other prime movers, as in most BONE and FLINT mills.

Edinburgh, Lothian, Scotland Scotland's capital is well supplied with service industry and museums. The adjacent port of Leith provided the docks and much of the industry, but remained politically and administratively separate until 1920.

The city had eighteen breweries as recently as 1960: now there are three. Biggest and ugliest is the Fountain Brewery of William McEwan. Tennants' Heriot Brewery is mainly modern, sandwiched by a modest Italianate office and a four-storey brewhouse. The Caledonian Brewery, formerly Lorimer & Clark, was saved by a management buy-out in 1987. It is a pleasing brick complex, founded in 1869, with a four-storey malthouse and brewhouse. The three open coppers, one installed in 1869, were, until 1985, the last direct coal-fired coppers in Britain.

The above breweries are to the west of the city. The other main brewing areas, Holyrood and Craigmillar, ceased brewing in 1986 and 1987 respectively, but had the highest concentration of breweries in Britain apart from Burton-upon-Trent. Craigend Brewery (once Drybrough's) and a three-storey maltings on Calton Road have been converted to flats, and the maltings of St Anne's Brewery is a store for Historic Scotland. The Argyll (Cowgate) brewery closed long ago but appears externally unchanged, having a louvred brewhouse and chimney. A brewery on The Pleasance is now a university sports centre.

There are two grain whisky distilleries. The North British has a Jacobean office dated 1887 and large BONDS. The Caledonian Distillery was, when built in 1855, the largest in Scotland, and still impresses, having Scottish BARONIAL crow-stepped bonds, a tall curved-roofed stillhouse, maltings, and a tall chimney that dominates Haymarket. The Scotch Whisky Heritage Centre opened in 1988 in a former school by the Castle.

Leith has a striking collection of bonded and general warehouses, some converted to flats, notably the Vaults of 1682, enlarged in 1785, with their sixteenth-century undercroft housing the Scotch Whisky Society, the Cooperage and Maritime Court. A large warehouse in Wellington Place, with rope mouldings, awaits conversion. The Vat 69 bonds on Bonnington Road, which are converted to flats and offices, are startlingly austere eight-storey brick hulks, one pilastered with a cast-iron water tank, originally a sugar refinery of 1866. Crabbie's Green Ginger Wine is blended in bonds of the 1830s on North Junction Street and is occasionally open to visitors.

A substantial publishing industry in Edinburgh was supported by papermills and printing works. The former were originally water-powered rag-pulp mills of the late eighteenth and early nineteenth centuries, ten on the River Esk and two on the Almond. The survivors are considerably altered. Printing works within the city date from the second half of the nineteenth century. Edina Works, a long, two-storey polychrome brick building, built in 1878 for Morrison & Gibb, now houses a builders' merchant. The fronts of printing works at Tanfield and Brandon Street mask new developments.

Grain milling was another significant Edinburgh industry. A windmill tower of 1685 stands at Leith. Quayside Mills, still working, were founded in 1825, and incorporate the wooden ogee spire of a church of 1675. In Carpet Lane there is a large arcaded mill of 1828, and Leith is dominated by the concrete Chancelot Mills of 1953–4. On the Water of Leith the five-storey West Mill of 1805 was converted to flats in 1973, and the pedimented granary of Bell's Mills of 1807 is now a hotel.

The London Road Foundry of T. L. Miller & Co. still functions as an engineering works, having long machine shops, an arcaded front of 1890, and an office within an ornate Jacobean tenement. The nineteenth-century Mitchell Street lead works is long disused but retains its cupola, post-crane and assorted chimneys.

At Portobello Pottery the bottle kilns of 1906 and 1909, 7 m (23 ft.) in diameter and 11.89 m (39 ft.) high, are now the best examples in Scotland. Other buildings were demolished on closure in 1972. The nearby Portobello Chocolate Factory is a reinforced-CONCRETE building of 1908 on the E. P. Wells system.

Edinburgh's first power station, at McDonald Road, was built in 1899. It is in brick, with a pedimented stone front and an arched steel roof on cast-iron stanchions. The octagonal chimney has an arcaded top.

The National Museums of Scotland were formed in 1985 combining the Royal Scottish Museum (founded in 1854, and the Scottish equivalent of the South Kensington museums – *see* LONDON) and the National Museum of Antiquities, which is devoted to the history of the Scots. The Chambers Street building of 1861 by Francis Fowke has a cast-iron columned and galleried interior with a laminated timber roof. Exhibits include a BOULTON & WATT engine of the 1780s, an Aberdeen water wheel of 1826, and the locomotive *Wylam Dilly* of 1813, together with a

Figure 39 Bonnington Bond, Leith, Edinburgh, a bonded warehouse for whisky adapted from a sugar refinery built *c*.1870
Mark Watson

large collection of scientific instruments. Most displays consist of models made in the museum workshops.

At Huntly House, Edinburgh District Museums cover local trade and industry, while the Tolbooth opposite houses 'The People's Story', a social and labour history display.

The Scottish Telecommunications Museum, owned by British Telecom, is housed in a former telephone exchange, 4 Newbattle Terrace, built in 1924 to bring the automatic system to Edinburgh. It houses manual and automatic exchanges and other equipment.

Haymarket station was the terminus of the Edinburgh & Glasgow Railway in 1840. The train shed has been re-erected at BO'NESS, leaving a fine office with Doric tetrastyle portico and clock. Waverley station was rebuilt

in 1892–1902 with island platforms under an overall multi-ridge steel roof. The North British and Caledonian Hotels were the flagships of the rival railway companies.

Between 1888 and 1923 Edinburgh had the fourth largest cable-tramway system in the world. The original power station and depot are on Henderson Row. The second, of four, was built in 1898 at Shrubhill, and comprises brick and stone buildings with shaped gables, a large, two-aisled steam-engine house, and later work-shops, all with steel roofs on cast-iron stanchions. A dormant transport museum containing an Edinburgh cable tram and an Aberdeen horse tram is reputed to lie within this complex.

The South (1786), Regent (1816), George IV (1829) and North (1896) Bridges turn parts of Edinburgh into a two-tier city. More dramatic is THOMAS TELFORD's Dean Bridge of 1829, four arches spanning the ravine of the Water of Leith. The vertical lift bridge over the Union Canal at Leamington in Gilmour Park is unique in Scotland.

Leith Docks are now the most extensive and intensively used in Scotland. From medieval times the mouth of the Water of Leith was lined with warehouses and shipyards, one of which housed the first patent SLIP by Thomas Morton (1781–1832) in 1823. JOHN RENNIE's East and West Docks (1806 and 1811–17) have been infilled, leaving his long four-storey warehouses and a cast-iron swing bridge of 1842. The long East and West Piers, completed in 1829, allowed access to the Victoria (1847), Albert (1869), Edinburgh (1873–81) and Imperial (1896–1904) Docks. Albert Dock was the first in Scotland to have hydraulic cranes, one of which survives. The Prince of Wales Graving Dock of 1858–63 has a hydraulic power station, with an Italianate campanile accumulator tower, now the office of the Forth Port Authority. There are two later graving docks, and a bow-truss swing bridge of 1896. The Western Harbour, completed in 1943, was lined by earlier shipbuilding yards. The Custom House of 1810, by William Burn (1789–1870), severely neo-Classical, is now a store for the National Museum.

Tenements for the working and middle classes are larger and deeper than those in Glasgow: four to six storeys, sometimes with basements and attics, Baronial in Marchmont, simply Classical in the New Town, and unadorned elsewhere. Colonies of two-storey flatted terraces were built by co-operatives at Pilrig in 1849, Stockbridge from 1861, and Haymarket and Abbeyhill in the 1870s.

BIBLIOGRAPHY
General
Hume, 1976
Specific
Pipes, R. J. *The Colonies of Stockbridge*. Edinburgh, 1984.

LOCATIONS
[M] Huntly House Museum, 142 Canongate, Edinburgh.
[M] National Museums of Scotland, Chambers Street, Edinburgh EH1 1JF, and Queen Street, Edinburgh EH2 1JD.
[M] The Scotch Whisky Heritage Centre, 358 Castlehill, The Royal Mile, Edinburgh EH1 2NE.
[M] Scottish Telecommunications Museum, c/o British Telecom, 6 Atholl Crescent, Edinburgh.

MARK WATSON

Edison, Thomas Alva (1847–1931) The most prolific of American inventors, whose work has done much to shape twentieth-century civilization. Edison was born in Milan, Ohio. By 1868 he was working for a telegraph company in Boston, and in 1869 he formed a partnership with F. L. Pope and J. N. Ashley in New York, the three calling themselves 'electrical engineers', the first use of the term. He was bought out the following year, and used his capital to set up an 'inventions' factory, concentrating at first on improvements in telegraphy. In 1876 he devised the carbon telephone transmitter. The same year he established a laboratory at Menlo Park, N.J., now at Dearborn (*see* MICHIGAN). He devised the phonograph (*see* GRAMOPHONE) in 1877; and in 1879 showed that the incandescent electric lamp could be produced commercially. In the 1880s he devised the essentials of a system by which electric current could be distributed to consumers from a 'central' POWER STATION. In 1887 he moved his laboratory to West Orange (*see* NEW JERSEY), and built up the commercial companies later to become the General Electric Corporation. He concerned himself with CEMENT manufacture, electric traction, and COPIERS; and in the 1890s did much to effect the standardization that made possible the commercial development of cinematography.

BIBLIOGRAPHY
General
Dyer *et al.*, 1929; Josephson, 1959; McLaren, 1943; Passer, 1972.

BARRIE TRINDER

Edlach an der Rax, Lower Austria, Austria A town 72 km (44 mi.) SW of Vienna, where an ironworks was established *c*.1716 by the convent of Neuberg, and sold to K. K. Innerberger Hauptgewerkschaft in 1780. The shell of a furnace of 1716 which was rebuilt in 1793, with its 12 m (39 ft.) chimney, is preserved and used as a dwelling.

Egyptian A style of INDUSTRIAL ARCHITECTURE, derived from buildings erected in Egypt between the 3rd millennium BC and the Roman period, often incorporating palm capitals, deep cornices and such decorative motifs as sphinxes. It was popular chiefly in the first half of the nineteenth century.

Eidskog, Hedmark, Norway The principal town on Engebret Soot's Canal, a timber-floating waterway, on the Swedish border, 60 km (37 mi.) E. of Oslo, built in the 1840s and used until 1932. Construction involved damming lakes and building sixteen locks and a 3 km (2 mi.) horse-operated railway. The canal came to public attention with a well-publicized canoe tour in 1975. It is now the subject of a conservation project.

BIBLIOGRAPHY
Specific
Wiig, J. Restoration of Engebret Soot's floating canal. In Nisser and Bedoire, 1978.

Eidsvoll, Akershus, Norway A town 68 km (42 mi.) N. of Oslo, on the River Vorma, which flows into the River Glommen from Lake Mjøsa. Eidsvoll was the original terminus of the Norwegian Trunk Railway completed from Oslo in 1854. Eidsvollsverk, an ironworks 6 km (4 mi.) W., where the Norwegian constitution was adopted in 1814, is now conserved. The paddle steamer *Skibladner*, constructed in 1856 and known as the 'white swan of Lake Mjøsa', operates a daily return service to LILLEHAMMER during the summer.

[S] Eidsvoll Memorial, Highway 20, 2074 Eidsvollsverk, Akershus.

Eifel, North Rhine-Westphalia, Germany   The western part of the Rheinisches Schiefergebirge, the Eifel, lies between the Moselle, the Rhine and the Belgian border. It is undulating highland country with many volcanic formations, from which have been extracted basalt, pumice, tufa (a soft limestone used for building and cement), and trass (employed for millstones and hydraulic cement). Lead mining was important in the nineteenth century, especially at Mechernich, 42 km (26 mi.) SE of Aachen, but declined in the 1940s. Its last memorial is the octagonal MALAKOFF TOWER of 1870 on the Mechernich Schafberg, one of the few surviving examples outside the RUHRGEBIET. Limekilns are commonplace in the region, especially around Kall and Nettersheim, 40 km (27 mi.) SE of Aachen. The traditional iron industry of the Eifel began to decline early in the nineteenth century. By c.1860 the last manufacturers had moved to the major transport routes of the Rhine and the Ruhr, which were also closer to coal supplies. A rare relic of ironworking is the first gas-pipe factory in continental Europe, built in 1845 at Gemünd-Mauel, 12 km (8 mi.) W. of Mechernich. Many former water power sites remain in the valleys of the eastern Eifel.

The many dams of the Eifel were built only partly for providing water power. The Urft dam, completed in 1904, supplies one of the finest JUGENDSTIL power stations in Europe, but was designed principally to prevent flooding in the lower reaches of the river Rur east of Aachen. Other dams of interest include the Olef dam, Hellenthal, 40 km (25 mi.) SE of Aachen, a pier and cell construction of 1955–9, and the Dreilägerbach dam of 1911 at Roetgen, 16 km (10 mi.) SE of Aachen. Besides the ten dams in the German Eifel, there are four on the Belgian side, including the celebrated Gileppe dam, 9 km (5 mi.) E. of VERVIERS.

Water was important for the textile industry of the German Eifel. The magnificent seven-storey 'Rotes Haus' (red house) above the Laufenbach in the textile town of Monschau, 30 km (19 mi.) S. of Aachen, combines dwellings with workshops, and was built in 1756 by Johann B. Scheibler. The late Baroque carvings in the stairwell depict all the stages of cloth manufacture. It is now the Scheibler Foundation museum. The Wiesenthal factory of 1809 in Monschau now houses public offices.

The social history of the Eifel is illustrated in the open-air museum at Kommern, 44 km (27 mi.) SE of Aachen, established in 1958 and opened three years later: it includes buildings relating to such traditional manufacturing crafts as weaving, wood-turning and shoemaking.

BIBLIOGRAPHY
General
Barkhausen, 1925; Bömmels, 1924; Gunter, 1970; Timmermann, 1951; Zippelius, 1974.
Specific
Hähnel, J. *Rheinisches Freilichtmuseum Kommern: Museumsführer* (Guide to the Rhineland Open-Air Museum, Kommern). Cologne: Rheinland-Verlag GmbH, 1983.

Schumacher, M. Zweckbau und Industrieschloss. Fabrikbauten der rheinisch-westfälischen Textilindustrie vor der Gründungzeit (Functional buildings and industrial castles. Factory buildings of pre-industrial textile manufactures in the Rhineland and Westphalia). In *Tradition: Zeitschrift für Firmengeschichte und Unternehmerbiographie* (Tradition: papers in business history and biography), xv. Stuttgart, 1970.

[M] Rheinisches Freilichtmuseum – Landesmuseum für Volkskunde (The Rhenish Open-Air Museum: Provincial Museum of Folk Culture), 5351 Kommern (Kreis Euskirchen).
[M] Scheibler Foundation Museum, Laufenstrasse 10, 5108 Monschau.

AXEL FÖHL

Eiffel, Alexandre Gustave (1832–1923)   The most celebrated of French constructional engineers, Eiffel was born at Dijon and trained at the École Centrale des Arts et Manufactures, establishing his own practice in 1866–7. His early works included the 162 m (540 ft.) long Garabit viaduct over the River Truyère in the Cantal department in southern France, 90 km (55 mi.) S. of Clermont Ferrand. Built in 1870–4, it crosses the river at a height of 120 m (400 ft.). He also designed a 160 m (525 ft.) span steel arch bridge at OPORTO (*see* figure 103), completed in 1877. Eiffel was one of the first to employ COMPRESSED AIR in CAISSONS during civil-engineering projects. In 1885 Eiffel designed the wrought-iron frame of the Statue of Liberty, NEW YORK, while the 300 m (1000 ft.) high latticework wrought-iron tower in PARIS which commemorates his name was built in 1887–9 for the centennial exposition in celebration of the French Revolution.

Eindhoven, Noord Brabant, The Netherlands   A city standing in a region of sandy soils where profitable agriculture has always been difficult and where until the 1890s textiles and cigars were the principal manufactures, having been attracted by new roads and canals and by cheap labour. In the 1920s more than seventy cigar and tobacco manufactories were working in Eindhoven, although remains of the industry are now few. Many small factories in the 'cigar villages' of Valkenswaard and Bergeyk, 6 km (4 mi.) S. of Eindhoven, only closed after World War II.

Frederik Philips and his son Gerard founded their company for the manufacture of carbon-filament lamps in 1891. At the Emmasingel the original buildings are cherished, and serve as an information centre for what is now a multinational company. Eindhoven is dominated by Philips: as early as 1930 three-quarters of its population worked in the company's many factories, which illustrated changing styles in industrial architecture, from concrete buildings of 1911 in traditional style to functional designs of the 1930s. In 'Philipsdorp' are many workers' dwellings, together with educational and recreational facilities. The company maintains a museum and the 'Evoluon', a building in the shape of a flying saucer, with displays on science and technology and their impact on society.

The 'De Ploeg' weaving mill at Bergeyk was built in

1923 as part of a Utopian co-operative community. At Helmond, 10 km (6 mi.) NE, nineteenth-century textile and engineering works remain along the Zuid Willemsvaart canal, and the Municipal Museum specializes in paintings relating to industry and labour.

Best, 11 km (7 mi.) NW, is the principal clog-manufacturing centre in the Netherlands, with several small factories (some open to the public) using wood from local poplar plantations. There are bell foundries at Aarle Rixtel, 19 km (12 mi.) NE, and Asten, 18 km (11 mi.) SE. De Groote Peel, south of Asten, is an extensive peatland drained from 1856. There is a preserved nineteenth-century water mill at Spoordonk, 16 km (10 mi.) NW; and a stone tower mill of 1857 in Oirschot, 12 km ($7\frac{1}{2}$ mi.) NW, together with the 'Oirschotse Stoel', a massive wooden stool symbolizing the local furniture industry.

LOCATIONS
[M] Evoluon, Noord-Brabantlaan 1a, Eindhoven.
[M] Gemeentemuseum (Municipal Museum), Kasteel Helmond, Helmond.
[M] Nationaal Beiaardmuseum (National Carillon Museum), Asten.
[M] Nederlandse Klompen Museum (Netherlands Museum of Clogmaking), Broekdijk 16, Best.
[M] Philips Bedrijfsmuseum (Philips Company Museum), Emmasingel, Gebouw HCE, Eindhoven.

JURRIE VAN DALEN

Eire See IRELAND.

Eisenerz, Styria, Austria See STYRIAN IRON TRAIL.

elastic Elastic webbing and braid consist of threads cut from thin rubber sheets, made by spreading layers of India rubber solution, already charged with sulphur for vulcanizing, on a textile base prepared with adhesives. Vulcanization is affected by steam. A considerable industry utilizing elastic webbing had grown up in the LEICESTER area by the 1850s, supplying materials for boots and gloves.

BIBLIOGRAPHY
General
Smith, 1965.

Elba (Isola d'Elba), Italy Iron ore on this Mediterranean island was worked by the Etruscans from the sixth century BC, and opencast workings on the coast recommenced in the seventeenth century, becoming the source of ore for the blast furnaces at CAPALBIO and FOLLONICA. Quarrying developed in the eastern peninsula where the most important sites worked in the tenth century were (from north to south): Rio Albano, Vigneria, Rio Marina, Terranova and Point Calamita. Narrow-gauge railways and aerial ropeways brought the ore to jetties on the coast.

BIBLIOGRAPHY
General
Naval Intelligence Division, 1944–5.

Elbasan, Albania The chief Albanian metallurgical plants are located at Elbasan, a sensitive area where foreigners are forbidden to take pictures even from great distances. There is a museum of local history and ethnography within the fortress.

LOCATION
[M] Elbasan Museum, Elbasan.

electric arc furnace A refractory-lined furnace in which an electric arc is struck between the electrode and the metal to be melted. Sir WILLIAM SIEMENS patented the concept in 1878. Paul Héroult used an electric arc furnace to produce aluminium in 1886. An electric arc furnace was used to make steel, often called 'electrosteel', by F. Kjellin at Gysinge bruk, Sweden, in 1899. In 1904 Héroult invented an arc furnace that was to become the model for all arc furnaces now in use. The most common type has three electrodes placed in a triangle. The production of steel in such furnaces increased enormously during World War I, at the same time as the production of alloy steel (*see* STEEL) increased, and electric arc furnaces proved superior for that purpose to OPEN-HEARTH FURNACES. Today electric arc furnaces are used for the production of some alloy steels, but mainly for melting scrap. A furnace of 1905 is preserved at REMSCHEID.

BIBLIOGRAPHY
General
Gale, 1969, 1971.

electric induction furnace A refractory-lined vessel, set on trunnions for charging and pouring, with wire coiled round it. Current through the wiring establishes the secondary circuit used to melt metal within the vessel. The induction furnace is used for melting pig iron, scrap or steel in a foundry, or for adding alloying elements to molten steel, but not for producing steel from pig iron. The first such furnaces were built by Northamp in the USA. The first in Europe was used at Finspång (*see* NORRKOPING) from 1927. A furnace of 1932 at Hagfors (*see* MUNKFORS) is preserved.

BIBLIOGRAPHY
General
Gale, 1969, 1971.

electric locomotive Main-line railways developed at the same time as the first significant experiments with electricity, and as early as 1842 Robert Davidson made a trial of electric railway traction in Scotland. The first significant demonstration was by Werner von Siemens (1816–92), who used a locomotive now in the Deutsches Museum (*see* MUNICH) to pull passengers along a 277 m (303 yd.) line at the Berlin exhibition of 1879, and was also concerned with experiments in Ireland (*see* PORTRUSH). The first public electric railway was opened at BRIGHTON by Magnus Volk (1851–1937) in 1883, the year in which LEO DAFT built an electric locomotive, the *Ampère*, for the Saratoga & Mount McGregor Railroad. THOMAS EDISON built three demonstration lines in 1880–4.

The first major railway-electrification scheme involved a 4.5 mi. (7 km) section of the Baltimore & Ohio, largely in tunnels, electrified in 1894 at 650 V d.c. Other American lines followed this example, notably the New York, New Haven & Hartford operating from 1907, the 216 km (134 mi.) section of the Virginian RR from Mullens to Roanoke in 1924–5, and the Pennsylvania RR between New York and Philadelphia in 1933. American electric locomotives were mostly large, rod-driven machines. The most celebrated were the GG1 class, 2–Co+Co–2, streamliners built for passenger and freight work by the Pennsylvania RR from 1933.

In Europe early initiatives came in Hungary and Switzerland. In 1896 Koloman von Kando demonstrated a locomotive using 3000 V three-phase a.c. in Budapest, and in 1902 the Budapest builders Ganz (*see* BUDAPEST) built locomotives of this type for lines in Italy. The locomotives worked until the 1960s. Kando was later the electrical engineer for the SIMPLON Railway. The first Swiss electric railway was that between Burgdorf and Thun, electrified in 1899. The great mountain routes through the Simplon and Lötschberg tunnels, completed in 1906 and 1910, were electrified from the beginning. The Swiss standardized on a single-phase system, and were pioneers in the 1930s in the changeover from rod-driven locomotives to those with individual axle drive. Switzerland and Sweden, both rich in hydro-electric power, electrified most of their systems before 1939. The electrification of the main line from Berlin to Silesia was begun in 1911; while in France the line from Paris to Orleans was electrified by 1926, and had been completed to Bordeaux and Toulouse by 1939. In Britain several systems were tried before 1914, but apart from underground lines in London and Liverpool, and suburban routes from Manchester and Newcastle, electric traction remained of little significance on British railways. In the 1920s and 30s the 600 V d.c. third rail system of the Southern Railway was extended to cover much of South-East England. Since World War II most main lines and the majority of heavily used suburban railway systems in Europe have been electrified.

Electric locomotives and multiple units pick up current either from conductor rails laid alongside or between the running rails, or through a pantograph which makes contact with a catenary of overhead wires. Low voltage (600–750 V) d.c. systems with conductor rails are used on the Long Island Railroad, the Southern Region of British Rail (formerly the Southern Railway), and many other urban systems. Medium voltage (1500–3000 V) d.c. systems with overhead wires were much favoured in the 1920s and 30s and are used in the Netherlands, parts of France, Spain and Italy. The three-phase a.c. system developed by Kando has now been abandoned. High-voltage (11 000–25 000 V) a.c. with overhead wires was employed in the USA, Scandinavia, Austria, Germany and Switzerland before 1939, and since the 1950s 25 000 V at the standard industrial frequency has become standard in France and Great Britain.

It is conventional to refer to the wheel arrangement of electric locomotives by a system using letters rather than numbers. A is equivalent to a single driving axle, B to two axles, C to three, D to four. An 'o' is added (e.g. Co) if each driving axle has a motor of its own. Unpowered axles or carrying trucks are denoted by numbers. Thus a locomotive mounted on two six-wheel bogies with each axle powered is denoted Co–Co; one where the inner wheels of each bogie are unpowered as A1A–A1A; and a similar machine with carrying trucks at each end as 2–Co–Co–2. The same system is used for diesel locomotives.

See also MULTIPLE UNIT.

BIBLIOGRAPHY
General
Ashe and Keiley, 1905; Dawson, 1909; Haut, 1977; Hinde, 1948; Langdon, 1897; Westwood, 1983.

BARRIE TRINDER

electric power Electric current, the flow of electrons in suitable materials (conductors), which can be generated, channelled, controlled, and exploited as a means of doing work, was regarded as an entertaining curiosity from antiquity until the mid-eighteenth century. Scientific investigations by Alessandro Volta (1745–1817), Pieter van Musschenbroek (1691–1761), Luigi Galvani (1737–98) and others led to new departures in chemistry, and to the discovery of the relationship between electricity and magnetism by H. C. Ørsted (1777–1851), J. J. A. Ampère (1800–64) and Michael Faraday (1791–1867) between 1819 and 1831. Thereafter developments in DYNAMOS, ALTERNATORS and GENERATORS, and the construction of large POWER STATIONS, have pushed power output in 160 years from scarcely a quarter of a watt to hundreds of thousands of millions per annum. The first large-scale commercial uses of electricity were for telegraphs, from 1837; lighthouses, from 1857; arc lighting of streets and large buildings, from the 1870s; and tramways, from 1883. Such pioneering systems employed direct current, but improvements in electric motors and the increasing need for wide distribution networks brought alternating current to the fore, where it remains. Electricity is now an indispensable basis for civilization.

See figure 40; *see also* figure 30.

BIBLIOGRAPHY
General
Kloss, 1987.

CHRISTOPHER GREEN

electric tram Trams powered by compressed air, by naptha, by batteries, by gas, petrol and diesel engines, and even by clockwork were tried, but none could compare with the economy and efficiency of electric traction. Power generated at a remote station was supplied to the tramlines; the tramcar simply completed an electrical circuit between the rails and an overhead wire, or various forms of surface or underground contact devices. The current was fed to electric motors which drove the tramcar through a graduated series of reducing resistances housed in a driver-operated controller. First demonstrated in Berlin in 1881, electric trams were

Figure 40   A diorama in the Deutsches Museum, Munich, showing the transmission of electric power in 1891 from Lauffen to Frankfurt-am-Main; in the foreground is a 100 hp electric motor.
Deutsches Museum, Munich

developed in the USA, from where the use of overhead-wire current collection became almost universal. Legislation limited the development of British tramways (*see* CROMFORD; FYLDE) and most had been replaced by buses by the 1960s. Elsewhere in Europe the value of the electric tram as a mass carrier has long been appreciated, and its reintroduction into several American and British cities has been effected or is planned.

BIBLIOGRAPHY
General
Kay, 1968; Klapper, 1961.

PAUL COLLINS

electrolysis   The decomposition of a substance by means of an electric current. Passing electricity through acidulated water or a salt solution (known as an electrolyte) between two electrodes – the anode, positive, and the cathode, negative – causes the solution to decompose. Michael Faraday (1791–1867) showed in 1832–4 that molten sodium chloride could be electrolysed to produce chlorine and sodium. The principle of electrolysis as a

means of producing alkali metals from their chlorides was patented in 1851, but it was not until cheap hydro-electric power became available at the end of the century that the process became practicable. The first commercial operations were carried out near Frankfurt by Chemische Fabrik Electron AG in 1889–90, and the widely used CASTNER-KELLNER CELL was developed during the 1890s. Electrolysis is the basis of many twentieth-century chemical and metallurgical processes.

BIBLIOGRAPHY
General
Castner-Kellner, 1945; Partington, 1950; Warren, 1980.

electroplating   The plating of one metal or alloy with another, brought about by placing the piece to be coated in a solution of the other metal, and using it as the cathode by which an electric current is passed through the solution.

elevator   A term with at least three distinct meanings in industrial archaeology:

1. 'The means by which man colonized the air', as it was described in 1915. Before 1865 few people lived more than 21 m (70 ft.) from the ground: the elevator made possible the SKYSCRAPER. The true elevator has a car or platform for the accommodation of passengers or freight, operating among the floors of a multi-storey building: guided by a system of vertical rails, it is raised by dedicated mechanically-powered machinery, under the control of the operator on the car. The earliest known elevators, called 'teagles', were operating in England in Lancashire textile factories by the 1830s, and were powered by LINE SHAFTING, control being by means of a stationary endless rope running the height of the shaft. Operating elevators in buildings without power sources posed difficulties. In 1848 Jesse Hartley ordered two hydraulic hoists (*see* HYDRAULIC POWER) for warehouses in LIVERPOOL from WILLIAM ARMSTRONG, which were the precursors of the hydraulic elevators which became widely used in the USA as public water supplies were extended. In 1854 Elisha Graves Otis (1811–61) developed the safety brake, which stopped the car if the tension on the hauling rope slacked. He established a company at Yonkers, N.Y., which was developed after his death by his son Charles Rollin Otis (1835–1927), particularly after he had patented further improvements to elevator brakes and hoisting machinery from 1864. By the mid-1870s hydraulic elevators were being used in buildings of up to twenty storeys in New York. Werner von Siemens (1816–92) exhibited an electric elevator at Mannheim, Germany, in 1880, and the first electric passenger elevator in the USA was installed by William Baxter in Baltimore in 1887, although hydraulic elevators continued to be installed for another generation. In Britain elevators are commonly called lifts.

A horizontal-cylinder, rope-geared hydraulic elevator, installed in Boston in 1902 by E. Brewer & Co., is preserved in the National Museum of American History, Washington DC, together with several historic artefacts from the Otis company. There are museums of elevators at BUDAPEST, and Alphen aan de Rijn (*see* LEIDEN), and one which includes some elevators at Monroe, N.Y.

2. A grain elevator is a machine for raising grain to the upper storeys of a warehouse, and in North America the term came to be applied to a GRANARY. A floating elevator in a port (*see* ROTTERDAM) is a vessel equipped with machinery for transferring grain between a ship and a granary on shore.

3. An elevator is also the control surface of an AEROPLANE which allows the pilot to determine the aircraft's pitch. On modern aircraft it is always located on the tailplane.

BIBLIOGRAPHY
General
Baxter, 1910; Jallings, 1916; Ritchie-Noakes, 1980, 1984; Simmen and Drepper, 1984; Vogel, 1988.
Specific
Brown, T. E. Passenger elevators. In *Transactions of the American Society of Engineers*, LIV, 1905.

The vertical railway. In *Harper's New Monthly Magazine*, November 1882.

LOCATION
[M] Smith's Clove Museum, Monroe, New York.

ROBERT M. VOGEL

Elverum, Hedmark, Norway   Elverum, situated 150 km (90 mi.) N. of Oslo, on the banks of the River Glomma and amidst some of the most luxuriant woodlands in Norway, is one of the best places in the world for the study of forest industries. The Glomma is Norway's longest river, and one of its busiest timber-floating waterways, although it is supposed that 1985 will have proved to be the last summer when it was used for transporting logs. Elverum was the centre for a great annual horse and timber fair, the Grundsetmarket, held every March. A section of the Rørosbane (railway to Røros), opened in 1862, stimulated the town's growth, and a brewery from that period has been listed as a historic monument. A steel suspension bridge of 1936 crosses the Glomma.

The Norsk Skogbruksmuseum, the national museum of forestry, hunting and inland fisheries, was established in 1954. Its main building, completed in 1970 and situated on the southern edge of the town on the east bank of the Glomma, houses a library and photographic archive collections as well as displays. It stands within an 8 ha (20 ac.) site, part of which is used as an open-air museum in which re-erected buildings are displayed, and is linked by a bridge with Prestoya, a 6 ha (15 ac.) island situated between the Klokkerfossen and Prestfossen rapids, on which there are further re-erected buildings. The indoor displays deal comprehensively with forestry industries, including collections of felling, peeling and marking axes, saws, callipers, sleds and chains used to prevent skidding. Log-floating is illustrated, principally by models of dams and sluices, including one of the Kjerraten i Åsa (*see* RINGERIKE); there are also displays showing raft-construction, and the pike poles used by drivers in different regions for breaking up log jams. The manufacture of such forest products as tar, charcoal, planks and birch-bark shoes, baskets and rucksacks is portrayed in displays which include many tools. Collections of weapons and traps show the development of hunting, and the freshwater fishing industry is illustrated by varieties of spears, nets and lines.

The buildings in the open-air sections of the museum are mostly small structures that were temporary working or dwelling places for lumbermen, hunters and fishermen in remote areas. Among them is a sectionalized cabin, constructed in 1911 to a design patented five years earlier by Martin Bakken, the first in Norway for a movable wooden building. Other structures include a gate saw, a saw powered by a portable steam engine fired with sawdust, animal traps, tar kilns, boathouses and a timber floating dam. There is a monument by Johann Georg von Langen to the first Norwegian forest administration which was established at Kongsberg in 1739. A timber bridge, constructed according to traditional methods in 1964, links the island of Prestoya with the main site. The careful

Figure 41 Navvies using barrow runs during the construction of Boxmoor embankment on the London & Birmingham Railway, *c.*1837 (from J. C. Bourne, *Drawings on the London and Birmingham Railway*, 1839)
Ironbridge Gorge Museum Trust

siting of cabins amidst birches and firs, with the constant background noise of the rapids, the scuttering of red squirrels and the purposeful, disciplined activity of giant ants, portrays the context of forest industry as effectively as the indoor displays explain its technologies.

The Glomdalsmuseum was established in 1911 and is administered by a consortium of local authorities from the whole Glomma valley. It is situated on the west bank of the river and is linked with the Prestoya section of the Norsk Skogbruksmuseum by a bridge. A 16 ha (40 ac.) open-air section includes eighty-eight re-erected buildings grouped to show the characteristics of particular parts of the region. Most are farmsteads, but the collection includes a tannery from Elverum, which worked from 1817 until 1943 and used quebracho bark from South America as well as the native spruce bark; a drying house for corn, malt, flax and timber; a corn mill; and a gate saw. Indoor exhibits in an attractive modern building illustrate life in the Glomma valley between 1700 and 1900. There are displays on road transport, and on the impact of railways and steamships of the region; an outstanding collection of basketwork and timber products; and informative sections on flax processing and the early tourist industry. The library includes the vast and important collections of the scholar Helge Væringsaasen (1836–

1917), with 60 000 volumes, including many popular scientific works, about 20 000 printed ephemera, and several hundred maps.

BIBLIOGRAPHY
General
Matheson, 1979.
Specific
Et halvt sekel: Glomdalsmuseet 1911–1961 (A Half-Century: the Glomsdal Museum), Elverum, 1961.
Fra samling til museum: Glomdalsmuseet 1911–1971 (From Collection to Museum). Elverum, 1971.

LOCATIONS
[M] Glomdalsmuseum, N-2400 Elverum.
[M] Norsk Skogbruksmuseum, N-2400 Elverum.

BARRIE TRINDER

embankment A term used from the 1780s for a bank erected to confine the course of a river, and from *c.*1810 for a long bank carrying a road, canal or railway over low ground on the level or at a reduced gradient. THOMAS TELFORD's approach to the PONTCYSYLLTE AQUEDUCT, completed in 1805, was one of the first of major significance. A structure intended simply to raise a road above marshy ground is better described as a 'causeway'.

BIBLIOGRAPHY
General
Green and Morgan, 1924; Rolt, 1958.

emerald A green gemstone, a variety of the mineral beryl, usually found in limestone and mica-schist. It has been worked since ancient times, particularly in Egypt, but also in Central Africa and South America.

BIBLIOGRAPHY
General
McLintock, 1983; Webster, 1983.

emery A commonly-used abrasive, essentially a mixture of granular corundum (Al_2O_3) and magnetite (Fe_3O_4). Deposits of emery occur in crystalline limestone, chiefly in Naxos and the USSR.

BIBLIOGRAPHY
General
Jones, 1950.

Empire A term applied to a phase of neo-Classical architecture originating in the period of imperial rule in France in 1804–14, and influential throughout Europe. It derived from Roman practice, with abundant use of such Greek and Egyptian motifs as laurel wreaths and sphinxes.

enamelling The fusing of a vitreous glaze onto a metallic surface, for decorative purposes, as in the production of miniatures at Limoges, France, in the sixteenth and seventeenth centuries, or of various wares at Bilston (*see* BLACK COUNTRY), England, by George Brett in the eighteenth; in the production of watch and clock faces and other forms of jewellery; or as a protective covering for cooking and other household utensils. Enamel is based on easily fusible salts, usually silicates and borates of sodium, potassium or lead, to which metallic oxides are added: tin to produce a white colouring, lead or antimony to produce yellow, gold or iron to give red, and copper or cobalt to give blues or greens. Enamel is normally produced in 'cakes' which are ground up before being applied to the prepared surface of the metal, and fired in a MUFFLE FURNACE. The manufacture of domestic wares, advertising placards and so on was based largely on the patent of the Englishman Charles Henry Paris of 1850, and the British industry was largely concentrated in BIRMINGHAM. Surfaces to be treated were cleaned with sulphuric acid and coated with gum to aid adhesion. Powdered enamel was sifted onto the surface, after which the wares were dried in an oven, and then fired in an enamelling furnace. Paris's enamel consisted of 260 parts cullet, 41 parts of sodium carbonate and 24 parts of boracic acid, plus oxides for colouring. The term is also used in CERAMICS.

BIBLIOGRAPHY
General
Rees, 1802–20.

BARRIE TRINDER

energy The capacity for doing work. The various forms of energy are potential, kinetic, electrical, heat, chemical, nuclear and radiant. These are all theoretically interconvertible, but it took the machines of the Industrial Revolution, especially the steam engine – which attracted the attention of theorists like N. L. S. Carnot (1796–1832), J. P. Joule (1818–89), and William Thompson, Lord Kelvin (1824–1909) – to demonstrate this. The unit of energy was named after Joule in 1889.

The main sources of energy used in industry have been animal power (*see* DONKEY GIN; HORSE GIN; TREADMILL); ELECTRIC POWER; GAS; HYDRAULIC POWER; internal combustion (*see* DIESEL ENGINE; OIL ENGINE; PETROL ENGINE); the STEAM ENGINE; WATER POWER; and WINDMILLS.

See also BOILER; CHIMNEY; HORSE POWER; LINE SHAFTING; MILLWRIGHT; ROPE DRIVE.

Engelsberg, Västmanland, Sweden Engelsberg, 12 km (8 mi.) E. of Fagersta, is one of the most perfectly preserved ironworking BRUKS in Sweden, the restoration of which was one of the principal Swedish projects during European Architectural Heritage Year in 1975.

A peasant ironworks operated on the site in the first half of the seventeenth century but from the 1680s under the direction of a local landowner Per Larsson Gyllenhööl it became a characteristic estate ironworks. The complex centres round a mansion house of the 1740s, in the French style, with a MANSARD roof. The blast furnace, one of the few furnaces of earth and timber construction which remain in Sweden, dates from 1779, although it is on the site of earlier furnaces, and was raised to its present height of 12.6 m (41 ft.) in 1878. The furnace was blown out in 1919, at which time its output of pig iron was about 10 tons a day. It has a water-powered iron cylinder blower, and an ore crusher probably installed in 1859. Engelsberg's forge building was constructed to accommodate the LANCASHIRE FORGE process in 1845. It contains two hammers and three-cylinder blowing machine, all water-powered. Numerous workers' houses survive, together with two summerhouses near the mansion which are constructed of slag blocks. The central archives for the Axel Johnson Group are located in a former charcoal barn.

On a small island in Lake Amännigen at Angelsberg is preserved one of the world's oldest OIL REFINERIES of the same type as those built in the USA during the 1860s following Edwin Drake's discovery of oil at Titusville, PENNSYLVANIA.

Pehr August Alund, a farmer and farm manager began in 1871 to refine petroleum at Annelund near the Engelsberg ironworks. The works were twice ravaged by fire, after which Alund acquired the island of Barrön, now Oljeön (oil island) in Lake Amännigen, one of the many lakes which form part of the route of the STRÖMSHOLMS CANAL. A company, Engelsbergs Oljefabriks Aktiebolag was formed in 1874, and the refinery was constructed in 1875–6. It was furnished with eight retorts, together with storage facilities and workers dwellings. Initially the company was able to produce a maximum of 1000 barrels of inflammable oil a year, together with kerosene, lubricating oil and paraffin wax.

The main building, 20 m × 10 m (60 × 30 ft.) and 4 m (12 ft.) high, was situated on the northern part of the island. It was extended by 1890 to its present size, 67 m (200 ft.) long, with a wing 14 m (43 ft.) long and 4 m (11 ft.) wide. The eight original retorts were set in brickwork. Four were installed later. All twelve are made of riveted boiler plates, and each holds 300 gallons. Each retort has its own wood-fired furnace. There is also a walled-in steam boiler.

The company was financially successful: the annual turnover in the period 1877–1902 was between 100 000 and 150 000 Sw kr., and the annual net profit between 20 000 and 15 000 Sw kr. The situation changed when protective duties were taken away soon after 1900, and in 1902 production ceased, although the works continued to make lubricating grease, paint and varnish until it finally went into liquidation in 1927. A year later the island was bought by Consul General Axel Johnson, who had taken over the Engelsberg ironworks in 1916. The plant was preserved and is now a scheduled monument. Restoration work was carried out in the 1950s and again in the 1970s. It has been purchased by the OK petroleum company, who have undertaken to continue to conserve the building, and it now forms part of the BERGSLAGEN Ekomuseum.

BIBLIOGRAPHY
General
Nisser, 1979.
Specific
Agren, P. Engelsberg's Oil Factory: an early petroleum refinery. Daedalus, 1967.
Larsson, L. M. Oljeön, Angelsberg, Fagusta kommun. Ekomuseum Bergslagen, Falun, 1988.
Nisser, M. Engelsberg Ironworks, Bergslagen. In *Architectural Review*, London, January 1975.

MARIE NISSER

England   The growth of manufactures and mining in England in the eighteenth century, defined as the 'Industrial Revolution', has traditionally been seen as a pattern of economic development subsequently followed by many other countries. The changes in the course of the eighteenth century were profound. The process of transfer to a coal-based rather than a charcoal-based manufacturing technology, begun in the seventeenth century, was largely completed, and rising production of coal reduced the costs of energy. The steam engine was widely adopted, ironmaking technology was transformed, the manufacture of textiles became factory-based, and a new transport infrastructure was provided by turnpike roads, canals and – in the coalfields – by primitive railways. Nineteenth-century writers like Karl Marx (1818–83) and Arnold Toynbee (1852–83) regarded the growth of the factory system as a distinct stage in human history, and much subsequent writing has followed the same line, seeing the technological developments of the 1770s and 80s as stimulants to the growth of an altogether different type of society. The most commonly used metaphor in recent decades has been Rostow's view (1960) of the Industrial Revolution as a 'take-off into self-sustained growth'. Many historians would now define the changes of the eighteenth century in different ways, placing more emphasis on the preconditions for economic growth, and taking a less optimistic view of British economic developments after 1850.

The boundaries of England have been unaltered since the sixteenth century. For most political, legal and administrative purposes, Wales has been integrated with England since that time but there is a separate Welsh authority responsible for most matters relating to industrial archaeology, and Wales is treated separately in this encyclopaedia. Each monarch since 1603 has ruled both Scotland and England, and the Scottish and English parliaments have been united since the Act of Union 1707, but the Scottish legal and educational systems have remained distinct, and Scotland is similarly accorded separate treatment. Ireland was ruled by the British Crown from the thirteenth century, but it was not until 1800 that the parliaments of the two countries were united. The Irish Republic gained its independence in 1921, although the six counties of Northern Ireland remain a province under British rule. In terms of industrial history Ireland can be regarded as a single entity, and it is so treated in this encyclopaedia.

England extends over 600 km (400 mi.) from north to south, and 500 km (300 mi.) from east to west. The geology is varied, with the older rocks of the north and west creating a generally more rugged terrain than is to be found in the south and east. Coal is England's most significant mineral resource. The mines of Northumberland and Durham were already supplying coal to London and places along the east and south coasts by 1650. Iron ore is found in most of the English coalfields, and has been exploited on a large scale until recent decades. Deposits of lead, tin and copper ores were important in the eighteenth and nineteenth centuries.

The population of England and Wales increased from less than 6 million in 1700 to more than 9 million by 1801, and more than 17 million by 1851. Coal production is difficult to quantify, but had probably reached 15 million tons per year by 1800, about 1 350 kg (27 cwt.) for each inhabitant. The output of pig iron rose from about 25 000 tons per year in the 1720s to over 250 000 tons in 1800. Imports of raw cotton had reached 27 378 000 kg (60 million lb.) per year by 1800. The first practical steam engine was set to work by THOMAS NEWCOMEN in 1712. There were about a hundred working by 1733, and between 2500 and 3000 by 1800.

It is increasingly evident that the developments of the second half of the eighteenth century had earlier precedents. In the course of the seventeenth century coal had been substituted for charcoal in a succession of manufacturing processes. ABRAHAM DARBY I's use of coke to smelt iron in 1709 was as much the last act in a series of substitutions of coal for charcoal as the beginning of a revolution in the iron industry. In many other respects the English economy of the early eighteenth century was well

England

advanced. Textiles were manufactured throughout the country and most regions produced specialist fabrics which were marketed nationally. In many less fertile areas small-scale domestic manufactures flourished in open settlements on hillsides or heathlands (*see* BLACK COUNTRY; STOKE-ON-TRENT). Foreigners marvelled at the cheapness of coal, and in Shropshire and the North-East wooden railways were used to convey it to navigable water. A steady growth in trade was reflected in the improvement of trackways across the PENNINES, and by 1750 most of the radial roads from London to the principal provincial cities were being improved by turnpike trusts, established by acts of parliament. Coastal shipping flourished, and many rivers were made navigable.

The flourishing state of commerce owed much to the removal of artificial restraints on trade during the English Revolution of the 1640s, and to the 'financial revolution', involving the establishment in 1694 of the Bank of England, and of insurance companies and other financial institutions after the flight of James II during the 'Glorious Revolution' of 1688. Research in recent decades has thrown light on the changing moral climate of the eighteenth century, and the increasing acceptance, in spite of popular protest, of assumptions about property that made possible the development of industrial capitalism. It has also become evident that the growth of manufacturing was due as much to investment by old-established landowning families and by the City of London as to the enterprise of archetypal Dissenting ironmasters or mill-owners.

The Great Exhibition of 1851 is traditionally regarded as the apogee of British industrial power. A main-line railway network of 6000 route miles had been created within the previous two decades. The output of pig iron had recently reached 2 million tons per year, and by 1854 was to reach 3 million tons. Raw cotton consumption had increased ten times since 1800 and was rising rapidly. England remained one of the world's principal producers of non-ferrous metals. Steam power was being applied throughout the country, and locomotives, stationary engines, and machines for many aspects of manufacturing were being exported in large numbers.

There was a significant change in attitudes to industry during the first half of the nineteenth century. In the 1790s it had been possible to regard the achievements of engineers and entrepreneurs with wonder and astonishment. Writers and artists looked on Arkwright's mills at CROMFORD or the Iron Bridge (*see* IRONBRIDGE) with admiration. In the social crisis of the early 1840s, when attention was drawn to the factory system in general and to MANCHESTER in particular, writers like Friedrich Engels (1820–95), Alexis de Tocqueville (1805–59), Charles Dickens (1812–70) and Elizabeth Gaskell (1810–65) equated manufacturing with urban squalor.

Industry was thereafter regarded with a certain sense of shame. Several studies have shown how entrepreneurial families of the second half of the nineteenth century turned away from manufacturing towards the traditional pursuits of the English landed classes, to the professions

and to the government of the expanding British Empire. Britain remained one of the foremost industrial powers, but played a secondary role in the development of some of the new industries of the late nineteenth century, like chemicals, motorcars and processed foodstuffs, although in the twentieth century England was until the 1980s one of the world's leading producers of motor vehicles, and English engineers pioneered such developments in aviation as the jet airliner.

The Industrial Revolution marked a short-lived shift of England's centre of economic gravity from the South-East to the North and the Midlands. London remained as ever the centre of commerce and the source of most capital, as well as the largest single manufacturing centre, but such developments as the growth of textile communities along the Pennine valleys, and of mines and ironworks on the moorlands of south Durham, represented a significant shift of emphasis. In the twentieth century that process has been steadily reversed. During the 1920s and 30s, while many of the older industrial regions suffered from plant closures and high unemployment, new industries developed in the South-East: motorcar factories at Dagenham, Luton and Oxford, aircraft production in Surrey and Hertfordshire, and a variety of consumer goods and food-processing plants around London. World War II and the boom of the 1950s brought a renewal of prosperity to the Northern districts, but in recent years many of the patterns of manufacturing established during the Industrial Revolution have been totally destroyed.

There has been a profound change in attitudes to industrial history in England since World War II. Before 1939 'historical monuments' tended to mean abbeys, castles and stately homes. Industry was traditionally regarded with distaste, as something that polluted the landscape. In the post-war period there was an increasing concern to understand the history of the landscape, and by implication the elements within it connected with manufacturing, which formed the academic foundation for the growth of interest in what was first described in print as 'industrial archaeology' in 1955 (*see* RIX, MICHAEL). At the same time there was a growing movement to conserve those aspects of the industrial landscape which were most obviously threatened with destruction. A concern to protect the narrow canals of the English Midlands, which was stimulated by the publication of L. T. C. ROLT's *Narrow Boat* in 1944, received formal expression in the formation in 1946 of the Inland Waterways Association, which acted as a pressure group to keep waterways open. The closure of many canals has been prevented; others, which had become derelict, have been re-opened to traffic; and canal cruising has become a popular holiday pastime, although other commercial use of narrow canals has almost entirely ceased. Rolt and other Englishmen were responsible for the formation in 1950 of a preservation society for the TALYLLYN RAILWAY which set the pattern for many subsequent railway preservation schemes. Public passenger services are now provided by twenty-five private preservation companies. The 1960s saw the formation of many industrial museums, the majority of them private concerns like the

Ironbridge Gorge Museum (*see* IRONBRIDGE), the Gladstone Pottery Museum (*see* STOKE-ON-TRENT), and Ryhope (*see* SUNDERLAND). Since 1980 the most significant developments in industrial museums have tended to come from local authority initiatives (*see* LEEDS; MANCHESTER; WIGAN).

The national museums in England are concentrated in London, and, except for the British Museum and the National Maritime Museum, date from the aftermath of the Great Exhibition of 1851. All are now administered by independent boards of trustees. The Science Museum (*see* LONDON) has the principal responsibility for matters relating to industrial archaeology, and administers a fund upon which other museums can draw for the conservation of machinery. It has developed satellite museums in the provinces, notably the National Railway Museum at YORK and the Museum of Photography, Film and Television at BRADFORD. England has been divided since the Local Government Act 1972 into administrative counties and districts. Responsibility for museums can be assumed either by counties or districts, and there is no uniform structure to the museum service across the country. The same act established seven metropolitan counties, which were abolished in 1986. The museum services in two of them, Liverpool and Manchester, have since been accorded national status and receive direct support from central government.

The Museums Association sets standards for the profession throughout Britain. Most of the administrative counties operate record offices which act as repositories for private archives, including industrial archives, as well as for official records. The Public Record Office is the national repository for the records of government, and its vast holdings include much of value to historians of industry in such sources as the papers of the court of Chancery as well as in items directly relating to industry. Censuses have been taken every ten years since 1801, except in 1941, and the original detailed returns for those of 1841 and later become available for study after 100 years. The Ordnance Survey, formally established in 1791, published seven editions of 1:63 360 maps covering the whole country, together with 1:2500 maps from 1855 and 1:500 maps for large towns from the same date. An increasing concern for the built environment, marked by the formation of the Civic Trust in 1957, has led to the setting up of many 'heritage centres', which are concerned principally with providing guidance for visitors to historic towns, rather than with caring for collections.

Since 1 April 1984 responsibility for the protection of historic monuments in England has been devolved from a government department to a quasi-autonomous body, the Historic Buildings and Monuments Commission, or English Heritage. District councils are responsible for liaising with English Heritage on most conservation questions. Most county council planning departments maintain Sites and Monuments Records, detailing all known archaeological sites, not just those that are accorded protection.

The Royal Commission on Historical Monuments (England) is the national body responsible for recording historic structures. Until recently the Commission compiled inventories of historic structures on a county-by-county basis, but it now adopts a thematic approach, exemplified by a detailed survey of all textile mills in West Yorkshire. About a quarter of the Commission's recording work is now concerned with industrial buildings. The Commission has inherited the National Record of Industrial Monuments, a card-based inventory established at the University of Bath in 1965. The public archive of the Commission, the National Monuments Record, is based in London.

Buildings in England are accorded statutory protection by three different means: by scheduling as Ancient Monuments, by listing as historic buildings, and by their being situated within designated 'conservation areas'. Scheduling under the Ancient Monuments Act 1979 indicates a recognition of the historic importance of a site. Any alteration to the site requires consent from English Heritage. A proportion of scheduled monuments are held in 'guardianship', and access is directly administered by English Heritage. The listing of buildings is based on legislation of 1944, 1962, 1968, 1971 and 1990. A revision of the list began in 1984, and when completed it is estimated that some 25 000 industrial sites will be protected by this means. Listing is not intended to grant unconditional protection from demolition or alteration, but to ensure that appropriate consideration is given before such developments can take place. Notification of all applications for consent to demolish listed buildings must be sent to six statutory consultative bodies: the Ancient Monuments Society, the Council for British Archaeology, the Georgian Group, the Society for the Protection of Ancient Buildings, the Victorian Society, and the Royal Commission on Historical Monuments. Buildings are graded I, II* and II, the first two categories qualifying for grant aid from central government for necessary repairs, the last normally only for discretionary aid from local government. Under the Civic Amenities Act 1967, modified in 1972, local authorities can designate areas of special architectural or historical interest as 'conservation areas', which gives a greater degree of control over certain aspects of development. Demolition of any unlisted building within a conservation area requires the consent of the planning authority. The Association for Industrial Archaeology, established in 1973, is the national body concerned with the subject, and publishes a twice-yearly review. The Newcomen Society is concerned primarily with the history of technology. Many other national societies are concerned with historical studies that overlap with industrial archaeology, or with the protection of categories of buildings of which industrial structures form part. The Ironbridge Institute (*see* IRONBRIDGE) provides postgraduate courses in industrial archaeology.

The English came late to an appreciation of their industrial heritage. Many outstanding monuments of the late eighteenth and early nineteenth centuries were destroyed as recently as the 1950s and 60s, but much of what remains is now protected, and some of it is presented and interpreted with imagination and skill. The collections in the Science Museum (*see* LONDON), the mills of the

Derwent Valley (*see* CROMFORD), the landscapes of such cities as LEEDS, MANCHESTER and SHEFFIELD, and the varied monuments of the Ironbridge Gorge, have few parallels elsewhere in the world.

See also AMBERLEY; ASHFORD; BANBURY; BARROW-IN-FURNESS; BATH; BEAMISH; BEAULIEU; BEDFORD; BEWDLEY; BIRMINGHAM; BLACK COUNTRY; BLUEBELL RAILWAY; BOLTON; BRADFORD; BRIDGEWATER CANAL; BRIGHTON; BRISTOL; BROMSGROVE; BURTON ON TRENT; CHILTERN HILLS; CLEE HILLS; CORNWALL; COVENTRY; CREWE; CROMFORD; DERBY; DURHAM; EAST ANGLIA; EXETER; FAKENHAM; FAVERSHAM; FENS; FOREST OF DEAN; FROME; FYLDE; GLOUCESTER; GREAT WESTERN RAILWAY; HALIFAX; HALTON; HARWICH; HELMSHORE; HEREFORD; HUDDERSFIELD; HULL; IRONBRIDGE; KENNET & AVON CANAL; LAKE DISTRICT; LANCASHIRE; LEEDS; LEICESTER; LINCOLNSHIRE; LIVERPOOL; LONDON; LOUGHBOROUGH; LUTON; MACCLESFIELD; MANCHESTER; MEDWAY; MOIRA; MORWELLHAM; NEWCASTLE-UPON-TYNE; NORTHWICH; NORWICH; NOTTINGHAM; OXFORD; PENNINES; PLYMOUTH; PORTSMOUTH; PORT SUNLIGHT; RUDDINGTON; ST HELENS; SEVERN TUNNEL; SHARDLOW; SHEFFIELD; SHREWSBURY; SOUTHAMPTON; STICKLEPATH; STOKE-ON-TRENT; STOURPORT; STRATFORD-UPON-AVON; STREET; STROUD; STYAL; SUNDERLAND; SWINDON; TEESSIDE; WARWICK; WEALD; WEALD AND DOWNLAND MUSEUM; WIGAN; WOODBRIDGE; WORCESTER; YORK; YORKSHIRE MOORS.

BIBLIOGRAPHY
General
Albert, 1972; Dyos and Aldcroft, 1969; Engels, 1845; Harley, 1975; Hobsbawm, 1969; Kerridge, 1985; Klingender, 1968; Marx, 1867; Mitchell and Deane, 1962; Nef, 1932; Raybould, 1973; Rostow, 1960; Stratton, 1987; Stratton and Trinder, 1987a; Thompson, 1963; Toynbee, 1884; Trinder, 1982b; Wrigley and Schofield, 1981.
Specific
Falconer, K. Inventories of the Industrial Heritage: an English perspective. In *Inventaire Général*, 1986.

LOCATIONS
[I] The Association for Industrial Archaeology, Ironbridge Gorge Museum, Ironbridge, Telford, Shropshire TF8 7AW.
[I] The Council for British Archaeology, 112 Kennington Road, London SE11 6RE.
[I] English Heritage, Fortress House, Savile Row, London W1X 2BT.
[I] The Museums Association, 34 Bloomsbury Way, London WC1A 2SF.
[I] The Newcomen Society, Science Museum, Exhibition Road, London SW7.
[I] The Royal Commission on Historical Monuments England, Fortress House, Savile Row, London W1X 2BT.

BARRIE TRINDER and MICHAEL STRATTON

English glass cone   A conical structure enclosing a glass kiln or kilns, which acts as a funnel to increase the draught. Such structures came into use from the first half of the eighteenth century, and could be up to 15 m (50 ft.) in diameter, and up to 25 m (80 ft.) high. Examples survive at Alloa (*see* CLACKMANNANSHIRE), LE CREUSOT, NEWCASTLE-UPON-TYNE, SHEFFIELD, and Stourbridge (*see* BLACK COUNTRY).

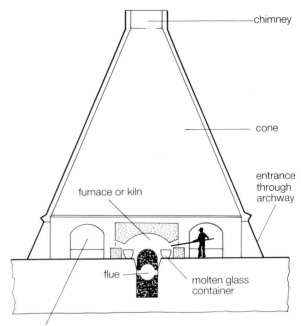

Figure 42   A diagrammatic section through a characteristic English glass cone: a glass blower is seen taking molten glass from a crucible in a furnace in which a strong draught has been created by the cone.

engraving   The incising of fine lines on wood, often box, or metal; either for decoration, as on armour or jewellery, or for printing illustrations, maps or music. Blocks for printing can be of wood or of metal – usually copper or, from 1819, steel. Engraving was the normal method of reproducing illustrations until well into the nineteenth century when it was superseded by LITHOGRAPHY.

BIBLIOGRAPHY
General
Ivins, 1943.

Entroncamento, Ribatejo, Portugal   A railway town at the junction of the Northern and Eastern Railways, 100 km (60 mi.) NE of Lisbon, where a railway museum may be established.

ephemera   A term applied to posters, handbills, paper bags, bill headings, tickets, trade cards and other printed items produced for short-term use, many of which contain illustrations and other information likely to be of use in historical investigations. They may reveal evidence of products (which may be depicted or listed), premises, vehicles used, modes of display or technical processes. The outstanding English source is the John Johnson Collection in OXFORD. In the USA the principal sources are the Bella Landauer Collection at the NEW YORK Historical Society, and the Collection of Business Americana incorporating the Warshaw Collection at the Smithsonian Institution, WASHINGTON DC.

BIBLIOGRAPHY
General
Apel and Dröge, 1980; Lewis, 1962; Turner and Vaisey, 1972.
Specific
The John Johnson Collection: catalogue of an exhibition. Oxford; Bodleian Library.
Laqueur, T. The John Johnson Collection in Oxford. In *History Workshop*, IV, 1977.

BARRIE TRINDER

Epinac, Saône-et-Loire, France   At the Hottinguer mine, Epinac, 24 km (15 mi.) W. of Beaune, is the only remaining French MALAKOFF TOWER, a square structure with four lateral wings, built in 1874–5 at a pit sunk in 1863. The semicircular and bull's-eye apertures add to its monumental appearance. The mine had a remarkable pneumatic lift mechanism, a 600 m (2000 ft.) metal tube in which the cage acted as piston. Its building remains and is occupied by a paint firm, but the machinery is gone.

BIBLIOGRAPHY
General
Daumas, 1980; Guiollard, 1989.

Erezée, Luxembourg, Belgium   The Tramway Touristique de l'Aisne is a 1 m (3 ft. 3 in.) gauge railway which extends 12 km (7½ mi.) from Erezée, which is 36 km (22 mi.) S. of Liège, to Lamorménil. It was closed in 1955, but reopened by a preservation group in 1965. Rolling stock includes a tramway locomotive by Grand Hornu of 1920.

LOCATION
[I] Tramway Touristique de l'Aisne, W. Ceuppenslaan 77, 1190 Brussels.

Erlach an der Pitten, Lower Austria, Austria   A village 10 km (6 mi.) S. of Wiener Neustadt, with a large limekiln built by the local brickmakers, Georg and Mathäus Kattinger, *c.*1877: it is said to comprise a million bricks. The kiln remained in use until 1945 and is now a protected monument. Rectangular in plan, it is built at the foot of a bank to facilitate loading from a wooden bridge.

Erzberg, Styria, Austria   *See* STYRIAN IRON TRAIL.

Esbjerg, Jutland, Denmark   Esbjerg is the principal port on the west coast of Jutland, its harbour having been built by the state in 1868–78 for the export of agricultural produce to Great Britain, following the loss of the ports further south in the Duchies after the war of 1864 (*see* DENMARK). Esbjerg soon became the most important fishing port in Denmark, with a large deep-sea fleet. The third sector in the city was industry, most of which grew up in connection with the harbour, bacon factories, corn mills, fish canneries, herring-oil works, boatyards, a large ropeworks, and several engineering works. Esbjerg now has a new function as the base for Danish oil activities in the North Sea.

The streets of the city were laid out to a grid pattern, presumably following American examples. Most of the older buildings date from *c.*1900, and are in a rather opulent historicist style. The city's principal landmark, the water tower of 1897, has a pyramid roof and four bay towers, and was inspired by the 'Nassauer Haus' in NUREMBERG. The railway station of 1904 is another example of this style.

The large Fishing and Shipping Museum covers local shipping, and fishing activities in general. The comprehensive collections include fishing equipment, boats, and petrol and diesel engines. Shipping has a long tradition in the region, and is particularly connected with the well-preserved skipper towns of Nordby and Sønderho on the nearby island of Fanø.

BIBLIOGRAPHY
General
Hyldtoft *et al.*, 1981; Sestoft, 1979.
Specific
Bruhn, V. *Esbjerg – by og borger* (Esbjerg – city and citizen). Esbjerg, 1972.
Dragsbo, P. Det industrielle miljø i Esbjerg (The industrial environment in Esbjerg). In *Mark og Montre*, 1978.
Rambusch, S. *Esbjerg havn 1868–1968* (Esbjerg harbour 1868–1968). Esbjerg, 1968.

LOCATIONS
[M] Esbjerg Museum, Finsensgade 1, 6700 Esbjerg.
[M] Fiskeri-og Søfartsmuseum, Saltvandsakvariet, Tarphagevej, 6700 Esbjerg.

OLE HYLDTOFT

escalator   Various kinds of moving staircase were demonstrated in the nineteenth century, but in 1910 the Otis Elevator Co. (*see* ELEVATOR), having acquired various patents, combined the best features of each to produce the practical design that has since been widely used in railway stations, department stores and airports.

BIBLIOGRAPHY
General
Tough and O'Flaherty, 1971.

Escaudain, Nord, France   The blast furnaces at Escaudain, 2 km (1 mi.) W. of Denain, were built in 1919–20 as an annexe to the original Denain ironworks which dated back to 1834. The furnaces have now been demolished, but one of the blowing engines survives: it is a producer-gas engine, using gases recovered at the throat of the furnace. Engines of this type, developed between 1905 and 1912, were installed at most blast furnaces built in France between 1920 and 1950. This example, bedded in 500 m³ (650 cu. yd.) of concrete foundations, and developing some 2000 hp, was built by the Belfort firm, Société Alsacienne de Construction Mécanique. It is one of the last remaining machines of its type surviving in France, and is now a protected monument.

BIBLIOGRAPHY
General
Hardy-Hémery, 1985.
Specific
Hardy-Hémery, O. Une nébuleuse en expansion au XIXe et XXe siècles: l'espace de l'usine sidérurgique de Denain (An expanding nebula during the nineteenth and twentieth centuries: the space of the Denain iron and steel works). In *Mouvement Social*, CXXV, 1983.

Eskilstuna, Södermanland, Sweden   Eskilstuna originated as a planned town of the seventeenth century, a community of smiths, manufacturing chiefly armaments. It was established in 1656 by Reinhold Rademacher, at the command of King Carl Gustaf, after whom the settlement was first named. The original twenty wooden smithy buildings, laid out on a grid plan, were designed by the leading Swedish architect, Jean de la Vallée. Eskilstuna gained municipal status in 1659, and within a few years 72 craftsmen, including nailers, locksmiths and cutlers were settled there, many of the skilled workers being German migrants. The people of Eskilstuna have continued to specialize in metalworking, and the city is now one of Sweden's leading engineering centres, with some important factory buildings surviving from the late nineteenth century and early twentieth century.

Six adjacent smithy buildings standing on the sites laid out in the 1650s have been restored, making up a museum complex known as Rademacher's Smithies; one is restored as a working iron smithy, one as a copper smithy, one a goldsmith's workshop, one housing a model of Eskilstuna as it was in 1788. Adjoining the forges is an exhibition hall in an adapted cutlery factory in which the current products of the Eskilstuna engineering industry are displayed. An industrial museum includes working steam engines and examples of the city's many engineering manufactures.

BIBLIOGRAPHY
General
Nisser, 1979.

LOCATIONS
[M] Faktorimuseet (Factory Museum), Faktoriholmarna, 631 86 Eskilstuna.
[M] Rademachersmedjorna (Rademacher's Smithies), Rademachergatan 50, 632 20 Eskilstuna.

BARRIE TRINDER

esparto grass   A species of rush, *Stipa tenacissima*, which originated in Spain where it was used for CORDAGE and for SHOES. It was employed as a raw material for PAPER manufacture from the 1860s.

Espinho, Beira Litoral, Portugal   A town on the Atlantic coast, 16 km (10 mi.) S. of Oporto, which has developed since the opening of the Northern Railway in 1867. The celebrated Brandão Gomes fish-canning factory, opened in 1894, has been reused as the local museum.

BIBLIOGRAPHY
Specific
Gaio, M. *Fábrica de Conservas 'Brandão Gomes'* (The Brandão Gomes canning factory). Espinho: Nascente, n.d.

Esposende, Minho, Portugal   A town at the mouth of the River Cávado, 50 km (30 mi.) N. of Oporto, with an iron bridge of 1891 built by Empresa Industrial Portuguesa company. A water-powered vertical-blade sawmill still works at Gemeses, 4 km (2½ mi.) E., and there are restored windmills operating at Abelheira. The windmills at the seaside resort of Apúlia, 6 km (4 mi.) S., are used as beach houses.

Essen, North-Rhine Westphalia, Germany   *See* RUHRGEBIET.

Estremoz, Alto Alentejo, Portugal   The centre of a region 135 km (85 mi.) E of Lisbon, with vast deposits of marble spread over an area 40 km × 6 km (25 mi. × 4 mi.). Reserves are estimated at 20 million tonnes. The marble is comparable in quality to that of CARRARA. Quarries are a prominent feature of the landscape, together with innumerable limekilns. There is a railway museum with steam locomotives and carriages of the nineteenth century as well as locomotives used in local mines. Exhibits include a Beyer Peacock 2–2–2 of 1862, exhibited in the London Exhibition of that year.

LOCATIONS
[M] Municipal Museum, Rossio do Marquês de Pombal 89, Estremoz.
[M] Railway Museum, Estremoz.

Esztergom, Komárom, Hungary   A historic town on the Danube, 50 km (30 mi.) NW of Budapest, with many historic buildings and long traditions of craft manufactures. A museum in a protected eighteenth-century building shows how the Danube has been controlled for purposes of navigation, water supply and irrigation. The history of coal mining at Dorog, 10 km (6 mi.) S., is illustrated in the Miners' Memorial House.

LOCATIONS
[M] Hungarian Hydraulics Museum, H-2500 Esztergom, Kolcsey u. 2.
[M] Miners' Memorial House, H-2510 Dorog, Sziklai S. u. 70.

Eta (Etur, Etera, Etar), Pleven, Bulgaria   The 'ethnographical park' at Eta is an open-air museum situated in a deep wooded valley south of Gabrovo, which has been an important centre of craft manufactures in Bulgaria since medieval times. In the nineteenth century it became a textile manufacturing centre and was known as 'Bulgaria's Manchester'. The museum was established in 1963

Figure 43 A water corn mill of 1874 at the ethnographical park at Eta, Bulgaria
Architekturno-Etnograficzeskij Kompleks 'Eter'

under the direction of Lazar Donkov, on the basis of research begun in 1949. It occupies 6 ha (15 ac.) of wooded land and contains about fifty buildings. Its aim is to illustrate the architecture, way of life and economy of the Gabrovo district during the period of the National Revival from the mid-eighteenth century to the liberation from the Ottoman yoke in 1878. Some examples of vernacular architecture are exhibited, but the main emphasis is on working crafts. Water power, derived from a leat fed by the River Sivek, which runs through the museum, is used to operate many of the exhibits. On the right bank of the river some of the individual workshops and buildings exhibited are *in situ*, and the remainder have been demolished and re-erected in the museum. They include a blacksmith's workshop, a cutler's (150 types of knife were said to have been produced in the Gabrovo district in the nineteenth century), a water-driven grinding shop, a fulling mill, a turner's lathe, a ribbon weaving shop, a dye house, a flourmill, a lathe for turning special containers for brandy and wine, a sawmill, and a wheelwright's shop. To these will be added an eighteenth-century farmhouse, charcoal kilns, a brandy still, and a workshop for preserving plums and apricots by pulping them and then drying the pulp in sheets. All the buildings on the left bank of the river are replicas, and crafts illustrated in a street of shops and workshops include those of the tanner, the potter, the goldsmith, the coppersmith, the confectioner, the bellmaker, the wind-instrument maker and the fur dresser. There is also a workshop for spinning and weaving goats' hair, a trade that has now vanished, surviving only in the museum. Proposed additions include workshops for making pack-saddles, wooden shovels and walnut oil. Eta is one of the most popular tourist attractions in Bulgaria, and receives half a million or so visitors a year.

BIBLIOGRAPHY
Specific
Bozikov, B. Die Freilichtmuseen Bulgariens (Bulgarian open-air museums). In *Ethnographica*, v, vi, Brno, 1963–4.
Der ethnographische architecturkomplex Etera (The ethnographic and architectural complex at Eta), Sofia, 1979.
Wildhaber, R. Das Bulgarische Freilichtmuseum in Etera (The Bulgarian Open-Air Museum at Eta). In *Schweizerisches Archiv für Volkskunde*, LXVI, 1970.

LOCATION
[M] Architekturno-Etnograficzeskij Kompleks 'Etera', Gabrovo.

TREFOR M. OWEN

ethanol (ethyl alcohol, C_2H_5OH) One of the family of organic compounds known as alcohols, present in alcoholic drinks. Ethanol is of major industrial importance as a solvent, a fuel, and a constituent of printing ink. Traditionally manufactured by the fermentation of starch or molasses, it is now obtained from petrochemical sources. METHANOL, which is poisonous, is added to ethanol to make commercial methylated spirits, used for lighting, cleaning and as a source of heat.

BIBLIOGRAPHY
General
Hardie and Pratt, 1966; Morgan and Pratt, 1938; Norman and Waddington, 1977.

ethene (ethylene, C_2H_4) A gas, now obtained from

243

petroleum, but previously from ethyl alcohol (*see* ETHANOL). Ethene is of prime importance as a source of organic compounds, particularly plastics (*see* POLYTHENE) and DETERGENTS.

BIBLIOGRAPHY
General
Hardie and Pratt, 1966; Norman and Waddington, 1977.

ethyl alcohol   *See* ETHANOL.

ethylene   *See* ETHENE.

ethyne (acetylene)   An important organic gas (C_2H_2), discovered in the 1830s but not utilized till the 1880s. It has traditionally been produced by the action of water on calcium carbide (CaC_2), which can only be produced economically in a furnace heated by cheap hydro-electric power:

$$CaC_2 + 2H_2O \rightarrow Ca(OH)_2 + C_2H_2.$$

Ethyne is used in lighting; in the synthesis of organic compounds; and in oxyacetylene welding, in which oxygen and acetylene (ethyne) are supplied separately to a blowpipe, producing a high-temperature flame. For cutting metals a third pipe with an additional oxygen supply is employed.

BIBLIOGRAPHY
General
Morgan and Pratt, 1938; Partington, 1950.

Euboea (Evia), Évvoiá, Greece   The second largest Greek island, at its nearest point only 60 m (200 ft.) from the mainland, with which it is linked by a swing bridge at Halkis (Khalkis), the capital. There are quarries of green marble at Styra, 42 km (26 mi.) SE of Halkis, and at Karystos, 124 km (77 mi.) SE of Halkis; and lignite mines near Kími, 50 km (30 mi.) E. of Halkis, which is also celebrated for the processing of figs.

Eupen, Liège, Belgium   A German-speaking city 30 km (19 mi.) E. of Liège, celebrated for brewing and textiles, Eupen was ceded to Belgium after World War I. Several breweries remain, and in Oestrasse is a large building the earliest parts of which date from 1745, constructed as a centre for domestic textile manufacture, comparable with the Rotes Haus in Mönschau (*see* EIFEL), 16 km (10 mi.) SE. A 65 m (215 ft.) high dam on the River Gileppe, 5 km (3 mi.) E., enlarged to its present size in 1935, is one of the largest in Belgium.

BIBLIOGRAPHY
General
Wehdorn and Georgeacopol-Winischhofer, 1990; Viaene, 1986.

excavation   Archaeological excavation is costly and destructive. The costs on site and in post-excavation work are frequently underestimated: several classes of indus-

trial sites, particularly those formerly water-powered, have incurred major overhead costs not always foreseen. In addition they are likely to yield residues requiring laboratory examination, as well as sizeable artefacts needing conservation: the justification for excavation relies on this work being properly resourced and competently executed. As with work on any period, the examination and successive removal of stratified deposits is an act of destruction, and, in planning a research strategy, a balance has to be struck between these losses, however well-kept and durable the record, and the confidence with which the amount of information that would be gained can be predicted. The use of field-walking and non-destructive geophysical survey methods is of particular importance in locating and characterizing below-ground features, as a preliminary or an alternative to full excavation: the size of many industrial features, the extent to which magnetic anomalies are created by kilns and furnaces, and the susceptibility of many waste deposits to geophysical survey makes such work essential.

Much excavation on industrial sites has arisen from the need to consolidate structures for conservation and often for display. This frequently requires the removal of destruction deposits, as well as residues accumulated against walls or over solid floors. Such work should proceed with no less care in recording than that done during problem-orientated or salvage excavation, and the penalty of destruction of stratification should be considered when choosing methods of stabilization or planning museum developments.

The need for excavation of post-medieval deposits is frequently seen to be in inverse proportion to the survival of the written, cartographic and iconographic record. In cases where excavation and archive material provide similar information, this argument is attractive: if plans and views of a works were to survive, if there were descriptions of the processes, of the experiments and failures as well as the successes, as well as catalogues of products, a detailed examination of the below-ground physical remains might have little to add. Such sources are rare, and the costs of excavation have to be weighed against the possibility of adding to the record. In a programme of research directed at a whole region, or into a particular phase of development of an industry, the issues are more complex: where a significant proportion of industrial units are poorly documented and have few standing remains, and where fieldwork provides significant information, there is a strong case for starting with excavation at the best-documented site in a group. In this way, as found at the start of research on early blast furnaces in the Weald, England, recorded costs of building or operation can be related to the size and characteristics of structures and plant; products, whether documented or surviving, can be related to excavated residues; and, of more general application to the archaeology of a region, dated groups of artefacts may be forthcoming. With such a basis, excavated information from the less well documented sites takes on additional meaning: size of building, quality of plant, quantities and characteristics of residues such as slags, cinders or discarded unfinished products

Figure 44 An overhead view of the excavation of the base of the charcoal-fuelled blast furnace at Pippingford, Sussex, England; to the right is a timber-lined casting pit.
David Crossley

may be related to the comprehensively researched example. With a basis of information of this kind, the need for further excavation is reduced: sampling, both of structures and deposits, can provide material for comparison, not only saving expenditure but preserving stratified deposits for the future, when questions now unforeseen may arise. Further, this yardstick approach frequently makes more sense of material recovered from field-walking on sites where excavation is impossible.

The case for salvage excavation may be stronger. If a site is to be destroyed by development, the argument for preservation of stratified deposits for future work cannot apply. But choices have to be made, and the best-documented example in a list of threatened sites must have priority, on the grounds set out above. If it is possible to combine salvage work with the establishment of a yardstick, scarce funds for rescue archaeology are well spent. If for one reason or another a poorly-documented example is to be investigated under rescue conditions, even if the investigator can only observe building excavation, the archaeologist is fortunate if he or she can compare his or her material, recovered under pressure of time, with information from a well-documented type-site.

There are many industries or areas for which little documentation survives, or indeed where little was created in the first place. With these, field evidence assumes the major role. This is particularly the case where units were small, and their proprietors had little need of accounts, and where mills, furnaces and the like were leased out by estates whose rentals record few details. Only when written or cartographic surveys were made, where disputes and litigation arose, or where correspondence survives do such archives come into their own, and even with these it frequently requires the location and dating of a site on the ground to provide the focus for

research into scattered references whose significance would otherwise go unrecognized.

Of the features recorded by excavation, those of structures, whether of mills, kilns or furnaces, have added considerably to knowledge, whereas experience has shown that the survival of more portable plant should not be too readily anticipated. It is important to recognize the extent of reuse of items such as water wheels, mill parts, forge hammers, bellows, moulds or indeed removable elements of buildings, transported at the termination of leases, or from abandoned works in declining industries. The extent of the secondhand trade in plant is something that has received little attention, but of which the excavator should be aware. In these cases it is necessary to recognize the emplacements for such equipment: bases of forge hammers and anvils, frames for bellows, boiler and engine bases, or underground flues at glass furnaces.

Excavation can play a vital part in gauging the efficiency of processes. A means of judging success or failure is by the examination of residues, for the written record is sparse. Before the nineteenth century it is exceptional for detailed comments to survive: the correspondence left by the Fullers, mid-eighteenth-century Sussex ironmasters, on the problems encountered at their Heathfield furnace (*see* WEALD) has few parallels. The key groups of residues whose context it is vital to record and that provide evidence for efficiency are abandoned products; process waste, composed of material such as unshaped glass fragments; and waste residues, such as ashes, slags and cinder, discarded during processes such as smelting or heating. With the first group, the products, the key question is how the objects excavated compare with marketed items, whether they have been discarded for falling short of acceptable quality or because of economic changes. Hence, acquaintance with contem-

245

porary artefacts from other sources is important, with due consideration given to the effects of burial on the excavated material. Industries varied in the extent to which second-grade products could find local markets, and hence in the amount of sub-standard artefacts discarded. Also, the use that could be made of discards varies: abandoned glass and metal could be returned to the pot as cullet or scrap, whereas pottery waste had little use except as hardcore.

Fragments discarded in the course of manufacture might likewise be reused. Their significance lies in information about the stages of production: runners of cast iron found on blast furnace waste tips are a good example of the problems of interpretation. If of acceptable quality, the larger runner could be refined at the forge in the same way as pig iron: if one is found, the question arises as to whether or how it was defective, and examination can provide information about operating difficulties rarely mentioned in written sources. In the glass industry, as another example, quantities of broken vessels may suggest failures at the annealing stage, although the extent to which material was recycled may result in only the final season's waste remaining in any quantity.

The third group comprises the by-product residues, examples being slags, ashes, bark from tanning pits, or fuller's earth. Some are more durable and identifiable than others, but, recorded in their stratified context, most can yield valuable information, related to phases in the life of a works. In the glass industry, for example, the amorphous lumps of bubbly material, often found on waste tips and wrongly named as slag, usually comprise scum ladled or spilled from the top of the melt in the crucible, and the quantity and composition of such waste has much to tell of the care taken in the selection of materials and the conduct of the melt. At the blast furnace, the composition of slags is a guide to the extent of separation of waste from iron, and slags taken from the base of the hearth at the end of a campaign often contain in microcosm the ore, fuel, iron and slag.

Such work is particularly important in the investigation of the difficulties experienced during periods of innovation, and the potential of excavation for recovering material generated in the formative stages of new processes is significant in deciding on priorities for fieldwork. In European terms, the introduction into the iron industry of the indirect process, the blast furnace and finery forge, is one such case, and the excavation of medieval furnace sites in Sweden is a notable example, to be followed, it is hoped, by comparable work in the southern Netherlands and in Italy, and the more widespread dissemination of excavation results from medieval German furnace sites. Likewise, the earliest use of coke in the blast furnace, and the attempts to develop alternatives to the finery forge, must rank high amongst priorities. The early stages of the introduction of mineral fuel into the production of glass, and the development of the closed crucible, are also examples where the examination of waste is of consequence, in indicating the consistency with which quality was achieved. From the former, residues from a mineral-fuelled furnace documentarily dated to the years 1617–

23 have been examined; in the case of the closed pot, the recent excavations at Bolsterstone, Yorkshire, have verified the use of the type of crucible referred to by the eighteenth-century French writer Bosc d'Antic as the 'English' pot. In ceramics an excellent example is the excavation of the Fulham pottery of John Dwight, the site not only of the first commercially successful attempt to produce stoneware in Britain, but of experiments in the production of porcelain.

Despite the potential demonstrated by past excavations, and the significance of shaping fieldwork priorities to match the possibilities of identifying key innovations and problems, we should guard against an assumption that verification comes easily from excavated material. The writings of contemporary observers of processes that were essentially empirical have shown the complexity of the variables. Bosc d'Antic is a good example, describing minute alterations in glass furnace structure which could make the difference between success and failure, and which would be hard for the excavator to detect from surviving fragments. It is indeed the third dimension, so often lost to the excavator, and in many industries so rarely surviving above ground, that can be vital, emphasizing the importance of combining contemporary iconographic evidence and recording fragments of standing buildings with the excavated record.

BIBLIOGRAPHY
General
Barker, 1982, 1986.
Specific
Ashurst, D. Excavations at the 17th/18th-century glasshouse at Bolsterstone, Yorkshire. In *PMA*, xxi, 1987.
Crossley, D. W. A 16th-century Wealden blast furnace: excavations at Panningridge, Sussex. In *PMA*, vi, 1972.
Crossley, D. W. Sir William Clavell's glasshouse at Kimmeridge, Dorset. In *Archaeological Journal*, 144, 1987.
Magnusson, G. Lapphyttan – an example of medieval iron production. In *Jernkontorets* (Stockholm) H34, 1985.
Newton, R. G. Who invented covered pots? In *Glass Technology*, xxix, 1987.

DAVID CROSSLEY

excavator A swivelling machine, originally based on a CRANE, designed to dig soil or ballast for civil engineering purposes. The first revolving shovel excavator is thought to have been a steam-powered machine mounted on a railway wagon, built in the USA in 1835. The steam 'navvy' was the invention of the French engineer Couvreux in 1861, and was employed on the Suez Canal from 1863. Steam navvies came into use in railway construction in the late nineteenth century, the Melton–Nottingham line of the Midland Railway, completed in 1880, being the first railway in Britain for which they were employed, reducing the cost of work by 80 per cent. The construction of the Nord-Ostsee, Panama and Manchester SHIP CANALS subsequently publicized the effectiveness of very large excavators. Chain-tracks were patented in the first decade of the twentieth century by David Roberts of the Hornsby company of Grantham, Lincolnshire; they were not taken up in Britain, however, and the rights were sold to the US company that became Caterpillar Tractor Ltd, one of the principal makers of excavators. A 100-ton Ruston Bucyrus steam navvy of 1931 is preserved at BEAMISH, and excavators are included in a museum near ARNHEM. In the twentieth century diesel has supplanted steam as the principal power source for excavators, whose operation is now usually controlled by complex hydraulic systems.

Dredges are excavators employed for digging materials from under water – silt from navigation channels, or alluvial mineral deposits (see MINING). Draglines combine the principles of the excavator and the AERIAL ROPEWAY and are employed in opencast mining and strip-mining.

BIBLIOGRAPHY
General
Grimshaw, 1985; Schulz, 1987; Wright, 1982.

BARRIE TRINDER

Exeter, Devon, England   A crossing point on the River Exe encouraged early settlement and by the eleventh century Exeter was the eighth largest town in Britain. It became the regional capital, a clothmaking centre and a significant port. An 8 km (5 mi.) ship canal was constructed in 1564–6, with the first pound locks in Britain. The terminal basin and riverside area has several buildings of interest and now houses the Exeter Maritime Museum. The six-arched iron bridge built in 1834–5 is an impressive reminder of nineteenth-century road improvements. Brunel's broad-gauge Bristol & Exeter Railway opened in 1844. The route to Plymouth continued westwards with the ill-fated South Devon Railway, operated on the atmospheric system until 1847. Atmospheric pumphouses survive at Totnes and Starcross (the latter now being a museum). St Thomas station in Exeter is in its original condition, as designed by ISAMBARD KINGDOM BRUNEL.

BIBLIOGRAPHY
Specific
Chitty, M. *Industrial Archaeology of Exeter: a guide*, n.d.

LOCATIONS
[M] Brunel Atmospheric Railway Museum, The Old Pumping House, Starcross, Exeter.
[M] Exeter Maritime Museum, Isca Ltd, The Quay, Exeter EX2 4AN.
[M] Royal Albert Memorial Museum, Queen Street, Exeter EX4 3RX.

JOHN POWELL

explosives   Until the 1860s GUNPOWDER was the only explosive available for military, civil engineering or mining purposes. Guncotton (nitrocellulose) was discovered in the 1840s, and manufactured in Britain after Sir Frederick Abel (1827–1902) had shown that it could be stabilized. ALFRED NOBEL was chiefly responsible for the growth of the 'high explosives' industry, based on nitrocellulose, nitroglycerine and a range of coal and petroleum derivatives, which transformed the manufacture of explosives into a research-based sector of the chemical industry, and enlarged the ambitions of civil engineers, as well as transforming the nature of warfare.

See also CORDITE; DYNAMITE; TNT.

Expressionism   Expressionism was the dominant artistic style in Northern Europe, particularly in Germany, in the period 1905–25: it was influential in painting, in films by such directors as Fritz Lang, and in architecture. Expressionist architectural forms were partly derived from ART NOUVEAU, and buildings tended to be freely shaped, often having the appearance of abstract sculpture. An outstanding Expressionist building is the Chilehaus, an office block in HAMBURG.

BIBLIOGRAPHY
General
Pehnt, 1974; Sharp, 1966.

F

factory The word 'factory' was used by the sixteenth century to refer to trading posts established by merchants in overseas countries, like those set up by European companies in India. As early as 1618 a place where books were made in London was called a factory, but the term did not generally refer to a manufacturing establishment until the late eighteenth century. It was accorded general recognition by the Factory Act 1802 which was the first of many attempts to regulate working hours and conditions in the TEXTILE MILLS that had evolved in previous decades, establishments often employing several hundred people, centred on large, usually multi-storey buildings, where power was employed for some processes, and where labour was specialized. By the early 1840s the merits of the 'factory system', a term first recorded in 1832, were being widely debated. With the spread of mass-production techniques to consumer-goods manufacturing in the second half of the nineteenth century, the word 'factory' was applied to places making shoes, furniture or shirts.

The precise meaning of 'factory' varies with circumstances, particularly in as far as it relates to the word MILL. In the Yorkshire woollen trade a 'mill' was where wool was prepared and spun: a factory produced the finished cloth. A similar distinction applied in the British linen industry. In the USA the term 'mill' refers to a place where bulk, semi-finished products are made, such as bales of cloth, steel coils, flour, cement or timber, while a 'factory' produces goods ready for the consumer: trousers, motor-cars, refrigerators or cigarettes.

The term 'factory village', meaning a COLONY dependent upon a factory, was used from the 1830s.

The term 'factory ship', indicating a large vessel on which fish or whalemeat is processed in the region where it is caught, was first recorded in the USA in 1932.

BIBLIOGRAPHY
General
Tann, 1970.

DAVID H. SHAYT and BARRIE TRINDER

Faeroe Islands (Føroyar), Denmark The Faeroe Islands in the North Atlantic are of volcanic origin, but were subjected to severe glaciation. The islands have a population of 46 000 inhabitants in an area of about 1400 km² (540 sq. mi.). Fishing is now the all-important occupation, and old boats and fishing equipment are exhibited at Bataøllin in Tórshavn, the capital of the islands.

On the island of Sudhuroy there are extensive coal seams in the parish of Frodba which have been mined until recently. The first hydro-electric power station was opened at Botnur on the same island in 1921, with two 400 hp Pelton turbines. A second power station was opened in the same year at Tórshavn (on Streymoy island), with its generator powered by a 150 hp diesel engine.

BIBLIOGRAPHY
Specific
Trap, J. P. *Danmark,* XXIX (Faeroe Islands). Copenhagen, 1968.

Fafe, Minho, Portugal A town 50 km (30 mi.) NE of Oporto, developed by Portuguese migrants who had returned from Brazil where they had set up some of the first cotton mills. A cinema of 1923 has a façade notable for its decorative features. The Regional Electricity Museum is in the hydro-electric power station at Santa Rita.

LOCATION
[M] Regional Electricity Museum, Santa Rita, Fafe.

Fagervik, Uudenmaan lääni, Finland Fagervik, near Inkoo (Inga), 60 km (40 mi.) W. of Helsinki, is perhaps the best-preserved and architecturally most distinguished ironworks in Finland. Carl Billsten, founder of the BILLNÄS ironworks, built a blast furnace and bar-iron forge at Fagervik in 1646. The Gustavian mansion, with its outbuildings (*see* FINLAND), was built to the design of Turku's city architect, C. F. Schröder, between 1762 and 1773. Adjacent to the mansion is a Baroque-style garden with greenhouses of the 1840s, and the country's oldest English-style garden, with extensive natural woodlands and Chinese pavilions. The wooden cruciform church at the ironworks dates from 1737 and the bell tower from 1766. On the road running past the church to the works is a compact group of well-preserved, red-painted workers' houses, dating from *c.*1800.

Of the production buildings, two forge buildings of 1758 and 1765 have survived, together with an old iron warehouse. Both the forges have been restored in recent years with the help of funding from the National Board of Antiquities, according to plans by the architect Merja Häro, as part of the most important study and restoration project so far undertaken on any industrial site in Finland.

There is no longer a blast furnace at Fagervik, but on its site is a grey stone mill building of 1769, and a water mill dating from the 1890s. A brick-built tin-plate mill situated next to the main road, dating from 1780, now functions as a shop; near to it is the old recreation room for the smiths who worked at the mill.

The Fagervik ironworks ceased production in 1902 but

248

one forge was used for other industrial purposes as late as 1927. The mansion is now a private agricultural and forestry centre.

LAURI PUTKONEN

faience   Classical and industrial archaeologists, and art historians, give differing definitions to this term, the only common ground being that they all refer to glazed ceramics. The word derives from Faenza, a town near the Adriatic coast of Italy that became famed in the late fifteenth century for the best majolica in Italy. Faience originated as the French name for tin-glazed earthenware of this type. Archaeologists use the word to refer to ancient Egyptian wares made of glazed, powdered quartz.

Industrial archaeologists usually use 'faience' to refer to large blocks or slabs of glazed ceramic, made to line the interiors or exteriors of buildings. Architectural faience evolved from the use of glazed panels to decorate portions of the Victoria and Albert Museum (*see* LONDON) in the 1860s. It was widely used in Britain as an adjunct to tiling in the interiors of commercial and public buildings in the 1880s and 1890s. The use of faience as external cladding for buildings was made technically possible by the development of finishes that could resist frost, a technique pioneered by Doulton of Lambeth, London, *c.*1889. Faience was used throughout Britain for facing public houses, CHAIN STORES and CINEMAS before 1939.

Faience was also widely used in Parisian architecture at the turn of the century, often to create brightly coloured façades with ART NOUVEAU detailing. The material gained its widest and most dramatic use in America, where it is known as glazed terracotta, possibly the finest examples being the Woolworth building, New York, designed by Cass Gilbert and completed in 1913, and the series of banks in the Midwest designed by Louis Sullivan (*see* SKYSCRAPER) in the early twentieth century.

See also figures 30, 145.

BIBLIOGRAPHY
General
Flemming and Honour, 1979; Hamilton, 1978.
Specific
Hodson, G. N. Architectural terracotta and faience. In *Transactions of the Ceramic Society*, xxxv, 1935–6.

MICHAEL STRATTON

Fairbairn, Sir William (1789–1874)   One of the most celebrated of Victorian mechanical engineers and a major contributor to the literature of the Industrial Revolution, Fairbairn was born in Kelso (*see* BORDERS). He became an apprentice millwright at a colliery in Northumberland, where he knew GEORGE STEPHENSON, and worked in Macclesfield in 1816 and in Manchester, initially for the millwright Thomas Hewes, from 1817. He designed and built more than a hundred bridges, and devised techniques for improving line shafting and for riveting boiler plates. In 1850 he patented a crane with a curving jib fabricated from wrought-iron plates, suitable for dockside use. He set up a yard to build IRON SHIPS at Millwall,

LONDON, in 1835, but soon gave it up. He was closely concerned in 1848–9 with the construction of the TUBULAR BRIDGES at MENAI and Conway, and was responsible for mechanical engineering aspects of the mill at Saltaire (*see* BRADFORD). He built two water mills at ZURICH in 1824, inspected government works at Constantinople (*see* ISTANBUL) in 1839, and advised on drainage works at HAARLEM in 1840. He was President of the Institute of Mechanical Engineers in 1854–5.

BIBLIOGRAPHY
General
Fairbairn, 1849, 1854, 1856, 1861; Pole, 1877; Smiles, 1863.

fairground   Early-nineteenth-century travelling shows offered few 'rides' except for swings and roundabouts for children, but by the 1890s steam and later electric power made possible flying machines and scenic railways, and permanent amusement parks were developed in resorts, combining such spectacular features with rifle ranges, coconut shies and slot machines. The pleasure beach at Blackpool (*see* FYLDE) originated in a gypsy encampment of the early 1890s. One of the characteristic rides of the mid-twentieth century, the 'dodgem', was introduced to Britain from America by Billy Butlin (*see* HOLIDAY CAMP) in 1928. Bushkill Park, Easton, Pa., is an amusement park of the early twentieth century, and includes a roundabout – a 'carousel' in North America – dating from 1904.

BIBLIOGRAPHY
General
Lindley, 1973.

Fairlie, Robert (1831–85)   Inventor of a double-bogie, double-boiler, but single-firebox locomotive for mountain railways, patented in 1864. *Little Wonder* of 1869 began the celebrated association with the FESTINIOG RAILWAY, where two are preserved. Examples were supplied to Burma, Mexico, Russia, Sweden and the USA where the type was taken up by William Mason (1803–83) and known as the 'Mason-Fairlie'.

BIBLIOGRAPHY
General
Abbott, 1970; Ahrons, 1927; Winton, 1986.

Fakenham, Norfolk, England   A town 40 km (25 mi.) NW of Norwich, the site of a complete small town gasworks, in the care of English Heritage (*see* ENGLAND). There was a works on the site in 1825, but the present retort house dates from 1846. The gasworks used horizontal retorts. Most plant is twentieth-century, but it reflects older practices.

Falkirk, Central, Scotland   A town famous for its foundries, some of which remain in operation: they are brick buildings with corrugated-iron cladding. The older parts of Carron Ironworks, founded in 1759, have been demolished, apart from the lade and the Baronial offices of 1876, but the company still operates and has a collection of its products including carronades.

The Forth & Clyde Canal runs through the town, and alongside it is the Rosebank (lowland malt) Distillery, founded in 1840, rebuilt in 1864, and still operating, although its round-ended BOND is now preserved as apartments and a restaurant. The main 'heritage' attractions of the district are at BO'NESS. Falkirk District Museums have preserved large-scale industrial items, from brick 'stupids' (wasters) to foundry and marine-engineering (punching and shearing) machines, and are constructing a working replica of the *Charlotte Dundas* (*see* STEAMSHIP).

LOCATION

[M] Falkirk Museums, c/o Public Library, Hope Street, Falkirk FK1 5AU.

MARK WATSON

Falkland Islands (Malvinas)   A small disputed archipelago in the South Atlantic, 1750 km (1100 mi.) S. of Montevedeo, Uruguay; it is ruled by Britain but claimed by Argentina. It is important for the hulks of historic ships, originally beached for storage and coaling purposes. SS *Great Britain* (*see* BRISTOL: IRON SHIP) was removed in 1970. Remaining hulks include:

- *Vicar of Bray*: a 282-ton wooden brig built at Whitehaven, England, in 1841, and used in the Californian Gold Rush of 1849.
- *Jhelun*: a 428-ton wooden barque, built at Liverpool, England, in 1849.
- *Charles Cooper*: a 977-ton wooden sailing ship, built at Black Rock, Conn., in 1856 for the New York–Le Havre PACKET BOAT service, beached at Port Stanley since 1866.
- *Egeria*: a 1066-ton wooden sailing ship, built in NEW BRUNSWICK, Canada, in 1859.
- *Garland*: a 599-ton iron barque, built at Liverpool, England, in 1864.
- *Fleetwing*: a 273-ton wooden brig, built at Portmadoc, Wales (*see* FESTINIOG RAILWAY) in 1874.

BIBLIOGRAPHY
General
Brouwer, 1985; Smith, 1973.

Falun, Kopparberg, Sweden   The origins of Falun, 240 km 150 mi.) N. of Stockholm, are closely associated with its copper mines. Falun was granted municipal privileges in 1643, but there is archaeological evidence of the extraction of ore from the eighth century AD, and the first document relating to the mine was signed on 16 June 1288. The company Stora, which only recently changed its name from Stora Kopparbergs Bergslags Aktiebolag, regards this date as the starting point of its history.

In the thirteenth century the Kopperberget – the copper mountain – had developed into a profitable enterprise, possibly under German influence. Raw copper had become a significant export commodity, and shares in the mine were eagerly sought after, not least by the Crown and the Church.

A succession of disastrous collapses in the early sixteenth century was followed by a drastic fall in production. King Gustav Vasa (r.1523–60) took vigorous action to restore output. German miners were brought to Kopparberget to construct hoisting devices, pump installations and other facilities. New and richer seams were discovered c.1579, which, with improvements in mining technology, opened the way to a great expansion of output. In 1650 copper-ore extraction and copper production reached a peak of about 3000 tonnes of raw copper, equivalent to about two-thirds of European copper output at that time. Sweden had almost a monopoly of the European copper trade. Mining operations were extended. Vertical shafts had to be driven to reach the ore, and the workings came to be increasingly undermined. There were severe collapses, and in 1687 came the worst disaster in the history of the mine when the walls between three large open cuts collapsed, transforming them into one vast pit, Stora Stöten, the bottom of which was covered by debris. From 1691 production never exceeded 1500 tons, and it declined further in the eighteenth century. Mining operations continued regardless, but Swedish copper lost its former dominant position on the world market, although until 1780 copper remained Sweden's second most important export commodity, after iron. The subsequent drop in output meant the inauguration of new lines of business. The production of sulphur and vitriol was revived, and from 1764 the Falun red paint was produced on an industrial scale, providing a use for the copper-free iron sulphide.

Stora is today an international enterprise. Copper ore is still mined, and the iron sulphide from the mine is the raw material for a profitable chemical concern. Falun red paint retains a faithful circle of customers. Gold ore has been extracted at Falun in recent years. Stora has wound up its iron and steel business, and is now one of Europe's leading forestry concerns.

As early as the 1890s the assistant manager at Falun, Carl Sahlin, had begun to put the company's mining history in order, and from c.1900 Stora has made great efforts to conserve its industrial monuments. The eighteenth-century Gruvstugan (mine building) near Stora Stöten was restored and inaugurated as a mining museum in the 1920s. Continuing mining operations in the 1960s made it necessary to move the old buildings, including the museum, from the brink of Stora Stöten. A replica of the museum building was built, and a wing added to house an auditorium and modern exhibits. Models of mining equipment by CHRISTOPHER POLHEM are amongst the museum's outstanding exhibits. Elsborg, the miners' housing district, made up of wooden houses covered with Falun red paint and standing on foundations of copper slag blocks, was restored during European Architectural Heritage Year in 1975. The older parts of the mine have been reinstated and opened to visitors. The constricted workings and the shafts, with their impressive timber structures, bear witness, in a centuries-long perspective, to the dangers faced by the miners. Stora Stöten, with its headframes, water wheel and a range of other buildings from various periods in the mine's history, forms one of the richest and most fascinating industrial landscapes in Sweden.

At Korså bruk, 12 km (8 mi.) NE of Falun, Stora has preserved Dalarna's last LANCASHIRE FORGE which dates from 1840 and ceased operation in 1930, together with its associated blast furnace of 1827–9 at Åg, which represents the technology of the 1890s, when it underwent its last major rebuilding before closure in 1927.

BIBLIOGRAPHY
General
Lindroth, 1955; Rydberg, 1988.

LOCATIONS
[M] Dalarnas Museum, Stiggatan 2-4, 791 21 Falun.
[M] Storas Museum (Mining Museum), Stora AB, 791 80 Falun.

MARIE NISSER

Faversham, Kent, England   A market town, port and railway junction, where the London–Dover road crosses Faversham Creek. From ancient times, the home of an oyster fishery. A heritage centre was opened in 1977, the third in Britain. Brewing has been important, the present Whitbread brewery dating from 1764; the even earlier Shepherd Neames brewery, from 1698, is open to visitors. There was also much brickmaking, for the London market, and there are many vitrified waste bricks throughout the town. There were gunpowder works in Faversham from the mid-sixteenth century, and the first gun-cotton factory was opened in 1846; by 1900 there were extensive factories for powder, cordite and nitroglycerine, which continued working until the 1930s. Chart Gunpowder Mills are preserved, with one mill surviving of a pair worked by a single water wheel.

LOCATION
[M] Fleur-de-Lis Heritage Centre, Preston Street, Faversham, Kent.

feathers   Bird feathers had two principal uses: the large tail feathers as quill pens, the remainder as bed fillings. Seventeenth- and eighteenth-century probate inventories in England show that feathers were collected and stored until enough had been accumulated to stuff a pillow or mattress, some of the latter weighing over 100 lb. (43 kg). The chief centre of commercial production in Britain was LINCOLNSHIRE, where geese were plucked five times a year, for quills and bed feathers. Cleaning works, where feathers were sorted, then heated to 90–120 °C, operated in the nineteenth century in Boston, LINCOLNSHIRE, and other towns. Waste was used as manure. Some companies also manufactured the mattresses in which their feathers were used.

Feathers of high quality, particularly the down or breast feathers of the eider duck (*see* DOWN), were an important product of the Arctic regions in the nineteenth century (*see* NORWAY).

BIBLIOGRAPHY
General
Wright, 1982.

Fehmarn, Schleswig-Holstein, Germany   An island 70 km (45 mi.) E of Kiel. It has several lighthouses which provide within a comparatively small area an illustration of the development of lighthouse-building between the 1830s and the 1930s. They include the Marienleuchte, a four-storey rectangular tower with two keepers' houses built onto the sides, dating from 1832; the Westmakelsdorf lighthouse of 1881–2; the Staberhuk lighthouse of 1903–4; the Flügger Ort of 1914–15; and the Strukkamphuk, a steel lighthouse built in 1935.

A museum of milling was opened in 1961 in Lemkenhafen. It occupies a Dutch-style windmill of 1787, which has a gallery, a tail pole, and latticed vanes for the sales. The island is crossed by the Vogelfluglinie (the bird's flight line), the rail and ferry route linking the German Federal Republic with the Danish island of Lolland (*see* LOLLAND-FALSTER); this was opened in 1963 following the severance of the routes used before World War II which went through DDR territory. The German terminus of the train ferries is at Puttgarden on Fehmarn.

BIBLIOGRAPHY
General
Slotta, 1975–85.

LOCATION
[M] Museum of Windmills, 2449 Lemkenhafen.

Feira, Beira Litoral, Portugal   Feira, 26 km (16 mi.) S. of Oporto, is the traditional centre of the paper industry in Portugal. Old papermills still work in the nearby villages of Paços de Brandão and Oleiros, while at Malaposta (Sanfins) is an old posting station.

Feiring, Akershus, Norway   An ironworks on the western shore of Lake Mjøsa, 35 km (22 mi.) N. of Eidsvoll, which operated in 1806–18. The stack of a blast furnace survives, with substantial remains of most other buildings. A programme of excavation and conservation began in 1956 and had been completed by 1978.

Felguera, La, Oviedo, Asturias, Spain   Construction of the Duro ironworks, at La Felguera, 16 km (10 mi.) SE of Oviedo, in the coal basin of the Nalón Valley, was begun in 1857 under the direction of its founder, D. Pedro Duro. Iron production began in 1862, and construction concluded in 1864 with the inauguration of HOT BLAST stoves and a second blast furnace, and the purchasing of a steamboat for transporting iron and raw materials. The works derived many advantages from its situation on the coalfield, and from the transport facilities provided by the newly-built Langreo railway. The Duro works has ceased iron and steel production, but only some of its structures have been demolished, pending the creation of a new technology park. The adjacent Urquijo workers' quarters and the Duro schools, built for employees at the ironworks, remain in use.

fellmonger   A merchant who bought sheepskins from a butcher, removed the wool for the manufacture of cloth or

251

felt, and sold the skin for TAWING or oil dressing (*see* CURRYING). A fellmonger's business was based in a yard, surrounded by single-storey sheds, often open on the yard side, and usually with a wool warehouse, a multi-storey building with taking-in doors, for bales of wool.

BIBLIOGRAPHY
General
Mayhew, 1850; Minnoch and Minnoch, 1970; O'Flaherty *et al.*, 1956.
Specific
Thomas, S., Clarkson, L. A. and Thompson, R. *Leather Manufacture through the Ages*. Northampton: East Midlands Industrial Archaeological Conference, 1983.

feltmaking   Felt is made from wool or hairs cut from animal fur. The best quality for hatmaking came from the beaver, but that from rabbits, hares, camels, seals, ostriches and goats was also employed. The hair was laid on a hurdle and vibrated by a bow up to 2.25 m (7 ft.) long, which crossed the fibres over one another so that their scales hooked them together, forming a mass called a batt. The batt was worked manually, then joined to another forming a conical shape. At a battery, an open iron boiler containing diluted sulphuric acid, the felt cone would be dipped and subjected to further pummelling on an adjacent bench. Hats were subsequently dyed, stiffened and shaped. The acid caused brain damage to the operatives, hence the traditional madness of hatters. Most felt was manufactured for HATMAKING, but some was used for such industrial purposes as papermaking.

BIBLIOGRAPHY
General
Book of Trades, 1839; Burkett, 1979; Tunis, 1965.

Fens, Bedfordshire, Cambridgeshire, Northamptonshire and Norfolk, England   An area along the Rivers Cam, Ouse, Nene and Welland, from Cambridge and Peterborough to the Wash, artificially drained from the 1630s when Sir Cornelius Vermuyden (?1595–?1683) created the Old and New Bedford Rivers. Many conflicts have arisen between drainage and navigation interests. The first steam engine was installed in 1821; drainage is now maintained by diesel and electric pumps. In Earith, 20 km (12 mi.) NW of Cambridge, at the southern end of the Bedford Rivers, there are several surviving pumphouses, including one at Willingham, 1 km ($\frac{1}{2}$ mi.) SE, where there is a preserved Ruston & Hornsby diesel pump and a 1902 turbine pump. At Denver Sluice, 45 km (28 mi.) NE of Cambridge, at the northern end of the Bedford Rivers, a sluice and lock of 1834 by Sir John Rennie (1794–1874) survive, with control gates of 1923. There is a restored six-storey tower mill nearby. Stretham pumping station, 16 km (10 mi.) N. of Cambridge, houses a pumping engine by Butterley Co. of 1831, a scoop wheel, and a 1925 Mirrlees diesel engine, on the original air-blast system. A smock mill pump at Wicken, 18 km (11 mi.) NW of Cambridge, dates from 1908, and has been preserved on the present site since 1955.

BIBLIOGRAPHY
General
Hills, 1967.
Specific
Summers, D. *The Great Ouse*. Newton Abbot: David & Charles, 1973.

LOCATION
[S] Stretham Engine, Stretham, Ely, Cambridgeshire.

BARRIE TRINDER

ferry   A place where passengers, animals and sometimes vehicles are conveyed by boat across a river or lake, a harbour or a narrow stretch of sea (*see* PACKET BOAT); from the sixteenth century the word has also been used as a synonym for ferry boat. Until the nineteenth century most ferry boats were built according to the customs of the inland navigation or coastal regions where they sailed, but the introduction of train and subsequently road vehicle ferries has led to standardization of the design of seagoing vessels.

River ferries are often hauled by chains or ropes fixed to posts on either side and passing between vertical rollers on the vessel. Horse ferries were established on some navigable rivers to enable beasts hauling barges to cross where towpaths change sides.

Several early twentieth-century steam ferries still work at Stockholm and Istanbul. Notable surviving ferry boats include:

- *Eureka*, 1890: a 2564-ton sidewheel steam ferry for passengers and trains, preserved at San Francisco, USA.
- *Berkeley*, 1898: a 1945-ton, steam, screw-propelled, double-ended San Francisco ferry, at San Diego, Calif., USA.
- *Trillium*, 1910: a 673-ton steam sidewheel ferry, working from Toronto, Canada.
- *Chief Wawatam*, 1911: a 2990-ton, steam train ferry still working between Mackinaw City and St Ignace, on Lake Michigan, USA.
- *Binghamton*, 1905: a 1462-ton, steam passenger and vehicle ferry, which crossed the Hudson River from New York, at Edgewater, N.J., USA.
- *Lady Denman*, 1912: a 65-ton wooden, diesel (formerly steam) Sydney Harbour ferry, at Huskisson, New South Wales, Australia, where she was built.
- *Bilfergen*, 1921: a 34-ton wooden, diesel-powered vessel, the first car ferry in Norway, at Søndeled.
- *Tattersall Castle*, 1934: a 556-ton River Humber paddle steamer, in London, England.
- *Zealand*, 1951: a 3046-ton train and road vehicle motor vessel, preserved in Copenhagen, Denmark.

BIBLIOGRAPHY
General
Andrews, 1975; Brouwer, 1985; Harlan, 1967; Murray, 1987; Ransome-Wallis, 1968.

LOCATION
[S] Søndeled Verteranskibsklubb, N-4990 Søndeled, Norway.

BARRIE TRINDER

fertilizers *See* AMMONIA; ARTIFICIAL FERTILIZERS.

Festiniog Railway, Porthmadog (Portmadoc), Gwynedd, Wales A 60.4 cm (1 ft. $11\frac{1}{2}$ in.) gauge railway, 33 km (21 mi.) S. of Bangor, built in 1836, linking the BLAENAU FFESTINIOG slate quarries in North Wales to Porthmadog harbour, 21 km (13 mi.) away. Originally it was gravity-operated, with horses returning the wagons; locomotives were introduced in 1863. The line was mostly closed in 1946 but was taken over by conservation volunteers in 1955, who now have a large collection of nineteenth- and twentieth-century locomotives. Porthmadog and Tremadog were planned towns, built during 1798–1828.

BIBLIOGRAPHY
General
Winton, 1986.
Specific
Boyd, J. I. C. *The Festiniog Railway*, 2 vols. Lingfield, Surrey: Oakwood Press, 1956, 1959.

LOCATION
[S] Festiniog Railway Co., Harbour Station, Porthmadog, Gwynedd LL49 9NF.

fibres The basic raw materials of textile production. Hair-like in appearance, they may be of animal, vegetable or mineral origin. All fibres, whether natural or synthetic, are polymers – long molecules of simple repeating units.

  See also COTTON; FLAX; HEMP; JUTE; SILK; SYNTHETIC FIBRES; WOOL.

BIBLIOGRAPHY
General
Bendure and Pfeiffer, 1946; Burnley, 1889; Montgomery, 1984; Wingate, 1979.

Fier, Albania An industrial town with cotton mills, brickworks, an oil refinery and chemical plant. The centre was designed by the French architect B.-F. de Barthélemy in the 1870s.

BIBLIOGRAPHY
General
Ward, 1983.

LOCATION
[M] Fier Museum, Fier.

Fierze, Albania Albania's largest hydro-electric power station, on the River Drin, 80 km (50 mi.) NE of Shkodër, with an output of 500 000 kW, and 6000 workers. The dam is 168 m (550 ft.) high.

Fife, Scotland A county, and in ancient times a kingdom, between the Rivers Forth and Tay. In the eighteenth century 90 per cent of Scottish salt production was on the shores of the Forth. Saltworks operated in conjunction with coastal collieries, consuming their small coals. Culross led the industry from the late sixteenth century, but later gave way to villages downstream. Fife's principal archaeological remains are the ruins on Preston Island of a combined coal mine (the Engine Pit) and salt-pan complex, built by 1813 and threatened by power station ash. At St Monance, 14 km (9 mi.) S. of St Andrews, is the tower of a windmill, which pumped to pans that have since been demolished. Inland at Thornton is an isolated early nineteenth-century three-storey colliery beam-engine house. Michael Colliery, East Wemyss, 9 km (6 mi.) NE of Kirkcaldy, was sunk in 1926 and closed by fire in 1967, but retains buildings, headgear and miners' rows. At Longannet, 12 km (7 mi.) E. of Dunfermline, four linked collieries supply a power station by an 8.8 km ($5\frac{1}{2}$ mi.) conveyor belt tunnel.

  Fourteen limekilns at Charleston, 8 km (5 mi.) S. of Dunfermline, built from 1761, form the largest group in Scotland. Lime was taken to Charleston Harbour, which has an eighteenth-century inner basin, by wagonway. An extensive alumina works in Burntisland, 12 km (7 mi.) W. of Dunfermline, with brick buildings and a large wooden water-cooling tower, was built *c.*1896 to supply Foyers and later aluminium works (*see* HIGHLANDS).

  The coal shipping installations at Burntisland of 1876 and 1901, and Methil, 11 km (6 mi.) NE of Kirkcaldy, of 1875, 1887 and 1913, were rarely used to capacity and are partially infilled. At Rosyth, 5 km (3 mi.) S. of Dunfermline, the newest of the Royal Naval dockyards, many of the structures, the cantilever cranes and the adjacent GARDEN CITY style housing date from the period of naval rivalry with Germany before and during World War I.

  The Scottish Fisheries Museum, Anstruther, opened in 1969 in a former ship's chandler's, with net-drying 'gallowses' and a wheelhouse in the yard. *The Reaper*, a Fifie of 1901, and *The Research*, a Zulu-class fishing boat of 1903, are still seaworthy. The collection includes Kelvin diesel and Gardiner semi-diesel engines, and all aspects of Scottish fishing are covered. Anstruther harbour has two basins, an octagonal light-tower and some stone and timber-boarded warehouses. The North Carr Light Vessel, in service during 1938–75, is open to the public. Wooden fishing boats are built at St Monance, 5 km (3 mi.) SW of Anstruther. Crail is the centre of crab and lobster fishing. Pittenweem harbour, 3 km (2 mi.) W. of Anstruther, home to the East Neuk fishing fleet, has eighteenth-century warehouses and chandlers' shops.

  Single-storey linen-weavers' cottages exist in such villages as Dairsie (originally called Osnaburgh after the coarse German fabric), 6 km (4 mi.) NE of Cupar; Freuchie, 16 km (10 mi.) N. of Kirkcaldy; and Ceres, 5 km (3 mi.) SE of Cupar, where the Fife Folk Museum, located in two cottages and a seventeenth-century weigh house, has displays relating to clay pipe-making as well as linen. Fife's first flax spinning mill was erected by James Aytoun in Kinghorn, 5 km (3 mi.) S. of Kirkcaldy, in 1792: it may be the tall, narrow mill, now a tenement, next to a mill of *c.*1860 in Overgate. Water-powered mills followed in the picturesque Dura Den. One of the Walker Company's Blebo Mills of 1803 survives as a dwelling, together with the owner's French Gothic house, a turbine house and a weir. Prinlaws Works, Leslie, 10 km (6 mi.) N. of

Kirkcaldy, in the late eighteenth century one of Fife's most extensive flax bleaching and spinning works, has been demolished except for the owner's house and an exceptional square brick stalk with a decorative top. New Mill near Cupar of *c*.1820, standing beside a grain mill, is now a farm. Small power-loom factories were built in the 1860s at Cupar and Kingskettle. The Lumsden Company's power-loom factory of 1860 at Freuchie stands adjacent to the owner's house and extensive rows of two-storey workers' housing.

Cardy Net Works, Lower Largo, 18 km (11 mi.) NE of Kirkcaldy, was built in 1867 by David Selkirk Gillies, descendant of Alexander Selkirk (1676–1721: Defoe's inspiration for Robinson Crusoe), and since closure has been a time capsule comprising warehouse, smithy, office and owner's house (each with Victorian furnishings), a walled garden, and an empty weaving shed.

Papermills in Fife originally depended on linen rags and plentiful water. Several mills using water supplied from Loch Leven by a cut made in 1827–33 to Markinch, 12 km (7 mi.) N. of Kirkcaldy, and Leslie are now continued by Tullis Russell & Co.: Rothes (1806), Auchmuty (1810) and Levenbank (1810), all substantially modernized. New raw materials prompted the Guardbridge White Pine Co. near Leuchars in 1872, which soon afterwards took up esparto grass, and Caldwell & Co.'s mills at Inverkeithing.

Bonthrone Maltings, Newton of Falkland, 14 km (8 mi.) NE of Kirkcaldy, has nineteenth-century ranges of malt floors, no longer used, each with a kiln, and linked to the remains of a brewery by a passage over a road. At Markinch, John Haig's Cameron Bridge grain distillery, founded in 1824, still functions, and sends its whisky to the large brick BONDS of the 1930s.

The Edinburgh, Perth & Dundee Railway opened in 1847, having train ferries across the Forth between Newhaven and Burntisland, and over the Tay, between Tayport and Broughty. The Burntisland terminus is neo-Classical; the stations at Markinch, Ladybank and Cupar a pleasing Italianate. A timber engine shed remains at Markinch.

See also DUNFERMLINE; FORTH BRIDGES; KIRKCALDY; and, for Tay Rail Bridge, DUNDEE.

BIBLIOGRAPHY
General
Hume, 1976; Whatley, 1984.

LOCATIONS
[M] Fife Folk Museum, Old High Street, Ceres, Fife.
[S] North Carr Light Vessel, c/o Director of Recreation, NE Fife District Council, County Buildings, Cupar, Fife.
[M] Scottish Fisheries Museum, St Ayles, Harbourhead, Anstruther, Fife.

MARK WATSON

Figueiró dos Vinhos, Beira Litoral, Portugal   A village 150 km (90 mi.) NE of Lisbon. Foz do Alge was an important metallurgical centre between 1692 and 1834. Remains of a cannon foundry are under the lake behind the Castelo do Bode dam, and can be seen in summer when the water level is low. There are archaeological remains of the nearby Machuca foundry.

BIBLIOGRAPHY
Specific
Carvalho, J. S. *A Ferraria de Foz do Alge* (The Foz do Alge ironworks). Oporto: Marânus.

file   Files, essential in most wood- and metal-working trades, have always been made of steel. First a piece of steel was hammered and re-hammered as close as possible to the final shape. It was then forged in dies, with hammers of two types, one cone-shaped, the other a large hammer with a face at each end. Next it was annealed; slowly cooled, with air excluded; and ground, usually on a large wheel. The surface was then cut with a small steel chisel, the file being held on a piece of lead on an anvil, which the smith sat astride, as if on a horse, holding the file with his feet by means of a strap. Finally the file was hardened. Filemaking machines were introduced in the USA from the early nineteenth century. Hand filemakers' shops survive in the SHEFFIELD and REMSCHEID regions.

BIBLIOGRAPHY
General
Barraclough, 1981–4; Treatise, n.d.

Filipstad, Värnland, Sweden   A small town at the northern end of Lake Daglösen, stands at the centre of a region rich in the remains of ironworks which were operating until the early twentieth century. Most were operated by the Uddeholm (*see* MUNKFORS) company. There are substantial remains of blast furnaces at Motjärnshyttan, 24 km (15 mi.) NW, Brattforshyttan, 9 km (6 mi.) SW, Storbrohyttan, 4 km ($2\frac{1}{2}$ mi.) NW, Saxåhyttan, 16 km (10 mi.) NW, and Torskebäckshyttan, 10 km (6 mi.) E., most of the surviving structures dating from the mid-nineteenth century. At Motjärnshyttan the blast furnace and calcining kilns are within the same structure. There are preserved remains of iron-ore mining operations at Långban, 18 km (11 mi.) NE, and Nordmark, 14 km (9 mi.) N.

film   All kinds of film shot on location are potentially useful to the historian of industry, as has been demonstrated by compilations from fiction films put together by the Museum of London as evidence of social history. Jean Renoir's *La Bête Humaine* of 1939 portrays the workings of a great railway terminus in the time of the steam locomotive more effectively than most documentaries on the subject. Humphrey Jennings's *Fires were Started* is more valuable to industrial archaeologists for what it shows about London's Dockland than for its portrayal of firefighting in World War II.

Manufacturing processes were recorded on film before 1900. PORT SUNLIGHT was filmed in 1898, and *A Visit to Peak Frean & Company's Biscuit Works* shot at a Bermondsey factory in 1906 lasts for more than thirty minutes. From the 1920s many films recording industrial processes were sponsored by companies, while increasing numbers were made for advertising purposes, often containing valuable information on manufacturing methods or the uses of products.

In the 1930s a distinct genre of documentary film

evolved, the term being defined by Paul Rotha (1939) as 'the use of the film medium to interpret creatively and in social terms the life of the people as it exists in reality'. In Britain the works of the Empire Marketing Board Film Unit, where John Grierson (1898–1972) began to work from 1928, and the GPO Film Unit, to which the staff of the unit transferred in 1933, set particularly high standards. *Night Mail* of 1936, directed by Basil Wright (1907–87), is the most celebrated documentary of the period. The tradition was continued during World War II by the Crown Film Unit, for whom the talented Humphrey Jennings (1907–50) made his best films, and after 1945 by the Shell Marketing Film Unit and British Transport Films. Another leading figure was Sir Arthur Elton (1906–73), whose works included *The Voice of the World*, of 1932, on the manufacture and social implications of radio; *Aero-Engine*, of 1933; *Housing Problems*, of 1935; and *The Cornish Engine*, of 1948. The documentary movement had many links with the revival of interest in industrial history in England. Jennings edited a selection of writings on industrialization, while Elton was responsible for a major collection of industrial art (*see* IRON-BRIDGE).

Elsewhere documentary developed in other ways. An outstanding French example is *En passant par la Lorraine* by George Franju (b.1912), an ironic study of a large steelworks. In Germany, Fritz Lang's *Metropolis* of 1929 is a diabolical, nightmarish evocation of an industrial hell. In the USA industrial settings have formed the basis for both documentary and dramatic film-making almost since the medium's appearance. The Library of Congress Motion Picture Collection includes a sizeable holding of industrial footage from the turn of the century, including invaluable reels of Westinghouse Co. shop and assembly-line activity of 1904.

BIBLIOGRAPHY
General
Barnow, 1974; Hardy, 1979; Hornsby, 1957; Huntley, 1969; Jennings, H., 1985; Jennings, M.-L., 1982; Rotha, 1939; Smith, 1976; Spottiswoode *et al.*, 1969; Sussex, 1975; Vigars, 1984.
Specific
British Film Institute. *Non-Fiction Films*, London: British Film Institute, 1980.
Whitney, R. Films in business archives. In *Business Archives*, May 1989.

PAUL COLLINS

finery-and-chafery forge A charcoal-fuelled FORGE, usually water-powered, where WROUGHT IRON was made from PIG IRON, used from the time of the introduction of the indirect process of ironmaking in the fifteenth and sixteenth centuries. Pig iron was decarburized with the aid of an air blast in a finery hearth, then SHINGLED under a hammer into 'half-bloom', then reheated in a chafery hearth before being hammered into a form suitable for slitting or some other method of reworking. This kind of forge was gradually superseded by puddling (*see* PUDDLING FURNACE) from the late eighteenth century.

The Osmund forge (*see* OSMUND IRON) and the GERMAN FORGE in Sweden, which were forms of this process, employed only a finery hearth in which the bloom was reheated for the refining stage.

See also LANCASHIRE FORGE; STAMPING AND POTTING; WALLOON FORGE.

BIBLIOGRAPHY
General
Beck, 1891, 1893–5; Belhoste *et al.* 1984; Bjorkenstam, 1984; Gale, 1969; Johannsen, 1953; Percy, 1864; Tylecote, 1986.
Specific
Morton, G. R. and Wingrove, J. The charcoal finery and chafery forge. In *Iron and Steel*, 1966.

BARRIE TRINDER

Finland Finland was a dominion of Sweden in 1650 as it had been since the crusades of the twelfth century. The seventeenth century saw on the one hand pressures of war and taxation, and on the other reforms of government and expanding trade based on mercantilism. Many new towns were founded to promote trade. At the same time a large proportion of the land was given to aristocrats, and large feudal estates grew at the expense of the peasants. Late in the seventeenth century the country suffered a serious famine, from which the nation had hardly recovered when it was plunged, in 1700, into the Great Nordic War. King Carl XII attacked first Denmark, and then Poland and Russia, where his luck ran out in 1709. The Russians invaded Finland, which remained under occupation until the Treaty of Uusikaupunki in 1721, which ceded the south-eastern corner of Finland, the province of Vyborg, to Russia. After the death of Carl XII, the estates who gathered for a parliamentary session in 1719 were proclaimed holders of power. The country began a new war against Russia in 1741 with the intention of winning back the areas it had lost, but the attempt failed, and the Treaty of Turku of 1743 ceded to Russia the land to the east of the River Kymijoki. Nevertheless the post-war period in Finland was one of development in many different spheres. The most important reform was the redistribution of the land, in which the old, fragmented field system was rationalized. The reign of King Gustav III, from 1771 to 1792, the so-called Gustavian Age, was a period of particularly vigorous innovation in Finland. In 1788 Gustav nevertheless instigated a war against Russia which provoked a rebellious spirit amongst Finnish officers. The war ended in 1790 with the Treaty of Värälä, in which the borders remained as before. Two years later Gustav III was killed by an assassin.

In the agreement signed by the Russian tsar, Alexander I, and Napoleon at Tilsit (Sovetsk) in 1807, Alexander promised to force Sweden to cease to involve itself in continental affairs. Sweden refused, and the result was the outbreak in 1808 of war between Russia and Sweden, which ended in 1809 in the Treaty of Hamina. Before this, Alexander I had called a session of the estates in Porvoo (Borgå), where he delivered a solemn promise: Finland was to become an autonomous grand duchy of Russia. Supreme authority was vested in an administrative

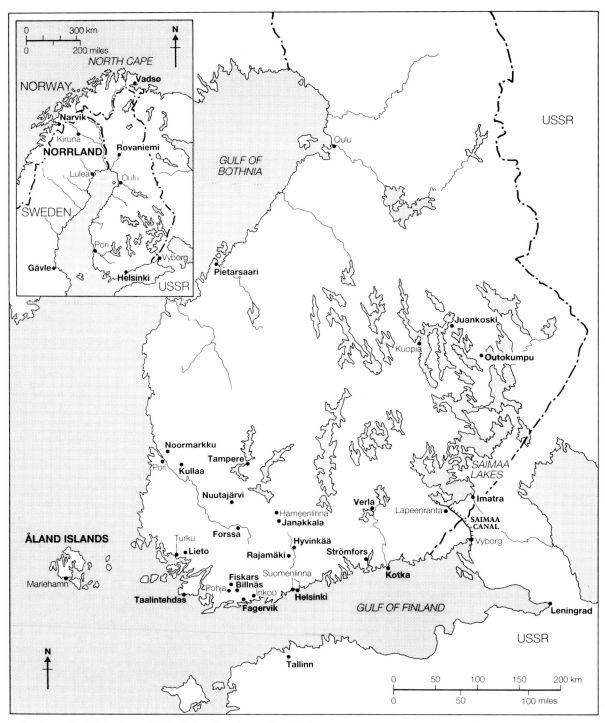

Finland, south of Oulu. Inset: Finland showing site north of Oulu

council, later the Senate. The territorial losses of 1721–32 were recompensed in 1811 by the restoration of the lands in the south-east to Finland. In 1812 HELSINKI was declared the capital of Finland. Although there was little in the way of economic development during the period of autonomy, the country gradually began to industrialize. It was only after the Crimean War that Tsar Alexander II (1818–81) enacted a number of liberal reforms, which gave a boost to the country's economic and intellectual development. Finnish was given an official position as a language of administration alongside Swedish. In 1865 Finland received its own currency, the mark, and in 1863, after a long period of suspension, the parliament was convened. During the 1870s local government was reformed and laws were passed establishing national service and complete freedom of trade. In 1885 the parliament was granted the right to legislate on its own account. But at the same time there was a Russian move to end Finland's special position within the tsarist empire, and restrictions were put into practice in the 1890s. During the reign of Nicholas II (1868–1918) these oppressive measures intensified, and a broad resistance was born in Finland, climaxing in a general strike in 1905, which led to reforms, the most important of them being the Parliament Act 1906. The Finnish parliament became unicameral; and universal suffrage was instituted at the same time. The situation changed in 1917 with the fall of the tsarist empire, and on 6 December 1917 the Finnish parliament declared independence.

The differing factions within the young nation led to civil war in 1918 between the so-called Reds and Whites, German forces contributing decisively to the victory of the latter. In 1919 Finland became a sovereign republic. Relations with the Soviet Union were regularized in the Treaty of Tartu in 1920. The 1920s marked the normalization of Finnish economic and political life, although the end of the decade saw the rise of radical right-wing politics, which culminated in an attempted revolution in 1932. Late in 1939 the Soviet Union began an attack on Finland which lasted until the following spring. In the Treaty of Moscow, Finland lost a large part of the province of Vyborg and Lapland. Just over a year later came another crisis in relations with the Soviet Union, and war was declared in the summer of 1941. This long-drawn-out campaign ended in the interim peace settlement of Moscow of September 1944, which was consolidated in Paris in 1947. In addition to the province of Vyborg, Finland lost the economically important Petsamo area in the north-east. In 1948 Finland and the Soviet Union signed a treaty of mutual friendship, co-operation and aid: this is still in force.

The post-war period has been characterized by Finland's policy of neutrality. Finland signed the General Agreement on Tariffs and Trade (GATT) in 1955; in the same year it became a member of the United Nations; and in 1961 it became an associate member of EFTA, and in 1986 a full member.

The economy of medieval Finland was based on slash-and-burn and field cultivation, and fishing and hunting; manufacturing activity was limited, long into the modern period, to domestic handicrafts, and shipbuilding in coastal areas. The first ironworks were founded in the mid-sixteenth century. The following century saw the foundation of fourteen ironworks, remains of most of which have survived. The governing factors in the choices of sites were supplies of wood for burning, availability of water power, and ease of transporting iron ore and pig iron, both of which were imported from Sweden. During the eighteenth century ironworks were also established in eastern Finland, and new processes enabled the exploitation of the region's BOG IRON ore deposits.

Finland's most important exports in the seventeenth and eighteenth centuries were tar and timber goods. There was a healthy export of ships from the shipyards of the Gulf of Bothnia to Sweden. During the eighteenth century trade diversified, with the establishment of glassworks, tobacco factories and of paper and textile mills.

Factories were established in Finland only at the beginning of the period of autonomy. TAMPERE, with its plentiful water power, became a centre for textiles, iron and paper. Machine shops, shipyards and food-processing centred around HELSINKI and Turku. The country's first engineering works was established in 1837 at FISKARS. Steam power was used industrially for the first time near Turku in 1842. The first steam sawmills began production in the mid nineteenth century, and multiplied rapidly. The value of the iron industry also grew rapidly after 1850 due to the development of puddling techniques for iron made from bog-iron ore, and because of demand from the engineering industry.

Modern wood-processing may be said to have started in Finland soon after the Crimean War when the country's first mechanical pulpwood mills were established. The first soda cellulose factory began production in 1876, and sodium sulphate was used for the first time in making pulp in 1886, although the sulphite cellulose method, also first used in 1886, became more common.

Although the speed of industrialization at the end of the nineteenth century was unparalleled, in 1914 over two-thirds of the population was still making its living from the land. The first years of the independent state were a difficult period for both agriculture and export trade. The deficit in the balance of trade led to inflation and in 1925 Finland adopted the gold standard, which partly stabilized the economy. The stresses of the civil war were relieved through land settlement legislation which led to the growth of agricultural modernization. Export drives directed towards the West, and a protectionist customs policy, soon began to effect the development of industry. The state itself became an industrial entrepreneur. Hydro-electric power stations were constructed and supplies of electricity to manufacturers improved. The boom in trade led to over-heating of the economy in the late 1920s, and in 1930–1 the country experienced its share of the worldwide depression. During the mid-1930s there was another boom, in which many industrial companies replaced old equipment and buildings.

The economics of the years after World War II were characterized by onerous war debts, reconstruction, and the resettlement of 400 000 refugees. The war debts led to the expansion of engineering, particularly of shipbuilding. The intense demand for processed-wood products in post-war Europe revived the timber industry, although international markets only opened up in the 1950s. The 1950s and 60s also saw the instigation of a hydro-electric power programme. The first nuclear power station began production in 1977.

In 1950 almost 50 per cent of the population still

derived its livelihood from agriculture and forestry. In the 1960s the proportion was 30 per cent, and in 1975 15 per cent. This reflects a change in economic structure that has been among the most rapid in Europe. At the same time the population has been concentrated in the towns, leaving the countryside deserted. Emigration to Sweden has been considerable in the post-war period, amounting to some 500 000 people. In industry change has been apparent in the contraction of labour-intensive manufactures. The textile industry in particular has seen a significant loss of jobs. Nevertheless there has been dramatic growth in services and in the public sector, and at the end of the 1980s unemployment was only 3–4 per cent, one of the lowest rates in the world.

The oldest roads still used in Finland are of medieval origin, but only the routes remain, with no traces of their former condition. Among the most important medieval routes is the King's Road, or Coast Road, from Turku to Vyborg, which may shortly be designed a 'leisure route'. Another important medieval route, the Häme Bull Road, led from Turku to Hämeenlinna. The Roads Museum administered by the Roads and Water Buildings Authorities, is concerned with Finland's historic roads and bridges, and conserves remains from nearly sixty of them.

Railways in Finland are a government responsibility. The construction of railways began in 1857, the 108 km (67 mi.) stretch between Helsinki and Hämeenlinna being completed in 1862, but the route to St Petersburg (Leningrad), completed in 1870, was to prove more important. At the end of the nineteenth century the network was improved, and the transverse network across the interior was finished in the early twentieth century. In 1965 5471 route km (3400 mi.) remained in use. The gauge in Finland is, for historical reasons, the same as in the Soviet Union, 1524 mm (5 ft.). The National Board of Antiquities, in co-operation with the railways authority, has drawn up a catalogue of 109 stations that are to be preserved, the oldest of them dating from 1852. The history of rail transport in Finland is displayed and documented in the Railway Museum, in HYVINKÄÄ.

The busiest ports in Finland are Helsinki, Kotka, Hamina, Hanko (Hangö), Turku and Naantali, and, in the far north on the Gulf of Bothnia, Oulu and Kemi. In winter sea channels are kept open by icebreakers, all built in Finnish shipyards. There are thirty-six lighthouses along the Finnish coast, many of which are of historic interest, the oldest dating from the early nineteenth century. The Maritime Museum in HELSINKI carries out studies and conservation connected with navigation and shipbuilding. The museum's collections include the lightship *Kemi* of 1901, and an English-built icebreaker, the *Tarmo* of 1907.

Finland has forty-six historic canals, but inland navigation has lost much of its economic importance in recent decades, except for the large Vuoksi waterway system, which is connected to the sea by the SAIMAA CANAL. The Heinävesi route, which belongs to the same system, has several well preserved sections of canal from the turn of

the century. The lock complex at Varistaipale, completed in 1915, has been a working canal museum since 1987.

The protection of ancient monuments and buildings in Finland is the responsibility of the National Board of Antiquities in conjunction with the Ministry for the Environment. A building protection law, which came into operation in 1985, devolved considerable responsibility to local authorities, with a requirement that in dealing with requests for planning permission councils should always explore options that retain old buildings. The emphasis of building preservation, according to the new law, lies precisely in areas where planning is controlled. Buildings outside planning areas can be protected by a special law that requires a decision from central government. There are currently more than a hundred such buildings in Finland, but it is expected that this law will be applied on more occasions in future. Industrial buildings have generally been protected through planning regulations since they are generally situated within planning areas. In addition to the building preservation law, an ancient monuments law can be applied to buildings of importance in industrial history in cases where the structures are no longer in use.

Both the National Board of Antiquities and the Ministry for the Environment have in recent years devoted increasing funds to the restoration of industrial buildings and structures. The Ministry for the Environment can, in addition, aid local authorities in acquiring old industrial buildings and areas of cultural-historical importance. Funding from provincial administrations and from employment authorities is important in many restoration projects.

The Finnish Road Museum was established by the National Board of Roads and Waterways in 1980. It is responsible for approximately sixty bridges and sections of road of various types which are restored and explained to the public. The museum publishes the results of its research into road transport history in the periodical *Tiemuseon Julkaisuja* (Transactions of the Road Museum).

Industrial archaeology is not yet taught in Finland on an organized basis. The Industrial Heritage Association has attempted to remedy this shortcoming by organizing annual seminars in conjunction with provincial museums. The Museum of Technology and other specialist museums are responsible for the documentation and study of machines, tools and industrial products. There are more than thirty open-air museums in Finland, composed principally of farmhouses, although most include buildings associated with manufacturing.

See also ÅLAND ISLANDS; BILLNÄS; FAGERVIK; FISKARS; FORSSA; HELSINKI; HYVINKÄÄ; IMATRA; JANAKKALA; JUANKOSKI; KOTKA; KULLAA; LIETO; NOORMARKU; NUUTAJÄRVI; OUTOKUMPU; PIETARSAARI; RAJAMÄKI; ROVANIEMI; SAIMAA CANAL; STRÖMFORS; TAALINTEHDAS; TAMPERE; VERLA.

BIBLIOGRAPHY
General
Ahvenainen *et al.*, 1982; Finnish Institute of Architects, 1952; Härö, 1979, 1987; Jutikkala *et al.*, 1980; Mattinen, 1985; Ministry of the Environment, 1987; National Board of Antiqui-

ties, 1982; Nisser and Bedoire, 1978; Putkonen, 1989a, 1989b; Zippelius, 1974.

LOCATIONS
[I] Museovirasto (The National Board of Antiquities), Nervanderinkatu 13, PL 193, SF-00101 Helsinki.
[I] Museovirasto, Rakennushistorian Osasto (The National Board of Antiquities, Department for Monuments and Sites), PL 187, SF-00171 Helsinki.
[I] Suomen Museoliitto (The Finnish Museums Association), Annankatu 16 D, SF-11020 Helsinki.
[I] Teollisuusperinneyhdistys – Industriminnesföreningen (Industrial Heritage Association – TICCIH Finland), c/o Elias Häro, PL 187, SF-00171 Helsinki.
[M] Tiemuseo (Finnish Road Museum), Tielaitos PL 33, SF-00521 Helsinki.
[I] Ympäristöministeriö, Kaavoitus-ja Rakennusosasto (Ministry for the Environment, Physical Planning and Building Department), PL 399, SF-00121 Helsinki.

LAURI PUTKONEN

firebrick *See* REFRACTORIES.

fireless locomotive A small STEAM LOCOMOTIVE with conventional mechanical parts, but with the boiler replaced by a steam reservoir, charged from steam-raising plant within the industrial complex in which it works. It is used where the risk of fire is high. It supposedly originated in New Orleans c.1872, and was built in Germany, the USA, Britain and France, where for a time 51-ton locomotives worked in Paris. The cylinder diameter was always greater than the stroke, so that for any given volume the area of cylinder wall was minimized. There are preserved examples at Quainton (*see* CHILTERN HILLS) and Carnforth, Lancashire, England.

BIBLIOGRAPHY
General
Civil and Baker, 1976; Westwood, 1983.
Specific
Reed, B. An apprentice at Hawthorn Leslie & Co. Ltd, 1921–5. In *Journal of the Stephenson Locomotive Society*, LXV, 1989.

fireproof Early iron-framed buildings (*see* INDUSTRIAL ARCHITECTURE; TEXTILE MILL) were designed to provide greater resistance to fire than conventional timber-framed structures. However, iron-framing was not proof against fire as was shown by fires at Stanley Mill, STROUD, and elsewhere. Nevertheless the term 'fireproof' is commonly used by industrial archaeologists as a synonym for the type of construction employing load-bearing walls, iron columns and iron beams carrying jack arches, which originated in Ditherington Mill, SHREWSBURY, in 1796–7; it is not used, by convention, to refer to later and more fire-resistant steel and concrete structures.

Between c.1830 and c.1910 many multi-storey industrial buildings in the USA were designed to be 'slow-burning', with a few large-section timber beams carrying thick – up to 10 cm (4 in.) – planks, thus creating few corners in which a fire could take hold and forming a frame that would burn only slowly and maintain structural integrity much longer than metallic framing.

BARRIE TRINDER and ROBERT M. VOGEL

fire-setting A method of fragmenting rock in metalliferous mines, employed before the extensive use of explosives. A fire was used to heat rock, after which the rock was quickly cooled by dousing with water, causing it to shatter on the surface. Traces can be observed in many preserved mines (*see* RØROS).

Fischbach-Camphausen, Saarland, Germany The Camphausen coal mine in Fischbach, 13 km (8 mi.) N. of Saarbrücken, is, like all the mines in the Saarland, part of the state-run company, Saar-bergwerke AG. The first two shafts were sunk in 1771, and in 1874 the pit was named after the Prussian finance minister Otto von Camphausen. It was the 40 m (131 ft.) high reinforced-concrete headstock, installed with two electrically-driven AEG engines (*see* BERLIN) for double winding, the first installation of its kind, that drew international attention to the pit. The headstock remains but the original engines were replaced in 1936–7.

fish A staple item of diet, whose consumption was encouraged by religious practices in Catholic Europe – 166 fast days, on which fish could be eaten, were observed each year in France in the seventeenth century. It was an important item of trade in the early eighteenth century, consignments of up to 28 barrels or two tons of herring being carried on the River Severn in England in 1715. Fishing was practised in most coastal regions, but by the seventeenth century the major sources off Iceland, Newfoundland and northern Norway were already being exploited by vessels from distant ports, and from c.1870 the trade in the most developed European economies came to be concentrated in specialist FISHING PORTS.

Fish can be preserved by drying (*see* NORWAY); smoking, which also enhances its flavour; CANNING (*see* BRITISH COLUMBIA; STAVANGER; VILA REAL DE SANTO ANTONIO); and freezing (*see* REFRIGERATION).

Many fishing vessels are preserved. Outstanding examples include the *Mary Joseph*, a herring and mackerel drifter of 1877 at Cultra (*see* BELFAST); the *Reaper*, a drifter of 1901 at Anstruther (*see* FIFE); the wooden schooner *American* of 1921 at Cape May, NEW JERSEY, and the 655-ton Grand Banks schooner *Creoula* of 1937 at LISBON.

See also BLOATER; FISHING PORT; FISH WEIR; SEALING; TRAIN OIL; WHALING.

BIBLIOGRAPHY
General
Ackerman, 1941; Braudel, 1981; Brouwer, 1985; Cutting, 1955.

BARRIE TRINDER

fishing port Traditional fishing ports from which relatively small vessels operate remain in use in most countries. The industrial-scale, specialist fishing port was the creation of the last quarter of the nineteenth century, examples including Boulogne, BREMERHAVEN, Cuxhaven, ESBJERG, Fleetwood (see FYLDE), Grimsby (see LINCOLN-SHIRE), HULL, Leghorn, Murmansk, OSTEND, Vigo and YMUIDEN.

The growth of such ports depended on the establishment of wholesale markets, linked to distribution points by rail across extensive hinterlands. The annual tonnage handled by rail at Grimsby, England, grew from 1514 tons in 1856 to 44376 tons in 1877. The rate of growth in England was subsequently accelerated by the development of fish-and-chip shops. Fish landings were increased by the employment of steam trawlers. At Grimsby there were 219 traditional fishing smacks in 1869 and 615 in 1881; but only 67 in 1901 due to increasing numbers of steam trawlers, of which there were 113 in 1897, 471 in 1901 and 619 in 1911. Successful fishing ports also needed factories able to process those parts of a fish, usually about 45 per cent, that were unfit for human consumption, into stock feed and fertilizer.

The components of a large fishing port might include quays for landing catches, areas for gutting the catch and for wholesale selling, railway sidings, ice factories, salt warehouses, smoke houses, net manufactories, coaling facilities, shipbuilding and repair docks, freezing plants and fishmeal plants. Fishing on this scale involved dangerous working conditions and much child labour.

Numerous artificial ponds are evidence of the raising of freshwater fish for human consumption in the Middle Ages. Commercial hatcheries for freshwater fish have developed since the late nineteenth century, particularly in the USA (see SOUTH DAKOTA).

See also REFRIGERATION.

BIBLIOGRAPHY
General
Alward, 1932; Beaujon, 1883; Cordeiro, 1989; Coull, 1972; Cutting, 1955; Wright, 1982.

BARRIE TRINDER

fish weir   A dam extending across, or part-way across, a river: usually of wattle, it incorporates a series of traps for fish, particularly eels. The fish weir was an important source of food in many regions. Such weirs obstructed navigation, and on rivers like the Severn channels were built to enable vessels to sail round them. Most fish weirs were of medieval origin. Some English examples survived into the twentieth century.

BIBLIOGRAPHY
Specific
Pannett, D. J. Fish weirs of the River Severn. In Aston, 1988.

Fiskars, Uudenmaan lääni, Finland   In 1649 the merchant Peter Thorwöste was granted permission to establish an ironworks at Fiskars, in the municipality of Pohja, 78 km (48 mi.) W. of Helsinki, and proceeded to construct a blast furnace and bar-iron forge. John Julin established an engineering works there in 1837, with the help of two expert mechanics, the Scot David Cowie and the Swede Anders Thalus Ericsson, both of whom had trained in Stockholm. The first Finnish steam engine was built in 1838 in the machine shop at Fiskars, a well-preserved red brick structure. The foundry building of 1836 is also of brick, and originally had two CUPOLA furnaces and a large crane. The rolling mill, completed in 1859, is a framed building with massive supporting pillars in the end walls. In addition to the buildings connected with the machine shop, the copper forge, whose oldest parts date from 1818, is preserved and adapted as an art gallery. The cutlery workshop, a two-storey brick structure, dates from 1888.

Structures preserved at Fiskars include distinguished residential as well as production buildings. The three-storey, EMPIRE-style mansion was built in 1816–18 to the design of Pehr Granstedt, Charles Bassi & C. L. Engel. An inn in the mansion park dates from 1836, and the brick school house by the road to the ironworks from 1826. In the late 1830s a large red-brick stable with a clock tower was built alongside it. The English architect, A. Peel, participated with Engel & Granstedt in the design of this building which became the emblem of the Fiskars works. The school house, the stable, the coach house, the two-storey workers' dwellings in Nya Kasernen, and the manager's house together form a harmonious neo-Classical streetscape. The oldest of the well-preserved workers' dwellings at Fiskars date from the early nineteenth century, and are currently being restored with government funding, after a decision taken in 1984 to preserve the site, together with that at BILLNÄS, 8 km (5 mi.) SE.

BIBLIOGRAPHY
General
Ryser and Rautsi, 1986.

LAURI PUTKONEN

flagstone   A fine-grained rock, usually a micaceous or sand limestone, that may easily be split along its bedding planes into paving slabs or sometimes for roofing (see SLATE).

BIBLIOGRAPHY
General
Challinor, 1986.

flannel   An open, loosely-textured woollen fabric, usually without nap, whose manufacture was concentrated in Montgomeryshire, Wales, and in some parts of LANCASHIRE from the early nineteenth century. The term also applies to garments made from the fabric.

flash lock   An obsolete form of lock on a river, which increased the depth upstream and had a gated opening. A staunch was such an opening with a vertical gate. The most common form was a beam swinging directly over a sill. Vertical baulks or rimers at intervals along the beam slotted into the sill, and square boards or paddles with long handles were set against them. As they were removed and the beam was swung open a flash of water would surge downstream, raising levels over shallows below, and enabling boats travelling upstream to be drawn through the gate, using winches if necessary. Flash locks were widespread in Western Europe in the Middle Ages but from the eighteenth century were gradually replaced by POUND LOCKS on rivers extensively used for navigation. About twenty survived in Britain in 1900, but there are now only fragmentary remains. In the late eighteenth and early nineteenth centuries flash locks were built on the Dnieper–Bug waterway, and on the River Mariinski in Russia. They were also used in early piecemeal attempts to make navigable such North American rivers as the James and the Roanoke in Virginia.

BIBLIOGRAPHY
General
Hadfield, 1986.
Specific
Lewis, M. J. T., Slatcher, W. N., and Jarvis, P. N. Flashlocks on English waterways: a survey. In *IA*, VI(3) 1969.

BARRIE TRINDER

flat There are two usages for this term in industrial archaeology:

1. The term used in Britain for APARTMENT, deriving from the Scottish word for a floor or storey within a house. It is not generally used in North America except in the term 'railroad flat', which means an apartment in a substandard building with a series of narrow rooms arranged in line.
2. A sailing vessel used in inland navigation. The term normally includes a prefix indicating the river on which the vessels works, as in 'Mersey flat' or 'Humber flat', or the commodity carried, as in 'deal flat', a vessel that conveyed softwoods.

flax The strong bast fibre within the stalk of the flax plant (*Linum usitatissimum*) is processed to make linen thread and yarn. Like all plant fibres, it is a form of CELLULOSE. The long flax fibres are called line; the shorter waste fibres produced during the initial stages of processing are called tow, hurds or nogs. Both are used to make different grades of cloth. Flax seed is crushed to make LINSEED OIL, and the seed hull is pressed into cake for livestock feed.

See also BRAKING; HACKLING; LINEN; RETTING; SCUTCHING.

BIBLIOGRAPHY
General
Horner, 1920.

flax cotton A nineteenth-century British development, flax cotton is the flax fibre chemically treated so that it may be mechanically processed more easily using machines devised for working cotton.

Flevoland, The Netherlands The youngest of the Neth-

erlands provinces, consisting of three of the four polders reclaimed from the former Zuiderzee since the completion of the enclosing dam (Afsluitdijk) in 1932: the Noordoost Polder of 1942, Oostelijk Flevoland of 1957, and Zuidelijk Flevoland of 1968. The Nieuwe Land information centre in Lelystad has displays on the reclamation projects, which have thus far drained 165 000 ha (65 000 ac.) of land and created a freshwater reservoir, the Ysselmeer. Two museums illustrate the region's maritime culture, with displays from the many wrecked ships found at the bottom of the former sea.

BIBLIOGRAPHY
General
Groen and Schmeink, 1985.

LOCATIONS
[M] Museum Schokland (Archaeological and geological collection), Middelbuurt 3, Ens Noordoost Polder.
[M] Museum voor Scheepsarcheologie (Museum of Ship Archaeology), Vossemeerdijk 21, Ketelhaven, Dronten.
[I] Nieuwe Land Information Centre, Oostvaardersdijk 1–13, Lelystad.

flint mill Flint is a variety of silica usually occurring in the form of pebbles; it is added in ground form to clay bodies, particularly for white ware such as bone china and porcelain, and used as a constituent for glazes. John Astbury (?1688–1743) is credited with introducing the use of flint to ceramics around 1720. Traditionally flint was calcined to make it easier to grind by hand or in primitive stamp mills (*see* STAMPERS). Partly in response to the health hazard of silicosis it became accepted practice to use stone blocks or balls in water for grinding. In many mills, blocks of chert, a flint-like quartz or siliceous rock, were moved around by oak paddles, thus grinding the calcined flints. The process is demonstrated at Cheddleton Flint Mill, near STOKE-ON-TRENT.

BIBLIOGRAPHY
General
Chandler, 1967; Hamer, 1986.
Specific
Horn, W. L. *Thwaite Mills*. Leeds: Thwaite Mills Society, n.d.

floating bridge A bridge that was essentially a roadway laid on the hulls of boats or pontoons, usually over a wide river. Such structures could be removed at times of heavy ice flow. In the nineteenth century floating bridges formed the crossings of the Rhine at Cologne, Koblenz, Mainz and Mannheim. Armies from the time of Julius Caesar have used temporary floating bridges. The Bailey bridge, a British development during World War II, devised by Sir Donald Bailey (1901–85), comprised a series of interchangeable truss panels that could be bolted together quickly, and erected either on pontoons or on the remaining foundations of wrecked bridges.

The name is also applied to a form of roll-on roll-off chain ferry devised by James M. Rendel (1799–1856) in 1831 and applied in England at Dartmouth, Southampton and elsewhere.

Figure 45   A sketch of a floating mill on the Danube in Romania (from B. Granville Barker, *The Danube with Pen and Pencil*, New York: Swan Sonnenschein, 1911)
Collection of Dr Mark Baldwin

BIBLIOGRAPHY
General
Horne, 1976; Murray, 1865.

floating mill   A mill powered by a fast-flowing river current, usually consisting of two boats, one with milling machinery, the other used for storage, with an undershot or 'current' water wheel between them. First used by the defenders of Rome during the Ostrogothic siege in AD 537, it was subsequently used in many parts of Europe, particularly on the Danube and its tributaries.
See also KOMÁRNO; SZENTENDRE.

CHRISTOPHER GREEN

floor cloth   A synonym for the type of OIL CLOTH used as a floor covering.

Florence (Firenze), Tuscany, Italy   Furniture and other luxury goods are still made in workshops in the centre of one of Europe's most cultured cities. Large-scale industry only became established in the inter-war period, in the suburb of Rifredi.

Florence has several buildings reflecting the Italian interpretation of the International Modern style. The Santa Maria Novella railway station of 1934 was built to a competition design by the Giovanni Michelucci group. Its severe angularity marks the acceptance of modern design by Mussolini's regime. The nearby central signal box by A. Mazzoni of 1931 is boldly streamlined, with rounded ends and a projecting canopy. The Stadio Communale in Campo di Marte is a concrete stadium of 1931 with a curved-section canopy boldly projecting over the seats, an early masterpiece by P. L. Nervi. Florence has many examples of cast-iron architecture, the most impressive being the Mercato Centrale de San Lorenzo of 1873, an arcade designed by Giuseppe Mengoni, who was responsible for the Galleria in MILAN.

The science museum accommodated in the Palazzo Castellani has a collection which includes objects owned by Galileo Galilei (1564–1642), some early bicycles, and a phonograph made by EDISON in 1890.

Impruneta, 15 km (9 mi.) S., is a major centre of the terracotta industry, as witnessed by the massive bright-red jars to be found round the small town and in the cloisters of the church. The firm of Angiolo Mariani still makes a wide variety of terracotta from earth excavated behind his workshops and burned in a charcoal-fired kiln.

BIBLIOGRAPHY
General
Gregotti, 1968; Orlandi, 1979.

LOCATION
[M] Museo di Storia della Scienza (Science Museum), Palazzo Castellani, Piazza dei Giudici, Florence.

MICHAEL STRATTON

Florida, United States of America   The nation's only peninsular state was colonized by the French, Spanish and English before its acquisition by the United States in 1822. The year-round warm climate and the rich alluvial soils of Florida have made it a prized location for agricultural industries. Tourism has long been the state's largest

Figure 46   Bolands Flour Mills, Grand Canal Dock, Ringsend, Dublin: the surviving structures illustrate the contrast between nineteenth-century methods of handling grain and flour in sacks, denoted by the taking-in doors in the buildings on either side of the complex, and twentieth-century methods using hoses and concrete silos.
Barrie Trinder

'industry', but the growing and processing of fruit (especially peaches, grapefruit and oranges), tobacco and sugar cane have been major contributors to Florida's economy. Other critical industries have included cigar-manufacture and the mining of FULLER'S EARTH.

Connecting parts of the island chain known as the Florida Keys at the state's southern tip is the 'over-sea railroad' bridge of 1912 by Henry Flagler (1830–1913), a low steel-girder bridge on concrete piers, now a highway route. A lighthouse of 1846 is preserved at Key West. In St Augustine the Bridge of Lions of 1927 crossing the Matanzas River is a 469 m (1538 ft.) steel-girder span segmented into twenty-two arches, with a double-leaf bascule at its centre.

An indication of both the dearth of historic industrial sites of the conventional sort, and the prominence of Florida's sunshine in its economy, is the designation by the American Society of Mechanical Engineers in 1983 of a twenty-four-head citrus fruit-juice extractor in Lakeland as an international mechanical engineering LANDMARK. The high-production machine of 1947 simultaneously squeezes the juice from twenty-four uncut oranges or grapefruit while extracting citrus oils from the peels. Icemaking machinery is displayed at the John Gorrie State Museum, and a sugar mill is displayed at Bunnell.

LOCATIONS
[S] Bulow Plantation Ruins, Bunnell, FL 32010.

[M] John Gorrie State Museum, Apalachicola, FL 32320.
[M] Lighthouse Military Museum, Key West, FL 33040.
[M] Thomas Edison Winter Home and Museum, 2350 McGregor Boulevard, Fort Myers, FL 33901.

DAVID H. SHAYT

flourmill   A loosely used term, often synonymous with CORN MILL, although the latter could also produce meal.

Flour can be made from many grains and root vegetables, and can be mixed with water into dough and baked to make loaves, with or without leavening. It can also be used for BISCUITS or pasta, or mixed with liquids to make gruel. The addition of bicarbonate of soda with an acid, usually tartaric, from the mid-nineteenth century produced self-raising flours, used particularly for CONFECTIONERY. Acid calcium phosphate ($CaHP_2O_8$) has been used for this purpose since the 1920s.

See also GRIST MILL; ROLLER MILLING.

BIBLIOGRAPHY
General
Amos, 1920.

flue   Specifically a chimney, but widely used to refer to any conduit for conveying smoke and gases heated in industrial processes. In glass manufacture 'flue' means an air intake. In industrial archaeology it refers particularly

263

to the long, nearly horizontal passages constructed to convey exhaust gases from CUPOLAS smelting lead, intended to conduct noxious fumes away from the smelter and to deposit on the walls solid materials, which could later be recovered and reworked. In this sense, the flue was first used in Derbyshire, England, in the late eighteenth century. Allen Smelt Mill, Allendale, 42 km (26 mi.) NW of Durham, has two flues, each 8 km (5 mi.) long, terminating in tall chimneys high on the Durham moors. Other outstanding English examples can be found at Grassington and Grinton, Yorkshire. They are the most spectacular industrial monuments to be found in remote upland regions.

See also figure 71.

BIBLIOGRAPHY
General
Stratton and Trinder, 1988.

fluorspar   Calcium fluoride (CaF_2), which is found associated with lead and zinc deposits in carboniferous limestone. It was used as a flux in steelmaking and the smelting of non-ferrous metals from the late nineteenth century; and in ceramics, enamelling, and the manufacture of hydrofluoric acid. A multicoloured form known as Blue John, from Derbyshire, England, was used for decorative purposes in the eighteenth and nineteenth centuries.

BIBLIOGRAPHY
General
Jones, 1950; Richardson, 1974.

flux   A substance mixed with metal to facilitate its fusion by lowering the melting point, or by combining with impurities and floating above the molten metal where it can be tapped off. Limestone is almost universally used as the flux in blast furnaces; lime and fluorspar are commonly employed in steelmaking.

flying boat   An AEROPLANE of relatively large size, if for civilian use one capable of carrying fare-paying passengers or freight. A smaller aircraft carrying only a pilot and two or three passengers is better described as a float plane. Flying boats were important in the development of air transport because they enabled long-distance routes – like those linking European states with their Asian and African colonies, those from the USA across the Pacific, and those connecting the principal Baltic cities – to be developed without the investment of capital in runways, and because the relatively large size of flying boats in the 1930s enabled the development of luxurious standards of service in heavier-than-air craft. Aircraft like the Short Empire class introduced in Britain in 1936, and the Boeing 314s of 1938 in the USA, offered cabins and promenade decks. Flying boats continued in use for long-distance commercial traffic after 1945, but on a diminishing scale; the last British services flew in 1958. A flying-boat hangar of the 1930s survives at Hythe, SOUTHAMPTON, where two terminal buildings also remain. A Short

Sandringham IV of 1946 is preserved at Southampton; a Short S.45 Solent 4 at Auckland, New Zealand; and Howard Hughes's remarkable *Spruce Goose* at Long Beach, CALIFORNIA.

BIBLIOGRAPHY
General
Allward, 1981; Hudson, 1972; Jackson, 1983.

JULIAN TEMPLE

Fohnsdorf, Styria, Austria   A coal-mining settlement from 1670, 38 km (24 mi.) SW of Leoben. A steam engine of 1923, by Friedrich-Wilhelm Hutte of Mühlheim (*see* RUHRGEBIET), was installed at the Wodzicki mine in a new engine house, utilizing the old headstock of 1884 which in 1923 was increased in height to 47 m (154 ft.). The mine closed in 1978, but the engine and headstock were accorded legislative protection, and have been preserved through the initiative of the Montanhistorische Verein für Österreich. The mine buildings now form a small OPEN-AIR MUSEUM.

BIBLIOGRAPHY
Specific
Wehdorn, M. Industrial archaeology in Austria. In Ferriot, 1981.

Foligno, Umbria, Italy   The Menotre Valley runs for 20 km (12 mi.) E. of Foligno, 16 km (10 mi.) SE of Assisi. Many water-powered corn and woollen mills operated in the valley during the period 1400–1800. Several fulling mills were converted to make woollen textiles, paper, rope or matches. The works still in operation are the Laurenzi flour mill, the Michaeli cotton mill at Scopoli, and a paper mill at Pale. At the bottom of the valley hydro-electric power stimulated the establishment of a box factory, an Italo-Belgian sugar refinery, and the state railway repair workshops.

BIBLIOGRAPHY
Specific
Bidovec, S. and Bartocci, F. 1985. La Valle del Menotre (The Menotre Valley). In *Archeologia Industriale*, II, 1985.

Follonica, Tuscany, Italy   A town 47 km (29 mi.) NW of Grosseto. It was the major centre for ironmaking in Tuscany prior to the erection of blast furnaces at Piombino in the late nineteenth century. Substantial remains of a furnace dating from 1836 are incorporated in a public works garage. The most dramatic monuments to Follonica's iron industry are an iron archway at an entrance to the works, with a shield flanked by two dolphins and surmounted by a blazing torch, and an arcade of cast iron erected in 1838 to designs by Carlo Reishammer outside the church of San Leopoldo.

BIBLIOGRAPHY
General
Jodice, 1985.

Fontinettes,   Pas-de-Calais,   France   The Fontinettes

BOAT LIFT on the Neufossé Canal at Arques, 4 km (2½ mi.) SE of Saint-Omer, was built in 1883–7 by the English engineer Edwin Clark (1814–94). The hydraulic lift replaced a flight of five locks between the Aa and Lys canal systems, raising vessels 13 m (43 ft.). The lift, unique in France, was replaced by a new lock in 1967 but is open to visitors. There is a display about its history with a working model.

BIBLIOGRAPHY
General
Grenier and Weiser-Benedetti, 1979; Hadfield, 1986.

LOCATION
[I] Syndicat d'Initiative de Saint-Omer, 52 rue Carnot, Saint-Omer.

food Grain and wine were traded in classical antiquity, and the production and processing of food for distant markets was one of the earliest industrial activities. Luxuries as well as necessities were important items of trade since every civilization needs dietary stimulants, which tended to be spices in the Middle Ages, alcohol from the sixteenth century, and tea, coffee and tobacco from the seventeenth century.

The nature of food manufactures began to change rapidly from the mid-nineteenth century, initially with the reorganization and expansion in response to technological developments of traditional activities like milling, brewing and dairying. Preserved foods like JAM and MARMALADE began to be marketed with vigour, and new manufactured products like BREAKFAST CEREALS and PICKLES were developed.

The food industry was transformed in the USA during the first three decades of the twentieth century, and the American example has been widely copied. The discovery of vitamins in 1911 led to an increased proportion of citrus in the diet, the slim figure became fashionable, and, as the numbers of jobs demanding heavy physical exertion diminished, fewer carbohydrates were consumed. The refrigerated railway wagon, and, from the 1920s, the refrigerated lorry, made it possible to ship perishable goods across all the states of the Union, no fewer than forty-two of the then forty-eight states supplying New York in 1927. In most developed countries the characteristic twentieth-century food factory is located in a suburb surrounded by grass, space and fresh air, and close to a road distribution network. In producing areas the characteristic buildings for preliminary cleaning and sorting processes are high sheds, with access for road or rail vehicles, often with specialist facilities such as grain silos or freezing plants.

For foods considered in this encyclopaedia, *see* CHOCOLATE; DAIRY; DRINK; FISH; FRUIT AND VEGETABLE PRODUCTS; GRAIN PRODUCTS; MEAT; SUGAR. For means of preserving food, *see* CANNING; REFRIGERATION; SALT; SALTPETRE.

BIBLIOGRAPHY
General
Boorstin, 1973; Braudel, 1981; Cummings, 1940; Drummond and Wilbraham, 1957; Ellsässer and Ossenberg, 1954; Hampe and Wittenberg, 1964; Hartley, 1954; Seignurie, 1904.

BARRIE TRINDER

Forbach an der Murg, Baden-Württemberg, Germany
The first large pump-storage hydro-electric power station and reservoir in Germany, now known as the Rudolf Fettweis plant, lies in the valley of the Murg in the northern Black Forest, 64 km (40 mi.) W. of Stuttgart. A combination, on the Swiss model, of hydro-electric power station and high-level barrage dam, it was built in two phases between 1914 and 1926. Seen from the south, looking down the River Murg, the first phase consisted of the Kirschbaumwasen dam with its headrace tunnel (cut through the rock), the surge chamber, and the metal penstocks linking it to the power station situated above Forsbach, which generated 22 MW. The reservoir, with its dam, and the works housing lay to the north. In the second phase of construction, which began in 1922, the Schwarzenbach dam was built to create a reservoir. It was 400 m (1312 ft.) long, 65.3 m (214 ft.) high, and had a capacity of 14.4 million m^3 (509 million cu. ft.). A penstock with a fall of 357 m (1171 ft.) leads to the power station, which generates 10.5 MW. Five turbines dating from 1917, made by Voith, are preserved, together with the three-phase generators by Brown, Boveri & Cie (*see* WINTERTHUR).

ROLF HÖHMANN

Ford, Henry (1863–1947) One of the great pioneers of the motorcar industry, and one of the first large-scale collectors of industrial artefacts, Ford worked for the EDISON Illuminating Co. of Detroit (*see* MICHIGAN) in 1891–9, after which he became involved in motorcar manufacture, forming the Ford Motor Co. in 1903. He pioneered the use of standardized parts and assembly-line production, and adopted a minimum wage for workers in 1914. His celebrated Model T was introduced in 1908, the Model A in 1928 and the V8 series in 1932. Ford assembly plants were set up in England (*see* MANCHESTER; LONDON), Denmark (*see* COPENHAGEN), Germany, Belgium, and elsewhere. The Henry Ford Museum was set up at Dearborn (*see* MICHIGAN) in 1929, to mark the fiftieth anniversary of Edison's incandescent lamp, and the Ford Foundation in 1936.

BIBLIOGRAPHY
General
Clymer, 1955; Nevins and Hill, 1954–63.

forest industry The ability to use wood – to build ships that could transport traders to Asia and colonists to America, to devise machines that could spin yarn, pump out mines or convey goods over long distances, and to create commodities like clocks or toys that could be traded from areas that had sparse agricultural resources – was one of the bases of European industrialization. The superiority of European forest resources to those of the Near East was one of the factors that ultimately limited the westward expansion of Islam. Wood was a major item of European trade by the seventeenth century (*see* RAFTS), and was one of the principal commodities imported to Europe from North America.

A forest economy can either be exploitative or managed. A forest can be felled and cleared, as a prelude to agricultural use of the land. If a forest is managed, some trees may be conserved for use as TIMBER for houses or ships, or as barrel staves (see COOPER). Others may be coppiced – cut so that they grow with many trunks, for use as poles or for CHARCOAL. Underwood and cuttings can be sold as fuel, or used for the manufacture of BASKETS, CHAIRS, CLOCKS or TOYMAKING. Ashes from wood burnt within forests are a source of POTASH. TAR can be made from wood in temporary kilns. The trapping of animals for FUR is also an important forest activity.

A log is the trunk of a felled tree. Logs were sawn into boards or LUMBER in a SAW PIT or, from the beginning of the seventeenth century, by wind or water power, and subsequently by steam or electric power (see SAWMILL).

Cleft staves, cut with the grain, are longer-lasting than sawn wood. They are used in such forms as palings, hurdles, and the frameworks of woven baskets. Bend ware – thin strips of ash or beech – was used to make various forms of household container, often called treenware, as well as the rims of sieves and riddles, used in BREWERIES, MALT, FOUNDRIES and other manufacturing processes.

WOOD CARVINGS and toys were characteristic products of regions like the Black Forest and the Erzgebirge in eastern Saxony where there is a notable museum at Seiffen. The products of CHILTERN HILLS beechwoods in the early twentieth century included wooden spoons, spades for the construction of sandcastles, hoops for children, and cheap cricket bats, as well as turned sycamore salad bowls, chairs and similar quality items.

From the second half of the nineteenth century the production of PULP, for use in the manufacture of paper, cardboard and synthetic fibres, became a dominant forest industry. The manufacture of plywood and fibreboard in large-scale sawmills was established by 1910 both in North America and in northern Europe, and expanded rapidly after World War II.

See also BOBBIN MILL; FUR; TURPENTINE.

BIBLIOGRAPHY
General
Hindle, 1975, 1981; James, 1981; Priestley and Fenner, 1985; Webster, 1919.
Specific
Sjunnesson, H. *Forest Industry*. In Nisser, 1981.

BARRIE TRINDER

Forest of Dean Gloucestershire, England, and Gwent, Wales An area between Monmouth, Cinderford and Chepstow, bounded by the Rivers Severn and Wye, and still heavily wooded. Coalworking by the Free Miners has ancient origins, and many early ironworks were established on tributary streams. Innovations were adopted tardily – the steam engine in 1777 and the coke blast furnace in 1795 – but heavy industry survived until the mid-twentieth century. Some small pits still operate. The region is crossed by the Severn & Wye Railway, and by a notable early nineteenth-century tramway from Lydney to Lydbrook with many branches.

Whitecliff Furnace, 10 km (6 mi.) NW of Lydney, which is well preserved, was worked for a few years only in the early nineteenth century. At Coed Ithel, 3 km (2 mi.) N. of Tintern, a seventeenth-century blast furnace is preserved in half section. There are many relics of forges and tin plate works near Tintern, where Germans established the first wire-drawing mill in Britain in 1566. Clearwell Caves, an iron-ore mine, are open to the public.

At Lydney Harbour, opened in 1813, plate rails and stone blocks in walls can be seen, and many tramroads traced. A spectacular tramroad inclined plane survives at Redbrook. The GWR station and signal box at Tintern are preserved as a visitor centre, and there is a steam centre on a colliery site at Norchard which has ex-GWR locomotives.

At Chepstow there is a five-span iron bridge of 1816, designed by JOHN RENNIE and erected by J. U. Rastrick (1780–1856). A bowstring tubular bridge by I. K. Brunel which carried the South Wales Railway was replaced in 1962.

BIBLIOGRAPHY
General
Nicholls, 1966; Paar, 1971, 1973.
Specific
Paar, H. W. *An Industrial Tour of the Wye Valley and the Forest of Dean*. London: West London Industrial Archaeological Society, 1980.

LOCATIONS
[S] Clearwell Caves, The Rocks, Clearwell Meend, Coleford, Gloucestershire.
[S] Dean Forest Railway, Norchard, Steam Centre, Lydney, Gloucestershire.
[M] Dean Heritage Museum Trust, Camp Mill, Soudley, Cinderford, Gloucestershire GL14 7UG.

BARRIE TRINDER

forge A term used to describe various types of ironworks, but best confined to a works where pig iron was converted into wrought iron, or to one where large pieces of wrought iron or steel were shaped by hammers or presses. A small-scale establishment of the latter kind, such as a blacksmith's workshop, is best defined as a SMITHY, and one where iron is made by a direct method as a BLOOMERY. The place containing the fire in which a blacksmith heats metal is best called a HEARTH.

See figure 47; *see also* CATALAN FORGE; FINERY-AND-CHAFERY FORGE; GERMAN FORGE; LANCASHIRE FORGE; PUDDLING FURNACE; SHINGLING; SMITHY; STAMPING AND POTTING; WALLOON FORGE.

Forges du St Maurice, Les, Quebec, Canada The remains of the first Canadian ironmaking industry, which operated from 1729 until 1883, are preserved within the historic park of the Forges du St Maurice, 13 km (8 mi.) N. of Trois-Rivières. The importance of this site was recognized as early as 1919 by the Commission for Historic Sites and Monuments National Board. Since 1966 archaeologi-

Figure 47   The Walloon Forge building at Osterby bruk, which contains two hearths and two water-powered hammers; the wrought-iron inscription within the gable records the rebuilding of the forge in 1794. It remained in operation until 1906.
Barrie Trinder

cal investigations, historical research and restoration have been successively undertaken by the Quebec Department of Cultural Affairs and by the Canadian Parks Service, the organization now responsible for the interpretation programme.

The ironworks utilized the water power of the St Maurice River, local supplies of wood, bog iron ore, and stone from the neighbouring regions of Batiscan, les Grès and Shawinigan. The works comprised three major structures which between them produced both cast iron and wrought iron. The blast furnace, constructed in 1736 according to a French design, was fired with charcoal. The furnace complex occupied an area of 825 m² (1000 sq. yd.) where there now remain traces of the masonry foundations of the bellows chamber, the power transmission system, the moulding floor, the tail race, the brick-built, circular hearth of the furnace, and a turbine chamber.

Two forges for refining the cast iron into wrought iron were constructed in 1739 and 1740. At the upper forge are traces of a water-powered hammer, of the bellows machinery; and of a second furnace and of the base of a steam engine, both dating from the 1880s. The lower forge, of which the finery chimney remains, was reorganized in 1872 for the manufacture of axes. There are remains of another chimney, a turbine, and a water-powered hammer.

The ironworks was concerned until about 1846 with the production of bar iron and of consumer goods –

kettles, nails, anvils, firebars, stoves and ploughshares – and also of armaments like bullets and cannon. Subsequently pig iron for casting as well as railway equipment was produced there.

Les Forges du St Maurice was an industrial community where work and residence were interdependent. There are traces of buildings concerned with administration, like the Grande Maison; of the provision of services, including sheds, a bakery, stables, storehouses and lavatories; of dwellings, houses and apartment blocks; and of the material culture of daily life around the centres of production, such as fragments of domestic objects, shards of pottery and clay tobacco pipes, glass and cutlery. In 1830 the population comprised 425 inhabitants, of whom the majority were engaged in part in agricultural or forestry work, or in such specialized occupations as those of furnace keepers, charcoal burners, forgemen, moulders and toolmakers.

In the Maurice region in the eighteenth and nineteenth centuries administrators and ironworkers who had worked at the Forges du St Maurice were responsible for the establishment of other ironworks. Forges were set up at Batiscan (1798–1812), Radnor (1854–1911), l'Islet (1856–78), St Tite (1878–88) and St Boniface (1878–81), where were found, with some variation, the same means of working metal, and the same forms of social organization as in the mother enterprise.

The interpretative programme at the Forges includes films, videos and guided tours.

267

Figure 48   The restored blast furnace at les Forges du St Maurice, Quebec: the sides of the mound support a roof which covers the excavated archaeological remains of the furnace and its surrounding buildings, which are accessible to visitors through the entrance to the right. The water wheel is a reconstruction. The scaffolding tower is located above the remains of the furnace and provides a viewpoint from which distant parts of the complex can be studied.
Barrie Trinder

BIBLIOGRAPHY
General
Trottier, 1980, 1983.

LOCATION
[M,S] Les Forges du St Maurice, Parc historique national, 10150 Boulevard des Forges, Trois-Rivières, Quebec G9C IBI.

LOUISE TROTTIER

forging press   A hydraulic press used to shape steel or wrought iron, invented in 1861 by John Haswell (*see* AUSTRIA), the railway engineer. The first such press, of which there is a model in the Science Museum (*see* LONDON), was built by the Kirkstall Forge Co. (*see* LEEDS) for the Cyclops works of George Cammell at SHEFFIELD, in 1863. In 1886 Sir Charles Davey developed the Duplex design, in which the side load is taken by a shaft sliding in a guide cylinder rather than by the necks of the hydraulic cylinders: this is the basis of many presses still in use. Outstandingly large presses have been built: there is one of 14 000 tonnes built by the Bethlehem Steel Corporation in the USA in 1893, and one of 15 000 tonnes by Krupp at Gusstahlfabrik, ESSEN, in 1928.
    See also figure 111.

BIBLIOGRAPHY
General
McNeil, 1972.

formaldehyde   *See* METHANAL.

Forsmarks bruk, Uppsala, Sweden   Forsmarks bruk is situated 25 km (16 mi.) NE of Dannemora, close to the Baltic coast in northern UPPLAND. Peasant ironmakers were active there in the Middle Ages, and in 1570 the bailiff Lars Hansson began to build blast furnaces and forges on behalf of the Crown. The bruk was leased to Gerhard de Besche and Peter Rochet, amongst others, in 1624, and they were allowed to acquire the property in 1646. Gerhard de Besche soon became sole owner of the bruk, which remained in his family until 1735.
    Forsmarks bruk produced cannon balls and other armaments at one period, but changed to produce bar iron by the Walloon method in the early seventeenth century. In 1660 there were three blast furnaces and three forges at Forsmark, and the bruk also included three blast furnaces and a forge at other places in the neighbourhood. The bruk suffered severely from the Russian attacks of 1719 (*see* UPPLAND). Most of the buildings were burnt down, and were rebuilt at the cost of some hardship to the owner.
    In 1751 the bruk was sold to a prosperous firm of iron merchants owned by Frans Jennings and Robert Finlay, who were of Scots origin. The firm became involved in various risky enterprises, and fell heavily into debt. It was dissolved, and John Jennings, son of Frans Jennings, became the sole owner of Forsmarks bruk. He proved to be a capable manager with great vision. He began a complete replanning of the bruk, including the construction of a new manor house and workers' dwellings, according to a 'general' plan by the architect Jean Eric Rehn. The renewal of Formarks bruk was continued by Count

Samuel of Ugglas, who had close connections with the royal court and bought the property in 1786. He built new forges and charcoal barns, commissioned a famous landscape architect to design the celebrated 'English' garden, and completed the 'general' plan for the bruk by building a church on the line of the main axis of the plan.

Forsmarks bruk produced Walloon iron, mainly for export. The bar iron from Forsmark was considered to be of top quality, but it could not compete with iron from LEUFSTA and Österby bruk and did not fetch quite such high prices.

Forsmark remained faithful to Walloon forging, and did not invest in more modern methods. In the 1890s the owner decided to stop iron production, and shift to pulp manufacture at nearby Johannisfors. The pulpmill caught fire in the early 1930s which brought industrial enterprise at Forsmark to an end. The woodlands were sold to Korsnäs AB. The buildings and farmland remained in the ownership of the Ugglas family until 1975, when the property was acquired by Forsmark Kraftgrupp AB, who started to build a nuclear power station on the coast a few kilometres away from the village. Forsmark Kraftgrupp AB has invested large sums in order to conserve the bruk with its old buildings and beautiful garden. The manor house is used by the company for hospitality, while many of the old workers' houses are now occupied by employees from the power station. Visitors are able to wander around the bruk, to see the local museum, and to eat at the restaurant.

BIBLIOGRAPHY
General
Ekman *et al.*, 1987; Janson and Janson, 1983; Norrby, 1983.

MARIE NISSER

Forssa, Turun ja Porin lääni, Finland   Industrial activity began in Forssa, 100 km (60 mi.) NW of Helsinki, in 1847, when the Swede A. W. Wahrén founded the Forssa Cotton-spinning Co. The first factory building, in brick, was completed in 1849. At the same time the wooden workers' houses in what is now Wahréninkatu Street were built. They are among the most important examples of early industrial workers' housing in Finland. The brick-built cotton warehouse in the same street, now the South-West Häme Museum, was built in 1849, an extra storey being added a decade later.

Forssa's old spinning mill was destroyed by fire in 1872, and a new brick mill was constructed the following year, according to designs ordered by Wahrén from England. This building has been extended from time to time, but always in sympathy with the original architecture. Part of the spinning mill, extended in the 1850s, and the dyehouse on the river bank survived the fire of 1872. During the 1870s Wahrén employed the expertise of the district architect, G. T. Chiewitz, in the design of his industrial buildings. Among the designs were houses for the factory director and the doctor and a factory school, all situated in the Factory Park which surrounded the spinning mill. Later in the 1870s housing for management was built in the park.

Wahrén extended his business in 1854 by constructing a separate weaving mill, which was destroyed by a fire in 1877. He ordered drawings for a replacement two-storey building, completed in 1878, from the Oldham architect Edward Potts. The mill was later extended both vertically and horizontally, in sympathy with the original design. Structurally the building is typical of its time, with cast-iron columns supporting brick vaulting springing from iron beams. The finishing building and dyehouse date mainly from the 1880s and 1890s.

In addition to the factory buildings, several areas of workers' housing are preserved in Forssa. The spinning complex is no longer used for manufacturing and the old factory buildings now house a library, museums, a school and a bowling rink. The buildings of the weaving plant remain in use.

LOCATION
[M] Lounais-Hämeen Museo, SF-30100 Forssa.

LAURI PUTKONEN

Forth Bridges, Scotland   The road and rail bridges between North and South Queensferry and the Kincardine-on-Forth Swing Bridge are amongst the world's great engineering feats.

The Forth rail bridge was built in 1882–90 by Tancred, Arrol & Co. to the designs of Sir John Fowler (1817–98) and Benjamin Baker (1840–1907). This, the world's first major structure in STEEL, employed tubular compression and latticed tension members to achieve its three characteristic twin cantilevers. The overall length is 2530 m (8296 ft.), the two main spans each reaching 521 m (1710 ft.) and giving a clearance for shipping at high water of 46 m (150 ft.). A visitor centre with access to the base of the north cantilever is under discussion.

The Forth road bridge, a suspension bridge with a central span of 1006 m (3300 ft.) is an accomplished if less pioneering design by Freeman, Fox & Partners, completed in 1964.

Kincardine-on-Forth Swing Bridge is a road bridge built in 1934–6 to the designs of Alexander Gibb & Partners, with a total length of 822 m (2696 ft.), including a 111 m (364 ft.) swing span, weighing 1600 tonnes, the longest in Britain. The bridge swung closed permanently in 1988, because of falling river traffic, but Bo'NESS Heritage Trust has taken on the upkeep of the electrical plant room.

BIBLIOGRAPHY
General
Westhofen, 1890.
Specific
McBeth, D. The Forth Rail Bridge. In Paxton, 1982.

LOCATION
[I] Bo'ness Heritage Trust, Bo'ness Station, Bo'ness EH51 0AD.

MARK WATSON

foundry   A works where metal is melted and poured into moulds to make castings. The word 'foundry', when unqualified, is normally understood to mean an iron

FOUNTAIN

foundry. If any other metal is being cast, it is usual to prefix the term: aluminium foundry, brass foundry, steel foundry, and so on. The part of a printing works where TYPE is cast is also known as a foundry.

From the sixteenth century (and much earlier in China) castings were made direct from the BLAST FURNACE, but by the 1660s there were distinct establishments in London remelting iron in AIR FURNACES and making castings, principally ordnance. From the late eighteenth century the use of the CUPOLA and improving transport facilities led to the growth of foundries in market towns across much of Western Europe, concerned initially with millwrighting work and agricultural machinery, and often extending their activities into other branches of engineering. A foundry would normally include a shop where patterns were made, traditionally of wood, but more recently of a variety of other materials, and often an extensive store for such patterns. Moulds were traditionally made on the foundry floor in a mixture of sand with a little clay, usually called 'greensand', the word 'green' referring to its unbaked state. Its colour was usually red before use and black afterwards. Moulds were also made of loam, a mixture of sand, clay, and straw, bonded with horse manure or a similar material. The moulding process has been mechanized in the twentieth century by the use of machines creating large numbers of identical moulds by ramming sand around mass-produced and often reusable patterns. A core is part of a mould, filling a space intended as a cavity within the casting, and foundries frequently have ovens for drying cores, since these are normally of thin section and so must be of a harsher sand composition, different from that of the rest of the mould body. The process of finishing castings is known as fettling; it may be done by simple hand processes like filing or grinding, or by modern techniques like shot blasting.

The word 'foundry' (like the French 'fonderie') is often misused, and applied to BLAST FURNACE complexes or FORGES.

See also AIR FURNACE; ART CASTINGS; STEEL FOUNDRY.

BIBLIOGRAPHY
General
Gale, 1969; Trinder, 1982.

BARRIE TRINDER

fountain   Originally a natural spring of water, the term came to mean a spring created artificially by pressure, particularly one intended for public WATER SUPPLY (often ornamented with sculpture) or one designed for ornamental effect. The word can also be applied to a reservoir for oil in a lamp, or for ink in a printing press.

Fourdrinier, Henry (1766–1854)   The English entrepreneur who was chiefly responsible for developing the manufacture of paper in continuous sheets by machine. Fourdrinier and his brother Sealy (*d.*1847) took out their first patent in 1801, began operating mills in Hertfordshire in 1804, and patented the continuous papermaking machine in 1807. Their ideas were copied and litigation brought Fourdrinier to bankruptcy, although the brothers were granted £7000 in 1840 in recognition of their achievements.

Fourier, (François-Marie) Charles (1771–1837)   A French social theorist, whose ideas influenced the CO-OPERATIVE MOVEMENT, and UTOPIAN COMMUNITIES generally. He argued that there was a natural social order, best achieved through communal associations called phalanxes. Several settlements based on Fourier's ideas were established in France, the most important at Familistère, GUISE, in 1859. Fourier's philosophy was taken by Albert Brisbane (1809–90) to the USA where over fifty phalanxes were set up, having an average life of two years. The most important were Phalanx, New Jersey, a colony based in a single large multi-storey building established in 1849, and Brook Farm, West Roxbury, near Boston, which operated from 1841 to 1847.

BIBLIOGRAPHY
General
Hayden, 1976; Hine, 1966.

Fourmies-Trélon, Nord, France   The Fourmies-Trélon region, 15 km (9 mi.) S. of Maubeuge, close to the Belgian border, has a rich industrial past. Extensive forests encouraged the development of ironworks and glassworks as early as the fifteenth century. Using coal from the Nord Pas-de-Calais coalfield, delivered by rail after 1880, these activities continued to prosper in the late nineteenth century and early twentieth century. The region had thirteen glassworks in 1880, and Fourmies also had a thriving woollen industry which grew rapidly in the second half of the nineteenth century.

The ÉCOMUSÉE devoted to the preservation and presentation of the region's industrial traditions occupies two old factories. At Fourmies the former Prouvost-Masurel wool-spinning mill, built in 1874 and active until 1970, now houses about a hundred old textile machines, thirty of them in running order. Most of the stages of wool production are illustrated: carding, combing, spinning and weaving. The machines come mainly from mills within the region and date for the most part from 1880–1900. The mill is a single-storey building, which was steam-powered. The detached engine house remains, along with a chimney stack with a remarkably ornate base.

The écomusée has a second branch located in the nearby Parant glassworks at Trélon, which dates from 1823. This was a bottle works, specializing after World War I in bottles for perfumes and pharmaceutical products. The factory ceased production in 1977, but several of the original buildings survive, including the glassmaker's residence, and the stables and storehouses. In the main furnace hall, which was rebuilt in 1889, there are two furnaces: a Boetius furnace of 1889, and a Stein furnace installed in 1923, when the semi-automatic production of perfume bottles was inaugurated. The écomusée organizes demonstrations of glass-blowing.

LOCATION
[M] Écomusée de la Région Fourmies-Trélon, 59610 Fourmies, France.

JEAN-FRANÇOIS BELHOSTE

Foynes (Faing), County Limerick, Ireland   The channel between Foynes and Foynes Island was the principal landing place for transatlantic flying boats in the 1920s. Few traces remain of installations connected with flying, but the terminus of the branch railway, now used for freight traffic, retains the grey limestone passenger station, together with the train shed, the signal box, and a water tank carried on six cast-iron pillars, installed by R. Graham of Waterford in 1892.

France   France today covers some 550 000 km² (212 000 sq. mi.). Starting from the Île de France around Paris, the country was pieced together gradually, progressively incorporating such independent feudal territories as Provence (1481), Brittany (1491) and the Bourbonnais around Moulins (1527). The provinces to the north-east were taken from the Habsburgs (*see* AUSTRIA) during the seventeenth century: a part of Alsace in 1648, Artois in 1659, Flanders in 1668 and Franche Comté in 1678. The independent duchy of LORRAINE was annexed in 1766. The country reached its present-day frontiers in 1860 when Savoy and Nice voted to join France. Between the Franco-Prussian war of 1870 and the end of the World War I, Alsace and a part of Lorraine were attached to the German Empire.

French political unity, patiently constructed over the centuries, brought together provinces which were of tremendous diversity in terms of climate and physical geography. For a long time the very size of the country constituted a serious obstacle to its economic integration, even though communication was facilitated by the major rivers flowing east to west, the Seine and the Loire, and north to south, the Saône and the Rhône. Reliable road communication was possible only between Paris and the principal provincial cities, like Lyons, Lille and Nancy, or along the Atlantic and Mediterranean seaboards. It was only during the nineteenth century that the country achieved real economic integration, thanks first of all to the creation of an extensive network of inland waterways, no less than 10 000 km (6200 mi.) being dug by 1840, and subsequently to the development of the railways, the growth of which was particularly important during the Second Empire between 1850 and 1870. Railway networks, all converging on Paris, reinforced the city's role as the country's economic capital.

In 1789, in terms of size and population, the kingdom of France was one of the leading European powers. Although 85 per cent of its population was still rural, the country had already witnessed considerable industrial development. It has been calculated that non-agricultural products already represented half of the goods produced, although this half includes food products and buildings, alongside manufactured goods proper, and the products of artisans.

The main industry of the Ancien Régime was textile manufacturing, with wool as its leading sector, thriving in the Champagne region, in Normandy and in Languedoc, and particularly dynamic in the production of high-quality broadcloth, using imported Spanish merino wools. During the second half of the seventeenth century broadcloth manufacture prospered in several towns, among them SEDAN, ABBEVILLE, Elbeuf and LOUVIERS, and also in the region between Carcassonne and Montpellier, notably at VILLENEUVETTE. A linen cloth industry also grew up in the north of France, at various locations in Flanders and Brittany, whilst the Lyons region saw the emergence of an important silk-weaving industry.

Where metallurgy is concerned, ironmaking was the essential sector. In 1789, the country had a total of some five hundred blast furnaces in operation, and in terms of gross output France probably rated second in Europe after Russia. It was at the turn of the fifteenth century that the indirect WALLOON FORGE process began to spread through France's major iron-producing regions in the north and the north-west, Normandy (*see* AUBE), Champagne, Burgundy (*see* BUFFON), Franche Comté (*see* AUVET) and the Nivernais region around Nevers. During the seventeenth century it reached the regions on either side of the Loire: Brittany (*see* ABBARETZ), the Berry (*see* SAINT-BONNET TRONÇAIS), and, further south, the Dordogne (*see* SAVIGNAC-LÉDRIER). Elsewhere earlier techniques, often better adapted to the physical and social conditions of mountain regions, persisted. In the Dauphiné and in Savoy, BERGAMASQUE FURNACES and finery forges were used from the beginning of the seventeenth century (*see* ALLEVARD), whilst in the PYRENEES and in CORSICA, as in the BASQUE COUNTRY and in northern Italy, the direct process, using a BLOOMERY furnace, survived well into the nineteenth century.

Alongside this primary iron production came a host of small ironworking establishments: nail production in Normandy, iron hardware around SAINT ÉTIENNE, or the arms factories at Charleville and NOUZONVILLE in the Ardennes. Special products such as steel or tin plate were less frequently made than in Germany or England. Some natural forge steel was produced around Rives in the Dauphiné (*see* ALLEVARD), and a major tin-plate manufacture began in Lorraine at BAINS-LES-BAINS in 1733.

Until the end of the nineteenth century, no other metal rivalled iron in importance, but in two areas not yet under French rule there was nonetheless some exploitation of copper and of argentiferous lead ores: in the Vosges, particularly up to the mid-sixteenth century (*see* SAINTE-MARIE-AUX-MINES), and in Savoy, mainly during the eighteenth century (*see* PEISEY). The copper industry took off in France in 1782, with the creation of a large factory at ROMILLY-SUR-ANDELLE, concentrating at first on the rolling of copper sheets for sheathing naval ships. Significant copper, brass and zinc industries subsequently developed in Normandy and in the Ardennes.

On account of its great economic and fiscal importance in France, salt may be counted amongst the leading extractive industries. Salt was produced from the salt marshes of Brittany, the Charente and Languedoc, but

France, excluding Corsica

there were also important underground salt mines in Lorraine and in Franche Comté at SALINS-LES-BAINS. As early as the fifteenth century slate was also mined from underground workings in ANJOU and in the Ardennes. The 'oilfield' of PECHELBRONN in Alsace was exploited from the mid-eighteenth century.

Glassmaking was another important industry of the Ancien Régime, and was often located in wooded regions not yet taken over by iron production: Lorraine, Thiér-ache, Languedoc and Normandy. This last region wit-nessed the fifteenth-century development of crown-glass production (*see* BEZANCOURT). Around 1688 the SAINT GOBAIN works began to cast plate glass on metal tables for the production of mirrors.

Other small-scale fire-based industries, potteries, brick and tile works, and limekilns were scattered throughout the country, mostly for the supply of local building markets (*see* ANJOU; COTENTIN; PAYS D'AUGE). One or two centres supplied larger markets: the Beauvais area, for example, specialized from the fourteenth century in STONEWARE, and LIMOGES became famous for its porcelain after 1770.

Tanning, another old industry, was similarly scattered throughout the country, but was particularly dense in the major livestock-producing areas, such as Normandy and the Massif Central. As for paper, the mills of the Dordogne and the region around Angoulême (*see* ANGOULÊME) were of particularly repute as early as the sixteenth century, but the main French paper works at CHÂLETTE-SUR-LOING was built near Montargis in 1738, far away from any traditional papermaking centre.

To conclude this survey of the country's old industries, those based on food and drink must also be mentioned. Alcohol often had its regional specificity: beer brewed in the north and the east (*see* AIRE-SUR-LA-LYS; STENAY), for example; brandy was a feature of trade at Cognac by the end of the eighteenth century. During the same century colonial produce, such as cane sugar from the French West Indies, gave rise to refineries at Bordeaux, Nantes and Orleans. Imported tobacco was prepared at royal manufactories located at Morlaix, in Brittany, at Dieppe, at Paris and in half a dozen other towns throughout the country. The tobacco factories, like the broadcloth factories already mentioned, the glass works at Saint Gobain, or the different manufactures at Langlée and Bains-les-Bains, were often large establishments installed in prestigious, purpose-built constructions. Associated with the mercantilist policies of Jean-Baptiste Colbert (1619–83), these privileged royal manufactures are one of the striking characteristics of the French industrial scene during the seventeenth and eighteenth centuries.

New industries

Alongside these traditional manufactures, new industries, the origins of France's nineteenth-century growth, began to develop during the second half of the eighteenth century. Following the English example, the cotton industry witnessed rapid early growth, particularly in the realm of calico production, located in Alsace around MULHOUSE. The first Arkwright water-frame in France was introduced at LOUVIERS in 1785, soon to be followed by many others, for example at the VALENÇAY mill in 1792.

Surface coal mining already existed on a small scale in ANJOU and the region around SAINT ÉTIENNE, but during the eighteenth century its physiognomy began to change as large-scale companies started to exploit seams up to 300 m (330 yd.) below ground. This tendency first emerged from 1720 at Anzin in the north, followed by the Bourbonnais region, Anjou, Normany, and at LE CREUSOT and in the Cevennes (*see* ALÈS).

These then were the main conditions from France's early industrialization. The country's industrial output was probably comparable to that of Britain at the end of the eighteenth century, but its structural organization was very different, which led to a different pattern of evolution during the nineteenth century. French industry remained a largely rural phenomenon, depending for its energy on water power and on burning wood rather than

coal. The number of steam engines in France grew only slowly: in 1850 – although France occupied second place in Europe on this count – their nominal horse-power stood at only 67 000 compared with 500 000 in Britain. Water power indeed remained the predominant source of mechanical power up to 1880, and several nineteenth-century French engineers pioneered new means of harnessing it: Jean-Victor Poncelet (1788–1867), in 1823 with his new overshot wheel; Alphonse Sagebien (1807–92), in 1851, who improved on the efficiency of the English breastshot wheel (*see* TRILBARDOU), and Benoît Fourneyron (1823–82) with his turbine.

Charcoal long remained the principal fuel used in ironmaking. In refining, the use of coal overtook it only in 1837, despite the construction of several large-scale integrated 'English-style' ironworks during the 1820s, notably those at Vrigne-aux-Bois in the Ardennes (*see* NOUZON) in 1821 or others on the Saint-Étienne coalfield. Coke became the predominant fuel for smelting only after 1856, although the earliest experiments with coke smelting in France date from 1782 at Le Creusot, and some large coke furnaces had been built between 1820 and 1840, for example at La Jahotière (*see* ABBARETZ) in 1827, or the six furnaces at LA VOULTE built between 1828 and 1845, and supplied with ores from PRIVAS. In the mid-nineteenth century, despite efforts to economize on fuel consumption, French iron and steel production was using one-third more wood than at the beginning of the century. Other industries – such as glassmaking, and brick and tile manufacture – went over to coal at an earlier date. By the eighteenth century, for example, most bottle works were located on or near coalfields (*see* ALÈS), or at sites easily accessible for imported coal (*see* ARLES).

The railway revolution – some 15 000 km (9300 mi.) were laid between 1845 and 1875 – gradually freed industry from its old ties to wood and water supply. The 1830s and 1840s witnessed relocation of heavy industry, which developed in particular on the coalfields of SAINT-ÉTIENNE, ALÈS-La Grand'Combe, DECAZEVILLE or Commentry, and subsequently from the 1850s, in the Nord Pas-de-Calais region (*see* DOUAI). Coal production in France rose from about 3 million tonnes to 19 million tonnes between 1840 and 1880.

During the nineteenth century the textile industry tended to concentrate in the north and the east, abandoning its traditional centres. The Lille-Roubaix-Tourcoing conurbation grew rapidly, Lille specializing in cotton goods and linen, Roubaix in wool. In eastern France it was primarily the region around MULHOUSE that witnessed the development of cotton production. Several engineering firms grew up, beginning by constructing textile machinery. Silk weaving remained a speciality of the Lyons region, but the production of raw silk in reeling and throwing mills occupied the women of many villages throughout the south-east, particularly in the CEVENNES and the department of Ardèche. The silk industry also stimulated the growth of satellite towns such as TARARE, near Lyons.

Even in a 'traditional' industry like tobacco production – which is still a state monopoly – mechanization

273

developed from the end of the 1820s, a new generation of factories being built during the second half of the century, starting with one at Strasbourg in 1848 (see below).

Nineteenth-century industrialization, amongst other effects, led to a marked increase in the proportion of the French population living in towns: from 26 per cent in 1851 to 36 per cent in 1886. Paris, in particular, witnessed considerable expansion, its three million inhabitants representing almost 10 per cent of the total population. Overall urban growth was also the result of the development of new industrial towns, based on coal, iron and steel: LE CREUSOT, DECAZEVILLE and ALÈS-La Grand'Combe. In these towns, as in older industrial centres like MULHOUSE or MONTLUÇON, industrialists often built houses for workers, sometimes with cultural, medical or educational facilities. One of the best-known initiatives was the 'Familistère' at GUISE, a community built between 1859 and 1880 by Jean-Baptiste Godin, who was inspired by the utopian socialism of CHARLES FOURIER. At NOISIEL, near his new chocolate factory, Emile Menier also built an estate of workers' houses, modelled on examples visited in England.

More new industries

The long crisis of French – and European – industry between 1870 and 1895 profoundly affected the country's industrial geography. The crisis was aggravated by the temporary 'loss' of Alsace and part of Lorraine to the German Empire. The structure, techniques and location of the country's old industries were all considerably modified. In the textile industry, the north continued to grow in importance, with wool – mechanized at last – overtaking cotton, particularly at ROUBAIX and Tourcoing, or in such new centres as FOURMIES-TRÉLON. After a long decline, charcoal iron production finally ceased, while coke steel production tended to concentrate in Lorraine, where the Gilchrist-Thomas OPEN-HEARTH process made possible the use of low-grade phosphoric iron ores.

A new industrial vitality at the end of the century was due largely to the appearance of new sectors, and in particular to the development of electric power. From the mid-1870s certain modern factories (Noisiel, from 1875, for example) already had electric lighting. In regions with good water supplies, like Normandy, small hydro-electric power plants were rapidly installed. By 1906 there were power stations on 175 of the 525 waterfalls in the department of Eure, some of them for public supply.

The most spectacular development of hydro-electric power occurred in the Alps; between 1885 and 1898, sixteen plants were created with a total capacity of 5000 kW (see DAUPHINÉ). Large coal-fired power stations were built on the country's coalfields, for example at La Grand'Combe (see ALÈS). Especially after 1920 the transmission of high-voltage current made possible the electrification of small-scale industries in small towns and villages throughout France. As early as 1905 a building was constructed at OYONNAX simply to provide individual comb producers with current from a nearby power station.

The new hydro-electric power of the Alps also brought growth to new chemical and metallurgical industries. In particular, the invention by Paul Héroult (1863–1914) in 1866 of the electrolytic furnace for aluminium production led to the birth of a powerful new industry, using the plentiful deposits of BAUXITE from the Var. Steelmaking was revitalized by the appearance of the electric furnace, the major Ugine factory in Savoy dating from 1909 (see DAUPHINÉ).

Amongst other new sectors, aircraft and motorcar manufacture were of particular importance. In 1913 France could already count ninety-three aircraft manufacturers, most of them operating on a small scale. Motorcar construction began during the 1890s, and up to 1906 France led the world in this promising new industry, and continued to lead Europe until the 1930s. One of the pioneers, G. A. Clément (1855–1928), who started as a bicycle manufacturer, built factories in the suburbs of Paris, at Levallois and in London. In 1898 another early starter, Louis Renault (1877–1944), launched the factory that was to become the largest in France between the two wars. His principal competitor, André Citroën, inspired by HENRY FORD's ASSEMBLY LINE techniques, built and then rebuilt the enormous Javel works in PARIS.

These new industries, with their heavy and specialized labour demands, tended to be located around the major cities, and principally in the Paris region. As well as being the political, administrative and financial capital of France, Paris in 1913 also contained one-sixth of the country's industrial workers. Twentieth-century industrialization has tended to encourage the growth of large suburbs, concentrating not only on these new industries, but also on older ones rejected by the city centre. This phenomenon is notable in Lyons, and in Paris, where dense industrial suburbs grew up, particularly to the north and east.

After the stagnation of the depression years and the destruction wrought by World War II, French industry enjoyed new prosperity during the thirty 'glorious' years of the post-war period. Many new enterprises were launched, whilst the more dynamic old ones engaged in ambitious modernization programmes. The state intervened here, keen to encourage industrial deployment away from the capital. This tendency, like the crisis of the last fifteen years, has progressively led to the disappearance of much obsolete industrial plant, generally unlamented, and, until quite recently, probably unrecorded.

The tobacco industry

With an interruption of less than two decades during the period of the Revolution, the French tobacco industry has been a state monopoly since a Colbertian decree of 1681. This monopoly was exploited by the Farmers General for most of the eighteenth century, then run directly by a 'State Manufactures Administration' attached to the ministry of finance during the nineteenth century.

Situated in the small Breton port of Morlaix (Finistère), easily accessible for the raw tobacco leaf shipped from America, one Royal Manufacture of the Ancien Régime survives intact, still used for the production of cigars and rolls of chewing tobacco. Built between 1736 and 1740 by one of the 'King's architects', Jean-François Blondel (1683–1756), and enlarged in the mid-nineteenth century, this factory also preserves a remarkable two-tiered battery of cast-iron leaf grinders installed in 1870 and still used to produce 'ordinary' snuff.

At the beginning of the nineteenth century, with the restoration by Napoleon of the tobacco monopoly, manufactures were opened in ten of France's major cities, sometimes occupying the old workshops of the General Farm, and in one case, at Toulouse, a religious building nationalized during the Revolution, a Benedictine convent, now an art school. These early factories were unable to keep up with developing demand, particularly for cigars, and proved difficult to adapt for the mechanization of certain production processes introduced from the late 1820s at the Paris factory, 'Gros Caillou', which was demolished in 1906.

During the second half of the nineteenth century a series of new, purpose-built tobacco factories were opened, the first at Strasbourg in 1848–50, designed by a local architect, J. A. Weyer, and the chief engineer of the tobacco administration, E. Rolland. The central building of this factory, which housed the mechanized operations, the chopping of tobacco leaf and the grinding of snuff, was destroyed by bombing at the end of World War II, but the three-storey 'exploitation' buildings around it, along with the director's pavilion, still stand, and are used for cigar production.

All together eighteen new tobacco factories were built between the 1850s and the 1920s, all of them closely following a model elaborated at Châteauroux (Indre) between 1858 and 1863. All tend to have the same forbidding barrack- or hospital-like appearance, being designed essentially for large concentrations of women workers – as many as 1500 per factory – producing cigars by hand. Solidly built, and laid out with obsessive and economy-producing symmetry, several have been successfully adapted to new uses, mostly converted into apartments: Issy-les-Moulineaux of 1900–4 in the suburbs of Paris, Nantes of 1861–4, Nancy of 1864–70, Orléans of 1885–1900, Toulouse of 1883–92, and soon, perhaps, Lyons of 1912–29. Two tobacco museums – one at Bergerac (Dordogne), the other at the headquarters in Paris of the SEITA, the heirs to the nineteenth-century tobacco administration – deal more with the objects used by the smoker than with the history of the industry.

The match industry

The state fiscal and industrial monopoly of MATCH production was added to the existing tobacco monopoly in 1890. In the context of agitation at this period about 'phossy jaw', the disease caused by the PHOSPHORUS used in making matches, state engineers developed a continuous match-making machine. The considerable floor space occupied by this machine, 8 m × 2.5 m (26 ft. × 8 ft.) necessitated new factory buildings. The factory of 1902 at Aubervilliers, a suburb to the north of Paris, is still used for storing official paper, whilst the factory at Aix-en-Provence (Bouches-du-Rhône), built in two stages between

1892 and 1906, has been adaptively reused as a public library.

The study and conservation of the industrial heritage

Although for more than thirty years a lively school of French historial research has been concerned with industrial history, it is not until the 1970s that the physical remains of industry began to be studied, protected, and, occasionally, rehabilitated and adapted as museums. The earliest efforts were primarily concerned with the better understanding of industrial monuments; the pioneering work of the ÉCOMUSÉE at LE CREUSOT, founded by Marcel Evrard in 1974, stands out here. The Écomusée's novel approach, soon adopted elsewhere, aimed at a total interpretation of the local environment; and at Le Creusot attention naturally turned to the sites and landscapes generated by industry. Le Creusot was soon followed by other écomusées, in particularly those at Beauvais, Roanne and FOURMIES-TRÉLON.

At this same period, around 1975, Maurice Daumas, a historian of technology working at the Paris Conservatoire National des Arts et Métiers (see PARIS), launched the first nationwide survey of eighteenth- and nineteenth-century industrial buildings, a survey that was to provide the raw material for his publication in 1980, L'Archéologie industrielle en France, still the principal reference book on the subject.

From the outset, the orientations of the new discipline differed slightly from those of the founding fathers on the other side of the English Channel. The French approach lays greater emphasis on sites and buildings, rather than on the machines in them, and tends to concentrate more on the structures relating to production than on the infrastructural elements relating to transportation: ports, canals, roads and railways. In terms of its chronological limits, the French approach is perhaps less exclusively concerned with the dramatic changes engendered by the Industrial Revolution of the eighteenth and nineteenth centuries. From the beginning, although not lacking its amateur enthusiasts, the discipline has been largely dominated by academic historians, often preoccupied by long-term secular movements. Perhaps for this reason, traces of earlier forms of industrialization were often afforded close attention. Such traces, dating back to the phase qualified by some historians as that of PROTO-INDUSTRIALIZATION, turn out to be particularly numerous and often well preserved in France's still extensive rural backwaters. The study of the French iron industry, for example, usually goes back to the late fifteenth century and the early sixteenth century, the period of the introduction of the blast furnaces, and also of the oldest surviving above-ground vestiges.

In 1978, in order to federate different research initiatives by individuals or by local industrial archaeology groups, a national association was founded: the Comité d'Information et de Liaison pour l'Archéologie, l'Étude et la Mise en Valeur du Patrimoine Industriel (The Committee for Disseminating Information concerning the Study, Archaeology and Value of the Industrial Heritage),

Figure 49 The péniche *Bonita* being hauled westwards out of Saverne along the Canal du Marne au Rhin by a narrow gauge electric locomotive, August 1964
Barrie Trinder

or CILAC. The aim of this association was to encourage the take-off and sustained growth of the new discipline in France; since 1979 it has organized a more or less annual national conference, and it publishes France's national review, *L'Archéologie industrielle en France* (Industrial archaeology in France).

At the beginning of the 1980s, the study of the industrial heritage received official recognition and support with the creation, in 1983, of a special industrial heritage group – the 'Cellule du Patrimoine Industriel' – within the Inventaire Général, an inventory research and documentation body dating from 1964, and attached to the heritage section of the Ministry of Culture. This small 'cell' has initiated two publicly-financed research programmes. A general, nationwide industrial heritage location survey was launched in 1986, aiming to locate, identify and describe all the existing industrial sites and buildings up to the cut-off date of 1950. The photographic coverage and historical documentation concerning each site is kept to a theoretical minimum, and the key information is entered into a national computerized database. This survey programme is presently under way in eleven of France's twenty-two regions, and at the present rate and on present budgets will go on well into the twenty-first century.

Prior to this general survey programme, the industrial heritage cell had already undertaken several thematic research and recording projects, concentrating on specific industrial techniques or sectors, and limited to defined geographical zones. Water-power installations, the iron and steel industry, glassworks, brick and tile works, coal mining and motorcar construction are the main areas tackled so far. For these projects, the documentary research is more thoroughgoing, often concerned with the contribution that the combination of literary and physical evidence can bring to a specific set of historical problems.

Outside the General Inventory, but often with its financial, moral or methodological support, several individual or group research projects have emerged during the 1980s: on the breweries of the STENAY region, for example, or on copper works in the Ardennes (*see* ROMILLY-SUR-ANDELLE). In the case of the metallurgical industries, several research projects have involved archaeological excavations, notably at the BUFFON ironworks, at AUBE, PAMPAILLY and PEISEY.

Without positing any causal relationship, the conservation and rehabilitation of industrial buildings is often facilitated by preliminary research projects of an essentially scholarly nature. Throughout the 1980s, local authorities and architects have often preferred reuse projects rather than demolition for redundant industrial buildings. Amongst the more remarkable of these, mention may be made of the Le Blan textile mill at Lille, converted into apartments in 1980, and, more recently, the rehabilitation of the livestock market at La Villette, PARIS, transformed by the same architectural partnership, Robert & Reichen, into a multi-purpose exhibition centre, next to the new science museum.

Of course, such prestigious adaptive reuse projects are not suitable for all kinds of industrial buildings, and other, less noble or less architecturally attractive sites have to depend for their preservation on administrative decisions. A few industrial buildings had been afforded statutory protection prior to 1985, but it was only after that date that the built industrial heritage received serious attention from the listing commission of the Historic Monuments administration. A special section, explicitly concerned with the industrial, scientific and technical heritage, is now attached to this administration, which has enabled some thirty major sites to be listed ('classés'): the TARARE silk mill, for example; the CORBEIL corn mills; and several forge sites in Normany and Britanny. Many other industrial sites have benefited from less binding protective measures ('inscription'), whilst some five hundred artefacts – essentially boats and steam locomotives – have also received statutory protection. Like those of the General Inventory, the documentary files prepared by the Historic Monuments Service are available for consultation by the general public at the regional headquarters ('Direction Régionale des Affaires Culturelles') of the Ministry of Culture.

The protection of a certain number of industrial monuments has been accompanied by a greater awareness of the importance of industrial archives. Public archive repositories in the departments are making greater efforts to save company archives, and a handful of companies – notably Saint Gobain, Renault and the state tobacco company (SEITA) – have taken coherent measures to safeguard their own 'paper' heritage. At Mulhouse (Centre Rhénan d'Archives et de Recherches Économiques) and at Lewarde (see DOUAI), private institutions are also concerned with the conservation of local industrial archives, whilst a new public centre for the archives of the world of work has recently been opened in the old Motte-Bossut mill at Roubaix (see LILLE).

Finally, some of the most remarkable French industrial sites have been transformed into site museums: an attractive solution, allowing collections of original or old production equipment to be shown in their context. Such museums have been successfully launched at Lewarde (see DOUAI), at FOURMIES-TRÉLON, at the BUFFON ironworks, at the ANGOULÊME paper museum, and in LORRAINE at the Neufchef and Aumetz iron-mining museum.

In proportion to its size and population, France probably has more motorcar museums than any other European country. The archaeology of the industry is, however, in its infancy, and other architectural traces of early motorcar civilization – garages of the Belle Epoque and the inter-war years in particular – remain inadequately recorded and appreciated. Amongst more than fifty car museums scattered throughout the country, including the national museum at MULHOUSE, two important non-Parisian company-related initiatives deserve special mention: the Museum of the Aventure Peugeot, sponsored by the Peugeot firm at Sochaux, and the Marius Berliet Automobile Foundation at Lyons, concerned with 'metallic' and documentary memory, not only of Berliet's vehicles, but of French industrial vehicles in general.

Sources

Since 1973 the whole of France has been covered by topographical maps on a scale of 1:25 000. Other scales are available, including 1 cm to 1 km, and 2 cm to 1 km, but the 4 cm maps are often the most useful, with specific symbols for such industrial landmarks as factory chimneys, windmills, blast furnaces, quarries and mines. Bookshops and newsagents stock maps of their localities. The complete series is available at the Paris shop of the Institut Géographique National (the French national geographical institute), which was founded in 1940, replacing the cartographic service of the army. The IGN also publishes facsimile versions of the Cassini maps of France published between 1760 and 1815 at a scale of 1:86 400, which are particularly rewarding for hunters of old water-powered industrial sites.

In France as elsewhere the earliest population counts were inspired by fiscal considerations, the first 'État des feux' (list of hearths) dating from 1328. For the historian, the information provided by such lists can be supplemented by the registers of births, marriages and deaths rendered obligatory by statutes of 1539 and 1579. It was only during the eighteenth century that population censuses began to be based more scientifically on numbers of births rather than on the fiscal notion of households. The first modern population census dates from 1801. It was thereafter repeated at more or less regular intervals – roughly every five years. The census of 1851 was the first to record socio-professional categories, and to provide information on numbers of workers.

Industrial statistics are more recent still. Some regional information features in the major enquiries undertaken by the 'Intendants' between 1697 and 1700. Such enquiries became more frequent during the eighteenth century, concentrating on particular, often strategic, industrial sectors. Wool production, for example, was recorded annually from the mid-seventeenth century by 'Inspectors of Manufactures'. In 1772 a national enquiry into the number and importance of the country's ironworks followed similar regional enquiries, and the national enquiry was renewed in 1788.

During the First Empire such sectorial statistical enquiries were pursued, whilst the idea of descriptive statistics gained strength. Between 1803 and 1808 a remarkable series of departmental monographs was produced. Unfortunately not all are complete. Each of the surviving surveys provides a very detailed picture of the industrial situation in the department concerned.

The nineteenth century saw only two major industrial censuses, in 1840–5 and 1860–5. Taking note of all industrial concerns employing more than ten workers, they resulted in published summaries in 1852 and 1873 which are of great value. In both cases Paris was given separate treatment, with specific census operations and publications, in 1852 and 1865. All these publications can easily be consulted at the Bibliothèque Nationale (National Library).

The idea of a regular statistical analysis of the country's industries emerged only during World War II. Since 1948 the Institut National de la Statistique et des Études

Economiques (INSEE) has kept up-to-date files on all industrial and commercial enterprises, and since 1968 there has been a special file on large-scale concerns with more than two hundred employees.

The nineteenth century also saw the production of a broad and interesting range of sectorial statistics, such as the annual returns on the mining and metallurgical industries, published from 1835 in *Statistiques de l'Industrie Minérale* (statistics of the mineral industries). The state tobacco monopoly similarly published highly detailed annual accounts from 1818.

See also ABBARETZ; ABBEVILLE; AIRE-SUR-LA-LYS; ALÈS; ALLEVARD; ANGOULÊME; ANJOU; ARLES; AUBE; AUVET; BAINS-LES-BAINS; BEAUCOURT; BEZANCOURT; BUFFON; CEVENNES; CHÂLETTE-SUR-LOING; CORBEIL; CORSICA; CORVOL-L'ORGUEILLEUX; COTENTIN; DAUPHINÉ; DECAZEVILLE; DOUAI; EIFFEL, ALEXANDRE GUSTAVE; EPINAC; ESCAUDAIN; FONTINETTES; FOURMIES-TRÉLON; GRAND CANAL; GUISE; LA VOULTE; LE CREUSOT; LILLE; LIMOGES; LORRAINE; LOUVIERS; LYONS; MARSEILLES; MONTLUÇON; MOSELLE; MULHOUSE; NANTES; NOISIEL; NOUZONVILLE; OYONNAX; PAMPAILLY; PARIS; PAYS D'AUGE; PECHELBRONN; PEISEY; PRIVAS; PYRENEES; RHINE; ROMILLY-SUR-ANDELLE; SAINT-BONNET TRONÇAIS; SAINT-ÉTIENNE; SAINT-GOBAIN; SAINT-LOUIS-ARZVILLER; SAINTE-MARIE-AUX-MINES; SALINS-LES-BAINS; SAVIGNAC-LÉDRIER; SEDAN; STENAY; TARARE; TRILBARDOU; VALENÇAY; VENTRON; VILLEDIEU-LES-POÊLES; VILLENEUVETTE; WITTELSHEIM.

BIBLIOGRAPHY
General
Asselain, 1984; Bergeron *et al.*, 1989; Braudel *et al.*, 1977–80; Daumas, 1980; Daumas *et al.*, 1962–79, 1978; Dreyfus, 1987; Dunham, 1955; Ficquelmont and Fontanon, 1990; Gille, 1964, 1978; Grenier and Wieser-Benedetti, 1979; Guiollard, 1989; Lautier *et al.* 1981; Lemoine, 1986; Loyer, 1983; Ministère de la Culture et de la Communication, 1987; Piettre and Smith, 1980; Price, 1973; Reddy, 1984; Rioux, 1971; Rives, 1925; Sütterlin, 1981.

Specific
Belhoste, J.-F. Les Manufactures de drap fin en France aux XVIIe et XVIIIe siècles (Broadcloth manufactures in France in the seventeenth and eighteenth centuries). In *Revue de l'Art*, LXV, 1984.

Belot, V.R. Guide des petits trains touristiques en France, Belgique, Luxembourg, Pays-Bas, Suisse (Guide to the tourist railways of France, Belgium, Luxembourg, the Low Countries and Switzerland). Paris: Pierre Horay Editeur, 1986.

Benoît, S. De l'hydro-mécanique à l'hydro-électrique (From hydraulic power to hydro-electricity). In *La France des Electriciens 1880–1980* (The electricians' France, 1880–1980): proceedings of the second national colloquium of the Association for the History of Electricity in France. Paris: PUF 1986.

Bergeron, L. L'Archéologie Industrielle (Industrial archaeology). In *Encyclopédie Universalis*, II. Paris, 1989.

Hamon, F. L'Architecture industrielle, travaux et publications, un bilan international (Industrial architecture, work in progress and publications, an international overview). In *Revue de l'Art*, LXXIX, 1988.

Institut National de la Statistique et des Études Economiques. Pour une historie de la statistique (For a history of statistics): transactions of a colloquium of 23–5 June 1976. Institut National de la Statistique et des Études Economiques, 1977.

BIBLIOGRAPHY
Specific
Buderath, 1990.

LOCATIONS
[M] Airport Exhibition, Rhein-Main Flughafen, 6000 Frankfurt.
[M] Bundespostmuseum (Museum of the Federal Postal Services), Schaumainkai 53, 6000 Frankfurt.
[M] Coin Collection of the German Federal Bank, Taunusanlage 4–6, 6000 Frankfurt.
[M] Historical Museum, Saalgasse 19, 6000 Frankfurt.
[M] Tramway Museum, Rheinlandstrasse, 6000 Frankfurt-Schwanheim.

ROLF HÖHMANN

Frederiksværk, Zealand, Denmark Frederiksværk, on the Roskilde Fjord in North Zealand, is one of the few distinctively industrial towns in Denmark. It is a relatively new foundation, dating from *c.*1750 when a bronze cannon factory was established, using water power from a specially cut canal from the nearby lake of Arresø to the fjord. In the next fifty years the dynamic owner, J. F. Classen, added several new products, the manufacture of gunpowder, the rolling of copper plates, and iron castings. Until *c.*1840 the iron foundry and engineering shops were the undisputed centre of iron manufactures in Denmark. Although for a long time the main customer was the state, the various plants, apart from the gunpowder mills, were at least nominally in private ownership. In 1942 the industrial importance of Frederiksværk was renewed when a large steel rolling mill, the only one in Denmark, was erected in the city.

The manufacture of gunpowder continued until *c.*1960. Most of the production area, which is near the city centre, is now a gunpowder museum, owned and operated by the Ministry of Defence. Many of the characteristic small mill buildings, drying houses and magazines have survived, some from the eighteenth century but most from the nineteenth.

Iron casting continues in the city, until recently in old premises. Among the more prominent surviving buildings is the monumental foundry Giethuset, built in the 1760s to the design of the famous architect N. Eigtved. It is proposed to restore the foundry as a national museum of ironmaking and engineering. The local history museum is housed in the arsenal of the former works.

The steelworks of 1942, the town's largest employer, is sited on the harbour, and is based on the use of domestic scrap. Originally it had two Siemens-Martin OPEN-HEARTH FURNACES, but in 1975 these were replaced by ELECTRIC ARC FURNACES.

BIBLIOGRAPHY
General
Nielsen, 1943–4; Sestoft, 1979.
Specific
Eriksen, E. *Frederiksværk, fra kanoner til kedler 1756–1956* (Frederiksværk, from cannons to boilers 1756–1956). Frederiksværk, 1956.
Eriksen, E. *Krudtværket pa Frederiksværk 1758–1958* (The gunpowder works at Frederiksværk 1758–1958). Frederiksværk, 1958.

Petersen, G. ed. *Historiske huse i Frederiksværk* (Historic houses in Frederiksværk). Frederiksværk, 1986.

LOCATIONS
[M] Frederiksværkegnens Museum (Local History Museum), Arsenalet, Torvet, 3300 Frederiksværk.
[M] Krudtværksmuseet (The Gunpowder Museum), Krudtværksalleen 3, 3300 Frederiksværk.

OLE HYLDTOFT

freehold land society A form of building society established in Birmingham by James Taylor (1814–87) from 1848, originally designed to create a class of owner-occupiers. It was popular in many English cities from 1850. A society raised money from subscribers to purchase land, which was then divided into plots, frequently distributed by ballot. Such societies often became vehicles for small-scale speculators rather than a means to owner-occupation. A characteristic freehold land society estate has houses on plots of uniform size, with a common frontage, often built in groups of two, three or four, of uneven height and area. Sometimes an investor who acquired several plots would keep one as garden ground.

BIBLIOGRAPHY
General
Chapman, 1971; Gauldie, 1974; Price, 1958; Trinder, 1982a, 1982b.

Freiberg and the Erzgebirge (Krusné Hory), Saxony, Germany This area, indicating by its very name – the Ore Mountains – that it is involved in the coal and iron industry, is about 150 km (90 mi.) long and 40 km (25 mi.) wide, and includes both German and Czech territory (*see* JÁCHYMOV). In 1168 miners from the HARZ MOUNTAINS began mining silver and iron ore in Freiberg, 32 km (20 mi.) SE of Dresden. This mining operation reached its peak in the fifteenth and sixteenth centuries. It declined during the Thirty Years War (1618–48), and later mining efforts were concentrated on rarer ores, such as lead, zinc and tin, and even later on nickel, cobalt, bismuth and uranium.

Monuments from all three main periods of the history of the coal and metal industry in the Erzgebirge have been preserved in and around Freiberg. In 1168 silver ore was discovered in the town, where one of the oldest academies of mining in the world was founded in 1765. Until about 1380 the silver ore was mined from depths of up to 100 m (330 ft.), with hammers and iron bars, and wound to the surface by hand. Barren rock was jettisoned as waste around the shafts, which thus grew progressively taller. Even today, the course of a vein of ore can easily be traced by the line of mounds on the surface; an example is the main drift between Freiberg and Tuttendorf, now a suburb of the city. Freiberg had municipal status from about 1210, and became the first free mining city in Germany when it was granted mining privileges in 1346–75.

It was at about this time that the first drainage adits were dug. The first, known as the Alte Tiefe Fürstenstolln (Old Deep Princely Adit) dates from before 1348. Its

279

entrance is preserved in eighteenth-century masonry work.

The second major period of mining in Freiberg typically produced poorer ore mined at greater depths. Details were recorded in one of the great works of technical literature and iconography, *De re metallica* by the Chemnitz physician GEORGIUS AGRICOLA, which was published in 1556 and translated from Latin into German in the following year.

Although only fragments of the machinery Agricola describes, among them stamp mills, horse gins and water wheels, have been preserved in museums, the peculiarities of the Freiberg mining region mean that to a certain extent the technology of the sixteenth century remained in use well into the nineteenth century, and even into the twentieth century. As late as 1856 a reversible water wheel for raising ore was installed at the 'Rote Grube' (red pit) in Freiberg, at a depth of 90 m (300 ft.). It was almost identical to a similar installation described by Agricola. The wheel remained in operation until 1944, and is well preserved, like the reversible water wheel built by Johann Christoph Roeder in 1805 in the 'Neuer Serenissimorum Tiefsten Schacht' (New, Most Serene, Deepest Pit) of the Rammelsberg mine in Goslar, now a part of the Goslar Museum of Mining (*see* HARZ MOUNTAINS).

The third epoch of mining at Freiberg began in 1765, after the Seven Years War of 1756–63, when attempts were made to consolidate the economy of the mines and the technology used in their operation. Evidence of this process is preserved in various 'Huthäuser' in and around Freiberg. These are the typical administrative buildings of the Erzgebirge mining area. The 'Huthaus' of the 'Herzog-August-Fundgrube' (Duke Augustus Mine) in Zug dates from the beginning of the eighteenth century. The building of the 'Beschert Glück' (Grant Fortune) mine in the same place dates from 1786, and had a bell-tower added in 1812.

The 'Abrahamschacht' (Abraham pit) of the 'Himmelfahrt' (Ascension) mine at Freiberg is a large complex dating from 1839, with a pithead building, smithy, administrative building, and miners' building, as well as sheds for ore dressing. Another extensive complex is formed by the buildings erected in 1847–9 at the mouth of the 'Alte Elisabeth' (Old Elisabeth) inclined shaft mine, which ceased operation in 1968 and is now used for teaching purposes by the Freiberg Academy of Mining. The machinery here is particularly interesting. The winding engine house contains the Watt steam engine made by the Chemnitz engineering concern of Constantin Pfaff, and installed in 1848–9. It was the fourth oldest steam engine in the DDR and the third oldest in the Freiberg mining region. Another room accommodates the water engine (*see* HYDRAULIC POWER) of shaft No. 8 of the 'Rothschönberger Stolln' (Rothschönberg Drift), built in 1875, which originally brought drinking water to the surface from a depth of 90 m (300 ft.) and pumped it into an overhead tank, in the village of Halsbrücke, 8 km (5 mi.) N. of Freiberg.

The Rothschönberg Drift represents one of the most remarkable achievements of mine surveying and construction in the world. The partly state-owned enterprise was completed between 1845 and 1877, and, including sections from all the Freiberg pits that profited by it, its total length was no less than 50.9 km (31.6 mi.). It remained in use until 1972.

As well as the hydraulic engine, the buildings of the 'Alte Elisabeth' mine also contain the steam blowing engine of the 'Morgenröthe' (Dawn) ironworks in the Vogtland, intended in 1829–31 for installation at the Antonshütte ironworks at Schwarzenberg, 40 km (25 mi.) SW of Freiberg. It stands in a building erected for the purpose in 1936. It was moved to the Halsbrücke works in 1862–3, and operated there until 1925. With its neo-Gothic decoration and beamless structure, it is an important monument of early German mechanical engineering.

In 1788 one of the first canal boat lifts was built of rubble masonry on the Grosschirma-Rothenfurt mining canal near Freiberg. A 6.3 m (20 ft.) difference in level was overcome by the use of five tackle blocks, which could raise and lower boats and move them laterally over both upper and lower water levels. Ore-carrying boats some 8 m (26 ft.) long, and weighing three tonnes, were moved in this way. They carried ore from the 'Churprinz' (Electoral prince) mine to the smelting works at Halsbrücke, 8 km (5 mi.) N. of Freiberg. The installation remained in use until 1868, when the water of the canal was required for other purposes, and the ore was thereafter carried by land.

These are only some of the many monuments preserved from eight hundred years of mining in Freiberg. The Freiberg Museum of Mining is the best starting point for a tour of the many historic relics of this industry, which also include the extensive networks of canals serving the mines, such as the system between Branderbisdorf, 5 km (3 mi.) SW of Freiberg and the 'Sankt Anna samt Altväter' (St Anne and the Patriarchs) mine, distinguished by its aqueducts. Toymaking in the Erzgebirge has been an important manufacture since the seventeenth century and is illustrated in the museum at Seiffen, 32 km (20 mi.) S. of Freiberg. Ironmaking in the region is commemorated in the museum at Schwarzenberg, and a restored forge in Frohnau, Annaberg. Elsewhere, the Zeitz 'Flossgraben' (raft ditch) with its eight viaducts and reservoir, is in no way inferior to the water-power system of the HARZ MOUNTAINS. Another monument to the mining industry of the Erzgebirge is the Annanberg 'Bergaltar' (mining altar) painted by Hans Hesse in 1521 for the Annenkirche, a church built between 1499 and 1525, and showing scenes depicting the mining techniques of the time. The sacred and secular architecture of Freiberg (the cathedral), Annaberg, 40 km (25 mi.) SW of Freiberg (the Annenkirche), and Schneeberg, 34 km (21 mi.) SW of Freiberg, are evidence of the economic importance of the mines – the industry enabled these towns to employ artists of outstanding talent.

BIBLIOGRAPHY
General
Agricola, 1556; Berger, 1980; Bleyl, 1917; Forberger, 1982; Schmidt and Theile, 1989; Slotta, 1983; Wagenbreth and Wächtler, 1983, 1986a, 1986b.

Specific

Hentschel, W. Aus den Anfängen des Fabrikbaus in Sachsen (Factory buildings in Saxony from the beginnings). In *Wissenschaftliche Zeitschrift der Technischen Hochschule Dresden* (Scientific papers of Dresden Polytechnic), III. Dresden, 1953–4.

LOCATIONS

[S] Alte Elisabeth Berg (Old Elisabeth Mine), 9200 Freiberg.

[M] Erzgebirge Museum: Department of Cultural History, Grosse Kirchgasse 16, 9300 Annaberg-Buchholz.

[M] Erzgebirge Toy Museum, Ernst Thälmann Strasse 73, 9335 Seiffen.

[M] Freiberg Bergbaumuseum (Freiberg Museum of Mining), Am Dom 1–3, 9200 Freiberg.

[S] Frohnauer Hammer, Schmatalstrasse 3, 9301 Frohnau, Kreis Annaberg.

[M] Museum for the Popular Art of the Mining Community, Rosa Luxemburg Platz 1, 9412 Schneeberg.

[M] Museum of the Erzgebirge Iron Industry, Obereschloss-strasse 36, 9430 Schwarzenberg.

[M] Scientific Collection of the Freiberg Mining Academy, Brennhausgass 14, 9200 Freiberg.

AXEL FÖHL

French stone   *See* MILLSTONES.

fretwork   A term with two meanings:

1. Ornamental woodwork, open designs appearing to be clusters of intersecting lines, cut with a fretsaw, a narrow-bladed, fine-toothed saw held under tension in a frame, and also known as a compass-saw. Fretwork became popular in the late nineteenth century as a means of adorning FURNITURE, and in Britain fretworking sets were marketed as educational toys (*see* EAST ANGLIA).
2. An architectural term for decorative work consisting of intersecting lines, used from *c.*1600.

Friedrichshafen, Baden-Württemberg, Germany   A city on Lake Constance (Bodensee), formerly a summer resort, which owes its present importance as an industrial centre to Count Ferdinand Zeppelin (1838–1917) and the dirigible AIRSHIP he developed. One of these aircraft first successfully took off from the lake in 1900, and about a hundred Zeppelins were built in Friedrichshafen before the disastrous fire which destroyed the *Hindenburg* at Lakehurst, New Jersey, in 1937. Other major concerns developed around the Zeppelin factory from the beginning of World War I, among them the Friedrichshafen gearwheel factory, the Maybach motor works, and the Dornier FLYING BOAT plant. Models and original parts illustrating the history of the Zeppelin are displayed in the municipal museum, where there are continuous showings of video copies of films of the epic voyages undertaken by the airships. All that remains of the works buildings is the Zeppelin village, a GARDEN CITY complex laid out by the architects Bonatz & Scholer as a present from the Count to his workers on his 75th birthday.

BIBLIOGRAPHY
Specific

Krins, H. Die Arbeitersiedlung 'Zeppelindorf' bei Friedrichshafen (The Zeppelin Village workers' colony near Friedrichshafen). In *Denkmalpflege in Baden-Württemberg*, II, 1979.

LOCATION

[M] Municipal Museum of Lake Constance, Adenauer Platz 1, 7990 Friedrichshafen.

RÖLF HÖHMANN

Friesland (Fryslân), The Netherlands   The bilingual (Dutch and Frisian) province of Friesland is known for its dairies, and industry in the nineteenth century was orientated around local raw materials and farm products. Harlingen (Harns) became an important port, exporting cheese, butter and cattle, and importing manufactures and coal. The Dokhaven of 1851 and the tidal harbour, Nieuwe Willemshaven, of 1877, extended the sixteenth-century basins. In Dokstraat are tiles with the names of English ports connected with Harlingen.

Kornwerderzand (Koarnwertersan), 10 km (6 mi.) S. of Harlingen, is on the Afsluitdijk, the dam enclosing the Zuiderzee, completed in 1932, giving access to the Ysselmeer through the Lorentz sluices of 1927–32. Makkum, 5 km (3 mi.) S., is a fishing port where a celebrated pottery and tile factory, established in the seventeenth century, remains in the ownership of the founding family. Visitors can tour the factory. Workum (Warkum), 10 km (6 mi.) S., is another former fishing port where the nineteenth-century De Hoop shipyard, which specialized in the construction and repair of wooden ships, has been restored. Staveren (Starum), 8 km (5 mi.) SW, is a former fishing port, once a member of the Hanseatic League, and a railway port in the 1880s on the route connecting Enkhuizen with Leeuwarden. The railway has been of less importance since the construction of the enclosing dam, but the ferry to Enkhuizen (*see* NOORD HOLLAND) still sails in summertime. Lemmer (De Lemmer), 24 km (15 mi.) E., was formerly a transit port, where passengers crossing the Zuiderzee from Amsterdam boarded the tramway to GRONINGEN. One of the ferry boats is preserved. There is a fine sluice complex of 1889; and 2 km (1 mi.) W. is the D. F. Woudagemaal pumping station of 1920, an example of the ultimate development of steam pumping, with four Jaffa compound engines, eight centrifugal pumps, and a capacity of 4000 m³ (14 000 cu. ft.) per minute. Since 1967 when it became an auxiliary pumping station oil fuel has been used instead of coal.

Leeuwarden (Ljouwert), the Frisian capital, has always been an administrative rather than a manufacturing city. The railway station has a roof of 1892, and a locomotive depot of 1886. The Hollanderwijk suburb was built in 1914 following GARDEN CITY concepts. The store of 1910 at Nieuweburen, locally called 'the skyscraper', is a building of cast concrete, which began to subside from the time of its construction. The Centrale Apotheek is an ART NOUVEAU chemist's shop in the centre.

Until the late nineteenth century most cheese and butter was produced at farmhouses, much of it being exported to England. Competition from Denmark stimulated the establishment of CREAMERIES. Modernization and concentration has forced many to close since 1945, but they remain a feature of the Frisian landscape, many now having other functions. At Veenwouden (Feanwalden), 12 km ($7\frac{1}{2}$ mi.) E. of Leeuwarden, the Freia creamery, founded in 1879, rebuilt in 1918 and working until 1969, remains intact with much of its equipment, parts having been removed to ARNHEM.

In south-east Friesland there was much reclamation of peatlands. Bontebok, Jubbega, 8 km (5 mi.) E. of Heerenveen, provides a good example of the landscape of peat digging.

The maritime history of Friesland is presented in a museum at Sneek (Snits), 21 km (13 mi.) SW of Leeuwarden. At Ylst (Drylts), 4 km ($2\frac{1}{2}$ mi.) SW, is an early example of industrialized woodworking, the Nooitgedagt skate factory. Joure (De greate Jouwer), 10 km (6 mi.) SE, was the birthplace of Douwe Egberts, now the largest tea and coffee concern in the Netherlands. The history of the company is shown in a store of 1896 and a coffee- and teashop of the 1930s. The restored Keverling brass foundry, which ceased production in 1983, is in the same street.

Schiermonnikoog (Skiermuontseach), one of the Frisian Islands, has two lighthouses of 1854, one of which has been used as a water tower since 1950.

BIBLIOGRAPHY
General
Thijsse, 1972.

LOCATIONS
[S] D. F. Woudagemaal (Pumping Station), Gemaalweg 76, Lemmer.
[M] Fries Aardewerkmuseum De Waag (De Waag Pottery Museum), Pruikmakershoek 2, Makkum.
[M] Fries Museum (Frisian Museum), Turfmarkt 24, Leeuwarden.
[M] Fries Scheepvaartmuseum (Frisian Maritime Museum), Kleinzand 14, Sneek.
[S] Geelkopergieterij Keverling (Keverling Brass Foundry), Geelgietersstraat, Joure.
[S] Johannes Hesselhuis (The Johannes Hessel House). Geelgietersstraat 1, Joure.
[S] Scheepswerf De Hoop (De Hoop Shipyard), Seburch 7, Workum.
[S] Tichelaars Tegelfabriek (Tichelaars Tile Factory), Postbus 11, Makkum.

JURRIE VAN DALEN

Frolov, Koz'ma Dmitrievich (1726–1800) and **Pyotr Kozmich** (1775–1839)   Koz'ma Dmitrievich was the son of an artisan of the Polevskoi metallurgical works in the Urals. He received training in mining engineering at the industrial school in Ekaterinburg and had a varied and inventive life before being transferred to the Altai region to work in a metal-refining works. Here he was responsible for many innovations, largely devoted to economizing on manpower. He was called upon to rescue the nearby Voznesensk silver mines from decline. The mines formed part of a gigantic water-power system most of which was completed in the 1780s. It involved a 2 km ($1\frac{1}{2}$ mi.) diversion of water from the River Smei, in the course of which it provided power for several works, including water-powered ore lifts. One of these lifts, serving the Preobrazhenskii mine, had its machinery, which included a 9 m (30 ft.) diameter water wheel, in a chamber more than 7 m (23 ft.) below the surface. At the Ekaterina mine an even larger and more grandiose underground chamber housed a 17 m (56 ft.) water wheel, the biggest in Russia, which through an ingenious system of rods and pumps could lift water from a depth of 210 m (700 ft.). The Voznesensk mine also had an underground chamber and wheel. Some of this system still exists, notably the underground chamber and the 17 m wheel at the Ekaterina mine. The Smei complex closed in 1893 but in due course a new metal-refining works was constructed which remains in use, its water supply assured by a dam and canal of Frolov's making. Frolov is best known not so much for his hydraulic engineering as for a system of internal railways in the mines, with wagons drawn by cables pulled by water wheels.

His son, Pyotr Kozmich, built a 2 km ($1\frac{1}{2}$ mi.) railway in 1809 to carry silver ore to the Zmeinogorsk works. This is believed to have been the first line in Russia to use horse traction, with one horse pulling 24 tons of ore in three wagons, a performance made possible by the extensive provision of cuttings and tunnels. There were cast-iron convex rails which matched grooves cut in the wagon wheels. The existence of the railway was scarcely known outside mining circles and when the tsar was shown a German model of a railway in 1816 his remarks suggested that he had no idea that Russia already possessed one. Relics of the line, including rails and wheels, are in the Altai Regional Museum in Barnaul, which was founded by P. K. Frolov to preserve for posterity knowledge of what had been achieved in the Altai mining complex.

BIBLIOGRAPHY
Specific
Virginskii, V. S. *Zamechatel'nyie russkiye izobretateli Frolovy.* Moscow, 1952.

JOHN WESTWOOD

Frome, Somerset, England   A centre of woollen manufactures from the seventeenth century. Workers' housing in the Trinity Street area west of the centre was laid out in the late seventeenth century. Two round wool stoves can be seen near the centre of Frome, as can a timber railway station of *c.*1850 with an overall roof. Mells, 5 km (3 mi.) W., has extensive remains of the Fussell water-powered edge-tool works, closed *c.*1890.

BIBLIOGRAPHY
General
Leech, 1981.

LOCATION
[M] Frome and East Mendip Museum, 1 North Parade, Frome, Somerset BA11 1AT.

Frövifors, Örebro, Sweden   Frövifors bruk, 30 km (20 mi.) N. of Örebro, is the site of a large modern board mill, completed in 1981, alongside a pulp and paper mill which originated in 1891. The commissioning of the new plant provided an opportunity for the preservation of the old board mill, something which had been foreseen in the early 1970s when the Swedish Pulp and Paper Association set up a historical group which brought together representatives of the industry with historians and archaeologists.

The earliest parts of the mill of the 1890s were constructed on the site of an ironworks, of which some slag tips remain. The outstanding interest of the site lies in two lines of red-brick machine shops which contain papermaking machinery installed by Karlstads Mekaniska Verkstad in 1907 and 1911; it is almost unaltered. The transmission shafts and belts that until 1942 conveyed power from water turbines to the machinery remain, as well as HOLLANDERS and other equipment used for grinding pulp. The mill was filmed and photographed when it was working in 1976, an oral history archive has been compiled, and the mill is well documented. The Frövifors Paper Mill Museum Foundation was established in 1984, and has plans to establish at the mill a museum which will have regional and national as well as local perspectives. Visitors to the museum are also able to enter the modern paper mill.

BIBLIOGRAPHY
General
Nisser and Bedoire, 1978.
Specific
Nisser, M. 1990. Frövifors Paper Mill. In *Teknik & Kultur*, II.
LOCATION
[M] Frövifors Paper Mill Museum.

BARRIE TRINDER

fruit and vegetable products *See* BANANAS; CANNING; CHEWING GUM; DRIED FRUIT; DRINK; JAM; MARMALADE; MUSTARD; OIL MILL; OLIVE OIL; PAPRIKA; PEA; PICKLE; POTATO; REFRIGERATION.

fuller's earth A form of fine-grained clay, usually consisting chiefly of hydrated aluminium silicate, with a high absorptive capacity, low plasticity, and strong decolorizing and degreasing properties. As the name implies, it has long been used in finishing woollen cloth, in order to remove grease from the fabric, and is also employed as an absorbent and bleaching agent in refining oils and fats. Fuller's earth is not a particular mineral but a name applied to any substance that can be used for these purposes. Most suitable clays result from the devitrification of volcanic glass, the chief sources in England being the Lower Greensand Beds in the WEALD, and quarries at Woburn near BEDFORD.

BIBLIOGRAPHY
Specific
Robertson, R. H. S. *Fuller's Earth: a history of calcium montmorillonite*. Hythe, Kent: Volturna Press, 1986.

fulling mill Fulling is a vigorous working of woollen cloth in a solution of water and a fulling agent (urine, FULLER'S EARTH or SOAP) to produce controlled shrinkage. It compacts and felts the fibres to provide a tight, smooth weave. Traditionally accomplished by workers' feet (hence the name 'walker' meaning a fuller), fulling was mechanized in medieval times. Fulling mills contained large wooden hammer beams called fulling stocks that pounded the cloth in solution; they were typically worked by water wheels. In the USA and Canada, and in the woollen cloth industry of Britain in the early nineteenth century, fulling and carding were often performed together in small, water-powered mills serving the needs of domestic woollen manufacture. Mechanical fulling mills in industry work by the action of beating, or by rollers within a tub.

BIBLIOGRAPHY
General
Pelham, 1958.
Specific
Dickenson, M. J. Fulling in the West Riding cloth industry, 1689–1770. In *TH*, x, 1979.

Fulton, Robert (1765–1815) An American inventor, born in Lancaster County, Pa., whose writings did much to publicize innovations on inland waterways, and who was responsible for the introduction of the steamboat to the USA. He began as an artist, and it was as a painter that he travelled to Europe in 1787. He became interested in canals, visited many British waterways, and in 1796 published a book on inland navigation, with many proposals which he claimed as his own. He built an experimental submarine in Paris in 1797, and returned to New York in 1806. The following year he established a steamboat service between that city and Albany which cut the journey time along the Hudson River from four days to 32 hours.

BIBLIOGRAPHY
General
Dickinson, 1913; Flexner, 1944; Fulton, 1796; Reigart, 1856.

functionalist A term applied to an architect or designer who interprets the satisfactory functioning of a building or object to be his or her prime objective. The term is often and somewhat misleadingly applied to the structures of the early Industrial Revolution, and is frequently used as a synonym for the INTERNATIONAL MODERN style.

Fundão, Beira Baixa, Portugal A town 210 km (130 mi.) NE of Lisbon, whose royal woollen factory ceased operation in 1821. Its building, renovated and enlarged in 1916, now houses the local council. Several woollen factories remain. Around the nearby Panasqueira tungsten mines are workers' dwellings arranged in a geometric plan on the mountainside.

funicular A railway ascending a steep gradient, in which a pair of cars is linked by a cable which passes several turns round a winding drum at the upper terminus, from which the operation is controlled. Usually there is a single track with a passing loop in the middle. Most are now electrically operated, although in the late nineteenth century many worked by means of a water balance. Lines more than about 2 km ($1\frac{1}{2}$ mi.) in length are usually divided into sections to avoid problems caused by too great a weight of cable. The funicular can climb a gradient steeper than 1 in 2, the maximum possible with a RACK RAILWAY. Large numbers have been built in Switzerland, the first of them in Lausanne in 1877. Funiculars form important parts of commuter transport networks in cities like Bilbao, Genoa, Cincinnati and Pittsburgh; in Pittsburgh two lines constructed in the 1870s remain in service.

See also CLIFF RAILWAY; INCLINED PLANE.

BIBLIOGRAPHY
General
Allen, 1965.

fur   The collection of furs was the principal activity that led to the European colonization of large parts of Canada and the USA, and was also an important trade in northern Europe. From the seventeenth century settlers in America established trading posts where skins from the beaver, marten, mink, racoon, fox and other animals hunted in the winter were bartered with native peoples. The trade was developed on a vast scale in the American West by John Jacob Astor (1763–1848), a migrant from Germany who reached New York in 1784 and died the richest man in America and founder of a dynasty of real-estate millionaires. Specialist warehouses were built to handle furs in LONDON and other ports, as well as specialist tanneries like the Maranda and Labrecque works in QUEBEC CITY.

See also SEALING.

BIBLIOGRAPHY
General
Chittenden, 1902; Hudson's Bay Company, 1920; Pinkerton, 1932.
Specific
Minnesota Historical Society. *Where Two Worlds Meet: the Great Lakes fur trade.* St Paul, Minn.: Minnesota Historical Society, 1982.

furniture   Furniture was traditionally made in towns by cabinet-makers. 'General' cabinet-makers concentrated on larger pieces like bookcases, but were capable of making smaller items like trays. 'Fancy' cabinet-makers specialized in portable items like workboxes, dressing cases and gaming tables. In large cities makers of frames for CHAIRS and bedsteads represented specialized branches of the trade. Many cabinet-makers in small towns were also upholsterers. By 1850 some branches were typically sweated trades, with men working at home and specializing in making such items as drawers for cabinets, the prelude to organization on a factory basis. Mass production of furniture began in the USA, particularly in cities supplying westbound migrants: in Cincinnati, OHIO, by 1854 one steam-powered, five-storey factory was employ-ing 250 men and making 125 000 chairs per annum; another was producing 52 000 bedsteads per annum.

BIBLIOGRAPHY
General
Boyce, 1986; Chambers, 1854; Hudson, 1980; Joy, 1977; Mayhew, 1850; Wells and Hooper, 1909.
Specific
Banham, R. Chairs as art. In Barker, 1977.

BARRIE TRINDER

fustian   A term applied from the fourteenth century to several kinds of fabric, including fustian of Naples which was a silk with two layers of pile of different lengths. From the 1590s when its manufacture was introduced into Ireland, fustian referred to a fabric with a linen warp and a cotton weft. By 1800 the word meant a coarse cloth made from cotton or flax and used for outer garments, essentially one with a cut pile like corduroy; 'fustian jackets' became a synonym for the English working class *c.*1840. The finishing of fustian involved sizing, and cutting the looped weft, processes carried on in small workshops in MANCHESTER and in large specialist establishments in north-west England, particularly in Lymm, Cheshire, where there are two rows of three-storey cottages with top-floor workshops, each extending over several cottages. Cloth was stretched for cutting on frames about 2 m (6 ft. 6 in.) long, with rollers at each end.

BIBLIOGRAPHY
General
Ashmore, 1982; BPP, 1863; Kerridge, 1985; Montgomery, 1984.
Specific
Chapman, S. D. James Longsdon (1745–1821), farmer and fustian manufacturer: the small firm in the early English cotton industry. In *TH,* I, 1970.

NANCY COX and BARRIE TRINDER

Fylde, Lancashire, England   The coastal plain between the Rivers Wyre and Ribble, on which there are many windmills: examples may be seen at Little Marton (1838), Lytham (1805), Clifton, and Thornton Cleveleys.

Fleetwood was planned as a packet port by Decimus Burton (1800–81) in the 1840s, but failed: a hotel, a terrace and two lighthouses survive. The L&YR built the docks in 1869–70 and there was subsequent development as a fishing port.

Blackpool, from the arrival of the railway in 1846, became the principal seaside resort of industrial Lancashire; its celebrated tower, 148 m (485 ft.) high, dates from 1891–4. Trams run the 22 km ($13\frac{1}{2}$ mi.) from Starr Gate in Blackpool to Fleetwood. A former Woolworth store of 1938, in the American style, can be seen on Blackpool front. Blackpool has three piers, with a fourth at Lytham, 10 km (8 mi.) to the south-east.

BIBLIOGRAPHY
General
Ashmore, 1982.

LOCATION
[M] Fleetwood Museum, Dock Street, Fleetwood FY7 6AQ.

G

Gakkel' (Haeckel), **Yakov** (1874–1945) A pioneer designer of diesel locomotives, Gakkel' was the son of the engineer who built the Vladivostok and Kronstadt harbour works. He trained as an electrical engineer, and worked for the WESTINGHOUSE Co. on the St Petersburg electric tramways. Financially secure from royalties inherited from his father-in-law, he dabbled in aviation, building his own machines, and making the first Russian inter-city flight. In 1918, while managing the Kiev tramways, he began to study the possibility of building diesel-electric locomotives, and later, encouraged by the government, he worked in the Institute of Power Engineering, where a diesel locomotive bureau was established. Two of his designs were built. One of these, No. Shch-el-1, was completed in Leningrad in 1924, and together with another Russian diesel-electric locomotive delivered at the same time, ranks among the world's pioneer main-line diesel locomotives. It is preserved and is normally on show outside the locomotive depot at Khovrino, in the northern outskirts of Moscow.

BIBLIOGRAPHY
General
Westwood, 1982.

gallery A word with a confusion of meanings in industrial archaeology.

In the sixteenth century the term meant a covered area for promenading, with a roof supported by pillars; from this developed the usage indicating a platform supported by columns in a place of public assembly, such as a church or theatre; and from this came the use of the word for a DEPARTMENT STORE with a central light well. Before 1600 the term also meant a place, then usually part of a house, where works of art were displayed. In England an institution called a gallery may be a museum of fine art, like the Tate Gallery in London, but the term is also applied to establishments where fine art is displayed and offered for sale, which is the usual meaning of the term in North America, and in France. The word is also applied to a section of the displays of a museum of any sort, so that an industrial museum may have galleries devoted to clocks or textiles.

By the 1630s the word was used to indicate part of a mine, usually a road giving access to the faces from which minerals were extracted. The Italian word 'galleria' means tunnel, and it and similar words in other languages are sometimes wrongly translated into English as 'gal-

lery'. The Italian 'galleria' also means ARCADE, while the French 'galéries' sometimes applies to a department store.

BARRIE TRINDER

galvanizing Galvanism, electricity generated by chemical action, takes its name from Luigi Galvani (1737–98) who observed the process in 1792. Galvanizing is the coating of metal by galvanic energy, but in practice the term is most commonly applied to the coating of iron or steel plates, strip or other sections, with zinc (*see* CORRUGATED IRON), which is not strictly speaking galvanizing.

Gánt, Veszprém, Hungary The chief centre of opencast bauxite mining in the Vertes Hills, 60 km (37 mi.) SW of Budapest. Before World War II, most of the bauxite produced was exported. A mining museum in a plant of 1926 forms part of the interpretative scheme established in 1976 for areas protected for their ecological interest.

LOCATION
[M] Bauxite Mining Museum, H-8082 Gánt.

garage Originally a place for the storage of motorcars. The first were used for overnight accommodation of vehicles belonging to inner-city residents, an example being the seven-storey building constructed in Denman Street, Piccadilly, London, in 1901. In America the term is applied to a building, usually multi-storey, in which cars are parked. In both Britain and America the term is applied to a building adjacent to or incorporated into a dwelling for the covered storage of a vehicle. In Britain 'garage' is commonly used as synonymous with SERVICE STATION or MOTORCAR SHOWROOM, particularly if the establishment incorporates a repair shop. Specially designed prefabricated domestic garages were on sale in England by the mid-1920s.

BIBLIOGRAPHY
General
Burgess-Wise, 1981; Conradi, 1931; Richardson, 1977; Ware, 1976.
Specific
Ricciati, J. W. *Garages and Service Stations*. Hainlin, 1952.

garden city Although the city of CHRISTCHURCH, New Zealand, was called a garden city almost from its beginnings in 1850, and although Alexander T. Steward established a suburb called Garden City on Long Island, New York, in 1869 which had been copied in ten other

Figure 50 Houses in the 'garden-city style' workers' quarter constructed by the Rotterdam Drydock Company in 1913–18 and renovated in the 1980s
Siem Pama

settlements in the United States by 1900, the term usually applies to the kind of balanced community envisaged in 1899 by Ebenezer Howard (1850–1928) in his book *Tomorrow: a Peaceful Path to Real Reform*, which was reprinted in 1902 as *Garden Cities of Tomorrow*. Howard envisaged cities with varied and strictly zoned industrial manufactures, low-density housing set in spacious gardens, a vigorous community life, and encircling green belts. Welwyn Garden City 38 km (24 mi.) N. of London, was defined in 1919 as 'a town designed for healthy living and industry; of a size that makes possible a full measure of social life, but not larger; surrounded by a rural belt; the whole of the land being in public ownership or held in trust for the community'. Howard's ideals were realized in Letchworth, 56 km (35 mi.) N. of London, England, where a site was acquired in 1903 for a town planned by RAYMOND UNWIN and Barry Parker, and at Welwyn Garden City, where building began in 1919. Strictly speaking these are the only garden cities built according to Howard's ideals, but the term 'garden-city style' is applied in most countries to suburbs, to company settlements like those in the RUHRGEBIET, and to the celebrated English examples of Bournville (*see* BIRMINGHAM), PORT SUNLIGHT and New Earswick (*see* YORK), which were laid out in similar ways.

The concept had a profound long-term influence on planning in Britain, particularly on NEW TOWNS. The Garden City Association, formed in 1899, became the Garden Cities and Town Planning Association in 1909, and the Town and Country Planning Association in 1941.

BIBLIOGRAPHY
General
Culpin, 1913; Darley, 1975; Fishman, 1977; Hartmann, 1977; Howard, 1946; Macfadyen, 1933; Meakin, 1905; Mumford, 1938, 1961; Purdom, 1913, 1925, 1963; Sennett, 1905; Soissons, 1989; Viet, 1960.

BARRIE TRINDER

garden suburb   A suburb laid out like the residential area of a GARDEN CITY, with low-density housing, often in historicist styles, many open spaces, many trees, and a profusion of communal buildings. The concept of a 'suburb', however, implying as it does dependence on a city, is in contradiction with Ebenezer Howard's ideal of the garden city as an economically balanced community.

BIBLIOGRAPHY
General
Howard, 1946.

gas   In a chemical sense, a substance that takes the form of a vapour at atmospheric temperature (*see* BUTANE; CARBON DIOXIDE; CHLORINE; ETHENE; ETHYNE; HELIUM; HYDROGEN; METHANAL; METHANE; NEON; NITROGEN; OXYGEN; PROPANE; PROPENE). In an industrial sense the term usually refers to a gas used as a fuel or illuminant (*see* COAL GAS; NATURAL GAS; PRODUCER GAS; TOWN GAS; WATER GAS), either artificially produced by distillation or carburation, or obtained naturally.

gas engine   A machine producing mechanical power by the internal combustion of a mixture of inflammable gas, in practice most commonly TOWN GAS, and air. The principle was described in 1809 by Sir George Cayley, who was seeking power for an aircraft, and developed by Christian Reithmann (1818–1909) in Munich in the 1860s and 70s. The first commercially successful gas

Figure 51   The brick-built gasholder house dating from 1888 at Concord, New Hampshire; this is the only structure of its kind in the United States with the gasholder surviving within. To its left is a more conventional steel-framed gasholder.
Barrie Trinder

engines were built by the Frenchman Étienne Lenoir (1822–1900), whose design, patented in 1860, was widely adopted. It was improved by Nikolaus August Otto (1832–91); after producing many oil engines with 'free-flying' pistons in association with Eugen Langen (1833–95) from 1867, Otto demonstrated a successful four-stroke engine in 1876, and had built more than 30 000 of them at a factory near Cologne by 1886. They were also built under licence in the USA and elsewhere. Most gas engines were of 12 hp or less, and were effective and economical sources of power for workshops and factories of modest size.

BIBLIOGRAPHY
General
Strandh, 1979.

gasholder   The most prominent features of most GAS-WORKS are the holders, which are used to store sufficient gas to compensate for fluctuations in load, and as a precaution against breakdown. Early holders were rectangular iron tanks inverted in water, which is universally used as an elastic, gas-tight seal. Most gasholders since 1814 have been in the form of inverted cylindrical bells, still set in tanks of water. The bells were most commonly held in place by a framework of cast-iron columns, later of steel sections, braced by horizontal girders and diagonal ties. In 1824 Tait devised a holder in which the bells, supported on guide-towers, telescoped into each other, accommodating more gas for the same

ground area. Small gasworks had single-lift holders, larger ones had telescopic, compound holders. The spirally guided holder with no external support was invented in Britain by W. Gadd, and first used in 1888. Some gasholders have been housed within brick, stone or timber buildings, as at Concord, NEW HAMPSHIRE, Troy, NEW YORK, Vienna and Warwick, England. A 'gasometer', the invention of Samuel Clegg in Britain in 1815, measured the gas as it passed from the holder to the mains.

BIBLIOGRAPHY
General
Meade, 1916.

CHRISTOPHER GREEN

gasoline   *See* PETROL.

gasworks   A works where coal gas is produced by heating coal in retorts to a temperature of 1350 °C, usually by using PRODUCER GAS. The basic pattern of works developed by WILLIAM MURDOCK (*see* COAL GAS) remained in use until the late twentieth century. Gas from the retort was collected into a submerged GASHOLDER. Early nineteenth-century horizontal retorts were of cast iron, but from 1850 REFRACTORIES were more generally used, and from the early twentieth century semi-vertical retorts like those of coke ovens were employed in Britain. Retorts were charged by hand in the early nineteenth century, a practice which continued at very small works, but by

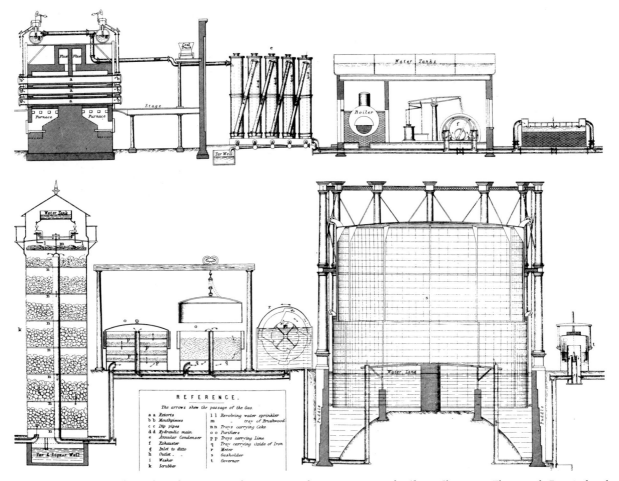

Figure 52 A section through a characteristic late nineteenth-century gasworks (from *Chemistry, Theoretical, Practical and Analytical, as applied to the Arts and Manufactures*, by 'Writers of Eminence', London: William Mackenzie, n.d., *c*.1870)

1900 mechanical charging of coal and unloading of coke was general in larger installations. During the nineteenth century increasingly sophisticated systems were added between production and storage. Gas from retorts was collected in hydraulic mains. Ammoniacal liquors (*see* AMMONIA) were removed by washing and by 'scrubbing' – passing gas through vessels filled with coke, wooden boards or ceramic drainpipes, to bring it into contact with large areas of wetted surface. Hydrogen sulphide (H_2S) was removed by passing the gas through beds of hydrated iron oxide and lime, the resultant iron sulphate being used for the manufacture of sulphuric acid. TAR deposits were collected from condensers, scrubbers and the hydraulic main. The gases from the retorts were diluted to produce TOWN GAS. Gas was stored in GAS-HOLDERS before distribution.

Most early gasworks were parts of such manufacturing complexes as textile factories, but by the mid-nineteenth century companies supplying domestic and industrial customers via networks of mains had been widely estab-

lished. Many became publicly-owned utilities, and city works of the late nineteenth century could be very large undertakings, that at Beckton, London, covering 254 ha (627 ac.).

See also ATHENS; BIGGAR; FAKENHAM; WARSAW; WARWICK; and figure 7.

BIBLIOGRAPHY
General
Coe, 1934; Davidson, 1923; Everard, 1949; Herring, 1893; Hornby, 1913; Meade, 1934; Morgan and Pratt, 1938; Stewart, 1958.
Specific
A day at the Westminster gasworks. In *Penny Magazine*, 1842.
Wilson, G. B. L. The small country gasworks. In *TNS*, XLVI, 1973.

CHRISTOPHER GREEN

Gateshead, Tyne and Wear, England   *See* NEWCASTLE-UPON-TYNE.

Gaudí, Antoni (1852–1926) A Catalan architect of remarkable imagination, whose buildings form a distinctive element in the landscape of CATALONIA, particularly of BARCELONA. He and his followers drew inspiration from Gothic and Moorish buildings to develop an original means of building, using sinuous, undulating shapes and polychromatic surfaces. In an international context his style can be interpreted as a Catalan and revolutionary development of ART NOUVEAU. Many of his important works were churches, but in Barcelona he was responsible for Güell Park, a housing development; a central market, the Sala de les Cent Columnes, built in 1900–14, where eighty-six Doric columns support an undulating ceiling ornamented with mosaics; and the Casa Batlló apartment block of 1905. Other notable Catalan architects working in the Art Nouveau style included Puigi Cadafalch, Cesar Martinell, Lluís Moncunill and Per Falquers.

BIBLIOGRAPHY
General
Martinell, 1960; Sweeney and Sert, 1960.

gauge A standard measurement. In an industrial context the word commonly refers to the distance between the inner running faces of the rails of a railway; the minimum width of locks and bridges on a canal or river; an instrument for measuring, particularly one showing the pressure of gas or liquid in a system; or a device used for checking the sizes of tools or workpieces in mass-manufacturing, or one employed for marking lines on wood or metal before cutting.

See also BROAD-GAUGE RAILWAY; LOADING GAUGE; NARROW-GAUGE RAILWAY; RAILWAY.

Gävle (Gefle), Gävleborg, Sweden A major port on the Baltic, 160 km (100 mi.) N. of Stockholm, with a current population of 90 000. It has flourished since the Middle Ages. Its historic trade in fish is now much reduced, although herring are still smoked with spruce twigs in the area. The principal exports have long been timber and pulp products, while oil is a significant import. Gävle has suffered four serious fires in its history. The broad boulevards which are a feature of the current town plan were laid out as fire breaks during the rebuilding after the last fire, in 1869. The so-called 'old town' which escaped the fire has many eighteenth-century houses lining its cobbled streets.

The Swedish Railway Museum has been located at Gävle since the 1970s. The collection includes several early examples of Swedish locomotive-building, among them a 1.1 m (3 ft. $7\frac{1}{2}$ in.) gauge 0–6–0 well-tank built in ESKILSTUNA in 1855; a 1.22 m (4 ft.) gauge 2–4–0T of 1865, the first locomotive built by Nydqvist & Holm of TROLLHÄTTAN; and *Carlsund*, a standard-gauge 0–6–0T of 1862, the first locomotive built by MOTALA Verstad. There are several locomotives by Beyer Peacock of MANCHESTER, the oldest dating from 1856; and a tiny 0–4–0T of 1873, one of the first products of Henry Hughes & Co. of LOUGHBOROUGH, a company which developed into the Brush Electrical Co. The larger twentieth-century locomo-

tives were mostly built in Sweden. A class Z electric locomotive of 1910, one of the first generation built for the iron-ore railways in Norrland, is also preserved.

The regional museum, founded in 1940 following a bequest by the Rettig family (who established a large tobacco business in the city in the nineteenth century), includes collections relating to shipping, textiles and the material culture of the region.

Silvanum is the principal Swedish museum of forestry. The site includes an arboretum.

LOCATIONS
[M] Järnvägsmuseum (Railway Museum), Rälsg 1, Box 571, 801 08 Gävle.
[M] Länsmuseet i Gävleborgs lä (Gävle Regional Museum), Sodra Strandgatan 20, Box 746, 8012 28 Gävle.
[M] Silvanum, Kungsbäcksvägen 32, S-802 28 Gävle.

BARRIE TRINDER

Gay-Lussac tower A coke-filled tower up to 20 m (64 ft.) high, and 5 m (16 ft.) in diameter, taking its name from the French chemist Joseph Louis Gay-Lussac (1778–1850), who devised the principle in 1827. Nitrous fumes from the lead-chamber process for making SULPHURIC ACID were dissolved in concentrated sulphuric acid to prevent their escape into the atmosphere. The process was used on a large scale from *c.*1860 in conjunction with GLOVER TOWERS, which enabled gases to be reused. The remains of one tower can be seen at HALTON.

BIBLIOGRAPHY
General
Partington, 1950.

Gdańsk (Danzig), Poland For centuries one of the principal ports of the Baltic, and a traditional source of grain for export. The Maritime Museum was established in 1960–5 on the initiative of the Society of Friends of the Maritime Museum. It was recognized in 1972 as the Central Maritime Museum for Poland. The collections include tools used in building boats, models of ships, life-saving equipment, fairway markings, and items illustrating the history of inland and coastal navigation. There are also displays concerned with yachting, water sports, tourism and marine art. The offices and some exhibits are located in the fifteenth-century Big Harbour Crane, which was originally one of the city gates, reconstructed to function as a crane for setting masts and handling cargo. Inside the crane there is a reconstructed wheel-hoist. Several old granaries on the Oławianka River are being reconstructed as exhibition rooms.

The Fishermen's Museum at Hel is a branch of the Central Maritime Museum, and is located in a fifteenth-century Protestant church by the outlet from the harbour. The museum is concerned only with sea fisheries, and exhibits include fishing nets, anchors and inshore fishing boats.

Another branch is the Museum of Lighthouses at Rozewie near Władysławowo, 56 km (35 mi.) NW of Gdańsk, established in 1962 in a nineteenth-century

289

lighthouse. The displays illustrate the development of lighthouses all over the world, and in Poland in particular.

The Big Mill in Gdańsk was built by the Teutonic knights on a channel of the Radunia River in the mid-sixteenth century and has been destroyed and rebuilt many times. Power was provided by eighteen overshot water wheels. In plan the building is an elongated rectangle. The walls are of brick and its seven storeys are covered with a large pitched roof. The first two floors were used for production, the remainder as warehouses. After modernization in the nineteenth century it operated until 1945. It was reconstructed in 1962–7, since when it has been used as a warehouse. All the milling equipment has been removed and only the water channels under the building now remain as reminders of its past.

The Oliwa ironworks, 12 km ($7\frac{1}{2}$ mi.) NW of Gdańsk, is the only works remaining of many mills which were erected on the Oliwski Stream from the fifteenth century onwards. In the seventeenth century there were about twenty mills, mostly working iron and copper, in the area. Iron was imported from Sweden and some local bog iron was also used. In 1870 there were twelve water-powered hammers in use in nine ironworks. The Oliwa works operated for a short time after World War II, and was opened to the public in 1978 as a branch of the Museum of Technology. Power was provided by three overshot water wheels, driven by water from a reservoir created by damming the Oliwski Stream. Equipment includes two two-ton water-powered hammers, bellows for forge hearths, and eccentric plate shears. All the equipment can be set in motion.

BIBLIOGRAPHY
Specific
Domańska, H. Młyny wodne Gdańska (Water mills in Gdańsk). In *Spotkania z zabytkami* (Encounters with Historical Monuments), 1985.
Smolarek, P. *Muzeum Morskie w Gdańsku* (The maritime museum in Gdańsk). Ossolineum, 1967.
Zbierska, E. Żuraw Gdański – Siedziba Muzeum Morskiego w Gdańsku (The Gdańsk crane – seat of the Maritime Museum in Gdańsk). In *Publikacje Muzeum Morskiego w Gdańsku* (Publications of the Maritime Museum in Gdańsk), II(1) 1964.

LOCATION
[M] Centralne Muzeum Morskie (Central Maritime Museum in Gdańsk), ul. Szeroka 67–8, Gdańsk.

PIOTR GERBER

gear-cutting machine A term applied to any of a family of MACHINE TOOLS employed to cut the teeth of gear wheels. The efficient transmission of power through trains of metal gears depends on the use of mathematical analysis to generate mathematically correct gear-tooth forms. Most early makers followed the adaptation by RICHARD ROBERTS in 1821 of the clockmakers' gear-dividing engine in which the blank can be variably adjusted to bring each tooth in line with a rotating or reciprocal cutter, guided onto the work by template or cam, or formed so as to produce the desired shape of tooth. The principle of meshing a hardened cutter gear with the

blank was introduced in the USA in the late nineteenth century: this dramatically reduced costs towards the end of the century, when the precision grinding of specially-shaped hardened cutters became practicable.

BIBLIOGRAPHY
General
Rolt, 1986; Steeds, 1969.

TIM PUTNAM

Gelsenkirchen, North-Rhine Westphalia, Germany *See* RUHRGEBIET.

generator A device for producing electricity. The earliest, in 1660, produced static electricity by friction of cloth against a variety of substances. Mechanical generators based on DYNAMOS were developed after 1831.
See also ALTERNATOR; POWER STATION.

BIBLIOGRAPHY
General
Dunsheath, 1962.

Geneva (Genève), Geneva, Switzerland A resort, the location for international conferences, and the capital of a canton renowned for its watches and jewellery, Geneva stands at the west end of Lake Geneva, and is divided into two parts by the River Rhône.

Five of the lake steamers dating from before 1927 have been converted to diesel operation, while four – *La Suisse* of 1910, *Savoie* of 1914, *Simplon* of 1920 and *Rhône* of 1927 – remain steam-powered. *Simplon* is the largest paddle steamer in Switzerland, 74 m (242 ft.) long, with capacity for 1500 passengers.

The city abattoir was restored by the city authorities in 1980 and adapted as an arts centre.

'La Coulouvrenière', a turbine-powered water-pumping station of 1883–6, remains with one original pumping unit installed by Escher Wyss.

BIBLIOGRAPHY
General
INSA, 1982–91.
Specific
Barblan, M.-A. and Riva, M. La maison du patrimoine industriel: une initiative orginale à Genève (The industrial heritage centre: an original initiative at Geneva). In *Museum*, CXLII, 1984.
Meystre, N. 100 years ago – a pioneering pump station in Geneva. In *Sulzer Technical Review*, LXVI, 1984.

LOCATIONS
[M] Musée d'Art et d'Histoire, Rue Charles-Galland 2, Geneva.
[M] Musée d'Horlogerie et de l'Émail (Museum of clock- and watchmaking), Route de Malagnou 15, Geneva.

HANS-PETER BÄRTSCHI

Genoa (Genova), Liguria, Italy The most important port in Italy, Genoa bristles with industrial archaeology, despite the damage inflicted by Allied bombardment during World War II. The most striking feature of the harbour is the Lanterna, a lighthouse built in 1139 and restored in 1543. The oldest quay in the centre of the bay, the Molo Vecchio, originally built in 1257, is covered by a long, double-pile warehouse, six bays deep and of four storeys. There were major extensions to the docks in 1876–88 and in the inter-war period. The liner terminal, the Stazione Marittima, includes a Renaissance-style block dating from the turn of the century, with an entrance under a symbolic longboat into a domed hall. Beyond is a long baggage hall dating from the 1930s, with murals portraying ships, hotels and aircraft. To the west is a newer terminal now used by ferries, the Stazione Marittima Ponte a Doria, a concrete modernist structure with oval towers.

Several metallurgical and engineering works developed in connection with shipbuilding. Ansaldo built their first railway locomotive near Genoa in 1854. The Ansaldo Cantieri Navali at Sestri Ponente, an industrial suburb to the north-west, became Italy's largest shipyard in the inter-war period. The firm developed a major manufacturing complex at nearby Cornigliano-Campi. Several of Ansaldo's factories were designed by Adolfo Ravinetta (1884–1968), who was responsible for industrial plants in many Italian towns. The Archivo Storico Ansaldo was founded in 1977 to collect documents and photographs relating to the company and to establish a documentation centre, now open to the public. A major erecting shop for armaments remains beneath the viaduct of the autostrada. It has Classical detailing in brickwork on the exterior, contrasting with an exposed concrete structure, including simply decorated balconies. Sestri Ponente is dominated by the Ilva Steelworks. The San Giorgio works is far smaller in scale; the factory was one constituent of a major firm which made cars and motor vessels, and which produced armaments during World War I. The office block of 1906 exemplifies the JUGENDSTIL decoration promoted by the Milan Exhibition of the same year. Gino Coppede (1866–1927) used symbols of wheels and geometrical patterns on the exterior and decorative metalwork in the entrance, and created an interior in the manner of a chalet.

Genoa's main railway station, Stazione Piazza Principe, dates from 1860. The richly decorated Renaissance façade, with its caryatids and griffins, signifies the role afforded to railways in unifying the Italian nation. To the west is the lower terminus of one of Genoa's funicular railways, the Ferrovia Principe Granarolo, opened in 1891, which takes the form of a miniature castle with a flagpole decorated with a wrought-iron eagle. It was designed by Coppede.

In the commercial centre, parallel to the Via Roma, is the Galleria Mazzini, built c.1875. It has a unique layout, the arcade running parallel to a main thoroughfare with a series of crossings, marked by large eagles and surmounted by octagonal domes. Several road tunnels ease traffic congestion in the city centre, the Galleria Giuseppe Garibaldi, dating from 1927, having the most grandiose and cavernous portals.

BIBLIOGRAPHY
General
Geist, 1983; Negri *et al.*, 1983; Selvafolta *et al.*, 1983.

LOCATION
[I] Archivo Storico Ansaldo (Ansaldo archives), Cornigliano-Campi, Genoa.

MICHAEL STRATTON

Georgia, United States of America As one of the ringleading Confederate states that sought secession from the Union in the 1860s, Georgia is home to a collection of industrial and engineering sites representing both the economic independence from the North which the state was capable of achieving, and the effort at separation itself. A face of the granite Stone Mountain in central Georgia was carved into deep relief by Gutson Borglum (1867–1941) in the 1920s to memorialize Confederate generals in the Civil War (hereabouts termed 'the War of Northern Aggression') and to demonstrate the possibilities of turning mountains into sculpture (*see* NORTH DAKOTA).

Georgia granite and marble for architectural cladding, bridgework and paving have long been major state exports. In 1828 one of the country's lesser gold rushes occurred in Lumpkin County. The Calhoun Mine in Dahlonega commemorates the event.

The streets of Savannah were laid out from 1733 on a modular grid pattern designed by James Oglethorpe (1696–1785), intermixing residential and public-use areas. This is the nation's earliest city plan still in use, and has been designated a historic civil engineering LANDMARK.

After the havoc of the Civil War, devastated cities like Columbus and Atlanta re-emerged as industrial centres, linked by a web of wartime railways with states north and west. In Columbus the Historic Riverfront Industrial Park contains a string of post-1865 industrial structures now put to commercial and residential uses. The production of textiles continues in structures at the river's edge, but the Columbus Ironworks of 1865 is now a convention centre.

At Fort Benning Army Base, the US Army's Infantry Centre, stand three of industrial archaeology's more unusual structures: parachute-practice jump towers of World War II erected by the Safe Parachute Jump Company.

Near Atlanta, the Tallulah Dam of 1913 channels water from its namesake river through penstocks into turbines under 180 m (600 ft.) of head.

The Savannah railway train shed of 1866, modified in 1877, is a fine example of American long-span trussed roofing, complemented by railway repair buildings of the same era.

BIBLIOGRAPHY
General
Brittain, 1976; Jackson, 1988.

LOCATIONS
[M] Dahlonega Gold Museum, Public Square, Box 2042, Dahlonega, GA 30533.
[M] Georgia Agrirama, Tifton, GA 31793.

[M] Ships of the Sea Museum, 503 E. River Street, Savannah, GA 31401.

[M] South-eastern Railway Museum, 3966 Buford Highway, Duluth, GA 30136.

[S] Stone Mountain Park, Box 778, Stone Mountain, GA 30086.

DAVID H. SHAYT

German Democratic Republic (GDR; Deutsche Demokratische Republik or DDR)   The German Democratic, the DDR, lay between the Baltic to the north, Poland to the east, Czechoslovakia to the south and the Federal Republic of Germany to the west. It extended over some 100000 km² (38000 sq. mi.) and had a population of 16 million. Its fifteen regions, comprising 27 urban and 191 rural administrative districts, were ruled from its capital, East Berlin, which comprised the former centre and the eastern half of the old imperial capital (see BERLIN; GERMAN FEDERAL REPUBLIC). Concentrations of population are found in East Berlin, with its 1.1 million inhabitants, in the Halle and Leipzig area, with two million, the area of Zwickau and Chemnitz (known in the years before 1990 as Karl-Marx-Stadt) with 1.6 million, and the area around Dresden, including the valley of the Elbe between Meissen and Pirna, with about two million.

The north of the former DDR is part of the North German lowlands; the south is part of the low mountain range of central Germany. The constitutional and political history of the DDR began in 1945, when the Soviet occupying power formed Communist and anti-Fascist parties in the most easterly of the four occupied zones of Germany, and a system of administration and government began to be constructed. As early as 1945 there were plans for the division of the old provinces of Brandenburg, Mecklenburg, Saxony, Saxe-Anhalt and Thuringia, and these were completed in 1952. In April 1946 the merging of the KPD (German Communist Party) and the SPD (German Socialist Party) led to the formation of the SED (the Socialist Unity Party of Germany), a significant step in the separation of the Soviet-occupied zone from the three western zones. With the Volksrat as constitutional assembly, and a separate currency reform, a basis for the foundation of a state was achieved. The constitution of the DDR was adopted in 1949. The nascent Cold War in which two social systems confronted each other gradually brought about the recognition of two German states on the territory of the former German Reich, against a background of their integration into the Western and Eastern economic, military and socio-political structures.

The economic and technical development of the DDR between 1945 and 1990 was shaped by the principles of the monopolistic power of the Socialist Unity Party, collective state ownership of the means of production, and a centrally-planned and controlled economic system.

The point of departure for this development was the commercial and industrial structure of the former provinces of the German Reich which made up the DDR. From north to south these were Mecklenburg, Brandenburg, Anhalt, Thuringia and Saxony. Their economic development, particularly their industrial growth in the late nineteenth century and early twentieth century, should be seen in connection with other parts of Germany, particularly the coal and iron region of UPPER SILESIA, and the industrial concentrations in southern and western Germany.

There were two approaches to the public presentation of industrial monuments in the DDR, the first concerned with the conservation and interpretation of structures like bridges which remain in use, and the other with those which no longer function, but which are presented to the public. Attempts have been made to secure the retention of significant numbers of relative common monuments, like the posts (see POST COACH) which marked miles on main roads. Some former industrial buildings have been consciously retained as 'show plants', depicting various aspects of major industries, including water supply in BERLIN and silver mining at FREIBERG. TRAILS have been devised in areas like the Erzgebirge which are rich in industrial monuments.

Within the DDR Saxony is notable for its historic bridges. The stone bridge in Plauen, 70 km (40 mi.) SW of Chemnitz, across the Weisse Elster river, was built in 1230–44, and the Rothenfurt bridge has carried the Freiberg–Meissen road across the River Mulde, 16 km (10 mi.) N. of Freiberg, since the sixteenth century. In 1690–1715 a twelve-arch aqueduct was built across it to carry water to supply power to the Sankt Anna mine in the Freiberg mining district. The aqueduct remained until 1893. A late Gothic stone bridge – the only one in the DDR – was built across the Mulde at Halsbach near Freiberg in 1576. There are two particularly famous railway bridges on the Leipzig–Nuremberg line, the Göltzschtal viaduct and the Elstertal bridge of 1846–51. The former, at Mylau, 50 km (30 mi.) SW of Chemnitz, is 574 m (1883 ft.) long in four ranges of 10, 13, 22 and 28 semicircular headed arches, and is brick-built, with two large central arches, each covering two of the storeys.

The bridges in Wörlitz Park, 20 km (12 mi.) SW of Wittenberg, make up a distinctive group. Duke Leopold Friedrich Franz of Anhalt-Dessau began laying out the park in 1764 with the aid of the architect, Friedrich Wilhelm von Erdmannsdorff, and was much influenced by their joint visits to England, where he saw neo-Gothic buildings and bridges. The wooden stepped bridge was built in 1773, modelled on a bridge at Kew, London, and was known as the Weisse Brücke (White Bridge). A chain bridge, 40 m (130 ft.) long, was built in 1781. In 1791 Duke Leopold had built an imitation of the Iron Bridge, constructed at Coalbrookdale (see IRONBRIDGE) in 1779: it is the earliest preserved iron bridge in Germany.

The iron industry is particularly well represented amongst the preserved industrial monuments of the DDR. The furnace at SCHMALKALDEN is one of the best conserved in Europe, while the Peitz furnace, an architecturally distinguished charcoal-fired blast furnace built in 1809–10, has been preserved at Cottbus, 100 km (60 mi.) SE of Berlin. With these buildings and various hammer forges of earlier periods which are now museums, protected monuments in the DDR provide a comprehensive picture of the history of ironmaking in the first half of the nineteenth century.

See also GERMANY.

BIBLIOGRAPHY
General
Berger, 1980; Schmidt and Theile, 1989, 1991; Wagenbreth and Wächtler, 1983, 1986a.

AXEL FÖHL

German Federal Republic   The German Federal Republic, consisting of those areas of Germany which had been occupied by Britain, France and the USA after 1945, was established in 1949, and became a fully sovereign state in 1955. The federal capital, where the Bundestag (parliament) meets is Bonn. The republic was divided into the Länder (provinces) of BADEN-WÜRTTEMBURG, BAVARIA (Bayern), Bremen, Hamburg, HESSE, Lower Saxony (Niedersachsen), NORTH RHINE-WESTPHALIA (Nordrhein-Westfalen), RHINELAND-PALATINATE (Rheinland-Pfalz), SAARLAND and Schleswig-Holstein. The Saarland only became part of the Republic in 1957. The Länder of Bremen, Hamburg, Lower Saxony and Schleswig-Holstein are discussed under the headword NORTH-WEST GERMANY. The local unit of government in the Federal Republic is the Landkreis or district, and the word 'district' is used in articles on places in the Republic as a translation of Landkreis.

The former Federal Republic included many of the principal industrial regions of Germany, including the RUHRGEBIET, and cities like HAMBURG, HANOVER, MUNICH, STUTTGART, NUREMBERG and AUGSBURG. West Germany experienced a remarkable economic revival, known as the Wirtschaftswunderjahre (economic miracle) between the late 1950s and the early 1970s, which made it the most prosperous of the European powers. It became a founder member of the European Economic Community in 1958.

Each of the Länder in the German Federal Republic is independent in cultural affairs, and consequently each has its own conservation, although there is much that is common between the laws of the various states. Typically a monument is defined as a man-made object, group of objects or part of an object, that is of such historical scientific or artistic value that its preservation serves a public interest. The terms 'historic', 'scientific' and 'artistic' are so interpreted as to include industrial monuments and features of urban design. The law also extends protection to the surroundings of a monument. A distinction is made in lists of protected monuments between built monuments, movable objects like sculpture or paintings, and archaeological monuments, whose valuable features are principally below ground. In the administration of conservation legislation a further distinction is made between the care of monuments (Denkmalpflege) and the protection and care of monuments (Denkmalschutz). The former is the responsibility of specific bodies, called Landesdenkmalamt or Landesamt für Denkmalpflege, in most of the states. The protection of monuments is seen as part of the powers of the state governments, and is usually delegated to state, city or district officials responsible for building matters and cultural affairs. From the early 1970s industrial monuments have increasingly figured as objects for listing and protection, following the appointment in North Rhine-Westphalia in 1973 of an inspector with specific responsibilities for the subject.

Outstanding amongst traditional museums in Germany dealing with industrial topics is the Deutsches Museum in MUNICH, one of the world's major repositories of technological artefacts (*see* MUSEUM). Many old-established city and district museums of local history are concerned to some extent with industries, particularly with such products as ceramics, domestic ironware and furniture. In the twentieth century, particularly the period since the 1950s, there has been a marked growth of traditional OPEN-AIR MUSEUMS in the Federal Republic, most of which include some buildings concerned with manufactures. From the early 1970s there was a marked change in policy relating to the portrayal of industry in museums, particularly in the Ruhrgebiet, where a strong emphasis came to be placed on the preservation *in situ* of historic industrial monuments as site museums, rather than on removing them to centralized museums. There have nevertheless been some innovative and imaginative interpretations of the industrial past in more conventional settings (*see* BERLIN; MANNHEIM).

About 250 former main-line steam locomotives are preserved in the former Federal Republic, including over fifty of the 2–10–0s built during World War II, together with about forty electric locomotives, among them several main-line locomotives of the 1930s, and about thirty diesels. There are over ninety railway preservation projects in the former Federal Republic.

The standard maps used in historical research in the Federal Republic are the Grundkarten, at a scale of 1:5000, produced by the cartographic offices in each of the states.

BIBLIOGRAPHY
General
Garvin and Fox, 1985; Henning, 1974b; Treue, 1970.

LOCATION
[I] Deutsche Gesellschaft für Eisenbahngeschichte (German Association for Railway History), Postfach 1627, 7100 Heilbronn.

AXEL FÖHL, NORBERT MENDGEN and BARRIE TRINDER

German forge   A type of forge employed in Sweden in which pig iron was melted in a finery hearth, bigger and deeper than that used in the OSMUND IRON process. The bloom was worked under the hammer, and then reheated in the finery hearth before being brought back to the hammer and worked into bars.

BIBLIOGRAPHY
General
Beck, 1891, 1893–5; Odelstierna, 1913.

Germany   The geographical limits of Germany have always been difficult to define. In the Middle Ages, the Holy Roman Empire extended over most of the German

Germany

lands, although the emperors, the Austrian Habsburgs, exercised little real power. Germany was devastated by the Thirty Years War, which ended with the Treaty of Westphalia in 1648. The treaty recognized over three hundred states, many of them very small, most of which

remained in existence until the armies of revolutionary France invaded Germany in the early 1790s.

During the eighteenth century Prussia rose to be the most powerful of the German states, a European power able to deal on equal terms with France or Britain. At the same time the Austrian Habsburgs extended their authority along the Danube and into the Balkans at the expense of the declining Turkish Empire. Both states gained further territories with the successive partitions of Poland in 1772, 1793 and 1794. In the Habsburg Empire especially, and to a lesser extent in Prussia, cultural as distinct from political boundaries were hard to define. The language of the Empire was German, and German was the language of trade in most towns. The families of many town-dwellers originated in areas that were unquestionably German. Yet most of those who lived in the countryside were of other nationalities. In other directions boundaries were frequently confused. There was no clear demarcation between Danish and German culture in Schleswig in the south of the Jutland peninsula. Alsace, where Strasbourg was annexed by King Louis XIV of France in 1681, long retained many elements of German culture. German is still the native language of parts of eastern Belgium, of some Swiss cantons, and of the South Tirol, which is now part of Italy.

Germany was thrown into confusion by the French invasions of the 1790s, and in 1806 the Holy Roman Empire was formally ended by Napoleon. The Treaty of Vienna of 1815 which brought a formal end to two decades of European conflict established a German Confederation of thirty-nine states, including Austria. Prussia gained substantial territories in the Rhineland and Westphalia in 1815, greatly increasing the state's industrial potential (*see* BERGISCHES LAND; COLOGNE; RUHRGEBIET; WUPPERTAL); and it was the Prussian-inspired customs union, the Zollverein, which was established in 1818 and covered most of Germany by 1834, that provided the main economic stimulus to unification. Rivalry between Prussia and Austria led to war in 1866 in which the Prussians were victorious; Prussia subsequently annexed Schleswig, Holstein, Hanover, Hesse-Cassel, Nassau and Frankfurt am Main. The remaining states north of the River Main joined the North German Confederation, in which Prussia was dominant. The states in southern Germany, Bavaria, Württemberg, Baden and Hesse-Darmstadt remained independent but joined the customs union, and participated with the Confederation in war against France in 1870. After victory in the war, which led to the annexation of Alsace and part of LORRAINE, the Confederation was transformed into a German Empire, with the King of Prussia as its Emperor. The southern states acknowledged the authority of the Emperor, but retained significant economic powers, including, in Bavaria and Württemberg, control of their own railways and postal services.

Germany's boundaries were reduced after the defeat of the Empire in World War I, principally by the re-creation of an independent Poland in the east, and the return of Alsace-Lorraine to France in the west. The victorious Allies in 1919 attempted to forbid the unification of Germany and AUSTRIA. Under the governments of the Weimar Republic in the 1920s and early 1930s, Germany suffered severe inflation and high unemployment. The coming to power of the Nazi Party of Adolf Hitler (1889–1945) in 1933, and the proclamation of the Third Reich

(empire) led to the renewal of expansionist foreign policies. Austria and Germany were united by the Anschluss of 1938; and before the end of the year the Sudetenland, part of the independent CZECHOSLOVAKIA created in 1919, had been annexed to Germany, with the connivance of the British and French governments, as a result of the Munich agreement. Further territorial demands on Poland led to the outbreak of World War II in September 1939. France, Belgium, Denmark and Norway were invaded in 1940, and Russia and the Balkans in 1941. For a short time the Third Reich extended from the Atlantic to the Urals and from the North Cape to the Crimea, and increasingly the economies both of Germany itself and of the occupied countries were given over to war production. Successive defeats in the east by the Red Army, and, after the invasions of Italy in 1943 and Normandy in 1944, by the armies of Britain, the USA and their allies in the west, led to the collapse of German power in May 1945. In the east the boundary of Germany was fixed along the Oder–Neisse line, Silesia being incorporated within the boundaries of Poland. Germany was divided into four zones of occupation, controlled by the USSR, the USA, Britain and France. Growing antagonism between the USSR and the other powers led in 1949 to the formation of two separate states, the GERMAN FEDERAL REPUBLIC in the west and the GERMAN DEMOCRATIC REPUBLIC (the DDR) in the east. The two were united in 1990.

Many parts of Germany had highly-developed economies long before the nineteenth century. The mining of metals in the Erzgebirge (*see* FREIBERG AND THE ERZGEBIRGE) and the HARZ MOUNTAINS, the production of tools in the BERGISCHES LAND, and the textiles manufactures based on AUGSBURG and AACHEN were of European importance long before the Industrial Revolution. The French Revolution of 1789, by dissolving old social restraints, proved an invigorating stimulus to the economies of the German states, and extension of Prussian power in the Rhineland by the post-war settlement of 1815 brought to a region with vast natural resources the authority of a government accustomed to using its efficient civil service to encourage economic growth. By 1850 the Ruhrgebiet had become one of the principal coal- and iron-producing regions of Europe, its development stimulated first by steamships on the RHINE and then by the growth of railways.

Main-line railways were largely responsible for the economic integration of Germany during the nineteenth century. The first was opened in 1835 between NUREMBERG and Fürth. The system reached its peak in 1914 when there were 62 410 route km (38 780 mi.) of railway in the then German Empire, worked by 32 798 locomotives. The various lines, some worked by private companies and some by state governments, were brought under the unified control of the Deutsche Reichsbahn Gesellschaft in 1924. Railways in the German Federal Republic were placed under the Deutsche Bundesbahn in 1949. Railways also greatly increased Germany's significance as a European power, since most of the routes between eastern and western, or northern and southern, Europe had to pass through German territory.

During the latter part of the nineteenth century

Germany became the dominant economic power in continental Europe, and was far outstripping Great Britain in technological innovation. The development of aniline dyes laid the foundation for many of the processes that have been of the greatest importance in twentieth-century chemical manufacturing. Engineering came to be a major industry in southern German cities like AUGSBURG, MUNICH, NUREMBERG and STUTTGART which were remote from the principal iron-making districts. German manufacturers sold railway locomotives in many European countries, and were prominent in the production of electrical apparatus, and later of motorcars. Above all, BERLIN became one of the world's greatest manufacturing cities.

A particular feature of German industrial development by the early twentieth century was the concern shown for architectural quality by such architects as PETER BEHRENS of the Deutsches Werkbund movement, and others associated with the BAUHAUS. In consequence the proportion of German industrial monuments of high artistic merit, whether railway stations, coal-mine headstocks, engineering works or toy factories, is much higher than in any other country.

See also AACHEN; ALFELD; ANHALT/SAXONY; AUGSBURG; BAD EMS; BADEN-WÜRTTEMBERG; BAD REICHENHALL; BAVARIA; BEHRENS, PETER; BENDORF; BENZ, KARL FRIEDRICH; BERGISCHES LAND; BERLIN; BRANDENBURG; BREMEN; BREMERHAVEN; BRUNSWICK; CHEMNITZ; CHIEMSEE; CLOPPENBURG; COLOGNE; DAIMLER, GOTTLIEB WILHELM; DANUBE, RIVER; DARMSTADT; DETMOLD; DRESDEN; DÜSSELDORF; EIFEL; FEHMARN; FISCHBACH-CAMPHAUSEN; FORBACH AN DER MURG; FRANKFURT AM MAIN; FREIBERG AND THE ERZGEBIRGE; FRIEDRICHSHAFEN; GERMAN DEMOCRATIC REPUBLIC; GERMAN FEDERAL REPUBLIC; GIENGEN AN DER BRENZ; GÖTTINGEN; GUTACH IM SCHWARZWALD; HAIGERLOCH-STETTEN; HAMBURG; HANOVER; HANSEATIC LEAGUE; HARZ MOUNTAINS; HEMFURTH; HESSE; IDAR-OBERSTEIN AND ASBACHERHÜTTE; KASSEL; KAUFUNGEN; KIEL; KOCHELSEE AND WALCHENSEE; KUCHEN; LAUCHERTHAL; LAUENBURG; LEIPZIG; LOLLAR; LÜNEBURG; MAINZ; MANNHEIM; MECKLENBURG; MELDORF; METTLACH; MIES VAN DER ROHE, LUDWIG; MINDEN-LÜBBECKE; MOSELLE; MUNICH; NECKAR; NENNDORF; NEUSTADT AN DER WEINSTRASSE; NIEDERFINOW; NORTH RHINE-WESTPHALIA; NORTH-WEST GERMANY; NUREMBERG; OBERURSEL; OCHSENHAUSEN; REINHARDSHAGEN; REMSCHEID; REUTLINGEN; RHEINBÖLLEN; RHEINFELDEN; RHINE; RHINELAND PALATINATE; ROSTOCK; RUHRGEBIET; RÜSSELSHEIM; SAARLAND; SALZGITTER; SCHINKEL, KARL FRIEDRICH; SCHMALKALDEN; SCHRAMBERG; SCHWÄBISCH GMÜND; SOLMS; STADTHAGEN; STUTTGART; THEUERN; THURINGIA; UNTERREGENBACH; VÖLKLINGEN; WALDALGESHEIM; WASSERALFINGEN; WEILBURG; WERRA; WETZLAR; WILHELMSHAVEN; WOLFSBURG; WRISBERGHOLZEN; WUPPERTAL; ZEITZ.

BIBLIOGRAPHY
General
Beer, 1949; Berthold *et al.*, 1985, 1988; Buddensieg and Henning, 1981; Drebusch, 1976; Föhl and Hamm, 1985, 1988; Henderson, 1975; Henning, 1973, 1974a, 1974b; IRB Themendokumentationen, 1986; Lindner, 1927; Lindner and Steinmetz, 1923; Matschoss, 1927–40; Müller-Wulckow, 1925; Paul, 1976, 1977, 1978, 1980a, 1980b; Paulinyi, 1975; Slotta, 1975, 1977, 1980, 1982, 1983, 1986, 1988; Sturm, 1977; Treue 1970, 1980.

Specific
Matschoss, C. and Lindner, W. ed. Technische Kulturdenkmale (Technical monuments). In *Auftrag der Agricola-Gesellschaft beim Deutschen Museum*. Munich: Verlag F. Bruckmann AG 1932.
Wolff, K. H. Guildmaster into millhand: the industrialization of linen and cotton in Germany to 1850. In *TH*, x, 1979.

AXEL FÖHL and BARRIE TRINDER

Ghent (Gand, Gent), Oost Vlaanderen, Belgium The capital city of East Flanders lies on the Rivers Scheldt (Schelde) and Leie and is intersected by numerous other natural and artificial waterways. Calico printing was established in the city in the mid-eighteenth century, but from c.1800 it grew rapidly, Ghent becoming a major European cotton-spinning city, sometimes known as the 'Manchester of Belgium'.

Several major textile buildings survive. A steam-powered mill of 1839–41 on the English pattern on Korianderstraat was closed in 1894 and later adapted to successive new uses. The J. de Hemptinne works on Opgeëistenlaan is a spinning mill with multi-storey blocks from 1853–4, later north-lit sheds, and two surviving Lancashire boilers. Two large Lancashire-style mills of the late nineteenth century are La Nouvelle Orléans spinning mill in Nieuwevaart, with buildings of 1896, 1899 and 1905, and the Filature de Roygem in Rooigemlaan, of 1897–1905. Other fabrics were also produced in Ghent, and some buildings relating to them remain. The Filature de Rabot in Frans Van Rijhovelaan is a jute-spinning mill of 1899, extended with ART NOUVEAU detailing in 1912. On Vogelenzan is the flax-spinning mill of La Société Linière Gantoise, dating from c.1840, with a vast neo-Classical house, and an adjacent director's house of 1862–4 in Second Empire style. There is an early spinning mule (called a jenny in Ghent) in the MIAT museum.

Much of the city's late-nineteenth-century industry was located on the canal to the north, including the former Laroche-Lechat rubber works on Edward Pyndertkaai, where the surviving buildings date from 1913, and the Belgian Paper Mills at Langerbrugge, of 1929–30. A power station at Langerbrugge, the Centrale Électrique des Flandres, is preserved as an energy museum. The building, designed by E. d'Huicque in 1913, has an elaborate brick façade with broad semicircular arched doorways, with a clerestoried lightweight steel truss roof. Two Brown Boveri generating sets have been retained.

Working-class housing of a highly distinctive type was built in Ghent from the 1820s until the early twentieth century. Houses were built in parallel ranges around courts known as Beluikencomplex, or inner blocks, and were approached by passages between larger buildings fronting onto main thoroughfares, often through arched entrances, one of which, dating from the 1860s, remains in Castellaan. There were about seven hundred such courts in the city in 1880, housing about a quarter of the population. Their layout was often shaped by earlier buildings which had grown up on the fringe of the city's built-up area, including medieval farmsteads, seventeenth-century suburban houses, and a former distillery. One such court, the Meerhembeluik, has been preserved.

Housing of a different nature is to be found in the vicinity of the main railway station where many middle-class villas of the turn of the century are decorated with ceramics in the Art Nouveau style, including several with faience from the Leeds Fireclay Company.

Two power station buildings in the INTERNATIONAL MODERN style by J. De Bondt remain in the city, one of 1934 in Gebr De Smetstraat, and one of 1935 in J. Van Stopenberghestraat.

Significant retailing buildings in Ghent include a large co-operative store of 1894 on Vrijdagsmarkt, and an arcade, the Vanderdoncttdoorgang, built in 1846–51 to designs by Louis Eyckens in the Late Empire style. The Coliseum, formerly the Valentino cinema, in Kuiperskaai is an Art Nouveau building of 1911. The Van Eyck bathhouse in Julius De Vigneplein dates from 1886, and is an early concrete structure by J. Monier & Co. A cast-iron bandstand of 1885 in Citadel Park is one of the most ornate in Europe.

St Peter's Station is a crenellated brick structure of 1908–12, by L. Cloquet, with polychrome stone arcading in the booking hall, completed for an exhibition of 1913. The city retains an extensive tramway network.

BIBLIOGRAPHY
General
Linters, 1986a; Viaene, 1986.
Specific
Debleeckere, G. Energeia: l'importance d'un Musée d'Archéologie Industrielle à Langerbrugge (Energeia: the importance of a museum of industrial archaeology at Langerbrugge). In *Électricité*, CLXXXVI, 1986.

LOCATIONS
[M] Archief en Museum van de Socialistische Arbeitersbeweging (Archives and Museum of the Socialist Workers' Movement), St Pietersnieuwstraat 23, 9000 Ghent.
[M] Electriciteitsmuseum Energeia, Langerbruggekaai 3, 9000 Ghent.
[M] Museum voor de Geschiedenis der Wetenschappen van de Rijksuniversiteit (Museum for Diffusion of Scientific and Technical Knowledge), Korte Meer 9, 9000 Ghent.
[M] Museum voor Industriële Archeologie en Textiel (MIAT; Museum of the Industrial Archaeology of Textiles), Gewad 13, 9000 Ghent.
[M] Museum voor Volkskunde (Folk-life Museum), Kraanlei 63, 9000 Ghent.

BARRIE TRINDER

Gibraltar   The rock of Gibraltar, on the northern side of the 13 km (8 mi.) straits that separate Europe and Africa at the western end of the Mediterranean, has been held by Britain since 1704, although Spain claims sovereignty. The area of the territory is only 7 km² (3 sq. mi.), and its industrial archaeological interest lies in its naval facilities. Installations in the eighteenth century were mostly of a rudimentary nature, but a hospital, which survives, was built before 1746. During the Napoleonic Wars in the first decade of the nineteenth century an underground drinking-water reservoir was built, lined with bricks which had to be carried from England; and a two-storey 60 m × 50 m (190 ft. × 160 ft.) storehouse for victualling supplies, which still stands, was commenced in 1807.

BIBLIOGRAPHY
General
Coad, 1983, 1989.

LOCATION
[M] Gibraltar Museum, 18–20 Bomb House Lane, Gibraltar.

Giengen an der Brenz, Baden-Württemberg, Germany   An architecturally revolutionary building forms part of the plant of the Steiff company, founded *c.*1880 in Giengen, 32 km (20 mi.) NE of Ulm, by Margarete Steiff for the manufacture of teddy bears and other soft toys. The building, made entirely of iron and glass, was erected by the Eisenwerke München in 1903: it is 30 m (98 ft.) long, 12 m (39 ft.) wide and 9.4 m (31 ft.) high. The outer shell consists of a continuous double-glazed wall and a flat roof. Inside are three floors, supported, like the roof, on six iron lattice-work columns. The corner columns comprise frameworks of riveted H-sections. Other buildings were erected between 1904 and 1910 in imitation of the original, but of wooden construction. This entirely plain building was a pioneering design in that it represents a very early use of the curtain-wall principle. It still serves its original purpose as a production plant and warehouse. Toymaking is illustrated in the town museum.

LOCATION
[M] Stadtmuseum (Town Museum), Rathus, 7928 Giengen an der Brenz.

Gijón, Oviedo, Asturias, Spain   On the Biscay coast of Asturias, 25 km (15 mi.) NE of Oviedo, Gijón developed as a port for the export of coal.

The Carbonera Highway was built in 1789 to carry coal to Gijón, and was followed in 1847 by the Langreo Railway, constructed under the patronage of the Duke of Riánsares, second husband of Queen Maria Cristina, which was intended to link the Nalón valley with the port. The railway was extended from its original terminus at Carbayín to Pola de Laviana, 32 m (20 mi.) S., in 1857. The railway facilities now belong to the state company FEVE (Ferrocarriles Españoles de Vía Estrecha). The route has undergone some minor alterations, but most of the original facilities remain intact, except for the terminus at Gijón, demolished in 1985.

The Lantero timber yard in Gijón is regarded as one of the most important industrial monuments in Asturias, and has recently been saved from destruction during the implementation of the town's planning scheme. The timber industry in Asturias was a key influence on mining and manufacturing in general. The main building in the Lantero yard measures 25 m × 66 m (82 ft. × 218 ft.), and is made up of twenty trusses of Finnish pine. The available evidence suggests that it was constructed *c.*1916 by the enterprise's own labour force and master carpenters. The first proprietor was Aquilino Lantero Bayón. As a result of reorganization within the company and the opening of new storage yards at Santander, Bilbao and Galicia, the facilities at Gijón were closed in 1980. In 1984 the town planning scheme proposed a new railway station in the vicinity. When the new station is completed the building will be dismantled and stored until a use is found. The architects designing a new Gijón Railway and Industry Museum have proposed to incorporate it as a machinery gallery displaying exhibits relating to industrialization in Asturias.

The La Camocha coal mine is in the parish of Vega in the Gijón district, 8 km (5 mi.) from the town centre, on the railway to San Martín de Huerces. The earliest prospecting for mines at La Camocha was in 1900. Coal was located at a depth of 160 m (520 ft.) in the following year. In April 1914 a second sounding began at a nearby site named Caldones, but at a depth of 563 m (1850 ft.) there was a sudden release of gas which caused a raging fire, known locally as the 'Caldones Flue', which left behind a derelict tower. In 1920 a steam winding machine was purchased from the German company Gütehoffnungshütte (GHH) of Oberhausen-Sterkrade, for the Santa Bárbara mine of the Turón company, but it was acquired by the Sociedad Anónima Felgueroso, owners of the La Camocha mine, who installed it at their Shaft No. 2, where it continues to operate, despite having sustained some damage. It is just over a century and a half ago that with the Vapor Bonaplata in Catalonia steam engines began to stimulate industrialization in Spain. Today, the La Camocha engine is evidence of the last chapter in this story.

CARLOS CAICOYA

Gilchrist Thomas, Sidney (1850–85) A Welsh amateur scientist, and inventor, in 1879, of the basic BESSEMER or 'Thomas' process for using non-phosphoric iron in large-scale steel production. He experimented at BLAENAVON and MERTHYR TYDFIL, developing linings for Bessemer converters that would absorb phosphorus. He thereby rescued steelmaking in areas with phosphoric ores, particularly in Britain, Germany and France. The resultant slag was widely used as a fertilizer.

BIBLIOGRAPHY
General
Gale, 1967.
Specific
Thompson, L. C. *Sidney Gilchrist Thomas*, 1940.

gilding A means of decorating ceramics using metallic gold. Gilding could be undertaken with burnished gold, whereby the metal after firing is rubbed with a smooth tool; matt gold, which is not burnished; or liquid gold.

gin Gin has two distinct meanings in industrial archaeology:

1. A source of power for machinery operated by an animal. (*See* DONKEY GIN; HORSE GIN.)

2. A spirit made from grain, which originated in the Netherlands in the sixteenth century, taking its name from the juniper (geneva) berries used for its flavouring. Unrestricted sale in early eighteenth-century England led to a surge in consumption, which caused such severe social problems that sales were restricted by legislation. (*See also* DISTILLING.)

BIBLIOGRAPHY
General
Watney, 1976.

girder bridge The word 'girder' was used from the mid-seventeenth century to refer to a main beam in a building that supported the joists carrying an upper floor, and from the mid-nineteenth century to an iron, steel or concrete longitudinal beam used to form the span of a bridge. Such a girder might be a simple rolled beam, or might be fabricated from iron or steel plates riveted (later welded) together, from smaller components forming a lattice structure, or from reinforced CONCRETE. Box girders, fabricated from steel, provide the light deck sections essential in modern long-span bridges. The technology was chiefly developed in Germany during reconstruction after World War II, but the principle dates from the TUBULAR BRIDGES of the nineteenth century. In England a rolled H-section joist (an I-beam in North America) is colloquially called a girder.

BIBLIOGRAPHY
Specific
Building with Steel: V – Bridgework, London: British Steel Corporation, 1970.

Gjirokastra (Gjirokastër, Argyrocastro), Albania A 'museum city' (*see* ALBANIA), in the south of Albania, birthplace of national leader Enver Hoxha and one of the most beautiful towns in the country. Some buildings date from the late seventeenth and early eighteenth centuries, but the majority are from between 1800 and 1860. Houses are solidly built with thick stone walls and tiny windows; the streets between them are narrow and cobbled. Inside the buildings niches, shelves, cupboards and window-seats are carved into the walls. Intricate wood carving, characteristic of the region, is displayed in many houses.

BIBLIOGRAPHY
General
Ward, 1983.

LOCATION
[M] Gjirokastra Museum, Gjirokastra.

Glarus, Switzerland A canton where domestic cotton manufacture flourished. Twenty-two cotton printing firms were established between 1740 and 1868, employing at their peak six thousand workers. The industrial landscape is impressive, with ten good specimens remain-

Figure 53 Linthouse Marine Engine Works of 1871–2, Glasgow, now being reassembled at Irvine by the Scottish Maritime Museum
Mark Watson

ing of more than forty cloth-drying towers. The cantonal museum has a section on the cotton industry.

LOCATION
[M] Museum of Glarus Canton, Freulerpalast, 8752, Näfels, Glarus.

Glasgow, Strathclyde, Scotland   One of the world's great manufacturing cities, Glasgow's industrial monuments were comprehensively catalogued by Hume in 1974.

In the early nineteenth century Glasgow was a cottonopolis second only to Manchester, but its position declined after 1860. Initially it was the merchanting centre for cotton yarn spun elsewhere, at places like Blantyre, 12 km (8 mi.) SE, where the counting house and tenements of a mill of 1785 now form the David Livingstone Centre. Glasgow's first steam-powered mill started in 1792. Few spinning mills survive intact. Scotland's first iron-framed building, probably modelled on the Salford Twist Mill, was Henry Houldsworth's cotton mill of 1804, demolished in 1969. It was followed in 1816 by two further fireproof mills, one of which, Humphrey's Mill, a six-storey brick building with cylindrical columns, survives in Old Rutherglen Road. Other cotton mills include the wooden-floored Falfield Mill of 1821, Barrowfield Spinning Factory

of 1846 which is M-roofed, and Alexander's thread mill of 1849 in Duke Street, a five-storey Italianate, concrete-floored fireproof building, converted in 1909 to the Great Eastern Hotel. On Carstairs Street is a mill of 1884–9 designed by Joseph Stott of Oldham, using his system of double brick arches on steel joists and cast-iron columns, six bays deep; it is being converted to the Laird Business Park, its twin having been demolished in 1986. When built these were the biggest spinners of cotton yarn in Scotland.

Dalmarnock's many weaving sheds have been reduced to a handful by comprehensive redevelopment. Barrowfield Weaving Factory of 1884–9 has north-lit sheds behind a two-storey front with a sky-blue chequer pattern in its brickwork.

James Templeton & Son came to own many carpet factories in the East End. Their Glasgow Green showpiece was William Leiper's Axminster Factory of 1888–92, in Venetian Gothic, the most colourful polychromy in Britain, with red terracotta, stone dressings, blue mosaic tympanum, and faience chevrons. Given the extensive wall planes, the interior has poor natural light. Additions by George Boswell have more glazing, horizontally banded in a 1934 block, and curving round corners of a

1937 block, which has a coloured zigzag parapet. The complex is now a Scottish Development Agency small business centre.

At the end of the nineteenth century Glasgow was Britain's principal centre of heavy engineering. Its buildings led the world in the enclosure of vast areas of space. The Clyde Foundry of Harland & Wolff, built as late as 1922 and demolished in 1967, was reckoned the biggest glass-clad structure in the world.

Prominent among the city's engineering firms was Randolph & Elder, millwrights, who patented a vertical compound marine engine in 1852, the assembly of which required great height for travelling cranes. The firm set up Fairfield Shipyard, Govan, in 1863, and in 1868–71 built an enormous cast-iron framed engine works behind a gigantic pilastered brick façade, four main fitting shops, with intermediate galleried bays on I-sectioned stanchions, bracing struts and girders all in cast iron, with 15.2 m (50 ft.) span timber roofs. Two Arrol (see below) steel-framed bays were added in 1906 and 1916. Govan Shipbuilders still operate at Fairfield, with a new fabrication shop, but older brass and woodworking shops, a model shop and a mould-loft, and a Beaux-Arts sculptured office of 1890. Fairfield supplied Govanites with Elder Park, Elder Cottage Hospital and the Pearce Institute.

Two other great iron-framed engine works are due for redevelopment. The fitting shop built at Linthouse Shipyard for Alexander Stephen & Sons in 1871–2 has two 16 m (53 ft.) span naves, three side aisles, and virtually no load-bearing walls. The cast-iron stanchions are longitudinally tied by timber and wrought iron. The building is being removed to IRVINE. The cast-iron framed boiler shop from Penman's Caledonian Ironworks is likewise being moved to BO'NESS. Originally the Machinery Hall for the Glasgow International Exhibition of 1888, the building has a main nave with tall cast-iron stanchions, side aisles and a wide timber roof.

Glasgow monopolized the export of sugar machinery. A. & W. Smith's Eglinton Engine Works dates from 1855. The original parts are a two- and three-storey fitting shop, a smithy and a four-storey pattern shop. To these were added an erecting shop in 1868 and a boiler shop in 1874, both with long timber-roofed bays, the travelling cranes on brick arcades. McOnie's Scotland Street Engine Works, founded in 1839 and now in multiple occupancy, has three-storey buildings of the 1850s and 70s, with yards for assembly, and big, fanlit doors. The Cranstonhill Foundry in Elliot Street has similar fanlights and tall windows. Kingston Engine Works in Portman Street of 1873, in polychrome brick, formerly made heavy machine tools and is now a printing works.

By 1900 most engineering works had standardized steel-framed buildings. The North British Diesel Engine Works of Barclay Curle & Co. of 1914 is outstanding, despite its new cladding. There are similarities between its high mansard roof with side galleries and PETER BEHRENS'S AEG turbine factory of 1909 (see BERLIN), perhaps because the German engineer Karl Bernhard worked on both buildings. The steel-framed Scotland Street Works of

James Howden & Co., dating from 1897–1908, is more typical and still functions, as does Weir's Holm Foundry, a building of 1912 and 1915 with ALBERT KAHN reinforced-concrete blocks. Fans and pumps are the respective products.

Locomotives from Glasgow were exported to all parts of the world, but the only remaining factory, the St Rollox works of the Caledonian Railway, dating in part from the 1880s, is threatened. Springburn College was built as the offices of the North British Locomotive Company in 1909, a four-storey Baroque block, steel-framed with giant columns. The Springburn Museum commemorates the great railway works of northern Glasgow.

Sentinel Works, Jessie Street, which produced the Sentinel steam lorry, includes a reinforced-concrete building of 1903, the first in Glasgow. The Albion Motor Works, Scotstoun, comprises a north-lit shed of 1903, an office of 1912 and a four-storey, American-styled reinforced-concrete office block of 1913–14. A smaller version of 1913 stands on Kilbirnie Street.

Sir William Arrol & Co., amongst the world's great structural engineers, built their last bridge in 1986, and only a part of their Dalmarnock Ironworks remains.

Scotland's biggest copper concern, Blair Campbell & McLean, supplied the brewing, distilling, sugar-refining and engineering industries from their steel-framed shops of 1900–14 in Woodville Street. Their Dutch gabled office is now 'Maritime House'.

Blacklock & MacArthur's Clydesdale Paint, Colour and Oil Works, rebuilt in 1888, has a Florentine Gothic towered, mass concrete-floored addition of 1900 by W. F. McGibbon. The grinding and mixing rooms are substantially intact. Next door Tradeston Paint Mills, now a toy warehouse, were converted in 1866 from a millwrighting shop of the 1850s. St Mungo Works, Broomloan Road, of 1901, has in its gable a gigantic example of a golf ball, its chief product. The Barras Market, with twin five-storey polychrome brick blocks and terracotta oriels, was built in 1877 as the clay tobacco pipe factory of W. White & Sons.

The City Grain Mills, a very long five- and six-storey range built in 1851–70, fronts the Forth & Clyde Canal terminus at Spier's Wharf. The adjacent seven-storey red and white brick Port Dundas Sugar Refinery of 1866 was converted to the Wheatsheaf Flour Mills in 1931. The entire range is to be converted to flats. Bishop Mills of 1853 at Partick have already been converted. Anderston Grain (later rice) Mills in Washington Street incorporate a vigorous red and white brick block of 1865 which may be similarly converted. Victoria Grain Mills in West Street of 1894–6, with Flemish gables and a crenellated tower, is now a clothes wholesaler's. The similar Scotstoun Flour Mills in Partick are still operating. The proportions of steam roller mills apparently suit the Italian castello look. The CNT Meadowside Granary of 1911–13 is a remarkable thirteen-storey brick hulk, half floored and half vertical silos, extended in 1937 and 1960. Gray Dunn & Co.'s biscuit factory with five-storey ranges of the 1870s and 1890s still operates. The Craigton Road Bakery, now a small business centre, dates from 1911 and has

'Kahncrete' (*see* KAHN, ALBERT) additions of 1923. The DCL Port Dundas Distillery, founded *c*.1820, remains amongst the largest in Scotland but both it and Tennant's Wellpark Brewery, founded in 1556, have been much altered.

Glasgow's Broomielaw and Merchant City contains several fine late eighteenth-century tobacco warehouses. In James Watt Street are four fine pedimented neo-Classical general, grain and bonded tobacco warehouses, the earliest a fireproof structure of 1847. The Bell Street railway warehouses of 1882–3, iron-framed with mass concrete arching, have been converted to flats.

Glasgow is celebrated for the application of cast iron and glass to its commercial buildings. Gardner's in Jamaica Street of 1855–6, by James Baird, with McConnel's patent internal and external iron frame, is the most graceful. Many prefabricated cast-iron buildings were exported from Glasgow, particularly by McFarlane's.

The Scottish Co-operative Wholesale Society had a remarkable group of warehouses and factories south of the Clyde. Co-operative House, Morrison Street, is a lavish Louis XIV-styled warehouse, crowned by a dome; it was built in 1893–7, with Flemish Gothic sides of 1887–93, all by Bruce & Hay. The main manufacturing estate from 1887 was at Shieldhall. By 1914, 3700 people were employed in sixteen factories for shoes, clothing and foodstuffs. Much has now been demolished, but the remarkably glazed Luma lightbulb factory of 1936 remains.

The famed Glasgow style of *c*.1900 was applied to few industrial buildings, except the *Glasgow Herald* building of 1893 by C. R. Mackintosh (1868–1928) and the white brick *Daily Record* works of 1901. J. J. Burnet's Wallace Scott tailoring building at Cathcart, with a glass and steel framework, has as modern an appearance as his Kodak building in LONDON. A more basic exposed HENNEBIQUE reinforced-concrete frame by Wylie & Blake housed the former Greenlees boot and shoe factory of 1910.

Most industrial buildings of the 1930s, like those on the tree-lined Hillington development of Scottish Industrial Estates, are not distinctively Glaswegian. The better modern buildings were purpose-built, examples being the fin-towered Leyland Garage at Salkeld Street, ironically now a mounted-police stables; and Sir E. Owen Williams's *Daily Express* (now *Glasgow Herald*) building of 1936, a longer version, with glass and vitrolite bands, of its Fleet Street senior (*see* LONDON). The W. D. & H. O. Wills tobacco factory on Alexandra Parade is equally close to the company's Newcastle-upon-Tyne works.

Dalmarnock gasworks has a cast-iron Doric gasholder of 1872. Govan Refuse Destructor has chimneys at each corner; initially it generated electricity. The smaller of Glasgow Corporation's first two electric power stations, St Andrew's Works, Pollokshaws Road, of 1889–90, is now partly a printing works. Several 'Steamies', public baths and wash-houses, retain old plant. The meat market has aisled spaces in wrought iron similar to La Villette (*see* PARIS).

Glasgow was not a notable port in the eighteenth century, most trade being handled at Greenock and Port Glasgow. The Clyde Navigation Trust, established in 1809, was responsible for moving operations up river. The Doric Customs House of 1840 is smaller than its contemporaries at Leith, Dundee and Greenock, reflecting Glasgow's lesser status. All berthage was quayside until the opening at Kingston Dock in 1867, followed by Queen's Dock in 1872–80, Prince's Dock in 1893–7 and King George V Dock in 1924–31. All but the last have since been filled in and replaced by an exhibition centre and housing. Only a few short stretches of transit sheds remain, notably Clyde Place of 1861, where a Babcock & Wilcox electrified steam crane still works. The 175 ton Stobcross Crane of 1932, a hammerhead cantilever-type crane for fitting marine engines and transshipping locomotives, is Glasgow's most characteristic landmark. Hydraulic power stations with Italianate accumulators survive at Queen's and Prince's Docks. Three dry docks at Govan, of 1869–75, 1883–6 and 1894–8, were each capable of holding the largest ships then afloat.

Two pedestrian flat-link chain suspension bridges cross the Clyde: Portland Street Bridge of 1851, with Classical stone pylons, and St Andrew's Bridge of 1853, with Corinthian cast-iron pylons. The lifts to Glasgow Harbour Tunnel of 1890–95 were in two steel-domed rotundas, now restaurants. The tunnels were infilled in 1985.

The Forth & Clyde Canal terminated in 1790 at Port Dundas where there is a Classical canal office of 1812. The Kelvin Aqueduct and two bascule bridges survive on the link to Bowling (*see* DUNBARTONSHIRE).

Central Station, the terminus of the Caledonian Railway, which opened in 1879, has an all-over ridge-and-furrow roof on big steel girders, obviating the need for columns. The North British Railway's Queen Street terminus of 1842 was rebuilt in 1878 under a 76 m (250 ft.) span arched train shed, now the only one in Scotland. Glasgow's circular Subway was, from 1896 to 1935, the only cable-hauled underground passenger system in the world. The twin engine house and tension run are now part of Howden's works in Scotland Street. The tram workshops on Albert Drive, vacated by the Museum of Transport, have become a theatre.

The Glasgow Museum of Transport, located since 1988 in Kelvin Hall, has comprehensive collections of road and rail vehicles and ship models. Its locomotives include a Highland Railway *Jones Goods*, the first British 4–6–0, and the Caledonian 4–2–2, No. 123. Other collections accumulated in Glasgow are displayed at IRVINE and SUMMERLEE HERITAGE PARK. The People's Palace and the Springburn Museum cover social and labour history. In Glasgow University's Hunterian Museum is a collection of scientific instruments, including the model Newcomen engine repaired by JAMES WATT in 1763 that inspired him to develop the separate condenser.

Stone-built tenement blocks of four storeys were the characteristic working- and middle-class dwellings of nineteenth- and early twentieth-century Glasgow. Many remain, and an apartment in a block of 1892 is preserved by the National Trust for Scotland.

BIBLIOGRAPHY
General
Butt, 1967; Hay and Stell, 1986; Hume, 1974.
Specific
Municipal Glasgow: its evolution and enterprises, Glasgow: Corporation of the City of Glasgow, 1914.

LOCATIONS
[M] Hunterian Museum, Glasgow University, Glasgow G12 8QQ.
[M] Museum of Transport, Kelvin Hall, 1 Bunhouse Road, Glasgow G3 8DP.
[M] People's Palace, Glasgow Green, Glasgow G40 1AT.
[S] The Tenement House, 145 Buccleuch Street, Garnethill, Glasgow.

MARK WATSON

glass Glass is made by heating a mixture of silica (usually in the form of sand), sodium carbonate (*see* ALKALI) and LIME at a very high temperature. Cullet or broken glass is often added, and RED LEAD is incorporated to produce crystal glass for tableware. Glass can be shaped by blowing, pressing, rolling, moulding, drawing out or spinning, and decorated by cutting and engraving amongst other techniques. Glass is annealed in ovens called lehrs.

In the thirteenth century pure, colourless, transparent glass was being produced in Venice, and used in the manufacture of objects of high value. Slowly glass came to be used in windows, the period of adoption being marked by the taxation of windows, in England from 1696 to 1851, in France from 1798 to 1917.

In 1700 most glass in continental Europe was made by blowing cylinders which were then opened out into sheets, which in turn were cut into various sizes. In England crown glass was more popular: this was made by cutting a blown cylinder, spinning it into a disc, annealing it, then cutting it into panes. Plate glass, made by casting, was made in France from 1688, and at Ravenshead, ST HELENS, from 1773. During the nineteenth century techniques for rolling and drawing glass using tank furnaces were developed. Sir WILLIAM SIEMENS used a gas-fired regenerative furnace to ensure a continuous flow of glass from a tank. Irving Washington Colburn (1861–1917) in the USA devised a means of ensuring a standard width of glass as it was continuously drawn from the furnace, enabling the mass production of plate glass of higher quality than previously available.

Laminated glass, used in motorcars, consists of two sheets of glass with a layer of tough plastic in between.

Glass is one of the principal building materials of the twentieth century, its potential to diminish the difference between indoors and outdoors having first been demonstrated in the Crystal Palace in 1851.

See also BOTTLE; ENGLISH GLASS CONE; STAINED GLASS; VITROLITE.

BIBLIOGRAPHY
General
Boorstin, 1973; McGrath and Frost, 1937; Powell, 1923.

BARRIE TRINDER

glazing While the application of clay slips to CERAMICS could only create simple colour contrasts, a glaze permitted a kaleidoscope of effects. A glaze is in essence a clear or coloured glass. Siliceous glazes consisting of soda glass were in use in Egyptian times, while lead glaze which had a greater adhesive power was being taken up from China to Rome by 200 BC. The preparation of lead compounds and the admixture of natural coloured earths containing iron, manganese and cobalt permitted a wide variety of colours.

A technique for creating a white opaque finish or enamel to cover dark bodies was developed by Lucca Della Robbia (1399–1482) in Italy in the early fifteenth century: tin ash was added to a lead glaze. By the middle of the seventeenth century Delft was the main centre for making tin enamel ware. The coating of a clay body with tin enamel marks a link between medieval Italian and Spanish wares and products directly relating to true porcelain. By the end of the seventeenth century DELFTWARE was being imitated by potteries in many English ports.

Articles for glazing must have the correct porosity for the adhesion of the glaze. The glaze may be applied by dipping, spraying, brushing, dusting or vaporizing in the kiln; it may be applied either to ware fired to biscuit form or when dry but unfired. The earliest form of glazing in Britain was with galena (*see* LEAD). SALT glazing was introduced into Britain from northern Europe about 1600. The proliferation of glaze effects depended on the adoption of lead glazes, the use of which was to be constrained within Britain from 1913 on account of health hazards.

BIBLIOGRAPHY
General
Hamer, 1986; Rhodes, 1969; Searle, 1929, 1929–30.

MICHAEL STRATTON

Gloucester, Gloucestershire, England The county town and a port on the River Severn, Gloucester increased in importance with the opening of the Gloucester & Berkeley Canal from Sharpness in 1827, and with the construction of docks, where many mid-nineteenth-century warehouses are preserved. Of interest are a museum of packaging in Albert Warehouse and the National Waterways Museum in Llanthony Warehouse. The Over Bridge across the Severn, built by THOMAS TELFORD in 1831, has a single stone arch of 50 m (164 ft.) span.

See also PORT BOOKS.

BIBLIOGRAPHY
General
Conway-Jones, 1984.

LOCATIONS
[M] City Museum and Art Gallery, Brunswick Road, Gloucester GL1 1HP.
[M] National Waterways Museum, Llanthony Warehouse, Gloucester Docks, Gloucester GL1 2EH.
[M] Robert Opie Collection of Packaging and Advertising, Albert Warehouse, Gloucester Docks, Gloucester GL1 2EH.

Glover tower   A squat tower, up to 9 m (30 ft.) high and 2.5 m (8 ft.) in diameter, lined with acid-resistant bricks and filled with coke or flint, part of the lead-chamber process for the manufacture of SULPHURIC ACID. The main function was to concentrate the acid by removing nitrous fumes which could then be reused in lead chambers. Glover towers were used in conjunction with GAY-LUSSAC TOWERS. They were the invention of John Glover (1817–1902), an acid manufacturer of Newcastle-upon-Tyne, England, in 1859.

BIBLIOGRAPHY
General
ICI, 1950; Morgan and Pratt, 1938; Partington, 1950.

gloves   The manufacture of gloves from LEATHER skins was widely practised in England in the seventeenth and eighteenth centuries, although there was some concentration in towns like Woodstock, 8 km (5 mi.) N. of Oxford. Gloves were made on a large scale in France, and exported to England, particularly after import duties were repealed in 1825. By the second half of the nineteenth century the principal gloving companies combined warehouses in London which handled imports, with modest-sized factories, chiefly in south and south-west England, many of which served as bases supplying domestic outworkers. Knitted gloves were also made by domestic outworkers, until from the 1890s machines were introduced that could produce tubes to which fingers could be added by hand.

BIBLIOGRAPHY
General
Hudson, 1980.

Gmunden, Upper Austria, Austria   The capital of the Salzkammergut, the imperial salt-working estate established by Maximilian I in the early sixteenth century, and situated at the point where the River Traun flows out of the Traunsee. The oldest surviving steam boat in Austria, the *Gisela*, built in 1870–1 by Gesellschaft der Freunde der Stadt Gmunden (Friends of the city of Gmunden) and restored in 1983–6, sails on the Traunsee. Two Bo–Bo electric locomotives of 1912 run on the private railway to Vorchdorf, 33 km (20 mi.) NE.

Gnosjö, Småland, Sweden   Töllstorps Industriemuseum at Gnosjö, 56 km (35 mi.) SW of Jönköping, has been established by a local heritage society, and effectively illustrates the development of industry within a rural setting. The open-air museum includes a farmstead, cottages and a flourmill, but its industrial focus is a series of wire mills which have been moved from elsewhere in the region to stand on sites that were originally occupied by wire mills. Other buildings include a wire-mesh weaving mill, and a workshop built in 1856 for the manufacture of hairpins, and later used as a tin-plate mill.

Also in Gnosjö is the J. E. Hyltens Industrial Museum, in a works established in 1879 by Johan Edvard Hylten, which proved to be the nucleus of one of Sweden's largest industrial companies. The factory manufactured a variety of wooden, metal and leather products. Features of the museum include a generator displayed at the Stockholm exhibition of 1897 and installed at Gnosjö in 1899, shops where FILES were made, a foundry with over 11 000 patterns, and a workshop with lathes and grinding, milling and drilling machines.

BIBLIOGRAPHY
General
Nisser, 1979.

LOCATIONS
[M] J. E. Hyltens Industriemuseum, Gnosjö.
[M] Töllstorps Industriemuseum, Gnosjö.

BARRIE TRINDER

Gois, Beira Litoral, Portugal   A town 120 km (75 mi.) SE of Oporto, with a papermill of 1828 and a hydro-electric power station of 1910.

gold   A metallic element and one of the earth's scarcest but most widely distributed metals, found in several forms including beds and veins. The working of gold has always been widespread, but in the nineteenth century there were notable 'gold rushes': to California in 1848, Colorado in 1858, Nevada in 1859, Ballarat (*see* SOVEREIGN HILL) in 1851, and Alaska and the Yukon in 1896–8. Much of the world's supply comes from 'native gold' ores, but it is also obtained as a by-product from smelting other metallic ores.

Gold occurs in alluvial deposits, such as those first worked in the 'rushes', because it is chemically unreactive and relatively dense (*see* ALLUVIAL MINING). Due to its density it is normally found towards the base of alluvial beds, and has to be removed with the deposit and then separated using water. These deposits may be found at depth (called 'deep leads') under newer sedimentary rocks; or even under lava flows as in parts of Australia, where they were mined by PILLAR-AND-STALL MINING techniques. Gold ores are also found in veins, which are worked like other vein deposits. Other sources have been found in large 'masses' or 'stockworks' containing fine particles, often associated with granite. These are worked by open pits. Minute quantities of gold have been drawn from clays and shales by the addition of MERCURY, which amalgamates with the gold.

In 1886 John Stewart MacArthur (1857–1920) devised the cyanide process for extracting gold from low-grade ores. Ore is crushed and dissolved in a weak solution of sodium cyanide (NaCN), from which the gold is precipitated by the addition of zinc shavings or dust (*see* NEW ZEALAND).

See also figures 18, 147.

BIBLIOGRAPHY
General
ICI, 1950.

IVOR J. BROWN

goldsmith   A tradesman who fashions gold into plate,

303

jewellery and so on. Until the development of banking networks, goldsmiths frequently acted as bankers within the local community. From the early nineteenth century the term SILVERSMITH or jeweller (*see* JEWELLERY MANUFACTURE) came to be applied more commonly to provincial tradesmen.

Gölsdorf, Karl (1861–1916) An Austrian locomotive engineer, the chief mechanical engineer of the state railways during 1893–1916. He was the son of Adolf Gölsdorf, the chief mechanical engineer of the Südbahn. He designed a two-cylinder compound locomotive in 1893, and is chiefly notable for devising a four-cylinder system of compounding, whereby two outside low-pressure cylinders and two high-pressure cylinders within the main frames were placed in line beneath the smokebox. He designed the first European 2–6–2 locomotive in 1904, and in 1911 produced a class 310, 2–6–4 tender engine, which came to symbolize the Austrian express locomotive. Nearly a thousand two-cylinder compound 2–8–0s were built to his design. Examples of most of Gölsdorf's important designs are preserved.

Gossage tower A coke-filled tower for dissolving the HYDROCHLORIC ACID gas produced during the first stage of ALKALI manufacture by the LEBLANC PROCESS. It was invented in 1836 by soapmaker William Gossage (1799–1877) and was much used in south Lancashire (*see* HALTON) after he moved there in 1850.

BIBLIOGRAPHY
General
Warren, 1980.
Specific
Chemical News, 4 April 1877.

Gotha Canal (Göta kanal), Sweden The Gotha Canal was constructed between 1810 and 1832, and links the Skaggerat with the Baltic. It was built according to the recommendations of THOMAS TELFORD, who spent about six weeks studying the route in 1808 and in a further spell in 1813. Telford's proposals were based on earlier plans by Swedish engineers. The scheme was realized through the energy of Count Baltzar von Platen (1766–1819). Vessels crossing Sweden leave Gothenburg along the Göta river, passing on to the TROLLHÄTTAN Canal, and subsequently into Lake Vänern. The Gotha Canal proper begins at Sjötorp on the eastern shore of the lake, then passes through Lakes Viken, Vättern, Boren and Roxen to the Baltic. Ships gain access to Lake Mälaren and to STOCKHOLM by the 3.2 km (2 mi.) Södertälje Canal, opened in 1819. The whole line of the waterway is 558 km (347 mi.) long from Gothenburg to Stockholm, of which only 97 km (60 mi.) consists of artificial cuts, on which there are 65 locks. The principal lock flights are at Borenshult at the west end of Lake Boren, 4 km (3 mi.) E. of Motala, and at Berg, 12 km (8 mi.) NE of Linköping, at the western end of Lake Roxen. Many lock gates, bollards and accommodation bridges were made, according to British practice, in cast iron. The headquarters of the canal company is at

Motala, where a dry dock of 1815 is conserved, and where the company archives are located. The establishment in the town in 1822 of a mechanical engineering works, Motala Verkstad, was a significant development in the history of the Swedish engineering industry. Under the direction of a Scots manager, Daniel Fraser, the works provided a grounding in engineering for a whole generation of Swedish workers. Parts of the Motala Verkstad premises are preserved.

The canal was never profitable, particularly after the opening of the railways, but it was important regionally for the transport of timber and agricultural produce, and now carries increasing numbers of pleasure craft. The Gotha Canal Shipping Co. operates cruises between Gothenburg and Stockholm.

BIBLIOGRAPHY
General
Hadfield, 1986; Rolt, 1958.
Specific
Meddelanden från Ostergötlands och Linköpings Stads Museum (Transactions from the Ostergötland and Linköpings City Museum). Linköping, 1969.
Nisser, M. *Industriminnen i Ostergötland* (Industrial monuments in Ostergötland). Ostergötland, 1969.
Nyström, B. The Göta Canal. In *Teknik & Kultur*, II, 1990.

LOCATIONS
[I] Gotha Canal Archives, S-591 46 Motala.
[M] Motala Museum, Charlottenborgs Slott, S-591 46 Motala.
[I] Rederiaktiebolaget Göta Kanal (Gotha Canal Shipping Company), PO Box 272, Hotellplatsen 2, S-401 24 Gothenburg 1.

BARRIE TRINDER

Gothenburg (Göteborg), Göteborg och Bohus, Sweden Sweden's second city and a major port, founded in 1619 by Dutch settlers at the invitation of King Gustavus Adolphus. Its planning around the Stora-Hamn-Kanal and the Ostra-Hamn-Kanal reflects that of some cities in the Netherlands. Gothenburg is the western terminus of the steamers that operate on the Gotha Canal.

The city is notable for its museums. The archeological and historical museum, which includes archive collections relating to the region, and domestic interiors, is located in the eighteenth-century warehouse of the Swedish East India Company. The Crown Arsenal (Kronhuset) of 1643 houses workshops where crafts, including glassmaking, are demonstrated. The Röhsskakonstslöjdmuseet illustrates the history of industrial design in Sweden and abroad, while the long history of shipping in Gothenburg is portrayed in the Maritime Museum. The Museum of Industry, in a working-class quarter of the town, has successfully investigated several aspects of Gothenburg's labour history.

LOCATIONS
[M] Göteborgs historiska arkeologiska och museums (Gothenburg's Archaeological and Historical Museums), 12 Norra Hamngatan, S-411 14 Gothenburg.
[M] Göteborgs industriemuseum (Museum for the History of Industry), Avägen 24, Box 5037, S-402 21 Gothenburg.
[M] Kronhuset, Kronhusgatan 1D, S-411 13 Gothenburg.

[M] Röhsskakonstslöjdmuseet (Röhss Museum of Applied Arts), 37–9 Vasagatan, 411 37 Gothenburg.
[M] Sjöfartsmuseet (Maritime Museum), Karl Johansgatan 1–3, S-414 59 Gothenburg.

BARRIE TRINDER

Gothic The architecture of pointed arches, rib vaults and buttresses, and skeletal structures with minimum infills. It was current in Europe from the late twelfth century until the sixteenth century, revived from the eighteenth century, and used in INDUSTRIAL ARCHITECTURE in the nineteenth century, in BLAST FURNACE complexes, RAILWAY STATIONS, PUMPING STATIONS, and in some TEXTILE MILLS and INDUSTRIAL COMMUNITIES. Early Gothic revival buildings tended to be Classical in plan, with delicate pointed arch ornamentation, a style sometimes called Gothick. By 1850 architects were trying, with high moral purpose, to imitate medieval styles. Subsequently, under the influence of William Butterfield (1814–1900), Alfred Waterhouse (1830–1905) and others, the Gothic style was imaginatively reworked in new materials. The main periods of English Gothic – Early English, Decorated and Perpendicular – were defined by Thomas Rickman (1776–1841).

BIBLIOGRAPHY
General
Clark, 1928; Rickman, 1817.

Göttingen, Lower Saxony, Germany The Luisenhall saltworks in Göttingen is now the only saltworks in Germany that still uses boiling pans. The first bore hole was sunk in 1851, and the first buildings constructed soon afterwards. After several bankruptcies, the buildings were extended in the 1890s to their present form. The pumps are driven by a water turbine, and heating for the pans is provided by burning wood waste. Luisenhall provides a complete illustration of a nineteenth-century saltworks. Its features include drilling towers with weatherboard facings, brick boiling houses with timber-framed superstructures, brine containers, an office block and a villa.

The locomotive repair shop of 1913, which covers an area of several hundred square metres, has a brick façade which shows the transition from neo-Classicism to modernism. The railway station of the 1850s has a largely unaltered exterior.

The Gartetal wool-spinning mill at Lengden, 15 km (9 mi.) E., is less notable for its building – a timber-framed former papermill – than for the completeness of its equipment, including carding machines, self-acting mules, ring-spinning machines and a Francis turbine, all from c.1900.

The Göttingen municipal museum holds more than twenty of the models of machines used c.1800 by Johann Beckmann (1739–1811) to illustrate his lectures on civil and mechanical engineering.

BIBLIOGRAPHY
General
Mende and Hamm, 1990; Slotta, 1975–85.

LOCATION
[M] Stadtmuseum (Municipal Museum), Ritterplan 7, 3400 Göttingen.

MICHAEL MENDE

Gottwaldov (Zlin), East Moravia, Czechoslovakia A town developed from the Bat'a shoe factory and company town, which were established in the 1920s. Production methods were adapted from American automobile production. Beginning as a collection of disparate buildings, the factory became a complex of functionally designed factory units. Le Corbusier's scheme for the new town was rejected as grandiose and idiosyncratic; the chosen designer was Frantisek Gahwa. The complex was planned to include a shoe factory and a shoemaking machinery factory, workers' housing and a hotel. The managing director's office is housed in an elevator. Gahwa's Community House was built in 1932–3. The Bat'a headquarters of 1937–8 was designed by Vladimir Karfik.

There is no exhibition on the growth of the town, though the factory has a museum of the history of shoes. Few old machines are preserved.

BIBLIOGRAPHY
General
Knox, 1965; Peichl and Slapeta, 1987.

LOCATION
[M] Museum of Shoemaking, Svit, Gottwaldov.

Gouda, Zuid Holland, The Netherlands A classic water town, built around a network of canals. The Waag (weigh-house) outside the Stadhuis (town hall) has bas-reliefs on the exterior, and a visitor centre within.

The manufacture of clay pipes flourished in the early nineteenth century, but declined by the 1860s owing to the popularity of cigars. Pipes, bricks and pottery are displayed in the 'de Moriaan' museum, with a pipemaker's workshop. The remains of a late-nineteenth-century stearine candle factory are incorporated in a modern chemical complex, which includes a museum.

Schoonhoven, a small town at the confluence of the Rivers Lek and Vlist, 17 km ($10\frac{1}{2}$ mi.) SE, is linked by ferry with Nieuwpoort on the south bank of the Lek. The Waag of 1617 is now a pancake restaurant. The national Gold, Silver and Clock Museum, in a chalet-style water tower of 1901, includes a silversmith's workshop.

LOCATIONS
[M] Kaarsenmuseum (Candle Museum), Turfmarkt 10, Gouda.
[M] Nederlands Goud, Zilver en Klokkenmuseum (Netherlands Gold, Silver and Clock Museum), Naterneplein 4, Schoonhoven.
[M] Stedelijk Museum 'de Moriaan', Westhaven 29, Gouda.

JURRIE VAN DALEN and BARRIE TRINDER

grain products See BAKERY; BISCUIT; BREAD OVEN; BREAKFAST CEREALS; CONFECTIONERY; CORN MILL; ELEVATOR; FLOURMILL; GRAIN SILO; GRANARY; GRISTMILL; MALT; ROLLER MILLING.

grain silo A cylindrical reinforced concrete grain bin, with a steel bottom, linked to a conveyor. The silo first appeared as a component of grain elevators (*see* GRANARY) in the USA in the late 1890s, in Buffalo, N.Y., and Minneapolis (*see* MINNESOTA). Earlier examples were rectangular, and of heavy timber construction. Storage of grain in bulk raises many engineering problems, since it can behave like a solid or a liquid, and collapses of 'walls' of grain can lead to implosions. The silo became one of the characteristic features of the landscape in the USA, particularly in the Midwest, and of grain PORTS elsewhere; it profoundly influenced the architects of the INTERNATIONAL MODERN movement in Europe. In recent decades the silo has been superseded by hangar-type structures where grain is handled by front-loader tractors, but many remain, and a celebrated group at Akron, OHIO, has been converted into a hotel.

BIBLIOGRAPHY
General
Banham, 1986.

gramophone One of the most characteristic domestic furnishings of the twentieth century, the gramophone became an industrial product largely due to THOMAS EDISON who in 1877 patented a machine that could record and play back the human voice. From 1894 he promoted the phonograph, the name by which the device is still known in America, as a means of entertainment, and by 1897 was selling machines for $20. Emile Berliner (1851–1929) developed the disc for recording, and also the means of making a master copy on zinc or nickel-plated copper for the mass production of records, introducing two-sided shellac records from 1904. It was Berliner's device, patented in 1887, which was first called the 'gramophone'. Berliner was also responsible for the development of what became the microphone: he applied for a patent in 1877 which was finally granted in 1891. The 33.3 rev./min. long-playing disc was introduced in 1948; it derived from wartime technology. Makers of gramophones and records were amongst the most dynamic companies of the inter-war period.

Magnetic recording was developed in the 1890s but given up as a commercial proposition; it was revived in World War II, and gradually introduced as a commercial product – the tape recorder – from the late 1940s.

BIBLIOGRAPHY
General
Gelatt, 1965; Reord and Welch, 1977.

BARRIE TRINDER

granary A place of storage for threshed grain. On a farm a granary was often raised from the ground on staddle stones or pillars to give protection from rats, as in those preserved at Avoncroft (*see* BROMSGROVE) and the WEALD AND DOWNLAND MUSEUM.

The term is also applied to storehouses for grain within manufacturing complexes, like the concrete structures built in the 1930s for the mills at Victoria Dock, London.

At a port the function of a granary unconnected with a manufacturing concern was to hold grain received by sea or by inland transport before dispatching it by the other mode. The eighteenth-century Grocer's Warehouse on the BRIDGEWATER CANAL in MANCHESTER is an early example of a specialist grain warehouse. Another was built at Duke's Dock, Liverpool, in 1811. Until the late nineteenth century granaries were designed for handling grain in sacks. Subsequently bulk handling methods were introduced. By the late nineteenth century a granary in a port might include silos as well as conventional warehouses, which, as in the Central Granary of 1899 at Millwall, London, were sometimes preferred for softer grains, like Black Sea wheat. Such warehouses were usually iron-framed, with roof-top watertanks for fire-fighting, and their floors were divided into compartments so that consignments could be kept separate. Bucket elevators, or rail-mounted or floating pneumatic elevators, might be used to unload ships. Loading was usually by spouts from conveyor belts. In North America the word ELEVATOR was synonymous with granary.

See also GRAIN SILO.

BIBLIOGRAPHY
General
Carr, 1984; Cunningham, 1923; Greeves, 1980; Mersey Docks and Harbour Board, 1960–1; Ritchie-Noakes, 1984.

BARRIE TRINDER

Grand Canal The name of three distinct navigations:

1. The Grand Canal from Hangzhou to Tianjin in China, built by the Sui Dynasty (AD 581–617), was the first summit-level canal, and had POUND LOCKS in the eleventh century. Although now used only for local traffic, it remains the longest canal in the world.

2. The Grand Canal d'Alsace is the lateral canal on the French bank of the Rhine between Basle and Strasbourg. It was begun in 1922, in conformity with the Treaty of Versailles. The first section, with locks and a hydro-electric power station at Kembs, was completed in 1932.

3. The Grand Canal is Ireland's most notable artificial navigation and one of the few canals in the world with substantial surviving monuments relating to passenger traffic. The project commenced in 1755 but the 127 km (79 mi.) main line from Dublin to Shannon Harbour, County Offaly, was only completed, with the advice of WILLIAM JESSOP, in 1804. The most important of several branches ran to Athy on the River Barrow, giving through navigation to Waterford. Barges 4.25 m (14 ft.) in beam could be accommodated. Commercial navigation continued until 1960, but the main line remains open for recreational use. The canal was distinguished for its passenger services. Six 'passage boats' were operating by 1790, and lighters with state and common cabins were introduced in 1834. The Grand Canal company owned five hotels, of which those at Portobello in Dublin, Robertstown, and Shannon Harbour remain.

Figure 54   One of the five hotels built in the first decade of the nineteenth century by the Grand Canal Company in Ireland, at Robertstown, near Prosperous, County Kildare, which is now a community centre
Barrie Trinder

BIBLIOGRAPHY
General
D'Arcy, 1969; Delany, 1973, 1986; Hadfield, 1986; Hadfield and
   Skempton, 1979; Rolt, 1949.

BARRIE TRINDER

Grande Dixence, La, Valais, Switzerland   One of the most ambitious pump storage hydro-electric power schemes in Switzerland, 54 km (33 mi.) SE of Montreux. Several proposals to utilize the water flowing down the Val d'Hérémence into the Rhône were made from 1900, but work did not begin until the Énergie de l'Ouest-Suisse (EOS) company was formed in 1927. A hollow concrete dam, 87 m (285 ft.) high, designed by Jean Landry, and then the highest in Switzerland, was completed in 1935. The dam was later submerged behind another much larger dam, 284 m (932 ft.) high, constructed between 1953 and 1961.

BIBLIOGRAPHY
Specific
La Grande Dixence. Geneva: Hydrodynamica, 1984.

Grängesberg, Dalarna, Sweden   The iron-ore deposits at Grängesberg, 16 km (10 mi.) SW of LUDVIKA in the BERGSLAGEN region, were known in the Middle Ages and the first documentary reference to the mine dates from 1584. The first of several prosperous periods of operation occurred in the seventeenth century. In 1670 there were twenty-two blast furnaces in the vicinity, producing pig iron from Grängesberg iron ore. The ore has a high phosphorus content, however, and the iron made from it was of poor quality. Extraction nevertheless continued, although it was not until the nineteenth century, with the introduction of the OPEN-HEARTH process for making steel, that the scale of mining was extended. The extraction of ore in the Bergslagen region became a matter of national importance, a source of great profits to landowners and to English capitalists who invested in foreign countries in order to obtain supplies of iron ore. Most of the English capital invested in Sweden was lost in trying to make profitable the mines in the far north, but in Bergslagen the capital invested returned substantial profits. The English financier Sir Ernest Cassel was one of the founders of a new mining company in Grängesberg in 1896, and had many other interests in Swedish ironworks. Ownership of the Grängesberg mine was later transferred back into Swedish hands.

When the iron-ore deposits in the far north of Sweden started to be profitable, the Grängesberg company acquired a majority of the shares in Luossavaara-Kiruna-vaara Aktiebolag (LKAB) in 1903, and continued to hold them until 1957, although in 1907 the company transferred about half its interests in the northern mines to the state. The export of iron ore from the Grängesberg mines, as well as from other iron-ore mines in Bergslagen, was very successful during the first five decades of the twentieth century, and in the 1940s Sweden was the leading exporter of iron ore on the world market. Some sixty mines were then in operation in Bergslagen, but conditions changed in the 1960s. The Bergslagen mines suffered from falling prices on the world market, and from rising costs in Sweden. Many had to close. In 1975 only eighteen remained in operation. Seven years later only two had survived: Grängesberg and DANNEMORA.

The pithead buildings and headstock are of modern concrete construction. In the south-eastern part of the village is a large area of workers' housing of the late nineteenth century, consisting of stuccoed wooden buildings, each containing four dwellings. The red-painted houses of the first decade of the twentieth century are examples of a more nationalistic wooden architecture. The cultural centre, with its monumental Classical portico designed by the Swedish architect Agi Lindegren, was built with money donated in 1896 by Sir Ernest Cassel, who directed that it was not to be used for political or religious meetings.

A railway museum at Grängesberg displays a collection of steam locomotives in a former locomotive depot and forms part of the Ekomuseum BERGSLAGEN.

BIBLIOGRAPHY
General
Meinander, 1968.

LOCATION
[M] Lokmuseet i Grängesberg (Locomotive Museum in Grängesberg), Grängesberg.

MARIE NISSER

granite A coarse-grained, acid, igneous rock, containing quartz, feldspar and usually MICA. It is used in civil engineering and for gravestones, kerbing, paving, precision-machine bases and surface plates, and sometimes building (*see* ABERDEEN). Vermont, North Carolina and New Hampshire granites are widely used in the USA. Granite was the basis of a sizeable industry in the west of England based on Penryn, but this suffered severe decline in the face of Scandinavian competition in 1905–10.

BIBLIOGRAPHY
General
Challinor, 1986.
Specific
Stanier, P. The granite-quarrying industry in Devon and Cornwall, Part 1: 1800–1910. In *IAR*, VII(2) 1985.

graphite A crystallized form of carbon, graphite is amongst the softest of minerals, although an allotrope of DIAMOND. Powdery concentrates of natural graphite have been found in deep rock formations in Canada, Mexico, Sri Lanka, and the USSR. Its fine, black, granular structure has allowed graphite to serve as a writing medium, when combined with clay; as dry lubrication; as a polish; as foundry mould facing; and as electrodes in electric furnaces. Artificial graphite manufacture began in the 1890s with successful experiments at Niagara Falls (New York), in which compacted rods of pure carbon powder were subjected to the action of electric arcs, the heat

generated fusing the carbon into a material that resembled graphite in certain applications.

graving dock 'Graving' is the cleaning of a ship's hull, by scraping and tarring. A graving dock was originally a DRY DOCK in which ships were placed to be graved, but the term came to mean any dry dock used for repairing ships.

gravity railway A railway where the predominant mineral traffic is downhill: loaded vehicles travel under gravity and momentum, controlled by brakesmen, with the empties hauled back by horses or locomotives. The FESTINIOG RAILWAY, engineered in 1836 by James Spooner, and lines linked with the Delaware & Hudson Canal are outstanding examples.

See also DANDY CART.

BIBLIOGRAPHY
General
Lewis, 1968.

Graz, Gratz, Styria, Austria   The capital of Styria, Graz stands on the River Mur, and is notable for its university, and the splendid complex of ancient buildings round the Landhaus. The city has a long industrial history. The Zeughaus (arsenal) of 1643–5 by Antonio Solar, part of the Landhaus complex, is now a museum with collections of arms and armour. A technical college was founded in 1811, and Graz became one of the principal engineering centres in the Habsburg Empire, the locomotive works of the Südbahn having been established there by the Englishman Joseph Hall.

Notable industrial buildings in Graz include a late-eighteenth-century cotton factory in Kasernstrasse; a Baroque factory for the mechanized production of nails, built by Franz Xavier Schafzahl in Korosistrasse in 1813; the Kienreich paper factory, adapted from a series of forge workshops in 1785; the soapworks of A. von Hohenblum and A. G. Gifford built in 1872 and enlarged in 1899; and the mustard, spirits and vinegar works of Albert Eckert with its office block of 1910 in the Secessionist style. The celebrated Puntigam brewery was founded in 1838 by Franz Knabl: a new brewhouse and two steam engines were installed in 1865–6, and the plant was substantially enlarged in 1893. The municipal slaughterhouse in Graz was built in 1876. A new refrigeration plant with a 36.5 m (120 ft.) tower was constructed in 1917. The plant was replaced in 1974 and is being adapted to new uses, one of the two main buildings having been converted to a wholesale greengrocery market. The east railway station (Östbahnhof) was built in 1872–3 as the terminus of the Hungarian Western Railway, which approached Graz from Raab. The restored building remains in use.

The railway to Köflach, the Graz Köflacher Bahn, dates from 1860 and was built to serve the lignite mines at Köflach, 40 km (25 mi.) W. The railway is now owned by the steelmaking combine Alpine Montan, and is worked by modern diesel locomotives; but it retains some steam locomotives, including No. 671, a double-framed 0–6–0 built for the Südbahn in 1860, which worked until the 1970s, and No. 56.3115, a two-cylinder Gölsdorf compound 2-8-0 of 1914.

BIBLIOGRAPHY
Specific
Roth, P. W. *Grazer Industriedenkmaler* (Industrial monuments in Graz). Graz: dbv-Verlag für die Technische Universität Graz, 1978.

LOCATIONS
[M] Joanneum Provincial Museum of Mining, Geology and Technology, Raubergasse 10, 8010 Graz.
[M] Joanneum Provincial Museum of Weapons and Armour, Herrengasse 16, 8010 Graz.

BARRIE TRINDER

Greathead, James Henry (1844–96) The inventor of the Greathead Shield, which enables tunnels to be driven through soft, non-self-supporting and water-laden ground. Greathead was born in Grahamstown, Cape Colony, South Africa. He moved to England in 1859, and worked for the Metropolitan Railway. His shield was circular in cross-section and developed from patents taken out in 1864 and 1868 by Peter W. Barlow, for whom he worked on the construction of the Tower Subway beneath the Thames in London in 1869. The shield was constructed of steel, with an enclosed section at the front housing the cutters (originally men working with picks and shovels), and pressed forward by hydraulic rams from the last completed section of tunnel. Spoil was passed through doors at the back to be taken out through the completed tunnel. The tunnel was circular and lined with cast-iron rings, joined by flanges on the inside: the space between tunnel walls and lining was grouted with concrete forced in under pressure.

BIBLIOGRAPHY
Specific
ILN, 7 November 1896.
Vogel, R. M. *Tunnel Engineering: a museum treatment*. Washington DC: Smithsonian Institution, 1964.

Great Western Railway, England The largest of the British railway companies before their grouping in 1923, with radial routes from London (Paddington) to Penzance, and through Birmingham to Birkenhead, and most routes between. Originating as a line from Bristol to London and sanctioned in 1835, the railway was designed by ISAMBARD KINGDOM BRUNEL and laid to a gauge of 7 ft. $0\frac{1}{4}$ in. (2.14 m); it was retained until 1892. The GWR has been notable in the twentieth century for its distinctive style of locomotive engineering, pioneered by G. J. Churchward (1857–1933). The Great Western Society at Didcot preserves and operates locomotives and carriages.
See also figure 159.

BIBLIOGRAPHY
General
McDermot, 1927; Rolt, 1957.

LOCATION
[I] Great Western Society, Didcot, Oxfordshire.

Greece Ancient Greece was the cradle of Western democracy, architecture, drama and historical scholarship, and for many centuries the Greeks formed one of Europe's most active trading communities, but the Greek economy was one of the least developed in Europe in the nineteenth century and industrialization has proceeded relatively slowly in the twentieth.

Modern Greece extends over some 132 000 km² (51 000 sq. mi.), over 80 per cent of which is mountainous, and has a population of over nine million. It is bounded by Albania, Yugoslavia, Bulgaria and Turkey. The country is divided into ten regions: Macedonia, Thrace, Epirus, Thessaly, Central Greece (Stereá Hellás) and Euboea, the Peloponnese, the Aegean Islands, the Ionian Islands, Crete and Attica. These are subdivided into fifty-one administrative units or 'nomi'. There are 1425 islands in the Aegean, of which over 160 are inhabited.

Most of modern Greece fell under Turkish occupation following the fall of Byzantium in 1453 (*see* ISTANBUL; TURKEY) and the Turkish capture of Athens in 1456. The exceptions were Venetian enclaves in the islands, most of which were taken by the Turks during the eighteenth century. Following the war of independence of the 1820s, a Greek state based on Athens was established as a sovereign kingdom under Otto of Bavaria in 1830. In 1864 the Ionian Islands, which had been a British protectorate since 1815, passed to the new state. Various parts of the Turkish empire came under Greek control in the decades before World War I: Thessaly and part of Epirus in 1881, Crete in 1908, and Thrace with the islands of Thasos, Imbros, Tenedos, Lesbos and Sámos in 1912–13. Annexation brought industrial centres like Thessaloníki under Greek rule and expanded the domestic market. Following the war with Turkey which ended in 1922, one and a half million Greeks from the cities of Asia Minor fled to Greece, while there was a similar movement eastwards of people of Turkish origin. The islands of Imbros and Tenedos were lost to Turkey. A settlement with Turkey was reached by the Treaty of Ankara of 1930. Between 1941 and 1944 Greece fell under German occupation, which was followed by civil war. In 1947 the Dodecanese islands, including Rhodes, which had been under Italian rule since 1912, passed to Greece.

The traditional exports of Greece included olive oil, wine, dried fruits, sponges and tobacco, conveyed on distinctive sailing vessels called caiques. In some areas enterprises of considerable size developed in the nineteenth century. The 1860s and 70s saw the beginnings of some large-scale ventures. There are large tobacco warehouses at KAVALA, and vast wine cellars in the PELOPONNESE, but in 1917 only 282 Greek industrial concerns employed more than twenty-five people.

The most important Greek mineral is marble, extensively quarried both on the mainland and in the islands. It was used in the construction of the Parthenon (*see* PENDELI), and for most theatres, temples and sculptures of the classical period; and in modern times in the construction of the dam on Lake Marathon. Greece has no significant deposits of coal, although lignite is mined at Alivérion on Euboea and at Ptolemaïs in Macedonia.

Greece

Bauxite is extracted at Distomon and Parnassós; and nickel, chromium, zinc, lead, pyrites and iron ore are worked on a modest scale.

Greek civilization has always been based on seafaring, and harbour installations of many periods survive, particularly in the islands. It is only in the twentieth century that an effective road network has been constructed. In 1867 there were 1625 km (990 mi.) of paved road, a total which had reached only 4012 km (2445 mi.) in 1910. Several roads were built by foreign engineers. The 40 km (25 mi.) route from Amfissa to Bralo (Lamía) was the work of British and French engineers in World War I, and is now used extensively by trucks carrying bauxite. The Greek railway system developed slowly, following the construction of the line between Athens and Piraeus in 1867–9. There were only 206 km (126 mi.) of railway by 1880. The system now totals some 2543 route km (1580 mi.). The first important long-distance route was the metre-gauge system linking Athens with the Peloponnese, built between 1882 and 1902. The standard-gauge 521 km (317 mi.) route from Piraeus and Athens to the north was built in 1904–8. Initially it terminated at the Turkish border: it was only in 1918, after Macedonia was liberated from the Turks, that the line with its 69 tunnels was completed for the full 521 km (317 mi.) to Thessaloníki, linking Greece with Istanbul and central Europe. Improved communications promoted industrial growth in the Greek hinterland from the 1920s.

Over the last 15–20 years the Greek public has shown a keen and growing interest in the preservation and maintenance of the country's architectural heritage. New attitudes have developed, not only towards the antiquities of classical times, or towards Byzantine and post-Byzantine churches and monasteries, Frankish castles and Venetian fortifications, but also towards vernacular architecture and neo-Classical structures all over the Greek mainland and the islands. Government policies concerning the listing, protection and preservation of buildings from the period after 1830 are based on Law No. 1469, issued in 1950. It is only the Ministry of Culture that has power, on the basis of this law, to implement programmes of conservation of historic sites and buildings, as well as the artefacts connected with them – the machinery, in the case of industrial buildings. Recently the stress in conservation policy has shifted from the preservation and restoration of specific monuments to the protection and development of historic and traditional settlements and sites in their full landscape context. Since 1977 the Ministry of Urban Planning has also had authority to list, protect and preserve complete sites, as well as specific buildings. The Ministry of Culture is promoting a number of inventories of industrial sites, commencing in Lávrion and Piraeus (see Athens). At an international conference, 'Industrial Archaeology, Industrial Civilization', held in Athens in November 1988 Melina Mercouri promised that a department would be established within the Ministry purely to promote the study and preservation of industrial sites. The Cultural Foundation of the Hellenic Bank of Industrial Development (ETBA), founded in 1981, is concerned with the history of Greek technology between c.1750 and 1950, and aims to further its objectives through publications, the encouragement of museums, the sponsorship of conferences and the development of popular interest in the subject. It publishes the journal *Technology*.

See also AMFISSA; ARTA; ATHENS; CORINTH; CRETE; EDESSA; EUBOEA; KAVALA; LÁVRION; LESBOS; MYKONOS; NÁXOS; PELOPONNESE; PENDELI; PIRAEUS; RHODES; SOUFLI; THESSALONÍKI.

BIBLIOGRAPHY
General
Campbell and Sherrard, 1968; Clogg, 1983; Clogg and Clogg, 1980; Hudson, 1973; Milward and Saul, 1977; Tipton and Aldrich, 1987a, 1987b.

MARIA FINE, MICHAEL STRATTON and BARRIE TRINDER

Greek Revival Part of the CLASSICAL revival in architecture. Greek architecture only became known in Western Europe from c.1750, one of its first exponents being Claude-Nicolas Ledoux (1736–1806: *see* SALINS). Greek styles were most fashionable in the 1820s and 30s, particularly in England, Scotland and Prussia.

Greenfield Valley, Holywell, Clwyd, Wales A 3 km (2 mi.) valley on the North Wales coast, 25 km (16 mi.) NW of Chester, notable for the concentration of early industries around a powerful stream. Other benefits of the site were proximity to coal, and to lead, zinc and copper ores, and access through Liverpool to colonial markets. Three wire mills, an iron forge, and a red lead mill were in use by 1728. Copper battery and rolling, pinmaking, and paper-milling were introduced in the 1750s and 60s. Before the end of the century a calamine and lead mine opened, several cotton spinning factories were built, and copper manufacturing expanded, especially with the development of copper-bolt making by THOMAS WILLIAMS. Several dams remain and one copper mill has been excavated.

BIBLIOGRAPHY
General
Harris, 1964.
Specific
Davies, K. and Williams, C. J. *The Greenfield Valley.* Holywell: Holywell Town Council, 1977.

Greenland, Denmark The huge Arctic island of Greenland for the most part consists of pre-Cambrian rocks covered by a permanent cap of ice. The total area is 2.2 million km^2 (850 000 sq. mi.) of which only 342 000 km^2 (132 000 sq. mi.) are free of ice. Most of the population of about 54 000 live along the southern two-thirds of the west coast. Fishing is the most important occupation, followed by hunting and farming.

A large mine for CRYOLITE has been worked at Ivittuut since 1856. Initially cryolite was used to make ALKALI, but later for aluminium smelting and enamelling. Further north on Disko island, coal has been mined on a small scale at Qutdligssat since 1924. On the east coast of Greenland lead and zinc were exploited in the 1950s and 60s at Mesters Vig. At Narsarsuaq in the south there are extensive remains of a large US air base constructed during World War II and revived during the Korean War.

BIBLIOGRAPHY
Specific
Banks, M. *Greenland.* Newton Abbot: David & Charles, 1975.
Trap, J. P. *Danmark,* xxx (Greenland). Copenhagen, 1970.

Greenock and **Western Renfrewshire,** Scotland The principal towns of Inverclyde District are Greenock, once known for 'ships, sugar and showers', and Port Glasgow, 5 km (3 mi.) E., established by the city of Glasgow from 1668 to deny the city's upriver trade to Greenock until the Clyde was made navigable.

A replica of the PS *Comet*, the first commercially successful steamship, stands in a pond in Port Glasgow. Shipbuilding continues there in Fergusson Ailsa's Newark Yard, and at Scott Lithgow's Glen and Kingston yards. Scott's were established in Westburn, Greenock, in 1711, and built their own engines from 1825, so Scott Lithgow is one of the longest-lived industrial concerns in Britain. Scott's Cartsburn yard in Greenock was demolished in 1988, leaving Steele's dry dock of 1818. Caird's (later Harland & Wolff's) Westburn shipyard possesses a big steel fabrication shop of 1919.

Marine engineering was begun in Greenock by Caird & Co. in 1826. Their Arthur Street works still stands. The finishing shop of the 1830s is probably the oldest purpose-built marine engineering building in the world. To this was added a fireproof brass foundry, and later cast-iron-framed machine shops, erecting shops and boiler shops, the cast-iron stanchions externally expressed with polychrome brick infill. J. G. Kincaid continue marine-engine manufacture on East Hamilton Street. In Renfrew the two-cylinder side-lever engine of the PS *Clyde* of 1851 is preserved on a pedestal.

Greenock has several early nineteenth-century warehouses with gables to the street and cast-iron columns inside, on Bogle, Dalrymple and Nicholson Streets, one now the Westburn Centre for small businesses. There is a later polychrome brick tobacco bond on Clarence Street.

The Inverclyde Initiative is developing office blocks, on the site of infilled docks and demolished warehouses near the Doric Customs House of 1818, designed by William Burn (1789–1870) and the finest in Scotland. The cast-iron, pilastered east transit shed at Custom House Quay may contain elements of Rennie's work. East India Harbour of 1805 by JOHN RENNIE has a dry dock and a handsome cast-iron-framed timber-clad transit shed of *c.*1860. Victoria Harbour of 1846–50 has a hydraulic power station with a small accumulator tower. James Watt Dock 1879–86 has the most dramatic multi-storey dockside warehouses in Scotland: three- and five-storey, 206 m (676 ft.) long, in polychrome brick, the columns doubling as chutes for grain or sugar. At the entrance is a giant Arrols cantilever hammerhead crane of 1907. Several over-ambitious projects, including the James Watt Dock, with the Garvel Graving Dock of 1871 and the Great Harbour of 1880, combined to drive Greenock Harbour Trust into bankruptcy in 1887.

JAMES WATT had carried out harbour improvements for his native town of Greenock, and supervised construction of the Berryards Reservoir, which is still used, in 1773. The more ambitious Shaw's Water Works was designed by Robert Thom in 1825-7, supplying drinking water to the town, and water power to a linear industrial estate, necessary for competition with Glasgow because there were no local supplies of coal. Among the concerns powered by the nineteen falls were Fleming & Reid worsted mills of 1840 and 1881 (the latter turbine-driven), the Eagle Foundry of Rankin & Blackmore, and Drummond's later Belfast-roofed polychrome brick joinery works. The Shaws water system was used in 1885-7 for the second public hydro-electricity supply in Britain.

Greenock had fourteen of the seventy-four British sugar refineries in 1864, and until the 1880s was the second sugar-refining centre in Britain. Berryards (renamed Westburn) Refinery was built in 1852, when it was water-powered; it was subsequently enlarged, and is still used by Tate & Lyle. It has a classic eight-storey, brick-piered building with a cast-iron roof tank and a triple-gabled sugar warehouse. Parts remain of two other refineries, Walker's of 1826 in Upper Nicholson Street, and Glebe, in Kerr Street, of 1831, with a five-storey, sharply wedge-shaped block of c.1870.

The Gourock Rope Works merged with the Port Glasgow Rope & Duck Co., established in 1736. At Port Glasgow the 400 m (1 300 ft.) ropewalk was demolished in 1976, leaving a striking fireproof eight-storey, polychrome brick, sailcloth factory, a former sugar refinery, acquired in 1868. It contains a nineteenth-century press packer and a rope race with pulleys. Residential and light industrial use is proposed.

Wemyss Bay Station, 11 km (7 mi.) SW, has a swirling glass and steel concourse with a half-timbered exterior, designed by James Miller, architect for the Caledonian Railway, in 1905.

BIBLIOGRAPHY
General
Hume, 1976; Shaw, 1984.
Specific
Clark, S. The Shaws Water Falls in Greenock. In *Scottish Society for Industrial Archaeology Newsletter*, 7(3) 1984, and 8(1) 1985.
Tucker, D. G. Hydro-electricity for public supply in Britain 1881-1894. In *IAR*, I, 1977.

MARK WATSON

Greymouth, Westland, New Zealand   A town settled in 1868, on the west coast, celebrated in the late nineteenth century for the manufacture of gold dredges at the Dispatch Foundry, established by a Scot, John Sewell, in 1873. The first boot factory in New Zealand was opened here in 1866 by Michael O'Brien, who subsequently became the leading entrepreneur in the industry, with factories in Christchurch. A building on Mawhera Quay survives. 'Greymouth special' cycles were manufactured by Albert Schultze from 1901.

Brunner coal mines, 8 km (5 mi.) to the E., were discovered by Thomas Brunner in 1848, and developed on a large scale from 1864. Many beehive ovens were built from 1868, producing coke for foundries in Christchurch and Wellington, and smelters in Australia and New Caledonia. A site including surface remains of mines and an extensive range of beehive ovens is now an industrial archaeology complex administered by the New Zealand Historic Places Trust. Massive hardwood coal tippling bins survive at Point Elizabeth Mine, Rewanui, part of the same mines.

Shantytown, 8 km (5 mi.) to the S. of Greymouth, is a re-creation of a typical gold mining town of the 1880s. Demonstrations of sluicing are given at the working face of a claim, and there are working panning tubs where the mineral is washed. Miners' accommodation includes an authentic 'den' for Chinese workers. A locomotive by Sharp, Stewart & Co. of Glasgow works passenger trains, and there are livery stables, a printing works, and various stores.

LOCATION
[M] Shantytown, New Zealand.

BARRIE TRINDER

grinding machine   A MACHINE TOOL that shapes metal surfaces by bringing them into contact with a rapidly rotating abrasive wheel. Depending on the design, either the wheel or the workpiece or both may revolve or be fed into contact. Grinding, actually a cutting process, is an ancient method for shaping metal, and by the early nineteenth century was widely employed to finish cylindrical surfaces and the hardened edges of tools and cutlery. Sandstone and crude emery grinding wheels fixed to the cross-slide of engine lathes sharpened the knives of woodworking tools and finished hardened surfaces in the mid-nineteenth century, but precision grinding as a manufacturing process depended on the development of stable synthetic abrasives of uniform composition in the 1870s. Synthetic wheels were employed in a variety of configurations: suspended in a calliper for finishing rollers; replacing the cutter in a universal milling machine or a gear shaper; or moving in a planetary plane for grinding internal surfaces. The 'centreless' grinder for producing extremely precise cylindrical surfaces was invented by Heim in 1915. Although grinding made possible the most precise machining of the hardest steels, it was still chiefly used as a finishing process until incorporated in the MASS PRODUCTION of automobile components in the early twentieth century.

BIBLIOGRAPHY
General
Rolt, 1986; Steeds, 1969; Woodbury, 1959.

TIM PUTNAM

grindstones   Stones, usually sandstones or sandy limestones, which can be shaped into a circular form and used for grinding edge tools (*see* MILLSTONES).

gristmill   'Grist' originally meant the action of grinding:

it came to mean grain to be ground, and the term 'gristmill' is synonymous with CORN MILL.

Groningen, The Netherlands   A province in the north-east Netherlands, the focus of modern natural gas and salt-extraction industries centred on the port of Delfzijl, 25 km (15.5 mi.) NE of the city of Groningen.

Groningen, the provincial capital, has long commercial traditions, and dominated the north-east of the Netherlands, particularly before 1900. The town was connected to the North Sea by the Reitdiep, a waterway west of the centre, until 1876 when its role was taken over by the Eemskanaal to Delfzijl, stimulating the movement of commercial activities to the east of the city. The Koren-beurs (corn exchange) of 1865 has a façade like the temple of Mercury, but its cast-iron pillars and glass walls resemble the Crystal Palace in London. There is a JUGENDSTIL shopping arcade. A CREAMERY and many warehouses in the centre and east of the city now serve as student apartments. East of the centre small farmhouses forming a distinct village were built in 1919 as a social housing project and renovated in the 1970s. There is an important tobacco manufacturing complex at Paters-woldseweg. The city has greatly changed in the 1980s because of the enforced transfer of public-sector offices to stimulate employment in the north. The new Museum of Printing displays nineteenth-century equipment and machines from local companies.

South-east of the capital much reclamation of peat lands took place between 1800 and 1860. Canals were built through areas where extraction had taken place since the seventeenth century. Characteristic villages grew up as ribbon developments along access roads, the first of them Hoogezand, 14 km (9 mi.) E. Peat ships were built at small shipyards, some of which still build modern coasters. In the nineteenth century peat was transported to the west of the country in exchange for household refuse that served as manure. Potato-flour factories were developed in the late nineteenth century, followed by strawboard plants. Changes in technology completely altered the agro-industrial economy after World War II. There are remains of strawboard factories in Hoogezand and at Scheemda, 28 km (17 mi.) E., are some buildings of the De Toekomst co-operative strawboard works built in 1899–1909, which closed in 1968. A museum at Veendam, 25 km ($15\frac{1}{2}$ mi.) SE of Groningen, portrays the history of the peat colonies.

Winschoten, 32 km (19 mi.) SE, has three surviving tower mills, and the last steam pumping station with an Archimedean screw, built in 1878–95, with a double compound engine of 1895 by the Landeweer company, which was electrified in 1929. A bell foundry of 1794 at nearby Heiligerlee was closed in 1980 and is now a museum. At Nieuwe-Pekela, 40 km (25 mi.) SE of Groningen, is a steam sawmill of 1875, partly modernized and still working, with a narrow-gauge railway. Along the Oosterdiep, Westerdiep, 40 km (25 mi.) SE, and the Pekel Aa (near Winschoten) are many imposing steel lifting bridges built between 1850 and 1945. Along the

Damsterdiep, constructed in 1650, industrial monuments include limekilns, 6 km (4 mi.) NE, and a brickyard, 10 km (6 mi.) NE.

At Nieuwe-Schans, 46 km (29 mi.) NE on the German border, the oldest locomotive shed in the Netherlands, dating from 1865, has served as a bus garage since 1948.

There is a Carriage Museum at Leek, 15 km (9 mi.) SW, and a Museum of Clothing at Bellingwolde, 40 km (25 mi.) SE of Groningen.

BIBLIOGRAPHY
General
Van der Ploeg, 1988.

LOCATIONS
[M] De Oude Wolden Streekmuseum (Clothing Museum), Hoofd-weg 161, Bellingwolde.
[M] Grafisch Museum (Printing Museum), Rabenhauptstraat 65, Groningen.
[M] Museum Behleezlil (Museum of Steam Pumping), Oostereinde 4, Winschoten.
[M] Nationaal Rijtuigmuseum (National Carriage Museum), Huis Nienoord, Leek.
[M] Noordelijk Scheepvaartmuseum (Maritime Museum) and Tabaksmuseum (Tobacco Museum), Brugstraat 24–6, Gron-ingen.
[M] Veenkolonial Museum (Peat Colony Museum), Kerkstraat 18, Veendam.

JURRIE VAN DALEN

Grossreifling, Styria, Austria   A village at the confluence of the Rivers Salza and Enns, 42 km (26 mi.) S. of Steyr. There are ironworks sites on the Enns. The Enns was much used for conveying timber to Hieflau, 9 km (6 mi.) upstream, where the timber was converted to charcoal and conveyed up the River Erzbach to Eisenerz (*see* STYRIAN IRON TRAIL) for use in furnaces. There are remains of the sixteenth-century timber-floating lock built by Hans von Gasteiger (d. 1577), a pioneer of this technology who was buried in a local church. The Österreichisches Holzmuseum (Austrian Forestry Museum), which is located in the Neuer Kasten (new storehouse) of Innerberger Hauptgewerkschaft, dates from 1771. Founded by forester and schoolmaster Adolf Grabner, it contains extensive displays on the qualities, utilization and transport of wood, with many models.

BIBLIOGRAPHY
General
Sperl, 1984.

LOCATION
[M] Österreichisches Holzmuseum (Austrian Forestry Museum), Forstmuseum Silvanum, Grossreifling, Austria.

guide-wheel railway   An edge-rail system, with four-wheeled wagons running on timber baulks, the wheels being broad with rollers rotating on the inside edges of the baulks. Horse haulage could be used. Such railways were observed in mines and on the surface in the mid-sixteenth century at Kremnica (Kremnitz) in Czechoslovakia and by the seventeenth century at several mines in the region. Similar systems were used at FALUN, Sweden, and in the

Harz region in the eighteenth century, and in the RUHRGEBIET, Germany, in the early nineteenth.

BIBLIOGRAPHY
General
Lewis, 1970.

Guimarães, Minho, Portugal   An industrial town 40 km (25 mi.) NE of Oporto, well known for cutlery, textiles and tanning. The first papermill to use wooden substances as its raw material was established at Caldas de Vizela, 8 km (5 mi.) S., in 1806, the Englishman Thomas Bishop being closely concerned with it. The factory was destroyed by the Napoleonic armies and nothing remains of it. Some water mills remain in operation on the River Vizela, and at Pevidém are some of the oldest textile mills of the county.

Guise, Aisne, France   If Jean-Baptiste Godin (1817–88) is a household name in France today, it is probably for his household appliances: enamelled bathtubs or, more especially, cast-iron stoves, still manufactured from nineteenth-century patterns. The original Godin foundry was established at Guise, close to its founder's birthplace, in 1846. Between 1859 and the 1880s, nestling in a meander of the River Oise, a whole self-contained industrial colony was established near the factory, its overall architectural conception and many of its practical details being inspired by Godin's reading of the utopian socialist CHARLES FOURIER. The 'Familistère', as this co-operative community was termed (Fourier wrote of a 'Phalanstère), offered its inhabitants, of whom there were some 1200 by 1880, the 'equivalents of wealth': educational, cultural, commercial, gardening and leisure facilities, and, of course, sanitary housing. The dwellings are organized on four levels, with galleries running around rectangular, glass-covered courtyards, conceived as places of fraternal gathering, of light, and also of mutual and moralistic surveillance.

Partially rebuilt after bomb damage during World War I, the housing pavilions and communal buildings, schools, day nursery, canteen and shop, are still intact and have recently been afforded official protection. A small museum in the former theatre presents the history of the site and of its founder.

BIBLIOGRAPHY
General
Brauman *et al.*, 1980; Delabre and Gautier, 1988; Paquot *et al.*, 1982.

PAUL SMITH

gun   A tube, closed at one end, from which projectiles are expelled at high velocity by the discharge of an explosive substance. Crude bamboo guns which used the detonation of GUNPOWDER to shoot clay balls appear to have been used in China around AD 1000. By the end of the sixteenth century the basic types of small arms (MUSKET, RIFLE and PISTOL) and heavy arms (CANNON, howitzers and mortars) had made their appearance. The potential of the new 'firepower' for the conduct of warfare

and the territorial disposition of power were first fully realized through the programme of technical innovation and military reorganization instigated by King Gustavus Adolphus (1594–1632) of Sweden.

The effectiveness of guns as weapons was dependent on several design considerations. The barrel had to be made strong, especially at the breech or firing end, to contain the explosive forces without the weapon becoming unwieldy; and its interior bore had to be made both round and straight to a high degree of precision. The large-scale production of identical projectiles, and an efficient means of loading the charge and firing it at the breech end were also important. Military efforts to achieve more rapid, mobile, dependable, accurate and destructive gunfire depended on, and encouraged the development of, metallurgy, MACHINE TOOLS and INTERCHANGEABLE PARTS. In 1663 the Royal Society in London discussed the principle of a gun that used the forces generated by its operation to reload automatically; its realization two hundred years later in the machine-guns of Maxim and Browning marked the maturity of metal-manufacturing culture.

BIBLIOGRAPHY
General
Greener, 1910; Hughes, 1974; McNeill, 1982.

TIM PUTNAM

gun metal   A form of BRONZE, usually also containing zinc to facilitate casting. Originally used for guns, from the nineteenth century gun metal has been used for bearings and pump bodies and for use with high-pressure steam.

BIBLIOGRAPHY
General
Alexander and Street, 1949.

gunpowder   A finely ground mixture of SALTPETRE, SULPHUR and CHARCOAL, in the proportion 75:15:10, otherwise called black powder; the only explosive available before the 1860s. Invented in China in the twelfth century, gunpowder was introduced into Europe in the thirteenth century and used in battle from the fourteenth. It was first used for blasting in mines in Hungary in 1627 and in England from the 1670s. Its use was further stimulated by the invention of the safety fuse by William Bickford of Tuckingmill, Cornwall, in 1805.

In a gunpowder mill, saltpetre and sulphur were refined, and charcoal pulverized, usually by a crushing mill with a stone-edge runner. The three ingredients were then 'incorporated', traditionally by pestle and mortar, but in the nineteenth century by steam or water-driven mills, producing 'mill cake', which was broken up and 'corned', i.e. pressed through sieves. The powder was glazed by tumbling in barrels to round the grains, black lead being added from the nineteenth century to increase water resistance. It was then dried, samples were proofed, and the remainder was packed in oak barrels. Buildings where it was made were widely spaced, with earth embankments on three sides and flimsy roofs, to minimize the effects of explosions. Powder has now been almost completely displaced by high explosives. Gunpowder factories were usually destroyed when production ceased but there are often extensive remains of earth banks and watercourses (*see* CORK; DELAWARE; FAVERSHAM; TASMANIA).

BIBLIOGRAPHY
General
Crocker, 1986; Patterson, 1986; Reader, 1970.
Specific
Howard, R. A. Black powder manufacture. In *Journal of the Society for Industrial Archeology*, I(1) 1975.

BARRIE TRINDER

Guntramsdorf, Lower Austria, Austria   A village 20 km (12 mi.) SW of Vienna, with a photographic engraving plant of Endler & Co., dating from 1910 and closed in 1986; the plant retains all its machinery, tools and moulds, as well as the power transmission plant. The Gesellschaft zur Förderung und Erforschung der Niederösterreichischen Industriekultur im Viertel unter dem Wienerwald (Association for the Promotion and Investigation of Industrial Culture in Lower Austria and the Wienerwald region) intends to preserve the workshops.

Gutach im Schwarzwald, Baden-Württemberg, Germany   Early, isolated electric power-supply systems, with small, often privately owned hydro-electric power stations are characteristic of Baden-Württemberg. Power stations, initially built by industrial firms for their own use, also contributed to the public supply. The firm of Gütermann in the Wildgutach valley of the western Black Forest, well-known as a manufacturer of sewing silks, and pioneers in electricity generation from 1866, supplied local communities from 1910 from a 160 kW power station. The Zweribach power station, with a small pumping plant and reservoir, was built by Gütermann in 1924, and is particularly interesting for its picturesque situation and design. The power station of a match factory in Haslach-Schnellingen fulfilled similar functions, the power of the Kinzig river being supplemented by a 1000 hp diesel engine which is preserved. Other examples that can still be seen are the Teinach power station, servicing the Calw district, and one in Hohebach, serving what were once the Jagst works.

The open-air museum of the Black Forest region in Gutach includes buildings relating to distilling, woodworking and shoemaking.

BIBLIOGRAPHY
General
Zippelius, 1974.

LOCATION
[M] Schwarzwälder Freilichtmuseum 'Vogtsbauernhof' (Vogtsbauernhof – the Black Forest open-air museum), 7611 Gutach im Schwarzwald.

ROLF HÖHMANN

gutta-percha   Latex or raw RUBBER produced from *Dichopsis gutta* and related plants from the East Indies, which insulates and remains unchanged in sea water and was used in submarine CABLES, as well as for tubes and pipes in hydraulic presses, washing pans and other apparatus used in the food and chemical industries. The first patent for working it dates from 1845.

BIBLIOGRAPHY
General
Clouth, 1903.

Gyoma, Békés, Hungary   A town on the River Körös, 160 km (100 mi.) SE of Budapest. The 100-year-old Kner printing works is now a printing museum containing every Hungarian type fount.

LOCATION
[M,S] Kner-print Museum, H-5500 Gyomaendrod Kossuth u. 16.

gypsum   A monoclinic form of calcium sulphate ($CaSO_4.2H_2O$), which occurs naturally and was a by-product of PHOSPHORUS manufacture. At 120–130 °C gypsum loses water and forms the hemihydrate, plaster of Paris ($2CaSO_4.H_2O$), which when mixed with water solidifies to gypsum, expanding slightly. Gypsum is used in the manufacture of PORTLAND CEMENT. Its opaque crystalline form is alabaster; the rhombic form ($CaSO_4$) is ANHYDRITE.

BIBLIOGRAPHY
General
Morgan and Pratt, 1938.

H

Haarlem, Noord Holland, The Netherlands A city which prospered in the seventeenth century through trade in linens, which were imported from Silesia and Friesland, bleached using the waters of Haarlemmermeer, and sold as 'Hollands', all over Europe. Silks and camlets (mixture fabrics, resembling silks) were manufactured in the late eighteenth century, and cotton factories were established after the secession of Belgium in 1830 (*see* THE NETHERLANDS), encouraged by King William I (1772–1843). The textile industry languished after 1850 and there are few remains. Several old-established printing companies, among them the Enschedé printing house near the cathedral, continue the tradition of Laurens Jansz Coster, one of the inventors of printing in the fifteenth century. Along the Spaarne river are two late nineteenth-century cocoa factories, one still in use, and remains of shipyards and engineering concerns, near a cast-iron swing bridge of 1902. Haarlem has a railway station of 1908, with magnificent tiled murals. Teyler's Museum, established in 1778 and the oldest museum in the Netherlands, displays scientific instruments.

At Halfweg, 7 km (5 mi.) E., is a steam pumping station of 1851 which is preserved with its equipment, including steam and water tube boilers, a Stork steam engine of 1923 (the third used in the station), and six scoop wheels.
See also CRUQUIUS.

LOCATIONS
[M] Museum Enschedé (Printing Museum), Klokhuisplein 5, Haarlem.
[S] Stoomgemaal Halfweg (Halfweg Steam Pumping Station), Haarlemmermeerstraat 4, Halfweg.
[M] Teyler's Museum, Spaarne 16, Haarlem.

JURRIE VAN DALEN

Haber-Bosch process *See* AMMONIA.

haberdashery A term applied to the goods sold by a haberdasher, originally hats and HOSIERY, and sometimes fabrics. From the seventeenth century 'haberdashery', if used precisely, meant small items relating to clothing, such as THREAD, RIBBON, LACE and TAPE.

hackling Hackling (also hatchelling or heckling) is a combing operation in the preparation of FLAX. The hackle (or hatchel or heckle) is a comb made of rows of metal teeth set upright into a wooden base, commonly measuring about 5 cm × 15 cm × 30 cm (2 in. × 6 in. × 12 in.); the metal teeth, which resemble nails or needles, rise about 10 cm (4 in.) high. The flax fibres are drawn through the metal teeth, usually in several stages, from coarse (the largest teeth, set widest apart), to fine (the smallest teeth, set closest together). In machine hackling, clamps hold the flax while it moves through sets of steel pins. This process continues the removal of residual stalk and sap, and separates the long-fibred flax from the shorter tow. Tow must first be carded, but long line fibres proceed from hackling to drawing, the first stage of spinning or yarn preparation.

A rippling comb, similar in size and configuration to a coarse hackle but with wider-spaced teeth, is used before RETTING and BRAKING to remove the seeds from the flax stalk. A wool comb takes essentially the same form as a hackle, but has much longer metal teeth, up to 25 cm (10 in.).

Hadfield, Ellis Charles Raymond (b.1909) Charles Hadfield has been chiefly responsible for the growth in understanding of waterways in Britain and further afield in the past forty years. With a background in publishing, he became an expert on firefighting during World War II, and subsequently Director of Publications for the Central Office of Information. His first book on canals was published in 1945, and he was one of the founders of the Inland Waterways Association in 1946, being expelled with L. T. C. ROLT in 1951. His *Canals of the British Isles* series, launched in 1955 and completed in 1977, has documented from original sources the history of almost every significant waterway in Britain. In 1960–4 he was partner with David St John Thomas in the publishing firm of David & Charles, which more than any other concern brought into print the exploding interest of the 1960s in British industrial and transport history. He served as a member of the British Waterways Board from 1963.

BIBLIOGRAPHY
General
Baldwin and Burton, 1984; Hadfield, 1950, 1955, 1960, 1966a, 1966b, 1967a, 1967b, 1968, 1986; Hadfield and Eyre, 1945; Hadfield and Skempton, 1979.

Hagen, North-Rhine Westphalia, Germany *See* RUHRGEBIET.

Hague, The ('s-Gravenhage, den Haag), Zuid Holland, The Netherlands The seat of the Dutch government, the function of The Hague has always been administrative rather than industrial. The Museum of the Book includes the equipment of an eighteenth-century printing company. Scheveningen, 3 km (2 mi.) NW, is a fishing port, with a harbour of 1904, and a packet station, linked with the capital by tramways. It is also a resort with a famous PIER, and a magnificent painted panorama portraying the port in 1880. A dodecagonal cast-iron lighthouse dates from 1875. At Voorschoten, 5 km (3 mi.) N., a former gold and silver factory, built as a mansion house in 1858, is a protected monument.

LOCATIONS

[M] Municipal Museum, Stadhouderslaan 41, The Hague.
[M] Nederlandse Postmuseum (Netherlands Postal Museum), Zeestraat 82, The Hague.
[S] Panorama Mesdag (Mesdag Panorama), Zeestraat 65b, The Hague.
[M] Rijksmuseum Meermanno-Westreenianum (Museum of the Book), Prinsessegracht 30, The Hague.

Haigerloch-Stetten, Baden Württemberg, Germany Baden-Württemberg lacks raw materials; only potassium mining is of any importance today. The oldest of three mines which produced rock salt is at Stetten, near Haigerloch, in the former Hohenzollern region, 56 km (35 mi.) SW of Stuttgart. Test drilling proved successful in 1852, and by 1854 a shaft had been sunk to 98 m (322 ft.). Of the original structures, the headstock building, the office and a dwelling house have been preserved, and stand on the slope above the River Eyach. Mines which were exploited by PILLAR-AND-STALL methods from 1877 remain accessible from this shaft.

hair Hair from many creatures has been used in FELTMAKING, in plastering, and for brushes. The long fibres in horsehair were combined with linen or cotton to be made into fabrics for seating; medium-length fibres were employed in fabric sieves for malting or dairying; and short fibres were carded, spun into a loose rope, soaked, heated and then unpicked, the process curling them to make them suitable for use in upholstery.

BIBLIOGRAPHY
General
Tomlinson, 1852-4.

Hakavik, Buskerud, Norway Hakavik Kraftverk is a hydro-electric power station built for the state railways in 1922 but soon afterwards taken over by the State Electricity Board, although still producing electricity for the railway system. It is preserved as an historical monument.

Halden, Østfold, Norway A town on the Swedish border, 90 km (56 mi.) S. of Oslo, at the mouth of the Tiste, an important timber-floating river. It was named Fredrikshald by King Frederick II in 1665, and known by that name until 1927. An iron pyramid of 1860 commemorates King Charles XII of Sweden. Halden is a centre for sawmilling and shoemaking, and the site of the Herrebø Faience Factory (1758-c.1775), whose products are displayed in Kunstindustrimuseet, OSLO. It is the terminus

of the Dalsland Canal to Skulerud, 50 km (30 mi.) long, constructed by Nils Ericsson in 1863-8.

BIBLIOGRAPHY
General
Forstrom, 1915.

Halifax, West Yorkshire, England An extensive Pennine parish. Domestic woollen manufacture was well established by 1700, and Halifax became one of the chief towns of the region, its population growing from 12 000 to 34 000 during 1801-51. There is a Piece Hall of 1777, the only surviving example in Yorkshire, built as a wholesale cloth market and later restored as shops. There is a pioneering project in the reuse of a textile factory as workshops at Dean Clough Mills. From 1859 Sir Edward Akroyd, a woollen manufacturer, built a model Gothic settlement, Akroyden, designed by GEORGE GILBERT SCOTT, adjacent to Haley Hill Mills and Scott's church of All Souls.

BIBLIOGRAPHY
General
Trinder, 1982b.

LOCATION

[I] Calderdale Museums Service, Bankfield Museum, Boothtown Road, Halifax HX3 6HG.

Hallein, Salzburg, Austria An ancient centre of saltworking on the western bank of the River Salzach, 18 km (11 mi.) S. of Salzburg. The museum in the former administrative building of the saltworks, of 1754, facing the river on Pflegerplatz, has a section on saltworks but is internationally celebrated for its collection of Celtic artefacts. The saltmine (Salzbergwerk) on Dürrnberg employed two hundred in 1903; it is approached from the town by cable car, and can be visited through an entrance now within the open-air museum of restored Celtic dwellings.

LOCATION

[M] Celtic Museum, Pflegerplatz, 5400 Hallein.

Hallingdal, Buskerud, Norway A valley extending north from Gulsvik at the northern end of Lake Krøderen, 165 km (103 mi.) N. of Oslo, through which passes the BERGENSBANEN.

Hallingdal Folkemuseum at Nesbyen, 40 km (25 mi.) N. of Gulsvik, founded in 1899 by agricultural official Gudbrand Tandberg on the promptings of local farmers, is now a museum for the whole region with large collections of artefacts and twenty-two re-erected buildings, mostly farmsteads with characteristic rose-painted interiors. Spinning wheels, looms and yarn winds provide evidence of domestic textile manufactures. Industrial buildings include a corn mill, a tar kiln, a shoemaker's cottage and a silver fox farm of the 1920s.

Oslo Lysverker, the electricity undertaking of the Norwegian capital, has nine power stations in Hallingdal. Water-power rights in the valley were obtained in 1916 but large-scale exploitation began after 1940 with the object of providing power to introduce electric heating in Oslo. The first power station, Hof I, began operation in 1949.

BIBLIOGRAPHY
General
Ljogodt, 1977.

LOCATION
[M] Hallingdal Folkemuseum, p.b. 87, 3541-Nesbyen.

BARRIE TRINDER

Hall in Tirol (Solbad Hall), Tyrol, Austria   The main source of salt in Tyrol, in the Inn Valley, 10 km (6 mi.) E. of Innsbruck. Brine was conveyed from as far as 10 km (6 mi.) away to evaporating houses in the Lower Stadt Platz which worked until 1967. The principal mines were on Haller Salzberg to the north. Hall in Tirol is also the site of the provincial mint, and a twelve-sided Münzerturm (mint tower) of 1486 still stands.

LOCATIONS
[M] Mining Museum, Fürstengasse, 6060 Hall in Tirol.
[S] Saltmine and Boiling Plant, 6060 Hall in Tirol.

hallmark   A term used from early in the eighteenth century for a distinctive mark put on gold or silver by an Assay office. Hallmarks enable pieces to be dated and their places of assay to be identified.

BIBLIOGRAPHY
General
Bradbury, 1975.

Hallstatt, Salzburg, Austria   A salt-working village on the west shore of the Hallstätter-See, which gives its name to an early European Iron Age culture of 1000–500 BC. A wooden pipeline, constructed in 1595 to take brine to Bad Ischl, 17 km (10 mi.) N., was extended to Ebensee, 29 km (18 mi.) N., in 1607, and is now a protected monument. The history of saltmines over several millennia is explained in the Museum of Prehistory. A funicular from the adjoining hamlet of Lahn gives access to Rudolfsturm, the home of the mine manager, of 1903, and the site of a castle built in 1284 to protect the saltworkings. The mines beyond are open to the public in the summer months.

LOCATION
[M] Museum of Prehistory, Markt, 4830, Hallstatt, Bezirk Gmunden.

Halton, Cheshire, England   A conurbation on either side of the River Mersey, including Runcorn and Widnes, the principal centre for the manufacture of sulphuric acid,

Figure 55   The River Mersey in the borough of Halton between Runcorn on the near bank and Widnes on the far bank in 1961, showing, from left to right, the Queen Aethelfleda railway bridge of 1868, the recently completed round bridge by Mott, Hay & Anderson, and the transporter bridge of 1905, which was awaiting demolition. The St Helens Canal appears in the top right corner, with the office building of the Gossage soap company, which in 1991 houses the headquarters of Catalyst, to the left of it. The Bridgewater Canal passes through Runcorn in the foreground, and the Manchester Ship Canal can be seen alongside the Mersey.
Catalyst

alkali and chlorine in Britain from the mid-nineteenth century. A museum based in a tower, once the office and laboratory for a soap works, provides a prospect and interpretation of the area which includes a section of the St Helen's Canal, opened in 1833; a basin at the terminus of the St Helens & Runcorn Gap Railway, a hybrid line completed in 1833; and the remains of condensing cisterns used in the manufacture of hydrochloric acid, pyrites kilns used in making sulphuric acid, a GAY-LUSSAC acid-absorption tower, and bases of Weldon chlorine stills. The Queen Aethelfleda wrought-iron lattice railway bridge across the Mersey, which has three 93 m (305 ft.) spans, is by William Baker, from 1868; and there are some traces of a transporter bridge of 1905–61.

BIBLIOGRAPHY
Specific
Greatbatch, M. L. and Mercer, P. J. *Spike Island.* Halton: Halton Chemical Industry Museum, 1985.

LOCATION
[M] Catalyst (Chemical Industry Museum), Gossage Tower, West Bank, Widnes, Cheshire.

Hamar, Hedmark, Norway Hamar, on the shores of Lake Mjøsa, 120 km (75 mi.) N. of Oslo, was founded by Pope Adrian IV in 1152, but destroyed by the Swedish army in 1567, and only revived as a municipality in 1848. The town prospered in the nineteenth century as a railway centre, where passengers on standard-gauge trains from Oslo changed to the 1067 mm (3 ft. 6 in.) trains that ran eastwards to ELVERUM from 1870, and from 1877 through to Røros and Trondheim. From 1921 standard-gauge trains ran to Trondheim from Hamar over Dovre summit. The railway company and a private concern, Jernstøper & Maskinfabrik, both established engineering workshops at Hamar. The latter are now closed. The railway company workshops are in Germanic style, with crenellated end gables and prominent round windows. The station is a distinguished building, of brick with heavy stone dressings: it has seventeen bays and two storeys, with a mixture of Gothic and Classical detailing.

The Norwegian Railway Museum (Norsk Jernbanemuseum) was established in a room at the station in 1896, but the collection was stored during 1912–26, and in 1956 moved to its present 30 ha (75 ac.) site on the lake shore, perhaps the most attractive setting of any railway museum. The state railway company took responsibility for the collection in 1946. The museum has followed the example of Scandinavian open-air folk museums in acquiring a collection of wooden buildings, including the stations from Kløften, on the Norwegian Trunk Railway, dating from 1854; Bestum, designed by G. Bull in 1890; Ilseng, designed by Paul Due in 1893; and Killingmo, from the 750 mm (2 ft. 5½ in.) Urskogs–Holands line, opened in 1896. The last now serves as a terminus for a 350 m (380 yd.) section of track on which visitors can travel in trains worked by a Chemnitz (2120) 0-6-0T of 1895 and a Henschel (24863) 2-6-2T of 1950 from the same line. The locomotive collection includes Nos. 16 and 17, 2-4-0s supplied to the Norwegian Trunk Railway in 1861 by

ROBERT STEPHENSON; No. 234, a two-cylinder 4-6-0 built at Hamar in 1911; No. 452, a four-cylinder compound 4-8-0 constructed at Hamar for the BERGENSBANEN in 1926; No. 470, a four-cylinder compound 2-8-4 built for the Dovrebane in 1942 by Krupps of Essen (identical locomotives were constructed by Thunes Mekaniske Verksted of Oslo); No. 21, a 1067 mm (3 ft. 6 in.) gauge Beyer Peacock 2-4-0T (992) of 1870; and No. 7, a 1067 mm gauge 4-4-0, the first locomotive built by Thunes in 1901. Other rolling stock includes two royal coaches, one of 1863 by J. Wright of Birmingham, England, and that used for the opening of the Rørosbane in 1877, constructed by Jackson & Sharp of Wilmington, Del., in the previous year; a CLERESTORY restaurant car with varnished wood body, built for the Bergensbanen in 1909–11; an Armstrong-Whitworth motorcar fitted with flanged railway wheels, built at Newcastle-upon-Tyne, England, in 1914 for the use of inspectors; and a primitive open fourth-class carriage built by the Metropolitan Railway Carriage and Wagon Co. in Birmingham in 1854. The track on which exhibits stand includes rails rolled in the late nineteenth century at Dowlais and Rhymney in Wales and at Bochum in Germany. A wheel lathe by Parr, Curtis & Madeley of Manchester, used from 1853 until 1953, is displayed with many smaller items of equipment.

The Hedmark county museum service (Hedmarksmuseet) and a collection of old farmsteads are located in a lakeside park adjoining the railway museum.

LOCATIONS
[M] Hedmarksmuseet (Hedmark County Museum), Domkirkeodden, 2300 Hamar.
[M] Norsk Jernbanemuseum (Norwegian Railway Museum), 2300 Hamar.

BARRIE TRINDER

Hamburg, Germany For centuries one of Europe's most important ports, an independent city until recent times, Hamburg, 120 km (75 mi.) SE of the mouth of the Elbe, retains many significant industrial monuments in spite of the bombing raids of World War II.

The quantitative increase in the movement of goods in the harbour between *c.*1770 and 1888 can be directly deduced by comparing the line of warehouses in the Reimerstwiete or the Deichstrasse with the buildings of the warehouse estate erected between 1882 and 1900. These are mostly five-storey brick buildings in the Gothic or Romanesque style, with gables providing shelter for winches. For heavy loads, the harbour authority ordered a new crane from the Kinthofen company in The Hague: this was originally steam-powered, and capable of lifting 15 tonnes. In outward appearance it is modelled on the LÜNEBURG crane.

Downstream on the Elbe, the St Pauli landing stages were built between 1903 and 1907 to plans by L. Raabe and O. Wöhleke. The two elevator towers for the Elbe tunnel were integrated into the complex a decade later.

Hamburg had a railway link as early as 1842, although the line connecting it with Altona was not opened until 1866, and the connection to Hamburg on the south bank of the Elbe came even later. Because of territorial fragmentation in the area and the activity of the various railway companies, a complex network of railways with several terminal stations developed in Hamburg. Once the railways had been taken over by Prussia there were changes, beginning in the late 1880s, and taking particular effect after 1903. They led to the building of the vast steel-girdered vault of the Hauptbahnhof, with its large, north-facing foyer, and to the well-lit, bright station hall of the Dammtor station, built well above the level of its surroundings. The broad, shallow arch of the Hauptbahnhof has one of the largest spans of any railway station. Its monumental effect is clearly visible from the Steintordamm, while on its other sides it is bordered by frontage buildings in a conservative style, partially faced in natural rough-hewn stone.

When the municipal waterworks were largely destroyed in a great fire in 1842, a new waterworks in Rothenburgsort were built in 1845–6 to designs by the English engineer William H. Lindley. They set a pattern for the new urban waterworks in Germany which were mostly constructed in the 1870s and 1880s. The Rothenburgsort works were later extended. Parts of the complex have been preserved as technical monuments. They include the pressure tower of 1845–6; the first engine house of 1857; a single-cylinder 40 hp compound steam engine of 1898, driving a d.c. generator by Schuckert, also of 1898; and a single-cylinder, four-stroke diesel engine of 1911. A two-cylinder steam piston pump of 1898 from the Villa Warburg is also on display in Rothenburgsort.

The oldest German lighthouse stands on the island of Neuwerk, 16 km (10 mi.) NE of Cuxhaven, which now belongs to Hamburg. It was built shortly after 1300 as a fortification tower. Lighting apparatus was installed in 1814; the present light dates from 1875. The emblem of Cuxhaven is the 'Kugelbake', a wooden beacon dating from the eighteenth century which stands on the tongue of land formed by the mouths of the Rivers Weser and Elbe.

The Chilehaus in Hamburg, a wedge-shaped, seven-storey office block, built to the design of Fritz Hoger in 1922–4, is one of the best examples of EXPRESSIONIST design.

The Museum of Work in Hamburg is accommodated in the buildings of the New York-Hamburg Rubber Goods Co. Shipping is illustrated in the Altona Museum, the electricity industry in the HEW Museum, tobacco processing in the Reemtsma Collection, and dairying in the Wilhelmsburg Regional Museum.

BIBLIOGRAPHY
General
Slotta, 1975–85.

LOCATIONS
[M] Altonaer Museum, Museumstrasse 23, 2000 Hamburg 50.
[I] Denkmalschutzamt der Freien und Hansestadt Hamburg (Monuments preservation department of the free Hanseatic city of Hamburg), Hamburger Strasse 45, 2000 Hamburg 76.
[M] HEW Museum, Klinikweg 23, 2000 Hamburg.
[M] Museum of Arts and Crafts, 1 Steintorplatz, 2000 Hamburg.
[M] Museum der Arbeit (Museum of Work), Maurienstrasse 19, 2000 Hamburg-Barmbek.

[M] Museum of the History of Hamburg, Holstenwall 24, 2000 Hamburg.
[M] Postal Museum, 36 Stephansplatz, 2000 Hamburg.
[M] Reemtsma Collection, Parkstrasse 51, 2000 Hamburg.
[M] Wilhelmsburg Regional Museum, 93 Kirchdorfer Strasse 163, 2000 Hamburg.

MICHAEL MENDE

Hamilton, Ontario, Canada   The chief steelmaking town in central Canada, whose most celebrated industrial monument is however its waterworks (now its museum), housing a pair of Cornish engines, built by John Gartshore & Co. of Dundas, Ontario, in 1858–9. It operated regularly until 1910, when electric pumps were installed, and intermittently until 1938.

LOCATION
[M] The Hamilton Museum of Steam and Technology, 900 Woodward Avenue, Hamilton, Ontario L8H 7N2.

Hanbury, John (1664–1734)   A leading member of a longstanding family of ironmasters. He developed the cylindrical rolling of iron plates at Pontypool, Wales, *c.*1720, thereby mechanizing and improving iron and tinplate manufacture and founding the modern tinplate industry, in which South Wales predominated for two centuries. He also revived the japanning of iron, a process invented by Thomas Allgood, Pontypool works manager in the seventeenth century.

BIBLIOGRAPHY
General
Minchinton, 1957.

handle house   Handles are wooden frames in which TEASELS are fixed for raising the nap on woollen cloth. Water was poured over them during the process and they were placed to dry in buildings through which air could flow through louvres or checkered brickwork. The only complete example in England is at Trowbridge, 12 km ($7\frac{1}{2}$ mi.) NE of FROME. Such buildings might also be used for storing unused teasels.

hand loom   A non-mechanized loom of any kind. Historical literature refers frequently to hand-loom weavers, particularly those whose threatened loss of employment in England in the first half of the nineteenth century was perceived as a major social problem.

BIBLIOGRAPHY
General
Bythell, 1969.

hangar   A shed in which aircraft can be stored and maintained: it must enclose a large, undivided space, and have entrances wide enough to move aircraft in and out. There is no clear distinction between military hangars and those used for civil aviation, and some of the older surviving examples have been used for both purposes. Some hangars have been used as AIRCRAFT FACTORIES.

Modern hangars are of steel construction, but earlier examples were of concrete, or had wooden frames or roofs.

One of the oldest surviving hangars is a concrete structure of 1912 at Schleissheim, MUNICH, originally built for military purposes. Three hangars of 1912–13 remain at Farnborough, Hampshire, and three timber-framed examples at Montrose (see ANGUS). A hangar of 1928 remains at Croydon, LONDON; a concrete-framed example of the 1930s at Heston, London, two of c.1936 at Gatwick Airport, and other good examples from the 1930s at Shoreham, Sussex, at Barton, Manchester, at Speke, LIVERPOOL, and at Blackpool (see FYLDE). In the USA a hangar of 1929 at Oakland, Calif., houses the Western Aerospace Museum, and three hangars of the 1920s at Quantico, Va., accommodate the US Marine Corps Air-Ground Museum. Several pre-World War II hangars remain at Le Bourget, PARIS.

See also AIRSHIP; FLYING BOAT.

BIBLIOGRAPHY
Specific
Sherman, R. W. Airplane hangars. In *Architectural Forum*, LIII, 1930.

JULIAN TEMPLE

Hanover (Hannover), Lower Saxony, Germany   A large city, the capital of one of the principal north German states, whose monarchs also ruled Great Britain between 1714 and 1837.

Towards the end of the 1860s the traditional use of water directly from the River Leine for drinking was increasingly dangerous. A large reservoir designed by Otto Wilsdorf was built on the Lindener Berg in 1876–8, together with the Ricklingen pumping station, which is no longer extant. Although the original equipment has been replaced, the outward appearance of the reservoir has been preserved. It measures 80 m × 40 m (262 ft. × 131 ft.) and rises fortress-like above a sloping rectangular terrace of natural stone. The waterworks of 1861–4, driven by two undershot water wheels, remains in Herrenhausen, replacing its eighteenth-century predecessors. Although it no longer supplies water for the fountains in the Grosser Garten park, it still fulfils important functions over and above its role as a technical monument. The two water wheels each drive two pumps with beams, originally intended to enable the Great Fountain to send a jet of water over 60 m (200 ft.) into the air. A small lock with wooden gates and a winch to operate them has also been preserved. Like its counterpart in Neustadt am Rübenberge, 30 km (19 mi.) downstream on the Leine, it dates in its present form from the first half of the eighteenth century. On the outskirts of the Grosser Garten, in the adjoining Georgengarten and in the Welfengarten, there are several road and foot bridges designed by Georg Ludwig Friedrich Laves between 1837 and 1843, making use of the split girder in wrought iron, which he developed. A small road bridge of riveted sheet steel, from the next decade, still crosses the Mühlenkanal to the monastery of Wienhausen in the district of Celle.

As early as 1826 Hanover had a gasworks, constructed by the Imperial-Continental Gas Association to provide its street lighting. Two large cast-iron lampposts of this period opposite the Leineschloss have been preserved, as has a gasholder of 1882 in the style of an Italian baptistry.

The development of factory architecture can be traced particularly clearly in Hanover, especially the construction of multi-storey buildings to accommodate different stages of production. These buildings are all, intentionally, of aesthetic merit, and were meant to serve as models. They include the König & Ebhardt accounts books factory (now Esselte Dymo), which Louis Frühling began to build in 1873; the biscuit factory of Hermann Bahlsen, built by the Siebrecht brothers in 1910–11 between Lister and Podbielskistrasse, part of which has late JUGENDSTIL terracotta ornamentation; the HANOMAG factory erected between 1917 and 1940 by A. Sasse and E. R. Mewes; and finally the plant of the Continental tyre factory built between 1923 and 1938 with a wide sweeping façade on Vahrenwalder Strasse, and a rather grand office block on the south side designed by PETER BEHRENS in 1912–14.

The Hindenburg Lock of the Mittelland Canal at Hanover-Anderten, 10 km (6 mi.) E. of the city centre, was built between 1919 and 1928 and was the largest inland waterways lock of its period in Europe. It is a double lock, 225 m (738 ft.) long and 15 m (49 ft.) deep, with fifty lateral storage reservoirs to prevent the loss of water as ships pass through. The most unusual characteristic of the lock is the use of twenty valve cabins arranged in rows along the sides of the lock chambers.

At Bredenbeck-Steinkrug, 20 km (12 mi.) SW, considerable parts of the glassworks of the Barons von Knigge, opened in 1838 and closed in the early 1920s, have been preserved, including the cone which covered the furnace, itself no longer extant. The glassworks were supplied with coal from their own mines in the nearby Deister area, where several spoil heaps remain.

Of the many potash mines in the rural districts around Hanover, Hildesheim and Celle, mention should be made of the complex in Sehnde, 18 km (11 mi.) SE of Hanover, with its own electric power station, winding engine house and pithead building, milling house and raw salts sheds, as well as its office block and watertower, most of which date from the first two decades of the twentieth century. There are also the Siegfried mine at Giesen, 26 km (16 mi.) S. of Hanover in the Hildesheim district, with its workshop, storage building and electric power plant of c.1910; and the Kaliwerk Niedersachsen-Riedel complex at Wathlingen, 35 km (22 mi.) NE of Hanover in Celle district, where the most notable features are the steel headstock of 1911, the pithead building, workshops and locomotives, and, not least, the workers' living quarters, a colony of five streets, the exteriors of which have scarcely been altered.

BIBLIOGRAPHY
General
Mende and Hamm, 1990; Slotta, 1975–85.

LOCATION
[M] Historisches museum am Hohen Ufor (Historical Museum), Pferdestrasse 6, 3000 Hanover.

MICHAEL MENDE

Hanseatic League An association of merchant guilds from cities in the Rhineland and the Baltic ports which was an important economic and political force in Northern Europe between the thirteenth century and the fifteenth century. The league had a membership of about a hundred towns, most of them German, in the late fourteenth century. It was responsible for the quelling of pirates, and for providing assistance to navigators by the construction of lighthouses. It established trading depots in foreign ports like BERGEN, Novgorod in Russia, and London. Its power declined in the sixteenth century as Dutch power increased in the Baltic, and its governing body met for the last time in 1669.

Hansom, Joseph Aloysius (1803–82) An architect, and the designer of BIRMINGHAM town hall, Hansom is best known as the promoter of a horse-drawn cab for urban use. Most carriages plying for hire in England *c.*1800 were second-hand private vehicles. Hansom designed a 'patent safety cabriolet' and in 1835 formed a company to manufacture it, but actually produced and sold a better design by John Chapman, which was standard in English cities until displaced by motor taxis after 1900. He also founded a journal, *The Builder*, in 1842, the principal source for the study of industrial and other buildings in Britain in the nineteenth century.

BIBLIOGRAPHY
General
Bird, 1969; Moore, 1902.

Hardanger, Hordaland, Norway An area around Hardanger Fjord, south of Bergen, with a long tradition of domestic manufacture of gold and silver trinkets, bed coverings and carpets. The restored Stekka sawmill at Tørvikbygd, 45 km (28 mi.) E. of Bergen, which was built before 1818 to service local needs, has a vertical blade operated by a water wheel.

BIBLIOGRAPHY
Specific
Wiig, J. Two Norwegian water-powered sawmills. In Nisser and Bedoire, 1978.

Hardwick, Philip (1791–1870) The most distinguished architect of the first phase of main-line railway construction. He was the son of Thomas Hardwick (1751–1819), and the father of Philip Charles Hardwick (1822–92), who were also architects. He designed buildings at St Katherine's Docks, LONDON, and the termini of the London & Birmingham Railway at Euston, which was demolished in the 1960s, and at Curzon Street, which remains (*see* BIRMINGHAM).

The Great Hall at Euston was by his son, who also designed the Great Western Hotel at Paddington Station, London.

Hargs bruk and Hargshamn, Uppsala, Sweden Hargs bruk lies 40 km (25 mi.) E. of DANNEMORA. It is a well-preserved Walloon BRUK which has remained private property, with vast forests and many hectares of farmland. The ironworkers' village, with its manor house of 1760 and eighteenth-century workers' dwellings, extends along two streets. A huge wooden GRANARY is now used as a museum. The exterior of the former upper forge is well preserved, but none of the plant remains. Hargs bruk produced Walloon iron from Dannemora iron ore, and was adapted to LANCASHIRE FORGING as late as 1904.

The property was created in the 1630s, and was bought by State-admiral Gustaf Otto Stenbock, who started ironmaking in the 1660s. The blast furnaces were located in neighbouring villages, one of them Bennebol, where a kiln and a late-nineteenth-century blast furnace are preserved. Like most of the UPPLAND bruks, Harg was ravaged by the Russian fleet in 1719. From 1730 to 1873 the bruk was in the possession of the Oxenstierna family, and then passed through marriage into the hands of the Beck-friis family, to whom it still belongs.

A few hundred metres south-east of the lower forge is a harbour with a notable five-storey warehouse in whitewashed stone. This was the bruk warehouse, built after the Russian invasion of 1719, when all the wooden warehouses along the coast were burnt down. Bar iron was stored on the lower floors, while imported grain and other products were kept on the upper floors. A similar warehouse belonging to LEUFSTA BRUK has been preserved on the coast about 25 km (16 mi.) N. Bar iron was loaded onto ships which conveyed it to Stockholm where it was checked and weighed before being exported.

MARIE NISSER

harness motion To achieve complex patterns in woven cloth, such as figures, fancy checks and twills, the warp threads on a loom must be raised and lowered in a related sequence determined by the designer. The harness is a frame across the top of the loom which holds the heddles, vertical cords or wires with loops in the middle through which the warp ends pass. The harness motion determines how the heddles control the shed or opening of the warp yarns to allow the shuttle to pass through, carrying the weft. The interlacing of the warp and weft determines the pattern.

The harness may be controlled by a roller or pattern chain motion, called a dobby, which acts by pins and levers to engage the wires that raise and lower the heddles.

Harwich, Essex, England A packet station for the Netherlands in the reign of William III (1688–1702), Harwich declined in the eighteenth century. A railway opened in 1854, and the GER constructed Parkeston Quay in 1882 and secured the mail contract in 1898. The High Lighthouse has a 27.4 m (90 ft.) octagonal tower: its construction was supervised by JOHN RENNIE in 1818; it was disused from 1862 but restored in 1975. A second, the 13.7 m (45 ft.) Low Lighthouse, can be seen on Harwich Green. A treadmill crane of 1667 from the Navy Yard was re-erected in 1930 on Harwich Green; its wheels are 4.8 m × 1.9 m (16 ft. × 3 ft. 10 in.). St Nicholas

Church, in Perpendicular style, of 1820–4, has internal columns, a gallery and window tracery of cast iron by Jacob Garrett of Ipswich. The Electric Palace of 1911 is an outstanding early cinema.

BIBLIOGRAPHY
General
Alderton and Booker, 1980.

Harz Mountains, Lower Saxony, Germany   One of the oldest of all industrial regions, which has many technical monuments. Their density is immediately striking, as are the many connections between mining and metalworking, water supply and distribution, mechanical engineering, technology, and the visual arts.

The Harz area now includes the districts of Goslar and Osterode; historically the Lower Harz, including Goslar, was distinct from the Upper Harz, including Clausthal and Zellerfeld. The eastern part of the Lower Harz was in the GERMAN DEMOCRATIC REPUBLIC.

Until 1988 the major centre of mining in the western part of the Lower Harz was Goslar, with the Rammelsberg. The development of mining and its subsidiary industries, and of miners' colonies, could be traced in this one mine alone from a series of sometimes unique examples, beginning underground with the Rathstiefsten Drift of *c*.1140; the Feuerzäher Vault, opened *c*.1360 and equipped by 1585 with a water wheel to drive a hoist; the Deep Julius Fortunatus Drift, superseding the drainage system of the Feuerzäher Vault; the New Serenissimorum Deep Pit of 1790 and later, with its reversible wheel which is still extant, and the linkage system to the hoist which leads from it; and finally the Roeder Drift, opened between 1798 and 1805, through which water to provide power was brought to the wheels from the Herzberger Pool. On the surface, the architecturally ornamented entrances to the drifts can be seen, as can the Maltermeister Tower, probably built in 1500 as a watchtower, but soon used almost exclusively as a signal tower. There is also the pithead building of eighteenth-century date, but restored in 1845. Of particular note is the graduated ore-dressing building, built on a downward slope in 1936–8 to plans by Fritz Schupp. The pithead gear towers over it, and it is surrounded by buildings from the first decade of the twentieth century, including the electric power plant of 1906.

The monuments of the Upper Harz are rather more scattered, and largely above ground, although they are equally varied – particularly in and around the centre of the region, the twin towns of Clausthal and Zellerfeld, 14 km (9 mi.) S. of Goslar. They include pools for water-power systems, some of which were constructed in the sixteenth century. In all sixty-three remain of seventy, which held sufficient water to provide power for fourteen weeks. The outlet tunnels from the pools are also partially preserved – the oldest, on the Wasserlauferteich, dating from before 1730 – as are the supply channels, parts of which ran over dams or through tunnels in dam walls. Fifteen pit buildings remain, mostly from the late seventeenth century and the eighteenth. They include the

Dorothee pit building of 1713, the Polsterberg winding house and the Rehberg pumping house at St Andreasberg, 26 km (16 mi.) SE of Goslar, which belong to the Samson Mine. Finally, the two oldest examples of steel headstocks in the Federal Republic are at the Ottilie Mine of 1876 and the Kaiser Wilhelm Mine of 1880. The two soughs – the 10.5 km ($6\frac{1}{2}$ mi.) Deep Georg sough of 1777–99, which surfaces in Bad Grund, and the 26 km (16 mi.) Ernst August sough in Gittelde, of 1851–64 – are part of the water-supply and distribution system of the Upper Harz, and the architecture of the entrance structures is typical of the time, and in scale with their importance. The great Harz Granary, a seven-storey structure built in Osterode, 24 km (15 mi.) SE of Goslar in 1720–3, was intended to supply miners and their families. The Samson mine in St Andreasberg was one of the first to have been preserved as a show mine. The pit went out of production in 1910. It was finally made safe in the 1950s, and now consists of a wooden pithead building, a rope drift, and the building holding the reversible winding drum. The hoist wheel which survives 18 m (60 ft.) below ground formerly drove the Fahrkunst (man engine) installed in 1847 along with the pumps. The Fahrkunst is still used for inspecting the hydro-electric plants 130 m (427 ft.) and 190 m (623 ft.) below the surface, installed respectively in 1922 and 1912. Silver was mined in the Samson mine from 1521.

While there are varied remains of non-ferrous-ore mining, the once equally important iron ore mines of the Harz Mountains have left few traces. However the Königshütte complex in Bad Lauterberg, 25 km (15 mi.) S. of Goslar, is a fine specimen of an ironworks of the 1830s and 40s. The neo-Classical buildings of the iron warehouse, with a portico of Doric cast-iron columns, the assay shed, the machine shop, the moulding shop, and the office block, as well as the works tavern and the great well, are evidence of the one-time importance of this Hanoverian ironworks. Only some fragments of the blast furnace, and of the foundry, which was built in the style of a Gothic church, are preserved in the masonry of the present foundry. A rough idea of a blast furnace of that time, and of its relationship to the rest of an ironworking complex, is given by the blast furnace and adjacent storehouse and administration buildings of the Wilhelmshütte ironworks at Bockenem-Bornum, 24 km (15 mi.) NE of Goslar, in the Hildesheim district on the western borders of the Harz, which date from the 1780s and 1830s.

The mining and local history museum in Zellerfeld includes an unusually extensive and comprehensive collection of late-eighteenth-century and early-nineteenth-century mining models, showing shaft installations, hoist wheels and transmission systems, and stamp mills, together with calcining and smelting furnaces.

BIBLIOGRAPHY
General
Mende and Hamm, 1990; Slotta, 1975–85.

LOCATIONS
[M] Bad Lauterberg Museum, Ritscherstrasse 13, 3422 Bad Lauterberg.
[M] Goslarer Museum, Königstrasse 1, 3380 Goslar.

[M] Oberharzer Bergbaumuseum (Upper Harz Regional and Mining Museum), Bornhardstrasse 16, 3392 Clausthal-Zellerfeld.
[M] Rammelsberg Mining Museum, Bergtal 19, 3380 Goslar.
[S] St Andreasberg Historisches Silbererzbergwerk (Historic Silver Mine), Grube Samson (Samson mine), 3424 St Andreasberg.

MICHAEL MENDE

Hasselt, Limburg, Belgium   The capital of Limburg is a long-established centre of the spirits industry and several distillery and former distillery buildings remain in the town: De Fransche Kroon and M. Prieken in Demerstraat; Lenen in Molenpoort, which dates from *c.*1850; Smeets in Raamstraat; and Frijns in Martelarenlaan, which has ART DECO ornamentation of *c.*1920. The museum in the former Stellingwerff-Theunissan distillery has comprehensive displays relating to the technology of the spirits industry, and to its packaging and marketing.

LOCATION
[M] Nationaal Jenevermuseum (National Spirits Museum), Thonissenlaan 73, 3500 Hasselt.

hatmaking   Most hats were traditionally made from felt (*see* FELTMAKING). Hatters worked in most market towns until the mid-nineteenth century, but in England there were concentrations of manufacturers in the Bristol and Manchester areas by the mid-eighteenth century. In London the trade was concentrated in Bermondsey, where one manufacturer employed up to three hundred people in 1850. Industrial-scale hatmaking gradually developed in the mid-nineteenth century, particularly in the Stockport area.

Straw hats were made by cutting straw to regular lengths, whitening it with smoke from sulphur, splitting it, and then working it into plaits. Straw hats were a traditional export of the Leghorn area of Italy, but manufacture was encouraged with success in the CHILTERN HILLS from the early nineteenth century.

BIBLIOGRAPHY
General
Mayhew, 1850.

Hattingen, North Rhine-Westphalia, Germany   *See* RUHRGEBIET.

Hawaii, United States of America   The island chain called Hawaii was annexed in 1898, entered the United States as a territory in 1900, and achieved statehood in 1959 as the nation's fiftieth. Hawaii is the southernmost state but does not reach as far west as the western coast of Alaska, despite its location in the central Pacific Ocean. On Hawaii's dozen major islands, sugar cane, sandalwood, coffee beans, pineapples and bananas have been keys to the native industrial life. All are treated modestly in Hawaii's Bishop Museum.

Whaling and sealing were intensively pursued in the last century, but little remains of these greasy industries in

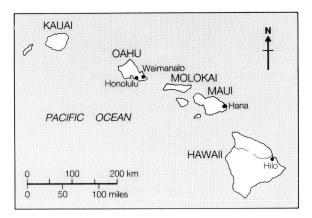

Hawaii

a state now given over largely to leisure and tropical agricultural pursuits.

The nation's earliest standing structure incorporating PORTLAND CEMENT in its concrete elements is seen in Honolulu's Kamehameha Post Office of 1871.

A recent example of the ways in which historic bridges may be accommodated to the requirements of modern loads is seen in the Hanalei River Bridge on the island of Kauai. This steel-truss span of 1912 was set for replacement in the 1970s, until local protests helped devise a scheme to reinforce the secondary trusswork and shift the bridge's load-bearing role away from the primary truss. Elsewhere on Kauai, a riveted truss bridge built in 1890 by Alexander Findlay & Co. of Motherwell, Scotland, is the only known British truss bridge standing in the USA. The 22 m (73 ft.) span crosses the Opaekaa Stream and is secured to lava-rock abutments.

See also figure 102.

BIBLIOGRAPHY
General
Jackson, 1988.

LOCATIONS
[M] Bishop Museum, 1525 Bernice Street, Honolulu, HI 96817.
[M] Pacific Whaling Museum, Sea Life Park, Waimanalo, HI 96795.

DAVID H. SHAYT

head race   A LEAT along which water is conveyed from a stream or reservoir to a water wheel or turbine.

hearth   A term with at least two meanings in industrial archaeology:

1. A fireplace, in the industrial sense particularly the structure in a FORGE or SMITHY that contains the fire in which metal is heated, sometimes with an air blast (*see* FINERY-AND-CHAFERY FORGE), and often with a hood above the flames.
2. The lower part of a blast furnace, in which the molten iron collects. The hearth stone formed the bottom of the furnace, and the section above it with vertical sides

was properly known as the crucible but often called the hearth.

BIBLIOGRAPHY
General
Gale, 1971.

heddle   *See* HARNESS MOTION.

helium (He)   An element and one of the 'rare gases', which together form less than one per cent of the atmosphere. Helium was discovered in 1895 by Sir William Ramsay (1852–1916). It is lighter than air and non-flammable, a safe alternative to hydrogen for use in balloons and AIRSHIPS. It is obtained by refrigeration from natural gas from oilfields at Medicine Hat, Canada, and in the USA, or by liquefaction of air.

Helmshore, Lancashire, England   The Museum of the Lancashire Textile Industry is housed in a condenser cotton mill, dating in its present form from 1859–60. Preparing, breaking-up and pickering machines and a scutcher are displayed; and breaker-carding engines, finisher-cards and Taylor Lang 714-spindle, self-acting mules are demonstrated on the first floor, which is preserved exactly as it was when working. The museum includes the adjacent Higher Mill of 1789, with its 5.5 m (18 ft.) diameter water wheel, scouring machines, teasle-raising gigs and working fulling stocks. An important collection of early textile machines includes an improved Hargreaves spinning jenny and a water frame from CROMFORD.

BIBLIOGRAPHY
General
Ashmore, 1982.

LOCATION
[M] Museum of the Lancashire Textile Industry, Holcombe Road, Helmshore, Rossendale BB4 4NP.

Helsingborg, Malmöhus, Sweden   Helsingborg, with a population of 100 000, lies at the narrowest point of the Sound (Oresund), and is the terminal of train- and road-vehicle ferries from HELSINGØR. The Fredriksdal Open-Air Museum, established as the result of a bequest of 1918, includes a water-powered stamping mill of the 1860s, which crushed bones for use as manure; a nineteenth-century water-powered sawmill; an octagonal tower mill of 1803; a late-eighteenth-century thatched malt kiln; extensive glovers' workshops, and a 2–8–2T locomotive which was built in the city. Pålsjö water mill, an outpost of the city museum situated in beechwoods on the northern edge of Helsingborg, dates from 1824.

LOCATIONS
[M] Fredriksdals friluftsmusem (Fredriksdal Open-Air Museum) 252 23 Helsingborg.
[M] Helsingborgs stadsmuseum (City Museum), Södra Storgatan 31, 252 23 Helsingborg.

Helsingør (Elsinore), Zealand, Denmark   The city of Helsingør has more to offer than just Hamlet's Kronborg castle. It is situated at the northern entrance to the Sound, only 3.9 km ($2\frac{1}{2}$ mi.) from Hälsingborg on the Swedish side. On account of the royal castle, and activities associated with the collection of tolls from ships passing through the Sound, Helsingør became at an early date one of the largest Danish provincial towns. Many merchants' houses and institutional buildings, now preserved, bear witness to its early prosperity. The abolition of the Sound tolls in 1857 was a hard blow to the city, only partly relieved by the beginning of industrial activities. In 1881 Helsingør gained new life through the establishment of the first large provincial shipyard in Denmark building steel ships, which until its recent closure was by far the largest workplace in the town. The harbour remains busy with ferry traffic.

Today Helsingør houses the Danish Technical Museum, which has extensive collections on science and technology from the eighteenth century to the present. Among the exhibits of international interest are Christian Sørensen's typesetting machine of 1855, Malling-Hansen's typewriter of 1867, and V. Poulsen's electromagnetic sound recorder of 1898. A pewterer's workshop furnished with its original equipment has been established. In the transport department exhibits include Hammel's Danish motorcar of 1888, which can still be operated, Ellehammer's aeroplane of 1906, the first to fly in Europe, and a 0–4–2 tender locomotive of 1868 by ROBERT STEPHENSON.

The Danish Maritime Museum is situated within Kronborg castle. The collections and displays cover the main features in the history of Danish ships, shipbuilding and navigation from *c*.1650 to the present. The collection includes many original drawings and models of ships. The museum is also the museum of the Danish colonies, with displays on trade with China, India, Africa, the West Indies and Greenland.

The first railway reached Helsingør in 1862, and the first station still survives. The present station was built in 1892 to service the newly established steam ferry to Hälsingborg. Kronborg castle inspired the architect N. P. C. Holsøe to use a Dutch Renaissance style for the building, which has often been called the most lavish railway station in Denmark. In 1897 the direct 'coast line' was opened to Copenhagen. Recently several of the intermediate stations along the line have been restored to their original appearance. A local railway association preserves several locomotives and carriages.

Hellebæk, 5 km (3 mi.) NW of Helsingør, is a factory colony founded in 1597 when the Danish king ordered the establishment of a small arms factory along a small river near the Kattegat. Later the workshops were privatized, and in the second half of the eighteenth century the premises were rebuilt and greatly enlarged. The works closed in 1870, but shortly afterwards a textile factory was established to continue Hellebæk's industrial traditions. The colony is well preserved, and its buildings are under legislative protection. They include the manor house, a hammer mill, a testing house and numerous dwellings for managers and workers.

BIBLIOGRAPHY
General
Andersen, 1969; Nielsen, 1943–4; Petersen, 1983–6; Sestoft, 1979.
Specific
Danmarks Tekniske Museums Årbog (Yearbooks of the Danish Technical Museum), 1952–.
Handels-og Søfartsmuseets Årbog (Yearbooks of the Danish Maritime Museum) 1941–.
Pedersen, K. Industrier i Helsingør før det 20 århundrede (Industry in Helsingør before the 20th century). In *Fra Frederiksborg Amt*, 1973.
Thalbitzer, V. Hellebæk in ældre tider (Hellebæk in olden times). In *Fra Frederiksborg Amt*, 1929.

LOCATIONS
[M] Danmarks Tekniske Museum, Ndr. Strandvej 23, 3000 Helsingør.
[M] Handels-og Søfartsmuseet, Kronborg, 3000 Helsingør.

OLE HYLDTOFT

Helsinki (Helsingfors), Uudenmaan lääni, Finland   The Finnish capital is of interest to industrial archaeologists principally for its railway station, its shipyards and its museums.

Helsinki's main railway station, designed by Eliel Saarinen (1873–1950) in 1904, and built in 1910–14, is one of the most distinguished of Europe's large termini, notable for the pioneering use of concrete in the roofs.

The islands of Suomenlinna in Helsinki harbour were strongly fortified in the second half of the eighteenth century. The construction of a dry dock began in 1749, and took ten years to complete. The basin was originally emptied by a windmill, but in the 1750s a new system was installed, with two shafts bored into the rock beneath the pump shafts, through which water was fed from a basin through a vaulted tunnel. Heating stoves enabled the system to be kept running until late in the autumn.

The period of Russian rule saw little activity at the Suomenlinna dock but the Russians began to renew the installations towards the end of World War I. The walls of the basin were lined with granite blocks, and a new workshop was built. When Finland became independent in 1917 the dockyard was finished, and in the 1920s the state aircraft construction company was located there. In the early 1930s the state shipyard company, later Valmet Oy, took over the dockyard, and the construction of the outer basin was finished. Valmet Oy continued to work the dockyard until the early 1980s, and in recent years it has been used as a repair dock for old, mainly wooden ships.

The Museum of Technology was founded in 1969 and opened to the public in 1975. It is located in the old buildings of the City of Helsinki Water Board, dating from the 1870s, and beautifully situated on Kuninkaankartano Island at the mouth of the River Vantaa. The island is named after a royal dwelling which stood there in the sixteenth century. The city of Helsinki was founded on the same spot in 1550, before being moved 6 km (4 mi.) to its present location in 1640.

The Museum of Technology currently has approximately 5000 m² (54 000 sq. ft.) of exhibition space. The displays trace the development of meteorology, printing, land surveying, sources of power, the chemical industries and sugar manufacture. The circular water-purification hall houses the departments of communications, forestry, mining and metallurgy, and building technology. The museum incorporates the power station, waterworks and mill, which are still housed in the Water Board buildings.

The open-air museum on Seurasaari island, founded in 1909 by the ethnographer Axel Olai Heikel (1851–1924), has exhibits from all parts of Finland, among them a tar boat from Oulu, a seventeenth-century water-powered sawmill, and a country store of 1871.

BIBLIOGRAPHY
General
Zippelius, 1974.

LOCATIONS
[M] Seurasaaren ulkomuseo (Seurasaari Folk Museum), Seurasaari, SF-00250 Helsinki.
[M] Suomen Kansallismuseo (National Museum of Finland), Mannerheimintie 34, Helsinki.
[S] Suomenlinna, SF-00190 Helsinki.
[M] Suomen Merimuseo (Maritime Museum of Finland), Hylkysaari, SF-00570 Helsinki.
[M] Tekniikanmuseo (Museum of Technology), Viikintie 1, SF-0560 Helsinki.

LAURI PUTKONEN

helve hammer   A heavy cast-iron hammer powered by a shaft from a water wheel or a steam engine, used for SHINGLING iron or making heavy forgings. A nose or frontal helve hammer used for shingling had the hammer head and anvil in the centre of the haft, the fulcrum at one end and the cams at the other; a belly helve, more commonly used for forgings, had the cam ring in the centre with the fulcrum and hammer head at each end.

See figure 56.

BIBLIOGRAPHY
General
Gale, 1969, 1971.

Hemfurth, Hesse, Germany   In 1905 the Prussian government decided to build a dam near Hemfurth, 32 km (20 mi.) SW of Kassel, to ensure water supplies for the extensive Dortmund-Ems and Mittelland Canal system, to generate electricity, and to give protection from flooding. At the time the dam, which created a reservoir with a capacity of 202.4 million m³ (more than 7 million cu. ft.) was the largest in Germany, and it remains the third largest. The construction of the Edertal dam continued from 1908 until 1914. The wall of the dam is 47 m (154 ft.) high, and it is 400 m (1300 ft.) long at the crown and 36 m (118 ft.) wide at the base. A bomb breached the wall in World War II, and the mass of water that poured out caused devastation in the Eder and Fulda valleys. The Edertal dam is now part of a complex system of reservoirs and storage basins. The oldest power station, at the foot of the dam, has been preserved with its original machinery of 1915.

hemp   The hemp plant (*Cannabis sativa*) has a woody

Figure 56 The belly helve hammer at the Walloon Forge at Aube (Orne), France; the wooden support structure of the hammer, typical of Walloon forges, is remarkably close to the description given in Diderot's *Encyclopédie*. An archaeological excavation beneath the anvil was conducted by T. Churin in 1983.

P. Corbierre, Inventaire général

stalk used for making coarse cloth and cordage. It is processed like FLAX, and was the traditional material used in ROPE manufacture.

BIBLIOGRAPHY
General
Horner, 1920.

Hennebique, François (1843–1921) A propagandist for reinforced CONCRETE. Born at Neuville St Vaast, in Belgium, he worked first as a labourer and later as a mason. He first used concrete in 1879, before conducting experiments to devise a system for linking together steel rods within concrete beams. Hennebique successfully defended patents for this against all comers, and created a successful construction company and publicity machine, based in Paris, that put the use of the material on an entirely new professional footing.

Hereford, Herefordshire, England   The county town, on the River Wye. A museum, formed in 1973 in the original Bulmer cider factory of 1888, illustrates cider manufacture in general and in Herefordshire in particular; it includes equipment from several closed works. The Bulmer factory is also the base for the preserved GWR locomotive *King George V*, built in 1927. The Waterworks Museum, formed in 1974, preserves steam engines of 1895 and 1906 in a pumping station with an adjacent ornamental water tower.

BIBLIOGRAPHY
General
Brook, 1977.

LOCATIONS
[M] Herefordshire Waterworks Museum, Broomy Hill, Hereford.
[M] The Museum of Cider, The Cider Mills, Ryelands Street, Hereford HR4 0LW.

Herend, Veszprém, Hungary   A village in the Bakony Mountains, 12 km ($7\frac{1}{2}$ mi.) W. of Veszprem, the site of a two-storey, twelve-bay porcelain factory built in 1839 by Mor Fischer, who exhibited a colossal Chinese-style dish at the Great Exhibition in London, 1851. The museum in the factory has displays relating to the history of the works. Nearby is a factory village.

BIBLIOGRAPHY
General
Kiss *et al.*, 1981.

LOCATION
[M,S] Porcelan-museum, H-8440 Herend, Kossuth u. 140.

heritage centre   A focus for interpretation, usually for an urban area or PARK: it may have graphic and audio-visual displays, but usually lacks a scientifically based collection of artefacts, although some centres are operated by museum services and display objects that belong to larger collections. Heritage centres may be starting points for guided tours or TRAILS. Many historic buildings, including some industrial structures, have been saved from demolition by conversion to heritage centres. Lowell (*see* MASSACHUSETTS) provides an outstanding example in the USA.

BIBLIOGRAPHY
Specific
Environmental Interpretation. Focus on Heritage Centres, March 1985.

Herning, Jutland, Denmark   With a history of less than a hundred years, Herning, in the middle of Jutland, is one of Denmark's youngest towns. Its basis was the textile industry, together with the cultivation of the extensive heathlands of the region. Stocking-knitting on a domestic scale has a long history in the area, as a by-occupation for farming families, working poor soils. Wool from local sheep was the raw material, and production flourished in the eighteenth century. From *c.*1870 traditional knitting yielded to a modern hosiery industry, which, especially from the 1930s, took a strong upturn. Herning remains the centre of a most important industrial region, with many hosiery factories in the city itself and the nearby small towns of Hammerum and Ikast. Textile history is well covered in the hosiery museum which forms part of Herning Museum. A shirt factory of circular design dating

from 1966 has been converted into the city's art museum, and a former dress factory now houses the Danish museum of photography.

The brown coal pits near the railway at Søby, 15 km (9 mi.) S., have thin seams, but were exploited during and after the two world wars because of the lack of foreign supplies. At boom times several thousand were employed there, but the area is now protected as a nature reserve, with one worker's dwelling of characteristically simple style serving as the museum of this Klondike-style venture.

BIBLIOGRAPHY
General
Johansen, 1988; Sestoft, 1979.
Specific
Knudsen, L. *Efter hosebinderne* (After the stocking-knitters). Herning, 1979.

LOCATION
[M] Herning Museum, Museumsgade 1, 7400 Herning.

OLE HYLDTOFT

Heslop, Adam (dates unknown)   An engineer, born in Cumberland, England, who in 1790, while working at the Ketley ironworks, Shropshire, patented an improved version of the NEWCOMEN engine. Heslop's engine had two cylinders, one of which worked as a single-acting steam-powered cylinder; the other, which condensed the steam, worked on the same principle as an atmospheric engine. Most Heslop engines were used for winding at collieries and some were still working in the twentieth century. The Science Museum, LONDON, has a Heslop engine, and the foundations of two are preserved at IRONBRIDGE.

BIBLIOGRAPHY
General
Trinder, 1981.
Specific
Leese, J. H. Old English power plants. In *Power* (New York), XXXVI, 1912.

Hesse (Hessen), Germany   Hesse, the most densely forested state in the Federal Republic, lies in the centre of the country, and is well placed for transport facilities. Industrialization did not begin until the region was opened up by railways in the mid-nineteenth century. The pace increased when Hesse became part of Prussia in 1866. Today, the greatest industrial activity in the region is in the Rhine-Main area, which lacks raw materials but has many chemical, electrical and motor plants. The iron ore of the Lahn-Dill region provided raw materials for iron-smelting, which gave rise to foundries and steelworks. North Hesse also produced iron in the early industrial period, and KASSEL was a centre for mechanical engineering, particularly the production of railway rolling stock. Potassium mining around WERRA in north-east Hesse, and opencast lignite mining at Borken and Wölfersheim, remain important industries.

See also DARMSTADT; FRANKFURT AM MAIN; HEMFURTH;

KASSEL; KAUFUNGEN; LOLLAR; OBERURSEL; REINHARDSHA-
GEN; RÜSSELSHEIM; SOLMS; WEILBURG; WERRA; WETZLAR.

LOCATION
[I] Hessisches Landesamt für Denkmalpflege (Hessian Department for Protecting Monuments), Schloss Biebrich/Westflügel,
6200 Wiesbaden-Biebrich.

Hieflau, Styria, Austria *See* STYRIAN IRON TRAIL.

Highlands, Scotland Manufactures in the north of
Scotland were for long supplied by itinerant tinkers. The
Highland Folk Museum, Kingussie, and the Auchindrain
Museum of Country Life, Inveraray, illustrate rural life
and crafts.

Caithness has some large grain mills, including Ach-
ingale Mill, Watten, of 1886, and John O'Groats Mill, built
in 1901 and still in use. The remains of horizontal mills
abound. Old Mills, Elgin, a meal mill of 1793, and Towie
Mill, Drumure, Dufftown, have been restored.

Cromarty retains several relics from the 'improvements'
of the 1770s, most notably the quadrangular hemp works
of 1772–3, comprising a two-storey, twenty-five-bay
range, converted to housing in 1984, and two shorter
ranges, one now a restaurant. A brewery was provided by
the local landowner *c.*1790 to counter local enthusiasm
for whisky. Nearby Resolis is an unlikely location for
Gordon's Mill of 1796, which made snuff.

A latrine turret and Venetian windows are amongst the
ruins of a cotton mill built in 1792–4 by David Dale
(1739–1806) at Spinningdale, Sutherland, to relieve local
poverty. It burned down in 1806. Carding mills supplying
hand spinners were widespread. One is now the visitor
centre of Tamnavulin distillery. Another, Knockando
Wool Mill, retains in working order a Platt mule, a
scribbler, a carder and a condenser of 1870, with two
Dobcross looms and a Tomlinson teasel gig of the 1890s.
On a larger scale Newmill, Elgin, founded in 1797, still
functions, having two two-storey blocks of the 1860s, one
Gothic and one Baronial. Kynoch's Isla Bank Mills, Keith,
founded in 1805, still employs mules.

Distilling equipment is still produced at New Mill of
Elgin Foundry. Rose Street Foundry had an iron-framed
fitting shop of 1895, with side galleries and elliptical
doors, now re-erected near Inverness as part of a supermarket.

Ironstone and magnesium were extracted at Lecht near
Tomintoul, lead around Loch Fyne, and coal at Brora.
Slate was worked from 1694 to 1955 at Ballachulish.
Elgin has two sandstone quarries, and pavement flags are
still worked in Caithness.

The British Aluminium Co. was attracted to the
Highlands by the prospects of hydro-electric power. A
waterfall was harnessed for the first works at Foyers on
the shores of Loch Ness. Built in 1896–8, it is now divided
into industrial units; it is a steel-framed building, with
louvred roofs and a stone crow-stepped front. The second
works of 1905–9, at Kinlochleven, is larger, the water
carried to it from Britain's first mass concrete dam. Garden

villages adjoin both works. Larger and still working, if less
attractive, is the post-war Fort William works. The hydro-
electric power stations for public supply, built by the
Scottish Hydro-Electric Board in 1950 at Fasnakyle and
Invergarry, are particularly fine. Many small oil engines
generating electricity remain in use. The Scottish
Museums Council Industrial Collections Survey has identified several extensive private collections of such engines.

The fishing industry required warehouses, ice and
curing houses in such harbours as Keiss, Whaligoe,
Rispond and Lybster, and kippering houses at Thurso and
Wick, the latter now having a heritage centre incorporating a cooperage. Simple fishing-fleet basins and ferry piers
by THOMAS TELFORD abound, as do fine lighthouses, many
designed by the STEVENSONS, built for the Commissioners
of Northern Lighthouses, a body established in 1786.

The Crinan Canal, which is 14.5 km (9 mi.) long, was
cut through the Mull of Kintyre in 1794–9 by JOHN
RENNIE. There are fourteen locks, four opening bridges,
and a hand-operated roller cantilever bridge of 1900 at
Dunardry. The Caledonian Canal was built through the
Great Glen in 1804–22 by Telford and WILLIAM JESSOP; it
incorporates four lochs, twenty-nine locks and three
aqueducts. There is a small museum in the canal
workshops at Fort Augustus.

The first roads in the Highlands were built to subjugate
the population after the rebellions of 1715 and 1745.
Later the Commissioners for Highland Roads and Bridges
engaged Telford to build the network which is largely that
in use today. Telford's bridge over the Spey at Craigella-
chie, a 46.2 m (151 ft.) segmental arched, four-rib, cast-
iron span, was erected in 1814–15 and restored in 1964.
Near the mouth of the Spey at Fochabers a masonry bridge
of 1804 was rebuilt with a main 56 m (184 ft.) span in
laminated timber in 1832, and with cast-iron ribs in
1853. The suspension footbridge of the late 1840s at
Bridge of Oich is the last of the Dredge type in Scotland.
Balmoral Castle is approached by a plate-girder road
bridge of 1857 by I. K. BRUNEL.

Much of the Highland railway system has been spared
closure, but neither the arched cast-iron bridge at Carron,
Aberlour, nor the more advanced lattice-truss bridge at
Ballindalloch, both built in 1863, now carries trains. A
290 m (950 ft.) bridge of 1886 at Speymouth, with a 30.5
m (350 ft.) central bow truss, is now a footbridge. The
Connel Ferry Bridge of 1903 by Sir William Arrol (1839–
1913) has a 150 m (500 ft.) steel cantilevered span across
the mouth of Loch Etive, and is now only a road bridge.
The Findhorn Viaduct near Forres of 1858, a major
wrought-iron box-girder bridge, remains in use, as does
the five-span wooden trestle Aultnaslanash Viaduct of
1897. The masonry Nairn Viaduct at Culloden Moor of
1898 is 550 m (1800 ft.) long. The Mallaig extension line,
opened in 1901, is most notable for its early mass-
concrete viaducts, built by 'Concrete Bob' McAlpine,
including the 40 m (127 ft.) crenellated span over
Borrodale Burn, and the curved, twenty-one arch, 380 m
(1250 ft.) long Glenfinnan Viaduct. The Strathspey
Railway runs steam locomotives between Aviemore and
Boat of Garten.

BIBLIOGRAPHY
General
Barclay-Harvey, 1949; Ellis, 1955/59; Hay and Stell, 1986; Hume, 1977; Telford, 1838; Vallance, 1938/63.

LOCATIONS
[M] Auchindrain Museum of Country Life, Inveraray, Argyll PA32 8XV.
[M] Highland Folk Museum, Duke Street, Kingussie, Inverness PH2 11JG.
[M] Strathspey Railway Association, Boat of Garten, Inverness PH24 3BH.

MARK WATSON

Himalaia, Manuel António Gomes (1868–1933) A Portuguese priest and scientist, the inventor of various devices, chief among them the Pyrheliophoro, an apparatus made up of a 75 m (200 ft.) high structure supplied with an 80 m^2 (940 sq. ft.) parabolic mirror and 6177 reflecting mirrors which attracted the sun's rays into a refractory capsule used as a crucible for melting metal. The structure followed the rotation of the earth around the sun, thanks to a clockwork device; and had a capacity for smelting superior to any existing electric furnace in 1904, when it obtained the Grand Prix, two gold medals and a silver medal at the World Fair at St Louis, Missouri, USA. Father Himalaia also developed smokeless powders (*see* EXPLOSIVES) and invented 'himalaite', an explosive more powerful than dynamite.

historical archaeology A term used chiefly in North America and Australasia for archaeology from the time of the first European settlements, in which the study of sites and artefacts interacts with documentary and oral evidence. The Society for Historical Archaeology in the USA was formed in 1967, and the Australian Society for Historical Archaeology in 1970. Industrial archaeology overlaps historical archaeology at many points; and in Australia, the learned society concerned with 'all aspects of settlement . . . from 1788 to the present' lists industrial archaeology and the engineering heritage among its specific interests.

BIBLIOGRAPHY
General
HuLan and Lawrence, 1970; South, 1977.
Specific
Australian Journal of Historical Archaeology, Australian Society for Historical Archaeology, 1983–.
Historical Archaeology, Society for Historical Archaeology, 1967–.

LOCATIONS
[I] Australian Society for Historical Archaeology, Box 220, Holme Building, University of Sydney, NSW 2006, Australia.
[I] Society for Historical Archaeology, PO Box 231033, Pleasant Hill, California, CA 94523.

BARRIE TRINDER

Historicist A style of architecture that draws in a scholarly and meticulous way upon styles used in the past.

Hjedding, Jutland, Denmark A small village near Ølgod, 40 km (25 mi.) N. of Esbjerg, where the first Danish co-operative creamery was established in 1882. The pioneering creameries were privately owned, but farmers' co-operatives soon became a dominant force, and by 1890 Denmark was covered by a network of about a thousand co-operative creameries. The co-operative movement was a significant factor in enabling Danish farmers to adjust to the new economic conditions of the period. The old creamery at Hjedding is now a museum furnished with relevant machines and equipment, and administered by the nearby museum at Ølgod.

BIBLIOGRAPHY
General
Johansen, 1988.
Specific
Bjørn, C. ed. *Dansk mejeribrug 1882–2000* (Danish dairying 1882–2000). Århus, 1982.

LOCATION
[M] Ølgod Museum, Vestergade 47, 6870 Ølgod.

Hlinsko, West Moravia, Czechoslovakia A town. The Vysočina Open-Air Museum owns various buildings in this area. The main 5 ha (2 ac.) site at Vesely Kopec forms a chiefly agricultural settlement, which includes a water-powered corn mill, sawmill and bleaching house. Svobodne Hamri is the site of an ironworks dating from the fourteenth century, with a tail HELVE HAMMER, a grinder, and separating trays which relate to its conversion to a corn mill.

BIBLIOGRAPHY
Specific
Štepán, L. *et al. Vysočina: Soubor Lidovych Staveb a Remesel* (Vysočina: a collection of wooden buildings). Hlinsko, n.d.

Hobart, Tasmania, Australia The Tasmanian capital was settled as a penal colony, first at Risdon Cove, then on the present site. The early timber and brick buildings were soon replaced by stone. John Lee Archer, an architect who worked in the colony from 1827 to 1839, was responsible for many distinctive buildings, military structures and public works, among them the Anglesea barracks and the Treasury. Sir Henry Hunter between 1855 and 1888 designed thirty-one Gothic buildings in the city. A SHOT TOWER remains at Sandy Bay.

Many whaling ships were built in the shipyards at Battery Point, where several slips remain. Whaling ships were provisioned at Hobart, and there are many traces of shore facilities for processing whale products.

BIBLIOGRAPHY
General
McCarty and Schedvin, 1978.

LOCATIONS
[M] Maritime Museum of Tasmania, 28 Cromwell Road, Battery Point, Hobart 7000.
[M] Tasmanian Museum and Art Gallery, GPO Box 1166M, 5 Argyle Street, Hobart 7001.

Hobøl, Østfold, Norway   A village, 40 km (25 mi.) SE of Oslo. Nordalen Sawmill in Hobøl represents the final development of the water-powered sawmill. The site has been used since the sixteenth century, but the equipment preserved there – a multi-blade saw with a cast-iron frame, probably by Myrens Verksted of Oslo – dates from 1890. Power was provided by two locally-made water wheels. Alongside is a turning shop which specialized in making handles for spades, shears and hoes. It is preserved through the agency of the county curator, and employed in cutting timber in authentic fashion for the restoration of historic buildings.

BIBLIOGRAPHY
Specific
Wiig, J. Two Norwegian water-powered sawmills. In Nisser and Bedoire, 1978.

Hoffman kiln   The first successful continuous circular KILN was developed by Friedrich Hoffman (1818–1900) in Austria in 1856, and introduced in Britain in 1858. The hearth was set beside the mouth of the kiln. The unfired pieces themselves acted as heating flues and the fire moved from opening to opening round the kiln; this design had been preceded by a continuous long chamber kiln erected at Constance in 1864. The Hoffman kiln was first developed with a circular brick tunnel; later examples were oval in plan, giving a greater length and hence greater economy. The fire gradually travelled forward, bricks being set at one 'end' of the circuit and withdrawn from the cooling end. A temporary paper partition was placed between the empty chamber and the one being filled, so that the draught flowed in the right direction. Various developments of the Hoffman kiln were introduced to reduce the discoloration of ware. Most Hoffman kilns were covered with roofs; early examples might have a central chimney but it became more typical to set the chimney at one end or one side of the kiln.

Hoffman kilns were adapted to burn LIME. There are surviving example in Britain at Llanymynech, 29 km (18 mi.) NW of Shrewsbury, at Minera, 8 km (5 mi.) W. of Wrexham, at Longcliffe, 2 km (1 mi.) N. of Settle, Yorkshire, and elsewhere.

See also figure 97.

BIBLIOGRAPHY
General
Searle, 1929.

MICHAEL STRATTON

hogshead   A container made by a cooper, usually equivalent in capacity to one and a half BARRELS or 48 gall. (2.18 hl), but a hogshead of wine, oil or honey held 63 gall. (2.86 hl) or half a PIPE, and a hogshead of cider or molasses, 110 gall. (5.00 hl).

BIBLIOGRAPHY
General
Zupko, 1968.

holiday camp   A residential centre for vacations, in Britain characteristic of the 1930s, 40s and 50s. The word 'camp' originally had military associations but during the nineteenth century it came to be associated with the American West, with the exploration of Africa and with gypsies.

The first permanent British holiday camp, open to all, is acknowledged to have been established by Joseph Cunningham of Liverpool, at Croudle Glen on the Isle of Man in 1894. It was moved to Douglas in 1904, where it remained until 1939. J. Fletcher Dodd established a Socialist camp at Caister-on-Sea, Norfolk, in 1906, using tents, later replaced by chalets. The first holiday camp organized by the CO-OPERATIVE MOVEMENT opened at Rothesay on the Isle of Bute in 1911. The concept became popular in the 1920s, utilizing bell tents surplus after World War I, and following precedents from France, Denmark and the USA; but it was in the 1930s that three ebullient entrepreneurs, Billy Butlin (1899–1980), Harry Warner (1889–1964) and Fred Pontin developed camps on a large scale, seizing the opportunities afforded by the growth of paid holidays. Butlin, originally a travelling showman, combined features from the pioneering camps, like chalets and mass catering, with centralized organization of entertainment. He opened an amusement park at Skegness, Lincolnshire, in 1927, adding to it his first camp in 1936. He built a second at Clacton, Essex, in 1936; and camps at Filey in Yorkshire, Pwllheli in North Wales and Ayr in Scotland were built to his specifications during World War II, initially for military use. Other camps were built by trades unions, including one at Cayton Bay, Yorkshire, which in 1933 displaced an earlier PLOTLAND holiday settlement. Architecturally the most distinguished holiday camp was that at Prestatyn, North Wales, designed by W. H. Hamlyn, which was largely in concrete with modernistic features like a control tower, and an ocean-liner-shaped structure for games. Holiday camps have declined since 1960, and those that remain have been substantially rebuilt.

BIBLIOGRAPHY
General
Butlin and Dacre, 1982; Holding, 1908; North, 1962; Schmitt, 1969; Ward and Hardy, 1986.
Specific
Bennett, F. Holiday camps: their design and planning. In *The Builder*, March/April 1939.

BARRIE TRINDER

Hollander beater   A beating machine consisting of a rectangular trough in which revolved a large roller fitted with knives. It was originally used to macerate and beat rags into pulp for the traditional manufacture of paper. The Hollander originated in the Netherlands *c*.1650, and was employed in Saxony by 1715, in France by 1738 (*see* CHALETTE-SUR-LOING), and in England by 1740. It worked more rapidly than STAMPERS. Adaptations of the machine remain in use.

BIBLIOGRAPHY
General
Shorter, 1971.

Specific
Hills, R. *Papermaking*. Manchester: North Western Museum of
Science and Industry, n.d.

Holme, Randle (1627–99)   A Cheshire gentleman, who
was responsible for a large collection of manuscripts
deposited in the British Museum by his son, Randle Holme
(d.1707). His *The Academy of Armory*, published in 1688,
was a guide to the composition of coats of arms, which
describes and illustrates almost every species of tool and
utensil employed in contemporary manufacturing.

BIBLIOGRAPHY
General
Holme, 1688.

Holmegård, Zealand, Denmark   The glassworks of Holmegård at Fensmark, 8 km (5 mi.) NE of Næstved, was
founded in 1825 by the Countess of Danneskjold-Samsøe.
Apart from several small works of *c.*1600 in Jutland, it
was the first glassworks in Denmark. It was located in
open countryside near a large bog which supplied peat for
the furnaces. Around the works the owner erected a
colony, including shops, a dining hall, a bakery, a school
chapel and dwellings for managers and workers. Holmegård installed its first automatic bottle machine as late
as 1935, but the factory has since been modernized
several times, and today it is once more the only
glassworks of considerable size in Denmark. Several
workers' dwellings of 1827–8 have survived. The oldest
production building is a glasshouse of 1874. A small
company museum illustrates the history of glass and
glassmaking.

In Næstved itself one of the biggest factories is Mag-
lemølle, founded in 1875, one of the few Danish papermills still in operation.

BIBLIOGRAPHY
General
Nielsen, 1943–4.
Specific
Buchwald, G. and Schlüter, M. *Kastrup og Holmegårds Glasværker
1825–1975* (Kastrup and the Holmegård Glassworks). Copen-
hagen, 1975.

LOCATION
[M,S] Holmegårds Glasværk, Fensmark, 4700 Næstved.

OLE HYLDTOFT

Holyhead Road, England and Wales   The best road of its
time in Europe, linking London with Dublin through
Coventry, Birmingham, Shrewsbury, Llangollen, Capel
Curig, Holyhead, and Howth. Coach services to Holyhead
had been developed by Robert Lawrence (d.1804) of
Shrewsbury from 1779. A demand for improvement
followed the Act of Union 1800 between Britain and
Ireland. The route was recommended to the parliamentary committee by THOMAS TELFORD in 1810–11: the
Holyhead Road Commission was appointed in 1815, and
in 1819 a Commission was appointed to take over the
existing road between Shrewsbury and Holyhead from the

turnpike trusts. East of Shrewsbury the Commission
continued to collaborate with the trusts. The road was
seen by Sir Henry Parnell (1776–1842), the Irish Member
of Parliament, as the precursor of a scheme to improve all
main roads. The road was meticulously documented in
annual parliamentary reports. Construction work began
under Telford's direction in 1815. The chief features west
of Shrewsbury include the ascent of Chirk Bank; the pass
of Glyn-diffwys; the ornate, cast-iron Waterloo Bridge at
Betws-y-coed; the pass of Nant Ffrancon; the MENAI
BRIDGE; and the road across Anglesey. Of the 106
mileposts, installed in 1828 for £5.5s.0d. each, many
remain, with several tollhouses of standard designs, and
many 'depots' for storage of road metals. The road west of
Shrewsbury was largely complete by 1830. Projects on
the English section continued in the 1830s. From 1837
traffic was reduced by railway competition; the Commission ceased work in 1850.

BIBLIOGRAPHY
General
Rolt, 1958.
Specific
Trinder, B. The Holyhead Road: an engineering project in its
social context. In Penfold, 1980.

LOCATION
[I] The Telford Collection, Ironbridge Gorge Museum, Ironbridge,
Telford, Shropshire TF8 7AW.

BARRIE TRINDER

hone   A type of stone, whose geological origins can be
quite varied, suitable when shaped for the finish-sharpen-
ing of edge tools (*see* MILLSTONES).

Hønefoss, Buskerud, Norway   A town at the head of
Tyrifjorden, 40 km (25 mi.) NW of Oslo, which grew to
prosperity through sawmilling. The Kistefoss Tresliperi is
the only preserved mechanical pulpmill in Norway; some
of the machinery dates from the 1880s. The millstones
with vertical shafts are coupled directly to water turbines,
those with horizontal shafts are electrically driven.

honey   The nectar and saccharine exudations of plants,
gathered, modified and stored in the comb by honey BEES.
The nature of honey varies widely according to its source.
It was the principal form of sweetening in some parts of
Europe into the twentieth century, but in most areas from
the sixteenth century was gradually displaced by sugar.
Until the development of canning it was used in the
preservation of fruit.

BIBLIOGRAPHY
General
Beeton, 1912; Crane, 1975.

horizontal engine   A steam engine in which a horizontal piston rod supplies power directly to the crankshaft of a
flywheel set in the same plane. It was developed first by
RICHARD TREVITHICK in 1802, but fear of uneven cylinder

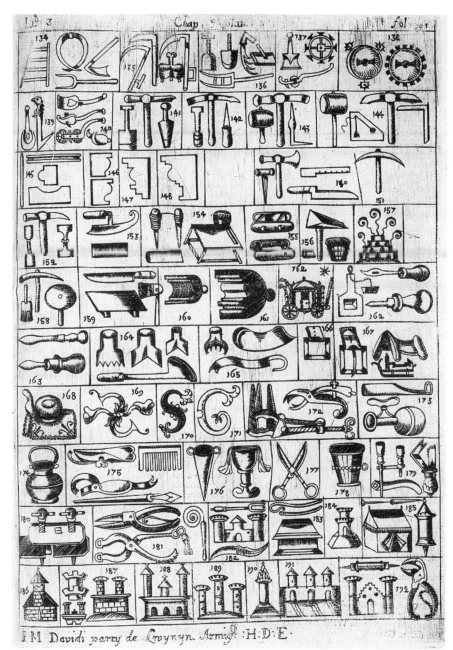

Figure 57 This typical page of illustrations from Book III of Randle Holme's *The Academy of Armory* shows the variety of information on trades provided in the volume: the top line depicts agricultural tools, including millstones in square 138, and drainage implements in 140. Masons' tools are illustrated in squares 142–8; those of slaters in 150–1; of bricklayers and brickmakers in 152–7; of plasterers in 158–60; of saddlers in 162–71, and of surgeons and associated occupations in 172–82. Square 157 shows a brick kiln, 161 a coach, and along the bottom line is a selection of towers, including a bridge of three arches in 191.
Bodleian Library, Oxford

wear impeded progress for half a century; thereafter it became one of the commonest forms of steam engine.

BIBLIOGRAPHY
General
Watkins, 1968.

horizontal windmill A type of TOWER MILL, either with turbine-type sails able to take wind from any direction, or with sails working with shrouds to direct wind from one direction. The sails directly drove millstones set beneath them. They were used in the Near East and in England, where they are said to have been introduced by Stephen Hooper in 1788.

horn The horns of cattle, a waste product from butchers, were important raw materials until the early twentieth century. Horns were left several months, then held over a wood fire and cut lengthwise with long

333

nippers; they were then pressed and hammered flat between hot, greased iron plates. They were used for COMBS, drinking vessels, spectacles, and tobacco boxes. Horn for lanthorn windows was soaked before cutting and shaved afterwards. Horn tips were used for knife handles and whipping tops, while shavings were used to make ornamental flowers, or as fertilizer. BEWDLEY was a centre of the horn trade in eighteenth-century England.

See also BONE MILL; COMB; SIZE.

BIBLIOGRAPHY
General
Houghton, 1692–1703; Tunis, 1965.

Hornblower, Jonathan (1753–1815) One of a family of Cornish engineers, and the originator of the compound steam engine. He was employed briefly by JAMES WATT. He devised, independently, a two-cylinder steam engine in 1781, and was immediately threatened by Watt for infringement of patents, although Watt's claims were never tested in the courts. The action probably impeded for more than a decade the development of compound and high-pressure steam. Fourteen Hornblower engines were built during 1790–8, all but two of them in Cornwall.

BIBLIOGRAPHY
Specific
Harris, T. R. The Hornblower family – pioneer steam engineers. In *Journal of the Trevithick Society*, IV, 1976.
Todd, A. C. Davies Gilbert – patron of engineers and Jonathan Hornblower. In *TNS*, XXXII, 1960.
Torrens, H. S. New light on the Hornblower and Winwood compound steam engine. In *Journal of the Trevithick Society*, IX, 1982.

Hornu, Hainaut, Belgium Le Grand Hornu, one of the most spectacular INDUSTRIAL COMMUNITIES in Europe, lies 8 km (5 mi.) W. of Mons, adjacent to the town of St Ghislain. A coal pit drained by a steam engine was operating in 1810 when the site was purchased by Henri de Gorge Legrand (1774–1832), who expanded the mines and in 1831 opened an engineering works, building steam engines and locomotives. The foundry, stores, offices and assembly shops, designed by the French architect Bruno Renard in the neo-Classical style, were laid out around an elliptical courtyard 140 m × 80 m (460 ft. × 260 ft.), and linked with continuous arcading. The buildings at the eastern end were converted into offices from 1971 by the architect Henri Guchez, and the remaining structures have been restored as ruins. The centre of the courtyard, with the cast-iron statue of Legrand in the centre, has been grassed over.

In 1820 Legrand wrote that he was 'trying to attract strong men by unheard-of comforts'. The construction of workers' houses began in 1819 and there were over four hundred when Legrand died in 1832. The brick, stuccoed houses, in the neo-Classical style, are of two storeys, with six rooms and a floor space of 55 m² (65 sq. yd.). There are pavilions at the ends of the terraces.

Tramway locomotives built at Hornu are exhibited at UTRECHT, EREZÉE, and BRUSSELS.

BIBLIOGRAPHY
General
Henderson, 1954; Hudson, 1979a; Linters, 1986b; Watelet, 1964a.
Specific
Bruwier, M., Meurant, A. and Pierard, C. Le Grand Hornu. In *Industrie*, 1968.

BARRIE TRINDER

horse The most important motive power for road transport before 1900, for railways before 1830, and for canals and some rivers before 1900, and a significant source of power for manufacturing. The horse was known in Europe from prehistoric times and was particularly prized in the Muslim world. The collar and most essential parts of the modern harness (*see* SADDLERY) were in use by the seventeenth century. Horses were supplied to urban and industrial regions from regions where breeding was a central part of the agricultural economy, like Naples, Andalusia, Brittany, Normandy, the Limousin, and the Welsh borders. Convoys could be seen entering Paris in the 1780s *en route* for the horse market in the rue St-Honoré, with ten or twelve animals in line, held together by shafts.

Horses were employed for riding, as pack animals, and as draught beasts for carts, wagons, and coaches. Accommodating horses was a dominant concern in every big city and in any town that had an extensive thoroughfare trade. A city cab needed two horses to keep it operating; a two-horse omnibus required an average of eleven; while a stage coach required as many as eight teams of four or six horses. While the use of horses for long-distance traffic decreased with the opening of main-line railways, traffic going to and from railway termini stimulated new demands for horse labour. Cities were packed with stables, hay carts and hay boats were continually delivering fodder, and the shallow parts of rivers were used for washing down coach horses.

In Britain the horse population between 1871 and 1901 grew proportionately faster than that of humans, since the import of grain had reduced the cost of feeding horses. By 1900 there were more horses working in British towns than in the countryside. A peak was reached in 1902 with 3.5 million horses working in Britain, as compared with 1.3 million in 1811. In the USA it was calculated that a horse ate 1.4 tons per annum of oats or corn and 2.4 tons of hay. The problems caused by the numbers of horses in great cities in Europe and America *c.*1900 were major concerns of municipal managers.

Horses of smaller breeds, usually called 'pit ponies', were used for underground haulage in mines, particularly as the scale of coal mining increased. In Britain the total so employed increased from 11 000 in 1851 to 70 000 in 1911, but gradually diminished after 1918.

See also BARGE; HORSE GIN; HORSE POWER; HORSE TRAM; LIVERY STABLE; OMNIBUS; PACKHORSE; POST COACH; RAILWAY; STAGE COACH; WAGGON.

BIBLIOGRAPHY
General
Braudel, 1981; Chartres, 1977; Edwards, 1988; Gordon, 1893;
    Grimshaw, 1982; Hey, 1980; Major, 1985; Thompson, 1972,
    1983.
Specific
Thompson, F. M. L. Nineteenth-century horse sense. In *EcHR*,
    XXIX, 1976.

BARRIE TRINDER

horse gin   A device or 'engine' powered by one or more
horses or donkeys walking round a circular track and
harnessed so as to turn a large toothed wheel, either in the
same plane or above, which turned smaller wheels
operating machinery. The device was extensively used for
raising materials from mines, in crushing mineral ores,
and in early textile factories. It can be adapted for
pumping, or for lifting heavy blocks of stone in a quarry, or
for working mechanical devices. A gin house is a building
accommodating the circular track around which the gin
horse walks. JAMES WATT developed the notion of HORSE-
POWER on the basis of a horse gin. In Germany dog wheels,
'tretmühlen', were employed in mines.
    See also COTTON GIN; CRUSHING CIRCLE.

Horsens, Jutland, Denmark   Horsens is a medium-sized
city on the east coast of Jutland. Several houses on
Søndergade, the unusually wide main street, bear witness
to the city's rich trading traditions, among them the
imposing merchant house, Lichtenbergs gård, now a
hotel, at No. 17, and the distillery house at No. 41, both
dating from the eighteenth century. During the nineteenth century Horsens developed into an important
industrial city with large textile mills, engineering works
and tobacco factories. The cotton concern of Crome &
Goldschmidt was the largest in Denmark from the 1880s
until its closure in the 1920s. Some characteristic mill
buildings with north-lit sheds have survived. Another
prominent example is the Bastian woodworking factory
erected in 1875, and notable for its unusual chimney of
German origin.
    Horsens was thus an appropriate place for the first
general industrial museum in Denmark, opened in 1977
with the name of 'The Museum of Workers, Craftsmen
and Industry', on the premises of the city's old power
station of 1906. The permanent displays include prime
movers, a printing workshop, a brewery, and two working-class apartments preserved *in situ*. The museum also
covers in detail the metal, tobacco, wood, graphics and
paper trades. Even if the machines are prominent, the
fundamental concept is to show them in conjunction with
the contemporary social environment.
    Vejle, 30 km (20 mi.) S., has a place in Danish industrial
history as an important centre for cotton spinning. Two
small rivers, Grejs Å and Vejle Å, flow out into the Vejle
Fjord, and on their relatively steep lower stretches have
driven considerable numbers of mills. A 6 km (4 mi.)
stretch of the Grejs once powered ten mills, among them
the Grejs textile factory and a hammer mill for iron; while

Figure 58   The chimney of the Bastian woodworking factory
at Horsens, dating from 1875; like many Scandinavian
industrial buildings of the nineteenth century, it reflects the
influence of German schools of architecture.
Jørgen Sestoft

335

the Vejle provided power for the Haraldskjær and Vingsted wood pulp mills, and the large Randbøldal textile mill. There are several remains of these mills, but Randbøldal has deteriorated in spite of legal protection.

BIBLIOGRAPHY
General
Johansen, 1988; Sestoft, 1979.
Specific
Bøcher, S. B. *Vandkraftens udnyttelse i det sydlige Nørrejylland* (The exploitation of water power in southern Jutland). Copenhagen, 1942.
Jensen, J. B. Industrialiseringen af Grejsdalen (The industrialization of the valley of Grejs). In *Fabrik og Bolig*, II, 1982.
Norn, O. *En købstads industrialisering* (The industrialization of a city). Horsens, 1973.

LOCATION
[M] Arbejder-, Håndværker-og Industrimuseet, Gasvej 17, 8700 Horsens.

OLE HYLDTOFT

horse power   A unit of power defined by JAMES WATT in 1782. Observing a 24 ft. (7.3 m) diameter HORSE GIN, he noted the revolution time as $2\frac{1}{2}$ minutes pulling 180 lb. (82 kg) or, rounded up, 33 000 ft.lb. per minute. The formal publication appeared in 1809. One horse power (hp) = 745.700 watts (W).

horse tram   A TRAMCAR in its simplest form. A four-wheeled single- or double-decked car would typically be hauled by a pair of horses supplemented by a pair of 'cock' horses on hills. The need to reverse at termini required the horses to be unhitched and reattached at the other end of the car, so that almost all horse tramcars were double-ended: cars whose bodies rotated were tried but not widely adopted. Horse trams were pioneered in New York in 1832 but did not reach Europe until the 1860s. Few horse tramways failed to adopt some form of mechanical traction, and some horse tramcars were converted into electric cars or served as trailers for steam, electric or cable trams. The horse trams in Douglas, ISLE OF MAN, are the only ones still working.

BIBLIOGRAPHY
General
Oakley, 1979.

Horten, Vestfold, Norway   A town on Oslofjord, 60 km (40 mi.) S. of Oslo, which grew up around Karl Johansvarn, Norway's principal naval dockyard. The Preus Fotohistorisk Museum, opened in 1967, was the creation of Leif Preus, head of a large photographic processing concern, in a three-storey factory vacated when the company moved to new premises. It shows the history of photography from its earliest times, and includes a complete daguerreotype set, a nineteenth-century studio, and a complete series of Kodak cameras.

BIBLIOGRAPHY
General
Baggethun, 1960.

LOCATION
[M] Preus Fotohistorisk Museum, Langgaten 82, 3190 Horten.

Hortobágy, Hajdú-Bihar, Hungary   A region 160 km (100 mi.) E. of Budapest, comprising 30 000 ha (75 000 ac.) of exceptionally flat land made barren after the Tartar invasions of the thirteenth century, but irrigated by the Tiszalök dam and power station, and by the Eastern Main Canal built under the first five-year plan (*see* HUNGARY). In the town of Hortobágy is a spectacular stone arched bridge designed by Ferenc Povolny in 1827–33; the bridge has nine arches, and is 167 m (545 ft.) long.

BIBLIOGRAPHY
General
Kiss *et al.*, 1981.

hosiery   Hose means an item of clothing for the leg, and hosiery most commonly refers to stockings or socks; but the term also denotes a range of clothing made by KNITTING, including breeches, handkerchiefs, waistcoats and various kinds of underwear. The hosiery industry in England, which was concentrated in NOTTINGHAM and LEICESTER, was controlled in the late nineteenth century from WAREHOUSES where items produced by domestic outworkers or small manufacturing units were finished and packed.

BIBLIOGRAPHY
General
BPP, 1863; Felkin, 1867; Pool and Llewellyn, 1955; Smith, 1965; Wells, 1935.
Specific
Chapman, S. D. The genesis of the British hosiery industry, 1660–1750. In *TH*, III, 1972.
Chapman, S. D. Enterprise and innovation in the British hosiery industry, 1750–1850. In *TH*, V, 1974.

hospital   The earliest large hospital buildings were either for the accommodation of the old, especially retired sailors or soldiers, as were Sir Christopher Wren's Royal Naval Hospital, Greenwich, London, of 1694, and Les Invalides, Paris, of 1670, or asylums for the mad. Increasing numbers of hospitals for the treatment of the sick were built in large cities during the eighteenth century. In the mid-nineteenth century, when hospitals were constructed in most towns of consequence, designers came to favour plans in which patients were dispersed in small, connected buildings rather than in single large blocks, thus lessening the dangers of infection, but this practice was abandoned as the causes of bacterial infection were recognized in the late nineteenth century.

BIBLIOGRAPHY
General
Grimshaw and Porter, 1989; Pevsner, 1976.

hot blast   The process by which air from the blowing engine of a BLAST FURNACE is heated in stoves before entering the furnace. It was developed by James Beaumont Neilson (1792–1865) of Glasgow, who first propounded the principle that the output of a furnace would be increased, and economies in fuel consumption made, with a heated blast. Neilson proved the effectiveness of his principle by using first wrought-iron, then cast-iron, pipe stoves, raising the blast temperatures to 315 °C. Such stoves were superseded by regenerative stoves developed by E. A. Cowper (*see* COWPER STOVE) from 1857.

BIBLIOGRAPHY
General
Gale, 1967, 1971; Percy, 1864.

hotching tub   *See* JIGGING.

hotel   A lodging place for travellers or longer-term resort dwellers, of superior status to an INN, used in this sense in English from the 1760s, before which the word denoted a large private residence, as in the French sense. The first hostelry in England so designated was 'The Hotel' in Exeter (now the Royal Clarence Hotel), so named in 1768. Hotels were built at English seaside resorts for middle-class customers, an example being the Albion, Broadstairs, of 1816, but the great period of seaside hotel building in Britain came in the 1860s, with the Grand, Brighton, of 1864, and Cuthbert Brodrick's (1822–1905) masterpiece, the Grand, Scarborough, of 1867.

While hotels in Europe copied the houses of the rich, in the USA they set new standards of luxury, which in turn influenced the ways in which people equipped their homes. In 1853 the Mount Vernon Hotel, Cape May, N.J., was by repute the first to fit every room with a bath, and the private bathroom had become the norm in American hotels by 1900. American hotels were much larger than those in Europe: the Metropolitan, New York, which opened in 1852, accommodated a thousand guests, and the Waldorf-Astoria of 1895–7 in the same city had more than 1500 rooms. The Statler, in Buffalo, N.Y., designed by G. B. Post & Sons in 1907–11, is regarded as the prototype of twentieth-century short-stay hotels.

The building of large hotels began in the principal European cities in the 1860s and 70s. The concept of the hotel was revolutionized in the late nineteenth century by Cesar Ritz (1850–1918), a Swiss who built the Ritz, Paris, in 1898; the Carlton, London, in 1899; and the Ritz, London, in 1904–6 – the city's first steel-framed building. Interiors were opulently fitted around palm courts, and bedrooms were lavishly furnished. By 1911 the principal hotels in European cities were offering ELEVATORS, electric lighting, central heating and garage accommodation, as well as private bathrooms. The Belgian coast is notable for its hotels of the inter-war period, which include the Grand at Nieuwpoort, built in the ART DECO style in 1924, and the Hôtel Normandie, Koksijde, constructed in the form of a boat in 1936.

See also BOARDING HOUSE; CARAVANSERAI; MOTEL; RAILWAY HOTEL.

BIBLIOGRAPHY
General
Boniface, 1981; Boorstin, 1973; Everitt, 1973; Hamburg-Amerika Linie, 1911; Pevsner, 1976; Rauers, 1942; Simmons, 1984; Taylor and Bush, 1974; Viaene, 1986; Williamson, 1930.

BARRIE TRINDER

house types   *See* APARTMENT; BACK-TO-BACK HOUSE; BARRACK HOUSE; BLIND-BACK HOUSE; BUNGALOW; BURGAGE PLOT; CATSLIDE; CLUSTER HOUSE; COTTAGE; FLAT; PREFABRICATED HOUSE; SEMI-DETACHED HOUSE; TENEMENT; TERRACE; TUNNEL-BACK HOUSE, VILLA.

Hronec, Central Slovakia, Czechoslovakia   An important ironworking town, especially noted for its bridges. A cast-iron bridge was built here in 1810, modelled on the bridge at IRONBRIDGE. Built across a canal, it was 4.7 m (18 ft.) long. The bridge was closed in 1962, and subsequently dismantled. Part of it is displayed in front of the ironworks in the town.

BIBLIOGRAPHY
General
Dusan, 1984.

Huddersfield, West Yorkshire, England   The town at the confluence of the Rivers Colne and Holme, whose valleys abound in domestic loomshops and textile mill complexes. Huddersfield Narrow Canal, opened in 1811, has seventy-four locks and the 4951 m (3 mi. 135 yd.) Standedge Tunnel, which is the longest in Britain. Most of the canal still holds water. Huddersfield has an outstanding railway station by J. P. Pritchett (1789–1868), built in 1847–8, in the Corinthian style. Caphouse Colliery, Flockton, 9.5 km (6 mi.) E., with its wooden headstock, and horizontal steam engine of 1876, is now a museum where visitors can go 120 m (390 ft.) underground.

BIBLIOGRAPHY
General
Rolt, 1950; Russell, 1982.

LOCATIONS
[I] Kirklees Leisure Services, Libraries, Museums and Arts Division, Red Doles, Huddersfield HD2 1YF.
[M] Yorkshire Mining Museum, Caphouse Colliery, New Road, Overton, Wakefield WF4 4AH.

Hudson, Kenneth (b. 1916)   An English writer and broadcaster, responsible in 1963 for the first book and the first specialist journal on industrial archaeology, published 'to draw attention to the surviving monuments of our industrial past', and proponent of the subject in many countries. Hudson is editor of several standard international reference works on museums, and is a distinguished 'museum critic'. He has always upheld the role of the amateur in industrial archaeology, and urged that serious attention be paid to workers as well as to machines, and to the industrial monuments of the twentieth century.

BIBLIOGRAPHY
General
Hudson, 1963, 1966, 1968, 1972, 1976, 1977, 1978, 1979a, 1979b, 1980, 1983, 1987; Hudson and Nicholls, 1981, 1987.

Specific
Journal of Industrial Archaeology, 1963–68.

hulk The beached hull of a sailing ship, used for storage, particularly of coal for steamships (*see* FALKLAND ISLANDS); or as accommodation for prisoners, as in the Thames Estuary in England and in the USA in the nineteenth century, or for construction workers.

Hull, Humberside, England The historic port at the mouth of the River Humber, with Humber Dock, built by JOHN RENNIE in 1809, and later docks built by railway companies. Paragon Station has an Italianate façade by G. T. Andrews, *c*.1848, and later but spectacular train sheds. Springhead Pumping Station houses a museum with a Cornish engine of 1876 by Bells, Lightfoot & Co. The Hennebique concrete building north-west of the centre was built by the engineering firm Rose, Downs & Thompson in 1900.

LOCATIONS
[I] Hull City Museums and Art Galleries Town Docks Museum, Queen Victoria Square, Hull HU1 3DX.
[M] Springhead Pumping Station Museum, Yorkshire Water Authority, Hull HU10 6RA.

Hull Landing, Quebec, Canada The site of Hull Landing in the Ottawa Valley, 207 km (129 mi.) SW of Montreal, became in the course of the nineteenth and early twentieth centuries the most significant place in Quebec for the development of the forest and paper industries. This has been revealed by multidisciplinary researches carried out by historians, ethnographers and archaeologists which began in 1972 under the auspices of the National Museum of Man (now the Canadian Museum of Civilizations) in Ottawa, the Canadian Parks Service and the National Capital Commission.

The large-scale exploitation of the forests of white pines and of hardwoods was first stimulated by the needs of Great Britain during the blockade imposed during the Napoleonic Wars of the early nineteenth century, and subsequently by the demands of the market in the USA. Exploitation during the nineteenth century was undertaken by British and American entrepreneurs, among them Philemon Wright (1760–1839), in the establishment of SAWMILLS. Between 1803 and 1850 the trees were assembled into RAFTS and transported along the river Outaouais and the St Lawrence and its tributaries to Quebec City where they were used in shipbuilding or loaded on to sailing ships destined for England.

Rescue archaeological work on the site in 1983 drew attention to the great pulp and paper complexes which were active between 1868 and 1972. Under the administration of the Wright, Baston & Currier Co. between 1868 and 1878 the installations comprised a sawmill, built in wood and stone, trimming and planing shops, a joiners' shop, a maintenance shop, a smithy, kilns for drying wood, stables, sheds, a grain silo, oil stores, and runways for timber. In the principal sawmill were reciprocating vertical saws, as well as circular saws, all worked with

steam from six tubular horizontal boilers, 12 m (40 ft.) long and 0·9 m (3 ft.) wide. The output in 1875 was 9.6 million metres (31.5 million ft.) of planks a year.

Most of the installations were destroyed in a fire in 1878 and in 1888 what was left became the property of E. B. Eddy, an entrepreneur already well known in the region as a maker of sulphur matches. He added to those buildings which remained intact a factory for making sulphite pulp: in 1891 this comprised twelve buildings – sawmills, warehouses, washing plants and four machine shops with horizontal digesters, among other equipment.

The complex was modernized in 1925 with the object of meeting the international demand for newsprint. Various new processes and machines were added in due course: watertube boilers, vertical digesters, acid accumulators, air compressors, drums for stripping bark, augurs for tearing apart wood, heat exchangers, centrifugal purifiers, sulphur kilns, cranes, conveyors, hoists, dehydration machinery, pumps, stripping presses, refiners, filters and the like. Wood and equipment were transported by 'alligators', special boats designed for the carriage of timber. The company still produces paper and provides guided tours of its plant.

BIBLIOGRAPHY
General
Lower, 1973; Nadon, 1984; Ruddel, 1983.

LOCATION
[S] E. B. Eddy Forest Products, Box 600, Hull, Quebec, J8X 3Y7.

LOUISE TROTTIER

hund By the sixteenth century, the generic name in Central Europe for a four-wheeled vehicle used in a mine, the word being derived from the Czech 'hyntow' or Magyar 'hinto' rather than from the German word for dog. A common type ran on two parallel planks, with a 'leitnagel' or guiding pin projecting below the front into the gap between the planks. Such vehicles were in use throughout the mining regions of Central Europe by the 1550s, when they were described by GEORGIUS AGRICOLA, and probably date from a century earlier. In the eighteenth century isolated examples were used in France, Switzerland and Russia and they were employed in the Ruhrgebiet in the nineteenth century. They weighed up to 69 kg (1 cwt. 40 lb.). Examples are preserved at LUCERNE, Eisenerz (*see* STYRIAN IRON TRAIL) and elsewhere. In some regions they were superseded by HUNGARIAN HUNDS.

BIBLIOGRAPHY
General
Lewis, 1970.

Hunedoara, Romania A region in the south-west of Romania, with long mining and metalworking traditions. Apart from Hunedoara city, the most important locations are Călan, Găvojdia, Ghelar, Lupeni, Nădrag, Teliuc, Titan, Topliţa and Uricani. A furnace for melting ores, which had been cut into rock in the ninth century, was found at Ghelar, and is now in the Science Museum,

Hungary

LONDON. It is in the shape of a truncated cone, with a diameter at the top of 0.65 m ($25\frac{1}{2}$ in.) and at the bottom of 0.33 m (13 in.), with a height of 1.8 m (70 in.). It is built with a cover at a charging platform, and air was let in through an opening in the lower part. Documents of 1681–2 mention that there were five blast furnaces in the region, provided with iron ore from Ghelar and Teliuc. A blast furnace with an annual output of 1200 tonnes was built at Topliţa in 1754. The engineering shops and foundry at Găvojdia were rebuilt in 1837, and in 1840 one of the first HOT BLAST systems was brought into operation at the adjoining blast furnace. Coke ovens were established at Lupeni and Uricani, 40 km (25 mi.) S. of Hunedoara, in 1857. Engineering workshops were built at Călan in 1863, and the first blast furnace was commissioned between 1869 and 1871. In the latter year the Victoria works came into operation, producing pig iron, iron castings and equipment for foundries. The Călan Ironworks began operation in 1882 and the first modern blast furnace was completed there in 1884.

There is also a tradition of working gold in the Hunedoara region which dates from pre-Roman times. In 1797 the master millwright Munteanu Urs built at the Săcărîmb mine a mill which was powered by the water used to wash the ore, and the following year he built a machine for washing ore. Felix Franzenau, the manager of the Săcărîmb mine, with Johan Huber, built further new machines for washing gold ore, and in 1806 he wrote a description of the mines and completed drawings of the machines.

BIBLIOGRAPHY
General
Bălan and Mihăilescu, 1985.

HORIA GIURGIUMAN

Hungarian hund A vehicle used in Central European mines from the mid-seventeenth century: it had four wheels, the back pair larger than the front, and ran on a single plank with the PUTTER pressing down at the back so that it ran on the rear wheels only, thus reducing friction. It was used instead of the HUND in some areas. Preserved examples at Clausthal-Zellerfeld (West Germany) and BANSKÁ BYSTRICA.

BIBLIOGRAPHY
General
Lewis, 1970.

Hungary Hungary is bounded by Austria, Czechoslovakia, USSR, Romania and Yugoslavia. It has a population of eleven million, of whom more than two million live in BUDAPEST. The country is divided into two parts by the Danube, which runs from north to south. Transdanubia is the area to the west of the river, and the great Hungarian plain lies to the east. The northern part of Hungary is mountainous and rich in minerals. From 1541 until the liberation of Budapest in 1686, Hungary was under Turkish occupation, but subsequently came under the control of the Habsburgs. The Hungarians asserted their independence in 1848 under the leadership of Lajos Kossuth, Ferenc Deák and others, the Habsburgs retaining power only with the assistance of Tsarist Russia. After 1867, under the Dual Monarchy (*see* AUSTRIA), Hungary had almost complete constitutional independence within the Empire, and its frontiers included Slovakia, Transylvania, now part of Romania, and Croatia with the port of Fiume (*see* RIJEKA), now in Yugoslavia. Hungary has substantial resources of lignite, bauxite, oil, and natural gas.

Hungary was dominated by the great estates of the nobility. There are rich traditions of folk art, including brightly coloured pottery, like the majolica made at Hódmezővásárhely (24 km (16 mi.) SE of Szeged), painted furniture, domestic linen weaving, and embroidery. Many of the ancient metal mines that are regarded historically as Hungarian are now within the borders of Czechoslovakia and Romania.

In the mid-nineteenth century modern communications improved links between Hungary and the West. Steam navigation on the Danube began in 1829 (*see* AUSTRIA) and shortly afterwards steamers were going up the Tisza to SZEGED. The Tisza is now navigable throughout its course in Hungary. The first railway, from Pest to VÁC, was opened in 1846, and by 1851 rail communication was established to Vienna. There was a boom in railway construction after 1867, when the state railway (MÁV) was constituted, and from 1880 government subsidies were provided for constructing secondary lines. There were 22 466 route km (13 960 mi.) of railway by 1914, but only 9382 km (5830 mi.) after the contraction of frontiers following World War I.

Economic development in the decades before World War I was very rapid. A substantial engineering industry was developed with state aid, which met 70 per cent of domestic demand by 1913. Many innovations were developed at the Ganz works in BUDAPEST. Steelmaking was developed, and a new open-hearth plant at Diósgyőr (*see* BÜKK), financed by the government, commenced in 1868; by 1913 it employed 8000 workers. Budapest developed particularly rapidly and Hungarians were active in the development of telecommunications and electric power. Tivadar Puskás set up the first telephone exchange in Paris. Kálmán Kandó was responsible for the electrification of the first main-line railway, the Valtellina line in Italy in 1898–1902, and for the development of phase-changing electric locomotives from 1923. M. Deri (1854–1938), K. Zipernovsky (1853–1942) and O. T. Bláthy (1860–1939) built the first serviceable electric transformers. Szilárd Zielinski (1860–1924) was a pioneer of the use of reinforced concrete, and is best known for designing the 40 m (130 ft.) span Sinka bridge on the Brassó–Fogaras railway in Transylvania, and the world's first reinforced-concrete weir on the River Körös at Gyula, 186 km (116 mi.) SE of Budapest, in 1905–6. Motorcar manufacture was also well developed in Hungary before 1914, the carburettor being the invention of Donát Bánki (1859–1922) and János Csonka (1852–1939). Nevertheless only 17 per cent of the population was engaged in industry in 1910. In the 1920s and 30s Hungarian architects like Farkas Molnár and Marcel Breuer led the Bauhaus-inspired Modern Movement in Eastern Europe. Diesel railcars built by Ganz became world-famous, and the engineer George Jendrassik (1898–1954) developed gas turbine traction for railway locomotives. The 1930s saw the beginnings of large-scale exploitation of the oilfields of the south-west. Under the Communist governments that ruled Hungary from 1948–90 there was an emphasis on heavy industry, developed during a succession of five-year plans, with the construction of steel, engineering and textile plants, and the production of wine, fruit brandies, and sausages for export.

As a result of resolutions of the Ministries of Agriculture, Building and Industry in the late 1970s, industrial monuments in Hungary are now well protected. Industrial concerns are charged with responsibility for presenting their own history to the public, and many now have their own museums. The railway authority has established a commission for preserving historic buildings and artefacts. The Technical Museum in Budapest has no displays but is a documentation centre which has a data bank relating to industrial history, on which were recorded by 1984 details of 100 000 artefacts, 200 000 photographs and 300 buildings. The museum publishes a periodical, *Rundschau für Technikgeschichte*, describing developments in industrial history. Mills have been studied in detail, and by 1984 seventeen windmills, fourteen granaries, thirteen water mills, four animal-powered mills and a floating mill (*see* SZENTENDRE) had been identified as industrial monuments. Important examples are a horse gin of Czech design of 1836 at Szarvas, 128 km (80 mi.) SE of Budapest; an eighteenth-century water mill with three wheels at Turistvánd in Szabolcs-Szatmár province; and a six-sail windmill of 1840, typical of those used on the Great Plain, which is preserved at Tes in Veszprém province. Open-air museums portraying folk culture have developed on a considerable scale since the late 1950s (*see* NYÍREGYHÁZA; SZENTENDRE), and in addition to the major museums some eighty buildings or small complexes are conserved for their ethnographical importance. Postcards are regarded as an important historical source; the collection of the late Dr Petrikovits in Szerencs totals over 600 000 cards.

See also AJKA; BALATON; BUDAPEST; BÜKK; DUNAÚJVÁROS; ESZTERGOM; GÁNT; GYOMA; HEREND; HORTOBÁGY; KALOCSA; KAPOSVÁR; KISKŐRÖS; KISKUNHALAS; NAGYCENK; NYÍREGYHÁZA; OROSZLÁNY; PÁPA; PÉCS; SALGÓTARJAN; SIÓ CANAL; SOPRON; SZEGED; SZÉKESFEHÉRVÁR; SZENTENDRE; SZENTGOTTHÁRD; TATA; VÁC; VÁRPALOTA; VESZPRÉM; ZALAEGERSZEG.

BIBLIOGRAPHY
General
Hoensch, 1984; Kiss *et al.*, 1981; Milward and Saul, 1977; Zippelius, 1974.
Specific
Kubinszky, M. Industrial archaeology in Hungary. In Victor and Wright, 1984.

LOCATIONS
[M] Műszaki Muzeum (Technical Museum), Kaposvári út 13, Budapest XI.
[M] Transport Museum, Városligeti Körút 11, Budapest.

MIHÁLY KUBINSZKY and BARRIE TRINDER

Hurum, Buskerud, Norway   On Drammensfjord, 20 km (12 mi.) SE of Drammen. The Engene Dynamite and Explosives Museum (Sprengtoff Historisk Museum) opened in 1983 in the only surviving factory that used the original process of ALFRED NOBEL. Seven buildings are preserved in the original condition of 1875. The museum shows Nobel's career and the history of the company.

LOCATION
[M] Sprengtoff Historisk Museum, c/o Dyno Industrier a/s, p.b. 779 Sentrum, 0106 Oslo 1.

hush Hushing is a method of exposing veins of ore, surface soil being removed by means of a torrent of water, usually accumulated in a reservoir behind a dam at the head of a gulley. Evidence of hushing has often been destroyed by subsequent mining. Traces remain in England (*see* PENNINES) and Wales (*see* ABERYSTWYTH).

BIBLIOGRAPHY
General
Stratton and Trinder, 1988.

Hüttenberg, Carinthia, Austria   A mining region northeast of Klagenfurt, with many remains of eighteenth- and nineteenth-century ironworks. At Urtl, 45 km (28 mi.) NE of Klagenfurt, there are ruins of a blast furnace built in 1578 and used until 1834. The stack is intact.

hybrid railway   A term applied by historians to railways built in Britain between 1800 and 1840, which marked a transitional phase between mineral and main-line railways (*see* RAILWAY). They typically had iron rails, sometimes plate rails (*see* PLATEWAY), and like canals were often engineered with inclined planes, which might be powered or self-acting. They usually ran over the land of several owners, therefore requiring legislative sanction, and often along the verges of public roads. They were usually open to anyone who wished to work wagons. Such engineers as THOMAS TELFORD and JOHN RENNIE were often consulted over their construction.

See figure 59; *see also* CROMFORD; DURHAM; FOREST OF DEAN; STRATFORD-UPON-AVON.

BIBLIOGRAPHY
General
Lewis, 1968; Priestley, 1831; Trinder, 1982a; von Oeynhausen and von Dechen, 1974; Wood, 1825.

hydraulic cement   A cement that will set under water. It is made from argillaceous limestone (a clayey limestone, with hydrated aluminium silicate) or chalk marl, which, when calcined, produces an impure form of calcium oxide which slakes with only feeble heat. JOHN SMEATON made hydraulic cement from limestone from Aberthaw, South Wales, when building the Eddystone Lighthouse (*see* LIGHTHOUSE) in 1756.

BIBLIOGRAPHY
General
Morgan and Pratt, 1938.

hydraulic crane   A crane whose winding mechanism was operated by hydraulic JIGGERS, patented by W. G. ARMSTRONG on 31 July 1846 following the experimental conversion of cranes on quays at Newcastle-upon-Tyne. Armstrong sold about 1200 cranes in the following twelve years.

BIBLIOGRAPHY
General
McNeil, 1968, 1972.

hydraulic power   The principles of hydraulic engineering – that power could be transmitted through liquids (in the first instance through water), and that a small input force could be multiplied into a large output force – were defined by Blaise Pascal (1623–62), but the first practical applications were probably hydraulic engines used to pump water from mines in the Harz Mountains, Saxony and Hungary in the mid-eighteenth century. Columns of water from reservoirs fed cylinders; pistons within were thereby raised until valves were tripped, causing the water to discharge and the pistons to fall, creating a lifting motion which operated pumps. WATER ENGINES were used to drain mines in Britain from 1765.

JOSEPH BRAMAH patented a hydraulic press in London in 1795, which initiated the development of hydraulic power. Bramah's press was used for crushing oil seeds, baling cotton and wool, and printing textiles. Within a wooden frame was mounted a large cast-iron cylinder in which worked an accurately fitted piston. Water was forced into the cylinder by a small-bore force pump, which raised the piston, and so achieved a considerable magnification of forces.

Hydraulic presses were developed by Matthew Murray and others for testing anchor chains for ships, and hydraulic power was used for some moving bridges in the second and third decades of the nineteenth century, but the next stages of its development were due principally to SIR WILLIAM ARMSTRONG (1810–1900), who completed his first experimental hydraulic engine, now in the Museum of Science and Industry at NEWCASTLE-UPON-TYNE, in 1836. In 1846 he patented a HYDRAULIC CRANE and in 1847 established a works at Elswick, Newcastle-upon-Tyne, which rapidly gained a market for its hydraulic machines. Hydraulic power came to be widely used in ports, for cranes, hoists, capstans, railway wagon traversers, conveyor belts, lifting bridges and dock gates. Centralized sources of power were constructed, at first towers like that of *c.*1851 at Grimsby (*see* LINCOLNSHIRE), into which water was pumped by a steam engine in order to create pressure in the mains for the operation of hydraulic machines, but from 1851 by ACCUMULATORS. Many important bridges, including Tower Bridge, LONDON, and the Swing Bridge at NEWCASTLE-UPON-TYNE, as well as various BOAT LIFTS, incorporated hydraulic power systems; and hydraulic power was employed on an increasing scale for shaping metal (*see* FORGING PRESS), drilling and riveting, particularly after the development by Ralph Tweddell (1843–95) of the hydraulic intensifier.

Hydraulic power was widely used in nineteenth-century civil engineering projects, for lifting structures into place, as with the Britannia Bridge over the Menai Straits (*see* MENAI BRIDGES) in 1849, the FORTH BRIDGE in 1885–9, or the launching of BRUNEL's *Great Eastern* in 1857.

341

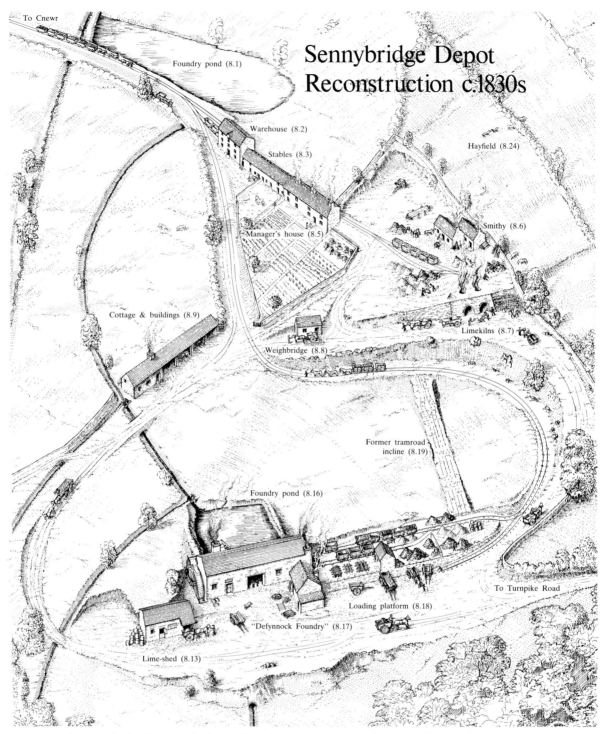

To Cnewr

Foundry pond (8.1)

Sennybridge Depot Reconstruction c.1830s

Warehouse (8.2)

Hayfield (8.24)

Stables (8.3)

Smithy (8.6)

Manager's house (8.5)

Cottage & buildings (8.9)

Limekilns (8.7)

Weighbridge (8.8)

Former tramroad incline (8.19)

Foundry pond (8.16)

To Turnpike Road

Loading platform (8.18)

"Defynnock Foundry" (8.17)

Lime-shed (8.13)

Figure 59 The Sennybridge Depot on the Brecon Forest Tramway as it was in the 1830s, showing the characteristic practices of a hybrid railway: the Defynnock Iron and Brass Foundry, with its cupola furnace and water-driven bellows, was opened in 1832, and the warehouse spanning the plateway sidings was build to handle general cargoes. The drawing (from Stephen Hughes, *The Brecon Forest Tramroads*, Aberystwyth: Royal Commission on Ancient and Historical Monuments in Wales, 1991) shows how the recording of archaeological features can enable past industrial landscapes to be re-created.
Royal Commission on Ancient and Historical Monuments in Wales

Bramah had envisaged the public supply of hydraulic power but this was not achieved until 1877 when a power company began operation in HULL, England. E. B. Ellington, consultant to the Hull company and managing director of a leading supplier of hydraulic equipment, was largely responsible for the growth of public supply companies. In 1882 the London Hydraulic Power Company was set up: by 1927 it had 296 km (184 mi.) of mains, including a tunnel under the Thames. Similar systems were established in Manchester, Birmingham, Liverpool, Glasgow, Antwerp, Bremen, Frankfurt-am-Main, Hamburg, Melbourne and Sydney, and were used to operate ELEVATORS and hoists, and even to move the cabaret platform at the Savoy Hotel, London. Such systems suffered severely from bombing in World War II.

It was also in Hull, in the city's oil mills, that oil came to replace water as the fluid medium in hydraulic systems. In the twentieth century many sophisticated mechanical engineering systems are hydraulically operated.

The French expression 'une roue hydraulique', meaning a water wheel, can lead to confusion in translation. Other Latin languages use similar expressions.

See also JIGGER.

BIBLIOGRAPHY
General
Jarvis, 1985; McNeil, 1968, 1972; Smiles, 1878.

BARRIE TRINDER

hydrochloric acid (HCl) 'Spirit of salt'. An acid produced during the LEBLANC PROCESS for making ALKALI, and recovered by means of a GOSSAGE TOWER. Its chief uses are in the manufacture of CHLORINE and BLEACHING POWDER, in TINPLATING, in GALVANIZING, and in the manufacture of dyestuffs.

hydro-electric power station The generation of electricity by water was first tried at Sir WILLIAM ARMSTRONG's home at Cragside, 42 km (26 mi.) NW of Newcastle-upon-Tyne, in 1880; then at Godalming, England, for a street-lighting system, in 1881; and was demonstrated at the Munich Exhibition of 1882. It depends on suitable topography, and on the availability of effective TURBINES. Most hydro-electric power stations depend on water impounded by a DAM and fed to the turbines by PENSTOCKS, but some of modest dimensions, and some large ones at such sites as NIAGARA (where power has been generated since 1886 and Fourneyron and Jonval turbines installed since 1895), have a sufficiently steady flow to obviate the need for large reservoirs. Some are situated in the bases of dams, dispensing with the need for penstocks. The height (or head) of water above the power station generally determines the type of turbine used. Impulse turbines such as that devised by PELTON in 1889 work best with heads above 200 m (660 ft.), while the reaction turbine developed in 1855 by J. B. Francis of Lowell, Mass., USA, is applied to heads of 5–100 m (15–330 ft.). For the Austrian engineer Viktor Kaplan in 1908 this seemed inadequate, and his vertical, propellor-shaped turbine of 1913 is capable of working with heads of 50 m (165 ft.) or

less. By 1950 these three types produced most of the power generated at hydro-electric stations. Hydro-electricity has been important in the development of regions where fossil fuels are non-existent or not easily exploitable, such as Ontario, Quebec, Sweden and Switzerland, and in such grand projects as the TENNESSEE Valley Scheme, from 1933, where irrigation, flood control and drinking-water supply were also important objectives. The low cost of hydro-electricity also made possible rapid developments in processes with large energy requirements, notably in the manufacture of certain chemicals and in refining certain metals, notably ALUMINIUM.

See also figures 22, 113, 142.

BIBLIOGRAPHY
General
Dunsheath, 1962; Koester, 1915; Rushmore and Lof, 1923.
Specific
Tucker, D. G. Hydro-electricity for public supply in Britain, 1881–1894. In *IAR*, I, 1977.

CHRISTOPHER GREEN

hydrogen (H) An element and the lightest known gas, with many industrial uses including the synthesis of AMMONIA, the reduction of metallic oxides, the annealing of alloys, and the hardening of fats; it was formerly used in AIRSHIPS. There are many methods of manufacture, including ELECTROLYSIS of CAUSTIC SODA or water, and preparation from water gas (*see* AMMONIA), or from METHANE obtained in the cracking of petroleum.

BIBLIOGRAPHY
General
Morgan and Pratt, 1938; Partington, 1950.

Hyvinkää, Uudenmaan lääni, Finland The Finnish Railway Museum is at Hyvinkää, a town 54 km (34 mi.) N. of Helsinki. It was established in the capital in 1898 and was located at the main station until 1974 when an old station and depot at Hyvinkää were restored to house it. The exhibition hall for rolling stock was opened in 1987. The collections include the oldest steam locomotive remaining in Finland, a Beyer Peacock 0–4–2 saddle tank of 1868; a Neilson 0–6–0 built in Glasgow in 1869; a wood-burning 4–4–0 built in Helsinki in 1875; a two-cylinder compound 2–6–0 with an axle load of only 8.3 tonnes, built at Tampere in 1903; and an American 2–10–0, supplied in 1947. Rolling stock includes a Fiat tramcar of 1914, an imperial coach built for the tsar in 1870, one constructed for the tsarina in 1875, and an imperial saloon of 1876. In addition to a large variety of rolling stock, the museum displays models of stations and trains, uniforms, and artefacts relating to the everyday lives of railway workers. An extensive library and a photographic archive are available for scholars. The museum has its own series of publications.

LOCATION
[M] Rautatiemuseo (Railway Museum), Hyvinkäänkatu 9, SF-05800 Hyvinkää.

LAURI PUTKONEN

I

icehouse A means of retaining ice during the warmer part of the year, for use in the preservation of meat, fish and dairy products, and as an ingredient for desserts. Some remain in use in Portugal, using ice collected from mountain tops. The principle was introduced into England *c*.1650. Icehouses are brick-lined, circular chambers with domes, either dug into a level surface and covered with soil or built into a slope. Plans and sections vary widely. All have drains to take away melt water. Ice, harvested in winter or, from the mid-nineteenth century, imported from Norway or North America, was packed into the chamber with straw. Icehouses themselves were rarely used for the storage of food as frequent access accelerated melting.

BIBLIOGRAPHY
General
Cummings, 1949.

Iceland Iceland has a land area of just over 100 000 km² (40 000 sq. mi.) with a population of less than 250 000 and lies immediately south of the Arctic Circle. Iceland was first permanently settled by Vikings from Norway in AD 874. In 1387 it came under Danish rule, and from 1602 a Danish monopoly company, the Horkraemmer, controlled its trade. The Horkraemmer's authority was overthrown in 1787 by Skuli Magnusson

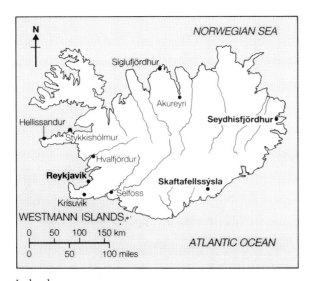

Iceland

(1711–94), who established woollen and fulling mills, a ropery and a tannery at Reykjavik, although these lasted for scarcely more than twenty years. During the nineteenth century ties with Denmark were loosened. Trading restrictions were removed in 1854, and in 1904 home rule was agreed, although Denmark retained responsibility for Iceland's defence and foreign policy until 1940.

Before 1900 Iceland's economy was in most respects underdeveloped but it has since been transformed by hydro-electric power and geothermal energy. Manufacturing industry is now varied, and Icelandic society is largely urban. Fishing has always been important. The first fish-freezing factory was set up in the Westmann Islands in 1907, and the first fishmeal-processing mill at Siglufjördur in 1910. Several herring-processing plants were established in the 1920s and 30s but all have now been closed, and some of the buildings adapted to new uses. Most fish is now processed in modern plants, but some fish-drying on traditional frames can still be observed. Norwegian companies established whaling stations in West Iceland in the 1880s and 90s of which only foundations now remain. The collection of eider down is a traditional industry, and a down-cleaning factory was built at Stykkishólmur in the early twentieth century. Several wool-processing factories were established in the late nineteenth century. Many co-operative dairies were set up in the early years of the twentieth century. Iron was made in bloomeries in the north and east of the island, and the National Museum contains relics of the manufacture of iron from bog ore. Sulphur was mined until the twentieth century at Krysuvik. China clay for the Copenhagen porcelain factory was worked in the eighteenth century. Iceland spar for optical instruments was mined at Helgustadir from 1850.

Traditional buildings in Iceland have bases of stone or lava blocks, with turf walls and roofs set in timber framing. Corrugated iron has been extensively used since the 1870s, and most twentieth-century structures are of concrete. The first major bridge of the modern road system was a 75 m (250 ft.) span steel structure built by a British company near Selfoss 48 km (30 mi.) SE of Reykjavik, in 1890. Very few remains of windmills and water mills have been found. No pottery has been made in Iceland and the few bricks used have been imported. The country has never had a passenger railway.

The principal museums are in Reykjavik and Seydhisfjördhur. There is a municipal museum at Akureyri and a seafaring museum at Hellissandur. The Iceland Geodetic Survey produces nine 1:250 000 maps which cover the whole country, and 1:25 000 sheets for certain areas.

344

Figure 60 The headstocks of St Hilda's Colliery, Wallsend, near Newcastle-upon-Tyne, as depicted by Thomas Hair, one of the principal British artists who portrayed industrial scenes (from T. H. Hair, *A Series of Views of the Collieries of Northumberland and Durham*, London: J. Madden, 1844); in the centre and to the right are characteristic chaldron wagons.
Elton Collection: Ironbridge Gorge Museum

See also REYKJAVIK; SEYDHISFJÖRDHUR; SKAFTAFELLS-SÝSLA.

BIBLIOGRAPHY
General
Annandale, 1905; Naval Intelligence Division, 1942; Williams, 1985.
Specific
Facts about Iceland, Reykjavik, 1970.
Magnusson, T. Conservation of industrial monuments of Iceland. In Nisser and Bedoire, 1978.
Tucker, D. G. The history of industries and crafts in Iceland. In *JIA*, IX, 1972.
Tucker, D. G. The stockfish industry in Iceland: living industrial archaeology. In *JIA*, IX, 1972.
Tucker, D. G. Windmills and watermills in Iceland. In *JIA*, IX, 1972.

LOCATION
[M] Icelandic Geodetic Survey, Laugavegur 178, Reykjavik.

BARRIE TRINDER

iconography The depiction of mines and manufactures falls into two major traditions, both of which reflect popular attitudes to industry as well as contemporary artistic tastes and fashions.

In the eighteenth century some major artists concerned themselves with industrial subjects. The Swede Pehr Hilleström (1732–1816) completed 124 paintings of copper mines, blast furnaces and glassworks. The Liègeois Léonard Defrance (1735–1805) depicted mines, rolling mills and the process of tobacco pressing. Joseph Wright (1734–97) of Derby was 'the first professional painter to express the spirit of the Industrial Revolution', painting the mills at CROMFORD in much the same way as he depicted the eruption of Vesuvius. A slightly later generation of painters working in England, Philip James de Loutherbourg (1740–1812), John Sell Cotman (1782–1842) and Paul Sandby Munn (1773–1845), saw industrial scenes as an element of the sublime, exciting the same horror as rugged mountains or tumultuous seas. The paintings of J. M. W. Turner (1775–1851) are a valuable documentary source for the study of river navigations and unimproved harbours, but his views of the river at Newcastle-upon-Tyne and his celebrated *Rain, Steam and Speed* reflect a subtle and sensitive response to the complexities and ambiguities of industrial landscapes. The work of such painters was popularized through many prints, by such publishers as John Boydell (1719–1802) and his nephew Josiah Boydell, as well as by images on ceramics, glass and textiles.

A documentary tradition depicting industrial processes by carefully delineated drawings extends from GEORGIUS AGRICOLA through the works of DENIS DIDEROT and ABRAHAM REES to those of J. C. BOURNE. An important early example in England was the drawing by Henry Beighton (d.1743) of a Newcomen engine, published in 1717, in which sections of the walls are broken to reveal details. JOHN SMEATON set a fashion for a freer style in published engineering drawings, which were intended to be aesthetically pleasing as well as accurate and instructive. Between 1790 and 1850 many drawings were produced to appear as plates in printed books. George Walker's (1781–1856) *Costume of Yorkshire*, the engravings of scenes in the Wye Valley and of windmills and trekvaarten boats in the Netherlands in the works of Samuel Ireland (d.1800), the plates in W. H. Pyne's *Microcosm*, the engravings in THOMAS TELFORD's *Autobiography*, and the views by Thomas Bury (1811–77) of the Liverpool & Manchester Railway are all notable examples.

By 1840 concern at the social consequences of the factory system and of the problems of urbanization was changing attitudes to industry. J. C. Bourne, the many artists who were inspired by the Crystal Palace in London, and George Hawkins (1810–52) who depicted the construction of the Menai and Conway bridges in Wales, continued to view technological developments with optimism. The more general feeling was one of melancholy, which is to be found even in the superb drawings of pit headstocks and staithes by Thomas Hair (d.1875), while the depiction of London from *c*.1869 by Gustave Doré (1832–83) verges on the hysterical. Artists tended to turn away from industry to other subjects, and PHOTOGRAPHY and subsequently FILM became the principal means of depicting mining and manufacturing.

In the twentieth century artists' responses to industry have varied from country to country. In the USSR the depiction of mining and manufacturing scenes was the established art of the Stalinist era. In England artists like John Nash (1893–1977) and John Piper (1903–) have been influential in creating a new interest in the industrial past, while L. S. Lowry (1887–1976) displayed a unique sensitivity to the ironies of the urban landscapes of the North-West.

See also EPHEMERA; FILM; MODEL; PHOTOGRAPHY; POSTCARD; TRADE TOKEN.

For examples of the various types of iconography used to depict industrial subjects see figures 35, 41, 45, 52, 60, 61, 65, 76, 85, 86, 98, 118, 131, 150, 172, 174.

BIBLIOGRAPHY
General
Bayley, 1978; Bellini *et al.*, 1986; Booker, 1963; Bury, 1831; Clark, 1850; Darby, 1974; Davies and Collier, 1986; Elton, 1968; Evrard, 1955; Falk, 1838; Gerdts, 1979; Gobert, 1906; Gray and Kanefsky, 1982; Hair, 1844; Ireland, 1795, 1797; Ivins, 1943; Jerrold and Doré, 1872; Klingender, 1968; Mathis *et al.*, 1988; Newcomen Society, 1950; Nicholson, 1968; Pyne, 1808; Rees, 1980; Shanes, 1981; Smith, 1979; Walker, 1885.
Specific
da Costa Nunes, J. M. The industrial landscape in America 1800–1840; ideology into art. In *IA*, XII, 1986.
Wright, H. E. The image makers: the role of the graphic arts in industrialization. In *IA*, XII, 1986.

BARRIE TRINDER

Idaho, United States of America   Gold was discovered in Idaho in 1860, resulting in the kind of boomtown settlement and subsequent industrial diversification seen earlier in California and Colorado. The mining of precious metals, lumbering, and the growing of potatoes and sugar beet had become staples of Idaho industry by 1900. Silver, mercury, cobalt, lead and zinc continue to issue from long-established deep-shaft mines in the Idaho panhandle.

In the arid south, dam construction transformed desert into fertile plain, beginning in 1904 with the rockfill Milner Dam across the Snake River at Murgaugh, still furnishing irrigating water to 260 km (160 mi.) of feeder canals, and thence to 146000 ha (360000 ac.) of farmland. Near Boise, the state capital, the 106 m (349 ft.) high Arrowrock Dam of 1916 was for a decade the world's tallest dam. The gravity-arch concrete structure is lodged in the steep Sawtooth Mountains, and remains in full service as flood control for melting snows and irrigation support for the plains below.

LOCATION
[M] Coeur D'Alene District Mining Museum, 509 Bank Street, Wallace, ID 83873.

DAVID H. SHAYT

Idar-Oberstein and **Asbacherhütte,** Rhineland-Palatinate, Germany   Idar-Oberstein, 48 km (32 mi.) E. of Trier, is the centre of the German jewellery trade. Around 1900 seventy gem-cutting works were still being operated by water power from the River Nahe and the River Idar, processing the agates found in the area. Today gems are imported and traded on the local jewellery exchange, which also houses museum of jewels. Two of the historic water-powered cutting works have been preserved: the restored Weiher works in Idar-Oberstein itself, and the works of the firm of E. Biehl in the Harfenmühle in Asbacherhütte on the Hunsrück range. Here the two cutting seats, designed to be operated in either a sitting or a lying position, are accommodated in the basement of the modest mill building. Power is provided by a small overshot water wheel. The works have been run by the family for four generations, changing very little, and are still in commercial use. They give an authentic idea of the state of gemstone working, the cutting technology and the power-systems used in the nineteenth century.

BIBLIOGRAPHY
General
Custodis, 1990.

LOCATIONS
[M] Mineral Museum, Hauptstrasse 436, 6580 Idar-Oberstein.
[M] Museum of Jewels, Gewerbehalle, Dr Liesegangstrasse, 6580 Idar-Oberstein.
[M] Regional Museum, Hauptstrasse 440, 6580 Idar-Oberstein.

ROLF HÖHMANN

Idrija (Idria), Slovenia, Yugoslavia   A historic centre of mercury and zinc mining, 35 km (22 mi.) SW of Ljubljana. Cinnabar (*see* MERCURY) deposits discovered in 1497 were worked by the Habsburg government from 1500. Smelters were operated on the right bank of the River Idriza north-east of the town. Between 1725 and 1788 some 5500 workers were employed. Around 1900, fifteen hundred miners lived in a community regulated by the mine management, who provided employment in lacemaking for the miners' wives and daughters. Collections relating to mercury extraction can be seen in the museum.

BIBLIOGRAPHY
General
Baedeker, 1903.

LOCATION
[M] Municipal Museum, ul. Prelovcena 9, 65280-Idrija.

Igualada, Barcelona, Catalonia, Spain   A leather-working and textile town, 51 km (32 mi.) NW of Barcelona, where the Igualadina Cotonera (the Igualadina cotton factory), built in 1840 in the English style and considered one of the oldest steam-powered factories in Catalonia, still survives. The Museu Comarcal occupies a late-nineteenth-century textile factory. A section is being installed dealing with the treatment of leather hides. Beside the museum stands the Teneria (tannery) de cal Granotes, an eighteenth-century building which opened as a museum in 1989. Two ART NOUVEAU tanneries still operate in the town.

LOCATION
[M] Museu Comarcal (Town Museum and Leather Museum), Carretera de Manresa, Igualada.

Île des Moulins, Quebec, Canada   One of the principal monuments of the pre-industrial period in Quebec, the Île des Moulins (the Island of Mills) is situated near to the town of Terrebonne, 30 km (18 mi.) SE of Montreal. On the island are sawmills and corn mills which were working between 1723 and 1922. Since 1974 the complex has been the property of the Quebec government, which has carried out programmes of research, conservation and interpretation in collaboration with local groups.

Some structures, among them two locks and a water-powered sawmill, were constructed by the French regime and powered by water from the Thousand Islands River; no trace of them now remains.

At the end of the eighteenth century the MacTavishes, Scots merchants engaged in the fur trade and associated with the North West Company, transformed the Île des Moulins into what amounted to an industrial and commercial complex. The buildings they constructed between 1784 and 1832 included sawmills, flourmills, mills for carding wool and fulling woollen cloth, a bakery, and sheds for storing skins. Specialist workers like joiners and tanners, as well as travellers and merchants, were drawn to the island.

Joseph Masson (1791–1847), a politician celebrated in the timber trade, together with his descendants, controlled the Île des Moulins between 1833 and 1883. Replanned according to the plans of the architect John Atkinson, the community then comprised industrial buildings, including flourmills, sawmills, carding and fulling mills, two forges, a kiln for drying grain, subsidiary buildings, houses and an administrative centre, and an infrastructure of services, a wooden bridge, two locks and

a fire pump. Some structures disappeared while some new ones were established, among them macadamized roads.

The coming of the industrial era brought to an end the operation of the mills, although the sawmill was still working in 1900. The buildings fell into decay and lost their historical significance until they were taken over by the Quebec government, which is undertaking the restoration of two flourmills, dating from 1846 and 1850, the administrative centre, some dams and the bridge.

BIBLIOGRAPHY
General
Daoust and Viau, 1979

LOUISE TROTTIER

Ílhavo, Beira Litoral, Portugal   A town 65 km (40 mi.) S. of Oporto, a centre of salt extraction but chiefly famous for the porcelain works, the Fábrica de Porcelanas da Vista Alegre, established in 1824. Documents relating to the works and a display of porcelain wares can be seen in the factory museum. The Ílhavo Museum has collections of Vista Alegre stained glass and porcelain, as well as displays relating to fishing and shipping.

LOCATIONS
[M] Museu Marítimo e Regional (Regional and Maritime Museum), Ílhavo.
[M] Vista Alegre Historical Museum, Ílhavo.

Illinois, United States of America   Direct access to both the Mississippi River and the Great Lakes in the heart of America's 'breadbasket' has made Illinois a leader in the production and distribution of agricultural and dairy products, transport vehicles, and farm machinery. Illinois industries have run the gamut from primary iron and steel works to textile manufacture, furniture-making and the production of railway wagons, machine tools and tractors. By 1924 Illinois was second only to Texas in the extent of its railway network, which totalled 19 371 km (12 037 mi.). A station of 1854 is preserved at Batavia.

Bituminous coal has been the state's chief mined product since the mid-nineteenth century, but petroleum, DIMENSION STONE, lead and zinc have also been extensively extracted.

Chicago remains one of the nation's premier industrial fountainheads, and home to a strong assortment of historic engineering sites, many publicly accessible. Chicago was completely rebuilt after a destructive fire in 1871, and its constricted site and its prosperous trade with the west gave birth to the SKYSCRAPER. The city retains many of the key buildings by Louis Sullivan (1856–1924) and others which exemplify the 'Chicago style'. Mail-order trading (*see* RETAILING) in the USA came to be centred in Chicago, which also developed pioneering DEPARTMENT STORES, and MEAT packing plants. The downtown's elevated railway network of 1897, termed the 'Loop', receives scores of thousands of commuters each morning, trains circling a thirty-five-block area to unload at the network's several Italianate revival stations, rendered in riveted steel. Within the Loop stands one of the nation's most picturesque watertowers. The Cheesbrough Tower and pumping station of 1869 is a crenellated pile of Romanesque granite, now dwarfed by the surrounding skyscrapers, but once the centrepiece of the city's water supply, drawn from Lake Michigan through a 3 km (2 mi.) subaqueous tunnel.

The narrow Chicago River has drained surrounding lands into Lake Michigan since 1900, passing through the city centre, and bridged by a bridge fancier's dream of movable bridge types. Among the swing, lift and draw spans, the native-born Scherzer rolling lift bridge of 1906 at Cermak Road, a bascule double-leaf span, is most distinctive. Another heavyweight bascule stands immobilized over the Chicago River at Cortland Street.

Some 18 m (60 ft.) beneath Chicago's downtown lies a maze of vaulted brick tunnels that rank among the country's more unusual engineering works. The Chicago transport tunnels were dug for narrow-gauge rail freight services as a response to the formidable traffic problems in the streets above. The network served merchant houses which funded its construction. Today access remains private, and the rolling stock has given way to storage and utility lines, but tours are available by request.

In South Chicago the structural remains of the quintessential American company town of Pullman may be seen, including housing and shops occupied by generations of railway passenger-car builders. The neighbourhood's Historic Pullman Foundation commemorates what became the nation's best-known MODEL COMMUNITY, built for workers of the PULLMAN Palace Car Company in 1881.

Chicago's Museum of Science and Industry of 1926 is housed in one of the few remaining exhibition buildings of the great World's Columbian Exposition of 1893. Its traditional reliance on corporate funding and exhibition gives it a distinctive position among the US's major industrial museums.

Over the last two centuries, rich veins of high-quality limestone in south-central Illinois have yielded excellent dimension stone for architectural and engineering works. One early bridge of the local stone is Waterloo's Fountain Creek Bridge of 1849, a 12.8 m (42 ft.) span, now retired, but typical of many such stone-arch bridges throughout Monroe County.

Bisecting Illinois south of Chicago is the Illinois & Michigan Canal, also called the Sanitary & Ship Canal in its passage through Chicago. The canal links natural and artificial waterways to provide crucial navigable communication between Lake Michigan and the Mississippi River. It passes through a landscape of industrial settlements and activities, many dating from the canal's early years. Zincville, a largely abandoned town along the canal, reveals in its name the origins of its establishment.

BIBLIOGRAPHY
General
Bensman and Lynch, 1988; Zukowsky, 1987.

LOCATIONS
[M,S] Batavia Depot Museum, 155 Houston, Batavia, IL 60510.
[M] Chicago Maritime Museum, 60 W. Walton Place, Chicago, IL 60610.
[M] Great Lakes Naval and Maritime Museum, 600 E. Grand Avenue, Chicago, IL 60611.
[M] Hartung's Automotive Museum, 3623 W. Lake Street, Glenview, IL 60025.
[S] Historic Pullman Foundation, 11111 S. Forrestville Avenue, Chicago, IL 60628.
[M] Illinois Railway Museum, Olson Road, Union, IL 60180.
[M] Monticello Railway Museum, Interstate 72 at Exit 63, Monticello, IL 61856.
[M] Museum of Science and Industry, 57th Street & Lake Shore Drive, Chicago, IL 60637.
[M] Rock Island Arsenal Museum, Rock Island, IL 61299.
[M] Telephony Museum, 225 W. Randolph Street, Lobby 1C, Chicago, IL 60606.
[M] The Time Museum, 7801 E. State Street, Rockford, IL 61125.
[M] Volo Auto Museum and Village, 27640 W. Highway 120, Volo, IL 60073.
[M] West Chicago Historical Museum (RR), 132 Main Street, W. Chicago, IL 60185.

DAVID H. SHAYT

Imatra, Kymen lääni, Finland   A town in eastern Finland, 12 km ($7\frac{1}{2}$ mi.) from the border of the USSR, on the Vuoksa River, which forms part of the Vuoksa inland navigation system. The river falls over 18 m (60 ft.) at Imatra, which in the nineteenth century was an internationally recognized beauty spot. The Finnish government harnessed the rapids for hydro-electric power between 1921 and 1929. The power station was extended in the 1930s and in 1952, when the earlier Francis turbines were replaced with seven Kaplan turbines. Today the output of the power station is 156 000 kW, making it the country's largest source of hydro-electric power. The buildings and the stone-faced dam were designed by Oiva & K. S. Kallio. Close to the power station are some fine, integrally planned residential areas for workers, dating from the 1920s and 1950s.

inclined plane   A slope, usually with rails, across which a vehicle can be moved between two relatively flat stretches of railway, or by which a boat can be transferred from one level of waterway to another. Slipways of wooden construction were used to transport boats between different levels of water in the Netherlands in the Middle Ages, and the principle was applied on continental railways by the 1720s. Self-acting railway inclined planes were in use in Shropshire, England (*see* IRONBRIDGE), by 1746, although the balanced, self-acting plane was patented in Britain by Michael Meinzies in 1750. The first powered inclined plane on the railways of north-east England was built at Black Fell, County Durham, in 1805. Inclined planes were used on many HYBRID RAILWAYS, and on some early standard-gauge lines, particularly for giving access to city centre termini like Euston in London.

Primitive forms of inclined plane using rollers were employed on waterways in ancient China, and in the Netherlands in the seventeenth century. The principle of carrying a boat on a cradle was applied in Italy before the end of the sixteenth century. Davies Ducart built three planes on the COALISLAND Canal in Ireland, but they were unsuccessful and the waterway was converted to a railway from 1789. Six successful inclined planes were built on the tub boat canals in Shropshire (see IRONBRIDGE) in 1788–96, two operating for more than a century; and there were several successful installations on the small canals of the West of England, some lifting vessels dry in cradles, some with wheeled boats and others with CAISSONS. The caisson incline at Blackhill on the Monkland Canal in Scotland worked from 1850 until 1887, and the Foxton Lift in Leicestershire on the Grand Junction Canal, which also employed caissons, was opened in 1900 but proved expensive to work and closed a decade later. Inclined planes that remain in use were built on the Oberland Canal in East Prussia between 1844 and 1860; and one on the Canal de l'Ourcq in France worked from the 1880s until 1922. The Morris Canal in NEW JERSEY, opened in 1831, had twenty-three planes, some of which remained in use in modified form until 1924. The most notable incline in the USA was at Georgetown on the Chesapeake & Ohio Canal: designed by W. R. Hutton in 1874 to take 250-ton boats, it worked only for three years. Since World War II inclined planes capable of lifting very large vessels have been constructed at SAINT LOUIS-ARZVILLER in France, RONQUIÈRES in Belgium, and Krasnoyarsk in the USSR.

BIBLIOGRAPHY
General
Hadfield, 1986; Lewis, 1970; McCutcheon, 1965, 1980; Tew, 1984; Trinder, 1981; Zonca, 1607.
Specific
Gardner, P. and Foden, F. *Foxton: locks and barge lift.* Leicester: Leicestershire County Council, 1979.
Hadfield, C. The evolution of the canal inclined plane. In *JRCHS*, xxv (3), 1979.
Skramstad, H. The Georgetown canal incline. In *Technology & Culture*, x (4), 1969.
Wakelin, P. The inclined planes of the Kidwelly & Llanelly Canal. In *Bulletin of the South-West Wales Industrial Archaeology Society*, 37, 1984.

BARRIE TRINDER

Indiana, United States of America   The 65 km (40 mi.) Lake Michigan waterfront that forms Indiana's northwestern border has been one of the world's great industrial corridors, combining access to global shipping with rich sources of agricultural and extractive industry and many classes of heavy manufacturing in the port city of Gary. Indiana's oolitic limestone may be found in construction throughout the world, as a building stone of exceptional purity, quarried around Burlington.

Among Indiana's half-dozen major centres of industry, South Bend stands out as a diversified community, heavily industrialized by 1900, with clock and watch manufacturers, machine-tool builders, and producers of many classes of light machinery. The city's Studebaker National Museum contains a fine sampling of regional manufactures, including automobiles, their production wisely switched over from wooden, horse-drawn waggons early in the century.

In the industrial archaeology of confinement, the patent rotary jail of 1882 in Crawfordsville occupies a special position. This two-storey cylindrical iron cage is divided into wedge-like cells, the whole geared to a pinion cranked by a jailer to admit and release prisoners through ports. As with the only other rotary jail – in Council Bluffs, Iowa – the structure is fully retired, and protected as a local historic site. It was recorded by HAER (see UNITED STATES OF AMERICA) in 1974.

The Indianapolis Market House of 1886 is a prominent example of the city's prosperous past, elegant cast-iron columns and roof trusses still sheltering a thriving market commerce.

In Connersville a rich assortment of early metal fabrication shops in various stages of decay and adaptation reflects the region's transformation early in the century from carriage- and horse-related manufacturing to the production of automobile components. The Indiana Cotton Mills complex of 1850 in Cannelton once produced one of the largest lines of cotton sheeting in the Midwest. The towering Romanesque mill looks today like a transplant from Lancashire, England.

Indiana is home to one of the great concentrations of covered timber bridges. Superb restored examples stand in Milroy, Moscow, Rockville and Rushville. A rare long-span cast- and wrought-iron truss bridge, 90 m (300 ft.) long, crosses Laughery Creek in Aurora, but is now closed to traffic.

LOCATIONS
[M] Howard Steamboat Museum, 1101 E. Market Street, Jeffersonville, IN 47130.
[M] Indiana Transportation Museum, 325 Cicero Road, State Road 19, Noblesville, IN 46060.
[M] Old Jail Museum, 225 N. Washington, Crawfordsville, IN 47933.
[M] Old Lighthouse Museum, Heisman Harbour Road, Michigan City, IN 46360.
[M] Studebaker National Museum, 120 S. St Joseph Street, South Bend, IN 46601.
[S] Whitewater Canal Historic Site, Metamora, IN 47030.

DAVID H. SHAYT

indigo   A blue dyestuff obtained from the plant *Indigofera tinctoria*, by fermentation and distilling of the leaves. The resulting concentrate is dried and formed into cakes which must be ground for use as a dye. Grown only in tropical climates, indigo produced a better blue colour than woad, and superseded that native European dyestuff by the seventeenth century. A chemical form of artificial indigo was developed in the 1880s, but the natural form is still preferred for some applications. In importing indigo to Europe from India, a distinction was always made between the 'fine' or 'rich' grade from Lahore, and the 'flat' indigo from Gujerat.

BIBLIOGRAPHY
General
Hummel, 1888; Hurry, 1930; Lauterbach, 1905; Partridge, 1823; Perkins and Everest, 1918.

industrial archaeology   A term that means different things in different contexts. If the agenda of TICCIH conferences are any guide, it encompasses the ADAPTIVE REUSE of industrial buildings, the presentation of manufactured artefacts in museums, the operation of PRESERVED RAILWAYS, administrative procedures for the CONSERVATION of ancient buildings, and aspects of the study of economic history and the history of technology.

Industrial archaeology is also a systematized means of utilizing structures and artefacts in enlarging our understanding of the industrial past, a branch of a discipline which has been defined as 'being concerned with the recovery, systematic description and study of material culture in the past' (Clarke, 1978). The activities comprehended within industrial archaeology – EXCAVATION, the RECORDING of field evidence, the CONSERVATION, classification and analysis of artefacts – as within any other branch of archaeology, may be carried out well or badly, by amateurs or professionals. Amateur interest in industrial archaeology of itself neither enhances nor diminishes its status as a discipline.

Similarly the theoretical role of archaeological activities in relation to the study of the past through documents is no different from that which pertains in the study of Roman civilization, the Middle Ages in Europe, the colonization of America, or any other historical period from which there is written evidence.

It is conceptually impossible to divorce knowledge of the industrial past obtained from documents from that obtained from archaeological investigations. The choice of a site or a region for study in the field will almost certainly be made in the light of documentary evidence, or under the influence of what documentary evidence has revealed about similar sites or regions. Yet industrial archaeology is not merely the handmaid of some supposedly superior discipline called 'history'. The understanding of past mining and manufacturing activities can be enlarged by archaeological studies if they are undertaken with as few preconceptions as is theoretically possible. To plot the incidence of the remains of water-power systems in a valley, without regard, in the first instance, to the uses to which they have been put, in the same way as a prehistorian plots the incidence of round barrows, is likely to reveal more than a study undertaken from the outset as an investigation of textile mills. The Harris matrix, devised as a means of investigating prehistoric archaeology, has been effectively used to phase limestone quarries. The systematic analysis of rails and sleepers is certainly the most effective way of understanding the technology of early railways.

Yet in further analysis – and there is no last analysis, nor any final solution of any problem relating to humanity's past – such 'pure' archaeological studies must form parts of syntheses with other types of evidence. Industrial archaeology is a means of allowing the study of buildings, artefacts and stratigraphy to stimulate new questions and the formulation of new hypotheses. It is not a facile means of obtaining new and fashionable evidence in support of existing theories, nor is it an esoteric study, isolated from the concerns of researchers whose prime sources are accounts, maps, patents or photographs.

The study of the physical evidence of the industrial past has its origins in the nineteenth century, and it was the Portuguese FRANCISCO DE SOUSA VITERBO who first used the term 'industrial archaeology' in 1896, but its modern development as a systematized study stems from changes in popular attitudes to industrial history in Britain in the 1950s. MICHAEL RIX published an article on 'industrial archaeology' in 1955, which principally stressed the aesthetic values of industrial structures. In 1963 KENNETH HUDSON published the first book on industrial archaeology, and edited the first journal on the subject. The initial growth of interest in industrial archaeology in many countries stems from lectures by Hudson, and from the influence of books by such British authors as Angus Buchanan, Neil Cossons and ARTHUR RAISTRICK.

The scope of 'industrial' archaeology has been much debated, not always with clarity. It has been questioned whether it should be defined by period, or by the kinds of activity with which it is concerned. The answers to this question must be pragmatic: a particular *ad hoc* solution has to be formulated when, for example, the scope of a journal, the range of an academic course, or the interests of a learned society are being defined. Most such pragmatic decisions have accepted that the study of industrial archaeology is focused in some way on the British Industrial Revolution of the eighteenth century, which may be interpreted as the 'core' of the study or as its starting point. It is legitimate to make such *ad hoc* decisions, but not to deny the enlightening value of studies that bestride the centuries, examining the ways in which humans have kindled fire, woven cloth or fired ceramics from prehistoric times to the present. It may be preferable to regard such studies as part of something called the 'history of technology'.

Mines, manufactures and great cities have existed since antiquity, yet it is possible to interpret the changes in the economy and society in Britain in the eighteenth century, the involvement of an increasing proportion of the population in manufacturing, the development of units of production employing many hundreds of people in specialized forms of labour, and the creation of more powerful prime movers and of speedier and more capacious forms of transport, as a particular category of historical event, one which has subsequently occurred elsewhere, in part as a result of conscious imitation, which is akin to and as difficult to define as a political revolution, a war or a religious revival. Industrialization is not necessarily based on steam power, cotton spinning and coal, but is a change of social and economic organization based on the technology and resources of its time. At a macro-level it is still possible to view industrialization as a take-off into self-sustained growth – the economies and societies of the industrialized countries have, whatever the effects of inertia or the swing from manufacturing to services, changed in ways that distinguish them totally from peasant societies of earlier periods, or of present-day 'under-developed' countries. Yet at a micro-level, industrial archaeology demonstrates more eloquently than any other discipline the paradoxes and follies of human ambition. From PARYS MOUNTAIN, SOVEREIGN HILL or

Lowell (*see* MASSACHUSETTS), particular forms of industry appear as mere passing phases of human activity.

Only from a narrow nationalist viewpoint can the technology of the Industrial Revolution be interpreted as wholly innovatory or wholly British. Steam power was effectively demonstrated by a French scientist who had studied in Germany. Railway technology has its origins in metalliferous mines now in Czechoslovakia and Romania. The textile factory was an Italian innovation rather than an invention of RICHARD ARKWRIGHT. It is impossible therefore to establish a clear distinction in archaeological or technological terms between the Industrial Revolution and earlier 'non-industrial' modes of manufacturing. What distinguishes the industrial period is its forms of social and economic organization. If industrial archaeology has a *terminus a quo* it must in some senses be the British Industrial Revolution of the eighteenth century; yet if that revolution is to be understood, it must extend back in time to comprehend the origins of many of the processes involved in that revolution.

Industrial archaeology must logically have a *terminus ad quem*. It could be argued that the late nineteenth century saw the end of a distinct phase of industrialization, with the advent of mild steel, electric power and the mechanization and organization on a factory basis of the manufacture of consumer goods. Yet to draw a clear dividing line is impossible. Manufacturing came to rely increasingly on scientific research and on the rigorous application of logic and discipline in the development of products, epitomized in the career of THOMAS EDISON. Paradoxically the success of new products depended heavily on exuberant marketing genius, on the flamboyance of extrovert entrepreneurs like HENRY FORD, H. J. Heinz (1844–1919) and George Eastman (1854–1937), who often relied on the hunch rather than the research paper. The origins of manufacturing success were increasingly in the USA rather than in Europe. Since 1960 it might be argued that the springs of enterprise have been most abundant around the Pacific Rim. Yet many new manufactures rely heavily on old ones, and on the consumer markets created in earlier generations. The only theoretically satisfactory *terminus ad quem* for industrial archaeology must be the time when today's technology is discarded. Recording methods appropriate to much mid-twentieth-century industry will be different from those applicable to that of the eighteenth century, but the essential logic of the discipline, that the study of the site or the artefact is essential in the formulation of hypotheses that will increase understanding of the industrial past, will remain unchanged.

The horizontal scope of industrial archaeology, the range of human activities in the industrial periods that it covers, varies from country to country. The implications of the proposition that it should be the total study of the landscape and artefacts of the last two and a half centuries have nowhere been carried through. In practice industrial archaeologists have left some aspects of the history of industrial societies to other specialists: fortifications and fighting vehicles to military historians, the design of major buildings to historians of architecture, and of farm buildings to agricultural historians. These are decisions based on convenience and practice rather than logic. Housing presents a series of paradoxes. The study of well-defined INDUSTRIAL COMMUNITIES – Saltaire, Pullman, Margaretenhohe – would be accepted as industrial archaeology almost anywhere, but not, perhaps, the study of such housing types as the BUNGALOW. Prisons and churches are, in practice, rarely studied by industrial archaeologists, unless the former have TREADMILLS or the latter iron frames. Industrial archaeology does not have rigid frontiers. It is in practice not the study of the whole of the physical evidence of society in recent centuries, but one which centres on manufactures and mining and their associated transport systems, civil engineering works and services, and overlaps into many areas of concern that are shared with other disciplines.

For particular aspects of industrial archaeology, *see* CONSERVATION, EXCAVATION, LANDSCAPE, RECORDING.

For relationships with other branches of archaeology, *see* ARCHAEOMETALLURGY; COLONIAL ARCHAEOLOGY; HISTORIC ARCHAEOLOGY; NAUTICAL ARCHAEOLOGY; POST-MEDIEVAL ARCHAEOLOGY.

For documentary sources, *see* SOURCES.

For industrial archaeologists, *see* HADFIELD, CHARLES; HUDSON, KENNETH; RAISTRICK, ARTHUR; REES, DAVID MORGAN; RIX, MICHAEL; SOUSA VITERBO, FRANCISCO DE; WATKINS, GEORGE.

BIBLIOGRAPHY
General
Bruwier and Duvosquel, 1975; Clarke, 1978; Daniel, 1975; Harris, 1979.
Specific
Clark, C. M. Trouble at t'mill: industrial archaeology in the 1980s. In *Antiquity*, LXI, 1987.

BARRIE TRINDER

industrial architecture Buildings erected in the service of industry cannot be automatically classified under the heading industrial architecture. The practical demands of manufacturing, storage and transport do not in themselves necessitate those aesthetic qualities that characterize an architectural treatment. Indeed, there are probably no other building types in which practicality counts for so much and aesthetics for so little. But that is not to say that architecture has no place in the industrial realm. Many industrial buildings constructed without conscious architectural effort have displayed architectural effects that designers of other types of buildings have been pleased to emulate. In many instances the requirements of industry have been entrusted to architects, partly in the hope that the buildings produced would achieve a status higher than that of mere utility.

The history of industrial architecture is concerned first and foremost with the role that architects have played in meeting the need for industrial buildings: a contribution that has varied in importance at different times and places. A related question concerns the circumstances in which industrial clients, from parochial firms to international corporations, have sought the help of architects – in preference, or in addition to, the other building professions and trades. To speak of industrial architecture in these terms precludes buildings which, whatever their merits, have no identifiable architectural input: though close in spirit, they call for investigation of a slightly different kind.

As one of the leading sectors of the English Industrial Revolution of the eighteenth century, the textile industry called forth the most interesting constructional developments of the period. The risk of combustion in textile mills hastened the introduction of fireproof systems of construction, relying on cast- and later wrought-iron components. Architects played no part in these innovations which arose from urgencies better understood by the mill owners themselves. The pioneering use of iron in Derbyshire mills, in Derby from 1792–3, and the West Mill, Belper, from 1793–5, was the work of the entrepreneur William Strutt. He used cruciform section iron columns supporting timber beams and brick arches. From 1796–7 Charles Bage, a partner in the flax-spinning concern which built Ditherington Mill, Shrewsbury, improved on Strutt's system by incorporating iron beams. The subsequent development of iron-framing refined and adapted Bage's example, principally by altering the section and profile of the beams and by substituting round for cruciform columns. These advances owed much to the engineering contractor WILLIAM FAIRBAIRN, whose firm rose to prominence as specialists in the construction of fireproof mills.

However sophisticated their internal structures, all these mills still depended on masonry exterior walls pierced by regular window openings. Their workmanlike façades, usually executed in local materials, expressed the regularity of their interiors, and only occasionally were they given architectural embellishment. The addition of a pediment or a run of blank arcading, if called for, could easily be handled by the builder or mason responsible for the work.

The same unselfconscious dignity characterized late eighteenth-century dockyard building in Britain, such as the roperies at Portsmouth and Chatham, of 1770 and 1785 respectively, and storehouses of the same date. These were not intended to draw attention to themselves, whereas the industrial buildings for which London was famous strove intentionally for greater effect. The massive breweries, whose mechanization so impressed foreign visitors, were designed to a formula that followed a gravitational logic for the handling of bulky materials; to fit that formula to a particular site, where publicity for the brewery was a further consideration, was regarded as a legitimate task for an architect. In London George Gwilt (1746–1807) was employed at the Anchor Brewery, Southwark, and Francis Edwards (1784–1857) gave the Lion Brewery, Lambeth, a full palazzo treatment on its Thameside elevation. Likewise the commercial pride of the London dock companies found expression in the grandeur of their architect-designed warehouses.

Iron-framed construction was adopted in both breweries and warehouses where necessary, though the use of iron presented a potential threat to the role of architects in the design of such buildings. At the most famous English dock complex, the Albert Dock in LIVERPOOL of 1841–5,

the engineer Joseph Hartley (1780–1860) employed an iron frame supporting brick-arched floors on the textile mill system, plus an ingenious stressed skin design of iron roof. The Doric treatment of the dockside colonnade may have been one result of Hartley's consultation with the architect PHILIP HARDWICK, but there is a feeling in this case and often thereafter that engineering was gaining the upper hand. The basic rules for the use of cast iron were easy enough to grasp, but the introduction of wrought iron from the mid-1840s required a more specialized expertise than most architects possessed. Engineers, or engineering contractors, could answer the architectural needs of industrial users more readily than architects could take on the engineers' role.

Architects' fear of usurpation by the other building professions helps account for the readiness with which they put their faith in historicist styles. The adoption of alternatives to Classicism, at first for the sake of visual diversity, but after the 1840s with more earnest intentions, enabled architects to claim expertise through their knowledge of past architectural eras. Under the ideological banners of A. W. N. Pugin (1812–52), John Ruskin (1819–1900) and Eugène-Emanuel Viollet-le-Duc (1814–79), far-reaching claims were made for the social and emblematic functions of historicism. Such ideas were most obviously applicable to buildings of a civic or social reforming kind, but their potential was also recognized by industrialists anxious about the reputations of their enterprises. The most obvious variation upon the Classical theme drew upon Italianate motifs to create a less austere effect. That was the method used by Lockwood & Mawson to modulate the colossal length of the Saltaire mill (see BRADFORD) of 1851–3, for which William Fairbairn supplied the basic structure. More exotic themes were occasionally displayed: an Egyptian temple at Marshall's Mill, Leeds (1838–40); or a version of the Doge's Palace, Venice, at Templeton's carpet factory, Glasgow (1889). In the case of the Menier chocolate factory (1871–2) at Noisiel-sur-Marne, east of Paris, the exterior bracing of the iron frame was adapted for the sake of architectural effect, and the polychromatic infill to the bracing incorporated plaques depicting ripening chocolate plants. For Émile-Justin Menier, as for other industrialists, the factory became the embodiment of the firm's identity. (See figure 28.)

The frequent dichotomy in factory design between the architectural front and the more utilitarian structure behind was repeated in the design of major railway stations, where the rival claims of corporate display and functionalism were even more evident. The classic of its kind, the Midland Railway's terminus of 1866–77 at St Pancras, London, was applauded in Building News on 11 February 1869 as being 'practical proof . . . of the advantages that accrue from the united working of architects and engineers'. But it was just as often referred to for the apparent discordance, rather than unity, between its train shed and the frontage offices and hotel. Architects successfully kept themselves in the forefront throughout the railway building boom in Britain, but were supplanted by engineers in the more cost conscious years towards the end of the century. In France the *Beaux-Arts* architectural tradition, with its emphasis on logical and integrated building layouts, gave architects a stronger hold over the supervision of station protects.

The strategy that architects used to secure their role in the design of industrial buildings presupposed that they would continue to hold a position as disinterested mediators between clients and building contractors. That claim was as important a part of their professional authority as their ability to supply the artistic ingredient in building design. However there were always those who, while still calling themselves architects, never aspired to quite such an other-worldly ideal, but were content to be more closely involved in the hard realities of the business world. For example, textile mill design a century after Strutt and Bage tended to follow standard patterns so predictable that the overall building cost could be calculated in terms of the number of spindles and the lengths of the mules. Architects such as the Stott dynasty of Oldham, Lancashire, were not only content to live by such rules, but themselves took stakes in new enterprises, and even sometimes acted as the chief promoters.

It was in the United States that architects' obedience to industrial requirements regardless of aesthetic priorities produced their most dramatic results. The German-born ALBERT KAHN developed a practice famous for its innovative and rapidly erected factories, especially ones supplied for the Detroit car industry. Using a reinforced concrete system devised by his brother Julius, Kahn's Packard Plant No. 10 of 1905 showed how concrete construction could produce better lit, more flexible interiors. Concrete framing was again used for the 179 m (860 ft.) long, four-storey Highland Park plant, completed in 1910 for the production of Model T Fords. But the multi-storey day-lit factory was obsolete almost from the beginning, as was shown by the Ford River Rouge complex, where a single storey, steel-frame shed predominated. Whatever grandeur these possessed was incidental to their workaday performance and adaptability.

The factories of Kahn and his contemporaries, plus the even more photogenic North American grain silos, attained a status that their creators never dreamed of when they were singled out by European architects as models of a post-historicist functionalist aesthetic. Le Corbusier exclaimed in 1923: 'The American engineers overwhelm with their calculations our expiring architecture.' Yet he and his contemporaries knew full well that the new architecture they were promoting would be based on far more than just calculation.

The emergence of a new aesthetic for industrial architecture was exemplified by two German projects: the turbine factory of Allgemeine Elektricitäts-Gesellschaft (AEG) of 1908–10 in BERLIN, and the Fagus shoe-last factory at ALFELD of 1911–14. At AEG, Peter Behrens (1868–1940) translated the machine hall with its travelling gantry into an industrial temple by projecting the three-hinged arched roof beyond the end bay, and by inclining the glazing between the stanchions along its main side elevation. For the Fagus factory, Behrens's pupil Walter Gropius (1883–1969) adopted a yet more radical form. Having taken over another architect's design, the plan of which he hardly altered, he turned the office block section into a glass box by setting the stanchions behind the window line, and by extending the glazing around the corner.

The attention that these projects attracted in the pioneering years of the modern movement helped secure for architects a greater part in the provision of industrial architecture than they had previously enjoyed. The association of modernism with the benefits of corporatism and industrial efficiency, symbolized by Germany's achievements before World War I, helped architects claim an enlarged role as agents of economic reform. Thanks to that reputation, most twentieth-century industrial buildings carry an architectural attribution, though the architectural element in their appearance may not always be as evident as it is in their nineteenth-century predecessors.

BIBLIOGRAPHY
General
Banham, 1986; Brockman, 1974; Buddensieg and Henning, 1978; Hildebrand, 1974; Holme, 1935; Jones, 1985; Lemoine, 1986; Nijhof, 1985; Pevsner, 1976; Richards, 1958; Tann, 1970.
Specific
Anderson, S. Modern architecture and industry: Peter Behrens and the AEG factories. In *Oppositions*, XXIII, 1981.
Fitzgerald, R.S. The development of the cast iron frame in textile mills to 1850. In *IAR*, x, 1988.
Spiller, B. The Georgian brewery. In *Architectural Review*, 122, 1957.
Sutherland, R.J.M. The introduction of structural wrought iron. In *TNS*, XXVI, 1963–4.
Wallis, T. Factories. *Journal of the RIBA*, 3rd series, XL, 1933.

ROBERT THORNE

industrial art   *See* ICONOGRAPHY.

industrial community   A community in which the predominant economic activity is related to manufacturing, mining or associated transport systems. Such communities range in size from large cities to isolated groups of railway workers' cottages. Industrial archaeologists have tended to concentrate their attention on the relatively small, easily identified colonies created by entrepreneurs (*see* COMPANY TOWN), but of late there has been increasing recognition of squatter communities, and of culturally distinct communities within conurbations (*see* COLONY). Much writing on the subject of industrial communities has concentrated on the study of housing. Lowe (1977) has shown in his study of the ironworking community of Blaenavon that the archaeological study of housing has the potential to add substantially to historical understanding. Lewis and Denton (1974) and Horton (1989) have also illuminated the history of industrial settlements with a broad-ranging archaeological approach, incorporating excavation as well as the surveying of upstanding remains. Oral sources too have been used extensively in the investigation of industrial communities.

The subtle distinctions between the English words used to describe house types or forms of social organization cannot be translated into other languages. The entries in this volume relating to industrial communities are necessarily largely concerned with British practice, and with English words commonly used in discussion of such communities.

See also COLONY; COMPANY TOWN; HOUSE TYPES; MODEL COMMUNITY; SQUATTER SETTLEMENT; SUBURB; UTOPIAN COMMUNITY.

BIBLIOGRAPHY
General
Horton, 1990; Lewis and Denton, 1974; Lowe, 1977; Samuel, 1975, 1977; Sutcliffe, 1981.
Specific
Jones, K., Hunt, M., Malam, J. and Trinder, B. Holywell Lane: a squatter community in the Shropshire coalfield. In *IAR*, VI, 1982.
Lowe, J. Housing as a source for industrial history: a case study of Blaenafon, a Welsh ironworks settlement, 1788–c.1845. In *IA*, VIII, 1982.

BARRIE TRINDER

industrial espionage The acquisition of technical expertise by unauthorized observation of processes, by arranging the export, often illegally, of machines, and by the enticement of skilled workers to emigrate. Espionage was one of the principal means by which technology was transferred from one country to another in the eighteenth century and the early nineteenth century; and when done with the sanction of government, as in France, or through a national agency like the Jernkontoret (ironmasters' association) or Bergskollegium (board of mines), as in Sweden, produced substantial archives which are prime sources for the industrial history of both the spying countries and those spied upon. Early in the eighteenth century Britons gained knowledge of silk-throwing in Italy and of ironworking in Sweden by such means, but by the end of the century Britain was the main source of technological innovation and knowledge of processes was sought by spies from France, Sweden, Russia, the Habsburg Empire and, after 1784, the USA.

See also TRANSFER OF TECHNOLOGY.

BIBLIOGRAPHY
General
Henderson, 1954; Jeremy, 1981; Rémond, 1946.
Specific
Birch, A. Foreign observers of the British iron industry during the eighteenth century. In *Journal of Economic History*, XXV, 1955.
Flinn, M. W. The travel diaries of Swedish engineers of the eighteenth century as sources of technological history. In *TNS*, XXX, 1957–8, 1958–9.
Freudenberger, H. Technologischer Wandel im 18 Jahrhundert (Technological change in the 18th century) *Wolfenbuttler Forschungen*, Band 14 (Research at Wolfenbuttel, vol. 14). Wolfenbuttel, 1981.
Harris, J. R. Technological transfer between England and France in the eighteenth century: the case of the hardware industry. In *The History and Sociology of Technology, Proceedings of the 24th Annual Meeting of the Society of the History of Technology*. Milwaukee, 1981.
Harris, J. R. Eighteenth-century industrial espionage. In *IAR*, VII, 1985.
Jeremy, D. Damming the flood: British governmental efforts to check the outflow of technicians and machinery, 1780–1843. In *Business History Review*, LI, 1977.
Mathias, P. Skill and the diffusion of innovations from Britain in the eighteenth century. In *Transactions of the Royal Historical Society*, XXV, 1975.
Musson, A. E. The Manchester School and the exportation of machinery. In *Business History*, XIV, 1972.
Robinson, E. International exchange of men and machines. In *Business History*, I, 1958.
Robinson, E. The transference of British technology to Russia. In Ratcliffe, 1975.

BARRIE TRINDER

industrial estate An area of land owned by a developer, whether a private entrepreneur or a public authority, and divided into plots for leasing or sale to manufacturing or commercial concerns, which may share some common services. The term first came to notice in England when applied to the Trafford Park Estate in MANCHESTER from 1896, and was commonly applied to World War I military bases around London (such as that at Slough) that were adapted for industrial use in the 1920s. The term is frequently applied to industrial zones in NEW TOWNS and other modern developments, including many on sites vacated by heavy industry.

See also TRADING ESTATE.

BIBLIOGRAPHY
General
Hall, 1962.

industrial railway A railway within or uniquely serving a mining or manufacturing plant, often a NARROW-GAUGE RAILWAY. Many steam locomotives from such systems remain on PRESERVED RAILWAYS. Some lines serving mines in remote regions of North America and Australia are of considerable length.

BIBLIOGRAPHY
General
Industrial Locomotive Society, 1967; Westwood, 1983.
Specific
White, J. H. Industrial locomotives: the forgotten servant. In *Technology and Culture*, XXI, 1980.

industrial school A boarding or day school for children who had committed minor crimes or who lived in circumstances where they were likely to commit crime, and distinct from a reformatory school, which was for those who had committed crimes for which an adult would be punishable by imprisonment. Most were privately run, but in Britain courts were empowered to commit individuals to them by the Industrial Schools Act 1857. Such schools were intended to create attitudes favourable to work, but provided little technical training. The first is reckoned to have been established in Aberdeen in 1841, and the idea was energetically propounded by Mary Carpenter (1807–77), who set up a school in Bristol in 1859. There were similar institutions in many countries, Houses of Refuge in New York and Philadelphia, farm schools in Belgium and Russia, and the 'Rauhehaus' of 1833 in Hamburg.

BIBLIOGRAPHY
General
Carpenter, 1851; Manton, 1976; Murray, 1854; Tobias, 1967; Watson, R. S., 1867; Watson, W., 1851.
Specific
Royal Commission on Reformatories and Industrial Schools, XLV, BPP, 1884.
Thomas, D. H. *Reformatory and Industrial Schools: an annotated list of schools approved by the Home Office, 1854–1933*. Newcastle-upon-Tyne: Newcastle Polytechnic, 1984.

BARRIE TRINDER

inland navigation A term applied to commercial operations on rivers, lakes and canals.

For vessels used on such waterways, *see* BARGE; FERRY; FLAT; KEEL; NARROW BOAT; PÉNICHE; RAFT; STARVATIONER; TUB BOAT; TUG.

For civil engineering features of inland waterways, *see* AQUEDUCT; BOAT LIFT; CAISSON; CANAL TUNNEL; CHAIN HAULAGE; FLASH LOCK; INCLINED PLANE; LOCK; POUND LOCK; SLUICE; STOP LOCK; WEIR.

BIBLIOGRAPHY
General
Whitworth, 1766.

inn An establishment providing refreshment and overnight accommodation for travellers, differing from a tavern, which provided only refreshment, and a hotel, which might provide accommodation on a long-term as well as an overnight basis. Originally 'inn' meant a dwelling place, and it is used in that sense in universities, legal establishments and orders of knighthood (*see* RHODES).

The development of the turnpike road system stimulated the construction of large inns in England in the second half of the eighteenth century. An inn that catered for MAIL COACHES, STAGE COACHES and POST COACHES was traditionally of courtyard plan, and required extensive stabling, which was often on a separate site. In England most of the inns in large cities have gone, but a few provincial examples survive – including the Mitre at Oxford and the Lion at Shrewsbury – and there are concentrations in small towns which subsisted on the thoroughfare trade, like Benson, Oxfordshire, and Stone, Staffordshire.

By the early nineteenth century inns were subject to regulation in most European countries. Some might be posting stations. In Prussia it was obligatory for the landlord to hang up in each bedroom the tariff for rooms, meals and the employment of servants.

See also HOTEL; PUBLIC HOUSE.

BIBLIOGRAPHY
General
Everitt, 1973; Monckton, 1969.

BARRIE TRINDER

Innsbruck, Tyrol, Austria The capital of the Tyrol, hemmed in by bold and fissured limestone mountains, and ruled by the Tyrolean line of the Habsburgs who held their own independent court in the city until 1665. Innsbruck stands on the main route south to the Brenner Pass, and on the railway linking Vienna with western Austria, making it one of the country's principal railway junctions. The Volkskunstmuseum (Museum of Folk Art) includes important collections of ceramics, pewter, basketwork and traditional textiles.

LOCATION
[M] Volkskunstmuseum (Museum of Folk Art), Universitätsstrasse 2, 6020 Innsbruck.

institute Within an INDUSTRIAL COMMUNITY an institute was usually a building designed for adult education, which might have lecture rooms, a reading room for newspapers, a library, and sometimes a museum or drawing studio. Institutes might be concerned primarily with vocational training, or with recreational learning. In England and in the USA, 'mechanics institutes' were organizations that promoted education for their members, and often organized periodic exhibitions of members' works.

insurance records Fire insurance began in England in the late seventeenth century, and was in widespread use in Europe and America by 1800. Two classes of records are of particular value to industrial historians.

Policy registers record and describe the properties accorded protection by insurance companies, and can provide evidence of capital accumulation and of the technology employed on particular sites. Over 150 series of records are preserved in Britain, containing many thousands of policies. The Guildhall Library is the main repository. They have been used in studies of textile factories, brewing, and the growth of towns.

Fire insurance plans of urban areas were produced by specialist companies and loaned to insurance companies when they had need of them. They provide remarkably detailed records of industrial land use. Their production in Britain has been dominated by one company, Charles E. Goad, who published 126 volumes between 1886 and 1970. There are substantial collections in the British Library and in the Guildhall Library (*see* LONDON).

BIBLIOGRAPHY
General
Cockerell, 1976; Rowley, 1984.
Specific
Beresford, M. W. Building history from insurance records. In *Urban History Yearbook*. Leicester: Leicester University Press, 1976.
Chapman, S. D. Fixed capital formation in the British cotton industry, 1770–1815. In *EcHR*, XXIII, 1973.
Chapman, S. D. Enterprise and innovation in the British hosiery industry, 1750–1850. In *TH*, V, 1974.
Donnachie, I. Sources of capital and capitalisation in the Scottish brewing industry, *c.*1750–1830. In *EcHR*, XXX, 1977.
Jenkins, D. T. Early factory development in the West Riding of Yorkshire, 1770–1800. In Harte and Ponting, 1973.

Schwarz, L. D. and Jones, L. J. Wealth, occupations and insurance in the late eighteenth century: the policy registers of the Sun Fire Office. In *EcHR*, XXXVI, 1983.

Thomas, J. H. Short guides to records, 19: fire insurance policy registers. In *History*, LIII, 1968.

Wright, H. E. Insurance mapping and industrial archeology. In *IA*, XI, 1983.

LOCATION
[I] Guildhall Library, London EC2P 3EJ.

PETER WAKELIN

interchangeable parts Mechanical components sufficiently standard in shape and size to be interchangeable in use, and therefore assembled rather than fitted. They are essential to modern manufacturing practice. Interchangeability relates to product-specific tolerances and may thus be said to have emerged historically at various points. The interchangeability of all the parts within a system made possible by elaborate sets of gauges, as adopted for strategic reasons in arms manufacture, must be distinguished from piecemeal or nominal standardization resulting from the mechanization of processes in, for example, clockmaking.

Intensive efforts to develop special-purpose machinery for small-arms parts in the *ante bellum* USA achieved economic viability after half a century, and fitting continued to be employed on close tolerances (*see* AMERICAN SYSTEM OF MANUFACTURE). High tooling costs limited the appeal of systemic interchangeability until measuring technology improved, a range of generic machine tools adapted for volume production emerged, and a new culture of professional mechanical engineering was formed in the later part of the nineteenth century. After 1900 these developments were brought together to serve large markets in MASS PRODUCTION of goods designed with interchangeable parts.

BIBLIOGRAPHY
General
Battison, 1976; Gilbert, 1965; Hounshell, 1984; Rolt, 1986; Smith, 1977.
Specific
Musson, A. E. Joseph Whitworth and the growth of mass production engineering. In *Business History*, XVII, 1975.

TIM PUTNAM

Interlaken, Bern, Switzerland   A resort on a spit of land between Lakes Thun and Brienz, with many classic nineteenth- and twentieth-century hotels, Interlaken is an important railway centre, served by the standard-gauge line from Bern along the north bank of Lake Thun, the metre-gauge SBB line across the Brunig pass to Lucerne, and the metre-gauge Berner Oberlandbahn line to Mürren. The last connects via Zweilütschinen and Grindelwald or through Lauterbrunnen and Wengen, to Kleine Scheidegg, lower terminus of the line opened in 1912 to Jungfraujoch, 3454 m (11 331 ft.) above sea level.

The paddle steamer *Lötschberg* which plies on Lake Brienz was built by Escher Wyss of Zurich in 1914.

BIBLIOGRAPHY
General
Allen, 1965.

intermittent kiln   A KILN with a single chamber which is heated and cooled alternately. The fire may be directed through the ware upwards, downwards or horizontally. It is more wasteful of fuel than a CONTINUOUS-CHAMBER KILN but is cheaper to build and more flexible in use.

BIBLIOGRAPHY
General
Rhodes, 1968; Searle, 1929.

international and national exhibitions   The Great Exhibition of 1851 held in the Crystal Palace in Hyde Park, London, is often regarded as the first of the great international exhibitions, although there were earlier precedents. Since that time there has been a succession of major exhibitions and fairs intended to attract international audiences, although some have intentionally limited their scope to single nations. An international convention of 1928 led to the establishment in Paris in 1931 of the Bureau International des Expositions, which controls the classification of such events. The catalogues of exhibitions of this sort provide valuable illustrations of the products of manufacturing industry, and of current attitudes to design and production methods. The most notable exhibitions have been in Dublin, 1852; New York, 1853–4; Paris, 1855; London, 1862; Paris, 1867; Vienna, 1873; Philadelphia, 1876; Paris, 1878; Glasgow, 1888; Paris, 1889; Chicago, 1893; Paris, 1900; St Louis, 1904; San Francisco, 1915; Wembley, London, 1924–5; Paris, 1937; New York, 1939; London, 1951. Exhibitions provided opportunities for architectural innovation, and some exhibition buildings have passed into industrial use or have been adapted as museums, as has the Palace of Fine Arts from the Exhibition of 1915, which now houses San Francisco's Exploratorium.

BIBLIOGRAPHY
General
Allwood, 1977; Frieleg, 1985.

BARRIE TRINDER

International Modern   The architectural style of the mid-twentieth century, characterized by generally cubic shapes, the use of concrete, steel frames and glass curtain walls, by close relationships between form and function, and by a shunning of ornamentation. The received interpretation of the Modern Movement, which derives from Pevsner's work of 1936, sees an evolution from the industrial structures of the early nineteenth century, the ART NOUVEAU style, and the work of such Americans as Louis Sullivan (1856–1924), to such buildings of the years before 1914 as those designed by PETER BEHRENS for AEG (*see* BERLIN; INDUSTRIAL ARCHITECTURE). Through the influence emanating from the BAUHAUS in the 1920s, the style came to be adopted by progressive architects in many

Figure 61   The opening by Queen Victoria of the Great International Exhibition of all Nations in Sir Joseph Paxton's Crystal Palace in Hyde Park, London, on 1 May 1851 (etching by George Cruikshank, published by David Bogue, London, 1851)
Elton Collection: Ironbridge Gorge Museum

countries in the 1930s and was widely used in the years after World War II.

The style is generally referred to in this volume as 'International Modern', although some contributors have preferred the terms 'modernist', 'cubist', 'FUNCTIONALIST', or 'Bauhaus'.

BIBLIOGRAPHY
General
Pevsner, 1936, 1960; Richards, 1958, 1962.

interpretation   Industrial archaeological monuments are most effectively interpreted *in situ*, but the subject is also interpreted through MUSEUMS. For other approaches to interpretation, *see* HERITAGE CENTRE; INTERNATIONAL AND NATIONAL EXHIBITIONS; PARK; PRESERVED RAILWAY; TRAIL; UNESCO WORLD HERITAGE SITE.

interurban   A TRAMWAY providing a link between separate towns or cities, distinguished from a suburban or rural tram route by its promoters' intent, and from a RAILWAY by its concentration upon passenger traffic, use of electric traction, and, usually, lower fares. Interurbans originated in 1893 in Portland, Oregon, and were most common in the USA where route mileage totalled 18 000 by the 1920s, but they were also built in England, Austria,

Germany, Egypt, Australia, the NETHERLANDS and BELGIUM, where the vast SNCV 'Vicinal' network radiated from BRUSSELS. Interurban tramcars were larger and heavier than ordinary trams, typically single-decked, and capable of speeds around 96 km (60 mi.) per hour. Most lines succumbed to road competition in the 1940s. Restored interurban tramcars operate over 30 route km (20 mi.) at Yakima, Washington. Preserved Belgian and Dutch examples can be seen at BRUSSELS, UTRECHT and Weert (*see* THE NETHERLANDS).

BIBLIOGRAPHY
General
Rowsome, 1956.

LOCATION
[M] Yakima Interurban Trolley Barn, 507 South 4th Avenue, Yakima, Washington, USA.

PAUL COLLINS

inventory   In North America, the usual term applied to a comprehensive survey of a particular class of historical monuments, including industrial monuments, within a defined region. The term is rarely so used in England, where, amongst historians, 'inventory' is often assumed to mean probate inventory (*see* PROBATE RECORDS). In

357

France, the 'Inventaire' is the national body charged with responsibility for historical monuments.

See also Sites and monuments record.

Inverbervie, Grampian, Scotland   A small burgh 15 km (9 mi.) S. of Stonehaven. In it is Scotland's first flax-spinning mill, probably the oldest extant in the world, dating from 1787 – Upper Mill, a two-storey building, later a flock mill and now empty. Seven flax mills followed in Inverbervie, of which Bervie Mill now makes wire ropes, Linty Mill processes fish, and the Spring and Klondyke Works are in tenemented industrial use. Craview Mill of 1907 is one of Scotland's two working flax mills, spinning tow and blends for furnishing and wall-covering fabrics. The later mills each comprise a single-storey preparing building and a two-storey spinning mill, with winding on the upper timber floor. They are as small as the 'system' can allow. Selbie Works, Gourdon, 1.5 km (1 mi.) S., is a series of north-lit spinning sheds that can still alternate between flax and jute – a small and highly specialized operation.

Inverbervie's bridge of 1799 is a dramatic single arch, 31 m (103 ft.) in span and 24 m (80 ft.) high, bypassed in 1933 by a reinforced-concrete bridge. Nearby Gourdon and Johnshaven have small but active fishing harbours.

BIBLIOGRAPHY
General
Hume, 1977.

MARK WATSON

Ionic   One the orders of Classical architecture, in which columns are topped with scrolled capitals.

Iowa, United States of America   Industry in this river-bounded Midwestern state has long been dominated by farming and its support activities. Grain storage elevators (silos), some of historic vintage and materials, pierce the skies above the rolling Iowa farmlands. Freight railways network the state, their mid-continent steam traffic having spawned sixty-one major locomotive and car repair shops by 1925.

Muscatine, Iowa, on the banks of the upper Mississippi River, has been a major centre of the American pearl button industry. At its height in the 1920s, forty-three pearl-working plants operated in the city, the shell supply harvested from shoals along the Mississippi and its nearby tributaries.

Further south along the river, the vast Keokuk Dam of 1913 was the first to back up the Mississippi, flooding a notorious series of whitewater rapids, and furnishing hydro-electric power in a great arcaded stone power-house. The straight-crested overflow dam spans 1430 m (4696 ft.) and is bypassed by an adjacent set of navigation locks.

In Council Bluffs is Pottawattamie County's three-storey rotary jail of the 1880s, like its only brother in Indiana, a geared iron cylinder with pie-slice cells, central

sewerage around the pivot shaft, and disguised from the outside world in an ornate Victorian brick structure.

BIBLIOGRAPHY
General
Gradwohl and Osborn, 1984; Schweider, 1983.
LOCATIONS
[M] Jefferson Telephone Museum, 105 W. Harrison, Jefferson, IA 50129.
[M] Keokuk River Museum, Johnson Street, Keokuk, IA 52632.
[S] Pottawattamie County Jail, 226 Pearl Street, Council Bluffs, IA 51501.
[M] Woodward Riverboat Museum, 2nd Street Harbour, Dubuque, IA 52001.

DAVID H. SHAYT

Ireland   Ireland comprises the western part of the British Isles. Mountain ranges around the coast surround a central plain, where fertile agricultural land is mingled with large areas of bog. There are few mineral deposits.

Ireland has a long history of political, social and religious unrest, having been under the British Crown since the Middle Ages. Ireland had its own parliament until, under the Act of Union 1800, it became part of the United Kingdom. Nationalist feeling erupted from time to time during the nineteenth century, and the Easter Rising of 1916 began a period of unrest which resulted in 1921 in the division of the country between the Free State – the twenty-six counties of Southern Ireland (Eire), which became an independent republic in 1949 – and the six counties forming Northern Ireland, which remains a province of the United Kingdom.

The Irish economy was traditionally based on agriculture, and the export of such products as flax and hides. The population in 1660 was about a million. Ironmaking flourished briefly in the late seventeenth century. There were ten blast furnaces and twenty forges in 1672, but lack of fuel soon caused the industry to contract. Fragments of a furnace survive at Whitegate, County Clare. There was a steady growth in trade in the eighteenth century, in spite of English legislation which impeded Irish commerce. During the 1760s Irish farmers concentrated increasingly on growing grain for the English market. Large mills along the valleys of such rivers as the Barrow, the Blackwater and the Suir, and tall stone warehouses at ports like Clonakilty and New Ross, reflect a vast export trade in grain and flour handled in sacks. In Galway City a power canal was constructed from which water passed through mill leats into a parallel navigable stream. Several five- and six-storey water-powered corn mills were built, providing models for a short-lived generation of cotton mills, constructed from the 1780s (*see* Cork; Prosperous; Slane). Many nascent industrial activities in the southern counties were destroyed by the Great Famine of 1845–9, which, through death and enforced emigration, reduced the population of the island from 8 million in 1841 to 6.5 million a decade later. The population continued to fall, and totalled only 4.3 million by 1911. There were moves towards concentration in traditional industries, and large roller mills were constructed at the principal ports. Industry prospered most in the north-

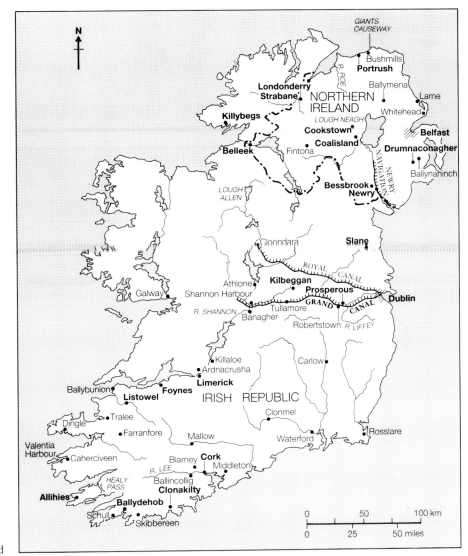

Ireland

eastern counties, and the political settlement of 1921 reflected, albeit crudely, an economic as well as a religious divide.

Natural power sources have always been important in a country which lacks coal. Animals were the main source of power for most mining operations long after the first steam pumping engines had been installed in Irish mines in the mid-eighteenth century. There was a concentration of wind-powered corn mills along the cereal-growing eastern seaboard in the eighteenth and early nineteenth centuries; examples – at Ballycopeland, County Down, and Tacumshin, County Wexford, 11 km (7 mi.) SW of Rosslare – are in the care of the respective governments. The Irish windmill has a characteristic form, with a movable thatched cap containing the windshaft, resting on a fixed stone tower, circular in plan.

Water was the characteristic source of power for milling

operations in most parts of Ireland. The Irish developed a unique water-power technology, particularly relating to the processing of flax. Horizontal mill wheels were used from early times for grinding corn, and in about 1740 the principle was adapted for scutching flax. In primitive scutching mills four boxed-in scutching blades were driven on a vertical shaft, propelled by the direct impulse of water on vanes or blades at its base. By 1800 most mills were powered by vertical water wheels, often designed and built by local foundries. The breaking of dried retted flax stems prior to scutching might be effected by vertical or, later, horizontal rolling frames, the latter developed by MacAdam Bros. of Belfast from c.1850. Another application of water power in linen manufacture was the beetling engine, introduced early in the eighteenth century. Rotating webs of linen were pounded by falling wooden 'beetles' to close the weave and produce a sheen on the fabric. Other examples of water power in the Irish countryside include sawmills, spade mills, oil mills and papermills.

The water turbine was first used to generate hydro-electric power in Ireland in 1896, when the 'Dog Leap' station was built on the River Roe, 22 km (13$\frac{1}{2}$ mi.) E. of Londonderry. It remained in use until the 1960s and is now preserved within the Roe Valley Country Park. A principal objective of energy policy in the Republic in the 1920s and 30s was to secure independence from British supplies of coal. The major hydro-electric scheme at Ardnacrusha, 5.6 km (3$\frac{1}{2}$ mi.) N. of Limerick, was built in 1925–9.

Ireland has extensive deposits of peat, usually called 'turf'. The Bord na Mona (state turf organization) was established in 1946 and built many 3 ft. (0.91 m) gauge railways across the bogs. Processing plants to manufacture turf briquettes were established, and turf-fired power stations were built at Portarlington, Ferbane, 20 km (12 mi.) W. of Tullamore, at Shannonbridge, 16 km (10 mi.) SW of Athlone, and elsewhere.

Ireland gained a network of inland transport facilities in the eighteenth and nineteenth centuries sadly in excess of the demand arising from native industry. Between the 1730s and the 1750s many TURNPIKE roads were constructed; but subsequently, between 1766 and 1898, most new roads were financed through the 'presentment system', by which the Grand Jury of a county could grant to an individual authority to improve a road, and reimburse him from public funds on completion. Many turnpike mileposts survive, varying from crudely carved blocks of stone, like those on the road from Cork to Mallow, to such neat iron posts as those on the route from Cork to Waterford. From 1831 the Irish Board of Public Works further improved trunk routes, like the Great Coast Road from Larne to Ballycastle, County Antrim, built by William Bald in 1832–43. A feature of Irish road transport in the nineteenth century was the network of 'car' services, for the most part on cross-country rather than radial routes, operated by Charles Bianconi (1786–1875) from Clonmel, County Tipperary, with specially designed 'bians', two- and four-wheeled vehicles, on which passengers sat back-to-back in two rows looking towards the roadsides, on either side of a central luggage well. By 1840 Bianconi's cars were achieving 3000 route miles a day. His example was copied by other entrepreneurs and it was not until the last quarter of the century that car services were superseded by branch railways. An outstanding feat of road building, commenced as relief work during the Famine and completed between 1928 and 1931, is the pass between Kerry and Cork which takes its name from Tim Healy (1855–1931), first Governor-General of the Irish Free State.

Many river-improvement and canal schemes were projected in the eighteenth century. The first plans to make the Shannon navigable date from 1715, although work was not completed until after the coming of the railways. Dublin was linked with Cloondara on the Shannon by the Royal Canal, and with Shannon Harbour by the Grand Canal. In the North inland navigation was focused on Lough Neagh, the largest freshwater lake in the British Isles. The Newry Navigation opened in 1742, providing a means by which coal from east Tyrone could be taken to the coast and Dublin; it was the first major canal in the British Isles. The COALISLAND Canal, also begun in the 1730s and similarly associated with the traffic in coal, posed greater engineering difficulties and was not completed until 1787. A short extension from Coalisland to Drumglass was designed for tub boats and incorporated INCLINED PLANES known as 'dry hurries', designed by Daviso de Arcort (Ducart), the first in Britain. Canal building in Ireland, in contrast to that in the rest of the British Isles, was carried out under state supervision, not in response to industrial growth but in the hope of stimulating it.

East Tyrone was the principal source of coal in Ireland, but the mines, which reached their peak of production in 1830–50, never attracted substantial investment: methods were always primitive and productivity from narrow seams was low. Mining has been spasmodic since 1850. There were also coal mines at Castlecomer, County Kilkenny, and New Birmingham, County Tipperary. Limestone quarrying and limeburning were widespread. Iron ore and bauxite were mined in County Antrim. A kiln of 1844 for calcining iron ore survives at Skerry East, near Newtown Crommelin, 15 km (9 mi.) NE of Ballymena. Lead ore was mined near Ballyvergin, County Clare, and at Silvermines, County Tipperary; and there were copper workings at ALLIHIES, around BALLYDEHOB, and at Coad Mountain, County Kerry. Avoca, County Wicklow, was an important source of pyrites for the English chemical industry. Slate was quarried at Benduff, near Ross Carbery, County Cork; SERPENTINE at Carrowtrasna, County Donegal; and millstones at Burns Mountain, County Donegal.

Ireland's principal manufacturing activity, the linen industry, was concentrated around BELFAST and the counties of Armagh and Down to the south, with a less dense scatter of mills across Antrim, Londonderry and Tyrone. Domestic manufactures were well established in the north of Ireland by 1700 and spread across almost the whole country in the course of the next 100 years. The countryside of the northern counties retains many monuments of the pre-factory stage of linen manufacture: bleaching houses, scutch mills (see DRUMNACONAGHER), beetling mills (see COOKSTOWN), and huts from which fabrics laid out on bleach greens were guarded, like those at Tullylish, County Down, and that in the Ulster Folk Museum (see BELFAST). Characteristic terraced housing survives in such flaxworking villages as Gilford, County Down; Ligoniel, now part of north-west Belfast; and BESSBROOK. The introduction of wet spinning, patented in 1825, provided the stimulus to the development of a large factory-based industry, whose buildings remain throughout the region. The linen industry has suffered decline in recent decades but still employs about 6000 people. Several late nineteenth-century steam engines have been retained in mill buildings. Engineering and subsequently shipbuilding developed in Belfast on a scale that was internationally significant.

Manufactures elsewhere, even in the great cities of Dublin and Cork, were essentially those of market towns: malting, brewing, distilling, tanning and flour milling, with just a few textile enterprises. The Congested Districts Board, set up in 1891, encouraged domestic textile manufacturing, with some success in Donegal (see KILLY-BEGS). Distilling is now concentrated at Bushmills (see PORTRUSH) and Midleton, County Cork. Beet sugar refineries were established at Carlow, Mallow, Thurles and Tuam in the 1930s as part of moves towards self-sufficiency in the south.

The growth of main-line railways spread still more thinly the limited amount of inland commodity traffic. First to open was the Dublin & Kingstown in 1834, followed by the Ulster Railway between Belfast and Lisburn in 1839. During the 1840s a gauge of 5 ft. 3 in. (1.92 m) was adopted. Many railways were built with little economic justification. The relative profitability of the Great Northern Railway of Ireland arose from the disproportionate concentration of manufacturing in Belfast. Late in the nineteenth century narrow-gauge lines were constructed, many serving regions of sparse population that could offer little hope of financial viability. Since World War II the railway system, both in the Republic and in Northern Ireland, has been drastically pruned, although there has been investment to ensure the efficient use of the remaining network. The remains along the west coast of lines like the Tralee & Dingle and the Farranfore, Cahirciveen & Valentia Harbour are amongst the most evocative monuments of the optimism of the railway age.

From 1882 the Irish Commissioners of Public Works were responsible for all the country's ancient monuments, but new arrangements were made on both sides of the border after partition in 1921. In the Republic the National Monuments Acts 1930–87 placed the responsibility for historic buildings and sites with the Commissioners of Public Works, who exercise their authority through the Office of Public Works. Some historic monuments are owned by the Commission, and some are held in guardianship while remaining the property of their original owners. Other buildings and sites are included in a Register of Historical Monuments, which prevents demolition or alteration without due consultation. The National Monuments Advisory Council advises the Commissioners and local authorities on all matters relating to historic sites and buildings. In Northern Ireland through the Ancient Monuments Act (Northern Ireland) 1926 the Department of the Environment (NI) has exercised responsibility for historic buildings and monuments, having powers to list, schedule and acquire buildings similar to those enjoyed by the parallel bodies in mainland Britain. In 1948 Queen's University, Belfast, appointed a lecturer in archaeology who also served as the province's first Inspector of Ancient Monuments, and in 1950 the Ministry of Finance established an Ancient Monuments Branch. Scholars in Northern Ireland have subsequently been prominent in the development of industrial archaeology as a discipline. Green's book on County Down (1949) was one of the earliest regional surveys of

industrial monuments, while McCutcheon's massive study (1980) of the whole province has no equal anywhere in the world. A register of business archives is maintained in Dublin.

The Northern Ireland committee of the National Trust has also been involved in the conservation of industrial monuments, like the beetling mill at Wellbrook, near Cookstown. The Railway Preservation Society of Ireland operates the *Portrush Flyer*, the only scheduled steam-hauled service regularly run on a public main-line track in the British Isles, and has six locomotives from north and south of the border at its depot at Whitehead, County Antrim, including a J15 0-6-0 of 1879, an example of the most numerous type of Irish steam locomotive, and Beyer Peacock 4-4-0s of 1913 and 1932. The Great Southern Railway Preservation Society, with depots at Tralee and Mallow, has steam and diesel rolling stock on both broad and narrow gauges.

Most aspects of manufacturing industry in the North-East are covered in the Ulster Museum (see BELFAST). The Ulster Folk and Transport Museum has buildings and collections that relate to the whole of the northern part of Ireland, not just to the six counties of the province. The associated transport museum is concerned with the whole of Ireland, and includes the notable 4-6-0 locomotive 800 *Maedhbh* (Maeve), built at Inchicore, Dublin, in 1939; a narrow-gauge 2-6-4T of 1912 from the County Donegal system; and the last horse tramcar in the British Isles, which was pulled from Fintona Junction to Fintona, County Tyrone, until 1957.

A series of 1:126 720 maps covering the whole of Ireland is published by Ordnance Survey (Suirbheireacht Ordanais) in Dublin.

See also ALLIHIES; BALLYDEHOB; BELFAST; BELLEEK; BESSBROOK; CLONAKILTY; COALISLAND; COOKSTOWN; CORK; DRUMNACONAGHER; DUBLIN; FOYNES; GRAND CANAL; KILBEGGAN; KILLYBEGS; LIMERICK; LISTOWEL; LONDONDERRY; NEWRY; PORTRUSH; PROSPEROUS; SHANNON; SLANE; STRABANE.

BIBLIOGRAPHY
General
Barry, 1985; Bianconi and Watson, 1962; Conray, 1928; Crawford, 1972, 1987; Cullen, 1987; Delany, 1986; Edwards, 1981; Gill, 1925; Green, 1949, 1963; Kennedy and Ollerenshaw, 1983; Lee, 1981; Lewis, 1837; Lyons, 1971; MacManus, 1967; McCutcheon, 1980; Meenan, 1970; Middlemass, 1981; Moody et al., 1982; Moody and Vaughan, 1986; Morton, 1962; O'Brien, 1918; Popplewell, 1981; Rolt, 1949; Shaw-Smith, 1984.

Specific
Bowie, G. Surviving stationary steam engines in the Republic of Ireland. In *IAR*, VI(1) 1979–80.
Clarkson, L. A. The writing of Irish economic and social history since 1968. In *Economic History Review*, 2nd ser., XXXIII, 1980.
Cullen, L. M. Eighteenth-century flour milling in Ireland. In *Irish Economic and Social History*, IV, 1977.
Johnson, D. S. The economic history of Ireland between the wars. In *Irish Economic & Social History*, I, 1974.
McCutcheon, W. A. The use of documentary source material in the Northern Ireland Survey of Industrial Archaeology. In *EcHR*, 2nd ser., XIX(2) 1966.

McCutcheon, W. A. Water-powered corn and flax scutching mills in Ulster. In *Ulster Folklife*, XII, 1966.

McCutcheon, W. A. Water power in the North of Ireland. In *TNS*, XXXIX, 1966–7.

McCutcheon, W. A. The corn mill in Ulster. In *Ulster Folklife*, XV/XVI, 1970.

McCutcheon, W. A. The stationary steam engine in Ulster. In O'Danachair, C. ed. *Folk & Farm*. Dublin: Royal Society of Antiquaries of Ireland, 1976.

LOCATIONS

[I] Office of Public Works, 51 St Stephen's Green, Dublin 2, Ireland.

[I] Ordnance Survey Office, Phoenix Park, Dublin, Ireland.

[I] Railway Preservation Society of Ireland, Whitehead, County Antrim, Northern Ireland.

[I] Survey of Business Records, Irish MSS Commission, 73 Merrion Square, Dublin 2, Ireland.

SARAH HILL

iron 'Iron is not only the seat of every other manufacture but the mainspring, perhaps, of civilized society,' wrote the Englishman Francis Horner in the early nineteenth century. The manufacture of iron and steel is one of the key factors in industrial growth. Iron is the most abundant and useful of metals, its ores occurring in many forms, as solid seams, as nodules in strata of clay or shale, and as sand. Carbonate ores ($FeCO_3$) occur widely, particularly within the Coal Measures. Haematite ores (Fe_2O_3) have been worked in many countries, and in the nineteenth century were particularly valued for their phosphorus content (*see* SIR HENRY BESSEMER). Limonite ores are mostly made up of goethite ($Fe_2O_3.H_2O$ or $FeO.OH$). Iron ore is also found associated with deposits of non-ferrous metallic ores, and in the form of BOG IRON.

From a metallurgical point of view furnaces for reducing iron ore can be divided into two main groups: bowl and shaft furnaces. In England any kind of furnace used to produce wrought iron by a direct method is called a BLOOMERY. The variety of such furnaces was wide, and some continued in use long after the development of the BLAST FURNACE from the fifteenth century. The CATALAN FORGE was a sophisticated bowl furnace which used ores low in phosphorus and was therefore competitive with the blast furnace, while in Germany Zerennfeuer furnaces produced iron by direct reduction well into the eighteenth century. The blast furnace is a form of shaft furnace, which was developed in Europe in the Middle Ages. Excavations in Sweden have revealed a blast furnace producing PIG IRON in the twelfth century. There were many other forms of shaft furnace developed to suit particular local conditions. The Chinese had furnaces producing CAST IRON at an earlier date than those in Europe, but these are properly termed cast-iron furnaces, not blast furnaces.

In the seventeenth and eighteenth centuries WROUGHT IRON, made in a FORGE from PIG IRON, itself the product of the blast furnace, was the most commonly used form of the metal, but structural and engineering applications of cast iron developed rapidly after 1750. From the mid-nineteenth century MILD STEEL incorporating many of the properties of both wrought and cast iron came to be the most commonly used form. A FOUNDRY is a works at which cast iron and steel can be shaped into castings. Wrought iron or steel can be shaped by a ROLLING MILL, WIRE MILL, TUBE MILL, or FORGING PRESS, or by hammers (*see* DROP HAMMER; HELVE HAMMER; OLIVER; STEAM HAMMER; TILT HAMMER). Iron and steel can be treated by coating with tin (*see* TINPLATE), electroplating, enamelling, galvanizing and japanning. Traditional iron and steel products include CHAINS; CUTLERY; FILES; locks (*see* LOCKSMITH); NEEDLES; PINS; RAZORS; SAWS; SCYTHES; SPRINGS.

BIBLIOGRAPHY

General

Beck, 1891, 1893–5; Bjorkenstam and Fornander, 1985; Bjorkenstam and Magnusson, 1988; Fairbairn, 1861; Gale, 1967, 1969, 1971; Johannsen, 1953; Schuhmann, 1984; Sperl, 1985; Tylecote, 1986.

BARRIE TRINDER

iron bridge   Iron was used in bridges in medieval China. There were plans for an iron bridge in Lyons, France, in the 1750s, and a small structure was probably completed at Kirklees, Yorkshire, England, in 1770. Nevertheless, in the late eighteenth century and for decades thereafter the bridge across the River Severn near Coalbrookdale in Shropshire, England, designed by Thomas Farnolls Pritchard (1723–77) and built by Abraham Darby III (1750–89), was recognized as the first iron bridge. The project was mooted by Pritchard to JOHN WILKINSON in 1773, parliamentary sanction was gained in 1776, and after much hesitation construction began late in 1777. The ironwork was erected in the summer of 1779 and the bridge opened on 1 January 1781. It was much celebrated and reproduced in many engravings, as well as on TRADE TOKENS and pottery. The bridge was a five-rib semicircular arch, but no subsequent bridge of consequence took this form. A replica in wrought iron was built at Worlitz, 12 km (8 mi.) E. of Dessau, Germany, in 1791, to be followed by major bridges in Prussia, France and Hungary. Several iron arches with cast-iron VOUSSOIRS on a principle devised by Rowland Burdon (1756–1836) and Thomas Wilson of Sunderland, England, were built, the most celebrated at Sunderland. Examples remain at Stratfield Saye, Hampshire, Newport Pagnell, Buckinghamshire, in England; and in Jamaica. THOMAS TELFORD's first iron bridge was completed at Buildwas, Shropshire, in 1796. In 1800 Telford put forward a design for a single iron arch to replace London Bridge, but confidence had been diminished by the collapse of several iron bridges, and the development of SUSPENSION BRIDGES brought an end to proposals for colossal arches in iron. Arches up to 50 m (170 ft.) in span continued to be built for major road and river crossings until the 1880s, as did many small iron bridges which could be erected around DOCKS, while the decorative qualities of cast iron led to its use for ornamental bridges in parks. From the 1880s the use of iron bridges was supplanted by steel or concrete structures. Iron was extensively used in truss, girder and suspension bridges

Figure 62   The Wellington or Halfpenny Bridge across the Liffey in Dublin, designed by John Windsor with iron ribs cast by the Coalbrookdale Company in 1816
Barrie Trinder

but the term 'iron bridge' normally implies a cast-iron arch.

See also figures 73, 166.

BIBLIOGRAPHY
General
Cossons and Trinder, 1979; Ruddock, 1979; Smith, 1979; Trinder, 1981.
Specific
James, J. G. Thomas Wilson's iron bridges. In *TNS*, L, 1978–9.
James, J. G. Russian iron bridges to 1850. In *TNS*, LIV, 1982–3.
Northcliffe, D. *A Preliminary Report on the Kirklees Iron Bridge of 1769 and its Builder*. Privately published, n.d.
Trinder, B. The first iron bridges. In *IAR*, III, 1979.

BARRIE TRINDER

Ironbridge, Shropshire, England   The Ironbridge Gorge, where the River Severn cuts through the high land of the Coalbrookdale coalfield, was the centre from which the British iron industry expanded during the Industrial Revolution. The achievements of the Ironbridge Gorge Museum in conserving the area were acknowledged when the Gorge was designated a UNESCO World Heritage Site in 1986. The 5 km (3 mi.) length of the Gorge includes the settlements of Ironbridge, Coalbrookdale, Coalport, Caughley, Blists Hill and Jackfield.

Large-scale exploitation of coal began in the late sixteenth century, and in the early seventeenth century wooden railways were used to carry coal to the river, and the LONGWALL system of mining coal was introduced. By c.1700 there were potteries, clay pipe manufactories, saltworks, glass houses, and lead smelters in the area. In 1708 ABRAHAM DARBY I (1678–1717) leased a derelict blast furnace at Coalbrookdale, and in 1709 began to smelt iron ore using coke instead of charcoal. The iron industry expanded in the 1750s as companies were established which leased land for mining, and produced coal, bricks and lime in addition to iron and iron products. The Iron Bridge, universally acknowledged at the time to have been the first of its kind, was built in 1777–81 to the design of Thomas Farnolls Pritchard (1723–77), under the supervision of Abraham Darby III (1750–89). Iron railways were introduced in 1767, and a network of tub-boat canals with six inclined planes was constructed. Lord Dundonald (1749–1831) experimented with the destructive distillation of coal and with the production of alkali in the area, while RICHARD TREVITHICK built a steam railway locomotive at Coalbrookdale in 1802. Porcelain factories were established at Caughley in the 1770s and at Coalport in the 1790s. For a time the Ironbridge Gorge attracted visitors from overseas, and many artists recorded the area. In the nineteenth century the region lost its pre-eminence in the iron trade, but the production of art castings in iron (introduced at Coalbrookdale c.1838) and the manufacture of decorative tiles both prospered. After 1880 the iron trade declined rapidly. Lack of development in the early twentieth century ensured the survival of many monuments of the Industrial Revolution.

In 1959, on the occasion of the 250th anniversary of the introduction of coke-smelting, the owners of the

Figure 63 Rolling of wrought iron in progress at the Blists Hill Open Air Museum, part of the Ironbridge Gorge Museum, where the puddling process was revived in 1986
John Powell

Coalbrookdale ironworks uncovered the Old Furnace used by Abraham Darby I, and established a small museum. The Ironbridge Gorge Museum Trust was set up in 1967 when redevelopment was imminent. It took over the museum in Coalbrookdale in 1970, established a museum in the former porcelain factory at Coalport in 1976, and in 1977 opened a visitor centre in a riverside warehouse in the Gothic style of *c*.1840. In 1979 the Trust established a new Museum of Iron in the Great Warehouse, Coalbrookdale, replacing the museum of 1959. It has displays illustrating ironmaking, and portraits of ironmasters of the Industrial Revolution, many nineteenth-century art castings and iron artefacts of all dates. The Old Furnace was enclosed in a modern cover building in 1982. The Trust began to restore the Craven Dunnill tileworks at Jackfield in 1983, and holds large collections of tiles, moulds and designs there. An open-air museum has been established on a former industrial site at Blists Hill, where there are remains of nineteenth-century blast furnaces, a brick and tile works, and the Hay inclined plane on the Shropshire Canal. The museum portrays the way of life of a late nineteenth-century industrial community. Its outstanding feature is an ironworks where wrought iron is manufactured in puddling furnaces, shingled under a

steam hammer, and rolled into bars. Other exhibits include a working foundry; a factory making candles by dipping; a sawmill where a horizontal reciprocating saw is worked by a Fielding & Platt oil engine of *c*.1914; a tollhouse designed by THOMAS TELFORD for the HOLYHEAD ROAD; and a squatter cottage. Three stationary steam engines are operated, and non-working engines include two beam engines built by Murdoch, Aitken & Co. of Glasgow in 1851 to blow blast furnaces at Priorslee, Shropshire. The Trust has responsibility for the Bedlam ironworks, a group of blast furnaces of the 1750s, of which there are substantial remains, and for the Tar Tunnel, a 300 m (330 yd.) tunnel driven into the side of the Gorge in 1786, where natural bitumen was exploited. The Trust collaborates with the University of Birmingham in the Ironbridge Institute, which provides postgraduate programmes in industrial archaeology.

BIBLIOGRAPHY
General
Cossons and Trinder, 1979; Smith, 1979; Trinder, 1981.
Specific
Cossons, N. Ironbridge – the first ten years. In *IAR*, III, 1979.
Raistrick, A. The old furnace at Coalbrookdale, Shropshire. In *IAR*, IV, 1980.

LOCATION
[I] Ironbridge Gorge Museum Trust, Ironbridge, Telford, Shropshire TF8 7AW.

BARRIE TRINDER

Iron Gates (Porţile de Fier), Romania and Yugoslavia   The name Iron Gates has traditionally been given to the gorges by which the River DANUBE passes through the Southern Carpathian Mountains (the Transylvanian Alps). In the nineteenth century this stretch of the river was bounded by Hungary and Serbia. It now forms the boundary between Romania and Yugoslavia. The 'cataract region' begins below Moldova Island, 130 km (80 mi.) downstream from Belgrade, and extends for 120 km (75 mi.), over which distance the natural fall of the river is 30 m (100 ft.). At Baziaş, upstream from the gorges, the Danube is 2 km (1.1 mi.) wide, but it contracts to less than 100 m (330 ft.) in the gorges. The highest cliffs, at Sterbez, rise some 683 m (2240 ft.) sheer from the surface of the river. Where the slope allows it, the sides of the gorges are thickly wooded. The Danube runs in a north-easterly direction through the Kazan Gorge and past the Tabula Trajana. At the modern town of Orşova it is joined by the River Cerna, and then turns to flow towards the southeast. It is much wider than in the gorges, but the rapid rate of flow is maintained, and the Iron Gates, 10 km (6 mi.) SE of Orşova, was a long line of rocks like black teeth sticking out of the fast-running water.

A towing path, partly on a shelf cut out of the cliffs, and partly cantilevered on wooden beams, was cut through the gorges by the Emperor Trajan and his successors between AD 28 and 102, an event commemorated by the inscription known as the 'Tabula Trajana'. Commercial traffic was sparse on this section of the river before the nineteenth century. The first steamship to pass through the Iron Gates was the DDSG vessel (*see* AUSTRIA) *Argo* in 1834. Some improvements to the channel were made by the DDSG from 1847, and by the Austrian Army from 1854. Three primitive cuts at Djevrin, Sip and Mali Djerdap assisted the passage of steamers through the gorges. In 1878 the Hungarian government was empowered by the Congress of Berlin to improve the navigation and to charge tolls, its activities being supervised by the International Danube Commission. A channel 2 m (6 ft. 6 in.) deep and 60 m (200 ft.) wide was cut through the rocks, and at the Iron Gates the Sip Canal, 2.5 km ($1\frac{1}{2}$ mi.) long and with a fall of 3.7 m (12 ft.), was built on the southern side of the river in 1895–8. A railway track was laid alongside and vessels were hauled upstream by heavy locomotives. The passage of boats through the gorges trebled between 1900 and 1912. After World War II Romania and Yugoslavia agreed to build a hydro-electric barrage at the Iron Gates with staircase pairs of locks on each side. The scheme was completed in 1972, a masterpiece of twentieth-century technology, but it has submerged both the works of Trajan and the late nineteenth-century attempts to ease the river passage between Eastern and Western Europe.

BIBLIOGRAPHY
General
Farson, 1926; Hadfield, 1986.

LOCATION
[M] Museul Porţile de Fier (Iron Gates Museum), str. Independentei 2, Drobeta Jurnu-Severin.

BARRIE TRINDER

iron ship   The first practical iron vessel was probably the *Trial*, a Severn barge launched by the ironmaster JOHN WILKINSON near IRONBRIDGE in 1787, but neither it nor subsequent iron NARROW BOATS built by Wilkinson showed any cost advantage over wooden vessels.

ISAMBARD KINGDOM BRUNEL's 3270-ton SS *Great Britain* of 1843, which began to work between Liverpool and New York in 1845, effectively demonstrated the suitability of iron for ocean going ships. The vessel ran aground at Dundrum Bay, Ireland, in 1846, but from 1852 until 1876 was successfully employed in the Australia trade. Brunel's 18 915-ton *Great Eastern*, built at Blackwall, London, in 1854–8 by John Scott Russell (1808–82), represented a vast increase in size, but she was operated with success only between 1865 and 1874 when she was laying transatlantic cables, and was not exceeded in size until the end of the nineteenth century. Iron was certainly not the normal material for ships in 1860, but the Liverpool barque *Altcar* of 1864 was the first substantial vessel to have a steel hull, and from the 1880s the use of steel for sailing as well as steam ships was widespread. Apart from the SS *Great Britain*, preserved at Bristol, important surviving iron-built vessels include the *Hipparchus*, a transitional sail-carrying, iron-hulled steamer built at Newcastle-upon-Tyne in 1867 and survives at PUNTA ARENAS, and HMS *Warrior* of 1860, the first ironclad in the British Royal Navy, preserved at PORTSMOUTH. Iron construction aided prefabrication, and on Lake Titicaca, Chile, are the *Chucuito* and the *Puno*, two British iron-hulled steamers taken there in parts in 1862 and 1871; while at Kigoma on Lake Tanganyika is the *Liemba*, a 1575-ton steel German steamer of 1914.

BIBLIOGRAPHY
General
Baker, 1965; Brouwer, 1985; Corlett, 1975; Emmerson, n.d.; Lubbock, 1927; Trinder, 1981; Walton, 1902.
Specific
Caldwell, J. B. The three great ships. In Pugsley, 1976.

BARRIE TRINDER

Irvine, Strathclyde, Scotland   A NEW TOWN, where the river mouth is being developed as a leisure attraction. The Scottish Maritime Museum, an independent museum established in 1983 when the West of Scotland Boat Museum moved to Irvine, has thirty-eight boats beside wood-piled quays, including the MV *Spartan* of 1942 and the coaster *Kyles* of 1872, both now diesel-engined. The museum is re-erecting a cast-iron-framed Linthouse engine shop (*see* GLASGOW) of 1872 to house turbines of 1901 from the *King Edward* (*see* TURBINE PROPULSION), the

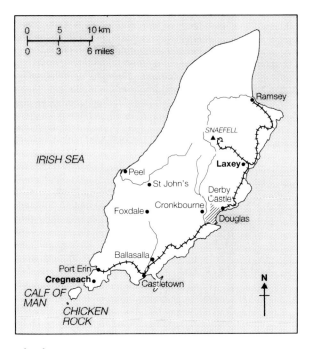

Isle of Man

cylinder of the *Comet* of 1812 (*see* STEAMSHIP) by Henry Bell (1767–1830), ropewalk equipment from Gourock Ropeworks, and a collection of large machine tools, punching and shearing machines, plate edge planers, steam hammers, and a pipe-bending machine. The museum is also responsible for a re-created shipbuilder's flat, the small Customs House, and the office and test house of the firm Laird Forge, established in 1881, which manufactured BLOCKS. (*See also* DUNBARTONSHIRE.)

Railway monuments in Irvine include a late nineteenth-century railway signal works, a station of 1839, and a six-arch stone viaduct.

LOCATION
[M] Scottish Maritime Museum, Laird Forge, Gottries Road, Irvine, Ayrshire KA12 8QE.

MARK WATSON

Isle of Man The Isle of Man lies in the Irish Sea some 120 km (75 mi.) NW of Liverpool and the same distance NE of Dublin. It extends 56 km (35 mi.) north–south and 16 km (10 mi.) east–west, with a range of hills in the centre rising to 621 m (1034 ft.) at the summit of Snaefell. The island is a lordship of the British crown, but has never been part of the United Kingdom, being governed by the Tynwald, its 800-year-old parliament, under statutes which date from 1866. The resort of Douglas on the east coast is the capital and centre of administration. The island's archaeology reflects a rich mixture of Scottish, English, Norse and Irish influences.

The island's many lighthouses are amongst the most important in the British Isles, the first, on the Calf, the small island to the south, having been built by ROBERT STEVENSON in 1818. The Granite Tower on Chicken Rock to the south of the Calf was constructed in 1869–75. The Isle of Man Steam Packet Company which links the island with Britain was founded in 1830. The nautical museum at Castletown displays the island's maritime past. Exhibits include a completely equipped sail loft and a ship's biscuit machine.

Lead and zinc ores have been extensively mined, mostly near Laxey, site of the water wheel that is the island's best-known landmark, and in the Foxdale area, 10 km (6 mi.) W. of Douglas. At Beckwith's lead mine, 3 km (2 mi.) W. of Foxdale, which was worked by the Isle of Man Mining Co. from *c*.1831–70, there are remains of a Cornish engine house and a crusher.

A water-powered cotton mill was built in 1780 at Ballasalla, 3 km (2 mi.) NE of Castletown, but worked only until *c*.1792. At St John's, 11 km (7 mi.) NW of Douglas, is the Tynwald mill, a three-storey building once used for the manufacture of blankets. The most impressive monument of the Manx textile industry is the village of Cronkbourne, 2 km (1 mi.) NW of Douglas, where forty-two one- and two-storey houses were built to accommodate the employees at William Moore's Tromode flax works.

Communications across the island were poor until the second half of the nineteenth century when most of the present road system was constructed. The first railway on the island, the 3 ft. (0.9 m) gauge, 25 km (15 mi.) route from Douglas to Peel, was opened in 1873 but no longer operates. The present Manx Steam Railway from the capital to Port Erin is still worked by Beyer Peacock 2–4–0T locomotives designed in 1873. The Douglas Horse Tramway, along the capital's elegant promenade to Derby Castle, is also of 3 ft. gauge and opened in 1876. Derby Castle is the terminus of the 20 km (12 mi.) Manx Electric Railway which opened to LAXEY in 1893 and to Ramsey in 1899.

Significant numbers of tourists were visiting the island as early as the 1830s, and railways and steamships brought a boom in the 1860s and 70s. Among the manufactures stimulated by tourism was brewing, and two notable breweries survive: Clinch's Lake Brewery on the North Quay at Douglas, which originated in 1779 but has buildings dating from 1868, and the Castletown Brewery dating from *c*.1830, which has a crenellated tower brewhouse.

The principal museums together with various other properties are administered by the Manx Museum and National Trust, constituted in 1886. The headquarters is the Manx Museum in Douglas, where there is a card index of industrial archaeological sites, with branches at CREGNEACH, the open-air folk museum, and Castletown (see above). Maps of the Isle of Man are published by the Ordnance Survey in Britain.

See also CREGNEACH; LAXEY.

BIBLIOGRAPHY
General
Garrad *et al.*, 1972.

BARRIE TRINDER

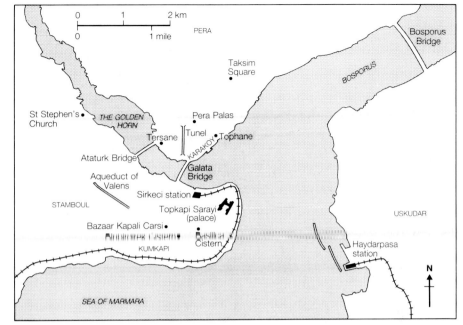

Istanbul

Isola del Liri, Latium, Italy   A centre of papermaking from the sixteenth century, 90 km (60 mi.) E. of Rome, with an abundance of water provided by a confluence of rivers. Sixty-four firms were operating in 1800. Mechanized production was introduced in 1812. The small Mancini works on the main island in the river has workshops behind the owner's villa, together with a sluice and a small hydro-electric power station. The Fibreno factory has neo-Classical detailing; while the Tiburtina works has one roof truss resting on the arcade of a temple of the first century BC.

BIBLIOGRAPHY
General
Negri *et al.*, 1983

Istanbul (Byzantium, Constantinople), Turkey   For sixteen centuries Constantinople was the capital of two successive empires, each, at its peak, the greatest in the world. The city was the largest in the world and its location made it a major centre of commerce.

Byzantium was founded in 667 BC. Constantine the Great chose in AD 330 to remove the capital of the Roman Empire to what became Constantinople. The Empire has subsequently been labelled Byzantine. By the fifteenth century the Empire was seriously weakened and in 1453 the city was captured by Mehmet II, 'the Conqueror', who made it the capital of the Ottoman Empire, renaming it Istanbul, a corruption of the Greek for 'in the city'. The Ottoman Empire reached its peak during the reign of Suleiman the Magnificent, between 1520 and 1566. It thereafter declined, as did Istanbul's predominance in the arts and trade.

Istanbul's interest to the industrial archaeologist lies in the monuments from its mercantile past, in the persist-

ence of traditional handicrafts and small workshops, in the efforts to modernize in the nineteenth and twentieth centuries, and in the foreign contributions to those efforts.

Today the city sprawls out into two continents, contains about 7 million inhabitants, and has on its outskirts every kind of factory, including one whose sole product is statues of Ataturk. This account is concerned with the old city of Stamboul itself, with Pera on the north side of the Golden Horn, traditionally the foreign quarter, and with Uskudar on the Asian shore of the Bosporus.

The Byzantines bequeathed to Istanbul a fascinating system of underground cisterns which were used throughout the Ottoman period. The largest, the Yerebatan Saray or Basilica cistern, was built by Justinian in the 530s and served the imperial palaces. Brick domical vaults are carried on Corinthian capitalled columns across an area 140 m × 70 m (425 ft. × 210 ft.). The system is open to the public. The second largest, Binbirdirek, is now dry, and was used for spinning, probably of silk, in the nineteenth century. The aqueduct of Valens built around AD 375 retains two-thirds of its 1000 m (1100 yd.) length, and was in use until *c.*1900. The Ottomans added water distribution points called 'taksim', most notably that at Taksim Square, built in 1731 and repaired in 1785; pyramidal water balance towers called 'suterazi', which reduced the velocity of flowing water; and ornamental drinking fountains called 'fesme'. In the 1880s the Compagnie des Eaux de Constantinople improved the supply of water from Lake Derkos (Durusu), 48 km (30 mi.) NW.

Istanbul's BAZAARS are prototypes for every covered shopping arcade but are surpassed by none. The Kapali Carsi is a labyrinthine bazaar established soon after the Ottoman conquest, and much rebuilt after earthquakes and fires. It contains several kilometres of shops beneath

Figure 64 The church of St Stephen, Istanbul, built for the Bulgarian Exarchate in 1871; the building was constructed of iron parts, cast at a foundry in Vienna, and shipped along the Danube.
Mark Watson

vaulted and domed masonry. Attached to some of them are 'hani', secure courtyards for the storage of goods and the accommodation of travelling merchants and their pack animals. Some date from the late nineteenth century and have galleries on cast-iron columns. The craft workshops of the old city are concentrated on the fringes of the bazaar, notably the Bakircilar Caddesi, where coppersmiths still hammer; and, to the north, the silk, cotton and wool exchanges where great bundles are still carried on human backs, and the click of the hand loom is still heard.

In the sixteenth century Tersane, the arsenal and shipyard in the Golden Horn, could accommodate 120 ships and was unparalleled in the world, but less survives from that period than at VENICE. A naval school was formed under British guidance *c.*1870 to build steam-powered ironclads. The first was said to be the most expensive ever constructed. A three-aisle marine engine works from that period has similarities to works in Scotland: an apparent two-storey exterior, probably masking a cast-iron frame, and wide, hipped timber roofs. Some ancient dry docks are flanked by gabled single-storey workshops from which a tall, square chimney stack protrudes. This most interesting shipyard remains in use, servicing ferries as well as naval craft.

Tophane, the gun foundry, is on the site adopted for the purpose soon after 1453, but the present building was built in 1803 by Selim III as part of his attempt to modernize the army. It appears from the exterior like an overscaled Turkish bath, having eight large domes on three piers, with eight tall ventilators. It is still occupied by the army and is inaccessible to visitors.

Other attempts by nineteenth-century sultans to modernize the Ottoman economy resemble those of the absolute monarchs of the *ancien régime*, working from the top downwards, and trying to set high standards in the manufacture of luxuries. So Istanbul has the Yildez Porselen Fabrikasi, still making porcelain inspired by the vulgar wares sent to the palace from Europe. The artistic standards achieved are deplorable when set against the indigenous sixteenth-century İznik tiles, now being revealed beneath early nineteenth-century Baroque frescos in Topaki Saray.

The Press Museum was opened in May 1988 in celebration of the freedom of the press. It contains British and German printing machines, including an Augsburg of 1892 driven by a Blackstone oil engine, a linotype machine, and a reconstructed hand printer's office. Small printing machines of great antiquity are to be found in many working printers' shops.

The ancient bridge of boats across the Golden Horn linking Stamboul with Pera was replaced in the late nineteenth century by a floating wrought-iron bridge of German design. Each morning the central Moorish arcaded section was floated on its pontoons out and to one side to allow ships to pass in and out of the Horn. The lower section provided a ferry landing stage, shops, and fish restaurants. It was replaced in 1988, when the old bridge was floated to a mooring further upstream. The first Bosporus suspension bridge, opened in 1973, has a span of 1074 m (3523 ft.), the fourth largest in the world.

The railway terminus for European trains, Sirkeci Gar, has a long brick and stone façade with a central domical entrance. The platforms have new concrete shelters. A steam tank locomotive of 1874 by Krauss of Munich is displayed outside. Haydarpasa station serves trains for Anatolia and is much larger. Pera Palas in Tepebasi, the luxury hotel for travellers on Georges Nagelmacker's Orient Express was far from the stations. Its 1890s opulence still attracts nostalgic travellers. Tunel, a French-built underground funicular railway, was opened in 1875 and has recently been modernized. The Tram Museum in an old tramway depot contains horse-drawn and electric trams and other vehicles, including some of the original Tunel carriages.

Whereas Byzantine buildings are characterized by layers of rubble and brick, the Turks introduced much timber into Istanbul's domestic architecture. Districts like Kumpapi that have escaped serious fires have many nineteenth-century timber-fronted houses, frequently with ornate jettied balconies. Metal plates coat some houses. The Gothic-Baroque church of St Stephen between Mursepasa Caddesi and the Golden Horn was built in 1871 for the Bulgarian Exarchate. It is entirely of cast iron, prefabricated by the Wagner company in Vienna, and shipped down the Danube. The roof is of sheet metal and many of the interior fittings are also metallic.

BIBLIOGRAPHY
General
Brosnahan, 1988; Freely, 1983; Murray, 1900; Summer-Boyd and Freeby, 1974.

LOCATIONS
[M] Maritime Museum, Barbaros parki yani Besiktas, Istanbul.
[M] Municipal Museum, Srachanebasi Fatik, Hayezit Square, Istanbul.
[M] Museum of Carpets and Kilims, Sultanhamet, Istanbul.
[M] Museum of Tiles and Ceramics, Sultanhamet, Istanbul.
[M] Press Museum, Basin Muzesi, 83 Yenicerila Caddesi, Istanbul.
[M] Tram Museum, Kusdili Tramvay Deposu, Kadikoy, Istanbul.

MARK WATSON

Italianate A style of ARCHITECTURE, derived from various historical periods of Italian building, which was popular in the mid-nineteenth century, often incorporating CAMPANILE and ARCADING on exterior walls. It was associated particularly with commercial buildings such as banks. The Italianate was a practical style for long façades as it readily accommodated repetition.

Italy Italy tends to be classified in industrial archaeology as a Mediterranean also-ran; but although large-scale industrialization only followed unification in 1861, the constituent states played crucial roles in the development of Western technology, through Roman aqueducts, Renaissance technology, and the foundation of the silk industry. Austrian, French and Spanish control of the various states was reflected in the pattern of early industrialization, while railway and engineering technology was imported from Britain. During the last hundred years Italians have made key contributions to the generation and application of electricity, to the use of concrete, and more latterly in industrial design.

Italy became united primarily through accretions by the principality of PIEDMONT, and incorporates the large islands of SICILY and SARDINIA. Numerous changes in boundaries occurred both before and after the Risorgimento, the national resurgence of the 1850s and 60s, the most significant being the addition of the Alpine areas of Trentino, upper Adige and Friuli-Venezia Giulia since World War I. The port of TRIESTE was ceded to Italy in 1920, the current boundaries with Yugoslavia being agreed in 1954. Italy surrounds two small independent states, San Marino near Ancona, and the Vatican City in Rome.

Population growth has only become rapid in the twentieth century. In 1800 about 18 800 000 people lived within the current boundaries of Italy. The figure doubled between 1825 and 1925 to around 39 million, and is now over 56 million. In the late nineteenth century the greatest growth was in the 'heel' of Apulia and Sicily;

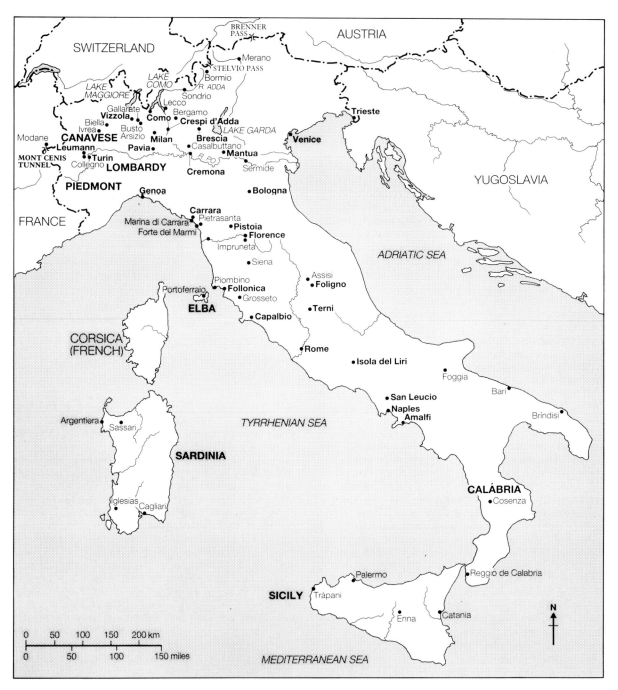

Italy

in the twentieth it has been in the industrial north. Emigration, particularly heavy in the first decade of the twentieth century, has been supplanted by a movement from south to north on a permanent or seasonal basis; up to 10 million moved to the northern industrial regions in the two decades after 1945.

The Romans left to posterity a series of massive aqueducts, while among the monuments of the Renaissance are formal systems of fortifications and extensive road systems. Cloth-making and -finishing and the production of paper, glass, silk and armaments had developed by the late medieval period. Complemented by a system of bank credit and money exchange, such trades supported large urban populations of around 200 000 in MILAN and

VENICE in the mid-fourteenth century. The inventions and writings of Andrea del Verrocchio (?1435–88) in engineering, of Leone Battista Alberti (1404–72) in applied science and of Michelangelo Buonarroti (1475–1564) in fortification, and the futuristic inventions of Leonardo da Vinci (1452–1519), were to inspire developments throughout Europe as a result of printing, which came to be widely practised during the Renaissance.

Silk offers an important example of the pre-eminence and transfer of Italian technology. From the thirteenth century throwing mills were established in Piedmont, with undershot water wheels powering machines that drew and wound the silk thread. These were supplanted by multi-storey factories accommodating tall cylindrical frames carrying spindles and reels. Mills built c.1700 in the foothills of the Alps in Piedmont and Lombardy, and in BOLOGNA, pioneered the layout and form of the factories and warehouses associated with the Industrial Revolution in Britain. The Italian form of the silk-throwing mill was patented by Thomas Lombe (1685–1739) in 1718 and applied in his mill in DERBY, arguably Britain's first factory.

The French invasions of Italy from 1494 precipitated almost four centuries of relative stagnation, with the silk industry actually declining in the seventeenth and eighteenth centuries. In the eighteenth century 80 per cent of Italy's working population were employed in agriculture, most manufacturing production being at a handicraft level. Growth was constrained by a lack of natural resources, the country lacking both fertile land and coal. The Italian iron industry used the technology of Provence or Spain rather than that of northern Europe, with blast furnaces supported by towers and blown by water TROMPES (see CAPALBIO).

Large-scale industrial development first occurred in the textile industry, partly because of its close relationship with agriculture, but also in response to the abundance of water power in the sub-Alpine regions of Lombardy and Piedmont. The flying shuttle was introduced at Schio in Venetia in 1738. In the early nineteenth century stagnation in the farming economy and low wages stimulated the development of mills. The silk industry started to expand around COMO in Lombardy and TURIN in Piedmont, while cotton production grew around Milan, the first large mill being established at Gallarate in 1812 (see LOMBARDY). A woollen industry also became established on the edge of the Alps, especially in Piedmont, though with less mechanization.

The early stages of industrialization in the Kingdom of Naples were marked by royal initiatives, the Bourbon monarchs in the eighteenth century promoting silkmaking at SAN LEUCIO, armaments manufacture at Torre Annunziata and engineering at Pietrarsa near NAPLES.

During the period of Risorgimento, from 1815 to 1861, economic development was slow. There was investment in some branches of agriculture, such as sugar refining and the processing of pasta, and foodstuffs were to constitute Italy's major export in the late nineteenth century. The pottery industry developed larger domestic and export markets, the working of the red-burning clays

being concentrated around MILAN, BOLOGNA and FLORENCE. Papermaking expanded around Fabriano and Bologna, and further south at ISOLA DEL LIRI. Metal- and glass-working developed in many towns, but heavy industry was largely restricted to armaments factories at GENOA, Turin and Naples, and shipyards at Genoa and Sestri Ponente near Naples.

Railways were fundamental to the policy of Camillo Cavour (1810–61) of creating a unified nation. They also triggered a late but dramatic industrial revolution. The first line to be opened was in the south, linking Naples and Portici in 1839. Most of the early lines were in the north, initially in Lombardy and Venetia. Cavour promoted the connection of Piedmont with France through the Alps, the Mont Cenis tunnel being started in 1857. After 1862 the newly established Kingdom of Italy promoted a spate of construction. Concessions were granted to companies, the costs of constructing lines being refunded once the lines were opened. By a law of 1885 Italy's railways were allocated to three large companies; in 1905 came the formation of the state railway, the Ferrovie dello Stato (FS). The first locomotives to operate in Italy were mostly 2-2-2s built in England. Later Italian-built locomotives were characterized by innovative technology, often giving them rather bizarre appearances. Italian developments applied elsewhere during the last decades of steam included Caprotti valve gears, and Crosti boilers, in which combustion gases passed through large pre-heaters.

Italy was at the forefront of railway electrification in the 1890s, with high-voltage systems operating north of Milan from 1901. After 1918 extensive schemes were implemented using the 3000 V d.c. system, and promoted by Benito Mussolini (1883–1945), whose policy was to reduce the country's dependence on imported coal.

Alessandro Volta (1745–1827), Luigi Galvani (1737–98) and GUGLIELMO MARCONI were key figures in the development of electric power and telecommunications. Antonio Pacinotti is less well known although it was he who in 1860 made the first effective dynamo, and who appreciated that this, when wired in reverse, formed an electric motor. The Italian commitment to electricity followed from the shortage of coal, and the abundant potential for hydro-electric power, both in the Alps and the Apennines. The Tivoli plant, opened in 1855, was one of the first to generate electricity from water power, and probably the first to furnish light and power from a distance. By 1892 it was supplying Rome, some 26 km (16 mi.) away. By 1895 there were 1240 power stations in Italy. Subsequent investment concentrated on fewer and larger plants. Several of those built on the River Adda to supply Milan from 1898 were given flamboyant architectural expression (see CRESPI D'ADDA; VIZZOLA), severer designs characterizing the stations in the higher mountain regions during the inter-war period.

Railways and electricity promoted heavy industry, most developments being co-ordinated by the state. Blast furnaces were erected at Portoferráio on ELBA in 1899. Steelworks developed at Savona, Genoa and Naples, pig iron smelted from ore from Elba being combined with scrap in OPEN-HEARTH FURNACES. Some plants were sited as much for strategic as economic reasons, an example being the works established at the secure inland location of TERNI, Umbria, in 1886. The largest engineering firms were primarily involved in making ships or armaments, most of them dependent on government contracts and on re-working British technology. The Ernesto Breda company in Milan made railway equipment and small vessels, including submarines. Armaments were also made at Naples, at Turin and at the Ansaldo plant in Genoa. Large shipyards were laid out at Genoa and Sestri Ponente near Naples, while the fleet of the Habsburg Empire was maintained at Trieste and Monfalcone. Turin developed as a major motorcar manufacturing centre. In 1898 Michele Lanza displayed Italy's first motor vehicle in the city, and in 1899 Giovanni Agnelli (1866–1945) opened his first works, soon to be trading as Fiat. At Ivrea, also in Piedmont, Camillo Olivetti established his typewriter works in 1911. Tariffs contributed to this industrial boom, growth being particularly rapid in the years before 1914.

Italy achieved rapid developments in the chemical industry, using such indigenous raw materials as the sulphur deposits of SICILY. The manufacture of ARTIFICIAL FERTILIZERS began in 1875. The Pirelli company was established in 1872, and led the development of the manufacture of tyres and other rubber products. The chemical, motorcar and commercial vehicle industries expanded dramatically during World War I. The establishment of a dictatorship under Benito Mussolini in 1926 led to economic policies aimed at self-sufficiency and overcoming the north–south imbalance. There was some exploitation of oil and natural gas. More dramatic was the major investment in roads from 1928, and in water supply, involving bold use of concrete for bridges and aqueducts. Such construction, and the building of aircraft hangars and underground petroleum stores as parts of the rearmament programme, resulted in concrete being used to impressive effect by a group of architects and engineers led by Pier Luigi Nervi (1891–1979).

One of the 'miracles' of post-war reconstruction was the application of concrete to such public and commercial buildings as the railway terminus in ROME designed by Montuori & Calini. This confidence also emerged in motorcar design, and in the making of stylish electrical appliances. From a late start, Italy had industrialized with a rush and with considerable panache to become renowned for the design of its commercial and public buildings, and its motorcars, typewriters and furniture.

Conservation legislation dates from the early twentieth century, but until recently has been cumbersome, and there have been insufficient staff for it to be effective. A law of 1909 allowed for the designation of monuments by the state, the notification being announced by a public crier. It deemed that any work on such monuments needed the permission of the Inspectorate of Monuments. By a law of 1939 the Minister of Public Instruction can compulsorily purchase a building when it is for sale, by matching the price accepted from a private buyer. This law also introduced protection for the surroundings of a monument. The provisions introduced for ensuring the repair of

monuments by the intervention of the state proved largely ineffective except with buildings owned by such corporate bodies as the Church, and were replaced in 1961 by a system whereby the Ministry can give restoration grants of up to 50 per cent.

The listing of buildings has been slow since the restrictive covenant has to be closely tied to the pattern of ownership; buildings in corporate ownership have gained greater protection than those in private hands. Recently the State Historic Preservation Office has proved more willing to afford protection to such industrial monuments as a blast furnace in Val Trompi, or a lime plant in Brescia. The greatest progress in conservation has been achieved in particular provinces, such as Milan, where monuments have been purchased for restoration by communes, and Bologna, where conservation has become an integral element of Communist local government. Some southern provinces have also been active in identifying and protecting industrial sites.

Until recently Italy could boast few industrial museums beyond the typical railway and scientific collections like those at the Leonardo da Vinci National Museum of Science and Technology in Milan. There are several current proposals for museums of 'material life'. A mining museum with strong community involvement is planned for Massa Marittima, 60 km (40 mi.) SW of Siena, and another at Inglesias on Sardinia. There are projects for industrial museums in Bologna, Naples, Rome and Terni, and for a silk museum at San Leucio.

There is growing commercial and public interest in adaptive reuse, great interest having been roused by plans for the rehabilitation of the Arsenale in VENICE, and the Lingotto factory in TURIN. Many redundant buildings in Turin and Milan have been converted, often with support from the municipal governments.

Italy is witnessing great vitality in industrial archaeology, extending from large-scale recording of products to stylish publications. Interest in the subject reached maturity in 1977 with an exhibition in Milan on the manufacturing community of San Leucio and an international conference on the industrial heritage. The Societa Italiana per l'Archaeologia Industriale (SIAI) was established in 1979, initially focusing on Milan but it no longer functions. It concentrated on research, inventories of sites, and the production of publications. The pace of research has been stimulated in recent years by funding from local government in Lombardy, Umbria, Abruzzi and Lazio.

Perhaps the most remarkable indication of Italian interest in industrial archaeology is in the publication of volumes illustrated exclusively in colour, one three-volume set being sponsored by a major bank, and another book being produced by the Italian Touring Club, an association for the promotion of tourism. The SIAI co-produced *Archaeologia Industriale*, a glossy and authoritative journal presenting recent research: this has now unfortunately ceased publication but a new magazine, *Il Coltello di Delfo*, was launched in 1987. Books and articles are characterized by an approach that integrates science and technology, and which takes a remarkably broad approach to the study of technology, working practices and industrial architecture.

See also AMALFI; BOLOGNA; BRESCIA; CALÁBRIA; CANAVESE; CAPALBIO; CARRARA; COMO; CREMONA; CRESPI D'ADDA; ELBA; FLORENCE; FOLIGNO; FOLLONICA; GENOA; ISOLA DEL LIRI; LEUMANN; LOMBARDY; MANTUA; MILAN; NAPLES; PAVIA; PIEDMONT; PISTOIA; ROME; SAN LEUCIO; SARDINIA; SICILY; STELVIO; TERNI; TRIESTE; TURIN; VENICE; VIZZOLA.

BIBLIOGRAPHY
General
Gregotti, 1968; Milward and Saul, 1977; Mioni *et al.*, 1981–3; Naval Intelligence Division, 1944–5; Negri *et al.*, 1983.

MICHAEL STRATTON

Ivančice, South Moravia, Czechoslovakia   The site of a viaduct over the River Jihlava, 25 km (15 mi.) W. of Brno, built in 1868–70 to carry the railway to Brno and now out of use. Of wrought- and cast-iron girder construction, 38 m (125 ft.) above the river, it has a total length of 394 m (1395 ft.).

BIBLIOGRAPHY
General
Dusan, 1984

ivory   A term now applied chiefly to the hard substance of tusks large enough to be of industrial use, from such animals as the elephant, the walrus and certain species of whale. Tusks from the African elephant can be up to 3 m (10 ft.) long, and each tusk can weigh up to 70 kg (160 lb.). Ivory has been used for decoration since antiquity. By the nineteenth century it was extensively used for PIANO keys, for the handles of CUTLERY, for COMBS, for chessmen and for the handles of UMBRELLAS. Shavings, turnings and other residues were rendered into gelatine, or calcined to make animal CHARCOAL, providing a black PIGMENT used in printing ink.

Izegem, West Vlaanderen, Belgium   An industrial town 10 km (6 mi.) NW of Kortrijk, where a 1640 hp horizontal tandem compound steam engine of 1936 is preserved in a tiled engine house at a power station. There are museums for the brush and shoe industries. The Éperon d'Or shoe factory of *c.*1930 in Kon Albertlaan has elaborate, finely finished brickwork, with a series of offset doorways in the street façade in an ART DECO style. Inner court housing of the 1860s like that in GHENT survives in Droge Janstraat.

BIBLIOGRAPHY
General
Linters, 1986b; Viaene, 1986.

LOCATIONS
[I] Izegemse Werkgroep Industriele Archeologie (Izegem Industrial Archaeology Group), Stadhuis, Korenmarkt 9, 8700 Izegem.
[M] Nationaal Borstelmuseum (National Brush Museum), Wolvestraat 2, 8700 Izegem.
[M] Nationaal Schoeiselmuseum (National Shoe Museum), Wijngaardstraat 9, 8700 Izegem.

İzmir (Smyrna), İzmir, Turkey   Turkey's third city and second port, founded in the third millennium BC. In Ottoman times a principal point of access to the Empire for western merchants. There are remains of Byzantine and Ottoman aqueducts on the Kemer river. Its population was more Christian than Muslim until the expulsion of the Greeks in 1922 when most of the old city was burned, although several merchants' houses do survive. Notable among the Ottoman 'hans' around Anafartalar Caddesi is the eighteenth-century Kizlaragasi Han, a courtyard CARAVANSERAI designed for the comfort of merchants and the security of their goods. Multi-storey stone tobacco warehouses of the nineteenth century, with characteristically small windows, survive at Murselpasa Bulvari and around Alsancak. At Cennetoglu on the southern side of the city are many tanneries, three- or four-storey reinforced concrete buildings, where skins are hung to dry on the open-sided top floors. Gunes is İzmir's leatherworking and shoemaking quarter.

Other industries and the city's coal-gas works are in the harbour area. Turkey's largest oil refinery, Aliağa, lies to the north. Several brickworks with HOFFMAN KILNS operate on the edges of the city. A waterfront redevelopment at Konak may involve retention of the old ferry terminal buildings.

The railway stations at Basmane and Alsancak have a late nineteenth-century Germanic appearance. A small German steam tank locomotive is displayed outside Alsancak station, and German-built steam locomotives still operate goods trains in the regions. The city is served by a network of trolley buses.

MARK WATSON

İznik (Nicaea), Bursa, Turkey   A small and ancient city, 85 km (53 mi.) SE of Istanbul, famous for its creed and its tiles. Most of the architectural ceramics that embellish Turkish mosques came from İznik: their manufacture was established in the early sixteenth century by Selim I, 'the Grim', with captured Persian craftsmen, and is considered to have reached its artistic peak in 1570–1620. Decline set in, with European fashions, in the eighteenth century. Passable imitations are now being made, but the secret of the red colour has not been rediscovered. There is a tile collection in the museum.

BIBLIOGRAPHY
General
Brosnahan, 1988.

LOCATION
[M] Nilufer Hatun Imareti, İznik, Turkey.

J

Jablonec, North Bohemia, Czechoslovakia   The centre of the decorative glass industry, and of modern costume jewellery manufacture. The town owes much of its character to the late nineteenth-century development of light engineering works, and was largely rebuilt in an ART NOUVEAU style. The Museum of Glass and Jewellery shows the phases of glass production and styles of wares, and also administers the nearby Kristianov glassworking settlement.

The Novosvetske glassworks at Harrachov, 20 km (12 mi.) NE, was founded before 1712. Painted, etched, cut and solid glass objects are still produced.

Zelezny Brod, 20 km (12 mi.) SE of Jablonec, is another old glassmaking town where manufacture still continues, and where there is a Glass Museum.

LOCATIONS
[M] Glass Museum, Glass Technical School, Zelezny Brod.
[M] Museum of Glass and Jewellery, Jiraskova Ulice c.4, Jablonec nad Nisou.

SIMON DERRY and TIM PUTNAM

Jáchymov, North-West Bohemia, Czechoslovakia   A centre of silver mining, which in the mid-sixteenth century became a royal mining town with rights to mint its own coin: at that time it was the second biggest town in Bohemia, and the most important silver-producing district in Europe. A school of mining was established in 1716. In the twentieth century, it found a new importance in uranium mining: the radioactive character of local mineral deposits was discovered in 1896, and uranium ore from the region was used in the first successful isolation of radium by Marie Curie (1867–1934). It then developed as a spa, where radioactivity was used in spa treatment for the first time. One radium mining site, Svornost, is preserved.

Also in the region are Doupnak-Cibousov, a protected site where semi-precious minerals were extracted in the Middle Ages, and Chomutov, where there is a mining museum. Horní Blatná, 10 km (6 mi.) W. of Jáchymov, is a tin and copper mining town laid out on a grid pattern between the early sixteenth century and the late seventeenth. A reconstructed metal-mining site is conserved. There is also a trail which takes in the remains of opencast mining on a hill outside the town.

Horní Slavkov, 20 km (12 mi.) S. of Jáchymov, was the centre for a tin-mining district in nearby forests. Tin was mined from the fourteenth century, but during the sixteenth century workings became extensive following new mining ordinances of 1480–90. A tin shaft was opened up in 1509, and in 1516 production from two shafts was 400–500 tons a year. At their peak in c.1560, the mines were producing 750 tons a year, but with the crash of tin prices, and the increasing expense of extraction, production fell away thereafter, and was not significant after 1620. Tin mining covered some 830 ha (340 ac.). In 1530–6 a 24 km (14 mi.) canal, 2 m (6 ft.) wide, was built to power waterworks for crushing, washing and separating ore. The sixteenth century saw improvements to lifting gear and drainage and in 1590 a new level was opened. In the sixteenth century there were ninety-one dressing plants and thirty-two smelters in the area, and in 1581 between 3000 and 4000 people were employed, 350 of them miners.

Krásno, 10 km (6 mi.) S. of Horní Slavkov, is another tin-mining town where evidence of early large-scale underground mining survives, together with the associated water-power systems.

LOCATIONS
[M] Mining Museum, Námęsti I maje ç 1, Chomutov.
[M] Museum of Atomic Energy, Jáchymov.

JUDITH ALFREY and SIMON DERRY

Jacobean   The architectural style characteristic of the reign of James I in England between 1603 and 1625. Its typical features are brick exteriors with stone quoins, hipped gables, onion-topped towers and turrets, mullioned and transomed windows, and elaborate chimney stacks. The style was revived in the nineteenth century and applied to railway stations (*see* STOKE-ON-TRENT) and other commercial and industrial buildings.

Jacquard loom   Extremely complicated patterned weaving requiring the control of many groups of warp and weft yarns. In the draw loom the warp threads were manually raised and lowered (drawn) by an attendant (the draw boy) seated above the loom. The invention by J. M. Jacquard (1752–1834) in c.1800, which improved on an earlier design by his fellow-Frenchman Vaucanson, involved the use of perforated pattern cards through which needles passed to lift and lower the warp ends, according to the pattern punched in the pasteboard cards. Jacquard-style hand looms are still in operation in the Croix Rouge district in LYONS, near the Musée des Tissus, where original examples of Vaucanson's and Jacquard's looms are on display. Industrial Jacquard looms are displayed in a workplace setting at the Calderdale Museum, HALIFAX, and in other museums, and Jacquard weaving remains an important process in the contemporary textile industry.

jam A preserve of semi-liquid consistency, made by boiling the pulp of fruits, and sometimes part of the rinds, with sugar. Jam is made from the more juicy berries such as strawberries, raspberries, and red- and blackcurrants. Jam was traditionally made in the home, but by 1900 factory-made jam, made in England at factories like those at Aintree, Liverpool, and Tiptree, Essex, was affordable by all but the poorest, although it was 'seldom both cheap and good' (Beeton, 1912).

(*See also* MARMALADE.)

BIBLIOGRAPHY
General
Beeton, 1912.

Janakkala, Hämeen lääni, Finland The Tervakoski papermill at Janakkala, 80 km (50 mi) NW of Helsinki, was founded in 1818 and is the oldest business of its kind in Finland still functioning. The mill originally manufactured handmade paper, and began mechanical production only in 1853. The manufacture of banknote paper for the Bank of Finland began in 1887.

The oldest industrial building in the area is the water-cleansing plant of 1872, an octagonal brick structure which now houses the factory's handmade-paper department. The majority of the mill buildings date from the early twentieth century. Close to the factory building are the Tervakoski mansion of the 1880s, and a representative group of managers' and worker's dwellings of different periods.

japanning The process of applying a black varnish of exceptional hardness, originally from Japan and used in Britain from the seventeenth century. It is made by heating asphaltum with linseed oil, or by mixing shellac, linseed oil and turpentine. It can be used to provide a protective coating for iron, and in the manufacture of papier mâché.

Jędrzejów, Kielce, Poland A town 38 km (27 mi.) S. of Kielce on the road to Kraków. Przypkowski Museum houses a collection of sundials, old astronomical prints and bookplates; the collection is amongst the richest in the world. The collection was founded by Feliks Przypkowski in 1895, and donated by his family to the state in 1962. Part of the museum is housed in a perfectly preserved monastic pharmacy dating from 1712. The collection includes three hundred sundials, dating from the fourteenth century to the twentieth; five hundred sixteenth-, seventeenth- and eighteenth-century astronomical prints; non-mechanical chronometers like sand-glasses and fire clocks; pharmaceutical equipment; and mechanical clocks, amongst them a pendulum clock of the late seventeenth century which is amongst the oldest in the world. There are further sections on the history of cooking, the Reformation in Poland, and the history of Jędrzejów.

BIBLIOGRAPHY
General
Lorentz, 1973.
Specific
Przypkowski, T. Państwowe Muzeum im Przypkowskich w Jędrzejowie (The Przypkowski Museum in Jędrzejów). In *Rocznik Muzeum Świętokrzyskiego* (Świętokrzyskie Museum yearbook), IV, 1966–7.

LOCATION
[M] Państwowe Muzeum im Przypkowskich (The Przypkowski Museum), Rynek 7–8, Jędrzejów.

JAN KĘSIK

Jenbach, Tyrol, Austria A railway junction and resort, 32 km (20 mi.) NE of Innsbruck, formerly the centre of non-ferrous-metal smelting on the River Inn, and on the main line from Innsbruck to Kufstein. The Achenseebahn, a 1000 mm (3 ft. 3 in.) gauge railway, partly on the Riggenbach RACK RAILWAY system, extends 12 km (7 mi.) N. and employs three 0–4–0T locomotives of 1899. The Zillertalbahn, a 760 mm (2 ft. 6 in.) gauge railway, extends 31 km (19 mi.) S. to Mayrhofen. Locomotives include three 0–6–2Ts by Krauss of Linz, the earliest of 1900, which typify Austrian narrow-gauge practice, as well as a Bo–Bo diesel of 1940.

Jessop, William (1745–1814) Described in 1793 as the 'first engineer of the Kingdom', Jessop was an outstanding civil engineer whose skills in handling water and earth contributed to many canal and river navigation schemes before 1800, and to dock and harbour projects afterwards. Born in Plymouth, England, he was apprenticed with JOHN SMEATON from 1759, working with him until 1772. Thereafter he provided advice on the CROMFORD, the Grand Junction, the Rochdale and the Barnsley canals amongst others in England, and on the GRAND CANAL in Ireland. His was the decision to build high-level aqueducts at Chirk and PONTCYSYLLTE on the Ellesmere Canal. He was responsible for land-drainage schemes in the FENS, Holderness and the Trent Valley; and was a pioneer of iron railways, and a leading investor in the great Butterley ironmaking concern in Derbyshire. In the last fifteen years of his life he achieved distinction as the engineer of improvements in the ports of LONDON and BRISTOL.

BIBLIOGRAPHY
General
Hadfield and Skempton, 1979.

jewellery manufacture A jeweller was originally one who set precious stones, but by the early nineteenth century the term had come to mean anyone who made rings, bracelets, brooches and the like, whether or not they worked in precious metals or with precious gems. A jeweller's tools normally included small hammers, pliers, drills, shears and saws, an anvil, a wire-drawing bench, and a flatting mill for rolling wire. By the mid-nineteenth century the trade was organized on an industrial basis particularly in Birmingham, England, where it still flourishes in a mixture of old and modern buildings in the Jewellery Quarter; around Casalmaggiore, 22 km (14 mi.) N. of Padua, Italy, where it was established by Giulio Galluzzi (1855–1932) from 1878; and at Idar-Oberstein, in the southern Eifel in Germany.

BIBLIOGRAPHY
General
Book of Trades, 1839.
Specific
Loffi, F. Casalmaggiore: la capitale del Bijou (Casalmaggiore: capital of jewellery manufacture). In *Il Coltello di Delfo*, VIII, 1989.

jib crane   A CRANE with a projecting arm, usually one that can be raised and lowered. The term was used from the 1760s, but became common from the mid-nineteenth century as dockside cranes with iron and later steel jibs came into use. Many ran on rails in ports; there were smaller, fixed, swivelling examples at railway and canal wharves. Some jib cranes are mobile, being mounted on motor lorries, railway wagons or even steam locomotives.

jig   A device employed to mount guide tools on a MACHINE TOOL, especially useful if successive or repetitive operations are to be performed. The devices used to hold the work in place are known as fixtures. The use of elaborate, specially-made jigs, fixtures and GAUGES was important in the early manufacture of INTERCHANGEABLE PARTS, and continued so in repetitive machining for mass production.

BIBLIOGRAPHY
General
Hounshell, 1984.

jigger   A hydraulic machine used to magnify the stroke of a hydraulic piston, invented by W. G. ARMSTRONG; it is also known as a hydraulic pulley multiplying gear or 'hydraulic devil'. The pulleys and chain of a crane or other lifting device are attached to a hydraulic piston, and multiply the stroke of the cylinder on the haulage chain.

BIBLIOGRAPHY
General
McNeil, 1968, 1972.

jigging   The separation of metallic ores from waste material by shaking crushed material in water. A 'hotching tub' was a means of jigging in which material placed in a sieve was vigorously jerked up and down in a tank of water, causing the heavy ore-bearing material to pass through the sieve into the tub, whence it would be transferred to a BUDDLE. Some jigging machines were powered by water wheels. (*See* figure 65.)

Jilove, South Bohemia, Czechoslovakia   A town where precious metals have been mined since the Middle Ages. In it is the Museum of the Production and Processing of Gold, established by the National Technical Museum in 1960. Displays are housed in an old mint, with models of various mining methods and geological maps. No visible mining remains survive. Nearby, in Mnišek and Cisovice, medieval precious-metal mining remains include large earthworks and settling ponds which have been surveyed by the Prague Archaeological Institute.

LOCATION
[M] Museum of the Production and Processing of Gold, Namesti c.16, Jilove u Prahy.

Jönköping, Jönköping, Sweden   Jönköping, a regional capital with over 100 000 inhabitants, lies at the southern end of Lake Vättern. It is the historic centre of the Swedish match industry, which dominated world markets in the early twentieth century. Its history is commemorated in a museum. Ironmaking in the region is illustrated in the county museum, and an open-air museum includes a WIRE MILL.

The township of Huskvarna to the east is an engineering centre historically dependent upon power derived from a waterfall. It was famous for its involvement in the development of SEWING MACHINES in the late nineteenth century, and its long association with the manufacture of sporting guns is commemorated in a museum.

BIBLIOGRAPHY
General
Cederschield and von Feilitzen, 1946.

LOCATIONS
[M] Friluftsmuseet (Open-Air Museum), Stadsparken, S-550 02 Jönköping.
[M] Huskvarna vapenmuseum (Huskvarna Armoury Museum), Smedbygatan 3c, S-561 42 Huskvarna.
[M] Jönköpings läns museum (Jönköping County Museum), Slottsgatan 2, PO Box 2133, S-550 02 Jönköping.
[M] Tändsticksmuseet, Storgatan 18a, S-551 89 Jonköping.

journal bearing   *See* BEARING.

Juankoski, Kuopion lääni, Finland   The Juantehdas ironworks at Juankoski, 42 km (26 mi.) NE of Kuopio, founded in 1746, was the first in Finland built specifically for smelting BOG IRON ore. At first it was only modestly successful, but the business fared better in the latter part of the nineteenth century when it produced cast-iron and engineering products. Between 1906 and 1908 there was a change of direction, and a mechanical pulpmill was built on the eastern bank of the river, followed a little later by a cardboard factory. At the same time production at the ironworks slackened, and the foundry was the last of its buildings to be closed, in 1928.

In the area of the ironworks west of the river a mid-nineteenth-century brick building is preserved, together with a forge (designed to accommodate puddling furnaces and rolling mills) built in 1858, and an engineering shop, dating in its current form from the 1890s. The red-brick foundry shop was built in 1875, and the engine house in

Figure 65   A system of sieves and jigging tubs for extracting copper ore from mine waste, used in the Carpathian Mountains and in Bohemia, and recorded by Georgius Agricola in the sixteenth century

Elton Collection: Ironbridge Gorge Museum

1904. All in all a distinguished collection of buildings has survived from this bog-iron works.

Several dwellings associated with the works also survive, including the houses of the supervisor, of 1826, and the manager, of 1864. The wooden church dates from the same year, and there is a late-nineteenth-century club house.

LAURI PUTKONEN

Judendorf-Strassengel, Styria, Austria   A cement factory, 10 km (6 mi.) NW of Graz, built in 1868 by Ignaz Walter, who experimented with the manufacture of PORTLAND CEMENT there in the 1870s. The works was taken over by Josef Priebsch on Walter's death in 1882 and three new kilns were built. Two further kilns were subsequently added. By 1898 output had reached approximately 10 000 tons per annum of Portland cement. Production ceased after 1945, but the buildings are still used by a chemical company.

Jugendstil   Literally, the 'young style': a German term for ART NOUVEAU, named after the Munich journal *Jugend*.

junction   A place where two or more railway tracks join.

The word was used in a railway context from *c.*1840, and gradually came to comprehend all the railway installations at such a place: sidings, a passenger station, a locomotive depot, even the community itself. A RAILWAY TOWN like CREWE may be referred to as a junction, as may a larger city like BASLE which has many other urban functions. In the USA the term frequently became the place name, as at Annapolis Junction, Wayne Junction and White River Junction.

A flying or burrowing junction is one where by means of bridges, cuttings and embankments it is arranged that trains leaving or joining one line do not block traffic on another. An example may be seen at Aynho, 8 km (5 mi.) S. of BANBURY.

BIBLIOGRAPHY
Specific
Simmons, J. *Rugby Junction*. Stratford-upon-Avon: Dugdale Society, 1969.

jute   The jute plant (*Corchorus*) has a woody stalk used for making coarse cloth, especially burlap bagging, linoleum and carpet backing, and CORDAGE. It is processed like FLAX.

K

Kahn, Albert (1869–1942)   The outstanding designer
of factory buildings of the twentieth century, Kahn was
born in Westphalia, spent his childhood in Luxembourg,
and migrated to Detroit in 1880. There he worked as a
fruit pedlar before going to art school, becoming an office
boy to an architect in 1885, and establishing his own
practice in 1902. His first major commission in 1904 was
the Engineering Building at the University of Michigan.
Kahn came to realize the shortcomings of contemporary
means of using concrete, and his brother Julius developed
the Kahn bar, a concrete-reinforcing bar with the shear
members rigidly attached, which was used in 1905 in the
Packard No. 10 car plant in Detroit, the first reinforced-
concrete factory in the USA. In 1909–14 Kahn designed
the Highland Park plant for HENRY FORD, beginning a long
association with the Ford company. By 1919 his practice
had a staff of four hundred, and designed many buildings
in Detroit in the 1920s and 30s. He was responsible for
over five hundred factories in the USSR, the drawings for
twelve of which were completed in Detroit, the remainder
in Moscow under the supervision of Kahn's staff. Kahn
designed two of the largest factories built during World
War II: the 30 ha (70 ac.) Willow Run bomber plant at
Ypsilanti, Michigan, built for Ford in 1941–3, and the
Chrysler tank arsenal, Detroit, of 1941. His practice in
Detroit continues.

See also figure 91.

BIBLIOGRAPHY
General
Ferry, 1968, 1970; Hildebrand, 1974; Kahn, 1936; Nelson,
1939.

BARRIE TRINDER

Kalinin (Tver'), USSR   An important city on the River
Volga, 100 km (60 mi.) NW of Moscow, owing its
development to the construction of the St Petersburg–
Moscow railway, routed through Tver' rather than
Novgorod, the latter losing its importance almost overnight. Kalinin was one of Russia's early centres for the
factory production of textiles. The Morozov Textile Works,
founded in 1858, is now part of a much larger complex.
A railway bridge over the Volga was built in 1851, but
until 1900 road traffic had only a floating bridge. In that
year a new bridge designed by L. I. Mashek was opened, a
cantilevered girder structure on stone piers now known as
the Staryi (old) Bridge.

Near Kalinin, at kilometre post 133 on the Moscow–
Leningrad highway, is the village of Radchenko, named
after a scientist who worked there in the 1920s, continuing experiments which for decades had been devoted to
the utilization of Russian peat reserves. In 1927 a peat-
fired electric generating station was opened which still
operates and formed the prototype for other, larger, peat-
fired stations. The local history museum dealing with the
peat industry was founded in 1913, dispersed in 1917, reopened in 1928, then largely destroyed in World War II
and not re-established until 1955. It is not a working
museum, but its 400 m² (480 sq. yd.) premises contain
some genuine artefacts to supplement the pictures and
models.

LOCATION
[M] Museum of Local History and Fine Art, Sovietskaya ul.3,
Kalinin.

JOHN WESTWOOD

Kalocsa, Bács-Kiskun, Hungary   A town east of the
Danube and 105 m (62 mi.) S. of Budapest. It is celebrated
for folk art, painted furniture and embroidery, all of which
are illustrated in the town museum. The entire railway
station is decorated with folk paintings, and a museum is
devoted to the study of paprika.

LOCATIONS
[M] Kalocsa House, Tompa utca, Kalocsa.
[M] Paprika Museum [Marx t.6,] H-6300 Kalocsa.

Kamienna Góra (Landeshut), Wrocław, Poland   A village 100 km (62 mi.) SW of Wrocław, containing the
Museum of the Lower Silesian Weaving Industry. The
region was one of the principal centres of flax weaving in
Europe in the seventeenth and eighteenth centuries, with
over 30 000 hand looms in use by 1800. Displays include
weaving shops of the eighteenth and nineteenth centuries, Jacquard looms of the nineteenth century, and various
power looms used in Lower Silesia.

BIBLIOGRAPHY
General
Maisner-Nieduszyński and Pawłowska-Wilde, 1986.

LOCATION
[M] Muzeum Tkactwa Dolnośląskiego (Museum of the Lower
Silesian Weaving Industry), Pl. Wolności 29, Kamienna Góra.

Kaniere Forks, Westland, New Zealand   A power
station, 40 km (25 mi.) S. of Greymouth, built in 1907–9
to supply power for pumping water from the Ross
Goldfields mines, utilizing races built for sluicing gold ore.
The timber turbine house was replaced after the fire in

1979, but the main 500 kW turbines by James Gordon & Co. of London, with twin 1 m (40 in.) Pelton wheels, remain. Kaniere Forks now supplies power to the West Coast Electric Power Board.

BIBLIOGRAPHY
General
Thornton, 1982.
Specific
Mort, M. *Ninety Years of Electric Power Supply on the West Coast.* Greymouth: West Coast Electric Power Board, 1978.

Kansas, United States of America   Within the borders of this farm state sits a squat stone obelisk marking the precise geographic centre of the forty-eight contiguous United States. Its position at Fort Riley, Kansas, helps symbolize the historic central role that agriculture has played in the US economy and physical geography.

Despite the state's historically rural character, the recovery of zinc, coal, natural gas, gypsum and petroleum helped Kansas prosper early this century. The mining of rock salt and its surface harvesting by the LIME method have long been other vital industries, overshadowed by the rolling fields of grain made famous in Hollywood's *Wizard of Oz*.

Kansas may lay claim to the largest concentration of reinforced-concrete rainbow-arch bridges in the USA – giving new meaning to an Ozian theme – with seventy-three recorded in a recent survey. The typical March patent rainbow bridge of 1912 resembles an iron bow-string TRUSS rendered in concrete, one fine example of the type, built in 1927, crossing Cedar Creek in Elgin.

By the mid-twentieth century Kansas had become the nation's chief producer of liquefied helium, while Winchita was a leading centre of small aircraft manufacture. In West Mineral the 5500 tonne Big Brutus powered mining shovel of 1962 was declared a national mechanical engineering LANDMARK in 1987. Its drop-leaf bucket could scoop out 135 tonnes of overburden, and in just over ten years of service it excavated 9 million tonnes of bituminous coal from depths of 6 m to 12 m (20 ft. to 40 ft.) for local electric power generation. It has since been handed over to a local group for restoration and preservation.

LOCATIONS
[M] Barbed Wire Museum, 614 Main Street, La Crosse, KS 67548.
[M] Harvey House Railroad Museum, 408 W. 7th Street, Florence, KS 66851.
[M] Oil Patch Museum, Interstate 70 at Highway 281, Russell, KS 67665.

DAVID H. SHAYT

Kaposvár, Somogy, Hungary   The centre of the region between Lake BALATON and the Yugoslav border, celebrated for peasant embroidery and wood carving. The nineteenth-century Golden Lion pharmacy is preserved. There is a large spinning mill established under the first five-year plan (*see* HUNGARY).

Karlholms bruk, Uppsala, Sweden   Karlholms bruk is situated on the shores of Lövstabukten, a deep inlet of the Baltic, 60 km (37 mi.) NW of Dannemora. Its history is closely connected with that of LEUFSTA BRUK and the de Geer family. It was founded soon after the Russian raids along the coast of UPPLAND in 1719. For several reasons scarcity of wood had become a problem for Leufsta bruk, and the foundations for a new bruk with enough woodlands to supply a blast furnace replacing one of those at Leufsta were laid out in 1727–8. A manor house and workers' dwellings were built around the furnace, and the forge was named after its owner Charles de Geer, the Swedish 'Carl' or 'Karl' being the equivalent to the French 'Charles'. A Walloon forge was built in 1735 but was soon replaced by a forge with an associated plate mill (*see* ROLLING MILL).

In 1879 a new LANCASHIRE FORGE was built, and Karlholms bruk shifted from the Walloon to the Lancashire method of forging bar iron. The Lancashire forge closed in the early 1930s but has been well preserved ever since. There were hardly any alterations while the forge was working, and it looks today almost as it did in the 1880s, with its Lancashire hearths, water-powered hammers, two steam-driven hammers, a rolling mill, water wheels, and a steam engine. The forge was restored in 1973 and has since been well maintained.

Besides the forge, one of Sweden's most significant industrial monuments, the village is well worth visiting, with its workers' dwellings, the manor house, and a wooden bell tower. Karlholms bruk remained in the possession of the de Geer family and Leufsta bruk until 1917. For some years it belonged to the newly-formed company Gimo Österby bruks AB. A large sawmill had been built in 1910 and forestry was to become the future of Karlholms bruk. In 1937 Karlholm was sold to Korsnäs Sågverks AB and the co-operative federation Kooperativa Förbundet (KF). A plant for the production of fibreboard was established and KF became the sole owner of the bruk in 1943.

BIBLIOGRAPHY
General
Molin, 1955.

MARIE NISSER

Karlovy Vary (Karlsbad), West Bohemia, Czechoslovakia   A spa town since the fourteenth century, but also an important centre for the ceramics industry, which used clay mined locally at Slavkov, Chodov, Loket and Ostrov. Several spa buildings remain but the Spudel colonnade, made in BLANSKO in 1878, was scrapped during World War II and replaced.

LOCATION
[M] Museum of Karlovy Porcelain, Tovární Ulice, Karlovy Vary, Brezov.

Kassel, Hesse, Germany   The French physicist Denis Papin (1647–?1712) carried out his experiments with steam power in Kassel and Marburg, his proposals for the improvement of the SAVERY engine appearing in 1707. Although Papin had no direct influence on the development of industry in Kassel, the city did become the home of Henschel, the largest locomotive manufacturer in Europe. Georg Christian Henschel was granted a licence to set up as a metal founder in 1785. He moved in 1836 to a larger site, which, known as the 'Henschelei', is now occupied by Kassel University. A foundry which dates from the time of the firm's foundation, a domed building 16 m (52 ft.) in diameter, is now used as an exhibition centre. The firm of Henschel, now part of the Thyssen group, has several historic locomotives on display at its modern premises.

The electrically-powered Neumühle pumping station has been preserved in its original condition, with a turbine generator of 1892, and an a.c. generator which is no longer in use. It was the work of Oskar von Miller, the German pioneer of electric power.

LOCATIONS
[M] Hesse Museum Brüder-Grimm Platz 5, 3500 Kassel.
[M] Rheinstahl-Henschel Works Museum, Henschelstrasse, 3500 Kassel.
[M] Deutsches Tapetenmuseum (German Wallpaper Museum), Brüder Grimm Platz 5, 3500 Kassel.

ROLF HÖHMANN

Kaufungen, Hesse, Germany   One of the few HORSE GINS in Germany preserved *in situ* is the 'Rossgang' in Oberkaufungen, 12 km (8 mi.) SE of Kassel. Until 1884 it worked the winding gear for the shaft of the small Freudenthal lignite mine. The building erected over the gin and the shaft, with a regular fourteen-sided plan and in the local timber-framed style, dates from 1820. The entire site was placed under a preservation order in 1974 and was renovated. Other local industries, including glassmaking and brassworking are illustrated in the St Georg Museum.

LOCATION
[M] St Georg Museum, 3504 Kaufungen.

Kaunas, Lithuania, USSR   An open-air museum at Rumsiskes (Rayon Kaisiadorys), east of Kaunas, dating from 1966, on a 190 ha (470 ac.) site, with over a hundred buildings, many of them concerned with such manufactures as weaving, pottery, joinery and shawlmaking. The tradition of open-air museums in Lithuania dates from 1909.

BIBLIOGRAPHY
General
Zippelius, 1974.
Specific
Klemensas, C. Die Litauischen Freilichtmuseen (The Lithuanian open-air museums). In *Ethnographica* (Brno), 5 and 6, 1963–4.

LOCATION
[M] Lietuvos TSR liaudies buities muziejus (Open-Air Museum of Lithuania), Kaunas, Muziejaus g.Nr.13.

Kavala (Kaválla), Macedonia, Greece   The second city of Macedonia, 166 km (103 mi.) E. of Thessaloníki. Tobacco production started before the War of Independence in the

1820s. Large tobacco warehouses in stone and wood were built later in the century, typically facing the harbour, and decorated in a neo-Classical style. Much demolition has occurred and most of the survivors are derelict.

BIBLIOGRAPHY
Specific
Ageloudi, S. Kavala as a tobacco city. In *Archaeology*, XVIII, 1986.

Kawau Island, Auckland, New Zealand   An island 50 km (30 mi.) N. of Auckland. Manganese ores were worked here in the early 1840s, leading to the discovery of copper ores, first shipped to England in 1844. By 1848 the mine was very productive, with 220 Cornish miners and Welsh smelthouse workers employed. The mines were flooded by 1851 and mining had ceased. Ruins of a Cornish engine house of 1847 and of a copper smelter are conserved by the Hauraki Gulf Maritime Park.

BIBLIOGRAPHY
General
Thornton, 1982.
Specific
Bloomfield, G. T. The Kawau copper mine, New Zealand. In *IA*, XI(1) 1974.

keel   A word with two meanings in industrial archaeology:

1. An open, oar-propelled boat, used to carry coal from up-river wharves in Tyne and Wear, England, to seagoing ships moored on lower stretches, particularly at Shields or Sunderland. The usual capacity was eight CHALDRONS, or about 21 tons, and the word keel was also a measurement, meaning that amount (*see* DURHAM; NEWCASTLE-UPON-TYNE). The name was also applied to river craft on the River Humber and its associated waterways, a typical vessel measuring 17.68 m × 4.27 m (58 ft. × 14 ft.). Keel-boats on the Mississippi and its tributaries were vessels sharp both in stem and stern, used from *c.*1810 until *c.*1840.
2. The longitudinal member of the frame of a ship, on which the rest of the frame is built up.

BIBLIOGRAPHY
General
Hadfield, 1986; Tomlinson, 1979.

kelp   Ashes yielding ALKALI, made by burning seaweed of species *Fucus* or *Laminaria*. The chief sources are the northern and north-western coasts of Britain, from which kelp was supplied to glassmakers by the early eighteenth century. Kilns and storehouses were built around the Scottish coast. The peak of Scottish production, *c.*1825, was 25000 tonnes per annum; there was a sharp decline after 1850.

BIBLIOGRAPHY
General
Warren, 1980.
Specific
Clow, A. and N. The natural and economic history of kelp. In *Annals of Science*, V(4) 1947.

Kennet & Avon Canal, England   The southernmost cross-country canal in Britain, connecting earlier navigations on the Rivers Kennet and Avon. Engineered by JOHN RENNIE, it was opened in 1810. It suffered severe competition from the GREAT WESTERN RAILWAY, opened in 1841, which paralleled its route and later purchased it. Features at the east end include turf-sided locks and preserved Cornish beam pumping engines at Crofton, Wiltshire. At the western end are a spectacular flight of twenty-nine locks at Devizes, two fine stone aqueducts across the River Avon at Avoncliff and Dundas, 4 km (2 mi.) SE of Bath, and a unique water-powered beam pumping engine at Claverton, near Bath. The canal was disused from the 1940s, but restoration began in 1952 and was completed in 1990.

BIBLIOGRAPHY
Specific
Clew, K. R. *The Kennet & Avon Canal: an illustrated history.* Newton Abbot: David & Charles, 1968.

Kentucky, United States of America   The Bluegrass State was the first region west of the Allegheny Mountains settled by American pioneers. Kentucky's industrial backbone has long been coal mining and tobacco-growing. The state's more distinctive commodities have included baseball bats, whisky, stringed musical instruments, and racehorses.

In Louisville, the state's largest city, stands the waterworks of 1875, an early sand-filtration site, lacking its original massive steam pumping engines, replaced by a later but now inactive pumpworks, but distinguished by the pristine Classical Revival style of its temple-like structures. Elsewhere in the city the High Victorian Gothic gatehouse of the Crescent Hill water-purification plant fronts a reservoir established for the city in the 1870s. Louisville's Union Station of 1891 is an outstanding example of Romanesque stonework in the style of H. H. Richardson (1838–86), adapted today as the headquarters of the local transport authority. The large Colgate-Palmolive soap factory in Louisville was a reformatory before its conversion in 1923, four-storey soap kettles now filling a former cell block. Several historic Bourbon distilleries still function in Louisville, supported by a concentration of mechanized cooperages.

One of the nation's more majestic high-level bridges has carried rail traffic 75 m (250 ft.) over the Kentucky River since 1911, a 340 m (1125 ft.) steel-truss cantilever span near the town of High Bridge.

Despite the national store of gold bullion at Fort Knox, gold mining has never been practised in Kentucky. Coal today makes up 90 per cent of the state's extracted minerals.

LOCATION
[M] Kentucky Railway Museum, Ormsby Station, LaGrange Road & Dorsey Lane, Louisville, KY 40223.

DAVID H. SHAYT

kerosine (kerosene)   An alternative name for the PARAF-FIN series of hydrocarbons, and for a refined petroleum product, intermediate in volatility between gasoline and gas oil, named kerosine from the Greek 'keros' (wax) by Abraham Gesner (1797–1864), who established a manufactory for lamp oil in New York. It was the first major substitute for whale oil in lamps, and ultimately the most widely used of the many liquid illuminants. It was known as 'coal oil' in the USA. Kerosine is used for domestic heating and as a constituent of fuel for gas turbines and jet engines. It is widely called 'paraffin' in England.

BIBLIOGRAPHY
General
BP, 1958.

kervanseray   *See* CARAVANSERAI.

kibble   A bucket used to draw minerals or waste from a mine, either a separate container or one of a series attached to a continuous rope. In the seventeenth century kibbles were usually made of wooden staves, resembling a half-barrel; by the mid-nineteenth century they were of wrought-iron plates riveted together.

Kidwelly (Cydweli) Dyfed, Wales   The most substantial remains of early tinplate manufacture in Wales, 30 km (19 mi.) NW of Swansea; reputedly this was the second tinplate mill, after HANBURY's of *c.*1720. Tinplate production began in 1737 at a forge dating from 1719; the forge was largely rebuilt in 1801. Like all Welsh mills before the 1950s, Kidwelly was a handmill, where wrought iron (or steel, from the 1880s) was passed repeatedly between hot rollers using handheld tongs. Sheets were pickled, washed, annealed and cold-rolled, then treated again before dipping in tin. The mill was closed in the 1940s following foreign competition from steel-strip mills and electrolytic tinning. A museum displays hot- and cold-rolling mills, pickling and annealing areas, and a horizontal oil engine to power the rollers.

BIBLIOGRAPHY
General
Minchinton, 1957; Rees, 1969.

LOCATION
[M] Kidwelly Industrial Museum, Kidwelly, Dyfed SA17 4LW.

Kiel, Schleswig-Holstein, Germany   As early as the sixteenth century plans were drawn up in Denmark to link the North Sea and the Baltic by a canal from Kiel, making use of the River Eider where it flows into the North Sea at Tönning. However, it was not until between 1777 and 1784 that any plan was put into practice, and then it was confined to the link between the Kiel fiord and the Eider at Rendsburg, a length of 43 km (27 mi.). In order to provide a source of water, the canal passed through the Upper Eider lakes. Although the Eider Canal proved increasingly unable to cope with navigation from the mid-nineteenth century, it was of great importance in the process of industrialization, particularly in Rendsburg, where there were foundries, as well as a shipyard. Various monuments testify to the importance of the Eider Canal: the double lock of 1781 at Rathmannsdorf near Kiel Projensdorf in the Rendsburg-Eckernförde district; Klein-königsförde (1777–84) on the Kiel Canal, 16 km (10 mi.) E. of Rendsburg; the lock of 1782–4 at Kluvensiek, 10 km (6 mi.) E. of Rendsburg which has ornate filigree cast-iron gates and a bascule bridge made at the Rendsburg Carlshütte ironworks in 1849–50; the large brick canal warehouses at Tönning, Rendsburg and Kiel-Holtenau, dating from the early 1780s; and the customs house in Rendsburg, with its cast-iron staircase, dating from the same period.

The problem of creating a short and efficient waterway between the North Sea and the Baltic became particularly urgent once Kiel had become Germany's main naval base on the Baltic, with its infrastructure of docks and ARSENALS. Between 1887 and 1895 what was then called the Kaiser Wilhelm Canal was built. It is now known in Germany as the Nord-Ostsee-Kanal, and elsewhere as the Kiel Canal. Locks were built at Brunsbüttel at the mouth of the Elbe, and at Kiel-Holtenau to maintain the water level in the canal, independent of the tides. These were the Alte Schleusen (old locks), built in 1895; and the larger Neue Schleusen (new locks), built in 1907–14 to make it possible for the then new Dreadnought battleships to pass through the canal. The old locks have mitred gates, the new locks sliding gates. The entrances to both sets are indicated by beacons dating from the 1890s. The beacon on the north side of Holtenau lock was installed as a monument to the successful completion of the canal. The outstanding bridge over the canal is that at Rendsburg, built in 1911–13 to plans by Friedrich Voss, the rail tracks of which are approached on the north by a long, looping ramp. A transporter suspended beneath the rail tracks conveys road vehicles over the canal. There are other notable bridges at Levensau near Kiel, built in 1893–4, and at Hochdonn, built in 1914–20; as well as the Prinz Heinrich road bridge in Kiel-Holtenau of 1909–12.

The Kiel Municipal and Maritime Museum is now housed in the Fischhalle (fish market), built in dark brick with a wooden truss roof in 1909–10, to plans by the city architect.

The Schleswig-Holstein open-air museum has been located in Molfsee, a suburb of Kiel, since the 1960s. Besides farm buildings it includes a post mill from Algermissen in the Hildesheim district, a Dutch-style windmill, and a CREAMERY of the 1870s.

BIBLIOGRAPHY
General
Slotta, 1975–88; Zippelius, 1974.
Specific
[M] Kamphausen, A. *Das Schleswig-Holsteinische Freilichtmuseum: Häuser und Hausgeschichten* (The Schleswig-Holstein Open-Air Museum: houses and their history). Neumünster: Karl Wachholtz Verlag, 1986.

LOCATIONS
[M] Municipal and Maritime Museum, Dänischestrasse 19, 2300 Kiel.

[M] Schleswig-Holsteinisches Freilichtmuseum (The Schleswig-Holstein Open-Air Museum), Rammsee, 2300 Kiel 1.

MICHAEL MENDE

Kiev, Ukraine, USSR   Capital of the Ukraine. There is a large open-air museum at Perejaslaw-Chmelnizki, displaying the history of the Dnieper Plains: it has many industrial buildings, including six windmills, a horse mill that was part of a tannery, a water mill, and a pottery.

BIBLIOGRAPHY
General
Zippelius, 1974.

LOCATION
[M] Etnopark-Musei prosto neba (Ethnographic Park and Open-Air Museum), Perejaslaw-Chmelnizki, Kiewska oblast.

Kilbeggan, County Westmeath, Ireland   A market village where the main road from Dublin to Athlone crosses the River Brosna. Locke's Distillery, being preserved by a Development Association formed in 1982, is the only example left in Ireland of a small pot-still distillery. Many eighteenth-century buildings survive. Some equipment was removed on closure in 1957, but remaining features include an undershot waterwheel, 4.7 m (15 ft. 6 in.) in diameter and 3.4 m (11 ft.) wide; a cross-compound, condensing steam engine of 1887 by Turnbull, Grant & Jack of Glasgow; two cast-iron mash tuns of 1892; one of four oak brewing vats; three oak fermentation vats; and a corking machine by W. G. Edmonds of Dublin. A collection of local bygones is displayed in the 40 m (130 ft.) grain loft.

LOCATION
[M,S] Kilbeggan Development Association, Locke's Distillery, Kilbeggan, County Westmeath.

Killybegs (Na Cealla Beaga), County Donegal, Ireland   A village 22 km (13 mi.) W. of Donegal, with a herring fishing station. Manufacture of hand-tufted carpets was introduced from Scotland in 1898 by Alexander Morton, with the aid of the Congested Districts Board, and still continues. Kilcar, 13 km (8 mi.) to the W., is another centre of cottage industries, including tweed manufacture, embroidery and knitting.

BIBLIOGRAPHY
General
Shaw-Smith, 1984.

kiln   A type of furnace used for burning, or firing, ceramic and other types of article or material. They transform a dry but weakly friable mass to hard, durable form. Brick and tile manufacturers generally refer to 'kilns' while potters have tended to use the term 'ovens', especially where the ware is protected by saggars or muffles from the products of combustion by a lining of refractory bricks, albeit at the expense of a greater use of fuel.

Firing involves fundamental chemical and physical

changes, their nature being dictated by temperature and the amount of free oxygen in the atmosphere. Firing temperatures were usually lower in Mediterranean countries because of the lack of frost and the shortage of coal for fuel. In northern Europe plentiful forests and later coal allowed kilns to be heated to 1200–1400 °C.

Clamps are not permanent structures at all but an arrangement of bricks, whereby at least part of the fuel has been mixed into the clay prior to making it into bricks. Clamps were used into the twentieth century for making stock bricks in south-east England. Circular kilns or ovens were built in increasingly large sizes in north Staffordshire during the eighteenth century; the period was also characterized by many initiatives in the control of temperature. During the second half of the nineteenth century H. Seger brought about a more scientific understanding of the effects of firing on bodies and glazes, developing pyrometric cones for measuring temperatures in the kiln.

From about 1855 various experiments were made using gas for firing kilns; while gas or oil are now likely to be used in large kilns, electricity heats the majority of smaller designs.

Advances in kiln technology have led to more sophisticated approaches to the drying of ware; humidity drying, which reduces the danger of cracking, was introduced in England around 1881. Tunnel driers, working on a similar principle to a TUNNEL KILN, were gradually adopted from the last quarter of the nineteenth century.

Outside the ceramics industry kilns are used for making GLASS and lime (see LIMEKILN), for calcining ores (see CALCINING KILN), and for making wood TAR and MALT.

BIBLIOGRAPHY
General
Rhodes, 1968; Searle, 1929.

MICHAEL STRATTON

Kinderdijk, Zuid Holland, The Netherlands   A unique and amazing landscape, the most powerful evocation of the appearance of the western provinces of the Netherlands in the period when they were drained entirely by wind power. Kinderdijk lies north of Alblasserdam, at the confluence of the Rivers Lek and Noord, 12 km ($7\frac{1}{2}$ mi.) SE of Rotterdam and 8 km (5 mi.) N. of Dordrecht. The dike called Kinderdijk follows the right bank of the River Noord. On the outside of the dike there are several shipyards and dredging contractors' yards with surviving nineteenth-century elements, and along the dike are workers' dwellings of the turn of the century. There are two principal ranges of windmills on either side of the drainage canals. One range of eight brick-built tower mills with outside scoop wheels was built for the drainage board of the Nether Polders in 1738. The second range, of eight octagonal tower mills, faced with reeds, also working outside scoop wheels, was built for the drainage board of the Upper Polders in 1740. Two similar mills, one of 1740 and one of 1760, served the Nieuw Lekkerland Polder, and one of 1740 was built for the Blokmeer Polder. The Molenkade is a walkway which gives access to the mills, some of which are open to the public. A nearby steam pumping station of 1868, which worked scoop wheels, is out of use.

LOCATION
[I] Molencommissie Kinderdijk (Kinderdijk Mill Commission), p/a VVV Dordrecht, Stationsweg 1, Dordrecht.

BARRIE TRINDER

Kingston upon Hull   *See* HULL.

Kirkcaldy, Fife, Scotland   A flax-spinning town which developed into a major centre for the production of linoleum. The first steam-powered spinning mills were built *c.*1806–9. From north to south the principal sites are Provost Swan's at Coal Wynd: two mills, one early, with Y-shaped cruciform columns, now a Pentecostal church, and another from the mid-nineteenth century, fireproof, now converted into industrial units. On Niccol Street the small Abbotshall Mills of James Aytoun, 'Father of the flax-spinning trade', were built in 1822 and 1825, spinning tow, and, from 1833, jute. These mills later became a dyeworks. There is a Gothic schoolhouse, and the oldest mill has cruciform columns and short iron beams. The biggest spinning mill in Fife is at West Bridge, founded in 1806 and rebuilt by J. & W. Hendry in 1856; it is fireproof with a Gothic cast-iron roof and quatrefoils. Acquired by Forth & Clyde Roperies in 1936, it is now derelict but was saved at a public enquiry in 1988.

Linen-weaving factories include Normand's in Dysart of *c.*1850; Abden of 1864; Sinclairtown Factory of 1866; Lockhart's of 1884; and the Hawkleymuir and Victoria Works, where Peter Greig Ltd still weave linen.

In 1828 Michael Nairn established a four-storey hand-loom factory, which is still standing, in Coal Wynd. He took up the manufacture in Pathhead of floor cloth in 1847; and of linoleum (patented by F. Walton of Staines in 1863) in 1877, becoming the world's biggest manufacturer of linoleum in a complex which in 1933 extended to 18 ha (45 ac.). It is now one of only three linoleum factories in the world. A mobile planer CALENDER dates from the 1890s, as do the brick-built 15 m (50 ft.) drying stoves in the North Factory. Part of the South Factory of the Scottish Linoleum Works of 1883 is of four storeys, with tall windows rising through three floors to light the painting of floor cloth. The impressive office of 1939 by James Miller has been adapted as apartments. St Mary's Canvas Works of 1869, a Renaissance-fronted weaving shed, with a three-storey concrete-floored addition of 1914, is now Kirkcaldy College of Education.

Rival linoleum manufacturers Barry, Ostlere & Shepherd, established in 1871, had a scattering of factories, much altered or demolished except for the Renaissance head office next to Kirkcaldy Museum, which is now occupied by the local authority. It was originally a linen factory.

Douglas & Grant, founded in 1854, were notable steam-engine makers who made the first British Corliss valves in 1863. Their Dunnikier Foundry is cast-iron-framed. The decaying rubble and pantiled buildings and stalks of

Figure 66 The chemical woodpulp and papermill at Klevfos, Norway, built in 1888, rebuilt after a fire in 1909, closed in 1976, and now a museum
Barrie Trinder

Whitebank Engine Works belong to the first half of the nineteenth century. Fife Forge is later, with a curved polychrome front to the railway; it was closed in 1987. Dysart Foundry still operates in Victorian engineering sheds.

East Bridge Flour Mill has a Palladian office, and was originally water- and horse-powered. A circular horse-gin house remains. The Harbour Maltings of Robert Hutchinson & Co, possess three- and four-storey ranges of malt floor with pyramidal kilns, the two conical kilns having recently been demolished, and modern silos. Further north, Curror Brothers' Maltings was established in 1880. Both still function, with modern techniques.

Balwearie and Hole Flint Mills, *c.*1840 and *c.*1860, were water-powered with calcining kilns. Some derelict machinery remains.

Kirkcaldy's medieval harbour was extended in 1843 and converted to a wet dock, with original gates, in 1906–8. Dysart harbour is basically seventeenth-century, built for coal shipment; it was gated in 1831. The tramway electricity generating station of 1903 on Victoria Road is derelict.

The Frances (*c.*1880) and Seafield (1954–9) Collieries at either end of Kirkcaldy were linked under the sea and worked the steepest seams in Britain (1 in 1.2 gradient). They closed in 1988.

Kirkcaldy Industrial Museum holds a linoleum block printing bench; small items of mining, textile and coopering equipment; and a collection of horse-drawn vehicles.

BIBLIOGRAPHY
General
Hume, 1976; Muir, 1956.
Specific
Stephen, W. M. Two flint mills near Kirkcaldy, Fife. In *IA*, III, 1966.

LOCATION
[M] Kirkcaldy Museum and Art Gallery, War Memorial Gardens, Kirkcaldy, Fife KY1 1YG.

MARK WATSON

Kiskőrös, Bács-Kiskun, Hungary   A town on the main routes to Belgrade, 110 km (70 mi.) S. of Budapest. The museum of road transport has displays showing the life of those employed in road transport and maintenance, and the tools and machines used in road-building.

LOCATION
[M] Road Museum, H-6200 Kiskőrös, Dózsa György u. 38.

Kiskunhalas, Bács-Kiskun, Hungary   A town 120 km (75 mi.) S. of Budapest on the railway to Belgrade, famous for 'Halas' lace in which fifty-six different stitches are used. There is a local lace museum, and a windmill is preserved.

Klagenfurt, Carinthia, Austria   The capital of Carinthia, linked with the Wörther See by the Lend Canal, constructed in 1527. It has a mining museum. There is an open-air museum of Carinthian buildings at Maria Saal, 14 km (9 mi.) N.

LOCATIONS
[M] Bergbau Museum (Mining Museum), Kreuzbergl, 9020 Klagenfurt.
[M] Kärntner Freilichtmuseum (Carinthian Open-Air Museum), 9063 Maria Saal, Klagenfurt.

Klausen-Leopoldsdorf, Lower Austria, Austria   A lumber-working settlement on the River Schwechat, established by Emperor Leopold I (1640–1705) in 1680. About 2 km (1½ mi.) downsteam is the main floodgate of a timber-floating lock of 1756, which operated until 1939, and has been preserved since 1965. It controlled a 20 km (12 mi.) stretch of the river to the rake at St Helena near Baden. The dam is of ashlar construction and is 5.2 m (17 ft.) high; the water is controlled by two wooden gates, each 1.7 m (5 ft. 7 in.) square.

Klevfos, Hedmark, Norway   The Klevfos Industrimuseum, 20 km (12 mi.) E. of Hamar, is a chemical wood pulp and paper mill. It produced about 3000 tons per annum of sulphate pulp, which was used to make various grades of wrapping paper. The mill was built in 1888, but suffered a fire in 1909, and the surviving equipment dates from its rebuilding two years later. Production of cellulose stopped in 1970, but papermaking continued until 1976.

The initiative to preserve the mill came from local people, and gained support from local and national government. The project is administered by the Hedmark county museum service, but has its own manager. The plant, with a floor space of 4000 m² (4800 sq. yd.), was a small one, but for that reason it can be preserved more easily than some of the larger factories elsewhere in Norway. Wood for the mill came at first by river, then along a siding from the Rørosbane, and was shunted between 1919 and 1953 by the ROBERT STEPHENSON 2–4–0 locomotive No. 17 *Caroline* of 1861, preserved at HAMAR. The machinery of the mill is largely complete, and illustrates the whole process, from the mills that cut the wood into chips, and the boilers in which the chips were heated with caustic soda (NaOH), to the guillotines used for cutting paper before dispatch. The plant includes a Hollander machine of 1910 by Drammen Jernverk. The machinery was driven direct by two 80 hp turbines, the only use of electricity being for lighting. When the mill was in production the smell sometimes reached Hamar.

The conservation project also encompasses an apartment block, in which there were eight two-room dwellings for workers, and a group of houses built in the 1920s for the accountant and the two shift foremen.

At nearby Løten is a distillery whose thirty-bay, three-storey building, of 1855 with additions in 1890, 1934 and 1941, displays on the front in wrought-iron letters the chemical formula for making spirits: $C_6H_{10}O_5 + H_2O \rightarrow 2C_2H_6O + 2CO_2$.

LOCATION
[M] Klevfos Industrimuseum, Postboks 1068, N2345 Ådalsbruk.

BARRIE TRINDER

knitting A process by which one continuous yarn is used to form a fabric, as distinct from weaving, where two sets of yarn are interlaced. Knitting originated in the Middle Ages, and was a common domestic occupation in Europe by the sixteenth century when the STOCKING FRAME was introduced.

Koblenz (Coblence), Rhineland-Palatinate, Germany *See* BENDORF; MOSELLE; RHINE; RHINELAND-PALATINATE.

Kochelsee and **Walchensee**, Bavaria, Germany The Walchensee and Kochelsee lakes lie about 75 km (46 mi.) S. of Munich in the foothills of the Alps, with a difference of about 200 m (660 ft.) between their levels. This difference was exploited as early as 1904 for the construction of a 25 000 hp hydro-electric power plant. However it was not until June 1918 that Oskar von Miller, founder of the Deutsches Museum, MUNICH, succeeded in realising his ambition of a power station with an output of over 100 000 hp, establishing the 'Bayernwerke' (Bavarian works) by combining existing power stations into a linked series of plants supplying electricity to the whole of Bavaria.

Between the end of 1918 and 1924, the Rivers Isar and Rissbach were diverted for this purpose into the Walchen-

see, through tunnels respectively 8 km (5 mi.) and 6 km (4 mi.) long. From there the water is fed through inlets and a pressure tunnel into the surge tank, a chateau-like structure built into the slope, and containing some 10 000 m³ (350 000 cu. ft.). Six penstocks carry water to the power house, 180 m (600 ft.) below, where it drives ten turbines of varying capacities, which generate both three-phase and single-phase current. The latter process made possible the electrification of part of the Bavarian railway network from 1924, and in general the Walchensee power station fostered the principle of using very large generating stations to supply electricity to extensive areas.

BIBLIOGRAPHY
General
Bayernwerk AG, 1975; Bott, 1985; Grimm, 1985.

AXEL FÖHL

Kolín, East Bohemia, Czechoslovakia A town with an Esso power station of 1929–31 and a Tatra car showroom of 1932, both by Jaruslav Fragner. A railway and a road cross the Labe on a reinforced concrete bridge of 1925–7: it is 150 m (160 yd.) long, and incorporates a hydro-electric power station.

BIBLIOGRAPHY
General
Dusan, 1984; Peichl and Slapeta, 1987.

Komárno, South Slovakia, Czechoslovakia A polyglot community facing the Hungarian town of Komárom across the River Danube. There has been shipbuilding activity here since the mid-eighteenth century, though no early buildings survive. There is a modern shipyard dating from after 1945. A replica FLOATING MILL was built in the yard, but as it had to fulfil modern safety standards it is not an exact replica of the mills that were common on this stretch of the Danube until the early years of this century.

Kongsberg, Buskerud, Norway Kongsberg, 86 km (53 mi.) W. of Oslo on the River Numedalslågen, was founded by King Christian IV in 1624 to smelt silver ores discovered in the region the previous year. In the eighteenth century the population exceeded 10 000 and the Baroque church of 1761 seats 2400. Over 130 mines were worked between 1623 and 1900. A mint and an arsenal were established, and the first forestry administration in Norway was set up at Kongsberg in 1739 (*see* ELVERUM).

Mining ceased in 1957. At the mine at Saggrenda, 7 km ($4\frac{1}{2}$ mi.) W., visitors are taken 2300 m (2500 yd.) underground along a narrow-gauge railway. The Bergverksmuseum in the former smelthouse buildings in the town centre includes silver nuggets and bars, coins struck at the mint, many hand tools, maps, and models of pumping systems. Opposite the church is the building constructed in 1786 to house the Royal School of Mining, established in 1757 and the first institution of its kind in Europe.

The Lågdal Museum, with twenty-two reconstructed

buildings, portrays the history of the region, and includes the workshops of an optician, a shoemaker, a clock repairer and a wood turner.

BIBLIOGRAPHY
General
Bergwitz, 1924; Brunnich, 1826; Moen, 1967.

LOCATIONS
[M] Lågdalsmuseet, Tillischbakken 8, 3600 Kongsberg.
[M] Norsk Bergverksmuseum Solvverket, Hyttegatan 3, 3600 Kongsberg.

BARRIE TRINDER

Kopaonik, Kosovo, Serbia, Yugoslavia   A mountain chain rising to 2000 m (6600 ft.) in the northern part of the autonomous province of Kosovo, 200 km (125 mi.) S. of Belgrade, with rich and varied mineral resources in a region 70 km by 40 km (43 mi. by 25 mi.). Products include ores of lead, zinc, iron, chromium, manganese, nickel, arsenic, tungsten, molybdenum, gold and silver, as well as asbestos, coal, limestone and granite. The chief town, Titova Mitrovica (Kosovska Mitrovica), at the confluence of the Rivers Sitnica and Ibar, is a medieval settlement which prospered after the opening of the railway in 1873: it also has mines and steel plants. Trepča, 10 km (6 mi.) N., has the largest lead and zinc mines in Yugoslavia, and a museum with mining collections.

BIBLIOGRAPHY
General
Hudson, 1973.

LOCATIONS
[M] Municipal Museum, 38330-Kosovska Mitrovica.
[M] Museum of Science, Technology and Mineralogy, 38226–Stari Trg, Trepča.

Koprivnice, East Moravia, Czechoslovakia   The site of the Tatra factory, started in 1852 by Ignac Sustala, first making coaches, then railway wagons and coaches after 1881, motorcars from 1897, and lorries from 1898. Railway production ceased in the 1950s and today the plant produces heavy-duty trucks, and air-cooled engines. Few early buildings remain, and none are protected. The company museum exhibits a representative selection of the vehicles produced at the factory.

BIBLIOGRAPHY
Specific
Rosencranz, K. *Auto Album Archive: Tratra.* Brno: Technical University, 1987.

LOCATION
[M] Technical Museum, Janackovy Sady, c. 226, Koprivnice.

Korcë (Korça, Koritsa), Albania   A town in eastern Albania, with a factory where tourists are shown weavers working on hand looms to produce Persian carpets at 360 000 knots to the square metre. Most of these carpets are for export, but cheaper types are produced for the home market.

BIBLIOGRAPHY
General
Ward, 1983.

LOCATION
[M] Korcë Museum, Korcë.

Kortrijk (Courtrai), West Vlaanderen, Belgium   A town that in the nineteenth century supplied linen, particularly high-quality table DAMASK, to all parts of Europe. The city stands on the River Leie (Lys), whose waters possess qualities favourable for bleaching as well as for retting flax. From *c.*1850 mechanical scutching was commonly practised in the region. In the 1920s and 30s many companies installed concrete tanks in which flax could be retted with hot water. Since the 1960s the industry has collapsed. Most of the two hundred factories have been demolished or reused, but many retting tanks and bleaching yards remain in the surrounding countryside. A windmill used for flax processing survives at Heule, 3 km (2 mi.) N. The National Flax Museum illustrates the history of the industry, and there are examples of flax products in the city art museums.

On Visserkaai are the colossal drying sheds of several brickworks and tileworks of *c.*1900, one being a five-storey range which extends for seventy bays.

At Deerlijk, 7 km ($4\frac{1}{2}$ mi.) NE, stands the preserved tower windmill 'Te Geest en ter Zande' (The Spirit of the Sand), constructed in 1888, with an adjacent steam mill of *c.*1900.

BIBLIOGRAPHY
General
Linters, 1986; Viaene, 1986.
Specific
De Vlasvallei en Haar Kanalen (The flax valley and its canals). Ghent: vvv, 1987.
Foulon, F. Vlasfabrieken: productiewijze-beschrijving-herbruik (Flaxmaking: production, technology, finance). In *Ons Industrieel Ergoed* (Our Industrial Heritage), I, 1982.

LOCATIONS
[M] Museum voor Oudheidkunde en Sierkunst en Museum voor Schone Kunsten (Fine Art Museum), Broelkaai 6, 8500 Kortrijk.
[M] Nationaal Vlasmuseum (National Flax Museum), Etoemme Sabbelaam 4, 8500 Kortrijk.

BARRIE TRINDER

Košice (Kaschan), East Slovakia, Czechoslovakia   The second largest town in the old kingdom of Hungary, and an important trading centre before the nineteenth century, when both magnesite (*see* MAGNESIUM) and iron ore were found in the surrounding region, and Košice started to develop as an industrial town. Magnesite was first exploited in 1886. Košice also became an important centre for the machine-tool industry. The most rapid period of growth was after 1948, with the setting up of the East Slovakian Steelworks and several heavy engineering plants. Recent exploitation has covered the traces of the earlier magnesite workings. The Technical Museum houses exhibits from throughout Slovakia, with a display

Figure 67 The Sunila Pulpmill, Kotka, designed by Alvar Aalto in 1937–8
National Board of Antiquities, Finland

relating to the East Slovakian Steelworks and an underground mining exhibition.

LOCATION
[M] Technical Museum, Leninova Ulice 94, Košice.

Kotka, Kymen lääni, Finland   The Sunila Pulpmill at Kotka in south-eastern Finland was erected in 1937–8 for the production of cellulose sulphate. The plant, with a large village for its employees, was designed by the architect Alvar Aalto (1888–1976). The village, begun when the mill was nearly finished, has housing for all categories of plant staff, with houses scattered in rows along the woody hillsides. Sunila is considered one of the outstanding examples of the International Modern style in Finland. The pulpmill still operates, and there have been alterations in the mill building, but under a plan of 1987 the residential area is protected, and there is a recommendation that the general appearance of the industrial plant should be preserved.

Kotor (Aeruvium, Cathara), Montenegro, Yugoslavia   A walled town at the head of the Boka Kotorska gulf, in a fjord-like bay amid the Karstic hills. The town has many medieval and Renaissance buildings. It was severely damaged by an earthquake in 1979. It was ruled by Venice from 1420, and was part of the Habsburg Empire in the nineteenth century. Though a port with three hundred ships in the eighteenth century, the introduction of steam ships from the mid-nineteenth century brought decline. The spectacular road around Kotor Bay to Cetinje was built by the Austrian engineer, J. Slad, in 1876–81; it has seventeen hairpin bends in 15 km (9 mi.). The Maritime Museum features the history of the Kotor Sailors' Guild. Perast, 10 km (6 mi.) NW, has been a shipbuilding centre since the sixteenth century. There are saltworks at nearby Prevlaka and Salinsko Polje.

LOCATION
[M] Maritime Museum, Palata Grgurina, Trg Bokeljske mornarice, 391, 81330-Kotor.

Kragujevac, Serbia, Yugoslavia   A town on the River Lepenica, 95 km (60 mi.) SE of Belgrade, now the principal centre of motor vehicle production in Yugoslavia, and historically a centre of armaments manufacture. Weapons and motorcars are displayed together in a museum in a former arsenal.

LOCATION
[M] Crvena Zastava Factory Museum, ul. Spanskich boraca 2, 34000-Kragujevac.

Kraków (Cracow), Kraków, Poland   Kraków, capital of

Poland until the end of the sixteenth century and the country's third largest city, is a place of outstanding beauty. It is one of the few Polish cities to have emerged relatively undamaged from World War II.

An extensive network of electric tramways links the centre of Kraków with the suburbs, and with the surrounding industrial region.

The Museum of Aviation and Astronautics is housed in a hangar at Rakowice Airport, Kraków, and was founded by the Aeroclub of the Polish People's Republic. The collection of exhibits started in 1946, although it was not officially opened until 1963. The museum houses seventy-five aircraft, two motorized gliders, and seven helicopters. The aircraft include some very early examples, chiefly of German origin, some Polish aircraft dating from before World War II and examples of every type built subsequently, together with foreign aircraft from before the war and some of wartime origin. A collection of 109 aircraft engines ranges in date from the earliest days of powered flying to the present. There are also collections of rockets and aircraft equipment. Other sections relate to important builders of aircraft and to outstanding Polish aviators. The museum has a library.

The origins of the Museum of Pharmacy at the Medical Academy in Kraków go back to the first half of the nineteenth century but the present museum was founded in 1946 on the initiative of the Provincial Chamber of Chemists, and was intended as a regional museum. After 1951 it came under the authority of the Ministry of Health and Social Welfare, and today it is a national establishment specializing in collecting items illustrating pharmaceutical science and techniques. It has about 15 000 exhibits, and a library of 6000 volumes. Most of the artefacts are items used in old laboratories and chemists' shops. They include the complete equipment of a chemist's cellar; items used in the manufacture of wax candles in the eighteenth century; a collection of casks for storing medicinal wine, dating from the seventeenth and eighteenth centuries; a collection of richly ornamented wooden containers for medicaments from the same period; weights made in Poland, Italy and Germany; Meissen pots; mortars from the fifteenth and sixteenth centuries; and the complete equipment of a chemist's shop of the early nineteenth century. The museum also has manuscript collections, including a grant made by King Stanisław August in the mid-eighteenth century, and a rich collection of prints, some from the sixteenth century.

BIBLIOGRAPHY
General
Krzyżan, 1983.
Specific
Roeske, W. Dzieje, zbiory, ekspozycje Muzeum Farmacji (History, collections and displays of the Museum of Pharmacy). In *Muzealnictwo*, 20, 1972.
Roeske, W. Zbiory Muzeum Farmacji w Krakowie (Collections of the Museum of Pharmacy in Kraków). In *Kwartalnik Historii Kultury Materialnej* (Quarterly Journal of the History of Material Culture), 2, 1968.

LOCATIONS
[M] Museum of Pharmacy, ul. Basztowa 3, Kraków.

[M] Muzeum Lotnictwa i Astronautyki (The Museum of Aviation and Aeronautics), Rakowice-Czyżyny, ul. Planu 6-letniego 17, Kraków.

Kranj (Carnium, Krainburg), Slovenia, Yugoslavia An ancient town 25 km (16 mi.) NW of Ljubljana, with modern metallurgical, textile, electronics and rubber industries, at the centre of the Kranjska mining region in the valleys of the River Sava and its tributaries. Metal mining was known in the region in the Middle Ages, and was of particular importance in the eighteenth century. Collections in the Gorenjski Museum include examples of the traditional painted furniture of the region.

Škofja Loka, 10 km (6 mi.) S. of Kranj, is an old town with many buildings under legal protection. An open-air museum around a castle, opened in 1962, includes a water mill and fruit-drying kilns.

At Kropa, 8 km (5 mi.) W. of Kranj, smiths still produce decorative ironwork; two rolling mills and a forging shop are preserved, and there are numerous ironworkers' houses.

Jesenice, 32 km (20 mi.) NW of Kranj, is a town with long ironmaking traditions, where steel has been made since the seventeenth century. The history of local mining and metallurgical technology, as well as of workers' movements among miners and railwaymen, is portrayed in the works museum.

Zelezniki, 12 km ($7\frac{1}{2}$ mi.) W. of Kranj, ceased to be an ironmaking centre in 1901, but the old works and houses of the ironworkers are preserved.

BIBLIOGRAPHY
General
Zippelius, 1974.

LOCATIONS
[M] Gorenjski Muzej, Trg Titov 4, 64001-Kranj.
[M] Loski Muzej-Škofja Loka, Postbox 9, Škofja Loka, SR Slovenia.
[M] Metallurgical Museum, Zelezniki.
[M] Smithy Museum, 64245-Kropa.
[M] Technology Museum of the Jesenice Steel Mill, C. Zelezarjev 8, 64270-Jesenice.

JERZY ROZPĘDOWSKI

Krefeld (Crefeld), North Rhine-Westphalia, Germany *See* NORTH RHINE-WESTPHALIA.

Kremnica, Central Slovakia, Czechoslovakia A gold-mining centre where the earliest workings date from the tenth century. One mine remains in production. In the seventeenth century there were thirty-five registered mining companies. The level of investment in the mines is illustrated by the water-power systems installed from the fifteenth century: water was supplied by pipe to the mines across a distance of over 20 km (12 mi.). Many of the mines are preserved as technical monuments, but the Municipal Museum is largely concerned with numismatics. During the nineteenth century there were thirty-five water mills in the area, and hydro-electric power was generated from 1921.

LOCATION
[M] Municipal Museum, Hellensteinovsky dom, Namesti 1 Maja, Kremnica.

Kristiansand, Vest Agder, Norway   The principal harbour on the south coast of Norway, and a planned town founded by King Christian IV in 1641. It suffered a succession of fires, the last in 1891. Vest Agder Fylkesmuseum is the largest open-air museum in Norway. The Valhalla soap factory and several limekilns in the vicinity are listed.

The pharmacy where the dramatist and poet Henrik Ibsen (1828–1906) was employed in 1847–50 is preserved at Grimstad, 45 km (28 mi.) NE.

BIBLIOGRAPHY
General
Trastader, 1972–3.

LOCATION
[M] Vest Agder Fylkesmuseum, p.b. 4048, 4601 Kristiansand.

Krøderen, Buskerud, Norway   A town at the south end of Lake Krøderen, 55 km (34 mi.) NW of Oslo, terminus of the 26 km (16 mi.) standard-gauge railway from Vikersund in MODUM parish, opened in 1872. Before completion of the Bergensbanen it was part of the route from Oslo to Bergen via HALLINGDAL on which passengers changed from railway to steamer at Krøderen. The line is now operated in the summer season by the Norsk Jernbaneklub (Norwegian Railway Club). The station of 1872 by Georg Bull is preserved in its original condition with the adjacent goods shed, locomotive depot and signal box, and a sales kiosk from Nesbyen station. The line is worked by No. 225, a Thunes 2–6–0 of 1911, a typical Norwegian branch-line locomotive, and No. 236, a Thunes 2–8–0 of 1912.

LOCATION
[S] Norsk Jernbaneklub, Krøderbanen, 3515 Krøderen.

BARRIE TRIINDER

Krujë (Kruja), Albania   A 'museum city' (*see* ALBANIA), centred on the fortress of Gjergj Kastrioti Skenderbeg (1405–68), a national hero. A restored Turkish bazaar of *c*.1800 resembles a working museum, with craftsmen demonstrating such traditional skills as basketmaking, shoemaking, silversmithing, and the manufacture of the distinctive white felt caps worn by men.

BIBLIOGRAPHY
General
Ward, 1983.

LOCATION
[M] Krujë Museum, Krujë.

Kuchen, Baden-Württemberg, Germany   When the textile manufacturer Arnold Staub set up his mechanized cotton spinning and weaving factory at Kuchen, 48 km (32 mi.) W. of Stuttgart in the upper Fils valley, he wanted it to be a model of its kind in every way – in its management and production techniques, socially, and architecturally. His architect, the railway engineer Georg von Morlok, drew up plans in 1857 showing the entire layout of the factory and the workers' accommodation designed as a self-contained unit, independent of existing village communities. The close connection of factory, living quarters and social institutions was not just an act of social benevolence: it served also to encourage loyalty among the workers, and was a particularly clear type of patriarchal regimentation. Part of the factory has been demolished, but the dwelling houses, bathhouse, washhouse, and a dining hall have been preserved. The buildings, timber-framed and plastered, are grouped around a tree-lined square, and still convey an authentic impression of a factory colony of the mid-nineteenth century.

Kullaa, Turun ja Porin lääni, Finland   The ironworks at Leineperi (Fredriksfors), near Kullaa, in western Finland, were established by Major Berndt Johan Hastfer in 1771, consisting at first of two forges and a works for manufacturing iron objects. In 1787 a blast furnace was added, and sawmilling began from 1877. The manufacture of iron ceased in 1908.

The most striking of the remaining structures at Leineperi is the tall blast furnace of 1861, the best-preserved of its kind in the country. The red-brick bar-iron forge on the south bank of the river dates from the same period, and has an extension of 1883 built of slag blocks. The workshop was converted into a sawmill, of which the saw frames, manufactured by the Swedish Bolinder company, remain as a memorial. The mansion, set in a park, dates from the 1860s, as does a group of ten small, regularly planned workers' houses, and a bakery built out of clay. Many old farm buildings which served the needs of the ironworks also survive. The council at Kullaa, in association with the National Board of Antiquities and Historical Monuments and the private landowner, has begun to restore the ironworks, and plans to use the site for museum, educational and recreational purposes.

LAURI PUTKONEN

Kutná Hora (Kuttenberg), Central Bohemia, Czechoslovakia   A silver-mining centre, a city that was second only to Prague in the Middle Ages. The importance of mining is reflected in the scale of civic and ecclesiastical building in the town, which acquired municipal status at the end of the thirteenth century. A royal mint was set up *c*.1300, and commerce and craft manufactures developed alongside mining. Surface extraction gave place to deeper shaft mining, using shafts of 50–150 m (180–500 ft.) in the late thirteenth century, and of 400 m (1300 ft.) by the end of the fourteenth. Associated with the mines there were smelting and dressing plants in the neighbouring Vrahlice and Bylanska valleys. At the end of the fourteenth century, these complexes were employing about 2500 people.

There was some decline during the fifteenth century, as

the costs of extraction increased. The mines under the town itself were closed as new areas to the north and south were opened up. The area was an important centre for innovations in mining techniques, and there was a complex water system associated with the mines, as well as a river navigation bringing in timber from the Krkonoše (Giant Mountains), some 50–100 km (30–60 mi.) to the north. The town remained prosperous until the end of the sixteenth century but new investment was unable to compensate for exhaustion of the resource and increasing costs. The mint was transferred to Prague in 1726. There was intermittent mining activity in the area during the nineteenth and twentieth centuries, including the exploitation of lead and zinc during World War II.

The medieval mines under the town have been partially rediscovered, and were re-opened in 1968. Kutná Hora's urban development and street pattern still reflect the medieval settlement pattern, originally a series of separate hamlets connected to each other, and to the mines, by a network of footpaths. Much of the town is laid out on deep layers of mining waste, and Sankturinovsky House is built on the site of a rare fortified manufacturing centre of the late fourteenth century.

The scale of Kutná Hora's mining activity stimulated growth and development in settlements over a very wide area. An example is Mala Upa (Krkonoše), a dispersed hamlet founded in the sixteenth century when timber was felled for the mines at Kutná Ora, which is now a holiday resort. The coal mines at Zacler in the Krkonoše were first worked by miners from Kutná Hora in 1796.

BIBLIOGRAPHY
Specific
Bilek, S. ed. *Kutná Hora v Banske Historii* (Kutná Hora in the History of Mining). Kutná Hora: Oblastni Muzeum, 1968.

LOCATION
[M] Oblastni Muzeum, Hradec, Barboiska Ulice, Kutná Hora.

JUDITH ALFREY and TIM PUTNAM

L

lace The word 'lace' has two principal meanings: cords for fixing shoes or garments like bodices, or delicate openwork fabrics, made from linen, silk, cotton or synthetic fibre, with patterns worked into them, used for borders, edgings, trimmings and semi-finished components of clothing like collars and cuffs. Lace of the latter kind can be made by working the patterns and then linking them together with bars or mesh, in the traditions established in Milan, Brussels and Devon, or made as a continuous fabric in a single operation, as was customary in Genoa, Antwerp, Mechelen, Valenciennes, Lille, Nottingham and Bedfordshire. Lace was made by hand in many parts of Europe in the seventeenth, eighteenth and nineteenth centuries.

The principal pioneer of the machine-made lace industry was John Heathcoat (1783–1861) who, following the destruction of his Loughborough factory by machine-breakers in 1816, moved his concern to a six-storey mill at Tiverton, Devon, where he employed 1600 people by 1822. Nevertheless the centre of the British lace industry remained in Nottingham, where steam-powered machinery almost completely replaced hand-operated machines between 1820 and 1860, and where the organization of late nineteenth-century production, as in the HOSIERY industry, was based on WAREHOUSES, some of which had rooms up to 100 m (350 ft.) long to allow lengths of lace to be spread at full length to be dried after mending, stiffening, bleaching and dyeing.

BIBLIOGRAPHY
General
Back, 1981; Felkin, 1867; Lowe and Richards, 1982; Stratton and Trinder, 1989b; Varley, 1959.
Specific
Oldfield, G. The Nottingham Lace Market. In *TH*, xv, 1984.
Varley, D. E. John Heathcoat (1783–1861): founder of the machine-made lace industry. In *TH*, i, 1968.

BARRIE TRINDER

Lachine Canal, Quebec, Canada *See* MONTREAL.

lade A channel along which water is conveyed to a mill wheel, a word etymologically unrelated to the synonymous LEAT.

Lajes do Pico, Azores, Portugal The Pico and Flores islands, belonging to the Azores archipelago, were formerly bases for whaling. The Whalers' Museum displays numerous artefacts connected with the industry.

LOCATION
[M] Whalers' Museum, Lajes do Pico, Azores.

Lake District, Cumbria, England The English Lake District, made famous by the Romantic poets of the early nineteenth century, is an area rich in minerals and has a long industrial history. At Duddon, Broughton-in-Furness, is a blast furnace which worked from 1736 until 1867. The complete stack survives, together with the charcoal barn and ore store. The furnace at Backbarrow, 11 km (7 mi.) NE of Ulverston, dating from 1711, was rebuilt into its present form in 1870, and was fired with charcoal until 1926. The ruins of the Stony Hazel finery-and-chafery forge at Satterthwaite, 9 km (6 mi.) SW of Windermere, are fragmentary, but they are the most substantial remains in Britain of a forge of this type. In the Copper Mines Valley north-west of Coniston are remains of massive water-power installations of the nineteenth century, as well as traces of sixteenth-century mining. The ex-Furness Railway station at Ulverston has magnificent cast-iron platform canopies of 1873. The outstanding monument to the many woodland industries of the Lake District is the Stott Park Bobbin Mill, Finsthwaite, 12 km ($7\frac{1}{2}$ mi.) SW of Windermere, dating from 1835, which is preserved by English Heritage; here nineteenth-century equipment, including several products of Lakeland foundries, is displayed and demonstrated. Weatheriggs Pottery, Clifton, 5 km (3 mi.) S. of Penrith, the best-known traditional pottery in England, produces Westmorland salt-glaze earthenware. To the north of the region the coalfields of Cumberland prospered from trading with Ireland. At Workington the industry is commemorated by the spectacular crenellated chimneys and engine house at Janes Pit, built by Henry Curwen c.1843. The 'candle-stick' chimney built by Sydney Smirke (1798–1877) c.1850 is a similar structure in the Lowther family's model coal port of Whitehaven. Barracks Mill, Catherine Street, Whitehaven, is an iron-framed, steam-powered linen factory of 1809. Several of the steam launches used on the lakes in the nineteenth century are preserved at Windermere, and another plies on Coniston Water.

BIBLIOGRAPHY
General
Davies-Shiel and Marshall, 1969; Shaw, 1972.

LOCATIONS
[M] Whitehaven Museum and Art Gallery, Market Place, Whitehaven, Cumbria CA28 7JG.
[M] Windermere Steamboat Museum, Rayrigg Road, Windermere, Cumbria LA23 1BN.

BARRIE TRINDER

Lancashire, England The historic county of Lancashire was the centre of the British cotton industry from the early nineteenth century. In 1974 parts of Lancashire were incorporated into Greater Manchester, Merseyside, Cheshire and Cumbria, and the modern county has a more rural aspect. Water power, coal, a disciplined labour force well accustomed to work in textiles, and the commercial skills gained both in domestic and overseas trading brought prosperity to the cotton industry in the early nineteenth century, and new industries, particularly engineering, developed subsequently. Towns of the Industrial Revolution grew chiefly along the valleys, with easy access to the high moorland. Many mill buildings remain, though most have been adapted to new uses. Shaw, near Oldham, has the best remaining concentration of large, steel-framed, red-brick mills of c.1890–1910. Distinctive types of early nineteenth-century weavers' cottages in lowland central Lancashire have been identified by Timmins (1977). Many mills, once water powered, remain in the rural north of the county along the River Lune and its tributaries.

See also BOLTON; FYLDE; LIVERPOOL; MANCHESTER; PENNINES; ST HELENS; WIGAN.

BIBLIOGRAPHY
General
Timmins, 1977.

LOCATION
[M] Lancashire County Museum, Stanley Street, Preston.

BARRIE TRINDER

Lancashire forge A modification of the FINERY-AND-CHAFERY FORGE process, used in Sweden to refine wrought iron from pig iron, with charcoal as the fuel. The Swedish metallurgist Gustaf Ekman saw a forge near Ulverston in the Furness portion of Lancashire, which he later adapted to Swedish conditions, converting an open WALLOON FORGE hearth, and closing it in. In 1845 he introduced his 'koltornsvallugn', a welding furnace where charcoal was used as fuel in a gas generator. In the Lancashire process the pig iron was refined and smelted in a closed finery hearth, and then reheated in a chafery or welding furnace. It was then hammered or rolled to bar iron. Numerous examples are preserved in SWEDEN, where in 1936 the process was recorded on a film, *Iron*, at the Uddeholm works (*see* MUNKFORS).

BIBLIOGRAPHY
General
Odelstierna, 1913.

land drainage A term that encompasses four activities: the control and management of rivers in their valleys, the provision and maintenance of ditches and other small watercourses, the reclamation of land from the sea, lakes and marshes, and the underdraining of farmland. Land drainage relates most closely to the history of industry in the last two categories. Substantial watercourses and embankments constructed in land reclamation schemes have strong affinities with canals and other civil engineering structures, while the prime movers employed in PUMPING STATIONS are essentially the same as those used in mining and manufacturing. The underdraining of farmland was dependent on the large-scale manufacture of the necessary materials and plant.

In England modern underdraining was pioneered in the 1760s by Joseph Elkington, inventor of the boring iron. The mole plough was the invention of Adam Scott in Essex in 1797, and the automatic mole plough, normally worked by TRACTION or PORTABLE ENGINES, was developed by John Fowler (1826–64), the principal British manufacturer of drainage plant in the mid-nineteenth century. The chief German supplier was Ottomeyer of Bad Pyrmont, a firm established in 1887 to provide peat ploughs. A system of shallow, parallel drains was developed in England by James Smith from c.1800, but mechanized production of DRAINAGE PIPES from the 1840s, together with a programme of government grants, enabled the adoption in the following decades of the system of deep, parallel drains proposed by Josiah Parks.

See also FENS; NETHERLANDS; POLDER; PUMPING STATION.

BIBLIOGRAPHY
General
Ayres and Scoates, 1939; Darby, 1956; Denton, 1883; Found *et al.*, 1974; Hills, 1967; Kendall, 1950; Lane, 1980; Nicholson, 1946; Phillips, 1989.

BARRIE TRINDER

landmark Originally, a boundary mark; subsequently, a point of guidance on a journey. By the mid-nineteenth century 'landmark' was used figuratively to indicate an important stage in a historical process.

In the USA in the twentieth century the importance of historical monuments has been marked by according them the status of 'landmarks'. Several of the professional engineering societies annually select a small number of noteworthy domestic (and occasionally international) structures or machines as engineering landmarks – providing no real legal, but often considerable psychological, protection – by bestowing recognition through bronze plaques, speeches and commemorative booklets. The ultimate honour the US government's National Park Service can give a site is designation as a National Historic Landmark, a level above listing on the National Register of Historic Places. Neither elevation safeguards a site from the threat of demolition, unless federal funds are involved in the proposed demolition or alteration, but the tax relief and civic honour they afford usually work to save sites so designated.

DAVID H. SHAYT

landscape The study of landscapes as part of industrial archaeology springs from two principal sources: from attempts by prehistorians to use archaeological evidence to reconstruct landscapes of the very distant past, and from the work of W. G. Hoskins (1908–) and other geographers whose concern has been to explain the

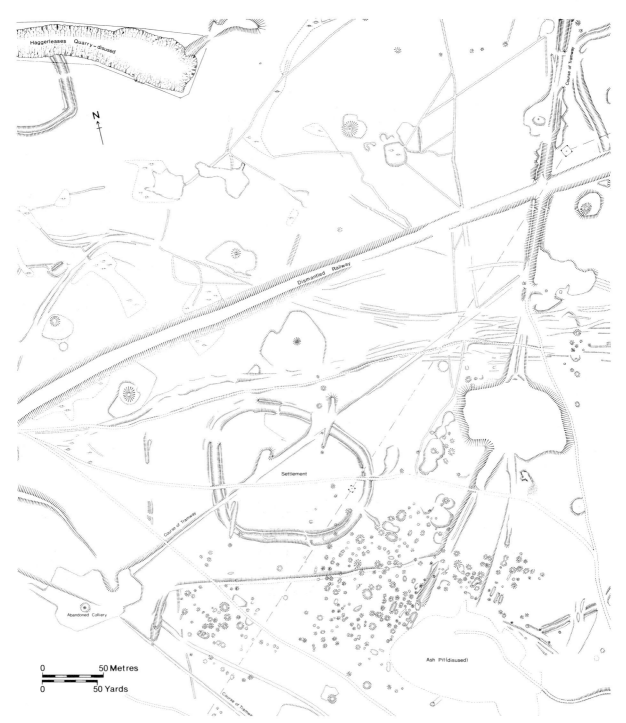

Figure 68 Analytical field survey adds clarity to the interpretation of an industrial LANDSCAPE which can be obtained from aerial photography: on Cockfield Fell, in County Durham, a subcircular late-prehistoric defended settlement is surrounded by a well-preserved coalfield landscape. To the right of the enclosure, subsidence craters outnumber the scattered bell-pits. The disused and quarried ash-pit of the village lies at bottom right, almost masking an adit, dug before 1897, of the Millfield Grange colliery. A spoil-tip from this colliery covers its own tramway from an earlier phase at lower left, and the later tramway crosses the prehistoric defences. In the centre, multiple trackways, leats and drains are cut by the Barnard Castle and Bishop Auckland branch of the North Eastern Railway, which operated between 1863 and 1962.

Royal Commission on the Historical Monuments of England

Figure 69 An aerial photograph, looking West, across Cockfield Fell in County Durham, England. A roadside quarry, 27 m deep, follows the line of a dyke of dolerite, a dense igneous rock. Extraction began in the mid-nineteenth century and ended in the 1950s. The line of the Bishop Auckland railway of 1863 is crossed by a colliery tramway; this intersection is also shown on Figure 68 (upper right). In the angle between these two are the earthworks of a late prehistoric enclosure. Scattered bell-pits give way to densely packed subsidence craters (on the extreme right) over shallow coal workings. To the left of the quarry, trackways cross the Fell. They are overlain (lower left) by a polygonal enclosure which seems to have been a garden; it gave its name to the adjacent Potato Garth Pit, part of the spoil from which is also visible. This, in turn was cut by the quarry. 'Crows-feet' tips of overburden from the quarry are also visible.
Royal Commission on the Historical Monuments of England

evolution of particular landscapes over long periods of time. A landscape approach to industrial archaeology brings many advantages. It can increase understanding of a site by avoiding too close a concentration on particular technological processes, and posing questions about sources of raw materials, transport facilities, power systems, the dwellings of entrepreneurs and employees and the disposal of waste products. On a micro-level it can stimulate an appreciation of the subtleties of particular sites, by developing an awareness of such features as the use of waste products as building materials, or the effects of property boundaries. A landscape approach also places industry in its broad historical context, showing its relationship to natural resources, and to historical events in the pre-industrial past, and in the period since industrial activity ceased on particular sites. Above all a landscape approach is a means of insuring that easily obtained archaeological evidence is not used simply to support accepted interpretations. It can identify new, often paradoxical, evidence which can stimulate more rigorously based syntheses.

See figures 68, 69; *see also* figures 8, 11, 55, 137, 146, 171.

BIBLIOGRAPHY
General
Aston, 1985; Hoskins, 1957; Trinder, 1982a.
Specific
Clark, C. M. Trouble at t'mill: industrial archaeology in the 1980s. In *Antiquity*, LXI, 1987.

BARRIE TRINDER

Lapphyttan, Västmanland, Sweden   Near Norberg, 18 km (11 mi.) SW of Avesta, Lapphyttan is the site of one of the most important excavations in the relatively short history of industrial archaeology. Six seasons of investigation under the direction of Ake Hyenstrand and Gert Magnusson in the late 1970s and early 1980s revealed a medieval ironworks, with samples of ore, calcining pits, water-power systems, and a reduction furnace of blast-furnace type. Carbon-14 tests showed that the furnace was in use as early as the twelfth century, and that it probably ceased operation in the mid-fourteenth century. The excavation completely revised accepted views of the location and of the chronology of the development of the blast furnace. Remains of refining furnaces for forging wrought iron were also discovered. This was the first complete medieval works to be investigated in Sweden.

BIBLIOGRAPHY
Specific
Magnusson, A. The medieval blast furnace at Lapphyttan. In Rockwell and Garcia, 1985.
Nisser, M. and Bedoire, F. Industrial heritage activities in Sweden, 1981–84. In Victor and Wright, 1984.

lathe   A machine for 'turning', by gradually feeding a single-point cutting tool against work rotating about a horizontal axis, producing principally cylindrical, but also flat and conical or threaded surfaces. Shaping materials while they are being rotated on a spindle is one of the oldest and most widely diffused techniques of manufacture. Simple drive mechanisms were provided by bows or sprung poles and cutting tools were hand-held and propped against the body or supports fixed to the frame. The desire to shape metal castings or forgings into mechanical parts led to the development of stable and adjustable mechanisms for rotating the work and holding the cutting tool. By the beginning of the nineteenth century a cluster of innovations has been consolidated into the type-form of the basic industrial or 'engine' lathe. A rigid frame, usually of cast iron, supported a spindle in bearings at the head above a bed machined with ways parallel to the axis of rotation on which was mounted an adjustable tail support bearing and a sliding tool-rest or carriage. A rack or lead screw was used to move the carriage along the bed and a similar principle was used to adjust the depth of cut by controlling the movement of a cross slide on the carriage. Power was supplied to the spindle and the carriage lead screw through stepped pulleys and change gears.

Using newly available carbon-steel tools, these features dramatically increased the speed and accuracy with which turned forms could be produced in iron, and revolutionized the cutting of screws. Engine lathes were employed wherever the mechanical workshops of manufacturing industry were to be found, in a variety of sizes and of bearing, chucking and tool mounting arrangements. For general engineering, a 'swing' or working diameter of 30–50 cm (12–20 in.) and a bed length of 1.2–2.4 m (4–8 ft.) were common. Many boring and grinding operations were performed with the aid of special attachments. After 1850 the mounting of toolsets in a 'turret' on the carriage or a separate 'capstan' or 'ram' facilitated repetitive chucked work such as the turning of small screws. Bar stock fed through a hollow spindle and power drive to the turret then opened the way to single and multi-spindle cam-actuated automatics. At the turn of the century new designs such as the flat-turret were introduced to achieve the greater rigidity and flexibility of arrangement required in mass-production precision machining of larger pieces under the greater stresses made possible by high-speed tungsten-carbide cutting tools.

Lathes are also used in wood- and leather-working, and in the ceramics industry for turning and giving an exact form to dried but unfired ceramic articles. Simple designs are treadle-driven, but powered lathes have been employed for such mass-produced utilitarian items as STONEWARE jars for MARMALADE.

BIBLIOGRAPHY
General
Battison, 1976; Rolt, 1986; Searle, 1929; Steeds, 1969; Woodbury, 1961.

TIM PUTNAM

Latrobe, Benjamin Henry (1764–1820)   The leading architect and engineer in the USA of the early nineteenth century, and father of a dynasty of engineers. Latrobe was born at the Moravian COLONY at Fulneck, LEEDS, England:

Figure 70 A small screw-cutting lathe with its accessories, designed by Henry Maudslay (1771–1831)
Science Museum, London

he studied in Germany and returned to England to work with the architect S. P. Cockerell and the engineer JOHN SMEATON. He emigrated to the USA in 1796, where he worked on the water supply of Philadelphia before going to WASHINGTON DC as Surveyor of Public Buildings in 1803. From 1814 he took charge of the rebuilding of the Capitol. He was engineer of the Chesapeake & Delaware Canal from 1799.

His son, John H. B. Latrobe (1803–91), was trained as an engineer but became a lawyer; he was a promoter of the Baltimore & Ohio Railroad, and recommended the installation of the MORSE telegraph between Baltimore and Washington; he also invented the Latrobe stove for room heating. The other son, Benjamin Henry Latrobe (1806–78), was also a civil engineer, and the father of Charles H. Latrobe (1834–1902), who worked for the Baltimore & Ohio Railroad and the Baltimore Bridge Company.

Laucherthal, Baden-Württemberg, Germany   The iron-works in the Laucher valley, 8 km (5 mi.) E. of Sigmaringen, was built on the site of an earlier works from 1707, when a BLAST FURNACE, a forge and the associated water-power systems and workers' housing were constructed on the initiative of the princes of Hohenzollern-Sigmaringen. These were followed in 1803 by a rolling mill, and a larger blast furnace with an associated casting house. The first CUPOLA furnace was added in 1853. Local mines provided iron ore, and the company produced its own charcoal. Competition brought about the closure of the blast furnace in 1879, but the rolling mill remains in operation. Five timber-framed dwelling houses have been preserved,

together with the large blast furnace of *c.*1830, which retains its forehearth, tapping hole and crane.

Lauenburg, Schleswig-Holstein, Germany   What is probably the oldest surviving lock in Europe is situated in Lauenburg, 48 km (32 mi.) SE of Hamburg: the Palmschleuse, last renovated in 1724, but of much earlier date. It represents the transition from the flash lock, with only one gate – as it can be seen in Witzeese, north of Lauenburg – to the later pound lock. The Palmschleuse forms the entrance to the Stecknitz Canal to Lübeck, and was built between 1391 and 1398 for the transport of salt and lime from Lüneburg. In the city of Lübeck, 56 km (35 mi.) N. of Lauenburg, the fourteenth-century salt warehouses by the Holsten gate on the River Trave are reminders of the importance of the salt trade.

Among the exhibits at the Museum of Elbe Shipping in Lauenburg are the coal-burning paddle steamer *Kaiser Wilhelm*, built in Dresden in 1900 for passenger traffic on the Upper Weser, which remains in working order, and a marine steam engine of earlier date.

BIBLIOGRAPHY
General
Slotta, 1975–88.

LOCATION
[M] Lauenburger Elbschiffahrtsmuseum (Museum of Elbe Shipping), Elbstrasse 59, 2058 Lauenburg.

laundry   Washing clothes for town-dwellers was traditionally the occupation of inhabitants of poor outer suburbs, or, in very large cities, of recent immigrants. By

Figure 71   The flue of a disused lead smelter at Lávrion, Greece, leading to the monumental plinth of a chimney on top of the hill
Michael Stratton

the mid-nineteenth century some laundries had evolved into small-scale industrial concerns, like that serving AMSTERDAM, preserved at ARNHEM, where there were boilers, coppers, tubs sunk into the floor for rinsing and soaking, and a horse gin working pounding machinery. The preparation of new garments for presentation in shops was an important part of the laundry industry. By 1900 larger-scale concerns had developed, usually with steam engines as prime movers, driving, through line-shafting and belts, rotary washers, collar and cuff ironing machines, and other specialized equipment supplied by such companies as the American Laundry Machinery Co. of Cincinnati, the Adams Laundry Machinery Co. of Troy, N.Y., and Manlove Alliott & Co. of Nottingham. Laundries have declined in the twentieth century with the growth of the domestic washing machine.

BIBLIOGRAPHY
General
Benjamin, 1900; *Laundry Journal*, 1896; Samuel, 1977.
Specific
Thomas, D. G. and Sowan, B. J. *The Walton Lodge Sanitary Laundry*. London: Greater London Industrial Archaeological Society, 1977.

BARRIE TRINDER

La Voulte, Ardèche, France   Six blast furnaces were built at La Voulte on the Rhône, 16 km (10 mi.) S. of Valence, between 1828 and 1845, in order to exploit local iron ores and coke from Rive-de-Gier (Loire) to make pig iron for the

Terrenoire ironworks at SAINT-ÉTIENNE. Four of the 15 m (49 ft.) high furnaces remain, two dating from 1828 and two from 1845. They were inspired by English technology, with blast provided by high-pressure steam engines, and served as models for a whole generation of French metallurgical engineers. The site also retains vestiges of iron-ore mines, calcining kilns and transport installations.

BIBLIOGRAPHY
General
Belhoste, 1991.
Specific
Peyre, P. Contribution à l'étude des mécanismes de l'innovation: l'exemple des fonderies de la Voulte (Ardèche) (A contribution to the study of innovatory mechanisms: the example of the La Voulte ironworks). In *Actes du 112è Congrès national des Sociétés Savantes*, II. Paris: Bibliothèque nationale, 1987.

Lávrion (Ergasteria), Attica, Greece   A major centre of lead and silver mining, both in classical antiquity and in modern times, 54 km (34 mi.) SE of Athens, on the Aegean. At the summit of the hills beyond Ag Konstandinos is a broken mining landscape where some shafts are still worked. The best group of mines is 5 km (3 mi.) W., at the head of a shallow valley running eastwards to the sea. There are extensive remains of classical silver working, parts of which have been excavated, including dressing floors and square-sectioned shafts descending almost vertically to galleries up to 500 m (1640 ft.) long. The ore was broken down with hammers, then washed and

Figure 72   Train of the Manx Electric Railway at Laxey
Michael Stratton

ground between stones. Tanks, channels and cisterns for separating out light waste materials are in a near-perfect state of preservation. A large cistern was used to collect rainwater, since the area lacks springs. The channels and the cisterns were lined with litharge (lead oxide, PbO), one of the by-products of the smelting process. Smelting took place at a distance from the mines where there was good ventilation. Production at the mines in classical times reached a peak *c.*483 BC, ceased in 413 with the incursion of the Spartans, resuming on a modest scale *c.*355 BC. There was a major revival in the mid-nineteenth century. Modern exploitation was largely by French and Greek companies.

Inland from Lávrion are the remains of the works of the Greek company. A large gable end wall survives, with a more modern washing house closer to the hillside. A small office block incorporates a mineralogical museum. Both the French mining company and the Greek company provided housing and social facilities for their workers. The music hall built by the Greek company remains in use. On the edge of the town is the works of the French company. The lower part includes a workshop with rubblestone walling and a series of wide internal arches. The western end accommodates a machine shop with hearths and machine tools. Approximately 200 m (220 yd.) up the hill is a modern lead-smelting works that still operates using imported ore to produce 40 000 tonnes of lead per annum, utilizing a long FLUE running up to a chimney stack.

Part of the lead-working area has been destroyed to make way for a large modern textile mill producing synthetic fabrics.

MICHAEL STRATTON

Laxey, Isle of Man   The most celebrated and reputedly the largest wheel in the world is the 200 hp Lady Isabella at Laxey, 10 km (6 mi.) NE of Douglas, designed by Robert Casement, and brought into use on 27 September 1854. The wheel, which is 22 m (72½ ft.) in diameter, worked on the pitch backshot principle, and has 168 buckets.

Large-scale mining for lead in the Laxey Valley seems to have begun with the digging of a lengthy ADIT in the early 1780s. A new company was formed in 1822 and subsequently the first water wheels were constructed to pump out the mines, being supplemented by a steam engine from 1846. A large water wheel was constructed in the late 1840s, but had a short life, being replaced by the Lady Isabella in 1854. The intended purpose of the vast wheel is not wholly certain. It has an estimated power output of 200 hp, yet required only 40–60 hp to work the pumps to which it was attached. A spare crank suggests that Casement originally intended it to pump with dual pump rods. Turbines were installed later in the nineteenth century, and in 1881 a MAN ENGINE worked by a water-pressure engine was constructed, the last known installation of such a system. The mines closed in 1929.

The Lady Isabella is the most spectacular of many industrial monuments in the Laxey Valley. There is a viaduct to carry the pump rods, originally of thirty-four stone arches, of which thirty-one survive, each of 4.1 m (13 ft. 5 in.) span. Several tunnels survive, including the 120 m (394 ft.) river tunnel built in 1846–8 when the original course of the River Mooar was diverted. The beam engine house still stands, together with a machine house of 1862 with a Fourneyron turbine built by McAdams Brothers of the Soho Foundry, Belfast, used for winding the shafts. A complex system of lades intersects the valley, and there are extensive remains of dressing floors.

399

From the first the Lady Isabella was brightly painted, and the wheel is depicted on many postcards and other souvenirs. It was clearly intended to be a spectacular feature of the landscape as well as a working part of the mine. Visitors were being charged to see the mill as early as the 1870s. In 1890 the Browside tramway was constructed to take visitors to the wheel.

The Manx Electric Railway climbs the Laxey Valley round a lengthy bend, crossing the Mooar on a curving stone viaduct. Laxey station, a pleasant timber building, is the terminus of the 1.07 m (3 ft. 6 in.) gauge railway opened in 1895 using the Fell rack system to climb to Snaefell summit. Several terraces of stone cottages, once occupied by miners still stand in Laxey village. West of the viaduct carrying the new road and south of the Glenroy river is the four-storey Laxey Glen Mill of 1860, which still works with early roller equipment.

The Lady Isabella was acquired by the Manx government in 1965 and the government has recently decided to acquire as much land as possible in the valley and to create an industrial archaeology trail.

BIBLIOGRAPHY
General
Clark *et al.*, 1985; Jespersen, 1970.
Specific
Cowin, F. *Laxey Mines Trail*. Douglas: Manx Conservation Council, 1973.
Stratton, M. *Laxey Glen Flour Mills and the Interpretation of Laxey*. Ironbridge, Ironbridge Institute, 1986.

BARRIE TRINDER

LD process A steel-making process in which molten pig iron is decarburized by the insertion of oxygen lances, first successfully demonstrated at Linz in 1949 (*see* AUSTRIA). Originally known as the Linzer Dusenverfahren process it is also supposed to take its name from its use at the Linz and Donawitz steelworks (*see* STYRIAN IRON TRAIL). It is now used almost universally: it can accommodate large quantities of steel scrap, and has many variations. The process is known in the USA as BOP (Basic Oxygen Process).

BIBLIOGRAPHY
General
Gale, 1967, 1969.

lead (Pb) A metallic element, and one of the bases of industrial civilization. It is found in several ores from which it is easily separated. The principal source is galena (lead sulphide, PbS), which often contains silver and is usually found in association with zinc ore. Deposits have been worked in Britain (*see* DURHAM; CROMFORD; SHREWSBURY), Australia, Canada, France and the USA (*see* COLORADO; IDAHO). Most lead deposits are in veins within sedimentary rocks, but deposits can be found as replacements and disseminations in limestones and dolomites, as in Colorado. The deposits are generally worked using conventional STOPING methods, but open-pit techniques are increasingly employed. Ore dressing is relatively simple due to the high density of galena. As lead has a high density, it has usually been crushed and concentrated by flotation (*see* BUDDLE; CRUSHING CIRCLE; DRESSING FLOOR; JIGGING).

Lead was smelted in the Middle Ages in wind-blown bole furnaces, but from the sixteenth century the ORE HEARTH was in use. The CUPOLA was introduced in the late seventeenth century, and for two hundred years both methods were employed in Britain. Various forms of blast furnaces have also been employed for smelting lead. Early means of smelting lead were often inefficient, and in the nineteenth century substantial works were established to extract metal from the SLAGS and SLIMES of previous generations.

Lead has many uses: in storage batteries, building construction, paints and ammunition.

See also RED LEAD; WHITE LEAD; PEWTER; SHOT TOWER; TYPE.

BIBLIOGRAPHY
General
Clough, 1980; Rowe, 1983; Stratton and Trinder, 1988.

IVOR J. BROWN

Leadhills, Strathclyde, Scotland *See* WANLOCKHEAD AND LEADHILLS.

leat A watercourse conveying water to the point where it is to be used, most often to a mill. Usually the leat is an artificial channel cut around a natural fall on a river or stream.

See also HEAD RACE; LADE; POWER CANAL; TRENCH.

leather The skin of an animal, stabilized by TANNING or treatment with alum or oils (*see* CURRYING; TAWING) to prevent decay. The skin of a mammal is composed of three layers; the outermost being the epidermis, composed of cells containing the hair system, the middle layer the corium, and the inner layer the flesh. Leather is made from the corium.

Leather is prepared from 'hides', the skins of fully-grown cattle, horses or buffalo; 'kips', the skins of calves and foals; or 'skins', which come from sheep, pigs, goats or deer. Untanned hides were traded internationally in the seventeenth century, temporarily conserved by drying, drying and salting, or by being packed in casks containing brine.

Leather was and is used in boots, shoes, clothing, gloves, and saddles; and also in belting for power transmission in factories and workshops, in the suspension and canopies of carriages, and to provide smooth surfaces in textile machines.

See also FELLMONGER; GLOVES; SADDLERY; SHOES; TANNING.

BIBLIOGRAPHY
General
Minnoch and Minnoch, 1970; O'Flaherty *et al.*, 1956; Procter, 1903, 1914; Stevens, 1891; Waterer, 1944.
Specific
Jenkins, J. G. *The Rhaeadr Tanner*. Cardiff: National Museum of Wales, 1973.

Thomas, S., Clarkson, L. A. and Thompson, R. *Leather Manufacture through the Ages*. Northampton: East Midlands Industrial Archaeological Conference, 1983.

BARRIE TRINDER

Leblanc process The principal source of alkali in the second and third quarters of the nineteenth century, when the world market was dominated by British producers who operated 120 works in 1880, and exported 347 000 tons of alkali in the peak year of 1883. The process was devised by the French physician Nicholas Leblanc (1742–1806) in 1787, employed in France during the Napoleonic Wars, introduced to Britain in Newcastle in 1796, and developed on a large scale in south Lancashire from the 1820s, owing to the initiative of James Muspratt (1792–1866) and J. C. Gamble (1776–1848).

The first of the two stages took place in a cast-iron pot called a saltcake or decomposing furnace, and depended on the reaction of sulphuric acid with salt to produce 'saltcake' (sodium sulphate, Na_2SO_4) and hydrochloric acid gas (HCl):

$$2NaCl + H_2SO_4 \rightarrow Na_2SO_4 + 2HCl$$

The saltcake was then heated in a revolving furnace with coal and limestone (calcium carbonate, $CaCO_3$) to produce 'black ash', a mixture of calcium sulphide (CaS) and sodium carbonate (Na_2CO_3):

$$Na_2SO_4 + CaCO_3 + 2C \rightarrow 2CO_2 + Na_2CO_3 + CaS$$

The sodium carbonate was dissolved in water, then evaporated to produce soda ash. In the early nineteenth century the calcium sulphide was discarded as 'alkali waste'.

The fumes of hydrochloric acid made the first stage dangerous and caused severe atmospheric pollution. Subsequently acid was recovered in GOSSAGE TOWERS, which led alkali manufacturers to become involved in making bleaching compounds (*see* BLEACHING POWDER). Some developed this as the main aspect of their business, selling the sodium sulphate to glassmakers who used it instead of soda ash. In 1835 A. N. Chance of Oldbury, near Birmingham, developed a method of recovering sulphur by charging the waste calcium sulphide into cylindrical iron vessels and passing carbon dioxide over it, producing hydrogen sulphide (H_2S), from which sulphur could be extracted in a kiln in which ferric oxide (Fe_2O_2) was employed as a catalyst. In 1868 Henry Deacon (1822–76) devised a means of producing chlorine from the waste hydrochloric acid gas by mixing it with air and passing it over a heated copper salt. By such means the economy of alkali production improved, and a mechanized furnace for producing saltcake was patented in 1875; but the process remained basically inefficient, being complicated and slow, and needing large dumping grounds for solid waste. It was superseded by the ammonia-soda process (*see* ERNEST SOLVAY).

Leblanc plants were characteristically small and ill-built and there are few significant remains (*see* HALTON).

BIBLIOGRAPHY
General
Allen, 1906; Clow, 1952; Morgan and Pratt, 1938; Partington, 1950; Reader, 1970; Warren, 1980.

BARRIE TRINDER

Le Creusot, Saône-et-Loire, France The first ironworks at Le Creusot was built between 1782 and 1787 under the direction of William Wilkinson, brother of JOHN WILKINSON, to supply the Indret cannon foundry near Nantes with pig iron. The four blast furnaces were the first in France to use coke and to have steam-powered blowing apparatus. The coal was found at Le Creusot, where deep mining had begun in 1769. The presence of coal also explained why the Cristallerie de la Reine (the Queen's crystal glassworks) moved to Le Creusot from its original site at Sèvres, near Paris, in 1787. Both industries also took advantage of the new Canal du Centre, dug between 1783 and 1793, linking the Loire to the Saône.

The early years of the ironworks were difficult ones. In 1826 the works was taken over by two English entrepreneurs, Aaron Manby and Daniel Wilson, who had been running an ironworking establishment, foundry, puddling furnaces and mechanical engineering works, at Charenton, near Paris, since 1822. From 1827 they built a new integrated, English-type ironworks at Le Creusot, which was taken over in 1836 by the Schneider family. The Schneiders ran Le Creusot for almost a century and a half, specializing in railway rolling stock, armaments, and subsequently in electrical equipment. The development of the factory induced the growth of a new town, which began with early-nineteenth-century barrack-like tenement blocks and came to include twentieth-century GARDEN CITY style estates with semi-detached houses for white-collar workers. Almost every type of housing generated by industry is represented at Le Creusot.

In 1973 the richness and exemplary nature of this industrial past led to the foundation of the ÉCOMUSÉE of Le Creusot–Montceau-les-Mines. The first operation undertaken by this novel museum was an inventory of the industrial monuments of the region, which pioneered the discipline of industrial archaeology in France. This example launched a movement of écomusées, those of the Beauvais region, of Roanne and of North Dauphiné being similarly concerned with the study of their local industrial heritage.

At Le Creusot, the écomusée is located in a part of the former Schneider residence, itself the château of the crystal glassworks until its closure in 1832. The collections of the museum include tools, models and works of art related to the theme of work, along with some 60 000 books and periodicals donated by the Society of French Civil Engineers.

The winding-up of the Creusot-Loire Company in 1984 led to the demolition of most of the buildings on the Riaux plain, the site in front of the château where the works had first been established. One building has been preserved here: the old crane and locomotive workshop, a brick structure of 1848–50, with large, round-arched win-

401

dows. Closer to the château, the outer shells of two conical English glass cones survive from the crystal glassworks. The cones were reused c.1870, one for a private chapel, the other for a water reservoir, subsequently a theatre. The large rolling-mill building – an iron-framed structure, 360 m × 100 m (1180 ft. × 330 ft.), erected by the Schneiders between 1861 and 1867 – also survives, as do the machine assembly shops built in 1900, with their north-lit roofing, and arcade façade on the town side, and the artillery workshop at the Breuil annexe, put up at the end of World War I and roofed with a thin vault of reinforced concrete. At the entrance to the town a 1300-tonne steam hammer, the most powerful in the world when it was built in 1876, has been erected as a monument. The oldest workers' dwellings, a row of cottages known as the 'Combe des Mineurs', were built in 1826 by Manby and Wilson for their English workers, and have many English features.

Montceau-les-Mines, 10 km (6 mi.) S. of Le Creusot, where the Chagot family of coal-owners had a similar influence to that of the Schneiders, also has interesting industrial sites. Over the former Saint-Claude mine, opened between 1857 and 1868, a twentieth-century steel headstock has been re-erected as a monument. The former winding-engine house, dating from 1877 and subsequently used as a dwelling, now contains a small mining museum. Nearby, the Lucy II coal-fired power station, a reinforced-concrete structure of 1920, has an interesting façade with a pediment and pilasters. Montceau also boasts one of the earliest French examples of a 'garden estate', the Cité des Alouettes, built between 1834 and 1854.

Alongside these monuments associated directly with industrialization, mention should also be made of the Canal du Centre, the main means of industrial transport until 1861 when the Paris–Lyon–Mediterranean railway was inaugurated. At Ecuisses, 10 km (6 mi.) W. of Le Creusot, an eighteenth-century lock still survives, with a canal museum nearby. The Torcy leat, 2 m (6.5 ft.) wide, which took water from the canal to the Creusot works also survives, passing through a tunnel 1.3 km (1400 yd.) long, still partially roofed with late-eighteenth-century brick vaulting.

BIBLIOGRAPHY
General
Clément, 1990; Devillers and Huet, 1981; Schneider, 1912.
Specific
Combe, M. J.-M. 150 e Anniversaire de la 1re locomotive construite au Creusot. Paris: Alsthom Creusot Rail, 1988.
Écomusée de la Communauté Le Creusot-Montceau. *L'espace de la Communauté urbaine à travers les Ages* (The environment of the Communauté Urbaine through the ages). Le Creusot, 1974.
François, P. *Itinéraires industriels* (Industrial itineraries, guidebook). Montceau-les-Mines, Le Creusot: Écomusée de la Communauté Le Creusot, 1982.
Hudson, K. A living museum. In *New Society*, 27 February 1975.
Trinder, B. Impressions of Le Creusot. *IAR*, v, 1981.

LOCATION
[M] Écomusée de la Communauté Urbaine, Château de la Verrerie, 71200 Le Creusot.

JEAN-FRANÇOIS BELHOSTE

Leeds, Yorkshire, England   Leeds stands on the borders of the Yorkshire coalfield and the Pennine textile region, and at the head of navigation on the River Aire, made passable to shipping in 1699. Leeds was a prosperous town by the early eighteenth century and grew rapidly thereafter as the commercial centre of the Yorkshire textile industry, becoming notable in the nineteenth century both for the grandeur of its civic buildings, particularly the town hall by Cuthbert Brodrick (1822–1905) of 1853–8, and for the squalor of some of its working-class quarters. John Marshall (1764–1845) established Leeds as a centre of factory-based flax manufacture, and in the nineteenth century the city was important for leather processing, engineering, iron and steel manufacture, and ceramics. In 1856 John Barron introduced a band knife which could cut several layers of cloth, and, stimulated by immigration in the 1880s of Jewish refugees from persecution in Eastern Europe, the Leeds clothing industry grew rapidly. Joseph Hepworth & Sons, the first company to manufacture clothing on a large scale for their own shops, began business in Leeds in 1883.

The Leeds end of the Leeds & Liverpool Canal opened in 1777 and several substantial warehouses stand near to the confluence of the canal and the Aire. Leeds became an important railway centre in the nineteenth century. To the west Thomas Grainger (1794–1852) built several elegant stone arched bridges carrying lines into the former Central station. The east side of the city is dominated by a viaduct built in 1866–9, carrying lines to Selby and York. The Middleton Railway, which originated with a colliery line in 1755, has been preserved from 1959 and has a collection of shunting locomotives including an ex-LNER SENTINEL. A roundhouse built for the Leeds & Thirsk Railway survives adjacent to a crescent-shaped workshop of c.1870 and a row of smiths' forges.

The mill by Ignatius Bonomi (1796–1878), built for JOHN MARSHALL & Co. in 1838–40 in the EGYPTIAN style, is important not just as a spectacular eccentricity but as a pioneer of the single-storey textile mill. Of equal curiosity is T. W. Harding's pin works, which includes a chimney of 1864 modelled on the tower of the Palazzo de Signore in Verona, and a square dust-extraction tower which is a copy of Giotto's campanile at the Duomo in Florence. The outstanding twentieth-century industrial building in Leeds is the clothing factory of Montague Burton (1885–1952) in Hudson Road.

Firebrick production began in Leeds c.1845. Manufacturers gradually expanded into terracotta, the leading company being Wilcock and Co., who altered their name to the Burmantofts Co. Ltd c.1888. From the 1880s until 1904 the company made art pottery of high quality. In 1889 the company was one of the constituents of Leeds Fireclay Ltd, which pioneered the use of large blocks of architectural terracotta, working closely with such architects as Alfred Waterhouse and with clients like the Prudential Insurance Co. (*see* LONDON). The company developed a considerable export trade. Buildings in Leeds that used its products included the Metropole Hotel of 1897–9 and the city markets in Kirkgate, rebuilt in 1904.

BACK-TO-BACK terraced houses were almost universal in the nineteenth century working-class areas of Leeds. The type probably derived from houses built on the BURGAGE PLOTS of the medieval town, and was particularly suited to the dense development of the enclosed fields onto which the town spread in the late eighteenth century when the first back-to-backs were built. While other cities prohibited the type, construction in Leeds continued, and well over half the plans approved by the corporation between 1900 and 1905 were for back-to-backs. Even after the Housing Act 1909 made the type illegal, permissions already granted enabled builders to continue erecting them until 1937. By 1970 most back-to-backs constructed before 1850 had been demolished, but many later terraces remain.

The Leeds industrial museum is in Armley Mills. The iron-framed mill building (except for its roof) dates from 1805, and was used primarily for scribbling and fulling, the water wheels being supplemented in the late nineteenth century by steam engines and a turbine. There are comprehensive displays of textile machinery and leather manufacture. Machine tools include a lathe made by JOHN SMEATON, and there are two four-column beam engines of c.1820 by Matthew Murray (1765–1826) and Benjamin Hick, as well as cranes by Balmforth, Smith and Booth, and products of John Fowler (1826–64), pioneer of steam ploughing. There is a display relating to the Leeds clothing industry, and a collection of optical equipment by the firm of Kershaws, pioneers of cinematography. Trail guides link the museum with the city centre and with sites to the west, including Kirkstall Power Station of 1928–30, Kirkstall Forge with the tilt-hammers of c.1676 and c.1740, a slitting mill and two drop hammers of the 1850s, and an iron bridge of 1819 at Newlay.

See also figure 98.

BIBLIOGRAPHY
General
Beresford, 1988; Briggs, 1963; Rimmer, 1960.
Specific
Beresford, M. W. The back-to-back house in Leeds, 1787–1937. In Chapman, 1971.
Brears, P. *The Museum of Leeds Trail*, 1981.
Brears, P. *Armley Mills: the Leeds Industrial Museum*. Leeds: Leeds Industrial Museum, 1981.

LOCATIONS
[M] Leeds City Museums, Calverley Street, Leeds LS1 3AA.
[S] The Middleton Railway, Tunstall Road, Leeds.

BARRIE TRINDER

Leicester, Leicestershire, England   The county town, on the River Soar, linked to the River Trent by the Leicester Canal in 1794, and to waterways to the south by the completion of the Grand Union Canal in 1814. The chief industries in the nineteenth century were hosiery and then shoemaking and elastic. Domestic workshops survive at Wigston Magna, 5 km (3 mi.) S. Most factories are unspectacular, although the Cooperative Wholesale Society Wheatsheaf Works, dating from 1891, is considered to be the largest footwear factory in the world, once employing over 2000. Surviving features of the hybrid Leicester & Swannington Railway of 1832 include the portal of Glenfield tunnel, 6 km (4 mi.) E., and the route of the inclined plane at Bagworth, 11 km (7 mi.) E. The Museum of Technology, housed in the sewage-pumping station of 1891 with four Gimson Woolf compound beam engines and one surviving Lancashire boiler, includes displays on hosiery, and the reconstructed Soar Lane lifting bridge of 1876. The John Doran Gas Museum is situated in the town's second gasworks of 1878. Leicester Midland Station, of 1892, has stylish work in brick and terracotta; while the blue-brick viaducts of the Great Central Railway London Extension, opened in 1899 and closed in 1967, still stride across the west of the town. Photographs of the building of the line taken by Francis Newton in the city museum form one of the best pictorial records of railway construction.

BIBLIOGRAPHY
General
Rolt, 1971a; Smith, 1965.

LOCATIONS
[M] John Doran Museum, Aylestone Road, Leicester.
[M] Leicester Museum of Technology, Abbey Pumping Station, Corporation Road, Leicester.
[M] Leicestershire Museums, Art Galleries and Records Service, New Walk, Leicester LE1 6TD.

BARRIE TRINDER

Leiden, Zuid Holland, The Netherlands   The principal Dutch university city, on an old course of the Rhine. Woollen cloth made Leiden one of the largest manufacturing centres in Europe in the seventeenth century but restrictions imposed by other countries caused decline, and mechanization in the nineteenth century was unsuccessful. Industrial history is displayed in the Lakenhal (cloth hall). *De Valk* (The Falcon) is a tower mill built on the ramparts in 1743, now a museum. A wind-powered sawmill operates nearby.

Pijpenkabinet is a privately-owned museum of clay pipes whose collections of samples and moulds are probably the best in the world.

In the dunes near Katwijk, 7 km (5 mi.) NW, is a narrow-gauge railway, using small steam locomotives from brickyards. The route follows the Atlantic Wall defences built by the Germans in World War II.

At Alphen aan den Rijn, 12 km ($7\frac{1}{2}$ mi.) E., is a collection of Dutch elevators, which includes a hydraulic lift of 1898.

LOCATIONS
[M] De Lakenhal (Cloth Hall), Oude Singel 28–32, Leiden.
[M] *De Valk* Molen (The Falcon Mill Museum), 2e Binnenvestgracht 1, Leiden.
[I] Dutch Narrow-Gauge Foundation NSS, c/o Dunantstraat 337, Zoetermeer.
[M] Liftenmuseum (Lift Museum), Hoorn 380, Alphen aan de Rijn.

[M] National Museum for the History of the Physical Sciences, Steenstraat 1a, Leiden.

[M] Pijpenkabinet, Oude Vest 159a, Leiden.

JURRIE VAN DALEN and BARRIE TRINDER

Leipzig, Saxony-Anhalt, Germany   The city of Leipzig, which stands on the Rivers Pleisse, Elster and Parthe, was the second largest in the DDR with well over half a million inhabitants. Since the twelfth century trade and trade fairs have been dominant in the economic life of this central German city, which is well served by all means of transport. The markets, held three times a year after 1458, made Leipzig a place of interchange between producers in Western Europe and consumers in the east, so that it developed into an international trading centre, a position which it retained until World War I. It was still the most important commercial centre in Germany until World War II. From the eighteenth century it was also prominent in the fur trade and in the production and marketing of books. The Börsenverein des Deutschen Buchhandels (Association of the German Book Trade) was founded in the city in 1825. Leipzig became the centre of the railway network in Saxony, and in 1863 Ferdinand Lassalle founded there the Allgemeinen Deutschen Arbeiterverein (the German General Workers' Association), the forerunner of modern trades unions. The city is surrounded by extensive lignite mining areas – such as Bitterfeld, 30 km (19 mi.) to the north, and Borna/ Meuselwitz, 26 km (16 mi.) to the south – much to the detriment of the quality of its atmosphere. Lignite has provided the basis for power stations at Thierbach and Böhlen-Lippendorf, respectively of 800 MW and 600 MW capacity.

The most interesting industrial buildings in Leipzig are two railway stations. The Bavarian station dates from the early period of railways in Germany, in which the city played a pioneering role, the Leipzig–Dresden line having been built in 1837–9. The station was constructed in 1842 as the terminus of the line running from Leipzig through Plauen and Hof to Nuremberg. The small village station dating from 1842 at Niederau, on the line to Dresden, has also been preserved. The Bavarian Station is the oldest main-line terminus in Germany and has been preserved unaltered. A triumphal portico across the rail approach to the station is pierced by four arches: these gave access to the arrival and departure platforms, the locomotive sidings and the carriage sidings. The portico, which has the appearance of a triumphal arch, is still an impressive structure although some of the adjacent office and residential buildings have been removed. A guardroom and the stairs giving access to a clock were accommodated in the towers flanking the portico. Eduard Poetzsch of Leipzig designed the station, in a mixture of Renaissance and neo-Classical styles. It displays the coats of arms of Anhalt, Bavaria and Saxony, the three states concerned with the railway.

The people of Leipzig completed a great undertaking in 1915 with the help of the state of Prussia. In 1902 it had been decided that the six stations in the city, originally run by different railway companies, should be combined, and so the mighty building of Leipzig Hauptbahnhof came in existence, a station exceeded in size in Europe only by the Stazione Centrale in MILAN. The Prussian and Saxon lines each had a large concourse building; between them lies an area 100 m (110 yd.) long, with waiting and dining rooms on the first floor, and further communicating passages and storage areas for luggage on the ground floor. A part of these sections is located on the outer side of the two concourse buildings, so that the entire façade is 298 m (978 ft.) in width. The platform level is reached by flights of granite stairs, and through an underpass 265 m (870 ft.) wide with a reinforced concrete vault above it; this leads to the thirteen island platforms, which give access to twenty-two running lines and four bays. These twenty-six tracks are spanned by an eight-section steel-trussed train shed, six of the sections being 45 m (148 ft.) wide and two 19 m (62 ft.) wide, the whole being 240 m (787 ft.) in length. The guidelines for the competitive invitation to tender plans, won by the architects Kühne & Lossow, had stated that the new railway station was to be 'an impressive architectural monument of the city of trade fairs', and evidence of the economic progress of Germany. In this it is characteristic of German architecture of the time of Kaiser Wilhelm II. Completed during World War I, the station suffered severe damage in air raids in World War II, particularly in the underpass hall. It was restored and back in full operation by 1960, its original form having been largely respected.

BIBLIOGRAPHY
General
Berger, 1980; Binney *et al.*, 1984; Schmidt and Theile, 1989; Wagenbreth and Wächtler, 1983.

LOCATIONS
[M] City Historical Museum, Altes Rathaus, Markt, 7010 Leipzig.
[M] Museum of Arts and Crafts, Johannisplatz 5–11, 7010 Leipzig.

AXEL FÖHL

Lely, Cornelis (1854–1929)   A Dutch civil engineer and Progressive Liberal politician who profoundly influenced twentieth-century land-drainage policies in the Netherlands. After doing research in the 1880s on the practicability of draining and enclosing the Zuiderzee, and on silting in rivers, Lely was a minister in the Department of Public Works for three spells in 1891–4, 1897–1901 and 1913–18, during which he was responsible for the legislation by which the Zuiderzee was subsequently drained and enclosed, and for establishing the economic and social framework for the exploitation of the coal resources of LIMBURG province. He was governor of Surinam in 1902–5.

BIBLIOGRAPHY
General
Jansma, 1954.

Leningrad (St Petersburg, Petrograd), USSR   Founded on virgin mud by Tsar Peter I (Peter the Great) in 1703,

Figure 73   One of eleven late-eighteenth-century wrought-iron bridges which survive in the Pushkin park, formerly known as Tsarkoe Seloe, near Leningrad; this example was designed by the Italian architect Giacomo Quarenghi (1744–1817) and erected in 1786.
Hugh Torrens

the capital of Russia from 1712 to 1918, Leningrad is a well-planned and dignified city with its centre on the south side of the River Neva, near the latter's estuary on Gulf of Finland. It became Russia's main port and hence an early centre of shipbuilding and engineering. Being the capital, it also became the cultural and educational centre of the Empire, although rivalled by Moscow. Its population was 200 000 in 1800, 2.2 million in 1914 and 4.58 million in 1979.

The earliest shipyard was the Admiralty Yard, situated close to the architecturally distinctive Admiralty building. The yard developed and expanded over succeeding centuries, so that there is little trace of its beginnings. The same may be said of the other great shipyards of the city which, before the Revolution, were building Super-Dreadnoughts and other naval craft. An example of their output is the cruiser *Avrora*, which is anchored in the Neva and open to the public. A veteran of the Russo-Japanese War and World War I, this vessel has been preserved thanks to its role in the 1917 Revolution, and is the world's only surviving example of an early twentieth-century cruiser. Another monument, preserved for its architectural merits, is the complex of warehouses on the island of New Holland, the island having been created by the cutting of the New Admiralty Canal in 1717. These brick warehouses were built tall to permit timber to be stored vertically instead of horizontally, and thirty barges could be unloaded simultaneously in the canal dock in the

centre. The complex was built between 1780 and 1840, the block facing the Moika Canal being the oldest.

The army as well as the navy relied on St Petersburg for its equipment, and the textile industry originated in Peter the Great's need for military uniforms. Substantial enterprises grew from the armaments works of Peter's time, among them the Obukhov Works, which still exist and were famous for guns, and the Izhora Works, which among other things produced armour plate. By the twentieth century the Putilov Works (see below) were renowned for heavy engineering. Foreign capital and foreign technology were frequently absorbed by these enterprises.

Foreign companies also set up subsidiaries in Russia. The present day Elektrosila factory was once part of the Siemens group, and another remainder of foreign industry can be seen on the main street, Nevskii Prospekt, where the distinctive building topped by a globe and now known as Dom Knigi was once the St Petersburg headquarters of the Singer Sewing Machine Company (*see* SEWING MACHINE). Other buildings on this street include No. 29, a sports shop surmounted by a pentagonal tower: originally a fireman's watchtower, this was transformed in 1853 into a semaphore point, the first of 149 providing communication between St Petersburg and Warsaw. Nevskii Prospekt ends at the Moscow station which retains its original mid-nineteenth century façade.

The Warsaw Station also retains its original appearance, but the Finland Station on the northern side of the river has been modernized, although it does contain the Finnish locomotive that Lenin used to escape from his pursuers in 1917, probably the only full-size locomotive to be entirely enclosed in a glass case. The Warsaw Station has been named as a suitable location for the future Russian railway museum. The existing Leningrad Railway Museum, founded in 1864 as part of the St Petersburg Institute of Railway Transport Engineers, is cramped and in no way suitable for its national role. In particular it cannot house rolling stock, a collection of which has now been accumulated, including most standard Soviet-built locomotive types, but only a few pre-Soviet designs.

Other specialized museums include the Central Naval Museum, whose prize exhibit is the small sailing craft reputed to be Peter the Great's first warship. There is also the Popov Museum, near the General Post Office, which is a museum of Russian telecommunications. Its exhibits include early radio equipment by Alexandr Stepanovich Popov (1859–1906) and Shilling's telegraph apparatus of 1830. There are many other museums in the city, as there always have been: Peter the Great was so keen that citizens should learn from museums that in his first, the 'Kunstkammer' – a kind of science museum whose original building survives – visitors seriously bent on self-improvement were given glasses of vodka.

What are now known as the Kirov Works, situated in the southern outskirts of Leningrad, 5 km (3 mi.) from the centre, originated in 1801 when the state metalworks were transferred from Kronshtadt to become the St Petersburg Iron Foundry. They were sold to N. I. Putilov in 1868, at which time they were still producing guns and ammunition. In 1873 locomotive and railway carriage construction began. The manufacture of rails and a substantial shipbuilding output guaranteed the company's prosperity, and in World War I it was Russia's biggest producer of munitions. It was nationalized after the Revolution, locomotive production ceasing in the 1920s as tractor building began on a massive scale. Relics of the early years are mainly submerged by later rebuilding, but one preserved object is the lathe at which Mikhail Ivanovich Kalinin (1875–1946), a Bolshevik leader and formal head of the USSR during 1919–46, worked in his revolutionary days, which is conserved *in situ* in an operating workshop.

The nearby village of Vyra has a two-hundred-year-old posting station, believed to be the setting for Pushkin's novelette, *The Stationmaster*. An attempt is being made to create a museum complex here, and in the mid-1980s the old inn adjoining the station was serving period cuisine in a period setting.

BIBLIOGRAPHY
Specific
Petunin, P. *et al. Nash Kirovskii zavod*. Moscow, 1951.
Pilyavoskogo, B. I. *Arkhitekturnyi putevoditel' po Leningradu*. Leningrad, 1971.
Leningrad: Entsiklopedicheskii spravochnik. Moscow, 1957.

LOCATIONS
[M] Academician F. N. Chernyschev Central Scientific, Geological and Prospecting Museum, Sredni Prospekt 72B, Leningrad.
[M] Central Naval Museum, Pushkinskaya pl. 4, Leningrad B-164.
[S] Cruiser *Avrora*, Petrogradskaya nab., Leningrad.
[I] House of Scientific and Technical Propaganda, Nevskii pr.58, Leningrad.
[M] Museum of the College of Decorative Arts, Solyanoi per.13, Leningrad.
[M] Museum of the G. V. Plekhanov Mining Institute, 21 Liniya 2, Leningrad.
[M] Museum of Porcelain, Pr.Obukhovskoi oborony 151–2, Leningrad.
[M] Museum of Railway History, Ul. Sadovaya 50, Leningrad.
[M] A. S. Popov Central Museum of Communications, Ul. Soyuza svyazi 7, Leningrad.
[M] State Circus Museum, Nab. reki Fontanki 3, Leningrad,
[M] State Museum of Ethnography of the Peoples of the USSR, Inzhenernaya ul. 4/1, Leningrad.
[M] State Museum of the History of Leningrad, Nab. Krasnogo Flota 44, Leningrad.

JOHN WESTWOOD

Leoben, Styria, Austria   *See* STYRIAN IRON TRAIL.

Leonida, Dimitrie (1883–1965)   A Romanian engineer and professor, who was responsible for numerous projects relating to power stations and telecommunications. In 1928 he founded the technical museum in BUCHAREST which since 1935 has been situated in the Park of Liberty. The museum was reorganized and extended in 1954.

BIBLIOGRAPHY
General
Bălan and Mihăilescu, 1985.

Lesbos (Lésvos), Aegean Islands, Greece   The largest of the Aegean islands, close to Asia Minor. The main industries are olive-oil refining, soapmaking, tanneries and textiles. The nineteenth-century olive mills contained steam-powered pressing machines. Soap factories were built on a more grandiose scale of stonework with brick dressings: boilers were located on the ground floors with cutting and cooling areas above. Approximately one hundred soap factories survive on the island: one has been restored with displays and a meeting room.

BIBLIOGRAPHY
General
Sifounakis *et al.*, 1986.

Leśna (Leschna), Jelenia Góra, Poland   The oldest hydroelectric plant in Silesia. A dam and a 140 ha (346 ac.) reservoir were built on the Kwisa River during 1901–5, and a power plant with five Francis turbines and five three-phase current generators together, of 2.4 MW output, were installed in 1905–7. Original equipment is preserved and is still in operation, together with the contemporary control and measuring devices. Leśna is one of the most important plants in Europe for the study of the history of hydro-electric power.

Leufsta bruk, Uppsala, Sweden   Leufsta bruk is situated

25 km (16 mi.) N. of the DANNEMORA mines. The Crown founded an ironworks at Leufsta in the early seventeenth century, and the bruk was leased to Willem de Besche and Louis de Geer in 1616. In 1643 Louis de Geer bought Leufsta bruk, together with Gimo and Österby bruk. This was the beginning of a glorious period in the history of Leufsta bruk. Louis de Geer had already introduced Walloon forging as a leaseholder, and soon Leufsta was to become the most important and the largest ironworking bruk in Sweden. It also became one of the targets for the Russians in 1719, who ravaged the UPPLAND ironworks in order to give advantages to their own iron producers. Leufsta already had buildings of distinctive architectural quality before the Russian attacks. Reconstruction started immediately after the raids, and the houses were rebuilt following the original regular plan.

Leufsta bruk was allowed to produce between 850 and 1000 tonnes of bar iron a year. Almost the entire production was exported to Sheffield. Bar iron from Leufsta was, together with that from Österby bruk, considered to be the best for steelmaking. A Swedish metallurgist, C. J. Heljestrand, visited England in 1844 and 1845, and reported that ordinary soft iron had been supplanted in the market by the superior and less expensive English puddled iron, but that Swedish iron still had the best reputation in steelmaking, as the raw material of blister steel (see STEEL), both for direct fabrication and for re-melting using the CRUCIBLE PROCESS. The best blister steel for manufacturing purposes was made from Leufsta iron, while blister steel from Österby iron was mostly used in the production of crucible steel. These 'steel irons', marked 'Hoop L' and 'Double bullet' respectively, fetched the highest prices.

Leufsta bruk has remained in the hands of the de Geer family until recently – for more than three hundred years. Many of the owners were not just successful industrialists but also notable statesmen, politicians, scientists and humanists. Charles de Geer was one of the most successful Swedish industrialists of the eighteenth century, but also a famous scientist with a special interest in entomology. His library included valuable collections of books on natural science, manuscripts and drawings.

The last forge at Leufsta ceased operation in 1926 and was soon afterwards demolished. The woodlands were sold to Korsnäs AB, a forestry company, and none of the industrial buildings remains except for an old brewery. The village is nevertheless worth visiting. A trust has been created to take care of the buildings and the collections, including valuable books, manuscripts and drawings. The bruk archives are well preserved, and scholars are able to consult social, economic and technological records back to the seventeenth century. At times there were as many as eight or nine hundred employees at Leufsta, including not only workers at the blast furnaces and forges but also charcoal burners and peasants; all can be traced in the archives. The manor house was rebuilt after the Russian attack in 1719, as was the chapel, which is furnished with an exceptionally fine organ. These buildings are regularly open to visitors. The fine architecture of the bruk, with its manor house, stables, grain stores, chapel, workers'

dwellings, gardens and pools, places Leufsta amongst the most important industrial heritage sites in Sweden.

MARIE NISSER

Leumann, Collegno, Piedmont, Italy   A MODEL COMMUNITY 10 km (6 mi.) W. of Turin, developed from 1875 by Napoleone Leumann around his cotton mill. Two areas of workers' housing were built between 1890 and 1911, many designed by an engineer, Pietro Fenoglio, and characterized by rich decoration. Leumann was motivated not so much by paternalism as the pursuit of a pre-industrial ideal of egalitarianism. This philosophy is demonstrated by his provision of educational and library facilities.

BIBLIOGRAPHY
General
Negri *et al.*, 1983; Selvafolta *et al.*, 1983.

Liberty Ship   The standard Allied cargo ship of World War II, and the backbone of merchant shipping for a generation afterwards, the Liberty Ship was based on a design by Joseph L. Thompson & Son of Sunderland. It employed welding, with many sections prefabricated for rapid construction, and was intended for simplicity of operation, with two decks and seven transverse watertight compartments, all personnel being berthed in one section amidships. It was powered by a single triple-expansion engine. Altogether, 2580 of the standard cargo version and 130 adapted for special purposes were constructed in Britain, the USA and Canada. The standard tonnage was 7176 tons gross. The *Jeremiah O'Brien* of 1943 is preserved at San Francisco; the *John W. Brown* of 1942 is intact on James River, Va.

BIBLIOGRAPHY
General
Baker, 1965; Brouwer, 1985; Sawyer and Mitchell, 1970.

Lichtenwörth, Lower Austria, Austria   A village 6 km (4 mi.) NW of Wiener Neustadt, with long traditions of metalworking. In 1747 Johann Christian Zug opened a needle factory, which was taken over by the imperial authorities in 1751. By 1756 workers' dwellings, known as 'Nadelburg' (needle castle), had been built to the design of the court architect, Nikolaus Pacassi (1716–90). Originally there were about eighty houses, of which forty-five, with several communal buildings, remain in use. A high wall surrounded these dwellings: part of it survives, with one of the three baroque entrances, topped by an imperial eagle flanked by cherubs.

Liège, Liège, Belgium   At the confluence of the Rivers Meuse and the Ourthe, Liège, the principal city of eastern Belgium, was the seat of independent Prince Bishops until the French Revolution. It has been a major centre for ironmaking and weapons manufacture for many centuries, and in the nineteenth century became the metropolis of a region whose industrial landscapes were and remain some of the most dramatic in Europe.

The steelworks at Seraing, 8 km (5 mi.) W. of the city, extending 5 km (3 mi.) along the banks of the Meuse, has developed from an ironworks established by the Englishman John Cockerill (1790–1840) in 1816 in the former palace of the Prince Bishops of Liège, which was claimed to be the largest manufactory of machines in the world by the 1860s. The site of the original blast furnaces is marked on the rue du Passage d'Eau alongside the Meuse. Val St Lambert, which adjoins Seraing, is a glassmaking community established in 1826, where glass furnaces, together with terraces of two-storey workers' cottages and the eighteen bay chateau home of the owner, have been preserved.

Former weapons factories remain in rue Chéri and rue de Bayards in Liège, but the principal armaments works is Fabrique National, the state-owned complex, established at Herstal, 6 km (4 mi.) N., in 1889: it is entered through a spectacular gateway of 1890. A works museum displays locks, tools and products of the company.

The zinc smelter of VIEILLE MONTAGNE, on the quai St-Paul-de-Sincay alongside the Ourthe, originated in 1835 but has been totally rebuilt several times. The extensive locomotive and carriage works of the Belgian state railways are on the south bank of the Meuse in Angleur, where a typical 350-tonne barge is preserved next to an iron lifting bridge over the Ourthe Canal.

In the early twentieth century the municipality built many dwellings for industrial workers, including brick terraces of 1910 on the rue Port Grumsel, and low-rise concrete apartment blocks of the 1920s and 30s on boulevard Ernest Solvay.

At St Nicolas, 4 km ($2\frac{1}{2}$ mi.) W., the Maison du Peuple is a cinema with an impressive concrete façade, designed by Joseph Moutschen in 1931, now adapted as a cultural centre.

The Museum of Iron and Coal in Liège includes the forehearth from a seventeenth-century charcoal blast furnace from Gonrieux (Entre-Sambre-et-Meuse), two hearths from finery forges, and two water-powered hammers. Many characteristic iron products of the region are displayed, together with models portraying ironworking processes developed by Walloons, documentary evidence concerning the migration of ironworkers, and important collections of keys, nails and iron works of art.

The Weapons Museum has a collection of more than ten thousand firearms, probably the largest in the world. The Curtius Museum displays the decorative arts and ceramics of the region. The Diocesan Museum is important for its Dinanderie (see DINANT), while the Glass Museum portrays the history of the industry in an international context.

At Blegny-Trembleur, 12 km ($7\frac{1}{2}$ mi.) NE, the provincial government established a museum at the former coal mine in 1980, as the last pit in Wallonia was on the verge of closure. Visitors are able to go underground, and trains link this museum to small museums concerned with vehicles, cheese and regional life, and with the abbey of Val Dieu.

Sprimont, 16 km (10 mi.) S., is a stone-quarrying town where there are remains of several large quarries, whose activities are recorded in a museum in a power-station building of 1910. A preserved narrow-gauge railway runs through the quarries.

At Wanze, 30 km (19 mi.) W., a large sugar refinery dating from 1870, with two huge silos of 1929, lines the banks of the Meuse.

BIBLIOGRAPHY
General
Linters, 1986a; Viaene, 1986; Wirtgen-Bernard and Dusart, 1981.

LOCATIONS
[S] Chemin de Fer de Sprimont (Sprimont Railway), rue d'Aywaille 91, 4170 Comblaine-au-Pont.
[S] Cristalleries du Val Saint Lambert (Val Saint Lambert Glassworks), 4ue de Val Saint Lambert 245, 4100 Seraing.
[M] Musée Communal de Herstal (Herstal Local Museum), Place Licour 15, 4400 Herstal.
[M] Musée Curtius, Quai de Maestricht 13, 4000 Liège.
[M] Musée des Armes (Weapons Museum), Quai de Maestricht 4, 4000 Liège.
[M] Musée de la Vie Wallone (Museum of Walloon Life), Cour des Mineurs, 4000 Liège.
[M] Musée des Mines (Mining Museum), rue Lambert 23, 4570-Blegny.
[M] Musée des Transport en Commun au Pays de Liège (Liège Museum of Public Transport), rue Richard Heinz 9, 4020 Liège.
[M] Musée Diocesain (Diocesan Museum), Bonne-Fortune 6, 4000 Liège.
[M] Musée du Fer et du Charbon (Museum of Iron and Coal), Boulevard R. Poincare 17, 4000 Liège.
[M] Musée du Verre (Glass Museum), Quai de Maestricht 13, 4000 Liège.
[M] Musée (Fabrique National) d'Archeologie Industrielle (Industrial Archaeological Museum of Fabrique National), 63 Rue en Bois, 4400 Herstal.
[M] Musée Régional de la Pierre (Regional Stone Museum), rue J. Potier 136, 4060 Sprimont.

BARRIE TRINDER

Lieto, Turun ja Porin lääni, Finland   The roots of the Littoinen woollen cloth factory at Lieto, 14 km (9 mi.) NE of Turku, are in a cloth manufacturing workshop established in Turku in 1738 by the dyer Esaias Wechter. A little later he founded a finishing works and fulling mill at Littoinen, Lieto, which in the following century developed into an important woollen cloth factory.

The oldest of the surviving buildings is a red-brick structure of 1824, originally in three storeys. In its original form it was a typical structure of its time, employing water power. In 1844 the first steam engine in Finland to be used as a source of power for manufacturing was installed here. Many new buildings were constructed in the late nineteenth century and early twentieth century. In the early 1920s the architect Valter Jung drew up ambitious plans for the area, as part of which a workers' residential area was built to high standards in a parkland setting at Kotimäki. This housing and the building of the Littoinen factory are protected by preservation orders.

lift The customary British term for ELEVATOR.
See also BOAT LIFT.

lifting bridge A term properly applied to a truss bridge with a movable span, the whole of which can be raised vertically by lifting equipment in two large towers at either end, but sometimes applied to a BASCULE BRIDGE. 'Lift bridge' is the more common term in the USA. An outstanding pioneering structure was the South Halsted Street Bridge, Chicago, 40 m (130 ft.) long: it was designed by J. A. L. Waddell and completed in 1893. By the 1930s bridges with lifting spans of up to 150 m (500 ft.) were being constructed in the USA.
See also SWING BRIDGE.

lighter A small vessel of shallow draught into which goods were unloaded from seagoing ships, or which were used generally for movement of goods within a port, the word probably deriving from 'lightener'. Originally lighters were used because seagoing ships drew too much water at quays, but with the introduction of DOCKS they were often employed to speed unloading.

The name is also applied to the dumb barge, 42 ft. × 10 ft. (12.8 m × 3.05 m) used on navigations in the FENS in England, and to the 62 ft. × 14 ft. (18.9 m × 4.27 m) standard craft of the waterways in the north of Ireland.

The Tyne lighter *Elswick* is preserved at Hebburn, 4 km (3 mi.) E. of NEWCASTLE-UPON-TYNE, England, and the Tagus lighter *Fragata do Tejo* at Belém, Lisbon, Portugal.

BIBLIOGRAPHY
General
Brouwer, 1985; Tomlinson, 1979.

lighthouse The 'Pharos' of Alexandria was one of forty ancient lighthouses around Europe and the Mediterranean, the oldest still working being at La Coruna, Spain. Medieval ecclesiastical lights, and those of secular bodies like the British Trinity House (established in 1514) were first built like any other round towers. In 1756 JOHN SMEATON devised for Eddystone Rock the system of dovetailing stone blocks that became standard practice in dozens of subsequent sea-washed towers. Alternative materials have been brick, wooden piles, cast iron (1805–1920) and, since 1853, concrete. Fires, candles and varieties of oil lamp were tried before KEROSINE became standard after 1845, the use of gas being rare. Reflectors were used at Liverpool from 1763, but it was Augustin Fresnel (d.1829) who revolutionized lighthouse optics with complex combinations of lens and prisms. Revolving lights for identification appeared first in France in 1790. Lighthouse technology was greatly advanced in the early nineteenth century by ROBERT STEVENSON and his sons.

BIBLIOGRAPHY
General
Beaver, 1971; Hague and Christie, 1975; Jackson, 1975; Majdalany, 1959; Parker, 1975; Stevenson, A., 1959; Stevenson, A. S., 1848, 1850; Stevenson, T. S., 1881.

CHRISTOPHER GREEN

lightship First used in the Netherlands in the fifteenth century and in Denmark in 1683. Early vessels, like that of 1732 at the Nore, England, had lanterns strung on a yard arm. From 1807 lamps encircled the mast, gimbals ensuring horizontal beams.

Many lightships are preserved, including the *Thomas F. Bayard* of 1880 at Vancouver, British Columbia, the *Fyrskib XVII* of 1895 at Roskilde, Denmark, the *Barnegat* of 1904 at Philadelphia, USA, *Bull* of 1909 at Hull, England, and *Chesapeake* of 1931 at Baltimore, USA.

BIBLIOGRAPHY
General
Brouwer, 1985.

lignite A brown, soft coal, often bearing traces of its constituent woody plants. Deposits are usually thick and close to surface, and are therefore ideally suited to STRIP MINING. Only occasionally are lignite deposits now worked by underground mining, although this practice was common in the past. Lignite is now worked in twenty-five countries. The principal deposits are in Poland and Germany, where estimated reserves in the Rhineland total 55 billion tonnes, and deposits as much as 100 m (300 ft.) thick are workable to depths of 600 m (2000 ft.).

Lille, Nord, France The principal centre in France for wool, cotton and linen textiles, the conurbation around Lille, Roubaix and Tourcoing developed during the nineteenth century around an old city and two small market towns which long retained their semi-rural patterns of landownership. Lille specialized in the spinning and weaving of linen and cotton, whilst Roubaix and Tourcoing concentrated on worsteds, with carpet manufacturing an added specialism at Tourcoing.

Until the mid-nineteenth century the organization of production still followed early patterns, like those at LOUVIERS and SEDAN, work being put out to small-scale units in which living and working spaces were generally combined, like the attic workshops of the linen thread makers at Lille, the handloom weavers' cottages at Roubaix, or the large town houses of the Tourcoing woolcombers and merchants with their typically wide carriage gateways. The successive mechanization of wool and linen spinning in the 1840s, of woolcombing in the 1850s, and more gradually of weaving, gave birth to successive generations of steam-powered textile factories, the earliest clearly copied from English models: simple, rectangular multi-storey brick structures, with rows of cast-iron columns supporting the floors.

From the 1860s larger mill buildings with more lavish architectural embellishments were built. The leading textile concerns were trying not only to concentrate the different stages of production, integrating spinning, weaving, finishing and dyeing processes, but also to bring these processes together for different fibres. The end of the century saw the construction of monumental mill complexes, with soaring, ornately-crowned chimneys, staircases concealed in medieval turrets, and decorative brickwork, mills which are today often termed the

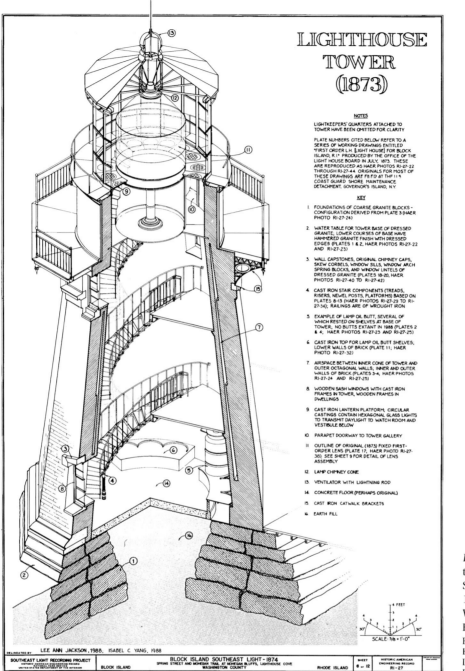

LIGHTHOUSE TOWER (1873)

NOTES

LIGHTKEEPERS' QUARTERS ATTACHED TO TOWER HAVE BEEN OMITTED FOR CLARITY

PLATE NUMBERS CITED BELOW REFER TO A SERIES OF WORKING DRAWINGS ENTITLED 'FIRST ORDER L.H. [LIGHT HOUSE] FOR BLOCK ISLAND, R.I.' PRODUCED BY THE OFFICE OF THE LIGHT HOUSE BOARD IN JULY, 1873. THESE ARE REPRODUCED AS HAER PHOTOS RI-27-22 THROUGH RI-27-44. ORIGINALS FOR MOST OF THESE DRAWINGS ARE FILED AT THE U.S. COAST GUARD SHORE MAINTENANCE DETACHMENT, GOVERNOR'S ISLAND, N.Y.

KEY

1. FOUNDATIONS OF COARSE GRANITE BLOCKS - CONFIGURATION DERIVED FROM PLATE 3 (HAER PHOTO RI-27-24)

2. WATER TABLE FOR TOWER BASE OF DRESSED GRANITE, LOWER COURSES OF BASE HAVE HAMMERED GRANITE FINISH WITH DRESSED EDGES (PLATES 1 & 2, HAER PHOTOS RI-27-22 AND RI-27-23)

3. WALL CAPSTONES, ORIGINAL CHIMNEY CAPS, SKEW CORBELS, WINDOW SILLS, WINDOW ARCH SPRING BLOCKS, AND WINDOW LINTELS OF DRESSED GRANITE (PLATES 18-20, HAER PHOTOS RI-27-40 TO RI-27-42)

4. CAST IRON STAIR COMPONENTS (TREADS, RISERS, NEWEL POSTS, PLATFORMS) BASED ON PLATES 8-13 (HAER PHOTOS RI-27-29 TO RI-27-34); RAILINGS ARE OF WROUGHT IRON

5. EXAMPLE OF LAMP OIL BUTT, SEVERAL OF WHICH RESTED ON SHELVES AT BASE OF TOWER; NO BUTTS EXTANT IN 1988 (PLATES 2 & 4; HAER PHOTOS RI-27-23 AND RI-27-25)

6. CAST IRON TOP FOR LAMP OIL BUTT SHELVES; LOWER WALLS OF BRICK (PLATE 11; HAER PHOTO RI-27-32)

7. AIRSPACE BETWEEN INNER CONE OF TOWER AND OUTER OCTAGONAL WALLS; INNER AND OUTER WALLS OF BRICK (PLATES 3-4, HAER PHOTOS RI-27-24 AND RI-27-25)

8. WOODEN SASH WINDOWS WITH CAST IRON FRAMES IN TOWER, WOODEN FRAMES IN DWELLINGS

9. CAST IRON LANTERN PLATFORM; CIRCULAR CASTINGS CONTAIN HEXAGONAL GLASS LIGHTS TO TRANSMIT DAYLIGHT TO WATCH ROOM AND VESTIBULE BELOW

10. PARAPET DOORWAY TO TOWER GALLERY

11. OUTLINE OF ORIGINAL (1873) FIXED FIRST-ORDER LENS (PLATE 17, HAER PHOTO RI-27-38); SEE SHEET 9 FOR DETAIL OF LENS ASSEMBLY

12. LAMP CHIMNEY CONE

13. VENTILATOR WITH LIGHTNING ROD

14. CONCRETE FLOOR (PERHAPS ORIGINAL)

15. CAST IRON CATWALK BRACKETS

16. EARTH FILL

4 FEET

SCALE: 3/8" = 1'-0"

DELINEATED BY: LEE ANN JACKSON, 1988, ISABEL C. YANG, 1988

SOUTHEAST LIGHT RECORDING PROJECT / HISTORIC AMERICAN ENGINEERING RECORD / NATIONAL PARK SERVICE / UNITED STATES DEPARTMENT OF THE INTERIOR | BLOCK ISLAND SOUTHEAST LIGHT - 1874 / SPRING STREET AND MOHEGAN TRAIL AT MOHEGAN BLUFFS, LIGHTHOUSE COVE / WASHINGTON COUNTY | BLOCK ISLAND | RHODE ISLAND | SHEET 6 — 12 | HISTORIC AMERICAN ENGINEERING RECORD RI-27

IF REPRODUCED, PLEASE CREDIT: HISTORIC AMERICAN ENGINEERING RECORD, NATIONAL PARK SERVICE, NAME OF DELINEATOR, DATE OF THE DRAWING

Figure 74 The LIGHTHOUSE tower of the Block Island Southeast Light, built in 1873 at Mohegan Bluffs, Washington County, Rhode Island

Historic American Engineering Record, National Park Service, Lee Ann Jackson and Isabel C. Yang, 1988

'châteaux of industry'. Examples include the Motte-Bossut mill at Roubaix, the Wallaert and Le Blan mills of 1898 and 1900 at Lille, the Thiriez mill and laundry works of 1896 and 1898, and the Delbart-Mallet mill of *c.*1890 at Loos near Lille. The same period saw the construction by FRANÇOIS HENNEBIQUE of the first textile factories in reinforced concrete, the Six Mill at Tourcoing in 1895 and the Barrois Mill at Lille in 1896, opening the way to a new functionalist phase in industrial architecture.

The crisis in the textile industry in France has led to the closure of most of these factories, and to the demolition of many. Several of the mills are of outstanding architectural quality, incorporating features of the local Flemish style, and some have been adapted to new uses. The Le Blan factory was transformed into apartments in 1980 by Reichen and Robert, an architectural practice subsequently responsible for the rehabilitation of the Blin & Blin factory built between 1870 and 1947 at Elbeuf.

The Motte-Bossut cotton-spinning mill at Roubaix was built between 1864 and 1905, replacing an earlier 'monster mill' opened in 1843 on the opposite side of the Roubaix Canal, and destroyed by fire in 1866. The millowner, Louis Motte, husband of Adèle Bossut, had visited Manchester in 1842, returning with the design principles of RICHARD ROBERTS's self-acting spinning mule.

The first building of 1864 already incorporated the two emblematic octagonal crenellated towers, which dominate what is today the boulevard Gambetta. One tower houses a staircase, the other is the envelope for the chimney. A new building with three stepped gables on the boulevard side went up in 1875; followed by a long, five-storey building with an attic above on the rue la Tuilerie; and finally, between 1891 and 1905, two more towers, one on either side of the main entrance, and again crenellated. The last important modifications, dating from 1920, brought new window openings to the gabled façade. The use of the different working areas is well documented for this period, from the taking-in and stock rooms for raw cotton, to the packing rooms for the finished thread.

The Motte-Bossut mill was closed in 1981. In 1984 it was decided to use the building for the first of five planned regional archive centres. The mill is being restored and adapted for this new use, with respect for the architectural qualities of at least some its façades. The centre will be able to accommodate 50 shelf km (30 mi.) of archives from industrialists, trades unions and the 'world of work' in general.

A museum at Comines, just over the Belgian frontier, 10 km (6 mi.) NW of Tourcoing, portrays the history of ribbon manufacture in the region.

See also AIRE-SUR-LA-LYS.

BIBLIOGRAPHY
General
Daumas, 1980; Grenier and Wieser-Benedetti, 1979; Viaene, 1986.
Specific
Culot, M., Grenier, L. & Wieser-Benedetti, H. L'Architecture industrielle de la région lilloise (The industrial architecture of the Lille region). In *Les Monuments Historiques de la France*, III, 1977.
Grislain, J. & Le Blan, M. L'Usine de la ville: l'example de Tourcoing (Nord) (The factory and the town: the example of Tourcoing). In *L'Archéologie Industrielle en France*, XVII–XVIII, 1989.
Lebrigand, Y. Les Archives du Monde du Travail (The archives of the world of work). In *L'Archéologie Industrielle en France*, XVII–XVIII, 1989.

LOCATIONS
[M] Industrial and Commercial Museum, 2 rue du Lombard, 59000 Lille.

[I] Le Centre des Archives du Monde du Travail (Archives centre of the world of work), Carrefour de l'Europe, 59100 Roubaix.
[M] Musée de la Rubanerie, rue du Fort, 7780 Comines, Belgium.

JEAN-FRANÇOIS BELHOSTE

Lillebæltsbroen, Funen (Fyn) & Jutland (Jylland), Denmark   The bridge across the Lillebælt (Little Belt) connecting Funen with Jutland, the first of the big Danish bridge projects of the 1930s, was opened in 1935. It is a 1.2 km ($\frac{3}{4}$ mi.) combined road and railway bridge, a cantilever structure of steel lattice girders. It was designed by A. Engelund and built by Monberg & Thorsen, in collaboration with the German companies of F. Krupp, L. Eilers and Grün & Bilfinger. In 1970 it was relieved by the new Lillebælt bridge, a 1.7 km (1 mi.) suspension bridge carrying a motorway. Recently work has begun on the Storebæltsforbindelse (Great Belt Connection) project, linking Zealand and Funen with a combined tunnel and bridge system more than 10 km (6 mi.) long, for road and railway traffic.

BIBLIOGRAPHY
Specific
DSB. *Lillebæltsbroen* (The Little Belt Bridge). Copenhagen: DSB, 1935.
Møller, I. *et al.* eds *At slå bro – paa dansk* (To bridge in Danish). Copenhagen, 1986.

Lillehammer, Oppland, Norway   Lillehammer is a resort town in central Norway, 180 km (110 mi.) N. of Oslo, on the east shore of Lake Mjøsa, at the south end of Gudbrandsdalen, a valley through which passes the ancient route from Oslo to Trondheim. The steamer quay, a protected monument, is served in summer by services from EIDSVOLL. There are several important industrial monuments in the area north of Lillehammer, including a nickel smelter at Espedalen, 64 km (40 mi.) N.

On the southern edge of Lillehammer is Maihaugen, the museum incorporating the collections of Anders Sandvig (1862–1950), son of a fisherman from Romsdal who trained as a dentist in Berlin and moved to Lillehammer when his life was threatened by consumption. In 1887, inspired by romantic nationalism and Darwinian theory, he began collecting buildings and artefacts, and Maihaugen opened in 1904. Sandvig conceived it as 'a collection of homes, where one can almost meet the people who lived there, understand their way of life, their tastes, their work, for the design and furnishing of a home give a picture of the people themselves . . .' The museum remains a private foundation but is supported by government grants. It extends over 36 ha (90 ac.) and includes over a hundred re-erected buildings, mostly from Gudbrandsdalen. A modern building contains forty-four exhibition rooms, most of them reconstructed workshops showing such traditional occupations as shoemaking, tailoring, umbrella manufacture, gunsmithing, wood engraving, bookbinding, basket making, and violin making. The open-air museum displays in a remarkably effective manner the architecture, arts and material culture of Gudbrandsdalen. Industrial buildings include a corn mill, a dyehouse and fulling mill, a tannery, a brass foundry and a posting station, but Maihaugen is chiefly important to the historian of industry for what it shows of manufactures carried on within isolated farmhouses. The storehouse of 1775 fitted up for the making of spinning wheels, the brewery in the Bjørnstad farmhouse, and the spinning wheels and looms found alongside beds and cooking facilities in many farmsteads all vividly illustrate manufacturing before the Industrial Revolution. Maihaugen portrays the history and culture of a mere 15 000 km² (1950 sq. mi.) district of central Norway, but it does so in a way that gives profound insights into all pre-industrial societies.

BIBLIOGRAPHY
General
Frolich, 1919; Halvorsen, 1965–9; Sandvigske Samlinger, 1948, 1952, 1957, 1961, 1964, 1975, 1979; Valen-Sendstad, 1982.

LOCATION
[M] De Sandvigske Samlinger-Maihaugen, 2600 Lillehammer.

BARRIE TRINDER

Limburg, Belgium   The Flemish-speaking province of Limburg in the north-east of Belgium consists largely of sandy heathlands, and saw little industrial development in the nineteenth century, apart from the distilleries of HASSELT, some sugar-beet factories, and the zinc works at Overpelt (*see* LA VIEILLE MONTAGNE). At Nerem, 4 km (2½ mi.) NW of Tongeren, is the Rosmeulen chocolate factory, built *c.*1900 in the ART NOUVEAU style. There is an industrial museum for the province at St Truiden.

Rising coal prices in the 1890s stimulated prospecting for coal, and in 1901 André Dumont established that about 25 m (80 ft.) of exploitable coal lay beneath the heathlands of the Kempen. Concessions were granted from 1907, but production did not begin until 1917 at Winterslag, most of the mines commencing work during the 1920s, with the coalfield reaching its maximum output of 7.2 million tonnes in 1939. The region was sparsely populated, and villages on GARDEN CITY principles were constructed to house immigrant miners, with the companies providing roads, churches, schools, and football grounds, and exercising a strict measure of social control. Concrete blocks were used in most of the buildings built before 1914, but as demand for such blocks for tunnel vaulting declined, bricks from colliery brickworks were used instead. The mines closed during the 1980s, but the villages and some pithead installations remain. The pit at Blegny-Trembleur (*see* LIÈGE) is preserved as a museum. At Beringen, 16 km (10 mi.) NW of Hasselt, there is a steel headstock of 1919–28, while the village includes the impressive church of St Theodard, the 'miners' cathedral', built in 1939–43. At Waterschei, 16 km (10 mi.) NE of Hasselt, the headstocks of 1922 and a concrete screening plant and conveyors of the André Dumont colliery have been retained, although apart from the office block the complex is threatened with demolition. At Winterslag, 12 km (8 mi.) NE of Hasselt, is the oldest pit headstock in the province, dating from 1915.

See also BOCHOLT; BOKRIJK.

BIBLIOGRAPHY
General
van Doorslaer, 1983; Viaene, 1986.
Specific
Vandebergh, L. *et al.* The Mining Towns of Limburg: General Situation and the example of Beringen. St Truiden: Provincial Museum, n.d.
Jenever en Steenkool (Gin and coal). Ghent: VVIA, 1987.

LOCATION
[M] Provincie Limburg Museum voor het Industrieel Erfgoed (Provincial Limburg Museum for the Industrial Heritage), Begijnhof 59, B-3800 St Truiden.

BARRIE TRINDER

Limburg, The Netherlands   The most southerly province of the Netherlands extends in a 'pan handle' along the eastern border between Belgium and West Germany. From 1900 the region extending from Kerkrade, 30 km (19 mi.) E. of Maastricht, 30 km (19 mi.) NW to the River Maas, which had been a quiet rural area, was transformed into a densely populated, urbanized mining region, where extraction continued until the 1970s. Between 1965 and 1975 competition from oil and gas destroyed the industry with the loss of about 50 000 jobs, the last coal being mined on 31 December 1974, the year of the foundation of the Mining Museum in Kerkrade. An inventory of monuments was made in 1978, although many have been destroyed.

There is an artificial mine in the resort of Valkenburg, 7 km (4 mi.) SW of Heerlen. Valkenburg station, on the railway from Aachen to Maastricht, has three-bay, three-storey crenellated central block, with three-bay single-storey wings on either side, and is the oldest in the Netherlands.

Coal was dug in Kerkrade near Rolduc abbey in medieval times, and from the eighteenth century the abbey developed the Domaniale mine near the German border. After the French occupation it was state-owned until 1846, when a 99-year concession was given to the Aachen-Maastricht railway company. A headstock of 1907 became a protected monument after restoration in 1976.

After much prospecting, four state-owned and seven private mines were established between 1890 and 1928, the state enterprise supported by CORNELIS LELY, who aimed to make the Netherlands less dependent on foreign coal, and founded a model commercial company, the Dutch State Mines, in 1902, to stimulate private investment. All the private mines were owned by foreign companies, principally Belgian and French.

The state mines, Wilhelmina (1903–6), Emma (1912) and Hendrik (1918), were situated in the eastern part of the region near Heerlen and Kerkrade, which is now urbanized, with residential areas scattered between waste tips and opencast workings. The Catholic municipality of Heerlen was against industrial development which would lead to perdition and socialism, like that in contemporary Liège, which is why Heerlen developed not as a town but as an agglomeration of small GARDEN CITY style mining colonies. Significant remains include back-to-back housing of 1909 in Grasbroek and of 1918 in Beersdal, built by the Oranje Nassau Mine company, which built the Leenhof colony of 1909–12 in Kerkrade; Schaesberg in 1913; and Eikske, also in 1913, which has twenty-six houses of particular note for their ornamentation. The Laura company built the Hopel colony in 1906–10: this was restored and declared a national monument in 1979. The Dutch State Mines built the Terwinselen colony for the workers of the Wilhelmina mine; and the Treebeek colony, 6 km (4 mi.) N. of Heerlen, for the adjacent Hendrik and Emma pits. The waste tips of Wilhelmina and Hendrik are now used as artificial ski slopes. The steel headstock of Oranje Nassau I, built at the turn of the century, is preserved; and the company's office block of 1932, with glass and iron construction to prevent subsidence, is now an archives repository. The concrete headstock of the Hendrik mine remains in Brunssum. In Kerkrade are six cooling towers of a power station of 1937, and a chimney and other buildings from the Laura company's Julia mine of 1922. Several colliery power stations remain in use.

North-west of Kerkrade the Dutch State Mines opened the Maurits pit near Geleen, 13 km (8 mi.) NW of Heerlen, in 1926. It was then the most up-to-date mine in Europe. The company also developed chemical operations in the region, where the landscape is still dominated by petro-chemical plants, within which are several remnants of earlier coal-based processes. The spoil tip of Maurits is used for the deposit of toxic waste. Two colonies remain north-west of Geleen; Lindenheuvel of 1919 and parts of Lutterade, developed in 1918 by building societies guaranteed by the State Mines.

The 35 km (22 mi.) Juliana Canal east of Geleen was cut in 1928–34 to avoid obstacles on the Maas. The Dutch State Mines harbour at Stein, opened in 1934, had quays extending over 2 km (1 mi.), where coal from the three state mines was transferred from railway wagons to barges. The private companies used wharves at Born, 12 km ($7\frac{1}{2}$ mi.) N. of Stein. Maasbracht, 10 km (6 mi.) SW of Roermond, where there are locks into the Maas also developed as a coal-shipping harbour.

The Beatrix mine, 10 km (6 mi.) E. of Roermond, was begun in 1952, when two shafts were sunk, but work was abandoned pending the reorganization of the industry. One of the shafts, 720 m (2360 ft.) deep, is now a centre for deep-water research and training, of great value to offshore industries as it is independent of weather conditions.

Outstanding monuments near Roermond are the buildings of a pottery of 1880 in Tegelen, and a tile factory of 1892 at Belfeld.

South Limburg is the highest part of the Netherlands with hills of up to 300 m (1000 ft.), and was traditionally a region of water mills, of which examples remain at Mechelen-Witten, 16 km (10 mi.) E. of Maastricht, and Meerssen, 4 km ($2\frac{1}{2}$ mi.) N. of Maastricht.

Maastricht, the provincial capital, is an important port on the Meuse, which was linked to Den Bosch and other Dutch towns by the Zuidwillems Canal of 1826. The city was connected by rail to Germany in 1853 and to Belgium in 1856, but had links with the rest of the Netherlands only from 1865. Glass, pottery and tile production developed on an industrial scale from 1845, with English management and a Belgian workforce. The Bonnefanten Museum has 57000 pieces from the collections of the Sphinx and Céramique factories; the two works merged in 1958 after a century of competition. The Sphinx potteries dominated the Bassin on the left bank of the Maas, where a warehouse of the 1860s has been adapted as apartments, and a five-storey papermill of the 1850s also remains. The Céramique concern began a huge concrete complex on the right bank in 1912, but it was never finished. A four-storey concrete SANITARY WARE works of 1916 is now part of the Bonnefanten Museum.

BIBLIOGRAPHY
General
DIEN database, Raedts, 1974.
Specific
De Clerq, P. L'archeologie industrielle au Pays Bas. In Ferriot, 1981.
Inventarisatie Industriële Archeologie Limburg (Roerende objecten) (Inventory of the industrial archaeology of Limburg). Kerkrade: Stichting Mijnmuseum, 1987.
Inventarisatie Industriële Archeologie Limburg (Onroerende objecten) (Inventory of the industrial archaeology of Limburg). Maastricht: Sociaal Historisch Centrum, 1988.
Inventarisatie Mijnmonumenten: samenwerkingsverband sanering mijnterreinen oostelijk mijngebied (Inventory of mining monuments: co-operative housing and mining landscapes). Heerlen, 1978.
Linssen, G. C. P. Schachten, Mijnbergen en Wooncolonies: De Limburgse Mijnstreek (mines and living quarters: the Limburg coalfield). In Nijhof, 1986.

LOCATIONS
[M] Bonnefanten Museum, Dominikanerplein 5, Maastricht.
[M] Fransche Molen (Fransche Water Mill museum), Lindelaan 32, Valkenburg.
[M] Mijn Museum (Mining Museum), Abdij Rolduc, Heyendahlaan 82, Kerkrade.

JURRIE VAN DALEN

lime Calcium oxide or quicklime (CaO), obtained from LIMESTONE or CHALK in a LIME kiln. Until the nineteenth century lime was the commonest form of mortar (*see* PORTLAND CEMENT) and fertilizer; as a fertilizer, though, it has largely been replaced by crushed limestone.

lime kiln One of the most commonly surviving forms of industrial monument, widely used but now redundant in most countries. Most were intermittently-worked shaft kilns, charged with layers of LIMESTONE and fuel, in which lime (calcium oxide, CaO) was produced, and shovelled out from the base: $CaCO_3 \rightarrow CaO + CO_2$

Most modern examples are large rotary kilns within chemical complexes, in which the carbon dioxide produced is recovered and utilized.

HOFFMAN KILNS were adapted for burning lime and some kilns were fired with gas (*see* MAKARAEO).

413

Figure 75 The three nineteenth-century limekilns which form the symbol of the Zuiderzeemuseum at Enkhuizen
Barrie Trinder

BIBLIOGRAPHY
General
Doncaster, 1916; Eckel, 1928; Morgan and Pratt, 1938.

Limerick (Luimneach), County Limerick, Ireland   A walled city on the River Shannon where building outside the walls only began in the mid-eighteenth century, when new docks, quays and a Customs House of 1765–9 by Davis Ducart were constructed. Limerick is a traditional site of glove manufacture with examples in the museum, and in the late nineteenth century Taits garment manufacturers employed over a thousand people, principally on military contracts.

Ardnacrusha, a hydro-electric power station of 1925–30, is 5 km (3 mi.) to the N. It has a head of 34 m (110 ft.), was constructed with German equipment, and helped to reduce energy costs in the Republic.

At Barringtonbridge, 10 km (6 mi.) SE, the R506 road crosses a tributary of the River Mulkear on a cast-iron bridge 17.4 m (57 ft.) in span, ornamented with Gothic trefoils and with the inscriptions 'Erected in 1818 by Mr. Barrington', and 'J. Doyle Fecit'.

BIBLIOGRAPHY
General
Cossons and Trinder, 1979; Cullen, 1987; Manning and McDowell, 1986.

LOCATION
[M] Limerick City Museum, Pery Square, Limerick.

limestone   A rock found in most countries, a natural calcium carbonate ($CaCO_3$) which occurs in varied physical forms, some utilized as building stones (*see* BATH; FLAGSTONE). Limestone is a source of lime, calcium oxide (CaO), which is obtained from LIME KILNS, and is an important chemical.

Limoges, Vienne, France   The china-clay deposits discovered in 1768 at Saint Yrieix, 30 km (18 mi.) S. of Limoges, were to become the basis of France's porcelain industry. Porcelain wares were first manufactured in 1771 at the royal works at Sèvres near Paris, but Limoges rapidly became the main centre of production. The American manufacturer, David Haviland, settled in Limoges c.1840, opening a factory which combined porcelain kilns and decorating shops, and selling much of his china to the USA. In 1907 there were no fewer than 135 kilns in Limoges, and several factories remain in production today.

The Casseaux factory was founded in 1816 by François Alluaud, who was already one of the town's leading manufacturers. His establishment was situated near a dam on the River Vienne, at a spot where floated timber was landed. From 1876 to 1881 the factory was run by Charles Field Haviland. It was then taken over from 1884 by a firm calling itself GDA (Gérard-Dufraisseix-Abbot). These three partners immediately built a new circular reverberatory kiln of the downdraught type, developed in England by Herbert Minton in 1875, and subsequently improved upon by the Haviland firm in 1878. At the end of the nineteenth century GDA was famous for its ART NOUVEAU products.

Towards the middle of the twentieth century circular kilns were gradually replaced by gas-fired tunnel kilns.

The circular kiln of the Casseaux factory, dating from 1884, which miraculously survived a fire which destroyed most of the works in 1981, is now a protected historical monument. It is housed in a rectangular building, 28 m × 12 m (92 ft. × 40 ft.), with walls of granite rubble work. The building is divided into two, each half formerly containing one kiln. The surviving kiln is a cylindrical construction 7.74 m (25 ft. 8 in.) high, topped by a 20 m (66 ft.) chimney going through the roof. The inside of the kiln is divided into two compartments by a horizontal brick vault. The lower chamber was used for firing the porcelain at 1500 °C. It was heated from side hearths (alandiers), the flames being drawn towards the bed plate of the kiln, then up towards the chamber above through flues incorporated into the walls of the kiln. This is the principal characteristic of this downdraught type of kiln, the upper chamber or 'globe' being used to give the porcelain its first biscuit baking at 950 °C. Along with its kiln, the Casseaux factory has also preserved several thousand nineteenth-century moulds.

Two museums at Limoges, one of them associated with the Haviland works, exhibit collections of old Limoges porcelain.

BIBLIOGRAPHY
Specific
Robinne, P. Unpublished dossier on the GDA kiln. Limoges: Inventaire Général, 1986.

LOCATIONS
[M] Adrien Dubouché National Museum, Place Winston-Churchill, 87000 Limoges.
[M] Municipal Museum, Place de la Cathédrale, 87000 Limoges.

JEAN-FRANÇOIS BELHOSTE

Lincolnshire, England The second largest English county, chiefly important for the drainage systems of the Fens, for harbours, and for manufactures related to agriculture.

Bass Maltings, Sleaford, of 1899–1905, is a spectacular range of eight six-storey maltings with a central engine house. Many windmills survive, including Hoyles Mill at Alford, the Maud Foster mill of 1819 at Boston, the mill of 1833 at Burgh-le-Marsh, the six-sail mill of 1880 at Waltham, and eight-sail mill of 1830 at Heckington. There is a FEATHER processing factory in Trinity Street, Boston; and a pea-processing plant at Heckington is now a visitor centre.

Agricultural engineering was important in the nineteenth century. Fragments survive of the first foundry in Lincolnshire, built by William Howden at Boston in 1803. There are substantial remains of the foundries of Clayton & Shuttleworth of Lincoln, William Marshall & Co.'s Britannia Ironworks at Gainsborough, and the Spittlegate works of Ruston & Co. at Grantham.

The first dock at Grimsby, built by JOHN RENNIE, *c.*1800, has since been filled in. The later mid-nineteenth-century docks were the first to use hydraulic power. Pressure was provided from a 33 m (108 ft.) red brick tower by J. W. Wild (1814–92), built in 1851, which was modelled on the Palazzo Public in Siena. There is also a hydraulic

ACCUMULATOR of 1892. The bus garage incorporates a seaplane hangar.

Amongst the historic drainage works are a single-cylinder A-frame beam engine of 1833 at Pinchbeck, which formerly operated a scoop wheel; and the Dog Dyke beam engine of 1855 at Tattershall. Bridges include the 40 m (131 ft.) Hockstow suspension bridge of 1834 by John Rennie, with its original ironwork; two cast-iron footbridges of 1811 over Maud Foster Drain near Boston, by Butterley Co.; the Cross Keys hydraulic swing bridge of 1894–7 at Sutton Bridge; and the Scherzer rolling lift bridge of 1912–16 at Keadby. New Bolingbroke, a failed model town of the 1820s, is on Medlam Drain: the market house survives.

BIBLIOGRAPHY
General
Wright, 1982.
Specific
Wright, N. R. *A Guide to the Industrial Archaeology of Lincolnshire.* Ironbridge: AIA, 1983.

LOCATION
[M] Lincolnshire Museums, County Offices, Newland, Lincoln LN1 1YL.

BARRIE TRINDER

linen The term 'linen' refers to all yarns spun and fabrics woven from fibres derived from flax, and to many derived from hemp. The process of HACKLING separates the long 'line' fibres from the short tow. The heaviest forms of linen are sailcloth, canvas, sacking and tarpaulins. The medium range includes tenting fabric, towelling and huckaback. Fine linens include cambrics, lawns and hollands. DAMASK is one of many forms of twilled linen. In the eighteenth century tow was also known as hurds or nogs, and was used to produce coarse hurden or noggen fabrics. Weaving flax needs considerable strength. A damp atmosphere is preferable and domestic workers often had looms in cellars.

BIBLIOGRAPHY
General
Horner, 1920; Merrimack Valley Textile Museum, 1980.

liner A vessel sailing regularly between two or more ports, usually carrying mails and passengers in addition to freight. The great age of the liner was the first half of the twentieth century, but the term was employed from the 1830s when this type of shipping operation was established by entrepreneurs like Sir Samuel Cunard (1787–1865), a Nova Scotian who in 1830 established regular sailings between Liverpool, Halifax, Nova Scotia, and Boston, Mass.; after migrating to England in 1838 he set up the British & North American Royal Mail Steam Packet Co., which in 1839 gained a government mail contract. Regular mail services commenced in 1840 with the *Britannia*, one of four 1200-ton paddle steamers ordered from Robert Napier of Glasgow. Cunard's name became synonymous with this type of ship, which itself became a symbol of modernity, Charles Kingsley (1819–75) referring in 1848 to 'the railroad, Cunard's liners and the electric telegraph'. Cunard's first iron liner was the *Persia* of 1855. The White Star Line's *Teutonic* of 1889 was one of the first passenger vessels of 10 000 tons, the size that has subsequently been taken as the definition of a liner.

A period of Anglo-German competition commenced with the launching of the four-stack *Kaiser Wilhelm der Grosse* in 1897. The size of liners increased dramatically, reaching 32 000 tons with the Cunarder *Mauritania* in 1905; 46 000 tons with the White Star Line's *Titanic*, which sank on its maiden voyage in 1912; and 54 000 tons with the German *Vaterland*, the largest liner in use before World War I. The Cunard *Carmania* of 1905 was the first liner to be powered by steam turbines instead of quadruple-expansion steam engines, and the Swedish *Gripsholm* of 1925 the first liner built as a motor ship.

The principal employment of liners was across the North Atlantic, a service whose economic basis was the carriage of immigrants in the steerage class to the USA, over 1.2 million arriving in New York in 1907 alone. Some 210 ships of more than 10 000 tons were employed in the North Atlantic trade between 1900 and 1970. The luxurious first-class accommodation was more valuable as a means of advertising than as a source of profit. The *Celtic*, which commenced service in 1900, conveyed 347 passengers in the first class, 160 in the second, and 2350 in steerage. Liners also linked European powers with their overseas territories. From the early 1920s the North Atlantic immigrant trade diminished, but was replaced by the carriage of American tourists. The *Bremen* of 1928 set the pattern for the liners of the 1930s, with the superstructure designed to minimize wind resistance and a large bulb below water level at the bow. French, Italian and Swedish ships came to be prominent in the Atlantic trade. Liners became still bigger; the largest, the *Queen Elizabeth*, did not make her first civilian voyage until 1946.

Some liners were used for cruising, and the Cunarder *Caronia* of 1948 was the first liner to be designed for cruising. The liner remained the usual means of intercontinental travel in 1950. Cunard were working twelve liners in 1957, but trade dramatically diminished after the first transatlantic commercial jet flight in that year, and remaining services are parts of cruising itineraries. The 81 200-ton Cunarder *Queen Mary*, which crossed the Atlantic between 1936 and 1967, is preserved at Long Beach, Calif., while the 51 000-ton *United States* of 1952 lies at Norfolk, Va.

Liners required special onshore facilities for passengers. Most of these facilities have been destroyed, the outstanding surviving example being at GENOA. There were also special facilities for handling immigrant passengers in North America. The one-time barracks for immigrants at Quebec now houses the archaeological collections of Parks Canada; while on Ellis Island, in NEW YORK harbour, a museum in the main immigrant-processing building commemorates the passages made by millions of immigrants, landing under the gaze of the Statue of Liberty.

BIBLIOGRAPHY
General
Bowen, 1930; Brinnin, 1971; Brinnin and Galvin, 1988; Cairns, 1972; Fry, 1896; Gibbs, 1952, 1963; Miller, 1987, 1989; Wall, 1892; Watson, 1988a, 1988b.

BARRIE TRINDER

line shafting   A system for transmitting power in factory or workshops, extensively used before the development of small electric motors powering individual machines. One or more shafts ran along each working floor: from these, machines were driven by flat belts, usually of leather. Horizontal shafting might be powered through gearing from vertical shafts extending through a building, deriving power from water wheels or steam engines, or later from water turbines or large electric motors. Shafting could also be powered from a ROPE DRIVE system. Early shafting tends to be square in section; later examples are round.

Linköping, Ostergötland, Sweden   The capital of Ostergötland, Linköping lies on the main routes from Stockholm to the south. It has important aircraft and motorcar factories but is principally a commercial and administrative centre.

Old Linköping is an open-air museum on the edge of the town with eighty buildings removed from the centre, including a ropeworks of 1877; a pharmaceutical warehouse of 1857, adapted as a small chocolate factory; and a restored and operating general store of 1873.

BIBLIOGRAPHY
Specific
Meddelanden från Ostergötlans och Linköpings Stads Museum (Transactions from the Ostergötlands and Linköpings City Museum). Linköping, 1969.
Nisser, M. *Industriminnen i Ostergötland* (Industrial monuments in Ostergötland). Ostergötland, 1969.

LOCATIONS
[M] Gamla Linköping (Old Linköping), Kryddbodtorget 1, 582 46 Linköping.
[M] Ostergötlands länsmuseum (Ostergotland Provincial Museum), 16 Vasavägen, Box 232, 581 01 Linköping.

linoleum   A floor covering, patented by F. Walton in 1860–3, in which a preparation of linseed oil and ground cork was spread uniformly over sheets of rough jute canvas. Boiled linseed oil was oxidized by allowing it to trickle down calico sheets suspended from high ceilings. It was then crushed, re-boiled and run into slabs, in which it was stored. Special looms could weave jute backing up to 3.65 m (12 ft.) wide. By the 1890s linoleum could be made with elaborate patterns that did not disappear as the surface became worn. Linoleums often imitated other materials – tiles, parquetry, marble or woven fabrics. The principal manufacturing centre in Britain was KIRKCALDY.

linotype   A revolutionary type-composing machine casting lines of type from reusable matrices controlled by a keyboard. It was invented by Ottmar Mergenthaler (1854–99) in 1886, and was the culmination of many attempts at mechanizing the process of type-casting and composing. Linotype was of particular importance in NEWSPAPER PRINTING.

See also MONOTYPE.

BIBLIOGRAPHY
General
Thompson, 1902, 1904.

linseed oil　An oil extracted by crushing the seed of FLAX in an OIL MILL. It is used in PAINTS, varnishes, printing inks, and for other industrial purposes.

BIBLIOGRAPHY
General
Brace, 1960.

lint　A term that refers to the FLAX plant, to flax prepared for spinning, and, from the late nineteenth century, to a soft material for dressing wounds, originally made by scraping linen cloth, but in the twentieth century from cotton. In the USA the fine waste formed in textile processes is also called lint, and in the South 'linthead' is a term of abuse.

linter　*See* DELINTING MACHINE.

Linz, Upper Austria, Austria　Austria's principal centre of textile, steel and chemical manufacture. The first railway in Austria was the 53 km (33 mi.) line to České Budějovice on the Vltava, which provided links with Hamburg and the Elbe. It was opened in 1832 and worked by horses until 1854. A state tobacco factory was established in 1850, with a 228 m (750 ft.) concrete building of 1936–7 by PETER BEHRENS and Alexander Popp. The Museum of Upper Austria in Schloss displays provincial furniture, stoves, glass, ceramics and ironware, and has a section on railways. Several locomotives, including 0–6–0s of 1868 and 1869 built in Vienna and Wiener Neustadt, are displayed in the ÖBB garden.

LOCATION
[M] Museum of Upper Austria, Schloss Tummelplatz, 4020 Linz.

Lipiny, Katowice, Poland　The site of a zinc-plate mill, the 'Silesia' plant, Lipiny is in the western part of Katowice. The zinc mill 'Konstancja' was established on the site in 1847, the zinc-plate mill being added subsequently, together with a blende-roasting plant and a sulphuric acid plant. There were originally eleven steam engines driving eighteen rolling-mill stands of various types. The rolling-mill hall of 1885–1895 is well preserved, as are six mill stands of 1898–1901 driven by Wilhelmshütte steam engines of 1901, and an open-flame fired furnace of 1901 for refining zinc. The plant is still in use.

BIBLIOGRAPHY
General
Orłowski, 1984.
Specific
Januszewski, S. Zabytki hutnictwa województwa katowickiego (Old metallurgical objects of the Katowice province). In *Kwartalnik Historii Kultury Materialnej* (Quarterly of the History of Material Culture), I, 1984, Warsaw.

Lisbon (Lisboa), Estremadura, Portugal　The Portuguese capital is located on the left bank of the vast estuary of the River Tagus (Tejo), a location that has always been favourable to settlement, the site having been successively inhabited by Phoenicians, Greeks, Romans, Visigoths and Moors. Lisbon became the capital of Portugal in the mid-thirteenth century, and played an important role in commerce between northern and southern Europe in the Middle Ages, but it was in the Age of Discovery of the fifteenth and sixteenth centuries that it reached its zenith, becoming for a time one of the most important cities in the world. The fleets commanded by Vasco da Gama (?1460–1524) and Pedro Álvares Cabral (?1467–1520) sailed from Lisbon, the former to discover the sea route to India and the latter to reach Brazil, rewarding the efforts of several generations of Portuguese to discover the secrets of the sea and develop the techniques of navigation. The physical remains of this period are not abundant owing to the great earthquake that struck the city in 1755 and the fire that followed. There are no remains, for example, of the shipyard where hundreds of workers built the vessels for the Portuguese expansion in Africa, the Indies and America. The outstanding building that relates to traditional seafaring is the Fábrica Nacional de Cordoaria (National Rope Factory) of 1778.

In the early eighteenth century, in accordance with the philosophy of the period, many public works were constructed, among which the most notable was the 58 km (36 mi.) Aqueduct of Águas Livres, built between 1729 and 1748 to supply the city with drinking water. It crosses the Alcântara valley on thirty-five monumental arches, 62 m (203 ft.) high and 34 m (112 ft.) wide, along a 941 m (1030 yd.) extension. The aqueduct begins at the Mãe-de-Água reservoir, whose dam was completed only in 1833.

After the earthquake of 1755 the city was rebuilt to a plan devised by the Marquis of POMBAL (1699–1789), the lower part of a regular geometric plan, with a network of sewers, an innovation for the period. The new buildings were built around 'cages', wooden frameworks intended to provide support in case of further earthquakes. The scale of reconstruction stimulated the mass production of wooden building components, tiles and window glass.

The building of the workers' quarter in the Amoreiras (Mulberries) area dates from this period. The name is indicative of the proximity of the Real Fábrica das Sedas (Royal Factory of Silks), the most important Portuguese manufacture of the eighteenth century. Also in this quarter was the porcelain factory, the Real Fábrica de Porcelana do Rato, which tried to introduce technology from England. There were also small workshops in the area. The planning of this industrial quarter, named the Colégio Real das Manufacturas (the Royal College of Manufactures), where for the first time factories, workshops, houses for factory owners and five hundred workers' dwellings were concentrated in one place, shows that the Marquis of Pombal was one of the most imaginative economic thinkers in Europe.

Two heavily industrialized regions developed in Lisbon during the nineteenth century. The western area from Boavista to Pedrouços, along the Alcântara Valley, later became a primarily residential area, but some important industrial buildings remain, including the Tejo power station of 1919, the building of the former Companhia de Fiação e Tecidos Lisbonense (Lisbon Spinning and Weaving Company) of 1848 with its adjacent workers' dwellings, the building of the Companhia Nacional de Moagem of 1910, and the buildings and silos of the former Fábrica de Moagens Vieillard et Touzet (Vieillard & Touzet Mills) of 1909 at Alcântara. Apart from textiles and milling, the metallurgical industry developed in the area, the Promitente and Empresa Industrial Portuguesa, two of the first companies to produce iron frameworks for buildings, being of particular importance, together with the Fábrica Vulcano e Colares, which from the mid-nineteenth century produced agricultural machinery and steam engines.

The eastern area along the Chelas valley from Xabregas to Poço do Bispo retains its industrial tradition, although many of its early factories have been abandoned and not preserved. Of particular note are the 'Portugal e Colónias' (Portugal and Colonies) complex at Beato; the former 'A Tabaqueira' (Tobacco Box) at Matinha, an iron-framed building now integrated in the arsenal; the Fábrica de Material de Guerra (Armaments Factory) de Braço de Prata; and the former power house of the Barbadinhos steam pumping station.

Interesting examples of industrial architecture in other parts of Lisbon include the former 'Portugália' brewery of 1912, the pottery 'Viúva Lamego' of 1865, with a tiled facade, and the headquarters of the former 'Lusitânia' pottery factory where the plant was recently demolished in spite of vehement public opposition. The Auto-Palace, a motorcar showroom and garage, and the iron-framed exhibition palace of Tapada da Ajuda (Enclosure of Help) are of note, while the Ethnographic Museum of the Sociedade de Geografia (Geographical Society) also has an iron-framed exhibition gallery.

The second industrialization of Lisbon began after World War II, its most significant monument being the Standard Electric building of 1948, designed by Cotinelli Telmo, one of the most important Portuguese architects of the time.

Industrial development attracted migrants to the capital. In the mid-nineteenth century the working population was lodged in the so-called 'pátios' (courtyards), which could be in building yards, in old palaces or in former monasteries. The need to lodge skilled workers led some companies in the late nineteenth and early twentieth centuries to build dwellings near such plants as the Vila Cabrinha (Goat Villa) and the Bairro Grandela. Most

workers in the second half of the nineteenth century lived in 'vilas', apartment blocks located in all parts of the city, of which some of the most notable are the Vila Sousa of 1889, the group at Amoreiras comprising the Vila Bagatela of 1879 and the Pátio do Monteiro of 1890, the Vila Berta of 1902–8, the Bairro Estrela d'Ouro of 1908, and the Vila Cândida at Graça and the Vila Luz Pereira of 1881–2 at Mouraria.

About 1860 a piped drinking-water network, 77 km (48 mi.) long, was begun, but it was only with the construction of the Alviela Aqueduct in 1871–80 and the Barbadinhos Steam Pumping Station in 1880 that the capital's need for water was met. Barbadinhos pumping station became in 1987 the Manuel da Maia Water Museum, a tribute to the brigadier and skilled engineer who was responsible for the Águas Livres aqueduct (see above).

The first public tramways in Lisbon, with carriages drawn by mules, and known as 'americans', began to work in 1873. The first electric tramway opened in 1901 after an agreement between the council and the Companhia Carris de Ferro (Carris Iron Company) in 1897. In 1924 Lisbon possessed a network of 108 route km (67 mi.). The company's tram depot is at Santo Amaro. The topography of the city demanded the building of nine funiculars, eight of them constructed in the last two decades of the nineteenth century. Only four remain at work. The funiculars of Lavra of 1884 and Glória of 1885 were the first to be set up and were operated first by a water counterbalance system, then by steam, and from 1915 and 1914 respectively by electricity. The funicular of Bica of 1892 was also operated by water power and later by steam and electricity. The Santa Justa lift of 1902, the only remaining vertical lift, is in the neo-Gothic style, and the masterpiece of Raoul Mesnier du Ponsard, the Portuguese engineer who also built the funiculars. Its iron framework consists of a 25 m (82 ft.) viaduct, supported in the middle by a concrete pillar and on the end by a 7.5 m × 7 m (23 ft. × 24 ft. 6 in.), 45 m (148 ft.) high metalwork tower. It was originally worked by a steam engine which was replaced by electric power in 1907.

The Rossio station of 1875 and the Alcântara-Terra station of 1887, which is attributed to A.G. EIFFEL, are the most important examples of railway architecture in Lisbon. The former, in the Manueline style, is of three storeys, the second of which communicates with a platform which is roofed in iron and glass. At the end of the platform starts the 2610 m (2854 yd.) long Rossio tunnel, the longest in Portugal.

Lisbon harbour is well situated for trade with all five continents and has always had an important role in the life of the city. Its area is huge, extending for 110 km (70 mi.) along the Tagus, 50 km (30 mi.) on the right bank and 69 km (37 mi.) on the left. The improvement of the harbour began in 1887 with the construction of docks, shipyards and water regulation works, together with wooden and iron-framed warehouses, some of which remain. The air museum at Alverca, 20 km (12 mi.) NE, includes a Douglas DC4 Skymaster airliner of 1941.

The pottery factory at Sacavém, Loures, 15 km (9 mi.)

N., established in 1850, is one of the most celebrated in Portugal.

BIBLIOGRAPHY
General
Associação dos Arquitectos Portugueses, 1987; Custodio, 1990; Estrela, 1986; Nabais and Ramos, 1985; Ribeiro *et al.*, 1981.
Specific
Cordeiro, J. L. Lisboa: le quattro vite di una centrale elettrica (Lisbon: the four lives of a power station). In *Il Coltello di Delfo*, VII, 1988.
Rodrigues, M. J. M. Tradição, Transição e Mudança: a produção do Espaço Urbano na Lisboa Oitocentista (Tradition, transition and change: urban space in eighteenth-century Lisbon). In *Boletim Cultural, Assembleia Distrital de Lisboa* (Cultural Bulletin of the Lisbon Assembly District), 84, 1978.
Sousa, A. V. Museu da Electricidade, Lisboa (The Museum of Electricity at Lisbon). Associação Portuguesa de Museologia (Portuguese Association of Museums), 1983.

LOCATIONS
[M] City Museum, Palácio Pimenta, Campo Grande 245, Lisbon.
[M] Geological and Archaeological Museum, Rua da Academia das Ciências 19, Lisbon.
[M] Manuel da Maia Water Museum, R. do Alviela (à Calçada dos Barbadinhos) 12, Lisbon.
[M] Museum do Ar (Air Museum), Alverca.
[M] Museum Nacional do Azulejo (National Museum of Tiles), Convento da Madre de Deus, Lisbon.
[M] Museum of Popular Art (Ethnographic), Avenida Brasília, Lisbon.
[M] Museu de Etnologia (Ethnological Museum), Av. Ilha da Madeira, Restelo, Lisbon.
[M] Museu dos CTT (Postal Museum), R. D. Estefânia, 173, Lisbon.
[M] Museu Rafael Bordalo Pinheiro (Ceramics Museum), Campo Grande, 382, Lisbon.
[M] National Coach Museum, Praça Afonso de Albuquerque, Lisbon.
[M] National Museum of Archaeology and Ethnology, Praça do Império, Belém, Lisbon.

JOSÉ M. LOPES CORDEIRO

Listowel (Lios Tuathail), County Kerry, Ireland A market town 25 km (16 mi.) E. of Tralee, terminus of the unique MONORAIL to Ballybunion, a seaside resort at the mouth of the Shannon, 14.5 km (9 mi.) SE. The monorail was authorized in 1885–6, built by the Lartigue Construction Co. and opened in 1888. The company went bankrupt in 1897 and the line closed in 1924. Two overbridges remain, the goods shed is now a dwelling, and track foundations can be seen along the remarkable straight road from Listowel to Ballybunion. A section of permanent way has been constructed from surviving remains at Lisselton, 7 km (4½ mi.) NW of Listowel. A bell once used to indicate the impending departure of trains is preserved in the National School, Listowel.

BIBLIOGRAPHY
General
Guerin, 1988; Newham, 1967.
Specific
Goodman, F. The Listowel & Ballybunion Railway. In *Railway Magazine*, VII, 1900.

Tucker, D. G. F. H. Behr's development of the Lartigue monorail: from country trawler to electric express. In *TNS*, LV, 1983–4.
Tucker, D. G. The Listowel & Ballybunion Railway; some revisions and additions to its story. In *Railway & Canal Historical Society*, XXVII, 1984.

Lithgow, New South Wales, Australia One of the principal heavy industrial centres in Australia. There are extensive remains of a BLAST FURNACE complex which operated between 1907 and 1926, including the shell of the blowing engine house, the foundations of two furnaces, pig beds, bases for devices to lift and break pigs, and traces of the railways that delivered raw materials and took away molten iron and pigs. A full survey of the site was carried out in 1986. Lithgow was also the location of Australia's first steelworks, the site of which has been cleared and now serves as a sports field.

Some excavations have been carried out on industrial sites, including the Lithgow Pottery works of 1879, prior to redevelopment.

BIBLIOGRAPHY
General
Cremin *et al.*, 1987; Evans, 1981; Hughes, 1964; Power, 1912.

LOCATION
[M] Esk Bank House Museum, Inch Street, Lithgow.

lithography A method of reproducing illustrations, printing from a limestone block upon which a greasy image attracts the ink. Lithography was invented by Aloys Senefelder (1771–1834) of Munich in 1798, and widely adopted in the nineteenth century when zinc plates replaced limestone. Stone from a quarry at Solenhofen, BAVARIA, was always regarded as the best for lithography.

BIBLIOGRAPHY
General
Ivins, 1943; Robins and Pennell, 1915.

Liverpool, Merseyside, England The premier port of northern England, which prospered through the sugar, cotton, tobacco and slave trades in the eighteenth century, and became Europe's principal emigration port for America in the nineteenth. Salthouse Dock was completed in 1734, but the greatest period of dock construction was under the direction of Jesse Hartley (1780–1860) between 1824 and 1860. By 1900 docks extended 6 km (4 mi.) N. and 4 km (2½ mi.) S. of Pierhead. Few are still used, but the most notable of Hartley's works, the Albert Dock of 1841–5, after being a contentious conservation issue for many years, is being put to new uses. The 3.25 ha (8 ac.) dock is surrounded by ranges of five-storey warehouses of fireproof construction, with the walls carried on elliptical arches springing from cast-iron columns, and roofs on wrought-iron sheeting: these now accommodate shops, a television centre and an art gallery, as well as the Merseyside Maritime Museum. At Stanley Dock, north of Pierhead, are two further fireproof warehouses, together with a twelve-storey brick tobacco warehouse, designed by G. F. Lyster in 1900.

Liverpool's waterfront is a magnificent monument to the self-confidence of Edwardian imperialism. It is dominated by W. Aubrey Thomas's concrete Royal Liver Building of 1908–10, the same architect's Harbour Board offices of 1908, and the Cunard Building of 1913 by Willink & Thickness. The ensemble is completed by the ventilation tower of the first Mersey Tunnel, built in 1925–34. Other notable commercial buildings include the offices by Richard Norman Shaw (1831–1912) for the White Star Line of 1896, and Oriel Chambers, Water Street, with large plate-glass windows cantilevered from an iron frame, a revolutionary structure for 1864. Liverpool has two cast-iron churches, St George, Everton, and St Michael in the Hamlet, designed by Rickman & Cragg in 1812–15.

Birkenhead, on the west bank of the Mersey, began to develop in 1824 when William Laird established an engineering works which grew into a shipyard. Soon afterwards a planned town to the design of James Gillespie was commenced with Hamilton Square as its centrepiece. Birkenhead Park, the first to be provided at public expense, was laid out in 1843–7 by SIR JOSEPH PAXTON. The docks at Birkenhead were built in the 1840s and 50s. The hydraulic generating station of 1863 still operates. Ellesmere Port, 16 km (10 mi.) S., the terminus of Ellesmere Canal, has extensive trans-shipment basins and is the site of a museum with a major collection of inland navigation craft.

Some traces of the Liverpool & Manchester Railway, opened in 1830, can be seen near Edgehill station; and at Rainhill, 15 km (9 mi.) E., scene of the locomotive trials of 1829, is the skew bridge shown in early views of the line. Liverpool Museum includes the locomotive *Lion* of 1838.

Liverpool working-class housing in the nineteenth century consisted typically of BACK-TO-BACK terraces arranged around courts, with passages through frontage houses giving access to the street. All such courts have now been demolished. At Aintree is a small garden suburb built by Sir William Hartley, the jam manufacturer, with streets named after fruits.

Prescot, 14 km (9 mi.) E., was important for watchmaking until the early twentieth century. A museum is devoted to the history of the industry.

BIBLIOGRAPHY
General
Ferneyhough, 1980; Ritchie-Noakes, 1984.
Specific
Taylor, I. C. The court and cellar dwelling: the eighteenth-century origins of the Liverpool slum. In *Transactions of the Historical Society of Lancashire and Cheshire*, 1970–1.

LOCATIONS
[M] The Boat Museum, Dockyard Road, Ellesmere Port, South Wirral L65 4EF.
[M] Merseyside Museums, William Brown Street, Liverpool L3 8EN.
[M] Merseyside Maritime Museum, Pier Head, Liverpool L3 1DN.
[M] Prescot Museum, 34 Church Street, Prescot, Merseyside L34 3LA.

BARRIE TRINDER

livery stable An establishment that provided horses, with or without carriages, for hire, principally for local use, those for long journeys being provided by posting houses (*see* POST COACH). Livery stables existed in most English towns until the early twentieth century, and the term was also employed in the USA.

Ljubljana (Laibach), Slovenia, Yugoslavia The capital of Slovenia, and an important communications centre, ruled by the Habsburgs during 1282–1918. It was much damaged in the earthquake of 1895. Very rapid industrial growth has occurred since World War II. Many aspects of the city's industrial history are illustrated in museums.

LOCATIONS
[M] Geographical Museum of Slovenia, Trg francoske revolucije 7, 61000-Ljubljana.
[M] Municipal Museum Gosposka 15, 61000-Ljubljana.
[M] Slovenian Ethnographical Museum, Trg Herojev 1, 61000-Ljubljana.
[M] Technology Museum of Slovenia, Parmova 33, 61000-Ljubljana.

loading gauge The limits of height and width to which railway vehicles must conform to run on particular tracks in order to clear bridges, tunnels and other structures. Dimensional restrictions are greater in Europe than in America, and particularly so in Great Britain. The name is also applied to frames hanging above the tracks at freight depots to ensure that wagons have not been loaded beyond the limit necessary to pass through bridges and tunnels; these are alternatively known as gauge frames.

lock A word with at least two meanings in industrial archaeology.

1. A device for fastening a door, or part of a gun. *See* LOCKSMITH.
2. On a navigable river or canal, a means of carrying a boat over a shallow section, or of raising or lowering it between different levels of a controlled waterway; or of shutting off a section of the waterway to allow it to be drained for repair.

See also FLASH LOCK; POUND LOCK; STOP LOCK.

locksmith A locksmith works in iron and brass, forging, tempering and filing the metals, to make padlocks and rim locks for doors. In a lock a removable key is used to slide an enclosed dead bolt into a keeper and out again at will. 'Wards' are obstacles used to prevent the use of all but the right key. A lock is normally built up on a base plate around a key. Willenhall (*see* BLACK COUNTRY) was the centre of the British lock trade, although there were locksmiths in most towns in the nineteenth century. Velbert is the equivalent lockmaking town in Germany. Important improvements in lockmaking were made by Charles Chubb (d. 1845), his son John (1816–72), and JOSEPH BRAMAH; and the whole trade was revolutionized by Linus Yale (1821–68), who perfected the 'Yale Infallible Bank Lock' in 1851, developed the cylinder lock with a small flat key in 1860–5, and established the Yale Lock Manufacturing Co. at Stamford, Conn., USA, in the year of his death.

BIBLIOGRAPHY
General
Hopkins, 1928; Plot, 1685; Tunis, 1965.

locomotive and carriage works   The first factory for the construction and maintenance of railway rolling stock was established by ROBERT STEPHENSON at Newcastle-upon-Tyne in 1823. In Britain most railway companies owned their own works, and private builders like North British of GLASGOW and Beyer Peacock of MANCHESTER catered largely for overseas markets. In the USA private concerns like Baldwin of Philadelphia, the American Locomotive Co. (ALCO) of Schenectady, N.Y., and Lima of Lima, Ohio, predominated in the steam era, and subsequently General Motors Electromotive Division, established at La Grange, Ill., in the 1930s has been supremely successful in supplying much of the world with diesel locomotives. Many locomotive works were established by Britons in continental Europe in the early days of railways. From the 1880s German companies like Borsig of Berlin, Maffei of Munich and Henschel of Kassel became increasingly competitive in world markets.

A steam locomotive works usually included an iron, a brass and later a steel foundry, forges for fabricating wrought-iron and steel parts, a sheet-metal shop for cabs, a boiler shop with facilities for forging copper, machine shops and a wheel shop. All of these supplied parts to an erecting shop, in which locomotives were assembled or dismantled above pits, with the assistance of overhead traverser cranes. One of the largest erecting shops was the 'A' shop at SWINDON, of 45 000 m² (500 000 sq. ft.). Many locomotive works had separate shops for building TENDERS. For steam locomotives few items would be 'bought-in': they would include brake apparatus, gauges, and latterly roller bearings. With diesel and electric locomotives most mechanical and electrical parts are likely to be obtained from specialist suppliers.

A railway carriage works often shared the site of a locomotive factory owned by a railway company, but private companies were likely to be specialist concerns. Sawmills and trim shops were prominent among the departments supplying assembly shops.

Locomotive and carriage works were amongst the largest of all manufacturing establishments. SWINDON employed over 12 000 people in the 1930s. The workings of such establishments in Britain are illustrated in the films *Building the locomotive 'Prince of Wales' at Swindon*, made by Urbnora in 1911, and in *Building the Corridor Third*, made by the LMSR in 1932.

BIBLIOGRAPHY
General
Larkin and Larkin, 1988; Lowe, 1975; Reed, 1982; Warren, 1923; Weitzman, 1987; Westwood, 1983; White, 1982; Williams, 1915.

BARRIE TRINDER

locomotive depot   A steam locomotive usually needs attention at least once a day, for the removal of ash from the smoke box and clinker from the firebox, and the replacement of fuel and water supplies. Depots to carry out these tasks were established from the beginnings of main-line railways. Frequently facilities for carrying out repairs were added, in particular wheel drops to enable worn axle-bearings to be replaced; some workshops were equipped with lathes and other tools. Many had mechanical coaling plants where wagons could be unloaded and locomotive tenders and bunkers filled with coal: the first such plant was constructed by the LNWR at Crewe in 1913.

Some railway companies constructed large 'through' sheds for routine maintenance, others preferred ROUND-HOUSES.

Some steam depots remain in use for other forms of traction and on PRESERVED RAILWAYS. In Britain those at Didcot (*see* GREAT WESTERN RAILWAY) and Carnforth, Lancashire – which has the country's only remaining mechanical coaling plant – are particularly well preserved. Several have been adapted to new uses (*see* YORK).

See also figure 159.

BIBLIOGRAPHY
General
Locomotive Publishing Company, n.d.

BARRIE TRINDER

lodging house   A building in which overnight accommodation was provided, usually on a short-term, casual basis, for workers seeking employment, for families temporarily without home, for travelling showmen, and for the very old. Lodging houses had a bad reputation in mid-nineteenth-century England – largely because criminal elements were thought to corrupt honest migratory craftsmen – and were regulated by legislation in 1851 and 1853, the latter Act providing for regular inspection and whitewashing of rooms. The 1851 Act, by allowing lodging houses to be built with public funds, eventually provided precedents by which local authorities were able to build houses for families (*see* COUNCIL HOUSE). Several philanthropic bodies built model lodging houses in cities for single male workers.

BIBLIOGRAPHY
General
Gauldie, 1974.

Łódź, Łódź, Poland   In the 1820s the government of the Congress Kingdom of Poland launched a programme for developing the textile region around Łódź, then based entirely on domestic manufactures. Wendisch's spinning mill, one of the first mechanized mills in Łódź, was built in 1827, and that of L. Gayers in 1835. In the first half of the nineteenth century the textile industry in Łódź was based mainly on wool and to a smaller extent on flax. The lack of government orders after the November Uprising of 1830, and the imposition in 1833 of tariff barriers between Russia and the Congress Kingdom of Poland, hampered the development of the wool industry and output was halved. A change to the production of cheaper cotton articles stimulated the home market and proved a basis for the re-establishment of the industry. In 1851 tariffs were withdrawn, and rapid expansion followed. By 1900 Łódź was one of the major textile centres of continental Europe. Most of the large textile plants of the late nineteenth century in the Łódź region were based on investment from abroad, particularly from France and Germany. The population of Łódź rose from 18 000 in 1851 to 100 000 in 1878, reaching 329 000 in 1903. The average population density in the city in 1911 was 13 300 per km². The urban infrastructure could not match this dynamic growth. In 1900 Łódź had neither a water supply system nor mains sewers. After World War I development slowed down as Łódź was cut off from its Russian markets.

Many monuments of nineteenth-century industry can be recognized in Łódź. There are still some remnants of the first stages of the programme of industrial development launched by the government of the Congress Kingdom of Poland. Some weavers' houses of that period remain, and the original plan of the city can still be traced. It was based on Piotrowska Street, along which were located the industrial plants, the workers' housing and the estates of the factory owners. The industrial architecture of the late nineteenth and early twentieth centuries in Łódź is characterized by advanced methods of construction and highly ornamental façades. The Karol Scheibler plant established in 1855 was among the biggest in the world, with 232 000 spindles and 3600 looms. It covers an area of 168 ha (68 ac.). A spinning mill of 1873 in Księży Młyn is 200 m (656 ft.) long, and contained 88 000 spindles. Other buildings notable for their size were the I. K. Poznański cotton factory and the plants of T. Grohman, M. Silbestein and J. Heinzl. Apart from such major complexes there were some 514 smaller establishments. The exceptionally luxurious mansions of the industrialists, set in their own grounds, and such working-class settlements as the K. Scheibler housing in Księży Młyn are also of note.

The Central Museum of the Textile Industry was established in Łódź in 1960 at the initiative of the Ministry of Culture and Art, and is located in the well-preserved spinning and weaving mill built in 1835–7 by Ludwik Gayer. It is concerned with the history of the Polish textile industry in general and with the role of the Łódzki textile industry region in particular. It also features the development of textile machinery. The historical section deals with the origins and development of textile manufacture around Łódź, and includes contracts made between the Łódź manufacturers and the government of the Congress Kingdom of Poland, as well as a collection of works of art concerned with the industry. The 'history of technology' section shows the development of weaving and spinning, and the evolution of textile machines, with displays of original machines and models. A further section deals with the history of woven fabrics, with a collection that includes samples of baroque and rococo silk, specimens of early nineteenth-century cloth, and contemporary examples, as well as the fabrics produced in the Łódź factories. A section on folk weaving displays many examples of tools and equipment used in domestic weaving, as well as samples of fabrics.

BIBLIOGRAPHY
General
Jezierski and Zawadzki, 1966; Łukasiewicz, 1963; Popławska, 1973, 1974.
Specific
Centralne Muzeum Włókiennictwa (Central Museum of the Textile Industry, Łódź), 1977.
Informator Muzeum Historii Włókiennictwa (Guidebook to the Museum of the History of the Textile Industry, Łódź), 1969.

LOCATION
[M] Centralne Muzeum Włókiennictwa (Central Museum of the Textile Industry), ul. Piotrkowska 282, Łódź.

PIOTR GERBER

Lofoten Islands, Nordland, Norway   A string of islands 500 km (300 mi.) N. of Trondheim, extending about 150 km (90 mi.) into the Atlantic. Fishing was very profitable in the nineteenth century and villages huddle along the shore beneath vast cliffs. Nusfjord on Flackstad, one of the most southerly islands, is a preserved fishing settlement with examples of temporary huts used by fishermen from elsewhere, a fishing boat owner's house, fish stores and 'hjeller', the racks used for drying fish. At Kabelvåg, 35 km (22 mi.) N. on Austvågøy island, is a fisheries museum.

BIBLIOGRAPHY
General
Tschudi-Madsen, 1977.

LOCATION
[M] Lofotmuseet, Storvågan, 8310 Kabelvåg.

logwood   The inner red wood of a South American tree, *Haematoxylon campechianum*, used widely in dyeing. Imported in log form – hence its name logwood, or dyewood – it was cut or ground mechanically by a rotating cutter for use as a dyestuff.

BIBLIOGRAPHY
General
Partridge, 1823; Perkins and Everest, 1918.
Specific
Day, J. The last of the dyewood mills. In *IA*, III, 1966.

Lolland-Falster, Denmark   Two Danish islands lying south of Zealand, both of which consist of low-lying plains of clay, whose fertile soil makes the islands well suited for the cultivation of sugar beet. Sugar mills were for a long period the most prominent industrial concerns in the islands. The first was built at Højbygard near Holeby in 1873, and was followed by mills in Nakskov, Nykøbing, Maribo and Sakskøbing. The mills at Højbygard and Maribo have been adapted for new uses, but the remainder are still working. Lolland enjoyed a shipbuilding boom during World War I. Two large yards for building steel ships were established, a short-lived concern in Rødbyhavn, and one at Nakskov, which until its recent closure was the principal employer in the islands.

The rural nature of the islands meant that factory owners had to build new dwellings to attract new workers and staff. Several factory colonies have survived, including one of the 1870s at the Højbygard sugar mill, two GARDEN CITY style developments at the shipyards at Rødbyhavn and Nakskov, twenty dwellings at Skimminge in Maribo, built by a local engineering concern c.1900, and a so-called Polish barracks at Tågerup near Rødby, erected to accommodate seasonal workers from Poland.

Since 1937 the Storstrømmen bridge has connected Falster to Zealand. Part of a large project for direct motorway and railway links from Copenhagen to Germany, it was designed by A. Engelund, and built by Christiani & Nielsen, with the British firm of Dorman Long, as a steel beam bridge with plate girders, and foundations of reinforced concrete. With a length of 3.2 km (2 mi.) the bridge was in its time the longest in Europe. In 1985 the old bridge was relieved by new motorway bridges, cable-stayed structures in pre-stressed concrete.

At Ålholm Castle, 16 km (10 mi.) SW of Nykøbing, is Denmark's biggest car museum with a collection of about three hundred vehicles. A preserved railway links the small port of Bandholm, where the station is a protected monument, with Maribo, the location of the historical museum for the islands, which has a small open-air section.

BIBLIOGRAPHY
Specific
Boyhus, E.-M. *Sukkerroer* (Sugar beet). Maribo, 1973.
Bro, H. Storstrømsbroen – 50 år (The Storstrømmen – 50 years). In *Fabrik og Bolig*, II, 1987.
Jensen, H. T. and Axelsen, P. *Fabriksboliger pa Lolland-Falster* (Factory dwellings on Lolland-Falster). Copenhagen, 1982.

LOCATION
[M] Lolland-Falsters Stiftsmuseum (Local history museum), Jernbanegade 22, 4930 Maribo.

OLE HYLDTOFT

Lollar, Hesse, Germany   The first coke-fired blast furnaces in Hesse, named 'Minerva' and 'Vulkan', were constructed by the Buderus company in Lollar, 12 km (8 mi.) N. of Giessen, in 1864. A 20 m (66 ft.) high Scottish-style blast furnace was added to the complex in 1898. The furnaces were blown out in 1907, but the tower of the charging hoist has been preserved, its topmost storey, 5.6 m (18 ft.) high, having been added when the new furnace was built in 1898. The owner's neo-Gothic villa of 1868 also remains on the site, and the workers' dwellings of the early twentieth century survive on the outskirts of Lollar. A works museum illustrates the history of central heating.

See also WETZLAR.

LOCATION
[M] Zentralheizungsmuseum (Museum of Central Heating), Buderus AG, 6304 Lollar.

Lombardy (Lombardia), Italy   The most prosperous region in Italy, Lombardy's early industrial growth was based on textiles. The silk industry was established around Lake Como by the early sixteenth century, focused on Lecco and COMO. Cotton mills initiated a larger scale of industrialization from the late eighteenth century. Factories combining spinning, weaving, dyeing and printing were established in Milan by Adamo Kramer in 1782, and by Frederico Schutz in 1790. In 1854 Lombardy had thirty-three spinning mills, employing 3800 workers. With the growing need for water power for spinning, investment in the early nineteenth century was concentrated on the banks of the River Olona north-west of Milan, and especially at Busto Arsizio and Gallarate, 35 km (22 mi.) from the region's capital. Gallarate's most impressive sites are weaving factories dating from the turn of the century, especially the Tessitura Borgomaneri in Via Roma, dating from 1902–7, with a lavishly classical façade.

Integrated spinning and weaving mills were developed after 1870. The Cantoni mill at Castellanza, 6 km (4 mi.) SE of Gallarate, combines a spinning mill dating from just before 1850 with a large area of north-lit weaving sheds dating from 1898–1902. Other large mills can be seen at Varano Borghi, 10 km (6 mi.) NW of Gallarate, and at Bellano by Lake COMO. Casalbuttano, 10 km (6 mi.) NW of Cremona, has two major spinning works, the Jacini and Turina mills, both redundant. The latter dates from 1825 and has elevations consisting of three tiers of shallow-arched arcades.

See also BRESCIA; COMO; CREMONA; CRESPI D'ADDA; MANTUA; MILAN; PAVIA; STELVIO; VIZZOLA.

BIBLIOGRAPHY
General
Mioni *et al.*, 1981–3; Negri *et al.*, 1983; Regione Lombardia, 1983.

MICHAEL STRATTON

London, England   London, at the lowest crossing point of the Thames, has been the principal English city and the nodal point of the country's communications since Roman times. It is also England's most important single centre of manufacturing industry.

Until 1800 most of London's overseas and coastal trade was handled at riverside wharves. The West India Docks, opened in 1802, across the isthmus of the Isle of Dogs, were designed by WILLIAM JESSOP: they provided secure moorings, surrounded by spacious warehouses and high walls. By 1914 the enclosed dock system extended some 12 km ($7\frac{1}{2}$ mi.) downstream from the Tower of London to King George V dock on the north bank, with the Surrey Commercial Docks on the south bank. Since 1960 trade has been concentrated at Tilbury, 30 km (18 mi.) downstream, and dockland is undergoing massive redevelopment. Most of the docks are likely to survive as water features in landscapes of apartments and offices, and some original warehouses remain at the West India Docks. The Grand Junction Canal reached London from the Midlands in 1801, and its basin at Paddington was linked to the docks at Limehouse by the Regent's Canal opened in 1820. Outstanding amongst the historic ships

423

Figure 76 The Abbey Mills sewage pumping station in East London at the time of its completion in 1868: although the original beam engines were replaced in the 1930s by electric pumps, Abbey Mills remains one of England's most impressive 'temples of public health'.

Illustrated London News

preserved on the Thames is the clipper *Cutty Sark*, which rests at Greenwich.

London's first main-line railway was the London & Greenwich, opened in 1836, which approached London Bridge station on a 6 km (4 mi.) viaduct of 878 brick arches, the first urban railway viaduct. Most of London's termini are of interest, the outstanding examples being St Pancras, built in 1868–74, with a single 75 m (246 ft.) span train shed by W. H. Barlow and GEORGE GILBERT SCOTT's palatial Gothic hotel; Lewis Cubitt's elegant twin train sheds at King's Cross; Edward Wilson's Liverpool Street, built in 1872–5; and MATTHEW DIGBY WYATT's Paddington, of 1854. The Camden Town Roundhouse, now a theatre, is an LNWR locomotive depot of 1847. London's underground railways date from the completion in 1863 of the 'cut-and-cover' Metropolitan Railway from Paddington to Farringdon. The Greathead shield made possible the construction of deep 'tube' lines, the first of which, the City & South London, opened in 1900. By 1910 most underground lines were owned by one concern, and the formation of the London Passenger Transport Board in 1933 made possible an integrated system, given distinction by the high quality of design

initiated by Frank Pick (1878–1941), and the architecture of Charles Holden (1875–1960). Sudbury Town (1931), Osterley (1934) and Southgate (1933) are among the most distinguished of Holden's stations, the latter retaining many original fittings. The London Transport Museum, in Covent Garden, includes a Beyer Peacock 4–4–0T condensing locomotive of the type used when the Metropolitan Railway opened. The East London line crosses beneath the Thames through the tunnel built by Marc Brunel (1769–1849) between 1826 and 1843. The museum in the terminus at North Woolwich is concerned with the Great Eastern Railway.

London's airport in the inter-war period was at Croydon. Its International Modern style buildings of 1927–8 closed in 1959, and are now part of an industrial estate. The imposing Imperial Airways terminal by A. Lakeman of 1939 in Buckingham Palace Road has been adapted to new uses. A plaque over a railway arch in Walthamstow commemorates where EDWIN ROE assembled the triplane which made the first all-British powered flight in July 1909. Most of the many pioneers of aircraft construction in London occupied similarly unheroic premises.

Many of London's streets are the creation of Victorian

424

planning, designed to obliterate slums or aid drainage. Holborn Viaduct, built by William Heywood in 1863–9, and Kingsway, completed in 1906, are examples, the latter notable for its tramway tunnel. The most ambitious scheme was the Embankment, built by Sir Joseph Bazalgette (1819–91) in 1864–70, providing a cover for a sewer and for the District Railway. Most of London's older bridges have been extensively rebuilt. Tower Bridge, completed in 1894, now has a visitor centre. The George in Borough High Street is London's only surviving coaching inn, while the Victoria Coach Station of 1932, by Wallis, Gilbert & Partners, is the focus of twentieth-century road passenger transport, and the concrete Stockwell bus garage of 1953 is much admired and is listed.

Making London a healthy place to live in was one of the great achievements of Victorian civilization. Parts of the embankments of Bazalgette's Northern and Southern Outfall Sewers can be used as footpaths, and the Abbey Mills Pumping Station, West Ham, built in 1865–8 to house eight beam engines, is a monumental temple of public health. The most venerable feature of London's water supply is the New River extending some 38 km (24 mi.) along the 30 m (100 ft.) contour from springs near Hertford to Islington: built by Sir Hugh Myddleton in 1613, it has subsequently been much altered. There are remains at New River Head around Myddleton Square. At the water pumping station at Kew Bridge four beam engines of 1820–71 are exhibited and occasionally steamed. London's first major electric power station was built for the London Electric Supply Corporation by Sebastin de Ferranti at Deptford in 1887. The most celebrated of several architecturally distinguished riverside power stations is Battersea, built in stages between 1933 and 1953, with detailing by Sir Giles Gilbert Scott (1880–1960), now adapted to other uses. There is a gasholder of c.1830 at Sands End Lane, Fulham, and an impressive group dating from 1868–74 at Kings Cross; a ski slope now adorns the waste tips of Beckton Gasworks, once the largest in London.

The most distinctive feature of working-class housing in central London is the multi-storey apartment block, built originally by charitable societies, and from the 1890s by public authorities. The oldest surviving block, though not quite the first to be built, is the group of Model Dwellings for Families in Streatham Street, near the British Museum, designed by Henry Roberts (d.1876). Roberts's modular model houses displayed at the Great Exhibition of 1851 now stand in Kennington Park Road. The majority of the older blocks were constructed for the Trust established in 1862 by the American GEORGE PEABODY (1795–1869). The tradition was continued from the 1890s by the newly formed London County Council (LCC). The Boundary Street scheme in Bethnal Green by Rowland Plumbe of 1890s was the council's first major project. From the late 1860s the Artisans', Labourers' and General Dwellings Company developed cottage estates at Shaftesbury Park, Battersea, Queens Park, Kilburn and Noel Park, Hornsey, an example followed by the Peabody Trust in Tottenham, and by the LCC in twentieth-century developments like the Watling Estate at Hendon. Bedford Park, planned from 1875 by Richard Norman Shaw (1831–1912), is acknowledged as the earliest planned garden suburb. Hampstead Garden Suburb, inspired by Dame Henrietta Barnett (1851–1936), was planned from 1905, extending over 320 ha (800 ac.), with many houses designed by RAYMOND UNWIN, and its churches by Sir Edwin Lutyens (1869–1944).

Monuments of manufacturing industry are less plentiful in London. Many of the principal nineteenth-century enterprises like the Thames Ironworks on the Isle of Dogs have disappeared. Whitbread's Brewery in Chigwell Street has some eighteenth-century buildings, including the Porter Tun room built by JOHN RENNIE in 1784. Silk-weavers' housing of the early eighteenth century survives in Fournier Street and Elder Street in Spitalfields. Twentieth-century development was influenced by the huge depots created around the city during World War I, which became industrial concentrations like Slough and Colindale. The most spectacular developments of the inter-war period were the ostentatiously fronted factories for consumer goods along Western Avenue and the Great West Road, like those built for Gillette and Hoover. Fleet Street contains a range of newspaper-printing factories, amongst which the Daily Express building of 1931, in black and transparent glass set in chromium strips, is outstanding.

London's Victorian wholesale markets are steadily moving from their central locations. Covent Garden Market, by Charles Fowler, mostly dating from 1828–31, has become a focus for small specialist shops, but Smithfield Meat Market, a cast-iron structure of 1867–8, remains in operation.

London has many retail premises of interest. Woburn Walk contains a range of elegant small shop frontages dating from c.1822. The best Victorian shop front is probably that of James Smith & Sons, umbrella makers, at 32 New Oxford Street. Liberty's in Regent Street, with its magnificent galleried interior of 1924, is an outstanding department store, while Marks & Spencers' Pantheon store in Oxford Street of 1938 is one of the most significant inter-war shops.

London is dominated by the offices of large companies. Interesting examples include the fiery red brick Prudential Insurance building in Holborn, designed in four stages by Alfred (1830–1905) and Paul (1861–1924) Waterhouse between 1877 and 1897; Kodak House, Kingsway, by Sir John Burnet (1857–1938) of 1911, one of the earliest examples of modernism applied to office buildings; and J. Lomax Simpson's massive Unilever Building of 1931 at Blackfriars.

The history of industry in London is displayed in the Museum of London, whose research projects have thrown light on the City before the Great Fire of 1666 and on such twentieth-century industries as film-making. The Science Museum contains the world's best collections of early steam engines and of the first generation of locomotives, including a Watt rotative engine of 1788, the only surviving TREVITHICK engine and GEORGE STEPHENSON's *Rocket*. Textile machines include an ARKWRIGHT spinning

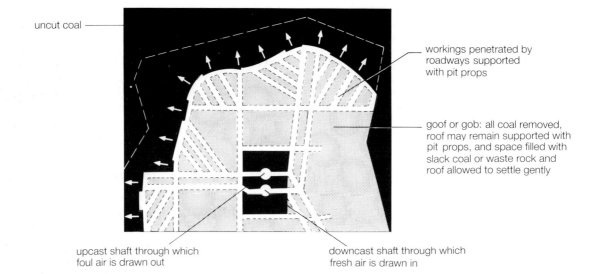

uncut coal

workings penetrated by
roadways supported
with pit props

goof or gob: all coal removed,
roof may remain supported with
pit props, and space filled with
slack coal or waste rock and
roof allowed to settle gently

upcast shaft through which
foul air is drawn out

downcast shaft through which
fresh air is drawn in

Figure 77   A plan showing the mode of operation of a mine utilizing a longwall system

frame of 1769 and a drawing frame of 1780. The collection of machine tools is of outstanding importance and there are galleries featuring bridges, chemicals, and most aspects of manufacturing. The Victoria and Albert Museum has rich collections of ceramics, glass and furnishings. Industrial history is illustrated in many of London's specialist museums.

See also figures 61 and 70.

BIBLIOGRAPHY
General
Barman, 1974; Hall, 1962; Jackson, 1969; NELP, 1986; Pudney, 1975; Simmons, 1986; Thomas, 1986.
Specific
Cochrane, R. *Landmark of London: the story of Battersea Power Station.* Central Electricity Generating Board, 1983.
Essex Lopresti, M. *Exploring the New River.* Studley, Warwickshire: Brewin, 1986.
Wohl, A. S. Housing of the working classes in London, 1815–1914. In Chapman, 1971.

LOCATIONS
[M] Bakelite Museum, 12 Mundania Court, Forest Hill Road, East Dulwich, London SE22.
[M] Clockmakers' Company Museum, Guildhall Library, Aldermanbury, London EC2P 2EJ.
[M] London Transport Museum, Covent Garden, London WC2E 7BB.
[M] Museum of London, London Wall, London EC2Y 5HN.
[M] National Postal Museum, King Edward Building, King Edward Street, London EC1A 1LP.
[M] North Woolwich Station Museum, Pier Road, North Woolwich, London E16 2JJ.
[M] Royal Armouries, HM Tower of London, London EC3N 4AB.
[M] The Science Museum, Exhibition Road, London SW7 2DD.
[M] Victoria and Albert Museum, Cromwell Road, London SW7 2RL.

BARRIE TRINDER

Londonderry (Derry), Londonderry, Northern Ireland   The fourth largest city in Ireland, developed from a walled town completed in 1618 by Sir Edward Donnington. Shirtmaking was important from the mid-nineteenth century, and several shirt factories remain including the five-storey brick premises of Tillie and Henderson, designed in 1856 by J. G. Ferguson, which dominate the north end of Craigavon Bridge. Port buildings along the River Foyle include a five-storey, seventeen-bay Rock flour mill of 1856.

BIBLIOGRAPHY
General
McCutcheon, 1980.

longwall mining   A system of mining, particularly for coal, which was developed in Shropshire, England, in the seventeenth century. In its earliest forms, the tunnels radiating from a shaft were planned in the shape of the letter T, the top of each T being the coalface, which connected with the ends of the faces of each of the adjacent tunnels. As the mineral was worked each T grew longer so that the distance between tunnels increased, and subsidiary tunnels were constructed to reduce face lengths. Several miners would enter each tunnel, and, dividing into two groups, would work from either side of the face. Typically, four miners might enter a tunnel heading with eight wagons, two would work into each side of the heading, each filling his share of the wagons. Any number of miners up to ten or so might work on each side of the heading, but more than this could prove unwieldy and unfair to the furthermost miner. The teams would be dependent on the slowest worker, in order that they could all leave together. There could also be problems relating to the supply and removal of wagons in the confined space of the tunnel at the face. Any waste material from immediately above or below the coal seam (often dug to give additional height to the roadways)

426

would be placed behind the T cross pieces as they advanced, thus providing additional support to the roof. Longwall working often involved division of labour between highly-skilled miners who cut coal and others who loaded and transported it; it was thus well suited to absorb migrant unskilled labour during periods of rapid growth. Longwall working was also well suited to mechanization. From the early twentieth century coal cutters and conveyors came into use, and from the 1940s various forms of cutter-loaders were introduced. The mechanized longwall system is now almost universal in large coal mines.

IVOR J. BROWN

loom A machine for making cloth by interlacing two parallel sets of yarn at right angles to each other (*see* TEXTILES). It consists of a frame in which the longitudinal warp yarn is wound between a pair of rolls or 'beams', making a 'shed' or opening through which the weft yarns are carried by a shuttle or shuttles passed from side to side. The speed of working was increased by the 'flying shuttle' of John Kay (d.1764), introduced in 1733. Weaving was first successfully mechanized in 1785–7 with the patenting by Edmund Cartwright (1743–1853) of the power loom, but it was many decades before the power loom could be applied to the manufacture of every type of fabric.

See also AUTOMATIC LOOM; CARPET LOOM; HAND LOOM; JACQUARD LOOM.

BIBLIOGRAPHY
General
Barlow, 1878.
Specific
Paulinyi, A. John Kay's flying shuttle: some consideration of his technical capacity and economic impact. In *TH*, XVII, 1986.

Lorraine, Meurthe-et-Moselle and Moselle, France The discovery of the GILCHRIST THOMAS process for using phosphoric iron in open-hearth steelmaking in 1878 led to the intensive extraction of low-grade iron ores, known as 'minette' in Lorraine. Until 1895, when the process ceased to be protected by patents, demand was generally satisfied by means of horizontal workings driven into the hillsides. The earliest such iron-ore mines in Lorraine date from the beginning of the nineteenth century, those at Hayange, 26 km (16 mi.) NW of Metz, and Moyeuvre, 19 km (12 mi.) NW of Metz, boasting remarkable masonry entrances. With the development of deep mining, both in the part of Lorraine annexed by Germany between 1870 and 1918 (the present-day department of Moselle) and in the part that remained French (Meurthe-et-Moselle), overall production rose from 7 million tonnes per annum in 1895 to 41 million tonnes in 1913. In that year there were some thirty-seven iron-ore mines in Lorraine with depths between 70 m and 140 m (230 ft. and 460 ft). Production rose above the 60 million tonne mark in 1962, declining thereafter, with the rate of closures accelerating dramatically after 1978. Only four mines remain in use, together producing about 10 million tonnes per annum.

Iron-ore mining made Lorraine the principal iron and steel region in France for almost a century, and since 1983 efforts have been made to conserve some traces of its heritage. Some abandoned pithead buildings, including office blocks, maintenance shops and power stations, have been reused, whilst two sites have been opened to the public as museums: the Bassompierre mine at Aumetz, and the Sainte-Neige mine at Neufchef, 40 km (25 mi.) N. of Metz.

The first was worked from 1897 until 1983. It retains a metal headstock built in 1940–2, and other characteristic structures from the first half of the twentieth century, housing the winding gear and the compressors. These buildings also had small-scale production facilities for liquid oxygen cartridges, explosive devices used in the mines from the 1920s.

At Neufchef the mine was a large adit, dating from the early nineteenth century. Nearly 2 km (1 mi.) are now open to the public, with a permanent exhibition of tools and machines depicting extraction techniques from the origins of the mines to today's electrified and computerized techniques. Particular attention is given to the period between 1920 and 1950 when compressed air was used. A modern museum building includes other exhibition rooms and a documentation centre.

BIBLIOGRAPHY
General
André, 1989.

LOCATION
[M] Musée des mines de fer (Iron Mining Museum), Site d'Aumetz, rue des Puits, 57710 Aumetz.

JEAN-FRANÇOIS BELHOSTE

Lothian, Scotland Coal pits on the Lothian coast between Joppa and Cockenzie and around Bo'ness were worked from an early date in conjunction with saltworks. The last Scottish saltworks closed at Prestonpans in 1959. An archaeological survey of the area has identified evidence of its eighteenth-century salt, sulphuric acid and other chemical operations. Limekilns were studied in the 1960s. Large examples are at Burdiehouse, 11 km (7 mi.) S. of Edinburgh, and Catcraigs, Dunbar, the latter restored by the Blue Circle Co. The SHALE OIL industry in West Lothian, established by James 'Paraffin' Young (1811–83) in 1851, peaked in 1910 and ceased in 1962. The distinctive red, flat-topped shale bings (waste tips) and company villages are linked by a heritage trail.

Papermills at Balerno, Currie, Newbattle, Polton and Penicuik, where Valleyfield Mill of 1708 was for long the largest in Scotland, have mostly undergone considerable alteration, but several date in part from the late eighteenth century or early nineteenth, and were water-powered.

Esk Net Mills, once the world's largest net-making concern, were founded in Musselburgh in 1854 by J. & W. Stuart, successors to James Patterson, inventor in 1820 of the jumper net-making machine. Hemp, and from 1857 cotton, was spun and then knitted by hand-powered machines in a large shed which forms one side of an ornamental garden. A square, fireproof four-storey cot-

427

ton-spinning mill was built in 1867, its façade embellished with statuary. Doubling and twisting sheds, a Greek-domed office, an iron clock tower, and a tall stalk and roping shed by Robert Lorimer complete the complex, where eight hundred people were employed.

Belhaven Brewery, Dunbar, is the oldest in Scotland, and one of the few surviving independent concerns, with stone vaults and wells claimed to be medieval. It was established as a commercial brewery in 1719, and largely rebuilt in 1814 following a fire. It has a three-storey maltings, two pyramidal kilns with wire-mesh floors, and a barley kiln of 1935. The brewhouse and chimney were reconstructed in 1887. A separate eighteenth-century three-storey maltings, with two kilns, stands by Dunbar harbour. Glenkinchie Distillery, Pencaitland, has a private museum of items culled from other Distillers' Co. distilleries: it is housed in the maltings of c.1840, which was twice enlarged and now lacks its kilns. The brick BONDS are of c.1900, the washback room was rebuilt in 1898, while the still room, with worm tubs, is quite modern. Linlithgow's St Magdalene's Distillery and Mains Maltings were each converted to housing in 1988–9, retaining their pagoda kilns.

Preston grain mill, 37 km (23 mi.) E. of Edinburgh, is cared for by the National Trust for Scotland. It has a detached circular barley kiln and machinery of the late nineteenth century and early twentieth. Sandy's Mill, Prestonkirk, of the late nineteenth century, is quite complete. Livingston Farm Mill, a water-powered grain and threshing mill of c.1770, is open to the public.

The Linlithgow Union Canal Society has a small museum in the stables of the Edinburgh & Glasgow Union Canal. This canal linked Edinburgh with the Forth & Clyde Canal at Falkirk via the twelve-span Avon and five-span Almond aqueducts, both cast-iron troughs on stone arches. The Edinburgh & Glasgow Railway paralleled these in 1842 with viaducts of thirty-six and twenty-three spans respectively. The route of the Cockenzie Wagonway of 1722 may still be traced. It was the first railway in Scotland and the only one to have featured in a battle, that of Prestonpans in 1745.

The Museum of Flight at East Fortune Airfield, 35 km (22 mi.) E. of Edinburgh, opened in 1975 at an airship station of 1915–16. The Callender-Hamilton hangars date from World War II, and contain aero engines, a Comet airliner, and a Weir W-2 Autogiro of 1934. The museum is administered by the National Museums of Scotland.

See also BO'NESS; EDINBURGH; FORTH BRIDGES; NEWTON-GRANGE AND PRESTONGRANGE.

BIBLIOGRAPHY
General
Hay and Stell, 1986; Hume, 1976; Whatley, 1987; Wood, 1985.
Specific
McMaster, C. A History of Belhaven Brewery. Scottish Brewing Archive, 1985.
Skinner, B. C. The Lime Industry in the Lothians. Edinburgh: University of Edinburgh Department of Adult Education, 1969.

MARK WATSON

Lötschberg, Switzerland   The abbreviated name of the 85 km (53 mi.) railway between Spiez and Brig, and of the Bern-Lötschberg-Simplon company, established in 1906, which operates it, with some associated lines. The object of the railway was to link the Swiss capital with Italy, by a tunnel through the Bernese Alps between the Kandertal and the Lötschental, running southwards into the Rhône valley. The 14.67 m (9 mi. 140 yd.) tunnel between Kandersteg and Goppenstein was begun in 1905 and opened after many difficulties in 1913. The line incorporates 43 other tunnels and 244 bridges and viaducts, outstanding examples of which are the 265 m (869 ft.) concrete viaduct over the Kander at Frutigen, and the Bietschtal Bridge, a steel arch of 95 m (312 ft.) span between two tunnels. The line was electrically worked from the start, with 1–E–1 locomotives of 2500 hp. The company pioneered the use of electric multiple units for services within Switzerland.

BIBLIOGRAPHY
General
Allen, 1965; Schneider, 1963.

Loughborough, Leicestershire, England   Textile, hosiery and engineering town on the River Soar, canalized in 1777. There are knitters' workshops at Kegworth, 18 km (10 mi.) NW, and Sutton Bonnington, 6 km (4 mi.) NW. Several mills survive. The Brush Traction plant of 1889 is on the site of the Henry Hughes locomotive works. John Taylor's bell foundry can be seen in Freehold Street. The Main Line Steam Trust operate steam trains on a 9 km (5 mi.) section of the former GCR London Extension. Hathern Station Brick & Terra-Cotta Company, 4 km ($2\frac{1}{2}$ mi.) NW, was established in 1878 and is still in production.

BIBLIOGRAPHY
General
Smith, 1965.

LOCATION
[M] Main Line Steam Trust, Central Station, Loughborough, Leicestershire LE11 1RW.

Louisiana, United States of America   Over a thousand miles of navigable lakes, tributaries, bayous and rivers, among them the Mississippi, interlace Louisiana, one of the Deep South's industrial hubs. The Industrial Canal of 1923 in south Louisiana gave Mississippi River shipping direct access to the Gulf of Mexico by way of Lake Pontchartrain.

Louisiana has a long record of diversified industry in the extraction of petroleum, natural gas, salt and sulphur, and the harvest of cotton and sugar cane. New Orleans grew as a focal point of commercial activity and French culture well before the acquisition of the 'Louisiana Purchase' territory from France in 1803, which multiplied the size of the nation several-fold. The lacy wrought- and cast-ironwork festooning many of the city's older downtown structures is the most characteristic architectural embellishment of the region, the product of a vigorous local network of foundries and forges.

Situated only a few feet above sea level, New Orleans has faced continual problems with flooding and with disease through impure water sources. In 1914 a system of novel low-head, high-volume screw pumps began servicing the city to drain canals and storm water during periods of high water. The machinery has been designated a National Historic Mechanical Engineering LANDMARK.

One of the nation's two extant streetcar lines runs through New Orleans, the Charles Avenue Line of 1835 which may rank as the oldest continuously operated street railway in the world. Motive powers for the line have included, in chronological order, horses, steam, humans, ammonia vapour, fireless superheated steam, and electricity, which continues to propel the cars along 24 km (15 mi.) of track between the city centre and the western suburbs.

In Shreveport stands one of the two surviving Waddell A-truss bridges in the country, a steel truss forming a near-equilateral triangle through which runs the roadway. The other Waddell A-truss stands in Missouri.

The monumental Huey P. Long Bridge of 1936 over the Mississippi River is a 6700 m (22 000 ft.) high-level tribute to a colourful state governor, which meets the dual needs of land and river traffic along the state's southern border.

BIBLIOGRAPHY
General
Franks and Lambert, 1982.

LOCATIONS
[I] Engineering Film Research Centre, Louisiana Technical University.
[M] The Rice Museum, Highway 90, Crowley, LA 70526.

DAVID H. SHAYT

Lousã, Beira Litoral, Portugal   The oldest papermill still operated in Portugal, founded in 1748, is located in this village 120 km (75 mi.) SE of Oporto. The Ermida hydro-electric power station is located, 5 km (3 mi.) SE.

Louvain (Leuven, Löven), Brabant, Belgium   A university city, most important as a manufacturing centre in the late Middle Ages. It stands on the River Dyle, and has a canal link to the River Rupel (*see* BOOM). Its neo-Classical railway station of 1879 has a long single-storey frontage, with a central and wing pavilions. There is a display of railway history from 1870 to the present in the locomotive depot in Kessel-lo, a suburb to the north-east. Louvaine is famous for its beer. An eight-storey brick maltings complex stands on Mechelsestraat, and there is a museum of brewing. Several courts of nineteenth-century workers' housing remain.

Tienen (Tirlemont), 18 km (11 mi.) SE, is the chief centre of sugar production in Belgium. The main refinery, Suikerraffinaderijen NY, dominates Aandorenstraat. Several water mills remain in the locality.

At Wijgmaal, 5 km (3 mi.) N., alongside the canal from Louvaine to the Rupel, is the former Remy starch factory, a mixture of brick and concrete buildings with one dominant concrete silo of 1920, topped by a tower bearing the company name.

BIBLIOGRAPHY
General
Viaene, 1986.

LOCATIONS
[S] Locomotivedepot Leuven, Brugberg, 3200 Kessel-lo.
[M] Stedelijk Brouwerijmuseum (Town Brewing Museum), Stad-huis, Grote Markt, 3000 Louvaine.
[M] Stedelijk Museum en Archief Het Toreke (Town Museum and Archives), Grote Markt, 3300 Tienen.

BARRIE TRINDER

Louvière, La, Hainaut, Belgium   The town at the heart of the Centre coalfield, in a landscape dominated by mines, steelworks and glassworks, most of which are now closed. The 19 km (12 mi.) Canal du Centre, which joins the Nimy–Scheldt Canal near Mons to the canal from Charleroi to Brussels and so links the Meuse and Scheldt basins, was begun in 1885 but not completed until 1917 when the area was under German occupation. The hydraulic pumping station for the canal, in brick with two four-storey crenellated towers, built in 1888, still stands in the rue de l'Ascenseur. The canal is celebrated for its four hydraulic lifts. No. 1, at Houdeng-Goegnies, 821 m (898 yd.) east of the road bridge near La Louvière station, was built in 1885–8, and raises vessels 15.397 m (50 ft. 6 in.). The three remaining lifts were completed in 1917. No. 2, at Houdeng-Aimeries, 2024 m (2213 yd.) west of the road bridge, rises 16.934 m (55 ft. 6 in.); as do No. 3, at Bracquegnies, 189 m (207 yd.) west, and No. 4, at Thieu, 3 km (1½ mi.) west. The lifts can raise vessels of up to 300 tonnes in their 45 m × 5.8 m (148 ft. × 19 ft.) tanks. A new line of canal has been built avoiding the hydraulic lifts, and capable of taking vessels of 1350 tonnes, with a single 73 m (239 ft.) vertical lift at Strépy-Thieu, but the original line has been retained. The canal is traversed by excursion boats operated by a voluntary organization. At a dry dock at Chapelle-lez-Herlaimont, 6 km (3½ mi.) E. of La Louvière, is a museum, where a barge of a type designed for the canal from Brussels to Charleroi by J. B. Vifquain, engineer of the government waterways department in the 1820s: the barge, which measures 19.8 m × 1.8 m (65 ft. × 6 ft.), is preserved.

Bois-du-Luc, a colliery village 2 km (1 mi.) SW of La Louvière, is the headquarters of the Écomusée du Centre. In 1685 local landowners combined to form the Société de Grand Conduit et du Charbonnage de Houdeng to drain mines and extract coal, functions that were inherited in 1807 by a new body, the Société des Charbonnage de Bois-du-Luc et d'Havre, which constructed a steam pumping engine in the same year. In 1838–53 a colliery village called Bosquetville was constructed, consisting originally of 166 houses, a number increased to 222 from 1866. Streets were laid out on a neo-Classical plan, with chamfered corners, blind arcading, and pilasters with stone capitals at the intersections. The two-storey brick cottages have semicircular headed arches over doors and windows with stone detailing. The last mine at Bois-du-

Figure 78   The vertical boat lift at Houdeng-Aimeries, La Louvière, Belgium, part of a series of four such lifts begun in the 1880s and completed in 1917; it has a vertical rise of 16.93 m (55 ft. 6 in.). The four lifts are being replaced by a lift at Strépy-Thieu, but will be preserved.
Barrie Trinder

Luc ceased work in 1973. The cottages have been renovated by a housing corporation. A late-nineteenth-century steam winding engine with classical pilasters, which was installed secondhand in its present engine house during the Great War, has been preserved. A range of pithead buildings, with a steel lattice headstock protruding through the roof of a five-bay, two-storey structure in brick, with giant pilasters, has been retained, together with the adjacent colliery power station, a brick building on a stone plinth, with Gothic and semicircular headed arcading. Two three-storey round watchtowers at the entrance to the colliery give it a fortress-like appearance. The tramway network around La Louvière is one of the most extensive in Belgium, and it is possible to travel for nearly 20 km (13 mi.) on such routes as that from Maurage to Trazegnies. A museum at Mariemont, 5 km (3

mi.) SE of La Louvière, has extensive displays of Belgian pottery and porcelain.

BIBLIOGRAPHY
General
Hadfield, 1986; Linters, 1986a; Viaene, 1986.
Specific
Roelants du Vivier, F. *Bois-du-Luc: une cité industrielle* (Bois-du-Luc: an industrial community). Brussels: Association Royale des Demeures Historiques de Belgique, 1973.

LOCATIONS
[I] Compagnie du Canal du Centre, Écluse No. 1, Rue des Peupliers 69, 7058 Thieu.
[M] Écomusée régional du Centre (Écomusée of the Centre Region), Ateliers du Bois-du-Luc, rue Sainte-Patrice, 7071 Houdeng-Aimeries.

[M] Musée Communale de la Louvière (La Louvière Town Museum), Chateau Gilson, rue de Bouvy 11, 7100 La Louvière.

[M] Musée de la Mine du Bois-du-Luc (Bois-du-Luc Mining Museum), rue Sainte-Patrice 1, 7071 Houdeng-Aimeries.

[M] Musée Royal de Mariemont (Royal Museum at Mariemont), chaussée de Mariemont 100, 6510 Morlawelz.

BARRIE TRINDER

Louviers, Eure, France Louviers, 40 km (25 mi.) S. of Rouen, is an old-established Norman town, already famous for its woollen cloth in the Middle Ages. During the sixteenth and seventeenth centuries the town was involved in linen bleaching, and around 1680, following the example of SEDAN and Elbeuf, it became engaged in the production of high-quality broadcloth, using Spanish wool imported via Rouen. At the end of the eighteenth century the town had more than a dozen prosperous cloth-manufacturing enterprises. It was in Louviers, too, that France's first mechanized cotton-spinning mill was constructed in 1785, with the help of two English technicians who had worked with RICHARD ARKWRIGHT. The well-known industrialist from Sedan, Guillaume Ternaux, introduced mechanized wool spinning in a mill erected c.1806. From 1820 many water-powered mills were built at Louviers for spinning yarn, and for fulling more ordinary woollen cloths, weaving being mechanized only towards the middle of the nineteenth century. This development also stimulated the growth of an important textile machinery concern, the Mercier company.

During a systematic study of the material remains of the Louviers textile industry, one of the difficulties lay in the precise identification of the production buildings, most of the eighteenth-century manufactures having no specific architectural or technological features which related them to particular processes. Most of them were also homes for manufacturers, and, where they survive, are still used as homes today. It is easy to recognize the manufactory built by Jean Baptiste Decretot in 1779 (in the rue de l'Hotel de Ville) on account of its monumental porch and dressed stone arcades, but the architecture of the former Frigard manufacture (at 33 rue Porte de Rouen), with its timber-framed façade, is indistinguishable from the neighbouring houses. Moreover, these 'manufactories' accounted only for a small fraction of the output of quality cloth, work processes being divided to the extreme. For weaving, the industrialists had small workshops scattered throughout the town. Spinning was entirely put out to domestic spinners in the surrounding villages, whilst the fulling mills were likewise out of town, upstream on the River Iton. Research has not enabled the spinners' houses to be identified, but the vestiges of an eighteenth-century fulling mill have been located at Amfreville-sur-Iton.

The buildings of several water-powered textile mills remain in the town, notably the brick structures of the Ternaux factory of 1806 at 19 rue Trinité, the two upper storeys of which were removed c.1950. From the outset this factory boasted gas lighting in its workshops. The buildings of the former Dievet factory (previously Jourdain), rebuilt c.1890, also survive.

BIBLIOGRAPHY
General
Chaplain, 1984.
Specific
Belhoste, J.-F. and Chaplain, J.-M. Les Manufactures textiles à Louviers de 1680 à 1830: architectures traditionnelles et révolution industrielle (Textile manufactures at Louviers, 1680–1830: traditional architecture and the industrial revolution). In *Comptes rendus du 104ᵉ Congrès national des Sociétés Savantes, Bordeaux, 1978.* (Proceedings of the 104th national congress of scientific societies). Paris: Bibliothèque nationale, 1979.
Belhoste, J.-F. and Chaplain, J.-M. Le Patrimoine industriel dans le département de l'Eure, XVIIIᵉ–XIXᵉ siècles (The industrial heritage of the Eure department in the eighteenth and nineteenth centuries). In *Connaissance de l'Eure,* XLVII, XLVIII, 1983.

LOCATION
[M] Musée Municipal (Municipal Museum), Place Ernest-Thorel, 27400 Louviers.

JEAN-FRANÇOIS BELHOSTE

LPG Liquefied petroleum gas, first sold in the USA in the 1930s, has since become widely used for domestic fuel, for internal combustion engines and as a raw material for chemical processes. BUTANE or PROPANE are both used, usually with other hydrocarbons. LPG is prepared from NATURAL GAS or during refining. Propane and butane are also obtained during the hydrogenation of coal to produce motor spirit (*see* PETROL).

See also WASHINGTON.

BIBLIOGRAPHY
General
BP, 1958.

Lucerne (Luzern), Lucerne, Switzerland The 'city of light', a cantonal capital in a spectacular setting amongst high mountains, in the north-west corner of Lake Lucerne (the Vierwaldstätter See), the most attractive and mysterious of the Swiss lakes, is bisected by the fast-flowing River Reuss. Steamers ascend the lake to Fleulen, where there is a station on the ST GOTTHARD railway. Stopping places include Gersau, where the silk factory of Schappe & Cordonnet is prominent on the waterfront. Five paddle steamers operate on Lake Lucerne: the *Uri* of 1901, the *Schiller* of 1906, the *Gallia* of 1913, the *Stadt Luzern* of 1928, and the *Unterwalden* of 1902 which has been restored with its original saloon fittings.

In the centre of Lucerne are the two oldest large covered wooden bridges in Europe, the Capellbrücke, 200 m (220 yd.) long, of the early fourteenth century, and the Spreuerbrücke, 80 m (90 yd.) long, with a cycle of pictures painted in 1611.

The Verkehrshaus de Schweiz is one of Europe's best transport museums, situated alongside the St Gotthard main line on the lakeside 1.5 km (1 mi.) E. of the centre, at a calling point for steamers. Steam locomotives include a replica of the 4–2–0 *Limmat*, built in Karlsruhe, Germany, in 1847 for the opening of the Zurich–Baden line; a four-cylinder 2–10–0 built at Winterthur in 1916 for freight

Figure 79   The paddle steamer *Stadt Luzern* of 1928 off Fleulen, Lake Lucerne, July 1987
Barrie Trinder

working on the St Gotthard line; a de Glehn four-cylinder compound 4–6–0 built at Winterthur in 1904 for express working on the Simplon line; and a four-cylinder 0–4–4–0 Mallet, built for the SCB in 1891–3. Electric locomotives include an Austrian-built 1–C–C–1 of 1924, similar to the original St Gotthard line electric locomotives, and a 'Crocodile', built for freight on the St Gotthard line in the early 1920s. A steam railcar from the Pilatusbahn (see below) and a vertical-boilered rack locomotive from the Vitznau–Rigibahn are also displayed. Other sections of the museum deal with posts and telecommunications, motor transport and aviation.

The Rigi is a much climbed and much visited mountain, 13 km (8 mi.) E. of Lucerne, where a hotel was erected on the summit in 1816. Two standard-gauge rack railways ascend to its 1979 m (5876 ft.) summit, one from the lakeside resort of Vitznau, the first pure rack railway in Switzerland (completed in 1871), the other from the main-line railway junction at Arth Goldau, opened in 1875. The Vitznau line was electrified in 1937, but two steam locomotives of 1923 and 1925 are retained for special trains.

Pilatus is a spectacular 2119 m (6952 ft.) summit, 9 km ($5\frac{1}{2}$ mi.) SW of Lucerne, ascended from Alpnachstad by the world's steepest rack railway, built on the Locher system (see RACK RAILWAY) in 1886–8, and worked by steam railcars until electrification in 1937. Cable cars ascend from Kriens in the south-west suburbs of Lucerne.

BIBLIOGRAPHY
General
Allen, 1965; INSA, 1982–91.

LOCATION
[M] Verkehrshaus de Schweiz (Swiss Transport Museum), Lidostrasse 3–7, 6006 Lucerne.

HANS-PETER BÄRTSCHI

Ludvika, Kopparberg, Sweden   A town lying in the heart of BERGSLAGEN. The most important industrial monuments within it are in the open-air Museum of Mining, initiated by Karl-Erik Forsslund and Gustaf Björkman, and opened in 1938, which includes pithead dressing plant for iron ore, water wheels, and associated rod transmission systems.

BIBLIOGRAPHY
General
Sörenson *et al.*, 1987.
Specific
Håkansson, N. G. *A Short Description of Ludvika Mine Museum.* Ludvika Hembygdsförening, Ludvika: n.d.

LOCATION
[M] Ludvika gruvmuseum (Mining Museum), Nils Nilsgata 7, Box 342, 771 03 Ludvika.

Łukasiewicz, Jan Józef Ignacy (1822–82)   A pharmacist, inventor of the kerosine lamp, and co-founder of the world's first petroleum-extraction concern. He was born near Mielec on 3 March 1822. After graduating from secondary school he worked at a chemist's shop in Łańcut, and then at a pharmacy in L'vov, where he began to take an interest in petroleum. The region at the foot of the Carpathian Mountains had long been renowned for its shallow deposit of petroleum, which was then used as grease and medicine for animals. In 1852 Łukasiewicz, assisted by Jan Zehm, distilled some petroleum and offered the product for sale as a patent medicine. When it failed to sell he conceived the idea of using it for lighting. By a process of fractional distillation he obtained pure kerosine, but had to design a new lamp that could use it. The world's first kerosine lamp was lit at Mikulasch's pharmacy in L'vov in March 1853, and at L'vov hospital the following July kerosine lamps were used to light the operating theatre. This date is regarded as the beginning of the Polish oil industry. In 1854, with Tytus Trzecieski and Karol Klobassa, he established the world's first oil wells in BÓBRKA. In 1856 he started the first Polish oil refinery in Ulaszowice. In 1870 he introduced jump drilling at the Bóbrka workings, and gave up his work as a chemist to devote himself to industry.

BIBLIOGRAPHY
General
Brzozowski, 1974.
Specific
Pilecki, J. Działalność i znaczenie Ignacego Łukasiewicza w pionierskim okresie przemysłu naftowego (Ignacy Łukasiewicz in the pioneering times of the oil industry). In *Studia i materiały z dziejów nauki polskiej* (Studies and Sources on the History of Polish Science), Series D, z 3, Warsaw, 1962.
Polski Słownik Biograficzny (Polish biographical dictionary) (Wrocław), XVIII, 1973.

JAN KĘSIK

lumber Originally, useless items; but by the late seventeenth century in North America the world 'lumber' was applied to timber sawn into rough planks ready to be used by craftsmen. A British statute of 1720 refered to 'wood and timber and the sorts of goods commonly called lumber, deals, balks, barrel staves and headings, spars for shipbuilding, oars, oak planks and wainscot, ebony'.

Lüneburg, Lower Saxony, Germany Nothing remains *in situ* of the Lüneburg saltworks which sent supplies all over northern Europe in the Middle Ages. The oldest remaining trace is a seventeenth-century saltpan in the regional museum. Those parts of the saltworks still extant in the city – operation finally ceased in 1982 – date from the nineteenth century and the early twentieth, and are now being made into a museum. They include a boiling house with open saltpans of 1924–5; two wooden brine containers, probably of nineteenth-century date, on what remains of the salt bank (there is a similar brine container in the lower drilling point of the Sülbeck saltworks at Einbeck in Northeim district, 20 km (12 mi.) N. of Göttingen); the donkey stable, originally built as a chemical works; and the neo-Classical wellhouse designed by G. L. F. Laves in 1832 to stand over the brine shaft drilled beneath Sonnin at the end of the eighteenth century.

The importance of the port of Lüneburg up to the mid-nineteenth century is shown by the harbour crane, erected in its present form at the end of the eighteenth century, and thoroughly renovated shortly before World War I.

BIBLIOGRAPHY
General
Mende and Hamm, 1990; Slotta, 1975–88.

LOCATIONS
[M] Deutsches Salzmuseum (German Salt Museum), Sülzforstrasse, 2120 Lüneburg.
[M] Museum für das Fürstentum Lüneburg (Regional Museum), Wandrahmstrasse 10, 2120 Lüneburg.

MICHAEL MENDE

Luton, Bedfordshire, England A town of fewer than 3000 inhabitants in 1800, Luton has grown to over 150 000 due to hatmaking in the nineteenth century and motor vehicle manufacture in the twentieth. Many traditional two-storey hatmaking workshops with one-way pitched roofs survive, attached to terraced cottages. The original top-lit shed of the Vauxhall car plant, built in 1902, still stands in a modern 120 ha (50 ac.) site, together with offices of 1907–15 on Kimpston Road, designed by H. B. Cresswell in William and Mary style.

BIBLIOGRAPHY
General
Bigmore, 1979; Collins and Stratton, 1986.

LOCATION
[M] Luton Museum and Art Gallery, Wardown Park, Luton, Bedfordshire LU2 7HA.

Luxembourg An independent state of 2600 km² (1000 sq. mi.) with a population of 350 000, bounded by France, Belgium and West Germany. Its situation at the meeting point of French and German cultures, and the supposed impregnability of the fortress of Luxembourg city, have given it strategic importance. From 1555 Luxembourg was part of the Spanish Netherlands: it came under the control of the Austrian Habsburgs after the Treaty of Utrecht in 1713. From 1795 until 1815 it was a French 'departement'; in 1815 it became an independent duchy which was given to the king of the Netherlands. The great powers guaranteed the neutrality of Luxembourg by the Treaty of London of 1867, and its fortifications were subsequently demolished.

Luxembourg joined the Zollverein (*see* GERMANY) in 1842–3, and remained a member until 1919. In 1926 it became the headquarters of the European Steel Cartel, and from 1952 of the European Coal and Steel Community.

The south of Luxembourg is rich in iron-ore deposits. Pig iron was being supplied to Liège armaments manufacturers by the late eighteenth century, but the region developed slowly. The first railway in the duchy was opened as late as 1859, and until 1858 all the ironworks used charcoal as their fuel. From the 1860s Luxembourg became one of the principal sources of iron in Europe. Grand ducal decrees laid down that ore could be mined only by companies who smelted within the duchy, thus forcing German companies to build blast furnaces in Luxembourg rather than take ore to Germany. By 1875

Luxembourg

there were twenty-four blast furnaces in the duchy, and the introduction of the GILCHRIST THOMAS process for making steel from iron smelted from phosphorus-rich ores made Luxembourg pig iron still more marketable. The output of iron ore rose from 368 000 tonnes in 1870 to 8 650 000 tonnes in 1913, and by 1900 the output of pig iron had reached 970 000 tonnes. The ironworks were concentrated along the French border, and attracted many Italian and German immigrants to such towns as Esch-sur-Alzette, Dudelange and Bettembourg.

The landscape of southern Luxembourg is dominated by steelworks, slag tips and towering orange cliffs of abandoned open-cast iron-ore workings. The Musée National des Mines des Roches Rouges at Rumelange, 18 km (11 mi.) S. of Luxembourg city, opened in 1973, is centred on a drift mine 650 m (2100 ft.) long, and high enough to have taken a standard-gauge railway. Visitors are conducted by ex-miners through galleries where machines remain *in situ*. A range of calcining kilns stands on the boundary of the museum.

The Chemins de Fer Luxembourgeois (CFL) is an independent railway system, although German, French and Belgian locomotives regularly work into the duchy. At Bettembourg, where the railway workshops are situated, a 2–10–0 locomotive of German design (DB class 52), built at Floridsdorf (*see* VIENNA) in 1947, one of twenty of the class sent to the CFL, is displayed in a park. A network of steam trams formerly extended from Luxembourg city as far as Mondorf-les-Bains, 16 km (10 mi.) SE; Remich, 18 km (11 mi.) SE; and Echternach, 30 km ($18\frac{1}{2}$ mi.) NE. A 5 km (3 mi.) mineral railway, built in 1873–9 between Minière Dhoil on the outskirts of Rodange, 22 km ($13\frac{1}{2}$ mi.) W. of Luxembourg city, and Fuhsbosch has been restored by L'Association des Musées et Tourisme Ferroviaires (AMTF). Three steam locomotives from the steel company Arbed are preserved, the passenger services being worked by an 0–6–0T built by Georg Egestorff of Hanover in 1900. The stations on the line give access to spectacular walks through abandoned iron-ore quarries. (*See* figure 80.)

The Moselle has been a commercial waterway for many centuries, but it was only in 1964 that it was made fully navigable from Thionville, along the southern border of Luxembourg, to the Rhine. Wasserbillig, at the confluence of the Sûre and the Moselle, on the Luxembourg/German frontier, is a traditional bargemen's town, and has a ferry across the Moselle to Oberbillig in Germany.

Luxembourg city is notable for its spectacular stone railway viaducts. The Musée d'Histoire et d'Art includes collections of pre-industrial manufactures. Wine cellars are open to the public at Remich on the Moselle and elsewhere, and a large hydro-electric station at Vianden, 36 km (22 mi.) N., can also be visited.

BIBLIOGRAPHY
General
Milward and Saul, 1977; Newcomer, 1984.

LOCATIONS
[M] L'Association des Musées et Tourisme Ferroviaires, 70 route de Peppange, Bettembourg.
[M] Musée d'Histoire et d'Art, Marche-aux-Poissons, Luxembourg.
[M] Musée National des Mines, Rumelange.

BARRIE TRINDER

Lyons (Lyon), Rhône, France   Lyons, at the confluence of the Rhône and the Saône has been a centre for the silk industry for several centuries, and many buildings relating to domestic manufacture remain in the city. It is also one of the leading French motor manufacturing cities, and has also been important for the manufacture of motorcar components, notably carburettors.

The city's museums cover most aspects of its varied industrial past, the manufacture of silk being the speciality of the Canut Museum.

LOCATIONS
[M] Berliet Museum, 69 Venissieux, 69001 Lyons.
[M] Canut Museum, 12 rue d'Ivry, 69001 Lyons.
[M] Fondation de l'automobile Marius Berliet, 39 avenue d'Esquirol, 69003 Lyons.
[M] French Motor Museum, Château de Rochetaillée, 69001 Lyons.
[M] Museum of Decorative Arts, 30 rue de la Charité, 69001 Lyons.
[M] Museum of the History of Lyons, 10 rue de Gadagne, 69001 Lyons.

Figure 80 Bo-Bo diesel locomotive No. 854 of the Société Nationale des Chemins de Fer Luxembourgeois, built by Brissoneaux & Lotz in 1957, adds a restaurant car operated by the Compagnie International des Wagons-lits et des Grands Express Européens to the *Italia Express*, the 15.24 from Rome Terminus to Brussels, at Luxembourg station, 17 May 1977
Barrie Trinder

[M] Museum of the History of Textiles, 34 rue de la Charité, 69001 Lyons.

[M] Museum of Printing and Paper Money, 13 rue de la Poulaillerie, 69001 Lyons.

[M] Museum of Stone, 101 boulevard des États Unis, 69000 Lyons.

Lyttelton, Canterbury, New Zealand   A port 10 km (6 mi.) W. of Christchurch. It has one of the world's four surviving TIME-BALL STATIONS (*see* figure 157), following the pattern of the original opened at Greenwich in 1833, and copied in all principal seaports throughout the world. The crenellated structure of 1876 was designed by Thomas Crane. A copper ball is hoisted above the tower at 12.59 p.m. daily, and dropped at 1 p.m., as a signal to allow ships' masters to check their chronometers. It has been restored to working order and is in the care of the New Zealand Historic Places Trust.

BIBLIOGRAPHY
General
Thornton, 1982.

M

McAdam, John Loudon (1756–1836)   A civil engineer whose name epitomized the improvement in roads brought about in Britain in the early nineteenth century. After travel in Europe and America he settled in Scotland in 1783 and became involved in highway administration. Subsequently he and his son became involved with work on over three hundred TURNPIKE TRUSTS. The verb 'macadamize' was in widespread use by 1820. He favoured a 6–10 in. (15–25 cm) surface of graded stone with a rise of 3 in. (8 cm) across an 18 ft. (5.5 m) width. His roadbuilding methods were regarded as cheaper than those of some of his civil engineering contemporaries.

See also TARMACADAM.

BIBLIOGRAPHY
General
Aitken, 1907; Bird, 1969; Boulnois, 1919; Devereux, 1936; McAdam, 1827; Parnell, 1835; Reader, 1980.

Macclesfield, Cheshire, England   A silk-manufacturing town of exceptional archaeological interest. Water-powered silk-throwing was introduced in 1743 by Charles Roe. Hand-loom weaving of silk began later in the eighteenth century. There were many silk mills in the Classical style; about thirty remain, among them Park Green Mill of 1785, and the elegant seventeen-bay Card Mill. Hand-loom weaving of silk on Jacquard looms is demonstrated in Paradise Mill. Many brick cottages have weaving attics, and the terrace in Paradise Street has been restored. Roe leased part of PARYS MOUNTAIN during 1764–85, and built copper smelters in Macclesfield. No traces remain, but smelters and Park Green Mill are depicted on Roe's tomb in Christ Church, built at his own expense in 1775–6. An imposing Sunday School building of 1813 contains a heritage centre. Macclesfield Canal, opened in 1831, crosses Bollin on an iron aqueduct. The Arighi Bianchi furniture shop has a fine cast-iron and glass front of 1882–3.

There are several cotton mills at Bollington, 5 km (3 mi.) NE, with over forty cottages at Lowerhouse Mill, dating from 1811.

BIBLIOGRAPHY
General
Ashmore, 1982; Malgren, 1985.

LOCATION
[M] Macclesfield Sunday School Heritage Centre Silk Museum, Roe Street, Macclesfield SK11 6XD.

machine tools   Tools that can perform a range of cutting and shaping operations in a controlled and calculable manner, deploying forces independent of and beyond the scope of the hand craftsman. The aid of such tools was necessary fully to utilize metals in manufacture, and the state of their development may be taken as an index of the qualitative and quantitative capabilities of manufacturing industry at any time. The basic types of machine tools have most often been identified by their operations, as with turning (*see* LATHE), DRILLING MACHINE; BORING MACHINE; MILLING MACHINE; GRINDING MACHINE; PLANER; SHAPING MACHINE and SLOTTING MACHINE. They may also be known by their products, as with the screw machine and GEAR-CUTTING MACHINE.

The lathe and drill, which depend on alternative uses of a revolving spindle, have antecedents in prehistory; as with most machine tools they have human-powered precursors in the late European Middle Ages. The idea of a system of machine tools capable of generating and reproducing calculable forms is elaborated in the notebooks of Leonardo da Vinci (1452–1519), although many of his ideas were not realized for some time. Before the emergence of a machine-tool industry, the devising and making of tools took place in the context of particular trades and industries. Before 1800 machine toolmakers were mining engineers like CHRISTOPHE POLHEM; armourers like Jan Verbruggen; clock, watch and instrument makers; millwrights like JOHN SMEATON; shipbuilders; carpenters; and ironmasters like WILKINSON.

During the eighteenth century, as new industrial processes began to demand accurately fashioned metal parts such as BEARINGS and journals, rollers, cylinders, gears, wheels and screws, mechanical workshops began to emerge both independently and within other enterprises. Where innovators had stuck close to the needs of a trade or, like Christophe Polhem, Jacques de Vaucanson (1709–82) or John Smeaton, applied themselves to a great variety of tasks, it became possible to devise and build sets of general-purpose machinery, not as an experiment or commission, but to be used to produce work for a number of different applications. This work was greatly advanced by the availability of carbon steel for cutting tools. Around 1800, men known primarily as machine toolmakers emerged in several countries but particularly in England where the demands of new industry were strong. HENRY MAUDSLAY's justly celebrated London workshop trained the most important British toolmakers of succeeding generations: RICHARD ROBERTS, James Nasmyth and JOSEPH WHITWORTH. Between them they established the basic patterns for the first engine lathes, planers, and drilling, slotting and shaping machines offered for sale.

In early nineteenth-century parlance, 'machine tools' were tools for making machines, and the 'machine shop' became an essential industrial department. The elegant work of Manchester and Leeds toolmakers applied Maudslay's concern with precision engineering to the needs of the textile machine and steam engine. More robust variants were developed for the special tasks of marine and railway engineering, often by engineering firms specializing in those trades. In addition to the major makers who often offered a comprehensive service, machine tools were sold by an increasing number of machine-using firms as by-products of their own engineering work.

In a period where the export of machinery from Britain was still subject to mercantilist legislation, mechanical ideas nevertheless circulated freely and were adapted to local conditions. In New England, state-of-the-art designs were embodied in wooden-framed machines, often built on site by uncelebrated makers. A US government programme for the manufacture of INTERCHANGEABLE PARTS for small arms spawned some tools that were capable of wider application, such as copy and turret lathes and the MILLING MACHINE, the principles of which were known but not exploited in Europe at this time. While armoury-related machine tool development by such firms as Robbins & Lawrence has been considered as pivotal in a distinctive AMERICAN SYSTEM OF MANUFACTURES, many early US machine shops, as in Britain, were closely bound up with textile machinery and steam-engine work. In the USA the story of Brown & Sharpe, which spanned instrument making, interchangeable manufacture and refined, innovative tool design, contains obvious echoes of MAUDSLAY. Like Maudslay's London workshop, the Providence, R.I. works of Brown & Sharpe became a preferred training and working ground for ambitious machinists after 1865.

International emulation and competition among the major makers increased in the last third of the nineteenth century. Improved versions of established types were built in France, Belgium, Sweden, Switzerland, Prussia and Saxony as well as in Britain, and important new designs emerged in the US, in association with the volume production of small mechanisms. JOSEPH BROWN, who had perfected the application of the turret principle to the repetitive manufacture of small crews, developed a universally adjustable milling machine in the manufacture of twist drills and applied the same principles in a universal grinding machine. The alloy steels and synthetic abrasives made it possible for machine shops to fashion harder materials to higher degrees of precision and increased the effectiveness of machine tools in quantity manufacture. This potential was explored in a series of experiments by F. W. TAYLOR and others as production engineering became an analytical discipline, working to abstract standards irrespective of volume and deploying a repertoire of machine tools in a complex variety of tasks.

Rapid growth in demand for such products as bicycles accelerated the international diffusion of milling and grinding. While the batch production of tools sold 'off the shelf' increased, making-to-order continued for a wide range of specialized requirements, and many companies maintained a strong identification with particular user groups. Larger firms consolidated their advantages in product development and marketing, while others faced marginality if unable to specialize in growth areas or established niches. The implications of a more intensive use of machine tools in manufacturing were realized at the turn of the century when harder cutting materials and direct electric drives exposed the limitations of existing designs. New, heavier machine-tool frames were developed to extend quantity manufacture into larger components at higher degrees of precision or to adapt established tools to accommodate fully automatic, multi-spindle operation.

The diffusion of the MASS PRODUCTION of automobiles and electromechanical goods in the twentieth century led to a rapid increase in the production of this new generation of machine tools, culminating in numerical control as part of a system of computer-integrated manufacture. However, the displacement of mechanical by electronic activation and of metals by polymers in many manufacturing applications have combined in recent years to circumscribe the technical and economic importance of the machine tool industry. Since 1960, many firms of long-standing in the industry have succumbed or disappeared within conglomerates, and leadership in the production of tools for general manufacturing has passed to the major Japanese electronics and engineering groups.

Machine tools are represented in the collections of most national and major municipal museums of technology. The Conservatoire in PARIS has early LATHES by Vaucanson, and the Science Museum, LONDON, holds several examples from the period in the early nineteenth century when English makers defined the classic form of many tools. The most important collection of American machine tools is that held by the American Precision Museum of Windsor, VERMONT, in the Armoury of 1848 where Robbins & Lawrence developed new designs in the course of interchangeable manufacture. The products of Brown & Sharpe are well represented in the NMAH in WASHINGTON DC.

Most machine tools are interpreted as isolated technical monuments. Slater Mill at Pawtucket, R.I., has re-created an early-nineteenth-century machine shop mill; machine shop reconstructions from later in the century may be found at the Hagley Museum in DELAWARE (c.1880), within the Technical Museum in STOCKHOLM (c.1875), and at Blists Hill Open-Air Museum, IRONBRIDGE (c.1890). Re-creations of general manufacturing involving ensembles of period tools are quite rare, and restricted to limited sets of operations as at the Hylltens brassworks in Gnosjo, Sweden.

See also FORGING PRESS; GAUGE; JIG; LINE SHAFTING; STEAM HAMMER; TOOLMAKING.

BIBLIOGRAPHY
General
Battison, 1976; Floud, 1976; Hounshell, 1984; Roe, 1916; Rolt, 1986; Steeds, 1969; Wagoner, 1968; Woodbury, 1958, 1959, 1960, 1961; Wüster, 1968.

Specific

Broehl, W. *Precision Valley*. Englewood Cliffs, N. J., 1966.

Putnam, T. The theory of design in the Second Machine Age. In *Journal of Design History*, I, 1988.

Rosenberg, N. Technological change in the machine tool industry, 1840–1910. In *Journal of Economic History*, XXIII, 1963.

Saul, S. B. The machine tool industry in Britain to 1914. In *Business History*, X, 1968.

TIM PUTNAM

Macintosh, Charles (1766–1843) The principal British pioneer of the RUBBER industry and the inventor of the waterproof fabric that bears his name. He was closely concerned with the development of BLEACHING POWDER by Charles Tennant (1768–1838), and of HOT BLAST by J. B. Neilson (1792–1865). In 1823 Macintosh patented a rubber waterproof fabric in which India rubber dissolved in naphtha was enclosed within two layers of cloth. From 1824 it was manufactured in a celebrated factory developed with the Birley family, near Little Ireland, the most notorious of MANCHESTER's slums. Later he was the partner of Thomas Hancock (1768–1865), whose claim to have invented the process of vulcanizing rubber with sulphur was contested by Charles Goodyear (1800–60).

BIBLIOGRAPHY
Specific

Levitt, S. Manchester mackintoshes: a history of the rubberized garment trade in Manchester. In *TH*, XVII, 1986.

madder A plant of the genus *Rubia tinctoria*, cultivated in Europe, the root of which was used for making red pigments and medicine. In CALICO PRINTING the madder style used a mordant first to print the design. After ageing, rinsing, and then passing the cloth through the madder solution, the design appeared only where the mordant had been applied.

Madeira, Portugal The chief island of an archipelago in the Atlantic, 1100 km (680 mi.) SW of Lisbon, noted for its fortified wines. At Machico, one of the chief fishing ports on the island, and elsewhere are many 'levadas', which drew water from many sources and conveyed it to the fields. The water flowing through some levadas was used to drive mills, including some in Machico. Porto da Cruz has an interesting harbour, and the Engenho do Porto da Cruz is one of the relics of the sugar industry. Former sugar factories, among them the Fábrica de Açúcar e Destilação de Aguardente, also survive at Funchal, the island's capital.

BIBLIOGRAPHY
Specific

Calver, N. G. Water mills on the levadas of Madeira. In *IAR*, III, 1978.

LOCATION
[M] Municipal Museum, R. da Mouraria 31, Funchal.

madras A plain woven, striped or check cotton fabric, with random checks or stripes in varying proportions, made with dyed yarns. It takes its name from the city in southern India.

Madrid, Castile, Spain Madrid, with its population of four million, has the highest altitude of any European capital. It is not primarily an industrial city, although its museums and public works have much to interest the industrial archaeologist. One of Europe's best concentrations of ART DECO cinemas lines the Gran Via.

The Delicias Station of 1880 is the oldest of the termini in Madrid. It was designed by the French engineer Cachelièvre, and is now the city's railway museum. It has a 170 m × 34 m (560 ft. × 110 ft.) train shed, whose design derives from buildings constructed for the Paris International Exhibition of 1878.

The first section of Madrid's underground railway was opened in 1919, a 4 km (2$\frac{1}{2}$ mi.) section from Cuatro Caminos to Puerta del Sol. The original system resembled the Paris Metro in many respects, but power was collected through an overhead pantograph rather than from a third rail. The system totalled 27 km (17 mi.) by 1957.

The Museum of Decorative Arts has collections of many characteristic Spanish manufactures: wallpapers from Cordova, tiles from Valencia, carpets and tapestries, while the Royal Tapestry Factory still operates. The Municipal Museum is notable for its eighteenth- and nineteenth-century maps.

BIBLIOGRAPHY
General

Civera, 1988; Marti *et al.*, 1982; Wrottesley, 1960.

LOCATIONS
[M] Municipal Museum, Calle Fuencarral 78, Madrid.
[M] Museo National del Ferrocarril (National Railway Museum), Estación de la Delicias, Madrid.
[M] Museum of Carriages, Palacio Nacional, Campo del Moro, Ribera del Manzanares, Madrid.
[M] Museum of the Mint and Stamp Printing works, Calle Dr Esquerdo 38, Madrid.
[M] Museum of the School of Mines, Calle Rios Rosas 21, Madrid.
[M] Museum of Science and Technology, Ciudad Universitaria, Madrid.
[M] Museum of the Spanish Village, Plaza de la Marine Española 9, Madrid.
[M] National Engraving Museum, Calle Alcalá 13, Madrid.
[M] Royal Carpet Factory, Calle Fuenterrabía 2, Madrid.

MERCEDES LOPEZ

magazine A term with three meanings in industrial archaeology:

1. A storehouse for EXPLOSIVES, particularly at a mine or quarry (*see* MINING). The magazine is often sited away from other structures, and built with a vaulted roof and sometimes earthen banks buttressing the walls. The word originally meant a store, and came to mean a place where armaments were kept.
2. A ship containing stores.
3. A storage chamber in various kinds of machines.

magnesium (Mg)   An elemental metal, important for its alloys, chiefly with ALUMINIUM, which are widely used in motorcar and aircraft manufacture and in optical apparatus. Before 1914 magnesium was produced on a significant scale only in Germany, by electrolysis of solutions of magnesium chloride from the salt deposits at Strassfurt. Subsequently it has been manufactured from sea water, of which it comprises one part in eight hundred; from the mineral magnesite ($MgCO_3$), which is also used as a refractory; and from DOLOMITE.

BIBLIOGRAPHY
General
Alexander and Street, 1949; Jones, 1950.

mail coach   John Palmer (1742–1818) developed letter-carrying coach services between Bath and London in 1784, and became Surveyor and Comptroller-General of the Post Office from 1786. Letters, and from 1791 passengers paying premium fares, were carried in coaches of improved design, rather smaller than most STAGE COACHES, all supplied by Besant & Vidler of Millbank, London, and hired out to contractors. Many innovations in coach design were pioneered on mail coaches which by 1820 weighed as little as 16 cwt. (800 kg) unladen. They had red wheels and running gear. The lower coach panels were maroon, most of the remainder being glossy black. Seven hundred were running in 1835. In Prussia the equivalent coaches were called 'Schnellposten': the mail and the coach office were often situated in the same inn, where a room called the Passagier Stube might be set aside for Schnellpost passengers.

See also INN; POSTAL SERVICES.

BIBLIOGRAPHY
General
Bird, 1969, De Quincey, 1956; Murray, 1865.

Maine, United States of America   Potato-growing, deep-sea fishing, lobster-trapping, logging, pulp and paper, and shipbuilding make up the more historic of Maine's industries. The quarrying and working of granite has been another longstanding activity in this heavily forested coastal state occupying the far north-eastern corner of the country.

With more than 90 per cent of its area forested, due in part to early efforts at reafforestation, Maine's woodworking industries have turned out products ranging from toothpicks to square-riggers. Shipbuilding is well commemorated at the Maine Maritime Museum in Bath; and in the real article at Bath Iron Works, which dates from 1826, and is today one of the nation's premier steelworking shipyards. At the lumbering museum in Patten stands an example of the Lombard steam log hauler, a rare steam-powered and tracked vehicle, today a National Historic Mechanical Engineering LANDMARK. Shipping, lumbering and railways are all well illustrated in the state's museums.

Maine's considerable number of offshore islands may explain the state's name ('the mainland'). On Vinalhaven Island are the remains of one of the nation's largest architectural stone-turning works, where outdoor lathes in the last century cut the island's granite into columns, some over 15 m (50 ft.) in length, for churches and public buildings. They were transported thence by ship.

Connecting other nearby islands is the 340 m (1120 ft.) Bailey Island Bridge of 1928, a unique stone crib causeway, built entirely of 3.65 m (12 ft.) 'baulks' of native granite. The open stone cribwork responded to the special conditions of the site: swift tides, severe salt-water exposure and ice flows.

Crossing the Carrabasset River in central Maine is the New Portland Wire Bridge of 1868, a rare survival of the light-duty, timber-towered suspension bridge. Shingle shrouding protects the towers, rising 7 m (23 ft.) above the roadbed. The 60 m (198 ft.) wire-cable span remains in service on a little-used side road.

Historic lighthouses dot the Maine coastline. The light of 1850 on Grinder Point near Islesboro houses a sailors' memorial museum. The 25 m (82 ft.) timber 'lighthouse' in Portland was actually an observation tower built in 1807. At Pemaquid Point a fishermen's museum keeps occupied a lighthouse keeper's dwelling of 1827.

BIBLIOGRAPHY
General
Candee, 1985; Jackson, 1988.

LOCATIONS
[M] Ashland Logging Museum, Box 348, Ashland, ME 04732.
[M] Bethel Steam Railroad Museum, Railroad Street, Bethel, ME 04217.
[M] The Fishermen's Museum, Lighthouse Park, Pemaquid Point, ME 04554.
[M] Grand Banks Schooner Museum, Boothbay, ME 04537.
[M] Maine Maritime Museum, 963 Washington Street, Bath, ME 04530.
[M] Maine State Museum, State House Complex, Augusta, ME 04333.
[M] Owls Head Transportation Museum, Route 73, Owls Head, ME 04854.
[M] Patten Lumbering Museum, Shin Pond Road, Patten, ME 04765.
[M] Penobscot Marine Museum, Church Street, Searsport, ME 04974.
[M] Seashore Trolley Museum, Long Cabin Road, Kennebunkport, ME 04046.
[M] Stanley Steamer Museum, School Street, Kingfield, ME 04947.
[M] Vinalhaven Historical Society Museum, High Street, Vinalhaven, ME 04863.
[M] Wells Auto Museum, Route 1, Wells, ME 04090.

DAVID H. SHAYT

Mainz, Rhineland Palatinate, Germany   The capital of RHINELAND PALATINATE, much damaged in World War II, is an important harbour on the RHINE but is chiefly significant in industrial history as one of the birthplaces of PRINTING.

The Gutenberg Museum has one of the world's most comprehensive collections relating to printing, from the fifteenth century to modern times. Bookbinding is illustrated in a separate museum within the same building,

Figure 81   The Malakoff Tower of 1856 at the Zeche Hannover 1/2 (Hanover mine) at Bochum in the Ruhrgebiet; within the building is winding machinery of 1892. The tower forms part of the Westphalian Museum of Industry.
Barrie Trinder

which also houses an institute concerned with the history of paper.

BIBLIOGRAPHY
Specific
Presser, H. *Gutenberg-Museum of the City of Mainz – World Museum of Printing.* Munich: Peter Winkler Verlag, 1974.

LOCATION
[M] Gutenberg Museum, Liebfrauenplatz 5, 6500 Mainz.

majolica   A decorated tin-glazed earthenware, traditionally fired at a low temperature giving a salmon-pink body colour, with a lead glaze made opaque by tin oxide. The name, sometimes 'maiolica', derives from Mallorca (*see* BALEARIC ISLANDS), where this kind of ware was made in the fifteenth century. It was subsequently produced in Spain and Italy where it was sometimes called FAIENCE and in the Netherlands where it was often known as DELFTWARE. English Majolica made in the late nine-teenth century comprised a range of highly-coloured wares made by different techniques.

Makaraeo, Otago, New Zealand   A town 64 km (40 mi.) N. of Dunedin, the most important limeworking site in New Zealand. Three conventional kilns were built *c.*1899 by the government, and a single, massive gas-fired kiln of German, 'Schmatolla' type, built by Milburn Lime & Cement Co. *c.*1909: the kiln is brick-built, and elliptical in plan.

BIBLIOGRAPHY
General
Thornton, 1982.

Malakoff tower   A term, used particularly in Germany (German: 'Malakow-Turm'), to describe a stone or brick tower at the top of a mine shaft and containing the winding gear. Towers are up to 30 m (100 ft.) in height, with wall thicknesses up to 2.5 m (8 ft.). Adjacent buildings containing winding engines or pumping engines or both are either in line with or at right-angles to the tower. Malakoff towers were used in the Ruhrgebiet from *c.*1850, but the name derived from Fort Malakoff in the Crimea, the storming of which on 8 September 1855 led to the fall of Sevastopol, which was much celebrated in Germany. Heights of towers increased as coal pits became deeper, their appearance became more sophisticated (elements of fortification architecture being applied), and corner towers with separate staircases were added as fire escapes. Later steel headstocks were often erected in or on top of Malakoff towers. Thirteen towers remain in the Ruhrgebiet, the oldest being those at the Carl mine in Essen of 1856–61, and Prosper II mine at Bottrop of 1872. They were also built in the Saarland, where none remain, and in UPPER SILESIA.

BIBLIOGRAPHY
Specific
Müller, R. Malakow-Türme auf den Schachtanlagen des Ruhrge-bietes, ein Überblick über ihre Entwicklung und den Stand ihrer Erhaltung (Malakoff towers, the pithead buildings of the Ruhrgebiet; an overview of their development, present condition and state of preservation). *Burgen und Schlösser* (Castles and mansions), i, 1982.

AXEL FÖHL

Maleniec, Kielce, Poland   Rolling mill and engineering shops, situated on the Czarna Konecka River 30 km (19 mi.) NW of Kielce, within the STAROPOLSKI INDUSTRIAL REGION. The ironworks on the site from the eighteenth century was modernized in 1835, with the construction of new sheet-mill stands (*c.*1850) which employed about forty workers. From 1856 the works went over to making nails, and in the early twentieth century was also producing spades and ploughshares. Until 1959 the original water-power system of the early nineteenth century remained in use. In 1967 the works was closed down and designated a museum, currently the responsibility of the Koneckie Farming Tools Plant (Koneckie Zakłady Narzędzi Gospodarczych), which co-operates with the Department of Metallurgy at the Silesian Technical University in Gliwice. Students from the department undergo part of their practical training while restoring machinery at the plant. The water-power system includes a dam, a 30 ha (12 ac.) reservoir, and two later wheels. The plant comprises a rolling-mill building of wooden construction, a brick-built spade mill, and an office block. In the rolling mill the complete sequence of the original equipment is preserved: the water wheel, the cast-iron transmission wheels taking the power to the roll stand, which were made in Starachowice in 1843, a two-chamber re-heating furnace, a plate-shearing machine, and a weighing machine. An old transmission system is also preserved in the spade mill, which includes a plate shearer, a grinding machine, a nailing machine of the mid-nineteenth century, rivetters, spring hammers, and drilling machines.

BIBLIOGRAPHY
General
Borsa, 1981.

PIOTR GERBER

Maliq, Albania   Formerly the Maliq Swamp in eastern Albania, the site of one of the principal land drainage schemes in post-war Europe. A 13 000 ha (32 124 ac.) state farm was created, specializing in the production of grain. The village of Maliq was founded in 1951 principally to serve the new sugar-beet processing factory.

malleable iron   CAST IRON that has been annealed by heating it with powdered iron ore for several days, making it possible to cast the iron into nails, hinges and the like. It is still widely used for many purposes where metal parts are subject to shock, as in vehicle parts and machine tools. Invented by René Réaumur (1683–1757) in France in 1722, the process was used in England by the 1790s but only patented by Samuel Lucas in 1804. A slightly different process was devised by Seth Boyden in the USA, producing iron that when fractured was dark in section and known as blackheart iron; iron made by the Lucas process was called whiteheart iron. (The term 'malleable iron' is sometimes misleadingly applied to WROUGHT IRON.)

BIBLIOGRAPHY
General
Gale, 1969, 1971; Schuhmann, 1984.

Mallet   A type of articulated steam locomotive patented in 1884 by Jules Anatole Mallet (1837–1919) of Geneva, with two sets of cylinders (usually compound) and driving wheels, with the boiler set rigidly on the rear unit, to which the front unit was pivoted. The type was designed for narrow-gauge mountain lines in Europe, but after the building of 2–6–6–2s for the Great Northern Railway (USA) in 1906 the principle was applied to the largest main-line locomotives in the USA, like the Union Pacific 'Big Boys', of which examples are preserved in Pennsylvania and California. A 0–4–4–0T for mountain lines is preserved at LUCERNE.

BIBLIOGRAPHY
General
Westwood, 1983.

Malmédy, Liège, Belgium   A town 38 km (24 mi.) SE of Liège, which became part of Prussia from 1815 and was ceded to Belgium in 1919. Water from local mineral springs has long been bottled and exported, and there are many former tannery buildings. Malmédy is important for the manufacture of paper, the history of which is portrayed in the national museum in the town.

BIBLIOGRAPHY
General
Viaene, 1986.

LOCATION
[M] Musée National du Papier (National Museum of Paper), Place de Rome, 4890 Malmédy.

Malmö, Malmöhus, Sweden   With a quarter of a million inhabitants, Malmö is Sweden's third largest city, whose growth in the modern period is due to a harbour constructed by a merchant Frans Suell in the late eighteenth century. A large TOWER MILL stands near the centre of the city.

The city museum service, based in the castle, includes sections concerned with shipping, particularly harbours, lighthouses, ferries and road carriages. The technical section has exhibits including a pump relating to Mårten Triewald (*see* DANNEMORA), and a small collection of railway vehicles, including a 2–2–0T locomotive built at Trollhättan in 1888.

LOCATIONS
[M] Malmö Museum, Slottsholmen (Castle), Malmöhusvägen 7, PO Box 406, S-201 24 Malmö.
[M] Malmö Museum, Sjöfartsmuseet (Maritime Museum), Malmöhusvägen 7, PO Box 406, S-201 24 Malmö.
[M] Malmö Museum, Tekniska museet (Technical Museum), Malmöhusvägen 7, PO Box 406, S-201 24 Malmö.
[M] Malmö Museum, Vagnmuseet (Carriage Museum), Malmöhusvägen 7, PO Box 406, S-201 24 Malmö.

malt   Grain, most commonly barley, in which germination has been stimulated by soaking, thus converting starch to sugar, and then arrested by heating, thus preserving the sugar. Malt is most commonly used in brewing and distilling.

In the traditional floor malting process barley is soaked in water in a tank, and then 'couched': laid out on a smooth floor, which is usually plastered. When it begins to sprout it is turned to ensure even growth. It is then placed in a kiln, on a floor which is often of specially-made tiles. The kiln is fired with a smokeless fuel: CHARCOAL, COKE or ANTHRACITE. The malt is dried on a hair cloth, placed across wooden ribs in a drying kiln, and fanned to remove dust. Malt is handled with a malt shovel, with a thin, wide blade, traditionally of wood. Floor maltings on a vast scale were built in the second half of the nineteenth century (*see* LINCOLNSHIRE), causing the closure of many small concerns, but only small concerns now persist with the process (*see* SCOTCH WHISKY).

From the late nineteenth century floor malting has gradually been superseded by mechanized pneumatic malting. In drum malting, the invention of the Belgian, Gallant, barley is germinated in air-conditioned drums, which can rotate to turn the grain. The process developed from 1876 by the French engineer, Jules Saladin, involves placing the steeped barley in compartments in a long chamber through which temperature-controlled moist air is blown, the grain being agitated by mechanical turners.

BIBLIOGRAPHY
General
Colyer, 1880; Gallaher, 1970; Mathias, 1959; Patrick, 1977; Reynoldson, 1808; Stopes, 1885; Wahl and Henius, 1908.

BARRIE TRINDER

Malta   The island of Malta and the adjacent Gozo lie at the western end of the straits between Sicily and North Africa, some 100 km (60 mi.) from the Sicilian coast. Malta was held by the Knights of St John until its capture

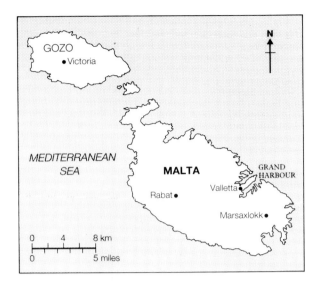

Malta

by the French in 1798. It was seized in 1800 by the British, who held it until the Maltese gained independence in 1964.

The islands consist entirely of limestone, which has been much quarried. The principal fishing port is Marsaxlokk, where the traditional Maltese vessel, the 'luzzu', still operates. There are salt evaporation pans on the shores of the small island of Gozo. A theatre from the time of the Knights, built in 1731, is preserved in Valletta (Valetta).

The principal industrial archaeological interest in Malta is in its dockyards. The British navy inherited from the Knights a waterside arsenal in Valletta harbour, of which there remains on Dockyard Creek a long stone-built range of chambers, all originally barrel-vaulted. Soon after 1809 the Royal Navy built an arcaded ropeworks on top of the range. Ropemaking continued until the 1870s, and most of the structure remains. The Navy completed a neo-Classical hospital in 1832, which was used until the 1960s. Malta's first dry dock was built in 1841–7, and still survives, although enlarged and altered. In 1841–5 a flour mill and bakery complex was built to the designs of William Scamp, an engineer from Woolwich Dockyard. It is a substantial structure, with a clock tower, which originally accommodated twelve circular ovens, ranged in groups of three, for baking biscuits.

BIBLIOGRAPHY
General
Coad, 1983, 1989.

LOCATIONS
[S] Manoel Theatre, Old Theatre Street, Valletta.
[M] National Museum, Kingsway, Valletta.

BARRIE TRINDER

Manchester, Greater Manchester, England   The metropolis of the Lancashire cotton trade, the focus of canal and railway systems, and a major engineering centre, Manchester was for some years around 1840 the symbol of the triumph of industry and of the social consequences of rapid urban growth. Visitors from Britain and abroad wrote many accounts of Manchester in that period, those of Friedrich Engels (1820–95) and Alexis de Tocqueville (1805–59) being the most memorable. Manchester has historically been administered separately from Salford on the north bank of the River Irwell, but essentially the two form one conurbation.

Manchester experienced a surge of civic pride in the second half of the nineteenth century, exemplified by its town hall, the Gothic masterpiece by Alfred Waterhouse (1830–1905) of 1868, and by the terracotta-clad Midland Hotel of 1898 by Charles Trubshaw. Whitworth Street is given a cavernous appearance by lines of tall warehouses, mostly in an Edwardian Baroque style, by H. S. Fairhurst. The former Central Station of 1876–9, with a single-arch train shed 64 m (210 ft.) in span and a vast brick vaulted undercroft, is now the G-Mex exhibition centre. The adjacent Great Northern Railway warehouse was a transfer point between rail, road and water transport. The Manchester Ship Canal, opened in 1894, made Manchester a port for ocean-going ships, but has declined since the 1970s. The Canal stimulated the development of Trafford Park, the first British industrial estate, from 1896. It became the site of many of Manchester's most significant twentieth-century industries, among them the Westinghouse electrical engineering works of 1901 (now GEC) and the first Ford motor factory in Britain (1911–29).

The main focus of industrial conservation is in Castlefield around the terminus of the BRIDGEWATER CANAL, opened in 1765, and its junction with the Rochdale Canal, opened in 1805. The area is dominated by warehouses, and by railway viaducts, notable for their decorative ironwork. The Greater Manchester Museum of Science and Industry, run by a charitable trust with the support of local and national government, incorporates Liverpool Road Station, the original terminus of the Liverpool & Manchester Railway, opened in 1830, and the world's oldest railway passenger station. An aerospace display, in which the role of the region in the development of aircraft manufacture is featured, is located in the iron and glass Lower Campsfield Market Hall of 1876–7. A traditional 'power hall' includes an Earnshaw & Holt horizontal mill engine of 1864, a Beyer Garrett locomotive built in Manchester which worked in South Africa, and a Vulcan Foundry locomotive which worked in Pakistan. A textile section includes an Arkwright carding engine of c.1800. Other sections feature electric power, paper-making and computers, the first stored-program computer having been made in Manchester in 1948. Visitors are able to observe the Museum's conservation workshops.

Castlefield is linked by the Rochdale Canal with Ancoats, where there are further early nineteenth-century warehouses around the basins in Ducie Street and Dale Street, and beyond them a series of important canalside mills, including Sedgewick Mill, designed by WILLIAM FAIRBAIRN for McConnell and Kennedy and completed in 1820, and Royal Mill, built in 1797 and rebuilt in 1912. Facing Oldham Road is Victoria Square, a five-storey, red-brick apartment block, built as a slum clearance project in 1889, and in Great Ancoats Street is the Daily Express building by Sir Owen Williams (1890–1969) of 1939, with an all-glass front, exposing the printing machinery inside.

Few working-class dwellings earlier than the TUNNEL-BACK terraces built according to local by-laws from the 1850s onwards can be found in Manchester, but some isolated examples of earlier housing have been surveyed. Garden suburbs on co-operative principles were built at Burnage, 5 km (3 mi.) SW, where J. Horner Hargreaves designed 136 houses built during 1907–10, and Fairfield, 6 km (4 mi.) E., where Sellers & Wood built 46 dwellings in 1914, adjacent to a Moravian settlement of 1785.

At Blackley, 6 km (4. mi.) NE, the ICI Organics Division houses a historical collection of dyestuffs.

BIBLIOGRAPHY
General
Aikin, 1795; Ashmore, 1969, 1982; Briggs, 1963; Engels, 1845; Fairbairn, 1877; Ferneyhough, 1980; Fitzgerald, 1980; Hadfield and Biddle, 1970; Harrison, 1967; Kellett, 1979; Malet, 1977; Tocqueville, 1958; Wadsworth and Mann, 1931.
Specific
Brumhead, D. *Castlefield: Britain's first urban heritage park*, 1984.
Roberts, J. *Working-Class Housing in Nineteenth-Century Manchester: the example of John Street, Irk Town 1826–1936*. Manchester: Neil Richardson, 1983.

LOCATION
[M] Greater Manchester Museum of Science and Industry, Liverpool Road, Castlefield, Manchester M3 4JP.

BARRIE TRINDER

man engine A system used from the early nineteenth century to enable miners to go to and from their work, principally in metalliferous mines. Systems of wooden rods were installed, sometimes in pairs, reciprocated by water-power, and later by steam engines in the same way as pumping rods. Steps were formed on the rods at intervals, and as they stroked up and down, for distances of 2–4 m (6–12 ft.), the miners stepped off at each change of direction, either on to staging affixed to the shaft wall or on to a similar step on a parallel rod at the end of its stroke. This motion would gradually carry a miner up or down the shaft. Man engines were used in CORNWALL, the ISLE OF MAN, and in the HARZ MOUNTAINS (*see* figure 82).

manganese (Mn) An elemental metal, used in steelmaking to deoxidize and desulphurize steel. About 1 per cent manganese increases the elasticity of steel for use in crushing apparatus and in rails. Its properties have been recognized since the eighteenth century. The chief sources are in India, Africa, and the USSR.

BIBLIOGRAPHY
General
Jones, 1950.

Manitoba, Canada The prairie province of Manitoba

Figure 82 A mine shaft in which a man engine has been installed: the rods to which the central platforms are attached are reciprocated by a prime mover, and the miner ascends or descends the shaft by stepping on and off the fixed platforms at either side.

was created in 1870 and enlarged to the west and north in 1881. The area had been opened up by the Hudson's Bay Company from 1670 but the main period of settlement, by Scots and Irish, was from 1812. Mechanization of farming has created many shrunken and deserted rural settlements; and numerous local railway lines, once the foundation of the province's prosperity, have been abandoned.

The province's most significant industrial monuments are situated at Port Nelson on Hudson's Bay, designated by the federal government in 1908 as the Arctic terminal for the prairie railway network. Despite known navigational problems created by strong tides, railway construction commenced and an artificial island was built in the estuary of the Nelson River and connected to the mainland by a bridge. Construction ceased in 1917 as a result of World War I, and when it was resumed in 1927 Churchill was selected as the railway terminal, eventually opening in 1932: the extensive civil engineering works around Port Nelson were abandoned.

BIBLIOGRAPHY
General
Morton, 1967; Stevens, 1962; Weir, 1960.

Mannheim, Baden-Württemberg, Germany   The landmark of this industrial city in northern Baden is an industrial monument: the neo-Baroque watertower built in 1889 at the centre of the city, which is laid out on a strict gridiron plan. The waterworks in the Käfertaler Wald, designed by O. Smreker in 1882 and brought into use in 1888, made it possible for the first time to provide a water supply independent of the Rhine. In 1906 the works had to be enlarged, as had been planned. The circular reservoir house for purified water, with its domed roof, the filtration plant buildings, and the associated living accommodation have been preserved. The sewage works in Neckerau, 3 km (2 mi.) SE, were built *c.*1890 and still employ the original pumping equipment. Local history is illustrated in the Reiss Museum in the arsenal building of 1777–9. The Baden-Württemberg Museum of Technology and Labour has extensive collections relating to the industrialization of the Federal Republic.

LOCATIONS
[M] Landesmuseum für Technik und Arbeit in Baden-Württemberg (Baden-Württemberg Museum of Technology and Labour), Museumsstrasse 1, 6800 Mannheim.
[M] Reiss Museum, Zeughaus C5, 6800 Mannheim.

ROLF HÖHMANN

mansard roof   A roof with a double slope, the lower longer and steeper than the upper. It takes its name from the French architect François Mansart (1598–1666).

BIBLIOGRAPHY
General
Smith and Braham, 1972.

Mantua (Mantova), Lombardy, Italy   A city sited where the River Mincio widens into three lakes, connected by locks and canals. The silk industry was established by 1543 when an edict granted privileges to foreigners who had introduced silk-throwing to the city. Large-scale water-powered corn mills developed in the eighteenth century. The main industrial development is in the Porta Catera district facing Lago Inferiore. There are numerous surviving brick kilns on the outskirts of the city, with some intermittent kilns dating from the eighteenth century.

At Sermide, 40 km (25 mi.) E. on the River Po, is a grandiose pumping station for land drainage, a palatial structure flanked by two chimneys built in the 1900s.

BIBLIOGRAPHY
General
Mioni *et al.*, 1981–3.

maps Maps and plans are, for good reason, the documentary tools most widely used by industrial archaeologists. Modern maps are essential equipment in fieldwork, and historical maps are fundamental primary sources. However, maps were not created for industrial archaeologists, and it is important to understand their origins and differences in order to interpret them.

Manuscript estate plans are amongst the oldest large-scale maps. These begin at varying dates; in England they were produced from the 1570s, but few were drawn in Scotland before the mid-eighteenth century. In North America hardly any early estate plans were drawn in northern New England, but many in South Carolina. Typically they show land belonging to individuals or organizations at about 1:5000, and were used as aids to estate management, to settle disputes, or as status symbols. The most detailed show buildings (sometimes with architectural details), roads, watercourses, mills, mines and other industrial activity; but some, like most eighteenth-century estate plans in Ireland, show little more than boundaries.

Some other large-scale maps of rural areas before the advent of national surveys were drawn for particular administrative purposes. Cadastral surveys were made of much of continental Europe from the seventeenth century; and from the eighteenth, many maps were drawn to administer the enclosure of common fields and waste. These and other historical maps were often accompanied by such documents as leases, legal cases, particulars of sale, or schedules of plot ownership and land use which provide valuable information.

Plans of buildings and urban areas have been drawn since the Renaissance. The largest-scale ones give internal layouts of buildings and were often drawn when property was changing hands or being altered. Such maps and plans are most common from the end of the nineteenth century, and burgeoned with the growth of planning and building regulations. Surveys of industrial complexes are common from this period; engineers' and architects' plans often survive in company archives, and fire insurance plans, on both sides of the Atlantic, give details of the construction and use of buildings, and the locations of boilers, engines and furnaces. Maps on smaller scales were produced to show the extent of specific industries in particular countries, like forest products in the USA and Canada.

Many large-scale strip maps were drawn to show lines of transport: for example, road books for travellers, or plans showing property affected by proposed canals and railways. In England and Wales the law provided for such plans to be deposited with county authorities from 1792. Many illustrate the landscape on either side as well as the route itself. Similarly, coastal charts made from medieval times show inland features as well as coastal waters. Those of the British Admiralty have been issued since 1795 and have worldwide coverage.

The first widely available maps were printed regional or county maps drawn at a scale of about 1:50000. Especially common in England from the eighteenth century, they show selected industrial activities. Important roads were almost always marked, windmills (used as triangulation points) were often carefully recorded, and features like ENGLISH GLASS CONES were landmarks to be noted; but areas of settlement or mining were shown only in generalized ways. At a larger scale, topographical maps of towns were published from the eighteenth century, and insurance plans of whole districts from the mid-nineteenth century.

The British Ordnance Survey, founded in 1791, and organizations like it all over the world, co-ordinate standardized surveys of whole countries. Successive editions of their maps are invaluable in showing changes during the past century and more. Modern editions show topographical features, contours, and either a national grid or lines of latitude and longitude. They are widely available at varied scales, sometimes from 1:1000000 up to 1:500. Those most used in archaeology are the largest-scale with national coverage: usually around 1:25000, like the United States Geological Survey 'Quads'. Such maps are regularly updated: for example the Swiss Office of Topography updates its maps every six or seven years. Specialist maps superimposed on national survey sheets show information about geology, soils, land use and other subjects.

Perhaps the first use of maps by industrial archaeologists is in preparing for detailed studies. Sites that may repay investigation can be identified by features like stream diversions at the likely locations of mills, or by place names (such as 'pandy' in Wales, meaning a site of fulling), as well as by explicit annotations. The relation of sites to surrounding features on maps may suggest important interpretations: for example, they might indicate that particular coal mines supplied blast furnaces, or suggest reasons for the route of a railway. Specialist modern maps can provide important information: geological maps are invaluable in interpreting extractive industries, and land-use maps can shed light on historical farming. The grid-reference systems of modern maps have important uses in fieldwork, to define exactly and permanently the locations of sites and excavated trenches. This is standard practice in report writing, and provides the basic method of identification in all archaeological sites and monuments records.

As documentary sources, maps help to interpret sites studied archaeologically, and provide comparative evidence about others now lost or not examined. Where a succession exists for the same place, they can show changes in features like buildings, transport routes or watercourses. They often identify industrial activities by name or by symbol (for example, a cross within a circle often indicates an ironworks). Associated schedules, if available, provide information as detailed as the functions of individual buildings and the association of waste dumps with particular manufacturers. The nationally-available English tithe map schedules of c.1836–50 are so detailed as to permit conclusions about regional land-use patterns. Ownership is often indicated by such schedules, or by shading to identify the property of an individual, or by labels like 'Rose & Co. Copper Works' or 'Smith's brick-field'.

Interpreting maps can be hazardous. All maps are selective representations, and features that were not considered important by the surveyor may have been omitted or sketched roughly. For instance, only one tramroad out of dozens in MERTHYR TYDFIL was marked on Yates's map of 1799, and areas of some tithe maps were left blank if land was not tithable. Elements of a landscape may have been deliberately distorted: for example, land-owners' houses were aggrandized on estate maps, and maps of Jamaican sugar plantations show refining com-plexes in disproportionate detail. Accompanying sche-dules or legal cases, the archival location of a map, and careful analysis of its content should always be used to establish its original purposes.

Reading map symbols is not often straightforward. Maps seldom had keys before the late nineteenth century, and there were many different conventions. Only careful examination may reveal that asterisks with holes in the middle represent watermills, or that boundaries were drawn to show who maintained them. A map which had some buildings shaded and others in outline might be misinterpreted as showing a landscape of tiny fields. Many symbols were highly stylized: for example cottages often indicated areas of settlement rather than individual buildings. Finally, some features of interest to industrial archaeologists were not distinguished. Thus, there was no widely-used symbol for the railways that multiplied in some areas before the nineteenth century, and they must often be disentangled from adjacent roads as though following a maze.

The date of a map should not be taken on trust: a prominent date may represent the survey, a copy, the printing, or the most recent updating. Frequently, manu-script maps or printing plates were altered so that they contained a little new information, such as the correction of a previous error or the addition of a new road, and the dates of alterations must be noted. However it should not be assumed that all changes of importance were incorpor-ated. Care even has to be taken to be sure that some features actually existed: phantom canals are found on some maps brought out before schemes were finalized.

Maps are the most seductive of sources, seeming clear and comprehensive in their portrayal of the landscape; but they are complex documents, profoundly influenced by past events and personalities. To reach an understand-ing of any map and how it can be used, there is no substitute for many hours of familiarization.

Historical maps can be found in many places: national and local archives, museums and libraries, and private or company collections. Often only one or a few copies of maps exist, but some were widely published or appeared in books, and facsimile reproductions of many are now available, often prefaced with valuable information for their interpretation. To track down others it is necessary to consult published catalogues and bibliographies and to enquire at likely repositories. The quality of catalogues varies: some give full descriptions of each sheet, some are merely summary listings, and some collections remain uncatalogued. Maps in books or legal papers are not usually catalogued separately.

Aids to finding modern maps can list current maps in print, describe map-producing agencies and their work, refer to catalogues and indexes, and describe geological, administrative and thematic maps. The loose-leaf *Geokata-log* is easily updated, gives detailed indexes to map series and describes them (in German). Published catalogues of major collections, such as the catalogue of the map division of the New York Public Library, and the British Museum Catalogue of Printed Maps, indicate the range of maps available; the catalogue of holdings of the American Geographical Society gives a useful index of maps in books and periodicals.

BIBLIOGRAPHY
General
Geokatalog; Harley, 1975; Kain and Prince, 1985; Pannell, 1974; Parry and Perkins, 1987; Portinaro and Knirsch, 1988; Seymour, 1980; Smith, 1988.
Specific
Piardi, F. Cartografia e archeologia industriale (Cartography and industrial archaeology). In *Il Coltello di Delfo*, v, 1988.
Smith, D. The representation of non-extractive industry on large-scale county maps of England and Wales 1700–*c*.1840. In *Cartographic Journal*, XXVI, 1989.
Vogel, R. M. Quadrangular treasure: the cartographic route to industrial archaeology. In *IA*, VI, 1980.
Wright, H. Insurance mapping and industrial archaeology. In *IA*, IX, 1983.

SARAH BENDALL and PETER WAKELIN

marble In a loose sense, any decorative stone that will take a polish; but strictly a limestone, usually one recrystallized by heat or other means, the polished surface of which is a light-coloured mosaic of calcite crystals. Marble is widely used in architecture and for gravestones. The principal source in Europe was CARRARA, but there were many others; it was also quarried on a large scale in Vermont, USA.

BIBLIOGRAPHY
General
Challinor, 1986.
Specific
Viner, D. J. The 1776 marble quarry, Iona, Inner Hebrides. In *IAR*, I(1) 1976.

Marconi, Guglielmo (1874–1937) An Italian pioneer of radio who first experimented in Bologna; faced with official indifference, he emigrated to Britain. Using existing technology he developed his first radio in 1896 and thereafter successfully exploited its commercial potential. He was awarded the Nobel Prize for Physics in 1909.

BIBLIOGRAPHY
General
Baker, 1970.

margarine Margarine was first developed by Hippolyte Méges-Mouriés (1817–80) in 1870, in response to a demand from the French government for a substitute for butter. His process involved submitting beef fat to the action in an alkaline medium of juices extracted from the stomachs of sheep or pigs. The product was first called oleomargarine. Subsequently manufacture on a large scale was developed by such concerns as Van der Bergh & Jurgens in the Netherlands, using oils from coconuts, ground nuts and cotton seed, as well as palm oil and TRAIN OIL. Milk is used in the process to emulsify the fats and confer flavour.

BIBLIOGRAPHY
General
Clayton, 1920; Mathias, 1967; Morgan and Pratt, 1938.

Mariánské Lázně, West Bohemia, Czechoslovakia An important spa town, with a spectacular iron colonnade forming part of the spa buildings, made at BLANSKO in 1889.

Mariembourg, Namur, Belgium A village 49 km (30 mi.) S. of Charleroi, where the station is the terminus and museum of the preserved railway, the Chemin de Fer à Vapeur des Trois Vallées (Three Valleys Steam Railway), which runs 23 km (14 mi.) east to Treignes. The line reopened in 1976-7.

BIBLIOGRAPHY
General
Viaene, 1986.

LOCATION
[I] Le Chemin de Fer and Vapeur des Trois Vallées (Three Valleys Steam Railway), 20 rue des Houblonnières, 5000 Namur.

Marinha Grande, Estremadura, Portugal The town, 110 km (68 mi.) N. of Lisbon, to which the celebrated glassworks was transferred from Coina (*see* BARREIRO) in 1750-1. Later the brothers Guilherme and João Diogo Stephens managed the factory and were responsible for its great success. A museum displays documents and examples of the factory's work. At Pedreanes, 2 km ($1\frac{1}{4}$ mi.) SE, the remains of a blast furnace of 1866 are visible following an excavation which began in 1987.

LOCATION
[M] Glass Museum, Stephens Glassworks, Marinha Grande.

maritime museum Maritime museums fall into two groups. There are the long-established collections consisting chiefly of ship models and paintings, often backed with good archives; of these, the National Maritime Museum, Greenwich (*see* LONDON), is the prime example. The second group are generally of more recent origin and consist of collections of ships. The preservation of individual ships is a well-established practice, the majority being fighting ships of special significance, like the *Avrora* at LENINGRAD or the *Victory* at Portsmouth. A merchant example is the *Cutty Sark*, preserved at Greenwich but significantly not by the museum. Some ambitious new museums of ships like those at San Francisco, New York and Bremerhaven combine the two approaches. The major difficulty lies in the preservation of large vessels, almost all the merchant ships in museums being of less than 10 000 tonnes

displacement, the majority of very much less. No very large ship has yet been preserved for historical reasons – for example, much of the *Queen Mary* at Long Beach, CALIFORNIA has been adapted as a hotel and conference centre: she is not preserved as a historical artefact. Maritime museums are often proposed as parts of waterfront rehabilitation schemes: it is questionable whether ship preservation has benefited from such projects, although a ship can, as with the *Discovery* at Dundee, serve as a focus for such a scheme. Ships are an attraction in the early stages of a project, but their maintenance is rarely adequately funded. In some cases ships have been allowed to deteriorate, and their continued presence has been criticized by residents seeking moorings for yachts.

BIBLIOGRAPHY
General
Van Beylen, 1969; Howe, 1987

NEIL COSSONS

market Markets are as old as towns, and traditionally took place in the open, but in large nineteenth-century cities they came to be accommodated in large buildings. In 1891 about half of the 766 markets in England took place under cover. The pattern was set by the wholesale markets in LONDON, designed by Charles Fowler (1791–1867), of which Covent Garden of 1828-30 is the best surviving example. Iron and glass were employed in the construction of many markets, as in Les Halles Central, Paris, designed by Victor Baltard in 1853 and demolished in 1971. Most were gas-lit and had running water and cold stores to serve traders like butchers and fishmongers. Most incorporated stalls for food, such as eels, pies or the ham-filled soft rolls for which BRADFORD Market was famous. Temperance organizations sometimes provided SOFT DRINKS like sarsaparilla, while public houses or bars were often incorporated in market buildings.

Many large nineteenth-century market buildings have been adapted to new uses, the conversion in 1976-7 of Quincy Market, Boston, Mass., originally constructed in 1824-6, having set a fashion for ethnic eateries which has been copied throughout the Western world.

BARRIE TRINDER

marmalade A preserve made like JAM, but from the firmer kinds of fruit: the rinds of oranges, grapefruit, and the like. Samuel Johnson observed it in the Scottish Islands in 1773, and it is often regarded as a Scottish innovation. Keillers of DUNDEE were marketing marmalade nationally by the 1840s. One of the most successful industrial manufacturers of the late nineteenth century was Frank Cooper (1844–1927) of Oxford, who began selling marmalade in white stoneware jars *c*.1873, and opened a purpose-built factory in 1903.

BIBLIOGRAPHY
Specific
Allen, B. *Cooper's Oxford: a history of Frank Cooper Ltd.* Oxford: Archive Services, 1989.

Figure 83   An engraving by Blanchard of the docks and warehouses at Marseilles in 1864: the 'Grand Entrepôt', the principal warehouse building, dating from 1859–64, is to the right, behind the grandiose façade of the dock company offices
CDEM

Marseilles (Marseille), Bouches-du-Rhône, France   Ever since the foundation of the city in the sixth century BC, the economic life of Marseilles has turned around its port and around maritime trade, primarily with the Levant. Cloth from the VILLENEUVETTE manufactory was shipped from Marseilles, for example. From the late seventeenth century Marseilles also began to trade with the New World. With the advent of steam navigation in the 1830s, and with the promise of important colonial trade with France's newly-conquered colonies in North Africa, the drawbacks of the limited space and archaic organization of Marseilles' natural 'old' port became increasingly apparent. Seventeenth- and eighteenth-century warehouse buildings known as 'domaines', scattered throughout the town and so not necessarily close to the quays, still combined residential and storage functions, the latter necessitating endless carrying and handling by a long-established corporation of porters.

Starting with the Joliette dock, built between 1844 and 1853, Marseilles' new dock system turned its back on the city, gradually creeping northwards on an ever-larger scale, to occupy 8 km (5 mi.) of the coastline, entirely reclaimed from the sea. The sea wall, parallel to the coast, was made by immersion on the seaward side of 20-tonne blocks of prefabricated concrete, a dock construction system first tried out in 1833 for the new port of Algiers.

In 1854 the concession for the exploitation of the port facilities was granted by the city of Marseilles to the Compagnie des Docks et Entrepôts (Dock and Warehouse Company), which pursued the construction of new docks, along with wharfside warehouses and dry-dock installations for ship-repairing. This company, launched with Parisian capital, was founded by Paulin Talabot (1799–1885), an engineer who followed the political philosophy of Saint-Simon and who was also one of the pioneers of French railway construction, responsible in particular for the line between Beaucaire and ALÈS opened in 1837 for carrying Grand'Combe coal towards the Mediterranean, and for the Avignon–Marseilles line of 1843 which linked the Rhône with the Mediterranean port. Talabot went on, in 1862, to found the Paris–Lyon–Méditerranée railway company, the PLM.

The principal warehouse building in the new Marseilles docks was erected by the company between 1859 and 1863. Directly inspired by similar buildings studied at Liverpool and London (especially the Victoria Docks of 1853–6 in London), it was the largest such edifice ever seen in France. Six storeys high and measuring 365 × 37 m (1200 ft. × 120 ft), its fireproof construction and modular conception made it, in turn, a model for warehouse buildings elsewhere. The English engineer SIR WILLIAM ARMSTRONG was called upon by the company to

448

design the dock's hydraulic cargo-handling system: some forty quayside cranes and as many warehouse lifts and hoists, all powered from a single hydraulic power station.

The main innovation introduced in the Marseilles docks was the penetration of the railway onto the quayside, eventually necessitating much lighter sheds and hangars, temporary cover for merchandise which spent less and less time in money-wasting immobility. The container revolution after 1950 was but another stage in this process, finally rendering warehouse buildings obsolete. While nothing remains of Armstrong's hydraulic cranes, the 'Grand Entrepôt' of Marseilles still stands, part of it – the former head offices of the Dock Company, behind a monumental Louis XIII-style façade – now used as offices. Most of the remaining warehouses now await both reuse proposals and some form of legislative protection.

Many pre-industrial manufactures, ceramics, furniture and ironware from the city and the region are displayed in the Cantini, Old Marseilles and Grobet-Labadie museums.

BIBLIOGRAPHY
General
Association culturelle des travailleurs de la Réparation navale, 1986; Bonillo and Borruey, 1990.
Specific
Bonillo, J. L. & Borruey, R. Du 'Domaine' au Dock: le rationalisation de l'espace portuaire Marseillais au XIXᵉ siècle (From the 'domaine' to the dock: the rationalisation of space in the port of Marseilles during the nineteenth century). In *L'Archéologie Industrielle en France*, XIV, 1986.

LOCATIONS
[M] Cantini Museum, 19 rue Grignan, 13001 Marseilles.
[M] Grobet-Labadie Museum, 140 boulevard Longchamp, 13001 Marseilles.
[M] Marseilles Maritime Museum, Palais de la Bourse, 13001 Marseilles.
[M] Museum of Old Marseilles, Maison Diamantée, rue de la Prison, 13001 Marseilles.

PAUL SMITH

Marshall, John (1765–1845)   The pioneering entrepreneur of the flax industry, who established the production of linen yarn, thread and ultimately cloth on a factory basis. Marshall, with partners, opened his first works, the Scotland Mill, near Leeds, in 1789 utilizing machines patented by their principal mechanic, Matthew Murray, 1765–1826. They built a mill in Leeds in 1791; then Marshall and his new partners, Benjamin & Thomas Benyon, constructed another in 1795; and then a third in SHREWSBURY in 1796–7, the first multi-storey, iron-framed building, designed by Charles Bage (d.1822). Marshall bought out his partners in 1804 and continued to develop the company in Shrewsbury and LEEDS, where he built a single-storey mill in the EGYPTIAN style in 1840. In 1826 he was the first mill-owner to be elected as Member of Parliament for the West Riding of Yorkshire. The company failed to prosper in the hands of his sons and grandsons, who lived as landowners in the LAKE DISTRICT, and its winding up in 1886 is often quoted as evidence of the 'decline of the industrial spirit' in nineteenth-century England.

BIBLIOGRAPHY
General
Macleod *et al.*, 1988; Rimmer, 1960.

marshalling yard   A series of parallel railway sidings on which goods wagons originating from different locations can be sorted or re-sorted into new trains before being dispatched to their next destinations or sorting points. Sidings generally converge into a single track at each end of the yard, thus allowing maximum control over shunting movements. Larger yards often have a 'hump', enabling wagons to enter sidings under their own momentum after being pushed over the hump by a locomotive. They are controlled by mechanical retarding apparatus operated from a control cabin. Many marshalling yards operate continuously, and have pylons to floodlight night-time working. The growth of container traffic and of 'piggy-back' systems for carrying road trailers, and the concentrations on block trains ('unit trains' in the USA) has greatly reduced the number of operating yards.

BIBLIOGRAPHY
General
Bulkeley, 1930; Burtt, 1923; Rhodes, 1989; Robbins, 1962.

JOHN POWELL

Marshlands, Marlborough, New Zealand   A town where there is a flax mill of *c*.1888, disused since 1963. Most buildings survive. There is a 25 hp two-cylinder steam engine, with scutcher, retting tank and bale press. An adjacent sawmill uses the electric-power system installed for the flax mill in 1926.

BIBLIOGRAPHY
General
Thornton, 1982.

Maryland, United States of America   The tortuous outline of this mid-Atlantic coastal state, appearing like spillage off the lip of some great vat, is due in part to the work of two British astronomers. In 1767 Charles Mason (?1730–87) and Jeremiah Dixon (d.1777) solved a bitter dispute among the colonial governments of Pennsylvania, Maryland and Delaware by replotting the boundary line between the three along a previously unmarked stretch of land. The resulting 'Mason and Dixon Line' (at 39° 43′ 26.3″ N.) came to identify not only the political boundaries but the traditional separation between the American 'South' and the 'North'.

Straddling Chesapeake Bay between the nation's capital and the northern urban centres, Maryland has been at the centre of some of the nation's earliest industrial stirrings, notably in the area of transportation. The Baltimore & Ohio Railroad of 1827, the Chesapeake & Ohio Canal of 1824 and, to a lesser degree, the Chesapeake & Delaware Canal of 1829 were designed to connect the commerce of the Ohio Valley and other internal areas with the Atlantic Coast trade. All three survive today in considerably altered forms, but following original align-ments, and passing over or through some of the original civil engineering works.

The C&O Canal's century of active service through Maryland is not adequately presented in any formal canal museum, but locks, lock keepers' dwellings, and various lesser structures remain along its length. Several miles of its lower reaches are still in water, and the towpath is well maintained. Baltimore's B&O Railroad Museum at Mount Clare fills one of the railroad company's old turntabled car-building and maintenance shops with a fine assortment of early and re-created locomotives, wagons and carriages of a past era.

The C&D Canal's most celebrated site is not a museum, nor the canal itself, widened and deepened in the 1960s, but a steam pumping station at Chesapeake City, Maryland. Preserved *in situ* at what was once the 13 km (8 mi.) ship canal's summit are the 11.9 m (39 ft.) scoop wheel and tandem Merrick steam engines of the 1850s that replaced canal water lost through lockage and evaporation in the period before the entire canal had been dug down to sea level.

The Chesapeake Bay Maritime museum in St Michaels has developed collections that chart the region's long attachment to the sea in shipping and fishing, while Baltimore's Museum of Industry has pioneered since 1981 the concept of the city industrial museum, with robust collecting, research and exhibition endeavours.

Baltimore City remains one of the nation's most diverse industrial centres, maintaining or reusing in altered forms a considerable array of structural types in the fields of power generation, manufacturing and public utilities. Baltimore's SHOT TOWER of 1828, the downtown sewage-pumping station of 1910, which is now a museum of public works, a massive harbourside power plant of 1904, and a score of wharf-related commercial structures have been effectively integrated into the city's new business economy and tourist-based service industry. Bethlehem Steel Corporation's much-diminished Sparrows Point works, dating from 1890, remains a robust smoking presence on the city's south-eastern horizon.

Elsewhere in the state stone blast-furnace remains stand at Principio, Nassawango, Lonaconing and Catoctin, while in the town of Savage stands the last surviving example of Wendel Bollman's once commonplace iron-truss railway bridges, wrought-iron straps radiating from the end posts as suspension ties. Prior to using the Bollman design for most of its short spans – which was its policy between 1852 and 1873 – the B&O Railroad built several early masonry-arch bridges, such as the Thomas Viaduct of 1835 over the Patapsco River, and the Carrollton Viaduct of 1829, claimed to be the nation's first railway bridge, which is now surrounded by Baltimore's urban sprawl. Both remain in full service.

LOCATIONS

[M] Baltimore & Ohio Railroad Museum, Mt. Clare Station, Pratt & Poppleton Streets, Baltimore, MD 21230.

[M] Baltimore Museum of Industry, 1415 Key Highway, Baltimore, MD 21230.

[M] Baltimore Streetcar Museum, 1901 Falls Road, Baltimore, MD 21211.

[M] Chesapeake Bay Maritime Museum, Navy Point, St. Michaels, MD 21663.

[M] Chesapeake & Ohio Canal Tavern Museum, 11710 MacArthur Boulevard, Potomac, MD 21782.

[M] Mount Vernon Museum of Incandescent Lighting, 717 Washington Place, Baltimore, MD 21201.

DAVID H. SHAYT

maslin In the seventeenth century, alloys resembling either silver or gold, used for salt cellars, spoons, candlesticks and the like. In the eighteenth century, seemingly a bright brass used mainly to make kettles (pans with hooped handles). By 1900 jam-making utensils made of cast iron or brass, and later of aluminium, were called maslin kettles.

Massachusetts, United States of America One of the first areas of the USA to be settled by Europeans, and one of the first to be subject to the influences of the British Industrial Revolution. The cluster of export-based industries that characterized America's earliest industrial life remain at the core of the state's industrial heritage. In textile production, ironworking, whaling, quarrying, shipbuilding and light manufacturing (like the shoe-making industry commemorated at Lynn), the small New England state is home to some of the best industrial archaeology in the nation.

The early-nineteenth-century profusion of specialized water-powered textile mills in America finds expression today at the Lowell National Historic Site, north of Boston. Refurbished mill buildings and methods of site interpretation at this urban multi-structure preserve, established in the late 1970s, have become models for other cities worldwide. The state's – and the nation's – broader involvement with textile manufacture is handled by the nearby Museum of American Textile History, located appropriately in the state that shares with Rhode Island the national title as birthplace of the cotton mill, in the 1780s, and of the woollen mill, in the 1790s.

Few of the diversion dams and power canals that fed the textile mills have been obliterated in the region, leaving a power-supply network in the landscape of rare dimensions. Canals receive treatment in Lowell's Middlesex Canal Museum, focused on the canal of 1803 that connected Lowell with Charlestown, Mass., through twenty locks and nine aqueducts. Along the Atlantic coast, the New Bedford Whaling Museum is one of the nation's major repositories of artefacts and documents preserving the history of industries associated with American whaling.

The nation's colonial ironworking roots in service to Britain have been 'commemorated' since 1954 at the Saugus Ironworks National Historic Site in Saugus, north of Boston. The Saugus Ironworks operated from 1646 until 1670, laying claim to the earliest commercially successful reduction and refining of iron in the New World. Bog ore was smelted in a blast furnace, and the resultant pig fined into wrought iron, and worked at a trip hammer and slitting mill into a range of sizes which could be forged into useful products. All but some portions of the orginal foundations have been completely rebuilt.

Much of Massachusett's energetic clock-making and watch-making activity was centred about the town of Waltham, west of Boston. Adaptation of factories to new uses was one of the industrial archaeological success stories of the 1970s, and the adaptations include two structures now occupied by industrial museums, one a former cotton mill.

In Boston the subway system of 1897 rivals New York's in the nightmarish decrepitude of its trackage, as well as the rocking, screeching yet exhilarating rides through the tunnels, no matter how new or rebuilt the cars themselves. Above ground, active and inactive examples of steam-powered water-pumping and sewage-pumping stations stand in corners of the city. The vast Charlestown Navy Yard is today a dazzling conversion from industry to posh housing, former foundry and machine-shop structures now broken up into jazzy, high-end condos. Amidst all, the important anchor-chain forge shop and ropewalk stand largely unchanged, with representative machinery spread through both.

Near the town of North Adams in western Massachusetts the Hoosac Tunnel of 1875 cuts through Hoosac Mountain in a 7.5 km (4mi. 1230 yd.) bore that was the longest transportation tunnel of its time in the western hemisphere. Its twenty-two-year excavation introduced to tunnelling pneumatic drills, the use of nitro-glycerine explosives, and the utilization of ventilation and construction shafts.

Minot's Ledge lighthouse, off the state's coast at Cohasset, was one of the most daring lighthouse constructions on the Atlantic, its foundation being in a state of continuous submersion. The success of the masonry tower at resisting open-sea wave action, depending on massive interlocking granite blocks laid in 1855–60, continues to be tested in gales that occasionally send waves crashing over its light. Beneath the waves, the Atlantic telegraph cable of 1879 is commemorated at nearby Orleans.

Old Sturbridge Village, opened in 1946, is an open-air museum portraying New England in the early nineteenth century, where such crafts as coopering, shoemaking, printing, and tinsmithing are demonstrated. Water-powered structures include a carding mill, a sawmill and a flour mill, and there is a well-stocked country store.

The Canton Viaduct of 1835, crossing 187 m (615 ft.) of a shallow river basin at Canton, carried the major railway linking Boston with Providence, Rhode Island. The viaduct's six stone arches appear to be masonry-filled but are in fact hollow, the 1.5 m (5 ft.) thick stone infill walls admitting river waters, and, beneath one arch, a four-lane highway.

BIBLIOGRAPHY
General
American Society of Mechanical Engineers, 1980; Comp, 1974; Kulik *et al.*, 1982; Molloy, 1976; Robbins and Jones, 1959; Sande, 1971.
Specific
Beaudry M. C. and Mrozowski, S. A. The archeology of work and home life in Lowell, Massachusetts: an interdisciplinary study of the Boott Cotton Mills Corporation. In *IA*, XIV, 1988.
Cooper, C. C. A whole battalion of stockers: Thomas Blanchard's production line and hand labor at Springfield Armory. In *IA*, XIV, 1988.
Gordon, R. B. Material evidence of the manufacturing methods used in armory practice. In *IA*, XIV, 1988.
Gross, L. F. Building on success; Lowell Mill construction and its results. In *IA*, XIV, 1988.
Larkin, J. and Sloat, C. *The Four Seasons at Old Sturbridge Village: a guidebook*. Sturbridge, Mass.: Old Sturbridge Inc.
Malone, P. M. Little kinks and devices at Springfield Armory, 1892–1918. In *IA*, XIV, 1988.
Raber, M. S. Conservative innovators, military small arms, and industrial history at Springfield Armory, 1794–1918. In *IA*, XIV, 1988.

LOCATIONS
[M] Charles River Museum of Industry, 154 Moody Street, Waltham, MA 02154.
[M] Chatham Railroad Museum, Depot Road, Chatham, MA 02633.
[M] Essex Shipbuilding Museum, Main Street, Essex, MA 01929.
[M] French Cable Station Museum, Cove Road, Orleans, MA 02653.
[S] Iron Work Farm, Acton, MA 01270.
[S] Lowell National Historic Site, PO Box 1098, Lowell, MA 01853.
[I] Lynn Historical Society, 125 Green Street, Lynn, MA 01902.
[M] Middlesex Canal Museum, University of Lowell, Lydon Library, 1 University Avenue, Lowell, MA 01854.
[M] Museum of American Textile History, 800 Massachusetts Avenue, North Andover, MA 01845.
[M] Museum of Transportation, 15 Newton Street, Brookline, MA 02146.
[M] New Bedford Whaling Museum, 18 Jonney Cake Hill, New Bedford, MA 01740.
[S] Old Schwamb Mill, 17 Mill Lane, Arlington, MA 02146.
[M] Old Sturbridge Village, Sturbridge, MA 01566.
[S] Saugus Ironworks, 244 Central Street, Saugus, MA 01906.
[S] Springfield Armory National Historic Site, 1 Armory Square, Springfield, MA 01105.
[I] Waltham Historical Society, 190 Moody Street, Waltham, MA 02154.

DAVID H. SHAYT

mass production The high-volume manufacture of standardized goods. In the broadest sense 'mass production' can be found in the machinery by Sir Marc Brunel (1781–1849) and HENRY MAUDSLAY for the manufacture of ships' blocks, or ARKWRIGHT's spinning works. However, the term appears to have been introduced by a FORD publicist to refer to the design of the Model 'T' as a 'people's car' and to its assembly from INTERCHANGEABLE PARTS on an ASSEMBLY LINE as a means of producing it cheaply. In this sense 'mass production' employed the culmination of nineteenth-century developments in mechanical engineering, MACHINE TOOL design and the corporate organization of production and distribution in the satisfaction of basic needs through the production of universal goods.

Subsequently, the term has been used as a general designation for the design and manufacturing strategy that made motor-cars and complex electromechanical consumer durables accessible to the working class that produced them. There have been attempts to understand mass production as the outgrowth of a distinctive AMERICAN SYSTEM OF MANUFACTURE committed to inflexible standardization, a now outmoded 'Fordism'. However, the capability for mass production results from the maturing of manufacturing practice internationally, and recent developments in management information systems have shown that flexibility and variety need not be incompatible with high quality and high volume.

BIBLIOGRAPHY
General
Chandler, 1977; Gilbert, 1965; Hounshell, 1984.
Specific
Musson, A. E. Joseph Whitworth and the growth of mass production engineering. In *Business History*, XVII, 1975.

TIM PUTNAM

mast   Masts for sailing ships were traditionally of pine, a British statute of 1710 referring to 'white or any other pine trees fit for masts'. The British gained control of superior supplies from the Baltic in the eighteenth century; in the nineteenth century these were replaced by pine from North America. Poles for masts were stored in mast ponds, sometimes held underwater by brick arches. They were shaped on trestles in mast houses, often the ground floors of buildings with MOULD LOFTS or SAIL LOFTS above, like that of 1753–5 which survives at Chatham, Kent (*see* MEDWAY).

BIBLIOGRAPHY
General
Braudel, 1981; Coad, 1983, 1989.

matches   Matches became the principal means of kindling fire in the early nineteenth century. A match is essentially a splinter of wood, dipped in sulphur or paraffin, and coated with a compound, which, when struck, takes fire.

Several forms of match were used in Europe from *c.*1805. The chemical match was coated with a material containing potassium chlorate ($KClO_3$), and took fire when it was dipped in SULPHURIC ACID, which the user carried in a small bottle. The friction or Congreve match, named after the rocket scientist Sir William Congreve (1772–1828), was invented in 1827 by John Walker of Stockton on Tees, England: this had a potassium chlorate coating, and was ignited by being pulled between folds of sandpaper. Phosphorus matches, known in Paris at the beginning of the century, were produced commercially in several European countries *c.*1833, Austria and the south German states becoming important centres of manufacture. The safety match, in which red rather than white PHOSPHORUS was employed, and applied to the striking surface rather than to the coating, was made by the brothers Carl and Frans Lündstrom from 1855, their factory at Jönköping becoming one of the world's largest. The process was introduced into Britain by Bryant & May. In 1898–9 a composition of phosphorus sesquisulphide and potassium chlorate was introduced in France, pro-

ducing a strike-anywhere surface which, unlike red phosphorus coatings, was neither poisonous nor explosive.

Matchmaking in the nineteenth century was highly dangerous. White phosphorus was poisonous, and exposure to it caused a severe disease of the jaw.

Match manufacture became a state monopoly in France from 1872, and in the USA and other countries matches were heavily taxed. There is a museum wih international coverage at BYSTRZYCA KŁODZKA.

BIBLIOGRAPHY
General
Cederschield and von Feilitzen, 1946; Threlfall, 1951.

BARRIE TRINDER

Matosinhos, Douro Litoral, Portugal   *See* OPORTO.

Maudslay, Henry (1771–1831)   One of the leading British mechanical engineers of the early nineteenth century, Maudslay was born at Woolwich and worked at the Royal Arsenal before a period of employment making locks with JOSEPH BRAMAH. Maudslay established his own engineering concern in Oxford Street, London, in 1798, and subsequently made the celebrated BLOCK-making equipment designed by Sir Marc Brunel for Portsmouth Dockyard. He took out patents for a TABLE ENGINE in 1807, and for calico printing in 1805 and 1808. From 1810 he moved to Westminster Bridge Road, where Joshua Field (1787–1863) became his partner, and concentrated on the improvement of the lathe, and of marine engines. Among those who worked for him were James Nasmyth (*see* STEAM HAMMER), RICHARD ROBERTS and Sir JOSEPH WHITWORTH.

See also figure 70.

BIBLIOGRAPHY
General
Gilbert, 1971.

Maurzyce, Łowicz, Warsaw, Poland   The world's first all-welded steel bridge, completed in 1928, across the Słudwia River not far from the Warsaw–Poznań main road. It was designed by Stefan Bryła, celebrated in the inter-war period for many outstanding civil engineering designs, and author of the first published code of practice on the electrical welding of steel structures. The bridge has a span of 27 m (89 ft.) and weighs 59 tonnes. It is built from two framework beams on which are placed a truss supporting a concrete deck, 6.2 m (20 ft.) wide. The bridge is no longer used and is to be a feature of an open-air museum of bridges (*see* figure 84).

BIBLIOGRAPHY
Specific
Most drogowy na rzece Słudwi (Road bridge on the Słudwia River). In *Spotkania z Zabytkami* (Encounters with Historical Monuments), VI, 1981.

Mayhew, Henry (1812–87)   A pioneer of sociological

Figure 84   The first all-welded steel bridge; crossing the Słudwia River at Maurzyce, it was designed by Stefan Bryła and completed in 1928.

investigation, whose published works on mid-nineteenth-century London are a prime source for industrial history. He provides information on the traditional divisions of labour, and on the impact of new technologies like mechanical sawmills and treadmills in prisons, and he describes industrial buildings in some detail. His best work and that of his collaborators appeared in the *Morning Chronicle* in 1849–50. He saw interviewees in their own homes, and had a profound understanding of the conditions of the poor. Much of the latter part of his life was spent in Germany.

BIBLIOGRAPHY
General
Mayhew, 1850, 1861–2; Mayhew and Binny, 1862; Razzell and Wainwright, 1973.
Specific
Bédarida, F. Londres au milieu du XIXe siècle: une analyse de structure sociale. In *Annales*, 1968.

meat   A dominant part of the European diet in the Middle Ages, the consumption of meat fell between 1550 and 1850, particularly in the Mediterranean region, although it rose in eighteenth-century England. From the mid-nineteenth century the application of scientific agriculture and the extension of pastoral farming in America and Australasia brought a renewed growth in meat eating.

Meat was traditionally preserved by salting. Considerable quantities of salted meat were exported from countries like Ireland to southern Europe. Parts of animals other than the flesh had many industrial applications (*see* DOWN; FEATHERS; HAIR; HORN; LEATHER; MARGARINE; TALLOW).

Traditionally meat was prepared by BUTCHERS, but the nature of the meat trade was transformed in the USA from the 1870s. Gustavus Franklin Swift (1839–1903), a butcher from New England who moved to Chicago in 1875, began to convey dressed carcasses to the eastern seaboard in refrigerated railway wagons. An effective design for these was perfected in 1881, which enabled carcasses hung on rails in the wagons to be conveyed straight along connecting rails into cold stores. The pioneer of disassembly-line techniques for dressing hog carcasses was Philip Danforth Armour (1832–1901) who established a business in Chicago in 1875. Swift, Armour and traders like Nelson Morris (1838–1907) built packing factories in the Chicago stockyards and elsewhere in the USA, acquired ranches in the West, and developed export trades to Europe and Asia.

See also ABATTOIR; CANDLE; CHANDLER; PET FOODS; SAUSAGE; SLAUGHTERHOUSE.

BIBLIOGRAPHY
General
Braudel, 1981; Critchell and Raymond, 1912; Gerrard, 1909; Harrison, 1963; Swift, 1927.
Specific
Hill, H. C. The development of Chicago as a center of the meat-packing industry. In *Mississippi Valley Historical Review*, 1923.

BARRIE TRINDER

mechanical engineering   The word 'mechanical' has a complex derivation; it was at one time applied to people, and meant 'of a low social class'. The term 'mechanical engineering', applying to that branch of engineering concerned with the making and operation of machines, came into use in the early nineteenth century, a period when many of the pioneers of the science in Britain were connected with the works of HENRY MAUDSLAY in London, and when it was developing in the USA through the work of such pioneers as ELI WHITNEY. In Britain the Institution of Mechanical Engineers was constituted in 1847, its first president being GEORGE STEPHENSON. Several specialist professional organizations subsequently diverged from it, although in other countries engineers retained unified professional organizations.

For techniques relating to mechanical engineering, *see* AMERICAN SYSTEM OF MANUFACTURE; ASSEMBLY LINE; INTERCHANGEABLE PARTS; MACHINE TOOLS; MASS PRODUCTION; PUMP; RIVET; TOYMAKING; VALVE.

For the products of mechanical engineering, *see* AIR-CRAFT FACTORY; ARMAMENTS; BICYCLE; BUSINESS MACHINES; CLOCK; LOCOMOTIVE AND CARRIAGE WORKS; MACHINE TOOLS; MINT; MOTORCAR FACTORY; PUMP; SEWING MACHINE; SHIPYARD; TOYMAKING; TEXTILE MACHINERY.

For mechanical engineers, *see* ARMSTRONG, SIR W. G.; BALL, E. B.; BRAMAH, J.; BRINDLEY, J.; BROWN, J. R.; BRUNTON, W.; CEGIELSKI, H.; CHEREPANOV, E. A. AND M. E.; CORLISS, G. H.; DONKIN, B.; EDISON, T.; FAIRBAIRN, SIR W.; FORD, H.; FROLOV, K. D. AND P. K.; GAKKEL', Y.; GÖLSDORF, K.; HESLOP, A.; HORNBLOWER, J.; MAUDSLAY, H.; MORRIS, W. R.; MURDOCK, W.; NEWCOMEN, T.; OTIS, E. G.; PARSONS, SIR C. A.; PELTON, L. A.; POLZUNOV, I.; ROBERTS, R.; ROE, SIR E. A. V.; ROLT, L. T. C.; SADLER, J.; SAVERY, T.; SIEMENS, C. W.; SPRAGUE, F. J.; STEPHENSON, G.; STEPHENSON, R.; SYMINGTON, W.; TAYLOR, F. W.; TREVITHICK, R.; VLAICU, A.; VUIA, T.; WAILES, R.; WATT, J.; WHITNEY, E.; WILKINSON, J.; WILLANS, P.

BIBLIOGRAPHY
General
Armytage, 1961; Ball, 1987; Buchanan, 1989; Calvert, 1967; Ludwig, 1981; Parsons, 1947.
Specific
Buchanan, R. A. Institutional proliferation in the British engineering profession. In *EcHR*, XXXVIII, 1985.

BARRIE TRINDER

Mecklenburg, Germany   Along the Baltic coast of Germany, Mecklenburg, had little industry apart from the processing of timber, some harvested locally, some imported. Other industrial activities were mostly associated with agriculture: brickworks, sugar-beet refineries, flourmills. In the days of sail there was an import and export trade on the coast, based on the ports of Rostock/Warnemünde and Wismar. After 1945 the ROSTOCK region developed a considerable shipbuilding industry, totalling 90 per cent of shipbuilding capacity in the DDR, and expanded into mechanical engineering and motorcar manufacture. Fishing and fish processing are natural companions of the shipbuilding industry, and 75 per cent of all East German canned fish comes from Sassnitz and Marienehe.

BIBLIOGRAPHY
General
Berger, 1980; Schmidt and Theile, 1989; Wagenbreth and Wächtler, 1983.

Medway, Kent, England   The lower Medway Valley around Chatham and Rochester, where the river is bridged by the London–Dover road, is one of the most heavily industrialized areas of southern England. From *c.*1820 bricks were supplied by barge to London, an industry which reached its peak in the third quarter of the nineteenth century. From *c.*1850 the Medway Valley became the most important area in Britain for the production of Portland Cement. Medway also became an engineering centre, through the firm of Thomas Aveling, a repairer of farm machinery in Rochester from *c.*1850, who began making agricultural steam engines in Strood *c.*1861; Aveling took Richard Porter into partnership in 1862, and became 'the father of the traction engine' by making the portable engine self-propelling. By 1900 about 1000 were employed at Aveling & Porter's Invicta works. Short Brothers moved from London to make Wright aircraft in Rochester in 1909, produced the first successful British seaplane in 1912, and built flying boats in the late 1930s.

The ex-Royal Navy dockyard at Chatham is one of the most important historic industrial sites in Britain, the upstream part comprising a complete shipyard of the age of sail. The main gate dates from 1719 with a COADE STONE hatchment bearing the arms of George III. Buildings within the high boundary walls include a 350 m (1150 ft.) ropery of 1786, two restored eighteenth-century timber-seasoning sheds, a fully equipped smithy, a SAWMILL of 1811–14 by Marc Brunel (1769–1849), and several nineteenth-century covered SLIPS. The MOULD LOFT above the mast house in a building of 1753 provides a clear space 37 m × 17 m (120 ft. × 56 ft.), where cross-sections of warships were drawn out full size, so that templates could be formed for shipwrights. The SAIL LOFT of the 1720s is a long three-storey building which served as a canvas store and sail workshop. The dockyard closed in 1984 and is conserved by a trust.

Sheerness naval dockyard, 19 km (12 mi.) E. at the mouth of the Medway, was closed in 1960 but the iron-framed boat store designed by Col. C. T. Green in 1858–60 still stands.

The 3642 m (3983 yd.) Strood Tunnel was built for the Thames & Medway Canal in 1824 and converted to railway use in 1844.

The Blue Circle Heritage Centre at Northfleet, 14 km (9 mi.) W. has sections on cooperage and the paper sacks used for cement, as well as a reconstruction of a nineteenth-century cement works laboratory. Adjacent is a cement kiln of the 1840s, built by William Aspin, son of the patentee of Portland Cement.

BIBLIOGRAPHY
General
Coad, 1983; Preston, 1977.

LOCATIONS
[M] Blue Circle Heritage Centre, The Creek, Northfleet, Kent DA11 9AS.
[M] Chatham Historic Dockyard Trust, The Old Pay Office, Church Lane, Chatham Historic Dockyard, Chatham ME4 4TQ.

BARRIE TRINDER

Medzev, East Slovakia, Czechoslovakia   A settlement associated with ironworking since the thirteenth century, when the king of Hungary invited Flemish, Dutch,

Walloon and German settlers because of their skills in ironworking. The people of the town still speak a dialect derived from these languages. Two forges with water-powered hammers are preserved in Medzev. One is owned and maintained by the technical museum at Košice; the other still functions as part of a private business. The museum's mill is water-powered and the building and its equipment are constructed entirely of wood. Demonstrations are given during the summer. The privately-run mill uses an old boiler as a water reservoir and the equipment is largely of iron. Demonstrations are given all year round.

Melbourne, Victoria, Australia The state capital, renowned for its architecture and for being the only Australian capital city to have retained its electric tramways. First settled illegally in 1834 on the banks of the Yarra, the town was formally laid out in 1837 by Robert Hoddle to Governor Darling's regulations (SEE AUSTRALIA), with wide main streets on a grid pattern. Gold-rush prosperity and a booming population in the second half of the nineteenth century resulted in major buildings of great quality. Of the 8 ha (20 ac.) of buildings constructed for the Melbourne International Exhibition of 1880, only the main hall with its Florentine dome remains.

Notable industrial buildings include a 50 m (165 ft.) campanile-style SHOT TOWER of 1889–90, with much of its equipment intact. The largest of the brick warehouse complexes which served the river trade was the five-storey Goldsbrough Mort Buildings, by John Gill, of 1862. Major industrial plants include the Carlton Brewery, established in 1864, and the Swallow & Ariel Steam Biscuit Manufactory of 1858, which made ships' biscuits. Melbourne is the chief motor-engineering centre in Australia, with four motorcar factories. At Williamstown stand a TIME-BALL STATION and a lighthouse of 1852, one of the earliest in the state. In north Melbourne stands one of several cable tramway engine houses built in 1889–90 and operated until 1935. The first steam railway in Australia was inaugurated in 1854 between Melbourne and Sandridge, and the domes and arches of Flinders Street Station, built in 1909, remain one of Melbourne's most distinctive architectural features. The locomotive and carriage works of Victorian Railways at Newport was built during the railway boom of 1886–8, with buildings of a high standard. It remains in operation. At Belgrave, 32 km (20 mi.) E. of the centre, the preserved 2 ft. 6 in. (0.76 m) gauge railway to Emerald is the only survivor of many of that gauge built to open up sparsely populated parts of Victoria in the 1890s.

The Living Museum of the West, an écomusée in the Maribyrnong valley west of Melbourne provides guidance to the remains of a meat cannery of 1867, and the Humes plant for the manufacture of centrifugally-spun concrete pipes, which operated between 1911 and 1979.

BIBLIOGRAPHY
General
Briggs, 1963; Grant and Serle, 1957; Heritage of Australia, 1981; Keating, 1970; McCarty and Schedvin, 1978; Newnham, 1956; Pike, 1957; Robertson, 1960; Turner, 1904.

LOCATIONS
[M] The Living Museum of the West, 42–4 Ferguson Street, Williamstown 3016.
[M] National Museum of Victoria, 328 Swanston Street, Melbourne 3000.
[M] Railway Museum, Champion Road, North Williamstown, Melbourne 3000.
[M] Science Museum of Victoria, 304–28 Swanston Street, Melbourne 3000.

KATE CLARK

Meldorf, Schleswig-Holstein, Germany The process of industrialization in a rural area, which involved the transition from crafts to small-scale manufactures, can be traced very clearly in the Local History and Agricultural Museum at Meldorf, 90 km (56 mi.) NW of Hamburg, which includes several complete shops and workshops. A similar range of fully-equipped craft workshops intended for the needs of the rural population may be found in the museum at Brome, in the Gifhorn district, 28 km (17 mi.) N. of Brunswick.

LOCATIONS
[M] Dithmarscher Landesmuseum und Landwirtschaftmuseum (Local History and Agricultural Museum), Bütjestrasse 4, 2223 Meldorf.
[M] Local History Museum, Junkerende, 3127 Brome.

Menai Bridges, Menai Bridge, Anglesey, Gwynedd, Wales The Menai Straits, 3 km (2 mi.) W. of Bangor, which separate the Isle of Anglesey from North Wales, are crossed by two engineering masterpieces on the key route to Ireland. A wide crossing was needed, with headroom for shipping. The Menai Bridge, built by THOMAS TELFORD in 1826 as part of the Holyhead Road, was the first successful major suspension bridge. It has a span of 178 m (579 ft.) with a 30 m (100 ft.) clearance above the water. The deck, a timber platform 9 m (30 ft.) wide, was suspended from flat iron chains by wrought-iron rods. The bridge was rebuilt in steel in 1939–40. The Britannia Bridge, by ROBERT STEPHENSON, was built in 1850 for the Chester & Holyhead Railway. It was of revolutionary construction: the two main spans of 141 m (459 ft.) and two approach spans of 70 m (230 ft.) were enclosed in girders fabricated from riveted wrought-iron plates in which trains ran. Thereafter plate girders were used widely. The bridge was rebuilt after a fire in 1970. (*See* figure 85.)

Similar but smaller bridges built contemporaneously by the same engineers survive as more intact monuments at Conwy, Gwynedd, 22 km (14 mi.) E. of Bangor.

BIBLIOGRAPHY
General
Morgan, 1971; Pannell, 1967.

Meppel, Drente, The Netherlands The most important town in the province in the nineteenth century, and a waterway centre since the fifteenth century, which expanded from the 1850s when peat deposits to the north and south-east were developed. Peat was shipped through Meppel, which was served by several canals, among them

Figure 85 The construction of the tubes for the Britannia Bridge across the Menai Straits (hand-coloured tinted lithograph by S. Russell, published in 1848)
Elton Collection: Ironbridge Gorge Museum

the Drentse Hoofdvaart of the 1760s. Activities related to peat included limekilns in Meppel and near Diever, 20 km (13 mi.) N. Several old-established printing companies founded a museum in the town; and the Scania-Vabis Museum owns a collection of commercial vehicles, including a steam lorry. Near the railway station, itself of 1868, is a pharmaceutical factory whose original buildings date from *c.* 1900.

LOCATIONS
[M] Grafisch Museum Drente (Drente Printing Museum), Kleine Oever 11, Meppel.
[M] Scania-Vabis Museum, Industrieweg 20, Meppel.

mercury (Hg) An elemental metal, liquid at room temperature, also called quicksilver. Metallic mercury is used in scientific instruments, in electrolytic processes, and in the recovery of GOLD from earth and gravel. There are many uses for mercuric compounds. Mercury is manufactured from the mineral cinnabar, a red sulphide of mercury (HgS), found in Italy, Spain, YUGOSLAVIA, California and elsewhere.

See also CASTNER-KELLNER CELL.

BIBLIOGRAPHY
General
Jones, 1950.

Merthyr Tydfil, Mid Glamorgan, Wales A town likened in 1844 to 'the fiery city of Pluto' on account of the wondrous noise and fiery skies from its furnaces and mills. It was probably the largest ironmaking town in the world, with an output a quarter that of the USA. Sweeping adoption of coal as fuel permitted the conglomeration of numerous furnaces and forges, transforming it from a village in the 1750s to the largest town in Wales by 1801. As the first town to grow up from the iron industry, its character presaged others across the world.

Merthyr's Dowlais Ironworks, established in 1759, was probably the first to use coke in South Wales. The other great works were all established by English immigrants in the next thirty years: Plymouth in 1763, Cyfarthfa in 1765, and Penydarren in 1782. Growth was largely concentrated within these following the adoption by RICHARD CRAWSHAY at Cyfarthfa *c.*1786 of Henry Cort's processes of rolling iron sections and of puddling (soon known as 'the Welsh Method'). Expansion was assisted by connection to Cardiff by canal in 1794 and by railway in 1841. By 1807 there were seventeen furnaces. By 1840 the largest of the works, Dowlais, had eighteen furnaces and employed 10 000 people.

Merthyr's death knell was sounded in 1856 by BESSEMER steelmaking. Dowlais was one of the first companies to licence the Bessemer process, only to find that it did not work satisfactorily with local ores. Dowlais and Cyfarthfa became steelworks, but could not compete with plants where imported ores were cheaply available; Dowlais itself began a works at CARDIFF in 1888. When SIDNEY GILCHRIST THOMAS made possible the use of phosphoric ores in 1879, Merthyr's decline was well under way, and local ores were depleted.

The character of Merthyr in the Industrial Revolution leaves many remnants, despite extensive clearance. The town retains an incoherent pattern between the separate ironworks' communities. The Crawshays, who owned the town, eschewed planning, permitting building wherever it would not obstruct ironmaking. Numerous streets simply followed tramroads; and vast slag heaps, like that at Dowlais, impeded development. Most early housing, built as terraces using the sandstone dug with the iron ore, has been cleared, but one typical late-eighteenth-century Cyfarthfa works terrace survives at Chapel Row. Overlooking it is the Crawshay residence, Cyfarthfa Castle, built in 1825. A few public buildings provided by the ironmasters remain: notably an octagonal chapel of 1788, and the library, school and hall erected at Dowlais in the 1840s to 1860s.

Little remains of the ironworks: the furnace bank at Cyfarthfa, and the characteristically polychromatic sandstone engine house and furnace arches at Ynysfach works, a Cyfarthfa subsidiary built in 1801. At Dowlais the Palladian stables built in 1820 and the vast brick blowing engine house have found new uses. Next to Cyfarthfa stands an iron bridge, Pont-y-Cafnau, built in 1793 by works engineer Watkin George for a tramroad and water-power leat: it is the earliest known iron railway bridge or aqueduct. Several tramroads, including the PENYDARREN, can be traced, and railways that crossed the valleys in the 1860s have left several graceful viaducts.

BIBLIOGRAPHY
General
Davies, 1933; Lowe, 1977; Rees, 1969, 1975; Riden, 1987.
Specific
Hague, D. and Hughes, S. Pont-y-Cafnau: the first iron railway bridge and aqueduct? In *Bulletin of the Association for Industrial Archaeology*, IX(4) 1982, 3–4.

LOCATIONS
[M] Cyfarthfa Castle Museum, Cyfarthfa Park, Merthyr Tydfil, Mid Glamorgan.
[M] Ynysfach Ironworks Interpretation Centre, Merthyr Tydfil, Mid Glamorgan.

PETER WAKELIN

Mértola, Baixo Alentejo, Portugal   A town of Roman origin, 180 km (110 mi.) SE of Lisbon, with manganese, copper and lead mines. The São Domingos mine was worked for copper pyrites during 1864–1965, and remaining buildings include miners' dwellings, workshops, an electric power station and two dams. Ore was transported by a private 18 km (11 mi.) railway of 1863, originally horse-operated, which ran to the port of Pomarão on the Guadiana river. The former metallurgical centre of Achada do Gamo was connected to the mine by a 3 km (2 mi.) branch railway. The partially submerged remains of water mills can be seen in the Guadiana river.

methanal (formaldehyde, HCHO)   A gas, obtained formerly from coal tar, but now synthetically from METHANOL. It is important in the manufacture of dyestuffs, pharmaceuticals, plastics and resins, and is a powerful disinfectant, hence its use in solution, as 'formalin', in preserving organic materials.

BIBLIOGRAPHY
General
Morgan and Pratt, 1938.

methane (CH_4)   A highly flammable gas, and the main component of NATURAL GAS. Methane reacts with steam to form 'synthesis gas', the basis for making METHANOL, carbon dioxide and hydrogen which can be used in making AMMONIA.

Methane occurs commonly in coal mines, where it is known as 'fire damp' (*see* MINING).

BIBLIOGRAPHY
General
BP, 1958.

methanol (methyl alcohol, CH_3OH)   An alcohol, first made by heating wood in retorts, hence its other names, 'wood spirit' and 'wood alcohol'. It was synthesized in Germany by I. G. Farbenindustrie in 1924, by combining hydrogen and carbon monoxide from water gas in the presence of a zinc or copper catalyst. It has also been obtained from natural gas and steam, using a nickel catalyst. Methanol is important as a solvent, in anti-freeze, in motor fuels, and as a source of METHANAL. Naturally-occurring methanol is called wood naphtha.

BIBLIOGRAPHY
General
Morgan and Pratt, 1938; Norman and Waddington, 1977.

methyl alcohol   *See* METHANOL.

methyl benzene (toluene, $C_6H_5CH_3$)   An aromatic hydrocarbon, the source of saccharin and TNT. It is extracted from NAPHTHA, produced from coal tar, or during the CRACKING of PETROLEUM.

BIBLIOGRAPHY
General
Morgan and Pratt, 1938.

metro   An urban passenger railway, often underground. The term originated in PARIS and was applied in BELGRADE, MOSCOW, WASHINGTON DC and elsewhere.

Mettlach, Saarland, Germany   The Benedictine abbey of Mettlach, 42 km (26 mi.) NW of Saarbrücken, founded in 690 for the nobility of the diocese of Trier, stands on the banks of the Saar some distance from the coal and iron works of the region. The abbey was dissolved after being looted by French troops in 1794. Its Baroque buildings had been constructed during the last years of its prosperity in 1738–80. The abbey was acquired in 1809 by Johann Franz Boch-Buschmann, who converted it into an earthenware factory; it still accommodates some production processes, the display areas, and the central offices of the firm of Villeroy & Boch. After 1811 the earthenware made at Mettlach was fired entirely in coal-burning furnaces. A wide range of architectural ceramics was manufactured there from the mid-nineteenth century. Although the buildings were adapted for manufacturing purposes, and extensions of many kinds were necessary, the abbey has been largely preserved and is an outstanding example of adaptive reuse, something which could scarcely have been foreseen in 1794.

BIBLIOGRAPHY
Specific
100 Jahre Mosaikfabrik Mettlach (100 years of mosaic manufacture at Mettlach). Mettlach: Villeroy & Boch, 1969.

NORBERT MENDGEN

Meyer's *Lexicon*   Meyer's *Konversations-Lexikon* is the standard dictionary of the German language, produced by the Bibliographisches Institut, which was established in 1826, and published in Leipzig and Vienna from 1840. The sixth edition, published between 1902 and 1909, is notable for its informative definitions of technical terms and for its high-quality illustrations of industrial processes.

AXEL FÖHL

mica A semi-transparent, readily-cleaved material, which occurs in sheet-like 'books' in quartzite formations, offering a variety of commercial applications. India, Argentina, Canada, Madagascar, and South Dakota in the USA have been the principal sources of the several mica species, distinguished by their colours and inclusions. As a see-through, heat-resistant material with decorative characteristics and poor electrical conductivity, micas have been used as stove windows and in furnace peep-holes ('Muscovy glass'); as packing for boilers and steam piping; and as insulation in electrical equipment. Mica has been supplemented from the 1930s by such substitutes as Formica ('for mica'). Mica is also used, in a pulverized form, as glitter in artists' paper and paints.

BIBLIOGRAPHY
General
Cirkel, 1912.

Micheldorf, Upper Austria, Austria A centre of scythe manufacture since the sixteenth century, 46 km (27 mi.) S. of Linz. Sensensmeide Am Gries (Gries scythe-making forge), dating in its present form from *c*.1830, opened as a museum in 1975, and is the best centre in Austria for studying the craft.

Michigan, United States of America Mining, inland navigation and the manufacture of vehicles characterize the industrial heritage of this dismembered state, the only mainland state to be split into separate major land masses. Michigan is draped by the Great Lakes Superior, Michigan and Huron, the centrelines of Superior and Huron forming an undulating boundary with Canada.

In the 1840s massive iron and copper ore deposits in Michigan's remote Keweenaw Peninsula began to dominate American sources and met much of the world's needs, being shipped out via the Lakes to the Atlantic. Deep shaft and surface mines grew across and beneath the land, and several generations of headstocks and various support structures remain in the now reforested 'UP' (Upper Peninsula), still home to a hardy independent breed of Michigander, with recognizable patterns of folk expression and culture.

The UP's distinctiveness is strengthened by some gigantic steel constructions, unique in the nation. The Quincy Mine Hoist of 1920 hauled ten-ton loads of copper ore from great depths, and sits today in its winding house at Hancock, Mich., attended by its two, now inactive, Corliss cross-compound steam engines, the hoist itself featuring a cylindro-conical winding drum 0.9 m (30 ft.) in diameter. Also retired, the Redridge Steel Dam of 1901 is a 307 m (1006 ft.) wide multiple-arch structure, using steel plates and girders atop a concrete foundation which once impounded water to service the UP's ore-stamping mills.

While the Iron Mountain Iron Mine Museum in Vulcan and the new Michigan Iron Industry Museum at Carp River cope with Michigan's rich ironworking history, the Lake Michigan Maritime Museum addresses the full range of navigational themes, including wrecks, raised by two centuries of industrial activity on and near some of the world's largest lakes.

On the outskirts of Detroit stands one of the nation's pre-eminent industrial museums, the Henry Ford Museum and the Edison Institute at Dearborn. Not surprisingly, the museum began as a function of the automobile industry in and around Detroit, when Henry Ford sought to preserve in physical forms the world the auto was leaving behind. The accumulations of everyday nineteenth-century and early-twentieth-century artefacts amassed for the museum remain its core, including many tonnes of industrial machinery. New approaches to history and to museums are severely modifying the nostalgic approach Ford took to his museum, using the material culture of an industrializing society to reveal the good but the bad and the ugly as well.

Michigan was the nursery of the twentieth-century automobile plant, the location of the most important works of ALBERT KAHN, who pioneered the techniques of concrete construction (*see* figure 91) which culminated in the mammoth-scale plants of World War II, including Ford's Willow Run bomber plant of 1941–3, on a 28 ha (70 ac.) site near Ypsilanti, and the Chrysler tank arsenal of 1941 in Detroit. The automobile industry remains one of Detroit's principal sources of employment. Along side roads around the towns of Dearborn, Highland Park and Hamtramck may be seen altered or decrepit remains of the long, heavily-windowed production and assembly plants of the 1920s and 30s that put Detroit on the map as 'Motor City' and provide crucial archaeological evidence for the evolution of the twentieth-century factory. Echoing the omnipotence of the auto industry in the area is the stupefying mural series of the 1930s by Diego Rivera (1886–1957) at the Detroit Institute of Arts, portraying the systems of production and dehumanizing labour brought on by the motorcar.

The Detroit Windsor Tunnel of 1931 beneath the Detroit River connecting the city with Canada used all three of the principal subaqueous tunnelling methods then available: cut-and-cover, compressed air and shield, and sunken tube. It also pioneered the use of arc welding in tunnel construction. A sweeping set of concrete helical entry ramps add a flourish to the Detroit approach.

Over the same river the Ambassador Bridge of 1929, an impressive long-span suspension bridge, was for a brief period the world's longest, with a clear span of 564 m (1850 ft.).

Michigan's once robust logging and lumber industries are captured in the survival of White's Covered Bridge at Smyrna, a structure of 1867 heavy with beams and posts of native timber through its 36 m (119 ft.) length: the bridge is open today only to pedestrians.

BIBLIOGRAPHY
General
Ferry, 1968, 1970; Hyde, 1978, 1986; Nelson, 1939; Reynolds, 1982.

LOCATIONS
[S] Coppertown USA, 101 Red Jacket Road, Calumet, MI 49913.
[I] Detroit Institute of Arts, 5200 Woodward Avenue, Detroit, MI 48202.
[M] Henry Ford Museum, 20900 Oakwood Boulevard, Dearborn, MI 48121.
[M] Iron County Museum, Museum Lane, Caspian, MI 49915.
[M] Iron Mountain Iron Mine Museum, US Highway 2, Vulcan, MI 49801.
[M] Lake Michigan Maritime Museum, Dyckman at Bridge, South Haven, MI 49090.
[M] Michigan Iron Industry Museum, Carp River, MI.
[M] Michigan Transit Museum, 200 Grand Street, Mt. Clemens, MI 48043.

DAVID H. SHAYT

Midleton, Cork, Ireland   The modern distilling complex at Midleton, 15 km (9 mi.) E. of Cork, was commissioned in 1975, and is the only commercial distillery in Ireland apart from that at Bushmills (*see* PORTRUSH). Adjacent to it the entire plant of an earlier distillery is preserved as a monument by Irish Distillers Ltd. The complex originated with a building intended to be a woollen mill, constructed *c*.1796, but never used for manufacturing textiles (*see* figure 86). It became the nucleus of a distillery in 1825, numerous large buildings – chiefly granaries, maltings, and bonded warehouses – being added in the following century. The internal structure of the main mill has been destroyed, but the exterior remains, a four-storey main block of nineteen bays, 48 m (150 ft.) long, with projecting wings at each end, the space between them having been filled with other buildings. The complex includes a water wheel, 5 m (16 ft.) wide and 6 m (19 ft.) in diameter, a beam engine in the Classical style, and a vast copper structure which is supposedly the world's largest pot still.

BIBLIOGRAPHY
Specific
Trinder, B. Midleton Distillery, County Cork: Observations on the archaeological implications of proposed developments. Telford: Ironbridge Institute, 1990.
LOCATION
[S] Irish Distillers Ltd, Midleton Distillery, County Cork.

BARRIE TRINDER

Mies van der Rohe, Ludwig (1886–1969)   One of the most influential of twentieth-century architects and designers, Mies was born in Aachen, was apprenticed to a furniture designer in Berlin in 1905, worked in the office of PETER BEHRENS from 1909, and established his own architectural practice in 1912. His early work was influenced by K. F. SCHINKEL, but by the 1920s he was proposing glass skyscrapers and was an acknowledged modernist. He designed the German pavilion at the Barcelona exhibition of 1929 and directed the BAUHAUS in 1930–3, after which he was forced into exile. He directed the architecture school at the Illinois Institute of Tech-

nology for twenty years from 1938. His works included apartments on Lake Shore Drive, Chicago, in 1948–51, the Seagram Building, New York, in 1954–8, and office buildings in Montreal and Toronto.

BIBLIOGRAPHY
General
Blake, 1960.

Mikulov, South Moravia, Czechoslovakia   The centre of a wine-producing region. Winemaking is featured in the local museum, and small 'colonies' of wine cellars have been restored and remain in use.

LOCATION
[M] Regional Museum, Zamek, Mikulov.

Milan (Milano), Lombardy, Italy   Milan is the industrial and commercial capital of Italy and the focus of Lombardy's prosperity. Its rapid growth after the Risorgimento (*see* ITALY) produced distinctive architecture, philanthropic housing, and a series of major factories. At the outbreak of World War II the principal engineering firms were Alfa Romeo and Eduardo, making motor vehicles and aircraft; Caproni, producing aircraft; and Osram, the light-bulb manufacturers. The rubber industry was dominated by Pirelli, with 12 000 employees.

Two districts within the city provide a concise insight into Milan's industrial development, and the growth of its public utilities and working-class housing. Walking west from Stazione Centrale, in Via De Castillia, one of the works of Italiano Brown Boveri is used for making electric motors, turbines and other electrical equipment. The factory of *c*.1900 is a long range with high windows lighting two storeys. Opposite, Via De Castillia 26 includes the four-square offices of the goods depot built by 1906 for the Milan–Monza railway. The original station of this, the first line into Milan, is in Viale Monte Grappa 12 and 12a, designed in the form of a palazzo by Giuseppe Sarti, with the architect Luigi Broggi, and built in 1840. Almost opposite, at Viale Monte Grappa 8, is the communal kitchen for the poor, built in 1883, a focus of Milanese philanthropy, and built in the Lombardic style popular in the years after unification. Slightly to the south, in Via Moscova, Via Montebello and Via San Marco, is the first major model housing project in Milan, three ranges of four and five storeys, built in 1862–8 and providing four hundred apartments with workshops on the ground floors. Further west at Via Bramante 42, the Officina Elettrica is a power station built in 1896, largely to supply the electric tram system inaugurated the following year. At Via Procaccini 4, the design of the office block of the Società Italiana Carminati-Toselli, dating from 1904–5, reflects the firm's production of rolling stock. Their architects created a façade incorporating bogies, couplings, and, at the end of the elevation, buffers.

South of the city centre industry used the canal system both for water supply and for transport. The papermill of Ambrogio Binda is located by the Pavia Canal at Alzaia Naviglio Pavese 160. Having been established in 1857, the works had developed by 1869 into a colony of a

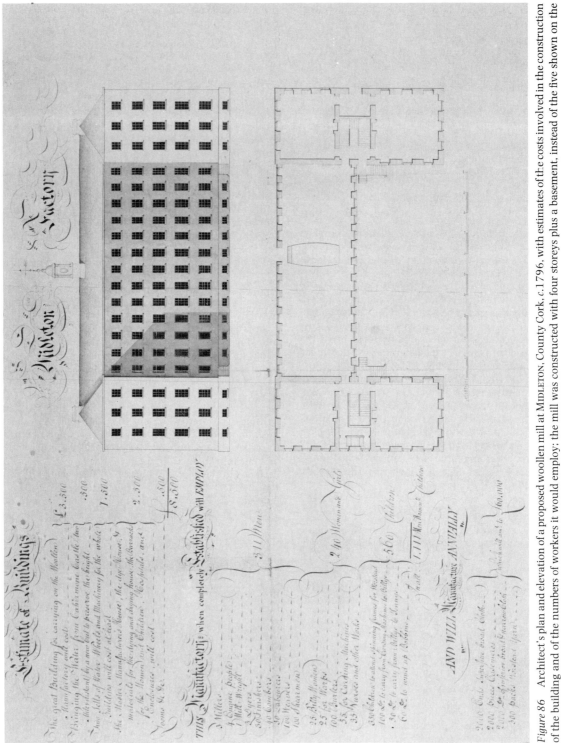

Figure 86 Architect's plan and elevation of a proposed woollen mill at MIDLETON, County Cork. *c*.1796, with estimates of the costs involved in the construction of the building and of the numbers of workers it would employ: the mill was constructed with four storeys plus a basement, instead of the five shown on the elevation. It was never used for the production of textiles. but served as a distillery from 1825 until 1975. Irish Distillers Ltd

thousand people, with its own shops, school and church. Much was destroyed in a fire of 1871, but one of the original housing blocks survives, a simple, rendered three-storey structure, together with evidence of the use of water wheels, turbines and steam power. On the east bank of the Pavia Canal, 1 km ($\frac{1}{2}$ mi.) N. at Via de Sanctis 10, is the Milan warehouse of the Certosa Mill, c.1925. A large gantry spans the road to an opening in the Renaissance façade, which is an interpretation in miniature of the front of the Stazione Centrale.

At the junction of Via Lincoln and Via Franklin, east of the city centre, is a secluded area of philanthropic housing with small gardens, dating from 1883. The small houses are enclosed by long ranges of apartment blocks.

The Galleria Vittorio Emanuele II, leading from the Piazza del Duomo, is the ultimate amongst nineteenth-century arcades, and a powerful symbol of Italian unification. The design by Giuseppe Mengoni of Bologna was adopted after a competition in 1860. It became an international project, with funding from an English consortium, the City of Milan Improvement Company; the dome was designed by a French engineer, and manufactured by Henry Joret of Paris. It opened in 1867, its triumphal arch to the Piazza del Duomo being completed later. Its ground plan takes the form of a Latin cross. It is seven storeys high, with a dome of the same diameter as that of St Peter's, Rome. Mengoni used extensive allegorical decoration, including frescos illustrative of science, art, industry and agriculture, and twenty-four statues of famous Italians.

The Stazione Centrale is one of Europe's largest termini and the last to be built with a Victorian-style train shed, made of steel in the form of five arches, the largest with a span of 73 m (240 ft.). Work to designs by Ulisse Stacchini began in 1906, resumed after the war in 1923, and was finished in 1931. The last phase included the massive PORTE-COCHÈRE, the concourse and the flights of stairs. The concourse is lined with marble and tile panels and is awesomely monumental.

Milan has been the focus for the study of Italian industrial archaeology since the 1970s, but its museum interpretation is highly traditional. The Leonardo da Vinci Museum, in a restored convent, presents important objects as dusty relics. There are galleries on clocks, computers, electricity, and textile machinery; a reconstruction of a foundry of the period after 1600; and extensive displays of prime movers including turbines. The large railway gallery has a replica of the first locomotive to run in Italy, the *Bayard*, a 2–2–2 supplied by Longridge & Co. of Newcastle-upon-Tyne for the line in the Bay of Naples. A 4–6–2 of 1911 and a 2–8–2 of 1923–4, both by Breda of Milan, demonstrate such characteristics of Italian railway technology as air brakes and Caprotti valve gear. There is also a Bo-Bo electric locomotive built in Budapest in 1900 for the Valtellina line. A modern gallery has displays of boats and aircraft.

BIBLIOGRAPHY
General
Binney *et al.*, 1984; Mioni *et al.*, 1981–3; Negri *et al.*, 1983; Selvafolta *et al.*, 1983.

Specific
Negri, A. and Selvafolta, O. Archeologia industriale a Milano (Industrial archaeology in Milan). In *Archeologia Industriale*, I, 1983.
Selvafolta, O. La casa operaia a Milano (Masterpiece in Milan). In *Parametro* (Descriptions), XI, 1980.
Selvafolta, O. La Galleria Vittorio Emanuele II di Milano (The Victor Emmanuel II Gallery in Milan). In *Costuire in Lombardia-Aspetti e Problemi di Storia Edilizia* (Building in Lombardia-Aspetti and Problems in Building History), 1983.
Selvafolta, O. I progetti e la realizzazione della stazione centrale di Milano (The birth of the concept and the realization of the central station in Milan). In *Construire in Lombardia – Infrastrutture Territoriali* (Building in Lombardy – the Local Infrastructure), 1984.

LOCATION
[M] Leonardo da Vinci Museum of Science and Technology, Via San Vittore 21, Milan.

MICHAEL STRATTON

mild steel *See* STEEL.

milepost A sign indicating distance along a road, most commonly a carved stone (hence 'milestone', the commoner English term) but by the nineteenth century often of cast iron. Most European main roads were marked with mileposts by 1800, although the length of a mile varied from country to country. In Rhenish Prussia the mile (4.66 English mi. or 7.5 km) was divided into one hundred parts marked by small roadside stones. Parnell thought mileposts necessary for timekeeping by coach drivers, for measuring by surveyors, and for the convenience of travellers. Most open-air museums have examples, and many survive *in situ*.

See also STOOP.

BIBLIOGRAPHY
General
Parnell, 1838.

military uniform Military uniforms have to be manufactured in large quantities, and often in advance of demand rather than to individual orders. Their supply provided important precedents for the development of the CLOTHING FACTORY. During the nineteenth century, in cities as remote as Gabrovo, BULGARIA, specialist workshops developed to supply uniforms for soldiers. In 1830 Thimonnier SEWING MACHINES were used for the first time to sew uniforms in Paris, and the American Civil War was an important stimulus both to the development of standard sizes and to the use of the sewing machine.

BIBLIOGRAPHY
General
Boorstin, 1973.
Specific
Smith, D. J. Army clothing contractors and the textile industries in the 18th century. In *TH*, XIV, 1983.

mill A term with a wide range of meanings in industrial

archaeology, being used both as verb and noun. It originally meant a building where corn was ground into flour and the word 'mill' is frequently used as an abbreviation for CORN MILL, WATER MILL or WINDMILL. The word later came to denote any series of machines or operations for grinding (that is, reducing solid substances to powder), as in the manufacture of snuff from tobacco, or pulp, as in the manufacture of paper from rags or wood. In this sense the mill might be either the machine for carrying out a particular process, or the establishment in which the machine, often with others, was located. By the sixteenth century the term 'mill' was being applied to mechanically-powered, non-grinding processes like fulling and sawing, and later to machines like 'blunging mills' and 'pug mills' used in CLAY PREPARATION. It was applied, duly qualified, to specific mechanized stages in ironmaking, as in ROLLING MILL and SLITTING MILL.

It is likely that the application of the term to places where textiles were manufactured arose from the use of water power for FULLING, and later for CARDING and SPINNING. The first recorded reference to a 'cotton mill' dates from 1791, and the term 'mill' came to be applied in a loose sense to almost any establishment where cotton was manufactured. In particular contexts, in the Yorkshire woollen industry or in the linen industry throughout Britain, a mill was where materials were prepared and spun, and a factory was where yarn was woven into cloth.

The word 'mill' also came to be used in a more general sense. In the USA it tends to apply to a large establishment where semi-finished products like rolled steel beams, flour, cement, or textiles are made, while a FACTORY makes goods ready for the consumer. In England the term is also applied to establishments like TINPLATE mills, where some stages of production may not be mechanized; or to lead mills, smelters not necessarily employing any form of mechanical power. Occasional uses of 'mill' have persisted long after any association with production has ended, as in the TREADMILL, once an integrated system of human-powered materials processing, and today nothing more than an endless belt put to some very non-industrial purposes.

See also MILLING MACHINE.

DAVID H. SHAYT and BARRIE TRINDER

milling machine A machine tool that shapes work by feeding it to a revolving toothed cutter. While milling was practised in the late Middle Ages, the development of a machine for milling was closely connected with the making of flat surfaces on parts for small arms, as a substitute for planing or filing, or both. Early milling machines – such as the one employed by Simeon North (1765–1852) in the manufacture of interchangeable pistol-lock parts in Connecticut in 1816 – adapted the headstock and cross slide of the engine LATHE to drive the cutter and move the work across its axis against the direction of rotation.

For good results milling requires robust, powerful machines and hard, well-shaped and maintained cutters. In the early nineteenth century its use was limited to taking rough cuts on pieces too small to plane, where labour was short or where standard patterns were followed. The introduction in 1848 of a 'plain' milling machine with double bearings, a knee-and-column milling machine with 'universal' flexibility in 1862 (*see* JOHN BROWN), and cutters of improved design and hardness in 1864, allowed milling machines to become accepted as standard machine tools. They are extensively employed in the manufacture of INTERCHANGEABLE PARTS.

BIBLIOGRAPHY
General
Battison, 1976; Rolt, 1986; Steeds, 1969; Woodbury, 1960.
Specific
Battison, E. A. Eli Whitney and the milling machine. In *Smithsonian Journal of History*, I, 1966.
Smith, M. R. John H. Hall, Simeon North and the milling machine. In *Technology and Culture*, XIV, 1973.

TIM PUTNAM

millstones Principally stones used for grinding grain, although the term is sometimes applied to GRINDSTONES. The Millstone Grit of the Derbyshire PENNINES, England, a sandstone with a high density of small, rounded quartz pebbles, is the principal source. An export trade was well established by the seventeenth century. Many partly-formed stones remain around former quarries. Millstone-makers identified their stones with individual marks about 15 cm (6 in.) long. British millstones are monolithic (all in one piece).

Small millstones of blue lava from the Eifel, Germany, were imported into England, as were French burr stones, which became increasingly popular in the eighteenth and nineteenth centuries as demand increased for finer grades of flour. They were made by cementing together segments of special stone.

British sources have been thoroughly documented by Tucker (1987).

See also CORN MILL.

BIBLIOGRAPHY
General
Sass, 1984.
Specific
Gleisberg, H. Millstone quarries. In *Transactions of the 4th Symposium, The International Molinological Society*, 1977.
Major, J. K. The manufacture of millstones in the Eifel Region of Germany. In *IAR*, VI, 1982.
Tucker, D. G. Millstones, quarries and millstone-makers. In *Post-medieval Archaeology*, XI, 1977.
Tucker, D. G. Millstone-making in the Peak District of Derbyshire: the quarries and the technology. In *IAR*, VIII(1), 1985.
Tucker, D. G. Millstone-making in England. In *IAR*, IX(2), 1987.
Ward, O. H. French millstones. In *Wind and Water Mills*, III, 1982.
Ward, O. H. The making and dressing of French-burr millstones in France in 1903. In *Wind and Water Mills*, V, 1984.

BARRIE TRINDER

millwright A craftsman responsible for the design, building and repair of mills, both wind and water. His most difficult task was making cogwheels, but he also dressed millstones. In the late eighteenth century mill-wrights became involved in the development of early textile factories in Britain, particularly with power-transmission equipment. The advantages of meshing wooden with iron cogwheels led some millwrights to make iron castings, and ultimately to establish foundries and engineering concerns.

Minden-Lübbecke, North Rhine-Westphalia, Germany
The Mittelland Canal, linking the Dortmund–Ems Canal (*see* RUHRGEBIET) with the Elbe and Berlin, was authorized in 1905. It crossed the Weser at Minden, 80 km (50 mi.) E. of Osnabruck, on a 375 m (1230 ft.) reinforced concrete viaduct of eight arches, which was completed in 1914. Pumping stations lift water from the river to the canal, and the two waterways are linked by locks.

The district of Minden-Lübbecke is a fertile agricultural region, notable for its mills. A programme of restoration with the object of restoring at least one mill in each of the eleven towns and villages in the district began in 1976, and an innovative mill trail (Mühlenstrasse) has been established by which visitors can take a route that enables them to see more than thirty mills, mostly windmills (*see* figure 177) but including some water and horse mills, some of which are regularly open to the public.

BIBLIOGRAPHY
Specific
Brepohl, W. *Die Westfälische Mühlenstrasse* (The Westphalian mill trail). Kreis Minden-Lübbecke, n.d.

LOCATION
[I] Kreisverwaltung Minden-Lübbecke (District Authority of Minden-Lübbecke), Postfach 1580, 4950 Minden.

mining The presence of minerals and the ability to work them economically has been the foundation of industrialization in such countries as Germany, Sweden and Britain, and more recently the USA, Australia, Canada and South Africa. Mining has been defined as the process of extracting minerals of economic value from the earth's crust. It is an ancient industry.

The technique of mining depends on the mineral and its mode of occurrence. Surface mining includes quarrying (for stone, clay or aggregates), strip and opencast mining (for coal or iron ore), open-pit mining (for base metals and non-metals), the harvesting of lake deposits (salt, sulphur and iron ore), and ALLUVIAL MINING. Underground mining is basically in two forms: STOPING for near-vertical vein deposits, and pillar (*see* PILLAR-AND-STALL MINING) and 'wall' (*see* LONGWALL MINING; SHORTWALL MINING) methods in near-horizontal bedded deposits such as coal, limestone, chalk, ironstone, sandstone, sand, oil shale, and fireclay. All these methods are of early origin. Since the 1850s attempts have been made to avoid human entry, methods have included wells (for extracting oil, gas, brine and water), solution mining (mainly for salt and sulphur, but also for the leaching of certain metal ores), and, for coal, the use of augering and underground gasification. Except for non-entry methods and the introduction of mechanization, the basic methods of mining

have changed little over the last three centuries; they have been refined, though, and locally-used methods have often been superseded by others from further afield. For example, the longwall methods of mining coal have almost completely displaced the pillar-and-stall methods in the larger British coal mines. No method can be given a definite 'era' as most variations are still in use somewhere today. The sequence of development can however often be followed – for example from pillar-and-stall to shortwall, to tubstall longwall, then to mechanical longwall – even within a single mine.

Surface-mining methods have hardly changed over the centuries except in scale and in the degree of mechanization. Modern dimension-stone quarries can look very similar to those of a hundred years ago. Except for the sources of power for holing or cutting tools all operations are undertaken basically by hand, or with the use of simple tools or derricks. Flame-cutting lances have replaced drills in some quarrying operations.

This article deals with aspects of mining common to most minerals. For variations concerning particular rocks or minerals, refer to individual entries such as ALUMINIUM; COPPER; DIAMOND; EMERALD; GOLD; LEAD; OIL INDUSTRY; RUBY; SALT; SILVER; STONE; TIN; URANIUM; ZINC. For methods of mining bedded deposits, *see* COAL MINING.

Access to mines
All underground methods of mining require a means of access. This can be by near-horizontal ADITS, crosscuts, day-holes or drifts, by near-vertical or vertical shafts, or by inclined shafts, slope shafts or declines. Adits have been used mainly to follow the mineral underground where the deposits have been shallow, and in mountainous areas. Shafts have been used to provide short-length access to deeper deposits in hilly areas, and where, in the past, adits were uneconomic due to the depth of deposit and the flatness of the country. Slope shafts and declines have been constructed as the result of a more recent need to accommodate specific methods of haulage. Once access to the deposit has been obtained a series of underground tunnels or haulage ways have to be developed so that an area of mineral-bearing material can be conveniently and safely exploited using one of the STOPING, wall or pillar methods referred to above. The layout has to allow for the ancillary processes of haulage, hoisting, drainage and ventilation. The actual techniques of breaking ground and forming tunnels are described separately below.

See also ALLUVIAL MINING; BELL PIT; HUSH; QUARRY; RAKE; STRIP MINING.

Underground haulage
Underground haulage tended to be over fairly short distances in metal mines compared with those from which coal was extracted. In early times leather bags were carried or baskets were dragged, but by the sixteenth century wheelbarrows and wheeled and wheel-less trucks running on planks were used (*see* HUND; HUNGARIAN HUND). By the late eighteenth century iron railways were in use (*see* RAILWAY). Timber edge rails, grooved planks, planks carrying metal strips, metal edge rails, flanged

rails, and vertical metal-strip rails were all used underground in the nineteenth century.

Ore cars, manually-propelled wheeled boxes, have been commonly used in mines. They are either discharged into an underground ore pocket near the shaft, or run into cages to be raised to the surface. In larger mines haulage was on rails, the containers being drawn by horses, and from the nineteenth century by locomotives, each animal or locomotive hauling several cars or trucks (often called a rake, a journey, or a set). Electric trolley-type locomotives were in use in Britain, the United States and Germany by the 1890s. In modern mines the cars are often permanently coupled, and tip while still connected. For lighter loads electric-battery and diesel locomotives have been used.

Ropes have also been used extensively for underground haulage, usually driven from a static engine, the engine being on the surface if a steam engine, and underground if powered by compressed air or electricity. Only occasionally were steam engines installed underground. Ropes could travel down shafts, through boreholes and along considerable lengths of tunnel. Where heavy loads were to be taken downhill, self-acting gravity inclines were sometimes used. There were three principal systems of rope haulage: direct single rope, main and tail ropes, and endless ropes. In some instances chains were used instead of ropes. Rope and chain systems were manpower-intensive as it was necessary to couple and uncouple the individual wagons forming sets, and to clip wagons on and off the ropes not only at the end-points but also wherever there were major changes of direction. Rope and chain systems were extensively used from the mid-nineteenth century until the 1960s.

Minerals have also been conveyed underground by boat on canals. These were mainly in use between 1750 and 1850, although some remained in use into the twentieth century. Examples included the BRIDGEWATER CANAL, several systems in the HARZ MOUNTAINS, and that at TARNOWSKIE GORY. Many large mines now use load–haul–dump systems, with articulated, tyred, multi-purpose machines, which transport minerals over short journeys to chutes or ore pockets. Others use dump trucks to haul from the working place or chute direct to the surface via an adit or a steeply graded decline.

See also PUTTER.

Hoisting

Minerals can be removed from mines either by direct tramming using small trucks or by tyred trucks, through an adit or decline as described above. Alternatively, some form of shaft transport can be used. In early times minerals were raised in baskets or leather bags, either by hand, using some form of steps or a ladder, or by means of a rope or chain using a simple machine. Such machines have included windlasses (winches or stowes); a gin-run or whip, in which a horse walks away from a shaft hauling the rope over a pulley; and a HORSE GIN, in which a horse walking in a circle rotates a drum on a vertical spindle, and a rope is wound on to the drum. A bucket-like container (known as a hoppit or KIBBLE) or a wheel-less

wooden box was often used in conjunction with a gin. Balancing tanks of water and water wheels have also been used as power sources for hoists, particularly in Wales and Germany.

Chains have been used for hoisting in deeper mines since the seventeenth century, but became more popular from the late eighteenth century. Their chief disadvantages are their weight and bulk. Wire ropes were in use in Germany from *c*.1850, and had replaced chains in most mines by 1900.

By the end of the eighteenth century steam engines were used to power hoists, and they were in common use by 1850. They permitted a considerable increase in output if used in conjunction with large containers or skips, or if cages were adopted, which could carry one or more wagons. Greater efficiency was achieved by operating skips or cages in 'balanced' pairs, driven from a single drum, and were safer if the cages were prevented from spinning by using shaft guides, either of wood or of wire. Steam hoists used reels or drums on which the ropes were alternately stored and paid out as the rope was hoisted up or down the shaft with its load. Sometimes this was done on a single drum, sometimes two drums were used; or a drum could have sections of two diameters (bi-cylindrical), the smaller providing the greater force needed when the load was at the bottom of a deep shaft and the engine rope had to be lifted. An alternative was the Koepe system, which utilized a number of ropes passing over pulleys at the top and bottom of the shaft. This system was adopted in Germany in the 1860s and subsequently spread to Britain and other countries. Since the 1920s most large hoists have used electric power, either a.c. or d.c., but many steam hoists remained in service well after 1950.

Headstocks – alternatively, headframes, headgears, or poppet heads in areas of Cornish influence – are the most easily recognizable, and the most commonly preserved, large-scale structures relating to mining. Each was unique, to suit the circumstances of its location, history, shaft depth and diameter, the type of winding engine and the method of operation. The earliest were of timber cut locally and fashioned into simple hand winches, horse-gin frames like those at Wollaton Park (*see* NOTTINGHAM) and Magpie Mine (*see* CROMFORD); and A- and H-frame structures. As mines increased in size, stays were added to resist the horizontal portion of the hoist's pull, and frames were combined as 'tandem headgears'. By 1850 cast-iron frames were in use in Staffordshire and Shropshire, England, but Mines Inspectors considered them unreliable. By the late nineteenth century wrought-iron lattice and steel frames became common. At most upcast ventilation shafts, and sometimes on other shafts, the frames were boxed in, using timber, stone or brick; and on occasion, as at Caphouse Colliery, Yorkshire, part of the headframe itself might be of stone, supporting the timber structure above it. In rare cases the solid rock might be used to support the winding pulley, as at Snailbeach, Shropshire (*see* SHREWSBURY), the decking level for the cage being at a lower level, entered by an adit. Rock-supported pulleys were also common in underground winding shafts. The practice in continental Europe has been to have a more solid headframe, often clad with bricks or timber. The Koepe winding towers of the twentieth century are mostly of reinforced concrete. The primary mineral-preparation plant was often attached to the headframe, but this could be a fire hazard when all the structures were of timber. Legislation was passed in Britain in 1911 preventing any new or replacement headstock being built of timber, but some earlier examples like that at Caphouse have remained in use. The height of the headframe was often such as to allow an elevated unloading platform which would provide gravity feed to simple dressing equipment or railway wagons. In some cases the great height of a headframe was due to its having been built over a previous installation so that working continued uninterrupted during replacement.

Systems of transporting men developed in parallel with the hoisting of minerals. Up to the seventeenth century most miners entered and left shaft mines by ladders. By the early nineteenth century they usually stood in baskets, kibbles or boxes, or sat in loops of chain. From the 1830s cages were used, but many metalliferous mines used MAN ENGINES.

See also MALAKOFF TOWER; ROPE.

Drainage

Shallow mines are generally affected only seasonally by water but those below the water table have a continuous problem. Adit or SOUGH drainage, which uses a tunnel driven into a hillside below the mine workings, has been used since early times. It is expensive at first cost, but it is highly effective and can be extended. The principal drainage adit in Cornwall, begun in 1748, was extended to a length of 50 km (30 miles) within fifty years. When sough drainage is not possible some form of pumping is necessary, although many mines have been kept clear of occasional water by bailing, using buckets on the hoist mechanism.

AGRICOLA described six types of pump used in the sixteenth century. Some consisted of series of open containers on continuous chains that raised water from sumps as they rotated. Others had rags or 'blocks' that acted as a series of pistons, pushing water up enclosed pipes. In the mid-seventeenth century plunger pumps, operated by water wheels, on the surface or underground, were well developed in Germany. Plunger pumps used long wooden rods to transmit movement, and extensive systems were developed. In England in 1712 THOMAS NEWCOMEN was the first to be successful in using steam to operate pumping mechanisms, and by 1730 Newcomen engines were employed in mines in Austria, Belgium, France, Hungary and Sweden (*see* STEAM ENGINE). Steam pumping was developed further by RICHARD TREVITHICK and other Cornish engineers (*see* CORNWALL) in the early nineteenth century, and by the 1820s depths of 120 m (400 ft.) could be pumped and kept dry.

Windmills have been used for pumping, as at Mona in Anglesey where water was once raised from 120 m (400 ft.) at the rate of 400 l (90 gall.) per minute. In the 1850s attempts were made to use COMPRESSED AIR to move water and to operate reciprocating pumps, but progress was slow. Only from the late 1860s were there serious suggestions that compressed air should replace steam underground, and a variety of techniques evolved during the 1890s spurred by the development of portable air-compressors and large stationary plants. By 1900 compressed air was in general use, not only as an alternative to steam in reciprocating pumps, but also as a means of forcing water along pipes. Electricity was used to power some reciprocating pumps before 1900, but as rotary-action pumps were developed during the twentieth century these became the principal means of draining mines.

Ventilation

Natural ventilation (*see* COAL MINING) has often been sufficient for metal-mining operations as most mines are in hilly districts and many have lower entrances for drainage. It is only in the twentieth century, as greater depths have been reached and it has been necessary to provide more acceptable working conditions, that mechanical ventilation systems similar to those employed in coal mines have been used.

See also WADDLE FAN.

Methods of working

The miner's basic tools since early times have been the shovel and the hammer or pick, but before hard rock can be moved it must be loosened. Crowbars and wedges were used when the rock was suitably fractured or holed; recourse has otherwise to be had to alternative means of fragmentation such as FIRE-SETTING. Gunpowder was probably first used in the seventeenth century, and it was quickly discovered that it could best be employed by boring a hole into the rock and sealing in the powder with clay packing or stemming. Most of the improvements since that time have been in the techniques for making holes and in the development of new explosives. Holes can be formed in rocks by means of hand-held drills, or by jumpers struck by hammers, a procedure practised in Welsh slate mines into the twentieth century. From the 1850s muscle was replaced by rotary drilling machines, and from the 1870s by COMPRESSED AIR drills. Early machines used solid drill-bits and the work was done 'dry', producing dusty, unhealthy conditions for the miner, but by 1900 hollow drill-rods that could carry water into the hole were being developed. Improvements were also made to the drill-bits that struck the rock, reducing the amount of dust generated.

'Nitro' explosives and a suitable detonator were invented by ALFRED NOBEL in 1866, and by 1875 he was producing DYNAMITE and blasting gelatine, the latter being extensively used still. Developments in drilling and blasting revolutionized both tunnelling techniques and the breaking of mineral at the face, and working methods to suit particular types of rock were developed. In the twentieth century compressed-air props to aid the driller have been developed; diamonds and tungsten carbide have been used in drill-bits; and electrically-powered drills have been introduced, particularly for use in softer rocks and in exploration.

See also COAL MINING; LONGWALL MINING; PILLAR-AND-STALL MINING; SAFETY LAMP; SHORTWALL MINING.

Surface treatment

Extracted minerals have to be 'dressed', to extract market-able products. These processes range from purely mecha-nical separation to techniques involving magnetism, chemical affinity, varying specific gravity, and heat. Since dressing processes depend upon the properties of the mineral they are considered in the entries on particular minerals (*see* ALUMINIUM; COAL; COPPER; GOLD; LEAD; SILVER; TIN; URANIUM; ZINC).

See also BUDDLE; CRUSHING CIRCLE; DRESSING FLOOR; JIGGING; SHAKING TABLE; STAMP.

BIBLIOGRAPHY
General
Agricola, 1556; Davies, 1902; Gregory, 1980; Hunt, 1887; Temple, 1972.

IVOR J. BROWN

mining museum Mining, like other industries, is amongst the interests of the principal museums of science and technology. Usually exhibits are confined to portable equipment and models, but the Deutsches Museum, MUNICH, was a pioneer in the provision of a replica mine. Many exhibits in the major geological museums also relate to mining. A few mining museums have substantial archives and research facilities. The Deutsches Bergbau Museum, Bochum (*see* RUHRGEBIET) is the outstanding example in Europe. Some museums, often with geological collections, are appendages of schools of mining.

Increasing numbers of mining museums offer under-ground experiences. Problems of drainage and roof sup-port often make it difficult to present underground workings in coal mines as exhibits, but this has been done with success. British examples include the Big Pit, Blaena-von, and the Yorkshire Mining Museum (*see* HUDDERS-FIELD). Even where workings remain accessible, it is difficult to convey a sense of a working mine. Some museums, among them the Black Country Museum and Chatterley Whitfield Mining Museum (*see* STOKE-ON-TRENT) in England, have opted for sophisticated replica mines near the surface. Metalliferous mines in hard rock present fewer difficulties of access, and many are displayed to the public (over thirty in Germany alone); some 'show mines' lack the collections that would entitle them to claim to be museums. Even with audio-visual aids used in some underground displays, the demands of public safety make it impossible to recreate the atmosphere of a working mine: nevertheless, the best such museums, like the Great Copper Mine at FALUN, offer some of the most moving experiences available in any kind of industrial museum.

Closely allied with mining museums are tunnelling museums. The Hall of Civil Engineering at the Smith-sonian Institution, Washington DC, features detailed dioramic models depicting the various tunnelling strategies that have evolved for the boring of transport and water passageways.

DAVID SHAYT and BARRIE TRINDER

mining town Mining towns are often, of necessity, isolated. In many cases their initial growth was rapid and their size has subsequently remained static, so that, in such diverse settlements as RØROS in Norway and the coal mining villages of the 1920s near NOTTINGHAM, England, they retain the essential planning and architectural characteristics of the period in which they were built. Deserted mining communities like those of the Gold Rushes in Canada and the USA (*see* BOURLAMAQUE; CALIFORNIA) can, when conserved, provide important evidence of the living conditions of the times in which they were built, of a kind lost in settlements that have remained prosperous.

BIBLIOGRAPHY
Specific
Stelter, G. A. and Artibise, A. F. J. Canadian resource towns in historical perspective. In *Plan Canada*, XVIII, 1978.
White, P. H. Some aspects of urban development by colliery companies, 1919–39. In *Manchester School*, XXIII, 1955.

Minnesota, United States of America   Although four-teenth among the states in land area, Minnesota may be the first among them in weight, with iron ore reserves in the north continuing to yield some 60 per cent of the nation's needs after almost a century of continuous production. Since the discovery of deposits late in the nineteenth century, high-grade iron ores from the Mesabi, Cuyana and Vermilion ranges have been fed to blast furnaces throughout the North-East, typically being shipped through the Great Lakes.

Commemorating and furthering the state's iron-ore heritage is the Iron Range Research Center in Chisholm. Three historic iron-mining sites remain as evidence of the pioneering years of the industry: the Hull-Rust-Mahoning Open Pit near Hibbing, the Soudan Iron Mine Shaft near Tower, and the Mountain Iron Mine of 1890–1956, north of the village of Mountain Iron.

Minnesota's Lake Superior coastline extends for 240 km (150 mi.). The ore town of Duluth embraces the nation's largest inland harbour, bridged in 1910 by a rare aerial lift (transporter) bridge, rebuilt in 1929 as a conventional vertical lift span. Access to such deep-water shipping also facilitated the development of manufactur-ing and agricultural processing in the state, making the principal city of Minneapolis the commercial centre of the upper Midwest.

Limestone quarrying, timber harvesting and flour milling have been other long-dominant industries in Minnesota, the quintessential timber-frame grain elevator (silo) a familiar but endangered aspect of the landscape. In 1927 the state's sixty-six elevators had a collective capacity of 63.5 million bushels, the greatest in the nation. In Minneapolis stands the Peavy-Haglin Experi-mental Concrete Grain Elevator of 1900, the first such circular structure, built to demonstrate the capacity of reinforced concrete to sustain loads of grain to a height of 38 m (125 ft.).

Numerous railway carriage and wagon works, masonry railway bridges, and depots dot the 'Twin Cities' of Minneapolis and St Paul, historic testimony to the once controlling influence of the railways linking this productive northern outpost with the outside world. Diverse manufactures and a solid base of natural resources to draw upon, chiefly ores and timber, have helped Minnesota to maintain a breadth of industrial activity, especially important in times of decreasing demand for steel.

BIBLIOGRAPHY
General
Dominick, 1982.

LOCATIONS
[S] Forest History Center, 2709 County Road 76, Grand Rapids, MN 55744.
[I] Iron Range Research Center, PO Box 392, Chisholm, MN 55719.
[M] Minnesota Transportation Museum, 4832 York Avenue, St Paul, MN 55343.

DAVID H. SHAYT

mint A factory where coins are made, by striking blank discs of the appropriate metal alloys in dies which restrict their lateral flow. Most are government-controlled, but some, like that in BIRMINGHAM, are commercial concerns working for several governments, and producing medals and the like for private customers. The production of banknotes has always been a specialized branch of PRINTING.

Miranda de Ebro, Logroño, Castile, Spain A town 64 km (40 mi.) S. of Bilbao, notable for its railway station, which was built in 1862 from the design of the English architect, Charles Vignoles (1793–1875). The station building, on an island platform, is an 87 m (285 ft.) long structure of twenty-one bays, from which iron platform awnings, prefabricated by Frederick Braby & Co. in London, project on either side.

BIBLIOGRAPHY
General
Civera, 1988.

Mississippi, United States of America Until the 1890s, one of the nation's least industrialized states, with more than half the inhabitants making their living from the soil. Not only have cotton, rice and sweet potatoes distinguished this Deep South state's agricultural record, but Mississippi wheat, peaches, beef, hogs and catfish have been major exports as well.

The state lacked an adequate shipping port on the Gulf of Mexico, but between 1901 and the 1920s a major dredging project created the artificial harbour at Gulfport, which remains the state's only deep-water facility.

Mississippi's thick forests of loblolly pine and lowland swamp pine have long furnished resins for one of the nation's largest producers of turpentine.

Near the Yazoo River, a tributary of the Mississippi River which forms the state's western border, lies one of the more important maritime remains of the early industrial era, the Civil War gunboat *Cairo.* The ironclad,

steam-powered vessel was one of several built by the Union forces (the 'North'), to wrest control of the lower Mississippi River from the Confederacy (the 'South'), a plan drawn up by the noted bridge engineer James B. Eads (1820–87). The *Cairo*'s power plant and hull, and remnants of its enclosed paddlewheel, stand preserved at a National Park Service site near the banks of the Yazoo from which they were raised in 1964, after sinking some 102 years earlier, a victim of Confederate river mines.

LOCATIONS
[M] Cairo Museum, Vicksburg National Military Park, 3201 Clay Street, Vicksburg, MS 39180.
[M] Casey Jones (Railroad) Museum, Main Street, Vaughan, MS 39179.

DAVID H. SHAYT

Missouri, United States of America Shoes, lead, corn and beer are among the more enduring products issuing from this state, situated in the nation's heartland. Warehouses remain as evidence of the pioneering role St Louis played in the fur trade. Well into the twentieth century, Missouri led all the states west of the Mississippi River in general manufacturing. It was and remains the only source for genuine corncob pipes.

In the town of Lawson is a rather unlikely but significant industrial survival: the Watkins Woolen Mill, active from 1861 until the turn of the century, when it was boarded up and forgotten. Reopened as an historic site in 1964, it stands as it looked at closure, a period collection of *in situ* carding, spinning, weaving, fulling and napping machines, belt-driven from steam-powered line shafting.

Crossing the Mississippi River at St Louis stretches the great Eads Bridge, completed in 1874. This pioneering iron and steel multiple-arch span used no centring in its cantilevered growth from the piers, each about 150 m (500 ft.) apart. The unprecedented clear spans for such a bridge, the use of pneumatic caissons to sink the piers and steel to jacket the arch ribs, and the latticed ironwork of the arch spandrels distinguish this as one of the pioneering works of American civil engineers, which induced other nations to take serious account of them.

No less than twenty-two rail lines terminated at St Louis Union Station on its completion in 1894. It is a Romanesque edifice, with a majestic clock tower and interior spaces dripping with filigree of the gilded age. In the mid-1980s, after a few decades of decay and near-demolition, the station re-emerged, restored to its old glory as a hotel and convention centre, with a new shopping arcade sheltered beneath the train shed.

The county-funded National Museum of Transport attempts to fill the gap caused by the absence of any federally-supported museum devoted exclusively to land transportation, a glaring omission in view of the centrality of rail and auto to the nation's growth, prosperity and continued survival. This museum's collections span the range of vehicle types from locomotives, rolling stock and buses, to motorcycles, trucks, tractors and bicycles, housed in part inside two railway tunnels of the 1850s, the first such bored west of the Mississippi.

See also figure 150.

BIBLIOGRAPHY
General
Scott and Miller, 1979.

LOCATIONS
[M] National Museum of Transport, 3015 Barrett Station Road, St Louis, MO 63122.
[S] Watkins Woolen Mill State Historic Site, Highway 69, Lawson, MO 64062.

DAVID H. SHAYT

Mjøndalen, Buskerud, Norway A town 12 km ($7\frac{1}{2}$ miles) W. of Drammen. Knudson's Smie, a five-bay, single-storey brick smithy, was built in 1907 in the 'V' of a road junction. Tools remain in place. This was a specialist manufactory which supplied marking axes, used to put identification marks on felled logs, to the whole of Scandinavia and to customers as far away as Africa.

Mladá Boleslav, North Bohemia, Czechoslovakia A town with important modernist buildings of the mid-1920s by Jiří Kroha: a technical school, officers' houses, the Gellner department store, and the Hotel Venec. A Skoda car factory was established in 1945.

model A model is a scaled-down three-dimensional representation of a machine or product or manufacturing process. A full-scale copy is best called a replica. Models pose questions to the industrial archaeologist; in their power to stimulate thought, they are second only to the examination of original artefacts and landscapes.

Models, whether contemporary or well-researched modern reconstructions, are often the best three-dimensional evidence for historic machines and processes. The huge collections of ship models at museums in GLASGOW and elsewhere, for example, represent the history of shipping in some ways more effectively than the relatively small numbers of preserved vessels.

Historical models were made for various purposes. Some were presented as parts of PATENT applications. Others, like those of CHRISTOPHE POLHEM preserved at FALUN and elsewhere, made complex processes comprehensible. Some civil engineering models were made to rehearse the order of construction of bridges; while others, like that in the Science Museum (*see* LONDON) of the Iron Bridge, were celebrations of the successful completion of projects.

Toy models may be crude, but even the simplest can convey historical evidence not available elsewhere; and the best, like the railway locomotives of Basset-Lowke or Fleischmann, are works of art comparable with high-quality topographical prints.

Models, whether made by industrial companies of their own sites, or by museums, have traditionally been employed to make comprehensible large manufacturing plants like oil refineries or steelworks.

Models and replicas have been used in recent years as means of investigating past processes. Italian scholars have gained new understanding of seventeenth-century silk-throwing machinery by the construction of half-scale models. The construction of full-scale replicas of locomotives began with the *Stourbridge Lion*, built in 1927 to celebrate the centenary of the Delaware & Hudson Railway, and the *Rocket*, which marked the centenary of the Liverpool & Manchester Railway in 1930. Replicas of early locomotives were built in several European countries to celebrate centenaries in the 1930s. Full-scale replicas recently constructed include those of a Newcomen engine, at the BLACK COUNTRY Museum, and of a TREVITHICK locomotive, at IRONBRIDGE.

BIBLIOGRAPHY
General
Dow, 1972.

BARRIE TRINDER

model community The word 'model' when applied to industrial communities is used with at least four subtly different meanings. There are thus four uses of the term 'model community':

1. A community planned to provide accommodation for workers at a particular industrial plant, even if in architectural terms the accommodation is little more than neatly ordered.
2. An industrial community whose architecture is designed to make a strong impression, whatever its style (*see* HORNU; PORT SUNLIGHT).
3. A community within which particular ethical standards are applied, which may be intended as a model for society at large (*see* UTOPIAN COMMUNITY).
4. A settlement such as New Earswick, YORK, where buildings are designed with the deliberate intent that they should be copied and are therefore priced at levels that may be affordable in less favourable circumstances.

BIBLIOGRAPHY
General
Curl, 1983; Gaskell, 1987; Jonas *et al.*, 1975; Meakin, 1905; Rowntree, 1954.

Modum, Buskerud, Norway COBALT ore was discovered at Modum, 30 km (20 mi.) NW of Drammen, by Ole Witloch in 1772, and in 1776 a royal decree established a blue colouring works (Blaafarveverk). It was operated for many years under German management, and from 1822 was in German ownership. The colouring manufactured was a mixture of potassium carbonate (K_2CO_3), quartz (SiO_2) and cobalt oxide (CoO). The product was poured into water in a molten state, which caused it to form droplets. It was then ground by quartzite millstones. The colouring was used in potteries, GLASS and PAINT manufactories. ARSENIC and sulphur compounds were removed from the ore in roasting kilns, and some of the arsenic compounds were distilled and sold. For several years around 1840 Modum, with over five hundred employees,

Figure 87 The mill pond at Brede on the Mølleåen, or Mill Stream, north of Copenhagen, where one of the best-preserved factory colonies in Denmark is concentrated round the former woollen-cloth factory in the centre of the picture; the buildings now house the modern departments of the National Museum.
Jørgen Sestoft

was the largest industrial enterprise in Norway, but production of colouring ceased in 1855 following the discovery of ultramarine, which displaced cobalt in paint-making. Mining continued until 1898. In the 1970s a trust was formed to conserve the remaining buildings which are now used as restaurants, shops and galleries.

BIBLIOGRAPHY
Specific
Wiig, J. The Blue Dye Works at Modum. In Nisser and Bedoire, 1978.

LOCATION
[M] Modum Blaafarveverk-Bygdemuseet Modum, 3340 Åmot.

BARRIE TRINDER

mohair Mohair yarn is made from the wool of the Angora goat from Turkey. It is used to weave a brilliant, white lustrous fabric of great elasticity, known in Western Europe in the eighteenth century but not used on a large scale until after 1836 when Sir Titus Salt (*see* BRADFORD) demonstrated the potential of the similar ALPACA wool. Mohair was subsequently much used in long-piled fabrics like PLUSH and in braids.

BIBLIOGRAPHY
General
James, 1857.

Moira, Leicestershire, England A coalfield settlement, 9 km (6 mi.) SE of BURTON-UPON-TRENT. A short-lived blast furnace of 1804–6 survives with the main structure complete, although the engine house was demolished in the 1960s. It has been extensively excavated. A New-comen engine house of *c.*1805 and limekilns can be seen nearby.

BIBLIOGRAPHY
General
Cranstone, 1985.

Mo i Rana, Nordland, Norway A steelworking town on the west coast, 360 km (220 mi.) N. of Trondheim, on the railway to Bodø. The steelworks is open to visitors. The local museum has a collection of re-erected buildings from the region.

LOCATION
[M] Rana Museum, Kulturhistorisk avd., Hans A. Meyers Sam-linger, 8600 Mo i Rana.

Mølleåen, Zealand, Denmark Mølleåen, the Mill Stream, north of Copenhagen, is often called the cradle of Danish industry. Along this river, only 12 km (8 mi.) long, with a total fall of only 20 m (70 ft.), stood nine watermills, which for three hundred years played important indus-trial roles. The intensive development of the river was mainly due to the nearness of the Copenhagen market and the entrepreneurial resources of the capital. The old medieval corn mills that lined the river in the seventeenth century were converted to various industrial uses, and most were further enlarged in the decades before 1800. To meet increasing power requirements, steam engines and water turbines were installed in the nineteenth century, and on this basis several mills continued to expand well into the twentieth century. Today all industrial produc-tion has ceased, but many remains from the area's industrial past have survived, and with their beautiful surroundings the mills constitute one of Copenhagen's major recreational assets. From the river's source in Furesøn, the nine mills are: Frederiksdal, Lyngby, Fugle-vad, Brede, Ørholm, Nymølle, Stampen, Rådvad and Strandmøllen.

The mill at Frederiksdal continued as a corn mill until its closure in 1885. The only important surviving building is the manor house of 1745. At Lyngby corn-grinding was for a long time supplemented by the fulling of cloth from several Copenhagen factories. The two mills at Lyngby burned down about 1900, and in 1903 the southern mill was re-erected in its present form. Recently the northern mill has been re-created as a water corn mill with undershot wheels.

At Fuglevad the mill was used for grinding corn well into the twentieth century, but in the eighteenth century this work was supplemented by iron and brass manufactures. Several buildings have survived, together with a Fourneyron water turbine of 1874. As early as 1814 the owner erected a large windmill to increase his power supplies. This now forms the only *in situ* building at the nearby Frilandsmuseet (National Open-Air Museum), where many old farmsteads and rural cottages from different parts of Denmark are displayed, among them a post mill, a large water mill from Funen and a tiny splash mill from the Faeroes.

The next mill, Brede, forms the centre of one of the largest and best-preserved factory colonies in Denmark. In the seventeenth century the corn mill was converted into a gunpowder mill, and then into a copper and brass works. From 1832 until 1956 the site was occupied by one of the biggest textile concerns in Denmark. The successive enlargement of the mill culminated *c*.1900 in the establishment of a large, paternalist factory colony, with its own dwellings for workers and managers, a dining hall, a grocery shop, a day nursery, a school, and gas and water works. Many buildings have survived, the oldest being the mansion house of 1797. Brede now houses the modern department of the National Museum, with extensive workshops, stores and exhibition galleries.

At Ørholm and Nymølle the water power from 1793 until 1921 was used to make paper. The seventh mill, Stampen, was used for fulling and other textile purposes for about three hundred years. Recently the National Museum has moved an old spinning works from Jutland to the cleared site, and re-erected it as a working factory, furnished with nineteenth-century machinery.

The mill community at Rådvad is another example of a well-preserved factory colony. Several of the buildings that are now protected date from the eighteenth century. Between 1759 and 1972 the mill manufactured hardware, most of the time under the direction of the Copenhagen Guild of Ironmongers. Today several of the buildings accommodate workshops educating young people in crafts that had died out but that are essential for future restoration projects.

The final mill, Strandmøllen, situated near The Sound, was the centre of Danish paper manufacturing from 1643 almost up to its closure in 1899. By 1821 the owner was supplementing his water power with a steam engine, and in 1829 he revolutionized production by installing the first papermaking machine in Scandinavia. The surviving papermill was restored in 1918.

BIBLIOGRAPHY
General
Nielsen, 1943–4; Sestoft, 1979.
Specific
Kayser, K. *Rådvad*. Copenhagen, 1980.
Møller, J. *Mølleåen*. Copenhagen, 1971.
Ottosson, P. *Bede Werck*. Copenhagen, 1971.
Tønsberg, J. *Industrialiseringen af Lyngby 1840–1916* (The industrial history of Lyngby 1840–1916). Lyngby, 1984.

LOCATIONS
[M] Frilandsmuseet ved Sorgenfri (National Open-Air Museum), 2800 Kongens Lyngby, Kongevejen 100.
[M] Nationalmuseet (National Museum), 3 afd., Brede, 2800 Lyngby.

OLE HYLDTOFT

molybdenum (Mo)   An elemental metal, chiefly used in the production of special STEELS but also as a chemical reagent and in electric fittings. The chief source is the mineral molybdenite (MoS_2). The principal mines are in the USA (particularly Climax, Colo.) and Canada.

BIBLIOGRAPHY
General
Alexander and Street, 1949; Jones, 1950.

monorail   A transport system with guided vehicles operating on a single rail, first proposed by Henry Robinson Palmer in 1821. The Langen principle (*see* WUPPERTAL and figure 178) uses an overhead rail carried on sheer legs from which cars are suspended. A system devised by Frenchman Charles François Marie-Thérèse Lartigue had the track elevated 1 m (39 in.) from the ground on triangular trestles. Locomotives (designed by Anatole Mallet), carriages and freight vehicles were balanced like panniers, with half of each vehicle on either side of the rail. Monorails have been demonstrated in most European countries and the USA.

The Lartigue Company, established in 1886 with Fritz Bernhard Behr (1842–1927) as managing director, built lines in Ireland (*see* LISTOWEL); in France, where a 17 km (10 mi.) line from Panissere to Feurs, north-west of Lyons, was built in 1896 but never operated successfully; and in Argentina and in Algeria. The company was wound up in 1906. From 1892 Behr put forward ideas for a high-speed electric monorail: he demonstrated the principle on a 5 km (3 mi.) line at Terveuren, Brussels, in 1897, and in 1899–1907 promoted a line between Liverpool and Manchester, which was never built.

BIBLIOGRAPHY
General
Guerin, 1988; Newham, 1967.
Specific
Behr, F. H. The Lartigue single-rail railway. In *Transactions of the Society of Engineers*, 1888.
Behr, F. H. *Lightning Express Railway Service: 120 to 150 miles per hour*. London: 1893.
Behr, F. H. and Petit, G. The Lartigue elevated single rail railway (London, 1886), reprinted as 'The complete Lartigue', Merioneth Railway Society, 1982.
Tucker, D. G. F. H. Behr's development of the Lartigue Monorail: from country crawler to electric express. In *TNS*, LV, 1983–4.

BARRIE TRINDER

Monotype   A type compositor or casting machine, casting individual letters. It was invented by Tolbert Lanston, and used from the 1880s. The type-caster is controlled from a keyboard by a perforated paper tape.

See also LINOTYPE.

Mons (Bergen), Hainaut, Belgium   A city devastated in successive wars, which stands at the centre of a landscape dominated by coal mining, ironmaking, cementworks and ceramics manufactures, all featured in the Industrial Museum. The ceramic products of the Faiencerie de Nimy, 4 km ($2\frac{1}{2}$ mi.) N. are displayed in a works museum (Musée de Vieux Nimy). The Road Museum has comprehensive displays on road construction. A mining museum at Colfontaine-Wasmes, 9 km (6 mi,) SE, is located in the buildings of a former colliery. A memorial commemorates the pastorship of the painter Vincent Van Gogh (1853–90) at Wasmes in 1878–9, and the house where he lived in Mons in 1879–80, a typical worker's dwelling of the period, is preserved.

BIBLIOGRAPHY
General
Viaene, 1986.

LOCATIONS
[S] Maison de Van Gogh, rue de Pavillon 53–5, 7000 Mons.
[M] Musée de la Mine 'Les Wagnaux' (Mining Museum), rue du Pont d'Arcole 14, 7200 Colfontaine-Wasmes.
[M] Musée de la Route (Road Museum), Casemate No. 4, place Nervienne, 7000 Mons.
[M] Musée de l'Industrie (Industrial Museum), Institut Superieur de Commerce de la Province de Hainaut, 17 place Warocque, 7000 Mons.
[M] Musée de Vieux Nimy (Old Nimy Museum), rue Mouzin 31, 7450 Nimy.

Montana, United States of America   As with most of the western states, Montana's great land area offered up a wealth of minerals once the means were available to locate and recover the ores. Soon after its organization as a territory in 1864, Montana zinc, gold, lead, coal, silver, arsenic and blue sapphires, but especially copper, began to emerge in quantity. The mining town of Butte, sitting atop 'the richest hill in the world', once supplied half the country's annual need for copper.

Nearby in the Montana mountains the once bustling company town of Anaconda has managed to retain its most important world-class relic – the 178 m (585 ft.) tall smokestack of the Anaconda Copper Mining Co., built in 1919. It is regarded as the tallest masonry stack in the Western world, although a higher stack is said to stand somewhere in the Soviet Union, and there is a 381 m (1251 ft.) concrete stack at Sudbury, Ontario. Much else from the boom days of copper has disappeared with the decline of the world copper industry.

Butte's World Museum of Mining and Hell Roarin' Gulch captures some of the hard-scrabble flavour of life and work in the mining camps around this state. The collection includes a Nordberg double-drum hoist, head-stocks, and the trappings of a mining camp of 1900.

Every mine, every factory, every bridge in Montana seems isolated. The state's vastness is accentuated by its sparse population, high, rocky terrain, and its lack of urbanization, making all the more delightful the discovery of such out-of-the-way engineering achievements as the Dearborn River High Bridge of 1897, a 49 m (160 ft.) in-service span, with its highway deck situated within the iron trusswork rather than above or below it.

LOCATIONS
[M] Copper Village Museum, 110 E. 8th Street, Anaconda, MT 59711.
[M] Mineral County (Gold Mining) Museum, 2nd Avenue East, Superior, MT 59872.
[M] World Museum of Mining and Hell Roarin' Gulch, West Park & Granite Streets, Butte, MT 59702.

DAVID H. SHAYT

Montluçon, Allier, France   A town of medieval origins which became an industrial centre *c.*1840 when the newly-cut Berry canal opened up access to the nearby Commentry coalfield. Coal was also brought to Montluçon by a railway, built from 1844. Industries sprang up along the canal: limekilns; a glassworks of 1840; a mirror factory of 1846; and two ironworks using Berry ore, the Hauts-Fourneaux works of 1842 and the important Saint Jacques works of 1845.

On the left bank of the River Cher a new working-class neighbourhood developed – la Ville Gozet – which today boasts two noteworthy monuments. Saint Paul's Church, built in 1864–7 by the architect Louis-Auguste Boileau (1812–96), has metallic domes supported by cast-iron columns, like those of the architect's other major church, Saint Eugène in Paris. Opposite the church stands a community centre of 1897–9, built by Gilbert Talbour-deau at the instigation of Jean Dormoy, Montluçon's well-known socialist mayor. The centre has a remarkable decorated façade and an imposing iron-framed assembly hall with a vast semicircular window.

Despite the destruction of the two ironworks – the Saint Jacques works disappeared in 1974 – the town retains numerous traces of its past industrial glory: mid-nineteenth century limekilns, the buildings of the first glassworks of 1840, some of 1861 from the mirror factory, and those of a chemical works opened in 1892 by the SAINT-GOBAIN company who were already owners of the mirror factory. These sites have been studied since 1983, and it is hoped to exhibit the objects and machines recovered, in particular those from the Saint-Jacques works, in the old 'Fers creux' factory, an iron-framed building with brick infill, built in 1866 for the manufacture of iron tubes.

BIBLIOGRAPHY
General
Bourgougnon and Desnoyers, 1986.

LOCATION
[M] Municipal Museum, 03100 Montluçon.

JEAN-FRANÇOIS BELHOSTE

Montmorency, Quebec, Canada   The manufacturing complex of Dominion Textile Inc. is located in the town of Montmorency, 30 km (18 mi.) NE of Quebec. The enterprise was chiefly orientated towards cotton production, and resulted from the merger in 1905 of the

Dominion Cotton Co., the Montmorency Cotton Mills, the Merchant Cotton Co. and the Colonial Bleaching and Printing Co. By 1913 the company was the dominant force in the Canadian textile industry. It became a multinational in 1980 and now has forty or so plants scattered across the world, ten of them in the province of Quebec.

The protectionist policies of the Canadian government, the Civil War in the USA, the heavy demand for certain fabrics during World War I, and the development of synthetic fibres were the factors that seem to have been responsible for its rapid growth. Equally the company benefited from its proximity to the Canadian National Railway route from Quebec City to Montreal along the north shore of the St Lawrence.

The Dominion Textile complex occupies an area of over 50 000 m² (533 000 sq. ft.) at the foot of the Montmorency Falls which provided it with hydro-electric power. It comprises about fifteen buildings constructed between 1889 and 1935, which are characterized by a rectangular style of architecture, with flat roofs and large numbers of windows. They include the principal mill, with its boiler-house, in brick and concrete; there are also subsidiary wooden buildings, sheds, covered sidings and maintenance workshops. To these may be added the many workers' dwellings and residential neighbourhoods – notably at Beauport and Boischatel – which were built as a result of the establishment of the factory.

The closure of the complex in 1986 may perhaps be explained by the transfer of textile production to the Far East. The machinery and equipment were dispersed to other factories or to the scrapyard, although the plant was modernized in 1961 and again in 1982. The owners of the complex are currently seeking to put it to profitable use and with property developers are intending to transform it into a residential and commercial centre.

BIBLIOGRAPHY
Specific
Brunelle, S. *Un volet muséologique au projet de réutilisation de la Dominion Textile de Montmorency* (A museological view of the project to reuse the Dominion Textile factory at Montmorency). Quebec: unpublished document, 1987.

LOUISE TROTTIER

Montreal, Quebec, Canada   One of the principal industrial cities of North America, one of the world's most important river ports, and a stimulating and rewarding setting for the study of industrial archaeology.

The development of Montreal as a port has been due to the successive work of three organizations, the Montreal Harbour Commission from 1830 to 1936, the National Council for Canadian Ports from 1936 until 1983, and since then to La Société du Port de Montréal.

The first port installations, constructed between 1830 and c.1880 according to a plan compiled by the British engineer Robert S. Piper and the Harbour Commission, consisted of quays and jetties in the Place Royale and old market areas. Enlarged annually between 1851 and 1880, these quays eventually had a total length of some 1.72 km (1.07 mi.). Retaining walls and embankments were also constructed during this period along the rue de la Commune and the rue des Commissionaires, in order to prevent damage from the spring floods, to raise the level of the water around the quays, and to allow the passage of ships of greater draught. Dredging operations between 1840 and 1880 increased the depth of the channel to 8.25 m (27 ft.) which improved the navigation between Montreal and Quebec City. The port facilities were greatly improved by the construction of land transport links between the island of Montreal and the south shore of the St Lawrence, notably the Victoria Bridge (see below) in 1853–60 and the Jacques Cartier Bridge in 1933.

In many respects the port installations at Montreal at the end of the nineteenth century were much as they are today, but subsequent additions have included steel and concrete sheds, built between 1900 and 1930, grain elevators dating from 1905–60, a refrigerated warehouse of 1928, and a container terminal of 1968–84. The clock tower was constructed in 1921 in commemoration of sailors lost at sea. During the past decade the port of Montreal has become a residential and recreational area. Its location near the historic district of Old Montreal, the increase of tourism and the effervescence of cultural activities in the city have led to the construction of condominiums in the area, and to the conversion of transit sheds into exhibition halls and theatres.

The establishment of commercial navigation between the St Lawrence River and the Great Lakes as well as the need for a line of defence against the threat from the USA led to the construction of the Lachine Canal between 1821 and 1825. The government of Lower Canada paid for the project, which was carried out by the British companies Bagg & White, McKay & Redpath and Phillips & White, and the British engineer Thomas Burnett. Between the port of Montreal and Lake St Louis the canal saw such intense activity between 1825 and 1968 that it may be considered the principal axis of industrial development in Canada.

The waterway became navigable in 1824, the canal being 13.4 km (8⅓ mi.) long, 14.4 m (47.24 ft.) wide, and 1.35 m (4.43 ft.) deep. Its seven locks, built in ASHLAR, were 30.8 m (101 ft.) long and 6.1 m (20 ft.) wide, with a draught of 1.5 m (5.92 ft.): these were its principal structures. They comprised double gates of composite wood and metal construction, operated by windlasses. The canal was crossed by thirteen bridges and several sewers went beneath it. Between 1843 and 1848 the growth of maritime traffic – due to the heavy demand for wood and grain in Canada and the USA, as well as the stimulus provided by the Erie Canal – made necessary the enlargement of the canal. It was widened to 6 m (19.7 ft.) with a draught of 2.7 m (8.86 ft.). A quay of 1.41 km (1542 yd.) was constructed, and five locks were retained, each of them measuring 61.6 m (202 ft.) long by 13.8 m (45.3 ft.) wide, by 2.9 m (9½ ft.) deep. They were built of stone, and had gates of wood and iron, opened by chains worked by capstans. During this period the St Lawrence navigation was extended by the construction of new

Figure 88   Locks Nos. 1 and 2 on the Lachine Canal in the port of Montreal, *c*.1930, showing a variety of shipping and a range of grain silos on the right
Public Archives, Canada

canals, the RIDEAU CANAL in 1832, the Chambly in 1843 and the Beauharnois in 1845.

From 1850 textile mills, foundries, flourmills and sawmills were erected along the banks of the Lachine Canal. Other factories were concentrated around the Saint-Gabriel lock and in the Côte Saint-Paul. Some, including the Redpath sugar refinery, established in 1854, and the Belding textile mill, built in 1876, have now ceased operation, but others are still working, including the Phillips Electrical Works, established in 1888, and the Canadian Switch and Spring factory of 1898. Many of these vast steel and concrete buildings are faced with ashlar and adorned with ART DECO ornamentation.

The last widening of the canal was undertaken from 1874. The locks were lengthened to 83 m (272 ft.) but their width remained unaltered. A new quay, 1.86 km (1 mi. 300 yd.) long, was constructed at Lachine.

Great numbers of small craft used the canal. Sailing ships were gradually supplanted by steamers from the 1880s, and those in turn by the 'canallers' after the

lengthening of the locks. These last building works allowed commercial navigation to reach a peak between 1930 and 1950. After this time commercial navigation turned towards the St Lawrence Seaway which, from its completion in 1959, favoured the high-capacity vessels, the 'lakers' chartered for the transport of raw materials in bulk.

The concentration of so many industrial plants along the Lachine Canal was due largely to the labour force of Irish migrants. Living in rented accommodation in wooden and brick houses, which were often insanitary, they populated successively the suburbs of Pointe-Saint-Charles, Saint-Henri and Côte Saint-Paul, as well as those to the north-west, Victoriatown and Griffintown which have since been destroyed by the construction of the Bonaventure highway.

The area between the highway, the port of Montreal, the municipality of Lachine and Lake St Louis is the responsibility of the Canadian Parks Service, which has undertaken a programme of research, restoration and interpretation. There is an 11 km (7 mi.) cycle track between the port of Montreal and Lake St Louis (which can be used by skiers in winter), an interpretation centre, and picnic areas.

The industrial expansion of Montreal and the growth of its population, especially between 1850 and 1920, are well illustrated by the district of Hochelaga-Maisonneuve in the south of the city. A programme of research, conservation and interpretation supported by the Quebec government is now in progress in the area; it is being carried out by a local organization, the History Workshop of Hochelaga-Maisonneuve, which works in collaboration with scholars at the University of Quebec in Montreal. Maisonneuve originated as a suburban municipality, and was literally created by a group of landed proprietors, some of them well-known politicians, who wished to take advantage of its position near to the port and the railways. Inspired by contemporary ideas about urban development in the USA, above all by the CITY BEAUTIFUL movement, the municipality came to favour the construction of grandiose public buildings – a market, a town hall, and a fire station – and the laying out of roads to attract new industries. About forty factories were established in the area between 1880 and 1917, most of them in the consumer goods sector: food, leather, soap, cutlery, tobacco, ice, engineering, iron and steel, construction materials like wood, cement, stone and terracotta, paper, textiles, electricity, chemicals and transport. Largely because of the high cost of these developments the municipality became insolvent, which led to its annexation to Montreal in 1918, but many enterprises established in the last century remain active in the area, particularly those concerned with food and transport.

The majority of the workers' houses built in the Hochelaga-Maisonneuve area in this period still remain. The dwellings of the late nineteenth century are in rural styles, whether in wood with pointed roofs, or in red brick in two storeys with a flat roof. Houses constructed between 1880 and 1920 are also in red brick, but with façades in grey stone, usually with three storeys linked by external wrought-iron staircases. Most of these houses accommodated large families, who often lived in insanitary conditions, but public health programmes and various social services were energetically provided by the city of Montreal from the early twentieth century.

Windsor Station in the south-west part of the city was built at the end of the nineteenth century as the terminus of Canada's first transcontinental railway, and also as the headquarters of its owners, the Canadian Pacific company. The station was constructed in three stages under the direction of the architects Bruce Price in 1888–9 and Edward Maxwell in 1900–6, and the engineer William Painter in 1910–12. It remains in use as a commuter train terminal and as headquarters of Canadian Pacific. The station is one of the most eloquent expressions of railway architecture in Canada, and draws its inspiration from the Romanesque style, shown by the use of grey stone which ultimately covered completely the steel framework, the predominance of semicircular arcading, the many arches, the tympana on the three interior storeys and on the façades onto the rue Saint-Antoine, the

columns and vertical windows grouped in threes on the top storey, the turrets, the dormers and the balustrade that embellishes the line of the roof on the lodge. The ticket hall, which now opens on to the rue de la Gauchetière, was originally covered with arcading and cornices in stone resting on granite columns. The increase in the number of platforms has necessitated the rearrangement of the space given over to passengers and in 1913 a new hall was created, constructed of iron, steel and glass. It is notable for its marble walls lined with wainscot panelling in walnut. Other new sections including one used for telecommunications were incorporated into the station after 1950, but they were not part of Price's original plans. Canadian Pacific and the Friends of Windsor Station are now jointly responsible for the conservation and interpretation of this great monument to the railway age and of the documents that relate to it.

The Victoria Bridge was the first means of railway communication linking the island of Montreal with the south shore of the St Lawrence river, and was built between 1853 and 1860 by the Grand Trunk Railway which was also responsible for its rebuilding in 1897–9, renaming it the Victoria Jubilee Bridge. In 1923 it was taken over by Canadian National, which is now responsible for its maintenance and for the archives relating to it. The bridge was designed by ROBERT STEPHENSON and constructed by the British company Petts, Brassey & Petts: it was originally a wrought-iron TUBULAR BRIDGE, some 2 km (1 mi. 430 yd.) long, comprising twenty-five spans of 4.8 m (15 ft. 9 in.), 6 m (19 ft. 8 in.) high, which rested on twenty-four limestone piers. Two factors, the use of coal as locomotive fuel and the increase in railway traffic, made reconstruction necessary after 1870. The work was carried out by the Detroit Bridge & Ironwork Co. and Dominion Bridge of Lachine (see above). The bridge was transformed by the erection of steel spans, the widening of the deck to 20 m (65 ft. 7 in.), the strengthening of the piers, and the addition of a second railway track. During the present century tracks for electric tramways and lanes for motor traffic have been added, and in 1986 it was carrying 38 freight trains, 18 passenger trains and 44 000 motor vehicles per day.

For the construction of the Victoria Bridge the Grand Trunk Co. employed a British labour force, consisting principally of Irishmen, and undertook to provide living accommodation for them. Consequently in 1857 the company built seven terraces of houses on the rue de Sebastopol near to its workshops. The houses were occupied by these workmen until 1868, and subsequently by employees of Canadian National. Since 1970 these houses, much altered over time, were taken over by property speculators and partially demolished, and in 1985 only three were still occupied. The houses are similar in style to those built by British railway companies, and to the two-storey flats of NEWCASTLE-UPON-TYNE. They are 16.5 m (54 ft.) long and extend back 10 m (33 ft.) from the frontage. They are constructed in red brick, and are of two storeys with low façades topped with double-pitched roofs.

The Canadian Railway Museum is located 16 km (10

mi.) SW of Montreal in the towns of Delson and St Constant near the route of the first railway in the British North American colonies, which was opened in 1836. The museum was founded in 1961 by the Canadian Railroad Historical Association, and is now managed by members of the Association, together with professional staff and volunteers. The museum's structures include a turntable, a length of track on which trains and tramcars run in summer, and the nineteenth-century Barrington station. Two large buildings house rolling stock. The collection is accessible to visitors and includes more than a hundred items of rolling stock – steam and diesel locomotives, passenger cars, freight wagons and tramcars – coming principally from the Canadian National and Canadian Pacific railways and the Montreal Transit Corporation. Exhibits of outstanding importance include a typical Canadian 4-4-0 locomotive of the 1880s; a Canadian Pacific 'Royal Hudson' 4-6-4, used on transcontinental trains from the 1930s; a Canadian National 'Hudson' 4-6-4, used on high-speed trains between Montreal and Toronto in the same period; a 365-ton Selkirk 2-10-4, built in 1949 for use in the Rocky Mountains; a diesel railcar built in Ottawa in 1926; a sleeping car of 1921; a tank wagon of 1916; several INTERURBAN cars of the second decade of the twentieth century; and the British streamlined 4-6-2 *Dominion of Canada*, built for the LNER in 1937. Further exhibits associated with the development of railway technology are displayed in an interpretation centre.

BIBLIOGRAPHY
General
Bouchard, 1980; Charbonneau, 1980; Forget, 1985; Linteau, 1981; Pinard, 1986.
Specific
Canadian Railway Museum Working Group. *The Next Spike: a report on the development of a concept for the expansion of the museum*. Ottawa: Canadian Railroad Historical Association and National Museums of Canada, 1979.
Chevrefils, Y. Il y a un siècle le pont Victoria (For a century there was the Victoria Bridge). In *Continuité*, XXVIII, 1985.
Labelle, E. Le port de Montréal, un siècle et demi de construction (A century and a half of development of the port of Montreal). In *Architecture Québec*, XXIX, 1986.
Lagué, J. *Proposition pour le canal de Lachine: écluses Saint-Gabriel* (Proposals for the Lachine Canal: the Saint-Gabriel Locks). Montreal: Heritage Montreal, 1985.
Sicotte, A.-M. and Thériault, R. *De la vapeur au velo: le guide du canal de Lachine* (From steam to bicycle: the guide to the Lachine Canal). Montreal. Association les Mil Lieues, 1986.
Willis, J. *The Lachine Canal, 1840–1900: preliminary report*. Quebec: Environnement Canada-Parcs, 1983.

LOCATIONS
[M] Canadian Railway Museum, PPO Box 148, St Constant, Quebec JOL 1XO.
[M] Centre d'interprétation de l'histoire du Canal de Lachine, Pavillon Monk, 711 Boulevard Saint-Joseph, Lachine.
[I] Service Canadien des parcs, secteur de Lachine, 200 ouest Boulevard René Levesque, suite 025, Montreal H2Z 1X4.

LOUISE TROTTIER

mordant A chemical used to bring about the colour change in dyeing processes involving such dyestuffs as MADDER and LOGWOOD. The colours obtained from dyes differ with different mordants. Madder by itself stains wool pale brown: with ALUM it gives a red colour, varying with the concentration; with iron in the form of copperas $(FeSO_4.7H_2O)$, a brown. Mordants can be bound firmly to the cloth before the application of dye by substances containing tannin; suitable substances include sumach, the dried and chopped leaves of the *Rhus* genus, and galls from oak trees.

BIBLIOGRAPHY
General
Partridge, 1823.

Morris, William (1834–96) A poet, designer, printer, conservationist and philosopher, one of the most penetrating critics of the capitalist industrial society of the nineteenth century, and one of the most subtle prophets of that which has evolved in the twentieth century. Morris was born to a rich bourgeois family on the eastern outskirts of London, and at Oxford in the early 1850s was influenced by medievalism. In 1856 he was articled for a short time to the architect, George Edmund Street (1824–81). In 1861 he established a design 'firm' with D. G. Rossetti (1828–82), F. M. Brown (1821–93) and E. Burne Jones (1833–98). He continued the concern after the partnership was dissolved in 1875, producing wallpapers, furnishings and carpets. In 1877 he was one of the founders of the Society for the Protection of Ancient Buildings. In 1890 he established the Kelmscott Press, producing books in which typefaces and illustrations were in harmony. In 1876–8 he became an active socialist, and his most important philosophical and prophetic works were published in the late 1880s and 1890s.

BIBLIOGRAPHY
General
Briggs, 1962; Morris, 1910–15; Pevsner, 1960; Thompson, 1955.

LOCATIONS
[S] Kelmscott Manor House, Witney, Oxfordshire.
[S] Red House, Red House Lane, Bexleyheath, Kent.
[M] William Morris Gallery, Lloyd Park, Forest Road, Walthamstow, Essex.

BARRIE TRINDER

Morris, William Richard, 1st Viscount Nuffield (1877–1963) One of the founders of the British motor industry, who began a bicycle firm in OXFORD at the age of sixteen, started to repair motorcars c.1902, and produced his first car, the bull-nosed Morris Oxford, in 1913. He made Oxford a major car-producing centre. Morris Motors Ltd was incorporated in 1919, and prospered by cutting prices during the slump of the 1920s. He joined with others in 1926 to form the Pressed Steel Co. to make car bodies, and his group acquired many other companies, notably the Austin concern in 1952. He was renowned as a philanthropist.

BIBLIOGRAPHY
General
Andrews and Brunner, 1955.

Morse, Samuel Finley Breese (1791–1872) An American artist, who became interested in telegraphy on a return voyage from Europe in 1832. In his electric telegraph, patented in 1837, an intermitting current caused coded marks on paper. After much frustration he opened a public line between Washington and Baltimore in 1844–5, using a dot and dash code devised by his assistant Alfred Vail. Latterly the use of sound only became widespread, although Morse himself opposed this.

BIBLIOGRAPHY
General
Morse, 1914.

Morwellham, Devon, England A port at the head of navigation on the River Tamar, 37 km (23 mi.) N. of Plymouth, where copper, arsenic and manganese ores from nearby mines were shipped in the mid-nineteenth century. The port declined from *c*.1870. A Dartington Hall Trust enterprise operates a museum. Features include the 2322 m (2539 yd.) tunnel on the 6.5 km (4 mi.) Tavistock Canal, opened in 1817; an inclined plane, which lowered canal boats 72 m (236 ft.) to river quays; and a train which takes visitors into a copper mine.

BIBLIOGRAPHY
General
Booker, 1971; Hadfield, 1967a.

LOCATION
[M] Morwellham Quay Open-Air Museum, Morwellham, Tavistock, Devon PL19 8JL.

mosaic A decorative effect on a pavement or wall, achieved in the ancient world by arrangements of small polychromatic stone cubes called tesserae. Mosaic was revived in the nineteenth century by CERAMICS companies. They produced first stoneware quarries (*see* TILES), which could be broken up and used as tesserae. Later they produced 'pseudo-' or geometric mosaics, square tiles made up of cubes of clay of different colours, assembled on plates; when completed these had deeply incised lines like those of a true mosaic.

BIBLIOGRAPHY
General
van Lemmen, 1979.

Moscow (Moskva), USSR The Capital of Muscovy, and then Russia, until 1712; then the 'second capital' after the rise of St Petersburg (later LENINGRAD), and capital of the USSR from 1918. From the fourteenth century it was the seat of the Russian Orthodox church. Moscow's population in 1800 was about 200 000, rising to a little over a million in 1897, making it the biggest Russian city, a distinction it has retained; the 1970 population exceeded seven million. It is situated on both banks of the River Moskva, which connects with the Volga system. This ready access to the main waterways was the crucial factor in the city's rise to political, religious and then commercial supremacy. From the sixteenth century a large population of craftsmen settled and worked in Moscow; many were foreigners, who tended to live in the Kitaiskii Gorod district. Larger-scale manufacturing appeared in the eighteenth century, but modern industry, initially textiles and engineering, began only in the 1830s. An engineered water supply was provided at the end of the eighteenth century and mains sewers in the late nineteenth. The electric tramways originated in 1899 and still flourish. The underground railway (Metro) was begun in 1932 and is still being extended. Although Moscow was only the 'second capital' in the railway age, the new lines tended to radiate more from Moscow than from St Petersburg.

Because most early buildings were wooden, few have survived. The Kremlin is a brick defensive wall on the north side of the river with a radius of about 1.6 km (1 mi.), enclosing old official and church buildings. On show within the walls are a 200-ton bronze bell, cast in Moscow in 1735 but damaged by fire soon afterwards, and a bronze cannon of 1586, each representing the peak Russian achievement in bronze casting of its period. They also illustrate the Russian penchant for size: the bell is 6.6 m (21 ft. 8 in.) in diameter, while the cannon barrel is 5.34 m (17 ft. 6 in.) long, with an inside diameter of 0.89 m (35 in.). Red Square is flanked on one side by the GUM department store, which was formerly an enclosed market designed by V. G. S. SHUKHOV. The Lenin Museum nearby is the former town hall, built in the late nineteenth century in the neo-Slavic style then becoming fashionable. Another representative of this style is the Rizhskii railway terminus, formerly the Vindava Station. On Railway Square are three termini, of which the oldest is the Leningrad Station terminus of the St Petersburg–Moscow Railway opened in 1849, which still has its original façade. Alongside is the Yaroslavl' Station of the early twentieth century which incorporates north Russian architectural features; and opposite is the much bigger Kazan Station which dates mainly from 1913–40, and combines traditional features of Muscovite and Kazan architecture. Of the other termini, the Kursk Station is a modern structure, and the Byelorussian is largely in its original condition, as is the Kiev Station. The Pavelets Station, built *c*.1900, imitates the French Louis XIV style. Outside it is a museum containing the 4–6–0 locomotive and baggage car that brought Lenin's body to Moscow. The locomotive is a rare example of a preserved passenger locomotive of the tsarist period, while the baggage car is even rarer, very few other examples of railway passenger stock having been preserved in Russia.

Other old surviving structures include the Printing House of 1679, and several bridges. The brick-arch Troitskii Bridge, believed to have been built in 1516 and restored several times, once spanned a river outside the Troitskii Gate of the Kremlin. The Lefortovo Bridge is the former Dvortsovyi Bridge, built in 1781 and rebuilt in 1940. This stone arched structure is interesting in that its roadway slopes down towards the centre, producing a fine

Figure 89   The GUM department store, Moscow, from Red Square, constructed from 1888 to 1893 on a site previously occupied by an open-air market
Novosti

cascade of drainwater in rainy weather. The 356 m (389 yd.) Rostokino Aqueduct is officially preserved although still in use: built at the end of the eighteenth century, it remains part of Moscow's water-supply system.

There are numerous specialized museums within the city, but even those that deal with specific industries have few artefacts, their main displays centring on pictures and documents. This is true to a large extent even of the Polytechnical Museum, founded in 1872, although this does have good collections of scientific apparatus and also an interesting collection of about thirty foreign and Russian-built motorcars, including an Armstrong Siddeley of 1912 and a home-built Russo-Balt K/12/120 of 1911. The Mining Institute has its own museum, as do certain factories, but these are not always open to the public.

Of the Moscow factories, the Dinamo electrical engineering works are the best known. Founded in 1897 by a Belgian, they received their present name in 1913 when they were bought by a Russian company. The Dinamo historical museum was established in 1964, and, like many similar museums, places greatest emphasis on the political activities of its workers.

Outside the city, the Ostankino estate museum includes a machine shop not untypical of those set up by landowners on their estates in the eighteenth and nineteenth centuries. Adjoining it is a museum of serf production, which is not entirely devoted to traditional handicrafts because Russian serfs sometimes became involved in industrial and technological progress. Another estate museum in the Moscow region is at Muranovo. This is

mainly concerned with literature, but is housed in the former Ashukinskaya station on the one-time Moscow–Yaroslavl' railway. In the northern suburbs, the locomotive depot at Khovrino displays the diesel locomotive built by Y. Gakkel'.

BIBLIOGRAPHY
Specific
Fal'kovskii, N. *Moskva v istorii tekniki*. Moscow, 1950.
Mikhailov, B. *Ostankino*. Moscow, 1976.
Moskva-Entsiklopediya, Moscow, 1980.
Nadezhin, B. *Mosty Moskvy*. Moscow, 1979.

LOCATIONS
[M] Exhibition of Soviet Economic Achievement, Pr.Mira, Moscow.
[M] A. E. Fersman Mineralogical Museum, Leninski pr.14–16, Moscow.
[M] M. V. Frunze Central Museum of Aviation and Astronautics, Ul.Krasnoarmeiskaya 14, Moscow.
[M] Kolomenskoye Estate Museum, Moscow.
[M] Museum of Decorative Arts, Ul.Razin 18/2, Moscow.
[M] Museum of Folk Art, Ul.Stanislavskogo 7, Moscow.
[M] Museum of History and of the Reconstruction of Moscow, Novaya pl.12, Moscow.
[M] Museum of Industrial Safety, Leninski pr.86, Moscow.
[M] Museum of Soil Sciences of Moscow State University, Moscow State University, Moscow.
[M] Ostankino Palace Museum of Serf Art, Ul.1 Ostankinskaya 5, Moscow.
[M] Permanent Exhibition of the Soviet Construction Industry, Frunzenskaya nab.30, Moscow.
[M] Pharmaceutical Museum, 1 Dubrovskaya ul.8/12, Moscow.
[M] Polytechnical Museum, Novaya pl.34, Moscow.

[M] State Museum of Ceramics and Kuskovo Estate, Kuskovo, Moscow.

JOHN WESTWOOD

Moselle, River (Mosel), France and Germany   The River Moselle rises near Épinal in the Vosges and flows through LORRAINE and to the south of the EIFEL to join the Rhine at Koblenz. It has been an important route between France and Germany since Roman times. Tolls on the river were removed in 1863, but navigational difficulties restricted traffic in the early twentieth century to only 6 million kilometre-tonnes per annum. Canalization of the Moselle began in 1952 with the 270 km (170 mi.) section from Koblenz to Thionville in France, and was extended in the 1970s to Neuves-Maisons, 394 km (245 mi.) from Koblenz.

Like the Rhine, the Moselle cuts deeply through slate mountains and, also like the Rhine, its valley is a wine-growing area and contains several important technological monuments connected with that trade. Two harbour cranes of different dates, used chiefly for loading casks of wine, are preserved in Trier. The so-called Old Crane dates from 1413, while the Toll Crane was built in 1744 on the model of the older one. Both have massive cylindrical bodies, and movable conical roofs. A peculiarity is the double arm, 13 m (43 ft.) long, which could be used to serve ships on the river and the road on the bank at the same time. Each crane was powered by two treadwheels, 4.2 m (13 ft. 9 in.) in diameter and 1.2 m (3 ft. 11 in.) wide.

The railway up the Moselle valley from Koblenz to Trier was opened in 1879. It was not always able to follow the meanders of the river. The loop at Cochem, 40 km (25 mi.) SW of Koblenz, had to be cut short by the 4200 m (4600 yd.) Kaiser Wilhelm tunnel. Until the construction of lines for high-speed trains in the 1980s this was the longest tunnel in Germany. The use of steam locomotives caused ventilation problems and a steam-powered ventilating system was installed at Cochem in 1904, to be replaced in 1937 by electric ventilators which remain extant. The building that housed the steam ventilation plant and the tunnel portal, which is decorated with imperial eagles, have been preserved. The steep slopes of the Moselle valley made it necessary to build a viaduct a kilometre long opposite the village of Pünderich, 44 km (27 mi.) SW of Koblenz.

Cable ferries have been used to link the banks of the river since Roman times. An octagonal stone ferry tower of 1863, from which the cable extended to the opposite bank, is preserved in Hatzenport, 18 km (11 mi.) SW of Koblenz. The cable pulleys and winch are still in place at the foot of the tower.

Bruno Möhring, architect of the machine shop of the Zollern 2/4 mine in Dortmund (see RUHRGEBIET), designed several JUGENDSTIL buildings in Traben-Trarbach, 56 km (35 mi.) SW of Koblenz. In 1897 he won a competition to design the Moselle bridge, a four-span arched structure; this was destroyed in World War II, although the portal building on the Trarbach bank has been preserved, with its two towers and an arch over the carriageway of the road. The wine cellar building designed by Möhring for the firm of Julius Kayser & Co. in 1906 is more severe in style.

BIBLIOGRAPHY
General
Custodis, 1990; Hadfield, 1986.

ROLF HÖHMANN

Mostar, Bosnia-Hercegovina, Yugoslavia   Capital of Hercegovina, on the River Neretua. Industrialization began after the Habsburgs took over territory from the Turks in 1878. Turkish Bridge, completed by the architect Hairudin on the orders of Suleiman the Magnificent in 1566, has a 30 m (100 ft.) arch of white limestone. There are mosques and early nineteenth-century houses of Turkish merchants, some of which are open to the public. There is a tradition of crafts manufactures, particularly of gold and silver. Mostar has a modern aluminium plant.

LOCATION
[M] Museum of Hercegovina, ul. Marsala Tita 160, 79000-Mostar.

Motala, Ostergötland, Sweden   *See* GOTHA CANAL.

motel   A form of hotel catering for travellers by motorcar (*mo*tor ho*tel*), usually a group of single-storey buildings, originally called 'cabins', for overnight accommodation, with central dining facilities. The first was built at Douglas, Arizona, in 1913, and the first chain was established in California from 1925–6, but the main period of growth in North America was in the 1930s. The first in Europe appeared in the 1950s.

BIBLIOGRAPHY
General
Baker and Funaro, 1955; Pevsner, 1976.

motorcar   A self-propelled wheeled vehicle, with steam, electric, gas or diesel power, but most commonly with a PETROL ENGINE. The motorcar has come to dominate twentieth-century manufacturing industry and social life. GOTTLIEB DAIMLER worked for a time in the Otto and Langen (*see* GAS ENGINE) factory at COLOGNE, and by 1881 had established his own works in STUTTGART where he adapted the Otto engine to power a moving vehicle. KARL BENZ was pursuing parallel developments, and in the late 1880s both applied improved forms of engine to four-wheeled vehicles. In 1890 Daimler built 350 cars, and began to grant licences for production in other countries. The first in the USA was built in 1893, and in due course that country came to dominate world production. The first volume-produced motorcar, the Oldsmobile, appeared in 1902, and HENRY FORD's Model T in 1908. Production in most countries expanded rapidly in the 1920s and 30s. Of the most significant components of the twentieth-century motorcar, the differential was devised by Onésiphone Pecqueur in France in 1827, the electric self-starter by Charles F. Kettering (1874–1958) in the

USA in 1912, the use of brakes on four wheels in the USA in 1923, and the use of safety glass in the USA in 1926.

See also AUTOMOBILE; CAR; GARAGE; MOTORCAR FACTORY; MOTORCAR SHOWROOM; SERVICE STATION.

BIBLIOGRAPHY
General
Anderson, 1950; Andrews and Brunner, 1955; Barker, 1988; Barker and Harduce, 1971; Dyos and Aldcroft, 1969; Flink, 1972; Kidner, 1946; Ling, 1990; Nevins and Hill, 1954 63; Oliver and Berkebile, 1968; Plowden, 1971; Rae, 1965; Sedgwick, 1970; Ware, 1976.

BARRIE TRINDER

motorcar factory The first cars were built in modest workshops. Prototype and first-production cars were usually hand-built, often by small engineering firms in specially cleared or unused parts of their premises. With modest capital injection, such firms were well equipped to develop prototype vehicles and make the transition to low-volume car production, although larger-scale production normally necessitated new building.

The first purpose-built car factories were completed around 1900. Two design approaches can be discerned: a series of single-storey workshops, and, on more constricted sites, multi-storey factories. In the former, production flowed towards the assembly and erecting shops situated at the centre of the site. The major drawbacks to this 'fixed shop' arrangement were the excessive effort required in moving materials and components among the shops and the cluttered nature of the site; space to expand the size and output of one shop had often to be gained at the expense of the future expansion or the very existence of adjacent shops. Multi-storey factories allowed more logical flows of components between production stages, with the manufacture of such major components as the chassis and body, and the major stages in production, like final assembly, and painting and trimming, each being allocated to a separate storey. Drawbacks to this form arose from the difficulties of expanding production, and the need to move items between storeys using lifts.

Before 1920 many different arrangements were tried. In one, best termed the 'flexible shop', production was ordered in a large, single-storey, rectangular NORTH-LIT SHED; this provided a massive space to house the various processes, which could easily be reallocated as required. Production flowed through the building in a U-shaped pattern. Others ordered production stages along adjacent rows of north-lit sheds, some separating those involving heat from those involving combustible materials by siting them on opposite sides of a service road.

The increased output levels required for the aviation, armament or military vehicle work undertaken by most car manufacturers during World War I introduced flow-production methods into many car factory machine shops for the first time. Following this experience they were put to good use when car production resumed. American manufacturers, notably Ford, had also adapted flow-production methods to the assembly of main component sub-assemblies, and to the final assembly of cars down long production tracks. These techniques spread first to Britain and then to Germany, through the opening of Ford subsidiaries in 1911 and 1931. They were embraced by other manufacturers, notably WILLIAM MORRIS (Lord Nuffield), who rebuilt their factories to accommodate them.

See figures 90, 91; *see also* ASSEMBLY LINE; INTERCHANGEABLE PARTS; KAHN, ALBERT; MASS PRODUCTION; and figures 107, 162.

BIBLIOGRAPHY
General
Chandler, 1964; Collins and Stratton, 1986; History Workshop, 1985, Oliver, 1981; Rae, 1959; Rolt, 1950a; Thomas and Donnelly, 1985.
Specific
Collins, P. H. and Stratton, M. J. From trestles to tracks: the development of the British car factory. In *Journal of Transport History*, 18 1988

PAUL COLLINS

motorcar showroom An establishment where motorcars are displayed and sold. The outstanding examples of the 1920s and 30s presented a modernist image, with vitrolite sheeting on the exterior, and large plate-glass display windows, tilted or curved to avoid distracting reflections. Showrooms were often multi-storey, with ramps or ELEVATORS connecting the floors, the uppermost of which might be used for servicing and repairs or for the storage of secondhand vehicles. Small-scale showrooms are often incorporated in SERVICE STATIONS.

BIBLIOGRAPHY
General
Conradi, 1931; Munce, 1960; Vehlefeld and Jacques, 1956; Ware, 1976.

motorcoach The development of the motorcoach resembles that of the motor OMNIBUS. Early examples were single-deck vehicles, open to the elements or with retractable hoods, and were often called 'charabancs', being used chiefly for private-hire pleasure trips. The first timetabled services in England began in 1921. In the 1920s and 30s, as standards of speed and comfort improved, networks of services were developed which rivalled those of railway companies. In North America the services of Greyhound and other companies prospered in the 1930s and are now the basic means of cheap, long-distance passenger transport. In Europe motorway services, using fast, powerful vehicles with underfloor engines, observation decks, on-board toilets, air-conditioning and catering, continue to compete with railway passenger services.

BIBLIOGRAPHY
General
Anderson and Frankis, 1970.

motorcycle A motorized bicycle or tricycle, powered by a petrol engine mounted on the frame. Some of the earliest powered vehicles were tricycles, and various machines were manufactured on an industrial scale in the years before World War I. By 1918 a standard configuration

Figure 90   Citroën '5CV' and Kégresse caterpillar-track vehicles on the trial track at the Clément-Bayard/Citroën factory at Levallois-Perret, *c.*1921
Citroën

Figure 91   Buffing, final trim and preliminary inspection in progress on a segment of the final assembly line at the Chevrolet plant of General Motors Corporation, at Flint, Michigan, 1947; the concrete-framed factory building was designed by Albert Kahn.
Albert Kahn Associates, Architects & Engineers, Detroit, Michigan

had been adopted, the rider being behind the petrol tank, beneath which was located the engine (attached to or forming part of the frame), which drove the rear wheel. In the 1920s and 30s motorcycles, often with side cars, were a significant form of transport, and remained so after World War II. Since the 1950s their significance has lessened, small machines providing inexpensive means of everyday personal transport, and the larger examples being kept primarily as means of fulfilling various recreational needs.

Motorcycle manufacture involves the bringing together of engines and cycle parts, including frames, mudguards, saddles, drive chains and suspension units, and general components like wheels and instruments. Motorcycle factories characteristically had closely-packed lines of machine tools, either in NORTH-LIT SHEDS or in well-lit multi-storey blocks, in which floors were linked by ELEVATORS, often located in corner towers. Frames were made from steel alloy tubes, bent and fitted together by brazing, and then cleaned and enamelled. Trestle assembly was still commonplace in the 1920s and 30s, although some companies were by then using ASSEMBLY LINES. The principal works were in COVENTRY in England, in Italy, in Germany and in the USA. From the 1950s Japan came to dominate world markets for all but the heaviest classes of motorcycles, which still emanate from Harley Davidson in the USA.

BIBLIOGRAPHY
General
Ayton, 1979; Caunter, 1982; Ixion, 1951; Smith, 1981; Tragatsch, 1979; Walford, 1931.
Specific
The Works of the BSA Co. Ltd. In *Automobile Engineer*, XVIII, 1928.
The Works of the Triumph Co. In *Automobile Engineer*, XIX, 1929.
The Ariel Motor Cycle Works. In *Automobile Engineer*, XXII, 1932.

BARRIE TRINDER

motor lorry   The main means of carrying freight in most countries of the world in the 1990s. Companies in the USA, Germany and France were beginning to produce specialist motor vehicles for conveying freight by the mid-1890s, but Britain lagged behind due to its preference for steam vehicles, and legislation restricting the speed of powered road vehicles which was only repealed in 1896. Early vehicles usually weighed no more than about three tons, and were petrol-engined. Vast numbers were built for military use in World War I, and many surplus vehicles became available at low cost for commercial use from 1918. Major developments of the 1920s were the adoption of pneumatic tyres, and, more importantly, the introduction of the heavy oil or diesel engine, although the use of petrol engines persisted rather longer in the USA. The development of heavier, longer chassis and improved braking systems enabled the establishment of long-distance services which threatened railway traffic. Further improvements were stimulated by military demands in World War II; they included all-wheel drive, and the development of extra-large vehicles for transport-

ing tanks and aeroplanes. Since 1945 the trend has been towards larger, heavier vehicles, almost exclusively diesel-powered, many being articulated vehicles with detachable tractor units and multi-axle trailers.

Networks of refreshment houses for long-distance lorry drivers have grown up in most countries, reflecting different cultures – transport cafés in Britain, 'truck stops' in the USA. Often the first generations were ephemeral buildings and are recorded only in photographs or films. Lorry driving, although a solitary occupation, has developed a repertoire of ballads.

See also STEAM LORRY; TRUCK.

BIBLIOGRAPHY
General
Hollowell, 1968; Klapper, 1973; Kuipers, 1972.

JOHN POWELL

motor museum   Motorcars are the most widely collected large artefacts of industrial civilization, and the number of collections open to the public is large. Of this number, some fulfil in every respect the requirements of MUSEUM status, and some, like the National Motor Museum, BEAULIEU, the Henry Ford Museum at Greenfield, MICHIGAN, or the Daimler-Benz Museum, STUTTGART, have displays and visitor facilities of the highest standards. Even the best have thus far made few attempts to interpret the significance of the motorcar, displaying large numbers of individual examples but rarely giving any indication of how they were made, or of the social benefits and problems which arise from use of the motorcar. Examples of most significant types of motorcar are preserved, but the emphasis in museums tends to be on the more spectacular vehicles built for the wealthy, or for special purposes.

BIBLIOGRAPHY
General
Nicholson, 1970.
Specific
Hyde, C. K. The automobile in American life: an exhibition at the Henry Ford Museum. In *Technology & Culture*, XXX, 1989.

BARRIE TRINDER

motor spirit   *See* PETROL.

motor vessel   A term usually applied to a vessel powered by a DIESEL ENGINE. The first was the triple-screw river tanker *Vandal* used in the Nobel company's petroleum enterprise in Russia from 1903 (*see* NOBEL, ALFRED). Since early diesel engines could not be reversed, the engine drove a generator powering electric motors that *could* be reversed. The first ocean-going motor ship is generally acknowledged to have been the 1940-ton *Selandia*, constructed by Burmeister & Wain of Copenhagen in 1911–12, built without a funnel to emphasize her means of propulsion. The Swedish *Gripsholm*, of 17 993 tons, built at Newcastle-upon-Tyne in 1925, was the first diesel-powered Atlantic liner. Since World War II the large marine diesel engine has come to replace both the triple-expansion steam engine and the steam turbine. The 26.6-ton wooden vessel *Helge* still sails from Svendborg (*see* ODENSE) and the 206-ton motor cargo ship *Wolfe Islander* of 1946 is preserved at Kingston, Ontario.

See also IRVINE.

BIBLIOGRAPHY
General
Baker, 1965; Brouwer, 1985; Burmeister & Wain, 1943; Lehmann, 1937.

BARRIE TRINDER

Motril, Granada, Andalusia, Spain   A city on the Mediterranean coast, 48 km (30 mi.) S. of Granada: the centre of the last sugar-cane growing area in Europe. The city's sugar refinery has ceased production, but its processing machinery and steam engines remain *in situ*.

mould loft   A room in a SHIPYARD in which the body plan of a ship is drawn out as a series of cross-sections at full size. From the body plan are taken all the templates and measurements required to build the ship, and the plan proves a constant series of checks on the ship's lines and dimensions. A mould loft has extensive floor space, is well-lit, and is unimpeded by upright columns: it is often situated on the top floor of a building with other workshops on the lower floors. A mould loft performed similar functions in the construction of both wooden and iron ships, but these are now fulfilled by optical and electronic equipment. An example of 1753–5 remains at Chatham (*see* MEDWAY).

BIBLIOGRAPHY
General
Coad, 1983, 1989.

moulds   Moulds are used in FOUNDRIES and many other industrial processes, but principally in CERAMICS. Perhaps the most fundamental development in ceramic technology was the adoption of moulds to permit the economical and accurate replication of forms. Wooden moulds were used for coarser ware, especially bricks from classical antiquity. They are retained in some brick and tile yards for coping and ridge tiles. Moulds supplanted the use of throwing techniques in the STOKE-ON-TRENT region *c.*1740–50. Cast metal was quickly supplanted by plaster, which absorbed moisture from the clay, aiding drying. The widespread adoption of plaster moulds for table and ornamental ware formed the basis of the mass production and mass marketing of stock designs replicated in large factories.

BIBLIOGRAPHY
General
Chandler, 1967; Searle, 1929.

Moura, Bento de (1702–76)   A Portuguese scientist, responsible for inventions in the fields of hydraulics, mechanics and chemistry, a member of the Royal Society of London to whom in 1752 he presented a paper on the development of the steam engine. Bento de Moura Portugal, as he is still known, died at the Fort of Junqueira, a victim of the Inquisition and of political persecution.

BIBLIOGRAPHY
Specific
Philosophical Transactions. London: Royal Society, 1752.

mousetrap   The manufacture of mousetraps on an industrial scale began in the mid-nineteenth century, and a mousetrap factory in PAISLEY was large enough to be converted later into apartments, but perhaps the chief significance of the mousetrap in industrial history is its place in the saying of Ralph Waldo Emerson (1803–82): 'If a man write a better book, preach a better sermon or make a better mousetrap than his neighbour, though he build his house in the woods, the world will make a beaten path to his door.'

muffle furnace   A furnace containing fire-resistant arches, which protect wares from coal and ashes while allowing heat to circulate and the operator to observe them. The muffle furnace is used particularly in assaying precious metals, and in ENAMELLING.

BIBLIOGRAPHY
General
Rees, 1802–20.

mule   A term with two meanings relevant to industrial archaeology:

1. The progeny of a male ass and a mare. (The term is also applied to the offspring of a stallion and a female ass, which should more properly be called a hinny.) Having both the strength of a horse and the endurance of an ass, the mule is used as a pack animal in mountainous regions, sometimes for operating machinery (*see* HORSE GIN), and was once widely used as a draught beast in the American South.
2. In the textile industry the word 'mule' is most commonly used as an abbreviation of SPINNING MULE.

Mulhouse, Haut-Rhin, France   Mulhouse was a free city until 1798 when it became part of France. Its industrial prosperity was founded in the eighteenth century, first on the production of printed cotton goods, then on mechanized spinning, which in turn engendered a mechanical engineering industry, and subsequently locomotive and carriage works. The first technical museum was opened at Mulhouse in 1857: a collection of drawings established by the Mulhouse Industrial Society. Its aim was to preserve the designs and samples produced by local calico printers. The collections were put into store in 1870, but in 1955 a new textile-printing museum was opened. This was followed in 1983 by a museum of wallpaper designs, set up in the former headquarters of the Order of Teutonic Knights – a magnificent building of 1735–8, which Jean Zuber had transformed into a wallpaper factory in 1797.

The museum has a complete collection of the designs produced by this factory.

This tradition of industrial museums has been continued in Mulhouse. The French Railway Museum opened in new buildings to the north of the city in 1976. Exhibits include *701*, de Glehn's first four-cylinder compound locomotive, a 4-2-2-0 of 1885; a de Glehn Atlantic compound of 1904; a giant 4-8-2 of 1925, Le Continent; a Crampton 4-2-0 of 1852; *232-U.1*, a 4-6-4 of 1949; *3-1192*, a Chapelon Pacific of 1936; an electric locomotive E.1 P.O. of 1900; a variety of railcars and multiple units, called 'autorails' in French; and numerous items of coaching stock, including sleeping cars and a Pullman car of 1926.

In 1982 a new motorcar museum was inaugurated, the former private collection of two textile magnates, the brothers Hans (b.1904) and Fritz (b.1906) Schlumpf. It is displayed in one of their former weaving shops. The collection numbers over five hundred vehicles, 123 of them Bugattis.

Electropolis, the museum of electrical energy, has amongst other objects a remarkable generating set dating from 1900, and incorporating a Brown & Boveri alternator, and a steam engine built by Sulzer in Switzerland. The whole weighs 70 tonnes and comes from the Dolfus-Mieg textile mill where it worked from 1901 until 1947. The steam engine has been restored and is operated at regular intervals.

The cité ouvrière at Mulhouse is one of Europe's outstanding model housing projects. It resulted from an initiative by a young textile manufacturer, Jean Zuber, who, appalled by overcrowding in the city, formed a limited company in 1853 to encourage owner-occupation. By 1870 the company's three thousand houses accommodated a third of the population of Mulhouse. The architect Emile Muller studied all available English and other models, and produced three basic designs, one of them a CLUSTER HOUSE or quadruplex arrangement. The earliest houses were built east of the Ill Canal. The extension to the west was a pioneering development in which traffic streets were differentiated from service lanes. Communal facilities included a market, baths, laundries, kindergartens and a library. It is a tribute to the planners that the area no longer has the appearance of a model colony, but simply that of an area where people enjoy living. Smaller developments on the same model took place at Guebwiller, Colmar and BEAUCOURT.

BIBLIOGRAPHY
General
Blumenfeld, 1971; Jonas, *et al.*, 1975; Leuillot, 1959.
Specific
Beamish, C. T. M. The Schlumpf Collection of Automobiles. In *TH*, VIII, 1977.
Schmitt, J. M. Relations between England and the Mulhouse textile industry in the 19th Century. In *TH*, XVII, 1986.

LOCATIONS
[M] Mulhouse Energy Centre, Electropolis, BP 2453, 68057 Mulhouse.
[M] Musée de l'Automobile, 192 avenue de Colmar, 68100 Mulhouse.
[M] Musée de l'Impression sur Étoffes (Museum of Printing on Fabrics), 3 rue des Bonnes-Gens, 68100 Mulhouse.
[M] Musée du Papier Peint (Wallpaper Museum), 18 rue Zuber, 68170 Rixheim.
[M] Musée Français du Chemin de Fer (French Railway Museum), 2 rue Alfred de Glehn, 68200 Mulhouse-Dornach.

JEAN-FRANÇOIS BELHOSTE

multiple unit A passenger train consisting of carriages with power units, either in compartments above the main frames or suspended below them, thus not requiring a locomotive. Multiple units usually have electric, diesel-electric or diesel-mechanical traction. The development of the multiple unit is attributed to F. J. Sprague (1857–1934), who applied the principle on the Chicago South Side Elevated Railroad in 1897. The term is also applied in the USA to diesel-electric locomotives working in multiple.

The multiple unit derived from the nineteenth-century railmotor, which was a small locomotive that provided support for one end of a bogie coach, in the opposite end of which was a cab from which it could be driven. An auto train worked in similar fashion, but the passenger coach or coaches did not depend for support on the locomotive, which could be removed for other duties. The term 'push-and-pull' train refers to a longer train with a separate locomotive at one end and a driving cab at the other, a system much used in France, Germany and Switzerland. A railcar was a single carriage, usually powered by a diesel engine, like the RDC (Rail Diesel Car) in the USA, but sometimes by steam (*see* SENTINEL): it was pioneered in the 1920s and 30s by the Budd company in the USA and by the GREAT WESTERN RAILWAY in Britain, but is perhaps most widespread in France where it is called an 'autorail'. A four-wheeled version, the railbus, was much used in Germany after 1945, most being built by the Uerdingen company.

Historic vehicles preserved include GWR railcars at Didcot and SWINDON and a Bugatti railcar at Mulhouse.

BIBLIOGRAPHY
General
Russell, 1985; Westwood, 1983.

BARRIE TRINDER

mungo The poorest grade of SHODDY, made especially from hard rags or felted materials. New mungo was made from unused waste materials like tailors' clippings; old mungo from used garments. The term was first recorded in 1857.

BIBLIOGRAPHY
General
Beaumont, 1919.

Munich (München), Bavaria, Germany Munich's importance in the study of the history of technology derives primarily from the existence of the Deutsches Museum von Meisterwerken der Naturwissenschaft und

Technik (German Museum of the Masterpieces of Natural Science and Technology). The first collections were exhibited in 1906 in provisional accommodation, and the foundation of a large new building was laid on the Kohleninsel the same year. While the concept of this institution – founded long after such similar museums as the Conservatoire des Arts et Métiers in PARIS and the Science Museum in LONDON – sprang from a sociopolitical desire for recognition for the achievements of German technologists and industrialists, the moving spirit and intellectual founding-father of the enterprise, the Munich industrialist Oskar von Miller, was motivated by wider aims. First, he wanted the museum to arouse widespread curiosity about the technology which, as he saw it, brought prosperity and progress; and second, he wanted that curiosity satisfied by an educational institution directly attached to the museum and open to all classes of society. With typical determination, and defying attempts by economists and politicians to exert influence on the project, he succeeded in these aims in the years between 1925, when the museum was opened, and the opening of the library in 1932. The Deutsches Museum has technological and industrial collections matched only by those of the Science Museum, London, and the Smithsonian Institution in WASHINGTON DC. Its extensive displays include galleries devoted to mining, motorcars, aeronautics, machine tools, textiles, plastics, industrial chemicals and railways. Particular items include the first dynamo, devised by Werner von Siemens in 1866, the first diesel engine of 1897, and KARL BENZ's first motorcar of 1886. The museum's library contains 700000 volumes. There is a large photographic archive, and a research institute and a further education establishment form part of the museum. The museum publishes the journal *Kultur & Technik* (Culture and technology).

There are two important works museums with exhibits illustrating the industrial development of Munich. The museum of Bayerische Motoren Werke (Bavarian Motor Works: BMW), opened in 1984, has an exhibition entitled 'Zeitmotor' (Motor of the times) which employs the methods of Hollywood to illustrate the technical and sociohistorical development of the motorcar in the twentieth century. In 1973 BMW erected a building of monocoque construction for this museum. It was designed by the architect Karl Schwanzer in the shape of a cylinder piston, and stands next to BMW's main administrative building. The Siemens works museum, founded in 1922 in Berlin where the firm was situated at the time, subsequently moved with it to Munich. It uses such inventions of Werner von Siemens as the pointer telegraph and the dynamo-electric principle to illustrate the history of electrical engineering. The Werner von Siemens Institute provides information on the work of Siemens and of the company he established, and promotes research on the history of electrical engineering and the electricity industry, as well as demonstrating modern equipment. The Institute holds extensive archives and photographic collections.

The public electricity supply of Munich, which did not begin operating until 1889, is represented by the buildings of the Muffat works, constructed in and around a wellhouse of 1833, and the Maximilian works, built in 1895 in the style of a Baroque garden pavilion, because of its inner-city location. The Maffei locomotive works opened in the north-east of the city in 1837. The hydroelectric plant built on the site in the Hirschau over the Eisbach now acts as a distribution centre for the civic electricity supply, and has three Francis TURBINES of 1900. The Südwerk I power station was built in the south of the city centre over the Isar Canal in 1907, and the Südwerk II station, in similar style, was added in 1922. Both are examples of a rather conservative Bavarian functionalist style.

The civic authorities also built the Maximilians-Getreide-Halle (Maximilian Corn Hall), known as the Schrannenhalle (cornmarket). It was constructed in the provisions market in 1851–3 by the Bavarian firms Cramer-Klett of Nuremberg and Maffei of Munich, on Parisian models. The building was originally 430 m (1400 ft.) long, with stone corner and central sections, and two glazed, cast-iron framed linking sections, each 164 m (540 ft.) long. The corner section was preserved within the provisions market and part of the connecting section was moved to Dachauerstrasse in the north of the city in 1924, as an early specimen of iron-and-glass construction.

The one-time royal porcelain works still operates at Nymphenburg palace, 6 km (4 mi.) W. of the city centre, where there is also a large collection of carriages and other vehicles that once belonged to the Bavarian court. Joseph von Baader (1763–1835), a Bavarian engineer who stayed in England from 1786 to 1794, from 1807 constructed water-pumping installations at Nymphenburg that still exist. They supplied the palace and fountains in the park and combined modern technology with Rococo architecture.

The Bavarian military airport at Schleissheim, 12 km (8 mi.) N. of the city, was built in reinforced concrete in 1917–18. Because of its proximity to the Baroque castle of Schleissheim the control tower was constructed in 1912 in the local style, but on a small scale. With the unpretentious hangar this complex is a monument to the pioneering period of German aviation.

See also figures 40, 92, 149.

BIBLIOGRAPHY
General
Bayerisches Landesamt für Denkmalpflege, 1978; Bott, 1985; Grimm, 1985.
Specific
Petzet, M. Die Halle des ehemaligen Militärflughafens Schleissheim (The hangar of the former military air base at Schleissheim). In *ICOMOS Germany 1979*, 1985.

LOCATIONS
[M] BMW (Bayerische Motoren Werke) Museum, Petuelring 130, 8000 Munich.
[M] Deutsches Brauerei-Museum (German brewery museum), St Jakobsplatz 1, 8000 Munich.
[M] Deutsches Museum, Postfach 160102, Museums Insel, 8000 Munich.
[M] Munich City Museum, St Jacobs Platz 1, 8000 Munich.

[M] Museum of the Sewing Machine, Heimeranstrasse 68–70, 8000 Munich.

[M] Royal Stables Carriage Collection, Schloss Nymphenburg, 8000 Munich 19.

[M] Werner von Siemens Institute of Siemens Corporate and Technical History, Prannerstrasse 10, 8000 Munich 2.

AXEL FÖHL

Munkfors, Värmland, Sweden Munkfors, 52 km (32 mi.) N. of Karlstad, is the site of the works where, for the first time in Sweden, mild steel was made by the OPEN-HEARTH process in 1868. A building constructed in 1877 to house open-hearth furnaces, which remained in operation until 1941, is preserved. The works belongs to the Uddeholm company, which takes its name from the ironworking community of Uddeholm, 20 km (12 mi.) N. of Munkfors. In 1936 the company commissioned a film entitled *Iron*, which is one of the most important visual records of the Swedish iron industry of the early twentieth century. Sequences shot at Munkfors include the operation of LANCASHIRE FORGES, open-hearth steel furnaces, and a ROLLING MILL of 1932 which extended over 2 ha (5 ac.). The film shows BLAST FURNACES, BESSEMER converters and a CHROMIUM steel furnace in operation at the company works at Hagfors, 6 km (4 mi.) E. of Uddeholm; and also illustrates iron-ore mining, a TUBE MILL, and the application of the company's steel in the manufacture of RAZOR blades, SAWS and springs for GRAMOPHONES. A Bessemer converter and an ELECTRIC-INDUCTION FURNACE of 1932 are preserved at Hagfors.

Murdock, William (1754–1839) The inventor of coal-gas lighting, Murdock was employed from 1777 by BOULTON & WATT as a steam engine erector, many of his letters and drawings remaining in the company archive. He set up an experimental gas-lighting system at the Soho Manufactory, BIRMINGHAM, in 1800, and subsequently developed the manufacture of lighting equipment by the company. He took out a patent in 1810 for stoneware pipes. He was involved with experiments on steam engines, and has been credited with design of the sun-and-plant motion (*see* WATT, JAMES).

museum There are relatively few major museums devoted specifically to science, technology and industry, although many historical and archaeological museums include items relating to such subjects in their collections. In London the Science Museum (the National Museum of Science and Industry) and in MUNICH the Deutsches Museum are the only two of significance as national museums, although the Smithsonian Institution's National Museum of American History in Washington contains important material relating to the history of technology and industry. There are important industrial collections held in museums of technology in several European capitals, notably STOCKHOLM, COPENHAGEN and VIENNA.

In PARIS, the Conservatoire des Arts et Métiers has important scientific material and some of industrial and engineering interest, including the steam carriage by Nicholas Cugnot (1725–1804) of 1769. The Chicago Museum of Science and Industry (*see* ILLINOIS) has some material of significance but one of the most outstanding collections in the USA is held by the Henry Ford Museum, Dearborn, MICHIGAN. It includes many steam engines both of American and European origin. The associated open-air museum, Greenfield, includes buildings and equipment relating to the work of HENRY FORD, the Wright brothers and THOMAS ALVA EDISON.

Figure 92 A reconstruction of the coalface of a nineteenth-century mine, modelled on a mine at Hausham, Upper Bavaria (part of the original display of the 1920s at the Deutsches Museum, Munich)
Deutsches Museum, Munich

Figure 93 A 700 hp Corliss compound engine from the Harle Syke Mill, Burnley, Lancashire, in steam in the East Hall of the Science Museum, London, where it forms part of a display system completed in 1988; the engine was built by the Burnley Ironworks in 1903, and drove about 1700 looms until 1970. It was installed in the museum in 1979.
Science Museum, London

A modern museum including industrial collections with applied arts is the Power House in SYDNEY. In AUCKLAND, New Zealand, the Museum of Transport and Technology (MOTAT) has extensive industrial collections.

The collections of the Science Museum, London, are outstanding, especially reflecting the role of Britain as an industrial power in the late eighteenth century and the first half of the nineteenth century. Important steam engines include a BOULTON & WATT rotative beam engine of 1788. There are the first steam TURBINES developed by CHARLES ALGERNON PARSONS in the 1880s for electrical power generation, and his marine turbine for *Turbinia* (*see* TURBINE PROPULSION) of 1894; WILLIAM SYMINGTON's marine steam engine of 1788; and the engine from the paddle steamer *Comet* of 1812, the first steam engine to power a commercial vessel. Further examples from the important marine engineering collections include the *Swan* and the *Raven* of 1867, the original ship hull models used by William Froude to establish the experimental

basis of ship hydrodynamics. Textile machinery, including RICHARD ARKWRIGHT's WATER FRAME of 1769, and BLOCK machinery of 1802–7 by Marc Isambard Brunel (1769–1849), are amongst the production machinery in the museum. The machine-tool collections include a PLANER of 1817 by RICHARD ROBERTS and one of 1842 by JOSEPH WHITWORTH, as well as lathes, screw-cutting machines, shaping, mortising and slotting machines exemplifying the work of JOSEPH BRAMAH, HENRY MAUDS-LAY and James Nasmyth. In its pictorial collection, the Science Museum holds *Coalbrookdale by Night* (*see* IRON-BRIDGE) by Philip de Loutherbourg (1740–1812), one of the most vivid and expressive contemporary paintings of Britain during the Industrial Revolution. The Science Museum also holds the National Railway Collection, most of which is displayed in its satellite museum, the National Railway Museum at York. The collection includes *Puffing Billy* of 1813, the world's oldest surviving steam locomotive, and GEORGE STEPHENSON's *Rocket* of 1829, both of which are normally displayed in London. At York there are some 150 items of railway motive power and rolling stock, and numerous smaller exhibits illustrating the history of railways and railway engineering in Britain.

Collections in the Deutsches Museum, Munich, reflect especially the growing industrial power of Germany in the late nineteenth century and early twentieth century. They include motorcars by KARL BENZ and GOTTLIEB DAIMLER, early DIESEL ENGINES, Werner von Seimens' dynamo of 1866, and notable chemical and mining collections.

Most representations of industry in museums concentrate on technology, on the operations of machines or processes. There is increasing interest in the portrayal of work as a human activity, exemplified in museums in COPENHAGEN, STEYR, HAMBURG and NORRKÖPING.

Important aspects of industry are portrayed in AIRCRAFT MUSEUMS, ÉCOMUSÉES, MARITIME MUSEUMS, MINING MUSEUMS, MOTOR MUSEUMS, OPEN-AIR MUSEUMS, RAILWAY MUSEUMS, TEXTILE MUSEUMS and TRANSPORT MUSEUMS, and in numerous specialist institutions dealing with such diverse subjects as peas, cider, slate, brushes, dredging, and maple sugar.

See figures 92, 93; for examples of practice in the conservation and interpretation of industrial topics in museums, see figures 29, 31, 32, 40, 43, 48, 53, 63, 66, 70, 75, 87, 144, 147, 148, 149, 154, 175, 176.

BIBLIOGRAPHY
General
Follett, 1978.
Specific
Science Museum Review London: Science Museum, 1988–.

NEIL COSSONS

music hall A type of THEATRE, designed for variety shows presided over by a chairman occupying a 'pulpit', which developed from the entertainments provided in public houses in the mid-nineteenth century. There were twenty-eight in London by 1868. The outstanding specialist buildings were constructed *c.*1900, mostly to the design of Frank Matcham (1854–1920), and included the Empire Palace, Leeds, of 1898, and the Empire, Hackney, London, of 1900. Many music halls were used for early cinema performances.

BIBLIOGRAPHY
General
Bailey, 1986; Bratton, 1986; Lowerson and Myerscough, 1977; Osborne, 1974; Pevsner, 1976; Walvin, 1978.

musket A long-barrelled, smooth-bored GUN of approximately 0.70 calibre (17 mm; 0.67 in.), held against the shoulder to fire a lead ball of some 25 g (0.88 oz.). During the sixteenth century, spark-generating 'locks' replaced mechanisms that applied 'matches' (tapers) to firing holes in the breech, and made shoulder arms a practical weapon. King Gustavus Adolphus of Sweden (1594–1632) used a lightened musket charged with pre-packed powder cartridges as the basis for a new infantry formation which remained little changed for two hundred years. To gain effective firepower with weapons capable at the most of three shots per minute, it was necessary to deploy concentrations of well-drilled troops who fired volleys in alternate ranks. The loose tolerances employed to ensure easy muzzle-loading reduced the effective range of musket fire to some 100 m (110 yd.); this was nevertheless preferred to the more accurate but difficult to load RIFLE until satisfactory breech-loading mechanisms, employing metal cartridges with percussion caps and integral bullets, were developed in the nineteenth century. The capacity to manufacture such precision weapons derived to a large extent from the attempts to mechanize the production of muskets with INTERCHANGEABLE PARTS, which began in the late eighteenth century.

BIBLIOGRAPHY
General
Hughes, 1974; McNeill, 1982.

TIM PUTNAM

mustard As an industrial product, mustard is either the milled flour of brown mustard (*Brassica juncea*) and white mustard (*Sinapis alba*), or a preparation of such flour blended with other ingredients and VINEGAR or grape juice, as in Dijon mustard. The husk is separated and used in OIL MILLS, while the kernel is milled. Several wind-powered mustard mills remain in the Low Countries (*see* ZAANDAM) while there is a large complex of industrial mills at NORWICH.

Mykonos (Mikonos), Aegean Islands, Greece An island celebrated for its windmills and handwoven fabrics, 130 km (79 mi.) SE of Athens, and held by the Venetians until 1718. Characteristic windmills, with cylindrical thatched towers and white triangular sails, were built in great numbers from the seventeenth century to grind grain. Some near the harbour have been restored, but there are many derelict towers across the island.

LOCATION
[M] Folklore Collection, Mykonos.

N

Nagycenk, Györ-Sopron, Hungary   12 km ($7\frac{1}{2}$ mi.) SE of Sopron stands the castle of the Széchenyi family. Count István Széchenyi (1791–1860) was a famous statesman and a pioneer of the national revival, founder of the Hungarian Academy of Sciences, instigator of steam navigation on the Danube and of the Chain Bridge in BUDAPEST. He installed a British gas-lighting system in the castle in 1830 after a visit to London. The retort house and its chimney remain. Part of the castle is a museum of Széchenyi's work, illustrating his concerns with railway construction, water power, and the manufacture of coinage; the remainder is an hotel. Adjacent to the castle is an open-air museum of narrow-gauge railways, with locomotives and rolling stock from all parts of Hungary and a 5 km (3 mi.) working line.

BIBLIOGRAPHY
General
Kiss *et al.*, 1981.

LOCATION
[M] Memorial Museum of Count István Széchenyi, H-9485 Nagycenk, Kiscenki u.3.

nails   The traditional method of making nails by hand was to heat a rod from a slitting mill in a hearth, commonly one shared by several nailers, and to put on the point by hammering, often with an OLIVER on a small anvil, the nail then being cut to length using a hammer with a wedge-shaped face. The nail was then put into a cavity, either a hole in the surface of the anvil, or a bore, a dumb-bell shaped steel tool with cavities in each end, so that the head could be shaped with a hammer. The first nail-making machines were introduced in the late eighteenth century, cutting nails from thin plates of iron. Later, machines making nails from iron wire were introduced, and from *c.*1850 most nails were made by machine. In Europe nailing was often a specialized occupation distinct from that of the BLACKSMITH, and was widespread, although there were areas like the BLACK COUNTRY where there were concentrations of nailers supplying national and export markets. In North America hand nailing was often part of the work of the blacksmith.

BIBLIOGRAPHY
General
Bodey, 1983; Treatise, n.d.

Nantes, Loire Atlantique, France   The LU biscuit factory at Nantes is a striking example of how firms in the food industries are often highly conscious of their architectural image, using this image in the promotion of their products. The LU factory (the name is an abbreviation of Lefèvre-Utile, the founder and his wife) dates from 1885 when a small family confectionery, in existence since the 1850s, bought up an old textile mill on the banks of the Loire. New workshops were soon added to this building to house modern equipment purchased from Vicars, the English oven manufacturers. The commercial success of the 'Petit Beurre' biscuit, launched in 1888, led to further development, and by 1909 the main façade of the factory along the Loire, opposite the castle and the railway station, had been totally transformed. Two ornate towers, topped with beacons and decorated with sculptures of trumpeted 'Renown', formed a monumental gateway, either to the factory itself or to the city of Nantes, depending on one's point of view. Designed by the Parisian architect Auguste Bluyssen in a style inspired by ART NOUVEAU, these towers served no productive function but featured in the idealized aerial views of the factory that adorned LU's biscuit tins and advertisements (*see* fig. 94).

If the 'Petit Beurre' biscuit is still going strong, the old factory was superseded by modern plant in 1986 and largely demolished. Only one of the towers, minus its dome, still survives, but a rich collection of photographs, many of them taken for the Paris exhibition of 1937, provides detailed information both on the production processes and the evolution of the factory's buildings.

BIBLIOGRAPHY
General
Kérouanton, 1989.

PAUL SMITH

naphtha   An ambiguous term, first applied to the light, flammable oil from the distillation of coal tar or shale, which has been used in lamps, as a solvent and as a source of BENZENE and TOLUENE. The word is also applied to one of the principal fractions from the CRACKING OF petroleum, an important chemical feedstock. 'Wood naphtha' is naturally-occurring METHANOL.

BIBLIOGRAPHY
General
BP, 1958; Morgan and Pratt, 1938.

Naples (Napoli), Campania, Italy   The growth of Naples into the main industrial centre in southern Italy was based on developments in armaments and later in railway engineering to the east of the city. Torre Annunziata, 20 km (12 mi.) SE on the River Sarno, was chosen as the site

Figure 94 An in-built hoarding on the LU factory on the quai Baco at Nantes, designed in 1888, advertising the 'Petit Beurre' biscuit; the photograph dates from 1895.
Collection of l'Inventaire général

of an arms factory in 1753. Luigi Vanvitelli (1700–73) designed the water-power system while his pupil, Francesco Sabatini, laid out the works. A formal block in the form of a palazzo was set in a courtyard. William Robinson, a Scots officer in the Neapolitan navy, established a gunpowder plant in parts of the works *c.*1830. Remaining buildings include a foundry and a lathe shop with cast-iron columns, and a museum of armaments dating from 1821 is located within the works.

Urban and industrial development to the east of the city followed the construction in 1839 of the Naples–Portici railway, the first in Italy. Robinson's works was transferred *c.*1840 to Pietrarsa, a coastal battery near Portici, where Colonel Vincenzo Uberti began a large engineering works and a technical training school. A foundry was built in 1843–5, and Pietrarsa began to make railway locomotives and wagons, and marine engines, and was run by the State railway, Ferrovie dello Statie, until its closure in 1975. This prime monument of southern Italian industrialization is now a railway museum, which opened in 1982 with locomotives displayed in the airy space of the late nineteenth-century assembly shop. The boiler shop and other buildings are in the course of restoration.

Heavy industrial plants, including an oil refinery, a cement works, and aircraft and motorcar factories line the Bay of Naples from the Ilva steelworks, Bagnoli, 9 km (6 mi.) W. of Naples, to Castellammare di Stabia, 24 km (15 mi.) E. The harbour was severely damaged in World War II, after which the Stazione Marittima on Molo Angioino was largely rebuilt. Several funiculars run from the harbour to the area called the Vomero.

The Galleria Umberto I, built in 1887–92 to designs by Emanuele Rocco, is a major arcade rivalling those in northern Italy. The main entrance, with its extensive sculpture, is opposite the San Carlo theatre by the Piazza Trenzo e Trieste. The roof structure is bold, with wings of the arcade having glazed barrel vaults supported by arched lattice trusses. A more modest arcade, the Galleria Principe di Napoli, leads from the Piazza Museo Nazionale. Designed in 1876 by Breglia & de Novelli, it was closely modelled on the Galleria Vittorio Emanuele II in Milan. After years of decay, exacerbated by the earthquake of 1980, Naples is developing a variety of conservation projects, some of which relate to the city's industrial monuments.

BIBLIOGRAPHY
General
Negri *et al.*, 1983.
Specific
Alisio, G. L'insediamento industriale nella Napoli dell' ottocento (The beginnings of industry in Naples in the eighteenth century). In *Archeologia Industriale*, I, 1983.

LOCATIONS
[M] Museum of Armaments, Sala d'Armi, Torre Annunziata, Naples.
[M] Railway Museum, Pietrarsa, Naples.

MICHAEL STRATTON

narrow boat A typical vessel of the canals of the English Midlands, deriving from boats used on the BRIDGEWATER CANAL in the 1760s. Its dimensions were probably settled at a meeting of canal proprietors at Lichfield on 15 December 1769. Typically the narrow boat is 70 ft. (21.34 m) long and 7 ft. (2.13 m) in beam, with a cabin 10 ft. (3.05 m) long in the stern, and has a cockpit giving access to the tiller. A triangular board called a cratch, 7 ft. (2.13 m) from the stem, marked the beginning of the cargo space. The capacity was up to 35 tons. From the 1820s if not earlier boats were worked by families who lived on board, although many boats were used only on a daily basis. Living conditions on narrow boats became a cause for concern in the 1870s, and registration was required from 1877. Narrow boats were traditionally decorated with rose, castle and floral motifs. Wooden boats were being built as late as the 1950s, but wrought-iron vessels were made from *c*.1788 (*see* IRON SHIP), and steel vessels and some of composite construction from the late nineteenth century. The first steam-powered narrow boat was the *Dart* of 1864, but horse haulage continued into the 1960s. Diesel engines were commonly used from the 1920s. A powered narrow boat often worked with an unpowered 'butty' vessel, of the same dimensions. The *Northwich*, preserved at Stoke Bruerne, Northampton-shire, is an example. Specialized forms were developed to carry tar and oil, like the *Giffard*, preserved at Ellesmere Port, Merseyside. Owner-operators of narrow boats were known as 'Number Ones'.

BIBLIOGRAPHY
General
Hadfield, 1986; Hanson, 1975; Lewery, 1974; Rolt, 1944; Smith, 1875; Tomlinson, 1979.
Specific
Chaplin, T. *A Short History of the Narrow Boat*. Norwich: Dibb, 1967.
On the canal. In *Household Words*, 11 September 1858.
Pacey, P. The poor man's Claude Lorraines: unravelling the story of the dissemination of an image. In *Visual Resources*, V, 1988.
Wilson, R. J. *The Number Ones: the story of the life of owner boatmen on the Midland canals*. Robert Wilson, 1972.

BARRIE TRINDER

narrow-gauge railway A term that usually refers to a line with a gauge narrower than the standard 1.435 m (4 ft. $8\frac{1}{2}$ in.) used in most countries (*see* RAILWAY), but many gauges were used in the 1830s and 40s, and there was no difference in principle between those of standard gauge and those with the rails slightly closer together. The term is best used to describe lines with significantly narrower gauges, less than 1 m (3 ft. 6 in.), designed to penetrate mountain regions, or for cheapness. Extensive narrow-gauge systems were built in the USA, Africa and Japan, as well as in such mountainous parts of Europe as Switzerland, Yugoslavia and NORWAY, where the CAP system (1067 mm) was developed. Narrow-gauge railways have been used in quarries, within industrial plants, and on pipeline and road construction projects, where they have now largely been replaced by tyred vehicles. Large networks were built on the European battlefronts of World War I.

BIBLIOGRAPHY
General
Bishop and Davies, 1972; Household, 1989; Lee, 1945; Lewis, 1968.

BARRIE TRINDER

Narvik, Nordlund, Norway A port for export of iron ore from the Kiruna mines in Sweden, established by a British company in the 1880s, originally named Speargarden after the manager, William Spear, later renamed Victoria-havn. It received municipal status in 1892. It was the terminus of the Ofot railway, which ran 489 km (304 mi.) to Luleå on the Baltic. The railway was opened in 1902, but much damaged in World War II. A 4-4-0 well-tank locomotive of 1882, by Nydquist worked at Narvik during 1900–64, is preserved.

BIBLIOGRAPHY
General
Schneider, 1963.

natural gas Gas found under pressure in the earth, alone or in association with CRUDE OIL, from which it has to be separated before either can be processed. It is used domestically for heating and cooling, and as raw material in the chemical industry. BUTANE and PROPANE are normally removed as LPG before natural gas is distributed as 'town gas'.

BIBLIOGRAPHY
General
BP, 1958.

nautical archaeology The study of wrecks, termed 'underwater archaeology' in the USA. It provides evidence not just of past shipbuilding methods but of wide ranges of manufactured artefacts from ships' cargoes and equipment, precisely dated to particular periods, and thus highly relevant to industrial archaeology. The potential of nautical archaeology is perhaps best illustrated in the *Vasa*, the seventeenth-century warship raised from the floor of STOCKHOLM harbour. In recent decades the availability of diving equipment at modest cost has led to the identification of many more wrecks, raising complex questions of archaeological ethics. Many countries have adopted legislation akin to the Protection of Wrecks Act 1973 in Britain and the Historic Shipwrecks 1976 in Australia, intended to control the unscientific removal of artefacts from wrecks.

BIBLIOGRAPHY
General
Cleere, 1989.
Specific
Muckelray, K. *Discover a Historic Wreck*. London: HMSO, 1981.

Náxos, Cyclades, Greece   A fertile and beautiful island, 30 km ($18\frac{1}{2}$ mi.) long and 19 km (12 mi.) broad, which is the world's chief source of a hard type of EMERY, used in grinding wheels. The quarries, east of Koronis at the north end of the island, are linked to the coast by an aerial ropeway. Náxos is also important for its marble quarries.

Neath Abbey, Neath, West Glamorgan, Wales   The site of the most complete surviving examples of late-eighteenth-century British blast furnaces, 9 km (6 mi.) NE of Swansea. Two stone furnaces 20 m (60 ft.) high were built by Quaker industrialists in 1792 with a Watt blowing engine between them. The Neath Abbey Iron Company integrated iron smelting with engineering: making renowned steam engines, locomotives, gasworks equipment and iron ships. Two of its steam engines from *c.* 1845 survive *in situ* at Glyn Pits, Pontypool, Gwent 12 km (7 mi.) N. of Newport. The works closed in the 1880s.

BIBLIOGRAPHY
Specific
Ince, L. *The Neath Abbey Iron Company*. Eindhoven: De Archaeologische Pers, 1984.
Palmer, M. and Neaverson, P. The steam engines at Glyn Pits Colliery, Pontypool: an archaeological investigation. In *IAR*, XIII, 1990.

Nebraska, United States of America   A prairie state west of the Missouri, that claims to grow the nation's greatest number of forage grasses, Nebraska lacks a substantial history of industrial activity. While the manufacture of mobile homes (caravans) and electrical components today occupies workers in some of the commercial centres of this Mid-western state, farming and its various support activities have long predominated.

The construction of the Union Pacific's rather misnamed Transcontinental Railroad began in Omaha in 1865, creating a steel artery for the subsequent rail network that fed Nebraska farm produce to distant markets. The nation's only museum devoted solely to the fur trade was opened in Chadron in 1949.

BIBLIOGRAPHY
General
Rapp and Beranek, 1984.

LOCATIONS
[M] Museum of the Fur Trade, East Highway 20, Chadron, NE 60337.
[S] Neligh Flour Mills Historic Site, North Street 7 Wylie Drive, Neligh, NE 68756.
[M] Union Pacific Historical Museum, 1416 Dodge Street, Omaha, NE 68179.

DAVID H. SHAYT

Neckar, Baden-Württemberg, Germany   After World War I an agreement between the German Reich and the then adjoining states of Baden, Hesse and Württemberg established a project to make the River Neckar a major commercial waterway. The industries of the Stuttgart region needed access to the Rhine and it was anticipated that long-term financial support could come from the profits of hydro-electric plants on the weirs. There was resistance to the scheme in the river valley, particularly in Heidelberg, and the architect Paul Bonatz was employed to ensure that weirs and power stations of aesthetically pleasing quality were built to fit in with the landscape. His buildings in Mannheim, Heidelberg, Neckarsteinach, (30 km (19 mi.) SE of Mannheim), and Hirschhorn in Hesse (32 km (20 mi.) E. of Mannheim), all of which were completed in the 1920s, show the influence of the INTERNATIONAL MODERN style, and were for many years models for similar constructions in Europe.

needles   Needles were traditionally made from steel wire, often drawn by water power within a needle mill. The wire was cut into lengths, bundled and rolled in bundles on a cast-iron table, or 'rubbed'. Individual needles were then pointed on small grindstones running dry; they were cut into exact lengths, the ends were flattened, and the eyes inserted, on an anvil, with very small punches and hammers. The 'gutters', the thread channels on either side of the eye, were added with small files. Needles were then straightened, heated in a small enclosed furnace, re-straightened, and then put into large lengths of cloth, each holding up to 50 000 needles, and scoured in beds of pebbles with TRAIN OIL, soap suds or EMERY in a water-powered machine, rather like a box mangle, first used *c.*1730. They were washed and given a final polish by 'blue pointing' on small grindstones. Manufacture was specialized, concentrated in such places as Hathersage near SHEFFIELD and Redditch in England, LICHTENWÖRTH in Austria, and around AACHEN in Germany.

491

BIBLIOGRAPHY
General
Rees, 1802–20; Rollings, 1981; Treatise, n.d.
Specific
Jones, S. R. H. The development of needle manufacturing in the West Midlands. In *Economic History Review*, 2nd ser., XXXI, 1978.

LOCATION
[M] Forge Mill Museum, Forge Mill, Needle Mill Lane, Redditch, Hereford and Worcestershire.

BARRIE TRINDER

Nenndorf, Lower Saxony, Germany   Several rural brick-works in Lower Saxony survived into the 1960s, but only those at Nenndorf in the Wittmund district, 30 km (19 mi.) W. of Wilhelmshaven, and Drochtersen, 15 km (9 mi.) N. of Stade, which both include a circular peat-fired Hoffman kiln, remain in operation. The original sheds for drying the raw bricks are still used.

neon (Ne)   A elemental rare gas. It is obtained by the fractional distillation of air. Neon gives a red glow when an electrical discharge is passed through it at low pressure, and is therefore used in display lighting, AIR-CRAFT BEACONS and the like.

Nes Jernverk, Aust Agder, Norway   An ironworks in the Tevedestrand commune on the south-east coast, 75 km (45 mi.) NE of Kristiansand. Established in the seventeenth century, it was modernized by Thomas Cranford from Carron (*see* FALKIRK) in 1799–1806. The works specialized in high-quality cast-iron stoves. Production of crucible steel commenced in 1850. A blast furnace was blown out in 1910, but steel production continued until 1950. A trust established in 1966 conserves the blast furnaces, the crucible steel plant, a hammer forge, the owner's mansion and some workers' housing. At nearby Fosstveit, Holt, is a footbridge of 1836 cast at the works.

net   A fabric of thread, twine or cord, the intersections of which are firmly knotted to form meshes of fixed dimensions. Nets were traditionally made from cords derived from hemp or flax, but cotton was increasingly used in the nineteenth century, and synthetic fibres have been employed in the twentieth century. Industrial-scale production of nets began with the establishment by James Patterson of a factory using netting machines at Mussel-burgh, near Edinburgh, c.1820.

Bobbin net, the foundation of machine-made LACE, is made by the intertwisting rather than the knotting of intersecting threads.

BIBLIOGRAPHY
General
Lawrie, 1948.

Netherlands, The   The history of industry in the Netherlands provides a valuable corrective to the view that manufacturing must necessarily be based on iron, coal and textiles, the materials that formed the foundations of the British Industrial Revolution. The economy of the Netherlands has developed in a way totally different from that of Britain, experiencing great prosperity in the seventeenth century and relative decline in the eighteenth, and showing signs of backwardness in the early nineteenth century. The second half of the nineteenth century can be interpreted as the time of the 'take-off' of industrialization, with the appearance of new manufactures from the 1870s.

The area of the Netherlands is some 40 000 km^2 (15 500 sq. mi.), of which 25 per cent is reclaimed land, 40 per cent of it below sea level. About 370 000 ha (915 000 ac.) were reclaimed from the sea and from open heaths between 1833 and 1911. The Netherlands is bordered to the east by the German Federal Republic and to the south by Belgium. The North Sea coastline has undergone substantial change over the centuries as land has been reclaimed, a continuing process especially in the area where the port of ROTTERDAM is expanding. In the present century the Zuiderzee (*see* FRIESLAND; NOORD-HOLLAND) has been enclosed by a 32 km (20 mi.) dam completed in 1932, and new polders have been drained to the east, north-west and south (*see* FLEVOLAND; ZEELAND).

Politically the Netherlands took its present form during the sixteenth century, when the Republic of the Seven United Provinces, originally led by William the Silent, revolted against Spanish rule. The Netherlands fell under French rule in the 1790s, when remaining feudal dues were abolished, and from 1815 until 1830 it was united with Belgium.

As a trading nation the Netherlands derives many natural advantages from its situation at the mouth of the Rhine and the fact that its location is suited for trading with the Baltic and Great Britain. By contrast the country is seriously deficient in natural resources. Energy was derived largely from the ingenious use of wind power in the seventeenth and eighteenth centuries. In the nineteenth century colonization of peat bogs (*see* BARGER-COMPASCUUM; EINDHOVEN; GRONINGEN) provided fuel for other districts as well as bringing more land into agricultural use. For most of the twentieth century the coalfields of LIMBURG have been an important source of energy. Since the 1930s oilfields of modest extent have been exploited in Drente (*see* BARGER-COMPASCUUM), and since the 1950s the Netherlands has enjoyed the use of the natural gasfields of GRONINGEN. Gas and oil have been successfully extracted from the North Sea since the 1970s. Water power has been significant only in some parts of the east and south.

Amsterdam was the principal financial centre in Europe in the seventeenth century and for much of the eighteenth, until its prosperity was largely destroyed during the French occupation. The prosperity of the Dutch 'golden age' was based on the country's ability to import raw materials from all parts of the world, to add significantly to their value, and to re-export them. This made the Netherlands vulnerable to changes in the policies of more powerful neighbours. Many industrial processes were

The Netherlands

based on wind power, and there were concentrations of windmills in such places as ZAANDAM. Before the end of the sixteenth century wind power was being used to drain and reclaim land, to saw timber and to make paper. The import of timber from the Baltic and the Upper Rhine was the foundation of the Dutch shipbuilding trade, and consequently of the country's large merchant fleet. Grain was imported from the Baltic for the home market and sustained the brewing and distilling industries. Linens from Silesia were taken to HAARLEM for bleaching and traded throughout Europe. Tobacco, rice and sugar from the Tropics were processed and sold abroad. Amsterdam merchants carried on a substantial trade in iron from Sweden and Russia. The dense network of canals in the Netherlands gave the country the best internal system of communications of any state in Europe. Of particular importance were the 'trekvaarten', waterways, with towpaths, on which vessels up to 15 m (50 ft.) long and 2.6 m (8 ft. 6 in.) in beam, carrying passengers or light freight consignments, could operate throughout the year

(except when the water was frozen). The first true 'trekvaart' was that between Haarlem and Amsterdam, built in 1631. The network totalled 658 km (408 mi.) by the 1660s. Traffic levels fell in the eighteenth century, but the final decline of the trekvaarten came only with the building of railways, and in remote areas they continued in use until the late nineteenth century. Some 2850 km (1770 mi.) of new roads were built in the Netherlands in the eighteenth century, and Dutch road carriers travelled long distances into Germany (*see* ZWOLLE).

The polders established in the eighteenth century were drained by wind power. The nineteen mills at KINDERDIJK form the only surviving landscape where this can be appreciated. In 1846 some 12 000 windmills generating 60 000 hp were employed in draining polders. Steam pumping engines gradually became the norm in the nineteenth century, and about four hundred were at work by 1877 (*see* CRUQUIUS; GRONINGEN; ZWOLLE). The first steam pumping engine was built in ROTTERDAM on the initiative of Steven Hoogendijk (1698–1788), a local watchmaker, who paid for an engine erected on the city wall by James Carter Hornblower in 1775–7. It was unsuccessful because the pumping system was faulty. The first BOULTON & WATT pumping engine in the Netherlands was installed on Hoogendijk's initiative to drain the Blijdorp polder near Rotterdam in 1787, and the second to pump out the dry dock at the military port of Hellevoetsluis in 1800–2. (A working model of the former was completed in Rotterdam in 1987.) Steam pumping engines gradually became the norm in the nineteenth century (see CRUQUIUS; GRONINGEN; ZWOLLE). The first steam engines used in manufacturing were installed in a flour mill in Amsterdam and a distillery in Rotterdam in the 1790s, but subsequent growth of steam power was slow. There were seventy-two steam engines in the Netherlands in 1837, and almost four hundred in 1853.

Some of the old-established Dutch manufactures benefited from changes of location in the first half of the nineteenth century. Pottery moved from DELFT to Maastricht (see LIMBURG), where government policy and the low costs of fuel and labour created favourable conditions for modern processes. In paper manufacturing there was a similar move from ZAANDAM to LIMBURG. Woollen cloth manufacture moved away from LEIDEN, which in the seventeenth century had been one of the principal industrial centres in Europe. Attempts to modernize, including the introduction of steam power in 1819, were unsuccessful, largely because of outmoded marketing structures, and the high wages in the coastal provinces. Woollen manufacturing in Noord Brabant prospered, especially in TILBURG, having been stimulated by French military orders. There was a concentration on coarse fabrics. The first steam engines were introduced in 1827 and in the second half of the nineteenth century there was a general transition from traditional to steam-powered factories.

The Netherlands cotton industry began to expand about 1830, stimulated by the Belgian secession. The country's first steam-powered cotton mill was erected at Almelo in 1820. Weavers had to be introduced to the use of the flying shuttle. The government encouraged the transfer of foreign (that is, Belgian) companies to the Netherlands by means of subsidies and guaranteed orders. The British-born entrepreneur Thomas Wilson moved to Haarlem from Ghent in 1833, to be followed by two other substantial Belgian firms. The complete manufacture of cotton fabrics could be carried out in HAARLEM by 1834.

Cotton manufacturing developed on a larger scale in TWENTE, developing from traditional domestic manufactures. The Englishman Thomas Ainsworth and the Belgian Charles de Maere introduced factory-based cotton manufacturing to the province. New canals and roads, built to supply fuel for steam engines, stimulated the modernization of the economy of the region, particularly from the 1860s. It is only since the 1960s that the textile industries of Twente and Noord Brabant have suffered serious decline.

The growth of modern engineering began in the 1820s when the development of steamboats led to the establishment of two shipbuilding concerns, in Rotterdam and Amsterdam. Until 1830 growth was retarded by Belgian competition, particularly from the government-protected works of John Cockerill at Seraing. After the Belgian secession both firms moved into the production of steamships. Throughout the nineteenth century they had to rely on the government both for orders and for loan finance, because their range of products was narrow and they were heavily dependent upon foreign orders. Dutch shipbuilding has continued to rely upon government support in the twentieth century. Foundries of some importance were established in LEIDEN, DORDRECHT and Deventer in the nineteenth century.

Railways developed slowly in the Netherlands. The first line, from Amsterdam to Haarlem, was opened in 1839 and extended to Rotterdam by 1847, but by 1850 there were only 170 route km (110 mi.) of railway, a total that had grown only to 355 km (220 mi.) by 1861. After 1860 the government took a direct role in railway construction, leasing lines for fifty years to operating companies. There were 3000 route km (1900 mi.) by 1910. Many roadside tramways were constructed in rural areas as well as towns. Some, like that from Zutphen to Emmerich and the 750 mm gauge line from Weert to Maaseik, crossed national frontiers.

The development of the ports of AMSTERDAM and ROTTERDAM was threatened in the 1820s by the increasing size of ocean-going ships, and by the limitations of traditional dredging methods. The Great North Holland Canal, linking Amsterdam directly with the North Sea at Den Helder, was dredged by sixteen horse-operated 'mud-mills' and opened in 1825. The Voorne Canal, opened in 1830, gave Rotterdam a better connection to the sea. Each canal was important only for a short time. The Nieuwe Waterweg (New Waterway) linking Rotterdam with the sea was built in 1866–72, but because of technical problems it did not come fully into use until the 1890s, making possible the subsequent rapid growth of the port. The North Sea Canal, which gave access to Amsterdam, was opened in 1876. Modern equipment, including wooden suction dredgers and steam bucket- and hopper-dredgers, were used for these projects and for land reclamation work like the drainage of the Haarlemmermeer (see CRUQUIUS), stimulating the growth of dredging companies (see SLIEDRECHT) which have been employed in the twentieth century on the Zuiderzee reclamation (1925–80), and the Delta works in Zeeland and Zuid Holland from 1954.

Dutch industry began to grow rapidly in the 1890s. In part this was an acceleration of the development of existing industries like textiles and shipbuilding. In part it was due to the growth of manufactures based on agriculture. The processing of potatoes to produce sago, glucose, dextrine, starch and meal had begun as early as 1841, but many new factories were built in Groningen province using crops from reclaimed peatlands. Strawboard factories came into existence in the same area, but the region's economy changed radically after World War II. From the 1850s sugar beet was grown on a large scale in Noord Brabant and Zeeland, and by 1912 twenty-seven processing factories had been constructed. One of the first modern

Dutch creameries was built in Friesland in 1897 (*see* ARNHEM; FRIESLAND). By 1899 there were sixty-three factories making condensed and powered milk. Cheese-making remained an important craft until the 1960s.

The commercial production of margarine was begun by the Jurgens Brothers in the 1870s (*see* ROTTERDAM). They set up factories all over Europe to make the basic material, oleo, from beef tallow, although from 1906 imported oils were employed. Traditional marketing links built up by the butter trade were used to sell margarine. By 1914 there were twenty-eight margarine factories in the Netherlands, employing 2400 people, and the majority of factories in Germany were Dutch-owned.

The growth of output did not necessarily depend on mechanization. Around 1900 there was growing standardization in the production and marketing of shoes, confectionery and cigars, but, particularly in poorer areas, manufacturing was often still organized on a domestic basis.

Some new manufactures owed nothing to past traditions. Chocolate manufacture, based on the Van Houten process for preparing a fat-free cocoa powder, patented as early as 1828, expanded rapidly, the number of cocoa beans consumed increased from 3.4 million a year in 1887–96 to 18 million in 1907–11. The Dutch were notable pioneers in the manufacture of diesel engines. Oil was discovered in the Dutch East Indian island of Sumatra in 1884, the Royal Dutch Company was formed in 1890, and the first oil obtained in 1892. In 1907 the company merged with the British Shell Company to form Royal Dutch Shell. By 1914 Rotterdam was the principal European port for the import of oil. Chemical plants were established near the ports, and the manufacture of fertilizers, rayon and pharmaceuticals was particularly stimulated during World War I. The manufacture of electric lamps (*see* EINDHOVEN) developed from the mid-1890s.

Dutch industry in the twentieth century has followed the pattern established in the 1890s. ROTTERDAM remains the centre of the European oil trade. Coal mining in LIMBURG began in 1899, and eleven mines were opened by 1927. The last mine closed in 1974 due to competition from oil and natural gas. Reserves of natural gas have been exploited since the 1950s, while peat extraction has virtually ceased. A modern blast furnace complex was built at YMUIDEN in 1924.

There were more than twenty tile factories in the Netherlands in the eighteenth century, but only four by 1900, although tiles can still be seen in buildings of many kinds. The restrained use of brick by Dutch architects in the 1920s, exemplified in the town hall at Hilversum and the second generation of houses at Agneta Park (*see* DELFT), was influential elsewhere, particularly in the work of Charles Holden (1875–1960) and Frank Pick (1878–1941) in LONDON.

The protection of historic monuments in the Netherlands dates from a wartime decree of 1940, which remained in force until the passing of a temporary Act in 1950, and of the Monuments Act 1961. Under the 1961 Act structures that are at least fifty years old can be listed by the Minister of Culture on the advice of the Monuments Council. Responsibility for monuments has subsequently been passed from central to regional and local government authorities. Some modifications were made by the Monuments Act 1988. There are some 43 000 listed monuments of all classes in the Netherlands, and about four hundred specially protected towns and villages. Protected national industrial monuments include some forty water mills, over a thousand windmills, twenty lighthouses, twenty-three railway stations, and twelve steam pumping stations. The Dutch Industrial Heritage Documentation Centre (DIEN) is collecting information for a computerized database, although the withdrawal of subsidies from the Ministry of Culture in 1988 halted the project. The database contains descriptions of eight thousand industrial objects and buildings. The Dutch Federation for the Industrial Heritage (FIEN) was formed in 1984 and meets informally once or twice a year. The journal *Industriele Archeologie*, published by the Stichting Industriele Archeologie in Nederland (Association for Industrial Archaeology), appears four times a year.

There are about eight hundred museums in the Netherlands, although the title 'museum' is not protected in law. Most towns have local-history museums, and many specialist museums are devoted to topics related to industrial history. Some, like the tramway museum in the garden of a suburban house at Weert (Limburg), which has five preserved tramcars, are entirely private concerns. Museums and other conservation projects rely heavily on volunteers, and the national agency has an officer specially appointed to organize voluntary efforts. An inventory of railway monuments has been made; though incomplete, it is a testament to voluntary effort. Volunteers have succeeded in producing inventories of industrial monuments in Rotterdam, and of several classes of monuments, among them bridges and factories. In Groningen province a survey of bridges by volunteers was extended by the provincial planning office to cover the socio-historical and landscape values of the structures. There are six preserved railways, while eight twentieth-century German locomotives are preserved by private societies at Rotterdam and Apeldoorn to work excursions. Some older waterways like the peat canal between Goredijk, Friesland, and Smilde, Drenthe, have been reopened to pleasure traffic following a report by the National Tourist Board of 1976.

There are some notable examples of adaptive reuse of industrial buildings in the Netherlands. Shopping centres have been created in a textile mill in Delden, Overijssel, and a margarine factory in Oosterhout, Noord Brabant. A water tower at Hellevoetsluis, Zuid Holland, a textile factory at Enschede, Twente, and two parallel ranges of brick kilns at Wageningen, Gelderland, have been put to residential use. A gasholder in Rotterdam is used as a day-nursery.

See also AMSTERDAM; ARNHEM; BARGER-COMPASCUUM; CRUQUIUS; DELFT; DORDRECHT; EINDHOVEN; FLEVOLAND; FRIESLAND; GOUDA; GRONINGEN; HAARLEM; HAGUE, THE; KINDERDIJK; LEIDEN; LELY, CORNELIS; LIMBURG; MEPPEL; NOORD HOLLAND; RHINE; ROTTERDAM; SLIEDRECHT; TILBURG;

Twente; Utrecht; Willemsoord; Ymuiden; Zaandam; Zeeland; Zwolle.

BIBLIOGRAPHY

General

Balk, 1985; Bos, 1974; Burke, 1956; Deelstra and Stehouwer, 1987; De Jonge, 1976; Dhondt and Bruwier, 1970; Everwijn, 1912; Feis and Nijhof, 1973; Griffiths, 1979; Groen and Schmeink, 1985; Ireland, 1795; Janssen, 1987; Jansen, 1984; KLM, 1928; Kossman, 1978; Lucas, 1905; Milward and Saul, 1973, 1977; Mokyr, 1976; Nederland Museumland, 1989; Nijhof, 1978, 1982, 1983, 1985, 1987; PTT, 1981; Reinink and Vermeulen, 1981; Stevens, 1986; Van Dalen, 1984; Van Dalen and Boon, 1983, 1986; Van de Meene and Nijhof, 1985; Van den Eerenbeemt, 1989; Van der Pols, 1984; Van der Veen, J. 1962; Van der Veen, R. 1981.

Specific

Van Dalen, J. 1977. Industrieel erfgoed in de computer: DIEN als service station (Industrial heritage in the computer: DIEN as a service station). In *Tijdschrift Industriële Archeologie* (Industrial Archaeology Review), XXIII, 1987.

Van den Eerenbeemt, H. F. J. M. Inleiding: 'Industriële Archeologie' (Introducing industrial archaeology). In *Tijdschrift Industriële Archeologie*, I and II, 1981-2.

Van den Eerenbeemt, H. F. J. M. Industriële Archeologie in Nederland: verleden, heden en toekomst (Industrial archaeology in the Netherlands: past, present and future). In *Tijdschrift Industriële Archeologie*, XI, 1984.

Van den Eerenbeemt, H. F. J. M. Industriële archeologie; waar hebben wi het over? Herbezinning en de kunst van het herbestemmen (Industrial archaeology: what are we talking about? Reflections on the art of adaptive reuse). In *Tijdschrift Industriële Archeologie*, XXXII, 1989.

Van den Eerenbeemt, H. F. J. M. Reflecties over roerend industriel erfgoed (Reflections on the movable industrial heritage). In *Tijdschrift Industriële Archeologie*, XXXIII, 1989.

Van der Pols, K. De introductie van de Stoommachine (The introduction of the steam engine to the Netherlands). In *Ondernemende geschiedenis* (Business History). The Hague, 1977.

Vercauteren, J. B. M. Industriële archeologie en de herbestemming van het culturele erfgoed (Industrial archaeology and the adaptive reuse of the cultural heritage). In *Tijdschrift Industriële Archeologie*, XXXI, 1989.

LOCATIONS

[I] DIEN (Dutch Industrial Heritage Documentation Centre), Postbus 2038, 3000 CA, Rotterdam.

[I] FIEN (Dutch Federation for the Industrial Heritage) c/o Zomervaart 106F, 1033 DN, Haarlem.

[I] Nederlandse Museumvereniging/Sectie Technische en Transportmusea (Netherlands Museums Association, Section for Technical and Transport Museums), c/o Nederlands Openluchtmuseum, Postbus 603, Arnhem.

[I] Rijksdienst voor de Monumentenzorg (State Service for the Protection of Monuments), Broederplein 41, Postbus 1001, 3700BA Zeist.

[I] Stichting Industriele Archeologie in Nederland, c/o Prof. Dondersstraat 23, 5017 HG, Tilburg.

JURRIE VAN DALEN and BARRIE TRINDER

Neuchâtel, Switzerland The chief clockmaking canton in Switzerland, also important in the pre-industrial stage of the textile industry. There is an important museum of horology, with a large collection of Swiss, French and British clocks, musical boxes, mechanical toys, automata, marine chronometers, and the machine tools required to make them, at La Chaux-de-Fonds, 16 km (10 mi.) N. of Neuchâtel; it was opened in 1902, and has an innovative museum building of 1972–4. There are other collections in the cantonal capital and at Le Locle, 16 km (10 mi.) NW. There is a museum of printed fabrics at Colombier, 8 km (5 mi.) SW of Neuchâtel; and at Cortaillod, 8 km (5 mi.) SW, are the buildings of Fabrique Neuve, a cotton-printing factory, with the owner's house in ornamental grounds, built in 1765–1815.

BIBLIOGRAPHY

Specific

Chollet, J.-P. *et al. L'Homme et le Temps.* La Chaux-de-Fonds: Musée International d'Horologerie, 1977.

LOCATIONS

[M] Château de Colombier, 2013, Colombier, Neuchâtel.

[M] Musée d'Art et d'Histoire (Museum of Art and History), Quai Leopold Robert, 2001 Neuchâtel.

[M] Musée d'Histoire et d'Horlogie (Museum of History and Clockmaking), Château des Monts, Monts 65, 2400 Le Locle, Neuchâtel.

[M] Musée International d'Horologerie (International Museum of Horology), rue des Musées 29, 2300 La Chaux-de-Fonds, Neuchâtel.

HANS-PETER BÄRTSCHI

Neustadt an der Weinstrasse, Rhineland-Palatinate, Germany In the locomotive depot built in 1846 just opposite the station concourse at Neustadt, 28 km (18 mi.) SW of Mannheim, by the Palatinate Railway, there is a railway museum. Locomotives and rolling stock from the museum work on the nearby branch line from Lambrecht, 6 km (4 mi.) W., to Elmstein, 14 km (9 mi.) W.

The remains of log-floating installations devised for transporting the wealth of timber produced in the Palatinate Forest can still be seen in the Elmstein valley. The Bavarian administration extended the installations in two stages of building, c.1780 and c.1830. In the catchment basin of the Speyerbach near Neustadt, log-floating was made possible on 140 km (87 miles) of waterway so that timber could be floated down to Speyer and Frankenthal on the Upper Rhine. Currents were controlled by sandstone walls, and many storage ponds were laid out besides the channels for the timber. Structures of this kind can still be seen in eastern Hesse at the forester's lodge at Breitenstein and in the Breitenbach, 75 km (45 mi.) S. of Kassel.

BIBLIOGRAPHY

General

Custodis, 1990.

LOCATION

[I] Deutsche Gesellschaft für Eisenbahngeschichte e V (DGEG: German Association for Railway History), Postfach 100318, Hindenburgstrasse 12, 6730 Neustadt an der Weinstrasse 1.

ROLF HÖHMANN

Nevada, United States of America Beneath Nevada's arid flatlands and craggy mountains have been reserves of mineral wealth that place this western state in the top rank of the nation's ore producers. This large, sparsely populated state has yielded consistent quantities of gold, silver, copper, lead, zinc, mercury, manganese, tungsten, gypsum, borax and oil through this century, and earlier. Nevada opal and turquoise mines have also produced in volume.

The MacKay School of Mines Museum in Reno treats the state mining heritage, highlighted in the 1850s by the blockbuster discovery of the Comstock Lode near Virginia City, a mammoth multi-metal find that between 1859 and 1890 produced $300 million in gold and silver. Virginia City retains the traditional appearance of the nineteenth-century mining boom town, with enormous High Victorian residences picked out in Steamboat Gothic woodwork, set against the arid, high-mountain desert.

Inside the US Mint building of 1869 in Carson City, the state capital, the Nevada State Museum chronicles the state's railway history, distinguished by the four transcontinental railways that once passed through the state. In a convenient piggy-back arrangement, the state-run museum also comprises the Nevada State Railroad Museum, where responsibilities are divided between state government workers and a core of volunteer railfans.

One of the greatest American engineering achievements of all time nestles into a narrow canyon in the southern tip of Nevada. The Hoover Dam was completed in 1935, impounding the waters of the Colorado River for use in irrigation, city water-supply systems, and the production of hydro-electric power, principally for residents in Southern California to the west. It remains the nation's thickest concrete dam, 180 m (600 ft.) thick at its base, and for a period was the world's highest at 221 m (726 ft.). The ART DECO treatment of the dam's crest and the adjacent power house, together with the majestic setting, have made the dam a popular destination for travellers *en route* to or from the Grand Canyon, the Las Vegas gambling casinos, and the recreational areas surrounding Lake Mead, the dam's vast reservoir.

The gambling industry, still Nevada's biggest, was inaugurated by the state in 1931, giving rise to a specialized manufacturing industry: slot-machine production, that exports worldwide.

LOCATIONS
[M] Mackay School of Mines Museum, University of Nevada, Reno, NV 89507.
[M] Nevada State Museum, 600 North Carson Street, Carson City, NV 89710.
[M] William Harrah Automobile Museum, 970 Glendale Street, Sparks, NV 89515.

DAVID H. SHAYT

New Brunswick (Nouveau Brunswick), Canada   A province on the Atlantic seaboard of North America, south of the Gulf of St Lawrence, and north of MAINE. There were both English and French settlements in modern New Brunswick by the early eighteenth century. A formal colonial structure was established in 1784 after an influx of loyalists fleeing from the USA. The Acadians,

descendants of French settlers, retain their distinct culture. New Brunswick prospered from British tariff preferences for timber during the Napoleonic Wars, and the forests that cover 87 per cent of the province remain a valuable industrial resource. Zinc has been the province's chief mineral resource. Marysville is a small but well-preserved textile community.

In the 1860s the capital, Saint John, was the fourth largest port in the British Empire. It remains a harbour vital to the Canadian economy, a convenient ice-free outlet from the industrial regions of Quebec and Ontario. At shipyards in Saint John, the many sailing vessels built on beaches along the coasts of New Brunswick were rigged, fitted with sails, and furnished with metal and other fittings that could not be made in shipbuilding outposts. A store of the 1860s has been preserved.

BIBLIOGRAPHY
General
Innis, 1940; MacNutt, 1963; Matthews and Panting, 1978; Wynn, 1981.

LOCATIONS
[M] Barbour's General Store, King Street E., Saint John, New Brunswick E2L 4L1.
[M] The New Brunswick Museum, 227 Douglas Avenue, Saint John, New Brunswick E2K 1E5.

DERYCK HOLDSWORTH

Newcastle, New South Wales, Australia   Newcastle grew up in response to the demands of industry. The first coal in Australia was discovered there in 1795, and mined from adits using convict labour. The Australian Agricultural Co. took over the mines and dug the first shallow shafts, but much deeper workings were opened from the 1870s. Extensive pithead buildings remain of the Stafford Main No. 2 Colliery of the 1920s, including a ventilation fan, coal conveyors and the power station building. A further group, including an explosives magazine, the power station and the transformer house, survives at the flooded Richmond Main Colliery, Cessnock, 48 km (30 mi.) W. A breakwater completed in 1846 stimulated the growth of Newcastle as a coal port, which drew new business with the railway to Maitland, 32 km (20 mi.) NW of Newcastle, opened in 1857.

BIBLIOGRAPHY
General
Hughes, 1964; Power, 1912.

Newcastle-upon-Tyne, Tyne and Wear, England   The metropolis of North-East England and of Britain's historically most productive coalfield, Newcastle stands at the lowest bridging point on the River Tyne: with Gateshead on the south bank, it flourished as a port for coal, and, in the nineteenth century, as one of the world's principal engineering centres, specializing in shipbuilding, locomotives, armaments and electrical equipment. The city has suffered severe recession in recent decades but much remains of the landscape of wharves, docks and cranes over the 20 m (12 mi.) between the city and Tynemouth. The prospect of the Tyne bridges remains one of the most breathtaking of all industrial landscapes.

The oldest surviving bridge is ROBERT STEPHENSON'S double-deck High Level Bridge of 1845–9, which carries the main-line railway on six cast-iron arches, with a roadway suspended beneath. It was supplemented in 1906 by C. A. Harrison's two-span, lattice-girder King Edward VII Bridge. The 86 m (282 ft.) Swing Bridge, on the site of the oldest crossing of the Tyne, was built in 1876 by W. G. Armstrong & Co. It retains its original hydraulic pumps, but they are now electrically powered. The Tyne Bridge of 1925–8 is a typical steel arched structure of the period.

Dunston Staithes, 3 km (2 mi.) W. on the south bank of the river, built by the NER in 1890 and 525 m (1722 ft.) long, were used for transferring coal from railway wagons to ships and are typical of many such structures built from the seventeenth century onwards. The 3 km (2 mi.) Victoria Tunnel, 2 km (1 mi.) NW, was driven in 1839–42 as part of a tramroad taking coal from Leazes Main Colliery to the Tyne, and is occasionally accessible.

Glassmaking was important on the Tyne in the eighteenth and early nineteenth centuries. The Lemington Glass cone, 8 km (5 mi.) W., some 33 m (108 ft.) high, is one of the industry's few monuments.

The characteristic working-class houses of the region were 'Newcastle flats', TERRACED dwellings with separate APARTMENTS on ground and first floors. The type had evolved by the mid-nineteenth century, and continued to be built in the twentieth.

The Central Arcade of 1905 contains magnificent faience by Burmantofts, while in Grainger Market is the only surviving Marks & Spencer 'penny bazaar'.

Newcastle Central is one of the outstanding stations in Britain, with train sheds with curved iron ribs of 1850, by John Dobson (1787–1865). Two viaducts on the Newcastle & North Shields Railway, at Ouseburn and Withington Dene, were originally in laminated timber, which was replaced in 1869 by wrought iron from the Weardale Ironworks. GEORGE STEPHENSON'S birthplace is preserved at Wylam, 20 km (12 mi.) W.

Outstanding features of the Museum of Science and Engineering are the world's first turbine-driven ship, the *Turbinia*, built by C. A. PARSONS in 1894, and a George Stephenson 0–4–0 locomotive of 1830.

BIBLIOGRAPHY
General
Atkinson, 1974; Muthesius, 1982.

LOCATION
[M] Museum of Science and Engineering, Blandford House, West Blandford Street, Newcastle-upon-Tyne, Tyne and Wear.

BARRIE TRINDER

Newcomen, Thomas (1663–1729) An ironmonger, from Dartmouth, England, who was impressed by the need to drain mines in CORNWALL, and devised the first automatic steam engine (*see* SAVERY) at Coneygre, Dudley (*see* BLACK COUNTRY), in 1712. Its piston propelled a balanced beam, to which the pump was attached, by admitting steam at atmospheric pressure into a cylinder. The steam was then condensed by a water jet within the cylinder, allowing the piston to be forced into the cylinder by atmospheric pressure – hence the name 'atmospheric' engine, by which it is often known. The Newcomen engine was deemed to be covered by the patents granted to THOMAS SAVERY, which were controlled by a consortium until the expiry of the patents in 1733, by which time almost a hundred engines had been installed in Britain. In the second half of the century the Newcomen engine, often called a 'common engine' or a 'fire engine', formed the basis of the far more efficient WATT engine, but it was such a cheap and reliable source of power within the coalfields, where the cost of fuel was negligible, that construction of new engines continued even after the Watt engine ceased to be protected by patents in 1800. Some Newcomen engines continued to work well into the twentieth century. The first in North America was erected by Josiah Hornblower (1729–1809) who migrated from England in 1753.

An engine from Hawkesbury, near COVENTRY, has been removed to Dartmouth, Devon, as a memorial to Thomas Newcomen. An early nineteenth-century engine is preserved *in situ* at Elsecar (*see* SHEFFIELD), and several remain within museums. The engine house that accommodated a Newcomen engine built by Martin Triewald in 1727 is preserved at DANNEMORA (*see* figure 34).

BIBLIOGRAPHY
General
Rolt and Allen, 1977.
Specific
Allen, J. S. The introduction of the Newcomen engine from 1710 to 1733. In *TNS*, XLII, 1969–70; *TNS*, XLIII, 1970–1; *TNS*, XLV, 1972–3.
Davey, H. The Newcomen engine. In *Proceedings of the Institution of Mechanical Engineers*, 1903.
Hollister-Short, G. J. The introduction of the Newcomen engine to Europe. In *TNS*, XL, 1976–7.
Mott, R. A. The Newcomen engine in the eighteenth century. In *TNS*, XXXV, 1962–3.
Nelson, W. *Josiah Hornblower and the First Steam Engine in North America*. Newark, New Jersey, 1883.

CHRISTOPHER GREEN

Newfoundland (Terre-Neuve), Canada The island of Newfoundland was discovered by the explorer John Cabot (1450–98) in 1497, and in succeeding centuries was settled by Europeans, mostly Britons, concerned with fishing on the Grand Banks to the south. Modern Newfoundland, which became a province of Canada in 1949, consists of the island together with the territory of Labrador on the mainland to the north-west.

The first shipment of iron ore from Belle Island, Newfoundland, took place in 1895, and the massive iron-ore body subsequently supplied most of the ore used in the furnaces on CAPE BRETON ISLAND. Mining ended in 1966 as

OPEN-HEARTH steelmaking was being abandoned, and the pig iron from the phosphoric ore is unsuitable for the LD PROCESS of steelmaking. Labrador has been an important source of iron ore, mined in places like Labrador City.

Many characteristic fishing settlements of scattered wooden houses remain on the Avalon Peninsula; and Trinity, 100 km (60 mi.) NW of St John's, has been restored as a heritage district, showing the domestic context of the traditional Atlantic seaboard fishing communities. The first Atlantic CABLE is commemorated at Heart's Content and the first transatlantic RADIO communication at Signal Hill, St John's.

BIBLIOGRAPHY
General
Innis, 1940; Matthews and Panting, 1978.

LOCATIONS
[S] Heart's Content Cable Station, Heart's Content, Newfoundland
[M] Newfoundland Museum, 287 Duckworth Street, St John's, Newfoundland A1C 1G9.
[S] Signal Hill National Historic Park, Signal Hill, St John's, Newfoundland A1C 5X4.

DERYCK HOLDSWORTH

New Hampshire, United States of America   The small New England mountain state of New Hampshire illustrates the general American law of industrial constriction: that the size of a state is inversely proportional to the intensity, diversity and historical interest of its industrial activity. New Hampshire has been home to a host of vital primary industries, both in the extractive and manufacturing fields. The state's natural endowments in stone and timber have been coupled with the acquired resources of a skilled immigrant population, and a location amidst the heavily populated centres of activity between Boston and the lower Canadian belt of commercial activity in Ontario and Quebec.

Quarries holding several varieties of granite, in addition to gneiss and mica deposits, have yielded stone for structural, monumental and architectural uses for well over a century. Timber resources have supplied the state's pulp and paper industries, but the mountainous terrain laced with rushing streams established New Hampshire as the fountainhead of water-powered woodworking and metal-cutting industries early in its history. The *Zeitgeist* of the proverbial 'Yankee ingenuity' lies somewhere in the remains of the small, independent, precision wood-turning, leather-cutting, and machine shops that still dot the southern half of New Hampshire: many of the works still operate, generating high-technology instrumentation for the computer and defence industries. Few if any of the water-power sources, however, remain in full cry. Companies once active in the towns of Nashua and Keene helped to establish the American machine-tool and woodworking-machine industries, drawing from foundry and metal-cutting skills developed in supplying textile machinery to the vast complexes of cotton and woollen mills that once filled New Hampshire and today still crowd Manchester, Nashua and Dover.

Harrisville is one of the finest surviving nineteenth-century mill villages in the nation, with several brick woollen mills with cupolas and clerestories, and one outstanding stone mill; and workers' housing grouped around the pool that was the source of water power. Several mill buildings are used by a manufacturer of specialist pumps, and another by a textile design concern.

The gasworks at Concord, the state capital, retains the most intact surviving gasholder house in the USA, a handsome circular brick structure of 1888, 26 m (86 ft.) in diameter and 8.5 m (28 ft.) high to the base of its conical roof, which was in service until 1952 (*see* figure 51). The wrought-iron tank, by Deily & Fowler of Philadelphia, remains in place.

Another clue to the longevity and dogged endurance of the state's work life exists on the slopes of Mount Washington, where the famous cog railway climbs its 37 per cent maximum grade. Built in 1869, this was the world's first such mountain-climbing RACK RAILWAY, a push-type steam line with self-levelling passenger carriages, and a rack system between the rails. The 5.6 km ($3\frac{1}{2}$ mi.) line furnishes access to the scenic vistas available at the summit, where today a small museum stands, dedicated to the history of the line and the surrounding White Mountains.

BIBLIOGRAPHY
General
Comp, 1974; Kulik *et al.*, 1982; Sande, 1971; US Bureau of Mines, 1976.
Specific
Taylor, W. L. The Concord (New Hampshire) gasholder: last intact survivor from the gas-making era. In *IA*, xi, 1984.

LOCATION
[M] Mount Washington Museum, 1 Washington Street, Gorham, NH 03581.

DAVID H. SHAYT

New Jersey, United States of America   No state could be better positioned than New Jersey to benefit and to suffer from northern industry and commerce, and from the sources of markets and raw materials to the south and west. New Jersey ranks forty-sixth out of the fifty states in land area, but its central location along the Atlantic coast and bountiful native resources have placed it in the upper tier of industrialized states.

Almost from the outset of European occupation in North America, the northern half of this hourglass-shaped state has been thick with industry, while in the south the rich, alluvial soil has produced a vast cornucopia of garden fruits and vegetables. Tying the state together is one of the nation's earliest railway networks, starting with the Camden & Amboy of the 1820s, on which ran the second British-made steam locomotive in North America, the *John Bull* of 1831, now in the Smithsonian Institution (*see* WASHINGTON DC).

Winding intermittently through the state's far north, segments of the now-dewatered Morris Canal can still be found. The canal was completed in 1835 to connect industries around Newark with sources of anthracite in

Pennsylvania, and was abandoned in 1922. Among the canal's distinctions were its INCLINED PLANES, up and down which canal boats passed on rails to negotiate the hilly terrain which the canal traversed. While not as popular as conventional lockage, due to the greater mechanical power required to raise undisplaced weight, the Morris Canal inclines were feats of pioneering mechanical ingenuity. Notable among them is the incline that survives at Stanhope, which still shows remains of the water turbine that powered the winch for pulling boats up the grade.

Along the canal, and in quantities through the gritty towns of Newark, Trenton, Passaic and Paterson, grew industrial works of an unending diversity, many of whose brick factories survive, either in altered forms or as abandoned shells. Structural evidence of the varnish works, shoe factories, scissor forges, knitting mills, cooperages, tanneries, watchworks, foundries, blast furnaces, gasworks and oil refineries still fill the landscape. The air in the region betrays the continuing presence of many of the more noxious trades.

In West Orange, preserved as a National Park Service site, THOMAS EDISON's extensive original laboratories and machine shop keep the memory of the inventor's life and work in good order, focusing principally on his work on lightbulbs and cinematography. In Morristown the telegraphic work of SAMUEL F. B. MORSE is celebrated at Historic Speedwell, a privately-sponsored site occupying the structures and grounds of the nineteenth-century Speedwell Iron Works, where Morse developed and tested the telegraph in 1838.

In a downtown Newark park stands a bronze statue of local hero Seth Boyden (1788–1870), who pioneered the manufacture of MALLEABLE IRON. Many of the more delicate fruits of such industry and invention stand and hang on the walls in the adjacent Newark Museum, still home to one of the state's best collections of fine art. It contrasts today with Newark's economic tailspin in the wake of civil unrest and a creeping industrial exodus to the South over recent decades.

The great sweeping curves of the trussed-arch Bayonne Bridge, completed in 1931 and now black with industrial grime, link the state with New York's Staten Island. The bridge affords a panoramic view of the Jersey industrial flats across the Hudson River from New York City. At the other bridge-building extreme, passing serenely over the quiet Raritan River on a side road in Clinton, is the Lowthorpe Truss Bridge, built in 1870, a dainty iron span fitted with endposts of an Italianate order, and displaying all the confident zeal of the small-town iron-truss bridge boom of the late nineteenth century.

BIBLIOGRAPHY
General
Jackson, 1988; Procter and Matuszeski, 1978.
Specific
Brady, B. J. Paterson, New Jersey: birthplace of the American Industrial Revolution. In *Archeology*, XXXIV, 1981.
Rutsch, E. S. Salvage archeology in Paterson, NJ, 1973–75. In *North-east Historical Archaeology*, IV, 1975.

LOCATIONS
[M] American Labor Museum, 83 Norwood Street, Haledon, NJ 07508.
[M,S] Edison National Historic Site, Main Street at Lakeside Avenue, West Orange, NJ 07052.
[M,S] Historic Speedwell, 333 Speedwell Avenue, Morristown, NJ 07960.
[M] Newark Museum, 49 Washington Street, Newark, NJ 07102.
[M] Ringwood Manor House Museum of the Iron Industry, Sloatsburg Road, Ringwood, NJ 07456.
[M] Volendam Windmill Museum, Adamic Hill Road, Milford, NJ 08848.

DAVID H. SHAYT

New Lanark, Strathclyde, Scotland A spectacularly sited and well-preserved company village, 1.5 km (1 mi.) S. of Lanark, the scene of ROBERT OWEN's first social experiments. New Lanark Conservation, founded in 1974, is 'revivifying' the village rather than turning it into a museum. Restored housing will accommodate three hundred, as opposed to the two thousand who lived there in 1800. Founded in 1785 by David Dale (1739–1806), with brief participation by RICHARD ARKWRIGHT, the tenemental housing was built by 1798. Owen took over the company and village in 1799, and added Nursery Buildings and the apprentice house in 1810, the co-operative store in 1813, the Institute for the Formation of Character in 1809–16, and the School in 1817.

Mill No. 1 was rebuilt with a Venetian centrepiece after a fire in 1788, and cut down from five storeys to three in 1945. No. 2 was widened *c.*1914. No. 4 burned down in 1883. No. 3, of *c.*1826, is fireproof and brick-arched, and has a cast-iron-plated top floor.

The mills, the institute and the school were sold to a scrap-metal firm in 1970, and after being acquired by compulsory purchase in 1983, passed to a charitable trust. The mills will house a hotel and computing and publishing companies. Restoration of the school dyeworks, foundry and mechanics' shop is complete.

The Falls of Clyde powered the mills via a tunnel and LADE. Lanarkshire Hydro-electric Power Co., Britain's first large public hydro-electric concern, also utilized the Falls with power stations at Bonnington (1927) and Stonebyres (1928). Both retain the original Francis turbines.

BIBLIOGRAPHY
General
Butt, 1971; Cole, 1930; Owen, 1972.
Specific
Butt, J., Donnachie, I. and Hume, J. R. Robert Owen of New Lanark, 1771–1858. In *Industrial Archaeology*, VIII, 1971.
Owen, R. *A Statement regarding the New Lanark Establishment.* 1812, rep. Glasgow: Molendinar Press, 1973.

LOCATION
[S] New Lanark Conservation, The Counting House, New Lanark, Lanark ML11 9DG.

MARK WATSON

New Mexico, United States of America While New Mexico has followed the conventional development pattern of the western states in yielding up a bounty of minerals, chiefly copper, tin, zinc, gold, silver, oil, lead, bituminous coal and uranium, the state has also been home since the 1940s to some of the nation's pioneering work in nuclear energy research. New Mexico's forbidding desert and mountain ranges were attributes seized upon by the federal government search for a quiet land in which to develop an atom bomb. Today, that enterprise and subsequent events are interpreted at the Los Alamos County Museum, situated among what remains probably the most isolated massing of American scientists currently at work.

Of the low-cost highway suspension bridges thrown across many western rivers of small width during the nation's first great response to the long-distance automobile, the Otowi Suspension Bridge of 1924 across the Rio Grande is a prime example, with pre-cast concrete towers and a timber-and-steel truss, none of the elements especially attractive. Together they present a welcome sign of civilization in a barren, inhospitable terrain, recalling the sudden new reach of automobiles into regions where city folk had never before travelled.

Several early-twentieth-century dams reflect the overriding hydro concerns in New Mexico – the supply of water for irrigation on the one hand and the impoundment of excess flood waters on the other. The Elephant Butte storage dam of 1916 and Conchas Waste Water Dam of 1938 – both of concrete – are massive exponents of their types. Remains of several stone-filled dams of the 1880s, built on private land for the use of their owners, stand north of Carlsbad.

Among the last of the nation's in-use narrow-gauge railways winds through northern New Mexico. A stretch of the Cumbres & Toltec Scenic Railway of 1880 is today a part of the Denver & Rio Grande Railway.

A sizeable archive of silver mining photographs and an early twentieth-century silver mining town in model form may be found at the Silver City Museum, together with documentary source material on the boom years of 1875–85.

LOCATIONS

[M] Los Alamos County Museum, 1921 Jupiter Street, Los Alamos, NM 87544.

[M] National Atomic Museum, South Wyoming Avenue, Building 10358, Kirtland Air Force Base East, Albuquerque, NM 87115.

[M] Silver City Museum, 312 West Broadway, Silver City, NM 88061.

[M] Telephone Pioneer Museum, 1209 Mountain Road, Albuquerque, NM 87110.

DAVID H. SHAYT

Newry, County Down, Northern Ireland A seaport on the coast road, 105 km (65 mi.) N. of Dublin and 61 km (38 mi.) S. of Belfast. It has been linked by canal to Lough Neagh from 1742. Warehouses, of local granite, remain on Canal Quay, Sugar Island, Merchants' Quay and Buttercrane Quay. Sands' Mill, a six-storey, ten-bay flour mill of 1876, alongside the canal, is listed. The ship canal linking Newry with the sea was built during 1759–67 and subsequently improved, but was closed in 1974.

BIBLIOGRAPHY
General
Green, 1963; McCutcheon, 1980.

New South Wales, Australia The most populous of the Australian states, with 5.5 million inhabitants, and the one whose industrial history is the most significant, with rich resources of coal, iron, tin, copper and gold, as well as some important urban industrial complexes.

The main coalfields are in the east, where early developments at NEWCASTLE were followed by the opening up of the LITHGOW area. Wollongong, where early miners' housing survives, forms the centre of the Illawarra field south of Sydney.

The first ironworks in Australia was the Fitzroy complex near Mittagong, which operated between 1848 and 1878. Only the furnace bases and slag tips survive, but iron from the works was used in the Gundagai Bridge of 1865 and the Bathurst Bridge of 1870. Blast furnaces were later established at Lithgow but smelting moved to Port Kembla in 1926.

Copper was mined at Cadia, 210 km (130 mi.) NW of Sydney, where a Cornish engine house of the 1870s is well preserved. Ore from the opencast workings at Cobar, 550 km (370 mi.) W. of Sydney, was exported through Port Adelaide between 1871 and 1920. The town is surrounded by a landscape of steel headstocks, cyanide tanks, and other remains of processing plants.

At Sunny Corner, 150 km (90 mi.) NW of Sydney, is an abandoned silver mine, where shafts, flues, a weighbridge and a manager's house of slag blocks can still be seen. The discovery of ore near Broken Hill in 1883 led to the Great Silver Boom of the 1880s. Gold-mining sites include the town of Hill End, where there are numerous remains of mines dating from the 1870s.

The stretch of land from Tingha in northern New South Wales to Stanthorpe in QUEENSLAND became the most productive tin-mining area in the world from *c.*1873, with both alluvial and shallow underground workings. Foundations of a Cornish-style smelter, which worked between 1874 and 1906, survive at Tent Hill near Emmaville.

Oil shale for the manufacture of kerosene, paraffin wax and lubricating oil was exported from Australia between 1865 and 1952. Most was mined from remote areas, and initially all was exported as shale although some processing later took place at most sites. The popular scenic railway at Katoomba originated in the 1870s as an incline for the Glen Mines. Because most sites were simply abandoned there are extensive remains. At Joadja, at the Kerosene Oil Shale Refinery, which operated for thirty years from 1873, there are retorts and workers' housing. Newnes in the Wolgan valley was developed in the first decade of the twentieth century to produce shale for motor spirit, with a refinery which was operating by 1911, but high costs brought closure in 1922. Only a public house remains of what was once a large town.

Figure 95 A stamper
battery at the Sunny
Corner silver and lead
mine, New South Wales
Kate Clark

Many of the landscapes and structures created by the extensive brick industry in the state in the late nineteenth century remain around Morpeth and Maitland.

New South Wales had a wool textile industry in the mid-nineteenth century. Eight woollen mills were working in the state in 1877, but economic depression in the 1890s brought about their closure. There were breweries in thirty-four of the country towns in the state in the course of the nineteenth century, one of the earliest being that of Andrew Thompson at Windsor, established in 1806. Bradley's Brewery at Goulburn dating from 1836, is now a private house, but its 28 hp steam engine is preserved in SYDNEY. A beam engine by Appleby of London of 1883 in a pumping station on the Wollondilly River at Goulburn still operates *in situ* as part of the Marsden Steam Museum, which also holds an English-built colliery winding engine of 1888 from a colliery at NEWCASTLE.

Old Sydney Town, near Goulburn, is a re-creation of buildings from the early period of the city's settlement, including convict gang huts, a dockyard, and a replica of the prefabricated building brought from London as the governor's residence in 1788.

Whaling sites at Twofold Bay are within the bounds of the Ben Boyd National Park, named after an early whaling captain. Try pots for rendering down blubber, capstans and blubber tanks are preserved at nearby Boydtown.

BIBLIOGRAPHY
General
Baker, 1986; Birmingham *et al*, 1979; Department of Main Roads, 1976; Heritage of Australia, 1981; Hughes, 1964; Jeans, 1972; Power, 1912.
Specific
Industrial Archaeology – a National Trust policy paper. Sydney: National Trust of Australia (NSW), 1988.

502

LOCATIONS
[I] Heritage Council of New South Wales, 4th Floor, Remington Centre, 175 Liverpool Street, Sydney, NSW 2000.
[M] Marsden Steam Museum, Marsden Bridge, Crookwell Road, Goulburn, NSW 2416.
[I] National Trust of Australia (New South Wales), Observatory Hill, Sydney, NSW 2000.
[I] New South Wales National Parks and Wildlife Service, 189 Kent Street, Sydney, NSW 2000.
[I] Old Sydney Town Pty Ltd, Somersby, New South Wales.

KATE CLARK

newspaper printing   Newspapers were first produced in the seventeenth century on hand presses, and were continually promoting innovations, as large print-runs of material with a short reading-life demand speed of production. *The Times* of London took the lead, employing Friedrich König (*see* PRESS). American newspapers introduced the first fully automatic rotary presses in 1865, and the Linotype machine in 1886. Fleet Street, London, had until the 1980s the greatest concentration of newspaper printing works in the world. A small town newspaper printing works is preserved at RØROS.

BIBLIOGRAPHY
General
Barson and Saint, 1988; Dunnett, 1988; Hutt, 1973.
Specific
Musson, A. E. Newspaper printing in the Industrial Revolution. In *EcHR*, x, 1958.

Newtongrange and Prestongrange, Lothian, Scotland   The Scottish Mining Museum is a two-site museum of coal mining, its related industries and communities, located at Lady Victoria Colliery, Newtongrange, Midlothian, and Prestongrange Colliery, East Lothian, 13 km (8 mi.) NE. Lady Victoria Colliery was sunk as the showpiece of the Lothian Coal Co. in 1890–4 and closed in 1981; it is being preserved in its entirety. The winding engines – of 2400 hp with twin 40 in. (1.016 m) cylinders with drop valves, by Grant Ritchie & Co. of Kilmarnock – and the eight Lancashire boilers are in working order. An extensive tub circuit and screening plant remain in the steel-framed brick surface complex, the ground floor of which, formerly railway sidings, will house the 'underground experience', the shaft having been filled in. Newtongrange is an intact company village, the largest in Scotland, with long brick terraces, an Institute, and the Dean Tavern, run on Gothenberg principles with the profits recycled for community projects. Rosewell, 5 km (3 mi.) W., is a smaller village built by the same company.

Prestongrange Colliery, the oldest documented coal-mining site in Britain, illustrates the earlier history of coal. Monks worked coal here in 1184. A new shaft with cast-iron tubbing was sunk in 1829, and in 1874 Harveys of Hayle supplied a Cornish pumping engine, with a second-hand 70 in. (1.78 m) cylinder of 1853. It is now unique in Scotland and was preserved through the efforts of its manager after the pit closed in 1962. Other surface buildings have been demolished, apart from the baths of

1952, and the power station of *c.*1910 which displays coal cutters, a high-speed engine of 1925 and a d.c. generator. A Howden fan, a compound winding engine, and the Hoffman kiln of a related brick and pipe works are also preserved. Volunteers operate a 'pug' shunting locomotive and a steam navvy (*see* EXCAVATOR).

LOCATIONS
[M] Scottish Mining Museum, Lady Victoria Colliery, Newtongrange, Midlothian.
[M] Scottish Mining Museum, Prestongrange, Prestonpans, East Lothian EH22 4QN.

MARK WATSON

new town   The concept of a settlement on an open site, planned from the outset, was known in the Middle Ages, and has remained common throughout the industrial period, but the term 'new town' is most generally applied to the state-financed British towns projected under the New Towns Act of 1946. These bear many resemblances to Ebenezer Howard's ideal of the GARDEN CITY, with populations of between 60 000 and 100 000, and rigidly zoned industrial and domestic areas. Examples are Stevenage, Harlow and Crawley, near London, Washington and Peterlee in County Durham. Milton Keynes in Buckinghamshire, Telford (*see* IRONBRIDGE) in Shropshire, all in England, and Cumbernauld and East Kilbride in Scotland.

BIBLIOGRAPHY
General
Hall, 1966; Osborn and Whittick, 1963; Schaffer, 1970; Self, 1972.

New York, United States of America   The state of New York extends some 500 km (300 mi.) from New York City to the Adirondacks and the Canadian border, incorporating some of the most sparsely inhabited as well as some of the most populous regions of the USA. Beyond the extremely dense banks of metamorphic rock that make up the island of Manhattan, the rise of New York as a commercial and industrial centre may be attributed in large measure to the extensive networks of canals and railways dug and laid across this large north-eastern state. The national government established itself in New York City at the time of independence, but relocated to Washington in 1790; New York then took off as the country's pre-eminent centre of international commerce and industry.

In 1807 the first successful demonstration of a steam-powered vessel, by Robert Fulton (1765–1815), occurred on an excursion up the Hudson River to Albany, an appropriate waterway, given its navigability for 240 km (150 mi.) upriver. Rivers, lakes and canals interconnect the state's other major cities – Rochester, Syracuse, Buffalo and Utica. The Erie Canal, completed in 1825, was the trendsetter for much of the nation, linking the Hudson River at Albany with the Great Lakes at Buffalo some 587 km (365 mi.) distant. The canal's homegrown design and construction under Benjamin Wright (1770–1842), regarded as the father of American civil engineering,

Figure 96   Brooklyn Bridge, New York, designed by John A. Roebling, photographed in the year of its centenary, 1983
Jet Lowe, HAER

opened the East to the ready availability of Western goods, the West to newly-arrived immigrants, and the world to the capabilities of American engineers. The much-enlarged canal remains in use, largely for pleasure boating. Its privately-run museum at Syracuse is housed in a canal weighing-lock building of 1850. The Champlain Canal and the Oswego Canal are other major New York waterways dug in the decade of ditches, the 1820s.

On the heels of canal construction, railways began to crisscross the state of New York, first linking ports with canal termini, and soon competing directly with the canals for traffic. In the north, the Erie Railway built a vast honeycomb of rails, stations, tunnels, bridges, cuttings and roundhouses, much of which remains scattered about several counties in various stages of ruin or reuse. Some of the largest of the state's railways pass through or terminate at New York City, in what might be the most densely packed accumulation of track outside Europe. The city's Grand Central Terminal of 1913, and the late Pennsylvania Station, open from 1910 to 1964, served as suitably awe-inspiring gateways for passengers arriving from abroad, destined for points inland, and for those rough folk from the American interior entering the metropolis.

The rail and automobile tunnels that run beneath the Hudson River into and out of New York City were significant engineering achievements of their times, but are difficult to appreciate firsthand today since the rail tunnels are unlit, and few automobile drivers can focus on anything but the traffic flow in the Lincoln Tunnel and the Holland Tunnel of 1927. Over both the Hudson River and East River on either side of Manhattan pass a remarkable family of bridges, representing some of the supreme engineering workmanship and design of their days: Brooklyn Bridge of 1883, Williamsburg Bridge of 1907, Manhattan Bridge of 1903, and the Queensboro Bridge of 1909, the George Washington Bridge of 1931, and, crossing New York Harbour, the Verrazano-Narrows Bridge of 1964, for several years the world's longest-span suspension bridge.

Elsewhere in the harbour stands one of the world's more poetic engineering LANDMARKS – the copper-sheathed, wrought-iron-framed Statue of Liberty of 1885, the largest metal statue in the world. A museum recounting her French birth and American restoration in the 1980s stands in the masonry base, while another museum on nearby Ellis Island, where many millions entered the country, preserves the physical evidence and the architecture of immigration.

Within New York City the industrial heritage abounds, the vintage subway stations, lower Manhattan's cast-iron building façades, Central Park's ornamental cast-iron bridges, several generations of skyscraping office buildings (*see* SKYSCRAPER and figure 145), the Croton water-supply aqueduct, and the old manufacturing districts of the lower downtown and Brooklyn being a few of the more conspicuous examples. Since the lamentable demolition of the monumental Penn Station in 1964, stiff new land-marking laws (*see* LANDMARK) have held in check the destruction of countless building exteriors and occasional interiors, while such flavourful neighbourhoods as the South Street fish market area and the industrial loft district of Soho, below Greenwich Village, have been transformed into up-scale, service-orientated commercial havens, pushing out the older trades and tradespeople.

Among the state's many outstanding preserved examples of early civil engineering works, the modest Cleft Ridge span in Brooklyn's Prospect Park ranks as the nation's earliest concrete bridge, a 7.3 m (24 ft.) arched span built in 1872 without any internal reinforcement, its portals dripping with cast Gothic ornament.

Buffalo, Rochester and Syracuse have been passing through periods of economic upheaval as shifts in major industries undercut their bases of employment and income. 'Industrial preservation' has taken on a new unsavoury meaning in the economically blighted parts of these smokestack cities, the historic steelmaking, textile and transport structures now embarrassing reminders of a used-up past, one which city administrators are seeking to replace with the new high-technology service industries that offer such promise.

The conurbation at the confluence of the Hudson and Mohawk rivers, north of the state capital of Albany, which incorporates Cohoes, Troy, Waterford and Watervliet, has one of the richest concentrations of industrial monuments in the nation, and one which has figured prominently in the development of the discipline of industrial archaeology. Few locations were so well-endowed with water power and transport facilities. Notable structures in Troy include the round gasholder house of 1873 built for the Troy Gaslight Co., a factory built for the International Shirt & Collar Co. in 1893, the Lion shirt and collar factory of 1884–97, and the Italianate works of W. & L. E. Gurley, makers of surveying instruments, built in 1862. Cohoes is dominated by the vast Harmony Mills cotton complex, constructed between 1837 and the 1870s, with its associated power canals and company housing. Watervliet Arsenal was established to provide ordnance for the United States Army in 1812. Among its historic structures are the 'Cast Iron Building' of 1859, which now houses a museum, the 400 m (1300 ft.) long Big Gun Shop of 1889–93, and powder magazines of 1818 and 1849.

In the far north of the state, the Adirondack Iron & Steel Co., established in 1826, built a blast furnace at Adirondack, 38 km (24 mi.) NE of Blue Mountain Lake, in 1855. It operated for only one year. Its stack and other remains, including a blowing machine, lie hidden in the woodlands beside the infant Hudson River, and have been surveyed by HAER (*see* UNITED STATES OF AMERICA).

Outside those parts of the state that have the means to preserve the fragile fabric of their distinctive industrial pasts, the collections of the New York State Museum at Albany are becoming increasingly representative of the materials-processing and manufacturing industries that propelled the state for its first two hundred years. Other museums illustrate particular industries: lumbering and mining at The Adirondack Museum, Blue Mountain Lake; whaling at Cold Spring Harbor and Sag Harbor; glass at Corning; woodworking at Hanford Mills, East Meredith; and salt at Liverpool. Despite the best efforts of developers, the marks of several generations of hydro-electric power and abrasives (carborundum) manufacture at Niagara Falls, and of the production of hand-made gloves in Gloversville, remain dominant features of the state's landscape.

BIBLIOGRAPHY
General
Gable, 1974; Jackson, 1988; Latimer *et al.*, 1984; Leary and Sholes, 1987; McCullough, 1972; Procter and Matuszeski, 1978; Stott, 1974; Vogel, 1973; Waite, 1972.
Specific
Chamberlin, W. P. The cleft-ridge span: America's first concrete arch. In *IA*, IX, 1983.
Seely, B. E. *et al. Drawings of the Adirondack ironworks, NL Industries.* Tahawus, NY 12879, n.d.
Waite, J. G. and Waite, D. S. Industrial Archeology in Troy, Waterford, Cohoes, Green Island and Watervliet. Troy, N.Y.: Hudson-Mohawk Industrial Gateway.

LOCATIONS
[M] Adirondack Museum, Blue Mountain Lake, NY 18112.
[M] American Museum of Immigration, Liberty Island, New York, NY 10004.
[M] Corning Museum of Glass, Museum Way, Corning, NY 14830.
[M] Erie Canal Museum, 318 Erie Boulevard, East Syracuse, NY 13202.
[M] Hanford Mills Museum, East Meredith, NY 13757.
[M] International Museum of Photography, George Eastman House, 900 East Avenue, Rochester, NY 14607.
[M] New York Museum of Transportation, 6393 East River Road, West Henrietta, NY 14586.
[M] New York State Museum, Empire State Plaza, Albany, NY 12230.
[M] New York State Transit Museum, Boerum Place and Schermerhorn Street, Brooklyn, NY 11201.
[M] Quarryman's Museum, 7480 Fite Road, Saugerties, NY 12477.
[M] Sag Harbor Whaling Museum, Main Street, Sag Harbor, NY 11963.
[M] Salt Museum, Onondaga Lake Park, Liverpool, NY 13088.
[M] South Street Seaport Museum, 107 Front Street, NY 10038.
[M] Statue of Liberty National Monument, Liberty Island, NY 10004.
[M] Whaling Museum, Cold Spring Harbor, NY 11724.

DAVID H. SHAYT

New Zealand   New Zealand was first settled by Polynesians in the tenth century AD. Their land was purchased by British settlers following the visits of James Cook and other western explorers. Under the Treaty of Waitangi of 1840 the country became a British colony. It continued as such until 1907 when it was recognized as a self-governing dominion. This article deals only with the

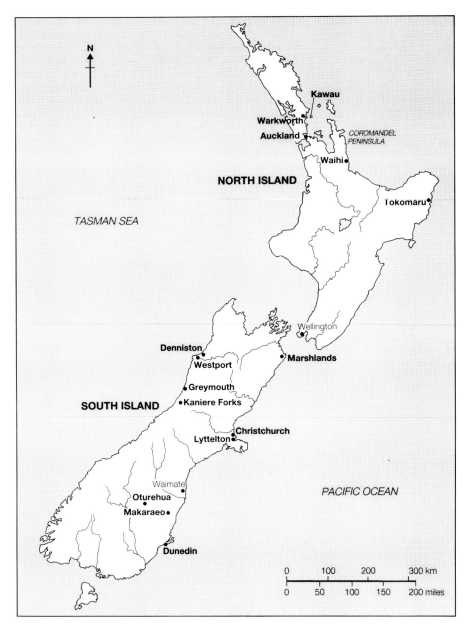

New Zealand

industrial technologies that emanated from Western Europe, and not with the complex strategies developed by the Maoris for utilizing and processing raw materials, which is beyond the scope of this encyclopaedia.

New Zealand consists of two main islands, extending together some 1600 km (1000 mi.) from north to south, and about 450 km (280 mi.) at the widest point from east to west. The country has a temperate climate. Its soils support huge areas of native forest and wide expanses of agricultural pastures, while in other parts there are vast mountainous tracts, swamps and glaciers.

New Zealand's industrial history has been shaped by its former colonial status. The industrial heritage is not one of large-scale manufacturing in urban factories: rather, the early settlers utilized forest and pasture, and to a lesser extent, such minerals as gold and coal. There was also some whaling and sealing, with associated boat-building, and utilization of native flax for ropes and nets. Milling was the first significant manufacturing activity, and the pioneer mills, like contemporary farm buildings, were constructed in a distinctive style in timber and corrugated iron.

An island nation, with an interior that was often impenetrable, New Zealand was primarily dependent on sea transport. Native timber was plentiful, and the first commercial shipyard was established c.1819 at Hokianga Harbour, an established port in the extreme north of North Island. Steamships were being built from the 1850s. New Zealand shipyards gained worldwide fame for scows, shallow-draught vessels, construction of which began in the 1870s. Several nineteenth-century lighthouses of British design remain, like that at Farewell Spit, and a time-ball station remains at LYTTELTON.

New Zealand's rivers are notoriously prone to flash floods, and despite the priority given by governments to surveying for roads and railways, the development of road and railway networks proceeded slowly; it was not until the 1870s and 80s that secure road links across the interior were established. Railways were built to a gauge of 1.07 m (3 ft. 6 in.), the network totalling 5455 route km (3390 mi.) by 1939. The principal engineering features are the steel viaducts of the North Island main line, built c.1900. The station at DUNEDIN represents the high point of New Zealand railway architecture. Its Scottish architect, George Alexander Troup, also designed a windmill for pumping water into the tenders of locomotives, which was used in standardized form throughout the railway system. The road system was extended rapidly in the 1930s to accommodate motor traffic, the total length of made-up roads rising from 77762 km (48321 mi.) to 101524 km (63086 mi.) between 1929 and 1939. The first airline began operation in 1934, and the first radio broadcasts were made in 1924.

The first Merino sheep were imported from Australia in the 1830s, and large-scale development of sheep farming followed in the 1850s. Huge sheep stations of 20000 ha (50000 ac.) in Otago, Canterbury and Marlborough represent the classic unit of production. The largest and most characteristic building of a sheep station was the woolshed, where shearing, sorting, baling, and storage of fleeces took place. Wooden woolsheds of 1856 survive at Te Waimate 40 km (25 mi.) S. of Timaru and Coldstream 40 km (25 mi.) NE of Timaru. Stone woolsheds are characteristic of the Otago region. A woolshed characteristically has a high gable or raised square tower to accommodate the tall screw press used for compressing wool into bales, and as many as forty-eight shearing stands. Mechanical handpieces were operated from overhead drive shafts along the sides of the sheds, but from the 1890s electrical shearing was developed. Sheep were reared not just for their wool but for their carcasses, which were boiled down for tallow or processed in a freezing works. The New Zealand Refrigeration Company was established in 1881 in association with the New Zealand Shipping Co., following the patenting by Bell & Coleman of Glasgow of refrigeration plant which could be used on board ships, and the first cargo of frozen mutton was conveyed to Britain in the sailing ship *Dunedin* in 1882. Land-based REFRIGERATION plants were established, using Haslam's dry-air process, plant for which was made in New Zealand.

As a result of New Zealand's isolation, flourmilling quickly became a widespread industry, most commonly using the water mill, the first recorded example of which was built at Waimate Mission Station in 1834. There were important groups of mills on the Wanganui and Waikato rivers on North Island, and the Avon on South Island. The earliest surviving mill is the preserved Kawana Flour Mill, Matahiwi, 40 km (25 mi.) N. of Wanganui, which dates from 1854. Water power was also important in the exploitation of New Zealand's timber resources. A water-powered sawmill was established at Mercury Bay in the Coromandel Peninsula in 1838, and by the late 1860s there was a major timber industry centred around Picton and Havelock in Marlborough province. In the 1870s the government encouraged Danes and Norwegians in forest breaking, and some relics of their sawmills survive at settlements like Norsewood and Dannevirke. Kauri dams (named after New Zealand's most celebrated timber tree), which are loose plank dams, probably based on American practice, were widely used for the transport of timber until the 1930s. Logs were retained behind the dam until there was sufficient water to carry them down to a mill in a controlled rush. There is a preserved example in the Kauaeranga Forest Park. Kauri-gum, the solidified turpentine of the kauri tree, used in the manufacture of oils, varnishes and linoleum, was a major export before 1914.

New Zealand had many areas of flax swamp, and flax mills directed towards the export trade developed from an early date at ports like Foxton.

Gold mining is the classic extractive industry in New Zealand. There were gold rushes in the early nineteenth century, to alluvial goldfields (see ALLUVIAL MINING), stimulating the growth of shanty towns of amateur prospectors. Some towns continued to prosper after the rushes were over but many survive only as 'ghost' towns. Gold mining became an industry with the discovery of gold in quartz reefs in Thames in 1867. Obtaining gold from quartz ores was usually undertaken by large companies which erected huge and distinctive stamper batteries for crushing ores. They were commonly in remote areas, built on steep hillsides for ease of loading, and they used water both as a source of power and for washing. Ores were fed into rock breakers (or 'grizzlies') for coarse crushing, and then to sequentially working stamp heads for finer reduction. The Phoenix Mining Co., Bullendale, Otago, used hydro-electric power in 1885 to drive thirty stamper heads, two air compressors and a rock breaker, the first time that electricity had been used in mining operations. Stamper battery development culminated in the huge two-hundred stamper head, electrically-powered Waikino batteries on the Ohinemuri River, built by the Waihi Gold Mining Co. in 1902. The nearby Martha Mine was the largest gold mine in New Zealand, with more than 160 km (100 mi.) of underground workings, and producing 35500000 ounces of gold between 1890 and 1952. The development of the cyanide process from the late 1880s doubled the efficiency of the processes used for recovering gold from ore. Much gold was also obtained by dredging, over two hundred dredges, employing more than two thousand men, being in operation in 1903. A dredge used on the Upper Taieri River in the 1890s has been preserved.

Large-scale coal workings began in the second half of

the nineteenth century. The largest concern was the Westport Coal Co. in Nelson province which was responsible for constructing the celebrated incline at DENNISTON. Other coal-mining centres included Greymouth, Huntly and North Otago. Large coal-tippling bins, which loaded graded coal from elevated tramways into railway wagons beneath, are characteristic structures, and many remain.

Manganese and copper ores were being mined in the 1840s on Kawau and Waikeke islands. Some antimony was mined at Endeavour Inlet and in Central Otago.

Many limekilns dating from the second half of the nineteenth century remain, all built into hillsides to facilitate loading. Lime burning was made obsolete by the introduction of Portland cement, introduced to New Zealand in 1884 by Nathaniel Wilson (see WARKWORTH). Concrete construction was used from 1850s, and had become very common by 1900. Many disused brick kilns survive, including a fourteen-chamber rectangular HOFF-MAN KILN of 1916 at Palmerston North and a circular Hoffmann kiln at Ashburton.

Woollen cloth manufacture was introduced to New Zealand in 1871 when A. J. Burns & Co. opened a steam-powered mill at Mosgiel, Otago, using British machinery, and operated by Scottish millhands.

New Zealand's engineering industry developed in the second half of the nineteenth century, concentrating on roller milling machinery for flourmills and pumps for mines. Railway workshops were established in the major centres by the 1880s, and the first locomotive to be built in New Zealand was completed in 1889.

The Edendale Dairy Factory established in 1882 was the country's pioneer dairy factory, utilizing the centrifugal cream separator, invented in 1878, and applying pasteurizers and curd agitators.

New Zealanders showed great flair for innovation in the use of hydro-electric power. A small power station on the Maraetotara Stream, built in 1892, remains in use. In 1891 a gold dredge measuring 24.3 m × 5.5 m × 1.3 m (80 ft. × 18 ft. 3 in. × 4 ft. 6 in.) was constructed on the Shotover River, deriving its power from a hydro-electric station, from which it was powered by a copper wire. In 1909 hydro-electric power was used for pumping water from gold mines from the Kaniere Forks power station, which still operates. Most of the main cities had electric power systems by 1900. The large-scale use of the thermal resources of the volcanic plateau on North Island began in the 1950s.

The New Zealand Historic Places Trust was inaugurated in 1955 with the coming into effect of the Historic Places Act 1954. It now operates under the Historic Places Act 1980 which charges it with powers to identify, investigate, record and interpret historic places and areas in New Zealand. It co-ordinates official and voluntary efforts in conservation, and works through twenty regional committees. The Trust owns some sixty properties including several industrial sites. From 1987 the Trust was linked for administrative purposes with a new Department of Conservation, which also incorporates parts of other government departments responsible for national parks. Many important industrial monuments are isolated and are in urgent need of recording before they are destroyed by decay.

See also AUCKLAND; CHRISTCHURCH; DENNISTON; DUNE-DIN; GREYMOUTH; KANIERE FORKS; KAWAU; LYTTELTON; MAKARAEO; MARSHLANDS; OTUREHUA; TOKOMARU; WAIHI; WARKWORTH; WESTPORT.

BIBLIOGRAPHY
General
Blair, 1887; Diamond and Hayward, 1975; Prichard, 1970; Salmon, 1963; Thornton, 1982, 1986; Williams, 1965.
Specific
New Zealand Historic Places Trust, Thirty Years 1955–85, Wellington: New Zealand Historic Places Trust, 1985.
Thornton, G. Industrial archaeology in New Zealand. In *IAR*, x(1) 1987.

LOCATION
[I] New Zealand Historic Places Trust, Antrim House, Boulcott Street, Wellington.

SARAH HILL

Niagara, Ontario, Canada, and New York, United States of America   One of the world's great natural wonders, the Niagara Falls are on the 34 km (21 mi.) river flowing from Lake Erie to Lake Ontario. The falls stimulated the growth of a celebrated resort with remarkable waxworks and fairgrounds; they were the setting for JOHN ROEBLING's railway suspension bridge of 1855; and they were the location of some of the most important early hydro-electric power stations and electrochemical plants. The hydro potential of the Falls has been estimated to be 3.73 million kilowatts (5 million horse power).

The isthmus between the two Great Lakes has been crossed by four successive versions of the Welland Canal, running parallel to the Niagara, and avoiding the Falls. The first was built by a company established in 1818 by William Hamilton Merritt (1793–1862). Navigation between the two lakes, utilizing the Welland and Niagara, was established in 1829. The canal, with forty timber locks, was completed in 1833. It was enlarged and completely rebuilt in 1842–51. After a further enlargement in 1873–81, there were twenty-five locks with electrically-powered gates, and a minimum depth of 3.7 m (12 ft.). The fourth Welland Canal was built in 1913–32. It was 44.3 km ($27\frac{1}{2}$ mi.) long, 8.2 m (27 ft.) deep, and had only seven locks. After the completion of the St Lawrence Seaway in 1959, a bypass taking the canal around the city of Welland was built in 1967–73. There are canal-viewing and information centres at Lock 3, St Catharines, and Lock Eight, Port Colborne; and displays relating to the canal in the museums at St Catharines and Port Colborne. The Merrittrail is a 22 km (14 mi.) bicycle and walking trail giving access to twenty-one locks of the second canal.

At St Catharines there are numerous remnants of the first three Welland Canals and of the industrial buildings that lined their banks. At the Lake Ontario end of the waterway are lighthouses of 1879 and 1898. In Merritton, south of St Catharines, near Lock 10 of the former canal, is a building which was part of the calcium carbide plant, utilizing electric power generated by the waters of the canal, established in 1892 by Thomas Leopold Wilson, patentee of the process. Further south at Thorold the Welland Mills, established in 1846, was once Canada's largest flourmilling complex. The mill closed in 1932 and its buildings are now used by a paper company for storage.

BIBLIOGRAPHY
General
Barnet *et al.*, 1982; Burtniak and Turner, 1980; Christensen *et al.*, 1976; Greenwald *et al.*, 1976; Hadfield, 1986; Jackson and Addis, 1982; Jackson and Burtniak, 1978; Jackson and White, 1971; Seibel, 1967.
Specific
Archaeological Excavation of Lock 24, First Welland Canal. London, Ontario: Historica Research, 1988.
Jackson, J. N. *The Four Welland Canals: A journey of discovery in St Catharines and Thorold.* St Catharines: Vanwell Publishing, 1989.

LOCATIONS
[M] Niagara Historical Society Museum, 43 Castlereagh Street, Niagara-on-the-Lake, Ontario.
[I] Niagara Parks Commission, Box 150, Niagara Falls, Ontario L2E 6T2.
[M] Port Colborne Historical and Marine Museum, 280 King Street, Port Colborne, Ontario.
[M] St Catharines Historical Museum 343 Merritt Street, St Catharines, Ontario.
[M] Welland Historical Museum, 65 Hooker Street, Welland, Ontario.
[I] Welland Canals Foundation, 215 Ontario Street, PO Box 745, St Catharines, Ontario L2R 6Y3.

DERYCK HOLDSWORTH

nickel (Ni)   A metal, which is usually found in association with copper, and is difficult to smelt. It is similar to iron, but resistant to corrosion. First isolated by Axel F. Cronstedt in 1751, nickel has since been used in the form of nickel-copper alloys or ferrous alloys, and especially in stainless steels. The carbonyl smelting process developed by Ludwig Mond, Carl Langer and H. Hirtz in 1890 was first applied commercially at Swansea, Wales, in 1901. The chief sources of nickel are New Caledonia and Canada; some deposits are found in Norway, where a smelter is preserved (*see* RINGERIKE).

BIBLIOGRAPHY
General
Morgan and Pratt, 1938.

Niederfinow, Brandenburg, Germany   The Oder–Havel Canal meets the River Oder 60 km (37 mi.) NE of Berlin. The difference in level of 36 m (118 ft.) between the two courses of these important waterways linking Berlin with the Baltic was overcome in 1914 by a series of four locks. These were replaced in 1927–32 by a boat lift of steel construction. A caisson, 85 m (279 ft.) long and 12 m (40 ft.) wide, about 4300 tonnes in weight, hangs from 156 wire cables running in pairs over guide pulleys in the upper parts of the frame, and attached to counterweights at the other end, which are of the same weight as the trough and its contents. Four 75 hp electric motors move the trough up and down over the racks, the lifting process taking about five minutes.

BIBLIOGRAPHY
General
Hadfield, 1986; Schmidt and Theile, 1989; Tew, 1984; Wagenbreth and Wächtler, 1983.

Nitra, South Slovakia, Czechoslovakia   A large and expanding town, and an important centre for agriculture. The National Agricultural Complex includes exhibition space and a showground and also has a museum of rural life, with reconstructions of traditional buildings. A narrow-gauge railway illustrates the transport of timber. An old bakery and distillery produce bread and slivovitz (plum brandy) by traditional methods.

nitric acid (HNO_3)   'Aqua fortis'. A chemical agent of prime importance, particularly in the manufacture of explosives, fertilizers and dyestuffs. Nitric acid was known in the Middle Ages but its chemical formula was understood only in the late eighteenth century. It was made in the nineteenth century by treating sodium nitrate ($NaNO_3$, or Chile saltpetre) with sulphuric acid (H_2SO_4) in cylindrical cast-iron retorts, and condensing the fumes in sorption towers:

$$2NaNO_3 + H_2SO_4 \rightarrow Na_2SO_4 + 2HNO_3$$

Nitric acid is also made by the BIRKELAND AND EYDE PROCESS, and by the Ostwald process, the oxidation of ammonia over a platinum catalyst.

BIBLIOGRAPHY
General
Morgan and Pratt, 1938; Partington, 1950.

nitrogen (N)   A largely unreactive elemental gas, which comprises about four-fifths of the atmosphere. It is commercially produced, with oxygen, from the distillation of liquid air. Nitrogen is used in various industrial processes that demand an inert atmosphere, but chiefly in the synthesis of AMMONIA.

BIBLIOGRAPHY
General
Morgan and Pratt, 1938; Partington, 1950.

Nivå, Zealand, Denmark   At Nivå brickyard on the Sound, 12 km (8 mi.) SW of Helsingør, a monumental fifteen-chamber circular brick kiln has recently been restored as a museum. It was built in 1870 on the HOFFMAN KILN principle, and was in continuous use until 1967. It represents the first generation of circular kilns in Denmark, of which the earliest was erected by G. Kähler at Korsør in 1867. The tradition of brickmaking in the Nivå area dates from *c.*1800. In the mid-nineteenth century several larger brickworks were established, taking advantage of suitable deposits of clays in glacial moraines, and easy transport by coastal shipping to Copenhagen.

Figure 97 The fifteen-chamber Hoffman kiln of 1870 at the brickworks at Nivå, Denmark, which was in use until 1967 and is now preserved.
Jørgen Sestoft

At Usserød, 5 km (3 mi.) S., an old textile mill, run from 1810 until 1981 by the Ministry of Defence, has been converted into the headquarters of the electronics firm S. T. Lyngsø. Among the surviving buildings is the spinning mill of 1803.

BIBLIOGRAPHY
Specific
Danstrup, E. B. *Den militære klædefabrik i Usserød* (The military uniform factory at Usserød). Horsholm, 1987.

Strømstad, P. *Ringoven ved Nive å* (The circular kiln at Nive å). Karlebo, 1985.

Nobel, Alfred Bernhard (1833–96) Creator of the modern explosives industry. A Swede, he spent much of his early life in Russia, where his father manufactured armaments for the government, and where he began to develop nitroglycerine in 1859 following its preparation by Ascanio Sobrero (1812–88) of Turin in 1846. Nobel returned to Sweden in 1863, but from the mid-1860s began to create a multinational enterprise with factories in Germany, Norway, Scotland and elsewhere. He left much of his fortune to endow the Nobel prizes.

Nitroglycerine was prepared by treating purified glycerine with a mixture of concentrated nitric and sulphuric acids. It was highly unstable, until in 1866 Nobel combined it with kieselguhr to make DYNAMITE. By 1865 Nobel had established the principle of the detonator, using mercury fulminate ($Hg(ONC)_2$). In the mid-1870s he developed blasting gelatine, incorporating nitrocellulose in nitroglycerine. The fourth of his major innovations was 'smokeless powder', developed as Ballistite from 1889, which could be used as a propellant for military purposes.

The only Nobel factory in its original condition is preserved at HURUM.

BIBLIOGRAPHY
General
Bergengren, 1962; Reader, 1970; Schluck and Sohlman, 1929.

BARRIE TRINDER

Noisiel, Seine-et-Marne, France   The Menier chocolate factory at Noisiel, 15 km (9 mi.) E. of Paris near the new town of Marne-la-Vallée and the Eurodisneyland, is situated on the River Marne, on the site of a corn mill dating back to the twelfth century. The mill was purchased in 1825 by Jean Antoine Brutus Menier (1795–1863) for the preparation of pharmaceutical products. His son, Émile Justin Menier (1812–81), concentrated on chocolate production, founding a vast chocolate empire with its own plantations in Nicaragua and its own commercial fleet. He extended the Noisiel site, transforming it into a model factory which was much visited and well publicized, and a company town, built from 1874 with housing inspired by examples from Leeds and BRADFORD.

All this construction was primarily the work of the engineer Jules Logre and the architect Jules Saulnier (1817–81); the latter's mill building astride the Marne, completed in 1872, which houses the Girard turbines and the chocolate-grinding and mixing equipment, is acknowledged as a landmark in architectural history (*see* figure 28). The building's revolutionary iron frame is left visible, contributing to the rich decorative effects of polychromatic brickwork and ceramic tiling, which depicts cacao flowers and the letter 'M'.

The site also includes a building known as the 'cathedral', designed in a Louis XV-style in 1907 by Stephen Sauvestre, architect of Eiffel's tower. Linking it to the workshops on the opposite bank is a single-span footbridge in iron-banded concrete, designed by the pioneering concrete engineer, Armand Considère.

The whole site, including factory buildings, municipal buildings, workers' housing, the Menier château and the model farm, is remarkably well preserved although production ceased in 1991. An association working with the municipality of Noisel organizes group visits to the site. 'Noisiel, Ville d'Histoire' is an organization concerned with the town's history.

BIBLIOGRAPHY
General
Marrey, 1984.
Specific
Valentin, M. and Michel, R. Le Fait municipal dans les politiques spatiales et sociales du patronat: les Menier et Noisiel entre 1871 et 1914 (Municipal considerations in the politics of spatial and social organisation: the Meniers at Noisiel, 1871–1914). In 1848 Révolutions et Mutations au XIXe siècle, IV, 1985.

LOCATION
[I] Noisiel, Ville d'Histoire, Mairie de Noisiel, BP 35, 77426 Marne-la-Vallée.

PAUL SMITH

Noord Holland (North Holland), The Netherlands   The province bordering the North Sea, which includes AMSTERDAM, HAARLEM and YMUIDEN, east of which lay the Zuiderzee, formerly a large inlet of the sea, around which were situated many small fishing and shipping ports. The drainage of the northern part of the province between Den Helder and Amsterdam has a long and complex history. Lakes were being reclaimed from the twelfth century, and many dams and dikes remain, with some eighty windmills.

A dangerous flood which followed the bursting of a dike in 1916, and the shortage of arable land experienced during World War I, ended discussions about the enclosure of the Zuiderzee which had gone on since the nineteenth century. In 1918 the Dutch parliament accepted a scheme to enclose and drain 350 000 ha (870 000 ac.) in four polders, with a 120 000 ha (300 000 ac.) freshwater reservoir. The enclosure dam (Afsluitdijk) was completed on 28 May 1932, after which the resultant freshwater lake was designated the IJsselmeer. The engineer CORNELIS LELY is commemorated by a statue by the ship locks at Den Oever at the south end of the dam, near to which the Leemans pumping station retains its 1200 hp diesel engine of 1929. The Wieringermeer Polder was enclosed in 1927–30, the Noordoostpolder in 1937–41, and Oostelijk and Zuidelijk FLEVOLAND in the post-war period. Drainage has brought a rich archaeological harvest in the form of more than two hundred shipwrecks.

Enkhuizen is a former fishing port at the north end of the dike from Lelystad, Flevoland, with a museum established in 1948 to portray the economic and social changes brought about by the enclosure of the Zuiderzee in 1932. The indoor section includes twelve ancient sailing vessels, many ship models, and a section on cartography. The open-air museum, opened in 1985, portrays life in the whole Zuiderzee region between 1880 and 1932, with 130 buildings constructed along streets, alleyways and canals, including fish-smoking kilns, lime-kilns, a variety of shops, a steam laundry and a shipyard. The museum is approached by ferry from the road across the dike. At Broekerhaven, 3 km (2 mi.) W., is an intact ship lift of 1922 for small, flat-bottomed vessels.

At Medemblik at the south end of Wieringermeer Polder, north of the Vier Noorderkoggen Polder, drained in the nineteenth century, is the National Steam Engine Museum. It was opened in 1986 in a former steam pumping station, 'De Vier Noorderkoggen', built in 1869, with symmetrical scoop wheels which in 1897 were replaced by four centrifugal pumps. The pumping station was extended in 1907, and the following year all but one of the twenty-four windmills on the polder were demolished. It was re-equipped from 1924 with a steam engine and two Lancashire boilers made in Breda and a centrifugal pump made in Utrecht. Exhibits moved in from elsewhere include three marine engines, boilers, pumps and generators. The Lely pumping station of 1929 has pumps driven by 3000 hp electric motors, and the Jaagin station has an American wind pump built in Groningen in 1927. The preserved railway from Medemblik to Hoorn, 12 km ($7\frac{1}{2}$ mi.) S., is operated with a mixture of branch line and tramway rolling stock, including nine steam locomotives ranging in date from 1897 to 1943, and five diesels, the earliest a Schwartzkopf of 1931. The Oudendijk pumping station of 1877, 7 km (4 mi.) SW of Hoorn, retains an oil engine.

Den Helder was established as a naval port in 1811 during the French occupation, and became the terminus of the 80 km (50 mi.) Great North Holland Canal (Noordhollands Kanaal) from AMSTERDAM in 1824. Fears of piercing the dunes led to the decision to run the canal northwards behind the dunes. There was a short boom in the 1870s, after which the opening of the North Sea Canal (see YMUIDEN) led shipping companies to leave the port.

The celebrated cheese trade of Alkmaar is portrayed in a museum, where traditional methods are shown alongside modern production techniques. South-east of the city is the Overdie pumping station with a Werkspoor diesel engine of 1913, which worked until 1988. At Akersloot, 8 km (5 mi.) S., the electric motors of 1918 at the Limmen pumping station of 1879 remain in use.

See also CRUQUIUS.

BIBLIOGRAPHY
General
Balk, 1985; DIEN database; Thijsse, 1972.
Specific
Van der Gragt, F. *Stoomtram Hoorn–Medemblik: gids en rollend materiaal* (The Hoorn–Medemblik steam railway: a guide to the rolling stock). Hoorn: Stoomtram Hoorn–Medemblik, 1979.

LOCATIONS
[M] Hollands Kaasmuseum (Dutch Cheese Museum), Waagplein 2, Alkmaar.
[M] Nederlands Stoommachinemuseum (Dutch Steam Engine Museum), Oosterdijk 4, Medemblik.
[S] Stoomtram Hoorn–Medemblik (Hoorn–Medemblik Steam Tram), PO Box 137, Tramstation, Van Dedemstraat 8, Hoorn.
[M] Zuiderzeemuseum, Wierdijk 18, Enkhuizen.

JURRIE VAN DALEN

Noormarkku, Turun ja Porin lääni, Finland   A municipality whose industrial traditions began with sawmilling in the 1740s. In 1806 a bar-iron forge was established on the banks of the river. The forge ceased production in 1920, although the sawmill functioned until 1956. Today the main office of the wood-processing company, A. Ahlström Ltd, is situated in Noormarkku, its JUGENDSTIL head office, completed in 1916 to the design of Emil Fabritius, standing in a large park.

Some representative buildings belonging to the owners of the works have survived from three different periods: the oldest, the wooden Isotalo by E. Lagerspetz, dates from 1881; the Jugendstil Havulinna by G. A. Lindberg is of 1901; the most distinguished is the Villa Mairea, designed by Alvar Aalto (1888–1976) in 1939.

The best-preserved of the old mill buildings is the water-powered sawmill which dates from the 1870s and was designed by the state agronomist, Henry Gibson. On the site of the sawmill's water wheel is a flourmill of the early twentieth century. Much of the rest of the mill, together with its equipment, has survived. The water-powered hammer of the bar-iron forge remains within a building of 1894. The brick-built, stuccoed power station dates from 1914. The oldest workers' accommodation on the site dates from the 1870s.

LAURI PUTKONEN

Norrköping, Ostergötland, Sweden   A port and city of 120 000 inhabitants, which lies where the River Motala emerges into the inlet called Bråviken. From the 1840s it was for more than a century Sweden's principal textile-manufacturing city, but most of the mills which lined the river closed in the 1960s and 70s. An inventory was prepared of the mills, prior to their being demolished or adapted for new uses.

The growth of the textile industry is portrayed in the city museum, while the dyeworks museum illustrates mid-nineteenth-century technology, concerned not just with dyeing but with fulling and the cultivation of flax. A museum of work has been established with the support of local trades unions in a former textile mill of 1917, and is operating through History of Work Councils to assist workers to investigate their own history.

Finspång, 30 km (20 mi.) W., is an ironworking centre, established by the Walloon Wellam de Wijk in the late sixteenth century. The water-powered ironworks came to specialize in the production of armaments, and was energetically developed by the Walloon Louis de Geer (d.1652) and his son, also Louis de Geer (1622–95). ART CASTINGS became significant products from the 1820s when the German ironfounder C. F. J. W. Mertens (d.1882) was employed there. In the twentieth century the works has been concerned chiefly with electrical engineering. Surviving monuments include the chateau constructed by de Geer in 1668, and ranges of workers' housing from the second half of the eighteenth century, each block bearing the date of construction in wrought-iron letters. A small eighteenth-century building houses a works museum, which includes cannon and art castings.

In the Kolmården forest, 35 km (22 mi.) NE, is the Reijmyre Glassworks which was founded in 1810. Some original buildings remain, and the modern works is open to the public.

BIBLIOGRAPHY
Specific
Meddelanden från Ostergötlands och Linköpings Stads Museum (Transactions of Ostergötlands and Linköpings City Museum). Linköping, 1969.
Nisser, M. *Industriminnen i Ostergötland* (Industrial monuments in Ostergötland). Ostergötland, 1969.

LOCATIONS
[M] Arbetets museet (Museum of Work), Laxholmen, S-602 21 Norrköping.
[M] Färgargården (Dyeworks Museum), Västgötegatan, 21, Norrköping.
[M] Norrköpings Stadsmuseet (Norrköping City Museum), Kristinaplatsen, Norrköping.

BARRIE TRINDER

Norrland, Sweden The Swedish provinces north of the 61st parallel – Jämtland, Västernorrland, Västerbotten and Norrbotten – are known collectively as Norrland. They comprise some two-thirds of the land area of Sweden, but sustain only a tiny proportion of the population. The population was even more sparse until the mid-nineteenth century when exploitation of the region's timber resources began, stimulating the growth of the ports on the Baltic. Monuments from eighteenth-century ironworks in Västerbotten are preserved at Olofsfors and Robertsfors. Towards the end of the nineteenth century the extensive iron-ore deposits in the Kiruna region were discovered, and exploitation on a large scale by the Luossavaara-Kirunavaara Aktiebolag (LKAB) company began following the completion in 1902 of the 489 km (302 mi.) railway from Luleå to NARVIK in Norway. In Kiruna LKAB constructed a notable estate of workers' houses from 1901. Since 1924 Boliden 24 km (15 mi.) W. of Skelleftea has been the chief source of non-ferrous ores in the region, particularly of ARSENIC.

Large-scale hydro-electric power generation began in the region with the construction of the power station at PORJUS which opened in 1914. Part of the Klabböle station at Umeå, which opened in 1899, is also preserved.

There are OPEN-AIR MUSEUMS at many of the principal towns in Norrland, examples being the regional museum at Härnösand, the Hantverks museum at Sundsvall, and the museum at Gammelstad. The development of industrial society is a particular theme of the town museum at Sundsvall, and the role of forest industry in the region is displayed in a museum at Lycksele.

BIBLIOGRAPHY
General
Nisser, 1979.

LOCATIONS
[M] Friluftsmuseet Gammelstad kyrkby (Open-air Museum of Gammelstad), S-954 00 Gammelstad.
[M] Hantverksmuseet, Norra Stadsberget, S-852 50 Sundsvall.
[M] Klabböle kraftsverksmuseet (Klabböle Power Station Museum), Umeå Energiverk, Box 224, S-901 04 Umeå.
[M] Länsmuseet-Murberget (Murberget Regional Museum), Box 2007, S-871 02 Härnösand.
[M] Olofsfors bruksmuseum, S-914 00 Nordmaling.
[M] Robertsfors bruksmuseum, Herrgårdsvägen, S-915 00 Robertsfors.
[M] Skogsmuseet (Forestry Museum), S-921 00 Lycksele.
[M] Sundsvalls Museum, Storgatan 29, S-852 30 Sundsvall.

BARRIE TRINDER

Norse mill The horizontal or SPLASH MILL, the name deriving from its supposed Viking origin. There are examples in many Scandinavian open-air museums.

North Carolina, United States of America Granite, tobacco, furniture and peanuts are four of the more traditional products of this southern state. While the North Carolina of the 1980s was the nation's largest producer of bricks, textiles and tobacco products, the state's industrial diversity is further embellished with the mining of coal, gold, iron ore and mica, and the production of rosins, turpentine and tar – a substance that may explain the state's nickname, the 'Tar Heel State'.

The earliest surviving navigable canal in the USA passes from South Mills, North Carolina, north into Virginia. The seven-lock, hand-dug Dismal Swamp Canal opened in 1805 after twelve years of construction. It remains as a scenic waterway along the Atlantic seaboard. Another canal, the Roanoke, was completed in 1823, but its dewatered native stone locks and a fine aqueduct over Chockoyotte Creek are all that remain of a key artery of commerce and water power in the state's industrial north-east.

Several of the more historic and more successful furniture factories remain active in their original brick buildings among the hardwood forests around Mount Airy in central North Carolina; this is also the state's granite-quarrying district, where much of the nation's granite curbing originates.

A great variety of substantial nineteenth-century cotton mills stand in various states of decay, reuse or continued textile service. In Durham and Winston-Salem, heavily corbelled brick tobacco warehouses have found new lives as downtown business and retail complexes, typical of the tobacco industry generally as it seeks to diversify away from cigarette production.

The first gold rush in the nation occurred in central North Carolina when nuggets were found in Cabarrus County in 1799. A museum and standing remains of dressing and stamping machinery testify to subsequent events, with special attention to the Reed Gold Mine, a principal source of gold for the nation prior to the Civil War.

North of the gold region, the state's early iron industry is acknowledged by the remains of several stone furnaces and their ancillary machinery. They are periodically shrouded by the ever-encroaching Southern vine, kudzu, with its alarming capacity to carpet entire structures and forest groves in a single growing season.

North Carolina's rocky Atlantic shore has sprouted a cluster of monumental lighthouses, from early tapered brick octagons to the tallest lighthouse in the USA, the conical 63 m (208 ft.) Cape Hatteras light, built in 1870.

An effective lighthouse-preservation campaign in the state has worked with the US Coast Guard and local authorities to ensure the continued well-being of the structures after their unmanning or darkening. In Raleigh, the state capital, stands another tower, the city water tower of 1887, its 0.92 m (3 ft.) thick octagonal brick walls now enclosing the state offices of the American Institute of Architects.

BIBLIOGRAPHY
General
Glass, 1975.

LOCATIONS
[M,S] Reed Gold Mines State Historic Site, Reed Mine Road, Stanfield, NC 28163.
[S] Wright Brothers National Memorial, Kill Devil Hills, NC 27948.

DAVID H. SHAYT

North Dakota, United States of America   Among fifty states, North Dakota is the most heavily agricultural, with some 90 per cent of its industry traditionally related one way or another to the growing and processing of wheat, barley, oats, flax, sugar beet and hay. The state also has a long but comparatively tiny history of lignite mining and oil production. In a state where the domesticated animal population far outnumbers the human inhabitants, the preservation of historic industrial sites is not a high item on the agenda. Accordingly the one trade that is accorded a measure of historical husbandry is the American fur trade, its role in early North Dakota well documented and preserved with collections of traps and stuffed animals at the Fort Union Trading Post, Williston, a National Park Service site.

LOCATION
[M,S] Fort Union Trading Post National Historic Site, Buford Road, Williston, ND 58801.

Northern Ireland   *See* IRELAND.

Northern Territory, Australia   Six times the size of Britain, with a population of only 134000 and harsh living conditions, the northern part of Australia became a Commonwealth territory in 1911 and attained self-government in 1978. It suffers from extremes of temperature, but while commercial crops are not viable, beef cattle are important. Gold, bauxite, manganese ore, copper, silver, iron ore and uranium are mined today. First settled in the 1820s, many early settlements – like Port Essington, inhabited only between 1838 and 1849 – were soon abandoned and are now important archaeological sites. The North Australian Railway from Palmerstone to Pine Creek was opened in 1887.

The impetus for the opening up of the state was the construction from 1870 of the overland telegraph, which was linked to a submarine cable from Java. Several repeater stations were built along the route and that at Alice Springs has been preserved. During World War II the territory was of great strategic importance. The Stuart Highway was built between Alice Springs and Darwin, and several decoy towns were constructed to confuse bomber crews.

BIBLIOGRAPHY
General
Heritage of Australia, 1981.

LOCATION
[I]   Museums and Art Galleries of the Northern Territory, PO Box 4646, Darwin, Northern Territory 5794.

KATE CLARK

north-lit shed   A single-storey building, often of considerable width as well as length, often with windowless walls, and with columns of cast iron, steel or concrete, carrying a steel-framed roof of saw-tooth pattern, aligned so that the fenestration incorporated within it faces north (in the northern hemisphere) to avoid glare from sunlight within the workplace. This building type appears to have originated in English textile factories before 1850, an early example being a structure of 1848 at Swan Meadow Mill, WIGAN. In the second half of the nineteenth century north-lit sheds came to be associated particularly with weaving complexes, especially those of north-east Lancashire, like the preserved Queen Street Mill, Burnley; but they were common components of textile complexes of all sorts and in all places, and in the twentieth century have been employed for many kinds of light manufactures. In early examples power was distributed by LINE SHAFTING.
See figure 98.

North Nation Mills, Quebec, Canada   The site of North Nation Mills, 5 km (3 mi.) N. of Plaisance, is one of the most important monuments of the paper industry which developed in the Outaouais valley in the nineteenth century. Taking advantage of the water power provided by the Petite Nation river, the first sawmill was built in 1817 by Joseph Papineau (1752–1841) and carried on from 1820 until 1882 by various entrepreneurs.

North Nation Mills is equally celebrated as an industrial community which evolved between 1882 and 1903 under the direction of the W. C. Edwards company. Documents and pictorial records, together with what remains on the ground, show the existence of a variety of buildings. In addition to the sawmill they included a smithy, a butter factory, and a cheese-making concern, as well as houses for workers and managers, a general store also used as a post and telegraph office, a school and a church. After 1903 the closure and dismantling of the sawmill led to the progressive abandonment of the village. Most of the buildings were eventually destroyed by the Gatineau Power Co. which acquired the Edwards property in 1920. Some were rescued and rebuilt by residents in Plaisance along the road between Hull and Montreal.

Since the beginning of the 1980s archaeologists and ethnographers have investigated the site of North Nation Mills and an interpretative programme has been established jointly by the Quebec government and the municipality of Plaisance.

Figure 98   An early range of north-lit sheds forms part of the flax mills of Wilkinson & Co. on the banks of the River Aire at Hunslet, Leeds, *c*.1861: the complex comprises a mixture of buildings of different styles and dates characteristic of most textile mills. Also of note is the seven-storey block on the right, with its turret containing staircases and lavatories. (From G. Meason, *The Official Illustrated Guide to the Great Northern Railway*, London: Griffin, 1861.)

Elton Collection: Ironbridge Gorge Museum

BIBLIOGRAPHY
General
Whitlock and Leclerc, 1984.

LOUISE TROTTIER

North Rhine-Westphalia (Nordrhein-Westfalen), Germany   The state of North Rhine-Westphalia was created in the west of the German Federal Republic in 1946–7. Its national frontiers border on the Netherlands and Belgium. From north to south it adjoins the federal states of Lower Saxony, Hesse and RHINELAND-PALATINATE. Its territory comprises the former Prussian provinces of Westphalia and North Rhineland and the 'land' of Lippe. In 1975 it was economically the strongest and most densely populated of the federal states, with 17.2 million inhabitants living in an area of 34 000 km² (13 000 sq. mi.). It has a maritime climate with cool summers and mild winters. Two-thirds of the state is level land, between 25 m and 100 m (80 ft. and 300 ft.) above sea level, and one-third is mountainous or hilly. The RHINE, its main waterway, cuts through the low mountain ranges of the EIFEL and the Rheinisches Schiefergebirge from south to north. There are other rivers – the Ruhr, the Weser and the Ems – but more important from the point of view of navigation is the network of canals built in the nineteenth century: the Dortmund–Ems Canal, the Ruhr Canal, the Rhine–Herne Canal and the Wesel–Datteln–Hamm Canal.

Although the coal and steel industries shaped the age of industrialization, even before 1850 there were major industries within the boundaries of the present state, producing for export markets. They included the cutlery industry of Solingen, the making of woollens in and around AACHEN, the linen manufactures of the Lower Rhine, and silk-working at Krefeld. Important urban centres include the coal and steel towns of the RUHRGEBIET including Duisburg, Essen, Bochum and Dortmund; the city of Cologne, a major commercial centre since the Middle Ages; the city of DÜSSELDORF, which has been the headquarters of industrial administration since 1900; and Bonn, seat of the federal state's government since 1949. In all, nineteen cities each with more than 100 000 inhabitants account for more than half the population.

North Rhine-Westphalia is well provided with transport facilities. In 1838 the second German railway was built from Düsseldorf to Erkrath, 8 km (5 mi.) E. Intense economic activity led to the development of dense railway, canal and road networks. Düsseldorf has had an airport since 1926, which today is second only to Frankfurt among German airports for the handling of scheduled passenger traffic, and holds first place for charter flights and air freight. In the 1990s it is to be linked by magnetically-operated express railway to the other international airport, Cologne-Bonn, 50 km (30 mi.) SE.

See also BERGISCHES LAND; COLOGNE; WUPPERTAL.

BIBLIOGRAPHY
General
Claas, 1939; Föhl, 1976; Günter, 1970; Klapheck, 1928; Landesvermessungsamt Nordrhein-Westfalen, 1968; Rhei-
nischer Verein für Denkmalpflege und Heimatschutz, 1910; Wildemann, 1928–9.
Specific
Lehmann, M. *Industriearchitektur in Westfalen: Zeugen der Technikgeschichte – Ausstellungskatalog* (Industrial architecture in Westphalia: evidence of the history of technology – exhibition catalogue). Münster, 1975.
Metternich, W. G. Die Pflege technischer Kulturdenkmale (The protection of technical monuments). In *Jahrbuch der Rheinischen Denkmalpflege* (Yearbook of Rhenish monuments protection), VIII. Düsseldorf, 1936.
Schumacher, M. Zweckbau und Industrieschloss: Fabrikbauten der Rheinisch-Westfälischen Textilindustrie vor der Gründungzeit (Functional buildings and industrial castles: factory buildings of pre-industrial textile manufactures in the Rhineland and Westphalia). In *Tradition: Zeitschrift für Firmengeschichte und Unternehmerbiographie* (Tradition: papers in business history and biography), XV. Stuttgart, 1970.
Spiegelhauer, D. Fabrikbau: Nutzbau-Zweckbau-Industriearchitektur (Factory buildings: functional and industrial architecture). In Trier and Weyres, 1980.
Technische Denkmäler (Technical monuments). Borken: Kreisverwaltung Borken, 1983.
Technische Denkmäler im Märkischen Kreis – Karte mit Information (Technical monuments in the Mark district, map with information), Märkischer Kreis, n.d.
Wildemann, T. Die Erhaltung technischer Kulturdenkmäler unter besonderer Berücksichtigung der Verhältnisse in den Rheinlanden (The conservation of technical monuments, taking into consideration in particular the conditions in the Rhineland). In *Zeitschrift für Denkmalpflege*, III. Düsseldorf, 1928–9.
Wildemann, T. *Technische Kulturdenkmäler in den Rheinlanden und ihre Erhaltung* (Technical monuments in the Rhineland and their preservation). Düsseldorf: Rheinischer Verein für Denkmalpflege, 1931.

LOCATIONS
[M] Deutsches Textilmuseum (German textile museum), Andreasmarkt 8, 4150 Krefeld.
[I] Rheinisches Amt für Denkmalpflege (Rhineland Monuments Protection Department), Abtei Brauweiler, Ehrenfriedstrasse 19, Postfach 2140, 5024 Pulheim 2.
[I] Westfälisches Amt für Denkmalpflege (Westphalian Monuments Protection Department), Erbdrostenhof, Salzstrasse 38, 4400 Münster/Westfalen.

AXEL FÖHL

North-West Germany, Germany   The federal states of Schleswig-Holstein and Hamburg, Lower Saxony (Niedersachsen) and Bremen now make up the north-western part of the German Federal Republic from the natural as well as the historical viewpoint. Schleswig was entirely a part of Denmark until 1864, while Holstein and Lauenburg were represented by Denmark in the German Federation. From 1866 until 1946–7 Schleswig-Holstein was a province of Prussia. In 1937 Lübeck and the Oldenburg district around Eutin were incorporated, while the industrial cities of Altona and Wandsbek and their suburbs became part of Hamburg. In the south the Hanoverian industrial towns of Harburg and Wilhelmsburg became part of Hamburg in exchange for Cuxhaven, which had hitherto belonged to the city, and similarly in 1939 the Hanoverian towns of Hemelingen, Grohn and

Blumenthal became part of Bremen. In 1947 Bremen was further extended in the area of what is now Bremerhaven to include the former Prussian industrial towns of Lehe, Geestemünde and Wulsdorf at the mouth of the Weser. Lower Saxony was created in 1946 from the states of Hanover (which had been a province of Prussia from 1866), Brunswick, Oldenburg and Schaumburg-Lippe.

Geologically, the east of Schleswig-Holstein belongs to an area of recent moraine deposits, its North Sea coast, like that of Lower Saxony, comprises a marshy landscape, adjoining older moraine areas to the east in Schleswig-Holstein and to the south in Lower Saxony. These areas are known as the Geest, a countryside of swamps and lines of dunes. In the south of Lower Saxony, roughly along the line of the Mittelland Canal between Osnabrück and Helmstedt, lies the extremely fertile region of Boerde, which merges into the Harz Mountains and other uplands along the southern fringe of the region.

Large areas of Schleswig-Holstein and Lower Saxony are involved in agriculture and its related, usually small-scale, industries. In both states industry is concentrated in urban centres, and does not extended into larger industrial regions except in the south-east of Lower Saxony, between Hanover, Brunswick and Salzgitter. Development of industry in north-west Germany has tended to arise from mining, shipping and agriculture. Mining in particular, and also the manufacture of linen and woollen textiles, had acquired importance beyond the immediate locality before 1800. The development of industrial companies, and with it the decline of the traditional linen-weaving and ironworking industries of the Harz and the mountains along the River Weser, was affected by the construction of railways, by the entry of individual states into the Zollverein (see GERMANY), by the establishment of the German Empire, and by the Third Reich's ambitious projects directed towards economic self-sufficiency. By the late 1840s the south of Lower Saxony, Bremen, Hamburg and Schleswig-Holstein were connected to southern Germany by railways running through Magdeburg or Berlin, but membership of the Zollverein tended to come later: Hanover and Oldenburg entered the organization in 1854, Schleswig-Holstein and Lübeck in 1867, Bremen and Hamburg not until 1888. The customs frontier around the Hanseatic towns encouraged the rise of industrial communities in neighbouring Holstein, Oldenburg and Hanover.

As early as the eighteenth century there was market-orientated agriculture, with distinctive subsidiary industries like flax and wool manufactures, lime-burning and brickmaking, around Hamburg, in the Artland area near Osnabrück, and on the Boerde. During the nineteenth century the range of such industries grew. The distilling of grain spirit expanded, and the manufacture of sugar from beet began in Brunswick in the mid-1840s, and in Hanover from the mid-1850s, expanding into a major industrial sector in the former state and providing a stimulus to mechanical engineering – as did lignite and potash mining after the 1870s. Even in the nineteenth century the majority of steam engines in Lower Saxony were being used in distilleries and sugar factories. Most of the large inland corn mills built after the 1850s, like the mining installations of the Harz mountains, depended on water power. The particular agricultural and horticultural traditions of Brunswick enabled the state to become a centre of the canning industry after the 1870s.

The maritime traffic of the region led to the development of an extensive and varied shipbuilding industry, with such attendant supply trades as sawmills and ropeworks, as well as foundries and engineering works when the building of iron ships commenced in the 1870s. At the same time (during the second half of the nineteenth century) a variety of industries developed around the processing of imported raw materials. They included wool and jute spinning mills in Neumünster, Blumenthal and Delmenhorst; cotton mills in Nordhorn and Schuettorf; tobacco factories in Hamburg and Bremen; rubber factories in Harburg and Hanover; bottle-glass works in Oldenburg, Uttersen, Geesthacht, Obernkirchen and Rinteln; cork and later linoleum manufacture in Delmenhorst; copper smelting in Wilhelmsburg; wholesale milling in Bremen; and coffee roasting in Hamburg and Bremen. In the early twentieth century blast furnaces were built in Lübeck and Bremen. Transport between the ports and the interior was initially by river, but from the late fourteenth century the rivers were supplemented by artificial waterways like the Stecknitz canal. By 1850 the major roads to the seaports were paved, although the railway was to remain the most important means of transport until the 1960s. After the 1850s Hanover became an important railway junction, and then, from the 1920s, a centre of canal shipping on the Mittelland Canal.

Mining in the region goes back to the Middle Ages, particularly in the HARZ MOUNTAINS. The ores mined were principally silver and lead, but copper and iron ores were also extracted, and there was an increase in the mining of zinc blende (sphalerite) from the late nineteenth century. By 1800 iron ore was being mined near Osnabrück, and in the Vorharz area and on the Boerde. Large coke-fired blast-furnace complexes were built to smelt the iron ore. They included the Georgsmarienhütte and Ilsede works of the late 1850s, the steel rolling mills in Osnabrück, those in Peine from the 1870s, and the Salzgitter-Watenstedt works of the 1930s. The coal mined near Osnabrück, that extracted to the south-west of Hanover, and that from Schaumburg between c.1500 and 1960, was of scarcely any value to the iron and steel industry, although there was an early coking plant in Schaumburg, at Nienstedt near Stadthagen, from 1810. Nevertheless local supplies of coal were the basis of glass manufacture, using ENGLISH GLASS CONES, in Obernkirchen and Bredenbeck-Steinkrug. LÜNEBURG was a saltworking centre of more than local importance. Potash was mined in Brunswick from the 1870s and in Hanover from the 1890s, in the districts of Hanover, Hildesheim and Celle. Schleswig-Holstein had almost no history of mining, except for limestone quarrying and drilling for oil which began in the southern Dithmarschen area in the 1880s. German oil production began in Lower Saxony near Peine (Ölheim) and Celle (Wietze) in the mid-1850s.

See also ALFELD; BRUNSWICK; BREMEN; BREMERHAVEN;

CLOPPENBURG; FEHMARN; GÖTTINGEN; HAMBURG; HARZ MOUNTAINS; HANOVER; KIEL; MELDORF; NENNDORF; SALZGITTER; STADTHAGEN; WILHELMSHAVEN; WOLFSBURG; WRISBERGHOLZEN.

BIBLIOGRAPHY
General
Mende and Hamm, 1990; Slotta, 1975–88.

LOCATIONS
[I] Amt für Denkmalpflege der Hansestadt Lübeck (Department for Monuments Protection in the Hanseatic City of Lübeck), Schloss Rantzau, Parade 1, 2400 Lübeck 1.
[I] Denkmalschutzamt der Freien und Hansestadt Hamburg (Monuments Preservation Department of the Free Hanseatic City of Hamburg), Hamburger Strasse 45, 2000 Hamburg 76.
[I] Landesamt für Denkmalpflege Bremen (Bremen Monuments Protection Department), Sandstrasse 3, 2800 Bremen.
[I] Landesamt für Denkmalpflege Schleswig-Holstein (Schleswig-Holstein Monuments Protection Department), Schloss, 2300 Kiel 1.
[I] Niedersächsisches Landesverwaltungsamt-Institut für Denkmalpflege (Lower Saxony Provincial Institute For Monuments Protection), Scharnhorststrasse 1, 3000 Hanover.

MICHAEL MENDE

Northwich, Cheshire, England   An ancient salt-working town, dominated by the Solvay and soda-crystal plants of ICI. A museum in a former workhouse displays much salt-working equipment. Lion Saltworks is the last open-pan works; all buildings remain. The River Weaver was linked with the Trent & Mersey Canal, 2 km (1 mi.) to the northeast, by the Anderton Lift of 1872–5, which was hydraulically operated until 1903–8, when an electric drive was installed.

BIBLIOGRAPHY
General
Ashmore, 1982.

LOCATION
[M] The Salt Museum, 162 London Road, Northwich, Cheshire CW9 8AB.

Norway   Norway has been shaped by glaciation, only a small portion of its land surface – along the rivers, fjords and lakes – being capable of cultivation. Nevertheless some of its principal centres of mining and manufacturing illustrate the history of industrialization with particular clarity.

The Norwegians emerged as a distinct people during the Viking period, and from the late fifteenth century were united with Denmark. From 1814 until 1905 Norway formed a union with Sweden but had a separate currency. BEAR ISLAND and SPITZBERGEN are Norwegian possessions.

The population of Norway in 1664 was only 450 000, but it had risen to 883 000 by 1801, had exceeded a million by 1850, and was more than two million by 1900. Migration, particularly to the USA, was at a high level in the nineteenth century. From 1870 a boom in exports brought rising living standards; and traditionally high educational attainments, resulting from the early development of compulsory schooling, ensured that Norway was well placed to benefit from the opportunities presented by hydro-electric power.

Timber was Norway's chief source of wealth in the eighteenth century. By 1840 there were 712 chartered sawmills, permitted to engage in the export trade, with many others serving local needs. Log-floating systems were developed on such rivers as the Glomma and the Drammens-elva, canals were built to carry timber (*see* EIDSKOG; HALDEN; SETESDAL), and several major engineering structures carried logs over valleys and across watersheds (*see* RINGERIKE; SETESDAL). Wood pulp was first made mechanically in Norway in 1863, and subsequently chemical plants using both sulphate and sulphite processes were established. By 1900 pulp exports were twice the value of timber exports. In the twentieth century production has been concentrated in larger sawmills and paper plants. A mechanical pulp mill is preserved near HØNEFOSS and a sulphate plant at KLEVFOS. The Stekka mill (*see* HARDANGER) is a typical local sawmill, while that at HØBOL represents the final development of the water-powered sawmill. The whole range of forest industries is illustrated in the National Museum of Forestry at ELVERUM.

Fishing was the other means by which Norway traditionally earned foreign exchange. During the nineteenth century there was a substantial growth of exports of barrelled herring, dried and salted cod, roes, cod-liver oil, and, at the end of the century, of canned brisling and sardines. The industry extended along the whole west coast, and in the north many steamer quays, oil boiling plants and deserted settlements remain to be recorded. The fishing industry is portrayed in museums at STAVANGER, BERGEN and elsewhere, and Nusfjord (*see* LOFOTEN ISLANDS) is preserved as a traditional fishing settlement.

Two mining concerns of European significance developed in Norway in the early seventeenth century. The silver mines at KONGSBERG and the copper mines at RØROS are subject to conservation schemes, and several smelters of non-ferrous metals have been protected by listing. Cobalt compounds were mined at MODUM.

The predominant building tradition in Norway involved the use of timber, but in the Fredriksstad region brickmaking was important from the seventeenth century, and a brickworks is among the nineteenth-century industrial buildings surviving in TRONDHEIM. Several limekilns have been preserved, including two at BÆRUM and one at Cape Lindesnes, the most southerly point of Norway.

The first blast furnace in Norway was blown in at Bærum in 1622, but the iron industry remained modest in scale. It lost protection against Swedish imports in 1825 and subsequently declined, although in the late nineteenth century iron-ore mining expanded, and the port of NARVIK, a British enterprise, was developed for the export of Swedish ores. Remains survive of eight seventeenth- and eighteenth-century furnaces (*see* EIDSVOLL; NES JERNVERK; TELEMARK CANAL).

The foundry products of the eighteenth century were largely armaments and stoves. By the early nineteenth century bridge castings were being produced (*see* BÆRUM;

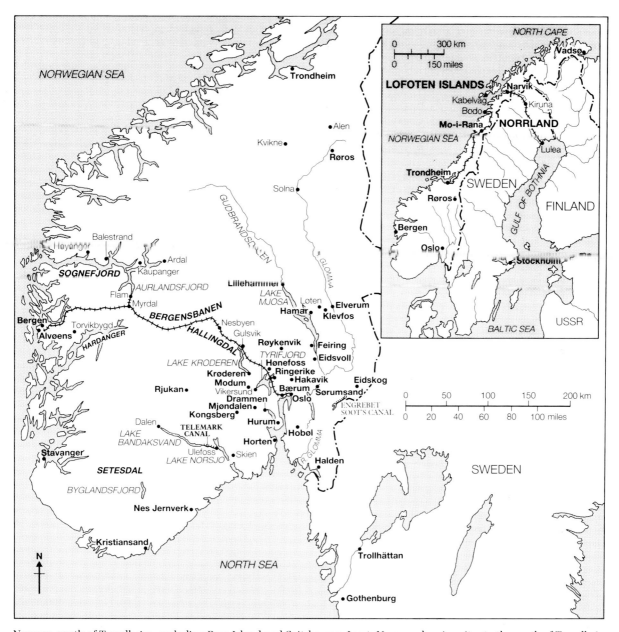

Norway, south of Trondheim, excluding Bear Island and Spitzbergen. Inset: Norway showing sites to the north of Trondheim

NES JERNWERK), and from the 1840s engineering works were established in Bergen, Drammen, Oslo and other towns.

Cotton spinning was introduced at HALDEN in the 1830s and in the Åker valley on the eastern side of Oslo in the 1840s. The latter is an area of prime importance for studying the whole process of urbanization and the impact of industry upon the landscape.

In the twentieth century industry has been transformed by hydro-electric power. It is possible to visit most power stations in the country. The low cost of power stimulated the growth of metallurgical and chemical plants. The Norsk Hydro company was formed in 1905 to manufacture calcium nitrate $(Ca(NO_3)_2)$ or Norge saltpetre, using the arc process devised by Samuel Eyde and Kristian Birkeland to make nitric oxide. In 1906–7 the British Aluminium Company built a smelter at Tyssedal.

Transport developments in the nineteenth century helped to unify Norway by linking cities that had previously been isolated. The steamships *Constitution* and *Prins Carl* were imported from England in 1827 to work between Oslo and Bergen. Regular services developed which made possible the growth of fishing settlements right up the west coast. A paddle steamer of 1856 still plies on Lake Mjøsa (*see* EIDSVOLL). Road transport remained the norm throughout the nineteenth century, and construction continued on an ambitious scale. Roads were toll-free, and the proprietors of posting 'stations' (Skydsstation) along the main routes were obliged to provide horses and vehicles at set rates. Norway's first railway, the Norsk Hoved Jernbane (the Norwegian Trunk Railway), was built to standard gauge by ROBERT STEPHENSON and opened from Oslo to Eidsvoll in 1854. Some railways were built to the 1067 mm (3 ft. 6 in.) gauge devised by Carl Abraham Pihl (1825–97) for use in difficult terrain, which was adopted, as the 'CAP system', in India, Russia and the Americas. In 1883 the Norwegian railway system amounted to only 1552 route km (946 mi.), but by 1954 there were 3968 route km (2419 mi.). Bergen and Trondheim were not linked with Oslo by standard-gauge routes until the twentieth century. Norway's railway museum is at HAMAR, and there are preserved lines at KRØDEREN, SETESDAL and SØRUMSAND.

The first legislation in Norway affording protection to historical monuments came into effect in 1905. The Building Heritage Act 1920 provided for the protection of listed buildings and enabled several industrial monuments to be preserved. The Ancient Monuments Act 1951 afforded further protection. The Cultural Heritage Act, which came into effect in 1979, supersedes previous legislation: it enables protection to be given to the complete environment of an historic structure and to certain of its internal fittings. The State Council for the Cultural Heritage is charged with advising the government on measures covered by the legislation. The administration of the law is the responsibility of the Central Office of National Antiquities (Riksantikvaren). In each of the eighteen Norwegian counties a curator is responsible for the application of the law, as well as for the museums administered by the authorities. The most comprehensive listing of buildings and sites of significance in the industrial history of Norway is that prepared for the Cultural Council (Norsk Kulturråds utvalg for Teknisk og Industrielt Kulturvern). The Norwegian Technical Museum (*see* OSLO) has been listing sites since 1943 and has recorded monuments like the aluminium smelter in Tyssedal which are now demolished. Many manufactures of the pre-industrial period are illustrated in the open-air museums established since the late nineteenth century (*see* OSLO; LILLEHAMMER). The National Grain Board has been responsible for the preservation of some fifty early corn mills. Many projects that now enjoy support from the state or county administrations were initiated by local voluntary organizations.

Regular censuses of population detailing occupations have been taken since 1801. The Norges Geografisk Oppmaling, founded in 1773, publishes a series of 1 : 50 000 maps which covers the whole country.

See also ALVØENS; BÆRUM; BERGEN; BERGENSBANEN; DRAMMEN; EIDSKOG; EIDSVOLL; ELVERUM; FEIRING; HAKAVIK; HALDEN; HALLINGDAL; HØBOL; HØNEFOSS; HORTEN; HURUM; KLEVFOS; KONGSBERG; KRISTIANSAND; KRØDEREN; LILLEHAMMER; LOFOTEN ISLANDS; MJØNDALEN; MODUM; MO I RANA; NARVIK; NES JERNWERK; OSLO; RINGERIKE; RJUKAN;

RØROS; RØYKENVIK; SETESDAL; SOGNEFJORD; SØRUMSAND; STAVANGER; TELEMARK CANAL; TRONDHEIM; VADSØ.

BIBLIOGRAPHY
General
Berg, 1968; Holt, 1974; Milward and Saul, 1973; Saetren, 1907; Wasbert and Svendsen, 1969.
Specific
Cultural Heritage Act, 1979. Oslo, Norway. Ministry of Environment.
Jorberg, L. The Industrial Revolution in Scandinavia, 1850–1914. In Cipolla, 1970.

LOCATION
[I] Riksantikvaren, Akershus Festning, Bygn. 18, Oslo MIL, Oslo 1.

BARRIE TRINDER

Norwich, Norfolk, England   The regional capital and a port on the River Yare; the third city in England in 1700. Worsted manufacture was important till the early nineteenth century. A six-storey mill of Norwich Yarn Co., from 1829, now Jarrolds' printing warehouse, was the last attempt to revive the trade. The Carrow mustard works of J. J. Colman, originated in 1854, has many multistorey red and white brick mills of the late nineteenth century, with a 1913 mill in reinforced concrete on the HENNEBIQUE principle. Norwich is now principally a service centre, exemplified by C. J. Skipper's Royal Arcade, with ART NOUVEAU tulip and heart motifs in glass, and the same architect's BAROQUE Norwich Union Insurance building. Thorpe Station, the imposing terminus by John Wilson, dates from 1886. The Coslany iron bridge of 1804 is by James Frost. Bridewell Museum features local industries.

BIBLIOGRAPHY
General
Alderton and Booker, 1980.

LOCATIONS
[M] Bridewell Museum, Bridewell Alley, Norwich NR2 1AQ.
[M] Colman's Mustard Museum, 3 Bridewell Alley, Norwich.

Nottingham, Nottinghamshire, England   The county town, and the market centre for much of the East Midlands, particularly for the coalfield to the north and east. Lace Market, the commercial area in the centre, is dominated by buildings in a heavily ornate style by T. C. Hine. Nottingham's growth was constrained by the survival of open fields, and in the early nineteenth century it was one of the most overcrowded of English cities. Its typical working-class houses before the mid-nineteenth century were BACK-TO-BACKS, but none survives.

The stocking frame was invented in 1589 by the Rev. William Lee at Calverton, 9 km (6 mi.) NE, where stockingers' cottages in Windles Square are preserved. Other domestic worshops survive at RUDDINGTON; Hucknall, 10 km (6 mi.) N.; Stapleford, 8 km (5 mi.) SW; and Bramcote, 7 km (4 mi.) W. Large mills for hosiery and lace manufacture survive at Draycot 15 km (9 mi.) W.; Sandiacre, 10 km (6 mi.) W.; Beeston, 5 km (3 mi.) SW;

and Long Eaton, 10 km (6 mi.) SW. A BOULTON & WATT engine was applied to work in a cotton mill for the first time at Papplewick, 12 km (7 mi.) N., where some mill buildings are now converted into dwellings, and there are extensive remains of reservoirs and leats. The factory by Sir Owen Williams (1890–1969) at Beeston, 5 km (3 mi.) SW, for Boots the Chemist, built in 1931, with mushroom concrete columns and glass curtain walls, is one of the most important British industrial buildings of the period.

A vertical colliery winding engine of 1873 is preserved at Bestwood, 8 km (5 mi.) N. The Dukeries coalfield developed in the 1920s, with villages in the GARDEN CITY style at such places as Blidworth, Ollerton, New Clipstone and Edwinstowe.

The Papplewick water pumping station, one of the most ornate in Britain, with two James Watt & Co. beam engines of 1884, set amidst stained glass and decorative tiles, is preserved by a trust.

Bennerley Viaduct of 1876–7, 11 km (7 mi.) NW, is 500 m (1640 ft.) long, and one of only two wrought-iron latticework railway viaducts surviving in Britain. Nottingham Midland station is a magnificent brick and terracotta building of 1903, while the Sun Inn, Eastwood, 13 km (8 mi.) NE, was the birthplace of the Midland Railway in 1832.

The Nottingham City Museum Service is based at the Castle Museum, where there are collections of Nottinghamware pottery and other local products. Branches include the industrial museum at Wollaton Hall, 5 km (3 mi.) W., with collections of laceworking machinery and a replica horse gin; the Brewhouse Yard Museum, which is concerned with social history; and the canal museum, in a former Fellows, Morton & Clayton warehouse.

BIBLIOGRAPHY
General
Chapman, 1971; Smith, 1965; Waller, 1983.
Specific
Greatrex, N. The Robinson enterprises in Papplewick, Nottinghamshire. In *IAR*, IX, 1986.

LOCATIONS
[M] Nottingham Castle Museum, The Castle, Nottingham NG1 6EL.
[S] Papplewick Engines Trust, off Longdale Lane, Ravenshead, Nottingham NG15 9AU.

BARRIE TRINDER

Nouzonville, Ardennes, France   The Royal Arms factory at Nouzonville was built in 1688 by Victor Fournier, who was already operating an armaments works at Charleville, 6 km (3½ mi.) S. The new factory was opened on the site of a sixteenth-century ironworks. Surrounded by a polygonal wall with eight fortified towers, the establishment incorporated all the manufacturing processes necessary for arms production. Some of them, like hammering and the drilling of barrels, were water-powered whilst others, the welding of gun barrels and the production of mountings, were carried out by hand in individual 'boutiques'.

The understanding of the site today is facilitated by the

survival of numerous plans, including a remarkable bird's-eye view of 1697. It is possible to follow the fortified wall, which had cannon pointing towards the Luxembourg frontier. One of its towers survives, along with the drilling shop building, remnants of the château, and a building which housed twenty-two welders' boutiques, with their living quarters, along a central corridor. This building had probably been the charcoal store of the former ironworks.

Around Charleville the buildings erected by the great Ardennais ironmaster Jean-Nicolas Gendarme are still relatively well preserved. At Aumont, the Vendresse blast furnace has a remarkable monumental façade, while at Vrigne-aux-Bois, at sites known as 'The Upper Forge' and 'The Slitting Mill', are the buildings of one of the earliest forges in France to have PUDDLING FURNACES and ROLLING MILLS.

BIBLIOGRAPHY
General
André *et al.*, 1978.

JEAN-FRANÇOIS BELHOSTE

Nova Scotia (Nouvelle-Écosse), Canada   The province of Nova Scotia consists of a 400 km (250 mi.) long peninsula with a 30 km (20 mi.) boundary with New Brunswick, and the island of Cape Breton to the north-east, to which the peninsula is linked by a causeway at Port Hastings. Nova Scotia was settled by the French from 1605 and by Scots from 1621, and was one of the founder provinces of the Canadian federation in 1867. The Acadian descendants of the French settlers retain a distinct culture.

The fisheries of the nineteenth century are commemorated in the Museum of the Atlantic at Halifax and the Fisheries Museum at Lunenburg, 65 km (40 mi.) SW, which once had the largest fleet of schooners engaged in the Grand Banks trade. Both contain old trawlers and schooners, exhibits of fishing gear, and archives relating to the trade. A modern fish-processing plant in Lunenburg, opened in 1964, is one of the largest in North America.

Timber is an important resource. About 75 per cent of the province is now forest, and in the nineteenth century the province produced many wooden ships (*see* CANADA). Historic vessels preserved at Lunenburg include the *Reo II*, a 125-ton rum runner of 1931, the *Theresa E. Connor*, a 185-ton schooner of 1938, and the *Cape North*, a 245-ton wooden trawler of 1945. Among the twenty restored buildings in the Historic Village at Sherbrooke, 140 km (85 mi.) NE of Halifax, is a sawmill which still operates with water power. The Sutherland Steam Mill at Denmark, 125 km (75 mi.) N. of Halifax, is a conserved steam-powered factory of the 1890s which manufactured carriages, sledges, and 'gingerbread'-style FRETWORK for wooden houses.

The Balmoral Grist Mill of 1874, 115 km (70 mi.) N. of Halifax, still grinds oats and buckwheat with its original milling machinery.

Coal mining on a significant scale was developed by an English syndicate from the 1820s, using English migrant workers and technology from DURHAM and Northumberland (*see* NEWCASTLE). The rows of miners' housing were based on English models. Despite the considerable resources in the two coalfields on CAPE BRETON ISLAND, and those at Stellarton, 130 km (80 mi.) NE of Halifax, and at Springhill, 120 km (75 mi.) NW of Halifax, and the adjacent iron ore mines at Ferrona and Londonderry, the era of industrialization in the province was relatively short. Nova Scotian coal never penetrated the Ontario market, where coal and ore from Pennsylvania and Michigan was always cheaper. At Stellarton early rows of housing from the British era and from later Canadian companies contribute to one of the best industrial landscapes in Canada. At Londonderry, 100 km (60 mi.) N. of Halifax, much evidence of iron-ore working, beehive coke ovens and slag tips remains *in situ*. The ironworks in Londonderry were established in the 1840s by entrepreneurs from SHEFFIELD, but surviving evidence dates mainly from *c.*1900. Other minerals – silver, copper, lead, gold, tin and zinc – now come mainly from one mine at Walton, 75 km (45 mi.) NW of Halifax.

The Museum of Industry at Stellarton is designed to provide a focus for the interpretation of industry in the province. Its exhibits include the excavated remains of coke ovens, steam and diesel locomotives, a tea-packaging machine, a machine shop from an engineering works and a steam crane.

Textile manufactures are commemorated at the Wile Carding mill of *c.*1860 at Bridgewater, 80 km (50 mi.) SW of Halifax, and the woollen mill of *c.*1884 at Barrington, 200 km (120 mi.) SW of Halifax.

The Shubenacadie Canal, an 86 km (53 mi.) waterway between Halifax and Maitland on the Minas Basin, in which artificial cuts link a series of lakes, was begun in 1826, with Samuel Cunard (*see* LINER) as the principal shareholder. Construction was abandoned in 1831, resumed in 1854, and completed in 1861, the revised line incorporating two inclined planes. Railway competition brought early abandonment, in 1870, but the provincial government began restoration in 1984. Interpretation centres have been established at the entrance to the system at Dartmouth on the eastern side of Halifax harbour, on the site of one of the inclined planes, and at Fairbanks to the north. An original wooden lock gate was found during excavations in 1989.

BIBLIOGRAPHY
General
Innis, 1940; Matthews and Panting, 1978; Robertson, 1982; Wayman, 1990.
Specific
Shubenacadie Canal Guide. Dartmouth: Shubenacadie Canal Commission, 1989.

LOCATIONS
[M,S] Balmoral Grist Mill, Balmoral Mills off Route 311, Nova Scotia.
[M,S] Barrington Woolen Mill, Barrington, Nova Scotia.
[M] Fairbanks Interpretive Centre, 54 Locks Road, Dartmouth, Nova Scotia, B2X 2W7.
[M] Fisheries Museum of the Atlantic, Lunenburg Route 3, Nova Scotia.
[M] Maritime Museum of the Atlantic, Lower Water Street, Halifax, Nova Scotia.
[M] Nova Scotia Museum, 1747 Summer Street, Halifax.
[M] Shubenacadie Interpretive Centre, 140 Alderney Drive, Dartmouth, Nova Scotia.
[M,S] Sutherland Steam Mill, Denmark Route 326, Nova Scotia.
[M,S] Wile Carding Mill, Bridgewater Route 325, Nova Scotia.

DERYCK HOLDSWORTH and MICHAEL STRATTON

Novi Sad, Vojvodina, Serbia, Yugoslavia   Capital of the autonomous province of Vojvodina, on the River Danube, 72 km (45 mi.) NW of Belgrade. Settled by Serbs and Slovenians in the seventeenth century, it was known in the nineteenth century as the 'Serbian Athens'. It is at the junction of the Mali Canal (*see* YUGOSLAVIA) and the Danube. Industries include shipyards building river craft, textiles, agricultural engineering, and natural gas extraction, the last of which is illustrated in a special museum.

LOCATION
[M] Collection of the Nafta Gas Company, 21000-Novi Sad.
[M] Museum of Vojvodina, Petrovardin-Tvrdjava, 21000-Novi Sad.

Novy Jáchymov, West Bohemia, Czechoslovakia   An integrated ironworks, established in 1820 by Count Furstenberg, with two charcoal blast furnaces which produced monumental castings, but were blown out in the 1880s through lack of timber and remoteness of the site. The mine entrance is a café and the administration block survives, but most features have disappeared, though a relic mining landscape remains. Many cast-iron grave monuments survive locally.

Nowa Ruda (Neurode), Wałbrzych, Poland   Until 1980 the mines at Nowa Ruda were the world's leading source of refractory shale, used in powdered forms for furnace linings. Prospecting in the region began in the 1860s. Production started in 1879, and in 1898–1900 the C. Kulmitz Company from Żarów built a range of twenty-four shaft furnaces, which was later extended until there were thirty-two furnaces by the 1930s. Originally shale was roasted in the kilns before being refined and this process remained in use until 1979. After 1930 it was employed alongside a process using rotary kilns, developed by Dr Eberhard Goebel, in which the shales were pre-roasted, then refined, and then subjected to a final roasting. In 1980 both the mines and the shale-processing concern were closed down. All the surviving remains, including the great bank of thirty-two shaft furnaces, are now preserved and under legislative protection. The staff of the Nowa Ruda colliery are developing the site as an open-air museum of technology and it will be included within the Lower Silesian écomusée (see Wałbrzych).

Nuremberg (Nürnberg), Bavaria, Germany   The terminus of the first main-line railway in Germany, the line to Fürth, 6 km (4 mi.) NW of Nuremberg, which was opened in 1835; fittingly, the city is the location of Germany's principal transport museum.

Railways are the museum's main concern. Steam locomotives include a replica of *Adler*, the first locomotive to run on the line to Fürth, a 4-4-4 locomotive built by Maffei in Munich in 1907, and *05 001*, a streamlined 4-6-4 express passenger locomotive built in 1934-5. Amongst the rolling stock is a second-class coach built for the Nuremberg–Fürth line in 1845, and a motorcoach of the Fliegender Hamburger (Flying Hamburger) diesel multiple-unit train built for high-speed services between Hamburg and Berlin in 1932.

There are extensive displays on signalling and on railway electricification, and a huge HO-gauge model railway layout, which includes a working hump MARSHALLING YARD. An extensive collection of large-scale static models includes not only locomotives but goods wagons, railway carriages, a Krauss double-decker steam railcar of 1882, and a coaling plant of 1901 from a LOCOMOTIVE DEPOT in Munich. The museum also includes some nineteenth-century models of vehicles and buildings illustrating the system of road transport prevailing in Bavaria before the building of main-line railways (*see* DILIGENCE; POST COACH; WAGGON). The collection is modest but authentic, and is probably the best museum representation of this phase of road transport history.

Nuremberg's imposing main railway station, in the BEAUX ARTS style, was designed by Carl Ritter von Zenger in 1906.

Nuremberg was the chief European TOYMAKING city by the late nineteenth century. The industry is commemorated by rich collections in the toy museum, and is magnificently illustrated each December by the Christkindlesmarkt (Christ-child's market) in the Hauptmarkt.

BIBLIOGRAPHY
General
Bott, 1985; Glaser *et al.*, 1983; Grimm, 1985.

LOCATIONS
[I] Centrum Industriekultur (Centre for Industrial Culture), Guntherstrasse 45, 8500 Nuremberg 40.
[M] Germanisches Nationalmuseum (German National Museum), Kornmarkt 1, 8500 Nuremberg.
[M] Spielzeugmuseum (Toy Museum), Karlstrasse 13, 8500 Nuremberg.
[M] Verkehrsmuseum Nürnberg (Nuremberg Transport Museum), Lessingstrasse 6, 8500 Nuremberg.

BARRIE TRINDER

Nuutajärvi, Hämeen lääni, Finland   A town in southern Finland, notable for its glassworks, founded in 1793 to produce bottles and window glass, the oldest in Finland still in production. In the mid-nineteenth century the production base was broadened with the advice of French and Belgian experts. In 1855 the district architect, G. T. Chiewitz, drew up a plan for the area and designed new buildings, including the ornate office block, a stone-built warehouse and a shop. The oldest workers' housing dates from the 1860s, and there is an integrated workers' residential area of the 1940s. The main building of the mansion dates from 1822, its present neo-Renaissance façades, designed by L. I. Lindqvist, having been added in 1869. It stands in an English-style park. Since 1977 the Nuutajärvi Glass Museum, displaying the products of the works, and designed by Professor Kaj Franck, has been housed in the old works buildings.

LOCATION
[M] Nuutajärvi lasimuseo (Nuutajärvi Glass Museum). SF-31160 Nuutajärvi.

Nyíregyháza, Szabolcs-Szatmár, Hungary   One of the most important open-air museums in Hungary, 230 km (140 mi.) NE of Budapest, and established in 1970. It now has more than seventy re-erected buildings, including premises for a bootmaker, saddler, ropemaker, potter, weaver and candlemaker.

BIBLIOGRAPHY
General
Zippelius, 1974.

LOCATION
[M] Jósa András Museum, Egyház u.15.

nylon   A manufactured fibre based on hexamethylene diamine and adipic acid, developed in the USA by Wallace Hume Carothers (1896–1937), a chemist employed by the du Pont corporation from 1928. His work represented the first controlled synthesis of a POLYMER, in which organic materials were combined to produce a specific set of properties. Laboratory work began in 1935, ultimately producing a resin, given the name nylon, that could be extruded, chipped, melted, and spun into strong filaments. Du Pont erected a pilot plant in 1938, and its manufacturing plant at Seaford, Del., purpose-built for nylon production, began operation in January 1940. Lightweight but strong, nylon was introduced especially to be used for women's stockings.

During World War II nylon was made into other goods, such as parachutes and tyre cord, that took advantage of its properties. Manufacture in Britain began in Coventry in the winter of 1941-2 in a factory that had been used for filling shells during World War I, but production was disrupted by bombing and a second plant was established during 1942 in a former paint factory at Stowmarket, Suffolk. The factories at both Coventry and Stowmarket closed in 1948 when British production was concentrated in a new plant at Pontypool, South Wales, built on the site of huts erected during World War II to accommodate workers from an armaments factory. An obsolete RAYON factory at Doncaster, Yorkshire, was adapted for nylon spinning in 1955 and in 1959-60 a third plant was established at Huclecote, Gloucestershire, in buildings which had been erected during World War II for the manufacture of aircraft engines.

See figures 99, 100.

BIBLIOGRAPHY
General
Hounshell and Smith, 1988; Hudson, 1978; Stevens, 1975.

MICHAEL STRATTON and HELENA WRIGHT

Figure 99   Spinning Unit No. 4 of the du Pont nylon plant at Seaford, Delaware, opened in 1938; the photograph dates from April 1939.
Hagley Museum & Library, Pictorial Collections

Figure 100 Charging
polymer into a hopper at
the du Pont nylon plant at
Seaford, Delaware,
photographed in April
1939
Hagley Museum & Library,
Pictorial Collections

O

Oberhausen, North-Rhine Westphalia, Germany *See* RUHRGEBIET.

Oberursel, Hesse, Germany   The Seck Brothers' foundry and engineering works was built in 1883 on the Wiemersmühle site in the Urselbach valley, 20 km (12 mi.) N. of Frankfurt. Wilhelm Seck, then a student of 22, developed a single-cylinder, four-stroke petrol engine in 1891, which was so successful that the motor factory of W. Seck & Co. was founded in 1892, and renamed the Oberursel Motor Works in 1898. In World War I production expanded when the Secks' 'Gnom' engine was used for aircraft. New buildings erected in 1916–18 – an aircraft engine factory, an office block and the façades of the production sheds – have been preserved. After World War I there was a drop in production which led to a takeover by the rival concern, Deutz of Cologne. Since 1938 the factory has been known as the Oberursel Works of Klöckner-Humboldt-Deutz.

Ochsenhausen, Baden-Württemberg, Germany   A village 38 km (24 mi.) S. of Ulm, the terminus of a preserved 750 mm (2 ft. $5\frac{1}{2}$ in.) gauge railway, typical of many state-built narrow-gauge lines once working in Württemberg. Opened in 1899 and closed by DB in 1983, the 19 km ($11\frac{1}{2}$ mi.) line to Warthausen is now operated by a private museum association with stock from Austria, Switzerland and Poland, and an original MALLET locomotive of 1899, No. 99 633. Ochsenhausen station is a characteristic terminus of a branch line in Württemberg, with examples of the standardized buildings constructed on such lines. (Another example of a line of this type is the private Jagst valley railway between Möckmühl, 35 km (22 mi.) NE of Heilbronn and Dörzbach.)

LOCATIONS
[I] Öchsle-Schmalspurbahn e V (Öchsle-Schmalspur Railway Company), Postfach 1228, 7955 Ochsenhausen.
[I] Südwestdeutsche Verkehrs-Ag, Jagsttalbahn, Bahnhofstrasse 8, 7119 Dörzbach.

Odense, Funen, Denmark   Odense, in the middle of the fertile island of Funen, is the island's undisputed capital. Remains of a ring fort show that its history extends back to the Viking age. Odense is one of the biggest regional centres in Denmark, and throughout the industrial period has vied with Århus for the status of the most important manufacturing region in Denmark after Copenhagen. Several innovations were introduced into Denmark at Odense, among them steam-powered water supply from 1852, street lighting by gas from 1852, and large-scale public electricity supply from 1891. The city has a varied industrial structure, with food, textiles and iron as the main sectors. During the Second Industrial Revolution (*see* DENMARK) Odense gained a cotton spinning mill, a large electric motor factory, and, from 1916, a steel shipyard.

Examples of pre-industrial activities on Funen are displayed at Odense's open-air museum, Den Fynske Landsby, on Skjerskovvej south of the centre, where exhibits include a large water mill; a Dutch-style windmill; a weaver's house; and a kiln of 1889 from the traditional brickworks at Bladstrup, north of Odense, the only survivor of hundreds of similar, single-chamber intermittent kilns once spread throughout Denmark.

From the industrial period, the large woollen cloth mill of M. K. Brandt was recently converted into a cultural centre, with an art gallery, cinema, concert hall and bars. It also houses the national Graphics Museum, which has collections of machines, products and photographs from the printing and paper industries. Among the few other buildings in the city surviving from the early period of industrialization is the Albani brewery, built in 1859 and 1875 in a mixture of Romanesque and Gothic styles. The old cattle market has recently been adapted to house the headquarters of the second national television channel.

Frederiksbro, the first Danish iron bridge, an arched structure of 1844 made by the local foundry of M. P. Allerup, survives in Odense. A former locomotive depot adjacent to the main station houses the National Railway Museum, originally founded in 1875 by Danish State Railways (DSB). There are many late nineteenth- and early twentieth-century locomotives, mostly by German manufacturers, including No. 931, a compound Atlantic of 1907 by Schwartzkopff, and No. 125, an 0-4-4 back tank locomotive of 1882 by Hohenzollern of Düsseldorf.

A current project has the object of restoring an old brickworks with a circular kiln at Lilleskov near Tommerup, 16 km (10 mi.) SW. Steenstup, 30 km (20 mi.) S., is the chief centre of brickmaking on Funen, due to a large deposit of clay from a glacial lake. The Sound of Svendborg, 40 km (25 mi.) S., with its many islands, is an important shipping area. The old fleet of sailing ships has now been replaced by coasters, tankers and other vessels owned by such companies as the Mærsk Line. A 26.6 tonne wooden motor vessel of 1924, the *Helge*, sails from Svendborg to the nearby islands in summer time.

BIBLIOGRAPHY
General
Bay, 1977; DSB, 1947; Johansen, 1988; Ransome-Wallis, 1971; Sestoft, 1979.

Specific

Johansen, H. C., Boje, P. and Møller, A. M. *Fabrik og bolig: Det industrielle miljø i Odense 1840–1940* (Factory and dwelling: the industrial environment in Odense 1840–1940). Odense, 1983.

LOCATIONS

[M] Jernbanemuseum (Railway Museum), Dannebrogsgade 24, 5000 Odense.

[M] Møntergaarden (Historical Museum), Overgrade 48–50, 5000 Odense. [This is also the correspondence address for Den Fynske Landsby.]

OLE HYLDTOFT

office block   The term 'office', meaning the place where the clerical work of an establishment is done, was first applied in royal and noble households, but was used in commercial contexts by the seventeenth century, sometimes being qualified to indicate the kind of business transacted, as in 'insurance office'. The 'office block', often separate from any manufacturing establishment, developed from the beginning of the nineteenth century with the growth of the professions and of services like banking and insurance, and as large manufacturing corporations sought to have a presence in city centres. Some of the first were insurance offices in London, like that built for the County Fire Office in 1819 in Regent Street. In many twentieth-century manufacturing complexes office blocks may have architectural pretensions lacking in buildings concerned with production.

See also COUNTING HOUSE; SKYSCRAPER.

Ohio, United States of America   Perhaps no state better exemplifies the economic importance of early industrial diversification than Ohio. This compact state, straddling the frontier between the eastern American states and 'the West', has benefited from a combination of highly skilled immigration, access to navigable rivers and lakes, and a rich reserve of natural resources, notably arable lands, coal and natural-gas fields, and seams of quality building stone. The state has an extensive record of heavy industrial output concentrated along its Lake Erie shore, and at urban centres inland, from rubber products, automobile parts and business machines to refractory bricks, high-grade natural grindstones, and machine tools.

Near Akron, home of the state's rubber industry, the Goodyear Airdock of 1919 is sited on private land, its 5.1 million m³ (55 million cu. ft.) of uninterrupted volume making it for years the world's largest interior, one capable of generating cloud formations and rain. The Goodyear blimp AIRSHIP occasionally uses the dock as home base, allowing a portion of the structure to maintain its original purpose.

In Cincinnati, the Ingalls Building is a narrow sixteen-storey office block squeezed into the downtown that lays claim to being the world's earliest standing reinforced concrete SKYSCRAPER. Completed in 1903, it demonstrated that concrete, properly mixed and reinforced, was both economical and structurally safe.

Elsewhere in Cincinnati, largely archaeological remains exist of the city's five inclined railways built between 1873 and 1892. All were of double-track, non-funicular construction, with levelled passenger cars carried on angular undercarriages. Street-crossing pier foundations of the lines remain in several residential neighbourhoods. Several of Cincinnati's older suburbs still depend on public gaslight to illuminate a number of their streets, a tradition dating from 1841. The Cincinnati Union Terminal, a vast ART DECO creation of 1919–33, is one of the nation's great railway terminal rebirths: it has been adapted to reuse as a commercial property, after falling on some very hard times in the 1960s and 70s.

One of JOHN A. ROEBLING's more important suspension bridges, completed in 1866, passes over the Ohio River at Cincinnati. As a harbinger of the Brooklyn Bridge (*see* NEW YORK; SUSPENSION BRIDGE), the Cincinnati span employs Roebling's classic heavy stone towers, diagonal stays and anchoring eye-bars in a powerful yet open design that kept the river free for steamship navigation.

Youngstown has used the dark days of the modern steel industry to reflect and act on the region's steelmaking and steelworking heritages by establishing the nation's only museum built solely and intentionally to focus on the steel industry. Artefacts are drawn from across the nation, but are used to embellish the social and technological history of steelmaking in the Ohio Valley, a stop not to be missed on any tour of the American 'rust belt'.

On Lake Erie, Cleveland's massive industrial past in heavy manufacturing and bulk materials processing has given way to the medical and educational professions as the re-education of steelworkers into computer jockeys seeks to uplift a depressed employment base. 'The Flats' was once a neighbourhood on the shores of Cleveland's Cuyahoga River, jammed with foundries, ships' chandleries, sailors' dives and warehouses. In the 1970s it was reborn as a swank enclave of pricy eating, drinking, and dancing establishments, in the shadow of Cleveland's towering railway terminal of 1929, still in use for a few local trains.

Fittingly, standing in Cleveland's Lakeview Cemetery is a bronze tribute to the steel industry and Henry Chisholm, one of the city's more benevolent steel barons. Paid for by his grieving workers, the monument includes scenes from the blast furnace and rolling mill cast in bas-relief into the base which surrounds the figure of Chisholm, who leans Hercules-like against a rolling-mill housing.

Crossing the Cuyahoga is a good respresentative selection of bridge types raised for rail and automotive uses, from the heavily-trussed lift bridges, one of the last built being entirely of aluminium, to the high-level bridge of 1918, a 180 m (590 ft.) steel arch, anchored by twelve arcaded concrete arches reminiscent of Roman aqueducts.

Quaker Square, Akron, is one of the nation's most innovative adaptive reuse projects. A cluster of thirty-two 37 m (120 ft.) grain silos with 17 cm (7 in.) thick concrete walls, built in 1932, was converted to the Quaker Square Hilton hotel, which opened in 1980, as the capstone of a range of restaurants and boutiques. The silos were built by the Quaker Oats Co., successor to an oatmeal enterprise established in Akron in 1854 by Ferdinand Schumacher (1822–1908), a pioneer of BREAKFAST CEREAL manufacture.

Figure 101   The four surviving Hulett unloaders, built in 1911–12 to transfer iron ore from the holds of ships to railway wagons or the stocking yard at the Pennsylvania RR Ore Dock, Cleveland, Ohio; the Hulett unloader, used at all the iron ore ports on the Great Lakes, was patented by George M. Hulett (1846–1923) in 1898. W. D. Ellis remarked in 1966, 'In repose, this monster is the ugliest, ungainliest machine ever made. In action, it's sheer poetry!'
Robert M. Vogel, Smithsonian Institution

One of the nation's more curious historic composite bridges still serves the small town of Baltimore: a hybrid chain suspension and wooden arch span of 1881, crossing Poplar Creek, and capped by a gabled sheet-metal roof.

The closest Ohio comes to a state-wide industrial museum is in Cleveland at the Western Reserve Historical Society, where significant archival records and artefacts pertaining to Ohio's industrial past are collected and placed in regular display.

See also figures 1, 2, 6.

BIBLIOGRAPHY
General
Bluestone, 1978; Ohio Department of Transportation, 1983; Procter and Matuszeski, 1978.
Specific
Miller, C.P. Industrial Archaeology in the USA: documenting the Pennsylvania Railway Ore Dock at Cleveland, Ohio. *World Archaeology*, xv, 1985.

LOCATIONS
[S] Buckeye Iron Furnace Historic Site, Wellston, OH 45692.

[M] National Road Museum, Zanesville, Ohio.
[M] Ohio Railway Museum, 990 Proprietors Road, Worthington, OH 43085.
[M] Western Reserve Historical Society, 10825 East Boulevard, Cleveland, OH 44106.

DAVID H. SHAYT

oil cloth   A form of floor covering, widely used in the nineteenth century until superseded by LINOLEUM. Lengths of canvas, up to 7 m × 23 m (8 yd. × 25 yd.) were first sized and then covered with paint (which was applied with trowels), before being subjected to streams of moist air at a temperature of *c*.32 °C. They were then dried and smoothed with pumice. Next the back was painted, before three additional coats of paint were applied with trowels. After further pumicing, patterns were printed on the sheets. Kamptulicon, invented *c*.1843 and marketed from *c*.1862, was a development of oil cloth in which the fabric was treated with a preparation of india rubber with ground cork, which was applied by rolling. The name 'oil cloth' is also applied to table coverings of woven cotton treated with linseed oil and a pigment, which remain in production. Manufacture of oil cloth was the foundation of the linoleum industry in KIRKCALDY.

oil engine A motive system deriving its power from the combustion of vaporized oil within an engine's cylinder, hence the term 'internal combustion engine'. Its ancestor, the GAS ENGINE, pioneered by Jean Joseph Lenoir (1822–1900) in 1860–5, in which coal gas, ignited by an electric sparking plug, drove a doube-acting piston, was thermally inefficient. Nikolaus August Otto (1832–91) in 1876 improved the fuel efficiency of the internal combustion engine by the introduction of a four-stroke cycle: (a) induction of the fuel mixture into the cylinder by the retreating piston; (b) its compression on the piston's return; (c) its ignition, forcing away the piston; (d) its exhaustion on the next return. For more flexibility and independence from mains supplies, liquid-fuel engines were developed by, among others, Priestman of Hull in 1886, but more successfully by Hornsby and Stuart in 1890. Their engines initiated the cycle by externally heating a 'hot-bulb' vaporizer, which vaporized the fuel. Oil engines powered the earliest motor carriages of Lenoir in 1863, BENZ in 1883, and DAIMLER in 1884–5, but were soon replaced with PETROL ENGINES.

BIBLIOGRAPHY
General
Strandh, 1979.

CHRISTOPHER GREEN

oil industry The oil industry has become one of the dominant forces in the world economy in the second half of the twentieth century. The term usually refers to the location, extraction and refining of PETROLEUM, and the production of useful materials from its fractions. The date 27 August 1859, when Edwin Drake (1819–1880) successfully drilled an oil well at Titusville, Pa., USA, is often taken as the beginning of the modern industry, and, in that it was the beginning of a process that led directly to the multi-national corporations of today, the claim has some justice. But there was already a considerable manufacture of lighting oils before Drake went to Titusville. The Argand lamp (*see* OIL LAMP) had stimulated demand in early nineteenth-century Europe for lighting oils, which were produced from CANNEL COAL in Scotland, from shale in Scotland and France, from LIGNITE in Germany, and from wood tar in Scandinavia. Oils were widely produced from vegetable and from animal sources, including sperm whales. In many parts of Europe, Alsace, Sicily, Galicia and Baku, petroleum had long been extracted from natural seepages and used for lighting, lubrication and medicinal purposes. A substantial oil industry producing lubricants, solvents and lighting oil, which was at first wholly independent of contemporary developments in the USA, grew up in Eastern Europe from the 1850s. A refinery was built at Lucacesti in Romania in 1840. J. J. I. ŁUKASIEWICZ established the first Polish

refinery in 1856; a refinery was built in Vienna in 1862 (*see* AUSTRIA); and the first in Azerbaydzhan began operation at Baku in 1863. Lighting oil was also manufactured in the USA from coal, whale oil and turpentine. Drake's discovery was followed by the establishment of refineries like that at Corry, Pa., which opened in 1861; but the 1860s were marked by confusion in the industry, and quarrels over land rights.

In 1870 John D. Rockefeller (1839–1937) and his associates in Cleveland, Ohio, formed the Standard Oil Company. By 1878 they controlled 90 per cent of the refinery capacity in the USA, and from 1886 became involved in extracting crude oil. The company dominated the American industry until 1911 when anti-trust legislation enforced the separation of some subsidiary companies.

World output of crude oil in 1910 was 44 million tonnes: 64 per cent from the USA, 23 per cent from Russia, and 7 per cent elsewhere in Europe. Production on a significant level in the Middle East began with the first exports from Iran in 1911. Sources in Indonesia and the Caribbean were developed, and the large companies began to operate on a multi-national basis. World output in 1936 totalled 244 million tonnes: 60 per cent from the USA, 5 per cent from the Middle East, 12 per cent from the USSR, and 4 per cent from the rest of Europe. By 1956 output had increased more than three times to 824 million tonnes, only 42 per cent coming from the USA, 21 per cent from the Middle East, 10 per cent from the USSR, and 5 per cent from the rest of Europe. From the 1920s, and increasingly after World War II, the oil companies dominated the CHEMICAL INDUSTRY.

See also CRUDE OIL; DIESEL ENGINE; DIESEL FUEL; DIESEL LOCOMOTIVE; LPG; MOTOR VESSEL; NATURAL GAS; OIL ENGINE; OIL LAMP; OIL PIPELINE; OIL REFINERY; OIL WELL; PETROL; PETROLEUM; SHALE OIL.

BIBLIOGRAPHY
General
Anderson, 1984; Beaton, 1957; BP, 1958; Forbes, 1958, 1959; Gale, 1860; Giddens, 1938, 1948; Harvard, 1960; Hidy and Hidy, 1955; Hofer, 1888; Jouan, 1949; Talbot, 1914; Thompson, 1908, 1910; van der Have and Verver, 1957; White, 1962; Williamson and Daum, 1959.

BARRIE TRINDER

oil lamp A means of lighting which gradually ousted the candle in developed countries during the nineteenth century, and initiated the growth of the petroleum industry.

The oil lamp developed from the cruse, a grease-filled dish from which protruded a wick. Betty lamps had wicks set in small troughs, and a hinged cover to limit the size of the flame. Benjamin Franklin (1706–90) made the discovery that three wicks on one lamp produced almost as much light as four single-wick lamps; because the wicks heated each other, the oil was vaporized more thoroughly. From about 1800 turpentine distilled over quicklime was used for lamps, but this caused explosive gases to accumulate, although from the 1820s this problem had been reduced by diluting the turpentine with alcohol.

In 1782 Pierre Aimé Argand (1750–1803) produced a lamp that allowed air to pass over both the inner and the outer surfaces of the flame. The lamp was widely used in British textile mills in the 1840s. The first lamp to burn kerosene was developed by J. J. I. Łukasiewicz in 1853. John Austen of New York, who was involved with the sale of kerosene, sought a lamp suitable for burning it and found a cheap flat-wick metal lamp with a glass chimney in Vienna, which was widely copied in the USA as the 'Vienna lamp'.

BARRIE TRINDER

oil mill The function of an oil mill is to extract oil from seeds, originally those of flax (*Linum usitatissium*), rape (*Brassica rapa*), coleseed (*Brassica oleifera*) or Gold of Pleasure (*Cemelina sativa*). The essential elements of the mill were brought together by the Dutchman Cornelis van Uytgeest in the 1590s. Mills might be water-, wind- or horse-powered. Seeds were crushed by rollers or drop stamps to produce 'seed-meal': this was heated in a pan over a fire, before being put into woollen bags, which were then placed in leather case lined with horse hair. The case was squeezed in a press to force out the oil. The residue was usually reworked to remove further oil, after which the remaining 'cake' was cut up and used as cattle feed. Industrial-scale mills were developed in the USA in the mid-nineteenth century, the first of the type in Britain being built at Gainsborough, Lincolnshire in 1873: such mills had large presses dealing with many kinds of seed used in the manufacture of Soap, Margarine, and the like. A horse-powered mill is preserved at Arnhem, and a water-powered example at Bokrijk.

BIBLIOGRAPHY
General
Brace, 1960; Kempers, 1979; Wright, 1982.

BARRIE TRINDER

oil pipeline Sometimes pipelines offer the cheapest means of transporting crude oil or petroleum products, in single-line pipes, up to 0.81 m (32 in.) in diameter by the 1950s, or in multiple lines. The first successful pipeline, in 1864, ran from Plumer, Pennsylvania, to the Allegheny River, a distance of 5 km (3 mi.). Early development was mostly in the USA where pipelines over 2500 km (1600 mi.) long were operating by 1914. Examples include the Big Inch, conveying crude oil 2010 km (1250 mi.) from Texas to Pennsylvania; the Little Big Inch, taking products 2390 km (1485 mi.) from Texas to New York; and the Plantation, a multiple line taking products 2030 km (1260 mi.) from Louisiana to North Carolina. The pipeline from Băicoi to Constanţa, Romania, was completed in 1916 (*see* Prahova).

BIBLIOGRAPHY
General
BP, 1958; Williamson and Daum, 1959.

oil refinery A works distilling crude oil into its fractions

or 'cuts', which originated in the USA and Eastern Europe in the 1850s and 60s. Originally crude oil was distilled from simple batch stills into rough, impure fractions, usually gasoline, kerosine, lubricating oils and fuel oils. The 'shell still', resembling the cylindrical boilers used for steam-raising, introduced in 1885, was standard until the development in 1911 of the 'pipe still', a furnace heated by gas or oil burners, with pipes carrying the crude oil running through it. Thermal Cracking was introduced *c.*1912 by William Burton of Standard Oil Co. (Indiana), and catalytic cracking was widely used from the 1930s. The first bubble-plate distillation column, used in 1920, was the beginning of major developments as demand switched from lighting oil to motor spirit.

The typical fractions into which crude oil was collected in the 1950s were:

(a) natural gas, mixed with the oil, rich in Methane and Ethene, used as a refinery fuel;
(b) primary flash distillate (PFD), boiling at 30–100 °C, yielding Propane and Butane for use as Lpg or refinery fuel, with some butane used for motor spirit (*see* Petrol);
(c) straight-run Benzine, boiling at 80–130 °C, used in motor spirit;
(d) naphtha, also known as heavy benzine or heavy gasoline, boiling at 120–80 °C, used in jet-engine fuel and as a raw material for chemical manufactures;
(e) Kerosine, boiling at 170–250 °C, for use as burning oil and as a source of aromatic hydrocarbons;
(f) atmospheric gas oil, boiling at 170–350 °C, used for Diesel fuel;
(g) atmospheric residue, the waxy remains, from which fuel oils can be extracted.

By the 1950s most refineries had extensive ranges of cracking and other processes. The precise range depended on the raw material and on the end-products. Most of the area of any refinery is taken up with the tank farm, cylindrical tanks up to 16 000 tonnes capacity being used by the 1950s, with spherical tanks for volatile liquids or liquefied gases.

An oil refinery is one of the most difficult industrial installations to conserve, and none has yet been retained as a monument apart from the Pioneer Oil Refinery of 1867 at Newhall, California.

See also Bóbrka; Cracking; Pennsylvania; Prahova.

BIBLIOGRAPHY
General
BP, 1958.

BARRIE TRINDER

oil tanker A vessel specially built for the carriage of crude oil or refinery products. The first was the *Gluckauf*, 91 m (300 ft.) long, of 2307 tons, launched at Newcastle-upon-Tyne, England, for Deutsches Amerikanische Petroleum Gesellschaft in 1886; in the tradition of later tankers she had all her machinery aft. Previously oil was shipped in barrels in ordinary cargo vessels, although there were fixed tanks in the Manx *Ramsey* of 1862 and the Belgian

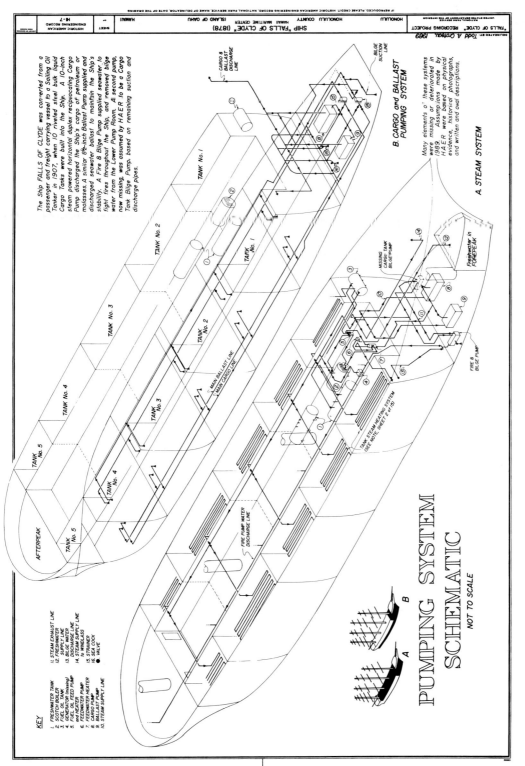

Figure 102 A schematic drawing by HAER showing the pumping system on the *Falls of Clyde*, an iron four-masted sailing ship built at Port Glasgow in 1878 and converted to an oil tanker in 1907; it survives at Honolulu, Hawaii.
Historic American Engineering Record. National Park Service, Todd A. Croteau, 1989

Vaterland of 1872. Total world capacity in 1914 was 2 million deadweight tons: this had risen to 17 million by 1939, and 44 million by the mid-1950s, when there were 2860 tankers working. The largest tanker before 1914 was the 9196-ton *Narragansett*, built at Greenock in 1903. the *Paul Paix*, built at Middlesbrough in 1908, was the first with longitudinal framing. By 1930s most tankers had three tanks abreast, divided by two longitudinal bulkheads. Before 1940 there were few vessels larger than 12 000 deadweight tons. No early mechanically powered tanker remains, but the *Falls of Clyde*, an iron four-masted sailing ship built at Port Glasgow in 1878 and converted to an oil tanker in 1907, survives at Honolulu, Hawaii.

BIBLIOGRAPHY
General
Baker, 1965; BP, 1958; Brouwer, 1985; King, 1956; Lisle, 1936.

BARRIE TRINDER

oil well An oil well is drilled from a derrick, a steel or in earlier times a wooden tower. A platform raised above ground level supports the 'draw-works', a winch used for raising and lowering the 'travelling-block', suspended from the 'crown block', the pulley mounted at the top of the tower. The cutting tool is attached to drill pipes and to the 'kelley', a square hollow shaft which engages in the 'rotary table', the housing for a geared ring driven by a power unit: through this assembly rotary motion is transmitted to the drill pipe. As the drill goes deeper the hoisting apparatus allows more sections to be added to the top of the drill pipe. Wells up to 6900 m (22 500 ft.) had been drilled by the 1950s. Drilling technology developed in the late nineteenth century in the USA and Romania (*see* PRAHOVA), where wells up to 300 m (1000 ft.) were being drilled by 1901.

When a well is producing, natural pressure may suffice to force up a column of oil, but it is usually necessary to raise oil to the surface mechanically. This is achieved either by using a simple plunger-type pump such as a 'nodding donkey', or by applying pneumatic pressure.

Natural gas and salt water are normally separated from the oil near the well top.

Several museums have collections of well-head equipment (*see* BOBRKA; PENNSYLVANIA; PRAHOVA).

See also figure 163.

BIBLIOGRAPHY
General
Anderson, 1984; BP, 1958.

BARRIE TRINDER

Oklahoma, United States of America Oil and gas have kept Oklahoma afloat almost since the establishment of the Oklahoma Territory in 1845. Both continue to dominate the economy, supporting the machine-building and repair industries in the principal cities of Tulsa and Oklahoma City. Bituminous coal, lead, zinc, copper and silver have been other prominent state extractives.

Two state museums, in Drumright and Healdton, preserve the heritage of artefacts from Oklahoma's oil industry, explaining the state's hard-won motto, *Labor omnia vincit* (Labour conquers all things).

On a sadder note, the remains of a rare American dam failure stand on either side of Turkey Creek in southwestern Oklahoma. William Fullerton's masonry block dam of 1895 diverted water to local farms until its destruction by flood in 1919 and subsequent abandonment.

LOCATIONS
[M] Drumright Oilfield Museum, East Broadway on Highways 99 & 33, Sante Fe Depot, Drumright, OK 74030.
[M] Healdton Oil Museum, 315 East Main Street, Healdton, OK 73438.

DAVID H. SHAYT

olive oil The basis of cooking in large parts of the Mediterranean world, and an important item of trade from classical antiquity. The fruits of the olive were traditionally crushed in edge runner mills like the preserved example at CAPALBIO. Olive oil is also used in CANNING fish and in SOAP manufacture.

Oliveira de Azemeis, Beira Litoral, Portugal A glass-making centre, 40 km (25 mi.) S. of Oporto, which flourished chiefly in the late nineteenth and early twentieth century. Papermaking and the manufacture of woollen hats also flourished in the county.

A glass furnace at nearby Covo was operating as early as 1528, but only the palace of the counts of Covo, a chapel of 1862, some workshop ruins, and the clock and bell now remain.

oliver A treadle-powered hammer used by smiths, particularly in the manufacture of nails, locks and other small objects made of wrought iron. A spring device, originally a pole of ash or a similar wood and latterly a metal coil spring, returns the hammer to its rest position. Surviving examples can be seen at IRONBRIDGE, the BLACK COUNTRY Museum, and Avoncroft (*see* BROMSGROVE).

BIBLIOGRAPHY
General
Gale, 1971.

omnibus From the Latin 'for all', the word 'omnibus' is generally applied to vehicles following set timetables and routes, which for a small fee, are accessible to all passengers without pre-booking, boarding and alighting taking place in the street. It is usually abbreviated to 'bus'.

Horse buses began to operate in Paris in 1819 and the first route in London, worked by George Shillibeer (1797–1866), began on 4 July 1829, being at once an encouragement to tradesmen and merchants to live 5–10 km (3–6 mi.) from their places of work. The Stage Carriage Act 1832 put such operations on a legal basis, and legislation of 1838 required registration of vehicles and the licensing of drivers. The first vehicles carried eighteen inside passengers but by the early 1840s buses with seats on the roofs were in operation. In 1847 the 'knife board' bus was introduced, with a longitudinal back-to-back seat on the top. 'Garden seat' style vehicles, with cross seats on the top, were general by the 1890s. Iron rungs initially gave access to the top deck, but were replaced from 1881 by curving staircases with 'modesty' boards which allowed females access to upper decks without embarrassment. By c.1860 buses with up to twenty-six seats were operating but the limited pulling power of a pair of horses impeded significant growth in size. By 1900 there were 4000 horse buses in London alone, most being distinguished by yellow wheels and bright company liveries. There were some 25 000 horse buses in Great Britain in 1890, and perhaps as many as 400 000 horses used to draw buses by 1900.

The first profitable motor bus service in Britain was operated in the Clevedon area of Somerset from 1899, the year in which the first tentative experiments were made in London. From 1903 the GREAT WESTERN RAILWAY began to operate motor buses from its Helston terminus to the Lizard Peninsula in CORNWALL. In 1905 the principal horse bus undertaking in London began to convert to motor operation, and by 1914 horse buses had largely disappeared in the city. Few remained anywhere after 1918.

The motor omnibus normally had a petrol engine at the front of its chassis, with wooden bodywork forming one or two decks, often open to the elements. As with the MOTOR LORRY, major improvements came in the 1920s with the introduction of oil and diesel engines, pneumatic tyres and metal bodywork. In many European and American cities the motor omnibus failed to compete successfully with tramcar networks and railways, but in places it came to reign supreme, the famous red double-decker bus of London Transport, introduced in 1923, becoming a symbol recognized throughout the world. In recent years there have been experiments with the position of engines in motor buses, and they are now usually located under the floor or at the rear, rather than at the front. Similarly front- or dual-entrance vehicles have replaced the open-plat-formed rear-entrance buses except in London. Mass car ownership has contributed to the demise of bus services in most developed countries, but urban congestion may lead to their revival. The bus is the most important form of transport in most Third World countries.

See also BUS DEPOT; BUS STATION; HORSE; MOTORCOACH.

BIBLIOGRAPHY
General
Booth, 1977; Hibbs, 1968, 1971; Lee, 1962, 1968; Thrupp, 1877.
Specific
The Omnibuses, In *Chambers's Edinburgh Journal*, IV, 1836.

JOHN POWELL

Ontario, Canada   Ontario, or Canada West, was established as a British colony ruled from Quebec in 1774. After an influx of loyalists fleeing from the USA it became in 1791 the separate colony of Upper Canada. The pioneering period of canoeing and fur-trading is commemorated at Old Ford William near Thunder Bay, and at nearby Grand Portage, Minnesota.

Ontario's development was made possible by the gradual improvement of navigation between the St Lawrence and the Great Lakes (*see* NIAGARA; RIDEAU CANAL). The Trent–Severn waterway, connecting Trenton on Lake Ontario with Port Severn on Lake Superior, through Lake Simcoe, was begun in 1896 but not opened throughout until 1920, when it was clear that the waterway would not be used for the large-scale carriage of grain. It has since developed as one of North America's most popular cruising waterways. Its most notable engineering feature is the hydraulic boat lift at Peterborough (usually called the lift lock), completed in 1904, which raises vessels 19.8 m (65 ft.): it is the highest lift for a structure of this kind, and is supposedly the world's largest mass concrete structure. A second lift at Kirkfield and two inclined planes, called marine railways, were built on the canal. One of the latter was replaced in 1965 by a lock, while the other at Big Shute was replaced by an enlarged incline in 1978. The rapids between Montreal and Lake Ontario were bypassed between 1843 and 1851 by the Beauharnois, Cornwall and Williamsburg Canals, but it was not until the completion of the St Lawrence Seaway in 1959 that a uniform depth of 8.23 m (27 ft.) was established, enabling large ocean-going craft to reach the Great Lakes. Locks at SAULT STE MARIE gave access to and from Lake Superior.

The prosperity of nineteenth-century agriculture in Ontario is reflected in numerous grist mills, built wherever there were falls on a river. Good examples are preserved by the National Capital Commission at Wakefield in the Ottawa valley, and at Black Creek Pioneer Village, Toronto. Brewing using malt from locally-grown barley prospered in cities like London. Many CREAMERIES are evidence of the growth of commercial dairying in the late nineteenth century, a development displayed in the province's first cheese factory at Ingersoll, 120 km (75 mi.) SW of Toronto. Most of the tobacco grown in Ontario is processed at Delhi, 125 km (75 mi.) SW of Toronto, where there is a museum of the tobacco industry.

The lumbering industry is portrayed in the Pioneer Logging Exhibit in the 7500 km^2 (3000 sq. mi.) Algonquin National Park, 240 km (150 mi.) N. of Toronto. At Upper Canada Village near Morrisburg, 56 km (35 mi.) SE of Ottawa, exhibits include a water-powered sawmill and a woollen mill.

SUDBURY is one of the world's principal mining cities, but minerals have been produced in many other parts of Ontario. Early oil extraction is commemorated at Petrolia (*see* SARNIA). The Niagara escarpment produced shale which was ground for brickmaking, as well as sandstone and limestone for building, industries which are commemorated in the Fork of Credit Provincial Park, 60 km (40 mi.) NW of Toronto.

Agricultural engineering in Canada was dominated by the company established by Daniel Massey (1798–1856), who opened a foundry at Newcastle, Ontario, in 1847. His son, Hart Almerrin Massey (1823–96), and grandson, Chester Daniel Massey (1850–1926), established works at Toronto and later at Brantford, 100 km (60 mi.) SW, from which they developed a worldwide reputation for tractors, reapers and, subsequently, combine harvesters. Many of

533

the company's products are displayed at the Ontario Agricultural Museum.

From the late nineteenth century industrial plants in Ontario were able to substitute hydro-electric power for power derived from imported coal. The government-run Ontario Hydro-Electric Power Commission (now Ontario Hydro) was established in 1906 to regulate the production, transmission and sale of electricity, particularly from NIAGARA, from which factories throughout south-western Ontario were receiving power by 1914. Early hydro-electric power generation is displayed at the Historical Museum at Magnetawam, 230 km (140 mi.) N. of Toronto, which is housed in an operational power station of 1925.

Windsor and Oshawa, 56 km (35 mi.) E. of Toronto, became the chief centres of motorcar manufacturing in Canada, and a large car museum has been established at the latter. Windsor stands on the peninsula between Lake Erie and Lake St Claire, south-east of Detroit (see MICHIGAN), to which it is connected by a tunnel. It was the gateway not just to Canada, but to the whole of the British Empire, for the motor manufacturers of Detroit. HENRY FORD opened a factory in the city in 1906, to be followed by Chrysler and General Motors. ALBERT KAHN built several factories in the city.

See also HAMILTON; OTTAWA; SARNIA; TORONTO; WATERLOO.

BIBLIOGRAPHY
General
Angus, 1988; Bowering, 1988; Burnham and Burnham, 1972; Careless, 1967, 1971; Cuming, 1983; Dean, 1969; Denison, 1949; Fram and Weiler, 1981; Hadfield, 1986; Leung, 1981; Mika, 1987; Newell, 1986a; Newell and Greenhill, 1989; Wayman, 1990.
Specific
Mika N., Mika, H. and Thompson, G. Black Creek Pioneer Village. Belleville, Ontario: Mika Publishing, 1988.

LOCATIONS
[M,S] Black Creek Pioneer Village, 1000 Murray Ross Parkway, North York (Toronto) M3J 2P3.
[M] Canadian Automotive Museum, 99 Simcoe Street South, Oshawa.
[M,S] Ingersoll Cheese Factory, Historical Museum and Sports Hall of Fame, Highway 19, Ingersoll, Ontario.
[S] Old Fort William, Vickers Heights Post Office, Thunder Bay, Ontario P0T 2Z0.
[M] Ontario Farm Museum, Milton, Ontario L9T 2Y3.
[I] Ontario Heritage Association, 7th Floor, 77 Bloor Street West, Toronto, Ontario M7A 2R9.
[I] Ontario Society for Industrial Archaeology, c/o 88 Upper Canada Drive, North York, Ontario M2P 1S4.
[M] Ontario Tobacco Museum, Delhi, Ontario.
[M,S] Upper Canada Village, St Lawrence Parks Commission, Box 740, Morrisburg, Ontario K0C 1X0.

DERYCK HOLDSWORTH

onyx A precious stone, a variety of quartz, distinguished by having regular bands of sharply contrasting colours, the most prized being of black and white.
See also ARIZONA.

opal A precious stone, a natural form of hydrated silica, the 'noble' form of which produces startling polychromatic effects as light passes through. Slovakia (see DUBNIK) and QUEENSLAND are important sources.

Opatówek, Kalisz, Poland A small town 10 km (6 mi.) E. of Kalisz, where industrial development was fostered by the Congress Kingdom of Poland. The Fiedler brothers established a textile plant at Opatówek in 1824–6. Tanneries and printing works operated around Kalisz, and the long-established 'Calisia' piano factory is in Kalisz. The Museum of Industrial History in Opatówek was established in 1981 to document the development of industry in the Kaliski region in the nineteenth and twentieth centuries, and was located in the well-preserved premises of a mill built by the Fiedler brothers in 1824–6. The museum includes reconstructions of processes used in the region, relating to textiles, tanneries, printing, and piano-making. A collection of local products includes samples of cloth, knitted articles, haberdashery and leather.

BIBLIOGRAPHY
Specific
Hauk, R. Muzeum Historii Przemysłu w Opatówku (The Museum of Industrial History in Opatówek). Opatówek, 1981.

LOCATION
[M] Muzeum Historii Przemysłu w Opatówku (The Museum of Industrial History in Opatówek), Opatówek.

open-air museum A collection of buildings removed from their original sites and re-erected within an enclosed museum, although within a given museum some buildings may remain in situ, some may be reconstructions, assemblages of parts from different sources making up an historical authentic exhibit, and some may be replicas, or scientifically designed copies. Open-air museums have traditionally been concerned with buildings relating to peasant cultures. The concept originated in Scandinavia in the late nineteenth century, when, under the influence of Romantic Nationalism, people interested in folk life began to move old wooden houses into their gardens. The acknowledged founder of open-air museums is Artur Hazelius (1833–1901), who began collecting artefacts in 1872, and in 1891 opened a museum on a fortified island in the Stockholm archipelago, which took the name 'Skansen' from the Swedish plural for fortifications (see STOCKHOLM). In some European languages the word 'Skansen' now means this type of museum. Similar national museums were set up on the edges of all the Scandinavian capitals before 1914 (see COPENHAGEN; HELSINKI; OSLO), and in Norway and Sweden many regional and local museums were established. Open-air museums were also opened in the Netherlands and the Baltic states before 1914. During the 1920s and 30s similar museums were opened in Germany, and since World War II there has been a marked expansion of open-air museums in Germany, in the Communist states of Eastern Europe, and in Great Britain. In Canada and the USA, where open-air museums similarly became popular in the 1920s and 30s, the dividing line between museums, historic villages and 'theme parks', consisting of replicas, is difficult to locate. The term 'open-air museum' is sometimes applied to industrial monuments preserved *in situ*, like Sloss Furnaces, Birmingham, ALABAMA.

The special status of open-air museums was recognized by the setting up of a commission by the fourth general conference of ICOM in 1956. The commission met in Denmark and Sweden in July 1956, and published a declaration in 1957 that was approved at the fifth general conference of ICOM in 1959. The Association of European Open-Air Museums was established in 1966, and was responsible for the framing of a revised declaration that was adopted at the thirteenth general conference of ICOM in August 1983. The declaration defines an open-air museum as 'a scientifically planned or directed or scientifically supervised collection, illustrating settlement, building, living and economic patterns, presented as entities in the open air in a dedicated part of the landscape, which is declared to be museum ground'. It is acknowledged that most such institutions are ethnographic or folk museums, and that most consist of buildings that have been moved. The declaration includes standards to be applied in moving buildings.

The educational effectiveness of open-air museums is widely acknowledged. They are attractive to the public and can convey an understanding of the past that can be gained in few other ways. Such museums can decline rapidly if funding for their maintenance is insufficient, and some Scandinavian museums, chiefly smaller examples, are visibly decaying. Some would argue that the existence of an open-air museum makes it more difficult to preserve buildings *in situ*, since developers may offer to such a museum structures that they wish to destroy. Purists argue that the archaeological integrity of a structure is totally destroyed if it is uprooted from its social and economic surroundings.

Many open-air museums preserve important evidence of domestic textile manufacture, hand metalworking, the leather trades and millwrighting. Upper Canada Village (*see* ONTARIO) includes a woollen mill with SPINNING MULES. Relatively few are directly concerned with the industrial heritage (*see* IRONBRIDGE; MICHIGAN; WUPPERTAL), and it seems doubtful whether the open-air museum as defined above will be an effective means of conserving the larger-scale monuments of late nineteenth and twentieth century industry.

BIBLIOGRAPHY
General
Ahrens *et al.*, 1984; Peate, 1948; Zippelius, 1974.
Specific
Selected Living Historical Farms, Villages and Agricultural Museums in the United States and Canada. Smithsonian Institution, Washington DC: Association for Living Historical Farms and Agricultural Museums.

BARRIE TRINDER

opencast mining   *See* STRIP MINING.

open-hearth furnace   A method of making mild steel developed by Sir WILLIAM SIEMENS, an alternative to the BESSEMER process. Siemens developed several types of regenerative furnace, with the aim of achieving economies in fuel consumption. In France in 1863 Pierre-Émile Martin (1824–1915) used one of his furnaces to make steel. Siemens patented the open-hearth process in 1866, and in 1869 opened a works at Landore, Swansea, making seventy-five tons of steel a week. Iron was melted in a hearth, fired from the opposite ends by coal gas, or, in more recent times, by oil. The waste combustion gases passed from the hearth through a range of refractive regenerators *en route* to the flue. When the direction of firing was reversed, the combustion air would be preheated by passing through the regenerators before mixing with the fuel. A second set of regenerators would be heated as the waste gases passed out of the hearth, and would be used in turn to heat combustion air when the direction of firing was again reversed. Fluxing materials used included limestone, fluorspar or iron ore. An open-hearth furnace, like the Bessemer process, could be used for either phosphoric or non-phosphoric irons, by the use of a basic or acid lining. An open-hearth process worked less rapidly than the Bessemer process, but it was easier to control precisely the carbon content of the steel. The Siemens-Martin process takes its name from Sir William Siemens and Pierre Martin, and is a term sometimes used to denote any form of open-hearth steelmaking: it should strictly be confined to a particular form of the process in which wrought iron or steel scrap formed part of the charge. An open hearth plant is preserved at MUNKFORS where the first steel from a regenerative furnace was made in 1864.

BIBLIOGRAPHY
General
Gale, 1969, 1971; Schuhmann, 1984.

MARIE NISSER and BARRIE TRINDER

Oporto (Porto), Douro Litoral, Portugal   The second city of Portugal, frequently known as 'the capital of work', Oporto is located on the right bank of the River Douro. It is the entrepôt for the external trade of the area, and the centre for the export of port wine. It has 450 000 inhabitants.

Oporto has a long industrial history, and remains of its early manufactures are to be seen everywhere. From the nineteenth century such districts as Bonfim, Campanhã, Massarelos, Lordelo do Ouro and Francos have been engaged in such industries as textiles, ceramics and metallurgy. Some buildings of that period remain, among them the pottery works of Massarelos, which is partially in ruins although retaining two conical kilns, one of the plants of the important metallurgical company Companhia Aliança, the woollen factory of Lordelo do Ouro, and the metal smelting works of the Companhia Aurifícia. Development has led to the destruction of many industrial buildings, particular Oporto's huge textile mills and foundries. The first iron-framed building in Portugal, the Oporto Crystal Palace, designed by the English architect T. Dillen Jones for the International Exhibition of 1865, was pulled down in the 1950s. Other iron-framed build-

Figure 103 A barge conveying barrels of port wine, moored in the shade of the two-decked Luiz I Bridge of 1886 on the River Douro at Oporto
Douglas Stoddart

ings remain, among them the Ferreira Borges Market of 1888, recently renovated as a council exhibition gallery, and the 'Pátio das Nações', a remarkable framework over the cloister of the Pálacio da Bolsa, designed by the Portuguese architect Tomas Soler in 1882. The two iron bridges over the Douro are the outstanding monuments of the industrial era in the city. The Maria Pia Bridge of 1877 has a 344 m (1129 ft.) deck for a railway track, 60 m (200 ft.) above the river, and enabled its designer, GUSTAVE EIFFEL, to gain the experience that later enabled him to

build the Garabit viaduct in France. The Luiz I Bridge, opened in 1886, has two decks for road traffic, with two spans of 392 m (1286 ft.) and 174 m (571 ft.). It was designed by T. Seyrig, and built by the Belgian company, Societé Willbroeck of Brussels, replacing an iron suspension bridge of 1843 of which two granite columns remain on the right bank of the river. In 1870 the council of Oporto gave a concession for an urban railway line from Boavista to Foz to what became in 1873 the Companhia Carril Americano do Porto à Foz (Oporto–Foz American Tram-

536

way Company), and at the same time allowed others to establish the Companhia Carris de Ferro do Porto Oporto Tramway Company to develop tramways within the city. In 1878 the 'americanos', the animal-powered carriages on the Boavista line, were replaced by cars pulled by Henschell locomotives. The two companies merged in 1893 and the first experiments with electric traction were carried out at the turn of the century, with the building of a power station at Massarelos, a building which has recently been renovated. At its peak the tramway network extended for 80 route km (50 mi.), but most of the lines have been dismantled. The huge tram depot is at Boavista.

São Bento railway station of 1915, planned by the Marques da Silva, has a remarkably elegant iron and glass 'marquise' (awning), as well as a large waiting room with tiles by Jorge Colaço, portraying the evolution of transport.

Important buildings relating to public utilities include the Freixo power station, and the pioneering water pumping station of 1886 at the mouth of the River Sousa, 8 km (5 mi.) SE.

The British Factory House by the River Douro, built in 1785, which includes a club as well as commercial offices, symbolized the close relationship with England that developed through the port wine trade.

Matosinhos, 6 km (4 mi.) NW, is a centre of the canning industry, whose commercial harbour (the Leixões harbour), constructed by Denderni, Duparchi & Co. between 1884 and 1892, is the most important in northern Portugal for the export of manufactured goods and port wine. It possesses two remarkable 50-ton CRANES, built by the French company Fives-Lille in 1888 and employed in the construction of the harbour and, until recently, in the operation of the port (*see* figure 33).

Vila Nova de Gaia on the south bank of the Douro has had important ceramics factories since the eighteenth century, as well as remarkable warehouses, some of eighteenth-century date, belonging to companies exporting port wine. The new wine is brought in casks to the warehouses in April, and left there for maturing and blending before shipment abroad. The Companhia Geral da Agricultura e Comércio dos Vinhos do Alto Douro, trading as the Royal Oporto Wine Company, was founded by royal charter in 1756 by King D. José I, under the auspices of the Marquis of POMBAL (1699–1789). Its museum contains many historical documents relating to the company and to the port wine trade in general, as well as oil paintings of D. José I and the Marquis of Pombal. At Crestuma, 16 km (10 mi.) SE of Oporto, there have been textile factories since 1857, among them one founded in 1890 by Augusto Moraes, inventor of the 'Moraes differential', the patent of which was purchased by John Hetherington & Sons of Manchester.

BIBLIOGRAPHY
Specific
Cordeiro, J. M. L. *Património Industrial de Matosinhos* (The industrial heritage of Matosinhos). Matosinhos: Câmara Municipal.
Cordeiro, J. M. L. A Indústria Conserveira em Matosinhos (The Matosinhos fish canning industry). Matosinhos: Câmara Municipal, 1989.

Martins, F. Subsídios para a História da Fábrica Cerâmica do Carvalhinho. In *Gaya*, II, 1984.

LOCATIONS
[M] Museum of Ethnography and History, Largo de São João Novo 11, Oporto.
[M] Royal Oporto Wine Company Museum, R. Azevedo Magalhães, 314, Vila Nova de Gaia.

JOSÉ M. LOPES CORDEIRO

oral history Some historians of industry have always made use of oral evidence, but its employment on a scientific basis for historical studies is a relatively recent development in most countries, which has arisen principally through the availability of cheap and effective tape recorders. Substantial and well-documented archives of recordings are now held by numerous institutions. Many contain evidence that relates to industrial history, whatever the original purposes for which they were collected. The principal collections in Britain are at the Universities of Essex and Lancaster.

BIBLIOGRAPHY
General
Evans, 1956, 1970; Humphries, 1981; Roberts, 1984; Thompson, 1978.

LOCATIONS
[I] Centre for North-Western Regional Studies, University of Lancaster, Bailrigg, Lancaster.
[I] Oral History Society, National Sound Archive, 19 Exhibition Road, London SW7 2AS.

Örebro, Örebro, Sweden A town at the centre of the heavily wooden region of Närke, which was completely rebuilt after a fire in 1854. The town's industrial history is illustrated in the Technical Museum, where there are important displays relating to nail manufacture and food packaging.

At Pershyttan, 24 km (15 mi.) NW of Örebro, are the scattered remains of an ironworks established in the fourteenth century, including a charcoal store, the headstock of an iron-ore mine, an 11 m (36 ft.) diameter water wheel, and a rod run to convey power from it to the pumps at the head of the mine shaft. The blast furnace on the site was completely rebuilt in 1896, modernized in 1940, and worked until 1953.

A museum of agricultural history at Karlslund, 5 km (3 mi.) W., has large collections of tractors and other farm machinery, as well as a working corn mill.

LOCATIONS
[M] Landbruksmuseet (Agricultural History Museum), Kvarnen, Karlsland, 705 90 Örebro.
[M] Örebro Läns museet (Provincial Museum), Engelbrektsgatan 3, 702 12 Örebro.
[M] Tekniska museet (Technical Museum), Hamnplan 1, 702 12 Örebro.

Oregon, United States of America Dominating the state's few industrially-inclined museums are the artefacts of the logging, deep-sea-fishing, shipping and rail-transport industries that have directed Oregon's non-agricultural economy. Oregon's lumber and fishing trades have also supported secondary industries, in woodworking machinery manufacture, and shipbuilding.

A string of lighthouses along Oregon's rocky coast occupy some of the most treacherous, wave-swept shoreline on the continent. Vicious tides, rock outcroppings, and the cold currents of the North Pacific have kept the island lighthouses relatively safe from the vandalizing and scrap removal that plague sites in more hospitable surroundings.

In the shadow of its traditional raw materials industries on the surface of the earth and beneath the sea, Oregon emerged in the mid-twentieth century as the nation's principal source of native nickel.

The state's great bisecting waterway, the Columbia River, has been host to the largest hydro-electric system in the world found along a single river. Fifty-five installations, beginning with the 375 m (1230 ft.) wide concrete Bonneville Dam in 1937, have been bringing electrification to much of the Pacific North-west. Benneville's fish hatchery of 1936, adjacent to the dam, pioneered the mitigation of the negative effects of dam construction on fish breeding, and is today a principal tourist attraction.

The imposing McCullough Bridge of 1936, which spans Coos Bay in southern Oregon with two sweeping steel cantilevers, joins a fine assortment of early-twentieth-century bridges of steel, timber and concrete throughout the state. The Bridge of the Gods, built across the Columbia River in 1926, borrows structurally from the QUEBEC and FORTH cantilever spans in its use of steel in a remote mountain setting.

BIBLIOGRAPHY
Specific
LaLande, J. M. Sojourners in search of gold: hydraulic mining techniques of the Chinese on the Oregon Frontier. In *IA*, XI, 1985.

LOCATIONS
[M] Collier Logging Museum, Route 2, Box 450, Chiloquin, OR 97624.
[M] Columbia River Maritime Museum, 1792 Marine Drive, Astoria, OR 97103.
[M] Oregon Electric Railway Museum, Glenwood, Forest Grove, OR 97116.

DAVID H. SHAYT

ore hearth   A furnace for smelting lead ore, in which the ore and the fuel were mixed. Sometimes the same hearth was used for calcining ore. The fire was blown with bellows, which were usually water-powered. The fuel is usually WHITE COAL or a mixture of peat and charcoal. By the nineteenth century the part of the furnace where smelting took place was usually a cast-iron box, typically measuring 58 cm × 53 cm × 30 cm (23 in. × 21 in. × 12 in.), contained within a small brick or stone stack. The ore hearth was probably in use in Germany by the sixteenth century. Some were still operating in the late nineteenth century in England, where the best surviving example is at Froggatt Wood, 13 km (8 mi.) SW of Sheffield.

BIBLIOGRAPHY
General
Clough, 1980; Kiernan, 1989; Percy, 1861; Stratton and Trinder, 1988.

organic compounds   Organic chemistry deals with hydrocarbons (compounds of carbon and hydrogen) and their derivatives, usually obtained from COAL or PETROLEUM. For the main articles dealing with organic compounds, *see* ASPHALT; BENZENE; BITUMEN; BUTANE; CREOSOTE; DETERGENTS; ETHANOL; ETHENE; ETHYNE; KEROSENE; METHANAL; METHANE; METHANOL; METHYL BENZENE; NAPHTHA; PARAFFIN; PHENOL; PHENYLAMINE; PROPANE; PROPENE; SOLVENT. Chemicals are referred to by the IUPAC nomenclature. Older names are cross-referenced.

Oroszlány, Komárom, Hungary   A coal-mining centre in the Vértes Mountains, 80 km (50 mi.) W. of Budapest, which has grown rapidly since World War II. Recent extraction has been largely by strip mining but mine No. 16, which operated between 1940 and 1971, has been preserved. Surface installations, including the electrically-worked headstock, the ventilation machinery, the control room and the engine room, have been retained. The museum has displays on the history of mining in the region, and on mines rescue services.

BIBLIOGRAPHY
General
Kiss, *et al.*, 1981.

LOCATION
[M] Mining Museum of Oroszlány, 16-os akna, H-2840 Oroszlány.

Oslo, Norway   The Norwegian capital is situated where the Aker river flows into the Oslo fjord. A town called Oslo was founded about AD 1050 on the east bank of the river. After its destruction by fire in 1624 a new settlement was laid out on the west bank by King Christian IV of Denmark, which he named 'Christiana'. The city was known by that name until 1925.

Until the nineteenth century Oslo was a small city by the standards of other European capitals, its population in 1800 being little more than 20 000. It grew rapidly during the course of the century, reaching 40 000 by 1860, and exceeding 150 000 thirty years later. Its present population is about half a million. The city is very dispersed, with a low population density. Its suburbs are linked by several tramways, of which the steeply-graded Holmenkollbanen, equipped with matchboard-sided cars built for the 1952 Winter Olympics, is the most notable.

Until the nineteenth century Oslo was a largely wooden city, and suffered several destructive fires. Few old buildings survive in the central business district, which is dominated by stone and stucco-fronted buildings of the late nineteenth century, mostly in a classical style derived from German schools of architecture.

The textile industry set the pattern for the industrialization of Oslo. The first cotton factories were established in the 1840s at Sagene on the Aker river to the north of the

Figure 104 A single-storey wooden cabin in Sandakerveien at Sagene on the eastern side of Oslo; the house must have been completed before 1857, when the construction of wooden dwellings in Oslo was forbidden. It is surrounded by apartment blocks in the neo-Classical style typical of those built in Oslo in the late nineteenth century.
Barrie Trinder

city. By 1855 there were seven water-powered mills in the vicinity. By 1865 there were 1507 textile workers in Oslo, more than 40 per cent of the city's industrial labour force. The Sagene area had many of the characteristics of an urban fringe before the 1840s, with sawmills and artisan workshops mixed with the villas of wealthy citizens. The Nedre Vøien spinning mill was built in 1845 and replaced after a fire in 1859 by a larger building of 1860 designed by Olof Nicolai Roll. It was further enlarged in the 1870s, and in 1897. Roll was also the architect of the Hjula weaving mill, built in 1855. He received his architectural training in Hanover and both buildings conform to the Rundbogen style, with steeply stepped gables. In 1873 the Hjula complex was enlarged to incorporate adjacent farm and papermill buildings, and in 1889 a single-storey extension accommodating 112 looms was added. The cotton mills have been adapted as offices, apartments and a restaurant. Many adjacent buildings provided evidence of the history of the community, among them an eighteenth-century farmhouse which was converted into apartments for skilled English workmen; a three-storey, five-bay wooden block of 1848, which contained twelve apartments and is galleried with external staircases at the rear; and some later tenements of brick. By the 1890s the surrounding area was covered with three- and four-storey apartment blocks in the Classical style. Amongst them survive some single-storey cabins dating from before 1857 when the construction of timber dwellings was prohibited in Oslo, as well as apartment blocks of the 1920s in the International Modern style. The area around the mills became a corridor between the outer surburbs and the city centre by 1900, and housing standards fell as workmen moved to better dwellings elsewhere. After a period of neglect it now has a

prosperous air, and is one of the best places in Europe in which to gain an understanding of the complex process of urban growth.

During the second half of the nineteenth century Oslo also developed an engineering industry, the first Norwegian steam engine being constructed in 1850 by the Myrens Mekaniske Verksted company, just north of the textile mills of the Aker valley. The buildings of the 1870s are the earliest structures surviving of this concern which was best known for its sawmilling equipment. The Akers Mek Verksted, established near the West station in 1854, was particularly concerned with shipbuilding, and closed in the early 1980s. Thunes Mekaniske Verksted, best known for its railway locomotives, ceased work at the same time, and its extensive workshops still line the railway to Drammen.

The Kunstindustrimuseet, established in 1877, contains collections from many Norwegian factories, including the Herrebø Faience factory (*see* HALDEN).

The Norwegian Folk Museum (Norsk Folkemuseum), founded by Dr Hans Aall in 1894, opened its collection of re-erected buildings on the island of Bygdoy in 1902. Houses are grouped by regions, and the collection illustrates well the long, unbroken traditions of Norwegian peasant life, particularly the making and decoration of such wooden items as chests and corner cupboards, and the domestic manufacture of linen. Industrial buildings include a late nineteenth-century fulling mill from Nordfjord; an eighteenth-century sawmill from Hardanger; a drying kiln for grain, flax and hemp, and a potter's workshop from Østfold; two corn mills; and several lumbermen's huts. The Old Town, a distinct part of the Museum illustrating urban history with buildings drawn chiefly from Oslo itself, includes seventeenth-, eighteenth- and nineteenth-century artisans' houses, an early twentieth-century grocer's shop, and the Norsk Farmasihistorisk Museum, comprising the furnishings of several pharmacies, including one from the 1920s organized for large-scale production. Ten mileposts, some in cast iron, are scattered through the Museum.

The Norwegian Museum of Science and Technology (Norsk Teknisk Museum), founded in 1914, moved in 1986 to a specially designed building adjacent to Kjelsas railway station on the north side of the city. The various galleries are devoted to 'Energy', 'Telecommunications', 'Road Transport', 'Aeronautics', 'Industry and Society' and 'Science and Industrial Development'. The Museum is involved with the preservation of industrial monuments throughout Norway, and has a large archive and library.

BIBLIOGRAPHY
General
Engh and Gunnarsjaa, 1984; Hoel Malmstrom, 1982; Lie and Opstad, 1976.

LOCATIONS
[M] Kunstindustrimuseet Oslo, St Olvavsgt.1, 0165 Oslo 1.
[M] Norsk Folkemuseum (Norwegian Folk Museum), Museumsveien 10, Bygdoy, Oslo 2.
[M] Norsk Sjofartsmuseum (Norwegian Shipping Museum), Bygdoynesvn.37 0286 Oslo 2.
[M] Norsk Teknisk Museum (Norwegian Museum of Science and Technology), Kjelsasveien 143, 0491 Oslo 4.
[M] Norsk Vegmuseum (Norwegian Road Museum), c/o Vegdirktoratet, p.b.6390 Etterstad, 0604, Oslo 6.

BARRIE TRINDER

Osmund iron A form of wrought iron made in Sweden from the Middle Ages. Osmund iron is a product of pig iron refined in an Osmund forge. The bedrock ores of Central Sweden are very rich, with low phosphorus and sulphur contents, but are dense and impossible to reduce except in BLAST FURNACES. In the Osmund forge the pig iron was converted to wrought iron or steel. The bloom was hammered to a cake and cut into pieces called Osmund, the weight of 24 pieces being exactly one Swedish pound (at that time 6.8 kg), so that the theoretical weight of each piece was 283 g. One Osmund was worth one Swedish penny. The first known reference to the word Osmund is in a British text of 1280, when 48 Osmunds were equal in weight to 30 lb., and worth one English shilling or two Swedish öre. Osmund iron was exported from Sweden from the thirteenth century to the sixteenth, when Osmund forges came to be superseded by forges with larger furnaces and HELVE HAMMERS producing wrought iron in the form of bars.

BIBLIOGRAPHY
General
Björkenstam and Fornander, 1985; Ekman *et al.* 1987; Hildebrand, 1987; Rogers, 1850–66; Tylecote, 1986.

MARIE NISSER

Ostend (Oostende, Ostende), West Vlaanderen, Belgium A fishing port and packet station from which the ferry service to Dover, England, was established in 1846. There are warehouses of concrete construction dating from 1906. The imposing baroque railway station dates from 1912–13. The de Smet de Nayer Brug (bridge) over the channel between the inner and outer harbours is a triple-hinged truss bridge of 1905, with ornate decorative ironwork, and columns at each corner. The tramways to De Panne and Knokke-Heist extend along almost the entire length of Belgian coastline. There are many interesting buildings of the 1920s and 30s along the coast, including a concrete motorcar showroom on a corner site at Blankenberge; the ART DECO Hotel de Sablon at De Panne; and the Hotel Bellevue, a rotunda at Middelkerke. There is a fishing museum at Knokke-Heist.

BIBLIOGRAPHY
General
Viaene, 1986.

LOCATIONS
[M] Heemkundig Museum (Local History Museum), Feest en Cultuuraleis, Wapenplein, 8400 Ostend.
[M] Heemkundig Museum Sincfala Voor Polder en Visseri (Sincfala Local History, Polders and Fishing Museum), Pannestraat 140, 8390 Knokke-Heist.

Österby bruk, Uppsala, Sweden *See* DANNEMORA.

Ostrava, North Moravia, Czechoslovakia The centre of iron-ore and coal mining for plants at Vítkovice, Třinec and Kuncice. The area is contiguous with the ironworking region of UPPER SILESIA. The first adit for coal was opened in 1782 and the first shaft sunk to 500 m (1600 ft.) in 1832. There is an open-air museum of coal mining, set up by the local mining company, and a town museum at the Anslem shaft in Ostrava. There are also plans for an underground museum of mining history with new adits, due to open *c.*2000: the museum will also include the mine administration block, the director's house, the pithead baths, working engineering shops, a headstock, and an engine house of 1914 which lacks its winding engines. A power station of 1894 called Carolinium, now without its machinery, houses a museum store. An educational trail takes in two hundred adits and shafts.

Vítkovice ironworks was founded in 1828. Puddling began in 1831, when a rolling mill was constructed. Coke smelting was introduced here for the first time in the Czech lands in 1836, though it was not until after its introduction at Kladno that the iron industry developed on a large scale. Vítkovice, together with Kladno and Třinec, was an important centre for innovation in the industry, partly owing to aristocratic entrepreneurship, and the concentration of resources in a large plant. The BESSEMER converter was introduced in 1866. There is still a large ironworking plant at Vítkovice. A steel arch suspension road bridge of 90 m (300 ft.), constructed at Vítkovice in 1913, joins 'Silesian' and 'Moravian' Ostrava.

BIBLIOGRAPHY
General
Dusan, 1984; Jeníček, 1963; Komlos, 1983.

LOCATION
[M] Museum of the Vítkovice Ironworks, Zamek VZKG, Vystavni c.99, Ostrava-Vítkovice.

JUDITH ALFREY, SIMON DERRY and TIM PUTNAM

Otis, Elisha Graves (1811–61) The pioneer of the ELEVATOR, Otis was born in Vermont. He became a mechanic at a bedstead concern at Bergen, N.J., which later moved to Yonkers, N.Y., where Otis devised a device for the company's new factory which prevented the elevator from falling if the rope broke. He established at Yonkers a workshop which built elevators, but it employed only twelve at the time of his death. The Otis Elevator Co. was largely the creation of his son, Charles Rollin Otis (1835–1927), who patented a new form of elevator brake in 1864.

Ottawa, Ontario, Canada   The settlement of Bytown, at the confluence of the Gatineau, the Ottawa and the Rideau rivers, established by the engineer of the RIDEAU CANAL, became the Canadian capital after confederation in 1867. The imposing style of the government buildings was matched by that of the Château Laurier, a hotel built by the Grand Trunk Railway. The city is linked to HULL LANDING in Quebec by several bridges, most notably by the Alexandra Bridge, a cantilever structure of 1900.

The National Museum of Science and Technology has large displays on communications, including a highly imaginative television section, and other sections on railways, power and energy, horse-drawn transport, and mechanical engineering. The Museum's landmark is a cast-iron lighthouse which stood on Cape North on Cape Breton Island from 1908 until 1980.

The National Aviation Museum, located in modern purpose-built premises, has a rich collection of airliners, including a Canadair Argus 1, a Canadair North Star, a Boeing 247D, a Lockheed 10a Electra and two Douglas DC3s. Special attention is given to the pioneering of bushflying by Canadian aviators.

LOCATIONS
[M] Canadian Museum of Civilization, 100 Laurier Street, Box 3100, Station B, Hull, Quebec, Canada J8X 4H2.
[M] National Aviation Museum, PO Box 9724, Ottawa Terminal, Ontario, K1G 5A3.
[M] National Museum of Science and Technology, 1867 St Laurent Boulevard, Ottawa, Ontario K1A 0M8.

DERYCK HOLDSWORTH

Oturehua (Rough Ridge), Otago, New Zealand   A settlement 100 km (60 mi.) NW of Dunedin. The 'Windmill Works' engineering shops were established by Ernest Hayes in 1895, making cutters for cutting pollard, a poison in strip form used for killing rabbits. A stone workshop was erected in 1908 and subsequently extended. Power was provided by windmill from 1905, and a larger mill erected in 1910. This was replaced in 1927 by a Pelton water turbine which remains in use, powering forty-seven drive shafts. One of the company's celebrated products was its

Figure 105   A characteristic farm windmill manufactured by the company established in 1895 by Ernest Hayes at Oturehua, Otago, New Zealand
Geoffrey Thornton, New Zealand Historic Places Trust

farm windmill. The original mill of 1912 remains at the works, which is now in the care of the New Zealand Historic Places Trust.

BIBLIOGRAPHY
General
Thornton, 1982.

Oudenaarde (Audenarde), West Vlaanderen, Belgium Oudenaarde is an ancient town on the Scheldt (Schelde), 24 km (15 mi.) SW of Ghent, long associated with the textile industry, the outstanding monument of which is the Gevaert mill in J. Lacopsstraat, an ornate polychrome-brick structure now adapted as offices and a library. Gabled workers' housing nearby dates from *c.* 1905. Oudenaarde railway station, an eccentric adaptation of RUNDBOGENSTIL, with a massive clock tower, dates from *c.*1900. A museum of the CIRCUS is located in the town.

BIBLIOGRAPHY
Specific
Industrielle Archeologie in de Vlaamse Ardennen (Industrial archaeology in the Flemish Ardennes). Ghent: VVV, 1987.

LOCATIONS
[M] Circusmuseum (Circus Museum), Broodstraat 24, 9700 Oudenaarde.
[M] Stedelijk Museum (Town Museum), Markt 1, 9700 Oudenaarde.

Outokumpu, Pohjois-Karjalan lääni, Finland   Copper was found at Outokumpu in eastern Finland early in the twentieth century by the German-born geologist Otto Trüstedt (1866–1929), and mining began in 1913. Significant output commenced in 1927–8, and most of the buildings associated with the mine date from this period. For a time Outokumpu was among the most important copper mines in Europe, but output has slackened and its many subsidiary mines have been exhausted in recent years. Outokumpu's mining museum was opened in 1982, with exhibition areas in old mine buildings, including the winding room, the crushing plant and the headstock tower. The museum portrays the development of mining and prospecting in Finland, and the establishment and everyday life of mining communities.

LOCATION
[M] Outokummun kaivosmuseo (Outokumpu Mining Museum), Outokummun Matkailu Oy, Sepänkatu 6, SF-83500 Outokumpu.

oven   *See* KILN.

Owen, Robert (1771–1858)   A factory master, philanthropist, pioneer of co-operation, and the founder of British Socialism, Owen was one of the most influential figures of the Industrial Revolution. Born in Newtown, Wales, he became a partner in the Chorlton Twist Co. in Manchester, which in 1799 acquired mills at the village of NEW LANARK which Owen managed, with great success. He married the daughter of the founder of the settlement, David Dale (1739–1806). In the second decade of the nineteenth century Owen established the Institution for the Formation of Character at New Lanark, and in speeches and pamphlets drew attention to the educational and social ideals he was applying. His proposals for 'villages of unity and co-operation' were particularly influential. At least sixteen Owenite colonies were set up in the USA, and during 1825–8 Owen himself was involved with New Harmony, Indiana, which had originally been established by followers of the German Protestant George Rapp. Seven Owenite settlements were established in Britain, the most important being at Orbiston, 3 km (2 mi.) N. of Motherwell, Scotland, which lasted from 1825 to 1829, and Harmony Hall, Queenswood, East Tytherley, 22 km (14 mi.) NW of Southampton, England, which operated from 1830 to 1845, with a large and luxurious communal building,

constructed to the designs of JOSEPH HANSOM. Owen withdrew from the New Lanark partnership on his return to England in 1829, established the Grand National Consolidated Trade Union in 1833–4, and propounded his views through the *New Moral World* between 1834 and 1841.

BIBLIOGRAPHY
General
Bestor, 1950; Cole, 1953; Cullen, 1910; Garnett, 1972; Harrison, 1969; Hayden, 1976; Owen, 1972.
Specific
Haworth, A. Planning and philosophy: the case of Owenism and Owenite socialism. In *Urban Studies,* XIII, 1976.

BARRIE TRINDER

Oxford, Oxfordshire, England   A university city and an inland port. Some houses survive at Fisher Row of the boating community, originally concerned with upstream navigation on the River Thames, but from the opening of the Oxford Canal in 1790 with canal boats.

The University Press, Walton Street, by David Robertson, built in 1826–30, is an outstanding example of Classical style applied to an industrial building. The University Museum, by Benjamin Woodward (1815–61) of 1853–9, is remarkable for the combination of Gothic tracery in wrought iron with exquisite stonework. The Ashmolean Museum has important collections of English seventeenth- and eighteenth-century ceramics. Marlborough Road, Grandpont, follows the route of the line to the original GWR station of 1844, and the nearby Hinksey pools were created by excavations for railway ballast. The LNWR station at Rewley Road, by Fox & Henderson in 1851, now a tyre depot, has a cast-iron frame similar to that of Crystal Palace. There is a polychrome brick power station building of 1893 in the western suburb of Osney. The University Surveyor's office in Tidmarsh Lane, converted from a malthouse in 1956, is an early and much commended example of adaptive reuse. A music hall in the Cowley Road has been converted to a publisher's offices.

Oxford has been transformed in the twentieth century by the motor industry. William Morris (1877–1963), later Lord Nuffield, moved from a cycle shop at 48 High Street to a purpose-built garage at 21 Longwall Street in 1910, and assembled the first Bullnose Morris there in 1912. In 1913 he began to build cars in the Oxford Military College, Cowley (the college being by T. G. Jackson (1835–1924), of 1877–8), and from 1914 in an adjacent 'tin shed'. The works was extended in 1920s and 30s. Morris's original showroom at 36–7 Queen Street moved to Morris Garages (now law courts) in St Aldates in 1932.

BIBLIOGRAPHY
General
Collins and Stratton, 1986; Prior, 1982; Victoria History, 1979.

LOCATIONS
[M] Ashmolean Museum of Art and Archaeology, Beaumont Street, Oxford OX1 2PH.

[M] The Museum of Oxford, St Aldates, Oxford.

[M] The University Museum, Parks Road, Oxford OX1 3PW.

BARRIE TRINDER

oxygen (O)   A gaseous element identified in 1771 by CARL SCHEELE (1742–86) and in 1774 by JOSEPH PRIESTLEY (1733–1804), of major importance in many modern industrial processes, particularly in metalworking (see LD PROCESS). A process for manufacturing oxygen by heating barium monoxide (BaO) to 540 °C, when it absorbed oxygen, which it released when further heated to 870 °C, was discovered by Jean-Baptiste Boussingault (1802–87) in 1851, and patented and developed in England by the brothers Brin, who kept the temperature at a constant 650 °C, effecting the release of oxygen by changing pressures. The Brins established the British Oxygen Co., which set up manufacturing plants in the principal British cities. From 1896 oxygen was obtained by the fractional distillation of liquid air, using the Linde process of 1902 and the Claude process of 1906, and by the ELECTROLYSIS of water.

BIBLIOGRAPHY
General
Morgan and Pratt, 1938; Partington, 1950.

Oyonnax, Ain, France   The 'Union Electrique' factory known as 'La Grande Vapeur' at Oyonnax, 35 km (21 mi.) E. of Bourg-en-Bresse, was built *c*.1905 in order to make electricity available to small-scale craftsmen producing celluloid combs. The craftsmen hired individual workshops inside the factory, their machines being linked by belt transmission to the building's main engine shaft.

The mechanization of comb production dates from the 1850s when horn began to replace boxwood as the raw material. New machines were used to cut the teeth and grooves and to sand the finished products. The energy required for this early mechanization exceeded the region's water-power capacity, and in 1865, in order to prevent their industry from leaving Oyonnax, the comb producers formed their first co-operative, the Société du Moteur Industriel, ou Grande Vapeur (the Industrial Motor Company, or the 'Great Steam'). The power of a single steam engine was distributed through 56 cell workshops, housing some 280 groove cutters and polishers. The 'Union Electrique' factory, erected in 1905, was thus a renewal of a well-tested organizational model.

The electricity came from the Saint-Mortier hydro-electric power station on the River Ain, 25 km (15 mi.) N. of Oyonnax, which opened in 1901. The new factory was specifically designed for the production of celluloid combs, this material having replaced horn from the 1880s.

Some elements of the first 'Grande Vapeur' building of 1865 still survive, now housing a cinema. The factory of 1905 remains entirely intact, although production there was gradually abandoned from the 1940s. It is the work of an architect from Saint Claude, A. Chanard (1878–1934), and belongs to the first generation of reinforced-concrete structures. Its ground plan is in the form of a letter 'V', each of the two wings housing thirty individual cell workshops on two storeys. The tower at the centre houses the administration. The flat roof has an original system of water tanks connected to the cells in order to be able to put out fires as rapidly as possible. The building is a protected monument in which it is planned to open a comb and plastics museum.

BIBLIOGRAPHY
Specific
Chanal, P. 'La Grande Vapeur': Usine de l'Union Electrique, 1905. Étude de faisabilité (The Grande Vapeur factory of Union Electrique, 1905: reuse feasibility study).
Dyvrande, B. L'Eau et l'industrie dans la région d'Oyonnax (Water and industry in the Oyonnax region). In *Revue Géographique de l'Est*, 1954.

JEAN-FRANÇOIS BELHOSTE

oyster   The mollusc *Ostrea*, which breeds in stony-bottomed stretches of shallow sea water, has long been regarded as a delicacy. Oysters are gathered with nippers, tongs or dredges. Pickled oysters were being traded in lots of as many as a hundred barrels in early eighteenth-century England, where the traditional sources were the beds near Colchester and Whitstable. By 1900 the chief sources were France, where the culture of oysters was pioneered from the 1860s, and the USA, where 50 000 worked in the industry, which was centred around the Chesapeake Bay. Oyster reservoirs where hauls from beds could be stored pending favourable market conditions were constructed at Ostend and Hasum in Schleswig-Holstein, among other ports. Discarded shells from oyster packeries were used for LIME and as road metal.

Many oyster-fishing vessels are preserved in the USA.

See also PEARLS.

BIBLIOGRAPHY
General
Brouwer, 1985; Ingersoll, 1881.

P

packet boat A packet was originally a vessel plying at regular intervals between two ports for the conveyance of mails, particularly diplomatic dispatches, as well as goods and passengers Vessels from Holyhead, Wales to Howth, Ireland, were called packets by the early seventeenth century, and by 1800 monthly packets were sailing from England to India. The first privately-owned packet line between North America and England was established in 1816, with three ships sailing in rotation. Steamships operating transoceanic services tended to be called LINERS, but the term packet was retained for cross-channel services, until superseded by FERRY.

The sailing packet *Charles Cooper* of 1856 survives in the FALKLAND ISLANDS.

The word 'packet' was also applied to passenger boats on canals like the coches d'eau working in France by the 1740s. Passenger travel on British canals continued for over a century after it commenced on the Bridgewater Canal in 1766, and the carriage of passengers was also important in Scotland, in Ireland (*see* GRAND CANAL), and in the USA.

BIBLIOGRAPHY
General
Baker, 1965; Brouwer, 1985; Bucknall, 1957; Hadfield, 1986; Head, 1968.
Specific
Malet, H. The packet boat age: a study in sources and resources. In *JRCHS*, XVII(2) 1981.

BARRIE TRINDER

packhorse A horse that carries freight on its back, in pannier baskets (most commonly used for minerals), in leather pack saddles, or tied to its harness (as with pieces of cloth). In eighteenth-century England an average load might be 560 lb. (254 kg). A packhorse was normally muzzled to prevent wayside grazing, and the leader of a team might have a collar fitted with bells. One such collar is displayed in Bankfield Museum, HALIFAX. Many bridges for packhorses were built in the PENNINES in 1660–1740, one of the best being at Oxspring, 18 km (11 mi.) NW of SHEFFIELD.

BIBLIOGRAPHY
General
Dyos and Aldcroft, 1969; Edwards, 1988; Hey, 1980.

paddle steamer The first working paddle steamer and the first practical STEAMSHIP was the *Comet*, designed by Alexander Hart, which pulled two 70-ton barges on the Forth & Clyde Canal in Scotland in 1802. The *Clermont* (from 1808 the *North River*), designed by Robert Fulton (1765–1815), began commercial operation on the Hudson River in the USA in 1807. The *Comet* (*see* IRVINE), designed by Henry Bell (1767–1830), which began operation as a tug between Glasgow and Greenock, Scotland, in 1812, was the first to work commercially in Europe. The *Margery* (later the *Elise*) was the first on the River Thames in 1814 and the first to cross the English Channel two years later. The *Rob Roy* in 1821 began the first regular steam service between Dover and Calais. The *Savannah* crossed the Atlantic in 1819, using its paddles to supplement its sails; but the *Sirius*, which just beat BRUNEL's *Great Western* across the ocean in 1838, was the first vessel to do so using sustained steam power. Paddle steamers on European rivers and lakes did much to stimulate economic growth in the early and mid-nineteenth century, while those used on American rivers like the Hudson and the Mississippi, where 125 were employed between New Orleans and Pittsburgh as early as 1825, were essential in the opening up of new areas for settlement. Stern paddlewheels were adopted instead of side wheels on the Mississippi from *c*.1850. Paddle steamers also played an important role in opening up the interior of Australia, particularly on the Murray River.

From the 1860s, ocean-going paddle steamers were largely replaced by vessels using SCREW PROPULSION, the last paddle-driven transatlantic liner being a French vessel delivered in 1865, but paddle tugs, ferries and excursion vessels continued to be built well into the twentieth century.

Many historic paddle steamers remain in use, including a fleet of five, the earliest of 1901, on Lake LUCERNE, in addition to the *Rigi* of 1847 which is preserved; a fleet of eight plus a preserved vessel on the Elbe at DRESDEN; and five preserved and two working vessels on the Murray River, SOUTH AUSTRALIA. In the USA the *Belle of Louisville* of 1914 is the last sternwheel paddle steamer active on the Mississippi. The *Hjelen* of 1861 works on the SILKEBORG, Denmark, lakes; the *Skibladner*, built at Motala in 1856, on Lake Mjøsa in Norway (*see* EIDSVOLL); the *Motala Express* of 1895 on Lake Wettern, Sweden, and many vessels on the Finnish lakes. The *Gisela* of 1872 sails on the Traunsee, Austria (*see* GMUNDEN), and the *Schonbrunn* of 1912 at Vienna. The 693-ton *Waverley* of 1947, the last seagoing paddle steamer, operates cruises from many British ports. The 673-ton *Trillium* works from TORONTO, while the 994-ton *Sicamous* of 1914 is preserved at Penticton, British Columbia.

See also figure 79.

BIBLIOGRAPHY
General
Andrews, 1976; Baker, 1965; Brouwer, 1985; Burtt, 1934; Dumbleton, 1973; Hambleton, 1948; Parsons and Tolley, 1973; Spratt, 1958, 1968.

LOCATION
[I] Waverley Steam Navigation Co., Anderston Quay, Glasgow.

BARRIE TRINDER

paint 'Liquid vehicles which hold in suspension solid colouring matters or pigments, so blended that such mixtures can be evenly applied to surfaces for protective or decorative purposes.' The liquids so used before 1950 were principally TURPENTINE or turpentine substitute, or LINSEED OIL. Benzene, petrol, naphtha or shale oils were used as thinners. In water-based paints pigments were compounded with water and SIZE or other adhesives. Gums, which are soluble in water, and resins, which are not, were used to confer hardness. The manufacture of resins began in Britain *c.*1790, but by the 1930s most such materials were developed from coal tar. The availability of material derived from petrochemicals has transformed paint-making since 1945. Lacquers based on nitrocellulose were extensively used from the 1920s. In the eighteenth century most paint would have been made up by the painters who were to apply it, but specialist manufacturing concerns were established in the nineteenth century.

BIBLIOGRAPHY
General
Mander, 1955; Morgan and Pratt, 1938; Smith, 1901.

Paisley, Strathclyde (Renfrewshire), Scotland Paisley, with adjacent parts of Eastern Renfrewshire, comprised Scotland's cotton-spinning centre. Hand weaving is represented by a hand-loom cottage in Kilbarchan, 8 km (5 mi.) W., built for a linen weaver, later a cotton weaver, in 1723, and now cared for by the National Trust for Scotland. Other hand-loom shops survive, some with external stairs.

The oldest surviving spinning mill in Scotland is in Johnstone, 6 km (4 mi.) W.: the Old End Mill is a six-storey building, with wooden floors and cast-iron columns, built in 1787, and now a bootlace factory. Nearby Cartside Mill, Milliken Park, is a fine six-storey mill of 1792, with Venetian windows. The Barbush linen thread mills of Finlayson, Bousfield & Co. include a cut-down fireproof mill, and some mid-nineteenth-century mills that once employed two thousand and are now in multi-occupation.

In Lochwinnoch, 14 km (9 mi.) SW, the 5 m (13.7 ft.) high arch dam survives from the Calderpark Mill of *c.*1790; and a wing of 1837 of Calderhaugh Mill, later a silk mill, is being converted to flats.

Broadlie Mill at Neilston, 8 km (5 mi.) S., was begun in 1790, rebuilt fireproof *c.*1850 and is now a tannery. Crofthead Mill was founded in 1792 but rebuilt in the late nineteenth century as two large, whitewashed, Oldham-

type (*see* LANCASHIRE) five- and six-storey deep fireproof mills which are still operated. The late-nineteenth century Netherplace dye works, originally used for bleaching, is also still operational.

Paisley was famous for its shawls, first of silk and then of cotton, woven to Indian-inspired Jacquard patterns. Paisley Museum has a large collection of shawls and a resident hand-loom weaver.

The world's biggest thread-spinning company was a combination in 1896 of Clark & Co., Anchor Mills, founded in 1812, and J. & P. Coats, Ferguslie Mills, founded in 1826. Operations have contracted to the Mile End Mill of 1899, with copper-clad towers and a huge chimney. The remainder of Anchor Mills is being developed into a business centre with seventy small concerns housed in the wooden-floored Old Shawl Factory of *c.*1840. The most striking block is the Domestic Finishing Mill of 1886, a five-storey polychrome brick cube, with concrete floors and a light well. Ferguslie Mills, once Britain's grandest cotton-mill complex, employing five thousand in 1890, has been less fortunate. The colossal concrete-floored, five-storey No. 1 spinning mill of 1886 has been vandalized; it was more ornate (in a French Renaissance way) and more advanced than any Lancashire mill. Some gatehouses, the counting house, the ornate half-timers' school of 1887 (now a wine bar), and the last stretch of the Glasgow, Paisley & Ardrossan Canal of 1806–10, remain here.

Abercrombie's polychrome brick Nethercommon Carpet Works, now apartments, dates from 1911–12. The Abercorn Ropeworks of 1884 was the last working ropewalk in Scotland. Still operating are the louvred Seedhill Tannery, and the Soho Engine Works of Campbell & Calderwood, which has a cast-iron frame of *c.*1880. At Johnstone, once a notable centre for machine tools, the simple brick Empress Works remains in production. Johnstone also has what is probably the only mouse-trap factory yet converted into apartments.

Municipal enterprise in Paisley is represented by the gasworks, with a fine cast-iron gasholder; and Black Hall Street electric power station, which worked between 1889 and 1930. Gilmour Street station was rebuilt in the 1890s behind its Tudor crenellated front of 1837. A railway bridge at Blackhall was originally an aqueduct built *c.*1810 by JOHN RENNIE for the Glasgow, Paisley & Ardrossan Canal.

The most colourful art deco building in Scotland, on the road from Glasgow to Renfrew Airport, is the now derelict India of Inchinnan tyre factory, designed by Wallis Gilbert, architects of the Hoover factory (*see* LONDON) in 1929–30. It has a sleek, white, two-storey pilastered façade with green, orange and black tiled details, fronting a former aircraft factory of 1916.

BIBLIOGRAPHY
General
Hume, 1976; McKean, 1987.

LOCATIONS
[M] Paisley Museum and Art Gallery, High Street, Paisley, Strathclyde PA1 2BA.

[S] Weaver's Cottage, The Cross, Kilbarchan, Paisley, Strathclyde.

MARK WATSON

Palladian An architectural style based on the work of the Italian architect Andrea Palladio (1518–80), the first great professional architect, which was revived in Italy, England, Germany and the Netherlands in the eighteenth century. It was employed in English country houses from c.1720, and subsequently in some TEXTILE MILLS modelled upon them.

BIBLIOGRAPHY
General
Guinness and Sadler, 1976; Palladio, 1570; Tann, 1970.

Pampailly, Rhône, France Silver was mined at Pampailly, 30 km (18 mi.) W. of Lyons, from the end of the fourteenth century, and mine accounts survive for the years 1455–6, after the king had confiscated the mine from its owner, the financier Jacques Coeur. Exploitation ceased before 1525, but was revived on a limited scale between 1764 and 1772. Since 1980 the shafts and galleries have been systematically explored, the tooling forge has been excavated, and the reduction and refining installations have been located.

BIBLIOGRAPHY
Specific
Benoit, P. L'Évolution d'un paysage minier et métallurgique, Pampailly au XVe siècle (Evolution of a mining and metalurgical landscape, fifteenth century Pampailly). In *Annales de Bretagne et des Pays de l'Ouest*, XCVI, 1989.

Pamplona, Navarre, Spain The ancient capital of the kingdom of Navarre, which was demoted to the status of a province only in 1841. Its principal industrial monument is the Noain Aqueduct which conveys water a distance of 14 km (9 mi.) into the city. The first project to achieve this object, by means of pipes, was proposed by François Gency in 1774 but rejected. The municipal authorities then approached the architect Ventura Rodriguez (1717–85), who took charge of the project in 1780 and completed it within ten years. The aqueduct includes a 97-arch, 1245 m (4085 ft.) viaduct. Another part of the aqueduct has been cut by the Navarre motorway. Luis Paret was responsible for the installation in 1788 of neo-Classical fountains at each of the water collection points in the city.

At Orbaiceta, 33 km (21 mi.) NE of Pamplona, is a royal ordnance factory, founded in 1784 by King Charles III, on an old-established ironworking site, well supplied with both minerals and water power. A new industrial colony was created around a square, with workers' dwellings and a church, lying between the iron-ore stores and the blast furnaces and their adjacent casting houses. Water to power the furnace bellows flowed along a stone aqueduct from a reservoir behind an ashlar stone dam. Many of the structures from the factory still remain.

EUSEBI CASANELLES and BARRIE TRINDER

panopticon The name given by the English social philosopher Jeremy Bentham (1748–1832) to a basic design for PRISONS or WORKHOUSES, with ranges of cells or wards radiating from central 'wells': supervisory staff could watch all the inmates or cell doors from one position. The outstanding example was Millbank Penitentiary, London, completed in 1821, but the concept influenced the design of numerous workhouses and other institutions.

Pápa, Veszprém, Hungary A city 180 km (110 mi.) W. of Budapest, celebrated for its textiles. The Kluge-Kékfestő-Textilmúzeum was established in 1962 to display the techniques of indigo-dyeing, in a dyehouse established by Karl Kluge who moved to Pápa from Saxony in 1786. The dyehouse worked until 1957. Most of the equipment is preserved, including a steam engine installed in 1905, a fifteen-vat dye room, and horse-operated mangles. There are museum displays on the printing of textiles.

BIBLIOGRAPHY
General
Kiss *et al.*, 1981.

LOCATION
[M] Kluge-Kékfestő-Textilmúzeum, Március 15 tér 12, H-8500 Pápa.

paper The name given to felted sheets formed by breaking down individual CELLULOSE fibres from rags, straw or wood, and mixing them in water, which is drained off through a screen. Papermaking originated in ancient China, and spread to the West along the Silk Route through Central Asia to the Middle East, reaching the Arab world by the seventh century AD, and Europe during the eleventh century. Its manufacture was of increasing importance after the invention of printing in the 1450s, with Germany, Italy, France and the Netherlands developing significant production capacity. Papermaking began in Britain by the 1490s. The number of papermills in England increased from about one hundred in 1700 to about four hundred in 1800.

Most traditional papermills were water-powered. Paper was made by beating rags in water with wooden STAMPERS or HOLLANDER BEATERS. The resultant pulp or 'stuff' – a dilute solution of less than two per cent fibres – was mixed in vats, which from the eighteenth century might be heated and agitated. The 'vatman' made sheets of paper on a mould, consisting of a wooden frame, the 'deckle', which kept the fibres from draining away with the water. He dipped the mould and deckle together into the vat, scooping up a supply of watery pulp. He then gave the mould a practised shake to set the fibres, and drained away most of the water. The deckle frame was removed, and the mould turned with a quick rocking motion to deposit the wet sheet of paper onto a piece of felt. When a 'post' of 144 sheets of paper and interleaved felts was built up, it would be pressed in a large wooden screw press. The paper then was hung to dry on ropes or poles in a drying loft, where shutters in the exterior walls controlled the air flow. The dry paper was smoothed by pressing with metal plates, and treated with SIZE if to be used for writing. A final finishing step polished the surface with hammers or agate burnishers.

The mechanization of papermaking was achieved by 1800, and machinery in use today still consists of the two basic machine types developed in the first half of the nineteenth century. The FOURDRINIER machine was invented in France in 1798 by Nicholas-Louis Robert (1761–1828) and sold to two English papermakers, Henry and Sealy Fourdrinier in 1801. The Fourdriniers employed BRYAN DONKIN to make numerous improvements. The machine poured liquid pulp onto a continuous web of wire screen, forming a sheet as the water drained away. The newly formed sheet was passed onto a moving felt, pressed between several pairs of rollers, and wound damp into a roll. The Fourdriniers used the machine in their Hertfordshire mill from about 1804, and exported many machines to Europe following their patent of 1807. Quite independently another English papermaker, John Dickinson (1782–1869) developed the cylinder-mould machine, patented in 1809, in which a screen-covered cylinder revolved in and out of the vat, forming a sheet through the action of suction within the cylinder. The cylinder-mould machine is still used for making CARD-BOARD and other types of sheet-formed products. The Gilpin brothers of Delaware copied Dickinson's cylinder-mould machine, and Thomas Gilpin patented it in the USA in 1816, claiming a significant alteration in the suction mechanism. The Gilpins were making paper by machine from 1817. The Fourdrinier machine, first used in the USA at Saugerties, New York, in 1827, was by far the more popular of the two machines.

The USA rapidly adopted papermaking machinery and soon led the world in the production and use of paper, leading to an extreme shortage of rags for raw material. Well into the nineteenth century there was a considerable international trade in rags for papermaking, stimulating even the export of Egyptian mummies for the sake of their linen wrappings. Experiments with substitute pulps had begun in the eighteenth century. Matthew Koops made paper from straw in England in 1800, and straw paper was made in many parts of the USA after 1829, utilizing agricultural waste to make cheap wrapping paper and board. In the 1850s Thomas Routledge (1819–87) of Sunderland, England, began to employ ESPARTO GRASS, which is still used for some grades of paper, but it was the use of wood PULP that transformed the industry in the second half of the century.

Mechanical or groundwood pulp processing reduced wood to pulp by grinding logs against a revolving wet grindstone. The resulting paper, cheap and brittle, was (and still is) used primarily for newsprint. Friedrich Keller in Saxony developed a wood-grinding machine in 1840, which was improved by Heinrich Voelter, a papermaker from Bautzen, Saxony, and displayed at the Crystal Palace in 1851 and at subsequent international exhibitions. A Keller-Voelter-type grinder was exported to Massachusetts where the first groundwood pulp was produced in 1867. Subsequent experiments led to the development of better-quality wood pulp through boiling with various chemicals, primarily using the SODA process and the sulphite process. Hugh Burgess patented the soda process in England in 1852, and in the USA in 1854. Burgess migrated to Philadelphia, where he became manager of the American Wood Paper Company in the 1860s. About the same time two Philadelphia chemists, Richard Tilghman (1824–90) and his brother Benjamin, developed the sodium sulphite process, which was greatly improved and used commercially by the Swedish chemist, Carl Eckman of Bergvik, in the early 1870s. Others further modified and improved the sulphite process.

By 1890 most paper was made from wood pulp, and the focus of papermaking moved to remote water-powered sites, in the vast forest areas of Scandinavia and North America. Large pulpmills could produce wood pulp which could be used to make PLASTICS or SYNTHETIC FIBRES as well as paper. Cheap hydro-electric power made it possible to operate huge papermills in such locations. Mills of this kind receive logs, which are reduced to chips or pulp by grinding against large revolving stones: the pulp is digested under pressure with chemicals; washed and bleached; and made into paper on machines which may be able to produce over a thousand metres a minute.

See also CELLOPHANE; PAPIER MÂCHÉ; and figure 35.

BIBLIOGRAPHY
General
Boorstin, 1973; Clapperton, 1951, 1967; Coleman, 1958; Hunter, 1947; Shorter, 1971; Toale, 1983; Vocabulaire, 1983; Voorn, 1960; Warren, 1980.

BARRIE TRINDER and HELENA WRIGHT

papier mâché Pulped paper which has been shaped, dried and usually japanned or varnished, to make boxes, trays and furniture, of a kind fashionable in the late eighteenth century. The term could also apply to objects made by pasting together thin sheets of paper over a mould. Unvarnished papier mâché is still used for egg cartons.

paprika *Capsicum annuum*, a pepper which thrives in warm temperate climates, is a native of America but is grown particularly in Hungary, where a mill is preserved at SZEGED and where a museum at KALOCSA is devoted to the subject.

BIBLIOGRAPHY
General
Prescott and Proctor, 1937.

paraffin An ambiguous term, first used by Reichenbach in 1830 to apply to the wax-like mixture of hydrocarbons made by distilling wood, coal or petroleum. Paraffin waxes from the crude-oil residue left after CRACKING are used for candles, waterproofing and polishes, and as a source of DETERGENTS. The British candlemakers Price & Co. (*see* PORT SUNLIGHT) began to use paraffin wax in 1855. The series of hydrocarbons that includes METHANE and PRO-

PANE has been known since 1872 as paraffins. In England KEROSINE is often called paraffin.

BIBLIOGRAPHY
General
BP, 1958.

parasol   *See* UMBRELLA.

Paris, France   Already a capital city for the Romans, for Clovis in the fifth century and for the Capetian dynasty between the tenth century and the fourteenth century, Paris developed at an important crossroads of land and water communications, situated near the confluence of the rivers Seine and Marne, at the heart of a rich wheat-growing basin. The strongly centralizing tendencies which characterized not only the governments of the Ancien Régime, but also those of the revolutionary period after 1789, the Empire and the nineteenth-century succession of restorations, the constitutional monarchies, the Second Republic, the Second Empire and the Third Republic, made Paris the undisputed political, administrative, financial, religious and cultural capital of France. The advent of railways in the 1840s – the first line into Paris, from Saint Germain, being opened in 1837 – reflected and strengthened this centralism, the lines radiating from the capital to all corners of what is often called the 'hexagon' of the French mainland. Their existence also helped confirm the city's position as France's industrial capital, although this aspect of Parisian history is rarely featured in guidebooks.

The city acquired much of its present-day physical appearance, and also reached its present-day administrative limits, during the Second Empire (1852–70), a period of prosperity and of far-reaching urban remodelling: 'slum clearance' in the historic centre around the Louvre and Tuileries palaces and on the Île de la Cité; installation of gas and water mains; creation of an efficient network of sewers; new covered markets; new parks, inspired in part by those of London; and broad new avenues cutting through the existing urban fabric to open up access to railway termini, to strategically-located military barracks, to existing monuments like the Arc de Triomphe, and to new ones like the Opéra.

In 1859 the Emperor Napoleon III and Baron Georges Haussmann (1809–91), prefect of the Seine (the department of Paris) and the energetic agent of many of these transformations, decided to have the suburban communes surrounding Paris 'annexed', more than doubling the size of the city. These eleven communes, wholly or partially absorbed, lay between the city's late-eighteenth-century frontier – the line of barriers and tollgates built from 1784 by C.-N. Ledoux (*see* SALINS-LES-BAINS), and the outer ring of fortifications developed at the instigation of King Louis Philippe's prime minister, Adolphe Thiers (1797–1877). The fortifications, essentially a green belt some 400 m (440 yd.) wide and 33 km (20 mi.) long, were abandoned only in 1919. To the north, east and south of the city much of the land freed was used between 1920 and 1936 for the construction of low-cost housing,

'hygienic' buildings of seven or eight storeys, like many of those in central Paris, often with decorative brickwork and faience. Paradoxically, these inter-war municipal housing projects are today less urgently in need of rehabilitation than many post-World War II social housing 'ensembles'. The land recovered from the fortifications was also used by motor vehicles: a broad, tree-lined avenue, which was supplemented from the mid-1960s by a six-lane ring road, the 'périphérique'.

This frontier, thus defined by the defence preoccupations of the 1840s, still clearly separates the city of Paris from its suburbs. Opened from 1900, to coincide with the Universal Exhibition of that year, the capital's first underground railway lines (the 'Métropolitain'), with their seductive ART NOUVEAU entrances designed by the architect Hector Guimard (1867–1942), did not venture outside these limits. Within them, covering 105 km² (40 sq. mi.), are the twenty 'arrondissements' or districts of what is still termed Paris 'intra-muros' (within the walls). Its population of 2 170 000, much the same as at the end of the nineteenth century, is declining today after forty years of stability (at 2 850 000 inhabitants) that ended in 1954. Beyond these limits, covering nearly 2000 km² (770 sq. mi.) and comprising 280 communes, the Parisian metropolitan region is the largest urban agglomeration of continental Europe. With more than ten million inhabitants, 18 per cent of the population of France, the region as a whole accounts for a quarter of French industrial production.

Few industrial sites of importance survive within the city itself. Founded by Jean-Baptiste Colbert (1619–83) in 1667, the famous Gobelins tapestry manufacture at 42 Avenue des Gobelins, in the 13th arrondissement, was installed in a dyeworks opened at the end of the fifteenth century on the banks of the Bièvre – a small tributary on the south bank of the Seine now lost in the sewers – where there was a concentration of such thirsty and polluting activities as tanning, bleaching and starch manufacture. One of several public buildings burned down during the last days of the commune in 1871, the tapestry manufactory was partially and pompously rebuilt in 1913. Several older buildings, associated either with the Gobelins manufacture or with a nearby seventeenth-century broadcloth factory, also survive; they are good examples of the non-specific architecture that the early textile industry could put to use, and of the consequent difficulties faced by those trying to identify such buildings today.

Another survival from the eighteenth century is the monumental and austerely neo-Classical Hôtel de la Monnaie, the mint. It was built from 1768 by Jacques-Denis Antoine (1733–1801) on the quai de Conti – on the left bank in today's 6th arrondissement. The workshop section, modernized and extended during the nineteenth century, continued to mint coinage until 1973, when a new plant was opened at Pessac near Bordeaux. The workshops, like those of the Gobelins, are open to visitors. Medals, decorations, collectors' limited series and the dies for the Pessac mint are still produced in Paris, and the recently renovated museum holds an interesting selection of eighteenth- and nineteenth-century manual and

Figure 106 A small metalworking establishment in the 11th arrondissement in Paris, the Maison Bedu, founded in 1868; the photograph dates from *c*.1905.
Private collection (Paris)

steam-powered coining presses, as well as a curious collection of nineteenth-century medals commemorating various industrial achievements.

The largest industrial enterprise in Paris for much of the nineteenth century, employing more than two thousand workers during the 1880s, was the state tobacco manufacture in the Gros-Caillou quarter in the 7th arrondissement. Partly as a result of the international exhibitions of 1878, 1889 and 1900 – which occupied the nearby Champ de Mars, where GUSTAVE EIFFEL's 300 m (1000 ft.) tower stands as a reminder of the 1889 exhibition – this neighbourhood lost its industrial vocation. After the workshops had been transferred to a new factory in the suburb of Issy-les-Moulineaux, to the west of Paris, the

Gros-Caillou factory was demolished in 1906, the site being developed for luxury residential buildings. A little downstream to the west, at Javel, in the 15th arrondissement, Paris's biggest twentieth-century factory, the main Citroën car plant (see below), was demolished during the 1980s to make way for the universal exhibition of 1989, which in the event was cancelled.

The most extensive industrial site inside Paris today is located to the north at 34 rue Championnet in the 18th arrondissement. Nine hectares (22 ac.) are occupied by the central bus maintenance depot of the RATP, the Paris public transport authority. Half of this site comprises repair shops and a spare parts centre built in 1948. The other half still has the workshops first erected by the

'Compagnie Générale des Omnibus' in 1882 for the construction of omnibuses and tramcars, which were used for making shells and aircraft during World War I. The company used in these shops hollow cast-iron columns and other structural elements recovered after the dismantling of the buildings which housed the international exhibition of 1878.

The rarity of important industrial sites within Paris is a reflection not only of the capital's present-day concentration on the tertiary sector of the economy and of its high land values, but also of the traditional nature of Parisian industry which is essentially small-scale. Far from natural mineral resources, the city's industrial strength has always resided in its abundant skilled labour, engaged primarily in satisfying an enormous, fashion-conscious consumer market with a broad range of basic necessities and luxury items – many of the latter, including clothing accessories, buttons, fans, umbrellas, artificial flowers, straw hats and combs, being known, significantly, as 'Paris articles'.

Although the comparisons are by no means straightforward, statistics for 1847–50 and 1896 reveal in each case that not more than one enterprise in ten employed more than ten workers; and less than one per cent employed more than a hundred workers. The abstract statistical analysis of the capital's evolving industrial geography has yet to be complemented by detailed surveys of the built vestiges of Parisian industry. Small workshops, each occupying half-a-dozen skilled workers, often located at the ends of closed courtyards or down passages behind residential blocks on street frontages, constitute a heritage that is rarely spectacular and often fragile. The outer arrondissements, particularly those to the east – the 11th for example, which is still host to a multitude of small metalworking concerns, or the faubourg Saint-Antoine, astride the 11th and 12th, centre of furniture-making since the fifteenth century – still have large numbers of such workshops and small urban factories. Art galleries, advertising agencies and computer-assisted architects are increasingly their present-day occupants, however, particularly in the newly-glamorous Bastille neighbourhood, in the brightly-lit shadow of the new Opéra house.

The close intermixture of living and working space has an original architectural manifestation in the rue des Immeubles industriels (the street of industrial buildings), located at the eastern end of the faubourg Saint-Antoine in the 11th arrondissement. This group of nineteen more or less identical buildings, occupying both sides of a short street completed in 1873, was designed by the architect E. Leménil (1832–1913). It was apparently a speculative venture, boasting none of the collective service elements that might place it in a fourierist (*see* FOURIER, CHARLES) tradition. The ground floor and mezzanine level, with a cast-iron structure left visible on the street, comprised workshop spaces; the four floors above, in brick and stone, constituted the living quarters. In 1881 the street had two thousand inhabitants. Power was distributed throughout the workshops from a 200 hp steam engine located in the basement, with the boilers beneath the back courtyard. This group of buildings has recently been given statutory

protection, though neither the engine nor the original belt transmissions are extant.

French industrial development had other effects on the capital than the appearance and disappearance of various forms and sites of production. The first iron bridge in Paris, the Pont des Arts between the Louvre and the Collège des Quatre Nations, seat of the French Academy, was built in 1801–3, and rebuilt in steel, with one arch less, in 1980. It is a precocious continental example of the use of a new and still costly structural material, increasingly employed from the 1820s in a broad variety of architectural programmes. The iron-and-glass covered shopping arcades ('passages') – of which many fine pre-Haussmannian examples survive, particularly in the 2nd and 9th arrondissements, on either side of the 'Grands Boulevards' – offer one of the more acceptable faces of nineteenth-century French capitalism, and also a structural foretaste of the subsequent programme of covered-market construction. The Halles Centrales, the central market built from 1853 under the direction of Victor Baltard (1805–74), was one of the earliest and most frequently imitated of the iron-and-glass 'umbrellas'. The widespread regret that followed its demolition during the summer of 1971 – one of the pavilions was kept and rebuilt at Nogent-sur-Marne, a suburb to the east of Paris beyond the Bois de Vincennes – probably helped to preserve several others of the thirty-one specialized or general market halls built in Paris up to the 1880s. Five of these, including the Marché du Temple of 1863–5 in the 3rd arrondissement and the flower market of 1874 on the Île de la Cité in the 4th arrondissement, are still functioning today; whilst nine others have been adapted, with more or less respect for their structures, for new uses. The vast cattle market hall at La Villette (see below), built by Baltard & Janvier in 1864–8 and recently transformed by the architects Robert & Reichen into a flexible congress and exhibition centre, emerges as one of the more successful examples of adaptive reuse.

Iron structures, often concealed behind more decorous stone façades, are to be found in many other nineteenth-century Parisian buildings. These are often prestigious public edifices, including libraries, such as Sainte-Geneviève in the 5th arrondissement, built by Henri Labrouste (1801–75) in 1844–50, or the National Library in the rue de Richelieu in the 2nd arrondissement, built by the same architect between 1858 and 1868, and department stores, such as Le Printemps of 1881–5, with extensions of 1907 and 1921, or the Samaritaine, in the 1st arrondissement, near the Pont Neuf opposite the Monnaie. The last is a metal-framed building with late Art Nouveau features, built between 1905 and 1910 by Frantz Jourdain (1847–1935); it was concealed in 1924 behind a more staid stone-faced extension designed by H. Sauvage (1873–1932). Amongst museums, the most notable example is probably the zoology gallery of the Museum of Natural History in the 5th arrondissement, built between 1877 and 1889 by Labrouste's pupil Jules André (1819–90). It is presently undergoing a renovation programme which can but put an end to the cavernous and dusty poetry of the place, closed to the public for over twenty years. A handful of churches also have metal structures, most notably the Saint-Eugène church in rue Sainte-Cécile in the 9th arrondissement, built by L. A. Boileau (*see* MONTLUÇON), with polychromatic cast-iron columns and Gothic-style cast-iron tracery in the windows. The sparser, more 'functional' Notre Dame du Travail (Our Lady of Labour) built by Jules Astruc in 1892–1902, is located in the 14th arrondissement, behind the Montparnasse railway station.

To turn from places of worship to railway stations – those other cathedrals of the nineteenth century – is logical, stations also fronting their vast metallic sheds with urban façades, stone buildings inspired by the architectural styles of the day. The Parisian selection of main-line stations covers the period from the late 1840s up to the present day, represented by the recent transformations for the use by TGV (très grande vitesse) trains of the 1990s of the nondescript Montparnasse station of the early 1970s. The earliest surviving main-line station is the Gare de l'Est, whose western half dates from 1847–52. Two exuberantly ornate stations built with the 1900 Universal Exhibition in mind also survive: the Gare de Lyon, in the 12th arrondissement, and the Gare d'Orsay near the heart of the city, opposite the Tuileries gardens on the left bank in the 7th arrondissement. This station was transformed from 1984 to house a new museum of nineteenth-century art. The Gare du Nord in the 10th arrondissement, built by J. I. Hittorff (1792–1867) between 1863 and 1865, may also be singled out for special mention. In 1861, the façade of the first station on the site was transferred, stone by stone, to Lille, where it is still a recognizable part of that city's station. Hittorff's edifice has a remarkable train shed with four rows of cast-iron columns, curving out at the summit in neo-Gothic brackets which support the central nave, structured with trusses of the type conceived in 1837 by Camille Polonceau, and used in many other train sheds, notably those of the Gare de l'Est. The monumental stone façade of the Gare du Nord is something of a Second Empire masterpiece, replete with erudite classical quotations and twenty-three female figures by thirteen eminent sculptors, representing the principal towns and cities served by the Nord railway company.

Architects designing public service buildings, such as waterworks and electricity power stations and sub-stations between 1895 and 1911, often made more unshamed use of the structural possibilities of metallic construction. Since the recent dismantling of the water-pumping station of 1888 by the Pont d'Austerlitz in the 12th arrondissement (the engine house of which, built to pump water 6 km (4 mi.) from the Seine to a reservoir on Montmartre, is supposedly to be rebuilt in the gardens at La Villette), one of the most interesting edifices of this sort is the factory, at 13 quai de la Gare in the 13th arrondissement, of the SUDAC company, which was established to distribute compressed air. Built in 1891, the factory had three halls, the central one, still intact, housing the generators for compressed air. They were originally installed by an Austrian engineer and entrepreneur, Victor Popp, to send uniform time impulses to

several of the capital's public clocks and to a host of other time-conscious private subscribers. The building, with steel framework, diagonal latticework reinforcements and brick-and-glass infill, has a stained-glass panel of the arms of Paris set in its main façade. Its pneumatic clock has been removed. Despite the building's imposing chimney and extensive infrastructural 'roots' – several hundred kilometres of air conduits installed for the most part in sewers, and subsequently serving many industrial functions other than time-keeping – it is unlikely to survive the redevelopment planned for this neighbourhood, a 130 ha (320 ac.) site upstream on the Seine, behind the Gare d'Austerlitz, earmarked for the glass towers of the new national library.

Where the suburbs of Paris are concerned, their period of industrial growth coincides with the century between 1860 and 1960. Development was so intensive in some of the communes near Paris that the terms 'suburb' and 'industry' easily became synonymous: in 1890, 90 per cent of the Plain of Saint Denis, immediately to the north of Paris, was occupied by industrial users. Although the division between Paris and its suburbs is palpable on the ground and in public transport, their segregation in economic and industrial terms is clearly artificial. A centrifugal movement, which gained momentum at the time of the 'annexation' of 1860, saw space-hungry industries moving out from the city to the new territories of the 'first crown', the ring of communes surrounding the fortifications. Often keeping office and sales buildings inside Paris, these companies were joined at their new suburban addresses by a roughly equal number of newly-created enterprises, giving rise to industrial 'corridors' largely determined by water transport: on the Seine, both downstream and upstream towards the Marne, and around the right bank canal and dock system, the Villette port, and the canals of the Ourcq, Saint-Denis and Saint-Martin, opened between 1802 and 1826. Up to the end of the 1880s rail transport played a less decisive role, local industrial requirements, particularly for freight depots, being largely ignored by the five major railway companies. An exception which underlines this rule is the 'Industrial Railways Company' at Saint-Denis. In 1884 this company was authorized to link up with the networks of the Nord and Est companies. A web of private sidings, still in private hands, opened up the Plain of Saint-Denis both to heavy industry, particularly metallurgical and engineering concerns, and to an extensive warehouse domain, spread over the communes of Saint-Denis and Aubervilliers at the gates of Paris, between La Chapelle and La Villette. More than ninety buildings, dating for the most part from between 1884 and 1903, are still in use here, some of them for their original entrepôt purposes.

Along with the attraction of easier communications and readier availability of cheaper square metres, Napoleonic legislation dating from 1810, concerning a broad range of insalubrious, incommodious or dangerous activities, was another factor contributing to the general movement of industry out of the capital. Intended to isolate the most dangerous of these activities from existing residential zones, the legislation authorized the creation of factories only after detailed administrative enquiries, which are rich sources where archives have survived. Authorization was in fact rarely refused – in less than 5 per cent of cases at the turn of the century – and the legislation did nothing to prevent housing from creeping up to the factories once they had been opened.

By 1900 industrial production in the suburbs had overtaken that of Paris, which was practically encircled by an industrial belt, interrupted only to the west by residential Neuilly and the Bois de Boulogne. Some suburban communes were relatively specialized, many chemical industries, for example, concentrating in the northern surburbs of Aubervilliers and La Courneuve – the backyards, so to speak, of the La Villette slaughter-houses, source of many raw materials. At the beginning of the twentieth century the communes on either side of the Seine to the west of Paris, already home to such luxury industries as perfumery and coach-building, became the main centres of the new, high-technology industries like aircraft construction, mechanical and electrical engineering, and motorcar manufacture, all stimulated by World War I. Other communes – Montreuil to the east, for example, a prolongation of the furniture-producing faubourg Saint-Antoine – had more traditional and diversified industrial activities, a diversity that became more widely characteristic as electrification and the growth of road transport between the wars freed many industries from earlier locational constraints. The main road heading out of Paris to Le Bourget, site of an international airport dating from 1919 and now used for air shows and for an AIRCRAFT MUSEUM, became a new industrial corridor during the inter-war years.

Starting in the late 1950s, partly as a consequence of government efforts to relocate industry away from the capital into the 'desert' of the French provinces, but mainly as a result of the deeper structural transformations generally known as 'the crisis', the Paris suburbs entered a period of industrial decline, particularly dramatic in the 'first crown' of communes industrialized during the nineteenth century. The now definitive end of motorcar manufacture in the Paris region (see below), accompanied by mushrooming office development in the surburbs to the west around La Défense, is symptomatic of this evolution. Elsewhere, it leaves dense and complex urban tissues spotted with decaying or abandoned factories and punctuated by even more problematic monumental ruins, such as those of the huge coal-fired power stations of the first half of the twentieth century – that at Saint-Denis, on the Seine, for example, dates from 1905 and 1933 and was closed in 1981; and the one-time 'most powerful power station in the world' at Vitry-sur-Seine, to the south-east, built in 1932 by J. A. Arrighi de Casanova and the architect G.-H. Pingusson, closed down in 1980.

It is impossible to single out all the important industrial sites in the Paris region. The industrial heritage has so far been recorded and studied only in a relatively piecemeal fashion. One reminder of the need for recording is the rate of change: of 115 varied sites identified in an inventory made in 1985 of the factory architecture of five communes along the Seine immediately to the south-east of Paris, eleven disappeared during the survey, and another twenty-four prior to the publication of its results in 1988. Throughout the Paris region zones of abandoned industrial buildings are still too easily labelled and then cleared as 'friches industrielles' (industrial wastelands) before being adequately recorded and thought about as industrial heritage.

Motorcar manufacture

Until recently, Paris was one of Europe's principal motorcar manufacturing centres. Situated astride the Seine 3 km (2 mi.) downstream from the city centre are the Renault car plants at Boulogne-Billancourt, which at their greatest extent during the 1950s covered nearly 100 ha (260 ac.) and employed up to 40 000 people. Founded in 1898 by Louis Renault (1877–1944) and his two brothers, the firm became the leading motorcar manufacturer in France within ten years thanks largely to big contracts for Parisian and London TAXIS, which brought with them the organization and economies of mass production. World War I brought further growth, with the area of workshops more than doubling to meet state orders for shells, aircraft, aero-engines, lorries, artillery, tractors, ambulances, and, from 1917, light tanks. With this diversification came greater, Ford-inspired vertical concentration, pursued by Renault throughout the 1920s and 30s. As well as cars, in a broad range of models, the Billancourt plant produced its own machine-tools, its own bricks and even its own paper.

In January 1945, shortly after Renault's death, the enterprise was nationalized, soon coming out with its popular '4CV' model, designed during the war, and in 1952 inaugurating its first 'decentralized' factory at Flins, Yvelines, 42 km (27 mi.) W. of Paris on the Seine. The 'Régie Nationale des Usines Renault' became a showcase enterprise, much analysed by sociologists and acquiring a symbolic importance in contemporary French social history on a par with its industrial and commercial pre-eminence: 'when Renault sneezes', it used to be said, 'France comes down with a cold'.

For the industrial archaeologist, the Billancourt site today offers a heterogeneous catalogue of factory architecture and construction techniques from 1898 up to the 1980s. The oldest building, the tool shed at the bottom of his parents' garden where Louis Renault knocked together his first car around a De Dion Bouton tricycle motor, is piously preserved amidst the trees in front of a two-storey brick office block of 1917, which now houses the firm's voluminous archives and photographic library. The most recent addition, the '57 Metal Shop', with its strikingly post-modern and cost-ineffective north-lit roofs was inaugurated in 1984.

Most of the workshop buildings date from World War I and the 1920s, although many were hastily rebuilt after bombing by the Royal Air Force in March 1942. The site grew in sporadic bursts as the market developed in France and abroad, and as new property could be acquired around Billancourt. The Île Seguin, more than 1 km long and 150 m (165 yd.) wide, was purchased in patient stages from 1909. The level of the island had to be raised

Figure 107   An aerial view of the Renault motorcar factory at Boulogne-Billancourt, Paris, taken in 1948: the earliest workshop, dating from 1898, still stands amidst the trees visible between the buildings on the right bank (Billancourt); the Île Seguin, in the foreground, was entirely covered with workshop buildings between 1928 and 1947, while the main five-storey building in the middle of the island dates from 1928 to 1930.
Renault

by 6 m (20 ft.) above the level of the floods of 1910 before it could be entirely covered with new buildings. Most notable among these is a coal-fired power station at the western tip of the island, built in 1928 and reclad in a late 'paquebot' (packet-boat) style in 1949. In the centre of the island, between the two bridges linking it to Billancourt to the north and to Meudon to the south, a five-storey reinforced-concrete structure, 225 m × 28 m (738 ft. × 92 ft.), erected in 1929, housed production lines for chassis assembly, body building and mounting, painting and finishing, and upholstery. A two-tiered covered track ran around most the island for testing finished vehicles.

The Île Seguin workshops are still in use but the Régie has announced its intention to close them in 1992. Some of the buildings on the Billancourt mainland will probably be retained for office use, but the extensive foundries and forge buildings have already been demolished, as has the old aircraft works, the 'O' factory, closer to Paris on the quai du Point du Jour. The closure of the 'workers' fortress' of the Île Seguin will mark the end of a tradition of motorcar manufacture in Paris and its suburbs that goes

back to the early 1900s when France briefly led the world in this quintessential twentieth-century industry.

Other emblematic motorcar sites have already bitten the dust. André Citroën (1878–1935), Renault's meteorically successful rival during the 1920s and 30s, came to car production only after World War I, during which, like Renault, shell manufacture had afforded him an apprenticeship in the organization of mass production. Occupying 19 ha (47 ac.) at Javel, on the Seine in south-western Paris, Citroën's was the largest factory ever seen within the capital. In six months in 1933 it was entirely rebuilt, the better to accommodate assembly-line production. These buildings were abandoned in 1974 and demolished in 1983, soon to be followed by other Citroën factories in the Parisian suburbs. The forge and foundry works at Clichy in the northern suburbs of Paris, built in 1924–6, were demolished in 1989, at the same time as the Citroën plant at Levallois-Perret, another suburb on the Seine, 2 km (1 mi.) NW of the centre of Paris.

This last factory, acquired by Citroën in 1921, and used from 1949 until 1989 for assembling the well-known

'2CV', dated from 1897 and was one of the earliest purpose-built motorcar factories in the world. It was constructed for Gustave Adolphe Clément (1855–1928), known as Clément-Bayard, a self-made tycoon who started, characteristically, as a bicycle manufacturer before going on to motorcars, motorcycles, aeroplanes and dirigibles. His association in 1902 with the Earl of Shrewsbury and Talbot lay behind the construction of the Clément-Talbot automobile works in Barlby Road, Notting Hill, London. Despite its very different, lavishly Edwardian street façade, the formal layout of this factory of 1903, in particular its rectangular trial track running around the roofs of the NORTH-LIT SHEDS, is clearly a direct copy of the now-demolished Levallois works.

Museums

Paris boasts two technical museums, one dating from the end of the eighteenth century, the other opened in 1986. The Musée National des Techniques (National Technical Museum) goes back to a decree of October 1794 which created a national conservatory of arts and trades ('Conservatoire National des Arts et Métiers'), which was conceived as a public repository for 'machines, tools, models, drawings, descriptions and books relating to arts and trades of all kinds'. It opened in 1799 in the former Saint-Martin-des-Champs priory, already having absorbed the collection of machines gathered or built since 1746 by the mechanic Jacques Vaucanson. Other collections came to enrich the holdings: those of the clockmaker Fernand Berthoud (1727–1807) and of the chemist Antoine Lavoisier (1743–94); the archives and artefacts previously held by the Academy of Science; and objects from successive international exhibitions. Up to the 1880s the conservatory was involved with the patent system, and its collections were considerably increased by inventors depositing their scientific instruments and machines, or models of them.

The collection today numbers nearly 80 000 items, dating mainly from the nineteenth century and the early twentieth century. About eight thousand objects are on permanent display in a succession of thematic rooms: textiles, clockmaking, mechanical engineering, energy, photography. Alongside its collection of objects the conservatory has a rich archive of drawings of industrial subjects, including, in particular, Vaucanson's industrial portfolio of the eighteenth century, and the nineteenth-century drawings of Le Blanc and Armengaud, teachers at the industrial drawing school which ran courses at the conservatory until 1874.

The new 'Cité des Sciences et de l'Industrie' at La Villette, opened on the site of the former meat market and abattoir near the canals of Saint-Martin and the Ourcq to the north-east of Paris, also holds collections of machines and scientific instruments, relating particularly to computer science, telecommunications, robots and printing. Some two thousand objects form the basis of a collection used for temporary exhibitions either at the Cité or elsewhere.

See also figures 90, 121.

BIBLIOGRAPHY
General
Bergeron, 1989; Bonnefous, 1987; Bowie, 1987; Chemetov and Marrey, 1976; Cinqualbre *et al.*, 1988; Daumas, 1976; Fourcaut, 1988; Fridenson, 1972; Garrioch, 1986; Gille, 1990; Hatry, 1982; Hillairet, 1963, 1972; Laux, 1976; Lemoine, 1986; Schweitzer, 1982; Sutcliffe 1970, 1983.

Specific
Actes du IXe colloque national sur le patrimoine industriel (Transactions of the Ninth National Congress on the Industrial Heritage), In *L'Archéologie industrielle en France*, xx, 1991.
Baruch-Gourden, J.-M. Un inventaire du patrimoine industriel bâti dans la banlieue nord de Paris, Aubervilliers, La Courneuve; repères méthodologiques (An inventory of the built industrial heritage in the northern Paris suburbs, La Courneuve and Aubervilliers; methodological implications). In *L'Archéologie industrielle en France*, xiv, 1987.
Cinqualbre, O. and Cohen, Y. L'Usine de la grande série; Citroën, quai de Javel (The mass-production factory Citroën, quai de Javel). In *Monuments Historiques*, cxxxiv, 1984.
Fridenson, P. L'Usine Renault de Flins (The Renault factory at Flins). In *Monuments Historiques*, cxxxiv, 1984.

LOCATIONS
[M] Cité des Sciences et de l'Industrie, 30 avenue Corentin-Cariou, 75930 Paris.
[M] Conservatoire National des Arts et Métiers (National Conservatory of Arts and Crafts), 270 rue Saint-Martin, 75003 Paris.
[M] French Postal Museum, 34 boulevard de Vaugirard, 75015 Paris.
[M] Museum of Air and Space, Le Bourget Airport, 93350 Le Bourget.
[M] Museum of the Cinema, Palais de Chaillot, Place de Trocadéro, 75016 Paris.
[M] Museum of Materials, Palais de Chaillot, Aile, 75016 Paris.
[M] Museum of Urban, Interurban and Rural Transport, 60 avenue Sainte-Marie, 94160 Saint Mandé.
[M] Museum of the Wood Industry, Bois de Vincennes, Route circulaire sud, 75000 Paris.
[M] Société d'Histoire du Groupe Renault, Expo-Musée, 27 rue des Abondances, 92100 Boulogne-Billancourt.

PAUL SMITH

park Originally, an area enclosed for hunting, the word came to mean the ornamental surroundings of great houses, including the royal parks of London to which the public were allowed access by the eighteenth century. The first of many parks created at public expense in nineteenth-century cities was laid out at Birkenhead, England, by JOSEPH PAXTON in 1843–7. Late-nineteenth-century parks might have lakes with boating, bandstands and facilities for games, as well as flowerbeds and ornamental trees.

In the USA from the 1870s the word was applied to very large areas subjected to planning constraints on account of their natural beauty. The designation 'national park' has subsequently been applied to sites like Lowell, Mass., of industrial archaeological interest. The concept of national parks has been copied in Canada, the United Kingdom and elsewhere.

Figure 108 The opencast workings at Parys Mountain, Anglesey, where copper mining began in the 1760s; on the horizon is a windmill, once employed in pumping water from the workings.
Barrie Trinder

Parsons, Sir Charles Algernon (1854–1931) Regarded in his lifetime as the most original British engineer since JAMES WATT, Parsons took out more than three hundred patents, and was responsible for the development of TURBINE PROPULSION for ships. He was apprenticed in 1877 to WILLIAM ARMSTRONG at Elswick, Newcastle-upon-Tyne, and from 1884 worked for Clarke, Chapman & Co., makers of dynamos, taking out his first patents for the steam turbine that year. Two hundred turbo-dynamos were made by 1888, chiefly for lighting ships. He established his own company in Newcastle in 1889, and built there the first power station with turbo-generating plant in 1890. In 1894 he set up a company to build steam turbines for ships, demonstrating the *Turbinia* at a naval review in 1897, and providing plant for the *King Edward*, in 1901 the first turbine-driven passenger ship.

Parys Mountain, Anglesey, Gwynedd, Wales From the discovery of copper on Parys Mountain (25 km (16 mi.) NW of Bangor) in 1761 until the early nineteenth century the adjacent Mona and Parys copper mines were the most

productive in the world. Mining began with adits and pits, but opencasting from the 1780s enabled the proprietor, THOMAS WILLIAMS, to command the world copper market. The huge opencast is still an awesome sight, and the colourful soils, impregnated with copper, lead and sulphur, have little vegetation. Remains can be seen of dressing floors where ore was broken by hand, and kilns where it was roasted to draw off sulphur. Green pools exist where copper was precipitated out of water pumped from the opencast by windmill and steam engine. Nearby, at Amlwch, is the harbour from which ore was shipped for smelting in Lancashire and Swansea.

BIBLIOGRAPHY
General
Harris, 1964; Rees, 1975.
Specific
Rowlands, J. *Copper Mountain.* Llangefni, Gwynedd, 1966.

PETER WAKELIN

Paspébiac, Quebec, Canada On the shore of the Chaleur Bay in the Gaspé Peninsula, 600 km (375 mi.) NE of Quebec City, the community of Paspébiac developed between 1800 and 1886 to serve the dried cod industry. During this period merchants from Jersey in the CHANNEL ISLANDS, the Robin and Le Bouthillier families, constructed a hundred or so buildings connected with the landing, conserving and processing of fish: workshops, warehouses and dwellings, with shops and other community buildings. They also encouraged a large-scale migration of Jerseymen from whom were drawn the specialist workers for the shipyards they established, the crews of ships, and the harbourmasters. The native Gaspésienne population was largely confined to fishing, using principally the techniques of the rod and line, the jigger, and the net and tackle.

The companies also established a system of truck trading under which the fisherman could obtain all the goods and equipment necessary for their work at the start of the season, on condition that they paid for it with their catch. These measures, added to other social and economic factors, enabled the Robin and Le Bouthillier families to create in the dried cod trade a virtual monopoly that extended through Europe and the USA.

The site of Paspébiac was partially burned in 1964, and was taken over in 1977 by a local association which is now acting in collaboration with the Quebec government and the municipal authorities to establish an interpretative programme. These developments have led to the restoration of several buildings and their use as a documentation centre on the fishing industry, a library and an exhibition gallery.

BIBLIOGRAPHY
General
Lepage, 1980; Moussette, 1979; Soucy and Roy, 1983.

LOUISE TROTTIER

passementerie A French term, for which there is no precise English equivalent, denoting a variety of braids, cords, ribbons and other trimmings for garments, made from silk, cotton or linen, whose manufacture was a speciality of the BASEL region.

BIBLIOGRAPHY
General
Diderot, 1959.

pasteboard   *See* CARDBOARD.

patent   Originally an open letter, usually from a sovereign, granting a licence or privilege to an individual or group. From *c*.1700 the term was applied to a right of protection granted by government to the inventor of a manufacturing process. The rate of granting of patents has often been taken as a means of assessing the innovatory skills of a particular society. Applications for patents, records of litigation arising from patents, and sometimes models produced to support applications, are prime sources for industrial history. Before the nineteenth century many patents – like granted that to THOMAS SAVERY for a means of 'raising water by fire' – were vaguely worded.

BIBLIOGRAPHY
General
Boehm, 1967; Davenport, 1979; Macleod, 1989.

pattens   *See* CLOGS.

pauper colony   Proposals to create colonies where paupers from cities could be settled on smallholdings, and thus support themselves, possibly with the aid of a measure of manufacturing employment, aroused much interest in Western Europe in the early nineteenth century. ROBERT OWEN in 1817 advocated 'villages of co-operation' with populations of up to 1500, and up to 600 ha (1500 ac.) of land, designed for those who were currently a direct financial burden on the public. In the Netherlands such schemes were put into effect (*see* WILLEMSOORD). While they attracted much attention they were not widely copied, although there was a settlement in Belgium, begun in 1822 when the country was under Dutch rule, at Wortel, 34 km (21 mi.) NE of Antwerp.

BIBLIOGRAPHY
General
Butt, 1971; Macgregor, 1835; Woolf, 1987.

Pavia, Lombardy, Italy   A province, whose main industrial products are related to agriculture, but in which in 1939 over 4000 workers were employed in textiles. The province contains several dramatic structures. The massive brick- and cementworks of C. Palli & Sons at Via 4 Novembre, Bressana Bottarone, was begun *c*.1800 and developed into a formal complex with pedimented gable ends. Several major bridges span the River Po, the finest being the iron trestle structure at Tornello between the city of Pavia and Stradella, 19 km (12 mi.) S., completed in 1912 and ornamented with a heraldic crest and flags in iron. At Vigevano, 35 km (22 mi.) NW, is the Ursus rubber factory, built in 1935–7 with a campanile, and a 2 m (6 ft. 6 in.) Wellington boot over one entrance.

Near the Certoza di Pavia, 8 km (5 mi.) N., a seven-storey turbine-powered flourmill, to the design of Cesare Luzzatto, was built *c*.1886. It has cast-iron columns with wooden beams and was sited for both water and rail transport to Milan. New granaries were built in 1888, and large silos had been constructed by 1900. The expression of the red brickwork and the round and segmental windows follow the idiom of north European commercial architecture. The mill still works and is well maintained.

BIBLIOGRAPHY
General
Negri *et al.*, 1983; Negri and Negri, 1982.

MICHAEL STRATTON

Paxton, Sir Joseph (1801–65)   The designer of the Crystal Palace, the iron, wood and glass structure that housed the Great Exhibition of 1851, and that more than any other building symbolized the importance which manufacturing industry had attained in Britain at that time. In 1826 he became superintendent of gardens at Chatsworth, Derbyshire, the seat of the Dukes of Devonshire, and built there a cast-iron and glass greenhouse. He designed Birkenhead Park, laid out in 1843–7, the first park to be created at public expense. He was a director of several railway companies.

BIBLIOGRAPHY
General
Chadwick, 1961.

Pays d'Auge, Calvados, France   The Pays d'Auge, north of Caen, is a region rich in clay, and tile manufacture is known to have flourished here as early as the fourteenth century. The greatest period of growth of brick- and tileworking dates, however, from the first half of the nineteenth century. Many of the factories were small-scale concerns, catering for a local market and using simple updraught kilns for batch production. The industry witnessed considerable modernization from the 1780s, stimulated by demand from the new seaside resorts along the Normandy coast. Clay preparation was mechanized and Hoffman-type continuous kilns were introduced, in particular at the Fresne d'Argences tileworks, 20 km (12 mi.) W. of Caen.

A few vertical kilns still survive, notably at the Sanneville tileworks, 10 km (6 mi.) E. of Caen, and the Cressonnière brickworks, 20 km (12 mi.) SE of Lisieux. The kiln at the latter was built in 1887, and had two drying chambers and one firing chamber capable of producing batches of 50000 bricks. Hoffman kilns survive with greater frequency, and good examples can be seen at brickworks at Glos (1902), 5 km (3 mi.) SE of Lisieux, and at Beaumont-en-Auge (1906), 20 km (12 mi). NE of Lisieux, and at tileworks of Mesnil at Bavent,

15 km (9 mi.) NW of Caen, and of Ussy (1913), 30 km (19 mi.) SE of Caen.

BIBLIOGRAPHY
Specific
Bernouis, P. Les Tuileries et briqueteries des arrondissements de Caen et Lisieux, XIXᵉ et XXᵉ siècles (Tile and brickworks in the arrondissements of Caen and Lisieux of the nineteenth and twentieth centuries). In *L'Homme et l'industrie en Normandie* (Man and industry in Normandy), *Bulletin spécial de la Société historique et archéologique de l'Orne.* Alençon, 1990.

JEAN-FRANÇOIS BELHOSTE

pea   The pea, *Pisum sativum*, is a highly-regarded vegetable, one of the first to be preserved on an industrial scale, first by dehydration, and subsequently by canning and freezing (*see* REFRIGERATION). One of the earliest preserved buildings associated with pea processing is a sorting shed of 1890 at Heckington, LINCOLNSHIRE. Machines for packeting dried peas are displayed at WIGAN Pier.

Peabody, George (1795–1869)   Born in Massachusetts, Peabody prospered as a merchant and in 1827 moved to London. He financed the US exhibits at the Great Exhibition of 1851, and in 1862 established the Peabody Trust, the most successful of the philanthropic organizations providing apartment blocks intended for LONDON's working class.

pearl   A concretion formed around a foreign body, like a grain of sand, within the shell of a mollusc. Lustrous pearls used in jewellery are found only in molluscs with naturally pearly linings to their shells, notably *Pinctada margaritifera*, the pearl oyster of the Indian Ocean, which is closer to the scallop than to the edible oyster. The main sources of natural pearls are the Persian Gulf; the Gulf of Mannar, between Sri Lanka and India; Thursday Island, on the north coast of Australia; and various locations in Mexico and Venezuela. Pearl mussels have been fished in Bavaria and the USA for their shells which are used in the manufacture of pearl buttons. Cultured pearls, made by inserting beads in oyster shells, were first produced in Japan in the early twentieth century.

peat   Decayed and partially carbonized vegetable matter, usually deposited in bogs or mosses from which it can be cut with appropriate tools into lengths suitable for handling and firing. Peat has been the principal source of energy in IRELAND, where it is usually called 'turf', and is still used in power stations. In the nineteenth century ambitious attempts were made to exploit peat deposits in the Netherlands (*see* BARGER COMPASCUUM), Belgium (*see* BOKRIJK), Denmark (*see* VIBORG), QUEBEC, Germany and Russia (*see* KALININ).

Peat was extensively used for smelting lead ore in the PENNINES, England, where remains of a large peat store survive at Old Gang, 18 km (11 mi.) W. of Richmond, Yorkshire. Experiments were made in England in the eighteenth century with the use of peat for smelting iron and in the early nineteenth century in forging wrought iron with peat, and it was used in glassmaking in Denmark (*see* HOLMEGÅRD).

BIBLIOGRAPHY
General
Percy, 1875.
Specific
Morton, G. R. The use of peat in the extraction of iron from its ore. In *Iron and Steel*, XXXVIII, 1965.
Mutton, N. *The use of peat in finery forges*, Wolverhampton: Wolverhampton College of Advanced Technology, 1966.

Pechelbronn, Bas-Rhin, France   Bituminous sands around Pechelbronn, 40 km (25 mi.) N. of Strasbourg, were mined from the mid-eighteenth century. Oil was extracted from shafts between 30 m and 100 m (100 ft. and 330 ft.) deep and used, after refining, for lubricating carriages and machinery. Progress in drilling, particularly the introduction of the Fauvelle system in 1879, made possible exploitation by wells or pumping, but mining techniques were still used up to 1918, with shafts up to 400 m (1300 ft.) deep. Exploitation ceased in 1956. A museum displays models and plans showing different drilling techniques, and ruins of old refineries are still visible among the mining installations of the 1920s and 30s. The workers' colony at Boussingault dates from the early twentieth century.

BIBLIOGRAPHY
General
Chambrier, 1919.
Specific
Merckwiller-Pechelbronn: La Commune centenaire et le pétrole (The hundred-year-old commune and petroleum). In *L'Outre-Forêt*, LXI, 1988.

Pécs (Funfkirchen), Baranya, Hungary   The chief town in southern Hungary, and a long established centre for the manufacture of leather, tobacco, beer, and agricultural machines. An apartment block of 1860, associated with an adjacent tannery, is being restored as a museum of working-class life. A wooden entrance hall gave access to the homes of thirty families. The tannery has been converted into the town museum.

The factory established by Vilmos Zsolnay (1828–1900) in 1851 produced richly coloured majolica, Delft-ware and porcelain, and architectural ceramics like the frost- and fire-resistant Pyrogranite used for stoves and external ornamentation in the ART NOUVEAU style. There are displays of these in the museum.

Coal mining in the region is centred on Komló, 10 km (6 mi.) N., which expanded with the growth of DUNAÚJVÁROS. A museum displays the history of ore and coal mining in the region, with underground galleries on the associated site open to visitors. The steel headstock of the Andras pit is preserved.

LOCATIONS
[M] Janus Pannonius Museum, H-7621 Pécs.
[M] Mining Museum of the Mecsek Region, H-7621 Pécs, Déryne u.9.

[M] Underground Exhibition, H-7621 Pécs Káptalan u.3.

pediment   A characteristic feature of CLASSICAL architecture, a pediment is a low-pitched gable above a door, window or PORTICO. In BAROQUE architecture a pediment may be curved, or broken in the centre.

Peggau, Styria, Austria   One of the most remarkable concentrations of industrial monuments in Austria is situated around Peggau, 16 km (10 mi.) N. of Graz.

The Badlwandgalerie viaduct formed part of the original route of the Südbahn linking Vienna with Trieste, by way of the Semmering Pass, the Mur valley and Graz. The line through the defile of Badlwand was built in 1843–4 and a road was constructed to run over the tracks on a viaduct of thirty-five arches, 367 m (440 yd.) long. The road was subsequently removed to the side of the gallery, and the railway was realigned on the other side of the valley in 1977–8. The gallery is protected as a unique historical monument.

On the western side of the valley, at the mouth of the Uebelbach valley, is the former lead and zinc smelting settlement of Deutschfeistritz, where in 1906–8 the Swiss company Albert Buss & Cie of Basel constructed a hydro-electric power station to the design of Josef Hötzel of Graz on the site of a former silver mine. It was taken over by the Steiermarkischen Elektrizitats-Gesellschaft (Styrian Electric Power Company) from 1910. The machinery was removed following the completion of a new station in 1965, but the concrete building remains.

There were many forges in the district and the scythe forge of Johann Pachernegg dating from the early nineteenth century has been protected as a historical monument since 1985. It worked until 1984, when it was producing some four hundred scythes a day, using two water-powered hammers.

The Steiermarkische Landesbahnen (Styrian local railway network) operates a 10.25 km (6 mi.) branch from Peggau to Ubelbach, on which two electric railcars of 1936 are employed.

The Österreiches Freilichtmuseum (Austrian Open-Air Museum) is a traditional open-air museum established in 1962 on the Scandinavian model, with some eighty mainly rural buildings from all over Austria arranged in provincial groups. Exhibits include four corn mills, an oil mill, a sawmill, and working demonstrations of shoe-making, weaving and hatmaking.

BIBLIOGRAPHY
General
Zippelius, 1974.

BARRIE TRINDER

Peisey, Savoie, France   Argentiferous lead was mined at Peisey from 1740 when the Duke of Savoy granted mining rights to an English company. It was used as a local centre for the Imperial Mining School in 1802, and in 1807 there were about four hundred workers. Production ceased in 1866. The building of the mining school

remains, together with various mining structures, and vestiges of water TROMPES for the smelting installations. There are remains of two smelting furnaces, probably dating from 1762.

BIBLIOGRAPHY
Specific
Chapon, P. *Fonderies de plomb argentifere de Peisey-Nancroix. Étude d'Archéologie industrielle* (Argentiferous lead smelters at Peisey-Nancroix: an industrial archaeological study). Conseil Général de Savoie: unpublished study, 1988.

Pejão (Castelo de Paiva), Douro Litoral, Portugal   A coal-mining settlement dating from 1884, 32 km (20 mi.) SE of Oporto, with a 7 km ($4\frac{1}{2}$ mi.) narrow-gauge railway, between the mines and the River Douro. It is now closed but some of its locomotives are preserved in museums at SANTARÉM and ESTREMOZ.

Pelješac, Croatia, Yugoslavia   A peninsula on the Adriatic coast, 70 km (45 mi.) long, linked to the mainland by ferries. There are oyster beds in its bays. Historically it was part of the republic of Ragusa (*see* DUBROVNIK) till 1806. There was a naval harbour at Mali Ston from 1490, but from the eighteenth century Orebic has been the principal city of the peninsula. The shallow waters on the shores of the Stonski Kanal bay prompted the establishment of a saltworks by the early fourteenth century: the works still operates using essentially the same technology, with evaporation pans, a Renaissance warehouse, and a nineteenth-century narrow-gauge railway. There is a fortified salt warehouse of 1462–81 at Mali Ston, nearby. Orebic is a lively seaport, with a Maritime Museum rich in exhibits from the period of transition between sail and steam, and two important private collections of material relating to seafaring.

LOCATION
[M] Maritime Museum, Orebic.

Peloponnese (Pelopónnisos), Greece   A mountainous promontory of some 21 440 km^2 (8280 sq. mi.) linked to mainland Greece by the isthmus of CORINTH. Traditional manufactures include the drying, processing and packing of currants at Corinth and Patras (Pátrai), and figs at Kalamáta (Kalámai). About 8 km (5 mi.) SW of Patras are the Akhaia-Klauss wine cellars, built by the Hellenistic Viniculture Company in 1861. The metre-gauge railway system constructed between 1886 and 1902, extending from Corinth around the north and west coasts, and crossing the centre of the peninsula to Kalamáta, includes some of the most spectacular sections of mountain railway in Europe. An equally spectacular 750 mm gauge line built in 1885–95, with three rack sections, extends 13 km (8 mi.) through a deep gorge from Diakopton on the north coast to Kalávrita.

BIBLIOGRAPHY
General
Schneider, 1967.

Figure 109 A view of the city of Ston on the Pelješac peninsula, Yugoslavia, showing the extensive salt pans on the shore of the Adriatic
Piotr Gerber

Pelton, Lester Allen (1829–1908) A California gold prospector, who did not find gold but devised a hydraulic impulse turbine, which he patented in 1889, in which water jets strike hemispherical bifurcated buckets around a wheel, developing up to 500 hp. Many Pelton wheels remain in use.

penal colony There were several settlements in Western Europe in the early nineteenth century like that at Ommerschans, near Meppel (*see* WILLEMSOORD), where felons were set to bring waste land into cultivation, as well as working at manufactures.

Several European countries, most notably Britain in Australia, established settlements overseas peopled by convicted felons. Several such settlements have been excavated and provide evidence of the early stages of colonization.

BIBLIOGRAPHY
General
Kerr, 1984.

pencil Originally, a fine brush used in painting, but by the seventeenth century the word applied to a graphite rod enclosed in wood, usually cedar, and used for writing or drawing. Originally graphite blocks from Borrowdale in the LAKE DISTRICT, for a long time the only source in Europe, were cut into veneers, then into rods. The Lake District pencil industry is commemorated at Keswick. The Faber company in Nuremburg in 1761 began to use a cemented compound of pulverized graphite, and from 1795 the Condé company in Paris pioneered modern pencil manufacture by extruding fine-ground graphite and clay, and subsequently heating it. Nuremburg, where there were twenty-six factories *c.*1900, became the chief centre of manufacture in Europe.

BIBLIOGRAPHY
General
Petroski, 1990.

LOCATION
[M] Cumberland Pencil Museum, Southey Works, Keswick, Cumbria CA12 5NG.

Pendeli (Pendelikón, Pentelikon, Penteli), Attica, Greece A much quarried mountain, 18 km (11 mi.) NE of Athens, the source of the marble used in the Parthenon and for numerous purposes since. The Greek National Trust has devised a trail which links the principal quarrying sites; this includes a 137 m (450 ft.) inclined paved way along which large blocks were slid down to lower levels. The quarries were owned by the monastery of Pendeli.

péniche The standard French canal barge of 300 tonnes, fitting within minimum dimensions laid down by Charles de Freycinet (1828–1923), Minister of Public Works from 1877, to pass through locks 38.5 m (126 ft.) long and 5 m (16 ft. 5 in.) wide, with a draught of 2 m (6 ft. 6 in.). This is now the minimum size of vessel normally used for long-distance traffic in continental Europe.

559

Figure 110   High Kinders at Greenfield, Saddleworth, near Manchester, one of the best examples of the rural 'proto-factory' in the Pennine textile region; the three- and four-storey buildings date from the mid-seventeenth to the mid-nineteenth centuries. The building in the foreground is a former dyehouse. The complex was once occupied by seven families.
Barrie Trinder

See also figure 49.

BIBLIOGRAPHY
General
Hadfield, 1986.

Pennines, England   The range of limestone and grit-stone hills which extends north and south through the centre of England between the Scottish border and the River Trent. Industrial activity in the northern Pennines was dominated by lead mining (*see* DURHAM). The southern part of the range, the White Peak in southern Yorkshire and Derbyshire, divided the industrial regions of Lancashire and West Yorkshire. Hey (1980) has shown that growing trade in the late seventeenth and eighteenth centuries was reflected in the construction of many new paved ways and packhorse bridges. Turnpike roads crossed the range by the mid-eighteenth century, to be followed by three canals and four principal railway routes in the nineteenth. There were distinctive patterns of housing with long, stone-mullioned windows, associated with textiles on both sides of the Pennines: they are best observed at Saddleworth and Milnrow on the west, and along the Holme and Calder Valleys in Yorkshire. Museums at Golcar and Saddleworth portray the area's industrial past, and there are many small but significant industrial monuments like the stone tenterposts at Marsden. Hebden Bridge, with Heptonstall, a typical example of a paired hilltop and riverside settlement, has set the pattern for conservation in the region and has become the centre for Pennine studies.

BIBLIOGRAPHY
General
Ashmore, 1982; Hey, 1980.
Specific
Smith, W. J. The architecture of the domestic system in South-East Lancashire and the adjoining Pennines. In Chapman, 1971.

LOCATIONS
[M] Colne Valley Museum, Cliffe Ash, Golcar, Huddersfield HD7 4PY.
[M] Pennine Heritage Network, Birchcliffe Centre, Hebden Bridge HX7 8DG.

[M] Saddleworth Museum and Art Gallery, High Street, Uppermill, Oldham OL3 6HS.

BARRIE TRINDER

Pennsylvania, United States of America Despite its dubious distinction as what some regard as the buckle on the 'rust belt', the centre of those heavy industries most subject to late twentieth-century decline, Pennsylvania has long reigned as the nation's largest producer of structural metal shapes and anthracite. They are just two of a host of products issuing from this very industrial state.

Pennsylvania probably has more standing early blast furnaces per square mile than any other state, including two sites heavily restored and interpreted as all-star LANDMARKS of the American ironmaking heritage. Both the Hopewell Furnace, built in 1820–40, and the Cornwall Furnace, built in 1742 and rebuilt in 1856, display relatively complete charcoal iron-smelting systems, including blowing machinery and charging assemblies, albeit heavily restored at Hopewell with new materials. Centralized state government preservation programmes have helped such efforts with inventories of iron furnace sites and material assistance with the preservation of the more significant. Lock Ridge Iron Furnace, built in 1868, marks the emergent use of ANTHRACITE as furnace fuel.

Structural evidence of Pennsylvania's prominent role in the US steel industry stands in the vicinities of Harrisburg, Bethlehem and Lehigh, while in a Pittsburgh railyard hangs the nation's only surviving BESSEMER converter, for lack of a more appropriate setting.

Across north-eastern Pennsylvania, the headstocks, breaker houses and company towns of the anthracite coal industry stand as silent witnesses to this once dominant industry, addressed through collections and programmes at Ashland and Eckley, and the Anthracite Museum at Scranton. The gritty social fabric of the miner's world is still alive in the houses and public buildings of such coal COMPANY TOWNS as Star Junction, Windber and Colver.

In the oilfields around Titusville (*see* OIL INDUSTRY), isolated oil-pumping stations are some of the more distinctive features of this heavily forested region, a landscape overseen by the Drake Oil Well Historic Site, one of the state's many satellite sites managed from Harrisburg.

Pennsylvania's deep-water ports, to the east at Philadelphia and to the west at Erie, have provided crucial outlets for state products and travellers, resulting in concentrations of railway networks, support structures and commercial enterprises dedicated to such traffic. Both cities contain patches of the golden eras of rail and ship transport in the scruffy corners of their downtowns. The other major Pennsylvania nexus at Pittsburgh occurs at the confluence of three major navigable rivers: the Ohio, Monongahela and Allegheny. The city underwent a glamorizing face-lift in the 1980s, transforming a sooty brick and iron downtown into glass and steel canyons of global commerce. Train depots have become restaurants and clubs, while many of the steel mills on the outskirts of Pittsburgh have been broken up to feed the scrap-hungry mini-mills carrying the steel industry forward elsewhere in the nation.

In the river towns of Homestead, McKeesport, Duquesne and others, east and west of Pittsburgh, the rich heritage of life in and around the steel mills awaits proper attention by local museums. An ingot-mould memorial stands in a town park across from the site of the once celebrated Homestead Works of US Steel in Homestead, not far from the highly-ornamented Eastern European churches, row houses and downtown district frequented by the immigrant workers who populated the mills.

Philadelphia's classically-inspired Fairmount Waterworks, dating from 1815, presents a far different picture of industrial health. The restored waterworks park contains several generations of pumping structures but precious little pumping machinery: it nevertheless symbolizes the first successful urban water-distribution effort in the country.

The passage of water – not for consumption but for buoyancy – also figured in the establishment of the Delaware & Hudson Canal through north-eastern Pennsylvania in 1828, as a connector between the anthracite coalfields and New York City. The waterway used a series of AQUEDUCTS to carry the canal boats over major rivers, the sole surviving one of these being a creation of JOHN ROEBLING, which is regarded as the earliest wire-cable suspension 'bridge' in the world still retaining its principal original elements. The aqueduct carried traffic across the Delaware River at Lackawaxen. Years after the canal's closure and the aqueduct's conversion to a private road bridge, the entire structure underwent a meticulous rebuilding in the 1980s to strengthen the deck structure and improve its physical state as a new addition to the National Park Service's roster of national historic sites.

Among Pennsylvania's other outstanding spans, highlights include Pittsburgh's double-lenticular truss Smithfield Street Bridge of 1883–91; the great steel Kinzua Viaduct of 1900, which crosses a river valley near Kushequa; the equally bucolic Starrucca Viaduct of 1848 near Lanesboro, which in its foundations embodies an early use of structural concrete; and in Brownsville the modest Dunlap's Creek Bridge of 1839, proclaimed as the first iron-arch bridge built in the USA. The world's longest concrete viaduct, the Tunkhannock of 1915, dominates the landscape at Nicholson (*see* figure 167).

BIBLIOGRAPHY
General
Oblinger, 1984; Paskoff, 1983; Procter and Matuszeski, 1978.
Specific
Miner, C. *Homestead: the Story of a Steel Town.* Pittsburgh: Historical Society of Western Pennsylvania, n.d.

LOCATIONS
[M] Allegheny Portage Railroad Museum, Cresson, PA 16630.
[M] Canal Museum, 200 South Delaware Drive, Easton, PA 18044.
[M,S] Cornwall Iron Furnace, Rexmont Road at Boyd Street, Cornwall, PA 17016.
[M] Drake Oil Well Museum, RD 3, Titusville, PA 16354.
[M] Eckley Miners' Village, Main Street, Eckley, PA 18255.

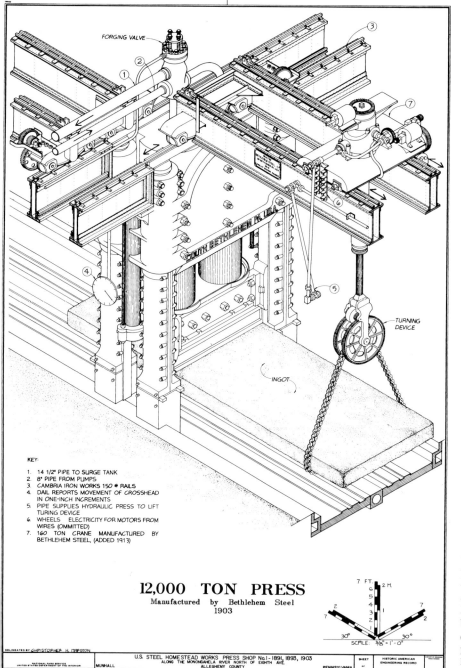

KEY:
1. 14 1/2" PIPE TO SURGE TANK
2. 8" PIPE FROM PUMPS
3. CAMBRIA IRON WORKS 150 # RAILS
4. DAIL REPORTS MOVEMENT OF CROSSHEAD
   IN ONE-INCH INCREMENTS
5. PIPE SUPPLIES HYDRAULIC PRESS TO LIFT
   TURING DEVICE
6. WHEELS   ELECTRICITY FOR MOTORS FROM
   WIRES (OMMITTED)
7. 160 TON CRANE MANUFACTURED BY
   BETHLEHEM STEEL, (ADDED 1913)

FORGING VALVE

TURNING DEVICE

INGOT

12,000 TON PRESS
Manufactured by Bethlehem Steel
1903

SCALE: 3/8" = 1'-0"

U.S. STEEL HOMESTEAD WORKS PRESS SHOP No.I-1891, 1893, 1903
ALONG THE MONONGAHELA RIVER NORTH OF EIGHTH AVE.
ALLEGHENY COUNTY

MUNHALL

PENNSYLVANIA

IF REPRODUCED, PLEASE CREDIT HISTORIC AMERICAN ENGINEERING RECORD, NATIONAL PARK SERVICE, NAME OF DELINEATOR, DATE OF THE DRAWING

Figure 111 A drawing by HAER of a 12 000-ton press at the US Steel Co.'s Homestead Works, Allegheny County, Pennsylvania; it was built by the Bethlehem Steel Corporation in 1903.
Historic American Engineering Record, National Park Service, Christopher H. Marston, 1989

[M,S] Hopewell Furnace Site RD 1 Box 345, Elverson, PA 19520.

[M] Museum of Anthracite Mining, Pine & 17th Streets, Ashland, PA 17921.

[M] Pennsylvania Anthracite Museum, Scranton, Pennsylvania.

[M] Pennsylvania Lumber Museum, Galeton, PA 16922.

[M] Railroaders' Memorial Museum, 1300 9th Avenue, Altoona, PA 16602.

[M] Railroad Museum of Pennsylvania, PO Box 15, Strasburg, PA 17579.

[M] Rough and Tumble (steam traction) Engineers Museum, PO Box 9, Kinzers, PA 17535.

[M] Saylor Park Portland Cement Industry Museum, North 2nd Street, Coplay, PA 18037.

[S] Steamtown, Scranton, PA 18505.

[M] Thomas Newcomen Library and Museum, 412 Newcomen Road, Exton, PA 19341.

DAVID H. SHAYT

penstock Originally a sluice to control the outflow of water from a 'pen' – such as a millpond – where it had been stored, to a mill. The term now refers to a pressure conduit for water from a dam inlet to a turbine or group of turbines in a HYDRO-ELECTRIC POWER STATION; it is usually a steel tube, although wrought iron, concrete and wood have been used. Even in the first decade of the century penstocks could be of great length, as are the 720 m (2360 ft.) tubes used at RJUKAN.

Penydarren Tramroad, Abercynon, Mid Glamorgan, Wales Situated 21 km (13 mi.) NW of Cardiff, this was one of many horse-drawn tramroads serving the South Wales iron industry c.1780–1850. It was completed in 1802, covering the 16 km (10 mi.) from MERTHYR TYDFIL. RICHARD TREVITHICK demonstrated the first use of a steam locomotive to draw a load on this railway on 21 February 1804; the locomotive pulled five wagons with 10 tons of freight and 70 men, but was not used subsequently as the locomotive was too heavy for the rails. The route, some stone sleepers, two tunnels, and the Trevithick memorial survive.

BIBLIOGRAPHY
General
Rees, 1975.

Pernes, Santarém, Ribatejo, Portugal A remarkable group of twelve water mills, rare in Portugal, 85 km (53 mi.) NE of Lisbon, with several dams and a network of canals. Works deriving power on the site, the first of which dates from 1756, made tools and, later, steel wire.

Perspex The commercial name for acrylic sheet, a clear, hard and tough polymer made from methyl 2-methylpro-penoate, used for aircraft windows and cockpit canopies, for shop and road signs, for baths and sinks, in medical apparatus, and for jewellery. Perspex was discovered by ICI scientists during research to develop safety glass for motorcars, for which it ultimately proved unsuitable. The process for its manufacture was patented in 1932, and the first sheets were produced in 1933, commercial production being transferred to Billingham, TEESSIDE, in the following year. In the USA acrylic sheet, originally a proprietary product of the Du Pont company, is called flexiglass.

BIBLIOGRAPHY
General
ICI, 1962.
Specific
Harness, A. *The Story of Perspex*. Loughborough: ESPI, n.d.

Perth and **Fremantle,** Western Australia, Australia Perth is the state capital, established in 1829 by free settlers on the banks of the Swan River, although little construction took place until convicts were brought to the site in 1850. An international exhibition was held in the city in 1881. Electric trams were introduced in 1899.

Perth was served by the port of Fremantle, 20 km (12 mi.) S., where government warehouses and wharves have been preserved. The earliest surviving building is the 'Round House' a twelve-sided stone gaol, built by Henry Reveley in 1830–1. The Maritime Museum specializes in the study of the many wrecks off the shores of Western Australia. Large-scale modern industries, oil refining, and the smelting of aluminium and nickel, are located at Kwinana to the south.

The Old Mill Museum in Perth is centred around a tower mill of 1835, which was adapted in 1880 as the focus of a suburban picnic resort, which proved unsuccessful. The museum has a substantial collection of road carriages.

BIBLIOGRAPHY
General
McCarty and Schedvin, 1978.

LOCATIONS
[M] The Old Mill Museum, Mill Point Road, South Perth.
[M] West Australia Maritime Museum, Cliff Street, Fremantle.
[M] The Western Australian Museum, Francis Street, Perth 6000.

Perthshire, Tayside, Scotland A county centred on the city of Perth, the traditional gateway to the Highlands. It contains some of the most important monuments of the Scottish textile industry, including Stanley Mills, 9.5 km (6 mi.) N. of Perth, where Bell Mill of 1786 is the least altered of RICHARD ARKWRIGHT's mills, a mill of five storeys and a basement, brick-built with a bell cupola. Adjacent are East Mill of 1802–9, extended in 1823–8, when the fireproof Mid Mill was built, with ancillary buildings; and a 237 m (776 ft.) tunnelled LADE that fed seven water wheels, replaced by turbines in 1921, which were scrapped in 1974. Cotton belting and endless cigarette tape were later specialties, but the mill closed in 1989. The company village has two-storey terraces laid out on a grid plan, and a church of 1828.

At Deanston Mills, 11 km (7 mi.) NW of Stirling, founded in 1785, the most striking buildings date from c.1827: an unfinished L-plan five-storey mill, and a buttressed single-storey weaving shed with brick and stone dome-vaulted roofs, the model for Marshall's Mill, LEEDS. In 1967 the complex became a distillery, which has since closed, but the buildings remain in use as a BOND. The weir, lade and some two-storey housing remain from the mill.

Glenruthven Mills, Auchterarder, 21 km (13 mi.) SW of Perth, were built in 1877 as a small cotton-weaving, later woollen-weaving, establishment, which on closure in 1980 was the last steam-powered mill in Scotland. The slide-valve tandem compound engine, installed c.1919 but as old as the mill, is regularly steamed.

Auchterarder Heritage Centre displays two Hattersley looms in part of the mill. The rest of the Anderston looms have been scrapped to make room for the 'Great Scots Visitor Centre and computerized lighting sensation'. The shafting remains. Two small woollen mills at Kilmahog are now primarily mill shops. One retains a water wheel; the other has three Hattersley demonstration power

Figure 112 Bell Mill, part of the Stanley Mill complex in Perthshire, the least altered of Richard Arkwright's cotton mills
Barrie Trinder

looms. Tod & Duncan's works at Kinross, founded in 1846, are the biggest cashmere mills in the world.

A circular eighteenth-century lint-scutching mill is restored at Invervar, Glenlyon, 18 km (12 mi.) W. of Aberfeldy. The Muckle Hoose, Spittalfield, 8 km (5 mi.) SW of Blairgowrie, dating from 1767, may have been a spinning school, but was long ago converted to housing. Textile mills in Blairgowrie were the last to use water wheels in Britain in the 1960s. Here the River Ericht powered eleven small mills built between 1798 and 1872. Oakbank (the first to try jute), Westfield and Keithbank mills contain wheels installed in 1865 and 1872, the last also having a standby Carmichael single-cylinder horizontal steam engine. Wallace Works, Perth, a fine single-storey weaving factory of 1868, now weaves synthetic fabrics.

The tributaries of the River Tay north of Perth offered some of the best bleaching sites in Britain. There are nineteenth-century stone and timber structures at Huntingtower, Stormontfield, Tulloch and Luncarty; the last,

founded in 1732 and at 50 ha (130 ac.) one of the largest in Britain, still operates. Workers' housing survives here and at Ashfield silk-dyeing and printworks. Pullars Dyeworks, Perth, was the largest in Scotland with pedimented, Italianate three-storey ranges of 1865 linked to a Baronial range of 1901 by a Bridge of Sighs. Part is used for dry-cleaning; the remainder has been sympathetically converted into a supermarket.

Scotland's best surviving urban mills turn on a fifteenth-century lade. Perth's Upper City Mills, for malt, corn and flour, were rebuilt in 1787, and converted in 1971 to a hotel, where two low-breast wheels adorn the foyer. Lower City Mills were rebuilt in 1802, and the later nineteenth-century machinery has recently been restored. Aberfeldy Mill of 1825, with Gothic detailing, was restored in 1987. Blair Atholl Mill, built *c*.1830, was last rebuilt after a fire in 1982. Both grind oatmeal and are open to the public.

Blackford's breweries can be traced from the fifteenth century. In 1900 there were three: only the office survives of Sharp's which was closed in 1927, and Eadie's was converted in 1949 to Tullibardine Distillery. W. B. Thomson's, however, remains as Gleneagles Maltings, the last commercial floor maltings in Scotland: it has four storeys, with a grain loft, a double kiln, and a Shanks oil engine. The product, ground at Craigie Mill, Perth, goes into 'Veda' malt loaves. Both the maltings and the tall, louvred brewhouse, closed in 1915 and now a potato store, were built in 1896–8.

Perth waterworks is a remarkable Ionic building with a domed cast-iron roof tank, cast in 1832 by Dundee Foundry, and a chimney topped by an urn. Conversion to a tourist information centre in 1973 involved the scrapping of the last steam pumping engine in a Scottish waterworks.

Perth railway station, of 1847, by Tite & Trotman, is in a Tudor style. A large goods station remains. Dunkeld Station, of 1856, in bargeboarded Gothic, and Pitlochry Station of 1882, which is Baronial, are fine examples of their types. Gleneagles, rebuilt in 1919, has steel cantilevered awnings, and was built to serve the nearby railway hotel which was completed in 1926, but reflects the style of the Edwardian era in which it was begun.

Perthshire's bridges are among the finest in Britain. The showpiece along the military roads of General George Wade (1673–1748) was designed by William Adam (1689–1748) at Aberfeldy, a 91 m (300 ft.), five-span bridge, of 1733, the same date as the two-span Wade bridge at Amulree. JOHN SMEATON built the 244 m (800 ft.) seven-span bridge at Perth in 1766–71; each spandrel has three hollow voids to reduce the overall weight. The contemporary Couttie Bridge has a handsome five-span hump. At Dunkeld is THOMAS TELFORD's 209 m (685 ft.) Gothic-detailed bridge with five main and two lesser arches. Smaller bridges include the early nineteenth-century Tudor cast-iron Chinese Bridge at Taymouth Castle, and the wrought-iron suspension bridge at Haughs of Drimmie, near Blairgowrie, with its 32 m (105 ft.) span; the latter has affinities with that at Kirkton of Glenisla (*see* ANGUS). Victoria Road Bridge, Caputh, erected by Sir William Arrol (1839–1913) in 1887–8, is thought to contain material from the Tay Bridge, DUNDEE, then under reconstruction.

Doune Motor Museum has forty vintage and classic cars, including a Rolls Royce of 1905. Strathallan Aero Park, Auchterarder, has historic aircraft of the 1930s, 40s and 50s, and a collection of aero engines.

See also SCOTCH WHISKY.

BIBLIOGRAPHY
General
Hay and Stell, 1986; Hume, 1977; Wood, 1985.
Specific
Cooke, A. ed. *Stanley: its history and development.* Dundee: University of Dundee, 1977.
MacMaster, C. *Scottish Brewing Archive Newsletter*, VII, 1986.

LOCATIONS
[M] Doune Motor Museum, Doune, Perthshire FK16 6HD.
[S] Glenruthven Mill, Abbey Road, Auchterarder, Perthshire.
[M] Perth Museum and Art Gallery, George Street, Perth PH1 5LB.

[M] Strathallan Aero Park, Strathallan Airfield, Auchterarder PH31 1LA.

MARK WATSON

Pêso da Régua, Alto Douro, Portugal   The economic centre of the Região (region) known as Demarcada do Douro, 70 km (43 mi.) NE of Oporto. The town owes its development to the Marquis of POMBAL (1699–1789) who established there in 1756 the headquarters of the Real Companhia Geral da Agricultura e Comércio dos Vinhos do Alto Douro (*see* OPORTO). This company soon became one of the largest of its kind in Europe, and from 1770 built huge warehouses for its wine along the banks of the River Douro, which is crossed by two bridges, one of them of iron. Visitors can visit the former Royal Oporto Wine Company house in the R. Marquês de Pombal, the lower floor of which is filled with modern wine producing equipment.

pet food   The canning of waste products from meat processing, for consumption by cats and dogs, began in the early twentieth century but its growth was due to the marketing skills of entrepreneurs like the American Forrest E. Mars. In England in 1934 Mars bought a Manchester company, Chappel Brothers, which canned meat for dogs, but soon transferred production to Slough (*see* LONDON). Products were marketed as Chappie and Kit-E-Kat, and sales developed rapidly (although the boom in pet food sales in Europe came after 1950).

Petrokrepost' (Shlisselburg, Shlussel'burg), Leningrad, USSR   Famous in revolutionary annals for its fortress, and used in tsarist times to imprison many noteworthy dissidents, Petrokrepost' is 60 km (37 mi.) E. of Leningrad. Part of the Nevskii shipbuilding complex is located there, and from the time of Tsar Peter I (Peter the Great) it has been a port of the Ladoga canal system, which connects the River Volga with the Baltic Sea, enabling craft to bypass the treacherous waters of Lake Ladoga. The idea of the bypass dates at least from 1712, and in 1718 Peter ordered its construction to ensure the passage of food and naval supplies to Petersburg and Kronshtadt. Completed in 1731, it had double locks at the terminal points of New Ladoga and Shlussel'burg. In the nineteenth century this system was replaced by a new, parallel New Ladoga system, but original locks survive at Petrokrepost'.

BIBLIOGRAPHY
Specific
Bolshaya sovietskaya entsiklopediya (Great Soviet Encyclopaedia), vol. 32, Moscow, 1953.

petrol   Motor spirit, or, in the USA, gasoline. The word 'petrol', colloquial in Britain, is not used in the industry. The spirit is a mixture of volatile liquid hydrocarbons which is vaporized before entering the cylinder of an engine. The product is a fraction distilled from CRUDE OIL, and enriched with compounds made from other fractions. Motor spirit can be manufactured from other sources, and in the 1920s and 30s was frequently made by hydrogenation of benzole or coal.

BIBLIOGRAPHY
General
BP, 1958; Morgan and Pratt, 1938.

petrol engine A motive system deriving its energy from the combustion of vaporized PETROL within the cylinder of an engine; it is therefore categorized, like the OIL ENGINE, as an 'internal combustion engine'. The crucial difference between the petrol engine and the oil engine, which it otherwise closely resembles, lies in the vaporization and ignition systems. CARL BENZ developed electric ignition, a battery and trembler coil system, with a spark plug. In the motor cars built by Benz and GOTTLIEB DAIMLER in 1886, petrol was carburized from the surface of flat trays. In 1893 Daimler's collaborator, William Maybach, devised a carburettor that atomized the fuel by spraying. Of the alternative systems, only the use by F. W. Lanchester (1868–1946) in 1895 of wicks had, in the days of impure fuel which clogged jets, a distinct advantage over the Maybach carburettor.

Daimler's ignition system, an externally heated tube, was used by other engineers but was superseded by Benz's development of electric ignition, a battery and trembler coil system with a spark plug which was improved by the Sims-Bosch magneto in 1895. Subsequent developments followed from the high-speed engines devised in 1895–9 by Albert de Dion and Georges Bouton, which attained up to 2000 rev/min, compared with the 800 rev/min of Benz and Daimler engines.

BIBLIOGRAPHY
General
Strandh, 1979.

CHRISTOPHER GREEN

petroleum Solid, liquid and gaseous hydrocarbons, occurring naturally in the earth. They have been exploited from seepages in many parts of Europe from early times, and produced incidentally from salt wells in the USA in the first half of the nineteenth century. In 1859 Edwin Drake (1819–80) at Titusville, Pennsylvania, was the first to drill a successful well specifically to obtain petroleum (*see* OIL INDUSTRY).

BIBLIOGRAPHY
General
BP, 1958; Harvard, 1960.

petrol locomotive Petrol engines have been applied both to railway locomotives and railcars, and several motor cars with flanged wheels used as inspection saloons are preserved (*see* HAMAR). In Britain the NER introduced a petrol-electric railcar in 1903, and several companies built similar vehicles before 1914. A mechanical drive locomotive was introduced in the USA in 1904, followed by a petrol-electric in 1906. Some shunting locomotives were built in the 1920s, but the diesel engine has proved a superior power unit for railway use.

pewter An alloy of tin, usually with lead (lay pewter) or copper (fine pewter). Small additions of bismuth were added from *c.*1600 to give hardness, and of antimony from *c.*1700 to produce a better colour. Pewter was used for dishes, hollowware, candlesticks, buttons, and the like. A low melting point made manufacture possible on simple hearths in small workshops, though the brass or bronze moulds were expensive. Cast pieces were easily soldered, and hammered or turned (or both). London was the main centre of production in England, but most British towns had at least one pewterer. From *c.*1740 the use of pewter declined, probably due to competition from pottery, iron, brass and tin plate.

BIBLIOGRAPHY
General
Hatcher and Barker, 1974.

pharmaceuticals Large companies producing drugs and other products for sale by chemists were established in most developed economies from the late nineteenth century. Substantial capital was required for research and testing, as well as for marketing. Such companies had various origins. In Britain Smith & Nephew developed from a business dealing in TRAIN OIL, and Boots from a retail herbal medicine concern. Friedrich Bayer (1825–80), inventor of aspirin, and founder of the Bayer company in WUPPERTAL and Leverkusen, was a dyestuffs manufacturer. BASEL came to have the greatest concentration of pharmaceutical factories in Europe, and the most significant artefacts of the early stages of the pharmaceutical industry are in the city.

Several pharmaceutical factories are of particular architectural distinction. The Boots factory at Beeston, NOTTINGHAM, by Sir Owen Williams (1890–1969), dates from 1935 and is of CONCRETE construction with mushroom columns. The multi-storey building is divided into a wet section for the production of liquids, creams and pastes, and a dry section for powders, tablets and lozenges. The prominent square clock tower of the Hoechst plant at Frankfort am Main, designed by PETER BEHRENS in 1920, became the company's logo.

BIBLIOGRAPHY
General
Bennett and Lever, 1981.

BARRIE TRINDER

pharmacy The practice of dispensing drugs for use as medicines, or a shop where such preparations are sold.
See also APOTHECARY; CHEMIST; DISPENSARY; DRUGGIST; DRUG STORE.

phenol (carbolic acid, C_6H_5OH) First isolated from coal tar in 1834, phenol has been used in the manufacture of plastics, nylon, resins, weedkillers and antiseptics. It is derived from BENZENE.

phenylamine (aniline) The simplest aromatic amine

Figure 113 The plant for the electrothermal manufacture of phosphorus on the Lièvre River at Buckingham, Quebec, established from 1893 by William Taylor Gibbs (1863–1910) and controlled by the British company Albright & Wilson from 1902
Barrie Trinder

($C_6H_5NH_2$), isolated in the 1830s by the destructive distillation of indigo and from coal tar, which was the main source in the nineteenth century. It forms the basis of aniline dyes, development of which began in England in 1856 with the production by Sir William Perkin (1838–1907) of a purple dye, mauveine, from aniline sulphate. Derivatives are widely used in plastics and medicines.

BIBLIOGRAPHY
General
Hardie and Pratt, 1966; Norman and Waddington, 1977.

phosphorus (P) An element which occurs in two principal forms. White phosphorus is poisonous and liable to inflame. The amorphous form, red phosphorus, is non-toxic and more stable. Both forms have been used in MATCHES and compounds of phosphorus are employed in medicine, DETERGENTS and plastics, and in preparing food.

Phosphorus was discovered in the seventeenth century and was manufactured from bone ash in 1777 by CARL SCHEELE (1742–86), but commercial production was begun by the Coignet company at Lyons in 1838, and by Arthur Albright (1811–1900), a Birmingham manufacturing chemist, in 1844 using bone ash from South America and the Balkans. Albright's company, Albright & Wilson of Oldbury, held a monopoly of British production in the nineteenth century.

The bone ash was softened and degreased with hydrochloric acid. Phosphoric acid was liberated from the ash with sulphuric acid, also forming calcium sulphate ($CaSO_4$), or GYPSUM; the phosphoric acid (H_3PO_4), was mixed with coal or charcoal, dried, ground, then placed in refractory retorts 1.2 m × 0.2 m (4 ft. × 8 in.), twenty-four of which were grouped inside a coal-fired furnace. Phosphorus was collected in condensers, treated with oxidizing agents and dilute sulphuric acid, and cast into blocks. Phosphorus rock or apatite ($3Ca_3(PO_4)_2.Ca(OH)_2$) was in due course substituted for bone ash.

Red phosphorus, discovered by Anton Von Schrotter of Vienna in 1845, was made from 1849 by heating white phosphorus in closed cast-iron pots, to which Arthur Albright added small open-ended tubes which acted as safety valves.

A gas-fired Siemens regenerative furnace (*see* SIEMENS, SIR WILLIAM) was used to make phosphorus in 1882, but in 1888 J. B. Readman patented the electrothermal process for the manufacture of phosphorus from apatite in an electric furnace. This is a continuous process in which

Figure 114   An example of the wealth of historical detail to be found in a very ordinary photograph: this view of central Halifax was taken in the late 1920s and sent to the Council for the Preservation of Rural England as an example of bad urban planning. It shows the Alexandra Hall, the ground floor of which is occupied by the chain store F. W. Woolworth & Co. In the centre is the enterprise of Hebble Motor Services, a combination of bus station and service station; in the former a motor omnibus prepares to depart for Leeds, while petrol prices are prominently displayed in the latter. Telephone cables carried on telegraph poles cross the area. In the foreground can be seen rails of the Halifax Corporation Tramways, a 3 ft. 6 in. (1.07 m) gauge system, which operated with electric traction between 1898 and 1939; while the wires at the top of the picture appear to be tramway cables, including, on the left, in front of the roof of the Alexandra Hall, a frog point.
CPRE Collection, Institute of Agricultural History and Museum of English Rural Life, University of Reading

phosphate rock, silica and carbon are fed into an electric furnace producing a gas from which phosphorus is condensed, and a slag, mostly calcium silicate. The retort process was quickly discarded, and plants using hydro-electric power were established at NIAGARA and at Buckingham, Quebec.

Until the twentieth century most phosphorus was used in making matches. Compounds used in food preparation include acid sodium pyrophosphate ($Na_2H_2P_2O_7$), mixed with bicarbonate of soda to make baking powder, and acid calcium phosphate ($CaHP_2O_8$), which is employed in self-raising flour.

BIBLIOGRAPHY
General
Coignet, 1900; Morgan and Pratt, 1938; Threlfall, 1951.

BARRIE TRINDER

photography   Literally 'writing with light'. CAMERAS had been used by artists for two hundred years before attempts were made by Thomas Wedgwood (1771–1805), Nicephore Niepce (1765–1833) in 1822, and others, to fix the image chemically. William Fox Talbot (1800–77) had achieved this by 1835, but his results were poor and his methods cumbersome. The initial boost to the subject came from the work of Louis Daguerre (1789–1851), whose 'Daguerreotypes' (high-quality unique images on silver) were launched on an enthusiastic public in 1839. A combination of this high resolution with the versatility of multiple copies was achieved in 1851 by J. Scott Archer's 'wet collodion' process, which also reduced the exposure time. Dry gelatine plates followed in 1871. George Eastman (1854–1932) devised a paper roll with a film of gelatine and collodion in 1884; and with the launch of the mass-produced Kodak No. 1

camera in 1888, the age of the snapshot had arrived. The photographic industry was well established by the 1870s and grew rapidly in most developed countries in the early twentieth century, the Kodak Company setting the pace, manufacturing cameras that were simple to use, and processing as well as manufacturing and selling films. CELLULOID film followed in 1889. Colour, first tried in 1868, was available by 1907, and safety film in 1948.

Photographs form one of the most important sources for the industrial history of the last 150 years. Photographers recorded what were regarded as modern wonders, like the construction of railways, of the Crystal Palace, and later of the FORTH BRIDGE, but from the late 1850s photography came to be used as a management tool in manufacturing. From the late 1850s the Manchester photographer James Mudd recorded every locomotive built by the Beyer Peacock (see BEYER GARRETT) company, a practice that became standard in many heavy-engineering concerns. Trade catalogues were illustrated with photographs from the 1860s. From World War I, companies in Britain set up their own photographic departments to produce material for internal use and for public relations purposes. Other photographers, often working surreptitiously, recorded working conditions for use in propaganda.

See also CAMERA; CINEMA; FILM; POSTCARD. For examples of historic photographs which provide industrial archaeological evidence see figures 13, 18, 20, 36, 38, 55, 88, 90, 91, 94, 107, 114, 142, 159, 164.

BIBLIOGRAPHY
General
Boorstin, 1972; Davies and Collier, 1986; Jenkins, 1966; Lowe, 1986; Newhall, 1964; Oliver, 1989; Powell, 1985; Taft, 1938; Whimster, 1990; Wilson, 1982.

CHRISTOPHER GREEN

piano The drawing-room piano was the principal musical product of the Industrial Revolution, a mark of prosperity which was one of the chief indicators of respectability in the late nineteenth century.

Piano manufacture was well established on an industrial scale in London by the 1840s, when the firm of Broadwood's occupied four parallel ranges of three-storey buildings in Westminster, and employed up to four hundred people in addition to outworkers, with specialist departments for turning legs, making hammers and sounding boards, cutting keys, sawing veneers, and cutting fretwork. Major developments in the second half of the nineteenth century were in Germany and the USA, where development was largely due to Henry Engelhard Steinway (Steinweg; 1797–1871) who migrated from Germany in 1851, set up a piano manufacturing concern, and in 1855 exhibited a piano with a cast-iron frame and cross strings. In 1866–7 he built the Steinway Hall on 14th Street, New York, which incorporated his offices and retail showrooms as well as a concert hall.

The mechanical piano was popular in the late nineteenth century and the early twentieth century, and two pianola roll factories survive, the QRS works at Buffalo, N.Y., and the Mastertouch factory at Petersham, N.S.W.

BIBLIOGRAPHY
General
Dolge, 1911; Ehrlich, 1976.

BARRIE TRINDER

pickle A preparation of fruit or vegetables, particularly cucumbers, steeped in vinegar, and boiled with spices, salt and sugar. It is used to give flavour to meat or cheese. Manufacture on an industrial scale developed in the late nineteenth century to such an extent that a writer in 1912 commented, 'Pickles may now be purchased in such variety and so cheaply that very few, save those who grow vegetables they cannot utilize in any other way, think of preparing them at home.' The pioneer of industrial pickle manufacturing was Henry John Heinz (1844–1919), who began to make pickles in Pittsburgh, Pennsylvania, in 1876 and devised his '57 varieties' slogan in 1896. Heinz employed 6500 people by 1919, and owned twenty-five factories with eighty-five pickle stations, together with bottle, box and can factories, and seed farms.

BIBLIOGRAPHY
General
Wright, 1982.

Piedmont (Piemonte), Italy The development of textiles in this region indicates the advanced state of some aspects of Italian industry in the 150 years before unification. Silk was being made on a modest scale at the end of the sixteenth century, many of the early factories being established by French merchants, although Francesco Galleani of Bologna was responsible for some of the first large water-powered mills, like those in Turin of 1667, Venaria of 1675, and Cavaglià of 1675. On the edge of the Alps, Cuneo had four silk mills by 1700.

At Collegno, 10 km (6 mi.) W. of Turin, is the four-storey, seventeen-bay Caccia silk mill, established in 1708 by the Provana family, who occupied the medieval castle which looks over the mill. By 1750 this was an impressive industrial colony. The regular fenestration and bare, rendered walls pre-date the 'functionalist' expression, regarded as being a pioneering feature of British INDUSTRIAL ARCHITECTURE of the 1780s and 90s.

Biella, 65 km (40 mi.) NE of Turin, has been one of the chief woollen towns of Italy since the Middle Ages. Several nineteenth-century mills with rendered walls and hipped, pantiled roofs survive, with five large cotton mills built in the inter-war period.

See also CANAVESANE; LEUMANN; TURIN.

BIBLIOGRAPHY
Specific
Patrimonio Edilizio Esistente: un pasato e un futuro (The heritage of standing buildings: the past and the future). Turin: AA. VV, 1980.

MICHAEL STRATTON

pier A term with three distinct meanings relevant to industrial archaeology:

Figure 115 The Strengberg tobacco works at Pietarsaari: the three-storey building with the clock tower was built in 1909 to designs by the Swedish architect Torben Grut.
Lauri Putkonen

1. A structure supporting an arch or any other type of span of a bridge, or one supporting an arch within a building.
2. A breakwater or embankment built out from the land such that it partially encloses a harbour.
3. A landing stage built from the land into water deep enough to allow ships to moor, whether on the side of a river or in the sea. At seaside resorts in the nineteenth century such a pier might be transformed into a promenade across the water on which concert halls, shops and assembly rooms were constructed. One of the first was the Chain Pier at BRIGHTON of 1823, which included shops and shelters as well as steps to give access to ships. Fantasy and function were remarkably combined in such structures as the west pier at Brighton of 1863–6, the north pier at Blackpool of 1862–3, and Clevedon pier of 1867–8. The outstanding designer was Eugenius Birch (1818–84). Many British piers have been lost since World War II but their historic importance has been recognized and considerable resources have been put into the conservation of outstanding examples. Pleasure piers are a characteristically British phenomenon, but the 354 m (1160 ft.) structure at Scheveningen (*see* THE HAGUE) is an outstanding continental example. Adamson (1977) provides a definitive list of British piers. Atlantic City's famous 'Steel Pier' of the 1920s remains a popular tourist attraction in NEW JERSEY.

BIBLIOGRAPHY
General
Adamson, 1977; Bainbridge, 1986; Lindley, 1973.

BARRIE TRINDER

Pietarsaari (Jakobstad), Vaasan lääni, Finland   A town on the west coast of Finland, the site of the Strengberg factory, which dates from 1762, the oldest tobacco factory in the country still in use. A red-brick building completed in 1898 to the designs of Grahn, Hedman & Wasastjerna has been adapted as council offices. In 1909 the factory was extended with a three-storey building designed by the Swedish architect, Torben Grut. Its dominant feature is a tower topped by a huge globe-shaped clock. The old and new factories were connected by an arcade bridging Alholminkatu Street, forming a gateway to the extensive area of wooden houses, originally occupied by tobacco workers. Next to the tobacco factory is an elegant fire station of 1912, also designed by Torben Grut. The history of the Strengberg complex is characterized by the strenuous efforts that have been made to produce architecture of distinction: these are reflected in the prominence that has been given to the buildings in the marketing of the company's products.

LAURI PUTKONEN

pig iron   CAST IRON in the form in which it comes from the BLAST FURNACE, ready for remelting in a FORGE or FOUNDRY. The name derives from the shape of the moulds into which it was cast when tapped. A runner was cut into a sand bed: into this ran molten iron from the furnace. The runner branched into side channels called sows, from which extended smaller channels at right angles, said to resemble pigs feeding from the sow. The first recorded use of the term was in England in 1665. In other ironmaking traditions, iron from the furnace was cast into different forms: in seventeenth- and eighteenth-century France into a single piece in the shape of a long, shallow fin; in Styria (*see* STYRIAN IRON TRAIL) into a flat sheet, later broken up by hammering. The pig-casting machine, in which molten iron is run into shallow moulds on an endless conveyor, and cooled by water sprays before being turned out, was invented in the USA in 1895 and has superseded old methods of casting pig; but in the twentieth century most molten pig iron is not cast but run into torpedo shaped ladle cars before being transported for use in molten form in steel making furnaces.

BIBLIOGRAPHY
General
Gale, 1967, 1969.

pigments Colouring matters which form the solid ingredients of paint. 'Lakes' are insoluble pigments derived from dyestuffs. Pigments were traditionally prepared for house painters by paint grinders, often in water-powered mills, of which there were many in the CROMFORD region, or for artists by 'artists' colourmen'.

White colouring was obtained from WHITE LEAD, zinc oxide, calcium carbonate or WHITING, BARYTES, CHINA CLAY, or GYPSUM. The last four are also widely used as fillers. Since the 1930s titanium dioxide slag has become the principal source of white pigments, the main source being the deposits of ilmenite near Havre St Pierre, 950 km (600 mi.) NE of Montreal: ilmenite is a mixture of iron oxides and titanium dioxide. The ore is transported to a plant at Sorel on the St Lawrence, 80 km (50 mi.) N. of Montreal, established in 1944, where electric furnaces are employed to extract both iron and titanium dioxide. Yellow pigments come from various ochres or iron oxides, or from chromium compounds. Blue is obtained from cobalt (*see* MODUM), silicates of sodium or aluminium. Red comes from ochres or RED LEAD.

BIBLIOGRAPHY
General
Morgan and Pratt, 1938.

pig mould A stone mould into which molten lead was cast from an ORE HEARTH, SLAG HEARTH or CUPOLA, usually a large block of sandstone with space hollowed out to receive the lead.

BIBLIOGRAPHY
General
Stratton and Trinder, 1988.

pilaster A pier or rectangular column projecting slightly from a wall, and in a CLASSICAL building conforming with one of the orders.

pillar-and-stall mining A method of mining, used principally for shallower, less gassy seams of coal, but also used in some deep seams; the commonest technique in extracting such bedded industrial materials as limestone, salt, and fireclay. The method is also known as 'room-and-pillar mining'. Tunnels or headings are driven into the solid mineral leaving pillars to support the roof. Often pillars were split by cross-tunnels to provide ventilation, and frequently the whole of a pillar was removed as the miner worked back towards his shaft and had no further need to support workings. The 'goaf' or 'gob' from which coal had been extracted would then subside. The dimensions of headings and pillars, their direction and their sequence of development are all subject to regional variation. The technique is still employed in some small mines but is not easily mechanized and has largely been superseded by LONGWALL MINING.

pin A pin is essentially a short length of stiff, straight wire, with a head at one end and a point at the other. Pinmaking was an early form of mass production, by the late eighteenth century being an operation of twenty-five stages, usually performed by different people. Pins were made from brass or iron, drawn into wire, cut into lengths and ground; a section of coiled metal for the head was attached by blows from a tiny drop hammer, then the pin was washed, tinned, washed again, and polished in a turning barrel partly filled with bran. Pins were sold in papers. Pinmaking on an industrial scale developed from the 1803s, after Lemuel W. Wright, an American, patented a pinmaking machine in England in 1824. John Ireland How (1793–1876) perfected a rotary machine for making pins in the USA in 1838. It was patented in 1841 and an example is held in the National Museum of American History, WASHINGTON DC. The chief pinmaking centre in nineteenth-century Britain was BIRMINGHAM, where the pioneer manufacturer was Daniel Foote Tayler.

BIBLIOGRAPHY
General
Tunis, 1965.

Pinhão, Alijó, Alto Douro, Portugal The centre of the port wine trade on the River Douro, 90 km (55 mi.) E. of Oporto and 18 km (11 mi.) SW of Alijó, with many commercial buildings connected with the trade and an iron bridge over the river. The exterior of the railway station is hung with tiles portraying grape cultivation and winemaking.

pipe A container made by a cooper, usually with a capacity of half a tun, or 126 gall. (5.73 hl), used for wine, cider, dried fruit, salt, oil, honey, peas and salmon. It is usually synonymous with 'butt'.

See also BARREL; DRAINAGE PIPE; HOGSHEAD; TOBACCO PIPE.

BIBLIOGRAPHY
General
Connor, 1987; Zupko, 1968.

Piraeus (Piraiévs), Attikí, Greece The port of ATHENS.

Pistoia, Tuscany, Italy To the north of this substantial city is the Lima Valley, with several surviving papermills located to use locally available straw, wood pulp and

571

water power, which previously used waste products of hemp and flax manufactures. Several steel plants were established around Pistoia by the Societa Metallurgica Italiana, founded in 1899. A TROMPE remains in use in a blacksmith's shop at Maresca.

BIBLIOGRAPHY
Specific
Antoci, C. Val di Lima (The Lima valley). In *Archeologia Industriale*, II, 1984.

pistol   A hand-held short-barrelled GUN, for use at very short range. While muzzle-loaded flintlock pistols became important personal weapons from the sixteenth century, they offered limited firepower or accuracy. In the 1840s, employing the techniques of the AMERICAN SYSTEM OF MANUFACTURE, Samuel Colt (1814–62) perfected a revolving breech-chamber using integral percussion cartridges. This dramatically increased the pistol's rate of fire and became the basis of the mechanized operation of larger guns.

pitch   A general term covering materials obtained as residues from the distillation of coal tar or turpentine. Pitch is used to seal the seams of ships and to bind small coal in making briquettes; it is also dissolved in naphtha for use in paints. The term is sometimes misleadingly applied to crude TURPENTINE or ASPHALT.

pithead baths   Buildings where coal miners changed into and out of their working clothes. They reflect a growing concern from the late nineteenth century for the health of miners and for the improvement of the landscapes of coal-mining districts. Pithead baths were introduced in Germany from the 1880s, and became obligatory from March 1900. In Germany, and in neighbouring mines in Belgium and Holland, baths consisted of halls containing hoists on which home or working clothes were suspended above changing areas surrounded by shower cubicles. Tub baths were usually available for supervisory staff, and there were segregated areas for those under 18. British baths were fitted with lockers rather than hoists, and the washed man and his clean clothes were segregated from the unwashed and his pit clothes. During the 1930s the Miners' Welfare Committee was responsible for erecting baths at the largest British pits. Their designs were inspired by the buildings of W. M. Dudok in the Netherlands and marked an early acceptance of modernism in Britain, paralleling the work of Frank Pick for the LONDON Underground. There were usually showers for miners, tub baths for supervisory staff, and separate areas for those under 18.

BIBLIOGRAPHY
General
Unverferth and Kroker, 1981.
Specific
Kemp, C. G. Recent developments in the design of colliery and miners' welfare buildings. In *Building Digest*, 1949.

MICHAEL STRATTON

planer   A machine tool designed to produce smooth flat surfaces, clamped to a reciprocating table and fed via a rack or screw against a single-point cutting tool fixed to a cross rail in a vertical frame. Cutters were fed incrementally across the work at the same depth at the end of each stroke. Drawings exist for a planer employed at Versailles after 1751, but the earliest surviving machine was built in 1817 by RICHARD ROBERTS, whose Manchester firm did much to establish the pattern widely built and employed in nineteenth-century machine shops in the making of heavier machinery. Planing began to be supplanted by milling and grinding machines when alloy steels and synthetic abrasive wheels became available in the latter part of the nineteenth century, but some planers were still being built in the 1950s. Similar machines are used in woodworking.

BIBLIOGRAPHY
General
Rolt, 1986; Steeds, 1969.

TIM PUTNAM

plastics   Substances that contain, at some stage, long chains of carbon atoms or arrangements of carbon atoms with oxygen, hydrogen and other atoms, that can be deformed under mechanical stress without losing their cohesion, and that keep the new forms that are given to them. At a certain temperature a plastic is capable of flow, and can be shaped by the application of heat and pressure. A thermoplastic material can be softened and resoftened indefinitely by heat and pressure, as long as the heat does not alter its chemical composition. A thermosetting plastic undergoes chemical changes with heat and pressure, and is converted into a mass that cannot readily be re-formed.

Natural plastics include shellac, and various derivatives of PITCH and BITUMEN, like the once familiar black stopper for beer bottles.

The first manufactured plastic was CELLULOID, demonstrated in 1862 by Sir Alexander Parkes (1813–90) and developed in the USA by John Wesley Hyatt (1837–1920). XYLONITE was a subsequent development.

Less flammable cellulose acetate resins were patented by C. F. Cross (1855–1935) and E. J. Bevan in 1894, and their production greatly increased during World War I when they were used as aircraft dope, the varnish employed to stiffen and seal fabrics used to cover airframes. After 1918 some of the plants concerned went over to the production of RAYON, but cellulose acetate became the most commonly used thermoplastic of the 1920s and 30s. Thermosetting phenol-methanal resins were patented by BAEKELAND in 1907. Casein plastics, based on milk protein, were developed in the early twentieth century in Britain and Germany. Means of manufacturing polyvinyl chloride (PVC) were perfected in both the USA and Germany *c.*1928. Polystyrene, which can be used as a substitute for rubber, was developed in the 1930s in Germany, where by 1939 it was the leading thermoplastic moulding material, and in the USA during World War II. The theoretical basis of plastics technology was established in the 1920s by Herman Staudinger, and a substantial industry developed as a result, an essential supplier to the motorcar and electrical industries. Sales of plastics in 1939 reached 125 000 tonnes in the USA, 75 000 tonnes in Germany and 30 000 in Britain. By 1945 over 400 000 tonnes were produced in the USA.

Thermosetting plastics are mostly sold as powders for compression with hydraulic presses or for extrusion moulding. Thermoplastic materials are produced as sheets, rods or tubes. The widely used injection moulding process, patented by A. Eichengrün in 1919, involves the feeding of a thermoplastic material in semi-liquid form, via a nozzle, into a two-part mould which opens to allow the ejection of the finished moulding. Plastics are also produced as films, between 1 mm and 15 mm in thickness, and as foils, which are less than 1 mm thick, and laminated with paper or wood substitutes.

Since World War II the plastics industry has grown rapidly. Many of the innovations of the 1930s, like POLYTHENE, have come into commercial production. Petroleum and natural gas have superseded coal as the principal sources of materials, a process begun in Britain in 1942.

See also NYLON; PERSPEX; RUBBER.

BIBLIOGRAPHY
General
Gloag, 1945; ICI, 1962; Kaufman, 1963; Yarsley and Couzens, 1945.
Specific
Harness, A. *The Story of Polythene*. Loughborough: ESPI, n.d.

BARRIE TRINDER

plateway A railway consisting of iron rails with upright flanges, on which worked smooth-wheeled wagons. First used in 1787 by John Curr (d. 1823) in the Duke of Norfolk's mines at Sheffield, they quickly spread, particularly in Shropshire (*see* RAILWAY; IRONBRIDGE). Plateways were perceived to have advantages over earlier forms of railway in cheapness and adaptability but became outmoded as new forms of edge rail developed. Existing systems continued and were extended through the nineteenth century, and were used in the twentieth. Rails were of cast or wrought iron, with some rolled from steel in the late nineteenth century. Sleepers were cast-iron, wrought-iron, wooden or stone blocks. Gauges varied. There were few applications outside Britain. There is a comprehensive collection of rails and sleepers at Ironbridge. *See* figure 116.

BIBLIOGRAPHY
General
Baader, 1882; Curr, 1797; Lewis, 1970; Wood, 1825.

plotland A development of housing on marginal land, whether in the countryside or on the edges of towns, often employing makeshift building materials, reused railway carriages, tramcars or buses, redundant military huts, or prefabricated buildings. Some developed from the summerhouses traditionally built on garden plots on the edges of cities, which remain in large numbers in the Netherlands, Germany, Austria (*see* VIENNA), and Denmark. Plotland development was a significant feature of housing in Britain in the 1920s and 30s, but was stopped by postwar planning legislation. It was concentrated on coastal and riverside sites, and in areas near cities where land values were low. Plotlands were closely associated with recreation, and their development in England foreshadowed such phenomena as HOLIDAY CAMPS and working-class owner-occupation. Sometimes, as at Peacehaven, 8 km (5 mi.) E. of Brighton, and in many places in California and Australia, plots were laid out by commercial developers, often on grid patterns. Second homes on plotlands are commonplace around such East European cities as Prague, Zagreb and Warsaw, as well as in Russia, where the bourgeois tradition of keeping a dacha (country home) has spread down the social scale. The shanty towns around Third World cities have much in common with plotlands.

BIBLIOGRAPHY
General
Hardy and Ward, 1984.

BARRIE TRINDER

plush A fabric with a long, rather sparse, stiff pile, all cut. Originally of wool, it was being made from silk and linen in the 1580s, and in the early nineteenth century from mohair and worsted. It was used for liveries and for upholstery.

BIBLIOGRAPHY
General
Kerridge, 1985; Montgomery, 1984.

Plymouth, Devon, England A port and naval base where the Rivers Tamar, Tavy, Lynher and Plym enter the English Channel. Plymouth Dock was established by the Royal Navy in the late seventeenth century, and renamed Devonport in 1823. The outstanding surviving naval feature is the Royal William Victualling Yard, Stonehouse, built by JOHN RENNIE in 1824–30 in the Classical style, with much use of iron framing. The Cornwall Railway, carried over the Tamar by I. K. BRUNEL's Royal Albert Bridge, formed of two 136 m (445 ft.) trusses on either side of a central pier, was completed 1859. The upper part of JOHN SMEATON's Eddystone Lighthouse of 1759 was rebuilt on Plymouth Hoe when the present lighthouse was constructed in 1882.

BIBLIOGRAPHY
General
Booker, 1971; Coad, 1983.
Specific
Shirley-Smith, H. Royal Albert Bridge, Saltash. In Pugsley, 1976.

LOCATION
[M] Plymouth City Museum and Art Gallery, Drake Circus, Plymouth PL4 8AJ.

Plzeň (Pilsen), West Bohemia, Czechoslovakia A centre of iron and steel production, which has specialized since the nineteenth century in heavy engineering and the

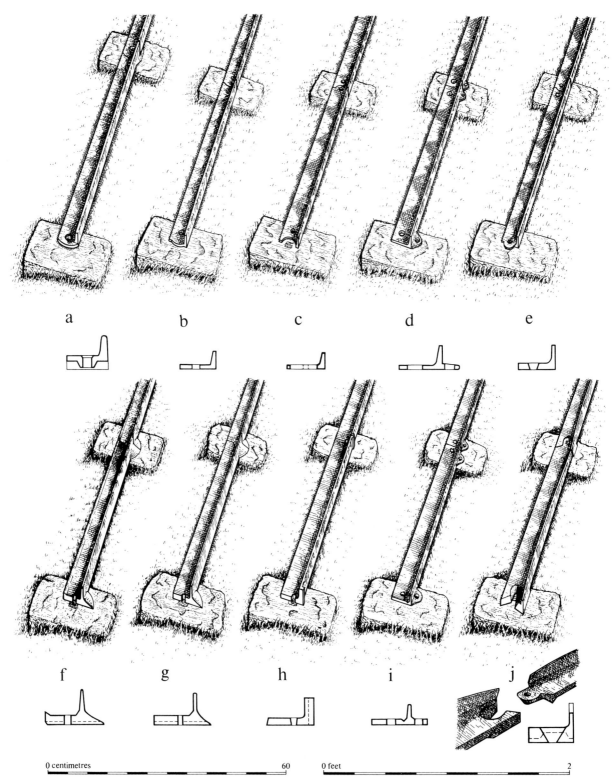

a   b   c   d   e

f   g   h   i   j

0 centimetres   60   0 feet   2

Figure 116   Rails from plateways in South Wales: the five rails in the top row of the drawing are all of relatively light weight and probably of eighteenth-century date; those in the lower row represent the variety of types found during archaeological investigation of the Brecon Forest Tramroad. (From Stephen Hughes, *The Brecon Forest Tramroads*, Aberystwyth: Royal Commission on Ancient and Historical Monuments in Wales, 1991.)

Royal Commission on Ancient and Historical Monuments in Wales

production of armaments. One of the most important foundries associated with the development of coke-fired ironworks in Central Europe is the Skoda works: originally founded at Sedlec by Count Wallenstein, it was moved to Plzeň in 1859 in order to be nearer to its markets. It was sold in the late 1860s to Émile Skoda, who extended the iron foundry, and built a non-ferrous foundry and a pattern shop. In 1886, a steel mill with open-hearth furnaces and crucible furnaces was established; this continued to expand until World War I when it became a major armaments works, with nine open-hearth furnaces. In 1919 it became part of Schneider & Cie, who introduced greensand mould casting in the 1920s. Today electric-arc furnaces are replacing pre-war open-hearth furnaces, but the iron foundry survives as in the inter-war period. The Skoda Museum documents the history of the plant, but does not preserve larger artefacts and structures.

Plzeň is also renowned for its brewing: there has been a significant brewing industry here since the Middle Ages, but the outstanding period of its development was in the early nineteenth century, when the first limited company was formed. There is a museum of brewing in an old brewery building.

BIBLIOGRAPHY
General
Jeníček, 1963.
Specific
Hucka, J. From the history of steel production in the Skoda Plzeň Concern. In *Skoda Review*, Prague, 1987.

LOCATION
[M] Museum of Western Czechoslovakia and Museum of Brewing, Veleslavinova Ulice c.6, Plzeň.

SIMON DERRY, JUDITH ALFREY and TIM PUTNAM

pneumatic dispatch A system of sending written messages through long narrow tubes by air pressure. It was devised in 1853 by J. Latimer Clark (1822–98) to link the Central and Stock Exchange stations of the Electric & International Telegraph Co. in London. The Post Office developed a network in London, abandoned in 1880, of which the longest tube extended 3541 m (3873 yd.), and similar systems were built in Berlin, Paris, Vienna and New York. Modified pneumatic systems were used in large shops from the late nineteenth century to dispatch cash from serving points to central tills and to return receipts and change. They were rendered redundant from the 1950s by electromechanical CASH REGISTERS.

BIBLIOGRAPHY
General
Ternant, 1881.

Podbrdo Railway (Wocheimerbahn), Slovenia, Yugoslavia Part of the Habsburg Empire route to Trieste in Italy from Klagenfurt and Villach in Austria, opened on 1 October 1906, now the Jesenice–Nova Grica route of the Yugoslav railways. There are thirty-two tunnels. The principal mountain section is between Podbrdo (Piedicolle) and Gorica. The 6339 m (6932 yd.) Podbrdo

(Wocheimer) tunnel under the Julian Alps passed under the boundary between Italy and Yugoslavia till 1945. Most international trains now take other routes.

LOCATION
Schneider, 1967.

Poland Poland is bordered on the east, south and west by the USSR, Czechoslovakia and Germany, and has a northern coastline of 524 km (325 mi.) on the Baltic Sea. The total area of the country is 312 510 km² (120 660 sq. mi.), and the population over 36 million. Of the land area 75 per cent is up to 200 m (656 ft.) above sea level, and 22 per cent is over 500 m (1640 ft.) above sea level. Most of the uplands, including the Sudeten and Carpathian Mountains, are along the southern border. Most (88 per cent) of Poland is drained by the Odra and Vistula (Wisła) rivers. Poland is divided into forty-nine administrative districts.

Poland is rich in minerals. There are three coal basins, the largest of which, in Upper Silesia, covers about 4500 km² (1750 sq. mi.) and is among the richest in the world. The coal deposits there are at a depth of about 1000 m (3300 ft.), and reserves are estimated at 70 million tonnes. The Lower Silesian coal basin covers an area of about 500 km² (200 sq. mi.) and produces high-quality coking coal. There are rich opencast workings for brown coal near Turoszów in Lower Silesia and near Konin and Bełchatów in Central Poland. Small quantities of crude oil have been extracted near Krosno and Jasło in the southeast for more than a century. Non-ferrous metals, mainly copper, are mined in Lower Silesia between Lubin and Głogów and near Złotoryja. Rich zinc ore deposits are exploited near Chorzów, Bytom and Olkusz in Upper Silesia. Iron ore is mined in Częstochowa province and in the Staropolski ore fields. Rich deposits of sulphur are exploited near Tarnobrzeg. Rock salt has been mined since the thirteenth century at Bochnia and Wieliczka, near Kraków, and in the north around Inowrocław, Kłodawa and Wapno.

The contemporary frontiers of Poland are very different from those of 1650 when Poland was a vast multinational country stretching further to the east, and incorporating Kurland, part of Inflants, the Ukraine and White Russia. Administratively it was divided into two parts, the Kingdom of Poland and the Grand Duchy of Lithuania. Poland was then an elective monarchy with the king chosen by the peers of the realm. Authority was shared by the monarch and a two-house Seym, or parliament.

The increasing power of Russia and Prussia, together with serious internal military and political weaknesses, led to the tragic dismemberment of Poland in the eighteenth century. In 1772, 1793 and 1795, Russia, Prussia and Austria carried out the three partitions of Poland. The largest share, 62 per cent, went to Russia. Prussia received 20 per cent, including the most-developed regions, Pomorze Gdańskie, Wielkopolska and Mazowsze. The Austrian empire received 18 per cent, including Małopolska with Kraków and part of the eastern provinces. Poland had lost Silesia in the fourteenth

Poland

century: it belonged to Austria until 1740, and then to Prussia.

In 1815 the Congress of Vienna imposed a new partition of Poland, abolishing the Grand Duchy of Warsaw which had been set up by Napoleon. Prussia regained the Grand Duchy of Poznań together with Silesia, Pomorze and Warmia. Part of Małopolska, which had been included in the Grand Duchy of Warsaw in 1809, again fell to Austria. Much of the territory that had comprised the Grand Duchy of Warsaw was established as the Kingdom of Poland, which until 1830 had a degree of autonomy, with its own Seym, government and army, but was afterwards entirely subordinated to Russia. The partition of 1815 proved stable and survived until World War I.

The policy of the governments that ruled Poland was aimed not only at the economic integration of the annexed lands, but also at the Russification or Germanization of the Polish people. Polish universities were closed down and the Polish language was banned from schools and offices. It was only in the Austrian-controlled areas after 1860 that the Poles gained a measure of independence.

Although after 1795 Poland was divided between three different alien countries the sense of nationality never disappeared, and the people managed to preserve and even to develop their own culture. The nineteenth century saw numerous struggles for national independence as the Poles showed their determination to resist the extermination of their culture.

In 1918, after 123 years of subjection, Poland regained its independence. Only a part of the territory that had formerly belonged to Poland came within the frontiers of the new state, but as a result of the Silesian uprisings of 1922, those parts of Upper Silesia where the Polish language predominated were also incorporated. On 1 September 1939 the German invasion of Poland marked the beginning of World War II. During the war Poland was occupied by the Germans and by the Russians, and suffered unparalleled devastation, reducing the population by one-sixth. Polish servicemen fought against the Germans on both eastern and western fronts and a strong resistance movement grew up within the country itself. After 1945, according to the international agreements made at Yalta and Potsdam, the boundaries were greatly changed and there were substantial movements of population. About a third of the Polish territory in the east was incorporated within the borders of the USSR. In the west Poland gained the former German territories of Warmia, Masuria and north and west Pomerania, together with Silesia. The post-war governments pursued policies intended to bring about rapid economic change.

In the seventeenth and eighteenth centuries Poland was largely an agricultural country, with 80 per cent of the inhabitants making their livings from farming, and the remaining 20 per cent involved in crafts, manufactures, commerce and services. Poland was one of the major exporters of agricultural products. During the Industrial Revolution of the nineteenth century there was no Polish economy: the three parts of the country functioned within the economies of the occupying powers. The Polish lands were generally underdeveloped. The feudal system prevailed in most areas until the mid-nineteenth century, and despite the introduction of capitalist modes of farming, the continued prevalence of smallholdings did not encourage industrial development. Poland lacked a strong middle class, and there were few sources of capital for the establishment of industrial plants. The growth of manufactures was often hampered by the policies of the occupying powers.

Industry flourished most in Silesia, where large-scale enterprises were established making use of local mineral resources. Such development was stimulated by protective tariffs established by the Prussian government and by investments from landowners. Nevertheless, compared with industrial regions in the western parts of Germany Silesia remained underdeveloped. Wielkopolska and Pomerania were treated as the bread-basket for industrializing Germany, and while agriculture prospered, the only important industries were the manufacture of agricultural machinery and food-processing.

In the Russian sector the principal industrial region was within the Congress Kingdom of Poland, where ambitious attempts were made between 1815 and 1840 to develop the metallurgical and textile industries, projects that benefited from the accessibility of the Russian markets. Investment was handled by the state through the Polish Bank, established in 1828, which co-ordinated industrial development through its control of credits. The Kingdom remained one of the most developed of the industrial provinces of Russia until World War I.

The Austrian sector of Poland was the least well developed of the three.

Despite the economic problems of the inter-war period, Poland's twenty years of independence after 1919 were marked by extensive economic developments. A modern harbour was built at Gdynia and the Central Industrial Region was developed on an ambitious scale.

Iron ore was already being mined on a considerable scale in the Świętokrzyskie Mountains by 1650, while lead and silver ores were being worked in the Olkusz region in the thirteenth century and in the Tarnowskie Mountains in the fourteenth. Saltmining in Bochnia and Wieliczka is recorded in the thirteenth century. The mining of hard coal in Lower Silesia began as early as the fourteenth century, and attained its peak between 1850 and 1880 when output reached 2 640 000 tonnes per annum. The first hard-coal mine in Upper Silesia was established at Ruda Śląska in 1751. A century later seventy-one mines in the region were producing a million tonnes of coal per annum, after production had been stimulated by demand from the iron and zinc industries. By 1880 coal production in Upper Silesia had reached 10 million tonnes per annum. The combination of coal mining, iron and zinc smelting, and engineering transformed Upper Silesia into one of Europe's principal industrial regions.

The Polish iron industry reached a turning point in the seventeenth century when primitive technology was replaced by the blast furnaces. Iron production was concentrated in the Staropolski and Częstochowski regions, and flourished between 1815 and 1830, when the November uprising brought a stop to investment. From 1833 control of the administration of mining and ironmaking was assumed by the Polish Bank, which thereafter controlled investment in those industries. Investment was concentrated particularly on the development of coke-based iron production in the Dąbrowski region, although even in the 1880s iron production in the Kingdom of Poland was based largely on charcoal fuel. In other respects there had been considerable progress in technology. Plate rolling mills were established in 1820, and the first puddling furnaces were built in 1833. From 1835 steam engines became more widely used, although even in 1876 there were fifty-two steam engines with a total power capacity of 1200 hp compared with the 3000 hp generated by all the water wheels operating in metallurgical plants in the Kingdom. A further turning point in the development of the iron industry in the Kingdom came in the 1880s. Pig-iron production increased from 35 000 tonnes per annum in 1878 to 221 000 tonnes in 1896, but the region's industry was ruined by World War I and production in 1920 was only 10 per cent of that recorded in 1913.

Upper Silesia became a major iron-producing centre in the course of the nineteenth century. In 1866 90 per cent of all iron-working plants in Upper Silesia were using hard coal as their fuel. The first Bessemer converter in Poland was set to work at the Huta Królewska, in 1863, beginning a process of concentration and modernization of ironworking in Upper Silesia. From the beginning of the twentieth century steam turbines, gas engines and electrification were introduced. From 1922 most of the iron and steel plants in Upper Silesia were within the boundaries of Poland, but the inter-war period proved to be a difficult period for the industry. The highest level of production, 879 000 tonnes, was achieved in 1938. During the war the plants fell into German hands, and after 1945 they were nationalized.

Zinc-smelting has played a most important role in the Polish economy since the early nineteenth century. In 1800 Jan Ruchberg, administrator of the lands and the glassworks of the Duchy of Pszczyńskie built the first muffle furnace for extracting metallic zinc from galena (lead sulphide, PbS) at Wesoła near Tychy. This marked the beginning of the zinc industry in Upper Silesia, the Dąbrowski Industrial Region and in Galicia. In the mid-nineteenth century about forty plants in Upper Silesia were producing over 30 000 tonnes of zinc a year, some 40–5 per cent of European output. Such a rapid growth was due largely to local deposits of galman (zinc carbonate, ZnO_3). In the 1870s important changes took place as a richer ore, zinc blende, was substituted. The more complex technology involved necessitated considerable investments of capital which led to the concentration of production in a smaller number of larger plants. After 1922 all the zinc plants were under Polish administration. A peak output was achieved in 1928 when Poland ranked third amongst the world's zinc producers, after the United States and Belgium.

A substantial engineering industry developed in Upper Silesia and the Congress Kingdom during the first half of the nineteenth century, following the establishment in the 1820s of a substantial plant near Warsaw. Many engineering plants were established by ironmaking concerns as outlets for their cast and wrought iron. Warsaw was the leading engineering centre in the Kingdom, with factories building trams, railway rolling stock, vessels for river and canal navigations, agricultural machinery, and plant for food-processing, particularly for sugar factories. In the late nineteenth century some 65 per cent of the Kingdom's output of machines was being exported to Russia. The CEGIELSKI agricultural machinery works in Poznań, in the Prussian sector of Poland, was of great importance in the latter part of the nineteenth century. Engineering in the Kingdom was devastated during World War I, and its restoration during the inter-war period was closely associated with the establishment of the Central Industrial Region. World War II brought ruin to many plants, particularly in the Warsaw region.

Textile manufacturing traditionally formed a strong sector within the Polish economy from the seventeenth century, when it used native raw materials like flax and wool. Lower Silesia, then outside Poland, was the world's leading exporter of flax products. In the late eighteenth century production was based on twenty thousand rural weaving shops. The introduction of cotton products and the mechanization of the production process brought an end to the flax industry in Lower Silesia in the early nineteenth century. From the 1820s textile manufacture flourished at Łódź and Kalisz in the Congress Kingdom of Poland, due to the ready markets available in Russia. The first cotton-spinning mills were built in the 1830s, when the first power looms were also installed in Geyer's plant in Łódź, although weaving was not mechanized on a large scale until the 1860s. By the end of the nineteenth century the Łódź Textile Industry Region was one of the principal centres of cotton production in Europe.

The first mechanized woollen-spinning mills in the Kingdom of Poland were established in Warsaw, Zgierz and Ozorków in the 1820s. In Galicia the main centre of woollen production was in Bielsko-Biała. The introduction of mechanization into the Lower Silesian flax industry was comparatively slow. In 1818 the brothers Alberti set up a mechanized flax-spinning mill in Wałbrzych, the first of its kind in continental Europe. One of the largest textile plants in Europe by the end of the nineteenth century was the linen factory at Żyrardów in the Congress Kingdom. The textile industry in the Kingdom in the nineteenth century produced mainly for export, and suffered considerably in the inter-war period when access to Russian markets was restricted.

Polish agriculture developed considerably in the course of the nineteenth century, together with such associated manufacturing concerns as flour mills, sugar factories and distilleries. The first factory in the world for processing sugar beet was built by Aschard in Lower Silesia in 1802, but for the most part mechanization of food-processing only began in the second half of the nineteenth century.

Before the industrial revolution the principal form of transport in Poland was river navigation. The construction of canals began in the second half of the eighteenth century. The Bydgoski Canal, connecting the Vistula with the Odra, was completed in 1774 and remains in use. The construction of the Królewski Canal connecting the Rivers Bug and Dnieper and the Ogiński Canal linking the Niemen with the Dnieper also began in the 1770s. The AUGUSTOWSKI CANAL was built during the period of intensive industrial development within the Congress Kingdom of Poland between 1815 and 1840. The building of a network of macadamized roads also began in the early nineteenth century. The first railway in Poland, connecting Wrocław with Oława in Lower Silesia was opened in 1842, and in 1848 Warsaw was linked by rail with Vienna. Most of the important railways in Poland were constructed in the 1860s and 70s. By 1900 the best-developed railway systems were in Silesia and in the Congress Kingdom of Poland, with the network in Galicia being much inferior. Each railway system had been built primarily to serve the needs of the occupying powers, and the Polish government after World War I faced complex problems in adapting the railway network to the needs of the newly-formed state. Many new branches were built in the inter-war period. Narrow- and standard-gauge steam locomotives still operate in Poland, and in the Bieszczady mountains a narrow-gauge line of 1895 remains a popular tourist attraction in the summer months, while another narrow-gauge line still links Trzebnica with Milicz near Wrocław.

Poland has rich traditions in the conservation of its industrial heritage. The first technical museum, the Museum of Technology and Industry, was established in Kraków in 1868 at the initiative of Dr Adrian Baraniecki. The Museum of Industry was established in Lvov in 1872. In the Russian sector a Museum of Industry and Farming was set up in Warsaw in 1875. The lack of freedom in political, economic and social spheres restricted such museums to teaching and popularizing new technical achievements. They were able to organize some special courses for women, as well as teaching in the technology of the sugar industry and in chemistry, and the Museum of Industry and Farming was one of the first in Europe to organize a seed-certification station. The prime concern of the museums was with education, so that most of the items collected were contemporary industrial products rather than historic artefacts. Polish technical museums retained this character until 1918. The Museum of Industry and Technology established in Warsaw in 1929 played an important role in the conservation of the industrial heritage. A spectacular achievement of the Museum was to succeed in putting under legal protection the early nineteenth-century puddling furnaces and rolling mill at SIELPIA WIELKA, which were opened to the public in 1934. Experience gained in this project led to the formulation of a methodology for future conservation schemes and during the 1930s plans were made to set up a museum of mining in an old silver mine at TARNOWSKIE GORY, and to open to the public the historic saltmine at WIELICZKA. During World War II the majority of the museums were severely damaged, the Museum of Industry and Technology being completely destroyed during the Warsaw Uprising.

After 1945 the conservation of the industrial heritage could not be accorded a high priority as the Polish government strove to rebuild the economy after the devastation caused by the war. Despite these difficulties two museums of technology were set up. In 1948 a Museum of Mining was established in Sosnowiec, although it has since closed down, and in 1949 the saltworks museum was set up at Wieliczka. The turning point in attitudes to industrial conservation came in 1955 when the Museum of Technology, affiliated to the Chief Technical Organization, was established in Warsaw. A systematic inventory of all technical artefacts was begun and the results published in the form of a catalogue. Such activities were supported by legislation. There are now some fifty-five museums of technology in Poland, some administratively subject to the Chief Technical Organization, some to the department concerned with the management of museums and the conservation of historical monuments at the Ministry of Culture and Art, and others to the management of industrial plants. The conservation of the industrial heritage is the concern of special sections at the provincial offices of Conservators of Monuments. The conservation of technological monuments and artefacts in Poland requires co-operation between scientific and technical organizations, industrial concerns and the authorities responsible for ancient monuments. Despite these efforts many industrial monuments in Poland are damaged, and there is no complete list of all the objects of importance in the history of technology in the country. There is a lack of specialists in this field, and no overall national programme for development. Voluntary initiatives are thus of the utmost importance and on various occasions they have stimulated official action. It is thanks to M. Radwan that many artefacts illustrating the history of metallurgy in the Staropolski Industrial Region have been preserved, and it was through the work of Alfons Długosz that the saltmine at Wieliczka was saved.

The Museum of Technology in Warsaw in the Chief Technical Organization fulfils the function of the central, co-ordinating institution for conserving the industrial heritage on a national scale. There are also national museums covering particular branches of industry: the Central Maritime Museum in GDAŃSK, the Museum of the Textile Industry in ŁÓDŹ, the Museum of Railway Engineering in WARSAW, the Museum of Posts and Telecommunications in WROCŁAW, and the Museums of Farming in Szreniawa and Ciechanowiec. The existing museums of technology reflect the fundamental branches of Polish industry, mining metallurgy and textiles. They include the Museum of Iron-Ore Mining in CZĘSTOCHAWA, the Museum of Hard-Coal Mining in ZABRZE, and the regional museums of the textile industry in BIELSKO-BIAŁA, KAMIENNA GÓRA, Białystok and Turek. The history of metallurgy from ancient times until the twentieth century is featured by a network of museums in the STAROPOLSKI INDUSTRIAL REGION. Regional industrial and technological traditions have led to the establishment of the Museum of Pharmacy in Kraków, the Museum of Silesian Trade in Swidnica, the Museum of the History of Industry in OPATÓWEK, and the Przypkowskich Museum in JĘDRZEJÓW. The post-war period has also seen the establishment of open-air museums following Scandinavian traditions in such places as Radom, Kielce, Lublin, Nowy Sącz and Sanok, most of which feature aspects of manufacturing before the industrial revolution. Many industrial monuments are preserved *in situ*, amongst the most interesting being the seventeenth-century papermill in DUSZNIKI ZDRÓJ, the paper-board plant at DOŁY BISKUPIE, the flour mill and ironworks in GDAŃSK, the hydro-electric plant at LÉSNA, the world's first welded road bridge at MAURZYCE, the gasworks in WARSAW and the flax-processing plant and workers' housing in ŻYRARDÓW. More recently a concern has grown to conserve not just the monument itself but also its wider environment. There are interesting plans to create an écomusée on the Kamienna River in the Staropolski Industrial Region. An area of oil workings has been preserved within the Open-Air Museum of Shale-Oil Mining in BÓBRKA and the écomusée in WAŁBRZYCH is developing a centre for displaying old and new mining technology. The profound political and economic changes of 1989–91 have necessitated a reappraisal of attitudes to the industrial heritage.

Poland has several unique technological monuments, most notably the Wieliczka saltmine, which is a UNESCO World Heritage Site, and the eighteenth-century silver mine at Tarnowskie Gory. The salt-graduation towers in Ciechocinek are unique, and there are few waterways as perfectly preserved as the AUGUSTOWSKI CANAL of the 1820s.

See also AUGUSTOWSKI CANAL; BIAŁOGON; BIELSKO-BIAŁA; BÓBRKA; BOBRZA; BYSTRZYCA KŁODZKA; CHEŁMSKO ŚLĄSKIE; CHLEWISKA; CIECHANOWIEC; CIECHOCINEK; CZĘSTOCHOWA; DOŁY BISKUPIE; DUSZNIKI ZDRÓJ; GDAŃSK; JĘDRZEJÓW; KAMIENNA GORA; KRAKÓW; LEŚNA; LIPINY; ŁÓDŹ; MALENIEC; MAURZYCE; NOWA RUDA; OPATÓWEK; SAMSONÓW; SIELPIA WIELKA; STARACHOWICE; STARA KUŹNICA; STAROPOLSKI INDUSTRIAL REGION; SWIDNICA; SZRENIAWA; TARNOWSKIE GORY; UPPER SILESIA; WAŁBRZYCH; WARSAW; WENECJA; WIELICZKA; WROCŁAW; ZABRZE; ŻYRARDÓW.

BIBLIOGRAPHY
General
Bocheński, 1984; Czajkowski, 1981; Dziekoński, 1963; Jasiuk, 1976; Jezierski and Zawadzki, 1966; Kaliński and Liberadzki,

1974; Krygier, 1958; Łukasiewicz, 1963; Mączak, 1981; Maisner-Nieduszyński and Pawłowska-Wilde, 1986; Maślakiewicz, 1965; Misztal, 1970; Molenda, 1972; Muzea, 1970; Orłowski, 1963; Orysiak, 1977; Pazdur, 1956, 1957, 1985, 1960–1; Pietrzak-Pawłowska, 1970; Pisarski, 1974; Popiołek, 1965; Radwan, 1963; Wielka Encyklopedia, 1967.

Specific
Jasiuk, J. Aktualne problemy ochrony zabytków techniki w Polsce (Problems of industrial heritage conservation in Poland). In *Materiały Muzeum Budownictwa Ludowego w Sanoku* (Journal of Material Culture of the Open-Air Museum in Sanok), XXIV, 1978.
Jasiuk, J. Chlubna karta ochrony zabytków techniki w Polsce (Glorious pages in the history of the conservation movement in Poland). In *Kwartalnik Historii Kultury Materialnej* (Quarterly Journal of the History of Material Culture), XXVIII (4) 1980.
Jasiuk, J. Ochrona materialnych źródeł do historii techniki w Polsce (Conservation of artefacts illustrating the history of technology in Poland). In *Kwartalnik Historii Nauki i Techniki* (The History of Science and Technology Quarterly), XXVIII(1) 1982.
Muzeum Przemysłu i Techniki w Warszawie, Przewodnik-Informator (Museum of Industry and Technology in Warsaw, Guide Book), 1933.

JAN KĘSIK

polder A Dutch word used in England from the early seventeenth century to refer to a piece of low-lying land reclaimed from the sea or from a lake, usually surrounded by dikes. The dikes receive drainage water from the polder, which is then lifted at a PUMPING STATION to flow away along a watercourse at a higher level.

Polhem (Polhammar), Christopher (1661–1751) The most famous of Swedish mining engineers, a scientist and at the same time a technologist, who was responsible for numerous imaginative innovations, and who had connections with mining developments throughout Europe. Born on the Swedish island of Gotland, he lived in Stockholm from 1669 and studied at the University of Uppsala from 1687. He became a skilled clockmaker, and in 1693 built at the FALUN copper mine a water-powered hoist for raising barrels of ore which became internationally famous. In 1694–6 he studied in Germany, the Netherlands, England and France, and after his return was appointed Director of Mining Engineering in Sweden, a post which gave him particular responsibilities at Falun. He visited mines in the HARZ in 1707. In 1700 he established a works near his home at Stiersund, near Husby in southern Dalarna, where such small metal items as scissors, knives and locks were made mechanically, although this visionary venture was never wholly successful. In 1718 he signed a contract to build a canal, which was never actually constructed, across Sweden from the Baltic to Gothenburg, a project which anticipated the GOTHA CANAL. Polhem's models of his machines are displayed in the National Museum of Science and Technology in STOCKHOLM and at Falun.

BIBLIOGRAPHY
Specific
Sörbom, P. *Christopher Polhem 1661–1751: the Swedish Daedalus.* Stockholm: Tekniska museet, 1985.

BARRIE TRINDER

polychrome The decorative effect in a building created by the use of different coloured materials, most commonly stones, bricks or architectural ceramics.

polymer The term 'polymer', derived from the Greek *polyus* (many) and *meros* (part), refers to a chemical compound whose molecule is formed from a large number of identical repeating units. The theory of polymerization, the chemical union of many similar molecules, was developed in the 1920s and 30s by W. H. Carothers (1896–1937) in the USA and by Hermann Staudinger in Germany. Polymers are synthesized from comparatively simple organic compounds like METHANOL, ETHENE and PHENOL. Polymers include many PLASTICS and such synthetic fibres as NYLON. To make a successful textile fibre, the polymer must have a high length-to-diameter ratio, the potential to be orientated, temperature resistance, a structure that permits secondary bonds to form, and strength. Polyester is an appropriate polymer for textile use: polystyrene is not. Since 1950 new polymer fibres have been developed, including polyesters such as Terylene (UK) and Dacron (US), both brand names of polyethylene terephthalate, which was identified in Britain by J. R. Whinfield and J. T. Dickson in the early 1940s, and went into commercial production in the USA in 1953 and in Britain in 1955.

BIBLIOGRAPHY
General
Hounshell and Smith, 1988; Stevens, 1975.

JANE HUTCHINS and BARRIE TRINDER

polythene The commonly used name for poly(ethene), a plastic discovered by ICI researchers in 1933, patented in 1936, first produced commercially at NORTHWICH in 1939, and used extensively as an insulator in RADAR apparatus in World War II. It was first used for household buckets and bowls in 1948, and has been extensively developed since.

BIBLIOGRAPHY
General
ICI, 1962.
Specific
Gibson, R. O. *The Discovery of Polythene.* London: Royal Institute of Chemistry, 1964.
Harness, A. *The Story of Polythene.* Loughborough: ESPI, n.d.

Polzunov, Ivan Ivanovich (1730–66) The designer and builder of the first Russian-made steam engine. As a supervisor in the state metallurgical complex in the Altai region, he suggested in 1763 a wholesale conversion from water to steam power, thereby solving the problem of industrial location in a region with few rivers. At the same time he submitted a design for a steam engine, which, unlike existing steam installations, actuated machinery directly, rather than by pumping water for water wheels. The project was approved by management, and ultimately by Empress Catherine II (Catherine the Great, 1729–96). For his initiative Polzunov was promoted to the rank of mining engineer, and some money and skilled personnel were allocated to the project. Not just the engine parts but also the tools to make them had to be manufactured, and it was not until late in 1765 that an engine rated at 32 hp was more or less ready. Basically it was an improved Newcomen engine, but with two cylinders of 80 cm (31 in.) diameter and 3 m (10 ft.) stroke, and two balancing beams. It differed from Polzunov's original design by being linked directly to bellows to provide a continuous draught for a furnace smelting non-ferrous metals. It was so used after Polzunov's death, probably for a short time only. While the engine was successful, its boiler was a weakness, and it was taken out of service after a few months. Local government officials resisted suggestions that it should be brought back into service, or that improved versions should be built. It was dismantled, and it is doubtful whether any parts remain, although there were reports in the nineteenth century that the cylinders were still in existence. A model in the Altai Regional Museum in Barnaul, built on the instructions of Polzunov's near contemporary K. D. FROLOV, was constructed from the drawings of his first, more versatile design.

BIBLIOGRAPHY
Specific
Danielevskii, V. V. *I. I. Polzunov*. Moscow, 1940.

JOHN WESTWOOD

Pombal, Sebastiao José de Carvalho e Mello, Marquês de (1699–1789) Pombal was virtually the ruler of Portugal between 1750 and 1777, during which period he held a position of ascendancy over King Joseph I. He organized the reconstruction of Lisbon after the great earthquake of 1755. His enlightened ideas did much to stimulate manufacturing industry in Portugal. He created a national basis for the organization of the silk industry, and established chartered companies to develop sardine and tunny fishing, hatmaking, and cutlery manufacture.

Ponta Delgada, Azores, Portugal   A city on São Miguel island in the eastern archipelago of the Azores, whose porcelain industry, dating from the mid-nineteenth century, is of particular interest. Tobacco processing began in the city in the late nineteenth century. Some furnace buildings remain from the Calheta foundry.

LOCATION
[M] Carlos Machado Museum, R. João Madeira, Ponta Delgada.

Pontcysyllte Aqueduct, Trefor, Clwyd, Wales   The most spectacular achievement of waterway engineering in Britain and a pioneer of cast-iron construction, the Pontcysyllte aqueduct was built in 1795–1805 to carry the Ellesmere Canal by nineteen arches 38 m (126 ft.) over the Dee valley in North Wales, 7 km (4½ mi.) E. of Llangollen. The height necessitated light construction with hollow masonry piers and spans, and a trough of iron plates. It was the third iron canal aqueduct to be built, but its daring and elegance made it the most influential. The relative roles of THOMAS TELFORD and WILLIAM JESSOP in its design are disputed, but most credit is usually paid to Telford, who designed a prototype at Longdon-on-Tern, Shropshire, in 1795–6.

BIBLIOGRAPHY
General
Hadfield and Skempton, 1979.
Specific
Cohen, P. Origins of the Pontcysyllte aqueduct. In *TNS*, LI, 1979–80.

PETER WAKELIN

Pontypridd, Mid Glamorgan, Wales   A town, 16 km (10 mi.) NW of Cardiff, with a magnificent single-arched bridge over the River Taff, built in 1755 by the self-taught Welsh mason, William Edwards (1719–89). Its span of 43 m (140 ft.) was the widest before the Sunderland Bridge of 1796, and the widest in stone until London Bridge of 1831. The first attempt was washed away and the second collapsed. Circular voids in the spandrels were introduced to relieve the weight. Edwards built other bridges in Wales, and in SWANSEA designed quays, copperworks and the settlement of Morriston.

BIBLIOGRAPHY
General
Pannell, 1967.

porcelain   A collective name for claywares with more or less translucent bodies. Porcelain was first made in China in or before the ninth century. Manufacture in Europe developed as a result of efforts to imitate Chinese productions which had been brought into Europe by the Portuguese and the Dutch. Rediscovery of the means of making true hard porcelain is credited to Johann Friedrich Bottger (d. 1719) who worked at Meissen near Dresden, who added a fluxing agent, alabaster or marble, to the clay; the Meissen porcelain works was established in 1710. In France the Sèvres works was founded at Vincennes in 1738, but only produced proper porcelain from c.1768. In same year William Cookworthy (1705–80) pioneered British efforts to manufacture a true porcelain; his patent covered a ceramic body in the form of china clay and a glaze made of china stone to which lime might be added. CHINA CLAY or kaolin is produced by the decomposition of granite. China stone, found in similar deposits, is a fine white powder of granite which is not fully kaolinized.

True porcelains are made of materials which when fired produce white-bodied wares. The materials must be very finely ground before use. Hard porcelains have clay bodies; feldspar within the clay body acts as the flux. Soft porcelains are earthenwares that have been made translucent by the addition of flux in the form of soda, potash, marble or bone ash. A series of British factories, such as the Chelsea Porcelain Works in London, used bone ash from around 1755. Worcester Works, from its foundation in 1751, used a paste of soapstone, the same approach being adopted at Caughley and Liverpool.

Figure 117 The Tysksebryggen or German Quay at the port of Bergen, a range of timber warehouses rebuilt after a fire in 1702, and now designated a UNESCO World Heritage Site
Barrie Trinder

BIBLIOGRAPHY
General
Atterbury, 1982; Boger, 1971; Burton, 1902; Chaffers, 1965; Cushion, 1980; Danckert, 1981; Godden, 1980; Jewitt, 1878; Searle, 1929–30; Weiss, 1971; Wynter, 1971.

MICHAEL STRATTON

Porjus, Norrbotten, Sweden Porjus, 190 km (120 mi.) NW of Luleå, and 100 km (60 mi.) S. of Kiruna, is a hydro-electric power station, the world's first major power plant with underground generating halls, completed in 1914, and sometimes known as the 'temple in the wilderness'. It was constructed 50 km (36 mi.) from the nearest village. Building materials were carried along a specially constructed railway. A 1250 m (4100 ft.) dam was built to control the supply of water, a 525 m (1720 ft.) headrace tunnel was blasted into the rock, and the 70 m × 11 m (230 ft. × 36 ft.) generating hall was cut into the rock some 50 m (160 ft.) below the surface. The station was designed by Erik Josephson, who also built the power stations at ALVKARLEBY and TROLLHÄTTAN. Josephson was responsible for the monumental switchgear building on the surface. The initial capacity of the station, when it had five turbines, was 38 MW, which has since increased to 530 MW. The station provided power for the electrification of the railway to the north, linking Luleå with the iron-mining town of Kiruna, and with the Norwegian port of NARVIK. The huts of the construction camp were replaced by elegant villas, the population of Porjus reaching about 3000 between 1920 and 1950. It has since fallen to around 600. The expansion of power generation on the Lule River in the 1970s made the switchgear building redundant. It has been converted into offices and facilities for the local community, and is visited by some 20 000 visitors a year.

BIBLIOGRAPHY
Specific
Nisser, M. Porjus water power station. In *Teknik & Kultur*, II, 1990.

MARIE NISSER

port A harbour, usually one where there are facilities for the loading and unloading and sometimes for the repair of ships. The term often refers to a town or city with port facilities. Harbours fall into four principal categories:

(a) natural harbours, like SYDNEY or Milford Haven;
(b) river ports, like LONDON or GLASGOW, some, like EXETER, gaining access to the sea by canals;
(c) PIER ports or artificial coves, like Dover or Portreath (*see* CORNWALL), usually within sheltered bays;
(d) harbours of refuge, usually entirely artificial, on inhospitable shores, like Gulfport, MISSISSIPPI.

Until the eighteenth century most loading and unloading took place alongside quays, but the construction of DOCKS transformed most large ports. Warehouses were built lining docks, which were enclosed with high walls. Sometimes warehouses were used as boundary walls. Until the nineteenth century most goods were handled in containers such that a strong man could lift them, although some windlass or treadmill (*see* HARWICH) cranes were employed. Steam cranes were generally unsuccessful in ports, but the HYDRAULIC CRANE, demonstrated by Sir W. G. ARMSTRONG in 1846, was widely adopted, and hydraulic power was also used to work bridge and dock gates, as well as hoists for bulk cargoes like coal. Electric cranes were used from the early twentieth century, but hydraulic power continued to be used in many European ports until the container revolution of the 1960s.

The coming of railways stimulated the building of single-storey transit sheds, of which those at ANTWERP are the most notable survivors. In many ports new docks were constructed which were served by rail from the beginning. Such docks often lacked substantial warehousing capacity.

Many new forms of cargo handling developed in the late nineteenth and early twentieth centuries. Grain silos were built first in North America, and then as exports of prairie grain developed, in European ports. Grain was unloaded by suction at Millwall Docks in London from 1904. From the 1920s overhead rail systems were used for handling animal carcasses, and conveyors were also developed for such commodities as coal and bananas. Specialized oil handling facilities with tank farms, and often with ships discharging at jetties rather than in docks, developed in the 1920s.

Methods of handling cargoes in ports have completely changed since 1950 and many nineteenth- and early twentieth-century docks are no longer used. Hydraulic power systems have been abandoned. The system of cargo handling that developed during the Industrial Revolution has been superseded by container systems, bulk carriers and their associated conveyors and pipelines, and by roll-on, roll-off FERRIES.

See also BREAKWATER; CRANE; CUSTOMS HOUSE; DOCK; DRY DOCK; FISHING PORT; HYDRAULIC POWER; LIGHTHOUSE; LINER; PIER; VICTUALLING YARD; WHALING; WHARF; and figures 83, 88.

BIBLIOGRAPHY
General
Greeves, 1980; Hunter, 1921; Jackson, 1983; Pudney, 1975; Stevenson, 1874; Vernon-Harcourt, 1885.
Specific
Swann, D. The engineers of English port improvements, 1660–1830. In *Transport History*, I, 1968.

BARRIE TRINDER

portable engine A self-contained steam engine that could be used as a mobile power unit for agricultural, forestry or industrial purposes, ranging in power from *c*.2 hp to 80 hp. The idea became practicable with TREVITHICK's high-pressure engine of 1802, but it was not until the 1840s that the firm of Ransomes of Ipswich, England, and others devised the type that became standard. A locomotive-style boiler was placed on wheels with an engine on top. Thousands were made in the next eighty years.

BIBLIOGRAPHY
Specific
Watkins, G. Steam power: an illustrated guide. In *Industrial Archaeology*, IV, 1970.

Portalegre, Alto Alentejo, Portugal A traditional centre of woollen manufacture, 160 km (100 mi.) SE of Lisbon.

The royal factory dating from 1772 was one of the most important in the country. The manufacture of tapestries began in the royal factory buildings in 1947, and Portalegre is now regarded as the largest tapestry centre in Europe.

BIBLIOGRAPHY
General
Queirós, 1981.

LOCATION
[M] Municipal Museum, R. José Mariá da Rosa, Portalegre.

port books An extensive group of documents recording the collection of national Customs duties (as opposed to local or 'petty customs' at ports), especially in the seventeenth and eighteenth centuries. The most detailed series include the Swedish *Stora Sjötullen*, and the English Port Books. The latter recorded coastal and overseas voyages in and out of 122 English and Welsh ports during 1565–1799. Overseas books registered duties paid and coastal books verified domestic movements. Most state the vessel's master, the home port, the vessel's name and tonnage, merchants' names, the date, origin and destination of the voyage, and the quantities and types of cargo. About 20 000 books in the Public Record Office, LONDON, describe millions of voyages. Their accuracy has been questioned, owing to customs evasion, but they are widely used to study trade and industry, English coastal shipping, the Anglo-Baltic trade in iron, English pottery production and coal output. Computerization of some records now enables intensive use.

See also SOUND TOLLS.

BIBLIOGRAPHY
General
Nef, 1932; Willan, 1938.
Specific
Aström, S.-E. From cloth to iron, Anglo-Baltic trade in the late 17th century. II: The customs accounts as sources for the history of the trade. In *Societas Scientiarum Fennica, Commentationes Humanarum Litterarum*, XXXVII, 1965.
Jarvis, R. C. Sources for the history of ports. In *Journal of Transport History*, III, 1957–8.
Wakelin, P. Comprehensive computerisation of a very large documentary source: the Portbooks Project at Wolverhampton Polytechnic. In Denley and Hopkin, 1987.

PETER WAKELIN

porte-cochère Originally a gateway for carriages, but the term more commonly applies to a porch large enough for vehicles to pass through.

portico An elaborate porch in the Classical style, usually projecting from the building, comprising columns supporting an entablature, topped by a PEDIMENT.

Portimão, Algarve, Portugal A port and an important fish-canning centre, 180 km (110 mi.) S. of Lisbon. The elegant bridge of Vau was begun in 1875 by the French company Fives-Lille. The town council has established a museum displaying the machinery and tools used in the canning industry.

Portland cement   The most widely used form of mortar since *c.*1900, and the principal material used in CONCRETE. It was patented in 1824 by Joseph Aspdin, and named Portland cement because of its resemblance to Portland stone. Aspdin's first works was at Gravesend (*see* MEDWAY). Portland cement is made from clay and some form of calcium carbonate, normally limestone or chalk: materials are mixed and ground, then fired up to 1540 °C in a kiln, where the lime, alumina and silica combine to form a clinker, which is cooled, mixed with GYPSUM to stabilize the cementitious compounds, and then pulverized in ball mills. Intermittently-worked shaft kilns were first used for firing (*see* JUDENDORF-STRASSENGEL) but were replaced by the rotary kiln, patented in the USA in 1885, which greatly increased the average size of cementworks.

BIBLIOGRAPHY
General
Brown, 1916; Cement Marketing Company, 1909; Doncaster, 1916; Eckel, 1928; Morgan and Pratt, 1938; Preston, 1977.

Portrush, County Antrim, Northern Ireland   A seaside resort, with harbour installations (1827–36) by John Rennie, which are now listed. It was served by steamer services from England before 1914. It is the terminus of the branch railway from Coleraine, opened in 1855, and has a spectacular station (1892–3) by Berkely Deane Wise, a mixture of red brick and timber framing with a 15 m (50 ft.) clock tower, a large concourse, and a restaurant seating three hundred. This was the first building in Northern Ireland to be listed. The building has since been adapted to new uses, while trains use a functional station nearby.

The depot, stumps of catenary posts, and the former Bushmills station remain of the 3 ft. (0.91 m) gauge hydro-electric tramway. This was opened to Bushmills in 1883, extended to the Giant's Causeway in 1887, and closed in 1949. The Salmon Leap power station, now derelict, housed two Alcott water turbines driving a Siemens generator. The tramway originally utilized a side conductor rail but adopted an overhead trolley system in 1899. A tramcar is preserved in the Ulster Folk and Transport Museum (*see* BELFAST).

Bushmills Distillery, 8 km (5 mi.) E., is reputed to date from 1608. While most of the buildings post-date a fire of 1885, Bushmills probably has the longest continuous history of any distillery in Britain.

BIBLIOGRAPHY
General
Barnard, 1887; McCutcheon, 1970, 1980.
Specific
Lee, C. E. The Giant's Causeway electric line. In *Railway Magazine*, 467, May 1936.
McGuigan, J. H. *The Giant's Causeway Tramway*. Lingfield: Oakwood Press, 1964.

BARRIE TRINDER

Portsmouth, Hampshire, England   A safe anchorage off the Solent has made Portsmouth an ideal harbour, and a naval dockyard was established by King John in the early thirteenth century. Its strategic importance increased and probably reached its zenith during the Napoleonic Wars when the town was considered so vital that it was fortified on the landward side for fear of invasion. The youthful THOMAS TELFORD designed the Commissioners' House in the Dockyard in the 1790s, and Marc Isambard Brunel (1769–1849) installed his celebrated block-making machinery there in the early nineteenth century. Major attractions are chiefly naval, and include HMS *Victory*, Nelson's flagship from Trafalgar; the *Mary Rose*, a warship of the reign of Henry VIII raised from the seabed in 1982; and HMS *Warrior*, the first screw-driven, ironclad warship, dating from 1860. Restored sewage beam-pumping engines can be seen in the suburb of Eastney.

BIBLIOGRAPHY
General
Moore, 1984, 1988.

LOCATIONS
[S] Eastney Pumping Station, Henderson Road, Eastney, Portsmouth PO4 9JF.
[M] HMS *Warrior*, The Hard, Portsmouth.
[M] Mary Rose Museum, No. 5 Boathouse, Main Road, HM Naval Base, Portsmouth PO1 3PX.
[M] Royal Naval Museum, HM Naval Base, Portsmouth PO1 3LR.

Port Sunlight, Merseyside, England   An industrial village in GARDEN CITY style, built from 1888 by soap manufacturer W. H. Lever (1851–1925). Four hundred houses had been erected by 1900, and ultimately there were over a thousand. The factory and the first houses were by Warrington architect, William Owen. Sir Edwin Lutyens (1869–1944), Ernest Newton (1856–1922) and other London and provincial architects provided a bewildering variety of designs for houses; there are also a church, a public house, many meeting halls, and the Lady Lever Art Gallery. Bromborough Pool Village, 1 km ($\frac{1}{2}$ mi.) E., is a settlement laid out by Price's Patent Candle Co. from 1853: for the time it was a remarkably spacious plan.

LOCATION
[M] Lady Lever Art Gallery, Port Sunlight Village, Wirral, Merseyside.

Portugal   Portugal lies on the western coast of the Iberian tableland, bordered by Spain to the north and east and by the Atlantic Ocean to the west and south. The land border is 1215 km (755 mi.) long while the coastline measures 832 km (517 mi.). The mainland area is some 88 944 km² (34 341 sq. mi.). Portugal's borders are the most ancient in Europe. Traditionally the country is divided into eleven counties, to which must be added the archipelagos of the Azores and Madeira, which are politically autonomous areas. They have an area of 3140 km² (1212 sq. mi.), making the total area of Portugal 91 560 km² (35 553 sq. mi.). The country has a population of 10 206 000, of whom about 20 per cent live in Lisbon.

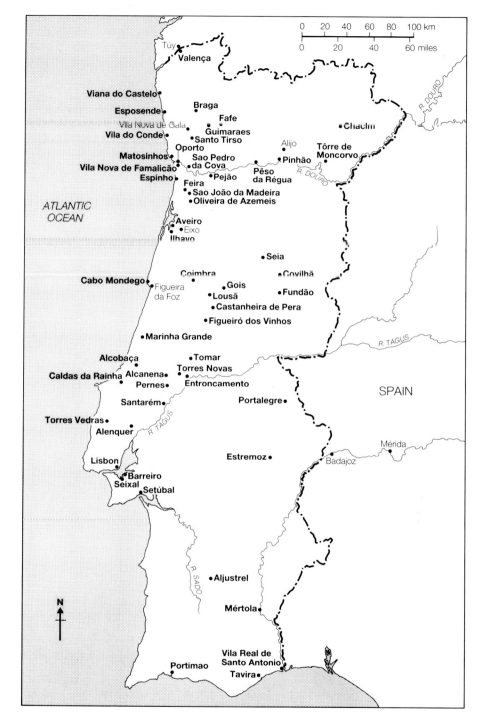

Portugal

In the early seventeenth century Portugal with its colonial empire was ruled by the Habsburgs, having lost its independence in 1580 due to the dual monarchy of Philip II (1527–98) of Spain; but in 1640, taking advantage of a European political situation that was unfavourable to Spain, independence was recovered through a rebellion led by the aristocracy who proclaimed the Duke of Bragança king with the title of John IV (1604–56). The break-up of the Iberian Union was not accepted by Spain, and war between the two nations lasted until 1668, Portugal receiving help from France and Britain. After the peace treaty with Spain the country enjoyed a

585

period of governmental stability and external peace which lasted until the end of the eighteenth century. The dominant political feature was a gradual centralization of power which under John V (1706–50) and Joseph I (1750–77) reached absolutism. In 1755 an earthquake destroyed part of Lisbon. In the reconstruction of the capital the Marquis of Pombal (1699–1789), a minister of Joseph I, played an important role, giving the city a new appearance in accordance with the principles of enlightened despotism. In the closing years of the eighteenth century political stability was shaken as the country became involved in European conflicts, and the hesitation of John VI (r. 1816–26) in accepting Napoleon's Continental System led to the Peninsular War (1808–14), which followed the French ruler's invasion of Portugal, where his army remained until it was driven out by a Portuguese-British army in 1810.

The proclamation of a constitutional regime in 1820 began a period of intense struggle between liberals and absolutists, which ended in 1834. In the second half of the nineteenth century the country went through a period of political stability and relatively rapid economic development. The spread of republican ideas in the closing years of the nineteenth century signalled the beginning of a crisis for the constitutional monarchy. The acceptance of an ultimatum presented by Great Britain, which demanded that Portugal should renounce its plan of extending its two colonial possessions across southern Africa, caused a nationwide protest, and eased the spread of a republican patriotism. After a fruitless attempt in 1891, a republican regime came to power in 1910, one of its first measures being the drafting of a new parliamentary constitution in 1911.

By participating on the Allied side in World War I, Portugal avoided the loss of its colonies but worsened the political situation of the republic. The instability brought about by inter-party struggles and the deterioration of the economic situation reached a climax with a *coup d'état* in 1926, which dissolved Parliament and established a military dictatorship. In 1933 a new constitution was drafted and with it the so-called 'Estado Novo' (New State), which was to align the country ideologically with Spain and Germany. The new regime, whose inspiration was the extremely right-wing Catholic professor of economics, António de Oliveira Salazar (1889–1970), forbade political parties, trades unions and strikes, imposed censorship of the press, and organized a political police force. With the victory of the Allies in World War II, organized opposition to the regime increased. In 1961 guerrilla wars broke out in the Portuguese colonies of Angola, Guinea-Bissau and Mozambique, which demanded independence. The regime replied by sending out troops. On 25 April 1974 a military *coup d'état* overthrew the oldest dictatorship in Europe, and restored the democratic constitution.

Most of Portugal is hilly, but there are no especially high mountains, some 11.6 per cent of the land area being over 700 m (2300 ft.) above sea level, and 43.1 per cent belong 200 m (650 ft.). The River Tagus (Tejo) divides it into two principal regions, mountainous to the north and prairie land to the south. The coast is generally shallow and flat.

The landscape is varied. Portugal has a great variety of metallic ores, but they are generally of low quality and many deposits have been exhausted. Tin and TUNGSTEN are found at Panasqueira and Fundão in the centre. The TÔRRE DE MONCORVO area has important deposits of iron ore although they are not currently exploited. Iron and copper pyrites are found around São Domingos and Aljustrel, and there are uranium deposits at Urgeiriça in the centre of the country. Coal is little exploited, the main beds being situated in Cape Mondego, São Pedro da Cova and Pejão. Quarrying, of limestone, marble, granite and china clay is important.

The fishing industry exists along the whole coastline, and is one of Portugal's traditional resources, contributing substantially to the feeding of the population as well as supplying the canning industry.

Many survivals of traditional manufacturing activities have disappeared in recent years, but some remains of the shipbuilding tradition developed during the period when Portuguese explorers were opening up Africa can be seen at places like VILA DO CONDE. Many coopers still work in OPORTO, and throughout the country there are attempts to revive local traditions in ceramics and textiles.

A particularly important aspect of the pre-industrial heritage is the exploitation of wind and water power in windmills, water mills, tide mills, sawmills, grinding mills and papermills. In 1960 Portugal had over 30 000 windmills and water mills, of which about a third were in use: 3000 windmills and 7000 water mills, 5000 of the latter having horizontal wheels. Now they are being destroyed rapidly and most will probably disappear in the near future. The most widespread windmills are Mediterranean-type tower mills, usually placed on the hills near the coast. They display many regional variations. Watermills are found all over the country, with horizontal wheels or overshot or undershot vertical wheels, although the power transmission systems are identical. Tide mills were quite important, and were used in Portugal as early as the fourteenth century. A particularly good example survives near SEIXAL at the mouth of the Tagus.

In the seventeenth and eighteenth centuries many decorative tiles were used in both religious and secular buildings, and subsequently railway stations were decorated with glazed tile panels with regional motifs. Most tile production is now industrialized, but many products of traditional tilemakers still adorn Portuguese buildings.

From the end of the seventeenth century Portugal, in accordance with current mercantilist theories, attempted to encourage industrial development with the aim of limiting imports. Tanneries, glassworks and silk manufactories were set up, while traditional manufactures like weaving were modernized. Gold was discovered in Brazil, then a Portuguese colony, c.1696, and the first gold smelting works were established. About 1000 tonnes of gold came to Lisbon before 1760, when the mines gave signs of exhaustion. The exploitation of Brazilian gold, together with the export of port wine to Great Britain in exchange for cotton and woollen cloth (according to the Methuen Treaty of 1703), hindered the Crown's policy of encouraging industrial development, although it did not prevent the setting up of some important manufacturing centres.

The depression arising from the exhaustion of the Brazilian gold mines stimulated a new period of industrialization, in which the Crown played a prominent role; this led to equilibrium in the balance of trade by the end of the eighteenth century. The first modern Portuguese factories, equipped with British machinery, were set up in this period. The water-frame was introduced between 1792 and 1794, and the first mule-jenny at the Real Fábrica de Alcobaça in 1789. The ironworks of Nova Oeiras was built in Angola in 1767. The steam engine only arrived in Portugal in 1819, although some had been operating in Brazil since 1811. Although Portugal was a latecomer to industrialization, it was sometimes involved in pioneering technological innovations. In 1742 BENTO DE MOURA made a primitive steam engine work before the assembled royal court. A drawing was published nine years later in *Philosophical Transactions*. In 1805 the Real Fábrica de Papel on the Vizela river became the first mill in the world to produce paper partly from wood, an initiative that was discontinued owing to the Napoleonic invasion in 1808 (*see* GUIMARÃES).

The French invasion – and the consequent exile of the royal family in Brazil between 1807 and 1820, and the various political and economic rights granted to the colony, including the ability to set up factories and to enjoy free trade with foreign countries – destroyed completely the precarious industrial structure in Portugal. Constitutional struggles between 1820 and 1834 delayed industrial development, but it was during this period that the first chemical factory was set up, in 1823, and Jacquard looms were introduced between 1824 and 1828.

Between 1850 and 1914 the pace of industrial development was fairly steady, accelerating after 1870. The opening of railways, from 1854, the building of macadamized roads, and the introduction of the telephone and telegraph were amongst the important developments of that period. HENNEBIQUE built a concrete bridge at Vale de Meoês (Mirandela) in 1906. Manufacturing was still less important than agriculture, and Portugal could not yet be regarded as a developed economy.

Coastal shipping and inland navigation provided the basic means of transport before the development of an adequate road system in the nineteenth century. The building in 1798 of the road from LISBON to COIMBRA made possible the commencement of stage-coach services, and in the first half of the nineteenth century a network of roads was established, mainly based on the capital, but also in the Entre-Douro e Minho region, and in the port wine area. River and coastal transport remained important, however, and in 1821 a regular connection by steamship was established between Lisbon and OPORTO. Stage coaches began to operate between the two cities only in 1855, along a macadamized road, commenced in 1824. Road building continued on a considerable scale throughout the second half of the nineteenth century.

The first railway was opened in 1856 and by 1932 a network totalling 3450 route km (2144 mi.) had been constructed, but it heavily favoured the coastal regions, and railways failed to reach some industrialized inland areas, making it difficult for them to find markets for their goods. Nor did the railway stimulate ironmaking. Locomotives, carriages and rails could be imported free of duty, so that the growth of iron- and steelmaking was delayed almost until the second half of the twentieth century.

The main commercial ports are located in the estuaries of the principal rivers, Lisbon on the Tagus, SETÚBAL on the Sado, and Leixões near Oporto on the Leça, the last an artificial harbour built at the end of the nineteenth century. There are numerous fishing ports which lack sufficient depth of water to be commercial harbours.

The Instituto Português do Património Cultural (Portuguese Institute of the Cultural Heritage) is responsible for the preservation and conservation of historic buildings. There is no specific legislation to protect the industrial heritage, although some industrial buildings are classified, and the ironworks at Nova Oeiras in Angola was classified in 1925, certainly one of the first industrial buildings in the world to be accorded legislative protection. The public sector museums are divided into three groups, national, regional and local council museums, and there are innumerable private museums.

The term 'industrial archaeology' first appeared in print in Portuguese in 1896, but it was not until the late 1970s that there was a marked surge of interest in the industrial heritage. Many local councils are now active in protecting industrial monuments, and there are displays relating to industrial history in the Museu Nacional da Ciência et da Técnica (National Museum of Science and Technology) at COIMBRA, and in local council and factory museums. The Portuguese railway authorities have established a network of museums where steam locomotives, carriages and other relics are preserved.

Windmills and water mills remain the characteristic

Figure 118 An Angolan stamp depicting the Fabrica de Ferro de Nova Oeiras, an ironworks built by the Portuguese in 1767–72; it was classified as a historic monoment by the Portuguese government as early as 28 May 1925, one of the first industrial structures to receive such protection
Michael Worthington

feature of the Portuguese industrial landscape, and the restored tide mills at SEIXAL are of particular interest. Apart from LISBON and OPORTO, the two main manufacturing cities, the industrial landscapes of the rivers Ave and Nabão are worthy of study, and COVILHÃ, a town traditionally devoted to the production of woollen cloth, has one of the most significant urban industrial landscapes.

The Serviços Cartográficos do Exército (Army Mapping Service) publishes maps at scales of 1:250 000 and 1:25 000, and the Instituto Geográfico e Cadastral (Geographical and Surveying Institute) is publishing the aerial survey of the country at a scale of 1:15 000. Some local councils have published maps on large scales.

See also ALCANENA; ALCOBAÇA; ALENQUER: ALJUSTREL; AVEIRO; BARREIRO; BRAGA; CABO MONDEGO; CALDAS DA RAINHA; CASTANHEIRA DE PÊRA; CHACIM; COIMBRA; COVILHÃ; ENTRONCAMENTO; ESPINHO; ESPOSENDE; ESTREMOZ; FAFE; FEIRA; FIGUEIRÓ DOS VINHOS; FUNDÃO; GOIS; GUIMARÃES; HIMALAIA, MANUEL ANTÓNIO GOMES; ÍLHAVO; LAJES DO PICO; LISBON; LOUSÃ; MADEIRA; MARINHA GRANDE; MÉRTOLA; MOURA, BENTO DE; OLIVEIRA DE AZEMEIS; OPORTO; PEJÃO; PERNES; PÊSO DA RÉGUA; PINHÃO; POMBAL, MARQUÊS DE; PONTA DELGADA; PORTALEGRE; PORTIMÃO; SANTARÉM; SANTO TIRSO; SÃO JOÃO DA MADEIRA; SÃO PEDRO DA COVA; SEIA; SEIXAL; SETÚBAL; SOUSA VITERBO, FRANCISCO DE; TAVIRA; TOMAR; TÔRRE DE MONCORVO; TORRES NOVAS; TORRES VEDRAS; VALENÇA DO MINHO; VIANA DO CASTELO; VILA DO CONDE; VILA NOVA DE FAMALICÃO; VILA REAL DE SANTO ANTONIO.

BIBLIOGRAPHY
General
Associaçao Portuguesa de Arqueologia Industrial, 1990; Cordeiro, 1989; Justino, 1988–9; Matos, 1980; Nabais and Ramos, 1987; Neto, 1985; Oliveira and Galhano, 1977; Oliveira *et al.* 1978, 1983.
Specific
Arqueologia Industrial, Braga: Universidade do Minho, 1987–.
Hume, J. Industrial archaeology in Portugal. In *Industrial Archaeology*, VII, 1970.
Reis, J. Industrial development in a late and slow developer: Portugal 1870–1913. In *Rivista di Storia Economica* (Papers in Economic History), 2nd ser., III, 1986.

JOSÉ M. LOPES CORDEIRO

port wine Port is a fortified wine from the upper Douro valley in PORTUGAL, exported, traditionally in PIPES, through OPORTO, particularly to England and the USA. Portuguese red wines were exported to England from the late Middle Ages, and trade was encouraged by the Methuen Treaty of 1703 (*see* PORTUGAL), but it was only from about 1820 that port wine took its present form, with an alcohol content of about 20 per cent.

postal service Couriers for royal and private business correspondence have existed since antiquity. Public postal systems derived from the official networks, but were often run for private profit. European posts were dominated by the Counts of Thurn and Taxis between 1450 and 1865, but national state-run systems gradually developed, in France in 1464, in England in 1635, in Russia in 1639, in Portugal in 1798, in Italy in 1818, in Switzerland in 1847, and in the Zollverein (*see* GERMANY) in 1850. In the USA, Congress gained power to establish post offices and post roads in 1787, stamps were adopted in 1847, and free deliveries in cities in 1863. After much political contention free rural deliveries were finally implemented in 1906. By 1897 most countries had joined the Universal Postal Union, formed to standardize rates. The underlying principles of modern postal systems – prepayment by the sender, denoted by a stamp, a uniform tariff by weight regardless of distance, and free delivery – were first successfully combined in Britain between 1840 and 1859. Postal organizations have utilized all kinds of transport, including horse, pigeon, coach, canal-barge, railway, ship, balloon, sledge, bicycle, pneumatic tube, pedestrian postman, aircraft, submarine, rocket and even floating zinc sphere (the last in Paris in 1870).

See also MAIL COACH; POSTBOX; POSTCARD; SORTING OFFICE; TRAVELLING POST OFFICE.

BIBLIOGRAPHY
General
Austen, 1978; Daunton, 1985.

CHRISTOPHER GREEN

postbox At first postboxes were carried by bellmen through streets, while post offices mostly had slotted receiving windows. Street boxes for outgoing mail were introduced briefly in Paris in 1653, but the first successful system was developed in Britain. Cast-iron upstanding boxes were installed in the Channel Islands in 1852, and all over Britain in the next two years. A 'pillar box' is freestanding and usually of cast iron. A 'wall box' is set into the side of a building or wall. Coin-operated stamp vending machines first appeared in 1884, but were not adopted by the Post Office until 1889. In the USA, the standard rural mailbox for delivered mail was adopted as part of the rural free-delivery system in 1898.

BIBLIOGRAPHY
General
Farrugia, 1969; Hudson, 1979a; Warren, 1978.

postcard Originally a plain correspondence card with a printed stamp, introduced in 1861 in the USA by John P. Charlton of Philadelphia, in Austria-Hungary in 1869, in Prussia and in Great Britain in 1870, and in France in 1873. It immediately became popular. In 1875 the First International Postal Treaty agreed that postcards could be sent between members at half the letter rate. Postcard sending developed most rapidly in Germany where 88 million were dispatched in 1899, compared with only 5 million in Britain in 1902. Postcards were produced by lithography, collotype, or half-tone relief (that is, photoengraving); the first two could be printed directly from the late 1860s, the last from the 1880s.

The leading postcard publisher in Britain was Francis Frith (1822–98), an early-retired printer who from 1856 was able to live on invested income. After travelling in Egypt he began to market photographs of exotic places and in 1860 set up a photographic business in Reigate which traded until 1972. Its collection of 60 000 glass-plate negatives survives and is accessible. The Curt Teich Co. archive in Lake County, Ill., USA, includes factory and mercantile establishments. The files include the original photographs from which postcards were made, correspondence about corrections, and samples of items used for colour correction. There are also large collections in HUNGARY.

BIBLIOGRAPHY
General
Byatt, 1978; Wilson, 1985.

LOCATIONS
[I] The Francis Frith Collection, Charlton Road, Andover, Hampshire SP10 3LE, England.
[I] Lake County Historical Society, Illinois, USA.

CHRISTOPHER GREEN

post coach A coach that could be hired by a private individual, to be driven either by himself or by a postilion. By 1800 there were systems in most European countries whereby 'post houses', inns or roadside farmhouses, were granted licences under which they were obliged to provide carriages for hire and to have available replacement horses for carriages hired elsewhere, as well as refreshments for travellers. By the mid-nineteenth century in Germany a written order called a 'laufzettel' could ensure that relays of horses would be ready along the route of a journey extending throughout the German states. Inferior services, known as 'Lohnkutscher' in the German states, 'voiturier' in France and 'Vetturino' in Italy, provided coaches seating four or five people inside and one outside, which would convey travellers up to 90 km (50 mi.) in a day, with no change of horses. Prices were normally regulated, and charges set by the 'post', a set distance within a given country: 5555 m (6075 yd.) in the Netherlands, 5 km (3 mi.) in Norway, and 15 km (9.3 mi.) in the Habsburg Empire. Prices were affected also by such factors as whether the postilion rode the horse or controlled it from a driving seat. In England, where posting was a monopoly until 1780, the cost was approximately three times that of the stage coach fare. In the Netherlands posting regulations were introduced by the French during the Napoleonic occupation, and abandoned in 1863. Posting was usually destroyed by railway competition, but it survived into the twentieth century in countries like Norway where railway development was slow. Post houses survive in open-air museums (*see* LILLEHAMMER) and several are preserved *in situ* (*see* LENINGRAD).

See also DILIGENCE; INN; MAIL COACH; STAGE COACH.

BIBLIOGRAPHY
General
Bird, 1969; Crofts, 1967.

BARRIE TRINDER

post-medieval archaeology A term used only in Britain. The Society for Post-Medieval Archaeology was formed in 1967, developing from an earlier Post-Medieval Ceramics Research Group: it defined its interests as the archaeology of the three centuries between 1450 and 1750, the period before industrialization. The society's journal first appeared in 1968, and from the beginning dealt with some industrial topics, in particular the glass and iron industries of the sixteenth and seventeenth centuries (*see* EXCAVATION). In recent years the scope of the journal has expanded to encompass topics like the growth of the pottery industry from 1660 to 1815, a Gloucestershire woollen mill built in 1813, and a Bristol tobacco pipe manufactory of the nineteenth century, which might certainly be regarded as industrial archaeological subjects.

BIBLIOGRAPHY
General
Crossley, 1990.
Specific
The Journal of Post-Medieval Archaeology, 1968–, London.

LOCATION
[I] The Society for Post-Medieval Archaeology, Museum of London, London Wall, London EC2Y 5HN.

BARRIE TRINDER

post mill The first type of European WINDMILL, the entire body of the mill revolving to face the wind on a vertical post (or stair tree) supported by a trestle or sill. On surviving examples the trestle is often supported on masonry or brick piers, and it is sometimes covered by a roundhouse.

potash A term often used to apply to any compound of potassium, but chiefly to two distinct substances: potassium carbonate (K_2CO_3), used as an alternative ALKALI to sodium carbonate; and potassium hydroxide (KOH), or caustic potash, which can be used instead of CAUSTIC SODA. Potassium salts have been extracted from the Dead Sea, and from mines in Alsace and Saxony, where solutions of potassium chloride are pumped, and subjected to ELECTROLYSIS to produce caustic potash.

BIBLIOGRAPHY
General
Morgan and Pratt, 1938; Partington, 1950.

potato The potato, *Solanum tuberosum*, which was brought to Europe from America in the seventeenth century, forms the world's most valuable vegetable crop, and significantly influenced the economy of regions like the west of IRELAND: in the nineteenth century its yield could be five times that of grain grown on the same ground.

Potatoes have been extensively used in industry, particularly for the production of ETHANOL, the production of starch, and as SIZE in textile manufactures. Starch manufacture involves the cleaning, grinding and sieving of potatoes to form a filtrate from which starch is extracted by successive settling and agitation in wooden vats, prior to drying.

Potato crisps, called 'chips' in North America, were first made in England by a Frenchman whose business was bought in 1919 by Frank Smith, who became the pioneer of a substantial industry. In 1921 he began making crisps in a former Handley Page aircraft factory at Cricklewood, London, and in 1928 constructed a specially-designed factory at Brentford. Until the late 1940s crisps were made in small copper pans each holding 27 litres (6 gallons) of oil.

The sweet potato, *Ipomoea batatas*, a native of tropical America unrelated to the common potato, is used as a vegetable in the USA (*see* MISSISSIPPI) and as a source of starch and alcohol in the USSR and Japan.

BIBLIOGRAPHY
General
Hudson, 1978; Prescott and Proctor, 1937; Salaman, 1949.

BARRIE TRINDER

potbank   The characteristic ceramics factory of the STOKE-ON-TRENT region. Typically it had a formal front to a road or, as in the case of JOSIAH WEDGWOOD's Etruria, to a canal, which was pierced by a waggon arch, often with a Venetian window illuminating the proprietor's office above. The arch gave access to a yard lined by an informal scatter of kilns, hovels and workshops.

BIBLIOGRAPHY
General
Tann, 1970.
Specific
Smith, D. M. Industrial architecture in the Potteries. In *North Staffordshire Journal of Field Studies*, v, 1965.

Pottendorf, Lower Austria, Austria   The first important centre of mechanized textile production in the Habsburg empire, 36 km (22 mi.) S. of Vienna. In 1801 Englishman John Thornton was placed by Kommerz Leih- & Wechsel Bank in charge of a yarn-manufacturing company at Pottendorf which by 1811 was working 38 800 spindles and employing 1800 workers. There were 47 460 spindles in the mills by 1828. In 1838 Thornton constructed a flax-spinning mill at Pottendorf which by 1845 was the largest in the empire, utilizing 8000 spindles. The factories were rebuilt in the 1890s but largely destroyed in World War II. Some early workers' dwellings remain.

BIBLIOGRAPHY
General
Milward and Saul, 1977.

potter's wheel   A machine used to shape ceramic articles from a plastic mass of clay while it is revolving.

Powered designs were widely adopted in the nineteenth century, and led to the fully mechanized jiggers and jollyers still in use; simpler foot-treadle-operated designs are pedalled in many craft potteries.

pottery   A term used from the fourteenth century to refer to a potter's workshop, and from the eighteenth to all kinds of ceramic wares for domestic use.

See also DELFTWARE; EARTHENWARE; FAIENCE; MAJOLICA; PORCELAIN; SALT GLAZE; SLIPWARE; STONEWARE; TERRACOTTA.

pound lock   Since the Rennaissance, the principal means employed in Europe of transferring boats between different levels of canals or rivers. A pound lock consists of a chamber, whose walls are usually set on piles and tied together with cross-beams, enclosed at either end by gates. Water is let in or out through sluices, usually set in the gates, so raising or lowering boats in the lock. Gates may be vertical or may swing horizontally.

The pound lock originated in China, probably in the tenth century AD, and may have been used in the Netherlands by the fourteenth century. The first in Italy was built at Milan in 1420, and mitre gates – which meet to form an apex facing the direction from which the water pressure comes, thus being held tight against each other and minimizing leakage – were drawn by Leonardo da Vinci (1452–1519) between 1498 and 1503. The first summit-level canal in Europe, the Canal du Midi in France completed in 1642, had forty-one locks. The first in England was on the EXETER Canal in 1564–6.

In the late nineteenth century powered lock gates were introduced, operated hydraulically or with water turbines, principally on such important rivers as the Seine, the Weaver and the Main, and side ponds came to be employed to store water for use in the next operation.

BIBLIOGRAPHY
General
Hadfield, 1986.
Specific
Needham, J. China and the invention of the pound lock. In *TRNS*, XXXVI, 1963–4.
Thelu, R. Les écluses avant le 17 siecle – Recherches sur les origines des écluses a sas (Locks before the 17th century – research on the origins of the pound lock). In *Navigation, Ports et Industries*, 631, 1978.

BARRIE TRINDER

power canal   A LEAT, usually on a large scale. The term is particularly applied to channels around falls on major rivers in the USA, built as speculations by companies who leased out industrial sites on the banks of these rivers with which they could then provide water power.

power station   A plant for generating electricity, com-

Figure 119   One of the Jugendstil entrances to the generator hall of the power station at the Zollern 2–4 mine at Dortmund-Bövinghausen in the Ruhrgebiet, designed by Bruno Möhring and Reinhold Krohn and dating from 1904; the mine forms the headquarters of the Westphalian Museum of Industry.
Barrie Trinder

prising a GENERATOR and source of motive power. Such equipment was easily accommodated in adapted structures, in Paris in 1875, in London and Brighton in 1881, and in New York in 1882, until demand had increased sufficiently to require large-scale buildings. EDISON's Pearl Street station in New York of 1882 was the first generator plant to which the word 'central', meaning 'for public use', was applied. Most stations of the 1880s had many small engines belted to many small d.c. generators. Between 1890 and 1910 stations were developed with fewer, larger engines, mostly of the CORLISS or WILLANS types, connected to large, slow-speed a.c. or d.c. generators. From *c.*1910 steam turbines of all types were used in most new installations, directly connected to high-speed alternators. The large installation by Sebastian de Ferranti (1864–1930) at Deptford, London, of 1889, where the machinery occupied some 3200 m^2 (40 000 sq. ft.), and included eighty Babcock & Wilcox boilers and provision for four 10 000 hp Corliss engines to drive the generators, stretched technology to the limit and beyond. The PARSONS turbine was first used in a power station in 1888. In power stations the source of motive power for the generators has almost always occupied more space than the generators themselves. Almost every form of motive power has been used to generate electricity, but the commonest form is the TURBINE, using steam generated by

coal, oil or peat, or water power, as in a HYDRO-ELECTRIC POWER STATION.

See also ALTERNATOR; DYNAMO.

BIBLIOGRAPHY
General
Carr, 1944; Dunsheath, 1962; Hennessey, 1972; Parsons, 1939.

CHRISTOPHER GREEN

Prague (Praha), Central Bohemia, Czechoslovakia   The long-established centre of Bohemia, Prague is Czechoslovakia's capital, spread round a pocket in the hills surrounding a bend in the River Vltava. The early modern city comprised five distinct settlements, with the royal (Hradcany) and aristocratic (Mala Strana) towns joined to the 'old' (Staré Mesto) and 'new' towns (Nove Mesto) and the fortress of Vysehrad by the 515 m (1689 ft.) Charles Bridge of 1357–1402. Prague became a unified city in 1784, incorporated its major industrial suburbs in 1883, and was extended to 'Greater Prague' in 1922.

Of the early industrial development in the city, most that survives relates to the River Vltava. A system of weirs was established after the Thirty Years War of 1618–48, facilitating the building of grain mills, tanneries and baths. The Old Town Mill was destroyed by fire in 1878 but smaller mills can be seen upstream of the western end

591

of the Charles Bridge on the Čertovka channel. The breadth of the river and its fall have continued to influence the pattern of development. Heavy industry and port facilities have concentrated downstream and the construction of new bridges has been a key to suburban development. A second crossing, the Chain Bridge of 1839–41 designed by Bedrich Schnirch, was built by Joseph Lanna, a shipowner, to form a link with the industrial suburb of Smichov.

Development in Prague in the nineteenth century was also shaped by the coming of railways. In 1845 it was linked to the Vienna railway system, and the central station (Nadrazi Praha Stred) was built.

Lines to Dresden and northern Bohemia were brought into the station in 1850. The Negrelli viaduct, which carries the line to Dresden 1100 m (3610 ft.) across the Vltava on 87 arches from Karlín to Holesovice is preserved. Hlavni Nadrazi, the Art Nouveau main station of 1901–9, is protected, as is the old central station.

Although the 'old town' contained many workshops and industrial sites in the early modern period, manufacturing soon spread to the 'new town' and formed the basis of suburbs. The Westphalian Reinhard von Westerhold, secretary to the Bohemian Commercial Council and inspector of the fustian trade, established, with government support, a 'garden' outside Prague containing a fustian factory of 1749, a tannery of 1750, and a wire-drawing works. Textile production brought in associated industries, and there were cotton printing works at Karlín and Smichov in the early nineteenth century, and a machine-building factory at Karlín.

After 1866, with the dismantling of the city walls and a spurt of road, rail and bridge building, the centre of the city lost many of its manufacturing activities. Boulevards were constructed along the line of the old town walls and the river embankments were renewed and lined with Empire-style tenements. Cheap accommodation for workers in central Prague became scarce during the 1850s and 60s, and subsequent industrial development focused on the suburbs of Smichov, Karlín, Vysochany and Holesovice, where owners' residences, industrial plants, and workers' housing were initially closely linked. The small machine and railway wagon works opened by C. Danek in Smichov in 1854 combined all three in one structure, with the workers' and the owner's apartments overlooking the courtyard workshops. However, as larger firms developed, such as the Prvni Ceskomoravska machine works established at Vysochany in 1871, housing and workplaces were dispersed.

Suburban expansion and industrial growth were both rapid after 1865, bringing improvements in sanitation and transportation: horse-drawn trams were introduced in 1875 following extensive street improvements, and several new bridges across the Vltava were constructed. Electric trams were introduced in 1896, linking the industrial suburbs to the old urban core, but neither these nor the upheavals of World War I broke the close links between workplace and residence in the industrial suburbs.

Prague has been an important centre for ironworking, engineering, and science-based industry. The Ringhoffer iron works manufactured structural iron like that used in the 1859 Tyl Theatre. The exhibition hall, designed by B. Munzburger for the 1891 International Exhibition, is one of the earliest steel-framed buildings in Czechoslovakia. Its future is uncertain. Prvni Ceskomoravska's output of machinery for sugar manufacture, mining and metal-working grew and diversified during the 1870s and in the following decade production of water turbines and bridge sections began, and a substantial export business developed. Refrigerators were added to the company's products in 1896, steam locomotives in 1899, motor cars in 1907, and a range of armaments in the approach to World War I. The expansion and technical development of this firm and others had been underpinned by the Czech Industrial Bank (Zivnostenska Banka), and the new terms of competition in the inter-war period led to mergers under the leadership of the Bank. Prvni Ceskomoravska and Breitfeld-Danek merged in 1921, and in 1927 they were joined by Kolben's electrical engineering company to form present day ČKD (Československa-Kolben-Danek).

Emil Kolben's electrical engineering works was founded in 1896 and recapitalized two years later under the control of the Industrial Bank. Kolben had gone from the Prague Technical High School through Western Europe to the USA where he had worked in the Edison laboratories, moving on to develop polyphase current devices for a Swiss firm before returning to Prague. His company rapidly expanded and by 1900 was building complete power stations and water turbines for export.

Other industries developed in the city in response to the large market it provided: breweries were established at Branik and Smichov in the later nineteenth century, and there was an ice factory at Branik. Transport equipment and precision-instrument making were located in the capital because of its market as well as the access it offered to government, and to scientific institutions. The residential development of the city generated its own engineering and industrial requirements: the first gasworks was established in Karlín in 1846, and others followed in Smichov and Zizkov in 1865. Prague was quick to take up electrical engineering. Arc lighting of the main streets was introduced in 1881, and the telephone in the following year. By the end of the century, many of the new suburban factories were using electric power from the outset.

The Stromovka Channel, now a preserved technical monument, is a 1 km (1000 yd.) stone-lined underground drift channel from the Vltava to fountains and lakes in the Stromovka gardens. It was built by Emperor Rudolf II in 1584–93, yet it was only in the 1880s that a civic steam-pumped water supply made it possible to bring water into individual apartments, thereby dramatically raising housing standards. The early twentieth-century central drainage plant, built by Henry Lindley to a British plan, comprised water storage tanks, two Breitfeld-Danek boilers built in 1903, and two steam engines. It is no longer in use but one pump survives, along with underground vaulted slurry tanks. Other important examples of urban engineering include the Palackého (1876–8), Privniho Maje (1899–1901), Svatopulja Čecha (1905–8) and Hlávkův (1908–12) bridges; the harbour and recanalization of the Vltava at Holesovice, which developed after 1875; and the New Town river embankments. A weir, lock and hydro-electric plant at Stavanice have been preserved.

Following independence, Prague became a centre for modernist architectural education with fierce polemics raging between the Technical University, the Academy of Fine Art and the School of Industrial Art, and strong links with French, Dutch, German and Russian circles. Kysela's late twenties department stores for Lindt and Bat'a set a pattern for open space and light developed by Kiltrick and Hruby's Bila Labut Store ten years later, which incorporated air conditioning. Janak's Hotel Julis of 1933 in Wenceslas Square and shopping arcades by Tyl & Bondy and Cerny showed how the same principles could be applied to restricted sites.

The National Technical Museum was founded in 1908 and established in the Schwarzenberg Palace, moving to its present site in 1940. Its precursors included the Museum Mathematicum founded by Jesuits in 1722, the short-lived Technological Museum, founded in 1799, and Naprstek's Industrial Museum of 1873. It houses collections concerning cars, aeroplanes, steam engines, motor cycles and model locomotives, and has a large collection of old locomotives which are not exhibited. It also has collections on the history and development of science, polygraphy, music boxes and electric motors which are kept in store. There are collections on the history of photography and cinematography, on time-measuring devices and electronics. An exhibition of mining with life-size mock-ups of mining and metallurgical machines and equipment is housed beneath the museum, and there is also a large model of a colliery and an ore mine. Other displays include a metallurgical exhibition, mechanical engineering and nuclear technology. In conjunction with the technical museums at Brno and Bratislava, it is responsible for several sites and smaller museums throughout the country.

At Mirejovice, 25 km (15 mi.) N., a 288 m (945 ft.) six-span steel-truss road bridge of 1900–4 crosses the Vltava.

BIBLIOGRAPHY
General
Dusan, 1984; French and Hamilton, 1979; Knox, 1965; Peichl and Slapeta, 1987.
Specific
Carter, F. W. ČKD employees, Prague, 1871–1920: some aspects of their geographical distribution. In *Journal of Historical Geography*, i, 1975.
Carter, F. W. The cotton printing industry in Prague, 1766–1873. In *Textile History*, VI, 1975.
Jilek, F. and Majer, J. *National Technical Museum, Praha*, Prague, 1980.
Kohout, J. and Vancura, J. Praha: 19 a 20 Stoleti, Technicke

Promeny (Prague in the 19th and 20th centuries: technical changes). In *SNTL*, 1986.

LOCATION
[M] Národní Technické Muzeum (National Technical Museum), Letné, Kostelní 42, Prague 7.

JUDITH ALFREY, SIMON DERRY and TIM PUTNAM

Prahova, Romania The Romanian district north of Bucharest centred on the cities of Ploiești, which is documented from 1545, and Cîmpina; it is chiefly important for its oil industry. Petroleum was extracted there from about 1550 and used for medical and lubricating purposes. The first documentary mention of the extraction of petroleum is in 1676; but there is an even earlier reference, in 1442, to oil-working in Moldavia. At first petroleum was extracted by digging ditches on the surface, in which it accumulated, or by sinking pits from which it was taken out in wooden buckets or leather bags, wound up by ropes coiled round wooden drums and worked by hand or with the aid of horses. Ventilation of the pits was by means of bellows, and they were lit up by mirrors which reflected the sunlight.

Marin Mehedinteanu built the first oil refinery in Romania, and the third in the world, at Rîfov, near Ploiești. It produced 2700 tonnes of kerosine per year, which was used for lighting the city of Bucharest. The first mechanical well-drilling machine was constructed at Drăgăneasa in 1883. It had wooden rods, but they were replaced the following year by metal rods following the patent of W. C. Allisson of 1881. More and more innovations were made which together increased the rate of extraction of petroleum and improved the means by which it was refined. Between 1893 and 1896 Anton Raky developed a new machine for rapid drilling, which is now displayed in the Deutsches Museum in Munich; and in 1904 he applied a flexible coupling between the motor and the drilling bit, which enabled the speed of the drill to be substantially increased. The first refinery on modern principles was built at Cîmpina in 1897. It had a capacity of 1200 tonnes a day. The Calyx-Drill rotative drilling rig was introduced in the Prahova region in 1901, enabling wells to be sunk to depths of 300 m (1000 ft.). In 1904 an oil refinery at Ploiești came into operation, and at Cîmpina attempts were made to extract oil from its deposits by pumping in gas, a method applied in California in 1911, which became commonplace in Romania between 1925 and 1935. Cîmpina was also the scene of experiments by the engineer Cantili in 1912, when he built an extendible drill, with two trucks and an electric motor, with which it was possible to drill dry to the bottom of a well. In 1916 the first oil pipeline from Băicoi to Constanța on the Black Sea was completed.

All the old installations relating to the oil industry in Prahova were destroyed in World War II, but the National Oil Museum in Ploiești has numerous historic artefacts, including a horse capstan used for lowering workers into wells and drawing out crude oil in buckets, leather bellows for ventilation, and lever arms from a Canadian-type drill.

BIBLIOGRAPHY
Specific
Un Secol de Industrie Petroliera in Romania (A century of the oil industry in Romania). Bucharest, 1971.

LOCATION
[M] National Oil Museum, Str. Dr E. Bagdazar 8, Ploieşti.

HORIA GIURGIUMAN

Pravia, Oviedo, Asturias, Spain   A city lying 26 km (16 mi.) NW of Oviedo, on the estuary of the River Nalón. The port of San Esteban has been notable for its commercial activity since the late eighteenth century, and as early as the fifteenth century was celebrated for its shipbuilding. In 1792 an attempt was made, under the direction of the engineer Fernando Casado de Torres, to make the River Nalón navigable, using the port of San Esteban at Pravia. The principal exports were coal from the inland mines and arms from the royal armaments factory at TRUBIA. The scheme was only temporarily successful. In 1797 the engineer Josef Müller submitted a design for a port project which utilized a system of sluices to maintain a constant water level in the harbour. A project directed by Pérez de la Sala in 1868 improved shipping facilities and rendered the River Nalón navigable from the port of San Esteban to the city of Pravia. Further improvements to the shipping channel and the wharfs were carried out between 1904 and 1923 under schemes prepared by Pedro Díaz and J. R. de Rivera. The port survives but it is no longer used for coal shipments and its facilities, along with those at Muros del Nalón and the town of San Esteban, are given over to fishing and the scrapping of ships.

Pravia's sugar refinery, between the Cudillero highway, the River Araguín and the Angones Bridge, was built in 1900 to serve the sugar-beet growing region extending to Candamo, Belmonte and Salas. The factory occupies a site of 3 ha (1.2 ac.). It consists of three main blocks with a 45 m (148 ft.) chimney, four weighing machines with their cabins, stores for sugar and molasses, a lime kiln, a sugar-beet yard, and stores for froth and pulp. The whole complex is surrounded by distinctive perimeter walls, rendered on the outer sides. The factory could process three hundred tonnes of sugar beet a day, using German 'Braunschweig' machinery.

CARLOS CAICOYA

precipitation   The extractive process whereby metals, particularly copper, are deposited from mineral-rich solutions by adding scrap of a more reactive metal, usually iron. At PARYS MOUNTAIN are remains of pits where copper sludge was obtained by placing scrap iron in copper sulphate solutions pumped from the mine.

prefabricated house   Timber prefabricated cottages were exported from Britain to the colonies in the early nineteenth century, and prefabricated hospitals and military storehouses were sent to the Crimea in the 1850s. The first timber prefabricated BUNGALOW intended for permanent occupation was erected in 1877, by which time prefabricated timber and CORRUGATED IRON stores, barns, factories and churches (*see* IRONBRIDGE) were relatively commonplace. The mass production of timber cabins in Scandinavia began in the 1900s (*see* ELVERUM), and this type of dwelling has also been extensively used in North America. In Britain in the late 1940s various types, some imported from Scandinavia, were used to relieve the post-war housing shortage, and were commonly called 'prefabs' (*see* BROMSGROVE). Although some designs were successful, there has been a general return to traditional building methods.

Among the most enduring forms of 'prefab' in the USA was the Quonset hut, a large section of arched corrugated steel with a plywood floor, originally developed by the US Navy at Quonset Point, Rhode Island, from the more austere British Nissen huts of the early twentieth century. Quonset huts proliferated on military bases in the 1940s and many remain in use elsewhere as warehouses, residences, repair shops and garages.

BIBLIOGRAPHY
General
Herbert, 1978; King, 1984.

DAVID H. SHAYT and BARRIE TRINDER

preserved railway   A term most commonly applied to lines that have been re-opened after closure by their original operators; it is sometimes applied to tourist-orientated lines like the Snowdon Mountain Railway in Wales which retain their original operating methods. There are examples in most European countries, but the numbers are particularly large in the USA and Britain, where the pattern set by the TALYLLYN RAILWAY and the FESTINIOG RAILWAY in the 1950s – of a reconstituted operating company backed by a separate organization for volunteer workers and enthusiast supporters – has been widely copied. There were six societies providing passenger services in Britain in 1965, four of them narrow-gauge, a total which had risen by 1989 to twenty-six, more than half of them standard-gauge, with about three hundred former main-line locomotives in addition to many from industrial railways. The principal lines, like the Severn Valley (*see* BEWDLEY) and the BLUEBELL RAILWAY, have developed into major tourist attractions; although profitable in accounting terms, they depend heavily on voluntary labour and the meeting by locomotive owners of the capital costs of restoration. On some lines standards of restoration and presentation approach those that would be expected in a first-rank museum; others work purely for the amusement of the operators. Market research has suggested that the success of preserved lines owes more to their appeal as venues for family outings than to their length or the variety of their steam locomotives.

The many preserved railways in the USA include several electric 'trolley' lines, an INTERURBAN, and two logging railways, the Cass Scenic RR in West Virginia, and the California Western RR at Fort Bragg, which offers an opportunity to 'ride the skunks' – direct-drive logging locomotives – 'through the redwoods'. Some American

Figure 120   The headstock
of 1879 at the Sevciny coal
mine in Príbram, Bohemia
Simon Derry

lines are of considerable length, like the 56 km (35 mi.) of
the Oregon Pacific & Eastern RR or the 72 km (45 mi.) of
the narrow-gauge Durango & Silverton RR in Colorado,
but many rely heavily on gift shops, 'journeys into history'
and meals on board, like those provided on the 'chew-
chew special' operated by the Wolfboro RR, N.H.

Many railway locomotives and vehicles are preserved in
other contexts: in museums, where in some cases they
may not be operated for conservation reasons; at 'steam
centres' or in working railway depots, from which they
may operate trains on tracks now normally used by other
forms of traction; or 'plinthed' as monuments in public
places. There has been some international interchange of
preserved locomotives. The GWR 4–6–0 *Pendennis Castle*
is in Australia and the LNER 4–6–2 *Dominion of Canada* in
MONTREAL. The stock of the Nene Valley Railway at
Peterborough, England, includes a French 4–6–0 and a
Norwegian 2–6–0; and an Austrian locomotive works on
the Welshpool & Llanfair Railway. British-built locomotives have been returned to their place of manufacture
from Australia, China and India, as have several preserved British locomotives exported to the USA in the
1960s.

BIBLIOGRAPHY
General
Baker and Harris, 1986; Body, 1981; Boyd, 1988; Ransome-
    Wallis, 1971; Rolt, 1953; Winters, 1986.
Specific
Draper, M. Can preservation survive? In *Steam Railway*, May
    1981.
Wilcock, D. Still on course to self-destruct. In *Steam Railway*, Nov.
    1984.

BARRIE TRINDER

press   The hand printing press, based on the linen-press,
simply screwed down a platen onto paper, pressing it
against a forme of type. With slight variations (*see*
COLUMBIA PRESS; STANHOPE PRESS) this remained widespread even after Friedrich Konig (1774–1833), a German working in London, devised steam presses using
cylinders instead of flat platens in 1810–18. The first true
rotary press appeared in 1851.

See also FORGING PRESS.

BIBLIOGRAPHY
General
Moran, 1973.

Prestongrange, Lothian, Scotland   *See* NEWTONGRANGE
AND PRESTONGRANGE.

Príbram,   South-West Bohemia, Czechoslovakia   A
silver- and gold-mining centre since the fourteenth century, currently exploited for opencast uranium mining.
There are many visible remains of nineteenth-century
workings, with a mining museum which opened in 1978
when mining ceased, comprising three buildings from the
extension of the Sevciny colliery in the 1870s: a headstock, an administration building in the English style, and
an engineering workshop. Workers' housing remains
nearby. In the administration building is a chronological
display illustrating the history of mining in Príbram.
Nearby two nineteenth-century ore mines are currently
being dismantled. Vozzech dates from 1857, and was the
first mine in the world to go to a depth of 1000 m (1100
yd.). The headstock and engine house are listed as
monuments. At the Anna mine two Breitfeld-Danek
compound winding engines of 1913 are preserved but

other features are not protected. Some other buildings relating to mining survive locally, including a steel-rope maker's shop. The museum is intended to become the central museum of ore mining in Bohemia, and will include cultural and social as well as technical exhibits.

LOCATION
[M] District Museum, Brezove Hory, Príbram.

JUDITH ALFREY and SIMON DERRY

Priestley, Joseph (1733–1804) A theologian and scientist, the discoverer with CARL SCHEELE of OXYGEN, and a pioneering researcher into electricity. Priestley knew and influenced many of the principal figures in the Industrial Revolution in Britain. He was ordained in 1762, and married the sister of JOHN WILKINSON. He identified oxygen in 1774, announcing his discovery in 1775. In 1780 he moved to Birmingham, where JOSIAH WEDGWOOD provided him with money and scientific apparatus, and where through the Lunar Society he knew Matthew Boulton (*see* BOULTON & WATT) and JAMES WATT. He welcomed the French Revolution, as a consequence of which his house was sacked by a 'Church and King' mob in July 1791, which was one of the reasons why in 1794 he migrated to the USA where he settled at Northumberland, Pennsylvania.

BIBLIOGRAPHY
Specific
Priestley Correspondence. Warrington, Cheshire: Warrington Public Library.

Prilep, Macedonia, Yugoslavia An ancient town outside the Markove Kule fortress, relocated to a new site by Turks in the fifteenth century. Traditional crafts are still practised in 'čaršija' (workshops) in the town centre. Prilep is an important centre for tobacco growing and processing, as is illustrated in a works museum. Many traditional water mills (*see* YUGOSLAVIA) can be seen at Zrza, between the village and the Archangela monastery.

LOCATIONS
[M] Monastyr Archangela Branch Museum, 97000-Prilep.
[M] National Museum, Mose Pijade 138, 97000-Prilep.
[M] Tobacco Works Museum, 97000-Prilep.

prime mover A machine that converts one form of energy into another, so acting as the source of the power conveyed through a transmission system. The term is used chiefly as a means of classifying such stationary sources of power as GAS ENGINES, HORSE GINS, OIL ENGINES and STEAM ENGINES.

printing The elements of book printing – type, a PRESS, and a production infrastructure – all pre-dated their combination by Johannes Gutenberg (?1397–1468) in fifteenth-century MAINZ. Almost immediately printing took on an industrial aspect, with large capital investment, interchangeability of parts, wide retail distribution networks and even some of the earliest trade unions. In England printing spread to most towns of note in the course of the eighteenth century. Mechanization was slow until NEWSPAPER PRINTING promoted such innovations as rotary presses, stereotyping, MONOTYPE and LINOTYPE. Printing and burgeoning literacy created attitudes critical of authority, so that official curbs were, and are, always threatening. The works founded by Christophe Plantin (?1520–89), which operated from the sixteenth century until the 1870s, is preserved in ANTWERP, and there is equipment from small nineteenth-century works in many museums.

See also COPIERS; ENGRAVING; LINOTYPE; LITHOGRAPHY; MONOTYPE; NEWSPAPER PRINTING; PRESS; TYPE; TYPEWRITER.

BIBLIOGRAPHY
General
Eisenstein, 1979; Glaister, 1960; Lewis, 1970; Moran, 1973.

CHRISTOPHER GREEN

prison A building in which convicted or suspected lawbreakers are confined, the term originally applying to the abstract state of confinement. Prisons came to have particular characteristics in the industrial period. The Englishman John Howard (?1726–90) visited prisons in most European countries and influenced the building of new prisons in most English county towns at the end of the eighteenth century, recommending the separation of prisoners supposed to be redeemable from those regarded as beyond reclaim. In several countries there was much interest in radial designs, whereby many prisoners or cells could be observed from a central point, the prototype being the Maison de Force of 1772–5 at Ackerghen near Ghent. The political economist Jeremy Bentham (1748–1832) advocated the adoption of a PANOPTICON plan for Millbank Penitentiary, completed in 1821, which became one of the sights of early-nineteenth-century London. Two American systems influenced the building of prisons in Europe: that in which prisoners were separated from each other, adopted in the Eastern Penitentiary, Philadelphia, of 1825, and the 'silent' system used at Auburn, N.Y., from 1816–25. The separate system became the ideal in England, and was applied in new prisons and extensions of the mid-nineteenth century. Labour, in England picking oakum for rope manufacture or sewing mailbags, formed part of many prison regimes. TREADMILLS were built and operated in some prisons, either for the power they could provide, or as a means of punishment in 'silent' regimes where infringements of rules were numerous. Cylindrical iron rotary jails are preserved in INDIANA and IOWA.

BIBLIOGRAPHY
General
Bentham, 1791; Burn, 1964; Clay, 1862; Howard, D. L. 1960; Howard, J. 1784; Mayhew and Binny, 1862; Pevsner, 1976.

BARRIE TRINDER

Privas, Ardèche, France Some 5 km (3 mi.) W. of Privas, which itself is 30 km (18 mi.) NW of Montélimar, stands the masonry headstock built in 1868 for the 100 m (330 ft.) deep No. 9 shaft of the Saint-Priest iron-ore mine. The winding gear and the steam engine were installed within the structure, and there are remnants of a rail link which conveyed ore wagons direct to the LA VOULTE blast furnaces.

BIBLIOGRAPHY
General
Belhoste, 1991

probate records Wills and probate inventories, lists of people's possessions made after their deaths, are significant sources for some aspects of industrial history before the mid-nineteenth century. The nature of such lists varies from country to country. Most include household goods, farm stock and tools and materials used in manufacturing, but landed property may be excluded, and the definition of movable possessions may vary between periods and between countries. They have been used in England, France, Germany, the Netherlands, Spain, Maryland (USA), Quebec (Canada), and Virginia (USA), to study the rates of diffusion of such manufactures as clocks and curtains, changing room uses, farm tools, and the transfer from wood to coal fuel. In England they throw light on such industries as fishing in Lincolnshire, the forest trades of the Chilterns, shipping in Yorkshire, mining in Shropshire, metal manufactures in Sheffield and the Black Country, domestic textiles in Yorkshire and the Thames barge trade. In the USA probate records have been used by historians more than by industrial archaeologists.

BIBLIOGRAPHY
General
Ambler and Watkinson, 1987; Burn, 1797; Moore, 1976; Reed, 1988; Trinder and Cox, 1980; Vickers, 1986; Woude and Schuurman, 1980.
Specific
Les actes notariés: source de l'histoire social XVI°–XIX° siècle. Actes due colluque de Strasbourg, Mars 1978 (Legal transactions as a source for social history: transactions of a seminar at Strasbourg, March 1978). Strasbourg: ISTRA, 1979.
Cox, N. and J. Probate inventories: the legal background, I & II. Valuations in probate inventories, I & II. In *The Local Historian*, XVI, 1984–6.
Garden, M. Les inventaires après décès: source globale de l'histoire social lyonnaise ou juxtaposition de monographies familiales? (Probate inventories: a source for a total social history of Lyons or a juxtaposition of genealogical monographs?) In *Cahiers d'Histoire*, XII, 1967.
Hey, D. G. The use of probate inventories for industrial archaeology. In *Industrial Archaeology*, X, 1973.
Paquet, G. and Wallot, J.-P. Les inventaires après décès à Montréal au tournant du 19° siècle: préliminaire à une analyse (Probate inventories at Montreal at the turn of the nineteenth century: a preliminary analysis). In *Revue d'Histoire de l'Amerique Française*, XXX, 1976–7.
Trinder, B. La vie d'une région en cours d'industrialisation: le Bassin houiller du Shropshire 1660–1760 (The material life of an emerging industrial region: the Shropshire coalfield 1660–1760). In *CILAC*, 1985.
Wiedmer, L. Le cadre de vie matèriel dans le campagne genevoise au XVIII° siècle (The standard of living in the countryside around Geneva in the 18th century). In *Revue du Vieux Genève*, XII, 1982.

BARRIE TRINDER

producer gas A mixture of carbon monoxide and NITROGEN, formed by passing air through red-hot coke. It is a poor source of energy, but is cheaply made in GASWORKS where it was used for heating RETORTS and added to TOWN GAS. It is used in glass and pottery manufacture, in the HABER-BOSCH PROCESS for making AMMONIA, and in the production of SMOKELESS FUEL. It was effectively manufactured first in SIEMENS's producer of 1861.

BIBLIOGRAPHY
General
Dowson and Larter, 1906.

proof house An establishment where barrels of GUNS of all kinds are tested by firing, and, if satisfactory, stamped, before sale or use: this is a legislative requirement in most countries. Completed guns are fired, in booths, with precisely measured charges, and subjected to inspection before stamping. Most proof houses have ranges in which unmounted barrels can be tested with charges of gunpowder. The proof house at BIRMINGHAM is a building of particular distinction.

propane (C_3H_8) A hydrocarbon gas, produced from natural gas or during the distillation of petroleum. It is distributed as LPG, and can be used in combination with oxygen for cutting metal.

BIBLIOGRAPHY
General
BP, 1958.

propene (propylene, C_3H_6) A hydrocarbon, and a gas at room temperature. Propene is formed by passing propane over a heated catalyst. It is used in the production of plastics.

BIBLIOGRAPHY
General
BP, 1958; Norman and Waddington, 1977.

propylene *See* PROPENE.

Prosperous (An Chorrchoill), County Kildare, Ireland A cotton-spinning settlement established by Robert Brooke on the Bog of Allen in 1780, and the scene of fierce fighting in the rising of 1798. The mill was destroyed but a terrace of workers' cottages, dated 1780, remains to the north of the unbending turnpike road across the Bog from Clane to Allenwood. One of the hotels built by the Grand Canal Company at Robertstown lies 4 km ($2\frac{1}{2}$ mi.) SW, and the Leinster Aqueduct of five stone arches over the Liffey is 6 km ($3\frac{1}{2}$ mi.) SE.

BIBLIOGRAPHY
General
Cullen, 1987; Pakenham, 1969.

proto-industrialization A concept developed from the early 1970s, especially after the publication of the article by Mendels (1972): it describes a phase of economic activity in which production is typically organized in cottage workshops in the countryside, in pastoral rather than arable regions, by families combining manufactures with agricultural activities. Towns in such regions served as distribution centres for goods *en route* for national and international markets. Products might include wooden wares, like toys, clocks and watches, small metal manufactures, and leather goods; above all, though, the practice applied to textiles. Proto-industrialization can be seen as a pre-condition for industrial growth, stimulating rapid population growth, the development of technical skills, and acquaintance with commerce. It can also be interpreted as a stage of immiseration or proletarianization, making the rural population dependent upon capitalist middlemen.

The concept has been subjected to criticism, particularly since it appears to encompass only a limited range of occupations. Treated flexibly, and as a social rather than a purely economic phenomenon, the model may be a usefully enlightening means of analysing early industrialization, by posing questions about the types of community where settlement is easy and population growth rapid, and where manufactures may flourish. Such communities may take up small-scale manufactures, or they may provide services, transport, or the manufacture of tools, containers or ropes, for capital-intensive activities like iron-smelting or coal-mining. Industrial archaeology, by identifying and analysing the physical remains of early industrial communities, can contribute significantly to the debate on proto-industrialization.

BIBLIOGRAPHY
General
Berg *et al.*, 1983; Clarkson, 1985; De Vries, 1976; Jones, 1974; Kriedte *et al.*, 1981; Levine, 1977; Pollard, 1981.
Specific
Houston, R. and Snell, K. Proto-industrialization? Cottage industry, social change, and industrial revolution. In *Historical Journal*, XXVII, 1984.
Hudson, P. Proto-industrialization: the case of the West Riding wool textile industry in the 18th and early 19th centuries. In *History Workshop Journal*, XII, 1981.
Jorberg, L. Proto-industrialization in Scandinavia. In *Scandinavian Economic History Review*, XXX, 1982.
Medick, H. The proto-industrial family economy: the structural function of household and family during the transition from peasant to industrial capitalism. In *Social History*, I, 1976.
Mendels, F. F. Proto-industrialization: the first phase of the industrialization process. In *Journal of Economic History*, XXXII, 1972.
Thirsk, J. Industries in the countryside. In Fisher, 1961.
Trinder, B. S. The open village in industrial Britain. In Nisser 1981.
Trinder, B. S. La vie d'une région en cours d'industrialisation (The

material life of an emerging industrial region: the Shropshire Coalfield 1660–1760. In CILAC, 1985.

BARRIE TRINDER

public house A term used in England from the late seventeenth century, sometimes referring to any type of hostelry licensed to sell alcoholic drinks, but usually to a tavern that did not provide overnight accommodation. A beerhouse, under the Beer Act 1830, was able to supply only beer, whereas a licensed public house also supplied spirits and wine. From the early nineteenth century many public houses came to be owned by brewing companies. Public houses were providers of recreational facilities, and venues for public meetings. Pressures in the 1890s to make them respectable led to the closure of many, and the erection of smaller numbers of architecturally distinctive buildings, like those in BIRMINGHAM.

See also HOTEL; INN.

BIBLIOGRAPHY
General
Clark, 1983; Crawford *et al.*, 1986; Dixon and Muthesius, 1978; Harrison, 1971.
Specific
Harrison, B. H. Pubs. In Dyos and Wolff, 1973.

public utility Since the early twentieth century services provided for the population – often, although not necessarily, those provided in large cities by government agencies – have been described as public utilities. Water was considered a responsibility of government in the ancient world (*see* ISTANBUL; SEVILLE) and remained so in many medieval and early modern communities. A mid-twentieth-century American work asserted that 'A water supply is a public necessity and a public enterprise. It is a recognized government activity' (Babbitt and Doland, 1939). Urban growth in the industrial period created new technical, administrative and political problems. Creating effective government agencies and providing satisfactory means of controlling private companies proved as difficult as devising methods of draining heavily populated urban areas. In regions like the RUHRGEBIET neighbouring cities developed co-operative agencies for services like water supply and sewage disposal. The need for public utilities was often argued on health grounds, and sustained by statistical evidence of the kind used in England by Edwin Chadwick (1800–90) in justifying the improvement of drainage and water supplies. In most countries the role of government in the provision of services has fluctuated, one of the peaks of government involvement being in Birmingham, England, in the late nineteenth century when Joseph Chamberlain (1836–1914) thought that the existence of the corporation should be justified by its role as an agent of improvement. The necessity of providing services came to be one of the primary determinants in twentieth-century town planning.

The services generally considered to be public utilities include ABBATOIRS; AIRPORTS; BATHHOUSES; COMPRESSED AIR supply; DOCKS; ELECTRIC POWER supply; short-distance FERRIES; gas supply (*see* COAL GAS; GASWORKS; TOWN GAS);

Figure 121 One of the more unusual types of public utility: the SUDAC compressed-air plant in the 13th arrondissement in Paris, dating from 1891, from which compressed air was supplied to numerous industrial customers; the building was designed by Victor Popp, director of the company, and Joseph Leclaire, the company engineer. The photograph was taken in 1891.
C. Decamps, Inventaire général

HOSPITALS; HYDRAULIC POWER; MARKETS; PNEUMATIC DISPATCH; POSTAL SERVICES; certain types of railway (*see* FUNICULAR; METRO; TUBE RAILWAY; UNDERGROUND RAILWAY); some aspects of road transport (*see* OMNIBUS; TRAMWAY; TROLLEY BUS); some maritime services (*see* LIGHTHOUSE; LIGHTSHIP); SEWAGE DISPOSAL; TELECOMMUNICATIONS; water power in certain circumstances (*see* POWER CANAL); and WATER SUPPLY.

BIBLIOGRAPHY
General
Babbitt and Doland, 1939; Clark, 1962; Finer, 1952; Fraser, 1976; Hoy, 1976; Lewis, 1952; Simon, 1890.

BARRIE TRINDER

Puchberg, Lower Austria, Austria   A resort 25 km (16 mi.) W. of Wiener Neustadt, with a 760 mm gauge rack railway (Schneeburgbahn) to Hochschneeberg, worked by six 0–4–2T locomotives built in 1893–9 by Krauss of Linz.

puddling furnace   A REVERBERATORY FURNACE used for forging wrought iron from pig iron, with coal as its fuel, patented by Henry Cort (1740–1800) of Fontley, Hampshire, England, in 1784. There were earlier experiments in the use of reverberatory furnaces for this purpose by George and Thomas Cranage in the 1760s and Peter Onions in 1784. For about twenty years Cort's method of making wrought iron was employed in Britain alongside

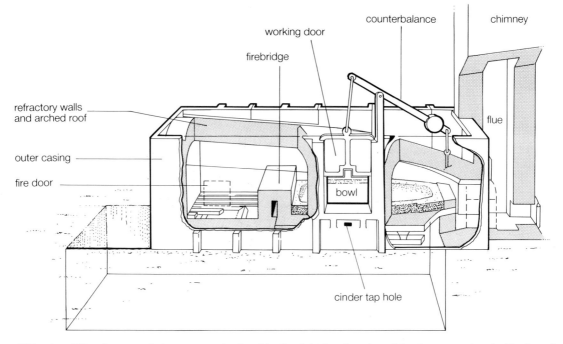

Figure 122   A puddling furnace: pig iron or scrap is placed in the right-hand section of the furnace and melted by heat drawn across the firebridge from coal burned in the section on the left; after a time decarburization begins and bubbles of carbon monoxide break through the surface for about half an hour. When this 'boiling' stage is complete the iron has ceased to be a liquid and takes the form of a pasty mass, which is quartered and removed through the fire door to be hammered into blooms of wrought iron.

the STAMPING AND POTTING process but by 1810 puddling was the predominant method, and had spread to North America and continental Europe. From *c*.1816 the process was improved by adding an oxidizing agent, usually forge slag, to melted pig iron, an innovation credited to Joseph Hall (1789–1862) and generally called 'wet puddling' as distinct from 'dry puddling' (the original Cort method). Attempts to mechanize puddling met with little success in Europe although they were used commercially in the USA. The output of wrought iron diminished after the introduction of mild steel in the second half of the nineteenth century, and ceased altogether in 1976. There are restored puddling furnaces at IRONBRIDGE and SIELPIA WIELKA.

BIBLIOGRAPHY
General
Gale, 1967, 1969; Mott, 1983.
Specific
Morton, G. R. and Mutton, N. The transition to Cort's puddling process. In *Journal of the Iron & Steel Institute*, 205, 1967.

BARRIE TRINDER

Pullman, George Mortimer (1831–97)   An entrepreneur who improved the railway sleeping car and introduced other innovations that eased travel during the second half of the nineteenth century. The first carriage converted by him into a sleeping car appeared in 1859,

and his first purpose-built sleeping car in 1865. In 1869 he introduced a dining car. Pullman cars were operated by railway companies, but managed by the Pullman Company who collected a supplement from passengers for their use. In the USA the word 'Pullman' became synonymous with sleeping car. Pullman developed his own manufacturing company, and accommodated his workers in a MODEL COMMUNITY 23 km (14 mi.) S. of Chicago (*see* ILLINOIS) from 1880, although the company had to dispose of it after riots in 1897.

Pullman carriages were used in several European countries. The first in Britain were introduced in 1874, and in 1881 the first all-Pullman train linking London with seaside resorts began to work, inaugurating a tradition which lasted until the 1960s. A works for assembling Pullman cars was established at Brighton by 1881, taken over by the British Pullman Car Co. under Sir Davidson Dalziel (1854–1928) in 1906, and began building carriages in 1908.

It was through Pullman cars that many innovations in railway carriage design were introduced into Europe, among them bogies, heating, better lighting, and daytime saloons. The term 'Pullman' is still used in Britain to indicate exclusive luxury trains. About a hundred Pullman cars remain in Britain, including the 'Topaz', built in 1914, in the National Railway Museum (*see* YORK), and there is a British-built car from the French *Golden Arrow* train of the 1920s at MULHOUSE.

BIBLIOGRAPHY
General
Behrend, 1962a; Harding, 1951; Husband, 1917; Morel, 1983.

BARRIE TRINDER

pulp Since the 1860s wood pulp has been the principal raw material for making PAPER: it is also used in the manufacture of PLASTICS and SYNTHETIC FIBRES. Pulp is made mechanically by shredding and grinding wood in running water so that the fibres are separated, sieving the liquid, then pressing it into pulp, which may be transported for further processing. Friedrich G. Keller in Germany patented a means of preparing pulp from wood by mechanical means in 1840. It was purchased in 1845 by Heinrich Voelter, who began production on a commercial scale. In 1864 Charles Watt and Hugh Burgess patented a process for the treatment of wood with caustic soda to produce pulp for papermaking. At many large modern papermills logs are shredded and the resultant suspension used in papermaking without being pressed and dried. Newsprint and other weaker grades of paper, made from mechanically-ground pulp, are often called simply 'pulp'. Alternatively pulp may be made by chemical methods: part of the cellulose which binds the wood fibres together is dissolved by boiling under pressure, originally with CAUSTIC SODA and subsequently with other chemicals that produced papers less liable to deteriorate.

See also figures 26, 66, 67.

BIBLIOGRAPHY
General
Shorter, 1971.

BARRIE TRINDER

pump A mechanical device for raising or moving liquids or gases. The most common form is the reciprocating pump, usually cylindrical in form, in which a piston, moved by a rod, creates pressure or suction. Reciprocating pumps take many forms, ranging from large installations used for draining mines or in water-supply systems to the injectors of diesel engines. The centrifugal pump, which works with a steady rotary action, was produced from *c.*1818 in the USA, where early examples were known as Massachusetts pumps. It became known in Europe after developed versions were exhibited by J. G. Appold at the Great Exhibition of 1851.

See also SHOES.

BIBLIOGRAPHY
General
Barr, 1983; Bowden-Smith, 1920; Butler, 1922; Hasluck, 1907; Westcott, 1932.

pumping station A pumping station is needed in almost every water supply system and in some sewage disposal systems.

Pumping stations in LAND DRAINAGE systems may take the form of WINDMILLS operating scoop wheels or Archimedean screws, or steam-, diesel- or electrically-powered pumps: these raise water that has drained into one watercourse into another at a higher level, along which it can flow into a natural drainage channel.

Prime movers in pumping stations tend to work well within their capacity for most of their time, and to be well maintained. In consequence many are preserved. In 1987 there were eighty pumping stations in Britain, with historic machinery dating from before 1939, including sixty-one with steam engines, three with water turbines, three with gas engines, two with steam turbines, nine with diesel engines and two with ram pump installations.

See also figure 76.

BIBLIOGRAPHY
General
Water Authorities Association, 1987.

Punta Arenas A Chilean port with many hulks of historic ships, once anchored to allow the coaling of ships going round Cape Horn. The hulks include:

- *Hipparchus*: a 1840-ton transitional sail-carrying, iron-hulled steamer, built at Newcastle-upon-Tyne in 1867.
- *Falstaff*: a 1465-ton iron sailing ship built at Barrow-in-Furness in 1875.
- *Munzo Gamero (County of Peebles)*: a 11 691-ton iron sailing ship, built at Glasgow in 1875.

BIBLIOGRAPHY
General
Brouwer, 1985.

putter Literally 'one who pushes', a term used in England from the early eighteenth century for one who pushed vehicles loaded with mineral in a mine. In central Europe in the seventeenth century the work was often done by a youth who had graduated from shovelling, but was not yet able to hew. In English coal mines the task of the putter was recorded in folk song as having been made easier by the introduction by John Curr in the late eighteenth century of plate rails (*see* PLATEWAY).

putty A filler: the usual means of securing window panes to their frames, and for setting plumbing fixtures. It is traditionally made from WHITING and oil in edge runner mills, although synthetics have replaced it for many purposes. LINSEED OIL putty was used for wooden window frames, quick-setting putty for metal frames, and rubber-based putty for VITROLITE panels. A putty mill is preserved at LEEDS.

LOCATION
[S] Thwaite Putty Mill, Stourton, Leeds LS10 1RP.

Pyrenees (Pyrénées), Ariège, France Although as early as the sixteenth century there were many forges in the part of the Pyrenees which now forms the department of Ariège, the CATALAN FORGE only appeared in the area at the end of the seventeenth century. In the Catalan forge iron was obtained directly from the ore, without the

Figure 123   Ore shutes at Rio Tinto station, 1982: installations of this sort, containing stone-built hoppers, were used to transfer PYRITES and other ores from railway wagons on high-level tracks to those on the 'main line' at a lower level.
Lyn Willies

intermediate state of cast iron from a blast furnace. A distinguishing feature was the use of water TROMPES to provide blast, a system which appeared in the DAUPHINÉ region *c.*1650, and reached the Ariège some forty years later.

A typical Catalan forge comprised a building of 150–200 m² (2150 sq. ft.) covering the bloomery furnace, which was an open, square hearth set in a masonry foundation between 70 cm and 90 cm (2ft. 3 in. and 2 ft. 10 in.) high. The tuyère bringing air into the hearth was connected to the wooden or stone 'wind chamber' into which the water fell. A bloom of iron weighing about 150 kg (330 lb.) was extracted every six hours or so, then taken to the nearby hammer which was driven by a small undershot water wheel. The water-power system would include an upper reservoir built to provide 7 m (23 ft.) of fall in the trompes. Near the furnace building were generally a charcoal storehouse, an iron warehouse, and sometimes dwellings for workers.

Production of iron from Catalan forges reached its peak in the nineteenth century when there were some seventy forges throughout the French Pyrenees in the departments of Aude, Pyrénées-Orientales and, above all,

Ariège. Around 1830 these departments accounted for more than 10 per cent of all French iron production.

The forge at Montgaillard was built on the Sios river at the end of the eighteenth century. It was operated for between eight and ten months of each year, and could produce about 100 tonnes of iron during such a season. Like most of the other Catalan forges of the Ariège department, it ceased production around 1865, and was converted by 1886 into an edge-tool workshop, the tilt hammer remaining in use until quite recently. This reuse has ensured the survival of many remains of the old forge. Although a turbine was installed to drive the grinding wheels, presses and shearing machines, the original water-power system was kept to drive the forge hammer, which was similar to that used in the original Catalan forge. The leat, the reservoir and the walls of the forge remain quite recognizable.

Elsewhere there are many other traces of this mountain iron production. At the Saint-Paul-de-Jarrat forge, 10 km (6 mi.) SE of Foix, there are remains of the leat, the reservoir and the half-ruined forge building. At Saint-Quentin-La-Tour, 30 km (18 mi.) NW of Foix, the water-supply system of the Queille tilt hammer forges still survives, along with elements of the trompe (built here, exceptionally, in stone) and its 'wind chamber'.

After 1815 some efforts were made to modernize iron production in the Pyrenees. Rolling mills and cementation furnaces were built for steel production, and in the 1850s the first charcoal-fired blast furnaces appeared at Pamiers, 20 km (12 mi.) N. of Foix, and at Prades, 40 km (25 mi.) W. of Perpignan. This latter site, the Ria works, was acquired in 1859 by the J. Holtzer firm of Unieux near SAINT-ÉTIENNE, which used the manganese-rich cast iron for its new puddled steel. In 1913 these were the last French blast furnaces still using charcoal. The battery of three small furnaces, about 12 m (39 ft.) high, still remains. Elsewhere in the Pyrenees there are traces of the spathic iron-ore mines of the Canigou mountain, in particular at Corneilla-de-Conflent, where there are late-nineteenth-century inclined planes, storehouses and railway tracks.

BIBLIOGRAPHY
Specific
Bonnenfant, M.-Th. Les Forges à roue hydraulique et à martinet de Montgaillard (Ariège) et la fabrication d'outillage pour la viticulture en Rousillon (The water-powered forge and tilt hammer of Montgaillard and the fabrication of tools for Rousillon wine-growing). In *Colloque d'Archéologie industrielle, Comptes rendus du 105ᵉ Congrès national des Sociétés Savantes, Caen, 1980*. Paris: Bibliothèque nationale, 1980.
Bonhote, J. and Cantelaube, J. Inventaire des vestiges de la métallurgie catalane ariègeoise au XIXᵉ siècle: étude d'archéo-logie industrielle (Inventory of the remains of Catalan metallurgy in the Ariège during the nineteenth century). In *Bulletin de la Société Ariègeoise, Sciences, Lettres et Arts*, 1989.
Lapalus, A. Le Haut Fourneau de Ria et la métallurgie fine de la Loire (The Ria blast blast furnace and high-grade metallurgy of the Loire). *Comptes rendus du 106ᵉ Congrès national des Sociétés Savantes, Perpignan, 1981*. Paris: Bibliothèque nationale, 1982.
Lapassat, R. L'Industrie du fer dans les Pyrénées orientales et ariègeoises au XIXᵉ siècle: les forges catalanes (The iron industry in the Pyrenees during the nineteenth century: Catalan forges). In *Confluent*, xx, 1983.

JEAN-FRANÇOIS BELHOSTE

pyrites Iron pyrites (iron disulphide, FeS_2) and copper pyrites ($CuFeS_2$) are important sources of sulphur and sulphuric acid in Europe. Iron pyrites has a golden appearance, and is sometimes called 'fool's gold'. The chief sources are in southern Spain (*see* RIO TINTO).

BIBLIOGRAPHY
General
Jones, 1950.

Q

quadruplex *See* DUPLEX.

quarry An open excavation or subterranean mine from which stone is cut or blasted. The word derives from the Latin 'quadraria', places from which squared stones were cut, and usually refers to sources of DIMENSION STONE, aggregate – whether a loose rock like sand or gravel, or a solid rock like BASALT that may be crushed for use on roads – or a rock like LIMESTONE that may be extracted on a large scale for its chemical properties. Strip mining is preferable as the term by which to refer to the open extraction of bedded or stoped deposits.

Quebec, Canada The most extensive of the provinces of Canada, Quebec occupies an area of 1 540 681 km² (594 857 sq. mi.) on the eastern coast, bounded to the west by the Hudson River and the province of Ontario, to the east by the provinces of New Brunswick and Newfoundland (Terre-Neuve), and to the south by the American states of Maine, New Hampshire, New York and Vermont. The name 'Quebec', originally coming from Algonquin language, means 'the place where the river gets narrower'.

The province includes three principal geological regions: the plateau of the Laurentian Shield in the north; in the centre the Laurentides mountains; in the south the valley of the St Lawrence, where the most productive land and consequently most of the population is concentrated. Along the south shore of the St Lawrence between QUEBEC CITY and Lake Champlain is the region of the Appalachians, which includes the fertile plains of the Eastern Townships. Quebec has an undulating landscape with hills rising to between 300 m and 600 m (980 ft. and 1970 ft.).

Quebec's drainage pattern is dominated by the St Lawrence river with its estuary and gulf, extending some 3600 km (2250 mi.) from west to east. On the south shore its principal tributaries are the Richelieu, Yamaska, Chaudière and Matapédia, and on the north shore the Ottawa, St Maurice, Saguenay and Manicouagan. The rivers which flow into James Bay and Hudson Bay, and those flowing into Ungava Bay, complete the pattern.

The climate of Quebec is characterized by summers that are short, hot and wet, and winters that are long and rigorous. These extreme fluctuations depend to a great extent on the pattern of relief, on the liberty of movement of the cold winds coming from the north and west, and of masses of warm air from the south. Frequently these masses of air come into conflict, giving rise to heavy falls of snow in winter and rain in summer.

Climatic variations have made an impact on the vegetation. North of the 52nd parallel in the Arctic tundra and taiga only shrubs and lichens are able to grow. The Laurentian Shield remains covered by the northern forests, composed principally of conifers, spruce, larches, pines and firs. In the most dense forests, in the valleys of the Ottawa River (Outaouais), the St Lawrence, and the Saguenay, around Lac Saint-Jean and in the Eastern Townships, conifers are mixed with such broad-leaved trees as maple, oak, beech and wild cherry.

Before the arrival of Europeans, the present territory of Quebec was occupied by several native tribes, the Iroquois and Algonquins in the valley of the St Lawrence, and Abenakis, Micmacs and Montagnais towards the east.

Between 1534 and 1536 expeditions led by Jacques Cartier (1491–1557) in the Gulf and up the River St Lawrence as far as Quebec (Stadacona) and Montreal (Hochelaga) claimed possession of the territory in the name of France.

Between 1608, when the first permanent settlement was established at Quebec by Samuel de Champlain (?1570–1635) and 1660, New France was predominantly concerned with trading, and particularly with the fur trade. Emigration was not encouraged by the French authorities. Between 1608 and 1760 only 10 000 migrants came to Quebec, originating principally from Burgundy, Brittany, Normandy and Picardy, producing a population by 1760 of nearly 75 000.

Most of these colonists established themselves along the banks of the St Lawrence and its tributaries. The French favoured a seigneurial system of settlement. Land was divided into a series of long narrow strips (between 2000–2500 m long by 200–250 m wide (2190–2730 yd. by 220–275 yd.) at right angles to the river. This 'rang' system came to characterize the landscape and social structure of Quebec. The population did not become as hierarchical as that of metropolitan France since the 'seigneurs' performed in the same way as other inhabitants the tasks of farmers, soldiers and traders.

The period between 1608 and 1760 was marked by many armed conflicts, at first with the Iroquois tribes and, after 1686, with British fleets which constituted a continuing threat to the colony. In order to counter these attacks the French created a permanent military presence; the regiment of Carignan-Sallières reached there in 1665, and was followed in 1683 by the 'troupes de la marine'.

Two decades of peace followed the Treaty of Utrecht of

1713, which had taken away from New France the territories of Nova Scotia (Acadie), Newfoundland (Terre-Neuve) and Hudson's Bay. After 1745 hostilities were resumed between France and Great Britain, which had repercussions in their respective colonies. In 1759, in the memorable battle of the Heights of Abraham, British troops captured Quebec. The surrender of the French armies at Montreal in 1760 marked the end of New France, after which the majority of the political leaders and commercial classes returned to metropolitan France. The later development of French-Canadian society was to be deeply marked by this rupture.

The British colonization of Quebec was marked by three principal stages. Between 1760 and 1774 the first rulers showed a spirit of tolerance, recognizing the French language and the Roman Catholic religion, although the French Canadians were kept out of administrative posts. In this context the Quebec Act 1774 sought to bring to the support of the government the power of the local authorities and the clergy. Alterations were introduced with the massive immigration of loyalists who sought refuge in Canada during the American Revolution. These changes originated in the constitutional act of 1791 by which the young English colony was to be divided into two provinces, Lower Canada (Quebec) and Upper Canada (Ontario), each having its own independent government. The role of the British merchants in Montreal who had prospered through the fur trade must be emphasized. Refusing to be treated as a minority in a province where they formed the majority, and wishing to obtain political representation by the device of an Assembly, the French-Canadians mounted a strong political opposition. It was this that provoked a rebellion between 1837 and 1839.

Following the Royal Commission conducted by Lord Durham (1792–1840) in order to reconcile the opposing groups, new arrangements were introduced by the Union government created in 1840, which brought together Canada East (Quebec) and Canada West (Ontario). English was recognized as the only official language of the country, while the French Canadians formed the majority of the population, and had to assume responsibility for a large percentage of the massive debts of Canada West. Their existence and even their survival was more than ever threatened in the 1840s when there was a severe economic crisis. Many of them sought exile in the USA, while Canada welcomed large numbers of migrants from the British Isles, above all from Ireland. All this brought about a considerable diminution in the French-Canadian population.

It was in this context that the Canadian Confederation was created in 1867. Its object was to define the respective limits of the jurisdiction of the central and provincial governments. Certain measures particularly affected Quebec. It became the official place of residence of the French-Canadians. The special status of their language, religion and civil law were recognized, and they obtained the means for economic, social and cultural self-development. In fact, due to a high birth rate and a reduction in British immigration, the French-

Canadian population underwent a remarkable expansion between 1867 and about 1960. During these decades Quebec, like Western civilization as a whole, experienced industrialization and urbanization.

Quebec's first phase of industrial activity occurred between 1730 and 1850. Favoured with an abundance of natural resources, water, wood, deposits of iron ore, and by the availability of human resources, both financial and technical, this pre industrial period was marked by the beginnings of mills, bakehouses, breweries (around Montreal and Quebec City), forges, foundries, charcoal kilns (in the region of Mauricie), the cutting and transport of wood (in the valley of the Ottawa River, and along the St Lawrence and its tributaries), as well as by shipbuilding at Quebec City. Brickmaking and ceramics were developed around Montreal, and fishing ports and fish processing grew up around Chaleur Bay.

The process of industrialization was strongly maintained after 1850, above all due to the political and economic stability brought about successively by the Union government and then by the coming of the Canadian Confederation. The state was amongst the contributors to the development of communications, to the improvement of the port of Montreal and the Lachine and Beauharnois canals on the St Lawrence, to the organization of the first railway network (composed of the Grand Trunk and Intercolonial companies), and to the construction of the Victoria Bridge. Well provided with capital, most of it British, the great financial institutions invested in consumer industries like sugar refining and flourmilling, in tobacco, in foundries, and in shoemaking. Most of these developments were concentrated in Montreal, which benefited from its position at the heart of the transport and financial systems. Furthermore the exhaustion of the forest of white pine, the heavy cost of squaring logs into planks, and the demands for sawn timber in the USA, stimulated the rise of the sawmilling industry. Consequently sawmills were established in almost every village in the province.

After the economic crisis of 1873–8 the process of industrialization entered a second phase after 1880. The establishment of preferential tariffs with England, the growth of the internal market in Canada, the construction of new railways and the general reorganization of rail transport were the principal causes. Thus in 1885 Montreal and Vancouver were linked by the Canadian Pacific Railway, and between 1920 and 1923 the other principal networks, the Grand Trunk, the Intercolonial, the National Transcontinental and the Canadian Northern were nationalized and regrouped as the Canadian National.

The period between 1880 and 1945, considered by some historians as a second Industrial Revolution, saw the development of new sectors based on the exploitation of natural resources: pulp and paper, hydro-electricity, electrochemicals, electrometallurgy and mining. This phase was characterized by the construction of huge manufacturing complexes near to sources of energy and raw materials, by the development of technologies relating to their operation, by growing specialization of labour, and by the attraction of capital from financial institutions in the USA. These three sectors underwent a considerable expansion after World War II. For example mining was to benefit from the massive exploitation of deposits of iron ore, asbestos, copper, gold, silver and molybdenum.

Manufacturing industry began to grow from the beginning of the twentieth century, partly due to the high rate of immigration before World War I, and partly to the introduction of new technologies, which, principally after 1945, were to encourage diversification. Between 1900 and 1959 the manufacturing sector came to include food and drink, and products derived from wood, paper, petroleum, coal, rubber, iron and steel, as well as tobacco, leather, chemical products, electrical equipment and appliances, clothing, textiles and transport equipment. The coming of the motorcar, the integration of the railway with road and river transport, the opening of the St Lawrence Seaway in 1959, the building of aircraft, the development of air transport, and the growth of a television network (in 1952) were the principal developments in communications in this period.

The consequences of industrialization on the environment in Quebec have led, in the first place, to spatial restructuring. The movement of population from the parishes on the shores of the St Lawrence associated with forestry or mining has contributed to the development of new regions, Haute-Mauricie, Saguenay-Lac Saint Jean, Upper Ottawa, the lower St Lawrence Gaspésie, Abitibi-Témiscamingue, and the north shore of the St Lawrence. The establishment of particular industries, notably in the pulp and paper sector, electrometallurgy and hydroelectricity, has led to the creation of new towns, notably Clarke City and Baie Comeau in the 1950s, SHAWINIGAN in 1901, and Arvida in the 1940s. Furthermore mining developments led to the establishment of Val d'Or and Rouyn in the 1930s, and Gagnon and Shefferville in the 1950s, and have given an urban character to some rural regions, particularly in the Eastern Townships. Secondly the development of transport facilities has permitted the relocation of economic activities in such cities as Quebec and Trois-Rivières. After 1896 they benefited from the reorganization of their port installations, from the construction of a bridge joining the two shores of the St Lawrence, and from the integration of the railway networks. Thirdly this period has seen the phenomenon of urbanization. Montreal, recognized at the time of the Confederation as the metropolis of Canada, has maintained this status in the succeeding decades. To industrial growth has been added geographical expansion. Since 1900 the city has taken in previously rural suburbs, St Henri on the banks of the Lachine Canal, and Hochelaga-Maisonneuve and Rosemont to the east. Montreal has followed a pattern of growth comparable to that of the great cities of the USA, and in 1961 had a population of more than a million.

Urbanization led to the formation of two social groups, the bourgeoisie and the working class. In this context several class conflicts broke out around the turn of the century, principally at Montreal, in the textile, tobacco and clothing factories, in the building trade and in railway construction, and in Quebec in the footwear industry. In response to the abuses suffered by the workers, trades unions were formed, among them the Knights of Labor, in 1883, which had its origins in the USA, and the Canadian Catholic Confederation of Labor (CCCL) in 1921. Legislation was applied progressively by the provincial government from 1909 to deal with industrial accidents, hours of work, the employment of children, conciliation and arbitration services, and the recognition of professional trades unions.

Recent historical studies have shown that it took more than a century to establish the industrial structure of Quebec. In all probability it was between 1850 and 1963, if one includes the nationalization of electricity, that most of the sectors that now contribute to the economic diversity of the province came into being: the exploitation of raw materials, the processing industries, and the manufacture of consumer goods.

The conservation and development of the industrial heritage in Quebec are to a considerable extent the responsibility of departments of the provincial government. The Department of Cultural Affairs for Quebec remains the principal agency in the field since it exercises powers under the Law of Cultural Properties passed in 1972 and amended several times since. The department receives and studies recommendations which are presented to it by a consultative body, the Commission for Cultural Properties. In this context the department has initiated in recent years several research projects in history, ethnology and industrial archaeology which have led to detailed surveys and in some cases to interpretative programmes. Examples include the pulp-works of CHICOUTIMI, the mining village of BOURLAMAQUE, the fish-processing plant of PASPÉBIAC, the tug *T. E. Draper* (see ANGLIERS), the hydro-electric power station on the Soulanges canal, and L'ILE DES MOULINS at Terrebonne.

In this work the Department of Cultural Affairs has generally operated in collaboration with the appropriate municipalities, with community groups, with companies with regional and local interests, and with the Department of Leisure, Hunting and Fishing, on such projects as that at VAL JALBERT. Support has also come from the regional offices of the Quebec national archives, notably in Mauricie, Abitibi-Témiscamingue and Saguenay-Lac Saint Jean. Furthermore Hydro-Quebec, which possesses an important collection of archives, has developed a scheme to take inventories of, to protect and to find new uses for some of its installations, and for the technical equipment therein.

Environment Canada is among the federal government organizations engaged in the conservation and interpretation of industrial monuments. It exercises jurisdiction over the historic national parks, including LES FORGES DU SAINT-MAURICE; over several canals and locks on the St Lawrence Seaway, among them Lachine, Côteau-du-Lac, Carillon and Sainte-Anne; and over the interpretation centre of the port of Quebec City. The Canadian Pacific and Canadian National corporations are responsible for the conservation of certain structures like the Victoria Bridge and the Windsor Station at Montreal, and for the documentation relating to them. On this last point they have been followed by the Air Canada corporation which is supporting the publication of scholarly works tracing its evolution.

The municipal authorities have been given responsibility in recent years for the restoration of former factories or for the diffusion of an understanding of the techniques of adaptive reuse. Among them are the Société Immobilière du patrimoine architectural (SIMPA) and the Commission d'initiative et de développement culturel (CIDEC) at Montreal as well as the Service d'urbanisme of the city of Quebec.

Several museums, like the Canadian Railway Museum at Saint-Constant and the Mining and Mineral Museum at Thetford, provide protection for, and present to the public, collections concerning specific industries. To this can be added the work of interpreting the landscapes of working-class districts, and developing oral-history programmes, carried out by l'Atelier d'Histoire Hochelaga-Maisonneuve and by an écomusée, la Maison du fier monde, both situated in heavily industrialized areas of MONTREAL.

The promotion of the study, understanding conservation and development of the industrial heritage in Quebec is the specific object of AQPI (l'Association québecoise pour le patrimoine industriel) which was established in 1988. This objective is shared in a general fashion by such voluntary organizations as the Quebec Federation of Historical Societies and the Quebec Association for Covered Bridges.

Teaching institutions, among them Concordia University and McGill University, both located in Montreal, provide courses concerned with the industrial history of the province. At Laval University in Quebec City research projects in industrial archaeology are carried out in collaboration with the municipality.

Finally one should not pass in silence the action taken by companies broadly concerned with preserving their archives and collections of plant, notably Alcan, Bell Canada and Domtar at Montreal, and Bombardier at Valcourt. Others have been concerned to adapt their installations to new uses, notably Domtex at MONTMORENCY, Johnson & Johnson, the Molson brewery and the Macdonald tobacco works at Montreal.

See also BAIE STE-CLAIRE; BOMBARDIER, J. A.; LES CÈDRES; HULL LANDING; NORTH NATION MILLS; THETFORD; QUEBEC CITY; WILSON FALLS and figures 18, 113.

BIBLIOGRAPHY
General
Trottier, 1985.
Specific
Arbour, A. *Les ponts couverts du Québec* (Covered bridges in Quebec). St.-Eustache, Quebec: Société québecoise des ponts couverts (Quebec Society for Covered Bridges), 1988.
L'Archéologie au Québec (Archaeology in Quebec). Québec: Ministère des Affaires culturelles, 1985.

LOCATION
[I] Association québecois pour le patrimoine industriel (Quebec

Association for the Industrial Heritage), CP 5225, Succ 'C'. Montreal (Quebec) H2X 3N2.

LOUISE TROTTIER

Quebec City, Quebec, Canada   The capital of the province, and the site in the seventeenth century of the first French settlement.

In the historic quarter of Old Quebec, the area bounded by the rue Saint-Nicolas, rue Saint-Vallier and rue Vallières, industrial activities concerned with the brewing of beer developed sporadically between the seventeenth century and the twentieth. This has been shown by archaeological research carried out on the site since 1982 by Laval University in collaboration with the municipality and the provincial Department of Cultural Affairs. The first brewery began to operate between 1669 and 1675 at the instigation of the French colonial authorities, its remains being traces of the walls, of a tower and a malt kiln resting on stone paving flags. Part of the building was later used as a residence by the Intendants of New France, and part as a warehouse. It was destroyed by fires in 1713 and 1845, by bombardments during the siege of Quebec by the British in 1759, and during the American invasion in 1775. The site continued in industry use with the breweries established by John Knight Boswell and his descendants between 1852 and 1952, and by the Dow company between 1952 and 1970. Cold stores, warehouse complexes, a bottling plant, boilers, covered sidings and stables were among the buildings constructed during this period. The site underwent many transformations which can be traced through the remains of concrete floors, walls, pillars, pump shafts, vaults, hoists and pipes. The ending of brewing activities by the Dow company, which was taken over by a multinational, led to the demolition of the buildings. The City of Quebec came to own the site in 1977 and encouraged the archaeological investigations and at the same time installed an historical interpretation centre within the vaults of the Intendant's palace.

Quebec Bridge links the two banks of the St Lawrence, about 8 km (5 mi.) upstream from the city. Its construction, which was financed by the federal and provincial governments, took place in two stages, from 1897 until 1907, and from 1907 until 1917. The provincial Department of Transport is currently responsible for the maintenance of the bridge and for the custody of the documents relating to it. On account of mistakes in the drawing up of the plans and in the methods of construction employed, the first structure collapsed in 1907, causing the deaths of 70 workers and the loss of $5 million. Subsequently a consortium of three engineers – the Canadian H. E. Vautelet, the American Ralph Madjeski, and Maurice Fitzmaurice, who was British – oversaw the application of new plans. The bridge is of the cantilever type, its design based on the use of nickel steel. It consists of a central truss flanked by suspended sections, which are carried on six piers. The whole bridge is 988 m (3241 ft.) long, 28.84 m (88 ft.) wide, and 33.5 m (110 ft.) high, the two extremities of the piers being separated by an

Figure 124   Quebec Bridge, the cantilever structure which crosses the St Lawrence about 8 km (5 mi.) upstream from Quebec City, constructed between 1897 and 1917; originally a railway bridge, it has carried both road and rail traffic since 1929.
Barrie Trinder

arch of 549 m (1801 ft.). From 1917 Quebec Bridge carried two railway tracks, to which a lane for motor traffic was added in 1929. In 1949 the removal of one of the railway tracks allowed the roadway to be enlarged.

BIBLIOGRAPHY
General
Dallaire *et al.*, 1974; Ville de Québec, 1986.

LOUISE TROTTIER

Queen Anne   A term applied to an architectural style practised in England between 1860 and 1900, and in the USA, which was a light-hearted and original mixture of elements from the seventeenth and eighteenth centuries, with a fondness for red brick, white woodwork, and curving gables. It was used in office blocks, schools, hotels and notably in the LONDON suburb of Bedford Park. It was associated with progressive causes, its principal exponent being Richard Norman Shaw (1831–1912). The name comes from the reign of Queen Anne (1702–

14), although some of its inspiration came from buildings built during the reign from 1689 of William III (1650–1702) and Mary II (1662–94) – the term 'William and Mary' sometimes being used almost as a synonym – or from earlier in the seventeenth century.

BIBLIOGRAPHY
General
Girouard, 1977; Saint, 1976.

Queensland, Australia   The arid interior of the state, which has a population of only 2.5 million, contrasts with the fertile south and east which produce wool, grain, sugar, cheese and butter, cotton and timber. Many historial homesteads remain, built of timber or corrugated iron, and set on high timber stilts. Jondaryan Woolshed was, when built in 1859–60, the largest woolshed in the state with fifty-six stands for shearers and a vast open interior. The chimney and ruined buildings of one of the earliest sugar mills in Queensland can be seen at Yengarie, 260 km (160 mi.) NW of

608

Brisbane. It was built in 1865 as a beef-extract plant. At Burketown on the Gulf of Carpentaria machinery from a plant of 1866 for boiling down beef extract remains. Sugar was introduced in the 1880s, using imported labour from the Pacific as it was considered too hot for Europeans to work. Today at Bundaberg, 310 km (190 mi.) N. of Brisbane, sugar refining and distilling are undertaken together.

Gold was found in the 1870s and there are several isolated towns with incongruous Victorian streetscapes, Ravenswood, 80 km (50 mi.) S. of Townsville, and Charters Towers, 110 km (70 mi.) SW of Townsville, being good examples. At the latter survives the Venus Gold Battery of 1872, the first permanent battery on the goldfields, with a seventy-five-head stamper. There are other batteries at Kidston, 350 km (220 mi.) NW of Townsville, Kingsborough. The Tyrconnel gold mine of 1876–1942 has remains of the full range of extractive and treatment processes. Copper mining began in the 1880s and remains of smelters survive at Chillagoe, 130 km (80 mi.) W. of Cairns. Iron ore is still being extracted at Mount Morgan, 40 km (25 mi.) SW of Rockhampton, from one of the world's largest artificial holes, begun in 1882. There are remains of tin mining near Heberton, 72 km (45 mi.) SW of Cairns. At the Rhondda Colliery near Ipswich is a large collection of nineteenth-century mining equipment. Mount Isa is now one of the world's most productive silver and lead mines.

At Longreach Airport is the original hangar built in 1923 for the Queensland and Northern Territory Aerial Service, which evolved into QANTAS, Australia's international airline. Australia's first aircraft were assembled there in 1926. Railways were vital to the state's development. Emerald has a wonderfully ornate chamferboard station, and at Rockhampton is a ROUNDHOUSE with capacity for seventy-eight locomotives. H. C. Royce designed the unusual Victoria swingbridge in Townsville, which pivots on a central cast-iron drum.

See also BRISBANE.

BIBLIOGRAPHY
General
Bell, 1984, 1987; Birmingham *et al*, 1979; Heritage of Australia, 1981.

KATE CLARK

quicksilver *See* MERCURY.

R

rack railway A railway climbing steep gradients on which is an extra rail with teeth or slots that engage with a toothed wheel on the locomotive or railcar. A pure rack railway usually climbs a continuous steep gradient for a relatively short distance, often directly up a mountain (*see* LUCERNE). A rack-and-adhesion line like the Furka–Oberalp line has a varied gradient profile with only some sections fitted with rack rails.

The Mount Washington Railway in New Hampshire, designed by Sylvester Marsh and opened in 1866, was the first rack railway. The rack rail was (and remains) formed of two parallel rolled-angle irons, with teeth formed by round steel sections riveted between. The first in Europe was the Vitznau–Rigi line, designed by Nikolaus Riggenbach and opened in 1871. Riggenbach rack rails are of cast iron with rectangular slots and have the appearance of a ladder. In Eduard Loch-Freuler's system which had horizontal teeth and slots, the teeth on one side matched the slots on the other; it was used only on the Pilatus Railway, opened in 1884. Emil Viktor Strub's system using rack rails with milled out teeth and U-shaped slots

Figure 125 The four types of rack rail: from top to bottom, Riggenbach 'ladder'; Locher system; Strub system; Abt system (twin bar)
Sulzer Brothers Ltd, Winterthur

610

between them, was applied on the Jungfrau line in 1912 and is widely used in Italy. Roman Abt's system uses twin or triple rails, with the teeth staggered to provide a smoother action between racks and the driving pinions. The system devised by the American G. E. Sellers and the Englishman John B. Fell, and improved in France by J. Hanscotte, had a third rail between the running rails against which ran horizontal wheels on the locomotive.

BIBLIOGRAPHY
General
Schneider, 1967.
Specific
Loosli, H. E. The rack railway: characteristics and scope of applications. In *Sulzer Technical Review* (Sulzer, Winterthur), 66(2) 1984.

BARRIE TRINDER

radar A method of establishing the range and direction of an aircraft in flight using ultra-high-frequency radio waves which reflect back to the source transmitter. Developed in Britain in the 1930s, tested successfully during the Battle of Britain in 1940, and extensively used in AIR-TRAFFIC CONTROL since World War II. Early 'Chain Home' radar masts remain at Canterbury, Dover and Stenigote, Lincolnshire. German 'Wurzburg' radar dishes are held by the Imperial War Museum in London and at Duxford, and a collection of British equipment is at the Science Museum outpost at Wroughton, near SWINDON.

BIBLIOGRAPHY
General
Bowen, 1987.

radio The physicist Heinrich Hertz (1857–94) in 1886 was the first to transmit electrical signals without intervening wires. Following this lead GUGLIELMO MARCONI demonstrated a practical system in 1897, and research thereafter was rapid, the basic problems of transmission, reception, tuning and amplification being successfully confronted. The Dane, Valdemar Poulsen, improved transmission with his arc generator of 1903; while the 'diode' radio valve of 1904, invented by J. A. Fleming (1849–1945), and the 'triode' of 1906, by Lee De Forest (1873–1961), both improved reception and amplification. The earliest messages were exclusively MORSE; speech and music were first broadcast in 1906, and regularly from 1913. Radio-sensitive crystals, using cats' whiskers to make adjustable connections, were used from 1906, and also formed the basis of the transistor introduced in 1948.

See also RADIO RECEIVER; RADIO STATION; TELEVISION.

BIBLIOGRAPHY
General
Fleming, 1910; Tyne, 1977.

radio receiver The earliest, like those of GUGLIELMO MARCONI of 1896, comprised an aerial, a 'coherer' (a glass tube filled with nickel and silver filings) and a MORSE sounder. Marconi improved the coherer but soon replaced it with a 'magnetic detector' and later with valves. A major step was the development of improved amplification, leading to the introduction of 'loudspeakers'. Radio receivers were marketed on a large scale from the early 1920s, and developed as items of furniture with substantial wooden cabinets in the 1920s and 30s. The introduction of the transistor in 1948 stimulated miniaturization and what Banham called 'defurnituriation'.

BIBLIOGRAPHY
General
Tyne, 1977.
Specific
Banham, R. Chairs as art. In Barker, P. 1977.

radio station The first was set up in 1897 by GUGLIELMO MARCONI in Britain for maritime communication. A trans-Atlantic link was established in 1901, but entertainment stations did not come on the air until 1919–20. Radio broadcasting, whether by private companies or public corporations, developed into a major industry in the 1920s and 30s.

BIBLIOGRAPHY
General
Barnouw, 1966, 1968, 1970; Briggs, 1961; Maclaurin, 1949.
Specific
Rowland-Jones, M. Two-Emma-Toc. In *WIH*, v, 1988.

raft Rafts have traditionally been used to float timber for constructional uses, fuel and exports, from mountainous areas to lowlands and the coast. Jean Rouvet, who in the sixteenth century began floating timber down the River Yonne into the Seine and to Paris, is commemorated in France as the inventor of 'flottage'. The principle was employed in most European countries, including Great Britain, where rafts were floated down the River Severn until the end of the eighteenth century. Rivers incapable of taking normal craft were often used for rafts, the French employing the word 'flottable' to describe such waterways. The principle was adopted in Russia in the time of Tsar Peter the Great (1672–1725), and by the 1880s 61 000 km (38 000 mi.) of waterway were used for rafts in addition to those sections open for conventional navigation. In 1881 47 272 rafts were floated down the Volga, and in 1893 some 20 000 went down the Niemen to Memel (Klaipėda). In the 1860s logs from Perm and the Urals were floated along the River Kama to the Caspian. Rafting was important on Siberian rivers like the Angara, where migrants often travelled to new settlements on rafts.

Rafting is a highly economic form of transport. It continued in many countries in spite of railway competition, and in Finland there has been a change from log- to raft-floating since World War II. Rafting was widely practised in North America. Steam tugs were used in the nineteenth century to push log rafts on the Mississippi and its tributaries. The most important use in nineteenth-century Europe was on the Rhine, where rafts of oaks and deals grew, snowball-like, on the Neckar, Moselle, Main and other tributaries and were floated to Dordrecht where the timber was sold. The journey from Bingen in the Rhine Gorge to Dordrecht took about eight days. In the 1860s such rafts were up to 210 m (700 ft.) long, and had previously been up to 275 m (900 ft.) long. The maximum width of 76 m (250 ft.) was regularly checked at Caub. The crew of such a raft could number up to five hundred, and eight or ten huts were normally erected on board for their accommodation. The owner normally had a superior residence on board. Steering was by means of anchors, and by rowers in four ranks fore and aft. A Rhine raft was composed of several layers of trees fastened with chains and rivets and planked with rough deals to form a deck. The wives of rowers often travelled on board, and practised by-employments like spinning. Such a raft could be worth up to £30 000 in the 1860s, and was normally owned by many shareholders. Rafting is still practised in Scandinavia.

BIBLIOGRAPHY
General
Braudel, 1981; Hadfield, 1986; Murray, 1865.

BARRIE TRINDER

railcar In England, a railway passenger carriage with an integral source of power (*see* MULTIPLE UNIT). In North America, a contemporary media term for freight wagon.

railroad A word for RAILWAY commonly used in Shropshire, England, and in areas that adopted the Shropshire type of railway from *c*.1700; but not in North-East England till the late eighteenth century. For many years it was used on an equal footing with the word 'railway', and was supplanted by the latter only after the evolution of the main-line system. In North America 'railroad' is the standard term, although a few large companies, like the Norfolk & Western, used 'railway' in their titles.

BIBLIOGRAPHY
General
Lewis, 1970; Wexler, 1955.

railway A prepared track which so guides the vehicles running on it that they cannot deviate from it. Railways originated in the metalliferous mines of Central Europe in the late Middle Ages, and were illustrated by AGRICOLA in the mid-sixteenth century. HUNDS, HUNGARIAN HUNDS and GUIDE-WHEEL RAILWAYS continued in use with minor modifications until the nineteenth century or later. Such methods may have been taken to England by Germans employed by the Mines Royal in the LAKE DISTRICT from 1564, but the mainstream of railway development seems to have originated independently with the use of wooden rails for surface transport in the English coalfields from the early seventeenth century.

The first wooden railway for the carriage of coal for which there is sound evidence was built by Huntingdon Beaumont at Wollaton, Nottinghamshire, between October 1603 and October 1604. From 1605 Beaumont leased coal workings in Northumberland and built railways to serve them. By 1605 railways had also been built in Shropshire (see IRONBRIDGE) and during the seventeenth century two distinct traditions of railway building emerged in the North-East and in Shropshire. In Shropshire gauges varied between 18 in. and 3 ft. (46–91 cm), and in the North-East from 3 ft. 10 in. to 5 ft. (1.17–1.52 m). The former used flat wagons, with loads held in place by iron hoops, and marshalled in trains; the latter, high-sided wagons discharged from the bottom, used individually until the late eighteenth century. Iron wheels were used in Shropshire from 1729, and iron rails – 6 ft. $\times$ $3\frac{1}{4}$ in. $\times$ $1\frac{1}{4}$ in. (1.82 m $\times$ 8.25 cm $\times$ 3.17 cm) cast-iron plates, forming the top sections of DOUBLE WAYS – from 1767. Wrought-iron edge rails were developed in England from 1789, but PLATEWAYS with flanged rails were initially adopted more widely. The T-sectioned rolled rail patented by John Birkinshaw in 1820 was more suitable for further development. The STEAM LOCOMOTIVE was developed rapidly between 1800 and 1830. From 1800 HYBRID RAILWAYS were built in considerable numbers. Motive power on most railways was provided by horses until the use of steam locomotives became widespread from the 1820s.

The Liverpool & Manchester Railway, engineered by GEORGE STEPHENSON and opened in 1830, broke with previous practice in that it had specialized track and mechanical traction, was subject to public control, and accommodated public traffic and passengers. No previous line had fulfilled all these criteria, which were the essentials of the main-line network that spread across Europe and North America in the following decades. There were 6000 mi. (9700 km) of railway in Britain by 1850, and over 20 000 mi. (32 000 km) by 1911. Main-line railways were opened in France in 1832, in Germany and Belgium in 1835, in Austria in 1837, in Italy and the Netherlands in 1839, and in Spain in 1848. By 1914 there were 38 000 mi. (61 000 km) in the German Empire, of which half were built after 1880, 29 000 mi. (47 000 km) in the Habsburg Empire, and 40 000 mi. (64 000 km) in Russia.

Robert L. Stevens designed the first H-section rail for the Camden and Amboy Railroad in 1830, and it gradually became the standard section, being rolled in wrought-iron and from the 1860s in steel. A common gauge in north-east England, 4 ft. $8\frac{1}{2}$ in. (1.44 m later 1.435 m) was adopted as standard in most countries (see BROAD-GAUGE RAILWAY; NARROW-GAUGE RAILWAY).

A distinctive tradition of railway building and operation developed in the USA, where there were 250 000 route miles (400 000 km) by 1914, generally employing lighter constructional methods, with trestle rather than masonry viaducts, locomotives with bogies and more accessible working parts, and large freight cars. Most significant developments in passenger comfort originated in North America.

In most countries the first closures of lines in remote areas came in the 1920s and 30s, but the same period saw new standards in long-distance passenger services, and the railway remained the dominant form of long-distance freight carriage. Since World War II road competition has brought about massive cutbacks of lightly-used lines, and, in North America, the severe curtailment of long-distance passenger services. Nevertheless in some highly developed countries, like Japan, France and West Germany, large-scale railway construction has continued. The network in Britain was reduced to 17 000 mi. (27 000 km) in 1963 and to 10 000 mi. (16 000 km) by 1988.

For the various types of railway, see ATMOSPHERIC RAILWAY; BROAD-GAUGE RAILWAY; CLIFF RAILWAY; DOUBLE WAY; FUNICULAR; GRAVITY RAILWAY; GUIDE-WHEEL RAILWAY; HYBRID RAILWAY; INDUSTRIAL RAILWAY; INTERURBAN; METRO; MONORAIL; NARROW-GAUGE RAILWAY; PLATEWAY; RACK RAILWAY; RAILROAD; TRAMWAY; TUBE RAILWAY; UNDERGROUND RAILWAY; WAGONWAY.

For structures associated with railways, see CAPSTAN; COAL DROP; CROSS-TIE; GAUGE; INCLINED PLANE; JUNCTION; LOADING GAUGE; LOCOMOTIVE DEPOT; MARSHALLING YARD; RAILWAY BRIDGE; RAILWAY FREIGHT DEPOT; RAILWAY HOTEL; RAILWAY SIGNAL; RAILWAY STATION; RAILWAY TUNNEL; ROUNDHOUSE; SIGNAL BOX; SLEEPER; STAITHE.

For railway motive power, see DANDY CART; DIESEL LOCOMOTIVE; ELECTRIC LOCOMOTIVE; HORSE; PETROL LOCOMOTIVE; STEAM LOCOMOTIVE.

For railway vehicles, see AIR BRAKE; CABOOSE; CHALDRON; CLERESTORY; HUND; HUNGARIAN HUND; MULTIPLE UNIT; PULLMAN, GEORGE; RAILWAY CARRIAGE; RAILWAY WAGON; REISEN; RESTAURANT CAR; ROYAL CARRIAGE; SLEEPING CAR; TRAVELLING POST OFFICE; VACUUM BRAKE; WAGON-LIT.

BIBLIOGRAPHY
General
Lewis, 1970; Marshall, 1938; Ottley, 1965; Robbins, 1962; Schivelbusch, 1986; Simmons, 1986; Union International des Chemins de Fer, 1975; Wexler, 1955.

BARRIE TRINDER

railway bridge The main-line railway systems of the mid-nineteenth century included many thousands of bridges. In Britain, as in most West European countries, most bridges were masonry arches or girder structures of relatively short span. In America the TRUSS BRIDGE was widely used. Railway engineers built major bridges of many kinds, lengthy VIADUCTS, large cast-iron arches, TUBULAR BRIDGES, elaborate latticework structures, and astonishing composites like the High Level Bridge at NEWCASTLE-UPON-TYNE. The enquiry into the collapse of a cast-iron girder bridge on the railway outside Chester, England, on 24 May 1847 led to a report of major importance in engineering history, which drew attention to the weakness of cast iron used in tension. The earliest surviving railway bridge is the Causey Arch of 1727 (*see* DURHAM). The iron Gaunless Viaduct of 1825 is preserved at YORK.

BIBLIOGRAPHY
General
BPP, 1849; Pottgiesser, 1985; Walters, 1966.

railway carriage The earliest first-class railway carriages, as used on the Liverpool & Manchester Railway, had iron frames with stage-coach-style bodies mounted in tandem upon them. Third-class carriages were simply open wagons with benches, and second-class were similar but covered in. The screw coupling patented in 1838 by Henry Booth of the L&MR brought significant improvements in comfort and safety. Most early carriages had leather-covered buffers, but various forms of spring buffers were gradually developed. By 1845 the first six-wheeled vehicles had appeared in Britain. Most carriages were lit by oil lamps and heated only by foot warmers made of cans filled with hot water and later with sodium acetate. In the USA there was increasing use of bogies by the 1850s, and the usual layout became the saloon; the compartment remained in general use in Europe. Vestibule connections between carriages were introduced in Connecticut in 1853 and developed by PULLMAN, the first carriages so equipped in Europe being Pullmans bought by the Midland Railway in England in 1875. Lavatories first appeared in British railway carriages in 1873. The Baker system of heating carriages developed in the USA had an oil-fired boiler operating a hot-water circuit in each carriage, but steam heating using radiators supplied by the locomotive was introduced in 1881 and became general. The first British train to have corridor and gangway connections throughout began to work on the GWR in 1891. An oil gas-lighting system was developed by Julius Pintsch in Prussia, and gas lighting was quite common by the late 1870s, but pressurized containers of inflammable gas were dangerous in crashes. The first electrically-lit carriage operated on the LBSCR in 1881 and derived its power from batteries, a similar system being used in the USA from 1885. In 1894 J. Stone developed a system using a small generator under each coach. Emergency communication between passengers and driver, using a cord with a gong, was employed in Britain from 1869, and applied universally with direct links to VACUUM BRAKE or AIR BRAKE systems from 1899. Specialist passenger vehicles like RESTAURANT CARS and SLEEPING CARS were developed in the late nineteenth century. In the 1920s and 30s passenger carriages reflected the function of railways as carriers over very long distances. Since World War II their design has been simplified and standardized, with new designs of bogie and suspension systems, and lightweight body construction. In America railway carriages are called 'passenger cars'.

Several examples of very early railway vehicles survive, as well as replicas built for various commemorations. The National Railway Museum (*see* YORK) has Bodmin & Wadebridge Railway vehicles of 1834, while at HAMAR is an open fourth-class carriage built in Birmingham in 1854. Many later examples are also preserved.

See also CLERESTORY; MULTIPLE UNIT; ROYAL CARRIAGE; TRAVELLING POST OFFICE; WAGON-LIT.

BIBLIOGRAPHY
General
Ellis, 1965; Lynes, 1959; Mencken, 1957; White, 1978.

BARRIE TRINDER

railway freight depot Large urban depots for freight traffic were built from the early years of main-line railways. The huge depot of the LNWR at Camden, London, was begun in the early 1840s and extended to 5.5 ha (14 ac.) by the 1880s. From the beginning it was equipped with steam cranes and capstans. Such depots were essentially interchanges between long-distance rail and local road transport, and most had extensive stabling for horses employed with road vehicles. Some – like those constructed by the GNR at King's Cross, London, and Deansgate, Manchester – also interchanged traffic with navigable waterways. Most urban freight depots include huge buildings for transferring merchandise between rail and road vehicles. In the mid-nineteenth century such buildings usually had cast-iron columns supporting timber or composite truss roofs, subsequently they were of steel-framed or concrete construction. Some railway companies subcontracted merchandise traffic to specialist freight-handling concerns, which might operate their own warehouses within such depots: the LNWR, for example, used Pickfords and Chaplin & Horne, and the Netherlands railways used Van Gend & Loos. There might also be specialist warehouses for grain or potatoes, and coal drops or equipment for handling other bulk commodities such as road metals. Most such depots would employ specialist devices like capstans, wagon turntables and traversers for moving wagons without the aid of locomotives. HYDRAULIC POWER systems might be installed to operate this machinery, and to work cranes. Most such depots are now redundant. Some, like Listley Street, Birmingham, are now used for road transport purposes, while others are being adapted to entirely new uses.

Between 1850 and 1950 almost every settlement of consequence in Europe and North America had at least one railway freight depot. The components might include goods sheds which, though of more modest dimensions than the great urban depots, fulfilled the same essential purposes: cattle docks, ramps for loading road vehicles onto flat wagons, hand-operated cranes, weighbridges for road vehicles, privately-operated specialist warehouses for commodities like tea, and loading gauges. Most had facilities for unloading coal, either by hand onto platforms, or by direct discharge from hopper wagons on miniature STAITHES. The essentials of a small freight depot are preserved at BEAMISH.

Figure 126   The end gables of the vast railway freight depot of Tours & Taxis in Brussels, dating from 1904, where goods were transferred between barges and rail and road vehicles
Barrie Trinder

BIBLIOGRAPHY
General
Bulkeley, 1930; Burtt, 1923; Duckworth and Jones, 1988.

BARRIE TRINDER

railway hotel   The first railway hotel was perhaps the Bridge Hotel, adjacent to the London Bridge terminus of the London & Greenwich Railway, an independent concern, projected in the same year as the railway and completed to provide entertainments at its opening in 1832. The first hotels owned by a railway company flanked PHILIP HARDWICK's arch at Euston in 1838. In the USA a distinctive type of hotel accommodating long-distance travellers by trains that ran only in daylight hours developed before sleeping cars became commonplace from the 1860s. The North Euston Hotel, Fleetwood (*see* FYLDE), is an example of this type of hotel in England. Hotels were built as parts of most principal termini in the second half of the nineteenth century. Many railway companies built hotels at resorts to promote traffic; the Zetland Hotel, Saltburn, North Yorkshire, designed by

William Peacher for the North-Eastern Railway in the early 1860s, and the Gleneagles Hotel, Auchterarder, Scotland, completed in 1926 but reflecting the luxury of the Edwardian era, are notable examples. The last British railway hotels were built in the 1930s, the Queens at Leeds, of 1937, exemplifying the first tradition, and the Midland at Morecambe, of 1933, the second.

BIBLIOGRAPHY
Specific
Monkhouse, C. Railway hotels. In Binney and Pearce, 1979.

BARRIE TRINDER

railway museum The presence of GEORGE STEPHENSON'S *Rocket* in the Science Museum in London shows how the conservation of railway artefacts became a cause for concern early in the history of railways. Early steam locomotives are found in most of the national museums of technology established before 1914. Museums specifically devoted to railways originated in the closing years of the nineteenth century, the Norwegian collection now displayed at HAMAR, dating from 1897, being one of the first. In Britain the pattern was set by John B. Harper (1853–1935), stationmaster at York from 1890, who developed the collection of vehicles assembled by the NER for the celebration of the Jubilee of the S&DR in 1875. Interest in the collection was stimulated by the centenary celebrations of the same railway in 1925, and it was largely due to Harper's energies that in 1928 a railway museum was opened at York in a former machine shop. The previous year the Stephenson Locomotive Society purchased the LBSCR locomotive No. 214 *Gladstone* of 1882, probably the first locomotive to be privately preserved. In the post-war period the demise of the steam locomotive has led to the creation of national railway museums in most European countries, and there are several major railroad museums in the USA. Some, like those at YORK, ODENSE and Baltimore (*see* MARYLAND), are in adapted locomotive depots. The boundaries between railway museums, PRESERVED RAILWAYS and steam centres, where locomotives are restored and operated, are often difficult to define. Some of the most important collections of locomotives and rolling stock are held by non-specialist museums like the Science Museum, LONDON, the National Museum of Science and Technology, OTTAWA, and the Chicago Museum of Science and Industry (*see* ILLINOIS).

BIBLIOGRAPHY
General
Simmons, 1970.

BARRIE TRINDER

railway signal Railways first relied on hand signals to ensure the avoidance of collisions, supplemented with lanterns at night, but semaphore arms in slotted posts were introduced on the London & Croydon Railway in 1839, and adopted on most networks until superseded on those with dense traffic by colour light systems in the twentieth century. In the nineteenth century, alternatives – such as flags or bars and discs – were also widely

used. Locking between signals was introduced in 1840, but it was not until 1860 that the first fully interlocking points and signals system appeared, and in Britain such systems only became compulsory in 1889. Pneumatic and hydraulic-assisted signals appeared in the USA and Italy in the 1880s. Track circuiting, introduced in 1901, led to automatic warning signals, and by 1928 electronic control systems, with illuminated line-diagram panels replacing direct views of the track, were becoming increasingly popular. Advances in electronics have enabled the development of ever more sophisticated systems.
See also SIGNAL BOX.

CHRISTOPHER GREEN

railway station One of the principal symbols of the industrial and urban age, representing the application of steam power to mass travel, the growth of great cities, and the dramatic application of iron and glass in architecture.

The station emerged as a building type around 1830, with the construction of the Liverpool & Manchester Railway in England, and the opening of the Baltimore & Ohio Railroad in the USA. The architecture of the surviving Liverpool Road terminus at MANCHESTER betrays the influence of TURNPIKE tollhouses, the ticket office having some restrained classical detailing.

The prime concern in designing the first generation of termini was with layout. Various plans were adopted, with buildings beside or at the ends of the tracks, to ensure segregation of arriving and departing trains, and later of passenger and freight traffic. Long single-platform stations had a vogue, two of the best surviving examples being Cambridge, England, by Francis Thompson in 1845, and Limerick Junction, Ireland.

The train shed emerged as a cult structure around 1850. The aim was to achieve wide spans that would cover several tracks and platforms with a minimum of intermediate columns and cross bracing. Laminated timber was used at King's Cross, London, by L. Cubitt in 1851–2, but wood was vulnerable to sulphurous soot and sparks. Paddington, built by I. K. BRUNEL and M. D. WYATT in 1852–4, marked the adoption for London termini of arched iron roofs. The culmination of this tradition was the single sweeping arch at St Pancras, of 1863–5, by W. H. Barlow and R. M. Ordish, which reached 74 m (243 ft.). Wider spans were achieved in later American stations, the largest being the 90 m (300 ft.) span of 1892–3 at the Pennsylvania RR, Broad Street Station, Philadelphia, by Wilson Bros. Most European termini of the late nineteenth century and early twentieth were covered by series of near semi-circular steel arches, the most striking groups being those at Frankfurt-am-Main, by G. P. H. Eggert & Faust of 1879–88, and Stazione Centrale, Milan, by U. Stacchini, of 1913–20.

Most Parisian termini and many other European examples expressed the arch form of the train sheds in their main street elevations. In Britain most of the major termini were fronted by enormous hotels, the finest being the Gothic fantasy at St Pancras, designed by GEORGE GILBERT SCOTT, and completed in 1876. The feature given greatest emphasis in American termini of the early twentieth century was the concourse, which at Cincinnati Union Station of 1929–33, by Fellheimer & Wagner, was roofed by a massive half dome.

The design of modest 'through' stations became conditioned by the desire of companies to adopt house styles, whether for reasons of economy or identity or to pacify local landowners through the adoption of compositional forms and materials appropriate to the region. H. A. Hunt designed a series of brick-built Jacobean-style stations for the North Staffordshire Railway (see STOKE-ON-TRENT), while I. K. Brunel favoured stone and Tudor motifs for 'through' stations on the GWR.

The concept of a corporate identity in station design emerged most strongly in urban railway networks. The tube lines built in London after 1900 were given tile-lined platforms and faience-clad entrances, to designs by Leslie Green. The almost contemporary stations designed by Otto Wagner (1841–1918) for VIENNA show a refined use of Secessionist forms and detailing. The concept of a completely integrated approach to design, from rolling stock to staff uniforms, emerged during the inter-war years when Frank Pick (1878–1941) managed the LONDON transport system. Under his supervision Charles Holden (1875–1960) designed a series of modernistic stations, some with concrete cantilevered canopies and high, well-lit concourses, the most dramatic examples being on the outer portions of the Piccadilly Line.

See also figures 132, 168, 175.

BIBLIOGRAPHY
General
Berger, 1980, 1987; Biddle, 1973; Biddle and Spence, 1977; Binney and Pearce, 1979; Dethier, 1978; Föhl and Hamm, 1984; Kellett, 1969; Krings, 1985; Kubinszky, 1969; Meeks, 1956; Schivelbusch, 1986.

MICHAEL STRATTON

railway town A community in which employment is dominated by a railway company's LOCOMOTIVE AND CARRIAGE WORKS or by employees operating a railway. In southern England the practice whereby most companies built their own rolling stock led to the rise of railway engineering communities, either on new sites or as appendages to older, non-industrial settlements. The outstanding examples were ASHFORD, CREWE, Eastleigh (see SOUTHAMPTON), SWINDON and Wolverton, which have been analysed as a distinctive type of settlement in which railway companies built housing until a point of economic 'take-off' had been reached. There were some distinctive railway communities within large cities, like Springburn in GLASGOW, Gorton in MANCHESTER, and the Great Eastern Railway's new town at Stratford in east LONDON. The economies of some smaller towns were centred on the engineering works of the lesser railway companies, like Melton Constable in Norfolk, Oswestry in Shropshire, Inverurie (see ABERDEEN) in Scotland, or Caerphilly in South Wales, as well as company villages associated with private locomotive works, like Vulcan Village, Lancashire, and villages like Woodford Halse, Northamptonshire,

which grew to accommodate the staff of locomotive depots and marshalling yards.

BIBLIOGRAPHY
General
Simmons, 1986.
Specific
Turton, B. J. The railway towns of Southern England. In *Transport History*, II, 1969.

BARRIE TRINDER

railway tunnel The underground origins of railways make it difficult to distinguish between an ADIT that has a railway going into it, and a TUNNEL built for communication. There were short tunnels on some HYBRID RAILWAYS, one of the earliest being the East Kenton tunnel, Newcastle-upon-Tyne, England, which was built by Christopher Bedlington in 1796. Tunnels were essential components of the first generation of main-line railways, those at Kilsby on the London & Birmingham and Box on the Great Western being of particular note. The latter was one of the first to have an ornate entrance. Most railway tunnels came to have invert arches below the tracks, and oval walls forming arches above. By the 1880s it was reckoned in Britain that a tunnel was usually economical when the depth of a CUTTING would exceed 20 m (60 ft.) for a considerable distance. The first major tunnel through the Alps, the Mont Cenis, 13.67 km (8 mi. 870 yd.) long, was completed in 1871. Most of the great feats of subsequent tunnelling were on mountain railways, the four longest in 1950 being the SIMPLON, 19.823 km (12 mi. 560 yd.); the Apennine, 18.51 km (11 mi. 880 yd.); the ST GOTTHARD, 14.987 km (9 mi. 550 yd.); and the Lötschberg, 14.6 km (9 mi. 130 yd.). The longest in North America was the 12.554 km (7 mi. 1410 yd.) Cascade Tunnel on the Great Northern Railway. Continuous tunnels on some urban UNDERGROUND RAILWAYS, like the 26.75 km (16 mi. 1100 yd.) line between Golders Green and Morden in London, are rather longer.

BIBLIOGRAPHY
General
Blower, 1964.
Specific
The Picture of Newcastle-upon-Tyne, Newcastle, 1807.
Walker, T. *The Severn Tunnel: its construction and difficulties*, 1891. Reprint Bath: Kingsmead, 1969.

BARRIE TRINDER

railway wagon The earliest freight wagons developed from those used on HYBRID RAILWAYS, principally CHALDRON and flat wagons, on which merchandise was protected by tarpaulins. The Liverpool & Manchester Railway, which was not a significant carrier of minerals, developed a range of specialist vehicles in the 1830s, including high-sided open wagons and horse boxes. By the 1850s covered vans for merchandise, flat bolster wagons for timber and lengths of iron (later steel), and cattle wagons were in widespread use.

In north-east England bottom-discharge wagons for

minerals originated in the seventeenth century (*see* CHALDRON) but it was not until the 1960s that they were generally employed for carrying coal in other parts of the country.

By the 1880s 30-ton vehicles were commonplace in the USA, which took the lead from 1897 in the application of AIR BRAKES to freight vehicles. By the early twentieth century all American freight wagons ran on bogies, and the standard vehicle for grain had a capacity of 100 tons. In Europe companies persisted with wagons of smaller capacity. In Britain and Belgium large proportions of the wagon fleets were controlled by private owners. There were few continuously braked wagons in Britain by 1914, and while the capacity of the typical mineral wagon had increased from about 6 tons in 1870 to 13 tons by the 1950s, there had been little change in its essential characteristics.

By 1900 further specialist wagons had been developed: tankers for oil, tar, chemicals, milk and vinegar, and refrigerated vehicles for fruit, meat and fish. From the mid-nineteenth century, containers were used for furniture, coal, and china clay.

A vehicle at the rear of a train from which brakes can be applied is essential if the train lacks continuous braking. At first a guard travelled in an open wagon, but from the late 1840s specialist brake vans were developed. (*See also* CABOOSE.)

Railway wagons are universally known as 'freight cars' in the USA.

Few freight wagons have been preserved relative to their past numbers and importance – there were 400 000 in Britain in 1881, and 664 000 in 1938 – but there are sets representing early twentieth-century practice on such preserved lines as the Severn Valley (*see* BEWDLEY).

BIBLIOGRAPHY
General
Bulkeley, 1930; Burtt, 1923; Essery *et al.*, 1970; Lynes, 1959; Simmons, 1986.

BARRIE TRINDER

Raistrick, Arthur (1896–1991) A distinguished British writer on industrial history, before the subject became fashionable, and a leading exponent of the view that industrial archaeology should be the study of particular technologies across the whole span of history, rather than the study of the industrial period. Raistrick was born at SALTAIRE, took degrees in civil engineering and geology, lectured at the University of Durham until 1956, and to university adult groups until 1970. He directed various archaeological excavations and encouraged many voluntary groups investigating industrial archaeology and mining history. A Quaker, he always dressed as a 'plain Friend', and was a pacifist. He was closely associated with the origins of the IRONBRIDGE Gorge Museum.

BIBLIOGRAPHY
General
Raistrick, 1950, 1953, 1972, 1975.

Specific
Raistrick, A. The Rolt Memorial Lecture 1979: the old furnace at Coalbrookdale, Shropshire. In *IAR*, IV, 1980.

Rajamäki, Uudenmaan lääni, Finland In 1888 factories were established at the town of Rajamäki, 40 km (25 mi.) N. of Helsinki, to manufacture yeast and to distil spirits. In 1919 the establishment was sold to the state and became part of the state alcohol company, which was known from 1932 as Alko Ltd. The oldest phase of the complex is represented by a brick distillery of the 1890s, which now houses the Rajamäki factory museum. After the repeal of Prohibition (imposed in Finland from 1919 until 1931), the factory was extended in 1935–8 according to designs by Erkki Huttunen, with new production buildings and extensive ranges of accommodation for workers and management. The church, completed to Huttunen's design in 1938, is one of the most important in Finland in the INTERNATIONAL MODERN style. Viewed as a whole, Rajamäki is a faithful representation of the planning principles of the 1930s.

rake A term with two meanings relevant to industrial archaeology:

1. A vertical vein of metallic ore, usually lead, occurring between walls of rock and cutting through the bedding. Often rakes have been worked from early times, leaving deep trenches several kilometres long, with adits leading off and shafts sunk at the sides. Dramatic examples can be seen in England at Dirtlow and Tideswell, Derbyshire, and at Charterhouse, Somerset; and in Germany at Mühlenbach, 3 km (2 mi.) E. of Koblenz.
2. A line of haulage trucks drawn by a horse or locomotive.

BIBLIOGRAPHY
General
Stratton and Trinder, 1988.

Rance, Hainaut, Belgium A marble-working town, 32 km (20 mi.) SW of Charleroi, from which stone was supplied for the palace at Versailles and the cathedral of St Peter's, Rome. Several former mines and cutting shops remain, and the industry is depicted in the National Museum of Marble.

BIBLIOGRAPHY
General
Viaene, 1986.

LOCATION
[M] Musée National de Marbre (National Museum of Marble), rue St Hubert 40, 6478 Rance.

Ravne na Koroškem (Gutenstein), Slovenia, Yugoslavia An open-air museum, 50 km (30 mi.) W. of Maribor, opened in 1953 at the Missthal Ironworks, in an area with many ancient iron and lead workings. Exhibits include a water-powered hammer from the ironworks, a mechanized lead-melting furnace, a rolling mill, and a drying oven which could be used for flax, apples or pears.

BIBLIOGRAPHY
General
Zippelius, 1974.

LOCATION
[M] Delavski Muzej Ravne na Koroškem, Na Gradu 1, 62390-Ravne na Koroškem.

rayon A manufactured fibre, once called artificial silk, made from regenerated cellulose such as processed wood pulp and cotton linters. A key innovation was the viscose process, patented in 1892. Viscose rayon, cellulose sodium xanthate, is made by treating wood pulp with caustic soda and then with carbon bisulphide, C_2S. The dissolved sodium cellulose xanthate is pumped through numerous small holes in discs called spinnerettes, extruding the liquid into an acid bath where it coagulates into filaments which can then be processed into yarn.

The first rayon factory was established at Besançon, France, in 1892, and the material was soon being produced under licence in several other countries. In 1898 C. H. Stearn patented a process for making filaments from viscose, establishing a pilot plant at Kew, 16 km (10 mi.) W. of London. The development of rayon manufacture in England was the achievement of the Courtauld company, whose main plant at Foleshill, COVENTRY, began commercial production in 1908. Courtaulds also established the first major plant in the USA, at Marcus Hook, Pennsylvania.

A rayon plant typically consisted of single-storey sheds for the chemical processes, with high roofs and complex systems for extracting the highly explosive carbon bisulphide, together with conventional multi-storey blocks for the less hazardous spinning and, where appropriate, weaving processes.

BIBLIOGRAPHY
General
Coleman, 1969; Courtaulds Ltd., 1957; Hounshell and Smith, 1988; Stevens, 1975; Ward-Jackson, 1941.
Specific
Harrop, J. The international rayon industry between the wars. In *TH*, I, 1969.

JANE HUTCHINS and MICHAEL STRATTON

razor A traditional, 'cut-throat' razor is a form of knife, and was usually made by a cutler. By the nineteenth century razors often had concave sides, and were said to be 'hollow ground'. The 'safety' razor, having a rectangular blade with a guard on one edge, fitting on to a hoe-shaped instrument, was developed in SHEFFIELD and in the USA from *c*.1828. King Camp Gillette (1855–1932), who had been advised when a young businessman to invent 'something that would be used and thrown away', combined the hoe-shaped razor with a double-edged replaceable blade. He established the Gillette Safety Razor Co. in the USA in 1901, which was producing 12.4 million blades a year by 1904, and set up plants in other countries, including Britain, where the factory on the Great West Road (*see* LONDON), designed by Sir Bannister Fletcher (1856–1963) in 1936 was architecturally one of the most notable of its time.

BIBLIOGRAPHY
Specific
Origin of the Gillette razor, In *Gillette Blade*. Feb./Mar. 1918.

recording The stuff of which industrial archaeology is made. It is the strongest link industrial archaeology has with field archaeology of the traditional type, and indeed with the field sciences generally. The essential character of a record is that it should be accurate, concise, and as complete as practicable or desirable. In the early years of industrial archaeology the perceived purposes of the record were two: firstly to make a statement about the current state of a site or group of sites, and secondly to accumulate summary information on a larger scale to allow assessment of relative importance. Both amateurs and professionals became involved in Britain, and the published results of their efforts may be seen in the *Journal of Industrial Archaeology* and its successors, and in the series published by David & Charles and Batsford.

The unpublished summary records in Britain include the National Record of Industrial Monuments (NRIM), compiled at the University of Bath and now held as a closed record by the Royal Commission on the Historical Monuments of England. Specialist groups have developed the concept, introduced by the NRIM, of using pro forma record cards or data sheets. Experience suggests that if used consistently, this type of record can be very valuable. To make the best use of it a photograph or photographs – and preferably some kind of sketch plan, if the layout is not obvious from the photographs – is essential. The card or data sheet approach lends itself to computer manipulation. My own view is that in this context the computer functions best as a mechanized index, and that it is a mistake to try to put too much onto the machine. The paper record, not the computer print-out, is irreplaceable. For computerization to function effectively, systematic classification is essential. Standard classifications are helpful, and should be based on experience of sites rather than on abstract considerations. Experience suggests a three-level classification: for example, textiles–cotton–weaving. It is difficult to be rigorously consistent, and multi-function sites pose particular problems. Here multiple entries are probably best, for example a corn and saw mill would appear under both grain milling and woodworking. It is better to duplicate and cross-reference than to overburden a system whose prime objective should be clarity of presentation and speed both of inputting and processing.

The more detailed recording of sites or objects can be tackled in a number of ways. For some excellent models, Hay and Stell (1986) on Scotland cannot be bettered. A thorough record would include enough photographs (including aerial photographs) adequately to define the subject; drawings, at least in the form of measured sketches; a written description, including a summary of

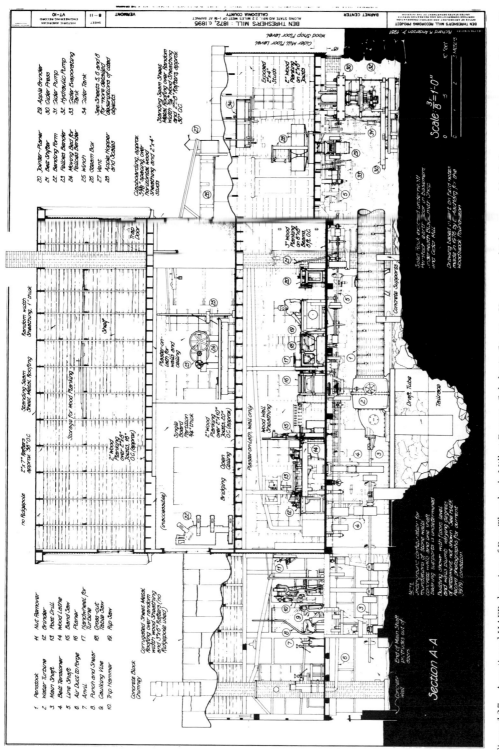

Figure 127 A sectioned HAER drawing of Ben Thresher's Mill at Barnet, Caledonia County, Vermont, which was used both for working wood and for making cider

Historic American Engineering Record. National Park Service. Richard K. Anderson. 1981

history, and reference to supporting information, such as product photographs, catalogues, advertisements and stationary samples; and map evidence. The objective should be to have a rapid visual sift: onto this can be grafted, according to the completeness and importance of the site, everything from a complete archive of business records to a monograph. It is essential to have a recording strategy, and to keep in mind that the best may be the enemy of the good: adequate recording of a number of sites is probably preferable to recording in great detail a single site, unless that site is of outstanding importance; dimensioned sketches may be just as useful as scaled orthographic projections.

For EXCAVATIONS, there are excellent models for recording in traditional archaeological practice, and there is no reason why the standards adopted in industrial archaeology should be any lower than those for other periods.

Photography, the most cost-effective medium, should take account of possible uses of the record. Many users will be content with a good perspective view, but 'straight on' views can be most valuable, especially for comparative purposes and for preparing finished drawings, should this be necessary. Constructional details are often useful. Photographs taken with lenses of different focal lengths do, of course, give different information, as well as different aesthetics. While it is often desirable to exclude people and vehicles from photographs, it is often these features which give life and scale to a view. In choosing between different types of film and camera format compromises must be made. For long it was rigidly held that black and white photography with a large-format camera was the ideal, and there is still much to commend this view. The convenience, flexibility and relative cheapness of the 35 mm format is, however, quite compelling. Smaller formats are frankly unsuitable. Colour is also an option. Experience suggests that colour is a desirable extra, and that the first preference would be for colour negative. Slides are preferable for colour reproduction but not essential. The decision here is a fine one. Slides used for projection will lose colour, and a master should, for preference, be kept purely for record. Prints are best mounted or stored in transparent envelopes, as repeated handling quickly reduces quality. Acid-free mounting card and storage envelopes are highly desirable. Each print should be identified clearly and unambiguously.

The traditional approach has often been to make written descriptions, photographs and drawings largely free-standing. The nature of industrial recording, however, is such that an integrated approach is commonly preferable, with annotated photographs, plans marked to show location of photographs, sketches, and finished drawing forming a unified record. Written description should always be as concise and clear as possible. Oral evidence is commonly an excellent way to clarify and amplify views based on observation.

Finally, it should be borne in mind that recording is not an end in itself; it is a means to the end of understanding that group of human activities, some very important indeed, which supply people with the essentials of life and death, and with various ways of making both more

bearable. To that end the record, whether it be a professional, public one, or an amateur, private one, should be as easy to use and as informative as possible. Microcomputers can be enormously helpful in organizing data. Any kind of system is better than none: a simple topographical one is often as easy to use as any, especially if a card or computer index can be used for thematic cross-reference. A good, simply arranged, well-maintained record is a pleasure both to the creators and the users.

For examples of excellence in the recording of industrial monuments see figures 5, 14, 28, 59, 68, 69, 74, 102, 111, 116, 127, 143, 155, 156, 174.

BIBLIOGRAPHY
General
HAER, 1981; Hay and Stell, 1986; Major, 1975; Pannell, 1974; Whimster, 1990.
Specific
Lankton, L. D. Three dimensions reduced to two: using measured drawings as a means to record IA sites. In Newell, 1978.
Recording Industrial Sites: a review. Council for British Archaeology, London, 1981.

JOHN HUME

red lead Lead oxide (Pb_3O_4), which was used in glass manufacture and varnishes. It was made in two stages in a colouring oven. First an air draught was played onto molten lead, which oxidized to form lead oxide (PbO); this was then cooled, removed, ground, and heated in another oven at a lower temperature until red lead was obtained.

BIBLIOGRAPHY
General
Stratton and Trinder, 1988.

reeling The term applied to the unwinding of the silk filament spun by the silkworm and its rewinding into skeins. The cocoons are boiled, steamed or soaked in hot water to loosen their natural gum. In hand reeling, the operative selects filaments from several cocoons, usually four to six, to reel simultaneously to form one strand of silk yarn. The operative sets the reel in motion and joins new cocoons as necessary to complete a skein of several thousand metres. The skeins are then twisted into standard bundles and sent to yarn manufacturing plants where the reeled silk is twisted or thrown into proper yarn. Some silk is sufficiently strong after reeling not to require THROWING and is only rewound as needed for weaving.

BIBLIOGRAPHY
General
Bendure and Pfeiffer, 1946.

Rees, Abraham (1743–1845) A Presbyterian minister whose *Cyclopaedia* is one of the principal sources for the technological history of the Industrial Revolution. It was published in British and American editions in forty-five volumes, each of two parts, between 1802 and 1820. Rees began his work as a cyclopaedist by re-editing the cyclopaedia of Ephraim Chambers (d.1740), originally published in 1728. His own great work is distinguished by the quality of its illustrations. Subsequent works by Sir David Brewster (1781–1868), C. F. Partington (d.1857) and C. Tomlinson (1808–97) followed the same tradition.

BIBLIOGRAPHY
General
Brewster, 1830; Collison, 1964; Partington, 1835; Rees, 1802–20, 1972; Tomlinson, 1852–4.
Specific
Harte, N. B. On Rees's *Cyclopaedia* as a source for the history of the textile industries in the early nineteenth century. In *Textile History*, V, 1974.
Jackson, B. L. An attempt to ascertain the actual dates of publication of the various parts of Rees's *Cyclopaedia*. In *Journal of Botany*, XXXIV, 1896.

Rees, David Morgan (1913–78) A major figure in industrial archaeology in Wales from the 1950s. In *Mines, Mills and Furnaces* (1969) he surveyed the main industries of Wales, analysing selected sites to provide a model of minute observation combined with general deduction. His *Industrial Archaeology in Wales* (1975) remains the standard introduction to the subject. As a member of the Ancient Monuments Board and the Royal Commission on Historical Monuments he helped gain official recognition of industrial conservation and recording. As the first Keeper of Industry at the National Museum of Wales he was responsible for establishing a slate-quarrying museum at DINORWIC and the Welsh Industrial and Maritime Museum at CARDIFF.

See also figure 172.

BIBLIOGRAPHY
General
Rees, 1969, 1975.
Specific
Day, J. and Day, R. Obituary: David Morgan Rees. In *Bulletin of the Association for Industrial Archaeology*, VI(2) 1978.

PETER WAKELIN

refinery A HEARTH used to reduce the carbon, manganese and silicon content of pig iron before it was used in a dry PUDDLING FURNACE, thus reducing the time taken for the process. It was fired with charcoal or coke.

See also OIL REFINERY.

BIBLIOGRAPHY
General
Gale, 1969, 1971; Trinder, 1981.

refractories The word 'refractory' originally meant stubborn: from the eighteenth century it was applied to substances that were difficult to fuse and resistant to heat, particularly those used for lining KILNS, crucibles, furnaces and the fireboxes of boilers. Various forms of sandstone were used for lining early BLAST FURNACES. Bricks made from selected clays, like those from STOURBRIDGE (*see* BLACK COUNTRY), came into use during the eighteenth century and are commonly called firebricks. Magnesite was used in the BESSEMER process for steelmaking from 1856. Austrian magnesite was exported to the USA for this purpose from 1885. Dolomite was used as a cheaper though not ideal substitute. Saggars, dishes in which wares are placed to prevent their being distorted by undue exposure to heat in the kiln, are made from refractory clays, as are other items of kiln furniture used in stacking wares. In Poland shales have been extensively used in making refractories (*see* NOWA RUDA).

BIBLIOGRAPHY
General
Norton, 1949; Searle, 1924.

refrigeration Ice cropped in winter was used on a considerable scale by 1800 for the preservation of food (*see* ICE HOUSE), and an international trade in ice, sometimes called Arctic Crystal, developed in the mid-nineteenth century. It was used in England for the preservation of fish at Grimsby, and in bacon factories in Wiltshire. In the USA there was a substantial trade in ice for home iceboxes, the first effective example of which – an oval cedar tub with a tinplate vessel inside, a hinged wooden lid lined with cloth, and joints sealed with rabbit fur – was invented by Thomas Moore in Maryland in 1803.

In the 1850s machine-made ice was used in the meat trade between Australia and England, but the pioneer of the large-scale commercial production of ice was the German, Carl von Linde (1842–1934), who invented the AMMONIA compression machine in 1876. Two hundred ice plants had been established in the USA by 1889, and there were two thousand by 1909, supplying ice for icebox refrigerators, for refrigerated railway wagons, and for industrial purposes, particularly in breweries, FISHING PORTS and MEAT packing centres. By 1921 domestic mechanical refrigerators were in production. Five thousand were manufactured in the USA in that year, a million in 1931, and three million in 1937.

The twentieth-century frozen-food industry was established by Clarence Birdseye (1886–1956), a New Yorker prompted to experiment with preserving food by experiences in Labrador, who invented a machine for freezing by pressing food between metal plates cooled to $-25\,°C$. In 1924 he built the first automatic quick-freezing machines and set up a company to market packaged frozen fish in compact blocks. This was so successful that he was able to sell out in 1929 and continue with his experiments, in 1949 perfecting an anhydrous process which cut the time taken to freeze food from 18 to $1\frac{1}{2}$ hours. The trade in frozen food in the USA was valued at $150 million a year by 1940, but its influence did not reach Europe until after 1945.

BIBLIOGRAPHY
General
Anderson, 1908, 1953; Boorstin, 1973; Critchell and Raymond, 1912; Hall, 1974; Hudson, 1965; Jones, 1984; Macintyre, 1928; Wright, 1982.

BARRIE TRINDER

Reinhardshagen, Hesse, Germany In the eighteenth

Figure 128   A water corn mill of the Renaissance period at Sloup, near Znojomo, Moravia
Simon Derry

and nineteenth centuries the state ironworks in the Veckerhagen quarter of Reinhardshagen, 22 km (14 mi.) NE of Kassel, was the largest industrial concern in Hesse-Kassel. It produced cast iron, especially coal ovens for export to northern Europe and the USA. The ore came from a nearby mine, and the charcoal used as fuel from surrounding forests. Production reached its peak in the mid-nineteenth century. In 1823–33 a large neo-Classical building was erected to accommodate locksmiths and pattern-makers. The foundry building was enlarged, probably in 1838, and a neo-Gothic gable was added. Production is estimated to have averaged 600 tonnes per annum. Subsequently the ironworks went through a period of crisis. It operated purely as an engineering works from 1868, and closed in 1903. The buildings still present an unusually complete impression of a nineteenth-century industrial concern, illustrating particularly well the industrial architecture of the 1850s.

Reisen   A term used in Slovakia and Transylvania from the seventeenth century to refer to a surface (as distinct from an underground) railway, or to the wagons that worked on such a railway, which might have guide wheels (*see* GUIDE-WHEEL RAILWAY) or, later, flanged wheels. Originally it was a forest slide, and sometimes a road cart.

BIBLIOGRAPHY
General
Lewis, 1970.

relay power station   A telegraphic installation passing on a signal to a more distant station. Devised by Edward Davy (1806–85) in 1837, it obviated the need for large currents.

Remscheid, North Rhine-Westphalia, Germany *See* BERGISCHES LAND.

Renaissance   The term generally applied to Italian art and architecture between *c.*1420 and *c.*1560, and to the styles derived therefrom in northern European countries. Many aspects of Renaissance architecture were revived for commercial and industrial buildings in the nineteenth century (*see* BEAUX-ARTS).

Rendsburg, Schleswig-Holstein, Germany   *See* KIEL.

Rennie, John (1761–1821)   One of the leading civil engineers of the Industrial Revolution, Rennie worked for BOULTON & WATT from 1784, and on his own account from 1791. He designed many canals, harbour installations and bridges, including the KENNET & AVON CANAL, Waterloo and Southwark bridges in London, and the PLYMOUTH breakwater. His sons, George Rennie (1791–1866) and Sir John Rennie (1794–1874), were also civil engineers, the latter completing his father's design for London Bridge in 1831 (*see* ARIZONA).

BIBLIOGRAPHY
General
Rennie, 1875.

Replica   *See* MODEL.

reservoir   A place for storing water, normally on a large scale for drinking or power supply; the term can apply more generally to a part of a machine where any kind of fluid is contained. Impounding reservoirs are for the primary storage of water before it passes through a WATERWORKS, and are usually created by damming streams or rivers. Impounding reservoirs allow suspended material to settle out of the water as the first stage of its treatment at a waterworks. Service reservoirs provide pressure for mains distribution systems, and may take the form of WATER TOWERS.

BIBLIOGRAPHY
General
Babbitt and Doland, 1939; Burton and Dumbleton, 1928; Turneaure and Russell, 1924.

Reşiţa, Caraş-Severin, Romania An area with long metalworking and engineering traditions, developing from a group of artisan workshops in existence by 1740, and working together by 1767. In 1771 a blast furnace came into operation, together with the first blister steel (*see* STEEL) furnace. A plate mill worked by a steam engine and a steam hammer were installed in 1846. The first railway rails to be made in Romania were rolled at Reşiţa in 1851. Coke production commenced in 1864, and a Bessemer converter was installed in 1868.

Pelton turbines of 1906 from the Grebla hydro-electric power station are displayed in the Reşiţa district museum, which is also to have sections on the metallurgical and mechanical engineering industries of Caraş-Severin. The first Romanian-built steam locomotive was completed at Reşiţa in 1923, and almost every type of Romanian steam locomotive is displayed in the museum.

BIBLIOGRAPHY
Specific
Doua Secole de Siderurgie la Reşiţa (Two centuries of ironmaking at Reşiţa). Bucharest, 1971.
Wollmann, V. Romania. In Georgeacopol-Winischhofer *et al.*, 1987.

LOCATION
[M] Museul regional Reşiţa (District Museum), 50 str. 7 Noiembrie, Reşiţa.

HORIA GIURGIUMAN

restaurant car Meals were served for the first time in a Pullman car on the Great Western Railroad of Canada in 1867, and PULLMAN constructed the first purpose-built dining car in 1868, although food had been served as early as 1835 on some American railways. The first restaurant cars in Britain appeared on the GNR in 1879, and their use spread across Europe as carriages with corridor connections came into use. The first buffet for light refreshments appeared on LBSCR Pullman trains in 1889.

Preserved restaurant cars include a magnificent vehicle of MR design of 1914 at YORK, and one built for the opening of the Bergenbanen in 1909–11 at HAMAR.

BIBLIOGRAPHY
Specific
Kitchenside, G. *The Restaurant Car: a century of railway catering.* Newton Abbot: David & Charles, 1979.

retailing The sale of goods in small quantities to those who use or consume them. In the pre-industrial period most goods were purchased from producers, whether in SHOPS, as was the case with most manufactured items, or MARKETS, the usual source of food in towns. In seventeenth-century England a mercer, who provided most goods brought to a town from elsewhere, normally sold fabrics, haberdashery, hosiery, paper and books, groceries (imported goods like spices and dried fruit), tobacco, and saltery, commodities like CANDLES, TAR and WHITING. Outside the towns there were probably few shops, most needs being met by travelling pedlars and occasional visits to fairs. The general store in a village or industrial community was probably an innovation of the late eighteenth century.

Nineteenth-century urban retailing tended to be formal, with restrained window and internal displays, negotiation with shopkeepers across counters, and settlement by long credit. In markets and on the open streets, selling was informal, with brash displays, vigorous promotion of goods, and cash settlement. The most innovative retailers of the late nineteenth century, whether in DEPARTMENT STORES or CHAIN STORES, brought the two traditions together. Plate GLASS made possible more inviting window displays, while CASH REGISTERS and sometimes PNEUMATIC DISPATCH systems transformed the process of selling. In the USA the isolation of farming families stimulated the development of mail-order concerns in the 1870s and 80s by such entrepreneurs as Aaron Montgomery Ward (1843–1913) and Richard Warren Sears (1863–1914), both of whom began to operate from Minnesota and then moved to Chicago.

Until the 1920s most retailing involved packaging, such as the weighing out of sweets into bags or the cutting and wrapping of butter. From the 1920s the growth of the packaging industry restricted the role of many retailers to selling. The size of units has increased, and their numbers have diminished, with growing numbers of motorcars. The out-of-town 'shopping centre' – the first of which was the Country Club Plaza Shopping Centre, Kansas City, designed by James C. Nichols in 1922 – grew rapidly in the inter-war period in the USA, accounting for a quarter of all retail purchases by 1940, but did not take root in Europe until after 1950.

Catalogues, such as the reprints edited by Adburgham, are a valuable source for the history of retailing.

See also APOTHECARY; ARCADE; BAKERY; BAZAAR; BUTCHER; COMPANY STORE; CONFECTIONERY; CO-OPERATIVE MOVEMENT; DEPARTMENT STORE; DISPENSARY; DRUG STORE; PHARMACY; SADDLERY; SHOES; STORE; SUPERMARKET; TRUCK SHOP.

BIBLIOGRAPHY
General
Adburgham, 1969, 1972, 1974; Alexander, 1970; Boorstin, 1973; Dean, 1970; Emmett and Jeuck, 1950; Jeffreys, 1954; Latham, 1972; Mui and Mui, 1989; Priestley and Fenner, 1985; Sears, Roebuck, 1897, 1902; Spufford, 1984; Trinder and Cox, 1980; Weil, 1977; Winstanley, 1983.
Specific
Lancaster, H. V. The design and architectural treatment of the shop. In *Journal of the Royal Society of Arts*, LXI, 1913.

Yamey, B. S. The evolution of shopping. In *Lloyds Bank Review*, XXXI, 1954.

BARRIE TRINDER

retort   In an industrial context, a container in which coal and other substances are heated. In GASWORKS early retorts were cylindrical, vertical vessels, charged and cleared from the top, but a horizontal mode was later adopted, and circular, elliptical and finally D-shaped cross-sections were tried. Retorts were at first of cast iron, but this distorted after continued heating and by 1822 refractory clay with iron doors was preferred. Various methods of increasing output were tried: charging the retort at one end and clearing the coke from the other appeared in 1831, and automatic stoking machines in 1868. But it was only in the Woodall–Duckham vertical retort of 1903, in which the coal was charged at the top and coke was removed from the bottom, that carbonization could be carefully controlled and continuous charging become economically viable.

retting   The most critical step in flax processing. The flax is soaked in order to decompose the gum that binds the usable bast fibres to the rest of the stalk. Traditionally flax was left to ret in a stream or pond, or even in a field heavy with dew, the famous Belgian Kortrijk linen being retted in the River Lys. Industrial processors use carefully monitored tanks.

Reutlingen, Baden-Württemberg, Germany   Some important buildings were erected *c.*1900 at the Louis Gminder textile works in Reutlingen, 40 km (25 mi.) S. of Stuttgart, including a large spinning mill with a cotton warehouse, a machine shop, and an ambitious housing development for the workers, known as Gmindersdorf. The architect Theodor Fischer (1862–1938) drew up the plans for the village, and the factory buildings were designed by P. J. Manz, who was responsible for many other industrial buildings in Württemberg. The Gminder company was taken over by Bosch in 1964. The spinning mill was converted to produce electrical components and the machine shop became a canteen. Part of the works village has been privatized. Some detached houses and a semicircular group of old people's dwellings have been preserved.

reverberatory furnace   A furnace in which the flame is directed onto the material being heated, which is separated by a wall made of REFRACTORY materials from the fuel and any contaminating elements that it may contain. The reverberatory furnace is used in melting metal or the smelting of metallic ores. It usually comprises two chambers, with fuel burning in one, and metal or ore in the second, at the end of which is the flue.

See also AIR FURNACE; CUPOLA; PUDDLING FURNACE.

revolving fund   A means of financing the rehabilitation of buildings in a particular area judged to be of historical or architectural interest: money is granted to an organization, often a charitable trust, and is used to purchase and renovate a building; this is then sold, and the proceeds used to buy and restore others.

Reykjavik, Iceland   The capital of Iceland originated as a trading settlement on Holmurinn island in the sixteenth century. In the 1750s Skuli Magnusson established the first industrial estate with a row of houses that came to form the main street of the first town, which received its charter in 1786. In 1858, when the population was only about 700, Reykjavik was described as 'a collection of wooden sheds and a suburb of turf huts'. There were 6000 inhabitants by 1900, 11 600 by 1910, 28 000 in 1930, and 84 000 by 1980. The city's prosperity has been due to deep-sea fishing and to the harbour, whose breakwaters were constructed between 1913 and 1917 under the direction of the Danish engineer N. P. Kirk, using *Minor* and *Pioner*, two 0–4–0 locomotives built in 1892 by Arn Jung of Jungenthal bei Kirchberg, Germany. *Pioner* is now at the Reykjavik Museum, and *Minor* is preserved by the harbour authorities.

There are few historic industrial buildings in Reykjavik. Iceland's first commercial brewery, set up in 1913, survives at 19–21 Njalsgata; and the city's first hydroelectric power station, built in 1921, is retained as a standby source of power.

The National Museum in the city centre has collections of iron artefacts of all periods, querns made from volcanic lava, rope-spinning machinery, woven fabrics and warp-weighted looms, as well as pictures of windmills, sulphur mining and fish-processing.

The open-air museum, Arbæjarsafn, 7 km (4 mi.) E. of the centre, dates from 1957. Sixteen buildings have been re-erected around the ancient farmstead of Arbær, including a turf and stone smithy, labourers' houses in stone and corrugated iron from Reykjavik, a lattice-work fish-drying shed, and warehouses built *c.*1820 at Vopnafjördhur in north-east Iceland by a Danish trading company. Other exhibits include the locomotive *Pioner*, an Aveling & Porter steamroller taken to Iceland in 1912, and a German gold drill, imported in 1922 and used until 1965 for prospecting for hot water.

BIBLIOGRAPHY
Specific
Arbæjarsafn. *Arbæjarsafn: Reykjavik Museum*. Reykjavik, 1981.
Arbæjarsafn. *Jarnbrautin i Reykjavik* (The locomotives in Reykjavik). Reykjavik, 1982.
Tucker, D. G. The history of industries and crafts in Iceland. In *JIA*, IX, 1972.

LOCATIONS
[M] Arbæjarsafn, Reykjavik Museum, IS 1 30 Reykjavik, Iceland.
[M] Thjodminjasafnid (National Museum), Sudurgotu, Reykjavik.

BARRIE TRINDER

Rheinböllen, Rhineland-Palatinate, Germany   The site of the Rheinböllen ironworks, 40 km (25 mi.) S. of Koblenz, is known to have been used for ironworking since the early Middle Ages, and the first documentary evidence dates from 1598. The present buildings were mostly erected in the first half of the nineteenth century. Like the Sayn ironworks at BENDORF, the works is an important and typical example of the practice of the period. From the eighteenth century the works was owned by the Utsch family, and subsequently by the related Puricelli family. In the seventeenth century the plant consisted of a blast furnace, a charcoal-fired FINERY AND CHAFERY forge, and a hammer mill. It was extended in the early nineteenth century, a blast furnace and two CUPOLA furnaces being added in 1835, and another blast furnace in 1840. The blast furnaces were blown out in 1893, but the ironworks continued as a foundry.

The old equipment is no longer in existence but the buildings in the valley, largely preserved in their original condition, convey a good impression of the external appearance of a large nineteenth-century ironworks. Looking down the valley, the first sight to meet the eye is the mausoleum of the owner's family, built in 1857, in the late Romantic style of the Rhineland. Next come the foundry building, the canteen, workers' dwelling houses, the stamping mill, the hammer mill, the blast-furnace building, a warehouse for cast-iron goods, and the old dwelling house of the Puricelli family. All these buildings are constructed of coarse brown rubble masonry. The newer and larger Puricelli house, on the other hand, is stuccoed, and with its neo-Classical design and extensive gardens, bears witness to the prosperity of the ironmasters of the time. The grounds now belong to the works of a large car-brake manufacturer further up the valley.

BIBLIOGRAPHY
General
Custodis, 1990.

ROLF HÖHMANN

Rheinfelden, Aargau, Switzerland, and Baden-Württemberg, Germany The first large hydro-electric power station in Europe to use running water was built in 1898 opposite the Swiss town of Rheinfelden, 16 km (10 mi.) E. of Basel, on the upper Rhine, which forms the border between Switzerland and Germany. Large industrial firms from both countries participated in the construction of the weir and the power station complex, including Escher Wyss, Zschokke and Oerlikon from Switzerland, and AEG from Germany. The channel running to the dam, and the building housing the turbines and generators (146 m (479 ft.) long and 24 m (79 ft.) high), are in Baden on the German side, as are the main users of the electricity, plants making aluminium and sodium. The original equipment of the power station consisted of twenty 840 hp Francis turbines, with ten three-phase generators and ten d.c. generators (for the aluminium works) mounted on their vertical shafts. Rheinfelden, like the contemporary complex at Niagara, NEW YORK, displays the transition to three-phase generation of electricity. The whole complex has been preserved, with certain technical modifications.

On the Swiss side of the river the vast Feldschlösschen brewery dominates the landscape. Dating from 1890 and

progressively extended until 1955, it resembles a castle in every detail. The central steam engine house and other parts of the interior are decorated with ceramic tiles, marble pillars, brass handrails and stained-glass windows. The works railway is still in working order and has its own steam locomotives. Timber-floating is among the industries illustrated in the Fircktaler Museum.

BIBLIOGRAPHY
General
Baldinger, 1987.

LOCATION
[M] Fircktaler Museum, Marktgasse 12, 4310 Rheinfelden, Aargau, Switzerland.

HANS-PETER BÄRTSCHI and ROLF HÖHMANN

Rhine, River (Rhein, Rhin, Rijn), France, Germany, The Netherlands and Switzerland The most important artery of European trade, the River Rhine is now a commercial navigation between BASLE and ROTTERDAM but its course through the Netherlands has been much changed over the centuries, and the extent of trade on the river as a whole has varied considerably. The many tolls on the river began to be removed by the Treaty of Vienna of 1815, which set up the Rhine Commission, the last tolls being withdrawn following the Convention of Mannheim of 1868. The first steamboat on the river, the British *Defiance*, reached Cologne in 1816; and in 1817 the *Caledonia*, commanded by the son of JAMES WATT, reached Koblenz. Regular steamboat services were established between Rotterdam and Cologne in 1823, and in 1826 the forerunner of the Köln-Düsseldorfer Rheinschiffahrt AG shipping line established a passenger service, which was to be popular with tourists going to Switzerland. Steam towing for freight vessels was introduced between Rotterdam and Mannheim in 1825. Railway competition brought a contraction of freight services, for which the head of the river was effectively Mannheim from 1855, but the channel was improved for smaller vessels by Colonel Gottfried von Tulla; to Strasbourg in 1876 and subsequently to Basel, where the first train of barges arrived in 1904, in which year there were 1183 steamers on the river. Traffic has grown in the twentieth century. In 1913 97000 craft passed Emmerich on the Dutch/German border, a total that reached 180000 by 1983. Improvements have also continued. Summertime passenger services operate from Amsterdam and Nijmegen to Basel.

The most beautiful and romantic landscapes of the Rhine lie in RHINELAND-PALATINATE. As it cuts through the Rhineland Slate Mountains, the river narrows to a width of 115 m (377 ft.); its functions as a major shipping route always entailed dangers here, particularly near the Loreley Rock, and the so-called Bingen Loch. Only since 1974 has a safe shipping channel been guaranteed by the corrective work, including dredging and blasting, repeatedly carried out on the riverbed. After 1827, when a deep enough channel had been blasted out of the rock at St Goar and Bingen, steamers were able to ply regularly between Cologne and Mainz. An important influence was that of Karl Ludwig Althans (*see* BENDORF). To make the Rhine navigable was a great historic achievement in engineering technology, not least because it meant that there was no further need for locks from the Upper Rhine to the mouth of the river.

Once ease of shipping was assured, many harbour and crane installations were built. The cranes in Bingen and Östrich-Winkel (Hesse), 8 km (5 mi.) E. of Bingen, both with massive square bodies and roofs that swivel with the arms of the cranes, are technological monuments from the pre-industrial period. Like the crane at Andernach, 16 km (10 mi.) NW of Koblenz, they date from the mid-sixteenth century, and their driving mechanisms, each equipped with two treadwheels, are still extant. The crane in Koblenz, dating from 1609, retains its tower shaft, with the historic gauge of 1785 for measuring the water level of the Rhine. Early industrial harbour complexes remain at Mainz (the Winterhafen and its swing bridge of 1877), and at Ludwigshafen (the Luitpoldhafen, which has a gauge tower dating from 1900). Large mill buildings, often romantically designed to resemble castles, were a common part of the picture in the harbours of the Rhine over a long period, but only one remains in Rhineland-Palatinate, at Niederlahnstein, 3 km (2 mi.) SE of Koblenz. Erected in 1890, the mill has an internal frame of cast-iron columns.

The railways too used the Rhine valley as a natural route. The line from Bingen to Cologne through Koblenz, on the left bank, and the connection from Wiesbaden to Oberlahnstein, opposite Koblenz, were opened in 1859 and 1862 respectively. Shortage of space in the narrow valley, and the convoluted windings of the river, made heavy civil engineering work essential. Tunnels, like the Loreley Tunnel, tend to have romantically designed portals. The station at Rolandseck, 44 km (27 mi.) NW of Koblenz, opened in 1856, is of especial historical importance. It is a neo-Classical building, reminiscent of a villa, with a colonnade around it and a terrace looking down to the Rhine. The building was long threatened with demolition, but is now used for private art exhibitions and is known as the 'artists' station'.

Another important economic factor in the Rhine valley, besides shipping and wine-growing, was the extraction of minerals, particularly the mining of slate. In Kaub, 45 km (28 m.) SE of Koblenz, the merging of fourteen pits in 1837 created the Wilhelm-Erbstollen joint mining company. The firm of Puricelli (*see* RHEINBÖLLEN) took over the business in 1870, and it closed in 1972. The surface buildings have been largely preserved, and the pithead building with the mouth of the adit lies on the steep bank of the Rhine, together with an area where roofing slates were dressed, a crushing mill, and dwelling houses. Access to the bank of the Rhine was by an elevator built into a medieval fortress tower in the town of Kaub.

The many Rhine bridges were almost entirely destroyed in the closing stages of World War II, but their characteristic shape is retained in the Theodor Heuss Bridge at Mainz, which was rebuilt after the war using old parts, in the manner of the original bridge of 1882, with half-timbered arches in the lower part of the structure.

BIBLIOGRAPHY
General
Banfield, 1846; Custodis, 1990; Hadfield, 1986.

LOCATIONS
[M] Museum of the Lower Rhine, Friedrich Wilhelm Strasse 64, 4100 Duisburg.
[M] Regional Museum, Burg Klop, 6530 Bingen.
[M] Rheingau Wine Museum, Brömserburg, Rheinstrasse 2, 6220 Rüdesheim.
[M] Rhine Museum, Festung Ehrenbreitstein, 5400 Koblenz.

ROLF HÖHMANN and BARRIE TRINDER

Rhineland-Palatinate (Rheinland-Pfalz), Germany   The federal state of Rhineland-Palatinate was created artificially after World War II by merging the Bavarian Palatinate, the Prussian regions of Koblenz, Trier and parts of Hesse-Nassau, and Rhenish Hesse on the left bank of the RHINE. Acting as an important traffic artery, the Rhine divides the state approximately north to south, with the Moselle and Lahn forming an east–west link across it the other way. The three rivers were and remain the backbone of commercial, economic and industrial development in the area. Even today, the country is very thinly populated outside the river valleys. It is predominantly given over to agriculture and forestry; the Palatinate Forest is the largest unbroken forested area in Germany. Cutting and exploiting timber therefore developed on an industrial scale at an early date, as is shown by the log-floating installation in the Elmstein valley and the paper-mills at Lambrecht (*see* NEUSTADT AN DER WEINSTRASSE). Wine-growing along the Rhine, the Moselle, the smaller tributary rivers of the Ahr and Nahe, and in Rhenish Hesse, make the Rhineland Palatinate the major German wine-growing area, although the intensively-run small companies seldom reach an industrial scale.

Today raw materials are extracted only for the building industry. Basalt lava of volcanic origin from the Eifel and Westerwald area is important for these purposes. Earthenware is made mainly in the Ransbach-Baumbach area, 24 km (15 mi.) NE of Koblenz; the manufacture of roofing tiles and terracotta at Jockgrim, 14 km (9 mi.) NW of Karlsruhe, once a large industry, ceased when the supply of clay ran out. Large-scale mining of iron ore in the Siegerland, Westerwald and Waldalgesheim areas has also ceased, as has the mining of lead, silver and zinc in BAD EMS and Braubach, 8 km (5 m.) SE of Koblenz.

Early smelting works, usually on the sites of old water-driven bloomeries, were built to process the ore, and were often run by several generations of the first owner's family, like the Gienanths in Hochstein and Eisenberg near Grünstadt, 24 km (15 mi.) NW of Mannheim, the Puricellis in RHEINBÖLLEN, and the Remys of BENDORF, who had an interest in the lead and silver mining and smelting of Bad Ems. The Prussian state ironworks at Sayn (*see* BENDORF) was of especial importance.

A centre of shoe manufacturing developed in Pirmasens, 68 km (42 mi.) SW of Mannheim, and the major textile industry was centred on the worsted spinning mill in Kaiserslautern, 50 km (30 mi.) W. of Mannheim, now adapted for new uses. More recently industrial sites without any significant remaining monuments have developed at Ludwigshafen, on the west bank of the Rhine opposite Mannheim, with the coming of the chemical industry on the Rhine (BASF, the Badische Anilin- und Soda-Fabrik), and in the Mainz and Bingen areas.

Also important are the many spas, with their saline springs and mineral water industry; the saltworks, retained in production for their medicinal properties, and the extensive spread of salt-graduation houses between Bad Kreuznach, 32 km (20 mi.) SW of Mannheim, and Bad Münster am Stein, 4 km (2½ mi.) S.

See also BAD EMS; BENDORF; IDAR-OBERSTEIN AND ASBACHERHÜTTE; MAINZ; MOSELLE; NEUSTADT AN DER WEINSTRASSE; RHEINBÖLLEN; RHINE; WALDALGESHEIM.

BIBLIOGRAPHY
General
Custodis, 1990.

LOCATIONS
[I] Landesamt für Denkmalpflege Rheinland-Pfalz (Rhineland-Palatinate Provincial Monuments Protection Office), Auf der Bastei 3, 6500 Mainz 1.
[M] Rhine Museum, Festung Ehrenbreitstein, 5400 Koblenz.
[M] Rhine-Palatinate Collection of Technology, Festung Ehrenbreitstein, 5400 Koblenz.

ROLF HÖHMANN

Rhode Island, United States of America   The smallest of the states, Rhode Island emerged as a textile producer, water-powered mills happily depending on a very uneven terrain across the state. Other key industries have been jewellery manufacture, machine-tool building, and the production of silver flatware and cutlery. A diverse family of masonry lighthouses dots the state's heavily trafficked Atlantic coastline.

Rhode Island's textile industry, growing out of prosperous maritime and agricultural trades, began in 1790 with English immigrant SAMUEL SLATER's introduction of ARKWRIGHT carding and spinning machines in Pawtucket, the site today of a national engineering LANDMARK, the Slater Mill of 1793, and its adjacent Wilkinson Machine Shop of 1811. The shop is a working, water-powered evocation of American machine usage in its formative state. Nearby, the town of Slaterville recalls the early-nineteenth-century emergence of the planned INDUSTRIAL COMMUNITY.

Rhode Islanders also pioneered the introduction of the power loom to the nation, at a mill in Peacedale fitted with the machinery in 1813. Small-scale, wood-framed cotton and woollen mills sprouted throughout Rhode Island between 1790 and the 1830s, the scarce labour supply and occasional embargoes promoting machine innovation and proliferation. Mill villages such as Georgiaville and Lonsdale symbolize the subsequent congealing of mill interests into concentrations of carding, spinning, weaving, worsted and threadmaking operations in single plants, supported by complex social infrastructures built around mill life.

As with most New England seaboard states, Rhode Island developed a granite industry at sites of surface outcroppings. Towns in the vicinity of Westerly County contain disused structural and mechanical remains of the quarrying and cutting operations, now gracefully working their way into the surrounding rural landscape.

Lost amid the profusion of textile mill buildings dotting the land are such sites as the twelve-sided brick gasholder house of 1860 in Woonsocket; the ornamental concrete-and-tile standpipe of 1910 in Westerly; and the stately Mount Hope Suspension Bridge of 1929, connecting Bristol and Portsmouth over the bustling Naragansett Bay.

Predictably for a state with a high level of early industrial density, Rhode Island boasts a fine series of suitably-orientated museums, led by the Slater Mill complex in Pawtucket, and the New England Wireless and Steam Museum, East Greenwich, home to copious collections of radio and telegraph equipment and steam prime movers, including a rare CORLISS engine actually built by the Corliss company in Providence. The Blackstone Valley museum, Lincoln, surrounded by several generations of textile mills and related transport structures, houses itself in a turnpike tollbooth of 1804.

See also figure 74.

BIBLIOGRAPHY
General
American Society of Mechanical Engineers, 1980; Jackson, 1988; Kulik et al., 1982; Kulik and Bonham, 1978.

LOCATIONS
[M] Blackstone Valley Historical Society, North Gate, Louisquisset Pike, Lincoln, RI 02864.
[M] New England Wireless and Steam Museum, Frenchtown Road, East Greenwich, RI 02818.
[M,S] Slater Mill Historic Site, Roosevelt Avenue, Pawtucket, RI 02860.

DAVID H. SHAYT

Rhodes (Ródhos), Dodecanese, Greece   An island 78 km (48 mi.) by 30 km (19 mi.), with a population of 67 000, the seat of the Order of St John from 1309 until the Turks seized the island in 1522. Rhodes came under Italian rule from 1912, and only became part of Greece in 1947. The island is noted for its ceramics, particularly plates from Lindos and vases from Arkangelos. Its most spectacular monument is the Odos Ippoton (the street of the knights) in the city of Rhodes, which is a unique Gothic street of the fifteenth and early sixteenth centuries, with 'inns' of the French, Provençal, Spanish and English knights.

LOCATION
[M] Decorative Arts Collection of the Museum of Rhodes, Plateia Arghyrokastrou, Rhodes.

Rhondda Valleys, Mid Glamorgan, Wales   The Rhondda Fach and Rhondda Fawr, 25 km (16 mi.) NW of Cardiff, were the most important of the valleys developed in the South Wales coal boom of c.1850–1913. Others included the Ebbw, Rhymney, Taff, Cynon, Ogmore and

Afan. Barren and sparsely populated before the mid-nineteenth century, the valleys developed quickly as deep shaft operation improved and demand rose for high-quality steam coal, especially for shipping. Mining for the outside market began in 1819 and grew with improved transport to Cardiff from *c*.1840. In 1851 the BUTE Estate demonstrated that deep seams were workable. Rapid development followed, from the 1860s, by Welsh industrialists like DAVID DAVIES: there were 32 collieries in 1884, producing 5.5 million tons a year. At the peak in 1938, 68 pits were producing 10 million tons, but the market was already contracting with the loss of foreign markets and the conversion of ships to oil. Only 12 pits remained in 1958, and none today. A government attempt in 1934 to stimulate employment at the Treforest Trading Estate brought light manufacturing.

The Rhondda valleys afford an awesome landscape of deep valleys, barren hillsides and spoil heaps (though these have mostly been cleared since the tragic Aberfan landslip in 1966). Pit villages were constricted into continuous ribbon townships with railways, pit sites and marshalling yards on narrow valley floors. Housing was almost exclusively of a well-built terraced form, provided by collieries to attract an immigrant workforce. Long terraces snake along valley sides, interspersed with schools, shops and a proliferation of Nonconformist chapels and miners' institutes. Few colliery buildings have survived, but there is a preserved group with late nineteenth-century headgears and buildings at Lewis Merthyr colliery, now the Rhondda Heritage Park.

BIBLIOGRAPHY
General
Morris and Williams, 1958.
Specific
Lewis, E. D. *The Rhondda Valleys*. London: Phoenix House, 1959.

LOCATION
[M,S] Rhondda Heritage Park, Porth, Rhondda, Mid Glamorgan.

PETER WAKELIN

ribbon A narrow band of a woven fabric, usually silk, satin or an imitation thereof, used in the ornamentation of garments or of the person, rather than for closing garments (for which TAPES, often made in the same regions, were employed). Types include caddis and galloons, and ribbons are often referred to by the fabric type, such as satin and taffeta. Historically, true ribbons had two selvedges, both edges woven to prevent unravelling.

See also PASSEMENTERIE.

Rideau Canal, Ontario, Canada A series of artificial cuts linking lakes: with the Ottawa River, it provides an alternative route for vessels travelling between the Great Lakes and the lower St Lawrence. It was built for the British Government, in order to avoid rapids on the St Lawrence and to prevent interference by the US military with traffic on the St Lawrence. Planned by Colonel John By (1779–1836) and supervised by officers of the Royal Engineers, it runs 198 km (123 mi.) from the small settlement of Bytown (the nucleus of present-day OTTAWA) to Kingston, Ontario. Originally forty-seven locks were built at twenty-two lock stations. Water supply was controlled by stone dams. The canal was opened in 1832 and remained a busy commercial waterway, particularly for vessels returning to Lake Ontario from Montreal, until the last of the deep-water canals around the rapids in the St Lawrence was completed in 1849. Some commercial traffic continued, but finally ceased in the 1920s. The canal has been developed as a recreational waterway since its transfer to the Canadian Parks Service in 1972. Structures have been renovated, interpretation centres established, and a range of publications produced.

BIBLIOGRAPHY
General
Forbes, 1981; Passfield, 1982; Tulloch, 1981.

DERYCK HOLDSWORTH

rifle A shoulder-fired, long-barrelled GUN, which by means of spiral grooves 'rifled' into its bore imparts a spin to a tight-fitting bullet. While rifles were used as accurate hunting arms from the sixteenth century the difficulty of muzzle-loading a tight-fitting bullet limited their military role to that of skirmishing until repeat-fire breech-loading mechanisms were devised in the early nineteenth century, and produced in quantity under the AMERICAN SYSTEM OF MANUFACTURE.

BIBLIOGRAPHY
General
Hughes, 1974.

Riga, Latvia, USSR An ancient port on the Baltic, and capital of Latvia. An open-air museum stands on a 97 ha (239 ac.) site 12 km ($7\frac{1}{2}$ mi.) E. of the centre. More than seventy buildings can be seen there, including a windmill and a water mill, a fishery, a pottery, and tar kilns. The tradition of open-air museums in Latvia dates from 1896 when the ethnographer M. Skruzizis established a small museum on the Scandinavian model, for the All-Russian Archaeological Congress held that year in Riga. The present museum was established in 1924, when Latvia was independent, and opened in 1932. Smaller open-air museums in Latvia, dating from the 1950s, can be found at Cēsis, Jēkabpils, Ludza and VENTSPILS.

BIBLIOGRAPHY
General
Zippelius, 1974.
Specific
The Latvian Ethnographic Open-Air Museum, Riga. 1964.
Strods, H. Die Entwicklung der Freilichtmuseen Lettlands (The development of open-air museums in Latvia). In *Ethnographica* (Brno), 5 and 6, 1963–4.

LOCATION
[M] Latvijskij Etnograficzeskij Muzej (Latvian Ethnographic Open-Air Museum), Bukulti 10, Rizskij Rajon, Riga.

Rijeka (Rieka, Fiume), Croatia, Yugoslavia A port on the Adriatic, once the capital of the Italian province of

Figure 129 The so-called Bessemer Smelter at Rio Tinto, constructed in 1904; the open arches along each side allowed for ventilation. In the background is the Marismilla Dam, behind which is a reservoir that provided process water. The surrounding hills are almost entirely lacking in vegetation as a result of many years of exposure to sulphur dioxide fumes from the smelters.
Craig Meredith

Carnaro, ruled by the Habsburgs from the late fifteenth century but a free port from 1709, and a seaport of Hungary until 1918 (*see* AUSTRIA; HUNGARY). A free state from 1920, Rijeka was invaded by Italian legionnaires in 1922, and handed to Italy in 1924. After World War II it became part of Yugoslavia. Foreign specialist workers were introduced in 1772 to develop shipbuilding. A sugar refinery, established in 1751, came to employ a thousand workers by 1800. Much industrial growth has taken place since 1945.

LOCATION
[M] Maritime and Historical Museum, Guvernervoa Palaca, Zrtava Fasizma 18, Rijeka.

Ringerike, Buskerud, Norway   A parish 30 km (20 mi.) NW of Oslo. The Kjerraten i Åsa is one of the few installations in Norway designed to carry floating logs across a watershed: a series of ten lifts, by which logs were raised 386 m (1266 ft.) on continuously moving chains, worked by water wheels, from Steinsfjord, the northeastern part of Tyrifjorden, through several lakes and stretches of rivers, to Lysaker on Oslofjord. An eleventh lift worked west of Lake Storflatan. Designed by Samuel Bagge, it worked throughout 1808–50 but was never profitable. The courses of leats powering water wheels and the foundations of the lifts are still visible, and some lengths of chain survive. There is a large scale model at ELVERUM. Other preserved industrial monuments in the parish include limekilns, a nickel smelter, and the ruins of the Sogndal ironworks.

ring spinning   The ring spindle patented in the USA in 1828 by John Thorp (1784–1848) achieved a much higher speed than the U-shaped flyer employed on other continuous spinning frames. A small metal loop called the traveller carried the yarn, which was twisted as it passed around a stationary ring surrounding the rotating spindle. Ring spinning displaced most other forms of continuous spinning frames during the nineteenth century, for both wool and cotton spinning.

Rio Tinto, Huelva, Andalusia, Spain   The Rio Tinto mines, 80 km (50 mi.) W. of Seville and 80 km (50 mi.) N. of Huelva, have been some of the most productive in Europe, and past activities have left an awe-inspiring landscape of polychromatic tips of mine waste and slag, most of them totally inert. The mines have been chiefly worked for copper, and for pyrites used as a source of SULPHURIC ACID, but silver and gold have also been obtained. There is extensive archaeological evidence of Roman and earlier workings, but large-scale operations began with the aid of British capital in the late nineteenth century, the Rio Tinto Co. being established in 1873. Much of the ore was obtained from opencast workings. Crushing plants, precipitation pits, calcining kilns, smelters, flues, a power station, reservoirs for process water, a copper smelting works and a sulphuric acid plant were built, and from 1876 until 1974 a metre-gauge railway linked the workings with the port of Huelva. A mining colony, Minas De Rio Tinto, was established, but the present town is the third to bear that name, its predecessors having been abandoned to allow the expansion of workings. Continuing exploitation and reclamation schemes have damaged the archaeology of the site.

See also figure 123.

BIBLIOGRAPHY
General
Avery, 1974; Checkland, 1967; Salkield, 1987.
Specific
Thorburn, J. A. The industrial archaeology of Rio Tinto and the Iberian pyrites belt. In *Bulletin of the Peak District Mines Historical Society*, XI, 1990.
Willies, L. The industrial landscape of Rio Tinto, Huelva, Spain. In *IAR*, XII, 1989.

BARRIE TRINDER

river navigation   Rivers have been used for the conveyance of passengers and freight since antiquity. By the seventeenth century the navigation of many European rivers had been improved by the installation of FLASH LOCKS and in some cases POUND LOCKS, but the interests of navigation often conflicted with those of millers. Many English rivers, some of them quite narrow or steep, were improved by means authorized by legislation in the century between 1660 and 1760, stimulating an interest in the engineering problems relating to inland navigation which provided one of the foundations for the ninety years of CANAL construction which followed and which tended to overshadow river improvement in most parts of Europe. From the 1820s steam tugs were widely used on the larger rivers in Europe, North America and Australia, and the second half of the nineteenth century saw a general expansion of river navigation. Obstacles to navigation were removed, often by steam-driven 'snag-boats' in the USA on the bigger rivers, and new canal connections were constructed, capable of taking the river-size vessels. This tendency has continued in the twentieth century and rivers like the Rhine, the Danube, the Mississippi and the St Lawrence have remained vital commercial arteries.

BIBLIOGRAPHY
General
de Salis, 1904; Dyos and Aldcroft, 1969; Hadfield, 1986; Priestley, 1831; Willan, 1936.
Specific
Skempton, A. W. The engineers of the English river navigations, 1620–1760. In TNS, XXIX, 1953.

BARRIE TRINDER

rivet   A means of fastening together pieces of metal. The rivet consists of a solid bar with a head at one end: it is inserted, after heating, through two or more holes in the pieces to be fastened, and the end is beaten out. The technique is used in many kinds of metalworking and is of considerable antiquity; it was employed, for example, by medieval makers of armour, but was of particular importance in the fabrication of WROUGHT IRON boilers, bridges and ships, as the limitations of the PUDDLING FURNACE restricted the size of pieces that could be rolled or forged. Hydraulic riveting, which was particularly important in shipbuilding and bridge construction, was developed in 1865 by Ralph Hart Tweddel (1843–95) of Newcastle-upon-Tyne. He patented the process in 1866, and intro-

duced a portable riveting machine in 1871. From the 1940s welding and bolting, which offered greater degrees of control, replaced riveting in many applications.

BIBLIOGRAPHY
General
Begeman, 1952; Lineham, 1907.

BARRIE TRINDER

Rix, Michael M. (1913–81)   A lecturer at the University of Birmingham, who in 1955 was the first to use the term 'industrial archaeology' in print. Michael Rix was an anthropologist by training, who became acquainted with IRONBRIDGE in the 1950s, and from 1957 ran influential summer schools on industrial archaeology. He was involved with the foundation of Ironbridge Gorge Museum, the Association for Industrial Archaeology and the Historical Metallurgy Group (now Society), and was one of the *animateurs* who, in the 1950s and 60s, radically altered British perceptions of the industrial past.

BIBLIOGRAPHY
General
Rix, 1967.
Specific
Association for Industrial Archaeology Bulletin, IX(1) 1982.
Rix, M. M. Industrial archaeology. In *The Amateur Historian*, II, 1955.
Rix, M. M. A proposal to establish national parks of industrial archaeology. In *Journal of Industrial Archaeology*, I, 1964.

Rjukan, Telemark, Norway   Vemork power station, 70 km (40 mi.) NW of Kongsberg, near the head of a river which flows eastwards into Lake Tinnsjø, was commenced in 1907 and completed in 1911. With a 300 m (980 ft.) head of water, carried through a tunnel more than 4 km ($2\frac{1}{2}$ mi.) long, and eleven 720 m (2360 ft.) penstocks, it was one of the first power stations to utilize high falls, and was considered the largest in the world. The main building, 110 m × 22 m (361 ft. × 72 ft.), built in concrete with a façade of hewn granite, was designed by Olaf Nordhagen. The ten 14 500 hp twin Pelton turbines were supplied by J. M. Voith of Heidenheim and A/G Escher Wyss of Zurich. The original purpose of the station was to provide current for Birkeland-Eydes furnaces for making nitric oxide (NO) as a stage in the manufacture of calcium nitrate ($Ca(NO_3)_2$). In 1927 the furnaces were replaced by a Haber-Bosch process for which hydrogen was manufactured by electrolysis. A building housing the hydrogen plant was built alongside the power station, and the heavy-water plant which formed part of it was destroyed in a celebrated raid during World War II. Production of hydrogen stopped in 1970, and the power station was replaced by a new underground installation.

The hydrogen plant was demolished in 1977, giving an unimpeded prospect of the façade of the power station, which is now a museum administered by a trust on which are representatives of trades unions, local authorities, the workers' educational association and the national electricity board. Much of the machinery remains *in situ*. The

Figure 130   Riveted steelwork at the base of one of the arches of the Harbour Bridge, Sydney, built between 1923 and 1932
John Clark

displays in the main turbine hall are concerned with the theme of energy, while a section in an adjacent building features the past, present and future life of the industrial worker.

BIBLIOGRAPHY
General
Partington, 1950.

Specific
Lindtveit, T. Vemork Hydro-electric Power Station. In Nisser and Bedoire, 1978.

LOCATION
[M] Industriarbeidermuseet Vemork, p.b. 43, 3661 Rjukan.

BARRIE TRINDER

road The development of roads along which it was possible to travel long distances in wheeled vehicles at reasonable speeds was one of the most important preconditions of industrialization. In the Turkish Empire it was possible to go by carriage from Istanbul to Belgrade in the sixteenth century, and by the mid-seventeenth the road from Paris to Orléans, the nearest port on the Loire, was paved. In France and England the extent of well-surfaced roads increased markedly in the mid-eighteenth century, a critical stage in England coming with the extension of the TURNPIKE system between 1745 and 1760.

In 1700 most roads had unbonded surfaces, which readily absorbed water. The best roads by 1800 had cambered surfaces with cross drains, and neatly dressed with broken stones bigger than a hens' eggs, with uniform sized larger stones for foundations. In urban areas from early nineteenth century paved strips were for heavy vehicles in wide macadamized (see MCADAM) roads. In LANCASHIRE paved roads costing up to £2000 a mile were laid in the late eighteenth century, providing the only surface that would withstand the impact of the heavy use generated by mining and manufacturing activities. In the Netherlands in the nineteenth century, shortage of stone led to the use of bricks called 'klinker' for surfacing roads. Gaps were filled with sand. Many roads in Belgium were surfaced with 'pavé', a form of COBBLES. SLAG has frequently been used for roads in metalworking regions. Cobbles, setts and FLAGSTONES have been used to surface roads and pavements – 'sidewalks' in North America – in towns and cities.

In the USA Congress gained power to build post roads as early as 1787, and from 1916 used them to create a nationwide network of roads suitable for motor traffic, for which a uniform numbering system, denoted on standardized shields, was devised from 1925.

Road surfaces in England in the 1880s were still unbonded but pressure from middle-class cyclists led to improvements. From the 1840s TAR was used on a small scale for bonding surfaces in England, the USA and France, and crude oil in California from 1894. Tarring became widespread in England after 1900. Pneumatic tyres on motor vehicles drew out the dust which previously had acted as the binding medium. R. E. B. Crompton (1845–1940) of the National Physical Laboratory showed the advantage of mixing hot tar with road metal and laying the mixture while it is plastic. Expenditure on roads in England increased by 85 per cent in 1890–1902, reflecting the influence of the motorcar. In 1909 the Road Board was set up with substantial finance for road improvements, and what had been known as 'the white roads of England' became black with bitumen. The first mass concrete road in Britain, Blackwood Crescent, Edinburgh, was laid in 1873. The Brooklands race track of 1907 in Surrey, England, brought concrete to public attention, and the first reinforced concrete public road was laid in Chester in 1913. From the 1920s new roads designed to carry heavy motor traffic were designed. Many of the first multi-carriageway routes were in the USA, but in Britain bypasses round towns were being constructed in the 1920s, and the German autobahnen and Italian autostrada of the 1930s set altogether new standards.

In recent decades the importance of road traffic in fostering the growth of trade in the seventeenth century has been increasingly recognized, as has the scale of the industry in the decades before the advent of main-line railways in the 1830s. There were about four thousand mail and stage coaches in Britain in 1835, employing 35 000 and 150 000 horses.

For buildings and engineering structures associated with road transport, see BRIDGE; BUS DEPOT; BUS STATION; CARAVANSERAI; CAR BARN; CAUSEY; COACH STATION; GARAGE; INN; LIVERY STABLE; MILEPOST; MOTEL; MOTORCAR SHOWROOM; POST COACH; SERVICE STATION; STOOP; TOLLGATE; TRAM DEPOT; TRAM STOP; TUNNEL; TURNPIKE; WEIGHING MACHINE.

For road surfaces, see BITUMEN; COBBLES; CONCRETE; FLAGSTONE; MCADAM, J. L.; SETTS; TAR; TARMACADAM.

For vehicles that are not mechanically powered, see BICYCLE; CAR; CARAVAN; CARRIAGE; CART; DILIGENCE; HANSOM, JOSEPH; HORSE; MAIL COACH; OMNIBUS; PACKHORSE; POST COACH; STAGE COACH; TAXI; WAGGON.

For mechanically-powered vehicles, see AUTOMOBILE; CAR; MOTORCAR; MOTORCOACH; MOTORCYCLE; MOTOR LORRY; OMNIBUS; STEAM CARRIAGE; STEAM LORRY; STEAM-ROLLER; TAXI; TRACTION ENGINE; TRAMCAR; TRUCK.

BIBLIOGRAPHY
General
Aitken, 1907; Ballen, 1914; Bird, 1969; Boulnois, 1919; Copeland, 1968; Gregory, 1938; Holt, 1795; Jeffreys, 1949; Labatut and Lane, 1972; Law and Clark, 1901; McAdam, 1827; Murray, 1865; Webb, 1913; Whitehead, 1975.

BARRIE TRINDER

road traffic signal In Britain roadside warning signs were first erected in the 1880s by cycling clubs, with some SEMAPHORE traffic control signals appearing later. One gas traffic light was used in Westminster in 1868–9, but the first electric signals appeared in the USA in 1914.

See also MILEPOST; STOOP.

Roberts, Richard (1789–1864) A mechanical engineer who made substantial contributions to many branches of technology, Roberts was born at Carreghofa, Montgomeryshire; worked as a patternmaker for JOHN WILKINSON at Bradley; and settled in Manchester from c.1816, becoming a partner in Sharp, Roberts & Co. He developed a screw-cutting lathe, a planing machine (an example of which is preserved in the Science Museum, London), a self-acting SPINNING MULE, and an oscillating and rotating wet gasometer. In 1826 he moved for a time to MULHOUSE. Subsequently he devised a steam brake for railway locomotives, a system of standardized gauges for engineers, and a machine using JACQUARD principles for punching holes in bridge and boiler plates, originally intended for fabricating the TUBULAR BRIDGE at Conway. He received a medal for a turret clock at the Great Exhibition of 1851, but died in poverty.

Roe, Sir Edwin Alliott Verdon (1877–1958) One of the leading British pioneers of aircraft production, who was experimenting at Brooklands, Surrey, from 1907, and who in 1909 built a triplane which is now in the Science Museum (*see* LONDON). In 1910 he designed the first aeroplane with an enclosed cabin, and established the AVRO company in MANCHESTER, which became one of the principal British aircraft production concerns.

Roebling, John A. (1806–69) The most innovative of American civil engineers of the nineteenth century, who applied a ruthlessly scientific approach to his work. Roebling was born at Mulhausen, Prussia, and qualified as a civil engineer in Berlin in 1826. After migrating to Pennsylvania in 1831 he farmed until 1837 when he obtained work surveying the railway for Harrisburg to Pittsburgh, subsequently obtaining further civil engineering commissions. From 1848 he established a company at Trenton, N.J., initially to manufacture wire rope for INCLINED PLANES, and later wire and wire ropes of all kinds. He designed several notable suspension AQUEDUCTS with wooden troughs, among them the 49 m (162 ft.) Pittsburgh Aqueduct of 1845, on the Pennsylvania State Canal, abandoned in 1860, and the Delaware Aqueduct on the Delaware & Hudson Canal at Lackawaxen, PENNSYLVANIA, which still survives. In 1855 he designed a railway suspension bridge at Niagara, which was replaced in 1897–8, and between 1856 and 1867 a suspension bridge was constructed to his design at Cincinnati, OHIO; but his greatest achievement was the Brooklyn Bridge, NEW YORK, completed in 1883 by his son Washington Roebling (1837–1926), which set the pattern for all major twentieth-century SUSPENSION BRIDGES.

BIBLIOGRAPHY
General
Jackson, 1988; Plowden, 1974.

BARRIE TRINDER

Roebuck, John (1718–94) One of the leading chemists of the British Industrial Revolution, Roebuck studied at the universities of Edinburgh and Leyden. He made innovations in the refining of precious metals and in SULPHURIC ACID manufacture, for which purposes he set up a works at Prestonpans (*see* LOTHIAN) in 1749. He became a partner in the Carron Ironworks (*see* FALKIRK) in 1760, and subsequently a partner of JAMES WATT. Roebuck's bankruptcy led to Watt's moving to Birmingham as partner of Matthew Boulton (*see* BOULTON & WATT).

roller bearing *See* BEARING.

roller milling The first practical flourmill with steel rollers instead of stones was established by the Swiss Jacob Sulzberger in 1834, and the process was subsequently employed extensively in Hungary. Roller milling was established in the main milling centres in the USA, where it is often called the 'Hungarian Process', by 1875. In Britain it was popularized by a demonstration in the Agricultural Hall, Islington, in 1881, and by 1887 a leading mill engineer claimed that stone milling had effectively been replaced. The introduction of roller milling led to the construction of very large mill buildings both in Europe and North America.

A water-powered mill converted to roller milling is preserved at Rowsley (*see* CROMFORD), and an early roller-milling plant is displayed in the Ganz Foundry Museum, BUDAPEST.

BIBLIOGRAPHY
General
Giedion, 1948; Glaumer, 1939; Kuhlmann, 1929.

rolling mill A rolling mill consists of two or more sets of rolls set in housings, and rotated by water, steam or electric power, in which hot or cold metal, principally iron or steel, is elongated and formed into particular shapes according to the form of the rolls. Rounds, squares, angles, plates, sheets, H-sections (I-beams) and many other structural sections can be produced by rolling.

The simplest form is a 'two-high' mill, consisting of two rolls, which, if designed for rounds or squares, have series of matching grooves in descending order of size cut into them. After each 'pass' of the metal the rolls are screwed closer together, although some mills have tracks in precalculated series of diminishing area which make adjustment unnecessary. The metal is usually returned over the rolls in a 'dead pass', but some two-high mills are reversible, rolling in each direction. A 'three-high' mill, in which metal is rolled in the return pass enabling the production of long lengths of small section, was developed from the early nineteenth century. The guide mill, developed at much the same time, enables small sections to be made without 'fins' along the sides. The penultimate pass is of the same cross-sectional area as the final pass but of a slightly different shape. An oval might be rolled for a round section, or a diamond for a square. The piece is guided into the final pass through a metal box which ensures that it is correctly aligned for the pass.

A forge train was the mill used for the initial rolling of puddled blooms of wrought iron after they had been shingled. A cogging mill in a steelworks is used for the initial rolling of an ingot.

A universal mill, first used in Britain in 1878 although applied earlier on the continent, is one that rolls plates or sections with rolls operating on the sides of the piece as well as above and below it. The universal beam mill, producing 'H-beams' or 'I-beams' was invented by Henry Grey (1849–1913) in the USA in 1897, but first applied commercially at Differdingen, Germany. In the continuous or tandem mill, patented by Charles While of Pontypridd, Wales, in 1861, and improved by George Bedson of Manchester, England, is one in which the piece passes along a series of stands arranged in a line. Bedson arranged the stands so that the piece was alternately rolled horizontally and vertically. The first continuous wide strip mill, which rolls a slab of steel into a very long strip at great speed in a series of tandem stands, was

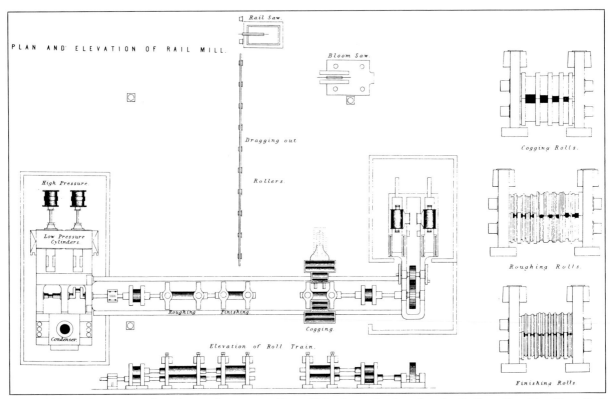

Figure 131 A characteristic late nineteenth-century rolling mill for the production of steel rails (from *Chemistry, Theoretical, Practical and Analytical, as applied to the Arts and Manufactures*, by 'Writers of Eminence', London: William Mackenzie, n.d., c.1870)
Collection of Dr Jeff Cox

developed in the USA by John B. Tytus in the 1920s. The first British mill of this kind began operation at Ebbw Vale, Wales, in 1938. Many such mills were built after World War II, and the steel they produce, the raw material for motor cars and domestic appliances, is now normally coiled after passing through the final pass of the mill.

The mechanical traverser for handling hot pieces on either side of a rolling mill stand was developed in the early 1860s by Sir John Alleyne (1820–1912) of Butterley, Derbyshire. Robert W. Hunt in the USA perfected a mechanical means of lifting pieces for the return pass through a three-high mill stand in 1884. By 1900 rolling mills were being powered by electric motors, although many steam-driven mills remained in operation after 1950.

See also figure 63.

BIBLIOGRAPHY
General
Gale, 1967, 1969, 1971; Lewis, 1976.

BARRIE TRINDER

Rolt, Lionel Thomas Caswall (1910–74) Rolt grew up in the Welsh Marches, and was apprenticed as an engineer at Kerr Stuart, STOKE-ON-TRENT. He worked for several companies in the 1930s, before deciding at his marriage in 1939 to live on a NARROW BOAT, the *Cressy*, embarking on a voyage from BANBURY which was cut short by the outbreak of World War II. Before going to the Talyllyn Railway, he worked as an industrial civil servant; he then worked as a writer. Rolt was responsible for three major achievements in industrial conservation. His first book, *Narrow Boat*, published in 1944, was the foundation of the movement to conserve Britain's narrow canal network that developed in the post-war period, and Rolt contributed substantially to the founding in 1946 of the Inland Waterways Association, although he was forced by internal differences to resign from it in 1950. In the early 1950s as manager of the TALYLLYN RAILWAY he demonstrated that railway preservation was practicable, showing that the line could be sustained by voluntary labour and by income from tourists. Finally, his biographies of the great engineers of the Industrial Revolution aroused interest in the period and fostered the growth of industrial archaeology. He was the first Chairman of the Association for Industrial Archaeology.

BIBLIOGRAPHY
General
Mackersey, 1985; Rogerson and Maxim, 1986; Rolt, 1969, 1970, 1971a.

BARRIE TRINDER

Romania

Roman cement A form of HYDRAULIC CEMENT, made before the introduction of PORTLAND CEMENT, and patented by J. Parker of Sheppey, England, in 1796. It is often used as STUCCO. Roman cement is made by calcining 'natural cement rocks', such as nodules found in southern England that contain both clay and calcium carbonate. Tournai, Belgium, is an important centre of production.

BIBLIOGRAPHY
General
Eckel, 1928; Morgan and Pratt, 1938.

Romanesque A style of architecture current in Europe from the tenth century to the twelfth century, Romanesque architecture is characterized by round arches, often ranged in ARCADES. The style was revived in the nineteenth century, but in Europe to only a limited extent for industrial buildings. It was a principal inspiration for the great American architect Henry Hobson Richardson (1838–86), who applied it to WAREHOUSES and RAILWAY STATIONS as well as to churches and libraries.

Romania Romania, in the north of the Balkan Peninsula, is a country of varied relief, possessing rich natural resources which have profoundly influenced its economic, political and social history. The Danube flows 1075 km (668 mi.) through Romania, and along much of its course the river forms the country's southern boundary with Yugoslavia and Bulgaria. The three Romanian provinces, Transylvania, Moldavia and Wallachia (Muntenia) emerged as independent principalities between the ninth

and the fourteenth centuries. The first attempt to establish a national state took place under the leadership of Prince Michael the Brave in the summer of 1600 but lasted for only three months. By 1650 most of modern Romania was within the Ottoman Empire, but by the mid-eighteenth century Transylvania had become part of the domain of the Austrian Habsburgs. In 1859 Moldavia and Wallachia formed a union known as 'The United Principalities', and in 1867 were united as Romania, although remaining under nominal Turkish suzerainty. A national state, independent of the Ottoman Empire, was established in 1877, and the Kingdom of Romania was proclaimed four years later; but it was not until after World War I and the demise of the Habsburg Empire that all the Romanian territories – Wallachia, Moldavia, Transylvania, Banat, Bucovina and Dobrogea – were united in one state. Various modifications to the frontiers took place in 1940, to the advantage of Hungary, Bulgaria and the USSR, but after World War II northern Transylvania was again returned to Romania. In 1947 Romania became a Popular Republic, and in 1965 the country was declared a Socialist Republic. Romania is divided into thirty-nine administrative districts, and in 1988 had a population of 23 million.

The Romanian people trace their ethnic origins from the Dacians, who have lived in the same territory since neolithic times. Between 106 and 275 AD the Dacian territory was occupied by the Romans, and the mixture of these two people, forming the Romanian nation, can be observed up to the present day. The Dacians practised agriculture, kept herds of cattle, and cultivated the vine. They exploited salt, gold, silver, iron and petroleum, as

635

well as working with wood and leather, and producing ceramics of remarkable quality. Their understanding of metallurgy led them to make a variety of bronze tools and weapons. They produced fabrics from flax and hemp. The Romans built paved roads, bridges and aqueducts in Dacia, and developed the area's mineral resources, particularly its gold. During the post-Roman period of the great migrations the people of the region continued to grow cereals, which in due course were ground in water mills; to breed cattle and horses; to extract minerals, particularly gold; and to smelt iron ore (*see* HUNEDOARA). Between the fourteenth and the eighteenth centuries agriculture was diversified by the introduction of maize, potatoes, rice, aniseed and chick peas, and the exploitation of minerals continued to develop. In 1775 the production of salt in Wallachia alone reached 31 250 tonnes. Gold and iron were extracted and worked, particularly in the HUNEDOARA area, in the West Carpathian (Apuseni) Mountains, and in northern Moldavia; while petroleum was extracted in PRAHOVA, Buzău, Hunedoara and Moldavia.

The traditional manufactures of Romania were associated with wood, iron, wool, hides, foodstuffs, salt and stone. Guilds of artisans were active in Transylvania as early as the twelfth century (*see* CLUJ-NAPOCA; SIBIU) but there is no evidence of them in Moldavia and Wallachia until the sixteenth century. The first evidence of large-scale units of production comes in the sixteenth century when armaments, paper, glass, river boats, textiles, iron and leather were all being manufactured on a considerable scale.

Through familiarity with working in wood there developed a tradition of millwrighting, leading to the construction of complex machinery powered by water, wind and animals. The use of horizontal mill wheels with 'spoons' or cups on the paddles was already widespread in the west of Romania in the fourteenth and fifteenth centuries. Such mills were used principally for grinding grain, but also for crushing metallic ores and sawing wood. Since they were constructed entirely of wood the earliest surviving examples are from the seventeenth and eighteenth centuries. The best-known comes from the commune of Cîineni in the Vîlcea district, and is exhibited in the Deutsches Museum in Munich, having been donated in 1905 by Gustav Thälman of Sibiu. This wheel is 1.2 m (47 in.) in diameter, and with a supply of 20 litres of water per second and a fall of 1.2 m (47 in.) produced between 0.5 and 1 hp. Usually the water ran onto such wheels from a height of two or three metres (4–6 ft.) along launders inclined at 45 degrees. The power of the water was used very efficiently due to the design of the paddles. The turbine invented by LESTER ALLEN PELTON in 1884 worked in the same way. Other examples of such mill wheels can be seen in the Museum of Popular Technology at SIBIU and the Technical Museum in BUCHAREST. A survey in 1957 revealed that there were 509 mills with horizontal wheels in the Banat district, 304 in Oltenia, 24 in Transylvania and Moldavia. There were 2787 mills with vertical wheels in Transylvania, 272 in Oltenia and Muntenia, 239 in Moldova, 74 in Banat and 14 in Dobrogea. At that time 35

floating mills remained working on the Rivers Mureş, Olt and Someş.

In 1887 153 factories were recognized in Romania, but in that year a law giving protection from foreign imports was introduced and the number increased to 769 by 1912, most of them concerned with cereals, and the processing of wood and petroleum. The production of petroleum, which stood at 134 185 tonnes in 1887, had increased thirteenfold by 1914 (*see* PRAHOVA). In Banat and Transylvania mining, the metallurgical industries and engineering continued to develop at REŞIŢA, Hunedoara, Arad, Satu Mare, Sibiu and Braşov. Agriculture continued to dominate the economy, but between 1924 and 1938 industrial production doubled. In 1930 the working population totalled 10 544 000, of whom 78 per cent were employed in agriculture and 10 per cent in industry.

Romania has some of the most extensive salt deposits of any country in the world, and traces of exploitation have been dated to 3500 BC. At first salt was extracted by evaporation on the surface rather than by underground workings. The Romans worked salt at Turda and Ocna Mureş in Transylvania, and in Maramureş in the north of Romania, extracting surface deposits and mining from parallelepipedal underground chambers, 20 m (66 ft.) high, 4–8 m (13–26 ft.) wide and 15–30 m (50–100 ft.) long. From the seventh century onwards chambers shaped like cones, bottles or bells were used in all three Romanian provinces. The bell system was used at Slănic Prahova. The shaft giving access to the salt deposits was 6–12 m (20–40 ft.) deep. From the base of the shaft a chamber was dug out, 4–6 m (13–20 ft.) high and 2–3 m (6–9 ft.) wide, and consolidated with wooden curbs. These curbs were protected with buffalo hides or clay in order to protect them from the decay caused by brine working its way into the chambers. Water was extracted from the pits by pumping or in pails. The salt was obtained by cutting blocks 2–5 m (6–15 ft.) long, 0.6–1.5 m (2–5 ft.) wide and 0.3–0.5 m (12–18 in.) high. The salt was brought to the surface with the aid of a machine called a 'crivac', which had a cylindrical drum 2–3 m (6–9 ft.) in diameter on a vertical axis, worked by horses through two beams placed in the form of a cross, and describing a circle 12 m (40 ft.) in diameter. A hemp rope that had been dipped in tallow was wound round the drum, and its two ends could be used to lower or raise loads in the shaft according to the direction in which the drum was rotated. At one end was hung a leather bag with which it was possible to lift out blocks of salt at a speed of 0.3–0.5 m (12–20 in.) per second. It was possible to lift out up to 80 tons a day from a depth of 100 m (30 ft.). Lighting in such mines was originally provided by earthenware lamps in which wicks burned in vegetable oil, and later by candles. Ventilation was improved by fires, which created currents of air. In the eighteenth century in Transylvania, and in the nineteenth century in the other Romanian provinces, salt mining was modernized in such places as Slănic Prahova, Sighet, Doftana and Tîrgu Ocna through the adoption of the method of mining using separate chambers which were pointed or trapezoidal in profile. The mechanical cutting of salt was introduced in 1889. There is a salt museum complex at Slănic Prahova. Old mines, with both bell-shaped and parallelepipedal chambers have been preserved at Turda.

Romania has a difficult terrain, and varied means of transport, by land, by river and by air, have been adopted to meet particular circumstances. The first timetabled passenger services, and the first to carry mail, were provided by 'diligences' from the beginning of the nineteenth century. The first effective transport in the cities was by horse omnibus; then, from 1872, by horse tramways; and from 1894 by electric tramways. The first railway, the 52 km (32 mi.) line between Oraviţa and Baziaş in Banat province, then ruled by the Habsburgs, was built in 1854–6. The first railway in the united provinces was that between Bucharest and Giurgiu on the Danube, opened in 1869. Between 1869 and 1888 the total route length of railway grew from 172 km to 2469 km (107 mi. to 1534 mi.), and by 1900 it totalled some 3100 km (1930 mi.).

The first evidence of water transport dates from 1183 when there are references to the carriage of salt on the Rivers Mureş and Olt. Boats for use on rivers and on the Black Sea were built in shipyards on the Danube at Giurgiu, Galaţi and BRĂILA. The first naval vessels in Moldavia were built in 1843, and the country's first steam warship for use on the river was launched at Giurgiu in 1861. River communication with Austria-Hungary and Germany was gradually improved as action was taken to ease the passage of ships through the Carpathian gorges (see IRON GATES).

Romanians have made vital contributions to the development of aeronautics. The first heavier-than-air machine to climb into the air through its own power was built by TRAIAN VUIA. AUREL VLAICU built some ingenious aircraft with which he accomplished remarkable feats in 1911–12, and as early as 1910 Henri Coandă (1886–1972) exhibited the first jet aircraft.

The first evidence of postal services in Moldavia dates from 1675–8, and in Wallachia from 1775 when a link with Constantinople was established. Post offices were opened in the principal towns of Wallachia and Moldavia between 1832 and 1858. The first electric telegraph was established in 1853, at first between Sibiu, Timişoara and Vienna, and then between Iaşi and Vienna through Bucovina. Romania joined the International Communications Union when it was established in 1865, the same year in which a law concerning postal and telegraph services was passed. The first telephone link between towns dates from 1890, and wireless telegraphy was introduced in 1905.

Printing first appeared in Wallachia in 1508 when several religious books were produced in the Slavonic language. In Transylvania the first printers were working at Sibiu in 1528 and at Braşov in 1535. After 1600, numerous printers were working in all the Romania provinces, producing books in Romanian, German, Greek, Arabic and Turkish.

The Commission for Historic Monuments in Romania was set up in 1860. It was transformed in 1874 into the Commission for Public Monuments, which had the task of listing, conserving and restoring monuments relating to the history of the Romanian people. In 1974 the law for the conservation of the national cultural heritage was adopted, under which offices were set up in the various districts with the tasks of listing, evaluating and ensuring the conservation and restoration of historic relics of all kinds. Some industrial monuments are situated as much as 15 km (9 mi.) from metalled roads, which poses particular problems of conservation. The National Museum in Bucharest, principally an art museum, and the Museum of Natural History in Iaşi both date from 1834, and various other museums were established during the nineteenth century, but the great period of expansion of the Romanian museum service was between 1955 and 1970 when 204 new museums were established. In 1985 there were 361 recognized museums in Romania, of which 6 were technical museums, 73 were historical museums, 43 were ethnographical museums and 70 were art museums. The four OPEN-AIR MUSEUMS at Bucharest, Banat, Cluj-Napoca and Sibiu, otherwise known as 'Museums of Popular Technology', are of particular importance for their collections illustrating Romanian technology.

See also BRAD; BRĂILA; BUCHAREST; CERNAVODĂ; CÎMPIA TURZII; CLUJ-NAPOCA; HUNEDOARA; IRON GATES; LEONIDA, DIMITRIE; PRAHOVA; REŞIŢA; ROŞIA MONTANĂ; SEBEŞ; SIBIU; VLĂHIŢA; VLAICU, AUREL; VUIA, TRAIAN.

BIBLIOGRAPHY
General
Klemm, 1979; Milward and Saul, 1977; Moroianu and Stefan, 1976; Otetea, 1985; Stamatiu, 1943.
Specific
Wollmann, V. Romania. In Georgeacopol-Winischhofer *et al.*, 1987.

HORIA GIURGIUMAN

Romantic Nationalist An approach to architecture in the late nineteenth century which paralleled movements in music and other arts. Architects sought inspiration from vernacular traditions, often applying the decorative features of modest farmhouses to large industrial and commercial buildings or housing developments. Particular manifestations include TUDOR in England, BARONIAL in Scotland, and 'Viking' in Denmark (see COPENHAGEN).

Rome (Roma), Latium, Italy A political and religious capital rather than an industrial centre. Printing, and such art-based manufactures as furniture, predominated at the turn of the century. By 1939 the largest employers were the Cisa rayon works and the armaments plant of S. A. Ernesto Breda.

There is a major concentration of historic industry on the banks of the River Tiber, 3 km (2 mi.) SW of the Colosseum. Most of the works were concerned with the provision of food and services and were established in the late nineteenth century to take advantage of rail and river transport. The old abattoir, 'Stabilimento di Mattazione', is the most impressive. It was built in 1888–90 at the

637

Figure 132 The concourse of Rome Terminus railway station, built from 1947 to the designs of Montuori & Calini
Michael Stratton

eastern end of the Testaccio bridge by the engineer Gioaccino Ersoch. A formal three-arched entrance is surmounted by a figure grappling with an enraged bull. To one side is the later refrigerated warehouse. Behind the archway are free-standing blocks in restrained classical form. The southern area consists of an enclosed stockyard with cast-iron canopies. The future of the site has been a drawn-out conservation issue.

Further south in Via del Commercio is the city's main gasworks, with two large gasholders, a group of warehouses, and gantries for off-loading coal brought up the Tiber. On the same road are the customs house, the ironmongery warehouse of C. Cantini, and the cheese warehouse of the Società Romana. A workhouse dating from 1735 fronts Piazza di Porta Portese, part of its long, four-storey range having been adapted as offices. Two blocks from the river, facing Piazza Mastai, is the palatial frontage of the state tobacco factory of 1863.

Rome's railway terminus is one of the most widely appreciated modernist buildings in Europe. The old station was demolished in 1937, and two lateral wings of monumental design were built by 1941. This scheme was supplanted by the winning entry of a competition held in 1947, submitted by Montuori & Calini and supported by a team of engineers. The entrance concourse is a thrillingly bright space, with sheer, glazed ends. It is covered by a sweeping concrete roof, supported by slender columns, and extending into a cantilevered canopy. Behind the entrance is a long six-storey block, with two bands of thin windows for each floor, giving a sense of greater size. The design was plagiarized in many European stations built in the 1950s and 60s.

LOCATIONS
[M] Museum of Historical Apparatus for the Reproduction of Sound, Via Michelangelo Caetani 32, Rome.
[M] Museum of Postal History and Telecommunications, Via Andreoli 11, Rome.
[M] Museum of Transportation, Stazione di Roma Termini, Rome.

MICHAEL STRATTON

Romilly-sur-Andelle, Eure, France   The copper works at Romilly, 18 km (11 mi.) SE of Rouen, was founded in 1782 for refining and rolling 'blister' copper imported from England or Sweden. One of the first works of its type in France, its principal product was sheet copper, used to sheath the hulls of vessels of the royal navy. It was owned by a powerful company, whose director, Michel Louis Lecamus de Limare, had visited England in 1781 to study contemporary copperworking technology.

The first buildings, known as the Perpignan works, were located on the River Andelle, and included a smelting plant with reverberatory furnaces, and a large, water-powered rolling mill. In 1788, 1816 and 1823 additional sites were established above the original works, as the company branched into brass production and zinc rolling. The rolling mill of the Perpignan works was entirely rebuilt in 1834, when it was equipped with a Poncelet water wheel, 5.5 m (18 ft.) in diameter. The organization of production in the building was, like that in contemporary French ironworks, modelled on English practice. When metal production ceased in 1896, the Perpignan works was adapted for glassmaking, which continued until 1956.

The archaeological study of the site has led to the precise dating of the surviving buildings, one of which was part of a fulling mill which flourished on the site before the copper works. The rolling-mill hall of 1834 is partially conserved.

Similar works were built in France at Avignon, in Vaucluse, in 1795 and at Imphy, in the Nièvre, in 1815, and in the region of Givet, in the Ardennes, there are significant remains of works built at Landchamps in 1787, Fromelennes in 1806 and Flohimont in 1817.

BIBLIOGRAPHY
General
Locci, 1988.
Specific
Belhoste, J.-F. and Peyre, P. L'Une des premières grandes usines hydrauliques: les fonderies de cuivre de Romilly-sur-Andelle (One of the first large water-powered factories: the copperworks of Romilly-sur-Andelle). In *Actes du IVᵉ colloque national sur le patrimoine industriel, Beauvais, Octobre 1982*. Écomusée du Beauvaisis, 1983.
Paris, A. Deux wallons dans la pointe de Givet ou les débuts de la métallurgie non-ferreuse (Two Walloons at Givet, or the beginnings of non-ferrous metallurgy). In *Revue Historique Ardennaise*, XXIII, 1988.
Paris, A. Une usine à cuivre dans la vallée de la Houille (Ardennes): Flohimont, 1817–1987 (A copperworks in the Houille valley in the Ardennes: Flohimont, 1817–1987). In *L'Archéologie industrielle en France*, XIX, 1989.

JEAN-FRANÇOIS BELHOSTE

Ronquières, Hainaut, Belgium   A village 28 km (17 mi.) S. of Brussels, on the Canal de Bruxelles à Charleroi. The canal was opened in 1832 for 70-tonne boats, and gradually enlarged to take 300-tonne vessels by 1914. Conversion to take 1350-tonne barges in the 1960s involved the construction of an electrically-driven inclined plane, begun in 1962: it is 1432 m (1566 yd.) long, with a 68 m (223 ft.) rise, and caissons 91 m × 12 m (300 ft. × 40 ft.). Facilities were provided for visitors from the start, and boat trips traverse a section of the canal, with locks and a tunnel, that was bypassed when the incline was constructed.

BIBLIOGRAPHY
General
Hadfield, 1986.
Specific
Gallez, A. *The 'sloping lock' at Ronquières*. Mons: Tourist Federation of Hainaut, 1971.

LOCATION
[I] Tourist Federation of the Province of Hainaut, 31 rue des Clercs, B-7000 Mons.

Ronse (Renaix), Oost Vlaanderen, Belgium   A small town 39 km (24 mi.) S. of Ghent, where the original railway station from Bruges, dating from 1837–8, was re-erected in the late nineteenth century. It has a three-storey, three-bay central block, linked by single-storey ranges with parapets along the roofs to pedimented pavilions at each end, with Corinthian pilasters. The Hotond windmill, a tower mill, is preserved to the north of the town.

BIBLIOGRAPHY
Specific
Industriele Archeologie in de Vlaamse Ardennen (Industrial archaeology in the Flemish Ardennes). Ghent: VVV, 1987.

LOCATION
[M] Museum voor Folklore en Plaatselijk (Folk-Life Museum and Local History), Priestersstraat 15, 9600 Ronse.

rope   Ropes were traditionally made from HEMP, the best for the purpose coming from regions that have long summers such as parts of Russia. From the mid-nineteenth century Manila 'hemp', from a plant of the banana family grown in the Philippines, was employed. Subsequently coir fibre from coconut husks and sisal from East Africa have been used.

Yarn for traditional hemp rope was produced from a bundle of heckled hemp wrapped around the waist of a roper who backed away from a revolving hook turned by an assistant. Strands of rope were made by passing the yarns through spiral grooves cut into bullet-shaped wooden blocks called tops, a process known as laying ropes. Thicker cables could be made by laying three strands or groups of strands. Until c.1800 most rope manufacturers used open-air ropewalks for making yarn and laying rope. Mechanized rope laying, using moving carriages with sets of horizontal wooden grooved cones and running on rails, was perfected by Captain Joseph Huddart (1741–1816) in 1799, and subsequently used in all large rope concerns, which thereafter tended to be very long buildings of three or four storeys. The best survivals are in naval dockyards, particularly the 350 m (1140 ft.) long building at Chatham, London, which retains its machinery of 1811 by HENRY MAUDSLAY. When ropes needed to be protected from water by TAR this was usually done by treatment of the yarn. Cotton ropes were employed in many of the ROPE DRIVE power-transmission systems, used in textile factories and elsewhere from the late nineteenth century.

Wire ropes were first used in the 1820s and became available commercially in Germany in the mid-1830s. Manufacturers of wire rope subsequently employed much of the technology used in CABLE manufacture. Wire ropes became essential components of AERIAL ROPEWAYS, CABLE-

CAR, ELEVATORS, SUSPENSION BRIDGES and of excavating and dredging equipment.

BIBLIOGRAPHY
General
Book of Trades, 1839; Hipkins, 1896; Lawrie, 1948; Tunis, 1965.
Specific
Coad, J. G. Chatham ropeyard. In *Post-Medieval Archaeology*, VII, 1973.
Dickinson, H. W. A condensed history of rope making. In *TNS*, XXIII, 1942–3.

BARRIE TRINDER

rope drive A means of transmitting power from the source to the point of use. Typically it was employed in Britain in a multi-storey factory through which ropes conveyed power from a steam engine, the ropes normally running round the flywheel in V-shaped grooves, through a space called a rope race, to pulleys driving LINE SHAFTING on the various floors. Usually there was a separate rope for each groove on the flywheel. An alternative system was to have a single continuous rope passing in turn around every groove. The rope drive was extensively used in LANCASHIRE cotton mills from the 1870s until steam power was superseded. It was also used for ROLLING MILLS and in brickworks.

BIBLIOGRAPHY
Specific
Watkins, G. Steam power: an illustrated guide. In *Industrial Archaeology*, IV, 1970.

Røros, Sør-Trøndelag, Norway A town of painted wooden farmsteads, built by miners on a plateau 600 m (2000 ft.) above sea level, which has been made desolate by the felling of trees to fuel copper smelters. Røros stands beneath cliffs of inert slag, by a waterfall on the Hitter river, 160 km (100 mi.) SE of Trondheim, and 10 km (6 mi.) from a lode of copper ore discovered in 1644. Smelting furnaces were built by the waterfall, and the plantation of the town dates from 1646. It was destroyed by the Swedish army in 1678, and subsequently rebuilt to its present plan. By 1700 its population had reached about 2000. Two main streets, Bergmannsgata and Kjerkgata, run down a slope parallel to the river, and are linked by narrow alleys making up a grid pattern. The church, designed by Peter Neumann in the Baroque style, was completed in 1784, replacing an earlier building. At the top of the hill is Malmplassen (Ore Square), where the smelthouses stood alongside the river. On the fringes of the town the pattern of building is less ordered, and streets like Sleggveien are lined with tiny, ramshackle wooden cabins. Ore was extracted from the many mines in the vicinity and taken to Røros for smelting, at first by horse and ox carts, and in the twentieth century by AERIAL ROPEWAYS. Most of the workers in Røros came from neighbouring rural parishes, and kept animals for haulage and for milking on the land around the town. Grain was obtained from a COMPANY STORE which functioned until the opening of the Rørosbanen (railway) in 1877 stimulated the growth of other shops. Røros was one of the principal sources of copper in Europe, and in 1840 the industry employed more than five hundred full-time workers, and took on another five hundred casual labourers each summer.

For much of the twentieth century the copper mines have been in decline, and they finally ceased work in 1977. The history of Røros in recent decades illustrates vividly how attitudes to conserving industrial monuments have changed. In 1910 Åspås House, one of the most distinguished buildings in Røros, was moved to the Trøndelag open-air museum in TRONDHEIM. The town's buildings were commended in 1922 as 'among the most unusual and interesting' in Norway. The following year eight were accorded protection by listing, but subsequently the five buildings making up the homestead of Aamund Prytz, made famous in a painting of 1903 by Harald Sohlberg, were demolished to make way for a filling station, and removed to the Norwegian Folk Museum in Oslo. In 1936 a site was acquired for an open-air museum in Røros, and the first building was re-erected there in 1946, but attitudes were changing. In 1939 two important conferences were held in Røros, and in a celebrated speech, Harry Fett, Director of the Central Office of Historical Monuments, called for the conservation of whole streetscapes, urging that with the obvious decline of mining, new uses should be found for the historic buildings of Røros. A new organization, 'Den gamle Bergstad' (The old mining town), was formed to promote conservation. Eighty buildings are now under legislative protection. In 1977 the state acquired the smelthouse and the adjacent properties, which are being restored by Røros Museum. In 1975 Røros was one of three pilot conservation schemes undertaken in Norway as part of European Architectural Heritage Year, and in 1982 the town was designated a UNESCO World Heritage Site. The Museum holds large collections of mining maps, and remarkably full records from the mining company. The Prytz houses, which had never been re-erected in Oslo, have been returned to Røros, where they stand as Harald Sohlberg saw them, giving rise to pressure to bring back the Åspås House from Trondheim, since its original site stands vacant. The object of conservation is now to show Røros in its total environment, which has raised such issues as whether new buildings should be permitted on the rough pastures on the edges of the town, and whether the encroachment of vegetation on the slag tips should be prevented.

Olavsgruva, 13 km (8 mi.) E., is a mine which supplied ore to the Røros smelters. It operated over many periods from the seventeenth century onwards, but was particularly important in the last decades of the industry, after new ores were discovered in 1935. Mining ceased there in 1972, but following an initiative by the trades unions the workings were opened to the public in 1979, a display at the entrance, which is particularly informative on working conditions, being completed two years later. The outstanding feature of the mine is the 'great hall', 50 m (160 ft.) below the surface. Many tools are displayed in authentic settings, and evidence of fire setting can be seen.

The Røros Museum is also conserving the office of a

Figure 133   The copper smelter alongside the Hitter river at Røros, Norway
Barrie Trinder

local newspaper (*see* NEWSPAPER PRINTING) which houses a press by Nebiolo Macchine, and LINOTYPE machines from Mergenthaler and Intertype of New York.

Several other sites of copper smelters worked by the Røros company are being conserved, among them the Eidet works at Ålen, 30 km (20 mi.) N., where a mid-nineteenth-century furnace and refining hearths have been restored; the Louise smelthouse at Solna in Alvdal, 65 km (40 mi.) SW, where there are dams, watercourses, and ruined buildings of an enterprise which operated from 1848 until 1879; and the Nåverdal smelter at Kvikne, 35 km (22 mi.) W., where a shaft-type furnace which worked for only a few years from 1867 is intact and has been restored.

BIBLIOGRAPHY
General
Dahle, 1894; Guldal, 1944; Tschudi-Madsen, 1977, 1983.
Specific
Fjell-Folk (Year books of Røros Museum), 1976–.
Odegaard, S. *Om Kjerka pa Røros* (Røros Church). Roros, 1984.

LOCATION
Rørosmuseet, 7460 Røros.

BARRIE TRINDER

Roşia Montană, Alba, Romania   A gold-mining district where ancient and modern methods have long co-existed.

An open-air museum includes Roman excavations, an eighteenth-century tower for the storage of gunpowder, two stamping mills, one with nine and one with twelve stamps, a 'Californian' type of stamping machine made by the English firm of Fraser & Chambers, and an electric winder of 1910 recovered from underground.

BIBLIOGRAPHY
General
Wollmann, V. Romania. In Georgeacopol-Winischhofer *et al.*, 1987.
Specific
Sintimbreanu, A. and Wollmann, V. Complexul muzeistic al exploatarii miniere Roşia Montană jud. Alba (The mining museum complex at Roşia Montană in the district of Alba). In *Revista muzeelor şi monumentelor* (Bucharest), 7, 1980.
Sintimbreanu, A. and Wollman, V. Noi valori in patrimoniul muzeistic al exploatarii miniere Roşia Montană (New values in the museum heritage of the mines of Roşia Montană). In *Revista muzeelor şi monumentelor* (Bucharest), 7, 1985.

rosin   *See* TURPENTINE.

Roskilde, Zealand, Denmark   At the end of the Roskilde Fjord, 30 km (20 mi.) W. of Copenhagen, lies the ancient city of Roskilde, in the Middle Ages the religious centre of Denmark. In 1962 five Viking ships were discovered at Skuldelev, 16 km (10 mi.) N., and are now displayed at the

Viking Ship Museum. Of special interest are two unique cargo vessels used by the Vikings for coastal trade and long-distance journeys. Among the industrial monuments of seventeenth- and eighteenth-century Roskilde are a brewhouse, a dyeworks and a sugar refinery. In the eighteenth century one of the city's nine water mills, Maglekilde, was adapted as a papermill, and in 1811 it was further extended and converted to cotton spinning, utilizing the first Danish steam engine outside the Copenhagen area.

The city entered a new era in 1847 when the first railway in Denmark was opened, linking Roskilde with Copenhagen. The original railway station survives, little altered, and is now a protected monument. The city has two fine examples of engineering workshops of the late nineteenth century. One is Maglekilde Maskinfabrik which has preserved buildings dating from 1867 onwards. The firm gained a wide reputation in 1878 when the workshop foreman, L. C. Nielsen, invented the continuous cream separator which revolutionized the dairy industry. The other is Roskilde Maskinfabrik, near the railway station, and built in a simple RUNDBOGENSTIL in 1908. The city is known for its distilleries, and the headquarters of Danish Distilleries, dating from 1881, is another example of Rundbogenstil.

The small coastal steamer *Skælskør* of 1915, which worked to the islands of Agersø and Omø, is preserved in Roskilde Fjord.

BIBLIOGRAPHY
General
Sestoft, 1979.
Specific
Romu 1987 (Yearbook of Roskilde Museum), Roskilde, 1988.

LOCATIONS
[M] Roskilde Museum (Local History Museum), Sct. Olsgade 18, 4000 Roskilde.
[M] Vikingeskibshallen (Viking Ship Museum), Strandengen, 4000 Roskilde.

OLE HYLDTOFT

Rostock, Mecklenburg, Germany   The history of shipbuilding within the bounds of the DDR, as defined in 1949, is illustrated by several preserved ships in the Baltic port of Rostock. Many years earlier, in 1903, the seagoing merchant vessel *Grete Cords*, of 1250 tonnes, was built in Rostock. Under the name of *Vorwärts* (Forward) she served as the DDR's first merchant ship, and is now a training ship, moored in the harbour. The first German submarine, built by Wilhelm Bauer, was overhauled in 1960 at the Neptune yard in Rostock, and has since been cared for by the Army Museum. The DDR commissioned the building in Rostock of a 10000 tonne freighter, the *Frieden*, in 1957, the fifth in a series of fifteen, constructed in sections, with four four-stroke 1800 hp diesel engines. The freighter has been lying up on the Warnow bank in Rostock since 1970. Her holds accommodate a museum of the history of shipbuilding on the Baltic coast, and in particular the history of shipbuilding in the DDR. The ship also has a sports hall and a youth hostel on board, and her engine rooms are preserved as part of the museum tour.

Next to the freighter stands the steam-powered *Langer Heinrich* (Tall Henry) pontoon crane, built in Gdansk (Danzig) in 1890. A steam tug built in 1908 in Hamburg, entirely of riveted construction, and a wooden fishing cutter built in the DDR in 1949 are also on exhibition. In the heyday of sail 378 vessels were registered at Rostock, the third largest German fleet; a slipway built c.1870, 30 m (100 ft.) long, for vessels of up to 100 tonnes, is a monument of that period.

BIBLIOGRAPHY
General
Schmidt and Theile, 1989; Wagenbreth and Wächtler, 1983.
Specific
Gesellschaft für Denkmalpflege im Kulturbund der DDR (Association for the Protection of Monuments within the Cultural Union of the DDR), and Ab Kultur im Rat der Stadt Rostock (Cultural Organization for the City of Rostock). In *Technische Denkmale in Rostock* (Technical monuments in Rostock). Rostock, 1986.

LOCATIONS
[M] Maritime Museum, August Bebel Strasse 1, 2500 Rostock.
[M] Museum of Cultural History, Steintor, 2500 Rostock.
[M] Museum of Shipbuilding, *Frieden*, 2520 Rostock-Schmerl.

AXEL FÖHL

Rotterdam, Zuid Holland, The Netherlands   Rotterdam, on the north bank of the Nieuwe Maas, was only a small port until the sixteenth century, when artificial harbours were constructed, following support given to William of Orange against the Spanish when the larger ports of Amsterdam and Antwerp were made inaccessible by the war. During the French occupation in the 1790s Rotterdam grew as a transshipment port for goods passing between England and Germany. In the 1830s growth was stimulated by the secession of Belgium (*see* THE NETHERLANDS), and Rotterdam came to handle nearly 40 per cent of Dutch East Indian trade.

The struggle against the silting-up of the links to the North Sea has been a constant factor in the history of Rotterdam. In 1821 plans were approved for the Voornse Kanaal, built in 1827–9, giving a direct connection to the sea at Hellevoetsluis, 35 km (21 mi.) SW, reducing the distance to the coast from 95 km (58 mi.) to 40 km (25 mi.). King William I financed the canal, which was opened in 1830, but its success was limited: the entrance silted up and the canal's dimensions were too small. Until the construction of the Nieuwe Waterweg in 1866–70 larger ships could reach Rotterdam only by devious routes of up to 115 km (70 mi.). The inlet of the Voornse Kanaal was dammed off north of Hellevoetsluis in 1950, but a 10 km (6 mi.) section was preserved. The plan of the civil engineer Pieter Caland to restore to the Nieuwe Maas its former outlet at Hoek van Holland was adopted by the government and the work, the construction of the Nieuwe Waterweg, carried out in 1866–70. After the opening problems arose and the original plan for scourage by tidal currents had to be abandoned because sand was deposited

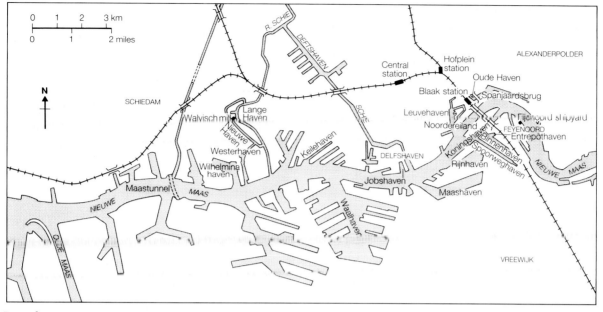

Rotterdam

in the entrance to the waterway. The engineer W. F. Leemans made many alterations in 1878–83, and used nineteen steam hopper dredgers (combinations of dredgers, tugboats and barges), some of which remained active until the 1950s. By 1896 vessels drawing up to 8.6 m (28 ft.) could reach Rotterdam, but the adaptation of the Nieuwe Waterweg has been a continuous process through the twentieth century.

Until 1850 Rotterdam was a commercial staple port where quick dispatch was not considered important. Companies were slow to adopt innovations like steamships, railways and bonded warehouses. Only 346 000 tonnes were handled in 1850. From 1879 Rotterdam developed into an international port. Remarkably in a time of liberalism, the city government stimulated the metamorphosis of the city by developing infrastructure, extending docks and quays, providing hydraulic, steam-powered and electric cranes, and erecting sheds for temporary warehousing. Gerrit Jan de Jongh, director of the harbour and municipal works from 1879 to 1910, played a prominent role in these developments, and is commemorated by a monument at Westzeedijk. By the 1980s up to 300 million tonnes of goods were being handled each year in modern installations at the end of the shortest route between the industrial heart of Europe and the rest of the world, situated at the combined mouth of the Rivers Rhine and Maas, with direct lock- and bridge-free access to the sea, and a sophisticated network of inland waterways, roads, railways and pipelines. Port activities have moved continually towards the North Sea since the 1890s, and now extend some 45 km (27 mi.) west of the city centre, and along the Nieuwe Waterweg, Nieuwe Maas, Lek, Noord and Merwede rivers. In the twentieth century petrochemicals have replaced ship-

building as the main manufacturing activity of the port area.

Massive damage was done to the centre by German bombing in 1940, and to parts of the port area during the German retreat in 1945. Rotterdam does not have a tradition of preserving its industrial buildings, but from the 1980s the city government began to demand that developers contribute towards the preservation or adaptive reuse of the cultural heritage.

During the second half of the nineteenth century the city, which had remained much the same size for two centuries, began to expand, as its industrial hinterland in Germany began to seek routes to the sea. After existing docks and quays were adapted, new canals and harbours were constructed with facilities for loading and unloading ships near to newly-erected factories. Many such developments took place outside the city walls and on the south bank of the Maas where several villages were absorbed from 1869 to enable the expansion of the port.

The Fijenoord shipyard started with royal support in a former isolation hospital in 1823, and remained in use until 1930; it was the only modern industry on the south bank until the 1870s when some impressive developments were completed. The 400 m (1300 ft.) railway bridges by Cail & Cie of Paris were built in 1874–7 as part of a project to make a north–south connection through the city on an iron viaduct. To save space the bridges, viaduct and the iron awnings of Blaak station are to be replaced in the 1990s by a tunnel. The railways to Amsterdam of 1847, and to Utrecht of 1855, were connected with those to Dordrecht and Antwerp to the south in 1877. South of the railway bridges the Koningshaven was constructed to re-establish trade on the river, establishing the artificial island, Noordereiland.

Several bridges were constructed or replaced to shorten waiting time at Koningshaven. A double bascule bridge of 1929 remains, as well as the 67 m (220 ft.) lifting railway bridge, built by the Gute Hoffnungshütte of Oberhausen in 1925–7, which is scheduled to remain in use until the tunnel is completed.

In this area, called Feyenoord, at the time when the alleged failure of the Nieuwe Waterweg was giving rise to pessimistic forecasts, the Rotterdam Trading Company began to establish modern facilities, which were taken over by the city when it became bankrupt in 1879. These comprised a revolutionary combination of hydraulic and steam power, railways, transshipment sheds, quays for deep-sea vessels, and a direct connection to the sea – the optimum conditions for quick dispatch and transit. The project won a gold medal at the Paris Exhibition of 1878. At the 1 ha (2.46 ac.) Entrepôthaven of 1879 a bonded warehouse was constructed in 1875–8, the Vijf Werelddelen (five continents): it is 198 m long, 37 m wide and 15 m high (650 ft. × 121 ft. × 49 ft.), with 192 cast-iron columns, and hydraulic cranes and winches which have been replaced. Figee electric cranes of 1908–30 remain in use. The complex is being adapted as artists' workshops. The impressive office building, the Poortgebouw of 1879, is now adapted as apartments; and an area around the inner harbour, the 6 ha (15 ac.) Binnenhaven, once the core of the company's activities, is being redeveloped, chiefly for housing. To the west the government and city authorities developed the Spoorweghaven (railway port) in 1873–9, which formed, with the complex of the Rotterdam Trading Company, the first industrial zone centred on the docks. From the landscape of the early twentieth century, 80 per cent of which was occupied by industry and transport facilities, there remain a Unilever margarine factory, which is still in use; the silos, brewhouse and fermenting cellars of the former Oranjeboom brewery, now used for storage; the Fijenoord shipyard, now an aluminium works; a creamery, still worked by the Nestlé company; the head office of a cement brickworks of 1898; and two small, quayless industrial harbours of 1900–1. Several buildings have been reused. The station of the Rotterdam Tramway Company, built in 1904, which until 1965 was the terminus of steam trams running to the Zuid Holland islands, is now a medical centre. The remaining buildings of a monumental nineteenth-century margarine factory, later the Hulstkamp distillery, are now used by a party centre and a museum. South-east of Feyenoord along the river bank are several slipways, and a special cross-slipway built for Rhine and inland craft, together with the engineering shops and foundries of two late-nineteenth-century shipyards, adapted as housing and business accommodation. The Burgerhout engines, once made here, are preserved at Medemblik (see NOORD-HOLLAND). The concrete Feyenoord football stadium, which has a capacity of 60 000, was built to relieve unemployment in 1936.

In accordance with G. J. De Jongh's maxims 'ships follow the dredger' and 'quays can wait for ships but ships cannot wait for quays', to the west of Feyenoord and on the north bank of the river the construction of docks and

Figure 134   A telephone cable junction house of 1911 on Noordsingel, Rotterdam, restored as an industrial monument in 1983–4
Siem Pama

quays continued, until by 1910 there were 210 ha (517 ac.) of wet docks, and 40 km (25 mi.) of quays of which 75 per cent were on the south bank. The equivalent totals in 1985 were 2200 ha (5410 ac.) and 38 km (23 mi.), excluding 43 km (27 mi.) of stone slopes. Because the nature of activities in the port was changing, from trade to transit, new types of installation were required. Instead of the canal-harbours large basins serving inland shipping were constructed, like the 30 ha (70 ac.) Rijnhaven of 1894, the 60 ha (150 ac.) Maashaven of 1905, and the 220 ha (541 ac.) Waalhaven, begun in 1906, delayed by World War I, and completed in 1930. Rotterdam was the most important European port for the import of petroleum by 1914, and three small specialist installations for handling oil were constructed in 1880–93. Six harbours on the north bank, which remain in use, were constructed in 1909–16, mainly for general cargo, and made necessary by competition from Antwerp. Concrete caissons were used in quay construction for the first time at Jobshaven in

1909, employing techniques developed by Dutch engineers in the Chilean port of Talcahuano in 1904.

At the Rijnhaven the power station of 1893 that provided power for the first electric crane in continental Europe still provides 600 V direct current for nearby installations. Other survivals include a monumental office block of 1901–7, once the headquarters of the Holland America Line, a five-storey tobacco warehouse of 1898, and the Santos coffee warehouse of 1903. At Maashaven large concrete grain silos built between 1910 and 1931 remain in use, with several modernized floating elevators. There was a violent strike when steam elevators were founded in 1907. As a result of an initiative by the city government in the 1870s, four iron floating dry docks, with steam-operated pumps, were ordered between 1883 and 1902, replacing a privately-owned wooden dry dock. Two remain in use, the 90 m × 27 m × 3 m (295 ft. × 89 ft. × 10 ft.) dock II by Kloos, Kinderdijk, of 1883 in the Brink shipyard in Waalhaven, and the 170 m × 36 m × 4 m (558 ft. × 118 ft. × 13 ft.) dock IV by Klönne, Dortmund, of 1902 in the Niehuis shipyard in Eemhaven, as well as a concrete floating dry dock of 1943 in the Brink shipyard, used during the Allied landings in Belgium.

The Rotterdam Drydock Company was established on a remote piece of land on the south bank in 1902 and was once an important shipbuilding and repair yard. It is now concerned with submarines, off-shore installations and turbines. Several machine shops and slipways of the early twentieth century remain, together with a GARDEN CITY style workers' quarter of 1913–18, with over four hundred dwellings and three churches, which has recently been renovated (see figure 50). The seaward movement of the oil industry transformed the agricultural landscape of the south bank. Pernis, once a quiet fishing port, was dominated from the late 1920s by oil installations, the first refinery, where some original structures remain, being constructed by Shell. A seemingly endless modern landscape of petrochemical installations, tank farms and wharves stretches along the south bank of the Nieuwe Waterweg and is still developing.

The few remains of the coffee and tobacco industries, which were important in the nineteenth century, include the restored De Lelie snuffmill, and its workshops of the 1840s which produced chewing-tobacco until the closure of the LIMBURG mines in the 1960s. The Van Nelle company, established in 1782, created a complex of coffee-roasting, tea-packing and tobacco plants in 1927–9 along the Schie, with tennis courts and football grounds for its two thousand workers. A monolithic building in concrete, glass and steel remains in use and is a protected monument. A steam-powered rice mill dating from 1857 is protected and may be adapted as student flats.

There are some interesting remains of the cotton industry, including a house of 1723 which was part of a printworks at Gravenweg. The creation in 1867 of the Alexanderpolder, 6 m (20 ft.) below sea level, brought an end to the use of surface water for the printing process. The Kralingen Cotton Company erected an enormous complex near Oostzeedijk in 1882 for producing imitation batik fabric. It closed in 1931 as a result of Japanese competition in the Dutch East Indies. Part of the oldest remaining building is now tenemented for business use. A fireproof concrete cotton warehouse on Keilehaven is now used for storage. The Van Klaveren varnish factory of 1923, with its 45 m (150 ft.) chimney, remains in use, with two boilers of the 1920s preserved in the varnish distillery.

A cholera epidemic in 1866 stimulated the provision of a new water-supply system, for the first time using surface water, filtered through sand, instead of underground water. The complex remained in use until 1977, when it was adapted to provide 2800 new homes, the watertower of 1871 being converted to offices. The filtration buildings of the 1930s were turned into apartments. Four original filter basins were kept in water, and the surrounding buildings used as artists' studios. A machine shop, a boiler house and other nineteenth-century buildings were adapted as workshops.

A new sewage system was created in the 1890s, also in part through the fear of cholera. At Westersingel is the monumental machine shop of a steam pumping station of 1891, which was electrified in 1923 and modified in 1985. The buildings of the steam pumping station at Admiraliteitskade are protected, and used for retailing.

There are few remains of the first gasworks of 1825. Two gasholders of 1897 remain at the Feyenoord municipal works and are now used as a youth centre. Two gasholder pits at the Kralingen gasworks of 1852–1926 now serve as gardens. A gasholder at the Keilehaven gasworks of 1913 has been adapted as a warehouse.

The Hofplein railway station remains the terminus of the electric railway to The Hague, built in 1905–8: the railway enters Rotterdam on a 1900 m (1700 yd.) concrete viaduct. A former railway carriage and tramcar factory on Kleiweg is now a tramway depot. Just one cast-iron feeder box by Penn & Bauduin of Dordrecht remains, in Mathenesserlaan, from the electrification of the tramway system in 1906, although two others remain as 'street furniture'.

The Maastunnel of 1937–42 was the first rectangular-section sunken tunnel in the world. The 17 m (58 ft.) escalators to the pedestrian and cyclists' tunnels retain their original equipment. There are two 60 m (200 ft.) high ventilation buildings, each with eight large exhausters and six ventilators supplied by Werkspoor, equipment for monitoring carbon monoxide, and a traffic control centre.

At picturesque Delfshaven, which was annexed to Rotterdam in 1886, are several former distillery buildings of 1850–80, now converted to new uses. The Piet Heyn cast-iron drawbridge was made in 1873 by the Enthoven foundry. The Dubbelde Palmboom Museum on the social history of Rotterdam occupies a warehouse of 1825 which was later a distillery and a furniture factory. It includes a working model of the BOULTON & WATT engine, the first steam engine in the Netherlands, installed in 1787 to pump a nearby polder. The museum was funded by the Batavian Society of Experimental Philosophy. The Zakkendragers Huisje Museum has tools from a pewter foundry of the seventeenth and eighteenth centuries.

The historic collection of the municipal telephone company, which operated between 1882 and 1950, is

Figure 135 The 'De Vijf Werelddelen' (five continents) bonded warehouse of 1875–8 in the Binnenhaven (inner harbour) at Rotterdam; the Figee electric crane dates from 1908 to 1930.
Siem Pama

displayed in the world's first Ericcson automatic telephone exchange (type AGF), built in 1923 on Korenaarstraat. The last telephone cable house built in the city in 1911 has been restored and remains *in situ* at Noordsingel.

The growth of Rotterdam's population has been impressive: 72 000 in 1830; 320 000 in 1900; 450 000 in 1915. The built-up area expanded to nine times its original size between 1850 and 1900, as workers were attracted by the prospects of jobs in the port. Large-scale speculation led to low-quality housing. One of the first social initiatives was the construction of rentable back-to-back houses for workers in Feyenoord, of which 1e and 2e Stampioend-

warsstraat of 1895 have been renovated. Garden-city style developments on the south bank include Vreewijk of 1916–38, now renovated, and Kossel and Stulemeyer of 1921–4, where the concrete houses are preserved. Other restoration projects have concerned housing of 1925–9 at Kiefhoek, of 1916 at Patrimoniumhof, and concrete dwellings of 1923 at Walravenbuurt. On the north bank remains a complex of galleried houses of 1917, where the galleries form veritable streets, one above the other, which were once accessible to the vehicles of bakers, milkmen and greengrocers.

The Rotterdam municipal archives include the records

of several shipyards and factories, and a collection of posters of 1890–1950 promoting companies. Technical drawings from the Fijenoord shipyard are shared with the Maritime Museum in AMSTERDAM.

The Maritime Museum at Leuvehaven, a harbour created in 1598, has a collection of twenty vessels, including *de Buffel*, an ironclad, steam-powered warship built by Robert Napier & Sons of Glasgow in 1867–8; a floating, steam-powered grain elevator of 1928 by Luther of Brunswick, used in Antwerp until 1980; three steam tugs of the 1920s; the peat boat *Annigje*; and the Frisian spritsail barge *Gruno*, which worked as a tramp on the Zuiderzee. Also on show are a cast-iron lighthouse of 1899, the 'Het Lage Licht' from Hoek van Holland; and several cranes, including a 2-tonne hydraulic crane of the 1890s from Antwerp by La Meuse of Liège.

The oldest harbour in Rotterdam, the Oude Haven of 1328, is now a mooring for privately owned vintage ships. A reconstructed slipway is surrounded by playful modern architecture, including the first Dutch skyscraper, the Witte Huis (white house) of 1898, and the restored hydraulic bridge, the Spanjaardsbrug, built by Fijenoord in 1885 to the design of G. J. de Jongh, which is powered from the drinking-water mains.

At Capelle aan den Yssel, 5 km (3 mi.) NE, remains the Beyerink steam pumping station of 1869, with two centrifugal pumps. It was electrified in 1927. A carpet factory with a watertower of 1926 survives at Moordrecht, 20 km (12 mi.) NE.

Schiedam, on the north bank of the Nieuwe Maas, west of Rotterdam, was important for gin manufacture in the eighteenth and nineteenth centuries. From *c*.1900 alcohol was made from sugarbeet instead of corn, the larger scale of production making small distilleries obsolete. There are four restored distillers' cornmills, of which the 'Walvisch' (Whale), 33 m (108 ft.) high, is one of the tallest in the world. Most of the distilleries and maltings around the harbours, Noordvest, Nieuwe Haven, Lange Haven and Westerhaven, have been adapted as apartments and warehouses. The corn exchange of 1792 remains, as does the Hollandia distillery and yeast factory of 1909. The Distillery Museum includes apparatus for distilling and cooper's tools. There is a private museum collection in Kuypers' distillery of 1911, where six stills remain in use. A grocer's shop of the 1920s on Lange Haven serves as a small museum of the CO-OPERATIVE MOVEMENT. Four floating dry docks of 1911–26 remain in use at the Wilton Fijenoord shipyard.

A 60 m (200 ft.) bridge of 1910 by Werkspoor remains from the former Westland steam tramway at Schipluiden, 7 km (4 mi.) NW of Schiedam, where the tramway station is now a museum. The Gaagweg pumping station was built in 1876 with a steam-powered scoop wheel, but now has electric equipment of 1919, including a belt-driven Pannevis centrifugal pump.

At Vlaardingen, 10 km (6 mi.) W. of Rotterdam, the herring fishery profited from the construction of the Nieuwe Waterweg. Herring warehouses and cooperies remain near the Oude Haven and the Wilhelminahaven of 1890–1905, and were connected to the Schiedam–Hoek van Holland railway built in 1891–3. The Fishery Museum presents a synopsis of all aspects of the Dutch North Sea fishery since the fourteenth century. Industrial development in the region started *c*.1900, with chemical factories on the Nieuwe Waterweg, the Lever Brothers' (*see* PORT SUNLIGHT) factory of 1901 on Wilhelminahaven, a magnesite and emery works of 1900, and a shipyard of the 1920s which remains partly in use. The office and laboratory buildings of the Hollandia Anglo Dutch milk and food company of 1897 are now a cultural centre.

The harbour at Maassluis, 15 km (9 mi.) W., is a base for tugs, and a small museum shows the development of towing services. A steam pumping station of 1882, 1 km ($\frac{1}{2}$ mi.) E., has a Ruston oil engine of 1930. Some 3 km (2 mi.) N. is a windmill of 1718, with a flight of 30 m (100 ft.), perhaps the largest in Europe, as well as a cast-iron top shaft of 1862 by the Enthoven foundry, a cast-iron watershaft of 1879 by the Prins van Oranje foundry, and a 6.5 m (21 ft.) scoop wheel. The pumping station is still used in emergencies. The adjacent steam pumping station dates from 1873, and now has an electrical installation of 1919.

Hoek van Holland, 30 km (19 mi.) W., is a part of Rotterdam that originated as the construction camp for the Nieuwe Waterweg, and developed as a PACKET BOAT station with the completion of the railway from Rotterdam in 1893. A cast-iron lighthouse of 1893 is a protected monument.

Hellevoetsluis, 35 km (22 mi.) SW on the former island of Voorne-Putten, was a naval base from the seventeenth century. The National Firefighting Museum occupies eighteenth-century dockyard buildings. In an attempt to create a base that could accommodate large warships that could not reach Rotterdam, a graving dock, one of the first of its kind (based on French examples at Brest), was constructed by Jan Blanken in 1802–6. It could be closed by a wooden 'bateau-porte', and was equipped with a Boulton & Watt engine, ordered via Hamburg as the Dutch republic was at war with England. The bateau-porte was replaced by a steel copy in the twentieth century, and the docks, now protected, remained in use until the 1950s. The Gesigt van 't Dok museum includes models of the docks made in 1805 and 1834.

The Rotterdam tramway company played an important role from 1898 in the development of the once isolated islands of Zuid Holland and Zeeland. Vehicles are being restored at the tramway harbour where trips are operated on a 2 km (1 mi.) section of the 1047 mm (3 ft. 5 in.) gauge line. On the Haringvlietdam, 7 km (4 mi.) SW, is an exhibition on the Delta Works project, which began in the 1950s. In the Delta harbour a 48 m × 27.4 m × 20.4 m (157 ft. × 90 ft. × 67 ft.) floating dry dock of 1883 by Kloos of Kinderdijk, once the first municipal dock in Rotterdam harbour, remains in use.

BIBLIOGRAPHY
General
Balk, 1985; Daalder *et al.*, 1985; DIEN database; Ringlever *et al.*, 1911; Rotterdamse Kunstichting, 1982; Van Dalen and Boon, 1983, 1986; Wattjes and ten Bosch, 1941; Ysselsteyn, 1908.
Specific
Bollerey, F. Von der 'Wasserfabrik' zum Wohngebiet: wohnem am

wasser umnutzung des geländes der Rotterdamer wasserwerke (From waterworks to living quarters: the transformation of the Rotterdam waterworks). In *Bauwelt* (Building World), XVII, 1984.

Ysselsteyn, H. A. van. De havenwerken van Rotterdam (The harbour works of Rotterdam). In *De Ingenieur*, XXI and XXII, 1887.

LOCATIONS

[M] Collectie Historische Telecommunicatie (Telecommunications Collection), Korenaarstraat, Rotterdam.

[M] De Dubbelde Palmboom (museum on living and working in Rotterdam), Voorhaven 12, Rotterdam.

[M] Distillery De Kuyper (private collection), Buitenhavenweg 98, Schiedam.

[M] Gemeente-archief (Municipal Archives), Robert Fruinstraat 52, Rotterdam.

[M] Haringvliet Expo (Exhibition of the History of the Delta Works), Haringvlietplein 3, Stellendam.

[M] Historical Museum of Rotterdam, Korte Hoogstraat 31, Rotterdam.

[S] Kralingse Karottenfabriek (Snuff mill), Plaszoom 356, Rotterdam.

[M] Maritiem Museum 'Prins Hendrik' (Maritime Museum 'Prince Hendrik'), Leeuwhaven 1, Rotterdam.

[M] Museumbranderij De Tweelingh (Distillery Museum), Noordvest 93, Schiedam.

[M] Museum Gesigt van 't Dok (Museum of dry docks), Oostzanddijk 20, Hellevoetsluis.

[M] Nationaal Brandweermuseum (National Firefighting Museum), Gallasplein 5, Hellevoetsluis.

[M] Nationaal Cooperatie Museum (Museum of co-operative Production and Stores), Lange Haven 84, Schiedam.

[M] Nationaal Gedestilleerd Museum (National Distillery Museum), Hoogstraat 112, Schiedam.

[M] Nationaal Sleepvaartmuseum (National Towing Service Museum), Hoogstraat 1, Maassluis.

[M] Rijdend Tram Museum (Tramway Museum), Tramhaven, Hellevoetsluis.

[M] Visserijmuseum (Fishery Museum), Westhavenkade 53, Vlaardingen.

[S] Zakkendragers Huisje (Porter's House), Voorstraat 13–15, Rotterdam.

JURRIE VAN DALEN

Roubaix, Nord, France   *See* LILLE.

roundhouse   A circular or polygonal building forming part of a LOCOMOTIVE DEPOT, with tracks radiating from a central turntable on which a locomotive can stand. One of the earliest, 50 m (160 ft.) in diameter, holding twenty-four locomotives on the various tracks, was built in the 1840s by the LNWR at Camden, LONDON. Roundhouses were used by many railway companies, both in Europe and America, for their larger depots.

Rovaniemi, Lapin lääni, Finland   In 1962 the Lapland Forestry Museum Association founded a museum at Rovaniemi in northern Finland, 94 km (58 mi.) N. of the port of Kemi on the Gulf of Bothnia. The need for a forestry museum was felt during the 1960s as traditional forestry was being radically changed through mechanization and the decreasing use of lakes for log movement. The Museum

aims to give a comprehensive picture of the traditions and working practices of Lappish forestry and log driving. It is situated close to the Arctic Circle on the shores of the beautiful Lake Salmijärvi. A lumberjacks' bunkhouse of the early twentieth century, the large so-called Luiro's cabin of 1939, an old shop, a stable, a tool shed, a smoke sauna and a log drivers' bunkhouse of 1904 have been relocated at the museum. Other exhibits include a steam tractor of 1889, a traction engine made in the USA which was used in remote locations during World War I.

LOCATION

[M,S] Lapin Metsämuseo (Lapland Forestry Museum), Metsämuseontie 7, SF-96400 Rovaniemi 40.

LAURI PUTKONEN

roving   A rove is a slive of a textile FIBRE, usually cotton or wool, which has been drawn out and slightly twisted. The term 'roving' is applied to what is usually the last process in the preparation stage of TEXTILE production, the one that immediately precedes spinning. The word 'roving' is also a synonym for 'rove', the product of the roving process.

royal carriage   Railway carriages for the use of royalty are preserved in many countries. Their constructional and mechanical details provide evidence of practice at particular periods, although their internal furnishings are scarcely typical. At YORK an LNWR vehicle incorporates two six-wheeled saloon bodies of 1869, while Queen Adelaide's coach exemplifies the better British carriages of the 1840s.

See also RUSSE.

BIBLIOGRAPHY
General
Kingston, 1985.

Røykenvik, Oppland, Norway   A small town 60 km (40 mi.) N. of Oslo. A distillery where spirits were made from potatoes, typical of many small Norwegian distilleries, is preserved with its complete equipment. The Jevnaker glassworks, 20 km (12 mi.) S., established in 1762 and still in production, admits visitors.

Rožňava, East Slovakia, Czechoslovakia   A mining town at the centre of an ironmaking region. A regional museum covers the history of iron-ore extraction in the area. There is an underground mining display, and an exhibition showing the local ore-mining sites, some of which can be visited; the blast furnace complex at Vlachovo, 15 km (9 mi.) NW, is in an advanced state of disrepair. It was built by the Andrassi family in 1843 and worked until 1907. The ore mines were directly behind the furnace and ore was brought in by inclined wagonway. The whole complex is built in a neo-Classical style.

At Nižná Slaná, 11 km (7 mi.) NW, a huge modern processing plant extracts ore from the 80 million tonnes of remaining reserves. A blast furnace which worked between 1867 and 1907 survives within the complex.

Figure 136 The blast-furnace complex dating from 1867 at Nižná Slaná, near Rožňava, Slovakia
Simon Derry

LOCATION
[M] Mining and Metalworking Museum, Rožňava.

Rožnov Pod Radhostem, North Moravia, Czechoslovakia   A former mountain spa which now includes a complex of open-air museums of the Wallachian region. The earliest was founded in 1914, and comprises several buildings from the old town conserved in the 1920s. Later additions include an upland village, and four mills: an eighteenth-century water-powered corn mill, a sawmill of 1789, a fulling mill of 1828, and a hand-powered nut-oil mill. The town is now dominated by a large chemical works.

BIBLIOGRAPHY
General
Zippelius, 1974.

LOCATION
[M] Wallachian Museum of Ethnography, Rožnov Pod Rahostem.

rubber   India rubber or caoutchouc is the dried, coagulated, milky juice of various tropical trees, used in unprocessed form for pencil erasers in eighteenth-century England. It was used for waterproofing by CHARLES MACINTOSH in the 1820s, but for most purposes rubber needs to be hardened or vulcanized so that it withstands extremes of temperature. Charles Goodyear (1800–60) took out a patent in the USA in 1841 for vulcanizing rubber with sulphur, thereby preventing it from becoming sticky at high temperatures and breaking at low temperatures.

In processing rubber the impurities are removed before the rubber is sliced in hot water, then dried and masticated, and heated and rolled, before being treated with sulphur to achieve vulcanization, for which long, cylindrical boilers and hydraulic presses are often employed. A substantial rubber industry grew up during the second half of the nineteenth century; its products, often of canvas impregnated with rubber, included hoses, driving belts, surfaces for rollers used in industrial processes, SHOES, ELASTIC webbing, and waterproof fabrics, as well as battery cases, syringes and other items made from hard rubber or ebonite. In the twentieth century the ranges of engineering applications has grown, particularly in motorcar manufacture, not just for TYRES but for many other purposes in hydraulic and suspension systems. Synthetic rubber (*see* PLASTICS) was being made in Germany before 1914, but was developed principally in that country in the 1930s and in the USA during World War II.

See also GUTTA-PERCHA.

BIBLIOGRAPHY
General
Clouth, 1903.

BARRIE TRINDER

ruby   A red variety of the mineral corundum, sapphire being a blue form. Corundum is found in rock and alluvial deposits, chiefly in Burma and Sri Lanka.

BIBLIOGRAPHY
General
McLintock, 1983; Webster, 1983.

Ruddington, Nottinghamshire, England   A village, 6 km (4 mi.) S. of Nottingham, in which a domestic knitting industry flourished. Thirty-eight stockingers' cottages were identified in a survey in 1967. In 1971 a charitable trust acquired a complex built as four tenanted homes in

1829, and converted it to a museum which illustrates the change from domestic production to a factory system. The bolts that secured the original frames to the floors are still *in situ* and twenty-three frames from elsewhere have been fixed to them. Twelve still operate. A frame smithing workshop has been established within the complex.

BIBLIOGRAPHY
Specific
Shrimpton, D. Ruddington framework knitters' cottages. In *IAR*, VIII(1) 1985.

LOCATION
[M] Ruddington Framework Knitters' Museum, Chapel Street, Ruddington, Nottinghamshire.

rug A length of loosely woven and often patterned woollen fabric, in the eighteenth century usually a bed covering or a means of keeping warm when travelling. In the nineteenth century the term came to be applied to floor coverings extending over areas less than a whole room.
See also CARPET.

Ruhrgebiet, North Rhine-Westphalia, Germany The largest concentration of industry in Europe, the Ruhr district, has an area of almost 5000 km² (1900 sq. mi.) in eleven towns and four districts, making up a third of the population of North Rhine-Westphalia. The Hellweg, the old east–west trade route, crosses the Rhine, the longest river in Germany running from north to south, at its confluence with the Ruhr. These are the two main transport routes of Central Europe. The Rhine links the Ruhr district to ROTTERDAM, the world's largest seaport. In the north and east of the Ruhrgebiet broad canals have assisted the bulk carriage of industrial goods since 1899. In the west lies the largest inland port in Europe, and to the east one of the largest marshalling yards. A dense road and railway network crisscrosses the entire district.

The Ruhrgebiet comprises part of the north-west European coal belt. With 3° inclination, the Upper Carboniferous strata stretch north from the outer heights of the Ruhr valley, reaching a depth of 1000 m (3300 ft.) at its northern edge by the River Lippe. The average depth of mining is 830 m (2700 ft.) and the average seam thickness 1.1 m (3 ft. 7 in.). Moving from the southern Ruhr valley after the Middle Ages, coal mining shifted north, east and west from *c.*1830, taking in the area between the Ruhr and the Lippe from Kamp-Lintfort on the left bank of the Rhine in the west, to Ahlen in Westphalia in the east. The number of mines, which used to be hundreds, was drastically reduced from 1968 with the founding of the Ruhrkohle company after a mining crisis which had been simmering since 1958. In 1976 there were thirty-five mines, mostly centralized collieries, producing 78 million tonnes of coal a year. The Ruhr was producing 30 per cent of the world's output of high-grade coking coal in 1975. The coal crisis of the 1960s, which was partly responsible for the founding of the nationalized Ruhrkohle, was followed by another slump from the late 1970s. High production costs made it impossible without subsidies for German coal to compete with imported coal. The drop in steel production and the

unwillingness of the electric power companies to continue guaranteeing sales of a large proportion of home-produced coal are leading to further pit closures, and it is possible that after the year 2000 there will not be a single mine left in production. Those concerned with industrial archaeology and the care of ancient monuments are therefore trying to preserve a number of pits and pithead buildings typical of various periods and regions. The structures around some adits, typical of the southern Ruhrgebiet and the earliest phases of mining, have already been preserved in the Mutten valley and in Blankenstein on the Ruhr.

There are hardly any pithead buildings remaining from the period before *c.*1850, although evidence of the use of steam engines remains, with an engine house of 1841 preserved at the former Carl Funke pit, and one of 1836 at the Mönkhofsbank pit in Essen. At the Vereinigte Wallfisch pit, Witten, the pithead building of 1850 and the ruins of the powerhouse have been preserved. The next and particularly striking phase of mining in the Ruhr, the period from *c.*1855 to *c.*1880 when deep mining was much on the increase, is rather better recorded by a series of the MALAKOFF TOWERS, typical of the period. The oldest of these massive structures, with walls up to 2.5 m (8 ft. 2 in.) thick, is the particularly fine Malakoff tower of the Carl pit of 1856–61 in Essen-Altenessen. It represents evidence of the period when banking capital from Cologne was being invested in mining in the Ruhr. An important specimen amongst the other twelve towers still preserved is that of Shaft 1 of the former double Malakoff tower at the Hannover pit, Bochum (*see* figure 81). The progressive Koepe winding system, dispensing with cable drum or sheave, was developed at this Krupp-owned mine. Finally, there are examples from the period when the architectural treatment of Malakoff towers was at its most opulent, in the two gigantic towers at the Hansa pit; Dortmund, of 1873, and the tower above Shaft 2 of the Prosper pit, Bottrop, of 1872. The first steel pit headstock in the Ruhrgebiet dates from 1869, and this form, in many variations with many dozens of examples, was typical of the next hundred years. One pithead gear of the Thyssen Colliery complex of 1907 in Duisburg-Hamborn is under a preservation order, as is the plate-girder structure of the headstock at the central shaft 12 of the Zollverein mine in Essen-Katernberg, which dates from 1932. Two sets of pithead gear from the turn of the century were moved from Gelsenkirchen and Herne for the museum at the Zollern 2–4 mine in Dortmund. The winding engine room of this pit, with the rest of the buildings above ground, form a complex which is one of the most important monuments of mining architecture of the period between 1890 and 1910. At this time coal was not only brought to the surface but also washed, sorted, coked and manufactured into by-products, so that there was a wide variety of buildings at the pithead. Complexes consisting of headstocks, engine rooms, pithead baths and wages offices, as well as workshops and other subsidiary buildings, have been preserved as industrial monuments in Duisburg (the Rheinpreussen 1–2 pit), in Moers (Shaft 4 of the Rheinpreussen pit), in Essen (the Bonifatius 1–2 pit), and in Gelsenkirchen (the Consolidation pit, Shaft 8). The spectrum of architectural styles used after 1870 for

Figure 137   The three blast furnaces of the Thyssen AG plant at Duisburg-Meiderich in the Ruhrgebiet which are to form a centrepiece for the Duisburg-Nord landscape park; the furnaces were built and rebuilt between the 1950s and the 1970s, but some of the buildings within the complex date from the early years of the twentieth century. In front of the furnaces are the massive concrete bunkers into which raw materials were fed by bottom-discharge railway wagons.
Barrie Trinder

industrial building thus extends from neo-Romanesque and Gothic revival to the JUGENDSTIL. The Bonifatius pit, in the Gothic style, and the Hansemann pit, Dortmund, in the brick Gothic style common east of the Elbe, are good examples. The Baroque Jacobi pit in Oberhausen has been destroyed.

The breakthrough of new architectural ideas shows in the generating hall of the Zollern 2–4 pit, completed in 1904, a building with a steel skeleton and Jugendstil decoration (*see* figure 119). No more pithead buildings were erected until the late 1920s and then mainly as extensions to existing mines. In 1928–32 the architects Schupp & Kremmer set a high standard with the functional design of the Zollverein 12 central shaft, and this remained the norm until *c*.1960. Plate-girder construction made the pithead gear itself part of the mine's architecture. The pithead frame, often designed as a 'hammerhead' tower, in which the winding machinery was in a tower high above the shaft (a space-saving device), also contributed to this effect. Shaft 3 of the Erin pit, Castrop-Rauxel, and Shaft 4 of the Osterfeld pit, Oberhausen, are good examples. Examples of headstocks built of plate girders or concrete after 1960, particularly in the Lippe area to the north of the Ruhrgebiet, are neither homogeneous nor impressive in form.

Little historic mining machinery has been preserved outside museums. There is some disused winding machinery of 1892 at the Hannover pit, Bochum, and of 1910 at the Consolidation 8 pit, Gelsenkirchen. The steam engine at the Lohberg pit, Dinslaken, of 1914, remains in use. Early electric-powered winding machinery dating from 1902 is preserved at the Zollern 2–4 pit, Dortmund, and some dating from 1910 at the Bonifatius mine, Essen.

Information on the history of mining can be found in the Deutsches Bergbaumuseum (German Mining Museum), Bochum, the biggest specialized mining museum in the world, founded in 1930 and financed by the mining industry. Access to the model mine, which is not an original working, is past the pithead gear brought to Bochum from Dortmund in 1973. A branch of the Westphalian Museum of Industry in the old Nachtigal pit in the Mutten valley near Witten has exhibits from the period around 1850–70, and nearby is a series of outdoor exhibits showing the history of mining, with replicas of horse-operated gins and adit mouths. There will be a similar display in the Deilbach valley, Essen. Both are in the extreme south of the Ruhrgebiet. The Bochum branch of the Westphalian Museum of Industry and the Duisburg-Homberg branch of the Rhenish Museum of Industry illustrate the Malakoff period. The mining boom of *c*.1900 is recorded by the main centre of the Westphalian Museum of Industry in Dortmund, at Zollern 2–4. The State Museum of Local History and Industry has a section on the history of mining, an interesting relic of the GESOLEI exhibition held in Düsseldorf in 1926 (the name being an abbreviation of 'Gesundheit, Soziales und Leibesübungen' – 'health, social and physical exercises'), a non-profitmaking and educational exhibition which attracted seven million visitors.

The second mainstay of the economy of the Ruhrgebiet was the concentration of iron and steel plants, which depended on the availability of fuel in the region and on its good transport facilities. From 1850 to 1912 the district itself was raising enough coal and iron ore to be self-sufficient. Large smelting centres grew up, especially in the towns of Duisburg, Oberhausen, Hattingen, Essen, Gelsenkirchen and Dortmund, where the firms of Thyssen,

Hoesch, Mannesmann, Krupp and Klöckner remain today. In 1974 21 million tonnes of steel were produced in the western Rhenish area, and 11 million tonnes in the eastern part, but the production curve, despite occasional leaps, is sinking steadily. In 1956 there were 156 shafts in the Ruhrgebiet, with 440 000 miners producing 124 million tonnes of coal. In 1980 there were only 180 000 men working at thirty pits, bringing up 68.7 million tonnes of coal. In the same period, steelmaking in the Ruhrgebiet rose from 16.4 million tonnes in 1955 to 25.3 million tonnes in 1979, still 20 per cent of the entire output of the EC, but in 1974 the figure had been over 30 million tonnes.

There is a better chance of finding monuments of early iron- and steelworking in the 'Mark region' and the Siegerland, east and south-east of the Ruhrgebiet, than in the Ruhr district itself. In 1938 the Luisenhütte smelting works, at Wocklum near Balve, 32 km (20 mi.) SE of Dortmund, which ceased operating in 1865, was made into a museum by the German Ironworkers' Association. The entire works has been preserved, and it contains the best example of a charcoal blast furnace in the Federal Republic. Not far off, in Menden, 12 km (8 mi.) SE of Dortmund, is a reconstructed charcoal blast furnace with original eighteenth-century ancillary buildings. Nothing has been preserved in the traditional ironworking district of the Siegerland, nor are there any good monuments of iron- and steelmaking between 1850 and 1900. Two twentieth-century blast-furnace complexes have been preserved: the Duisburg-Meiderich plant of Thyssen AG, and parts of the Henrichshütte plant in Hattingen. Now disused, the Duisburg plant has three blast furnaces, and the Hattingen plant one, along with blowing engine houses and ancillary buildings, all protected by conservation orders. Furnaces dating from the 1950s to the 1970s, with older component parts, are soon to be opened as showplaces of heavy industry – a development which, if one also takes into account the proposed preservation of two blast-furnace complexes in the SAARLAND, the other great steelmaking area of the Federal Republic, is a luxury no other industrial country in the world has yet allowed itself.

Such a vast industrial capacity could not have developed without the corresponding extension of transport facilities. Until 1860 the River Ruhr, with its port of Ruhrort on the Rhine, was the central axis of coal transport from the district. The Prussian administration recognized this from 1776 in its river engineering. Many locks preserved from the time of their rebuilding c.1844, at Mülheim, Essen, Hattingen and elsewhere still bear witness to that fact. Then the railways displaced shipping as the main carriers of bulk freight. However, that did not prevent the harbour of Ruhrort, and later on the neighbouring town of Duisburg, linked with it in 1905, from growing into the biggest inland port in the world, with private harbours and shipyards on both sides of the Rhine. The semicircular remains of the shipyard basin of 1820 at Duisburg-Ruhrort have been preserved. This was also the site of the shipping business of the coal and steel industrialist Franz Haniel. In 1842 another harbour basin was laid out around the elliptical ring of 1820. The harbour was enlarged again in

1860–8 and in 1872–90, and the River Ruhr was diverted south. In 1869 1.3 million tonnes of coal were shipped from the port. In 1890 the railway brought 2.6 million tonnes of coal to it. From this time Ruhrort became the transit station for imported ore from Spain, Italy and Canada. Three new harbour basins, A, B and C, were built in 1903–8, exclusively for coal transport, and in 1913 the quantity they handled had reached 18.7 million tonnes.

The port of Duisburg, independent until 1905, had as much as 34.7 ha (14 ac.) of enclosed water in 1893. In 1912, when the port authorities of Duisburg and Ruhrort were merged, there were 189 ha (76.5 ac.) of enclosed water, 477 ha (193 ac.) of land, quays measuring 43 km (26 mi.) in length, and 311 km (189 mi.) of railway network. Many mills in the inner port of Duisburg, and a lifting bridge of 1950 of great architectural merit at the Schwanentor, are monuments of this development. The Ruhrort part of the port, by the shipyard basin, preserved two original buildings from the old Haniel shipyard, dating from 1860 and 1871. Many masonry bases show the sites of former coal tipplers working on various systems. There was never a central hydraulic network, all the tipplers being individually operated.

On the left bank of the Rhine, opposite Ruhrort, one of two crenellated brick towers of 1852 still stands. With its partner on the opposite bank, now gone, it accommodated elevator machinery made by W. G. ARMSTRONG of Newcastle-upon-Tyne, for a ferry taking railway wagons loaded with coal to the power-hungry textile-manufacturing region on the left bank of the Lower Rhine.

There are two museums in Duisburg-Ruhrort providing information about the port, the German Inland Navigation Museum and the Haniel Museum, the latter a private museum set up by the Haniel company in its historic eighteenth-century warehouse.

A group of fine monuments relating to inland navigation is preserved on the opposite, eastern, side of the Ruhrgebiet, where a canal network was constructed from the late nineteenth century to take coal out of the region to the east and north-east and to bring in other bulk goods. In all four large constructions for raising boats are concentrated at Henrichenburg near Waltrop, 16 km (10 mi.) NW of Dortmund, where the Dortmund branch canal joins the Rhine–Herne Canal. Traffic then goes north through the Dortmund–Ems Canal to reach the North Sea at Emden. At Rheine the Mittelland Canal branches east; since 1915 it has taken shipping to Hanover and Wolfsburg, and since 1939 to Berlin. The most impressive feature at Henrichenburg is the boat lift of 1899, with a vertical rise of 14 m (46 ft.); a single caisson, 68 m × 8.6 m (186 ft. × 28 ft.), kept in equilibrium by five floats in deep wells (see figure 16). Since 1979 it has been part of the Westphalian Industrial Museum. A few metres away is a lift operating on the same principles, built in 1962 and still in use. In between is a lock of 1917 with ten reservoir basins, also of architectural interest. Further north a new lock is being built, capable of taking the standard 1350-tonne Europa BARGE. This is a complex of canal buildings unique in Germany, comparable only with the Belgian complex at La Louvière and Ronquières (see BOAT LIFT; INCLINED PLANE).

Another major feat of civil engineering was the solution of the fresh-water supply and sewage-disposal problems in the Ruhrgebiet, with the initial decision to use the River Emscher as the main waste-water accumulator, and to build dams to provide drinking water for the region. The structure of the circular waste-water pumping station on the Emscher, built by Alfred Fischer in 1913, is a monument to the great achievements of the water companies of the Ruhrgebiet since 1900. Fourteen dams along the upper course of the Ruhr and fifty-one water-works with 117 treatment works provide for the private and industrial water consumers of the region.

The workers' colonies of the mining and ironworking plants form one of the unique features of the Ruhrgebiet. Specimens have been preserved showing their development from the bleak barrack-like dwellings of the Gutehoff-nungshütte in Oberhausen-Eisenheim, built in 1844, to the early miners' dwellings of 1867 in Essen-Altenessen; and the post-1900 complexes showing the influence of Ebenezer Howard's GARDEN CITY movement, such as the Hüttenheim settlement in Duisburg, or the Gottfried-Wilhelm miners' settlement in Essen. Around 1920 those towns and communities that were trying to overcome the housing problems of industrial workers often had architecturally progressive ideas, as witnessed by the Vittinghoff settlement in Gelsenkirchen, and the Dickelsbach settlement in Duisburg-Wanheimerort. These complexes experimented with centralized facilities for laundry, heating and the like.

The coal and steel firm of Krupp of Essen occupies a special position in the Ruhrgebiet, showing both a sense of architectural quality and a paternalist initiative on the part of the employers. The Krupp settlements for the old and disabled, Altenhof I and II, which are partly preserved, and in particular the famous Margarethenhöhe, founded by Alfred Krupp's daughter-in-law Margarethe in 1906, are remarkable evidence of comfortable and responsibly-planned workers' dwellings. It is obvious that all these dwellings were of better quality than those not provided by entrepreneurs, and also that linking work to the offer of a home was an effective means of imposing discipline.

The private residences of employers are also indicative of the attitudes of the coal and steel entrepreneurs of the Ruhrgebiet. The Villa Hügel in Essen-Bredeney, owned by Alfred Krupp (who refused to accept a noble title), is now a museum. August Thyssen's Landsberg Castle at Essen Kettwig can be viewed from the outside.

The Ruhrland Museum of the city of Essen displays the industrial and social development of the region. The open-air museum at Hagen, established on a 38 ha (94 ac.) site in 1960, illustrates the pre-Industrial Revolution manufactures of north-west Germany rather than the industrialized conurbations of the nineteenth century, but includes some important technological exhibits nevertheless. These include a paper mill, a brewery, a battery mill for working copper, a brassworks, a wire mill, and a zinc rolling mill. Since the early 1970s the emphasis in the conservation of industrial buildings has been on the retention of monuments *in situ*. The Westphalian Industrial Museum and the Rhineland Industrial Museum, in the east and west of the region respectively, are both responsible for buildings and other structures retained and interpreted in their original locations.

BIBLIOGRAPHY
General
Abelshauser, 1984; Achilles, 1985; Banfield, 1846; Becher *et al.*, 1977; Biecker and Buschmann, 1986; Bollerey and Hartmann, 1978; Buddensieg, 1984; Busch *et al.*, 1980; Föhl, 1976; Gebhardt, 1957; Grunsky, 1975; Günter, 1970, 1980; Henderson, 1975; Hermann and Hermann, 1981; Hinz, 1977; Huske, 1987; Kastorff-Viehmann, 1981; Klapheck, 1928; Kösters, 1981; Landeskonservator Rheinland, 1972; Socha, 1985; Tew, 1984; Wiel, 1970; Wüstenfeld, 1978.

Specific
Buschmann, W. *Zeche Zollverein in Essen* (The Zollverein mine in Essen). Cologne: Rheinische Kunststätten, 1986.

Die Abstiegsbauwerke Henrichenburg (The boat lifts at Henrichenburg), Wasser- und Schiffahrtsdirektion West (Western Water and Shipping Authority), n.d.

Günter, R. Zu einer Geschichte der technischen Architektur im Rheinland: Textil – Eisen – Kohle (Towards an architectural history of technical monuments in the Rhineland – textiles, iron and coal). In *Beiträge zur rheinischen Kunstgeschichte und Denkmalpflege*, XVI. Düsseldorf, 1972.

Landschaftsverband Rheinland, Rheinisches Industriemuseum (The Rhineland Museum of Industry), Cologne: Rheinland-Verlag GmbH, 1984.

Metternich, W. G. Die Pflege technischer Kulturdenkmale (The protection of technical monuments). In *Jahrbuch der Rheinischen Denkmalpflege* (Yearbook of Rhenish Monuments Protection), VIII. Düsseldorf, 1936.

Müller, R. Malakow-Türme auf den Schachtanlagen des Ruhrgebietes. Ein Überblick über ihre Entwicklung und den Stand ihrer Erhaltung (Malakoff towers, the headstocks of the Ruhrgebiet: an overview of their development and of the state of their preservation). In *Burgen und Schlösser* (Castles and palaces), I. Koblenz, 1962.

Schumacher, M. Zweckbau und Industrieschloss. Fabrikbauten der rheinisch-westfälischen Textilindustrie vor der Gründungzeit (Functional buildings and industrial castles: factory buildings of pre-industrial textile manufactures in the Rhineland and Westphalia). In *Tradition: Zeitschrift für Firmengeschichte und Unternehmerbiographie* (Tradition: papers in business history and biography), XV. Stuttgart, 1970.

Sonnenschein, F. H. and Kleinert, C. *1000 Jahre Technik- und Handwerksgeschichte* (A history of 1000 years of handicrafts and technology). Hagen: Linnepe Verlagsgesellschaft, 1984.

Tatort. Das Rheinische Industriemuseum im Aufbau (The places concerned: the building up of the Rhenish industrial museum). Cologne: Rheinisches Industriemuseum, n.d.

Wildemann, T. Die Erhaltung technischer Kulturdenkmäler unter besonderer Berücksichtigung der Verhältnisse in den Rheinlanden (The conservation of technical monuments, taking into consideration in particular the conditions in the Rhineland). *Zeitschrift für Denkmalpflege*, III. Düsseldorf, 1928–9.

Wildemann, T. *Technische Kulturdenkmäler in den Rheinlanden und ihre Erhaltung* (Technical monuments in the Rhineland and their preservation). Düsseldorf. Rheinischer Verein für Denkmalpflege, 1931.

LOCATIONS
[M] Bochum-Dahlhausen Eisenbahnmuseum (Bochum-Dahlhausen Railway Museum), Dr C. Otto Strasse 191, 4630 Bochum-Dahlhausen.
[M] Deutsches Bergbau-Museum, Am Bergbaumuseum 28, 4630 Bochum.

[M] Haniel Museum, Hanielplatz 3, 4100 Duisburg-Ruhrort.

[M] Historical Museum, Ritterhausstrasse 34, 4600 Dortmund.

[M] Municipal Museum, Leineweberstrasse 1, 4330 Mülheim.

[M] Museum Eisenheim, Berliner Strasse 10–12, 4200 Oberhausen-Eisenheim.

[M] Museum of Inland Navigation, Friedrich Wilhelm Strasse 64, 4100 Duisburg.

[M] Regional Museum, Altes Rathaus, Untermarkt 2, 4320 Hattingen.

[M] Regional Museum, Im Stadtgarten 20, 4250 Bottrop.

[M] Rheinisches Industriemuseum (Rhineland Industrial Museum), Hansastrasse 18, 4200 Oberhausen.

[M] Ruhr Regional Museum, Bismarckstrasse 62, 4300 Essen.

[M] Villa Hügel, 4300 Essen.

[M] Westfälisches Freilichtmuseum Technischer Kulturdenkmäler (Westphalian Open-Air Museum of Technical Monuments), Mäckingerbach, 5800 Hagen 1 – Selbecke.

[M] Westfälisches Industriemuseum (Westphalian Industrial Museum), Zeche Zollern, Grubenweg 5, 4600 Dortmund 72.

AXEL FÖHL

rum A spirit with a high alcohol content, never less than 70 per cent by weight, made in the West Indies, the southern USA and elsewhere, from molasses and other waste products of cane-sugar cultivation, using pot stills or continuous processes (*see* DISTILLING).

BIBLIOGRAPHY
General
Rogers and Aubert, 1915.

Rundbogenstil A German term meaning 'round arch style', which is applied to a style of historicist architecture, deriving its inspiration from early Renaissance work in northern Italy. It was widely used for industrial buildings between 1850 and 1914, in Germany, Scandinavia and wherever architects who had trained in Germany were employed.

Russe (Ruse, Rustchuk), Russe, Bulgaria A major port of the Danube and the administrative centre for the northern part of Bulgaria. The first railway in Bulgaria was constructed in 1866 from Russe to Varna on the Black Sea, a distance of 221 km (137 mi.). From the first this line had greater strategic importance, and it was only the second line to be built in the Ottoman Empire. With the construction in 1954 of the Friendship Bridge, which carries both road and railway over the Danube to Romania, an impressive new railway station was built at a higher level than the original building, the latter being converted into a National Museum of Transport, administered by the Ministry of Transport. The present form of the station buildings dates from an extension of *c*.1879. Several steam locomotives are displayed in sidings, the oldest being No. 148, an 0-6-0 built in Newcastle-upon-Tyne in 1866.

Most of the other locomotives are of German origin. There is a collection of carriages from the years 1888–1903, as well as a wagon used for cereal transport. The official railway carriage of the Sultan Abdul Aziz is perhaps the museum's most distinctive exhibit. It is oriental in appearance, and has accommodation for the Sultan at one end and a saloon for the harem at the other, with an open galleried space in between. The carriage built for King Ferdinand of Bulgaria includes timepieces showing Central European Time as well as local time. Another royal carriage is that constructed in Wrocław in 1911 for his son, later King Boris. The carriage used by the Russian Marshal Tolbuhin as his mobile headquarters during the Red Army's Bulgarian campaign of 1944 is also exhibited: it dates from 1902. The station's former waiting rooms and ticket halls, as well as the locomotive and rolling-stock repair shops built by Messrs Gladstone in 1866, are used for exhibitions of photographs and models. The museum also gives attention to the history of the Danube navigation, with models of such vessels as the Austrian steamship *Radetsky*, which is associated with the 1876 uprising, and of the *Dimitri Bagoyff*, a passenger vessel built in 1941 which plied between Russe and Vienna.

LOCATION
[M] Museum of Transport, ul Bratya Obretenovi 13, Russe.

TREFOR M. OWEN

Rüsselsheim, Hesse, Germany Adam Opel (b.1837) began making sewing machines in Rüsselsheim, a town 14 km (9 mi.) W. of Mainz, in 1862. From 1866 to 1937 his concern also produced bicycles, and he began to manufacture motorcars in 1898. The cars were his greatest success, and by 1914 he was regarded as the largest motor manufacturer in Germany. The General Motors Corporation of the USA took a majority interest in Adam Opel AG in 1929, and today the Rüsselsheim works is the largest European plant owned by GM. Between 1916 and 1930 the long southern frontage of the plant was built in several phases, and more and more buildings were erected in the same style, culminating in 1930 with the striking 52 m (171 ft.) high Opel Tower. The façade and tower have been preserved complete. The town of Rüsselsheim has established a museum in the former fortress, which has a particularly good section on industrial history, and won a Council of Europe prize in 1980.

LOCATION
[M] Municipal Museum, Hauptmann Scheuermann Weg 4, 6090 Rüsselsheim.

Russia *See* UNION OF SOVIET SOCIALIST REPUBLICS.

S

Saarland, Germany   The Saarland was the smallest and youngest state in the German Federal Republic, has about a million inhabitants and adjoins Lorraine, in France, and Luxembourg.

The Saarland's development into a major mining, ironworking and glassmaking region began in the nineteenth century with the increasing use of coal, as well as through the improvement of the transport system with the growth of the railway system after 1850 and the partial canalization of the River Saar after 1871 to link it with the Rhine–Marne Canal.

Until 1794 most of the Saar region was part of the county of Nassau-Saarbrücken. Industrial development was first encouraged by its ruler, Prince Wilhelm Heinrich (r.1741–68). Specialists in ironworking and other manufactures were recruited abroad, and in 1754 coal mines were brought under government control so that exploitation could be systematically developed.

When the armies of revolutionary France invaded in 1793 the region became and remained a bone of contention between German and French economic interests. The customs frontiers were repeatedly shifted, so that the economic development of the area was frequently disrupted, particularly after the two World Wars. Economically, the area was integrated with France during the periods 1798–1815, 1919–39 and 1945–57, the state-owned coal mines becoming French property on each occasion.

In 1957 the Saarland was reunited with Germany as a state within the Federal Republic. Since the early 1980s there has been considerable reconstruction of the area's coal and iron industries.

See also FISCHBACH-CAMPHAUSEN; METTLACH; VÖLKLINGEN.

BIBLIOGRAPHY
Specific
Bünte, H. *300 Years of Dillinger Steelworks: an historical review.* Dillinger: Dillinger Hüttenwerke, 1989.

LOCATIONS
[M] Saarland Museum, Alte Sonnenburg, Bismarckstrasse 16, 6600 Saarbrücken.
[I] Staatliches Konservatoramt, Schlossplatz 16, 6600 Saarbrücken.

NORBERT MENDGEN

saddlery   A saddler is a manufacturer of riding saddles, harness for draught beasts and equipment for PACK-HORSES, making such items as stirrups, bridles, whips and collars, and working with girth cloth, a coarse form of linen, as well as leather. A 'brown saddler' made equipment for riding horses, a 'black saddler' for draught horses. A saddler's metalwork was normally made by specialist craftsmen called lorimers, who in England were concentrated in Walsall (*see* BLACK COUNTRY). A saddler's principal tools are awls and other piercing implements, knives and pincers, with punches and branding irons used for decorating leather. Numbers of saddlers increased in developed countries in the late nineteenth century as more HORSES were employed in urban areas.

A saddle was built up around a wooden framework called a saddle tree, which was sometimes made by a specialist craftsman. Sheepskin (known as 'basils') or horsehair was used for lining.

BIBLIOGRAPHY
General
Book of Trades, 1839; Holme, 1688.
Specific
Waterer, J. W. *A Short History of Saddles in Europe.* Northampton: Museum of Leathercraft, n.d.

Sadler, James (1753–1828)   The first English aeronaut, ascending in a balloon at Oxford in 1784, and a pioneer of steam power. He lectured on chemistry before undertaking research for the Admiralty in 1796–1810. His two-cylinder steam engine, for which he was threatened with prosecution by BOULTON & WATT, was an important step in the evolution of the TABLE ENGINE. His engines were used on railway inclined planes near IRONBRIDGE in 1792–3, and one of them was the first steam engine to be installed in PORTSMOUTH dockyard.

safety lamp   A means of lighting a mine, particularly a coal mine, without igniting METHANE gas. Sir HUMPHRY DAVY (1778–1820) first produced a practical lamp, which utilized wire gauze. The air/methane flame would not propagate through the gauze (see COAL MINING).

saggar   *See* KILN; REFRACTORIES.

sailcloth   A form of CANVAS used for the sails of ships or windmills, usually manufactured by specialist weavers. Sails were prepared for use in a SAIL LOFT. The chief centre of manufacture in England was Bridport, Dorset.

See also LINEN.

sailing ship   The European wooden three-masted sailing ship, perhaps the most important means of transport in human history, was perfected in the fifteenth century and carried most of the continent's seaborne trade until the late nineteenth century. The masts of such ships were usually in three parts, from each of which square sails were set from spars called yards. Sails on a square-rigger could be trimmed only to the front of the mast so the wind acted only on the back surface. On SCHOONERS, built in increasing numbers from the mid-eighteenth century, sails could be adjusted so that the wind acted on either side, enabling a ship to sail closer to the wind.

The Suez Canal (*see* SHIP CANALS), completed in 1869, posed a considerable threat to transoceanic sailing ships. Sailing ships continued to be built, and their design was refined (*see* CLIPPER; SCHOONER) between 1870 and 1914, but increasingly the successful new vessels were schooners of steel construction. Wooden square-riggers ceased to be built by the mid-1870s, and iron and steel square-riggers were no longer being constructed by 1900. The latter years of World War I saw a boom in schooner construction in North America, Scandinavia, the Netherlands and Italy, but sailing ships were gradually abandoned as a means of commercial transport between 1921 and 1939, although a few, notably the fleet of Gustaf Erikson, based in the ÅLAND ISLANDS, continued to work for some years after 1945.

Notable surviving square-riggers include:

- *Polly Woodside*, Belfast 1885: a 647-ton iron barque, preserved at MELBOURNE, Australia.
- *Balclutha*, Glasgow 1886: a 1862-ton steel square-rigger, preserved at San Francisco, CALIFORNIA, USA.
- *Sigyn*, Gothenburg 1887: a 359-ton wooden barque, preserved at Turku, Finland.
- *Pommern*, Greenock 1904: a 2376-ton four-master steel barque, preserved at Mariehamn, ÅLAND ISLANDS, Finland.
- *Passat*, Hamburg 1911: a 2888-ton (net) four-master built for the Chilean nitrate trade, preserved at Lübeck, Germany.

See also CLIPPER; FALKLAND ISLANDS; OIL TANKER; PUNTA ARENAS; SCHOONER; SOUTH GEORGIA.

BIBLIOGRAPHY
General
Brouwer, 1985; Chapelle, 1936; Greenhill and Manning, 1988; Kemp, 1972; Lubbock, 1927; Lundstrom, 1961, 1969; Underhill, 1938, 1958.
Specific
Graham, G. S. The ascendancy of the sailing ship, 1850–85. In *English Historical Review*, IX, 1956.

BARRIE TRINDER

sail loft The part of a shipyard where sails are laid out and sewn: a large, unencumbered floor space, where sailmakers sit on low benches with blocks with holes for tools at one end. A loft of 1860 remains at Bermuda. In naval yards sail lofts might be used for making flags.

BIBLIOGRAPHY
General
Coad, 1983, 1989.

Saimaa Canal, Kymen lääni, Finland The first attempt to join the Saimaa Lake navigation system to the Baltic was made in the early sixteenth century, and another a century later, but neither was successful. The canal from the city of Lappeenranta to the Baltic at Vyborg (Viipuri) was completed in 1845–56, according to designs by Carl von Rosenkampff, the work being supervised by the Swedish engineer Nils Ericson. On completion it was 60 km (40 mi.) long, with twenty-eight locks, and could take 250-tonne vessels. Work on rebuilding the canal for larger vessels began in 1926 but was interrupted by World War II, during which Vyborg and the eastern section of the waterway were ceded to the USSR. The canal was rebuilt in 1963–8, the section in the USSR being leased to Finland for fifty years. Parts of the old, granite-lined sections, and some locks, have been preserved on the Finnish side, and at the western end of the canal is a large area of sawmill-workers' housing of the 1920s.

BIBLIOGRAPHY
General
Hadfield, 1986.

LAURI PUTKONEN

Saint-Bonnet Tronçais, Allier, France The Tronçais ironworks, 40 km (25 mi.) N. of Montluçon, is the last of a series of some thirty ironmaking establishments built during the seventeenth and eighteenth centuries in and around the Berry, the region in the centre of France corresponding more or less with the present-day departments of Cher and Indre. Most of these ironworks were installed on major seigneurial estates, on tributaries flowing north into the Loire. The development of ironmaking in this region is associated with that of Atlantic trade, particularly out of the port of Nantes. Several works were suppliers of the 'Compagnie des Indes' (Indies company) which had trading installations and ships to be fitted out at Lorient. Many of them were launched in the time of Jean Baptiste Colbert (1619–83), several by landowners in the Berry who were members of his circle. In 1682 Colbert himself created the works known as the 'Forge Neuve' at Saint-Baudel, 25 km (16 mi.) S. of Bourges, in his barony of Châteauneuf.

The Clavières works around Ardentes in the Indre, 12 km (7 mi.) SE of Châteauroux, was built from 1670 in the Duchy of Châteauroux which then belonged to the Prince of Condé. There were three different sites comprising three blast furnaces – one of them with a double shaft for cannon production – three finery forges and rolling and slitting mills. For a long time this establishment was the largest ironworks in France.

Fewer ironworks were opened during the eighteenth century. The main ones were at Luçay and at Vierzon. The former was built in 1767 by the Farmer General, Philippe Charles Legendre de Villemorien, who had a château nearby at VALENÇAY, where, around 1789, his son opened a textile mill equipped with WATER FRAMES. The latter was created in 1776 on property belonging to the king's brother, the Comte d'Artois. The Tronçais works, finally, were built from 1788 to take advantage of the 2600 ha (64 000 ac.) royal forest of Tronçais. The initiative here came from Nicolas Rambourg, former manager of the Charleville arms manufactory (see NOUZONVILLE), and then of the Indret cannon foundry, both run by Ignace François de Wendel (1778–1825), one of the founders of LE CREUSOT.

During the nineteenth century the ironworks in the western part of the Berry evolved very little, except at Vierzon where a large-scale, integrated 'English-style' forge was opened in 1839, supplied with pig iron by the old charcoal-fired furnaces of the surrounding countryside. The group of ironworks to the east, previously of little importance, witnessed considerable development. This was particularly the case for the sites in the Aubois valley, influenced by the large-scale works created in 1821 at Fourchambault, 8 km (5 mi.) NW of Nevers. The blast furnaces at La Guerche and at Le Chautay, for example, were rebuilt during the 1840s. At the old Torteron works, the main annexe of Fourchambault, an important second foundry was created, which was active until 1882. To the south of the Berry, the proximity of the Commentry coalfield (see MONTLUÇON) also encouraged modernization. The owners of the Tronçais works, for example, built a small 'English-style' forge in the 1820s, and in 1839 a larger one was opened in the existing Mareuil works, 30 km (19 mi.) SW of Bourges. Most of the old charcoal furnaces ceased their activities during the 1860s, whilst the factories at Vierzon, Tronçais and Mareuil went over to other metal products such as wire and cables, which were produced until the 1980s and the closure of Vierzon.

The old forge site at Tronçais still has many of its original buildings. It is particularly remarkable for the beauty of its well-preserved setting, at the edge of the Tronçais forest, by a large lake. The stack of the blast furnace of 1788 still stands, along with an adjacent building which formerly housed the bellows, set in well-appointed masonry. The building which housed the finery forge also remains, although the site's subsequent industrial activities have modified it considerably. The old iron store building, with large, semicircular windows, and a charcoal barn on top, built in 1814, also remains. The site also has a two-storey building of the 1830s erected to house mule drivers. It contains four two-room dwelling units. There are also vestiges of associated brickworks, tileworks and a limeworks. At the nearby annexe, known as Sologne, some eighteenth-century housing remains; while at Morat there is a building of the 1820s which accommodated the small 'English-style' forge.

There are some remains of buildings and structures on most of the other old ironmaking sites of the Berry. At the site known as the 'Forge Haute' (upper forge) at Ardentes, belonging to the Clavières forge, the building of the slitting mill still stands, along with a housing block which probably dates from the seventeenth century, and a communal bakery. The development of three sites along the Indre gave rise to a road network, and to an entirely new village at Clavières, laid out with strictly geometrical streets and squares, planned at the end of the eighteenth century and retaining all its essential features.

The main nineteenth-century remains are in the east of the region, particularly in the Aubois valley. They include blast furnaces of the 1840s at Le Chautay, La Guerche and Saint-Florent-sur-Cher, the last known as Les Lavoirs, with its casting house intact. At Torteron are several ruined buildings and a small town created almost entirely in the 1850s around metallurgical activities. In the neighbouring village of Champ-de-la-Croix a fine ensemble of iron-ore miners' houses still stands. At the Grossouvre ironworks, further south in the Aubois valley is a splendid forge building of the 1840s, together with a galleried tenement block built about 1830.

BIBLIOGRAPHY
General
Tournaire, 1990.
Specific
Léon, P. Les Forges du Cher (Ironworks in the Cher). In *Berry: une terre à découvrir*, VIII, 1988.
Tournaire, J. Les Forges de l'Indre (Ironworks in the Indre). In *Berry: une terre à découvrir*, VII, 1988.
Villepreux, G. Un maître des forges sous quatre régimes: Nicolas Rambourg (an ironmaster under four regimes: Nicolas Rambourg). In *Revue d'Histoire des Mines et de la Métallurgie*, III, 1971.

JEAN-FRANÇOIS BELHOSTE

Sainte Croix, Vaud, Switzerland   A town near the French border in a region with long traditions of toy manufacture. At CIMA music boxes and automata, the ingenious mechanical toys made in the area since the eighteenth century, are exhibited, manufactured and repaired.

LOCATION
[M,S] CIMA (International Centre of Mechanical Art), Rue de l'Industrie 2, 1450-Sainte Croix, Vaud.

Saint-Étienne, Loire, France   Until the mid-nineteenth century the Saint-Étienne and Rive-de-Gier coalfield was the most productive in France. At the end of the eighteenth century and at the beginning of the nineteenth this coal stimulated the development of prosperous glassmaking and ironmaking industries, the latter also being encouraged by older traditions of armaments and ironmongery manufacture. The earliest railway lines in France were built here, to carry coal to the Loire and to the Rhône: Saint-Étienne to Andrézieux from 1823 and Saint-Étienne to Lyons in 1827. Alongside these coal-based industries, Saint-Étienne also had a prosperous textile manufacture which specialized in ribbons.

Industry in the region has been in dramatic decline for about fifteen years, the last coal mine closing in 1984. The Saint-Étienne Museum of Art and Industry keeps a record of local industrial life, with a collection of firearms, 300 000 ribbon samples, and several generations of power looms, either full-size or scale models.

Vestiges of mining activities have been preserved at the Couriot mine, sunk in 1913 and closed in 1972. This was one of the earliest mines where the surface installations were electrified. Its winding gear was equipped with a

Koepe pulley. Today a demonstration gallery on the surface, some 350 m (1148 ft.) long, shows nineteenth- and twentieth-century coal-extraction techniques. At Saint-Chamond, 10 km (6 mi.) NE of Saint-Étienne, the old Combélibert mine is one of the few pits in France to preserve a wooden headstock, along with an engine house dating from the second half of the nineteenth century.

Traces of the iron and steel industry are still to be found along the Gier valley towards Saint-Chamond and in the Ondaine valley towards Firminy, 10 km (6 mi.) SW of Saint-Étienne. A few late-eighteenth-century and early-nineteenth-century buildings survive: the former slitting mill of Unieux, the Sauvanière wire-drawing mill on the Cotatay and the Begon works, specializing, until the early 1980s, in fencing foils for competitions. Most of the buildings date from after 1860, however. At Unieux the old Jacob Holtzer factory, famous for the development of special steels at the end of the nineteenth century, conserved several of its old buildings until 1990, including one in brick with a wooden frame, dating from before 1878, and another with a metal framework dating from 1900. The 'Vigneron' tenement building, containing thirty-eight flats, built next to the factory in 1862, was restored in 1976.

The Unieux steelworks also owned the 'Alliance' scythe factory at Pont-Salomon on the Semène River. Its buildings of c.1860 were probably among the first in France to have north-lit roofs. In the Gier basin, the Terrenoire, the Lorette, Saint-Chamond and Rive-de-Gier works still retain some of their nineteenth-century timber-framed and iron-framed buildings. Finally, at Chambon-Feugerolles there is still the Crozet-Fourneyron factory where, in 1850, Benoît Fourneyron began industrial production of the turbine he had invented between 1823 and 1832. The old foundry building dating from 1852 still survives, along with the testing shop, with its interesting remains of a very early travelling crane.

BIBLIOGRAPHY
General
Belhoste, 1991; Bravard, 1981; Daumas, 1980.
Specific
Itinéraire Saint-Étienne–Ondaine–Haut Beaujolais (Guide produced for TICCIH conference 1981). Paris: CILAC, 1981.

JEAN-FRANÇOIS BELHOSTE

Sainte-Marie-aux-Mines, Haut-Rhin, France The Saint-Louis-Eisenthur silver mine at Sainte-Marie-aux-Mines, 54 km (33 mi.) SW of Strasbourg, is located on the lodes of Neuenberg, and was particularly important in the late sixteenth century. Two mines – one called Eisenthur, the other die Aych ('the oak') – were opened separately in 1549, merging in 1569. Their ores were probably soon worked out, although mining resumed on a small scale during the eighteenth century.

The Saint-Louis lode has now been studied for more than twenty years, more particularly since 1983, with the combined development of pot-holing and mining archaeology. These studies have enabled 4 km (2½ mi.) of headings and working faces to be plotted with precision,

giving a clearer understanding of the underground architecture of the mines, the techniques of working and timbering the shafts and galleries, drainage methods, and the development of underground transport and extraction techniques. A network of almost 1 km of underground galleries can be visited.

The mine belongs to the major orefield of the Vosges, where about 80 km (50 mi.) of workings have now been plotted. There were probably more than 600 km (365 mi.) dating from the period of intense exploitation which lasted from c.1500 to the outbreak of the Thirty Years War. Apart from studies of the underground evidence, several headstock sites have been excavated, notably the Tiergarten Mine at Silberwald, Munster, 35 km (21 mi.) NW of Mulhouse, and the Samson mine at Saint-Croix-aux-Mines in the Vosges. Ore dressing and washing installations, tool forges and housing have been brought to light.

The nearby sector of the old Comté of Rosemont also witnessed some mining activities in the seventeenth and eighteenth centuries, particularly after 1659 when the Comté became the property of the Mazarin family. Silver was mined, along with copper and lead. A small mining museum has recently opened at Giromagny, 14 km (8½ mi.) N. of Belfort.

BIBLIOGRAPHY
General
Ancel and Fluck, 1988; Société industrielle de Mulhouse, 1990.

LOCATION
[M] Mineralogical and Mining Museum, 70 rue Wilson, 68160 Sainte-Marie-aux-Mines.

JEAN-FRANÇOIS BELHOSTE

St Fagans, South Glamorgan, Wales The Welsh Folk Museum at St Fagans, 4 km (2½ mi.) W. of Cardiff, which was begun in 1950 by Iorwerth C. Peate, is the oldest British open-air museum of re-erected buildings. It aims to represent the culture of Wales by buildings 'maintained in living order' within 40 ha (100 ac.) of parkland. Several buildings represent Welsh industries: a woollen mill employs nineteenth-century machinery to demonstrate processes from raw wool to dyed cloth, and a tannery, a corn mill, and a pottery kiln have been re-erected. Other buildings include ironworkers' houses of c.1800 from MERTHYR TYDFIL, a quarryman's cottage, a turnpike road toll house, a school, and agricultural buildings. Galleries display an unsurpassed collection of Welsh folk artefacts.

BIBLIOGRAPHY
Specific
Peate, I. C. *Open-Air Museums.* Cardiff: National Museum of Wales, 1948.

LOCATION
[M] Welsh Folk Museum, St Fagans, Cardiff, South Glamorgan CF5 6XB.

St Gallen, Switzerland The cantonal capital, and one of Switzerland's principal industrial cities, specializing in the late nineteenth century in embroidered cotton goods. The first mechanized cotton mill in Switzerland was established in the buildings of a monastery in St Gallen, but it was unsuccessful. The history of textiles is illustrated in the town's museums, together with the work of the city's locksmiths and pewterers, while the domestic stage of textile manufacture is well displayed in the Toggenburg Museum at Lichtensteig, 24 km (15 mi.) SW.

The railway station, with a lengthy street frontage in a neo-Baroque style, is one of the most imposing in Switzerland. Substantial stone warehouses remain within the station perimeter. At Brüggen, 4 km (2½ mi.) W., the SBB main line (see SWITZERLAND) crosses the River Sitter on a masonry viaduct 191 m (627 ft.) long, while a nearby 366 m (1200 ft.) iron and stone viaduct carries the track of the Lake Constance–Toggenburg railway. The 19 km (12 mi.) rack and adhesion railway to Appenzell is one of the most attractive minor lines in Switzerland. The railway connects with the Schwägalp–Säntis Luftseilbahnnen (see AERIAL ROPEWAY) which ascends 1121 m (3677 ft.) to the 2483 m (8146 ft.) summit of Säntis. It was completed in 1935, one of the first large-scale installations of its kind, its cars each carrying thirty-five passengers.

LOCATIONS
[M] Historical Museum, Museumstrasse 50, 9000 St Gallen.
[M] Museum of Industrial and Applied Arts, Vadianstrasse 2, 9000 St Gallen.
[M] Toggenburg Regional Museum, Rathaus, 9620 Lichtensteig, St Gallen.

HANS-PETER BÄRTSCHI

Saint-Gobain, Aisne, France   The production of plate glass for mirrors may be considered to have begun in France in 1665, when the Royal Manufactory of Mirror Glass was founded at Reuilly, then just outside Paris, in the eastern faubourg (suburb) of Saint-Antoine. In 1667 another establishment was opened at Tourlaville, on the edge of the Brix forest, 4 km (3 mi.) E. of Cherbourg, in Manche. The glass at this period was blown into a cylindrical form, cut into sheets while still hot, then flattened and annealed. These semi-manufactured products were then sent to the Reuilly establishment for fine grinding with abrasive sand and EMERY powder, and polishing with cloth-covered boards, before being backed with tin leaf. Between 1688 and 1692 a new process was developed: molten glass was cast onto a metal table and flattened out by a copper roller. This process enabled much larger sheets of glass to be made, and led, in 1693, to the opening of a new manufactory, built inside the remnants of a former castle located in a clearing of the Saint-Gobain forest, 16 km (10 mi.) S. of Saint-Quentin. The different establishments of Reuilly, Tourlaville and Saint-Gobain were merged into a single concern in 1695.

Most investment in the eighteenth century was concentrated at the Saint-Gobain works. In 1769 some of the grinding and polishing workshops were transferred from Reuilly to Saint-Gobain, and in 1775 dwellings were built to accommodate the workers who, until that time, had lived in the tower of the old castle and in lodgings along its ramparts. The Reuilly workshops were finally closed

down at the beginning of the nineteenth century, to be followed by the Tourlaville factory which was abandoned in 1834. From 1822 part of the production process was moved to Chauny, 12 km (8 mi.) E. of Saint-Gobain on the River Oise, near to its junction with the Saint-Quentin canal. This new works took over the production of SODA and the grinding and finishing stages, which were increasingly mechanized.

The Saint-Gobain factory is still in use, although far-reaching modifications were made in the 1920s when Siemens basin furnaces were introduced for continuous production, finally replacing the traditional method of pouring the molten glass onto a table. Despite these changes, the factory has several vestiges of its eighteenth- and nineteenth-century installations, not least its monumental entrance porch. The factory still retains traces of the original layout of the castle, which was quarried for building materials when the first manufactory was opened in the seventeenth century. The eighteenth-century workers' dwellings have been demolished.

At Tourlaville several of the old buildings, in particular a former polishers' workshop, survived until April 1944 when they were destroyed by bombing. A chapel, a COUNTING HOUSE and two workers' dwellings remain, however, and a small museum installed in a nearby farmhouse displays several old artefacts associated with the manufactory.

BIBLIOGRAPHY
General
Hamon, 1988; Lepetit, 1987.
Specific
Hamon, M. La Manufacture royale des glaces de Saint-Gobain. In Monuments Historiques, III, 1977.

JEAN-FRANÇOIS BELHOSTE

St Gotthard, Ticino and Uri, Switzerland   The most important of the passes through the Alps, linking the southern extremity of Lake Lucerne with the Ticino valley and northern Italy. The canton of Uri replaced the packhorse trail over the St Gotthard Pass with a paved road in 1819. The Teufelsbrücke (Devil's Bridge) and the 'Urnerloch' tunnel in the Schollenen Gorge north of Andermatt are preserved as monuments from this period.

The Gotthard Railway between Lucerne and Chiasso is the busiest of all European mountain railways, and its scenery the most memorable. Originally planned at an international conference in 1869, it was opened to traffic in 1882. No original bridges remain but the whole of the line, particularly the northern approaches to the main 15 km (9.3 mi.) tunnel, with spiral tunnels at Wassen, Rodi-Fiesso and Pianotondo, still offers the train traveller an unforgettable experience. The tunnel was built with great difficulty. The principal engineer, Louis Favre (1826–1879) died from a heart attack while inspecting the tunnel. A memorial to the 177 who died and the 403 who were injured during construction stands on Airolo station south of the tunnel. The line was electrified in 1920. Lake Ritom, an artificial reservoir 5 km (3 mi.) E. of Airolo, was

Figure 138 A barge being conveyed in the caisson of the inclined plane of Saint-Louis-Arzviller on the Canal de la Marne au Rhin, which was opened to traffic in 1969
Collection of Dr Barrie Trinder

created as part of the construction of the associated power stations.

BIBLIOGRAPHY
General
Schneider, 1967.

LOCATION
[M] Museo Nazionale del San Gottardo (National Museum of the St Gotthard), Vecchi a Sesta, CH-6718 San Gottardo.

HANS-PETER BÄRTSCHI

St Helens, Merseyside, England   A principal centre of flat glass manufacture in Britain, on the eastern edge of the Lancashire coalfield. The nineteenth-century town grew from scattered industrial settlements; the market square dates from 1833, the town hall from 1838. The manufacture of pottery (illustrated in the St Helens Museum) and glass had been established by the late seventeenth century. Mining was stimulated by the Sankey Brook Navigation, constructed by John Ashton and Henry Berry in 1757, which linked the coalfield with the Cheshire saltworks and Liverpool: the navigation is disused but much is still in water. Through the initiative of coalmaster John Mackay, the British Cast Plate Glass Co. was established at Ravenhead in 1773–6, using French technology, and the PARYS MOUNTAIN company set up copper smelters and rolling mills. Glass manufacture expanded rapidly in 1830–45. William Pilkington, a doctor, took a share in the St Helens Crown Glass Co. in 1826, and his family came to dominate the industry in the twentieth century. The Pilkington company introduced the float glass process in the 1950s, and the company museum has comprehensive displays relating to local and wider aspects of the industry.

BIBLIOGRAPHY
General
Ashmore, 1982; Barker, 1977; Barker and Harris, 1954.

LOCATIONS
[M] Pilkington Glass Museum, Prescot Road, St Helens, Merseyside WA10 3TT.
[M] St Helens Museum and Art Gallery, College Street, St Helens, Merseyside WA10 1TW.

BARRIE TRINDER

St Hubert, Luxembourg, Belgium   St Hubert is a small town huddled around a medieval abbey in the midst of dense forests on the Ardennes plateau. The Fourneau St-Michel, 6 km (4 mi.) N., is a charcoal-fired, water-powered blast furnace of 1771, essentially complete with stack, charcoal barn and casting house. The Museum of Iron in an adjacent timber-framed house contains fire backs, plaques (including the 'Last Supper'), nail-making equipment, and a dog-powered hammer. The open-air Museum of Walloon Rural Life is adjacent. Buildings, including a clogmaker's shop and other artisan workshops, have been moved to the site and grouped in zones.

LOCATION
[M] Fourneau St-Michel, Musée de la Vie Rurale en Wallonie (Museum of Walloon Rural Life), 6900 St. Hubert.

Saint-Louis-Arzviller, Moselle, France   The 310 km (190 mi.) long Canal de la Marne au Rhin, from Vitry-le-François to Strasbourg, was built between 1846 and 1853, and was notable for the use of pusher tugs between 1855 and 1875, and subsequently for the employment of the traditional French system of 'halage', or towing by electric locomotives running on a metre-gauge railway laid on the towpath. During improvements in the 1960s a stretch that included seventeen locks near the villages of Saint-Louis and Arzviller, 62 km (38 mi.) NW of Strasbourg, was bypassed by a new cut which includes an inclined plane with a vertical rise of 44.5 m (146 ft.), in which barges are carried sideways in a CAISSON (*see* figure 138). It opened to traffic in 1969. Visitor facilities are provided at the inclined plane.

BIBLIOGRAPHY
General
Hadfield, 1986.

LOCATION
[I] Syndicat d'Initiative, Plan Incliné, Saint-Louis, 57820 Lutzelbourg.

St Peter-Freienstein, Styria, Austria   *See* STYRIAN IRON TRAIL.

St Petersburg   *See* LENINGRAD.

Sala, Västmanland, Sweden   The town of Sala lies 120 km (75 mi.) NW of Stockholm. The Sala mine, 2.5 km ($1\frac{1}{2}$ mi.) W. of the town, has been Sweden's principal source of silver.

The ore consists of galena, with silver encrusted in dolomite and zinc in some parts of the mine. The ore has a silver content of about 1 per cent. By means of complex extraction processes, the annual output of silver rose to about 4000 kg (8800 lb.) at the peak of the mine's prosperity in the 1530s. The total output of silver from *c.*1500 until the silver mine closed in 1908 has been estimated at around 500 tonnes.

The ore deposit was discovered in the late fifteenth century, and in 1512 the first charter relating to it was signed, enabling the Crown to claim control over the mine, although this control was scarcely effective since the miners had their own furnaces in the surrounding woods for smelting silver. Nevertheless the state and the Church acquired more and more shares in the mine, which was characterized as 'Riksens förnämste Clenodium' (the most important treasure of the state). The mine was favoured with many privileges, especially during the reign of King Gustavus Vasa (1496–1560) when it was estimated that about a thousand people lived in the adjacent village. In the early seventeenth century the village was destroyed when the inhabitants had to move to the newly-established town of Sala.

After great success in the 1530s, the prosperity of the mine declined. The shafts suffered severe collapses, and it was difficult to keep the workings free from water. The output in 1609 was no more than 9.05 kg (20 lb.) of silver. Seventeenth-century kings showed much interest in improving the mine. With the help of German miners, new shafts were opened, new pumping machinery installed, and production increased, but it reached only about half the levels of the late sixteenth century. In 1682 the ownership of the mine and the silver works was taken over by Sala bergslag, a miners' co-operative. The com-

pany had difficulty in maintaining the mine. Several efforts were made to improve its operation and raise production, some more successful than others. In 1908 silver mining was abandoned, and the production of zinc expanded.

Many of the old installations at the Sala remain. Some workings can be visited, and on the surface there are buildings of many periods, from the late sixteenth century to the late nineteenth century, including wooden headstocks of great architectural significance, the office building, a clock tower, the manor house which was the home of the mine director, and the building in which the miners used to assemble. Artefacts relating to the mine are displayed in a museum.

BIBLIOGRAPHY
General
Granström, 1940; Norberg, 1978.

LOCATION
[M] Sala Silver Mine Museum.

MARIE NISSER

salami   *See* SAUSAGE.

Salford, Greater Manchester, England   *See* MANCHESTER.

Salgótarjan, Nógrád, Hungary   A mining town in the valley of Tarján, near the northern border of Hungary, 80 km (50 mi.) NE of Budapest. Coal was discovered in the 1850s, and ironworks, engineering factories and potteries developed to use it. There is a preserved mine with underground galleries 200 m (650 ft.) deep, with many remains of horse haulage systems.

BIBLIOGRAPHY
General
Kiss *et al.*, 1981.

LOCATION
[M,S] Bothornik Jozsef Mining Museum, H-3100 Salgótarjan, Bajcsy Zs. u. l.

Salins-les-Bains, Jura, France   Salt has probably been produced in the Franche-Comté region since Roman times, and the saltworks at Salins are known to have existed in the sixth century. They remained active, practically without interruption, from the twelfth century until 1962. The industry was based on the canalization of underground saltwater springs, the brine being brought to the surface and run into large, open, oval or rectangular evaporation pans, the furnaces beneath which were kept alight for 12–18 hours. After the evaporation of all the water, the salt was moulded into loaves for sale or transport.

In about 1750 the old noria at Salins was replaced by a modern pumping system driven by a water wheel. The scarcity of wood in the vicinity led to the opening of new works nearer to the extensive forests of Chaux. Located at Arc-et-Senans, they were built between 1775 and 1779, the brine from Salins being piped there through 21 km (13 mi.) of 'saloduct' made of hollowed-out pine trunks. The pipeline led directly to evaporation sheds which raised the salinity level of the brine prior to boiling.

The saltworks at Salins have been transformed into a museum. A vaulted underground chamber still houses the spectacular water-powered pumping system, which is little changed since 1750. Four salt pans also survive. The well-known neo-Classical buildings which make up the saltworks at Arc-et-Senans were designed by Claude-Nicolas Ledoux (1736–1806) for his employers at the General Farm; they too are well preserved, and are designated a UNESCO World Heritage Site. The semicircular layout of the buildings – two large boiling houses, a monumental entrance porch and twenty-four dwellings for workers in two curved wings – is remarkable. Long since emptied of all industrial equipment, as salt production ceased in 1895, Ledoux's buildings now house a congress centre and futurology research institute. The nearby evaporation building, nearly 500 m (1650 ft.) long, was destroyed early this century.

The museum at Salins is one of a circuit in the region devoted to economic history and working life, which also includes a tileworks at Malbrans, an ironworks at Baignes, and a small rural edge-tool factory at Nans-sous-Sainte Anne which retains a remarkable pair of wooden bellows in working order.

BIBLIOGRAPHY
General
Brelot, 1985; Brelot and Locatelli, 1981; Brelot and Mayaud, 1982; Deming, 1986.

LOCATION
[M] Salt Museum, 39110 Salins-les-Bains.

JEAN-FRANÇOIS BELHOSTE

salt Sodium chloride (NaCl) was perhaps the most important traded commodity before the Industrial Revolution, being the most readily available food preservative, a source of taxation revenue for governments, an easily applied glaze for ceramics, and in some societies a form of currency. In seventeenth-century Europe salt was readily produced in the Catholic south and formed a convenient item of exchange with the fishermen of the Protestant north. It was used for preserving beef, pork and butter, and gave savour to the farinaceous gruels on which many subsisted. In several countries its manufacture became a royal monopoly.

Salt is the predominant mineral in sea water, and has traditionally been produced by evaporation in the Mediterranean and Adriatic (*see* PELJEŠAC), and on the Atlantic coasts of Spain and Portugal. The liquid led into pans for evaporation is called 'bittern'. Salt is also found inland in sedimentary deposits, from which it is extracted either by conventional mining, or by dissolving it underground and pumping up brine. The traditional means of evaporating such brine was by boiling in wrought-iron pans, adding blood supplied by butchers to speed the process. An open pan works is preserved at NORTHWICH. From the 1880s processes using vacuum pans heated by steam were developed in Austria by Sigismund Pick; at Manistee, Mich., USA, by George R. Ray; and subsequently in Cheshire, England.

Sodium chloride, solid or in solution, forms the raw material for many chemical processes (*see* LEBLANC PROCESS; SOLVAY, ERNEST). The electrolysis of salt is the starting point of such very large chemical plants as those at Tavaux in France Compté and Borth Wallach near Cleves in Germany.

See also HALLEIN; HALL IN TIROL; HALLSTATT; NORTHWICH; SOLIVAR; WIELICZKA.

BIBLIOGRAPHY
General
Agricola, 1950; Braudel, 1981; Kaufmann, 1971; Lefond, 1969; Morgan and Pratt, 1938; Multhauf, 1978; Whatley, 1987.
Specific
Morrison, J. *Chemical Uses of Salt.* Northwich: Salt Museum, n.d.
Morrison, J. *The Development of the Vacuum Process for the Evaporation of Brine.* Northwich: Salt Museum, n.d.
Twigg, G. *Open-pan salt-making.* Northwich: Salt Museum, n.d.

BARRIE TRINDER

Saltaire, West Yorkshire, England *See* BRADFORD.

salt glaze A term applied to EARTHENWARES or STONEWARES glazed by salt thrown into the kiln with water during the firing process. Salt-glaze saggars (*see* REFRACTORIES) are distinguished by having holes in the sides to allow the salt to affect the wares. Salt glazes were used in the Rhineland from the fourteenth century, and were popular in England in the late seventeenth century and early eighteenth century.

BIBLIOGRAPHY
General
Rhodes, 1969.

saltpetre Potassium nitrate (KNO₃), sometimes called nitre: a food preservative, but historically its chief use has been in the manufacture of GUNPOWDER. Saltpetre was imported to Europe from India through Venice, and during the seventeenth century through Dutch and British East India companies. It was produced organically in 'nitre beds' filled with earth and manure.

Norge saltpetre is calcium nitrate (Ca(NO₃)₂; *see* BIRKELAND AND EYDE PROCESS.

Chile saltpetre, or sodium nitrate (NaNO₃), extracted from natural deposits in Chile, was imported to Europe from *c.*1840 and was chiefly used as a fertilizer.

BIBLIOGRAPHY
General
Crocker, 1986; Partington, 1950.

Salzburg, Salzburg, Austria A trading city on the River Salzach on the Bavarian border. It was an independent ecclesiastical principality until secularization in 1802, then briefly part of Bavaria, but was within the Habsburg empire from 1816. Alm-Kanal, beneath the city centre, a system of tunnels built from the twelfth century to provide power for water mills, remains in use as part of the sewer system. Defences were removed permitting suburban expansion from the 1870s. Neuthor tunnel, 128 m (140 yd.) long, between Sigmundsplatz and Hildmansplatz, was driven in 1764–7 under the direction of Archbishop Sigismund III, giving access to the suburb of Riedenburg. The archbishop's horse trough, of monumental design by Michael Bernard Mandl of 1695, is at the northern end. There are remains of houses in the conglomerate rock of Mönchsberg, west of the Franz-Josef Quay on the left bank of the Salzach. Several railways and lifts ascend surrounding hills. The Salzburger Stadtwerke Verkehrsbetriebe (Salzburg City Transport service) operates a 25 km (16 mi.) railway from outside the ÖBB station to Lamprechtshausen, and has some early electric locomotives.

Salzgitter, Lower Saxony, Germany The present-day urban district of Salzgitter, 16 km (10 mi.) SW of Brunswick, was an almost entirely agricultural region until 1937. In the course of the Third Reich's efforts to achieve self-sufficiency, it was chosen as the site of a gigantic iron and steel works, with thirty-two blast furnaces. Twelve had been completed by 1945, and all but three were demolished in 1947–50. The raw materials were ore from the Lower Cretaceous measures, and after the 1950s oolitic ores from the Konrad pit, which has tandem steel headstocks. The mining of ores has now stopped, but several buildings have been preserved for other uses, and such examples as the office block and pithead buildings of Shaft 2 of the Hannoversche Treue mine at Salzgitter Calbecht, and Shaft 1 of the Haverlahwiese pit serve to illustrate the conformist architecture of the Third Reich, as do the mine buildings, which include the loading area, at Salzgitter-Ohlendorf. The ore-preparation plants in Othfresen, 10 km (6 mi.) N. of Goslar, and at the Emilie pit of 1939 at Adenstedt-Bülten in Peine, 30 km (19 mi.) N., are preserved. They consist of massive brick buildings dominating the surrounding countryside, with steel-barred strip windows. The blast furnace plant itself, with its coke ovens, a sinter plant and a power station of 1940, is similarly a dominant feature of the landscape. An underground vault beneath the road accommodated prisoners of war and other prisoners in 1942–5, and is now a memorial.

BIBLIOGRAPHY
General
Mende and Hamm, 1990; Slotta, 1975–85.

MICHAEL MENDE

samovar A Russian tea urn, often provided to supply guests in a hotel or travellers on a long-distance train.

Samsonów, Kielce, Poland The site of a blast furnace, 20 km (12 mi.) N. of Kielce, in the STAROPOLSKI INDUSTRIAL REGION. Construction of the state-owned plant began in 1816 at the suggestion of STANISŁAW STASZIC. The charcoal blast furnace with casting house and cupola

furnace were finished in 1823; cylinder bellows were installed in 1829, with a water wheel which was replaced in the 1850s by steam engines. The plant was closed after a fire in 1866; the preserved ruins are now open to the public. The main part of the plant was designed on classical principles following the plan of a palace. The hoist tower dominates the whole complex: behind it a casting house is flanked by a pattern shop, a drying shop and an enamelling shop. Adjoining the hoist tower are the blowing house and the water-wheel house, water being fed from a nearby reservoir after being drawn from the Bobrza river.

BIBLIOGRAPHY
General
Krygier, 1958.

Sandviken, Gävleborg, Sweden A steelmaking town established alongside the railway from Gävle to Falun in 1862, and, after a bankruptcy, taken over by the ancestors of the present company, Sandvik AB, in 1866. The city remains an important engineering centre. Living quarters in the early years were primitive, but from the 1880s the company began to provide good-quality housing for its workers.

Many of the structures associated with an OPEN-HEARTH steelworks of the late nineteenth century remain intact, including rolling mill buildings of 1886 and 1893, the building which once housed the open-hearth furnaces, which dates from 1896, and an engineering workshop of 1862. Twenty-five of the original single-storey workers' cottages have been restored and remain in use.

Rosenlöf's Printing Works, Kungsgården, 10 km (6 mi.) W. of Sandviken was closed in 1974 after operating with few essential changes for nearly a century. The works was preserved as a museum by the municipality, and opened in 1983. At the peak of its prosperity the works employed about fifteen people, and manual and mechanical typesetting plant, presses and bookbinding equipment are displayed.

Gysinge bruk, 34 km (21 mi.) S., is an ironworking community established in 1668, where production continued until 1927. Surviving monuments include a clock tower of 1751, an inn of the 1780s which was a posting station, and dwellings used by workers from the WALLOON FORGES. At Gysinge Bruk in 1900 steel was made for the first time in an electric furnace, and the 'Kjellinska induction furnace' remains in the power station building. A museum displays log floating.

Ironmaking began at Hammarby bruk, 14 km (9 mi.) SW, in the sixteenth century, but ceased in 1885 when a pulpmill using the sulphite process was established, which continued until 1983. A manor house of 1850 and two rows of ironworkers' houses remain.

The Smedsgården museum shows workers' dwellings built during the first fifty years of the twentieth century. The textile museum at Högbo, 6 km (4 mi.) N., is concerned particularly with the products of domestic craft textile associations in the early twentieth century.

Edsken blast furnace, 40 km (25 mi.) W. of Sandviken

was built in 1664 to supply Högbo bruk with pig iron, but it is principally remembered for its role in the Swedish steel industry. Göran Fredrik Göransson (1819–1900), shareholder at Högbo bruk, and part-owner of the Elfstrand iron merchandizing house in Gävle, bought a one-fifth share in the rights in Sweden to the Bessemer patent for making steel, and began in November 1857 to try to make steel in two trunnion-mounted converters which he had received from England. The results were unsatisfactory. He acquired two new converters from England and enlarged the apertures of the tuyeres, thus allowing more air to pass through the molten iron. The first charge was made on 18 July 1858 and produced excellent steel, showing that best results were given when MANGANESE was present. In due course SIR HENRY BESSEMER accepted Göransson's improvements, which were incorporated in Bessemer converters as they were adopted throughout the world. Bessemer production continued at Edsken until 1866, with pig iron production ceasing in 1880. Nothing of the blast furnace plant now remains, but a plate has been set up commemorating the first successful charge of Bessemer steel. Göransson became manager of the new steelworks at Sandviken which subsequently became one of the leading companies in Sweden.

BIBLIOGRAPHY
General
Attman, 1986; Nisser and Bedoire, 1978; Nisser 1979.
Specific
Carlberg, P. Bessemermetodens genombrott vid Edsken och Högbo (Bessemer steelmaking at Edsken and Högbo). In *Med Hammare och Fackla* (With Hammer and tongs), Stockholm, XXII, 1962.
Wahlberg, A. G. F. Göransson och bessmerprocessen (G. F. Göransson and the Bessemer process). In *Ett svenskt jerverk* (Swedish ironworks), Uppsala, 1937.

LOCATIONS
[M] Dalälvarnas Flottningsmuseet (Log-floating Museum), Gysinge, S-180 20 Osterfärnebo.
[M] Rosenlöfs Tryckery (Rosenlöf Printing Works Museum), Korsikavägen 23, Sandviken.
[M] Textilmuseet (Textile Museum), Gruvvägen 4, Högbo.
[M] Smedsgården (Smiths' houses), Smedgatan 2, 811 80 Sandviken.

MARIE NISSER

sanitary ware A term employed to describe a variety of ceramic products used for domestic and industrial sanitation. Most is in the form of glazed brick and tiles, sanitary pipes, and sanitary tanks, baths, sinks, urinals and water closet basins. The coarser types of wares, such as sewer pipes, have been made with a vitrified body, while forms requiring a more attractive appearance have generally been executed in an earthenware body covered with a white glaze.

The manufacture of sanitary ware expanded rapidly as the movement for sanitary reform developed in the cities of Europe and North America in the mid-nineteenth century. In England firms like Doulton of Lambeth, London, and Gibbs & Canning of Tamworth, Staffordshire, took the lead in supplying sewer pipes in mains drainage schemes in towns. The rapid growth of American cities supported such firms as Gladding-McBean of Lincoln, Calif., which pioneered the technology of extruding sewer pipes. They adopted a machine that could extrude vertically pipes up to 1.03 m (42 in.) in diameter.

The best glazed sanitary ware has been made with fireclay, which is less liable than other clays to crack and craze when used to make large articles. The major British firms were located near LEEDS and STOKE-ON-TRENT and on the Lancashire coalfield. Important developments were made c.1900 in slip casting, pouring liquid clay into plaster moulds to enable the economic production of large and complex slabs and bowls. Humidity driers were adopted from the 1920s to control the drying of such wares.

BIBLIOGRAPHY
General
Searle, 1929–30.

MICHAEL STRATTON

San Leucio, Campania, Italy A silkmaking centre, 33 km (20 mi.) N. of Naples, outside the formal grounds of the Palazzo Reale, the Neapolitan equivalent of Versailles, completed by King Ferdinand I in 1774 from plans by Luigi Vanvitelli (1700–83). Ferdinand IV developed San Leucio as a model industrial town. The focus is the Casino Reale di Belvedere, a miniature palace, approached up a formal flight of steps, and built from 1775 to designs by Francesco Collecini, a pupil of Vanvitelli. The courtyard accommodated workshops for hand looms. Silk was being woven by 1782 and in 1785 housing was constructed below the Casino, which itself was adapted as offices. The two long terraces of workers' housing, in Via Giardini Reali and Via Vaccheria, are separated by a formal approach to the Casino under a classical archway.

San Leucio was part of a royal exercise in paternalistic management, embracing agriculture and based on principles of equality among the workers. Utopianism gave way to commerce in the nineteenth century. A long water-powered silk-throwing factory to the design of Giovanni Patturelli was built behind the Casino in 1823. The nineteenth-century works is now largely derelict, but artificial silk and nylon are still made and hand looms are still used in the Palazzo dello Stabilimento. Research on San Leucio has been undertaken by the Faculty of Architecture at Naples University, and a film has been produced by the Dipartimento Scuole Educazione. The Belvedere palace is being restored as a museum covering the technology of silkmaking and the history of the settlement.

BIBLIOGRAPHY
General
Negri *et al.*, 1983.
Specific
San Leucio: archeologia, storia, progretto (San Leucio: archaeology, history, project). Naples: AA.VV, 1977.

MICHAEL STRATTON

San Sebastián (Donostia), Gipuzkoa, Basque Country, Spain   A resort of some 200 000 inhabitants and the principal city of the province of Gipuzkoa. It has a rich industrial heritage. The Museum of San Telmo, located in a former Dominican abbey, has ethnographical collections relating to the BASQUE COUNTRY, including wooden and iron artefacts, pottery and water wheels.

The Agorregi ironworks in the Pagoeta National Park, 18 km (11 mi.) SW of San Sebastián, is a forge located at the confluence of two small streams, with a complex water-power system operating the hammers and bellows. The forge building is a distinguished eighteenth-century structure, alongside which is a calcining kiln. The whole complex has been restored.

At Bedua on the Zumaia estuary, 21 km (13 mi.) W. of San Sebastián, is a harbour with a warehouse and a cement works. The harbour was used in the Middle Ages to unload iron ore from Vizcaya consigned to ironworks in the Urola valley. A Baroque mansion of the early seventeenth century also served as a warehouse. The water-powered cement works, 'Uriarte, Zubimendi, Corta & Cía' was established in the mid-nineteenth century, one of several in the Urola valley.

Zumaia, 22 km (14 mi.) W. of San Sebastián, is the coastal terminus of the railway to Zumárraga, 22 km (14 mi.) S., which, with many bridges and tunnels, passes through the spectacular scenery of the Urola valley. The line was built from 1921 under the direction of the engineer J. M. Alomso Zabala, and operated until 1987. The stations at the two termini, together with those at Balneario de Cestona, 7 km (4 mi.) S. of Zumaya, and Azpeitia, where the locomotive and carriage depots are situated, 12 km ($7\frac{1}{2}$ mi.) S. of Zumaya, are particularly notable.

The Ferreria Mirandaola (Mirandaola ironworks), 6 km (4 mi.) S. of Zumárraga, is a water-powered CATALAN FORGE, restored to working condition in 1958.

BIBLIOGRAPHY
General
Gomez *et al.*, 1990.

LOCATIONS
[S] Ferreria Mirandaola, Patricio Echeverría, SA-Legazpia.
[M] Museum of San Telmo, Plaza de Zuloaga, Donostia, San Sebastián.

EUSEBI CASANELLES

Santarém, Ribatejo, Portugal   A city on the River Tagus (Tejo), 70 km (43 mi.) NE of Lisbon. The river is crossed by a viaduct of stone and iron, 1214 m (3983 ft.) long and 22 m (72 ft.) high, built in 1876–81. The railway museum at the station includes royal carriages of 1858 and 1877. An iron bridge attributed to A.G. EIFFEL crosses the Asseca brook. What was probably the only Portuguese canal, built for drainage purposes in the mid-eighteenth century, ran from Santarém to Azambuja, 26 km (16 mi.) SW. It was rebuilt in 1848.

BIBLIOGRAPHY
Specific
Custódio, J. As pontes metálicas da era industrial em Portugal

(Metal bridges of the industrial period in Portugal). In *História*, XLII, 1982.

Santo Tirso, Douro Litoral, Portugal   The buildings remain of the first of the great textile mills of the Ave valley, established at São Tomé de Negrelos, 24 km (15 mi.) NE of Oporto, in 1845. At Pereiras, Monte Cordova, 4 km ($2\frac{1}{2}$ mi.) SE of Santo Tirso, is a preserved water-powered vertical-blade sawmill.

BIBLIOGRAPHY
Specific
Cordeiro, J. M. L. A serra hidráulica de Pereiras, Monte Córdova, Santo Tirso (The water-powered saw at Pereiras, Monte Córdova, Santo Tirso). In *Cadernos de Arqueologia*, 2nd ser., III, 1986.

LOCATION
[M] Abade Pedrosa Museum, Santo Tirso

São João da Madeira, Beira Litoral, Portugal   A traditional hat-making centre, 31 km (19 mi.) S. of Oporto. The first factory making felt hats was founded in 1802, and in 1867 there were fifteen works using hair from different animals. Two felt hat manufacturers continue to operate.

BIBLIOGRAPHY
Specific
Lima, A. and Ribeiro, J. *Indústria de Chapelaria em São João da Madeira*. Câmara Municipal, São João da Madeira, 1987.

São Pedro da Cova, Douro Litoral, Portugal   A coal mine 10 km (6 mi.) E. of Oporto, discovered in 1795, and exploited during 1804–1970, with 20 km ($12\frac{1}{2}$ mi.) of galleries, in an area 3 km × 2 km (2 mi. × $1\frac{1}{4}$ mi.).

BIBLIOGRAPHY
Specific
Almeida, M. M. O transportador aéreo–São Pedro da Cova, Rio Tinto, Porto (The aerial ropeway at São Pedro da Cova, Rio Tinto, Oporto). In *Revista ARPPA*, I, 1987.

LOCATION
[M] Museu Mineiro de São Pedro da Cova (Mining museum of São Pedro da Cova).

sapphire   A blue form of the mineral corundum (*see* RUBY).

Sarajevo, Bosnia-Herzegovina, Yugoslavia   The capital of Bosnia and Herzegovina on the River Miljacka, ruled by the Turks during 1463–1878. Traditional crafts are practised in 'čaršija' (workshops) in the city centre, the buildings of which have been modernized.

Ocevije, 34 km (21 mi.) N., is the centre of a district with many iron forges, as well as traditional mills and tanneries, with an ethnographical branch of the Sarajevo museum.

LOCATION
[M] Zemaljski Muzej, Vojvode Putnika 7, 71000-Sarajevo.

Sarandë, Albania   A town on the coast in the extreme

south of Albania, with two important hydro-electric power stations, Bistrice 2 and Stalin, within 20 km (12 mi.) of Sarandë.

Sardinia (Sardegna), Italy   An island, which was in the possession of the House of Savoy, rulers of PIEDMONT from 1720. The main industries have been mining, metallurgy and the extraction of salt from sea water. Mining activity dates from the Bronze Age, and lead and zinc workings were developed on a large scale in the nineteenth century, some fifteen major mines being established around Iglesias, 56 km (35 mi.) W. of Cagliari. A large dressing plant survives at Nedida, 16 km (10 mi.) SW of Iglesias, a town whose lavish domestic architecture and public buildings reflect industrial wealth.

Argentiera, 35 km (22 mi.) W. of Sassari on the northwest coast, has remains of lead mines dating from c.1890. The future of the workers' village of Miniera Vecchia has become a major issue, the SIAI (see ITALY) urging conservation rather than redevelopment as tourist accommodation.

BIBLIOGRAPHY
Specific
Il luogo del lavoro (Workers' habitations), AA.VV, 1986.
Togni, R. Il complesso minerario dell'Argentiera (The mining complex at Argentiera). In *Archeologia Industriale*, II, 1984.

MICHAEL STRATTON

Sarnia, Ontario, Canada   Sarnia, on Lake Huron, developed as the refinery and later the petrochemical centre for the Ontario oilfields. In 1942 the Polymer Corporation was established on the shore of the St Clair River south of Sarnia to produce synthetic rubber for armaments manufacture. Subsequently other industries using petroleum products became established there. Sarnia became known as 'Chemical Valley', and for many years a picture of its industrial installations appeared on Canadian $10 bills.

Petrolia, 32 km (20 mi.) SE, became Canada's first oil boom town after the discovery of a gushing oil well in the nearby community subsequently called Oil Springs. The well was discovered in 1862 by James Miller Williams (1818–90), who had begun extracting and refining oil in the district in 1858. Petrolia Discovery is a 24 ha (60 ac.) oilfield, operating as it did at the end of the nineteenth century. At Oil Springs the Williams Well, the first to product oil commercially in the area, is an outdoor section of the Oil Museum of Canada, whose other exhibits include nineteenth-century drill rigs.

BIBLIOGRAPHY
General
Ball, 1987.
Specific
Newell, D. Technological innovation and persistence in the Ontario oilfields: some evidence from industrial archaeology. *World Archaeology* XV, 1985.
O'Meara, M. *Oil Springs: the birthplace of the oil industry in North America*, 3rd edn. Oil Springs, Ontario: privately published, 1976.

LOCATIONS
[M] Oil Museum of Canada, Kelly Road, Oil Springs, Ontario.
[S] Petrolia Discovery, Blind Line, Petrolia, Ontario.

CHRIS ANDRAE

sauce   When produced on an industrial scale, a sauce is a vinegar-based preparation for adding flavour to food, typically containing a purée of vegetables or fruit, particularly tomatoes, as well as salt, spices and sugar, usually prepared in vacuum pans. Most well-known sauces owe their fame to inspired marketing. The recipe and the name of HP Sauce, made in Birmingham by Edwin Samson Moore, who established a vinegar factory in 1875, were obtained from a Nottingham shopkeeper in 1901. The company's French labels first appeared in 1917. In England the manufacture of tomato ketchup (also known as 'catchup' and 'catsup' in North America) was concentrated near Boston, Lincolnshire, taking advantage of the tomato-growing areas of the FENS.

BIBLIOGRAPHY
General
Landen and Daniel, 1985.

Sault Ste Marie, Ontario, Canada, and Michigan, United States of America   The twin US and Canadian cities on either side of the St Mary's River. The river, the link between Lakes Huron and Superior, is one of the busiest inland waterways in the world. The first wooden lock on the river was constructed by the North-West Company in 1798 and destroyed in 1812, but a replica stands near its site. The 1650 m (1800 yd.) Sault Canal on the US side, with a staircase pair of locks, was opened in 1855; it was supplemented by the 18.3 m (60 ft.) wide Weitzel lock in 1881. The original staircase was replaced by the 30.5 m (100 ft.) Poe lock in 1896. The MacArthur lock replaced the Weitzel lock in 1943, and the old Poe lock was replaced in 1968. The first lock on the Canadian side of the river was completed in 1895. It is now administered by the Canadian Parks Service, which provides cruises through the lock systems.

Sault Ste Marie is a major lumbering centre, and one of the chief Canadian sources of steel. The Algoma Central Railway offers diesel-hauled tours through the spectacular scenery of the Agawa Canyon.

BIBLIOGRAPHY
General
Hadfield, 1986; Passfield, 1989.

LOCATION
[M] Sault Ste Marie Museum, 107 East Street, Sault Ste Marie, Ontario.

BARRIE TRINDER

sausage   A means of preserving MEAT and of making use of parts of a carcass that would otherwise be inedible, the sausage is a mixture of finely chopped meat, duly seasoned, sometimes cured, and enclosed in a cylindrical skin, originally from the intestines of an animal but

Figure 139 The bascule bridge at Sault Ste Marie, Michigan; at the time it was constructed, in the 1930s, it was the longest in the world.
Jet Lowe, HAER

latterly of a synthetic material. Sausages may be intended for boiling or frying and eating as they are; they may be for containing a paté; or they may be for slicing and eating cold, when they are normally called salami. Almost any kind of meat, offal or animal blood can be used. There are strong regional traditions in most countries, particularly in France, Germany, Hungary and Italy, and over two hundred varieties are recognized in the USA. Industrial-scale concerns making sausages were widespread by 1900. A salami factory is preserved in SZEGED.

BIBLIOGRAPHY
General
Babet-Charton, 1954; Laloue, 1954.

Savery, Thomas (?1650–1715)   A British military engineer and holder of a patent for an engine whose function was defined as 'raising water by fire'. The patent, granted in 1698, was judged to be infringed by the very different

form of steam engine developed by THOMAS NEWCOMEN. In the Savery pump steam from a boiler was condensed by cold water outside the vessel, the resulting vacuum drawing up the water. Savery pumps were labour-intensive, fuel-expensive, and temperamental, but enjoyed a revival in the late eighteenth century. The pulsometer pump, used in the USA from the 1870s for raising noxious liquids, worked on precisely the same principle.

BIBLIOGRAPHY
General
Savery, 1702.

Savignac-Lédrier, Dordogne, France   This nineteenth-century ironworks on the River Auvézère, 50 km (31 mi.) NE of Périgueux, is remarkably well preserved, with a blast furnace 11 m (36 ft.) high, complete with a waste-gas recovery system, two puddling furnaces, a cementation furnace and a stamping mill. There are other well-preserved ironworking sites in the vicinity, at Ans, Les Eyzies, Reilhac, Fayolle and La Mothe Feuillade (Charente), a reminder of Périgord's pre-eminence in the seventeenth and eighteenth centuries as a supplier of cast-iron naval cannon.

BIBLIOGRAPHY
General
Lamy, 1987; Sütterlin, 1981.

sawmill The cutting of logs into LUMBER was traditionally the work of sawyers working in SAW PITS. There were four main branches of the trade in the mid-nineteenth century: the cutting of hardwoods like mahogany into veneers, of softwoods for CARPENTERS to use in building, of staves for COOPERS, and of planks for shipbuilding. From the late eighteenth century hand-sawing was gradually replaced in England by mechanized saw mills. The first horse-powered mills in London began work in the 1790s, and the first steam mill in 1806–7. There were sixty-eight steam mills by 1850, most having two steam engines of about 10 hp, working three frames, each with three vertical saws. The band saw was patented in England in 1808 by William Newberry. The circular saw was invented in the USA by Eli Terry (1772–1852) in 1816. Machines for making tongues and grooves in boards were introduced in London from c.1830, and equipment for making mouldings for cornices and skirtings from the late 1840s. Many companies in Western Europe developed steam mills, some firms growing to considerable size, like that of W. Brügmann & Son, established in Dortmund by 1867, which eight years later had mills at Duisburg, Mannheim, Papenburg and Lübeck. Large drying sheds, often with louvred or open sides, were usually components of such complexes.

The wind-powered sawmill or paltrok, in which three vertical blades are worked by cranks from the main shaft of a windmill, with a winch drawing logs up to them, was a Dutch invention of c.1600. There are examples at LEIDEN and ARNHEM.

In the nineteenth century thousands of water-powered mills were constructed in the USA, Norway, and other timber-rich countries. Most had a reciprocating saw, with a water-powered mechanism propelling logs against it. There are notable preserved examples at Sturbridge (*see* MASSACHUSETTS), and at Denmark, NOVA SCOTIA. There was a great expansion of sawmilling from the 1870s in Scandinavia, particularly along the Baltic coast of northern Sweden.

BIBLIOGRAPHY
General
Apel and Dröge, 1980; Bale and Bale, 1924; *Book of Trades*, 1839; Mayhew, 1850; Sims, 1985.

BARRIE TRINDER

saw pit A saw pit is the traditional means of cutting logs into boards. Logs are placed on rollers spanning a brick-lined pit about 2 m (6 ft.) deep and 1.5 m (4ft. 6 in.) wide.

In the pit stands the pit man, who holds one end of a whip- or sash-saw, the other end being held by the top sawyer or top man who stands on the log. The pit man – a name also applied to the crank of a powered, reciprocating sawmill – pulls down on the cutting stroke, and lubricates the blade. A scaffold 'pit' operated on the same principles but was a timber construction raised from the ground, in contrast to an excavated or a 'sunk' pit. Numbers declined in the nineteenth century with the building of mechanized SAWMILLS. Working examples remain at Avoncroft (*see* BROMSGROVE) and the WEALD AND DOWNLAND MUSEUM.

BIBLIOGRAPHY
General
Book of Trades, 1839; Mayhew, 1850.

saws Handsaws have been used since classical antiquity, and mechanically powered saws, using wind or water power, were used from the late Middle Ages. Steam and later electrically powered sawmills came into operation during the nineteenth century. The principles of manufacture are similar for all saws, from the massive blades of sawmills to small handsaws.

Saws were traditionally made either of wrought iron hardened by hammering, and planished on an anvil to give stiffness and elasticity, or of cast steel. The teeth would be cut with steel cutters and filed in a vice, before the saw was heated in a small reverberatory furnace with some kind of fat, whale oil, rosin, tallow or beef suet, with which it became encrusted. It was next cooked, and the encrustations were then burned off over a coke fire, the blazing liquid giving the requisite temper. It was hammered again, and ground on a large wheel, up to 2 m (7 ft.) in diameter, and then buffed like a piece of CUTLERY or 'glazed' by working against blocks of hardwood. Finally it was 'blocked' (hammered for the final time) by a highly skilled workman, before being cleaned and having the teeth 'set', or slightly bent, alternate teeth to either side. Sawmaking was always a specialist occupation, being concentrated in such centres as SHEFFIELD and SANDVIKEN.

BIBLIOGRAPHY
General
Barraclough, 1981–4; Treatise, n.d.

BARRIE TRINDER

Sázava, South Bohemia, Czechoslovakia The site of a museum of glassmaking technology, established in 1952 as part of the National Technical Museum. It incorporates exhibitions of glassmaking originally created for the national museum.

LOCATION
[M] Museum of Glass Technology, Zamek, Sázava.

Schaffhausen, Schaffhausen, Swizerland A city on the Rhine, near the Rhine Falls, the site in 1887–90 of one of the first aluminium smelters, which drew its power from a hydro-electric installation. The smelting concern subsequently moved to CHIPPIS.

The Georg Fischer Foundation established the Eisenbibliothek (Iron library) in the Paradies monastery, Schaffhausen, in 1948. It holds over 27 000 volumes relating to iron and associated subjects.

In the eighteenth century the brothers H. and J. U. Grubenmann gained an international reputation for wooden bridges. H. Grubenmann built the Rhine bridge at Schaffhausen, with two 50 m (165 ft.) spans in 1755-7, exemplifying the 'Schaffhausen principle', with the arch rising to form the parapet. It has been replaced, but a bridge built by Johann Ulrich Grubenmann (1707-71) in 1766-7 at Oberglatt, 34 km (21 mi.) S., has been restored.

BIBLIOGRAPHY
General
Baldinger, 1987.

LOCATIONS
[M] Allerheiligenmuseum (All Saints' Museum) Klosterplatz 1, 8200 Schaffhausen.
[I] Eisenbibliothek, Klostergut Paradies, CH-8246 Langwiesen, Schaffhausen.

HANS-PETER BÄRTSCHI

Scheele, Carl Wilhelm (1742-86)   A Swedish chemist, apprenticed as a pharmacist in Göteborg in 1757, who from 1770 to 1775 worked at Uppsala and thereafter at Köpling. At much the same time as JOSEPH PRIESTLEY he discovered OXYGEN. He also discovered CHLORINE, and experimented with FLUORSPAR.

BIBLIOGRAPHY
General
Urdang, 1958.

Schinkel, Karl Friedrich (1781-1841)   Schinkel, the creator of modern BERLIN, was employed from 1810 by the Prussian Department of Works where he was chief architect from 1815 and Director of Works from 1831. Although celebrated as an exponent of neo-Classicism, Schinkel also worked in the Gothic style, and utilized cast iron and terracotta as well as traditional materials. He had a profound influence on building activity throughout the Prussian domains at a time when the state was taking a leading role in the promotion of industry. During his visit to England in 1826 he was strongly impressed by such industrial buildings as the cotton mills in Ancoats, MANCHESTER, and the smithy at Woolwich Dockyard, now preserved at IRONBRIDGE.

BIBLIOGRAPHY
General
Schinkel, 1986; Watkin and Mellinghoff, 1987.

Schmalkalden, Thuringia, Germany   The history of ironworking in Schmalkalden in Thuringia dates from the fourteenth century. The Neue Hütte or Happelshütte works at Schmalkalden, 40 km (25 mi.) SE of Eisenach, has been restored as a monument to the industry. In 1835 a charcoal-fired BLAST FURNACE of rubble masonry, about 10 m (33 ft.) high was erected. It was surrounded by a half-timbered building with Classical detailing. Of its early equipment a HOT BLAST stove and a blowing engine have been preserved. In 1870 the furnace was raised about two metres and another, smaller furnace was installed beside it. The restoration undertaken in 1965-80 removed the casing of this later furnace to show the pleasing architectural form of the furnace of 1835 to better advantage. Local industry is illustrated in a museum in the castle.

BIBLIOGRAPHY
General
Schmidt and Theile, 1989; Wagenbreth and Wächtler, 1983.

LOCATION
[M] Schloss Wilhelmsburg, 6080 Schmalkalden.

schnapps   A German term used in other countries, deriving from a word meaning a quick gulp; it applies to almost any beverage with a high percentage of alcohol, whether made from grain or potatoes.
   See also AKVAVIT.

Schönerer, Matthias (1807-81)   The principal railway entrepreneur of the Habsburg Empire. In 1834 he advised Rothschilds, the bankers, that steam locomotives should be used on the Nordbahn. He studied railways in the USA, and returned to Vienna with the steam locomotive *Philadelphia* in 1838, bringing American engineers to train Austrian railway staff. He worked closely with bankers who financed Austrian railways and with the directors of the Südbahn and the Kaiserine Elisabeth Bahn. He was ennobled in 1860, and, unusually for an Austrian entrepreneur, he purchased a feudal estate at Rosenau, Lower Austria.

schooner   One of the principal types of sailing ship used in the Industrial Revolution period, employed in many deep-water and coastal trades. Schooners were built in England and the Netherlands by the early seventeenth century and in colonial North America by the early eighteenth. American shipbuilders, particularly those of Prince Edward Island, profoundly influenced European practice in the nineteenth century. A schooner had at least two masts, each of two parts, and was powered by gaff and boom sails, both receiving the wind on either side according to the direction of the wind relative to the direction in which the ship was sailing. Schooners were economical in labour: a large American schooner of the late nineteenth century could be worked with three or four skilled men and five or six ordinary seamen. British schooner construction reached a peak between 1870 and 1914, most vessels being three-masters with square topsails, constructed in rural yards on the south and west coasts. The schooners developed in the USA from the 1860s had three or four times the cargo capacity of contemporary British vessels, four-masters being built by the late 1870s, the first five-master in 1898 and the first six-master in 1900. Some iron and steel schooners were constructed in this period. Trades in which schooners were used included the carriage of oranges from the

Azores and timber from the Baltic to Britain, slate from North Wales to Germany, salt from Europe to Newfoundland, returning with dried fish, and lumber along both east and west coasts of North America. The larger schooners were obsolete by 1914 but World War I enabled many to survive. Smaller vessels up to 250 tons continued to be built into the 1940s, and some were still trading in the Danish islands and the Aegean in the mid-1950s. Notable surviving schooners include:

- *Ernestina*, New England 1894: wooden, preserved at New Bedford, Mass., USA.
- *C. A. Thayer*, California 1895: 452 tons, wooden, preserved at SAN FRANCISCO, Calif., USA.
- *Shamrock*, 1899: preserved at Cotehele Quay, Cornwall.
- *Kathleen and Mary*, Connah's Quay, 1900: preserved at St Katherine's Dock, LONDON.
- *Alma Doepel*, Bellinger River 1903: 117 tons net, wooden, preserved in Melbourne, Australia.
- *Anna Moller*, 1906: preserved at COPENHAGEN, Denmark.
- *Fulton*, 1915: now a training ship in Norway.

BIBLIOGRAPHY
General
Brouwer, 1985; Greenhill, 1980.

BARRIE TRINDER

Schramberg, Baden-Württemberg, Germany   Schramberg, 80 km (50 mi.) SW of Stuttgart, is a traditional centre of Black Forest watchmaking, as are the twin towns of Villingen and Schwenningen, 20 km (12 mi.) S. Several buildings belonging to the firm founded by Erhard Junghans in 1861, constructed during World War I when the principal production was of mechanical ignition systems for military use, have been preserved on the original site at Geisshalde. An earlier rival firm, the Hamburg-American Clock Factory, founded in 1875, merged with Junghans in 1930 and the large self-contained factory complex in the Gottelbach valley is no longer in use.

LOCATION
[M] Town Museum, 7230 Schramberg.

Schwäbisch Gmünd, Baden-Württemberg, Germany The manufacture of gold- and silverware, an important craft industry in Baden and Württemberg, and originally organized by guilds, was developed on an industrial scale in the mid-nineteenth century when commercial capital was invested in machinery, and methods adopted that involved the division of labour. This transition is documented in the silverware factory in the town of Schwäbisch Gmünd, 54 km (34 mi.) E. of Stuttgart. The factory was erected by Nikolaus Ott in 1845, in the style of a traditional merchant's house, with space for forty workers. The Josef Pauser company took over the firm in 1925, and when it was closed in 1984 nothing was altered.

LOCATION
[M] Municipal Museum, Johannisplatz 3, 7070 Schwäbisch-Gmünd.

Schwaz, Tyrol, Austria   A town on the River Inn, 26 km (16 mi.) NE of Innsbruck. Silver and copper mines here were worked from the fifteenth century. Copper smelters were still in production in the early twentieth century, and provided the roof for the church. Iron ore was also extracted. An imperial tobacco factory employed 1200 women in 1900; and there were majolica works of note.

Scotch whisky   Scotland's most celebrated export and most successful industrial-archaeological attraction is the malt whisky industry of the Highlands, concentrated especially in Speyside. Distilling in the Highlands in the eighteenth century was almost entirely carried on illicitly. In 1822–3 a reduction of duty and heavier penalties combined to foster an increase in licensed distilling. Expansion was steady in the 1870s and 80s, reaching a peak in the 1890s, when twenty-one new distilleries were built in Speyside alone. The first half of the twentieth century was a time of depression, and the unusually-designed distillery built at Tormore in 1958–60 was the first to be built since 1900. About ninety distilleries now exist in the Highlands, including a dozen that have recently ceased production.

The best-preserved have the functions of the various parts clearly discernible from the outside. The older distilleries, such as Edradour and Glenturret, tend to be strung out along burns, whereas the typical distillery of the 1890s is more likely to have a courtyard layout, alongside a railway.

Campbeltown is the exception, a town full of early nineteenth-century distilleries that thrived on sea links to Glasgow but faded when railways opened up the Highlands. Only Springbank Distillery (1828, rebuilt 1889) still operates, but Hazelburn (1837) and Lochend are bonded stores, and Benmohr Distillery is an attractive bus depot.

The process begins at the maltings, a long two- or three-storey block with a single or double kiln. Inside, cast-iron columns carry wooden floors with concrete or stone slabs on the lower floors where the barley germinates and is turned by hand shovels. Only the following distilleries still do floor malting: Balvenie, Benriach, Longmorn, Glendronach, Glengarioch (Highland), Highland Park (Orkney), Springbank (Campbeltown), Bowmore and Laphroaig (Islay). The first pneumatic drum maltings was at Speyburn, a three-storey brick and concrete building of 1897 which ceased work in 1968. The later French system of Saladin maltings is to be seen in Tamdhu, Millburn and Dalmore distilleries. Most malt is now supplied by modern centralized maltings.

Germination is halted in the malt kiln by a peat and anthracite fire, the peat flavouring the malt. The older type of pyramidal kiln terminated in tall, louvred ventilators, such as can be seen at Edradour, Bowmore and Glengarioch. The distinctive pagoda kiln evolved in the

1890s, with a pyramid roof sweeping up into an oriental cap. This is so much a distillery trade mark that it is even repeated over the stillhouse of the Braes of Glenlivet distillery of 1973.

Some distilleries, such as Dalwhinnie, Strathisla and Glentauchers have paired kilns. Others, like Coleburn and Cardhu, have standard malt kilns and separate, smaller, differently shaped barley kilns. The malt is ground and mixed with hot water in mash tuns and fermented in washbacks, before passing to wash stills and then spirit stills. These vessels have limited lifespans but are generally replaced by stills of similar patterns to maintain the distinctive flavour of each distillery. Riveted as opposed to welded stills can only be found in such distilleries as Balblair and Caperdonich that have reopened after periods of closure, and their eventual replacement is inevitable. The following distilleries have coal-fired stills: Strathisla, Glen Grant, Longmorn, Glendronach, Ardmore and Glenfiddich, the last having been re-converted from steam. The vapour is condensed in condensers, but a few distilleries, such as Dalls Dhu, Mortlach and Edradour, retain tapering worm tubs for this purpose.

The renewal of mash tuns and stills has led to the reconstruction of the mash-, wash- and still-houses of most distilleries. Only a few, such as Strathisla, retain nineteenth-century still-houses. Parkmore, Dufftown, has the most complete series of buildings because since 1931 it has served as a store.

Only a small amount of power is required in a distillery. Rummagers in stills at Glen Grant and Longmorn are driven by tiny water wheels turned by the overflows from washbacks. Most late-nineteenth-century distilleries had small steam engines. Those at Longmore, Ardmore and Auchentoshan remain in working order.

The universal feature of every distillery is the bonded store. Whisky must be stored for at least three years, and usually for much longer, under the supervision of Customs and Excise. Extensive ranges of one-, two- and three-storey warehouses occupy much more space than the buildings used for production. The presence of maturing whisky in several distilleries that have recently ceased operation ensures that they will be maintained, and they may reopen if demand increases.

The opening of distilleries to visitors is a recent development, pioneered by Glenfiddich, whose reception centre in the maltings, opened in 1969, has become Scotland's major industrial archaeological attraction, with over 50 000 visitors a year.

The following Highland malt distilleries are open to visitors:

Auchentoshan Old Kilpatrick, Dunbartonshire. Founded in 1825, rebuilt in 1875 and again recently. It uses triple distillation; and contains a preserved steam engine.

Blair Athol Pitlochry, Perthshire. Founded in 1826, but mainly modern.

Cardhu Knockando, Morayshire. Founded in 1884, it has three-storey bonds and maltings, and two kilns.

Dallas Dhu Forres, Morayshire. Built in 1899 and closed in 1983. Preserved as a guardianship monument (*see* SCOTLAND) by Historic Buildings and Monuments. It is quite complete, with worm tub condensers.

Edradour Pitlochry, Perthshire. The smallest distillery in Scotland, founded in 1825. The plant was renewed in 1982. A visitor centre has been housed in the maltings. A unique Morton refrigerator of 1933 may be seen, as may worm tubs.

Glendronach Huntly, Aberdeenshire. Founded in 1826. Floor maltings are still in use; the stills are coal-fired.

Glenfarclas Ballindalloch, Banffshire. Founded in 1837 and rebuilt in 1897, 1960 and 1976; it is mainly modern, with no kilns.

Glenfiddich Dufftown, Banffshire. Built in 1886. The stillhouse was rebuilt in 1974 with small coal-fired stills. There is a bottling hall.

Glengarioch Old Meldrum, Aberdeenshire. Founded in 1797. There are floor maltings, shafting, and waste-heat greenhouses.

Glengoyne Drumgoyne, Stirlingshire. Founded in 1833 and rebuilt in 1966.

Glen Grant Rothes, Morayshire. Founded in 1840 and extended in the 1870s and 1970s. There are four coal- and six gas-fired stills and a rummager water wheel, but no kilns.

The Glenlivet Glenlivet, Banffshire. Founded in 1824, it moved to this site in 1858, and was rebuilt in 1958 and 1972. Gothic bonded stores date from 1880 and 1897; there are no kilns. Dark grains are converted to animal feed in a special plant.

Glenturret Crieff, Perthshire. Founded illicitly in 1775, closed in 1923 and reopened in 1959, this distillery retains early buildings.

Royal Lachnagar Crathie, Aberdeenshire. Built in 1825 and the 1880s and little altered. A chain suspension bridge of 1834 can be seen nearby.

Strathisla Keith, Banffshire. Converted from a brewery in 1786. The Complex includes eighteenth-century buildings and an M-roofed still-house with two coal-fired stills.

Tamdhu Knockando, Morayshire. Founded in 1896 and closed during 1927–47, it was largely rebuilt in 1975. Saladin maltings can be seen. A visitor centre is housed in Knockando railway station.

Tamnavulin-Glenlivet Ballindalloch, Banffshire. Built in 1966. A visitor centre is sited in a small wool-carding mill, with a water wheel.

See also ANGUS; DUMFRIES AND GALLOWAY; EDINBURGH; FALKIRK; LOTHIAN; SCOTTISH ISLANDS.

BIBLIOGRAPHY
General
Barnard, 1887; Moss and Hume, 1985.
Specific
Scotland's Distilleries: a visitor's guide, Famedram, 1984.

MARK WATSON

Scotland

Scotland The northern constituent of the United Kingdom. The crowns of England and Scotland were united by James VI of Scotland (James I of England) in 1603 and the respective parliaments merged in the Act of Union 1707. Thereafter Scottish political history became bound up with that of Great Britain. Provincial adminis-

tration was by burgh and county. Local government reorganization in 1975 combined these into 'Districts' within larger 'Regions'.

Scotland is divided by diagonal geological faults into the Highlands, the Lowlands and the Southern Uplands. The Lowland region, to which urban industrialization was largely confined, focuses on the Clyde, Forth and Tay Rivers, and the strip of land by the North Sea. Scotland is one of the most northerly of the industrialized countries. It shares many characteristics with the Scandinavian and Baltic states besides that of latitude. Trans-Atlantic trade from the seventeenth century led to the growth of the Clyde as a trading artery.

Scotland's famous heavy industries have long histories. Coal was mined near the east coast by Cistercian monks in the twelfth century and was particularly important in the production of salt in LOTHIAN and FIFE in the sixteenth, seventeenth and eighteenth centuries. Scottish iron ore was first smelted with coke at Carron in 1759 (see FALKIRK), and the charcoal blast furnaces (see BONAWE) were superseded. The major ironmaking boom occurred in the Lanarkshire blackband ironstone region (see DAL-MELLINGTON, SUMMERLEE HERITAGE PARK); with the development of HOT BLAST from 1828. Coal production peaked in 1913 and the mines were nationalized in 1947. In the 1990s it is expected that Scotland will retain only one big coal mine, the Longannet complex, 40 km (25 mi.) NW of Edinburgh, apart from twelve small private mines. Scottish steelmaking was centralized from 1956 at Ravenscraig, Motherwell, one of three British integrated iron and steel works, with continuous casting and a hot strip mill.

Shipbuilding and the making of marine and stationary engines, locomotives, and sugar-milling and machine tools were fields in which GLASGOW led the world, but are now reduced in importance. Major engineering firms are also found at ABERDEEN, DUNDEE, EDINBURGH, GREENOCK AND WESTERN RENFREWSHIRE and KIRKCALDY, and in AYRSHIRE and DUNBARTONSHIRE.

After World War I the decline of heavy industry demanded efforts, still pursued, to bring 'sunrise' industries – motorcars, tyres, cash registers – to Scotland. These too have left industrial monuments (see DUMFRIES AND GALLOWAY; DUNBARTONSHIRE; DUNDEE; GLASGOW; PAISLEY). The Board of Trustees for Fisheries and Manufactures similarly set itself in 1727 the task of improving standards in the linen trade, by stamping approved qualities and distributing awards for inventions. Its activities were to be overshadowed by the explosion of Arkwright's cotton spinning mills in the 1780s (see NEW LANARK; PERTHSHIRE). Cotton manufacture concentrated in the early nineteenth century in Renfrewshire (see PAISLEY) and Glasgow, bleaching and dyeing in the east (see ABERDEEN; ANGUS; DUNDEE; DUNFERMLINE; FIFE; INVER-BERVIE; KIRKCALDY; PERTHSHIRE) and Scotland became a springboard for the phenomenal growth of jute manufacture (see ANGUS; DUNDEE) and linoleum (see KIRKCALDY). The paper industry required supplies of linen rags and water (see ABERDEEN; FIFE; LOTHIAN; EDINBURGH). The woollen industry was more diffuse (see ABERDEEN; AYR-SHIRE; BORDERS; CLACKMANNANSHIRE; DUMFRIES; HIGH-LANDS; SCOTTISH ISLANDS), and experienced fewer dramatic ups and downs. A reliance on quality markets has helped surprisingly small units with historic machinery to survive in operation.

The same may be said of the SCOTCH WHISKY industry,

but not of the brewing industry, which once exported great quantities. All but three full-size working breweries are now part of large combines (see CLACKMANNANSHIRE; EDINBURGH; GLASGOW; HIGHLANDS; LOTHIAN; PERTHSHIRE). The industry supports the Scottish Brewing Archive in Heriot-Watt University, Edinburgh. Its collection of artefacts may become the kernel of a museum of brewing in an Edinburgh brewery.

Scotland's major docks are at Leith (Edinburgh), Green-ock, Dundee and Aberdeen. Glasgow is no longer a significant port. Long stretches of canal are limited to two 'remainder waterways', the Forth and Clyde, of 1768–90 (see DUNBARTONSHIRE; FALKIRK; GLASGOW), and the Union from Falkirk to Edinburgh, of 1818–22 (see LOTHIAN); and the Caledonian and Crinan Ship Canals (see HIGHLANDS), still operated and managed by the British Waterways Board. Civil engineering monuments are, thanks to Scotland's topography, spectacular (see FORTH BRIDGES; HIGHLANDS). British Rail operates steam trains between Mallaig and Fort William in summer. The Scottish Railway Preservation Society, based at BO'NESS, also organizes steam excursions. The world's last ocean-going paddle steamer, the Waverley, is based in Glasgow.

Responsibility for the protection of the built heritage has devolved on Historic Buildings and Monuments, Scotland (renamed Historic Scotland in 1991), which is directly responsible to the Secretary of State for Scotland. Some 36 000 buildings are listed, of which perhaps five hundred are industrial, and may not be altered or demolished without planning permission from District Councils and the Secretary of State. Most listed buildings date from the nineteenth century or earlier, but some may only be thirty years old. A re-survey is taking in more recent and industrial buildings. Some structures may be scheduled as Ancient Monuments – examples being the engines belonging to the Scottish Mining Museum, NEW-TONGRANGE, and the glass cone at Alloa (see CLACKMAN-NANSHIRE) – and subject to slightly different legislation. Grants are given for repairs (as to NEW LANARK), and some, like BONAWE Ironworks, are in state care and are known as 'guardianship monuments'.

The recording of buildings – and increasingly of industrial processes – that are under threat is a responsibility of the Royal Commission on the Ancient and Historic Monuments of Scotland (RCAHMS). The records fill the National Monuments Record of Scotland or appear in publications. The two staff of the Scottish Industrial Archaeology Survey, which was founded in 1978, were absorbed into the RCAHMS in 1985, bringing with them their rapid survey techniques. Thematic studies have included wind and water mills and the heavy ceramics industry. The Scottish Industrial Archaeology Panel brings together many of the bodies professionally involved in industrial archaeology.

The Scottish Industrial Heritage Society was formed in 1984 from the Scottish Industrial Archaeology Society and the Scottish Society for the Preservation of Historic Machinery. The Scottish Vernacular Buildings Working Group studies such topics as folk life, traditional construction, agriculture, and food processing.

Scotland has four hundred museums: technology and ethnology are covered nationally by the National Museums of Scotland, based in Edinburgh, but with outstations including BIGGAR gasworks and East Fortune Airfield, Lothian. The local museum structure is at District level. Some small Districts are unable to employ museum professionals. The majority of museums are independently run and small. The biggest employers are some of the independent industrial museums and heritage sites (the Scottish Maritime and Mining Museums at IRVINE and NEWTONGRANGE AND PRESTONGRANGE, BO'NESS, DALMELLINGTON, NEW LANARK, SUMMERLEE, and WANLOCKHEAD AND LEADHILLS). The Scotttish Museums Council (SMC) provides support and training for all of Scotland's museums. A recent project under SMC auspices has been to catalogue industrial collections held in Scottish museums and private collections, revealing surprising gaps, overlaps, and a wealth of unusual collections, of (for example) oil engines.

Scottish census records and Ordnance Survey maps are similar to those in ENGLAND, but many other classes of documentary source material, particularly records of property, are totally different from those south of the border.

See also ABERDEEN; ANGUS; AYRSHIRE; BIGGAR; BONAWE; BO'NESS; BORDERS; CLACKMANNANSHIRE; DALMELLINGTON; DUMFRIES AND GALLOWAY; DUNBARTONSHIRE; DUNDEE; DUNFERMLINE; EDINBURGH; FALKIRK; FIFE; FORTH BRIDGES; GLASGOW; GREENOCK AND WESTERN RENFREWSHIRE; HIGHLANDS; INVERBERVIE; IRVINE; KIRKCALDY; LOTHIAN; NEW LANARK; NEWTONGRANGE AND PRESTONGRANGE; PAISLEY AND EASTERN RENFREWSHIRE; PERTHSHIRE; SCOTCH WHISKY; SCOTTISH ISLANDS; SUMMERLEE HERITAGE PARK; WANLOCKHEAD AND LEADHILLS.

BIBLIOGRAPHY
General
Butt, 1967; Butt *et al.*, 1968; Hay and Stell, 1986; Hume, 1976, 1977; Lindsay, 1968; Smout, 1969, 1986.

LOCATIONS
[I] Historic Scotland, 20 Brandon Street, Edinburgh EH3 5RA.
[I] The Royal Commission on the Ancient and Historical Monuments of Scotland, 52–4 Melville Street, Edinburgh EH3 7HF. (This incorporates the National Monuments Record. Communications to the Scottish Industrial Archaeology Panel may be sent here.)
[I] Scottish Brewing Archive, Heriot-Watt University, Chambers Street, Edinburgh EH1 1HX.
[I] Scottish Industrial Heritage Society, c/o Eric Watt, 129 Fotheringay Road, Glasgow G41 4LG.
[I] Scottish Vernacular Buildings Working Group, c/o Elspeth Dalgleish, 19 York Place, Edinburgh.

MARK WATSON

Scott, George Gilbert (1811–78) One of the most celebrated British architects of the nineteenth century, whose first job after qualification was as superintendent of works during the construction of Hungerford Market, London, in 1831, where he was employed by the great contractor Samuel Morton Peto (1809–89). He then worked for a time with Henry Roberts (d.1876): Roberts who was particularly concerned with working-class housing and who designed the modular cottages exhibited in the Great Exhibition of 1851 (*see* LONDON). Then with his partner W. B. Moffat he developed a practice which specialized in designing WORKHOUSES, of which fifty were built before 1845, among them those at Belper (*see* CROMFORD) and MACCLESFIELD. In 1844 he won a competition to design the church of St Nicholas, HAMBURG, whose gaunt, ruined tower remains in an area devastated by bombing in World War II. He planned the INDUSTRIAL COMMUNITY at Akroyden at HALIFAX, and from 1865 designed the station buildings and hotel at St Pancras, LONDON, his greatest secular achievement.

Sir Giles Gilbert Scott (1880–1960), designer of Battersea Power Station and of the Guinness Brewery, Park Royal, London, was his grandson.

BIBLIOGRAPHY
General
Clark, 1928.

BARRIE TRINDER

Scottish Islands, Scotland The islands comprise Orkney and Shetland, the Inner and Outer Hebrides, and the Islands in the Clyde Estuary.

Meal milling was performed in hundreds of SPLASH MILLS whose sites are readily found dotting streams, particularly in Uig, Lewis and Shetland. Dounby Click Mill, Orkney, is a guardianship monument (*see* SCOTLAND). Landlords seeking to make improvements encouraged islanders to bring their meal to larger nineteenth-century mills, like the disused examples on Mull (Benessand, Kilmore) and Colonsay. The thatched Glendale Mill on Skye has been restored. Large mills on Orkney include the complex of grain and threshing mills at Boardhouse, where one of 1873 still works. The exposed landscape of Orkney was well situated for windmills, wind-pumps and wind-powered threshing machines.

Mineral salt pans at Ascog, Bute, of c.1650, and Cock of Arran, c.1710, are the best preserved in Scotland, although economically far less significant than those of the Forth. Each had pans in their rounded seaward gables. Alkali was extracted by burning KELP on most of the Hebrides. Slate quarries and quarrymen's housing can be seen on Belnahua and Easdale. Marble was quarried on Iona, where there is an abandoned gas engine and a frame saw of 1907; limestone at Lismore (where there are extensive kilns) and elsewhere; and millstones at Port Ellen on Islay and Griburn on Mull. A roofless beam-engine house remains from the Mulreesh leadmines, Islay. Ironstone mines at Raasay were developed from 1913–14 by William Baird & Co., and worked by prisoners of war. The pier and the bases of four calcining kilns for ore are of reinforced concrete.

Scotland's second cotton mill was erected at Rothesay, Bute, in 1779, to be followed by four others, driven from 1821 by canals designed by Robert Thom. One mill is now weaving furniture fabrics. The water-powered woollen mill at Bridgend, Islay, is a remarkably well-preserved, integrated mill, numbering a near-unique piecing machine, a SLUBBING BILLY and two SPINNING JENNIES amongst its *in situ* machinery. The famous Harris tweed came to the island in the late nineteenth century and is woven on treadle-powered Hattersley looms.

Each of Islay's malt whisky distilleries has its own pier for sea transport. The renowed peatiness of the whisky is achieved in part by floor malting, carried on at distilleries like Bowmore (1779), Lagavulin (1816) and Laphroaig (1820) to a greater extent than anywhere else in Scotland. Bruichladdich of 1881 is of precast concrete. Bowmore, Lagavulin and Bunnahabhainn receive visitors. Ledaig Distillery, Mull, opened in 1823, closed as a result of prohibition in the USA in 1924, and reopened in 1972. It has a big four-storey BOND. Talisker, Skye, is much rebuilt. In Kirkwall, Orkney, Highland Park Distillery still uses floor maltings, and Scapa Distillery has a water wheel.

There are short lighthouse towers of 1757 and 1793 at Little Cumbrae. The Stevenson (*see* STEVENSON, ROBERT) family constructed several for the Commissioners of Northern Lighthouses, including Rinns of Islay (1825), Lismore (1833) and the Skerryvore, Tiree (1838–44). Keepers' houses in the Egyptian style and bridges of cast iron accompanied some of these.

The Commissioners for Highland Roads and Bridges secured the services of THOMAS TELFORD in the early nineteenth century to organize the road network in Skye, which remains much the same today, and to construct a prodigious number of bridges, harbours and ferry piers. A cast-iron bridge between Bowmore and Laggan Bay, Islay, had stood 'for several years' before 1811.

BIBLIOGRAPHY
General
Hay and Stell, 1986; Hume, 1977.
Specific
Viner, D. J. The Marble Quarry, Iona, Inner Hebrides. In *IAR*, I, 1976.
Whatley, C. A. An early 18th century Scottish saltwork: Arran, c.1710–35. In *IAR*, VI, 1982.

MARK WATSON

screw propulsion Experiments in working ships by propellers were carried out in Britain in 1836–7 by Francis Pettit Smith (1808–74) and John Ericsson (1803–99). Ericsson took out a patent in 1836, and emigrated to the USA, where he designed a screw-propelled warship in 1842. The first practical screw-propelled ship was the *Archimedes*, a schooner built in 1838 by Henry Wimhurst which circumnavigated Britain in 1840. The use of screw propulsion on the SS *Great Britain* (*see* BRISTOL) in 1843 showed its potential, and it was employed on the Cunard liners *Alpes* and *Andes* in 1852. By the 1870s it was the normal means of propelling an ocean-going steamship. Surviving examples of early screw-propelled vessels include the *Sir Walter Scott* of 1899, which works on Loch Katrine, Scotland; the *Segwun* of 1887, which works on Lake Muskoka, Ontario; and the *Keewatin*, shipped in

prefabricated form from Glasgow to the Great Lakes in 1907, and preserved at Douglas, Michigan. John Stevens's double-screw steam engine and boiler of 1804 stand preserved in the National Museum of American History, WASHINGTON DC.

BIBLIOGRAPHY
General
Baker, 1965.

BARRIE TRINDER

scutching A stage in the preparation of FLAX, scutching (or swingling) continues the BRAKING process, as the flax is struck with a flat wooden blade to scrape away gummy residue and hard pieces of the stalk. In hand processing, the scutching knife is a single wooden blade used against an upright support for the flax. Mechanical scutchers operate in combination with the brakers, and employ metal blades to beat and scrape away the woody portions of the flax.

scythe A scythe is a tool used in mowing, with a curved blade, traditionally of wrought iron with a steel edge, joined at right angles to a long pole, to which a handle called a cog is attached. A scythe is made by more than thirty hammering, cooling and grinding processes, the latter often on wheels up to 2.5 m (8 ft.) in diameter. Specialist manufactures in most countries served national markets, important centres being Norton and Eckington near SHEFFIELD, Bellbroughton, Worcestershire, and Mells, Somerset, in England; Styria (*see* PEGGAU), in Austria; and Leverkusen, in Germany. Sickles, reaping hooks and hay knives were made by similar methods. Swedish-made acid BESSEMER steel was exceptionally well suited for scythemaking and was exported in great quantities to Britain for this purpose.

See also STICKLEPATH.

BIBLIOGRAPHY
General
Barraclough, 1981–4; Rees, 1802–20; Sylvester, 1972.

sealing The seal (*Phoca vitulina*) is a gregarious marine mammal, hunted for its hair, oil, and fur. The Newfoundland sealing trade, concerned chiefly with the harp seal, was established early in the nineteenth century and employed up to 10000 people by 1900. Another important area was between Spitzbergen and Jan Mayen island, where large-scale hunting began in 1840. Sealers used small boats to locate seals on ice floes. Young seals were killed, and the skins with the layers of fat beneath removed and collected. Seal oil was used for the same purposes as TRAIN OIL. Fur seals do not breed in the North Atlantic and were sought off Alaska and the southern coasts of Africa and South America. London was the centre of the seal fur trade.

Aarvak, a sealer of 1912, is preserved at Hareid, Norway.

BIBLIOGRAPHY
General
Brouwer, 1985; Busch, 1988.

LOCATION
[I] Hareid Historical Society, 6060 Haried, Norway.

sea transport The sea has been the prime means of international trade throughout the industrial period, and in 1950 remained the principal means of intercontinental passenger transport, the swing to air travel dating from the late 1950s.

For the various types of vessel employed, *see* BARGE; CLIPPER; DREDGER; FERRY; LIBERTY SHIP; LIGHTER; LINER; OIL TANKER; PACKET BOAT; TENDER; TRAMP STEAMER; TUG. For the various forms of construction and propulsion of ships, *see* IRON SHIP; MOTOR VESSEL; PADDLE STEAMER; SAILING SHIP; SCHOONER; SCREW PROPULSION; STEAMSHIP; TURBINE PROPULSION. For installations on land that relate to sea transport, *see* BEACON; BREAKWATER; CRANE; CUSTOMS HOUSE; DOCK; HYDRAULIC POWER; LIGHTHOUSE; PIER; PORT; VICTUALLING YARD; WAREHOUSE; WHARF. *See also* BUOY; CABLE; FISHING; LIGHTHOUSE; LIGHTSHIP; SEALING; TIME-BALL STATION; WHALING.

Before 1854 a ship's capacity was based on the number of TUNS of wine that could be carried. From 1854 a system devised by George Moorsom was used, calculating the actual internal capacity of a ship. Gross tonnage is normally quoted in this volume. Net tonnage is the gross tonnage less an allowance for machinery, crew's quarters and so on. Deadweight tonnage, usually quoted in wartime, is the difference between the full-load displacement when floating at an assigned water line and the ship's light weight.

Brouwer (1985) has provided the standard work of reference on preserved vessels of all kinds.

BIBLIOGRAPHY
General
Baker, 1965; Brouwer, 1985; Davis, 1962; Fayle, 1933; Lindsay, 1874–6.

BARRIE TRINDER

Sebeş, Alba, Romania A hydro-electric power plant of 1906, preserved with the aqueduct that conveyed water to the turbines: the aqueduct is 1783 m (5850 ft.) long, of which 930 m (3050 ft.) is carried on concrete arches. The aqueduct is protected as a technical monument. It supplied power for the papermill at Petreşti of 1854, which was the first modern paper-making plant in Transylvania.

BIBLIOGRAPHY
General
Wollmann, V. Romania. In Georgeacopol-Winischhofer *et al.*, 1987.

Secessionist A Viennese variation of ART NOUVEAU, which takes its name from a small building built in 1897–8 by Joseph Maria Olbrich (1867–1908) as headquarters for a group of young progressive artists including Joseph Hoffmann (1870–1956) reacting against the Classical styles that persisted in Viennese design.

Sedan, Ardennes, France The Dijonval cloth manufacture at Sedan was the first created in France for the production of high-quality broadcloth made from the wool of Spanish merino sheep, and intended to compete with imported Dutch cloths. It was founded in 1646 at Sedan, not long after this principality had become a part of France. Until the early nineteenth century the manufactury produced high-quality cloths, then more ordinary fabrics up to the closure of the works around 1960. Nineteenth-century mechanization and extension had little effect on the buildings erected a century earlier. Despite their apparent architectural unity, however, these buildings date from several different periods. The main building with its fifteen bays, its three storeys and its central block surmounted by a pediment and bell-cupola, dates from 1755. The left wing was constructed in 1788, but the twin right wing was destroyed by a fire at the end of the eighteenth century, and rebuilt to exactly the same plans in the early nineteenth century.

Several production processes, the preparation of the wool, dyeing and fulling, were effected outside the manufactory. There are some much altered remains of the fulling mill about 500 m (550 yd.) from the factory, at Rivage, on a branch of the Meuse; whilst an old scouring basin still survives at Fraîche-Eau, Floing, 3 km (2 mi.) NE of Sedan.

Within the town of Sedan are many other vestiges of woollen cloth factories, of which there were no fewer than thirty in the late eighteenth century. The buildings of the old Cunin-Gridaine factory in rue Bayle, which date from the first part of the nineteenth century, are still visible, as is part of the Manufacture des Gros Chiens in rue de Ménil, opened in 1688 in the former residence of an ironmaster from Liège, which was built c.1629. This manufactory also occupied the buildings of the former military academy, the Académie des Exercices of 1607, which also still stand. At Bazeilles, near Sedan, the buildings of an old fulling mill, probably dating from 1764, are particularly well preserved.

The Dijonval Manufacture has been acquired by the municipality and the buildings, entirely renovated, now have statutory protection (*see* figure 140).

BIBLIOGRAPHY
General
Belhoste *et al.*, 1984.

JEAN-FRANÇOIS BELHOSTE

Segovia, Segovia, Castile, Spain Segovia, 92 km (57 mi.) NW of Madrid, is one of Spain's most attractive historic cities. Its Roman aqueduct, a mortarless granite structure of 165 arches, rising 29 m (96 ft.) above the Plaza del Azoguejo, still carries water, and is a UNESCO WORLD HERITAGE SITE.

The Royal San Ildefonso Glassworks at La Granja, 10 km (6 mi.) SE, near the eighteenth-century palace of San

Figure 140   The central building of the Dijonval cloth manufactory at Sedan, built in 1755 and housing the preparation and finishing processes; with its pediment and bell cupola, it is the most architecturally ornate part of the complex.
J. C. Stamm, Inventaire général

Ildefonso which is known as Little Versailles, is a complex of major importance in the development of industrial architecture. It dates from 1772 and was designed by Juan de Villanueva (1739–1811), architect of the Prado museum in Madrid. The building is in the neo-Classical style with a central nave topped with two domes in the style of a basilica. The building is being restored to accommodate the National Glass Centre.

MERCEDES LOPEZ

Seia, Beira Alta, Portugal   A town east of the Estrela mountains, 110 km (68 mi.) SE of Oporto, with many old textile factories, some now in ruins. At Valezim, 8 km (5 mi.) S., are two water mills with undershot wheels. There

are two early hydro-electric power stations in the region, at Senhora do Desterro, with buildings dating from 1909, and Sabugueiro, 20 km (12 mi.) E. of Seia, the highest in Portugal, which still has plant from the early twentieth century.

Seixal, Estremadura, Portugal   The centre of a heavily industrialized region at the mouth of the River Tagus (Tejo), 14 km (9 mi.) S. of Lisbon, with archaeological monuments of major importance. The gunpowder works of Vale de Milhaços still operates, and employs a steam engine. The woollen factory of Arrentela of 1855 was equipped with one of the first steam engines made in Portugal, by the Colares company. The glass bottle factory

Figure 141 A Sentinel S4 steam lorry, built in Shrewsbury in May 1937, two months before the Sentinel company ceased to manufacture steam lorries (although a batch was constructed for Argentina in 1950); this vehicle worked for the Castle Firebrick Co. of Buckley, Flintshire, until 1957, and was subsequently employed by Early Transport of Wareham, Dorset. It is now ' in private ownership in Shropshire.
Barrie Trinder

of Amora, of 1888–1930, was the first industrial site in Portugal to be excavated. A group of ten tide mills is being restored by the council, and that at Corroios, dating from 1403, is already open to the public. The mills form part of the county ECOMUSÉE, which has already restored a yard where wooden ships were built, together with several traditional vessels.

BIBLIOGRAPHY
Specific
Nabais, A. J. *Moínhos de Maré: património industrial* (Moínhos de Maré: industrial heritage). Seixal: Câmara Municipal, 1986.
Seixal–Ecomuseu (Seixal: écomusée). Seixal: Câmara Municipal. 1987.

LOCATION
[M] Seixal-Ecomuseu, Câmara Municipal, Seixal.

semaphore One of the first military visual telegraph systems was established along the French coasts in 1803. SIGNAL TOWERS fitted with central masts used three movable arms to send up to three hundred coded phrases. Britain (1815–49), the USA (1816, 1821), Prussia (1832–52) and Russia (1834–54) adopted similar systems. 'Semaphore' now usually implies hand-flag or batten signalling, or RAILWAY SIGNALS.
See also SIGNAL BOX; SIGNAL TOWER.

BIBLIOGRAPHY
General
Wilson, 1976.

semi-detached house A term used from the mid-nineteenth century to refer to pairs of houses joined together in distinct blocks, a form of building used from *c.*1800, but particularly popular in the suburbs built in Britain between 1919 and 1939, when over four million dwellings were added to the housing stock. For long disparaged and unfashionable, semi-detached suburban houses have recently been reassessed with sympathy.

BIBLIOGRAPHY
General
Jackson, 1973; Oliver *et al.*, 1981.

Semmering, Lower Austria and Styria, Austria A pass between the valleys of the Rivers Schwarza and Mürz; the boundary between the provinces of Lower Austria and Styria. The road on the slope above Gloggnitz was built in 1842 with a maximum grade of 1 in 7. Gloggnitz–Mürzzuschlag is a 58 km (33 mi.) section of the Südbahn (the railway from Vienna to Trieste): built in 1848–54, with its summit at 897 m (2943 ft.), it was the first of the great European mountain railways. There is a monument on the rocks near Semmering station to the designer, Karl Ritter von Ghega (1802–60). The line has sixteen tunnels, the longest being 6.036 km (3 mi. 63 yd.); and sixteen viaducts, that over the Kalte Rinne being 184 m (201 yd.) long and 46 m (151 ft.) high. The sites of many historic ironworks can be seen in Mürztal, below Mürzzuschlag. There is a huge hotel, the Südbahnhotel-Semmering, on the slope of Kartnerhogel, 2 km ($1\frac{1}{2}$ mi.) N. of Semmering station.

BIBLIOGRAPHY
General
Schneider, 1963.

Sentinel The Sentinel company, based in SHREWSBURY from 1915, were makers of STEAM LORRIES, and from the 1920s built shunting locomotives up to 200 hp and steam-power units for railcars, with vertical boilers, small high-pressure cylinders with poppet valves, and chain drive to wheels. Over 120 steam lorries are preserved, together with a railcar in Spain and more than 20 locomotives in Britain, including examples at IRONBRIDGE, Quainton (see CHILTERN HILLS) and LEEDS.

BIBLIOGRAPHY
General
Hughes and Thomas, 1973; Thomas and Thomas, 1987; Westwood, 1983.
Specific
Sentinel Patent Locomotives, Sentinel Wagon Works, Shrewsbury, 1931. Reprint EP, Wakefield, 1974.

serpentine The Lizard Peninsula, CORNWALL, England is largely composed of metamorphic rocks, among which is serpentine, which ranges in colour from dark green to greyish brown, and is often streaked and blotched with red iron oxide and such white minerals as talc. The rock was used in medieval churches, and was being worked commercially by the 1820s. Queen Victoria ordered a table and other pieces for her home at Osborn in the Isle of Wight in 1846. The London Penzance Serpentine Company was formed in 1851 with a works at Poltesco, Careleon Cove. The proprietors of the Wherrytown Works, Penzance, formed in 1848, exhibited at the Great Exhibition in 1851. The industry produced candelabra, tables, chimney pieces, pulpits, shop fronts and monuments, as well as increasing numbers of souvenirs for tourists, model crosses, model lighthouses (based on the nearby Lizard Lighthouse), jewellery, vases, inkstands and barometers. Most of this ware was turned on a lathe and highly polished. The stone does not weather well in the British climate and its use for external decoration was limited. Factory production ceased although some workshops still operate at Lizard Point. This was a localized industry comparable with Whitby jet and Blue John wares, which flourished under Queen Victoria's patronage. Examples of early serpentine objects, in deep red, are now highly sought after. The ruins of the Poltesco Factory, now on National Trust property, include a water wheel pit, a sawing floor, and the remains of the engine house. Serpentine has also been extracted in the USA, where it clads churches and many private homes of the nineteenth century along the Atlantic seaboard of the USA, but is subject to severe flaking in wet weather.

STUART B. SMITH

service industries Those sectors of an industrial economy not directly related to production. The most substantial are COMMUNICATIONS and TRANSPORT. Buildings relating to services include those concerned with administration (see COUNTING HOUSE; OFFICE BLOCK; SKYSCRAPER) and storage (see WAREHOUSE), although such structures may be components of manufacturing complexes. Other service sectors include RETAILING; entertainment (see BATHHOUSE; CINEMA; CIRCUS; FAIRGROUND; MUSIC HALL; PARK; PIER; SPA; THEATRE); the accommodation of travellers (see BOARDING HOUSE; CARAVANSERAI; HOLIDAY

CAMP; HOTEL; INN; LODGING HOUSE; MOTEL; PUBLIC HOUSE; RAILWAY HOTEL); and the provision of cleaning services (see DRY CLEANING; LAUNDRY). Buildings concerned with government, education, religion and accommodation of the sick, the criminal and the poor (see BATHHOUSE; HOSPITAL; INDUSTRIAL SCHOOL; INSTITUTE; PRISON; SPA; WORKHOUSE), are included in this book where their roles in industrial communities are significant.

BARRIE TRINDER

service station A service station is a roadside establishment where, amongst other facilities, fuel is available for private cars. Motor spirit was first distributed through ironmongers and similar trades, in Britain in two-gallon rectangular cans which could be fitted to the running boards of motorcars. Sylvanus F. Bowser, in St Louis, who developed a hand pump for water in 1885 from 1905 used it, fitted with a glass gauge and hose hook-up, to fill cars with fuel. The first service station for motor spirit was opened in Detroit in 1911. The first kerbside pump in England was supposedly installed in Shrewsbury in 1914, and the US Army brought many more to Europe during World War I. Electrically-driven pumps were introduced from the 1930s. The first motor tanker to be used in Britain for delivering fuel in bulk, rather than in drums, began work in 1919.

In most countries many service stations of the 1920s were adapted from existing buildings, and many old-style kerbside pumps remained in use in 1950. The first purpose-built service station in Britain was opened by the Automobile Association at Aldermaston, Berkshire, in 1919. The term 'filling station' was first used in the USA, c.1921. By the 1930s most service stations in North America and continental Europe sold fuel from one company only, and consequently adopted the house styles of the oil companies. In Britain many sold fuel from several sources, but were nevertheless dominated by company images. In the 1920s and 30s increasing numbers of purpose-designed service stations were constructed, often on corner sites – in Europe they were in three principal styles: the 'olde worlde cottage', the neo-classical and the international modern. In the USA the most bizarre architectural fantasies were realized in service stations – giant oil cans, crinolined ladies and a colossal giraffe, for example. From the 1940s it became normal practice to group pumps on 'islands' in pairs. Concrete, made oilproof by additives, became the standard surface. Many service stations came to incorporate repair shops and showrooms (see GARAGE; MOTORCAR SHOWROOM).

BIBLIOGRAPHY
General
Anderson, 1984; Boorstin, 1973; BP, 1958; Burgess-Wise, 1981; Liveing, 1959; Munce, 1960; Richardson, 1977; Segers, 1984; Vehlefeld and Jacques, 1956; Vieyra, 1979; Ware, 1976.
Specific
Garage and Motor Agent, December 1922.
Ricciati, J. W. *Garages and Service Stations*. Hainlin, 1952.

BARRIE TRINDER

Setesdal, Aust and Vest Agder, Norway   A valley extending 230 km (140 mi.) N. of Kristiansand, which includes the 36 km (22 mi.) Byglandsfjord. The railway, 58 km (36 mi.) of 1067 mm (3 ft. 6in.) gauge from Kristiansand to the fjord, was closed in 1962, but 9 km (6 mi.) of it, from Grovane, 18 km (12 mi.) NE of Kristiansand, is preserved by Setesdalsbanen Hobby Club, with the support of local authorities. Locomotives include a Thunes 2–4–2T of 1902 built for the line, 2 Dubs 2–6–2Ts of 1895, and an identical locomotive by Thunes of 1902. The Steinsfoss Tonmerrenhein Vennesla, 12 km (8 mi.) N. of Kristiansand, is an aqueduct formerly used for floating timber across the valley. At Evje, south of the fjord, are remains of the nickel works that operated during 1872–1946, feldspar quarries, and the preserved Fennefoss Paper Mill.

LOCATION
[S] Setesdalsbanen, Grovane, 4700 Venesla.

setts   Regularly shaped blocks, typically of stone or wood, making up a road surface, usually in a city, and particularly associated with TRAMWAY systems. GRANITE setts from ABERDEEN costing £920 a mile for an 18 ft. (5.5 m) width, were in use in London in the early nineteenth century. BASALT quarried in the CLEE HILLS, and stone from Mountsorrel, Leicestershire, and Penmaenmawr, North Wales, were widely used for setts. Wooden blocks bound with pitch, first employed in Russia, then in Berlin, New York and Philadelphia, were laid in London in 1838, and widely used thereafter. Rubber setts were used in OXFORD in the 1930s and 40s.

BIBLIOGRAPHY
General
Whitehead, 1975.

Setúbal, Estremadura, Portugal   A commercial and fishing harbour, 32 km (20 mi.) SE of Lisbon, once the most important canning centre in Portugal. The canning industry is featured with other industries in the Museum of Work. The railway terminus, at the end of a branch of the former South & South-East Railway, dates from 1861. The public market of 1876 has an elegant iron frame. There are also interesting workers' houses. The Sado salt works, extending some 40 km (25 mi.) along the River Sado, comprises some 380 evaporating pans.

BIBLIOGRAPHY
Specific
Abreu, M. *A Indústria Conserveira em Setúbal* (Industrial conservation in Setúbal). Setúbal: Museu do Trabalho/Câmara Municipal, 1988.

LOCATIONS
[M] Archaeological and Ethnographical Museum, Av. Luisa Todi, 162, Setúbal.
[M] Museu do Trabalho (Museum of Work), Câmara Municipal, Setúbal.

Severn Tunnel, Avon, England, and Gwent, Wales   One of the outstanding feats of railway engineering, con-structed between Pilning, 14 km (9 mi.) N. of Bristol, and Sudbrook, 7 km (4 mi.) SW of Chepstow, for GWR by T. A. Walker from 1879, after trial headings commenced in 1873. The headings met in 1884, and the first trains passed through in January 1886. The tunnel was drained by six Cornish engines with 70 in. (178 cm) cylinders in the engine house at Sudbrook, now destroyed. The tunnel is still heavily used.

BIBLIOGRAPHY
General
MacDermot, 1927.

Seville (Sevilla), Sevilla, Andalusia, Spain   The chief city of Andalusia in southern Spain, and the centre of a region notable for its copper, lead, iron ore and coal deposits, as well as for the production of sherry. Seville for long enjoyed a monopoly of trade with Spain's American colonies. The Archives of the Indies, containing the official documents relating to the colonies, stands near the cathedral, while many buildings remain in one of the city's parks from the Spanish-American exhibition of 1929.

Seville's outstanding industrial monument is the tobacco factory of 1769, a vast building in the neo-Classical style, whose modular plan anticipated the English textile factories of the Industrial Revolution. It has been adapted as a university hall of residence.

The railway station in the Plaza de Armas was designed in 1899–1901 by Santos Silva y N. Suárez. It is a synthesis of French and Moorish styles, with polychromatic ornamentation derived from that of the Alhambra, the great Moorish palace at Granada.

Sherry is made from grapes grown across the 95 km (60 mi.) of countryside between Seville and Jerez da la Frontera, where the principal 'bodegas', open-fronted warehouses are situated.

BIBLIOGRAPHY
General
Civera, 1988.

EUSEBI CASANELLES

sewage disposal   Sewage is the liquid conveyed in SEWERS, comprising excreta, household waste, industrial waste or storm water. 'Separate systems' are those in which surface water and domestic sewage are separated. Until the nineteenth century human excrement accumulated in earth closets or middens and was removed in the hours of darkness by 'night soil men' and used as fertilizer. Dr John Snow in London in the 1850s established that cholera, which had struck Western Europe in successive epidemics since *c*.1830, was caused by drinking polluted water. Sanitary reformers, among them Edwin Chadwick (1800–90), advocated water-carriage for sewage, using the water-closet, reinvented by JOSEPH BRAMAH, and pipes glazed on the inside. Most major cities had systems of sewerage – networks of pipes – before 1900. Initially they discharged directly into watercourses or the sea, but later to sewage TREATMENT WORKS. There were only ten municipal systems in the USA in 1860, but over two hundred in 1880.

See also PUMPING STATION.

BIBLIOGRAPHY
General
Adams, 1930; Boorstin, 1973; Escritt, 1939; Föhl and Hamm, 1985; Reid, 1908; Steel, 1953; Wohl, 1983.

JEFF COX

sewer A pipe or conduit for the conveyance of sewage, now normally closed in, although open sewers were commonplace in the nineteenth century and earlier. A sewer is laid on a gradient to ensure an adequate rate of flow.

Sewers before the nineteenth century were usually large masonry structures, often streams that had been arched over. There were 133 km (83 mi.) of such sewers in London in 1841, used almost entirely for rainwater.

From the 1850s as SEWAGE DISPOSAL systems for foul household effluent were developed, tubular glazed earthenware pipes were commonly used for smaller sewers, while large main sewers were of cast iron, wrought iron or brick, and later of concrete. Circular pipes aid the velocity with a small rate of flow and are most resistant to the pressure of the surrounding earth, but egg-shaped sewers were common in the nineteenth century and earlier. It is usual to provide manholes giving access to inspection chambers wherever sewers change direction, gradient or size.

Sir Joseph Bazalgette (1819–91) was responsible for the construction of the Northern and Southern Outfall Sewers in London in 1858–65. These were interception sewers, which ran west–east, cutting across the existing systems which ran north–south or south–north into the Thames.

'Sewerage' is a collective term meaning a system of sewers.

BIBLIOGRAPHY
General
Babbitt, 1940; Cohn, 1966; Escritt, 1939; Steel, 1953; Wohl, 1983.

BARRIE TRINDER

sewing machine The first effective tailor's sewing machine was introduced in France by Bartholemy Thimonnier in 1830, and used for the production of MILITARY UNIFORMS. Many inventors subsequently contributed to the development of machines used in clothing manufacture and in shoemaking. Walter Hunt in New York in 1832 developed the principle of moving a needle by means of a vibrating arm in conjunction with a shuttle which carried a second thread to make an interlocking stitch. The sewing machine was further developed by Elias Howe (1819–67), who took out a patent in 1846, and by Isaac Merit Singer (1811–75). Legal disputes between the two culminated in the formation in 1856 of the Sewing Machine Corporation, in which the resources of the patent owners were pooled. Mass production began in the USA, where some 700 000 per year were being made by the early 1870s, and the Singer Corporation subsequently established plants in Europe, notably at Clydebank (*see* DUNBARTONSHIRE), where the works opened in 1884 was claimed to be the largest in the world. The sewing machine was one of the first mass-produced consumer durables. It transformed the manufacture of shoes, and stimulated the growth of CLOTHING FACTORIES. The most important collection of sewing machines is in the Smithsonian Institution, WASHINGTON DC.

BIBLIOGRAPHY
General
Cooper, 1976.

Specific
Lewton, F. L. The servant in the house: a brief history of the sewing machine. In *Smithsonian Institution Annual Report 1929*, 1930.

BARRIE TRINDER

Seydhisfjördhur, Iceland A town 380 km (240 mi.) NE of Reykjavik, site of the East Iceland Technical Museum. Fjardarselsvirkjun, the first hydro-electric power station in Iceland, dating from 1913, is designated part of the museum. The head of water is approximately 50 m (160 ft.). The original equipment – a turbine by J. M. Woeth of Württemberg, and a generator by Siemens & Schuckert – is still used when demand is heavy. Additional machinery includes a turbine by R. T. Gilkes & Gordon of Kendal, and a generator installed in 1947.

shaking table A means of separating finely-crushed particles of metallic ores, particularly those of tin, from waste. On an inclined surface, typically vibrated by water power, the heavier ore particles would shake downwards, leaving the waste at the top.

shale oil Oil was extracted from bituminous shales in many countries, following the discovery, *c.*1850 by Dr James Young (1811–83), that oil could be obtained from Scottish shale. Young began the sale of KEROSINE in 1856. Shale was crushed, and heated externally in retorts into which steam was introduced, producing oil, ammoniacal liquors and gas which was recovered and used for further heating. The shale oil was distilled by processes similar to those employed for crude oil (*see* OIL REFINERY). Dumps of spent shale, called 'bings', are a feature of the landscape of the south bank of the Forth (*see* LOTHIAN). Shale oil was also extracted in Dorset and, with less success, in Norfolk.

BIBLIOGRAPHY
General
Morgan and Pratt, 1938.

Shannon, Ireland The longest river in the British Isles, draining much of the centre and west of Ireland. It rises south of Enniskillen, and flows south through a succession of loughs to a broad estuary west of LIMERICK. Work to make the Shannon navigable began in 1755 but it was only perfected in first half of the nineteenth century, after

Figure 142   The installation of a rotor and generator in Shawinigan 2A power station, Quebec, in 1911
Hydro-Québec

the GRAND CANAL Company, which relied on it for access to Limerick and Athlone, took responsibility for the section from Lough Derg to Lough Ree. Some sections of parallel canal were built, but abandoned when the main navigation works were carried out in the 1840s. Traces remain at Athlone and Banagher. Steamers were introduced in 1825–6 by John Grantham (1775–1833), who is commemorated in Killaloe Cathedral. The head of the present navigation is at Battlebridge, but Lough Allen above it is also navigable. Navigation of the lower reaches was altered by construction of the power station at Ardnacrusha (*see* LIMERICK).

BIBLIOGRAPHY
General
Delany, 1966, 1973, 1986.

shaping machine or **shaper**   A machine that shapes flat or contoured surfaces by means of a cutter fed across the face of the secured work, which is indexed beneath the cutter on the return stroke.

BIBLIOGRAPHY
General
Rolt, 1986; Steeds, 1969.

Shardlow, Derbyshire, England   An inland port on the Trent & Mersey Canal (completed in 1777), 2 km ($1\frac{1}{2}$ mi.) W. of the junction with the Trent at Derwentmouth, where the London–Manchester road crossed the canal. Goods were transshipped between river and canal craft. Shardlow has many late eighteenth-century warehouses, several converted to cornmills after the decline of canal sundries traffic in the nineteenth century. It is now a centre for pleasure cruising. Features include warehouses for malt, iron and salt, a boatyard, inns, cast-iron mileposts, and a wharf crane. The Clock Warehouse of 1780 is now a visitor centre.

BIBLIOGRAPHY
General
Cossons, 1988.

LOCATION
[I] Arkwright Society, Canal Shardlow, 1976.
[S] The Clock Warehouse, London Road, Shardlow, Derbyshire.

Shawinigan, Quebec, Canada   The town of Shawinigan, 166 km (103 mi.) NE of Montreal, was one of the birthplaces of heavy industry in Quebec, particularly in hydro-electric generation, electrometallurgy, and pulp- and papermaking. The town was planned from 1900 by the Shawinigan Water & Power Corporation. Other concerns that required water power were attracted to the site: the Northern Aluminium Co. (now Alcan), and the Belgo-Canadian Pulp & Paper company (now Stone-Consolidated).

After the nationalization of the electricity industry by the provincial government in 1963, the property of the Shawinigan Water & Power Corporation passed to Hydro Québec, which since 1982 has been carrying out a programme of conservation and development of its installations in collaboration with university scholars and local and regional organizations.

Fed by the powerful falls of Shawinigan on the St Maurice river and situated in a magnificent rural landscape, the industrial installations at Shawinigan include dams, bridges and a railway, but principally five hydro-electric power stations built between 1900 and 1948, of which two remain in operation.

Shawinigan 2 comprises an original section, built in 1914, in the style of an Italian Renaissance palace, with balconies and semicircular headed windows, and an extension dating from 1922 inspired by the ART DECO style. It accommodates five sets of horizontal-shaft turbine alternators of 15 000 watts, designed on the Francis principle (see TURBINE) and installed in 1914; and three vertical-shaft ALTERNATORS of 30 000 kW, which were added between 1922 and 1929. At the rear of the building are the metal penstocks. Shawinigan 3 was designed between 1946 and 1949 in a functional modernist style, and is sited on a steep slope, ascended by a funicular which is used for the transportation of heavy equipment.

The former works of the Northern Aluminium Co., constructed in 1901, where aluminium was smelted in Canada for the first time, is to be an interpretation centre. The industrial monuments and the modern technological installations, as well as the natural features of the environment, are to be integrated within a circuit which should lead to the development of the tourist potential of this vast industrial complex.

BIBLIOGRAPHY
General
Hogue *et al.*, 1979; Larose, 1982.

LOUISE TROTTIER

shawl manufacture A shawl is a rectangular piece of light fabric, worn around the neck, shoulders or head, chiefly by women. It was introduced to Europe from India in the eighteenth century, and is often of CASHMERE. Production on a large scale was the speciality of PAISLEY, where a substantial factory-based industry grew up in the nineteenth century from earlier domestic manufactures.

BIBLIOGRAPHY
General
Butt, 1987.

Shchusev, Alexei Viktorovich (1873–1949) The architect responsible for a surprising number of the Russian public buildings of the ponderous, monolithic, classical style, popularly and derogatively known as the Stalinist style. In his earlier career he was attached to Russian national and traditional models, as demonstrated by his design for the Kazan Station in Moscow, with its echoes of old Muscovite themes. This design, which was well suited functionally to the requirements of a station handling an enormous passenger traffic, was drawn up before the Revolution, and largely built between the wars, finally being completed with some modifications in the 1980s. Of his later 'Stalinist' period, examples in Moscow are the Moskva Hotel; the Komsomol'skaya Ploshchad' Metro station, which looks like a mausoleum; and the Lenin Mausoleum on Red Square, which could be mistaken for a Metro station.

BIBLIOGRAPHY
Specific
Bolshaya sovietskaya entsiklopediya (Great Soviet Encyclopaedia), vol. 48, Moscow, 1957.

JOHN WESTWOOD

Sheffield, South Yorkshire, England One of the world's principal centres for the manufacture of cutlery, saws, scythes, files, razors and silver plate, Sheffield, at the confluence of the Rivers Don and Sheaf, prospered in the seventeenth and eighteenth centuries as a result of abundant water power, the availability of local coal and iron, and the ease with which Baltic iron could be imported. Sub-contracting was a feature of the cutlery trades, many processes being carried on by outworkers known locally as 'little mesters'. Sheffield's urban pattern was partly shaped by a grid of streets laid out by the Duke of Norfolk from *c.*1770. The population of Sheffield grew from 46 000 in 1801 to 409 000 in 1901. In 1864 240 people were killed by a flood following the collapse of Dale Dike dam, 12 km (8 mi.) NW, which was owned by a private water company, an event that led to reconsiderations of methods of constructing earth dams. Steelmaking was important in the region from the Middle Ages, and it was at Sheffield in 1740 that Benjamin Huntsman (1704–76) perfected the CRUCIBLE PROCESS of steel manufacture. In 1861 Henry Bessemer demonstrated his process for steelmaking to the ironmaster Sir John Brown (1806–96), and from that time there grew up along the banks of the Don a series of large steelworks, specializing in armaments.

Most of the large works of the late nineteenth century have been demolished. Some cutlery workshops remain in operation in the centre. A cementation furnace survives in Hoyle Street, and a cross-section of another in Russell Street. Typical file shops survive at Ecclesfield, 6 km (4 mi.) N., and there are cutlers' shops at Grenoside, 6 km (4 mi.) NW. At Low Mill, Silkstone, 19 km (12 mi.) N., is a well-preserved small blast furnace of *c.*1820, while at Rockley, 15 km (9 mi.) N., is a blast furnace of 1652 which has been excavated: it has a crenellated top and a lining of sandstone blocks. Alongside is a Newcomen engine house of the mid-eighteenth century. At Elsecar, 13 km (8 mi.) N., a Newcomen engine, built by John Burgh of Chesterfield *c.*1795, is preserved in its original engine house.

683

Glassmaking was important in the eighteenth century and at Catcliffe, 6 km (4 mi.) E., is an English glass cone of *c*.1740, 18 m (60 ft.) high. Sharrow Snuff Mill, 6 km (4 mi.) S., is still in operation with an overshot wheel driving pestle-and-mortar mills.

Sheffield's industrial museum on Kelham Island is in the former generating station for the city's electric trams, built in 1899. It includes displays relating to products made in the city over the past three hundred years, ranging from steel through silver to liquorice allsorts. There is a courtyard of 'little mesters' workshops. The 12 000 hp River Don engine, formerly used in an armour plate mill, is regularly turned, and films are shown of it operating *in situ*. A Bessemer converter stands outside the museum. Abbeydale Industrial Hamlet, 5.5 km (3½ mi.) S., is a group of cottages and workshops on the Sheaf, dating from the late eighteenth century, including grinding shops for scythes, two water-powered tilt hammers, and a crucible steel shop. Shephard Wheel, 5.5 km (3½ mi.) SW, is a water-powered grinding shop typical of those used by 'little mesters' with a 5.5 m (18 ft.) cast-iron wheel. Wortley Top Forge, 14 km (8½ mi.) NW, is an old ironworking site, used from the nineteenth century for making railway wagon axles: there is a 4 m (13 ft.) breast-shot water wheel, together with a belly helve hammer and three jib cranes. Two shops in the city specialize in locally produced hardware.

BIBLIOGRAPHY
General
Pollard, 1959; Walton, 1948.
Specific
National Coal Board, *The Newcomen Type Engine at Elsecar*, 1984.

LOCATIONS
[M] Abbeydale Industrial Hamlet, Abbeydale Road South, Sheffield S7 2QW.
[M] Sheffield Industrial Museum, Kelham Island, off Alma Street, Sheffield S3 8RY.

BARRIE TRINDER

Sheffield plate A sheet of silver fused to copper by heating, and then rolled into a thinner sheet and used like silver. It is also called 'fused plate'. It was invented by Thomas Bolsover in 1742.

shingling The process of hammering wrought iron in order to weld together the particles of metal, to expel slag and to shape the metal into a form in which it could be rolled. A HELVE HAMMER or STEAM HAMMER might be used for shingling. A shingler normally wore sheet iron 'armour', a leather apron, and a gauze mask as protection against flying particles of slag.

BIBLIOGRAPHY
General
Gale, 1969, 1971.

ship canal A canal that can accommodate ocean-going ships, usually built across an isthmus or to give access to a river port.

The pattern for ship canals was set by the Frenchman Ferdinand de Lesseps (1805–94), who in 1869 completed the 164 km (102 mi.) canal across the isthmus of Suez linking the Mediterranean and the Red Sea. In the Netherlands the New Waterway giving access to Rotterdam was opened in 1872, and the North Sea Canal from Ijmuiden to Amsterdam in 1876. In Russia the Morskoy Canal from Kronstadt to St Petersburg (*see* LENINGRAD) was completed in 1884. The ship canal that made MANCHESTER a port was opened in 1894, the year before the completion of the canal across Jutland linking Kiel with the North Sea. Ships began to use the CORINTH Canal in 1893, while the route across the isthmus of Panama, begun by De Lesseps in 1881, was completed by the US government in 1914. The joint US/Canadian project to open up the Great Lakes to seagoing ships began in 1895. The new Welland Canal, with 27 ft. (8.23 m) locks, was opened in 1932, but the ambitious St Lawrence Seaway scheme was not completed until the 1950s.

BIBLIOGRAPHY
General
Bunau-Varilla, 1913; Hadfield, 1986; Hammond and Lewin, 1966; McCullough, 1976; Mack, 1944; Makepeace, 1983; Mills, 1913; Miner, 1940; Siegfried, 1940.

BARRIE TRINDER

shipyard An establishment where ships are constructed and repaired. Yards building wooden ships were widely dispersed, but the growing popularity of IRON SHIPS and later steel ships in the nineteenth century led to concentration on sites that could readily be supplied from ironworks. The standards of construction of naval ships have traditionally been more demanding than those for merchant vessels, and naval shipyards have been characterized by the monumental quality of their architecture. Most of the outstanding remains of the shipbuilding industry are in such yards, whether they reflect, like Chatham, the nature of wooden shipbuilding in the eighteenth century, or, like Boston, Mass., that of steel-ship construction in the first half of the twentieth century.

Wooden ships were built in much the same way as wooden houses. A modeller executed the plan of the naval architect, and the templates were prepared in a MOULD LOFT. The shipwright shaped pieces roughly cut by a ship's sawyer, and erected the frame, made up of the keel, the middle timbers or futtocks, and the top timbers. The frame was left for a month before being 'skinned' or covered with planks. Traditional wooden ships were either of carvel construction, with the planks all flush and smooth, or of clinker construction, with each external plank overlapping the one below, and fastened with copper nails. Caulkers were employed to fill the gaps between the planks with oakum, which was covered with pitch. The ship's joiner fitted out the vessel, constructing the cabins and holds, and employing the skills of the cabinet maker to furnish the former. Specialist workers included MAST makers, BLOCK makers, and the builders of ships' boats. Characteristic components of a yard building wooden ships were SLIPS, ponds for masts and boats, seasoning sheds, sawpits and later sawmills, carpenters' shops, a mould loft and SAIL LOFT, a mast house, a block-making shop and store, a hemp store, a tar house, a ROPE walk, a smithy, and a water tower for firefighting. The danger of fire led to the early use of iron-framing for shipyard buildings, many of which had upper floors of stone slabs laid on cast-iron joists.

The development of iron and later steel ships brought about an increase in the size of shipyards, since iron ships could be built much longer than the 80 m (260 ft.) reckoned to be the maximum length of a wooden vessel. The preparatory stages of making a ship were completely changed, as steel stockyards, preparation plants and fabrication areas replaced seasoning sheds and sawmills. Mould lofts were still used. Slips or berths for building ships were more likely to be surrounded by cranes, and the range of outfitting trades was extended to include painters, pipeworkers, engineers and subsequently electricians. Most shipyards came to have DRY DOCKS where vessels were checked after outfitting but before sea trials. Iron and steel ships were first constructed using riveting, but in 1885 Nicholas de Barnados obtained a patent in Russia for electric welding with a carbon arc, and by 1914 welding was widely used for ship repairs and for some new construction. The first all-welded ship was the 389-ton coaster *Fullargar* built at Birkenhead in 1920. Since 1945 riveting has been almost totally displaced by welding.

In France from the late eighteenth century models of ships' hulls were tested in tanks, and the practice was developed further by William Froude (1810–79) in experiments for the British Admiralty between 1856 and 1870. Such ideas were adopted slowly, and there were only five model tanks in the world by 1900, one of which survives at DUNBARTONSHIRE.

See also GRAVING DOCK.

BIBLIOGRAPHY
General
Coad, 1983, 1989; Haldane, 1893; Laing, 1985; Mayhew, 1849–50; Murray, 1861, 1863; Walton, 1902, 1921.

BARRIE TRINDER

shirt manufacture The shirt was, apart from hosiery and the felt hat, the first male garment whose manufacture was industrialized. There were shirt factories in the USA by 1832, and some very large examples by the late nineteenth century (*see* NEW YORK). The British industry developed in the second half of the nineteenth century, one of the chief centres being LONDONDERRY.

shoddy A woollen fabric made from yarn produced by tearing woollen rags to shreds, with the addition of some new wool. The process was established in Batley, Yorkshire, by Benjamin Law in 1813. Earlier, recycled waste materials were used for padding. The chief concentration of shoddy mills was south-west of LEEDS, in Dewsbury and Batley, which was known in the 1860s as 'the great Shoddy Metropolis'. Shoddy was made from soft rags, MUNGO from hard rags. Shoddy yarn was produced on a rag machine, whose principal part was a swift. The term 'shoddy' may derive from a word meaning small stones, the waste product of a quarry. It has come to mean of inferior quality. *See* figure 143.

BIBLIOGRAPHY
General
Beaumont, 1919.

shoes In the pre-industrial period shoemaking was the most common craft occupation. Manufacture on an industrial scale began in the second half of the nineteenth century, and retailing was completely reorganized in the early twentieth century with the growth of CHAIN STORES.

A shoe made by traditional methods was shaped around a last, either for an individual's foot, or a 'foot-type'. Until the nineteenth century most shoes were 'straights': each shoe could be worn on either the right or the left foot. In larger cities shoemakers specialized in men's or women's footware, or in making fashionable boots, these shoemakers being the élite of the trade. The word 'cordwainer', originally meaning a worker in leather from Cordova, was more or less synonymous with 'shoemaker' by the eighteenth century. A cobbler was a repairer rather than a maker of shoes.

Marc Brunel (1769–1849) set up a boot factory with machines in London in 1812, but it was unsuccessful. By 1850 shoes made in Northampton were being marketed on a large scale in London, where footwear imported from France was also widely available. Factory production of ready-made shoes in the mid-nineteenth century was led by firms like C. & J. Clark of Street, Somerset, established in 1829, who rough-cut the leather in their factory, but put it out to domestic workers to be made into shoes. The principal change was brought about by the development of the SEWING MACHINE. From 1854 Lyman Reed Black, in Massachusetts, used the lock-stitch sewing machine invented by Elias Howe (1819–67) in 1847 to fix uppers to soles. Black's machines became commercially available from 1864. Gordan McKay, who also worked in Massachusetts, perfected in 1862 a machine to sew uppers to soles. He profited from military demand during the Civil War, and production of ready-made shoes for the American working class greatly expanded in the late 1860s. Riveting machines were developed for fixing uppers to soles from the 1860s. The cementing of soles to uppers, which began in the 1860s, was commonplace by the 1920s. Factory production came to be concentrated in towns like Offenbach, in RHINELAND-PALATINATE; Northampton, where the museum houses a major collection of shoes, NORWICH, STREET, and LEICESTER in England; and Lynn, MASSACHUSETTS.

'Pumps', shoes with single soles and no heels (otherwise called running shoes), and slippers, shoes without heels, were being made in England by the 1680s. Shoes with vulcanized rubber soles, developed by CHARLES MACINTOSH, were shown in the Great Exhibition in London in 1851, and from *c*.1868 canvas shoes with rubber soles came on the market. Shoes were also made of jute (*see* ANGUS) and ESPARTO GRASS.

One of the more distinguished industrial buildings

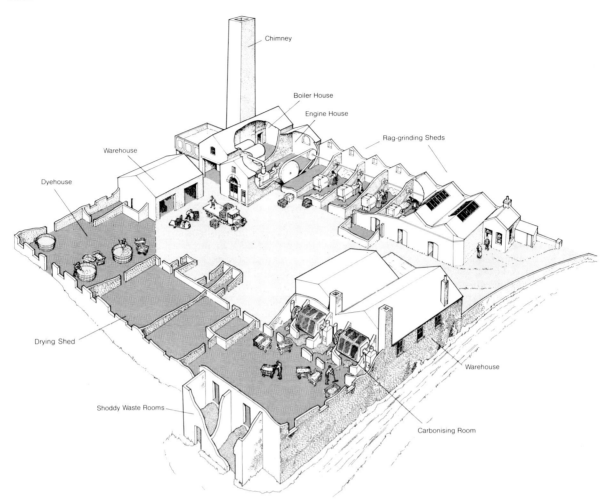

Chimney

Boiler House

Engine House

Rag-grinding Sheds

Warehouse

Dyehouse

Drying Shed

Shoddy Waste Rooms

Warehouse

Carbonising Room

Figure 143 A cut-away perspective of Runtlings Mill, Ossett, Yorkshire, showing the typical form of the SHODDY and mungo mill; the courtyard is bounded by ranges of sheds for sorting, carbonizing, rag-grinding and dyeing.
Royal Commission on the Historical Monuments of England

connected with shoe manufacture is the shoe last (Schuh-leisten) factory by Walter Gropius (1883–1969) at ALFELD.

See also CLOGS.

BIBLIOGRAPHY
General
Boorstin, 1973; Long, 1956; Sparks, 1949; Sutton, 1979; Swaysland, 1905; Wheldon, 1946.
Specific
Mountfield, P. R. Early technological innovation and the British footwear industry. In *IAR*, II, 1977.

LOCATION
[M] Central Museum and Art Gallery, Guildhall Road, Northampton.

BARRIE TRINDER

shop A building, or a part of one, where goods may be made, prepared for sale, or sold. In a manufacturing establishment the word 'shop' is usually qualified so as to indicate function, as in 'paint shop', 'pattern shop', 'erecting shop'. In England the term more commonly refers to a RETAILING establishment, to which the word STORE might be applied in North America.

See also APOTHECARY; ARCADE; BAKERY; BAZAAR; BUTCHER; CASH REGISTER; CHAIN STORE; COMPANY STORE; CONFECTIONERY; CO-OPERATIVE MOVEMENT; DEPARTMENT STORE; DISPENSARY; DRUG STORE; MARKET; PHARMACY; PNEUMATIC DISPATCH; SADDLERY; SHOES; SUPERMARKET; TRUCK SHOP.

BIBLIOGRAPHY
General
Dean, 1970; Jeffreys, 1954; Winstanley, 1983.
Specific
Lancaster, H. V. The design and architectural treatment of the shop. In *Journal of the Royal Society of Arts*, LXI, 1913.

Yamey, B. S. The evolution of shopping. In *Lloyds Bank Review*, XXXI, 1954.

shortwall mining A method of mining coal, and a variation of LONGWALL MINING. A short face is used up to 20 m (63 ft.) wide, with a single access roadway maintained behind it. A similar method, known as 'single entry' working, is now being introduced in British mines to work small remnant areas of coal.

shot tower A tower used for making lead shot of uniform size, the characteristic feature of a lead-processing works, and patented by William Watts of Bristol, England, in 1782. It was typically 55 m (180 ft.) high, although a tower of 1838 in Baltimore was 71 m (234 ft.), tapering from 10 m (33 ft.) in diameter at the base to 5 m (15 ft.) at the top. Pig lead was melted in small furnaces at different heights according to the size of shot required, with some arsenic added to prevent the lead falling as a continuous stream. Molton lead was poured from various heights through perforated copper screens, falling as spheres into a vat of water below. Sometimes the fall was increased by excavation of a pit at the base of the tower. The shot was rolled down inclined glass panels to remove any misshapen pieces. The towers of 1799 at Chester, England, of 1907 at Edmonton, London, and of 1909 at Hartford, Conn., USA, all remain in use.

BIBLIOGRAPHY
General
Stratton and Trinder, 1988; Tunis, 1965.

Shrewsbury, Shropshire, England   A market town on the River Severn. The first iron-framed textile mill was constructed in 1796–7 in the northern suburb of Ditherington, designed by Charles Bage for John Marshall and partners: it is 54.56 m × 12.04 m ($179\frac{1}{2}$ ft. × $39\frac{1}{2}$ ft.), has five storeys, and has load-bearing brick walls between which run three lines of cruciform-section cast-iron columns carrying iron cross beams, from which spring arches carrying floors above. It served as a flax mill till 1886, then as a maltings from *c.* 1900 until 1987. Alongside ran the Shrewsbury Canal, which at Longdon, 12 km ($7\frac{1}{2}$ mi.) E., crossed the River Tern on a cast-iron aqueduct constructed by THOMAS TELFORD, in 1795–6. 5–8a Severn Street are houses converted from the iron-framed outbuilding of a second flax mill complex, of which the main building built by Bage in 1804–5, was demolished in 1836. The Sentinel Wagon Works of 1915–20, with adjacent GARDEN CITY style housing, is now a diesel engine works. Snailbeach, 16 km (10 mi.) SW, was the centre of a lead mining region; in it are the remains of engine houses and a 2 ft. 4 in. (71 cm) gauge railway. Atcham, 6 km (4 mi.) E., has a seven-arch stone bridge of 1769–71 by John Gwynne (d.1786), with a concrete bridge of 1929 alongside, and the remains of an eighteenth-century lock at the confluence of the Tern and the Severn.

See also figure 141.

BIBLIOGRAPHY
General
Brook and Allbutt, 1973; Rimmer, 1960; Trinder, 1981, 1984.
Specific
Denton, J. H. and Lewis, M. J. T. The River Tern Navigation. In *Journal of the Railway and Canal Historical Society*, XXIII, 1977.
Skempton, A. W. and Johnson, H. R. The first iron frames. In *Architectural Review*, CXXXI (751). 1962.

BARRIE TRINDER

Shukhov, Vladimir Grigorevich (1853–1939)   One of the most original and versatile of modern Russian engineers. His main work was in the Baku oil industry, where he developed many solutions to the problems encountered by this new technology. He built Russia's first oil pipeline, from the Balakhanskii fields to Baku, and the world's first heavy oil pipeline, using exhaust from the steam pumps to heat the oil. The Shukhov watertube boiler can still be encountered in Russia.

He also pursued an interest in metal construction, endeavouring to bring a new lightness to architecture. His net-form steel roofs, covering large areas in relation to the density of pillars, were used in several covered markets and the Kiev Station in Moscow. His light metal arches, similarly designed on mathematical principles, were also an asset to architects and have survived in several places, notably in the building that is now the GUM department store on Red Square in Moscow. He built around five hundred bridges on the same principles. Among other surviving examples of his work are the metal framework of Moscow's General Post Office, and the revolving stage of the Moscow Arts Theatre. In the difficult years of 1921–4 the Bolshevik government enlisted his help to design wooden structures because of the steel shortage.

His most spectacular innovations were the so-called Shukhov towers, for which he was granted a patent in 1896, and of which about two hundred were built. They were of steel lattice construction, circular in cross-section, but with concave sides. They were used successfully as masts for US battleships, and, less successfully, on two Russian warships, but their main use was for supporting water towers. The one that survives at Nikolaev, which was not untypical in weighing six times less than the water in its tank, was built in 1906–7. In 1944 the retreating German army exploded a demolition charge beneath it, which simply overturned it. It was then replaced in its vertical position and resumed its function. Another, at 148 m (486 ft.) the highest built, was erected in Moscow in 1921, and in 1945 was used as the transmitting tower for the USSR's first television broadcasts.

BIBLIOGRAPHY
Specific
Konfederatov, I. Ya. *Vladimir Grigorevich Shukhov*. Moscow, 1950.

JOHN WESTWOOD

Sibiu, Sibiu, Romania   A city in the south of Transylvania, documented from the late twelfth century, and an ancient centre of guild-based artisan manufactures. There were nineteen guilds in 1376, and in about 1700 the first workshops making weapons and paper were established. The town possesses many buildings in a simple Baroque style, among them the Brukenthal palace, completed in 1785, which since 1817 has been the town museum. The museum of popular technology, Dumbrava Sibiu, is a branch of the town museum. It includes machines and workshops from the whole of Romania, among them a gold ore stamping mill, a foundry where steel bells were cast, a great variety of wind and water mills, and floating mills from the rivers Olt and Someş. The first hydro-electric power station in Transylvania was built at Sadu in 1896 to supply the city of Sibiu.

BIBLIOGRAPHY
General
Giurescu, 1973.
Specific
Museul Tehnicii Populare Complexul muzeistic Dumbrava Sibiu (The Museum of Popular Technology: the museum complex at Dumbrava Sibiu). Sibiu, 1986.

LOCATION
[M] Museul Bruckenthal (Brukenthal Museum), Piata Republicii 4, Sibiu.

HORIA GIURGIUMAN

Sicily (Sicilia), Italy   An island, whose most important industrial sites relate to sulphur working. They are concentrated in the centre of the island in a belt 120 km (75 mi.) long and 40 km (25 mi.) wide, around Enna. Mining commenced around 1730, and for many years Sicily had a world monopoly in the production of sulphur. Gypsum and limestone containing sulphur were excavated and purified at three types of plant. The most primitive were circular kilns about 25 m (80 ft.) high in which the sulphur melted and ran out into moulds. Examples survive in ruined form at the Floristella mine, Valguarnera, 24 km (15 mi.) SE of Enna, where there is also a ruined mansion built by the owner of the mine. Gill's kilns were introduced in 1886 using technology comparable to that employed by Hoffman for burning bricks. The sulphur is set in four cells, and gases are passed from one chamber to another before being exhausted through a central flue. An example survives at the Trabia Tallarita mine, near Caltanissetta, 35 km (22 mi.) W. of Enna. Modern plants purify sulphur with superheated steam, a process patented in 1865, but only adopted widely from the 1880s.

At the western tip of Sicily, Trápani, 90 km (55 mi.) W. of Palermo, is surrounded by the remains of windmills, which were used for pumping brine. A few still have their sails, but in most cases only the towers survive. Bonagia, 9 km (6 mi.) N. of Trápani, has been a major centre for processing tuna fish from the nineteenth century. Remains of saltmining can be found around Gela on the south coast, 90 km (55 mi.) SW of Catania.

BIBLIOGRAPHY
General
Negri *et al.*, 1983.

Specific
Il luogo del lavoro (Workers' habitations). AA.VV, 1986.

MICHAEL STRATTON

sickle   A tool used for reaping: *see* SCYTHES.

Sielpia Wielka, Kielce, Poland   The museum of the STAROPOLSKI INDUSTRIAL REGION, 40 km (25 mi.) NW of Kielce. It includes a puddling forge and rolling mill built during 1825–42, a water-power system, workers' housing, a school, and offices, all in the classical style. The plant of the early nineteenth century was in use until 1934 when it was closed down, recognized as a site of historical interest, and opened to the public as a branch of the Warsaw Museum of Technology. The original rolling stands and puddling furnaces were displayed, together with other machines from different parts of the Staropolski Industrial Region, including Filip Girard's water turbine. During World War II the museum was destroyed. A proposal to re-establish it was put forward by the Warsaw Museum of Technology in 1956. The buildings were restored and plant from elsewhere in the region was put on display. The museum now has an original water wheel and a rich collection of other machines, including a lathe by James Fox which worked in Białogon until 1955, a steam pump of 1858, an early nineteenth-century steam-blowing engine, and various other lathes and drilling machines. There is also an exhibition of art castings made by foundries in the Staropolski Industrial Region. The reconstruction of the rolling mill and puddling furnaces destroyed in the war is now in progress.

BIBLIOGRAPHY
General
Jasiuk, 1962, 1973.
Specific
Jasiuk, J. 50 lat Muzeum Zagłębia Staropolskiego w Sielpi (50 years of the Museum of the Staropolski Industrial Region in Sielpia). n.d.

PIOTR GERBER

Siemens, Sir William (Carl Wilhelm) (1823–83)   A scientist, the inventor of many industrial processes, and the holder of 113 patents. Born in Hanover and educated at various German universities, he visited England in 1843 to find a market for an electroplating device patented in Prussia, and subsequently developed other processes, acting as the London agent of the electrical firm of Siemens & Halske, established by his elder brother Werner. In 1858 he established an English branch of the company at Millbank, London, moving to Charlton in 1866; at the works there over 2000 were subsequently employed, especially in the manufacture of equipment for long-distance telegraphs. In 1857 he suggested that his regenerative furnace, originally applied in glassmaking, could be used to melt steel. He developed the concept into a process using an OPEN HEARTH FURNACE for steelmaking, which he patented and applied in an experimental works at Birmingham in 1866, and at the works at Landore,

Figure 144 A steam pump made in 1858 by Rudolf Siebert of Friedland-in-Maehren in the collection of machines held by the Museum of the Staropolski Industrial Region at Sielpia Wielka
Piotr Gerber

Swansea, during 1869–88. In 1878 he patented the ELECTRIC ARC FURNACE. In 1867 he announced the principle of the dynamo, simultaneously with Sir CHARLES WHEATSTONE and C. F. Varley. He applied electric power to the PORTRUSH tramway in 1883. Resident in Britain for much of his life, and naturalized in 1859, Siemens was knighted in 1882, and honoured throughout Europe.

BIBLIOGRAPHY
General
Pole, 1888.

Siemens-Martin process *See* OPEN HEARTH FURNACE.

signal box An elevated structure situated adjacent to a railway from which signals, points, level-crossing gates and so on can be operated. In the USA it is known as a signal tower. Such structures began to be built from the mid-nineteenth century at intervals along lines as railways became too complex to signal by hand. Levers controlling points were first grouped together in 1843 at Bricklayers' Arms, London, where the first interlocking frame, ensuring that signals and points could not be set in conflict, was installed in 1856. The characteristic two-storey box, with control levers above and locking mechanisms below, was devised by John Saxby in 1857. Signal boxes often reflect the distinctive architectural style of the railway company or signalling contractor responsible for building them. Some companies, like the Midland Railway in England, built prefabricated signal boxes.

A signalman can communicate with his colleagues in adjacent boxes by telegraphic instruments or telephone before allowing a train to proceed safely into the territory or 'section' controlled by an adjacent box. Signals, points and the rest are operated by means of wires or rods connected to levers inside the signal box; as layouts have become more complicated, sophisticated locking and interlocking devices have been developed to prevent conflicting movements or the operation of apparatus in an incorrect sequence. In recent times electrically-powered signals and colour lights have replaced manual systems and semaphore signals, and these in turn are being superseded by computerized electronic systems and radio signalling. These networks are controlled from regional centres, and in many countries the traditional signal box is disappearing.

Some railway companies manufactured their own signalling equipment (*see* IRVINE), but many were supplied by international engineering concerns like the Westinghouse company.

Working signal boxes with traditional block equipment remain on several PRESERVED RAILWAYS.

BIBLIOGRAPHY
General
Nock, 1962; Signalling Study Group, 1986.

JOHN POWELL

signal tower   A term with two applications in industrial archaeology:

1. A link in a SEMAPHORE communication system. Often three-storey buildings on hills in line-of-sight, signal towers provided working and living space, usually for two crewmen with their families. There are surviving examples at Chatley Heath, 2 km ($1\frac{1}{2}$ mi.) SW of Chobham, and Guildford, both in England; at Köln-Flittard (*see* COLOGNE) in Germany; and at LENINGRAD in the USSR.
2. A North American term for SIGNAL BOX.

BIBLIOGRAPHY
General
Falconer, 1980.

silk   The fine soft thread secreted by silkworm caterpillars (*Bombyx mori*) in forming their cocoons. The silkworms are fed mulberry leaves until they enter the pupa stage. The larvae are killed by heating or boiling the cocoons, prior to winding off the silk thread they have spun. Silk is an animal fibre, a protein – not cellulose, as all the plant fibres are. Floss silk is made from rough thread broken off while winding off cocoons. It is carded like wool and used to make cheaper varieties of silk fabric and in embroidery.

The Italian silk industry of the seventeenth century pioneered several aspects of the factory system.

See also ARTIFICIAL SILK; REELING; THROWING; and figure 25.

BIBLIOGRAPHY
General
Schober, 1930.

Silkeborg, Jutland, Denmark   The city of Silkeborg in mid-Jutland owes its existence to a papermill, built in 1844 on the banks of the Gudenå, the largest river in Denmark, by the Drewsen family, who owned several papermills at MØLLEÅEN, where water supplies were inadequate. The new mill had abundant water power and occupies a central place in Danish industrial history. From the beginning it had a 60 hp iron water wheel, for two decades the largest in the country, and when it was extended in 1847 it was equipped with a water turbine, the first in Denmark. The oldest surviving buildings date from 1864, but some workers' dwellings of 1847 remain. The paddle steamer *Hjejlen* (Golden Plover), built by Baumgarten & Burmeister in 1862, serves tourists on the beautiful Silkeborg lakes. A water tower of 1902 partly of reinforced concrete, and designed by Anton Rosen, is a protected monument.

At Klostermølle, 20 km (12 mi.) S., on the Gudenå, an old corn mill was converted in 1873 into a pulp mill. Driven by two Jonval water turbines the mill used wood from local forests, and from 1933 until its closure in 1975 it combined wood pulping with the manufacture of cardboard. The turbines have survived, together with various buildings, including the large cardboard drying barn, built in wood, and they are now restored as an historical monument. A little further south at Vestbirk a hydro-electric power station of 1924, with two double turbines giving a total capacity of 1800 hp, remains in normal operation. The biggest hydro-electric power station in Denmark is on the Gudenå at Tange, 20 km (12 mi.) N. of Silkeborg. Opened in 1921, its building was stimulated by power shortages during World War I. It is equipped with three Francis turbines, each with a capacity of 2000 hp. The Danish electricity museum has recently been established in the station, which continues to operate.

BIBLIOGRAPHY
General
Brouwer, 1985; Johansen, 1988; Sestoft, 1979.
Specific
Larsen, K. D. *Papirarbejdernes historie i Silkeborg 1844–1982* (The history of the paper workers in Silkeborg 1844–1982). Silkeborg, 1983.
Nielsen, P. B. Klostermølle. In *Fabrik og Bolig*, II, 1988.

LOCATIONS
[M] Elmuseet, Bjerringbrovej 44, 8850 Bjerringbro.
[M] Silkeborg Museum, Hovedgårdsvej, 8600 Silkeborg.

OLE HYLDTOFT

Silvanum, Styria, Austria   *See* GROSSREIFLING.

silver (Ag)   A metallic element which has always been regarded as a precious metal, and at times comparable in value with gold. In the 1850s gold was about sixteen times more valuable, but as the mining of lead, zinc and copper expanded after 1900, silver, produced as a by-product (*see* CUPELLATION), flooded on to the market, and its value fell to one-thirtieth that of gold.

Silver ore is rarely found alone, but is usually carried in other metal ores. European sources included KONGSBERG in Norway, and mines in the TAUERN. Mexican and Peruvian silver was brought to Europe from the sixteenth century, and in the nineteenth century major discoveries were made in Australia (*see* BROKEN HILL) and the USA (*see* COLORADO; IDAHO).

Silver ores are usually worked from veins with other metals by STOPING or open pits. The chief source is the mineral silver sulphide argentite (Ag_2S), commonly found in galena, the principal lead ore. The other principal source is cerargyrite (AgCl). A large proportion of silver production comes as a by-product from lead, zinc and copper mines. After the ore has been dressed, using methods similar to those employed for other metals, silver must be separated from lead, copper or other metals. This was formerly achieved by cupellation, but other methods – blast furnaces, flow furnaces and electrolytic processes – have been developed since the 1850s.

Silver is used in coinage and electrical engineering as well as in jewellery, the making of mirrors and the plating of cutlery. Its compounds are extensively employed in photographic materials.

See also figure 154.

BIBLIOGRAPHY
General
Jones, 1950; Percy, 1880.

IVOR J. BROWN

silver plate   A term that can apply either to a piece of flatware or a dish made of pure silver, or to objects of base metal with a thin coating of siliver.

See also SHEFFIELD PLATE.

silversmith   A tradesman who works in silver, and often in gold and with jewels. To form tankards, silver was usually cast or cut to pattern and soldered together. Smiths use dies to produce such items as spoons; and draw wire for strengthening hollow ware, and for decorative purposes. Surfaces can be ornamented by chasing or engraving.

BIBLIOGRAPHY
General
Tunis, 1965.

Simplon, Lombardia, Italy, and Valais, Switzerland   The pass between Brig and Domodossola, linking the Rhône Valley and the Valle d'Ossola, giving easy access to Milan and other cities of northern Italy. The first road for vehicles was built under Napoleon I. Railways had reached Brig and Domodossola by 1878, but the decision to build the 42 km (26 mi.) line between the two, incorporating a tunnel, was not taken until 1895. Construction commenced in 1896 under Alfred Brandt

(1845–99) and Carl Brandau (1849–1917), and the 19.8 km (12.3 mi.) long tunnel, then the longest in the world, opened in May 1906. The tunnel section was electrified in July 1906.

BIBLIOGRAPHY
General
Schneider, 1963.

sintering   The agglomeration and concentration of metallic ores into lumps of open texture suitable for penetration by gases in smelting furnaces, achieved by burning small coke with finely crushed ore. Developed by A. S. Dwight and R. L. Lloyd in the USA in 1905 as a means of dealing with ore dust. A sinter plant of 1928 survives at VÖLKLINGEN.

BIBLIOGRAPHY
General
Gale, 1967, 1969.

Sió Canal, Tolna, Fejér, Somogy, Hungary   A navigation incorporating sections of the River Sió, linking Lake Balaton to the Danube. It was used in the Roman and medieval periods, but the valley became marshland when mills were constructed under Turkish rule. Improvement was stimulated when the railway was built along the south shore of the lake in 1858, but the navigation was not completed until 1950. A museum at Siofók shows the work of the civil engineer József Beszédes (1787–1852).

BIBLIOGRAPHY
General
Hadfield, 1986.

LOCATION
[M] József Beszédes Museum, H-8600 Siófok, Sió u.2.

sites and monuments record   A database of all the known archaeological sites, compiled to serve as a planning tool within a defined region, in England usually a county. Inclusion on such a record does not imply protected status, although protected monuments are included. In the USA the record is termed the National Register of Historic Places.

See also INVENTORY.

size   A semi-solid glutinous substance, resistant to water and aiding adhesion, used in dressing YARN and such fabrics as FUSTIAN, and on all PAPERS designed for writing and most for printing. In traditional papermaking, size was made by preparing a resin soap from resin and CAUSTIC SODA, to which ALUM was added. Size can be made from bones and most gelatinous substances from animals used in glue manufacture, and from starches like those extracted from potatoes.

Skaftafellssýsla, Iceland   An area of south Iceland, 240 km (150 mi.) E. of Reykjavik. It is notable for farms with home-made electric power plants, built between 1910 and 1930, usually with turbines made by local craftsmen and generators from wrecked ships. Some of these are still in use.

BIBLIOGRAPHY
Specific
Magnusson, T. Conservation of industrial monuments in Iceland. In Nisser and Bedoire, 1978.

skew bridge An ARCH, TRUSS BRIDGE or CONCRETE BRIDGE, carrying one line of way over another crossing at an angle other than a right angle. In a skew arch every piece of stone has to be worked to a compound curvature which is different from that of every other piece. An early and celebrated example is at Rainhill, 16 km (10 mi.) E. of Liverpool, on the Liverpool & Manchester Railway.

Skopje (Skupi, Uskup), Macedonia, Yugoslavia The capital of Macedonia, ruled by the Turks throughout 1392–1912. It was severely damaged in an earthquake in 1963. Of interest are the Turkish stone bridge of ten arches, dating from the fourteenth century; and Daut Pasha Hamman, a domed Turkish bathhouse. A BAZAAR houses many leather and wood workers. An archaeological museum in Kursumlihan, a former CARAVANSERAI, occupies an arcaded building with a central courtyard, once the resort of merchants travelling within the Ottoman Empire. An ethnological museum is sited in an old railway station.

LOCATIONS
[M] Archaeological Museum, Kursumlihan, Skopje.
[M] Ethnological Museum, Plostad Marsala Titoa 18 III, Skopje.

skyscraper The symbol of American enterprise in the first half of the twentieth century: a very high building, given over largely to office accommodation, sometimes mixed with APARTMENTS, and often with shops on the lower floors. (In the mid-nineteenth century the word 'skyscraper' denoted a very tall man or a high horse.) The skyscraper was a response to the demand for office space in city centres where land values were high, from banks, professional practices, insurance companies and mail-order concerns. Skyscrapers came to be associated with the most dynamic American corporations.

The three essentials of a skyscraper are the use of an iron or steel frame and ELEVATORS, and emphasis on the vertical elements in the elevations. The Equitable Building in New York, built in 1870 by Gilman & Kendall, with six storeys and 40 m (130 ft.) high, was the first office block to contain an elevator. But it was Chicago that was the birthplace of the skyscraper, a vibrant city where architects like Louis Sullivan (1856–1924) saw it as a form of building expressing American dynamism. A writer in 1888 commented 'the skyscrapers of Chicago out-rival anything of their kind in the world'. The cast-iron- and wrought-iron-framed, ten-storey Home Insurance Building, built in Chicago in 1883–5 by William LeBaron Jenney (1832–1909), is sometimes regarded as the first

skyscraper, although some later and taller buildings, like the sixteen-storey Monadnock Building of 1891 by Daniel Burnham (1846–1912) and John Wellborn Root (1850–91), lacked steel frames. Sullivan's Wainwright Building in St Louis of 1891 was one of the first in which the vertical elements in the elevations were emphasised. Skyscrapers in New York tend to reflect historic European styles. The first steel frame in the city was not erected until 1889, and the most spectacular of the first-generation skyscrapers appeared just before World War I: the Metropolitan Life Tower of 1909, by Napoleon Le Brun (1821–1901) & Son, a 210 m (700 ft.) high replica of the campanile in St Mark's Square, Venice; and the 241 m (792 ft.) Woolworth Building of 1913, designed by Cass Gilbert (1859–1934), which included twenty-nine elevators, was ornamented internally and externally with Gothic detailing, and accommodated 14 000 workers. In the 1920s and early 30s outstanding examples were built in other American cities, including the 210 m (700 ft.) Terminal Tower in Cleveland of 1931 by Anderson, Probst & White; but the most significant developments were in New York, where William Van Alen's 319 m (1048 ft.) Chrysler Building of 1930 and the 381 m (1250 ft.) Empire State Building of the following year by Shreve, Lamb & Harmon, marked a peak of achievement before building was curtailed by the slump and World War II. The latter remained the world's highest building in 1950, after which skyscrapers came to dominate the centres of most of the world's principal cities.

BIBLIOGRAPHY
General
Condit, 1952, 1964; Goldberger, 1981.
Specific
Webster, J. C. The skyscraper: logical and historical considerations. In *Journal of the Society of Architectural Historians*, XVIII, 1959.

BARRIE TRINDER

slag The waste product of smelting or forging metal, most commonly a vitreous material with a high silica content. The analysis of slag is increasingly used as a means of understanding historic metal working processes (*see* ARCHAEOMETALLURGY). Slag was often reused. Copper slag was cast into blocks and used as bricks (*see* CORNWALL; FALUN). Iron slag is often too brittle for constructional use, but was employed in other ways: in boundary walls; in houses at Ironville, Derbyshire, England, and Troy, N.Y., USA, and summer houses at ENGELSBERG and elsewhere in Sweden; and very commonly as road metal or railway ballast. Slags from early, inefficient processes have often been reworked for metal.

Tips of mining waste are often wrongly called slag heaps.

See also figures 23, 152.

BIBLIOGRAPHY
General
Tylecote, 1986.

Figure 145 One of the world's most notable skyscrapers: the Woolworth Building, 233 Broadway, New York, built in 1913 to the design of Cass Gilbert; the intricate Gothic detailing is in faience.
Michael Stratton

slag hearth A small furnace for extracting lead from slag, usually associated in Britain with ORE HEARTHS, but in Savoy with reverberatory furnaces. By the nineteenth century the working part consisted of cast-iron plates: a typical example, observed at Alston, County Durham, in 1830, was parallelepipedal in form, 0.91 m (3 ft.) high with base 0.66 m × 0.56 m (25 in. × 22 in.), and there was a horizontal tuyère in the rear wall. After the metallic lead had been tapped, the slag was run into water, where rapid cooling caused granulation of further metallic lead, which was separated by STAMPS and washing.

BIBLIOGRAPHY
General
Clough, 1980; Coste and Perdonnet, 1830; Kiernan, 1989; Stratton and Trinder, 1988.

Slane, County Meath, Ireland A town on the River Boyne, which is crossed by the main road from Dublin to Londonderry on a multi-arched stone bridge. A flour mill, begun in 1763, was completed in 1767; 45 m × 8 m (148 ft. × 28 ft.), it had five storeys and was the first major industrial building in Ireland. It was followed in the 1780s by cotton spinning mills. The main surviving building is a nine-bay, five-storey mill, the central three bays projecting beneath a pediment, together with an elegant house and later top-lit sheds.

BIBLIOGRAPHY
General
Cullen, 1987.

slate A rock that splits readily into thin plates. In a loose sense the term is applied to any hard argillaceous rocks that have been used for roofing, like the 'stone slates' of the PENNINES, England, or the 'slate' from Stonesfield, 8 km (5 mi.) N. of Oxford, in the Jurassic measures, where the cleavage is due entirely to stratification. Geologists would now use the term to mean rocks that have been further hardened by lateral pressures, and have at the same time had imposed upon them a cleavage at right angles to the pressure. Slate was extensively quarried in the nineteenth century in WALES, whence it was widely exported; in VERMONT, USA; and in ANJOU in France. In addition to its use for roofing it has also been employed in chemical apparatus, and for other purposes where flat surfaces are essential.
See also figure 146.

BIBLIOGRAPHY
General
Belhoste, 1988; Challinor, 1986.

Slater, Samuel (1768–1835) The founder of the American cotton industry, who was born at Belper (*see* CROMFORD), Derbyshire, and apprenticed with JEDEDIAH STRUTT from 1783. In 1789 he emigrated in disguise to the USA, and the following year began building WATER FRAMES. He opened a cotton factory at Pawtucket, RHODE ISLAND, in 1793, and subsequently established works elsewhere in Rhode Island, MASSACHUSETTS and NEW HAMPSHIRE.

BIBLIOGRAPHY
General
Bagnall, 1890.

slaughterhouse A place where cattle are killed, and their carcasses cut up and distributed to BUTCHERS and other users (*see* MEAT). A slaughterhouse may be part of a butcher's establishment. One that is open for public use is properly called an ABATTOIR.

sleeper A word with at least two meanings in industrial archaeology:
1. A support for rails on a railway, usually placed at right angles to the rails, but sometimes, as on BRUNEL's BROAD-GAUGE RAILWAY, longitudinally. Stone blocks were used on early WAGONWAYS, and cast-iron sleepers

on some PLATEWAYS. Most railways before 1950 used softwood baulks impregnated with CREOSOTE, but concrete sleepers are now standard. In North America sleepers are called cross-ties, or simply ties, and longitudinal sleepers are known as stringers.
2. A colloquial term for SLEEPING CAR.

BIBLIOGRAPHY
General
Westwood, 1983.

sleeping car There were first-class compartments in which seats could be extended for sleeping on the London & Birmingham Railway in England in the 1840s, and carriages with bunks were introduced on the Cumberland Valley RR in the USA in 1837, but purpose-built sleeping cars were working by the 1850s when GEORGE PULLMAN began to improve the levels of comfort they provided. The first sleeping cars in Britain began to operate between London and Glasgow in 1873. Development in Western Europe was due largely to the WAGON-LIT company.

BIBLIOGRAPHY
General
Simmons, 1978.

Sliedrecht, Zuid Holland, The Netherlands A small town on the River Merwede, 14 km (9 mi.) NE of Dordrecht, where most Dutch dredging companies originated. As early as the sixteenth century the best navvies were found in this area. They used rushes and osiers from the nearby Biesbos woodlands to protect soft shores against erosion. Several dredging companies are located along the river. An overview of the industry is provided by the National Dredging Museum, which has detailed models of cutter-suction dredgers, and demonstrations with working models of all kinds of dredging methods. One of the last wet gasholders remaining in the Netherlands is in use as a store. Along the Merwede Kanaal, built in 1826 and extended in 1893, are several nineteenth-century swing bridges and sluices.

At Gorinchem, 10 km (6 mi.) E., a sugar factory of 1871, which had its own harbour, is now used as a chemical plant.

BIBLIOGRAPHY
General
Bos, 1974.

LOCATION
[M] Nationaal Baggermuseum (National Dredging Museum), Molendijk 28, Sliedrecht.

slimes Mixtures of finely-grained ore and mud drained from DRESSING FLOORS in processing non-ferrous ores. The fine grains of ore, once extracted from the mud, were termed sludge. Often slimes once dumped as waste have later been reworked for their remaining ore content.

BIBLIOGRAPHY
General
Stratton and Trinder, 1988.

slip A berth in a SHIPYARD where a ship is constructed. There were covered examples at Karlskrona, Sweden, by 1807, and in British and American yards soon afterwards. Some roofs of slips were up to 20 m (60 ft.) wide and 90 m (300 ft.) long, and employed similar constructional forms to those used in the train sheds of large railway stations and later of aircraft hangars.

The term 'slip' is also applied to berths for FERRY boats, usually double-ended vessels crossing rivers or short stretches of sea.

BIBLIOGRAPHY
General
Coad, 1983, 1989.

slipware Pottery decorated with slip, a suspension of fine particles in water. In Britain the slip was most likely to be of a white or buff colour, and to be applied to beakers, cups and large dishes. Production of slipware was established in Germany by the end of the sixteenth century and became common in France, in particular around Lezoux; it came to prominence in Britain about the middle of the seventeenth century, the most prominent potters to use this approach being the Toft brothers in North Staffordshire. Slipware was introduced to North America by colonists who settled in PENNSYLVANIA.

BIBLIOGRAPHY
General
Searle, 1929–30.

slitting mill A two-stage process for the production of narrow rods for nailers and other smiths from blooms of wrought iron, used in the Liège region by 1500, and patented in England in 1588. A bloom was first hammered into the shape of a bar and rolled into a strip between two plain cylindrical iron rolls, powered by a water wheel. The strip was then passed through a pair of counter-rotating shafts, on which were collars which acted as rotary shears. There is a replica at Saugus MASSACHUSETTS.

BIBLIOGRAPHY
General
Gale, 1969, 1971.

slotting machine or **slotter** A specialized SHAPING MACHINE with a vertically reciprocating tool for cutting slots, especially key ways. Work is fed linearly or rotated slowly to produce circular forms. Early slotting machines were built by ROBERTS, and Nasmyth (*see* STEAM HAMMER) introduced both a slot milling machine and a version of the reciprocating machine which fed the cutter from below the work table.

BIBLIOGRAPHY
General
Rolt, 1986; Steeds, 1969.

Sloup, South Moravia, Czechoslovakia The site of a water-driven corn mill in the Renaissance style of quite outstanding elegance, on an artificial channel fed from the River Dyje (*see* figure 128). The mill, which has four undershot wheels, dates from 1512. It is now preserved. Its nineteenth-century milling equipment is being renovated to illustrate the development of corn milling in Moravia. The Museum also owns a fisherman's house. Sloup was the site of the first cotton printing factory in the Czech lands, in 1763.

slubbing billy Early CARDING MACHINES for wool did not produce continuous roving (*see* TEXTILES) of sufficient strength to be spun. An intermediate machine, the slubbing billy, was developed to piece short slivers together. A moving wooden carriage drew out the slivers and wound them on rotating spindles in a gentle motion akin to that of a SPINNING JENNY.

sluice 'To sluice' means to let out: a sluice is thus a complete structure for impounding water, with a gate or other means by which its outward flow can be controlled. The word also means a paddle or slide for controlling the flow of water, a component of such a gate, or of a WEIR or lock gate. It is applied too to an overflow channel for water. The English word sluice, unlike 'sluis' in Dutch or 'schleuse' in German, is not synonymous with POUND LOCK, although a sluice gate is the upper gate of such a lock.

Smeaton, John (1724–92) The first of the outstanding British civil engineers of the Industrial Revolution, Smeaton was born and died at Austhorpe, near Leeds, where he also lived for much of his life. He began his career as a maker of scientific instruments. He designed a coffer dam for Westminster Bridge (*see* ARCH) in 1748, and in 1755 studied Dutch mills, canals and harbours. He made significant improvements to windmills and water mills, and to the NEWCOMEN engine. He built the third Eddystone lighthouse (*see* PLYMOUTH) in 1756–9, and many notable stone arch bridges including those at Banff, Coldstream and Perth. He was engineer of the Forth & Clyde Canal; of the land-drainage scheme at Hatfield Chase, Yorkshire; and of the harbours at St Ives, Portpatrick, Ramsgate and elsewhere. He established the Society of Civil Engineers (*see* CIVIL ENGINEERING), the 'Smeatonians', in 1771.

BIBLIOGRAPHY
General
Skempton, 1981.

Smiles, Samuel (1812–1904) The great Victorian apostle of self-help, a surgeon who became a railway administrator in London from 1854, and subsequently the prolific author of morally improving works, which contain material of significant historical value relating to the self-made engineers and entrepreneurs of the Industrial Revolution, some of it based on original sources no longer available.

BIBLIOGRAPHY
General
Smiles, A., 1956; Smiles, S., 1857, 1859, 1861–2, 1863, 1866, 1871, 1875, 1880, 1883a, 1883b.

smithy The workshop of a smith, but the term can mean a smith's HEARTH. Sometimes, particularly in shipyards, it refers to a large building where forgings are made from wrought iron or steel, as in the Navy Yard, Boston, Mass., USA, or the Woolwich Dockyard, England, whose iron-framed smithy, designed by JOHN RENNIE in 1815, has been re-erected to house the wrought-iron works at IRONBRIDGE.

smock mill A type of WINDMILL, usually of wooden construction and of polygonal, especially octagonal, plan. The sails are set in a revolving cap, as on a TOWER MILL. The type originated in the Netherlands in the sixteenth century, and was well known in England, the English name referring to the traditional garb of the farm worker.

smokeless fuel The conversion of coal to a smokeless solid fuel, with oil as a by-product, was a twentieth-century development, the most significant advances having taken place in the 1920s. Coal was subject to low-temperature carbonization, being heated to 600 °C in steel retorts by the radiation from burning PRODUCER GAS. Three products resulted: the fuel itself, whose characteristics were determined by a careful blending of coals; low-temperature gas, richer in hydrocarbons than that produced in a gasworks, and much of it being reused as fuel; and paraffinoid oils, which could be purified and used as aircraft or motor fuel.

Snowdonia, Gwynedd, Wales A mountainous region of North Wales, significant for mineral extraction. Massive slate quarries, like Penrhyn, DINORWIC and BLAENAU FFESTINIOG, were linked to improved harbours from the 1780s. Output reached 26 000 tons in 1793, then 489 000 tons in 1898, satisfying British and foreign urban expansion before the mass production of tiles. Copper mining in the eighteenth and nineteenth centuries has left water-power systems, adits, pumping and winding equipment, dressing and crushing areas, barracks, tramways and aerial ropeways: for example at Sygun and Drws-y-coed mines. Gold was discovered north of Dolgellau in 1843: it was mined mainly in the 1850s, 60s and 90s. Snowdon Mountain Railway was constructed for tourists in 1894, taking them to the highest summit in Wales, 1078 m (3500 ft.); it uses Swiss rack-and-pinion locomotives.

BIBLIOGRAPHY
General
Dodd, 1971; Lindsay, 1974.
Specific
Bick, D. *The Old Copper Mines of Snowdonia*. Newent, Gloucestershire: The Pound House, 1982.

snuff Tobacco, either leaves or stalks, or a mixture of the two, ground to powder and often perfumed; it is taken by sniffing. Snuff was used in Europe by the 1550s when it was available in Lisbon. Most snuff mills were equipped both with edge runners and pestle-action machines. The principal centres of production in Britain were Mitcham, on the River Wandle, and Devizes, the origin of grinding stones now preserved in BRISTOL Industrial Museum.

BIBLIOGRAPHY
General
Braudel, 1981; Dodd, 1843.

soap 'The quantity of soap consumed by a nation', wrote Justus Liebig (1803–73), 'would be no inaccurate measure whereby to estimate its wealth and civilization'. Soaps act by lowering the surface tension between water and an oil or other insoluble material. Soft soap, made from potash, is used for industrial purposes, like the finishing stages of textile production; hard soap, made from soda, is for personal use.

Soap is made by heating natural fats containing the glycerides of saturated carboxylic acids with caustic soda, to form the sodium salts of the acids (the soaps), which are precipitated by the addition of sodium chloride. Until supplies of caustic soda became readily available, alkali, whether sodium carbonate or potassium carbonate, in the form of ash, was steeped with lime, calcium oxide, and water, to make lye, a solution of caustic soda ($NaOH$). In any soap-boiling process, caustic soda (or potash) is run, with steam, into vats of boiling fat. Soap gradually forms on the surface, salt is added to speed the separation, and the soap and lyes are separated. The soap is then remelted in another lye, boiled with steam and cast into blocks. Glycerin is a by-product of soap manufacture. White soap is normally made with olive oil, yellow soap with tallow and yellow rosin, and Castile soap with oil and iron sulphate.

The historic centre of the European soap manufacturing was MARSEILLES, but small-scale soap makers worked in most market towns. The production of soap increased sharply in Britain between 1700 and 1850, in spite of excise duties, most of it being made by small-scale soap boilers. The growth of alkali manufacture led some alkali makers into soap production.

William Gossage (1799–1877) established a works at Widnes (*see* HALTON) from 1850, a pioneer large-scale manufacturer using brand names like 'Magical' and 'Restu'. New fats like palm oil and cotton seed oil were employed, and in the late nineteenth century soap came to be sold in individual tablets (or cakes), under branded names, rather than in blocks to be cut by the retailer. In Britain the leader of this revolution was W. H. Lever (*see* PORT SUNLIGHT), maker of Sunlight Soap, but the change had American precedents. Manufacturers produced new products. In 1894 Lever brought out 'Lifebuoy' soap, using carbolic acid and the 'nigre', or waste fatty acids, produced during the manufacture of 'Sunlight' soap. Milled soap flakes were sold in packets, one of the pioneering brands being Lever's 'Lux', launched in 1899–

Figure 146 Cutting the roof of the world in Snowdonia: quarrying to over 616 m (2000 ft.) at Dinorwic in North Wales provided roofing slates for Britain's towns and for export markets from the late eighteenth century. The slate was worked in terraces up the mountainside, with sawmills and slate-splitting workshops built onto banks of waste edge-tipped by ephemeral tramroad tracks on either side. Each ton of finished slates left 30 tons of waste. Vertiginous counterbalanced inclines, also built of slate, connected the terrace tramroads and carried the product to the valley.

Aerofilms Ltd

1900. Soap powders – mixtures of milled soap, powdered soda and bleaching agents – were developed in Germany, 'Persil' being registered by Henkel & Co. of Düsseldorf in 1906, and marketed in England by Joseph Crossfield & Co. from 1909. Scouring powders, like Lever's 'Vim', launched in 1904 – mixtures of milled soap, soda and silica – were another new product of the early twentieth century.

The growing scale of soap production in the late nineteenth century led manufacturers towards vertical integration: to the production of their own caustic soda, to the processing of their own fats (like Lever's establishment of an oil and cake mill at Port Sunlight in 1896), and to the production of oils in Africa, Lever acquiring a concession on nearly 810 000 ha (2 000 000 ac.) for the production of palm oil in the Belgian Congo in 1911.

BIBLIOGRAPHY
General
Book of Trades, 1839; Musson, 1965; Wilson, 1954.

BARRIE TRINDER

soda A confusing chemical term, most commonly applied to sodium carbonate (Na_2CO_3), otherwise called soda ash, or ALKALI. A solution of sodium carbonate on evaporating forms large crystals of washing soda ($Na_2CO_3 \cdot 10H_2O$). Bicarbonate of soda, also known as sodium hydrogen carbonate or sodium bicarbonate ($NaHCO_3$), is formed in large quantities in the Solvay process, but is all converted to carbonate, commercial bicarbonate being prepared by treating the carbonate with carbonic acid (carbon dioxide + water). Soda is used in medicine, and since the late nineteenth century in baking powder (*see* PHOSPHORUS). CAUSTIC SODA, or sodium hydroxide ($NaOH$), is a chemical important in many industrial processes. Soda water, or carbonated water, an early invention of Joseph Priestley (1733–1804), is water in which carbon dioxide has been dissolved so that it is 'aerated'.

BIBLIOGRAPHY
General
Partington, 1950.

soft drinks The term 'soft drinks' normally applies to non-alcoholic cold drinks. SPA water was a significant item of trade in Europe by 1700. The manufacture of non-alcoholic drinks was stimulated by the invention, by JOSEPH BRAMAH and others of processes for making carbonated water. An important pioneer of the trade was Jacob Schweppe (1740–1821), born in Hesse, who set up works in Geneva, using the 'Geneva system' of manufacture which utilized compression pumps. He established a company in England during a visit in 1792–9, which in due course built large factories at Hendon, London, in 1896, and Colwall, using spa water from Malvern, in 1892. The mid-nineteenth century saw the growth of other large concerns supplying railway companies and hotels, like the Ellis Soda Water Works at Ruthin, North Wales, which sustained a considerable local basketmak-ing industry supplying the hampers in which bottles were dispatched. By the late nineteenth century a soft drinks factory included departments for producing flavouring essences and colourings, and oils like those of aniseed and ginger; syruping machines; machinery for aerating water; and filling and bottling plants.

BIBLIOGRAPHY
General
Hayward-Tylor, 1910; Kirkby, 1902; Riley, 1972; Simmons, 1983.

Sognefjord, Sogn og Fjordane, Norway   The most extensive of the Norwegian fjords, north of Bergen, 180 km (110 mi.) long. There is a regional open-air museum at Kaupanger: Kvikne's Hotel, Balestrand, one of the last of the great wooden hotels built for nineteenth-century tourists, with an Anglican church nearby, built in 1887 for English visitors and modelled on the traditional stave church. A combined corn and saw mill, with a vertical multi-bladed saw, is preserved at Offerdale in Årdal parish. There is a hydro-electric power station with an adjacent aluminium plant at Høyanger.

Flåm, a small village with a quay, at the head of the precipitous Aurlandsfjord at the eastern end of the Sognefjord, is the terminus of a 20 km (12 mi.) branch railway opened in 1942 linking the fjord with Myrdal on the BERGENSBANEN. The line rises 865 m (2840 ft.), passing many waterfalls and giving spectacular views of the Flåmsdal. The road that climbs the valley, itself a notable work of civil engineering with seventeen hairpin bends, was built in the 1890s to aid the construction of the Bergensbanen.

BIBLIOGRAPHY
General
Schneider, 1963.

Soignies (Zinnik), Hainaut, Belgium   A town 37 km (23 mi.) SW of Brussels, important for its limestone quarries, which employed 2700 men in 1900. Former quarries and limekilns dominate the surrounding landscape, and in the town are two interesting quarry-company headquarters buildings. The three-storey office block of the Wincqz quarries is in brick, with a vast commemorative stone of 1855. The Paternoster quarries were administered from an elegant neo-classical chateau in rue Mademoiselle Hannicq. There are terraces of two-storey workers' houses of 1830–50 in the Soignies-Carrières district. The Durobor glassworks in rue Mademoiselle Hannicq is a thirteen-bay concrete structure of 1928–30, in 1931 the first in Europe to have an automatic glass-blowing machine.

BIBLIOGRAPHY
General
Viaene, 1986.

LOCATION
[M] Musée du Vieux Cimetière (Old Cemetery Museum), Parc du Vieux Cimetière, rue H. Leroy, 7400 Soignies.

Sokolov, North Bohemia, Czechoslovakia   A centre for

LIGNITE mining and chemical industries, as well as glassworks, textiles and porcelain manufacture. An industrial museum was established in 1960 by the National Technical Museum.

LOCATION

[M] Museum of Mining History, Zamek, Sokolov.

Solikamsk, Perm, USSR Possibly the earliest permanent Russian settlement in the Urals, Solikamsk, lies on the River Kama about 180 km (110 mi.) N. of Perm. Its saltworks date from c.1430, and it is now a centre of the Soviet potash, fertilizer and paper industries. The Perm District Museum holds the original annual chronicles of the settlement from 1500 to 1796, a selection from which has been published. The nineteenth-century saltworks, only recently closed, were at Ust-Borovskii, in the northern outskirts of the town, and have been largely preserved, partly in working order. About fifty buildings are included in the complex, two of which are timber towers for raising the salt solution, whose architecture derives directly from Muscovite fortress towers. Eight evaporation houses are also preserved, as well as several salt barns. Part of the works, comprising one 'technical cell' (that is one of each unit of the production process) has been removed to the Khokhlovsk Open-Air Museum of Architecture and Ethnography.

BIBLIOGRAPHY
Specific
Berkh. V. N. *Puteshestviya v goroda Cherdyn' i Solikamsk.* St Petersburg, 1821.
Solikamsk: putevoditel, Perm. 1980.

Solingen, North Rhine-Westphalia, Germany *See* BERGISCHES LAND.

Solivar, East Slovakia, Czechoslovakia Salt mining in the region to the south of Prešov has been important since at least the thirteenth century. The surviving remains are largely those of the industry that grew up after the flooding of the rock salt deposits in 1752. They include the pit headstock, a horse gin, the 'ceterne' or settling tank, the 'varna' or 'kitchen', the 'frantisek' or salt warehouse, and the 'klopacha', the wooden bell for calling the miners to work. The rectangular pithead building has an octagonal horse-gin house at one end. The saline solution was hauled out of the mine in an 800-litre (175-gallon) oxhide bag and sent down channels to the settling house. This is a brick and slatted plank building sloping downhill along the direction of the flow: inside are twelve timber settling tanks. The solution was then taken by pipe to the 'kitchen' to be boiled. The boilers and pans are in the process of reconstruction. A wagonway then took the salt to the warehouse, a Baroque building partly destroyed by a fire in 1986. Solivar is a National Cultural Monument which has the potential to show the links between all the processes from salt mining to final production, in an urban context which also includes examples of workers' housing.

BIBLIOGRAPHY
Specific
Kosova, K. and Gojodic, I. *Solivar: problems in conserving the National Cultural Monument.* Pamiatky Priroda, 1981.

SIMON DERRY

Solms, Hesse, Germany The Fortuna iron-ore mine near Oberbiel, in the Lahn valley, 60 km (40 mi.) NE of Koblenz, was one of the most productive in the Lahn-Dill area. Mining continued there until 1983. In 1849 Prince zu Solms-Braunfels acquired the mine to supply his ironworks, the Georgshütte in Burgsolms. In 1906 the mine passed into the possession of the firm of Krupp, which extended the surface buildings. The winding-engine house is one of the largest mine buildings in the region. A peculiarity of the Fortuna mine was that the vertical shaft was linked, after 1908, to a large horizontal haulage tunnel; 1.6 million tonnes of iron ore had passed along this by 1983. The entire complex has been preserved as a show mine, and a mining museum has been set up on the surface.

Solvay, Ernest (1838–1922) The first to succeed commercially in operating the ammonia-soda process for the production of ALKALI (sodium carbonate). His first small plant in Brussels began operation in 1861, large-scale production starting at Couillet, east of Charleroi, in 1865. In 1873 he constructed a works at Dombasle, south of Nancy, where 200 000 tonnes per annum of alkali were being made by 1879. The process was introduced in Britain by John Brunner (1842–1919) and Ludwig Mond (1839–1909) at NORTHWICH in 1874, and the Solvay Process Co. began production in North America at Syracuse (N.Y.) in 1884. The Solvay process dominated the world's alkali trade by 1900, and many plants remain in production.

The process begins with brine, which is saturated with ammonia, producing ammoniacal salt solution. This in turn is saturated with carbon dioxide under pressure, producing sodium bicarbonate and ammonium chloride. At the high concentrations used, sodium bicarbonate precipitates, and is collected and heated to produce soda ash.

This is a complex process which is not divided into clear-cut steps, but it may be represented by the following equations:

$$NaCl + NH_4HCO_3 \rightarrow NaHCO_3 + NH_4Cl$$
$$2NaHCO_3 \rightarrow Na_2CO_3 + CO_2 + H_2O$$

The carbonizing of the ammoniacal solution takes place in a Solvay tower, in which the stream of carbon dioxide is brought into contact with the solution. The first Solvay tower, 25 m (80 ft.) in height, was built in 1869.

Carbon dioxide for the process is produced in kilns charged with limestone and coke.

BIBLIOGRAPHY
General
Bolle, 1963; Cohen, 1956; Morgan and Pratt, 1938; Partington, 1950; Reader, 1970; Warren, 1980.

Specific
Mason, W. The manufacture of ammonia soda. In *Chemical Trades Journal*, 7 November, 1908.

BARRIE TRINDER

solvent   A substance that dissolves some other substance or substances. The term is usually applied to an organic solvent, a volatile liquid used to dissolve a solid during the manufacture of paint, polishes and the like.

BIBLIOGRAPHY
General
Morgan and Pratt, 1938.

Sønderborg, Jutland, Denmark   Sønderborg is a port and market town of medieval origin, situated partly on the east coast of southern Jutland and partly on the island of Als. Industry was established in the town in the nineteenth century, and in 1921 a large worsted spinning mill was established there. Since World War II industrial development has been more varied, but principally in the engineering sector.

Around the small town of Egernsund, 10 km (6 mi.) W., is the largest concentration of brickworks in Denmark, grouped around extensive deposits of stoneless clay from a glacial lake, and benefiting from easy sea-borne transportation of the products and of the fuel needed for the kilns. In the first half of the nineteenth century some of the brickyards at Egernsund were the most developed in Scandinavia, and in 1840 the first tunnel kiln in the world was patented and operated in the yard of Hans Jordt near Flensburg, on what is now the German side of the fjord (*see* DENMARK). The brick industry in the area grew rapidly in the nineteenth century, reaching a peak of thirty-eight operating brickworks in 1880. Eight brickyards still operate around Egernsund, and the circular kiln and some workers' dwellings at the closed Cathrinesminde works are being restored as a museum of bricks and tiles.

The largest factory in Denmark, the Danfoss engineering concern, is situated, contrary to the usual rules of industrial location, at the former village of Havnbjerg on the island of Als. Founded in 1933 by M. Clausen at his father's farm, the firm has developed into a multinational company specializing in the production of regulating devices for heating and cooling.

BIBLIOGRAPHY
General
Johansen, 1988.
Specific
Adriansen, I. *et al. Teglværker ved Flensborg Fjord* (Brickworks at Flensborg Fjord). Gråsten, 1984.
Askgaard, H. *Den sønderjyske industris udvikling fra 1920 til 1970* (The development of industry in South Jutland 1920–1970). Copenhagen, 1970.
Askgaard, H. *En fabrik og dens omgivelser* (A factory and its environment). Copenhagen, 1976.

LOCATION
[M] Museet på Sønderborg Slot (Historical Museum), 6400 Sønderborg.

OLE HYLDTOFT

Sopron (Ödenburg), Györ-Sopron, Hungary   An ancient city with Roman remains, medieval walls, and many Baroque buildings, on the eastern slopes of the Alpine foothills, 220 km (140 mi.) W. of Budapest, 65 km (40 mi.) SE of Vienna. The chief Hungarian mining museum has collections relating to the mining of oil, natural gas, minerals and DIMENSION STONE, artists' depictions of mining, and the history of the Hungarian mint. There are also historical displays at the Brennbergbánya mine, 10 km (6 mi.) SE, where coal is said to have been first mined in Hungary. The Franz Liszt Museum includes sections on industrial history as well as on pottery and folk art. The national forestry museum is being established in the palace of the Esterházys, and there is a museum in a bakery of 1749. The international private railway, Györ–Sopron–Ebenfurthi Vasut (*see* AUSTRIA), has a museum at the south station, which dates from 1847. There are spectacular pillar-and-stall workings in the Fertörákos quarry 6 km (4 mi.) N., which are the location for an operatic festival each June.

LOCATIONS
[M] Bakery Museum, Bécsi u. 5, H-9400 Sopron.
[M] Central Mining Museum, Templom u. 2, H-9400 Sopron.
[M] Forestry Museum, Templom u. 4, H-9400 Sopron.
[M] Liszt Ferenc Museum (Franz Liszt Museum), H-9400 Sopron.

MIHÁLY KUBINSZKY

sorting office   A sorting office is a building where mail is sorted for transmission onwards or for distribution. Most sorting is still by manual pigeonholding, as in the nineteenth century, but in some countries mechanization by electronic tagging with postcodes has been introduced.

See also TRAVELLING POST OFFICE.

Sørumsand, Akershus, Norway   A town on the eastern bank of the River Glomma, 40 km (25 mi.) E. of Oslo. It is the terminus of the 56 km (35 mi.) Urskog–Hølandsbanen railway, a 750 mm gauge branch of the state railway to Skulerud, which carried freight and passengers in 1895–1960. A 3.5 km (2 mi.) section to Fossum is preserved and operated by a voluntary group, A/L Hølandsbanen, with support from the local authorities. Two identical 2–6–2T locomotives by Chemnitz of 1909 and 1925, and original passenger coaches, are in use.

LOCATION
[S] A/L Urskog–Hølandsbanen, p.b. 711, Sentrum Oslo 1.

Soufli, Thrace, Greece   A small town on the Turkish border, with many ancient timber-framed houses, in a region celebrated for wine and silk. The history of silk production and processing, in both domestic and factory-based periods, is illustrated in a museum located in the family home of the politician and intellectual, K. Kourtidis (1870–1944). Oral, documentary and photographic evidence of silk manufacture was collected during a research project in 1987.

BIBLIOGRAPHY
Specific
Oikonomou, A. Silk Cultivation in Soufli. In *Technology*, II, 1988.

LOCATION
[M] Arkhontiko Kourtidhi, Soufli.

sough A slightly sloping tunnel, perhaps several kilometres long, driven into a hillside below mine workings to drain away water.

Sound tolls The toll books for the Sound, the strait between Denmark and Sweden, form one of the most important sources for industrial history in Europe. Tolls were collected from Kronborg Castle, Helsingør, by the rulers of Denmark from the sixteenth century until 1857. The records are held in the Royal Archives in COPENHAGEN, and have been extensively used – among other purposes, for quantifying exports of wood and tar from Sweden and Finland.

BIBLIOGRAPHY
General
Bang and Korst, 1906–53; Johansen, 1983.

sources The prime source of evidence for the industrial archaeologist is the structure, site or artefact. Other sources include the writings of classic authorities (*see* AGRICOLA, GEORGIUS; BOURNE, J. C.; DIDEROT, DENIS; FAIRBAIRN, WILLIAM; HOLME, RANDLE; MAYER'S LEXICON; MAYHEW, HENRY; REES, ABRAHAM; SMILES, SAMUEL; TELFORD, THOMAS); documents (*see* ACCOUNTS; BUSINESS RECORDS; CENSUS; DESIGN REGISTRATION; INSURANCE RECORDS; MAP; PATENT; PORT BOOKS; PROBATE RECORDS; SOUND TOLLS); ICONOGRAPHY; INDUSTRIAL ESPIONAGE; INVENTORY of monuments; ORAL HISTORY; TRADE SECRET; and VIDEO HISTORY.

BARRIE TRINDER

Sousa Viterbo, Francisco de (1845–1910) A Portuguese historian, journalist and poet, author of books extending over many disciplines, including literary history, archaeology, medicine, ethnography, nautical studies, the fine arts, industrial history and biography. His article 'Portuguese industrial archaeology: the mills', published in the August–September issue of 1896 of *O Arqueólogo Português*, was one of the first studies to use the expression 'industrial archaeology'. Sousa Viterbo not only laid the foundations of a new discipline but showed how the study of the physical remains of past manufacturing activities, and people's memories of their operation, could be of relevance in the modern world.

BIBLIOGRAPHY
General
Sousa Viterbo, 1896.

Southampton, Hampshire, England A medieval port, which from the 1830s grew to be Britain's premier ocean liner terminal. There are some remains of medieval warehouses, one of which was used for the construction of 'Moonbeam' aircraft before 1914. The east docks were constructed from 1836; the west docks, including Ocean Dock for passenger liners, in the 1920s and 30s. Ocean Dock is no longer used for passengers. Terminus Station, by Sir William Tite (1798–1873), from 1839, and the former LSWR hotel are the principal monuments of passenger services.

Aircraft manufacture has been important in the area, and Southampton was the principal terminal for flying boats linking England with its overseas empire in the 1930s and 40s. Hythe was used by flying boats during 1937–50, and a passenger pier survives alongside World War I hangars. Imperial House, a timber-framed terminal building with observation balconies, was used in 1937–48, and the Maritime Air Terminal, now HMS Wessex, during 1948–58, when flying-boat services ceased. A Sandringham flying boat is preserved by the Museum service.

Eastleigh, 9.5 km (6 mi.) N., is a railway town where the LSWR established a locomotive and carriage works in 1888. Parts are now incorporated in the Barton Park industrial estate. Of the company-built workers' accommodation, Dutton Cottages of 1892 and some houses of 1899 survive.

BIBLIOGRAPHY
General
Moore, 1984, 1988.
Specific
Moore, P. The industrial archaeology of the regions of the British Isles: No. 2, Hampshire. In *IAR*, VII(1) 1985.
Turton, B. J. The railway towns of Southern England. In *Transport History*, I(2) 1969.

LOCATION
[M] Southampton City Museums and Art Gallery, Civic Centre, Southampton SO9 4XF.

BARRIE TRINDER

South Australia, Australia An arid state with few climatic advantages, although it is rich in metallic ores. Silver and lead were discovered in 1841, and Australia's first mining and smelting concern was established at Glen Osmond, where the flue remains, although the operation ceased in 1848. The Olympic Dam Company is now the world's largest producer of copper and uranium. Copper was found in 1842 at Kapunda, and in 1845 at Burra, where the mine directors laid out Kooringa, the first COMPANY TOWN in Australia. Most ore was exported to SWANSEA, Wales, although smelting began at Burra in 1849. Cottages with Welsh and Cornish characteristics remain, as well as engine houses and flues. The narrow-gauge Pichi Richi railway, built in 1882 to carry copper, continues in operation, retaining some original cranes and buildings. It is the oldest intact railway in Australia and one of the longest of its kind in the world. Blast furnaces and a steel works operate at Whyalla, where a large shipyard flourished between 1939 and 1978. Ore is mined at Iron Knob and Iron Monarch, 50 km (30 mi.) N. of Whyalla.

No convicts meant no cheap labour, so that innovations in food-processing were adopted quickly. Wheat was the basis of early prosperity. A windmill tower of 1842 survives at Hahndorf, 40 km (25 mi.) E. of Adelaide, and a water wheel made in Glasgow in 1860 at Bridgewater Mill. Lutherans from Prussia settled in the Barossa Valley in 1851 and established vineyards, orchards and olive groves, with distinctive patterns of settlements. Australia's oldest irrigation area is around Renmark, where there are now canneries and juice factories.

Paddle steamers on the Murray River were an important factor in the development of the eastern part of the state. Several are preserved, including the 55-ton *Enterprise* of 1878, which still operates; the 118-ton *Gem* of 1876, at the Swan Hill Folk Museum, Victoria; the 157-ton *Marion* of 1897, at Mannum, 60 km (36 mi.) E. of Adelaide; and the 83-tonne *Oscar W.* of 1908, at Murray Bridge.

Australia's largest motor museum, at Birdwood, 24 km (15 mi.) E. of Adelaide, has over three hundred motor vehicles, including 160 motorcycles, and the oldest running Australian-made power road vehicle, a Shearer Steam Car of 1899.

Kangaroo Island has important remains of the short-lived sealing industry which ended after the seals had been virtually exterminated in the 1830s.

At Gawler, 30 km (19 mi.) N. of Adelaide, the James Marting & Co. engineering works, the largest in Australia, produced bridges, mining equipment and locomotives. The Eagle Foundry in King Street remains, together with the Albion flour mill of 1868, and remnants of gasworks, brickworks and limekilns.

See also ADELAIDE.

BIBLIOGRAPHY
General
Birmingham *et al.*, 1983; Brouwer, 1985; Donovan and Kirkman, 1986; Hammerton, 1986; Heritage of Australia, 1981; Ioannou, 1986; Parsons and Tolley, 1973; Williams, 1974.
Specific
Bannear, D. The interpretation of structural remains at Bolla Bollana copper smelting works, South Australia. In *Australian Journal of Historical Archaeology*, VI, 1988.

LOCATIONS
[M] Birdwood Mill National Motor Museum, Birdwood, South Australia 5234.
[M] Swan Hill Folk Museum, Horseshoe Bend, Swan Hill, Victoria 3585.

KATE CLARK

South Carolina, United States of America   This state's transition late in the nineteenth century from an agricultural to an industrial economy is manifest in the cotton and lumber mills that pepper the South Carolina countryside. The cheap, plentiful water power of streams descending from the piedmont plateau spurred the creation of bulk-materials processing in the very regions of their extraction. Native-grown cotton and timber have been further enriched as industrial commodities by the pres-

ence of easily navigable rivers, giving ocean access to goods in both raw and finished forms.

South Carolinian plantation life and its companion slave trade yielded some surprising proto-industrial spin-offs. Charleston's town jail contained one of the few American prisoner TREADMILLS, of the kind common in Great Britain. In use between 1823 and the 1840s, it was trodden by captured runaway slaves to grind grain for consumption within the jail.

Elsewhere in the state capital, the Charleston Railroad Artifacts Museum honours the state's dense network of small railway lines that threaded through the hills servicing plantation communities isolated from urban centres. The Charleston–Hamburg Railroad, constructed in 1833, was the world's longest at the time, extending some 219 km (136 mi.).

One of the nation's few trade-specific museums stands in a market of 1842 in Georgetown, devoted to the state's substantial involvement with the production of rice. And at Tigerville, the earliest surviving engineered bridge in the American South-East crosses Gap Creek. The Poinsett Bridge is a small stone-arch span built in 1820 to carry a highway into North Carolina. The noted engineer and architect Robert Mills (1781–1855) may have been its designer. Not known for their modesty, Southern museums occasionally offer spectacular claims of attribution, such as the one by Branchville's Railroad Shrine and Museum that their depot of 1877 sits at the site of the first railroad JUNCTION in the world.

LOCATIONS
[M] Branchville Railroad Shrine and Museum, 102 N. Main Street, Branchville, SC 29432.
[M] Charleston Railroad Artifacts Museum, 3534 Admiral Drive, Charleston, SC 29405.
[M] The Rice Museum, Lafayette Park, Front and Screven Streets, Georgetown, SC 29440.

DAVID H. SHAYT

South Dakota, United States of America   Deep in the American breadbasket, South Dakota is one of the more solidly agricultural states, although gold, silver and tungsten have been mined from deep shafts in the state's Black Hills for most of the century. Among these finds, the most prominent has been the great Homestake Mine in Lead City, which had yielded some $200 million worth of metals by 1927.

Carved into one of these Black Hills is the famous ode to the pneumatic chisel by Gutson Borglum (1867–1941). The gigantic heads of Presidents George Washington, Thomas Jefferson, Abraham Lincoln and Theodore Roosevelt began to emerge from the fine, dense granite of Mount Rushmore in the mid-1920s, the single-minded drive of Borglum and the tenacity of his carvers overcoming a host of obstacles, natural, political and technological. Both the mountainside and its nearby museum are National Park Service property, the museum housing some eight hundred of the hand-driven and machine-powered tools used in the job.

The equipment of deep-shaft gold mining as well as the

shaft itself may be examined at the Big Thunder Gold Mine of the 1880s in Keystone. And what may be the nation's only historic fish hatchery site and museum stand in a hatchery structure of 1899 at Spearfish.

LOCATIONS

[M,S] Big Thunder Gold Mine, Box 706, Keystone, SD 57751.

[M,S] D. C. Booth Historic Fish Hatchery and Museum, 722 Main Street, Spearfish, SD 57783.

[M] Mount Rushmore National Memorial, Keystone, SD 57751-0268.

[M] Lead Mining Museum, Lead, South Dakota.

DAVID H. SHAYT

South Georgia   An archipelago 1400 km (870 mi.) SE of the FALKLAND ISLANDS from which it is administered. Hulks of historic ships can be seen at several locations. They include:

- *Bayard*: a 1319-ton iron barque, built at Liverpool in 1864.
- *Louise*: a 1065-ton copper-sheathed wooden sailing ship, built at Freeport, Maine, in 1869.
- *Brutus*: a 1686-ton steel sailing ship, built at Port Glasgow in 1884.
- *Petrel*: a 245-ton steam whaler, built at Oslo in 1928.

BIBLIOGRAPHY
General
Brouwer, 1985.
Specific
Headlund, R. K. Wrecks and remains at South Georgia. In *British Antarctic Survey*, LXV, 1900.

Sovereign Hill, Victoria, Australia   Sovereign Hill at Ballarat vividly commemorates the gold boom of the early 1850s which created the town. It is a re-creation of a gold-mining settlement, in which all the buildings are based on detailed research into the originals. It was opened by the Ballarat Historical Park Association in 1970. Mining methods are displayed in the Red Hill Gully Diggings, where goldpanning is demonstrated, and there are horse gins, ore-dressing machinery, gold-diggers' dwellings, and a reconstruction of the Gold Commissioner's tent. The town area contains premises relating to various trades, including a newspaper office, a coachbuilder's shop, a bakery, a foundry and a confectionery manufactory. A third section of the museum is concerned with the methods used to mine gold in Victoria between 1860 and 1918, as a substantial industry grew out of the work of the early prospectors. It is centred around the surface buildings, including the headstock, of the Sovereign Quartz Mine. Exhibits include a large ten-head stamper battery, worked by a compound steam engine built in Ballarat in 1904. Sovereign Hill attracts some 250 000 visitors a year and is one of the most imaginative of all interpretations of industrial history.

BIBLIOGRAPHY
Specific
Glover, B. *Sovereign Hill Goldmining township, Ballarat.* Richmond, Victoria: Scancolor. 1982.

Reid, J. *Gold Museum: Ballarat's museum of man's heritage of gold.* Sydney: A. H. & A. W. Reed, 1980.

LOCATION

[I] Ballarat Historical Park Association, Sovereign Hill Goldmining Township Post Office, Ballarat, Victoria 3350.

KATE CLARK

spa   Originally, a settlement around a spring of mineral water where invalids sought cures, but the word came to mean a town of resort, where those with independent sources of income settled, or which the wealthy visited for holidays. The word, used from the sixteenth century, comes from Spa in eastern Belgium, one of the principal European watering-places. The archetype in eighteenth-century England was BATH, but the most important nineteenth-century spas were in Germany, where they were encouraged and controlled by state authorities. The essential components were boarding houses, hotels, facilities for drinking and bathing in the water, an assembly room, a casino, a library and routes for walks or rides on donkeys or ponies. Spa water was widely traded in England by the early eighteenth century, and that from Spa, and Seltzer in Nassau, was exported in large quantities by the 1860s.

BIBLIOGRAPHY
General
Granville, 1837, 1841; Murray, 1865.

Spa, Liège, Belgium   The town, 22 km (14 mi.) SE of Liège, that gives its name to all resorts with mineral springs. It was long celebrated for its traditional manufacture of lacquered woodwork, particularly ornamental boxes, which began in the seventeenth century, and is featured in the local museum. The buildings constructed for those taking the waters include several notable applications of cast iron. The covered promenade of 1878 in the parc des Sept Heures, the Galérie Léopold II, has a glass roof supported by cast-iron columns with neo-classical detailing. The bathhouse, the 'Pouhon Pierre-le-Grand', of 1880, has a roof with a delicately traceried iron frame.

BIBLIOGRAPHY
General
Viaene, 1986.

LOCATION

[M] Musée de la Ville d'Eaux (Museum of the town of water), avenue Reine Astrid 7, 4880 Spa.

Spain   Seventeenth-century Spain was characterized by growing regional imbalances. The population rose by 50 per cent during the century, but this overall increase masked considerable differences between regions. The rise in population persisted until well into the nineteenth century.

In the eighteenth century the interior was overwhelmingly agrarian. Production rose gradually due to an increase in the range of crops and an expanding working

Figure 147 The boiler house, headstock, winding house and other pithead buildings at Sovereign Hill: these buildings have been constructed since 1970 to house the museum's working machinery and are based on research into those which operated in this area between 1861 and 1915.
Ballarat Historical Park Association

population. Cereal production predominated. The interior market remained poorly organized, and crises in food production occurred with monotonous regularity since the peasant was able neither to stock nor invest nor even market his produce.

In Catalonia (Cataluña) and the Basque country, the situation varied markedly. There were textile manufactures in Catalonia in the eighteenth century which, with the Catalan commercial tradition, proved a sound foundation for the textile industrialization of the nineteenth century. Catalonia was the first part of Spain to compare with the industrial regions of other advanced European countries. The heyday of the Catalan cotton industry began in 1832 with the introduction of the power loom, and in 1835 with the construction of the first steam-powered textile factory. This sector stimulated other branches of textile manufacture, and Catalonia came to assume a commanding position within the Spanish

economy, particularly in the manufacture of flour, oil, leather and even porcelain. The weak point in the Catalan economy was the lack of coal and iron mines.

Two important canals were begun in Spain in the eighteenth century, the Imperial Canal of Aragón, between TUDELA and Saragossa (Zaragoza), and the Imperial Canal of Castile, which was designed to link the port of Santander with central Spain, as well as for irrigation and water-power purposes. It was begun in 1753, but construction ceased in 1791. It was not resumed until 1831, and the first barges only reached Valladolid in 1835, and Medina de Rioseco in 1849. Most of the 207 km (129 mi.) long canal is now in a ruinous state.

Spain's greatest contribution to civil engineering was the development of dam-construction technology. Continuity has been traced from Roman dams near Mérida, 54 km (34 mi.) E. of Badajoz; through those constructed by

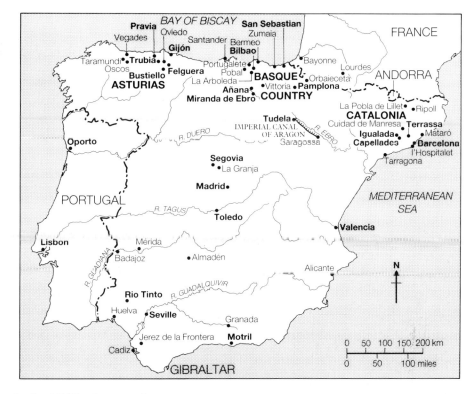

Spain

both Christians and Moors in the Middle Ages; to the curving dam across the Monegre River at Alicante built between 1579 and 1594, and to the prototype of all modern buttress dams, the 120 m (400 ft.) long, 22 m (72 ft.) high structure at Almendralejo, 52 km (32 mi.) SE of Badajoz, which was constructed in 1747. A corn mill was installed within the body of the dam. Its machinery has been removed, but the dam remains in use for water supply.

In the Basque country the export of wrought iron to other European markets, to the colonies and to Castile, stimulated the accumulation of capital and the creation of an enterprise mentality which was to bear fruit in the last thirty years of the nineteenth century.

Reforms in the early nineteenth century brought a gradual end to the *ancien régime* in Spain which aided the growth of capitalist methods of production and the rise of the bourgeoisie. Changes in systems of cultivation, and the sale of large areas of land, gave rise to an enormous increase in agricultural production.

Economic developments in the second half of the nineteenth century were dominated by the growth of railways, the agrarian crisis of the closing decades of the century, and the industrialization of the Basque country.

The first railway in Spain, from Barcelona to Mataró, opened in 1848. Railway construction was stimulated by massive injections of foreign capital. A gauge of 1.674 m (5 ft. 6 in.) became standard, although many narrow-gauge lines were constructed in mountainous regions, many of them now closed. Spain's railway museums display a rich and varied inheritance of steam locomo-

tives, originating in Britain, Germany, France and the USA, as well as magnificent locomotives built and designed in Spain in the twentieth century.

Agrarian output shrank from the early 1880s, as exports declined, imports increased and prices began to fall. The crisis affected Spain more than most European countries, because of the backwardness of agricultural techniques, the high cost of transport and the lack of investment. Estate revenues fell, land went out of production, markets were lost and the living standards of the peasantry declined. Emigration increased, more than two million Spaniards leaving the country between 1882 and 1906. Only wine-producing continued to flourish, particularly in Catalonia, and in the Valencia area.

The response to the crisis in Spain was the raising of tariffs. The depreciation of the peseta reinforced protectionist attitudes, and there was a marked recovery of agrarian prosperity from the beginning of the twentieth century, but in 1920 58 per cent of the working population were still involved in the agricultural sector.

Legislation of 1868 relating to mines, which remained in force until 1944, brought about the heyday of the Spanish mining sector. Growth was stimulated by foreign capital. In Vizcaya the mine-owners made considerable profits through their association with foreign interests, but this was not the case elsewhere. A significant factor was the existence in the Basque province of Vizcaya of a coherent, native bourgeoisie. Elsewhere, in copper mines of the south (*see* RIO TINTO), exploitation of mining resources by English and French companies had almost a colonial aspect. Spain became an important source of

705

other metallic ores: Almadén, for example, 205 km (127 mi.) SW of Madrid, was the principal European source of cinnabar for MERCURY.

The development of modern iron- and steelmaking in Spain falls into three phases. First came the industrialization and early deindustrialization of the south-east, where the first blast furnaces were installed c.1830. The second phase began in 1860 with modernization in the north, particularly in Asturias, which lowered prices, and brought ironmaking in Andalusia to an end. The third stage began in the late 1870s in Vizcaya, and was centred on BILBAO. The reasons for development in Vizcaya were the existence of non-phosphoric ores (essential at that time for the production of steel), the richness of the ore, the ease of extracting it from opencast workings, and the low cost of labour, which ensured that Vizcayan ore was very cheap. Its availability attracted foreign, particularly English, capital, and British coal was imported to smelt Vizcayan ore, in spite of the existence of coal in nearby Asturias: ships delivering coal could return with cargoes of ore for British furnaces.

Neutrality in World War I had positive consequences for the Spanish economy. Exports rose in response to demand from the countries fighting the war, and because Spain was able to supply neutral countries that had previously been markets for the warring states. Products which had previously been imported came to be supplied by Spanish producers. The balance of trade had thus changed markedly in Spain's favour by 1919.

Between 1923 and 1930 controls, monopolies and commissions for the regulation of production dominated economic activity, but such economic nationalism conflicted with the concessions granted to such foreign concerns as AEG Iberica, Siemens and ITT. The 'great crash' of 1929 affected foreign trade and the financial sector, but cereal production and the growth of such consumer goods industries as textiles were sustained, and the effects of the crisis on the Spanish economy were modest. The proclamation in 1931 of the Second Republic began a more serious crisis, as capital began to flow abroad, public and private investment declined, and industrial output fell, with growing lack of bourgeois confidence in the regime.

The Civil War of 1936–9 and the subsequent installation of the dictatorship of General Francisco Franco (1892–1975), which lasted from 1939 until 1975, signalled a radical change in politics and in the economy. Economic autonomy, social repression and a high degree of profit accumulation are the distinctive features of the first period of the dictatorship. Economic reconstruction took many years and it was not until 1956 that real incomes again matched those of 1935. The period was characterized by inflation, prices rising by 250 per cent between 1939 and 1950.

The failure of the policy of economic autonomy, which almost depleted Spain's foreign currency reserves, necessitated a period of liberalization, the beginning of which was marked in 1957 with strikes in Catalonia and the Basque country. It was then that a Stabilization Plan brought new policies which achieved some success. The peasant population declined, about five million people abandoning the land between 1960 and 1975, and the large-scale mechanization of agriculture began. The end to the Franco period began in an economic sense in 1973 with the rise in the price of crude oil, the repercussions of which dominated political discussions in Spain following the death of the dictator. Spain entered the European Economic Community in 1986, and now has a distinguished position amongst the industrialized nations, having been transformed from a collection of backward economies in the space of a decade.

Spain is divided into Comunidades Autonomas (autonomous communities), which are themselves divided into provinces. Both communities and provinces appear in the headings for articles relating to towns in Spain.

Concern for the conservation of the industrial heritage grew rapidly in Spain during the 1980s. National conferences were held in Bilbao in 1982, in Barcelona in 1985 and in Seville in 1990, and societies concerned with the subject have been established in Catalonia and Madrid.

See also AÑANA; ASTURIAS; BALEARIC ISLANDS; BARCELONA; BASQUE COUNTRY; BILBAO; BUSTIELLO; CAPELLADES; CATALONIA; FELGUERA, LA; GAUDÍ, ANTONI; GIJÓN; IGUALADA; MADRID; MIRANDA DE EBRO; MOTRIL; PAMPLONA; PRAVIA; RIO TINTO; SAN SEBASTIÁN; SEGOVIA; SEVILLE; TERRASSA; TOLEDO; TRUBIA; TUDELA; VALENCIA.

BIBLIOGRAPHY
General
Armas, 1980; Civera, 1988; Generalitat de Catalunya, 1988; Gomez *et al.*, 1990); Hadfield, 1986; Hudson, 1979a; Marti *et al*, 1982; Milward and Saul, 1977.
Specific
Smith, N. Early Spanish dams. In *Endeavour*, XXVIII, 1969.

LOCATIONS
[I] Associació del Museu de la Ciencia i de la Tècnica i d'Arqueologia Industrial de Cataluya (Association of Museums of Science, Technology and Industrial Archaeology in Catalonia), Via Laietana 39, Barcelona 8003.
[I] Associacion Española del Patrimonio Industrial y de la Obra Publica (Spanish Association for the Industrial and Civil Engineering Heritage). Museo Nacional del Ferrocarril (National Railway Museum), Estacion de la Delicias, Madrid.

RAFAEL ARACIL

spandrel The triangular space between an arch and a straight-sided figure enclosing it: in industrial archaeological writing, most commonly the abutment and deck of a bridge.

spelter An alternative name for zinc or zinc alloys, particularly in the seventeenth and eighteenth centuries.

spinning jenny The first practical multiple-spindle spinning machine was invented by James Hargreaves (d.1778) and patented in England in 1770. While the operator moved the carriage out, the roving (*see* TEXTILES) was drawn and twisted; when the carriage was moved back, the yarn was wound onto the rotating spindles. Hand-powered, it was applicable to either wool or cotton, in home, workshop or factory. Jenny workshops multiplied rapidly in England in the late eighteenth century.

BIBLIOGRAPHY
General
Jeremy, 1981.
Specific
Aspin, C. New evidence on James Hargreaves and the spinning jenny. In *TH*, I, 1968.
Shimwell, D. W. Capital investment in the expansion of the jenny workshop industry in the Derbyshire leadmining village of Bradwell, 1799–1801. In *TH*, IV, 1973.

spinning mule Invented by Samuel Crompton (1753–1827) in England in the 1770s, the mule combined the drafting rollers of ARKWRIGHT'S WATER FRAME with the moving carriage of Hargreaves's SPINNING JENNY. Its intermittent spinning method provided the most uniform yarn and the widest range of counts or sizes. The self-actor, a fully mechanized version, was developed in England by RICHARD ROBERTS between 1825 and 1830. Mule spinning was a highly skilled and demanding task, and mule spinners were amongst the most militant of textile workers. A floor of 714-spindle mules with the appropriate carding and doubling machines is preserved at HELMSHORE, and a few mules remain in use, chiefly for wool spinning.

BIBLIOGRAPHY
General
Catling, 1970; French, 1859; Jeremy, 1981.
Specific
Rose, M. E. Samuel Crompton (1753–1827): inventory of the spinning mule. In *Transactions of the Lancashire and Cheshire Antiquarian Society*, LXXV and LXXVI, 1965–6.

spinning wheel The principal means of spinning yarn in Europe and America between the late Middle Ages and the Industrial Revolution. Like the reel and other earlier forms of spinning, it was essentially a rotating spindle, given regular motion by a treadle-powered flywheel. The flier, which twists the yarn before it is wound on the bobbin, was known by the early sixteenth century. Seventeenth- and eighteenth-century documents distinguish between the long, large or great wheel, which was used for spinning wool, and the small, little or short wheel, employed to spin flax or hemp.

spirits A spirit is the product of concentrating an alcoholic drink by distilling. In the Middle Ages distilled alcohol was regarded as a medicine, and prepared by APOTHECARIES in stills or alembics. In the sixteenth century it came to be used as a beverage, and became popular as such in the seventeenth and eighteenth centuries. Trade in spirits was promoted by Dutch merchants. The reputations of Cognac and Armagnac (*see* BRANDY) were established, and spices like aniseed were increasingly used as flavouring. Technological innovations made possible the growth of distilling on an industrial scale. Weigert's still of 1772 made continuous cooling possible; while the Coffey Still, patented by the Irishman Aeneas Coffey in 1830, allowed the continuous production of whisky, in contrast to the pot still which was an intermittent process.

See also AKVAVIT; BRANDY; CIDER; GIN; RUM; SCHNAPPS; SCOTCH WHISKY; VODKA; WHISKY.

BIBLIOGRAPHY
General
Braudel, 1981; Thomson, 1849.
Specific
Mathias, P. Agriculture and the brewing and distilling industries in the eighteenth century. In *EcHR*, V, 1952–3.

Spitzbergen (Spitsbergen, Svalbard), Svalbard, Norway The archipelego of Spitzbergen extends over 62 000 km^2 (24 000 sq. mi.) and lies in the Barents Sea 950 km (580 mi.) N. of NARVIK. Eighty per cent of the land is under permanent ice, and nearly half is under legal protection for ecological reasons. The archipelago was put under Norwegian jurisdiction in 1920 by the Treaty of Sèvres, which confirmed Russian rights to mine coal there.

The main island, West Spitzbergen (Vestspitsbergen) has rich coal resources. Coal was used from the seventeenth century for boiling whale blubber, and small quantities were exported to northern Norway from the 1820s, but large-scale exploitation only began c.1900. There are many remains of mining activity around the settlements of Ny-Ålesund and Longyearbyen (which was named after the American mining engineer J. M. Longyear, 1850–1922) but few buildings date from before 1945. The principal buildings in the Russian settlements, Pyramiden and Barentsburg, are in a pompous Baroque style. In the north of the archipelego are remains of whaling activity, which began in the early seventeenth century, including the Dutch settlements of Amsterdamoya and Smeerenburg.

BIBLIOGRAPHY
General
Greve, 1975; Sugden, 1982.

LOCATION
[M] Svalbard Museum, 9170 Longyearbyen, Svalbard.

splash mill The earliest form of watermill, also known as the Norse mill, in which a horizontal wheel at the foot of a vertical shaft (tirl) and fitted with vanes horizontal to the flow of a stream. The motion of the vanes and wheel directly turns a millstone above, an inflexible means of transmission which is difficult to control. Variations include the Tuscan mill and those found in ROMANIA, which have spoon-shaped blades. Examples exist throughout much of Europe and the Near East (*see* BITOLA).

Split, Croatia, Yugoslavia A town dominated by the palace of Diocletian (245–313), built in about AD 300, around which in later centuries refugees from the nearby Greek city of Salonae established themselves amidst ruins. Skopje was held by Venice till 1797, then by Austrians during 1813–1918. It is now a major port, industrial centre and resort.

At Salonae, 8 km (5 mi.) NE, a disused grain mill on the River Jadro has sixteen separate pairs of millstones, each pair driven by a separate horizontal water wheel.

LOCATIONS
[M] City Museum, Papaliceva 1, 58000-Split.
[M] Ethnographical Museum, Narodni trg 1, 58000-Split.
[M] Maritime Museum, Palaca Milesi, 7 Trg Brace Radica, 58000-Split.

Sprague, Frank Julian (1857–1934) A pioneer of electric traction, born in Connecticut, who resigned from the US Navy in 1883 to work with THOMAS EDISON. He soon formed the Sprague Electric Railway & Motor Co. to make traction motors for electric TRAMCARS, but it was absorbed by Edison's General Electric Co. in 1890. In 1982 he established the Sprague Electric Elevator Co., which built about six hundred elevators before it was sold to the OTIS company. His experience with elevators led him in 1897 to devise a system of MULTIPLE UNIT control for railway trains, in which wheel slip was virtually eliminated by having many powered axles at intervals along the train, controllable from cabs at either end.

spring A piece of metal, usually carefully selected steel, used in a machine such as a clock to give motion by its tendency to unwind, in vehicles to absorb shocks, in weighing machines, and for many other engineering applications. In the eighteenth century a spring was traditionally shaped and heated, and then dropped into hot fat of some kind. It would be re-heated to a violet hue, before being hammered, filed, and finally polished. A coiled spring was normally shaped on a lathe. From c.1850 specialist spring manufacturers grew up in Europe and America, although many engineering concerns continued to make their own springs. Since 1900, as means of heat treatment have become more sophisticated and machines like the universal automatic coiler (patented in 1919) have been developed, most springs have been made by specialist manufacturers.

BIBLIOGRAPHY
General
Barraclough, 1981–4; Carlson, 1978; Rees, 1802–20.

squatter settlement A house or houses built on common land of which the builder lacks the legal title, a phenomenon that contributed substantially to the growth of industry in England and Wales. Similar developments took place elsewhere in Europe with variations arising from different legal systems. In Britain it was widely, although in law mistakenly, believed that if a house could be constructed with smoke arising from its hearth within one day, the builder had a right to remain. Common land belonged to the lord of the manor although he could not alienate it. A squatter settlement could be controlled by the annual imposition of fines in a manorial court; conventional rents could not be charged. Squatter plots

were usually irregular in shape, and bounded by low earth ramparts on which were planted such useful trees as crab apple, hazel, damson and holly. Urban sprawl has engulfed such substantial areas of industrial squatter settlement as the BLACK COUNTRY, while the landscape of others was changed by enclosure. In Britain the best-preserved region of industrial squatting is in the CLEE HILLS.

BIBLIOGRAPHY
General
Stamp and Hoskins, 1963; Trinder, 1982a.
Specific
Bettey, J. Seventeenth-century squatters' dwellings – some documentary evidence. In *Vernacular Architecture*, XIII, 1982.
Jones, K., Hunt, M., Malam, J., and Trinder, B. Holywell Lane: a squatter community in the Shropshire coalfield. In *IAR*, VI, 1982.
Trinder, B. The open village in industrial Britain. In Nisser, 1981.

BARRIE TRINDER

Stadthagen, Lower Saxony, Germany Coal mining in the Schaumburg district around Stadthagen, 44 km (27 mi.) W. of Hanover, was a principal source of income for the Counts, later the Princes, of Schaumburg-Lippe from the fifteenth century. Several monuments of the industry remain, most of them from the late nineteenth century and the early twentieth, providing a good illustration of the transition from adit to shaft mining, and of the ideas of a model mine current at the turn of the century. In spite of decay, and the destruction of headstocks and coking plant, these ideas are particularly well illustrated in the two phases of building at the Georgschacht mine, one of 1902, the other of 1925. The mine ceased operation in 1960. Remaining buildings include the locomotive sheds, the carpentry and engineering workshops, the water-tower, the boiler house and power station, the transformers, the pithead building and baths, the crusher for the coke ovens, and the benzene plant. In Nienstedt, 6 km (4 mi.) SW, a building housing a headstock of the 1840s remains, together with a shale calcining furnace of c.1870; and at Obernkirchen the building erected at the entrance to the Liethstolien drift mine in 1902 survives, together with the impressive ruins of a briquette factory of 1907. In the Schaumburg valley are further remains of mine buildings whose exteriors have largely been preserved while the buildings have been adapted to new uses, such as structures of 1910 at Tallensen, of 1935 at Beckedorf and Blyinghausen, and of 1953–7 at Lüdersfeld.

BIBLIOGRAPHY
General
Mende and Hamm, 1990; Slotta, 1975–88.

LOCATION
[M] Stadtmuseum (Municipal Museum), 3060 Stadthagen.

MICHAEL MENDE

stage coach A coach that ran at specific times between specific places. The term was first used in the late seventeenth century to describe a network which in the

1630s extended only thirty miles from London, but which by 1705 linked the English capital with 180 towns throughout the country. The term was used in North America, and similar services operated in most European countries. Horses were normally changed after each 'stage' of about 20 km (12 mi.). In England the system grew vigorously in the eighteenth century as TURNPIKE roads were extended. Between London and Birmingham there was one coach a week in 1740, thirty a week in 1783, and thirty-four a day by 1829. By 1830 the average speed was rather less than 10 mph (16 km/h) including stops. In England William Champion (1787–1859) was the principal owner of coaches, which he leased out to operators. He owned 1300 horses in the early 1830s. Outside passengers were conveyed from c.1750, and by 1830 as many as eleven might be riding on the top. Stage coaches were quickly driven from the roads by railway competition, but they were substantial vehicles and many are preserved.

See also DILIGENCE; HORSE; INN; MAIL COACH; POST COACH; WAGGON.

BIBLIOGRAPHY
General
Bates, 1969; Dyos and Aldcroft, 1969.

BARRIE TRINDER

stained glass A term loosely applied to coloured glass used for architectural purposes, usually in the form of mosaics of different colours set in leaded lights. Glass is coloured by coating it with a fusible pigment and then firing it, and by adding chemicals to a molten glass mix, producing 'solid' coloured glass. Specialist manufacturers produced on a large scale the coloured leaded glass which was popular in the bourgeois homes of the late nineteenth century and the first three decades of the twentieth century.

stainless steel *See* STEEL.

staithe A platform, often roofed, that carried a railway above a river or the sea: from it coal from wagons with bottom-door discharge could be directed through chutes into ships. There was often space at an intermediate level where coal could be stored when no vessels were docked. Staithes originated in north-east England before 1700; they were adapted to successive developments in railway technology and used until the 1980s. Dunston Staithes are preserved (*see* NEWCASTLE-UPON-TYNE).

BIBLIOGRAPHY
General
Lewis, 1970.

stamp A form of water-powered machine for crushing metallic ores, particularly those of tin, copper and gold, used from the early eighteenth century. Heavy wooden 'stampers', often with cast-iron heads, held upright in wooden frames, were raised by the action of a cam on a horizontal shaft driven by a water wheel, and allowed to fall on to the material to be crushed. There is an example at Tolgus (*see* CORNWALL). Massive direct-powered steam stamps were widely used to crush copper ore in the USA (*see* MICHIGAN).

See also figure 95.

stampers Ranges of up to five cam-operated wooden hammers, used for beating rags in troughs, through which there was a flow of water, in the traditional process of PAPER manufacture. The troughs were so arranged that the rags could be moved from one to another as they were pulped. The hammers on the first trough were shod with spikes to fray the cloth. The last in the sequence had plain wooden heads so that fine fibres would not be lost. Large, complex stampers were in use in Italy by the sixteenth century. A few remained in use in the 1920s for making fine-quality paper.

stamping and potting A coal-fired method making WROUGHT IRON from PIG IRON, patented by John Wright and Richard Jesson of West Bromwich in 1773 (patent No. 1054). Broken pieces of pig iron were heated in clay pots. The method was much used in England until soon after 1800, when it was generally superseded by the PUDDLING FURNACE.

BIBLIOGRAPHY
General
Hyde, 1977; Trinder, 1981.
Specific
Morton, G. R. and Mutton, N. The transition to Cort's puddling process. In *Journal of the Iron & Steel Institute*, 205, 1967.

Stanhope press The first hand printing press with an iron frame, which required only a single pull. It was designed in 1800 by the third Earl Stanhope (1753–1816), who also revived stereotyping, the reproduction of blocks of text set in type by making impressions in clay, or casts in plaster, which served as moulds for lead castings. Stanhope's original contribution was a system of compound levers to increase the efficiency and pressure of the single pull.

BIBLIOGRAPHY
General
Moran, 1973.

staple A term with two meanings in industrial archaeology:
1. Natural FIBRES, such as COTTON, WOOL and FLAX, are described as being of long or short staple according to the length and fineness of the individual fibres of which they are composed.
2. A traded commodity, specifically one of importance in a particular context, like wool in medieval England or oil in twentieth-century ROTTERDAM, or a trading centre or port where such commodities are traded.

Starachowice, Kielce, Poland An ironworks on the

Kamienna River, 35 km (22 mi.) S. of Radom, the pivotal point of STANISŁAW STASZIC's programme in the early nineteenth century to encourage industrial development of what became the STAROPOLSKI INDUSTRIAL REGION. Charcoal-fired blast furnaces were built in 1838–41 and modernized from time to time until 1901. After the opening in 1885 of a railway that linked the Staropolski region to the Dąbrowski and Doniecki coal basins in Russia a coke-fired furnace was built in Starachowice and worked until 1968. Due to the initiative of local people the plant has become an open-air museum, and a site of about 7 ha (14 ac.) is now under legal protection. It included the blast furnace with Cowper stoves and hoist tower, a boiler house, a blowing house with a steam engine of 1885, and parts of the complex of 1838–41. Work is in progress to develop the site as the Central Museum of Iron and Steel.

BIBLIOGRAPHY
General
Jasiuk, 1973; Wojewódzki, 1983.

Stara Kuźnica, Końskie, Kielce, Poland   A water-powered ironworks, 10 km (6 mi.) NE of Końskie, 65 km (40 mi.) SW of Radom, in the STAROPOLSKI INDUSTRIAL REGION. Equipment is in the style of the eighteenth century although dating from the second half of the nineteenth. It includes wooden box bellows and a water-driven hammer. After several years of restoration the ironworks opened to the public in 1961. The machinery can be set in motion. The ironworks is now a branch of the Museum of Technology.

BIBLIOGRAPHY
General
Jasiuk, 1973.

Staropolski Industrial Region, Poland   This region, bounded by the rivers Vistula (Wisła), Pilica and Nida, has many advantages as a centre for industrial development: accessible deposits of iron ore, copper, zinc, silver and building stone, together with rivers providing water power, and extensive ranges of forest. Mining and metallurgical industries developed at an early date, most of the plants being concentrated along the Czarna and Kamienna rivers and using water power. Charcoal was employed for the smelting of ores as the region lacked hard coal. Government schemes of the late eighteenth century to set up an armaments industry in the region were cancelled when Poland lost its independence, but the idea of creating a modern industrial centre in the Staropolski region was reactivated by the government of the Congress Kingdom of Poland after 1815. Projects devised by STANISŁAW STASZIC and Ksawery Drucki-Lubecki, the Minister of Finance, provided for industrial development in the region. Staszic's programme, drawn up in 1817, proposed a metallurgical complex of linked plants along the Kamienna River. Plants along the upper reaches were to supply those downstream with raw materials and semifinished products. STARACHOWICE was designed as the centre of the operation. The November uprising of 1830 halted these plans. While the previous pace of develop-

ment was never equalled, government efforts ensured that a series of metallurgical and ore-treatment plants was eventually established, each employing 80–100 workers. In the 1850s thirty-two blast furnaces produced about 11 000 tonnes of iron per annum. In the second half of the nineteenth century the industry stagnated as iron-ore resources became depleted and less charcoal could be obtained from the forests. By the end of the century the region had lost its leading position in the Polish iron industry to the Dąbrowski Region of Upper Silesia. Between the wars large-scale production continued only at Ostrowiec and Starachowice, and the industry was back to the scale of the early nineteenth century.

The Staropolski Industrial Region is rich in historic industrial monuments. The oldest are the Neolithic flint mines at Krzemionki Opatowskie. There are remains of ancient iron-ore workings in the Kamienna valley, and some traces of ancient bloomeries have survived to modern times. These periods are illustrated in the Museum of Ancient Metallurgy in the Świętokrzyskie Mountains at Nowa Słupia. Many traces of seventeenth- and eighteenth-century furnaces, slag tips and water systems can still be seen. There are substantial remains of blast furnaces at SAMSONÓW and Kuźniki. The charcoal-using iron-making plant at CHLEWISKA, dating from the nineteenth century and still in use during World War II, is well preserved. Many historic features are preserved in the ironworks at BIAŁOGON, where installations dating from the first half of the nineteenth century for working copper and lead can still be seen, but only traces of the water systems and some slag tips survive as witnesses of the once numerous forging shops on the site. A forge at Stara Kuźnica remains in its original condition, and the rolling mill and engineering workshops at MALENIEC are also preserved. The rolling mill and puddling furnaces at SIELPIA WIELKA were put under legal protection before World War II. Machines and plant from various other works in the region have been brought together at this site. A new programme, the 'Écomusée of the Staropolskie Agglomeration', has been devised to protect sites associated with Stanisław Staszic's project to construct a metallurgical complex on the Kamienna River.

See also BIAŁOGON, BOBRZA, CHLEWISKA, DOŁY BISKUPIE, MALENIEC, SAMSONÓW, SIELPIA WIELKA, STARACHOWICE, STARA KUŹNICA.

BIBLIOGRAPHY
General
Jasiuk, 1973; Pazdur, 1956.

PIOTR GERBER

starvationer   A simple, double-ended boat used to carry coal on the BRIDGEWATER CANAL and in its associated mines. The largest version was 50 ft × 7 ft. (15.25 m × 2.13 m). The name probably came from the skeleton-like appearance of the vessels caused by their exposed ribs.

BIBLIOGRAPHY
General
Smith, 1979; Tomlinson, 1979.

710

Staszic, Stanisław Wawrzyniec (1755–1826) A politician and one of the outstanding minds in eighteenth- and nineteenth-century Poland. Born in Piła in 1755, his mother intended him to enter the priesthood. He attended the theological seminary in Poznań, where he was ordained in 1779, and also studied natural science at the Collège de France. Shortly before the partition of Poland Staszic won fame as a political publicist, notable for his reforming ideas. He occupied high positions in the Grand Duchy of Warsaw and, after its fall in 1815, in the Congress Kingdom of Poland. He was director of the Division of Industry and Mining during 1816–24, and chairman of the Board of Directors for Mining in Kielce. Staszic encouraged the development of the Staropolski coalfield, and as a geologist he carried out prospecting work and planned new pits, increasing the number of iron-ore mines in the region from nine to thirty-seven. He discovered hard coal deposits in Dąbrowa Górnicza and began mining there. He formed the Cadre of Miners, an organization which initially took much of its discipline from military traditions. In 1816 he founded the Academy of Mining in Kielce. His interest in metallurgy led to the publication of many research papers on metallurgy and to fame as an explorer of the Tatra Mountains. His book *O ziemiorództwie Karpatów i innych gór i równin Polski* reflects his experiences as an explorer and contains much information about the geology and minerals of the Tatras, with many maps and tables comparing sources of iron ore according to their petrographic characteristics. He indicated the depths, technical details, output and other data of saltmines, comparing them with mines in Hungary, Romania and Transylvania. Staszic is commemorated by a museum in Piła.

BIBLIOGRAPHY
General
Szacka, 1966.
Specific
Goetel, W. *Stanisław Staszic na 50 lecie Akademii Górniczo-Hutniczej im Stanisława Staszica w Krakowie* (The fiftieth anniversary of the Stanisław Staszic Academy of Mining and Metallurgy in Kraków). Kraków, 1969.

JAN KĘSIK

Stavanger, Rogaland, Norway The third city of Norway, with a charter of 1426, on a superb natural harbour on a branch of the Stavangerfjord, on the west coast, 160 km (100 mi.) S. of Bergen. Stavanger's population in 1801 numbered only 2460, but the growth of the fishing industry, and particularly of sardine canning, increased it to over 30 000 by 1900. In 1914 over half the working population was employed in fish canning. In spite of fires, substantial numbers of wooden houses and warehouses survive, particularly in the harbour area. Since 1970 Stavanger has become the principal centre of the Norwegian oil industry. Fish canning has ceased in the city, but a museum (Hermetikkmuseet) has been established in an old factory, showing how brisling and sardines were canned between 1880 and 1920. The oil industry already has museum.

BIBLIOGRAPHY
General
Kongsthogskolans Arkitekturskola, 1972; Tschudi-Madsen, 1977.

LOCATIONS
[M] Hermetikkmuseet i Stavanger, Stavanger Museum, Musegt.16, 4000 Stavanger.
[M] Norsk Oljemuseum, Lovdahlsgt.1, 4000 Stavanger.

BARRIE TRINDER

steam carriage The first full-scale road vehicles to move by steam were built in Paris between 1765 and 1770, and one from this period, built by Nicolas Cugnot (1725–1804), survives in PARIS. WILLIAM MURDOCK and RICHARD TREVITHICK and others experimented with steam carriages in the early nineteenth century but difficulties were encountered with crankshafts and with small high-pressure boilers. Sir Goldworthy Gurney (1793–1875) built several vehicles between 1825 and 1831, and in 1828 achieved some fame for a run from London to Bath with a fourteen-seat vehicle, but this was by no means a triumphant success, and interest in steam carriages waned with the coming of railways. There was a revival in the late nineteenth century as motor transport developed, and many steam carriages were built commercially, before the viability of the MOTORCAR was established.

BIBLIOGRAPHY
General
Bird, 1969; Davison, 1953; Fletcher, 1891, 1904; Gladwin, 1988.
Specific
Cossons, N. The Grenville steam carriage. In *Transport History*, I, 1968.

BARRIE TRINDER

steam engine A power source deriving its energy from fossil fuel, which is used to boil water in an almost closed vessel, producing steam which moves one or more pistons in tight-fitting cylinders. The energy is transmitted by a piston rod to a diversity of devices. The vital power source for the Industrial Revolution, the steam engine was developed to operate at atmospheric pressure by THOMAS SAVERY, THOMAS NEWCOMEN, ADAM HESLOP, JAMES SADLER, and most famously by JAMES WATT; and subsequently, using higher pressures, by JONATHAN HORNBLOWER, RICHARD TREVITHICK, HENRY CORLISS, PETER WILLANS, BELLIS & MORCOM, and many others. Between 2500 and 3000 steam engines were installed in Britain before 1800, by which time engines had been erected in many parts of continental Europe and in North America. The efficiency of the steam engine was greatly improved during the nineteenth century with new configurations, higher steam pressures, compounding, and means like the UNIFLOW principle of avoiding heat loss through condensation.

Most eighteenth-century steam engines were BEAM

Figure 148 A steam hammer, built by James Nasmyth's company at Patricroft, Manchester, and used in an ironworks in New Jersey, displayed in the Smithsonian Institution, Washington DC
Smithsonian Institution

ENGINES. For other types and configurations, *see* COM-POUND ENGINE; CORNISH ENGINE; HORIZONTAL ENGINE; PORT-ABLE ENGINE; STEAM LOCOMOTIVE; TABLE ENGINE; TRACTION ENGINE; VERTICAL ENGINE.

See also BOILER; CHIMNEY; STEAM LOCOMOTIVE; STEAM-SHIP; TURBINE; and figures 93, 170, 174.

BIBLIOGRAPHY
General
Farey, 1827; Hayes, 1981; Matschoss, 1908; Pursell, 1969; Storer, 1969; Thurston, 1878; Tunzelmann, 1978; Wagen-breth and Wächtler, 1986a; Watkins, 1970–1, 1978–9.
Specific
Harris, J. R. The employment of steam power in the eighteenth century. In *History*, LII, 1967.
Kanefsky, J. and Robey, J. Steam engines in eighteenth-century Britain: a quantitative assessment. In *Technology and Culture*, XII, 1980.
Musson, A. E. Industrial motive power in the United Kingdom, 1800–1870. In *EcHR*, 2nd Ser., XXIX, 1976.
Robinson, E. H. The early diffusion of steam power. In *Journal of Economic History*, XXXIV, 1974.
Watkins, G. Steam power – an illustrated guide. In *Industrial Archaeology*, IV, 1967.

CHRISTOPHER GREEN

steam hammer A hammer operating vertically, pow-ered by a steam cylinder in the apex of an A-frame, with the anvil located between the two members of the frame. It was invented by James Nasmyth (1808–90) in 1839, and was intended for the forging of a paddle shaft for the SS *Great Britain* (*see* BRISTOL), which was eventually screw-driven. It was first used at LE CREUSOT, and manufactured at Nasmyth's works at Patricroft, Manchester (*see* BRIDGE-WATER CANAL). The steam hammer was used for SHIN-GLING wrought iron, and in making forgings. The original version was single-acting, but a double-acting version giving a heavier blow was introduced by Nasmyth in

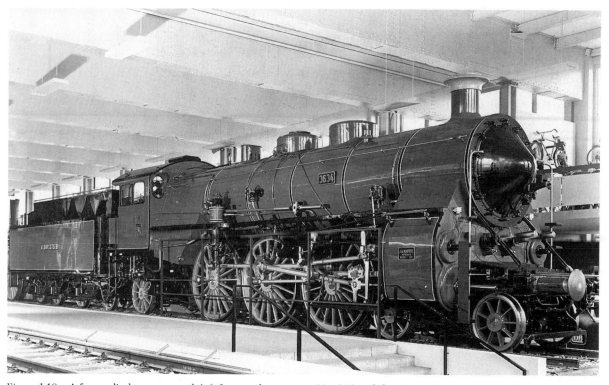

Figure 149 A four-cylinder compound 4-6-2 steam locomotive, No. 3634 of class S3/6 of Bavarian State Railways and later No. 18.451 of Deutsches Bundesbahn, built in 1912 by J. A. Maffei AG of Munich: between 1908 and 1931, 159 locomotives of this class were constructed, the last forty of them for Deutsche Reichsbahn Gesellschaft, which employed them in many parts of Germany, including the haulage of the Rheingold express through the Rhine valley from the Dutch frontier to Basle. They were among the first European main-line locomotives to have American-style bar frames. This locomotive was placed with much ceremony in the Deutsches Museum, Munich, in 1958, but other members of the class remained working until May 1965. Deutsches Museum, Munich

1843. Many static examples survive (*see* LE CREUSOT); there is a working example at IRONBRIDGE.

BIBLIOGRAPHY
General
Nasmyth, 1883.

steam locomotive The most potent icon of the Industrial Revolution, seen in the nineteenth century as the ultimate symbol of progress. The first steam locomotive was built by RICHARD TREVITHICK at Coalbrookdale (*see* IRONBRIDGE) in 1802, and the first one known to have worked, also designed by Trevithick, was used on the PENYDARREN TRAMROAD in 1804. The locomotive developed rapidly in north-east England in the next two decades, and at the Rainhill trials of 1829 on the Liverpool & Manchester Railway (*see* LIVERPOOL; MANCHESTER), most of its essential principles were demonstrated on GEORGE STEPHENSON's *Rocket*.

A steam locomotive consists of a frame, usually constructed of two parallel wrought-iron or steel plates – but in North America often of bars – or occasionally in later years of a single steel casting. To the frame are attached the boiler, and the cylinders and motion by which the locomotive is propelled.

The boiler, which may have parallel sides or be tapered, consists of a firebox with an inner layer of copper, later of steel, enclosing the fire, separated by stays from the outer shell and protected by fusible plugs and by safety valves. Early fireboxes had round tops, but in the twentieth century the flat-topped boiler invented by Alfred Belpaire (1820–93), which provides a greater heating surface, has been widely employed. Smoke and hot air from the fire pass through tubes, a principle patented by Marc Seguin in France in 1827. Steam is usually collected in a dome on top of the boiler and may be further dried in a superheater, a tube with several bends passing back through the boiler tubes, first employed by R. & W. Hawthorn in 1839. Steam then passes to the steam chest, from which it is admitted to the cylinders through valves controlled by the valve gear, the commonest forms of which are the link motion devised by ROBERT STEPHENSON and that developed in 1844 by Égide Walschaerts (1820–1901). The cylinders may be located within the frames, driving a crank axle through connecting rods, or outside the frames, conveying motion to crank pins on the main

713

driving wheels. Multi-cylinder locomotives, with two cylinders outside the frames and one or more between them, were developed from the 1840s; and compound locomotives, with two, three or four cylinders of different pressure, were widely employed in continental Europe and the USA. Exhaust steam passes through a blast pipe into the chimney, creating in the process a draught which draws the fire in the firebox through the boiler tubes. The driving wheel axles were carried in axleboxes set in hornblocks attached to slits in the frames. Driving wheels were normally spoked, with the tyres shrunk on, but disc wheels were employed, chiefly in the USA, in the twentieth century.

The main controls of a locomotive are injectors, introduced by the Frenchman Henri Giffard (1825–82) in 1859, which force water into the boiler; the regulator or throttle valve, which controls the amount of steam entering the cylinders and is usually located in the steam dome on top of the boiler; and the reversing gear which determines the point in the stroke of the piston at which steam is cut off and the valve gear thrown into reverse. Water for a locomotive was conveyed in a TENDER or in tanks (see TANK LOCOMOTIVE) attached to the frame or boiler.

Most railways used steam locomotives until after World War II, except for some urban lines and those in countries where there was cheap hydro-electric power, but since 1945 they have been replaced by diesel and electric traction throughout Europe, North America and Australasia. The last steam locomotives were built in the USA in 1953, the USSR in 1956, Australia in 1958 and Great Britain in 1960. Many remain in use in Africa and Asia, and they are still manufactured in China.

The British and American system for referring to locomotives is to give the numbers of leading, driving and trailing wheels (for example, 2–4–2, 4–6–2, 0–8–2), with the suffix 'T' to indicate a tank locomotive (thus 0–4–2T, 0–10–0T); this system is used throughout this encyclopaedia. In continental Europe it is usual to use a system based on the number of axles (thus 1.2.1, 2.3.1, 0.4.1 rather than 2–4–2, 4–6–2, 0–8–2).

Steam locomotives are preserved in large numbers in many countries.

See also BEYER GARRETT; CONDENSING LOCOMOTIVE; FAIRLIE, ROBERT; FIRELESS LOCOMOTIVE; MALLET; PRESERVED RAILWAY; SENTINEL; SWITCHER; and figures 27, 159, 175.

BIBLIOGRAPHY
General
Ahrons, 1927; Bell, 1950; Bruce, 1952; Jones, 1969; Marshall, 1953; Sinclair, 1907; Snell, 1971; Westwood, 1983; White, 1968.
Specific
Nock, O. S. Steam Locomotive. London: British Transport Commission, 1962.

BARRIE TRINDER

steam lorry A steam-powered vehicle with a platform for carrying loads. The overtype had a locomotive boiler at the front, on which was mounted a compound engine from which the rear wheels were driven by means of chains. The undertype had the engine and transmission mounted below the load platform. The more successful manufacturing companies continued to supply steam lorries into the 1930s (see SENTINEL and figure 141).

BIBLIOGRAPHY
General
Clark, 1960; Fletcher, 1891; Gladwin, 1988; Klapper, 1973; Kuipers, 1972; Norris, 1906.

steamroller Horse-drawn rollers were used quite widely on water-bound road surfaces in the early nineteenth century, particularly in Prussia. The first patent for a steamroller was taken out by Louis Lemoine of Bordeaux in 1859. Experiments on rolling roads on the royal parks in London in the 1860s led the MEDWAY engineer Thomas Aveling to adopt for production designs by William Clark (1821–81) and William F. Batho (1828–86) for a three-point roller, with two large-diameter rolls on the rear axle, and a smaller, wider roll on a subframe at the front, rotated by chains and used for steering. Aveling exported steamrollers to New York and Philadephia in 1868–9, the first to be used in the USA. The first American-built rollers were made by Andrew Lindelhof in the early 1870s. Tandem rollers had rolls of equal size at front and rear. Steamrollers made possible improved methods of road construction (see ASPHALT; ROAD; TARMACADAM). From c.1890 scarifiers for breaking the surfaces of roads to be treated were mounted on the offsides at the rear. Water sprayers and scrapers were usually fitted to keep rollers clean. Steamrollers commonly towed ancillary equipment – tar boilers, water carts, and accommodation vans for crews. Companies hiring rollers and crews to local authorities pioneered the principle of contract hiring in British civil engineering.

About 500 steamrollers had been built in Britain by 1889, and about 1700 by 1900. A further 1700 were delivered for home use in the next decade. By 1930 about 5750 had been built for British customers, two-thirds of them by Aveling & Porter (see MEDWAY). A further 200 were made after 1930, but by 1960 steamrollers were no longer of commercial importance, having been displaced by motor rollers. Many steamrollers are preserved, one of the earliest being Aveling & Porter No. 1457 of 1878 in the Norwegian Technical Museum in OSLO.

BIBLIOGRAPHY
General
Whitehead, 1975.

BARRIE TRINDER

steamship The steamship was seen as one of the symbols of a new civilization in the early nineteenth century. The first successful experiments in steam propulsion were carried out in 1788 on Dalswinton Loch (see DUMFRIES AND GALLOWAY) by WILLIAM SYMINGTON. The earliest steam vessels were wooden PADDLE STEAMERS. I. K. BRUNEL's SS Great Britain of 1843 embodied the transition to iron construction and screw propulsion, although it was not until the late nineteenth century that most ocean-going vessels were iron (or steel) propeller-driven ships. The potential of steam cargo vessels was demonstrated by the 437-ton screw-propelled London collier *John Bowes* of 1852 which did the work of two sailing colliers and remained in operation until 1933. Steam turbine propulsion was first effectively demonstrated by Sir Charles Parson's yacht *Turbinia* (*see* NEWCASTLE-UPON-TYNE; TURBINE PROPULSION) in 1894, but the triple-expansion engine, introduced in France in 1871, remained the standard means of propulsion for most merchant ships until the 1940s (*see* LIBERTY SHIP). MOTOR VESSELS have gradually replaced steamships for most purposes in the course of the twentieth century.

The oldest surviving complete steam vessel is probably the 12.5 m (41 ft.) long *Dolly* of 1850, preserved at Windermere (*see* LAKE DISTRICT).

BIBLIOGRAPHY
General
Baker, 1965; Brouwer, 1985; Buchanan, 1956; Fletcher, 1910; Hadfield, 1986; Haldane, 1893; Hunter, 1949; Marestier, 1957; Spratt, 1958; Stanton, 1895.
Specific
Hughes, J. R. T. and Reiter, S. The first 1945 British steamships. In *Journal of the American Statistical Association*, 1958.

BARRIE TRINDER

steam tram Steam traction was the most readily adaptable form of motive power for tramways in the late nineteenth century. Self-propelled steam tramcars were abandoned in favour of separate steam tram engines: compact, coke-fired, double-ended, four-wheeled locomotives, with enclosed sides and ends, and roofs bearing condenser devices to reduce smoke emission (*see* HORNU; UTRECHT). Each was driven by one man, who also did the firing. Initially used to haul horse trams, steam's excess power led to divergence in tramway practice between Britain, where large bogie-mounted, double-decked trailers became the norm, and continental Europe, where multiple trailers were used. Most urban steam tramways were converted to electric traction around 1900, but they were retained longer in rural areas. Much of Belgium's SNCV network remained steam-operated until the 1940s (*see* EREZÉE); the Chiemsee-Bahn in Bavaria still uses tram locomotives built by Krauss in 1887 (*see* figure 27); and British-built steam trams still work at Surabaya, Indonesia.

BIBLIOGRAPHY
General
Webb, 1983.

PAUL COLLINS

steel Steel is an alloy of iron and carbon; it may also incorporate other elements, like manganese, chromium, copper or nickel, in which case it is normally called alloy steel. The addition of carbon to steel enables it to be hardened and tempered, making it suitable for weapons and tools. Carbon steel normally contains between 0.5

and 1.3 per cent carbon. By contrast WROUGHT IRON contains virtually no carbon, and CAST IRON between 3 and 4 per cent.

Until the 1860s steel was differentiated from wrought iron or cast iron only by its carbon content. Before the development of the BLAST FURNACE steel was made either by modifying the conditions in a BLOOMERY so that some carbon was retained in the bloom, in this way producing 'natural steel', or by heating bloomery iron in a bed of charcoal so that carbon would diffuse into the iron.

When cast iron became available, steel could be made by melting the iron and burning out from it just sufficient of the carbon. Blister steel could be made in a CEMENTATION FURNACE, by case-hardening layers of wrought iron interspersed with powdered charcoal in large sealed chests. Steel could also be produced in a modified PUDDLING FURNACE, melting cast iron and burning out sufficient carbon to produce steel. All these methods provided steel in a bloom, not in liquid form. From 1740 steel suitable for casting into ingots could be obtained by the CRUCIBLE PROCESS, remelting blister steel in refractory clay pots.

'Mild steel' is an altogether different product, which between the 1850s and the 1970s supplanted wrought iron, becoming one of the characteristic features of twentieth-century civilization, the raw material of motor-cars and domestic appliances, of machinery of all kinds, and an essential element in constructional engineering. Mild steel was first manufactured by Sir HENRY BESSEMER in 1856, and in the 1860s the OPEN-HEARTH FURNACE process was developed by Sir WILLIAM SIEMENS. From the 1880s the work of S. G. THOMAS enabled iron made from phosphoric ores to be used in steelmaking. Since World War II most mild steel has been made by the LD PROCESS.

During the present century alloy steels have been developed on a large scale for specialist purposes. Manganese steel was perfected by Sir Robert Hadfield (1858–1940); and stainless steel, which has a chromium content of about 12.5 per cent, was discovered by Harry Brearley (1871–1948) in 1913. Alloy steels are usually made in ELECTRIC-ARC FURNACES or ELECTRIC INDUCTION FURNACES, or in modern times by the argon–oxygen–decarburization (AOD) process.

Late nineteenth- and twentieth-century steel plants are of great size and complexity and difficult to conserve. Several relatively small works are conserved in Sweden, including a Bessemer plant at Hagfors and an open-hearth plant at MUNKFORS. The history of various types of steel manufacture is displayed in SHEFFIELD.

BIBLIOGRAPHY
General
Barraclough, 1981–4; Gale, 1967, 1969; Lewis, 1976; Schuhmann, 1984.

MARIE NISSER and BARRIE TRINDER

steel bridge The first major bridge to make extensive use of steel was the three-span deck arch structure at St Louis, MISSOURI, completed by James Buchanan Eads (1820–87) in 1874, the longest span being of 158 m (510 ft.). It is

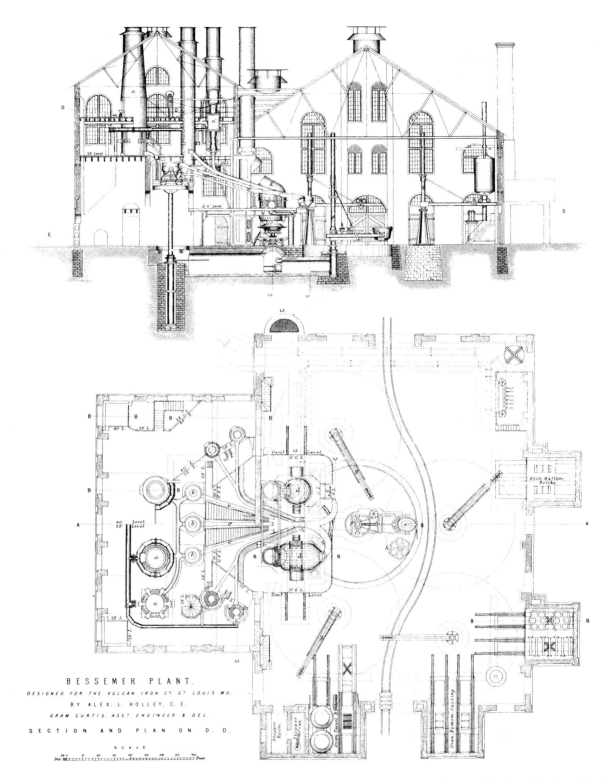

Figure 150 Section and elevation (top) and plan (bottom) of a Bessemer steelmaking plant, designed for the Vulcan Iron Co. of St Louis, Missouri, by Alexander L. Holley (from *Chemistry, Theoretical, Practical and Analytical, as applied to the Arts and Manufactures*, by 'Writers of Eminence', London: William Mackenzie, n.d., *c.*1870)

Collection of Dr Jeff Cox

ranked with the Brooklyn Bridge, NEW YORK, amongst the greatest achievements of American civil engineering. In Britain the first major demonstration of the constructional potential of steel was the FORTH BRIDGE, completed in 1890. Some of the principal bridges of the early twentieth century, like those at SYDNEY and NEWCASTLE-UPON-TYNE are steel arches, but the principal use of steel in bridge-building is now in suspension and box-girder structures, and as reinforcement in concrete.

See also figures 84, 153.

BIBLIOGRAPHY
General
Scott and Miller, 1979.
Specific
Building with Steel: V – Bridgework, 1970. London: British Steel Corporation.

steel foundry Manufacture of steel castings originated in continental Europe *c*.1845. The first British steel foundry was that of Naylor, Vickers & Co., Sheffield, opened in 1855; the size was limited by the capacity of the CRUCIBLE PROCESS. The first open hearth steel castings were made at Terre Noire, France, in 1875. Many steel foundries developed in the twentieth century. Small Bessemer converters have sometimes been used for melting steel for castings, and subsequently ELECTRIC-ARC FURNACES or ELECTRIC INDUCTION FURNACES.

BIBLIOGRAPHY
General
Gale, 1969; Schuhmann, 1984.

Steierische Eisenstrasse, Styria, Austria *See* STYRIAN IRON TRAIL.

Stelvio, Lombardy, Italy The Stelvio pass, 75 km (47 mi.) NE of Sondrio, links Merano and Bormio, and was constructed by the Habsburg government in 1820–5, with a summit 2758 m (9048 ft.) above sea level, the highest carriage road in nineteenth-century Europe, and still the second highest road pass in the alps. The Italian side shows the most impressive feats of road construction, with stunning views into the Tyrol. The route is impassable in winter.

Stenay, Meuse, France The Beer Museum at Stenay, 40 km (25 mi.) N. of Verdun, was opened in 1986 in a former maltings, in use from 1879 until 1914. This northern part of the Meuse department, near the Belgian border, had no fewer than twenty-one breweries and maltings between 1800 and 1914, eleven of them dating from the eighteenth century, if not earlier, the remainder creations of the nineteenth century. Most were small, artisan-scale enterprises, brewing according to traditional high-temperature fermentation techniques. Most disappeared during World War I.

The maltings where the museum is situated was opened in 1879 by Henry & Co., a group of leading brewers operating in the northern part of the Meuse department

and the Ardennes. The malting enterprise was not directly linked with any particular brewery, a feature that is typical of the Meuse brewing industry during the years following the Franco-Prussian War, which brought an end to malt imports from Germany.

The Stenay maltings was opened in a former storehouse in the citadel, built *c*.1610. It was about 65 m (210 ft.) long, and had three levels, one underground. Its use for malting necessitated the addition of another floor and the construction of malt kilns at each end of the building. The malt was dried in these tower-like structures by an updraught of hot air. The germination of the barley and its transformation into malt was carried out in the vaulted chambers of the cellars and the ground floor. After World War I the site was occupied first by a mushroom-grower and then by a fibreboard manufacturer, neither of whom tampered much with the building.

The museum traces the history of the production and consumption of beer. It also houses a centre holding photographic records and archives from some thirty-three brewing concerns in Stenay and its region. Many of the buildings of these old breweries survive, the best preserved being those of the former Quinard brewery, which operated at Stenay between 1834 and 1852.

BIBLIOGRAPHY
Specific
Voluer, P. Unpublished study for the Inventaire Général, Paris, 1985.

LOCATION
[M] Musée de la Bière (Beer Museum), rue de la Citadelle, 55700 Stenay.

JEAN-FRANÇOIS BELHOSTE

Stephenson, George (1781–1848) The self-taught fireman of a colliery winding engine, who made the greatest single contribution to the development of the main line RAILWAY. In 1814 he built his first locomotive and the following year produced a SAFETY LAMP for mines. He was engineer of the Hetton Colliery Railway of 1822 and the Stockton & Darlington Railway which opened in 1825. From 1824 he was employed as engineer of the Liverpool & Manchester Railway, where, at the Rainhill trials on 6 October 1829, his locomotive *Rocket* was shown to be superior to those of his competitors. He was subsequently engineer of the Grand Junction and North Midland railways, and invested his fortune in landed estates in the east Midlands where he developed collieries and lime works.

BIBLIOGRAPHY
General
Davies, 1977; Rolt, 1960; Smiles, 1857.

Stephenson, Robert (1803–59) The son of GEORGE STEPHENSON, Robert when he was twenty was managing the locomotive works established by his father at Newcastle-upon-Tyne. After visiting South America in 1824–7, he superintended the building of the *Rocket* locomotive. He was engineer of the London & Birmingham Railway, whose construction was portrayed by J. C. BOURNE. His subsequent works included the High Level Bridge at NEWCASTLE-UPON-TYNE, the Royal Border Bridge at Berwick (see BORDERS), the MENAI and Conway tubular bridges, and the Victoria Bridge, MONTREAL.

BIBLIOGRAPHY
General
Rolt, 1960; Rowland, 1954.

Stevenson, Robert (1771–1850) The founder of a dynasty of Scots engineers, Stevenson is particularly known as a designer of lighthouses although he also built roads and bridges. He became engineer to the Northern Lighthouse Board before 1800 and held the office until 1843, constructing twenty new lighthouses, the most important of them that on Bell Rock (see ANGUS) of 1807–12, for which he devised a movable JIB CRANE. The lightship used during the construction of the lighthouse was the first to have a lantern surrounding the mast.

Robert Stevenson was the father of Alan Stevenson (1807–1865), who succeeded him at the Northern Lighthouse Board in 1843 and who designed the Skerryvor lighthouse near Tyree in 1838–43; of David Stevenson (1815–66), an authority on river improvements who also developed the use of paraffin for illuminating lighthouses; and of Thomas Stevenson (1818–87), who with his brother David jointly took on the duties of engineer to the Northern Lighthouse Board in 1853, and was father of the author Robert Louis Stevenson (1850–94).

BIBLIOGRAPHY
General
Stevenson, A. S. 1848, 1850; Stevenson, D. 1838, 1845; Stevenson, R. L. 1912; Stevenson, T. 1874, 1881.

Steyr, Upper Austria, Austria   A city at the confluence of the Rivers Steyr and Enns, the principal commercial centre for the iron trade of Styria. Iron from Eisenerz (see STYRIAN IRON TRAIL) was conveyed to Steyr down the Enns from Heiflau, 70 km (43 mi.) upstream – a trade illustrated in the Flössermuseum at Kastenreith, 22 m (14 mi.) S. Magnificent merchants' houses in Gothic, Baroque and Classical styles, stand in the Hauptplatz. There were many water-powered forges in the vicinity, making edge tools, cutlery and nails. The municipal museum in the gatehouse, Innerberger Stadl, has representations of a scythe forge and a nail forge and many other exhibits relating to the iron trade. Josef Werndl (1831–89), the 'saviour of Steyr', retrieved the prosperity of the town when it was threatened by the decline of the traditional iron trade by establishing the Österreichische Waffenfabriks Gesellschaft (Austrian Rifle Factory) which made a breech-loading gun that he had invented. The company developed into Steyr-Daimler-Puch, producing bearings, bicycles, commercial vehicles, and, in the 1930s, motorcars (see VIENNA). As the result of an initiative by Werndl, Steyr was one of the first cities in Europe to be lit by electricity, a supply company being established in 1884. The Museum Arbeitswelt (Museum of Work) was established in a nineteenth-century small-arms factory in 1987, and has

displays on the theme 'Work–Man–Machine'. The Wehrgrabenviertel is a nineteenth-century suburb of working-class housing which is being restored, in one of the largest projects of this kind in Austria.

BIBLIOGRAPHY
General
Sperl, 1984.

LOCATIONS
[M] Innerberger Stadl (Gatehouse), Grünmarkt 26, A-4400 Steyr.
[M] Museum Arbeitswelt (Museum of Work), Wehrgraben, A-4400 Steyr.

BARRIE TRINDER

Sticklepath, Devon, England   A works on the River Taw, 5 km (3 mi.) E. of Okehampton, miscalled a 'foundry'. It made scythes, reaping hooks, hay knives, axes and the like during 1814–1960, and was worked by the Finch family. One water wheel operated a pair of tilt hammers, another provided blast for the hearths, and a third worked grindstones. The works has been conserved by a trust from 1966.

LOCATION
[M] Finch Foundry, Sticklepath, Okehampton, Devon.

Stockholm, Sweden   The Swedish capital, and the country's principal centre of consumer goods manufactures, is built on a series of islands where Lake Mälaren flows into the Baltic. The city's influence extends across an archipelago which stretches 60 km (40 mi.) to the east.

Stockholm grew rapidly from the mid-nineteenth century, its population rising from 100 000 in 1850 to 300 000 in 1900, and 420 000 in 1920. It now has about a million inhabitants. The city acquired over 10 000 ha (4000 ac.) of land from neighbouring communities between 1880 and 1920. The development on a large scale of public utilities led to the creation of new municipally-owned settlements around waterworks and hospitals on the fringe of the city. Consumer goods manufactures expanded rapidly in the city in the same period. Shanty-type wooden dwellings erected on the edges of the city were quickly replaced by apartment blocks, often in the neo-Classical style. Stockholm is particularly rich in photographic records of this period of expansion.

Industrial buildings in central and suburban Stockholm were documented in the early 1980s and the inventory published in 1986.

The München Brewery, Söder Mälarstrand, on the banks of Lake Mälaren, was established in the 1850s, and was the first brewery in Sweden in which a steam engine was employed. The present imposing buildings, in a Gothic style influenced by German architects, were built in 1893–1909. At that time this was the largest brewery in Sweden and employed some 350 workers. The brewery ceased operation in 1971 and has been adapted for a variety of new uses.

The earliest buildings of the Hjorthagen power station

date from 1900–5. The power station has been enlarged several times, and some turbines of the 1920s remain.

The first part of the city's underground railway system was completed in 1933 when an existing electric tramway was extended from Skanstill to Slüssen. In the 1940s the line was reconstructed to take full-size electric trains. Further extensions to the system have incorporated remarkable stations excavated from the solid rock.

The *Vasa*, a newly-built and ornately-decorated warship which capsized in Stockholm harbour in 1628, was located in 1956, raised to the surface in the 1960s and placed on public display in 1962. The exhibition has subsequently been extended, and the many artefacts recovered and conserved now provide the most vivid impression anywhere in the world of life on a large wooden sailing ship. The collections of glass, ceramics, cooper's wares and pewter are of particular importance.

The Tekniska museet (Technical Museum) established in 1936 has displays relating to most aspects of Swedish industry, including a large gallery concerned with electric power inaugurated in 1983, and exhibitions relating to the forest and construction industries.

Skansen, the first significant OPEN-AIR MUSEUM, was opened by Artur Hazelius (1833–1901) in 1891. It now extends over 30 ha (75 ac.), and its collection numbers some 150 buildings, including an ironmaster's farmstead from Västmanland, a chipping house used by grindstone makers at Orsa in Dalarna, a scutching mill from Forsa in Hälsingland, several windmills, numerous mileposts, a water-powered felting machine from Härjedalen, and a tannery from Småland, as well as various buildings associated with the latter stages of Swedish industrialization, including the 'old men's retreat', a restaurant and bar from Stockholm, an industrial worker's dwelling of the 1880s, and a Social Democratic hall of 1907. Skansen has proved a successful means of educating people of all ages, and has attracted more than two million visitors per year since 1938. Skansen originally formed part of the same foundation as the Nordiska museet, which holds large collections of the kinds of artefacts displayed in their authentic settings in the houses in Skansen, but two separate foundations were established in 1963.

Subjects covered by the city's other museums include photography, brewing, postal communications, shipping, the underground railway, tobacco, wines and spirits, and the scientist Jons Jakob Berzelius (1779–1848), discoverer of the principle of the catalyst.

The ceramics works at Gustavsberg, in the archipelago, 40 km (25 mi.) E. of the city centre, is the most celebrated in Sweden, and dates from 1825. A museum displays not just the wares produced and the processes used since 1825, but also the plastics and modern ceramics made by the company.

BIBLIOGRAPHY
General
Hammarström 1970.
Specific
Hall, T. Swedish Urban Environment: a presentation. In *Industrial Buildings and Dwellings*, II, 1978.
Kleingardt, B. *Wasa*. Stockholm: Wasavarvet, 1974.

Scharp, B. Small communities located by Stockholm outside the city borders, 1880–1920. In CILAC, 1985.

LOCATIONS
[M] Berzeliusmuseet (Berzelius Museum), Roslagsvägen, Box 50005, 104 05 Stockholm.
[M] Bryggerimuseet 'Pripporama' (Brewery Museum, 'Pripporama'), Voltavägen 29, Bromma.
[M] Drottningholms teater och teatermuseum (Drottningholm Court Theatre and Museum), 102 511 Stockholm.
[M] Fotografiska museet (Photographic Museum), Skeppsholmen, 102 27 Stockholm.
[M] Historiska museet (Museum of National Antiquities), Narvavägen 13-7, 114 84 Stockholm.
[M] Keramiskt centrum (Ceramics Centre), AB Gustavsbergs Febriker, 134 00 Gustavsberg.
[M] Nordiska museet (Nordic Museum), Lejonslätten, Djurgården, 114 21 Stockholm.
[M] Postmuseum (Postal Museum), Lilla Nygatan 6, 103 11 Stockholm.
[M] Sjöhistoriska museet (National Maritime Museum), Djurgårdsbrunnsvägen 24, 115 27 Stockholm.
[M] Skansen, Djurgården, 115 21 Stockholm.
[M] Spårvägsmuseet (City Transport Museum), Odenplans Tunnelbanestation, AB Storstockholms Lokaltrafik, Box 6301, 113 81 Stockholm.
[M] Stockholms Stadsmuseum (Stockholm City Museum), Peter Myndes Backe 6, 116 46 Stockholm.
[M] Sveriges Arkitekturmuseum (Swedish Museum of Architecture), Skeppsholmen, 111 49 Stockholm.
[M] Tekniska museet med telemuseum (National Museum of Science and Technology with the Telecommunications Museum), Museivägen 7, 115 27 Stockholm.
[M] Tobaksmuseet (Tobacco Museum), Gubhyllan, Box 17007, 104 62 Stockholm.
[M,S] Regalskeppet Wasa Wasavaret (The Wasa Dockyard), Djurgården, 115 27 Stockholm.
[M] Vin- och Sprithistoriska museet (Wine and spirit museum), St Eriksgatan 121, 113 43 Stockholm.

BARRIE TRINDER

stocking frame   The stocking frame, the invention of the Revd William Lee (d.?1610) of Calverton, Nottinghamshire, in 1589, is a machine, originally mostly of wood, for knitting woollen stockings. As first devised, it knitted flat fabrics which were sewn into tubular form, but Lee improved the machine so that it could be adjusted to produce fabrics fashioned like legs, now known in the trade as 'full fashion' hosiery, and so that it could knit silk as well as worsted yarn. Lee took his invention to France, where he died in 1610.

The frame was improved during the seventeenth century, becoming a complex machine of 3500 components. From 1730 cotton yarn was knitted on frames. In England, London was the main centre for framework knitting in the seventeenth century, but subsequently the industry was concentrated in Nottinghamshire. Until the 1850s it was primarily a domestic industry, which took root particularly in open communities, which tended to have high proportions of poor inhabitants and rapid rates of population growth. The first factory in which mechanically-powered knitting frames were effectively used was that of Hine & Mundella in Nottingham, which opened in

719

Figure 151 One of the bottle ovens at Price's National Teapot Works, on the banks of the Trent & Mersey Canal at Longport, Stoke-on-Trent
Barrie Trinder

1851; but it was not until the 1870s that most hosiery was produced in such establishments, and some hand frames remained in use for special purposes well into the twentieth century. Stocking frames are effectively displayed in the museum at RUDDINGTON.

BIBLIOGRAPHY
General
Felkin, 1867.
Specific
Lewis, P. William Lee's stocking frame: technical evolution and economic viability, 1589–1750. In *TH*, XVII, 1986.
Mills, D. R. Rural industry and social structure: framework knitters in Leicestershire, 1670–1851. In *TH*, XIII, 1982.

BARRIE TRINDER

Stoke-on-Trent, Staffordshire, England   A city with a population of 250 000, on the coalfield extending through the Vale of Trent, and one of the world's principal centres of ceramic manufacture. Open settlement characterized the area in the seventeenth century, and traces of squatter-type settlement remain in areas like Sneyd Green, but otherwise there are few working-class houses dating from before the late nineteenth century. The Industrial Revolution in pottery manufacture is often said to have originated with JOSIAH WEDGWOOD's factory at Etruria in Stoke-on-Trent of 1769, although there were in fact earlier precedents. Industrial growth was stimulated by the Trent & Mersey Canal, opened in 1777. In the nineteenth century the towns of Stoke, Burslem, Fenton, Longton, Hanley and Tunstall competed in the provision of town halls and markets; they were amalgamated in 1908. The Wedgwood Memorial Institute of 1863–9, with its terracotta panels showing scenes of pottery manufacture, and the Baroque Burslem Town Hall of 1852–7 are the most notable of such buildings. Of several hundred bottle kilns once used to fire wares only *c*.40 remain, together with some calcining kilns, both bottle-shaped and rectangular, and many traditional potbanks, factories with formal street frontages, often with Venetian windows over wagon arches, and yards untidily lined with kilns and workshops behind. Middleport Pottery and Price's National Teapot Works at Longport are good examples. Only a round building, of which the purpose is obscure, remains of Wedgwood's Etruria, together with Etruria Hall, the mansion built for him by Joseph Pickford (1736–82). The Wedgwood works was relocated in 1938–50 to a garden village at Barlaston, 8 km (5 mi.) S., where demonstrations, a large ceramic collection, and historical displays can be seen at the Wedgwood Centre.

The Gladstone Pottery Museum, Longton, is a typical late nineteenth-century potbank, where the relationship of the various component buildings of a pottery manufactory can readily be understood. The City Museum and Art Gallery, a building completed in 1981, houses one of the world's largest ceramics collections, superbly displayed. Collections of wares are also displayed at the Gladstone Museum, and at visitor centres at the Coalport, Minton and Doulton works. About a dozen manufacturers accept parties of visitors at their factories, and there are more than twenty factory shops.

The preparation of materials for pottery manufacture can be studied at Shirley's Bone and Flint Mill on the Trent & Mersey Canal, an out-station of the City Museum dating from 1856, where a steam engine worked the grinding pans, and at Cheddleton Flint Mill, 12 km (8 mi.) NE on the Caldon Canal, where kilns, water wheels and grinding pans have been restored.

Chatterley Whitfield Mining Museum, Tunstall, conserves a Wordsley Mesnes steam winding engine of 1914, together with realistic representations of working conditions underground. Many colliery spoil tips have been made into parks.

The area was served until 1923 by the North Staffordshire Railway, a company with a strong sense of local identity. Most of its stations are in a Jacobean style in brick, designed by H. A. Hunt. The company's headquarters was at Stoke station, completed in 1849, which stands alongside the North Stafford Hotel of 1850, in a similar style. Good examples of the style applied to small stations are Longport and Stone, 11 km (7 mi.) S.

The canal network provides the best means of studying the Potteries landscape, its outstanding features being the 3000 m (9840 ft.) Harecastle Tunnels north of the conurbation, one by James Brindley (completed 1777), the other by THOMAS TELFORD (1827).

BIBLIOGRAPHY
General
Brook, 1977; Sherlock, 1976; Weatherill, 1971.
Specific
Green, T. *et al.* Jesse Shirley's Etruscan bone and flint mill, Stoke-on-Trent. In IAR, IX (1) 1986.

LOCATIONS
[M] Chatterley Whitfield Mining Museum, Tunstall, Stoke-on-Trent ST6 8UN.
[S] Cheddleton Flint Mill, Cheadle Road, Leek, Staffordshire.
[M] City Museum and Art Gallery, Bethesda Street, Hanley, Stoke-on-Trent ST1 3DE.
[S] Coalport Craft Centre, Park Street, Fenton, Stoke-on-Trent ST4 3JB.
[M] Gladstone Pottery Museum, Uttoxeter Road, Longton, Stoke-on-Trent ST3 1PQ.
[M] Minton Museum, London Road, Stoke-on-Trent ST4 7QD.
[M] The Sir Henry Doulton Gallery, Nile Street, Burslem, Stoke-on-Trent ST6 2AJ.
[M] Wedgwood Visitor Centre and Museum, Josiah Wedgwood & Sons Ltd, Barlaston, Stoke-on-Trent ST12 9ES.

BARRIE TRINDER

stone The quarrying of stone has been important from the time when man first constructed buildings. Europe is well endowed with stone suitable for use as DIMENSION STONE: limestones, sandstones, granites and slates. With the coming of the railways in the nineteenth century the movement of materials increased, and stone quarrying expanded. By 1900 over 100 000 people were employed in quarrying building stones in Britain.

Most limestones, sandstones and igneous rocks were worked from open pits, but substantial quantities have been worked from mines. Underground workings in France and the Netherlands are extensive, and some mining continues there and in England (near Bath) and Scotland. SLATE has been extensively worked by underground operations, and some mines are still working. The introduction from the 1870s of compressed-air drilling and steam shovels meant that overburden could be removed more cheaply, so that many underground workings were converted to open pits. Both surface and underground sources were worked using systems of shallow benches, the stone being removed in blocks as near rectangular as possible. In most quarries a groove was chiselled, or holes were drilled, along the line where the split was required. The holes were made by hand or machine, and a device known as a plug was hammered in between 'feathers' until a split occurred. Steam-powered channelling machines and saws were developed to help in chiselling the grooves. Light charges of explosive have also been used.

Before sale stone had to be dressed to shape, usually with chisels, but at large quarries saws, planers, lathes and rubbing beds have been employed since the mid-nineteenth century, the appearance of the pneumatic chisel late in the century being of particular importance. Many hand skills remain essential.

During the last century there has been a vast increase in the amount of crushed stone produced as aggregate for road construction, railway ballast and concrete products.

See also BASALT; DIMENSION STONE; FLAGSTONE; GRANITE; LIMESTONE; MARBLE; SERPENTINE.

BIBLIOGRAPHY
General
Greenwell and Elsden, 1913.

IVOR J. BROWN

stoneware A variety of clayware with a hard and glassy or vitrified body, impervious to water. It is made of fat clays, moderately rich in silica and fluxes; stoneware does not lose its shape when fired to vitrification. Stoneware is fired to a higher temperature than earthenware so that the body becomes vitrified. Stoneware shares the chemical composition of hard porcelain but is more plastic and can thus be formed into such articles as large insulators.

Manufacture of stoneware on a large scale was initiated in Germany before the seventeenth century. Large quantities of jugs and beer mugs were made near Hohr and Grenzhausen into the twentieth century. The manufacture of stoneware in Britain developed in the eighteenth century, new standards being achieved by JOSIAH WEDG-

WOOD. Large-scale mass production was initiated by Doulton with their Lambeth Works in London, making stoneware jugs in brown colours or with brighter decoration from 1839.

BIBLIOGRAPHY
General
Jewitt, 1878.

stoop   A carved rectangular block of stone 1.6–2.0 m (5–6 ft.) high, giving directions at crossings of packhorse routes in the PENNINES. Installation was stimulated by legislation of 1697, and many stoops survive.

See also MILEPOST.

BIBLIOGRAPHY
General
Hey, 1980.

stoping   Mining by steplike excavation, the basic method of mining veined ores of the metals COPPER, SILVER, GOLD, LEAD, ZINC and TIN. The veins may be inclined or nearly vertical, at a width varying from 1–2 m (3–6 ft.) to 30 m (100 ft.) or more, and may continue across the country for many miles. From early times veins have been located at the surface by simple prospecting and then followed by sinking shafts or driving adits into the hillsides. From the shafts or adits the veins would be cut out in series of steps, or stopes, either above or below a haulage tunnel. Any waste encountered would be stacked in the worked-out voids which would be supported by large blocks of stone or timber. If the steps were formed below the haulage way, small shafts would be formed and the ore raised to the haulage way by bucket or KIBBLE: this was called underhand stoping. If the steps were formed above the haulage way, work could continue by standing on broken ore or wooden supports known as stemples, but chutes would have to be maintained down which the ore could pass: this was known as overhand stoping.

As mechanized mining has been introduced since the nineteenth century, stoping methods have become more effectively systematized, but basically they remain much the same. Proved vein lengths are now 'blocked out' by driving tunnels. In order to provide for easier and safer working many of the tunnels and shafts are now driven parallel to and in the solid alongside the veins, with short crosscuts into them. Excavation above these crosscuts is now carried out by such methods as shrinkage stoping, which allows broken ore to be removed as it is required but leaves enough to support the walls of the stopes and for miners to work on. When the solid is worked from beneath, a 'cut-and-fill' stoping method may be used in this, waste is imported to provide a solid base. In modern metal mines, some of which are over 3500 m (12 000 ft.) deep, purpose-designed mechanized drilling, loading and hauling systems are employed.

IVOR J. BROWN

stop lock   A means of shutting off water from a section of canal or navigable river, usually by means of boards dropped into slots in stone, timber or ironwork lining the banks.

store   The term 'store' was used by the sixteenth century to mean the stock of a tradesman, and by *c.*1650 for a place of storage or WAREHOUSE. In America by *c.*1740 a 'store' had come to be a place where merchandise was sold, a typical example being preserved at Sturbridge (*see* MASSACHUSETTS). In England the term was used from *c.*1850 to mean a retailer's premises, but was usually qualified, as with Co-operative store (*see* CO-OPERATIVE MOVEMENT) and DEPARTMENT STORE.

BIBLIOGRAPHY
Specific
Carson, G. *Country stores in early New England*. Old Sturbridge Village, Sturbridge, Mass. 1955.

Stourport, Worcestershire, England   An archetypal canal town at the junction of the Staffordshire & Worcestershire Canal (completed in 1772) and the River Severn. Three of six transshipment basins survive, with warehouses; they are linked to the river by broad and narrow lock flights. There are many eighteenth-century domestic buildings with the same brick detailing as those of the canal company. Stourport is the head of navigation on the Severn since the improvements of the 1840s.

BIBLIOGRAPHY
General
Porteous, 1977.

Strabane, County Tyrone, Northern Ireland   A market town of prime importance in the history of printing, 21 km (14 mi.) S. of Londonderry, at the confluence of the Foyle and the Finn. Two newspapers were published in the town in the late eighteenth century. Gray's Printing Press is preserved by National Trust; and a double-fronted stationery shop on Main Street, with bowed windows, operates commercially. A two-storey printer's workshop across the courtyard includes Columbia and Albion presses, and quantities of wooden poster type. John Dunlop (1747–1812), pioneer American newspaper publisher, and printer of the American Declaration of Independence, was apprenticed in this works.

BIBLIOGRAPHY
General
Gallagher and Rogers, 1986.

Strässa, Västmanland, Sweden   The iron-ore mine at Strässa, about 10 km (6 mi.) N. of Lindesberg and 210 km (130 mi.) NW of Stockholm, was regarded as the second greatest iron-ore deposit in Central Sweden, after that at GRÄNGESBERG. Mining operations started in the seventeenth century, ceased in the 1920s, and were resumed in the 1950s, when highly specialized equipment was installed, enabling production to rise to 11 tons of iron ore per man-hour, a record for shaft mining. The mine closed in 1982 and has subsequently been opened to the public.

At a depth of 195 m (640 ft.) a small train takes visitors to various parts of the workings. The modern surface installations have been preserved.

BIBLIOGRAPHY
General
Serning *et al.*, 1987.

Stratford-upon-Avon, Warwickshire, England The head of navigation on the River Avon, with a transshipment basin at the terminus of Stratford Canal, completed in 1816 and restored in the 1960s. An eight-arch brick viaduct of 1826 carried the Stratford & Moreton Railway across the river. A wagon from the railway is preserved in the open. Near Bearley, 7 km (4$\frac{1}{2}$ mi.) NW, the canal crosses the valley on an iron aqueduct.

BIBLIOGRAPHY
Specific
Hadfield, C. and Norris, J. *Waterways to Stratford*. Newton Abbot: David & Charles, 1962.

Strathclyde, Scotland *See* AYRSHIRE; BIGGAR; BONAWE; DALMELLINGTON; DUNBARTONSHIRE; GLASGOW; GREENOCK AND WESTERN RENFREWSHIRE; HIGHLANDS (for Argyll); IRVINE; NEW LANARK; PAISLEY; SCOTTISH ISLANDS; SUMMERLEE HERITAGE PARK; WANLOCKHEAD AND LEADHILLS.

streaming A form of ALLUVIAL MINING, applied particularly to methods for working tin in CORNWALL, and during nineteenth-century gold rushes.

Street, Somerset, England A model settlement, largely of Gothic terraces of the late nineteenth century, associated with the shoe factory of the Quaker Clark family, which includes a museum of footwear. Wookey Hole, 12 km (7 mi.) N., has spectacular caves where the River Axe emerges from the Mendips. A paper mill with traditional technology is part of the tourist attraction, which also includes a collection of fairground equipment.

LOCATIONS
[M] The Shoe Museum, C. & J. Clark Ltd, Street, Somerset BA16 0YA.
[S] Wookey Hole Caves Ltd, Wells, Somerset.

streetcar 'Streetcar' is a North American term for TRAMCAR. 'Streetcar suburbs' were those that grew up along the tracks of tramway systems in the late nineteenth century.

stringer *See* SLEEPER.

strip mining The working of minerals from vast open trenches or pits, alternatively known as 'opencast mining'. The digging of minerals from outcrops was the earliest form of mining, but the term is chiefly applied to methods employed in the twentieth century. Contour strip-mining is used chiefly in the United States, where outcrops of a seam are stripped in the form of a bench around the hillside. In this, and in other methods used in the US and in some brown-coal operations in Europe, the overburden – the overlying rocks above the pay-mineral– are not replaced in the void, but stacked in nearby valleys or formed into new hills. The original void can later be reclaimed by regrading the land and replacing subsoils and soils, now at lower levels.

Bucket-chain or bucket-wheel excavators or large scoop draglines are used in strip-mining, often in conjunction with extensive conveyor or dump-truck systems. Open-cuts or opencasts are used where minerals lie rather deeper. A progressive system is established in which the overburden is removed separately, and then replaced systematically after the pay-mineral has been mined. In the case of coal a long trench is formed by removing soil, subsoil, mudstones and shales using draglines, mechanical shovels and trucks. The first cut is taken and the coal removed; thereafter the second cut is taken parallel to it with all the overburden being placed in the first cut. Material from the third cut then goes into the second cut, and so on. Where the mineral is so deep that a cut reaching it is too wide to be crossed by a dragline, a system of dump trucks or bridging conveyors can be used. In recent years programmes of restoration have been adopted, in which subsoils and soils are replaced on the back-filled cuts and the land progressively restored, albeit at a lower level; in many countries, however, strip-mining systems of the late nineteenth century and early twentieth have left land in a state in which it is of little use.

IVOR J. BROWN

Strömfors, Uudenmaan lääni, Finland The Strömfors ironworks, founded in 1698, near the south coast of Finland, 22 km (14 mi.) W. of KOTKA, is one of the best preserved in the country. At first there was no blast furnace, only a forge complex, using pig iron brought mainly from Sweden. The old German forges were replaced in 1865 by a Franche-Comté forge, a charcoal finery process which originated in eastern France and was widely used in Belgium and Scandinavia. The forge continued in use until 1950 when iron production at Strömfors ceased.

The oldest surviving building on the site is the octagonal church of 1772. On the east bank of the river is a group of eighteenth-century workers' dwellings, and also much accommodation from the nineteenth century and the early twentieth century. The mansion was built in 1892.

Of the old production buildings, the most notable is a red-brick bar-iron forge of 1871, extended with a blacksmith's workshop in 1896. When production ceased in 1950 the workshop was converted into a museum which still contains a hammer with the water wheel which powered it, and a nailer's workshop removed from the main forge building, a brick structure of 1846 and 1857, where the hearth in which bundles of iron rods were heated is preserved, together with its water-power system.

723

A water-powered sawmill, with ornate gabled windows, dates from 1887.

BIBLIOGRAPHY
General
Percy, 1864.

LOCATION
[M] Ironworks Museum, SF-07970 Ruotsinpyhtää.

LAURI PUTKONEN

Strömsbergs bruk, Uppsala, Sweden Strömsbergs bruk is situated on the River Tämnarån, about 30 km (20 mi.) NW of DANNEMORA. At Strömsbergs bruk can be seen all the components of a traditional BRUK: the industrial buildings as well as the manor house, the farm buildings and the workers' dwellings. The buildings do not all date from the same period but they are concentrated in a fairly small area around a pool, and give a good illustration of the past life of this kind of community.

Strömsbergs bruk was founded in 1643–5 by Welam Vervier, a Walloon. He also bought another bruk, Västland, a few kilometres upstream, and the two ironworks henceforth remained in the possession of the same owners. Vervier produced sheet iron for the gun manufactory at Söderhamn further north on the Baltic coast, and also produced bar iron for export. In 1734 Strömsbergs bruk, together with many other bruks, was acquired by Charles de Geer of LEUFSTA. He built the manor house as a dower house for his wife, who moved there after his death in 1778. The workers' houses were rebuilt in the early nineteenth century, and are placed along a street on one side of the pool, with the manor house on the other side.

Strömsbergs bruk was large by the standards of other bruks, but the quality of its Walloon iron did not qualify it for a place amongst the leading Öregrund (*see* UPPLAND) ironworks in the nineteenth century. However the bruk expanded in the second half of the nineteenth century. The blast furnace was modernized and new installations in the forge made it possible for the bruk to shift to LANCASHIRE FORGING.

The enormous bruk property of the de Geer family was split up in 1861 when Charlotta de Geer, on her marriage to Count Baltzar von Platen, became the owner of Strömsberg and three nearby bruks. The property was later taken over by the Wachtmeister family, who sold it in the 1920s to Stora Kopparbergs Bergslags AB (*see* FALUN). The ironworks were insufficiently profitable and the company stopped production, but it retained the woodlands for other purposes and continued farming, although in 1977 the farmland and the manor were sold into private ownership. The Lancashire forge was restored in 1978.

BIBLIOGRAPHY
General
Molmberg, 1917.

MARIE NISSER

Strömsholms Canal, Kopparberg, Västmanland, Sweden The 110 km (70 mi.) Strömsholms Canal, built in 1777–95, links Smedjebacken, through fourteen lakes and twenty-six locks, with Strömsholm on the Mälaren river which flows through Stockholm. After a period of disuse the canal was reopened for pleasure traffic in 1970 and now forms part of the Ekomuseum BERGSLAGEN.

Industrial archaeological sites along its route include the ironworks at ENGELSBERG, a mill museum at Stenhuset, museums of ironworking and of motor cycles at Surahammar, and a canal museum at Hallstahammar. The canal is navigated by a variety of vessels from canoes to a 70-seater trip boat, which operates between Smedjebacken and Hallstahammar.

BIBLIOGRAPHY
General
Hadfield, 1986.

LOCATIONS
[M] Kanalmuseet (Canal Museum), Skantzen, 734 00 Hallstahammar.
[M] Surahammars bruksmuseet, Herrgårdsvägen, 735 00 Surahammar.

Stroud, Gloucestershire, England Stroudwater Valley and its tributaries, with the area around Wotton-under-Edge, 15 km (9 mi.) SW, were the chief centres of the Gloucestershire woollen industry, which changed to the factory system early in the nineteenth century. Some production continues. There are many early nineteenth-century mills, chiefly of stone. Stanley Mill, 5 km (3 mi.) SW, is of outstanding quality: partially iron-framed, of brick and in the Palladian style, with a full range of outbuildings including a piered building originally for drying (*see* figures 155, 156). The valley forms the route of the Stroudwater Navigation and the Thames & Severn Canal, opened in 1789 and closed early in the twentieth century; two ornate portals of Sapperton Tunnel, 10 km (6 mi.) SE, survive.

BIBLIOGRAPHY
General
Stratton and Trinder, 1987b.
Specific
Stratton, M. and Trinder, B. Stanley Mill, Gloucestershire. *Post-Medieval Archaeology*, XXII 1988.

LOCATION
[M] Stroud District Museum, Lansdown, Stroud, Gloucestershire GL5 1BB.

Strowger, Almon B. (1839–1902) An American undertaker who at LaPort, Indiana, devised a rotary stepping switch which made possible the first automatic TELEPHONE EXCHANGES in 1889–96. He described them as 'weightless, girlless, and cussless'.

BIBLIOGRAPHY
General
Casson, 1910.

Strutt, Jedediah (1726–97) A prominent English entrepreneur in the cotton spinning and hosiery industries in the east Midlands, who was responsible for improvements to the STOCKING FRAME. He was a partner of RICHARD ARKWRIGHT in several ventures. He built mills at Belper, 10 km (6 mi.) SE of CROMFORD. His business was continued by his sons, Joseph Strutt (1765–1844) and William Strutt (1756–1830), pioneer of iron-framed buildings.

BIBLIOGRAPHY
General
Fitton and Wadsworth, 1958.

stucco Plaster used to cover the exterior walls of a building, sometimes fashioned in imitation of stone. It was made in the sixteenth century from GYPSUM and pulverized MARBLE, but subsequently from various mixtures of LIME, PORTLAND CEMENT and fine aggregates.

Stückofen The German name for a form of BLOOMERY, with a tall shaft for the direct reduction of roughly crushed iron ore, used in such alpine regions as Styria (*see* STYRIAN IRON TRAIL) and Carinthia from the Middle Ages until the eighteenth century. The arch leading into the furnace, through which went the TUYÈRES, was stopped with lime during the blowing process. The blocking was knocked away when blowing was complete, the lump of iron being pulled out horizontally. The main product was a bloom of wrought iron, but sometimes pig iron was obtained as a by-product. A Stückofen was water-powered, with a single tuyère. The interior form was that of two truncated cones placed base to base. The last Stückofen in Austria was blown out in 1775, by which time the furnaces were relatively large, some more than 7 m (23 ft.) high, and producing blooms of 300–1000 kg (660–2200 lb.).

BIBLIOGRAPHY
General
Sperl, 1985; Tylecote, 1986.

Stuttgart, Baden-Württemberg, Germany Industry developed in the capital of Württemberg only after the city was linked to the railway network, and initially on only a small scale. In 1882 Stuttgart's industrial production occupied only the eighth place among the towns of Württemberg. Over the next two decades GOTTLIEB DAIMLER (1834–1900) and Robert Bosch (1861–1942) laid the foundations for the motor manufacturing and electrical industries which still dominate the middle Neckar valley. After working at Cologne-Deutz, Daimler collaborated with Wilhelm Maybach (1846–1929) to develop the first high-speed internal combustion engine in 1883, and successfully incorporated it in various vehicles. Independently KARL BENZ (1844–1929) had done the same in Mannheim. The two of them formed Daimler-Benz in 1926. Robert Bosch is also closely connected with the development of the internal combustion engine and the motorcar. His precision machine shop became one of the major suppliers of the motor vehicle industry, and developed into a large electrical business when it began producing electric ignition systems for Daimler's and Benz's engines. The building in which Daimler's first

engine ran – the greenhouse of the inventor's villa in Cannstatt – is preserved as a reminder of his experiments. Another major car-manufacturing firm, Porsche, founded after World War II in Zuffenhausen, has its roots in Daimler, where Ferdinand Porsche (1875–1951) was head of the design office from 1923 to 1929. He had the prototype of the Volkswagen built in 1934 in the garage of his villa, which was designed by the architect Paul Bonatz.

The Daimler-Benz Museum, within the company's manufacturing complex on the eastern side of Stuttgart, is one of the most stylish of the world's motor museums, with a collection which includes vehicles of 1886 by both Benz and Daimler, and many others of outstanding interest and quality, as well as aircraft and marine engines. The Porsche company also has a motor museum; and brewing is well illustrated in another of the city's museum. The best collection of agricultural machinery in Germany is at the country life museum at Stuttgart Hohenheim.

Stuttgart Hauptbahnhof (the central station), built by Paul Bonatz in 1914–21, is one of Europe's outstanding railway termini, a subtle and humane exercise in the creation of vast yet unintimidating spaces in which people can circulate.

LOCATIONS
[M] Bad Cannstatt Museum, Wilhelmstrasse 7, 7000 Stuttgart-Bad Cannstatt.
[M] Daimler-Benz AG Museum, Mercedes Strasse, Postfach 6002 02, 7000 Stuttgart 60.
[M] Daimler Memorial Museum, Taubenheimerstrasse 13, 7000 Stuttgart.
[M] Deutsches Landwirtschafts Museum (German Country-Life Museum), Garbenstrasse 9A, 7000 Stuttgart 70 (Hohenheim).
[I] LGA Design Centre, Kanzleistrasse 19, 7000 Stuttgart.
[M] Museum of the History of Stuttgart, Konrad Adenauer Strasse 2, 7000 Stuttgart.
[M] Porsche Museum, Porschestrasse 42, 7000 Stuttgart.
[M] Postal Museum, Friedrichstrasse 13, 7000 Stuttgart.
[M] Schwäbisches Brauereimuseum (Swabian Brewing Museum), Robert Koch Strasse 12, 7000 Stuttgart 80.

ROLF HÖHMANN

Styal, Cheshire, England Quarry Bank Mill, a celebrated textile factory colony, established by Samuel Greg in 1784, is owned by the National Trust and administered as a museum by a charitable trust. The original water-powered five-storey mill, subsequently extended, contains displays and working machines. The adjacent community includes an apprentice house, a school, a shop, a chapel, cottages adapted from earlier buildings, and terraces built by the Gregs.

BIBLIOGRAPHY
General
Ashmore, 1982; Faucher, 1845; Rose, 1986.
Specific
Seckers, D. Quarry Bank Mill: growth of a museum on a shoestring. In *Museums Journal*, 84(2) 1984.

LOCATION
[M] Quarry Bank Mill Trust Ltd, Quarry Bank Mill, Styal, Cheshire SK9 4LA.

Styrian Iron Trail (Steierische Eisenstrasse), Styria, Austria   The Erzberg, or 'iron mountain', has been one of the principal sources of iron ore in Europe since the twelfth century, if not from the traditional date of its discovery in 712. The traditional routes from the mountain have been southwards along the Vordernbergerbach to the Mur valley at Leoben and thence to Graz; and northwards along the Erzbach, which joins the River Enns at Hieflau, and thence through the gorges of the Enns to Steyr and Linz. Since 1978, through the initiative of the archaeologist Dr Gerhard Sperl, the 40 km (25 mi.) route from Leoben to Hieflau has been promoted as the Styrian Iron Trail.

By the thirteenth century the primitive BLOOMERY furnaces of the region (rennofen) were replaced by shaft bloomeries (stückofen), which remained in use until BLAST FURNACES (flossofen) and FINERY-AND-CHAFERY FORGES were constructed between 1751 and 1763. Archduke Johann (1782–1859) took a close interest in the Styrian iron trade and was responsible for a substantial reorganization from 1822. In 1881 the mines and ironworks between Leoben and Hieflau were brought under the control of Österreichische Alpine-Montangesellschaft (Austrian Alpine Coal and Iron Co.) which now forms part of the Voest-Alpine combine. Historically the manufacture of iron has been organized in a highly formal way, with specific roles being allocated to those who worked water-powered furnaces (radmeister), those who operated forges and mills (hammerherren), and the iron merchants (eisenverleger). In addition to iron ore, copper and mercuric ores and lignite have been mined in the region.

From the fourteenth century the city of Leoben enjoyed monopolistic privileges in the iron trade, and many ironmasters' houses remain there. In 1849 the school of mines was transferred there from Vordernberg to form the core of the present university. The Göss brewery, situated in a former nunnery, dates from 1860. The city museum in Leoben contains exhibits relating to the iron industry.

Donawitz to the north-west was the site of a water-powered puddling forge in the mid-nineteenth century, but in 1878 a steelworks using the Siemens-Martin OPEN HEARTH process was built there, to be followed in 1891 by a coke-fired blast furnace, and the older processes were given up. Since World War II Donawitz has been one of the world's principal steelworks. The LD PROCESS of steelmaking was introduced in 1953, and there are now three LD-melting furnaces, fed by two modern blast furnaces.

At St Peter-Freienstein, 5 km (3 mi.) N., there is a collection of historic salt-mining tools in the Schloss Friedhofen, and a fine ironmaster's house survives at the Jandl sheet mill. At Trofaiach, 8 km (5 mi.) N. of Leoben, is a further local history museum with displays of traditional ironworkers' costumes.

Vordernberg, 18 km (12 mi.) N. of Leoben, was the main smelting centre south of the iron mountain, and there are few places in the world with a richer inheritance of monuments of ironmaking and houses of ironworkers. Iron was worked in the area from the early Middle Ages,

but most of the surviving monuments date from the reorganization of the trade by Archduke Johann in the nineteenth century. The centre of the town is the market well with an elaborate wrought-iron cover of 1668. Adjacent to it is Radwerk (blast furnace) IV, dating from 1846, which is preserved intact, with its charcoal barn, calcining kilns, bellows and casting house; it is now a museum. Less than 100 m north is Radwerk III, where the nineteenth-century steam engine that powered the furnace bellows is preserved. Just 150 m (165 yd.) north is Radwerk I, where the charcoal barns and all the buildings apart from the furnace stack remain. About 250 m (275 yd.) south of the market square is the mining academy of 1840, used until 1849, and adjacent to it the Lehrfrischhütte, or training forge, where apprentice forgemen were taught their trade. Finally 200 m (220 yd.) further south is the stack of the furnace of Radwerk X. Several buildings are decorated with figures in traditional mining costumes.

The ironmasters in Vordernberg obtained their ore from the iron mountain. By the late eighteenth century a special track for ore carts had been established alongside the post road. A primitive railway with two inclined planes was constructed by Johann Dulnig in 1831–48. Substantial remains of this route can be seen to the north of Vordernberg, and alongside the track, 2 km (1 mi.) N. of the town, is the monumental ruin of the Laurenti ore-calcining plant. Dulnig's line was replaced in 1891 by a standard-gauge rack railway, on which steam traction was employed until 1981. An 0–6–2T locomotive of 1908 is preserved in the square at Vordernberg; and a 2–12–2T built for the line in 1941 is at the main station to the south of Vordernberg, which is the terminus of an electrified branch from Leoben. An 0–6–2T of 1892 and an 0–12–0 of 1912 from the line are preserved at Strasshof (see DEUTSCH-WAGRAM).

The Erzberg, known as the Styrian loaf of bread ('Steierischen Brotlaib), rises to 1250 m (5000 ft.). The Siderite ore deposits were worked by hammer and wedge until the introduction of gunpowder in 1720. Until the nineteenth century much of the ore was conveyed away by sack haulers, but about 1810 a system of dumping shafts and galleries was established, extensive remains of which survive. The town of Eisenerz is situated at the foot of the mountain, and contains many ironmasters' houses, together with the shift tower (Schichtturm), which houses a bell formerly used for calling miners to work. The town museum contains displays relating to ironmaking and mining including a HUND.

The iron trail ends at Hieflau, 14 km (9 mi.) N. of Eisenerz, where the Erzbach flows into the Enns. A wood rake was constructed there on the latter river in 1572 by Hans von Gasteiger (see GROSSREIFLING). Jewellery was made there for many centuries from 'Achstein', a type of coal found in the vicinity. The town is the beginning of the 'Eisenwurzen', a region where iron was traditionally worked into useful products, extending along the Enns to Steyr.

The Styrian Iron Trail presents many contrasts. The Donawitz works has set the pattern for steelmaking throughout the world during the past thirty years. Yet at

Vordernberg and Eisenerz it is possible to experience a tradition of ironmaking that lasted many centuries, and that is quite different from any that has grown up since the Industrial Revolution. Charcoal fuel and water power were used until well into the twentieth century. Traditional symbols and images are preserved on buildings as well as in museums, and traditional costumes are still worn.

BIBLIOGRAPHY
General
Schneider, 1963; Schuster, 1978; Sperl, 1984.

LOCATIONS
[M] Gemeindemuseum (Parish Museum) in Ausbau, Hieflau.
[M] Heimatmuseum (Local Museum), Museumsstiege 2, Eisenerz.
[M] Heimatmuseum (Local Museum), Rebenburggasse, Trofaich.
[M] Radwerk IV (Blast Furnace IV), Hauptplatz, Vordernberg.
[M] Stadtisches Museum (City Museum), Kirchgasse, Leoben.
[M] Zahnradbahnmuseum (Rack Railway Museum), Haptstrasse 85, Vordernberg.

STUART B. SMITH and BARRIE TRINDER

suburb A term originally applied to the areas immediately outside the bounds of a city, whether built-up or not, but which in the nineteenth century came to mean a residential area dependent upon a city, although many suburbs that began as mere dormitories developed their own commercial and industrial bases. Many suburbs of Australasia and North America were laid out in uniform building plots, and the commonest house type was often the BUNGALOW or 'rambler'. In European cities the construction of permanent dwellings might be preceded by the establishment of gardens, pleasure grounds, brickyards and quarries, and sometimes of PLOTLAND settlements, all of which may have left archaeological traces. Development might be haphazard, with the building of VILLAS preceding by several decades the construction of more numerous dwellings in TERRACES. Twentieth-century British suburbs have been characterized by SEMI-DETACHED HOUSES.

BIBLIOGRAPHY
General
Dyos, 1973; Jackson, 1973, 1985; Oliver *et al.*, 1981.

Sudbury, Ontario, Canada Nickel was discovered at Sudbury, 350 km (220 mi.) NW of Toronto, during the construction of the Canadian Pacific Railway in 1883. Gold, silver, cobalt and platinum ores have since been worked in addition to the nickel deposits, which are the world's largest. The landscape is dominated by huge smelter chimneys. A further landmark is a 9 m (30 ft.) high Big Nickel, a colossal replica of a Canadian coin of 1951. A visit to the Big Nickel Mine includes a tour of underground workings. The early years of the city are portrayed in the Copper Cliff and Flour Mill Heritage Museums; while Science North is a snowflake-shaped science centre, portraying many aspects of the sub-Arctic regions.

LOCATIONS
[M,S] Big Nickel Mine, Loren Street at Big Nickel Mine Road, Sudbury, Ontario.

[M] Copper Cliff Museum, Balsam Street, Copper Cliff, Ontario.
[M] Flour Mill Heritage Museum, St Charles Street, Sudbury, Ontario.
[M] Science North, Ramsey Lake Road and Paris Street, Sudbury, Ontario.

sugar Sugar cane, *Saccharum officinarum*, grows only in hot climates, knowledge of it reaching Europe after the Crusaders had encountered it in Cyprus in the thirteenth century. Between 1600 and 1750 sugar became the principal form of sweetening in Western Europe, as imports from the Americas slowly supplanted honey. British consumption rose from 10 000 tonnes per annum in 1700 to 150 000 tonnes in 1800. Cane is usually crushed in a SUGAR-CANE MILL on the plantation where it is grown, and further processed in a SUGAR REFINERY in the country of consumption. Extraction from beet in BEET SUGAR REFINERIES developed on a large scale in the nineteenth century.

In the USA there was great pressure from packaging firms from the 1920s to sell sugar in bags, but by 1928 only 10 per cent of American sugar was sold in this way, although packaging has since become almost universal.

The extraction of sugar from maple, *Acer saccharinum*, is a significant industry in the northern USA, Quebec and Ontario.

See also JAM; HONEY; MARMALADE.

BIBLIOGRAPHY
General
Boorstin, 1973; Braudel, 1981; Brooks, 1983; Deer, 1950; Galloway, 1988; Prescott and Proctor, 1937.

BARRIE TRINDER

sugar-cane mill In the nineteenth century, a sugar mill meant a mill with three, four or five sets of heavy, close-set iron rollers – usually steam-powered, although earlier examples were worked by animals – used for extracting juice from sugar cane on or near the plantation where it is grown. The outstanding surviving mills are in the Virgin Islands and have been surveyed by HAER (*see* UNITED STATES OF AMERICA). The manufacture of rolls for mills was an important trade for British foundries (*see* GLASGOW). Modern mills employ shredding apparatus before the cane is crushed, and treat crushed cane with water to extract the maximum amount of sugar. Raw sugar was traditionally dispatched to SUGAR REFINERIES in HOGSHEADS, then in jute bags, but subsequently in bulk.

BIBLIOGRAPHY
General
Prescott and Proctor, 1937.

sugar refinery Sugar-refining technology was developed in Venice, where Egyptian cane was employed. Until the early nineteenth century the moist cane, imported in HOGSHEADS, was dissolved in water with a little limewater, filtered, and then boiled fast to concentrate the liquid. By 1840 the solution was usually evaporated under pressure in vacuum pans: the sugar crystals which formed in the thick juice were separated in centrifuges before being washed and dried to form granulated sugar. The juice that remains is molasses, which has several industrial uses (*see* ETHANOL; RUM). Most sugar refineries are concentrated in ports like Baltimore, MARYLAND; LONDON; LIVERPOOL; MONTREAL; New Orleans, LOUISIANA; Philadelphia, PENNSYLVANIA and ROTTERDAM.

See also BEET SUGAR REFINERY.

BIBLIOGRAPHY
General
Brooks, 1983; Deer, 1950; Prescott and Proctor, 1937.

sulphur (S)   An element with many important compounds, and one constituent of GUNPOWDER. Mined in Sicily, Poland, Louisiana, Texas and elsewhere, it is extracted from pyrites and produced in various chemical processes (*see* LEBLANC).

sulphuric acid (H_2SO_4)   Benjamin Disraeli remarked that there was 'no better barometer to show the state of an industrial nation than the figure representing the consumption of sulphuric acid per head of population'. In the nineteenth century sulphuric acid, then more commonly called vitriol or oil of vitriol, was used in a high proportion of chemical manufacturing processes. Its relative importance has diminished with the use of ELECTROLYSIS but it remains essential in many processes. In 1950 the annual consumption was 2 million tonnes in Britain, 1.5 million in France and 10 million in the USA.

Sulphuric acid was made in large quantities from the early nineteenth century for use in the LEBLANC PROCESS. It was produced in England from 1746 by the lead-chamber process developed by John Roebuck (1718–94) in which copper pyrites (CuS_2; and later iron pyrites, FeS_2) was burned in kilns (*see* HALTON), producing sulphur dioxide: this was fed, with steam and nitrous oxide, into lead chambers, where they reacted with oxygen from the air to form fine mists of dilute sulphuric acid. From 1850 waste sulphur dioxide from the calcining of copper ores was also employed. By 1900 a lead chamber could be as large as 60 m × 9 m × 7.5 m (200 ft. × 30 ft. × 25 ft), and manufacture had developed from an intermittent to a continuous process, GAY-LUSSAC and Glover towers being used to recycle waste gases. Until 1914 most British sulphuric acid was manufactured by this method, but the principle of the contact process – by which a mixture of sulphur dioxide and oxygen is passed over a heated platinum catalyst, producing sulphur trioxide which can be dissolved in water to form sulphuric acid – was propounded in 1831 by Peregrine Phillips, a Bristol vinegar maker, and vigorously developed in Germany from the 1870s.

BIBLIOGRAPHY
General
Morgan and Pratt, 1938; Partington, 1950; Warren, 1980; Williams, 1953.
Specific
Clow, A. & N. Vitriol in the Industrial Revolution. In *EcHR*, xv.

Dickinson, H. W. The history of vitriol manufacture in England. In *TNS*, I.

BARRIE TRINDER

Summerlee Heritage Park, Coatbridge, Strathclyde, Scotland   An independent industrial museum 15 km (9 mi.) E. of Glasgow, founded in 1984 with items from the Glasgow Museums and the Scottish Society for the Preservation of Historic Machinery. It is on the site of the Summerlee Ironworks, founded in 1835 by Wilson & Co., and from 1857 controlled by the family of J. B. Neilson (1792–1865), patentee of HOT BLAST, who turned Coatbridge into 'the Iron Burgh'. Excavations have revealed the foundations of four furnaces and five heating stoves. Furnaces went out of blast in the 1930s, and in the 1950s were replaced by a crane-works: this is now an exhibition hall for a collection of machine tools, including Shanks horizontal and vertical planing machines, equipment from Hudson's Boiler Works and a brass foundry, a Tropenas-type steel converter and a rolling mill. Exhibits include two winding engines – an atmospheric rotative beam engine of *c*.1810 from Rutherglen, and a 1926 compound piston valve engine from Cardowan Colliery – and a double-beam McNaughted engine (*see* COMPOUND ENGINE) from a Glasgow cotton mill. A restored stretch of the Monkland Canal carries a steel replica of *Vulcan* of 1819, Scotland's first iron-hulled boat.

LOCATION
[S] Summerlee Heritage Trust, West Canal Street, Coatbridge, Lanarkshire.

MARK WATSON

Sunderland, Tyne and Wear, England   A coal shipping port and later a shipbuilding town at the mouth of the River Wear, first crossed by a 73 m (240 ft.) iron bridge built by Rowland Burdon in 1792–6; this was replaced by a steel-girder structure in 1929. Monkwearmouth station on the north bank, designed by Thomas Moore in 1848, with its Doric pilasters and Ionic portico, is the outstanding small station in Britain. Ryhope, 5 km (3 mi.) S., has a water pumping station of 1868, with two original R. & W. Hawthorn beam engines and three Lancashire boilers of 1908. Characteristic working-class houses were single-storey terraced cottages, built until the early twentieth century.

BIBLIOGRAPHY
General
Atkinson, 1974; Cossons and Trinder, 1979; Muthesius, 1982.
Specific
Linsley, S. M. *Ryhope Pumping Station: a history and description.* Newcastle: Ryhope Engine Trust, 1973.

LOCATIONS
[M] Ryhope Engines Trust, Ryhope, Sunderland, Tyne and Wear SR2 0ND.
[M] Sunderland Museum and Art Gallery, Borough Road, Sunderland, Tyne and Wear SR1 1PP.

supermarket   A shop selling food and often other goods, where customers make choices of goods from shelves, and pay at a 'check-out' till, in effect being compelled to see the whole stock, and encouraged to buy on impulse. The first to use the principle was 'Piggly-Wiggly', established by Clarence Saunders (1881–1953) at Memphis, Tenn., in 1916. The first very large supermarket was Crystal Palace, San Francisco, a steel-framed building of 6300 m² (68 000 sq. ft.), opened in 1923, with parking for 4350 cars. Customers in the first supermarkets collected goods in baskets. The first shopping trolley was adapted from a push-along toy in Houston, Texas, in the early 1920s. Such carts were being manufactured on a large scale by 1930. Supermarkets spread rapidly in the USA in the 1920s and 30s. The first in Britain was opened in St Albans after Jack Cohen (1898–1979), founder of the Tesco company, had visited the USA in 1936, but it was not until the easing in the early 1950s of wartime rationing that the supermarket became established in Europe. Supermarkets stimulated the growth of the packaging industry. The development of refrigeration enabled them to sell perishable and frozen foods in the same way as other goods.

BIBLIOGRAPHY
General
Boorstin, 1973; Corina, 1971; Franken and Larrabee, 1928.

BARRIE TRINDER

superphosphates *See* ARTIFICIAL FERTILIZERS.

suspension bridge A bridge in which the deck is hung from cables slung between two anchorages over towers or piers at either end. This form of construction was known in ancient China, introduced on a small scale in the West in the eighteenth century, and developed with some sophistication in France, Scotland, Switzerland, and by James Finley in the USA, in the early nineteenth century. In 1826 THOMAS TELFORD demonstrated at MENAI the potential of suspension bridges for spanning great distances beyond the capabilities of other forms of construction, and the type was developed to perfection by John A. Roebling (1806–69) in the USA.

The stability of the deck in relation to wind pressures is a critical factor in the design of suspension bridges. Menai was severely damaged in a storm in 1839, but Telford had foreseen the eventuality and spare parts were to hand for its speedy repair. The Tacoma Narrows Bridge in WASHINGTON state, which was opened on 1 July 1940, collapsed on 7 November 1940, after its plate-girder deck developed oscillations.

Early suspension bridges had wrought-iron chains, that at Conway being the best preserved example. Roebling pioneered the use of iron wire cables with his Pittsburgh bridge of 1846, his Delaware & Hudson Canal aqueduct of 1848, and his Niagara Falls bridge of 1855. Most nineteenth-century suspension bridges had masonry towers, although Finley in the USA often used wood, but concrete and steel have been used for this purpose in the twentieth century. Roebling's Brooklyn Bridge, completed by his son, Washington Roebling (1837–1926), in 1883 has a span of 480 m (1595 ft.) and for forty-six years was the longest suspension bridge in the world (*see* figure 96). The Golden Gate Bridge, San Francisco, completed in 1937, with a span of 1280 m (4200 ft.), remained the longest in 1950.

BIBLIOGRAPHY
General
Jackson, 1988; McCullough, 1972; Peters, 1987; Prade, 1990; Pugsley, 1957.

BARRIE TRINDER

Swansea (Abertawe), West Glamorgan, Wales Swansea is the principal city of south-west Wales, the centre of a conurbation extending from Port Talbot to Llanelli. Its position at the intersection of the South Wales coalfield with the sea meant that mining developed as the demand for coal increased from the seventeenth century, and continued with the growing demand for anthracite in the twentieth century. The first British copper-smelter was established at Aberdulais near Neath in 1584. A steam winding engine house of before 1782 – possibly the oldest in the world – survives at Gwernllwynchwith, and a typical anthracite mine of the 1920s is preserved at Crynant. In the eighteenth and nineteenth centuries the area led the world in non-ferrous metals, with numerous copper, nickel, silver, lead and zinc works using local coal, and ores shipped from south-west England, from ABERYSTWYTH, from THOMAS WILLIAMS's mines in North Wales, and from overseas. The greatest concentration was in the Lower Swansea Valley, which became despoiled by slag heaps and noxious fumes. A massive landscaping programme has cleared most industrial remains, but areas of slag survive and the plan of Morriston township, built by a copper-magnate from the 1780s, can be traced. Ironmaking developed from the late eighteenth century, for example at NEATH ABBEY, and further north after the experiments of DAVID THOMAS in the 1830s. Steel production grew with tinplate, world production of which was dominated by numerous handmills between Llanelli and Port Talbot for much of the nineteenth century. Production declined in the twentieth century and concentrated in electrolytic tinning mills from the 1950s, but remains of handmills survive at Aberdulais and KIDWELLY. Chemical refining started with the establishment of Llandarcy Oil Refinery in 1922 and expanded into the 1960s. Transport services focused on several natural harbours, superseded by wet-dock facilities from the 1850s, mainly at Swansea, where one dock is now a marina with a museum of industry alongside. Inland transport was by roads, several early wooden railways, horse-drawn tramroads, a series of canals up the valleys, and steam railways along the coast and into the coalfield to the north and west. The Oystermouth or Mumbles railway, built in 1806 to limestone quarries along Swansea Bay, was the route of the world's first regular rail passenger service, instituted in 1807 by Benjamin French using horse-drawn carriages. The route now forms the foreshore.

729

BIBLIOGRAPHY
General
John, 1950; Rees, 1975.
Specific
Hilton, K. J. ed. *The Lower Swansea Valley Project*. London: Longman, 1967.
Lee, C. E. *The Swansea & Mumbles Railway*, 3rd edn. South Godstone, Surrey: Oakwood Press, 1970.

LOCATIONS
[S] Aberdulais Falls, Aberdulais, Neath, West Glamorgan SA10 8EU.
[M,S] Cefn Coed Colliery Museum, Crynant, Neath, West Glamorgan SA10 8SN.
[M] Swansea Maritime and Industrial Museum, Museum Square, Maritime Quarter, Swansea SA1 1SN.

PETER WAKELIN

Sweden Sweden in the late twentieth century enjoys a high standard of living and has one of the world's most industrialized economies. It has long traditions of mining and manufacturing, based not just on rich mineral resources but on the ability of the Swedes to adapt to changing conditions. Sweden also possesses some of the world's most remarkable industrial monuments, many of them located within communities that have been continuously concerned with mining or manufacturing for many centuries.

Sweden was one of the leading European powers in the first half of the seventeenth century when under King Gustavus Adolphus II (1594–1632) its armies were influential in the Thirty Years War of 1618–48. At the end of the war the southern provinces of Halland and Skåne remained part of Denmark, but Sweden held FINLAND, Baltic territories including Estonia and Livonia, and lands around Bremen and Verden in north-west Germany. Continuing conflicts in Scandinavia led to the Treaty of Copenhagen of 1660 which confirmed Swedish possession of Skåne and Halland, and established the boundaries between Norway, Sweden and Denmark as they have remained until the present day. The Great Northern War of 1700–21, in which Sweden was in conflict with Russia, led to the loss of the Baltic and German territories. Control of Finland, and of the ALAND ISLANDS, was ceded to Russia in 1809. In 1814 a dynastic union was established with NORWAY which lasted until 1905.

Sweden extends over an area of 450 000 km² (175 000 sq. mi.) and has a population of over 8 million. It extends 1500 km (930 mi.) from south to north, and has land frontiers with Norway and Finland. For administrative purposes it is divided into 24 provinces. The northern provinces, beyond the 61st parallel, comprising two-thirds of the total land area and collectively called Norrland, are sparsely inhabited, and were of little economic importance until the nineteenth century when first their woodlands, and later their iron-ore resources and hydro-electric power potential, began to be exploited.

By the seventeenth century Sweden was one of the principal European producers of copper (*see* FALUN) and silver (*see* SALA), but iron was the country's most significant product. In the mid-eighteenth century roughly half the iron produced in Europe was smelted in Sweden, much of it in the BERGSLAGEN region. Patterns of production in central Sweden established before 1700 were to remain remarkably little changed until the latter part of the nineteenth century, and the ironworking BRUKS, located in rural settings, proved to be remarkably stable communities. The state controlled the iron trade, forbidding the export of iron ore or pig iron, and controlling the trade in wrought iron. The forests of the BERGSLAGEN were conserved in order to secure charcoal supplies for the blast furnaces. A complex system of inland navigation was developed to transport iron. Its monuments include notable warehouses like those at Grangärde, 16 km (10 mi.) NW of LUDVIKA, which are partially built of blast-furnace slag (*see also* HARGS BRUK AND HARGSHAMN). Observers, sent to England and elsewhere to secure information about the iron trade and ironworking technology, left records which are sources of the utmost importance for industrial historians in the countries they visited.

Although a Newcomen engine was installed at DANNEMORA in the 1720s, and the GOTHA CANAL shows the influence of THOMAS TELFORD, the British Industrial Revolution of the late eighteenth century at first had little effect on Sweden. The export of iron was affected by the increased availability of coke blast iron in Britain, but such was the quality of the Swedish iron that many British and other steelmakers continued to buy it. The major changes in ironmaking technology introduced in Britain in the eighteenth century were not adopted in Sweden, although the LANCASHIRE FORGE introduced from the 1820s was based on an atypical British practice. Factory-based textile production began in the nineteenth century in STOCKHOLM, BORÅS and NORRKÖPING, and mechanical engineering works were established at such places as TROLLHÄTTAN and Motala (*see* GOTHA CANAL).

Sweden in 1850 thus remained a relatively poor country, largely dependent upon agriculture. The vitality of the iron industry had few secondary consequences within the economy. From the mid-nineteenth century important steps were taken which made possible the subsequent modernization of Swedish society. There were extensive agricultural reforms, which increased productivity; and schooling became compulsory from 1842. Railways came late to Sweden. Only 527 route km (327 mi.) had been completed by 1860 and the system was complicated by a diversity of gauges, but the strategic main lines were of standard gauge and from the 1860s contributed substantially to economic growth.

In 1870 three-quarters of the Swedish people depended upon agriculture for their livelihoods, and only 13 per cent of the population lived in cities. The basic economic structure of the country changed substantially in the following decades, during which the population rose from 4 million to 5.5 million by 1914, which hastened the exodus from the countryside to the cities, and stimulated the rate of emigration. By 1900 the industrial sector of the economy provided a greater proportion of gross national product than the agricultural sector. In part this resulted

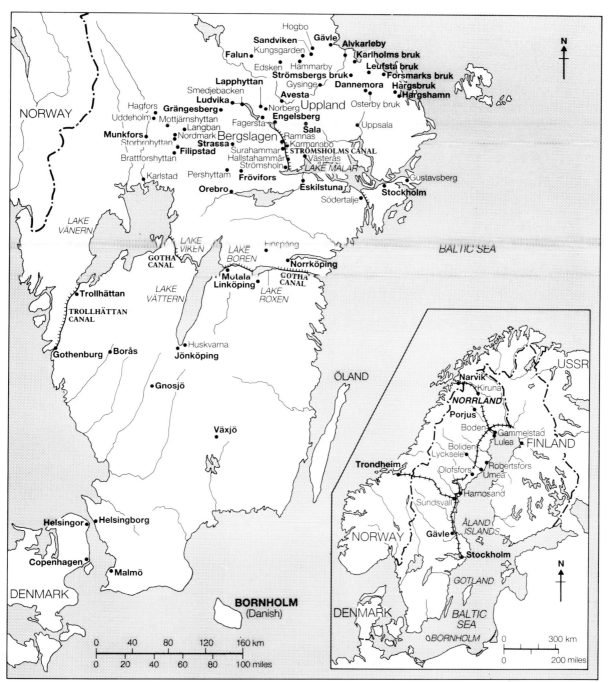

Sweden, south of Gävle, excluding Gotland. Inset: Sweden, showing sites north of Gävle

from the growth of traditional iron- and wood-based industries, in part from the expansion of consumer goods manufactures like sugar-refining and the production of ready-made clothes, and in part from wholly new activities, particularly in engineering.

The traditional Swedish iron producers faced increasing competition during the nineteenth century from iron made in coke-fired blast furnaces of the type developed in Great Britain in the eighteenth century. Many small furnaces and forges were closed from the 1870s, some of the sites being reused by manufacturers of paper and timber (*see* FRÖVIFORS; KARLHOLMS BRUK); at others new

731

Figure 152   A warehouse for storing iron, constructed of blocks of iron slag, at Grangärde in Dalarna, Sweden, from which a succession of lakes, rivers and canals formed a through navigation to Stockholm; the village was the location in 1978 for the third international conference on industrial monuments, at which the TICCIH organization was formally constituted.
Barrie Trinder

ways of making steel in Open hearth and Electric furnaces were adopted, while a few, some of which have been preserved, continued traditional processes into the twentieth century. The number of works with blast furnaces declined from 107 in 1876 to 86 in 1912, while the number of forges making wrought iron fell from 327 to 49 in the same period. The most important technological development for the central Swedish iron industry was the open-hearth process, which made it possible to use phosphoric iron-ore deposits to make pig iron for steelmaking. The first electric furnace to be used for making steel was set to work at Gysinge (*see* Sandviken) in 1900. Vast reserves of ore were exploited from the end of the nineteenth century in northern Sweden. Mines were established in Kiruna and elsewhere, from which ore was moved by rail to the Norwegian port of Narvik, whence steamers carried it to ironworks throughout Europe, but particularly to the Ruhrgebiet.

The nature of forest industry also underwent a fundamental change. At first producers concentrated on sawn timber, exports of which tripled between 1830 and 1850. From 1849, when the first Swedish steam-driven sawmill was established in Norrland, log-floating facilities were developed and the region became a substantial producer of timber. Exports of timber increased by over 50 per cent between 1850 and 1855, and multiplied by two and a half times during the 1860s. Later in the century, as the emphasis of production moved from sawn timber to pulp and newsprint, the same facilities were adapted to take logs to pulpmills. The country's first mechanical pulpmill

was set up in 1857, and the world's first chemical pulpmill came into operation at Bergvik, 70 km (40 km) N. of Gävle, in 1872. Many ironworking companies threatened by the development of new methods of steelmaking transferred their capital to pulp-making enterprises, and in some cases set up new timber or pulp plants alongside old ironworks. Many young people from the south of Sweden migrated to work in the forests and mills of Norrland, where some substantial industrial communities were created in regions which had previously sustained only sparse populations.

Sweden also saw the growth of new industries in the closing years of the nineteenth century. Engineering flourished, drawing in some cases upon the accumulated skills of centuries in communities like Eskilstuna, in others developing foundries established earlier in the nineteenth century for the manufacture of agricultural machinery, sawmill equipment and locomotives (*see* Eskilstuna, Trollhättan). Sweden was among the world leaders in the manufacture of such products as Cream separators, Telephones, Ball bearings and electric Generators. Companies involved in such manufactures had of necessity to look to international markets. In more recent times Swedish companies have made distinctive contributions to the development of aircraft and motorcar manufacture.

Like the houses of the peasantry, the ironworks of central Sweden were seen in a Romantic light in the late nineteenth century. They were celebrated by poets and artists who conjured up visions of blast furnaces in forest clearings on dark winter nights, their stacks silhouetted by the flames bursting from their throats, and by sweating forgemen hammering bars of wrought iron. Many works closed but were maintained in the hope of better times, and in due course came to be preserved as monuments by the large companies which owned them, or in some cases by local historical societies. At LUDVIKA the local historical society set up an open-air museum of the mining industry which opened in 1938, while at FALUN the Stora Kopparberg company opened a museum as early as 1922.

There are probably more BLAST FURNACES preserved in Sweden than in any other country. The majority are relatively small charcoal-fuelled, water-powered structures, reflecting seventeenth- or eighteenth-century practice, although they may well have continued operation until the late nineteenth century or even the early twentieth century. One of the best examples is at ENGELS-BERG. The number of surviving late-nineteenth-century or early-twentieth-century blast furnaces is smaller, but again Sweden probably has more preserved examples than any other country, the most significant being those at AVESTA, Ag (see FALUN) and Pershyttan (see ÖREBRO). Many water-powered forges also survive although relatively few retain their equipment (see DANNEMORA; ENGELSBERG; KARLHOLMS BRUK; STRÖMSBERGS BRUK). Sweden also has more significant monuments than any other country of the early period of mild steel manufacture. A Bessemer converter, for example, is preserved at the ironworks at Iggesund, 130 km (80 mi.) N. of Gävle, and another at Hagfors (see MUNKFORS). There are also many notable monuments of iron-ore mining (see DANNEMORA; GRÄNGESBERG; STRÅSSA). A documentation project begun by the National Board of Antiquities in 1920 has identified some seven thousand ironworking sites, including a thousand where blast furnaces were operated.

Wood has been Sweden's other major natural resource. Several sawmills are preserved, including the water-powered example at Blåvik in Västernorrland. An early mechanical pulpmill has been reserved at Forsvik bruk, on the Gotha Canal, 8 km (5 mi.) W. of Lake Vättern, while a museum of the pulp and paper industry has been established at FRÖVIFORS.

Sweden quickly took advantage of the opportunities presented by hydro-electric power in the late nineteenth century. One of the country's first hydro-electric power stations, at Nås, 52 km (32 mi.) W. of Borlange, dating from 1896–9, has been preserved. In 1908 the government set up the State Power Board, which was responsible for the three important power stations built at TROLLHÄTTAN in 1909, ÄLVKARLEBY in 1911, and PORJUS in 1914. Finnforsen hydro-electric power station, in Västerbotten province, 32 km (20 mi.) W. of Skellefteå, was inaugurated as a museum in 1983.

Early industry in Sweden is probably better documented than that of any other country. Many enterprises have runs of accounts which date from the seventeenth century, while parish registers and taxation returns enable the compilation of unusually comprehensive studies of industrial communities. There are numerous scholarly histories of Swedish companies, while from the

1970s Swedish intellectuals, notably Gunnar Sillén in *Stiga vi mot ljuset* (We rise towards the light) and Sven Lindqvist in *Gräv där Du star* (Dig where you stand) have encouraged working people to co-operate in the production of their own history, not just in the form of books but as dramatic productions and exhibitions. Such activities build on long traditions of adult education through study circles organized by the ABF (the Swedish Workers' Educational Association). Notable examples have included studies of builders, office workers and dockers.

Sweden has a comprehensive network of public and private museums. In 1977 the SAMDOK (contemporary documentation) project was inaugurated with the object of stimulating curators to document aspects of life that are still flourishing, rather than just activities that are on the verge of disappearance. Some fifty museums with major concerns with the history of technology or industry came together to establish a co-operative council (TIM3A) in 1983. Sweden's principal industrial collections are in the Tekniska museet (Technical Museum) in Stockholm which was founded in 1923, and developed under the direction of Torsten Althin. Its main concern has always been with the history of engineering, but in the 1940s it was responsible with the Nordiska museet for a pioneering oral historical project entitled 'Workers' Memories'. There have been other notable examples of innovation in museums and in the interpretation of *in situ* monuments in Sweden, most notably the institution of the ekomuseum BERGSLAGEN in the mid-1980s.

Sweden's greatest contribution to museology has probably been the development of the OPEN-AIR MUSEUM, which was part of the Romantic Nationalist movement of the late nineteenth century. The first major open-air museum, Skansen in STOCKHOLM, was opened by Artur Hazelius (1833–1901) in 1891. His example was followed elsewhere in Sweden, and hundreds of open-air museums were opened in the first forty years of the twentieth century. Most were collections of less than ten moved buildings, often administered by local historical societies; but some, like Kulturen in Lund or Fredriksdals in HELSINGBORG, developed into substantial institutions. Most of the buildings in such museums are farmsteads but many museums have mills and other early industrial buildings, and some (see GNOSJÖ; LUDVIKA) are devoted primarily to portraying the history of industry.

The Historic Buildings Act 1960 affords protection to buildings in private ownership, including industrial monuments, although the protection it provides for the landscapes surrounding individual buildings is limited. Buildings in public ownership are protected by legislation of 1920, while ruins and buried sites are the subject of an Act concerning Ancient Monuments and Finds, revised in 1942. The Central Office of National Antiquities was responsible for a survey of preservation and recording activities relating to the industrial heritage; this was published in 1985, and has been followed up by regional initiatives. The Office is also involved in preservation schemes for industrial monuments.

There have been notable examples of adaptive reuse schemes applied to industrial buildings in Sweden since

733

the 1970s. A brewhouse of 1910 at the Hamburger brewery on Norrtullsgatan in Stockholm was converted to a public meeting place, while one of several early-twentieth-century shoe factories in Örebro, designed by Wilhelm Nissen in 1906–7, was adapted as offices in 1973. Subsequently an early-twentieth-century flourmill in Kalmar was converted to municipal offices, and a cement factory in Hällekis adapted as grain silos. A Swedish view of the ethics of reusing industrial buildings is provided by Törnquist (1986).

Employers' organizations and trades unions have played particularly active roles in the conservation of the Swedish industrial heritage. The Jernkontoret (Ironmasters' Association) holds important collections of documents at its Stockholm offices, and has sponsored research projects into various aspects of the history of the Swedish iron and steel industry, as well as projects recording contemporary changes. The Association of the Swedish Pulp and Paper Industry provided support in the late 1970s for the compilation of a record of all pulp and paper mills in the country, and it was the association that decided to concentrate preservation resources within the industry on the Frövifors mill. The state railway company has carried out a survey of all stations and railway buildings in the 1970s, and the state hydro-electric power company formulated a conservation plan for its power stations during the same period. Swedish companies also have a long tradition of commissioning and publishing accounts of their own histories.

Some important excavations of industrial sites have been carried out in Sweden – notably that at LAPPHYTTAN – which have radically altered views of the chronology of the introduction of the blast furnace.

A Swedish National Committee for the History of Technology, aiming to encourage research which can put Swedish history in its international context, was established in 1981, and published the journal *Polhem*. The journal *Teknik & Kultur* (Technology and culture), published quarterly in Stockholm, surveys the industrial, technological and labour history of all the Scandinavian countries. Labour history is covered in the journal *Arbetarhistoria*.

See also ÄLVKARLEBY; AVESTA; BERGSLAGEN; BORÅS; DANNEMORA; ENGELSBERG; ESKILSTUNA; FALUN; FILIPSTAD; FORSMARKS BRUK; FRÖVIFORS; GÄVLE; GNOSJÖ; GOTHA CANAL; GOTHENBURG; GRÄNGESBERG; HARGS BRUK AND HARGSHAMM; HELSINGBORG; JÖNKÖPING; KARLHOLMS BRUK; LAPPHYTTAN; LEUFSTA BRUK; LINKÖPING; LUDVIKA; MALMÖ; MUNKFORS; NORRKÖPING; NORRLAND; ÖREBRO; POLHEM (POLHEM), CHRISTOPHER; PORJUS; SALA; SANDVIKEN; STOCKHOLM; STRÅSSA; STRÖMSBERGS BRUK; STRÖMSHOLMS CANAL; TROLLHÄTTAN; UPPLAND; VÄXJÖ.

BIBLIOGRAPHY
General
Andersson, 1970; Hecksher, 1956; Jörberg, 1961, 1970; Lindquist, 1978; Milward and Saul, 1973; Montgomery, 1939; Nisser, 1981; Nisser and Bedoire, 1978; Rockwell and Garcia, 1985; Sillen, 1977; Soderlund, 1952.

Specific
Bebyggelsehistorisk tidskrift, Konsthögskolans arkitekturskola, Skeppsholmen, 111 49 Stockholm.
Bohm, I. 1972. *Den Svenska Masugnen under 1800-talet* (The Swedish blast furnace in the nineteenth century). Stockholm: Jernkontoret.
Nyström, B. Sweden. In Georgeacopol-Winischhofer *et al.*, 1987.
SAMDOCK, 1982. *Spread the Responsibility for Museum Documentation*. Stockholm: Nordiska museet.
Soderlund, E. F. The impact of the British Industrial Revolution on the Swedish iron industry. In Pressnell, 1960.

LOCATIONS
[I] Riksantikvarieämbetet (Central Office of National Antiquities), Stockholm.
[I] Teknik & Kultur, Upplandsgatan 74, S-113 44 Stockholm.

BARRIE TRINDER

Swidnica (Schweidnitz), Wrocław, Poland A medieval town in Lower Silesia, 50 km (31 mi.) S. of Wrocław, on the traditional trading route between eastern and western Europe, and famous for its brewing. The Museum of Historic Trading, established in 1967, collects items illustrating trade in the town, including scales, weights, measures, price lists, wholesalers' advertisements, and old shop equipment. The collection of weighing equipment includes one-pan scales, two-pan scales and spring scales.

BIBLIOGRAPHY
Specific
Matuszkiewicz, A. *Muzeum Dawnego Kupiectwa w Swidnicy* (The Museum of Historic Trading in Swidnica). Swidnica, 1977.

LOCATION
[M] Muzeum Dawnego Kupiectwa Śląskiego (The Museum of Historic Trading), Swidnica.

Swindon, Wiltshire, England An archetypal railway town, for a century dominated by the locomotive works of the GWR. Swindon's population grew from 1198 to 45 006 during 1801–1901. A village for works employees, designed by MATTHEW DIGBY WYATT from 1842, was extensively restored in the 1970s: it has terraces of small, stone cottages, with pavilions around a square at the centre. The church of St Mark is by GEORGE GILBERT SCOTT in 1842; the Mechanics' Institute dates from 1853–4. The GWR Museum is in a building that was formerly a lodging house and chapel: it includes the 4–4–0 locomotive *City of Truro*, the 4–6–0 *Lode Star* and the *Dean Goods* 0–6–0 2516. An adjacent cottage has been restored as part of the museum.

BIBLIOGRAPHY
General
Simmons, 1986; Victoria History, 1959; Williams, 1986.

LOCATION
[M] Great Western Railway Museum, Faringdon Road, Swindon, Wiltshire.

swing bridge A bridge of truss or girder configuration, usually carrying a road or railway over a waterway, in which one section pivots around a central pier to allow the passage of vessels.

Switzerland

switcher A North American term for a locomotive that shunts in a MARSHALLING YARD or station, or undertakes short trips, but that does not pull trains on main lines (as a 'road engine' does). A switcher invariably has neither leading nor trailing wheels.

Switzerland Switzerland often appears as a clean and efficient resort for tourists, without industrial cities in the mode of Manchester or Pittsburgh, or mineral resources of international significance. The country is nevertheless one of great interest to the industrial archaeologist. Domestic manufactures developing in areas of sparse agricultural resources were of particular importance in providing foundations for the growth of large-scale manufacturing concerns. Switzerland's textile manufacturers were in the vanguard of the first Industrial Revolution in continental Europe, and Swiss makers of textile machines founded companies that remain among the most prominent in the international engineering industry. Swiss railway engineers in the nineteenth century and early twentieth established a system that provided a foundation for the growth of tourism, encouraged international transit traffic, and gave opportunities for innovation in electrical engineering.

The year 1648 brought to an end 120 years of religious warfare in Switzerland between the predominantly urban Protestant regions and the largely rural Catholic districts. During the preceding time of schism, however, a new work ethic was developing, with an economic base in the growth of domestic manufactures. The Peace of Westphalia of 1648 brought international recognition of the Swiss Confederation, which dates its own independence from the Letter of Federation of 1291. Switzerland, subdivided into subject territories – eight Catholic and seven Protestant cantons – did not, however, achieve

lasting religious peace until two more wars had been fought. In the second battle, at Villmergen in 1712, the Protestant forces defeated the Catholics and subsequently religious questions were settled by a court of arbitration. A positive result of the religious peace was the Confederation's willingness to accept religious refugees. After the Revocation of the Edict of Nantes, many French Protestant refugees migrated to Switzerland, bringing the country considerable economic stimulus.

In the eighteenth century north-east Switzerland developed into a proto-industrial area with a high proportion of domestic textile workers. In many communities of the Zürich Oberland over 50 per cent of the population lived by spinning and weaving. Trade in raw cotton, yarn and cloth was monopolized by town-based merchants, who put out the work and dominated the country dwellers through their middlemen, known as 'Fergger' or forwarding agents. This urban hegemony was oppressive to the peasant, and to commercial initiatives in rural areas, creating tensions reflected in the Swiss Peasants' War of 1653, the Geneva riots of 1707, the Lausanne rising of 1723, the riots around Basle from 1726, and conspiracies in Berne and Ticino, culminating in countrywide insurrections from 1790, which came under the ideological and political influence of the French Revolution. In 1797 the Diet which had hitherto ruled the Confederation met for the last time. In 1798 Napoleon occupied the old Confederation, in the face of some violent opposition, particularly from the interior of the country, and proclaimed the Helvetian Republic, which survived three *coups d'état*, and was dissolved after five years.

The Congress of Vienna of 1815 reorganized Switzerland as a confederation of twenty-two sovereign cantons, without subject territories, but also ushered in a conservative period of fifteen years, the 'Restoration', during which liberal forces increased in strength with the growth of industrialization. In 1830–1 they took over the government of seven cantons, abolished land taxes and tithes for the second time by the capitalization of the land, extended the economic infrastructure, and established compulsory primary education, technical institutes and new universities. In 1844 the disagreements between the liberal cantons and the conservative, Catholic cantons came to a head, leading to the last civil war in Switzerland, which ended with the victory of the liberals in 1847 and the establishment of the modern Confederation in 1848. Twenty years later the almost unlimited power of the liberals was threatened by the democratic movement, which led in 1874 to the revised Federal constitution which remains in force.

The period before World War I (in which Switzerland remained neutral) was notable for the strengthening of the labour movement, and the rise of a multiplicity of political parties. An electoral system was set up using proportional representation after 1918, with all the large parties being represented in government. In the 1920s and 30s there was radical change on both left and right, tendencies checked after 1936 by the need to defend the country against Fascism. In 1936 Switzerland began to arm. In 1937 the leading engineering trade union made a peace treaty with management, and in 1939 there was a general mobilization of the militia to face the threat of Hitler. The fact that Switzerland survived World War II almost unharmed was a reason for the economic boom of the post-war period when the country assumed a leading position in many areas of world trade (which has been retained, thanks to modernization, a high standard of general education, and also what is, in an international context, a high proportion of foreign workers.

Switzerland is famous for the variety of geographical and linguistic features within its small area of 41 293 km² (15 943 sq. mi.). It has no direct access to the sea, its main topographical feature being the Alps, which occupy 60 per cent of the surface area. The Mittelland, where most of the larger towns are situated, comprises 30 per cent of the surface area, and the Jura 10 per cent. Abundant water power has shaped the development of trade and industry over the years, and the variety of building materials is reflected in the urban areas. Switzerland is regarded as a country with few raw materials, but industrial archaeological research shows that iron ore, lead, zinc, nickel, copper, lignite, silver and even gold have been dug from hundreds of mines in the Alps and Jura from Roman times to the twentieth century. The salt mines of the Chablais were famous, but between 1869 and 1966 all other mines in the country were closed. The coal mines in particular were not productive and worked only in a time of scarcity. Consequently the exploitation of water power in Switzerland has continually expanded right up to the present.

In 1933 water rights remained for over six thousand mills. Thousands of mill ponds and leats bear witness to the 'mechanical revolution of the Middle Ages' when mills were built all over the country. Particularly well-preserved examples are the three-level underground mill at Col-des-Roches, Neuchâtel, and the Neerach mill in Zürich canton. Five small mills at St Luc in the Valais have

become an open-air museum. A sawmill with a Zuppinger wheel remains in Roggwil, 10 km N. of St Gallen, while at Böttstein, 9 km NE of Baden, are an oil mill and a restored corn mill.

The watch and clockmaking industry was a speciality of Neuchâtel. Swiss watchmakers rivalled the watchmakers of London in the development of small clockwork devices, illustrated in museums at La Chaux des Fond, Le Locle, Neuchâtel, Geneva and Winterthur.

The pre-industrial stages of textile manufacture are illustrated at St Gallen. Silk was manufactured around Zurich and Basle, and in the interior. In the eighteenth century cotton manufacturing developed, particularly in the Zürich Oberland, where there are hundreds of houses of spinners and weavers, known as 'Flarzhäuser', each accommodating up to twelve families of domestic workers. A Flarzhaus at Undel, near Bauma, Zürich, is conserved as a monument, and the domestic cotton industry is illustrated at Lichtensteig (see St Gallen). These proto-industrial activities were carried out for town-based merchants by domestic workers, first as a sideline, then as their sole means of earning bread. The merchants had the products of their labours finished in the first real factory buildings, which were constructed near towns. The technique of colour printing on cloth was brought to Switzerland by Protestant refugees from France in the eighteenth century, and cotton printing works were among the first factories in the country, some of them employing over five hundred workers. Cotton printing is illustrated in the museums at Colombier (see Neuchâtel) and Näfels (see Glarus), while factories remain at Cortaillod (see Neuchâtel) and Zurich, and drying towers in the canton of Glarus. Ribbon-weaving, or 'passementerie', was particularly prevalent in the Basel-Land sub-canton (see Basle).

This highly developed system whereby spinning and weaving of cotton was put out to domestic workers constituted the basis of the industrial revolution in Switzerland. The first mechanically-powered cotton mill was opened in 1800, with the help of the government of the Helvetian Republic, in the monastery of St Gallen, but it was unsuccessful. The first purpose-built cotton manufactory was constructed at Hard near Winterthur in 1802. All the buildings of the factory community survive. Similar complexes, with owners' houses and dwellings for workers were built all over the north-east of Switzerland from 1805. The valleys of the Töss and the Aa in the canton of Zürich developed into textile manufacturing areas from the 1820s. Spinning mills were constructed wherever a river could provide water to power them. Along the 9 km (6 mi.) of the Aabach between Robenhausen, Wetzikon and Niederuster, 10 km (6 mi.) SE of Zurich, some twenty factories were built, and are now linked by 'The Industrial Trail of the Zürich Oberland' (see Zurich).

Spinning-mill construction reached a peak in the 1830s and for a time Switzerland was a leading cotton-manufacturing country, but in that decade began a shift of investment into heavy engineering. During the Napoleonic Wars many spinning mills started workshops for building spinning frames. The Escher Wyss machine factory in Zurich was the leading works. The Rieter works in Winterthur became the most important for the manufacture of spinning frames. The Honegger loom factory at Rüti in the Zürich Oberland, and the firm of Saurer at Arbon on Lake Constance, specialized in embroidery machines and later in motor lorries. Engineering works also grew from foundries, often developed in remote places with their own workers' housing. The firm of Georg Fischer made the Muhletal near SCHAFFHAUSEN a centre of the foundry industry, while the Sulzer foundries made Winterthur the leading engineering centre in the country. Industrialists from Winterthur were also concerned with one of the first aluminium works in the world, opened in 1887 at Schaffhausen. The son of Charles Brown (1827–1905), an English engineer who played a leading role in Winterthur, gave his name to Brown Boveri in Baden.

Early mining is best illustrated in the salt mines at BEX and at the museum in a former silver and lead mine at DAVOS. Remains of a blast furnace at Filisur (see DAVOS) are preserved, and there are plans to open up former coal workings near ZURICH. With the opening of railways minerals could easily be imported and only large Swiss mines survived, like the iron-ore mine at Gonzen near Sargans, in St Gallen canton, which worked until 1966 and is now a museum.

Extractive industries were concerned principally with clay, stone and aggregates. Supplies of limestone and gypsum are inexhaustible and Switzerland came to have the highest consumption of concrete per head of population of any country in the world. A concrete industry developed as early as the 1890s in the Jura region. PORTLAND CEMENT was first made in Switzerland in 1871, and large plants built at Wildegg and Holderbank. These, with vast gravel pits like those at Rafz, show the impact of the industry. What might be called the 'concrete age' came into being in the twentieth century. Concrete was used for countless flood-protection schemes in the mountains, and for huge dams. The engineer Robert Maillart (1872–1940) gained an international reputation for his concrete bridges, and thanks to his concrete buildings the Swiss Le Corbusier became the best-known architect of the twentieth century.

Switzerland was prominent in the mechanization of food processing, particularly in the construction of flour mills and the manufacture of chocolate and baby foods (see VEVEY). In 1834 Jakob Sulzberger developed the first practical roller mill in Frauenfeld, 16 km (10 mi.) E. of Winterthur, his plant being made by the Ganz company (see BUDAPEST). As a result of the change from stone to roller grinding about three thousand mills went out of business. Some early roller mills (see ZURICH) still operate, making partial use of belt-driven transmission. Brewing is also important in Switzerland; and many breweries, like that at RHEINFELDEN, are crenellated. The textile finishing and pharmaceutical trades developed into the vast Swiss chemical industry from the 1880s (see BASLE).

Switzerland has played a leading role in the development of electric power, and the country's power stations are amongst its most notable industrial monuments. All the larger watercourses are used to generate electricity,

some 75 per cent of economically productive waterfalls being exploited. The first power stations began to operate in 1881–2 in St Moritz and Lausanne, providing electric lighting. In Lausanne over 50 km (30 mi.) of direct-current cabling were installed for this purpose. A 1500 hp plant was built at Taulan in 1887 for the first electric tramway in Switzerland between Vevey and Montreux. In 1887–90 the town of Schaffhausen built a power station with d.c. generators by the Moser dam above the Rhine Falls. It has been replaced, but several important early power stations are preserved (see BADEN; GENEVA; ZURICH). In 1898–1920 three of the biggest power stations in the world at that time were built on the Rhine, each with a spacious turbine hall of high architectural quality. Of these, the station at Laufenburg, 20 km (12 mi.) NW of Baden, which began operating in 1913–14 with six turbines and a capacity of 39 000 hp, has been preserved. The early twentieth century also saw the first large water-storage power stations. Lake di Poschiavo served as a natural reservoir for the Campocologno power station, which was opened in 1906; it has twelve turbines and a capacity of 36 000 hp. The contemporary station at CHIPPIS is of similar size. In 1920 another series of power stations was built for the electrification of the main railways. The artificial Lake Ritom was constructed on the St Gotthard Pass and has a capacity of 27.5 million m^3 per annum. The Piotta-Ritom power station was designed for a capacity of 56 000 hp, and the second power station for the Swiss Federal Railways, built in Amsteg in 1924, had a capacity of 81 600 hp. The 100 000 hp barrier was passed in the 1930s with the Ryburg-Schwörstadt Rhine–Black Forest station, and the pumped storage stations of Chandolin-Dixence (see LA GRAND DIXENCE); Etzel, 28 km (17 mi.) S. of Zürich; and Oberhasli-Innertkirchen, 16 km (10 mi.) SE of Brienz. Earth dams were built for the first artificial storage reservoirs like that at Lake Klöntal, of 1908–10, which consists of 110 000 m^3 (144 000 cu. yd.) of clay, earth and rock brought up the valley by horses. The first concrete dam had been built as early as 1869–72 at Fribourg-Pérolles, but it was only after 1916 that arched dams of a design suited to the new material were built. The first Jorgensen arched dam in Europe, 55 m (180 ft.) high and 115 m (377 ft.) long, was built in 1919–20 at Montsalvens near Fribourg. Energy requirements during World War II led to a boom in power-station and dam construction which lasted until the 1960s, and saw the building of what were then the biggest embankment dams in the world, the 237 m (778 ft.) high Mauvoisin barrier of 1957, and the 284 m (932 ft.) high La Grande Dixence dam of 1962.

In Roman times there was a network of roads between Lake Constance and Lake Geneva with three passes over the Graubünden Alps and one over the Valais Alps. In the Middle Ages the St Gotthard pass was opened with bridges boldly flung over the Schollenen gorge for packhorse traffic. In the seventeenth century pack and post-messenger traffic increased, but there were no roads to carry wheeled traffic. Between 1711 and 1798 several cantons extended their road systems to take carts and carriages, and a network of posting stations and country inns developed, laying the first foundations of the tourist industry. Rivers had to be bridged for the new main roads, and the Grubenmann brothers (*see* SCHAFFHAUSEN) gained international celebrity, having designed several large covered wooden bridges. Today Switzerland has over 150 wooden bridges of the eighteenth and nineteenth centuries, some of the most important being those in Bremgarten, in Wangen on the Aare, in Lütisburg in the Toggenburg, at Sevelen and Diessenhofen on the Rhine, and in LUCERNE.

The Swiss began to build roads for wheeled traffic over the Alpine passes from 1798. Napoleon used conscript labour to construct the first high-level road, over the SIMPLON pass in the years up to 1805. The cantons continued to extend the road network after the French occupation. In the years up to 1823 the canton Graubünden built the roads of the San Bernardino and Splügen passes, making it possible for the first time for carriages to go between northern and southern Switzerland. The canton of Uri replaced the pack trail over the St Gotthard pass with a paved road in 1819. As through roads were built, access to the cities was improved with new bridges. The world's first cable suspension bridge, constructed by Henry Dufour over the city moat in Geneva, and the two suspension bridges in Fribourg, one with a span of 273 m (898 ft.), built by Joseph Charly in 1832–40, have been demolished, and only masonry structures like the Münster bridge in Zurich survive from this period. The two steel-arch truss bridges over the Aare in Bern are outstanding examples of late nineteenth-century Swiss engineering.

The railway age began in Switzerland in 1846. Railways attracted the major share of investment in transport for seventy years, and for a time in the 1850s absorbed the larger part of domestic investment. Until nationalization began in 1902 the principal companies were the Nordostbahn (North-Eastern Railway) or NOB, with a network between Zurich, Basle, Lucerne and Lake Constance; the Schweizerische Centralbahn (Swiss Central Railway) or SCB, running out of Basle to Berne and Lucerne; the Vereinigte Schweizerbahnen (United Swiss Railways) or VSB, centred on St Gallen; the Gotthardbahn (Gotthard Railway) or GB, between Lucerne and Chiasso; and the western railways united under the name of the Jura-Simplon company, or JS. The most important NOB station is in Zurich. This company, its constituents and associates were responsible for constructing some important iron truss bridges. The small mesh lattice truss bridge at Koblenz (Aargau) dates from 1859, and was one of the last bridges built in this way. The truss bridge at Ossingen, built in 1875, is 328 m (1076 ft.) long; and that at Hemishoften, completed in the same year, 252 m (827 ft.) long. The stone and iron viaduct at Eglisau is 440 m (1444 ft.) long, of similar composite construction to the approaches to Zurich station. Outstanding structures on the VSB are the station and Sitter viaduct in ST GALLEN. Outstanding structures on the JS system are the viaduct at Grandfrey near Fribourg – 383 m (1257 ft.) long, originally of iron, but replaced by a concrete bridge in 1925–6 – and the station in Lausanne. The St Gotthard tunnel,

completed in 1882, is 15 km (9.3 mi.) long, a length exceeded in 1906 by the 19.8 km (12.3 mi.) of the Simplon. A new private railway, the Bern-Lötschberg-Simplon-Bahn (BLS) began operating in 1913 with some equally impressive civil engineering: it was electrified from the start, a pioneering achievement, using single-phase alternating current. Another important mountain railway network is the metre-gauge Rhätische Bahn (Rhaetian Railway), built from 1888, which incorporated the Albula Railway; it had loop tunnels, hairpin bends, and what remained for a long time the highest railway in Switzerland, over the Landwasser river. The Bernina Railway, the highest through mountain railway in Europe, climbs 1824 m (5984 ft.) between Tirano and the head of the Bernina pass, 2253 m (7392 ft.) above sea level. Other purely tourist lines, like those to Jungfraujoch (*see* INTERLAKEN) and the Cornergrat Railway, which climbs from Zermatt to a height of 3089 m (10 134 ft.) above sea level and was built in 1898–9, have equally dramatic engineering features. Switzerland has a particularly interesting railway system since no lines of any significance have been closed, and it is the only country that has fully electrified a railway network of such size. Both the SBB and private lines run excursions with steam locomotives and old electric stock. The principal preserved railways are the Bloney–Chamby narrow-gauge and Hinwil–Bauma (*see* ZURICH) standard-gauge lines. There is a large collection of railway rolling stock in Lucerne. Several mountain railways keep steam locomotives for special workings or for the erection and dismantling of catenaries in spring and autumn, and many steam locomotives have been 'plinthed' at stations. The Swiss have also been pioneers in the technology of cable cars. There are innumerable small systems giving access to shelf villages, often with cars conveying no more than six people, as well as spectacular high-capacity operations developed since World War II, like those taking visitors to such peaks as Titlis, 3239 m (10 626 ft.), and Schilthorn, 2970 m (9744 ft.).

The Swiss lakes were incorporated within the Roman road networks, the packhorse trail system, and the national roads, but lost their importance for freight transport as railways were built along their shores. Passenger steamship operation began as early as 1823 with the launch of the *Guillaume Tell* in Geneva, and from 1836 the Swiss were building their own steamships, and exporting paddle steamers to neighbouring countries. Twelve paddle steamers built between 1901 and 1927 remain in use on the Swiss lakes (*see* GENEVA; LUCERNE; ZURICH), two are conserved out of use with their machinery intact, and five have been converted to diesel operation. The principal inland waterway system in Europe, the Rhine navigation, terminates at BASLE. The first steamship arrived there in 1832, but large-scale navigation did not commence until 1904.

Switzerland has a long tradition of aviation, and as early as 1910, 100 000 people assembled to celebrate the 'heroes of the aeroplane'. The aerodrome at Dübendorf (*see* ZURICH) is an important site in aviation history.

Industrial archaeology is not officially taught or researched in Swiss universities, although historical courses in building construction are offered by the Eidgenössische Technische Hochschule (Swiss Federal Institute of Technology) and some courses at the universities of Basle and Zurich give consideration to industrial history. Most preservation initiatives stem from the cantonal and municipal offices for the preservation of monuments. The canton of Zürich, for example, now systematically takes account of industrial monuments. The preservation of technical monuments can now be supported or wholly financed at public expense, as is the case with the fittings of the Rhine papermill in Basle, or the 'mühlerama' in Zurich. The principal museum in the field is the Verkehrshaus der Schweiz in Lucerne, while others of importance are the 'Technorama' in Winterthur and the open-air museum at Ballenberg (see BRIENZ).

The foundation of industrial archaeology in Switzerland is provided by societies, established to conserve particular monuments, a mill, a steam locomotive, an aircraft or a collection of road and rail vehicles. The national societies of railway enthusiasts are particularly active, and the 'Pro Vaporama' society of Thun collects steam engines. Such societies are often supported by private finance, by local authorities and by cantonal offices for the preservation of monuments. Inventories of monuments have also been made on a private or partly private level. The Gessellschaft für Kunstdenkmäler (Society for Artistic Monuments) has for some time been including monuments of technological history in its records. They are listed in the 'Inventar neuerer Schweizer Architektur' (Inventory of Recent Swiss Architecture) under their respective towns. The Schweizer Heimatschutz (Swiss Regional Preservation Society) and other associations support such inventories. The journal *Industriearchäologie* (Industrial archaeology) has been published since 1977, while *Ferrum*, published by the Iron Library, includes historical material. Some large companies have their own historical collections or museums, such as the Honnegger (Sulzer) weaving-frame collection of Rüti, 28 km (17 mi.) SE of Zurich (*see also* SCHAFFHAUSEN; VEVEY); and the federal railways and Rhaetian Railways have made inventories of their stations. It is more likely that in the future companies will support the activities of societies interested in industrial archaeology than that they will take initiatives themselves.

The Federal Office of Topography publishes maps at 1:25 000, 1:50 000 and 1:100 000 and smaller scales.

See also AIGLE; BADEN; BASLE; BERNE; BEX; BRIENZ; CHIPPIS; DAVOS; GENEVA; GLARUS; LA GRANDE DIXENCE; INTERLAKEN; LÖTSCHBERG; LUCERNE; NEUCHÂTEL; RHEINFELDEN; RHINE; SAINTE CROIX; ST GALLEN; ST GOTTHARD; SCHAFFHAUSEN; SIMPLON; VALLORBE; VEVEY; WINTERTHUR; ZURICH.

BIBLIOGRAPHY
General
Allen, 1965; Baldinger, 1987; Bergier, 1983; Bodmer, 1960; EJS, 1947; Gruner, 1968; Hauser, 1961; INSA, 1982–91; Mathys, 1954; Milward and Saul, 1973; Rappard, 1914; Schneider, 1967; Stutz, 1976; Swiss National Tourist Office, 1981; Wyssling, 1946.

LOCATIONS
[I] Federal Office of Topography, CH-3084 Wabern.
[I] *Ferrum*, Klostergut Paradies, CH-8246 Langwiesen.
[I] *Industriearchäologie*, Oskar Baldinger, Aarestrasse 83, 5222 Umiken.
[I] Schweizerische gesellschaft für Technikgeschichte (The Swiss association for the history of technology), Institut für geschichte, ETH-Zentrum, 8092 Zurich.

HANS-PETER BÄRTSCHI

Sydney, New South Wales, Australia   The settlement of Sydney began under the direction of Governor Arthur Phillips (1738–1814) in 1788 but early growth was haphazard. Governor Lachlan Macquarie (1762–1824), in office between 1810 and 1821, reorganized the town and was responsible for many public works including Hyde Park Barracks and the Mint, both now preserved. The city subsequently grew to be the largest in Australia, with the greatest concentration of urban industry.

Buildings from the early period of settlement have been preserved at 'The Rocks', and some of the old docks have been redeveloped as arts or leisure facilities. Goat Island in Sydney Harbour was the site of a munitions store, begun in 1826, which was adapted from the 1870s to store high explosives. Surviving buildings include coopers' and shipwrights' workshops.

The Harbour Bridge, the city's best-known landmark, is a 503 m (1650 ft.) span steel arch, built between 1923 and 1932, by the English firm Dorman, Long & Co (*see* figure 130). The design was conceived by Dr J. J. C. Bradfield, and developed by Sir Ralph Freeman (1880–1950).

Randwick Tramway Workshops, established in 1881, once employed over a thousand people in maintaining tramcars and overhead wiring, but have operated on a much reduced scale since the tramcars were replaced by buses in 1961. A tramcar shed is now a civil engineering laboratory of the University of New South Wales.

The Quarantine Station, now part of the Sydney Harbour National Park, was built in 1837 in response to a cholera epidemic, extended in the 1850s and 1870s, and closed in 1984. It is conserved by the National Parks and Wildlife Service, the surviving structures including housing for different classes, a mortuary and a railway system. Sydney's second source of water was Busby's Bore, a 3.4 km (2.125 mi.) tunnel driven from Centennial Park under the Victoria Barracks in 1827–37, which remained in use until 1858. The Pier Street pumping station in Ultimo, a three-storey Italianate structure, with the remains of a huge cast-iron tank made by 'Coalbrook . . .' (presumably Coalbrookdale – *see* IRONBRIDGE) on the roof, was built for the Sydney and Suburban Hydraulic Power Company, which operated from 1891 until 1965. Two hydraulic accumulators remain in the building, which has been converted to a restaurant.

Sydney retains many nineteenth-century terraced houses with cast-iron balustrades on their balconies.

Figure 153 The Harbour Bridge, Sydney, from the north-west; the 503 m (1650 ft.) steel arch was erected between 1923 and 1932. On the left is the Luna Park fairground.

John Clark

Goodman's Buildings on the Parramatta Road, the main artery to the west of Sydney, is a notable shop and apartment development of 1893–1912, designed by Joseph Sheerin, with striking two-storey over-footpath verandas. Tooths Kent Brewery, established in 1835, continues to operate on its original site. The Mastertouch Factory at Petersham is the best-preserved pianola-roll factory in the world.

The Power House, opened in 1988, is Australia's principal museum of science and technology. Located in the Ultimo Power Station which provided electricity for the city's trams for sixty years until 1963, its major themes include 'Creativity and Australian Achievement', 'Everyday Life in Australia' and 'Science, Technology and Perception'. One of the centrepieces of the museum is a BOULTON & WATT steam engine built for Whitbread's brewery, London, in 1785, which was shipped to Sydney for the Museum of Applied Arts and Sciences, forerunner of the Powerhouse, in 1888. A second beam engine, of 16 hp, by HENRY MAUDSLAY of London, was imported in 1837, and worked at a flour mill and brewery near Goulburn (*see* NEW SOUTH WALES) for 84 years. Other exhibits include steam locomotives, motorcars and aircraft. There are sections on information technology and brewing, and a re-creation of a cinema of the 1930s.

BIBLIOGRAPHY

General

Broomham, 1987; Heritage of Australia, 1981; Kelly, 1981; Kerr, 1984; McCarty and Schedvin, 1978; Stanbury, 1979.

Specific

Hutton, M. Sydney's hidden water source. In *Heritage Conservation News*, III, 1986.

Kerr, J. S. *Goat Island: an analysis of documentary and physical evidence and an assessment of significance*. Sydney: Maritime Services Board of NSW, 1985.

The Power House: a museum for us all. Power House Museum, Sydney, 1985.

Temple, H. Sydney's hidden and forgotten power source. In *Heritage Conservation News*, II, 1984.

LOCATIONS

[M] The Australian Museum, 6–8 College Street, Sydney 2000.

[M] Geological and Mining Museum, 36 George Street North, Sydney 2000.

[M,S] Power House Museum, Harris Street, Ultimo, Sydney, New South Wales.

[M] Rail Transport Museum, Enfield Locomotive Depot, Sydney.

KATE CLARK

Symington, William (1763–1831)   A pioneer of the use of steam power for road vehicles and boats, Symington was born at Leadhills and educated at Glasgow and Edinburgh. He constructed a steam road carriage in 1786. At the suggestion of James Taylor (1753–1825), he patented in 1787 a steam engine for a boat which was tried on Dalswinton Loch (*see* DUMFRIES & GALLOWAY) in 1788. The engine is preserved in the Science Museum, London. A second patent in 1801 proved to be the basis of the system of transmitting power used in most subsequent PADDLE STEAMERS, including the *Charlotte Dundas* in 1802.

BIBLIOGRAPHY
General
Harvey and Rose, 1980.

synthetic fibres   Textile fibres made from materials other than the traditional wool, cotton, silk, hemp and flax are described as synthetic or artificial. These polymeric materials were developed to replicate, enhance or combine the properties of natural fibres. Control of each step of manufacture enables the producer to create a particular set of desirable properties, eliminating the possibility of undesirable properties in natural fibres that may be the result of poor weather conditions or variations in an animal's diet. Synthetic fibres are sometimes classified as either man-made cellulosic or man-made non-cellulosic fibres, to distinguish those of vegetable origin, such as rayon or acetate, from those that are based on petrochemicals, such as polyester or nylon. The first synthetic fibre to be produced on a commercial scale was RAYON, which is derived from wood pulp, and is thus cellulose-based. NYLON was the first man-made non-cellulosic fibre.

Synthetic fibres consist of an enormous group of materials developed to provide products as diverse as space suits and tennis rackets. Among the manufactured cellulosic fibres are acetate and triacetate. The manufactured non-cellulosic fibres include those with an animal base, such as casein; those with a vegetable base, such as peanuts or soyabeans; and those with a mineral base, such as fibreglass. With the exception of fibreglass, these last are of limited application for textile use. Far more important commercially are those fibres based on petrochemicals, widely referred to as synthetics. Among them are acrylics, and olefins such as polyethylene and polypropylene.

BIBLIOGRAPHY
General
Hounshell and Smith, 1988; Stevens, 1975.

JANE HUTCHINS and BARRIE TRINDER

Szeged, Csongrad, Hungary   A city at the confluence of the Rivers Tisza and Maros, on a salt-trading route from Transylvania. Szeged was destroyed in the flood of 1879, after which it was developed again on a new plan of concentric boulevards designed by Lajos Tisza. The linen industry was established in the city by N. Bakay, and is commemorated in a museum.

Kiskundorozsma, 6 km (4 mi.) N., contains a textile works established in the late 1930s with hand-operated spinning frames in the converted stables of a cavalry

barracks. The town developed into a great centre of the post-war Hungarian textile industry, with huge cotton mills.

Szeged is a traditional centre for the manufacture of highly-coloured slippers, and for paprika-processing and sausage-making. A salami factory and a paprika mill are preserved. There is much river fishing, particularly for carp, and a majolica factory makes wine flasks and tulip-patterned jugs.

LOCATION
[M] Hemp Industry Museum, H-6724 Szeged, Rigo u. 5–7.

Székesfehérvár (Stuhlweissenburg), Fejér, Hungary One of the oldest cities in Hungary, 65 km (40 mi.) SW of Budapest on the highway to Lake Balaton, with fine architectural wrought-iron work and a preserved Baroque pharmacy of 1758. There is an important aluminium plant there, with an associated museum. An ornate cast-iron exhibition pavilion or bandstand, with the roof supported on sixteen Corinthian columns, which was designed by Antal Platzer, remains from the National Exhibition held in the city in 1879.

BIBLIOGRAPHY
General
Boldizsár, 1959; Kiss, *et al.*, 1981.

LOCATION
[M] Hungarian Aluminium Museum, H-8000 Székesfehérvár, Zombori út 12.

Szentendre, Pest, Hungary   A town 15 km (10 mi.) N. of Budapest. In it is the Szabadtéri Néprajzi Muzeum, an open-air museum and overall the most important in Hungary, on a 47 ha (116 ac.) site. The museum was established in 1967 to show buildings of the Kisalföld and Tisza regions, and includes spinning and weaving shops, leather-workers' premises, wind and water mills, and limekilns. There are demonstrations of charcoal burning.

An exhibit of particular importance is the FLOATING MILL from Ráckeve on the Danube, 40 km (25 mi.) S. of Budapest. The mill, dating from *c.*1870 and restored in 1961–2, is one of the few surviving in Europe. The paddle wheel is situated between the 'house ship', which contains the milling machinery, and the 'store ship', or floating granary.

BIBLIOGRAPHY
General
Kecskés, 1990; Kiss *et al.*, 1981; Zippelius, 1974.

LOCATION
[M] Szabadtéri Néprajzi Muzeum, Szabadságforrás, Postafiók 3, H-2000 Szentendre.

Szentgotthárd (St Gotthard), Vas, Hungary   A town on the River Rába (Raab) on the Austrian border, 40 km (25 mi.) SW of Szombathely. It is the site of an important preserved scythe forge, converted from a corn mill in 1900, with two early nineteenth-century tilt hammers, originally worked by a water wheel, then by a water turbine, next by electricity, and now by a diesel engine.

BIBLIOGRAPHY
General
Kiss *et al.*, 1981.

Szreniawa, Poznań, Poland   A town 10 km (6 mi.) S. of Poznań. The National Museum of Farming was established in 1964 on the premises of the 'Szreniawa' state farm. It is the central museum of farming in Poland, building on the tradition of the Museum of Technology and Farming established in 1875 in Warsaw, and covering the history of Polish farming from the earliest times until the present. Exhibits include tools, machines, and nineteenth-century agricultural engines manufactured in the HIPOLIT CEGIELSKI plant.

BIBLIOGRAPHY
General
Orysiak, 1977.
Specific
Muzeum Rolnictwa w Szreniawie (The Museum of Farming in Szreniawa). Warsaw, 1974.

LOCATION
[M] Muzeum Narodowe Rolnictwa w Szreniawie kołto Poznania (The National Museum of Farming in Szreniawa near Poznań), 62–952 Komorniki, Szreniawa.

T

Taalintehdas (Dalsbruk), Turun ja Porin lääni, Finland The Taalintehdas ironworks near Dragsfjärd on the west coast, 50 km (30 mi.) S. of Turku, was founded in 1686, and in the eighteenth century worked closely with the nearby Björkboda works. Taalintehdas became an independent company in 1856, when puddling furnaces and a rolling mill were built. In the 1870s the Swiss, Jakob Stillitz, installed Finland's first open-hearth steelmaking plant.

Industrial traditions are clearly visible in the Taalintehdas area. Of the blast furnace of 1850, the grey stone base and the brick middle section, with its curved openings, have survived. Close by are the red-brick foundry and machine shops. The former was restored for the use of the museum in 1986. The latter houses a fire station and laundry. At nearby Norrbacken are found eighteenth-century blocks of workers' dwellings of wooden construction, one of which was restored in 1983 and is now used by the museum. A representative selection of workers' dwellings from other periods survives at Taalintehdas, including a two-storeyed, stuccoed 'barracks' building of the 1830s, and a two- and three-storeyed 'barracks' built of slag blocks, dating from 1873 and 1880. Gallery access apartments are another characteristic form of workers' accommodation at Taalintehdas.

The twelve coke ovens by the river, made of slag blocks, are unique in Finland. Like the old foundry, and the examples of workers' accommodation, they have been in the care of the Taalintehdas Museum Foundation since 1982. On the old quay is an elegant group of EMPIRE-style buildings, including a stable, a granary and a warehouse.

LOCATION
[M] Taalintehdas Museum Foundation, SF-25900 Taalintehdas.

LAURI PUTKONEN

table engine A steam engine in which the vertical cylinder is supported on a metal table and the piston works a crankshaft beneath the table. Patented in 1807 by Henry Maudslay (1771–1831), it was self-contained, portable, and efficient, and was a popular source of power for small workshops. Many are preserved in museums.

BIBLIOGRAPHY
General
Watkins, 1968.

Tábor, South Bohemia, Czechoslovakia   A Hussite town and the centre of domestic textile manufacture. There are several early reinforced concrete bridges in the area. In Tábor itself a bridge of 1934–5 carries the road to Bechyně across the Luznice. At Bechyně, 25 km (15 mi.) SE, is a 190 m (725 ft.) reinforced concrete arch of 1925–8 over the Luznice, 38 m (125 ft.) above the river at its highest point. At Poldolsko, 40 km (28 mi.) W. of Tábor, a 510 m (1675 ft.) structure crosses the Orlická Nádrž reservoir. It has a principal arch and a series of lesser side arches, and was built in 1938–40 to carry the Tábor–Písek road.

BIBLIOGRAPHY
General
Dusan, 1984.

tailor A maker of clothes, particularly outer garments, traditionally for men, women's attire being manufactured by dressmakers. Most clothing was made by tailors until the advent of CLOTHING FACTORIES in the second half of the nineteenth century. Work was traditionally divided between men who measured customers and cut out cloth, and those who sat cross-legged on benches, sewing together the components of garments. A smoothing iron called a goose was used to press down seams. Traditional tailoring continues on a small scale as a luxury trade.

BIBLIOGRAPHY
General
Book of Trades, 1839.

tail race A channel through which water that has been used in a mill to turn a water wheel or turbine returns to the stream from which it was earlier diverted.

Tallinn, Estonia, USSR   The capital of Estonia and a port on the Gulf of Finland. The open-air museum for the Soviet Republic of Estonia was established on a 64 ha (158 ac.) site in 1957 and opened in 1964. Exhibits include windmills and water mills, smithies and fisheries, and there are collections relating to textiles, forestry, furniture manufacturing, and toolmaking.

BIBLIOGRAPHY
General
Zippelius, 1974.

LOCATION
[M] Eesti Riiklik Vabauhumuuseum (Estonian National Open-Air Museum), Vabauhumuuseumi tee 12, Tallinn.

tallow Solid fat, usually from cattle or sheep, which has been separated – most commonly by rendering in a pot and pressing – from the fibrous matter, the 'greeves' or

743

'cracklings', the latter being fed to pigs or ducks. Tallow is also extracted from TRAIN OIL. Tallow was a much-traded commodity by 1700, and in the 1850s some 60 000 tons was imported to Britain annually from Russia. Most tallow was used for making CANDLES, the term 'tallow chandler' being almost synonymous wih candlemaker, but it was also used in making cheaper forms of soap and as a lubricant.

BIBLIOGRAPHY
General
Tomlinson, 1852–4.

Talyllyn Railway, Tywyn, Gwynedd, Wales A 69 cm (2 ft. 3 in.) gauge line, 19 km (12 mi.) N. of Aberystwyth, authorized in 1865 and opened 1866, reaching 11.6 km ($7\frac{1}{4}$ mi.) from the slate quarries at Bryn Eglwys to Tywyn on the coast. From the beginning, passengers were carried. From 1951 the line was run by a holding company backed by a Preservation Society, setting the pattern for other conservation schemes. This was the first industrial conservation project to become a significant tourist attraction, carrying 57 000 passengers a year by 1957. Stock includes two original locomotives by Fletcher Jennings of Whitehaven, two locomotives from the Corris Railway, 16 km (10 mi.) E., and some original coaches.

BIBLIOGRAPHY
General
Rolt, 1953.

LOCATION
[S] Talyllyn Railway Company, Wharf Station, Tywyn, Gwynedd LL36 9EY.

Tampere, Hämeen lääni, Finland The most emphatically industrial of Finnish cities. The first manufacturing plants to use the water power of the rapids of Tammerkoski were established in the late eighteenth century, and many more were built in the nineteenth century. Many have recently closed or moved, and new uses are being found for the old buildings.

In 1820 a Scot, James Finlayson, received permission to set up a foundry and forge on the banks of the Tammerkoski river at Tampere, as well as full rights over the ground and water power. Finlayson also wove woollen cloth in his complex, but began to manufacture cotton fabrics on a significant scale only from 1828. In 1836 ownership of the company was transferred to a group of St Petersburg (Leningrad) businessmen, who began an energetic renewal of its activities.

In 1838 the so-called Old Factory, a six-storey building designed by Carl Leszig, and representing the new industrial architecture, both in size and building technique, was opened. A decisive part in the planning of the building was taken by John Barker, a recent arrival in Finland, who had become acquainted with modern textile-factory design in Belgium. The wooden joists and intermediate floors of the building were supported by eighteen cast-iron columns on each floor, which themselves formed a vertical support system. All the machines used in the Finlayson factory were made in the company's own machine shop. Barker ordered working drawings of the machines from the Cockerill works at LIÈGE, which represented the latest technology of the time.

The original organization of the cotton factory was as follows. The weaving workshops were situated on the two lowest floors. The third floor housed the warp-spinning section. The fourth was used for cleansing and carding new wool, and the fifth for weft-spinning. The warehouse and a large water tank, into which water was pumped with the aid of a large water wheel, were situated in the attic. In the event of fire it was possible to direct water along iron pipes to every floor.

In the 1850s the Old Factory was extended at both ends, with buildings which still survive. In the 1870s a staircase tower attached to the building received its crenellated top. The 1850s also saw the completion of the so-called River Factory, on the banks of the Tammer, and in the early 1860s the so-called Clock Tower Building, ornamented with Gothic stepped gables, was faced in white stucco, like the Old Factory.

The large Plevna weaving mill, a range of north-lit sheds, was completed in 1877. The original design was by the Bolton architect George Cunliffe, but the final drawings for the façade were made by Tampere's city architect, F. L. Calonius. Plevna was the first factory building of its kind in Finland, and is also of importance in the history of technology as the first place in which electric light was used in Finland, in 1882. At the turn of the century Plevna was extended with the so-called New Cloth Mill, according to the designs of the Swiss architect C. Sequin-Bronner, who also designed the four-storey carding and spinning building, Siperia. The factory's handsome red-brick office block was completed in 1895 to designs by the city architect, Lambert Petterson. The director's palatial mansion, situated in an English-style park and completed in 1899, is also to his design.

Twentieth-century architecture is represented in the Finlayson plant by a hydro-electric power station and dye works designed by Jarl Eklund in the 1920s, and Heikki & Kaija Siren's sewing room of 1960.

In the 1980s output decreased dramatically, and the company relinquished its properties. The most important factory buildings have been retained, and new homes and offices will be built in the area.

The Tampella industrial complex at Tampere originated with a blast furnace built on the east bank of the Tammerkoski River in 1843. In 1856 an engineering shop was constructed, and construction of a linen factory was commenced alongside it. Four years later the two works were united as the Tampere Linen & Iron Industrial Co.

The linen factory, completed in 1859 to plans by the district architect, G. T. Chiewitz, was a five-storey brick building, with cast-iron pillars supporting brick-arches on the two lower floors, with wooden frames and flooring above. In 1883 a fire damaged the weaving mill, after which it was lowered by one storey. The building survives, surrounded by later additions. Most other production buildings date from the late nineteenth century and early twentieth century, and there is a group of JUGENDSTIL workers' houses. Production of linen will cease in the early 1990s.

The Lapinniemi woollen mill, founded in 1897, is closely linked with the Tampella complex. The five-storey brick spinning mill on the lake shore was completed in 1899 to plans by the architect Berndt Blom. It is dominated by a tall, crenellated water tower. The building was extended several times. It is now adapted to new uses. Only the façades remain of many of the buildings, the interiors having been used as apartments.

BIBLIOGRAPHY
General
Nisser and Bedoire, 1978.

LAURI PUTKONEN

tank locomotive A STEAM LOCOMOTIVE that has receptacles for water and fuel on its own frame rather than on a separate TENDER. Coal is most commonly carried in a bunker behind the cab, but in some small locomotives it is carried in bins mounted on either side of the boiler, in front of the cab. Water tanks are commonly carried on the frames on either side of the boiler (when they are known as side tanks) but they may also be mounted astride the boiler (saddle tanks), between the frames (well tanks), or in tanks cantilevered from the sides of the boiler (pannier tanks). A back tank has the water tank and coal bunker behind the cab as on a tender locomotive, but mounted on the same frame as the boiler and motion. In the British notation for referring to steam locomotives by their wheel arrangements, it is usual to add the suffixes 'T' to indicate a side tank, 'ST' a saddle tank, 'PT' a pannier tank and 'WT' a well tank: 2–6–2T, 0–4–0ST, 0–6–0PT, 0–6–2WT. In Scotland a small tank engine is called a 'pug'.

tanning The process by which hides (*see* LEATHER) are preserved by steeping in infusions of tannic acid. In the traditional tannery hides were suspended in pits containing lime solutions which loosened the hair and outer tissues, and separated the fibres of the corium, the inner portion of the hide. Salt had to be washed from imported, salted hides. After soaking, the loosened material was removed by a two-handled knife on a beam, a bench with a convex surface. Hides were then made supple by infusions of birds' or dogs' dung. They were next tanned in solutions of oak bark, first in a weak liquor, then in solutions of greater strength, in each of which they might remain for a month or more, the total process taking up to two years, and concluding with the drying of the leather.

A traditional tannery commonly consisted of two-storey buildings containing shops for preparing, drying and CURRYING, around a courtyard in which the lime and tanning pits are situated, together with stores for bark and dung, and a bark mill (which may be a hopper-fed grinding mill) or a horse-powered edge runner. An example is preserved at ST FAGANS. Tanneries in large ports like London, where the industry was concentrated in Bermondsey, were much larger: they had long, often high

black louvred, windowless buildings where leather was hung to dry, and pits surrounded by low sheds with red-tiled roofs, with stacks of new bark, spent bark waiting to be carried away as manure, heaped HORNS and parings destined for gluemakers, all grouped around a high chimney.

The tanning process came to be organized on an industrial basis during the second half of the nineteenth century. In 1850 there had been tanneries in most European and North American market towns. By 1900 there was an increasing concentration near ports, and around meat packing centres. In Germany the main concentration was at Mülheim in the Ruhrgebiet. New tanneries were highly mechanized, and employed chemical processes. Through the work of Augustus Schultz in the USA and others, CHROMIUM compounds came to be used in tanning, and machines, like that of Alpha Richardson of Boston, Mass. of 1856, were developed to split hides into layers. Band knife machines were employed to stretch out irregularly shaped skins, the first being built by John Baring in 1818.

BIBLIOGRAPHY
General
Lamb, 1923; Mayhew, 1850; Minnoch and Minnoch, 1970; O'Flaherty *et al.*, 1956; Procter, 1903, 1914; Stevens, 1891; Tunis, 1965; Walsh, 1964.
Specific
Clarkson, L. A. The English bark trade, 1660–1830. In *Agricultural History Review*, XXII, 1974.
Jenkins, J. G. *The Rhaeadr Tanner*. Cardiff: National Museum of Wales, 1973.
Thomas, S., Clarkson, L. A. and Thompson, R. *Leather Manufacture through the Ages*. Northampton: East Midlands Industrial Archaeological Conference, 1983.
Thompson, R. S. Tanning – man's first manufacturing process? In *TNS*, LIII, 1981–2.

BARRIE TRINDER

tape A term with two meanings in industrial archaeology:

1. A narrow, woven strip of fabric, an item of haberdashery, used in closing or fixing garments, as distinct from RIBBONS, which were employed for decoration. Tapes were also used for binding edges of such fabric goods as blankets. Varieties were distinguished by colour, as with Carnation Tape or Coventry Blue, or function, as with stay tapes. The meaning of terms denoting types of tape, like ferret or inkle, often changed with fashion. In England manufacture was concentrated in Coventry, although the outstanding surviving site is at Upper Tean, 14 km (9 mi.) S. of STOKE-ON-TRENT, where a range of manufacturing buildings from the seventeenth to the early twentieth centuries remains intact.
2. From the 1880s the word 'tape' was applied to the paper strips on which messages are received on certain types of TELEGRAPH instrument.

tapestry A fabric designed to be hung as a wall

covering, curtain or seat cover: the design on it may be painted, embroidered or woven. Traditional tapestries, like those produced in fifteenth-century Flanders, were made with no visible weft, the design being formed by short stitches on the warp. The celebrated Gobelin works was established in Paris under royal patronage in 1603. Production of traditional tapestries continued as a luxury trade into the industrial period, and the term has also been applied to embroidered furnishing fabrics and to Jacquard-woven figured upholstery cloth.

BIBLIOGRAPHY
General
Geijer, 1979.

tar A thick, dark, viscous liquid, a mixture of hydrocarbons, resins and alcohols, obtained by the destructive distillation of wood or coal. Natural tars are found in CALIFORNIA and the Athabasca Sands in ALBERTA. Tar has been used from early times for preserving timber and cordage.

Coal tar, obtained from GASWORKS, COKE OVENS or SMOKELESS FUEL plants, is important as a source of many chemicals. By thermal distillation, usually in iron or steel tanks, it can be fractionated into NAPHTHA (up to 110 °C); light oil (up to 180 °C); carbolic oil or light creosote (up to 230 °C), producing PHENOL; creosote (up to 270 °C), which is used as a preservative; and anthracene (up to 360 °C). The development of ANILINE dyes in the late nineteenth century stimulated the growth of distinct tar-distilling concerns, which collected raw materials from gasworks and elsewhere.

Tar was first used for bonding road surfaces in NOTTINGHAM in the 1840s, and employed in Paris from 1854, and in the USA from 1866. Systematic tarring of ROADS in England began c.1910, and distilled tar for the purpose came to be manufactured on a considerable scale. Thomas Aitken of Cupar, Fife, patented the most successful tar sprayer for use in roadmaking, first demonstrating it in 1907.

BIBLIOGRAPHY
General
Bunbury and Davidson, 1925; Gardner, 1915; Lunge, 1909; Warnes, 1914; Whitehead, 1975.

BARRIE TRINDER

Tarare, Rhône, France The Beaujolais region, north of Lyons, was an important textile-producing area during the Ancien Régime, first for woven cotton goods and subsequently for silk throwing and weaving. The silk industry was run by producers from Lyons who found it more economical to establish their workshops out of the city. During the second half of the nineteenth century the region was France's main producer of muslins and fine silk cloth.

Jean-Baptiste Martin (1801–67) was a Lyons merchant who began by designing an improved loom for plush and light velvet. From 1843 he built the 'Vert Galant' textile mill at Tarare, 30 km (19 mi.) NW of Lyons. The factory had two main buildings, one used for throwing the raw silk, the other for weaving. Other establishments were soon associated with the Tarare works, in particular a dyeworks at Roanne, 44 km (27 mi.) NW, and retail outlets at Lyons and Paris. One of the firm's specialities, and the basis of its reputation, was plush used for top hats. This product used raw silk imported from Asia rather than that produced in the CEVENNES. The factory went into decline after World War I and the weaving building was demolished.

The silk-throwing mill had a particular form of organization, being run, so to speak, as a 'boarding factory' (usine internat). In the time of J.-B. Martin about twenty nuns were in charge of five hundred young girls, 'poor' girls aged between 13 and 16, attached to the factory as apprentices. The factory gave them board and lodging, dormitories, a kitchen with a vegetable garden, rooms for study and sewing, and a large chapel. These elements of the factory were carefully separated from the weavers' shops where men from the town came to work. From the outset, particular attention was paid to details of security and hygiene, details which much impressed contemporary observers.

The silk-throwing mill is now a protected monument. It is a four-storey stone structure, with two small wings at each end forming a courtyard. On the second floor of one wing, the former chapel, with a floor area of 400 m² (4300 sq. ft.), has a remarkable multi-coloured wooden framework.

The town of Cours, 20 km (12 mi.) N. of Tarare, specialized during the nineteenth century in blanket weaving. The former Poizat factory has recently been adapted as apartments and craft workshops. Two nineteenth-century Corliss steam engines have been conserved, one of them being restored to working order.

JEAN-FRANÇOIS BELHOSTE

tarmacadam The name, derived from JOHN LOUDON MCADAM, applied to mixtures of road metal and tar applied in a plastic state. Some experiments were made with crude TAR in the nineteenth century, but between 1903 and 1914 mechanical mixing plants were developed, and distilled tar became available as the use of pneumatic tyres on motor vehicles made bonded surfaces essential (*see* ROADS). E. Purnell Hooly, who established a works in 1903 at Denby, Derbyshire, pioneered the use of crushed blast-furnace SLAG as the aggregate in tarmacadam.

BIBLIOGRAPHY
General
Whitehead, 1975.

Tarnowskie Gory (Tarnowitz), Katowice, Poland A mining town, 25 km (16 mi.) N. of Katowice. There have been silver mines in the Tarnowski region since medieval times, and they have flourished particularly since the second half of the eighteenth century after the installation of a steam engine, one of the first in continental Europe. A complex system of navigable levels was constructed in the

Figure 154 The navigable level in the museum of silver and lead mining at Tarnowskie Gory, Poland
Piotr Gerber

first half of the nineteenth century. When the mining of silver ceased, lead and zinc ores were worked. The mines closed early in the twentieth century, by which time about 20 000 shafts and adits and hundreds of kilometres of galleries had been driven. Shortly before World War II an inventory of the surviving remains was compiled and ideas for making the mines accessible to the public were put forward. These re-emerged in the 1950s when the Public Committee for the Reconstruction of the Mine Museum was established. In 1958 a 600 m (660 yd.) section of a drain adit, 'Czarny Pstrag', was opened to the public. In 1976 the workings between the 'Aniol', 'Szczęść Boże' and 'Żmija' shafts were made accessible. Visitors can travel through the mine along a 1700 m (1860 yd.) route through chambers and galleries 40 m (130 ft.) below ground level. Between the 'Szczęść Boże' and 'Żmija' shafts they are conveyed in boats along 270 m (295 yd.) of the drainage adit, one of the outstanding experiences offered in any mining museum in the world. On the surface a hoist tower has been constructed, with displays and a library. An open-air museum has been established alongside, with steam locomotives and stationary steam engines.

BIBLIOGRAPHY
Specific
Gerber, P. Zabytkowa Kopalnia Rud Ołowiu i Srebra w Tarnowskich Górach (Old silver and lead mines in the Tarnowski Mountains). In *XXIII Symposium, Hornicka Príbram ve Védé a Technice*. Príbram, 1984.

LOCATION
[S] Kopalnia Zabytkowa w Tarnowskich Górach (Old silver and lead mines in Tarnowskie Gory), ul. Robotnicza 52, Tarnowskie Gory.

PIOTR GERBER

tartan A cloth of wool, silk or other fibres woven in stripes of various colours, crossing one another at right angles so as to form a regular pattern. Tartan is particularly associated with Scotland, where patterns indicate tribal affiliations. The word possibly derives from the French 'tirtaine', although this was a wool-linen mixture.

BIBLIOGRAPHY
General
Kerridge, 1985.

Tasmania, Australia An island 240 km (150 mi.) from the south coast of Australia, Tasmania was settled by Europeans as a penal colony, of which the structures in and around Port Arthur, dating from 1830–77, including several industrial remains, are graphic reminders. Notable engineering achievements of the convicts, supervised by the Royal Engineers, included Australia's oldest bridge, the Richmond Bridge of 1823. The state has a population of less than half a million.

Coal was first mined by convicts near Port Arthur where shafts had replaced adits by 1836. Remains of the prison including the stone barracks and chapel survive.

Mining developed on the west and north-east of the island as a by-product of the search for gold. Almost every precious and semi-precious mineral is found in Tasmania. The peak of activity was in the late nineteenth century, and most mines had closed by the 1950s. The denuded landscape of Queenstown is a powerful illustration of the effects of mining. At Strahan on the west coast are remains of an Abt RACK RAILWAY which served the copper mines at Mount Lyell. At the foot of the Blue Peaked Hills is one of Australia's few charcoal blast furnaces, operated by the Ilfracombe Iron Co. in the 1870s. Tin mining, and the Chinese miners employed in Tasmania, are commemorated at the Derby mine in the north-east of the island, which opened in 1876.

Hydro-electricity is now a major source of power, and the earliest public hydro-electric power station in the southern hemisphere survives at Duck Reach, Launceston. It operated from 1895 until 1956. Launceston Gasworks of *c.*1890 is the best preserved in Australia.

The *Enterprise*, a characteristic Tasmanian ketch built in 1902, is preserved at Bicheno on the west coast; and the *Excella*, a 174-ton steam passenger ferry of 1912 is preserved at HOBART where she was built.

BIBLIOGRAPHY
General
Blainey, 1954; Heritage of Australia, 1981; Kerr, 1984; Kerrison, 1963; Morris-Nunn and Tassell, 1982; Rae, 1983.

LOCATIONS
[M] Derby Tin Mine Centre, Derby, Tasmania 7254.
[M] Queen Victoria Museum, Launceston, Tasmania.

KATE CLARK

Tata, Komárom, Hungary   A town 56 km (35 mi.) W. of Budapest, with two important water corn mills: the Cifra mill, rebuilt in 1753 in a style that combines the Baroque with the Hungarian vernacular, the wooden structure being ornamented throughout with carvings; and the Nepomucenus mill of 1758, designed in the Baroque style by Jakab Felluer. There is a museum containing works by the eighteenth-century ceramicist Domonkos Kuny (d.1749).

Tatabánya, 10 km (6 mi.) SE, is a lignite-mining town which was enlarged when power stations were constructed during the first five-year plan (*see* HUNGARY).

LOCATION
[M] Domonkos Kuny Museum, Öregvár, Tata.

Tauern, Salzburg and Carinthia, Austria   The Alpine range of Hohe Tauern divides the provinces of Salzburg and Carinthia. The 81 km (50 mi.) Schwarzach–St Veit–Spital–Millstätter see section of the railway from Salzburg to Villach was built in 1901–9 to the design of Karl Wurmb (1850–1907). It passes through an 8.5 km ($5\frac{1}{4}$ mi.) tunnel between Böckstein and Mallnitz. The Tauern range is an important source of gold. A gold-dressing plant at Böckstein was established in 1741 but was disused from *c.*1900; the buildings have been converted to dwellings. Montanhistorische Verein für Österreich (Association for the History of the Austrian Coal and Iron Industry) began a scheme in 1975 to conserve dwellings, and to use buildings not used as houses for displays. A working-class house and a salt warehouse were opened to the public from 1981. The older buildings in Böckstein

were put under legislative protection from 1977. There is a further museum relating to gold mining in Tauern at Döllach-im-Mölltal, 20 km (12 mi.) W. of Mallnitz, at the foot of the Grossglockner Hochalpenstrasse, the road route through the mountains.

BIBLIOGRAPHY
General
Schneider, 1963.
Specific
Wehdorn M. Archéologie industrielle en Autriche (Industrial archaeology in Austria). In Ferriot, 1981.

LOCATION
[M] Regional and Gold Mining Museum, Schloss Grosskirchheim, 9843 Döllach-im-Mölltal, Bezirk Spital an der Drau.

tavern   *See* INN.

Tavira, Algarve, Portugal   An important tuna-fishing port, 220 km (136 mi.) S. of Lisbon. A study on the possibility of establishing a museum of the industry in Arraial Ferreira Neto, a complex of warehouses, shipyards and workshops, is in progress.

LOCATION
[M] Museum of the Fishing Industry, Tavira.

tawing   The process by which leather was made from skins (*see* LEATHER) by treatment with ALUM or oils. Skins were prepared by liming, as in the TANNING process, although sheep skins were normally hung in wood smoke. They were placed in a solution of alum, SALT, flour and egg yolks, or covered with a paste made from these substances. They were then hung and became hard, after which they were softened by damping and beating.

BIBLIOGRAPHY
Specific
Jenkins, J. G. *The Rhaeadr Tannery*. Cardiff: National Museum of Wales, 1973.
Thomas, S., Clarkson, L. A. and Thompson, R. *Leather Manufacture through the Ages*. Northampton: East Midlands Industrial Archaeological Conference, 1983.

taxi   The word 'taxi' was originally an abbreviated form of 'taximeter' (earlier 'taxameter'), an automatic device, the invention of the German Wilhelm Bruhn in 1891, indicating to a passenger in a cab the distance traversed and the fare due. By 1907 the term meant a motor vehicle in which such a device was employed. In London, motor vehicles, for thirty years principally Renaults with English bodies, effectively displaced horse cabs from *c.*1907. The London 'black cab', specifically designed as a taxi, appeared in the 1930s. In most cities standard production cars are employed.

BIBLIOGRAPHY
General
Bird, 1969; Georgano, 1972.

Taylor, Frederick Winslow (1856–1915)   The American pioneer of scientific methods of work study, a Quaker whose evangelistic zeal for efficiency revolutionized systems of production in many industries. Born in Philadephia, Taylor worked as a labourer, pattern maker and machinist after defective eyesight allegedly cut short his academic career. From 1893 he operated as a management consultant, except between 1898 and 1901 when he was retained by the Bethlehem Steel Corporation. His *magnum opus* on management was published in 1911. Taylor was also a notable engineer, who, in 1890, designed and built one of the largest steam hammers to work successfully in the USA; and an inventor, who took out about a hundred patents, and was the joint developer of the Taylor-White process of heat treatment for tool steel.

BIBLIOGRAPHY
General
Doorstin, 1966, 1973; Copley, 1973; Kakar, 1970; Taylor, 1911; Taylor and Thompson, 1905.
Specific
Taylor, F. W. A piece rate system. In *Transactions of the American Society of Mechanical Engineers*, XVI, 1895.
Taylor, F. W. Shop management. In *Transactions of the American Society of Mechanical Engineers*, XXIV, 1903.

BARRIE TRINDER

tea A drink which originated in China, made from the leaves of the plant *Thea sinensis*. It was imported to Western Europe *c*.1610, and became popular in the Netherlands, Britain and Russia from the 1720s. PORCELAIN pots in which to brew it, and cups from which it could be drunk, were imported alongside the leaves. There was a large trade in tea from Canton to England, the Netherlands, Sweden and Germany by the 1760s, when 6 million lb. (2.7 million kg) were exported in English vessels and 4.5 million lb. (2 million kg) in Dutch. In the nineteenth century this was one of the most important transoceanic trades (*see* CLIPPER).

Tea drinking was a symbol of working-class affluence in England by the late eighteenth century. Most tea was sold loose and blended by retailers, those denominated 'tea dealers' being grocers with pretensions rather than specialists. Packeting, regarded as a precaution against adulteration, was begun by Hornimans before 1850, but it was well into the twentieth century before this became a universal practice. Tea bags were being sold by the 1920s.

See also SAMOVAR.

BIBLIOGRAPHY
General
Braudel, 1981; Forrest, 1973; Winstanley, 1983.

teasel The plant *Dipsacus fullonum*, whose burr-like seed heads are ranged in frames called handles and employed to raise the nap on woollen cloth before shearing. Handles are often arranged on a large roller in a machine called a teasel gig.

Teesside, England A nineteenth-century conurbation,

extending 20 km (12 mi.) along the south bank of the River Tees from Stockton to Redcar, and 25 km (15 mi.) northwards to Hartlepool. The Stockton & Darlington Railway of 1825 stimulated the use of the Tees for coal exports. Middlesbrough, the new terminus of the railway, is on a site purchased in 1829. There were 154 inhabitants in Middlesbrough in 1831, but 40 000 by 1861. The first dock was built in 1842; the Bocklow & Vaughan foundry and forge in 1841. Ores were discovered in the Cleveland Hills to the south in 1848–50. The first blast furnaces were built in 1853, and Teesside grew to become one of the principal ironmaking areas in Britain. A modern blast furnace complex can be seen at Redcar, but there are few remains of the nineteenth-century works.

Middlesbrough Transporter Bridge of 1911, by G. C. Insbault, is 259 m (850 ft.) long. The Tees Bridge, Newport, is a lifting bridge with a 2500 ton deck, built in 1934 by a local company, Dorman Long.

The Billingham (Haverton Hill) ICI plant originated as the Brunner Mond synthetic ammonia works of 1923. There are remains of anhydrite mine shafts.

The port of Hartlepool, 10 km (6 mi.) N. of Middlesbrough, developed from a dock of 1840. Seaton High Light, a lighthouse bearing the date 1838, is now obscured from the sea by intervening buildings.

BIBLIOGRAPHY
General
Briggs, 1963; Harrison and Almond, 1978.

LOCATIONS
[M] Green Dragon Heritage Centre, Green Dragon Yard, Finkle Street, Stockton-on-Tees, Cleveland TS18 2DE.
[M] Hartlepool Maritime Museum, Northgate, Hartlepool, Cleveland.
[M] Preston Hall Museum, Preston Park, Yarm Road, Stockton-on-Tees, Cleveland TS18 3RH.

BARRIE TRINDER

telecommunications Literally, communication over long distances, in practice a term normally applied to systems employing electric wires and cables (*see* TELEGRAPH; TELEPHONE), RADIO waves, or combinations of the two.

telegraph After the use of BEACONS in ancient and medieval times, a visual telecommunications system was first developed using rotatable T-shaped masts, by Claude Chappe (1763–1805). Operating successfully in France between 1793 and 1856, this was distinct from the SEMAPHORE system and another shutter system, used in Britain in 1795–1814 and in Scandinavia in 1795–1881. Gradually these systems were replaced by electric telegraphs, first successfully promoted by W. F. Cooke (1806–79) and CHARLES WHEATSTONE in 1837–9, and, independently, by SAMUEL MORSE. The greatest expansion accompanied the building of railway networks in Britain and the USA. In continental Europe civilian use was often restricted until the 1850s. As well as being invaluable commercially, telegraphs promoted innovations in CABLES and equipment, and stimulated and sustained provincial newspapers.

See also ATLANTIC TELEGRAPH; CABLE; DUPLEX; MORSE, SAMUEL; RELAY POWER STATION; TELEGRAPH OFFICE; TELEGRAPH POLE; TELEGRAPH RECEIVERS AND TRANSMITTERS; WHEATSTONE, CHARLES.

BIBLIOGRAPHY
General
Herbert, 1916; Kieve, 1973; Marland, 1964; Thompson, 1947.

CHRISTOPHER GREEN

telegraph office The main offices of telegraph companies were often light and airy, containing rows of tables set with MORSE sounders, keys, relays and other equipment. On one side were pigeonholes for telegram dispatch. In most countries posts in such offices were considered 'respectable' situations for respectable females.

telegraph pole A pole, usually of larch or pine impregnated with CREOSOTE, carrying cables on glass or ceramic insulators. Telegraph poles are usually set beside railways or roads, and in the 1860s were often felled by rival companies. Concrete or steel poles are sometimes employed.

BIBLIOGRAPHY
General
Herbert, 1916.
Specific
Brent, W. H. The telegraph pole. In *Journal of the Institute of Post Office Electrical Engineers*, 154, 1933–4.
Gibbon, A. O. The telegraph pole. In *Journal of the Institute of Post Office Electrical Engineers*, 3, 1910.

telegraph receivers and transmitters Early electrical telegraphs used multiple wires, one for each letter, but in 1819 the Dane, Hans Christian Oersted (1777–1851) discovered the deflection of a needle by a current. Thereafter numerous needle telegraph systems were developed: the needles pointed to letters or code numbers. To these CHARLES WHEATSTONE added his easily operated ABC system, with a pointer or pointers indicating individual letters. In most offices these were back-ups to MORSE sets.

BIBLIOGRAPHY
General
Herbert, 1916; Marland, 1964.

Telemark Canal, Telemark, Norway The upper section of this canal links Dalen at the head of Bandaksvand lake with Ulefoss, 110 km (70 mi.) SW of Oslo, on Lake Norsjø, providing 75 km (50 mi.) of navigation, with fourteen locks. It was completed in 1892. The lower section, engineered by Engrebret Soot (*see* EIDSKOG) and completed in 1861, links the lower end of Lake Norsjø with Skien and the sea. It has been principally used for the conveyance of timber. The remains of a blast furnace, established in 1625, can be seen at Fossum near Skien.

telephone The transmission of speech by wire was discussed by CHARLES WHEATSTONE in 1831, but it was the careful work of ALEXANDER GRAHAM BELL in the USA in 1870–7 that fully demonstrated the possibilities. Inventors in Britain and America improved subscribers' equipment, but the main problems centred around the development of efficient TELEPHONE EXCHANGES capable of coping with an explosion in demand. By 1884 there were 148 000 telephones in the USA and 11 000 in Britain. In 1910 there was one telephone for every 11 people in the USA, for every 68 in Britain, 65 in Germany and 186 in France. There were 1.5 million telephones in the USA in 1900, and 17.5 million in 1932.

See also BELL, ALEXANDER GRAHAM; STROWGER, ALMON B.; TELEPHONE BOX; TELEPHONE EXCHANGE; TELEPHONE RECEIVERS AND TRANSMITTERS and figure 134.

BIBLIOGRAPHY
General
Boettinger, 1977; Bradfield and John, 1928; Casson, 1910; Hall-Ellis, 1986; Robertson, 1947; Watson, 1926; Young, 1983.

telephone box A kiosk containing a telephone for public use, worked by placing coins, tokens ('jetons' in France, 'jettoni' in Italy), or, more recently, magnetic cards in slots. Telephone boxes are some of the most characteristic features of the streetscapes of particular countries.

The first in Britain was installed in 1884 but it was not until 1921 that standardized designs for kiosks were adopted. The first concrete designs were unsuccessful, but in 1924 the K2 design by Sir Giles Gilbert Scott (1880–1960) was introduced, a cast-iron structure, with fluted corners, domed top and square glazing bars. Fewer than two hundred survived in 1985, when there were still many thousands of Scott's smaller, more streamlined, K6 design of 1935–6.

BIBLIOGRAPHY
Specific
Aslet, C. and Powers, A. The British Telephone Box – Take it as Red. London: Thirties Society, n.d.

telephone exchange The first exchanges, opened in the USA in 1878 and in Britain in 1879, required two operators to receive and pass on each call. Successive developments were multiple-line plugs introduced by C. B. Scribner in 1880; central battery exchanges to eliminate batteries in subscribers' telephones, first used in 1892; and automatic switching, the invention of ALMON STROWGER in 1889–96.

BIBLIOGRAPHY
General
Boettinger, 1977; Casson, 1910; Hall-Ellis, 1986.

telephone receivers and transmitters Following Faraday's electrical research, the principle explored by ALEXANDER GRAHAM BELL, and independently by the German Philip Reis in 1863, was that a vibrating membrane could vary a magnetic field to produce a transmittable alternating current that could be turned back into sound by a distant receiver. Bell's transmitter was improved by D. E. Hughes's 'microphone' in 1878. THOMAS EDISON in 1877 and subsequently others introduced carbon components to enhance quality. Receivers were given far less attention. Dial phones first appeared in 1897.

BIBLIOGRAPHY
General
Boettinger, 1977; Bradfield and John, 1928.

television A means of transmitting pictures using the photo-sensitive element selenium was first suggested in 1875. Development accompanied that of RADIO. Some still pictures had been sent by 1907. Two rival methods emerged for breaking down images into transmittable form: a mechanical spinning disc, developed by J. L. Baird (1888–1946) in 1926, and the 'Ionoscope', an electric cathode scanner developed in the USA in 1924–31. The latter became the basis for modern television. The first public television service came into operation from Alexandra Palace, London, on 2 November 1936.

BIBLIOGRAPHY
General
Barnouw, 1968, 1970; Fielding, 1967.

Telford, Thomas (1757–1834) The most prolific civil engineer of the Industrial Revolution period, whose bridges, roads, harbours and buildings are marked by an unfailing elegance and regard for the nature of the materials employed. The son of a Dumfriesshire shepherd, he worked as a mason in Edinburgh before going to England, where in 1788 he became county surveyor for Shropshire. He completed the SHREWSBURY Canal in 1797, and was responsible for the construction of the Ellesmere Canal, including the aqueducts at Chirk and PONTCYSYLLTE completed in 1801 and 1805. He built many new roads and harbours in Scotland and designed the Caledonian Canal (*see* HIGHLANDS). He visited Sweden to advise on the construction of the GOTHA CANAL in 1808 and 1813. He was engineer to the HOLYHEAD ROAD Commission, for whom his works included the MENAI BRIDGE, and late in life designed bridges of exceptional quality at Tewkesbury and GLOUCESTER. In 1818 he was founder-President of the Institute of Civil Engineers. His life was devoted almost wholly to his work, and his single-mindedness and thorough attention to detail are evidenced by his voluminous surviving correspondence. A complete documentation of his activities in copied form is held at IRONBRIDGE, in Telford, the NEW TOWN named after him.

BIBLIOGRAPHY
General
Gibb, 1935; Penfold, 1980; Rolt, 1958; Telford, 1838.

BARRIE TRINDER

tender A word with two meanings in industrial archaeology:

1. A vehicle forming part of a STEAM LOCOMOTIVE, used for carrying supplies of fuel (coal, oil or wood) and water, a term used from the earliest days of the steam locomotive. From 1860 many British and American main-line locomotives had tenders fitted with scoops to enable water to be picked up from troughs between the rails, without the necessity to stop. On the LNER some locomotives had tenders with corridors through which crews could pass to and from the trains enabling non-stop running over the 632 km (393 mi.) between London and Edinburgh.
2. A small vessel used to service a large ocean-going ship, for example to bring in mail or passengers from a liner which is calling at, but not berthing at, a port.

tenement In origin a legal term meaning a freehold estate that can be inherited, or a house used as a dwelling, 'tenement' came to apply to a separately occupied room or set of rooms within a subdivided house, in which sense the word is now applied to units within a large factory which has been adapted to new uses. In Scotland the term applies to the multi-storey blocks of working-class dwellings characteristic of DUNDEE, EDINBURGH and GLASGOW, and to individual APARTMENTS within such blocks.

BIBLIOGRAPHY
General
Burnett, 1978; Gauldie, 1974.

Tennessee, United States of America In a state with three major museums devoted to the life and work of Elvis Presley, and a couple of dozen other historic homes and halls of fame celebrating the country music 'industry', industrial preservation has not been a hot item in Tennessee. The methodical destruction of Chattanooga's proud industrial heart in the 1970s made room for such theme pieces as the Chattanooga Choo-Choo Hilton Hotel, wherein railway passenger cars have been long-stationary guest rooms. Cute, but no cigar.

In the twentieth century, Tennessee has ranked first in the nation in the extraction of marble, zinc and pyrites; and first in the South in copper and coal. Both river and canal transport were well developed in Tennessee by the century's turn. The pioneering steam railways that networked the state are well represented in a pair of state rail museums, while the Mississippi River Museum takes Civil War riverboat activity as its dominant theme, using engines, models and boat hardware to represent the roles of rivers and riverine engineering in the state's growth.

Norris Dam, the first of the great Tennessee Valley Authority concrete dams that tamed the destructive Tennessee River in the 1930s, began providing hydroelectric power in 1936 to the backward hill folk who once were thought to characterize the state's population. The Montgomery Bell Tunnel of 1818 in Cheatham County is the earliest known rock tunnel of significant size in the USA, while the Memphis Cantilever railway bridge, erected in 1892 over the Mississippi, is built entirely of the newly-developed basic open-hearth steel, its 241 m (791 ft.) main span the longest railway truss on the continent at the time.

BIBLIOGRAPHY
Specific
Honerkamp, N. Innovation and change in the antebellum Southern iron industry: an example from Chattanooga, Tennessee. In *IA*, XIII, 1987.

LOCATIONS
[M] American Museum of Atomic Energy, 300 South Tulane Avenue, Oak Ridge, TN 37830.
[M] Casey Jones Railroad Museum, Jackson, TN 38305.
[M] Mississippi River Museum at Mud Island, 125 Mid-America Mall, Memphis, TN 38103.
[S] Mount Lookout Railway Incline, Chattanooga, Tennessee.
[M] Tennessee Valley Railroad Museum, 4119 Cromwell Road, Chattanooga, TN 37421.

DAVID H. SHAYT

tenter frame A structure made of wooden bars, erected outdoors to act as a drying and stretching frame for finishing woollen cloth. Metal hooks called 'tenterhooks' hold the cloth in place, to make sure it dries evenly and squarely. Within a textile mill tentering machines stretch the fabric laterally along moving belts and convey it by rollers to drying cylinders.

Teplice, North-West Bohemia, Czechoslovakia A spa town, which also has a place in Czech industrial history as the centre of a region of flat glass manufacture and the scene of important developments in the iron industry in the late nineteenth century. Teplice rolling mills were aggressive in obtaining rights to use the latest technology. They installed a Siemens remelting furnace in 1873, and in 1892 the Rudolf ironworks built one of the earliest known continuous strip-rolling mills.

BIBLIOGRAPHY
General
Jeníček, 1963.

Terni, Umbria, Italy In the late nineteenth century water power from the River Nera and a secure inland location encouraged the development of large textile, steel and electro-chemical plants in and around Terni, 92 km (57 mi.) N. of Rome. Woollen mills were established in the 1860s, and from 1873 Stafano Breda initiated the construction of the first steel plant, which by the 1890s supplied over 60 per cent of national steel production and employed three thousand workers. Long ranges of building lined Viale Brin, but most of the earliest examples have been demolished due to war damage and rationalization. The most impressive feature in old photographs, an octagonal building housing a 108-ton steam hammer, was demolished in 1957. One of the workshops now accommodates a display of armaments made at Terni. Another structure, entirely of iron and used for bullet production, is now a warehouse. Other buildings dating from the early period of the steelworks include the offices of the hydro-electric undertaking, with a crenellated campanile, the building which housed the library, and a block of workers' flats of 1888.

BIBLIOGRAPHY
General
Negri *et al.*, 1983.
Specific
Covino R. and Gallo, G. Terni insediamenti industriali e struttura urbana fra otto e novecento (Terni – the establishment of manufacturing and of the urban structure from the 1880s). In *Archeologia Industriale*, I, 1983.

MICHAEL STRATTON

terrace A row of houses of uniform style, the characteristic form of housing in England during the nineteenth century. It is estimated that 83 per cent of all dwellings in England and Wales in 1911 were terraced, varying from the single-storey miners' cottages of the Sunderland region to the four-storey blocks with basements and attics occupied by the rich in the West End of London. Many terraces consisted of BACK-TO-BACK HOUSES or TUNNEL-BACK HOUSES. One of the longest recorded was Silkstone Row, Lower Altofts, Yorkshire, which was built in the 1860s and was 244 m (800 ft.) long.

BIBLIOGRAPHY
General
Daunton, 1983; Dyos, 1973; Muthesius, 1982.

terracotta Large blocks of pressed clay, typically buff or red in colour. The word may be applied to any form of ware but is most widely associated with statues, garden ornaments and building façades. Terracotta was used in Renaissance Italy and revived in Germany with the RUNDBOGENSTIL; in Great Britain it was widely made in the last quarter of the nineteenth century and dominated the architecture of such cities as Birmingham and Leeds. In Britain terracotta was supplanted by FAIENCE after 1900. The technology of terracotta manufacture was exported from Britain to the USA with the construction of the Boston Museum of Fine Arts, and manufacture on a large scale began in New York and Chicago. Terracotta was extensively used in SKYSCRAPERS. Its popularity waned in the USA with the Great Crash and in Britain with World War II. A parallel industry was the production of porous terracotta for fireproofing.
See also figures 24, 145.

BIBLIOGRAPHY
General
Hamilton, 1978.

MICHAEL STRATTON

Terrassa (Tarrasa), Barcelona, Catalonia, Spain A textile manufacturing town, 24 km (15 mi.) NW of Barcelona, whose industrial monuments include the Vapor Aymerich i Amat, one of Europe's most spectacular and least conventional textile factories. Designed by Lluís Moncunill and completed in 1909, the steam-powered factory's 10 000 m² (110 000 sq. ft.) single-storey weaving shed has a remarkable helical chimney, and a roof of parabolic Catalan arches supported by cast-iron columns. The arches are intricately interwoven, to create large glazed areas in the roof, an imaginative reworking of the concept of the NORTH-LIT SHED. The factory now accommodates the Catalonian Museum of Science and Technology, a federal organization with responsibility for several sites in the province, including the paper museum at CAPELLADES. The main display in Terrassa includes sections on energy, textiles, communications, metallurgy, plastic, transport, and technology in the home. The Museum publishes a regular bulletin on industrial archaeology in Catalonia.

The Vapor Amat, an old dyeworks near the museum, has been converted into a municipal exhibition hall, while the Vapor Catex factory is now the headquarters of a theatrical institute. Moncunill also designed two other buildings in the area, the Casa Freixa, an industrialist's mansion in the style of GAUDÍ, and a power station. The textile museum, founded in 1946, has collections of fabrics, particularly from the pre-industrial period, of international significance.

BIBLIOGRAPHY
General
Generalitat de Catalunya, 1988; Marti *et al.*, 1982.
Specific
El Gran Projecte del Museu de la Ciéncia i de la Técnica de Catalunya. Generalitat de Catalunya Department de Cultural, 1987.

LOCATIONS
[M] Museu de la Ciéncia i de la Técnic de Catalunya (The Catalan Museum of Science and Industry), Rambla d'Egara 270, 08221 Terrassa.
[M] Museu Téxtil, C. Salmerón 19–21, 08222 Terrassa.

EUSEBI CASANELLES

Texas, United States of America Black gold, or Texas tea, also known as oil, is the substance that comes to mind in the popular conception of Texas industry. Lots of it, gushing out in great geysers that have kept afloat another mythic image, that of the cigar-chomping, cowboy-booted Texan millionaire. In reality, Texas has ranked third among the oil-producing states.

While the state's underground riches have indeed placed it first in overall mineral extraction, other Texas industries have been uniformly large as well, from cotton-processing, silver-smelting, and water-supply systems, to vast bridge- and dam-building projects. With a land mass exceeding that of France by 129 500 km² (50 000 sq. mi.), Texas is second in size only to the state of Alaska.

Along the shoreline of the Gulf of Mexico in Texas stand two of the world's tallest and sturdiest iron-clad lighthouses, the Matagorda light of 1852 at Pass Cavallo, rebuilt in 1872, and the Point bolivar light of 1873 near Galveston. Inch-thick riveted iron plate is bonded to brickwork in these brave structures, built to withstand hurricane-force winds and waves.

Two of the more significant Texan bridges are the Waco Suspension Bridge of 1869, a crenellated tower and wire-rope suspended span, rebuilt in 1914; and the Orange–Port Arthur High Bridge of 1938, a steel-trussed 2362 m (7750 ft.) span, 54 m (176 ft.) over the Neches River at Bridge City.

Major railway stations in Texas have been especially well fitted to receive the great numbers of steam rail passengers who once could crisscross most of the state. Union Terminal, Dallas, completed in 1916, is a sleek BEAUX-ARTS structure, finished with cast-iron chandeliers, rechristened the Dallas Transportation Center in 1974. In San Antonio, the International and Great Northern Railroad Station of 1907 still looms as one of the great Spanish Mission-revival styled stations of the West, now retired from rail service, but protected.

The remains of the Alamo Portland and Roman Cement Works in 1881 also stand in San Antonio as the first such activity west of the Mississippi. After closure, the stone kilns and stack were incorporated into a public promenade garden.

Historic oil sites in Texas take several forms. The sheet-iron refining still of an oil refinery of 1898 has LANDMARK status at Corsicana. A pair of petroleum museums interpret the field at Midland and Fort Worth. And in the ghost town of Thurber, a 46 m (150 ft.) brick chimney, reminiscent of British design, with its massive octagonal form and elaborate corbelling, remains a solitary monument to the Texas & Pacific Oil Company which once operated a string of mines, wells, refineries and kilns throughout the north-western corner of the state.

LOCATIONS
[M] Age of Steam Railroad Museum, Fairgrounds, Dallas, TX 75226.
[M] Burlington-Rock Island Railroad Museum, 218 Elm Street, Teague, TX 75860.
[M] National Museum of Communications, 6305 North O'Connor Street, Irving, TX 75039.
[M] The Petroleum Museum, 1500 Interstate 20 West, Midland, TX 79701.
[M] Western Company Petroleum Museum, 6000 Western Place, Fort Worth, TX 76107.

DAVID H. SHAYT

textile machinery The first stage of industrialization in many countries has been the manufacture of textiles, which has typically been followed by the production of textile machinery, sometimes by machine shops within textile mills, sometimes by independent concerns, many of which have in due course turned to other aspects of engineering. Examples can be identified in Great Britain, Germany and the USA, but the history of the ZURICH and WINTERTHUR region provides the clearest examples.

See also BLEACHING; CALENDER; CALICO PRINTING; CARDING MACHINE; CLOTHING FACTORY; CONDENSER CARDING MACHINE; COTTON GIN; COTTON PRESS; DELINTING MACHINE; DEVIL; DYEHOUSE; FULLING MILL; HACKLING; LOOM; REELING; RING SPINNING; SCUTCHING; SEWING MACHINE; SLUBBING BILLY; SPINNING JENNY; SPINNING MULE; STOCKING FRAME; TEXTILE MILL; TEXTILES; THROWING; WATER FRAME.

textile mill The textile mill or FACTORY was one of the symbols of the Industrial Revolution. It set a pattern for the application of mechanical power, and for the concentration and specialization of labour. From the late

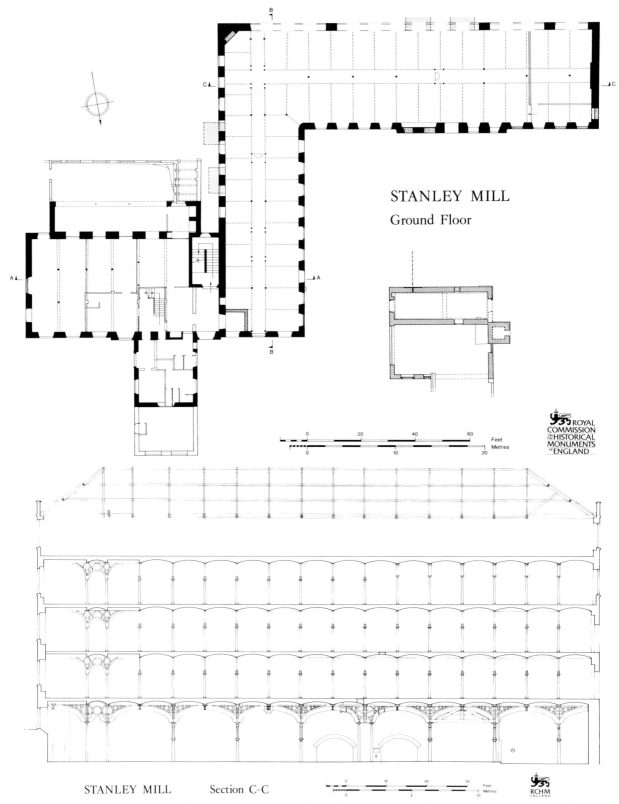

STANLEY MILL

Ground Floor

ROYAL
COMMISSION
ON THE HISTORICAL
MONUMENTS
OF ENGLAND

STANLEY MILL   Section C-C

RCHM
ENGLAND

Figure 155   (top) Plan of the original buildings at Stanley Mill, Stroud, Gloucestershire: the building to the south and the central building are iron-framed; that to the left is of conventional construction. (bottom) A section, C-C, through the more southerly of the original iron-framed buildings, showing iron-framing, a wooden roof and blocked archways for headraces of water wheels
Royal Commission on the Historical Monuments of England

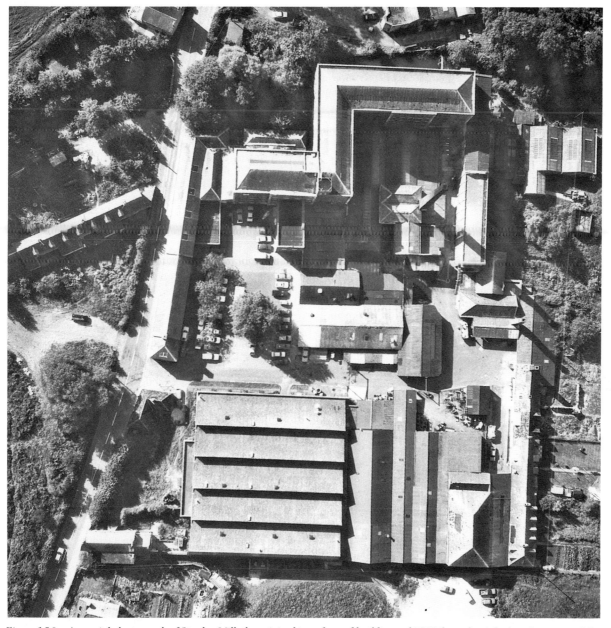

Figure 156   An aerial photograph of Stanley Mill: the original iron-framed buildings of 1813 form the right-hand portions of the straightened 'Z' at the top of the picture, in the angle of which stands the two-bayed, hipped-roofed steam-engine house of 1822.
Royal Commission on the Historical Monuments of England

eighteenth century, when Joseph Wright (1734–97) of Derby painted Arkwright's mills at Cromford, to the mid-twentieth century when the landscapes of Lancashire towns dominated the works of L. S. Lowry (1887–1976), textile mills have powerfully influenced artists and writers.

The development of the textile factory may be portrayed as the evolution of the multi-storey mill building, from seventeenth-century Italian origins, through Lombe's silk

mill at Derby, Richard Arkwright's cotton mill of 1771 at Cromford, and Charles Bage's iron-framed flax mill at Shrewsbury of 1796–7, through Saltaire, Manningham Mill (*see* Bradford), New Harmony Mills, Cohoes, New York, and other vast works of the mid-nineteenth century, and ultimately to the great steel-framed mills built in Lancashire *c.*1900 and widely copied, and the multi-storey rayon factories of the 1920s. The evolution of iron and later of steel frames is one critical factor in such a pattern. Another is the development of systems of power transmission: first, power from water wheels and beam engines was transmitted through vertical shafts and LINE SHAFTING, which drove machines by belts; later, power from the same sources was transmitted through ROPE DRIVE systems; later still, electric motors drove shafting attached to machines; and latterly electric motors powered individual machines. The development of service systems is a further theme. Staircases and lavatories were accommodated in turrets, thus freeing floor space for machines, from the late eighteenth century until the 1920s. Archaeological investigation has identified evidence of early heating systems, involving open fires and flues, in some eighteenth-century factory buildings. Subsequently hot-water systems provided an alternative which was less of a fire hazard. Textile factories in Britain were pioneering users of GAS lighting, although many persisted with candles and oil lamps until the mid-nineteenth century. Such a heroic saga is only one approach to the subject.

A textile factory is more than a multi-storey building. It may be defined as a complex in which take place at least two of the major stages in the manufacture of textiles – preparation, spinning, weaving or knitting, and finishing. From the 1770s some processes in at least one stage would be mechanically powered, although processes that did not require power might be concentrated around those that did. A further characteristic of a factory is that it is usually clearly defined and demarcated by boundary walls, with lodges and gates, like those of the country houses of the aristocracy, controlling entrances. Few textile factories consist only of a powered multi-storey block. Most complexes include warehouses, some of which may be single-storey structures. Most will have engineering workshops, stables, garages, office blocks, and several houses for key workers. Many will have distinctive DYEHOUSES or GAS plants. A textile factory is a dynamic institution, whose functions habitually change over time. In some cases a factory may grow towards integration, until it encompasses all four major stages in textile manufacture, expanding in extent until it is able to take in raw materials and dispatch finished fabrics. In other instances growth within a company may dictate a narrowing of the range of processes or stages carried on within a particular complex. Integration has been important in some areas and in some branches of the industry, but predetermined progress towards integration is an unhelpful model.

One approach to an understanding of the evolution of the textile factory is to see it as the concentration of processes and stages of manufacture around particular nuclei. One such nucleus was the water-powered, and later steam-powered, multi-storey spinning mill of late-eighteenth-century England; but it was not the only one, and such buildings should be regarded not as factories but as components of factories, as should the water-powered silk-throwing mills of seventeenth- and eighteenth-century Italy, from which the English cotton mills probably derived.

Another nucleus was a building which served as a base for the distribution of raw materials to domestic spinners and weavers, which might grow in scale, and come to accommodate production processes. An outstanding survival of this type of building is the Rotes Haus, Monschau (see EIFEL), built by J. B. Scheibler in 1756, an eight-bay, five-storey building, which was the centre of employment for four thousand people, most of them working in their own homes. The mansion houses, the homes of the woollen clothiers of the STROUD area of England, similarly developed from centres of distribution into locations of production, and remained as essential components of factories in the mid-nineteenth century, long after the adoption of mechanical power and the concentration of the various stages of manufacture. Loom houses, which provided space in which numbers of hand-loom weavers could work, and jenny shops, where small numbers of SPINNING JENNIES were concentrated, provide other examples of this type.

In areas that produced woollen cloth the FULLING MILL was another nucleus around which other mechanically-powered stages of production, particularly CARDING, might be concentrated, leading to the emergence of factory complexes. For much of the nineteenth century in parts of Yorkshire the preparation and finishing stages of woollen cloth manufacture were carried out in mills, while spinning and weaving operations were performed by domestic workers.

In many textile regions the factory did not simply supersede domestic production: to assume that it did is again to adopt a misleading model. Textile manufacture continued to be an important industry in London in the mid-nineteenth century, but was organized almost entirely on a domestic basis. The plight of some HAND LOOM weavers in England in the second quarter of the nineteenth century has tended to obscure the continuing role of domestic workers in, for example, the manufacture of woollen cloth in Gloucestershire, or hosiery in Nottinghamshire. It is more helpful to consider the hypothesis that in many branches of textiles there were lengthy periods during which in particular regions some stages of manufacture were carried on in factories and some by outworkers.

The textile factory presents formidable challenges to industrial archaeologists. Reasons for building factories in particular ways can rarely be found in documentary sources. In many textile regions large numbers of mills survive, although some will have been demolished and many adapted to new uses. Straightforward mapping of surviving evidence, undertaken in the same way that prehistorians plot burial mounds, will bring to light patterns that cannot be perceived in documentary sources. Some mills have constantly been adapted to new processes. Some, like the classic Lancashire spinning mills of the late nineteenth century, served several generations in the form in which they were designed. To understand a textile factory it is essential to relate form to function, to appreciate that a building was designed for a particular manufacturing purpose, and not primarily as a means of developing the art of architecture, nor of advancing constructional technology. In DUNDEE, for example, flax and jute mills were iron-framed to provide strength for carrying heavy machines, and had Gothic-style three-bay nave-and-aisle layouts to accommodate the spinning frames normally employed in them. The approach of the archaeologist to this area of study is potentially more rewarding than that of the historian of architecture or technology.

See also MILL; TEXTILES and figures 86, 98, 110, 112, 140, 143.

BIBLIOGRAPHY
General
Darwell, 1978; Stratton and Trinder, 1989; Tann, 1970; Watson, 1989.
Specific
Fitzgerald, R. The development of the cast-iron frame in textile mills to 1850. In *IAR*, x, 1988.
Giles, C. and Goodall, I. H. Framing a survey of textile mills: RCHME's West Riding experience. In *IAR*, ix, 1986.
Stratton, M. and Trinder, B. Stanley Mill, Gloucestershire. In *Post-Medieval Archaeology*, XXII, 1988.

BARRIE TRINDER

textile museum The principal collections of historic textile machinery tend to be held by national museums of science and technology, like the Science Museum, London, the Smithsonian Institution, Washington DC, or the Deutsches Museum, Munich. Major collections of fabrics, the products of the textile industry, are often held by museums of applied arts, like the Victoria and Albert Museum, London. Museums of costume are also important as repositories of textiles, which may be dated and of clear provenance.

Amongst specialist textile museums some are primarily research institutions, holding large collections of which only small proportions are displayed. Such museums may take a broad approach to the scientific study of the industry and its products, as does the Merrimack Valley Textile Museum, Mass. Others, often supported by the industry, are concerned with the close study of particular aspects of textiles, like the museum of textile printing in MULHOUSE, or that concerned with dyestuffs in BRADFORD.

A further category of textile museum is that established in a notable textile mill, often with the prime aim of preserving the building. In some cases, as at HELMSHORE, Lancashire, it has been possible to preserve substantial areas of a mill virtually complete, with all the machinery in use when it last functioned in operating condition. Such museums can usually portray only some of the principal phases of textile manufacture. In other cases, as at STYAL, all the machinery was removed before the mill became a museum, and a variety of equipment portrays the whole range of textile production.

BIBLIOGRAPHY
Specific
Merrimack Valley Textile Museum: the housing of a textile collection, North Andover, Mass.: Merrimack Valley Textile Museum, 1968.

BARRIE TRINDER

textiles Since ancient times people in every culture have processed plant and animal fibres into cloth for garments, shelter and furnishings. Preferences for particular fibres have been based on the availability of raw materials and the nature of the climate. Flax, from which linen cloth is made, may be the oldest plant fibre to be spun and woven. Cotton, the other major plant fibre, may be almost as ancient; archaeological evidence suggests that cotton cloth was in use in India and Peru as far back as 3500 BC. From well before the Christian era the Chinese made and traded silk, eventually developing a distribution network – the Silk Road – through Central Asia to the Mediterranean. Mesopotamia, in so many respects the cradle of civilization, also gave rise to the working of wool, and the Middle East remains a centre of carpet production (*see* TURKEY).

Roman and Arab conquests in Europe carried the knowledge of textile processing north and west. By the Middle Ages sophisticated textile manufacturing existed in Spain and Italy. England became a centre of the woollen cloth trade by the seventeenth century, and led the industrial revolution in textiles in the eighteenth. Domestic production of linen and woollen cloth continued in most countries through much of the nineteenth century, but from the late Middle Ages more specialized manufacture of fine-quality woollens and silks had developed outside the home. Craft guilds, small artisan shops, and substantial, integrated manufactories throughout Europe produced a remarkable variety of goods. Surviving piece halls (*see* HALIFAX) and the 'wool churches' of Flanders provide physical evidence of the mature capitalist organization and great wealth of the cloth trade. Numerous machines produced yarn and cloth for an active market economy. Visual resources (such as engravings) can help identify the application and progress of water-powered machinery even where the physical evidence no longer survives.

Dyed and painted Indian cottons reached Europe in large quantities after the Portuguese began trading with the sub-continent by sea in the sixteenth century. Augsburg was known for its printed cottons and linens in the seventeenth century, about the same time that Huguenot refugees from France brought the art to England. Spurred by the great interest in manufactured cotton goods, the English began to revolutionize the production of textiles from the 1730s. The industrialization of textiles involved several key inventions that created demand and stimulated responses in other stages of the manufacturing process. The flying shuttle of 1733 by John Kay (d.1764), was a relatively simple arrangement of cords that propelled the shuttle between boxes at either side of the loom; it dramatically increased the speed and productivity of HAND-LOOM weaving. Greater amounts of yarn were needed, and improvements in spinning machinery followed, such as the SPINNING JENNY of James Hargreaves (d.1778) and RICHARD ARKWRIGHT'S WATER FRAME. Several experiments with power weaving, such as the processes patented by Edmund Cartwright (1743–1823) in Britain in the late 1780s, came to successful completion early in the nineteenth century. Power-loom weaving

757

became fully realized on both sides of the Atlantic by 1820. Applied first in the cotton manufacture, these innovations were translated to wool, flax and silk production by eager industrialists and talented machine builders in America and throughout Europe by the middle of the nineteenth century. Mechanization of textile manufacture began with the FULLING MILLS of the Middle Ages, and was continued with the silk-throwing mills of seventeenth-century Italy. The TEXTILE MILL, one of the most potent symbols of early industrialization, developed in the English cotton industry from the 1770s and was widely copied, although in some textile regions factories and domestic manufactures co-existed for many decades.

Each type of FIBRE – cotton, wool, silk and the flax/hemp/jute family – is worked into yarn or cloth according to a system developed to accommodate the fibre's physical properties and most suited to its intended finished products. Cotton, especially, could be processed mechanically more easily than other fibres, and often led the way in technological developments. Chemical developments capitalized on the qualities of cellulose fibres that could be worked on the cotton system. FLAX COTTON, chemical cotton and regenerated wood pulp (*see* RAYON) preceded a whole new group of synthetic fibres extruded from chemical compounds, including PETROLEUM derivatives.

Preparation

The processing of textile fibres into woven cloth consists of four basic stages of production: preparing, spinning, weaving and finishing.

The first processes prepare the raw material to be worked. The fibres are cleaned and separated from their seeds or natural coverings (*see* COTTON GIN), and if necessary from their shipping containers, such as bales. The compressed bale of cotton, formed in the COTTON PRESS, passes through a bale breaker, a spike-covered conveyor which pulls the fibres apart. Opening machines further separate and clean the cotton.

Wool sacks or bales contain whole fleeces that must be sorted by hand according to grade, length and quality of fibre. Once graded, wool is picked to open the matted fibres and remove dirt, sticks and burrs. Both cotton and wool manufacture use a machine called the DEVIL (or picker, in American usage) which employs toothed cylinders to separate and clean the fibres. Devils fitted with long metal teeth tear rags as the first stage in reprocessing woven cloth into SHODDY or MUNGO. Virgin wool must next be scoured with soap, water and acids to remove oil (lanolin) and perspiration (suint). A variety of chemical methods, depending on the final use of the wool, is employed in the scouring train, a series of bowls or tanks.

The woody stalk of the flax plant has been worked into linen yarn and cloth since ancient times. The Near East, especially Egypt, was known for linen production. Flanders became an important centre from medieval times, followed by some parts of Germany, including Silesia, Osnabruck and Tecklenburg, the latter best-known through its product, anglicized as ticking. The Russians exported flax; the Dutch gained a reputation for bleaching and finishing linen cloth; and the Belgians and

the Irish developed the linen manufacture into a major industry that has continued into the twentieth century. Processing the flax plant to free the inner core of fibre suitable for spinning involves several steps. The entire plant is pulled from the ground and dried. Next the seeds are removed by rippling, drawing the plants through a toothed comb. The seeds are crushed to make LINSEED OIL. The stalks are then retted (soaked), broken, and HACKLED to free the fibre for processing.

Wool, flax and cotton fibres are carded on CARDING MACHINES. Rotating cylinders covered with closely-spaced wire teeth set in leather separate and straighten the fibres. Wool to be worked on the WORSTED system, usually the longer-fibred varieties, is then combed (*see* COMBING MACHINE). Cotton for fine spinning, flax and short-fibred Australian (Botany) wools can also be combed after carding (*see* CARDING MACHINE).

The term WORSTED denotes yarn or fabric (stuffs) made from long-fibred wools on a separate preparatory system. Designed to take advantage of the longer fibres, worsted processing involved separating the longest and best fibres, called 'tops', from the shorter waste fibres, called 'noils'. The tops were carded separately and then combed to lengthen the fibres and keep them parallel. In hand combing, hanks of tops were attached to a post and combed with a heated metal comb, made of 20–30 cm (8–10 in.) iron teeth set in a wooden handle. Worsted machinery includes carding machines and combs of several patented designs (*see* COMBING MACHINE). Worsted yarns were used for knitting and for weaving fine cloth with little or no nap.

The preparation of silk from the cocoon of the silkworm has been practised in China since 4000 BC and remained a closely guarded secret for three thousand years. India seems to have learned the trade before the time of Christ. Japan, leader in the industry since the nineteenth century, gained knowledge of silk via Korea about AD 200. Gradually, through trade along the caravan routes of Central Asia known as the Silk Road, knowledge of working silk came to the West. Italy was an important centre of silk production from the Middle Ages, eventually superseded by LYONS in the seventeenth century. There the draw-loom weavers created formal patterned silks used for garments and furnishing fabrics throughout Europe. By the eighteenth century the Spitalfields district of London emerged as a rival to Lyons, but both were overcome by competition from the new preference for cotton goods.

Silk never entirely lost its popularity. There were many nineteenth-century attempts to raise silkworms in various parts of the world. Industrialization brought the promises of more cheaply woven silks, and the Japanese and American silk industries grew apace, the firms of Cheney Brothers of South Manchester, Conn., and Belding Brothers of Belding, Mich., being particular examples. The enormous demand for silk between 1900 and 1920 led directly to the improvement of artificial silk (*see* RAYON) and the development of other SYNTHETIC FIBRES.

Silk is naturally produced by silkworms, fed fifty times their weight in mulberry leaves until they are ready to spin cocoons in preparation for their emergence as moths. The cocoons are heated to kill the larvae, whose emergence would damage the silk, and then the silk filaments are wound off and plied together to form silk yarn (*see* REELING; THROWING).

Spinning

Several steps constitute the spinning of all or any YARN: drawing, twisting and winding. Preliminary forms of spinning machinery include slubbing (*see* SLUBBING BILLY) drawing and roving frames, which accomplish preliminary stages of drawing, twisting and winding. They produce ROVING. In spinning, the fibres are drawn out and simultaneously twisted into a continuous filament that will maintain sufficient integrity as it is wound onto a spindle.

Two basic methods evolved: intermittent and continuous spinning. In intermittent spinning, the drawing and twisting motions are separated from and precede the winding of the yarn onto the spindle. Machines for intermittent spinning include the SPINNING MULE and the SPINNING JENNY. Mule spinning in particular produces very uniform yarn and has been used for both cotton and wool.

In continuous spinning, the three functions occur in one continuous motion. Machines for continuous spinning include the WATER FRAME and cap, ring and throstle spinning frames. The earliest, Richard Arkwright's water frame of 1769, drew the yarn out through two sets of drafting rollers revolving at different speeds. It twisted the yarn over an inverted U-shaped flyer, and wound it onto a bobbin. The throstle frame, a variant developed in the 1790s and used until the 1850s, drove each spindle by means of a band from a long tin drum. The cap spinner, or cap spinning frame, patented in the USA by John Danforth in 1828, substituted an inverted metal cup for the inverted U-shaped flyer. The RING SPINNING frame, patented in the USA by John Thorp (1784–1848) in 1828, exchanged a stationary metal ring for the flyer and added twist to the yarn, which is pulled through a small metal loop called a traveller. A twisting frame combines several strands of yarn, twisting them into thicker yarn, such as two- or four-ply.

Various machines have been devised to apply coatings (including sizing and dressing for warp preparations) and other finishing products to yarn. Some processes, such as mercerizing, can be applied either to yarn or to cloth. Mercerizing involves immersion in a CAUSTIC SODA solution, and increases the lustre of the yarn or cloth, giving better dyeing results.

Weaving

Weaving is the process of forming cloth by interlacing two parallel sets of yarn at right angles to each other. It is performed on a loom, a frame of wood or metal in which the warp yarn is wound between a pair of 'beams' front and back. Harnesses attached to the upper members of the loom raise and lower the warp yarns to permit passage of the weft or filling yarn.

The necessary preparatory steps for weaving are warp and weft winding, processes that package the yarn and make it ready to be woven. The warp yarns are the longitudinal series held in place on the loom; the weft or filling yarns are carried transversely in the shuttle or shuttles passed from side to side. Warping is the name given to several steps of rewinding and measuring yarn to be used for the warp. Spooling is the process of taking yarn from the package prepared by the spinning machine and winding it onto spools. Winding involves rewinding yarn from the spool stand on to a warp beam, a single large spool set into the loom. Weft yarns also are wound onto bobbins called quills or pirns, carried inside the shuttles. Dressing or sizing is the process of applying a starch solution to the warp yarn to protect it from the abrasion of the weaving motion.

Other cloth fabrication methods include knitting and lace making. Knitting produces fabric by interlocking loops of a single strand of yarn carried on needles. The needles can be set into a frame, such as a STOCKING FRAME, in use in Britain for hosiery manufacture from the sixteenth century until *c.*1900, or in knitting machines that produce both flat and tubular goods (*see* RUDDINGTON). Lace is an open-work fabric produced by twisting two or more sets of threads, usually quite fine in diameter.

Finishing

Woven cloth requires several finishing operations after weaving to provide suitable surface qualities and more decorative finishes. Any cloth may be dyed in the piece to alter its colour. Cotton and linen cloth are often washed and bleached; these two fabrics are the most likely to be printed with designs, although woollen cloth and woven silk may also be printed.

The BLEACHING of cotton and linen yarn and cloth was performed outdoors by the action of sunlight, air and water, until the mid-eighteenth century when chemical improvements were introduced (*see* BLEACHING POWDER). A solution of chlorine or chloride of lime is used, alternating with washing, in large heated vats or kiers over several hours, even days. Before bleaching, the cloth is singed by heated plates, rollers, or an open flame, to remove any residual nap or fuzz from the surface.

Dyeing introduced colour; in addition to the dyestuff, it may require the use of chemical agents called MORDANTS, such as iron, alum or tin, to effect colour changes. It may occur in the preparatory stage, the fibre itself being dyed (hence the term 'dyed in the wool'); it may also occur following spinning, the yarn being dyed; or in the finishing process, as piece dyeing. It is carried out in vats through which the goods pass in continuous movement to achieve saturation, or by means of immersion. Plants such as INDIGO, WOAD, LOGWOOD and MADDER have been used for dyestuffs since ancient times. Synthetic dyes made from coal tar derivatives were introduced following the discovery by Sir William Henry Perkin (1838–1907) in Britain in 1856 of an ANILINE mauve. The German chemical industry developed rapidly to become the primary producer of synthetic dyes by 1900.

Patterns were produced on the surface of cloth after weaving by printing and embossing. Printing provided decorative cloth at less expense than elaborate figured weaving. Simple printing from carved wooden blocks was known to the ancients, but its application as elaborate patterns containing multiple colours developed into a highly skilled craft. By the seventeenth century engraved copper plates also were used to print cloth, and patterns in addition to colours could be applied by pressing cloth between embossed plates, as for moires and harateens. Machine-powered printing from engraved copper cylinders developed in Britain by the 1780s, and British calico printers were highly valued agents of the TRANSFER OF TECHNOLOGY to America and within Europe in the nineteenth century (*see* CALICO PRINTING).

Woven woollen cloth is washed and fulled by being beaten with hammers or passed through rollers while wet, to tighten the weave and raise a nap (*see* FULLING MILL). Napping is a brushing action that raises the cloth's surface fibres. Some cotton fabrics, such as cambric and flannel, also are napped. The hooked tips of the TEASEL plant were used for napping from antiquity, and in the eighteenth and nineteenth centuries used in frames called handles. Wire teeth, such as those used for carding, came to be applied to rotary machines or gigs, first developed with teasles about 1800.

Shearing evenly cuts the nap raised in the napping process. The use of large iron hand-shears operated by skilled craftsmen preceded early attempts to mechanize the process by setting smaller hand-shears into a power-driven frame. Rotary shearing machines successfully changed the method to one involving a series of blades rotating around a cylinder, patented by S. G. Dorr in the USA in 1792.

Calendering provides a hot or cold press finish and lustre to the fabric as it passes between the steel rolls of the calender. Before mechanization metal plates were laid between folds of cloth and the stack was pressed in a standing screw press. Linen and cotton fabrics were 'beetled' or stamped by rotating wooden mallets to glaze or burnish the finish.

For types of textiles, *see* FIBRES.

For fabrics and other textile products, *see* ALPACA; BLANKET; CALICO PRINTING; CANVAS; CARPET; CASHMERE; CORDAGE; DAMASK; FELTMAKING; FLANNEL; FUSTIAN; HOSIERY; LACE; LINEN; LINOLEUM; LINT; MADRAS; MOHAIR; MUNGO; OIL CLOTH; PASSEMENTERIE; PLUSH; RIBBON; RUG; SAILCLOTH; SHODDY; TAPE; TAPESTRY; TARTAN; TWEED; WOOLLENS; WORSTED.

For spinning, *see* MULE; RING SPINNING; SPINNING JENNY; SPINNING MULE; SPINNING WHEEL; THREAD; WATER FRAME; WET SPINNING; YARN.

For weaving, *see* LOOM.

For finishing, *see* BLEACHING; CALENDER; CALICO PRINTING; CLOTH STOVE; DYEING; FULLING MILL; HANDLE HOUSE; TEASEL; TENTER FRAME.

For buildings concerned with textiles, *see* CLOTH STOVE; COMPANY MILL; DYEHOUSE; FULLING MILL; HANDLE HOUSE; NORTHLIT SHED; TEXTILE MILL; WAREHOUSE; WOOLSTOVE.

For the manufacture of clothing, *see* CLOTHING FACTORY; HATMAKING; MILITARY UNIFORM; SEWING MACHINE; SHAWL MANUFACTURE; SHIRT MANUFACTURE; TAILOR.

See also TEXTILE MACHINERY.

BIBLIOGRAPHY
General
Baines, 1835, 1858; Beck, 1881; Bendure and Pfeiffer, 1946; Burnham, 1981; Burnley, 1889; Carmichael *et al.*, 1947; Daniels, 1920; Farnie, 1979; Jenkins and Ponting, 1982; Jeremy, 1981; Kerridge, 1985; Mauersberger, 1947; Montgomery, 1984; Reddy, 1984; Wilson, 1979; Wingate, 1979.

HELENA WRIGHT

theatre A place where dramatic productions can be performed to substantial audiences. It is usually divided into a stage, an auditorium and a foyer. The characteristics of theatres have been transformed in the industrial period. The earliest are court and civic theatres like the Residenz theatre, Bayreuth, of 1744–8 by Giuseppe and Carlo Galli Bibiena, and the court theatre, Drottningholm (*see* STOCKHOLM), of 1764–6 by C. F. Adelcrantz. Several theatres for public audiences were built in pre-Revolutionary France, including the Grand Théâtre, Bordeaux, of 1777–80 by Victor Louis, and the theatre at Besançon of 1778–84, by C.-N. Ledoux (1736–1806), which had graded seating and an orchestra pit. The Théâtre Français at the Palais Royal, Paris, built to the designs of Victor Louis in 1785–90, is notable for its wrought-iron roof and its fireproof floors of hollow ceramic pots. In the mid-nineteenth century theatres and opera houses of great complexity were built, the pattern being set by the Schauspielhaus in Berlin, built in 1818–21 by K. F. SCHINKEL. Richard Wagner (1813–83), the composer, was influential in demanding that a theatre should provide an atmosphere conducive to drama, and his Festpielhaus at Bayreuth, built in 1872–6 to designs by O. Brückwald, had amphitheatrical seating without boxes or galleries, a deep pit for the orchestra, and an auditorium which could be completely darkened. The subsequent use of steel and concrete construction removed objections to galleries, whose cast-iron columns had obstructed lines of vision. Great efforts were made in the late nineteenth century to achieve fireproof construction, by such means as installing iron fire curtains. The Savoy theatre, London, designed by C. J. Phipps (1835–97) for Richard D'Oyly Carte (1844–1901), was the first to use electric lighting, while D'Oyly Carte's opera house of 1889 (subsequently the Palace Theatre), designed by T. E. Collett (1840–1924), also incorporated cantilevered balconies, and hot and cold air ventilation. Many theatres were built in the great cities of Europe and North America in the decades before 1914, some of them, like the London Coliseum which seated four thousand, buildings of great size and complexity.

BIBLIOGRAPHY
General
Pevsner, 1976.

BARRIE TRINDER

Thessaloníki (Salonica), Macedonia, Greece The second largest city in Greece, although from the time of the Turkish invasion in 1430 until the eighteenth century the Greek inhabitants suffered systematic persecution. It was liberated by the Greek army on 8 November 1912. The Turkish inhabitants left in the early 1920s, to be replaced with Greek refugees from Asia Minor. The large Jewish community, which migrated to Thessaloníki from Spain c.1600, was exterminated by the Germans during World War II. The harbour was constructed by French engineers in the nineteenth century.

Much of the city was rebuilt after a major fire in 1917. Some tall flourmills survive, of which the most impressive example is the Allatini Mill. The most characteristic feature of the turn-of-the-century industrial architecture is the use of decorative and pierced brick. Thessaloníki has an active railway society with nineteen steam locomotives in various states of preservation prior to the establishment of a railway museum.

BIBLIOGRAPHY
Specific
Iatridis, M. Thessaloníki Technical Museum. In *Technology*, ii, 1988.
Kolona, I. V. and Traganou-Deliyanni, O. Beginnings of industry in Thessaloníki, 1870–1912. In *Technology*, ii, 1988.

LOCATION
[M] Folklore Museum of Northern Greece, 68 Vasilissis Olgas Street, Thessaloníki.

MICHAEL STRATTON

Thetford, Quebec, Canada The Mineral and Mining Museum of the Asbestos Region is located at Thetford, 105 km (65 mi.) S. of Quebec. It was founded in 1976 by an association of mineral collectors and geologists. Its object is to show how the region has made its living from mining, and its main focus is on the exploitation of asbestos. Collections include specimens of the mineral; finished products; maps and photographs of the principal workings; and mining equipment, filters, jaw crushers and a bucking hammer.

BIBLIOGRAPHY
Specific
Les musées du Québec. Quebec: Ministry of Cultural Affairs, 1981.

LOCATION
[M] Musée minéralogique et minier de la région de l'amiante (Mineral and Mining Museum of the Asbestos Region), 671 Boulevard Smith Sud, Thetford Mines, Quebec G6G 5T3.

Theuern, Bavaria, Germany A twin settlement with Kümmersbruck, which lies on the River Vils, 70 km (40 mi.) SE of Nuremberg. The Hammerherrenschloss (hammer castle) was built there in 1781, one of many structures of its kind, and a late reflection of the one-time importance of the area's iron industry. In 1387 the so-called 'great hammer agreement', signed by sixty-eight entrepreneurs, had laid the foundations of an iron industry which was to prosper by selling its products to all parts of Europe. The Bergbau- und Industriemuseum Ostbayern (East Bavarian Museum of Mining and Industry), housed in the castle, and its various branches provide documentation relating to the Bayrische Eisen-

strasse (Bavarian Iron Road) which ran from Pegnitz in the north to Regensburg in the south, with exhibits ranging from hoists used to bring ore out of mines to iron church gratings. Its displays are the best evidence of the historical importance of industry in the Upper Palatinate.

BIBLIOGRAPHY
General
Bott, 1985; Götschman, 1985; Grimm 1985.
Specific
Die Oberpfalz, ein europäisches Eisenzentrum. 600 Jahre grosse Hammereinung (The Upper Palatinate: a European ironworking centre: 600 years of the great hammer agreement). Theuern: Bergbau- und Industriemuseum Ostbayern (East Bavarian Museum of Mining and Industry) 1987.

LOCATION
[M] Bergbau- und Industriemuseum Ostbayern (East Bavarian Museum of Mining and Industry), Portnerstrasse 1, 8451 Theuern.

AXEL FÖHL

Thomas, David (1794–1882) A Welsh ironworks manager, responsible for developing smelting with anthracite. Anthracite was unusable until 1837 when experiments, conducted by Thomas with George Crane at Ynyscedwyn, near Swansea, used hot blast. The new process led to thirty-six new furnaces being established in south-west Wales. Thomas took the process to America in 1839, where it became the basis of the Pennsylvania iron industry. He established the Lehigh Crane Iron Company in 1840 and the Thomas Iron Company in 1854; the latter became the largest pig-iron producer in the USA.

BIBLIOGRAPHY
General
Rees, 1975.
Specific
Roberts, E. R. Notable men of Wales: David Thomas, the father of the anthracite iron trade. In *The Red Dragon*, October 1883.

Thomas Gilchrist, Sidney *See* GILCHRIST THOMAS, SIDNEY.

thread A thin, continuous filament of spun fibre: a yarn of such fineness as to suit it for sewing or lacemaking, not cloth production.

throwing The term applied to the process of twisting silk filament or rayon into yarn ready for weaving or knitting. A twist is put into cotton, woollen or linen yarn during the spinning process. As silk is already spun into a preliminary filament by the silkworm, it remains only to be wound off (*see* REELING) and twisted or thrown to strengthen it further. Throwing adds a twist; the doubling or plying of several strands together also occurs in the throwing process. The throwing mills of seventeenth-century Italy represented a crucial stage in the organization of textile manufacture on an industrial scale.

BIBLIOGRAPHY
General
Bendure and Pfeiffer, 1946.

Thuringia, Germany   Mining featured prominently in the economy of Thuringia, formerly the south-western part of the DDR, comprising the modern regions of Erfurt, Gera and Suhl. There was a historic iron-ore mining industry in SCHMALKALDEN until the mid-nineteenth century. Copper and manganese ores are found near Ilmenau, a region for which, as a minister of the state of Weimar, Johann Wolfgang von Goethe (1749–1832) was responsible. The large quantities of timber produced in the Thuringian forests were the basis for glass-blowing in Ilmenau, and papermaking in the Suhl region, which now also manufactures high-quality armaments.

BIBLIOGRAPHY
General
Berger, 1980; Schmidt and Theile, 1989; Wagenbreth and Wächtler, 1983.

LOCATIONS
[M] Municipal Museum, Stockfisch, Lininstrasse 169, 5000 Erfurt.
[M] Museum of Cultural History, Strasse der Republik 2, 6500 Gera.
[M] Museum of Local History, Amtshaus, Markt 1, 6300 Ilmenau.
[M] Weapons Museum, Wilhelm Pieck Strasse, 1160 Suhl.

TICCIH   The International Committee for the Conservation of the Industrial Heritage (TICCIH) was established in consequence of the First International Conference on the Conservation of Industrial Monuments, organized by Neil Cossons (b. 1939) and Barrie Trinder (b. 1939) at IRONBRIDGE in May 1973. After a second conference at Bochum (*see* RUHRGEBIET) in 1975, statutes were adopted at a third meeting in Sweden in 1978. Subsequent conferences were held in France in 1981, the USA in 1984, Austria in 1987, and Belgium in 1990. Representatives have attended from all the major European countries, the USSR, Japan, Australia, the USA and Canada; and the organization has links with Third World countries. The conference papers have been published, usually in two volumes: a set of national reports on progress in industrial conservation, produced at the time of the conferences, and a volume of edited working papers, published subsequently. TICCIH also organizes intermediate conferences on particular topics, makes representations to national governments and international organizations, and has a publishing programme.

BIBLIOGRAPHY
General
Cossons, 1975; CILAC, 1981; 1985; Georgeacopol-Winischhofer *et al.*, 1987; Kroker, 1978; Nisser, 1978, 1981; Nisser and Bedoire, 1978; Victor and Wright, 1984; Wright and Vogel, 1986.

LOCATION
[I] TICCIH Secretariat, Ironbridge Gorge Museum, Ironbridge, Telford TF8 7AW, England.

tide mill   A water mill deriving its energy from the tides. Using similar machinery to other water mills, it requires a tide-pond and sea-dam with one-way hatches to catch the tide as it turns. Water channels and regulators let the water out past the wheels.
See also WOODBRIDGE.

BIBLIOGRAPHY
General
Wailes, 1956.

Tilburg, Noord Brabant, The Netherlands   Until 1960, the principal centre of the woollen textile industry in the Netherlands: it was known as the Dutch Leeds. Since then many factories have disappeared, and local government has only recently shown interest in the remaining buildings.

Traditions of working with wool date from the Middle Ages when sheep were kept on the sandy heathlands. From the seventeenth century ribbon development occurred along the access roads. In the eighteenth century merchants from LEIDEN settled in the region stimulating factory production. The 'factory house' of 1792 near Bodehof is the only surviving monument of these early attempts at the concentration of production. Houses used for domestic weaving remain at Van Bijlandtstraat. In 1812, when 320 looms were in use, the industry employed about 4500 workers, due to heavy demand from France, particularly for military uniforms. After 1830 the industry lost its access to the Belgian market, and moved towards mass production. Dutch military orders stimulated growth. Wages were low, but most workers had strips of land for growing potatoes and raising goats or pigs. A further period of growth in the 1860s was stimulated in part by the American Civil War. An inventory of 1979 identified fifty-two surviving textile mills, of which the Mommers complex was chosen as the location for a textile museum. Restoration began in 1983 of buildings comprising spinning and warping sheds of 1885–94, an engine and boiler house of 1885, the owner's house of 1889, and the surrounding workers' houses. Some machines in the mill are still employed for commercial production. Traditional tapestry production and damask weaving are demonstrated on original equipment. Goirkestraat, where the museum is situated, was the focus of the textile industry until the 1960s. One of the few remaining factories, the AaBe plant, shows how such complexes developed between 1920 and 1960. The municipal archives in St Josephstraat, in a former flannel factory (the oldest part adapted from a military barracks of the 1840s), includes many documents from the textile industry.

The chief engineering works of the Dutch railways developed from the 1860s along Lange Nieuwstraat and Atelierstraat, and is the largest industrial complex in the town. The Scryption probably has the world's largest collection of typewriters and office equipment. The Koningshoeve brewery is one of the last surviving nineteenth-century monastic breweries, and now brews 'trappiste' for a large Belgian brewing company.

At Geertruidenberg, 27 km (17 mi.) N. where the River Donge joins the Bergse Maas, the Donge power station of the 1920s has been a distributor station since the completion of the much larger Amer station, 1 km ($\frac{1}{2}$ mi.) N., after World War II. The area extending 30 km (19 mi.) between Geertruidenberg and 's Hertogenbosch, 30 km (19 mi.) to the east, known as the 'Langstraat', was a major centre of leatherworking and shoemaking, with almost six hundred small companies active in the 1870s. Waalwijk, 15 km (9 mi.) N. of Tilburg, the chief shoemaking town, has a major museum of leatherworking.

At 's Hertogenbosch, the capital of the province, the original platform awnings of 1896 at the railway station are threatened by modernization plans. The Grasso Royal Machine Works west of the station remain in use, but local government policies have forced manufacturers to leave the city centre. The nineteenth-century cigar factory at Boschveldweg has been adapted as artists' workshops and a mosque. Several coffee-roasting factories have disappeared, but the Drie Mollen works of 1818 retains its original shop where coffee and tea are sold. The square watertower of 1885 contains youth workers' offices after four floors were created inside.

At Oss, 15 km (9 mi.) NE of 's Hertogenbosch, are several buildings linked with nineteenth-century margarine production. After the process of making margarine was discovered by the French chemist Mège Mouriès (1817–80) in 1870, Anthony Jurgens of Oss bought the patent for preparing 'butterine', as it was then known, in 1871. His competitor Van den Bergh started in 1873 but transferred his activities to ROTTERDAM. The two companies merged in 1921 and now form part of Unilever. Several villas and office blocks belonging to the two companies remain.

The Lips Autotron Transport Park at Rosmalen, 2 km (1$\frac{1}{2}$ mi.) NE of 's Hertogenbosch, has over four hundred vehicles, including an 1885 Benz.

A printing museum at Etten-Leur, 35 km (22 mi.) W. of Tilburg, has presses ranging in date from 1790 to 1921, and a complete printing office of c.1910. Research has shown traces of almost 300 km (200 mi.) of peat canals dug in the region before 1750.

BIBLIOGRAPHY
General
Griffiths, 1979; Kappelhof and Zeeuws, 1979; Leenders, 1989; Van den Eerenbeemt, 1977; Van Gorp, 1984, 1987.

LOCATIONS
[M] Autotron Themapark Vervoer (Transport Theme Park), Graafsebaan 133, Rosmalen.
[M] Drukkerijmuseum (Printing Museum), Leeuwerik 8, Etten-Leur.
[M] Nederlands Leer-en Schoenenmuseum (Netherland Leather and Shoe Museum), Elzenweg 25, Waalwijk.
[M] Nederlands Textielmuseum (Netherlands Textile Museum), Goirkestraat 96, Tilburg.
[M] Scryption (writing and typewriter museum), Spoorlaan 434a, Tilburg.

JURRIE VAN DALEN

tiles Thin slabs of clayware used for covering roofs, floors, walls and hearths, for lining sinks and other sanitary appliances, and tanks used for various purposes, and for the decoration of the interiors and exteriors of buildings. Floor tiles are often called quarries. Tiles may be hand-moulded, machine-pressed or extruded. The most ornamental tiles are floor and wall tiles. The Victorian revival of decorative tiles followed from experiments by Herbert Minton (1793–1858) in the 1820s. In 1830 Samuel Wright of Shelton, Staffordshire, patented a process for making encaustic tiles using medieval techniques: a slab of plastic clay was impressed with a pattern, the resulting recess being filled with a liquid clay slip of contrasting colour. Mass production became possible with the application of Thomas Prosser's patent of 1840 for using powdered dust clay which could be fed into hand- and later steam-powered machines. A variety of techniques was developed for decorating wall tiles: glazing over relief patterns, transfer printing and hand painting permitted a remarkable kaleidoscope of effects, used widely for house porches, public houses and large commercial and public buildings.

The largest British manufacturers included Minton of Stoke-on-Trent, and Maw & Co. of Jackfield, Shropshire. Maw & Co. introduced the steam-driven tile press in 1873. The technology and artistry of decorative tile manufacture was introduced to the USA about the time of the Philadelphia Centennial Exhibition of 1876 and further developed in the Boston region. In Portugal and elsewhere strong pre-industrial traditions of decorative tile manufacture have formed the basis of large, mass-production enterprises.

BIBLIOGRAPHY
General
Austwick and Austwick, 1980; Barnard, 1972; Berendson, 1957; Carter and Hidden, 1937; Hamilton, 1978; Lefèvre, 1900; Lockett, 1979; van Lemmen, 1979.
Specific
Herbert, A. T. *The Jackfield Decorative Tile Industry*. Telford: Ironbridge Gorge Museum Trust, 1979.
Herbert, A. T. Jackfield decorative tiles in use. In *IAR*, III, 1979.

MICHAEL STRATTON

tilt hammer The earliest form of powered hammer, used in the iron trade to deliver light blows in rapid succession. It comprised a hammer head at one end of a haft and a fulcrum in the centre, and is operated by cams on a shaft connected to a water wheel or steam engine at the opposite end. Usually it had a spring beam over the hammer head to increase the effectiveness of the blows, and sometimes a recoil block under the tail to increase the spring action.

BIBLIOGRAPHY
General
Gale, 1969, 1971.

timber Wood for the construction of houses or ships, usually after it has been trimmed and squared. 'Standing timber' is a term applied to growing trees capable of yielding wood for such purposes. A technical definition is the 'trunk, stem or body of a tree after it has attained the diameter of 8 in. [20.32 cm]' (Bale and Bale, 1924).

BIBLIOGRAPHY
General
Bale and Bale, 1924.

time-ball station An official establishment visually communicating the exact time to facilitate the correction of ships' chronometers. The concept was devised by Captain Robert Wauchope, RN, in 1818, tested at Portsmouth in 1829, and installed at Greenwich in 1833. A ball slid down a mast at exactly 1 p.m. (13.00 hrs). Invariably added to existing buildings such as telegraph towers, time-ball stations were soon established throughout the world: in Mauritius in 1833, St Helena in 1834, Cape Town in 1836, the USA in 1838, and Liverpool in 1844. Those at Dover, of 1855, and LYTTELTON of 1876 have been restored. Discs, boards and guns have also been used as time signals.

BIBLIOGRAPHY
Specific
Bartky, I. R. and Dick, S. J. The first time balls. In *Journal for the History of Astronomy*, XII, 1981.

tin (Sn) An elemental metal, and one of the first used by man, but as late as 1800 world production was no more than about 9000 tonnes per year. By 1900 it had increased to 75 000 tonnes and by 1940 to 238 000 tonnes, due largely to the growth of the CANNING industry. Previously tin had been used chiefly as a constituent of PEWTER and BRONZE, and for the manufacture of TINPLATE, as well as in solders, and in glazes and mordants. CORNWALL, where the ores occurred in close proximity to copper ores, was the principal European source. In more recent times Malaysia, Bolivia and China have been the major producers. 'Block tin' is metallic tin refined and cast into blocks.

Tin ores are found in alluvial deposits and in lodes. The principal ore is cassiterite, which in alluvial deposits has been deposited by natural processes of erosion from other rocks and transportation by water. Most of the world's tin, other than that in Cornwall and Bolivia, has been worked from such deposits, often using hydraulic monitors or dredging.

Cornwall has been the principal European source of tin ore from veins. In the 1850s Britain supplied about one-third of the world's tin from about three hundred mines, many of which were of considerable longevity. From the 1880s, with the development of new sources elsewhere, the British industry declined. It was from the Cornish tin mines that mining techniques were exported throughout the world. Steam engines for pumping, equipment for rockbreaking and dressing, and above all skills in STOPING were all highly developed in the Cornish mines of the nineteenth century.

From the early eighteenth century tin ore dressing began with crushing under powered STAMPS. The ore was then separated from waste materials by BUDDLES or other washing and flotation processes, including JIGGING and SHAKING TABLES.

Tin was smelted in BLOWING HOUSES until the late nineteenth century, and in coal-fired reverberatory furnaces from the late seventeenth century. It is now refined by electrolysis.

BIBLIOGRAPHY
General
Barton, 1968, 1971.

IVOR J. BROWN

tinplate Tinplate is wrought iron or steel sheet thinly plated with tin. It is the essential raw material of the canning industry. In the eighteenth century tinplate was used for many household utensils in the basic forms of the box, the cylinder and the cone. Sheet iron was first rolled for making tinplate by JOHN HANBURY *c*.1720, and the process of manufacture remained much the same until World War II. Plates are rolled to the gauge required and sheared to the desired width; they were then 'pickled' in a tank of acid, washed, annealed, cold-rolled with emery and oil, re-washed and scoured. Next they were put in a pot of grease before immersion in a bath of molten tin, and finally they were dried in a succession of other pots. The electrolytic tinning process introduced in World War II has completely superseded older methods, which are displayed at KIDWELLY. Traditional tinplate workers' shops can be seen at IRONBRIDGE and Sturbridge (*see* MASSACHUSETTS).

See also WHITESMITH.

BIBLIOGRAPHY
General
Ferrner, 1759–60; Gale, 1969; Percy, 1864.

Tiranë, Albania The capital of Albania, and location of the national museums and the national university. There is a vast Soviet-built Palace of Culture, housing the Museum of the Struggle for National Liberation, on Skenderbeg Square. Entrance is past a large statue of Enver Hoxha (*see* ALBANIA), and a display of anti-aircraft guns. There are excellent prehistoric, classical and medieval galleries. Twentieth-century galleries concentrate on the struggle for national independence, but contain few artefacts apart from Hoxha's Olivetti typewriter.

BIBLIOGRAPHY
General
Ward, 1983.

LOCATIONS
[M] Museum of Archaeology and Ethnography, Institute of Scientific Research in History and Linguistics, State University, Tiranë.
[M] Museum of the Struggle for National Liberation, Tiranë.

TNT Trinitro-toluene or Trotyl, a military explosive manufactured from toluene, itself derived from naphtha, and mixed with ammonium nitrate as 'amatols' in shells

Figure 157 The time-ball
station of 1876 at
Lyttelton, New Zealand,
which was designed by
Thomas Crane; it is in the
custody of the New Zealand
Historic Places Trust.
New Zealand Historic Places
Trust

Figure 158   Chopped and fermented tobacco leaf being ground into 'ordinary' snuff at the Morlaix (Finistère) manufactory of the SEITA, the French national tobacco monopoly; this particular mill was built in 1870.
E. Revault, CNMHS

and bombs. Production developed in Britain during World War I.

BIBLIOGRAPHY
General
Reader, 1970.

tobacco   The plant *Tabacum nicotiana*, the smoking of which was observed by Christopher Columbus (1451–1506) in Cuba and had spread throughout Europe by 1700. Tobacco was first taken as SNUFF through the nose or by chewing, then by smoking CIGARS. Tobacco was cultivated in Eastern Europe, where it remains an important crop, and in colonies like Virginia, where the leaves were cured on plantations and exported in HOGSHEADS. Until well into the eighteenth century imported bales of tobacco were processed in small towns prior to sale by mercers, and in large towns by specialist tobacconists, using 'tobacco engines' for cutting. Some processing took place in TOBACCO WAREHOUSES. In Seville, the 200 m (600 ft.) long Fabrica de Tabacos, now part of the university, was built from 1728, and by 1840 factories using steam-powered cutting machinery had been established in London, but it was the growing popularity of the CIGARETTE in the second half of the nineteenth century that brought about the concentration of tobacco processing in large factories. A machine for wrapping tobacco was patented by William Rose (*c*.1865–1929) of Gainsborough in 1885, and his company subsequently made packaging machinery for chocolate and blue for bleaching.

The tobacco trade has been a state monopoly in several countries including FRANCE, ITALY and AUSTRIA. Several twentieth-century tobacco factories are buildings of architectural distinction. They include the Yenidze factory in DRESDEN, a reinforced concrete building in oriental style with a glass dome flanked by minarets, designed by Martin Hammitzsch in 1909; the elegant steel and glass van Nelle factory at Rotterdam, by Brinkmann & van der Vlucht, of 1927–9; a concrete building of 1936–7 by PETER BEHRENS and Alexander Popp at LINZ; and a factory by Pier Luigi Nervi (1891–1979) of 1952, at Bologna. There is an important collection of tobacco-working artefacts in BRISTOL Industrial Museum.

BIBLIOGRAPHY
General
Dodd, 1843; Holme, 1688.

BARRIE TRINDER

tobacco pipe   The long porous stems of clay smoking

pipes absorb nicotine, and pipes were being made for smoking tobacco as early as 1570. The chief centre in England by the 1630s was Broseley (*see* IRONBRIDGE). There were two principal types: those made of a single piece, as used in northern and western Europe, and those used in eastern Europe where only the bowl was of ceramic. Pipes made of clay lacking iron oxide fire to a white colour. A clay tobacco pipe is shaped by hand-moulding and then forced into a metal mould with a wire inserted to form the stem. Pipes were typically fired in saggars in small KILNS.

BIBLIOGRAPHY
General
Searle, 1929–30; Walker, 1977.

tobacco warehouse A building designed specifically for handling tobacco might be a bonded warehouse (*see* BOND) and might contain facilities for removing tobacco leaves from the HOGSHEADS in which they were imported, and pressing them. On account of the danger of fire many warehouses were of iron-framed construction, and most had wall cranes – operated manually in the early nineteenth century and later by hydraulic power – for lifting hogsheads. Damaged tobacco was destroyed by Customs authorities, who might have an adjacent 'pipe' for burning it. A specialist 64 m × 55 m (210 ft. × 180 ft.) bonded warehouse which could accommodate 7000 hogsheads of tobacco was built at the King's Dock, Liverpool, as early as 1792–3, and the partly iron-framed 'New Tobacco' warehouse (later the Skin Floor) in London Docks in 1811–13. The twelve-storey warehouse at Stanley Dock, Liverpool, 221 m (725 ft.) long, 50 m (165 ft.) wide and 38 m (125 ft.) high, with 14.5 ha (36 ac.) of floor space, which was constructed by George Fosbury Lyster in 1900, was the world's largest tobacco warehouse in 1950.

BIBLIOGRAPHY
General
Ritchie-Noakes, 1984.
Specific
Thorne, R. Rebirth of a rogue: origins of the skin floor. In *Architectural Journal*, 23 July 1986.

BARRIE TRINDER

Tokomaru, Manawatu, New Zealand A steam-engine museum, developed from the mid-1960s in a region where there were seven flax mills in the early twentieth century, all powered by steam and served by railways. The collection includes a 138 hp Tangye sawmill engine of 1904; a 50 hp horizontal engine and winch by Appleby Bros., London, built for a patent shipbuilding SLIP, at Wellington, in 1869; an 0–4–4T geared locomotive from a logging railway, built by Climax of Pennsylvania in 1904; a similar locomotive built in New Zealand in 1920; and a New Zealand-built 20 hp portable log hauler by Vulcan Foundries of Napier, of 1925.

BIBLIOGRAPHY
Specific
Rennie, N. *The Tokomaru Steam Engine Museum.* Tokomaru, n.d.

LOCATION
[M] Tokomaru Steam Engine Museum, Main Highway 57, Tokomaru, Manawatu.

Tolbuhin (Tolbukhin, Tolbuchin, Dobritch), Varna, Bulgaria An old established market town in South Dobrudja on the main road and rail route from Varna to Constanta in Romania. The region was under Romanian control in the 1920s and 30s. The town takes its present name from the Red Army marshal who liberated Bulgaria in 1944. Tolbuhin's industrial development was chiefly linked with agriculture. Its post-war expansion has included the construction of a 'Street of the Crafts', opened in 1984 and inspired by the museum at ETA. It consists of rows of modern buildings on either side of an open street near the centre of the town. The complex includes a bakery, a hatter's shop, a wood turnery, a book bindery, spinning and weaving shops, a saddler's workshop, a pottery, and a workshop where bagpipes are made. An exhibition hall displays the work of some sixteen to twenty local craftsmen in coopering, copperbeating and other skills.

LOCATION
[M] Regional Historical Museum, Bul. Lenin, Tolbuhin.

Toledo, Toledo, Castile, Spain The former Spanish capital, 72 km (45 mi.) S. of Madrid, stands above a dramatic gorge on the River Tagus, which is crossed by one of the world's most celebrated stone arches, the Alcántara Bridge, constructed by the Romans and many times rebuilt. The station of 1914–17 was designed by the architect Narcisco Claveria and is inspired by Moorish influences. Craftsmen in Toledo continue to make the fine metalwork for which the city is famous, especially Damascene (*see* DAMASK), black steel inlaid with gold, silver and copper wire decoration.

tollgate A barrier at which tolls were collected from travellers, most commonly on a road (*see* TURNPIKE) but sometimes on a navigable waterway. The Irish politician, Sir Henry Parnell (1776–1842) considered that gates should never be at the top or bottom of a hill, that they should be painted white to aid visibility, and that they should be well lit. In most countries where turnpike styles of road administration prevailed, it was usual to build houses for tollkeepers alongside gates. Parnell argued that tolls could be increased if honest tollkeepers could be attracted by good-quality houses. Many tollgates and tollhouses are displayed in open-air museums (*see* ARNHEM; BOKRIJK; IRONBRIDGE; ST FAGANS).

BIBLIOGRAPHY
General
Parnell, 1838.

Specific
Kanefsky, J. *Devon Tollhouses*. Exeter: Exeter Industrial Archaeology Group, 1976.

toluene   *See* METHYL BENZENE.

Tomar, Ribatejo, Portugal   A spinning and weaving mill, 105 km (65 mi.) NE of Lisbon, the first cotton mill of the British type in Portugal, established in 1789 by J. Ratton and T. Lecusson Verdier. In 1882 an electric lighting plant, also the first in Portugal, was set up in the factory. Many other interesting industrial buildings remain in Tomar, including the sixteenth-century mills of El-Rei and old papermills, all powered by the River Nabão. The first hydraulic wine press in the region was installed in the late nineteenth century by M. Mendes Codinho, who, in 1912, constructed a modern corn mill which remains in operation.

BIBLIOGRAPHY
Specific
Guimarães, M. de S. *Historia de uma Fábrica* (The history of a factory). Santarém: Junta Distrital, 1976.

toolmaking   A term referring to the preparation of tool steel, frequently fixtures and JIGS, or dies for pressing, stamping, die casting or extruding metals, or for injection moulding and similar processes in plastic manufacture, to be used in the mass production of solid objects. A press working die, utilized in shaping sheet metal into predetermined shapes and configurations, is of two parts: the 'punch' and 'die', or 'male' and 'female'. The department within a factory where tools are prepared is called a toolroom.

Toronto, Ontario, Canada   Canada's principal commercial city, situated on the north shore of Lake Ontario, Toronto dates from the military post, Fort York, established in 1793 in the new colony of Upper Canada. The municipality of Toronto dates from 1834. Through the nineteenth century the city consolidated its position as the government and financial centre of the province and as a port for wheat exports, especially after railways linking the city with Georgian Bay and Lake Huron ports facilitated Midwest and later prairie linkages. Manufacturing developed to provision the prosperous agrarian hinterland; the firm of Massey-Harris (later Massey-Ferguson) prospered as a major agricultural implement firm after a move to Toronto from Newcastle, Ontario, in 1844. Meat-packing, brewing, flourmilling, and papermaking also developed in the city. Relatively few historic industrial buildings survive, one of the most important being the Gooderham & Worts Distillery of 1832. One of the first papermills in Ontario was at Todmorden, on the Don River, then a rural site but now within Toronto, where a brewery and sawmill had developed in the 1790s. Eventually three papermills developed in the valley, one of which (Todmorden Mills) is now maintained by the Borough of East York. Another functions nearby, having

shifted from rag sources to wood PULP after the invention of the sulphite process in the 1860s.

The focus of much of Toronto's economic activity was a vast lakeside complex of railway marshalling yards that served adjacent factories and warehouses. In recent decades the sidings have been replaced, symbolically, by other means of communication: the Canadian National telecommunications tower, a convention centre, the Canadian Broadcasting Corporation studios, a symphony hall, and a domed sports stadium. Many of the factories and warehouses survive, but retro-fitted for restaurants, studios and offices. The port function has diminished considerably, the lakeside elevators and warehouses now largely gone in the van of revitalization for 'urban festival venues' and luxury housing initiated by the federal government's Harbourfront park development since the 1970s. There are other concentrations of industrial buildings along the railway axis to the north-west of downtown, including the Massey-Ferguson works (now closed and likely to be demolished and redeveloped) and the Canada Packers meat-processing plants in Toronto Junction, and to the north-east the planned industrial suburb of Leaside, built after 1913 by the Canadian Northern Railway. Garment factories along Spadina Avenue date from the 1910s and 1920s and are still the core of the city's fashion district, but the extensive complex of factories, warehouses and mail-order departments associated at the beginning of the twentieth century with the national chain T. Eaton & Co. was demolished to make way for the extensive galleria-styled Eaton Centre in the 1970s.

Toronto has an extensive streetcar network, and an underground railway (subway) which opened in 1954, both built to the unusual gauge of 4 ft. $10\frac{3}{4}$ in. (1.492 m).

Toronto's principal historical monuments are its downtown office blocks. In few other great cities is it possible to see such clear evidence of the evolution of the administrative buildings used by banks, insurance companies and the headquarters staff of other large concerns. These range from rugged stone-built, non-frame-construction, historicist-styled, three- and four-storey blocks of the late nineteenth century, like the Confederation Life Building of 1889–91; through early steel-framed ten- to twenty-storey skyscrapers built before 1914 (several of which claimed the title 'Tallest Building in the British Empire' when completed), and the thirty-two-storey sleek Canadian Bank of Commerce tower of 1929–32; to the elegant purity of towers designed by MIES VAN DER ROHE in the 1960s, and other taller towers in the International style of the 1970s and 1980s. It was and still is in these King Street towers that enterprises capitalized and then managed mining, lumbering, railroads, real estate and financial services for the national economy. The Toronto street railway developers Mackenzie & Mann created an empire of utilities and railways, first in Ontario and the Canadian West, then in Spain and Latin America, especially Brazil (today's Brascan), managed from a number of office buildings along King Street.

Some grand houses associated with the city's plutocrats survive, the most fanciful being Casa Loma, a castle-like landmark built for Sir Henry Pellatt, who profited from Niagara-based utilities. Fort York records the earliest phases of the city's history, and barracks of a subsequent fort now house a marine museum. Discussions about a museum for the city have focused on transforming the Gooderham & Worts Distillery or the Depression-era former Stock Exchange on Bay Street.

BIBLIOGRAPHY
General
Kealey, 1980; Lemon, 1985; Newell and Greenhill, 1989; Russell, 1984.
Specific
Spelt, J. Toronto: the evolution of an urban landscape. In *Journal of Geography*, LXXXIII, 1984. Macombe, Ill.: Western Illinois University.

LOCATIONS
[S] Historic Fort York, Fleet Street and Strachan Avenue, Toronto.
[M] Marine Museum of Upper Canada, Exhibition Place, Lakeshore Boulevard West, Toronto M6K 3B9.
[M] Royal Ontario Museum, 100 Queen's Park, Toronto, Ontario M5S 2C6.
[M,S] Todmorden Mills Museum Park, 67 Pottery Road, Toronto.

DERYCK HOLDSWORTH

Tôrre de Moncorvo, Trás-os-Montes, Portugal   An iron-mining centre, 150 km (90 mi.) E. of Oporto. There were workings here in Roman times. The mines are now closed, but there is a small museum of iron at Carvalhal, 8 km (5 mi.) E. The remains of the ironworks of 1781 at Chapa Cunha were excavated in 1983. Other important industrial buildings in the town include a blanket factory, now disused, with its machinery remaining *in situ*; a communal wax press; and a fireworks factory at Felgar, 10 km (6 mi.) NE, regarded as one of the best in Portugal. At Pocinho, 11 km (7 mi.) SW, a steel bridge, 245 m (804 ft.) long, spans the River Douro.

BIBLIOGRAPHY
General
Custódio and Barros, 1984.
Specific
Júnior, J. R. dos Santos. Lagar comunitário de cera Felgueiras-Moncorvo (The communal wax press at Felgueiras-Moncorvo). In *Trabalhos de Antropologia e Etnologia*, XXIV, 1983.

LOCATION
[M] Museum of Iron, Carvalhal.

Torres Novas, Ribatejo, Portugal   A town with paper and cotton factories of the early nineteenth century, 110 km (68 mi.) NE of Lisbon. There are remains of dams and water mills along the River Almonda which supplied the factories with power. Local industries are depicted in the Ethnographic Museum.

LOCATIONS
[M] Carlos Reis Municipal Museum, Largo do Salvador, Torres Novas.
[M] Ethnographic Museum, Torres Novas.

Torres Vedras, Estremadura, Portugal   The main town of the Região do Oeste (Western Region), 40 km (25 mi.) N. of Lisbon. The region has one of the most important groups of windmills in Europe. An excavation in 1988 revealed remains of an ice manufactory, which a stone slab showed to have been that built by the Court ice-seller in 1782.

LOCATION
[M] Municipal Museum, R. Serpa Pinto 7, Torres Vedras

Tourcoing, Nord, France   *See* LILLE.

Tournai (Doornik), Hainaut, Belgium   A substantial town on the River Scheldt (Schelde) where the traditional manufacture of carpets for Brussels still employed over two thousand in the 1860s. Several former woollen and flax factories remain, among them the Château Boucher of 1834 which overlooks the river, and there is a neo-Classical former slaughterhouse of 1833–5 by Bruno Renard in the rue de l'Arsenal. Much nineteenth-century textile workers' housing survives, including single-storey terraces in the chaussée de Renaix. The valley between Tournai and Antoing, 7 km ($4\frac{1}{2}$ mi.) SE, was important for lime-burning, with more than a hundred kilns in the late nineteenth century, many of which survive. Tournai's historical museum includes a chemist's shop, looms, clogmaker's and pipemaker's workshops, and a dog mill. There are museums of building construction at Ramegnies-Chin, 12 km (7 mi.) NE and of stone-working at Antoing.

BIBLIOGRAPHY
General
Linters, 1986a; Viaene, 1986.

LOCATIONS
[M] Musée de Folklore (Folk-life Museum), Reduit des Sions, 7500 Tournai.
[M] Musée d'Histoire, d'Archéologie et des Arts Decoratifs (Museum of History, Archaeology and Decorative Arts), rue des Carmes 8, 7500 Tournai.
[M] Musée de la Pierre (Stone Museum), Stade d'Antoing, 7640 Antoing.
[M] Pré-musée des Arts et Métiers de la Construction (Museum of Building Construction), chaussée de Tournai 50, 7721 Ramegnies-Chin.

BARRIE TRINDER

tow   A string of barges, tied together with cables and pushed by teams of TUG boats. Tows are the form in which great masses of bulk cargo pass along major navigable rivers in North America.

tower mill   A type of WINDMILL, in which a stone, brick or flint tower supports a revolving cap in which the sails are set. It was introduced to Europe in about the fourteenth century. Towers were also used for HORIZONTAL WINDMILLS.

town gas   Gas that is distributed through mains for

domestic and general commercial and industrial use, whether COAL GAS (to which WATER GAS or PRODUCER GAS may have been added), gas produced from oil, METHANE obtained from coal workings, or NATURAL GAS. A typical mixture might be 56 per cent hydrogen, 23 per cent methane, and 11 per cent carbon monoxide.

toymaking   The term applied in Britain to the manufacture of small fancy goods in metal – such as enamelled boxes – that were made on a lathe, or in a stamping machine or press. Toymaking developed rapidly in BIRMINGHAM between 1710 and 1760: PROBATE RECORDS for that period refer to toys displayed on mantelpieces. Through Matthew Boulton (*see* BOULTON & WATT) the skills developed in toymaking came to influence the development of the steam engine. In the nineteenth century the term was applied to the manufacture of more utilitarian steel articles – hammers, pincers, button-hooks and so on.

The manufacture of toys in the sense of children's playthings was a characteristic FOREST INDUSTRY. A range of objects for the entertainment and education of the young was produced in the great cities of Europe in the mid-nineteenth century, including microscopes, model trains, and musical instruments. Their production employed a great range of woodworking and metalworking skills as well as arts akin to those of the upholsterer and seamstress. Workers in green wood, who made wheeled toys from willow, birch and poplar, were termed Bristol toymakers. Toys for the rich included complex toy theatres, of which the first is thought to have been made in 1813. Fancy toys, mechanical and moving animals were fashioned from paper, wire, wood and papier mâché. Copper models were sold of most household utensils, while tinplate toys included mugs, guns and musical instruments. Detonating crackers were made in London by Italians.

Toys were extensively traded even in the seventeenth century, when wooden tops, windmills and ninepins from Nuremberg and the Black Forest and ceramic Dutch figures were widely available in England. By 1850 most toy trumpets and the poorer qualities of magic lantern sold in England were French, while English manufacturers sent quantities of toy guns to Australia. Factory production of toys began in the second half of the nineteenth century. The manufacture of model trains was pioneered in England by W. J. Bassett-Lowke (d.1953), who made high-quality models in Northampton from 1899, and in Germany by the Bing brothers and the Fleischmann brothers, whose factories were established in Nuremberg in 1865 and 1887 respectively. Model cars became the speciality of Charles Rossignol, who started a toy factory in the Rue de Chemin Vert in Paris in 1868. The first manufacturer of high-quality teddy bears was Margaret Steiff (1847–1909), who published her first catalogue in 1894 (*see* GIENGEN AM DER BRENZ). The principal American toy concern was established by Louis Marx (b.1894), who specialized in mail-order sales. Frank Hornby (1863–1936) was the outstanding twentieth-century British manufacturer, setting up a factory in Liverpool to make Meccano construction kits, and producing Hornby model trains from 1920 and die-cast Dinky Toys from 1934. Since 1945 plastic has been increasingly used in toymaking, one of the outstanding products being Lego construction kits (*see* BILLUND).

BIBLIOGRAPHY
General
King, 1978; Mayhew, 1849–50; Priestley and Fenner, 1985; Richardson, 1981; Rowlands, 1975.
Specific
Robinson, E. The Boulton and Fothergill Manufactory. In *University of Birmingham Historical Journal*, VII, 1959.
Robinson, E. Eighteenth-century commerce and fashion. In *EcHR*, 2nd ser., XVI, 1965–6.

LOCATION
[M] Bethnal Green Museum, Cambridge Heath Road, London E2 9PA.

BARRIE TRINDER

traction engine   A self-propelling unit for hauling loads along roads, without a platform for carrying loads. It usually consists of a simple or compound engine with slide valves, mounted on a locomotive-type boiler, with two- or three-speed transmission to the rear wheels. Traction engines are often fitted with power take-offs, in the form of winches for timber clearing, or driving machinery. The most elaborate were FAIRGROUND engines, which often had dynamos to provide power and lighting for roundabouts and other machines.

BIBLIOGRAPHY
General
Clark, 1960; Hughes, 1968.
Specific
Watkins, G. Steam power: an illustrated guide. In *Industrial Archaeology*, IV, 1970.

trade secret   One method of according indefinite protection to innovative technical knowledge, other than by PATENTS, which have limited lives, has been to preserve trade secrets. Hidden knowledge has been declared in courts of law as a legitimate method of shielding manufacturing techniques or formulae from competitors, although no legal defence exists against accidental disclosure, or attempts to reverse-engineer a product to determine its constituents or method of manufacture. No registries of trade secrets exist, making problematical their direct use in historical research.

BIBLIOGRAPHY
Specific
Shayt, D. H. Manufacturing secrecy: the dueling cymbalmakers of North America. In *IA*, XV, 1989.

trade token   A token made by a tradesman to enable him to pay his workmen during shortages of legal tender; usually it has only local currency. In England tokens were used in the seventeenth century but were driven out by new issues of copper coins. There was a new outbreak of token-issuing between 1787 and 1817 by entrepreneurs like THOMÀS WILLIAMS and JOHN WILKINSON. Most tokens were of copper but a few silver tokens were struck in 1811–12. Tokens became illegal in 1817. Tokens illustrate many aspects of contemporary industry, including mine headstocks, looms, blast furnaces, glassworks, bridges, river and canal vessels, and road vehicles.

BIBLIOGRAPHY
General
Dalton and Hamer, 1910; Mathias, 1962.

trading estate An INDUSTRIAL ESTATE, particularly one built under the British government's Special Areas (Amendment) Act 1937, designed to reduce unemployment. There are notable examples at Treforest in South Wales, Team Valley in County Durham, and North Hillington, Glasgow. Most concerns on such estates engage in lighter forms of manufacturing or warehousing.

BIBLIOGRAPHY
General
Mowat, 1955.

trail A means of interpreting a historic landscape: an itinerary around a series of features of historic, architectural or ecological interest. Guidance on what can be seen is usually provided by a leaflet, but sometimes on graphic panels or by a tape player. Viewing points may be indicated by numbers or symbols. The use of trails is often linked with HERITAGE CENTRES.

train oil A term usually applied to oil obtained by boiling the blubber of whales, but occasionally applied to fish and seal oils. Stearin, or whale TALLOW, is separated by freezing. Train oil is used for treating wood, in TAWING and dressing FLAX, and in oil lamps. Oil from the sperm whale is used as a lubricant for particularly delicate machinery.

tramcar A single- or double-decked public transport vehicle, employing horse, steam, cable, electric or some other form of mechanical power to propel it along rails let into the road surface. Traditionally, although not exclusively, tramcars can be driven from either end, which eliminates turning at termini. In the USA, tramcars are called 'trolleys', 'trolley cars' or 'streetcars'.

See also CABLE TRAM; ELECTRIC TRAM; HORSE TRAM; STEAM TRAM.

BIBLIOGRAPHY
General
Central Electric Railfans' Association, 1986.

tram depot A building where TRAMCARS are stored and maintained when not in service: in the USA it is called a car barn. Most are single-storey, but there were multi-storey examples in New York City and elsewhere in the USA. Each features a series of parallel tramlines termed 'roads', capable of storing several trams, with inspection pits running beneath for all or part of their length, and a traverser at one end to permit trams to be moved between roads. Some form of tramcar washing facilities, plus stores and shops to permit running repairs, are usually found at each depot, although on larger systems these may be centralized. Depots built for HORSE TRAMS may retain the extensive stables, provender and manure stores required for this mode of operation (*see* VIENNA). A depot will usually be embellished with the name and insignia of the municipality or operating company.

tramp steamer A vessel that did not sail along regular routes (*see* LINER) but carried whatever cargoes were available to it. The term was used from the 1880s, and usually applied to steamers although sailing vessels also took part in this trade. Preserved vessels include:

- *Amadeo*, 1884: a 412-ton Liverpool-built, iron-hulled steamship, protected as a historical relic at Estancia San Gregorio, Chile.
- *Vorwarts*, 1903: a 8730-ton steamship, at Rostock, Germany, where she was built.
- *Hestmanden*, 1911: a 755-ton steamer, at Trondheim, Norway.
- *Skælskør*, 1915: a 49-ton coastal steamer, at Roskilde, Denmark.

BIBLIOGRAPHY
General
Brouwer, 1985; Metaxas, 1971.

tram stop Unlike the first buses, tramcars had authorized stopping places along each route, at which the tramway operator sometimes saw fit to place some kind of shelter. At first this might have been an old horse-tram body, but this would in time be replaced by a purpose-built shelter, constructed from local materials or prefabricated in cast iron. Larger town and city termini featured more elaborate shelter designs, often incorporating cast-iron columns, glass roofs, and coloured glass panels. Such shelters afforded protection from the elements. Stops along exposed tram routes, and on heavily-used lines like that along Blackpool (*see* FYLDE) seafront, were built on a scale approaching that of railway stations.

See also figure 38.

tramway A term used from the late eighteenth century to denote a small or temporary railway, employing man-, horse- or mechanical power. Laid in a mine, quarry or manufacturing establishment, it was used for the movement of freight (*see* PLATEWAY).

More commonly 'tramway' describes a system of public transport, usually using electrically-powered TRAMCARS which run on grooved rails set into and flush with the road surface, and draw current from overhead wires.

See also CABLE TRAM; CAR BARN; ELECTRIC TRAM; HORSE TRAM; STEAM TRAM; TRAMCAR; TRAM DEPOT; TRAM STOP.

transfer of technology Manufacturing on an industrial scale is a complex cultural process. The replication in one country of a process carried on with success in another

771

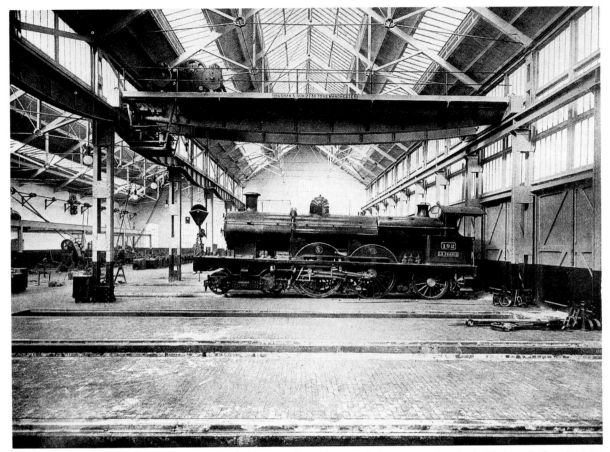

Figure 159 An example of the transfer of technology in the early twentieth century: the Great Western Railway's 4-4-2 compound locomotive No. 102 *La France*, to the design of Alfred de Glehn, ordered in 1903 by the company's Chief Mechanical Engineer, George Jackson Churchward, from the Société Alsacienne de Constructions Mécaniques of Mulhouse. The GWR operated four such locomotives, but the four-cylinder simple 4-6-0 became the company's standard express passenger traction. *La France* is depicted in the locomotive depot at Old Oak Common, London, in a catalogue issued by the Vaughan Crane Company of Manchester in 1920.

Ironbridge Gorge Museum Trust

depends on the availability of comparable raw materials, of an effective infrastructure providing tools, containers, and other essential equipment, and above all on amenable and appropriately skilled workers. Studies in recent decades have shown the complexity of the process by which the technologies developed in eighteenth-century England were transferred elsewhere, particularly in the establishment of coal-using ironworks in France, and of textile manufactures in the USA. Neither INDUSTRIAL ESPIONAGE, in the sense of obtaining information about processes, nor the acquisition of PATENT rights were sufficient bases for the establishment of new manufacturing concerns – the experienced practitioner was the most efficient agent of international diffusion of technology. Many industrial processes of the eighteenth and nineteenth centuries, such as the sinking of coal mines, the operation and maintenance of reverberatory furnaces, and the manufacture of refractory crucibles, depended on

visual and tactile experience, and on manual dexterity, which could not be taught from textbooks nor passed on by spies. The presence of migrant workers in an industrial community may be reflected by a variety of archaeological evidence. Lowe (1977) has observed practices from Shropshire and Yorkshire in ironworks housing in South Wales; and the Combe des Mineurs at LE CREUSOT, apart from some superficial Gallic features, could well have been built in Shropshire. The CLUSTER HOUSE, the characteristic home of the skilled textile worker, originated in England in the 1790s, but spread to MULHOUSE and thence to Spain and the Ruhrgebiet. Rock-built cottages and chapels which could have been built in Redruth or Gwennap, as well as Cornish engine houses, reflect the presence of Cornishmen in non-ferrous metal mines in many parts of the world. Archaeological evidence may also survive of equipment which skilled workers found essential, like the refractory bricks from Stourbridge (*see* BLACK COUNTRY), which have been identified on ironworking sites in Australia and Pennsylvania.

From the mid-nineteenth century the transfer of technological knowledge became in some ways less dramatic, as intercontinental travel became easier, as the diffusion of new ideas was accelerated by technical literature, as companies came to acquire patent rights from overseas, and, in the late nineteenth century, as multinational corporations developed. The transfer of technology remained a complex process, dependent on many cultural factors. Motorcar factory managers in the 1920s found that making vehicles in Europe was different from making the same models with the same equipment in Detroit. Japanese entrepreneurs in Europe are having similar experiences in the 1990s. To transfer technology is analogous to transplanting a seedling: not just the strength of the seedling but the nature of the new seedbed will determine the quality of the mature plant.

BIBLIOGRAPHY
General
Habakkuk, 1967; Harris, 1972; Jeremy, 1981; Lowe, 1977.
Specific
Chandler, A. Anthracite coal and the beginnings of the Industrial Revolution in the United States. In *Business History Review*, XLVI, 1971.
Harris, J. R. Skills, coal and British industry in the eighteenth century. In *History*, LXI, 1976.
Harris, J. R. Industrial espionage in the eighteenth century. In *IAR*, 1985.
Harris, J. R. The diffusion of English metallurgical methods to eighteenth-century France. In *French History*, II, 1988.
Mathias, P. Skills and the diffusion of innovations from Britain in the eighteenth century. In *Transactions of the Royal Historical Society*, XXV, 1975.
Yates, W. R. Discovery of the process for making anthracite iron. In *Pennsylvania Magazine of History and Biography*, 1974.

BARRIE TRINDER

transport *See* AIR TRANSPORT; CANAL; RAILWAY; RIVER NAVIGATION; ROAD.

transporter bridge A type of bridge developed in the late nineteenth century, in which a platform carrying vehicles and pedestrians moves backwards and forwards across a river or canal: the platform is suspended from a trolley which travels on a girder running between two towers. Sixteen are known to have been constructed, the first, to the design of Alberto Palacio Elisagüe (1856–1931), at Portugalete near BILBAO in 1893, having a 162 m (530 ft.) span (*see* figure 9). The largest was the 305 m (1000 ft.) span between Runcorn and Widnes (*see* HALTON and figure 55), opened in 1905 and demolished in 1961. Examples survive at RENDSBURG, Newport (Gwent), TEESSIDE and Warrington; and transporter bridges once stood at Rouen (1899–1940) and Nantes (1903–57) in France and Duluth (1905–29) in the USA. The structure is known in the USA as an aerial lift bridge.

BIBLIOGRAPHY
General
Ashmore, 1982; Cossons, 1988.
Specific
Forbes, N. N. *Transporter Bridges*. Cardiff: Light Railway Transport League, 1970.

transport museum Of all industries, transport is perhaps best represented in museums, although a museum portraying something that implies movement is in part a contradiction in terms. The concern for historic transport artefacts shown in the nineteenth century is reflected in the numbers of early railway locomotives preserved throughout Europe and North America. The history of transport is portrayed in various classes of museum.

The principal museums of science and technology, like the Science Museum, London, the National Museum of American History at the Smithsonian Institution, Washington DC, and the Deutsches Museum in Munich, all have large transport collections which include many of the world's most important preserved vehicles.

Many museums are concerned with specific aspects of transport. Some are discussed under the headwords AIRCRAFT MUSEUM, MARITIME MUSEUM, MOTOR MUSEUM and RAILWAY MUSEUM. Others deal with topics like motorcycles, canals, trams, trolley buses and carriages. Museums in this category range from publicly-funded organizations with high standards, extensive archives and reserve collections, to small, privately-run concerns, largely in tourist areas, with a few motorcars or railway locomotives, which are museums in name only.

Major museums devoted specifically to transport, rather than to one aspect of it, are relatively few in number, those in LUCERNE, NUREMBERG and GLASGOW being some of the best European examples, while in the USA that at St Louis (*see* MISSOURI) is outstanding.

Museums are not the only bodies concerned with the conservation of transport artefacts. Most of the historic motorcars which are preserved are in private hands. In Britain more steam locomotives are held by PRESERVED RAILWAYS than by museums, and the operation of a significant length of a railway or canal retains for posterity something that could not be conserved in a museum. The experience of flying in the 1940s can be recaptured by flights in DC3s in the YUKON or Ju52s in ZURICH, but not in aircraft museums.

The International Association of Transport Museums evolved from the ICOM Committee 17, which was concerned with transport, at a meeting in Cologne in July 1968. It holds an annual conference, and produces a yearbook.

BIBLIOGRAPHY
General
Garvey, 1982; Simmons, 1970.
Specific
International Association of Transport Museums. *Yearbook*. I, Gdansk, 1974–; XIII/XIV, Bremerhaven, 1986/87.

LOCATIONS
[I] Association of British Transport Museums, c/o The Science Museum, Exhibition Road, London SW7 2DD.
[I] International Association of Transport Museums, c/o

Deutsches Schiffahrtsmuseum, Van-Ronzelen-Strasse, D-1850 Bremerhaven, Germany.

BARRIE TRINDER

travelling post office In 1838 the GJR adapted a carriage for sorting mail, and for picking up and dropping pouches of letters; it ran between Birmingham and Liverpool. Subsequently travelling sorting offices were developed in France (from 1840) and in most European countries, and many still operate, although no longer picking up and setting down mail while in motion. An example of 1885 is preserved at YORK, together with a replica of the 1838 vehicle. Methods of operating in the 1930s are vividly illustrated in the film *Night Mail* of 1936. Armoured post-vans were a feature of railroads in the USA.

treadmill A device powered by a large vertical tread-wheel, turned, usually internally, by an animal, often by a man or men. Treadwheel cranes for lifting and lowering building materials were used in antiquity, and some survive in medieval cathedrals. They were also used as mine hoists and as port cranes (*see* HARWICH; MOSELLE; RHINE). William Cubitt later adapted the device as a broad, externally-powered wheel, for use in prisons. These raised water, turned millstones or powered windsail fans for ventilation or to increase prisoners' demoralization. A treadwheel remains in the gaol at Beaumaris, Anglesey. Three were installed in the USA but none survives. Small internal treadwheels were used for turning roasting spits, usually operated by dogs: such mills were called dog wheels.

See also WEALD AND DOWNLAND MUSEUM.

BIBLIOGRAPHY
General
Major, 1978.
Specific
Shayt, D. H. Stairway to redemption: America's encounter with the British prison treadmill. *T & C*, xxx, 1989.

treatment works An establishment where sewage (*see* SEWAGE DISPOSAL) is treated. Almost every works is unique but the usual basis of treatment is that sewage passes through screens and then into grit channels, where grit is settled out to protect pumps and valves in subsequent parts of the system. It then goes to primary sedimentation tanks where primary or raw sludge is settled out, leaving settled sewage, which has the appearance of cloudy water. The settled sewage is oxidized by bacteria either in the Activated Sludge Process, in which air is forced in, or by biological filtration. In the Activated Sludge Process sludge is settled and returned to the head of the tank to maintain the bacterial population. The humus that sloughs off the biological filters is settled and goes back to the primary sludge tank. The 'clear, sparkling effluent' is discharged into a watercourse, or given tertiary treatment so that it can be so discharged. The raw sludge goes for anaerobic digestion, yielding fuel gas and secondary or digested sludge which is more easily dewatered and has only a slight tarry smell. The sludge is used as fertilizer, dumped or incinerated. From the mid-nineteenth century sludge was often dumped and allowed to drain on 'sewage farms'. Treatment works proper developed in the late nineteenth century. Oxidation may be achieved in circular or rectangular filter beds, which act as biological filters (pioneered by J. W. Dibdin in London in 1892); by the Imhoff system using compressed air in rectangular tanks; or by agitation in open tanks – the Activated Sludge Process, developed in MANCHESTER and Lawrence (*see* MASSACHUSETTS) in 1912.

The concrete ART DECO installation at Krefeld is architecturally one of the most distinguished treatment works.

BIBLIOGRAPHY
General
Adams, 1930; Escrit, 1939; Föhl, 1976; Reid, 1908; Steel, 1953.

JEFF COX

trench At first, in England, a pathway through woodland, then a ditch; but in New England, USA, a synonym for LEAT.

Trevithick, Richard (1771–1833) One of the pioneers of the steam engine, responsible particularly for the application of high-pressure steam and for experiments with steam locomotion. The son of a mine manager in Cornwall, England, he was developing a high-pressure steam engine by 1796, which drove a land carriage with some success in 1801–2. In 1802 he built a steam locomotive at Coalbrookdale (*see* IRONBRIDGE) which was probably never set to work, but in 1804 one of his locomotives pulled a train on the PENYDARREN TRAMROAD, and other locomotives followed. The Penydarren and Coalbrookdale locomotives have been replicated at CARDIFF and IRONBRIDGE. Trevithick high-pressure stationary engines were built by John Hazledine at Bridgnorth, one of which is displayed in the Science Museum, LONDON. Trevithick's most enduring invention was the CORNISH ENGINE. He set out on an expedition in 1816 to erect engines in Peru, and returned penniless in 1828.

BIBLIOGRAPHY
General
Dickinson, 1938; Dickinson and Titley, 1934; Law, 1965; Storer, 1969; Trevithick, 1872; Trinder, 1981.
Specific
Tonkin, S. M. Trevithick, Rastrick and the Hazledine Foundry at Bridgnorth. In *TNS*, xxvi, 1947–9.

CHRISTOPHER GREEN

Trieste, Friuli-Venezia Giulia, Italy The industrial archaeology of Trieste hinges on its growth as a free port from 1719, its role as the principal port of the Habsburg Empire (*see* AUSTRIA), and the impetus of the opening of the Suez Canal in 1869. The Commune of Trieste was liberated from Austrian control when it was ceded to Italy in 1920. In 1947 Trieste and Istria were created a free territory, but in 1954 the city passed back to Italy.

Figure 160 The Lloyd Arsenal Works, Trieste, originally a shipyard of the Austrian Navy, designed by Theophil von Hansen and begun in 1862
Michael Stratton

The Canale Grande was built from 1754 as the focal point of the New Town, a project promoted by the Emperor Charles VI (1685–1740) and completed by Empress Maria Theresa (1717–80). The quays on this short, dead-end canal running inland from Corso Cavour were lined with warehouses which have since been adapted as shops and apartments. The last section, facing the church of San Antonio, was filled in during the inter-war period.

Corn mills, candle factories and other eighteenth-century industries were located north of the New Town. The two areas were connected and docks and warehouses added after the arrival of the first railway, the Sudbahn from Vienna, in 1857. The original station was rebuilt in 1877 with a Renaissance-style booking hall, which is incorporated into the current Stazione Centrale, whose overall roof was demolished in 1940. A workshop and warehouse were built between the station and the harbour *c.*1857, the two massive stone ranges of forty-four bays being joined into a U-form plan by the addition of a granary, eight bays in length and fronted by a projecting pediment, the whole group being 300 m (1000 ft.) long.

The warehouses are just inland from the Porto Vecchio, which was developed to handle the growth of traffic that followed the opening of the Suez Canal. Several stone-built warehouses, cranes and projecting jetties survive. Jetties and basins No. 1 and No. 2 were created in 1875; No. 3,

with a long warehouse with projecting gables and hydraulic cranes, whose buildings are now demolished, in 1887; No. 0 in 1889; and in 1893 the port was completed with basin No. 4. Some of the warehouses near the station, which have rusticated stonework, were designed by a French architect, *c.*1890. A group of warehouses dating from 1908 have balconies providing deck access at every floor, with derrick cranes set at intervals along the top storey. The hydraulic cranes at basins No. 1 and No. 4 were operated by pumping stations at either end of the range of docks. One pumping station survives, with its chimney, at basin No. 0.

Beyond and above the Porto Vecchio is the Vittoria lighthouse, built in 1927 to designs by Arduino Berlam. Commemorating those lost at sea during World War I, the ribbed column of limestone is fronted by the statue of a sailor, and an anchor with a winged figure surmounts the light.

By the early twentieth century the harbour south of Porto Vecchio and fronting the city centre was used primarily for passenger traffic. A railway ran along the quayside from 1887 until a tunnel under the city was completed in 1981. The Stazione Marittima was built in 1930 to designs by Umberto Nordio, in a stolid stripped classicism with nautical imagery. South of the station is the fishmarket of 1913 by S. Giorgio Polli, with a large corner tower, and an open interior of stone and concrete to dispel the stench of fish.

To the south of a second lighthouse is Campo Marzio railway station, opened in 1906. A stone frontage and side wings supported a crescent overall truss roof, which has been removed. The loss of Istria to Yugoslavia led to closure, but a railway museum was opened in 1984, with an excellent combination of locomotives, models, photographs and plans concentrating on the development of Trieste's railway and tramway networks. The station tracks hold twelve steam locomotives. A 2–6–2, No. 229.170, built in Austria, was the first to be restored. An electric locomotive of class E626, introduced in 1931, is also preserved. Neighbouring lines are filled with withdrawn locomotives.

The Porto Nuovo, east of the museum and south of the centre, developed from 1908, and came to be dominated by concrete structures of the inter-war period. Jetty No. 5 has large cranes running on overhead gantries. Off Via dei Calderai is the works of Lloyd Arsenal which originated c.1862 as a shipyard of the Austrian navy. The works was designed by the Dane, Theophil von Hansen, who designed the parliament buildings in Vienna. A dramatic towered entrance with a high bridge leaping a dockyard road at third-storey height gives access to the main building. Lower two-storey workshops run east–west. Further east in Via Bartolomeo d'Alviano is the gasworks of the Usina Comunale del Gas, established in 1864, which is dominated by a stone-built neo-Classical holder, the Sheldonian Theatre of gas-making.

From the Piazza Oberdan, tram line No. 2, constructed with Austrian backing and opened in 1902–3, provides a technologically fascinating and scenically dramatic route to Opicina. For most of the journey the tram propels itself, under electric traction, fed by a catenary. For the steepest section up to the crenellate Stazione Scorcola the car is coupled above a cable-hauled vehicle. The tramsheds are near to the head station at Opicina.

BIBLIOGRAPHY
General
Negri *et al.*, 1983.
Specific
Cordara, P. Trieste: industria e commercio all periferia di un impero (Trieste: industry and commerce at the margin of an empire). In *Archaeologia Industriale*, I, 1983.

LOCATIONS
[M] Historical Museum, Miramare Castle, Trieste.
[M] Maritime Museum, Via di Campo Marzio 1, Trieste.
[M] Mercantile Museum, Faculty of Economics, Trieste University, Trieste.
[M] Railway Museum, Campo Marzio Station, Trieste.

MICHAEL STRATTON

Trilbardou, Seine-et-Marne, France At Trilbardou, 30 km (19 mi.) E. of Paris, is a pumping station built in 1865–6 to raise water from the Marne into the Canal de l'Ourcq. This pumping station is notable for its Sagebien wheel, 11 m (36 ft.) in diameter and 6 m (20 ft.) wide, which drives four pumps, designed by the same engineer

(*see* figure 173). The Sagebien wheel was the last type of water wheel developed in France during the nineteenth century before progress in turbine design made new water wheels obsolete for industrial purposes. Invented in 1851 by Alphonse Sagebien (1807–92) it is a breastshot wheel with its blades angled in the same direction as the wheel's rotation, which enables the wheel to operate practically immersed in a substantial supply of water, where only a slight fall is available. The wheel's efficiency could be as high as 95 per cent. About three hundred Sagebien wheels were installed between 1851 and 1892, primarily in the north and west of France, and principally for modern corn mills, textile factories and papermills. From 1865 they were used in pumping stations supplying water to such cities as Amiens, Le Mans and Paris.

BIBLIOGRAPHY
Specific
Beguinot, P. Les Anciennes Installations de pompage du service des eaux de la Ville de Paris (Old water-pumping installations for Paris). In *L'Archéologie industrielle en France*, XIII, 1986.
Belhoste, J.-F. and Cartier, C. La Roue Sagebien, histoire d'une invention (The Sagebien wheel: history of an invention). In *Cahiers d'Histoire et de Philosophie des Sciences*. Paris, 1990.

JEAN-FRANÇOIS BELHOSTE

trip hammer An alternative name for the TILT HAMMER, sometimes incorrectly applied to the HELVE HAMMER.

BIBLIOGRAPHY
General
Gale, 1971.

Trofaiach, Styria, Austria *See* STYRIAN IRON TRAIL.

trolleybus The trolleybus began in the 1880s as an experimental vehicle in Germany where early development took place. By 1910 the basic form of the 'trackless trolley' had evolved: an electrically powered, 'free wheel' road vehicle, drawing its power, through twin trolley booms, from a pair of overhead wires. Much of the later development of trolleybuses took place in Britain. Services began in Leeds and Bradford in 1911, but the vehicles were heavy, slow and cumbersome, and it was the work of C. Owen Silvers at Wolverhampton, in converting petrol-engined buses into trolleybuses, that showed their potential. By 1928 Wolverhampton had the world's largest trolleybus network, and the town became a showpiece on which many European systems were based. Able, with slight modification, to use much of the power-supply system of the TRAMCAR, trolleybuses replaced trams in many British towns, although elsewhere both have continued to operate. The trolleybus combined the best features of the tramcar and the motor omnibus – electric power ensured that it was clean and efficient, while its ability to manœuvre led to freer traffic movement. All major British trolleybus systems have been replaced by motor vehicles, but networks in continental Europe include those at Arnhem, Nancy and Solingen, and several operate in the USSR. There is a trolleybus museum at Sandtoft, England.

BIBLIOGRAPHY
General
Kay, 1968; Klapper, 1961.

LOCATION
[M] Sandtoft Transport Centre, Belton Road, Sandtoft, Doncaster.

PAUL COLLINS

trolley car *See* TRAMCAR.

Trollhättan, Älvsborg, Sweden Trollhättan, 66 km (44 mi.) N. of Gothenburg, is one of Europe's foremost water-power sites, where six cataracts with a total fall of 33 m (108 ft.) extend over a distance of 1450 m (1600 yd.). The power of the water has been used for many industrial purposes, particularly for sawing timber, and is now utilized in hydro-electric power stations, of which the most significant historically is the Oliden station, opened in 1909. In the nineteenth century Trollhättan developed as one of Sweden's principal engineering centres, several locomotives built there being displayed at GÄVLE. The town's industrial history is featured in its museum.

The Trollhätte Canal, linking the Göta River, and thus the city of Gothenburg, with Lake Vänern, was opened in 1800. It formed part of the inland waterway route across Sweden that was completed by the opening of the GOTHA CANAL in 1832. The section parallel to the cataracts at Trollhättan, with eight locks in two staircases, was built by Erik Nordewall. A new flight of locks at Trollhättan, as wide as those on the Gotha Canal, was constructed by Nils Ericson in 1844. They in turn were replaced in 1916 by four locks able to accommodate 2000-tonne ocean-going ships. Another lock, constructed in 1749 by CHRISTOPHER POLHEM and abandoned in 1755, serves as a monument to an earlier scheme to create an inland waterway across Sweden.

BIBLIOGRAPHY
General
Hadfield, 1986; Nisser, 1979.

LOCATION
[M] Trollhättans museet, Magasingatan 15, S-461 30 Trollhät-tan.

BARRIE TRINDER

trompe A 'trumpet', through which a blast was created by falling water, enabling a furnace or hearth to be blown without moving parts. The trompe is believed to have originated in Italy in the first half of the seventeenth century. It was used in many blast furnaces and forges in the Mediterranean countries. Water from a cistern or aqueduct is allowed to fall some 6 m (20 ft.) through a pipe made from tree trunks, at the top of which is a throat formed from boards, and a series of holes or aspirators which incline inwards and downwards at an angle of *c.*45 degrees. The pipe terminates in a wooden, trapezoidal wind-chest, in which is a stone or a cast-iron plate to receive the full force of the falling water. A vertical pipe from the top of the wind-chest is connected by a leather tube to a blast pipe. The trompe was regarded as an efficient means of providing blast, but the saturation of the air with moisture was sometimes considered a disadvantage. The best-preserved trompes are probably those at CAPALBIO; remains of trompes can be observed at other ironworking sites in Tuscany, in Spain and in France, and there is a working example at a blacksmith's shop at Maresca near Pistoia, Italy. Trompes were employed at furnaces in southern France, and were universally used in the CATALAN FORGE process.

BIBLIOGRAPHY
General
Crossley and Trinder, 1983; Percy, 1864.

BARRIE TRINDER

Trondheim, Sør-Trøndelag, Norway The ancient capital of Norway is a multicoloured wooden city clustered around the cathedral of St Olof on a peninsula bounded by the Trondheim Fjord and the mouth of the River Nidelva. Weather-boarded warehouses of breathtaking beauty stand on the Kjobmandsgade and Fjordgade, their façades reflected in the Ostrekanslhavn and the Ovre Elvehavn. The population of the city in 1800 was less than 10 000, but after the railway link with Oslo was established by the completion of the Rørosbanen in 1877 and improved with the opening of the Dovrebanen in 1921, its prosperity increased. Trondheim has a rich legacy of nineteenth-century industrial buildings, including a brewery, engineering shops and the brickworks, 'Trondhjems Aktieteglverk', near the cathedral, which had a continuous history of brickmaking from 1227 until 1970. A fourteen-chamber Hoffman brick kiln built by Germans in the 1860s is preserved.

The Trøndelag Folk Museum, established in 1913, comprises some sixty re-erected buildings from the region on a 14 ha (6 ac.) site. The Hans Nissengarden of *c.*1720 is a typical Trondheim merchant's house. The Åspåsgarden from RØROS was removed to the museum in 1910. Buildings of industrial significance include a nineteenth-century posting station, a bath house which was used for drying flax and malt, and a coppersmith's workshop of 1911. The Museum of Applied Art (Nordenfjeldske Kunstindustrimuseum), established in 1893, has furnishings, textiles, ceramics and glass from the Renaissance to modern times. Its Art Nouveau pieces are of particular importance, and there is a complete interior of *c.*1900 designed for the museum by the Belgian Henry van de Velde. The Maritime Museum (Sjofartsmuseet), housed in a restored eighteenth-century prison building, holds the records of several Trondheim merchant houses.

BIBLIOGRAPHY
General
Mykland and Sogner, 1955–62.

BARRIE TRINDER

Trubia, Oviedo, Asturias, Spain   The arms factory at Trubia in central Asturias, 12 km ($7\frac{1}{2}$ mi.) W. of Oviedo, was founded in 1794 by a royal decree, requiring the relocation of some centres of armaments manufacture from the Basque country into Asturias to take advantage of local supplies of coal and iron ore, and to remove strategic manufactures away from the French border.

The establishment of the Trubia arms factory was directed by the military engineer Muñoz San Clemente, and it was built quickly. One of the first measures was the building of a dam to supply water power to the factory, the reservoir being fed by a canal from the River Trubia, a tributary of the River Nalón. At the same time two blast furnaces, 'el Volcán' and 'el Incendio' were constructed, each with a capacity of two tonnes of iron per day. The 'el Volcán' furnace was blown in for the first time in 1796, and was the first Spanish blast furnace to use coke instead of charcoal. The adoption of the process proved slow and costly since accurate metallurgical analysis was not then possible. In 1844, after a period of decline, an army officer, D. Francisco Antonio Elorza, was appointed director at Trubia, and added the manufacture of cannon to that of grenades and small arms. Elorza's reforms and technological innovations are well documented in the works archives.

During the years of the Franco dictatorship the Trubia factory, with its namesake producing small arms at Oviedo, where the Mauser rifle was manufactured, were directly dependent on military spending. The factory is now part of a group of state enterprises belonging to the National Institute of Industry.

CARLOS CAICOYA

truck   Originally, a small wooden wheel or roller, the word later came to mean a hand barrow. In England it was applied to railway wagons, and in North America to the bogies on which the bodies of railway carriages or wagons were carried. In North America, and increasingly in England, it is now applied to MOTOR LORRIES.

truck shop   'Truck', in an abstract sense, means 'exchange'. 'Truck shop' was a term used in England for a place where workers at an industrial plant, who were not paid in cash, could exchange whatever tokens they had been given for goods. Such shops were the cause of much resentment, and were a cause of industrial unrest in the 1830s and 40s, and a stimulus to the growth of the Co-OPERATIVE MOVEMENT.

See also PASPÉBIAC.

truss bridge   A bridge that is an assemblage of many relatively small structural members, some in tension and some in compression, comprising a series of interconnecting triangles. This form of construction was particularly suited to North American conditions in the nineteenth century. On a deck truss bridge traffic is carried across the top of the truss structure, while on a through truss traffic passes through the structure on plates laid on the bottom structural members. A pony truss is similar to a through truss but has no lateral bracing between the upper members.

Many American engineers developed variations of basic truss structures which were named after them. The earliest and simplest form was the king post truss. The popular Burr arch truss, patented in 1817 by Theodore Burr (1771–1822), was essentially a king post truss strengthened with an arch. The bowstring arch truss, patented by Squire Whipple (1804–88), has a curving top-chord compression member held together by bottom-chord members in tension, and was widely used on American rural roads. The Pratt truss, one of the most popular American bridge types, patented in 1844 by Caleb and Thomas Pratt (1812–75), has vertical compression members and diagonal tension members. It was originally conceived as a combination of wooden and metal members, but in practice was usually all metal. The lenticular truss is a form of Pratt truss in which both top and bottom chords are polygonal, forming the shape of a lens. The camelback, Baltimore and Pennsylvania trusses are variations of the Pratt truss. The Howe truss, developed by William Howe (1803–52) and commonly used on early American railroads, combined diagonal wooden compression members with vertical iron tension members. The Warren truss, patented by James Warren in 1848, has diagonal members which carry both tensile and compressive forces. It was not widely used until the early twentieth century.

Popular forms in Germany were those designed by F. A. von Pauli (1802–83), whose lenticular truss bridges were mostly on Bavarian railways, and J. W. Schwedler (1823–94), who devised a truss in which the diagonals acted as ties only: this was employed for many important railway crossings.

See figure 161; *see also* figure 19.

BIBLIOGRAPHY
General
Jackson, 1988; Mehrtens, 1900; Straub, 1949.
Specific
Comp, T. A. and Jackson, D. *Bridge Truss Types: a guide to dating and identifying.* Nashville: American Association for State and Local History, 1977.

BARRIE TRINDER

tub boat   A small vessel usually employed on a canal with INCLINED PLANES, measuring 5–6.5 m (18–21 ft.) long and about 1.5 m (5 ft.) wide, and often box-shaped. Tub boats were frequently worked in 'trains'. A preserved wrought-iron example and a wooden replica may be seen at IRONBRIDGE. A variation was the compartment boat or 'Tom Pudding', patented by W. H. Bartholomew and used

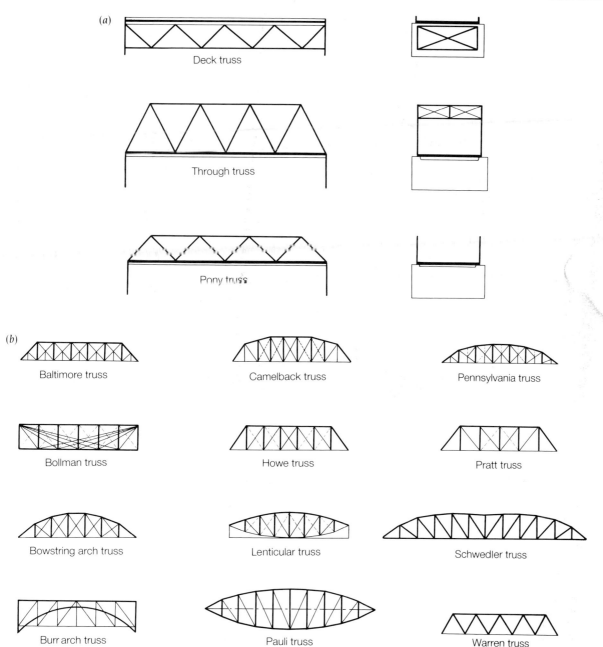

Figure 161 (a) Sections and side elevations of the three basic forms of truss bridge; (b) side elevations of some of the types of truss bridges most commonly used in the United States and Germany

on Yorkshire waterways, measuring 6.4 m × 4.5 m (21 ft. × 15 ft.), and usually pushed by steam tugs.

BIBLIOGRAPHY
General
Hadfield, 1986; Tomlinson, 1979.

tube mill Tubes can be made from steel or wrought iron by two methods: by forming a strip into a tubular shape and welding the joint, or by piercing and elongating a solid billet. In 1891 the brothers Reinhard and Max Mannesmann patented the 'pilgrim's step' process for seamless tubemaking, which involves the use of a special form of ROLLING MILL. The former file mill in REMSCHEID, where the process was first operated, still survives. Tubes or pipes can also be made in a foundry by centrifugal

779

casting, a process invented by the Brazilian S. de Lavana in 1914.

tube railway An urban UNDERGROUND RAILWAY made by tunnelling rather than 'cut-and-cover' methods, on which the use of electric traction was essential. Tubes were made possible by the Greathead Shield. The first tube ran under the River Thames in London near the Tower, and operated with cable traction during 1870–94 until superseded by Tower Bridge. The City & South London tube opened in 1890. The deepest point on the London system is 40 m (130 ft.) below the surface.

BIBLIOGRAPHY
Specific
Simmons, J. The pattern of tube railways in London. In *Journal of Transport History*, VII, 1965–6.

tubular bridge A bridge consisting of a colossal hollow beam with a road or railway running through it. The term is applied to the MENAI (*see* figure 85) and Conway railway bridges built in 1850 by ROBERT STEPHENSON, after much agonizing over the design with WILLIAM FAIRBAIRN and others. The type had few direct progeny, with the exception of Stephenson's bridge at MONTREAL, but the use of the flat-beam principle was of major importance for the future of bridge-building.

BIBLIOGRAPHY
General
Clark, 1850; Fairbairn, 1849.
Specific
Tyson, S. Notes on the historical development and use of tubes in the construction of bridges. In *IAR*, II, 1977.

Tudela, Navarre, Spain The principal industrial monument at Tudela, on the River Ebro, 83 km (52 mi.) S. of Pamplona, is the 'La Mejana' flourmill, built in 1847–9 under the direction of Don Domingo Auirre, on the site of an older mill. It was transformed in 1912 when the Austro-Hungarian company, Bühler Brothers, installed roller-milling equipment. The milling, sifting and bleaching plant is well preserved, and the site provides a full picture of the workings of a large, industrial-scale flourmill of the early twentieth century.

The Imperial Canal of Aragón is a bypass to the River Ebro between Tudela and Saragossa (Zaragoza), 85 km (53 mi.) downstream. Originally built in the sixteenth century for irrigation, it was made navigable for 100-ton vessels between 1770 and 1790. Its wharfs, locks and lock-keepers' cottages are well preserved.

BIBLIOGRAPHY
General
Generalitat de Catalunya, 1988; Hadfield, 1986.

Tudor An imprecise architectural term, applying literally to the styles used while the House of Tudor ruled England between 1485 and 1603, which were revived in the nineteenth century for industrial and commercial buildings and housing developments. In domestic buildings, Tudor implies mullioned windows, drip moulds and dormer windows; on larger buildings, it implies ornate strapwork decoration, curving gables and complex chimneys. The term Elizabethan, applying to the reign of Elizabeth I between 1558 and 1603, sometimes refers to this same style, and there is no clear dividing line between Tudor and JACOBEAN styles, still less between the two styles when revived.

tug A powered vessel designed to haul, or assist the manoeuvres of, other vessels. Some of the earliest steamships were employed for haulage purposes on the River Clyde in 1814, the River Tyne in 1822 and the Hudson River from 1826. Screw propulsion for tugs was introduced in the 1860s, but paddle tugs continued to be preferred for some purposes. European tugs generally had their towing hooks amidships, but it was customary in North America to place them well aft. In the USA tugs defy their name in being used predominantly to push rather than to tow or tug other vessels.

Tugs were used on canals to haul vessels through tunnels, sometimes drawing electric power from underwater cables or, as at Harecastle (*see* STOKE-ON-TRENT) during 1914–54, from overhead wires.

Many tugs, mostly of the twentieth century, are preserved in Canada, England, the Netherlands, the USA and elsewhere. Notable examples are the wooden *John Taxis* built at Chester, Pa., in 1869 now berthed at Wilmington, N.C.; the paddle tug *Eppleton Hall* built for Seaham Harbour (*see* DURHAM) in 1914, now in San Francisco; the steam tug *Baltimore* of 1920, at the Baltimore Museum of Industry; and the canal tugs *Mayflower* of 1861, at BRISTOL, and *Worcester* of 1908, at Ellesmere Port, Cheshire, England.

BIBLIOGRAPHY
General
Baker, 1965; Brouwer, 1985.

BARRIE TRINDER

tumbrel *See* CART.

tun The largest staved container traditionally used in the English wine trade, with a capacity of 252 gall. (11.46 hl). Until 1854 the capacity of a ship was based on the number of tuns of wine it could carry (*see* SEA TRANSPORT).

See also BARREL; HOGSHEAD; PIPE.

BIBLIOGRAPHY
General
Zupko, 1968.

tungsten (W) An elemental metal, known also as wolfram, and derived from the mineral wolframite ((Fe,Mn)WO$_4$) found in association with tin deposits. ROBERT MUSHET demonstrated its properties when alloyed with steel. Tungsten has the highest melting point of all metals, and is used in cutting tools, as tungsten carbide, as well as in dyeing and for filaments in electric lamps. It is mined in California, Nevada, and Portugal.

BIBLIOGRAPHY
General
Jones, 1950; Richardson, 1974.

tunnel A subterranean thoroughfare, although the word was not used in that sense until the late eighteenth century. The word is commonly used in mining (*see* ADIT; MINING; PILLAR-AND-STALL MINING; SOUGH; STOPING). Road tunnels were built from the early eighteenth century (*see* SALZBURG). Tunnels are essential parts of canals and main-line railways, and are occasionally used in urban tramway networks (*see* LONDON). They are employed for pedestrian use, under rivers as in GLASGOW, as parts of water-power and water-supply systems, and as thoroughfares for conveyor belts. The Thames Tunnel in LONDON of 1825–43, by Sir Marc Brunel (1769–1849), was the first to be driven with the use of a shield. The Hoosac Tunnel, Mass., USA, driven in 1851–75, was the fountainhead of such modern rock tunnelling techniques as COMPRESSED AIR drills and the use of high EXPLOSIVES.

See also CANAL TUNNEL; GREATHEAD, JAMES HENRY; RAILWAY TUNNEL.

BIBLIOGRAPHY
General
Blower, 1964; Copperthwaite, 1906; Hammond, 1959.
Specific
Vogel, R. M. *Tunnel Engineering: a museum treatment*. Washington DC: Smithsonian Institution, 1964.

tunnel-back house The characteristic working-class and lower-middle-class house of urban England between *c*.1850 and 1914, usually built in TERRACES with access to the backs via tunnels between the houses. This house type was a development from a four-room house by addition at the rear of an extension containing a third bedroom, with a scullery and often a water closet below. The style was adopted because of the perceived need for separate sleeping accommodation for male and female children, but proved to be an inefficient form of building, and was much disliked by reformers favouring GARDEN CITY styles. Many thousands remain in use.

BIBLIOGRAPHY
General
Chapman, 1971; Daunton, 1983; Meakin, 1905; Muthesius, 1982.

tunnel kiln A KILN in which goods travel on wagons past the heated gases. The goods are first warmed by escaping gas; they then gradually pass to the hottest part of the kiln, and finally they are cooled by a current of air which is subsequently used for the combustion of the fuel. In 1840 a Danish patent was granted to P. A. Jordt but the first examples to be erected may be French and date from the 1850s. Early tunnel kilns were too short to be effective. Later designs, such as those built in Holland, might be around 90 m (300 ft.) long. The first American tunnel kiln was installed in 1889 at Chicago for firing dry-pressed bricks. PRODUCER GAS was adopted as the most convenient fuel. A current of air might be drawn through the length of the tunnel in a direction opposite to that in which the goods travel, the air being heated by the fired goods and passing forward to pre-heat freshly set goods.

In a Dressler tunnel kiln, dating from *c*.1900, combusted gases pass through a pair of combustion chambers on either side of the cars. This system proved to be a satisfactory substitute for the muffle kiln in firing fine earthenware and glazed ceramics.

BIBLIOGRAPHY
General
Rhodes, 1968; Searle, 1929.

MICHAEL STRATTON

turbine A device that utilizes the kinetic energy of liquid or gas flow. In the impulse turbine the direct force of the fluid striking the blades provides most of the turning effect. In the reaction turbine most of the power comes from the pressure of the fluid against the blades as it leaves their curved surfaces. The earliest undershot wheels in WATER MILLS and SPLASH MILLS are essentially impulse water turbines, and steam turbines were considered in antiquity and in the Renaissance. A prototype water turbine was described by J. T. Desaguliers (1683–1744) but it was Benoît Fourneyron (1802–67) in 1827 who, working at LE CREUSOT, perfected a turbine with fixed inner vanes that directed water from a central source against outer vanes, thus producing the rotation. By 1837 Fourneyron was building turbines rotating at 2300 rev/min producing up to 60 hp. Many others, especially J. B. Francis in 1828 and L. A. PELTON produced improved designs.

CHARLES PARSONS produced the first effective steam turbine in 1884, using sets of vanes of increasing size through which steam flows, expanding as it does so. Other contemporary steam turbines were built by the Swede C. G. P. De Laval (1845–1913) and the American Charles G. Curtis (1860–1953).

Fourneyron turbines were first used for electric power generation at NIAGARA in 1895. Steam and water turbines remain the principal means of generating electric power.

Gas turbines were first considered as early as 1826, and developed in Germany and Czechoslovakia in the early twentieth century, but it was Sir Frank Whittle who realized their potential with the jet engine (*see* AEROPLANE).

See also TURBINE PROPULSION.

BIBLIOGRAPHY
General
Frankel, 1977; Kearton, 1922; Neilson, 1912; Richardson, 1911.

CHRISTOPHER GREEN

turbine propulsion The use of the steam turbine to power a ship was demonstrated by SIR CHARLES PARSONS in the *Turbinia*, a yacht completed in 1894, which raced at 34.5 knots through the British fleet anchored at Spithead in 1897. The first merchant vessel to be powered by a turbine was the 551-ton Clyde ferry *King Edward* (*see*

IRVINE) of 1901 which worked until 1951, while the first turbine-powered transatlantic liner was the Allan Line's 10 629-ton *Victorian* of 1904. Turbines became the standard means of propelling the larger merchant ships and remained so until after World War II.

BIBLIOGRAPHY
General
Baker, 1965; Richardson, 1911.

Turin (Torino), Piedmont Italy The most important industrial city in Italy after Milan. One of the major cotton centres, with many clothing factories, it gained railway workshops in the late nineteenth century, and came to be dominated by the motor industry in the twentieth century; it is also the focus for the Italian film industry.

The main nineteenth-century workshops were fed with power from canals, seven of which ran through the north-east of the city. In the middle of the century the major armaments concern, the Fabbriche d'Armi del Valdocco, had four water wheels and a turbine. Workshops and housing associated with them can be seen in the area between Corso Regina and the River Dora. In Piazza Borgo Dora is the Arsenale of 1867, with a central clock tower and arcaded front, executed in brick and terracotta. About 500 m (550 yards) S. of the Piazza Della Repubblica is a large octagonal space filled by a teeming conglomeration of markets, stalls, arcades and tram tracks. In the south-east and south-west corners are two stone and wooden roofed markets. To the north-east is a complex U-shaped iron and glass hall, dating from 1916, with a free-standing canopy behind. To the south-east an arcade, cruciform in plan with an additional transept, leads to Via Basilica.

In 1848 three engineering works combined to form the Strade Ferrate for repairing locomotives and making rolling stock. A new complex of workshops was built from 1884 just south of the prison, fronting Corso Vittorio. The buildings, in stone with brick dressings and stepped end gables, based on north European practice, are now largely unused. Later workshops of *c.*1900 have rendered exteriors. The locomotive shop has a traverser for linking a series of erecting bays.

The main railway station at Porta Nuova was erected in 1866–8, the concourse being rebuilt in 1954 with the retention of the original first-floor arcade of glass and lace-like iron tracery. The original train shed designed by Carlo Felice has been converted into a large booking hall, with the platforms located beyond the new concourse.

The motorcar industry, which came to be dominated by Fiat and Lancia, evolved from coachbuilding. Diatto, established as early as 1835 for making carriage wheels, pre-dated Fiat, whose first works was established in Corso Dante in 1899. Fiat's original offices west of Via Chiabrera were designed by Alfredo Premoli, with ART NOUVEAU decoration. To the east is another block, also carrying the Fiat name, and now occupied by the firm's social club. Additional works of brick pier construction were built in 1900–5 north of the centre in Via Cuneo and Via Dominiani, and laid out in orderly parallel ranges reminiscent of railway workshops. This works, the Grandi Motori, was extended *c.*1915 with concrete-framed buildings, marking the adoption by Fiat's Director of Production, Giacomo Matte-Trucco, of this form of American construction. The system can also be seen 700 m (760 yd.) east of Grandi Motori in the Nebiole works on the north-west corner of Via Bologna and Via Padova. Another factory illustrates the adoption of concrete construction before World War I. The Savigliano engineering workshops, erected in 1912 just north of the River Dora in

Corso Mortara, used the HENNEBIQUE system of construction in a design by Enrico Monicelli.

The culmination of Matte-Trucco's use of concrete is the Fiat Lingotto works, 3 km (2 mi.) S. of Stazione Porta Nuova, and west of Via Nizza. Construction commenced in 1916, and the works ultimately grew to comprise a block 507 m (2512 ft.) long, with five main storeys, and a test track on the roof. Motorcar manufacture progressed from the ground floor upwards. Lingotto is a dramatic expression of the continued belief in multi-storey car assembly, of the Italian enthusiasm for concrete, and of a futuristic conception of industry. The boldest use of concrete is in the ramp, built in 1924 and supported by a web of beams, which takes cars to the roof: it forms an oval circuit with banked curves. Part of Fiat Lingotto is now used for exhibitions, while an international competition held in 1984 was intended to find new uses for this colossus of industrial archaeology.

The products of Turin's motor industry can be seen in the Ruffia Motor Museum fronting Corso Unita d'Italia. The collection concentrates on Fiat and Lancia, and includes racing vehicles and motorcycles. There are modest attempts to interpret the development of engines, chassis and bodywork. Highlights amongst the lines of vehicles include the steam landau of 1854 by Virginio Bordino, a Peugeot of 1894, a racing Fiat of 1903, and a Lancia of 1923 demonstrating the use of combined body and chassis construction.

BIBLIOGRAPHY
General
Banham, 1986; Negri *et al.*, 1983.
Specific
Friedemann, A. Sviluppo urbano e industriale a Torino (Urban and industrial development in Turin). In *Archeologia Industriale*, I, 1983.

LOCATION
[M] Ruffia Motor Museum, Corso Unita d'Italia, Turin.

MICHAEL STRATTON

Turkey Turkey has traditionally been seen as the bridge between Europe and Asia, and since 1973 there has been a real bridge across the Bosporus. About 3 per cent of modern Turkey, Eastern Thrace, lies in Europe, and is bounded by Greece and Bulgaria. To the east of the straits lies Anatolia, bounded by the Black Sea, the USSR, Iran, Iraq, Syria, the Mediterranean and the Aegean. Modern Turkey extends some 1600 km (1000 mi.) from east to west, and occupies an area of 777 000 ha² (300 000 sq. mi.).

Two great empires had their centres within what is now Turkey (*see* ISTANBUL). The Byzantine Empire collapsed in 1453 when Constantinople fell to the Turks. Two centuries later the Turkish Ottoman Empire extended from the Caspian Sea and the Persian Gulf to Algiers and the approaches to Vienna, and from Egypt far north into the Ukraine. The Ottoman Empire had a culture and an economy quite distinct from that of the West. Trade revolved around such institutions as the BAZAAR and

the CARAVANSERAI. Road transport was based upon the seatless carriage in which passengers squatted on the floor. Typical houses lacked chimneys and derived heat from charcoal braziers. Horse-powered prime movers were well developed throughout the Empire (*see* ROMANIA). Coffee drinking passed into Western Europe from the Empire in the seventeenth century. During the eighteenth and nineteenth centuries the boundary of Turkish rule in the Balkans was slowly pushed back by the power of the Habsburgs, and by the growth of nationalist feeling. Economic development in the Empire was largely controlled by foreign banks, particularly French and German banks. Turkey supported Germany in World War I, at the end of which French and British troops occupied Constantinople. War with Greece followed, to be concluded in 1923 by the Treaty of Lausanne, which defined the frontiers of a new Turkish republic under Mustafa Kemal (Ataturk; d.1938) who began radical programmes of reform. The historic names of cities like Constantinople (*see* ISTANBUL) and Smyrna (*see* İZMIR) were changed to Turkish forms.

Tobacco has for long been Turkey's chief export, and one in which the state has always had a controlling interest. Stone warehouses in İZMIR and tall factories with pediments and chimneys in Ayvalık are amongst the few nineteenth-century industrial buildings in Turkey, and relate largely to the tobacco trade. Turkey exports large quantities of raw and manufactured cotton. Adana and Kayseri are the chief centres. Woollen manufacture is concentrated in İzmir and Istanbul, and Turkey is set to become the world's largest manufacturer of hand-woven carpets, much of the weaving being done by women. The Muradiye quarter of the city of Bursa is the chief centre for silk spinning. Some of the 'Fabrikas' were set up under French supervision to export silk to Lyon.

The magnificent tiles in the mosques of Istanbul came from İznik (Nicaea), the best being produced between 1570 and 1620. By the late eighteenth century inferior European tiles were the vogue. Manufacture of the İznik type has been revived at Kütahya.

Under the Ottoman Empire industrial development was sluggish. Some railways were built, mostly with foreign capital, and some textile factories were established. Breweries based on German practice were set up in the late nineteenth century. From 1923 Ataturk determined that Turkey should be as far as possible self-sufficient. An example of his policy is provided by his nurturing of an aircraft industry: the first Turkish aircraft factory was established with the assistance of the German Junkers company at Eskişehir in 1925 where eighty-seven military planes, based on American, German, Polish and British prototypes, were constructed between 1932 and 1936.

The first main-line railway in Turkey, running west from Istanbul, was begun in 1869, and by the mid-1870s had reached Plovdiv in modern Bulgaria. The present trunk route across Anatolia to Istanbul was begun by a French company, and taken over in 1880 by a British concern, from whom it passed in 1888 to a German company, under whose auspices it reached Ankara.

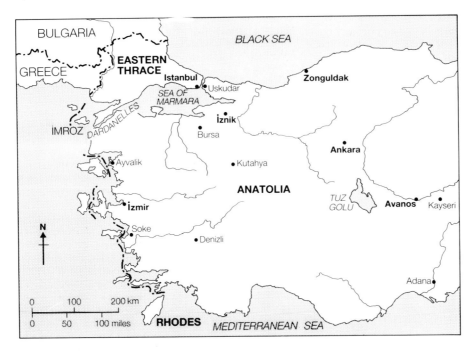

Turkey, west of Kayseri

Stations on the line have a Germanic appearance with steeply pitched roofs, not seen elsewhere in Turkey. Some steam locomotives still work freight trains.

Since prehistoric times Turkey has been an important source of metals, and mineral royalties formed a large part of the revenue of the Ottoman Empire. The Mines Regulations of 1861 ended the state monopoly of mining, allowing landowners to open up mines on their own land, and enabling the leasing of mining rights on state land to private entrepreneurs. This freedom resulted in the development of coal mines at ZONGULDAK; iron, lead, silver and copper mines in both Eastern Thrace and Anatolia; lignite mines near Cannakale; and lead mines on the island of İmroz, near Janina. Copper, chromium, bauxite, mercury, emery and sulphur are also produced, and oil is extracted on a considerable scale. Etibank, a state-owned organization formed in 1935, operates many non-ferrous metal mines, and is the only operator of non-ferrous smelting works.

Historic monuments in Turkey are the responsibility of the Ministry of Culture.

There are some large modern industrial plants in Turkey, like the Akeimento Cement Works, near Istanbul, the Aliaga Oil refinery near İzmir, and the modern cotton factories at Aydın and Kayseri, but the country's chief interest to the industrial archaeologist is that it provides opportunities to see processes that are no longer used in Western Europe or North America. There are many steam winding engines dating from the second half of the nineteenth century in the mines around ZONGULDAK. Many limestone quarries still use hand loading techniques. Limekilns can still be seen in operation in the hills around Söke, belching black, acrid smoke, and surrounded by corrugated iron awnings. Light perforated

bricks and roofing tiles are for the most part manufactured in rectangular HOFFMAN KILNS, some being of recent construction. They are often clad in stone with brick and sheet metal superstructures and outbuildings, and detached cylindrical chimneys. A small brickworks near Denizli observed in 1988 was employing a horse gin to grind clay, and firing its bricks by drying them in the sun. The manufacture of concrete blocks by pressing them and drying them in the sun can be observed in most parts of the country.

See also ANKARA; AVANOS; ISTANBUL; İZMIR; İZNIK; ZONGULDAK.

BIBLIOGRAPHY
General
Durrant, 1972; Goodwin, 1971; Ostrogorsky, 1968; Shaw, 1976–7; Summer-Boyd and Freeby, 1974; Tipton and Aldrich, 1987.
Specific
English, P. J. The Turkish connection. In *Industrial Past*, VII, 1980.
Etibank's role in the Turkish mining industry. In *Mining Magazine*, 1979.

LOCATION
[I] Kültür ve Tanitma (Ministry of Culture), Bakannigi, Ankara.

IVOR J. BROWN and MARK WATSON

turnpike Originally, a gate. The term was applied to the barriers erected across roads in England by trusts empowered by Act of Parliament to collect tolls from travellers and apply the income to the improvement of the roads. The first English turnpike road was created in 1663, but the system did not begin to spread until the 1690s. By *c*.1750 the principal radial routes from London to the provincial capitals had been turnpiked, and by *c*.1780 most main roads were subjected to legislation. In the early nineteenth century turnpike trusts built many completely new sections of road. Trusts had powers to collect tolls from drivers of vehicles or animals, at fixed rates; to contract out the collection of such tolls; to acquire land for improvements; and to borrow money on the security of future income, this being the principal source of capital for improvements. Regulations concerning vehicle weights and widths of wheels were codified in the General Turnpike Act 1773. Most turnpike acts had to be renewed after twenty-one years, and with the growth of railway competition in the nineteenth century many trusts allowed their powers to lapse. The Highways Act 1862 enabled the creation of over four hundred Highways Boards taking over parish responsibilities, and an Act of 1878 allowed main roads, most of which were formerly turnpikes, to come under their control. The last turnpike trusts ceased to exercise their powers in the 1890s.

There were similar systems of toll roads in most West European countries, in the Habsburg and Russian Empires, and in some parts of the USA, where the word has been applied to twentieth-century multi-carriageway toll roads.

BIBLIOGRAPHY
General
Albert, 1972; Dyos and Aldcroft, 1969; Parnell, 1838; Pawson, 1977; Reader, 1980.

BARRIE TRINDER

turpentine   The most widely used of traditional PAINT solvents, a volatile oil made from resin collected from conifers, *Pinus australis* and *Pinus taedra* in North America, *Pinus maritima* and *Pinus pinaster* in Portugal and southern France and *Pinus sylvestris* and *Pinus ledebourii* in Russia. On distillation, about 25 per cent of the resin is volatilized and then condensed as turpentine, the residue being rosin, used by musicians to treat the bows of their instruments.

BIBLIOGRAPHY
General
Morgan and Pratt, 1938.

turquoise   A precious stone, of bluish-green colour, consisting of hydrous phosphate of aluminium. European supplies came originally from the Turkish empire, from which the name derives.

tuyère   A nozzle, in modern times water-cooled, through which air is forced into a furnace. A tuyère pipe conveys air to a furnace from bellows or a blowing engine. In stone-built blast furnaces tuyères are set in tuyère arches. Alternative terms are tew iron, twire, and twear.

tweed   A twilled woollen cloth of rather rough appearance, originally made in southern Scotland. It was a trade name by *c*.1830, possibly coined from a misreading of

'tweel', the Scots form of 'twill', this misreading being helped by the cloth's association with the River Tweed.

BIBLIOGRAPHY
General
Kerridge, 1985.

Twente, Overijssel, The Netherlands   Twente, the most easterly of the three regions of Overijssel province, developed in the nineteenth century from a poverty-stricken heathland region, with few natural resources, into the principal cotton textile area of the Netherlands, with its centre at Enschede. The basis was a domestic manufacture which had developed during the eighteenth century.

The first spinning mill was established shortly before the Belgian secession in 1830 (*see* THE NETHERLANDS), which stimulated production for the East Indies market. In 1832 Thomas Ainsworth (1795–1841) from Lancashire advised that in a region where wages were low, hand-weaving would be preferable to the use of power looms, and in 1833 he established a school for weavers at Goor, 22 km (14 mi.) W. of Enschede. Fifteen associated weaving sheds were set up at other towns. There is a memorial to this 'useful man' at Goor, 'from grateful Overijssel'. In the 1850s Ainsworth founded a factory which later became part of the royal weaving company at Nijverdal, 30 km (19 mi.) NW. Weaving sheds of the nineteenth century and a JUGENDSTIL boilerhouse of 1911 remain, in this typical manufacturing village.

The textile industry in Twente concentrated on weaving, and imported much of its yarn. The industry enjoyed a boom in the 1890s, and by 1911 there were seven mills, employing more than a thousand workers each. Reorganization between 1967 and 1982 led to almost total closure with the loss of 25 000 jobs.

At Enschede the Lancashire-style Jannink factory of 1900, which closed in 1969, was in 1981 adapted as apartments; it also accommodates a museum illustrating the textile industry in Twente and Achterhoek between 1840 and 1930. Parts of the Van Heek factory are used as a business centre. The adjacent Empire-style mansion was built in 1834 for the entrepreneur Charles de Maere who came from Ghent to Enschede after the Belgian secession. Motor lorry manufacture is featured in the DAF museum. Pathmos Garden City, with almost nine hundred dwellings, was constructed in 1914–22 by a building society established by textile manufacturers.

At Hengelo, 8 km (5 mi.) NW, Lansink, a GARDEN CITY colony of three hundred dwellings of 1911, now a protected monument, stands alongside the nineteenth-century building of Stork, originally a textile concern which from the 1860s developed as a manufacturer of textile machines. There is an Industrial Museum in the former power station. Some original buildings of the Hengelo brewery of 1879 remain in use.

The AKZO chemical plant arose from the accidental discovery in 1885 of salt deposits in Delden, 4 km ($2\frac{1}{2}$ mi.) W. of Hengelo, where a museum illustrates the industry's history. After the completion of the Enschede–Zutphen canal in the 1930s the company moved to Hengelo where several wooden towers erected over salt boreholes survive at the south of the town. There were once over two hundred of them scattered across the countryside between Enschede and Hengelo. A watertower of 1894 remains in Delden.

At Borne, 3 km (1½ mi.) NW of Hengelo, some buildings of the Spanjaard spinning mill of the 1920s are used as a business centre, as are the concrete-framed buildings and watertower of the Twente mill in Almelo, 13 km (8 mi.) NW of Hengelo. Almelo was connected with Zwolle in the 1850s by the Overijssel Kanaal, and with Nordhorn in Germany by a canal of the 1880s, which was never successful but is a protected monument. At Vriezenveen, 7 km (4 mi.) N. of Almelo, is a museum concerned with the peat-cutting industry.

At Losser, 9 km (6 mi.) NE of Enschede, a brickyard is preserved. In 1926 a Hoffman kiln replaced twelve clamp kilns here. Also preserved are the drying huts and a narrow-gauge railway.

Three water mills have been preserved at Vasse, 24 km (15 mi.) N. of Enschede, *De Mast*, an oil mill converted to a corn mill, *Bels* of 1830, and *Frans* of 1870.

From Haaksbergen, 12 km (7½ mi.) SW of Enschede, a preserved railway runs 7 km (4 mi.) north to Boekelo. The station, dating from 1884, has been restored to its condition of 1900, and trains are worked by an 0-4-0T locomotive of 1901 by Backer & Rueb of Breda. The preserved Oostendorper water mill on the Buurser beek, a river 3 km (2 mi.) E. of Haaksbergen, is a sixteenth-century sandstone building, with two wheels, one for corn and one for oil. At Buurse, 8 km SW of Enschede, is a traditional pewter manufactory using sand moulds.

The Stoomhoutzagerij *Nahuis* at Groenlo, Gelderland, 30 km (19 mi.) S. of Enschede, is a steam sawmill, now run by a trust, with an engine, built in 1897 and installed in its present location in 1918, driving sixteen saws. A second engine of 1892 drives a dynamo for lighting. Steam is provided from a wood-fired boiler with a 28 m (92 ft.) chimney. The railway station of 1878 at the border town of Winterswijk, 10 km (6 mi.) SE of Groenlo, was restored in 1982 to a variety of uses. The once large marshalling yard has been dismantled, but a station building of 1908 houses a display on local railway history.

BIBLIOGRAPHY
Specific
De Natris, W. Textielfabrieken in Twente. In *Jaarboek Twente* (Yearbook of Twente Province), XVI, 1977.

LOCATIONS
[S] *Bels*, Bergweg 9, Vasse, Overijssel.
[M] DAF Automobielmuseum (DAF Motor Lorry Museum), Bentstraat 43, Enschede.
[S] *De Mast*, Denekamperweg 244, Vasse, Overijssel.
[S] *Frans*, Oosteriksweg 26, Mander, Vasse, Overijssel.
[M] HEIM (Hengelo Industrial Museum), Bornsestraat 7, Hengelo.
[S] Oostendorper Watermolen (Oostendorper Water Mill), Langelo, Haaksbergen, Overijssel.
[M] Railway Exhibition, Gols-station, Houtladingstraat, Winterswijk.
[M] Stichting Museum Buurtspoorweg (Museum Trust for Local Railways), Stationsstraat 3, Haaksbergen.
[S] Stoomhoutzagerij (Steam Sawmill), Winterswijkseweg 47, Groenlo.
[M] Textielindustriemuseum (Textile Industry Museum), Haaksbergstraat/Industriestraat, Enschede.
[S] 'Tingieterij Wilsor' (Wilsor pewter manufactory), Buurse, Overijssel.
[M] Veenmuseum (Peat Museum), Paterswal 9, Vriezenveen.
[M] Zoutmuseum (Salt Museum), Langestraat 30, Delden.

JURRIE VAN DALEN

type Movable printing type, derived from metalworkers' punches, reached a peak of artistic perfection in Europe in the sixteenth century, unsurpassed until the designs of John Baskerville (1706–75) of Birmingham. Type is usually cast from an alloy of tin, antimony and lead, which expands slightly on solidification, giving sharpness of character. Manual type-casting was superseded by the use of machines (*see* LINOTYPE; MONOTYPE) in the late nineteenth century.

BIBLIOGRAPHY
General
Jaspert et al., 1953; Morrison and Day, 1963.

typewriter The first commercially successful typewriters were produced in the USA in the early 1870s, although writing machines of many kinds had previously been made in Austria, Britain and France, and the word was first used by C. Latham Sholes (1819–90) from Wisconsin who took out a patent in 1868. From 1878 large-scale manufacture was pioneered by E. Remington & Sons of Ilion, N.Y., and by 1900 over 100 000 per year were being produced in the USA. The Remington typewriter was introduced to England by Ebenezer Howard (*see* GARDEN CITY).

The Remington typewriter utilized a keyboard which had earlier been used by SAMUEL MORSE for the transmission of writing over long distances: its keys when depressed worked levers called type bars which caused type to strike through an inked ribbon against paper wound around a roller, at the same time causing the roller to be moved automatically a short distance to the left. Many variations were tried in the late nineteenth century.

The typewriter became a highly significant development in communications. Its manufacture marked a significant stage in the development of MASS PRODUCTION techniques, while its use in offices opened careers in commerce to women.

BIBLIOGRAPHY
General
Bliven, 1954; Current, 1954.

BARRIE TRINDER

tyre A tyre is the outer circumferential part of a wheel, which falls on the road or rail. On WAGGONS, CARTS, CARRIAGES and coaches tyres were traditionally of wrought iron. Tyres on railway vehicles were also of wrought iron until superseded by steel.

Early motorcars and bicycles had solid rubber tyres. The pneumatic tyre was first applied by the Belfast veterinary surgeon John Boyd Dunlop (1840–1921) to a cycle in 1888, its immediate success bringing popularity to the 'safety' BICYCLE. Earlier, in 1846, it was Robert William Thompson (1822–73) who had produced pneumatic rubber tyres, but the lack of customers had prevented the commercial development of his idea. During the first decade of the twentieth century the pneumatic tyre incorporating THREAD and steel wire became an established component of the motorcar.

Companies like Dunlop in Britain, Goodyear in the USA and Michelin in France grew up principally to supply mass-produced tyres to motorcar manufacturers, and several built factories notable for their architectural style, like those of Firestone in LONDON, Dunlop in BIRMINGHAM, and Goodyear in Akron, OHIO.

BIBLIOGRAPHY
General
Pearson, 1906.

BARRIE TRINDER

U

Ul'yanovsk (Simbirsk), USSR   A city with an important aircraft museum, whose nucleus was initially redundant jet airliners, including the pioneer twin-jet Tu-104, but the Dushanbe Bureau for the Restoration of Aircraft is now seeking out and restoring the remains of earlier aircraft, both military and civil. In the mid-1980s several historic aircraft were added to the collection: an example of the R-5, which won a first prize in the 1930 Tehrān air display; of the Ant-4, which was one of the first twin-engined, all-metal monoplanes of the 1920s, and in 1929 flew from Moscow to New York; of the Ant-7; and of the Ak-1. It was estimated in 1987 that two hundred old aircraft had been identified, of which fifty-four would be restored.

BIBLIOGRAPHY
Specific
Gudok, 27 January 1987.

JOHN WESTWOOD

umbrella   A fabric screen to give protection from the elements, opening from a central stick. The term was first applied in the seventeenth century to devices brought to Europe from the tropics to give protection from the sun, later called parasols, but by the 1630s was used for those giving protection from rain. There were umbrella makers in many towns by the early nineteenth century. Manufacture on an industrial scale was pioneered in England by Samuel Fox (d.1887) of Stocksbridge, SHEFFIELD, who in 1852 patented the 'Paragon' rib, a thin strip of steel rolled into a U-section. Manufacturers in Solingen (*see* BERGIS-CHESLAND) specialized in rolling umbrella sections. The manufacture of umbrella silk, or lightweight mixture fabrics which could be substituted for it, was a speciality of east London and adjacent parts of Essex, Lyons, and Krefeld in the nineteenth century. A special fabric for umbrellas, zanella, was made in Germany from the early twentieth century.

underground railway   Railways originated underground, and the first uses of the term 'underground railway' appear to relate to colliery lines in North-East England, but the term is principally applied to urban passenger lines like the Metropolitan Railway in London, opened in 1863. Some, like the Metropolitan, much of the Paris Metro or the U-bahn in Vienna, were built by 'cut-and-cover' methods, following the streets; others in deeper 'tubes' (*see* TUBE RAILWAY).

BIBLIOGRAPHY
General
Nock, 1973.
Specific
Lindsey, C. F. *Underground Railways in London: a select bibliography.* London: privately published, 1973.

Unesco World Heritage Site   The General Council of Unesco (the United Nations Educational, Scientific and Cultural Organization) adopted in 1972 a 'Convention Concerning the Protection of the World Cultural and Natural Heritage' which by 1988 had been ratified by over a hundred member states. Under the Convention the World Heritage Committee can adopt as World Heritage sites those 'irreplaceable testimonies of past civilizations and natural landscapes of great beauty and significance' nominated by member states which fulfil criteria related to their cultural value and the adequacy of provision for their preservation. Nearly three hundred sites had been designated by December 1987. This total includes few industrial sites: those that are so designated include ARC-ET-SENANS; the quays at BERGEN; IRONBRIDGE; the tin mines at Potosi, Bolivia; and the salt mine at WIELICZKA.

   See also figures 63, 117, 176.

BIBLIOGRAPHY
Specific
Unesco Courier (Paris) XXXIII, 1980; XLI, 1988.

LOCATION
[I] The Secretariat, World Heritage Foundation, Unesco, 7 Place de Fontenoy, 75700, Paris.

BARRIE TRINDER

uniflow   A steam engine in which the steam, superheated and at high pressure, flows in one direction, entering at one end of the cylinder, and exiting in the centre via ports uncovered by the retreating piston. The American Jacob Perkins (1766–1849) first conceived the idea in the 1820s. The work was largely repeated by Leonard Jennet Todd in 1881, but it was the German Johann Stumpf (1862–1908) who designed the first practical uniflow engines, which became noted for their efficiency, being as economical as triple-expansion engines of the same power and occupying less space. Uniflow engines were built in both horizontal and vertical configurations.

BIBLIOGRAPHY
General
Frankel, 1977; Law, 1965.

Union of Soviet Socialist Republics, west of River Yenisey

Union of Soviet Socialist Republics Modern Russia emerged as the result of the steady expansion of the princedom of Muscovy during and after the Tartar occupation of the thirteenth and fourteenth centuries. By the sixteenth century Muscovite expeditions were penetrating into Siberia, although it was not until the nineteenth century that Russia was firmly established on the Pacific. Meanwhile, and especially in the eighteenth century, the Russian Empire expanded northwards and westwards at the expense of Sweden and Poland, and southwards at the expense of Turkey. Defeat in World War I, together with the 1917 revolution, resulted in a diminution of territory. Poland, Finland, Estonia, Lithuania and Latvia won their independence, although in the case of the latter three this lasted only up to their re-absorption by Moscow in 1939–40.

European Russia may be roughly divided into the fertile steppelands of the south, and the forested or marshy northern and central regions. The Caucasian republics of Georgia, Armenia and Azerbaydzhan, which are usually considered to be part of European Russia, are mainly mountainous. Except in these Caucasian parts, stone is relatively scarce in Russia, which has considerably affected both architecture and technology.

The Russian population was probably 41 million in 1812, rising to 125 million in the 1897 census; this figure covers the entire Empire, but the population is almost entirely concentrated in the European parts. The peak population of 1913 (166 million) was not regained until the late 1930s, war, territorial losses and various privations having cost the lives of more than 20 million citizens in 1913–21. Of the 1897 population, 56 million were Russian-speakers and could be regarded as Muscovite Russians. Another 23 million spoke Ukrainian, and there were 6 million White Russians and 8 million Poles. Despite growing emigration, there were about 5 million Jews. By the end of the century the 'two capitals', St Petersburg and Moscow, each had a population in excess of one million.

A feature of Russian society was the persistence of serfdom up to 1861. On the eve of their liberation serfs amounted to about 38 per cent of the population of European Russia, with the better-placed state peasants outnumbering them by a small margin. At that time, about 94 per cent of the population was rural. The abolition of serfdom did not end all the attitudes associated with it, which caused many problems when, in late tsarist and Soviet times, a Western-style industrialization was undertaken. The prevalence of state enterprise and state direction in both tsarist and Soviet Russia may be regarded partly as a consequence of these attitudes, but the general lack of enterprise, ambition and industrial thrust was probably also a consequence of the despotic nature of the Russian state and of the ethical traditions of the Orthodox Church.

State industry reached its first peak under Tsar Peter I (Peter the Great, 1672–1725) who, unable to rely on manufacturing concerns established by landowners on their estates, set up nearly ninety state factories during his reign. These were mainly concerned with the requirements of war: textiles and uniforms, sailcloth, sulphur and gunpowder, cannon and small arms, iron and copper. Individual entrepreneurs who set up their own factories did so with state help in the form of tax exemptions, bulk orders and allocation of labour. While peasants were conscripted for the factories, successful efforts were made to persuade foreign craftsmen and specialists to bring their skills and technology to Russia. After the death of Peter in 1725 these new industries tended to degenerate, partly because incompetent management, freed of Peter's strong hand, was left to itself.

An exception to this general decline was the iron industry. Under Peter ironmaking was developed in the Urals, and progressed so rapidly that by the end of the eighteenth century Russia was the world's biggest pig-iron producer, shipping much of her production to Britain, along with more traditional exports like ships' masts, sails and ropes. Hitherto, iron production had been mainly in Karelia, and, especially, central Russia, where a Dutchman had obtained a concession to build ironworks near Tula in the mid-seventeenth century. Tula later became a centre for finished metal products, including guns, cutlery

and samovars. The exhaustion of forest reserves and the impurity of central-region pig iron, which made difficult the manufacture of reliable cannon, required a fresh start in the Urals, where the forests were untouched, the ores were more pure, and water-power was abundant. It was Demidov, a blacksmith from Tula, who established several ironworks around Ekaterinburg (Sverdlovsk) in the Urals, while the local mines were placed under the supervision of a German expert.

In the late eighteenth century Russia was technologically well advanced in ironmaking, developing some innovations, and successfully operating blast furnaces which were larger than those elsewhere. However, as was to become characteristic of Russian industry generally, radical advances in Western technology were adopted only slowly, with the state alternating between indifference or even resistance to change, and breakneck efforts to catch up. As innovations transformed Western metallurgy in the early nineteenth century, the Russian iron industry fell behind. It was not until the 1870s, with the government's generous concession to the Welsh ironmaster John Hughes, that the ores of the Ukraine were exploited, with the establishment of a new metallurgical region around DONETSK. By 1900 Russia occupied fourth place amongst the world's iron producers, and the Urals iron industry was moribund. At least one blast furnace in the Urals, the Polevskoi near Sverdlovsk, has been preserved. In Soviet times a new ferrous metallurgical combine was established elsewhere in the Urals, exploiting the ores of Magnitogorsk.

The rise of metallurgy in the Ukraine brought with it the modern coal industry. Previously coal had been mined only on a small scale, with an annual output in the mid-nineteenth century of little more than 100 000 tonnes. The availability of wood and the cost of transport made coal a poor proposition before the railway age. By 1913 production had risen to 29 million tonnes, most of it from the Ukraine, although there were sizeable workings around Moscow, in Poland, and in the Urals. Donetsk coal retained its importance in Soviet times, despite the development of new mines in the Urals and Asian Russia.

Coal and oil grew concurrently, the Baku oil industry being developed by Ludvig and Robert Nobel from the 1870s. With the construction of oil refineries a new chemical industry emerged, in which the Nobels were also involved. Oil fuel (or rather the residue after the refineries had finished with the oil) was used as a coal substitute for steamships and locomotives. Robert Urquhart, a Scottish locomotive engineer employed by the Tsaritsyn–Gryazi Railway, played a key role in adapting locomotives for this kind of fuel. The Nobel enterprises were foremost in carrying oil not in barrels but in railway tank cars and steam tankers, the latter having their holds lined with cement for the purpose.

Despite abundant reserves of coal, wood and oil, other sources of energy were sought, notably peat, which in the twentieth century has been used sporadically for electricity generation. There is a notable peat-fired generating station near KALININ. Hydro-electricity was particularly exploited in Soviet times, with Russian engineers like M. O.

DOLIVO-DOBROVOL'SKII making important contributions to its development.

Steam power is supposed to have come to Russia with the import of a Newcomen engine to operate a palace fountain in the early eighteenth century. In the 1760s I. POLZUNOV designed a steam engine said to be an improvement over the Newcomen model. Towards the end of the century Russian mechanics visited Birmingham to familiarize themselves with the Watt engine. A steam engine of 1815 is preserved in its brick engine house at the Arkhangel'skoye open-air museum. A Briton, Charles Gascoyne, after establishing an iron foundry at Olonets, started an engineering works at St Petersburg which subsequently developed into the Izhora armaments works, and other large factories in the area and at the nearby naval centre of Kronshtadt. Another Briton established an agricultural machinery works in Moscow, and then the Alexandrovskii Works at St Petersburg, which made textile machinery. In the last quarter of the nineteenth century, a period of rapid industrial and technological development, the government encouraged home production of machinery, especially of railway equipment and factory plant. The main firms, which were often foreign-owned, belonged to cartels, which may have helped orderly development but did not encourage innovation.

Partly because of the strength, until Soviet times, of handicraft industry, and partly because of government policy, factory production of consumer goods lagged behind the levels of Western countries. This was less true of textiles than of other products. In the eighteenth century Ivanovo was a centre for cotton manufacturing, and its predominance was assured when the Moscow industry was ruined in a great fire. An anglicized German, Ludwig Knoop, gained a monopoly for the import of British spinning machinery into Russia, and thereby exercised a controlling influence on the industry. British workers were also imported, and some British specialists were active in the industry until 1917. At the outset factories were heavy consumers of Lancashire yarn, but after the construction of the railway into Turkestan they began to use cotton grown in the Empire's Central Asian territories. By 1900 Russia had more spindles for spinning cotton than any other continental European country.

Great distances, shortages of stone, and extremes of climate have meant that Russian roads have always been inadequate. To some extent this lack was made up in the pre-railway age by the numerous rivers of European Russia. At the annual trade fairs, of which the largest was at Nizhnii Novgorod, goods offered for sale had often travelled hundreds, sometimes thousands of kilometres, by water. The trunk route of water transport was, and remains, the River Volga with its numerous tributaries. To make better use of the rivers Russian rulers, starting in the twelfth century with an improvement scheme at Novgorod, built canals, a policy facilitated by the availability of serf labour. Peter the Great was an enthusiastic canal builder, initiating surveys, and building, among others, the Vyshnyi Volochek–Iver Canal, linking the Volga with the Baltic. His attempt to link the Don and the Volga failed,

although the project was eventually completed in Soviet times. At the end of the nineteenth century there were nine major canal systems in use. Here and there, as at PETROKREPOST', remnants of dams and locks from these systems remain, sometimes in service. By the end of the eighteenth century Russian government engineers had amassed vast experience in hydraulic engineering, which was put to good use in industrial projects. In 1700 there were already some two hundred dams providing water power for manufacturing concerns. The 17 m (56 ft.) diameter underground water wheel of K. D. FROLOV at Zmeinogorsk is still in existence.

Zmeinogorsk was also the site of what was probably Russia's first railway, a horse-drawn mineral line. The first public railway was from St Petersburg to the nearby town of Tsarskoye Selo (Pushkin), where the summer palace was located. The line was opened in 1838, after which there was some delay while the government determined its policy. The problem of how to exploit new technology without the usual accompaniment of new – and therefore potentially subversive – ideas was, and would remain, a characteristic Russian dilemma. In the early 1850s the state opened its St Petersburg–Moscow and Warsaw–Krakow lines. Henceforth railway policy revolved around the various building plans drawn up by the government, and around the permanent controversy about the most advantageous mix of wholly state control and state-assisted private enterprise in construction and operation. At the time of the revolution there were still six large private railway companies, although most routes belonged to the state.

The railway gauge was standardized at 5 ft. (1.524 m) in the 1850s although the line opened in 1838 had been 6 ft. (1.829 m) and the Warsaw–Krakow line of standard 4ft. $8\frac{1}{2}$ in. (1.435 m) gauge. Later, for the usual reasons, some lines of 2 ft. 6 in. (750 mm) gauge were built, some of which remain in use. The decade 1895–1905 was a great period for railway building, especially in Asiatic Russia, where the Trans-Siberian line and the eastern part of the Trans-Caspian line were completed. By 1913 there were 72 000 route km (44 740 mi.) of common carrier railway, and this doubled in the following seventy years. Narrow-gauge mileage reached a peak of over 6000 km (3700 mi.) in 1946, and in the 1950s new narrow-gauge lines in Kazakhstan compensated for closures and conversions elsewhere. Considerable lengths of narrow-gauge line remain in Latvia and Estonia.

Many buildings of the early railway age remain in use, including the two termini of the St Petersburg–Moscow line. Some original buildings of the locomotive works are also in daily use. The Alexandrovskii Works, which assembled and repaired the imported American locomotives used on the St Petersburg–Moscow line, became the Profintern Works in Soviet times. The Kilomna Works near Moscow, where locomotives were built from the 1860s, developed into one of the great engineering complexes of the USSR. Towards the end of the nineteenth century the state offered substantial inducements to encourage domestic locomotive building, which made it worthwhile for the Pultilov Works at St Petersburg (*see*

Figure 163   Off-shore oil rigs in Azerbaydzhan
Novosti

LENINGRAD) and the Sormovo Works at Nizhnii Novgorod (hitherto building river steamships) to begin locomotive construction, and for a new specialized locomotive works to be established at Lugansk. The Sormovo and Putilov works in the Soviet period turned to general engineering, while the Lugansk (Voroshilovgrad) Works are now the centre of the diesel locomotive industry.

The first electric tramway appeared in Kiev in 1892, and the technology spread rapidly. Foreign and notably Belgian companies participated, and in scores of towns the electric tram remains an essential element of urban transportation. The 5 ft. (1.524 m) gauge was favoured, although there are about half a dozen systems of 3 ft. 6 in. (1.067 m) gauge. Moscow and to an increasing extent other big cities use modern Czech-built tramcars, but in the smaller towns vintage vehicles remain in use. Several cities employ trolleybuses.

One of several distinctive features of Russian industrial archaeology is that many industrial relics remain within functioning complexes, and are therefore unremarked, or at least not open to outside visitors. Another is that until recently public appreciation of industrial monuments was non-existent. The period from the 1920s to the 1950s was a black age for preservation. The economy was so tightly pressed that resources devoted to conservation could be

seen as direct losses from the economy. Excessive concern with security meant that records were regarded as dangerous unless it could be proved otherwise. This is why, for example, photographic records of railway station layouts are practically non-existent for the 1930s, 40s and 50s, whereas there are hundreds of postcard views of pre-revolutionary railway scenes. The creditable achievement in Soviet times of multiplying the output of engineering graduates had the unfortunate side effect of producing 'vandals with diplomas', who would not allow antiquarian scruples to interfere with their quest for bonuses awarded for handing in metal scrap. In the 1920s there was a siding full of the original locomotives of the St Petersburg–Moscow railway, but despite metal plates announcing that they were earmarked for preservation, they were fed to furnaces. Similar events took place in later years and in other industries. Possibly the biggest factor, however, was a general lack of appreciation of the old in a period when all emphasis was on the new and revolutionary. It was in such an atmosphere that the Museum of the History of Science and Technology at Leningrad was broken up when its parent, the Academy of Sciences, was transferred from Leningrad to Moscow.

On the other hand the difficult economic situation meant that plant and machinery was kept in use well beyond its natural life. It is still possible to find nineteenth-century tools and equipment in use, which, with the current burgeoning interest in the past and its relics, means that in some fields the prospects for preservation are bright.

It was probably in the late 1960s that the tide began to turn. Possibly the more relaxed economic situation and greater time for leisure interests were factors in this. Another was the blossoming, especially on the part of Muscovite Russians, of a nationalistic but largely nostalgic interest in the past. A legislative basis for improvement came with the Law on the Preservation and Utilization of Memorials of History and Culture, passed in 1976. This amounted to official approval for efforts to preserve industrial and technical relics, and allowed the establishment of the unofficial All-Russian Society for the Preservation of Memorials of History and Culture ('VOOPIK'), with branches in several of the larger cities. Most have 'Sections for Memorials of Science and Technology'. Moreover, since 1980 the Institute of the History of Science and Technology of the Academy of Sciences has published a journal, *Voprosy istorii estestvozhaniyi i tekhniki* (Questions of the History of Science and Technology). So far this has been mainly interested in the history of Russian science, but technology has not been ignored.

Museums have been a much-appreciated feature of Russian society, both before and after the Revolution. Polytechnical museums exist in Moscow and LENINGRAD. There are more specialized museums which usually rely on documents and models. The LENINGRAD and Tashkent railway museums and the UL'YANOVSK civil aviation museum have promising futures. There are over seventy open-air museums in Russia; the majority have been established since 1945, although those in Latvia and Lithuania date from the 1920s and 30s, and interest in such museums in the Baltic states began as early as the 1890s. The concept of working museums arrived late in Russia and little has been done, but the material exists in several localities. Perhaps the most promising is in the Altai region of Central Asia, where many of the late eighteenth- and early nineteenth-century mining installations are still in place. The Baku oilfields, parts of the Donets Basin, and various sites in the older industrial cities also offer opportunities. Already, the idea of placing a whole industrial complex on public view has been accepted. The saltworks at SOLIKAMSK and the VENTSPILS fisheries museum are examples of a phenomenon that is still rare but that may be expected to multiply.

Russian and Soviet industrialists, inventors and scientists have shown great originality. Important advances were often made first by Russians, but, because of the difficulty of obtaining government approval, these often languished and were overtaken by Western innovations. Highly original solutions were sometimes proposed and occasionally carried into practice by Russians. Telegraphy, radio and aviation were just three fields in which Russians played leading roles. Hidden away inside Russia, sometimes in obscure museums, are the relics of great experiments and great enterprises which deserve wider appreciation.

See also BELOMORSK; CHEREPANOV, E. A. AND M. E.; DOLIVO-DOBROVOL'SKII, M. O.; DONETSK; FROVLOVS, K. D; GAKKEL', Y.; KALININ; KAUNAS; KIEV; LENINGRAD; MOSCOW; PETROKREPOST'; POLZUNOV, I.; RIGA; SHCHUSEV, A. V.; SHUKHOV, V. G. S.; SOLIKAMSK; TALLINN; UL'YANOVSK; VENTSPILS.

BIBLIOGRAPHY
General
Andrie, 1988; Blackwell, 1968; Lyaschenko, 1949; Westwood, 1982; Zippelius, 1974.
Specific
Museums in the USSR, Moscow: Ministry of Culture, 1977.

LOCATION
[M] Railway Museum, Railway Station, Tashkent.

JOHN WESTWOOD

United States of America

Industry is a central thread interwoven with the establishment of British colonies in North America and the emergence of the independent nation of the USA in 1776. Plentiful natural resources coupled with waves of skilled immigrants and systems of open commerce enabled the region to stir with industrial activity well before it won its independence.

Although self-sufficient agricultural pursuits occupied the first European settlers in America, the acquisition of raw materials by the mother country, and the creation of markets for finished goods produced in Europe served to stimulate interest in the development of American colonies. Soon after the first British settlement in the sixteenth century and the outright seizure of territory from the Dutch in 1664, the dual mercantile roles of the colonies as provider and consumer of British goods began to furnish a basis for the hostilities that resulted in the creation of an independent USA.

Company colonies organized for profit and controlled from England were established in Virginia in 1607 by the London Co., and in Massachusetts in 1664 by the Massachusetts Bay Co., as centres of export for North American furs, timber, fish and agricultural products. Independent colonial ventures, however, in the processing and manufacturing of goods for domestic use and export to other nations, met with restrictive legislation such as the Navigation Acts 1651, 1660 and 1663, which limited certain exports to passage in British ships bound for British ports alone. The Iron Act 1750 sought unsuccessfully to prevent colonial American ironworks from producing anything but pig and bar iron bound for British manufacturers. Despite these and other efforts to keep the colonies economically and politically dependent on England, an independent American commerce flourished in shipbuilding, trapping, textile manufacture, agricultural processing and the production of ironwares. Great Britain nevertheless remained the chief market for and source of many manufactured goods until well after American independence.

The new encouragements given to American manufactures after the War of Independence of 1775–83 dramatically increased the abilities of craft shops to produce goods, although a sparse population in a hostile, frontier environment continued to confine such growth largely to

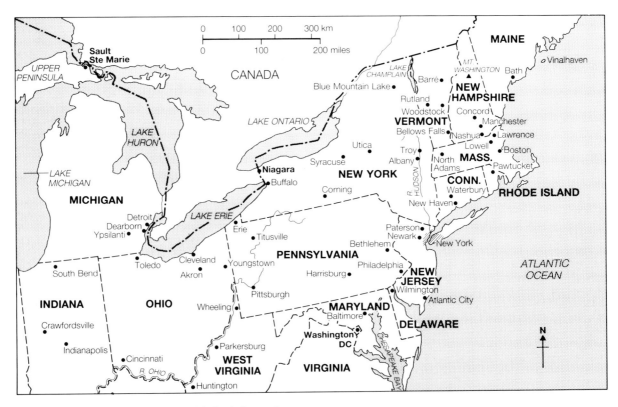

United States of America (above), and (below) the north-eastern states

agricultural activity. The establishment of an American system of patents for new inventions, the facilitation of interstate commerce with road, canal and, later, railway construction, and the creation of a central banking system to hasten the exchange of goods were among the incentives that encouraged a rising interest in American manufacturing. It was not, however, until the early nineteenth century, when the mills and factories of New England took on sizeable workforces, harnessed the region's water-power resources on a large scale and concentrated methods of production, that the term 'Industrial' first appeared in connection with manufacturing or processing enterprises.

By the 1790s, American 'industry', such as it was, comprised a scattering of water-powered mills and craft-workers' shops using many technologies and knowledgeable workers brought from Europe. While all but the most basic commodities continued to be imported from abroad, such manufacturing centres as Philadelphia and Boston were developing sophisticated networks of small-scale commercialization, supported by systems of transport whose bridges, roads and canals were increasingly products of a new, native-grown, American engineering community.

Population scarcity is considered one of the main incentives that pushed American manufacturing enterprise to mechanize early (*see* AMERICAN SYSTEM OF MANUFACTURES), spurring a host of supporting developments in the extraction and processing of raw materials, the development of transport networks, and the creation of armies of labour-saving woodworking and metal-cutting machines. Hand labour remained a major aspect of all early industrial endeavours, but burgeoning markets for finished goods placed a premium on the ability of labour to produce, by hand or by machine.

A rapidly expanding immigrant population and its accompanying commercial activity moved west and south of the Atlantic seaboard with the acquisition of vast tracts of land from Spain and France in the early and mid-nineteenth century. The original thirteen states of 1776 had grown to twenty-six by 1828, creating centres of commerce no longer wedded to coastal trade. British-built locomotives, modified to suit American terrain, steamed along iron-plated wooden trackage; steam engines also supplanted water wheels in manufacturing facilities from the 1830s, freeing mills from dependence on falling water as motive power. The replacement of iron gears with flat leather belts produced an American revolution in power-transmission systems, decreasing fabrication costs and power loss and increasing the adaptability of steam power to a broad range of enterprises.

As in Great Britain, a gradual geographical clustering of industries by type began to occur in the early nineteenth century, a function of resource availability and access to markets. Textile production and the precision metal-cutting industries became concentrated in the New England states. The iron and and steel industries, initially dispersed wherever ready sources of ore and fuel existed, concentrated in mid-century around the great seams of bituminous COAL in western Pennsylvania and northern Alabama. Specialized woodworking and leather industries sprang up in knots across lower New England and the heavily forested regions of the upper Midwest. The rough bridge- and building-construction methods that knitted these centres together, depending on craftsmen and designers who were often unskilled in classical techniques, yielded a reputation for quick work not necessarily envied by observers from abroad. The British construction journal, *The Builder*, commented in 1891 that 'in England we have had some differences of opinion as to whether architecture may be considered as an art or a profession, but it has been reserved for America to present us with architecture as a trade'.

With the acquisition of Louisiana from France in 1803, Texas and California from Mexico in the 1840s, Florida and further western territories from Spain in 1819 and 1848, and Oregon and Alaska from Russia in 1846 and 1867, the USA increased in size several times over. Abundant land and seemingly endless resources of every sort helped breed among the new Americans a sense of their 'manifest destiny' to create a pre-ordained civilization from ocean to ocean. Railways and rivers were providing for essential movement of people and materials across such expanses by mid-century, the steam-powered means passing through several series of innovations to develop power and speed. Such was the vigour of interest in steam power, mobile or stationary, that onlookers occasionally presumed a neglect of other worthy pursuits by Americans: 'No one who has passed his thirteenth year in the savage atmosphere of America can be a piano virtuoso', wrote Pierre Zimmerman in 1841, refusing admission of an American pianist to the Paris Conservatory: 'The best that country can do in the way of art is to turn out manufacturers of steam engines.'

As with the War of Independence, the American Civil War of 1861–5 had a strong basis in economic conflict. The largely agricultural but industrially aspiring Southern states saw their wealth, resources and traditions being drained by the encroaching mid-century influences of the Northern states, with their alien notions about the institution of slavery and Southern economics generally. With the war's costly suppression of the Confederate effort towards secession, national commerce became even more firmly rooted in the industrial north, although New Orleans and Charleston, among other ports, prospered as centres of manufacturing and Southern commerce. As with most wars, the Civil War also advanced industrial technologies, especially in metalworking. Between 1864 and 1868, more cotton spindles were placed in operation, more blast furnaces erected and iron smelted, more steel made, more lumber sawn and more factories constructed than in any previous four-year period in the nation's history.

With the completion of transcontinental railways in subsequent years, such vigour spread west to California, chequered with occasional economic slumps. With the support of massive federal tariff protections, the period from 1870 to 1920 saw America come of age as a world industrial power, admitting millions of European immigrants, while exporting American influence through the establishment of strategic territorial presences in the Pacific, the Caribbean and Central America.

In the headlong rush to produce and diversify, the exploitation of natural resources reached levels by the century's end that called for an arresting of unchecked industrial growth. The foul airs around the steel mills had caused one visitor to Pittsburgh in 1868 to describe it as 'hell with the lid taken off'. Animal species were disappearing. Virgin forests, once considered inexhaustible, had all but vanished from the eastern states. The sense of genuine limits on growth helped spark federal legislation in the early twentieth century to protect wilderness lands. The same protection was not afforded to the monopolizing industrialists and railway barons who sought to capitalize on the mushrooming demand for goods and services by slicing off enormous market shares for their exclusive control. Environmental and trust-busting legislation joined with new controls on workplace safety and sanitation to produce a new climate of industrial restraint in the century's early decades.

The craft-based immigrant labour forces were one of several forces behind the creation of a powerful organized American labour presence, beginning in the post-Civil War years. Protests over wage rates, working conditions, the length of the working day, hiring practices, and the introduction of labour-saving machinery stimulated market-wrenching union action, from which workers gained new powers, but such action also led to the closure of factories unable to cope with these demands.

An increasingly assertive work force provided an even greater spur to the development of specialized semi-automatic production machines by the century's end. Reliance on semi-skilled, cheaper workers tending greater numbers of metal-cutting or textile machines accelerated overall growth while feeding expanding consumer demand, trends considerably heightened by the two world wars, despite the new controls placed on industry by government.

Steel production and precision metalworking were fields upgraded to world-leading status by an enterprise that remains at the heart of American manufacturing activity: the automobile industry. The physical size of the nation and the population's mobility placed the automobile at the centre of a vast network of rubber, glass and metals manufactures, spinning off technologies that have affected a host of other industries.

The pervasive economic depression of the 1930s, with its fatal effects on much small-scale industry, precipitated massive government intervention in private business activity. Make-work programmes employed waves of destitute blue-collar and white-collar workers, not only propping up the economy but creating some of the most monumental and enduring architectural and civil engineering works of the age, poetic counterpoints to the waves of human destruction that followed in World War II.

After 1945 the new industrial age of streamlined building construction, together with an impatience with faded notions about the ornamentation of structures, especially industrial ones, placed the standing artefacts of the industrial past in considerable jeopardy. Post-war needs for inexpensive housing and rapid transit created additional excuses for the levelling of 'old-fashioned' structures in the great urban-renewal and interstate highway projects of the 1950s and 60s.

With the destruction of such conspicuous landmarks as Pennsylvania Station in New York City (built in 1910, razed in 1964) and early industrialized amusement parks like San Francisco's Playland at the Beach, locally fuelled outcries that developers should cease and desist resulted in protective federal, state and local legislation in the 1970s, aimed at safeguarding what remained of the oustanding examples of the architectural and industrial heritage. As a consequence of such grass-roots campaigns, which rallied support for an individual iron bridge or mill building, several of the professional engineering organizations established landmarking programmes (see LANDMARK) to add their belated voices to protests against the desecration of past engineering achievements. In the late 1960s the National Park Service established the Historic American Engineering Record (HAER) – a younger sister to the Historic American Buildings Survey (HABS) – as a documentary centre, recording by photograph and measured drawing the details of historic industrial structures.

National organizations like the Association for Preservation Technology, the National Trust for Historic Preservation, and especially the Society for Industrial Archeology (founded in 1971) began to act as clearing houses for news and background on an industrial heritage, attracting sizeable numbers of Americans from museums, universities, private industry and government. Museums newly involved in the field, led by the National Museum of American History in Washington, joined with a handful of universities to take up the considerable historical issues and problems raised by the transformation of the industrial landscape and such associated matters as the emasculation of the American steel industry. Recording and collecting in an environment of decrepit heavy industry have posed challenges that continue to perplex.

Such institutional momentum nevertheless helped to inaugurate a nationwide interest in reconsidering the usefulness of ill-used industrial structures, not simply as historic sites but as well-built surroundings for new corporate offices, food markets, housing for the elderly, and high-technology 'post-industrial' activities. Such interests received a big boost in 1981 with the passing of federal legislation that decreased taxes levied on developers who appropriately restored properties designated as historic.

At the federal level the US Department of the Interior administers programmes that set preservation standards, identify and certify historic properties, and occasionally acquire sites of national importance for custody by the National Park Service. Preservation initiatives not of a purely profit-making nature often receive funding through the National Endowment for the Humanities, another federal agency. At the state level, inventories of historic sites and preservation programme support rests with the state historic preservation offices, occasionally in

Figure 164 'The Niagara of Water Wheels,' 18.3 m (60 ft.) in diameter, and yielding a maximum of 482 hp, constructed in 1851 on the Wynantskill at Troy, New York, by Henry Burden, a Scotsman who developed a series of works producing such items as horse shoes and spikes for railway cross-ties; the photograph dates from *c*.1900. The wheel collapsed early in the twentieth century.

Smithsonian Institution, Engineering Archives

the form of state historical societies. Locally a variety of professional and volunteer organizations exist in most urban areas to champion specific structures and work with the developers, the effectiveness of these groups typically being dependent on the significance of the heritage resources and the resolve of the participants.

A systematic basis for survey work throughout the USA is provided by the 'general-purpose' maps published by the US Geological Survey since the early 1880s, originally at a scale of 1:62 500 but since the 1960s at 1:24 000. The maps are bounded on their four sides by parallels of latitude and meridians of longitude producing a near rectangle called a quadrangle. They are normally called 'quads'. The *Statistical Abstract of the United States*, published annually since 1878, provides essential data for studies of industrial history.

The new recognition being given to the structural

soundness of the built environment of ages past, matched with a reappraisal of much modern building construction, continues to breathe life into derelict canneries, textile mills, locomotive depots and sewage-pumping stations across the land, despite a reduction in 1986 to the tax relief available to preservation developers. Efforts to save the nation's many small historic bridges must contend with pressures from state and federal transportation bureaucracies, seeking high-profile upgrades of the transit infrastructure, targeting many spans for demolition and replacement. Many of the smaller iron bridges clearly unfit to carry modern traffic loads have been relocated to side roads or, with some imagination, placed in parklands. Other spans have held their ground, sympathetic applications of structural steel and hidden trusswork strengthening their decks and towers. As a tour of any American city's inner core or riverfront will reveal, a profusion of

797

industrial structures of the past stands in wait for the transforming effects of adaptive reuse.

See also ALABAMA; ALASKA; ARIZONA; ARKANSAS; CALIFORNIA; COLORADO; CONNECTICUT; DELAWARE; FLORIDA; GEORGIA; HAWAII; IDAHO; ILLINOIS; INDIANA; IOWA; KANSAS; KENTUCKY; LOUISIANA; MAINE; MARYLAND; MASSACHUSETTS; MICHIGAN; MINNESOTA; MISSISSIPPI; MISSOURI; MONTANA; NEBRASKA; NEVADA; NEW HAMPSHIRE; NEW JERSEY; NEW MEXICO; NEW YORK; NORTH CAROLINA; NORTH DAKOTA; OHIO; OKLAHOMA; OREGON; PENNSYLVANIA; RHODE ISLAND; SOUTH CAROLINA; SOUTH DAKOTA; TENNESSEE; TEXAS; UTAH; VERMONT; VIRGINIA; WASHINGTON; WASHINGTON DC; WEST VIRGINIA; WISCONSIN; WYOMING.

BIBLIOGRAPHY
General
Bishop, 1864; Boorstin, 1958, 1965, 1973; Clark, 1928; Ferguson, 1968; Finegold, 1978; Habakkuk, 1967; HAER, 1981; Hartenberg, 1979; Hazen and Hazen, 1985; Hindle, 1966, 1975, 1981; Hoy, 1976; Hunter, 1979, 1984; Jackson, K. 1985; Jackson, D. C. 1988; Jeremy, 1981; Kasson, 1976; Kidney, 1976; Knight, 1876; Koch, 1979; Lewis, 1976; Mayr and Post, 1982; Meeks, 1956; Montgomery, 1979; Munn, 1977; Nelson, 1975; Pursell, 1969; Sande, 1976; Shank, 1982; Vogel, 1973; White, 1968, 1980.

Specific
Comp, T. A. and Jackson, D. *Bridge Truss Types: a guide to dating and identifying*. Nashville, Tenn.: American Association for State and Local History, 1977.
Procter, M. and Matuszeski, W. *Gritty Cities*. Philadelphia, 1978.
Vogel, R. M. Quadrangular treasure: the cartographic route to industrial archeology. In *IA*, VI, 1980.

LOCATIONS
[I] Early American Industries Association, 60 Harvest Lane, Levittown, NY 11756.
[I] Friends of Cast Iron Architecture, 135 E. 87th Street 6C, New York, NY 10028.
[I] Historic American Engineering Record, National Park Service, PO Box 37127, Washington, DC 20013–7127.
[I] National Trust for Historic Preservation, 1785 Massachusetts Avenue NW, Washington, DC 20036.
[I] Society for the History of Technology, University of Chicago Press, 5801 South Ellis Avenue, Chicago, Illinois 60637.
[I] Society for Historical Archaeology, PO Box 231033, Pleasant Hill, California 94523.
[I] Society for Industrial Archeology, Room 5020, National Museum of American History, Smithsonian Institution, Washington, DC 20560.

DAVID H. SHAYT

Unterregenbach, Baden-Württemberg, Germany The covered wooden bridge over the Jagst in Unterregenbach, 40 km (25 mi.) NE of Heilbronn, built in 1821, is a fine monument to the carpenter's art. It has a truss-frame arch, 47 m (154 ft.) in length, and is among the largest preserved single-span wooden bridges.

Unwin, Raymond (1863–1940) One of the most influential of twentieth-century planners, Unwin designed the GARDEN CITY of Letchworth, Hampstead Garden Suburb in LONDON, New Earswick (*see* YORK), and

Gretna (*see* DUMFRIES & GALLOWAY). From 1896 he worked in partnership with Richard Barry Parker. His career from 1910 was chiefly in government and universities.

BIBLIOGRAPHY
General
Unwin, 1909.

Upper Silesia, Poland Upper Silesia is one of the principal industrial regions in Europe, extending over 5400 km^2 (2100 sq. mi.) of coal measures in the form of a triangle stretching from the Tarnowskie Mountains in the north to Czechoslovakia in the south. The coal deposits dip only slightly, making them easy to mine, and reach a depth of one kilometre. Coking-coal deposits are concentrated in the western and southern parts of the region. In the seventeenth and eighteenth centuries metal-working plants were all situated near to sources of ore, with iron being smelted at Kluczbork, Lubliniec and Opole, and silver and lead mined at Tarnowskie Gory and Bytom.

In the early nineteenth century the Upper Silesian Industrial Region was divided between the three powers who occupied Poland. The western part, Upper Silesia proper, belonged to Prussia and underwent rapid industrialization. The north-eastern part, the Dąbrowskie region, was under Russian administration and industry was concentrated mainly around Dąbrowa Górnicza, where a government plant for the development of metallurgical industries based on local coal supplies was put into operation in the 1830s. In the last thirty years of the nineteenth century the Dąbrowski region became the most important steel-producing area in the Congress Kingdom of Poland. Large quantities of steel were exported to Russia, and engineering, textile manufactures and glassmaking all prospered. The eastern part of the region, the Krakowskie area, was ruled by the Habsburgs whose policies impeded industrial development.

The growth of the Upper Silesian Industrial Region was stimulated in the early nineteenth century by the introduction of a new method of extracting metallic zinc from the rich deposits of galman ($ZnCO_3$) found in the Tarnowskie Mountains and in the vicinity of Bytom. By 1850 Upper Silesia was among the biggest producers of zinc in the world. Growing zinc production did much to stimulate coal mining.

In Gliwice a coke-fired blast furnace was built to the design of a Scot, John Baildon, in 1796. Coke smelting brought about changes in the geographical distribution of industrial plants during the nineteenth century. At the beginning of the century the largest plants were located at such places as Opole, Kluczbork and Lubliniec, far from the coalfields, but these declined as urban-industrial developments grew around Bytom, Chorzów, Gliwice, Katowice and ZABRZE, where most coal was mined, and where zinc works and ironworks were established. Supplies of iron ore in Upper Silesia were gradually exhausted during the second half of the nineteenth century, and ore was imported from the Ukraine, Sweden and Austria. Technological developments, new markets created by the construction of railways (beginning in 1845 and 1847 with the lines from Wrocław to Berlin and Kraków), capital investment from abroad, and the protective tariffs raised by the Prussian government all served to accelerate industrial growth in the second half of the nineteenth century. Between 1860 and 1913 the number of industrial workers in the Prussian part of Upper Silesia increased from 30 000 to 90 000. Coal production increased to eighteen times its starting volume over the same period, reaching 43 400 000 tonnes in 1913. Pig-iron output was multiplied eleven times and zinc production four times. The population of the region rose from 966 000 in 1849 to 2 200 000 in 1910, most of the workers in the Prussian sector being Polish. After World War I the Dąbrowski and Krakowski regions became part of independent Poland and in 1922 the greater part of Upper Silesia was incorporated into Poland.

The last iron-ore mines closed during the slump of 1930–3 but the region's industries revived in the late 1930s. After World War II the whole region was incorporated within Poland. The industrial scene within the region is now dominated by coal mining, metallurgy, coking plants, and engineering and chemical installations. Only a few industrial monuments and historical artefacts have been preserved. A hoist tower with winding gear of 1798 has been retained at the Machine Tool Plant 'Ponar' at Poręba, 20 km (12 mi.) NE of Katowice. At Palowice near Orzegów is a brickworks with a richly ornamented hoist tower of the mid-nineteenth century. In Ozimek on the Mała Panew River is the oldest suspension bridge in Upper Silesia, dating from 1827. Typical elements within the industrial landscape are vast and often richly ornamented production halls like the power-plant building of 1900–7 at the 'Bobrek' steel mill in Bytom, or the rolling mill at the 'Jedność' steelworks in Siemianowice, 10 km (6 mi.) N. of Katowice. Mining and metalworking traditions are well documented. At TARNOWSKIE GORY is a museum of silver and lead mining in old workings dating from the seventeenth to the nineteenth centuries. The rolling mill of 1901 from the 'Silesia' plant at LIPINY, near Katowice, has been placed under legislative protection, together with part of a zinc mill of 1908. At Szopienice, also near Katowice, muffle furnaces for zinc smelting are preserved, together with zinc furnaces dating from 1910, a blende warehouse, marking hammers, and a water tower of 1912. The Museum of Mining in ZABRZE is centred around the 'Guide' shaft of 1860. At the 'Pokój' mine in Ruda Śląska, 15 km (9 mi.) W. of Katowice, the buildings at the head of the 'Andrzej' shaft are well preserved, together with the buildings of c.1900 relating to the 'Franciszek' shaft at the 'Wawel' mine. In Katowice-Wełnowiec some of the buildings of the 'Alfred' mine of the 1870s were converted to apartments in the 1920s. One of the oldest power plants in the Upper Silesian region, 'Chorzów', built in 1896–8, is still in operation, and some important historic machines remain in use in modern industrial plants. There are steam hammers of the late nineteenth century at the F. Dzierżyński steel mill at Dąbrowa Górnicza, 20 km (12 mi.) NE of Katowice. Steam winding engines remain in use at several mines, the most impor-

tant being that of 1896 at the 'Bartosz' shaft of the 'Katowice' mine.

Many workers' settlements of historic interest can be found within the region. A good example of a development in the style of a garden city, based on English precedents, is 'Giszowiec' near Katowice, established in 1907–14, while 'Nikiszowiec' near Katowice is an example of a settlement consisting of large apartment blocks.

BIBLIOGRAPHY
General
Jaros, 1966; Jezierski and Zawadzki, 1966; Kowecka, 1978; Kwaśny, 1968.

PIOTR GERBER

Uppland, Uppsala, Sweden   The northern part of the old province of Uppland is largely a forest region. Iron ore was mined and smelted on a small scale in the Middle Ages, when peasant ironworkers produced OSMUND IRON. In the fifteenth century the discovery of the DANNEMORA iron ore mine completely changed the situation. During the reign of King Gustavus Vasa (1496–1560) the Crown became involved in the development of iron production in Sweden with the object of increasing state revenues. Great efforts were made to change from producing osmund iron to making bar iron. The Crown took over many of the existing small ironworks and appointed bailiffs to control production. At Dannemora a special company in which the king was a shareholder was formed in 1540. Skilled miners were brought in from Germany.

The ironworks around the Dannemora mines owned by the Crown started to increase their production, and the development of ironworking in the region was continued by the sons of Gustavus Vasa. In the early seventeenth century began a period of prosperity for the iron industry of northern Uppland which was to last for more than two hundred years. The state developed new policies to encourage iron production. The ironworks were at first leased out, and from the 1640s the leaseholders were allowed to acquire their works. Many of the tenants were foreigners, a great number of them prosperous Walloon merchants or technicians from the region around LIÈGE, who had been displaced during the Thirty Years War of 1618–48. Louis de Geer arranged their migration to Sweden. The migration of Walloons reached a peak in the 1630s and ceased completely in the 1650s, by which time some three hundred Walloon ironworkers and their families had settled in Sweden. They remained faithful to the French language, their Calvinist religion, and their cultural traditions. For generations sons inherited the jobs of their fathers, and were trained by them. Many Walloon names are still to be found in the BRUKS of Uppland. The expansion of ironworking continued during the seventeenth century, but with the ending of the Thirty Years War in 1648 it was necessary to find new markets, and the development of steelmaking in the SHEFFIELD area proved to be of the utmost importance to the Walloon ironworks of northern Uppland.

The exceptionally high quality of Dannemora iron ore, combined with the Walloon methods of producing pig iron and forging it, made the bar iron from the Walloon bruks especially suitable for steel manufacture. Walloon iron was highly esteemed by the Sheffield steelmakers, who paid almost twice as much for Walloon or 'Öregrund' iron as for other types. The bruks of Uppland grew in importance and prosperity. Leufstra and Österby became the two largest bruks in the country. Nevertheless only 10 per cent of Swedish bar-iron exports originated from the Walloon bruks, the remainder of the market being supplied by the ironworks in BERGSLAGEN which produced the so-called German forged iron.

The ironworks along the coast of Uppland were ravaged by the Russians in 1719. All the buildings were burnt down and iron production ceased for several years, but the rapid recovery of the industry was stimulated by an increasing demand for Walloon iron, and the bruks became even more successful than before. Capital could not be invested in advanced technological improvements since the State would not allow increased production. The owners of the ironworks therefore used their surplus capital to replan and rebuild the bruks as MODEL COMMUNITIES, and many of the Uppland communities in the mid-eighteenth century were adorned with buildings of high architectural quality. The ironmasters built not only fine new manor houses, designed by the best architects of the time, but also churches, workers' cottages, furnace and forge buildings, and ornamental gardens. These villages remain as evidence of the working and living conditions in Swedish ironworking communities of the pre-industrial period. Among the largest and best preserved are FORSMARKS BRUK, Hargs bruk (see HARGS BRUK AND HARGSHAMN), KARLHOLMS BRUK, LEUFSTRA BRUK, Österby bruk, 6 km (4 mi.) E. of DANNEMORA, and STRÖMSBERGS BRUK.

The advent of mild steel, made by the BESSEMER and OPEN-HEARTH processes, at first made little impact on the Walloon bruks. A few had turned to the use of LANCASHIRE FORGES but many continued with their small water-powered works using the Walloon process. There remained a market for Walloon iron which could be sold at a high premium, but the quantities exported could never match those from modern steelworks. The total amount of bar iron from the Walloon bruks amounted to between 7000 and 8000 tons in the late nineteenth century, a figure which was never surpassed.

Some of the Walloon forges closed down in the last decades of the nineteenth century. Others survived until the 1920s and 30s. The last Walloon forge in Uppland – at Österby bruk – ceased operation in the 1940s. The last of all the Walloon forges in Sweden – at Strömbacka in Hälsingland – closed down in 1947.

Only a few of the ironworks in northern Uppland turned to modern iron- and steelmaking. The export of pig iron from Sweden was never allowed until the mid-nineteenth century. When the ban was raised some of the larger enterprises in Uppland started to produce pig iron on a larger scale, and then built modern steelmaking plants. Gimo bruk, Söderfors bruk and Österby bruk thus continued with modern steelmaking into the twentieth century.

BIBLIOGRAPHY
General
Ehn, 1979; Ekman *et al.*, 1987; Nisser, 1979.

MARIE NISSER

uranium (U)   An elemental metal. Mining of uranium developed in the twentieth century in connection with the production of radium, but it was also used as a salt in glass and pottery manufacture. Demand increased following the development of atomic power during World War II. Uranium occurs in many forms, often in association with other metal ores, and deposits have been worked with similar techniques. The principal producers are Zaire, the USA, Canada, Australia, and Namibia, with some deposits in Europe (*see* JÁCHYMOV).

Utah, United States of America   The standard rollcall of Western extractive metallic ores – copper, gold, silver, lead, and zinc – does not avoid Utah, another of the large, rectilinear states of the mountain West. A vast open-pit copper mine, claimed to be the world's first – although PARYS MOUNTAIN was a precedent – was dug in 1904 near Salt Lake City, where it continues to yield a large portion of the nation's annual need. In Eureka stands the Tintic Mining Museum, surveying the state's entire mining heritage.

By the late twentieth century manufacturing had replaced mining as Utah's chief industry, while the state's central location in the West continued to make it a hub of land transportation systems.

Chief among these has been the railway. The first transcontinental trunk line passes through northern Utah, the famous joining of its two segments from east and west occurring in 1869 at Promontory. The resulting railway followed a circuitous course around lakes, mountains and other obstructions. Under new ownership, it was straightened and shortened in 1904, passing over an 18 km (11 mi.) timber trestle viaduct across the Great Salt Lake, known today as the Ogden–Lucin Cutoff Trestle.

One of John Eastwood's most eye-popping multiple-arch dams remains in active service across Parley's Creek, near Salt Lake City. The Mountain Dell Dam was built in 1917, and raised 12 m (40 ft.) in 1925: its massive concrete struts and buttresses are open to view on the downstream face.

In Ogden sits one of the nation's more unexpected wide-ranging industrial museums, the Ogden Union Station Museum. Its collection of locomotives, automobiles, construction equipment, machine tools and inventor's patent models is housed in the city's locomotive depot of 1924.

BIBLIOGRAPHY
Specific
Jackson, D. C. John S. Eastwood and the Mountain Dell Dam. In
   IA, v, 1979.

LOCATIONS
[M] Ogden Union Station Museum, 25th & Wall Avenues, Ogden,

Figure 165 The Mountain Dell multiple arch dam, near Salt Lake City, Utah, designed by John Eastwood; it was build in 1917 and heightened in 1925.
Jet Lowe, HAER

UT 84401.
[M] Tintic Mining Museum, Box 218, Eureka, UT 84628.

DAVID H. SHAYT

Utopian community 'Utopia' was the name given by Sir Thomas More (1478–1535), in a book written in Latin in 1515–16 and published in English in 1551, to an imaginary island with a perfect system of government. The term was applied from the early seventeenth century to any such imaginary country, region or settlement, and from the mid-eighteenth century to any idealistic scheme for the organization of society.

In the industrial period the term 'Utopian' has been applied both to theoretical proposals for MODEL COMMUNI-TIES, and to settlements based on particular ideas that have actually been established, of which there were many in the nineteenth century.

Among the most influential proposals were those of John Minter Morgan (1782–1854); James Silk Buck-

801

ingham (1786–1855), who suggested a city called 'Victoria', planned in concentric squares, with prefabricated iron houses and communal bathrooms and kitchens; Sir Benjamin Richardson (1828–96); and WILLIAM MORRIS.

Most Utopian settlements are based on religious or political ideals which implied some degree of common ownership of property. Some, like the CHARTIST land colonies in England, were based on more individualistic ideals. The Moravian church, established in 1457 and by the eighteenth century based at Herrnhut, Saxony, set up seven colonies in England and Ireland in 1744–85. Most of the buildings remain of those at Fulneck, 8 km (5 mi.) W. of Leeds, and Fairfield, 7 km (4 mi.) E. of MANCHESTER. Utopian colonies embodying the principles of ROBERT OWEN and CHARLES FOURIER were established both in Europe and America, while William Allen (1770–1843), an ex-Owenite Quaker, whose autobiography records many visits to continental Utopian settlements, established a successful colony at Lindfield, 22 km (13 mi.) N. of BRIGHTON, in the 1820s. Many small colonies were started in Britain in the 1880s and 90s, of which the most successful was Whiteway, 12 km ($7\frac{1}{2}$ mi.) SE of Gloucester, a settlement of Tolstoyan anarchists of 1898.

Many hundreds of Utopian settlements, both religious and secular, were established in the United States in the nineteenth century. Shaker colonies and others based on Protestant ideals emanating from Germany were established in the north-eastern states in the first half of the century, and seventeen major settlements were founded in California between 1850–1950. The great bridge designer JOHN A. ROEBLING established a Utopian agricultural community, Saxonburg, Pennsylvania, before turning his energies entirely to civil engineering.

Few Utopian settlements have been successful in practical terms. Their financial bases have often been insecure, and both managers and settlers have often found it difficult to implement the founding ideals. The influence of such settlements on the broader development of planning has nevertheless been profound.

BIBLIOGRAPHY
General
Allen, 1846–9; Armytage, 1961b, 1965; Bell, 1969; Bestor, 1950; Buckingham, 1849; Darley, 1975; Fishman, 1977; Hardy, 1979; Harrison, 1969; Hayden, 1976; Hine, 1966; Jones, 1947; Morgan, 1826, 1834; Morris, 1891–2; Richardson, 1876; Shaw, 1935.
Specific
Abercrombie, P. Ideal cities, no. 2: Victoria. In *Town Planning Review*, IX, 1921.
Albertson, R. A survey of mutualistic communities in America. In *Iowa Journal of History and Politics*, XXXIV, 1936.
Bushee, F. A. Communistic societies in the United States. In *Political Science Quarterly*, XX, 1905.

BARRIE TRINDER

Utrecht, Utrecht, The Netherlands Utrecht did not become a major industrial city until the last quarter of the nineteenth century when new railways and waterways and the demolition of the city walls opened up new possibilities for manufacturers. Utrecht had a rail connection to Amsterdam in 1843 but it took thirty years to build connections with other Dutch cities and with Germany. By the 1870s four of the eighteen Dutch railway companies had stations in the city.

The oldest station is Maliebaan of 1874, east of the centre, which houses the national Railway Museum. Locomotives include a replica built in 1938 of *De Arend*, the first locomotive to work in the Netherlands, supplied by Longridge of Bedlington, Northumberland, in 1839; Beyer Peacock 2-4-0s of 1863 and 1881; a Sharp Stewart of Glasgow 4-4-0 of 1881 and a 2-10-0 built by the North British Company in Glasgow in 1945; a Borsig 2-4-0 of 1880; a Schwartzkopff 4-4-0 of 1914; a large 4-8-4T of 1931, built to work coal trains in Limburg; and a Henschel tram locomotive of 1907.

The present central station has a roof of 1895, and to the north-west is a large complex of running sheds and railway warehouses including several nineteenth-century buildings. Three office blocks, of 1871, 1895 and 1921, form the headquarters of the Netherlands Railways.

The Merwede Kanaal of 1892, west of the city, linked Utrecht with Amsterdam, and with the great rivers to the south. The metallurgical industries that developed along it from the late nineteenth century and declined after World War II have left few traces, apart from the GARDEN CITY style colonies of Zuilen of 1910 and Elinkwijk of 1914. The Beatrix locks of 1938, 5 km (3 mi.) S., connect Utrecht via the Lekkanaal with the River Lek.

The Oudegracht (Old Moat) in the city centre is connected with the River Vecht and the Vaartsche Rijn, which dates from the twelfth century and is probably the oldest canal in the Netherlands. Many warehouse cellars along its wharves now serve as cafés. The Pelletier tobacco and cigar factory of 1844 and 1908, closed in 1933, is now an apartment block. A brewery of the 1860s, with its adjacent workers' housing, was once owned by the Catholic Church. Two early twentieth-century department stores remain, one still operating, one used as a bank; and a romantic grocer's shop of 1873 operates as a museum. The central abattoir of 1901 remains in use. The Lauwerhof watertower of 1895 houses a museum illustrating the history of water supply in the Netherlands. A cotton factory of 1811, used from 1816 as a school, remains in Biltstraat, and a meal and flour mill of 1874 and 1916 at Wittevrouwensingel. Douwe Egbert's coffee and tea factory on the Merwede Kanaal includes several early twentieth-century buildings, as well as a museum showing the history of coffee, tea and tobacco since the seventeenth century (*see* FRIESLAND). There is also a museum at the National Mint of 1911.

Soesterberg military airbase, 10 km (6 mi.) E., has a hangar of the 1920s with a roof of metal pipes. At nearby Soestduinen are a pumping station, built in 1902 by the city water company, and a railway station of 1865 of asymmetrical design, quite different from the chalet style of Soest station of 1897, 15 km (9 mi.) NW.

Nijkerk, Gelderland, 25 km (16 mi.) NE, is a former tobacco port connected to the Zuiderzee, with several eighteenth- and nineteenth-century warehouses. The

Arkenheem pumping station of 1883, with two scoop wheels, original engines by Backer & Rueb, and Stork boilers of 1908, was recently restored. The Dutch Electricity and Telecommunications Museum has a modest collection of equipment.

Woerden, 18 km (11 mi.) W., has a JUGENDSTIL railway station and a watertower of 1906 now used as an exhibition centre. The Teylingen pumping station of 1871 retains a tandem compound engine, which worked a centrifugal pump of 1907 until superseded by electric power in 1923. Woerden had the largest cheese market in the country in the 1920s, and several cheese warehouses are now used as apartments.

Leerdam, Zuid Holland, 24 km (15 mi.) S., is the centre of the Dutch glass industry, with workers' housing, and a museum in what was once a factory owner's house.

LOCATIONS

[M] Central Museum, Agnietenstraat 1, Utrecht.
[M] Douwe Egbert's Museum (museum of pipes, coffee and tea), Vleutensevaart 35, Utrecht.
[M] Museumwinkel (Grocer's Shop Museum), Hoogt 6, Utrecht.
[M] National Glasmuseum (National Glass Museum), Lingedijk 28, Leerdam.
[M] Nederlands Elektriciteits en Techniekmuseum (Electricity and Telecommunications Museum), Waagplein 2a, Nijkerk.
[M] Nederlands Spoorweg Museum (Netherlands Railway Museum), Johan van Oldenbarneveltlaan 6, Utrecht.
[M] Rijksmunt Museum (National Mint Museum), Leidseweg 90, Utrecht.
[S] Stoomgemaal Arkenheem (Steam Pumping Station), Zeedijk, Nijkerk.
[M] Waterleidingmuseum (Waterworks Museum), Lauwerhof 29, Utrecht.

JURRIE VAN DALEN

V

Vác (Waitzen), Pest, Hungary   A Baroque town on the Danube, 35 km (22 mi.) N. of Budapest. In it is a 33 m (110 ft.) two-arch stone bridge of 1753–8 over Gombás-patak brook, designed by Ignác Oracsek and decorated with statues of seven saints. The region is celebrated for the hand-loom weaving of linens. The Forte (formerly Kodak) photographic materials factory has a museum displaying photographic technology and a collection of works by pioneer photographer Jozsef Petzval (1807–91).

BIBLIOGRAPHY
General
Kiss *et al.*, 1981.

LOCATION
[M] Petzval Jozsef Collection, H-2600 Vác, Tragor Ignac u. 9.

vacuum brake   An automatic brake devised by James Graham (1836–1914) in 1878 for use on railways, in which a vacuum exhauster on the locomotive draws air through a pipe from the brake cylinders on the individual vehicles, until pistons move the brakes to the 'off' position. When air is admitted the brakes are applied. Vacuum brakes were used in Britain (particularly after legislation in 1889 which made automatic brakes compulsory for passenger trains from 1893), to some extent in Denmark, Norway, Spain and Portugal, in British territories overseas, on some American railroads between 1870 and 1900, and on the New York elevated lines over a longer period. Vacuum brakes were phased out in most of Europe from the 1960s.

BIBLIOGRAPHY
General
Ahrons, 1927; Westwood, 1983.

Vadsø, Finnmark, Norway   A settlement 900 km (560 mi.) N. of Trondheim, near the borders of the USSR and Finland, in a region celebrated in the nineteenth century for the collection of eider feathers and the hunting of ermine. A steel-lattice airship-mooring tower, the departure point for the voyages of Roald Amundsen (1872–1928) and Umberto Nobile (1885–1978) to America and the North Pole in 1926–8, stands near a medieval settlement site.

Valença do Minho, Minho, Portugal   A border town, 96 km (60 mi.) N. of Oporto, connected to Spain by an iron bridge of 1886. At the railway station is a small museum of railway relics dating from 1875 to 1891.

Valençay, Indre, France   The cotton mill at Valençay, 40 km (25 mi.) N. of Châteauroux, was put up at the beginning of the period of the French Revolution by Jean-Baptiste Legendre de Luçay (1752–97), a former Farmer-General, whose father had already used the vast family estates of Valençay and Luçay for an ironworks, opened in 1767. The construction and subsequent management of the mill was reputedly entrusted to a 'skilful mechanic' invited over from England by Legendre. From 1799 the mill was leased to the Belgian entrepreneur Liévin Bauwens (1769–1822), who also ran another large cotton mill at Passy, near Paris. In 1806 the mill, along with the estate and the château, was purchased by Napoleon's minister, Talleyrand, who enlarged and modernized it. A four-storey building, about 23 m × 8 m (75 ft. × 26 ft), with a collection of water frames and mules, equipped with approximately 2300 spindles, produced 10 tonnes of thread in 1810. Along with the associated hosiery works, the mill employed some 130 workers at this date.

The mill ceased production *c.*1845, and was transformed first into a corn mill, and then into a barn. The building still stands, retaining traces of these successive modifications. The two upper floors and the staircase have disappeared. In the two remaining rooms are remnants of the old transmission system, and a Poncelet-type water wheel, probably dating from the building's use as a corn mill.

BIBLIOGRAPHY
Specific
Unpublished study for Monuments Historiques, Ministère de la Culture. Paris.

JEAN-FRANÇOIS BELHOSTE

Valencia, Valencia, Spain   The centre of an agricultural region which irrigation has made one of the richest in Spain. Its fertility is celebrated in the city's brick and tile central market, the Plaza de Mercado, a huge domed structure, with stained-glass windows, extending over 8000 m² (86 000 sq. ft.).

Valencia Norte station, dating from 1915 and designed by Demetri Ribes, is one of the most magnificent in Spain, with a 196 m × 45 m (643 ft. × 148 ft.) train shed, and a two-storey, eleven-bay main building, with a central *porte-cochère*, and flanked by two four-storey, turreted pavilions, with an ornate interior inspired by the Viennese SECESSIONIST movement.

Valencia was an important centre for silk production in

the late Middle Ages, a trade reflected in the fifteenth-century 'Lonja de Seda' or silk exchange.

Valencia's predominance in the Spanish ceramic industry, particularly in the production of coloured tiles ('azulejos') and porcelain, is reflected in the National Ceramics Museum in the palace of the Marques de Dos Aguas.

BIBLIOGRAPHY
General
Aguilar, 1980; Civera, 1988; Marti *et al.*, 1982.

LOCATIONS
[M] City Historical Museum, Ayuntamiento, Plaza Candillo 1, Valencia.
[M] Gonzalez Marti National Museum of Ceramics, Rinconada Garcia Sanchez, Valencia.
[M] Museum of the Vancia Silk Industry, Call Hospital 7, Valencia.

BARRIE TRINDER

Val Jalbert, Quebec, Canada   The village of Val Jalbert was developed in the region of Lake St Jean, 250 km (155 mi.) NE of Quebec City, by a succession of five companies concerned with pulp and paper manufacture, principally the Chichoutimi Pulp company (*see* CHICOUTIMI) and the Quebec Pulp & Paper Corporation.

The complex drew its power from the Ouiatchouan Falls and its timber from the surrounding coniferous forests. The complex comprised a main building housing the plant necessary for the mechanical production of pulp: stripping machines, mills, defibring machines, hydraulic presses and sieves, as well as turbines and a generator which provided power for the operations. A dam and a sawmill were located 900 m (980 yd.) downstream from the falls.

The village of Val Jalbert, situated alongside the Quebec–Lake St Jean railway, had all the characteristics of an industrial community. Its population, which in 1913 comprised two hundred inhabitants, enjoyed essential services provided by the companies that owned the complex: houses, a general store, a post office, a bank, a school, a hotel, a chapel, a fire station and a water supply. In 1942 economic reasons led to the closure of the works and the suspension of public services. Val Jalbert became a veritable ghost village, but the Quebec government, which acquired the site in 1949, has transformed it into a historical and country park. Some of the dwellings and public buildings have been restored as part of the interpretative programme.

LOCATION
[I] Archives nationales du Québec à Chicoutimi; fonds de la Société historique du Saguenay (Quebec National Archives at Chicoutimi: collection of the Saguenay historical society).
[M,S] Village historique de Val-Jalbert, Case postale 34, Route 169, Roberval (Quebec) G8H 2N4.

LOUISE TROTTIER

Vallorbe, Vaud, Switzerland   A traditional watchmaking town on the Swiss/French border, mostly rebuilt following a fire in 1883. There are long traditions of ironworking in the district, where there were once three blast furnaces and thirty forges. The Iron Museum, showing how iron has been worked in the region for the last two thousand years, is on the site of 'les Grandes Forges', which date from 1495. There are three water wheels, one of which operates a trip hammer, with displays on the manufacture of saws, files and other tools by traditional and modern methods.

A museum of railway equipment at the station includes a French 4–8–2 (241P) locomotive, one of thirty-five built by Schneider in 1948–52.

At la Sarraz, 12 km ($7\frac{1}{2}$ mi.) SE, a comprehensive museum of the horse occupies an old castle, together with collections of clocks and furniture.

BIBLIOGRAPHY
General
Keller, 1979.

LOCATIONS
[M] Gyger Museum, Bahnhof, Vallorbe.
[M] Musée de Cheval, Château de la Sarraz, CH-1315 la Sarraz, Vaud.
[M] Musée de Fer, CH-1337 Vallorbe.

STUART B. SMITH

valve   In industrial archaeology a valve is a device for regulating the flow of a gas or a liquid in a machine or other circulation system. The word originally meant one or other of the halves of a double door. The forms of valves used in such diverse mechanisms as steam engines, water-supply systems and petrol engines are varied, but in most cases they are the parts of the system where the highest engineering standards are applied. Engineering companies specializing in the manufacture of valves developed from the late nineteenth century.

A thermionic valve, or 'tube' – a system of electrodes arranged in an evacuated or gas-filled glass envelope – controls circuits in a RADIO or other electronic system. In a radio a valve rectifies signals, producing a current varying in amplitude with the frequency of the sound waves fed to the transmitter; this current can be used to operate a loudspeaker, so reproducing the original sound. Most RADIO RECEIVERS were fitted with thermionic valves until the application of transistors became widespread in the 1950s.

BIBLIOGRAPHY
General
Barr, 1893; Butler, 1922; Westcott, 1932.

BARRIE TRINDER

vanadium (V)   An elemental metal, used to produce STEEL alloys which are used in high-speed tools, in springs, in earthmoving and ore-dressing machinery, and in many kinds of forgings used in mechanical engineering. Sources of vanadium ores include COLORADO, Norway and the USSR. Compounds of the metal, including vanadium pentoxide (V_2O_5), used as a catalyst in the production of sulphuric acid, can be recovered from the residues of various oils and bitumens.

BIBLIOGRAPHY
General
Jones, 1950.

Vancouver Island, British Columbia, Canada Vancouver Island, extending 430 km (270 mi.) north-west to south-east, was settled as a British colony in 1849, and united with British Columbia in 1866, becoming part of the Canadian federation in 1871.

The provincial museum in Victoria has comprehensive displays on logging, mining and salmon-canning in the province. The Cowichan Valley Logging Museum at Duncan, 50 km (30 mi.) N. of Victoria, interprets the vast increase in the scale of exploitation of the western Canadian forests in the twentieth century.

The island is rich in coal, first exploited on a large scale in the 1840s when the Hudson Bay Co. imported miners from Staffordshire, England, to Nanaimo, 96 km (60 mi.) N. of Victoria. Mines sunk later at Extension, Wellington and on Newcastle Island have left some surface structures as well as company housing, and some relics of the distinctive settlements established to accommodate the Chinese miners brought in by the mine owners to assist and often to undercut the costs of white labour. The coal-mining town of Cumberland, 180 km (110 mi.) N. of Victoria, has many surviving artefacts, especially housing, as well as a museum.

Outstanding buildings in the capital, Victoria, include the Empress Hotel of 1908, one of the series of château-style hotels which included the Château Frontenac in Quebec; a purpose-built chocolate shop and factory of 1903; Weiler's five-storey department store of 1898; and the Oriental Hotel, a prefabricated cast-iron building in the Italianate style of 1893, from the tower of which a beacon was kept burning as a navigational aid to ships.

BIBLIOGRAPHY
General
Haig-Brown, 1961.
Specific
Vickers, R. S. George Robinson: Nanaimo mine agent. In *The Beaver* (Winnipeg) Autumn 1984.
Walking Tour: Old Town, Victoria, Victoria BC: Heritage Tour Maps, 1979.

LOCATIONS
[M] British Columbia Provincial Museum, 601 Belleville Street, Victoria BC.
[M] Cowichan Valley Logging Museum, Trans-Canada Highway, Duncan BC, V9L 3W8.

DERYCK HOLDSWORTH

Varna, Varna, Bulgaria A major Black Sea port, founded by the Greeks in the sixth century BC. During the Middle Ages, it enjoyed a thriving trade with Genoa, Venice and Ragusa. It continued to grow during the Ottoman period, and was linked by rail with Russe in 1866 and Sofia in 1899. A modern harbour, constructed in 1906, consolidated Varna's position as Bulgaria's leading port. The Ethnographical Museum includes displays on fishing, crafts, and viticulture. The Marine Museum, opened in 1913, is given over entirely to naval exhibits in both indoor and outdoor displays, and includes the torpedo boat that sank a Turkish cruiser in the war of 1913. The laying of a cable between Varna and Sebastopol in 1868 by the British ship *Faraday* is commemorated. It is intended to extend the scope of the museum to include the Bulgarian mercantile marine.

LOCATION
[M] Maritime Museum, Bul. Tschervenoarmejski 2, Varna.

Várpalota, Veszprém, Hungary A town 75 km (45 mi.) SW of Budapest, developed during the first five-year plan (*see* HUNGARY) from three villages with lignite mines which produced fuel for power stations. A museum illustrates the production of coal over the past hundred years. The 'November 7 Power Station' was completed on 7 November 1951, having been built in less than two years. Also of interest are the aluminium smelters, which use bauxite from mines in the region; and the Pét fertilizer plant, which was destroyed in the war and later rebuilt.

LOCATION
[M] Museum of Mining in the Várpalota Region, H-8100 Varpalota, Hosok tér, Thury var.

Växjö (Wexiö), Kronoberg, Sweden The capital of the old region of Småland. The city was rebuilt after serious fires in 1830 and 1840. Småland was celebrated for glassmaking, and the regional museum displays the largest collection of glass in northern Europe, together with substantial collections of coins and textiles.

LOCATION
[M] Smålands museet, Järnvaägsgatan 2, PO Box 66, S-351 03 Växjö.

Velké Losiny, North Bohemia, Czechoslovakia The site of a preserved papermill, which still operates within a state castle. Paper has been manufactured by hand here since the sixteenth century. A large museum of paper manufacture was established in 1955, the displays being installed by the National Technical Museum.

BIBLIOGRAPHY
Specific
Jiled, F. and Majer, J. *National Technical Museum, Praha.* Prague, 1988.

Venetian Gothic An ornate style of architecture which enjoyed some popularity for industrial buildings in the nineteenth century (*see* GLASGOW). It derived principally from the Doge's Palace, Venice, built in the century from 1340.

Venetian window A feature of PALLADIAN architecture used in many industrial buildings: it has three openings, the central one arched and wider than the others. It is also

Figure 166 Iron footbridge at Fondamenta Priuli, Venice, cast at the Fonderia Veneta, San Rocco, in 1868
Michael Stratton

called a Serliana. Venetian doorways are of similar form, but are less common.

Venice (Venezia), Venetia, Italy   Venice's industrial history goes unappreciated by most tourists, although the municipality has identified 150 major sites. The Arsenale is the earliest, having been founded in 1104. At the height of Venetian prosperity in the fifteenth century it employed 16 000 workers. Its name, derived from the Arabic for workshop, was applied to many other shipbuilding yards. Situated 600 m (660 yd.) east of Piazza San Marco, the Arsenale is most easily seen from vaporetto route No. 5, which passes through arches in the crenellated walls. The formal entrance from the south is between two castellated towers, one bearing a clock, the other a sundial. Two covered slips and a series of warehouses incorporating classical columns front the Rio d'Arsenale. The most dramatic parts of the Arsenale, as yet inaccessible to the public, are the sixteenth-century ropeworks, and a square laid out in the eighteenth century. A survey has been made recording the main features, from the hydraulic cranes to the power station. Since the Italian navy transferred its Upper Adriatic base to Ancona the Arsenale has seen little use.

Just east of the Jewish quarter several iron bridges span some of the minor canals. At Fondamenta dei Ormesini, by the Madonna del Orto, an elegant single-span structure is made up of two ribs decorated with lions' heads. The parapet has strapwork decoration, and is marked 'E. G. Neville & Co., 1865, Fonderia Veneta, San Rocco, Venezia'. E. G. Neville engineered the iron version of the Accademia bridge, subsequently rebuilt in wood. Slightly to the south a virtually identical iron bridge by Fondamenta Priuli is dated 1868. Further east, Ponte dell' l'Acquavita is of comparable design, but has more curva-

ceous parapet decoration. 'Const. a.1854 A Spese Civiche Fond Berengo' is cast on the ribs.

The Guidecca is dominated by the towering Gothic bulk of the Stucky Mill. An original eight-storey block, with the name on a large pediment, faced the canal and was built in 1883 by Giovanni Stucky. It was extended to either side in a more Germanic style in 1895, the largest block of seven storeys having a tower and spire. Forming a group with the mill is the Bitterie Veneziane, a brewery of comparable scale, with Gothic doorways and crenellation, which has been adapted as flats.

BIBLIOGRAPHY
General
Negri *et al.*, 1983; Selvafolta, 1983.
Specific
Simoni, C. La Venezia dell'arsenale: un banco di prova. *Il Coltello di Delfo* (The Venice Arsenal proof house), II, 1987.

MICHAEL STRATTON

Ventron, Vosges, France   The Grand Ventron cotton mill, 1.5 km (1 mi.) E. of the town of Ventron, 40 km (25 mi.) SW of Colmar, was built *c*.1857 by the Germain brothers. Its main building is a rectangular, three-storey block, 12.5 m × 23 m (41 ft. × 75 ft), where thirty-three looms were housed on the first two floors. They were driven by a turbine which is still in place, making this mill typical of the Vosges textile industry. It was closed down in 1955 and now houses a museum of cotton spinning and weaving machinery.

LOCATION
[M] Musée du Textile (Textile Museum), Mairie de Ventron, 88310 Cornimont.

Ventspils (Windau), Latvia, USSR   A Latvian seaport

and fishing centre. The Museum of Ocean Fishing is noteworthy less for the fishery and fish-processing exhibits than for its railway, which originated from the unsolicited gift of narrow-gauge track and rolling stock from a line converted to broad-gauge. After these items were restored to working order for use in a feature film, it was decided to keep a section of track within the museum site for the operation of a period train.

BIBLIOGRAPHY
Specific
Gudok, 2 December 1984.

Verla, Kymen lääni, Finland   The mechanical pulpmill and cardboard factory at Verla, 68 km (42 mi.) N. of Kotka, was established in the 1870s by Hugo Neuman (1847–1906), a Finnish-born civil engineer, trained in Zurich, who had been involved in railway construction. The first buildings were of wood, but they were renewed in brick after a fire in 1892. The mill, cardboard factory and drying building, designed by the architect Edward Dippel, represent an unusually rich form of brick architecture. They have load-bearing walls, and intermediate floors supported by wooden pillars and beams. The factory has remained on its original site since the late nineteenth century and provides a unique picture of the industrial landscape of its time. The so-called Pehtoori's building, surrounded by parkland and designed in its present form by Dippel in the 1890s, is closely connected with the manufacturing area. The building has copious FRETWORK decoration, and a tower overlooking the river. The Verla factory ceased manufacture in 1964, but plans for a mill museum were put into action immediately, and it was opened in 1972, the owners, Kymmene Oy, one of Finland's biggest wood-processing companies, having funded the restoration and renovation programme. The workers' housing and Pehtoori's building are used as the company's holiday village. The mill museum is now administered by a trust.

All the machines and exhibits in the Verla Mill Museum appear in their original form. The museum traces the history of the manufacture of handmade card, which has remained astonishingly little changed from the early period of Finnish wood-processing to the present day. Exhibits include debarking machines, grinders, the drying lofts and calenders. Before touring the museum, visitors see a film of activity shot shortly before production at the mill ceased.

BIBLIOGRAPHY
Specific
Talvi, V. The Verla Mill Story. In *Kymi Kymmene Paper*, Kouvola, 1982.

LOCATION
[M] Verlan tehdasmuseo (Verla Mill Museum), SF-47850 Verla.

LAURI PUTKONEN

Vermont, United States of America   Perhaps it is only coincidental that the tapered states of Vermont and New Hampshire join like a set of machinist's levelling blocks.

The states are thick with small-town machine shops – originally water-powered – and much of the nation's history of early machine-tool development. Paying tribute to this heritage, with special emphasis on the cluster of manufacturers in and about Precision Valley, is the American Precision Museum in Windsor. The pre-eminent collection of early metal-cutting machines is housed in the Robbins & Lawrence factory of 1846, from which the Enfield armaments works in England obtained its first rifle-making machines in the 1850s. The adjacent rubble-filled Ascutney Dam of 1834, one of the few pre-1850 dams to survive in the nation, furnished water power for the factory.

Vermont's reputation as a state of quiet, hard-working, rock-solid characters is nowhere more evident than in the quarrying and stone-finishing towns of Rutland and Barre. One can barely swing one's arms in Barre without striking evidence of its grey granite industry, from the quarries surrounding the cities to the building façades, the granite-cutting sheds and the statuary in the town's Hope Cemetery. Nearby Rutland's stone heritage is of a more humble order, springing from its deep shelves of roofing slate and benches of marble, still a preferred material for architectural cladding. Rutland is home to the one-of-a-kind New England Maple Sugar Museum.

In the state's far north-western corner, the Shelburne Museum is berth to the dewatered sidewheel steamer *Ticonderoga* of 1906, plus a vast array of other transport artefacts and hand tools.

Beyond its diverse cluster of mid-nineteenth-century covered bridges, Vermont's iron Elm Street Bridge of 1879 over the Ottauquechee in Woodstock was the cause of a trail-blazing confrontation between bridge preservationists and highway officials in 1975. The precedent-setting compromise achieved, which brought the bridge into accord with modern highway standards, retained the important trussed arch panels while widening and reinforcing the deck; the changes were made using money slated for the span's demolition.

See also figures 19, 127.

BIBLIOGRAPHY
General
Comp, 1974; Jackson, 1988; Kulik *et al.*, 1982; Sande, 1971; US Bureau of Mines, 1976.

LOCATIONS
[M] American Precision Museum, 196 Main Street, Windsor, VT 05089.
[M,S] Chittenden Mills, Jericho, VT 05465.
[M] New England Maple Sugar Museum, PO Box 1615, Rutland, VT 05701.
[M] Shelburne Museum, US Route 7, Shelburne, VT 05482.

DAVID H. SHAYT

vertical engine   A steam engine in which a vertical piston rod supplies energy via a crankshaft directly to the crankshaft of a flywheel suspended above the cylinder. The vertical engine is extensively used for winding in mines, the design of Phineas Crowther of 1800 being much used in north-east England, where an example is preserved at BEAMISH. In some cases the cylinder is mounted above the flywheel.

BIBLIOGRAPHY
General
Storer, 1969; Watkins, 1968.

Verviers, Liège, Belgium   The principal woollen-cloth manufacturing town in Belgium owed its growth to abundant water power, and to the softness of the water. An English mechanic, William Cockerill (d.1832) built the first carding machines and power looms in Verviers early in the nineteenth century, and by 1846 13 615 in the city were employed making woollen cloth. Many buildings associated with the woollen industry remain, ranging from the Maison Closset, an eight-bay, four-storey apartment block for domestic workers, of the late seventeenth century to the mid-nineteenth century Houmour Gérard factory, with elaborate Gothic ornamentation, and many ranges of north-lit sheds. Verviers Central station is a distinguished neo-baroque building by Emile Barguet of 1925.

The sandstone Gileppe Barrage near Baelen, 8 km (5 mi.) E., 234 m (256 yd.) long at the top, 47 m (154 ft.) high, and surmounted by a colossal Belgian lion, was built in 1869–75, specifically to supply the mills with water for washing wool.

BIBLIOGRAPHY
General
Fehl *et al.*, 1991; Viaene, 1986.

LOCATION
[M] Musée National de la Laine (National Museum of Wool), rue de Séroule 8, 4800 Verviers.

BARRIE TRINDER

Veszprém, Veszprém, Hungary   A historic city, built on steep slopes in the Bakony mountains. Two important museums relate to the building industry: one, which is part of the Hungarian Architectural Museum, displays building technology; the other, in a protected building of 1772, is concerned with brick manufacture in Transdanubia.

LOCATIONS
[M] Brick Museum, H-8200 Veszprém, Vár u. 35.
[M] Building Industry Museum, H-8200 Veszprém, Házgyár u. 1.

Vevey, Vaud, Switzerland   A resort on the north shore of Lake Geneva, 6 km (4 mi.) NW of Montreux, with which it was linked by the first electric tramway in Switzerland in 1887. The town was celebrated for the manufacture of chocolate and baby foods by the 1890s. The Alimentarium, a food museum, established by the Nestlé company in 1985, informs visitors about past and present problems relating to food and nutrition. The scope is worldwide, with particular attention being given to four regions where important sources of food originated: the Philippines for rice, Anatolia for wheat, Cameroon for millet, and Peru for maize and potatoes. One section deals with

the impact of industrialization on eating habits, contrasting European diets of 1760 with those of 1900.

An important photographic museum opened in 1979 with the support of the Kodak company.

LOCATIONS
[M] Alimentarium, Musée de l'Alimentation (Food Museum) BP 13, CH-1800 Vevey.
[M] Musée d'appareils photographiques (Camera museum), 5 Grande Place, 1800 Vevey.

HANS-PETER BÄRTSCHI

viaduct   A multi-span bridge carrying a road or railway, which can be a series of arches in masonry, iron or concrete, timber structures between stone piers, or a succession of steel or wrought-iron lattice or girder spans. The principle was known in the ancient world. In urban areas railway viaducts, of which that at Greenwich (*see* LONDON) was the first, are dominant features of the industrial landscape and often provide accommodation for workshops and the like. *See* Figure 167.

BIBLIOGRAPHY
General
Kellett, 1969; Prade, 1990.

Viana do Castelo, Minho, Portugal   A commercial port, 62 km (38 mi.) N. of Oporto, at the mouth of the River Lima, which is crossed by an iron bridge built in 1878 by GUSTAVE EIFFEL's company, which has two 563 m (1841 ft.) decks, the upper for vehicles, the lower for trains; it was the first of its kind in Portugal. A funicular ascends from the railway station to a belvedere on Santa Luzia mountain. Other industrial monuments include the Dom Prior tide mill, the Alvarães pottery kiln, and two windmills with trapezoid sails at Carreço, 8 km (5 mi.) N.

LOCATIONS
[M] Alvarães Ceramic Museum, Alvarães, Viana do Castelo.
[M] Municipal Museum, Largo de S Domingos, Viana do Castelo.

Viborg, Jutland, Denmark   Viborg has Viking origins and was formerly the judicial and political centre of Jutland and the terminus of the old main road through the peninsula. It had a wide range of traditional crafts and early industrial activities, of which the most important monument is the Brænderigården (distillery house) of the early eighteenth century.

Just south of Viborg, a cardboard mill at Brunnshåb has recently been converted into a working factory museum. About 1820 the manufacturer Bertil Bruun extended a small corn and fulling mill to become what was then one of Denmark's largest textile mills. The present buildings were erected after a fire in 1909. In 1919 the textile mill was changed into a cardboard factory, which operated until 1986.

The limestone workings at Daugbjerg and Mønsted, 15 km (9 mi.) W., form another important industrial site, with one of the few real mines in Denmark. For centuries quarrying and burning limestone was an important by-

Figure 167   The world's longest concrete viaduct, the Tunkhannock RR Viaduct at Nicholson, Pennsylvania, constructed in 1915
Jet Lowe, HAER

occupation for local farmers, but from 1870 traditional quarrying was increasingly replaced by modern methods. Today examples of the old galleries can be visited at Dybdal, while the combined opencast and underground workings at Mønsted give an impression of the scale of modern industrial extraction.

The primary purpose of the open-air museum at Hjerl Hede, 35 km (22 mi.) W., is to portray the development of the traditional Danish village, but it has several monuments of interest to the industrial archaeologist, among them a post mill of 1778, a water mill of 1858, shops for a coach-builder, a cooper and a ropemaker, and a re-erected creamery of 1897 from the island of Mandø. Associated museums of forestry and bog cultivation include a sawmill powered by a portable engine, and peat-cutting machinery.

BIBLIOGRAPHY
Specific
Bruunshåb gamle papfabrik (Bruunshåb old papermill). In *Fabrik og Bolig*, II, 1988.
Jacobsen, C. Kalken i Daugbjerg og Mønsted (Chalk working at Daugbjerg and Mønsted). In *Fra Viborg Amt*, 1985.
Hjerl-Hansen, F. ed. *Hjerl Hede.* Vinderup: Hjerl Hedes Frilandsmuseum, 1980.
Lauridsen, H. R. *Viborgs industrihistorie 1742–1990* (The industrial history of Viborg 1742–1990). Viborg, 1990.

LOCATIONS
[M,S] Bruunshåb Gamle Papfabrik, Vinkelvej 97, 8800 Viborg.
[M] Hjerl Hedes Frilansmuseum, Hjerl Hedevej 14, 7830 Vinderup.

OLE HYLDTOFT

Victoria, Australia   Some of the most extraordinary industrial remains in Victoria are Aboriginal. At Mount William quarries and working floors document a vast greenstone axe industry whose products were traded over hundreds of kilometres. At Lake Condah Swamp and at Toolondo can be seen mazes of traps and artificial channels constructed for fish and eel harvesting.

The discovery of gold in 1851 brought a flood of people into rural Victoria, and although the boom was short-lived, many country towns retain a Victorian grandeur. Ballarat was one of the few such towns that continued to prosper with its foundry and locomotive works. Early mining technology was very basic, and little survives, but once the easily accessible gold was worked out, larger companies began to utilize more intensive processes. Head frames, winding gear and the Deborah mine can be seen at Ballarat, and a mixture of *in situ* monuments and reconstructions at SOVEREIGN HILL. Other mining museums are at Bendigo and Kyneton. Miners from overseas imported their own traditions, and CORNISH ENGINE houses survive at Fryerstown and the Duke of Cornwall mine, Chewton. The best monument of large-scale alluvial technology is the El Dorado gold dredge of 1935 at Beechworth. The contribution of the Chinese to mining is reflected in the cemetery at Beechworth and the Joss House at Bendigo. An open-air museum at Swan Hill portrays early pioneer life. Victorian coal mining is commemorated at Coal Creek, 110 km (67 mi.) SE of MELBOURNE.

A rare survival of the short-lived Victorian iron industry is the Lal Lal charcoal blast furnace complex of 1873–85, 24 km (16 mi.) SE of Ballarat, which includes hearths, slag heaps, quarries and tramways, as well as refractory bricks imported from Stourbridge, England. The furnace structure of 1880–1, is 7.5 m (25 ft.) square, 17 m (56 ft.) high, and of rubble construction with a brick lining.

The first steam railway opened in 1854 but private companies ran into difficulties and were nationalized in 1872. By 1900 there were 4800 km (3000 mi.) of railway. Many trestle bridges, like that of 1890 at Hanford's Creek, Pyalong, 140 km (85 mi.) N. of Melbourne, were constructed of local bush timber, and there are several fine stone arched bridges, one of the largest being at Malmsbury, 90 km (55 mi.) NW of Melbourne, of 1859. Echuca, 170 km (105 mi.) N. of Melbourne, on the Murray River was the terminus of the first rail link between Melbourne and the border with New South Wales, and there are remains of a huge timber wharf and associated railway facilities.

BIBLIOGRAPHY
General
Blainey, 1954, 1963; Heritage of Australia, 1981; Serle, 1972.
Specific
Lal Lal Blast Furnace, Forest Commission, Victoria, n.d.

LOCATIONS
[M] Coal Creek Historical Park, Korumburra, Victoria.
[M] Cobb & Company Historical Folk Museum, Bendigo, Victoria 3550.
[M] Kyneton Historical Museum, Piper Street, Kyneton, Victoria 3444.
[M] Museum of Victoria, 328 Swanston Street, Melbourne.
[M] Swan Hill Folk Museum, Horseshoe Bend, Swan Hill, Victoria 3585.

KATE CLARK

victualling yard A naval establishment where ships were supplied with provisions. Specialist establishments known as 'victualling yards' were established by the British Royal Navy at home and overseas from the eighteenth century, comprising rum stores, rum and gin distilleries, breweries, flour mills, bakeries, slaughterhouses, cooperages and vegetable stores. The outstanding surviving example is at PLYMOUTH, but a huge storehouse of 1807 remains at Gibraltar, and a mid-nineteenth-century mill and bakery on Malta. The complex of the 1850s at Bermuda has been restored.

BIBLIOGRAPHY
General
Coad, 1983.

video history The best work in ORAL HISTORY is being enhanced with the aid of the portable video camera. Beyond the voices and faces of the industrial workforce, video may record work processes, machine operations, and the structural interplay between the site and its surroundings. Such systematic study may become the ultimate form of industrial archaeological documentation.

Vieille Montagne, La (Altenberg), Liège, Belgium La Vieille Montagne (the old mountain) is situated in Kelmis (La Calamine), 16 km (10 mi.) NE of Verviers and 8 km (5 mi,) SW of Aachen. Zinc carbonate ($ZnCO_3$) or CALAMINE (Smithsonite) was mined there in the fourteenth century, and by the eighteenth La Vieille Montagne was the principal European source of the ore. Kelmis has been in Belgium since 1919, before which it had been neutral territory since the Treaty of Limits of 1816. Before the French Revolution it was in the Duchy of Limburg in the Austrian Netherlands. In 1806 Napoleon granted a monopoly of mining rights to Jean Jacques Daniel Dony, who had developed a continuously heated furnace for smelting metallic zinc. Dony's company was known as La Société Anonyme de la Vieille Montagne. Some calamine was smelted at Liège but in 1835 furnaces were constructed at Kelmis. In the late nineteenth century the company came to rely on imported ore and moved its operations to factories at Overpelt, 30 km (19 mi.) N. of Hasselt, in 1888; Lommel, 34 km (21 mi.) N. of Hasselt, in 1904; and Rotem, 30 km (19 mi.) NE of Hasselt, in 1911. Blende (zinc sulphate) and galena (lead sulphate) were mined at Kelmis, and zinc white was produced from waste dumps. Calamine was quarried from deep open pits which have since been filled with household waste. There are remains of a calcining kiln, dressing floors on the River Gohl (Geule), and banks of slag containing shards of ceramic retorts. The company headquarters of 1910 is now a garage but bears plates marked 'VM'. Many houses have roofs and walls covered with zinc tiles. The calamine violet, *Viola arvensis calaminaria*, grows profusely in Kelmis and is regarded as the symbol of the area's industrial past.

BIBLIOGRAPHY
General
Fehl *et al.*, 1991.
Specific
Day, J. The continental origins of Bristol brass. In *IAR*, VII(1) 1984.
Centenaire de la Société des Mines et Fonderies de Zinc de la Vieille Montagne. Liège, 1937.
L'Industrie du Zinc: Société de la Vieille Montagne 1837–1905. Liège, 1905.

BARRIE TRINDER

Vienna (Wien), Austria Vienna stands on the Danube (which formerly linked it with the domains of the

Figure 168   One of the twin pavilions which comprised Karlsplatz station on the suburban railway system in Vienna, designed by Otto Wagner; the pavilion was preserved when the station was rebuilt in the 1970s.
Barrie Trinder

Habsburgs in eastern Europe), at the point where the river is crossed by one of the historic routes between the Baltic and the Adriatic. Much of the city retains the atmosphere of an imperial capital of the late nineteenth century, with the vast Hofburg palace, the opera, and other imposing buildings along the Ringstrasse. Vienna grew rapidly in the second half of the nineteenth century, its population increasing from rather less than half a million at the time of the first census in 1859 to over a million in the 1880s, and, after the incorporation of suburbs like Floridsdorf previously outside the city boundary, to more than two million by 1910. Vienna was one of the most important manufacturing centres in Europe in the period before World War I, and one where civic pride in the provision of amenities for its people was scarcely equalled. Vienna lost its role as imperial capital in 1918 and suffered severe destruction at the end of World War II; its population is now only 1.5 million.

The old centre of the city is located about 3 km (2 mi.) from the Danube, south-west of the Danube Canal, an old branch of the Danube where the Romans had built fortifications. For a city of such political importance Vienna was remarkably unfashionable and relatively little visited until the mid-nineteenth century. In 1857 the Emperor Franz Josef (1830–1916) issued a decree authorizing the levelling of the broad band of fortifications that separated the city from its suburbs. The Ringstrasse was laid out along the line of the fortifications and lined with public buildings and apartment blocks in a distinctive style. Though these were not industrial buildings, the use of tiles, terracotta and faience is a valuable illustration of contemporary building technology.

For many centuries much of Vienna's grain was ground in FLOATING MILLS (schiffsmühlen) on the Danube, fifty-six of which were still in operation when relocation was necessary during flood-protection works in the 1870s. The last ceased work in 1935.

The Arsenal (Arsenalstrasse) is a massive complex which supplied the military needs of one of the largest European armies, and its architectural style reflects the power of the Habsburg empire. It was begun in 1849, the first major project of the young Emperor Franz Josef, the architects being Theophil Hansen and Ludwig Foster. The main block, which now houses the museum of military history, is in RUNDBOGENSTIL with dramatic polychromatic effects. Other buildings include a crenellated 36-bay engineering shop.

Floridsdorf, east of the Danube, was the principal centre

of heavy engineering in Vienna, following the construction of a locomotive works for the Nordbahn by the Englishman John Baillie in 1839. At the same time another Englishman, John Haswell, built a locomotive works for the Südbahn alongside that railway's terminus, which evolved into the Steg-Werkstätte engineering complex. The greatest concentration of late-nineteenth-century consumer-goods factories was in the suburb of Favoriten, south of the Südbahnhof, where notable buildings include a candy factory in Belgradplatz, an electrical equipment factory of 1890–1 in Gudrunstrasse, a sewing-machine factory of 1885 in Leebgasse, a lamp factory of 1896 in Pernerstorfergasse, the Gläser engineering works of 1888–9 in Quellenstrasse, and the Luzzatto engineering works of 1906–7 in Siccardsburggasse.

A series of notable public works began in the 1870s. The construction of a 90 km (56 mi.) aqueduct to supply the city with drinking water from Kaiserbrunn in the Styrian mountains was begun in 1870. The Rosenhügel reservoir at the end of the aqueduct, begun in 1870 and extended on several occasions, is in Hietzing, 6 km (4 mi.) SW of the centre. Extensive public works were undertaken in the late nineteenth century to control floodwaters on the Danube and its tributary, the River Wien. The massive flood-hold in Weidlingau, Hütteldorf, where the Mauerbach enters the Wien, was constructed in 1895–1900. Serious attention was given to the drainage of the city from the time of the cholera epidemic in the 1830s, after which sewers were constructed along both banks of the River Wien. These were extended when the limits of the city were enlarged from 1890, and in 1903–6 the stretch of the river in the Stadtpark was ornamented to become an elegant feature of the landscape. The lock at the northern entrance to the Danube Canal at Nadelwehr Nussdorf and the lock-gate building (schützenhaus) of 1908 on the east bank of the canal opposite the Schwedenplatz were both designed by Otto Wagner (see below).

The first street tramways in Vienna were privately financed horse systems. The first electric tramway was opened in 1897, and between 1898 and 1903 the entire system was electrified and brought under the control of the municipality. The tramway depot in Kreuzgasse was built for horse trams in 1883, and alongside it is a farmstead-style building with a high pitched roof; originally it consisted of stables on the ground floor and a hayloft above. The tramsheds from the 1890s were built in three stages, the first entirely in timber with king-post trusses, the second with cast-iron columns and wooden trusses, and the third with steel lattice construction. Other interesting tramways depots still in use are in Gerichtsgasse, Floridsdorf, where there is a Baroque-style administration block, and on the south side of Mariahilfer Strasse, north-east of Schönbrunn palace.

The architect Otto Wagner (1841–1918) came to prominence with the publication of a plan in 1893 for circumferential road and rail links around Vienna. Two years later he published *Moderne Architektur*, a decisive break with the 'outlived world of forms' of the Ringstrasse, and with his own previous and largely traditional work.

The book contained such sentiments as 'nothing that is not practical can be beautiful', and the buildings that he designed in the following years are rightly regarded as amongst the most elegant and humane precursors of a non-historicist decorative architecture.

Wagner was the chief architect of the city railway system, which was constructed between 1894 and 1901: he designed more than thirty stations, as well as viaducts, bridges and tunnel portals. Initially three lines were proposed: the 'Gürtel' line between Meidling-Hauptstrasse and Heiligenstadt, the 'Obere Wiental' line from the former station to Hütteldorf-Hacking, and the 'Untere Wiental' line between Landstrasse-Wien Mitte and Meidling-Hauptstrasse, all of which were completed by 1899. Subsequently the 'Donaukanal' line between Landstrasse-Wien was opened in 1901, and the Vorortelinie across the outer suburbs from Heiligenstadt to Penzing was completed in 1898. The first four lines passed under the control of the municipality in 1924, and were shortly afterwards electrified. The Vorortelinie remained the responsibility of the ÖBB, and was used only for freight services. The system has been radically altered in the last twenty years, but many of Wagner's stations remain in use, good examples being Stadtpark, Hütteldorf-Hacking, Pilgramgasse, and Friedens-brücke. Two stations on the system are of exceptional interest. The twin pavilions that formed the station in Karlsplatz are of quite astonishing elegance. During the rebuilding of the system in 1978 the station platforms were relocated, but the pavilions were rebuilt and one of them is now a café. Near Schönbrunn palace Wagner built the Hofpavilion, a special station for the imperial family, a domed building spanning the tracks east of the public station at Hietzing. The Vorortelinie has been restored and trains between Heiligenstadt, Penzing and Hütteldorf-Hacking began operating in May 1987. Such surviving stations as Ottakring and Gersthof have been sensitively restored, as have engineering features like the 114 m (374 ft.) bridge across the Wiental. A complete train of the early days of the Stadtbahn, three carriages and a Carl Gölsdorf two-cylinder compound 2–6–2T locomotive of 1897, is preserved at Strasshof.

Wagner's postal saving bank (Öst.Postsparkassenamt) of 1904–6, with its amazingly pure, glass-vaulted banking hall, was seen as a building that represented the Viennese citizen as opposed to the city's bankers.

The Prater is a 1300 ha (3200 ac.) park between the Danube and the Danube Canal. The 60 m (200 ft.) diameter Ferris wheel (Reisenrad) was built for the World Exhibition in 1897 by the English engineer Walter B. Basset. It was destroyed in World War II, but restored in 1946 and featured memorably in the film *The Third Man*. It is the only survivor of several wheels of the same kind.

The authorities in Vienna have a proud tradition of providing living accommodation for the city's working class, and numerous apartment blocks constructed since World War I carry inscriptions bearing the city's name and the date of building, with plaques in their entrances listing architects and others chiefly responsible for their construction. Late nineteenth-century working-class apartments were known as Mietkaserne (rent barracks), and were sometimes erected by industrial companies. An example is a block of twenty-four apartments built in Brunnerstrasse, Floridsdorf, in 1871–3 for Wiener Loko-motiv-Fabrik-Aktiegesellschaft (Vienna Locomotive-Building Company) and designed by F. Wilhelm. Typical of the housing provided in the period immediately after World War I is the Schlinger Hof, Floridsforf, designed by Hans Glaser and Karl Scheffel and built in 1925–6. These five-storey apartments are of rough-cast finish, with steeply pitched tiled roofs broken by dormer windows of varied size. The main frontage is on to Brunnerstrasse, where there are shops on the ground floor, while to the south is a covered market. Werndlgasse to the north includes a variety of blocks built in the 1930s. The Werkbundsiedlung (experimental housing) off Jagdsch-lossgasse, 2.5 km (1$\frac{1}{2}$ mi.) SW of the centre, includes apartments designed by architects of various nationalities including R. Bauer, Adolf Loos and E. Plischke.

The most celebrated of the Viennese municipal housing developments is the Karl Marx Hof, Heiligenstadt, a vast block containing over 1300 dwellings, designed by Karl Ehn and built between 1927 and 1930. The apartments in Karl Marx Hof are of concrete construction, mostly of

Figure 169 The Karl Marx Hof, Heiligenstadt, Vienna, of 1927–30, which contains more than 1300 dwellings and was designed by Karl Ehn
Barrie Trinder

five storeys, framing a series of irregular courtyards between Heiligenstrasse and Boschstrasse. One of these, the 12 February Platz (which takes its name from an anti-Fascist demonstration of 1934) is open to the west, and is bounded to the east by a six-storey range, pierced by four arched passageways and crowned by six towers. Vehicu-lar access to the courts is provided by massive arched entrances within six-storey towers. The rough-cast finish is relieved by brick dressings and projecting rectangular bays. Access to the apartments is provided by staircases, entered through elaborately framed doorways, and pro-jecting galleries. The pedestrian entrances to the court-yards are through portcullis-like wrought-iron gates. On the ground floor fronting onto Heiligenstrasse is a range of shops and doctors' surgeries. A kindergarten and a public baths are situated in Felix Braun Gasse, which cuts through the range.

Municipal apartment blocks designed by internation-ally celebrated architects contrast oddly with the PLOT-LAND housing in many parts of the city. In many cases such housing seems to have developed on municipal allotments. Most houses are well maintained and many are covered with modern materials, so that it is difficult to appreciate the original constructional materials. One substantial plotland area is off Flötzersteig, south of the Psychiatrisches Krankenhaus (mental hospital) and north of the Baumgarten cemetery. Others lie along the railway line north-east of Floridsdorf.

Vienna possesses a range of museums in accord with its former status as an imperial capital. Those that deal with the history of the city and its region tend to neglect the history of industry. There are important specialist collec-tions of clocks and carriages.

Das Technisches Museum für Industrie und Gewerbe (The Technical Museum) was established in 1908, as part of the sixtieth anniversary celebrations of the accession of the Emperor Franz Josef, but it was not opened until 1918. Its first director was Dr Ludwig Erhard. It is a traditional museum, of models, samples and pictures, with predict-able sections on posts and telegraphs, printing, aviation, ceramics and glass, and an apothecary's shop of 1720, but it includes many individual exhibits of quite outstanding importance. There is an original model of a Watt engine of 1795, with a variety of nineteenth-century steam engines, including one of 1856 built by Vincenz Prick of Landstrasse, Vienna. The many important items of electri-city-generating equipment of the late nineteenth century include a Wechselstrom generator, built by Ganz & Co. of Budapest in 1895. There are several marine engines, including a steam engine by J. & A. Blyth of London, supplied in 1853 for the river steamer *Victoria*, con-structed by Robert Napier of Glasgow for use on the Danube. Outstanding among the many machine tools is one designed by John Haswell in 1862 and used in the state railway workshops in Vienna until 1931. The sections on motorcars and bicycles are particularly impor-tant for machines made in Austria. There are bicycles by Johann Puch of Graz made from 1901, while the cars include a large sedan by Graf & Stift of Vienna built in 1911, and an open tourer by the same company of 1925, together with a Steyr 220 and Steyr 55 of 1938. There is an early petrol filling pump manufactured by G. Rumpel of Vienna. The manufacture of sewing machines was of considerable importance in Austria in the early twentieth century and is represented by a sizeable collection. Sections on mining, salt and chemicals consist largely of models. The building department includes some early models of GARDEN CITY style houses and apartments; while there is a model of the first type of multi-chamber kiln for firing ceramics devised by Friedrich Hoffman in 1858. A 1:25 scale model of the Zeppelin L21 of 1900 is outstanding amongst the aviation exhibits. The Technical Museum also serves as Austria's chief railway museum, and a collection of locomotives includes *Steinbrück*, an outside-cylinder 4–4–0 built by Haswell in 1848; *Ajax*, an 0–4–2 built by Jones, Turner & Evans of Warrington, England, for the Nordbahn in 1841; 1513, a Gölsdorf 2–6–2 tender engine of 1910; and 1570.01, a 1A Bo A1 electric of 1926.

There are several notable examples of the adaptive reuse of industrial buildings in Vienna. The Handelskai grain silo, one of the earliest concrete buildings in Austria, has been converted to a 742-bed hotel, while several imaginative schemes have been proposed for the adaptation of the four vast gasholders built for Wiener Stadtwerke Gaswerke in 1896–9 in the suburb of Simmering, and disused since 1981.

BIBLIOGRAPHY
General
Bobek and Lichtenberger, 1966; Hudson, 1971; Janik and Toulmin, 1973; Schorske, 1980; Wagner, 1895; Wagner-Rieger, 1970; Wehdorn and Georgeacopol-Winischhofer, 1990.

LOCATIONS
[M] Alte Backstube (Old Bakery), 34 Lange Gasse, Vienna 8.
[M] Alte Schmiede (Old Smithy), 9 Schönlaterngasse, Vienna 9.
[M] Museum of Horseshoeing, Harnessing and Saddling, 11 Linke Bahngasse, Vienna 3.
[M] Österr. Museum für angewandte Kunst (Austrian Museum of Applied Arts), 5 Stübenring, Vienna 5.
[M] Österr. Museum für Volkskund (Austrian Folklore Museum), 15–19 Laudongasse, Vienna 8.
[I] Österr. Nationalbibliotheck (Austrian National Library), 1 Josefsplatz, Vienna 1.
[M] Stadtmuseum (Historical Museum of the City of Vienna), Karlsplatz, Vienna 4.
[M] Technisches Museum für Industrie und Gewerbe (Technical Museum), 212 Mariahilfer Strasse, Vienna 14.
[M] Tobacco Museum, Messepalast, Vienna 2.
[M] Uhrenmuseum (Clock Museum), 2 Schulhof, Vienna 1.

MICHAEL STRATTON and BARRIE TRINDER

Vila do Conde, Douro Litoral, Portugal   A port at the mouth of the River Ave, 26 km (16 mi.) N. of Oporto, with one of the oldest Portuguese shipyards, which still builds wooden ships.

LOCATION
[M] Ethnographical Museum, Praça da República, Vila do Conde.

Vila Nova de Famalicão, Minho, Portugal   The centre of

a heavily industrialized region, 30 km (20 mi.) N. of Oporto. There are large textile factories of early date at Riba de Ave and Caniços. The railway museum at Lousado, 8 km (5 mi.) S., the most important in northern Portugal, includes a carriage presented by Benito Mussolini (1883–1945) in 1931. Lousado's clock factory, the only one in Portugal, was founded in 1894. The town councils of the region have established a museum portraying the textile industry of the Ave valley.

LOCATION
[M] Railway Museum, Lousado.

Vila Real de Santo Antonio, Algarve, Portugal   A planned town with a geometric layout, founded by the Marquis of POMBAL (1699–1789) in 1774, 220 km (135 mi.) SE of Lisbon, on the Spanish border. A commercial and fishing port, its importance has declined since the mines at São Domingos de Mértola were closed and tuna fishing was abandoned. As in other Algarve towns, a fish canning industry was established in the nineteenth century but is now undergoing a crisis. The town council has set up a fish-canning museum in a former factory.

villa   A suburban dwelling, detached or SEMI-DETACHED, and often in a relatively spacious setting. English writers in the early nineteenth century referred to 'villas for the habitation of people in genteel circumstances' and 'villas and ornamental cottages'; and to 'an advance of villas . . . seizing a few picked positions', which was the first stage of suburban development. Originally the term meant a country mansion, and referred particularly to those of the Roman Empire or Renaissance Italy. In an industrial colony with a hierarchical housing system, like CRESPI D'ADDA, villas normally accommodated the managers.

BIBLIOGRAPHY
General
Coffin, 1979; Dyos, 1973.

Villedieu-les-Poëles, Manche, France   A Norman town celebrated for its copper and brass, where craftsmen still beat useful and decorative wares from sheets of copper. There is a museum of copper and brass, and a bell foundry in the town is open to the public.

BIBLIOGRAPHY
Specific
Matilleu, J. *Promenades dans Villedieu-les-Poëles*. Condé-sur-Noireau: Editions Corlet, 1982.
Villedieu-les-Poëles: le musée de Cuivre. Condé-sur-Noireau: Editions Corlet.

LOCATIONS
[S] Fonderie des Cloches (Bell foundry), rue du Pont-Chigon, 50800 Villedieu-les-Poëles.
[M] Musée de Cuivre (Copper Museum), rue Général Huard, 50800 Villedieu-les-Poëles.

Villeneuvette, Hérault, France   The Royal Cloth Manufacture at Villeneuvette was the second royal enterprise in Languedoc for the production of high-quality broadcloth for the Levant market, following a first venture at Saptes, near Carcassonne in the Aude. Founded in 1673 near Clermont-l'Hérault, 30 km (18 mi.) W. of Montpellier, it was taken over in 1678 by investors from this town, financiers who were also involved in the cutting of the Canal du Midi and the building of a new port at Sète.

The Villeneuvette manufacture prospered until the 1770s. During the nineteenth century it was run privately by the Maistre family, producing lower-quality cloth but otherwise little altered in its organization. The factory ceased production in 1954.

The manufacture was created in a rural setting and entirely from scratch. Prior to its implantation, there was just a farmstead on the site with a modest corn and fulling mill. This is the exceptional characteristic of the site, the factory and its annexes being laid out as a little town, a new town ('villeneuve') which acquired autonomous municipal existence in 1677. There are many remains of the original manufacture: an impressive monumental arch leads onto the main square, where there is a chapel of c.1740. By the square there are five blocks of workers' dwellings, probably dating from the late seventeenth century, two-storey buildings divided into identical living cells, each comprising one room with an alcove. Most of the production was carried out in a single building, 40 m (130 ft.) long, with a central block topped by a bell tower. This building too probably dates from the foundation of the manufacture. Behind it an artificial reservoir, 100 m (330 ft.) long, was dug around 1740. An aqueduct and channel brought water from the River Dourbie, which was used both as a source of energy and for washing and dyeing wool and cloth. During the second half of the nineteenth century new buildings were added, particularly to house steam engines. The village today attracts many visitors. Some of the buildings remain occupied but others are in serious need of repair.

BIBLIOGRAPHY
General
Thomson, 1982.
Specific
Alberge, C. and Laurent, L.-P. *et al.* Villeneuvette, une manufacture en Bas-Languedoc (Villeneuvette, a manufactory in lower Languedoc). In *Etudes sur l'Hérault*, xv, 1984.
Belhoste, J.-F., Grandjouan M.-S. *et al.* La Cité de Villeneuvette, guide du visiteur (Villeneuvette: a visitor's guide). In *Archéologie du Midi Médiéval*, v, 1987.

JEAN-FRANÇOIS BELHOSTE

vinegar Acetic acid produced by the secondary fermentation of liquids derived from vegetables: it is used in preserving food, and is the basis of PICKLES and SAUCES. Vinegar can be made from malt liquors, WINE, CIDER, and fruit juices. The manufacture of malt vinegar on an industrial scale, by brewing a weak wort (*see* BREWERY), began in the early nineteenth century. There were five large works in London by 1840. Wort was produced in mash tuns and taken by hoses into casks laid in ranks in extensive 'fields', where bacterial action promoted acidification. An alternative method, later used universally, was

to use large casks in hot rooms, a process known as 'stoving'.

BIBLIOGRAPHY
General
Beeton, 1912; Dodd, 1843; Landen and Daniel, 1985; Meesom, 1860.

Virginia, United States of America Little remains of the experiment in iron manufacture along the Atlantic coast of this state that inaugurated the trade on the North American continent. The Falling Creek charcoal blast furnace and finery-and-chafery forge of 1623–5 is regarded as the first integrated ironworks west of the Atlantic, although it and all the inhabitants of the British settlement were wiped out by Indians before commercial success could be achieved. Archaeological evidence has indicated that successful reduction and casting of the rich bog ore did occur along the James River.

Iron mining and manufacture play intermittent, background roles in the rise of the Virginian economy, with the bulk of the activity occurring in the mountainous western half of the state. Tobacco-growing, textile manufactures and shipbuilding have occupied more central positions, acknowledged in Danville's National Tobacco–Textile Museum; although the capital city, Richmond, weighs in with a respectable collection of cast-iron building façades and funerary work in the Hollywood Cemetery, principally the ornate iron crypt of President James Madison (1751–1836).

Virginia's Jackson Ferry Shot Tower is the earliest and most unusual of the nation's SHOT TOWERS. Using lead from the nearby Austinville mines, this 48 m (150 ft.) rectangular stone structure remained in use well into the twentieth century, and is now a protected state LANDMARK.

Just upriver from Washington DC stands evidence of another early Virginian engineering experiment that, like Falling Creek, ultimately met with failure. The locks and walls of the Patowmack Canal, built between 1785 and 1799, occupy rugged stone outcroppings above Great Falls on the Potomac River, the considerable drop requiring a stupefying 21 m (70 ft.) tidelock below the falls. Proposed and planned by George Washington (1732–89), the canal was part of the first extensive system of joint canal–river navigations in the nation.

The 1300 m (4250 ft.) Crozet Railroad Tunnel of 1858 at Rockfish Gap represents the swansong of the hand method of rock drilling in North America. Three other noteworthy landmarks in this agricultural state are the remains of the Tredegar Ironworks in Richmond, notable for producing Confederate ordnance during the Civil War; a former World War II torpedo factory in Alexandria, now converted into art studios; and the Cape Henry Lighthouse of 1791 at Virginia Beach, the first commissioned public works structure in the nation.

Colonial Williamsburg is a restoration, begun in 1926 with support from John D. Rockefeller, Jr (1874–1960), of the city that was the state capital in the eighteenth century. Within the 70 ha (175 ac.) Historic Area, eighty-eight surviving buildings have been fully restored, and another fifty reconstructed. Archive resources are extensive and there is an active historic archaeology programme, which has included the replication of a working BLOOMERY. Printing, papermaking, gun manufacture, shoemaking, saddlemaking, coopering, wheelwrighting and brickmaking are among the trades practised.

LOCATIONS

[M] American Work Horse Museum, PO Box 88, Paeonian Springs, VA 22129.
[S] The Colonial Williamsburg Foundation, Williamsburg, VA 23187.
[M] Mariners' Museum, Museum Drive, Newport News, VA 23606.
[M] National Tobacco–Textile Museum, 614 Lynn Street, Danville, VA 14541.
[M] Portsmouth Naval Shipyard Museum, 420 High Street, Portsmouth, VA 23704.

DAVID H. SHAYT

visitor centre   *See* HERITAGE CENTRE.

vitriol   A sulphate of any of various metals, such as copper sulphate ($CuSO_4$), known as blue vitriol; a term widely used until after 1850. SULPHURIC ACID was known as 'oil of vitriol', although this was commonly abbreviated to 'vitriol'.

Vitrolite   A rolled opal glass, used principally for facing buildings, manufactured by adding fluorides to the glass. The first Vitrolite in England was made in 1930. Notable applications include the Daily Express building (*see* LONDON) and the dado in the Mersey Tunnel (*see* LIVERPOOL). It was widely used for shop fronts.

BIBLIOGRAPHY
General
McGrath and Frost, 1937.

Vizzola, Lombardy, Italy   Some of Italy's earliest hydroelectric power stations are on the River Ticino. Vizzola power station, 50 km (30 mi.) NW of Milan, was built in 1898–1900, with extensive concrete water channels, supported on large arcades with sweeping curves. Further down the Ticino at Vigevano, 35 km (22 mi.) SW of Milan, is a power station in Renaissance style of the early 1900s.

The Ticino became the focus of the development of the Italian aircraft industry. Gianni Caproni (1856–1957) developed a glider in Belgium, and with the support of the army established a factory for biplanes at Vizzola, which was expanded during the two world wars. Two buildings of the complex now accommodate a museum of flight, including aeroplanes, airships, propellers and other components. The nearby Villa Caproni, originally connected to the works by an avenue, was built in the 1920s with a grand central entrance; this was later adorned with an iron canopy saved from Milan's first central railway station, demolished in 1931.

Another pioneering aircraft factory was at Sesto Calende at the southern tip of Lake Maggiore, 15 km (9 mi.) N. of Vizzola. The SIAI (*see* ITALY) works was established in the town's sawmills, Luigi Cape using the sheds for the manufacture of FBA (Franco-British Aviation) seaplanes from 1915. A house converted into the company offices in the same year survives, along with several buildings erected before 1925. The eastern part of the complex, built after 1945, includes an impressive brick archway surmounted by an eagle with spread wings, and a recreation pavilion with decorative frescos and wrought-iron work.

BIBLIOGRAPHY
General
Negri *et al.*, 1983.

MICHAEL STRATTON

Vlăhiţa, Harghita, Romania   A water-powered forge, with three tilt hammers, which forms part of a modern ironworks, is still used to demonstrate the manufacture of hoes and shovels.

BIBLIOGRAPHY
General
Wollmann, V. Romania. In Georgeacopol-Winischhofer *et al.*, 1987.
Specific
Wollmann, V. Un Monument de tehnică preindustriala. Forja de la Vlăhiţa, jud.Harghita (A monument of pre-industrial technology, the forge from Vlăhiţa in the district of Harghita). In *Revista muzeelor si monumentelor* (Bucharest), 2, 1986.

Vlaicu, Aurel (1882–1913)   One of the most important pioneers of aeronautics, Vlaicu was born in the village of Binţinţi, near Hunedoara in Romania. He made his first flights in a glider of his own invention, which was lifted into the air by being pulled by men or horses. In 1910 at Bucharest he built the aeroplane Vlaicu I with which on 11 June he succeeded in making a 40–50 m (120–150 ft.) long flight at a height of about 1 m (3 ft.). On 16 August he climbed to a height of 150 m (490 ft.), flying at an average speed of 70 km (43 mi.) per hour. The fuselage of this aircraft was formed from an aluminium tube which supported all the other elements: the elevators at the rear, the nacelle with the controls and the engine, the wing, the rudder in the form of a cross at the tail, the two counter-rotating, coaxial propellers (which counteracted the pair for reversing), and the fuel tank. By placing the elevator at the rear and the centre of gravity in a lower position, Vlaicu gave the aircraft manœuvrability and stability. With the aircraft Vlaicu II, built in 1911, Vlaicu made some remarkable displays at Aspern near Vienna in 1912. In 1913 he built a third aircraft, Vlaicu III, which had an all-metal frame, but he died on 13 September of that year, when he crashed during an attempt to fly over the Carpathian Mountains.

BIBLIOGRAPHY
General
Gheorghiu, 1979.

HORIA GIURGIUMAN

Figure 170 The blowing engine hall at the Völklingen ironworks in the Saarland: since the closure of the adjacent blast furnaces in 1986 the hall has been used for rock concerts and other public performances.
Saarstahl GMBH

vodka A SPIRIT, often almost tasteless but of interesting consistency, made from rye malt or potato, traditionally in Russia, Poland and Finland, but now on an industrial scale in Britain and the USA. The distilling process is similar to that used for WHISKY, but the final stage is filtering through charcoal.

See also DISTILLING.

Völklingen, Saarland, Germany   A town 10 km (6 mi.) W. of Saarbrücken, the site of what is probably the last blast-furnace plant from the turn of the century to have been preserved in its entirety. Most of it was built in 1883–1916: it was modernized several times, and ceased production in 1986. This impressive complex is concentrated into a small space between the River Saar and the railway from Saarbrücken to Trier, close to the centre of Völklingen. On the other side of the railway is a rolling mill which still operates, with three stands, driven by steam engines of 1890, 1909 and 1912.

The ironworks originated in 1873 as a FORGE making puddled iron, and was taken over by the Röchling brothers in 1881. The blast furnaces built after 1883 supplied enough pig iron for business to expand rapidly, and the works was the major manufacturer of wrought-iron sections in Germany as early as 1889. At the end of World War I the blast-furnace complex with its six furnaces displayed, in all essentials, what is still its distinctive shape on the skyline. The ironworks was principally engaged in making armaments in both World Wars. The two German defeats and the periods of military administration that followed, together with the shifting of the customs frontiers, led to severe economic problems. At the beginning of the steel crisis in the early 1970s the ironworks merged with ARBED of Luxembourg; the firm of Röchling, its former owners, withdrew in 1978. The reconstruction of the industry led to the closure of the blast-furnace plant in 1986, after a life of 103 years.

The parts of the works that are still in operation, including a modern LD PROCESS steel plant and a rolling mill for sections, have been known as Saarstahl AG since 1989, and formed a single holding company with Dillinger Hütte AG, which was founded in 1685 and became a limited company in 1808.

818

The blast-furnace plant concentrates all the equipment for producing pig iron into a small space.

The coking plant, established in 1898, has four batteries of coke ovens and two coal towers. The oldest battery of ovens dates from 1934 and the oldest coal tower from 1898.

The dry gas-purification plant of 1912–25 consists of three sheds with filter blocks for purifying waste gases through cloth filters. It was the first large-scale dry gas-purification plant in the world, built according to the Halberg-Beth patent.

The electric conveyor system built between 1911 and 1918 has buckets that travel automatically along suspended rails to charge the blast furnaces, with cable haulage inclines which take them from the coke ovens and the sinter plant 27 m (89 ft.) up to the charging platforms.

The six blast furnaces were built between 1916 and 1976. Their internal height is about 19 m (62 ft.), and their eventual output was 1000 tonnes a day, compared with the 76 tonnes per day achieved with the first blast furnace on the site between 1883 and 1891.

The COWPER STOVES include one of 1885 with a riveted steel jacket, and nine others from before 1916. The most modern high-temperature stove has an external combustion chamber and dates from 1976.

The ore-preparation area, constructed between 1911 and 1918, consists of ore silos, ore and dust bunkers, a slag crushing and sifting plant, a slag cooler, and the slag conveyor plant of 1928–38 – a four-storey, steel-framed structure, with four slag conveyors, built according to the Dwight-Lloyd patent. This was the first large plant of its kind in Germany and one of the first in the world.

The blowing engine hall is a vast single-storey building, 150 m × 34 m (492 ft. × 116 ft.), built in stages between 1900 and 1938, which formerly contained ten blowing engines for the blast furnaces. Seven engines have been preserved, the oldest a double-acting, four-stroke twin tandem engine (MAN DTZ 13) of 1905 with an output of 17 000 m_3 (22 250 cu. yd.) per hour. The most recent are two double-acting, four-stroke tandem engines by Demag (DT 14/MAN DT 14) of 1914, each with an output of 62 000 m^3 (81 000 cu. yd.) per hour, which can also drive an electric generator of the SSW (Siemens-Schuckert-Werke) type.

Three steam engines of 1889–1912 drive the rolling mill stands V, VI and VII. The largest is a tandem triple reversing engine of 1909 by Ehrhardt & Sehmer of Saarbrücken, rated at 12 000 hp at 120 rev./min. The smallest is a single-cylinder, 'direct current' engine by Ehrhardt & Sehmer capable of 6800 hp at 83 rev./min. The engines operate daily.

Ancillary buildings include an office block of 1912; a services area with workshops for carpenters, fitters, ropemakers, painters and plumbers, built between 1898 and 1919; a pumphouse of 1910, with two gas engines of 1917 working centrifugal pumps by drive belts; and a reinforced-concrete watertower of 1918 holding cooling water for the furnaces.

The blowing hall and a workshop area next to it, as well as parts of the services area, have been adapted for cultural purposes since the plant went out of production; other parts of the complex are to be similarly converted.

BIBLIOGRAPHY
Specific
Nutzinger, R., Boehmer, H. and Johannsen, O. *50 Jahre Röchling Völklingen: Die Entwicklung eines Rheinischen Industrie-Unternehmens* (50 years of smelting at Völklingen: the development of a Rhenish industrial enterprise). Saarbrücken. Gebr Hofer AG, 1931.

NORBERT MENDGEN

Vordernberg, Styria, Austria   *See* STYRIAN IRON TRAIL.

voussoir   A wedge-shaped component of an ARCH or vault. It is usually of shaped stone, but the term can be applied to ceramic or iron components serving the same purpose.

Vuia, Traian (1872–1950)   An eminent innovator in aeronautics, born at Logoj near Timişoara, in the district of Timiş, Romania. He brought forward in Paris in 1902 a project for a flying automobile, which was granted French patent No. 332106. In 1905 he completed the construction of an aircraft with which on 18 March 1906 at Montesson near Paris he succeeded in making a 12 m (40 ft.) flight at a height of 0.6 m (2 ft.). This was the first self-propelled flight in a heavier-than-air machine. The original aircraft is conserved in the Aeronautics Museum in PARIS, and there is a copy in the Central Military Museum in Bucharest. Between 1916 and 1918 Vuia brought forward in Paris various military inventions, including a marine torpedo; and between 1918 and 1922 he built helicopters, propelled and kept in the air by rotors. In order to provide such machines with power he perfected in 1925 an internal combustion steam generator of 1 hp/1.15 kg.

BIBLIOGRAPHY
General
Carafoli, 1966; Moroianu and Stefan, 1968.

W

waddle fan One of several mechanical ventilators developed for use at mines after 1860, other types including the Guibal, Schiel, Walker and Sirocco systems. All operated on the principle of centrifugal force. (Other types, like the Lamielle Ventilator, operated by displacement and air-forcing.) The waddle fan was outstanding in its simplicity and because it could operate in the open. It had no external casing, but delivered to the atmosphere all around its periphery, drawing air from the mine at its centre or throat. Fans of this kind were directly driven by steam engines, and later by electric motors. The first waddle fan was installed in 1864, and by 1900 about 250 had been installed in Britain, ranging in diameter from 3 m (10 ft.) to 14 m (45 ft.). About eight were working in British mines in the late 1960s. Preserved examples remain at BLAENAVON and at BEAMISH. An 'Indestructible' steam-driven ventilation fan of 1910 is displayed at WIGAN Pier.

waggon A four-wheeled, horse-drawn vehicle, usually carrying freight on roads, but the term also applies to vehicles used on farms. (A railway vehicle is usually called a 'wagon' – see RAILWAY WAGON). In eighteenth-century England there was a distinction between a waggon and a wain which is not now fully apparent, except that a wain was more likely to be drawn by oxen. The front pair of wheels on a waggon is attached to the shafts, and turns on a bolster. Waggon-construction usually followed regional traditions.

In many countries regular if slow waggon services carrying small consignments over long distances were developing by 1700, and by 1800 there were quite extensive networks. In England and Wales in 1835 there were 14 000 regular weekly services of this kind. In England they were called stage waggons, in Germany Postwagen. Such vehicles normally had canvas hoods and punt-like containers slung between the axles.

BIBLIOGRAPHY
General
Dyos and Aldcroft, 1969.

wagon-lit La Compagnie Internationale des Wagons-Lits et des Grands Express Européens, established by the Belgian engineer Georges Nagelmackers (1845–1905) and his partners, operates sleeping cars across national boundaries. Nagelmackers visited the USA in 1868 and saw Pullman cars in operation. He registered a company in Liège but its operations were curtailed by the Franco-Prussian War of 1870. He formed a new company in Brussels in 1876, and operated restaurant cars in addition to sleeping cars from 1883. The company's cars were working in most European countries by 1900, operations including the Orient Express linking Paris with ISTANBUL from 1883 and the Moscow–Vladivostock route from 1898.

BIBLIOGRAPHY
General
Behrend, 1962b; CIWL, 1926.

wagonway A term used to describe a RAILWAY in north-east England from the early seventeenth century until the early nineteenth century. The term remained in use, referring to older types of line.

BIBLIOGRAPHY
General
Lewis, 1970.

Waihi, Auckland, New Zealand A gold mining settlement 110 km (70 mi.) SE of Auckland, built around the Martha Mine. There are important remains, including a group of six 17 m (55 ft.) high concrete cyanide tanks of c.1905, and the vast concrete shell of No. 5 Pumphouse of 1904, stripped of machinery. This pump could raise 22 730 000 litres (90 000 gallons) of water per hour from a depth of 470 m (1 550 ft.). Only the concrete foundations remain of a two-hundred stamp Victoria Battery at Waikino, 10 km (6 mi.) SW.

BIBLIOGRAPHY
General
Thornton, 1982.

Wailes, Rex (1901–86) An authority on mills, who was responsible for the establishment of the Industrial Monuments Survey in England for the Ministry of Public Building and Works, 1963–71. An engineer who began studying windmills while apprenticed to Robey & Co. of Lincoln, he subsequently worked for his family firm in London. He was President of the Newcomen Society in 1954–6.

BIBLIOGRAPHY
General
Wailes, 1948, 1967.
Specific
IA, XVIII, 1988.

Wałbrzych (Waldenburg), Wrocław, Poland A mining

centre, 40 km (25 mi.) S. of Wrocław. The Old and New Mining Technology Centre is one of the components of an écomusée planned for the Wałbrzysko-Noworudzkie coalfield in Lower Silesia, in which the Institute of the History of Architecture, Art and Technology at Wrocław Technical University and the management of the Wałbrzyskie mines are collaborating. Coal has been mined in the area since the fifteenth century, and the industry flourished particularly in the late eighteenth and early nineteenth centuries. Various working machines are being preserved.

The first stage of the project was accomplished in 1986, and included the conservation of two neighbouring mineshafts, the 'Irena' and 'Gabriel', dating from c.1900. The 'Gabriel' complex comprises an engine house with an electric winder of 1909 which is currently used for training winding enginemen, and a training adit which contains a display of modern mining machinery. The 'Irena' buildings house an exhibition featuring the development of the mine. In the engine house of the 'Irena' mine is a Leonardo-Ilgner electric winder of 1903, with all its original equipment in good condition. The 'Irena' shaft is still used for ventilation and access. An exhibition of mining machines and equipment for underground and vertical haulage has been arranged in the area between the two shafts. The site is also used as a training centre for miners and is managed by the Wałbrzyskie mines administration.

The project also includes the 'Wojciech' (former 'Wrangel') shaft at the 'Victoria' colliery in Wałbrzych, originally the winding shaft of the colliery, but from the early twentieth century the air shaft. In 1980 it was phased out, and was put under legislative protection. The brick-built Malakoff tower which contained the winding equipment dates from 1860 and is amongst the oldest preserved in Poland. The winding-engine house was erected in 1902 and until 1975 it contained steam-operated winding equipment, similar to that of 1898 which is preserved at the neighbouring 'Zbigniew' shaft.

The installations at the 'Wojciech' shaft were threatened by plans to build a new colliery, the 'Kopernik', but it was decided to incorporate the historic monuments into the new installations. Similar decisions were taken with the late nineteenth-century 'Powietrzny' shaft, and the early twentieth-century 'Tytus' shaft, and all three now survive as features of the historic landscape of the Wałbrzych coalfield.

It is also planned to include in the écomusée a drainage adit of 1794, some 800 m (875 yd.) long, which is being made safe for public access, and the refractory shale plant at Nowa ruda.

BIBLIOGRAPHY
General
Piatek, 1989.
Specific
Januszewski, S. Ochrona zabytków techniki górniczej Zagłębia Dolnośląskiego (The protection of mining technology relics in the Lower Silesian Coalfield). In *Górnictwo węgla kamiennego w procesie kształtowania środowiska ludzkiego* (Coal mining in the process of human-environment shaping). Wrocław: Wydawnictwo Politechniki Wrocławskiej, 1985.

LOCATION
[M] Ośrodek Dawnej i Nowej Techniki Górniczej w Wałbrzychu (Old and New Mining Technology Centre in Wałbrzych), ul. Św Józefa, Wałbrzych.

PIOTR GERBER

Waldalgesheim, Rhineland-Palatinate, Germany The Dr Geier manganese mine above Waldalgesheim, 4 km ($2\frac{1}{2}$ mi.) W. of Bingen, is one of Germany's outstanding mining monuments because of the scale of the planning of the complex and the unity of its architectural style. The first reference to manganese mining in the Bingen area dates from 1628. Concessions were granted from 1832. At first lumps of ore were mined from near the surface, but the architect Dr Geier of Mainz explored the area and acquired the Amalienhöhe field in 1883, commencing deep mining in 1886. The mines were merged in 1906 under the title of the Consolidierte Braunsteinwerke Dr Geier (Dr Geier Consolidated Manganese Works). A cable railway took the ore to the Rhine and a solution of manganese in water was taken through a tunnel to the river. After World War I the Mannesmann company took over the mine. It was converted to dolomite mining in 1954. By the time it ceased operation in 1971, 5.5 million tonnes of manganese ore and 2.6 million tonnes of dolomite had been mined.

In 1916, during the shortages in World War I, a start was made on the rebuilding of the Strauben mine and the entire installation was completed in 1920. The plans for the surface buildings were by the Darmstadt architects, Markwort & Seibert. The buildings are grouped around a courtyard, comparable to the arrangements at the Zollern 2/4 mine in Dortmund (*see* Ruhrgebiet). The grand scale on which the buildings are designed, in the neo-Baroque style of Darmstadt, is unique for a mining installation. Almost all the buildings of the castle-like complex are preserved. Behind the entrance, with its two pavilions, are the canteen and hall on the left, the pithead building and wages hall, both the pithead baths on the right, and then the ore silo, winding tower and cable railway installation. The power station stands at the back of the courtyard, with the cooling pool, shaped like a fountain, in front. The view of the plant, placed on a hilltop, is dominated from the valley by the large ore silo and the steeple-like headstock, the latter having a water tank fitted into its top store. Closely connected with the mining plant are new buildings of the same period in the village of Waldalgesheim, designed by the same architects, to replace parts of the village destroyed by mining subsidence. The surface buildings, which were falling into disrepair when the mine closed, passed into private ownership in 1977 and have since been renovated.

BIBLIOGRAPHY
General
Custodis, 1990.

ROLF HÖHMANN

Wales (Cymru) Wales is a historic nation within the

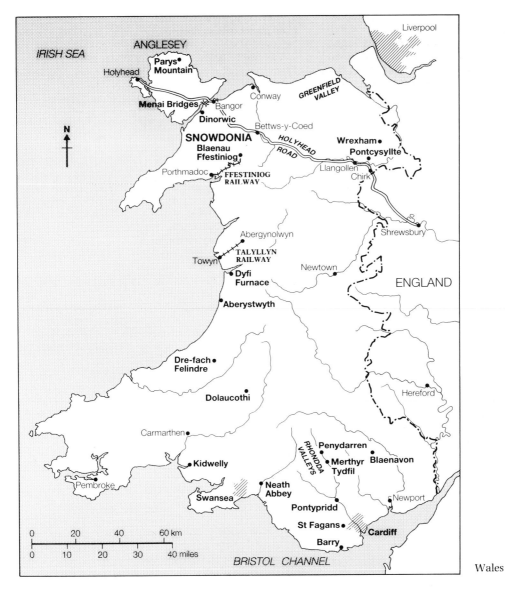

Wales

United Kingdom which has had a long history of industrial development, with a world significance in the extractive industries, especially coal, slate, lead and copper, and in heavy manufacturing, especially of non-ferrous metals, iron, steel and tinplate. Its eastern border with England has remained stationary, roughly following its upland perimeter, and it is bounded on all other sides by the sea. The country was subject to English rule from the thirteenth century and achieved legal union in 1536. However, it has maintained a strong national character, with an autonomous government department with a wide range of responsibilities, and some important national institutions. The Welsh language is still spoken, particularly in isolated areas.

The country has a land area of 21 000 km² (8000 sq.

mi.) and is approximately 225 km (140 mi.) from north to south and between 65 km (40 mi.) and 160 km (100 mi.) from west to east. It is largely upland in character, with 60 per cent of its land area over 150 m (500 ft.) above sea level and a series of mountain zones dominating the interior. The upland areas are suited mainly to forestry and pasture, but the coastal strip is more fertile and densely settled. Industrial minerals are mainly found in the upland areas, most notably in the North and South Wales coalfields, the North and Mid Wales non-ferrous-metals fields, and the slate massif of SNOWDONIA.

Wales had a poor and largely pastoral economy before its period of industrialization from the eighteenth century. A few of its significant industries were presaged in the pre-industrial period, but the chief industrialization of Wales is usually regarded as a pseudo-colonial process, dependent on English capital and entrepreneurship introduced in the eighteenth and nineteenth centuries, most notably in places such as MERTHYR TYDFIL and BLAENAVON. Most land was controlled by absentee aristocrats like the Marquesses of BUTE. Only a few exceptional Welshmen, like THOMAS WILLIAMS, were pioneers and profiteers of industrial development before the late nineteenth century when natives like DAVID THOMAS, or DAVID DAVIES and other RHONDDA coal-owners, were more frequently found in the ranks of industrialists. Such colonialism tended to restrict Welsh industries to basic extraction and processing, which was liable to sudden booms and depressions, with few subsidiary industries.

Before the Industrial Revolution the most important industry was woollen manufacture, the production of coarse cloth in domestic workshops throughout the country from the fifteenth century. In the seventeenth century the industry employed 100 000 people, or about a quarter of the population; but it declined with competition from Yorkshire and the West of England. It survived into the nineteenth century with the growth of water-powered factories, particularly in Montgomeryshire and Carmarthenshire (for example at DRE-FACH FELINDRE), but much production remained in smaller mills and workshops, like that at ST FAGANS open-air museum.

A Welsh iron industry was established in the sixteenth and seventeenth centuries when timber was short in south-eastern England. At least thirty blast furnaces existed across Wales in the charcoal era (for example DYFI FURNACE, and Bersham furnace near WREXHAM), but there was little manufacturing of the pig iron produced. However, with coke-smelting from the 1750s, and puddling from the 1780s, South Wales became the most important producer of iron in the world, making pig and bar iron and many simple cast-iron and wrought-iron goods. By 1796 it had twenty-six coke furnaces and overtook Shropshire in production. By 1830 it represented 40 per cent of British pig-iron output. The industry had been established afresh almost exclusively by English entrepreneurs. It was concentrated above all in MERTHYR TYDFIL, but a string of ironmaking centres by 1850 colonized the northern rim of the South Wales coalfield from Hirwaun to BLAENAVON, where iron ore, limestone and coking coal were available. A few works were built on the coalfield's southern rim, for example at NEATH ABBEY; and from the 1830s in the anthracite region around SWANSEA.

The iron industry was heavily damaged by the introduction of Bessemer steelmaking in 1856, since local ores were rendered unusable until the Thomas process (see GILCHRIST THOMAS) was introduced in 1879. By this time several inland works had closed, and others had been set up closer to imported ores, for example in CARDIFF. Most of the new works were small and specialized in steel-sheet manufacture for tinning. Mechanized tinplate manufacture was invented in Wales by JOHN HANBURY in the 1720s, and world tinplate production became firmly concentrated in South Wales, and especially on the coast around SWANSEA, in the nineteenth century, using local coal and iron and Cornish tin. Tinning mills, such as that

at KIDWELLY, were small and hand-operated. Competition from American steel-strip and electrolytic tinning processes caused severe decline in the twentieth century.

The two principal coalfields of Wales are in north-east Wales (extending from Point of Air to Oswestry) and in South Wales (from Pontypool in the east to Kidwelly in the west, with a narrow extension in Pembrokeshire). From the seventeenth century mining grew within reach of the sea, notably around SWANSEA and Tenby. During the Industrial Revolution these areas continued to develop, but greater changes were wrought elsewhere by English entrepreneurs: introducing coke ironmaking in the north from the 1760s, and building canals up the valleys to release new supplies for export from the 1790s. However the greatest boom came from the mid-nineteenth century with the opening up of the RHONDDA VALLEYS and other steam coal areas feeding CARDIFF's export markets. At its peak production in 1913 Wales exported 30 of its 56 million tonnes; this comprised one-third of world coal exports. A further boom occurred around SWANSEA when anthracite became used as a domestic coal from the 1920s; but the general decline was already under way, matching the decline in the metal trades and the conversion of shipping to oil.

Non-ferrous-metals mining was also long-established in Wales. Gold was mined by the Romans at DOLAUCOTHI, and then sporadically there and in SNOWDONIA, especially in the late nineteenth and early twentieth centuries. Lead ores were exploited from every county of Wales. Mining on a large scale was undertaken in the Mid Wales ore field, focused on ABERYSTWYTH, from the sixteenth century, and expanded especially there and in north-east Wales until the end of the nineteenth century. Copper was mined along with lead and zinc in many areas, but was chiefly concentrated in SNOWDONIA, and the prodigious PARYS MOUNTAIN mines, from the late eighteenth to late nineteenth centuries. The mines were seldom associated with processing of ores other than crushing or buddling (see BUDDLE) as, except in north-east Wales, they were not close to supplies of coal. Smelting took place at coastal parts of the coalfields: in the GREENFIELD VALLEY and in the area around SWANSEA. Swansea was the world centre of non-ferrous-metal smelting for a time, with works established in the eighteenth and nineteenth centuries to smelt copper from Cornwall and the Welsh fields diversifying into other non-ferrous metals and their by-products. Many works smelted South American and other ores with the decline of Welsh ore production; but most fell to foreign competition from the 1880s.

The last of the great Welsh industries was slate quarrying. Slates for roofing and other purposes were quarried in several areas, but the greatest production was in SNOWDONIA, at highly organized quarries like DINORWIC, Penrhyn and BLAENAU FFESTINIOG. Slate exports to roof the urban expansion of England grew rapidly throughout the nineteenth century, but fell disastrously after a peak in 1918 due to competition from mass-produced tiles and foreign slates.

Few other industries developed on a large scale in Wales. Bricks were produced on the coalfields during the

Figure 171 Sinuous settlement in a South Wales valley: this aerial view of the Taff valley at Aberfan, looking north to Troed-y-Rhiw, shows the typical arrangement of settlement, mining and transport facilities in coalfield valleys like the Taff, the Rhondda and the Rhymney which developed from the mid-nineteenth century. The narrow valley floor is dominated by the Taff (later Merthyr Vale) Colliery and its railway sidings in a loop of the river. The Glamorganshire Canal, the Taff Vale Railway and the main road to Cardiff all fight for space with schools, chapels and terraces of housing between the barren mountainsides. Waste tipping by aerial ropeways on the hillsides led to the Aberfan disaster in 1966, when a landslip buried people in their homes and children at school. This and other waste tips have now been drained and cleared.   Aerofilms Ltd

nineteenth century, notably at WREXHAM; earthenwares were made through the eighteenth century at Buckley; and porcelain was made briefly near Cardiff and Swansea. Brewing and baking developed in many industrial towns. In the nineteenth century dairies opened to supply English and Welsh cities with milk by train, and large reservoirs were built to send them water by pipeline. Resorts were also developed, mainly on the coast, for example in north Wales and at ABERYSTWYTH. Foundries were widespread, and there were a few more prestigious engineering works, such as NEATH ABBEY.

Many boosts to production in Welsh industries were associated with transport improvements. Roads were improved throughout the eighteenth and nineteenth centuries, but the HOLYHEAD ROAD was completely exceptional in quality. Harbours were improved to ship the products of growing industries, for example in SNOWDONIA for slate and at ABERYSTWYTH for lead; and the coal-ports, such as CARDIFF, SWANSEA and BARRY, built wet docks in the late nineteenth century. Canals were built from the 1790s, notably up the South Wales valleys in conjunction with horse-drawn tramroads built with iron plates or rails on stone sleepers, like the PENYDARREN TRAMROAD. Only the Ellesmere Canal network in North Wales joined the English canal system. Many miles of railways were built after the Taff Vale–CARDIFF line in 1841, mostly ramifying throughout the coalfield valleys. Several narrow-gauge mineral railways were built in North and Mid Wales, for instance the TALYLLYN RAILWAY and the FESTINIOG RAILWAY. Only a few long-distance lines were built, most notably the South Wales Railway linking the London route to Milford Haven by 1863, and the Cambrian Railway reaching ABERYSTWYTH a year later. It is typical of Welsh industrial development that these and other lines were concerned to link with England or the sea, and not to join one part of Wales to another.

Conservation of industrial sites and monuments is carried out by a variety of bodies, from government departments to commercial museums. The system of protection for important individual monuments is listing and scheduling, which imposes legal controls on their redevelopment. The compilation of lists of such monuments is undertaken by the Welsh heritage agency Cadw, frequently on the advice of the Royal Commission on Ancient and Historical Monuments in Wales. When protected sites are threatened, they may be recorded by either the Royal Commission or one of the county-level archaeological trusts.

Within this legal structure, various organizations play similar roles of conserving monuments and sites. Cadw directly maintains some sites, such as DYFI FURNACE and BLAENAVON ironworks. The state-funded National Museum of Wales operates museums which represent individual industries at important sites such as DINORWIC and DRE-FACH FELINDRE (largely thanks to the work of DAVID MORGAN REES in the 1960s) as well as a national museum of industry at Cardiff and an open-air museum at ST FAGANS. Local authorities act through their own museums, for example at SWANSEA and WREXHAM, but more often contribute to voluntary trusts, as at BLAENA-

VON's Big Pit mining museum, and KIDWELLY tinplate museum. A few industrial sites are preserved by the National Trust, for example at DOLAUCOTHI and Aberdulais near SWANSEA. There is also a growing number of commercial museums dependent on tourism, particularly in SNOWDONIA. Many of these have grown with the example of preserved railways, such as the TALYLLYN RAILWAY and FESTINIOG RAILWAY. However, many sites of world industrial significance are not sufficiently protected, for example at NEATH ABBEY or PARYS MOUNTAIN. In certain areas, too, a violent antipathy to the industrial heritage has resulted in massive clearances of important remains, most notably in MERTHYR TYDFIL and the Lower SWANSEA Valley up to the 1980s. A more balanced approach to conservation awaits much more wide-ranging research into the country's very significant industrial archaeology.

See also ABERYSTWYTH; BARRY; BLAENAU FFESTINIOG; BLAENAVON; BUTE, JOHN, 2ND MARQUIS OF; CARDIFF; CRAWSHAY, RICHARD; DAVIES, DAVID; DINORWIC; DOLAUCOTHI; DRE-FACH FELINDRE; DYFI FURNACE; FESTINIOG RAILWAY; GILCHRIST THOMAS, SIDNEY; GREENFIELD VALLEY; HANBURY, JOHN; HOLYHEAD ROAD; KIDWELLY; MENAI BRIDGES; MERTHYR TYDFIL; NEATH ABBEY; PARYS MOUNTAIN; PENYDARREN TRAMROAD; PONTCYSYLLTE AQUEDUCT; PONTYPRIDD; REES, DAVID MORGAN; RHONDDA VALLEYS; ST FAGANS; SEVERN TUNNEL; SNOWDONIA; SWANSEA; TALYLLYN RAILWAY; THOMAS, DAVID; WILLIAMS, THOMAS; WREXHAM.

BIBLIOGRAPHY
General
Dodd, 1971; Jenkins, 1969; Lewis, 1967; Lindsay, 1974; Rees, 1969, 1975; Riden, 1987.
Specific
Bowen, E. G. ed. *Wales: a physical, historical and regional geography.* London: Methuen, 1957.
Emery, F. V. *The World's Landscapes, 2: Wales.* London: Longman, 1969.

LOCATIONS
[I] Cadw, Brunel House, 2 Fitzaland Road, Cardiff CF2 1UY.
[I] Royal Commission on Ancient and Historical Monuments in Wales, Crown Building, Plas Crug, Aberystwyth, Dyfed SY23 2HP.

PETER WAKELIN

Walloon forge A process for forging pig iron from the blast furnace into wrought iron, which was the origin of the FINERY-AND-CHAFERY FORGE. It seems to have originated in the Eifel and the Ardennes from where it spread to the Liège region and to other countries in the seventeenth century. It was introduced to Sweden by Walloon immigrants in the early seventeenth century, almost all the Walloon forges in Sweden being situated in Uppland province. The iron ore from the DANNEMORA mines, combined with the Walloon methods of smelting and forging, gave an iron almost free from slag inclusions. Walloon iron from Sweden was of exceptionally high quality and was mainly used for manufacturing steel, most of it being exported. It fetched a premium price on the Sheffield market and was used in CEMENTATION FURNACES as well as for the CRUCIBLE PROCESS. The last bars of

Walloon iron were produced at Österbybruk in 1943 and at Strombackabruk in 1947.

The end of a bar (French: 'geuse') of cast iron was pushed forward through an opening in the outer wall of the finery hearth, above a bed of incandescent charcoal and opposite a TUYÈRE. Only as much of the bar was used as was needed to provide sufficient iron for a bloom. When the cast iron began to melt, it dripped through the blast from the tuyère to the bottom of the hearth which was covered with a deposit of slag, with some silicon and manganese, and was oxidized there, forming a bloom.

See also figure 56.

BIBLIOGRAPHY
General
Barraclough, 1981–4; Ekman *et al.*, 1987; Forsmark och vallon-jarnet, 1928; Hildebrand, 1987; Odelstierna, 1913.

MARIE NISSER

Wanlockhead, Dumfries & Galloway, and **Leadhills**, Strathclyde, Scotland   One of Britain's most isolated communities, where from the seventeenth century silver and lead were mined. Wanlockhead Museum Trust has remarkable achievements to its credit. A stretch of level at Loch Nell Mine, the remains of a smelt mill, foundations of the Bay Mine water wheel and Symington steam engine pumps have been excavated and consolidated. A unique water-powered beam pumping engine is a guardianship monument (*see* SCOTLAND). Other items of plant, including a hydraulic pumping engine at South Glencrieff Mine, survive underground. The Trust has acquired the village church and the Miners' Reading Society Library, formed in 1756: this and the library of 1741 in Leadhills are the oldest working-men's libraries in Britain.

BIBLIOGRAPHY
Specific
Downs-Rose, G. and Harvey, W. S. Water-bucket pumps and the Wanlockhead Engine. In *IA*, x(2) 1973.

LOCATION
[M] Museum of Scottish Lead Mining, Goldscaur Row, Wanlock-head, Dumfriesshire.

MARK WATSON

warehouse   Essentially, a place for the storage of raw materials or finished merchandise, but the term has more subtle connotations in particular circumstances.

Warehouses are traditionally found in PORTS. Some of the best examples from the pre-industrial period are in AMSTERDAM, BERGEN, DORDRECHT and TRONDHEIM. From the construction of the West India Docks in LONDON in 1800 warehouses in ports were primarily designed for security, sometimes forming the outer walls of dock complexes, and were increasingly equipped with steam and later with hydraulic mechanisms for cargo handling. Many techniques of iron-framed construction were pioneered in warehouses in the early nineteenth century, and they were later at the forefront of experiments in steel and concrete construction.

A warehouse is also a place where goods for a SHOP are stored before being sold or displayed. Such a warehouse might be a room, or a separate building.

In mid-nineteenth century England a retail establishment, particularly one selling goods that were just beginning to be produced for a national market, might be styled a 'boot and shoe warehouse'. A wholesale establishment selling salt to farmers, processors of food or other manufacturers might be termed a 'salt warehouse'. An 'Italian warehouse' was a shop where commodities like dried fruit and olive oil were sold.

A warehouse is also a component of various types of manufacturing complex. It may be a store for raw materials or parts; or the dispatching point for finished products, in which case the word 'warehouse' may be as much an accounting concept as a physical location.

The term has various meanings in the textile industry. In Britain a commercial concern has always been known as a 'house' (an abbreviation for 'warehouse'), and in lace, hosiery and cotton manufacture from the mid-nineteenth century the huge warehouses of Nottingham, Manchester and Leicester were places where goods were prepared by commercial concerns for dispatch rather than where they were simply stored. Cotton fabrics might be pressed, and lace would be wound and have odd ends removed.

See also BOND; ELEVATOR; GRANARY; TOBACCO WARE-HOUSE; VICTUALLING YARD; and figures 135, 152.

BIBLIOGRAPHY
General
Hudson, 1978; Stratton and Trinder, 1989b.
Specific
Lloyd-Jones, R. and Lewis, M. J. The economic structure of Cottonopolis in 1815. In *TH*, XVII, 1986.

BARRIE TRINDER

Warkworth, Auckland, New Zealand   A settlement on the east coast, 50 km (30 mi.) N. of Auckland. It is the site of the ruins of a massive works, the first in the southern hemisphere to manufacture Portland Cement, built by Nathaniel Wilson in 1884 and subsequently extended. The remains include the unreinforced concrete building of 1903 with 230 mm (9 in.) walls, 12 m (40 ft.) high and 18 m (60 ft.) long.

BIBLIOGRAPHY
General
Thornton, 1982.
Specific
Keys, H. J. *Mahurangi: The story of Warkworth, New Zealand.* Warkworth, 1953.

Warsaw (Warszawa), Poland   The Polish capital, on the River Vistula (Wisła), Warsaw suffered more severely than any other major city in Europe during World War II. The Old City has been heroically restored after virtual obliteration during the Warsaw Uprising of 1944, but few old buildings survive elsewhere in the city.

The Museum of Technology, which is administered by the Chief Technical Organization (Naczelnej Organizacji Techniezej), is located in the Palace of Culture and Science. It was established to continue the work of the

Museum of Industry and Technology which had operated between 1929 and 1939, and co-ordinates all initiatives in the field of industrial conservation. It has various local branches: the Museum of Ancient Metallurgy of the Świętokrzyskie Mountains Region in Nowa Słupia, the Museum of the STAROPOLSKI INDUSTRIAL REGION in SIELPIA WIELKA, the ironworks in CHLEWISKA, the water-powered forge at Oliwa, the water-powered ironworks in Stara Kuźnica, and the former Norblin plant in Warsaw itself, which is being reorganized to house a museum of the city's industry.

The main sections of the museum feature communications, mining and metallurgy, forestry and industries using wood, building materials, printing, musical instruments, chemicals, radio broadcasting, electronics, digital machines, astronomy, and astronautics. Permanent exhibitions illustrate a selection of contemporary scientific and technological topics, with special features of Polish achievements in the particular fields covered. There are displays of Polish motorcycles and cars, typewriters and other office equipment, radio receivers, geodetic instruments, cameras, telephones and telegraphic equipment, sewing machines, electronic digital machines, sound-recording and sound-reproduction equipment. There are excellent models displaying such complexities as the workings of large twentieth-century chemical plants. The museum organizes exhibitions for display in Poland and abroad, carries out research projects, and has a specialized library.

The Museum of Railway Engineering is located at the closed Warszawa Główna Osobowa railway station, and was established to carry on the traditions of a museum that was destroyed during World War II. In the hall of the station there are displays of the banners of the Polish railway workers' trades unions, uniforms, engines and equipment for locomotives, models of locomotives and carriages, and documents illustrating the history of the line from Warsaw to Vienna. Along the platforms are exhibited steam, diesel and electric locomotives, both standard-gauge and narrow-gauge, of Polish and foreign construction, together with a selection of carriages. Many steam locomotives are still operating in Poland and as they are withdrawn from traffic, selected examples are preserved. The museum takes responsibility for a train consisting of an armoured locomotive and carriages constructed by the Germans during World War II; this is preserved at Skarżysko. The museum has another branch under construction at Gryfice, near Szczecin, where exhibits relating to the history of narrow-gauge railways in Pomerania are displayed. Several steam locomotives from the years 1914–30 have been collected, together with supplies of spares.

The Museum of the Gas Industry is located in a former gasworks in the Wola municipal quarter, which was built in 1886 and closed in 1977. At the time of closure equipment dating from between 1860 and 1900 was still in use, including brick gasholders, a highly decorative control room, a water tower, and a warehouse. There are also rotational exhaust fans, ammonia scrubbers from 1893–1900, and a metering system of 1900. Many small items connected with the industry are displayed, including refrigerators, lamps, and cookers; and documents illustrate the history of gas engineering, and that of the Wola plant and its workers. The display concludes with a contemporary automatic distribution room, with up-to-date control and measuring apparatus.

BIBLIOGRAPHY
General
Jasiuk, 1976; Łepkowski, 1968; Muzeum Przemysłu, 1933.
Specific
Muzeum Kolejnictwa w Warszawie (The Museum of Railway Engineering in Warsaw), 1979.
Wann, E. Gazownia Wolska (The Wola Gasworks). In *Spotkania z Zabytkami* (Encounters with Historical Monuments), IV, 1983.
Wann, E. Muzeum Gazownictwa w Warszawie (The Museum of the Gasworks in Warsaw). In *Kwartalnik Historii Kultury Materialnej* (Quarterly of the History of Material Culture), II, 1983.

LOCATIONS
[M] Muzeum Gazownictwa w Warszawie (The Museum of Gasworks in Warsaw), ul. Kasprzaka 25, Warsaw.
[M] Muzeum Kolejnictwa w Warszawie (The Museum of Railway Engineering in Warsaw), ul. Towarowa 1, Warsaw.
[M] Muzeum Techniki w Warszawie (The Museum of Technology in Warsaw), Pałac Kultury i Nauki (Palace of Culture and Science), Warsaw.

PIOTR GERBER

Warwick, Warwickshire, England The county town, overshadowed from the early nineteenth century by the adjacent spa town of Leamington. The gas works of 1822, has a symmetrical façade with an entrance flanked by two octagonal brick towers which originally contained gasholders. A long flight of locks on the Warwick & Birmingham Canal can be seen at Hatton, 4 km ($2\frac{1}{2}$ mi.) W.

BIBLIOGRAPHY
General
Brook, 1977.

Washington, United States of America With some ninety dams throughout this north-western state, built for irrigation, power, water supply and flood control, Washington has become the nation's largest user of electrical power derived from dams for the purpose of producing aluminium. Beyond its falling-water fame, the state is a softwood-lumbering, freshwater-fishing and aircraft-building centre. The usual Western litany of gold, silver, copper, lead and zinc mining has played in Washington, as in adjacent states.

Seattle, fronting the vast natural harbour of Puget Sound, contains some novel experiments in industrial preservation and reuse. Gas Works Park, as an *in situ* collection of natural gas-refining, compression and distribution apparatus, stands on an island in the Sound opposite Seattle. The site became an eye-opening conversion in the 1970s, from polluted eyesore to colourful theme park complete with musical concerts and playgrounds amid the pipes and tanks. The site fell on hard times in later years with the discovery of persistent toxic wastes leeching up into the surrounding soil.

Seattle's Georgetown Power Plant, a power station of 1906, may be the only steam plant ever to have had a classical music score composed for it and played within it. Written by local conductor David Mahler in 1986, 'Powerhouse' received its premier within the plant, the strings, percussion and brass seated around and between the pair of Curtis vertical steam turbines, yielding a critically acclaimed 'cathedral-like' performance. The unspectacular brick plant itself is a well-preserved example of the work of time-and-motion guru Frank B. Gilbreth (1868–1924) during his building construction period.

Tacoma's Western Forest Industries Museum provides the last word in logging history collections in the American North-West. Holdings include a loggers' camp with bunkhouse, a long-hauling steam railway, and a broad assortment of axes and saws, both hand and chain. Another tribute to the state's pervasive lumbering crosses the Quinault River near Taholah. The Chow Chow bridge, built in 1952 to carry logging trucks, is a homegrown assemblage of heavy timber trusses tied to suspension cables strung over timber towers. The 60 m (190 ft.) span, now off-limits to loggers and absorbed into an Indian reservation, was a product of the Aloha Lumber Company.

True to the pattern elsewhere in the remote pockets of natural wealth in the Pacific North-West, Washington has had its share of COMPANY TOWNS, notably Dupont and Concrete. The town of Dupont near Tacoma remains a distinctive collection of worker housing and COMPANY STORES, together with a museum. It is separated from other development by a ring of open land, signifying the nature of the work that was under way within: the manufacture of explosives. Concrete, in the north-central part of the state, lays claim to being the centre of the American PORTLAND CEMENT industry, and one of its major suppliers for much of the twentieth century.

LOCATIONS

[M] Cle Elum Mining and Telephone Museum, 221 E. First Street, Cle Elum, WA 98922.

[M] Dupont Historical Museum, 125 Barksdale Avenue, Dupont, WA 98327.

[M] Klondike Gold Rush Museum, 117 South Main Street, Seattle, WA 98104.

[M] Museum of History and Industry, 2700 24th Avenue E., Seattle, WA 98112.

[M] Puget Sound Railroad Museum, 109 King Street, Snoqualmie, WA 98065.

[M] Western Forest Industries Museum, 5400 N. Pearl, Tacoma, WA 94801.

DAVID H. SHAYT

Washington DC (District of Columbia), United States of America Monumentality characterizes the significant industrial and engineering works of the nation's capital. Founded in 1787, as the republic's first planned city on the grand scale, the City of Washington, which today makes up the District of Columbia, attracted some of the nation's and Europe's premier architectural and engineering talent. Since the late nineteenth century little heavy private industry has existed in the capital, a function of the federal government's wish to separate itself from the grime and associated problems of industrial activity.

Although pockets of light industry prospered well into the twentieth century in various corners of Washington, little remains today. The principal exception to this trend was the US Naval Gun Factory in south-west Washington, which produced the largest classes of naval ordnance and instrumentation from the early nineteenth century until the 1960s. The Chesapeake & Ohio Canal, commenced in 1828, is the nation's narrowest national park, and was once the city's principal commercial artery from the West, bringing coal and other bulk products to Washington and points south until 1924.

The ribbed-section dome of the US Capitol building may be the largest accumulation of structural cast iron in the world. Probably cast in foundries in nearby Baltimore, the dome was added to the building in 1868; the earliest parts of the building date from 1793.

When the 169 m (555 ft.) Washington Monument was completed in 1885, the obelisk offered visitors a steam-driven elevator ride to what remains an unmatched view of the city. The squared spiral stairway wrapping round the elevator shaft is closed to the public today, but is one of the great stairclimbs, the caged elevator rising and falling on the inboard side, and outboard elaborately carved memorial stones from around the world, some with industrial subject matter, set into the monument wall. The obelisk's adjacent steam plant is today a police station.

Washington's water-supply aqueduct of 1853–63 is a 19 km (12 mi.) underground, gravity-fed waterway that continues to convey water to the city from intakes along the Potomac River. The aqueduct, among other works in the city, is a monument to the distinguished career of Montgomery C. Meigs (1816–92), one of Washington's pre-eminent civil engineers. Along with the Pension Building (today the National Building Museum), the Arts and Industries Building of the Smithsonian Institution, and the construction of the Capitol dome, Meigs's work included the aqueduct and its notable Cabin John Bridge. The bridge carries the city's water supply over a ravine in a 67 m (220 ft.) single-span stone arch, until 1903 the world's longest, and still the nation's. Further down the system the water crosses another valley in a cast-iron-pipe arch bridge over Rock Creek Park, the pipes serving both as conduit and structural support. The pipes, originally unclad, may still be spied through gaps in the twentieth-century concrete facing.

The nation's foremost museum of the history of industry, engineering and technology is the Smithsonian's National Museum of American History, opened in 1964. Formerly the National Museum of the History of Technology, the building is the home of the proverbial 'nation's attic', loaded with major collections in most fields of human activity. The collections of power and production machinery, bridge and tunnel models, hand tools, and engineering archival materials are continually being re-displayed and expanded. The collection of civil-engineering artwork is unrivalled. An attempt is made at the National Building Museum, a brick Victorian extravaganza elsewhere in Washington, to address the history of American architectural achievement.

Two masonry bridges crossing the Potomac along Washington's western border stand as monumental gateways to the city. Both are of reinforced concrete, but of contrasting symbolic roles. The Francis Scott Key Bridge of 1923 is a businesslike four-arch deck span connecting the Georgetown section of the city with communities in Virginia. The Arlington Memorial Bridge of 1932 is a neo-Classical ten-arch span, clad in granite, that presents a low, distinguished entry to the monumental core of the city. Its central cast-iron double-leaf bascule span no longer opens, given the disappearance of commercial river traffic above this section of the Potomac.

See also figures 31, 148.

LOCATIONS
[M] National Air and Space Museum, Smithsonian Institution, Sixth Street & Independence Avenue, Washington, DC 20560.
[M] National Building Museum, Pension Building, Judiciary Square, Washington, DC 20001.
[M] National Museum of American History, Smithsonian Institution, 14th Street & Constitution Avenue, Washington, DC 20560.
[M.S] Pierce Mill, 5000 Glover Road NW, Washington, DC 20015.

DAVID H. SHAYT

Wasseralfingen, Baden-Württemberg, Germany The Schwäbischen Hüttenwerke (Swabian Ironworks) in Wasseralfingen (3 km (2 mi.) N. of Aalen), with the associated plants at Königsbronn (16 km (10 mi.) S.), Ludwigstal and Wilhelmshütte, are among the oldest industrial concerns in the Federal Republic. Iron was being produced at Königsbronn as early as 1365; the first blast furnace was brought into use in 1651; and the modern ironworks began in 1832. The regular use of the blast furnaces ceased in 1888 because smelting on the site was no longer competitive, and the furnaces at the main works at Wasseralfingen were also subsequently blown out. The works then concentrated on working with pig iron brought in from outside, and particularly on hard chill casting, and on the production of rollers for papermaking. A pair of reverberatory air furnaces of 1854, with cast-iron walls and chimney stays, and a wooden crane have been preserved in the restored original building at Königsbronn. There is also an exhibit showing the first electricity-generating plant in Württemberg, including a Voith turbine.

LOCATION
[M] Ironworks Museum, Stadtteil Wasseralfingen, Wilhelmstrasse 67, 7080 Aalen.

ROLF HÖHMANN

watch A miniature CLOCK, to be carried on the person.

With the increasing importance given to timekeeping in early modern Europe, successive efforts were made to increase the accuracy and reliability of watches while reducing their size (especially for the fashion-conscious) or their cost (for the rest). The size and motion imparted to the watch case in use made accurate regulation more difficult to achieve than in a clock. Reducing friction – and thus the force required – and irregularities in the gear train helped; insulating the balance wheel from interference, and immobilizing the escapement except when released by a cam or pinion on the arbor of the balance wheel, proved most important. Refinements in mechanical watch design continued to be made, with diminishing returns after 1800. Wristwatches were popularized in Britain by military use in the Boer War of 1899–1902.

The delicate watchmaking tools of the eighteenth century prefigured many of the ideas later employed in the design of MACHINE TOOLS capable of precision manufacture to an abstract standard, but watchmaking long remained an art of fitting, even where the search for volume and cheapness led to dispersed divisions of labour. Quality-steel files were crucial tools. Factory production of mechanical watches with INTERCHANGEABLE PARTS was introduced at Waltham, Mass., USA, in the 1850s and reached its peak a century later, just before such watches were supplanted by quartz-regulated digital microelectronic circuitry.

BIBLIOGRAPHY
General
Ashton, 1939; Baillie, 1951; Crom, 1980; Jacquet and Japis, 1970; Landes, 1983; Weiss, 1982.

TIM PUTNAM

water crane *See* CRANE.

water engine The term usually applied to an early form of HYDRAULIC POWER, in which an engine, usually with a vertical cylinder (often situated at the base of a shaft but sometimes on the surface), used a head of water of about 50 m (165 ft.) to power pumps that drained lower levels. Such engines could be employed only where there were both a suitable head of water and drainage for the water used for power and for that pumped from the lower levels. The first in Britain was installed in a Durham lead mine in 1765. Development continued into the nineteenth century, much of the technology being derived from STEAM ENGINES. Notable examples are preserved at Matlock (*see* CROMFORD), WANLOCKHEAD, and Allenheads (*see* DURHAM) in Britain; and at Bad Reichenhall, and in the Deutsches Museum, MUNICH, both in Germany.

BIBLIOGRAPHY
General
Bjorling, 1894; McNeil, 1972; Strandh, 1979.

water frame A machine for spinning cotton, patented

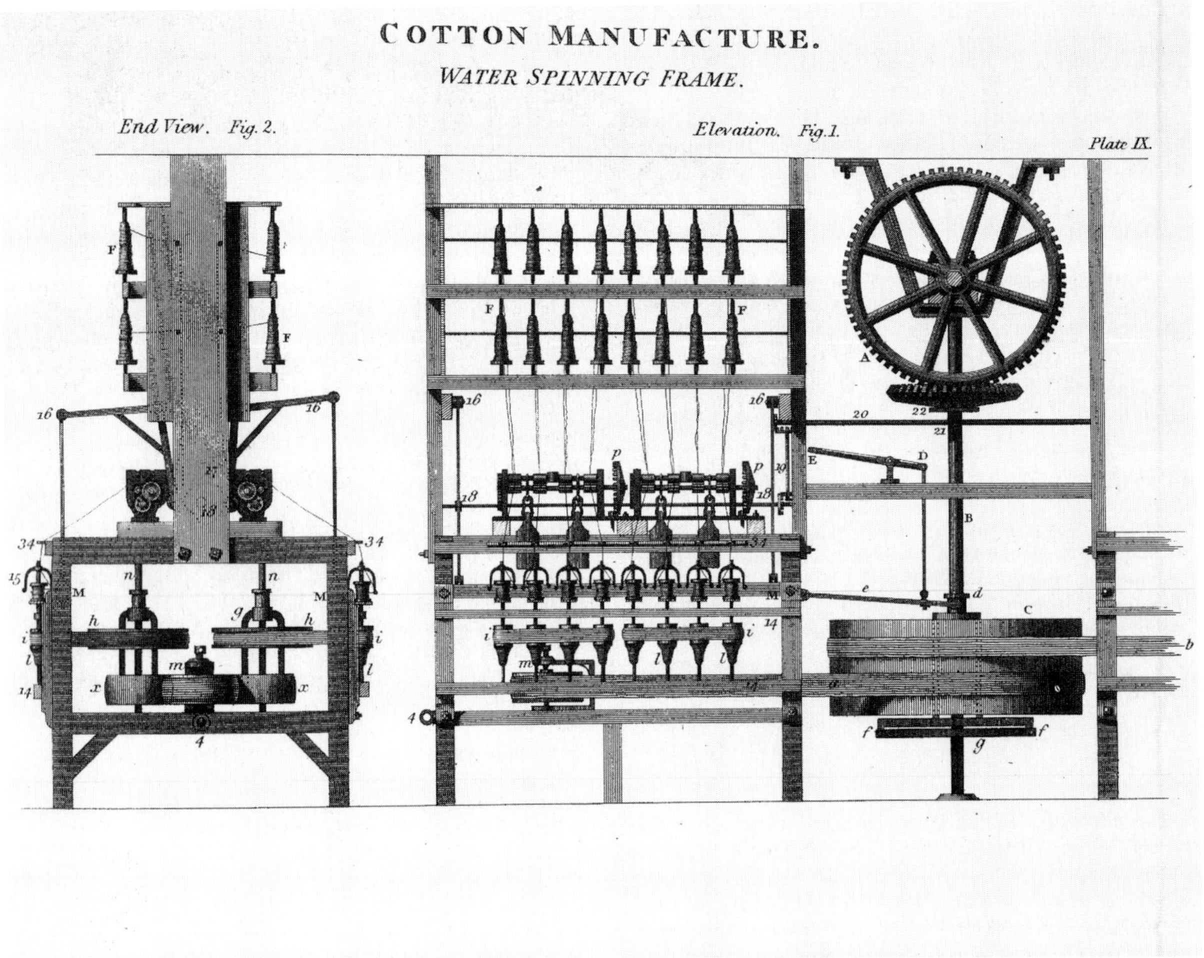

COTTON MANUFACTURE.
WATER SPINNING FRAME.

End View. Fig. 2.   *Elevation. Fig. 1.*   *Plate IX*

Figure 172   A water frame of *c.* 1800 (from Abraham Rees, *The Cyclopaedia; or Universal Dictionary of Arts, Sciences and Literature,* published between 1802 and 1820)
Ironbridge Gorge Museum Trust

by RICHARD ARKWRIGHT in England in 1769. Operating on the continuous spinning principle, in one continuous motion it drew the yarn out between sets of rollers turning at different speeds, and wound it by means of a flyer onto a rotating spindle. To achieve this it relied on water power, hence its name. Important early examples are preserved at HELMSHORE, the Science Museum (*see* LONDON), and, as built by SAMUEL SLATER *c.*1790, at NMAH (*see* WASHINGTON DC).

BIBLIOGRAPHY
General
Fitton, 1989; Hills, 1973; Jeremy, 1981.

water gas A mixture of HYDROGEN, carbon monoxide and CARBON DIOXIDE, formed by passing steam through incandescent coke. Water gas is made in GASWORKS and is added to TOWN GAS, and used also in the HABER-BOSCH PROCESS for making AMMONIA.

Waterloo, Ontario, Canada   Waterloo and Kitchener (formerly Berlin) are twin cities, 100 km (60 mi.) SW of Toronto. Berlin originated as a Mennonite settlement, and grew by 1900 to be an industrial city producing pianos, clocks and clothing. At Waterloo the Seagram Museum, housed in a former distillery warehouse of 1868, displays the technology of wine and spirit manufacture. Exhibits include a 10.7 m (35 ft.) high still. A 250 hp Ruston diesel engine of 1924 remains at the William Street water-pumping station in Waterloo; and a Corliss-type steam engine of 1910, which drives machines producing embossed rubber soles for shoes, stands in the Kaufman Footwear factory in Kitchener.

830

Figure 173 An example of the improved effiency of water power systems: the Sagebien breastshot wheel at the Trilbardou pumping station on the River Marne: installed in 1866, it was restored to working order in the late 1980s.
P. Fortin, Inventaire général

BIBLIOGRAPHY
Specific
McLaughlin, K. *Made in Berlin*. Kitchener, Ontario: Joseph Schneider Haus, 1989.

LOCATION
[M] Seagram Museum, 57 Erb Street West, Po Box 1605, Waterloo, Ontario N2J 4N6.

water mill The first water mills were powered by horizontal wheels (*see* NORSE MILL; ROMANIA; SPLASH MILL), known since antiquity in the Near East and Europe. By the first century BC the 'Vitruvian' vertical wheel was in use, with three basic types eventually emerging, named 'overshot', 'breastshot' and 'undershot', depending on the point at which the water flowed against the wheel. Variations such as the 'back-shot' (*see* LAXEY) can also be seen. The wheels – at first of wood, then from the eighteenth century of cast-iron, with many hybrid forms – were set with buckets or vanes depending on the water flow. In early times the energy was transferred to the machinery within the mill via a 'lantern' gear (a circular cage meshing with a vertical wheel), and later with toothed wheels and other gears. The most common form in England was a pit wheel on the same axle as the water wheel, driving a crown wheel set on a vertical shaft that extended through the building. Although water was the major source of power for all kinds of manufactures, water wheels developed very little until the scientific studies of Antoine Parent (1666–1716) in 1704 and JOHN SMEATON in 1759 showed that the overshot wheel was of vastly

superior efficiency to the undershot, with the breastshot as a compromise. Jean-Victor Poncelet (1788–1867) subsequently improved the undershot wheel in 1824, and WILLIAM FAIRBAIRN improved the design of buckets. Alphonse Sagebien (1807–92) (*see* TRILBARDOU) developed a wheel which could operate when it was almost submerged. The Poncelet wheel inspired the development of the turbine.

See also FLOATING MILL; HEAD RACE; LADE; LEAT; POWER CANAL; TAIL RACE; TIDE MILL; TURBINE.

BIBLIOGRAPHY
General
Finch, 1933; Hunter, 1979; Reynolds, 1983; Wölfel, 1987.

CHRISTOPHER GREEN

water power WATER MILLS of many types have been known for many centuries, but only the scientific work of Blaise Pascal (1623–62) and others enabled water to be utilized for transmitting power. Engineers such as JOSEPH BRAMAH and WILLIAM ARMSTRONG developed HYDRAULIC systems powering presses, rams, cranes and so on from the 1780s. In the second half of the nineteenth century changing demands for power prompted the development of water TURBINES, in due course used in HYDRO-ELECTRIC POWER STATIONS.

Water power was extensively used in the Industrial Revolution, in ironmaking; in textiles; and, in many countries, as a means of draining mines. It remained a major source of industrial power even in coal-rich Britain until after the middle of the nineteenth century.

See also figures 43, 87, 128, 164.

BIBLIOGRAPHY
General
Hunter, 1979; Reynolds, 1983.

water supply The need to supply drinking water to cities stimulated some of the greatest engineering achievements of classical antiquity, like the system which includes the Pont du Gard: some of these, like Justinian's cistern in ISTANBUL, have remained in use until modern times. Artificial watercourses constructed to convey drinking water over considerable distances, like the New River in LONDON, the Aqua Felice and Aqua Paola in ROME and the watercourse in Lisbon, have also remained in use for several centuries. From the sixteenth century large water wheels came to be used to raise drinking water into cisterns, at TOLEDO in 1526, AUGSBURG in 1548 and PARIS in 1603-8. A water wheel patented by John Hadley (1682–1744) in 1693, which could be raised and lowered to suit various water levels, was employed on London Bridge (*see* LONDON) in 1696, at Leeds in 1694 and at Exeter in 1695.

All systems of this kind involved the direct supply of water to the houses of the rich, via clay, wooden or lead pipes; the supply was often intermittent. The populace at large was supplied from conduits, like that constructed at the principal crossroads in Oxford in 1617 (which now stands in parkland at Nuneham Courtney, 8 km (5 mi.) S.), or by water carriers, who were often, by tradition, women. Bottled spa water was already traded on a considerable scale by the eighteenth century. The significance of water supplies was shown in some countries by ornate well-head installations, like those in POLAND, RHODES and VENICE, or ornate public fountains like those in ANTWERP, BERN and NUREMBERG. A steam engine was first employed to pump water for drinking at York Buildings, Chelsea, London, in 1720.

In the nineteenth century the threat of water-borne disease in industrial cities led to the construction of WATERWORKS in which water was purified in the process of transmission from source to consumer, while development of water-borne SEWAGE DISPOSAL systems greatly increased the demand for water. From 1850 large cities increasingly sought water from distant mountainous regions: Liverpool from Lake Vyrnwy, 84 km (52 mi.) SW, from 1880; and Birmingham from the Elan Valley, 110 km (68 mi.) W., from 1892. The first large-scale RESERVOIR for drinking water in Germany was built for the city of Remscheid in 1891 after much debate in the 1880s on the quality of reservoir water. Otto Intze (1843–1904), the father of German dam construction, showed the necessity of choosing the optimum level from which to extract water from a reservoir, and the need to clear vegetation from reservoir sites. It was acknowledged in most countries that securing a supply of clean water was a necessary function of government. Some civil engineers, like George Leather (1787–1870) in Leeds, James Leslie (1801–89) in Edinburgh and DUNDEE, and J. F. La Trobe Bateman (1810–89) in Manchester and Glasgow, came to specialize in water supply.

The first significant municipal water-supply undertaking in North America was established by Benjamin H. Latrobe (1764–1820) at Philadelphia in 1801. By 1850 most cities in the USA had supply systems. The bathroom became a necessity in most American middle-class homes by 1900, greatly increasing demand for water.

See also CISTERN; FOUNTAIN; PUBLIC UTILITY; PUMPING STATION; WATER TOWER.

BIBLIOGRAPHY
General
Babbitt and Doland, 1939; Blake, 1956; Binnie, 1981; Braudel, 1981; Burton and Dumbleton, 1928; Dixey, 1950; Föhl and Hamm, 1985; Hartley, 1978; Richards and Payne, 1899; Robins, 1946; Steel, 1953; Turneaure and Russell, 1924; Veal, 1931; Water Authorities Association, 1987.

BARRIE TRINDER

water tower The water tower is a container, raised to a relatively high altitude, made of wood, cast iron, steel or reinforced concrete, that acts as a buffer between a water supply and the place where it is used. Preferably placed at the highest point of a supply network, it also maintains the requisite pressure of the water supply. Its construction may be divided into three parts: the substructure of the tower, the shaft, and the actual container or tank.

The first wooden overhead water tanks, made in Nuremberg and Leipzig, Germany, in the sixteenth century, had capacities of only about 10 m³ (2200 gall.). In 1800 a wooden overhead tank holding 80 m³ (17 600 gall.) was built in Philadelphia, Pa., USA. Significant progress in the construction of water towers came only with the development of railways. Cast-iron overhead tanks, at first cylindrical and later rectangular in form, were made in England from 1830. In 1853–5 W. H. Lindley built a water tower in Hamburg which had a cast-iron container with a capacity of 2350 m³ (106 800 gall.). After c.1855 the form of the container base changed: in Aachen in 1883, for example, Otto Intze (1843–1904) found a structurally sound shape by combining the forms of a spherical tank and a conical base. By c.1910 several hundred Intze towers had been built to supply railway depots and towns.

Joseph Monier (1823–1906) began building the first reinforced CONCRETE overhead tanks c.1873, followed by Hennebique from c.1895. One of the first water towers made entirely of concrete was built at Newton-le-Willows, 20 km (12½ mi.) E. of Liverpool, in 1904. Both its substructure and the tank were of reinforced concrete. After 1920 the shafts of water towers in the USA were of monocoque construction; from 1950 the tanks, generally in the shape of blunted cones, were cast in concrete on the ground and lifted into place by hydraulic jacks as the supporting shafts were built up. This led to tanks of up to 9000 m³ (40 900 gall.). Steel tanks in the USA, which have no outer casings, are often spheroidal or elliptical in form.

The development of pressure-pump systems for water supplies has rendered water towers redundant in many networks.

BIBLIOGRAPHY
General
Becher, 1988; Föhl and Hamm, 1985; Merkl *et al.*, 1985.

AXEL FÖHL

waterworks An intermediate installation between a source of water and the consumers. The term was first applied to installations on supply systems in sixteenth-century London, but came into more general usage in the nineteenth century as purification came to be one of the functions of such works. Filtration of water for public supply began in the first half of the nineteenth century, one of the first applications being at PAISLEY in 1804, and became compulsory in LONDON from 1855. A waterworks usually pumps water to a distribution reservoir whence it flows to consumers by gravity. Water is drawn from wells, springs, boreholes or rivers, or from impounding reservoirs which may be at some distance. Suspended material is settled out in impounding reservoirs. The water is treated by slow sand filtration, or by coagulation followed by rapid sand filtration, or by microstraining. Rapid mechanical filtration was developed at Louisville, Ky., by Charles Hermany and G. W. Fuller from 1895–7. The water is then disinfected by chlorine. Water may also be softened, by treatment with lime, sodium carbonate (*see* ALKALI) or zeolites, sodium-iron or sodium-aluminium silicates. Pure water for distribution is held in service reservoirs before being conveyed through pipe systems to consumers. Since the mid-nineteenth century water-works have included facilities for sampling and analysis to ensure the quality of supplies.

Many nineteenth-century waterworks were designed with style and set in ornate landscapes, and considerable numbers have been preserved. British examples are listed by the Water Authorities Association (1987).

BIBLIOGRAPHY
General
Adams, 1938; Babbitt and Doland, 1939; Binnie, 1981; Burton and Dumbleton, 1928; Dixey, 1950; Flinn *et al.*, 1927; Föhl and Hamm, 1985; Richards and Payne, 1899; Robins, 1946; Steel, 1953; Taylor, 1927; Tudsbery and Brightmore, 1905; Turneaure and Russell, 1924; Uren, 1914; Veal, 1931; Water Authorities Association, 1987.

JEFF COX

Watkins, George Middleton (1904–89) The authority on the last generation of British steam engines. A boilerman in Bristol gasworks, from the 1930s he undertook tours by motorcycle, photographing and documenting steam engines of all kinds. From 1966 he was research assistant at the University of Bath, where he was awarded a master's degree in 1969. His archive is now in the custody of the RCHME (*see* ENGLAND).

Figure 174 A view of the steam winding engine at the Prestage and Broseley Tileries, Broseley, Shropshire, taken by George Watkins in 1936; this was a single cylinder rotative beam engine, of 20–25 hp, winding clay from approximately 110 m (330 ft.); it worked until *c*.1940. George Watkins described it thus: 'Very early engine of simplest construction. The pit was known to be at work in 1800, and the owners were satisfied that it was the original engine; there was no record of a change. The only known repair was a piston rod replacement in 1930. The slide valve was operated by bumpers on the plug rod, a very early feature, and the engine was reversed to lower the clay wagons into the Deep pit which had reached 100 yards by 1936. The gears were 14 in pinion to a gear 5 ft. 6 in. on the drum shaft; the drum was 6 ft. 6 in. diameter. The winding trip took about three minutes, but the incline was steep. It was worked by one man, who fired the small amount of coal used by the egg-ended boiler which was 4 ft. 6 in. in diameter × 24 ft. long. The engine frame was of timber.'

Royal Commission on the Historical Monuments of England: Watkins Collection

BIBLIOGRAPHY
General
Buchanan and Watkins, 1976; Watkins, 1968; Watkins and Buchanan, 1975.
Specific
Watkins, G. Some practical aspects of the preservation of steam engines. In Cossons, 1975.

Watt, James (1736–1819) An engineer and maker of mathematical instruments at the University of Glasgow. In 1763 or 1764, as he repaired a model of a NEWCOMEN engine, he perceived the fuel economy that would come from having a condensation vessel separate from the piston cylinder. A patent covering the separate condenser was taken out in 1769. In 1774 he moved to Birmingham and in 1775 became the partner of Matthew Boulton (*see* BOULTON & WATT). The partnership supplied its first steam engines to customers in 1776. Subsequently Watt developed an engine which could provide rotative as distinct from reciprocating motion, using 'sun-and-planet' gearing on the flywheel in 1781; a double-acting engine, in which steam propelled the piston in both directions, in 1782; and connecting rods between piston and beam – the parallel motion – which was perfected in 1784. Watt rated the capacity of his engines in HORSE POWER. The firm of Boulton & Watt provided designs of steam engines for their customers, together with the valves, but most parts had to be obtained from other suppliers. Payment was by an annual premium based on the notional saving as against the use of a Newcomen engine, the engine's output being measured by a sealed counting device designed by Watt. Watt's patents were extended in 1775 to expire in 1800, and were fiercely protected against 'pirate' engine builders. Newcomen engines continued to be built in large numbers in the closing decades of the eighteenth century, together with other varieties of steam engine, and in the last quarter of the century between 450 and 500 engines of Watt's design were installed in Britain, only about 30 per cent of the market for steam engines. Nevertheless Watt's contributions to the technology of the steam engine were to form the basis of its subsequent development.

Watt's genius extended into many fields. He surveyed several canals and developed an effective COPIER. His formal involvement in the engine partnership ended in 1800.

The model Newcomen engine that Watt repaired is in the Hunterian Museum, Glasgow. Watt reciprocating and rotative engines are displayed in the Science Museum, LONDON, together with the contents of his workshop, which include an experimental model of a separate condenser. The Smethwick engine supplied to the Birmingham Canal Navigation in 1779 is displayed in BIRMINGHAM.

BIBLIOGRAPHY
General
Dickinson, 1936, 1938; Dickinson and Jenkins, 1927; Farey, 1827; Hart, 1958; Law, 1965; Muirhead, 1854; Musson and Robinson, 1969; Robinson and Musson, 1969; Tann, 1981.
Specific
Dickinson, H. W. *The Garret Workshop of James Watt*. London: HMSO, 1929, reprint 1969.
Kanefsky J. and Robey, J. Steam engines in eighteenth-century Britain: a quantitative assessment. In *Technology and Culture*, 1980.
Law, R. J. *James Watt and the Separate Condenser: an account of the invention*. London: HMSO for Science Museum, 1969.
Tann J. and Breckin, M. The international diffusion of the Watt engine, 1775–1825. In *EcHR*, XXXI, 1978.

CHRISTOPHER GREEN

wax An easily-moulded substance produced by BEES, although the term is also applied to hydrocarbons with similar properties produced at an OIL REFINERY. Beeswax is traditionally used in making CANDLES, especially those for ecclesiastical use, and as a polish.

Weald, Kent and Sussex, England From the sixteenth century until the eighteenth the Weald was the most important ironmaking region in Britain. It is bounded by the North and South Downs, and by the chalk hills between Alton and Petersfield in the West. Ironstone occurs in the clays, silts and sandstones that comprise the Quaternary deposits of the Wealden Beds. Wealden iron was important in Roman times, and again from the introduction of the blast furnace to Ashdown Forest by Frenchmen from the Pays de Bray in the late fifteenth century. In 1653 there were thirty-six blast furnaces and forty-five forges, many fewer than in the 1570s, which drew on 80 000 ha (200 000 ac.) of coppices for their wood. During the Dutch Wars of the 1660s a specialism in ordnance developed, and over the next fifty years the number of furnaces remained the same, while many forges closed. Competition from the Carron ironworks led to a final downturn after 1763. The last furnace was blown out in 1813, and the last forge closed in 1820. The industry was the subject of a pioneering archaeological study by Straker (1931), and since 1968 has been investigated by the Wealden Iron Research Group, a combination of academic and volunteer interests, responsible for excavations. Water wheels, gun-casting pits and the base of a boring mill have been uncovered, and a boring bar from Stream Furnace, 9 km (6 mi.) W. of Battle, has also been found. There are cannon from Wealden furnaces at the Tower of London, and other artefacts in the museums at Hastings and Lewes. There are over thirty iron tombs in the parish church at Wadhurst, 8 km (5 mi.) SE of Tunbridge Wells.

BIBLIOGRAPHY
General
Cleere and Crossley, 1985; Crossley, 1975; Straker, 1931.
Specific
Crossley, D. W. Cannon manufacture at Pippingford, Sussex: excavation of two iron furnaces of c.1717. In *Post-Medieval Archaeology*, 9, 1975.
Crossley, D. W. A gun-casting furnace at Scarlets, Cowden, Kent. In *PMA*, 13, 1979.

LOCATIONS
[M] Museum of Local History, Anne of Cleves House, Southover High Street, Lewes, East Sussex BN7 1JA.
[M] Museum of Local History, Old Town Hall, High Street, Hastings, East Sussex TN34 1ET.
[M] Royal Armouries, HM Tower of London, London EC3N 4AB.

BARRIE TRINDER

Weald and Downland Museum, Sussex, England   A 16 ha (40 ac.) open-air museum of the traditional buildings of the Weald and Downland areas of South-East England, established in 1967 and operated by a charitable trust. Exhibits include the tread wheel from a 100 m (330 ft.) well, sawpits, a seventeenth-century stone water mill, a nineteenth-century wind pump, and a weatherboarded turnpike tollhouse of *c.*1807. There are regular charcoal burnings.

LOCATION
[M] Weald and Downland Museum, Singleton, Chichester, Sussex.

Wedgwood, Josiah (1750–95)   Born at Burslem near STOKE-ON-TRENT to a family of potters, Wedgwood was the most influential entrepreneur in the CERAMICS industry during the Industrial Revolution. From *c.*1752 to 1756 he worked with Thomas Whieldon (1719–95), and subsequently, on becoming a master at the Ivy House Works, Burslem, began to produce wares of a quality and uniformity remarkable for the period. In 1769 he opened a new, rationally-planned pottery at Etruria, which became one of the most visited industrial complexes in Britain. His products included cream and marbled wares, and black basalt wares in the Classical style. He employed John Flaxman (1755–1826) and other leading artists to design wares. He was one of the chief promoters of the Trent & Mersey Canal, on which Etruria was situated. His third son was Thomas Wedgwood (1771–1805), a pioneer of PHOTOGRAPHY. Manuscripts relating to Wedgwood are preserved at Keele, and pictures and artefacts at Barlaston.

BIBLIOGRAPHY
General
Burton, 1976.

LOCATIONS
[I] The Library, University of Keele, Keele, Staffordshire.
[M] Wedgwood Visitor Centre and Museum, Josiah Wedgwood & Sons Ltd, Barlaston, Stoke-on-Trent ST12 9ES.

weighing machine   A device used on TURNPIKE roads to ensure that vehicles were loaded within limits laid down by law. The earliest were gigantic steelyards, on which carriages were lifted up by chains slung beneath them. One such remains at Woodbridge, Suffolk, England. By 1800 most machines were weighbridges, platforms flush with the road, and supported in a pit by levers, in such a way that the weight could be calculated from an adjacent scale, or, in the machine patented by Robert Salmon (1763–1821) in 1796, on a dial. Similar machines were and are used to check the weights of loads leaving industrial premises in road vehicles.

BIBLIOGRAPHY
General
Cossons, 1988; Rees, 1802–20.

Weilburg, Hesse, Germany   When the River Lahn was made navigable in the nineteenth century, a 195.26 m (640 ft.) tunnel had to be built in Weilburg, 48 km (30 mi.) E. of Koblenz, to cut off a bend in the river. It took nine years to construct the tunnel, which was opened in 1847, but the canalization of the river proved unprofitable having been started too late and being designed only for small vessels. The Lahn Valley Railway, construction of which began ten years later, took over the transport functions of the river, and the locks and tunnel are now used only for leisure cruising. The tunnel is an important industrial monument, perhaps the world's only river tunnel. It was renovated in 1977. There is also a museum in Weilburg illustrating iron-ore mining in the Lahn-Dill region.

LOCATION
[M] Municipal and Mining Museum, Schlossplatz 1, 6290 Weilburg.

weir   A barrier across a waterway, intended to divert a flow into an alternative channel, or to maintain a particular level along a given stretch, usually distinguished from a DAM by having a continuous flow of water over the top. At a natural fall on a navigable river, the navigation channel passes through a lock, while the alternative stream normally crosses a weir. The term is also applied to the reservoir formed above a weir structure, particularly that for a WATER MILL.
See also FISHWEIR.

Wenecja, Żnin, Poznań, Poland   A museum of narrow-gauge railways, based on the 60 cm (2 ft.) gauge Żnin–Wenecja–Gąsowa line, at Wenecja near Żnin, 90 km (56 mi.) NE of Poznań, opened 1972. On display are working steam locomotives of 1899 and 1911, together with a set of contemporary passenger carriages and a postal car. The museum is housed in an old station.

BIBLIOGRAPHY
Specific
Muzeum Kolejnictwa w Warszawie, Informator (Museum of Railways in Warsaw, guidebook). Warsaw, 1979.

Werra, Hesse, Germany   Hesse's large deposits of potassium are concentrated in the region of the Werra, between Kassel, Fulda and Eisenach, and in Neuhof near Fulda. The expansion of potassium production was particularly intensive after World War II, when the partition of Germany left the largest of the Werra mines in the DDR. The mines are the Grimberg, Heringen and Herfa-Neurode pits, situated around Heringen, 48 km (30 mi.) NE of Fulda; the Hattorf and Heimboldshausen-Ransbach mines at Hattorf; and the Neuhof and Ellers mines at Neuhof. Each of the three groups retain some of its old buildings. The headstock building at Heringen of 1912, the small hydro-electric power stations at Lengers and Harnrode, of 1903 and 1908 respectively, and the workers' housing of 1926 at Philippsthal are especially worthy of note.

Western Australia, Australia   This largely desert state covers almost one half of Australia, and problems of poor land, water supply and large distances hindered develop-

835

Figure 175 A 4-6-0 locomotive of the West Australian Government Railways, preserved in the museum at Kalamunda, Western Australia; it was built by Dübs of Glasgow in 1897 to a design provided by Beyer Peacock of Manchester. In the background is the station building of 1927, which forms the headquarters of the History Village at Kalamunda.
E. G. Webb

ment. Nevertheless when the first settlers arrived, the area supported a large Aboriginal population whose industrial concerns included tidal fish traps at Oyster Harbour, and the Wilgie Mia ochre mine.

Today mining on a vast scale dominates the West Australian economy. The only significant early mine was the Geraldton copper and lead mine developed from 1849 by Cornish miners. Gold was discovered relatively late, in the 1890s, and such towns as Kalgoorlie display fine Victorian buildings, although many others are deserted. Demand for timber and coal created new industries, and one timber mill workshop at Yarloop still contains nineteenth-century equipment. The State Battery remains at Coolgardie, a corrugated iron-clad building of 1902, and still in use. At Cunderah stands one of the brick pumping stations of the pipeline built in 1902 to convey water from Perth to the goldfields, a distance of 560 km (350 mi.). An unusual flue, built in 1851 as part of a lead smelter, survives at Warribano. The chimney was built over a hole in the ground and lead removed from the base, in railway trucks. Today iron ore is mined in the Hamersley ranges and at Mount Tom Price.

The Ord River scheme intended to irrigate the Kimberley region has created the largest artificial lake in Australia.

The History Village, Kalamunda, is located in a railway station building of 1927, and includes two post office buildings, of 1900 and 1922, a sawpit, and a kerosene stationary engine of 1909.

Western Australia has an extraordinary collection of wrecks, the earliest of which was the *Trial*, an English ship wrecked in 1622.

There are remains of whaling stations at Malus Island, Babbage Island and Albany, where there are ruins of a plant for hydrogenizing whale oil for margarine manufacture.

See also PERTH AND FREMANTLE.

BIBLIOGRAPHY
General
Heritage of Australia, 1981.
Specific
Register of Classified and Recorded Buildings. Perth: National Trust (WA), 1977.

LOCATIONS
[I] Kalamunda and Districts Historical Society Inc., PO Box 121, Kalamunda 6076, Western Australia.
[M] Western Australian Museum, Francis Street, Perth, Western Australia 6000.

KATE CLARK

Westinghouse, George (1846–1914) The pioneer of the air brake, and one of the most innovative of American engineers, Westinghouse was the son of a Westphalian immigrant who made agricultural implements at Schenectady, New York. After service in the Civil War, Westinghouse took out his first patent, for a rotary steam engine, in 1865. He took out the first of over twenty patents relating to air brakes in 1869. In the manufacture of air brakes he insisted upon standardized INTERCHANGEABLE PARTS. He began to build up a railway signalling business in 1880 by buying up relevant patents, and from 1883 turned his attention to control systems for NATURAL GAS distribution, then being developed in Pittsburgh (*see* PENNSYLVANIA). From 1885 he became concerned with electric power generation and distribution in the city, establishing the Westinghouse Electrical Co. in 1886, and specializing in alternating current equipment. From 1889 his company built a model works and industrial community at Wilmerding, east of Pittsburgh. Westinghouse was responsible for the electric lighting at the Colombian World Fair in Chicago in 1893, and in the same year began to develop hydro-electric power at NIAGARA.

Westport, Nelson, New Zealand   A port at the mouth of the Buller River, which prospered through the coal trade (*see* DENNISTON). The Westport Coal Company formed in 1878 to work the mines on the plateau inland from the port, became the largest industrial concern in New Zealand. Coaltown Museum, established in 1972, has reconstructions of mines and sophisticated audio-visual presentations about coal mining. It incorporates part of the timber-framed, weatherboarded brewery, erected by William Nahr in 1896.

Charlestown, 26 km (16 mi.) S., is a gold mining 'ghost town' which once had a population of 20 000. Still visible are some ring bolts on rocks and the remains of the stamping battery.

BIBLIOGRAPHY
General
Thornton, 1982.

LOCATION
[M] Coaltown Mining Museum, Queen Street South, PO Box 216, Westport.

West Virginia, United States of America   In a mountainous, heavily-forested state that owes much of its economic and occupational life to coal mining, the lack of an adequate coal museum or preserved mine site in West Virginia may appear unusual. But, as the poet said, 'We don't know who invented water, but we can be sure it wasn't a fish', bituminous coal and its many good and evil influences have been and remain ever-present, omnipotent aspects of everyday life for many West Virginians. The washing of coal-stained clothes and the following of school sports on television are more predictable weekend pursuits for West Virginians than museum-going.

The state has ranked among the top five coal-producing states since Independence. Coal was discovered along Coal River in 1742 and quickly developed markets in the ironworks and later steelworks of Pennsylvania, and the commerce of the Midwest through the Ohio River Valley. The region's coal-based prosperity, among other factors, insured its separation from Virginia in 1861 as a new state.

Parkersburg and Huntington retain the dark, gritty richness of coal and its support industries, both relatively small river towns, but with canyons of brick factories pressed against the commercial downtowns and blackened iron bridges crossing the rivers that bisect them. Wheeling, by contrast, grew upon a more diverse manufacturing base into one of the least-recognized accumulations of high Victorian splendour in the nation. Block upon block of tall mansions outfitted in steamboat Gothic millwork back up against an equally frilly downtown commercial district. On the horizon stand the remains of the nail mills, glassworks, breweries, foundries and cigar works that boosted this city into the upper reaches of American industrial prosperity in the nineteenth century.

Necklacing the Ohio River at Wheeling is the famous suspension bridge of 1849 by Charles Ellet (1810–62), a long-span, stone-towered structure, improved and rebuilt in various ways in 1854, 1859 and 1872. The rather squat towers span 308 m (1010 ft.), and retain evidence of the sooty exhaust from the steamboats that once passed beneath.

Elsewhere in the state, the New River Gorge Bridge, a mid-twentieth-century span of arched steel trusswork several hundred feet over the New River, is given a special place in world bridge fame by an annual midsummer event at which parachute enthusiasts are invited by the state to jump off the bridge at mid-span, and, if all goes well, float down onto one of the river's sandbars.

BIBLIOGRAPHY
General
Smith, 1977.

LOCATION
[M] Jackson's Sawmill Museum, Route 1, State 4-H Camp, Weston, WV 26452.

DAVID H. SHAYT

wet spinning   A process used in the preparation of fine linen yarns, in which flaxen roving (*see* TEXTILES) passes through a trough of water heated to *c.*50 °C: this softens the pectose, the gum-like material that binds the flax cells together, enabling the fibre to be elongated to a finer strand without breaking. Wet spinning was invented by the Parisian Philippe de Girard and patented by two of his employees in 1815, but it was in LEEDS in the late 1820s that it was developed as a practical commercial process.

BIBLIOGRAPHY
General
Horner, 1920; Rimmer, 1960.

Wetzlar, Hesse, Germany   The most important industrial concern in central Hesse is the firm of Buderus, now over 250 years old. It was founded as a family business at Wetzlar, 12 km (8 mi.) W. of Giessen, and a feature of its entrepreneurial policy was that it acquired or leased the sites of many old iron-smelting works and foundries, as well as acquiring interests in mines and operating them to ensure supplies of ore to the main part of its production, smelting iron ore and making cast-iron products. The first blast furnace began operating in Wetzlar in 1872, and manufacture of foundry products began in 1901. As a result of the development of electric furnaces this last and largest of the Hessian blast-furnace complexes went out of production in 1981. As well as more recent buildings, the complex contains what was once the owner's house, now the company's archive repository. Wetzlar is also a centre of the precision-engineering and optical industries, its best-known firm, Leitz (makers of Leica cameras), being represented by the one-time owner's villa and a works museum.

See also LOLLAR.

ROLF HÖHMANN

whaling The Basques hunted whales in the Bay of Biscay in the Middle Ages, but the origins of modern whaling stem from the Arctic voyage of Henry Hudson (d. 1611) in 1607. Hudson's discoveries led first English then Dutch, German and Danish vessels to seek whales in the waters around SPITZBERGEN, where the principal catch was the Greenland or Arctic whale, *Balaena mysticetus*, capable of yielding 15 tonnes of oil and 750 kg (15 cwt.) of whalebone. The same whales were sought in the Pacific by vessels based in San Francisco. In the nineteenth century whalers hunted the blue whale, *Balaenoptera sibbaldii*, off the coast of northern Norway, using explosive harpoons; they towed the carcasses to depots on shore. The sperm whale, *Physeter macrocephalus*, was hunted in deep waters from Nantucket, Mass., from the early eighteenth century. Some 360 vessels were involved in the trade by 1774, and about 150 in the 1880s. Sperm oil is boiled at sea, and has less smell than other forms of whale oil. The industry is commemorated at Mystic Seaport, Conn. Whaling in the Antarctic developed in the early twentieth century.

By the late nineteenth century whales were hunted in sailing ships up to 500 tonnes, with auxiliary steam engines, and about fifty tanks each of which could hold up to 250 tons of blubber. Whales were killed from 8.2 m (27 ft.) boats, with harpoon platforms in the bows. Whale lines were ropes of $2\frac{3}{4}$ in. (0.07 m) diameter, up to 1280 m (4200 ft.) long. The explosive harpoon, the invention of the Norwegian Svend Foyn in 1865, required an 80-ton whaleboat with a 30 hp engine.

Whale oil is the principal form of TRAIN OIL and its use in oil lamps stimulated the growth of whaling in the first half of the nineteenth century. Its use in margarine led to a further increase in whaling activity after 1900. Whale bone was traditionally used in corsets and umbrellas, but in 1808 Samuel Crackes showed that it could be employed in strips for brushes used for such purposes as cleaning boiler flues, and this was its chief use by *c*.1900.

The sailing whaler *Charles W. Morgan* of 1841 is preserved at Mystic, CONNECTICUT and the steamer *Rau IX* at Bremerhaven, while the steam-powered *Petrel* survives on SOUTH GEORGIA.

BIBLIOGRAPHY
General
Jackson, 1978; Simpson and Goodman, 1986.
Specific
Pearson, M. The technology of whaling in Australian waters in the 19th century. In *Australian Journal of Historical Archaeology*, I, 1983.

BARRIE TRINDER

wharf A wall of timber, masonry or concrete, constructed along the edge of a stretch of water so that ships may be loaded and unloaded alongside. The term is often taken to include the flat area extending back from the wall, where goods might be stored, and to warehouses and the like which might be built within such an area. The term is also applied to installations for loading and unloading railway or road vehicles.

Wheatstone, Charles (1802–75) An English physicist of a retiring disposition: fascinated by electrical phenomena, his was the scientific brain behind the first successful electric telegraph in 1837–9. His major contribution was the Wheatstone automatic telegraph, transmitting and receiving via a perforated paper tape.

BIBLIOGRAPHY
General
Cooke, 1866; Herbert, 1916; Hubbard, 1965.

wheelwright Literally, a maker of wheels, but in practice a builder of carts and waggons, one of the most important of the traditional woodworking trades. The term was also applied to a specialist maker of wheels within a carriage-building concern. A traditional waggon wheel consisted of the nave, the boss in the centre, the spokes, and the felloes or fellies, the parts making up the rim. The felloes were bound by the stroke, a wrought-iron (later steel) rim, which was heated and shrunk on, being secured to the felloes by cart nails. In the USA a nave was called a 'hub', and the stroke a 'tire'. The nave was bound by iron hoops called nave-bands.

In the Netherlands specialist wheelwrights in rural areas produced wheels for use by coach and waggon builders in the cities. In the USA by 1870 large industrial-scale wheelwrights were catering for the needs of hundreds of small waggon and coachmakers. Such concerns employed purpose-built wheelmaking machines, manufactured by several of the leading American builders of woodworking machinery, and often used hydraulic presses to fit tires on wheels. Some continued to make 'artillery' style wheels for motor vehicles until the 1930s. The buildings of the last large-scale wheelmaking concern, Hooper, Brother & Darlington of Westchester, Pa., were recorded by HAER (*See* UNITED STATES OF AMERICA) in 1969–70.

BIBLIOGRAPHY
General
Book of Trades, 1839; Holme, 1688; Sturt, 1923; Tunis, 1965.

BARRIE TRINDER

whisky A spirit distilled from fermented mashes (*see* BREWERY), either from malt or mixtures of malt and unmalted cereals. In Britain the Scotch product is always called 'whisky', the Irish product being 'whiskey'. The term 'whisky' is used in Canada, but 'whiskey' is commoner both for Scotch and Irish spirits in the USA. In the USA the native whiskies are rye and bourbon, the former made from a mixture of rye or barley malt and unmalted rye, the latter from barley malt or wheat malt and maize.

See also DISTILLING; SCOTCH WHISKY.

white coal A term which has two distinct meanings in industrial archaeology:

1. Wood that was dried but not burned to form charcoal. It was used in the smelting of non-ferrous metals, particularly lead. White coal was produced on a white-coal hearth: the example at Froggatt Wood, 13 km (8 mi.) SW of Sheffield, England, consists of two large stone slabs across which lengths of wood were placed, to be dried by fires of twigs beneath.

2. The term in French is 'houille blanche', and in German 'Weisse Kohle', both of which literally mean 'white coal' but in practice are used to mean water power, often specifically hydro-electric power.

BIBLIOGRAPHY
General
Stratton and Trinder, 1988.

white lead Basic lead carbonate ($2PbCO_3$,$Pb(OH)_2$), until recent times the most important constituent of paint. The stack process of manufacture originated in Venice in the seventeenth century: thin plates of lead were rolled up and suspended above pots of vinegar, four hundred of which would be set out on a bed of horse dung, then covered with boards on which more pots were set. The stack was closed for three weeks, then dismantled and the corroded lead removed. The chamber process developed in Germany in the nineteenth century: in this, straps of lead were hung up and gas combining carbonic acid, acetic acid, oxygen and water was pumped through. The corrosion products were subsequently ground up for paint-making.

BIBLIOGRAPHY
General
Jones, 1950; Stratton and Trinder, 1988.

white metal Low-melting alloys whose principal components are lead, tin, copper and antimony. White metals are used chiefly for bearings, in which context they are sometimes known as 'brasses', but also as fusible plugs in boilers and as TYPE.

BIBLIOGRAPHY
General
Tuer and Bolz, 1984.

whitesmith A term sometimes applied to a smith specializing in finely finished work in wrought iron or steel, such as decorative fire irons, and often extending into bell-hanging or LOCKSMITHING; and sometimes to a craftsman making domestic utensils from tinplate.

BIBLIOGRAPHY
General
Book of English Trades, 1839.

whiting Finely graded CHALK, used in the pharmaceutical industry, in polishing pastes, PAINTS and PUTTY, and, in the nineteenth century, by unscrupulous bakers or prison governors, in breadmaking. In the traditional manufacturing process chalk was ground to a fine powder in an edge runner mill, mixed with water, and allowed to settle in tanks, the heaviest particles settling in the first tank. The resultant pastes were dried on solid chalk blocks which absorbed moisture. Powered grinding and drying machines were used from the late nineteenth century. Whiting mills are preserved at LEEDS and Hessle.

BIBLIOGRAPHY
Specific
Horn, W. L. *Thwaite Mills*. Leeds: Thwaite Mills Society; n.d.

LOCATIONS
[S] Hessle Whiting Mill, Hessle Foreshore, Hessle, North Humberside.
[S] Thwaite Putty Mill, Stourton, Leeds LS10 1RP.

Whitney, Eli (1765–1825) The pioneer of modern production engineering was born in Massachusetts and gained skills in making violins and nails before going to Yale in 1789. Soon after moving to Georgia in 1792 he devised a COTTON GIN for which he received a patent in 1794. He commenced manufacture of the gin in New Haven, Conn., shipping completed machines to the South; but by 1812, when the patent expired, litigation had drained away any potential profits. In 1798 he began the manufacture of firearms at Whitneyville near New Haven, and slowly developed, with contemporaries like J. R. BROWN and Simeon North (1765–1852), the concept of INTERCHANGEABLE PARTS. He contributed substantially to the development of the MILLING MACHINE and to tool-making generally.

BIBLIOGRAPHY
General
Olmsted, 1846; Roe, 1916.
Specific
Battison, E. A. Eli Whitney and the milling machine. In *Smithsonian Journal of History*, I, 1966.
Woodbury, R. S. The legend of Eli Whitney and interchangeable parts. In *Technology and Culture*, I, 1960.

Whitworth, Joseph (1803–87) One of the most talented of British mechanical engineers, Whitworth was born in Stockport and worked in a Derbyshire cotton factory before in 1821 taking a job as a mechanic in Manchester. From 1825 he worked for HENRY MAUDSLAY in London, where he developed means of making truly plane surfaces. Later he was employed in the workshop where calculating machines (*see* COMPUTER) designed by Charles Babbage (1791–1871) were being manufactured, before establishing himself as a toolmaker in Manchester in 1833. He displayed an array of machine tools at the Great Exhibition in 1851. He developed systems of standardized measures and gauges which were widely employed. The most important was his uniform system of screw threads, first suggested in 1841, which was in general use by 1860. From 1854 he was involved with the manufacture of armaments, and developed a means of casting ductile steel utilizing a hydraulic press. His works in Manchester became a limited company in 1874, and in

Figure 176   An eighteenth-century horse gin in the salt mine museum at Wieliczka
S. Januszewski

1897 was amalgamated with that in Newcastle-upon-Tyne established by Sir WILLIAM ARMSTRONG. The Whitworth Art Gallery in the University of Manchester is named after him.

BIBLIOGRAPHY
Specific
Musson, A. E. Joseph Whitworth and the growth of mass production engineering. In *Business History*, XVII, 1975.

BARRIE TRINDER

Wieliczka, Kraków, Poland   A town 15 km (9 mi.) SE of Kraków. Salt has been mined at Wieliczka for over seven hundred years. The rock-salt deposits comprise several folded salt beds, ranging in thickness from a few metres to several tens of metres. The upper salt bed contains large salt lumps, up to half a million cubic metres in volume. The structure of the deposits has determined the mining technology employed. The mine now has some 200 km (125 mi.) of excavated headings, and about 2040 chambers distributed throughout nine main working floors, ranging in depth from 57 to 327 m (187 to 1073 ft.). The area of mining activity is 5.5 km ($3\frac{1}{2}$ mi.) long and 1.5 km (1 mi.) wide, and the excavations amount to 7.5 million m³ (9.8 million cu. yd).

Until the partitions of Poland the Wieliczka saltmine had been under royal administration. As early as the sixteenth century, when it had a thousand employees, it was one of the largest mines in Europe. Salt was mined in cylindrical blocks, each weighing 500 kg (10 cwt.), or as chips or powder. It was taken from the mine by wooden hoists. From the fifteenth century onwards various horse-operated winding devices were employed, and with slight modifications this type of apparatus continued in use until the nineteenth century. After 1795 the mine fell into the hands of the Austrian government. Mining methods were modernized and the process of production reorganized. Blasting powder came into use and horse-driven winding equipment was replaced by steam engines. Underground railways were introduced, and in the 1920s and 30s new mining machines were employed.

The most interesting parts of the Wieliczka saltmine were opened to the public in the late nineteenth century. The mine was subsequently put under legislative protection, and in 1978 it was designated a UNESCO World Heritage Site. The founder of the museum and its director for many years was Professor Alfons Długosz.

The present route for visitors is 4 km (2.5 mi.) long. Starting at a depth of 63 m (207 ft.), and crossing three working floors, it descends to 135 m (443 ft.). It passes the St Antonio chapel of 1689, and the Blessed Kings' Chapel, both richly decorated with salt bas-reliefs of biblical subjects. It passes through several chambers as high as 70 m (230 ft.), where the roofs are supported with wooden scaffolds; here various types of old mining technology are exhibited. The museum itself is located on the third working floor, 135 m (443 ft.) deep, in thirteen chambers excavated in the nineteenth and early twentieth centuries. Exhibits include old mining tools and equipment from the mine: wooden winding gear for raising salt from the mine, as well as for transport between galleries and haulage on inclines, a seventeenth-century pulley, an eighteenth-century hoist wheel, an eighteenth-century horse gin, a Saxon type of horse gin of 1734–43, an eighteenth-century Hungarian horse gin, and a brake wheel from an early nineteenth-century incline. There are numerous devices for mining and processing salt, a nineteenth-century hand mill, a stamp mill, a paddle wheel of the late sixteenth-century, an eighteenth-century sled, and 'hunds' or wagons for transporting salt. There are also displays of documents and works of art connected with the Wieliczka mine, swords and side arms worn by miners on feast days, the silver Wieliczki horn, and plans of the mine, including those by Marcin German of 1638 and Jan Gotfryd Borlach of 1719. Visitors can also admire a collection of minerals found in salt deposits. The museum has a rich collection of books, maps and archives relating to saltmining, ranging from the fifteenth century to the present. There is a sanatorium for allergy sufferers in the underground workings.

BIBLIOGRAPHY
General
Długosz, 1958; Piotrowicz and Grzesiowski, 1977.
Specific
Długosz *Zabytki dawnych urządzeń transportowych w Muzeum Żup Krakowskich* (Old transport devices in the Museum of the Krakowskie Saltmine in Wieliczka).

LOCATION
[M] Muzeum Żup Krakowskich w Wieliczce (The Museum of the Krakowskie Saltmine), Park Kingi 1, Wieliczka.

PIOTR GERBER

Wiener Neustadt, Lower Austria, Austria   A city 58 km (36 mi.) S. of Vienna, the seat of a military academy since 1752, and an imperial manufacturing centre. It was linked with Vienna by the Wiener Neustadter Kanal, built by Sebastian von Maillard and Joseph Schemerl in 1797–1803, and extended to Pöttsching, 10 km (6 mi.) E., in 1810–11. The canal accommodated barges 22.7 m × 1.73 m (74 ft. × 5 ft. 6 in.). Navigation ceased in 1879: 35 km (22 mi.) of canal are still in water; 38 of the 52 locks survive, and 19 original bridges still stand. The lock at Kottingbrunn, 16 km (10 mi.) N., is preserved.

Emperor Franz Joseph's Aqueduct was built to supply water to the town in 1909–10: its 42 m (135 ft.) brick and reinforced-concrete tower holds 750 m³ (981 cu. yd.) water. Important nineteenth-century engineering works include a locomotive factory established in 1842 and sold to Georg Sigl in 1860: it became an armaments works from 1938. It was closed in 1965, but its entrance is preserved as a monument.

LOCATION
[M] Municipal Museum, Wienerstrasse 63, 2700 Wiener Neustadt.

Wigan, Greater Manchester, England   A town in the Lancashire coalfield, but also on the western edge of the cotton region. Through the writings of George Orwell (1903–50), Wigan came to symbolize the decay of the North in the depression of the 1930s. Wigan Pier, where coal was loaded onto the Leeds & Liverpool Canal, became a music hall joke, but since 1985 it has been the site of a heritage centre in former warehouses, linked by canal with the adjacent Trencherfield Mill, where there are a steam engine and rope race, and working ring spinning machinery.

BIBLIOGRAPHY
General
Orwell, 1936.

LOCATION
[M] Wigan Pier Heritage Centre, Wigan Pier, Wigan WN3 4EU.

Wilhelmshaven, Lower Saxony, Germany   A treaty between Prussia and Oldenburg gave Prussia the southern part of what is now Wilhelmshaven, and it was extended, principally in the 1870s, to become the main North Sea naval port. Despite severe damage during World War II, the entrance building to the Imperial Naval Dockyard, again a naval base, still stands. Dating from 1876, it is a three-storey brick building with a double gateway in the central projection. The first workers' quarters built by the Prussian Navy remain in the Huntestrasse. A technological monument of particular importance is the Kaiser Wilhelm Bridge over the Ems–Jade Canal, built in 1906–7, and the largest swing bridge in Germany. The 390 m (1280 ft.) long sea lock built in 1942, destroyed in 1945 and reopened in 1964, is one of the largest in the world.

At Dykhausen in the Friesland district, 20 km (12 mi.) SW of Wilhelmshaven, is a dredger mill with an Archimedean screw, built in the style of a Dutch mill with a tailpole.

BIBLIOGRAPHY
General
Mende and Hamm, 1990; Slotta, 1975–85.

LOCATION
[M] Maritime Museum, Rathaus, Rathausplatz 10, 2940 Wilhelmshaven.

MICHAEL MENDE

Wilkinson, John (1738–1808)   The most celebrated of

841

the ironmasters of the Industrial Revolution, Wilkinson was the son of the iron founder, Isaac Wilkinson (*c*.1704–84), and grew up near his father's works in the LAKE DISTRICT. From 1753 he worked at the Bersham furnace near WREXHAM, and in 1757 became a partner in the New Willey ironworks, Shropshire (*see* IRONBRIDGE). He subsequently operated other furnace complexes in Shropshire, and set up an integrated ironworks at Bradley, near Wolverhampton, in 1766, which became celebrated for its innovations. He was involved in manufacturing armaments, for which purpose he had a depot in London, and also had interests in lead mines in North Wales. He issued many TRADE TOKENS. He played a significant role in the construction of the Iron Bridge and launched a wrought-iron boat in 1787.

Wilkinson was closely involved with the development of the steam engine. In 1774 he patented a boring machine for cannon, which worked on the same principles as one introduced at Woolwich Arsenal by a Dutchman, Jan Verbruggen, in 1770. He also developed a machine for boring cylinders, which he believed to be protected by the same patent, but lost protection for it when the patent was revoked in 1779. In 1776 he used the second production BOULTON & WATT engine to provide direct power for the blowing apparatus of the Willey blast furnace, thus freeing ironworks from absolute dependence on water power: his Snedshill furnaces of 1777 were the first built without any provision for water power. Wilkinson supplied the cylinders for most Boulton & Watt engines built before the mid-1790s, when, as a result of disagreements with his brother William Wilkinson (?1744–1808), it became clear that he had built many engines that infringed JAMES WATT's patents. In spite of losses through litigation he retained a substantial fortune at the time of his death which was consumed in legal disputes among his descendants. His monument at Lindale, 15 km (9 mi.) SW of Kendal, was restored in 1984. One of his homes, Castle Head, 1 km S. of Lindale, is now a field study centre.

BIBLIOGRAPHY
General
Cossons and Trinder, 1979; Trinder, 1981.
Specific
AIA Bulletin, XII, 1985.

BARRIE TRINDER

Willans, Peter William (1851–92) A British engineer who patented in 1884 an enclosed high-speed steam engine with either two or three vertical cylinders, intended for the direct drive of electric generators. The steam entered from the top and was distributed via ports in central trunks, fitted with piston valves, all concentric with the pistons. Willans engines were machined to the finest tolerances with full interchangeable parts, and were highly successful in power stations before being rendered obsolete by the steam turbine. Willans introduced further developments in the 1860s, successfully overcoming problems relating to vibration, dynamics, lubrication and the heating of bearings, and thereby established the high-speed engine as a major type of steam engine.

BIBLIOGRAPHY
General
Frankel, 1977; Law, 1965.

Willemsoord, Overijssel, The Netherlands   Willemsoord, 6 km (4 mi.) NW of Steenwijk, is a well-preserved example of the Dutch pauper colonies which aroused international interest in the first half of the nineteenth century. The depression that followed the Napoleonic wars in the second decade of the nineteenth century led to an increase in pauperism, and in 1816–17 a charitable society, the Maatschappij van Weldadigheid (Benevolent Society), was formed in The Hague ('s Gravenhage), with the object of purchasing land on the heathlands of Drenthe and Overijssel for the settlement of paupers. The colonies of Willemsoord, Frederiksoord (6 km (4 mi.) NE of Steenwijk, in Drenthe), and Wilheminaoord (10 km (6 mi.) N. of Steenwijk, also in Drenthe) were established in 1818. Plots of 3 ha ($7\frac{1}{2}$ ac.), considered to be capable of supporting families of six, were laid out, and each family was given a house and a cow, and provided with free schooling and medical care. Much labour was expended in making the land cultivable, and in improving the navigation of the River Aa through to the Zuiderzee (Ijsselmeer). Hand-loom weaving was established in weaving sheds, and some inhabitants had looms at home. Bricks were made from clay dug on the spot, mortar was produced by calcining sea shells with turf from the heathlands, and most dwellings were roofed with reed thatch. The project was directed by General van der Bosch, whose name is commemorated in the principal building at Willemsoord, the Hoeve General van der Bosch, an enormous traditional farmstead, which stands alongside the elegant church of 1851. The plots and farmhouses of Willemsoord were laid out on a grid plan. Two types of farmhouse can be distinguished, both rectangular in plan, extending back from narrow road frontages, one with the entrance to the front and a semi-hipped roof, the other with an entrance on one side and an outshot on the other.

The same heathland was the setting for two other colonies. At Veenhuizen, in Drenthe, 14 km (9 mi.) NW of Assen, was a settlement for orphans and foundlings, with three large buildings about 800 m (880 yd.) apart, two for orphans and one for beggars; and at Ommerschans, near Meppel in Overijssel, was a penal colony for the idle and dissolute, established around an old fortress. Veenhuizen has served as a prison since 1918, and was modified in the 1950s. Its museum portrays the hard life endured by the colonists since 1823.

BIBLIOGRAPHY
General
Macgregor, 1835.

LOCATION
[M] Museum Veenhuizen, Hoofdweg 8, Veenhuizen.

BARRIE TRINDER

Williams, Thomas (1737–1802) Called the 'Copper King' for his role in the copper industry of the late eighteenth century, Williams controlled cheap ore supplies from PARYS MOUNTAIN in his native North Wales and diversified into smelting and manufacturing in Lancashire, SWANSEA, the GREENFIELD VALLEY and elsewhere to break the cartel governing the British copper market, then the largest in the world. Much of his wealth derived from developing effective bolts for copper sheathing of ships.

BIBLIOGRAPHY
General
Harris, 1964.

Wilson Falls, St-Jérôme, Quebec, Canada The pulpmill at Wilson Falls, 60 km (37 mi.) NW of Montreal, was a celebrated centre between 1881 and 1958 for the mechanical production of pulp, of cardboard and of newsprint. The development of the complex was the concern of three companies, Messrs Delisle between 1881–93, James C. Wilson between 1893 and 1920, and J. C. Wilson Ltd from 1920 until 1958. The principal mill building was constructed, burned and rebuilt twice between 1881 and 1900. Within was located all the plant necessary for the mechanical production of pulp: a sawmill, a stripping machine, and three ring grinders, each having three chambers coupled to two turbines, and a fixed filter. A weir with associated structures in wood, a dam of triangular construction, caissons, and penstocks bound together by wrought-iron bands, comprised the water-power system. Three turbines based on the Pelton model with horizontal axes were located on concrete supports by the water inflows. The workers' houses were also built on concrete foundations, as were the service buildings, the stables, warehouses, garage and bridge. Only traces of the foundations of these buildings now remain. The pulpmill was abandoned in 1958 and its walls and roofs gradually collapsed. Under the ruins archaeologists have found a basin for floating logs, a centrifugal pump, some underground cavities and the foundations of a pulp reservoir.

The site is now the property of the North River Regional Park Corporation, which brings together four municipalities, and since 1986 it has been the object of archaeological research carried out jointly by the Corporation and the Quebec government. This work also includes the conservation and interpretation of the remains.

BIBLIOGRAPHY
General
Arkeos Inc., 1986.

LOUISE TROTTIER

windmill A wind-driven source of power, the essential features being the sails, the 'luffing gear' (a means of turning the sails into the wind), and internal gearing to utilize the power for a practical purpose. Windmills probably originated in the Middle East and had been introduced to Europe by *c*.1150. The main types are the POST MILL, SMOCK MILL, TOWER MILL and HORIZONTAL WINDMILL, the first of which appeared in Europe in the

Figure 177 One of the windmills on the mill-trail in the district of Minden-Lübbecke in Westphalia, this tower mill at Sudhemmern can be operated and its sails are in place. From time to time the mill is open to the public, and on these occasions 'platenkuchen' are made for visitors in the adjoining bakery.
Barrie Trinder

twelfth century. Most windmills had four or more sail rods, poles fixed in a cross on the mill shaft. To the rods were attached bars or rails, on which the cloth sails were set. In 1772 Andrew Meikle (1719–1811) devised a 'spring sail', which comprised shutters that could be set, then held in place by springs. Improvements along similar lines were Hooper's 'Roller Reefing Sail' of 1789, using roller blinds instead of shutters, and Cubbit's popular 'Patent Sail' of 1807, which enabled adjustments to be made without stopping the mill. The use of cast-iron gearing, advocated by JOHN SMEATON, enabled more sails to be added, and mills with as many as eight sails have been operated (*see* LINCOLNSHIRE). Latterly the use of iron, steel and other forms of new technology gave rise to the vaned wheel of the annular sail in 1855, familiar in WIND PUMPS and most recently in aerogenerators.

Luffing was first achieved with a tail pole or chain, the mill or cap simply being dragged round by hand, though capstans and winches were also used. In 1745 Edmund Lee patented the fan-tail, a vaned wheel at right angles to the main sails, which turned them towards the wind automatically. Fan-carriages on post mills turned the whole mill.

Inside a corn-grinding windmill, millstones were over- or (more usually) underdriven; in the former the power was transferred via a spur wheel above the stones, in the latter, one beneath them. Crucial to successful working were effective brakes and especially 'tentering', the fine adjustment of the distance between the millstones. Since the late eighteenth century this has been achieved with a centrifugal governor controlling a beam on which one of the stones is supported.

Most windmills were CORN MILLS or were used in LAND DRAINAGE, but they were also employed as SAW MILLS, in making PAPER, as OIL MILLS, and for grinding MUSTARD, while a few provided power for TEXTILE MILLS. Most countries or regions had distinctive forms of windmill. Most had passed out of commercial use by 1950, but many are preserved *in situ* and in open-air museums.

See also figure 105.

BIBLIOGRAPHY
General
Finch, 1933; Wailes, 1948, 1954.

CHRISTOPHER GREEN

wind pump A machine for lifting water. Three types of water-lifting mills should be distinguished. The earliest, POST MILLS and TOWER MILLS fitted with simple scoop water wheels, were used extensively in the Netherlands (Wip Mills) and in the English FENS by the seventeenth century. Later, scoop wheels were replaced with archimedean screws, known in the Netherlands as polder, spider, and tjasker mills; a variant, the Dutch meadow mill, raises water by centrifugal force, created by a Norse wheel, a type of horizontal water wheel (*see* NORSE MILL).

Reciprocating pumps were also fitted to Dutch and English tower, post and smock mills, and formed the essential mechanism of wind pumps with annular sails in the USA, and Australia.

wine The fermented juice of the grape. French, Italian and German laws stipulate that wine may be made from fresh grapes only. In England the term is commonly applied to fermented drinks made from other fruits, and from vegetables; while 'barley wine' is a strong beer. Wine originated in antiquity, and was spread through the Mediterranean by the ancient Greeks. It was much traded in the Middle Ages, and by the seventeenth century was 'drawn as if by a magnet to the countries of the north' (Braudel, 1981). Three main types of wine were recognized in England in the eighteenth century: French; Rhenish, which included wine from the entire German-speaking world; and Spanish, which included Portuguese wine. Vintages were first established in the eighteenth century.

Grapes are crushed to form a 'must' which is fermented in vats, and then run into casks which are stored longitudinally on racks. Most wine is clarified by fining at this stage. Most is then quickly bottled, but a small proportion is matured and sold as vintage wine. The organization of the trade ranges from the estates of the small chateaux that produce the best wines of Burgundy, through the regional co-operatives that operate in Tuscany, to the large state enterprises found in Yugoslavia and Bulgaria.

The wine industry in the nineteenth century was afflicted by three major pests: the mildew *Oideum* from the 1850s, which was treated by dusting with sulphur, the aphid *Phylloxera vastatrix* from 1843, which was eventually countered by grafting European vines to resistant stocks from California, and the mildew *Peronospera viticola* from 1884, which was treated by spraying with copper salts.

Fortified wines like PORT WINE, to which extra alcohol, usually brandy, has been added, are more easily traded. Sparkling wines like champagne, which became popular in the first half of the eighteenth century, are cleared and bottled after normal fermentation is complete, and a second fermentation in the bottle is caused by the addition of yeast and sugar.

BIBLIOGRAPHY
General
Amerine and Cruess, 1960; Braudel, 1981; Genevois and Ribereau-Gayon, 1947; Johnson, 1971; Simon, 1921, 1972; Vogt, 1952.

BARRIE TRINDER

Winterthur, Zürich, Switzerland Winterthur, 20 km ($12\frac{1}{2}$ mi.) NE of Zurich, became the principal engineering centre in Switzerland in the mid-nineteenth century. In 1851 Jakob Sulzer-Hirzel (1806–83) brought the British engineer Charles Brown (1827–1905) to the city. In 1871 Charles Brown founded the Schweizerische Lokomotiv- und Maschinenfabrik (Swiss Locomotive and Engineering Works) in the city, and later became a founding partner of the Oerlikon electrical engineering works. The Sulzer works produced its first steam engine in 1854, and began to manufacture air and gas compressors in 1877, and diesel engines in 1903.

The engineering industry developed from the manufacture of machinery for the region's textile mills. The first purpose-built cotton mill in Switzerland was built above a waterfall at Hard, Winterthur. There were two spinning mills, a weaving mill, a flour mill, a farmhouse with a tavern and bakery, the owner's mansion, dwellings for workers, and a boarding house for women and children employed in the factory. The whole complex is preserved, although adapted to new uses.

The former textile factory at Winterthur-Wülflingen is a large Classical building with two wings, one with offices and one containing the owner's dwelling, and dates from 1818–26.

Technorama Schweiz is a large exhibition of over 6000 m² (65 000 sq. ft.), arranged in eight sections dealing with energy, materials, textiles, dwellings, information, physics and measurement, chemistry, and buildings. It is more a science centre than a museum, but contains some historical material.

The Kellenberg collection is one of the most important Swiss clock museums.

BIBLIOGRAPHY
General
Bärtschi, 1988, 1990.
Specific
Müller, U. Witnesses to 150 years of engineering science. In *Sulzer Technical Review*, LXVI, 1984.

LOCATIONS
[M] Kellenberger Collection, Rathaus, Martgasse 20, 8400 Winterthur.
[M] Technorama Schweiz (Swiss Technorama), Frauenfelderstrasse, 8400 Winterthur.

HANS-PETER BÄRTSCHI

wire mill Wire, whether made of iron or steel or any other metal, is manufactured by drawing a strand through a hole in a steel plate known as a draw plate, thus elongating it and reducing it in cross-section. It is usually drawn on to a drum at the far end of the draw plate, and linked to the drum by pincers attached to a chain. The drum can be hand- or power-operated. Fine wire is made from wire of larger section by repeated drawings. Metals lose their ductility while being drawn: annealing furnaces are used to restore it. In the twentieth century wires of larger section are produced in a rod mill. A water-powered wire mill known as the 'Pepper Mill' is demonstrated at HAGEN.

Wisconsin, United States of America For a state known most for its self-effacing production of cheese and milk, Wisconsin may contain the greatest number of specialized museums devoted to heavy industries. Paper, automobiles, furniture, beer and general machinery follow closely on the heels of cheese and milk in this large north-central state, neatly divided between traditional urban and rural industries.

While Wisconsin has shared with Michigan and Minnesota deep ranges of iron ore and seams of durable granite, lead mining occupies a strong position in the state's history. Three sites commemorate the trade: Pendarvis, at Mineral Point, with its mining camp of the 1840s and lead-mining tools brought over by Cornish immigrants; the Platteville Mining Museum's lead mine and head frame of the 1840s; and the Badger Mine of 1827 at Shullsburg.

Rhinelander's logging museum and the Paul Bunyan logging camp at Eau Claire celebrate the Scandinavian immigrant skills and mills that moved these northern woods into the furniture, window and door factories of Milwaukee and Sheboygan. Clintonville's Four Wheel Drive Museum is housed in a machine shop of 1906, while more traditional transport museums stand at Gills Rock, Green Bay, Manitowoc, and North Freedom. Mequon's Crafts Museum collects the tools and equipment of the ice-harvesting industry; while at Fish Creek the Eagle Lighthouse of 1868, which once guarded Green Bay's entrance

to Lake Michigan, is a splendid example of Great Lakes lighthouse preservation, housing a permanent exhibit on the subject.

LOCATIONS
[M,S] Badger Mine and Museum, Shullsberg, WI 53586.
[M] Crafts Museum, 11458 North Laguna Drive, Mequon, WI 53902.
[M] Door County Maritime Museum, 12950 Highway 42, Gills Rock, WI 54210.
[M,S] Eagle Lighthouse, Peninsula State Park, Fish Creek, WI 54212.
[M] Four Wheel Drive Museum, Foot of East 11th Street, Clintonville, WI 54929.
[M] Manitowoc Maritime Museum, 402 N. 8th Street, Manitowoc, WI 54220.
[M] Mid-Continent Railway Museum, Walnut Street, North Freedom, WI 53951.
[M] National Railroad Museum, 2285 South Broadway, Green Bay, WI 54304.
[M] Paul Bunyan Logging Camp, Carson Park, Eau Claire, WI 54703.
[S] Pendarvis, 114 Shake Rag Street, Mineral Point, WI 53565.
[M] Platteville Mining Museum, 385 E. Main Street, Platteville, WI 53818.
[M] Rhinelander Logging Museum, Pioneer Park, Rhinelander, WI 54501.

DAVID H. SHAYT

Wittelsheim, Haut-Rhin, France Potash was discovered at Wittelsheim in Alsace, 10 km (6 mi.) NW of Mulhouse, by Joseph Vogt, owner of the copperworks at Niederbruck near Massevaux, 20 km (12 mi.) E. of Mulhouse, who from 1895 had developed new prospecting techniques. Drill towers built and installed by his firm were capable of going more than 1000 m (3200 ft.) deep. At this date Alsace was under German rule, and the first industrial-scale potash exploitation developed around Wittelsheim after 1910 at the instigation of Deutsche Kaliwerke AG, owners of potash mines at Stassfurt in Saxony.

At the same time Vogt formed a company with a group of French industrialists to mine the Kali-Sainte-Thérèse concession around Ensisheim, 10 km (6 mi.) NE of Wittelsheim. After 1918 the former German mines came under the control of the French government. The inter-war period was one of rapid growth, the tonnage of potash mined at Kali-Sainte-Thérèse, for example, rising from 155 000 tonnes in 1920 to a million in 1930. A peak output of two million tonnes was achieved in 1959, followed by gradual decline. By 1976 the Kali-Sainte-Thérèse mines had closed, leaving only some mines around Wittelsheim still active.

The old 'Joseph-Else' site, south of Wittelsheim, offers the most interesting vestiges of this Alsatian mining activity. The two shafts, Joseph and Else, respectively 500 m and 550 m (1640 ft. and 1800 ft.) deep, were sunk in 1911 and 1912. The metal headstocks of the Joseph pit date from this period. The reinforced-concrete headstocks of the Else pit date from 1928. The surface buildings are of 1928–9, and are still used for storage, although no potash has been mined here since 1966. The nearby Graffen-wald-Joseph-Else housing estate has 504 dwellings dating from 1919. Six different types of building may be identified, incorporating one, two or four housing units; they were intended for engineers, clerical staff and mine workers. With its sloping roofs, the architecture of this estate has a decidedly rural air, coming in two distinct versions, German and Alsatian. The estate also has two schools, a co-operative store, a medical centre, bathhouses, and a refectory building which now houses the Alsatian Potash Miners' Association.

The former surface buildings of the old 'Carreau Rodolphe' near Ensisheim also survive, and are to be used by the Alsace Écomusée at Ungersheim.

BIBLIOGRAPHY
General
Jonas, 1977.
Specific
Jaeger, G. Joseph Vogt 1847–1921, Les Hommes et la potasse (Men and Potash). In *Review of the Maison du Mineur et de la Potasse*, I, 1985.
Zgud, M.-L. La Cité Graffenwald-Joseph Else. In *Review of the Maison du Mineur et de la Potasse*, I, 1985.

LOCATION
[M] Écomusée de Haute Alsace, BP 71, F-68190 Ungersheim.

JEAN-FRANÇOIS BELHOSTE

woad A blue dyestuff obtained from a plant of the mustard family, *Isatis tinctoria*. Cultivated throughout Europe, Asia and North Africa, woad leaves were pulped and formed into balls. Once dried and ground woad was moistened and allowed to ferment. Valued highly in the Middle Ages, woad was to a large extent replaced by INDIGO which produced a stronger blue colour.

BIBLIOGRAPHY
General
Hummel, 1888; Hurry, 1930; Lauterbach, 1905; Partridge, 1823; Perkins and Everest, 1918.

wolfram, wolframite *See* TUNGSTEN.

Wolfsburg, Lower Saxony, Germany The Volkswagen car plant at Wolfsburg, 75 km (45 mi.) E. of Hanover, was built on the banks of the Mittelland Canal in 1938–9 to designs by R. E. Mewes and K. Kohlbecker. 'Strength through joy' (Kraft durch Freude) was the catchphrase of the time, and the car was named KDF-Wagen accordingly. The plant is dominated on the Wolfsburg side by the administration and storage area, with the assembly and finishing plants adjoining them to the east, ending with a façade punctuated by twenty-three projecting staircases, and the power station. Since 1958 there has been an office tower block at the western end.

BIBLIOGRAPHY
General
Mende and Hamm, 1990; Slotta, 1975–85.

LOCATION
[M] Volkswagen Museum, 3180 Wolfsburg.

wood Wood from trees is one of the prime industrial raw materials. *See* BASKET; BOBBIN MILL; CARPENTER; CHAIR; CHARCOAL; COOPER; CORK; FOREST INDUSTRY; FRETWORK; FURNITURE; LUMBER; MOUSE TRAP; PENCIL; PULP; SAWMILL; SAW PIT; TAR; TIMBER; TOYMAKING; TURPENTINE; WHEELWRIGHT; WOOD CARVING.

It is also one of the most important constructional materials, used in buildings, bridges (*see* WOODEN BRIDGE), and for many specialist applications in manufacturing, notably for vats for materials like fruit juices, and fatty acids used in making margarine, both of which it would be dangerous to store in metal containers, or for making WHISKY, CIDER, WINE or VINEGAR, where the wood adds particular qualities to the liquid stored in it.

Woodbridge, Suffolk, England Notable for a surviving WEIGHING MACHINE and for a tide mill on the River Debden, 10 km (6 mi.) E. of Ipswich. Though it has medieval origins, the present structure dates from 1793. Timber-framed and clad with boards, it was worked until the 1950s, and is now preserved by a trust. A 3 ha (1.2 ac.) mill pond provides a 2 m (6 ft. 6 in.) head of water; and a wheel, 7 m (23 ft.) diameter and 2 m (6 ft. 6 in.) wide, drives four pairs of stones via a pit wheel, a wallower (*see* WATER MILL), an upright shaft and spur wheels.

BIBLIOGRAPHY
General
Alderton and Booker, 1980.

wood carving Toys and various forms of ornamental woodwork for domestic use were produced in many forest regions, and traded extensively from the late seventeenth century. Wood carving was also a city trade, a branch of cabinet-making. The London wood carvers in the mid-nineteenth century were an élite group of craftsmen who as a body owned a large collection of books and prints for models.

BIBLIOGRAPHY
General
Mayhew, 1850.

wooden bridge The term 'wooden bridge' is often taken to mean a TRUSS BRIDGE or beam bridge covered with a pitched roof to protect it from snow, of the type regarded with much affection in Austria, Switzerland (*see* LUCERNE), Quebec and the USA (*see* INDIANA). The propensity of timber to decay and to burn has destroyed most of the more ambitious structures of the past, including the Rhine bridge at Schaffhausen, Switzerland, built in 1755–7 by H. and J. U. Grubenmann (1709–83; 1707–81); the 104 m (340 ft.) Colossus Bridge over the Schuykill at Philadelphia, USA, completed by Louis Wernwag (1751–1821) in 1813; the Kew and Battersea bridges in LONDON; the timber arch viaducts built by John and Benjamin Green at NEWCASTLE-UPON-TYNE; and the many timber viaducts on the railways of the West of England designed by I. K. BRUNEL. A notable survivor, the Barmouth railway viaduct in North Wales, was saved from destruction by worms in the 1980s.

BIBLIOGRAPHY
General
Allen, 1957, 1959, 1970; American Society of Civil Engineers, 1976; Jackson, 1988; Pugsley, 1976; Ruddock, 1979.

wool The hair of sheep, goats, camels or other ruminant animals. Chemically it is a protein. Usually it is shorn or clipped annually from the animal, which need not be killed or skinned to furnish its wool. The pelt of a dead sheep may provide wool; in that case the skin is termed a 'fell' and the fleece is called pulled wool.

For wool preparation, *see* CARDING MACHINE; CARDING MILL; COMBING MACHINE; CONDENSER CARDING MACHINE; DEVIL; SLUBBING BILLY; WOOL STOVE.

BIBLIOGRAPHY
General
Bischoff, 1842; Burnley, 1889; Cole, 1926; Freudenberger, 1964; Heaton, 1920; James, 1857; Jenkins and Ponting, 1982; Lipson, 1953; Merrimack Valley Textile Museum, 1965; White, 1836.

woollens The term 'woollens' can be applied to any fabric woven from woollen yarn, but often, and particularly in England, it refers to fabrics made from short-staple (or short-fibred) wool, as distinct from WORSTED which is made from long-staple wool. Woollen yarn was prepared by carding so that the fibres were crossed and interlaced, and had high felting properties. In the mid-nineteenth century woollen yarn was spun on mules and most of the factories producing fine woollens were fully integrated.

BIBLIOGRAPHY
General
Beaumont, 1919; Bischoff, 1842; Heaton, 1965; Jenkins and Ponting, 1982; Lipson, 1953.

wool stove Wool and woollen fabrics cannot be bleached with chlorine, and the usual method of bleaching them in the eighteenth and nineteenth centuries was by wetting them and heating them in stoves with shallow pans of sulphur, known in Britain as wool stoves. Such structures remained in use for blanket making at Witney until the 1940s. A stove is also a building where wool is dried after scouring, or woollen cloth after FULLING, usually a long narrow building with wooden racks on which cloth was laid out, and with iron pipes to provide heating. Gloucestershire examples of the early nineteenth century were about 50 m (165 ft.) long. There were also circular cloth stoves in the form of stone towers, of which examples survive at FROME and at Melksham, 22 km (14 mi.) NE of Frome. A stove used for drying finished fabrics would probably be called a CLOTH STOVE.

BIBLIOGRAPHY
Specific
Tann, J. The bleaching of woollen and worsted goods, 1740–1860. In *TH*, I, 1969.

Worcester, Worcestershire, England The county town, on the River Severn. Porcelain manufacture was intro-duced in 1749; the present factory dates from 1792. Extensive displays can be seen in the Dyson Perrins Museum. Worcester is also celebrated for vinegar and sauce. The vinegar works at Lowesmoore, has a thirteen-bay, two-storey, red brick vat hall of the late nineteenth century. At Powick, 3 km (2 mi.) S., an early hydro-electric power built by the city corporation in 1894 worked until the 1920s, and some buildings remain.

BIBLIOGRAPHY
Specific
Tucker, D. G. Hydro-electricity for public supply in Britain. In *IAR*, I(2) 1977.

LOCATIONS
[M] Dyson Perrins Museum, Severn Street, Worcester WR1 2NE.
[M] Worcester City Museum, City Museum and Art Gallery, Foregate Street, Worcester WR1 1DT.

workhouse An English term for an establishment where the able-bodied unable to support themselves could find food and shelter in return for labour; the workhouse also provided accommodation for the old, sick, mad, orphaned, senile and illegitimate. A workhouse may also be called a House of Work, a House of Industry or a Poor House.

A change in attitudes to the destitute, leading to demands that relief should only be provided in return for work, can be observed in most West European countries in the sixteenth century, and the 'dépôts de mendicité' and 'alberghi dei poveri' of seventeenth- and eighteenth-century France and Italy had much in common with the workhouse. The work provided was usually of a simple nature, like spinning hemp or making nails, but had some economic importance in textile cities like Lyons and Bologna.

The English Poor Law 1601 obliged parish officials to provide work for the able-bodied poor and some work-houses were built in the seventeenth century, but an Act of 1722–3 formalized the right of parishes to erect workhouses, if appropriate in collaboration with other parishes, and to refuse relief to those who would not enter. Many were run by individuals on a contract basis. Larger establishments were built following the Act of 1786 promoted by Thomas Gilbert (1720–98) which encour-aged the parishes to work together on poor relief. Workhouse administration was criticized in the report on the Poor Law by Edwin Chadwick (1800–90) in 1832, and in the Poor Law Amendment Act 1834 relief was only to be given to the able-bodied inside the workhouse, where labour was to be 'less eligible' than that available elsewhere, and there was to be segregation of the sexes. The new law was unpopular and the many new work-houses were known as 'Bastilles'. Segregation of categor-ies proved less effective than had been anticipated, and most workhouses developed into hospitals for the chroni-cally sick and the senile, for which functions many remain in use.

At IRONBRIDGE 13 Belmont Road is a pre-1834 work-house that is now a private dwelling. One of the best preserved of the workhouses that followed the 1834 Act is

847

at Chipping Norton, Oxfordshire, a building on the panopticon principle, with an octagonal centre topped by a cupola, and radiating wings: it was designed by George Wilkinson (1814–90), with a chapel of 1856–7 by G. E. Street (1824–81).

In the USA 'workhouse' is a name applied from the 1880s to a prison or house of correction for petty offenders.

BIBLIOGRAPHY
General
Bagley, 1966; Checkland, 1973; Marshall, 1968; Poynter, 1969; Rose, 1971; Tate, 1969; Webb, 1929; Woolf, 1987.
Specific
Blaug, M. The myth of the old Poor Law and the making of the new. In *Journal of Economic History*, XXIII, 1963.
Blaug, M. The Poor Law Report re-examined. In *Journal of Economic History*, XXIV, 1964.
Coats, A. W. Economic thought and Poor Law policy in the 18th century. In *EcHR*, XIII, 1966.

BARRIE TRINDER

worsted   Well-twisted yarn made from long-staple (or long-fibred) WOOL, combed so that the fibres lie parallel to each other. It is employed in making HOSIERY and worsted cloth. Most suitings and speciality wool fabrics, including serge, crepe and gaberdine are worsteds. The term was used in the Middle Ages and derives from Worstead, a village 16 km (10 mi.) N. of Norwich. From *c*.1800 the chief centre of manufacture of worsted cloth was around BRADFORD, growth being particularly rapid in the 1830s. The worsted region was distinct from but contiguous with the Yorkshire WOOLLEN region whose centre was Leeds. Worsted spinning was less integrated with weaving than in the woollen trade, yarn being spun by modified WATER FRAMES called throstles rather than by SPINNING MULES.

BIBLIOGRAPHY
General
Beaumont, 1919; Bischoff, 1842; Heaton, 1965; James, 1857; Jenkins, 1975; Jenkins and Ponting, 1982; Lipson, 1953.

Wrexham, Clwyd, Wales   The principal town of the North Wales coalfield, where coal has been mined commercially since the seventeenth century. Bersham Ironworks was probably the first outside Coalbrookdale to convert from charcoal to coke, under Charles Lloyd in 1721. The works was run by the Wilkinsons from 1753: JOHN WILKINSON cast and bored cylinders for BOULTON & WATT from 1775, made armaments and built steam engines. The remains include an octagonal foundry, workers' housing, the furnace base, and the accounting house. Wilkinson also established an ironworks at Brymbo in 1795–8, of which a furnace of *c.* 1820 and earlier buildings survive. The works was rebuilt in 1885 as the first steelworks using the Thomas process (*see* GILCHRIST THOMAS). Brickmaking in the area from the nineteenth century used coal-measure clays, particularly for refractories, terracotta and faience. The works of J. C. Edwards (1828–96), in Ruabon, 8 km (5 mi.) SE,

specialized in bright red brick which was used throughout Britain from the 1860s until the 1940s and dominated local architecture.

BIBLIOGRAPHY
General
Riden, 1987; Trinder, 1981.
Specific
Stratton, M. The terracotta industry; its distribution, manufacturing process and products. In *IAR*, VIII, 1986.

LOCATION
[M,S] Bersham Industrial Heritage Centre, Bersham, Wrexham, Clwyd LL14 4HT.

PETER WAKELIN

Wrisbergholzen, Lower Saxony, Germany   The site of a faience factory, 20 km (12 mi.) SW of Hildesheim, which operated between 1734 and 1830 as part of a landed estate: it is one of the oldest manufacturing complexes in north-west Germany. Its buildings, essentially following regional architectural traditions, are grouped in three wings around a small courtyard, and are timber-framed, infilled with quarried stone. The manor house contains a room panelled with the large painted tiles produced in the factory, and showing emblematic figures.

BIBLIOGRAPHY
General
Mende and Hamm, 1990; Slotta, 1975–85.

Wrocław (Breslau), Wrocław, Poland   The principal city of Silesia, which ranked second after Berlin amongst the cities of Prussia before 1914. Wrocław stands on the River Oder, and on the railway from Berlin to Kraków.

The Jarhunderthall (People's Hall) was built in 1911–13 to the design of Max Berg, Trauer and Mayer, to commemorate the centenary of the Battle of Leipzig. It is a gigantic arched-ribbed structure of reinforced concrete, 67 m (220 ft.) in span, and can seat about 10 000 people. The building is in a self-consciously modern style and was seen as one of the great achievements of its time. It is now used as a sports hall and is open to the public as an example of the twentieth-century modernist style of architecture.

The waterworks in Na Grobli Street, in the eastern part of Wrocław, was established in 1867–71, and was originally designed to meet the needs of some 200 000 inhabitants. It consists of water intakes from the Odra, deep wells, filtration and water-treatment stations, and an intermediate pumping station. The outstanding feature is a monumental water tower which houses two richly ornamented 270 hp Wolf vertical double-compound engines of the 1870s, manufactured by the Ruffer Company in Wrocław. The upper part of the tower is occupied by two 21 000 m³ (750 000 cu. ft.) reservoirs. The tower is flanked by boiler houses which have been adapted to new uses. A scheme is in progress to convert the tower and steam engines into a museum. About 4 km (2.5 mi.) E. of the tower there is an intermediate pumping station of 1903, which feeds water from nearby wells to the waterworks. It remains in operation and has, apart from modern pumps, three horizontal Wolf steam engines driving plunger pumps, with a combined capacity of 60 000 m^3 (2.1 million cu. ft.) per day. In Wiśniowa Street is a water tower of 1905, richly decorated, with representations of traditional Germanic themes.

The Museum of Posts and Telecommunications dates from the first years of Polish independence in 1918. It was originally established in the building of the Head Office of Posts and Telegraphs in Warsaw in February 1919. During World War II the museum was destroyed but it was re-established in 1956 in the main post office of 1931 in Wrocław. It is the only establishment in Poland specializing in collecting items connected with posts and telecommunications. There are sections concerned with telegraphic apparatus, and with Morse equipment used between 1914 and 1950. There is Hungher apparatus from the inter-war period, a Wheatstone apparatus of 1857, a Greed teleprinter of 1950, and Baudat equipment of 1874. There are photographs and pictures, postal regulations, plans of postal connections, uniforms used by postmen in Poland, post boxes, post sign-boards, and scale models of mail coaches. The museum has a rich collection of postage stamps.

BIBLIOGRAPHY
Specific
50 lat Muzeum Poczty i Telekomunikacji 1921–71, Informator (50 years of the Museum of Posts and Telecommunications 1921–71, guidebook), 1971. Wrocław.
Śnieżko, A. *Muzeum Poczty i Telekomunikacji* (The museum of posts and telecommunications in Wrocław). Wrocław, 1965.

LOCATIONS
[M] Muzeum Poczty i Telekomunikacji (Museum of Posts and Telecommunications), ul. Krasińskiego 4, Wrocław.
[S] Hala Ludowa (The People's Hall), ul. Wróblewskiego, Wrocław.
[S] Zakłady Wodociągowe we Wrocławiu (Wrocław Waterworks), ul. Na Grobli, Wrocław.

PIOTR GERBER and JAN KĘSIK

wrought iron A commercially pure form of iron, containing virtually no carbon, and fibrous in texture due to threads of slag. It is the product of the BLOOMERY and, after development of the BLAST FURNACE, of the FORGE. Strong in tension, wrought iron can be welded, rolled (*see* ROLLING MILL), drawn, and shaped by hammering. Until the development of mild steel (*see* STEEL), it was the usual material for nails, locks and chains, for structural sections used in tension, and for machine parts. It was gradually superseded by mild steel from the mid-nineteenth century and is now manufactured only in museums (*see* IRONBRIDGE; SIELPIA WIELKA). Red or hot short iron has an excess of sulphur and tends to crumble when being worked hot. Cold short iron, with an excess of phosphorus, is brittle when worked cold.

BIBLIOGRAPHY
General
Gale, 1967, 1969.
Specific
Gordon, R. B. Metallography and the mechanical properties of wrought iron. In Ironbridge Institute, 1986.

Wuppertal, North Rhine-Westphalia, Germany Wuppertal was created in 1929 from the previously independent towns of Barmen and Elberfeld, and lies along an 18 km (11 mi.) stretch of the narrow valley of the River Wupper, to the north of Solingen and Remscheid. As early as 1850 it had more industries than any other town in Rhenish Prussia, with 236 textile firms, mostly manufacturing silk, cotton and silk-and-cotton ribbons and tapes. Yarn bleaching using the soft water of the Wupper and its tributaries was also a major industry from c.1400. There were over a hundred bleaching works by 1606. Linen and later cotton ribbon-weaving soon developed, and expanded rapidly after 1600 when the ribbon loom was introduced from the Netherlands.

The finishing of cloth stimulated the growth of an extensive chemical industry in the nineteenth century, originating in the dying of yarn, with a particular emphasis on the use of Turkish red. Friedrich Bayer and Friedrich Weskott founded a dyeworks in 1863. The development of synthetic dyes and the inventions of Carl Duisberg, who began working for Bayer in the fields of dyes and pharmaceuticals in 1883, were the beginning of a success story which was to cause the firm to move to the banks of the Rhine and sites well placed for transport facilities. It set up in Leverkusen in 1891, Dormagen in 1916, and Uerdingen in 1951, but the pharmaceuticals research department of this internationally famous firm remains in Wuppertal, as well as a pharmaceuticals and pesticides factory with 3500 employees.

The best way to appreciate the industrial archaeology of Wuppertal is to take the unique monorail, the Schwebebahn, which passes right over the Bayer works. The lack of level surfaces for transport in the narrow valley impelled the city to build an elevated railway even before 1900. It was constructed above the riverbed of the Wupper to a design by the Cologne entrepreneur and engineer Eugen Langen, as an overhead monorail supported by steel girders. Between 1898 and 1903 13.3 km (8 mi.) of track were built, with two carriage sheds, and twenty stations, mostly constructed above the river, and some preserved in their original condition. The city has other monuments relating to the history of transport, notably Elberfeld station, with its magnificent neo-Classical façade, built in 1846. The picturesque stations of Ottenbruch, Mirke and Loh were built along the Rhenish Railways line north of the Wupper in 1879. The high round-arched brick viaducts on this railway were built in the same year.

A historic industrial building in the Engelstrasse in Barmen now accommodates the Museum of Early Industrialization, which has exhibits showing the technical and social history of the industrial city of Wuppertal.

The three Wupper factories in Dahlerau, Vogelsmühle

Figure 178 The Schwebebahn in Wuppertal, with one of the monorail cars passing above the River Wupper.
Barrie Trinder

and Dahlhausen are living museums of textile history. They were built for cloth manufacturing between 1815 and 1900 and expanded many times. At Dahlerau there is a private works museum and a complete steam engine house of 1891. The main building of this factory, dating from 1836–72, retains its original construction with cast-iron columns and wooden beams, as well as interesting transmission systems, turbines and generators.

BIBLIOGRAPHY
General
Becker, 1980; Böse, 1948; Günter, 1970; Hoth, 1975; Schierk and Schmidt, 1976; Zeit, 1948.
Specific
Museum für Frühindustrialisierung: Materialienmappe (Museum of protoindustrialization: illustrative map). Wuppertal: Historisches Zentrum, n.d.

LOCATIONS
[M] Historisches Uhren-Museum (Historical Clock Museum), Postrasse 11, 5600 Wuppertal 1.
[M] Municipal Museum, Haus der Jugend, Geschwister Scholl Platz 6, 5600 Wuppertal.

AXEL FÖHL

Wyatt, Sir Matthew Digby (1820–77) An architect who trained in the office of his brother, T. H. Wyatt (1807–80), and set up on his own account from 1832. He was secretary to the executive committee of the Great Exhibition of 1851, and designed interiors for several of the courts in the Crystal Palace. His most significant works were for the GREAT WESTERN RAILWAY, including company housing at SWINDON, and Paddington station on which he worked with I. K. BRUNEL in 1854–5.

BIBLIOGRAPHY
General
Pevsner, 1950.

Wyoming, United States of America   Industrial history enthusiasts will be hard-pressed to spend a great deal of time in this wind-swept rectangle of mountains and plains, known fondly as 'the state of high altitudes and low multitudes'. Oil, natural gas, gold and uranium have been important extractive industries in Wyoming, but sheep-ranching and cattle-drives that pushed vast herds up from Texas for summer grazing have shaped the state's national reputation, immortalized in these lines from a cowboy refrain: 'Whoopee ti yi yo, git along little doggies for you know Wyoming will be your new home. . .'

Wyoming's Riverton Museum commemorates the state's mining, logging and trapping heritages, while the Saratoga Museum embraces the history of the transcontinental railway passing through the state, putting the city's Union Pacific locomotive depot of 1890 to a new but appropriate use.

Spanning the great North Platte River at Fort Laramie is the King Iron Bridge Company's three-span, 122 m (400 ft.) bowstring arch truss bridge of 1875, and at Cody and Alcova stand two impressive concrete arch dams from the experimental decade in concrete construction, the twentieth century's first. The 60 m (200 ft.) high Buffalo Bill Dam across the Shoshone River and the 66 m (218 ft.) Pathfinder Dam backing up the North Platte are both storage dams built for the irrigation needs of the vast Wyoming plain.

LOCATIONS
[M] Riverton Museum, 700 East Park, Riverton, WY 82501.
[M] Saratoga Museum, 106 Constitution Avenue, Saratoga, WY 82331.

DAVID H. SHAYT

X

xylonite A form of CELLULOID developed in Britain from Parkesine (*see* PLASTICS), capable of being worked into sheets, rods, tube and film. It was one of the most commonly used plastics of the 1930s and 40s. The Xylonite Company was formed in London in 1869.

BIBLIOGRAPHY
General
ICI, 1962; Kaufman, 1963; Yarsley and Couzens, 1945.

Y

yarn A continuous filament of drawn and twisted fibres: the primary product of the spinning process. It is used in knitting and the weaving of cloth.

Ymuiden, Noord Holland, The Netherlands One of the world's largest shipping locks, giving access to the North Sea Canal (Noordzeekanaal: *see* AMSTERDAM), was constructed in 1865–76 at Ymuiden, then called the 'cutting of Holland at its smallest' because the strip of dunes was then narrower than elsewhere. The Amsterdam Canal Company commissioned an English company to carry out the work. The piers, 1.5 km (1650 yd.) long, designed by an Englishman, were changed several times, and have been extended since. English workers who died during the project are buried at the Engelmundus churchyard in nearby Velsen. More than a thousand ships passed through the locks in the first year. Two cast-iron lighthouses of 1878 remain in use. The locks were restored after damage in World War II, when the Germans built an enormous submarine bunker on the south bank of the canal.

Shipping activity stimulated the growth of fishing and by 1900 Ymuiden was the largest fishing port in Europe. Four private fish auction houses competed until nationalization in 1902. Several refrigerated warehouses remain, one dating from 1911.

World War I stimulated the foundation of a national steel company, and on the north bank of the canal the Hoogovens blast furnace complex, which used easily imported raw materials, came into production in 1924, creating a whole new industrial landscape. Many old structures remain in use, including tidal and inland harbours, three gasholders, a cement factory of 1930 which uses blast furnace slag, two reinforced concrete watertowers of 1915, and more than 100 km (60 mi.) of industrial railway. Ymuiden is now the third port of the Netherlands.

BIBLIOGRAPHY
General
Balk, 1985.

JURRIE VAN DALEN

York, North Yorkshire, England A walled city, which became one of Britain's principal railway junctions. The station, with its curving glass and iron train sheds of 1872–7, is one of the most impressive in Britain. The National Railway Museum, a branch of the Science Museum, opened in 1975. Locomotives include the *Agenoria* of 1829, the LWNR *Columbine* of 1846, GNR *Atlantic* No. 251, GWR 2–8–0 No. 2818, and an LNER 4–6–2 *Mallard* which holds the world speed record for steam; they are displayed in a former locomotive depot. York Castle Museum, founded by John L. Kirk (1869–1940) in 1938, has reconstructed streets, and a valuable collection of tools and household artefacts.

New Earswick, 3 km (2 mi.) N., was an influential garden suburb, begun in 1902 by Joseph Rowntree (1836–1925), the Quaker chocolate manufacturer, with a trust being founded in 1904; houses were designed by RAYMOND UNWIN and Barry Parker.

BIBLIOGRAPHY
General
Rowntree, 1954; Simmons, 1986.
Specific
Brears, P. *The Dairy Catalogue.* York: York Castle Museum, 1979.
Brears, P. *The Kitchen Catalogue.* York: York Castle Museum, 1979.

LOCATION
[M] National Railway Museum, Leeman Road, York YO2 4XJ.
[M] York Castle Museum, Tower Street, York YO1 1RY.

Yorkshire Moors, England A national park, encompassing the Cleveland Hills where there are many mineral workings. The pithead complex of an iron ore mine survives at Skelton Park, 5 km (3 mi.) S. of Saltburn. At Rosedale, 18 km (11 mi.) NW of Pickering, there are two spectacular ranges of calcining kilns of the 1860s for iron ore. Rabbits still burrow in remnants of tips of red oxide dust, most of which was reclaimed in the 1920s. Alum quarries of 1672–1871 can be seen at Boulby, 12 km (7 mi.) E. of Saltburn. The North Yorkshire Moors Railway, from Grosmont to Pickering, is a preserved line with a collection of locomotives from the NER and the LNER, and coaches from the Great Central Railway and the Hull & Barnsley Railway.

BIBLIOGRAPHY
General
Harrison and Almond, 1978.

LOCATION
[S] North Yorkshire Moors Railway, Pickering Station, Pickering, North Yorkshire YO18 7AJ.

Yugoslavia Yugoslavia is a federal, multinational state,

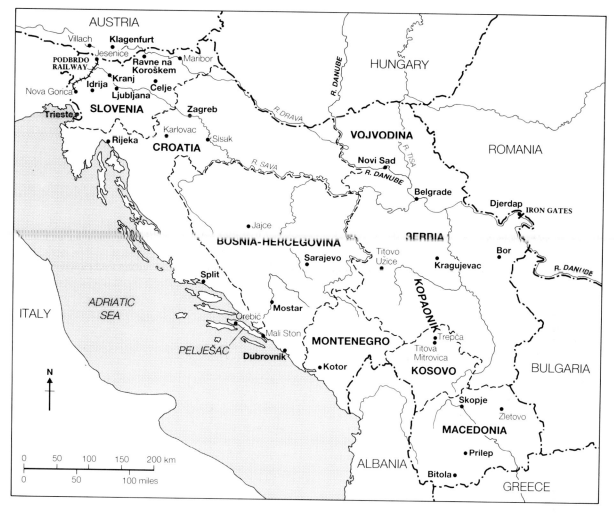

Yugoslavia

with a population of some 23 million, consisting of six socialist republics, Bosnia-Hercegovina, Croatia (Hrvatska), Macedonia (Makedonija), Montenegro (Crna Gora), Slovenia (Slovenija, Carniola) and Serbia (Srbija); within Serbia there are the autonomous provinces of Kosovo, which has a substantial Albanian population, and Vojvodina, where the predominant cultures are Hungarian and Slovak. Nearly 90 per cent of the population is Slavonic, but there are Romanian, Turkish, Bulgarian and Italian minorities.

Yugoslavia took its present form after World War I, and its constituent parts have undergone many political changes during the past three centuries. In 1650 most of present-day Yugoslavia was under Turkish rule. The North-West belonged to the Austrian Habsburgs, the coastal strip of Dalmatia with its offshore islands was under Venetian control, while Ragusa (later Dubrovnik) was effectively independent. The Habsburgs gained Croatia and Slovenia by the Treaty of Karlowitz of 1699, and later advanced their rule into Serbia, but in 1739 the

Turks regained the lands south of the Danube. Following national uprisings in the Napoleonic period the Serbs achieved internal self-government in 1830. Turkish garrisons were evacuated in 1867 and the independence of Serbia was recognized at the Congress of Berlin in 1876. Bosnia-Hercegovina was placed under Austrian control in 1878 and annexed in 1908. Montenegro had achieved a measure of self-government in 1796 and gained independence in 1878. With the creation of the dual monarchy of Austria-Hungary in 1867 (see AUSTRIA), Croatia became part of Hungary, with Fiume (see RIJEKA) serving as that country's outlet to the sea. The Kingdom of the Serbs, Croats and Slovenes emerged from the turmoils of the wars in 1918 and was renamed Yugoslavia in 1929. It consisted of Serbia and Montenegro, previously independent states, Bosnia-Hercegovina, Slovenia and Croatia which had been part of Austria-Hungary, and Macedonia, which had been under Turkish rule. The new country was dominated by the Serbs, and there were severe internal conflicts. In 1941 Yugoslavia was invaded by German forces, and much of its territory divided between surrounding states. A partisan movement under Josip Broz (Brod), later Marshal Tito (1892–1980), was established, and contributed substantially to the defeat of the Nazis in 1944–5. The Federal People's Republic of Yugoslavia was proclaimed, and a socialist constitution adopted in 1946. In 1948 Tito broke his alliance with the USSR, and Yugoslavia has since pursued a neutralist policy abroad. Differences over the frontier with Italy were resolved by successive agreements in 1947, 1954 and 1975.

The Yugoslav economy has undergone massive changes since the establishment of the socialist government after World War II. In 1939 75 per cent of the population were engaged in agriculture, a proportion reduced to less than 50 per cent by 1970.

Dams, watercourses, ruins of mills and even working mills are ubiquitous features of the landscape in Yugoslavia. Some windmills remain in Vojvodina, around Bačka Topola, 60 km (37 mi.) NW of Belgrade, and Orom, 75 km (46 mi.) W. of Belgrade, together with horse-driven mills used for grinding grain. In the North water mills with vertical wheels were employed from the Middle Ages, but in the south (see BITOLA) horizontal wheels in the Byzantine tradition drove grindstones directly. Sometimes many such mills were grouped together along a watercourse, as at Salona (see SPLIT), at Zrza (see PRILEP), or at Jajce, 105 km (65 mi.) NW of Sarajevo. An oil mill survives at Novi Kneževac, 135 km (84 mi.) N. of Belgrade. Forest products have always been important; in the 1930s there were 120 large sawmills in Croatia, Slovenia and Bosnia, 341 classified as of medium size and 1667 regarded as small.

Several retteries for flax remain, including one at Bački Petrovac, 90 km (55 mi.) NW of Belgrade. In nearby Vladimirovac is a large-scale horse-operated device of the early nineteenth century for raising water from wells. Traditional lime burning in conical kilns is still widely practised in Macedonia.

Salt has been produced on the Adriatic coast since classical times. The largest works are at Ston (see PELJEŠAC), Pag Island, 90 km (55 mi.) SE of Rijeka, and at Ulcinj, 150 km (95 mi.) SE of Dubrovnik. Salt warehouses of the eighteenth century remain at Stari Grade, 65 km (40 mi.) SE of Rijeka, and from the Napoleonic period at Portoroz, 24 km (15 mi.) SW of Trieste. Salt is produced by brine pumping at Tuzla, 150 km (95 mi.) W. of Belgrade.

Sugar has been made in Yugoslavia since the establishment of a cane refinery at Rijeka in 1751. Sugar manufacture from beet began early in the nineteenth century. There were nine beet refineries by 1927.

Traditional techniques of woollen manufacture are still employed in Macedonia (see BITOLA). The cultivation of silkworms was important by the seventeenth century, and in the eighteenth century there were manufacturing plants at LJUBLJANA and Maribor among other places. A woollen cloth manufactory was established in Ljubljana in 1725 and there was some development of cotton textiles in the mid-nineteenth century at Leskovac, 220 km (140 mi.) SE of Belgrade.

Yugoslavia produces substantial amounts of cotton, and there is a considerable tobacco industry based on Zletovo, 65 km (40 mi.) E. of Skopje, where there are innumerable tiny, square, brick sheds for drying and storing the crop. Yugoslavia has become a major wine exporter, and there are ancient and magnificent cellars at Maribor and at Kučevo, 100 km (60 mi.) SE of Belgrade.

Yugoslavia has important deposits of copper, bismuth, silver, mercury and bauxite. The principal concentrations of metallic ores are in Slovenia (see CELJE; IDRIJA; KRANJ); in Kosovo (see KOPAONIK) and around BOR in Serbia; and in Krotovo in Macedonia. Metallurgical industries have developed rapidly since 1945. In 1939 the output of pig iron was 667 000 tonnes per annum, a level that had risen to 5 million tonnes by the 1970s. Ironworking was widespread in earlier times. Coal extraction on a significant scale began in the eighteenth century, and was particularly important in the Istrian peninsula, from which coal was taken to the cities of Trieste and Rijeka. Oil has been extracted since 1885. The largest hydro-electric plants are those of 1947–52 on the Radica river.

Several important roads were built or improved during the Turkish occupation. The Carolinian Road from Karlovac to Rijeka was completed in 1726. In Dalmatia important road improvements were made in the Napoleonic period, while the roads in northern Serbia were improved in the late nineteenth century due to the initiative of Milan Obrenovic. Road building on a considerable scale was undertaken in the 1920s and 30s, while the modern route from Belgrade through Zagreb to Ljubljana was completed in 1950. Many notable bridges built by the Turks remain in use (see MOSTAR; SKOPJE).

Inland navigation has always centred on the Danube. There are now some 1900 km (1180 mi.) of navigable waterway in Yugoslavia. The River Drava is navigable for 138 km (86 mi.); the Sava for 595 km (370 mi.), to Sisak; and the Tisa (Theiss) for 764 km (475 mi.) to Tokay in Hungary, a distance shortened to 483 km (300 mi.) by drainage works between 1832 and 1879. The 123 km (76 mi.) canal from Bačko Gradište on the Tisa to the Danube near the present Hungarian border, variously called the Franzen, the Ferencz, the King Peter I or the Veliki Bačka canal, was built in 1795–1802. The lock at Bezdan, rebuilt in 1856, is claimed to be the first concrete lock in Europe. Another canal, the Ferencz Josef, King Alexander I or Mali canal, which is 69 km (43 mi.) long, was built in 1855–72 to link the Franzen Canal with the Danube at Novi Sad. This waterway was designed for irrigation and flood control, but in 1870 the Francis Canal Co. were given a 75-year concession to operate the navigation. They altered the Tisa end to terminate at Stari Bečej, and by 1914 were handling 432 990 tonnes of freight a year. The 74 km (46 mi.) Bega Canal, from the Tisa near its confluence with the Danube to Timişoara, then in Hungary but now in Romania, was completed in 1900. The Yugoslav government in the inter-war period carried out many improvements to inland navigation. The Sava was made navigable for standard Danube barges to Sisak, and further upstream for smaller vessels. Its tributaries, the Kupa and Una, were respectively made navigable 135 km (84 mi.) to Karlovac and 70 km (43 mi.) to Bosanski Novi. The Drava was made accessible for Danube barges to Osijek, and further for smaller craft. Danube barges operated up the Tisa to Csongrád in Hungary, with passenger services as far as Szeged. The canal system was disused after World War II but in 1947 the Danube–Tisa–Danube scheme began, for flood control and irrigation as well as navigation. It is based on the Bezdan–Bečej–Banatska (*see* IRON GATES) route, the former King Peter I Canal, and its 278 km (173 mi.) main route allows big barges to bypass the Danube's long loop through Belgrade.

Coastal shipping has always been important. Modern Yugoslavia has some 1500 km (900 mi.) of coastline, off which lie 914 islands. Shipyards are recorded from the Middle Ages, while that at Senj, 50 km (30 mi.) SE of Rijeka, was particularly important in the eighteenth century. The most important modern yards are at Rijeka and Pula.

Yugoslavia has some 10 000 route km (6200 mi.) of railways. The nature of the railway system was determined by the various administrations of the nineteenth century. In Croatia and Slovenia most lines were of standard gauge, while most in Bosnia-Hercegovina were of 76 cm (2 ft. 6 in.) gauge, those in Macedonia of 60 cm (2 ft.) gauge, and those in Serbia a mixture of standard and narrow gauge. Railway building continued in the 1920s and 30s, and while many narrow-gauge lines and routes have closed, having ceased to be viable because of frontier changes, construction has continued in the post-war period, the most notable achievement being the 476 km (296 mi.) line from Belgrade to the Adriatic at Bar, commenced in 1952 and completed in 1976. One of the most notable engineering works is the 7.975 km (4.95 mi.) tunnel near Hrusica on the Austrian border. Tramway systems were built in Belgrade, Osijek, Dubrovnik, Ljubljana, Niš, Novi Sad, Sarajevo, Subotica and Zagreb.

Yugoslavia suffered severely in World War II. There are few remains of major industrial plants predating the war but in the remoter regions are some outstanding survivals of pre-industrial manufacturing technology. There is a well-developed network of regional museums, and ten OPEN-AIR MUSEUMS have been opened following a recommendation by the Minister of Art and Culture in 1949.

The economy of Yugoslavia has always presented sharp contrasts. The mineral-rich Alpine areas of Slovenia have been as prosperous as adjacent parts of Austria and Italy, and were exposed for many centuries to cultural influences emanating from Vienna. At the other extreme is Macedonia, whose economy stagnated under centuries of Turkish rule: it remains one of the least developed parts of Europe, although one where extraordinary survival of pre-industrial manufacturing techniques can still be observed. Many villages still appear to outsiders to be like folk museums, and age-old crafts are still practised in the cities.

See also BELGRADE; BITOLA; BOR; CELJE; DJERDAP; DUBROVNIK; IDRIJA; KOPAONIK; KOTOR; KRAGUJEVAC; KRANJ; LJUBLJANA; MOSTAR; NOVI SAD; PELJEŠAC; PODBRDO RAILWAY; PRILEP; RAVNE NA KOROŠKEM; RIJEKA; SARAJEVO; SKOPJE; SPLIT; ZAGREB.

BIBLIOGRAPHY
General
Hadfield, 1986; Hudson, 1972; Milward and Saul, 1973; Savez Muzehskih Drustava Jugoslavije, 1962; Schneider, 1963; Zippelius, 1974.
Specific
Han, V. Regional and local museums in Yugoslavia. In *Museum*, XIV, 1961.

JERZY ROZPĘDOWSKI and BARRIE TRINDER

Yukon territory, Canada   Gold nuggets were found at Bonanza Creek on the Klondike River, a tributary of the Yukon, in 1898, and stimulated the last of the great gold rushes. A substantial mining industry developed in the wake of the prospectors, and the region was designated a separate territory within the Canadian federation in 1898. Several mines still operate at Bear Creek near Dawson, and the region is rich in industrial archaeology.

Dawson, capital of the territory until 1953, is an impressive mining town, restored by the Canadian Parks Service. The narrow-gauge White Pass & Yukon Railway connects Carcross in the south of the territory, where the tracks cross a wooden Howe truss swing bridge, with Skagway in ALASKA. Many of the region's transport needs were met by wooden, stern-wheel paddle steamers, of which preserved examples include the 1041-ton *Tutshi* 1917 at Carcross, the 1020-ton *Klondike* of 1937 at Whitehorse, and the 422-ton *Keno* of 1922 at Dawson. A vast dredge built in 1941 for the Yukon Consolidated Gold Co. is preserved at Bonanza Creek. Douglas DC3 airliners operate 'flightseeing' tours from Dawson.

BIBLIOGRAPHY
General
Phillips, 1967.

LOCATIONS
[I] Atlas Tours, 5th Floor, 609 West Hastings, Vancouver BC, V6B 4W4.
[M,S] Dawson City Historic Sites, Dawson City, Yukon Territory, Y0B 1G0.
[M] Dawson City Museum, Old Territorial Administration Building, 5th Avenue, Dawson City, Yukon Territory, Y0B 1G0.

DERYCK HOLDSWORTH

Z

Zaandam, Noord Holland, The Netherlands   The River Zaan, which joins the Y north-west of Amsterdam, was one of the principal centres of wealth in the Netherlands in the seventeenth and eighteenth centuries, its industries epitomizing the success of the Dutch in importing materials from all over the world, adding value to them by using wind power as well as skill, and selling the finished products in international markets. A visitor in 1789 described the 9 km (6 mi.) of the river valley upstream from its confluence with the Y as 'one of the greatest magazines of ships' timbers and naval stores in Europe', and counting nearly three hundred windmills. In the 1860s Zaandam was said to consist of a line of four hundred windmills, some of gigantic size, with the surrounding villages forming a street nearly 8 km (5 mi.) long. Wind power was used for grinding corn, pumping water from the polders, sawing timber, making paper, chopping tobacco, making oil, grinding colours for paints, crushing sandstone to make cleaning powder, and grinding volcanic rock from Andernach on the Rhine to produce HYDRAULIC CEMENT.

Zaandam declined under the French occupation but revived after the opening of the North Sea Canal (Noordzeekanaal: *see* AMSTERDAM) to which it has a direct connection. At Wormer, 4 km ($2\frac{1}{2}$ mi.) N. along the Zaan, is a concentration of multi-storey factories and concrete silos. The Veerdijk in Wormer still offers a unique view even after the demolition of bark-peeling mills and warehouses in 1979. Remaining buildings were protected in 1985 and include three wooden warehouses of 1875–80; warehouses with impressive cast-iron columns of the 1890s, named Batavia, Saigon, Bassein, Donau, and Koningsbergen; the Mercurius warehouse of 1919, with joist-less concrete floors integral with the frame; the Hollandia peeling mill of 1877 and 1913; and the Lassie concrete silo, 36.5 m (120 ft.) high, of 1912. Several buildings have been successfully adapted to new uses, including the Verkade chocolate factory of 1886 and a chemical works in 1913 in Zaandam, and the Adelaar soapworks of 1906 in Wormerveer.

The principal concentration of preserved mills is at the Zaanse Schans Museum, 3 km (2 mi.) N. of Zaandam, where on the west bank of the river, upstream from the Juliana bridge, an eighteenth-century mustard mill, a polder mill of 1869, a colour mill of 1781 and an oil mill of 1676 have been preserved in an open-air museum. On either side of the bridge stand the corn mill *De Bleeke Dood* of 1656 on the west bank and the oil mill *De Ooievaar* of 1622 on the east bank. An oil mill is preserved at Koog aan den Zaan, where there is also a Mill Museum in an eighteenth-century house. A grocer's shop of 1887 and the cottage where Tsar Peter the Great of Russia stayed incognito with a local boatbuilder in 1697 are preserved in Zaandam.

BIBLIOGRAPHY
General
Ireland, 1795; Murray, 1865.

LOCATIONS
[S] De Zoeker (Oil Mill), Kalverringdijk 31, Zaandam.
[S] Het Pink (Oil Mill), Pinkstraat 12, Koog aan den Zaan.
[M] Molen Museum (Mill Museum), Museumlaan 18, Koog aan den Zaan.
[M] Museumwinkel Albert Heyn (Shopping Museum) Kalverringdijk 5, Zaandam.
[S] Tsar Peter's Cottage, Krimp 23, Zaandam.
[M] Zaanse Schans, Kalverringdijk 25, Zaandam.

JURRIE VAN DALEN and BARRIE TRINDER

Zabrze, Katowice, Poland   A museum of coal mining, administered by the Ministry of Mining and Power, 15 km (9 mi.) W. of Katowice. It was established in 1979, when it took over some exhibits from the museum at Sosnowiec. The history section includes collections of lamps, tools, cutting machinery, underground transport equipment, draining and ventilation apparatus, miners' uniforms, and banners of miners' unions and associations. A section on the industrial uses of coal illustrates coke-making and various chemical processes involving coal. A third section is concerned with mining culture. The museum has a branch at the M-300 pilot mining plant, formerly the 'Guido' mine, where disused workings from the 1860s are accessible.

BIBLIOGRAPHY
General
Jaros, 1973; Maisner-Nieduszyńska and Pawłowski-Wilde, 1986.

LOCATION
[M] Muzeum Górnictwa Węglowego (Museum of Coal Mining), Zabrze, ul. 3 Maja 19, Zabrze.

Zagreb, Croatia, Yugoslavia   The capital of Croatia: a city of nearly half a million, on the River Sava. As well as an extensive tramway system, Zagreb has a rack railway of 1888 to the upper parts of the city. The city is an important textile centre, with technical and ethnographic museums dealing with the whole of Yugoslavia.

LOCATIONS
[M] Ethnographical Museum, Mazuranic trg 14, 41000-Zagreb.

[M] Museum of Arts and Handicrafts, Trg marsala Tita 10, 41000-Zagreb.

[M] Museum of Postal Services, Telegraphs and Telephones, ul.Juriseceva 13, 41000-Zagreb.

[M] Technical Museum, Savska c.18, 41000-Zagreb.

Zalaegerszeg, Zala, Hungary   The centre of the richly wooded Göcsej region between Lake BALATON and the Austrian border. Oil and natural gas were discovered in 1937, and production rapidly expanded during the first five-year plan (*see* HUNGARY). Development of the industry is shown in an open-air museum, with well-drilling and pumping rigs, a nodding-donkey pump, and gas separators. The traditional fabrics of the region are displayed in the Göcsej Museum.

LOCATIONS

[M] Göcsej Museum, H-8900 Zalaegerszeg

[M] Hungarian Oil Industry Museum, H-8900 Zalaegerszeg, Falumuzeum u.

Zeeland, The Netherlands   The arms of Zeeland show a lion struggling to escape from the sea, perfectly symbolizing the history of a province where many acres of fertile land have been reclaimed since the Middle Ages. The Delta Works project has dammed off estuaries and raised dikes to prevent repetition of the disaster of 1953, when breaches of the dikes caused floods and resulted in the loss of 1850 lives. The coastline between Zeeland and GRONINGEN which, including the Zuiderzee, extended for some 1900 km (1200 mi.) in 1840, is now reduced to about 600 km (400 mi.). Only the Westerschelde firth, the shipping route to Antwerp, and the Nieuwe Waterweg to ROTTERDAM remain tidal. A centre interpreting the Delta Works is located by the storm surge barrier of 1986 in the Oosterschelde firth.

In the nineteenth century the inhabitants of the islands that are now connected to the mainland by the Delta Works were largely concerned with agriculture and fishing. Several small harbours for shipping wool, madder, sugar beet and flax remain. The island of Schouwen-Duiveland became orientated towards Rotterdam, and was linked with the city from 1900 by a tramway: the tramway was severed in the flood of 1953, although a depot of 1900 remains at Brouwershaven, and a station of 1915 at Haamstede. On the coast near Haamstede is the West Schouwen lighthouse of 1837–40, more than 50 m (165 ft.) high. Its original lanthorn is preserved on the nearby harbour wall. The modest control tower and terminal of Haamstede airstrip were built in 1931 to improve communication with Rotterdam, and are now used as a hotel. The museum at Zierikzee, 12 km ($7\frac{1}{2}$ mi.) E., deals with the gathering of shellfish and the manufacture of sea salt.

The port of Flushing (Vlissingen) on Walcheren island, Napoleon's 'pistol to England's breast', has been a packet station since 1871 when a dam between Walcheren and Zuid Beveland enabled the establishment of railway connections. At Westkapelle, 20 km (13 mi.) NW, is the Noorderhoofd lighthouse of 1875, a round cast-iron, structure, by the Nering Bögel foundry.

On Zuid Beveland is a partly open watertower of 1910, once part of the country's first regional waterworks. From Goes a 16 km (10 mi.) preserved railway to Oudelande operates from a locomotive depot of 1924. On Tholen is a watertower, once known to the island's Calvinists, who preferred pure rainwater, as 'the pope with the red hat'.

Zeeuws-Vlaanderen, between the Belgian border and Westerschelde firth, can only be reached by boat or through Belgium. It developed from marshes in the sixteenth century. It is mostly rural, except for the industrial zone between the harbour at Terneuzen and the frontier. The Ghent–Terneuzen Canal, with two sea locks at Terneuzen of 1825–7, was initiated by King William I to stimulate the Ghent cotton industry before the separation of Belgium and the Netherlands. A third lock, for ships up to 10000 tonnes, which remains in standby use, was completed in 1910. Since the lifting of the Schelde tolls in 1863 the canal and locks have been enlarged several times to admit larger ships, from 1968 up to 60000 tonnes. Since 1900 the chemical industry has flourished in the canal zone, with the growth of a large nitrogen plant on the east bank, which had five large concrete buildings of the 1920s. A coke plant of 1911 was built to supply blast furnaces at Zelzate over the Belgian border. At the border town of Sas-Van-Gent are two sugar refineries of 1872 and 1899, flour mills, and glass and chemical plants, all with buildings from the early twentieth century. A steam compressor of 1926, once used for driving sugar-beet conveyor belts, is preserved by the municipality. On the coast, 3 km (2 mi.) W. of Breskens, is the 22 m (72 ft.) Nieuwe Sluis cast-iron lighthouse of 1866.

BIBLIOGRAPHY

General

Groen and Schmeink, 1985.

LOCATIONS

[M] Delta Expo, Neeltje Jans-Island, Burgh-Haamstede.

[M] Maritime Museum Zierikzee, Mol 15, Zierikzee.

[S] Stichting-Stoomtram Goes-Borsele (Goes-Borsele Steam Train Society), Postbus 250, Goes.

JURRIE VAN DALEN

Zeitz, Saxony-Anhalt, Germany   Since the seventeenth century, the main source of energy in eastern Germany has been LIGNITE or brown coal. It was mined from deep pits between c.1880 and 1925, from which period a headstock has been preserved at the Paul II mine in Theissen, but since then it has come mainly from OPEN CAST mining. North of the town of Zeitz, which has a mining section in its municipal museum, there is a whole complex of monuments of lignite mining, with subsidences from deep mining around the Paul II headstock, and relics illustrating the open-cast mining of the later period. Protected monuments illustrating the processing of the coal include the Groitzschen extraction plant, which used the Rolle process to extract tar, paraffin and other by-products from brown coal. The plant began operation in 1890 and is the last of its kind in the world. The Zeitz

857

briquette factory of 1889 contains the oldest preserved briquette press, which dates from 1883. The former DDR was the world's biggest producer of brown coal, with an output of 260 million tonnes a year in 1970, compared with 180 million tonnes in the USSR and 108 million tonnes in West Germany. The preserved plants provide a record of the history of the brown coal industry up to 1945.

BIBLIOGRAPHY
General
Berger, 1980; Schmidt and Theile, 1989; Wagenbreth and Wächtler, 1983.

LOCATION
[M] Municipal Museum, Schloss Moritz, 4900 Zeitz.

AXEL FÖHL

zinc (Zn)   An elemental metal. In the seventeenth and eighteenth centuries it was used, primarily in the form of CALAMINE, in the manufacture of brass; but with the development of GALVANIZING in the mid-nineteenth century demand for zinc greatly increased. Zinc alloy die-castings were much used from the 1930s. The ores, principally calamine and zinc blende (sphalerite), are usually found in association with LEAD and are worked in a similar manner. The principal source in Europe was formerly Kelmis (*see* VIEILLE MONTAGNE) but the USA, Canada and Australia are now the chief producers, together with an important deposit at Ammeberg, Sweden. Separation of lead and zinc ores by differential flotation was developed at Broken Hill, Australia, from 1922.

Metallic zinc is difficult to produce since the metal has a low boiling point and easily vaporizes. William Champion of Bristol was the first to smelt the metal on a commercial scale in the 1730s, the process remaining secret till the 1790s. Calamine and carbon were mixed in an enclosed fireclay crucible, and zinc vapour was distilled through an iron pipe in the bottom. A method using horizontal retorts was introduced by Jean Jacques Daniel Dony (*see* VIEILLE MONTAGNE) in the Liège area in 1806. Later in the nineteenth century vertical retorts were used. An electrothermic process was introduced in 1931, and electrolysis is now used. Some zinc is now smelted in blast furnaces like the 'Imperial Smelter' employed at Avonmouth, Bristol.

See also SPELTER.

BIBLIOGRAPHY
General
Ferrner, 1986; Jones, 1950; Richardson, 1974; Street and Alexander, 1949.

IVOR J. BROWN and BARRIE TRINDER

Zonguldak, Zonguldak, Turkey   The coal basin around Zonguldak on the Black Sea, 200 km (125 mi.) N. of Ankara, is the richest in the Mediterranean region. In some places there are fifty seams, giving a total thickness of 70 m (230 ft.) of coal. The area was first explored by Uzun Mehmet, who took samples to the royal palace in

1829. Responsibility for the mines was given to an exploitation company in 1848, and foreign investment followed. In 1940 the mines were nationalized and operated first by Etibank (*see* TURKEY) and then by Turkish Coal Enterprises. In 1865 production had reached 50000 tonnes per annum; by 1890 it was 150000 tonnes; in 1920, 400000 tonnes; by 1940, a million tonnes; and by 1969, 7.3 million tonnes. The coal is used in industrial plants, for firing railway locomotives and ships, and for domestic purposes.

In recent years eight large collieries have been in operation working seams that are generally very steep, sometimes using methods more common in metalliferous mining (*see* STOPING). Until 1952 only wood was used for underground supports, and ponies were universally used for underground haulage. Recently metal supports, modern forms of haulage and mechanized mining methods have been introduced. On the surface can be found the remains of steam winding engines of the second half of the nineteenth century by such manufacturers as Fraser Chalmers and the Mold Foundry.

BIBLIOGRAPHY
Specific
Ganey, M. Underground operations at Zonguldak coalfield, Turkey. In *The Mining Engineer*, 1967.
Mining Annual Review (London), 1982.

IVOR J. BROWN

Zurich, Zürich, Switzerland   Zurich is more celebrated as a financial than as a manufacturing centre, but the city and the canton of which it is capital contain one of the most interesting concentrations of industrial monuments in Europe. The city is situated at the north end of Lake Zürich, where the River Limmat flows out of the lake, to be joined by the Sihl 2 km (1 mi.) downstream.

Zurich has always been an important transport centre. The steamers *Stadt Rapperswil* of 1914 and *Stadt Zürich* of 1909, both restored with their original saloon fittings, work from the quay at Zürich-Wollishofen. The main station, Zürich Hauptbahnhof, originally the Nordostbahnhof, designed by J. F. Wanner and based on the concept of Gottfried Semper in 1861–71, is one of the most ornate in Europe. The main entrance is a triumphal arch, flanked by pavilions, with the train shed beyond, originally of nine but now of seven bays, with ridge and furrow roofs. Since 1894 trains have approached the station across viaducts over 800 m (2600 ft.) long of composite stone and iron construction. The aerodrome at Dübendorf, 6 km (4 mi.) NE, was Switzerland's most important airfield from the pioneering days of aviation until World War II. Several wooden-roofed hangars remain from the early twentieth century, together with an arched-roofed hangar of mixed construction of 1923, and an arched concrete hall, all now in military use, one containing the Swiss Air Force Museum. Three Junkers-52 airliners make regular pleasure flights from Dübendorf. Zurich retains an extensive network of electric tramways.

At Zürich-Wipkingen, an industrial quarter on the banks of the Limmat, north-west of the city centre, the former Hofmeister cotton-printing works is now a technical school. A 'Stadtkuche', a municipal soup kitchen for the poor, remains within the former Esslinger cotton-printing works, built in 1786. At Zürich-Wollishofen, on the west bank of the lake 2 km (1 mi.) S., the so-called 'red factory', a silk-weaving mill of 1893 designed by Carl Arnold Sequin, is now a cultural centre.

The industrial archaeology trail through the Zürich Oberland provides a means of exploring what was once one of Europe's principal textile-manufacturing regions, with many cotton- and silk-factory complexes, set in parkland with the owners' villas and workers' dwellings. Most are now adapted to new uses. The trail begins at the landing stage at Uster, 11 km (7 mi.) SE of Zurich on the Greifensee, and extends through Wetzikon to Bauma, 24 km (15 mi.) E. At Niederuster on the shore of the Griefensee is a magnificent complex of industrial buildings, constructed as a silk-throwing factory from 1853, and including housing for owners and workers. From 1907 until 1917 it was used for the manufacture of Turicum motor cars, and is now owned by an engineering concern. In Uster stands the first big spinning mill constructed by Heinrich Kunz, rebuilt in its present five-storey, fifteen bay form in 1831-4. A crèche building designed to accommodate the children of women workers (which still operates) and an apartment block for spinster workers also remain. Uster brewery, designed by Emanual Walcher in 1897-1901 has a steam engine of 1897 and is preserved by the municipality. Wetzikon, 6 km (4 mi.) SE of Uster, stands on the stream which flows from the Pfäffikon into the Greifensee. Its industrial monuments include the Stegenmühle, a water-powered copper mill, later an engineering works and now a cultural centre, and a small machine embroidery works of 1877, a two-storey building in polychrome brick. At Unteraathal, 2 km (1 mi.) NW of Wetzikon, is a five-storey cotton mill built by Heinrich Kunz in 1851: it worked until 1971 and is being adapted to new uses. In the Chämtnertobel gorge, 3 km (2 mi.) E. of Wetzikon, there were three transmission towers built to take a cable drive from turbines to weaving mills on a shoulder above the valley. At Stockrüti, 6 km (4 mi.) E. of Wetzikon, a water-powered sawmill is operated by the Vereins zur Erhaltung alter Handwerks- und Industrie-Anlagen im Zürcher Oberland (VEHI), an organization formed in 1979 to preserve manufacturing and industrial traditions in the region. Another sawmill, in an elegant building of 1794, is at Kempten, 2 km (1 mi.) NW of Wetzikon, at the mouth of the Chämtnertobel gorge. At Neuthal, 7 km (4 mi.) NE of Wetzikon, is a factory complex of 1827, including a spinning mill and the owner's house, workers' housing, three reservoirs, and a crenellated turbine house of the late nineteenth century, with a rope wheel drive system. It forms one of the most impressive textile complexes in Switzerland. The trail concludes at Bauma, 8 km (5 mi.) NE of Wetzikon, a former textile manufacturing town, which is the terminus of the preserved railway to Hinwil, 8 km (5 mi.) SW.

At Stäfa, 20 km ($12\frac{1}{2}$ mi.) SE of Zurich on the shores of Lake Zürich, is the Mies cotton factory, perhaps the finest weaving manufactory in Switzerland. At Käpfnach-

Horgen, 15 km (9 mi.) S., also on the lake, there are plans to open a former coal mine to the public.

The Tiefenbrunnen mill in Zurich was the last roller flour mill in Switzerland working entirely by mechanical power transmission. Some of its machinery dates from 1913. It is now a protected monument.

Zurich's municipal abattoir, built in 1905-9, had the reputation of being the best equipped in Switzerland. In the early 1980s it was restored and new buildings added in a style that blended with the old.

Several important early power stations can be seen in the city and canton. The old municipal power station of 1892 has been preserved, with the Letten canal from which it gained its power. Other preserved power stations are at Ottenbach, 14 km (9 mi.) SW, with Francis turbines and generators of 1920, and Bülach-Herrenwies, 16 km (10 mi.) N.

The Schweizerisches Landesmuseum (Swiss National Museum) includes important collections relating to mill-wrighting and water power.

BIBLIOGRAPHY
General
Bärtschi, 1983.
Specific
Bärtschi, H.-P. Industriearchäologie im Zürcher Oberland (Industrial Archaeology in the Zürich Oberland). In *Schweiz*, 11, 1985.

LOCATIONS
[S] Aerodrom Museum, Dübendorf, Zurich.
[M] Electric Power Station, Zurich-Höngg, Werdinsel, Zurich.
[M] Mühlerama Cornmill Museum, Seefeldstrasse 231, 8008 Zurich.
[M] Museum of Applied Art, Ausstellungstrasse 60, 8003 Zürich.
[M] Swiss National Museum, Museumstrasse 2, 8023 Zürich.

HANS-PETER BÄRTSCHI

Zwolle, Overijssel, The Netherlands   A Hanseatic town (*see* GERMANY) ringed by seventeenth-century canals: it served as an entrepôt for trade between the Netherlands and North Germany, and in the mid-eighteenth century as a base for carts which carried goods all over Germany. Zwolle had a direct link to the Yssel from 1819 with the completion of the Willemsvaart, a canal. The double locks, the Katerveersluis, south-west of the centre, are protected but no longer used.

Zwolle is an important railway centre, with a bridge of 1862 over the Yssel, a station of 1868 with its original platform awnings, a railway workshop of the 1870s now used by the Stork company, and a lenticular truss bridge of 1883 over the marshalling yard.

Kampen, 12 km ($7\frac{1}{2}$ mi.) W., is a port on the Yssel delta which flourished in the Middle Ages and entered the Hanseatic League in 1441. Over five hundred monuments in the town are listed. Kampen became an industrial town in the nineteenth century, notable for its cigar factories, and for many workers' dwellings where domestic manufacture took place because the factories lacked room to expand. There is a Tobacco Museum (Tabaksmuseum), and the once steam-powered De Olifant factory remains in operation, producing over a hundred types of tobacco. Features include a drying kiln, original warehouses, and remains of the steam engine. Modern techniques are used in an adjacent coffee factory whose building dates from 1906. A Bailey bridge (*see* FLOATING BRIDGE), a legacy of World War II, links the railway terminus of 1911 with the city.

Genemuiden, 16 km (10 mi.) NW, is a fishing port on the Zwarte Water (Zwartemeer), with a complete sluice of 1866 designed to protect the town against the Zuiderzee, together with a rolling bridge. The traditional manufacture was rush matting, and industrial matting and carpets are still made, giving employment to about a third of the population. The Mastenbroek pumping station at Kamperzeedijk, 4 km (2$\frac{1}{2}$ mi.) SW, has a horizontal steam engine of 1856 by the Atlas works of Amsterdam with a 7.5 m (24 ft. 8 in.) diameter flywheel and a Lancashire boiler of 1925. Until 1961 it worked a scoop wheel system which could raise up to 500 m³ (110 000 gall.) water per minute. East of Kamperzeedijk is the Rambonnet pumping station of 1897, and to the north is a diesel pumping station of 1927, the last to be built in the Netherlands. At Hasselt, 6 km (4 mi.) S., shell lime is commercially produced in three limekilns, renovated in 1982.

At Deventer, a Hanseatic town 25 km (15 mi.) S. of Zwolle on the Yssel, a carpet mill of 1907 remains in use. Several early-twentieth-century cigar factories have been put to new uses; along the river is an enormous late-nineteenth century flour-mill complex; while in Raamstraat are buildings of a contemporary chemical plant, and in Bergstraat the remnants of the Nering Bögel iron foundry.

At Dedemsvaart, 25 km (15 mi.) NE of Zwolle, is a preserved gasholder; while at Staphorst, 16 km (10 mi.) N., are two flourishing early-twentieth-century creameries where milk is still delivered in churns by members of co-operatives.

BIBLIOGRAPHY
General
Dekkers and Wiersma, 1986; Feis and Nijhof, 1983.

LOCATIONS
[M] Het Gotisch Huis (The Gothic House municipal museum), Oudestraat 158, Kampen.
[M] Nederlands Tapijtmuseum (Netherlands Carpet Museum), c/o Fabrieksstraat 13, Genemuiden.
[M] Provinciaal Overijssels Museum (Overijssel Provincial Museum), Voorstraat 34, Zwolle.
[S] Schelpkalkbranderij (Shell lime factory), Kalkovenseweg 3, Hasselt.
[S] Stoomgemaal Mastenbroek (Mastenbroek Steam Pump), Kamperzeedijk.
[S] Stoomtabakskerverij De Olifant (Elephant Steam Tobacco Works), Voorstraat 106, Kampen.
[M] Tabaksmuseum (Tobacco Museum), Botermarkt 3, Kampen.

JURRIE VAN DALEN

Żyrardów, Skierniewice, Poland   A textile centre, 50 km (30 mi.) SW of Warsaw. Flax-spinning and weaving mills were set up on this site in 1832–3, and the town of Żyrardów was named after Filip Girard, inventor of the first spinning machine for flax to be used in Poland. By 1900 Żyrardów was one of the principal centres of the flax industry in Europe, and the present-day flax plant continues to use the nineteenth-century buildings, some of which are under legal protection. The housing for the factory workers, built in the 1870s, is of great interest and contains many innovatory planning features. Some 95 per cent of the original buildings remain in use: 130 houses, eighteen shops and workshops, and some sixty other buildings. Żyrardów is an important example of a settlement from the time of the Industrial Revolution, containing as it does many features typical of twentieth-century planning ideals.

BIBLIOGRAPHY
Specific
Kubiak, J. *Żyrardów-osada fabryczna* (Żyrardów: industrial settlement). In *Spotkania z Zabytkami* (Encounters with Historical Monuments), 6, 1981.

Appendix: Guide to Contents by Subject

The articles on technology and on other aspects of industrial archaeology which are not site-specific (See Introduction p. xvii) have been planned in eighteen sections, with a selection of biographies in addition. The sections are set out below, and are sub-divided where appropriate.

1. TRANSPORT

1.1. Air transport

Structures and installations
aircraft beacon
aircraft
air-traffic control
control tower
hangar
radar

Aircraft
aeroplane
aircraft factory
aircraft museum
airliner
airship
balloon
flying boat

1.2. Sea transport

Seagoing vessels
clipper
dredger
ferry
hulk
iron ship
Liberty ship
lighter
liner
motor vessel
oil tanker
packet boat
paddle steamer
sailing ship
schooner
screw propulsion
ship canal
steamship
tender
tramp steamer
tug
turbine propulsion

Locations of historic vessels
Falkland Islands
maritime museum
Punta Arenas
South Georgia

Structures
breakwater
chandler
crane
customs house
dock
dry dock
fishing port
hydraulic power
lighthouse
lightship
pier
port
victualling yard
warehouse
whaling
wharf

1.3. Inland navigation

Types
canal
river navigation
ship canal

Structures and installations
accommodation bridge
aqueduct
boat lift
caisson
canal tunnel
chain haulage
flash lock
inclined plane
lock
pound lock
sluice
stop lock

Vessels
barge
ferry
flat
keel
narrow boat
packet boat
péniche
raft
starvationer
tow
tub boat

1.4. Rail transport

Types of railway
atmospheric railway
broad-gauge railway
cliff railway
double way
funicular
gravity railway
guide-wheel railway
hybrid railway
industrial railway
interurban
metro
monorail
narrow-gauge railway

plateway
rack railway
railroad
railway
tramway
tube railway
underground railway
wagonway

Railway installations and structures
ballast
capstan
coal drop
cross-tie
gauge
junction
loading gauge
locomotive depot
marshalling yard
railway bridge
railway freight depot
railway hotel
railway station
railway tunnel
roadhouse
signal box
sleeper
staithe

Railway motive power
Beyer Garrett
condensing locomotive
dandy cart
diesel locomotive
electric locomotive
Fairlie, Robert
fireless locomotive
Mallett
petrol locomotive
Sentinel
steam locomotive
switcher
tank locomotive
tender

Railway vehicles
air brake
caboose
chaldron
clerestory
hund
Hungarian hund
multiple unit
Pullman, George
railcar
railway carriage
railway wagon
Reisen
restaurant car
royal carriage

sleeping car
travelling post office
vacuum brake
wagon-lit

Railway preservation
preserved railway
railway museum

1.5. Road transport

Types of road
causey
road
turnpike

Road vehicles
automobile
bicycle
cable tram
car
carriage
cart
coachmaking
diligence
electric tram
Hansom, Joseph
horse
horse tram
mail coach
motorcar
motorcoach
motorcycle
motorlorry
mule
omnibus
packhorse
post coach
stage coach
steam carriage
steam lorry
steamroller
steamtram
streetcar
taxi
traction engine
tramcar
trolleybus
truck
waggon

Road transport structures
bitumen
bridge
bus depot
bus station
car barn
coach station
cobbles
concrete

flagstone
garage
inn
livery stable
McAdam, John Loudon
milepost
motorcar showroom
service station
setts
stoop
tar
tarmacadam
tollgate
tram depot
tram stop
tunnel
turnpike
weighing machine

2. CIVIL ENGINEERING

2.1. General terms

ballast
cutting
dam
embankment
excavator
weir

2.2. Structural techniques

concrete
fireproof
Hennebique, François

2.3. Bridge

accommodation bridge
aqueduct
arch
bascule bridge
caisson
cantilever bridge
concrete bridge
floating bridge
girder bridge
iron bridge
lifting bridge
skew bridge
spandrel
steel bridge
suspension bridge
swing bridge
transporter bridge
truss bridge
tubular bridge
viaduct
voussoir
wooden bridge

862

2.4. Tunnel

canal tunnel
Greathead, James Henry
railway tunnel
tunnel

2.5. Hydraulic power

accumulator
capstan
elevator
forging press
hydraulic crane
jigger

2.6. Air transport

airport

2.7. Sea transport

breakwater
dock
dry dock
hydraulic power
pier
port
ship canal
wharf

2.8. Inland navigation

aqueduct
boat lift
caisson
canal
canal tunnel
chain haulage
flash lock
lock
pound lock
river navigation
sluice
stop lock
weir

2.9. Railway

ballast
cross-tie
inclined plane
railway bridge
sleeper

2.10. Road

bitumen
bridge
cobbles

concrete
flagstone
McAdam, John Loudon
setts
tar
tarmacadam
tunnel

2.11. Rope-worked and allied systems

aerial ropeway
cable car
elevator
escalator
lift

2.12. Land drainage and irrigation

polder
pumping station

2.13. Water supply

aqueduct
cistern
fountain
pumping station
reservoir
water tower
waterworks

2.14. Sewage disposal

pumping station
sewer
treatment works

2.15. Crane

excavator
hydraulic crane
jib crane
treadmill

3. MECHANICAL ENGINEERING

3.1. General terms

American system of manufacture
bearing
pump
rivet
toymaking
valve

3.2. Machine tools

boring machine
drilling machine

gauge
gear-cutting machine
grinding machine
jig
lathe
milling machine
planer
shaping machine
slotting machine
steam hammer
toolmaking

3.3. Particular manufactures

Armaments
arsenal
cannon
gun
magazine
musket
pistol
proof house
shot tower

Business machines
cash register
computer
copier
typewriter

Shipyard
block
boilermaker
dry dock
graving dock
mast
mould loft
sail loft
slip

Clocks and watches
chronometer
clock
watch

3.4. Other manufactures

aircraft factory
coachmaking
locomotive and carriage works
motorcar factory
pump
sewing machine
textile machinery

4. EXTRACTIVE INDUSTRIES

4.1. Mining

Mining systems
adit

alluvial mining
bell pit
drift mine
gallery
hush
mining
opencast mining
quarry
rake
stoping
streaming
strip mining

Techniques of extraction
compressed air
fire setting
longwall mining
magazine
mining
pillar-and-stall mining
shortwall mining

Techniques of hoisting
horse gin
kibble
Malakoff tower
man engine
mining
rope
steam engine

Drainage techniques
mining
sough

Underground haulage
horse
hund
Hungarian hund
putter

Ventilation methods
mining
waddle fan

Pithead installations
buddle
crushing circle
dressing floor
horse gin
hotching tub
jigging
magazine
Malakoff tower
pithead baths
shaking table
stamp

Lighting of mines
candle
safety lamp

4.2. Metals

General terms
calcining kiln
slag
slime

Aluminium
bauxite
cryolite

Copper
Babbit metal
battery
bell metal
brass
Britannia metal
bronze
gun metal
maslin
pewter
precipitation
white metal

Lead, zinc and uranium
brass
calamine
condenser
cupola
flue
galvanizing
lead
ore hearth
pewter
pig mould
red lead
shot tower
slag hearth
spelter
type
uranium
white coal
white lead
zinc

Precious metals
assay
cupellation
gold
goldsmith
hallmark
jewellery manufacture
muffle furnace
silver
silver plate
silversmith

Tin
antimony
blowing house
canning

pewter
streaming
tinplate

Other metals
arsenic
bismuth
chromium
cobalt
magnesium
manganese
mercury
molybdenum
nickel
pyrites
quicksilver
tungsten
vanadium
wolfram

4.3. Oil

asphalt
bitumen
cracking
crude oil
diesel fuel
gasoline
kerosine
LPG
motor spirit
natural gas
oil engine
oil lamp
oil pipeline
oil refinery
oil well
petrol
petroleum
shale oil

4.4. Gems

diamond
emerald
jewellery manufacture
onyx
opal
pearl
ruby
sapphire
turquoise

4.5. Salt

brine

4.6. Stone

anhydrite

basalt
chalk
dimension stone
dolomite
emery
flagstone
granite
grindstones
gypsum
Hoffman kiln
hone
hydraulic cement
lime
lime kiln
limestone
marble
millstones
Portland cement
refractories
roman cement
sawmill
serpentine
slate
stucco

4.7. Other minerals

alum
asbestos
barytes
clay
fluorspar
fuller's earth
graphite
mica
potash
pyrites
saltpetre
sulphur

5. COAL

5.1. Types of coal

anthracite
brown coal
cannel coal
coke
lignite
peat

5.2. Coal mining

mining
pithead baths

5.3. Coal gas

bitumen
coke

coke oven
gasholder
gasworks
pitch
producer gas
retort
smokeless fuel
tar
town gas
water gas

6. IRON

6.1. Types of iron

bar iron
bog iron
cast iron
corrugated iron
malleable iron
Osmund iron
pig iron
steel
wrought iron

6.2. Extraction and preparation of ore

calcining kiln
sintering

6.3. Smelting

Bergamasque furnace
blast furnace
bloomery
Catalan forge
charcoal barn
coke oven
Cowper stove
flux
hearth
hot blast
refractory
slag
Stückofen
Trompe
tuyère

6.4. Refining and forging

finery-and-chafery forge
forge
German forge
hearth
Lancashire forge
puddling furnace
refinery
reverberatory furnace
shingling

stamping and potting
Walloon forge

6.5. Foundry

air furnace
art castings
cupola
steel foundry

6.6. Fabrication

annealing furnace
drop hammer
electroplating
enamelling
forging press
galvanising
hearth
helve hammer
japanning
muffle furnace
oliver
rolling mill
slitting mill
smithy
steam hammer
tilt hammer
tinplate
trip hammer
tube mill
wire mill

6.7. Steel

Bessemer, Sir Henry
cementation furnace
crucible process
electric arc furnace
electric induction furnace
Gilchrist Thomas, Sidney
LD process
open hearth furnace
oxygen
Siemens, William

6.8. Iron manufactures

blacksmith
nails
chains
cutlery
files
lock
mechanical engineering
needles
pin
razor
saws
scythes

spring
whitesmith

7. MANUFACTURING INDUSTRY

7.1. Food

Bee products
honey

Grain products
bakery
biscuit
bread oven
breakfast cereals
confectionery
corn mill
edge runner
flour mill
grain silo
grist mill
malt
millstones
mustard
roller milling

Dairy products
butter
cheese
condensed milk
creamery
cream separator
dairy
margarine

Drink
akvavit
aquavit
beer
brandy
brewery
chocolate
cider
cocoa
coffee
distilling
gin
port wine
rum
samovar
sauce
schnapps
soft drinks
spirits
tea
vinegar
vodka
whiskey
wine

Drugs
apothecary
chemist
cigar
cigarette
druggist
pharmaceuticals
pharmacy
snuff
tobacco

Fish
bloater
fishing port
fish weir
oyster
sealing
train oil
whaling

Meat
abattoir
butcher
pet food
sausage
slaughterhouse

Sugar
beet sugar refinery
sugar-cane mill
sugar refinery

Fruit and vegetable products
banana
chewing gum
dried fruit
jam
marmalade
oil mill
olive oil
paprika
pea
pickle
potato

Preservation of food
canning
icehouse
refrigeration
salt
saltpetre

7.2. Animal products

Bee products
honey
wax

Leather
boots

cobbler
cordwainer
currying
fellmonger
gloves
saddlery
shoes
tanning
tawing

Hair, fur and feathers
down
feathers
feltmaking
fur
hair
hatmaking

Horn and bone
bone mill
comb
horn
ivory
size

Meat products
abattoir
butcher
candles
chandler
pet food
sausage
slaughterhouse
tallow

7.3. Paper

cardboard
cellophane
celluloid
cellulose
esparto grass
Fourdrinier, Henry
Hollander beater
papier mâché
pulp
stampers

7.4. Rubber and plastics

Baekeland, Leo
elastic
gutta-percha
Macintosh, Charles
perspex
plastics
polythene
rubber
tyre

7.5. Wood and straw products

barrel
basket
bobbin mill
bung mill
carpenter
chair
charcoal
clogs
cooper
cork
esparto grass
floating mill
forest industry
fretwork
furniture
hogshead
lumber
mouse trap
pencil
pipe
sawmill
saw pit
timber
tun
turpentine
umbrella
wheelwright
white coal
wood carving
wood

7.6. Glass

bottle
English glass cone
stained glass
vitrolite

7.7. Ceramics

ball clay
bone mill
bottle oven
bricks
china clay
clay
clay preparation machines
coade stone
continuous-chamber kiln
Delftware
drainage pipe
earthenware
faience
firebrick
flint mill
gilding
glazing
Hoffman kiln

intermittent kiln
kiln
lathe
majolica
mosaic
porcelain
potbank
potter's wheel
pottery
refractories
salt glaze
sanitary ware
slipware
stoneware
terracotta
tiles
tobacco pipe
tunnel kiln

7.8. Paint and allied products

linseed oil
paint
pigments
putty
whiting

8. TEXTILES

8.1. Fibres and raw materials

artificial silk
condenser cotton
cotton
cotton gin
cotton press
delinting machine
flax
flax cotton
hemp
jute
nylon
polymer
rayon
silk
staple
synthetic fibres
wool

8.2. Fibre preparation

braking
carding machine
carding mill
combing machine
condenser carding machine
devil
hackling
slubbing billy
reeling

retting
scutching
textiles
throwing
wool stove

8.3. Spinning and yarn production

mule
ring spinning
roving
spinning jenny
spinning mule
spinning wheel
staple
textiles
thread
water frame
wet spinning
yarn

8.4. Weaving

automatic loom
carpet loom
hand loom
harness motion
Jacquard Loom
loom
textiles

8.5. Finishing

aniline
bleaching
calender
calico printing
cloth stove
dyehouse
dyeing
fulling mill
handle house
indigo
logwood
madder
mordant
teasel
tenter frame
textiles
woad

8.6. Knitting

hosiery

8.7. Lace and ribbons

haberdashery
lace
passementerie

ribbon
tape

8.8. Fabrics

alpaca
blanket
calico printing
canvas
carpet
cashmere
damask
flannel
fustian
linen
linoleum
lint
madras
mohair
mungo
oil cloth
plush
rug
sailcloth
shoddy
tapestry
tartan
tweed
woollens
worsted

8.9. Cordage

net
rope
sail loft

8.10. Clothing manufacture

military uniform
sewing machine
shawl manufacture
shirt manufacture
tailor

8.11. Textile mill

company mill
north-lit shed
warehouse

9. ENERGY AND POWER

9.1. General terms

energy
horse power
line shafting
millwright

prime mover
rope drive

9.2. Animal power

donkey gin
horse
horse gin
treadmill

9.3. Electric power

Generation of power
alternator
dynamo
generator
hydro-electric power station
penstock
power station

Applications of electric power
electric arc furnace
electric induction furnace
elevator

9.4. Gas

gas engine
gasholder
gasworks
retort
town gas

9.5. Internal combustion

diesel engine
gas engine
motorcar
motorcoach
motor lorry
oil engine
omnibus
petrol engine

9.6. Steam engine

beam engine
Bellis & Morcom
boiler
Boulton & Watt
chimney
compound engine
condenser
Corliss, George
Cornish engine
Heslop, Adam
horizontal engine
Hornblower, Jonathan
Newcomen, Thomas
portable engine

Savery, Thomas
steam carriage
steam locomotive
steam lorry
steamroller
steamship
steam tram
table engine
traction engine
Trevithick, Richard
turbine
uniflow
vertical engine
Watt, James
Willans, Peter

9.7. Water power

floating mill
head race
hydraulic power
hydro-electric power station
lade
leat
Norse mill
Pelton, Lester Allen
power canal
splash mill
tail race
tide mill
turbine
water engine
water mill

9.8. Wind power

horizontal windmill
post mill
smock mill
tower mill
wind pump
windmill

10. COMMUNICATIONS

10.1. Postal service

mail coach
pneumatic dispatch
postbox
postcard
sorting office
travelling post office

10.2. Printing

Columbia press
copier
engraving
linotype
lithography

Monotype
newspaper printing
press
Stanhope press
type
typewriter

10.3. Signals

aircraft beacon
beacon
buoy
lighthouse
lightship
milepost
railway signal
road traffic signal
semaphore
signal box
signal tower
time-ball station

10.4. Photography

camera
cinema
postcard

10.5. Telecommunications and
computers

Atlantic telegraph
Bell, Alexander Graham
cable
computer
duplex
Marconi, Guglielmo
Morse, Samuel
radio
radio receiver
radio station
relay power station
Strowger, Almon B.
telecommunications
telegraph
telegraph office
telegraph pole
telegraph receivers and transmitters
telephone
telephone box
telephone exchange
telephone receivers and transmitters
television
Wheatstone, Charles

11. SERVICE INDUSTRIES

11.1.   Accommodation of the sick,
criminals and the poor

apprentice house

hospital
industrial school
pauper colony
penal colony
prison
spa
workhouse

11.2. Accommodation of travellers

boarding house
caravanserai
holiday camp
hotel
inn
lodging house
motel
public house
railway hotel

11.3. Administration

counting house
office block
skyscraper

11.4. Cleaning services

dry cleaning
laundry

11.5. Education

institute

11.6. Entertainment

bathhouse
cinema
circus
fairground
gallery
music hall
pier
spa
theatre

11.7. Government

customs house

11.8 Retailing

apothecary
arcade
bakery
bazaar
butcher
cash register
chain store

chemist
company store
confectionery
co-operative movement
department store
dispensary
drug store
gallery
market
pneumatic dispatch
saddlery
shoes
shop
store
supermarket
truck shop

11.9. Storage

bond or bonded warehouse
grain silo
granary
staple
tobacco warehouse
victualling yard
warehouse

12. INDUSTRIAL COMMUNITY

12.1. Colony

pauper colony
penal colony

12.2. Company town

apprentice house
bruk
company store
mining town
railway town
truck shop

12.3. House types

apartment
back-to-back house
barrack house
blind-back house
bungalow
burgage plot
caravan
catslide
cluster house
cottage
cottage orné
flat
prefabricated house
semi-detached house
tenement

terrace
tunnel-back house
villa

12.4. Housing agencies

building society
council house
freehold land society

12.5. Industrial estate

trading estate

12.6. Model settlement

garden city
garden suburb
new town

12.7. Types of community

caravan
Chartist community
co-operative movement
Fourier, Charles
Owen, Robert
plotland
resort
spa
squatter settlement
suburb
Utopian community

13. CHEMICALS

13.1. Processes and terms

apothecary
Castner-Keller cell
catalyst
chemist
druggist
electrolysis
pharmaceuticals
pharmacy

13.2. Acids

Birkeland and Eyde process
Gay-Lussac tower
Glover tower
hydrochloric acid
nitric acid
sulphuric acid
vitriol

13.3. Alkalis

ammonia

ammonia-soda process
anhydrite
barilla
caustic soda
Gossage tower
Haber-Bosch process
kelp
Leblanc process
lime
limestone
salt
soap
soda
Solvay, Ernest

13.4. Gases and derivatives

bleaching powder
carbon dioxide
chlorine
cyanide
helium
hydrogen
neon
nitrogen
oxygen

13.5. Organic compounds

acetylene
alcohol
aniline
benzene
butane
creosote
detergents
ethanol
ethene
ethyl Alcohol
ethylene
ethyne
formaldehyde
kerosine
methanal
methane
methanol
methyl alcohol
methyl benzene
naphtha
paraffin
phenol
phenylamine
propane
propene
propylene
solvent
toluene

13.6. Explosives

cartridges

charcoal
dynamite
gunpowder
Nobel, Alfred
saltpetre
sulphur

13.7. Phosphorus

artificial fertilizers
detergents
fertilizers
matches
superphosphates

14. PUBLIC UTILITIES

abattoir
bathhouse
compressed air
electric power
gas
hydraulic power
lighthouse
lightship
market
omnibus
park
pneumatic despatch
postal service
power canal
road
sewage disposal
telecommunications
tramway
trolleybus
underground railway
water power
water supply

15. ARCHITECTURE

15.1. General terms

adaptive reuse
industrial architecture

15.2. Architectural styles

Art Deco
Art Nouveau
Ashlar
baroque
Beaux-Arts
Bauhaus
City Beautiful
Classical
Corinthian
cottage orné
Doric

Empire
Egyptian
Expressionism
functionalist
garden city
Gothic
Greek Revival
historicist
International Modern
Ionic
Italianate
Jacobean
Jugendstil
Palladian
Renaissance
Romanesque
Romantic Nationalist
Rundbogenstil
Secessionist
Tudor
Venetian Gothic

15.3. Architectural terms

arcade
campanile
clerestory
crenellation
cupola
fireproof
fretwork
mansard roof
panoptican
pediment
pilaster
polychrome
porte-cochère
portico
prefabricated house
Venetian window

15.4. Building materials

basalt
bricks
cement
Coade stone
concrete
dimension stone
faience
fireproof
granite
lime
limestone
majolica
marble
mosaic
paint
Portland cement
putty

Roman cement
sanitary ware
slate
stone
stucco
terracotta
tiles
timber

16. SOURCES

16.1. Classic works

Agricola, Georgius
Diderot, Denis
Mayhew, Henry
Rees, Abraham
Smiles, Samuel
Sousa Viterbo, F. de

16.2. Documentary and oral sources

accounts
business records
census
design registration
industrial espionage
insurance records
inventory
map
oral history
patent
port books
probate records
sites and monuments record
Sound tolls

16.3. Iconography

Agricola, Georgius
art
Bourne, John Cooke
Diderot, Denis
ephemera
film
industrial architecture
models
photography
postcard
trade token
video history

17. INTERPRETATION

17.1. Museum
(see index for further information on museums)

écomusée

gallery
maritime museum
mining museum
motor museum
open-air museum
textile museum
transport museum

17.2. Other aspects of interpretation

gallery
heritage centre
international and national exhibitions
model
park
preserved railway
TICCIH
trail
Unesco World Heritage Site
visitor centre

18. THEORY

18.1. Archaeology

archaeometallurgy
colonial archaeology
excavation
historical archaeology
industrial archaeology
nautical archaeology
post-medieval archaeology
recording

18.2. Conservation

Inventory
landmark
revolving fund

18.3 Industrial archaeological terms

factory
landscape
mill
proto-industrialization
transfer of technology

19. BIOGRAPHIES

Agricola, Georgius
Arkwright, Richard
Armstrong, Sir William
Baekeland, Leo
Ball, Edmund Bruce
Behrens, Peter
Bell, Alexander Graham

Benz, Karl
Bessemer, Sir Henry
Bombardier, J. Armand
Bouche, Thomas
Bourne, John Cooke
Bramah, Joseph
Brindley, James
Brown, Joseph Rogers
Brunel, Isambard Kingdom
Brunton, William
Bute, John 2nd Marquis of
Cegielski, Hipolit
Cherepanov, Efim Alexeevich &
   Miron Efimavich
Corliss, George Henry
Crawshay, Richard
Daft, Leo
Daimler, Gottlieb
Darby, Abraham
Davies, David
Davy, Sir Humphry
Diderot, Denis
Dolovi-Dobrovol'skii, M. O.
Donkin, Bryan
Edison, Thomas
Fairbairn, William
Fairlie, Robert
Ford, Henry
Fourdrinier, Henry
Fourier, Charles
Frolov, Koz'ma Dmitrievitch &
   Pyotr Kozmich
Fulton, Robert
Gakkel', Yakov
Gilchrist Thomas, Sidney
Gölsdorf, Karl
Greathead, James Henry
Hadfield, Charles
Hansom, Joseph Aloysius
Hardwick, Philip
Hennebique, François
Heslop, Adam

Himalai, Manuel Antonio Gomes
Holme, Randle
Hornblower, Jonathan
Hudson, Kenneth
Kahn, Albert
Latrobe, Benjamin
Lely, Cornelis
Leonida, Dimitrie
Łukasiewicz, Jan Józef Ignacy
McAdam, John Loudon
Marconi, Guglielmo
Marshall, John
Maudsley, Henry
Mayhew, Henry
Mies van der Rohe, Ludwig
Morris, William
Morris, William, 1st Viscount
   Nuffield
Morse, Samuel Finley Breese
Moura, Bento de
Murdock, William
Newcomen, Thomas
Nobel, Alfred Bernhard
Otis, Elisha Greaves
Owen, Robert
Parsons, Sir Charles Algernon
Paxton, Joseph
Peabody, George
Pelton, Lester Allen
Polheim (Polhammar), Christopher
Polzunov, Ivan Ivanovich
Priestley, Joseph
Pullman, George Mortimer
Raistrick, Arthur
Rees, Abraham
Rees, David Morgan
Rennie, John
Rix, Michael
Roberts, Richard
Roe, Sir Edwin Alliott Verdon
Roebling, John
Roebuck, John

Rolt, Lionel Thomas Caswall
Sadler, James
Savery, Thomas
Scheele, Carl Wilhelm
Schinkel, Karl Friedrich
Schonerer, Matthias
Scott, George Gilbert
Shchusev, Aleksei Viktorovich
Shukhov, Vladimir Grigorevich
Siemens, Sir William
Slater, Samuel
Smeaton, John
Smiles, Samuel
Solvay, Ernest
Sousa Viterbo, Francisco de
Sprague, Frank Julian
Staszic, Stanislaw
Stephenson, George
Stephenson, Robert
Stevenson, Robert
Strowger, Almon B
Strutt, Jedediah
Symington, William
Taylor, Frederick Winslow
Telford, Thomas
Trevithick, Richard
Unwin, Raymond
Vlaicu, Aurel
Vuia, Traian
Watkins, George
Watt, James
Wedgwood, Josiah
Westinghouse, George
Wheatstone, Charles
Whitney, Eli
Wilkinson, John
Whitworth, Joseph
Willans, Peter William
Williams, Thomas
Wyatt, Matthew Digby

Bibliography

The bibliography comprises a single alphabetical list of all works referred to in the text which are of major significance in the study of industrial archaeology, although many will be primarily concerned with different disciplines.

Where there is an English edition of a book originally or concurrently published in another language, it is the English edition which is normally quoted. Only the English title is quoted of bilingual works.

When a book has been published in more than one edition the date quoted will usually be that of the original publication, except in the case of works of historical scholarship which have been substantially revised in later editions, and technical works which have appeared in many editions. In both cases the edition which has been used for research will be quoted.

In the case of reprints of historical works, the original date of publication is normally given, but the date of the reprint is quoted in the bibliography.

Abbot, D. 1976. *The Lower Peninsula of Michigan, an Inventory of Historic Engineering and Industrial Sites.* Washington DC: HAER.

Abbot, R. A. S. 1970. *The Fairlie Locomotive.* Newton Abbot: David & Charles.

Abelshauser, W. 1984. *Der Ruhrohlenbergbau seit 1945: Wiederaufbau, Krise, Anpassung* (The Ruhr coal mining industry since 1945: rebuilding, crisis, adaptation). Munich: C. H. Beck Verlag.

Achilles, F. W. 1985. *Rhein-Ruhr Hafen Duisburg: Grösster Binnenhafen der Welt* (The Rhine-Ruhr harbour, Duisburg: the largest inland port in the world). Duisburg: Mercator Verlag.

Ackerman, E. A. 1941. *New England's Fishing Industry.* Chicago, IL: University of Illinois Press.

Adams, H. C. 1938. *Waterworks for Urban and Rural Districts*, 3rd edn. London: Pitman.

Adams, S. H. 1930. *Modern Sewage Disposal and Hygienics.* London: Spon.

Adams, W. B. 1837. *English Pleasure Carriages.* London: Spon. Reprint, 1971, Bath: Adams & Dart.

Adamson, S. H. 1977. *Seaside Piers.* London: Batsford.

Adburgham, A. ed. 1969. *Yesterday's Shopping: the Army and Navy Stores catalogue 1907.* Newton Abbot: David & Charles.

——1972. *Victorian Shopping: Harrods catalogue 1895.* Newton Abbot: David & Charles.

——1974. *Gamages Christmas Bazaar 1913, being a facsimile reprint of the 1913 Christmas Catalogue of A. W. Gamage Ltd. of Holborn, London.* Newton Abbot: David & Charles.

——1975. *Libertys: the biography of a store.* London: Allen & Unwin.

Agricola, G. 1556. *De Re Metallica* (Concerning metals), trans. H. C. and L. C. Hoover, 1912, London: Mining Magazine. Reprint, 1950, New York: Dover.

Aguilar, I. 1980. *Demetri Ribes.* Valencia.

Ahrens, C., Balassa, A. and Zippelius, A. 1984. *25 Jahre ICOM-Deklaration uber Freilichtmuseen* (Twenty-five years of ICOM-Declaration about open air museums). Budapest: Szabadteri Naprajzi Muzeum.

Ahrons, E. L. 1927. *The British Steam Railway Locomotive 1825–1925.* London: Locomotive Publishing. Reprint, 1987, London: Bracken Press.

Ahvenainen, J., Pihkala, E., and Rasila, V. 1982. *Suomen taloushistorica, II Tellistuva Suomi* (Finnish social history, vol. II: industrializing Finland). Helsinki.

Aikin, J. 1795. *A Description of the Country from Thirty to Forty Miles round Manchester.* London: John Stockdale. Reprint, 1968, Newton Abbot: David & Charles.

Aitken, T. 1907. *Road Making and Maintenance.* London: Charles Griffin.

Albert, W. 1972. *The Turnpike Road System in England, 1663–1840.* Cambridge: Cambridge University Press.

Alderson, F. 1972. *Bicycling: a history.* Newton Abbot: David & Charles.

Alderton, D. and Booker, J. 1980. *The Batsford Guide to the Industrial Archaeology of East Anglia.* London: Batsford.

Alexander, D. 1970. *Retailing in England during the Industrial Revolution.* London: Athlone Press.

Alexander, W. and Street, A. 1949. *Metals in the Service of Man.* London: Pelican.

Allen, C. J. 1965. *Switzerland's Amazing Railways*, rev. edn. London: Nelson.

Allen, G. C. 1919. *The Industrial Development of Birmingham and the Black Country, 1860–1917.* London: Allen & Unwin

Allen, J. F. 1906. *Some Founders of the Chemical Industry: men to be remembered.* London: Sherratt & Hughes.

Allen, R. S. 1957. *Covered Bridges of the North Eastern States.* Brattleborough, VT: Steven Greene.

——1959. *Covered Bridges of the Mid-Atlantic States.* Brattleborough, VT: Steven Greene.

——1970. *Covered Bridges of the Southern States.* Brattleborough, VT: Steven Greene.

Allen, W. 1846–9. *The Life of William Allen*. London: Charles Gilpin.

Allward, M. 1981. *An Illustrated History of Seaplanes and Flying Boats*. Ashbourne: Moorland.

Allwood, J. 1977. *The Great Exhibitions*. London: Studio Vista.

Alward, G. L. 1932. *The Sea Fisheries of Great Britain and Ireland*. Grimsby: Albert Gait.

Ambler, R. and Watkinson, L. 1987. *Farmers and Fishermen: the probate inventories of the ancient parish of Clee, South Humberside 1536–1742*. Hull: University of Hull.

American Society of Civil Engineers 1970. *The Civil Engineer: his origins*. New York: Committee on History and Heritage of American Civil Engineering.

——1976. *American Wooden Bridges*. New York: Committee on History and Heritage of American Civil Engineering.

American Society of Mechanical Engineers (Boston Branch) 1980. *A Record of Our Beginnings*. Boston, MA: American Society of Mechanical Engineers.

Amerine, M. A. and Cruess, W. V. 1960. *The Technology of Wine Making*. Westport, CT: Avi Publishing.

Amos, P. A. 1920. *The Process of Flour Manufacture*. London: Longmans Green.

Ancel, B. and Fluck, P. 1988. *Une exploitation minière du XVIè siècle dans les Vosges. Le filon Saint-Louis de Neuenberg (Haut-Rhin). Caractères et évolution* (A sixteenth century mine in the Vosges. The Saint-Louis lode of Neuenberg, characteristics and evolution). Paris: Maison des Sciences de l'Homme.

Anderson, J. W. 1908. *Refrigeration: an elementary textbook*. London: Longman.

Anderson, O. E. 1953. *Refrigeration in America*. Princeton, NJ: Princeton University Press.

Anderson, R. C. and Frankis, G. 1970. *The History of Royal Blue Express Services*. Newton Abbot: David & Charles.

Anderson, R. E. 1950. *The Story of the American Automobile*. Washington DC: Public Affairs Press.

Anderson, R. O. 1984. *Fundamentals of the Petroleum Industry*. London: Weidenfeld & Nicolson.

Anderson, T. R. 1969. *Danks biler og motorcykler 1900–20* (Danish motorcars and motorcycles 1900–20). Copenhagen: Hassing.

Andersson, H. O. 1978. *Industrinnen* (Industrial monuments). Stockholm: Sveriges Arkitekturmuseum.

Andersson, I. 1970. *A History of Sweden*, transl. C. Hannay. London: Weidenfeld & Nicolson.

André, L., Belhoste, J.-F. and Bertrand, P. 1978. *La Métallurgie du fer dans les Ardennes* (Ironmaking in the Ardennes). Paris: Ministère de la Culture.

André, L. et al. 1989. *Musées des Mines de Fer de Lorraine* (Lorraine iron-mining museums). Neutchef: Amomferior.

Andrews, G. 1975. *The Ferries of Sydney*. Sydney: Reed.

——1976. *Veteran Ships of Australia and New Zealand*. Sydney: Reed.

Andrews, P. W. S. and Brunner, E. 1955. *The Life of Lord Nuffield*. Oxford: Basil Blackwell.

Andrie, V. 1988. *Workers in Stalin's Russia: industrialization and social change in a planned economy*. Hemel Hempstead: Harvester.

Andrieux, J.-Y. 1987. *Forges et hauts fourneaux en Bretagne du XVIIè siècle au XIXè siècle* (Forges and blast furnaces in Brittany from the seventeenth century to the nineteenth century). Nantes: CID Editions.

Angus, J. T. 1988. *A Respectable Ditch: a history of the Trent Severn Waterway, 1833–1920*. Montreal and Kingston: McGill-Queen's University Press.

Annandale, N. 1905. *The Faroes and Iceland*. Oxford: Oxford University Press.

Apel, C. and Dröge, K. 1980. *Fabrik im Ornament: Ansichten auf Firmenbriefköpfen des 19 Jahrhunderts* (Manufactures illustrated: views on company billheadings of the nineteenth century). Munster: Westfälischen Museumsamt.

Architektenverein zu Berlin and Vereinigung Berliner Arkitekten 1896–. *Berlin und seine Bauten* (Berlin and its buildings). Berlin: Ernst.

Arkeos Inc. 1986. *Pulperie des chutes Wilson: archéologie, technologie, historie: étude préliminaire* (The Wilson Falls pump mill: a preliminary study of its archaeology, technology and history). Montreal: Ministry of Cultural Affairs.

Armas, A. R. de 1980. *Ciencia y Tecnologia en la España Ilustrade* (Spanish science and technology illustrated). Madrid: Ediciones Turner.

Armstrong, W. 1885. *Chimneys, Furnaces and Fireplaces: a book for the use of practical engineers*. London.

Armytage, W. H. G. 1961a. *A Social History of Engineering*. London: Faber.

——1961b. *Heavens Below: utopian experiments in England 1560–1960*. London: Routledge.

——1965. *Yesterday's Tomorrows: a historic survey of future societies*. London: Routledge.

Arnoux, M., Lecherbonnier, Y. et al. 1991. *La métallurgie normande et percheronne: la révolution du haut fourneau, XVè–XVIIè siècles* (The iron industry in Normandy and the Perche: the blast furnace revolution of the fifteenth to seventeenth centuries). Paris: Ministère de la Culture, Cahiers de l'Inventaire.

Arpin, M. 1948. *Historique de la meneurie et de la boulangerie* (History of flour-milling and bread-making). Paris: Le Chancelier.

Ashe, S. and Keiley, J. D. 1905. *Electric Railways Theoretically and Practically Treated*. London: Constable.

Ashmead, G. B. 1956. *Aircraft Production Methods*. Philadelphia, PA: Chilton.

Ashmore, O. 1969. *The Industrial Archaeology of Lancashire*. Newton Abbot: David & Charles.

——1982. *The Industrial Archaeology of North-west England and Where to Find It*. Manchester: Manchester University Press.

Ashton, T. S. 1939. *An Eighteenth Century Industrialist: Peter Stubs of Warrington*. Manchester: Manchester University Press.

Ashton, T. S. and Sykes, J. 1929. *The Coal Industry of the Eighteenth Century*. Manchester: University of Manchester Economic History Series.

Ashworth, W. 1986. *The History of the British Coal Industry*, vol. V: *1946–1982*. Oxford: Oxford University Press.

Asselain, J.-S. 1984. *Histoire économique de la France du XVIII*e *siècle à nos jours* (Economic history of France from the eighteenth century to the present day). Paris: Le Seuil.

Associaçao dos Arquitectos Portugueses 1987. *Guia Urbanistico e Arquitectónico de Lisboa* (A guide to the city and the architecture of Lisbon). Lisbon: AAP.

Associaçao Portuguesa de Arqueologia Industrial 1990. *I Encontro Nacional sobre o Patrimonio Industrial: Actas e Communicaçoes II* (Transactions of the first national seminar on the industrial heritage: proceedings II). Coimbra: Coimbra Editora.

Association culturelle des travailleurs de la réparation navale 1986. *Navires en forme: l'industrie de la réparation navale à Marseille* (Ships in dry dock: the naval refitting industry at Marseilles). Marseilles: Musée d'Histoire.

Aston, M. 1985. *Interpreting the Landscape: landscape archaeology in local studies*. London: Batsford.

—— 1988. *Medieval Fish, Fisheries and Fishponds*. Oxford: British Archaeological Abstracts.

Aston, R. L. 1957. *The Diesel Locomotive*. London: Thames & Hudson.

Atkinson, F. 1966. *The Great Northern Coalfield*. London: University Tutorial Press.

—— 1974. *The Industrial Archaeology of North-east England*. 2 vols. Newton Abbot: David & Charles.

Atterbury, P. ed. 1982. *The History of Porcelain*. London: Orbis.

Attman, A. 1986. *Sveskt järn 1800–1914* (Swedish iron 1800–1914). Stockholm: Jernkontorets Berghistoriska Skriftserie.

Atwell, D. 1980. *Cathedrals of the Movies*. London: Architectural Press.

Austen, B. 1978. *English Provincial Posts: a study based on Kentish examples*. Chichester: Phillimore.

Austwick, J. and Austwick, B. 1980. *The Decorative Tile: an illustrated history of English tile-making and design*. London: Pitman House.

Avery, D. 1974. *Not on Queen Victoria's Birthday*. London: Collins.

Ayres, Q. C. and Scoates, D. 1939. *Land Drainage and Reclamation*, 2nd edn. New York: McGraw Hill.

Ayton, C. 1979. *The History of Motor-cycling*. London: Orbis.

Baader, J. von 1822. *Neues System der Fortschaffenden Mechanik* (New systems of mechanical transport). Munich: Verlag des Verfassers.

Babbitt, H. E. 1940. *Sewage and Sewage Treatment*, 5th edn. New York: John Wiley.

Babbitt, H. E. and Doland, J. J. 1939. *Water Supply Engineering*, 3rd edn. New York and London: McGraw Hill.

Babet-Charton, H. 1954. *La Charcuterie à la Campagne* (Rural charcuterie), 6th edn. Paris: Maison Rustique.

Back, A. 1981. *Thomas Lester: his lace and the East Midlands industry 1820–1905*. Bedford: Ruth Bean.

Baedeker, K. 1903. *The Eastern Alps*. Leipzig: Karl Baedeker.

Baggethun, R. 1960. *Horten: ferjestedet som ble marinestasjon og by* (Horten: port and town). Horten: Horten kommune.

Bagley, J. J. and Bagley, A. J. 1966. *The English Poor Law*. London: Macmillan.

Bagnall, W. R. 1890. *Samuel Slater and the Early Developments of the Cotton Manufacture in the United States*. Middletown, CT: J. S. Stewart.

Bailey, P. 1986. *Music Hall: the business of pleasure*. Milton Keynes: Open University Press.

Baillie, G. 1951. *Clocks and Watches: an historical bibliography*. London: Holland.

Bainbridge, C. 1986. *Pavilions on the Sea: a history of the seaside pleasure pier*. London: Robert Hale.

Baines, E. 1835. *The History of the Cotton Manufacture in Great Britain*. London: Fisher, Fisher & Jackson. Reprint, 1966, London: Cass.

Baines, E. 1858. *An Account of the Woollen Manufacture of England*. Reprint, 1970, Newton Abbot: David & Charles.

Baker, D. S. 1986. *From Yeomen to Brickmasters*. Canberra: F. Baker & Sons.

Baker, G. and Funaro, B. 1955. *Motels*. New York: Reinhold.

Baker, M. and Harris, N. 1986. *Steam Echoes*. London: Silver Link.

Baker, W. A. 1965. *From Paddle Steamer to Nuclear Ship: a history of the engine-powered vessel*. London: C. A. Watts.

Baker, W. J. 1970. *A History of the Marconi Company*. London: Methuen.

Bălan, S. and Mihăilescu, S. N. 1985. *Istoria stuntei si tehnici in Romania* (History of science and technology in Romania). Bucharest: Editura Academia.

Baldinger, O. 1987. *Erhaltung Industrieller Kulturgüter in der Schweiz* (The preservation of industrial monuments and artefacts in Switzerland). Umiken: Verlag Industriearchäologie.

—— 1988. *Reiseführer Industriearchäologie Mallorca* (A guide to the industrial archaeology of Majorca). Umiken: Verlag Industriearchäologie.

Baldwin, M. and Burton, A. 1984. *Canals: a new look. Studies in honour of Charles Hadfield*. Chichester: Phillimore.

Bale, M. P. and Bale, A. P. 1924. *Saw-mills: their arrangement and management and the economical conversion of timber*. London: Technical Press.

Balk, J. T. 1985. *Onze Havens* (Our Ports). Soest: Publiboek.

Ball, N. R. 1987. *Mind, Heart and Vision: professional engineering in Canada 1887 to 1987*. Ottawa: National Museum of Science and Technology.

—— 1988. *Building Canada: a history of public works*. Toronto: University of Toronto Press.

Ballen, D. 1914. *Bibliography of Roadmaking and Roads in the United Kingdom*. London: Studies in Economic and Political Science.

Bancroft, R. M. and Bancroft, F. J. 1885. *A Practical Treatise on the Construction of Tall Chimney Shafts.* Manchester: John Calvert.

Banfield, T. C. 1846. *Industry of the Rhine.* London: Charles Knight. Reprint, 1969, New York: Augustus M. Kelley.

Bang, N. and Korst, K. 1906–53. *Tabeller over skibsfart og varetransport gennem oresund 1497–1783* (Tables of shipping and goods transport through the Sound 1497–1783). Copenhagen: Gyldendal.

Banham, R. 1986. *A Concrete Atlantis.* Cambridge, MA and London: MIT Press.

Banks, A. G. and Schofield, R. B. 1968. *Brindley at Wet Earth.* Newton Abbot: David & Charles.

Barblan, M.-A. 1985. *Il était une fois l'industrie* (Once there was industry). Carouge: Collection Patrimoine Industriel de la Suisse.

Barclay-Harvey, M. 1949. *A History of the Great North of Scotland Railway.* London: Locomotive Publishing Company.

Bardon, J. 1982. *Belfast: an illustrated history.* Belfast: Blackstaff Press.

Barker, A. and Harduce, A. 1971. *Automobile Design: great designers and their work.* Newton Abbot: David & Charles.

Barker, B. G. 1911. *The Danube with Pen and Pencil.* London: Swan Sonnenschein.

Barker, P. 1977. *Arts and Society.* London: Fontana.

Barker, P. A. 1982. *Techniques of Archaeological Excavation.* London: Batsford.

—— 1986. *Understanding Archaeological Excavations.* London: Batsford.

Barker, T. C. 1977. *The Glassmakers: Pilkingtons – the rise of an international company 1826–1976.* London: Weidenfield & Nicholson.

—— 1988. *The Economic and Social Effect of the Spread of Motor Vehicles.* London: Macmillan.

Barker, T. C. and Harris, J. R. 1954. *A Merseyside Town in the Industrial Revolution.* Liverpool: Liverpool University Press.

Barkhausen, E. 1925. *Die Tuchindustrie in Monjoie, ihr Aufstieg und Niedergang* (The cloth industry in Monschau: its rise and fall). Aachen: Aachener Verlags und Drückerei-Gesellschaft.

Barlow, A. 1878. *History and Principles of Weaving by Hand and Power.* London: Sampson Low.

Barman, C. 1974. *The Man Who Built London Transport: a bibliography by Frank Pick.* Newton Abbot: David & Charles.

Barnard, A. 1887. *The Whiskey Distilleries of the United Kingdom.* London: Harper's Weekly Gazette.

—— 1889. *The Noted Breweries of Great Britain and Ireland.* 3 vols. London: Sir Joseph Causton.

Barnard, J. 1972. *Victorian Ceramic Tiles.* London: Studio Vista.

Barnet, R. D. et al. 1982. *The Industrial Archaeology of the Electrical Development Company Generating Station at Niagara Falls.* Niagara Falls: Niagara Society of Industrial History.

Barnouw, E. 1966. *A Tower in Babel: a history of broadcasting in the United States to 1933.* New York: Oxford University Press.

—— 1968. *The Golden Web: a history of broadcasting in the United States 1933–1953.* New York: Oxford University Press.

—— 1970. *The Image Empire: a history of broadcasting in the United States from 1953.* New York: Oxford University Press.

—— 1974. *Documentary: a history of the non-fiction film.* New York: Oxford University Press.

Barr, W. M. 1983. *Pumping Machinery.* Philadelphia, PA: Lippincott.

Barraclough, K. C. 1976. *Benjamin Huntsman 1704–1776.* Sheffield: Sheffield City Libraries.

—— 1981–4. *Steelmaking before Bessemer.* London: Metals Society.

Barry, M. 1985. *Across Deep Waters: bridges of Ireland.* Dublin: Frankfort Press.

Barson, S. and Saint, A. 1988. *A Farewell to Fleet Street.* London: English Heritage.

Bartlett, J. N. 1969. *Carpeting the Millions: the growth of Britain's carpet industry.* Edinburgh: John Donald.

Barton, D. B. 1961. *A History of Copper Mining in Cornwall and Devon.* Truro: Barton.

—— 1967. *A History of Tin Mining in Cornwall.* Truro: Barton.

—— 1968. *Essays in Cornish Mining History,* vol. I. Truro: Bradford Barton.

—— 1971. *Essays in Cornish Mining History,* vol. II. Truro: Bradford Barton.

Bärtschi, H. P. 1983. *Industrialisierung, Eisenbahnschlachten und Stadtebau: die entwicklung des Zürcher industrie- und arbeiterstadtteils assersihl. Ein vergleichender beitrag zur architektur- und technick-geschichte* (Industrialisation, railway construction and urban growth: the development of industry and workers' communities in Zurich. A comparative study in agricultural and technical history). Basel: Birkhäuser Verlag.

—— 1990. *Winterthur: Industriestadt in Umbruch* (Winterthur: an industrial city in transition). Wetzikon: Buchverlag der Drukerei Wetzikon.

Basas, M. 1967. *Aspectos de la vida económica de Bilbao de 1861 a 1866* (Aspects of the economy of Bilbao from 1861 to 1866). Bilbao: Cámara de Comercio Industria y Navegación de Bilbao.

—— 1978. *Economía y Sociedad Bilbaínas en torno al Sitio de 1874* (Economy and society in Bilbao from 1874 until the turn of the century). Bilbao: Junta de Cultura de Vizcaya.

Bates, A. 1969. *Directory of Stage Coach Services, 1836.* Newton Abbot: David & Charles.

Battison, E. A. 1976. *From Muskets to Mass Production.* Windsor, VT.

Baumeier, S. 1983. *Westfälische Bauernhäuser: Vor Bagger und Raupe gerettet* (Westphalian peasant houses: retained by hook and by crook). Bielefeld: Westfalen-Verlag.

Bautens, R. 1984. *Industriele revoluties in de provincie Antwerpen* (The industrial revolution in the province of Antwerp). Antwerp: Antwerpen-Weesp, Standaard Uitg.

Bauters, P. 1979. *Vlaamse Molens: winde en watermolens in Vlaanderen, geschiedenis, bouw, werking, recht* (Flemish mills: windmills and watermills in Vlaanderen, history, construction, operation and legal aspects). Antwerp.

Baxter, W., Jnr 1910. *Hydraulic Elevators: their design, construction, operation, care and management.* New York: McGraw Hill.

Bay, W. 1977. *Denmarks damplokomotiver* (Denmark's steam locomotives). Copenhagen: Herluf Andersens Forlag.

Bayer-Desimond, M. von 1931. *Flughatenanlagen* (Investment in airports). Berlin.

Bayerisches Landesamt für Denkmalpflege 1978. *Vom Glaspalast zum Gaskessel: Münchens Weg ins technische Zeitalter* (From glasspalace to gasholder: Munich's development in the industrial period). Munich: Arbeitshefte des Bayerischen Amtes für Denkmalpflege, Verlag Lipp.

Bayernwerk A.G. 1975. *Das Walcheneekraftwerk* (The Walchensee power station). Munich: Bayernwerk AG.

Bayley, S. 1978. *Nature, Work and Art.* Milton Keynes: Open University.

BBC 1985. *British Broadcasting Data Publications 1922–1982.* London: British Broadcasting Corporation.

Beaton, K. 1957. *Enterprise in Oil: a history of Shell in the United States.* New York: Appleton-Century-Crofts.

Beaudry-Gourd, B. 1983. *La mine Lamaque et le village minier de Bourlamaque* (The Lamaque mine and the mining village of Bourlamaque). Rouen: Collège de l'Abitibi-Témiscamingue.

Beaujon, A. 1883. *The History of the Dutch Sea Fisheries.* London: William Clowes.

Beaumont, R. 1919. *Woollen and Worsted: the theory and technology of the manufacture of woollen, worsted and union yarns and fabrics,* 3rd edn. London: Library Press.

Beaver, P. 1971. *A History of Lighthouses.* London: Peter Davies.

Bech, S. et al. eds 1980–3. *Kobenhavens historie, I–VI* (The history of Copenhagen, vols I–VI). Copenhagen: Gyldendal.

Becher, B. and Becher, H. 1988. *Water Towers.* Cambridge, MA: MIT Press.

Becher, B., Becher, H., Günther, G. and Neumann, E. 1977. *Zeche Zollern 2. Aufbruch zur modernen Industriearchitektur und Technik* (The Zollern 2 mine: the beginnings of modern industrial architecture and technology). Munich: Prestel Verlag.

Beck, L. 1891. *Die Geschichte des Eisens (in technischer und Kulturgeschichtlicher Beziehung),* Erste Abeilung: *Von der ältesten Zeit bis um das Jahr 1500 n.Chr.* (The technical and cultural aspects of the history of ironmaking, vol. I: from the earliest times to the fifteenth century). Braunschweig: Friedrich Vieweg und Sohn.

—— 1893–5. *Die Geschichte des Eisens (in technischer und Kulturgeschichtlicher Beziehung),* Zweite Abeilung: *Das XVI und XVII Jahrhundert* (The technical and cultural aspects of the history of ironmaking, vol. II: the sixteenth and seventeenth centuries). Braunschweig: Friedrich Vieweg und Sohn.

Beck, S. W. 1881. *The Draper's Dictionary.* London: Warehousemen and Drapers' Journal Office.

Becker, H. 1980. *Die Wuppertaler Schwebebahn in der Bau-, Wirtschafts- und Sozialgeschichte des 19 Jahrhunderts, insbesondere die Hochbauten der Anlage* (The Wuppertal spider railway in the architectural, economic and social history of the nineteenth century, in particular its structural engineering and buildings). Munich: Selbstverlag.

Beckett, J. C. and Glasscock, R. E. 1967. *Belfast: the origin and growth of an industrial city.* London: British Broadcasting Corporation.

Beckett, J. C. et al. 1983. *Belfast: the making of the city.* Belfast: Appletree Press.

Beer, J. J. 1949. *The Emergence of the German Dye Industry.* Urbana, IL: University of Illinois Press.

Beeton, I. M. 1912. *Mrs Beeton's Every-day Cookery.* London: Ward Lock.

Begeman, M. L. 1952. *Manufacturing Processes,* 3rd edn. New York: Wiley & Sons.

Behrend, G. 1926a. *Pullman in Europe.* London: Ian Allen.

—— 1926b. *Grand European Expresses.* London: Allen & Unwin.

Belhoste, J.-F. 1982. *Histoire des forges d'Allevard* (History of the Allevard ironworks). Grenoble: privately published.

—— 1988. *Les Ardoisieres en Pays de la Loire* (The slate workings in the Loire region). Nantes: Service Regional de l'Inventaire General des Pays de la Loire.

—— 1991. *Fonte, fer, acier, XVè – debut XXè siècles, Rhone-Alpes* (Cast iron, wrought iron, steel, fifteenth century to early twentieth century, Rhone-Alpes). Paris: Ministère de la Culture, Images du Patrimonie.

Belhoste, J.-F., Bertrand, P. and Gayot, G. 1984. *La Manufacture de Dijonval et la draperie sedanaise 1650–1850* (The Dijonval Manufactury and the Sedan cloth industry 1650–1850). Paris: Ministère de la Culture, Cahiers de l'Inventaire.

Belhoste, J.-F., Maheux, H. et al. 1984. *Les Forges du Pays de Châteaubriant* (Ironworks of the Châteaubriant region). Paris and Nantes: Ministère de la Culture, Cahiers de l'Inventaire.

Bélisle, J. 1981. *La centrale hydro-électrique du canal de Soulanges, Les Cèdres* (The hydro-electric power station of the Soulanges Canal at Les Cèdres). Montreal: Ministry of Cultural Affairs.

Bell, A. M. 1950. *Locomotives: their construction, maintenance and operation.* London: Virtue.

Bell, C. and Bell, R. 1969. *City Fathers: the early history of town planning in Britain.* London: Barrie & Rockliff, Cresset Press.

Bell, P. 1984. *Timber and Iron: houses in North Queensland mining settlements 1861–1920.* Brisbane: University of Queensland Press.

—— 1987. *Gold, Iron and Steam: the industrial archaeology*

of the Palmer goldfield. Townsville: James Cook University.

Bellini, M., Travi, L. M. and Nicolin, P. 1986. *Il Luogo del Lavoro* (The depiction of work). Milan: Electa, Triennale di Milano.

Bendure, Z. and Pfeiffer, G. 1946. *America's Fabrics*. New York: Macmillan.

Benjamin, D. H. 1900. *The Launderer: a practical treatise on the management and operation of a steam laundry*. Cincinnati, OH: Starchroom Publishing.

Bennett, R. and Lever, J. A. 1981. *A History of Smith & Nephew 1856–1981*. London: Smith & Nephew.

Benoit, S. 1990. *La Grande Forge de Buffon* (The Buffon Ironworks). Montbard. Association pour las sauvegarde et l'animation des forges de Buffon.

Bensman, D. and Lynch, R. 1988. *Rusted Dreams: hard times in a steel community*. Berkeley, CA: University of California Press.

Benson, J. 1980. *British Coalminers in the Nineteenth Century: a social history*. Dublin: Gill & Macmillan.

Bentham, J. 1791. *The Panopticon or Prison Discipline*. London: T. Payne.

Bentley, T. 1779. *A Short View of the General Advantages of Inland Navigation*. London: privately published.

Behrend, I. and Ránki, G. 1977. *Economic Development in East Central Europe in the Nineteenth and Twentieth Centuries*. New York and London: Columbia University Press.

Berendson, A. 1957. *Tiles: a general history*. London: Faber.

Beresford, M. 1961. *New Towns of the Middle Ages*. London: Lutterworth Press.

——1988. *East End, West End: the faces of Leeds during urbanization 1684–1842*. Leeds: Thoresby Society.

Berg, A. 1968. *Norsk Gardstun* (Norwegian farmhouses). Oslo: Institut sammenlignende Kultursforskning.

Berg, M., Hudson, P. and Sonenscher, M. 1983. *Manufacture in Town and Country before the Factory*. Cambridge: Cambridge University Press.

Bergasse, J.-D. 1983. *Le Canal du Midi: trois siècles de bataillerie et de voyages* (The Canal du Midi: three centuries of struggles and journeys). Cessenon: Bergasse.

Bergengren, E. 1962. *Alfred Nobel: the man and his work*, transl. A. Blair. London: Nelson.

Berger, M. 1980. *Historische Bahnhofsbauten I: Sachsens, Preussens, Mecklenburgs und Thuringens* (Historic railway station buildings I: Saxony, Prussia, Mecklenburg and Thuringia). Berlin: VEB Verlag fur Verkehravesen.

——1987. *Historische Bahnhofsbauten II: Braunschweig, Hannover, Bremen, Hamburg, Oldenburg und Shleswig Holstein* (Historic railway station buildings II: Braunschweig, Hannover, Bremen, Hamburg, Oldenburg und Shleswig Holstein). Berlin: VEB Verlag fur Verkehravesen.

Bergeron, L. ed. 1989. *Paris, genèse d'un paysage* (Paris, genesis of a landscape). Paris: Picard.

Bergeron, L., Bourdelais, P. et al. 1989. *L'espace français* (The space of France). Paris: Le Seuil.

Bergier, J.-F. 1983. *Die Wirtschaftsgeschichte der Schweiz* (The economic history of Switzerland). Zürich.

Bergwitz, J. K. 1924. *Kongsberg: Som Bergkoloni, Bergstad og Kjopstad 1624–1924* (Kongsberg: mining colony and town 1624–1924). Oslo: Grondahl.

Berthold, R. et al. 1985. *Produktivkräfte in Deutschland I: 1870–1917/18* (Industrial production in Germany I, 1870–1917/18). Berlin: Akademie-Verlag.

——1988. *Produktivkräfte in Deutschland II: 1917/18–1945* (Industrial production in Germany II, 1917/18–1945). Berlin: Akademie-Verlag.

Berthollet, C. L. 1791. *Elements of the Art of Dyeing*. London & Paris: Couchman.

Bessemer, H. 1905. *Sir Henry Bessemer: an autobiography*. London: Engineering.

Bestor, A. E. 1950. *Backwoods Utopias*. Philadelphia, PA: University of Pennsylvania Press.

Betts, C. and Betts, D. 1973. *The Railways of Great Britain*. Newton Abbot: David & Charles.

Bianconi, M. O'C. and Watson, S. J. 1962. *Bianconi*. Dublin: Allen Figgis.

Bibliothèque Nationale 1951. *Diderot et L'Encyclopédie* (Diderot and the Encyclopedia). Paris: Bibliothèque Nationale.

Biddle, G. 1973. *Victorian Stations*. Newton Abbot: David & Charles.

Biddle, G. and Nock, O. S. 1983. *The Railway Heritage of Britain*. London: Michael Joseph.

Biddle, G. and Spence, J. 1977. *The British Railway Station*. Newton Abbot: David & Charles.

Biecker, J. and Buschmann, W. 1986. *Berbauarchitektur* (Mining architecture). Bochum: Studienverlage Dr N. Bruckmeyer.

Bigmore, P. 1979. *The Bedfordshire Landscape*. London: Hodder & Stoughton.

Bilbao, L. M. 1984. *La siderurgía vasca, 1770–1885* (Basque ironmaking, 1770–1885). San Sebastián: Eusko Ikaskuntza.

Binney, M., Hamm, M. and Föhl, A. 1984. *Great Railway Stations of Europe*. London: Thames & Hudson.

Binney, M. and Pearce, D. 1979. *Railway Architecture*. London: Orbis.

Binnie, G. M. 1981. *Early Victorian Water Engineers*. London: Thomas Telford.

——1987. *Early Dam Builders in Britain*. London: Thomas Telford.

Bird, A. 1969. *Roads and Vehicles*. London: Batsford.

Birmingham, J., Jack, I. and Jeans, D. 1979. *Australian Pioneer Technology: sites and relics*. Richmond: Heinemann Educational Australia.

——1983. *Industrial Archaeology in Australia: rural industry*. Richmond: Heinemann Educational Australia.

Bischoff, J. 1842. *A Comprehensive History of the Woollen and Worsted Manufactures*. London: Smith Elder. Reprint, 1968, London: Cass.

Bishop, D. and Davies, W. J. K. 1972. *Railways and War before 1918*. London: Blandford Press.

Bishop, J. L. 1864. *A History of American Manufactures*

from 1608 to 1860. 3 vols. Reprint, 1966, Fairfield, NJ: Kelley.

Bjorkenstam, N. and Fornander, S. 1985. *Metallurgy and Technology at Lapphyttan, Medieval Iron in Society.* Stockholm: Jernkontorets forskning.

Bjorkenstam, N. and Magnusson, G. 1988. *Ore as a Factor for the Development of the Indirect Process.* Vallecamonica: Conference La Siderurgia nell'Antiquita.

Bjorling, P. R. 1894. *Water or Hydraulic Motors.* London: Spon.

Black, W. 1849. *A Practical Treatise on Brewing.* London: Longman.

Blackwell, W. L. 1968. *The Beginnings of Russian Industrialization 1800–1860.* Princeton, NJ: Princeton University Press.

Blainey, G. 1954. *The Peaks of Lyell.* Carlton: Melbourne University Press.

—— 1963. *The Rush that Never Ended.* Carlton: Melbourne University Press.

Blair, M. 1981. *Once Upon the Lagan: the story of the Lagan canal.* Belfast: Blackstall Press.

Blair, W. N. 1887. *The Industries of New Zealand.* Christchurch: Press Company.

Blake, N. 1956. *Water for the Cities: a history of urban water supply in the United States.* Syracuse, NY: Syracuse University Press.

Blake, P. 1960. *Mies van der Rohe: Architecture and Structure.* London: Gollancz.

Bleyl, F. 1917. *Baulich und volkskuhnlich Beachtenswertes aus dem Kulturgebiet des Silberbergbaues* (Notable buildings and folklore features of the cultural region of the silver mines). Dresden: Landesverein Sächsischer Heimatschutz.

Bliven, B. 1954. *The Wonderful Writing Machine.* New York: Random House.

Blower, A. 1964. *British Railway Tunnels.* London: Ian Allan.

Bluestone, D. M. 1978. *Cleveland, an Inventory of Historic Engineering and Industrial Sites.* Washington DC: National Park Service.

Blumenfeld, H. 1971. *The Modern Metropolis: its origins, growth, characteristics and planning.* Cambridge, MA: MIT Press.

Bobek, H. and Lichtenberger, E. 1966. *Bauliche Gestalt und Entwicklung seit der Mitt des 19 Jahrhunderts* (Building structures: form and development since the mid-nineteenth century). Vienna: Graz-Böhlau.

Bochenski, A. 1972. *Dzieje i techniki Swietokrzyskiego gornictwa i hutnictwa kruszcowego* (The history and technology of ore mining in the Swietokrzyskie mountains). Warsaw: Wydawnictwo Geologiczne.

—— 1984. *Przemysł Polski w dawnych wiekach* (The history of Polish industry). Warsaw: Panstwowy Institut Wydawniczy.

Bodey, H. 1983. *Nailmaking.* Princes Risborough: Shire Publications.

Bodmer, W. 1960. *Die Entwicklung der schweizerischen Textilwirtschaft im Rahmen der übrigen Industrien und Wirtschaftszweige* (The development of Swiss textile manufactures in the context of other industries and economic factors). Zürich: Verlag Berichthaus.

Body, G. and Body, I. G. 1981. *Light Railways, Transport and Industrial Preservation.* Weston-Super-mare: Avon, Anglia.

Body, G. and Eastleigh, R. L. 1964. *Cliff Railways of the British Isles.* Newton Abbot: David & Charles.

Boehm, K. 1967. *The British Patent System.* Cambridge: Cambridge University Press.

Boettinger, H. M. 1977. *The Telephone Book: Bell, Watson, Vail and American life 1876–1976.* New York: Riverwood.

Boger, L. A. 1971. *A Dictionary of World Pottery and Porcelain.* London: A. & C. Black.

Bohm, I. 1972. *The Swedish Blast Furnace in the Nineteenth century.* Stockholm: Jernkontorets forskning.

Boissé, P., Tétu, O. et al. 1990. *Architecture et industrie à Aire-sur-la-Lys* (Architecture and industry at Aire-sur-la-Lys). Paris: Ministère de la Culture, Images du Patrimonie.

Boje, P. 1979. *Det industrielle miljo 1840–1940: kilder og litterature* (The industrial environment 1840–1940: sources and literature). Copenhagen: Akademisk forlag.

Boldizsár, I. 1959. *Hungary: a comprehensive guidebook.* Budapest: Corvina.

Bolle, J. 1963. *Solvay: l'invention, l'homme, l'enterprise industrielle, 1863–1963* (Solvay: the man, the invention, the industrial enterprise, 1863–1963). Brussels: Solvay et Cie.

Bollerey, F. and Hartmann, K. 1978. *Siedlungen aus dem Reg Bez Düsseldorf* (Workers' colonies in the Düsseldorf region). Essen: Kommunalverband Ruhrgebiet.

Bömmels, N. 1924. *Die Eifeler Eisenindustrie im 19 Jahrhundert* (The Eifel iron industry in the nineteenth century). Aachen: La Ruelle.

Boniface, P. 1981. *Hotels and Restaurants: 1830 to the present day.* London: HMSO for the Royal Commission on the Historic Monuments of England.

Bonillo, J. L., Borruey, R. et al. 1990. *Marseille, Ville et Port* (Marseilles, City and Port). Marseilles: Editions Parenthèses.

Bonnefous, E. 1987. *Le Conservatoire national des Arts et Métiers, son histoire, son musée* (The National conservatory of arts and trades, its history, its museums). Paris: CNAM.

Book of Trades 1839. *The Young Tradesman or Book of English Trades; being a Library of the Useful Arts for Commercial Education.* London: Whittaker.

Booker, F. 1971. *The Industrial Archaeology of the Tamar Valley,* 2nd edn. Newton Abbot: David & Charles.

Booker, J. 1974. *Essex and the Industrial Revolution.* Chelmsford: Essex County Council.

Booker, P. J. 1963. *A History of Engineering Drawing.* London: Chatto & Windus.

Boorstin, D. J. 1958. *The Americans: the colonial experience.* New York: Random House.

—— 1965. *The Americans: the national experience.* New York: Random House.

—— 1966. *An American Primer*. New York: New American Library.

—— 1972. *The Image*. New York: Harper.

—— 1973. *The Americans: the democratic experience*. London: Sphere Books.

Booth, G. 1977. *The British Motor Bus*, 2nd edn. London: Ian Allan.

Borsa, T. 1981. *Zakład w Maleńcu* (The Maleniec plant). Kielce.

Bos, W. 1974. *Van baggerbeugel tot sleepzuiger: een overzicht van de ontwikkeling van de Naderlandse baggerindustrie* (From bucket-dredging to grablines: an outline of the development of the Dutch dredging industry). Sliedrecht: Van Wijngaarden.

Böse, A. 1948. *Johann Wülfing und Sohn*. Lennep: Adolph Mann (printer).

Boswell, J. 1966. *JS100: the story of Sainsburys*. London: J. Sainsbury.

Bott, G. 1985. *Leben und Arbeiten im Industriezeitalter: eine Austellung zur Wirtschafts- und Sozialgeschichte Bayerns seit 1850* (Living and working in industrial times: an exhibition of the economic and social history of Bavaria since 1850). Stuttgart: Konrad Theiss Verlag.

Bouchard, A. 1980. *L'industrialisation à Hochelaga-Maisonneuve* (The industrialisation of Hochelaga-Maisonneuve). Montreal: Atelier d'Histoire Hochelaga-Maisonneuve.

Boucher, C. T. G. 1968. *James Brindley, Engineer: the great canal builder*. Norwich: Goose.

Boudier, J.-F. and Luquet, F. M. 1981. *Dictionnaire laitier* (Dictionary of dairying). Paris: Technique et Documentation.

Boulnois, H. P. 1919. *Modern Roads*. London: Edward Arnold.

Bourgougnon, R. and Desnoyers, M. 1986. *Montluçon au siècle de l'industrie: le temps du canal, du fer et du charbon* (Montluçon during the century of industry: the age of the canal, of iron and of coal). Montlucon: Moulins.

Bourne, J. C. 1839. *Drawings on the London and Birmingham Railway*. London: Ackerman. Reprint, 1970, Newton Abbot: David & Charles.

—— 1846. *The History and Description of the Great Western Railway*. London: Bogue. Reprint, 1981, Newton Abbot: David & Charles.

Bowden-Smith, E. C. 1920. *The Efficiency of Pumps and Ejectors*. London: Constable.

Bowen, E. G. 1987. *Radar Days*. Bristol: A. Hilger.

Bowen, F. C. 1930. *A Century of Atlantic Travel*. Boston, MA: Little, Brown & Co.

Bowering, I. 1988. *The Art and Mystery of Breweries in Ontario*. Burnstown, Ontario: General Store Publishing House.

Bowie, K. ed. 1987. *Les grandes gares parisiennes au XIXè siècle* (The main Paris railway stations during the nineteenth century). Paris: Délégation à l'action artistique de la Ville de Paris.

Boyce, C. 1986. *The Dictionary of Furniture*. New York: Facts on File.

Boyd, J. I. C. 1988. *The Talyllyn Railway*. Didcot: Wild Swan.

Boyne, W. J. 1988. *Power Behind the Wheel: the evolution of car design and technology*. London: Conran Octopus.

Boyson, R. 1970. *The Ashworth Cotton Enterprise: the rise and fall of a family firm 1818–1880*. Oxford: Oxford University Press.

BP (British Petroleum) 1958. *Our Industry*, 3rd edn. London: British Petroleum.

BPP (British Parliamentary Papers) 1840, XXIII. *Hand Loom Weavers. Report of the Assistant Commissioners on Eastern and South-Western England, the West Riding of Yorkshire and Germany*. London: HMSO.

—— 1849. *Report of the Commissioners appointed to inquire into the Application of Iron to Railway Structures*. London: HMSO.

—— 1863, XVIII. *First Report from the Commissioners on the Employment of Children and Young Persons in Trade and Manufactures*. London: HMSO.

—— 1868–9, XIV. *Report on the Printworks Act and on the Bleaching and Dyeing Works Acts*. London: HMSO.

Brace, H. W. 1960. *The History of Seed Crushing in Great Britain*. London: Land Books.

Bradbury, F. 1902. *Carpet Manufacture*. Belfast: Langdale House.

—— 1975. *Bradbury's Book of Hallmarks: a guide to marks of origin on British and Irish silver, gold and platinum and on foreign imported silver and gold plate 1544–1975*, 15th edn. Sheffield: J. W. Northend.

Bradfield, R. and John, W. J. 1928. *Telephone and Power Transmission*. London: Chapman & Hall.

Braet, G. 1883. *Note sur la construction et la stabilitée des cheminées en maconerie* (Note on the construction and stability of masonry chimneys). Brussels.

Brassil, A. 1980. *Industrial Archaeology Sites List*. 2 vols. Sydney: National Trust of Australia.

Bratton, J. S. 1986. *Music Hall: performance and style*. Milton Keynes: Open University Press.

Braudel, F. 1981. *Civilisation and Capitalism 15th–18th Century*, vol. I: *The structures of everyday life, the limits of the possible*. London: Collins.

—— 1982. *Civilization and Capitalism 15th–18th Century*, vol. II: *The wheels of commerce*. London: Collins.

—— 1984. *Civilization and Capitalism 15th–18th Century*, vol. III: *The perspective of the world*. London: Collins.

Braudel, F., Labrousse, E. et al. 1977–80. *Histoire économique et sociale de la France* (Economic and social history of France). 4 vols. Paris: PUF.

Brauman, A. et al. 1980. *Jean-Baptiste André Godin (1817–1888). Le Familstère de Guise ou les équivalents de la Richesse* (The Familistère at Guise or the equivalents of wealth). Brussels: Archives d'Architecture Moderne.

Bravard, J.-P. 1981. *L'Ondaine, valle du Fer* (The Ondaine, iron valley). Saint-Etienne: Le Heneff.

Brears, P. C. D. 1971. *The English Country Pottery: its history and techniques*. Newton Abbot: David & Charles.

Brears, P. C. D. and Harrison, S. 1979. *The Dairy Catalogue.* York: Castle Museum.

Brelot, C. I. 1985. *La Saline comtale de Salins (Jura)* (The Counts' Saltworks, Salins). Besançon: CRDP.

Brelot, C. I. and Locatelli, R. 1981. *Un millénaire d'exploitation du sel en France-Comté: contribution à l'archéologie industrielle des Salines de Salins* (A thousand years of Franche-Compté salt production: a contribution to the industrial archaeology of the saltworks at Salins). Besançon: CRDP.

Brelot, C. I. and Mayaud, J.-L. 1982. *L'Industrie en Sabots, la taillanderie de Nans-sous-Sainte Anne, Doubs* (Industry in clogs, the Nans-sous-Sainte Anne edge tool works, Doubs). Paris: Garnier.

Brent, R. D. 1933. *The History of British Aviation 1908–14.* Reprint, 1988, Surbiton: Air Research Publications.

Breschi, R., Mancini, A. and Tosi, M. T. 1982. *L'industria del Ferro nel territorio pistoiese* (The iron industry in the Pistoia region). Pistoia.

Brett, C. E. B. 1967. *Buildings of Belfast 1700–1914.* London: Weidenfeld & Nicolson.

Brewster, D. 1830. *The Edinburgh Encyclopedia.* Edinburgh: Blackwood.

Briggs, A. 1959. *Chartist Studies.* London: Macmillan.

——1961. *The Birth of Broadcasting.* Oxford: Oxford University Press.

——1962. *William Morris: selected writing and designs.* Harmondsworth: Penguin.

——1963. *Victorian Cities.* London: Odhams.

——1984. *Marks and Spencers 1884–1984: a centenary history.* London: Marks and Spencer.

Briggs, A. and Gill, C. 1952. *History of Birmingham*, vol. I: *to 1865*; vol. II: *1865–1939.* Oxford: Oxford University Press.

Bright, C. 1898. *Submarine Telegraphy.* London: Lockwood.

Brinnin, J. M. 1971. *The Swan of the Grand Saloon.* New York: Delacorte.

Brinnin, J. M. and Galvin, K. 1988. *Grand Luxe: the transatlantic style.* London: Bloomsbury.

British Association 1950. *Birmingham and its Regional Setting.* London: British Association for the Advancement of Science.

Brittain, J. E. 1976. *A Brief History of Engineering in Georgia and Guide to Seventy-six Historic Engineering Sites.* Atlanta, GA: Georgia Institute of Technology.

Broadbridge, S. 1974. *The Birmingham Canal Navigations 1768–1846.* Newton Abbot: David & Charles.

Brockman, H. A. N. 1974. *The British Architect in Industry 1841–1940.* London: Allen & Unwin.

Broehl, W. 1966. *Precision Valley.* Englewood Cliffs, NJ: Prentice-Hall.

Brogden, S. 1968. *Australia's Two Airline Policy.* Melbourne: Melbourne University Press.

Brongniart, A. 1844. *Traité des Artes Céramiques* (Treatise on the ceramic arts). Paris: Béchet Jeune.

Brook, F. 1977. *The Industrial Archaeology of the British Isles: the West Midlands.* London: Batsford.

Brook, F. and Allbutt, M. 1973. *The Shropshire Lead Mines.* Ashbourne: Moorland.

Brooke, S. 1984. *The Railways of Australia.* Sydney: Dreamweaver.

Brooks, C. M. 1983. *Aspects of the Sugar Refining Industry from the Sixteenth to the Nineteenth Century.* London: PMA.

Broomham, R. 1987. *First Light: 150 years of gas.* Sydney: Hale & Iremonger.

Brosnahan, T. 1988. *Turkey: a travel survival kit.* London: Lonely Planet.

Brothwell, D. and Higgs, E. 1969. *Science in Archaeology: a survey of progress and research.* London: Thames & Hudson.

Brouwer, N. J. 1985. *International Register of Historic Ships.* Oswestry: Anthony Nelson.

Brown, J. 1832. *Memoir of Robert Blincoe.* London.

Brown, R. C. and Cook, R. 1974. *Canada 1896–1921: a nation transformed.* Toronto: McClelland & Steward.

Brown, W. A. 1916. *The Portland Cement Industry: a practical treatise on the building, equipping and economical running of a Portland cement plant.* London: Crosby Lockwood.

Bruce, A. W. 1952. *The Steam Locomotive in America.* New York: W. W. Norton.

Bruce, R. V. 1973. *Bell: Alexander Graham Bell and the conquest of solitude.* London: Gollancz.

Brugmans, H. 1973. *Geschiedenis van Amsterdam, V–VI* (History of Amsterdam, vols V–VI). Utrecht: Spectrum.

Brunel, I. 1870. *The Life of I. K. Brunel, Civil Engineer.* Reprint, 1971, Newton Abbot: David & Charles.

Brunello, F. 1973. *L'arte della tintura nella storia dell'umanità* (The art of dyeing in the history of mankind). Vicenza: Neri Pozza.

Brunnich, T. 1826. *Kongsberg Solvebergverk i Norge* (Kongsberg silvermines in Norway). Copenhagen.

Bruwier, M. and Duvosquel, J.-M. 1975. *La règne de la machine: rencontre avec l'archéologie industrielle* (The reign of the machine: the meeting point with industrial archaeology). Brussels: Crédit Communal de Belgique.

Brzozowski, S. 1974. *Ignacy Łukasiewicz.* Warsaw: Interpress.

Buchanan, C. A. and Buchanan, R. A. 1980. *The Batsford Guide to the Industrial Archaeology of Central Southern England.* London: Batsford.

Buchanan, L. 1956. *Ships of Steam.* New York: McGraw Hill.

Buchanan, R. A. 1989. *The Engineers: a history of the engineering profession in Britain 1750–1914.* London: Jessica Kingsley.

Buchanan, R. A. and Cossons, N. 1969. *The Industrial Archaeology of the Bristol Region.* Newton Abbot: David & Charles.

Buchanan, R. A. and Watkins, G. 1976. *The Industrial Archaeology of the Stationary Steam Engine.* London: Allen Lane.

Buckingham, J. S. 1849. *National Evils and Practical Remedies.* London: Peter Jackson.

Bucknall, R. 1957. *Boat Trains and Channel Packets: the English short sea routes.* London: Stuart.

Buddensieg, T. 1984. *Villa Hügel: Das Wohnhaus Krupp in Essen* (The Villa Hügel: home of the Krupp family in Essen). Berlin: Siedler Verlag.

Buddensieg, T., Düwell, K. and Sembach, K.-J. 1987. *Wissenschaften in Berlin*, Band I: *Objecte*; Band II: *Disziplinen*; Band III: *Gedanken* (Science in Berlin, vol. I: objects; vol. II: discipline; vol. III: ideas). Berlin: Mann Verlag.

Buddensieg, T. and Henning, R. 1978. *Industriekultur: Peter Behrens und die AEG 1907–1914* (Industrial culture: Peter Behrens and the AEG 1907–1914). Berlin: Mann Verlag.

—— 1981. *Die Nützlichen Künste: Gestaltende Technik und Bildende Kunst seit der Industriellen Revolution* (Useful art: applied technology and fine art during the Industrial Revolution). Berlin: Quadriga Verlag.

Buder, S. 1967. *Pullman: an experiment in industrial order and community planning 1880–1930.* New York: Oxford University Press.

Buderath, B. 1990. *Peter Behrens: Umbautes Licht: Das Verwaltungsgebäude der Hoechst AG.* (Peter Behrens: enclosing light: the administrative buildings of the Hoechst company). Munich: Prestel Verlag.

Bulkeley, G. 1930. *Railway and Seaport Freight Movement with Examples of British and American Practice.* London: Crosby Lockwood.

Bunau-Varilla, P. 1913. *Panama: the creation, destruction and resurrection.* London: Constable.

Bunbury, H. M. and Davidson, A. 1925. *The Industrial Applications of Coal Tar Products.* London: Benn.

Bunsheath, P. 1962. *A History of Electrical Engineering.* London: Faber.

Burgess-Wise, D. 1981. *Automobile Archaeology.* Cambridge: Stephens.

Burke, G. 1956. *The Making of Dutch Towns.* London: Cleaver-Hulme.

—— 1971. *Towns in the Making.* London: Arnold.

Burkett, M. E. 1979. *The Art of the Felt Maker.* Kendall: Abbot Hall Gallery.

Burmeister and Wain 1943. *Burmeister and Wain Gennem Hunderede Aar* (Burmeister and Wain through one hundred years). Copenhagen: Burmeister & Wain.

Burn, R. 1797. *Ecclesiastical Law*, 6th edn. London: Butterworth.

Burn, W. L. 1964. *The Age of Equipoise: a study of the mid-Victorian generation.* London: Allen & Unwin.

Burnett, J. 1978. *A Social History of Housing 1815–1970.* Newton Abbot: David & Charles.

Burnham, D. K. 1981. *Warf and Weft: a textile terminology.* Toronto: ROM.

Burnham, H. B. and Burnham, D. K. 1972. *Keep Me Warm One Night: early handloom weaving in eastern Canada.* Toronto: University of Toronto Press.

Burnley, J. 1889. *The History of Wool and Wool Combing.* London: Sampson Low. Reprint, 1969, New York: Kelly.

Burtniak, J. and Turner, W. B. eds 1980. *Villages in the Niagara Peninsula.* St Catherines: Brock University.

Burton, A. 1976. *Josiah Wedgwood: a biography.* London: Deutsch.

Burton, W. 1902. *A History and Description of English Porcelain.* London: Cassell. Reprint, 1972, Wakefield: EP.

Burton, W. K. and Dumbleton, J. E. 1928. *The Water Supply of Towns and the Construction of Waterworks*, 4th edn. London: Crosby Lockwood.

Burtt, F. 1934. *Cross Channel and Coastal Paddle Steamers.* London: Tilling.

Burtt, P. 1923. *The Principal Factors in Freight Train Operation.* London: Allen & Unwin.

Bury, T. T. 1831. *Six Coloured Views of the Liverpool and Manchester Railway.* London: Ackermann.

Busch, B. C. 1988. *War against the Seals: a history of the North American seal fishery.* Gloucester: Alan Sutton.

Busch, W., Schupp, F. and Kremmer, M. 1980. *Berbauar-chitektur 1919–1974* (Mining architecture 1919–1974). *Arbeitshefte des Landeskonservatores Rheinland* XIII. Cologne: Rheinland Verlag.

Butler, E. 1922. *Modern Pumping and Hydraulic Machinery.* London: Griffin.

Butler, P. H. 1985. *British Isles Airfield Guide*, 10th edn. Liverpool: Merseyside Aviation Society.

Butlin, B. and Dacre, P. 1982. *The Billy Butlin Story.* London: Robson.

Butlin, N. G. 1964. *Investment in Australian Economic Development 1861–1900.* Melbourne: Cambridge University Press.

Butt, J. 1967. *The Industrial Archaeology of Scotland.* Newton Abbot: David & Charles.

—— 1971. *Robert Owen, Prince of Cotton Spinners: a symposium.* Newton Abbot: David & Charles.

—— 1987. *Essays in Scottish Textile History.* Aberdeen: Aberdeen University Press.

Butt, J., Donnachie, I. and Hume, J. R. 1968. *Industrial History in Pictures: Scotland.* Newton Abbot: David & Charles.

Buxton, N. K. 1979. *Economic Development of the British Coal Industry.* London: Batsford.

Byatt, A. 1978. *Picture Postcards and their Publishers.* Malvern: Golden Age.

Bythell, D. 1969. *The Hand Loom Weavers.* Cambridge: Cambridge University Press.

Cairns, N. T. 1972. *North Atlantic Passenger Liners since 1900.* London: Ian Allan.

Calhoun, D. H. 1960. *The American Civil Engineer: origins and conflict.* Cambridge, MA: Technology Press.

Calvert, M. 1967. *The Mechanical Engineer in America 1839–1910: professional cultures in conflict.* Baltimore, MD: Johns Hopkins University Press.

Campbell, J. and Sherrard, P. 1968. *A History of Modern Greece.* Cambridge: Cambridge University Press.

Canadian Port and Harbour Directory 1923. *Canadian Port and Harbour Directory.* Ottawa: Holland.

Candee, R. M. 1985. *Atlantic Heights: a World War One shipbuilders' community.* Portsmouth, NH: Portsmouth Marine Society.

Cantrell, J. A. 1984. *James Nasmyth and the Bridgewater Foundry: a study of entrepreneurship in the early engineering industry.* Manchester: Chetham Society.

Carafoli, E. 1966. *Rolul stiintelor tehnice in dezvoltarea economica a Romaniei* (The role of technology in the economnic development of Romania). Bucharest: Centum Anni Academicae.

Careless, J. M. S. 1967. *The Canadians 1867–1967*. Toronto: Macmillan.

—— 1971. *Colonists and Canadiens 1760–1867*. Toronto.

Carlson, H. 1978. *Spring Designer's Handbook*. New York: Marcel Dekker.

Carmichael, W. L., Linton, G. and Price, I. 1947. *Callaway Textile Dictionary*. Georgia: Callaway Mills.

Carne, J. E. 1908. *The Copper Mining Industry in New South Wales*, 2nd edn. Sydney: New South Wales Geological Survey.

Carpenter, M. 1851. *Reformatory Schools for the Children of the Perishing and Dangerous Classes and for Juvenile Offenders*. London: Gilpin.

Carr, R. J. M. 1984. *Docklands History Survey: a guide to research*. London: Greater London Council.

Carr, T. H. 1944. *Electric Power Stations*. London: Chapman & Hall.

Carter, C. and Hidden, H. R. 1937. *Wall and Floor Tiling*. London: Caxton.

Carter, F. W. 1972. *Dubrovnik (Ragusa): a classic city state*. London and New York: Seminar Press.

Case, J. 1921. *The Theory of Direct-current Dynamos and Motors*. Cambridge: Heffer.

Cassau, T. 1915. *The Consumer Co-operative Movement in Germany*. London: Fisher Unwin.

Casserley, H. C. 1979. *Irish Railways in the Heyday of Steam*. Truro: Bradford Barton.

Casson, H. N. 1910. *The History of the Telephone*. Chicago: McClurg.

Castner-Kellner 1945. *Fifty Years of Progress: the story of the Castner-Kellner Company*. Runcorn: Castner-Kellner Company.

Catling, H. 1970. *The Spinning Mule*. Newton Abbot: David & Charles.

Caunter, C. F. 1955. *The History and Development of Cycles*. London: HMSO.

—— 1982. *Motor Cycles*. London: HMSO.

Cederschield, G. and von Feilitzen, E. 1946. *The History of the Swedish Match Industry*. Stockholm: Natur och Kultur.

Cement Marketing Company 1909. *Everyday uses of Portland Cement*. London: Cement Marketing Company.

Central Electric Railfans' Association 1986. *The Colorful Streetcars We Rode*. Chicago, IL: Central Electric Railfans' Association.

Ceram, C. W. 1965. *The Archaeology of the Cinema*. London: Thames & Hudson.

Chadwick, G. F. 1961. *The Works of Sir Joseph Paxton 1803–65*. London: Architectural Press.

Chaffers, W. 1965. *Marks and Monograms on European and Oriental Pottery and Porcelain*, 2nd edn. 2 vols. London: William Reeves.

Challinor, J. 1986. *A Dictionary of Geology*, 6th edn, ed. A. Wyatt. Cardiff: University of Wales Press.

Chaloner, W. O. 1950. *The Social and Economic Development of Crewe, 1780–1923*. Manchester: Manchester University Press.

Chambers, W. 1854. *Things as they are in America*. Edinburgh: W. & R. Chambers.

Chambrier, P. de 1919. *Historique de Pechelbronn 1498–1918* (History of Pechelbronn 1498–1918). Neuchatel: Attinger Frères.

Chancellor, V. 1969. *Master and Artisan in Victorian England*. London: Evelyn, Adams & Mackay.

Chandler, A. 1977. *The Visible Hand. the managerial revolution in American business*. Cambridge, MA: Belknap Press of Harvard University Press.

Chandler, A. D. Jnr. 1964. *Giant Enterprise: Ford, General Motors and the automobile industry: sources and reading*. New York: Harcourt Brace.

Chandler, M. 1967. *Ceramics in the Modern World*. London: Aldus.

Chapelle, H. I. 1936. *History of American Sailing Ships*. New York: Norton.

Chaplain, J.-M. 1984. *La Chambre des Tisseurs, Louviers: cité drapière, 1680–1840* (The weaver's room, Louviers: a cloth-making town, 1680–1840). Seyssel: Champ-vallon.

Chapman, S. C. and Chassagne, S. 1981. *European Textile Printers in the Eighteenth Century: a study of Peel and Oberkampf*. London: Heinemann.

Chapman, S. D. 1967. *The Early Factory Masters: the transition to the factory system in the Midlands textile industry*. Newton Abbot: David & Charles.

—— 1971. *The History of Working-class Housing*. Newton Abbot: David & Charles.

—— 1974. *Jesse Boot of Boots the Chemist*. London: Hodder & Stoughton.

Charbonneau, R. et al. 1980. *L'histoire du logement ouvrier à Hochelaga-Maisonneuve* (The history of working class housing at Hochelaga-Maisonneuve). Hochelaga-Maisonneuve: Atelier d'Histoire Hochelaga-Maisonneuve.

Charlton, C., Hool, D. and Strange, P. 1971. *Arkwright and the Mills at Cromford*. Cromford: Arkwright Society.

Chartres, J. A. 1977. *Internal Trade in England 1500–1700*. London: Macmillan.

Checkland, S. G. 1967. *The Mines of Tharsis: Roman, French and British enterprise in Spain*. London: Allen & Unwin.

Checkland, S. G. and Checkland, E. O. A. 1973. *The Poor Law Report of 1834*. Harmondsworth: Penguin.

Chemetov, P. and Marrey, B. 1976. *Familièrement inconnues: Architectures, Paris, 1848–1914* (Familiar yet ignored: architecture in Paris, 1848–1914). Paris: Secrétariat d'Etat à la Culture.

Chittenden, H. M. 1902. *The American Fur Trade of the Far West*. New York: Harper.

Chitty, M. 1971. *Industrial Archaeology of Exeter: a guide*. Exeter: University of Exeter Industrial Archaeology Group.

Christensen, C. J., Di Giacomo, A. and Pohorly, J. E. 1976. *History of Engineering in Niagara*. St Catharines: Engineering Institute of Canada, Niagara Peninsula Branch.

883

Christiansen, R. 1973. *A Regional History of the Railways of Britain*, vol. VII: *The West Midlands*. Newton Abbot: David & Charles.

Church, R. 1986. *The History of the British Coal Industry*, vol. III: *1830–1913*. Oxford: Oxford University Press.

CIBA 1959. *The Story of Chemical Industry in Basle*. Olten and Lausanne: Urs Graf.

Ciekot, J. 1985. *Gomictwo wegla kamiennego w procesie ksztaltowania srodowiska ludzkiego* (Coal mining in the process of human environment shaping). Wroclaw: Wroclaw Polytechnic.

CILAC 1981. *ICCIH 81: The Fourth International Conference on the Conservation of Industrial Heritage*. Paris: CILAC.

——1985. *L'Etude et la mise en valeur du patrimoine industriel: 4è Conférence internationale Lyon-Grenoble, Septembre 1981* (The study and value of the industrial heritage: the fourth international conference, Lyon and Grenoble, September 1981). Paris: Centre National de la Recherche Scientifique.

Cinqualbre, O., Hamon F. et al. 1988. *Architectures d'Usines en Val-de-marne, 1822–1939* (Factory architecture in the Val-de Marne 1822–1939). Paris: Cahiers de l'Inventaire, Ministère de la Culture.

Cipolla, C. M. 1967. *Clocks and Culture 1300–1700*. New York: Walker.

——1970. *The Fontana Economic History of Europe*, vol. IV. London: Fontana.

——1983. *The Emergence of Industrial Societies*, vol. I. Glasgow: Fontana.

Cirkel, F. 1912. *Mica: its occurrence, exploitation and uses*. Ottawa: Mines Branch of Canada.

Civera, I. A. 1988. *La Estación de Ferrocarril Puerta de la Ciudad* (The development of the railway station, gateway to the city). Valencia: Consellería de Cultura, Educación y Ciencia.

Civil, A. and Baker, A. C. 1976. *Fireless locomotives: a history of all British-built examples with notes on the general history of the type and its principles of operation*. Tarrant Hinton: Oakwood Press.

CIWL 1926. *Cinquantenaire de la Compagnie Internationale des Wagons-lits et des Grands Express Européens 1876–1926*. Brussels: Compagnie Internationale des Wagons-lits.

Claas, W. 1939. *Die technischen Kulturdenkmale im Bereich der früheren Grafschaft Mark* (Technical monuments in the former principality of Mark). Hagen: Westfälische Verlagsanstalt.

Claer, C. and Philippe, M. 1991. *L'ancienne sidérurgie de la Haute Saône* (Historic ironmaking in the Haute Saône). Paris: Ministère de la Culture, Cahiers de l'Inventaire.

Clapperton, R. H. 1951. *Modern Papermaking*. Oxford: Basil Blackwell.

——1967. *The Papermaking Machine*. Oxford: Pergamon.

Clark, C., Horton, M. and Stratton, M. J. 1985. *The Great Laxey Wheel and Mine*. Telford: Ironbridge Institute.

Clark, E. 1850. *The Britannia and Conway Tubular Bridges*. London: John Weale.

Clark, G. K. 1962. *The Making of Victorian England*. London: Methuen.

Clark, K. 1928. *The Gothic Revival: an essay in the history of taste*. London: Constable.

Clark, M. 1983. *A Short History of Australia*, 2nd edn (illustrated). Melbourne: Macmillan.

Clark, P. 1983. *The English Alehouse: a social history 1200–1830*. London: Longman.

Clark, R. H. 1960. *The Development of the English Traction Engine*. Norwich: Goose.

——1963. *The Development of the English Steam Waggon*. Norwich: Goose.

Clark, V. S. 1928. *History of Manufactures in the United States from 1607*. New York: Peter Smith.

Clarke, D. 1978. *Analytical Archaeology*, 2nd edn. London: Methuen.

Clarkson, L. A. 1971. *The Pre-Industrial Economy in Britain, 1500–1700*. London: Batsford.

——1985. *Proto-Industrialization: the first phase of industrialization*. London: Macmillan.

Clay, W. L. 1862. *Our Convict Systems*. London: Macmillan.

Clayton, W. 1920. *Margarine*. London: Longman.

Cleary, E. J. 1965. *The Building Society Movement*. London: Paul Elek.

Cleere, H. and Crossley, D. W. 1985. *The Iron Industry of the Weald*. Leicester: Leicester University Press.

Cleere, H. F. 1989. *Archaeological Heritage Management in the Modern World*. London: Unwin Hyman.

Clegg, H. A., Fox, A. and Thompson, A. F. 1964. *A History of British Trade Unions since 1889*, vol I. Oxford: Clarendon Press.

Clément, B. 1990. *Le Creusot, la Plaine des Riaux, lectures du paysage industriel* (Le Creusot, the Riaux plain: readings of the industrial landscape). Montceau-les-Mines: Ecomusée de la Communauté Le Creusot.

Clogg, R. 1983. *Greece in the 1980s*. London: Macmillan.

Clogg, R. and Clogg, M. 1980. *Greece*. Oxford: Oxford World Bibliographies.

Clough, R. T. 1980. *The Lead Smelting Mills of the Yorkshire Dales and Northern Pennines*, 2nd edn. Keighley: privately published.

Clouth, F. 1903. *Rubber, Gutta-Percha and Balata*. London: Maclaren.

Clow, A. and Clow, N. 1952. *The Chemical Revolution*. London: Blatchworth.

Cluett, D., Nash, J. and Learmonth, B. 1980. *Croydon Airport: the Great Days 1928–1939*. London: London Borough of Sutton.

Clymer, J. F. 1955. *Henry's Wonderful Model T, 1908–27*. New York: McGraw-Hill.

CNRS 1985. *L'étude et la mise en valeur du patrimoine industriel* (The study of the industrial heritage). Paris: Editions du Centre National de la Recherche Scientifique.

Coad, J. G. 1983. *Historic Architecture of the Royal Navy: an introduction*. London: Gollancz.

——1989. *The Royal Dockyards 1690–1850: architecture and engineering works of the sailing navy*. Aldershot: Scolar Press.

Cockerell, H. A. L. 1976. *The British Insurance Business, 1547–1970: an introduction and guide to historical records in the United Kingdom.* London: Heinemann Educational Books.

Coe, A. 1934. *The Science and Practice of Gas Supply.* 3 vols. Halifax: The Gas College.

Coe, W. E. 1969. *The Engineering Industry of the North of Ireland.* Newton Abbot: David & Charles.

Coffin, D. R. 1979. *The Villa in the Life of Renaissance Rome.* Princeton, NJ: Princeton University Press.

Cohen, J. M. 1956. *The Life of Ludwig Mond.* London: Methuen.

Cohn, M. M. 1966. *Sewers for Growing America.* Ambler, PA: Certainteed Productions Corporation.

Coignet 1900. *Histoire de la Maison Coignet 1818–1900.* Lyons: A. Rey.

Cole, A. and Watts, G. 1952. *The Handicrafts of France as Recorded in the Descriptions des Arts et Métiers 1761–1788.* Cambridge, MA: Harvard University Press.

Cole, A. H. 1926. *The American Wool Manufacture.* Cambridge, MA: Harvard University Press.

Cole, G. D. H. 1930. *The Life of Robert Owen.* London: Macmillan.

Cole, M. 1953. *Robert Owen 1771–1858.* London: Batchworth.

Cole, P. R. 1926. *Pioneers of Australian Industry: Australian industries and their founders.* Sydney: G. B. Philip.

Coleman, D. C. 1958. *The British Paper Industry 1495–1860: a study in industrial growth.* Oxford: Clarendon.

—— 1969. *Courtaulds: an economic and social history.* Oxford: Clarendon Press.

Collier, B. 1974. *The Airship: a history.* London: Hart-Davis, MacGibbon.

Collins, E. J. T. 1978. *The Economy of Upland Britain, 1750–1950.* Reading: University of Reading.

Collins, J. H. 1924. *The Story of Canned Foods.* New York: Dutton.

Collins, P. and Stratton, M. J. 1986. *From Trestles to Tracks.* Telford: Ironbridge Institute.

Collison, R. 1964. *Encyclopaedias: their history throughout the ages.* New York: Hafner.

Colwell, M. 1970. *Whaling around Australia.* London: Angus & Robertson.

Colyer, F. 1880. *Breweries and Malting.* London: Spon.

Comp, T. A. 1974. *New England, an Inventory of Historic Engineering and Industrial Sites.* Washington DC: National Park Service.

Condit, C. 1952. *The Rise of the Skyscraper.* Chicago, IL: University of Chicago Press.

—— 1964. *The Chicago School of Architecture.* Chicago, IL: University of Chicago Press.

Connah, G. 1988. *"Of the Hut I Builded": the archaeology of Australia's history.* Melbourne: Cambridge University Press.

Connor, R. D. 1987. *The Weights and Measures of England.* London: Science Museum.

Conradi, H. 1931. *Grossgaragen* (Large garages). Leipzig: Bebhardt.

Conray, J. C. 1928. *A History of Railways in Ireland.* London: Longman.

Conway-Jones, H. 1984. *Gloucester Docks: an illustrated history.* Gloucester: Alan Sutton.

Cooke, W. F. 1866. *The Electric Telegraph: was it invented by Professor Wheatstone?* 2 vols. London: W. H. Smith.

Cooper, G. 1976. *The Sewing Machine: its invention and development,* 2nd edn. Washington DC: Smithsonian Institution Press.

Copeland, J. 1968. *Roads and Their Traffic 1750–1850.* London: Batsford.

Copeland, M. T. 1912. *The Cotton Manufacturing Industry of the United States.* Cambridge, MA: Harvard University Press.

Copley, F. B. 1923. *Frederick W. Taylor: father of scientific management.* 2 vols. New York: Harper.

Copperthwaite, W. C. 1906. *Tunnel Shields and the Use of Compressed Air in Subaqueous Works.* New York: Van Nostrand.

Cordeiro, J. M. L. 1989. *A Industria Conserveira em Matosinhos* (The canning industry of Matosinhos). Matosinhos: Câmara Municipal de Matosinhos.

Corina, M. 1971. *Pile it High, Sell it Cheap: the authorized biography of Sir J. Cohen, founder of Tesco.* London: Weidenfeld & Nicholson.

Corlett, E. 1975. *The Iron Ship: the history and significance of Brunel's 'Great Britain'.* Bradford on Avon: Moonraker.

Corredor, J. and Montaner, J. M. 1984. *Arquitectura industrial en Cataluña del 1732 al 1919* (Industrial architecture in Catalonia from 1732 to 1919). Barcelona: Creaciones Gráficas.

Cossons, N. ed. 1975. *Transactions of the First International Congress on the Conservation of Industrial Monuments, Ironbridge, 29 May to 5 June 1973.* Telford: Ironbridge Gorge Museum.

—— 1988. *The BP Book of Industrial Archaeology,* 2nd edn. Newton Abbot: David & Charles.

Cossons, N. and Trinder, B. S. 1979. *The Iron Bridge: symbol of the Industrial Revolution.* Bradford on Avon: Adams & Dart.

Coste, P.-L. and Perdonnet, A. A. 1830. *Smelting of Lead Ores in Reverberatory Furnaces as Performed in Great Britain.* Reprint, 1986, Eindhoven: De Archaeologische Pers.

Coull, J. R. 1972. *The Fisheries of Europe: an economic geography.* London: Bell.

Council of Europe 1987. *The Industrial Heritage: what policies? Report of the Lyons colloquy.* Strasbourg: Council of Europe.

Countryman, B. 1982. *The R100 in Canada.* Nobito: Boston Mills Press.

Court, W. B. 1938. *The Rise of the Midland Industries, 1600–1838.* Oxford: Oxford University Press.

—— 1965. *British Economic History, 1870–1914: commentary and documents.* Cambridge: Cambridge University Press.

Courtaulds Ltd. 1957. *The Manufacture of Viscose Rayon.* Coventry: Courtaulds Ltd.

Courtecuisse, M. 1920. *La Manufacture de draps Van Robais au XVIIe et XVIIIe siècles* (The Van Robais broadcloth manufacture in the seventeenth and eighteenth centuries). Abbeville.

Coutant, Y. 1986. *Moulins des Flandres* (Windmills of Flanders). Ingersheim-Colmar: Editions SAEP.

Cox, B. 1979. *Paddle Steamers*. Poole: Blandford Press.

Crane, E. ed. 1975. *Honey: a comprehensive survey*. London: Heinemann.

Cranstone, D. 1985. *Moira Furnace: a Napoleonic blast furnace in Leicestershire*. Coalville: North West Leicestershire District Council.

Crawford, A., Dunn, M. and Thorne, R. 1986. *Birmingham Pubs 1880–1939*. Gloucester: Alan Sutton.

Crawford, W. H. 1972. *Domestic Industry in Ireland*. Dublin: Gill & Macmillan.

—— 1987. *The Irish Linen Industry*. Belfast: Ulster Folk and Transport Museum.

Cremin, A., Jack, R. I., Murray, T., Poweel, C. and Schulstad, W. 1987. *Survey of Historical Sites Lithgow Area*. Sydney: Department of Environment and Planning.

Critchell, J. T. and Raymond, J. 1912. *The History of the Frozen Meat Trade*. London: Constable.

Crocker, G. 1986. *The Gunpowder Industry*. Princes Risborough: Shire Publications.

Crofts, J. 1967. *Packhorse, Wagon and Post*. London: Routledge & Kegan Paul.

Crom, T. H. 1980. *Horological Shop Tools 1700–1900*. Melrose, FL: T. R. Crom.

Crompton, R. J. 1972. *A Short History of Modern Bulgaria*. Cambridge: Cambridge University Press.

Crossley, D. W. 1975. *The Bewl Valley Ironworks*. London: Institute of Archaeology.

—— 1980. A Table of the United Kingdom blast furnace sites. In *Historical Metallurgy Society Newsletter* IX, 1–3.

—— 1984. The survival of early blast furnaces: a world survey. In *Journal of the Historical Metallurgy Society* XVIII(2), 112–131.

—— 1990. *Post-medieval Archaeology in Britain*. Leicester: Leicester University Press.

Crossley, D. W. and Trinder, B. S. 1983. *The Ferreira at Pescia Fiorentina, Tuscany*. Telford: Ironbridge Institute.

Crowley, T. E. 1982. *The Beam Engine: a massive chapter in the history of steam*. Oxford: Senecio.

Cullen, A. 1910. *Adventures in Socialism: New Lanark Establishment and Orbiston Community*. Glasgow: John Smith.

Cullen, L. M. 1987. *The Economic History of Ireland since 1660*, 2nd edn. London: Batsford.

Culot, M. 1980. *Inventaire visuel de l'architecture industrielle à Bruxelles* (Pictorial inventory of the industrial architecture of Brussels). 18 Vols. Brussels: Archives d'Architecture Moderne.

Culpin, E. 1913. *The Garden City Movement up to date*. London: Garden Cities and Town Planning Association.

Cuming, D. J. 1983. *Discovering Heritage Bridges on Ontario's Roads*. Erin: Boston Mills Press.

Cummings, R. O. 1940. *The American and his Food*. Chicago, IL: University of Chicago Press.

—— 1949. *The American Ice Harvests*. Berkeley, CA: University of California Press.

Cunningham, B. 1923. *Cargo Handling at Ports*. London: Chapman and Hall.

Curl, J. S. 1983. *The Life and Work of Henry Roberts, 1803–1876: the evangelical conscience and the campaign for model housing and healthy nations*. Chichester: Phillimore.

Curr, J. 1797. *The Coal Viewer*. Sheffield: for John Curr. Reprint, 1970, London: Cass.

Current, R. N. 1954. *The Typewriter and the Men who Made it*. Urbana, IL: University of Illinois Press.

Cushion, J. P. 1980. *Handbook of Pottery and Porcelain Marks*, 4th edn. London: Faber.

Custódio, J. 1990. *O Patrimonio Industrial e os Trabalhadores: o caso do Vale de Chelas, Lisboa* (Industrial heritage and the workers: the case of the Vale de Chelas, Lisbon). Coimbra: Coimbra Editora.

Custódio, J. and Barros, G. M. 1984. *O Ferro de Moncorvo* (The ironworks at Moncorvo). Lisbon: Ferrominas.

Custodis, G.-P. 1990. *Technische Denkmäler in Rheinland-Pfalz* (Technical monuments in Rhineland-Palatinate). Koblenz: Görres Verlag.

Cutting, C. L. 1955. *Fish Saving: a history of fish processing from ancient to modern times*. London: Leonard Hill.

Czajkowski, J. 1981. *Muzea skansenowskie w Polsce* (Open air museums in Poland). Poznań: Państowe Wydawnictowo Rolnicze i Leśne.

Daalder, R. van Dalen, J. et al. 1985. *Werkstad: 30 industriële monumenten in Rotterdam* (Working town: thirty industrial monuments in Rotterdam). Rotterdam: Stichting Industrieel Erfgoed Rijnmond.

Dahle, H. 1894. *Roros Kobbervaerk 1664–1894* (Roros copperworks 1664–1894). Trondheim.

Dahmen, J. 1930. *Das Aachener Tuchgewerbe bis zum Ende des 19 Jahrhundert* (The Aachen textile trade until the end of the nineteenth century). Berlin and Leipzig: Weiss.

Dallaire, T. et al. 1974. *Les ponts du Québec*. Quebec: Ministry of Transport.

D'Alpuget, B. 1987. *The Workers*. Sydney: Collins.

Dalton, R. and Hamer, S. H. 1910. *Provincial Token Coinage of the Eighteenth Century*. Bristol: privately published in parts.

Danckert, L. 1981. *Directory of European Porcelain*, 4th edn. London: NAG Press.

Daniel, G. 1975. *A Hundred and Fifty Years of Archaeology*. London: Duckworth.

Daniels, G. W. 1920. *The Early English Cotton Industry*. London: Longman Green.

Daoust, G. and Viau, R. 1979. *L'île des Moulins* (The island of mills). Quebec: Ministry of Cultural Affairs.

Darby, H. C. 1956. *The Draining of the Fens*. Cambridge: Cambridge University Press.

Darby, M. 1974. *Early Railway Prints from the Collection of Mr and Mrs M. G. Powell*. London: HMSO for Victoria and Albert Museum.

D'Arcy, G. 1969. *Portrait of the Grand Canal*. Dublin: Transport Research Associates.

Darley, G. 1975. *Villages of Vision*. London: Architectural Press.

Darwell, S. 1978. *The Run of the Mill: a pictorial narrative of the expansion, dominion, decline and enduring impact of the New England textile industry*. Boston, MA: David R. Godine.

Daumas, M. ed. 1976. *Evolution de la géographie industrielle de Paris et sa proche banlieu au XIXè siècle* (Evolution of the industrial geography of Paris and its close suburbs during the nineteenth century). Paris: Centre de Documentation d'Histoire des Techniques.

——1980. *L'Archéologie industrielle en France* (Industrial archaeology in France). Paris: PUF.

Daumas, M. et al. 1962–79. *Histoire Générale des Techniques* (General history of technology). 5 vols. Paris: PUF.

——1978. *Les bâtiments à usage industriel aux XVIIIè et XIXè siècles en France* (Buildings for industrial use in France in the eighteenth and nineteenth centuries). Paris: Centre de Documentation d'Histoire des Techniques.

Daunton, M. J. 1977. *Coal Metropolis: Cardiff 1670–1914*. Leicester: Leicester University Press.

——1983. *House and Home in the Victorian City: working class housing 1850–1914*. London: Edward Arnold.

——1984. *Councillors and Tenants: local authority housing in English cities 1919–1939*. Leicester: Leicester University Press.

——1985. *Royal Mail: the Post Office since 1840*. London: Athlone Press.

——1987. *A Property-owning Democracy? Housing in Britain*. London: Faber.

Davenport, N. 1979. *United Kingdom Patent System: a brief history*. London: Kenneth Mason.

Davidson, W. B. 1923. *Gas Manufacture*. London: Longmans Green.

Davies, D. J. 1933. *The Economic History of South Wales prior to 1800*. Cardiff: University of Wales Press Board.

Davies, E. H. 1902. *Machinery for Metalliferous Mines*, 2nd edn. London: Crosby Lockwood & Son.

Davies, H. 1977. *George Stephenson*. London: Quartet.

Davies, J. 1899. *Galvanised Iron*. London: Spon.

Davies, J. 1981. *Cardiff and the Marquesses of Bute*. Cardiff: University of Wales Press.

Davies, R. E. G. 1972. *Airlines of the United States since 1914*. London: Putnam.

Davies, S. and Collier, C. 1986. *Industrial Image*. London: Photographers' Gallery.

Davies-Shiel, M. and Marshall, J. D. 1969. *The Industrial Archaeology of the Lake Counties*. Newton Abbot: David & Charles.

Davis, J. G. 1965–75. *Cheese*. 4 vols. London: Churchill Livingston.

Davis, R. 1962. *The Rise of the English Shipping Industry*. London: Macmillan.

Davison, C. B. 1953. *The History of Steam Road Vehicles*. London: HMSO.

Dawson, P. 1909. *Electric Traction on Railways*. London: The Electrician.

Day, J. 1973. *Bristol Brass*. Newton Abbot: David & Charles.

Dean, D. ed. 1970. *English Shop Fronts from Contemporary Source Books 1792–1840*. London: Alec Tiranti.

Dean, W. G. 1969. *An Economic Atlas of Ontario*. Toronto: University of Toronto Press.

Deelstra, T. and Stehouwer, C. 1987. *Sloop of hergebruik* (Demolition or re-use). Utrecht: Uitgave Landelijk Ondersteuningsinstituut Kunstzinnige Vorming.

Deer, N. 1950. *The History of Sugar*. London: Chapman & Hall.

Deighton, L. 1978. *Airshipwreck*. London: Cape.

De Industrie in Belgie 1981. *Twee eeuwen ountwikkeling, 1780–1980* (Two centuries of evolution, 1780–1980). Brussels: Credit Communal de Belgique 1981.

De Jong, H. 1983. *Over Bruggen* (About Bridges). Delft: Delft University Press.

De Jonge, J. A. 1976. *De industrialisatie van Nederland tussen 1850 en 1914* (The industrialization of the Netherlands between 1850 and 1914). Nijmegen: SUN.

Dekkers, G. and Wiersma, H. eds 1986. *Oude fabrieks- en bedrijfsgebouwen in Overijssel* (Old factories and industrial buildings in Overijssel). Zwolle: Waanders.

Delabre, G. and Gautier, J.-M. 1988. *Vers une République du Travail: Jean-Baptiste André Godin 1817–1888* (Towards a Republic of Work: Jean-Baptiste André Godin 1817–1888). Paris: Editions de la Villette.

Delamain, R. 1936. *Histoire du Cognac* (History of Cognac). Paris: Stock.

Delany, R. 1973. *The Grand Canal of Ireland*. Newton Abbot: David & Charles.

——1986. *Ireland's Inland Waterways*. Belfast: Appletree.

Delany, V. T. H. and Delany, D. R. 1966. *Canals of the South of Ireland*. Newton Abbot: David & Charles.

De Maré, E. 1950. *The Bridges of Britain*. London: Batsford.

Deming, M. K. 1986. *La Saline royale d'Arc et Senans de Claude Nicolas Ledoux* (The royal saltworks of Claude Nicolas Ledoux at Arc et Senans). Besancon: CRDP-CNMHS.

Denfer, J. 1984. *Charpenterie métallique, menuserie en fer et serrurerie* (Metal frameworks, iron joinery and building hardware). Paris: Baudry.

Denison, M. 1949. *Harvest Triumphant: the story of Massey Harris*. New York: Dodd, Mead.

Denley, P. and Hopkin, D. 1987. *History of Computing*. Manchester: Manchester University Press.

Dennis, L. G. and White, A. V. 1911. *Water-powers of Canada*. Ottawa: Mortimer.

Denton, J. B. 1883. *Agricultural Drainage*. London: Spon.

Department of Main Roads 1976. *The Roadmakers: a history of main roads in New South Wales*. Sydney: New South Wales Department of Main Roads.

De Quincey, T. 1956. *The English Mail Coach*. London: Dent.

De Salis, H. R. 1904. *Bradshaw's Canals and Navigable Rivers of England and Wales*. London: Blacklock.

Dessauer, J. H. 1971. *My Years with Xerox: the billions nobody wanted*. New York.

Dessauer, J. H. and Clarke, H. E. eds 1965. *Xerography and Related Processes*. New York: Focal Press.

Dethier, J. 1978. *Le temps des gares* (All stations). Paris: Centre Georges Pompidou.

De Tocqueville, A. 1958. *Journeys to England and Ireland*, ed. E. P. Mayer. London: Faber & Faber.

De Vaillac, A. d'A. 1979. *Connaissance du Canal du Midi* (Understanding the Canal du Midi). Paris: Editions France-Empire.

Devereux, R. 1936. *John Loudon McAdam*. Oxford: Oxford University Press.

Devillers, C. and Huet, B. 1981. *Le Creusot: naissance et développement d'une ville industrielle, 1782–1914* (Le Creusot, birth and development of an industrial town, 1782–1914). Seyssel: Champ Vallon.

De Vries, J. 1976. *The Economy of Europe in an Age of Crisis 1600–1700.* Cambridge: Cambridge University Press.

Deyrup, F. J. 1948. *Arms Makers of the Connecticut Valley*. Northampton, MA: Smith College Studies in History.

Dherent, C. 1986. *Archives du Monde du Travail, Région Nord Pas-de-Calais, Guide de Recherch* (Archives of the world of work, the Nord Pas-de-Calais region, research guide). Lille: Archives départmentales du Nord.

Dhondt, J. and Bruwier, M. 1970. *The Industrial Revolution in Belgium and Holland 1700–1914*. London: Fontana.

Diamond, J. T. and Haywards B. W. 1975. *Kauri Timber Dams*. Auckland.

Dickinson, H. W. 1913. *Robert Fulton, Engineer and Artist*. London: John Lane.

——1936. *James Watt, Craftsman and Engineer*. Cambridge: Cambridge University Press.

——1938. *A Short History of the Steam Engine*. Cambridge: Cambridge University Press.

Dickinson, H. W. and Jenkins, R. 1927. *James Watt and the Steam Engine*. Oxford: Clarendon Press.

Dickinson, H. W. and Titley, A. 1934. *Richard Trevithick: the engineer and the man*. Cambridge: Cambridge University Press.

Diderot, D. 1751–77. *Encyclopédie, ou Dictionnaire Raisonné des Sciences, des Arts, et des Métiers* (Encyclopaedia, or reasoned dictionary of the sciences, the arts and trades). Paris: Le Breton.

——1959. *A Diderot Pictorial Encyclopaedia of Trades and Industry*, ed. C. G. Gillespie. New York: Dover.

DIEN database. DIEN (Dutch International Heritage Documentation Centre), Postbus 2038, 3000 CA. Rotterdam.

Dixey, F. 1950. *A Practical Handbook of Water Supply*, 2nd edn. London: Murby.

Dixon, H. 1975. *An Introduction to Ulster Architecture*. Belfast: Ulster Architectural Heritage Society.

Dixon, R. and Muthesius, S. 1978. *Victorian Architecture*. London: Thames & Hudson.

Długosz, A. 1958. *Wieliczka Magnum Sal* (Wieliczka salt mine). Krakow: Wydawnictowo 'Arkady'.

Dobson, E. 1893. *A Rudimentary Treatise on the Manufacture of Bricks and Tiles*, 9th edn. London: Crosby Lockwood.

Dobson, E. and Hammond, A. 1903. *The Practical Brick and Tile Book*. London: Crosby Lockwood.

Dodd, A. H. 1971. *The Industrial Revolution in North Wales*, 3rd edn. Cardiff: University of Wales Press.

Dodd, G. 1843. *Days at the Factories, or the Manufacturing Industry of Great Britain Described*. London: Charles Knight. Reprint, 1975, Wakefield: EP Publishing.

Dolge, A. 1911. *Pianos and their Makers*. Covina, CA: Covina Publishing Company.

Dominick, J. 1982. *Cold Spring Granite: a history*. Cold Spring, MN: Cold Spring Granite Company.

Doncaster, E. A. 1916. *Limes and Cements*. London: Spon.

Donnachie, I. 1971. *The Industrial Archaeology of Galloway*. Newton Abbot: David & Charles.

Donovan, P. and Kirkman, N. 1986. *The Unquenchable Flame: the South Australian Gas Company 1861–1986*. Adelaide: Wakefield Press.

Dorlay, J. S. 1978. *The Roneo Story*. Romford: Roneo Vickers.

Dornier GmbH 1983. *Dornier: a documentation of the Dornier company history*. Friedrichshafen: Dornier GmbH.

Douet, J. 1988. *Going up in Smoke: the history of the industrial chimney*. London: Victorian Society.

Dow, G. 1972. *World Locomotive Models*. Bath: Adams & Dart.

Dowling, R. 1926. *Sugar Beet and Beet Sugar*. London: Ernest Benn.

Dowson, J. E. and Larter, A. T. 1906. *Producer Gas*. London: Longmans Green.

Drebusch, G. 1976. *Industriearchitektur* (Industrial architecture). Munich: Heyne Verlag.

Dreyfus, M. 1987. *Les sources de l'histoire ouvrière, sociale et industrielle en France, XIXè et XXè siècle, guide documentaire* (The sources of working-class history in France, nineteenth and twentieth centuries, documentation guide). Paris: Les Editions Ouvrières.

Drummond, J. C. and Wilbraham, A. 1957. *The Englishman's Food: five centuries of English diet*, rev. edn. London: Jonathan Cape.

DSB 1947. *De Danske Statsbaner 1847–1947* (The Danish state railways 1847–1947). Copenhagen: DSB.

Duckworth, S. P. and Jones, B. V. 1988. *King's Cross Development Site: an inventory of architectural and industrial features*. London: English Heritage.

Dumbleton, B. 1973. *The Story of the Paddle Steamer*. Melksham, Wiltshire: Colin Venton.

Dunell, H. 1925. *British Wire-drawing and Wire-working Machinery*. London: Constable.

Dunham, A. L. 1955. *The Industrial Revolution in France, 1815–1848*. New York: Exposition Press.

Dunn, M. 1848. *A Treatise on the Winning and Working of Collieries*. Newcastle: privately published.

Dunnett, P. J. S. 1988. *The World Newspaper Industry*. London: Croom Helm.

Dunning, J. 1985. *Britain's Butchers: the trade through the ages*. London: International Thomson.

Dunsheath, P. 1962. *A History of Electrical Engineering.* London: Faber.

Duprat, B., Paulin, M. et al. 1985. *Moulinage de soie en Ardèche, l'architecture des usines traditionelles, atlas et catalogue raisonné* (Ardèche silk-throwing mills, the architecture of traditional factories, atlas and reasoned catalogue). Lyons: Ministère de la Culture et Ecole d'Architecture de Lyon.

Durand, G., Wienin, M. et al. 1991. *Au fil de la soie: architectures d'une industrie en Cévennes: Gard, Hérault, Lozère* (Unravelling silk: architecture of an industry in the Cévennes: Gard, Hérault, Lozère). Montpellier: Ministère de la Culture, Images du Patrimoine.

Durrant, A. E. 1972. *The Steam Locomotives of Eastern Europe.* Newton Abbot: David & Charles.

—— 1987. *Garratt Locomotives of the World.* Newton Abbot: David & Charles.

Dušan, J. 1984. *Naše mosty Historicke a Soucasne* (Our bridges: historical and contemporary). Prague: Nadas.

Dyer, F. L. Martin, T. C. and Meadowcroft, W. H. 1929. *Edison: his life and inventions.* New York: Harper.

Dyos, H. J. and Aldcroft, D. H. 1969. *British Transport: an economic survey from the seventeenth to the twentieth century.* Leicester: Leicester University Press.

—— 1968. *The Study of Urban History.* London: Edward Arnold.

—— 1973. *Victorian Suburb: a study of the growth of Camberwell,* 3rd edn. Leicester: Leicester University Press.

Dyos, H. J. and Wolff, M. 1973. *The Victorian City: images and realities.* London: Routledge & Kegan Paul.

Dzienkoński, T. 1963. *Metalurgia miedzi, ołowiu i sreba w Europie Srodkowej od XV do końa XVIII iweku* (Metallurgy of lead, copper and silver in Central Europe from the 15th century to the 18th). Wrocław: Ossolineum.

EJS 1947. *Ein Jahrhundert Scweizer Bahnen* (A century of Swiss railways). Frauenfeld: René Thiessing.

Earl, B. 1968. *Cornish Mining.* Truro: Barton.

Earle, J. B. F. 1971. *A Century of Road Materials.* Oxford: Basil Blackwell.

Eckel, E. C. 1928. *Cements and Plasters.* London: John Wiley.

Edwards, M. M. 1967. *The Growth of the British Cotton Trade 1780–1815.* Manchester: Manchester University Press.

Edwards, P. 1988. *The Horse Trader of Tudor and Stuart England.* Cambridge: Cambridge University Press.

Edwards, R. D. 1981. *An Atlas of Irish History,* 2nd edn. London: Methuen.

Ehn, O. 1979. *Järnhantering och järnbruck I: Vägvisare till kulturen i Uppsala län* (Iron and ironworking communities, vol. I: studies in the culture of the Uppsala region). Uppsala.

Ehrlich, C. 1976. *The Piano: a history.* London: Dent.

Eisenstein, E. 1979. *The Printing Press as an Agent of Change.* 2 vols. Cambridge: Cambridge University Press.

Eklund, J. 1975. *The Incompleate Chymist: being an essay on the eighteenth century chemist in his laboratory with a dictionary of obsolete chemical terms of the period.* Washington DC: Smithsonian Institute.

Ekman, W., Nisser, M. and Norrby, J. eds 1987. *Forsmark och Vallonjärnet* (Forsmark and Walloon iron). Stockholm: Forsmark Kraftgrupp AB.

Ellis, A. 1982. *The Sailing Barges of Maritime England.* Shepperton: Shepperton Swan.

Ellis, C. H. 1947. *The Trains We Loved.* London: Allen & Unwin.

—— 1955/1959. *The North British Railway.* London: Ian Allen.

—— 1965. *Railway Carriages in the British Isles from 1830 to 1914.* London: Allen & Unwin.

Ellison, T. 1968. *The Cotton Trade of Great Britain.* London: Cass.

Ellsässer, K. and Ossenberg, H. 1954. *Bauten der Lebensmittel-Industrie* (Buildings of the food industry). Stuttgart: Julius Hoffmann.

Elphick, G. 1988. *The Craft of the Bellfounder.* Chichester: Phillimore.

Elton, A. 1968. *Art and the Industrial Revolution, Exhibition Catalogue.* Manchester: City Art Gallery.

Emmerson, G. S. n.d. *The Greatest Iron Ship: SS Great Eastern.* Newton Abbot: David & Charles.

Emmett, B. and Jeuck, J. E. 1950. *A History of Sears, Roebuck and Company.* Chicago, IL: University of Chicago Press.

Engels, F. 1845. *The Condition of the Working Class in England,* ed. W. O. Henderson and W. H. Chaloner, 1958. Oxford: Basil Blackwell.

Engh, P. H. and Gunnersjaa, A. 1984. *Oslo en Arkitekturguide* (Oslo: an architectural guide). Oslo.

Eno, A. L. 1976. *When Cotton was King: a History of Lowell, Massachusetts.* Lowell, MA: Lowell Historical Society.

Erler, U. and Schmeidel, H. 1988. *Brücken. Historiches, Konstruktion, Denkmäler* (Bridges. History, construction and status as monuments). Leipzig: VEB Fachbuchverlag.

Escrit, L. B. 1939. *Sewage Engineering: an authentic work on current English practice and design.* London: Contractor's Record.

Essery, R. J., Rowland, D. P. and Steel, W. O. 1970. *British Goods Waggons from 1887 to the Present Day.* Newton Abbot: David & Charles.

Estrela, E. 1986. *Lisboa: a Cidade dor Elevadores* (Lisbon: city of elevators). Lisbon: Carris.

Evans, G. E. 1956. *Ask the Fellows who cut the Hay.* London: Faber & Faber.

—— 1970. *Where Beards Wag All: the relevance of the oral tradition.* London: Faber & Faber.

Evans, I. 1981. *The Lithgow Pottery.* Sydney: Flannel Flower Press.

Evans, S. G. 1960. *A Short History of Bulgaria.* London: Lawrence & Wishart.

Everard, S. 1949. *The History of the Gas, Light and Coke Company 1812–1949.* London: Ernest Benn.

Everitt, A. M. 1973. *Perspectives in English Urban History.* London: Lawrence & Wishart.

Everwijn, J. C. A. ed. 1912. *Beschrijving van handel en*

nijverheid in Nederland (A description of trade and industry in the Netherlands). 2 vols. The Hague.

Eves, E. and Burger, D. 1988. *Great Car Collections of the World.* London: Prion.

Evrard, R. 1955. *Les Artists et les usines à fer* (Artists and Ironworks). Liège: Editions Solédi.

Fabrik og Bolig (Factories and dwellings) 1979–. Copenhagen.

Fairbairn, W. 1849. *An Account of the Construction of the Britannia and Conway Tubular Bridges.* London: John Weale.

——1854. *On the Application of Cast and Wrought Iron to Building Purposes.* London: John Weale.

——1856. *Useful Information for Engineers.* London: Longman Green.

——1861. *Iron: its history, properties and processes of manufacture.* London: A & C Black.

——1877. *The Life of Sir William Fairbairn, partly written by himself and completed by William Pole,* ed. A. E. Musson. Reprint, 1978, Newton Abbot: David & Charles.

Falconer, K. 1980. *Guide to England's Industrial Heritage.* London: Batsford.

Falk, B. 1838. *Turner, the Painter: his hidden life.* London: Heinemann.

Farey, J. 1811–17. *Agriculture of Derbyshire,* vols I–III. London: Board of Agriculture.

——1827. *Treatise on the Steam Engine.* London: Longman. Reprint, 1971, Newton Abbot: David & Charles.

Farnie, D. A. 1979. *The English Cotton Industry and the World Market.* Oxford: Clarendon Press.

Farrugia, J. Y. 1969. *The Letter Box: a history of Post Office pillar and wall boxes.* Fontwell, Sussex: Centaur.

Farson, N. 1926. *Sailing Across Europe.* London: Hutchinson. Reprint, 1985, London: Century Publishing.

Faucher, L. 1845. *Etudes sur l'Angleterre* (Studies of England). Paris: Guillaumin.

Fay, C. R. 1920. *Co-operation at Home and Abroad: a description and analysis.* London: P. S. King.

Fayle, C. E. 1933. *A Short History of the World's Shipping Industry.* London: George Allen & Unwin.

Fehl, G., Kaspari-Küffen, D. and Meyer, L.-H. 1991. *Mit Wasser und Dampf: Zeitzeugen der frühen Industrialisierung im Belgisch-Deutschen Grenzraum* (With water and steam: evidence of early industrialization in the borderland between Belgium and Germany). Aachen: Meyer & Meyer.

Feigenbaum, E. and Feldman, J. 1963. *Computers and Thought.* New York: McGraw Hill.

Feilden, B. M. 1982. *The Conservation of Historic Buildings.* London: Butterworth.

Feis, B. R. and Nijhof, P. 1973. *Bedrijfsmonumenten in het groene hart van Nederland* (Industrial monuments in the green heart of the Netherlands). Zwolle: Waanders.

Felkin, W. 1867. *A History of the Machine-wrought Hosiery and Lace Manufacture.* Reprint, 1967, Newton Abbot: David & Charles.

Ferguson, E. 1968. *Bibliography of the History of Technology.* Cambridge, MA: MIT Press.

Ferneyhough, F. 1980. *The Liverpool and Manchester Railway, 1830–1980.* London: Hale.

Ferragni, D., Malliet, J. and Torraca, G. 1982. *Iron Factories of the Italian Maremma.* Rome: ICCROM.

Ferriot, D. 1981. *ICCIH 1981: Fourth International Conference on the Conservation of the Industrial Heritage: National Reports.* Paris: CILAC.

Ferrner, B. 1986. *Ferrner's Journal 1759–60: an industrial spy in Bath and Bristol,* ed. A. P. Woolrich. Eindhoven: De Archaeologische Pers.

Ferry, J. W. 1960. *A History of the Department Store.* New York: Macmillan.

Ferry, W. H. 1968. *The Buildings of Detroit.* Detroit, MI: Wayne State University Press.

——1970. *The Legacy of Albert Kahn.* Detroit, MI: Detroit Institute of Arts.

Ficquelmont, G.-M. de, and Fontanon, C. 1990. *Le guide du patrimoine industriel, scientifique et technique* (Guide to the industrial, scientific and technical heritage). Paris: La Manufacture.

Fielding, R. 1967. *A Technological History of Motion Pictures and Television.* Cambridge: Cambridge University Press.

Finch, W. C. 1933. *Watermills and Windmills: a historical survey of their rise, decline and fall as portrayed in those of Kent.* London: C. W. Daniel. Reprint, 1976, Sheerness: Arthur Cassell.

Findlay, W. P. K. 1971. *Modern Brewing Technology.* London: Macmillan.

Finegold, A. N. Inc. 1978. *Recycling Historic Railroad Stations: a citizen's manual.* Washington DC: US Department of Transportation.

Finer, S. E. 1952. *The Life and Times of Sir Edwin Chadwick.* London: Methuen.

Finnish Institute of Architects 1952. *Suomen teollisuuden arkkitehtuuria* (Finnish industrial architecture). Helsinki: Picture Archive.

Fischer, G. et al. 1985. *Bierbrauen im Rheinland* (Breweries in the Rhineland). Cologne: Reinland-Verlag GmbH.

Fischer, W. 1949. *Aachener Werkbauten des 18 und 19 Jahrhundert* (Working buildings of the eighteenth and nineteenth centuries in Aachen). Aachen: privately published.

Fisher, F. J. ed. 1961. *Essays in the Economic and Social History of Tudor and Stuart England.* Cambridge: Cambridge University Press.

Fishman, R. 1977. *Urban Utopias in the Twentieth Century: Ebenezer Howard, Frank Lloyd Wright and le Corbusier.* New York: Basic.

Fitton, R. S. 1989. *The Arkwrights: spinners of fortune.* Manchester: Manchester University Press.

Fitton, R. S. and Wadsworth, A. P. 1958. *The Strutts and the Arkwrights 1758–1830: a study of the early factory system.* Manchester: Manchester University Press.

Fitzgerald, R. S. 1980. *Liverpool Road Station, Manchester: an historical and architectural survey.* Manchester: Manchester University Press for Royal Commission on Historical Monuments.

Fleming, J. and Honour, H. 1979. *The Penguin Dictionary of the Decorative Arts*. London: Penguin.

Fleming, J. A. 1910. *The Principles of Electric Wave Telegraphy and Telephony*. London: Longman.

Fletcher, R. A. 1910. *Steamships: the story of their development to the present day*. Philadelphia: Lippincott.

Fletcher, W. 1891. *History and Development of Steam on Common Roads*. London: Spon. Reprint, 1972, Newton Abbot: David & Charles.

——1904. *English and American Steam Carriages and Traction Engines*. Reprint, 1973, Newton Abbot: David & Charles.

Flexner, J. T. 1944. *Steamboats Came True: American inventors in action*. New York: Viking.

Flink, J. T. 1972. *America Adopts the Automobile 1895–1910*. Cambridge, MA: MIT Press.

Flinn, A. D., Weston, R. S. and Bogert, C. L. 1927. *Waterworks Handbook of Design, Construction and Operation*, 3rd edn. London and New York: McGraw Hill.

Flinn, M. W. 1984. *The History of the British Coal Industry*, vol. II: *1700–1830*. Oxford: Oxford University Press.

Floud, R. 1976. *The British Machine Tool Industry 1850–1914*. Cambridge: Cambridge University Press.

Fogg, C. 1981. *Chains and Chainmaking*. Princes Risborough: Shire Publications.

Föhl, A. 1976. Technische Denkmale im Rheinland (Technical monuments in the Rhineland). *Arbeitshefte des Landeskonservatores Rheinland XX*. Cologne: Rheinland Verlag.

Föhl, A. and Hamm, M. 1984. *Bahnhöfe* (Railway Stations). Düsseldorf: VDI Verlag.

——1985. *Die Industriegeschichte des Wassers* (The industrial history of water). Düsseldorf: VDI Verlag.

——1988. *Die Industriegeschichte de Textils: Technik, Architektur, Wirtschaft* (The textile industry: technology, architecture, economics). Düsseldorf: VDI Verlag.

Follett, D. 1978. *The Rise of the Science Museum under Henry Lyons*. London: Science Museum.

Forberger, R. 1982. *Industrielle Revolution in Sachsen 1800–1861*, Band I: *Die Revolution der Produktivkräfte in Sachsen 1800–1830*; Band II: *Ubersichten zur Fabrikenwicklung 1800–1830* (The Industrial Revolution in Saxony 1800–1861, vol. I: the revolution in productivity in Saxony 1800–1830; vol. II: an overview of product development 1800–1830). Berlin: Akademie-Verlag.

Forbes, E. 1981. *Commercial Navigation on the Rideau Canal 1832–1981*. Ottawa: Parks Canada.

Forbes, R. J. 1958. *Studies in Early Petroleum History*. Leyden: Brill.

——1959. *More Studies in Early Petroleum History*. Leyden: Brill.

Förderverein Rettet den Leuchturm Rotersand 1986. *Denkmalshutz an Bauten der Schiffahrtsgeschichte* (The protection of buildings relating to the history of shipping). Bremerhaven: Förderverein Rettet den Leuchturm Rotersand.

Forget, M. et al. 1985. *Les maisons en rangée de la rue de Sébastopol. Étude historique, relevé photographique, analyse architecturale et évaluation patrimoniale* (The terraced houses of the rue de Sebastopol. History, photographic survey, architectural analysis and historical evaluation). Montreal: Ministry of Cultural Affairs.

Forrest, D. 1973. *Tea for the British*. London: Chatto & Windus.

Forsmark och vallonjarnet (Forsmark and Walloon iron making) 1928. Stockholm: Forsmarks Crafgrupp AB.

Forstrom, O. 1915 *Fredrikshald i 250 ar: 1665–1915* (Fredrikshald over 250 years: 1665–1915). Fredrikshald.

Foster, C. 1894. *A text book of ore and stone mining*. London: Charles Griffin.

Found, W. C., Hill, A. R., and Spence, E. S. 1974. *Economic and Environmental Impacts of Land Drainage in Ontario*. Toronto.

Fourcaut, A. ed. 1988. *Un siècle de banlieue parisienne 1859–1964: guide de recherche* (A century of Parisian suburbs, 1859–1964: a research guide). Paris: L'Harmattan.

Fram, M. and Weiler, J. 1981. *Continuity with Change: planning for the conservation of Ontario's manmade heritage*. Toronto: Ontario Ministry of Culture and Recreation.

Frankel, T. 1977. *Steam Engines and Turbines*. Washington DC: Smithsonian Institute.

Franken, R. B. and Larrabee, C. B. 1928. *Packages that Sell*. New York: Harper.

Franks, K. A. and Lambert, P. F. 1982. *Early Louisiana and Arkansas Oil: a photographic history*. Texas A and M University, TX: Montague History of Oil Series.

Frantz, J. B. 1951. *Gail Borden: dairyman to a nation*. Norman, OK: University of Oklahoma Press.

Fraser, D. 1976. *Urban Politics in Victorian England: the structure of politics in Victorian cities*. Leicester: Leicester University Press.

Freeland, J. M. 1968. *Architecture in Australia: a history*. Canberra: F. W. Cheshire.

Freely, J. 1983. *Istanbul*. London: Blue Guide.

Freeman, P., Martin, E. and Dean, J. 1985. *Building Conservation in Australia*. Canberra: RAIA Education Division.

French, G. J. 1859. *The Life and Times of Samuel Crompton*. Reprint, 1970, Bath: Adams & Dart.

French, R. A. and Hamilton, F. E. I. 1979. *The Socialist City: spatial structure and urban policy*. Chichester: Wiley.

Freudenberger, H. 1964. *Waldstein Woollen Mill*. Cambridge, MA: Harvard University Press.

Fridenson, P. 1972. *Histoire des usines Renault: naissance de la grande entreprise, 1898–1939* (History of the Renault factories, birth of the large-scale enterprise, 1898–1939). Paris: Le Seuil.

Frieleg, W. 1985. *Buildings of the World Exhibitions*. Leipzig: Editions Leipzig.

Frogg, C. 1981. *Chains and Chainmaking*. Princes Risborough: Shire Publications.

Frolich, T. 1919. *Lillehammer 1827–1918*. Lillehammer.

Fry, H. 1896. *The History of North Atlantic Steam Navigation*. Reprint, 1969, London: Cornmarket.

Fullaondo, D. 1969. *La arquitectura y el urganismo de la región y el entorno de Bilbao* (Architecture and urbanization in Bilbao and its region). Madrid: Alfaguara.

——1971. *La arquitectura y los arquitectos de la región y el entorno de Bilbao* (Architecture and architects in Bilbao and its region). Madrid: Alfaguara.

Fulton, R. 1796. *A Treatise on Canal Navigation*. London: I. & J. Taylor.

Gable, J. 1974. *Long Island, An Inventory of Historic Engineering and Industrial Sites*. Washington DC: National Park Service.

Gagnon, G. 1984. *La pulperie de Chicoutimi en évolution* (The evolution of the Chichoutimi pulp mill). Chicoutimi: City of Chicoutimi.

Gale, T. A. 1860. *The Wonder of the Nineteenth Century: rock oil in Pennsylvania and elsewhere*. Erie: Sloan & Griffeth. Reprint, 1952, New York: Ethyl Corporation.

Gale, W. K. V. 1952. *Boulton, Watt and the Soho Undertakings*. Birmingham: City of Birmingham Museum Service.

——1967. *The British Iron and Steel Industry*. Newton Abbot: David & Charles.

——1969. *Iron and Steel*. London: Longmans.

——1971. *The Iron and Steel Industry: a dictionary of terms*. Newton Abbot: David & Charles.

——1979. *The Black Country Iron Industry: a technical history*. London: The Metals Society.

Gallagher, L. and Rogers, D. 1986. *Castle, Coast and Cottage: the National Trust in Northern Ireland*. Belfast: Blackstaff Press.

Gallaher, H. St G. 1970. *Malt in the Beginning*. Newark: Associated British Maltsters.

Galloway, J. H. 1988. *The Sugar Cane Industry: an history geography from its origins to 1914*. Cambridge: Cambridge University Press.

Galloway, R. L. 1882. *A History of Coal Mining in Great Britain*. London: Macmillan. Reprint, 1969, Newton Abbot: David & Charles.

——1898. *Annals of Coalmining*. London: Macmillan. Reprint, 1971, Newton Abbot: David & Charles.

Garbrecht, G. 1987. *Historische Talsperren* (Historic dams). Stuttgart: Verlag Konrad Vittwer.

Gardner, W. 1978. *Chemical Synonyms and Trade Names*, rev. E. I. Cooke and R. W. I. Cooke. Oxford: Technical Press.

Gardner, W. M. 1915. *The British Coal Tar Industry: its origin, development and decline*. London: Williams & Norgate.

Garner, F. H. and Archer, M. 1948. *English Delftware*. London: Faber.

Garnett, R. G. 1972. *Co-operation in the Owenite Socialist Communities in Britain 1825–45*. Manchester: Manchester University Press.

Garrad, L. S. et al. 1972. *The Industrial Archaeology of the Isle of Man*. Newton Abbot: David & Charles.

Garrioch, D. 1986. *Neighbourhood and Community in Paris 1740–1790*. Cambridge: Cambridge University Press.

Garvey, J. 1982. *A Guide to the Transport Museums of Great Britain*. London: Pelham.

Garvin, B. and Fox, P. 1985a. *Deutsche Bundesbahn: German Federal Railways: the complete guide to all DB locomotives and multiple units*. Sheffield: Platform 5.

——1985b. *OBB: Austrian Federal Railways*. Sheffield: Platform 5.

Gaskell, P. 1835. *Artisans and Machinery*. London: J. W. Parker. Reprint, 1968, London: Cass.

Gaskell, S. 1987. *Model Housing: from the Great Exhibition to the Festival of Britain*. London: Mansell.

Gauldie, E. 1974. *Cruel Habitations: a history of working class housing 1780–1918*. London: Allen & Unwin.

Gautier, B. H. 1714. *Traité des Ponts* (A treatise on bridges). Paris.

——1717. *Dissertation sur les culées, voussoirs, piles et poussées des ponts* (Dissertation on the footings, voussoirs, poles and thrust of bridges). Paris.

Gebhardt, G. 1957. *Ruhrgebau. Geschichte, Aufbau und Verflechtung seiner Gesellschaften und Organisationem* (The Ruhr mining industry, its history, origins, integration, social fabric and organisation). Essen: Glückauf.

Geijer, A. 1979. *A History of Textile Art*. London: Passold Research Fund.

Geist, A. 1983. *Arcades*. London.

Geist, J. F. and Kürvers, K. 1980. *Das Berliner Mietshaus 1740–1862* (The tenement house in Berlin 1740–1862). Munich: Prestel Verlag.

Gelatt, R. 1965. *The Fabulous Phonograph*, 2nd edn. New York: Appleton-Century.

Generalitat de Catalunya 1988. *II Jornardes sobre la Protecció i Revalorització del Patrimoni Industrial* (Papers of the second conference on the conservation and evaluation of the industrial heritage). Barcelona: Generalitat de Caltalunya.

Genevois, L. and Ribereau-Gayon, J. 1947. *Le Vin* (Wine). Paris: Hermann.

Geokatalog (constantly updated). Stuttgart: GeoCenter.

Georgano, G. E. 1972. *A History of the London Taxicab*. Newton Abbot: David & Charles.

George, A. D. 1986. *Aircraft Factories: origins, development and archaeology*. Manchester: Manchester Polytechnic.

Georgeacopol-Winischhofer, U., Swittalek, P. and Wehdorn, M. 1987. *TICCIH: Industrial Heritage, Austria 1987, Transactions I, National Reports*. Vienna: Federal Office for the Protection of Monuments.

Gerdts, A. B. 1979. *The Working American*. Washington DC: Smithsonian Institute.

Gerrard, F. 1909. *The Book of the Meat Trade*. London: Caxton.

Gheorghiu, C. 1979. *Inventii si prioritatia romanesti in aviatie* (Romanian inventions and innovations in aviation). Bucharest.

Gibb, A. 1935. *The Story of Telford*. London: Alexander MacLehose.

Gibbons, H. 1926. *John Wanamaker*. 2 vols. New York and London: Harper.

Gibbs, C. R. V. 1952. *Passenger Liners of the Western Ocean*. London: Staples.

—— 1963. *British Passenger Liners of the Five Oceans*. London: Putnam.

Giddens, P. H. 1938. *The Birth of the Oil Industry*. New York: Macmillan.

—— 1948. *Early Days of Oil: a pictorial history of the beginnings of the industry in Pennsylvania*. Princetown, NJ: Princetown University Press.

Giedion, S. 1948. *Mechanisation Takes Command: a contribution to anonymous history*. Oxford: Oxford University Press.

Gilbert, K. R. 1965. *The Portsmouth Block-making Machinery*. London: Science Museum.

—— 1971. *Henry Maudslay, Machine Builder*. London: Science Museum.

Gill, C. 1925. *The Rise of the Irish Linen Industry*. Oxford: Clarendon Press.

Gille, B. 1964. *Les sources statistiques de l'histoire de France* (Statistical sources of French history). Geneva and Paris: Droz.

Gille, B. 1978. *Histoire des Techniques* (History of Technology). Paris: Gallimard.

Gille, G. ed. 1990. *L'Institut et la Monnaie, deux palais sur un quai* (The Institute and the Mint, two palaces on one bank). Paris: Délégation à l'Action artistique de la Ville de Paris.

Gillen, M. 1989. *The Founders of Australia: a biographical dictionary of the first fleet*. Sydney: Library of Australian History.

Girouard, M. 1977. *Sweetness and Light: the Queen Anne Movement 1860–1900*. Oxford: Clarendon Press.

Giurescu, C. C. 1973. *Contributii la istoria stiintei si teknicii romanesti in sec XV inceptul sec XIX* (Contributions to the history of science and technology in Romania from the fifteenth century to the early nineteenth century). Bucharest: Editura

Giurescu C. C. and Giurescu, C. D. 1975. *Istoria Romanilor* (The history of Romania). Bucharest.

Gladwin, D. 1988. *Steam Transport on the Roads*. Chichester: Phillimore.

Glaister, G. A. 1960. *Glossary of the Book*. London: Allen & Unwin.

Glamann, K. 1962. *Bryggeriets historie i Danmark intil slutningen af det 19 århundrede* (The history of the breweries in Denmark from the beginnings until the nineteenth century). Copenhagen: Gyldendal.

Glaser, H., Ruppert, W. and Neudecker, N. 1983. *Industriekultur in Nürnberg: ein Deutsch Stadt in Maschinenzeitalter* (Industrial culture in Nuremberg: a German city in the machine age). Munich: C. H. Beck.

Glass, B. D. 1975. *North Carolina, an Inventory of Historic Engineering and Industrial Sites*. Washington DC: National Park Service.

Glass, D. V. 1978. *Numbering the People: the eighteenth-century population controversy and the development of census and vital statistics in Britain*. London: Gordon & Cremonesi.

Glaumer, W. 1939. *Die Historische Entwicklung der Müllerei* (The historical development of milling). Munich and Berlin: Oldenbourg.

Glazebrook, G. P. de T. 1964. *A History of Transportation in Canada*, 2nd edn. Toronto: McClelland & Stewart.

Gledhill, D. 1981. *Gas Lighting*. Princes Risborough: Shire Publications.

Gloag, J 1945. *Plastics and Industrial Design*. London: Allen & Unwin.

Gloag, J. and Bridgewater, D. 1948. *A History of Cast Iron in Architecture*. London: Allen & Unwin.

Glynn, S. 1975. *Urbanisation in Australian History, 1788–1900*. Australia: Nelson.

Gobert, C. 1906. *Autobiographie d'un peintre Liègois* (Autobiography of a painter from Liège). Liège: Pierre Mardaga.

Goddon, G. A. 1980. *An Illustrated Encyclopaedia of British Pottery and Porcelain*, 2nd edn. London: Barrie & Jenkins.

Goknil, U. V. 1966. *Living Architecture: Ottoman*. London: Oldbourne.

Goldberger, P. 1981. *The Skyscraper*. New York: Alfred A. Knopf.

Gómez, M. I., Ezkerra, A. S. and Llanos, M. Z. 1988. *Arqueologia Industrial en Bizkaia* (Industrial Archaeology in Bizkaia). Bilbao: Universidad de Deusto.

Gómez, M. I., Gorbea, M. J. T. and Llanos, M. Z. 1990. *Arqueologia Industrial en Gipuzkoa* (Industrial archaeology in Gipuzkoa). Bilbao: Universidad de Deusto.

Gonzalez Portilla, M. 1981. *La formación de la sociedad capitalista en el País Vasco 1876–1913* (The formation of a capitalist society in the Basque country 1876–1913). Bilbao: Harámburu.

—— 1985. *La Siderurgia Vasca 1880–1901* (The Basque iron industry 1880–1901). Bilbao: Euskal Herriko Unibertsitatea.

Goodwin, G. 1971. *A History of Ottoman Architecture*. London: Thames & Hudson.

Gordon, G. 1986. *Regional Cities in the United Kingdom, 1890–1980*. London: Harper & Row.

Gordon, W. J. 1893. *The Horse World of London*. Reprint, 1971, Newton Abbot: David & Charles.

Górewicz, J. 1971. *Orłowski: Kanal Augustowski jego dzieje i presztosc* (The Augustowski canal: its origins and history). Warsaw: WP.

—— 1974. *Opowieść o Kanale Augustowskin* (The story of the Augustowski canal). Warsaw: Sport y turystyka.

Gosden, P. H. J. H. 1973. *Self-help: voluntary associations in nineteenth century Britain*. London: Batsford.

Götschman, D. 1985. *Oberpfälzer Eisen. Bergbau und Eisengewerbe im 16 und 17 Jahrhundert* (Upper Palatinate Iron: mining and the iron trade in the sixteenth and sevententh centuries). Theuern: Bergbau- und Industriemuseum Ostbayern.

Gradwohl, D. M. and Osborn, N. M. 1984. *Exploring Buried Buxton: archaeology of an abandoned coal mining town with a large black population*. Ames, IA: Iowa State University Press.

Granström, G. A. 1940. *Ur Sala silvergruvas historia* (History of the Sala silver mine). Västerås.

Grant, J. and Searle, G. 1957. *The Melbourne Scene, 1803–1956*. Carlton: Melbourne University Press.

Granville, A. B. 1837. *The Spas of Germany*. London: Henry Colburn.

——1841. *The Spas of England and Principal Sea Bathing Places*. 2 vols. London: Henry Colburn. Reprint, 1971, Bath: Adams & Dart.

Gray, D. and Kanefsky, J. 1982. *Coal: British Mining in Art 1680–1980*. London: Arts Council of Great Britain.

Green, E. R. R. 1949. *The Lagan Valley 1800–1850*. London: Faber & Faber.

——1963. *The Industrial Archaeology of County Down*. Belfast: HMSO.

Green, J. W. and Morgan, H. P. H. 1924. *Highway Engineering*. London: St Bride's Press.

Greener, W. W. 1910. *The Gun and its Development*. London: Cassell.

Greenhill, B. 1968. *The Merchant Schooners*. Newton Abbot: David & Charles.

——1980. *Schooners*. London: Batsford.

Greenhill, B. and Manning, S. 1988. *The Evolution of the Wooden Ship*. London: Batsford.

Greenwald, M., Levitt, A. and Peebles, E. 1976. *The Welland Canals: historical resource analysis and preservation alternatives*. Toronto: Ontario Ministry of Culture and Recreation.

Greenwell, A. and Elsden, J. V. 1913. *Practical Stone Quarrying*. London: Crosby Lockwood.

Greeves, I. S. 1980. *London Docks 1800–1980: a civil engineering history*. London: Thomas Telford.

Gregory, C. E. 1980. *A Concise History of Mining*. Oxford: Pergamon.

Gregory, J. W. 1938. *The Story of the Road*, 2nd edn. London: A. & C. Black.

Gregotti, V. 1968. *New Dimensions in Italian Architecture*. London: Studio Vista.

Grenier, L. and Weiser-Benedetti, H. 1979. *Les Châteaux de l'industrie* (Châteaux of industry). Paris and Brussels: Archives d'Architecture Moderne.

Greve, T. 1975. *Svalbard, Norway in the Arctic Ocean*. Oslo: Grondahl.

Gribbon, H. D. 1969. *The History of Water Power in Ulster*. Newton Abbot: David & Charles.

Griffin, A. R. 1971. *Coalmining*. London: Longman.

——1977. *The British Coalmining Industry*. Hartington, Derbyshire: Moorland.

Griffiths, R. T. 1979. *Industrial Retardation in the Netherlands 1830–1850*. The Hague: Nijhoff.

Griffiths, S. 1872. *Guide to the Iron Industry of Great Britain*. Reprint, 1969, Newton Abbot: David & Charles.

Grimm, C. 1985. *Aufbruch ins Industriezeitalter*, Band I–IV (The beginnings of the industrial period, vols I–IV). Munich: Oldenbourg Verlag.

Grimshaw, A. 1982. *The Horse: a bibliography of British books 1851–1976*. London: Library Association.

Grimshaw, L. and Porter, R. 1989. *The Hospital in History*. London: Routledge.

Grimshaw, P. N. 1985. *Excavators*. Poole, Dorset: Blandford Press.

Groen, K. and Schmeink, T. 1985. *Dijken* (Dikes). The Hague: Studio Druk.

Grosser, M. 1980. *Diesel: the man and the engine*. Newton Abbot: David & Charles.

Gruner, E. 1968. *Die Arbeiter in der Schweiz im 19. Jahr* (Swiss workers in the nineteenth century). Bern.

Grunsky, E. 1975. *Vier Siedlungen in Duisburg 1925–30* (Four settlements in Duisburg 1925–30). *Arbeitshefte des Landeskonservators Rheinland XII*. Cologne: Rheinland Verlag.

Gudok. (Daily newspaper, Moscow.)

Guerin, M. 1988. *The Lartigue: Listowel and Ballybunion Railway*. Listowel: Listowel Centenary Committee.

Guiard, T. 1917. *La Industria Naval Vizcaina* (The shipbuilding industry in Vizcaya). Bilbao: Rochelt.

Guinness, D. and Sadler, J. T. 1976. *The Palladian Style in England, Ireland and America*. London: Thames & Hudson.

Guiollard, P.-C. 1983. *En Cévennes quand tournaient les molettes* (In the Cévennes when the winding gear still wound). Tarbes: privately published.

Guiollard, P.-C. 1989. *Les chevalements des houillières françaises de 1830 à 1989* (The headstocks in French coalfields from 1830 to 1989). Brussels: P.-C. Guiollard.

Guldal, J. 1944. *Roros Bergstad og Kobbervaerk 300 ar* (Three hundred years of the mining town and copperworks of Roros). Ringerike: Weberg.

Gunston, B. 1989a. *World Encyclopaedia of Aero Engines*, 2nd edn. Wellingborough: Patrick Stevens.

——1989b. *Rolls Royce Aero Engines*. Wellingborough: Patrick Stevens.

Günter, R. 1970. *Zu einer Geschichte der technischen Architektur im Rheinland: Textil-Eisen-Kohle* (Towards a history of industrial architecture in the Rhineland: textiles-iron-coal). *Beiträge für rheinischen Kulturgeschichte und Denkmalplege XVI*.

——1973. *Rettet Eisenheim* (Save Eisenheim). Bielefeld: Fachhochschule.

——1980. *Leben in Eisenheim: Arbeit Kommunikation und Sozialisation in einer Arbeitersiedlung* (Living in Eisenheim: work, communication and socialization in a workers' colony). Weinheim and Basel: Beltz Verlag.

Gut, A. 1984. *Das Berliner Wohnhaus des 17 und 18 Jahrhunderts* (The Berlin dwelling house in the seventeenth and eighteenth centuries). Berlin: W. Ernst, VEB Verlag für Bauwesen.

Habakkuk, H. J. 1967. *American and British Technology in the Nineteenth Century: the search for labour-saving inventions*. Cambridge: Cambridge University Press.

Hadfield, A. M. 1970. *The Chartist Land Company*. Newton Abbot: David & Charles.

Hadfield, C. 1950. *British Canals: an illustrated history*. London: Phoenix House.

——1955. *The Canals of Southern England*. London: Phoenix House.

——1960. *The Canals of South Wales and the Border*. Cardiff: University of Wales Press.

—— 1966a. *The Canals of the East Midlands (including part of London)*. Newton Abbot: David & Charles.

—— 1966b. *The Canals of the West Midlands*. Newton Abbot: David & Charles.

—— 1967a. *The Canals of South-west England*. Newton Abbot: David & Charles.

—— 1967b. *Atmospheric Railways: a Victorian venture in silent speed*. Newton Abbot: David & Charles.

—— 1968, *The Canal Age*. Newton Abbot: David & Charles.

—— 1969. *The Canals of the West of England*. Newton Abbot: David & Charles.

—— 1986. *World Canals*. Newton Abbot: David & Charles.

Hadfield, C. and Biddle, G. 1970. *The Canals of North-west England*. 2 vols. Newton Abbot: David & Charles.

Hadfield, C. and Eyre, F. 1945. *English Rivers and Canals*. London: Collins.

Hadfield, C. and Skempton, A. W. 1979. *William Jessop, Engineer*. Newton Abbot: David & Charles.

Haegermann, G. 1964. *Von Caementum zum Sapmbeton* (From cement to pre-stressed concrete). Wiesbaden Bauverlag-GmbH.

HAER 1981. *Historic American Engineer Record Field Instructions*. Washington DC: National Parks Service.

Hague, D. B. and Christie, R. 1975. *Lighthouses: their architectural history and archaeology*. London: Gomer Press.

Haig-Brown, R. 1961. *The Living Land: an account of the natural resources of British Columbia*. Toronto: Macmillan.

Hainlin, T. 1952. *Forms and Functions of Twentieth Century Architecture*. New York: Columbia University Press.

Hair, T. H. 1844. *A Series of Views of the Collieries of Northumberland and Durham*. London: J. Madden.

Haldane, J. W. C. 1893. *Steamships and Their Machinery from First to Last*. London: Spon.

Hall, H. 1888. *The Ice Industry of the United States with a Brief Sketch of its History*. Washington DC: Census Office. Reprint, 1974, Washington DC: Early American Industries Association.

Hall, K. L. K. and Cooper, C. 1984. *Windows on the Works: industry on the Eli Whitney site 1798–1979*. Hamden, CT: Eli Whitney Museum.

Hall, P. 1962. *The Industries of London*. London: Hutchinson.

—— 1966. *The World Cities*. London: Weidenfeld & Nicholson.

Hall-Ellis, M. J. 1986. *The Early History of the Telephone in Bath*. Bristol: British Telecom.

Halvorsen, K. 1965–9. *Det gamle Lillehammer* (Old Lillehammer). 5 vols. Lillehammer: Mesna.

Hambleton, F. C. 1948. *Famous Paddle Steamers*. London: Marshall.

Hamburg-Amerika Linie 1911. *Guide through Europe*. Berlin: J. Hermann Herz.

Hamer, F. and Hamer, J. 1986. *The Potter's Dictionary of Materials and Techniques*, 2nd edn. London: A. & C. Black.

Hamilton, D. 1978. *The Thames & Hudson Manual of Architectural Ceramics*. London: Thames & Hudson.

Hamilton, J. 1967. *The English Brass and Copper Industry to 1800*, 2nd edn. London: Cass.

Hammarström, I. 1970. *Stockholm i Svensk ekonomi 1850–1914* (Stockholm in the Swedish Economy, 1850–1914). Stockholm.

Hammarström, I. and Hall, T. eds 1979. *Growth and Transformation of the Modern City*. Stockholm.

Hammerton, M. 1986. *Water South Australia a history of the Engineering and Water Supply Department*. Adelaide: Wakefield Press.

Hammond, R. 1959. *Tunnel Engineering*. London: Heywood.

Hammond, R. and Lewin, C. J. 1966. *The Panama Canal*. London: Muller.

Hamon, M. 1988. *Du soleil à la terre, une histoire de Saint-Gobain* (From the sun to the earth, a history of Saint-Gobain), Paris: Jean-Claud Lattòn.

Hampe, E. C. and Wittenberg, M. 1964. *The Lifeline of America: development of the food industry*. New York: McGraw-Hill.

Hansen, Sv. Aa. 1970. *Early Industrialization in Denmark*. Copenhagen: Akademisk forlag.

—— 1972–4. *Okonomisk vækst i Danmark*, I–II (Economic growth in Denmark, vols I-II). Copenhagen: Akademisk forlag.

Hansmann, W. and Zahn, W. 1971. Denkmäler der Stolberger Messingindustrie (Monuments of the Stolberg brass industry). *Arbeitshefte des Landeskonservators Rheinland* II. Cologne: Rheinland Verlag.

Hanson, H. 1975. *The Canal Boatmen 1760–1914*. Manchester: Manchester University Press.

Hardie, D. W. F. and Pratt, J. D. 1966. *A History of the Modern British Chemical Industry*. Oxford: Pergamon.

Harding, C. R. 1951. *George Mortimer Pullman and the Pullman Company*. London: Newcomen Society.

Hardy, D. 1979. *Alternative Communities in Nineteenth Century England*. London: Longman.

Hardy, D. and Ward, C. 1984. *Arcadia for All: the legacy of a makeshift landscape*. London: Mansell.

Hardy, F. 1979. *John Grierson: a documentary biography*. London: Faber & Faber.

Hardy-Hémery, O. 1985. *Industries, patronat et ouvriers du Valenciennois pendant le premier XXème siècle* (Industries, employers and workers in the Vallenciennes region during the early twentieth century). Paris: Messidor, Editions Sociales.

Harlan, G. H. 1967. *San Francisco Ferry Boats*. Berkeley, CA: Howell-North.

Harley, J. B. 1975. *Ordnance Survey Maps: a descriptive manual*. London: HMSO.

Härö, E.-S. 1979. *Asko. Ruukinmiljööt: Bruksmiljöer* (Early industrial milieux: exhibition). Helsinki: Museum of Finnish Architecture.

—— 1987. *Suomalaisen ruunkinmiljöön yleispiirteet* (General characteristics of early industrial milieux in Finland). Helsinki: Yliopistopaino.

Harris, E. C. 1979. *Principles of Archaeological Stratigraphy*. London: Academic Press.

Harris, J. R. 1964. *The Copper King: a biography of Thomas*

Williams of Llanidan. Liverpool: Liverpool University Press.

——1972. *Industry and Technology in the Eighteenth Century: Britain and France*. Birmingham: University of Birmingham.

Harris, R. C. and Matthews, G. 1987. *Historical Atlas of Canada*, vol. I. Toronto: University of Toronto Press.

Harris, R. C. and Warkentin, J. 1974. *Canada Before Confederation: a study in historical geography*. Toronto: Oxford University Press.

Harrison, B. H. 1971. *Drink and the Victorians: the temperance question in England 1815–72*. London: Faber.

Harrison, G. 1963. *Borthwicks: a centenary in the meat trade, 1863–1963*. London: Borthwick.

Harrison, J. F. C. 1969. *Robert Owen and the Owenites in Britain and America: the quest for the New Moral World*. London: Routledge & Kegan Paul.

Harrison, J. K. and Almond, J. K. 1978. *The Industrial Archaeology of Cleveland*. Middlesbrough: Cleveland County Library.

Harrison, W. 1967. *The History of the Manchester Railways*, ed. W. H. Chaloner. Manchester: Lancashire & Cheshire Antiquarian Society.

Harrods 1949. *Harrods Ltd.: a study of British achievement 1849–1949*. London: Harrods Ltd.

Hart, I. B. 1958. *James Watt and the History of Steam Power*. New York: Henry Schuman.

Harte, N. B. and Ponting, K. G. 1973. *Textile History and Economic History: essays in honour of Julia de Lacy Mann*. Manchester: Manchester University Press.

Hartenberg, R. S. 1979. *National Historic Mechanical Engineering Landmarks*. New York: American Society of Mechanical Engineers.

Hartley, D. 1954. *Food in England*. London: MacDonald.

——1978. *Water in England*. London: MacDonald & James.

Hartley, H. 1966. *Humphrey Davy*. London: Nelson.

Hartmann, K. 1977. *Deutsche Gartenstadtbewegung: Kulturpolitik und Gesellschaftsreform* (German garden cities: cultural politics and social reform). Munich: H. Moos Verlag.

Harvard 1960. *Oil's First Century: papers given at the Centennial Seminar on the History of the Petroleum Industry*. Cambridge, MA: Harvard Business School.

Harvey, W. S. and Rose, G. D. 1980. *William Symington*. London: Northgate.

Haselfoot, A. 1978. *The Batsford Guide to the Archaeology of South-east England*. London: Batsford.

Haslam, M. 1989. *In the Nouveau Style*. London: Thames & Hudson.

Hasluck, P. N. 1907. *Pumps and Hydraulic Rams*. London: Constable.

Hatcher, J. 1991. *The History of the British Coal Industry*, vol. I: *before 1700*. Oxford: Oxford University Press.

Hatcher, J. and Barker, T. C. 1974. *A History of British Pewter*. London: Longman.

Hatry, G. 1982. *Louis Renault, patron absolu* (Louis Renault, absolute boss). Paris: Lafourcade.

Hauser, A. 1961. *Schweizerische Wirtschafts- und Sozial Geschichte* (Swiss economic and social history). Zürich: Erlengach.

Haut, F. J. G. 1977. *Electric Locomotives of the World*. Truro: Bradford Barton.

Hay, G. D. and Stell, G. P. 1986. *Monuments of Industry: an illustrated historical record*. Edinburgh: Royal Commission of the Ancient and Historic Monuments of Scotland.

Hayden, D. 1976. *Seven American Utopias: the architecture of Communitarian Socialism, 1790–1975*. Cambridge, MA and London: MIT Press.

Hayes, G. 1981. *A Guide to Stationary Steam Engines*. Ashbourne: Moorland.

Hayward, K. 1989. *The British Aircraft Industry*. Manchester: Manchester University Press.

Hayward-Tylor 1910. *Aerated Water Machinery made by Hayward-Tylor & Co Ltd*. London: Hayward Tylor.

Hazen, M. H. and Hazen, R. M. 1985. *Wealth Inexhaustible: a history of America's mineral industries to 1850*. New York: Van Nostrand Reinhold.

Head, Sir G. 1968. *A Home Tour Through the Manufacturing Districts of England in the Summer of 1835*. Reprint, London: Cass.

Heaton, H. 1920. *The Yorkshire Woollen and Worsted Industries*. Oxford: Clarendon Press.

Hecksher, E. F. 1954. *An Economic History of Sweden*. Cambridge, MA: Harvard University Press.

——1956. *Den svenska arbetarklassens historia* (The history of the Swedish working class). Stockholm: Bonnier.

Henderson, W. O. 1954. *Britain and Industrial Europe 1750–1870*. Liverpool: Liverpool University Press.

——1975. *The Rise of German Industrial Power 1834–1914*. London: Maurice Temple Smith.

Hennessey, R. A. S. 1972. *The Electric Revolution*. Newcastle upon Tyne: Oriel.

Henning, F. W. 1973. *Die Industrialiesierung in Deutschland 1800 bis 1914* (The industrialization of Germany 1800 to 1914). Paderborn: Ferdinand Schöningh.

——1974a. *Die vorindustrielle Deutschland 800 bis 1800* (Pre-industrial Germany 800 to 1800). Paderborn: Ferdinand Schöningh.

——1974b. *Die Industrialisierung in Deutschland 1914 bis 1972* (Industrialization in Germany 1914 to 1972). Paderborn: Ferdinand Schöningh.

Herbarth, D. 1978. Die Entwicklung der optischen Telegraphie in Preussen (The development of the semaphore signalling system in Prussia). *Arbeitshefte des Landeskonservators Rheinland* XV. Cologne: Rheinland Verlag.

Herbert, G. 1978. *Pioneers of Prefabrication: the British contribution in the nineteenth century*. Baltimore, MD: Johns Hopkins University Press.

Herbert, T. E. 1916. *Telegraphy: a detailed exposition of the telegraph system of the British Post Office*. London: Whittaker.

Heritage of Australia 1981. *The Heritage of Australia*. Melbourne: Macmillan.

Hermann, W. and Hermann, G. 1981. *Die alten Zechen an*

der Ruhr (The old mines of the Ruhr district). Königstein: Karl Robert Langeviesche Nachfolge.

Herring, W. H. 1893. *The Construction of Gasworks Practically Described.* London: Hazell, Watson & Viney.

Hey, D. 1980. *Packmen, Carriers and Packhorse Roads: trade and communications in North Derbyshire and South Yorkshire.* Leicester: Leicester University Press.

Hibbs, J. 1968. *The History of the British Bus Services.* Newton Abbot: David & Charles.

——1971. *The Omnibus: readings in the history of road passenger transport.* Newton Abbot: David & Charles.

Hidy, R. W. and Hidy, M. E. 1955. *Pioneering in Big Business: the history of the Standard Oil Company, NJ, 1882–1911.* New York: Harper.

Higgs, E. 1989. *Making Sense of the Census: the manuscript returns for England and Wales 1801–1901.* London: HMSO.

Hildebrand, G. 1974. *Designing for Industry: the architecture of Albert Kahn.* Cambridge, MA and London: MIT Press.

Hildebrand, K.-G. 1987. *Svensket jarn. Sexton- och Sjutton-hundratal Exportindustri fore industrialismen* (Swedish iron in the sixteenth and seventeenth centuries: an exporting industry before industrialization). Stockholm: Jernkontorets forskning.

Hildebrandt, A. 1908. *Balloons and Airships.* London: Constable. Reprint, 1973, Wakefield: EP.

Hildebrandt, W., Lemburg, P. and Wewel, J. 1988. *Historische Bauwerek der Berliner Industrie,* Heft I (Historic industrial buildings in Berlin, vol. I). Berlin: Kiepert KG.

Hill, C. W. 1911. *Electric Crane Construction.* London: Charles Griffin.

Hillairet, J. 1963, 1972. *Dictionnaire historique des rues de Paris* (Historical dictionary of Paris streets). Paris: Editions de Minuit.

Hills, R. L. 1967. *Machines, Mills, and Uncountable Costly Necessities.* Norwich: Goose.

——1973. *Richard Arkwright and Cotton Spinning.* London: Priory Press.

Hinde, D. W. and Hinde, M. 1948. *Electric and Diesel Electric Locomotives.* London: Macmillan.

Hinde, H. L. 1938. *Brewing: science and practice.* London: Chapman & Hall.

Hindle, B. 1966. *Technology in Early America: a bibliography of early American technology.* Chapel Hill, NC: University of North Carolina Press.

——1975. *America's Wooden Age: aspects of its early technology.* Tarrytown, NY: Sleepy Hollow Restorations.

——1981. *Material Culture of the Wooden Age.* Tarrytown, NY: Sleepy Hollow Restorations.

Hine, R. V. 1966. *California's Utopian Colonies.* New Haven, CT and London: Yale University Press.

Hinz, F.-L. 1977. *Die Geschichte der Wocklumer Eisenhütte* (The history of the Wocklum ironworks). Wocklum: Altenaer Beiträge.

Hipkins, W. E. 1896. *The Wire Rope and its Applications.* Birmingham: J. & E. Wright.

History Workshop 1985. *Making Cars: a history of car making at Cowley.* London: Routledge & Kegan Paul.

Hoag, J. 1963. *Western Islamic Architecture.* London: Prentice Hall.

Hobsbawm, E. J. 1969. *Industry and Empire: an economic history of Britain since 1750.* Harmondsworth: Penguin.

Hoel Malstrom, K. 1982. *Fabrikk og Bolig ved Akerselva* (Factories and buildings of the Akerselva). Oslo: Norsk Teknisk Museum.

Hoensch, J. K. 1984. *A History of Modern Hungary 1867–1986.* London: Longman.

Hofer, H. 1888. *Das Erdol* (Petroleum). Brunswick: Bieweg.

Hogue, C. et al. 1979. *Québec, un siècle d'électricité* (Quebec, a century of electricity). Montreal: Libre Expression.

Holding, T. H. 1908. *The Camper's Handbook.* London: Simkin Marshall.

Holdsworth, D. ed. 1985. *Reviving Main Street.* Toronto: University of Toronto Press.

Hollingworth, B. 1979. *How to Drive a Steam Locomotive.* London: Astragal.

Hollowell, P. G. 1968. *The Lorry Driver.* London: Routledge & Kegan Paul.

Holme, C. G. 1935. *Industrial Architecture.* London: Studio.

Holme, R. 1688. *The Academy of Armory.* Chester: privately published.

Holt, J. 1795. *A General View of the Agriculture of Lancashire.* London: G. Nicol.

Holt, L. J. 1974. *Norges Historie* (The history of Norway). Oslo.

Holyoake, G. J. 1870. *The History of Co-operation in England: its literature and advocates.* London: Trubner.

Hopkins, A. A. 1928. *The Lure of the Lock.* New York: General Society of Mechanics and Tradesmen.

Hopkins, H. 1970. *A Span of Bridges.* Newton Abbot: David & Charles.

Hornby, J. 1913. *A Textbook of Gas Manufacture for Students.* London: G. Bell.

Horne, J. 1976. *Farewell to the Floating Bridges: a pictorial history of floating bridge operation in Southampton.* Southampton: Southampton University Industrial Archaeology Group.

Horner, J. 1920. *The Linen Trade of Europe during the Spinning Wheel Period.* Belfast: McCaw, Stevenson & Orr.

Hornsby, L. 1957. *The Film and Industry.* London: Newman Neame.

Horton, E. 1973. *The Age of the Airship.* London: Sidgwick & Jackson.

Horton, M. H. 1990. *Newdale: an industrial community of the mid-eighteenth century.* Telford: Ironbridge Institute.

Hoskins, W. G. 1957. *The Making of the English Landscape.* London: Hodder & Stoughton.

Hössle, F. 1935. *Alte Papiermuhlen der Provinz Schleisien* (Old papermills in the province of Silesia). Wrocław.

Hoth, W. 1975. *Die Industrielisierung einer Rheinischen Gewerbestadt-dargstellt am Beispiel Wuppertal* (The industrialization of a Rhenish commercial town described through the example of Wuppertal). *Schriften zur rheinisch-westfälischen Wirtschaftgeschichte* (Papers on economic history in the Rhineland and Westphalia) XXVIII. Cologne: Rheinisch-Westfälisches Wirtschaftsarchiv.

Houghton, J. 1692–1703. *A Collection of Letters for the Improvement of Husbandry and Trade.* London: privately published.

Hounshell, D. A. 1984. *From the American System to Mass Production.* Baltimore, MD: Johns Hopkins University Press.

Hounshell, D. A. and Smith, J. K. Jnr. 1988. *Science and Corporate Strategy: Du Pont R & D, 1902–30.* New York: Cambridge University Press.

Household, H. 1989. *Narrow Gauge Railways: England and the fifteen inch.* Gloucester: Alan Sutton.

Howard, D. L. 1960. *The English Prisons.* London: Methuen.

Howard, E. 1946. *Garden Cities of Tomorrow,* ed. with introduction by L. Mumford. London: Faber.

Howard, F. 1988. *Wilbur and Orville: the story of the Wright brothers.* London: Robert Hale.

Howard, J. 1784. *The State of the Prisons,* 3rd edn. Warrington: W. Eyres.

Howe, H. 1987. *The Maritime Museums of North America.* New York: Facts on File.

Howe, O. J. and Matthews, F. G. 1986. *American Clipper Ships 1833–58.* 2 vols. New York: Dover.

Hower, R. M. 1943. *The History of Macy's of New York 1858–1909: chapters in the evolution of the department store.* Cambridge, MA: Harvard University Press.

Hoy, S.E. 1976. *History of Public works in the United States.* Chicago, IL: American Public Works Association.

Hubbard, G. 1965. *Cooke and Wheatstone and the Invention of the Electric Telegraph.* London: Routledge & Kegan Paul.

Hubbard, H. V. 1930. *Airports: their location, administration and legal basis.* Cambridge, MA: Harvard University Press.

Hudson's Bay Company 1920. *The Governor and Company of Adventurers of England Trading into Hudson Bay during Two Hundred and Fifty Years 1670–1920.* London: Hudson's Bay Company.

Hudson, K. 1963. *Industrial Archaeology: an introduction.* London: John Baker.

—— 1965. *The Industrial Archaeology of Southern England.* Newton Abbot: David & Charles.

—— 1966. *A History of English China Clays.* Newton Abbot: David & Charles.

—— 1968. *Towards Precision Shoemaking.* Newton Abbot: David & Charles.

—— 1970. *Working to Rule.* Bath: Adams & Dart.

—— 1971. *A Guide to the Industrial Archaeology of Europe.* Bath: Adams & Dart.

—Hudson, K. 1972. *Air Travel: a social history.* Bath: Adams & Dart.

—— 1973. *A Guide to the Industrial Archaeology of Continental Europe.* Bath: Adams & Dart.

—— 1976. *Industrial Archaeology: a new introduction.* London: John Baker.

—— 1977. *Museums for the 80s: a survey of world trends.* London: Macmillan.

—— 1978. *Food, Clothes and Shelter.* London: John Baker.

—— 1979a. *World Industrial Archaeology.* Cambridge: Cambridge University Press.

—— 1979b. *Street Furniture.* London: Bodley Head.

—— 1980. *Where We Used to Work.* London: John Baker.

—— 1983. *The Archaeology of the Consumer Society.* London: Heinemann.

—— 1987. *Museums of Influence.* Cambridge: Cambridge University Press.

Hudson, K. and Nicholls, A. 1981. *The Directory of Museums.* London: Macmillan.

—— 1987. *The Cambridge Guide to the Museums of Britain and Ireland.* Cambridge: Cambridge University Press.

Hudson, O. R. 1953. *A Hundred Years of the Halifax: a history of the Halifax Building Society 1853–1953.* London: Batsford.

Hughes, B. R. 1974. *Firepower: weapons effectiveness on the battlefield.* London: Arms & Armour Press.

Hughes, E. and Eames, A. 1975. *Porthmadog Ships.* Caernarvon: Gwynned Archives Service.

Hughes, H. 1964. *The Australian Iron and Steel Industry 1848–1962.* Parkville: Melbourne University Press.

Hughes, H. W. 1917. *A Text-book of Coal Mining.* London: Griffin.

Hughes, W. H. 1968. *A Century of Traction Engines.* Newton Abbot: David & Charles.

Hughes, W. J. and Thomas, J. L. 1973. *The Sentinel: a history of Alley & MacLellan and the Sentinel waggon works,* vol. I: *1875–1930.* Newton Abbot: David & Charles.

HuLan, R. and Lawrence, S. S. 1970. *A Guide to the Reading and Study of Historic Site Archaeology.* Columbia, MO: University of Missouri Museum of Anthropology.

Hull, E. 1881. *The Coalfields of Great Britain.* London: E. Stanford.

Hume, J. R. 1974. *The Industrial Archaeology of Glasgow.* Glasgow: Blackie.

—— 1976. *The Industrial Archaeology of Scotland,* vol. I: *The Central Lowlands.* London: Batsford.

—— 1977. *The Industrial Archaeology of Scotland,* vol. II: *The Highlands and Islands.* London: Batsford.

Hume, N. 1970. *A Guide to the Artefacts of Colonial America.* New York: Knopf.

Hummel, J. J. 1888. *The Dyeing of Textile Fabrics,* 3rd edn. London: Cassell.

Humphries, S. 1981. *Hooligans or Rebels: an oral history of working class childhood and youth 1889–1939.* Oxford: Basil Blackwell.

Hunt, R. A. 1887. *Historical Sketch of British Mining.* London: Crosby Lockwood. Reprint, 1978, Wakefield: EP Publishing.

Hunter, D. 1947. *Papermaking: the history and technique of an ancient craft.* London: Pleiades.

Hunter, L. C. 1949. *Steamboats on the Western Rivers: an economic and technological history.* Cambridge, MA: Harvard University Press.

—— 1979. *A History of Industrial Power in the United*

States, 1780–1930, vol. I: *Waterpower in the century of the steam engine*. Charlottsville, VA: University Press of Virginia.

—— 1984. *A History of Industrial Power in the United States 1780–1930*, vol. II: *Steampower*. Charlottesville, VA: University Press of Virginia.

Hunter, W. H. 1921. *Dock and Lock Machinery: a technical manual*. London: Constable.

Huntley, J. 1969. *Railways in the Cinema*. London: Ian Allan.

Hurry, J. B. 1930. *The Woad Plant and its Dye*. Oxford: Oxford University Press.

Husband, J. 1917. *The Story of the Pullman Car*. Chicago, IL: McClurg.

Huse, N. 1989. *Verloren, gefährdet, geschütz. Baudenkmale in Berlin* (Lost, endangered, protected. Building conservation in Berlin). Berlin: Argon.

Huske, J. 1987. *Die Steinkohlenzerben im Ruhrrevier Datue und Fakten von den Anfagen bis 1986* (The coal mines in the Ruhr region: data and facts from the beginnings until 1986). Bochum: Deutsches Bergbau Museum.

Hutt, A. 1973. *The Changing Newspaper: typographical trends in Britain and America, 1622–1972*. London: Gordon Fraser.

Hyde, C. K. 1977. *Technological Change and the British Iron Industry*. Princeton, NJ: Princeton University Press.

Hyde, C. K. 1978. *The Upper Peninsula of Michigan, an Inventory of Historic Engineering and Industrial Sites*. Washington DC: National Park Service.

—— 1986. *The Northern Lights: lighthouses of the Upper Great Lakes*. Lansing, MI: Two Peninsula Press.

Hyldtoft, O. 1984. *Kobenhavns Industrialisering, 1840–1914* (The industrialization of Copenhagen, 1840–1914). Herning: Systime.

Hyldtoft, O. et al. 1981. *Det industrielle Danmark 1840–1914* (Industrial Denmark 1840–1914). Herning: Systime.

Hyman, A. 1982. *Charles Babbage, Pioneer of the Computer*. Oxford: Oxford University Press.

ICCROM 1974. *Conservation in Museums and Galleries*. Rome: ICCROM.

—— 1985. *Ironworks and Iron Monuments: study, conservation and adaptive uses, symposium, Ironbridge 23–25 October 1984*. Rome: ICCROM.

ICI 1950. *Ancestors of an Industry*. Birmingham: Kynoch Press.

—— 1962. *The Birth of an Industry*. London: ICI.

ICOMOS 1979, 1982, 1985. *Eisen Architektur: Die Rolle des Eisens in der historischen Architektur der ersten Halfte der 19. Jahrhunderts* (Iron architecture: the role of iron in the historic architecture of the first half of the nineteenth century). 3 vols. Hannover: Curt R. Vincente Verlag.

Industrial Locomotive Society 1967. *Steam Locomotives in Industry*. Newton Abbot: David & Charles.

Ingersoll, E. 1881. *The Oyster Industry*. Washington DC: US Department of the Interior.

Innis, H. A. 1923. *A History of the Canadian Pacific Railway*. Reprint, 1971, Toronto: Toronto University Press.

—— 1930. *The Fur Trade in Canada*. New Haven, CT: Yale University Press.

—— 1940. *The Cod Fisheries: the history of an international economy*. Toronto: University of Toronto Press.

INSA 1982–91. *Inventar der neuen Schweizer Architektur 1850–1920* (Inventory of new architecture in Switzerland 1850–1920). Berne: Gesellschaft für Kunstgeschichte.

Ioannou, N. 1986. *From Folk to Studio Pottery*. Adelaide: Wakefield Press.

IRB Themendokumentationem 1986. *Baudenkmäler: Erhaltung, Sanierung, Pflege: Eine Literaturdokumentation* (Built monuments: maintenance, conservation and preservation: a bibliography). Stuttgart: IRB Verlage.

Ireland, S. 1795. *A Picturesque Tour through Holland, Brabant and Part of France Made in the Autumn of 1789*. London: J. Egerton.

Ireland, S. 1797. *Picturesque Views on the River Wye*. London: R. Faulder.

Ironbridge Institute 1986. *Papers presented to the International Seminar on Wrought Iron, Ironbridge 14–17 July 1986*. Telford: Ironbridge Institute.

Irving, R. 1985. *The History and Design of the Australian House*. Melbourne: Oxford University Press.

Ivins, W. M. 1943. *How Prints Look*. New York: Metropolitan Museum of Art.

Ixion, 1951. *Motor Cycle Cavalcade*. London: Iliffe. Reprint, 1971, Wakefield: SR.

Jackson, A. 1973. *Semi-Detached London*. London: Allen & Unwin.

Jackson, A. A. 1969. *London's Termini*. Newton Abbot: David & Charles.

Jackson, A. J. 1987. *British Civil Aircraft 1919–72*, 3rd edn. 3 vols. London: Putnam.

Jackson, D. 1975. *Lighthouses of England and Wales including the Channel Islands*. Newton Abbot: David and Charles.

Jackson, D. C. 1988. *Great American Bridges and Dams*. Washington DC: Preservation Press.

Jackson, G. 1978. *The British Whaling Trade*. London: Black.

—— 1983. *The History and Architecture of Ports*. Tadworth: World's Work.

Jackson, J. N. and Addis, F. A. 1982. *The Welland Canals: a comprehensive guide*. St Catharines: Welland Canals Foundation.

Jackson, J. N. and Burtniak, J. 1978. *Railways in the Niagara Peninsula*. Belleville: Mika Publishing.

Jackson, J. N. and White, C. 1971. *The Industrial Structure of the Niagara Peninsula*. St Catherines: Brock University.

Jackson, K. 1985. *Crabgrass Frontier: the Suburbanization of the United States*. Oxford: Oxford University Press.

Jacquet, E. and Japis, A. 1970. *Technique and History of the Swiss Watch*. London: Hamlyn.

Jairazbhoy, R. A. 1971. *An Outline of Islamic Architecture*. London: JK Publishers.

Jallings, J. H. 1916. *Elevators: a practical treatise on the development and design of hand, belt, steam, hydraulic and electric elevators*. Chicago, IL: American Technical Society.

James, J. 1857. *A History of the Worsted Manufacture in England*. London: Longman. Reprint, 1968, London: Cass.

James, N. D. G. 1981. *A History of English Forestry*. Oxford: Blackwell.

James, W. H. N. 1916. *Alternating Currents in Theory and Practice*. Cambridge: Cambridge University Press.

Janik, A. and Toulmin, S. 1973. *Wittgenstein's Vienna*. London: Weidenfeld & Nicholson.

Jansen, G. H. 1984. *Cultuurgeschiedenis van de Hollandse stad: Een land van steden: Het spoor van de tijd* (A cultural history of Dutch towns: a country of towns: the track of time). The Hague: Staatsuitgeverij.

Jansma, K. 1954. *Lely: Bedwinger van de Zuiderzee*, 2nd edn. Amsterdam: H. J. Paris.

Janson, S. and Janson, A. eds 1983. *Forsmarks bruk: en herrgårdsmiljö* (Forsmarks bruk: a seignorial environment). Stockholm: Forsmark Kraftgrupp AB.

Janssen, G. B. 1987. *Baksteen fabricape in Nederland: van nijverheid tot industrie, 1850–1920* (Brickmaking in the Netherlands: from craft to industry, 1850–1920). Zutphen: Walburg.

Jaros, J. 1966. *Historia gornictwa weglowego w zaglebiu Gornoslaskim* (The history of coal mining in the Upper Silesia region to 1914). Wroclaw: Ossolineum.

—— 1973. Dzieje hutnictwa zelaza w rejonie Gliwic i Zabrza do 1945 (The history of the metallurgy of iron in the Gliwice and Zabrze regions to 1945). *Kwartalnik Historii Nauki i Techniki* (Quarterly of the history of science and technology), XVIII (4).

Jarvis, A. 1985. *Hydraulic Machines*. Princes Risborough: Shire Publications.

Jasiuk, J. 1962. Zabytki techniki w województwie kieleckim i ich naukowe oraz dydaktyczne znaczenie (Technological artefacts in Kieleckie province and their scientific and didactic significance). *The Swietokrzyski Annual* I.

—— 1973. Muzea Technili w Kielecczyźnie (The museuems of technology in Kieleckie province). *Roczniki Muzeum Swietokrzyskiejo* VIII.

—— 1976. Dzialalność Naczelnej Organizacji Technicznej w latach 1945–1974 (The works of the Chief Technical Organization in the years 1945–1974). Warsaw.

Jaspert, W., Berry, W. T. and Johnson, A. F. 1953. *Encyclopaedia of Type Faces*. London: Blandford Press.

JC 1708. *The Compleat Collier*. London: G. Conyers. Reprint, 1968, Newcastle: Frank Graham.

Jeans, D. 1972. *An Historical Geography of New South Wales to 1901*. Sydney: Longman Cheshire.

Jeffreys, J. B. 1954. *Retail Trading in Britain 1850–1950*. Cambridge: Cambridge University Press.

Jeffreys, R. 1949. *The King's Highway: an historical and autobiographical record of the developments of the past sixty years*. London: Batchworth.

Jelavich, B. 1983. *History of the Balkans*. Cambridge: Cambridge University Press.

Jeníček, L. 1963. *Metal Founding Through the Ages on Czech Territory*. Prague: National Technical Museum.

Jeníček, L. and Krulis, I. 1968. *British Inventions of the Industrial Revolution in the Iron and Steel Industry on Czechoslovak Territory*. Prague: National Technical Museum.

Jenkins, D. 1975. *The West Riding Wool Textile Industry 1770–1835*. Edington, Wiltshire: Pasold.

Jenkins, D. and Ponting, K. 1982. *The British Wool Textile Industry 1770–1914*. London: Heinemann.

Jenkins, J. G. 1969. *The Welsh Woollen Industry*. Cardiff: National Museum of Wales.

Jenkins, R. V. 1966. *Images and Enterprise: technology and the American photographic industry*. Baltimore, MD: John Hopkins University Press.

Jenkinson, D. 1988. *The National Railway Collection*. London: Collins.

Jennings, H. 1985. *Pandemonium 1660–1886: the coming of the machine as seen by contemporary observers*. London: Deutsch.

Jennings, M.-L. 1982. *Humphrey Jennings, Film-Maker/Painter/Poet*. London: British Film Institute.

Jennings, T. S. 1988. *Bellfounding*. Princes Risborough: Shire Publications.

Jeremy, D. J. 1981. *Transatlantic Industrial Revolution: the diffusion of textile technologies between Britain and America, 1790s–1830s*. Oxford: Basil Blackwell.

Jerrold, W. B. and Doré, G. 1872. *London*. London: Grant.

Jesperson, A. 1970. *The Lady Isabella Waterwheel*. Virum: privately published.

Jewitt, L. 1878. *The Ceramic Art of Great Britain*, ed. G. A. Godden, 1972. London: Barrie & Jenkins.

Jezierski, A. and Zawadzki, S. 1966. *Dwa wieki przymysłu w Polsce Zarys Dziejów* (Two centuries of industry in Poland). Warsaw: Wiedza Powszechna.

Jodice, R. 1985. *L'Architettura del ferro Italia 1796–1914* (Iron architecture in Italy 1796–1914). Florence.

Johannsen, O. 1953. *Geschichte des Eisens* (History of Iron). Dusseldorf: Verlag Stahleisen.

Johansen, H. Chr. 1983. *Shipping and Trade Between the Baltic Area and Western Europe 1784–95*. Copenhagen.

—— 1987. *The Danish Economy in the Twentieth Century*. New York: St Margaret's Press.

—— 1988. *Industriens vækst og vilkar 1870–1973* (Industrial growth and conditions 1870–1973). Odense: Odense Univ forlag.

John, A. H. 1950. *The Industrial Development of South Wales*. Cardiff: University of Wales Press.

Johnson, D. L. 1980. *Australian Architecture, 1901–51: sources of modernism*. Sydney: Sydney University Press.

Johnson, H. 1971. *The World Atlas of Wine*. London: Mitchell Beazley.

Johnson, R. W. and Lynch, R. W. 1932. *The Sales Strategy of John H. Patterson, Founder of the National Cash Register Company*. Chicago, IL: Dartnell.

Jonas, S. 1977. *La Fondation des Villages ouvriers des mines de Potasse du Haut-Rhin* (The establishment of workers' villages for the Haut-Rhin potash mines). Strasbourg: USHS.

Jonas, S., Heckner, P. and Knorr, J. M. 1975. *La cité de*

Mulhouse: étude critique d'un modèle d'habitat ouvrier historique (The cité ouvrière at Mulhouse: a critical study of an historic model workes' settlement). Strasbourg: University of Strasbourg.

Jones, E. 1985. *Industrial Architecture in Britain 1750–1939.* London: Batsford.

Jones, E. L. 1974. *Agriculture and the Industrial Revolution.* Oxford: Basil Blackwell.

Jones, H. D. 1917. *Communal Settlements in the United States.* Washington DC: Library of Congress.

Jones, J. C. 1984. *America's Icemen: an illustrative history of the United States natural ice industry 1665–1925.* Humble, TX: Jobeco.

Jones, K. P. 1969. *Steam Locomotive Development 1923–1962: a critical bibliography.* London: Library Association.

Jones, W. R. 1950. *Minerals in Industry.* Harmondsworth: Penguin.

Jörberg, L. 1961. *Growth and Fluctuations in Swedish Industry 1869–1912.* Lund: Lund University.

—— 1970. *The Industrial Revolution in Scandinavia 1850–1914.* London: Fontana.

Josephson, M. 1959. *Edison: a biography.* New York: McGraw-Hill.

Jouan, R. 1949. *Le Petrole: roi du monde* (Petroleum: king of the world). Paris: Monde Payot.

Joy, E. 1977. *Pictorial Dictionary of British Nineteenth Century Furniture Design.* Woodbridge: Antique Collectors Club.

Joyce, P. 1980. *Work, Society and Politics: the culture of the factory in late Victorian England.* Hassocks: Harvester Press.

Justino, D. 1988–9. *A Formaçao do Espaço Económico Nacional: Portugal 1810–1913* (The formation of the Portuguese economy 1810–1913). 2 vols. Lisbon: Vega.

Jutikkala, E., Kaukiainen, Y. and Åström, S.E. 1980. *Suomen taloushistorica* I: *Agraarinen Suomi* (Finnish economic history, vol. I: agricultural Finland). Helsinki: Tammi.

Kahn, I. 1936. *Industrial and Commercial Buildings.* Detroit, MI: Albert Kahn Inc.

Kahne, G. 1978. *The Last Tall Ships: Gustav Erikson and the Åland sailing fleets 1872–1947.* London: Conway Maritime Press.

Kain, R. J. P. and Prince, H. C. 1985. *The Tithe Surveys of England and Wales.* Cambridge: Cambridge University Press.

Kakar, S. 1970. *Frederick Taylor: a study in personality and innovation.* Cambridge, MA: MIT Press.

Kaliński, J. and Liberadzki, B. 1974. *Zarys dziejów transportu ladowego w Polsce XIX i XX wieku* (The history of land transport in Poland in the nineteenth and twentieth centuries). Warsaw: WP.

Kalla-Bishop, P. M. 1973. *Hungarian Railways.* Newton Abbot: David & Charles.

Kappelhof, A. C. M. and Zeeuws, T. 1979. *De ruimten van de werkende mens: resten van een Noorbrabants verleden* (Space for working people: episodes from the history of Noordbrabant). Den Bosch.

Kaser, M. C. 1985. *The Economic History of Eastern Europe 1919–1973.* Oxford: Oxford University Press.

Kasson, J. F. 1976. *Civilizing the Machine: technology and Republican values in America 1776–1900.* New York: Grossman.

Kastorff-Viehmann, R. 1981. *Wohnungsbau für Arbeite: das Beispiel Ruhrgebiet bis 1914* (Dwellings for workers: the example of the Ruhrgebiet up to 1914). Aachen: Klenkes Verlag.

Kaufman, M. 1963. *The First Century of Plastics: celluloid and its sequel.* London: Plastics Institute.

Kaufmann, D. W. 1971. *Sodium Chloride: the production and properties of salt and brine.* New York: Hafner.

Kay, D. 1968. *Buses and Trolleybuses since 1945.* London: Blandford.

Kealey, G. S. 1980. *Toronto Workers Respond to Industrial Capitalism, 1867–1892.* Toronto: University of Toronto Press.

Kearton, W. J. 1922. *Steam Turbine Theory and Practice.* London: Pitman.

Keating, J. D. 1970. *Mind the Curve: a history of the cable trams.* Melbourne: Melbourne University Press.

Kecskés, P. 1990. *The Museum of the Hungarian Village at Szentendre.* Budapest: Corvina.

Keilhau, W. 1951. *Norges Eldste Linje-Rederi: det Bergenski Dampskibs-Selskab 1851–1951* (Norway's oldest transport company: the Bergen steamship line 1851–1951). Bergen: Bergenski Dampskibs-Selskab.

Keller, G. 1979. *Propre en order. Habitation et vie domestique 1850–1930: l'exemple vaudois* (Cleanliness and order. Everday domestic life 1850–1930: the example of the Vaud). Lausanne: Editions d'En bas.

Kellett, J. R. 1979. *The Impact of Railways on Victorian Cities.* London: Routledge & Kegan Paul.

Kelley, D. W. 1986. *Charcoal and Charcoal Burning.* Princes Risborough: Shire Publications.

Kelly, A. 1990. *Mrs Coade's Stone.* Upton-upon-Severn: Self-publishing Association.

Kelly, M. 1981. *Plague Sydney 1900: a photographic introduction to the hidden Sydney.* Sydney: Doak Press.

Kemp, P. 1972. *The Oxford Companion to Ships and the Sea.* Oxford: Oxford University Press.

Kempers, A. J. B. 1979. *Oliemolens* (Oilmills). Arnhem: Netherlands Open Air Museum.

Kendall, R. G. 1950. *Land Drainage.* London: Faber & Faber.

Kennedy, L. and Ollerenshaw, P. 1983. *An Economic History of Ulster 1820–1945.* Manchester: Manchester University Press.

Kent-Jones, D. W. and Mitchell, E. F. 1962. *The Practice and Science of Bread Making.* Liverpool: Northern Publishing.

Kerr, D. and Holdsworth, D. 1990. *Historical Atlas of Canada*, vol. 3. Toronto: University of Toronto Press.

Kerr, G. J. 1974. *Australian and New Zealand Sail Traders.* Blackwood: Lynton.

Kerr, J. S. 1984. *Design for Convicts: an account of the design for convict establishments in the Australian colonies during the transportation era.* Sydney: Library of Australian History.

—— 1985. *The Conservation Plan: a guide to the preparation of conservation plans for places of European cultural significance*, 2nd edn. Sydney: National Trust of Australia (NSW).

Kérouanton, J.-L. 1988. *Les ardoisières en Pays de la Loire* (The slate quarries of the Pays de la Loire region). Paris: Ministère de la Culture.

—— 1989. *Lu: une Usine à Nantes* (Lu: a factory at Nantes). Nantes: Ministère de la Culture, Images du Patrimoine.

Kerridge, E. 1985. *Textile Manufactures in Early Modern England*. Manchester: Manchester University Press.

Kerrison, J. 1963. *Beaconsfield Gold*. Beaconsfield: Beaconsfield Rotary Club.

Kidder Smith, G. E. 1955. *Italy Builds*. London: Architectural Press.

Kidner, R. W. 1946. *The Early History of the Motor Car 1769–1897*. Chislehurst: Oakwood Press.

Kidney, W. C. 1976. *Working Places*. Pittsburgh, PA: Ober Park Associates.

Kidwell, C. B. and Christman, M. C. 1974. *Suiting Everyone: the democratization of clothing in America*. Washington DC: Smithsonian Insitute Press.

Kiernan, D. 1989. *The Derbyshire Lead Industry in the Sixteenth Century*. Chesterfield: Derbyshire Records Society.

Kietowicz, F. 1968. *Z dziejów pirzemysłu zapałczanego w Polsce* (The history of the match-making industry in Poland). Bystrzyca Kłodzka.

Kieve, S. L. 1973. *The Electric Telegraph: a social and economic history*. Newton Abbot: David & Charles.

Killanin, Lord and Duignan, M. V. 1967. *The Shell Guide to Ireland*. London: Ebury Press.

Kilmartin, L. and Thorns, D. C. 1978. *Cities Unlimited*. London: Allen & Unwin.

King, A. D. 1984. *The Bungalow: the product of a global culture*. London: Routledge & Kegan Paul.

King, C. E. 1978. *The Encyclopaedia of Toys*. London: Robert Hale.

King, G. A. B. 1956. *Tanker Practice: the construction, operation and maintenance of tankers*. Wokingham: Maritime Press.

Kingston, P. 1985. *Royal Trains*. Newton Abbot: David & Charles.

Kirichenko, E. 1977. *Moscow Architectural Monuments of the 1830s–1910s*. Moscow: Iskusstvo.

Kirkby, W. 1902. *The Evolution of Artificial Mineral Waters*. Manchester: Jewsbury & Brown.

Kiss, L., Kiszely, G. and Vajda, P. 1981. *Magyarorszag ipari Muemlekei* (Industrial monuments in Hungary). Budapest: Orszagos Muszaki Muzeum.

Klapheck, R. 1928. *Neue Baukunst in den Rheinlanden* (New architecture in the Rhineland). Düsseldorf: Schwann.

Klapper, C. 1961. *The Golden Age of Tramways*. London: Routledge & Kegan Paul.

—— 1973. *British Lorries 1900–1945*. London: Ian Allan.

Klemm, F. 1979. *Zur Kulturgeschichte den Technik* (The cultural history of technology). Munich: Deutsches Museum.

Klingender, F. 1968. *Art and the Industrial Revolution*, ed. Sir Arthur Elton. London: Paladin.

KLM 1928. *The Importance of Holland Seen from the Air*. Amsterdam: KLM.

Kloss, A. 1987. *Von der Elektricität aur Elektrizität: Ein Streifzug durch die Geschichte der Electroteknik, Elektroenergetik und Elektronik* (From electricity to electricity: a section through the history of electrical engineering, electric power generation and electronics). Basel: Birkhäuser.

Knight, E. H. 1876. *Knight's American Mechanical Dictionary: being a description of tools, instruments, machines, processes and engineering*. New York: Hurd & Houghton.

Knight, F. 1973. *The Clipper Ship*. London: Collins.

Knox, B. 1965. *The Architecture of Prague and Bohemia*. London: Faber.

Knudsen, T. 1988. *Storbyen stobes 1840–1917* (The casting of the big city 1840–1917). Copenhagen: Akademisk forlag.

Koch, J. E. 1979. *Industrial Archaeology: an introductory bibliography*. Monticello, IL: Vance.

Koester, F. 1915. *Hydroelectric Developments and Engineering*. New York: Van Nostrand.

Komlos, J. 1983. *Economic Development in the Habsburg Monarchy in the Nineteenth Century*. New York: Boulder.

Kongsthogskolans Arkitekturskola 1972. *Stavanger*. Stockholm: Kongsthogskolans Arkitekturskola.

Korff, G. and Rürup, R. 1987. *Berlin, Berlin. Die Ausstellung zur Geschichte der Stadt* (Berlin, Berlin. The exhibition of the history of the city). Berlin: Nicola Verlag.

Kossmann, E. H. 1978. *The Low Countries 1780–1940*. Oxford: Clarendon Press.

Kösters, H. 1981. *Dictung in Stein und Grün. Margarethenhöhe* (Poetry in stone and greenery. Margarethenhöhe). Essen: Beleke KG.

Kowecka, E. 1978. *Historia Kultury Materialnej* (The history of material culture). Wrocław: Ossolineum.

Kranzberg, M. and Pursell, C. eds 1967. *Technology and Western Civilization*. New York: Oxford University Press.

Kriedte, P., Medick, H. and Schlumbohm, A. 1981. *Industrialization before Industrialization*. Cambridge: Cambridge University Press.

Krings, U. 1977. Der Kölner Hauptbahnhof (The main railway station in Cologne). *Arbeitshefte des Landeskonservators Rheinland* XXII. Cologne: Rheinland Verlag.

Krings, U. 1985. *Bahnhofs architekture, Deutsche Gross stadtbahnhofe des Historismus* (Railway station architecture: historic stations in the cities of Germany). Munich: Prestel.

Kroetsch, R. 1969. *An Atlas of Alberta*. Calgary: University of Alberta.

Kroker, W. 1978. *SICCIM: The Second International Con-*

ference on the Conservation of Industrial Monuments: Transactions. Bochum: Deutsches Bergbau-Museum.

Krygier, E. 1958. *Katalog zabytków budownictwa przemys-lowego w Polsce zasady opracowania* (Catalogue of historic industrial buildings in Poland). Wrocław: Osolineum.

Krzyżan, M. 1983. *Samoloty w muzeach polskich* (Aircraft in Polish museums). Warsaw: Wydawnictura Komunikacji itacznosci.

Kubinszky, M. 1969. *Bahnhofe Europas: Ihre Geschichte, Kunst und Technik* (European railway stations: their history, architecture and technology). Stuttgart: Franckh'sche Verlagshandlung.

Kuhlmann, C. B. 1929. *Development of the Flour Milling Industry in the United States.* Boston, MA: Houghton Mifflin.

Kuipers, J. E. J. 1972. *Commercial Vehicles of the World.* Tingfield: Oakwood.

Kulik, G. and Bonham, J. 1978. *Rhode Island, an Inventory of Historic Engineering and Industrial Sites,* Washington DC: National Park Service.

Kulik, G., Parks, R. and Penn, T. 1982. *The New England Mill Village, 1790–1860.* Cambridge, MA: MIT Press.

Kwaśny, Z. 1968. *Hutnicto zelaza na Górnym Ślasku w pierwszej połowie XIX wieku* (The metallurgy of iron in Upper Silesia in the first half of the nineteenth century). Wrocław: Ossolineum.

Labatut, J. and Lane, W. J. eds 1972. *Highways in our National Life,* 2nd edn. Princeton, NJ: Bureau of Urban Research.

Labelye, C. 1739. *A short account of the methods made use of in laying the foundation of the piers of Westminster Bridge.* London: W. Strahan.

—— 1751. *A Description of Westminster Bridge.* Dublin: G. & A. Ewing.

Lacasse, R. 1988. *Joseph-Armand Bombardier, le rêve d'un inventeur.* Montreal: Libre expression.

Laing, E. A. M. 1985. *Steam Wooden Warship Building in Portsmouth Dockyard 1832–1852.* Portsmouth: Portsmouth City Council.

Lake, C. 1987. *Jersey Airport: the first fifty years, 1937–1987.* London: Michael Stephens.

Laloue, P. E. 1954. *Le Guide de la charcuterie: aide-memoire de charcuterie practique* (Guide and reference book to charcuterie). Montreuil-sous-Bois: Guide de la Charcuterie.

Lamard, P. 1988. *Histoire d'un capital familial au XIXè siecle: le capital Japy* (History of a family capital during the nineteenth century: the Japy capital). Montbéliard: Société belfortaine d'émulation.

Lamb, M. C. 1923. *The Manufacture of Chrome Leather.* London: Anglo-American Technical Company.

Lambert, R. S. 1938. *The Universal Provider: a study of William Whiteley and the rise of the London department store.* London: Harrap.

Lambrick, G. 1985. *Archaeology and Nature Conservation.* Oxford: Oxford University Department of External Studies.

Lamy, Y. 1987. *Hommes de fer en Périgord au XIXè siecle*

(Men of iron in Périgord during the nineteenth century). Lyons: La Manufacture.

Lancaster, B. and Mason, T. 1986. *Life and Labour in a Twentieth-century City: the experience of Coventry.* Coventry: Cryfield Press.

Landen, D. and Daniel, J. 1985. *The True Story of HP Sauce.* London: Methuen.

Landes, D. S. 1983. *Revolution in Time: clocks and the making of the modern world.* Cambridge, MA: MIT Press.

Landeskonservator Rheinland 1972. Technische Denkmäler: Arbeitsiedlungen 1 und 2 (Technical monuments: workers' colonies 1 and 2). *Arbeitshefte des Landeskonservators Rheinland* I, II. Bonn: Landeskonservators Rheinland.

Landesvermessungsamt Nordrhein-Westfalen 1968. *Topographischer Atlas Nordrhein-Westfalen* (Topographical Atlas of North-Rhine Westphalia). Bonn: Landesvermessungsamt Nordrhein-Westfalen.

Lane, M. R. 1980. *The Story of the Steam Plough Works: Fowlers of Leeds.* London: Northgate.

Langdon, W. E. 1897. *The Application of Electricity to Railway Working.* London: Spon.

Lankton, L. D. 1982. *Old Reliable: an illustrated history of the Quincy Mining Company.* Hancock, MI: Quincy Mine Historical Association.

Lardière, B. 1991. *Les Usines Japy en Franche-Comté* (The Japy factories in Franche-Comté). Besançon: Ministère de la Culture, Inventaire Général de Monuments et des Richesses artistiques de la France.

Larkin, E. J. and Larkin, J. G. 1988. *Railway Workshops of Britain 1823–1986.* London: Macmillan.

Larose, J.-F. et al. 1982. *Mauricie: étude du potential de polyvalence des propriétés riveraines d'Hydro Québec* (Mauricie: a study of the various uses of the riverside properties of Hydro-Québec). Montreal: Direction Environnement Hydro Québec.

Larson, H. M. 1948. *Guide to Business History: materials for the study of American buisness history and suggestions for their use.* Cambridge, MA: Harvard University Press.

Latham, F. B. 1972. *A Century of Serving Consumers: the story of Montgomery Ward.* Chicago, IL: Montgomery Ward and Co.

Latimer, M., Hindle, B. and Kranzberg, M. 1984. *Bridge to the Future: a centennial celebration of the Brooklyn Bridge.* New York: New York Academy of Sciences.

Laundry Journal 1896. *Laundry Management: a handbook for use in public and private laundries,* 3rd edn. London: Crosby Lockwood.

Lauridsen, H. R. 1990. *Viborgs industrihitorie, 1742–1990* (The industrial history of Viborg, 1742–1990). Viborg.

Lauterbach, F. 1905. *Der Kampf des Waides mit dem Indigo* (The struggle between woad and indigo). Leipzig: Vita.

Lautier, F., Schalchli, T. et al. 1981. *L'Usine et son espace* (The factory and its space). Paris: Editions de la Villette.

Laux, J. M. 1976. *In First Gear: the French automobile*

industry to 1914. Liverpool: Liverpool University Press.

Law, H. and Clark, D. K. 1901. *The Construction of Roads and Streets*. London: Lockwood.

Law, R. J. 1965. *The Steam Engine: a brief history*. London: Science Museum.

Lawrie, G. 1948. *The Practical Ropemaker*. Belfast: H. R. Carter.

Lawton, R. 1978. *The Census and Social Structure: an interpretative guide to nineteenth-century censuses for England and Wales*. London: Cass.

Leary, T. and Sholes, E. 1987. *From Fire to Rust: business, technology and work at the Lackawanna steel plant, 1889–1983*. Buffalo, NY: Buffalo and Erie County Historical Society.

Lebhar, G. M. 1963. *Chain Stores in America 1859–1962*. New York: New York Chain Store Publishing Corporation.

Lebrun, P. 1979. *Essai sur la Revolution Industrielle en Belgique*. Brussels: Academie Royale.

Lee, C. E. 1945. *Narrow Gauge Railways in North Wales*. London: Railway Publishing Company.

——1962. *The Early Motor Bus*. London: British Railways Board.

——1968. *The Horse Bus as Vehicle*. London: British Railways Board.

Lee, J. 1981. *Irish Historiography 1970–1979*. Cork: Cork University Press.

Leech, R. 1981. *Early Industrial Housing: the Trinity area of Frome*. London: HMSO for the Royal Commission on Historical Monuments.

Leenders, N. A. H. W. 1989. *Verdwenen venen. Een onderzoek naar de ligging en exploitatie tussen Antwerpen, Turnhout, Geertruidenberg en Willemstad 1250–1750* (Disappearing links. A review of the relationships between Antwerp, Tournhout, Geertruidenberg and Willemstad 1250–1750). Wageningen: Pudoc.

Lefèvre, L. 1900. *Architectural Pottery*. London: Scott Greenwood.

Lefond, S. J. 1969. *Handbook of World Salt Resources*. New York: Plenum.

Legatt, R. F. 1987. *Railways of Canada*. Newton Abbot: David & Charles.

Lehmann, J. 1937. *MS Selandia 1912–1937*. Copenhagen.

Leigh, E. 1873. *The Science of Modern Cotton Spinning*. Manchester: Palmer & Howe.

Lemoine, B. 1986. *L'Architecture du Fer, France, XIXè siècle* (Iron architecture, France, nineteenth century). Seyssel: Champvallon.

Lemon, J. T. 1985. *Toronto since 1918: an illustrated history*. Toronto: Lorimer.

Lepage, A. 1980. *Le banc de Paspébiac, site commercial et industriel* (The Paspébiac bank, a commercial and industrial site). Quebec: Ministry of Cultural Affairs.

Lepetit, H. 1987. *Sur les traces de la Manufacture des glaces, Tourlaville, 1667–1834* (On the tracks of the mirror manufactory, Tourlaville, 1667–1834). Cherbourg: Amis du Musée de la Glacerie.

Łepkowski, T. 1968. *Przemysł warszawski u progu epoki kapitalistucznej* (Industry in Warsaw on the threshold of the capitalist era). Warsaw: PWN.

Leuillot, P. 1959. *L'Alsace au début du XIXè siècle, II: les transformations économiques* (Alsace at the beginning of the nineteenth century, vol. II: the economic transformations). Paris: SEVPEN.

Leung, F. L. 1981. *Grist and Flour Mills in Ontario 1780s–1880s: from millstones to rollers*. Ottawa: Parks Canada.

Levaillant de la Fieffe, O. 1873. *Verreries de Normandie* (Glassworks in Normandy). Rouen: G. Lanctin.

Levine, D. 1977. *Family Formation in an Age of Nascent Capitalism*. London: Academic Press.

Lewery, A. J. 1974. *Canal Boat Painting*. Newton Abbot: David & Charles.

Lewis, J. 1962. *Printed Ephemera*. Ipswich: Cowell.

——1970. *Anatomy of Printing*. London: Faber.

Lewis, M. J. T. 1968. *How Festiniog Got its Railway*. Caterham: Railway and Canal History Society.

——1970. *Early Wooden Railways*. London: Routledge & Kegan Paul.

Lewis, M. J. T. and Denton, J. H. 1974. *Rhosydd Slate Quarry*. Shrewsbury: Cottage Press.

Lewis, R. A. 1952. *Edwin Chadwick and the Public Health Movement*. London: Longmans Green.

Lewis, S. 1837. *Topographical Dictionary of Ireland*. London: S. Lewis.

Lewis, W. D. 1976. *Iron and Steel in America*. Wilmington, DE: Eleutherian Mills-Hagley Foundation, Inc.

Lewis, W. J. 1967. *Lead Mining in Wales*. Cardiff: University of Wales Press.

Lie, I.-M. K. and Opstad, L. 1976. *Kunstindustrimuseet i Oslo* (The art industrial museum in Oslo). Oslo: Kunstindustrimuseet.

Lindgren, M. and Sorbom, P. 1985. *Christopher Polhem, the Swedish Daedalus*. Stockholm: National Technical Museum.

Lindley, K. 1973. *Seaside Architecture*. London: Hugh Evelyn.

Lindner, W. 1927. *Bauten der Technik: Ihre Form under Wirking* (Industrial buildings: their form and effect). Berlin: Wasmuth.

Lindner, W. and Steinmetz, G. 1923. *Die Ingenieurbauten in ihre guten Gestaltung* (Forms of engineering construction). Berlin: Wasmuth.

Lindquist, G., Thor, L. and Carlsson, T. 1984. *Museiboken Sverigeslänsmuseer* (The regional museums of Sweden). Stockholm.

Lindquist, S. 1978. *Gräv där Du star* (Dig where you stand). Stockholm.

Lindroth, S. 1955. *Gruvbrytning och kopparhantering vid Stora Kopparberget intill 1800-talets börjam* (Mining operations and copper working at Stora Kopparberg up to the eighteenth century). 2 vols. Uppsala: Almquistowicksell/Geber.

Lindsay, J. 1968. *The Canals of Scotland*. Newton Abbot: David & Charles.

——1974. *A History of the North Wales Slate Industry*. Newton Abbot: David & Charles.

Lindsay, W. S. 1874–6. *The History of Merchant Shipping and Ancient Commerce.* London: Sampson Low.

Lineham, W. J. 1907. *A Text Book of Mechanical Engineering.* London: Chapman & Hall.

Ling, P. J. 1990. *America and the Automobile: technology, reform and social change, 1893–1923.* Manchester: Manchester University Press.

Linge, G. 1979. *Industrial Awakening: a geography of Australian manufacture 1788–1890.* Canberra: Australian National University Press.

Linteau, P.-A. 1981. *Maisonneuve: comment des promoteurs fabriquent une ville* (Maisonneuve: how the promoters built up a town). Montreal: Boréal Express.

Linters, A. 1979. *Industriele Erfgoed in Limburg. Prov. Dienst voor het Kunstpatrimonium, St-Truiden* (Industrial heritage in Limburg: the provincial art history service, St-Truiden). Liège and Brussels: Pierre Mardaga.

——1985. *Spoorwegen in Belgie* (Railways in Belgium). Ghent: VVIA.

——1986a. *Industria: Industriele architectuur in Belgie* (Industry: industrial architecture in Belgium). Liège: Pierre Mardaga.

——1986b. *Industriele Archaeologie in Vlaanderen* (Industrial archaeology in Vlaanderen). Antwerp: EBES.

Lipson, E. 1953. *A Short History of Wool and its Manufacture.* London: Heinemann.

Lisle, B. O. 1936. *Tanker Technique 1700–1936.* London: World Tankship Publications.

Liveing, E. 1959. *Pioneers of Petrol: a century history of cars.* London: Cape & Leonard.

Ljogodt, L. 1977. *Oslo Lysverker* (The Oslo electric power company). Oslo: Oslo Lysverker.

Lloyd, H. 1975. *The Quaker Lloyds in the Industrial Revolution.* London: Hutchinson.

Lloyd, N. 1925. *A History of English Brickwork.* Reprint, 1983, London: Antique Collector's Club.

Locci, J.-P. 1988. *Fonderies et Fondeurs: histoire des etablissements métallurgiques en Vaucluse au XIXè et XXè siècles* (Foundries and founders: history of metallurgic establishments in the Vaucluse, nineteenth and twentieth centuries). Avignon.

Locke, R. R. 1978. *Les fonderies et forges d'Alais à l'époque des premiers chemins de fer, 1829–1874* (Foundries and forges at Alès during the early railway age, 1829–1874). Paris: M. Rivière.

Lockett, T. A. 1979. *Collecting Victorian Tiles.* Woodbridge: Antique Collectors' Club.

Locomotive Publishing Company n.d. *The Locomotive in Service.* London: Locomotive Publishing Company.

Long, J. V. A. 1956. *An Introduction to Shoemaking.* London: Shoe and Leather News.

Long, P. J. 1987. *The Birmingham and Gloucester Railway.* Gloucester: Alan Sutton.

Lord, J. 1923. *Capital and Steam Power 1750–1800.* London: P. S. King.

Lorentz, S. 1973. *Przewodnik po muzeach i zbiorach w Polsce* (Guidebook of Polish museums). Warsaw: Interpress.

Lossen, W. 1968. *Geschichte und Beschreibung der Reichenhaller Solequellen, der Soleleitungen von Berchtesgaden-Rosenheim, der Reichenhaler Saline* (History and description of the brine sprines at Reichenhall, the salt pipeline from Berchtesgaden to Rosenheim and the salt works at Reichenhall). Bad Reichenhall.

Lough, J. 1954. *The Enclycopèdie of Diderot and d'Alambert: selected articles.* Cambridge: Cambridge University Press.

Lovett, R. W. and Bishop, E. M. 1978. *Manuscripts in Baker Library.* Cambridge, MA: Harvard Graduate School of Business Administration.

Lowe, D. and Richards, J. 1982. *The City of Lace.* Nottingham: Nottingham Lace Centre.

Lowe, J. 1986. *Industrial Eye.* Washington DC: Preservation Press.

Lowe, J. B. 1977. *Welsh Industrial Workers' Housing 1775–1875.* Cardiff: National Museum of Wales.

Lowe, J. W. 1975. *British Steam Locomotive Builders.* Norwich: Goose.

Lower, A. R. M. 1973. *Great Britain's Woodyard: British America and the timber trade 1763–1867.* Toronto: McGill-Queen's University Press.

Lowerson, J. and Myerscough, J. 1977. *Time to Spare in Victorian England.* Hassocks: Harvester.

Lowry, T. M. and Cavell, A. C. 1944. *Intermediate Chemistry.* London: Macmillan.

Loyer, F. 1983. *Le Siècle de l'industrie* (The century of industry). Geneva: Skira.

Lubbock, B. 1927. *The Last of the Windjammers.* Reprint, 1969, Glasgow: Brown, Son & Fergusson.

——1929. *The Down Easterns: American deep water sailing ships 1869–1929.* Glasgow: Brown, Son & Fergusson.

——1932. *The Nitrate Clippers.* Glasgow: Brown, Son & Fergusson.

——1946. *The China Clippers.* Glasgow: Brown, Son & Fergusson.

Lucas, E. V. 1905. *A Wanderer in Holland.* London: Methuen.

Ludwig, K.-H. 1981. *Technik, Ingenieure und Gesellschaft: Geschichte des Vereins Deutscher Ingenieure 1856–1981* (Technology, engineering and society: the German Society of Engineers 1856–1981). Düsseldorf: VDI-Verlag.

Łukasiewicz, J. 1963. *Przewrót techniczny w przemyśle Królestwa Polskiego 1852–1886* (The revolution in industrial technology in the congress kingdom of Poland 1852–1886). Warsaw: PWN.

Lundstrom, B. 1961. *The Ship.* London: Allen & Unwin.

——1969. *Sailing Ships.* London: Allen & Unwin.

Lunge, G. 1909. *Coal Tar and Ammonia.* London: Gurney & Jackson.

Lunkenheimer, L. 1990. Schleifkotten, Mühlen und Hämmer an den Solinger Bächer (Grinding machines, mills and hammers on the streams of Solingen). *Arbeitshefte des Landeskonservators Rheinland XXXIII.* Cologne: Rheinland Verlag.

Lyaschenko, P. 1949. *History of the National Economy of Russia.* New York: Macmillan.

Lynch, P. and Vaizey, J. 1960. *Guinness's Brewery in the*

Irish Economy 1759–1876. Cambridge: Cambridge University Press.

Lynes, L. 1959. *Railway Carriages and Wagons: theories and practices.* London: Locomotive Publishing Company.

Lyon-Caen, J.-F. and Ménégoz, J.-C. 1989. *Cathédrales électriques, architecture des centrales hydrauliques du Dauphiné* (Electric cathedrals, the architecture of hydro-electric power stations in the Dauphiné). Grenoble: Musée Dauphinois.

Lyons, F. S. L. 1971. *Ireland since the Famine.* London: Weidenfeld & Nicolson.

McAdam, J. L. 1827. *Remarks on the Present System of Road Making.* London: Longman.

McCarty, J. W. and Schedvin, C. B. 1978. *Australian Capital Cities.* Sydney: Sydney University Press.

McCullough, D. 1972. *The Great Bridge.* New York: Simon & Schuster.

—— 1976. *The Path between the Seas: the creation of the Panama Canal 1870–1914.* New York: Simon and Schuster.

McCutcheon, A. 1965. *The Canals of the North of Ireland.* Newton Abbot: David & Charles.

—— 1969. *Railway History In Pictures, Ireland,* vol. I. Newton Abbot: David & Charles.

—— 1970. *Railway History In Pictures, Ireland,* vol. II. Newton Abbot: David & Charles.

—— 1977. *Wheel and Spindle: aspects of Irish industrial history.* Belfast: Blackstaff Press.

—— 1980. *The Industrial Archaeology of Northern Ireland.* Belfast: HMSO.

MacDermot, E. T. 1882/1964. *History of the Manchester Railways,* ed. W. H. Chaloner. Manchester: Lancashire & Cheshire Antiquarian Society.

—— 1927. *History of the Great Western Railway.* London: GWR. Revised and edited by C. R. Clinker, 1964, London: Ian Allen.

MacEwan, P. 1915. *The Art of Dispensing.* London: Chemist and Druggist.

Macfadyen, D. 1933. *Sir Ebenezer Howard and the Garden City Movement.* Manchester: Manchester University Press.

McGrath, R. and Frost, A. C. 1937. *Glass in Architectural Decoration.* London: Architectural Press.

Macgregor, J. 1835. *My Notebook.* London: Macrone.

Macintyre, H. J. 1928. *A Handbook of Mechanical Refrigeration.* New York: John Wiley.

Mack, G. 1944. *The Land Divided.* New York: Knopf.

McKean, C. 1987. *The Scottish Thirties.* Edinburgh: Scottish Academic Press.

Mackersey, I. 1985. *Tom Rolt and the Cressy Years.* Cleobury Mortimer, Shropshire: Baldwin.

McLaren, M. 1943. *The Rise of the Electrical Industry in the Nineteenth Century.* Princeton, NJ: Princeton University Press.

Maclaurin, W. R. 1949. *Invention and Innovation in the Radio Industry.* New York: Macmillan.

Macleod, C. 1989. *Inventing the Industrial Revolution: the English patent system 1660–1800.* Cambridge: Cambridge University Press.

Macleod, M., Trinder, B. S. and Worthington, M. 1988.

The Ditherington Flax Mill, Shrewsbury: a survey and historical evaluation. Telford: Ironbridge Institute.

McLintock, W. F. P. 1983. *Gemstones in the Geological Museum,* 4th edn, rev. P. M. Statham. London: HMSO.

MacManus, F. 1967. *The Years of The Great Test 1926–1939.* Cork: Mercier Press.

McNeil, I. 1968. *Joseph Bramah: a century of invention 1749–1851.* Newton Abbot: David & Charles.

—— 1972. *Hydraulic Power.* London: Longman.

McNeill, W. H. 1982. *The Pursuit of Power: technology, armed force and society since AD 1000.* Chicago, IL: Chicago University Press.

MacNutt, W. S. 1963. *New Brunswick: a history 1784–1867.* Toronto: Macmillan.

Maczak, A. 1981. *Encyklopedia Historii Gospodarczej Poloski do 1945* (Encyclopaedia of the economic history of Poland to 1945). Warsaw: Interpress.

Maddin, R. 1988. *The Beginnings of the Use of Metals and Alloys: papers from the Second International Conference on the Beginnings of the Use of Metals and Alloys, Zhengzhou, China, 1986.* Cambridge, MA: MIT Press.

Maisner-Nieduszyński, P. and Pawłowska-Wilde, B. 1986. *Muzea w Polsce* (Museums in Poland). Warsaw: Osrodek Dokumentacji Zabytów.

Majdalany, F. 1959. *The Red Rocks of Eddystone.* London: Longman.

Majer, J. et al. 1987. *Technicke Pamiatky Stredoceskeho Kraje* (Technical heritage of the central Czech region). Prague: National Heritage Museum.

Major, J. K. 1975. *Fieldwork in Industrial Archaeology.* London: Batsford.

—— 1978. *Animal-powered Engines.* London: Batsford.

—— 1985. *Animal-powered Machines.* Princes Risborough: Shire Publications.

Makepeace, C. 1983. *The Manchester Ship Canal: a short history.* Nelson: Hendon Publishing Company.

Malet, H. 1977. *Bridgewater: the canal duke, 1736–1803.* Manchester: Manchester University Press. 2nd ed., 1990, Nelson: Hendon Publishing Company.

Malinverno, B. et al. 1989. *L'Ancienne métallurgie dans le département des Vosges* (Old metalworking in the Vosges département). Nancy: Ministère de la Culture, Images du Patrimoine.

Molmberg, E. 1917. *Strömbergs bruks historia* (The history of Strömbergs bruk). Uppsala.

Malgren, K. 1985. *Silk Town: industry and culture in Macclesfield 1750–1835.* Hull: Hull University Press.

Mander, G. P. 1955. *The History of Mander Brothers 1773–1955.* Wolverhampton: Mander Brothers.

Manning, M. and McDowell, M. 1986. *Electricity Supply in Ireland: the history of the ESB.* Dublin: Gill & Macmillan.

Manton, J. 1976. *Mary Carpenter and the Children of the Streets.* London: Heinemann.

Marcosson, I. F. 1945. *Wherever Men Trade: the romance of the cash register.* New York: Dodd, Mead & Co.

Marestier, J. B. 1957. *Memoir on Steamboats of the United States of America.* Mystic, CT: Marine Historical Association.

Marks, E. C. R. 1904. *Notes on the Construction of Cranes and Lifting Machinery*, 3rd edn. Manchester: Technical Publishing Company.

Marland, E. A. 1964. *Early Electrical Communication*. London: Aberlard-Schuman.

Marrey, B. 1979. *Les Grands Magasins des Origines à 1929* (Great stores from their origins until 1929). Paris.

——1984. *Un Capitalisme idéal* (An ideal capitalism). Paris: Glancier-Guinaud.

Marrey, B. and Chemetov, P. 1976. *Familièrement inconnues: architutres Paris 1848–1914* (Familiar but not understood: architecture in Paris 1848–1914). Paris: ICOMOS.

Marsh, A. and Ryan, V. 1980. *A Historical Directory of Trade Unions*, vol. I. Aldershot: Gower.

——1984. *A Historical Directory of Trade Unions*, vol. II. Aldershot: Gower.

——1987. *A Historical Directory of Trade Unions*, vol. III. Aldershot: Gower.

Marshall, C. F. D. 1938, *A History of British Railways down to the Board of Agriculture*. Oxford: Oxford University Press.

——1953. *The History of Locomotive Design down to the End of the Year 1831*. London: Locomotive Publishing Company.

Marshall, J. D. 1958. *An Economic History of Furness 1711–1900, and of the Town of Barrow 1757–1897*. Reprint, 1981, Beckermet, Cumbria: M. Moon.

Marshall, J. D. 1968. *The Old Poor Law*. London: Macmillan.

Marshall, W. 1808. *Review and Abstract of Country Reports to the Board of Agriculture*, vol. I: *Northern Department*. London: Longman.

Marti, D. R. A. et al. 1982. *I Jornades sobre la Preotecció i Revalorització del Patrimoni Industrial* (Conference papers on the conservation and evaluation of the industrial heritage). Bilbao: Departamento de Cultura del Gobierno Vasco.

Martin, G. 1918. *Industrial and Manufacturing Chemistry (Organic)*. London: Crosby Lockwood.

Martin, W. 1989. *Manufakturbauten im Berliner Raum seit dem Ausgehenden 17 Jahrhundert* (Manufacturing buildings in the Berlin area since the end of the seventeenth century). *Bauwerke und Kunstdenkmäler von Berlin* (Architectural and artistic monuments of Berlin) XVIII. Berlin: Mann Verlag.

Martinell, C. 1960. *Antoni Gaudí*. New York: Universe Books.

Marx, K. 1867. *Das Kapital* (Capital). Ed. E. Paul and C. Paul, 1928, London: Allen and Unwin.

Maślakiewicz, K. 1965. *Z dzieków górnictwa solnego w Polsce* (The history of salt-mining in Poland). Warsaw: Wyd. Navkowo-Techniczne.

Masur, G. 1971. *Imperial Berlin*. London: Routledge & Kegan Paul.

Matheson, W. 1979. *Norsk Skogbruksmuseum skogbruk, jakt og fiske 25 ar 1954–1979* (The Norwegian museum of forestry, hunting and fishing, the first twenty-five years 1954–1979). Elverum: Norsk Skogbruksmuseum.

Mathias, P. 1959. *The Brewing Industry in England 1700–1830*. Cambridge: Cambridge University Press.

——1962. *English Trade Tokens*. London: Abelard-Schuman.

——1967. *The Retailing Revolution*. London: Longman.

Mathis, F. et al. 1988. *Das Bild der Industrie in Österreich* (Views of industry in Austria). Innsbruck: Galerie im Taxispalais & Institut für Kunstgeschichte der Universitatät Innsbruck.

Mathys, E. 1954. *Bieträge zur Schweizerischen Eisenbahngeschichte* (Essays on Swiss railway history). Bern: Kümmerley & Frey.

Matos, A. T. D. 1980. *Transportes e Comunicaçoes em Portugal, Açores e Madeira 1750–1850* (Transport and communications in Portugal, the Azores and Madeira 1750–1850). Ponta Delgada: Universidade dos Açores.

Matschoss, C. 1908. *Die Entwicklung der Dampfmaschine: Eine Geschichte der ortsfesten Dampfmaschine und der Lokomobile der Schiffmaschine und Lokomotive* (The development of the steam engine: a history of the stationary steam engine, the steam carriage, the marine engine and the locomotive). Berlin: Julius Spinger. Reprint, 1983, Moers: Steiger.

——ed. 1927–40. *Beiträge zur Geschichte der Technik und Industrie, Jahrbuch des Vereines Deutscher Ingenieure, Sektion Technische Kulturdenkmäler* (Papers on the history of technology and industry, yearbook of the German Association of Engineers, sections on technical monuments). Berlin: Vereines Deutscher Ingenieure.

Matthews, K. and Panting, G. eds 1978. *Ships and Shipbuilding in the North Atlantic Region*. St John's: Memorial University of Newfoundland.

Matthews, L. G. 1982. *Antiques of the Pharmacy*, vol. I: *Ceramics*. Bath: Merrell Medicines.

——1983a. *Antiques of the Pharmacy*, vol. II: *Metal and Glass*. Bath: Merrell Medicines.

——1983b. *Antiques of the Pharmacy*, vol. III: *Wooden Objects*. Bath: Merrell Medicines.

——1985. *Regional Guide to Pharmacy's Past*. Bath: Merrell Medicines.

Mattinen, M. 1985. *Teollisuusympäristöt. Teollisuusympäristöjen dokumentointi, tutkimus ja soujelu Suomessa* (Industrial milieux. The documentation, study and preservation of industrial milieux in Finland). Helsinki: Työväenperinne – Arbetartradition.

Mauersberger, H. R. 1947. *Matthews Textile Fibers*. New York: John Wiley & Sons.

May, R. 1977. *The Gold Rushes*. London: Luscombe.

Mayhew, H. 1850. *The Unknown Mayhew: selections from the Morning Chronicle*, ed. E. P. Thompson and E. Yeo, 1973. Harmondsworth: Penguin.

——1861–2. *The Life and Labour of the London Poor*. London: Griffin Bohn.

Mayhew, H. and Binny, J. 1862. *The Criminal Prisons of London*. London: Griffin Bohn.

Mayr, O. and Post, R. eds 1982. *Yankee Enterprise: the rise of the American system of manufactures*. Washington DC: Smithsonian Institute Press.

Mead, W. R. and Jaatinen, S. H. 1975. *The Åland Islands*. Newton Abbot: David & Charles.

Meade, A. 1916. *Modern Gasworks Practice*. London: Benn.

—— 1934. *The New Modern Gasworks Practice*. London: Eyre & Spottiswoode.

Meakin, B. 1905. *Model Factories and Villages: ideal conditions of labour and housing*. London: Fisher Unwin.

Meeks, C. L. V. 1956. *The Railroad Station: an architectural history*. New Haven, CT: Yale University Press.

Meenan, J. 1970. *The Irish Economy since 1922*. Liverpool: Liverpool University Press.

Meesom, G. 1860. *Great Westerns. The Official Illustrated Guide to the Great Western Railway*. London: Griffin.

Meinander, N. 1968. *Grängesberg: en krönika om svensk järnmalm* (Grängesberg: a chronicle of Swedish iron-working). Stockholm: Grängesberg.

Mellor, G. J. 1968. *The Northern Music Hall*. Newcastle upon Tyne: Frank Graham.

Mencken, A. 1957. *The Railroad Passenger Car*. Baltimore, MD: Johns Hopkins University Press.

Mende, M. and Hamm, M. 1990. *Denkmale der Industrie und Technik in Niedersachsen und Bremen* (Monuments of industry and technology in Lower Saxony and Bremen). Berlin: Nicolai.

Mendes, J. M. A. 1984. *A Area Económica de Coimbra* (The Coimbra economic region). Coimbra: Comissa de Coordenaçao da Regiao Centro.

Merestier, J. B. 1957. *Memoir on Steamboats of the United States of America*. Mystic, CT: Marine Historical Association.

Merhtens, G. 1900. *Der Deutsche Brückenbau im 19 Jahrhundert* (German bridge-building in the nineteenth century). Berlin: Klassika teknik. Reprint, 1984, Düsseldorf: VDI-Verlag.

Merkl, G. et al. 1985. *Wassertürme* (Water Towers). Munich: R. Oldenbourg Verlag.

Merrill, R. H. 1969. *Engineering in American Society 1850–1875*. Lexington, KY: University Press of Kentucky.

Merrimack Valley Textile Museum 1965. *Wool Technology and the Industrial Revolution*. North Andover, MA: Merrimack Valley Textile Museum.

—— 1980. *All Sorts of Good Sufficient Linen Cloth: linen making in New England 1640–1860*. North Andover, MA: Merrimack Valley Textile Museum.

Mersey Docks and Harbour Board 1960–1. *The Port of Liverpool*. Liverpool: Littlebury.

Metaxas, B. N. 1971. *The Economics of Tramp Shipping*. London: Athlone Press.

Metropolis, N., Houlett, J. and Rota, G. C. eds 1980. *A History of Computing in the Twentieth Century*. New York: Academic Press.

Middlemass, T. 1981. *Irish Standard Guage Railways*. Newton Abbot: David & Charles.

Mika, N. and Mika, H. 1987. *Historic Mills of Ontario*. Belleville: Mika Publishing.

Mikerry, L. 1979. *Aviation in Canada*. Toronto: McGraw Hill Rogerson.

Miller, D., Rowlands, M. and Tilley, C. 1989. *Domination and Resistance*. London: Unwin Hyman.

Miller, W. H. 1987. *Famous Ocean Liners: the story of passenger shipping from the turn of the century to the present day*. Wellingborough: Patrick Stephens.

—— 1989. *German Ocean Liners of the Twentieth Century*. Wellingborough: Patrick Stephens.

Mills, J. S. 1913. *The Panama Canal*. London: Nelson.

Milserry, E. 1979. *Aviation in Canada*. Toronto: McGraw Hill Rogerson.

Milward, A. and Saul, S. B. 1973. *The Economic Development of Continental Europe 1780–1870*. London: Allen & Unwin.

—— 1977. *The Development of the Economies of Continental Europe 1850–1914*. London: Allen & Unwin.

Milward, R. and Robinson, A. 1971. *The West Midlands*. London: Eyre Methuen.

Minchinton, W. E. 1957. *The British Tinplate Industry*. Oxford: Oxford University Press.

Miner, D. C. 1940. *The Fight for the Panama Route*. New York: Columbia University Press.

Mining Association of Great Britain 1925. *Historical Review of Coal Mining*. London: Fleetway.

Ministère de la Culture et de la Communication 1987. *Les Inventaire du patrimoine industriel, objectifs et méthodes* (Industrial heritage inventories, aims and methods). Proceedings of a round table discussion held in Paris, 13–14 March 1986. Paris: Direction du Patrimoine.

Ministry of the Environment 1987. *Rakennussuojelu* (Preservation of Buildings). Helsinki: Ministry of the Environment.

Minnoch, J. K. and Minnoch, D. A. eds 1970. *Hides and Skins*. Chicago, IL: Jacobsen.

Mioni, A. et al. 1981–3. *Archeologia Industriale in Lombardia* (Industrial Architecture in Lombardy). 3 vols. Milan: Mediocredito Lombardo.

Misztal, S. 1970. *Przemiany w strukturze przesterzennej przemysłu na ziemach polskich w latach 1860–1965* (Changes in the location of industry in Poland 1860–1965). Warsaw: DWN.

Mitchell, B. 1921. *The Rise of Cotton Mills in the South*. Baltimore, MD: Johns Hopkins University Press.

Mitchell, B. R. and Deane, P. 1962. *Abstract of British Historical Statistics*. Cambridge: Cambridge University Press.

Mock, E. B. 1949. *The Architecture of Bridges*. New York: Museum of Modern Art.

Moen, K. 1967. *Kongsberg Solvverk 1623–1957* (Kongsberg silverworks 1623–1957). Oslo.

Mokyr, J. 1976. *Industrialisation in the Low Countries 1795–1850*. New Haven, NJ.

Molenda, D. 1972. *Kopalnie rud ołowiu na terenie złóż slasko krakowskich w XVI-XVIII wieku* (Lead mines in the Krakow region of Silesia from the sixteenth century to the eighteenth). Wrocław: Ossolineum.

Molin, H. 1955. *Karlholms Bruks bok: en krönika kring ett upplandsbruk* (The book of Karlholms bruk: a chronicle of a bruk in Uppland). Stockholm: Esselle.

Molloy, P. M. 1976. *The Lower Merrimack River Valley, an*

Inventory of Historic Engineering and Industrial Sites. Washington DC: National Parks Service.

Monckton, H. A. 1966. *A History of English Ale and Beer.* London: Bodley Head.

——1969. *A History of the English Public House.* London: Bodley Head.

Montgomery, D. 1979. *Workers' Control in America: studies in the history of work, technology and labour.* Cambridge: Cambridge University Press.

Montgomery, F. M. 1970. *Printed Textiles: English and American cottons and linens, 1700–1850.* New York: Viking Press.

——1984. *Textiles in America 1650–1870.* New York: Norton.

Montgomery, G. A. 1939. *The Rise of Modern Industry in Sweden.* London: King.

Moody, T. W., Martin, F. X. and Byrne, F. J. 1982. *A New History of Ireland, vol. VIII. A Chronology of Irish History to 1976.* Oxford: Oxford University Press.

Moody, T. W. and Vaughan, W. E. 1986. *A New History Of Ireland, vol. IV: Eighteenth Century Ireland, 1691–1800.* Oxford: Clarendon Press.

Moore, H. C. 1902. *Omnibuses and Cabs.* London: Chapman & Hall.

Moore, J. S. 1976. *The Goods and Chattels of Our Forefathers: Frampton Cotterell and district probate inventories 1539–1804.* Chichester: Phillimore.

Moore, P. 1984. *A Guide to the Industrial Archaeology of Hampshire and the Isle of Wight.* Southampton: Southampton University Industrial Archaeology Group.

——1988. *The Industrial Heritage of Hampshire and the Isle of Wight.* Chichester: Phillimore.

Moran, J. 1973. *Printing Presses: history and development from the fifteenth century to modern times.* Berkeley: University of California Press.

Moreau, F. 1990. *Le roman vrai de l'Encyclopédie* (The real novel of the encyclopaedia). Paris: Gallimard.

Morel, J. 1983. *Pullman: the Pullman Car Co., its services, cars, and traditions.* Newton Abbot: David & Charles.

Morgan, B. 1971. *Civil Engineering: railways.* London: Longmans.

Morgan, J. M. 1826. *The Revolt of the Bees.* London: Longmans.

——1834. *Hampden in the Nineteenth Century.* London: E. Moxon.

Morgan, K. O. 1981. *Rebirth of a Nation: Wales 1880–1980.* Oxford: Clarendon Press.

Morgan, G. T. and Pratt, D. D. 1938. *The British Chemical Industry: its rise and development.* London: Edward Arnold.

Moroianu, D. and Stefan, M. I. 1963. *Focul Viu* (The living fire). Bucharest.

——1968. *Pasiunea Stuntei* (The passion for science). Bucharest.

——1976. *Maestrii ingeniozitatii romanesti* (Masters of Romanian Inventive Genius). Bucharest: Editura Didactica si Pedagogica.

Morris, J. H. and Williams, L. J. 1958. *The South Wales Coal Industry 1841–1875.* Cardiff: University of Wales Press.

Morris, M. ed. 1910–15. *The Collected Works of William Morris.* 24 vols. London: Longmans.

Morris, P. J. T. and Russell, C. A. 1988. *Archives of the British Chemical Industry, 1750–1914: a handlist.* Faringdon: British Society for the History of Science.

Morris, W. 1891–2. *News from Nowhere.* London: Reeves & Turner.

Morris Nunn, M. and Tassell, C. B. 1982. *Launceston's Industrial Heritage: a survey.* 2 vols. Launceston: Queen Victoria Museum.

Morrison, P. and Morrison, E. 1961. *Charles Babbage and his Calculating Engines.* New York: Dover.

Morrison, S. and Day, K. 1963. *The Typographic Book 1450–1935.* London: Benn.

Morse, E. L. ed. 1914. *Samuel F. B. Morse: his letters and journals.* New York: Houghton Mifflin.

Morsel, H. 1981. *Itinéraire Alpes* (Alpine excursion). Lyon-Grenoble. International Conference of TICCIH, CILAC.

Morton, J. 1983. *Thomas Bolton & Sons Ltd 1783–1983: the bicentenary history of a major copper and brass manufacturer.* Ashbourne: Moorland.

Morton, R. G. 1962. *Standard Guage Railways in the North of Ireland.* Belfast: Ulster Museum.

Morton, W. L. 1967. *Manitoba: a history,* 2nd edn. Toronto: University of Toronto Press.

Moss, M. S. and Hume, J. R. 1985. *Workshop of the World: engineering and shipbuilding in the west of Scotland.* London: Heinemann.

Mott, R. A. 1936. *The History of Coke Making and of the Coke Oven Managers' Association.* Cambridge: Heffer.

——1983. *Henry Cort: the great finer, creator of puddled iron.* London: The Metals Society.

Mott, R. A. and Wheeler, R. V. 1939. *The Quality of Coke.* London: Chapman & Hall.

Mouchel, L. T. and Partners 1909. *Hennebique Ferro-Conrete: theory and practice: a handbook for architects and engineers.* London: Mouchel.

Moussette, M. 1979. *La pêche sur le Saint-Laurent* (Fishing on the St Lawrence). Montreal: Boréal Express.

Mowat, C. L. 1955. *Britain between the wars 1918–1940.* London: Methuen.

Mui, L. and Mui, H.-C. 1989. *Shops and Shopkeeping in Eighteenth Century England.* London: Routledge.

Muir, A. 1956. *Nairns of Kirkcaldy: a short history of the company 1847–1956.* Cambridge: Heffer.

Muirhead, J. P. 1854. *The Origin and Process of the Mechanical Inventions of James Watt.* 3 vols. London: John Murray.

Müller-Wulckow, W. 1925. *Bauten der Arbeit und des Verkehrs aus deutscher Gegnwart* (Buildings associated with work and transport in present-day Germany). Leipzig: Königstein.

Multhauf, R. P. 1978. *Neptune's Gift: a history of common salt.* Baltimore, MD: Johns Hopkins University Press.

Mumford, L. 1938. *The Culture of Cities.* New York and London: Secker & Warburg.

——1961. *The City in History.* New York: Harcourt Brace.

Munce, J. F. 1960. *Industrial Architecture: an analysis of international building practice*. New York: Dodge.

Munn, R. F. 1977. *The Coal Industry in America: a bibliography and guide to studies*, 2nd edn. Morgantown, WV: West Virginia University Library.

Murray, A. 1861. *The Theory and Practice of Shipbuilding*. Edinburgh.

—— 1863. *Shipbuilding in Iron and Wood*. Edinburgh.

Murray, J. 1865. *A Handbook for Travellers on the Continent*. London: John Murray.

—— 1900. *Murray's Handbook for Travellers in Constantinople, Brusa and the Troad*. London: John Murray.

Murray, M. and Murray, L. 1987. *The Traveller's Guide to the Ocean Ferryliners of Europe*. 2 vols. Newton Abbot: David & Charles.

Murray, P. J. 1854. *Reformatory Schools in France and England*. London: W. F. & F. G. Cash.

Musson, A. E. 1965. *Enterprise in Soap and Chemicals: Joseph Crosfield and Sons Ltd 1815–1965*. Manchester: Manchester University Press.

Musson, A. E. and Robinson, E. 1969. *Science and Technology in the Industrial Revolution*. Manchester: Manchester University Press.

Muthesius, S. 1982. *The English Terraced House*. New Haven, CT and London: Yale University Press.

Muzea 1970. *Muzea i zabytki techniki w Polsce* (Museums and technological artefacts in Poland). Warsaw: WNT.

Muzeum Przemysłu 1933. *Muzeum Przemysłu i Techniki w Warszawie, Przewodnik-Informator* (Museum of Industry and technology in Warsaw, Guide Book). Warsaw: P. Tyzi Ska.

Mykland, K. and Sogner, B. 1955–1962. *Trondheim bys historie* (History of the city of Trondheim). 4 vols. Trondheim.

Myrant, G. 1977. *The Protection of Industrial Designs*. London and New York: McGraw Hill.

Myrdal, J. and Kessle, G. 1978. *Albania Defiant*. Stockholm: AB P. A. Norstedt & Soners Forlag.

Nabais, A. J. and Ramos, P. O. 1985. *Port of Lisbon*. Lisbon: Adminstraçao-Geral do Porto de Lisboa.

—— 1987. *Eiffel em Portugal* (Eiffel in Portugal). Lisbon: Institut Franco-Portugais.

Nadel, G. J. 1957. *Australia's Colonial Culture*. Melbourne: F. W. Cheshire.

Nadon, P. 1984. *Archéologie des sites du Musée de l'Homme et de la Galerie nationale* (Archaeology of the sites of the Museum of Man and of the National Gallery). Quebec.

Nasmyth, J. 1883. *James Nasmyth: an autobiography*, ed. S. Smiles. London: John Murray.

National Board of Antiquities 1982. *Suomen rautatieasemat vuosina 1857–1920* (Finnish railway stations 1857–1920). Helsinki: National Board of Antiquities.

Naval Intelligence Division 1942. *Iceland*. London: Admiralty.

—— 1944–5. *Geographical Handbook Series: Italy*. 4 vols. London: Admiralty.

Nederland Museumland 1989. *Stichting Museumjaarkaart* (Museums association yearbook). Wormer: Leiden/Inmerc.

Neere, H. and Crossley, D. W. 1985. *The Iron Industry of the Weald*. Leicester: Leicester University Press.

Nef, J. U. 1932. *The Rise of the British Coal Industry*. London: Routledge.

Negri, A. et al. 1983. *Archeologia Industriale* (Industrial archaeology). Bergamo: Touring Club Italiano.

Negri, A. and Negri, M. 1982. *Archeologia Industriale a Pavia* (Industrial archaeology in Pavia). Pavia: Amministrazione Provinciale di Pavia.

Neilson, R. M. 1912. *The Steam Turbine*. London: Longmans.

NELP (North East London Polytechnic) 1986. *Dockland: an illustrated survey of life and work in east London*. London: Thames & Hudson.

Nelson, D. 1975. *Managers and Workers: origins of the new factory system in the United States, 1880–1920*. Madison, WI: University of Wisconsin Press.

Nelson, G. 1939. *The Industrial Architecture of Albert Kahn Inc*. New York: Architectural Book Publishing Corporation.

Nemecek, V. 1986. *The History of Soviet Aircraft from 1918*. London: Collins, Willow Books.

Neto, J. D. M. 1790. *Methodo para Construir as estradas em Portugal* (Methods of building roads in Portugal). Reprint, 1985, Lisbon: Junta Autónoma das Estradas.

Neutze, M. 1977. *Urban Development in Australia*. London: Allen & Unwin.

Nevins, A. and Hill, F. E. 1954–63. *Ford: the times, the man, the company*. New York: Charles Scribner's Sons.

Newcomen Society, 1950. *A Catalogue of the Engineering Drawings of John Smeaton FRS Preserved in the Library of the Royal Society*. London: Newcomen Society.

Newcomer, J. 1984. *The Grand Duchy of Luxembourg: the evolution of nationhood 1963–1983*. Lanham, University Press of America.

Newell, D. 1978. *Industrial Archaeology in the Human Sciences*. Washington DC: SIA.

—— 1986a. *Technology on the Frontier: mining in old Ontario*. Toronto.

—— 1986b. *A Final Report on the Historical Research and Analysis Aspects of the British Columbia Salmon Canneries Project Industrial Archaeology*. Vancouver: University of British Columbia Press.

—— 1989. *Development of the Pacific Canning Industry: a grown man's game*. Kingston and Montreal: McGill-Queen's University Press.

Newell, D. et al. 1986. *SFU/UBC Inventory of Historic Salmon Cannery Sites*. 7 vols. Burnaby, British Columbia: SFU Geography Department.

Newell, D. and Greenhill, R. 1989. *Survivals: aspects of industrial archaeology in Ontario*. Erin: Boston Mills Press.

Newell, D. and Hovis, L. eds 1985. *British Columbia's Salmon Industry: a preliminary annotated guide to bibliographical and archival sources*. British Columbia.

Newhall, B. 1964. *The History of Photography*. New York: Museum of Modern Art.

Newham, A. T. 1967. *The Listowell and Ballybunion Railway*. Lingfield: Oakwood Press.

Newnham, W. H. 1956. *Melbourne, The Biography of a City*. Melbourne: F. W. Cheshire.

Nicholls, H. G. 1966. *Forest of Dean* (1858), *Ironmaking in Olden Times* (1866). Joint reprint, Wakefield: EP.

Nicholson, B. 1968. *Joseph Wright of Derby, Painter of Light*. London: Routledge & Kegan Paul.

Nicholson, H. H. 1946. *The Principles of Field Drainage*. Cambridge: Cambridge University Press.

Nicholson, T. R. 1970. *The World's Motor Museums*. London: Dent.

Nicol, E. W. L. 1923. *Coke and its Uses*. London: Ernest Benn.

Nielsen, A. ed. 1943–4. *Industriens historie i Danmark*, I-III (The history of Danish industry, vols I-III). Copenhagen: G. E. C. Gads forlag.

Nijhof, P. 1978. *Monumenten van bedrijf en techniek industriele archaeologie in Nederland* (Industrial and technical monuments in the Netherlands). Zutphen: De Walburg Pers.

—— 1982. *Watermolens in Nederland* (Watermills in the Netherlands). Zwolle: Waanders.

—— 1983. *Windmolens in Nederland* (Windmills in the Netherlands). Zwolle: Waanders.

—— 1985. *Oude Fabriedsgebouwen in Nederland* (Old factory buildings in the Netherlands). Amsterdam: De Bataafsche Leeuw.

—— ed. 1986. *Op zoek naar ons industrieel verleden* (Concerning the loss of our industrial heritage). Haarlem: Gottmer.

—— 1987. *Industrial Heritage and Recreation and Tourism: a Dutch Contribution*. Paper Presented to TICCIH conference, Vienna.

Nisser, M. 1978. *The Industrial Heritage: The Third International Conference on the Conservation of Industrial Monuments: Transactions I: National Reports: Europe except Scandinavia, North America, Japan*. Stockholm: Nordisja Museet.

—— ed. 1979. *Industriminnen, En bok om industri- och teknik-bebyggelselsmiljöer* (Industrial monuments: a book on the environments of industry and technology). Stockholm: Arkitekturmuseet.

—— 1981. *The Industrial Heritage: The Third International Conference on the Conservation of Industrial Monuments: Transactions III*. Stockholm: Nordisja Museet.

Nisser, M. and Bedoire, F. 1978. *The Industrial Heritage in Scandinavia: The Third International Conference on the Conservation of Industrial Monuments: Transactions II: Scandinavian Reports*. Stockholm: Nordisja Museet.

Nock, O. S. 1962. *Fifty Years of Railway Signalling*. London: Institute of Railway Signal Engineers.

—— 1973. *Underground Railways of the World*. London: A. & C. Black.

Norberg, P. 1978. *Sala gruvas historia under 1500- och 1600-talen* (The history of the Sala mine in the fifteenth and sixteenth centuries). Sala: Sala Kommun.

Norberg-Schulz, C. 1972. *Baroque Architecture*. New York: Harry N. Abrams.

Norman, R. O. C. and Waddington, D. J. 1977. *Modern Organic Chemistry*, 2nd edn. London: Mills & Boon.

Norrby, J. 1983. *När Forsmark bran* (Fires at Forsmark). Stockholm: Forsmark Kraftgrupp AB.

Norris, W. 1906. *Modern Steam Road Waggons*. London: Longmans.

North, R. 1962. *The Butlin Story*. Norwich: Jarrold.

Norton, F. H. 1949. *Refractories*, 3rd edn. New York: McGraw-Hill.

Oakley, E. R. 1979. *The British Horse Tram Era*. London: Tramway & Light Railway Society.

Oblinger, C. 1984. *Cornwall: the people and culture of an industrial Camelot*. Harrisburg, PA: Pennsylvania Historical and Museum Commission.

O'Brien, G. 1918. *The Economic History of Ireland in the Eighteenth Century*. Dublin: Maunsel. Reprint, 1977, Philadelphia, PA: Porcupine Press.

O'Connor, C. 1985. *Spanning Two Centuries: historic bridges of Australia*. Brisbane: University of Queensland Press.

Odelstierna, E. G. 1913. *Janets metallurgi* (The metallurgy of Iron). Stockholm: A. Bonnier.

O'Flaherty, F., Roddy, W. T. and Lollar, R. M. eds 1956. *The Chemistry and Technology of Leather*. New York: Reinhold.

Ogden, R. E. 1978. *Aircraft Museums Directory, European edition*. London: Battle of Britain Prints International.

—— 1983. *British Aviation Museums*. Stamford, NY: Key Publishing.

—— 1988. *Great Aircraft Collections of the World*. London: Multimedia Publications.

Ohio Department of Transportation 1983. *The Ohio Historic Bridge Inventory, Evaluation and Preservation Plan*. Columbia, OH: Ohio Department of Transportation.

Oliveira, E. V. de and Galhano, F. 1977. *Tecnologia Tradiconal Portuguesa: pisoes* (Traditional technology in Portugal: fishing). Lisbon: INIC.

Oliveira, E. V. de, Galhano, F. and Pereira, B. 1978. *Tecnologia Tradicional Portuguesa: o linho* (Traditional technology in Portugal: linen). Lisbon: INIC.

—— 1983. *Tecnologia Tradicional Portuguesa: sistemas de moagem* (Traditional technology in Portugal: milling systems). Lisbon: INIC.

Oliver, G. 1981. *Cars and Coachbuilding: one hundred years of road vehicle development*. London: Sotheby Parke Bernet.

—— 1989. *Photographs and Local History*. London: Batsford.

Oliver, P., Davis, I. and Bentley, I. 1981. *Dunroamin: the suburban semi and its enemies*. London: Barrie & Jenkins.

Oliver, S. H. and Berkbile, D. H. 1968. *The Smithsonian Collection of Automobiles and Motorcycles*. Washington DC: Smithsonian Institution.

Olmsted, D. 1846. *Memoir of Eli Whitney, Esq*. New Haven, CT: Durrie & Peck.

Ordish, H. G. 1967. *Cornish Engine Houses: a pictorial survey*. Truro: Bradford Barton.

Orlandi, G. L. 1979. *Ferro e Architettura a Firenze* (Iron and Architecture in Florence). Florence.

Orłowski, A. 1984. *Zarys rozwoju zakładow Metalurgicznych 'Silesia', zakład Lipiny w latach 1847–1885* (The history of the 'Silesia' steel mill at Lipany 1847–1885). Katowice.

Orłowski, B. 1963. *Tysiąc lat polskiej techniki* (One thousand years of Polish technology). Warsaw: Nasza Ksiegarnia.

Ormsby, M. A. 1971. *British Columbia: a history*. Vancouver: MacMillan.

Orwell, G. 1936. *The Road to Wigan Pier*. London: Gollancz.

Orysiak, S. 1977. *Muzealnictwo historyczne i historia techniki w Polsce Ludowej w latach 1945–1970* (Historical museology and museums of technology in the Polish People's Republic 1945–1970). Warsaw: Ośrodek Dokumentacji Zabytków.

Osborn, F. and Whittick, A. 1963. *The New Towns: the answer to Megalopolis*. London and New York: Leonard Hill.

Osborne, D. F. 1974. *Music Hall in Britain*. Newton Abbot: David & Charles.

Osborne, R. E. 1967. *East-central Europe: a geographical introduction to seven socialist states*. London: Chatto & Windus.

Ostrogorsky, G. 1968. *History of the Byzantine State*. Oxford: Basil Blackwell.

Otetea, A. 1985. *A Concise History of Romania*. London: Robert Hale.

Ottevanger, G. et al. 1985. *Molens, gemalen en andere waterstaatkundige elementen in Midden-Delfland* (Mills, associated buildings and other water-powered sites in mid-Delfland). The Hague: Prov Zuidholland.

Ottley, G. 1965. *A Bibliography of British Railway History*. London: Allen & Unwin.

Owen, C. C. 1978. *The Development of Industry in Burton-on-Trent*. Chichester: Phillimore.

Owen, R. 1972. *A New View of Society and Other Writings*, ed. J. Butt. London: Dent.

Paar, H. W. 1973. *The Severn and Wye Railway*. Newton Abbot: David & Charles.

——1971. *The Great Western Railway in Dean*. Newton Abbot: David & Charles.

Pagnamenta, P. and Overy, R. 1984. *All Our Working Lives*. London: British Broadcasting Corporation.

Pakenham, T. 1969. *The Year of Liberty: the story of the great Irish rebellion of 1798*. London: Hodder & Stoughton.

Palladio, A. 1570. *I quattro libri dell'architettura* (Four books concerning architecture). Venice. Reprint, 1965, New York: Dover.

Palmer, M. and Neaverson, P. 1987. *The Basset Mines: their history and industrial archaeology*. Sheffield: Northern Mines Research Society.

Pannell, J. P. M. 1967. *An Illustrated History of Civil Engineering*. London: Thames & Hudson.

——1974. *Techniques of Industrial Archaeology*. Newton Abbot: David and Charles.

Panshar, W. G. and Slater, C. C. 1956. *Baking in America*. Evanston, IL: Northwestern University Press.

Paquot, T., Epron, A. et al. 1982. *Le Familistère Godin à Guise: habiter l'Utopie* (The Godin Familistère at Guise: Living in Utopia). Paris: Editions de la Villette.

Parker, T. 1975. *Lighthouses*. New York: Taplinger.

Parker, W. J. L. 1948. *The Great Coal Schooners of New England 1870–1909*. Mystic, CT: Marine Historical Association.

Parnell, Sir H. 1838. *A Treatise on Roads*. London: Longman.

Parry, R. B. and Perkins, C. R. 1987. *World Mapping Today*. London: Butterworth.

Parsons, R. H. 1939. *The Early Days of the Power Station Industry*. Cambridge: Cambridge University Press.

——1947. *A History of the Institution of Mechanical Engineers 1847–1947*. London: Institution of Mechanical Engineers.

Parsons, R. H. and Tolley, J. C. 1973. *Paddle Steamers of Australasia*. Lobenthal, South Australia: privately published.

Partington, C. F. 1835. *The British Cyclopaedia of the Arts and Sciences*. London: Orr & Smith.

Partington, J. R. 1950. *A Textbook of Inorganic Chemistry*, 6th edn. London: Macmillan.

Partridge, W. 1823. *A Practical Treatise on Dyeing of Woollen Cotton and Skein Silk*. New York: W. Partridge. Reprint, 1973, Edington: Pasold.

Pasdermadjam, H. 1954. *The Department Store: its origins, evolution and economics*. London: Newman Books

Paskoff, P. F. 1983. *Industrial Evolution: organization, structure and growth of the Pennsylvania iron industry 1750–1860*. Baltimore, MD: Johns Hopkins University Press.

Pasold, E. W. 1977. *Ladybird, Ladybird: a story of private enterprise*. Manchester: Manchester University Press.

Passer, H. C. 1972. *The Electrical Manufacturers 1875–1900: a study in competition, entrepreneurship, technical change and economic growth*, 2nd edn. Cambridge, MA: Harvard University Press.

Passfield, R. W. 1982. *Building the Rideau Canal: a pictorial history*. Don Mills: Fitzhenry & Whiteside.

——1989. *Technology in Transition: the 'Soo' Ship Canal, 1889–1985*. Ottawa: Ministry of the Environment, Supply and Services.

Patrick, A. 1977. *Maltings in Nottinghamshire: a survey in industrial archaeology*. Nottingham: Nottinghamshire County Council.

Patterson, E. M. 1965. *The Ballycastle Railway*. Newton Abbot: David & Charles.

——1986. *Gunpowder Technology and Incorporation*. Faversham: Faversham Society.

Paul, W. 1976. *Technische Sehenswürdigkeiten in Deutschland*, Band I: *Schleswig-Holstein, Niedersachsen, Hamburg, Bremen* (Objects of technical interest in Germany, vol. I: Schleswig-Holstein, Niedersachsen, Hamburg, Bremen). Munich: ADAC Verlag.

——1977. *Technische Sehenswürdigkeiten in Deutschland*, Band II: *Nordrhein-Westfalen* (Objects of technical interest in Germany vol. II: Nordrhein-Westfalen). Munich: ADAC Verlag.

——1978. *Technische Sehenswürdigkeiten in Deutschland, Band III: Hessen, Rheinland-Pfalz, Saarland, Baden-Württemberg* (Objects of technical interest in Germany, vol. III: Hessen, Rheinland-Pfalz, Saarland, Baden-Württemberg). Muinch: ADAC Verlag.

——1980a. *Technische Sehenswürdigkeiten in Deutschland, Band IV: Bayern* (Objects of technical interest in Germany, vol. IV: Bayern). Munich: ADAC Verlag.

——1980b. *Technische Sehenswürdigkeiten in Deutschland, Band V: Berlin* (Objects of technical interest in Germany, vol. V: Berlin). Munich: ADAC Verlag.

Paulinyi, A. 1975. *Industriearchäologie: Neue Aspekte der Wirtschafts- und Technikgeschichte* (Industrial archaeology: a new aspect of economic history and of the history of technology). Dortmund: Gesselschaft für Westfällische Wirtschaftsgeschichte.

Pawson, E. 1977. *Transport and Economy: the turnpike roads of eighteenth-century Britain*. London: Academic Press.

Paxton, R. 1982. *A Heritage of Bridges between Edinburgh, Kelso and Berwick*. Edinburgh: Institution of Civil Engineers and East of Scotland Association.

Pazdur, J. 1956. Gornictwo i hutnictwo Zagłębia Staropolskiego w połowie XIX w 1846–1864 (Mining and metallurgy in the Staropolskie Industrial region in the mid-19th century, 1846–1864). In *Kwartalnik Historyczny* LXIII, 4–5.

——1957. Materiały do dziejów hutnictwa zelaza w Polsce e XVIII (Materials relating to the history of metallurgy in Poland in the late 18th century). In *Studia z dziejów górnictwa i hutnictwa* I. Wroclaw.

——1960–61. *Zarys dziejów górnictwa na ziemiach polskich* (The history of mining in Poland). Katowice: WGH.

——1985. Praktyka i teoria archeologii górniczej (Practice and theory of mining archeology). In *Kwartalnik Historii Kultury Materialnej* XXXIII, 1–2.

Pearcy, A. 1988. *Douglas DC3 Survivors*. Bourne End: Aston Publications.

Pearson, H. C. 1906. *Rubber Tires and all about them*. New York: India Rubber Publishing Co.

Pearson, M. and Temple, H. 1983. *Historical Archaeology and Conservation Philosophy: papers from the Historical Archaeology Session, ANZAAS Congress, Sydney, 1982*. Sydney: Heritage Council of New South Wales.

Peate, I. C. 1948. *Amgueddfeydd Gwerin* (Folk museums). Cardiff: University of Wales Press.

Peaty, I. P. 1985. *Brewery Railways*. Newton Abbot: David & Charles.

Pehnt, A. 1974. *Expressionist Architecture*. London: Thames & Hudson.

Peichl, G. and Slapeta, V. 1987. *Czech Functionalism 1918–1938*. London: Architectural Association.

Pelham, R. A. 1958. *Fulling Mills*. London: Society for the Protection of Ancient Buildings.

Pellew, C. E. 1913. *Dyes and Dyeing*. New York: McBride Nast.

Penfold, A. 1980. *Thomas Telford, Engineer*. London: Thomas Telford.

Penhallurick, R. D. 1986. *Tin in Antiquity*. London: Institute of Metals.

Percy, J. 1861. *Metallurgy*. London: John Murray.

——1864. *Metallurgy: iron and steel*. London: John Murray.

——1870. *The Metallurgy of Lead*. London: John Murray.

——1875. *Metallurgy: the art of extracting metals from their ores: introduction: refractory materials and fuel*. London: John Murray.

——1880. *Metallurgy: the art of extracting metals for their ores: gold and silver*. London: John Murray.

Perkins, A. G. and Everest, A. E. 1918. *The Natural Organic Colouring Matters*. London: Longmans.

Perren, R. 1978. *The Meat Trade in Britain 1840–1914*. London: Routledge & Kegan Paul.

Peters, E. D. 1907. *Principles of Copper Smelting*. New York: Hill.

Peters, T. F. 1987. *Transitions in Engineering: Guillaume Henri Dufour and the early nineteenth century cable suspension bridges*. Basel: Birkhauser.

Petersen, H. M. 1983–6. *Danske dampskibe indtil 1870, I–III* (Danish steamships until 1870, vols I–III). Esbjerg: Forlaget Bygd.

Petri, F. and Droege, G. 1979. *Rheinische Geschichte, Band III: Wirtschaft und Kultur im 19 un 20 Jahrhundert* (Rhenish history, vol. III: economy and culture in the nineteenth and twentieth centuries). Düsseldorf: Schwann.

Petroski, H. 1990. *The Pencil*. New York: Knopf.

Pevsner, N. 1936. *Pioneers of the Modern Movement*. London: Faber.

——1950. *Matthew Digby Wyatt*. Cambridge: Cambridge University Press.

——1960. *Pioneers of Modern Design*. Harmondsworth: Penguin.

——1976. *A History of Building Types*. London: Thames & Hudson.

Pevsner, N. and Wedgewood, A. 1966. *The Buildings of England: Warwickshire*. London: Penguin.

Phillips, A. D. M. 1989. *The Underdraining of Farmland in England during the Nineteenth Century*. Cambridge: Cambridge University Press.

Phillips, R. A. J. 1967. *Canada's North*. New York: St Martin's Press.

Phillipson, D. 1985. *African Archaeology*. Cambridge: Cambridge University Press.

Piatek, E. 1989. *Historia dolnoslaskiego gornictwa wegla kamiennego od XV do polowy XVIII* (History of coal-mining in Lower Silesia from the fifteenth century to the middle of the eighteenth century). Wroclaw: Wydawnictwo Politechniki Wroclawskiej.

Pickles, W. 1971. *Our Grimy Heritage*. Fontwell, Sussex: Centaur.

Pietrzak-Pawlowska, T. 1970. *Uprzemyslowienie ziem polskich w XIX i XX wieku* (The industrialization of the Polish territories in the nineteenth and twentieth centuries). Wroclaw: DWN.

Piettre, J.-H. and Smith, P. 1980. *Architecture des manufactures, tabac et allumettes 1726–1939* (Architectures

913

of manufactures, tobacco and matches 1726–1939). Paris: Musée du SEITA.

Pike, D. 1957. *Paradise of Dissent: South Australia, 1829–1857*. London: Longmans.

Pildas, A. 1980. *Movie Palaces*. New York: Charles N. Potter.

Pinard, G. 1986. *Montréal, son histoire, son architecture* (Montreal, its history, its architecture). Montreal: Éditions La Presse.

Pinkerton, R. E. 1932. *Hudson's Bay Company*. London: Butterworth.

Piotrowicz, J. and Grzesiowski, J. 1977. *Utworzenie i rozwoj Zup Krakowskich w Wieliczce: Studia i Materiały do Dziejów Żup Solnych w Polsce* (The origins and development of the Krakowskie salt mine: studies and materials concerning the history of salt mines in Poland). Warsaw.

Pisarski, M. 1974. *Koleje polskie 1842–1972* (Polish railways 1842–1972). Warsaw: WKL.

Plenderleith, H. J. and Werner, A. E. A. 1970. *The Conservation of Antiquities and Works of Art: treatment, repair and restoration*. Oxford: Oxford University Press.

Plot, R. 1686. *The Natural History of Staffordshire*. Oxford: at the Theatre.

Plowden, D. 1974. *Bridges: the spans of North America*. New York: Viking.

Plowden, W. 1971. *The Motor Car and Politics 1896–1970*. London: Bodley Head.

Plummer, A. and Early, R. E. 1969. *The Blanket Makers 1669–1969: a history of Charles Early and Marriott (Witney) Ltd*. London: Routledge & Kegal Paul.

Pole, W. 1844. *Treatise on the Cornish Pumping Engine*. London: J. Weale.

——ed. 1877. *The Life of Sir William Fairbairn, Bt*. Reprint, 1970, Newton Abbot: David & Charles.

——1888. *The Life of Sir William Siemens*. London: John Murray.

Pollard, S. 1959. *The History of Labour in Sheffield*. Liverpool: Liverpool University Press.

——1965. *The Genesis of Modern Management: a study of the Industrial Revolution in Great Britain*. London: Arnold.

——1981. *Peaceful Conquest: the industrialization of Europe 1760–1970*. Oxford: Oxford University Press.

Pool, A. G. and Llewellyn, G. 1955. *The British Hosiery Industry: a study in competition*. Leicester: Leicester University Press.

Pool, J. L. 1982. *America's Valley Forges and Valley Furnaces*. West Cornwall, CT: J. L. Pool.

Popiołek, K. 1965. *Gornóslaski przemysł górniczo-hutniczy w drugiej polowie XIX wieku* (The Upper Silesian mining and metallurgical industry in the second half of the nineteenth century). Katowice: PWN.

Popławska, I. 1973. *Architektura przemysłowa Łodzi w XIX wieku* (The industrial architecture of Łodz in the nineteenth century). Warsaw: PWN.

——1974. *Dawne Fabryki Łodzi* (Old factories in Łodz). Łodz: BBiDZ.

Popplewell, S. 1981. *Irish Museums Guide*. Dublin: Word River.

Porteous, J. D. 1977. *Canal Ports: the urban achievement of the canal age*. London: Academic Press.

Portinaro, P. and Knirsch, F. 1988. *The Cartography of North America*. Oxford: Facts on File.

Porto, M. 1982. *A Cerâmica em Coimbra* (Ceramics in Coimbra). Coimbra: Comissao de Coordenaçao de Regiao Centro.

Posener, J. 1979. *Berlin auf dem Wege zu einer neuen Architektur: das Zeitalter Wilhelms II* (Berlin on the way to a new architecture: the times of William II). Munich: Prestel Verlag.

Postma, T. 1979. *Fokker bouwer aan de wereldluchtvaart* (Fokker: aircraft builders of the world). English edition, 1980, London: Jane's.

Pottgiesser, H. 1985. *Eisenbahnbrücken aus zwei Jahrhunderten* (Two centuries of railway bridges). Basel: Birkhauser Verlag.

Pound, R. 1960. *Selfridge: a biography*. London: Heinemann.

Powell, H. J. 1923. *Glass Making in England*. London: G. Bell.

Powell, R. 1985. *Photography and the Making of History: Brunel's kingdom*. Bristol: Watershed.

Power, F. D. 1912. *The Coalfields and Collieries of Australia*. Melbourne: C. Parker.

Poynter, J. R. 1969. *Society and Pauperism: English ideas on poor relief 1795–1834*. London: Routledge & Kegan Paul.

Prade, M. 1990. *Ponts et viaducts remarquables d'Europe* (Remarkable European bridges and viaducts). Poitiers: Danièle Brissaud.

Pratt, V. 1987. *Thinking Machines: the evolution of artificial intelligence*. Oxford: Basil Blackwell.

Pratt and Witney Aircraft 1952. *The Aircraft Gas Turbine Engine and its Operation*. East Hartford, CT: United Aircraft Corporation.

Prescott, S. C. and Proctor, B. E. 1937. *Food Technology*. New York: McGraw-Hill.

Pressnell, L. 1960. *Studies in the Industrial Revolution*. London: Athlone Press.

Prest, J. 1960. *The Industrial Revolution in Coventry*. Oxford: Oxford University Press.

Preston, J. M. 1977. *Industrial Medway*. Rochester: J. M. Preston.

Price, J. M. 1973. *France and the Chesapeake, a history of the French tobacco monopoly 1674–1791, and of its relationship to the British and American tobacco trades*. Ann Arbor, MI: University of Michigan Press.

Price, J. S. 1958. *Building Societies: their origins and history*. London: Franey.

Prichard, M. F. L. 1970. *An Economic History of New Zealand up to 1939*. Auckland: Collins.

Priestley, J. 1831. *An Historical Account of the Navigable Rivers, Canals and Railways of Britain*. London: Longmans.

Priestley, U. and Fenner, A. 1985. *Shops and Shopkeepers in Norwich 1660–1730*. Norwich: Centre for East Anglian Studies.

Prior, M. 1982. *Fisher Row*. Oxford: Oxford University Press.

Procter, M. and Matuszeski, B. 1978. *Gritty Cities: a second look at Allentown, Bethlehem, Bridgeport, Hoboken, Lancaster, Norwich, Paterson, Reading, Trenton, Troy, Waterbury, Wilmington.* Philadelphia, PA: Temple University Press.

Proctor, H. R. 1903. *The Principles of Leather Manufacture.* London: Spon.

—— 1914. *The Making of Leather.* Cambridge: Cambridge University Press.

PTT 1981. *Honderd Jaar telefoon: Geschiedenis van de openbare telefonie in Nederland 1881–1981* (A hundred years of telephones: a history of telephones in the Netherlands 1881–1981). The Hague: PTT.

Pudney, J. 1975. *London's Docks.* London: Thames & Hudson.

Pugsley, A. 1957. *The Theory of Suspension Bridges.* London: Arnold.

—— 1976. *The Works of Isambard Kingdom Brunel: an engineering appreciation.* London: Institution of Civil Engineers.

Purdom, C. B. 1913. *The Garden City: a study of the development of the modern town.* London: Dent.

—— 1925. *The Building of Satellite Towns.* London: Dent.

—— 1963. *The Letchworth Achievement.* London: Dent.

Pursell, C. W. Jnr. 1969. *Early Stationary Steam Engines in America: a study in the migration of a technology.* Washington DC: Smithsonian Institution Press.

Putkonen, L. 1989a. *Kultuurihistoriallisesti arvokkaat teollisuusympäristöt* (Industrial milieux of cultural-historical importance). Helsinki: Ministry of the Environment.

—— 1989b. *Teollisuuden arkkitehtuuri 1809–1880* (Industrial architecture 1809–1880). Keuruu: Ars Suomen taide.

Pyne, W. H. 1808. *Microcosm: of a picturesque delineation of the arts, agriculture, manufactures etc. of Great Britain.* Reprint, 1974, Luton: Luton Museum.

Queirós, F. F. 1981. *A Real Fábrica de Lanificios de Portalegre em 1781* (The Establishment of the woollen factory at Portalegre in 1781). Portalegre: Assembleia Distrital.

Quimby, I. M. G. 1978. *Material Culture and the Study of American Life.* New York: Norton.

Radwan, M. 1963. *Rudy, kuźnice i huty żelaza w Polsce* (Ores, ironworks and metallurgical plants in Poland). Warsaw: WNT.

Rae, J. B. 1959. *American Automobile Manufacturers: the first forty years.* Philadelphia, PA: Chilton.

—— 1965. *The American Automobile: a brief history.* Chicago, IL: History of American Civilization.

Rae, L. 1983. *A History of Railways and Tramways on Tasmania's West Coast.* Hobart: Mercury Walsh.

Raedts, C. E. P. M. 1974. *De opkomst, de ontwikkeling en de neergang van de steenkolenmijnbouw in Limburg* (The rise, development and decline of coalmining in Limburg). Assen: Van Gorcum.

Raistrick, A. 1950. *Quakers in Science and Industry.* London: Bannisdale Press.

—— 1953. *Dynasty of Ironfounders.* London: Longmans.

—— 1970. *The Landscape of the West Riding of Yorkshire.* London: Hodder & Stoughton.

—— 1972. *Industrial Archaeology: an historical survey.* London: Eyre Methuen.

—— 1975. *The Lead Industry of Wensleydale and Swaledale.* 2 vols. Ashbourne: Moorland.

Raistrick, A. and Jennings, B. 1983. *A History of Lead Mining in the Pennines.* London: Longman.

Ramsaye, T. 1926. *A Million and One Nights.* New York: Simon & Schuster.

Randall, B. 1975. *The Origins of Digital Computers.* Berlin: Springer-Verlag.

Ransome-Wallis, P. 1968. *Train Ferries of Western Europe.* London: Ian Allan.

—— 1971. *Preserved Steam Locomotives of Western Europe.* 2 vols. London: Ian Allen.

Rapp, W. F. and Boranek, S. K. 1984. *The Industrial Archaeology of Nebraska.* Crete, NE: J.-B. Publishing.

Rappard, W. 1914. *La révolution industrielle et les origines de la protection légale du travail en Suisse* (The industrial revolution and the origins of the legal protection of working rights in Switzerland). Bern: Stæmpfli.

Ratcliffe, B. M. 1975. *Great Britain and her World 1750–1914: essays in honour of W. O. Henderson.* Manchester: Manchester University Press.

Rauers, F. 1942. *Kulturgeschichte der Gaststätte* (The cultural history of hotels). Berlin: Metzner.

Rawlinson, R. 1859. *Designs for Tall Chimney Shafts.* London: J. Weale.

Ray, C. 1973. *Cognac.* London: Harrap.

Raybould, T. J. 1973. *The Economic Emergence of the Black Country: a study of the Dudley Estate.* Newton Abbot: David & Charles.

Razzell, P. E. and Wainwright, R. W. 1973. *The Victorian Working Class: selections from letters to the Morning Chronicle.* London: Cass.

Reader, W. J. 1970. *Imperial Chemical Industries: a history.* Oxford: Oxford University Press.

—— 1980. *Macadam: The Macadam Family and the Turnpike Roads 1798–1861.* London: Heinemann.

Rechcizl, M. 1968. *Czechoslovakia Past and Present.* The Hague and Paris: Mouton.

Reddy, W. M. 1984. *The Rise of Market Culture: the textile trade and French society 1750–1900.* Cambridge: Cambridge University Press.

Redfern, P. 1913. *The Story of the CWS: the jubilee history of the Co-operative Wholesale Society 1863–1913.* Manchester: CWS.

Reed, B. 1982. *Crewe Locomotive Works and its Men.* Newton Abbot: David & Charles.

Reed, M. 1988. *Buckinghamshire Probate Inventories 1661–1714.* Aylesbury: Buckinghamshire Record Society.

Rees, A. 1802–20. *The Cyclopaedia: or Universal Dictionary of Arts, Sciences and Literature.* London: Longman.

—— 1972. *Rees's Manufacturing Industry (1819–20): a selection from The Cyclopaedia or Universal Dictionary of Arts, Sciences and Literature by Abraham Rees,* ed. N. Cossons. Newton Abbot: David & Charles.

Rees, D. M. 1969. *Mines, Mills and Furnaces: an introduction to industrial archaeology in Wales.* London: HMSO.

——1975. *The Industrial Archaeology of Wales.* Newton Abbot: David & Charles.

Rees, G. 1969. *St Michael: a history of Marks and Spencer.* London: Weidenfeld & Nicholson.

——1980. *Early Railway Prints: a social history of the railways from 1825–1850.* Oxford: Phaidon.

Regione Lombardia, I Monumenti Storica 1983. *Industriali della Lombardia, Censimento Regionale* (Industry in Lombardy: regional inventory). Milan: Regione Lombardia, I Monumenti Storico.

Reid, D. 1985. *The Miners of Decazeville: a genealogy of deindustrialization.* Cambridge, MA: Harvard University Press.

Reid, G. 1908. *Practical Sanitation.* London: Charles Griffin.

Reigart, J. F. 1856. *The Life of Robert Fulton.* Philadelphia, PA: G. C. Henderson.

Reinink, A. W. and Vermeulen, J. G. 1981. *Ijskelders, koeltechnieken van weleer* (Icehouses, refrigeration techniques of former times). Nieuwkoop.

Rémond, A. 1946. *John Holker, manufacturier et grand fonctionnaire en France au XVIIIe siècle* (John Holker, manufacturer and civil servant in eighteenth century France). Paris: Rivière.

Rennie, J. 1875. *Autobiography of Sir John Rennie, FRS.* London: Spon.

Reord, O. and Welch, W. L. 1977. *From Tin Foil to Stereo: evolution of the phonograph,* 2nd edn. Indianapolis, IN: Howard W. Sams.

Reynolds, T. S. 1982. *Sault Ste. Marie.* Washington DC: National Park Survey.

——1983. *Stronger than a Hundred Men: a history of the vertical waterwheel.* Baltimore, MD: Johns Hopkins University Press.

Reynoldson, J. 1808. *Principles of Making Malt.* London: Hage.

Rheinsicher Verein für Denkmalpflege und Heimatschutz 1910. *Industriebauten. Geschichtlich Industriebauten. Neuzeitlich Industriebauten* (Industrial buildings. Historical industrial buildings. Modern industrial buildings). Düsseldorf: Mittelungen des Rheinischen Vereins für Denkmalpflege und Heimatschutz.

Rhodes, D. 1968. *Kilns: design, construction and operation.* London: Pitman.

——1969. *Clays and Glazes for the Potter.* London: Pitman.

Rhodes, M. 1989. *The Illustrated History of British Marshalling Yards.* Oxford: Oxford Publishing Company.

Ribbe, W. and Schäche, W. 1985. *Die Siemensstadt: Geschichte und Architektur eines Industriestandortes* (Siemensstadt: the history and architecture of an industrial community). Berlin: Verlag Ernst und Sohn.

Ribeiro, I., Custodio, J. and Santos, L. 1981. *Arquelogia Industrial do Bairro de Alcântara* (Industrial archaeology of Bairro de Alcântara). Lisbon: Carris.

Rich, E. E. 1967. *The Fur Trade and the Northwest to 1857.* Toronto: McClelland & Stewart.

Richard, T. 1838. *Etudes sur l'art d'extraire immediament le fer de ses mineraux sans couvertir le metal en fonte* (Studies in the extraction of iron from its mineral without converting the metal into cast iron). Paris.

Richards, E. 1973. *The Leviathan of Wealth: The Sutherland fortune in the Industrial Revolution.* London: Routledge & Kegan Paul.

Richards, H. C. and Payne, W. H. C. 1899. *London Water Supply,* 2nd edn. London: King.

Richards, J. M. 1958. *The Functional Tradition in Early Industrial Buildings.* London: Architectural Press.

——1962. *An Introduction to Modern Architecture.* Harmondsworth: Penguin.

Richardson, A. 1911. *The Evolution of the Parsons Steam Turbine.* London: Engineering.

Richardson, B. 1876. *Hygeia: the City of Health.* London: Macmillan.

Richardson, J. B. 1974. *Metal Mining.* London: Allen Lane.

Richardson, K. 1977. *The British Motor Industry 1896–1939.* London: Macmillan.

Richardson, M. and Richardson, S. 1981. *Dinky Toys and Modelled Miniatures.* London: New Cavendish.

Richmond, L. and Stockford, B. 1986. *Company Archives: a survey of the records of the first registered companies in England and Wales.* London: Business Archives Council.

Richmond, L. and Turton, A. 1989. *The Brewing Industry: a guide to historical records.* Manchester: Manchester University Press.

Rickman, T. 1817. *An Attempt to Discriminate the Styles of English Architecture from the Conquest to the Reformation.* London.

Riden, P. 1978. Eighteenth-century blast furnaces: a new check list. *Journal of the Historical Metallurgy Society* XII(1).

——1987. *A Gazetteer of Charcoal-fired Blast Furnaces in Great Britain in use since 1600.* Cardiff: Philip Riden.

Rigg, J. B. 1970. *A Guide to Manuscripts in the Eleutherian Mills Historical Library.* Wilmington, DE: Eleutherian Mills Historical Library.

Riley, G. 1985. *Vintage Aircraft Discovery.* Bourne End: Aston Publications.

Riley, J. J. 1972. *A History of the American Soft Drink Industry.* New York: Arno Press.

Rimmer, W. G. 1960. *Marshalls of Leeds, Flax Spinners 1788–1886.* Cambridge: Cambridge University Press.

Ringlever, W. et al. 1911. *Rotterdam Album,* English edn. Rotterdam.

Rioux, J.-P. 1971. *La Révolution industrielle* (The industrial revolution). Paris: Le Seuil.

Ritchie-Noakes, N. 1980. *Jesse Hartley: Dock Engineer to the Port of Liverpool 1824–60.* Liverpool: Merseyside County Museums.

——1984. *Liverpool's Historic Waterfront: the world's first mercantile dock system.* London: HMSO.

Rives, M. 1925. *Le Monopole des Alumettes en France* (The match monopoly in France). Paris: privately published.

Rivière, G. H. 1989. *La Muséologie selon Georges Henri*

Rivière (Museology according to Georges Henri Rivière). Paris: Dunod.

Rix, M. M. 1967. *Industrial Archaeology.* London: Historical Association.

Robbins, M. 1962. *The Railway Age.* London: Routledge & Kegan Paul.

Robbins, R. W. and Jones, E. 1959. *Hidden America.* New York: Alfred A. Knopf.

Roberts, E. 1984. *A Woman's Place: an oral history of working-class women 1890–1940.* Oxford: Basil Blackwell.

Robertson, B. R. 1982. *Sawpower: making lumber in the sawmills of Nova Scotia.* Halifax: Nova Scotia Museum.

Robertson, E. G. 1960. *Victorian Heritage: ornamental cast iron in Melbourne.* Melbourne: Georgian House.

Robertson, J. H. 1947. *The Story of the Telephone.* London: Pitman.

Robins, E. and Pennel, J. 1915. *Lithography and Lithographers.* New York: Macmillan.

Robins, F. W. 1946. *The Story of Water Supply.* Oxford: Oxford University Press.

Robinson, E. and Musson, A. E. 1969. *James Watt and the Steam Revolution.* Bath: Adams & Dart.

Robson, R. 1957. *The Cotton Industry in Britain.* London: Macmillan.

Rockwell, C. and Garcia, M. 1985. *Ironworks and Iron Monuments: study, conservation and adaptive use.* Rome: ICCROM.

Roe, J. W. 1916. *English and American Tool Builders.* New Haven, CT: Yale University Press.

Rogers, A. and Aubert, A. B. 1915. *Industrial Chemistry: a manual for the student and manufacturer,* 2nd edn. London: Constable.

Rogers, J. E. T. 1850–66. *A History of Agriculture and Prices in England.* Oxford: Clarendon Press.

Rogerson, I. and Maxim, G. 1986. *L. T. C. Rolt: a bibliography.* Cleobury Mortimer, Shropshire: Baldwin.

Roll, E. 1930. *An Early Experiment in Industrial Organization.* London: Longmans. Reprint, 1968, London: Cass.

Rollings, J. G. 1981. *Needlemaking.* Princes Risborough: Shire Publications.

Rolls Royce Ltd 1969. *The Jet Engine.* London: Rolls Royce Ltd.

Rolt, L. T. C. 1944. *Narrow Boat.* London: Eyre & Spottiswoode.

—— 1949. *Green and Silver.* London: Allen & Unwin.

—— 1950a. *Horseless Carriage: the motor car in England.* London: Constable.

—— 1950b. *The Inland Waterways of England.* London: Allen & Unwin.

—— 1953. *Railway Adventure.* London: Constable.

—— 1955. *Red For Danger.* London: Bodley Head.

—— 1957. *Isambard Kingdom Brunel: a biography.* London: Longman.

—— 1958. *Thomas Telford.* London: Longman.

—— 1960. *George and Robert Stephenson: the railway revolution.* London: Longman.

—— 1969. *Waterloo Ironworks.* Newton Abbot: David & Charles.

—— 1970. *Victorian Engineering.* London: Allen Lane.

—— 1971a. *Landscape with Machines: an autobiography.* London: Longman.

—— 1971b. *The Making of a Railway.* London: Hugh Evelyn.

—— 1974. *The Potters' Field: a history of the South Devon ball clay industry.* Newton Abbot: David & Charles.

—— 1977. *Landscape with Canals: an autobiography.* London: Allen Lane.

—— 1986. *Tools for the Job,* rev. edn. London: HMSO.

Rolt, L. T. C. and Allen, J. S. 1977. *The Steam Engine of Thomas Newcomen.* Hartington: Moorland.

Ronnow, S. 1919. *Pehr Hillestrom och hans Brucks-och Bergverksmalningar* (Pehr Hillestrom and his depictions of bruks and mining instalations). Stockholm.

Rose, M. 1971. *The English Poor Law 1870–1830.* Newton Abbot: David & Charles.

Rose, M. B. 1986. *The Gregs of Quarry Bank Mill: the rise and decline of a family firm, 1750–1914.* Cambridge: Cambridge University Press.

Rosenberg, N. ed. 1959. *The American System of Manufactures.* Edinburgh: Edinburgh University Press.

Rosten, L. 1945. *Hollywood: the movie colony, the movie makers.* New York: Harcourt Brace.

Rostow, W. W. 1960. *The Stages of Economic Growth.* Cambridge: Cambridge University Press.

Roth, M. 1981. *Connecticut, an Inventory of Historic Engineering and Industrial Sites.* Washington DC: National Park Service.

Rotha, P. 1939. *Documentary Film,* 2nd edn. London: Faber & Faber.

Rotterdamse Kunstichting 1982. *Havenarchitectuur: een inventarisatie van industriële gebouwen in het Rotterdamse havengebied* (Port architecture: an inventory of industrial buildings in the Rotterdam harbour area). Rotterdam: Rotterdamse Kunstichting.

Roussinov, S. 1965. *Bulgaria: land, economy, culture.* Sofia: Foreign Language Press.

Rowe, D. J. 1983. *Lead Manufacturing in Britain.* London: Croom Helm.

Rowland, J. 1954. *George Stephenson: creator of Britain's railways.* London: Odhams.

Rowlands, M. 1975. *Masters and Men in the Small Metalware Trades of the West Midlands.* Manchester: Manchester University Press.

Rowley, G. 1984. *British Fire Insurance Plans.* Hatfield: Charles E. Goad.

Rowntree Trust 1954. *One Man's Vision: the story of the Joseph Rowntree Village Trust.* London: Allen & Unwin.

Rowsome, F. 1956. *Trolley Car Treasury.* New York: Bonanza Books.

Ruddel, D.-T. 1983. *Canadians and their Environment.* Ottawa: National Museum of Man.

Ruddock, T. 1979. *Arch Bridges and their Buildings 1735–1835.* Cambridge: Cambridge University Press.

Rugg, D. S. 1985. *Eastern Europe.* London: Longman.

Rushmore, D. B. and Lof, E. A. 1923. *Hydro-electric Power Stations*. New York: John Wiley.

Russell, F. ed. 1979. *Art Nouveau Architecture*. London: Academy Editions.

Russell, J. H. 1985. *GWR Diesel Railcars*. Didcot: Wild Swan.

Russell, R. 1982. *The Lost Canals of England*. Newton Abbot: David & Charles.

Russell, V. 1984. *Forging a Concensus: historical essays on Toronto*. Toronto: University of Toronto Press.

Rydberg, S. 1981. *Dannemora genom 500 år* (Dannemora through 500 years). Falun.

——1988. *Det Stora Kopparberget: en tidresa* (The great copper mine: a synopsis). Hedemora.

Ryser, J. and Rautsi, J. 1986. *The Pohja Case: a Finnish municipality in transition*. Helsinki: Ministry of the Environment.

Saetran, G. 1907. *Beskrivelse af Skiens Vasdrag* (Description of rivers and so on). Oslo.

Saint, A. 1976. *Richard Norman Shaw*. London: Yale University Press.

Salaman, R. N. 1949. *The History and Social Influence of the Potato*. Cambridge: Cambridge University Press.

Salaun, J-P. 1985. *Le four à chaux de Baie Sainte-Claire, Ile d'Anticosti, Québec* (The limekiln at Baie Sainte-Claire on Anticosti Island, Quebec). Quebec: Ministry of Cultural Affairs.

Salber, D. 1987. *Das Aachener Revier. 150 Jahre Steinkohlebergbau an Wurm und Inde* (The Aachen mining area. 150 years of hard coal mining on the Wurm and Inde). Aachen: Schweers & Wall.

Salkield, L. 1987. *A Technical History of the Rio Tinto Mines*. London: Institution of Mining and Metallurgy.

Salmon, J. H. M. 1963. *A History of Goldmining in New Zealand*. Wellington: Government Print.

Sametz, Z. W. 1964. *An Economic Geography of Canada*. Toronto: University of Toronto Press.

Samuel, R. 1975. *Village Life and Labour*. London: Routledge & Kegan Paul.

——1977. *Miners, Quarrymen and Saltworkers*. London: Routledge & Kegan Paul.

Sande, T. A. 1971. *The New England Textile Mill Survey: selections from the Historic American Buildings Survey* XI. Washington DC: HABS.

——1976. *Industrial Archaeology: a new look at the American heritage*. Brattleboro, VT: Stephen Greene Press.

Sandercock, L. 1975. *Cities for Sale*. Melbourne: Melbourne University Press.

Sandstrom, G. E. 1963. *The History of Tunnelling: underground workings through the ages*. London: Barrie & Rockliff.

Sandvigske Samlinger, Maihaugen 1948. *Arbok 1931–46* (Yearbook 1931–46); 1952. *Arbok 1950–2*; 1957. *Arbok 1953–6*; 1961. *Arbok 1957–60*; 1964. *Arbok 1961–3*; 1975. *Arbok 1969–75*; 1979. *Arbok 1976–9*. Lillehammer: Sandvigske Samlinger, Maihaugen.

Sanger, G. 1926. *Seventy Years a Showman*. London: Dent.

Santos, M. J. M. 1982. *O Complexo Industrial do Cabo Mondego* (The Cabo Mondego industrial complex). Figueira da Foz: Câmara Municipal.

Sanz, J. A. and Giner, J. 1984. *L'Arquitectura de la industria a Catalunya en els segles XVIII y XIX* (Industrial architecture in Catalonia in the eighteenth and nineteenth centuries). Vallès: Escola Técnica Superior d'Arquitectura del Vallès.

Sass, J. A. 1984. *The Versatile Millstone: workhorse of many industries*. Knoxville, TN: Society for the Preservation of Old Mills.

Saul, S. B. ed. 1970. *Technological Change: the United States and Britain in the nineteenth century*. London: Methuen.

Savery, T. 1702. *The Miner's Friend*. London: S. Crouch. Reprint, 1979, Edinburgh: Antiquarian Facsimiles.

Savez Muzehskih Drustava Jugoslavije 1962. *Muzeji Jugoslavije* (Yugoslav Museums). Belgrade: Savez Muzehskih Drustava Jugoslavije.

Sawyer, L. A. and Mitchell, W. H. 1970. *The Liberty Ships*. Cambridge, MA: Cornell Maritime.

Schade, C. 1980. *Woningbouw voor arbeiders in het 19de eeuwse Amsterdam* (Dwellings for workers in nineteenth-century Amsterdam). Amsterdam: Van Gennep.

Schaffer, F. 1970. *The New Town Story*. London: MacGibbon & Kee.

Schedvin, C. B. and McCarty, J. W. 1976. *Urbanisation in Australia: the nineteenth century*. Sydney: Sydney University Press.

Schefold, U. 1986. *150 Jahre Eisenbahns in Österreich* (One hundred and fifty years of railways in Austria). Munich: Sudwest Verlag.

Schierk, H.-F. and Schmidt, N. 1976. Die Schwebebahn in Wuppertal (The spider railway in Wuppertal). *Arbeitshefte des Landeskonservators Rheinland* XIX. Cologne: Rheinland Verlag.

Schinkel, K. F. 1986. *Reise nach England, Schottland und Paris im Jahre 1826* (Journey to England, Scotland and Paris in the year 1826), ed. G. Riemen and D. Bindeman. Berlin: Henschelverlag Kunst und Gesellschaft.

Schivelbusch, W. 1986. *The Railway Journey: the industrialisation of time and space in the nineteenth century*. Leamington: Berg.

Schluck, H. and Sohlman, R. 1929. *The Life of Alfred Nobel*, trans. B. Lunn and B. Lunn. London: Heinemann.

Schmidt, H. and Eilhardt, E.-M. 1984. *Die Bauwerke der Berliner S-Bahn* (The buildings of the Berlin S-Bahn). 2 Vols. Berlin: Wissenschaftsverlag Spiess.

Schmidt, W. and Theile, W. 1989. *Denkmale der Produktions- und Verkehrsgeschichte*, Teil I (Monuments of industrial and transport history, vol. I). Berlin: VEB Verlag für Bauwesen.

——1991. *Denkmale der Produktions- und Verkehrsgeschichte*, Teil II (Monuments of industrial and transport history, vol. II). Berlin: VEB Verlag für Bauwesen.

Schmitt, P. 1969. *Back to Nature: the Arcadian myth in urban America*. New York: Oxford University Press.

Schmitz, F. 1921. *Die Papiermühlen und Papiermacher des*

bergischen Strundeftales (The paper mills and paper makers of the Strundeft valley in the Bergisches Land). Bergisch Gladbach: Otto Lapp.

Schmutzler, J. 1962. *Art Nouveau.* London: Thames & Hudson.

Schneider et Cie 1912. *Les Etablissements Schneider: economies sociale.* Paris: Imprimerie Générale Lahure.

Schneider, A. 1963. *Gebirgsbahnen Europas* (Railways through the mountains of Europe). Zurich: Orell Fussli Verlag. English edn, 1967, London: Ian Allen.

Schneider, R., Hamm, M. and Kühne, G. 1980. *Berlin: Denkmäler einer Industrielandschaft* (Berlin: Monuments within an industrial landscape). Berlin: Nicolai Verlag.

Schorske, C. E. 1980. *Fin-de-siècle Vienna: politics and culture.* New York: Knopf.

Schreiber, A. 1925. *Das Krafwerk Fortuna II* (The Fortuna II power station). Leipzig: Spinner Verlag.

Schober, J. 1930. *Silk and the Silk Industry.* London: Constable.

Schubert, H. R. 1957. *History of the British Iron and Steel Industry.* London: Routledge & Kegan Paul.

Schulz, W. 1987. *Der Nord-Ostsee-Kanal: Eine Fotochronik der Baugerschichte* (A photographic history of the construction of the Nord-Ostsee Canal). Heide In Holstein: Verlag Boyem.

Schumacher, F. 1912. *Goderzlagerstatten und der Goldbergau der Rudaer Zwolf-Apostel-Gewerkeschaft zu Brad in Siburgen* (The Rudaer Zwolf-Apostel-Gewerkeschaft gold deposits and gold mines at Brad in Transylvania). Berlin: Bureau fur praktische Geologie, Verlagsabteilung.

Schuhmann, G. 1984. *Iron and Steel,* reprinted from *The Pilot,* official publication of the Philadelphia & Reading RR, YMCA, 1906. Washington DC: Society for Industrial Archaeology.

Schunder, F. 1968. *Geschichte des Aachener Steinkohlenbergbaues* (History of hard coal mining in the Aachen area). Essen: Verlag Glückauf.

Schuster, W. 1978. *Vordernberg und sein technischen Denkmale* (Vordernberg and its technical monuments). Vienna: Montan-Verlag.

Schwarz, K. 1981. *Berlin: Von der Residenzstadt zur Industriemetropole,* Band I: *Die Entwicklung der Industriestadt Berlin- das Beispiel Moabit;* Band II: *Leitfaden zum Lehrpfad zu Historischen Stätten des Berliner Nordens;* Band III: *Katalog* (Berlin from royal residency to industrial metropolis, vol. I: the development of the industrial city of Berlin – the example of the Moabit; vol. II: the main threads of the development of the historic states of the north of Berlin; vol. III: catalogue). Berlin: Technische Hochschule Berlin.

Schweider, D. 1983. *Black Diamonds: life and work in Iowa's coal mining communities, 1895–1925.* Ames, IO: Iowa State University Press.

Schweitzer, S. 1982. *Des engrenages à la chaîne, les usines Citroën, 1915–1935* (From gear-wheels to assembly lines, the Citroën factories, 1915–1935). Lyon: Presses Universitaires de Lyon.

Scott, Q. and Miller, H. S. 1979. *The Eads Bridge.* Columbia, MO and London: University of Missouri Press.

Scratchley, A. 1849. *Treatise on Benefit Building Societies.* London.

Searle, A. B. 1915. *Bricks and Artificial Stones of Non-plastic Materials: their manufacture and use.* London: J. & A. Churchill.

——1920. *Modern Brickmaking,* 2nd edn. London: Scott Greenwood.

——1924. *Refractory Materials: their manufacture and use.* London: Griffin.

——1925. *Clay and What We Get from it.* London: Sheldon.

——1929. *The Clayworker's Hand-book: a manual for all engaged in the manufacture of articles from clay,* 4th edn. London: Charles Griffin

Searle, A. B. 1929–30. *An Encyclopaedia of the Ceramic Industries.* London: Benn.

Sears, Roebuck 1897. *Sears, Roebuck Catalog.* Reprint, 1976, New York: Chelsea House.

——1902. *Sears, Roebuck Catalog.* Reprint, 1970, New York: Crown.

——1927. *Sears, Roebuck Catalog.* Reprint, New York: Crown.

Sebert, L. M. 1981. *The Maps of Canada.* Toronto.

Sedgwick, M. 1970. *Cars of the 1930s.* London: Batsford.

Segers, J. 1984. *Benzinestations* (Petrol stations). Nijmegen: Katholicke Universiteit.

Seignurie, A. 1904. *Dictionnaire encyclopédique de l'épicerie et des industries annexes* (Enclopaedic dictionary of the grocery trade and related manufactures). Paris: Éditions Nouvelle.

Self, P. 1972. *New Towns: the British experience.* London: Charles Knight.

Selvafolta, O. et al. 1983. *Supermappa dell'Archeologia Industriale* (Survey of Industrial Archaeology). Milan.

Sennett, A. R. 1905. *Garden Cities in Theory and Practice.* London: Bemrose.

Serle, G. 1972. *The Rush to be Rich: a history of the colony of Victoria, 1883–89.* Melbourne: Melbourne University Press.

Serning, B., Björkstedt, K.-A. and Westlund, C. 1987. *De mellansvenska järnmalmsgruvorna* (The iron ore mines of central Sweden). Stockholm: IVA-rapport.

Sestoft, J. 1979. *Arbejdets bygninger* (Industrial buildings). Copenhagen: Gyldendal.

Seton Watson, H. 1956. *The East European Revolution.* London: Methuen.

Seton Watson, R. W. 1965. *A History of the Czechs and Slovaks.* Hamden, CT: Archon Books.

Seymour, W. A. 1980. *A History of the Ordnance Survey.* Folkestone: Dawson.

Shanes, E. 1981. *Turner's Rivers, Harbours and Canals.* London: Chatto & Windus.

Shank, W. H. 1982. *Towpaths to Tugboats: a history of American canal engineering.* York, PA: American Canal and Transportation Center.

Shann, E. O. C. 1930. *An Economic History of Australia.* London: Cambridge University Press.

Sharp, D. 1966. *Modern Architecture and Expressionism.* London: Longmans.

Shaw, J. 1984. *Water Power in Scotland.* Edinburgh: John Donald.

Shaw, N. 1935. *Whiteway: a colony on the Cotswolds.* London: C. W. Daniel.

Shaw, S. J. and Shaw, E. K. 1976–7. *History of the Ottoman Empire and Modern Turkey.* Cambridge: Cambridge University Press.

Shaw, W. T. 1972. *Mining in the Lake Counties.* Clapham: Dalesman.

Shaw-Smith, D. 1984. *Ireland's Traditional Crafts.* London: Thames & Hudson.

Sherard, R. H. 1897. *The White Slaves of England, being true pictures of certain social conditions in the kingdom of England in the year 1897.* London: Bowden.

Shercliff, W. H. 1987. *Nature's Joys Are Free for All: a history of countryside recreation in north-east Cheshire.* Stockport: privately published.

Sherlock, R. 1976. *The Industrial Archaeology of Staffordshire.* Newton Abbot: David & Charles.

Shipway, J. S. 1987. *The Tay Railway Bridge 1887–1897.* London: Institution of Civil Engineers.

Short, J. B. 1928. *The Butcher's Shop: a study of a country butcher's business.* Oxford: Oxford University Press.

Shorter, A. H. 1971. *Papermaking in the British Isles.* Newton Abbot: David & Charles.

Seibel, G. A. ed. 1967. *Niagara Falls, Canada: a history of the city and the world famous beauty spot.* Niagara Falls: Kiwanis Club.

Siegfried, A. 1940. *Suez and Panama.* London: Jonathan Cape.

Sifounakis, N. et al. 1986. *Industrial Buildings on Lesbos of the Nineteenth Century and Early Twentieth Centuries: olive presses and soap factories.* Lesbos: Prefecture of Lesbos.

Signalling Study Group 1986. *The Signal Box: a pictorial history and guide to designs.* Oxford: Oxford Publishing Company.

Sillen, G. 1977. *Stiga vi mot ljuset* (We rise towards the light). Stockholm.

Silvan, L. 1982. *Cerámica del País Vasco* (Ceramics in the Basque country). San Sebastián: Caja de Ahorros Provincial de Guipúzcoa.

Simmen, J. and Drepper, U. 1984. *Der Fahrstuhl: die Geschichte der vertikalen Eroberung* (The Lift: a history of vertical conquest). Munich: Prestel.

Simmons, D. A. 1983. *Schweppes: the first 200 years.* London: Springwood.

Simmons, J. 1970. *Transport Museums in Britain and Western Europe.* London: Allen & Unwin.

—— 1978. *The Railway in England and Wales 1830–1914.* Leicester: Leicester University Press.

—— 1984. *The Victorian Hotel.* Leicester: Victorian Studies Centre, University of Leicester.

—— 1986. *The Railway in Town and Country 1830–1914.* Newton Abbot: David & Charles.

Simon, A. L. 1921. *Wine and the Wine Trade.* London: Pitman.

—— 1972. *The Gazetteer of Wines.* Newton Abbot: David & Charles.

Simon, J. 1890. *English Sanitary Institutions.* London: Cassell.

Simpson, M. and Goodman, R. B. 1986. *Whalesong: a pictorial history of whaling and Hawaii.* Honolulu, HA: Beyond Words.

Sims, W. L. 1985. *Two Hundred Years of History and Evolution of Woodworking Machinery.* Burton Lazars: Walers.

Sinclair, A. 1907. *Development of the Locomotive Engine.* Reprint, 1970, Cambridge, MA: MIT Press.

Skempton, A. W. 1981. *John Smeaton FRS.* London: Thomas Telford.

Slotta, R. 1975. *Technische Denkmaler in der Bundesrepublik Deutschland* (Technical monuments in the Federal Republic of Germany). Bochum: Deutsches Bergbau-Museum.

—— 1977. *Technische Denkmäler in der Bundesrepublik Deutschland: Elektrizitäts-, Gas- und Wasserversorgung* (Technical monuments in the German Federal Republic: electricity, gas and water undertakings). Bochum: Deutsches Bergbaumuseum.

—— 1980. *Technische Denkmäler in der Bundesrepublik Deutschland: Die Kali- und Steinsalzindustrie* (Technical monuments in the German Federal Republic: the potash and rocksalt industries). Bochum: Deutsches Bergbaumuseum.

—— 1982. *Einführung in die Industriearchäologie* (Guide to industrial archaeology). Darmstadt: Wissenschafl. Buchges.

—— 1983. *Technische Denkmäler in der Bundesrepublik Deutschland: Der Metallerzbergbau* (Technical monuments in the German Federal Republic: metal mining). Bochum: Deutsches Bergbaumuseum.

—— 1986. *Technische Denkmäler in der Bundesrepublik Deutschland: Der Eisenerzbergbau* (Technical monuments in the German Federal Republic: iron ore mining). Bochum: Deutsches Bergbaumuseum.

—— 1988. *Technische Denkmäler in der Bundesrepublik Deutschland: Der Eisenerzbergbau; die Hochofenpwerke* (Technical monuments in the German Federal Republic: iron ore mining; blast furnace complexes). Bochum: Deutsches Bergbaumuseum.

Słowiński, L. 1983. *Hipolit Cegielski 1813–1868.* Poznań: KAW.

Smiles, A. 1956. *Samuel Smiles and his Surroundings.* London: Robert Hale.

Smiles, S. 1857. *The Life of George Stephenson.* London: John Murray.

—— 1859. *Self-Help.* London: John Murray.

—— 1861–62. *Lives of the Engineers.* London: John Murray.

—— 1863. *Industrial Biography.* London: John Murray.

—— 1866. *Boulton and Watt.* London: John Murray.

—— 1871. *Character.* London: John Murray.

—— 1875. *Thrift.* London: John Murray.

—— 1878. *Industrial Biography: iron workers and tool makers.* London: John Murray.

—— 1880. *Duty.* London: John Murray.

——1883a. *James Nasmyth: autobiography.* London: John Murray.

——1883b. *Men of Industry and Invention.* London: John Murray.

Smith, A. 1872. *Air and Rain.* London.

Smith, B. M. D. 1981. *The History of the British Motor Cycle Industry.* Birmingham: University of Birmingham Centre for Urban and Regional Studies.

Smith, C. S. 1988. *A History of Metallurgy: the development of ideas on the structure of metals before 1890.* Cambridge, MA: MIT Press.

Smith, D. 1965. *The Industrial Archaeology of the East Midlands.* Newton Abbot: David & Charles.

——1988. *Maps and Plans for the Local Historian and Collector.* London: Batsford.

Smith, G. 1875. *Our Canal Populations: a cry from the boat cabins with remedy.* London: Houghton.

Smith, J. 1973. *Condemned at Stanley.* New York: National Maritime Historical Society.

Smith, J. C. 1901. *The Manufacture of Paint.* London: Scott Greenwood.

Smith, M. R. 1977. *Harpers Ferry Armory and the New Technology: the challenge of change.* Ithaca, NY: Cornell University Press.

Smith, N. 1971. *A History of Dams.* London: Peter Davies.

Smith, P. 1976. *The Historian and Film.* Cambridge: Cambridge University Press.

Smith, P. and Braham, A. 1972. *François Mansart.* London: Zwemmer.

Smith, P. L. 1979. *A Pictorial History of Canal Craft.* London: Batsford.

Smith, S. B. 1979. *A View from the Iron Bridge.* London: Thames & Hudson.

Smout, T. C. 1969. *A History of the Scottish People 1560–1830.* Glasgow: Collins.

——1986. *A Century of the Scottish People 1830–1950.* Glasgow: Collins.

Snell, J. B. 1971. *Railways: Mechanical Engineering.* London: Longman.

Socha, B. 1985. *Bestandsaufnahme: Stillgelegte Anlagen aus Industrie und Verkehr in Westfalen* (Taking stock: redundant industrial and transport installations in Westphalia). Hagen: Linnepe Verlagsgesellschaft.

Society of American Archivists, Business Archives Committee 1969. *A Directory of Business Archives.* Washington DC: Society of American Archivists.

Société industrielle de Mulhouse 1990. *Les techniques minières de l'antiquité à la fin du XVIIIe siècle* (Mining techniques from antiquity to the end of the eighteenth century), Colloquium, Strasbourg, April 1988. Mulhouse: Bulletin de la Société industrielle de Mulhouse.

Söderlund, E. F. ed. 1952. *Swedish Timber Exports 1850–1950.* Stockholm: Wood Exporter's Association.

Soissons, M. de 1989. *Welwyn Garden City: a town designed for healthy living.* London: Publications for Companies.

Sörenson, U., Backlund, A.-C., Hamrin, O. and Ahlgren, B. 1987. *Järn bryter bygd* (Iron and colonization). Stockholm: Rubicon.

Soucy, C. and Roy, J-L. 1983. *Le banc de Paspébiac, historie, patrimoine et développement regional* (The Paspébiac bank, history, heritage and regional development). Paspébiac: Centre de documentation et d'interpretation sur les pêches.

Sousa Viterbo, F. 1896. *Arquelogia Industrial Portuguesa: os moinhas* (Industrial archaeology in Portugal: the mills). Reprint, 1986, Guimaraes: Muralha.

South, S. 1977. *Method and Theory in Historical Archaeology.* New York: Academic Press.

Southby, E. R. 1885. *A Systematic Handbook of Practical Brewing.* London: Southby.

Spangenberg, F. and Saal, P. 1983. *Kijk op Stations Amsterdam* (Guide to the railway stations of Amsterdam). Amsterdam: Elsevier.

Sparks, W. L. 1949. *Shoemaking in Norwich.* Northampton: National Institute of the Boot and Shoe Industry.

Speil, G. 1984. *Steirische Eisenstrasse* (The Styrian Iron Road). Leoben: Montanhistorischen Vereines fur Österreich.

——1985. *De Technologie der dirkten Eisenherstellung im Alpenraum: der Stuckofenprozess* (The technology of the direction reduction of iron in the Alpine regions: the Stuckofen process). In Medieval Iron in Society, Stockholm: Jernkontorets Forskning.

Spielman, P. E. 1924. *The Constituents of Coal Tar.* London: Longmans.

Spiesz, A. 1961. *Manufaktur Obdobie na Slovake 1775–1825* (The period of manufacturing in Slovakia 1775–1825). Bratislava.

Spottiswoode, R. et al. 1969. *The Focal Encyclopaedia of Film and Television Techniques.* London: Focal Press.

Spratt, H. P. 1958. *The Birth of the Steamboat.* London: Griffin.

——1968. *Transatlantic Paddle Steamer,* 2nd edn. Glasgow: Brown, Son & Fergusson.

Spufford, M. 1984. *The Great Reclothing of Rural England: petty chapmen and their wares in the seventeenth century.* London: Hambledon.

Squires, R. W. 1983. *The New Navvies: a history of the waterways restoration.* Chichester: Phillimore.

Stacey, D. A. 1982. *Sockeyland Tinplate: technological change in the Fraser River Canning Industry 1871–1918.* Victoria: British Columbia Provincial Museum.

Stadler, K. R. 1971. *Austria.* London: Benn.

Stamatiu, M. 1943. *Istoricul metodelor de exploatare a zacamintelor de sare* (History of the methods of extracting salt deposits). Bucharest.

Stamp, L. D. and Hoskins, W. G. 1963. *The Common Lands of England and Wales.* London: Collins.

Stanbridge, H. 1978. *The History of Sewage Treatment in Britain.* Maidstone: Institute of Water Pollution Control.

Stanbury, P. 1979. *10,000 years of Sydney Life: a guide to archaeological discovery.* Sydney: Macleay Museum.

Stanley, C. 1979. *Highlights in the History of Concrete.* Slough: Cement and Concrete Association.

Stanton, S. W. 1895. *American Steam Vessels.* New York: Smith & Stanton.

Stapleton, D. H. 1987. *The Engineering Drawings of Benjamin Henry Latrobe.* New Haven, CT: Yale University Press.

Steeds, W. 1969. *A History of Machine Tools 1700–1910.* Oxford: Oxford University Press.

Steel, E. W. 1953. *Water Supply and Sewerage,* 3rd edn. New York and London: McGraw Hill.

Stelter, G. A. and Artibise, A. F. J. 1977. *The Canadian City: essays in urban history.* Toronto: McClelland & Stewart.

—— 1984. *The Canadian City: essays in urban and social history.* Ottawa: Carleton University Press.

Stevens, G. R. 1962. *Canadian National Railways.* Toronto: Clarke Irwin.

Stevens, H. 1986. *Hergebruik van oude gebouwen* (Understanding old buildings). Zutphen: Terra.

Stevens, J. W. 1891. *Leather Manufacture: a treatise.* London: Samson Low.

Stevens, M. P. 1975. *Polymer Chemistry: an introduction.* Reading, MA: Addison-Wesley.

Stevenson, A. 1959. *The World's Lighthouses Before 1820.* Edinburgh.

Stevenson, A. S. 1848. *An Account of the Skerryvor Lighthouse with Notes on the Illumination of Lighthouses.* Edinburgh: A. & C. Black.

—— 1850. *A Rudimentary Treatise on the History, Construction and Illumination of Lighthouses.* London: J. Weale.

Stevenson, D. 1838. *A Sketch of the Civil Engineering of North America.* London: J. Weale.

—— 1845. *Remarks on the Improvement of Tidal Rivers.* London: J. Weale.

Stevenson, R. L. 1912. *Records of a Family of Engineers.* London: Chatto & Windus.

Stevenson, T. S. 1874. *The Design and Construction of Harbours: a treatise on maritime engineering,* 2nd edn. Edinburgh: A. & C. Black.

—— 1881. *Lighthouse Construction and Illumination.* London: Spon.

Stewart, E. G. 1958. *Town Gas: its manufacture and distribution.* London: HMSO for Science Museum.

Stopes, H. 1885. *Malt and Malting.* London: F. W. Lyon.

Storer, J. D. 1969. *A Simple History of the Steam Engine.* London: John Baker.

Stott, P. H. 1974. *Long Island: an inventory of historic engineering and industrial sites.* Washington DC: National Park Service.

Straker, E. 1931. *Wealden Iron.* London: Bell.

Strandh, S. 1979. *Machines: an illustrated history.* London: Artists House.

Stratton, M. J. ed. 1987. *Interpreting the Industrial Past.* Telford: Ironbridge Institute.

Stratton, M. J. and Trinder, B. S. 1987a. *Industrial Monuments in England: an approach to legislative protection.* Telford: Ironbridge Institute.

—— 1987b. *Stanley Mill, King's Stanley, Stroud, Gloucestershire: an historical and archaeological evaluation.* Telford: Ironbridge Institute.

—— 1988. *Industrial Monuments in England: the iron and lead industries.* Telford: Ironbridge Institute.

—— 1989a. *Industrial Monuments in England: the copper, brass and tin industries.* Telford: Ironbridge Institute.

—— 1989b. *Industrial Monuments in England: the textile industry.* Telford: Ironbridge Institute.

Straub, H. 1949. *Die Geschcihte der Bauingenierukunst* (A history of civil engineering). Baschichte der Bauingenierukunst. Basel: Verlag Birkhauser. English edition, 1952, London: Leonard Hill.

Street, A. and Alexander, W. 1949. *Metals in the Service of Man.* London: Pelican.

Strohmeyer, K. 1980. *Warenhauser* (Department Stores). Berlin: Wagenbach Verlag.

Stroud, J. 1959. *Famous Airports of the World.* London: Mullcr.

—— 1980. *Airports of the World.* London: Putnam.

Stuart, D. 1975. *County Borough: a history of Burton-on-Trent, 1901–74.* Burton-on-Trent: Charter Trustees.

Stübben, J. 1898. *Neue Werft- und Hafenanlage zu Köln: Festschrift zur Eröffnung* (New shipbuilding and harbour works in Cologne: a symposium on their opening). Cologne: privately published.

Sturm, H. 1977. *Fabrikarchitektur-Villa-Arbeitersiedlung* (The architecture of factories, villas and workers' colonies). Munich: Moos Verlag.

Stursberg, E. 1964. *Geschichte des Hütten- und Hammerwesens im ehemaligen Herzogtum Berg* (History of the ironworks and hammer forges in the former dukedom of Berg). Beiträge für Geschichte Remscheids VIII. Remscheid: privately published.

Sturt, G. 1923. *The Wheelwright's Shop.* Cambridge: Cambridge University Press.

Stutz, W. 1976. *Bahnhofe der Schweiz* (Swiss Railway Stations). Zürich.

Sugden, D. 1982. *Arctic and Antarctic: a modern geographical synthesis.* Oxford: Basil Blackwell.

Summer-Boyd, H. and Freeby, J. 1974. *Strolling through Istanbul,* 2nd edn. Istanbul.

Supple, B. 1987. *The History of the British Coal Mining Industry,* vol. IV: *1913–1946.* Oxford: Oxford University Press.

Sussex, E. 1975. *The Rise and Fall of British Documentary.* Berkeley, CA: University of California Press.

Sutcliffe, A. R. 1970. *The Autumn of Central Paris: the defeat of town planning 1850–1970.* London: Edward Arnold.

—— 1981. *The History of Urban and Regional Planning: an annotated bibliography.* London: Mansell.

—— 1983. *London and Paris: capitals of the nineteenth century.* Leicester: Victorian Studies Centre, University of Leicester.

Sutcliffe, A. R. and Smith, R. 1974. *History of Birmingham,* vol. III: *1939–1970.* Oxford: Oxford University Press.

Sütterlin, C. 1981. *La Grand Forge* (Ironworks). Paris: Editions d'Assailly.

Sutton, G. B. 1979. *A History of Shoe Making in Street, Somerset: C. and J. Clark, 1833–1903.* York: Sessions.

Swaysland, E. J. C. 1905. *Boot and Shoe Design and Manufacture.* Northampton: Joseph Tebbutt.

Swedish Ironmasters' Association (Jernkontoret) 1982. *Svenskt och utlandskt jarn pa 1600-talets Europmark-*

nad (Iron and steel on the European market in the seventeenth century). Stockholm: Swedish Ironmasters' Association.

Sweeney, J. J. and Sert, J. L. 1960. *Antoni Gaudí*. London: Architectural Press.

Swift, L. F. 1927. *The Yankee of the Yards: the biography of Gustavus Franklin Swift*. Chicago, IL: A. W. Shaw.

Swiss National Tourist Office 1981. *Eisen, Le Fer in Suisse, Ferro, Iron*. Zürich: Swiss National Tourist Office.

Sykes, W. J. 1897. *The Principles and Practice of Brewing*. London: Charles Griffin.

Sylvester, J. W. H. 1972. *Scythemaking at Abbeydale*. Sheffield: Sheffield City Museums.

Szacka, B. 1966. *Stanisław Staszic*. Warsaw: PIW.

Taft, R. 1938. *Photography and the American Scene: a social history 1839–89*. New York: Macmillan.

Talbot, F. A. 1914. *The Oil Conquest of the World*. London: Heinemann.

Tann, J. 1970. *The Development of the Factory*. London: Cornmarket Press.

—— 1981. *The Selected Papers of Boulton and Watt*, vol. I: *The Engine Partnership 1775–1825*. London: Diploma Press.

Tate, W. E. 1969. *The Parish Chest: a study of the records of parochial administration in England*, 3rd edn. Cambridge: Cambridge University Press.

Taylor, D. and Bush, D. 1974. *The Golden Age of British Hotels*. London: Northwood Publications.

Taylor, F. J. 1927. *Modern Waterworks Practice*. London: Benn.

Taylor, F. M. H. 1939. *Production and Utilisation of Coke*. London: Walter King.

Taylor, F. W. 1911. *The Principles of Scientific Management*. New York: Harper.

Taylor, F. W. and Thompson, S. E. 1905. *A Treatise on Concrete, Plain and Reinforced*. New York: J. Wiley.

Taylor, R. C. 1848. *Statistics of Coal: the geographical and geological distribution of fossil fuel*. London: Chapman.

Telford, T. 1838. *The Life of Thomas Telford*, ed. J. Rickman. London: J. & L. G. Hansard.

Temple, J. 1972. *Mining: an international history*. New York: Praeger.

—— 1987. *Wings over Woodley: the story of Miles Aircraft and the Adwest Group*. Bourne End: Aston Publications.

Ternant, M. A. L. 1881. *Les Télégraphes* (Telegraphs). Paris: Hachette.

Teuteberg, H. J. ed. 1985. *Homo habitans*. Munster.

Tew, D. 1984. *Canal Inclines and Lifts*. Gloucester: Alan Sutton.

Thomas, A. R. and Thomas, J. L. 1987. *The Sentinel: a history of Alley & MacLellan and the Sentinel waggon works*, vol. II: *1930–1980*. Worcester: Woodpecker.

Thomas, D. and Donnelly, T. 1985. *The Motor Car Industry in Coventry since the 1890s*. London: Croom Helm.

Thomas, R. H. G. 1986. *London's First Railway: The London and Greenwich*. London: Batsford.

Thomas, S. ed. 1975. *Delaware, an Inventory of Historic Engineering and Industrial Sites*. Washington DC: National Park Service.

Thompson, A. B. 1908. *The Oil Fields of Russia*. London: Crosby Lockwood.

—— 1910. *Petroleum Mining and Oil Field Development*. London: Crosby Lockwood.

Thompson, E. P. 1955. *William Morris: Romantic to Revolutionary*. London: Lawrence & Wishart.

—— 1963. *The Making of the English Working Class*. London: Victor Gollancz.

Thompson, F. M. L. 1972. *Victorian England: the horse-drawn society*. London: Bedford College.

—— 1983. *Horses in European Economic History: a preliminary canter*. Reading: British Agricultural History Society.

Thompson, G. B. 1952. *The John Horner Collection of Spindles, Spinning Wheels and Accessories at the Ulster Museum*. Belfast: Belfast Municipal Art Gallery and Museum.

Thompson, I. M. A. 1983. *Manual of Curatorship*. London: Butterworth.

Thompson, J. S. 1902. *The Mechanisation of the Linotype*. Chicago, IL: Inland Printer Co.

—— 1904. *The History of Composing Machines*. Reprint, 1980, New York: Gardland Publishing.

Thompson, P. 1978. *The Voice of the Past: oral history*. Oxford: Oxford University Press.

Thompson, R. L. 1947. *Wiring a Continent: history of the telegraph industry in the United States 1832–66*. Princeton, NJ: Princeton University Press.

Thomson, J. K. J. 1982. *Clermont-de-Lodève, 1633–1789: fluctuations in the prosperity of a Languedocian cloth-making town*. Cambridge: Cambridge University Press.

Thomson, T. 1849. *Brewing and Distillation*. Edinburgh: A. & C. Black.

Thornton, G. 1986. *The New Zealand Heritage of Farm Buildings*. Auckland.

—— 1982. *New Zealand's Industrial Heritage*. Wellington: A. H. & A. W. Reed.

Threlfall, R. E. 1951. *The Story of 100 Years of Phosphorus Making 1851–1951*. Oldbury: Albright & Wilson.

Thrupp, G. A. 1877. *A History of Coaches*. London: Kirby & Endean.

Thurston, R. H. 1878. *A History of the Growth of the Steam Engine*. London: Kegan Paul. Reprint, 1939, Ithaca, NY: Cornell University Press.

Thÿsse, J. T. 1972. *Een halve eeuw Zuiderzeewerken, 1920–1970* (A half century of the Zuider Zee works, 1920–1970). Groningen: Tjeenk Willink.

Timmerman, R. 1951. *Die Talsperrem am Nordrande des Rheinischen Schiefergebirges: Ihre Bedeutung für den Abflussvorgang und ihre wirtschaftliche Ausnutzung* (The dams on the northern edge of the Rhine slate region: their significance for drainage patterns and their economic uses). Landshut: Verlag des Amtes für Landeskunde.

Timmins, J. G. 1977. *Handloom Weavers' Cottages in Central Lancashire*. Lancaster: University of Lancaster Press.

Timmins, S. 1866. *Birmingham and the Midlands Hardware District*. London: Hardwick.

Tipton, F. B. and Aldrich, R. 1987a. *An Economic and Social History of Europe, 1890–1939*. London: Macmillan Education.

——1987b. *An Economic and Social History of Europe from 1939 to the Present*. London: Macmillan Education.

Tizard, W. L. 1857. *The Theory and Practice of Brewing*, 4th edn. London: Tizard.

Toale, B. 1983. *The Art of Papermaking*. Worcester, MA: Davis.

Tobias, J. J. 1967. *Crime and Industrial Society in the Nineteenth Century*. London: Batsford.

Tocqueville, A. de 1958. *Journeys to England and Ireland*, ed. E. P. Meyer. London: Faber & Faber.

Tomlinson, C. 1852–4. *Encyclopaedia of Useful Arts and Manufactures*. 2 vols. London: Virtue.

Tomlinson, E. P. 1979. *Britain's River and Canal Craft*. Ashbourne: Moorland.

Torrens, H. 1978. *The Evolution of a Family Firm: Stothert & Pitt of Bath*. Bath: Stothert & Pitt.

Tough, J. M. and O'Flaherty, C. A. 1971. *Passenger Conveyors: an innovatory form of communal transport*. London: Ian Allan.

Tournaire, J. 1990. *Les forges de Clavières, 1686–1874* (The Clavières ironworks, 1686–1874). Châteauroux: privately published.

Towner, D. C. 1957. *English Cream-Coloured Earthenware*. London: Faber.

Toynbee, A. 1884. *Lectures on the Industrial Revolution*. London: Rivington.

Tragatsch, E. 1979. *The Illustrated History of Motor Cycles*. London: Temple Press Books.

Trastader, 1972–3. *Trastader i Norden* (Wooden Towns of Scandinavia). Stockholm: Konsthögskolans Arkitekturskola.

Treatise n.d. (c.1840). *A Treatise on the progressive improvement and present state of the Manufactures in Metal*. London: Spottiswoode.

Tredgold, T. 1895. *Elementary Principles of Carpentry*, 9th edn. London: Spon.

Treue, W. 1970. *Wirtschaftsgeschichte der Neuzeit: Im Zeitalter der Industriellen Revolution 1700 bis 1960* (The economic history of the new times: the era of the Industrial Revolution 1700–1960). Stuttgart: Alfred Kröner Verlag.

——1980. *Gesellschaft, Wirtschaft und Technik: Deutschland im 19 Jahrhundert* (Society, the economy and technology: Germany in the nineteenth century). Munich: Deutscher Taschenbuch Verlag.

Trevithick, F. 1872. *The Life of Richard Trevithick*. London: Spon.

Trier, E. and Weyres, E. 1980. *Kunst des 19 Jahrhunderts im Rheinland*, Band II: *Architektur* (Nineteenth century art in the Rhineland, vol. II: architecture). Düsseldorf: Schwann.

Trinder, B. S. 1981. *The Industrial Revolution in Shropshire*, 2nd edn. Chichester: Phillimore.

——1982a. *Victorian Banbury*. Chichester: Phillimore.

——1982b. *The Making of the Industrial Landscape*. London: Dent.

——1984. *Victorian Shrewsbury*. Shrewsbury: Shropshire County Council.

——1991. *The Darbys of Coalbrookdale*, 4th edn. Chichester: Phillimore.

Trinder, B. S. and Cox, J. 1980. *Yeomen and Colliers in Telford: the probate inventories of Dawley, Lilleshall, Wellington and Wrockwardine*. Chichester: Phillimore.

Tripp, B. H. 1956. *Renold Chains: a history of the company and the rise of the precision chain industry*. London: Allen & Unwin.

Trost, H. 1987. *Die Bau- und Kunstdenkmale der DDR, Haupstadt Berlin* (Architectural and artistic monuments in Berlin, capital of the DDR). 2 vols. Berlin: Henschel Verlag.

Trottier, L. 1980. *Les Forges, historiographie des Forges du Saint-Maurice* (Les Forges, the historiography of Les Forges Saint-Maurice). Montreal: Boréal Express.

——1983. *Évaluation du potential historique des fours à charbon de bois des Grandes Piles en relation avec quelques sites sidérurgiques de la Mauricie* (Evaluation of the historical potential of the charcoal furnaces of Grandes Piles in relation to some other ironworks in the Mauricie region). Quebec: Ministry of Cultural Affairs.

——1985. *Le patrimoine industriel au Québec* (The industrial heritage in Quebec). Quebec: Commission des biens culturelles.

Tschudi-Madsen, S. 1977. *Framtid for Fortiden* (Three European architectural heritage year projects). Nusford: Gullik Kollandsrud; Roros: Ola Overags; Stavenger: Finar Heden; Oslo.

——1983. *Fredede Hus og Anlegg III: Roros Bergstad* (Houses and landscapes, vol. III: the mining town of Roros). Oslo: Universitetsforlaget.

Tucker, D. G. 1983. *Ayrshire Hone Stones*. Ayr: Ayrshire Archaeological and Natural History Society.

Tudsbery, J. H. T. and Brightmore, A. W. 1905. *The Principles of Waterworks Engineering*. London: Spon.

Tuer, D. F. and Bolz, R. W. 1984. *An Encyclopaedic Dictionary of Engineering Technology*. London: Chapman & Hall.

Tulloch, J. 1981. *The Rideau Canal: defence, transport and recreation*. Ottawa: Parks Canada.

Tunis, E. 1965. *Colonial Craftsmen and the Beginnings of American Industry*. New York: Crowell.

Tunzelmann, G. N. von 1978. *Steam Power and British Industrialization to 1860*. Oxford: Oxford University Press.

Turkevich, J. and Turkevich, L. 1968. *Prominent Scientists of Continental Europe*. New York: American Eloisier Publishing Company.

Turneaure, F. E. and Russell, H. L. 1924. *Public Water Supplies: requirements, resources and the construction of waterworks*, 3rd edn. New York: John Wiley.

Turner, H. G. 1904. *A History of the Colony of Victoria*. London: Longman Green.

Turner, M. L. and Vaisey, D. 1972. *Oxford Shops and Shopping*. Oxford: Oxford Illustrated Press.

Turner, P. St J. 1968. *Handbook of the Vickers Viscount*. London: Ian Allan.

Tylecote, R. F. 1986. *The Prehistory of Metallurgy in the British Isles*. London: The Institute of Metals.

Tyne, G. F. J. 1977. *Saga of the Vacuum Tube*. Indianapolis, IN: Howard W. Sams.

Ukers, W. H. 1935. *All about Coffee*. New York: Tea and Coffee Trade Journal Co.

Underhill, H. A. 1938. *Sailing Ships, Trigs and Rigging*. Glasgow: Brown, Son & Fergusson.

——1958. *Masting and Rigging the Clipper Ship and Ocean Carrier*. Glasgow: Brown, Son & Fergusson.

Union International des Chemins de Fer 1975. *Lexique Général des Chemins de Fer* (General dictionary of railway terms). Stuttgart: Malsch & Vogel.

United States Steel Co. 1971. *The Making, Shaping and Treating of Steel*, 10th edn. Pittsburgh, PA: Association of Iron & Steel Engineers.

Unsal, B. 1973. *Turkish Islamic Architecture in Seljuk and Ottoman Times, 1071–1923*. London: St Martin's Press.

Unverferth, G. and Kroker, E. 1981. *Der Arbeitsplatz des Bergmanns in historischen Bilder und Dokumenten* (The working places of miners in historical pictures and documents). Bochum: Deutsches Bergbau Museum.

Unwin, R. 1909. *Town Planning in Practice*. London: Fisher Unwin.

Urdang, G. 1958. *The Apothecary Chemist: Carl Wilhelm Scheele, a pictorial biography*, 2nd edn. Madison: American Institute of Pharmacy.

Ure, A. 1835. *The Philosophy of Manufactures*. London: Bohn.

Uren, F. C. 1914. *Waterworks Engineering*. Bristol: Castle Litho.

US Bureau of Mines 1976. *Mining and Mineral Operations in the New England and Mid-Atlantic States*. Washington DC: US Bureau of Mines.

Valen-Sandstad, F. 1982. *The Sandvig Collections*. Lillehammer: Sandvigske Samlinger.

Vallance, H. A. 1938. *The Highway Railway*. London: Stockwell. 2nd edn, 1963, Newton Abbot: David & Charles.

Van Beylen, J. 1969. *Repertory of Maritime Museums and their Collections*. Antwerp: National Maritime Museum.

Van Dalen, J. 1984. *Nieuw gezicht op oud werk: Bijdrage tot de industriële archeologie in Nederland in het algemeen en in Rotterdam in het bizonder* (New visions on old work: a contribution to industrial archaeology in the Netherlands, particularly in Rotterdam). Rotterdam: Erasmus University.

Van Dalen, J. and Boon, W. 1983. *Oud werk, overzicht van industrieel erfgoed in Rotterdam* (Old work, an inventory of the industrial heritage in Rotterdam), 2nd edn. Rotterdam: Stichting Industrieel Erfgoed Rijmond.

——1986. *Nieuw Gezicht op Oud Werk: Industriele Archeologie: introductie en bibliografie* (New Visions on Old Work: industrial archaeology: an introduction and bibliography). Rotterdam: Stichting Industrieel Erfgoed Rijmond.

Van de Meene, J. G. C. and Nijhof, P. 1985. *Spoorwegmonumenten in Nederland* (Railway monuments in the Netherlands). Amsterdam: Uitgave Koninlijke Nederlandse Oudheidkundige Bond.

Van den Abeelen, G. 1973. *L'Archaeologie industrielle* (Industrial archaeology). Brussels.

Van den Branden, J. P. 1975. *Musées de Belgique* (Belgian museums). Brussels: Editions Creatif.

Van den Eerenbeemt, H. F. J. M. 1977. *Ontwikkelingslijnen en Scharnierpunten in het Brabants industrieel bedrijf 1777–1914* (Developments and turning points in industry in Brabant 1777–1914). Tilburg: Bijdragen tot de geschiedenis van het suiden van Nederland.

——1989. *In het spoor van de vooruitgang: het noderniseringsproces van de Nederlandse samenleving 1730–1980* (In the track of progress: the modernisation process in Dutch society 1730–1980). Tilburg: Tilburg University Press.

Van der Have, J. H. and Verver, C. G. 1957. *Petroleum and its Products*. London: Pitman.

Van der Ploeg, P. 1988. *Bruggen in Groningen: Inventarisatie van Bruggen voorkomend in het raamplan waterwegen van de provincie Groningen* (Bridges in Groningen: an inventory of the outstanding bridges of the waterways of the province of Groningen).

Van der Pols, K. 1984. *De ontwikkeling van het wateropvoerwerktuig in Nederland 1770–1870* (The Development of water-powered machinery in the Netherlands 1770–1870). Delft: Delft University Press.

Van der Veen, J. 1962. *Dredge, Drain, Recalim: the art of a nation*. The Hague: Nijhoff.

Van der Veen, R. 1981. *Vuurtorens: Over vierboeten, lichtwachters en markante bouwwerken* (Lighthouses: with lightships, beacons and other structures for warning). Bussum: De Boer Maritiem.

Van Doorslaer, B. 1983. *Steenkool in Limburg* (Coal in Limburg). St Truiden: Provinciaal Museum vor het Industrieel Erfgoed.

Van Gorp, P. J. M. 1984. *De Industriele Revolutie in de Nederlandse Wollenstoffenindustrie* (The Industrial Revolution in the Dutch woollen cloth industry). Tilburs.

——1987. *Tilburg eens de wolstad van Nederland: bloei en ondergang van de Tilburgse wollenstoffenindustrie* (Tilburg, once the wool towns of the Netherlands: the flowering and decline of Tilburg's woollen textile industry). Eidhoven: Bura.

Van Lemmen, H. 1979. *Tiles: a Collectors' Guide*. London: Souvenir Press.

Varley, D. E. 1959. *A History of the Midland Counties Lace Manufacturers' Association 1915–58*. Long Eaton: Lace Productions.

Veal, T. H. P. 1931. *The Supply of Water*. London: Chapman and Hall.

Veale, S. E. 1945. *Tomorrow's Airliners, Airways and Airports*. London: Pilot Press.

Vehlefeld, R. and Jacques, F. 1956. *Garagen und Tankstellen* (Garages and service stations). Munich.

Vernon-Harcourt, L. F. 1885. *Harbours and Docks*. 2 vols. Oxford: Clarendon Press.

Veyret-Verner, G. 1948. *L'Industrie des Alpes françaises*

(The industry of the French Alps). Grenoble: Arthand.

Viaene, P. 1986. *Industriele Archaeologie in Belgie* (Industrial archaeology in Belgium). Ghent: Museum voor Industriele Archaeologie en Textiel.

Vickers, N. 1986. *A Yorkshire Town of the Eighteenth Century: the probate inventories of Whitby, North Yorkshire, 1700–1800.* Studley: Brewin.

Victor, S. and Wright, H. 1984. *Industrial Heritage 84: National Reports: The Fifth International Conference on the Conservation of the Industrial Heritage.* Washington DC: SIA.

Victoria History 1959. *Victoria History of the Counties of England: Wiltshire*, vol. IV. Oxford: Oxford University Press.

Victoria History 1964. *Victoria History of the Counties of England: Warwickshire*, vol. VII. Oxford: Oxford University Press.

Victoria History 1979. *Victoria History of the Counties of England: Oxfordshire*, vol. IV. Oxford: Oxford University Press.

Viet, J. 1960. *Les Villes nouveaux* (New Towns). Paris: UNESCO.

Vieyra, D. I. 1979. *"Fill 'er Up": an architectural history of America's gas stations.* New York: Macmillan.

Vigars, N. 1984. *A Short History of the Shell Film Unit (1934–1984).* London: Shell International.

Vignobles, O. J. 1898. *Life of Charles Blacker Vignobles.* London: Longmans.

Vilaça, I. 1980. *A Indústria dos Damascos em Braga* (The damask industry in Braga). Braga: ASPS/CMB.

Ville de Québec, 1986. *Mise en valeur et interprétation du site du premier palais de l'Intendant* (The development and interpretation of the site of the first Intendant's palace). Quebec: Ville de Québec.

Vire, L. 1970. *La distribution publique d'eau à Bruxelles 1830–1970* (Public water supply in Brussels 1830–1970). Brussels.

Vistor, S. and Wright, H. 1984. *Industrial Heritage 84: National Reports.* Washington DC: Society for Industrial Archaeology.

Vocabulaire 1983. *Vocabulaire du Material papetier: Anglais: Français* (Wordbook of papermaking terms: English: French). Quebec and Trois Rivières: University Presses of Quebec and Trois Rivières.

Vogel, R. M. 1971. *Roebling's Delaware and Hudson Canal Aqueducts.* Washington DC: Smithsonian Institution Press.

——ed. 1973. *A Report of the Mohawk-Hudson Area Survey: a selective recording survey of the industrial archaeology of the Mohawk and Hudson River Valleys in the Vicinity of Troy, NY, June-September 1969.* Washington DC: Smithsonian Institution Press.

Vogel, R. M. 1988. *Vertical Transportation in Old Back Bay, a Museum Case Study: the acquistion of a small residential hydraulic elevator.* Washington DC: Smithsonian Institution Press.

Vogt, E. 1952. *Der Wein* (Wine). Stuttgart: Ulmer.

Von Oeynhausen, C. and von Dechen, H. 1974. *Railways in England 1826 and 1827*, ed. E. C. Lee. Cambridge: Newcomen Society.

Voorn, H. 1960. *De papiermolens in de provincie Noord-Holland* (Paper mills in the province of Noord-Holland). Haarlem.

Voppel, G. 1965. *Die Aachener Bergbau-und Industrielandschaft* (The mining and industrial landscape of the Aachen area). Wiesbaden.

Wadsworth, A. P. and Mann, J. de L. 1931. *The Cotton Trade and Industrial Lancashire.* Manchester: Manchester University Press.

Wagenbreth, O. and Wächtler, E. 1983. *Technische Denkmale in der Deutschen Demokratischen Republik* (Technical monuments in the German Democratic Republic). Leipzig: VEB Deutscher Verlag für Grundstoffindustrie.

——1986a. *Dampfmaschinen: Die Kolbendampfmaschine als historische Erscheinung und technisches Denkmal* (Steam engines: the piston steam engine, historical views and technical monuments). Leipzig: VEB Fachbuchverlag.

——1986b. *Der Freiberger Bergbau: Technische Denkmale und Geschichte* (The Freiberg mining area: technical monuments and history). Leipzig: VEB Deutscher Verlag für Grundstoffindustrie.

Wagner, O. 1895. *Moderne Architektur* (Modern architecture). Vienna: Schroll.

Wagner-Rieger, R. 1970. *Wiens Architektur im 19 Jahrhundert* (Viennese architecture in the nineteenth century). Vienna: Österreichischer Bundesverlag.

Wagoner, H. D. 1968. *The United States Machine Tool Industry from 1900 to 1950.* Cambridge, MA: MIT Press.

Wahl, R. and Henius, M. 1908. *American Handbook of the Brewing, Malting and Auxiliary Trades*, 3rd edn. Chicago, IL: Wahl-Henius.

Wahlund, J. 1879. *Dannemora grufvor: Historisk skildring* (The Dannemora mines: a historical portrait). Stockholm: Norstedt.

Wailes, R. 1948. *Windmills in England.* London: Architectural Press.

——1956. *Tide Mills.* London: Society for the Protection of Ancient Buildings.

——1967. *The English Windmill*, 2nd edn. London: Routledge & Kegan Paul.

Waite, J. G. 1972. *Iron Architecture in New York City: Two Studies in Industrial Archaeology.* Albany, NY: New York State Historic Trust.

Walford, E. W. 1931. *Early Days in the British Motor Cycle Industry.* Coventry: British Cycle and Motor Cycle Manufacturers' and Traders' Union.

Walker, G. 1885. *The Costume of Yorkshire*, ed. E. Hailstone. Leeds: Richard Jackson.

Walker, I. C. 1977. *Clay Tobacco Pipes, with particular reference to the Bristol industry.* Hull: Parks Canada.

Wall, R. 1977. *Ocean Liners.* New York: E. P. Dutton.

Wallace, W. 1976. *Czechoslovakia.* London: Ernest Benn.

Waller, R. J. 1983. *The Dukeries Transformed: the social and political development of a twentieth-century coalfield.* Oxford: Oxford University Press.

Wallis-Tayler, A. J. 1898. *Aerial or Wire-Rope Tramways: their construction and management*. London: Crosby Lockwood.

Walsh, P. C. 1964. *Tanning in the United States to 1850*. Washington DC: Smithsonian Institution.

Walters, D. 1966. *British Railway Bridges*. London: Ian Allan.

Walton, J. K. 1978. *The Blackpool Landlady*. Manchester: Manchester University Press.

——1983. *The English Seaside Resort*. Leicester: Leicester University Press.

Walton, M. 1948. *Sheffield: its story and its achievements*. Sheffield: Sheffield Telegraph and Star.

Walton, T. 1902. *Steel Ships: their construction and maintenance*. London: Charles Griffin.

——1921. *Present-day Shipbuilding*. London: Charles Griffin.

Walvin, J. 1978. *Leisure and Society 1830–50*. London: Longman.

Ward, C. and Hardy, D. 1986. *Goodnight Campers! The History of the British Holiday Camp*. London: Mansell.

Ward, P. 1983. *Albania: a travel guide*. London: Oleander Press.

Ward-Jackson, C. H. 1941. *A History of Courtaulds*. London: Curwen Press.

Ware, M. 1976. *The Making of the Motor Car 1895–1930*. Ashbourne: Moorland.

Warnes, A. R. 1914. *Coal Tar Distillation and the Working-up of Coal Tar Products*. London: Ian Allan.

Warnke, M. 1970. *Das Kunstwerk zwischen Wissenschaft und Weltanschauung* (Art between science and a view of life). Gutersloh: Bertelsmann.

Warren, A. 1988. *Barry Scrapyard: the preservation miracle*. Newton Abbot: David & Charles.

Warren, G. 1978. *Vanishing Street Furniture*. Newton Abbot: David & Charles.

Warren, J. G. H. 1923. *A Century of Locomotive Building by Robert Stephenson & Co*. Reprint, 1970, Newton Abbot: David & Charles.

Warren, K. 1980. *Chemical Foundations: the alkali industry in Britain to 1926*. Oxford: Clarendon Press.

Warschnitter, J. 1980. *A la Rencontre d'Hutchinson* (Getting to know Hutchinson). Paris: Chotard.

Wasbert, G. C. and Svendsen, A. S. 1969. *Industriens historie i Norge* (Industrial history in Norway). Oslo.

Watelet, H. 1964a. *Inventaire des Archives des Societaires et de la société civile des usines et mines de Houille du Grand-Hornu* (Inventory of the business and civic archives of the works and coal mines of Le Grand-Hornu). Paris.

——1964b. *Inventaire des Archives des Charbonnages de Mariemont-Bascoup*. Paris.

Water Authorities Association 1987. *The Water Heritage*. London: Water Authorities Association.

Waterer, J. W. 1944. *Leather in Life, Art and Industry*. London: Faber.

Watkin, D. and Mellinghoff, T. 1987. *German Architecture and the Classical Ideal 1740–1840*. London: Thames & Hudson.

Watkins, G. 1968. *The Stationary Steam Engine*. Newton Abbot: David & Charles.

Watkins, G. 1970–71. *The Textile Mill Engine*. 2 vols. Newton Abbot: David & Charles.

——1978–79. *The Steam Engine in Industry*. 2 vols. Ashbourne: Moorland.

Watkins, G. and Buchanan, R. A. 1975. *Man and the Steam Engine*. Hove: Priory Press.

Watney, J. 1974. *Beer is Best: a history of beer*. London: Peter Owen.

——1976. *Mother's Ruin: a history of gin*. London: Peter Owen.

Watson, M. H. 1988a. *Flagships of the Line*. Cambridge: Patrick Stephens.

——1988b. *US Passenger Liners since 1945*. Cambridge: Patrick Stephens.

Watson, M. S. 1989. *Jute and Flax Mills in Dundee*. Dundee: Hutton Press.

Watson, R. S. 1867. *Industrial Schools*. Newcastle Upon Tyne: Ragged and Industrial Schools.

Watson, T. A. 1926. *The Birth and Babyhood of the Telephone*. New York: American Telephone and Telegraph Company.

Watson, W. 1851. *The Juvenile Vagrant and the Industrial School*. Aberdeen.

Wattjes, J. G. and ten Bosch, W. T. H. 1941. *Rotterdam en hoe het bouwde* (Rotterdam and how it was built). Leiden: A. W. Sÿthoff.

Wayman, M. 1990. *All that Glitters: readings in historical metallurgy*. Toronto: Canadian Institute of Mining and Metallurgy.

Weatherill, L. 1971. *The Pottery Trade and North Staffordshire, 1660–1760*. Manchester: Manchester University Press.

Webb, J. S. 1983. *The British Steam Tram*. London: Tramway & Light Railway Society.

Webb, S. and Webb, B. 1906–1929. *English Poor Law History*, vols VII-IX. London: Longmans.

——1913. *The Story of the King's Highway*. London: Longmans.

Webber, R. 1971. *The Village Blacksmith*. Newton Abbot: David & Charles.

Webster, A. D. 1919. *Firewoods: their production and fuel values*. London: Fisher Unwin.

Webster, R. 1983. *Gems: their sources, descriptions and identification*, 4th edn, rev. B. W. Andeson. London: Butterworth.

Wehdorn, M. and Georgeacopol-Winischhofer, U. 1990. *Baudenkmäler der Technik und Industrie in Österreich* (Historical monuments relating to technology and industry in Austria). Vienne: Böhlau.

Weiher, S. von 1987. *Berlins Weg zur Elektropolis* (The development of Berlin into Electropolis). Göttingen and Zurich: Muste Schmidt Verlag.

Weil, G. L. 1977. *Sears, Roebuck, USA: the great American catalog store and how it grew*. New York: Stein and Day.

Weiner, M. J. 1981. *English Culture and the Decline of the Industrial Spirit, 1850–1980*. Cambridge: Cambridge University Press.

Weir, T. R. 1960. *The Economic Atlas of Manitoba.* Winnipeg: Department of Industry and Commerce, Province of Manitoba.

Weiss, G. 1971. *The Book of Porcelain.* London: Barrie & Jenkinson.

Weiss, L. 1982. *Watchmaking in England 1760–1820.* London: Hale.

Weitzman, D. 1987. *Superpower – the making of a steam locomotive.* Boston: David R. Godine.

Welch, C. 1894. *The History of the Tower Bridge.* London: Smith Elder.

Wells, F. A. 1935. *The British Hosiery Trade: its history and organisation.* London: Allen & Unwin.

Wells, P. A. and Hooper, J. 1909. *Modern Cabinet Work, Furniture and Fitments.* London: Batsford.

Wendt, L. and Cogan, H. 1952. *Give the Lady what She Wants!* Chicago, IL: Rand McNally.

Werner, E. 1975. Die Eisenbahnbrüke über die Wupper in Müngsten 1893–1897 (The railway bridges over the Wupper in Müngsten 1893–1897). *Arbeitshefte des Landeskonservators Rheinland V.* Cologne: Rheinland Verlag.

Westcott, G. F. 1932. *Handbooks of the Collections Illustrating Pumping Machinery.* London: Science Museum.

Westhofen, W. 1890. *The Forth Bridge.* Reprint, 1989, Edinburgh: Moubray House.

Westwood, J. N. 1982. *Soviet Locomotive Technology during Industrialization, 1928–52.* London: Macmillan.

Westwood, J. N. 1983. *The Railway Data Book.* Cambridge: Patrick Stephens.

Wexler, P. J. 1955. *La Formation du vocabulaire des chemins de fer en France 1778–1842* (The formation of railway vocabulary in France 1778–1842). Geneva: Droz.

Whatley, C. A. 1984. *That Important and Necessary Article: the salt industry and its trade in Fife and Tayside circa 1570–1850.* Dundee: Abertay Historical Society.

—— 1987. *The Scottish Salt Industry,* ed. J. Butt. London: Dent.

Wheldon, W. H. 1946. *A Norvic Century 1846–1946.* Norwich: Jarrold.

Whiffen, M. and Breeze, C. 1984. *Pueblo Deco: the art deco architecture of the Southwest.* Albuquerque, NM: University of New Mexico Press.

Whimster, R. 1990. *The Emerging Past: air photography and the Buried Landscape.* London: Royal Commission on the Historical Monuments of England.

White, G. S. 1836. *Memoir of Samuel Slater; with a history of the rise and progress of the cotton manufacture in England and America.* Philadelphia, PA.

White, G. T. 1962. *Formative Years in the Far West: a history of Standard Oil of California and predecessors through 1919.* New York: Appleton-Century-Crofts.

White, J. H. 1968. *American Locomotives: an Engineering History, 1830–1880.* Baltimore, MD: Johns Hopkins University Press.

—— 1980. *A History of the American Locomotive: its development, 1830–1880.* New York: Dover.

—— 1982. *A Short History of American Locomotive Builders in the Steam Era.* Washington DC: Bass.

—— 1978. *The American Passenger Railroad Car.* Baltimore, MD: John Hopkins University Press.

Whitehead, R. A. 1975. *A Century of Steam Rolling.* London: Ian Allan.

Whiteman, W. M. 1973. *The History of the Caravan.* London: Blandford.

Whitlock, L. and Leclerc, L. 1984. *Recherche ethnohistorique et du potential archéologique du site de North Nation Mills* (Ethnographical and historical research and an archaeological evaluation of the site of North Nation Mills). Quebec: Ministry of Cultural Affairs.

Whitt, F. R. and Wilson, D. G. 1982. *Bicycling Science.* Cambridge, MA: MIT Press.

Whitworth, R. 1766. *Advantages of Inland Navigation.* London: R. Baldwin.

Wiel, P. 1970. *Wirteschaftsgeschichte des Ruhrgebietes. Tatsachen und Zahlen* (The economic history of the Ruhrgebiet: facts and figures). Essen: Siedlungsverband Ruhrkohlendiren.

Wielka Encyklopedia 1967. *Wielka Encyklopedia Powszechna,* IX (The great encyclopaedia, IX). Warsaw: PWN.

Wiene, A. 1912. *Das Warenhaus* (The warehouse store). Berlin: Wasmuth Verlag.

Wildemann, T. 1928–9. *Die Erhaltung technischer Kulturdenkmäler unter besonderer Berücksichtigung der Verhältnisse in den Rheinlanden* (The conservation of technical monuments, taking into consideration in particular the conditions in the Rhineland).

Wilhelm, K. 1983. *Walter Gropius, Industriearchitekt* (Walter Gropius, industrial architect). Brunswick/Wiesbaden: Viebeg Verlag.

Wilhelmi, M., Kühne, G. and Rudolf, G. 1987. *Alte Pumpwerke in Berlin* (Old pumping stations in Berlin). Berlin: Nicolai Verlag.

Willan, T. S. 1936. *The English Coasting Trade.* Reprint, 1967, Manchester: Manchester University Press.

Willerslev, R. 1988. *Saadan boede vi Kobenhavn* (Workers dwelling conditions in Copenhagen). Copenhagen: Akademisk forlag.

Williams, A. 1986. *Life in a Railway Factory.* Newton Abbot: David & Charles.

Williams, D. 1985. *Iceland: the visitor's guide.* London: Stacey.

Williams, G. J. 1965. *Economic Geology of New Zealand.* Melbourne: Australasian Institute of Mining and Metallurgy.

Williams, M. 1974. *The Making of the South Australian Landscape.* Sydney: Harcourt Brace.

Williams, T. I. 1953. *The Chemical Industry.* Harmondsworth: Penguin.

Williamson, H. F. and Daum, A. R. 1959. *The American Petroleum Industry 1859–1959: the age of illumination.* Evanston, IL: North Western University Press.

Williamson, J. 1930. *The American Hotel.* New York: Knopf.

Wilson, A. M. 1957. *Diderot, the Testing Years, 1713–1759.* New York: Oxford University Press.

Wilson, C. 1954. *The History of Unilever: a study in economic growth and social change.* London: Cassell.

Wilson, D. 1985. *Francis Frith's Travels: a photographic journey through Victorian Britain*. London: Dent.

Wilson, D. R. 1982. *Air Photography Interpretation for Archaeologists*. London: Batsford.

Wilson, G. 1976. *The Old Telegraphs*. Chichester: Phillimore.

Wilson, K. 1979. *A History of Textiles*. Boulder, CO: Westview Press.

Wingate, I. B. 1979. *Fairchild's Dictionary of Textiles*, 6th edn. New York: Fairchild Publications.

Winkler, J. K. 1940. *Five and Ten: the fabulous life of F. W. Woolworth*. New York: McBride.

Winstanley, M. J. 1983. *The Shopkeeper's World 1830–1913*. Manchester: Manchester University Press.

Winton, J. 1986. *The Little Wonder: 150 years of the Festiniog Railway*, rev. edn. London: Michael Joseph.

Wirtgen-Bernard, C. and Dusart, M. 1981. *Visages industriels d'hier et d'aujourd'hui en Pays de Liège*. Liège: P. Mardaga.

Wiskemann, E. 1966. *Europe of the Dictators 1919–45*. London: Fontana.

Wohl, A. S. 1983. *Endangered Lives: Public Health in Victorian Britain*. London: Dent.

Wojewódzki, R. 1983. *Zagadnienia ochrony dziedzictwa kulturowego nad Kamienna* (The problems of industrial heritage conservation on the Kamienna river). Kielce: BBiDZ.

Wölfel, W. 1987. *Das Wasserad: Eine historische Betrachtung* (The water wheel: an historical consideration). Berlin: VEB Verlag fur Bauwesen.

Wood, J. 1985. *Sixty Industrial Archaeology Sites in Scotland*. Telford: Association for Industrial Archaeology and Scottish Industrial Archaeology Society.

Wood, J. W. 1940. *Airports: some elements of design and future development*. New York: Coward-McCann.

Wood, N. 1825. *A Practical Treatise on Railroads*. London: Longmans.

Woodbury, R. S. 1958. *History of the Gear Cutting Machine*. Cambridge, MA: MIT Press.

——1959. *History of the Grinding Machine*. Cambridge, MA: MIT Press.

——1960. *History of the Milling Machine*. Cambridge, MA: MIT Press.

——1961. *History of the Lathe*. Cambridge, MA: MIT Press.

Woodcock, F. H. 1938. *Canned Foods and the Canning Industry*. London: Pitman.

Woodford, J. 1976. *Bricks to Build a House with*. London: Routledge & Kegan Paul.

Woodforde, J. 1970. *The Story of the Bicycle*. London: Routledge & Kegan Paul.

Woolf, S. 1987. *The Poor in Western Europe in the Eighteenth and Nineteenth Centuries*. London: Methuen.

Woronoff, D. 1984. *L'Industrie sidérurgique en France pendant la Révolution et l'Empire* (The iron industry in France during the Revolution and the Empire). Paris: Editions de l'Ecole des Hautes Etudes en Sciènces Sociales.

Woude, A. van der and Schuurman, F. 1980. *Probate Inventories: a new source for the historical study of wealth, material culture and agricultural development*. Wageningen, The Hague: A. A. G. Bijdragen.

Wragg, D. W. 1973. *A Dictionary of Aviation*. Reading: Osprey.

Wright, H. and Vogel, R. 1986. *Industrial Heritage 86: Proceedings of the Fifth International Conference on the Conservation of Industrial Heritage*. Washington DC: SIA.

Wright, L. 1960. *Clean and Decent: the history of the bathroom and water closet*. London: Routledge & Kegan Paul.

Wright, N. R. 1982. *Lincolnshire Towns and Industry 1700–1914*. Lincoln: Society for Lincolnshire History and Archaeology.

Wrigley, E. A. 1966. *An Introduction to English Historical Demography*. London: Weidenfeld & Nicholson.

Wrigley, E. A. and Schofield, R. S. 1981. *The Population History of England 1541–1871*. London: Edward Arnold.

Wrottesly, A. J. F. 1960. *Famous Underground Railways of the World*, 2nd edn. London: Muller.

Wüstenfeld, G. A. 1978. *Die Ruhrschiffahrt von 1780 bis 1890* (The shipping on the Ruhr between 1780 and 1890). Wetter: Monographie zur Geschichte des Ruhrgebietes Schrift.

Wüster, E. 1968. *The Machine Tool: an interlingual dictionary of basic concepts*. London: Technical Press.

Wynn, G. 1981. *Timber Colony: a historical geography of early nineteenth century New Brunswick*. Toronto: University of Toronto Press.

Wynter, H. 1971. *An Introduction to European Porcelain*. London: Arlington.

Wyssling, W. 1946. *Die Entwicklung ser Schweizerischen Elektrizitätswerke* (The development of the Swiss electrical industry). Zurich.

Yarsley, V. E. and Couzens, E. G. 1945. *Plastics*. Harmondsworth: Penguin.

Yearsley, I. 1962. *The Manchester Tram*. Huddersfield: Advertiser Press.

Young, P. 1983. *Power of Speech: a history of Standard Telephones and Cables*. London: Allen and Unwin.

Ysselsteyn, H. A. van 1908. *De haven van Rotterdam* (The Port of Rotterdam), 3rd edn. Rotterdam: Nijgh & Van Ditmar.

Zeit, P. 1948. *Dahlhausen an der Wupper und seine industriellen Anlagen* (Dahlhausen on the Wupper and its industrial zone). Bonn: Göte Schwippert Kommissionsverlag.

Zippelius, A. 1974. *Handbuch der europäischen Freilichtmuseen* (Handbook of European open air museums). Cologne: Rheinland-Verlag GmbH.

Zonca, V. 1607. *Nuovo Teatro di Machine ed Edifici* (New Treatises on machines and buildings). Padova.

Zukowsky, J. ed. 1987. *Chicago Architektur 1872–1922: Die Entstehung der kiomopolitischen Architektur des 20 Jahrhunderts* (Architecture in Chicago 1872–1922: the origins of the cosmopolitan architecture of the twentieth century). Munich: Prestel-Verlag.

BIBLIOGRAPHY

Zupko, R. E. 1968. *A Dictionary of English Weights and Measures from Anglo-Saxon Times to the Nineteenth Century*. Madison, WI: University of Wisconsin Press.

8 Nentori 1980. *The People's Socialist Republic of Albania*. Tiranë: 8 Nentori Publishing House.

—— 1982. *The National Exhibition of the Material Culture of the Albanian People*. Tiranë: 8 Nentori Publishing House.

—— 1984. *Forty Years of Socialist Albania: statistical data on the development of the economy and culture*. Tiranë: 8 Nentori Publishing House.

Index

Alphabetical sorting is according to letter by letter, with the page numbers to the main entries indicated by bold type and positioned first in the list of numbers. Detailed entries to canals, museums and railways are to be found in the Index Supplement. Processes which derive from one person are indexed under the name of the relevant person (for example, the Bessemer process is indexed under Sir Henry Bessemer).

Index Supplement